PENGUIN HANDBOOKS

The New Penguin Guide to Compact Discs and Cassettes

This book is primarily about **compact discs** and the reader will imm[illegible]iately discover the remarkable range of music available in this new m[illegible] [illegible]ickly scanning through its pages. The **CDs** stand out clearly, a[illegible] [illegible]bers are printed in **bold** type, while *cassettes* are numb[illegible] [illegible] an alternative medium for more casual liste[illegible] [illegible] technical quality, and they cost much less [illegible] [illegible] the bargain-price range offer quite remarkable valu[illegible] [illegible] well on the way to obsolescence, so they are not included in [illegible]. Perhaps one day digital tape will take over from the standard musicas[illegible], but for the moment the normal cassette player, whether the domestic, personalized and portable version, or in its in-car format, has become a universal alternative to the CD player and is not likely to be supplanted easily. Normal cassettes are likely to remain the major alternative to CDs for the immediately foreseeable future.

EDWARD GREENFIELD has been Record Critic of the *Guardian* since 1954 and from 1964 Music Critic too. At the end of 1960 he joined the reviewing panel of *Gramophone*, specializing in operatic and orchestral issues. He is a regular broadcaster on music and records for the BBC and has a weekly record programme on the BBC World Service. In 1958 he published a monograph on the operas of Puccini. More recently he has writtten studies on the recorded work of Joan Sutherland and André Previn. He has been a regular juror on International Record awards and has appeared with such artists as Elisabeth Schwarzkopf and Joan Sutherland in public interviews.

ROBERT LAYTON studied at Oxford with Edmund Rubbra for composition and with Egon Wellesz for the history of music. He spent two years in Sweden at the universities of Uppsala and Stockholm. He joined the BBC Music Division in 1959 and has been responsible for such programmes as *Interpretations on Record*. He has contributed 'A Quarterly Retrospect' to *Gramophone* for a number of years and he has written books on Berwald and Sibelius and has specialized in Scandinavian music. His recent publications include a monograph on the Dvořák symphonies and concertos for the BBC Music Guides, of which he is General Editor, and the first two volumes of his translations of Erik Tawastsjerna's definitive study of Sibelius. In 1987 he was awarded the Sibelius Medal and in the following year was made a Knight of the Order of the White Rose of Finland for his services to Finnish music.

IVAN MARCH is a former professional musician and a regular contributor to *Gramophone*. He studied at Trinity College of Music, London, and at the Royal Manchester College. After service in the RAF Central Band, he played the horn professionally for the BBC and travelled with the Carl Rosa and D'Oyly Carte opera companies. Now director of the Long Playing Record Library, the largest commercial lending library for classical music on compact discs in the British Isles, he is a well-known lecturer, journalist and personality in the world of recorded music.

The New Penguin Guide to Compact Discs and Cassettes

Edward Greenfield, Robert Layton and Ivan March

Edited by Ivan March

Penguin Books

PENGUIN BOOKS

Published by the Penguin Group
27 Wrights Lane, London W8 5TZ, England
Viking Penguin Inc., 40 West 23rd Street, New York, New York 10010, USA
Penguin Books Australia Ltd, Ringwood, Victoria, Australia
Penguin Books Canada Ltd, 2801 John Street, Markham, Ontario, Canada L3R 1B4
Penguin Books (NZ) Ltd, 182–190 Wairau Road, Auckland 10, New Zealand

Penguin Books Ltd, Registered Offices: Harmondsworth, Middlesex, England

First published 1988

Made and printed in Great Britain by
Richard Clay Ltd,
Bungay, Suffolk
Typeset in 8 on 9½ pt Times

Contents

Editor's Comment

With the publication of *The New Penguin Guide to Compact Discs and Cassettes* it is fascinating to reflect that just thirty years ago we were preparing our first hardback *Stereo Record Guide*. Stereo was then very much in its infancy, although subsequent experience has shown that some of the most successful recordings dated from those very early days, when simpler techniques were used. Initially, the musical public was not convinced of the legitimacy of stereo in musical terms, fearing that the element of demonstration gimmickry was simply designed to sell more records (which it certainly did). Our first *Guide* helped to establish the now unquestioned premise that stereo produced a genuine revolution in the truthfulness of recorded sound in many ways even more profound than the improvements in realism and presence (together with the virtual disappearance of instrusive background) that came a quarter of a century later with the arrival of the compact disc. During the following two decades, and particularly in the vintage 1960s, an enormous amount of music appeared on records for the first time, much of it unfamiliar or even unknown in terms of live performance, and the gramophone established a combined documentary/archival role quite as important as that of the printed musical score. Moreover, many of the major recorded performances of the repertoire masterpieces made during that period were highly distinguished, creating a pre-digital legacy of the utmost musical importance.

The compact disc is now established as the major sound-carrier for pre-recorded music, with no serious rival in sight. Digital tape, with its less instantaneous access, has the sole added advantage of its domestic copying facility, and even this is minimized by the high current cost of the digital blank tape. As the extensive content of the current *Guide* readily demonstrates, there has been a further remarkable expansion of available repertoire to mark the success of the new medium, providing not only a huge number of new digital recordings but also delving well back into the past. This vast coverage encompasses not only the analogue LP era (mono as well as stereo) but also the heady days of shellac 78-r.p.m. discs, as far back as the earliest pre-electric recording, when the voice of Enrico Caruso, caught with amazing realism for the period (1902–4), first convinced a wide public that the gramophone was much more than a toy.

During the preparation of this book we have been constantly deluged – and at times nearly overwhelmed – by the flood of new CDs from every source (for smaller companies have been able to benefit from the new technology alongside the major international groups). With the phenomenal duplications of popular classical repertoire has come an adventurous growth in the area of little-known music: the symphonies of Gade and Tubin and the vocal works of Marc-Antoine Charpentier are striking examples, to say nothing of the widespread growth of British music on record. Thus the CD has already confounded the doubts of its early critics, who could never have foreseen how quickly the catalogue would multiply, or indeed anticipate the appearance of cheaper mid-priced reissues, made doubly attractive by their generous playing time. By now LPs, sadly, are well on their way to obsolescence. Excellent and inexpensive cassettes are taking their place, offering the less affluent an admirable alternative introduction to the basic classical repertoire.

Ivan March

Preface

The compact disc has caught the public imagination in a way its creators could hardly have anticipated when the first CDs were made available to the general public in the early months of 1983; nor could it have been guessed how quickly the new medium would come to dominate the world of recording. The newcomer to CD is usually first amazed by the magnetism and uncanny presence of a clear and realistically balanced digital recording, heard against a background of total silence. After this dramatic experience it is only a short step to discovering that a first-class analogue recording from the pre-digital era can be digitally remastered so that its (inevitable) background hiss is greatly subdued, often virtually silenced, while – if the operation is masterminded with skill and care – the quality of the sound can be considerably enhanced.

However, the compact disc is not the only modern sound-carrier which gives excellent reproduction. The pre-recorded chrome cassette, if not matching the CD in presence and realism, offers an alternative technology that is in essence more casual but equally useful in a different way. It too provides music against an undisturbed background, if not absolute silence. The best 'bargain' cassettes can offer up to an hour and a half of listening, while costing about a third as much as a compact disc.

To all intents and purposes, the LP is becoming obsolete as a music carrier – although, no doubt, used LPs will remain in the marketplace for many years to come. During 1987, the major manufacturers discontinued the re-pressing of their back catalogues and, as factory stocks ran down, most major recordings have ceased to be available in this format. It may be that certain esoteric material will remain available in black-disc form, if for a limited period; but it cannot be long before classical LPs disappear entirely from all but specialist shops, with the display space taken over by their CD and cassette alternatives.

The New Penguin Guide to Compact Discs and Cassettes surveys the available classical repertoire from this fresh viewpoint. It includes all major CDs and important bargain-priced cassettes. Usually premium-priced new issues are offered in tape formulations alongside their CD equivalents, but, after early demand has been satisfied, the cassettes are often withdrawn. We have therefore included references to tape quality where pertinent. Certain EMI tape issues must be approached with caution – as indicated in the text – as for a period this company misguidedly returned to the use of iron-oxide stock for its cassette manufacture, sometimes with considerable loss of fidelity. However, EMI have now reverted to chrome tape, and it seems likely that in due course back-catalogue items may be re-transferred. It is always clear from the spine of a cassette whether or not chrome tape has been used.

Since our last *Compact Disc Guide* was published, a growing area of controversy has arisen concerning the digital remastering of analogue recordings for their CD reissue. The object of such a process is to try and enhance an older recording within digital terms of reference, to improve clarity and presence and, at the same time, to remove most of the background noise inherent on the master recording. (The Philips label has even adopted a 'NoNoise' logo in reintroducing historical recordings to the CD catalogue.) But, alas, it is all too easy for an excellent analogue original to become degraded by this attempted facelift if it is clumsily applied. A sharp aural image is not always or necessarily a more musically agreeable one, and if the ambience of the original recording was fairly resonant, attempts to improve internal clarity can be false, so that a combination of added harshness plus a degree of fuzziness is the result.

Early digital transfers, made during the first two or three years of CD, were relatively modest in their aspirations and were usually highly successful. With later examples, where great care was taken (for instance, the Solti Decca recording of Wagner's *Ring* cycle, or Sir Thomas Beecham's Delius on HMV), the improvements in sound can seem almost miraculous. More recently, however, the results have too often achieved an unnaturally bright treble response, which brings glare to the violins, ill balanced by a reduction of the fullness and resonance in the bass. A curious effect is produced that can best be described as 'dehydration' in which the body and substance of the recording seem to evaporate, and this applies particularly to reissues on mid-priced labels, from EMI as well as from the Polygram group (Decca, DG and, rather less culpably, Philips). There seems to be a standard processing system applied to all these discs; this sometimes works to advantage and is often remarkably successful, but too often it produces a degree of edginess on top which it is difficult to smooth with the playback controls.

The enormous influence of the 'authentic' lobby in current recordings of baroque music (and now some nineteenth-century music too, with Beethoven's as well as Mozart's keyboard concertos available on the fortepiano) has brought an important element of choice between modern and period instruments. Although any form of authenticity must inherently add interest to a recorded performance, we are not always wholly convinced that the use of old instruments (or copies) and conjectural historical performance techniques (which can vary enormously in their emphasis) necessarily bring the listener closer to the spirit of the music. Players of early instruments sometimes seem to be intimidated by the letter of the text, which can take precedence over the breathing of life into phrases weighed down by arbitrary linear bulges, while textures can be made to sound desiccated or vinegary. It is salutary to remember that Anton Stadler, the clarinettist for whom Mozart wrote his *Clarinet quintet*, possessed a timbre which a contemporary described as 'so soft and lovely that nobody who has a heart can resist it'; it is no less reasonable to conjecture that the reason for Mozart's much-quoted dislike for the flute may have derived from the somewhat anaemic timbre which some early instruments can produce.

However, having experienced 'authenticity' of a more invigorating and life-enhancing character – such as one can expect, for instance, from performances directed by an artist like John Eliot Gardiner – one's listening ears are never quite the same again. The influence of the authentic movement has undoubtedly been profound, even if it does not diminish our loyalties to established interpretations of conductors of the calibre of Sir Thomas Beecham, Bruno Walter and, more recently, Sir Colin Davis or Sir Neville Marriner with his illustrious Academy. As to the use of the fortepiano for nineteenth-century music, here one's reactions must be more guarded, for all its revelations of freshness and clarity of texture. It is easy to believe that when Beethoven composed his *Hammerklavier sonata* or *Emperor concerto* his aural imagination suggested an idealized piano image, not unlike that of the modern Steinway concert grand.

Fortunately the CD offers a profusion of recordings representing all persuasions of performance and, with it, a new golden age of recorded music. While the price of new premium-priced CDs remains fairly high (for recording costs always have to be amortized) it seems likely that the future will provide more and more reissues in the lower price-ranges; these often offer up to seventy-five minutes of music and represent excellent value by any standards, especially when one remembers that in 1950 the first LPs cost £2, a far greater amount in real terms. For those with limited budgets, tape offers a real alternative, and here the cost for each minute of music is ridiculously low, making our universal musical heritage readily available to everyone.

Introduction

The object of *The New Penguin Guide to Compact Discs and Cassettes* is to give the serious collector a comprehensive survey of the finest recordings of permanent music, primarily on compact discs, but also on cassettes. As most CDs are issued almost simultaneously on both sides of the Atlantic and use identical international catalogue numbers, this *Guide* should be found to be equally useful in Great Britain and the USA. The internationalization of repertoire and numbers is increasingly applying to cassettes and CDs (though, notably in regard to cassettes, EMI/Angel remains an exception to this practice). The major European labels are imported in their original formats; thus we have BIS from Scandinavia, Erato from France, Harmonia Mundi from France, Hungaroton from Hungary, Supraphon from Czechoslovakia, Teldec from Germany, Olympia using masters from the USSR, all providing important recordings of international repertoire, often rare and uniquely valuable. The (relatively) smaller labels like ASV, Chandos, Hyperion, Meridian from Britain and Arabesque, Nonesuch and Pro Arte from the USA are marketed independently and, like the European issues, have international catalogue numbers. These small recording companies, because digital recording techniques and CD and tape mastering are readily available universally, are able to compete with the majors on both artistic and technical terms and, by imaginative choice of repertoire, have established a firm and expanding presence in the marketplace. Special mention must be made of Pickwick International, the British firm which has provided the first 'bargain-priced' compact discs, retailing at about two-thirds of the premium price with no apparent loss of standards, either artistic or technical, even if the artists' roster contains some presently unfamiliar names.

DG's justly famous Walkman series continues to dominate the field of extended-length chrome cassettes by continuing to produce some astonishing bargains. Its digital successor, the Pocket Music tape series, has perhaps not been as consistently successful, but still offers interesting modern recordings in the same price range. The technology of cassette transfer has now become highly sophisticated and, where chrome stock is used, the difference in sound between tape and the older LP format is minimal, any minor disadvantage in range being more than offset by the security from extraneous background noises offered by the former. With major issues and reissues the back-up documentation is now generally adequate, though sometimes suffering from miniaturization, with librettos often printed in a minuscule typeface. Yet CDs, too, are not always entirely free from this defect. Unfortunately many double-length bargain-priced cassettes incorporate only minimal documentation, offering merely a list of titles and performers. This represents a lamentable deterioration in standards, which is also reflected by the three-language presentation of musical notes with premium-priced issues, in both media, thus limiting the space available.

The sheer number available of records of artistic merit causes considerable problems in any assessment of overall and individual excellence. While in the case of a single popular repertoire work it might be ideal for the discussion to be conducted by a single reviewer, it was not always possible for one person to have access to every version, and division of reviewing responsibility inevitably leads to some clashes of opinion. Also there are certain works and certain recorded performances for which one or another of our team has a special affinity. Such a personal identification can often carry with it a special perception too. We feel that it is a strength of our basic style to let such conveyed pleasure or admiration for the merits of an individual recording come over directly to the reader, even if this produces a certain ambivalence in the matter of choice between competing recordings. Where disagreement is profound (and this has rarely happened), then readers will find an indication of this difference of opinion in the text.

We have considered and rejected the use of initials against individual reviews, since this is essentially a team project. The occasions for disagreement generally concern matters of aesthetics, for instance in the manner of recording balance, where a contrived effect may trouble some ears more than others, or in the matter of style, where the difference between robustness and refinement of approach produces controversy, rather than any question of artistic integrity.

EVALUATION

Most recordings issued today by the major companies, whether on compact disc or cassette, are of a high technical standard and offer performances of a quality at least as high as is heard in the average concert hall. In adopting a starring system for the evaluation of records, we have decided to make use of from one to three stars. Brackets round one or more of the stars indicate some reservations about its inclusion and readers are advised to refer to the text. Brackets round all the stars usually indicate a basic qualification: for instance, a mono recording of a performance of artistic interest, where considerable allowances have to be made for the sound quality, even though the recording may have been digitally remastered.

Our evaluation system may be summarized as follows:

*** An outstanding performance and recording in every way

** A good performance and recording of today's normal high standard.

* A fair performance, reasonably well or well recorded.

Our evaluation is normally applied to the record as a whole, unless there are two main works, or groups of works, on each side of the disc, and by different composers. In this case each is dealt with separately in its appropriate place. In the case of a collection of shorter works, we feel there is little point in giving a different starring to each item, even if their merits are uneven, since the record can only be purchased as a complete programme.

ROSETTES

To a very few records and cassettes we have awarded a rosette: ❀.

Unlike our general evaluation, in which we have tried to be consistent, a rosette is a quite arbitrary compliment by a member of the reviewing team to a recorded performance which, he finds, shows special illumination, magic, or a spiritual quality that places it in a very special class. The choice is essentially a personal one (although often it represents a shared view), and in some cases it is applied to an issue where certain reservations must also be mentioned in the text of the review. The rosette symbol is placed immediately before the normal evaluation and record number. It is quite small – we do not mean to imply an 'Academy Award' but a personal token of appreciation for something uniquely valuable. We hope that, once the reader has discovered and perhaps acquired a 'rosette' CD or tape, its special qualities will soon become apparent.

DIGITAL RECORDINGS

Many compact discs are actually recorded digitally, but an increasing number of digitally remastered analogue recordings are now appearing, and we thought it important to include a clear indication of the difference:

Dig. This indicates that the master recording was digitally encoded.

BARGAIN ISSUES

With the honourable exceptions of Pickwick's mid-priced series (issued on the aptly named 'Innovative Music Productions' label – IMP for short), certain EMI Eminence and Classics for Pleasure CDs and a sprinkling of others, most digitally recorded CDs continue to be issued at a fairly high premium price. However, since the publication of our last edition we have seen a huge expansion of the mid-priced CD range – usually standard repertoire works in excellent analogue recordings, digitally remastered. Often these reissue CDs are generous in playing time, increasing their value to the collector. The record chain stores are now also offering even cheaper classical CDs at super-bargain price, usually featuring second-line performances by artists whose names are not internationally familiar. Often in these cases the remastering leaves a good deal to be desired but, at the very low prices currently pertaining, some collectors may be tempted to explore this repertoire for themselves. For reasons of space, it has not been possible to include such material in this book. Without having to resort to this material of doubtful lineage, however, the collector still has plenty of scope to decide how much to pay for a recorded performance, with a CD range from about £5 up to well over twice that amount, and cassettes costing around half as much as their equivalent CDs and sometimes much less than that.

Our listing of each recording first indicates if it is not in fact in the premium-price range, as follows:

(M) Medium-priced label, with the CD costing around £7–£8 and the equivalent cassette between £3.50 and £4.50.

(B) Bargain-priced label, with the CD costing £5–£6 and the equivalent cassette about £2.50–£3.

Some chain stores, however, may from time to time have special offers when prices are even lower.

In the case of double-length cassettes, which contain the equivalent of the contents of two normal LPs, we have taken this into account in choosing the appropriate symbol. For instance, DG Walkman tapes have a list price in the region of £3.50 but usually offer up to ninety minutes of music.

It is possible that, in current inflationary times, prices may rise during the life of this book so that the above limitations become unrealistic, but the major manufacturers usually maintain the price ratios between labels when an overall increase is made.

LAYOUT OF TEXT

We have aimed to make our style as simple as possible, even though the catalogue numbers of recordings are no longer as straightforward as they once were, and we are now often dealing with a double format of **CD** and *cassette* relating to the same recording. So, immediately after the evaluation and before the catalogue numbers, the record make is given, usually in abbreviated form (a key to the abbreviations is provided on pages xvii–xix).

The compact disc catalogue comes first in **bold type** (unless there is no CD available at the time of going to print); then the cassette is indicated in *italics*.

With certain CDs the **CD** number consists only of digits, while the *cassette* has an alphabetical prefix; in other instances there are different alphabetical prefixes for each format and the number remains unaltered; in some examples the **CD** and *tape* have quite different catalogue numbers.

Here are some typical examples:

Decca Dig. **400 055-2**; *KSXDC 7562.*
CBS Dig. **MK 42124**; *IMT 42124.*
Chan. Dig. **CHAN 8541**; *ABTD 1161.*

The Polygram group (Decca, DG and Philips) now use the same basic catalogue number for both formats, with the final digit indicating **CD** or *tape*, viz. **410 507-2**; *410 507-4*; many companies are now moving towards using a hyphenated **-2** at the end of a catalogue number to indicate a **CD**.

In the case of a set of two or more **CDs** or *tapes*, the number of units involved is given in brackets after the catalogue number:

DG Dig. **423 079-2**, *423 079-4* (2).

AMERICAN CATALOGUE NUMBERS

The numbers which follow in square brackets are US catalogue numbers; here a similar differentiation is made between disc (in **bold** type) and cassette issue (in *italics*), while the abbreviation [id.] indicates that the American number is identical with the European, which is increasingly the case.

ABBREVIATIONS

To save space we have adopted a number of standard abbreviations in listing orchestras and performing groups (a list is provided below), and the titles of works are often shortened, especially where they are listed several times. Artists' christian names are sometimes not included where they are not absolutely necessary for identification purposes. We have also usually omitted details of the contents of operatic highlights collections. These can be found in the *Gramophone Compact Disc* and *Classical Catalogues* published by *Gramophone* magazine.

We have followed common practice in the use of the original language for titles where it seems sensible. In most cases, English is used for orchestral and instrumental music and the original language for vocal music and opera. There are exceptions, however; for instance, the Johann Strauss discography uses the German language in the interests of consistency.

ORDER OF MUSIC

The order of music under each composer's name broadly follows that adopted by the *Gramophone Catalogues*: orchestral music, including concertos and symphonies; chamber music; solo instrumental music (in some cases with keyboard and organ music separated); vocal and choral music; opera; vocal collections; miscellaneous collections.

The *Gramophone Catalogues* now usually include stage works alongside opera; we have not generally followed this practice, preferring to list, for instance, ballet music and incidental music (where no vocal items are involved) in the general orchestral group. Within each group our listing follows an alphabetical sequence, and couplings within a single composer's output are *usually* discussed together instead of separately with cross-references. Occasionally and inevitably because of this alphabetical approach, different recordings of a given work can become separated when a record is listed and discussed under the first work of its alphabetical sequence. The editor feels that alphabetical consistency is essential if the reader is to learn to find his or her way about.

CONCERTS AND RECITALS

Most collections of music intended to be regarded as concerts or recitals involve many composers, and it is quite impractical to deal with them within the alphabetical composer index. They are grouped separately, at the end of the book, in three sections. In each section, recordings are usually arranged in alphabetical order of the performers' names: concerts of orchestral and concertante music under the name of the orchestra, ensemble or, if more important, conductor or soloist; instrumental recitals under the name of the instrumentalist; operatic and vocal recitals under the principal singer or vocal group, as seems appropriate.

In certain cases where the compilation features many different performers it is listed alphabetically under its collective title, or the key word in that title (so *Favourite operatic duets* is listed under 'Operatic duets'). Sometimes for complicated collections only brief details of contents and performers are given; fuller information can usually be found in the *Gramophone Compact Disc* and *Classical Catalogues*.

CATALOGUE NUMBERS

Enormous care has gone into the checking of CD and cassette numbers and contents to ensure that all details are correct, but the editor and publishers cannot be held responsible for any mistakes that may have crept in despite all our zealous checking. When ordering CDs or cassettes, readers are urged to provide their record-dealer with full details of the music and performers as well as the catalogue number.

DELETIONS

Although, for the moment, CDs still seem relatively impervious to the deletions axe, it is likely that some cassettes will have been withdrawn in the period before we appear in print, and others are likely to disappear during the lifetime of the book. Sometimes copies may still be found in specialist shops, and there remains the compensation that most really important and desirable recordings are eventually reissued.

PRICES

As we go to press, prices of CDs are tending to fall, and during the life of this book some labels will come into the mid-price category. For instance, a sudden price-cut from Hyperion brings their CDs into the upper-mid-price range – though this does not yet apply to the equivalent cassettes. Hungaroton, too, have made an almost comparable reduction for CDs.

ACKNOWLEDGEMENTS

The editor and authors again express their gratitude to Roger Wells for his help in the preparation of this volume, which has proved quite indispensable. We also wish to thank Kathleen March for her zealous checking of the finished copy and each set of proofs, prior to its delivery to Roger Wells and the printers. Without her untiring efforts this book would be a good deal less accurate. Finally the authors gratefully acknowledge the many letters of encouragement and appreciation from readers which have helped to make our marathon task worth while, and whose comments about errata have helped to make the present text more precise in its detail than its predecessor.

E.G.
R.L.
I.M.

For American Readers

American catalogue numbers are included throughout this survey where they are known at the time of going to press. In each case the American domestic listing is given in square brackets immediately after the British catalogue number. The abbreviation [id.]. indicates that the American and British numbers are identical, or nearly so. For instance, a CBS number could use the same digits on both sides of the Atlantic, but have different alphabetical prefixes, and EMI/Angel use extra digits for their British compact discs. Thus the US number **CDC 47001** becomes **CDC 747001-2** in Britain (the **-2** is the European indication that it is a compact disc). The addition of (d.) immediately before the American number indicates some difference in the contents of the American issue. We have taken care to check catalogue information as far as is possible, but as all the editorial work has been done in England there is always the possibility of error; American readers are therefore invited, when ordering records locally, to take the precaution of giving their dealer the fullest information about the music and recordings they want.

The indications (M) and (D) immediately before the starring of a disc refer only to the British record, as pricing systems are not always identical on both sides of the Atlantic.

Where no American catalogue number is given, this does not necessarily mean that a record is not available in the USA; the transatlantic issue may not have been made at the time of the publication of this *Guide*. Readers are advised to check the current *Schwann* catalogue and to consult their local record store.

One of the more significant roles played by the international recording industry is to provide recordings of contemporary scores, and in this way the gramophone record becomes fundamental in establishing the reputation of music written in our own time. However, for understandable commercial reasons, the greater part of this output is permanently accessible only in its country of origin. Those recordings that are exported seldom remain available abroad for long periods (although there are honourable exceptions). Some important twentieth-century American music is not readily obtainable in recorded form in Great Britain, whilst modern British and European composers are much more generously favoured. The reflection of this imbalance within these pages is obviously not the choice of the authors.

An International Mail-order Source for Recordings

Readers are urged to support a local dealer if he is prepared and able to give a proper service, and to remember that many CDs and tapes involve perseverance to obtain. If, however, difficulty is experienced locally, we suggest the following mail-order alternative, which operates world-wide:

Squires Gate Music Centre
Squires Gate Station Approach
Blackpool
Lancashire FY8 2SP
England

Compact disc orders are patiently extended until they finally come to hand by this organization (which is operated under the direction of the Editor of *The New Penguin Guide to Compact Discs and Cassettes*. A full guarantee is made of safe delivery of any order undertaken. Please write for more details, enclosing a stamped, addressed envelope if within the UK.

American readers seeking a domestic mail-order source may write to the following address where a comparable supply service is in operation, (for both American and imported European labels). Please order from, or write for more details (enclosing a stamped, addressed envelope if within the USA) to:

PG Dept
Serenade Records
1713 G St, N.W.
Washington DC 20006
USA

Abbreviations

Ac.	Academy, Academic
AAM	Academy of Ancient Music
Amb. S.	Ambrosian Singers
Ang.	Angel
Ara.	Arabesque
arr.	arranged
ASMF	Academy of St Martin-in-the-Fields
ASV	Academy Sound and Vision
Bar.	Baroque
Bav.	Bavarian
BPO	Berlin Philharmonic Orchestra
Cal.	Calliope
Cap.	Caprice
CBSO	City of Birmingham Symphony Orchestra
CfP	Classics for Pleasure
Ch.	Choir; Chorale; Chorus
Chan.	Chandos
CO	Chamber Orchestra
COE	Chamber Orchestra of Europe
Col. Mus. Ant.	Cologne Musica Antiqua
Coll.	Collegium
Coll. Aur.	Collegium Aureum
Coll. Mus.	Collegium Musicum
comp.	completed
Concg. O	Concertgebouw Orchestra of Amsterdam
cond.	conductor, conducted
Cons.	Consort
CRD	Continental Record Distributors
(d.)	different coupling
Dept	Department
DG	Deutsche Grammophon
Dig.	digital recording
E.	England, English
ECO	English Chamber Orchestra
ed.	edited
Ens.	Ensemble
Fest.	Festival
Fr.	French
GO	Gewandhaus Orchestra
Gold	Gold Label

HM	Harmonia Mundi
HMV	His Master's Voice
Hung.	Hungaroton
Hyp.	Hyperion
L.	London
Lon.	London (Record Company)
LACO	Los Angeles Chamber Orchestra
LAPO	Los Angeles Philharmonic Orchestra
LOP	Lamoureux Orchestra of Paris
LPO	London Philharmonic Orchestra
LSO	London Symphony Orchestra
Mer.	Meridian
Met.	Metropolitan
movt	movement
N.	North
nar.	narrated
Nat.	National
None.	Nonesuch
NY	New York
O	Orchestra, Orchestre
Odys.	Odyssey
O-L	Oiseau-Lyre
Op.	Opera (in performance listings), opus (in music titles)
orch.	orchestrated
ORTF	L'Orchestre de la radio et télévision française
Ph.	Philips
Phd.	Philadelphia
Philh.	Philharmonia
PO	Philharmonic Orchestra
Pres.	Presence
PRT	Precision Records & Tapes
Qt	Quartet
R.	Radio
RCA	distributed in UK by BMG
ROHCG	Royal Opera House, Covent Garden
RPO	Royal Philharmonic Orchestra
RSO	Radio Symphony Orchestra
S.	South
Sar.	Sarabande
SCO	Stuttgart Chamber Orchestra
Sera.	Seraphim
Sinf.	Sinfonietta
SNO	Scottish National Orchestra
SO	Symphony Orchestra
Soc.	Society
Sol. Ven.	I Solisti Veneti
SRO	Suisse Romande Orchestra
Sup.	Supraphon
Tel.	Teldec

trans.	transcription, transcribed
V.	Vienna
Van.	Vanguard
Var.	Varese
VCM	Vienna Concentus Musicus
VPO	Vienna Philharmonic Orchestra
VSO	Vienna Symphony Orchestra
W.	West

Adam, Adolphe (1803–56)

Giselle (ballet): complete recording.
*** Decca Dig. **417 505-2**; *417 505-4* (2) [id.]. ROHCG O, Bonynge.

Giselle (ballet): original score (abridged).
(M) **(*) Decca **417 738-2**; *417 738-4* [id.]. VPO, Karajan.

The highly romantic story of *Giselle* (1841), the first of the great classical ballets, is based on the German legend of the Wilis, pale apparitions who dance in a gothic misty moonlight; maidens who have died before their nuptials could be celebrated, they return at night to inveigle any unwary male traveller into a dance which begins in passion but ends in death. In *Giselle*, the heroine has an abortive affair with Albrecht without knowing he is a prince. When the deception is exposed, she loses her mind and falls dead at her lover's feet. In Act II, summoned from the grave by the Queen of the Wilis and forced to tempt her lover into the fatal dance, she saves him by remaining near the cross of her tomb, which breaks the power of the spell. Adam's fine score may be melodramatic but it has balletic feeling in every bar, while Giselle's leitmotiv is hauntingly memorable.

Bonynge's performance offers the complete original score, exactly as Adam scored it, with all repeats. Also included are the *Peasants' Pas de deux* in Act I with music by Frédéric Bürgmuller, and two other insertions, possibly by Minkus. The two CDs and cassettes play for a total of nearly 126 minutes, and there is a good deal of unfamiliar material included. However, the invention is consistently agreeable, especially when the playing is so polished and warmly sympathetic. Bonynge's tempi are very much of the ballet theatre, but the overall tension is maintained well and detail is affectionately vivid. Recorded in London's Henry Wood Hall, with its glowing acoustics, the sound is richly coloured and sumptuous, the bass resonance almost too expansive. But the effect is undoubtedly beguiling in this very Romantic work, and this one of the most successful and satisfying of Bonynge's many ballet recordings made for Decca over the years. No one could complain that the strings lack fullness of timbre.

Karajan's performance offers sixty minutes of music (which will be enough for most listeners as it fits conveniently on to a single CD or tape): he effectively combines drama with an affectionate warmth, and the phrasing of the lyrical passages produces much lovely – if sometimes suave – playing from the Vienna strings. The more robust writing, including the horn calls of the huntsmen, has plenty of vigour and colour. John Culshaw supervised the recording, made in the Sofiensaal in 1961, and its original excellence is enhanced by the digital remastering, rather like the cleaning of a painting. Detail is refined but the brighter sound-image retains a balancing depth and resonance while adding to the feeling of vitality. String tone remains quite full (although the leader's solos seem a trifle thin in timbre, like those of the principal oboe) and there is plenty of ambient atmosphere and colour. Karajan is particularly good in the closing pages: when Giselle leaves her lover for ever, he creates a tellingly spacious romantic apotheosis.

Le Postillon de Longjumeau (complete).
*** HMV Dig. **CDS7 47554-8**; [Ang. **CDCB 47554**]; *EX 270435-5* (2). John Aler, June Anderson, Lafont, Le Roux, Laforge Ch. Ens., Monte Carlo PO, Fulton.

Adolphe Adam's opera, *Le Postillon de Longjumeau*, is best known for the hero's spectacular Act I aria with its stratospheric top notes; however, it does contain many other charming moments and is given an excellent complete recording on this EMI set. John Aler, heady in tone throughout his range and with no strain on those top notes, is outstanding as the postilion himself – who soon after singing that aria leaves his newly wed bride to become an opera singer.

As Madeleine, the abandoned wife, June Anderson is admirably agile, and she brings a vein of toughness to a heroine who, after inheriting a fortune, seeks revenge on her opera-singer husband. The voice, however, is a trifle raw.

The story is preposterous, but there is a spike behind the fun, which adds point to the music. Thomas Fulton with the Monte Carlo Philharmonic is very effective in giving the right spring to the many ensembles. The CD version adds clarity to the warmly atmospheric sound.

Adams, John (born 1947)

Shaker loops.

*** Ph. **412 214-2** [id.]. San Francisco SO, De Waart – REICH: *Variations for winds.****

Shaker loops is one of the more appealing of minimalist works. John Adams adapted the piece from an earlier string septet when he became composer-in-residence to the San Francisco orchestra. The inspiration was from the Shakers, the religious sect whose devotions regularly led to shaking and trembling. (The shaking was a substitute for sex, which they didn't believe in – so perhaps it is not surprising that the Shakers are no longer numerous. They are now best remembered for their hymnal – the source of inspiration for Copland's *Appalachian spring* – and also a much-admired cookery book.) In his four linked movements Adams reproduces the shaking in prolonged ostinatos and trills, making the result sound like Sibelius stuck in the groove. Whatever the limitations, there is a genuine poetic imagination here; both performance and recording are outstanding on CD.

Grand pianola music.

*** HMV Dig. **CDC7 47331-2** [id.]; *EL 270291-4* [Ang. *4XS 37345*]. Feinberg, Oppens, Wood, Bryden, Wheeler, Solisti New York, Wilson – REICH: *8 Lines; Vermont counterpoint.****

Even more than Adams's *Shaker loops*, this ambitious work seems likely to achieve a crossover between the worlds of concert and 'pop' music. It is in three sections, the first possessing the most fascinating aural detail, dominated by the piano filigree, but with vocal, orchestral and percussive interjections making a kaleidoscopic texture which is hypnotically compulsive in its climactic progress. After a more serene central movement the finale builds to a huge climax, using a simple but indelible phrase as its basis. Indeed the emotional and structural scope of the work is belied by its title, and one could imagine this piece creating a sensation at a promenade concert. The performance here has the feeling of a live occasion and the recording is very impressive in its CD format, the tape less so: the bass drum occasionally swamps the overall sound-picture.

Addinsell, Richard (1904–77)

Warsaw concerto.

*** Ph. Dig. **411 123-2**; *411 123-4* [id.]. Dichter, Philh. O, Marriner (with *Concert of concertante music* ***).
*** Decca Dig. **414 348-2**; *414 348-4* [id.]. Ortiz, RPO, Atzmon – LITOLFF: *Scherzo*; GOTTSCHALK: *Grande fantaisie*; RACHMANINOV: *Concerto No. 2.****

Richard Addinsell's pastiche miniature concerto, written for the film *Dangerous moonlight* in 1942, is perfectly crafted and its atmosphere combines all the elements of the Romantic concerto to great effect; moreover it has a truly memorable main theme. It is beautifully played here, with Marriner revealing the most engaging orchestral detail. The sound is first rate, with a kindly acoustic, admirably suited to the music, superbly caught on the CD. The chrome cassette is vivid and well balanced too.

The alternative from Cristina Ortiz is a warmly romantic account, spacious in conception, with the resonant ambience of Walthamstow Assembly Hall providing beguilingly rich string timbres. Although the opening is leisurely, Ortiz plays the main theme very tenderly; her approach is given an added evocation by the slightly backward balance of the piano. If the couplings are suitable, this is a rewarding collection, more substantial than Dichter's. The recording is first class in both media.

Aguado, Dionisio (1784–1849)

Adagio, Op. 2/1; Polonaise, Op. 2/2; Introduction and Rondo, Op. 2/3.
(*) RCA Dig. **RD 84549 [RCD1 4549]. Julian Bream (guitar) – SOR: *Fantaisies* etc.**(*)

Aguado was a contemporary of Sor, with whom his music is coupled – the two composers played duets together in Paris. Bream tells us that their techniques were quite different, Sor playing with his fingertips, Aguado using his nails. Neither wrote with a strong Spanish flavour, but Aguado's music is agreeable enough and inventive. The *Adagio* is the most striking piece, serene and introspective; it might have been even more effective had Bream been slightly less deliberate and reflective and chosen to move the music on a little more. However, the other pieces have plenty of life, and all are played with Bream's characteristic feeling for colour. The New York recording is truthful and realistic, and the programme overall is generous (64′ 39″).

Alain, Jehan (1911–40)

3 Danses; 2nd Fantaisie; Le jardin suspendu; Litanies; Suite; Variations on a theme of Clément Janequin.
*** Erato **ECD 88194** [id.]. Marie-Claire Alain (organ of St Christopher's Basilica, Belfort).

These recordings come from a comprehensive three-LP set issued at the beginning of the 1980s. Marie-Claire, the composer's sister, was only thirteen when her brother was killed in the last war, yet she retains vivid memories of his performances of his own music. They were very close, and there are special associations for her in many of the pieces. He could never have dreamed that she would grow up to become a distinguished organist of world fame and able to record definitive versions. The present selection includes some of the most frequently played pieces, notably the exuberantly inventive *Litanies* and the sensuously mysterious *Le jardin suspendu*. The *Three Dances* are particularly striking and original in scope: the composer was in the process of orchestrating them at the time of his death; the story of the loss of the manuscript – blown away into the fields of France – is particularly poignant. But the music itself remains, to blaze out inspiringly under the hands of his sister. The sound of the CD is first class.

Albéniz, Isaac (1860–1909)

Iberia (suite): *Evocaçión; El Abaicín; Fête-dieu à Séville; Triana* (orch. Arbós).
** Erato Dig. **ECD 88255**; *MCE 75316* [id.]. O de Paris, Barenboim – FALLA: *Nights in the gardens of Spain.****

Albéniz conceived *Iberia* for the piano. Arbós's orchestrations, by use of vivid orchestral colour emphasize the brightness and glare of the Spanish landscape. The languorous sophistication of Barenboim's approach is more in line with the French impressionistic view of Spain by Ravel. The conductor's cosily sentient imagery works well in the opening *Evocaçión* but misses much of the explosive gaudiness of the climax of *Fête-dieu à Séville*, while the dance rhythms of *Triana* are surely too cultivated. The Erato recording was made at a live performance, and this has not only restricted the range of the sound but added unwanted bronchial afflictions from the audience. There is one quite alarming cough in a quiet moment of *Fête-dieu à Séville*.

Cantos de España: Córdoba, Op. 232/4; Mallorca (Barcarola), Op. 202; Piezás caracteristicás: Zambra Granadina; Torre Bermaja, Op. 92/7, 12; Suite española: Granada; Sevilla; Cádiz; Asturias, Op. 47/1, 3–5.
*** CBS Dig. **CD 36679** [id.]; *40-36679* [*HMT 36679*]. John Williams (guitar).

Some of Albéniz's more colourful miniatures are here, and John Williams plays them most evocatively. His mood is slightly introvert, and the underlying technical skill is hidden in his concern for atmosphere. A most engaging recital, recorded with great faithfulness and not over-projected. The CD has striking presence, although it is not as beguiling as Julian Bream's RCA recital – see below – in catching the surrounding ambient effect. There is a good cassette.

Cantos de España: Córdoba, Op. 234/4; Mallorca, Op. 202. Suite española, Op. 47: Cádiz; Granada; Sevilla.
❀ *** RCA Dig. **RCD 14378** [id.]. Julian Bream (guitar) – GRANADOS: *Collection.**** ❀

Julian Bream is in superb form in this splendid recital, his own favourite record, vividly recorded in the pleasingly warm acoustic of Wardour Chapel, near his home in Wiltshire. The CD, with its background of complete silence, is electrifying, giving an uncanny impression of the great guitarist sitting and making music just beyond the loudspeakers. Perhaps the image is a fraction larger than life, but the effect is remarkable, and this issue was undoubtedly a landmark in recorded realism. The playing itself has wonderfully communicative rhythmic feeling, great subtlety of colour, and its spontaneity increases the impression that one is experiencing a 'live' recital. The performance of the haunting *Córdoba*, which ends the group, is unforgettable.

Suite española, Op. 47.
(*) ASV *ZCALH 949* [id.]. Alma Petchersky (piano) – FALLA: *Fantasia baetica* (with GRANADOS: *Allegro de concierto*).

Alma Petchersky is an Argentinian pianist, a sensitive and musical player of excellent credentials. Hers is at present the only available version of these justly popular salon pieces, and she is obviously thoroughly at home with them. She plays engagingly and with a natural spontaneity that gives pleasure. The recording is generally faithful, without being in the top bracket; the cassette is well balanced, but the use of iron-oxide stock means that there is some loss in the upper range.

Albinoni, Tommaso (1671–1750)

Adagio in G. min. for organ and strings (arr. Giazotto).
*** Ph. Dig. **410 606-2**; *410 606-4* [id.]. I Musici (with *Baroque Concert.****)
(M) *** Decca **417 712-2**; *417 266-4* [id.]. SCO, Münchinger – PACHELBEL: *Canon* ***; VIVALDI: *4 Seasons.***(*)
(M) *** Pickwick Dig. **PCD 802.** Scottish CO, Laredo (with *String masterpieces.****)
(*) Decca Dig. **411 973-2: *411 973-4* [id.]. SCO, Münchinger (with *Baroque concert.***(*))
** DG **415 301-2** [id.]. BPO, Karajan – CORELLI: *Concerto grosso, Op. 6/8*; VIVALDI: *4 seasons.***
(M) ** DG *419 488-4* [id.]. BPO, Karajan – PACHELBEL: *Canon and Gigue*; VIVALDI: *4 seasons.***

Albinoni's *Adagio* in Giazotto's cunning arrangement combines features from both the baroque and romantic eras, which have made it a world-wide hit with the musical public. It is much recorded in baroque and other collections, including at least one version using 'authentic' instruments which seems ironically perverse. I Musici gave it its CD début; collectors who have a soft spot for the piece will find this performance thoroughly recommendable, with nicely judged expressive feeling giving the melodic line a restrained nobility. The sound is excellent, too, in both formats, and the rest of the programme is equally successful.

No less telling is the mid-priced, digitally recorded Pickwick account, strongly contoured and most responsively played by the Scottish Chamber Orchestra under Jaime Laredo. Münchinger's two versions are also well judged, not opulent but expressive, and both the analogue and stereo recordings are of Decca's best quality. Karajan's analogue recording has, however lost some of its allure in the digital remastering. He has re-recorded it digitally with much better sound, but the performance is rather sombre – see Concerts (DG **413 309-2**).

Oboe concertos, Op. 7: Nos 3 in B flat; 6 in D.
(M) *** PRT **PVCD 8374** [id.]. Evelyn Rothwell, Pro Arte O, Barbirolli – CIMAROSA; MARCELLO: *Concertos.****

A warm welcome back to the catalogue for the first of Evelyn Rothwell's two outstanding collections of oboe concertos with her husband conducting. The early stereo still sounds well, with the oboe timbre nicely caught. The orchestral texture is not rich but the resonance provides enough fullness. Miss Rothwell's line in the two slow movements is ravishing without being overtly romantic, while the spiccato playing in the opening movement of Op. 7/6 and the sparkle of the same work's finale bring comparable pleasure. The companion collection combines Corelli with (attrib.) Haydn and Pergolesi – see below.

Alfvén, Hugo (1872–1960)

Midsummer vigil, Op. 19; The Mountain King, Op. 37; The Prodigal son, (i) Festive music, Op. 25.
** Swedish Soc. **SCD 1003** [id.]. Royal Op. O, Stockholm, Hugo Alfvén; (i) Westerberg.

Alfvén's historic recordings were made in 1954 when he was in his eighties, and they have great freshness. The Swedish Royal Opera Orchestra play with spirit and affection for him, and the recorded sound in both *Midsummer vigil* and *The Mountain King*, though dated, does credit to the Swedish engineering of the day. The charming ballet music to *The Prodigal son* fares less well for, although it was made as late as 1957, it is much less satisfactory. All this music is folk-inspired and popular – and deservedly so.

Symphony No. 1 in F min., Op. 7; A Legend of the Skerries, Op. 20.
** Swedish Soc. **SCD 1001** [id.]. Swedish RSO, Westerberg.

The recording of the symphony dates from 1972 and that of the tone-poem from 1967. The *First Symphony* is a young man's work, written in 1897; it is well crafted and has a good feeling for the received formal conventions. Its ideas are attractive without being either particularly individual or memorable. It is a thoroughly enjoyable, typically post-nationalist symphony, particularly when as alertly performed as here by the Swedish Radio Orchestra under Stig Westerberg. The tone-poem is a slightly later and rather Straussian evocation of the atmosphere of the Stockholm archipelago, dating from 1905.

Symphony No. 2 in D, Op. 11.
** Swedish Soc. **SCD 1005** [id.]. Stockholm PO, Segerstam.

The *Second Symphony* (1899) served to put Alfvén firmly on the Swedish musical map. It was first performed the day after the composer's twenty-seventh birthday, conducted by Stenhammar. Like its predecessor, the ideas are pleasing though they do not possess a particularly individual stamp. Leif Segerstam draws committed playing from the Stockholm Philharmonic, and the recording, like that of the *First Symphony*, made in 1972 is well transferred, though the acoustic is not quite ideal.

Symphony No. 4 in C min. (Från Havsbandet), Op. 11.
(*) Bluebell **ABCD 001. Söderström, Winbergh, Stockholm PO, Westerberg.

The *Fourth Symphony* (1919) evokes the other-worldly atmosphere of the beautiful archipelago that stretches out from Stockholm into the Baltic. Its subtitle is best translated as 'from the outermost skerries of the archipelago'. It has a highly romantic programme plotting the emotions of two lovers, which rather shocked contemporary opinion in Sweden as being excessively sensual. The score is opulent, sumptuous and at times rather derivative: Strauss, Reger and Debussy; with its lavish scoring (quadruple woodwind, eight horns, two harps, celeste and piano etc.) it calls to mind the *Alpine symphony*. It is no masterpiece, though there are some glorious sonorities. The wordless vocalise, prompted perhaps by the example of Nielsen in the *Sinfonia Espansiva*, is rather less satisfying. This performance does not find Söderström in best voice – her vibrato is unusually obtrusive – and the microphones lend a hard edge to Gösta Winbergh's voice. The 1979 recording, always impressively detailed, comes over splendidly in the CD format.

Alkan, Charles (1813–88)

30 Chants: Allegretto, Op. 38/2; 2 Barcarolles, Op. 65/6, Op. 70/6. Esquisses, Op. 63/4, 10, 11, 20, 21, 28, 29, 41. Gigue, Op. 24. Marche No. 1, Op. 37; Les mois: Gros temps; Carnaval; Promenade sur l'eau, Op. 74/1–3. Nocturne No. 1, Op. 22. Petit conte. Préludes, Op. 31/11, 12, 13, 15, 16. Le tambour, Op. 50/2. Toccatina, Op. 75.
(M) *** HMV *EG 270187-4* [Ara. **Z 6523**]. Ronald Smith (piano).

This collection of Alkan miniatures is certainly varied, though no one would choose to listen to it all at one sitting. Alkan collectors should note that most of these pieces have appeared before, though not in quite such realistic sound. Ronald Smith gives a dazzling account of *Carnaval* from *Les mois* at the beginning of the record, and he is in good form throughout. At the time of going to press, the CD version is available only in the USA (on the Arabesque label).

Allegri, Gregorio (1582–1652)

Miserere.
*** Gimell **CDGIM 339** [id.]. Tallis Scholars, Phillips – MUNDY: *Vox patris caelestis;* PALESTRINA: *Missa Papae Marcelli.****
(M) *** Argo *417 160-4* [id.]. King's College Ch., Willcocks (with Collection ***).
(*) DG Dig. **415 517-2; *415 517-4* [id.]. Westminster Abbey Ch., Preston – PALESTRINA: *Missa Papae Marcelli* etc.***
(M) ** Pickwick **PCD 806** [**MCAD 5847**]. Pro Cantione Antiqua, Mark Brown – TALLIS: *Lamentations* etc.**
** HMV Dig. **CDC7 47065-2** [id.]; *EL 270095-4* [Ang. *4DS 38086*]. King's College, Cambridge, Ch., Cleobury (with Concert **(*)).
** HMV Dig. **CDC7 47699-2**; *EL 270565-4*. Taverner Cons., Parrott (with *Music of the Sistine Chapel* **(*)).

Mozart was so impressed with Allegri's *Miserere* when he heard it in the Sistine Chapel (which originally claimed exclusive rights to its performance) that he wrote the music out from memory so that it could be performed elsewhere. On the much-praised Gimell version, the soaring treble solo is taken by a girl, Alison Stamp, and her memorable contribution is enhanced by the recording itself. The Tallis Scholars are ideally balanced in Merton College Chapel, Oxford, and Peter Phillips, their conductor, emphasizes his use of a double choir by placing the solo group in the echoing distance and the main choir directly in front of the listener. The contrasts are dramatic and hugely effective, and are even more telling against the background of the CD.

The earlier King's recording under Willcocks has a comparably arresting treble solo from Roy Goodman, which has genuine radiance; although the perspectives are less dramatic than on Gimell/CfP, this performance is also outstanding. It has been reissued on an excellent mid-priced cassette within a splendid collection of other King's recordings dating from the mid-1960s, including Tallis's 40-part motet, *Spem in alium* – see Concerts (Vocal Collections), below.

Preston's account with the Westminster choristers was not recorded in the Abbey but in the more intimate acoustic of All Saint's, Tooting. The performance is a fine one and, like the Argo and Gimell/CfP versions, uses the device of a double perspective to add evocation to the second group. The treble solo, though sung confidently, is more positive, less easeful in style; and the result is not quite so memorable as with its two main competitors. However, the coupling includes an outstanding performance of Palestrina's *Missa Papae Marcelli.* While the CD adds an extra sense of tangibility, the chrome cassette too is of the very highest quality.

None of the remaining versions is distinctive, although all are well sung. The Pickwick is excellently recorded and has a price advantage: the more recent King's version is acoustically mistier; Parrott's account, recorded in the Temple Church, London, is made to seem comparatively robust by the forward balance.

Alwyn, William (1905–85)

(i) *Rhapsody for piano quartet; String quartet No. 3; String trio.*
*** Chan. Dig. **CHAN 8440**; *ABTD 1153* [id.]. (i) David Willison; Qt of London.

These three works encompass half a century: the thick-textured *Rhapsody* comes from 1938, when Alwyn was in his thirties, while the *Third Quartet* was composed in 1984, the year before his death. The *String trio* comes in between, at a time when serial techniques were in vogue – but Alwyn's serialism (like Frank Martin's or Benjamin Frankel's) is skin deep and never strays far from a fundamentally tonal language. As one would expect, it is more expertly written than the earlier work and has many moments of real eloquence. The *Third Quartet* is the most important work on this record; like its two predecessors, it is a concentrated and thoughtful piece of very considerable substance, elegiac in feeling. The playing of the Quartet of London throughout (and of David Willison in the *Rhapsody*) is both committed and persuasive. As a recording, this is in the very first flight, and brings the musicians vividly into one's living-room.

String quartets Nos 1 in D min.; 2 (Spring waters).
*** Chan. Dig. *ABTD 1063* [id.]. Qt of London.

Both quartets are works of substance. The *First* comes from the mid-1950s and immediately precedes the *Third Symphony*, while its companion comes twenty years later and derives its subtitle, *Spring waters*, from Turgenev: *'My careless years, my precious days, like the waters of springtime have melted away'*. Its theme is the daunting prospect of old age, and there is a note of disillusion and resignation running through its pages. Both performances are thoroughly committed and the digital recording has clarity and presence. A rewarding issue, and in its chrome-cassette form the sound is of demonstration quality.

Fantasy-Waltzes; 12 Preludes.
(*) Chan. Dig. **CHAN 8399; *ABTD 1125* [id.]. John Ogdon (piano).

The *Fantasy-Waltzes* were written after a visit to Troldhaugen, Grieg's home near Bergen. They are highly attractive pieces, particularly the haunting *Third* in *E minor* and are excellently played by John Ogdon, who is also responsible for a perceptive insert-note. There is very occasionally a trace of roughness in his *forte* tone (in the Eighth piece, for example), but there is great delicacy elsewhere and a command of colour and atmosphere. The *12 Preludes* are fluent, inventive, beautifully wrought pieces that ought to be better known and well repay investigation. The recording, made at The Maltings, Snape, is first rate and carries the imprimatur of the composer in whose presence it was made. Recommended.

(i) *Invocations;* (ii) *A Leave-taking* (song cycles).
*** Chan. Dig. *ABTD 1117* [id.]. (i) Jill Gomez, John Constable; (ii) Anthony Rolfe-Johnson, Graham Johnson.

Almost as an offshoot from his opera, *Miss Julie*, Alwyn wrote these two song-cycles for the two singers who sang the principal roles of Julie and the Gamekeeper. In each, with a distinctive and unexpected choice of poems, Alwyn shows a keen ear for matching word-movement in music with a free arioso style. Notable in the tenor cycle, *A Leave-taking* (to words by the Victorian, John Leicester Warren), is *The Ocean wood*, subtly evocative in its sea inspirations. The soprano cycle (to words by Michael Armstrong) is almost equally distinguished, leading to a beautiful *Invocation to the Queen of Moonlight*, which suits Jill Gomez's sensuous high soprano perfectly. Excellent performances, not least from the accompanists, and first-rate recording.

Arensky, Anton (1861–1906)

(i) *Piano concerto No. 2 in F min., Op. 2;* (ii) *Egyptian nights, Op. 50a.*
(M) ** Olympia **OCD 107** [id.]. (i) Cherkassov; USSR R SO, (i) Alexeev; (ii) Demchenko – IPPOLITOV-IVANOV: *Caucasian sketches.***

Arensky's *F minor Concerto* is something of a rarity: its first subject could hardly be more Chopinesque and is obstinately memorable, and although the rather banal second theme is all too reminiscent of Liszt at his most rumbustious, the slow movement too is beautifully wrought. If the finale is less distinctive, the work is worth investigating, for the performance is a good one; Alexei Cherkassov brings sensibility and a convincing sense of rubato to the lyrical writing. The recording is somewhat two-dimensional and the piano timbre is not ideally rich but remains fully acceptable. For the most part Arensky's music has a salon pallor that robs it of freshness and vitality; but this concerto, though its debts to Chopin and Liszt are heavy, shows a vein of feeling, particularly in the slow movement, that is far from contemptible. The *Egyptian nights suite* is all that survives from a ballet, written for a visit by the Shah of Persia to St Petersburg in 1890. In the event its production was abandoned but later Diaghilev took it up, and Fokine's choreography involved the use of additional music by Glinka, Glazunov and Taniev. The six numbers which are Arensky's own are not the most potent of cheap music – they have something in common with Luigini's *Ballet Egyptien*, even if thematically much less indelible. The bright brash playing here projects the music quite effectively, though the recording has a degree of coarseness; the interest of the repertoire (including the coupling) and the generous overall playing time of this mid-priced CD (72′ 39″) earn the disc its place in the catalogue.

Violin concerto in A min., Op. 54.
(M) *** Olympia Dig. **OCD 106** [id.]. Stadler, Leningrad PO, Chernushenko – TCHAIKOVSKY: *Suite No. 3.****

This concerto, structured as a single movement, was introduced to the catalogue at the end of the 1970s by Aaron Rosand's pioneering Turnabout recording (long since deleted). It is a much later work than the *Piano concerto* and is a winning piece with a particularly endearing second-subject group theme, a tune which can be exorcized only with repeated hearing. The delicate use of waltz rhythms in the central section has great charm. The work is most persuasively played by Sergei Stadler, who has a firm rich line and a full understanding of the work's nostalgic feeling. The accompaniment by the splendid Leningrad Philharmonic Orchestra under Vladislav Chernushenko is quite admirable. If the soloist is balanced a shade closely, in all other respects the clear recording, which has excellent presence and detail, is worthy of the performance and should make many new friends for this engaging work which makes a refreshing change from the Bruch and Glazunov concertos. With its very attractive coupling, this disc, which is in the upper-middle price range, is well worth exploring.

Piano trio No. 1 in D min., Op. 32.
*** CRD *CRDC 4109* [id.]. Nash Ens. – RIMSKY-KORSAKOV: *Quintet.****
*** Chan. Dig. **CHAN 8477**; *ABTD 1188* [id.]. Borodin Trio – GLINKA: *Trio.****

Apart from the *Tchaikovsky variations*, Arensky is probably best known for this *D minor Piano trio*, published in 1894. The shades of Mendelssohn, Borodin and Tchaikovsky can clearly be discerned; while the invention is fertile and has an endearing period charm, at the same time the ideas have undoubted freshness. The account by members of the Nash Ensemble is first class in every way. These fine players capture the Slav melancholy of the *Elegia*, and in the delightful *Scherzo* Ian Brown is both delicate and nimble-fingered. The sound of the cassette is well up to CRD's usual very high standard.

On the also excellently recorded Chandos CD, the Borodins give a lively and full-blooded account of the *Trio*. The *Scherzo* comes off as well as it does on the Nash account. The chrome tape yields first-class results, too, and does justice to the Borodins' genial playing. However, the CRD issue remains the more attractive choice as it is coupled with the delightful Rimsky-Korsakov *Piano and wind quintet*.

Arne, Thomas (1710–78)

Symphonies Nos 1 in C; 2 in F; 3 in E flat; 4 in C min.
** Chan. Dig. **CHAN 8403**; *ABTD 1140* [id.]. Cantilena, Sheppard.

These four symphonies slipped from view for many years: their first publication since the original 1767 edition had to wait until the 1970s. Arne began writing them late in his career when Handel reigned supreme in England. Faced by the new-fangled symphonies of the Mannheim School and others, he was stimulated to produce works as electric in their way as those of Haydn's middle period; though there is an obvious influence by J. C. Bach, particularly in No. 3, there is much that is individual. It seems likely that the C minor, the most ambitious of the group, was not even performed in Arne's lifetime, so its rediscovery is doubly welcome.

The symphonies receive business-like performances from the Cantilena and Adrian Sheppard, perhaps a little short on charm and subtlety, though the rather close recording may exaggerate this defect. A serviceable issue that falls short of real distinction.

Cymon and Iphigenia; Frolic and free (cantatas)*; Jenny; The Lover's recantation; The Morning* (cantata)*; Sigh no more, ladies; Thou soft flowing Avon; What tho' his guilt.*
*** Hyp. Dig. **CDA 66237**; *KA 66237* [id.]. Emma Kirkby, Richard Morton, Parley of Instruments, Goodman.

Much of Arne's musical career was spent in the theatre or at the Vauxhall Pleasure Gardens because, as a Catholic, he could not find outlets for his talents in the Anglican Church. The present collection admirably shows the ingenuous simplicity of his vocal writing, very much in the mid-eighteenth-century English pastoral school with its 'Hey down derrys'. Emma Kirkby has the perfect timbre and all the vocal freshness to bring this music charmingly to life. Whether in the engaging cantatas or in the theatre songs she sparkles. *Cymon and Iphigenia*, with its tale of the 'clown' finding the ravishing Iphigenia asleep in an Elysian glade, her awakening, recognition and surprise at his expressions of ardour, then her realization that her suitor is 'comely, straight and tall' and 'might improve his awkward gait', is particularly winning. On his way to his destiny Cymon 'whistled as he went', and the flute innocently provides the whistle. Richard Morton sings well too, though his style has not always quite the easy manner of Kirkby; he is always responsive, and is suitably high-spirited in *Frolic and free* where the scoring for two flutes, two oboes, bassoon and strings is particularly felicitous. The recital ends with Emma Kirkby at her finest in *The Lover's recantation.* Excellent, warm recording, with the voices naturally projected. A most entertaining concert.

Arnold, Malcolm (born 1921)

(i; ii) *Beckus the Dandipratt: overture;* (iii; ii) *4 Cornish dances;* (i; iv) *8 English dances;* (iii; ii) *Peterloo: overture;* (i; ii) *Solitaire: Saraband; Polka.*
(M) *** HMV *TC-ESD 107780-4.* (i) Bournemouth SO; (ii) composer; (iii) CBSO; (iv) Groves.

Arnold is above all a miniaturist and his shorter pieces show his orchestral and melodic flair to best advantage. *Beckus the Dandipratt* is given a delightfully nonchalant portrayal here. The rhetoric of *Peterloo* does not quite come off, but the feeling of approaching menace at the opening is unforgettable. Best of all are the *English dances*, played by Groves with an admirable mixture of expressive feeling and gusto. What indelible little masterpieces they are. The *Solitaire* items (almost equally effective) were additional numbers added to turn the *Dances* into a ballet in 1956. The cassette is vivid, but loses a little of the sharpness and refinement of the upper range, although on side two – where the level rises a little – the *English dances* project well.

Clarinet concerto No. 1, Op. 20.
** Unicorn Dig. **DKPCD 9066**; *DKPC 9066* [id.]. Gary Gray, RPO, Newstone – COPLAND: *Concerto* *(*); LUTOSLAWSKI: *Dance preludes* **; ROSSINI: *Variations.* *(*)

Clarinet concerto No. 1; Horn concerto No. 2; Oboe concerto; Trumpet concerto.
*** HMV *EL 270264-4.* Hilton, Civil, Hunt, Wallace, Bournemouth Sinf., Del Mar.

Malcolm Arnold has more than eighteen concertos to his credit. Having been a trumpeter, he writes with uncommon skill for the instrument, and the same brilliance characterizes John Wallace's dazzling playing. The work is relatively recent, following the *Eighth Symphony* (1979); like so much of his music, it has broad appeal, but touches a richer vein of imagination in the slow movement. The *Oboe concerto* (1952), written for Leon Goossens, is played with quite superb panache and virtuosity by Gordon Hunt who is surely second to none among present-day players; Janet Hilton in the *First Clarinet concerto* (1948) and Alan Civil in the *Second Horn concerto* (1956) are hardly less brilliant. This music is well crafted, enormously facile and at times glib, but Arnold has many admirers and they will find much to delight them in these performances. The recordings are well transferred to tape.

Gary Gray gives Arnold's attractive *Clarinet concerto* its CD début; while he has the measure of the characteristically quirky secondary theme of the first movement and Harry Newstone provides a sympathetic accompaniment, the finale (and indeed the performance overall) could have had greater rhythmic lift; Janet Hilton on HMV is far preferable. The sound is very good, if resonant, and the clarinet is naturally balanced.

Guitar concerto, Op. 67.
(M) *(*) Pickwick Dig. **PCD 859**. Michael Conn, O of St John's, Smith Square, Lubbock – RODRIGO: *Concierto de Aranjuez*.**

Michael Conn gives Arnold's highly engaging *Guitar concerto* its CD début, but his performing personality is pale: he makes little of the 'lollipop' melody of the first movement and it is left to Lubbock and the orchestral strings to demonstrate its warmth. The *Adagio* is certainly atmospheric and the finale genially paced, with Lubbock's alert accompaniments adding more character than the solo playing. The digital recording is first class, naturally balanced and with vivid detail. A disappointment. We look forward to the arrival of Julian Bream's fine RCA version on CD.

(i) *Symphony No. 2, Op. 40;* (ii) *Symphony No. 5, Op. 74.* (i) *Peterloo: overture.*
*** HMV **CDC7 49513-2**. (i) Bournemouth SO, Groves; (ii) CBSO, composer.

The recoupling of two of Arnold's most impressive symphonies can be warmly welcomed. Both recordings date from the 1970s. The *Second Symphony* is one of Malcolm Arnold's best pieces, far more complex in structure than it may initially seem. Like Shostakovich, in the first movement Arnold opts for an easy-going *Allegretto*, but the undemanding open-air manner conceals genuine symphonic purpose. So with the rest of the symphony, including the beautiful slow movement – much the longest – where a haunting tune with a distant echo of the second subject of Tchaikovsky's *Pathétique* builds to a formidable climax. Arnold has developed the habit of hiding his deeper emotions behind a bright, extrovert manner, and his *Fifth Symphony* brings out this dichotomy very clearly. It is a consciously elegiac work, written in memory of friends who died young; it contains some of his most intense and emotional music but remains easily approachable. The *tempestuoso* first movement, starting with a solitary oboe, is punctuated with bursts of anger and with percussion adding brilliance; it is both tenderly valedictory and nostalgic. So too the gracefully lyrical slow movement before the dazzling scherzo and the drum-and-fife finale. The composer secures an excellent response from the Birmingham orchestra, as Groves, in Bournemouth, is equally dedicated. The compact disc transfer is outstandingly successful; indeed the sound approaches the demonstration class in its vivid detail, body and spaciousness. The *Overture* makes a highly effective encore.

Arriaga, Juan (1806–26)

String quartets Nos 1 in D min.; 2 in A; 3 in E flat.
*** CRD *CRDC 4012/3* [id.]. Chilingirian Qt.

Arriaga's three quartets serve admirably to demonstrate the strength of his musical personality. The *First* has a memorable slow movement that immediately evokes Haydn, and the opening movement of the *Second* shows a quite remarkable impulse and maturity. None of these three quartets has a bar of music not worthy of a musical mind of the highest order. The Chilingirian Quartet is one of the most polished and stylish to have emerged in the last decade; these performances impressively present a case for regarding these works as weightier than we have generally thought. If Arriaga stands at a pivotal point between the eighteenth and nineteenth centuries, the Chilingirians firmly plant him in a world that knew Beethoven. Quite apart from completeness and ample recording, these CRD performances – notably of the *Andante* of the *D minor*, here very measured – bring new illumination to a lost genius. The cassette quality is first class; the tape coupling Nos 2 and 3 approaches a demonstration standard in its vividness and excellent detail.

Auric, Georges (1899–1983)

L'Eventail de Jeanne: (complete ballet, including music by Delannoy, Ferroud, Ibert, Milhaud, Poulenc, Ravel, Roland-Manuel, Roussel, Florent Schmitt).
Les Mariés de la Tour Eiffel: (complete ballet, including music by Honegger, Milhaud, Poulenc, Tailleferre).
❀ *** Chan. Dig. **CHAN 8356**; *ABTD 1119* [id.]. Philh. O, Simon.

Composite works, such as *Les Vendredis*, or the *Sellinger's Round* of Britten, Lennox Berkeley, Tippett and others, rarely prove a satisfactory whole; such is undoubtedly the case in both of the ballets recorded here – but what a delightful and exhilarating assortment they make! Only two of the pieces in *Les Mariés de la Tour Eiffel*, the product of a collaboration between Cocteau and *Les Six*, are longer than three minutes and most are much shorter; similarly, the longest of the feathers in *L'Eventail* (*Jeanne's Fan*), the *Kermesse valse* of Florent Schmitt, runs to barely five minutes (and, incidentally, is the weakest). This ballet was the idea of a Parisian society hostess who presented ten composers with a feather from her fan and invited them to write a piece each for her ballet pupils. A carefree spirit and captivating wit run through both these inventive scores. The Ravel *Fanfare* is among the shortest and most original of the contributions to *L'Eventail de Jeanne*, and there are many other charming things apart from the best-known number, Poulenc's *Pastourelle*. Roland-Manuel's inventive *Canarie* is a real discovery and so, too, is Roussel's *Sarabande* – a haunting and lovely piece. Honegger's contribution to *Les Mariés*, a highly effective *Funeral march*, will also be new to most collectors; it incorporates the theme from Milhaud's *Wedding march* as well as the Waltz from Gounod's *Faust*. In fact these pieces are full of imagination and fun – even the Ibert *Valse* quotes the Ravel *Valses nobles*. Geoffrey Simon and the Philharmonia Orchestra give a very good account of themselves and the Chandos recording is little short of spectacular. Its detail is quite marvellously sharp on CD, and the chrome cassette is remarkably good, too.

Bach, Carl Philipp Emanuel (1714–88)

Flute concerto in D min., Wq. 22.
(M) **(*) ASV **CDQS 6012**; *ZCQS 6012*. Dingfelder, ECO, Mackerras – HOFFMEISTER: *Concertos Nos 6 & 9.***(*)

Those who are interested in the Hoffmeister coupling rather than a C. P. E. Bach collection will find Ingrid Dingfelder's playing both spirited and stylish, while Mackerras's accompaniments match polish with vigour. The sound-quality too is admirably vivid and this CD reissue is competitively priced. There is also a good (and cheaper) cassette.

Flute concertos: in D, Wq. 22; in A min., Wq. 166; in A, Wq. 169.
*** Capriccio Dig. **10 104** [id.]; *CC 27 146*. Eckart Haupf, C. P. E. Bach C O, Haenchen.

Flute concertos: in B flat, Wq. 167; in G, Wq. 169.
*** Capriccio Dig. **10 105** [id.]; *CC 27 147*. Eckart Haupf, C. P. E. Bach C O, Haenchen.

With Frederick the Great of Prussia a keen flautist himself as well as a composer, the flute was a favourite instrument with all the principal composers at the Berlin court in his time. C. P. E. Bach contributed strongly with these five concertos – though, with solo writing of such virtuosity, Frederick himself can hardly have been the intended performer.

This collection, with the five works presented in chronological order, squeezes the first three on to the first disc, the remaining two on to the second. If the second disc is the less generous, it does contain the last and finest of the concertos, a splendid work in G, written in 1755, which from its bold sweeping opening onward magnetizes the ear with its quick-changing argument. The central E minor *Largo* too is among the most moving of Bach's slow movements. Eckart Haupf gives lively, cleanly articulated performances, well supported by the strong, full-bodied and vigorous accompaniments of the C. P. E. Bach Chamber Orchestra under Hartmut Haenchen. Full, atmospheric recording from East German VEB engineers. There are excellent matching cassettes.

Harpsichord concerto in A, Wq. 29; Flute quartets Nos 1 in A min., 2 in D; 3 in G, Wq. 93–95.
*** Ph. Dig. **416615-2**; *416615-4* [id.]. Hazelzet, Peeters, Van der Meer, Amsterdam Bar. O, Ton Koopman.

The *A major Concerto* comes from the 1750s and is something of a rarity on record. Koopman gives a very spirited account of it, with all the brio one could ask for in the outer movements and a splendidly thoughtful *Largo*. He gets excellent and responsive playing from the Amsterdam Baroque Orchestra. The three *Flute quartets* are late, from the last year of Bach's life, and are given predictably sensitive performances by Hazelzet and his excellent colleagues. Koopman opts for the harpsichord rather than a fortepiano, but he plays with such panache that few will be worried. The Philips recording as usual is beautifully clean and finely detailed. The chrome tape too is cleanly transferred.

Harpsichord concertos, Wq. 43/1–6.
*** HMV Dig. **CDS7 49207-8** (2). Van Asperen, Melante 81 Orchestra.

These six concertos come from 1771 during Bach's Hamburg period, and they are disturbingly original and volatile in temperament. Period instruments are used to produce an excellently light and transparent texture. The playing of Bob van Asperen is a delight: bright, vital and intelligent; and the recording is very fine indeed. Another indispensable issue for collectors interested in this intriguing composer.

Harpsichord concerto in G, Wq. 43/5.
(*) CRD **CRD 3411 [id.]. Pinnock, E. Concert – VIVALDI: *Trial between harmony and invention* etc.**(*)

An excellent performance of an attractive work, using original instruments, nicely balancing the claims of modern ears and total authenticity. This is a bonus for a pair of CDs containing all the concertos of Vivaldi's Op. 8 except *The Four Seasons*. The CD transfer smooths the treble a little but maintains most of the original focus.

Double harpsichord concerto in F, Wq. 46.
*** DG Dig. **419 256-2** [id.]. Staier, Hill, Col. Mus. Ant., Goebel – W. F. BACH: *Double concerto* etc.***

Carl Philipp Emanuel composed some 52 keyboard concertos in all – the first in 1733 and the last in the year of his death, 1788. Wq. 46 comes from 1740 and is a particularly interesting piece. Its first movement sets out in a lively F major, but there is an almost immediate contrast in mood and a shift to the minor, after which he touches on different keys before returning to F. The ideas are full of variety and the slow movement is particularly thoughtful and introspective. This most inventive piece is played with vitality, imagination and dedication by these artists; the recording is exceptionally well balanced, with the two solo instruments taking up the right amount of aural space in relation to the orchestra. And how dazzling they are in the finale!

Oboe concertos: in B flat, Wq. 164; in E flat, Wq. 165.
** Capriccio Dig. **10 069** [id.]; *CC 27 119.* Glaetzner, New Bach Coll. Mus., Pommer – J. C. BACH: *Concerto.***

Max Pommer and his Leipzig players are less lively and imaginative in these C. P. E. Bach *Oboe concertos* than their Berlin colleagues in the flute works. Burkhardt Glaetzner's very reedy, piping oboe tone is distinctive but makes for monotony. The two works themselves – well supplemented here by an *Oboe concerto* of Johann Christian Bach – date from 1765, well after the *Flute concertos,* fine works both with their abrupt changes of mood. The recording, full but rather bass-heavy, emphasizes the discrepancy between Leipzig and Berlin performances in the Capriccio series. The cassette omits the J. C. Bach Concerto.

Organ concertos: in G; in E flat, Wq. 34–5; Fantasia and fugue in C min., Wq. 119/7; Prelude in D, Wq. 70/7.
*** Capriccio Dig. **10 135** [id.]; *CC 27 114.* Roland Munch, C. P. E. Bach C O, Haenchen.

C. P. E. Bach writing for the organ, at a time when that instrument had grown rather unfashionable with composers, inevitably sets up echoes of his father. They were written in 1755 and 1759 respectively, the first optionally for harpsichord, the second lighter in style and less ambitious in scale, with a lovely central *Adagio* to muted string accompaniment. With much of the writing involving simple alternation of orchestra and soloist, Hartmut Haenchen and his admirable C. P. E. Bach Chamber Orchestra reinforce the lively expressiveness of the writing, alongside the soloist, Roland Munch, on a Berlin baroque organ of the 1750s. The two solo pieces are impressive too, though here the J.S.B. echoes fail to expand satisfyingly, when the scale is so much less ambitious. Full, atmospheric recording as in the other Berlin recordings of Capriccio's C. P. E. Bach series. There is a good chrome tape.

Berlin sinfonias. in C; in F, Wq. 174/5: in E min.; in E flat, Wq. 178/9; in F, Wq. 181.
*** Capriccio Dig. **10 103**; *CC 27 105* [id.]. C. P. E. Bach C O, Haenchen.

This issue represents Volume 1 in an enterprising and ambitious series which aims to record all the music of C. P. E. Bach. The *Berlin sinfonias* are most welcome as they have not previously been recorded. They span the years between 1755 and 1762 when Bach was at Potsdam. The music has consistent vitality and colour – the use of flutes in the *Andante* of the *F major,* Wq. 151, makes an appealingly sensuous contrast to the reedier oboes in the outer movements. The playing of Haenchen's excellent C. P. E. Bach group is alert and vigorous, with airy textures and attractively sprung rhythms. Modern instruments are used in the best possible way so that, without any of the excesses of authenticism, the sounds have body, yet textures are not too ample for the period. Slow movements have expressive commitment without any suggestion of romanticism, and there is a fine sense of balance so that the boldness of Bach's inspiration is well projected. Excellent sound and a first-class matching chrome cassette.

6 Hamburg sinfonias, Wq. 182/1–6.
*** DG **415 300-2** [id.]. E. Concert, Pinnock.
*** Capriccio Dig. **10 106** [id.]; *CC 27 145.* C. P. E. Bach C O, Haenchen.
*** O-L **417 124-2**; *417 124-4* [id.]. AAM, Hogwood.

Hardly performed at all (even in C. P. E. Bach's lifetime), totally neglected until the 1930s and rarely heard even then, the six *Hamburg string sinfonias* have now triumphantly found their niche, thanks to records. Written for Baron von Swieten in 1773, they are magnificent examples of Bach's later style when, after the years at the Berlin court, he had greater freedom in Hamburg. They are particularly striking in their unexpected twists of imagination with wild, head-reeling modulations and sudden pauses which suggest the twentieth century rather than the eighteenth. The abrasiveness of such music comes out sharply in the kind of authenticity favoured by the Academy of Ancient Music. Hogwood continually has one responding as to new music, not least in the dark, bare, slow movements and this is reflected in the sharply focused sound. However, many listeners may find the angularity does not make for relaxed listening; they can turn to the English Concert under Pinnock which offers a performing style no less authentic than Hogwood's but with more concern for eighteenth-century poise and elegance. The 1960 analogue recording sounds splendidly fresh and clear in its remastered format. Hogwood's set dates from 1979 and has an excellent equivalent tape which smooths a little of the aggressiveness on the treble.

There is clearly still room for a further alternative, in the newest digital recordings which are part of Capriccio's integral series of C. P. E. Bach's music, using modern instruments. Hartmut Haenchen and the strings of the C. P. E. Bach Chamber Orchestra give attractively warm, red-blooded performances. Though ensemble is not always ideally refined, allegros are strong and vigorous, and the extra sweetness of the lovely *Adagios* is most welcome. Vivid, full recording to match and a lively chrome tape.

CHAMBER AND INSTRUMENTAL MUSIC

Flute sonatas: in D, Wq. 83; in E, Wq. 84; in G, Wq. 85; in G, Wq. 86.
(*) Denon Dig. **C37 7807 [id.]. András Adorján, Huguette Dreyfus.

These sonatas come from 1745–55 when Carl Philipp Emanuel was at Potsdam. They are less exploratory in idiom and less unpredictable than is often the case with this composer. Most inward-looking is the slow movement of the E major (given mistakenly as in E minor in the booklet). Each is entitled 'for harpsichord obbligato and flute', which explains why Alfred Wotquenne classified them as works for the keyboard, not flute. They are pleasing if somewhat bland. The recordings were made in Tokyo in 1976 and are well balanced, with the players neither too forward nor recessed. András Adorján, the Hungarian-born flautist, has an agreeably sweet tone. The CD offers a total playing time of 47 minutes.

Flute sonatas: in E min., Wq. 124; in G; in A min.; in D, Wq. 127–9; in G, Wq. 133; in G, Wq. 134.
*** Capriccio Dig. **10 101** [id.]; *CC 27 101*. Eckart Haupf, Siegfried Pank, Armin Thalheim.

This issue in the C. P. E. Bach series collects six of the composer's eleven flute sonatas in fresh, lively performances, well recorded. The early ones, written much more under his father's influence, prove the more original to modern ears. The opening *Adagios* with their chromatic progressions have overtones of Passion music within a small compass. The six pieces last, in all, less than 50 minutes, ending with one written in Bach's Hamburg period, two years before he died, altogether lighter and more conventionally classical, presenting an interesting perspective on the rest.

Sonatinas: in G, Wq. 98; in F, Wq. 104; in E flat, Wq. 105; in B flat, Wq. 110.
*(*) HMV Dig. **CDC7 47655-2**. Coll. Aur. with Virginia Black, Eric Lynn Kelley.

In all, C. P. E. Bach composed ten sonatinas for keyboard and various instruments, as well as two more for two keyboards. Of these only three (including the *F major*, Wq. 104) were published in his lifetime. The works on this disc were all composed in Berlin between 1762 and '64. They are something of an experiment in which Carl Philipp Emanuel combined elements of the concerto and the suite, setting the keyboard into an ensemble usually comprising two horns, two flutes, two violins, viola and bass. In the *G major*, Wq. 98, the harpsichord writing is confined to a predominantly decorative role; elsewhere the two players (harpsichord and fortepiano) almost approach the role of concerto soloists. The tonal progress of the first movement of the *E flat Sonatina*, Wq. 104, is Carl Philipp Emanuel at his most eloquent. The recordings are truthful and present, but the performances leave much to be desired: the two soloists are accomplished, but although the fast movements are generally lively, slow ones tend to be sluggish and plodding.

Trio sonatas: in A min., Wq. 148; in D, Wq. 151.
(*) Denon Dig. **C37 7093 [id.]. Nicolet, Holliger, Jaccottet – J. S. BACH: *Trio sonatas.***(*)

Originally written for flute and violin (or two violins) and continuo, these *Trio sonatas* sound attractive enough in the combination of flute and oboe, although one would have welcomed a greater degree of dynamic variation in the playing. This effect, however, is partly caused by the resonance. In spite of the catalogue numbering, the *D major Sonata* was probably written about a decade before the *A minor* work, yet it is undoubtedly the finer piece, showing Carl Philipp Emanuel's originality and flair to good effect. Both playing and recording are admirably vivid.

Trio sonata in G, Wq. 157.
*** CBS Dig. **MK 37813** [id.]. Rampal, Stern, Ritter, Parnas – J. C. F., J. S. and W. F. BACH: *Trio sonatas.****

A particularly attractive work, opening with a fine *Adagio* and with a memorably spirited central movement. The playing is distinguished and the balance excellent. The CD is very clear and believable, but could have been improved with a shade more ambience. A recommendable and rewarding collection.

Viola da gamba sonatas: in G min., Wq. 88; in C; in D, Wq. 136–7; Fantasia for fortepiano, Wq. 59.
* Capriccio Dig. **10 102** [id.]; *CC 27 102.* Siegfried Pank, Christiane Jaccottet.

In Capriccio's C. P. E. Bach series this collection is one of the less attractive items, with square, unimaginative performances of three viola da gamba *Sonatas*, the first two with clavichord (amplified to make it sound like toasting fork on birdcage), the last (including a beautiful central *Larghetto*) with more congenial accompaniment on fortepiano. Christiane Jaccottet, whose contribution till then is as stolid as Siegfried Pank's angular, rough-toned gamba playing, then suddenly blossoms in a thoughtful, imaginative performance of an improvisation-like *Fantasia.*

Die letzten Leiden des Erlösers (The Last Sufferings of the Saviour), Wq. 233.
*** HMV **CDS7 47753-8**. Schlick, Reyghere, Patriasz, Pregardien, Egmond, Coll Vac. Ghent, La Petite Bande, Kuijken.

The Israelites in the desert (1769) which Archiv issued some years ago alerted us to the quality of the oratorios C. P. E. Bach wrote in the late 1760s and '70s after he succeeded Telemann at Hamburg. *Die letzten Leiden des Erlösers* (1770) has moments of even greater inspiration than its immediate predecessor; its invention has nobility and originality – though it must be admitted that there are some passages which are routine. However, the restless intelligence and sensibility which pervade so much of his music are all in evidence. As Eugene Helm points out, the normal plan of the da capo aria is expanded to ABABA, with written-out varied repeats as in the fine aria, *Donner nur ein Wort der Macht* that ends the first disc. *Die letzten Leiden* has good claims to be considered one of Carl Philipp Emanuel's masterpieces, and it is given a first-class performance by the excellent team of soloists assembled here. The singing of the Collegium

Vocale of Ghent is also eloquent, and the playing of La Petite Bande under Sigiswald Kuijken is predictably vivid and alive. Fine, well-balanced recording, made in collaboration with West-Deutscher Rundfunk.

Bach, Johann Christian (1735–82)

Cello concerto in C min.; Sinfonia concertante in A for violin, cello and orchestra.
** Chan. Dig. **CHAN 8470**; *ABTD 1181* [id.]. Yuli and Eleonora Turovsky, I Musici di Montreal, Y. Turovsky – BOCCHERINI: *Cello concerto.***

The *Cello concerto* would seem to be a conjectural reconstruction; Warburton does not include it in his Grove work-list. Saint-Saëns made an arrangement of it for piano, but it is not clear who prepared the present transcription or reconstruction. The outer movements would seem to look backwards to baroque models though not its much later companion. The *A major Sinfonia concertante* comes from the mid-1770s and has all the charm and grace one associates with its composer. Yuli Turovsky's playing has warmth and good taste, though his intonation is not always completely true. He directs his Canadian ensemble with style and spirit, and the recording, too, is well defined and warm.

Oboe concerto in F.
(M) *** Ph. *412 354-4*. Heinz Holliger, ECO, Leppard – FIALA: *Cor anglais concerto*; HUMMEL: *Introduction, theme and variations.****
** Capriccio Dig. **10 069** [id.]. Glaetzner, New Bach Coll. Mus., Pommer – C. P. E. BACH: *Concertos.***

The manuscript for this work was rediscovered in the British Museum and its authenticity is not certain. It is an attractive, if not an especially individual, work, but with an appealing *Larghetto* and a florid finale, which Holliger dispatches effortlessly. Indeed the playing is of the highest quality and Holliger contributes his own cadenzas. The sound is fresh, full and well balanced.

This appealing concerto is also included with the recordings of Carl Philipp Emanuel *Oboe concertos* in Capriccio's integral series of that composer's music, but the performance, like those of its couplings, is acceptable rather than outstanding – see above.

Six 'favourite' overtures: Nos 1–3 in D; 4 in C; 5–6 in G.
*** O-L **417 148-2** [id.]. AAM, Hogwood.

J. C. Bach's *Six 'favourite' overtures* were published as a set in London in 1763 for use in the concert hall, although their original derivation was theatrical. They are all short and succinct Italian-style pieces in three movements (fast–slow–fast), and they show great variety of invention and imaginative scoring (using double wind, horns and strings). The performances here are characteristically alert and vivid and there are many features to stay in the mind: the trio for wind instruments in the finale of No. 1; the attractively robust outer movements of No. 3; the Vivaldi-like figuration of the finale of No. 4; the tripping strings in the *Andante* of No. 5. This is not an issue to play all at once; when dipped into, however, it offers delightful music played in a refreshingly spirited (and stylish) way. The analogue recording dates from 1978. It sounds impressively fresh in its CD format.

Sinfonia concertante in A for violin, cello and orchestra; Grand Overture in E flat.
(*) CBS **MK 39964; *IMT 39964* [id.]. Yo-Yo Ma, Zukerman, St Paul CO – BOCCHERINI: *Cello concerto* (arr. Grützmacher).***

The performance of the *Sinfonia concertante* is generally preferable to the Chandos alternative, although couplings may have to be considered, and there are some stylistic incongruities, notably the continuo added to the *Overture* for double orchestra which is a fine work, and could manage without such fanciful imitations. Generally, however, this is an enjoyable pairing and the playing of the soloists in the *Sinfonia concertante* establishes a fine musical interplay, although the cadenza is over-elaborated. Good sound, with excellent stereo effects.

Oboe quartet in B flat, Op. 8/6.
*** Denon Dig. **C37 7119** [id.]. Holliger, Salvatore Qt – M. HAYDN: *Divertimenti*; MOZART: *Adagio.****

The unpretentious elegance of J. C. Bach's *Oboe quartet* is beautifully caught by the incomparable Holliger and his stylish partners. An excellent coupling for even more compelling works, all vividly recorded.

Quintets: in C, Op. 11/1; in D, Op. 11/6; in D, Op. 22/1. Sextet in C.
*** DG Dig. **423 385-2** [id.]. English Concert.

This is a self-recommending collection. The music, delectably scored for unexpected combinations of instruments, is wonderfully fresh and inventive in these spirited performances, with the sounds of the original instruments adding bite and colour and readily finding the music's charm. This was one of the last recordings made by the fine oboist, David Reichenberg, whose playing is recognizably stylish and vivid. The sound has splendid realism and presence.

Bach, Johann Christoph Friedrich (1732–95)

Sonata for fortepiano, flute and violin in C, HWVII/7.
*** CBS Dig. **MK 37813** [id.]. Rampal, Stern, Ritter, Parnas – C. P. E., J. S. and W. F. BACH: *Trio sonatas.****

An engagingly inventive piece throughout its three movements, with the role of the fortepiano important enough to imply a solo concertante chamber piece. The artists play expertly and readily convey their enjoyment, while the balance is very adroit. The clarity of the recording is emphasized on CD without artificiality, but a little more ambient glow would have been welcome.

The Bach family before Johann Sebastian

Bach, Johann Christoph (1642–1703)
Bach, Johann Michael (1648–94)
Bach, Georg Christoph (1642–97)
Bach, Heinrich (1615–92)
J. C. BACH: Cantatas: *Ach, dass ich Wassers g'nug hätte; Er erhub sich Streit; Die Furcht des Herren; Herr wende dich und sei mir gnädig; Meine Freundin; Wir bist du denn.* J. M. BACH: Cantatas: *Ach bleib uns, Herr Jesu Christ; Ach, wie sehnlich wart' ich der Zeit; Auf lasst uns den Herren loben; Es ist ein grosser Gewinn; Liebster Jesu, hör mein Flehen.* G. C. BACH: Cantata: *Siehe, wie fein und lieblich.* H. BACH: *Ich danke dir, Gott.*
*** DG **419 253-2** (2) [id.]. Soloists, Rheinische Kantorei, Col. Mus. Ant., Goebel.

Johann Sebastian not only wrote a short family history, he also made a compilation of the family's music (*Altbachisches Archiv*), which he passed on to Carl Philipp Emanuel. These eventually found their way into the archives of the Berlin Singakademie and were published in 1935; the whole collection was destroyed during the war. These two CDs include all the cantatas and vocal concertos by Bach's forefathers that he preserved, with, in addition, a vocal concerto, *Herr, wende dich*, by Johann Christoph Bach. This survives in an autograph at the Berlin Staatsbibliotek and receives its first publication here in any form.

Johann Michael Bach, who was organist and parish clerk at Gehren for the last two decades of his life and died when Johann Sebastian was nine, is represented by his five delightfully fresh and inventive cantatas. He was obviously familiar with such models as Hassler and Praetorius. All are much shorter even than those of Buxtehude and much less ambitious than *Meine Freundin, du bist schön* by his older brother, Johann Christoph, the greatest of Bach's precursors. This is the most substantial of the works on the first disc, and the five other cantatas of his dominate its companion. Bach praised Johann Christoph as profound, and Carl Philipp Emanuel spoke of him as a 'great and expressive composer'. There are certainly many powerful and haunting passages to be found in *Meine Freundin, du bist schön* and the lament *Ach, dass ich Wassers g'nug hätte*. Only one work by his father, Heinrich Bach, survives, the vocal concerto *Ich danke dir, Gott* a short piece of some six minutes which calls to mind the Venetian style of Schütz. The last of the four Bachs represented in the set was his nephew Georg Christoph, a cousin of the brothers Johann Michael and Christoph. His charming wedding cantata, *Siehe, wie fein und lieblich*, records a happy family event. This set breaks new ground for the gramophone and does so with great distinction, for the performances and recording are of the very highest quality. An invaluable issue and indispensable for collectors with an interest in Johann Sebastian.

Bach, Johann Sebastian (1685–1750)

The Art of fugue, BWV 1080.
(M) ** Decca *414 326-4* (2). Stuttgart CO, Münchinger.

The Art of fugue; Canons, BWV 1072/8 and 1086/7; Musical offering, BWV 1079.
** DG Dig. **413 642-2** (3). Col. Mus. Ant., Goebel.

The Art of fugue; Canons, BWV 1072/8; 1086; Goldberg canons, BWV 1087.
**(*) DG *413 728-4* (2) [id.]. Col. Mus. Ant., Goebel.

How to perform *The Art of fugue* has always presented problems, since Bach's own indications are so sparse. The very fact that (with the exception of the items for two harpsichords) the whole complex argument can be compassed by ten fingers on one keyboard points to that option, but there is no doubt that for the listener at large, not following the score, a more varied instrumentation is both easier on the ear and clearer in its presentation of argument.

In the Cologne performance, the movements are divided between strings and solo harpsichord, and the two harpsichord players are often imaginative and expressive. The rhythmic vigour of the playing of Musica Antiqua confounds the scholarly idea that this is music *not* intended for public performance. But there are snags to the authentic style, notably the bite on the string tone and also the expressive bulges which are at times exaggerated. However, this is generally much to be preferred to the somewhat joyless *Musical offering* with which it comes in harness on the CD set, together with some newly found *Canons*, attractive shavings from the master's workbench. The recording is remarkably clean and present. The cassettes offer the *Canons* but are not hampered with the *Musical offering*. They are smoothly transferred.

For those seeking a mid-priced set of *The Art of fugue* alone, Münchinger's cassette alternative might be considered. It is a good deal mellower than the DG version and its essential sobriety has a cumulative effect. The instrumentation usually allots the fugues to the strings and the canons to solo woodwind, varied with solo strings. After the incomplete quadruple fugue, Münchinger rounds off the work with the chorale prelude, *Vor deinen Thron*, in principle quite wrong, but moving in practice. The recording comes from a vintage Decca period.

Brandenburg concertos Nos 1–6, BWV 1046/51; Orchestral suites Nos 1–4, BWV 1066/9; (i) *Triple concerto in A min., BWV 1044.*
(*) DG **413 629-2 (4) [id.]. E. Concert, Pinnock; (i) with Beznosiuk, Standage.

This package of four CDs continues the DG Archiv Bach Edition. The merits of Pinnock's *Brandenburg concertos* are enhanced on the present CD transfer which is made at a high level, giving the impression of vivid presence. As performances, the orchestral *Suites* are somewhat more controversial and, as so often in performances on period instruments, there is a distinct loss of breadth and grandeur. In the *Triple concerto*, for the same forces as the *Fifth Brandenburg* (flute, violin, harpsichord and strings), Lisa Beznosiuk and Simon Standage are both excellent and Pinnock himself is at his very best. The CD has wonderful clarity here. However, the alternative three-CD set omitting BWV 1044 is more economical – see below.

Brandenburg concertos Nos 1–6, BWV 1046/51; Suites Nos 1–4, BWV 1066/9.
(*) DG **423 492-2 (3) [id.]. E. Concert, Pinnock.
(*) HMV Dig. **CDS7 47881-8; *EX 270459-5* (3). ASMF, Marriner.

Marriner's latest, HMV digital recordings of the *Brandenburgs* and *Suites* are economically linked together on three CDs. The *Suites* are also available separately on tape – see below. If his earliest version of the *Brandenburgs* was marred by the eccentric edition used (attempting to re-create the original unamended text sent to the Margrave of Brandenburg) and the second involved star soloists who, with their strong instrumental personalities, may to some ears stand out too strikingly from the rest, this third essay is unexceptionable, with fine teamwork, superb ensemble and well-judged speeds, never too hectic. However, although the playing is freshly conceived, it also has a certain urbane quality (although this does not apply to George Malcolm's harpsichord contribution, notably in the special link provided in No. 3). Many will like performances with a little more eccentricity, not quite so safe, and they will turn to Marriner's earlier Philips set (see below) or, if original instruments are required, to Gardiner, or to Pinnock (the purchase of whose version involves a less economical package of four CDs including the *Triple concerto*, BWV 1044 – see above). Marriner's new recording of the *Suites* is a worthy successor to his earliest, Argo set, and the vividness of the playing is enhanced by the excellent sound, full in texture yet transparent, too.

Brandenburg concertos Nos 1–6, BWV 1046/51.
*** DG Dig. **410 500/1-2**; *410 500/1-4* [id.]. E. Concert, Pinnock.
*** Ph. **400 076/7-2**; *7654 058* (2) [id.]. ASMF, Marriner.
(M) *** Pickwick Dig. **PCD 830** (1–3); **PCD 845** (4–6). ECO, Ledger.
(M) *** Ph. **420 345/6-2**; *420 345/6-4* [id.]. ECO Leppard.
(*) HMV Dig. **CDC7 47045-2 (1, 2 & 6); **CDC7 47046-2** (3, 4 & 5) [id.]. Linde Cons., Linde.
(*) Erato Dig. **ECD 88054/5; *MCE 751342* (2) [id.]. Amsterdam Bar. O, Koopman.
(*) Ph. Dig. **412 790-2; *412 790-4* (2) [id.]. I Musici.
(*) O-L Dig. **414 187-2; *414 187-4* (2) [id.]. AAM, Hogwood.
(M) ** DG *419 654/5-4* [id.]. LAPO, Zukerman.
(M) *(*) Tel. **ZS8 43626/7** [id.]. VCM, Harnoncourt.

Brandenburg concertos Nos 1–6; Triple concerto in A min. for flute, violin & harpsichord, BWV 1044.
(*) DG Dig. **423 116-2** (2). Col. Mus. Ant., Goebel.

The current wide range of choice for the *Brandenburgs* (including Marriner's latest digital HMV set coupled with the *Suites* – see above) means that now there is surely a CD set to suit all tastes.

Pinnock continues to hold his place at the top of the list in offering the most exhilarating musical experience. His DG performances represent the peak of his achievement as an advocate of authentic performance, with sounds that are clear and refreshing but not too abrasive. Interpretatively he tends to opt for faster speeds in outer movements, relatively slow in *Andantes*, with a warm but stylish degree of expressiveness – as in the lovely account of the slow movement of No. 6 – but from first to last there is no routine. Soloists are outstanding, and so is the recording, with the CDs transferred at a very high level, giving the sound great immediacy. The chrome cassettes, too, are vivid and clear, if marginally less cleanly focused.

For those who still cannot quite attune their ears to the style of string playing favoured by the authentic school, there are several excellent alternatives. Marriner's analogue Philips set has been remastered since it was first issued and the sound is both natural and lively. Above all, these performances communicate warmth and enjoyment; and they are strong in personality, with Henryk Szeryng, Jean-Pierre Rampal and Michala Petri adding individuality to three of the concertos without breaking the consistency of beautifully sprung performances. George Malcolm is the ideal continuo player, as he is in the later HMV recording. There are good cassettes. However, this set has to face strong competition in the mid-priced range.

On Pickwick, Ledger has the advantage of fresh and detailed digital recording. He directs resilient, well-paced readings of all six concertos, lively yet never over-forced. The slow movements in particular are most beautifully done, persuasively and without mannerism. Flutes rather than recorders are used in No. 4.

Leppard's Philips set, also in the mid-priced range, is higher-powered than Ledger's, whose gentler manner will for many be easier to live with. But the exhilaration of the Leppard set is undeniable, even though the element of controversy remains surrounding the consistently fast tempi he adopts throughout. With sparkling solo playing (including John Wilbraham's crisp trumpet in No. 2 and a piquant recorder contribution from the late David Munrow in No. 4) there is much to enjoy here, though Leppard's own harpsichord solo in No. 5 is less flexible than would be ideal. The remastered analogue sound is full and ample – the horns in No. 1 especially so – but the forward balance ensures a good overall clarity on the CDs; the cassettes have more bass resonance and are not quite so sharply defined.

Among the other full-priced versions, the Linde and Koopman sets remain fairly competitive. The Linde Consort is one of the most stylish and responsive of authentic performing groups working in Europe and their recording sounds very fresh and vivid on CD. It can be warmly recommended with sprung rhythms and generally well-chosen tempi, and these compact discs deserve to rank alongside Pinnock's set.

Relaxed and intimate, Koopman's account is also among the most attractive using period instruments, another alternative to Pinnock's outstanding version for those who prefer expressive contrasts to be less sharply marked. Like Pinnock, Koopman is not afraid to read *Affettuoso* on the slow movement of No. 5 as genuinely expressive and warm, though without sentimentality. As with Pinnock, players are one to a part, with excellent British soloists included in the band. In the *Third Concerto*, Koopman effectively interpolates the *Toccata in G*, BWV 916, as a harpsichord link between the two movements. The sound on CD is immediate, but not aggressively so. There are good chrome cassettes but the quality is marginally less clean on top than in the disc versions.

I Musici are joined by distinguished soloists. Heinz Holliger brings expressive finesse (and nicely judged embellishments) to the principal oboe role, while Hermann Baumann leads the superb horn playing in No. 1. Guy Touvron's trumpet bravura is as arresting in No. 2 as it is stylish, and the recording balances him effectively with the oboe and recorder. The readings are strong and direct, with allegros powerfully energetic at generally fast speeds, the string playing heard at its finest in the extremely energetic finale of No. 3, which also reveals clear antiphonal detail. The sound is very vivid, close and immediate, without being aggressive, matching the performances. Where I Musici fall short is on rhythmic imagination in slow movements, with bass lines at times too evenly stressed, perhaps owing to the absence of a director, but the plainness and honesty of these invigorating accounts will appeal to many. The digital recording is strikingly 'present' on CD, but the slightly smoother chrome cassettes also make an excellent impression.

Though Hogwood's set of *Brandenburgs* is notably less persuasive than Pinnock's, also on period instruments, with often brisk speeds, more metrical and less well sprung, the distinctive point is that unlike most rivals he has chosen the original Cöthen score rather than the usual text as sent to the Margrave of Brandenburg. Besides many detailed differences, this version has no *Polonaise* in the *First Concerto*, and the harpsichord cadenza in No. 5 is much less elaborate, 'more convincingly proportioned' as Hogwood himself suggests. Some may prefer the extra directness of Hogwood's approach over Pinnock's, with charm never a part of the mixture, more abrasive string-tone and brisker, less expressive slow movements. Excellent recorded sound, with the expected added presence on CD. The chrome cassettes have a slight loss of refinement in the upper range.

Zukerman's performances are fresh and technically impressive, with good playing from soloists of the Los Angeles Philharmonic. Sometimes rhythms are a shade unrelenting, as in Nos 2 and 3, but No. 5 has a fine slow movement and a vivacious finale. The sound is good, but there are other finer sets in the mid-price range.

Harnoncourt's late-1960s analogue set (recorded in the Great Hall of the Schönburg Palace in Vienna) was an early adventure in authenticity; it has undoubted interest but is of uneven musical appeal. The excessive closeness of the sound-picture, which is consistent throughout, means there is nothing like a real *pianissimo*, and internal balances produce variable degrees of success: Nos 2 and 5, for instance, integrate better than No. 4. Generally tempi are traditional, but here and there – as in the plodding speed for the first movement of No. 2 and the insensitively fast first movement of No. 6 – the direction is less convincing.

Harnoncourt has re-recorded the *Brandenburgs* digitally, but the newer set is less attractive than the old. Speeds are slow, rhythms heavy (Tel. **ZK8 42823** and **42840**).

Reinhard Goebel's set with Musica Antiqua is one to have you disbelieving your ears. Even in an age of period performance that favours fast speed, his allegros are hectic to the point of recklessness, in several instances comically impossible. It is hard not to laugh out loud at the speeds for both movements of No. 3 (the second more than the first) and even more at the sketchy strumming which purports to be the first movement of No. 6, 'without tempo indication', as the booklet reminds us. At Goebel's headlong speed the semiquaver arpeggios are hardly audible and even the repeated quavers sound rushed. It is a tribute to the virtuosity of the Cologne ensemble that they otherwise cope so well, usually playing with a good rhythmic spring. As a curiosity the set is certainly worth hearing, and the speeds mean that, even with modest side-lengths, four *Brandenburgs* are fitted on to the first disc, with the *Triple concerto*, much less eccentrically done, as a substantial makeweight on the second. Slow movements, by contrast with fast, are taken relatively conservatively, though Goebel's squeezy style is often uncomfortable, with the ensemble characteristically edgy in its light, clear style. First-rate recording.

DG have also made available Karajan's polished and lively performances on CD (DG **415 374-2**). They are, of course, beautifully played and represent an orchestral tradition now likely to disappear, but they are strictly for admirers of Karajan. Marriner's second Philips set (reissued on inexpensive cassettes – Ph. *400 076/7-4*) must also be passed over, as his later versions have far greater appeal.

Flute concertos: in C (from *BWV 1055*); *in E min.* (from movements of *Cantata No. 35*); *in G min.* (from *BWV 1056*).
**(*) CBS Dig. *IMT 39022* [id.]. Rampal, Ars Rediviva, Munçlinger.

If you enjoy transcriptions of Bach for the flute – and they are easy to enjoy here – it is difficult to imagine them being played better than by Jean-Pierre Rampal. The *C major* and *G minor Concertos* derive respectively from the *A major* and *F minor Harpsichord concertos*. Rampal is wonderfully nimble in the opening allegro of BWV 1055 and gives a radiantly beautiful account of the slow movement cantilena of BWV 1056. Munclinger, who made the arrangements, provides sympathetic accompaniments with the Ars Rediviva of Prague, although rhythmically he does not quite display Rampal's lightness of touch. The recording is very good indeed and beautifully balanced on the chrome tape.

(i) *Flute concerto in E min.* (from *BWV 1059* and *BWV 35*; ed. Radeke); *Suite No. 2 in B min., BWV 1067;* (ii) *Trio sonata No. 4 in G, BWV 1039; The Musical offering: Trio sonata in C min., BWV 1079.*
(M) ** RCA **GD 86517 [RCA 6517-2 RG]**; *GK 86517*. Galway; (i) Zagreb Soloists, Ninic; (ii) Kyung-Wha Chung, Moll, Welsh.

These recordings were originally issued on two separate LPs, both of which contained an additional work. The digital remastering has brought an artificial brightening of the sound, without clarifying the orchestral group, and thinning textures instead. The flute timbre also sounds less rounded than originally. The eminently musical James Galway plays freshly in the concertante works and with his excellent partners seems equally at home in the *Trio sonatas*, although here the playing does seem at times understated. This mid-priced CD is offered without documentation, other than titles. The equivalent cassette is smoother on top and on the whole sounds better than the CD.

Concerto for flute, violin and harpsichord in A min., BWV 1044; Concerto for oboe and violin in C min., BWV 1060; Concerto for oboe d'amore in A, BWV 1055.
*** DG Dig. **413 731-2**; *413 731-4* [id.]. Beznosiuk, Standage, Reichenberg, Pinnock, E. Concert.

As in their other Bach concerto recordings for DG Archiv, Pinnock and the English Concert prove the most persuasive practitioners of authentic performance, both vigorous and warm with consistently resilient rhythms. This collection of works transcribed from better-known originals features two wind soloists with tone warmer and less abrasive than many using baroque instruments. The recorded sound is exceptionally vivid in its sense of presence in its CD format. The tape focus is good but less clean and sharp.

Guitar concerto in E (arr. from *Violin concerto, BWV 1042*). *Aria from BWV 1003.*
** CBS Dig. **MK 39560**; *IMT 39560* [id.]. John Williams, ASMF, Sillito – HANDEL; MARCELLO: *Concertos.***

This is not an especially effective arrangement: the guitar has to be artificially balanced with the modern string texture. Williams makes the strongest impression in the *Adagio* and in the *Aria* from the *A minor Sonata for unaccompanied violin*, which is offered as an encore. The recording is good. The chrome tape is less extended in the upper range.

Harpsichord concertos Nos 1–7, BWV 1052/8; No. 8 in D min. (reconstructed Kipnis), *BWV 1079; Brandenburg concerto No. 5, BWV 1050; Italian concerto, BWV 971.*
(B) **(*) CBS *MGT 39801/2* (available separately) [id.]. Kipnis, L. Strings, Marriner.

At the beginning of the 1970s Igor Kipnis undertook an intensive series of sessions with the London Strings (the St Martin's Academy under a pseudonym), recording not merely the well-known keyboard concertos but the fringe works too: the arrangements of the *Violin concertos in E* and *A minor* and of the *Fourth Brandenburg*, plus an eighth work reconstructed by Kipnis himself from a fragment of nine bars identical with the *Sinfonia* of *Cantata No. 35*. Kipnis scored that movement for concertante forces and added two other movements from the same cantata; that is typical of his eager approach to Bach. The recording, made in EMI's St John's Wood studio, is better balanced than many made by CBS at this time, and the sound of these tapes is vivid if not altogether refined. The music making is infectious, the accompaniments are characteristic of the vintage ASMF recordings and the cassettes are inexpensive. *MGT 39801* contains the first five concertos and makes a worthwhile independent purchase.

Clavier concertos Nos 1–7, BWV 1052/8.
(*) HMV Dig. **CDS7 47629-8; *EX 270470-5* (2). Gavrilov (piano), ASMF, Marriner.

In terms of dexterity and clarity of articulation Andrei Gavrilov cannot be faulted and he produces some beautiful sound when his playing is lyrical and relaxed. At times one feels he pushes on relentlessly and his incisive touch in the first movement of the *D minor* and the *A major* might strike some listeners as almost aggressive and hard driven. But if the momentum is a bit unremitting in some movements, there are a lot of memorable things, too. Indeed, in the slow movement of the *D minor* and *F minor concertos*, there is playing of real poetry and delicacy – and, for that matter, in the finale of the *A major*. The recordings are excellently balanced, with the piano well integrated into the overall picture. Gavrilov's admirers will want to investigate these undeniably accomplished performances for their many felicities. The iron-oxide cassettes are smooth and pleasing but lack the ultimate range of the CDs, though the piano timbre is truthful.

Harpsichord concertos Nos 1 in D min., BWV 1052; 5 in F min., BWV 1056; Double harpsichord concertos Nos 1–2, BWV 1060/1; Triple harpsichord concertos Nos 1–2, BWV 1063/4; Quadruple harpsichord concerto, BWV 1065. Violin concertos Nos 1–2; Double violin concerto, BWV 1041/3.
(*) DG Dig. **413 634-2 (3). Pinnock, Gilbert, Mortensen, Kraemer, Standage, Wilcock, E. Concert.

This compilation, which DG prepared for their tercentenary Bach Edition on CD, collects the major keyboard concertos plus the two violin concertos and the *Double concerto* in what are for the most part brilliant performances. In the violin concertos the tempi will be too extreme for some tastes, though these accounts are generally to be preferred to those of Jaap Schröder/ Christopher Hogwood, in which slow movements are fast and shorn of romanticism, and the nasal and raw string-tone is unpleasing. Of the period-instrument performances, this still leads the field, and the CD has great lucidity and presence.

Harpsichord concertos Nos 1 in D min.; 2 in E; 3 in D, BWV 1052/4.
*** DG Dig. **415 991-2** [id.]. Pinnock, E. Concert.

Harpsichord concertos Nos 4 in A; 5 in F; 6 in F; 7 in G min., BWV 1055/8.
*** DG Dig. **415 992-2** [id.]. Pinnock, E. Concert.

Trevor Pinnock plays with real panache, his scholarship tempered by excellent musicianship. There are occasions when one feels his tempi are a little too fast and unrelenting, but for the most part there is little cause for complaint. On the contrary, the performances give much pleasure and the period instruments are better played than on most issues of this kind. Both

CDs are digital and have the advantage of great clarity of texture. Apart from the very quick tempi (particularly in the finale of BWV 1055) which strike an unsympathetic note – and baroque violins are not to every taste – this set is thoroughly recommendable.

Clavier concertos Nos 1 in D min., BWV 1052; 3 in D, BWV 1054; 5 in F min., BWV 1056; 6 in F, BWV 1057.
*** Tel. Dig. **ZK8 43208** [id.]. Katsaris (piano), Liszt CO, Rolla.

The *F major*, BWV 1057, is the transcription of the *Fourth Brandenburg concerto* and the others also derive from earlier works. Cyprien Katsaris possesses the most remarkable technique and feeling for colour which are to be heard to excellent advantage in this vividly recorded and well-filled disc. He has an astonishingly vital musicality and keyboard resource. The playing of the Liszt Chamber Orchestra, surely one of the very finest chamber ensembles in the world, is splendidly supportive. Exhilarating and imaginative performances all round. A most distinguished issue.

Harpsichord concertos No. 1 in D min.; 4 in A; 5 in F min.; 6 in F, BWV 1052; 1055–7.
(M) *(*) Pickwick Dig. **PCD 864**. Ivor Bolton, St James Baroque Players.

Capable, though not exceptional, performances, well held together by Ivor Bolton who presides at the keyboard as soloist/director. They are let down by some lacklustre string-tone and a less than ideal balance. In the slow movement of the *D minor*, the strings are too near the microphone and the harpsichord too distant. This may be inexpensive and the digital sound vivid, but more enjoyable versions of these works are available.

Clavier concertos Nos 1 in D min., BWV 1052; 4 in A, BWV 1055; 5 in F min., BWV 1056.
*** Denon Dig. **C37 7236** [id.]. András Schiff (piano), ECO, Malcolm.

András Schiff never tries to pretend that he is not using a modern piano, and the lightness of his touch and his control of colour are a constant delight to the ear. George Malcolm's accompaniments are alert and resilient, and the actual sound of the strings is perfectly in scale. Outer movements have splendid vigour and transparency; slow movements are expressive and evocative in their control of atmosphere. Schiff's decoration in the *Larghetto* of the *A major* is admirable, as is his simple eloquence in the famous cantilena of the *F minor Concerto*. This is highly recommended, and it is an example of digital recording at its most believable, although it is very noticeable on CD that the upper strings are soft-grained and not brightly lit.

Clavier concertos Nos 1 in D min., BWV 1052; 5 in F min., BWV 1056; 7 in G min., BWV 1058.
*(*) Ph. Dig. **420 200-2**; *420 200-4* [id.]. Steuerman (piano), COE, Judd.

Jean-Louis Steuerman offers accomplished pianism and considerable refinement of touch – much needed, given his rhythmic inflexibility and otherwise joyless manner. In the end the unremitting metronomic tread induces monotony and there is little sense of spontaneity and sparkle, even in the finale of the *D minor*. There is spirited and neat playing from him and the Chamber Orchestra of Europe under James Judd, and the Philips recording is wonderfully transparent and present, the piano being reproduced with remarkable fidelity; but there is little here to challenge Schiff or Katsaris. The cassette is well managed but is less transparent than the CD.

Double harpsichord concertos: Nos 1 in C min.; 2 in C; 3 in C min., BWV 1060/2.
(*) DG Dig. **415 131-2 [id.]. Pinnock, Gilbert, E. Concert.

The character of the Pinnock performances is robust, with the balance forward and the performances very strongly projected. The combination of period instruments and playing of determined vigour certainly makes a bold impression, but the relatively unrelaxed approach to the slow movements will not appeal to all ears. The third of the double concertos, BWV 1062, is an alternative version of the *Concerto for two violins*, BWV 1043; though the keyboard format has a certain fascination, it is no match for the original, especially in the beautiful slow movement, with – as here – squeezed accompanying chords. The lively recording has very striking presence on CD.

Double clavier concertos Nos 1–3, BWV 1060/2.
** HMV Dig. **CDC7 47922-2.** Béroff, Collard (pianos), O de Paris Ens., Wallez.

The two instruments are well defined in the aural picture though they are a bit too close in the *C major*. Robust, straightforward playing from the two distinguished soloists, who are spirited but rather monochrome in the *C major*. They seem deliberately to eschew refinement of colour here but are more characteristically imaginative in the *C minor*, BWV 1060, whose slow movement is both sensitive and compelling. Rhythms are lively enough, but the orchestral playing under Jean-Pierre Wallez is not particularly inspired. The other *C minor Concerto* is transcribed from the D minor concerto for two violins, and here the orchestral playing is distinctly laboured.

Double clavier concertos Nos 1 in C min., BWV 1060; 2 in C, BWV 1061; Triple clavier concerto in D min., BWV 1063; Quadruple clavier concerto in A min., BWV 1065.
*** DG Dig. **415 655-2** [id.]. Eschenbach, Frantz, Oppitz, Schmidt (pianos), Hamburg PO, Eschenbach.

Helmut Schmidt, the German ex-Chancellor, joins his friends, Eschenbach and Frantz, alongside Gerhard Oppitz in the *Quadruple concerto*. This work opens the concert – and very enjoyable it is, with soloists and musical director Eschenbach showing they appreciate the colour of the Vivaldi work (Op. 3/10, originally for four violins) on which it is closely based. The other concertos are presented with comparable vigour (the finale of the *Triple concerto* is particularly exhilarating) with slow movements correspondingly thoughtful and responsive. The recording is rather resonant but it attractively bathes the music making in a genial glow, and the spirit of this record is the very opposite of that atmosphere of scholarly rectitude that too often pervades more authentic Bach playing. On CD the reverberation offers no problems and, although detail is not sharp, the overall sound-picture is believable.

Triple harpsichord concertos Nos 1 in D min.; 2 in C, BWV 1063/4; Quadruple harpsichord concerto in A min., BWV 1065.
(*) DG Dig. **400 041-2 [id.]. Pinnock, Gilbert, Mortensen, Kraemer, E. Concert.

Like the *Double concertos* above, this music was originally conceived for other instruments. The *C major Concerto*, BWV 1064, was based on a triple violin concerto, and in the *Quadruple concerto* Bach drew on Vivaldi's Op. 3/10, originally for four violins. The slightly aggressive style of the music making – everything alert, vigorously paced and forwardly projected – emphasizes the bravura of Bach's conceptions. The CD adds to the feeling of presence and the sound has added depth, but the aggressive sensation remains and the listener is conscious that the balance is artificial and microphone-aided.

Triple clavier concertos Nos 1 in D min., 2 in C, BWV 1063/4; Quadruple clavier concerto in A min., BWV 1065.
** EMI **CDC7 47063-2** [id.]. Béroff, Collard, Tacchino, Rigutto, Paris Ens., Wallez.

Another record for those who prefer their Bach on the piano, given such spirited if rather literal playing from this distinguished French team. The balance is skilfully managed and enables the keyboard part-writing to be heard with the utmost clarity and to vivid effect. The orchestral playing is not particularly distinguished, however; but the excellence of the pianists who dominate the proceedings outweighs any reservations. The sound-quality has additional clarity on CD.

Oboe concertos: in A (from *BWV 1055*); *in D min.* (from *BWV 1059*); *in F* (from *BWV 1053*).
*** Ph. Dig. **415 851-2** [id.]. Heinz Holliger, ASMF, Iona Brown.

Stylish, pointed performances (leaning at times towards Romantic expressiveness in slow movements) of two concertos better known in their harpsichord versions (BMW 1053 and 1055) and a third reconstruction from seemingly independent movements. The outer movements of the latter owe their origins to the *Cantata No. 35* – Bach was always transcribing cantata movements for his concertos – while the lovely slow movement is well known in two forms: as the central movement of the *F minor Harpsichord concerto* and as the *Sinfonia* from *Cantata No. 156*, where the oboe is soloist. Excellent recording, with the CD gaining from the silent background.

Violin concertos Nos 1–2, BWV 1041/2; in D min., BWV 1052; in G min., BWV 1056; (i) *Double concerto, BWV 1053,* (ii) *Double concerto for violin and oboe, BWV 1060.*
**(*) Ph. Dig. *416 412-4* (2) [id.]. Accardo, (i) Batjer; (ii) Boyd; COE.

Although this Philips tape box has the advantage of full and refined modern recording – albeit a little bass-orientated in its tape transfer – it seems uncompetitive beside other more generous anthologies on a single CD or cassette (see below). Salvatore Accardo uses various Cremonese instruments – the 1718 and 1727 Stradivarius that he owns and another one belonging to the city of Cremona – with his customary poise and lack of affectation, and these accounts in which he additionally directs the Chamber Orchestra of Europe are thoroughly enjoyable. Accardo gives a particularly thoughtful account of the slow movement of the *E major*. He also gives a spirited and well-shaped account of the *D minor Concerto*, BWV 1052, which he himself has edited. The playing of the Chamber Orchestra of Europe is very good, though they make rather heavy weather of the slow movement of the *A minor*.

(i) *Violin concertos Nos 1–2, BWV 1041-2;* (ii) *Violin concerto in G min.* (from *BWV 1056*); (i; ii) *Double violin concerto, BWV 1053.*
*** HMV **CDC7 47856-2** [id.]. (i) Perlman, (ii) Zukerman, ECO, Barenboim.

(i) *Violin concertos Nos 1–2, BWV 1041-2;* (ii) *Violin concerto in G min.* (from *BWV 1056*); (i; ii) *Double violin concerto, BWV 1053;* (i; iii) *Double concerto for violin & oboe in D min., BWV 1060.*
(M) *** HMV *EG 290530-4* [Ang. *4AM 34726*]. (i) Perlman, (ii) Zukerman, (iii) Black, ECO, Barenboim.

(i) *Violin concertos Nos 1–2, BWV 1041-2;* (i; ii) *Double violin concerto, BWV 1053;* (i; iii) *Double concerto for violin & oboe in D min., BWV 1060.*
❀ (M) *** Ph. **420 700-2**; *420 700-4* [id.]. (i) Grumiaux; (ii) Krebbers, (iii) Holliger; (i; ii) Les Solistes Romandes, Arpad Gerecz; (iii) New Philh. O, Edo de Waart.
** ASV Novalis **150 017-2**; *150 017-4* [id.]. (i) Sitkovetsky; (ii) Garcia; (ii) Neil Black; ECO.

Arthur Grumiaux has recorded the violin concertos before in stereo, but the present Swiss versions were made in 1978, when he was joined in the *Double concerto* by Hermann Krebbers.

The result is an outstanding success with the inspirational intertwining of the solo lines producing an intensely expressive account of the slow movement, and the timbres of the two artists individual yet inter-reactive in the outer allegros, with the finale irresistibly vivaçious. The way Grumiaux responds to the challenge of working with another great artist comes over equally clearly in the concerto with oboe, reconstructed from the *Double harpsichord concerto in C minor*. There the interplay of phrasing with Holliger is enchanting and, although the recording is earlier (1970), the sound is still good. Grumiaux's performances of the two solo concertos are equally satisfying. This is playing from one of the most musical and sensitive soloists of our time and, if anything, it is even finer than his earlier (1964) accounts (with Leppard), with a purity of line and an expressive response in slow movements that communicate very positively, so that the *Andante* of the *A minor* is made to seem almost as beautiful as the great *Adagio* of the *E major*. Les Solistes Romandes under Gerecz provide crisply rhythmic allegros and are sensitively supportive in the expressive music. The digital remastering produces transparently fresh yet warm sound and gives the soloists great presence, without robbing the playing of too much of its dynamic range – indeed this is a quite outstanding example of an analogue recording being enhanced. The cassette, softer-grained in the treble, is also outstanding and is in some ways even more natural than the compact disc.

The HMV CD was compiled in America and combines the Perlman/ Zukerman recordings of BWV 1041-3 that were originally issued separately in 1972 and 1975. Zukerman is soloist in the *G minor Concerto* (arranged from the *F minor Harpsichord concerto* with its sublime *Arioso* slow movement). The two famous violinists, with their friend and colleague Barenboim, are inspired to give a very fine account of the *Double violin concerto*, one in which their artistry is beautifully matched in all its intensity, with the slow movement in particular sounding ravishing. Perlman is also impressive in the *Adagio* of the *E major* solo *Violin concerto*, but neither he nor Zukerman in BWV 1056 is quite so impressive without the challenge of the other. The digital remastering provides a full and agreeable balance and the sound remains good, if not ideally transparent. The bass is drier and in the opening *E major Concerto* tends to thump a bit, though in the other concertos this emphasis subsides. The cassette, which costs a great deal less, has comparably good sound and yet offers an additional work, the *Concerto for violin and oboe* (also given on the Grumiaux CD). Here Neil Black makes a distinguished contribution: the outer movements tend to be fastish and the slow movement is expressive and eloquent, if not as magical as with Grumiaux and Holliger. However, Barenboim provides the most sympathetic support throughout and this is another Bach collection to cherish.

On Novalis, eminently well-recorded performances, lively and spirited with no lack of polish or finesse. On CD, the ECO sound is exceptionally realistic and vivid, and the acoustic is warm; on cassette, the solo violin timbre is made to sound rather thin because of the high-level transfer. Very good playing generally, let down a little in slow movements where a degree more imagination would be welcome; the performance of the *Concerto for violin and oboe* does not match the Grumiaux/Holliger version.

Violin concertos Nos 1 in A min.; 2 in E; Double concerto, BWV 1041/3.
*** HMV Dig. **CDC7 47011-2** [id.]; *TC-ASD 143520-4* [Ang. *4XS 37989*]. Mutter, ECO, Accardo.
*** DG Dig. **410 646-2**; *410 646-4* [id.]. Standage, Wilcock, E. Concert, Pinnock.
(M) *** HMV *ED 290146-4* [Ang. *4XG 60258*]. Menuhin, Ferras, Fest. CO, or Robert Masters CO.
(*) Ph. Dig. **416 413-2 [id.]. Accardo, Batjer, COE.
(M) **(*) Pickwick Dig. **PCD 808.** Laredo, Scottish CO.
(**) O-L Dig. **400 080-2** [id.]. Schröder, Hirons, AAM, Hogwood.

The three issues listed above by Grumiaux, Perlman/Zukerman and Sitkovetsky include more music. Alongside them the other CDs including only BWV 1041/3 seem ungenerous, even if they offer considerable artistic satisfaction.

Anne-Sophie Mutter's variety of timbre as well as the imagination of her phrasing is extremely compelling; while the degree of romantic warmth she adopts in her Bach playing is at odds with today's 'authentic' school, her performance of the slow movement of the *E major Concerto* is finer than any other version, except Grumiaux's, with marvellous shading within a range of hushed tones. Accardo's accompaniment here (as throughout this collection) is splendidly stylish and alert, as the opening of the first movement of BWV 1042 readily shows. In principle the slow movement of the *Double concerto* – where Accardo takes up his bow to become a solo partner, scaling down his timbre – is too slow, but the result could hardly be more beautiful, helped by EMI recording which gives body to the small ECO string band. The soloists are rather forwardly balanced, but in all other respects this issue is technically impressive. The CD is strikingly fresh and clear and gives the artists great presence. The equivalent cassette (though not chrome) is one of EMI's best.

If you want the three favourite Bach *Violin concertos* on original instruments, then Pinnock's disc is the one to go for. Rhythms are crisp and lifted at nicely chosen speeds – not too fast for slow movements – but, as so often with authentic performances of violin concertos, the edge will not please everyone. Good clear recording.

Menuhin's (1960) recording was made when he was in excellent technical form. He directs the orchestra as well as appearing as principal soloist, and it is in the accompaniments that these accounts fall slightly short, with outer movements not as rhythmically resilient as Accardo's. Nevertheless Menuhin's playing still gives great pleasure, with its balance of humanity and classical sympathy. Ferras matches his timbre to Menuhin's perfectly in the *Double concerto* and their playing cannot be faulted on minor points of style. HMV have freshened the recording, providing a sound-picture that belies its age.

Accardo has the advantage of full, modern digital sound. His performances are characteristically warm and polished, perhaps a shade understated at times. They are also available in a two-tape set with other concertos – see above.

On the mid-priced Pickwick CD, Laredo directs sympathetic traditional performances of the three concertos, which are lively in outer movements, warmly expressive without being sentimental in slow movements. The excellent Scottish Chamber Orchestra is well recorded with a realistic, well-judged balance except for the rather too prominent harpsichord continuo which, at times, in its relentlessness detracts from the generally well-sprung rhythms. Laredo's tone is a little thin at times, but that is a fault on the right side.

With authentic sound uncompromisingly abrasive and speeds generally brisk and inflexible, the Academy of Ancient Music's version of the *Violin concertos* is the opposite of Mutter's expressive approach. For some it apparently stands as a refreshing revelation, but sample the slow movement of the *Double concerto* –like a siciliana before you buy. Bright and clear recording to match, with the edge of string sound unrelenting throughout. The compact disc with its silent background puts the music making into even sharper relief.

Other compilations of the same three concertos include Kantorow (Denon **C 37 7096**) who plays with sweet timbre and fine imagination but is let down by stodgy accompaniments, and Kremer (Ph. **411 108-2**) who is too relentless to give much musical satisfaction.

Violin concertos: in D min., BWV 1052; in G min., BWV 1056; (i) *Double concerto for violin and oboe in D min., BWV 1060.*
*(*) HMV Dig. **CDC7 47073-2** [id.]. Perlman; (i) Ray Still; Israel PO.

All three concertos are better known in harpsichord versions. These recordings, dry and close to the point of aggressiveness, are far less acceptable than Perlman's own earlier versions of the two D minor works with the ECO under Barenboim – see above. Though he plays with imagination, he is heavier this time. The other concerto, the violin version of the *F minor Harpsichord concerto*, is even heavier in the first two movements, with the *Largo* almost coming to a halt.

Double violin concerto in D min., BWV 1043; Triple violin concerto in D, BWV 1064.
** HMV Dig. **CDC7 47900-2** [id.]. Menuhin, Ha Kun, Mi-Kyung Li, Camerata Lysy, Gstaad – VIVALDI: *Concertos.***

Despite the persuasive artistry of Menuhin and fresh, bouncy playing from the young orchestra, the version of the *Double concerto* with the Camerata Lysy is disappointing, largely because of the boxy, unhelpful recording which, as well as taking bloom from string tone, exposes flaws of ensemble. The arrangement of the delightful *C major Triple harpsichord concerto* for three violins makes an interesting curiosity, well played but suffering even more from edgy sound.

Double violin concerto, BWV 1043; Double concerto for violin and oboe, BWV 1060.
** CBS Dig. [**MK 37278**]. Zukerman, Stern, Killmer, St Paul CO, James – VIVALDI: *L'estro armonico: Double concerto.***

Zukerman – who is the music director of the St Paul Chamber Orchestra – has made this group a fair rival in its musical achievement to the Minneapolis Orchestra in the other city of the yoked pair of 'twins'. Unfortunately, the recording of his CBS digital collection underlines the weightiness of the bass which is uncomfortably heavy for Bach. Solo work is a delight, but there are better versions of all these concertos. This CD has been withdrawn in the UK.

Double concerto for violin and oboe in D min., BWV 1060; Easter oratorio: Sinfonia.
*** Ph. Dig. **411 466-2** [id.]. Holliger, Kremer – VIVALDI: *Oboe; Violin concertos.***(*)

Double concerto for violin and oboe in D min., BWV 1060.
(*) ASV Dig. **CDCOE 803; *ZC COE 803* [id.]. Blankenstein, Boyd, COE, Schneider – MOZART: *Sinfonia concertante*; VIVALDI: *Concerto, RV 556.***(*)

Double concerto for violin and oboe; Triple concerto for flute, violin and harpsichord in A min., BWV 1044.
(*) Denon Dig. **C37 7064 [id.]. Kantorow, Bourgue, Adorján, Dreyfus, Netherlands CO, Bakels.

Holliger is at his distinguished best in the *Double concerto*, and Kremer makes a good partner in a fresh performance with a serene central *Adagio*. But what makes this coupling memorable is the improvisatory quality which Holliger brings to his beautiful account of the solo in the *Sinfonia* from the *Easter oratorio* which sounds just like the slow movement of a concerto. The recording is first class, the ambience nicely judged, and the oboe is especially tangible in the CD format.

Maurice Bourgue is also an outstanding artist and in the Denon version the *Double concerto* is dominated by him, with phrasing and tonal nuances that consistently ensnare the ear. Jean-Jacques Kantorow makes another fine contribution, not quite so individual but producing immaculate playing. The *Triple concerto* is less compellingly done, and there one is more aware of the often inappropriately beefy style of the Netherlands Chamber Orchestra, as recorded here. The flautist András Adorján, Hungarian-born but trained in Denmark, is the leader, with Kantorow matching his rhythmic freshness and evenness of tone. Huguette Dreyfus's harpsichord is rather aggressively recorded, but otherwise the sound is first rate.

Recorded live, with stage and audience noises audible, the ASV version from the Chamber Orchestra of Europe is not immaculate, with the opening allegro rather sluggish of rhythm, but the solo playing from the oboist Douglas Boyd and the violinist Marieka Blankenstein is outstanding. Atmospheric recording, not ideally balanced.

The Musical offering, BWV 1079.
*** Ph. **412 800-2** [id.]. ASMF, Marriner.
*** HMV Dig. **CDC7 49199-2** [id.]. Linde Cons.

Sir Neville Marriner uses his own edition and instrumentation: strings with three solo violins, solo viola and a solo cello; flute, organ and harpsichord. He places the three-part *Ricercar* (scored for organ) at the beginning and the six-part *Ricercar* at the very end, scored for strings. As the centrepiece comes the *Trio sonata* (flute, violin and continuo), and on either side the *Canons*. Thurston Dart advocated playing the three-part *Ricercar* on the fortepiano (as it was probably heard in Potsdam). The actual performance here is of high quality, though some of the playing is a trifle bland. It is, however, excellently recorded and overall must be numbered among the most successful accounts of the work. Although originally an analogue master (1980), in its CD format it is given additional presence and clarity.

Hans-Martin Linde draws on the thinking of the American scholar, Ursula Kirkendale, whose conclusion favours the same sequence of movements as that adopted by Spitta – not that this is necessarily a first consideration since, with a little effort, the listener can exercise his own preferences in playing the disc. Generally speaking, Linde is as stylish and accomplished as any of his rivals, and he and his six colleagues are to be preferred to the Musica Antiqua of Cologne, and have a warmer sound too.

Orchestral suites Nos 1–4, BWV 1066/9; Suite in G min., BWV 1070 (spurious).
** DG Dig. **415 671-2** (2) [id.]. Col. Mus. Ant., Goebel.

Orchestral suites Nos 1–4, BWV 1066/9.
*** Erato Dig. **ECD 88048/9** (2) [id.]. E. Bar. Soloists, Gardiner.
*** HMV Dig. *EX 270310-5* (2). ASMF, Marriner.
(M) *** Decca *414 248-4* (2) [id.]. ASMF, Marriner.
(B) *** CfP *CFPD 41 4440-5* [Ang. Sera. *4X2G 6085* (2)]. Bath Fest. O, Menuhin.
(*) HMV **CDS7 47819-8 (2) [Pro **2CDD 205**]. Petite Bande, Kuijken.
(*) Capriccio **10 011/2 (available separately). Leipzig New Bach Coll., Pommer.
(M) ** Tel. **ZS8 43633/4**. VCM, Harnoncourt.

Gardiner's is an outstanding set using period instruments. In his characteristic manner, allegros tend to be fast and lightly sprung, with slower movements elegantly pointed. Though the edginess of baroque violins using a squeeze technique on sustained notes makes for some abrasiveness, Gardiner avoids the extremes which mark even Pinnock's English Concert version on CD (see above). Thanks to full and immediate recording, textures are fresh and clear, with trumpet and timpani biting through but not excessively.

Marriner's third and most recent version of the Bach *Suites* is linked in its CD format with his newest HMV recording of the Brandenburgs – see also above. This has the advantage of saving a disc. The cassettes are coupled normally and are of good quality although many tape collectors may feel the cheaper and earlier Argo version is more attractive. For his HMV set, Marriner uses an edition prepared by Clifford Bartlett which shows notable differences from both his earlier versions, the first one for Argo fresh, bright and brisk under the influence of Thurston Dart, the second for Philips far slacker and sometimes too smooth. The third one reveals some influence from the authentic movement; on one textual point, the double-dotting in the introduction to *Suite No. 3 in D*, he takes a more extreme view than the authentic specialists, turning the three semiquavers at the end of each half-bar into precise demi-semi-quavers. In the other introductions, too, there is a return to the clipped, clear manner of his first version – but not to speeds quite so fast. At times the new version may not be quite so precise of ensemble as the very first; but, with a slightly more relaxed manner and more spacious recording, it is more genial, a good choice for anyone wanting modern instruments and outstanding digital recording. As in both previous versions, William Bennett is the brilliant flute soloist in *Suite No. 2*.

Marriner's Argo recording, dating from the beginning of the 1970s, dominated the catalogue for over a decade. The remastered sound is even more vivid than the original on the new cassettes which are brightly lit in the treble. Thurston Dart was very much involved in this performance; the exuberance of the music making makes a fitting memorial to his scholarship which always sought to enhance, never to deaden, the music's spirit. For those not insisting on original instruments, this is still an excellent recommendation, very competitively priced. Marriner's 1979 Philips set has been reissued at mid-price in good modern chrome-tape transfers, with *Suites Nos 2* and *3* coupled together (*416 657-4*) to make a popular pairing and *Suites Nos 1* and *4* on *420 293-4*. But the Decca/Argo recording has strikingly more vitality.

Menuhin's set was recorded at the beginning of the 1960s. The sound was first class in its day, clear and well balanced, and it does not seem dated now, with excellent cassette transfers. Those who respond to Bach from the 'pre-authentic era' will find Menuhin's humanity shows an admirable balance between freshness and warmth, conveying the music's spirit and breadth without inflation. A first-rate bargain.

Kuijken with La Petite Bande shows that authentic performance need not be acidly over-abrasive. Set against a warm acoustic – more comfortable for the trumpet-sound if not always helpful to clarity – these are brightly attractive performances with their just speeds and resilient rhythms. Solo work is most stylish, though ensemble is not always immaculate and intonation is somewhat variable. Nevertheless a good alternative to Gardiner and the English Baroque Soloists if you are looking for performances on original instruments. The CDs are certainly impressive in their spaciousness, and definition is excellent.

Pommer's version, issued as part of the Leipzig Bach Edition to celebrate Bach's Tercentenary, brought the first complete set of the *Suites* on CD using modern pitch. Anyone not wanting authentic performance might consider these lively and fresh versions with generally brisk but not unfeeling speeds, rhythmically buoyant. Karl-Heinz Passin, the flute soloist in *Suite No. 2*, is not specially imaginative, but he gives a brilliant account of the dashing *Badinerie* at the end, in which Pommer encourages a hint of accelerando. Good atmospheric recording, but with a slightly boomy bass.

Goebel's set of the *Suites* with his virtuoso team is essentially for devotees of period performance. Abrasive, choppy of phrasing, using squeeze techniques on sustained notes, they present a clear and lively view of what constitutes authentic performance, but there are other versions using period instruments just as fresh and far easier on the ear. No. 2, recorded earliest, uses a single instrument per part, Nos 1, 3 and 4 a normal baroque orchestra with four first and four second violins. Despite the difference of scale, the style is recognizably similar, though allegros with the bigger band are often even more extreme, hectic to the point of frenzy. Fine vivid recording with plenty of presence on CD. The makeweight, *Suite No. 5* (using one instrument per part), is spurious, probably by Bach's son, Wilhelm Friedemann, attractive but very different in style from the rest.

Harnoncourt's newest digital recording with the Vienna Concentus Musicus (**ZK8 43051/2**) proved disappointingly lacking in finesse and not always convincingly balanced. Thus his earlier set from the late 1960s, which broke new ground in its pioneering of an authentic approach, is welcome back to the catalogue at mid-price. The effect is clean and literal, the acoustic bright and somewhat hard. Slow introductions are taken fast in allemande-style, minuets are taken slowly and – hardest point to accept – there is no concession to expressiveness in the famous *Air* from *Suite No. 3*. The *Sarabande* of No. 2 may sound a little disconcerting with its use of *notes inégales*, but the *Gigue* of No. 3 – and for that matter all the fast movements and fugues – are splendidly alive. The drawback is the prevailing *mezzo* *forte* of these performances, but admirers of the conductor will find his approach has all the usual hallmarks of his baroque style.

Münchinger and his Stuttgart players were also pioneers in a new approach to Bach on an apt scale in the early days of mono LPs, so it is sad that his latest Decca set of the *Suites* – for all the fullness and brilliance of the digital recording – is unattractively heavy, with rhythms unlifted (Decca **414 505-2**).

Orchestral suites Nos 1, 3 & 4, BWV 1066, 1068/9.
*** HMV Dig. **CDC7 49025-2**. Linde Consort, Linde.

Although one wonders who would want a CD of the Bach *Suites*, however generously full, which omits the famous B minor work for flute and strings, these Linde performances are undoubtedly attractive. The string style is less abrasive than that of the English Concert and the rhythmic spring in allegros generally lighter. The grandeur of the music is not missed either, for against a warm acoustic the intimate scale readily accommodates the panoply of trumpets in Nos 3 and 4. The famous *Air* is pointed and elegant. Good, warm recording.

Orchestral suites Nos 2–3, BWV 1067/8; (i) *Flute concerto, BWV 1056;* (ii) *Concerto for violin and oboe, BWV 1060.*
(M) **(*) Decca **417 715-2** [id.]; *416 282-4*. ASMF, Marriner; (i) with Bennett; (ii) Kaine, Miller.

These spirited and polished performances come from Marriner's Argo recordings of the 1970s. The digital remastering has emphasized the bright lighting of the recording in the *Suites*, the violin timbre is thin (some might feel the effect is more 'authentic') and the overall sound balance rather dry in the bass. The two concertos (which date from 1975) are noticeably more expansive in quality. The cassette matches the CD quite closely; if anything, the tape sound is slightly fuller.

CHAMBER MUSIC

(Unaccompanied) *Cello suites Nos 1–6, BWV 1007/12.*
*** HMV Dig. **CDS7 47471-8;** *EX 270077-5* (2). Heinrich Schiff.
*** HMV Dig. **CDC7 47035-2** (1, 4 & 5); **47036-2** (2, 3 & 6). Paul Tortelier.
(M) *** DG *419 359-4* (2). Pierre Fournier.
*** DG Dig. **415 416-2** (3). Mischa Maisky.
(*) Decca Dig. **414 163-2; *414 163-4* (2) [id.]. Lynn Harrell.
(*) CBS Dig. **M2K 37867 (2) [id.]. Yo-Yo Ma.

Schiff blows any cobwebs away from these dark and taxing works, not with consciously authentic performances that risk desiccation but with sharply direct ones, tough in manner and at speeds generally far faster than usual. For once one is constantly reminded that these are suites of dance movements, with Schiff's rhythmic pointing a delight. So even the *Sarabandes* emerge as stately dances, not unfeeling but freed of the heavy romanticism which is often plastered on them. Equally, the fast movements are given a lightness and resilience which make them sound fresh and new. Strong and positive, producing a consistent flow of beautiful tone at whatever dynamic level, Schiff here establishes his individual artistry very clearly. He is treated to an excellent recording, with the cello given fine bloom against a warm but intimate acoustic. The CDs have striking presence and realism, but the cassettes are also truthful and clear.

Recorded in the reverberant acoustic of the Temple Church in London, Tortelier's 1983 performances of the *Suites* present clear contrasts with his version of twenty years earlier. His approach remains broadly romantic by today's purist standards, but this time the rhythms are steadier, the command greater, with the preludes of each suite strongly characterized to capture the attention even in simple chattering passagework. Some will prefer a drier acoustic than this, but the digital sound is first rate, with striking presence on CD. Originally issued on three discs, Tortelier's set has now been reissued on two.

Fournier's richly phrased and warm-toned performances were recorded in 1961 and dominated the catalogue during the 1960s. They carry an impressive musical conviction. This is not refined, introverted playing – the cellist dwelling within himself – but a bold and vigorous reading obviously designed to project to a listener and convince him this is music to be listened to and enjoyed. The recording, made in a resonant but not overblown ambience, does not sound in the least dated, and the cassette transfer is highly realistic. A bargain.

The spareness and restraint of Harrell's performances contrast strongly with the more extrovert manner of most virtuosi, but rarely if ever is he guilty of understatement. The simple dedication of the playing, combined with cleanness of attack and purity of tone, bring natural unforced intensity. One might disagree with the occasional tempo, but the overall command is unassailable. Excellent, aptly intimate recorded quality. The realism of the sound is very striking in both media with the silent background giving a marginal advantage to the CD format.

Mischa Maisky is undoubtedly a master cellist; he produces an altogether sumptuous tone which is beautifully captured by the DG engineers. His issue is handicapped by being spread over three discs which is no doubt tidy and logical, but is also uneconomical in view of the fact that Decca with Harrell, CBS on CD with Ma and HMV in their recordings of Schiff and Tortelier have managed to put them on to two. Maisky's performances are beautifully cultured and at a high emotional temperature. He is rather less inclined to let the music speak for itself than some of his rivals and is at times even self-indulgent. The *Sarabande* of the *D minor Suite* is a little narcissistic and the impatient may find it interminable; nor is that of *No. 5 in C minor* free from affectation. There are times in the quicker dance movements when one longs for him to move on. However, there is no doubt that he makes an absolutely glorious sound and commands an unusually wide range of colour and tone.

Yo-Yo Ma gives deeply satisfying performances, not generally as weighty or improvisational as Tortelier's epic readings, less direct and positive than Schiff's, yet not as restrained as Lynn Harrell's. The effect is both strong and thoughtful. Ma commands the highest artistry, and his playing invariably offers both technical mastery and elevation of spirit. Moreover, the CBS engineers have given him truthful and well-balanced sound. However, his intonation is not always absolutely impeccable. This is not serious but, all the same, in so lofty a movement as the *Sarabande* from *Suite No. 5 in C minor* one does not want to be aware of any blemishes. In years to come, one feels Ma may find even more to say on these intensely demanding works – just as Tortelier has developed over the years – but although there is much to admire, his present set cannot be counted a first recommendation.

(Unaccompanied) *Cello suites Nos 1 in G, BWV 1007; 4 in E flat, BWV 1010* (arr. for flute).
(*) Denon Dig. **C 37 7383 [id.]. Aurèle Nicolet (flute).

Understandably, exponents of instruments other than the violin and the cello cast envious eyes on the violin partitas and the cello suites; Aurèle Nicolet, an excellent artist, makes a good case for translating two of the suites to the needs of an instrument with a compass two octaves higher. The one real gain is the extra flexibility, with brisk dance movements the most effective – but even there the extra ease is hardly consistent with what Bach intended. Nicolet overcomes the problem of the double-stopped chords with deft arpeggios. Good, undistracting recording.

Flute sonatas (arr. from *Trio sonatas*); *in G, BWV 525; in D min., BWV 527; in G, BWV 1038; in C min., BWV 1079.*
(*) Denon Dig. **C37 7058 [id.]. Aurèle Nicolet (flute), Michio Kobayashi (harpsichord).

These are all arrangements (BWV 525 and 527 come from organ sonatas), but effective enough. The playing is flexible and lively, and this duo certainly work well together as a team. The balance of the flute is a shade close, so that Nicolet dominates the proceedings, but the keyboard detail is not masked and the instrument is realistically recorded. The acoustic is resonant, but agreeable. The performances are very positive; a little more light and shade from the flute would have made them even more attractive, but allegros are never aggressive, and Kobayashi nimbly matches Nicolet in dexterity.

Flute sonatas Nos 1–6, BWV 1030/5; Partita, BWV 1013; Sonata, BWV 1020.
** CBS Dig. *12T 39746* (2) [id.]. Rampal, Pinnock, Pidoux.

Flute sonatas Nos 1 in B min, BWV 1030; 3 in A, BWV 1032; 5 in E min., BWV 1034; 6 in E, BWV 1035; Partita in A min., BWV 1013.
(*) Denon Dig. **C37 7331 [id.]. Nicolet, Jaccottet, Fujiwara.

In all, eight *Flute sonatas* are traditionally attributed to Bach, five of which are accepted as authentic by the editors of the *Neuen Bach-Ausgabe*, and it is these that are included on this well-filled Denon CD. The autographs of the *B minor* and the *A major* survive in Bach's own hand from about 1736, though that of the latter is not complete. (Nearly 46 bars are missing in the first movement of the *A major* and, although Alfred Dürr and others have made efforts to restore the missing passages, these artists play the movement as it stands.) The music itself comes from Bach's days at Cöthen. The later *E major sonata* was written when Bach visited Potsdam in 1741, and it is beautifully played, as for that matter are they all. Naturally when a modern flute is blended with harpsichord, it tends to dominate. The recordings were made in Switzerland in 1984 and are otherwise well balanced.

Rampal plays fluently and in good style. He is particularly impressive in his phrasing of slow movements, and his performance of the solo *Partita* is eloquent. The snag is the recording balance, with the flute timbre rich and forward, while the harpsichord (an attractive American instrument, after Hemsch) is relegated to the background. When Roland Pidoux's cello is added to the continuo, the combined sound tends to congeal and detail is opaque.

Lute suites (arr. for guitar)*: Nos 1–4, BWV 995/7 and 1006a.*
*** CBS **MK 42204** [id.]. John Williams (guitar).

With all four *Suites* conveniently fitted on to a single compact disc, this CBS issue offers a clear first choice in this repertoire. John Williams shows a natural feeling for Bach; the flair of his playing with its rhythmic vitality and sense of colour is always telling. His is a first-class set in every way: the linear control and ornamentation are equally impressive. The CD transfer is made at the highest level; but with the volume control turned down a bit, the guitar image has a real presence and the close balance does not affect the fullness of timbre. Background noise is not a problem. There is also a bargain-priced double-length tape (*MGT 39487*) which is not quite as refined as sound but includes also the *Prelude and fugue*, BWV 999/1000. But the superior technology of the compact disc is unquestioned.

Lute suites (arr. for guitar)*: Nos 1 in E min., BWV 996; 2 in A min.* (originally *C min.*)*, BWV 997;* (i) *Trio sonatas Nos 1 in E flat, BWV 525; 5 in C, BWV 529* (ed. Bream).
(*) RCA **RD 89654 [RCD1 5841]. Julian Bream (guitar/lute); (i) with George Malcolm.

Bream's compilation comes from records made in the 1960s: the *Lute suites* were recorded in Kenwood House in 1965 and the *Trio sonatas* at Bishopsgate Institute in 1969. The *Lute suites* are played with great subtlety and mastery on the guitar; the *Trio sonatas* are usually heard on the organ, but Bream's arrangement for lute and harpsichord is effective, even if one may prefer the originals. They are elegantly played and crisply recorded; the digital remastering provides a quiet background and adds to the sense of presence, though the harpsichord remains a shade less well defined in the bass register than is ideal.

Lute suites Nos 3 in G min., BWV 995; 4 in F (trans. of *Solo Violin partita in E*), *BWV 1006a; Prelude in C min. and fugue in G min., BWV 999/1000.*
(*) Saydisc Amon Ra **CD-SAR 23 [id.]. Nigel North (baroque lute).

Nigel North plays this music on a baroque lute and he is convincingly recorded in a slightly dry acoustic which is yet not too enclosed. These works lie awkwardly for the lute, and his style is freer and less rhythmically precise than John Williams using the guitar; some may prefer the firmer outline of the latter's playing. Nigel North is at his finest in the transcription of the *E major Violin partita*, which he plays in the key of F (even though the autograph is in the key of the original), as apparently E major offers problems for the lute. Certainly it is both enjoyable and very convincing in North's arrangement where there are a few minor changes in the chordal layout.

Trio sonatas Nos 1 in D min., 2 in C, 3 & 4 in G, BWV 1036/9.
*** HM Dig. **HMC 901173**; *HMC 40 1173* [id.]. L. Bar.

This disc contains two sonatas of established authenticity, the *G major*, BWV 1039, and (perhaps less certain) its companion in the same key, BWV 1038, which exists in a set of parts in Bach's own hand. The other two are of less certain authorship: the *D minor*, BWV 1036, is thought to be the work of either Wilhelm Friedemann or Carl Philipp Emanuel, and BWV 1037 by Bach's pupil, Goldberg. The playing of the London Baroque has great freshness and spirit, and readers wanting this repertoire need not hesitate. The recording is eminently satisfactory, too.

Trio sonatas Nos 2–4, BWV 1037/9; Movement in F, BWV 1040.
*(*) HMV **CDS7 49201-8** (2) [id.]. Linde Consort – HANDEL: *Trio sonatas.**(*)

The Linde Consort number some excellent players among their ranks; even so, one is aware of the imperfections and vulnerability of period instruments, and intonation and ensemble are not always perfect here. Well recorded though they are, these performances do not give unqualified pleasure and cannot be given a strong recommendation.

Trio sonatas: in C, BWV 529; in G, BWV 530; in C, BWV 1037; (from *The Musical offering, BWV 1079*).
*(*) Denon Dig. **C37 7953** [id.]. Nicolet, Blacher, Kobayashi, Fujiwara.

These accomplished but ultimately bland performances were recorded in Tokyo in 1985. Aurèle Nicolet is very much the dominant partner and certainly dominates the sound-picture in all four works. The *C major Trio*, BWV 1037, is thought to be by Bach's pupil, Goldberg, and the remaining two are transcriptions of the *Trio sonatas for organ* (BWV 529/30).

Trio sonatas: in G min., BWV 1029; in D min., BWV 1036; in F, BWV 1040 (for flute, oboe and continuo).
(*) Denon Dig. **C37 7093 [id.]. Nicolet, Holliger, Jaccottet – C. P. E. BACH: *Trio sonatas.***(*)

The *Sonata in D minor*, BWV 1036, although attractive, is almost certainly spurious; indeed, its content seems too mellifluously *galant* to come from the pen of Johann Sebastian. BWV 1029 certainly is Bach, as its opening movement makes obvious, deriving from a sonata for viola da gamba. All three are enjoyable when given performances so spirited and polished. One would have welcomed rather more light and shade, but the resonant ambience has contributed to this. In all other respects the recording is excellent.

Trio sonatas: in C min. (from *The Musical offering, BWV 1079*); *in G, BWV 1038.*
*** CBS Dig. **MK 37813** [id.]. Rampal, Stern, Ritter, Parnas – C. P. E., J. C. F. and W. F. BACH: *Trio sonatas.****

In this splendidly played group of *Trio sonatas* the *G major*, BWV 1038, is especially welcome, the excerpt from *The Musical offering* less so (as it will make a duplication for many collectors), even though the performance is full of vitality. The balance is good, but the CD suggests that the microphones were just a shade too close to the violin.

Viola da gamba sonatas Nos 1–3, BWV 1027/9.
*** HMV **CDC7 47964-2**. Wieland Kuijken, Gustav Leonhardt.
*** Simax **PCS 1024** [id.]. Laurence Dreyfus, Ketil Haugsand.
*** CBS Dig. **MK 37794** [id.]. Yo-Yo Ma (cello), Kenneth Cooper.
*** Decca Dig. **417 646-2**; *417 646-4* [id.]. Lynn Harrell (cello), Igor Kipnis – HANDEL: *Viola da gamba sonata.****
*** DG Dig. **415 471-2** [id.]. Mischa Maisky (cello), Martha Argerich (piano).

Viola da gamba sonatas Nos 1–3, BWV 1027/9; Trio sonata in G, BWV 1039.
(M) ** Tel. **ZS8 43772** [id.]. Nikolaus Harnoncourt, Herbert Tachezi; with Brüggen, Stastny.

The three sonatas for viola da gamba and harpsichord come from Bach's Cöthen period, and the G minor is arguably the highest peak in this particular literature. Wieland Kuijken and Gustav Leonhardt are both sensitive and scholarly, their tempi well judged and their artistry in good evidence. Their phrasing is finely shaped and natural, and there is no sense of the relentless flow that can so often impair the faster movements. The slow movement of the G minor is very slow but the tempo obviously springs from musical conviction and as a result *feels* right. This is among the best accounts of these sonatas to have appeared on the market for some years, and the recorded sound is faithful; it may be too immediate for some tastes, but adjustment of the controls gives a satisfactory result.

Laurence Dreyfus is an American scholar and player who studied with Leonard Rose at the Juilliard and subsequently with Wieland Kuijken in Brussels. He has published extensively on the music of Bach and teaches music history at Yale. He has prepared an edition of the viola da gamba sonatas which forms the basis for this recording. He plays a French-style seven-string gamba, and is hardly less eloquent a player than Kuijken; he has every bit as much polish and is superbly partnered by the Norwegian harpsichordist, Ketil Haugsand. They are beautifully recorded in a warm and spacious acoustic. Theirs is the more recent (and fresher) sound, which makes them a first choice alongside Kuijken and Leonhardt.

Yo-Yo Ma plays with great eloquence and natural feeling. His tone is warm and refined and his technical command remains as ever irreproachable. Kenneth Cooper is a splendid partner; collectors who prefer the cello to a gamba need not hesitate. The colour of the harpsichord does not blend with the cello quite as naturally as with a gamba and there is still a case to be made for the modern piano as a more appropriate partner. The CD has wonderful clarity and presence, and admirers of this cellist will undoubtedly want to acquire this issue.

Lynn Harrell uses gut strings (he is, however, not afraid of vibrato); he is quite successfully balanced with Igor Kipnis who plays an Italian harpsichord, tuned in unequal temperament, which is most naturally balanced and recorded. The cello timbre inevitably dominates the sound-picture, but Harrell's playing with its dedication and simplicity is most satisfying throughout, especially in slow movements which have a natural intensity. He offers an attractive Handel sonata as a bonus.

Mischa Maisky is also a highly expressive cellist and, unlike Yo-Yo Ma, he opts for the piano – successfully, for Martha Argerich is a Bach player of the first order. In fact the sonority of the cello and the modern piano seems a happier marriage than the compromise Ma and Cooper adopt. The recording is extremely well balanced too, and although the acoustic has struck some commentators as a little too reverberant, others will find it pleasingly warm. A most enjoyable account for collectors who do not care for period instruments.

Harnoncourt is brisk and full-blooded in the opening of the *G major* (he is twice as fast as either Kuijken or Dreyfus). Immediate comparison betrays the age of the recording (1969) though, taken in its own right, it is eminently acceptable. This gives a bonus in the form of the *G major Sonata* and, of course, enjoys a price advantage over the newer versions.

(Unaccompanied) *Violin sonatas Nos 1–3, BWV 1001, 1003 & 1005; Violin partitas Nos 1–3, BWV 1002, 1004 & 1006.*
*** ASV **CDDCD 454** (2) [id.]. Oscar Shumsky.
*** Orfeo **C 130853H** (2) [id.]. Dmitry Sitkovetsky.
(*) Denon Dig. **C37 7405/7 [id.]. Jean-Jacques Kantorow.
** DG Dig. **413 810-2** (3) [id.]. Schlomo Mintz.

Shumsky's clean attack and tight vibrato, coupled with virtuosity of the highest order, make for strong and refreshing readings, full of flair and imagination. If you want big-scale playing of Bach, this supplies the need splendidly, though the dry, close acoustic reduces the scale and undermines tenderness. Nevertheless, alongside Sitkovetsky's slightly less dramatic Orfeo set, this makes a primary recommendation in this repertoire.

Dmitry Sitkovetsky is not only a player of exceptional virtuosity but a real stylist. Although he offers all the *Sonatas* and *Partitas* on two compact discs, he also manages to include many repeats, though naturally some have to be omitted, given the constraints of space. This fine violinist conveys no sense of haste and he has a splendidly fluid sense of line and firm rhythms. The excellence and naturalness of the recording make the claims of this set very strong indeed.

Jean-Jacques Kantorow won the Carl Flesch Prize in 1962 at the age of seventeen but has made relatively few records until quite recently. This playing is refreshingly clean, and his well-paced and fluent accounts have much to commend them. They are vital, satisfying performances; though the recording lacks warmth, it is clear and present, even if there is a trace of edge at the very top. This gifted French artist may lack the grace and smoothness of Grumiaux, but the playing is in eminently good style and he does justice to Bach's contrapuntal writing. A highly recommendable set made uncompetitive by its uneconomical layout.

Schlomo Mintz takes all the technical difficulties in his stride and his excellently recorded accounts give much musical satisfaction. His playing has youthful vitality and power, but the famous *Chaconne* from the *D minor Partita* finds him wanting. Intonation is generally secure but goes seriously awry in the middle of the *G minor Fugue*. The sound is bold and clear, but the three-disc format makes this set very expensive.

(Unaccompanied) *Violin sonata No. 2, BWV 1003; Partita No. 2, BWV 1004.*
(M) ** Ph. *416 235–4* [id.]. Gidon Kremer.

Those looking for an inexpensive tape including the famous *Chaconne* from the second *Partita* will find the Philips recording truthful and the tape transfer provides plenty of presence. Kremer's playing is impressively assured technically, although its phrasing is unimaginative and he does not convey much sense of joy in the music. The *Partita* itself produces some rather aggressive bowing.

Violin sonatas (for violin and harpsichord) *Nos 1–6, BWV 1014/9.*
*** Ph. Dig. **410 401-2** (2) [id.]. Monica Huggett, Ton Koopman.

Monica Huggett, one of the outstanding exponents of authentic performance and first violin of Koopman's Amsterdam Baroque Soloists, plays with refined expressiveness in a beautifully unified conception of these six endlessly inventive works. Other versions may be more vigorous but, with excellent recording, detailed and well balanced, period instruments are projected most persuasively. The sound is strikingly 'present' in its CD format. Two alternative versions are given of the slow movement of BWV 1019.

Violin sonatas (for violin and harpsichord) *Nos 2–5, BWV 1021/4; Cantabile ma un poco adagio, BWV 1019a; Fugue in G min., BWV 1026.*
* HMV Dig. **CDC7 49203-2**. L. Bar.

These are charmless performances, the authenticity bringing unconvincingly squeezed lines in slow movements and spiky allegros; moreover, the sound is not very cleanly focused.

KEYBOARD MUSIC

The Art of fugue, BWV 1080; Italian concerto, BWV 971; Partita No. 7 in B min., BWV 831; Prelude, fugue and allegro in E flat, BWV 998.
*** HMV **CDS7 49130-8** (2) [Ang. **CDCB 49130**]. Gustav Leonhardt (harpsichord).

Versions of *The Art of fugue* in instrumental transcriptions of various kinds as well as on the organ have not been rare, but harpsichord performances are few. Gustav Leonhardt argues most convincingly that a 'glance at the compass of the alto voice (down to B, second octave below middle C) in the first twelve fugues suffices to make sure that none of Bach's nevertheless richly varied ensemble groups can be used for *The Art of fugue*'. The notation of polyphonic textures in full as opposed to short score was common in the seventeenth and eighteenth centuries (and even as early as 1580), and it has only been in the twentieth century that musicians have taken *The Art of fugue* as 'ensemble music'. Leonhardt uses a copy by Martin Skowroneck of a Dulcken harpsichord of 1745, a responsive and beautiful instrument. Convincing though Leonhardt's scholarly essay is, it is his playing that clinches the truth of his musical argument. Every strand in the texture emerges with clarity and every phrase is allowed to speak for itself. In the 12th and 18th fugues Leonhardt is joined by Bob van Asperen. The great Dutch artist-scholar argues that from the 'unsustained instruments with keyboard range larger than four octaves, the harpsichord claims first place in *The Art of fugue* (Bach left five harpsichords and no clavichord on his death), though organ and clavichord are not to be totally excluded, especially for certain pieces'. Leonhardt does not include the unfinished fugue, but that will be the only reservation to cross the minds of most listeners. This is a very impressive and rewarding set, well recorded and produced.

The Art of fugue, BWV 1080 (see also orchestral versions).
*** HM **HMC 901169/70**; *HM 40 1169/70* [id.]. Davitt Moroney (harpsichord).
*(*) Ph. **412 729-2** [id.]. Zoltan Kocsis (piano) (with Ferenc Rados).

Kocsis plays *The Art of fugue* on a well-timbred piano, boldly and clearly, but often favouring considerable cadential ritenutos. This will not be to all tastes, although the part-writing is made admirably clear. It must be said that the purposeful approach, coupled with the forward projection of the sound, can become a little taxing, and there is little variety of dynamic. The fugues are followed by the four canons and then, by way of supplement, the augmentational canon and the transcription for two keyboards of the three-part mirror fugue. Kocsis is joined here by Ferenc Rados, but they do not make a convincing case for the use of piano textures, as detail is not sharply defined. The recording itself is natural, but the persistent *martellato* of the playing becomes wearing.

After Kocsis, it is a relief to turn to Davitt Moroney's account of *The Art of fugue* on the harpsichord. He commands not only the intellectual side of the work but also the aesthetic, and his musicianship is second to none. Moroney makes some alterations in the order of the various contrapuncti but he argues his case persuasively. If you want an account of this work on CD, played on a keyboard instrument, this is unlikely to disappoint – and he is eminently well served by the engineers. Davitt Moroney has imagination as well as scholarship.

Capriccio in B flat on the departure of a beloved brother, BWV 992; Chromatic fantasia and fugue in D min., BWV 903; Fantasias and fugue in A min., BWV 904; in C min. (unfinished), *BWV 906; Prelude and fugue in A min., BWV 894.*
*(*) Ph. Dig. **420 176-2**. Jean-Louis Steuerman (piano).

After the success of Steuerman's earlier Bach recital – see below – this is disappointing. There is much that is unyielding in his *A minor Prelude and fugue*, BWV 894, that opens the recital. Yet the *Capriccio sopra la lontananza del fratello dilettisimo* is far from unimpressive and obviously the product of much thought. He eschews pianistic colouring – at times to some effect in the middle movement of the *Capriccio* where he comes close to the intimacy of a clavichord. There is little sense of mystery in the *A minor Fantasia* and again he proves quite inflexible in the *Chromatic fantasia and fugue*. There is an element of puritanism about this playing, as if enjoyment of its vitality or sheer sonority is to be avoided. Much though one would like to be welcoming to this artist – particularly as he includes the unfinished fugue, BWV 906, a rarity on disc – the narrow range of keyboard colour within which he chooses to operate and the rigid rhythms ultimately induce aural fatigue. He is marvellously recorded with great realism and in the best Philips traditions.

Capriccio in B flat, BWV 992; Chromatic fantasia and fugue in D min., BWV 903; French suite No. 5 in G, BWV 816; Italian concerto in F, BWV 971; Toccata and fugue in D min., BWV 914.
(M) ** Pickwick Dig. **PCD 817** [id.]. Robert Aldwinkle (harpsichord).

Robert Aldwinkle is a brilliant player, as the *Chromatic fantasia* immediately demonstrates; he is also thoughtful, and his articulation is the model of clarity. But his style lacks idiosyncrasy; thus the famous *Gavotte* in the *French suite* is very positive, yet is rather too sober. The harpsichord is faithfully recorded, but the microphones capture a bright treble and a lighter response from the bass. This may be the character of the instrument, which is not named; however, unless the volume control is set at *mezzo forte* there is at times a touch of aggressiveness.

Capriccio in B flat, BWV 992; Fantasia and fugue in A min., BWV 904; Prelude, fugue and allegro in E flat, BWV 998; Suite in E min., BWV 996 (originally for lute)*; Toccata in E min., BWV 914.*
*** Ph. Dig. **416 141-2**; *416 141-4* [id.]. Gustav Leonhardt (harpsichord).

Gustav Leonhardt plays a William Dowd harpsichord, modelled on an instrument by Mietke of Berlin dating from 1715. The sonorities are rich and the great Dutch player exploits them with characteristic resourcefulness. His well-planned recital has vitality, freshness and imagination, and everything comes vividly to life, thanks perhaps to a splendidly articulate recording. Collectors are advised to play at a low level setting for the most natural effect. There is a very good cassette, but it lacks the ultimate presence of the compact disc.

Chaconne in D min. (arr. Busoni from (unaccompanied) *Violin partita No. 2 in D min., BWV 1004*).
*** RCA **RD 85673** [**RCA 5673-2-RC**]. Artur Rubinstein – LISZT: *Sonata.***(*) (with FRANCK: *Prelude, chorale & fugue* ***).
*** Decca Dig. **417 372-2**; *417 372-4* [id.]. Alicia de Larrocha – HANDEL: *Suite No. 5*; MOZART: *Fantasy and sonata No. 14.****

Busoni's arrangement of the celebrated *Chaconne* for solo violin is a piece which has to be presented with flair as virtuoso piano music, and Rubinstein is an ideal choice of pianist. He recorded this performance in Rome in 1970, when he was already in his eighties, but the freshness and spirit are a delight. The recording is clangy but not unpleasantly so.

Alicia de Larrocha also gives a masterful account of the Busoni transcription, strongly held together and rich in sonority and subtlety. One of the finest performances of this pianistic showpiece we have had in recent years, and marvellously recorded, full-bodied and warm.

Chromatic fantasia and fugue in D min., BWV 903; Chorale Preludes: Ich ruf zu dir, BWV 639; Nun komm' der Heiden Heiland, BWV 659 (both arr. Busoni)*; Fantasia in A min., BWV 922; Fantasia and fugue in A min., BWV 904; Italian concerto in F, BWV 971.*
*** Ph. **412 252-2** [id.]. Alfred Brendel (piano).

Brendel's fine Bach recital originally appeared in 1978 and has been digitally remastered for the CD format. The performances are of the old school with no attempt to strive after harpsichord effects, and with every piece creating a sound world of its own. The *Italian concerto* is particularly imposing, with a finely sustained sense of line and beautifully articulated rhythms. The recording is in every way truthful and present, bringing the grand piano very much into the living-room before one's very eyes. Masterly.

Chromatic fantasia and fugue in D min., BWV 903; Fantasia in C min., BWV 906; Italian concerto in F, BWV 971; Prelude and fugue in A min., BWV 894.
(*) Denon Dig. **C37 7233 [id.]. Huguette Dreyfus (harpsichord).

Eminently straightforward accounts, perhaps a little unyielding at times but cleanly and truthfully recorded. Huguette Dreyfus plays with an admirable style and taste, without any ostentatious changes of registration. The recording is processed at a high level and for best results should be played at a low volume setting.

4 Duets, BWV 802–5; English Suite No. 6 in D min., BWV 811; Italian Concerto, BWV 971; Toccata in C minor, BWV 911.
*** DG Dig. **419 218-2**; *419 218-4* [id.]. Angela Hewitt (piano).

Angela Hewitt is a young Canadian pianist of great talent who won the 1985 International Bach Competition in Toronto. Her début record offers splendid vindication of the wisdom of the judges' decision. In both the *Italian concerto* and the *English suite* her playing is enormously alive and stimulating. Textures are clean, with every strand in perfect focus and every phrase clearly articulated. She plays with vital imaginative resource, totally free from idiosyncrasy and affectation. Handel, when questioned as to the purpose of his music, answered that it 'was to make people better' – and this is the effect one experiences after listening to these exhilarating performances. The piano is beautifully captured on this recording, which must be numbered as one of the most successful DG have given us, with fresh, life-like sound and vivid presence.

English suites Nos 1–6, BWV 806/11.
*** HMV Dig. **CDS7 49000-8** (2) [Ang. **CDCB 49000**]. Gustav Leonhardt (harpsichord).

*** HM *40.1074/5* [id.]. Kenneth Gilbert (harpsichord).
** CBS **M2K 42268** (2) [id.]. Glenn Gould (piano) (with *Partita, BWV 831*).

Gustav Leonhardt uses a 1755 instrument by Nicholas Lefebre of Rouen, recently restored by Martin Skowroneck, and very beautiful it sounds too in this clear but not too forwardly balanced recording. The *English suites* are thought to come from 1715, the year of Carl Philipp Emanuel's birth, or possibly a few years later, and to predate the *French suites*. Leonhardt's playing here has a flair and vitality that one does not always associate with him, and there is no doubt that he makes the most of the introspective *Sarabande* of the *G minor Suite*. He is better served by the EMI engineers than when he last recorded these for Philips, where he was too forward; his performances, too, are more flexible and relaxed. The CD transfer retains the atmospheric sound-balance; the harpsichord is present without being right on top of the listener. Kenneth Gilbert's alternative on Harmonia Mundi is also very fine, however, and when this is issued on compact disc will be a strong competitor.

Kenneth Gilbert uses a Couchet-Taskin of 1788 and is given a first-class recording. His playing has a fine sense of style, the rubato flowing naturally and never self-conscious, the ornamentation nicely judged. He is inconsistent in the matter of repeats, but this may be due to the desire to fit the six suites economically on to four sides. As the price is slightly lower than the premium range, this is excellent value, particularly as the recording itself is so realistic. The cassettes are transferred at the highest level and while the sound is admirably vivid, care will have to be taken with the volume control if a truthful image is to be obtained.

Glenn Gould often inspires the adjective wilful, and certainly his performances have much that is eccentric. At the same time the strength of his musical personality cannot be denied; the music is always alive, phrasing is often strikingly imaginative and textures have appealing inner clarity. On the other hand, there is some bizarre ornamentation and accentuation, and the vocalizations are tiresome. The sound is clean and dry but not unbelievably so.

English suites Nos 2 in A min.; 3 in G min., BWV 807/8.
*** DG Dig. **415 480-2**; *415 480-4* [id.]. Ivo Pogorelich (piano).

The young Yugoslav pianist plays both *Suites* with a welcome absence of affectation. He observes all repeats and, although some of the *Sarabandes* are really rather slow which may strain the allegiance of some listeners, there is generally speaking an impressive feeling of movement. The repeats, incidentally, are literal and there is barely a trace of the narcissism that afflicts him in the romantic repertoire. It is all beautifully articulate and fresh. The recording is one of DG's best, with natural piano sound and an excellent sense of presence. There is a first-class tape.

French suites Nos 1–6, BWV 812/7.
(*) HM **HMC 90437/8 [id.]. Kenneth Gilbert (harpsichord).
(*) HMV Dig. **CDS7 49293-2 [Ang. **CDCB 49293**]. Andrei Gavrilov (piano).
** CBS **M2K 42267** [id.]. Glenn Gould (piano).

French suites Nos 1–6; Suites: in A min., BWV 818a; in E flat, BWV 819; Allemande, BWV 819a.
*** O-L Dig. **411811-2** (2) [id.]. Christopher Hogwood (harpsichord).

Christopher Hogwood uses two harpsichords now in the possession of the Paris Conservatoire collection, a Ruckers of 1646 enlarged and modified by Taskin in 1780, and a 1749 instrument, basically the work of Jean-Jacques Goujon and slightly modified by Jacques Joachim Swanen in 1784. They are magnificent creatures and Hogwood coaxes superb sounds from them: his playing is expressive, and the relentless sense of onward momentum that disfigures so many harpsichordists is pleasingly absent. On CD, the tangibility and presence bring a successful balance of sound. These performances have both style and character and can be recommended with some enthusiasm. The genesis of the so-called *French suites* is a complicated matter which Hogwood discusses in his scholarly notes, included with this set. To the *French suites* themselves he adds the two others that Bach had obviously intended to include as Nos 5 and 6. The useful notes describe the tuning which was adopted for each suite.

Kenneth Gilbert's recording dates from the mid-1970s. He uses a 1636 Ruckers, rebuilt by Hemsch, which is made to sound full and robust by the forward balance. One needs to set the volume control cautiously and perhaps make further adjustments at times. As in his set of the *English suites*, the playing has a natural flow; there is an obvious feeling for the strongly rhythmic French style, yet his flexibility prevents any sense of rigidity. Tempi are well judged and ornamentation is discreet. This is fine playing, but Hogwood has the advantage of digital recording and offers more music. Gilbert's set is played a semitone lower than normal present-day pitch.

Gavrilov's set is full of interesting things, and there is some sophisticated, not to say masterly, pianism. The part-writing is keenly alive and the playing full of subtle touches. He draws a wide range of tone colour from the keyboard and employs a wider dynamic range than might be expected. There is an element of the self-conscious here and a measure of exaggeration in some of the *Gigues*, but there is much that is felicitous, too. One thinks longingly of Adolf Busch's dictum that the artist should draw attention to the beauty of the music and not to his own artistry. The recording is excellent.

Brilliant though Glenn Gould's playing is, it is far too idiosyncratic to justify an unqualified recommendation. Needless to say, there are revealing touches, marvellously clear part-writing and much impressive finger dexterity. There are some odd tempi and a lot of very detached playing that inspires more admiration than conviction. The recording is acceptable, rather dry and close.

Goldberg variations, BWV 988.
*** DG **415 130-2** [id.]. Trevor Pinnock (harpsichord).
*** Decca Dig. **417 116-2** [id.]. András Schiff (piano).
*** HM Dig. **HMC 901240**; *40.1240* [id.]. Kenneth Gilbert (harpsichord).
*(**) CBS **CD 37779** [id.]. Glenn Gould (piano).
(M) ** Tel. **ZS8 43652** [id.]. Gustav Leonhardt (harpsichord).
*(*) HMV Dig. **CDC7 47546-2**. Maria Tipo (piano).

Goldberg variations, BWV 988; Chromatic fantasia and fugue, BWV 903; Italian concerto in F, BWV 971.
(M) (**) HMV mono **CDH7 61008-2** [id.]. Wanda Landowska (harpsichord).

Trevor Pinnock uses a Ruckers dating from 1646, modified over a century later by Taskin and restored most recently in 1968 by Hubert Bédard. He retains repeats in more than half the variations – which seems a good compromise, in that variety is maintained yet there is no necessity for a third side. The playing is eminently vital and intelligent, with alert, finely articulated rhythm. If tempi are generally brisk, there are few with which listeners are likely to quarrel; Pinnock shows himself flexible and imaginative in the inward-looking variations such as No. 25. The recording is very truthful and vivid, especially in its CD format, though it benefits from a slightly lower level of setting than usual. In any event this can be recommended alongside Kenneth Gilbert's somewhat mellower Harmonia Mundi version, which has the advantage of digital recording.

For those who enjoy Bach on the piano, András Schiff's set can receive the most enthusiastic advocacy. His recording carries the imprimatur of no less an authority than George Malcolm, who used to maintain that 'the Goldberg variations were the one work of Bach which positively demanded the two keyboards of the harpsichord in order to achieve the contrapuntal clarity in the numerous hand-crossing passages'. This performance changed his mind, and Schiff's much-admired dexterity and musicianship will go far in persuading sceptics that this not only can but does give profound musical satisfaction in the hands of a perceptive artist. The part-writing emerges with splendid definition and subtlety: Schiff does not play as if he is performing a holy ritual but with a keen sense of enjoyment of the piano's colour and sonority – and devoid of vocal obbligato. The Decca recording is excellent in every way, clean and realistic.

Kenneth Gilbert gives a refreshingly natural performance of the *Goldberg*. He uses a recent copy of a Ruckers–Taskin, and it makes a very pleasing sound. His is an aristocratic reading; he avoids excessive display and there is a quiet, cultured quality about his playing that is very persuasive. His is an essentially introspective account, recorded in a rather less lively acoustic than is Pinnock on Archiv, and he is a thoughtful and thought-provoking player.

Glenn Gould made his recording début with the *Goldberg variations* way back in the mid-1950s; this latest version was among the last records he made. As in his earlier account, there are astonishing feats of prestidigitation and the clarity he produced in the part-writing is often little short of extraordinary. In his earlier record he made no repeats; now he repeats a section of almost half of them and also joins some pairs together (6 with 7 and 9 with 10, for example). Yet, even apart from his vocalise, he does a number of weird things – fierce staccatos, brutal accents, and so on – that inhibit one from suggesting this as a first recommendation even among piano versions. The recording is, as usual with this artist, inclined to be dry and forward (he engineered his own records and admired this kind of sound) which aids clarity. A thought-provoking rather than a satisfying reading – an award-winning disc, too; however, for all that, many readers will find the groans and croons intolerable and will be bewildered by many things he does. The withdrawn, rapt opening *Aria* is rather beautiful – but why, one wonders, does he emphasize the third part in many of the canons? The CD has admirable presence but emphasizes the vocalise.

Maria Tipo's recording was made in the Salle Wagram, Paris. Her approach is freely romantic in spirit with far from unpleasing variety and subtlety of tonal shading. She observes first repeats only (even so the CD runs to 64′) and generally speaking the playing is free from excessive idiosyncrasy, with rubati not overdone, though variations 22 and 26 are an exception. The recording is fresh and immediate; but with Schiff's account available on Decca, this could hardly be a first recommendation even for those who favour an uncompromisingly pianistic approach to this masterpiece.

Leonhardt's set of the *Goldberg* is now more than twenty years old, but the sound remains undimmed. Indeed the transfer to CD freshens it. It is eminently scholarly but without the vitality of Pinnock or the aristocratic finesse of Kenneth Gilbert.

Wanda Landowska's version from the 1930s was the first ever complete recording of Bach's *Goldberg variations*; though on a clangy Pleyel – not helped by the close recording – the result is aggressive, the imagination of the soloist is endlessly illuminating on her own terms, just as her classic performances of the two other favourite Bach keyboard works are.

Italian concerto in F, BWV 971; 4 Duets, BWV 802/5; Partita No. 7 in B min., BWV 831.
*** Ph. Dig. **416 410-2**; *416 410-4* [id.]. Jean-Louis Steuerman (piano).

Jean-Louis Steuerman's playing here is free, without seeming out of style, consistently imaginative and alive. The outer movements of the *Italian concerto* have infectious buoyancy, while the *Andante*, like the serene *Sarabande* in the *B minor Partita*, has a simple beauty which is most affecting. In both movements the sustaining powers of the piano are used to great effect, yet the music is not romanticized. The *Duets* (which derive from the so-called *Organ mass* in the third volume of the *Clavierübung*) are delightfully fresh, the rhythmic articulation consistently deft. The performance of the *B minor Partita* crowns the recital: this is Bach in terms of the modern instrument with no concessions to the harpsichord. With excellent, natural Philips recording, this is strongly recommended, though the chrome cassette brings a sound-balance that is fuller in the middle range and slightly less fresh on top. This is much more satisfying than some more recent issues from this artist.

15 2-part Inventions, BWV 772/786; 15 3-part Inventions, BWV 787/801.
*** Denon Dig. **C37 7566** [id.]. Huguette Dreyfus (harpsichord).
*** DG Dig. **415 112-2** [id.]. Kenneth Gilbert (harpsichord).
(*) Decca Dig. **411 974-2; *411 974-4* [id.]. András Schiff (piano).

The title Bach gave these pieces clearly denotes their pedagogic purpose: to impart an ability to play clearly in two and three parts and 'above all to attain a singing style of playing'. Begun in 1720 for his eldest son, ten-year-old Wilhelm Friedemann, they were originally placed in order of difficulty, but Bach subsequently arranged them in ascending key order. For those wanting a recording of these works played on the harpsichord, choice rests between Huguette Dreyfus and Kenneth Gilbert's Archiv set which is first class in every way. Dreyfus, however, is hardly less impressive; in some ways her playing is more relaxed, though no less rhythmically vital. Her instrument is a Hemsch and her recording was made at Notre Dame in 1978. To achieve a realistic result it is essential to reduce the dynamic level to the lowest point if the instrument is not to seem out of scale. Mme Dreyfus is a shade warmer and freer than Gilbert and some will prefer her record.

Kenneth Gilbert plays a magnificant 1671 harpsichord by the Antwerp maker, Jan Couchet, which was later enlarged, first by Blanchet and then by Taskin in 1778, and which was restored in 1980 by Bédard. It has a rich, almost pearl-like sound, which is enhanced by the acoustic of Chartres Museum where it was recorded. Once again the CD needs to be played at a much lower level of setting than usual if the dynamic capacity of the instrument is to register truthfully. Gilbert's playing has exemplary taste and sense of musical purpose. Strongly recommended, alongside the Denon version.

Readers who prefer their Bach on the piano will welcome András Schiff's excellent recording on Decca. His playing is (for this repertoire), rather generous with rubato and other expressive touches, but elegant in the articulation of part-writing. This is at times a bit overdone; such is his musicianship and pianistic sensitivity, however, that the overall results are likely to persuade most listeners. There is a lot of life and colour in the playing and much to enjoy. The recording is excellent in both formats; the instrument sounds extraordinarily lifelike, as if in one's very room, on CD.

15 2-part Inventions, BWV 772/786; 15 3-part Inventions, BWV 787/801. Toccatas Nos. 1–7, BWV 910/916.
*(**) CBS **M2K 42269** [id.]. Glenn Gould (piano).

By coupling the *Inventions* with the *Toccatas*, CBS have generously encapsulated some of Glenn Gould's most impressive Bach performances. He pairs each of the *Two-* and *Three-part Inventions* (with each pair in identical keys) and at all times the listener is conscious he is in the presence of a penetrating musical mind: the clarity of the individual strands is remarkable. The *Toccatas* are often quite complex in structure, but Gould has their full measure. His playing combines fastidious and remarkable pianism with some impulsive, not to say wilful, touches. But the music is always alive; slow sections often have striking thoughtfulness and serenity, and undoubtedly this is Bach playing of distinction. The recording balance is close and rather dry but truthful, with rather more bloom than its previous incarnations. The one overriding snag is the vocalise which is even more apparent against the quiet background. If one can accept this, there is much to admire here, with the contrapuntal strands beautifully balanced and clarified.

Partitas Nos 1–6, BWV 825/30.
*** DG Dig. **415 493-2**; *415 493-4* (2) [id.]. Trevor Pinnock (harpsichord).
(*) HMV **CDS7 47996-8 (2) [Ang. **CDCB 47996**]. Gustav Leonhardt (harpsichord).
(*) HM Dig. **HMC 901144/6; *40.1144/6* [id.]. Kenneth Gilbert (harpsichord).
*** Decca Dig. **411 732-2**; *411 732-4* (2) [id.]. András Schiff (piano).
** Ph. Dig. **416 616-2**; *416 616-4* (2) [id.]. Jean-Louis Steuerman (piano).
*(*) Denon Dig. **C37 7333/5**. Huguette Dreyfus (harpsichord).

Trevor Pinnock uses a copy of a Hemsch (*c.* 1760) by David Jacques Way, tuned to unequal temperament and sounding marvellously present in this recording. Tempi are generally well judged, rhythms vital yet free, and there is little to justify the criticism that he rushes some movements. He also conveys a certain sense of pleasure that is infectious and he has great spirit and panache. There are excellent chrome cassettes, although the harpsichord image loses a little of its sharpness of focus.

Leonhardt's set was not conceived as an entity but was recorded over a longish period (1964–71). The *Second Partita* is heard at today's pitch, the others are recorded a semitone lower, and there are some variations of quality in the recordings of different partitas. Nevertheless these are searching and often profound readings. There are occasional exaggerations (the *Allemande* of the *First Suite*) and some of the dotted rhythms are over-emphatic – or stiff might be a better expression. Yet this still remains an impressive achievement, for the thoughts of this scholar-musician are always illuminating and his artistry compels admiration.

There is no doubting the excellence of Kenneth Gilbert's set on Harmonia Mundi which, in terms of scholarship and artistry, has much to recommend it. All the same it is handicapped by being spread over three discs or cassettes. Professor Gilbert uses a Couchet–Taskin–Blanchet (1671–1778) and is well enough recorded – but most readers will doubtless want to know whether the differences between the Gilbert and the Pinnock versions justify the additional outlay, and it is difficult to argue that they do.

Schiff is a most persuasive advocate of Bach on the piano, consistently exploiting the modern instrument's potential in range of colour and light and shade, not to mention its sustaining power. Though few will cavil at his treatment of fast movements, some may find him a degree wayward in slow movements, though the freshness of his rubato and the sparkle of his ornamentation are always winning. The sound is outstandingly fine, particularly on CD, with the chrome cassettes in the demonstration class too.

Eminently straightforward and unfussy playing from Steuerman which some collectors may prefer to the more purely 'pianistic' version like Schiff's. He has a well-developed sense of style, as one might expect from a prizewinner at the Leipzig Bach Competition, and he does not cultivate beauty of sound for its own sake. At times Steuerman is a little inhibited – as if he mistrusts spontaneity – and there are others when he is a little prosaic and literal. He is also somewhat inconsistent about repeats. Nevertheless he remains a generally sound guide to the *Partitas* and he is certainly well recorded.

Huguette Dreyfus gives strong, purposeful performances which, with the harpsichord recorded close, quickly sound too heavyweight. Her rhythmic style is rather relentless, lacking the tonal variety, charm and point which make rivals so persuasive. The six *Partitas* are extravagantly laid out, with only two on each disc, where on CD three are easily possible.

8 Preludes for W. F. Bach, BWV 924/32; 6 Little Preludes, BWV 933/8; 5 Preludes, BWV

939/43; Prelude, BWV 999; Prelude, fugue and allegro in E flat, BWV 998; Preludes and fughettas: in F and G, BWV 901/2; Fantasia and fugue in A min., BWV 904.
(*) DG Dig. **419 426-2; *419 426-4* [id.]. Kenneth Gilbert (harpsichord).

Splendid artistry from this scholar-player; he is predictably stylish and authoritative. He uses a harpsichord by a Flemish maker, Jan Couchet, enlarged by Blanchet in 1759 and by Taskin in 1778, overhauled by Hubert Bédard. He is recorded in the Museum at Chartres: the acoustic is lively and the balance very close; on CD, the transfer is at a very high level indeed. Even played at the lowest setting, the sound seems a bit unrelieved and overbright. This really has 'presence' with a vengeance. The excellence of the playing is not however in question.

Toccatas Nos 1–7, BWV 910/16.
(M) *(**) CBS *M2T 42161* (2) [id.]. Glenn Gould (piano).

On compact disc, Glenn Gould's *Toccatas* are coupled with the *Inventions* – see above. Tape collectors are offered the *Toccatas* alone, although at mid-price.

The Well-tempered Clavier (48 Preludes & fugues), BWV 846/983.
*** DG Dig. **413 439-2** (4) [id.]. Kenneth Gilbert (harpsichord).

The Well-tempered Clavier, Book I, Preludes & fugues Nos 1–24, BWV 846/69.
❀ *** Decca Dig. **414 388-2**; *414 388-4* (2) [id.]. András Schiff (piano).
** HMV **CDS7 49126-8** [Ang. **CDCB 49126**]. Gustav Leonhardt (harpsichord).

The Well-tempered Clavier, Book II, Preludes & fugues Nos 25–48, BWV 870/93.
❀ *** Decca Dig. **417 236-2**; *417 236-4* (2) [id.]. András Schiff (piano).
** HMV **CDS7 49128-2** [Ang. **CDCB 49128**]. Gustav Leonhardt (harpsichord).

Gilbert has made some superb harpsichord records, but his set of the '48' crowns them all. By a substantial margin it now supplants all existing harpsichord versions, with readings that are resilient and individual, yet totally unmannered. Though Gilbert deliberately refuses to use the sort of wide changes of registration which are now thought unauthentic, the range of his expression and the beauty of his instrument, made originally in Antwerp in 1671 and later enlarged in France, give all the variety needed. There is a concentration and purposefulness about each performance over the widest range of moods and expression, and the quality of recording, immediate without being too aggressive, adds to that, although, even on CD, some might feel that the acoustic is just a shade too resonant.

There are no advocates of Bach on the piano more imaginative or persuasive than András Schiff. His set of the '48', conveniently divided into two boxes of two discs, one for each book, is a delight throughout. Schiff – who at an early age found a mentor in Bach with the harpsichordist, George Malcolm – often takes a very individual view of particular preludes and fugues but, as with a pianist like Wilhelm Kempff his unexpected readings regularly win one over long before the end. Consistently he translates this music into pianistic terms, rarely if ever imitating the harpsichord, and though his very choice of the piano will rule him out with those seeking authenticity, his voyage of discovery through this supreme keyboard collection is the more riveting, when the piano is an easier instrument to listen to over long periods. First-rate sound. Each prelude and fugue is separately banded on CD, but without any indexing of the fugues. The chrome cassettes are hardly less impressive technically, without such easy access, but wonderful for the car or for late evening listening, with the music divided into eight groups. The tapes have the same booklets as the CDs.

Gulda's 1973 recording on the piano (Ph. **412 794-2**) is eclipsed by the Schiff set, although it does have the advantage of separate bands for the fugues as well as the preludes.

Gustav Leonhardt plays a copy of a Taskin by David Rubio for Book I and an instrument of

Martin Skowroneck for Book II. It must be said straight away that the attractions of this issue are much diminished by the quality of the recorded sound. Both instruments are closely balanced and even when the volume is reduced the perspective seems unnatural, as if one were leaning into the instrument itself. Tastes in matters of 'registration' are bound to differ, but there is little with which to quarrel and much to admire. This distinguished player and scholar possesses both the effortless technique and the musical insights that are required, and even if there are moments that seem a trifle pedantic – the *C sharp major Fugue* of Book II is rather 'spelt out' – this version offers more rewarding interpretative insights than many of the previously available rivals. Were the sound more sympathetic and appealing, this would be a stronger recommendation, for Leonhardt combines scholarship, technique and sensibility in no small measure. But Kenneth Gilbert's set is preferable in almost all respects.

COLLECTION

(i) *Chromatic fantasia and fugue, BWV 902; French suite in B min., BWV 831; Italian concerto, BWV 971; Toccata in D min., BWV 913.* (ii) *Allabreve in D, BWV 589; Canzona in D. min., BWV 588; Passacaglia in C min., BWV 582; Pastorale in F, BWV 590; 6 Schübler chorales, BWV 645/50; Toccata, adagio and fugue in C, BWV 564; Toccatas and fugues: in D min., BWV 565; in D min. (Dorian), BWV 538; in F, BWV 540.*
(*) DG **413 638-2 (3). (i) Trevor Pinnock (harpsichord): (ii) Ton Koopman (organ).

Trevor Pinnock's performances come from the late 1970s and have been digitally remastered to excellent effect. He is impressive in the *Chromatic fantasia and fugue*, where his sense of style is matched by his technical expertise. A certain literalness of approach is less evident in the *Chromatic fantasy* than in the finale of the *Italian concerto*, which is relentless, and in the *Toccata*. Ton Koopman is allotted two of the three records here and his recordings are of more recent provenance. There is no want of vitality, but he can be austere in matters of registration, and at times, a little unyielding rhythmically. However, admiration far exceeds reservations, and the clarity of sound on CD is really quite outstanding.

ORGAN MUSIC

Adagio in C (from *BWV 565*)*; Chorales: Herzlich tut mich verlangen, BWV 727; Liebster Jesu, BWV 730; Wachet auf, BWV 645; Fantasia and fugue in G min., BWV 542; Fugue in E flat* (*St Anne*)*, BWV 552; Passacaglia and fugue in C min., BWV 582; Toccata and fugue in D min., BWV 565.*
(M) *** Decca **417 711-2**; *417 276-4* [id.]. Peter Hurford (various organs).

An admirable popular recital taken from Peter Hurford's outstanding Bach series. Performances are consistently alive and the vivid recording (the high-level tape almost as impressive as the CD) projects them strongly. A self-recommending issue that will surely tempt any purchaser to go on and explore the whole series when it is issued on compact disc.

Allabreve in D, BWV 589; Canzona in D min., BWV 588; Passacaglia and fugue in C min., BWV 582; Pastorale in F, BWV 590; 6 Schübler chorales, BWV 645/50; Toccatas and fugues in D min. (*Dorian*)*, BWV 538 and 565; Trio sonata in C, BWV 529.*
(B) **(*) DG Dig. *419 825-4*. Ton Koopman (various organs).

Ton Koopman uses two different organs here, principally the Grote Kerk, Massluis, but the *Schübler chorales* are recorded on the Waalse Kerk, Amsterdam, whose reeds are rather fiercely projected, emphasized by the high level of the tape transfer and indeed the emphatically rhythmic style of the playing. The recital opens with the famous *D minor Toccata and fugue*, BWV 565, and this performance has an engaging eccentricity in that Koopman introduces decoration into the opening flourishes. The performance has an excitingly paced fugue and is superbly recorded. Excellent contrast is provided by the *Pastorale* (an extended piece of some twelve minutes) where the registration features the organ's flute stops piquantly. The other performances are well structured and alive, if sometimes rather considered in feeling. The sound is generally first class, though occasionally there is just a suggestion that the tape is reaching saturation point.

Allabreve in D, BWV 589; Chorale prelude: Ach Gott und Herr, BWV 714; Preludes and fugues, BWV 532 and BWV 553/560; Toccata and fugue in D min., BWV 565.
*** Meridian **ECD 84081** [id.]. David Sanger (organ of St Catherine's College, Cambridge).

The organ at St Catherine's College, Cambridge, was completely rebuilt in 1978/9, but is partly based on the pipework of the Swell and certain ranks of the Great (Open and Stopped Diapason, the Principal, Open Flute and Trumpet) taken from an organ originally situated at the Unitarian Chapel, Little Portland Street, built just over a hundred years earlier. The resulting combination is a great success, and its reedy clarity and brightness of timbre are especially suitable for Bach, as is immediately shown in the famous opening *D minor Toccata and fugue* which David Sanger presents with fluent vigour. His playing throughout is thoughtful and well structured; registration shows an excellent sense of colour without being flamboyant. The *Preludes and fugues* are laid out simply before the listener and, although Sanger's style is essentially relaxed, the forward momentum is maintained convincingly and Bach's music is allowed to speak for itself. The *Preludes and fugues in D flat*, BWV 560, and *in D*, BWV 532 (which ends the recital) are particularly convincing, and the latter makes a fine demonstration item alongside BWV 565 for its delightful registration in the fugue as well as for the light clarity of Sanger's touch.

33 Arnstadt chorale preludes (from Yale manuscript).
*** HM Dig. **HMC 905158**; *40. 5158* [id.]. Joseph Payne (organ of St Paul's, Brookline, Mass.).

38 Arnstadt chorale preludes (Yale); 8 Short preludes & fugues, BWV 553/60.
*** HMV Dig. **CDS7 49296-2** (2) [Ang. **CDCB 49296**]. Werner Jacob (Silbermann organ, Arlesheim).

These pieces recently came to light in a volume of 82 chorale preludes in the Lowell Mason collection at Yale. Of the 38 Bach chorale preludes in the MS, 33 were previously unknown, and it is these that Joseph Payne gives us on his compact disc. As he points out, these were not intended to be heard consecutively; and he has arranged them in 'a sequence chosen for musical interest and contrast and not in the order of the manuscript'. The obvious advantage of CD, apart from clarity and presence, is of course the fact that one can isolate a short group to suit one's personal preference. Payne uses the 1983 Bozeman-Gibson organ at St Paul's Church, Brookline, near Boston, which makes very suitable noises. The sound has a splendid definition, though the acoustic is not particularly warm.

In addition to the 33 newly discovered chorale preludes authenticated by Christoph Wolff, Werner Jacob gives us the other five present in the collection but known from other sources. This entails going on to a second CD and offering a fill-up, the *Eight Short preludes and fugues*, BWV 553–60, attributed to Bach. Werner Jacob uses the Silbermann organ of Arlesheim Cathedral in Switzerland and has the advantage of an altogether more pleasing acoustic. It may not match the American recording in terms of clarity, but in every other respect it has much to recommend it, including a much warmer ambience and sense of atmosphere. It costs more than Payne's single disc; otherwise the choice may be left to individual taste; both offer illumination and neither will disappoint. The acoustic of Arlesheim Cathedral will sway some collectors in favour of the EMI recording.

The Art of fugue, BWV 1080 (see also above).
(M) ** Tel. **ZS8 43771** [id.]. Herbert Tachezi (organ of Ahrend & Brunzema, Bremen).

In an accompanying essay, Herbert Tachezi argues his case for playing *The Art of fugue* on the organ for, as he says, 'the performability of many fugues is technically considerably alleviated and simplified by the use of a pedal keyboard while the polyphony is elucidated; furthermore the pedal ensures the complete tonal independence of the bass part'. He also argues persuasively that the very notation is also attuned to the instrument, for organ works by Frescobaldi and others are notated in score form. However, in practice – and in spite of his excellence – there is greater aural fatigue here than in harpsichord, piano or strings. The incomplete final 'torso' of the triple fugue is omitted. The recording dates from 1977 and is excellent in every respect.

Chorale partita on Sei gegrüsset, Jesu gutig, BWV 768; Fantasia in G, BWV 572; 6 Schübler chorale preludes, BWV 645/50.
*** Ph. **412 117-2** [id.]. Daniel Chorzempa (Silbermann organ, Arlesheim Cathedral).

Both the *Sei gegrüsset Partita* and the *Schübler chorales* are admirably designed to demonstrate the palette of a fine organ in the hands of an imaginative player; and here Daniel Chorzempa is on top form, in matters of both registration and musical judgement. His playing is always alive rhythmically (the famous opening *Schübler chorale* has a characteristically genial articulation). The *Fantasia* is comparatively sober but ends with impressive, almost orchestral flair. The Silbermann organ at Arlesheim is justly famous for its colours and bright focus; it sounds splendid on the superbly balanced CD.

Chorale partita on Sei gegrüsset, Jesu gutig, BWV 768; Prelude and fugue in D, BWV 532; Prelude in G, BWV 568; Sonata No. 4 in E min., BWV 528.
*** Denon Dig. **C37 7376** [id.]. Jacques Van Oortmerssen (organ of Walloon Church, Amsterdam).

The organ of the Waalse Kerk is a magnificent instrument, dating originally from 1680 but extended in 1734 by Christian Müller. After various modifications through the years, in the mid-1960s the organ was restored as closely as possible to Müller's conception. The opening *Prelude in G* massively demonstrates the power and variety of timbre it commands and Jacques Van Oortmerssen, although not an international virtuoso, is fully its master in the buoyant performance of the *Prelude and fugue in D*. His registration in the *Andante* of the *E minor Sonata* is a delight; in the extended variations of the *Sei gegrüsset Partita* he is consistently imaginative in his choice of colouring. The playing, always alive, is traditional in the best sense, and the CD recording is superbly realistic. A most rewarding recital. The separate sections of the *Sei gegrüsset* variations are separately banded; in many ways, this is more effective than Chorzempa's performance (see above), partly because the various mixtures of Van Oortmerssen's registration are so naturally well defined.

Chorale preludes Nos 1–45 (Orgelbüchlein), BWV 599/644.
(*) Denon Dig. **CO 1711/2 [id.]. Jørgen Hansen (organ of Holmens Church, Copenhagen).

The forty-five chorale variations which make up the *Orgelbüchlein* (Little Organ Book) were devised by Bach to train organists in the working-out of chorale themes. The set follows the Church calendar from Advent through to Easter; most are quite short, many lasting a minute or less, but some (*O Lamm Gottes unschuldig* and *O Mensch bewein' dein' Sunde gross* – the latter runs to 5′) more ambitious. So that the chorale is absolutely clear to the listener, the melody invariably appears in the top line. Bach's elaborations are intended to illuminate the spirit of the text with which the melody is associated; Jørgen Hansen follows Bach's intentions with appropriate registration, erring on the side of sobriety in certain instances. However, his playing is consistently clear and direct and the chosen tempi are usually apt. A little more extroversion would have been welcome at times, but the simplicity of approach brings its own rewards. The colourful Danish organ (sometimes reedy, sometimes mellifluous) is rather closely observed by the engineers; a shade more ambient effect would have been ideal; however, the sound is not dry but very faithful and present. Separate cues give the listener access that was never possible before on LP and tape and, while this music should not be taken all at one go, it is possible to programme effective groupings and enjoy the imaginative diversity of Bach's writing.

Chorale preludes: Allein Gott in der Höh' sei Ehr, BWV 662/4; An Wasserflüssen Babylon, BWV 653; Schmücke dich, BWV 654; Von Gott will ich nicht lassen, BWV 658. Preludes and fugues: in B min., BWV 544; in E min., BWV 548.

(*) Erato Dig. **ECD 88174; *MCE 75250* [id.]. Marie-Claire Alain (organ of St Martin's Church, Groningen, Netherlands).

Marie-Claire Alain's way with Bach's *Preludes and fugues* is nothing if not magisterial. The sheer breadth of the *Prelude in E minor*, supported by massive sounds from the Schnitger organ, must engender a sense of awe, but when the fugue begins the florid detail engages the listener in its coruscation of brilliance, not sharply defined, but suggesting an element almost of fantasy. The chorale, *An Wasserflüssen Babylon*, which follows creates an agreeable, serene repose. The *B minor Prelude* flows along urbanely but the same weighty treatment to the coupled fugue brings a feeling of relentlessness. There is a hint of romanticism (use of tremolo) in the three closing variants on the chorale, *Allein Gott*, but the registration is attractive, particularly in the final treatment *as a trio*, which is intended as an invocation of the Holy Ghost. The organ is superbly recorded throughout, and although some of the passagework is blurred, clearly Mme Alain does not seek the sharpest articulation in the faster passages. She is very good at balancing the chorales and retaining their atmosphere.

Chorale preludes: Alle Menschen müssen sterben, BWV 643; Vater unser in Himmelreich, BWV 737; Fantasia and fugue in G min., BWV 542; Passacaglia and fugue in C min., BWV 582; Toccata in F, BWV 540.

** Telarc Dig. **CD 80049** [id.]. Michael Murray (organ at Methuen Memorial Hall, Mass.).

The sound here is first class. The acoustic is fairly reverberant, and this is an organ obviously intended by its builders to produce a wide panoply of sound rather than crystal-clear inner detail. The most impressive performance is of the *Passacaglia and fugue in C minor*, well paced and powerful with an effectively wide dynamic range. Michael Murray's approach to the *Fantasia and fugue* and *Toccata* is rather measured. The *Chorale preludes* are given serene and, it must be admitted, slightly static performances. The background is not quite silent, for the organ contributes its own characteristic sound as the air goes through the pipes.

Chorale preludes: Christe, du Lamm Gottes, BWV 619; Herr Christ, der ein'ge Gottes Sohn, BWV 601; Heut' triumphiret Gottes Sohn, BWV 630; Liebster Jesu, BWV 731; Preludes and fugues: in G, BWV 541; in A min., BWV 543; in C min., BWV 546; Toccata, adagio and fugue in C, BWV 564.

* Telarc Dig. **CD 80127** [id.]. Michael Murray (organ of St Andreas-Kirche, Hildesheim).

A disappointing follow-up to his two previous recitals, Michael Murray's playing here is wanting in vitality and the *Toccata, adagio and fugue in C* lacks a sense of awe or power. The chorale preludes are agreeably uneventful. The sound of this West German organ is faithfully massive, but opaque.

Chorale preludes: Kommst du nun, Jesu, BWV 650; Wachet auf, BWV 645; Pastorale in F, BWV 590; Passacaglia in C min., BWV 582; Toccata, adagio and fugue in C, BWV 564; Toccata and fugue in D min., BWV 565; Trio sonata in C, BWV 529.
(*) DG Dig. **423 200-2 [id.]. Ton Koopman (various organs).

This is a further assembly of Ton Koopman's performances which can be found listed above and below in other collections, both on CD and (less expensively) on tape. The present recital is generous; the sound is very good, varying between instruments.

Chorale preludes: Nun komm der Heiden Heiland, BWV 569; Wachet auf, BWV 545; Concerto in A min. (after Vivaldi), *BWV 593; Fantasia and fugue in G min., BWV 542; Passacaglia in C min., BWV 582; Toccata, adagio and fugue in C, BWV 564; Toccata and fugue in D min., BWV 565.*
(M) ** HMV **CDM7 69029-2** [id.]; *EG 769029-4*. Lionel Rogg (various organs).

Lionel Rogg has made three surveys of Bach's organ music in stereo, the first an integral set on the BACH label for Oryx in the 1960s, then again for Harmonia Mundi a decade later. These recordings come from his further HMV series, mostly from 1975/6, but with the two chorales recorded as recently as 1985. His style is relaxed and somewhat didactic, though he takes a brisk view of the famous *Toccata and fugue in D minor* which opens the programme. He is at his best in the works which gain from a measured pulse and a clear grasp of the architecture, like the *Passacaglia in C minor* and BWV 564, although the lighter *Concerto* after Vivaldi is also quite successful. The sound is very clear, but the digital remastering has brought an added dryness to the ambient effect: the originals had more warmth of sonority.

Chorale preludes: O Mensch bewein' dein' Sünde gross, BWV 622; Schmücke dich, O liebe Seele, BWV 654; Wachet auf, BWV 645; Fantasia and fugue in G min., BWV 542; Passacaglia and fugue in C min., BWV 582; Prelude and fugue in A min., BWV 543; Toccata and fugue in D min., BWV 565.
(*) HMV **CDC7 47645-2. Werner Jacob (various organs).

Werner Jacob uses a different organ for each piece and the ubiquitous *D minor Toccata and fugue*, played with some flair, sounds splendid on the Silbermann instrument at Arlesheim. He plays the chorale preludes reverentially but effectively, and his registration is unostentatious so that one's awareness of changes of venue is not emphasized. The passagework of the *Prelude and fugue in A minor* (St Bavo, Haarlem) is rather blurred, but that seems to come from the player's style of articulation; it is otherwise a fine performance. The powerfully spacious opening of the *Fantasia and fugue in G minor* serves to demonstrate the massive tone of the organ of Marienkirche Stralsund, but the similar grandeur of the *Passacaglia* of the *Passacaglia in C minor*, recorded in Brandenburg, is underlined by Jacob's purposeful and deliberately slow basic tempo. Nevertheless this is all fine playing in the German tradition.

Concerto in A min. (after Vivaldi), *BWV 593; Fantasia and fugue in G min., BWV 542; Fugue in G min., BWV 578; Passacaglia and fugue in C min., BWV 582; Toccata and fugue in D min., BWV 565.*
** Erato Dig. **ECD 88004**. Marie-Claire Alain (organ of Collégiale of Saint-Donat Drôme).

After a lively account of the famous *D minor Toccata and fugue* Marie-Claire Alain is heard at her most individual in the *Fugue in G minor*, BWV 578, which she registers delicately, giving the impression of orchestral woodwind. At the other end of the scale, she is weightily imposing in the *Passacaglia in C minor*, but a similarly massive approach to the *G minor Fantasia* seems a little overdone. The *Concerto* is buoyant in the outer movements, but the *Adagio* (again nicely registered) rather hangs fire. The organ sounds attractive with its throaty reeds and sonorous pedals which support but never confuse the texture.

Concerto in A min. (after Vivaldi), *BWV 593; Preludes and fugues: in D, BWV 532; in B min., BWV 544; Toccata and fugue in D min., BWV 565.*
** Telarc **CD 80088** [id.]. Michael Murray (organs at Congregational Church, Los Angeles).

The paired Skinner-Schlicker organs at the First Congregational Church of Los Angeles are widely separated, situated at opposite ends of the nave. They are controlled by twin consoles of four manuals; the effect in this recording is to spread the point source of the sound (there are no exaggerated antiphonal effects) in the most attractive way. The acoustics of the church are such that detail in the *Toccata and fugue* and the *Concerto* is never blurred, though in the *B minor Prelude and fugue* Michael Murray's mellifluous presentation produces over-smooth articulation. He and the organ both sound splendid in BWV 565, where the fast pacing generates lively bravura. The arrangement of the Vivaldi *Concerto* is pleasingly registered, especially the central *Adagio*, and is played with an agreeably light touch. In both preludes and fugues, however, the approach is more conventional.

Fantasia in C, BWV 570; Fugue in G min., BWV 578; Preludes and fugues: in C, BWV 545; in G min., BWV 535; 6 Schübler chorales, BWV 645/50; Toccata and fugue in D min., BWV 565; Trios: in C min., BWV 585; in D min., BWV 583.
** Denon Dig. **C37 7004** [id.]. Hans Otto (Silbermann organ, Freiberg).

A generous recital (55′ 37″) very well recorded. The attractively bright, reedy characteristic of the Freiberg organ is well suited to Bach's music, and the balance ensures inner clarity as well as a convincing overall perspective. Hans Otto, however, is a rather didactic player. He does not make a distinctive impression with the opening *Toccata and fugue in D minor*, and is rhythmically over-assertive in the famous opening *Schübler chorale, Wachet auf*. He is at his best in the *Prelude and fugue in G minor* (BWV 535) and the closing fugue of the recital (BWV 578) which are presented simply and straightforwardly.

Fantasia and fugue in C min., BWV 537; Prelude and fugue in G, BWV 541; Toccata and fugue in D min. (Dorian), BWV 538; Toccata and fugue in E, BWV 566.
** Ph. Dig. **416 363-2**; *416 363-4* [id.]. Daniel Chorzempa (organ of Bovenkerk, Kampen).

Although the *Dorian toccata* which opens this recital is buoyant enough, Daniel Chorzempa's performances here are otherwise heftily conceived and the fugues proceed in considered fashion without ever taking off. The massive sounds of the Bovenkerk organ contribute to this weighty impression and everything is caught spectacularly on CD. The chrome cassette is good, too, but has minor problems with the cadential climaxes of BWV 538 and BWV 566.

Fantasia in G, BWV 572; Preludes and fugues: in C, BWV 545; in C min.; in G, BWV 549/50; in G min., BWV 535; Pastorale, BWV 590; Toccata and fugue in D min., BWV 565.
(M) *** Ph. **420 860-2**; *420 860-4* [id.]. Wolfgang Rübsam (organ of Frauenfeld, Switzerland).

A splendid collection of early works, nearly all dating from Bach's Arnstadt and Weimar periods and full of exuberance of spirit. The *Fugue in G*, BWV 550, is especially memorable, but undoubtedly the highlight of the recital is the superb performance of the *Fantasia in G*. It opens with an exhilarating *Très vitement* and after a massive *Grave* middle section comes a brilliantly lightweight bravura finale. Wolfgang Rübsam's articulation is deliciously pointed. The recording of the Metzler organ has a fairly long reverberation period, and Rübsam anticipates this in his playing most successfully. The quality of the recorded sound is splendid, on tape as well as CD. Highly recommended.

Fantasia and fugue in G min., BWV 542; Prelude and fugue in F min., BWV 534; Toccata and fugue in D min., BWV 565; Toccata, adagio and fugue in C, BWV 564; Trio sonata No. 1 in E flat, BWV 525.
(M) ** DG **419 047-2**; *419 047-4* [id.]. Helmut Walcha (organ of St Laurenskerk, Alkmaar).

Fantasia and fugue in G min., BWV 542; Passacaglia and fugue in C min., BWV 582; Toccata and fugues: in D min., BWV 565; in F, BWV 540.
(M) ** DG *419 659-4*. Helmut Walcha (organ of St Laurenskerk, Alkmaar).

These recordings, made in 1963/4, sound extremely well in their CD format: the brightness is supported by an underlying depth and there is a sense of perspective too, particularly in the interplay of the famous *D minor Fugue* which shows Walcha at his most extrovert. The other performances are often very effectively registered, notably the *C major Fugue*, BWV 564, and the first movement of the *Trio sonata*, but Walcha's pulse seems determinedly steady in most of this music. Structures are well controlled and detail is lucid, but there is also a sense of ponderousness which will not appeal to everyone. The alternative collection is available on tape only (issued in DG's curiously uneven Focus series, in the lower-middle price range). Both tapes are well engineered.

Passacaglia and fugue in C min., BWV 582; Toccata and fugue in C, BWV 564; Toccata and fugue in D min. (Dorian), BWV 538; Toccata and fugue in D min., BWV 565.
*** Argo **411 824 2**; *411 824 4* [id.]. Peter Hurford (organs of Ratzeburg Cathedral, West Germany, and Church of Our Lady of Sorrows, Toronto, Canada).

Another excellent sampler of Hurford's Bach recordings, opening with his massively extrovert *Toccata and fugue in D minor*, BWV 565, but with a variety of mood in the other works, the *Dorian fugue* quite relaxed, the *C minor Passacaglia and fugue* unhurried but superbly controlled. The sound is first class in both formats, with the CD having that extra degree of presence; but the cassette is also demonstration-worthy.

Prelude and fugue in E flat, BWV 552; Prelude, Largo (BWV 529/2) and fugue in C, BWV 545; Toccata and fugue in D min., BWV 565.
*(*) Ph. Dig. **410 038-2** [id.]. Daniel Chorzempa (organ).

Daniel Chorzempa is splendidly recorded, but the performances are very measured, as is obvious from the famous *D minor Fugue*. In the big E flat work, the effect is massive but static, and the performance is too deliberate by half. The CD with its silent background creates a most spectacular impression on the listener and it is a pity that this recital offers playing of relatively little flair.

6 Schübler chorale preludes, BWV 645/50; Chorales: Jesu, joy of man's desiring (from *Cantata 147*); *Erbarm dich, BWV 721; Ich ruf' zu dir, Herr Jesu Christ, BWV 639; Nun freut euch, BWV 734a; Nun komm' der Heiden Heiland, BWV 659; O Mensch bewein, BWV 622; Wir glauben all an einen Gott, BWV 680.*
** Erato Dig. **ECD 88030** [id.]. Marie-Claire Alain (organ of Collégiale of Saint-Donat, Drôme).

Marie-Claire Alain's style here is often impulsive, and she registers exuberantly in the faster chorales. However, in the slower ones there are hints of romanticism. The rhythm of the first

Schübler chorale, Wachet auf, could be smoother, but at least the playing here is never dull. The organ is given striking presence on CD.

Toccata, adagio and fugue in C, BWV 564; Toccata and fugues; in D min. (*Dorian*), *BWV 538; in D min., BWV 565; in F, BWV 540.*
(*) DG Dig. **410 999-2 [id.]. Ton Koopman (organ of Massluis Grote Kerk).

Ears will prick up at the opening flourishes of the famous *D minor Toccata and fugue*, BWV 565, as Ton Koopman, who favours plenty of ornamentation, has added a brief trill. When this eccentricity is past, the performance is attractively buoyant and the *Toccata, adagio and fugue*, BWV 564, also goes well. However, a good deal of the fast passagework in the programme as a whole tends to get slightly blurred by the acoustic resonance, even on CD. The performances throughout are very positive, even if the last degree of imagination is missing in both execution and registration. If one accepts the spacious presentation and accompanying lack of sharp inner definition, the tangibility of the organ image is impressive.

VOCAL MUSIC

Cantatas Nos 1: Wie schön leuchtet uns der Morgenstern; 2: Ach Gott, vom Himmel; 3: Ach Gott, wie manches Herzeleid; 4: Christ lag in Todesbanden.
(M) *** Tel. **ZL8 35027** (2) [id.]. Treble soloists from V. Boys' Ch., Esswood, Equiluz, Van Egmond, V. Boys' Ch., Ch. Viennensis, VCM, Harnoncourt.

The remarkable Teldec project, a complete recording of all Bach's cantatas, began in the early 1970s and is now nearing completion. The first CDs appeared during the tercentenary year and the digital remastering proved consistently successful. There is no background noise to speak of, and the sound is clarified and refined, to bring striking presence to voices and accompaniment alike. The acoustic is usually not too dry and not too ecclesiastical either, and the projection is realistic. The original LP packaging included full scores. Inevitably, the CDs omit these but retain the English translations of the texts and excellent notes by Alfred Dürr. They are offered at upper mid-price. All new issues are made in CD format; this began with Cantata No. 147 (the source of the famous *Jesu, joy of man's desiring*); in the following box, beginning with No. 152, the number of cantatas included was increased, still within the paired CD format. The earlier volumes are now also being reissued; at the time of going to press, the first thirteen have already appeared. Most of the others should resurface during the lifetime of this book. They remain available for those willing to invest in LPs. It is a great pity that the trial issue of several volumes on chrome cassettes had to be aborted for lack of public response, for they were of the highest technical quality and lost little of the presence and clarity of the CDs.

The authentic character of the performances means that boys replace women, not only in the choruses but also as soloists, and the size of the forces is confined to what we know Bach himself would have expected. The simplicity of the approach brings its own merits, for the imperfect yet otherworldly quality of some of the treble soloists refreshingly focuses the listener's attention on the music itself. Less appealing is the quality of the violins, which eschew vibrato – and, it would sometimes seem, any kind of timbre!

Generally speaking, there is a certain want of rhythmic freedom and some expressive caution. Rhythmic accents are underlined with some regularity and the grandeur of Bach's inspiration is at times lost to view. Where there are no alternatives for outstanding cantatas, such as the marvellously rich and resourceful sonorities of the sinfonia to *Ach Gott, vom Himmel* (No. 2), with its heavenly aria, *Durchs Feuer wird das Silber rein*, choice is simple, and here the performance too is a fine one. There is more grandeur to John Eliot Gardiner's account of *Christ lag in Todesbanden* (No. 4), but there is so much fine music in Cantatas 2 and 3, not otherwise obtainable on record, that the first of these volumes is a must.

Cantatas Nos 4: Christ lag in Todesbanden; 26: Ach wie flüchtig, ach wie nichtig; 51: Jauchzet Gott in allen Landen; 56: Ich will den Kreuzstab gerne tragen; 61: Nun komm, der Heiden Heiland; 80: Ein feste Burge ist unser Gott; 106: Gottes Zeit ist die allerbeste Zeit (Actus tragicus); 147: Herz und Mund und Tat und Leben.
** DG **413 646-2** (3) [id.]. Soloists, Munich Bach Ch., Munich Bach O, Karl Richter.

As part of their CD Bach Edition issued in the tercentenary year, Archiv have collected eight cantatas from the vast number recorded by Karl Richter over the years. Thanks to him, we had the most comprehensive survey of the Bach cantatas to be put on record before the ambitious Harnoncourt–Leonhardt venture got into its stride. The earliest recording here, *Herz und Mund und Tat und Leben*, comes from 1962 and is among the best, while the most recent, *Ach wie flüchtig, ach wie nichtig*, comes from 1979. The choice seems quite arbitrary, though it does garner a particularly rich variety of singers, including Edith Mathis, Ernst Haefliger, Peter Schreier and Dietrich Fischer-Dieskau. The digitally remastered transfers sound very good indeed, and collectors need not worry on this score. Richter, of course, was rather heavy-handed at times – no one who puts his 1966 account of *Gottes Zeit* alongside the infinitely more imaginative and sensitive version made by Jürgen Jürgens with the Leonhardt Consort at about the same time would have any doubts on that score! Recommended, but with modified rapture.

Cantatas Nos 4: Christ lag in Todesbanden; 50: Nun ist das Heil und die Kraft; 118: O Jesu Christ, meine Lebens Licht; 131: Aus der Tiete rufe ich, Herr zu dir.
*** Erato Dig. **ECD 88117** (2) [id.]. Monteverdi Ch., E. Bar. Soloists, Gardiner – *Motets*.***

These performances first appeared in LP form in the early 1980s. The original LP set (alongside the *Motets* – see below) included the magnificent cantata movement, BWV 50, for double choir (used as an epilogue to the glorious *Singet dem Herrn*), together with BWV 118 and 131. To those the CD set – also two discs – adds one of the best loved of all cantatas, *Christ lag in Todesbanden*, BWV 4. Alongside this, the high point is probably *O Jesu Christ, meine Lebens Licht*, given in its second version and with genuine majesty. At other times Gardiner's tempi are characteristically brisk, but there is no question about the vitality of the music making here. The recording is truthful and present, without being in the demonstration category.

(i) *Cantatas Nos 5: Wo soll ich fliehen; 6: Bleib bei uns;* (ii) *7: Christ unser Herr zum Jordan kam; 8: Liebster Gott.*
(M) *** Tel **ZL8 35028** (2) [id.]. Esswood, Equiluz, Van Egmond, (i) Treble soloists from V. Boys' Ch., Ch. Viennensis, V. Boys' Ch., VCM, Harnoncourt; (ii) Regensburg treble soloists, King's College Ch., Leonhardt Cons., Leonhardt.

This is generally up to the standard of the series, although Richter's old recording of No. 8, *Liebster Gott*, on Archiv (now deleted) had greater breadth and vision than the Leonhardt version. No. 6, *Bleib bei uns*, has a fine alto solo with oboe obbligato, which is very well done; the solo treble also distinguishes himself. The wind embroidery for the opening chorus of No. 8 again shows the character of the early instruments to good effect, and Kurt Equiluz's solo, *Was willst du dich, mein Geist, entsetzen*, eloquently sung, is given an effective oboe d'amore decoration. The presence of the remastered sound is striking in these excellent CDs.

(i) *Cantatas Nos 9: Es ist das Heil; 10: Meine Seele erhebt den Herrn;* (ii) *11: Lobet Gott in seinen Reichen.*
(M) *** Tel. **ZL8 35029** (2) [id.]. Esswood, Equiluz, Van Egmond; (i) Regensburg treble soloists, King's College Ch., Leonhardt Cons., Leonhardt; (ii) Treble soloists from V. Boys' Ch., Ch. Viennensis, V. Boys' Ch., VCM, Harnoncourt.

Cantata No. 9 has a memorable opening chorus with a background embroidery by flute and oboe d'amore. Later there is a striking tenor aria, *Wir waren schon zu tief gesunken*, and a duet for soprano and alto, *Herr, du siebst statt, guter Werke*, again decorated by the flute and oboe d'amore. *Lobet Gott*, the Ascension cantata, is a large-scale work (it has a CD to itself) in which the joyful introductory chorus (with trumpets) set the mood for a strong performance that brings out the best in all the soloists.

Cantata No. 10: Meine Seele erhebt den Herrn.
(M) *** Decca *414 322-4*. Ameling, Watts, Krenn, Rintzler, V. Ac. Ch., SCO, Münchinger – *Magnificat*.***

An excellent coupling for a first-rate account of the D major *Magnificat*. This fine cantata is very well sung and played, with all the performers at their best. The recording too is freshly vivid on the excellent chrome tape. A bargain.

Cantatas Nos 12: Weinen, klagen; 13: Meine Seufzer, meine Tränen; 14: Wär Gott nich; 16: Herr Gott, dich loben.
(M) *** Tel. **ZL8 35030** (2) [id.]. Gampert, Hinterreiter, Esswood, Equiluz, Van Altena, Van Egmond, King's Coll. Ch., Leonhardt Cons., Leonhardt.

Cantata No. 12, *Weinen, klagen, sorgen, zagen* ('Weeping, lamenting, worrying, fearing') written for the third Sunday after Easter, has an understandable melancholy. The alto aria is particularly fine (*Kreuz und Krone sind verbunden*) and the oboe obbligato is beautifully done. No. 14, *Wär Gott nich mit uns diese Zeit*, has a splendid extended opening chorus, of considerable complexity and striking power. There is much wonderful music in all three works here; performances and recordings are first class.

Cantatas Nos 17: Wer Dank opfert; 18: Gleich wie der Regen; 19: Es erhub sich ein Streit; 20: O Ewigkeit, du Donnerwort.
(M) *** Tel. **ZL8 35031** (2) [id.]. Treble soloists from V. Boys' Ch., Esswood, Equiluz, Van Egmond, V. Boys' Ch., Ch. Viennensis, VCM, Harnoncourt.

Another fine set including superb music which is very little known. No. 17 has a long sinfonia and opening chorus combined; and in No. 19, the introductory fugal chorus is magnificent in its tumultuous polyphony. The closing chorus is simpler, but trumpets add a touch of ceremonial splendour. No. 20 also features trumpets not only in the choruses but no less effectively in the bass aria, *Wacht auf*. This work also includes a memorable alto/tenor duet, *O Menschenkind, hör auf geschwind*. The sound is first class, fresh, vivid and clear.

(i) *Cantatas Nos 21: Ich hatte viel Bekümmernis;* (ii) *22: Jesus nahm zu sich die Zwölfe; 23: Du wahrer Gott.*
(M) **(*) Tel. **ZL8 35032** (2) [id.]. Esswood, Equiluz; (i) Walker, Wyatt, V. Boys' Ch., Ch. Viennensis, VCM, Harnoncourt; (ii) Gampert, Van Altena, Van Egmond, King's College Ch., Leonhardt Cons., Leonhardt.

The magnificent *Ich hatte viel Bekümmernis* lacks something in flair and Leonhardt is a little rigid in No. 22, *Jesus nahm zu sich die Zwölfe*. Harnoncourt tends in general to be freer, but a constant source of irritation through the series is the tendency to accent all main beats. This was the final appearance of the King's College Choir which made a worthwhile contribution to many of the early performances in the series. The CD transfers are well up to the standard already set by this rewarding enterprise.

Cantatas Nos 24: Ein ungefärbt Gemüte; 25: Es ist nichts gesundes; 26: Ach wie flüchtig; 27: Wer weiss, wie nahe mir.

(M) *** Tel. **ZL8 35033** (2). Esswood, Equiluz, Van Egmond, Siegmund, Nimsgern, V. Boys' Ch., C. Viennensis, VCM, Harnoncourt.

This volume is worth having in particular for the sake of the magnificent *Es ist nichts gesundes*, a cantata of exceptional richness of expression and resource. No. 27, *Wer weiss, wie nahe mir mein Ende*, is altogether magnificent too, and the performances are some of the finest to appear in this ambitious and often impressive survey. Certainly for those dipping into rather than collecting all this series, Volumes 1 and 7 would be good starting-points, even though in the case of the latter all the cantatas are exceptionally short.

Cantatas Nos 28: Gottlob! nun geht das Jahr zu Ende; 29: Wir danken dir, Gott; 30: Freue dich, erlöste Schar!

(M) *** Tel. **ZL8 35034** (2). Esswood, Equiluz, Van Egmond, Nimsgern, V. Boys' Ch., Ch. Viennensis, VCM, Harnoncourt.

(i) *Cantatas Nos 31: Der Himmel lacht, die Erde jubilieret;* (ii) *32: Liebster Jesu, mein Verlangen; 33: Allein zu dir, Herr Jesu Christ;* (i) *34: O ewiges Feuer.*

(M) *** Tel. **ZL8 35035** (2). (i) Esswood, Equiluz, Nimsgern, V. Boys' Ch., Ch. Viennensis, VCM, Harnoncourt; (ii) Gampert, Jacobs, Van Altena, Van Egmond, Hanover Boys' Ch., Leonhardt Cons., Leonhardt.

Cantatas Nos 35: Geist und Seele wird verwirret; 36: Schwingt freudig euch empor; 37: Wer da glaubet und getauft wird; 38: Aus tiefer Not schrei ich zu dir.

(M) *** Tel. **ZL8 35036** (2). Esswood, Equiluz, Ruud Van der Meer, V. Boys' Ch., Ch. Viennensis, VCM, Harnoncourt.

These three albums continue the high standard that has distinguished this enterprise. Of the new names in the roster of soloists one must mention the stylish singing of René Jacobs, and Walter Gampert is the excellent treble soloist in *Liebster Jesu.* No. 34 is an especially attractive cantata and here, as throughout, one notes the liveliness as well as the authenticity of the performances, although the expressive writing is sensitively handled, too: the alto aria, *Wohl euch, ihr auserwahlten, Seelen* ('Blessed ye hearts whom God has chosen'), with its atmospheric obbligato flutes is particularly memorable. **ZL8 35036** is another set where the listener is struck again and again by the fertility of Bach's imagination. No. 35 features an outstanding concertante organ solo; No. 36 uses a pair of oboi d'amore, and there are oboes in duet in No. 38. Most enjoyable, with excellent solo singing, clear, well-balanced sound, made exceptionally vivid in the CD remastering.

(i) *Cantatas Nos 39: Brich dem Hungrigen dein Brot;* (i; ii) *40: Dazu ist erschienen der Sohn Gottes;* (iii) *41: Jesu, nun sei gepreiset; 42: Am Abend aber desselbigen Sabbats.*

(M) ** Tel. **ZL8 35269** (2). (i) Jacobs, Van Egmond, Hanover Boys' Ch., Leonhardt Cons., Leonhardt; (ii) Van Altena; (iii) Esswood, Equiluz, Van der Meer, V. Boys' Ch., VCM, Harnoncourt.

This is one of the less distinguished sets in this long and successful project. No. 41, *Jesu, nun sei gepreiset*, probably fares best: one admires the light tone of the baroque brass instruments and the general sense of style that informs the proceedings, even if intonation, as inevitably seems to happen with authentic instruments, is not always true. The music is quite magnificent. So, too, is Cantata 42, *Am Abend aber desselbigen Sabbats*, but these artists do little to convey the feeling of the opening sinfonia, the oboe melody losing much of its expressive fervour. There is a loss of breadth too in No. 39, *Brich dem Hungrigen dein Brot*, which is not altogether offset by the authenticity to which these performers are dedicated. No. 40 has some lively choruses, well sung, and there is also some excellent obbligato horn playing: here the music making is undoubtedly spirited. Throughout there is some very stylish and well-prepared singing by the soloists and, taking into account the quality of the music making, there is much to enjoy here, even if the performances sometimes radiate greater concern with historical rectitude (as these artists conceive it) than in communicating their pleasure in the music. The recordings are exemplary and the CD transfers marvellously managed: everything is fresh and clear, without exaggeration yet with excellent presence.

(i) *Cantatas Nos 43: Gott fähret auf mit Jauchzen; 44: Sie werden euch in den Bann tun;* (ii) *45: Es ist dir gesagt; 46: Schauet doch und sehet, ob irgend.*
(M) *** Tel. **ZL8 35283** (2) [id.]. (i) Jelosits, Esswood, Equiluz, Van der Meer, V. Boys' Ch., VCM, Harnoncourt; (ii) Jacobs, Equiluz, Kunz, Hanover Boys' Ch., Leonhardt Cons., Leonhardt.

Not all the volumes in this ambitious series have equal claims on the collector's pocket, but this is among the finest yet to appear. Cantata 43, *Gott fähret auf mit Jauchzen*, and its successor are for the Sunday of Ascension Day and the Sunday following, while No. 46 is the one that includes the original *Qui tollis peccata* of the *B minor Mass*. This and No. 43 are not otherwise available, and though the texture could be more revealingly laid out in 46, this is the only technical blemish in a very fine recording. The performances are of the highest standard and young Peter Jelosits, the boy treble, copes manfully with the very considerable demands of Bach's writing. He is really astonishingly fine, and his companions in these records are no less accomplished. Leonhardt takes the chorale in No. 46 a little on the fast side; but enough of quibbles – this is really a first-class box.

Cantatas Nos 47: Wer sich selbst erhöhet; 48: Ich elender Mensch; 49: Ich geh' und suche mit Verlangen; 50: Nun ist das Heil.
(M) *** Tel. **ZL8 35284** (2) [id.]. Jelosits, Esswood, Equiluz, Van der Meer, V. Boy's Ch., Ch. Viennensis, VCM, Harnoncourt.

This fine (if uneven) series continues its progress and reaches almost a quarter of the way through the complete cantatas. The same stylistic features of the set are to be found as in earlier boxes along with the same excellent presentation. The treble soloist in No. 49, *Ich geh' und suche mit Verlangen*, Peter Jelosits, really is remarkable. Perhaps the chorus in No. 50, *Nun ist das Heil*, is a shade overdriven, but by and large this is one of the best of the series, and the riches the music unfolds do not fail to surprise and reward the listener.

Cantatas Nos 51–146.
On CD, the reissue of earlier volumes of the Harnoncourt/Leonhardt series of Bach *Cantatas* has reached only Volume 13 although, as can be seen below, the later-numbered works are being issued immediately in compact disc format. As we go to press, the middle volumes including Nos 51–146 are still available in their LP format, but we understand that further reissues will appear on CD in 1988/9 until the whole project is complete.

Cantata No. 51: Jauchzet Gott in allen Landen.
*** Ph. Dig. **411 458-2**; *411 458-4* [id.]. Emma Kirkby, E. Bar. Soloists, Gardiner – *Magnificat*.***

Jauchzet Gott is one of Bach's most joyful cantatas; Emma Kirkby follows the example of the opening trumpeting (Crispian Steele-Perkins – in excellent form) when she begins. It is a brilliantly responsive performance, admirably accompanied and very well recorded in both formats.

Cantatas Nos 51: Jauchzet Gott in allen Landen; 140: Wachet auf, ruft uns die Stimme.
** O-L Dig. **417 616-2**; *417 616-4* [id.]. Baird, Minter, Jeffrey Thomas, Opalach, Bach Ens., Rifkin.

Wachet auf, ruft uns die Stimme is placed first and gives pleasure, for the artists seem to be enjoying themselves. As in his other Bach records, Joshua Rifkin goes for the one-to-a-part principle in his instrumental ensemble (save for the violins), resting his case on the number of copies of the parts surviving at Leipzig. Rifkin uses a later Leipzig text for *Jauchzet Gott*. The very opening is somewhat measured and bloodless and does not ring out as it does on some rival versions; generally speaking, his account is too judicious in spirit. Julianne Baird is an excellent singer who possesses a pleasing voice and has commendable technique. The recording is excellent in its CD format, but our copy of the cassette was faultily transferred, with an unacceptably low level on side one.

Cantatas Nos 80: Ein' feste Burg ist unser Gott; 140: Wachet auf, ruft uns die Stimme.
(*) Decca Dig. **414 045-2; *414 045-4* [id.]. Fontana, Hamari, Winbergh, Krause, Hymnus Boys' Ch., SCO, Münchinger.

Münchinger, who uses the trumpets and timpani added by Bach's eldest son, Wilhelm Friedemann, has the advantage of excellently transparent and well-detailed Decca digital recording and a fine team of soloists: both Gösta Winbergh and Tom Krause make positive contributions. Karl Münchinger does not bring quite the warmth or musicality that distinguishes the finest performances of Bach, but there is little of the pedantry that has at times afflicted his performances. On CD, extra pleasure is afforded by the attractive ambience – the concert-hall balance is expertly managed – and by the tangibility of the chorus, whose vigorous contribution is given striking body and presence. All the movements are separately banded. There is an excellent chrome cassette.

Cantatas Nos 80: Ein' feste Burg ist unser Gott; 147: Herz und Mund und Tat und Leben.
*(**) O-L Dig. **417 250-2**; *417 250-4* [id.]. Bryden, Minter, Jeffrey Thomas, Opalach, Bach Ens., Rifkin.

Both cantatas date from Bach's Leipzig years but grew through a process of expansion and revision from music that he had written during his time at Weimar. In a lengthy essay accompanying the disc, Joshua Rifkin sets out their history and the principles and assumptions upon which his interpretation rests. He not only goes for the one-to-a-part principle in his instrumental ensemble but also as far as the choruses are concerned. He opts for a female soprano rather than a boy, but an adult male alto. Not all will find his solutions congenial and one can well imagine his fast tempo for the *Jesu, joy of man's desiring* chorale that ends the first part of *Herz und Mund und Tat und Leben* will set the cat among the pigeons. In some ways it is both refreshing and convincing, though the use of one voice to a part in the chorales is not. There is also a loss of grandeur and body in such movements as the opening chorus. There is some good singing here and the playing is lively enough. Rifkin strips away much of the received conventions about Bach performance practice. A stimulating, thought-provoking performance rather than a completely convincing experience.

Cantatas Nos (i) *82: Ich habe genug;* (ii) *202; Weichet nur, betrübte Schatten.*
*(*) Hyp. *KA 66036*. (i) David Thomas; (ii) Emma Kirkby; Taverner Players, Parrott.

In *Ich habe genug* David Thomas gives a good but not inspired account of the solo part and although the odd intonation blemish is of little importance, memories of Hotter, Souzay, Fischer-Dieskau and others who have recorded it in the past are not banished. Emma Kirkby is more successful in *Weichet nur, betrübte Schatten* and as usual delights the listener though some may feel that the excellent Taverner Players under Andrew Parrott could bring greater flair and lightness of touch to this felicitous score. Good recording, sensibly balanced. The cassette is made at fractionally too high a level and the upper range is confused in focus.

Cantatas Nos 82: Ich habe genug; 169: Gott soll allein mein Herze haben.
(B) *** HMV *TCC2-POR 154592-9*. Baker, Amb. S., Bath Fest. O, Menuhin – *Arias*.***

Ich habe genug is one of the best-known of Bach's cantatas, while No. 169 is a comparative rarity. The performances are expressive and intelligent, though Dame Janet Baker does not achieve quite the same heights of inspiration here as in her Decca recording of No. 159. The sound is admirably lifelike and reproduces smoothly, with a natural bloom on the voice, and the coupling of this special double-length cassette issue is very attractive – see below.

Cantatas Nos 106: Gottes Zeit ist die allerbeste Zeit; 131: Aus der Tiefen.
*** O-L Dig. **417 323-2**; *417 323-4* [id.]. Monoyios, Rickards, Brownlees, Opalach, Bach Ens., Rifkin.

Both cantatas probably come from the early months of Bach's tenure as organist at Mulhausen in 1707. The one-voice-to-a-part principle is applied again, and readers who do not respond to it will doubtless take avoiding action. In doing so, however, they will miss a performance of considerable merit: the opening of *Gottes Zeit* is one of the most beautiful moments in all Bach and is beautifully done. Even those who find the avoidance of vocal vibrato an unnatural constraint may find themselves persuaded by this performance. *Aus der Tiefen* is hardly less fine, and the singers are all first class. One feels the needs for greater weight and a more full-blooded approach at times, but this is outweighed by the sensitivity and intelligence that inform these excellently balanced recordings.

Cantata No. 140: Wachet auf.
(M) *(*) DG **419 466-2**, *419 466-4* [id.]. Mathis, Schreier, Fischer-Dieskau, Munich Bach Ch. and O, Karl Richter – *Magnificat*.*(*)

The merits of Richter's performances are well enough known: his readings have a no-nonsense honesty, a certain plainness and sobriety. He has a distinguished team of singers in this cantata, but listening again after more than two decades, he does seem stolid and heavy-handed. The opening chorus plods heavily, and so does the duet, *Wann kommst du, mein Heil*. Collectors who are allergic to period instruments may want to consider this nevertheless; despite the distinction of the singing, however, Richter's direction is rigid and Teutonic. The recording comes from 1962 and is beginning to show its age, particularly in choruses. However, the sound is smooth enough: there is not a great deal to choose between CD and tape.

Cantatas Nos 140: Wachet auf; 147: Herz und Mund und Tat und Leben.
(*) Tel. **ZK8 43203 [id.]. Bergius, Rampf, Esswood, Equiluz, Hampson, Tölz Boys' Ch., VCM, Harnoncourt.

A coupling of two familiar cantatas, both made famous by their chorales. In No. 147, some may be a little disconcerted by the minor swelling effect in the phrasing of *Jesu, joy of man's desiring*, but otherwise the authentic approach brings much to enjoy. In No. 140 there are two beautiful duets between treble and bass soloists, representing dialogues between Jesus and the human soul, which are memorably sung. The production and recording are well up to the usual Telefunken standard.

Cantatas (i) *Nos 147: Herz und Mund und Tat und Leben; 148: Bringet dem Herrn Ehre seines Namens;* (ii) *149: Man singet mit Freuden vom Sieg; 150: Nach dir, Herr, verlanget mich; 151: Süsser Trost, mein Jesus kommt.*

(M) *** Tel. Dig. **ZL8 35654** (2) [id.]. Bergius, Hennig, Esswood, Equiluz, Van Egmond; (i) Tölz Boys' Ch., VCM, Harnoncourt; (ii) Ghent Coll. Vocale, Leonhardt Cons., Leonhardt.

The compact discs sound absolutely first class, with splendid definition and clarity in their favour. The best-known cantata here is the festive No. 147, *Herz und Mund und Tat und Leben*, part of which derives from Weimar; but 148, *Bringet dem Herrn Ehre seines Namens*, is relatively little heard and proves an inventive and rewarding score. Paul Esswood's aria, *Mund und Herz steht dir offen*, scored for two oboi d'amore and oboe di caccia, is a delight and is beautifully played (much better than in No. 154 in the next volume). No. 149, *Man singet mit Freuden vom Sieg*, is another festive cantata whose opening chorus draws on 208, *Was mir behagt*. Generally good playing here and some fine singing, particularly from the young treble, Sebastian Hennig. No. 150, *Nach dir, Herr, verlanget mich*, is not assigned to any specific Sunday or feast-day; if doubt has been cast on its authenticity, surely there can be none as to its merit. There is a marvellous bassoon obbligato in the bass aria, *Krafft und Starke sei gesungen Gott*, which is expertly played. (Not all the instrumental playing is flawless or tidy.) No. 151, *Süsser Trost, mein Jesus kommt*, is a Christmas cantata, and a delightful one, too.

Cantatas Nos 152: Tritt auf die Glaubensbahn; 153: Schau lieber Gott, wie meine Feind; 154: Mein liebster Jesus ist verloren; 155: Mein Gott, wie lang, ach lange; 156: Ich steh' mit einem Fuss im Grabe.

(M) **(*) Tel. Dig. **ZL8 35656** (2) [id.]. Wegmann, Bergius, Rampf, Esswood, Equiluz, Hampson, Tölz Boys' Ch., VCM, Harnoncourt.

The five cantatas in this box are designed for the two Sundays after Christmas and the first three of Epiphany. None are otherwise currently available in either tape or compact disc format. Unlike the majority of these boxes, all five cantatas are given to the Vienna Concentus Musicus under Nikolaus Harnoncourt. No. 152, *Tritt auf die Glaubensbahn*, is the earliest, dating from 1714, and has some particularly felicitous instrumental invention: the *Sinfonia* is a delight. The playing of the Concentus Musicus is eloquent and the performance as a whole very enjoyable. Unfortunately the young Christoph Wegmann is obviously beset by nerves, though the voice, if unsteady, is admirably pure. No. 153, *Schau lieber Gott, wie meine Feind*, is a rarity and is unusual in that it discards the usual opening chorus in favour of a simple chorale: indeed, the cantata has three chorales in all. No. 154, *Mein liebster Jesus ist verloren*, is a powerful and emotional piece. The oboi d'amore suffer from imperfect intonation in the fourth number, *Jesu, lass dich finden*. Generally speaking, however, this is an acceptable performance. No. 155, *Mein Gott, wie lang, ach lange*, is another early cantata (1716). The recording is very clean indeed, but perhaps a trifle dry, with relatively little ambience.

Cantatas Nos (i) *157: Ich lasse dich nicht, du segnest mich denn; 158: Der Friede sei mit dir; 159: Sehet, wir geh'n hinauf gen Jerusalem;* (ii) *161: Komm, du süsse Todesstunde; 162: Ach, ich sehe, jetzt, da ich Hochzeit gehe; 163: Nur jedem das Seine.*

(M) ** Tel. Dig. **ZL 35657** (2) [id.]. Eiwanger, Esswood, Equiluz, Van Egmond, Tölz Boys' Ch., (i) Wegmann, Ghent Coll. Vocale, Leonhardt; (ii) Iconomou, Holl, VCM, Harnoncourt.

Of the cantatas recorded here, the finest and most familiar is undoubtedly 159, *Sehet, wir geh'n hinauf gen Jerusalem*, with the moving combination of chorale and aria, *Ich folge dir nach*, and the highly expressive aria for bass and oboe. Hardly less impressive is No. 161, *Komm, du süsse Todesstunde*, for two treble recorders, strings, organ and continuo, a much earlier work from Weimer. So, too are its companions. No. 157, *Ich lasse dich nicht, du segnest mich denn*, is a chamber cantata for tenor, bass, strings, flute and oboe d'amore. It was written for a memorial service in 1727. The autograph does not survive, and the score used not the copy made in 1755 but a conjectural reconstruction made by Klaus Hofmann. To be frank, it is not inspired. Its companion, No. 158, *Der Friede sei mit dir*, is incomplete but far from routine Bach. Although the performances are touched by moments of inspiration and are beautifully recorded, they fall short of distinction. Wind intonation is less than ideal at times.

Cantatas Nos 159: Sehet, wir geh'n hinauf gen Jerusalem; 170: Vergnügte Ruh'.
❀ (M) *** Decca *410 170-4* [id.]. Baker, Tear, Shirley-Quirk, St Anthony Singers, ASMF, Marriner.

Sehet, wir geh'n hinauf gen Jerusalem is one of Bach's most inspired cantatas and surely ranks high on any shortlist of the essential Bach. Particularly glorious is the penultimate meditation, *Es ist vollbracht* ('It is finished'), with its poignant oboe obbligato. Both Dame Janet Baker and John Shirley-Quirk are in marvellous voice, and performance and recording are of high quality. The coupling, *Vergnügte Ruh'*, makes a worthy companion, and it is equally superbly performed. This is among the half dozen or so cantata recordings that ought to be in every collection.

Cantatas Nos (i) *164: Ihr, die ihr euch von Christo nennet; 165: O heiliges Geist und Wasserbad; 166: Wo gehest du hin?;* (ii) *167: Ihr Menschen rühmet Gottes Liebe; 168: Tue, Rechnung! Donnerwort; 169: Gott soll allein mein Herz haben.*
(M) ** Tel. Dig. **ZL8 35658** (2) [id.]. Esswood, Equiluz, Tölz Boys' Ch.; (i) Wegmann, Eiwanger, Van Egmond, Ghent Coll. Vocale, Leonhardt Cons., Leonhardt; (ii) Iconomou, Immler, Holl, VCM, Harnoncourt.

With the exception of No. 165, all the cantatas in this collection come from Bach's Leipzig period. In No. 164, *Ihr, die ihr euch von Christo nennet* the intonation of the two flauto traverso and Paul Esswood at the beginning of the aria, *Nur durch Lieb und durch Erbarmen*, is excruciating, and the direction here, under Leonhardt, laboured. Elsewhere things are much better and the aria, *Händen, die sich nicht verschliessen*, is spirited though the boy treble is rather swamped by Van Egmond. No. 165, *O heiliges Geist und Wasserbad* is a Weimar cantata, and of excellent quality. The treble copes well with the opening solo, which is fugal in character though a rondo in form. Though one of the more rarely performed cantatas, this is both inventive and varied, as indeed is its successor on this disc, *Wo gehest du hin?* It has an inspired tenor aria – well sung, too. (This is better known in its organ version, BWV 584.) No. 167 draws on material from the *E major Concerto*, BWV 1053 and is more pastoral in character; No. 168, *Tue Rechnung! Donnerwort*, opens with a very spirited aria that evokes a superb response from the Vienna Concentus Musicus and finds the bass soloist in excellent form. Elsewhere there are moments when the performances sound as if they would benefit from more rehearsal, though those under Harnoncourt are generally livelier. As usual, excellent recording and infinitely rewarding music.

Cantatas Nos (i) *170: Vergnügte Ruhe;* (ii) *171: Gott wie dein Name;* (i) *172: Erschallet ihr Lieder;* (ii) *173: Erhöhtes Fleisch und Blut; 174: Ich liebe den Höchsten von ganzem Gemute.*
(M) **(*) Tel. Dig. **ZL8 35659** (2) [id.]. (i) Esswood, Van Alterna, Van Egmond, Hannover Boys' Ch., Coll. Voc., Leonhardt Cons., Leonhardt; (ii) Equiluz, Holl, Tölz Ch., VCM, Harnoncourt.

No. 170, *Vergnügte Ruhe beliebte Seelenlust*, is for alto and instruments and without chorus or chorale. There is a moving alto aria, eloquently sung by Paul Esswood, who copes with the demanding role very impressively. Leonhardt makes heavy weather of the aria, *Die Welt das Sundenhaus*. No. 171 falls to Harnoncourt. It was written for the Leipzig New Year in 1729 and is festive in character – the aria will be familiar as Bach borrows it from *Der zufriedengestellte Äolus* (BWV 205), while the closing chorale comes from *Cantata No. 41*. The boy treble Helmut Wittek is quite remarkable in the aria, *Jesus soll mein erstes Wort*.

Nos 172–4 are all Whitsuntide cantatas: No. 172 receives a rather laboured performance from Leonhardt; 173, *Erhöhtes Fleisch und Blut*, is a reworking of an earlier secular cantata from Cöthen. *Ich liebe den Höchsten von ganzem Gemute* opens with the first movement of *Brandenburg No. 3*, scored for oboes, oboe di caccia, horns and strings, plus bassoon continuo. The first CD is shorter than 40 minutes, but there is a price adjustment in compensation. Excellent sound and eminently serviceable performances.

Cantata No. 205: Der zufriedengestellte Äolus.
*** Tel. Dig. **ZK8. 42 915** [id.]. Kenny, Lipovsek, Equiluz, Holl, Arnold-Schönberg Ch., VCM, Harnoncourt.

There is no alternative recording of *Der zufriedengestellte Äolus* (or *Aeolus propitiated*) which Bach composed in 1725 for the name-day of August Müller, a botanist at the University of Leipzig. Bach calls it 'Dramma per musica', and some of its invention comes as close to opera as anything he wrote. It is a long piece of fifteen numbers and is written for ambitious forces: three trumpets, two horns, drums, two flutes, two oboes, string continuo with obbligato parts for viola d'amore, viola da gamba and oboe d'amore, plus four solo voices and choir, all of whom serenade the learned scholar. Picander's libretto is slight, as for that matter is the plot. Aeolus plans to release the autumn gales, and resists the pleas of Zephyrus and Pomona to desist; however, Pallas finally persuades him that to do so will spoil the festivities she plans for August Müller. The performance is very good indeed, though the heavy accents in the opening chorus of the winds and the wooden orchestral tutti in the second number must be noted. Alice Harnoncourt's obbligato in *Angenehmer Zephyrus* ('Delightful Zephyr') is a model of good style and is beautifully articulated. The singers, particularly Yvonne Kenny's Pallas and Kurt Equiluz's Zephyrus, are good; the recording has a decently spacious acoustic and no lack of detail. Recommended.

Cantata No. 208: Was mir behagt, ist nur die muntre Jagd (*Hunt Cantata*).
*** Hyp. Dig. **CDA 66169**; *KA 66169* [id.]. Jennifer Smith, Emma Kirkby, Simon Davis, Michael George, Parley of Instruments, Goodman.

The number 208 indicates the order in which the cantatas were published by the editors of the Bach Gesamtausgabe and has no chronological significance. This delightful piece comes from 1713, when Bach was in his twenties, and celebrates the birthday of the Duke of Sachsen-Weissenfels, whose passion was hunting. It is a cantata rich in melodic invention of the highest quality. On this record the cantata is framed by movements from the *Sinfonia*, BWV 1046a, the original version of the *First Brandenburg concerto*. (One of the blessings of CD is that collectors who want only the cantata itself can programme their players accordingly – though few, having heard this, would want to do so.) The performance has the benefit of excellent soloists and first-class instrumental playing. As we go to press, this delightful piece is not otherwise represented on CD; however, even were a rival to appear, it would have to be very good to equal – let alone surpass – this. There is a splendid equivalent chrome cassette.

Cantatas (i) *Nos 208: Was mir behagt, ist nur die muntre Jagd* (*Hunt cantata*); (ii) *211: Schweigt stille, plaudert nicht* (*Coffee cantata*).
(M) ** HMV *ED 290370-4*. (i) Kupper, Köth, Wunderlich, Fischer-Dieskau, Berlin SO; (ii) Otto, Traxel, BPO, Forster.

Both recordings date from the early 1960s and benefit from remastering. Fischer-Dieskau is the finest of the soloists in the *Hunt cantata*; Erika Köth suffers from a consistent vibrato and Karl Forster does not bring the lightest touch to the proceedings. The *Coffee cantata* is another matter and again finds Fischer-Dieskau at his most persuasive. So conditioned are we to period-instrument performances that these accounts now seem distinctly overweight and the style heavy-handed, but there is a good deal of musical life in them. The recording sounds well enough in its tape format and is very generous in its content – the *Hunt cantata*, alone, takes 35 minutes, but the Hyperion version above is superior in almost all respects.

Cantatas Nos 211: Schweigt stille, plaudert nicht (*Coffee cantata*)*; 212: Mer hahn en neue Oberkeet* (*Peasant cantata*).
*** O-L Dig. **417 621-2**; *417 621-4* [id.]. Kirkby, Rogers, Covey-Crump, Thomas, AAM, Hogwood.
(M) *** Tel. **ZS8 43631** [id.]. Hansman, Equiluz, Van Egmond, VCM, Harnoncourt.
(B) ** CfP *TC-CFP 4516*. Lisa Otto, Traxel, Fischer-Dieskau, St Hedwig's Cathedral Ch., BPO, Forster.
** Hung. Dig. **HCD 12462** [id.]. Laki, Gati, Fulop, Capella Savaria, Németh.
** Mer. Dig. **ECD 84110.** Dawson, Robertson, Alder, Friends of Apollo.
*(*) Ph. Dig. **412 882-2** [id.]. Varady, Baldin, Fischer-Dieskau, ASMF, Marriner.

This coupling is surprisingly well served by the current catalogue. In Hogwood's Oiseau-Lyre version, the solo singing is of a high order. Emma Kirkby is particularly appealing in the *Coffee cantata* and her father is admirably portrayed by David Thomas. Hogwood opts for single strings (as do the Friends of Apollo on Meridian), and those accustomed to hearing these pieces with more substantial forces may find they sound thin. However, there is a corresponding gain in lightness and intimacy. The recording is altogether excellent and strikes an excellent balance between voices and instruments: the cassette, like the CD, is in the demonstration class, with voices and accompaniment caught with striking freshness.

Harnoncourt's coupling dates from 1968 and was the first to be recorded using original instruments or copies. The digital remastering has been entirely successful: the sound is not dated and the performances as fresh as the day they were made. The recording has an excellent ambience and space, as well as focusing detail in the right perspective. The performance of the *Peasant cantata* (which comes first) is totally unselfconscious and the singers are first class; in the *Coffee cantata* Max van Egmond's opening aria has great eloquence; throughout both pieces, Harnoncourt infuses his players with enthusiasm and a genuine sense of enjoyment.

Those who do not want a period-instrument performance have another alternative, but on cassette only. Karl Forster's accounts of this coupling come from the early 1960s and will strike younger (and not-so-young) listeners as somewhat old-fashioned. The acoustic is generous and warm, and there is nothing one-to-a-part about the strings of the Berlin Philharmonic. Older readers will find it eminently enjoyable – there is more life than in Richter's performances of that period – and very well sung. At its bargain price, it is well worth considering.

With Németh, in the *Coffee cantata* the famous aria, *Hat man nicht mit seinen Kindern*, goes much faster than usual – so as to reinforce the grumbling, snappish character of Schlendrian, no doubt, but oddly serving only to diminish it. (Fischer-Dieskau has infinitely more character here in Karl Forster's EMI reissue – see above.) The Capella Savaria use authentic instruments and, if the strings sound badly in need of a massive blood transfusion in the admired (but not by us) manner of 'authentic' groups, there is an accomplished flautist. These are decently recorded performances, not outstanding but eminently serviceable and, at times, quite spirited.

Lynne Dawson has a light and characterful voice, and she gives a good account of herself in both cantatas, though her partner, Stephen Alder, would seem to be less happily cast. The Friends of Apollo is a period-instrument group who in this instance play one-to-a-part.

Surprisingly, Julia Varady is the weak link in the Philips performance, for her account of the aria, *Heute noch, liebe Vater*, from the *Coffee cantata* is curiously wanting in subtlety and delicacy. There are good things in the *Peasant cantata* from Fischer-Dieskau and Marriner, but this is not in itself enough to earn more than a qualified welcome.

Christmas oratorio, BWV 248.

*** DG Dig. **423 232-2**; *423 232-4* (2) [id.]. Rolfe-Johnson, Argenta, Von Otter, Blochwitz, Bär, Monteverdi Ch., E. Bar. Sol., Gardiner.

(*) Ph. Dig. **420 204-2; *420 204-4* (3) [id.]. Donath, Ihle, Lipovsek, Schreier, Buchner, Holl, Leipzig R. Ch., Dresden State O, Schreier.

(M) **(*) Tel. **ZB8 35022** (3) [id.]. Treble soloists from V. Boys' Ch., Esswood, Equiluz, Nimsgern, V. Boys' Ch., Ch. Viennensis, VCM, Harnoncourt.

** Erato Dig. **ECD 880593** (3) [id.]. Schlick, C. Watkinson, Equiluz, Brodard, Lausanne Ens. and Ch., Corboz.

** DG **413 625-2** (3) [id.]. Janowitz, Ludwig, Wunderlich, Crass, Munich Bach Ch. and O, Karl Richter.

(M) ** Decca *414 445-4* (3). Ameling, Watts, Pears, Krause, Lübeck Kantorei, SCO, Münchinger.

John Eliot Gardiner in his Bach series for DG Archiv recorded the *Christmas oratorio* just after giving a series of live performances, spread – as Bach expected them to be – over six days of the Christmas period. The success of that project is reflected in the freshness of the singing and playing, with Gardiner's often brisk speeds sounding bright and eager, not breathless. Far more than usual, one registers the joyfulness of the work, from the trumpets and timpani at the start onwards. The haunting shepherds' music of the second cantata is lightly sprung and the celebrations of the third, with trumpets again prominent, are typical. Solo voices are light and clear, to match both the scale and resilient manner, adding to the freshness and precision. Anthony Rolfe-Johnson makes a pointful and expressive Evangelist, and also outstanding is Anne-Sophie von Otter with her natural gravity and exceptionally beautiful mezzo. Beauty of tone consistently marks the singing of Nancy Argenta and Hans-Peter Blochwitz; though Olaf Bär is a baritone rather than a bass, his detailed expressiveness, lieder-like, makes up for any lack of weight. The clinching point is a practical one: unlike previous rivals, the whole oratorio is neatly contained on only two discs and tapes, with three cantatas on each instead of two. The sound is full and atmospheric without clouding detail, a fine addition to an excellent series. The chrome cassettes offer a state-of-the-art transfer and a genuine (less expensive) alternative to the CDs.

Following up the success of his Dresden recording of the *St Matthew Passion*, Peter Schreier contributes a fine, fresh version of the *Christmas oratorio*, similarly taking on the double duties of conducting and singing the central part of the Evangelist. In that role there is no one currently quite to match him, particularly when (as here) he is in his sweetest, purest voice. As in the *St Matthew*, the Leipzig Radio Choir, one of the most accomplished in Europe, sings freshly and responsively, and though modern instruments are used, Schreier consistently shows how he has been influenced by new ideas of authentic performance on period instruments. Though the scale is larger than in a period performance; the speeds are regularly very fast, sprightly rather than breathless, with string articulation crisp and light. None of the other soloists quite matches Schreier, but they make a strong, consistent team. The contralto, Marjana Lipovsek, for example, has a rich, warm voice which verges on sounding too fruity for Bach, yet she sings movingly in the cradle-song of Part 2. Full, bright and atmospheric recording on both CD and cassette, but the layout on three CDs or tapes makes this issue uncompetitive alongside Gardiner.

Harnoncourt in his search for authenticity in Bach performance has rarely been more successful than here. It will not be to everyone's taste to have a boy treble and male counter-tenor instead of women soloists, but the purity of sound of these singers is most affecting. Above all Harnoncourt in this instance never allows his pursuit of authentic sound to weigh the performance down. It has a lightness of touch which should please everyone. The sound, as usual from this source, is excellent and has transferred to CD with conspicuous success, but the use of three discs, even at mid-price, is disadvantageous.

Festive with trumpets, superbly played, Corboz's version begins exceptionally well, with fresh and beautifully balanced sound from chorus and orchestra. All six cantatas are presented very attractively, with bright sound set within an intimate but helpful acoustic; however, Corboz falls too often into a rhythmic jogtrot to undermine the imaginative singing and solo playing. The four soloists all have clean, very attractive voices, marred only by Michel Brodard's heavily aspirated style. Carolyn Watkinson is outstanding, but the tenderness of her singing in the Cradle song in the second cantata is minimized when the accompaniment is pedestrian.

Richter's recording comes up impressively in the CD transfer prepared for DG Archiv's Bach Edition, but the performance as well as the recording have dated. Relatively stiff, Richter takes an unvarying view of the chorales; fine solo singing and good choral work are, however, some compensation, with Christa Ludwig especially beautiful in the Cradle song. The contribution of the late Fritz Wunderlich too is glowingly beautiful, but Franz Crass, the bass, is coarse and unyielding.

On tape Münchinger directs an admirably fresh performance, sharper in tone, brighter in recording (which dates from 1967) than Richter's set on DG Archiv. With an excellent team of soloists and with Lübeck trebles adding to the freshness, this is a good middle-of-the-road version, representative of modern scholarship as determined in the immediate pre-authentic era. The tapes are inexpensive too.

Magnificat in D, BWV 243.

*** Ph. Dig. **411 458-2**; *411 458-4* [id.]. Argenta, Kwella, Kirkby, Brett, Rolfe-Johnson, David Thomas, E. Bar. Soloists, Gardiner – *Cantata No. 51.****

(M) *** Decca *414 322-4*. Ameling, Watts, Krenn, Bork, Krause, V. Ac. Ch., SCO, Münchinger – *Cantata No. 10.****

(M) **(*) Decca *417 457-4* [id.]. Palmer, Watts, Tear, Roberts, King's College Ch., ASMF, Ledger – VIVALDI: *Gloria.***(*)

(M) *(*) DG **419 466-2**; *419 466-4* [id.]. Stader, Töpper, Haefliger, Fischer-Dieskau, Munich Bach Ch. and O, Karl Richter – *Cantata No. 140.**(*)

* Tel. Dig. **ZK8 42955** [id.]. Heichele, Esswood, Equiluz, Holl, V. Boys' Ch., Schoenberg Ch., VCM, Harnoncourt – HANDEL: *Utrecht Te Deum* *(*)

The better-known D major version of the *Magnificat* receives an exhilarating performance from John Eliot Gardiner. Tempi are consistently brisk, but the vigour and precision of the chorus are such that one never has the feeling that the pacing is hurried, for the singing has fervour as well as energy and, when there is need to relax, Gardiner does so convincingly. A splendid team of soloists, and the accompaniment is no less impressive, with a memorable oboe d'amore obbligato to embroider the *Quia respexit*. This is first class in every way, and the recorded sound is well balanced, fresh and vivid. The CD has that extra degree of presence, but the chrome cassette is outstandingly well managed, too.

Münchinger's Stuttgart recording dates from 1969 and was one of his finest Bach performances. It is still as impressive as any in the catalogue after the Gardiner version, which has a more authentic overall feel. But in its day, Münchinger's version was highly regarded. The soloists are uniformly good and so are the contributions of the Vienna Academy Choir and the Stuttgart Chamber Orchestra. Münchinger tends to stress the breadth and spaciousness of the *Magnificat* – though his reading has plenty of spirit – and the Decca engineers have captured the detail with admirable clarity and naturalness. Even though this is in Decca's lowest price range (and thus costs about a third the price of Gardiner's CD), the cassette is transferred on chrome stock. It is admirably focused and extremely vivid, with the trumpets sounding resplendent. A fine bargain.

Philip Ledger directs a lively and dramatic account. The warm acoustic of King's College Chapel creates problems of balance but surprisingly few of clarity, and with its generous Vivaldi coupling (the playing time for the two works together is about 65′) this is a most attractive version, provided that boys' voices in the chorus are preferred. The women soloists are outstanding, as is the St Martin's Academy. The four Christmas interpolations provide an additional attraction. The tape quality is excellent, vivid and lively.

Richter is a bit heavy-handed at times, but there is plenty of vigour and the chorus responds well to his direction. The soloists are very good, except for Hertha Töpper who lacks refinement in some of the florid writing. Sonically this sounds its age – it dates from the early 1960s – but the remastering is quite acceptable on CD and tape alike, though the opening chorus could do with greater freshness.

Harnoncourt's version is generously coupled with a major Handel piece, but the squareness of rhythm, with repeated quavers chugging instead of lifting, makes the result pedestrian, despite some excellent solo singing. The chorus is far less imaginative, pedestrian like the playing. The sound is clear but on the dry side, not at all atmospheric.

Magnificat in E flat (original version), *BWV 243a.*

*** O-L **414 678-2** [id.]. Nelson, Kirkby, C. Watkinson, Elliot, D. Watkinson, Christ Church Ch., AAM, Preston – VIVALDI: *Gloria.****

The original version of the *Magnificat* is textually different in detail (quite apart from being a semitone higher) and has four interpolations for the celebration of Christmas. Preston and the Academy of Ancient Music present a characteristically alert and fresh performance, and the Christ Church Choir is in excellent form. One might quibble at the use of women soloists instead of boys, but these three specialist singers have just the right incisive timbre and provide the insight of experience. The compact disc is now paired with Vivaldi's *Gloria*, a much more generous coupling than the original LP.

Mass in B min., BWV 232.

*** DG Dig. **415 514-2**; *415 514-4* [id.]. Argenta, Dawson, Fairfield, Knibbs, Kwella, Hall, Nichols, Chance, Collin, Stafford, Evans, Milner, Murgatroyd, Lloyd-Morgan, Varcoe, Monteverdi Ch., E. Bar. Soloists, Gardiner.

*** HMV Dig. **CDS7 47293-8** [Ang. **CDCB 47292**]; *EX 270239-5* (2) [Ang. *4D2S 3975*]. Kirkby, Van Evera, Iconomou, Immler, Kilian, Covey-Crump, David Thomas, Taverner Cons. and Players, Parrott.

*** Ph. **416 415-2** (2) [id.]. Marshall, Baker, Tear, Ramey, Ch. and ASMF, Marriner.

*** Eurodisc **610 089** (2). Popp, C. Watkinson, Bluchner, Lorenz, Adam, Leipzig R. Ch., New Bach Coll. Mus., Schreier.

*** None. Dig. **CD 79036-2** (2) [id.]. Nelson, Baird, Dooley, Minter, Hoffmeister, Brownlees, Opalach, Schultze, Bach Ens., Rifkin.

(M) **(*) Tel. **ZA8 35019** (2) [id.]. Hansmann, Iiyama, Watts, Equiluz, Van Egmond, V. Boys' Ch., Ch. Viennensis, VCM, Harnoncourt.

(*) HMV **CDS7 47595-8 (2). Poulenard, Laurens, Jacobs, Elwes, Van Egmond, Van der Kamp, Netherlands Bach Coll. Mus., La Petite Bande, Leonhardt.

(M) **(*) Decca *414 251-4* (2). Ameling, Minton, Watts, Krenn, Krause, Stuttgart Chamber Ch. and O, Münchinger.

John Eliot Gardiner makes an impressive start to his projected series of Bach choral works for DG Archiv with this magnificent account of the *B minor Mass*, one which attempts to keep within an authentic scale but which also triumphantly encompasses the work's grandeur. Where latterly in 'authentic' performances we have come to expect the grand six-part setting of the *Sanctus* to trip along like a dance movement, Gardiner masterfully conveys the majesty (with bells and censer-swinging evoked) simultaneously with a crisply resilient rhythmic pulse. The choral tone is luminous and powerfully projected. In the earlier parts of the *Mass*, Gardiner generally has four voices per part, but key passages – such as the opening of the first *Kyrie* fugue – are treated as concertinos for soloists alone. The later, more elaborate sections, such as the *Sanctus*, have five voices per part, so that the final *Dona nobis pacem* is subtly grander than when it appears earlier as *Gratias agimus tibi*. The regular solo numbers are taken by choir members, all of them pure-toned and none of them hooters, making a cohesive whole. The alto, Michael Chance, deserves special mention for his distinctively warm and even singing in both *Qui sedes* and *Agnus Dei*. On CD, the recording is warmly atmospheric but not cloudy, very well designed to present both breadth and clarity. There are excellent chrome cassettes.

Prompted by Joshua Rifkin's argument for one voice per part even in this most monumental of Bach's choral works, Parrott very effectively modifies that absolute stance – hoping to re-create even more closely the conditions Bach would have expected in Leipzig – by adding to the soloists a ripieno group of five singers from the Taverner Consort for the choruses. The instrumental group is similarly augmented with the keenest discretion. Though there was no live performance of the *Mass* in Bach's lifetime – it was considered a work of theory like the *Art of fugue*, a summation of a lifetime of study – this aims 'to adopt the conventions of a hypothetical performance by Bach himself at Leipzig'. Parrott's success lies in retaining the freshness and bite of the Rifkin approach while creating a more vivid atmosphere. Speeds are generally fast, with rhythms sprung to reflect the inspiration of dance; however, the inner darkness of the *Crucifixus*, for example, is conveyed intensely in its hushed tones, while the *Et resurrexit* promptly erupts with a power to compensate for any lack of traditional weight. Soloists are excellent, within the new conventions of authentic performance, with reduction of vibrato still allowing sweetness as well as purity. The three boy altos from the Austrian Tölzerchor are very well matched, sharing the alto solo role between them. If you want a performance on a reduced scale, Parrott scores palpably over Rifkin in the keener, more dramatic sense of contrast, clearly distinguishing choruses and solos. The recording, made in St John's, Smith Square, is both realistic and atmospheric. The compact discs are impressively clear and generously cued. They emphasize the comparatively forward balance and intimacy of scale.

For Neville Marriner this was a larger recording project than he had undertaken before, and he rose superbly to the challenge. Predictably, many of the tempi are daringly fast; *Et resurrexit*, for example, has the Academy chorus on its toes, but the rhythms are so resiliently sprung that the result is exhilarating, never hectic. An even more remarkable achievement is that in the great moments of contemplation such as *Et incarnatus* and *Crucifixus* Marriner finds a degree of inner intensity to match the gravity of Bach's inspiration, with tempi often slower than usual. That dedication is matched by the soloists, the superb soprano Margaret Marshall as much as the longer-established singers. This is a performance which finds the balance between small-scale authenticity and recognition of massive inspiration, neither too small nor too large, and with good atmospheric recording, not quite as defined as it might be on inner detail; this is fully recommendable. The remastering for CD has been able to improve the definition only marginally: the choral textures are realistically full but not ideally transparent.

The refreshing distinctiveness of Schreier's reading is typified by his account of the great *Sanctus*, dancing along lightly and briskly, not at all weighty in the usual manner. His speeds are consistently fast, but that does not prevent Schreier from capturing a devotional mood, as for example in the final *Dona nobis pacem* which, in powerful crescendo, begins in meditation and ends in joy. Though Schreier has opted for modern pitch and instruments, his performance gains from experience of the authentic movement; in the bass aria, *Quoniam*, for example, he has a corno di caccia playing the horn obbligato an octave higher than usual. With bright, keen choral singing and very good work from the soloists (Theo Adam occasionally excepted, with his sour tone), this is an excellent version for anyone wanting a resilient, lightweight view, using authentically small forces but without the problems of authentic performance. Good, spacious recording.

Whether or not you subscribe to the controversial theories behind the performance under Joshua Rifkin, the result is undeniably refreshing and often exhilarating. Rifkin – best known for playing Scott Joplin rags but a classical scholar too – here presents Bach's masterpiece in the improbable form of one voice to a part in the choruses. There are scholarly arguments in favour of suggesting that Bach, even for such grand choruses, employed that smallest possible ensemble. Certainly one gets a totally new perspective when, at generally brisk speeds, the complex counterpoint is so crisp and clean, with original (relatively gentle) instruments in the orchestra adding to the freshness and intimacy. The soprano, Judith Nelson, is already well known in the world of authentic performance; the other soloists also sing with comparable brightness, freshness and precision, even if lack of choral weight means that dramatic contrasts are less sharp than usual. An exciting pioneering set, crisply and vividly recorded, which rightly won *Gramophone*'s choral award in 1983. However, the newer set from Parrott's Taverner Consort, which has followed on directly from Rifkin's pioneering approach, will probably be preferred by most readers for its greater sense of drama and atmosphere.

Harnoncourt's version marked a breakthrough in the development of the authentic movement. The compact disc version of his performance is not just clearer but carries more impact. It confirms that, in parallel with his account of the *Christmas oratorio*, this is one of his most effective Bach performances on a chamber scale, with the choir, including boys' voices, projecting keenly. Rhythmically he is not as imaginative as his finest authentic rivals, and the brisk *Sanctus* is disappointing, but he rises warmly to the final *Dona nobis pacem*, given a real sense of occasion. First-rate solo singing, notably from Helen Watts, aptly firm and even. Nicely balanced recording, good for its late-1960s vintage.

Leonhardt's manner, unlike that of most advocates of period performance and authentic-sized forces, is relaxed at generally slow speeds. That underlines the devotional quality of his whole performance, its concentration. To that extent it provides a welcome alternative to the brisker performances of Gardiner and Parrott, but the slackness of much of the choral singing is a shortcoming when, in this of all Bach's works, the chorus provides the central focus. The team of soloists has no weak link, and La Petite Bande once again proves itself one of the most accomplished of baroque groups. Well-balanced recording too, originally designed for broadcast transmission through the European Broadcasting Union.

Münchinger's is a strong, enjoyable performance with an exceptionally fine quintet of soloists and first-rate recording. On balance it makes a fair recommendation; however, with fastish tempi and a generally extrovert manner it is efficient rather than inspiring. The chorus sings well but is placed rather backwardly. The recording dates from 1971 and has been successfully remastered, with the cassettes successful in their vividness. The chorus sounds vibrant and clear and the trumpets offer no transfer problems.

Masses: in F, BWV 233; in A, BWV 234; in G min., BWV 235; in G, BWV 236.

* HMV Dig. **CDS7 49222-8** (2). Åkerlund, Weller, De Mey, Varcoe, Basle Madrigalists, Linde Cons., Linde.

All Bach's Lutheran masses have the same ground plan: the *Kyrie* is distinguished by contrapuntal writing of some ingenuity, while the *Gloria* falls into two larger-scale movements that provide a festive framework for three solo sections. All the material is borrowed or 'parodied' from the cantatas BWV 72, 102, 179 and 187, only the recitatives and choruses being newly composed. These Linde performances are dutiful, neither vital nor particularly imaginative – and at times less than distinguished. The *Qui tollis* of the *A major Mass*, for example, suffers from frail intonation from the flutes and some insecurity from Lina Åkerlund, who phrases sensitively. There is some good singing, particularly from Sharon Weller and Stephen Varcoe, but these *Masses* need more persuasive advocacy and commitment. The recordings are well balanced and lifelike.

Motets: *Singet dem Herrn ein Neues Lied, BWV 225; Der Geist hilft unser Schwachheit, BWV 226; Jesu meine Freude, BWV 227; Der Gerechte Kommt um Fürchte dich nicht, BWV 228; Komm, Jesu Komm, BWV 229; Lobet den Herrn, BWV 230; Sei Lob und Preis mit Ehren, BWV 231.*

*** Erato Dig. **ECD 88117** (2) [id.]. Monteverdi Ch., E. Bar. Sol., Gardiner – *Cantatas Nos 4, 50, 118, 131.****

(*) HM **HMC 901231; *HMC40.1231* [id.] (without BWV 231). Soloists, Ghent Coll. Vocale, Chapelle Royale Ch. & O, Herreweghe.

(*) HMV Dig. **CDC7 49204-2 (2) (without BWV 231). Trebles of Hanover Boys' Ch., Hilliard Ens., L. Bar., Hillier.

John Eliot Gardiner's set of Bach's great motets, recorded for Erato in 1981, was one of his first major Bach recordings with the Monteverdi Choir. As well as bringing exceptionally strong and stylish performances, spaciously conceived with crisp, clean, resilient rhythms, the set has the attendant advantage of including not just the six motets regularly recognized in the Bach Gesellschaft edition but the motet-like works that have been counted as cantatas – see above. The CD set additionally adds a rarity, *Sei Lob und Preis mit Ehren*, BWV 231. It makes a superb collection in such performances, beautifully recorded in a helpful church acoustic.

Other recordings usually concentrate on the six regular motets, and under Philippe Herreweghe, responsible for a fine account of the *St Matthew Passion*, they are presented in fresh, meticulously clean performances, with instruments doubling vocal lines. One oddity is that the extended five-part motet, *Jesu meine Freude*, is sung by soloists and not the choir. Any gain in intimacy must be measured against an obvious loss of dramatic contrast in Bach's vivid setting of the words. Excellent sound.

Paul Hillier with the Hilliard Ensemble offers the same programme: these works were for generations known as Bach's 'unaccompanied' motets, though providing accompaniment is now regarded as the authentic course. Hillier opts for simple continuo instrumentation of cello, violone, organ and lute. That goes with small choral forces to match the intimate approach. The results are fresh, light and alert, thoughtful too, but, as with Herreweghe, the element of grandeur in the elaborate *Singet dem Herrn* is undermined. Very good atmospheric sound.

St John Passion, BWV 245.

*** DG Dig. **419 324-2**; *419 324-4* (2) [id.]. Rolfe-Johnson, Varcoe, Hauptmann, Argenta & soloists, Monteverdi Ch., E. Bar. Sol., Gardiner.

(M) **(*) Tel. **ZA8 35018** (2) [id.]. Equiluz, Van t'Hoff, Van Egmond, Villisech, Schneeweis, treble soloists from Vienna Boys' Ch., Ch. Viennensis, VCM, Harnoncourt.

(M) **(*) Decca *414 068-4* (2) [id.]. Ellenbeck, Berry, Ahrans, Ameling, Hamari, Hollweg, Prey, Stuttgart Hymnus Boys' Ch., SCO, Münchinger.

** DG **413 622-2** (2) [id.]. Lear, Töpper, Haefliger, Prey, Engen, Munich Bach Ch. & O, Karl Richter.

Gardiner conducts an exhilarating performance, so dramatic in its approach and so wide-ranging in the emotions conveyed it might be a religious opera. Speeds are regularly on the fast side but, characteristically, Gardiner consistently keeps a spring in the rhythm and urgently intensifies such points as the violence of the *Kreuzige* (Crucify) choruses and the section involving the casting of lots. The very opening chorus is made the more agonizing when the wind writing itself seems to suggest howls of pain. Yet Gardiner's refusal to dawdle even at the moment of the Crucifixion does not prevent the whole performance from conveying necessary dedication. Chorales are treated in contrasted ways, which may not please the more severe authenticists but, as with so much of Gardiner's work, here is a performance using authentic scale and period instruments which speaks in the most vivid way to anyone prepared to listen, not just to the specialist. Soloists – regular contributors to Gardiner's team – are all first rate, with Anthony Rolfe-Johnson light and resilient as the Evangelist, and Nancy Argenta exceptionally sweet-toned. The alto solos are beautifully taken by the counter-tenor Michael Chance, bringing necessary gravity to *Es ist vollbracht*. Warm and atmospheric, yet clear and detailed recording, with excellent matching chrome cassettes.

Harnoncourt's 1971 version using male voices only and period instruments makes a welcome reappearance on CD in Teldec's mid-price reissue series. In those early days of the new authentic movement, the determination to avoid a nineteenth-century meditative approach was extreme. This is a fresh, brisk tour through Bach's most dramatic choral work, helped by the light, distinctive narration of Kurt Equiluz and the bright singing of the Viennese choristers, men and boys. Soloists from the Vienna Boys' Choir sing the soprano and alto arias, the point most likely to disturb traditional listeners; but within its chosen approach this remains a positive and characterful reading, vigorous if not as resilient as some more recent performances using period instruments. The sound in the CD transfer is excellent, vivid and with fine presence.

Münchinger's set dates from 1975, and the recording is excellent. The dynamic range is strikingly wide and the sound itself fresh and full, with the tapes bright and clear. Münchinger's reading matches his other recordings of Bach's choral works, with a superb line-up of soloists, all of them clear-toned and precise, and with a fresh and young-sounding tenor, Dieter Ellenbeck, as the Evangelist. The musical balance of the score is pointed most satisfyingly without idiosyncrasy, using organ continuo with no harpsichord. This is preferable to Richter and is priced at not much more than a third of the cost of the DG compact discs.

The CD version of Richter's 1964 recording freshens and clarifies the inevitably limited sound. Though choral passages remain less well focused, the recitatives and arias have fine immediacy. This is a typical example of Richter's Bach style, sober and weighty and obviously dedicated, but wearing badly as the trend towards lightening the performance of Bach gains ground. Haefliger is outstanding among the soloists.

St John Passion: Choruses and arias (sung in English).

(M) **(*) Decca *414 645-4*. Harwood, Watts, Young, Alan, King's College Ch., L Philomusica, Willcocks.

A generous (fifteen items) and apt selection from Willcocks's excellent recording of the *St John Passion* in English, which dates from 1960. Contributions from chorus and soloists are well balanced to make satisfying listening, and the performance retains its freshness. Only the big opening chorus falls a little short of the rest in intensity. The chrome-tape transfer is clear, full and well focused.

St Matthew Passion, BWV 244.

*** Ph. Dig. **412 527-2** (3); *421 527-4* (3) [id.]. Schreier, Adam, Popp, Lipovsek, Holl, Dresden Children's Ch., Leipzig R. Ch., Dresden State O, Schreier.

*** HMV **CDS7 47241-8** (3) [id.]. Pears, Fischer-Dieskau, Schwarzkopf, Ludwig, Gedda, Berry, Hampstead Parish Church Ch., Philh. Ch. & O, Klemperer.

*** Decca Dig. **421 177-2**; *421 177-4* (3) [id.]. Te Kanawa, Von Otter, Rolfe-Johnson, Krause, Blochwitz, Bär, Chicago Ch., Children's Ch. & SO, Solti.

(*) Tel. Dig. **ZB8 35668 (3) [id.]. Equiluz, Holl, Augér, Greenawald, Rappe, Van Nes, Rosenshein, Van der Meer, Scharinger, St Baavo Knabenchor, Concg. Ch. & O, Harnoncourt.

(*) HM **HMC 901155/7 [id.]. Crook, Cold, Schluck, Jacobs, Blochwitz, Kooy, Chapelle Royale Ch., Ghent Coll. Mus., Herreweghe.

(*) DG **413 613-2 (3) [id.]. Schreier, Fischer-Dieskau, Mathis, Baker, Salminen, Regensburger Domspatzen, Munich Bach Ch. & O, Karl Richter.

(M) **(*) Decca *414 057-4* (3). Pears, Prey, Ameling, Hoffgen, Wunderlich, Krause, Stuttgart Hymnus Boys' Ch., SCO, Münchinger.

(M) ** Tel. **ZB8 35047** (3) [id.]. Equiluz, Esswood, Sutcliffe, Bowman, Rogers, Ridderbusch, Van Egmond, Schopper, Regensburger Boys' Ch., King's College, Cambridge, Ch., VCM, Harnoncourt.

** Erato Dig. **ECD 880633** (3) [id.]. Equiluz, Faulstisch, Margaret Marshall, C. Watkinson, Rolfe-Johnson, Huttenlocher, Lausanne Vocal Ens. & CO, Corboz.

(M) ** Ph. **420 900-2** (3) [id.]. Giebel, Höffgen, Haefliger, Berry, Ketelaars, Netherlands R. Ch., St Willibrod Boys' Ch., Concg. O, Jochum.

** DG **419 789-2** (3) [id.]. Schreier, Laubenthal, Fischer-Dieskau, Janowitz, Ludwig, V. Singverein, V. Boys' Ch., German Op. Ch., BPO, Karajan.

It is an astonishing achievement of Peter Schreier to conduct this most exacting of choral works as well as taking the leading vocal role of the Evangelist. His aim in Bach interpretation is to bring new lightness without following the full dictates of authentic performance and in this he succeeds superbly. Such meditative arias as the contralto's *Erbarme dich* or the soprano's *Aus liebe* bring a natural gravity and depth of expression, though Marjana Lipovsek has a tendency to sit on the flat side of the note, and Lucia Popp's silvery soprano is not always caught at its sweetest. The end result is a refreshing and cohesive performance, ideal for records, when there is no tendency for the piece to drag. The recording is first rate, with the choral forces well separated. The CD version takes three discs and the extra convenience offered by copious banding adds to the enjoyment of using the set. The cassettes are also well managed with a good choral focus, though not as impressively vivid and clear as on Münchinger's Decca tapes.

While it certainly will not appeal to the authentic lobby, Klemperer's 1962 Philharmonia recording of the *St Matthew Passion* represents one of his greatest achievements on record, an act of devotion of such intensity that points of style and interpretation seem insignificant. Klemperer's way is to take the chorales slowly, with pauses at the end of each line; he makes no concessions to recent scholarship on the question of introducing ornamentation. His dedication is immediately apparent in the first great chorus, *Kommt ihr Tochter*, with the chorale, *O Lamm Gottes unschuldig*, given to the trebles in ripieno. The recording allows clear separation between the first and second choruses on left and right, while ringing out from the centre is the pure tone of the boys of the Hampstead choir. There is a matchless team of soloists, with Peter Pears at his peak in the role of Evangelist and Fischer-Dieskau deeply expressive as Jesus. The professional Philharmonia Choir sings with the finest focus. The whole cast clearly shared Klemperer's own intense feelings, and one can only sit back and share them too, whatever one's preconceptions. Digitally remastered with enhanced clarity, this now fits on to three CDs against the four LPs of the original issue.

Solti uses a reduced-size Chicago Symphony Orchestra and himself hand-picked the choir. With him the *Passion* is less devotional than celebratory. With speeds on the fast side, resilient rhythms and bright choral tone he brings it closer than usual to the *St John Passion*, with its message of heavenly joy. Clean, fresh solo singing, too, with Hans-Peter Blochwitz the sweetest-toned Evangelist on record. Olaf Bär as Jesus is youthfully virile, Anne Sofie von Otter makes a radiant alto soloist giving natural gravity to *Erbarme dich*, and this should suit those who still fight shy of authenticity. It is comparable with his companion set of Handel's *Messiah*, which is successful in much the same way. Brilliant, full, Decca recording with fine presence and clarity – indeed the sound is of the highest order.

Recorded live in March 1985, Harnoncourt's Concertgebouw version, strikingly different from his earlier, trend-setting essay in period performance (also on Teldec and now reissued on mid-price CD), has many thrilling moments, beginning in the great first chorus when the boys enter with their chorale theme. Some of Harnoncourt's period performance mannerisms persist – the bulges on certain notes for example – but the squareness of rhythm that has sometimes afflicted his work is counterbalanced by his preference for fast speeds, at times too fast for comfort. With excellent choral singing and outstanding contributions from at least two of the soloists – the ever-responsive, light-toned Evangelist, Kurt Equiluz, and the brightly beautiful Arleen Augér – this is a dramatic account that can be recommended to any who fancy a live performance. The sound is vivid and immediate, with remarkably few audience noises.

With an outstanding team of solo singers, all clear-toned and mostly new to records, and with bright, immediate sound full of presence, Herreweghe's version presents a good choice for anyone wanting a performance on period instruments at lower pitch. Howard Crook is an excellent, fresh-toned Evangelist, and the other tenor, Hans-Peter Blochwitz, is first rate too. The alto part is taken by the celebrated counter-tenor, René Jacobs, rather hooty in *Erbarme dich*; but Barbara Schluck, with her bright clear soprano voice, sings radiantly. The instrumental group plays in authentic style but not abrasively so; Herreweghe's control of rhythm, however, tends to be too heavy. Chorales are often slow and over-accented, and heavy stressing mars the big numbers too. In lightness and point the Schreier version on Philips, which is only just on the other side of the authenticity barrier, at modern pitch and with modern instruments but adopting many authentic-performance practices, is consistently preferable.

Richter's version, replacing an earlier account, was the last of his major Bach recordings and arguably the finest, with an outstanding team of soloists and excellent choral singing (including splendid treble contributions from the 'Cathedral Sparrows' of Regensburg). Dame Janet Baker's singing of *Erbarme dich* crowns a totally dedicated performance, but the heaviness of Richter's approach to Bach is becoming more and more difficult to accept in an age when the extra illumination gained from treating Bach more lightly and resiliently is universally recognized. The CD transfer for the DG Archiv Bach Edition brings many benefits in convenience as well as in sound-quality but, if anything, the extra immediacy adds to the heaviness.

Münchinger's direction does not attain the spiritual heights of an interpretation such as Klemperer's, but his version is consistently fresh and alert, and it has the degree of authenticity of its period (1965) – although much has happened to Bach performances since then. All the soloists are excellent, and Peter Pears shows that no tenor of his generation rivalled his insight as the Evangelist. Elly Ameling is sweet-toned and sensitive. The recording is first class, clear and brilliant and very well balanced. The cassettes are particularly successful, with the chorus sounding incisive and well defined, with just the right degree of weight. Some may object to the deliberate closeness with which the voice of Hermann Prey as Jesus has been recorded.

Harnoncourt's earlier set emerges as freshly in its digital remastering as the others in the series, remarkable for its daring authenticity. The vocal sound remains unique in its total reliance on male voices (including boy trebles); the choral singing is incisive and lightweight. For many, the emotional kernel of Bach's great work lies in the solo contributions and here these are variable, with Karl Ridderbusch and Paul Esswood outstanding. Some of the other contributions are less reliable, and the use of boy trebles for the soprano arias produces a strangely detached effect, although the singing itself is usually technically good.

The scale and liveliness of the story-telling are very much in favour of the Corboz version. This is the *Matthew Passion* presented as a narrative rather than as a grand, spiritual event; it is enjoyable within limits but misses a sense of occasion and, with it, the spiritual depth of the work. Though the chorales are done lightly and expressively, it does not help that the choral sound is much cloudier than that of the solo voices, a first-rate team with Kurt Equiluz as ever an outstanding, lively and distinctive Evangelist. Chief blame for the limitations of the performance must rest with Corboz, who too often keeps rhythms too evenly stressed.

Jochum's set from the 1960s is a romantic view of the work, spiritual and intense but lacking the inner firmness which makes Klemperer's performances – similarly romantic by modern standards – so unforgettable an experience. This means that Jochum seems to encourage even as sensitive a singer as Ernst Haefliger to introduce moments of sentimentality into the Evangelist's part. Even so, the solo singing is strong and generally stylish, and the Netherlands Radio Chorus sings with great point and attack. The stereo perspectives are well managed, and in its remastered format the recording sounds remarkably fresh.

Karajan's Bach, always polished, grows smoother still with the years. His account of the *St Matthew Passion* is plainly aimed at devotees – of Karajan as much as of Bach. The result, concentrated in refinement, faithfully reflects the live performances which he has given in Berlin. With excellent singing and playing and with reverberant recording moulded to the interpretation, it represents an individual view pursued in the face of the current fashion, and many will enjoy it.

Mengelberg's legendary performance recorded in the Amsterdam Concertgebouw on Palm Sunday 1939 remains available and has undoubted historic interest. But the great German-born conductor indulges in ritardandi that are positively horrendous, and this is far too eccentric a performance for any but the specialist collector (Ph. mono **416 206-2** (3)).

Vocal collections

Aria: *Bist du bei mir.* Cantata arias: *No. 6: Hochgelobter Gottesshon; No. 11: Ach bleibe doch; No. 34: Wohl euch ihr auserwählten Seelen; No. 129. Gelobet sei der Herr; No. 161: Komm, du süsse Todesstunde; No. 190: Lobe Zion, deinen Gott. Christmas oratorio: Bereite dich. Easter oratorio: Saget, saget mir geschwinde. Magnificat: Et exultavit. St John Passion: Es ist vollbracht.*

(B) *** HMV *TCC 2-POR 154592-9.* Dame Janet Baker, ASMF, Marriner – *Cantatas Nos 82 and 169.****

Predictably, Dame Janet Baker gives beautiful and deeply felt performances of a fine inexpensive collection of Bach arias. Sweet contemplative arias predominate, and an excellent case is made for including the alternative cantata version, *Ach bleibe doch*, of what became the *Agnus Dei* in the *B minor Mass*. The accompaniments could hardly be more understanding (the gamba solo in *Es ist vollbracht* adding extra poignancy), and the recording is rich and warm. This issue in HMV's 'Portrait of the Artist' series is excellent value, with the arias coupled with two fine performances of cantatas.

Arias: *Bist du bei mir; Cantata 202: Weichet nur, Betrubte Schatten. Cantata 209: Ricetti gramezza. St Matthew Passion: Blute nur; Ich will dir mein Herze schenken.*

(*) Delos Dig. **D/CD 3026 [id.]. Arleen Augér, Mostly Mozart O, Schwarz – HANDEL: *Arias.***(*)

Arleen Augér's pure, sweet soprano, effortlessly controlled, makes for bright performances of these Bach arias and songs, ideally suited to *Bist du bei mir*, less so to such a dark aria as *Blute nur* from the *St Matthew Passion*, not helped by relatively coarse accompaniment, over-recorded. Still very recommendable for admirers of this delightful singer, well coupled with Handel arias.

Arias: *Mass in B min.: Agnus Dei; Qui sedes. St John Passion: All is fulfilled. St Matthew Passion: Grief for sin.*

(***) Decca mono **414 623-2**; stereo *414 623-4*. Kathleen Ferrier, LPO, Boult – HANDEL: *Arias.*(***) ❀

On 7th and 8th October 1952, Kathleen Ferrier made her last and perhaps greatest record in London's Kingsway Hall, coupling four arias each by Bach and Handel. The combined skill of John Culshaw and Kenneth Wilkinson ensured a recording of the utmost fidelity by the standards of that time; with the advent of stereo, Sir Adrian Boult and the LPO, who provided the original accompaniments, were persuaded by Culshaw to return and record a new orchestral backing, over the old, and the result was something of a musical and technological miracle. It might seem perverse, therefore, that for the CD issue Decca have returned to the original mono master tape, yet the results fully justify that decision. Close comparison between mono CD and stereo LP shows that in masking the earlier recording the voice became very slightly clouded, particularly in its upper range. Now it re-emerges with extraordinary naturalness and presence. The mono accompaniments were beautifully balanced and orchestral detail is clarified further, with the harpsichord continuo coming through the more transparent texture in *Grief for sin* and Ambrose Gauntlett's viola da gamba obbligato for *All is fulfilled* more tangible. Of course the upper strings sound thinner, but that adds an 'authentic' touch, and they are given a far more dramatic bite in the climax at the words: *The Lion of Judah fought the fight*. In stereo, on tape, the overall effect is richer; but the digitally remastered mono original, apart from enhancing the vocal realism, undoubtedly emphasizes the freshness of Boult's contribution. The pre-Dolby background noise is still apparent but is in no way distracting. The compact disc documentation, however, is inferior to that provided with the medium-priced LP, offering only a chatty biographical note about Kathleen Ferrier and nothing about the circumstances surrounding the recording, or its subsequent history. The excellent cassette carries the stereo version.

ARRANGEMENTS

BACH–STOKOWSKI

Toccata & fugue in D min., BWV 565; Suite No. 3, BWV 1068: Air; Chorales: Ein feste Burg, Komm süsser Todd. Christmas oratorio: Shepherd's chorus. English suite No. 2: Bourrée; Fugue in G min., BW4 578; Passacaglia & fugue in C min., BWV 582; Violin partita No. 1, BWV 1002: Sarabande. Violin partita No. 3, BWV 1006: Prelude.
(M) ** HMV **CDM7 69072-2** [id.]. Stokowski and his SO.

Stokowski's Bach arrangements are now assuming something like classic status, a fine antidote for those who fight shy of vinegary authenticity. Even when he goes over the top, his vulgarity has a unique conviction. Either you respond or you do not. Here, as ever, his orchestral palette turns baroque music into vivid splashes of romantic orchestral colour. In the *Passacaglia and fugue in C minor*, those rich, sawing double-basses, mellifluous woodwind fugal passages, echoing horns and resplendent cadences cannot help but make a strong physical impact, and indeed it is the lively music here that registers best, notably the 'Little' *Fugue in G minor*. The expressive pieces, played slowly and indulgently, sound sentimental. No doubt Stokowski is heard at his most compulsive in the arrangement of the *Toccata and fugue in D minor*, made famous by Walt Disney's *Fantasia*, and that is given a vigorously persuasive performance here. However, the digital remastering has robbed the early stereo (1957/8) of much of its sumptuousness, and those wishing to wallow in both this piece and the *G minor Fugue* in spectacular modern digital sound should turn to Erich Kunzel's outstanding Telarc CD. Stokowski began his career in Cincinnati, and it is appropriate that this city's orchestra should provide such a memorable collection of his transcriptions of music by a wide range of composers (Telarc **CD 80129** – see Concerts, below).

Bach, Wilhelm Friedemann (1710–84)

Double harpsichord concerto in E flat, Falck 46; Sonata in F for 2 harpsichords, Falck 10, BWV Anh. 188.
*** DG Dig. **419 256-2** [id.]. Staier, Hill, Coll. Mus. Ant., Goebel – C. P. E. BACH: *Double harpsichord concerto.****

The concerto comes from Bach's Dresden period (1733–46) and is something of a revelation. It begins in a rather festive spirit with trumpet and drums, which suggests a much later period and, alongside these forward-looking flourishes, there are typical baroque touches. The slow movement, for the two harpsichords alone, has an expressive depth that confirms the impression that Wilhelm Friedemann was potentially the most gifted of Bach's sons. The finale is certainly highly inventive and the playing has enormous sparkle. Readers normally allergic to period instruments should note that such is the liveliness and imagination of these performances that only the good things – clarity and lightness of texture, etc. – and none of the drawbacks, are in evidence. The *Sonata* comes from early in the composer's Dresden period and is actually termed 'concerto' in both Friedemann's autograph and in a copy made by Sebastian. Indeed, the old Bach-Gesellschaft edition attributed it to Sebastian, calling it a 'sonata' or 'duetto'. But thirty years before this, in an earlier edition, Brahms had got its authorship right. Yet undoubtedly both *Sonata* and *Concerto* are almost worthy of Johann Sebastian himself.

6 Duets for 2 flutes.
** Denon Dig. **C37 7287** [id.]. Aurèle and Christiane Nicolet.

Sixty minutes of flute duets is a daunting prospect but, taken individually and, it must be added, very occasionally, these pieces can give pleasure. Four of the six (F54, 55, 47 and 59) were composed while Wilhelm Friedemann was at Dresden (1733–46), and the remaining two after 1770 when he was unsettled. Aurèle Nicolet and his wife, Christiane, give highly accomplished and vividly recorded accounts of all six pieces, which are far from uninventive but hardly of great significance.

Trio sonata in A min. (incomplete).
*** CBS Dig. **MK 37813** [id.]. Rampal, Stern, Ritter, Parnas – C. P. E., J. C. F. and J. S. BACH: *Trio sonatas.****

This comes at the end of an attractive and very well-played recital of music by Bach and his musical sons. We are offered a tempting opening movement and then, after a few bars, the *Larghetto* peters out in a mood of gentle melancholy. Whether the rest of the piece was lost or never actually written we are not told. Admirably clear recording.

Baermann, Heinrich (1784–1847)

Adagio for clarinet and orchestra.
*** ASV Dig. **CDDCA 559**; *ZCDCA 559* [id.]. Emma Johnson, ECO, Groves – CRUSELL: *Concerto No. 2**** (🏵); ROSSINI: *Introduction, theme and variations****; WEBER: *Concertino.****
*** HMV Dig. **CDC7 47233-2**; *EL 270220-4*. Meyer, Württemberg CO, Faerber – MENDELSSOHN: *Concert pieces*; WEBER: *Clarinet quintet.****
(M) **(*) Decca **417 643-2** [id.]. Boskovsky, V. Octet (members) – BRAHMS: *Quintet*; MOZART: *Quintet.***(*)

Heinrich Baermann's rather beautiful *Adagio*, once attributed to Wagner, is offered here by two young clarinettists, both of whom have recently sprung to fame, Emma Johnson as the BBC's 'Young musician of the year' in 1984, and Sabine Meyer, who was involved in a tussle between Karajan and the Berlin Philharmonic when she was appointed principal in 1983. Both artists play the work warmly and sympathetically. Boskovsky, too, is particularly languorous – and all are well accompanied and recorded. Couplings should dictate choice here.

Balakirev, Mily (1837–1910)

Symphony No. 1 in C.
*** HMV Dig. **CDC7 47505-2**. CBSO, Järvi – LIADOV: *Polonaise*.**(*)

Balakirev occupied a dominant position in Russian musical life for many years after the death of Glinka, yet his reputation rests on a distinctly meagre output. In his music we have what Gerald Abraham once called 'the dawn and sunset of genius with little of its full day'. Yet there is surely no questioning the appeal of his ideas or the skill and richness of their presentation. The *First Symphony* is rarely heard in the concert hall and although it has been relatively neglected by the gramophone, both Karajan and Beecham have recorded it in the past, and no doubt one or both of these versions will in due course resurface on CD. Meanwhile Järvi's version can be confidently recommended. He gives a good performance, well prepared with excellent ensemble and responsive woodwind phrasing, securing an impressive sense of momentum in the first two movements. If the tension drops a little in the slow movement by comparison with the versions of his two famous predecessors, it is still convincingly shaped. The recording is extremely fine. The balance is a little close, but there is good sonority to the strings and, in truthfulness of timbre, strength of bass response and range, the sound is altogether first class.

Symphony No. 2 in D min; Tamara.
(*) HM Chant du Monde **LDC 278758 [id.]. USSR State Ac. O, Svetlanov.

The *Second Symphony* comes from the sunset of Balakirev's career and occupied him from 1900–1908, but it is a highly appealing score. The *Scherzo alla cossaca* is a particularly delightful movement, and Yevgeny Svetlanov makes out a very persuasive case for it on this CD. *Tamara*, perhaps his masterpiece, stands in much the same relation to the rest of his music as does Rimsky-Korsakov's *Scheherazade* in his output. The exotic hothouse atmosphere comes over well in Svetlanov's performance, although the recording is made in a very resonant acoustic. These recordings are not new and are hardly of demonstration quality but they are admirably serviceable. A very attractive issue that should enjoy much popularity.

Piano sonata in B flat min.
(*) Archduke Dig. **DARC2; *MARC2* [id.]. Donna Amato – DUTILLEUX: *Sonata*.**(*)

The Balakirev is arguably the greatest Russian piano sonata of the pre-1914 era, with the Tchaikovsky *G major* a close second. Its second movement was completed five years before the rest of the work and published independently as *Mazurka No. 5 in D*. (This itself had begun life almost half a century before, in 1856, as part of an earlier sonata, also in B flat minor.) The first movement is a remarkable fusion of sonata form and fugue, quite unique in Russian music, and the slow movement has a warmth and poetic feeling reminiscent of the *First Symphony*. Donna Amato gives a musicianly account of it, well paced and authoritative – not surprisingly, since she studied with Louis Kentner, who made the very first recording of it after the war. The recording, though not in the demonstration class, is very lifelike, both on CD and tape, and given the interest and rarity of the coupling, this is a most desirable issue, even if the playing time at 47′ is not particularly generous.

Bantock, Granville (1868–1946)

The Pierrot of the Minute: overture.
*** Chan. **CHAN 8373**; (M) *CBT 1018* [id.]. Bournemouth Sinf., Del Mar – BRIDGE: *Summer*, etc.; BUTTERWORTH: *Banks of green willow*.***

Bantock's overture comes from 1908 and was one of his most popular works. It is concerned with Pierrot's dream in which he falls in love with a Moon Maiden who tells him their love must die at dawn, but he will not listen. He wakes to realize that his dream of love lasted a mere minute. The writing is often delicate and at times Elgarian, and the piece is well worth investigating. The recording – originally issued on RCA – has now passed back to Chandos. It has been digitally remastered with great success and sounds remarkably fresh on CD. The cassette is excellent too and is offered at mid-price, so costs a great deal less than the CD.

Barber, Samuel (1910–81)

Adagio for strings.

*** Argo **417 818-2**; *KZRC 845* [id.]. ASMF, Marriner – COPLAND: *Quiet city*; COWELL: *Hymn*; CRESTON: *Rumor*; IVES: *Symphony No. 3.****

*** DG Dig. **413 324-2**; *3302 083* [id.]. LAPO, Bernstein – BERNSTEIN: *Candide overture*; COPLAND: *Appalachian spring*; SCHUMAN: *American festival overture.****

(*) HMV **CDC7 47521-2 [id.]. Stokowski & his SO – BARTÓK: *Music for strings, percussion & celesta*; SCHOENBERG: *Verklaerte Nacht.***(*)

(M) **(*) HMV *EG 290615-4*. Phd. O, Ormandy – LISZT: *Hungarian fantasia*; R. STRAUSS: *Also sprach Zarathustra.***(*)

Samuel Barber's *Adagio for strings* now has the kind of international currency afforded to very few twentieth-century masterpieces, having appeared as theme music in two widely successful films (*The Elephant Man* and *Platoon*). It received its pioneering recording from Toscanini. Marriner's 1976 performance all but matches Toscanini's intensity and has great eloquence and conviction. It is arguably the most satisfying version we have had since the war, although Bernstein's alternative has the advantage of digital recording. The quality of sound on the remastered CD retains most of the richness and body of the analogue LP, but at the climax the brighter lighting brings a slightly sparer violin texture than on the original LP, along with the extra presence and clearer detail. The splendid cassette equivalent remains for those who prefer the original analogue balance and a softer treble response.

Bernstein's version is also outstandingly eloquent. His reading has an expansively restrained elegiac feeling, but his control of the climax – in what is substantially a live recording – is unerring. The recording balance is somewhat close but full and clear, and the digital sound has a thrillingly wide dynamic range plus the advantage of complete background silence. There is also an extremely vivid chrome cassette. Bernstein's couplings are, like Marriner's, all highly desirable.

Stokowski recorded the Barber *Adagio* in 1967. It is a powerfully expressive performance, moving forward to its climax in a passionate single sweep, then falling back with little relaxation of tempo. His timing is 6′ 21″ against Marriner's 8′ 42″, yet Stokowski's pacing remains totally convincing. The sound too is full and vivid. This is a worthwhile reissue, and it is a pity it is not offered in EMI's mid-priced Studio series.

Ormandy's is a direct but involvingly passionate account with a powerful climax and a secure, beautifully gradated closing section, with the music's valedictory qualities well caught. The recording sounds impressive in its iron-oxide tape format, but although the couplings are generous, they are less aptly chosen.

Adagio for strings; (i) *Piano concerto, Op. 38; Medea's meditation and Dance of vengeance, Op. 23a.*
*** ASV Dig. **CDDCA 534**; *ZCDCA 534* [id.]. (i) Joselson; LSO, Schenck.

In this fine new recorded performance, Barber's *Concerto* emerges as a much stronger work than it previously seemed. Tedd Joselson is marvellously and dazzlingly brilliant, as well as being highly sensitive and poetic. What also shows this score to better advantage than before is the greater richness and detail of the ASV recording and the unforced and poetic orchestral contribution from the LSO under Andrew Schenck. The *Concerto*'s ideas are exuberant, neo-romantic and, if not quite as fresh as those of the *Violin* or *Cello concerto*, they have an abundant warmth; needless to say, the piano writing is as expert as one would expect from the composer of the celebrated *Sonata*. The LSO also give a singularly fine account of the *Medea* excerpt (not to be confused with the Suite) and a restrained and noble one of the celebrated *Adagio*. On cassette the resonance has caused problems and led to a relatively low transfer level, which means that detail is clouded.

Cello concerto, Op. 22.
*** Chan. Dig. **CHAN 8322**; *ABTD 1085* [id.]. Wallfisch, ECO, Simon – SHOSTAKOVICH: *Cello concerto No. 1.****

It has taken three decades for the Barber *Cello concerto* to resurface on record: the pioneering record by Zara Nelsova and the composer (Decca mono LX 3048) has long been a collectors' item. A new version by Raphael Wallfisch and the ECO under Geoffrey Simon comes in harness with the *Cello concerto No. 1* of Shostakovich and is all the more welcome for being so very much overdue. Of course the first movement is discursive and the invention throughout could be more strongly held together – but what invention! It has a vernal freshness and an affecting youthful innocence which never fails to exert its charm. It is an impressive and eloquent reading, and the elegiac slow movement is especially fine. Wallfisch is forwardly balanced, but otherwise the recording is truthful; the orchestra is vividly detailed on the excellent chrome tape. In its compact disc form, the sound is outstandingly realistic; given the excellence of the coupling, this must receive the strongest recommendation.

Violin concerto, Op. 14.
*** HMV Dig. **CDC7 47850-2**. Oliviera, St Louis SO, Slatkin – HANSON: *Symphony No. 2.****

(i) *Violin concerto; Essay for orchestra No. 2; School for Scandal: overture; Vannesa: Prelude and Intermezzo.*
*** Pro Arte Dig. **CCD 241** [id.]. (i) Silverstein; Utah SO.

Anyone who enjoys Barber's *Adagio for strings* must respond to the *Violin concerto*, whose slow movement has a comparable poignant melancholy. It is genuinely beautiful and the whole work is inspired; it has consistent warmth, freshness and humanity. Isaac Stern has made a fine record of it; perhaps Elmer Oliviera's version is on a smaller scale, but he is much better balanced and responds to the nostalgia of the *Andante* with a vein of bitter-sweet yearning that is most affecting. It is a fine performance overall with a brilliantly played finale and is warmly and realistically recorded, with Slatkin directing an entirely sympathetic accompaniment. Admirably coupled with Hanson's very rewarding *Second Symphony*, this can be strongly recommended. Isaac Stern's performance of the *Concerto* on CBS will no doubt appear on CD in due course – it is of superlative quality and the recording is good, but the close balance for the soloist is less than ideal (CBS *40-61621* [*MPT 39070*]).

The alternative version from Joseph Silverstein is in some ways an even stronger performance than Oliviera's, with the Utah orchestra providing a fervently passionate accompaniment. Both soloist and orchestra are forwardly projected by the extremely vivid Pro Arte recording, at the expense of some fierceness on the fortissimo massed violins, but in consequence Silverstein's image is bigger than Oliviera's, which suits the style of the playing. Silverstein also directs the other works, which are well worth having. In particular the vivacious *School for Scandal overture* provides a memorably lyrical tune to haunt the memory, but the *Essay* too is a considerable and inventive piece. The bright sound suits the orchestral works.

Summer music.
*** Crystal **CD 750** [id.]. Westwood Wind Quintet – CARLSSON: *Nightwings*; LIGETI: *Bagatelles*; MATHIAS: *Quintet*.***

Samuel Barber's *Summer music* is an evocative mood-picture of summer, ranging from its languid opening to the more restless middle section. It is a gloriously warm and lyrical piece whose neglect on record is difficult to understand. This is far superior to the earlier recording that was briefly in circulation; superbly committed and sensitive playing and vivid, warm recording.

Agnus Dei.
*** Hyp. Dig. **CDA 66129**; *KA 66129* [id.]. Corydon Singers, Matthew Best – BERNSTEIN: *Chichester Psalms*; COPLAND: *In the beginning* etc.***

Barber's *Agnus Dei* is none other than our old friend the *Adagio*, arranged for voices by the composer in 1967. Matthew Best's fine performance moves spaciously and expansively to an impressive climax. Voices can't create the same kind of tension as bows pressed passionately on strings, but they can produce a glowing radiance, as they do here. The sound is very fine, with the acoustics of St Jude-on-the-Hill, Hampstead, admirably suited to the music. There is an excellent chrome cassette.

Barrios, Agustin (1885–1944)

Aconquija; Aire de Zamba; La catedral; Choro de saudade; Cueca; Estudio; Una limosna el amor de Dios; Madrigal (Gavota); Maxixa; Mazurka apassionata; Minuet; Preludio; Sueño en la floresta; Valse No. 3; Villancico de Navidad.
**(*) CBS *40-76662* [*MT 35145*]. Williams.

Agustin Barrios is a little-known Paraguayan guitarist and composer who had the distinction of making (in 1909) the first known recording of a guitar. His music essentially belongs to the previous century. Its invention is fresh, if sometimes ingenuous, and the pieces here are well varied in style. In the expert hands of John Williams the collection provides a very entertaining recital, ideal for late-evening listening. Try the charming opening *La catedral* (sweet but not sugary) or the irresistible *Sueño en la floresta*, which ends the side in a breathtaking haze of fluttering figurations that remind one of Tarrega's *Recuerdos de la Alhambra*. The recording is excellent.

Bartók, Béla (1881–1945)

Concerto for orchestra.
(M) *** Decca **417 754-2** [id.]. Chicago SO, Solti – MUSSORGSKY: *Pictures*.***
** HMV **CDC7 47837-2**. Chicago SO, Ozawa – JANÁČEK: *Sinfonietta*.**

Concerto for orchestra; 2 Images, Op. 10.
(*) Ph. Dig. **411 132-2 [id.]. Concg. O, Dorati.

(i) *Concerto for orchestra; Music for strings, percussion and celesta.*
(*) CBS **MK 42397 [id.]. (i) NYPO or BBC SO, Boulez.
(*) DG **415 322-2 [id.]. BPO, Karajan.

Solti gave Bartók's *Concerto for orchestra* its compact disc début. The brilliantly clear recording was an early demonstration of the advantages of CD, with the silent background increasing the projection of the music making and (with superb definition in the bass) helping to create the listener's feeling of anticipation in the atmospheric opening bars. The upper range of the sound, however, is very brightly lit indeed, which brings an aggressive feeling to the upper strings. This undoubtedly suits the reading, fierce and biting on the one hand, exuberant on the other. With superlative playing from Solti's own Chicago orchestra and such vivid sound this will be an obvious choice for most readers, particularly as Decca have reissued the performance at mid-price, recoupled with a similarly brilliant version of Mussorgsky's *Pictures at an exhibition*. In the *Concerto* Solti has consulted original sources to suggest a faster speed than usual in the second movement, and this he makes entirely convincing.

Boulez's recording of the *Concerto* was made in 1972 in the Manhattan Centre, New York. The sessions were set up with quadraphonic sound very much in mind, and the remastered recording remains spaciously atmospheric. Though Boulez does not draw such precise ensemble from his New York players as Solti, for instance, this is a compulsive account, consciously expressive with plenty of colour. The *Music for strings, percussion and celesta* was recorded in Walthamstow five years earlier, but this recording too has a pleasing ambience although the balance is at times contrived – the piano in the second movement looms suddenly into the foreground and is out of perspective. Yet detail is vivid and, as in the coupling, the slight restriction of the upper range which has come with the background quiet ensures a comfortable effect. The performance is one of Boulez's finest. He gives an admirably hushed account of the opening and conveys its sense of mystery; the *Adagio* too is evocative, while the quick movements have plenty of attack and rhythmic vitality. The BBC Symphony Orchestra respond with genuine enthusiasm and their playing is often most sensitive. Altogether a thoroughly worthwhile if expensive reissue.

Dorati's is a surprisingly lyrical account of Bartók's most popular work, consistently bringing out the folk-dance element along with the fun of the inspiration. The bite and excitement are less prominent than in more brilliant and extrovert readings, but there is a clear place for this, warmly rather than brilliantly recorded, and well coupled with the two atmospheric *Pictures: Blossoming* and *Village dance*. The CD version is clear and faithful.

Karajan's recording of the *Concerto for orchestra* comes from 1966 and of the *Music for strings, percussion and celesta* from 1973; they have been very successfully remastered digitally for compact disc. In the *Concerto*, the Berlin Philharmonic, in superb form, give a performance that is rich, romantic and smooth – for some ears perhaps excessively so. Karajan is right in treating Bartók emotionally, but comparison with Solti points the contrast between Berlin romanticism and earthy Hungarian passion. With Solti, any rubato is linked with the Hungarian folksong idiom, where Karajan's moulding of phrases is essentially of the German tradition. The *Music for strings, percussion and celesta* also has well-upholstered timbre, and here Karajan's essentially romantic view combines with the recording to produce a certain urbanity. He avoids undue expressiveness in the opening slow fugue (except in a big rallentando at the end), but the third movement is given a performance of great atmosphere. Nevertheless, the playing of the Berlin strings is a pleasure in itself, and the sound is impressive and sumptuous.

Ozawa's HMV reissue produces dazzling playing from the Chicago orchestra and a bright but well-balanced sound-picture. There are more searching and more atmospheric performances available, but none more brilliant. The performance is full of life and energy. Even so, this early-1970s recording might have been more competitive at mid-price. It sounds rather two-dimensional on CD.

Hungaroton offer a compilation, joining the *Concerto* with choral music including the *Cantata profana*, but this is not really a memorable disc and the performances directed by Ferencsik and Lehel respectively are not distinctive (Hung. **HCD 1275902**).

Piano concertos Nos 1–3; Music for strings, percussion & celesta; Rhapsody for piano and orchestra; Scherzo for piano and orchestra.
*** Ph. Dig. **416 831-2**; *416 831-4* (3) [id.]. Kocsis, Budapest Fest. O, Fischer.

This outstanding new set dominates the catalogue in this repertoire. Kocsis recorded the *First* and *Second Piano concertos* in the early 1970s for Hungaroton; but these new versions are even more vibrant, and the *Third* is superbly done, to make it perhaps the finest on record. The inclusion of the *Music for strings, percussion and celesta* may be counted a disadvantage by some, particularly as the resonant acoustic and rather forward balance prevent an absolute pianissimo and detract from the feeling of mystery; but this is still an exciting and involving performance. We have had the *Rhapsody* before, and the account here is as fine as the *Concertos*; what is especially welcome is the *Scherzo*. It is an extensive piece (30′) dating from 1904, withdrawn by the composer after the first rehearsal and never performed in his lifetime. Its style is fascinatingly eclectic, but the writing is extremely spontaneous and the work springs to life when the performers are so obviously enjoying themselves. The full-bodied recording with a rich, tangible piano-image is very satisfying and there are excellent chrome cassettes, losing only a fraction of the upper range by comparison with the CDs.

Piano concertos Nos 1 in A; 2 in G.
*** DG **415 371-2** [id.]. Pollini, Chicago SO, Abbado.

Piano concertos Nos 1 in A; 3 in E.
(M) *** HMV *EG 290846-4*. Barenboim, New Philh. O, Boulez.

The DG issue forms a partnership between two of the most distinguished Italian musicians of the day, collaborating in performances of two formidable works which in their exuberance sweep away any idea that this might be forbidding music. Virtuosity goes with a sense of spontaneity. Rhythms in fast movements are freely and infectiously sprung to bring out bluff Bartókian high spirits, rather than any brutality. The Chicago orchestra, vividly recorded, is in superb form and the CD gives a new lease of life to the 1979 analogue recording.

There is plenty of electricity generated in the unexpected combination of Barenboim and Boulez, and though these are not the most polished performances of the concertos ever recorded they have a consistent dynamism. In the event it is Barenboim who seems to emerge the dominant partner, and the orchestra enters with enormous gusto into the task of following his mercurial playing. In the *First Concerto* there is a striking element of humour, entirely apt for Bartók's mellowed Indian summer; the jazz rhythms have a natural expressiveness. The hymn like slow movement has all the still intensity one expects from Barenboim when he is on top form, though in fact the tempo is not particularly slow. The recording is warmly atmospheric and the tape transfer copes well with the resonance. A good bargain.

Piano concerto No. 3 in E.
(*) Decca **411 969-2 [id.]. Vladimir Ashkenazy, LPO, Solti – PROKOFIEV: *Concerto No. 3.****

This Ashkenazy/Solti performance is a recoupling for CD (the original pairing was with the *Second Concerto*). The character of the performance follows very much the tone of voice of the tougher, earlier works, rarely relaxing. Tempi tend to be fast but, with the red-blooded Hungarian fire of the conductor matched by the Slavonic bite of the pianist, this performance sparks off the kind of energy and dash one would expect at a live performance, with the slow movement bringing hushed inner concentration. The transfer to CD is well managed, for the brilliance of the sound is the more striking, even if inner textures are not ideally detailed.

Concerto for 2 pianos, percussion and celesta.
*** Ph. Dig. **416 378-2** [id.]. Freire, Argerich, L. and J. Pustjens, Concg. O, Zinman – KODÁLY: *Dances of Galánta.****

(i) *Concerto for 2 pianos, percussion and celesta; Sonata for 2 pianos, percussion and celesta.*
*** HMV Dig. **CDC7 47446-2**; *EL 270418-4*. K. and M. Labèque, Gualda, Drouet; (i) CBSO, Rattle.

Though the differences are less vital than you might expect, it is an attractive idea to have on a single disc both the *Sonata for two pianos and percussion* and the *Concerto* which Bartók drew from it. Comparing the two, one might wonder why a full orchestra was needed to add relatively little extra. The Labèque sisters give brilliant, intense performances of both works which can be enjoyed equally; however, with the percussion relatively close in the *Sonata* the focus is sharper, with xylophone and timpani particularly impressive. Even in the slow movement, the *Sonata* brings a more hushed intensity, but in the *Concerto* it is good to have as imaginative a conductor as Simon Rattle. There is a well-managed XDR iron-oxide cassette, but the advantage of the absolutely silent background of the CD is obvious.

Martha Argerich with Stephen Bishop-Kovacevich recorded a fierily vibrant performance of the *Sonata*, and there is much of the same high-voltage electricity in her recording of the orchestral version with Nelson Freire. There is a wild urgency in the allegro of the first movement, subtle pointing in the slow movement, and lightness and wit in the finale, taken at a speed to allow spring in the rhythm. The recording with pianos placed relatively close is well detailed but lacks something in mystery.

Violin concerto No. 1, Op. posth.
*** Decca Dig. **411 804-2**; *411 804-4* [id.]. Kyung Wha Chung, Chicago SO, Solti – BERG: *Concerto.****

In Bartók's early *Concerto* – inspired, like Berg's late one, by a woman – the tender intensity of Chung's playing is established in the opening phrase, and the whole performance is comparably magnetic, brimming with poetry to make one forget the relative immaturity of the writing. Solti and the Chicago orchestra could not be more understanding, and the recording is brilliant and warm to match, whichever medium is chosen.

Violin concerto No. 2 in B min.
(M) *** HMV *EG 290322* [Ang. *4AM 37418*]. Perlman, LSO, Previn.

Perlman's is a superb performance, totally committed and full of youthful urgency, with the sense of spontaneity that comes more readily when performers have already worked together on the music in the concert hall. The contrasts are fearlessly achieved by both soloist and orchestra, with everyone relishing virtuosity in the outer movements. The slow movement is deliberately understated by the soloist, with the fragmentation of the theme lightly touched in, but even there the orchestra has its passionate comments. With no coupling, this is rather short measure, but no finer version of this masterly concerto has ever been available. The 1974 recording is full and lively, and the XDR cassette sounds well. When this arrives on CD it should prove unassailable.

Dance suite.
(*) ASV Dig. *ZCDCA 536*. LSO, Nowak – RAVEL: *Daphnis et Chloé: Suites 1 and 2.(*)

Grzegorz Nowak in a finely pointed account with the LSO brings out a surprising range of mood, witty in the third movement, affectionate in the fourth. The recording, made at the EMI

No. 1 Studio, is biting and brilliant without any harshness. The pity is that the Ravel coupling is far less imaginatively done. The cassette is well enough transferred, but there is some loss of upper range.

Divertimento for strings; Music for strings, percussion and celesta.
*** Hung. Dig. **HCD 12531** [id.]. Liszt C O, Rolla.

Divertimento for strings; Rumanian folk dances.
(*) DG **415 668-2 [id.]. Orpheus CO – JANÁČEK: *Mládi.***(*)

The *Music for strings, percussion and celesta* (1936) and the *Divertimento for strings* (1939) were both written for Paul Sacher's Basle Chamber Orchestra. The Liszt Chamber Orchestra comprises seventeen players, including Janos Rolla who directs from the first desk. These are both expert performances, and distil a powerful atmosphere in the slow movements of both pieces. They command beautifully rapt *pianissimo* tone and keen intensity. The sound is less reverberant than some rivals, but there is no lack of ambience. Readers who want an account that would not have greatly differed from Sacher's at the first performance will not be disappointed: indeed, this is the best available.

The American Orpheus Chamber Orchestra also give an eminently well-prepared account of the *Divertimento*, but they are not as sensibly (or competitively) coupled as the Liszt Chamber Orchestra on Hungaroton. Good though their performance is, it is not quite as idiomatic in its sense of mystery or intensity of feeling as the Hungaroton, even if it possesses both in good measure. The recording, though very clean and well balanced, is not so atmospheric. The differences are minute and to emphasize them would be wrong. The DG issue deserves a recommendation none the less, and readers attracted to the coupling can confidently invest in it. The popular *Rumanian folk dances* are also attractively done. The compact disc is of DG's finest quality, particularly vivid and clear.

(i) *The Miraculous Mandarin* (complete ballet), *Op. 19;* (ii) *2 Portraits, Op. 5.*
*** DG Dig. **410 598-2** [id.]. (i) Amb. S.; LSO, Abbado; (ii) with Minz – PROKOFIEV: *Scythian suite.****

(i) *The Miraculous Mandarin* (complete ballet), *Op. 19; Music for strings, percussion and celesta.*
(*) Decca Dig. **411 894-2 [id.]. (i) Kenneth Jewell Chorale; Detroit S O, Dorati.

The Miraculous Mandarin: concert suite; *Music for strings, percussion and celesta.*
(*) HMV **CDC7 47117-2 [id.]. Phd. O, Ormandy.

The Miraculous Mandarin (suite), *Op. 19; The Wooden Prince* (suite), *Op. 13.*
* Denon Dig. **CO 1330** [id.]. Toyko Met. S O, Hiroshi Wakasugi.

Abbado directs a fiercely powerful performance of Bartók's barbarically furious ballet – including the wordless chorus in the finale – but one which, thanks to the refinement of the recording, is texturally clear, except for the very opening which is a little clouded. This makes the aggressiveness of the writing more acceptable while losing nothing in power. The Prokofiev coupling, added for the CD issue, is highly appropriate and equally successful; before that, however, the ear is sweetened by Minz's warmth in the *Portraits*. If he is at times over-sweet, that is more acceptable when he is surrounded by music of such vehemence.

The range and brilliance of Decca's Detroit recording are spectacular, with the formidable bass response particularly impressive on CD. That makes up for any lessening of tension in the actual performance compared with Dorati's previous recordings of both works. Though the playing in the early ballet – the complete score, not the truncated text sanctioned in the so-called suite – is polished enough, it finally lacks the flamboyance needed, the bold display of controlled barbarism. The *Music for strings, percussion and celesta* lacks the final degree of intensity, too. Nevertheless, such an apt, attractive and generous coupling presented in superb sound should not be dismissed.

Ormandy and the Philadelphia Orchestra have recorded *The Miraculous Mandarin* before, but this 1979 version of the suite does full justice to the Philadelphia strings and the sonorities of their cellos and basses. *The Miraculous Mandarin* suite is dazzling; the only reservation to be made concerns the *Music for strings, percussion and celesta*, where greater mystery is needed (at least in the first and third movements). There is no want of eloquence and passion, but the dynamic range at the *pianissimo* end of the spectrum leaves something to be desired. That apart, there is so much to enjoy and admire here that this issue can be recommended: the orchestral playing as such and the recording, too, are of the very first order.

Wakasugi's version of the *suite* on Denon cannot compete as a performance or recording. The coupling of music from another early Bartók ballet, much more neglected, *The Wooden Prince*, is welcome, though there too the performance is undercharacterized.

Music for strings, percussion and celesta.
(M) **(*) HMV **CDM7 69242-2** [id.]. BPO, Karajan – HINDEMITH: *Mathis der Maler.****
(*) HMV **CDC7 47521-2 [id.]. Stokowski and his SO – BARBER: *Adagio*; SCHOENBERG: *Verklaerte Nacht.***(*)
** Hung. **HCD 12631-2** [id.]. Bav. RSO, Bernstein – BERNSTEIN: *Divertimento.***

Karajan first recorded the *Music for strings, percussion and celesta* in 1949; this HMV version comes from 1960. Though not so well recorded as the 1973 remake for DG (see above), it is a marvellously atmospheric and committed account, in some ways fresher and more spontaneous than the later version. The sound needs more body and colour in the middle and upper registers, but it is still acceptable and, given the excellence of the performance (and the coupling), this is still very well worth considering.

Stokowski's performance dates from 1959 and the quality is remarkably full, aided by the resonant acoustics of the Manhattan Center, New York. It is an unashamedly romantic view, but by no means indulgent. Some will want more bite in the allegros (the finale uses the folk elements good-humouredly), but Stokowski is at his best in the eerie nocturnal music. This CD has very good couplings, and it is a pity it is not offered alongside the Karajan in HMV's Studio series.

Recorded live – not with his usual post-edited technique but at an actual performance in Budapest – Bernstein's version has tremendous vigour, with some fine solo work from the Bavarian principals, though ensemble is often rough. The sound is atmospheric, capturing the feeling of a live occasion, but string tone is unrefined.

CHAMBER AND INSTRUMENTAL MUSIC

Contrasts.
(***) CBS **MK 42227**; *MT 42227* [id.]. Benny Goodman, Joseph Szigeti, composer – BERNSTEIN: *Prelude, fugue and riffs*; COPLAND: *Concerto*; STRAVINSKY: *Ebony concerto*; GOULD: *Derivations.*(***)

Benny Goodman's recording with Szigeti and the composer, from the 78 r.p.m. era, is part of an enterprising and worthwhile anthology demonstrating the remarkable range of this famous clarinettist in twentieth-century music. This Bartók work was written for him. The 1940 recording sounds fully acceptable and the authority of the music making is obvious.

Sonata for 2 pianos and percussion.
*** CBS Dig. **MK 42625**; *IMT 42625* [id.]. Perahia, Solti, Corkhill, Glennie – BRAHMS: *Variations on a theme by Haydn.****

An unexpected and highly creative partnership produces a vivid and strongly characterized performance. The combination of star conductor, taking time off from the rostrum, and his distinguished associate, each striking sparks off the other, with Solti bringing Hungarian flair to the proceedings, makes for great eloquence in this powerful work. The recording is vivid to match, giving the players great presence.

(i) *Sonata for 2 pianos and percussion;* (ii) (Solo) *Violin sonata.*
*** Accord Dig. **149047**. (i) Janka and Jurg Wyttenbach, Schmid, Huber; (ii) Schneeberger.

The Accord recordings were made in Basle in the wake of the Bartók centenary celebrations. Hans-Heinz Schneeberger is little known outside Switzerland, though he has recorded Willy Burkhard's beautiful *Concerto*. He is obviously an accomplished artist and his account can withstand comparison with most if not all rivals. The *Sonata for 2 pianos and percussion* receives an exhilarating performance though Janka and Jurg Wyttenbach are neither as subtle nor as imaginative pianistically as Argerich and Bishop-Kovacevich on Philips (see above). However, the CD recording is astonishingly good and also very natural. There is impressive range and the percussion players sound as if they are there in one's living-room. Well worth paying money for!

String quartets Nos 1–6.
*** HMV Dig. **CDS7 47720-8**; *EX 270611-5* (3) [Ang. **CDCC 47720**]. Alban Berg Qt.
*** ASV Dig. *ZCDCA 510* (1–2); *509* (3–4); *504* (5–6). Lindsay Qt.
(*) Astree **CDE 7717 (1–2); **7718** (3–4); **7719** (5–6). Végh Qt.
** Hung. Dig. **HCD 12502/4** [id.]. Takács Qt.

The Alban Berg Quartet is one of the great ensembles of the day; in terms of sheer virtuosity and attack, as well as great beauty of sound, they are unsurpassed. One would be bowled over in the concert hall, and it is all pretty dazzling on record. The finale of No. 5 is quite breathtaking, as for that matter are both the middle quartets. These are very impressive performances indeed, technically almost in a class of their own. They are very well recorded too, on chrome cassette as well as on CD, even though the sound is not superior to that DG provided for the Tokyo Quartet which, when it is transferred to CD, will sweep the board. At times the Alban Berg appear to treat this music as a vehicle for their own supreme virtuosity; and they lose the immediacy of feeling one found in the pioneering sets of Nos 5 and 6 by the Hungarians on shellac or the first mono LP set by the Végh.

The Lindsay Quartet on ASV are the only other version available on tape. Searchingly powerful and expressive, they are strongly projected readings given the advantage of first-class digital sound, warmly atmospheric but nicely focused. The quality of the tape transfers is outstanding.

The analogue Végh recordings date from 1972, but the CD transfers are splendidly managed – there is a fine sense of presence, yet the ambient fullness one associates with the best analogue recordings remains and there is no edginess on top. The Végh players sometimes respond with more expressive warmth than some may like; but others may find this the very quality in their music making that prevents this music from becoming too aggressive. On the whole they give very perceptive performances. They are not flawless technically, but they understand what this music is about.

The Takács Quartet is a Hungarian ensemble of high quality. But while they bring a youthful ardour and vitality to this repertoire and have excellent ensemble and attack to commend them, they tend now to be somewhat outclassed by the competition; they do not dispense the sense of mystery and atmosphere which the Lindsays bring to these works. There is, however, much more to admire than to cavil at: they have ample fire and are certainly not short on virtuosity. The recording is a trifle forward, and though it has plenty of presence it is not as refined as the best of its competitors.

Violin sonatas Nos 1 and 2.
(*) Hung. **HCD 11655-2. Kremer, Smirnov.

Both *Sonatas* come from the early 1920s and are among Bartók's most original compositions. They were conceived at a time when Bartók had been playing the Szymanowski *Mythes* and, fired by enthusiasm, had ordered all of the Polish composer's music to study. Some of the visionary, mystical intensity of Szymanowski permeates these concentrated works. Kremer and Smirnov play with total commitment and their performances can only be described as masterly. The recording (from the early 1970s) is rather closely balanced and the acoustic somewhat drier than is ideal, otherwise this would receive a full three-star recommendation, for the performances merit it.

(Solo) *Violin sonata.*
*** HMV Dig. **CDC7 47621-2** [id.]; *EL 270538-4.* Nigel Kennedy – ELLINGTON: *Mainly black.****

Nigel Kennedy gives a masterly, deeply felt reading of the Bartók solo *Violin sonata*, the work originally commissioned by his own early mentor, Yehudi Menuhin. With outstandingly vivid recording, full of presence, Kennedy draws beautiful sounds from his instrument, whether in the pure, poised lines of the *Melodia*, in the mysterious, elusive *Presto*, or even in the often craggy double-stopping of the *Chaconne*. With an unexpected but fascinating and apt Ellington coupling, it is one of Kennedy's most impressive recordings yet. There is a good XDR tape, but the CD undoubtedly brings added presence and range.

Dance suite; Hungarian peasant songs: 3 Rondos on folk tunes; Rumanian dances.
*** Denon Dig. **C37 7092** [id.]. András Schiff (piano).

András Schiff, whose reputation rests on his keenly imaginative readings in the classical repertory, here demonstrates his red-blooded Hungarian fervour. In the *Dance suite* his range of mood, tone and expression makes up for the lack of varied orchestral colours, and the popular *Rumanian dances* have rarely been played with such infectious rhythms, often light and witty. The other collections are just as persuasively played, and the piano sound is first rate, with plenty of bite and losing inner clarity only with the heaviest textures of the *Dance suite*. Though the CD has only four bands, it is most generously indexed with even the 15 tiny *Peasant songs* all separated.

For children, Books I and II (complete).
*(*) Hung. **HCD 12304-2** [id.]. Zoltán Kocsis.

Zoltán Kocsis is fully attuned to this music which has more depth and poignancy than it is given credit for, and his playing, as one would expect, is thoroughly idiomatic. However, the recording, made in Budapest in 1980, has a distinctly unglamorous acoustic (the effect is almost like an upright piano in a small music-room), and this undoubtedly diminishes the appeal of this record.

Out of doors; Suite, Op. 14.
*(**) Tel. **ZK8 43417** [id.]. Dezsö Ránki – STRAVINSKY: *3 Movements from Petrushka* etc.*(**)

Dezsö Ránki is a highly talented Hungarian pianist and a notable Bartók interpreter. Unfortunately his account of the *Suite* and *Out of doors*, recorded in 1981, is handicapped by dry recording which militates against atmosphere. The performances are first class and, were the recording of comparable quality, this would carry a three-star recommendation.

OPERA

Bluebeard's Castle (sung in Hungarian).
(M) *** Decca *414 167-4* [id.]. Ludwig, Berry, LSO, Kertesz.
(*) Hung. Dig. **MCD 12254 [id.]. Obraztsova, Nesterenko, Hungarian State Op. O, Ferencsik.

Bartók's idea of portraying martial conflict in an opera was as unpromising as could be, but in the event *Bluebeard's Castle* is an enthralling work with its concentration on mood, atmosphere and slow development as Bluebeard's wife finds the key to each new door. Its comparative lack of action makes it an ideal work for the gramophone, and there have been a surprising number of attempts to record it. Kertesz set new standards in his version with Christa Ludwig and Walter Berry, not only in the playing of the LSO at its peak, in the firm sensitivity of the soloists and the brilliance of the recording, but also in the natural Hungarian inflexions inspired by the conductor. The reissue of this 1966 recording was one of the first on Decca's mid-price London Enterprise label, which offers a cassette of high quality – indeed, it is in the demonstration class, refined as well as clear and vivid.

With two distinguished Soviet singers taking the roles of Bluebeard and Judith, Ferencsik's Hungaroton version (his fourth recording of the work) is vocally resonant and delicately atmospheric with the hushed pianissimo of the opening tellingly caught. Yet in musical weight and intensity, not to mention dramatic detail and technical virtuosity, this inevitably yields before the finest versions using Western orchestras. The digital recording is full and faithful.

Bax, Arnold (1883–1953)

(i) *Cello concerto; Cortège; Mediterranean; Northern Ballad No. 3; Overture to a picaresque comedy.*
*** Chan. Dig. **CHAN 8494**; *ABTD 1204* [id.]. (i) Wallfisch; LPO, Bryden Thomson.

The *Cello concerto* (1934) was Bax's first major work after the *Fifth Symphony*. Both the *Symphonic variations* (1918) and the *Winter legends* (1932) are concertante works, and Bax subsequently rechristened his viola concerto *Phantasy for viola and orchestra*. Like both the concertante works, the *Cello concerto* disappeared from the repertoire after a few years and had to wait more than half a century for this, its first recording. It is rhapsodic in feeling, tender and ruminative rather than epic, as are the concertante piano works, and more lightly scored. Raphael Wallfisch seems a totally convinced advocate and plays with marvellous sensitivity and finesse, given splendid support by the LPO under Bryden Thomson. The other pieces are of mixed quality: the *Third Northern Ballad* is a dark, brooding score, while the *Cortège* and *Mediterranean* are pretty commonplace. The *Overture to a picaresque comedy* is first-rate Bax, high-spirited and inventive, but Bryden Thomson sets rather too measured a pace for it to sparkle as it should. The recording maintains the high standards of the Bax Chandos series and as usual with Chandos, there is an excellent chrome cassette.

The Garden of Fand (symphonic poem).
(M) **(*) PRT **PVCD 8380** [id.]. Hallé O, Barbirolli – BUTTERWORTH: *Shropshire Lad*; VAUGHAN WILLIAMS: *Symphony No. 8*.**(*)

Barbirolli's vintage recording of *The Garden of Fand* is second only to Beecham's version; the 1957 recording has been marvellously freshened by Michael Dutton's digital remastering, with the body of Hallé string tone not diminished by the extra vividness and clarity. With equally outstanding couplings, this is an indispensable representation of Barbirolli's art. It is a pity that this disc offers no documentation.

The Garden of Fand; The happy forest; November woods; Summer music.
*** Chan. Dig. **CHAN 8307**; *ABTD 1066* [id.]. Ulster O, Bryden Thomson.

This excellent, highly enjoyable Chandos collection of Bax tone-poems, the first of a series, represents the work of the Ulster Orchestra at its very finest. The Celtic twilight in Bax's music is ripely and sympathetically caught in the first three items, while *Summer music*, dedicated to Sir Thomas Beecham and here given its first ever recording, brings an intriguing kinship with the music of Delius. The Chandos recording is superb, full, vivid and natural, with no unnatural close-ups. The chrome cassette has striking range and projection, but the massed upper strings lack body compared with the CD. The compact disc is outstanding, the bass firm and clean, while the sound has exceptional detail and range.

In the faery hills; Into the twilight; Rosc-Catha; The tale the pine-trees knew.
*** Chan. Dig. **CHAN 8367**; *ABTD 1133* [id.]. Ulster O, Bryden Thomson.

Outstanding as Bryden Thomson's records of Bax and others have been, this second collection of Bax tone-poems is among the finest. With recording of demonstration quality, exceptionally vivid and well balanced on CD, Bryden Thomson draws from the Ulster Orchestra playing not just of keen commitment but of great refinement and finesse, too. *The tale the pine-trees knew*, written in 1931, is one of the better-known as well as one of the most evocative of Bax's tone-poems, here done with total sympathy. The other three tone-poems, written between 1908 and 1910, form an Irish trilogy which Bax – long before the Irish Republic ever used the name – collectively called *Eire*. The first two are filled with typically Baxian Celtic twilight, but the last (*Rosc-Catha* meaning 'battle hymn') presents the composer in vigorous, extrovert mood, making an excellent contrast.

Malta G.C. (complete); *Oliver Twist: Suite* (film scores).
(*) Cloud Nine Dig. **ACN 7012. RPO, Alwyn.

Both these film-scores are in the form of a series of miniatures; on the whole, *Oliver Twist* stands up more effectively without the visual imagery. The use of concertante piano is effective in a brief nocturnal portrayal of Oliver and later in a sequence called *Oliver and Brownlow*. *Oliver and the Artful Dodger* and *Fagin's romp* both give rise to effective and inventive scherzando writing, and the finale brings a resplendent Waltonian jubilation. In *Malta G.C.* much of the score is concerned with wartime action: it is the gentler music, the *Intermezzo* and *Reconstruction* and again the final apotheosis, that brings the most memorable writing. Kenneth Alwyn conducts the RPO with fine flair and commitment, Eric Parkin is the brief soloist and the recording is brilliantly colourful and vivid, if at times a little lacking in the richest sonority.

On the sea-shore.
*** Chan. Dig. **CHAN 8473**; *ABTD 1184*. [id.]. Ulster O, Handley – BRIDGE: *The Sea*; BRITTEN: *Sea interludes*.***

Bax's Prelude, *On the sea-shore*, sensitively orchestrated by Graham Parlett from the composer's short-score, was originally intended as part of a saga-drama on an Irish theme. It makes a colourful and atmospheric companion to the masterly Bridge and Britten pieces on the disc, played and recorded with similar warmth and brilliance. The chrome cassette, too, is up to Chandos's usual high standard.

3 Pieces: Evening piece; Irish landscape; Dance in the sunlight.
*** HMV Dig. **CDC7 47945-2**; *EL 270592-4* [id.]. ECO, Tate – BRIDGE: *There is a willow***(*); BUTTERWORTH: *Banks of green willow, etc.***(*); MOERAN: *Lonely waters.****

The three Bax *Pieces* as attractive rarities make a welcome appearance in Tate's English recital. The first two are characteristically evocative, while the third is in Bax's brightest, most extrovert vein. Refined performances, warmly recorded, with the CD bringing good detail and presence without loss of atmosphere. There is also a well-managed iron-oxide tape.

Spring Fire; Northern Ballad No. 2; Symphonic scherzo.
*** Chan. Dig. **CHAN 8464**; *ABTD 1180* [id.]. RPO, Vernon Handley.

Spring Fire is an early work, predating *The Garden of Fand* and the *First Symphony*. In a way it is his Symphony No. 0: in four movements, two of which are almost worth putting alongside his best tone-poems. Their feeling is rhapsodic, and Bax's command of the orchestra is already richly in evidence. Although it dates from 1913 it was not actually performed until 1970, long after his death. The second *Northern Ballad* is also a valuable acquisition to the catalogue; it is held together powerfully and is both tauter and more coherent than much of his later music – including the *Seventh Symphony*! It is dark and bleak, still strongly tied to the landscape of the rugged northern coasts. The *Symphonic scherzo* is of less moment; it began life as a movement from a piano sonata and its thematic substance is less memorable that that of its companions. Highly idiomatic playing from Vernon Handley and the RPO, and a thoroughly lifelike and characteristically well-detailed recording from Chandos. The chrome tape, too, is outstandingly successful.

Symphonic variations for piano and orchestra; Morning Song (Maytime in Sussex).
*** Chan. Dig. **CHAN 8516**; *ABTD 1226* [id.]. Margaret Fingerhut, LPO, Bryden Thomson.

The *Symphonic variations* were written during the 1914–18 War when Bax's passion for Harriet Cohen was at its height. It is an ambitious score, almost 50 minutes in duration, to which Harriet Cohen had exclusive rights. Although she played it a great deal between the wars (it was briefly a favourite at the Proms), albeit without the first variation, *'Youth'*, and with certain emendations to accommodate her technique, the work fell into neglect. Its rescue by Margaret Fingerhut in this magnificent Chandos recording can only be hailed as a triumph. She reveals it as a work of considerable substance with some sinewy, powerful writing in the more combative variations, thoughtful and purposeful elsewhere. The balance between piano and orchestra could hardly be better judged and more natural; and the orchestral playing under Bryden Thomson is first class. In his later years, Bax was knighted and became Master of the King's Music, in which capacity he was commissioned to compose a piece to celebrate the present Queen's twenty-first birthday; the result was the amiable but discursive *Morning song*. This CD is in the demonstration class, and the same might be said of its equivalent chrome cassette.

Symphony No. 1 in E flat; Christmas Eve.
*** Chan. Dig. **CHAN 8480**; *ABTD 1192.* [id.]. LPO, Bryden Thomson.

Bax's *First Symphony* began life as a piano sonata in 1921. The following year he scored the outer movements and replaced the second with a powerful funeral oration. Bax spoke of the 'fierce, almost defiant character' of the main themes of the first movement, and there is an undoubtedly combative spirit to this score. However, it is the slow movement that lies at the core of this work – it is 'both mystic and elegiac'. Bryden Thomson is completely inside the idiom and is boldly expressive, relaxing his pace when the natural flow of the music suggests it; and the results carry total conviction. *Christmas eve* is an earlier work, coming from the

Edwardian era, but it is a less developed and less interesting piece. Bryden Thomson directs this richly textured, dark-hued score with total authority. Bax's splendid scoring is particularly rich in the tenor-baritone register; and the lower wind (such as bass clarinet, heckelphone (bass oboe) and the sarrusphone, a contrabassoon) are heard to excellent advantage on the new Chandos digital recording. On tape the sound is sumptuous rather than sharply defined.

Symphony No. 2; Nympholept.
*** Chan. Dig. **CHAN 8493**; *ABT 1203* [id.]. LPO, Bryden Thomson.

The *Second Symphony* comes from 1924–6; first performed in America, it was dedicated to Koussevitzky (Nos 4 and 7 also had their premières in the United States). It is a rich and engrossing work, closely related to nature and full of rich invention. The strength of Bryden Thomson's account lies in its breadth and sweep: its evocation of and identification with the natural and spiritual world of this composer. He seems totally at one with Bax's sensibility and secures orchestral playing of total commitment. *Nympholept* means 'possessed by nymphs' and is earlier, originally for piano and scored before Bax wrote *The Garden of Fand.* It, too, is an imaginative piece and, though not one of his finest works, its 18 minutes makes an admirable fill-up to the *Symphony*. As with other issues in the series, the recording is in the demonstration class, of spectacular clarity and definition. The chrome tape, too, is well up to Chandos's high standard, the sound rich and vivid, the focus excellent.

Symphony No. 3. Paean; the Dance of Wild Irravel.
*** Chan. Dig. **CHAN 8454**; *ABTD 1165* [id.]. LPO, Bryden Thomson.

The *Third* was the first Bax symphony ever to be recorded, by Barbirolli and the Hallé Orchestra, way back in 1943: it was recently reissued on HMV, but has now been withdrawn. It is arguably the best, though the *Second* also has strong claims to be so regarded. Even if the rumbustious opening of the finale does not wholly convince, everything else in this glorious work does. The opening is one of the composer's finest inspirations and has a searching, visionary quality about it. Bax's imaginative resources seem to be more richly stocked here than in almost any other of his major works, and the slow movement is wholly unlike anything else in English music. Bryden Thomson is closely attuned to the Bax idiom, and it would be difficult to overpraise him and his fine players. The two companion pieces, the *Paean* and *The Dance of Wild Irravel*, may perhaps strain the allegiance of some – but no matter, the symphony is a sufficient feast; it is Bax's longest at nearly 50 minutes. The Chandos recording has marvellous presence and vivid detail that does full justice to Bax's sumptuous and opulent orchestral textures. The chrome-cassette transfer is first class in every way.

Symphony No. 4; Tintagel.
*** Chan. Dig. **CHAN 8312**; *ABTD 1091* [id.]. Ulster O, Bryden Thomson.

The *Fourth Symphony* was written in 1930–31; part of the first movement was worked out at Bax's Irish refuge in Glencolumcille, but the seascapes that the score brings to mind are mainly those of the coast and islands of the Western Highlands where Bax spent each winter during the 1930s. The copious flow of ideas in the best of his symphonies (2, 3, 5 and 6) does not always go hand in hand with organic coherence, and the overall impression remains of a series of related episodes rather than a growing musical organism. The ideas may not be quite as memorable as those of the *Third* and *Fifth*, but the moods are still powerful and the colours vivid. The performance is altogether splendid; Bryden Thomson encourages his players to a scrupulous observance of dynamic nuance as well as a sensitive projection of atmosphere. The CD is a demonstration disc even by the high standards Chandos have established in this field. The chrome tape is also first class.

Symphony No. 6; Festival overture.
*** Chan. Dig. **CHAN 8586**; *ABTD 1278* [id.]. LPO, Bryden Thomson.

The *Sixth Symphony* of 1934 is the last major work to find Bax in the fullness of his creative poser. The invention is rich and formally the work is full of interest, its finale (Introduction – Scherzo and Trio – Epilogue) being particularly powerful. Bryden Thomson is scrupulously attentive to the dynamic and agogic markings of the score, and the LPO respond admirably. The makeweight is an early overture of 1912, never recorded before. First-class recording, well up to the high standard of this series.

Winter Legends; Saga fragment.
*** Chan. Dig. **CHAN 8484**; *ABTD 1195* [id.]. Margaret Fingerhut, LPO, Bryden Thomson.

The *Winter Legends*, for piano and orchestra, comes from much the same time as the *Third Symphony*, to which at times its world seems spiritually related. His critics claim that the Bax symphonies are episodic, and his musical thinking less organic than Elgar or Vaughan Williams, but still who cares when the episodes are so rich in colour and inspiration? The *Winter Legends* were originally composed for Harriet Cohen, and the keyboard writing is ambitious; this is in some ways a sinfonia concertante for piano and orchestra rather than a concerto proper. The piano part survives in no fewer than five different forms; the soloist has opened out the cuts made in earlier performances and made her choice among the versions where differences are to be found. She proves an impressive and totally convincing advocate for the score and, as far as the recorded sound is concerned, it would be difficult to imagine the balance between soloist and orchestra being more realistically judged. The companion piece came into being a few years later, in 1933: Bax required a short work for Harriet Cohen to play with a small orchestra, and this is a transcription of his one-movement *Piano quartet* of 1922. A quite outstanding disc. On the excellent chrome cassette the reverberation has meant a lower than usual transfer level but definition remains very good and the sound is truthful in timbre and balance.

CHAMBER AND INSTRUMENTAL MUSIC

Clarinet sonata.
** Chan. Dig. *ABTD 1078* [id.]. Janet Hilton, Keith Swallow – BLISS: *Clarinet quintet* (with VAUGHAN WILLIAMS: *6 Studies****).

Both artists are rather closely balanced in a very ample acoustic but they play the *Sonata* with sensitivity and conviction. It comes from 1934, the same year as the *Sixth Symphony*, and, despite its rhapsodic air, is a well-fashioned and succinct piece. For all its overt romanticism, it is not the best Bax and does not compare with the *Nonet* or the *Oboe quintet*, but its vein of lyricism and undoubted warmth will win it a following. The couplings, the *Clarinet quintet* of Bliss and the Vaughan Williams *Studies*, enhance its attractions on disc. The chrome cassette is of the highest Chandos quality, vivid and well balanced.

(i) *Harp quintet;* (ii) *Piano quartet. String quartet No. 1.*
*** Chan. Dig. **CHAN 8391**; *ABTD 1113* [id.]. (i) Skaila Kanga, (ii) John McCabe; English Qt.

All the music on this issue was written in the wake of the First World War: both the *Harp quintet* (1919) and the *Piano quartet* (1922) are one-movement works, and the *First String quartet* was composed in the closing months of the war. The latter piece is said to be Bax's response to criticism that his music was becoming over-complicated and for a time it was one of his most frequently played works. There is a strong folk element in the finale and the first movement comes close to the sound-world of the Dvořák quartets. Perhaps the finest of the three movements is its elegiac centrepiece. But it is all music with a strong and immediate appeal. The *Harp quintet* is more fully characteristic and has some evocative writing to commend it. The *Piano quartet,* with its winning lyricism, was reworked in the early 1930s for piano and small orchestra as was the *Saga fragment* (see above). These may not be Bax's most important scores, but they are rewarding; and the performances are thoroughly idiomatic and eminently well recorded. The chrome cassette, as usual from this source, is of such technical excellence as to make a fully recommendable alternative to the CD.

Oboe quintet.
*** Chan. Dig. **CHAN 8392**; *ABTD 1114* [id.]. Sarah Francis, English Qt – HOLST: *Air & variations*, etc.; MOERAN: *Fantasy Qt*; JACOB: *Quartet.****

Bax's *Oboe quintet*, written for Leon Goossens, dates from the time of the *First Symphony* and is a confident, inventive piece with a hauntingly inspired *Lento* and a gay Irish jig for its finale, though even this movement has a reflective inner core. After an almost oriental twist to the opening phrase, the work's introduction immediately establishes its depth of mood, and throughout the texture of the writing is rich without being prolix. Sarah Francis proves a most responsive soloist – though she is balanced too close; in all other respects the recording is up to Chandos's usual high standards, and the playing of the English Quartet is admirable. There is an excellent tape.

Piano trio in B flat.
*** Chan. Dig. **CHAN 8495**; *ABTD 1205* [id.]. Borodin Trio – BRIDGE: *Trio No. 2.****

The *Piano trio* was Bax's last chamber work; it was finished after the last war in 1946, when he had put the seven symphonies well behind him and his creative fires burned less fiercely. Lewis Foreman finds it 'less personal and expansive' than his earlier chamber works, but there is still much to which admirers of this long-neglected composer can respond – particularly the thoughtful slow movement. The playing of the Borodin Trio is very distinguished indeed and they seem completely attuned to the idiom. Even if it is not Bax at his best, this makes a welcome addition to his discography, particularly in view of the excellence of both performance and recording. There is a very good chrome cassette.

Rhapsodic Ballad (for solo cello).
*** Chan. Dig. **CHAN 8499**; *ABTD 1209* [id.]. Raphael Wallfisch – BRIDGE: *Cello sonata;* DELIUS: *Cello sonata*; WALTON: *Passacaglia.****

The *Rhapsodic Ballad* for cello alone comes from 1939 and is a freely expressive piece, played with authority and dedication by Raphael Wallfisch. The recording has plenty of warmth and range, and is a useful addition to the ever-growing Bax discography. As on the CD, the chrome tape gives the solo cello a natural presence.

Lullaby (Berceuse); Country Tune; Sonatas Nos 1 & 2; Winter waters.
** Chan. Dig. **CHAN 8496**; *ABTD 1206* [id.]. Eric Parkin (piano).

Bax was a formidable pianist and his writing is always both individual and idiomatic. The first version of the *Sonata No. 1* was written in the Ukraine, but was revised at the same time he composed its successor (1919–20). There is a Russian flavour to the *First*, and the opening of No. 2 momentarily suggests Medtner. Both are interesting pieces and they receive powerful performances from Eric Parkin, who is as persuasive an interpreter of this composer as he is of John Ireland. The recording is made in a very resonant (and not ideal) acoustic, with some unpleasing clangour – but, this reservation apart, this usefully fills a gap in the catalogue.

VOCAL MUSIC

I sing of a maiden; Mater ora filium; This world's joie.
*** HMV Dig. **CDC7 47663-2**; *EL 270440-4*. King's College Ch., Cambridge, Cleobury – FINZI: *God is gone up*, etc.***

Bax's ambitious setting of a medieval carol, *Mater ora filium*, is one of the most difficult a cappella pieces in the choral repertory. Here under Stephen Cleobury, the King's Choir gives it a virtuoso performance, with trebles performing wonders in the taxingly high passages. Perhaps the composer anticipated, when he wrote such a piece, that trebles would one day be able to cope with such writing, but the timbre of boys' voices adds to the poignancy of the piece. It is particularly apt too, when the original inspiration for the piece came from his hearing Byrd's *Mass in Five Voices*. The other two Bax pieces, also setting medieval texts, are most beautifully done too, with the unaccompanied voices vividly recorded against the spacious acoustic of King's Chapel. This brings some problems for the iron-oxide tape transfer which tends to blur the detail of the recording and is generally less sharply focused than the excellent CD.

Beethoven, Ludwig van (1770–1827)

Piano concertos Nos 1–5.
*** O-L Dig. **421 408-2**; *421 408-4* (3) [id.]. Steven Lubin, AAM, Hogwood.
(*) Telarc Dig. **CD 80061 (3) [id.]. Rudolf Serkin, Boston SO, Ozawa.
*(*) Ph. Dig. **411 189-2** (3) [id.]. Alfred Brendel, Chicago SO, Levine.
*(*) HMV Dig. **CDS7 47974-8**; *EX 270608-5* (3). Barenboim, BPO.

Piano concertos Nos 1–5; Andante favori; Polonaise in C, Op. 89.
(***) Arabesque mono **Z 6549** (*Nos 1–2*); **Z 6550** (*Nos 3–4*); **Z 6551** (*No. 5, Andante* and *Polonaise*) [id.]. Artur Schnabel, LSO or LPO, Sargent.

Piano concertos Nos 1–5; (i) *Choral fantasia, Op. 80.*
(M) ** DG **419 793-2** (3) [id.]. Pollini, VPO, Boehm, Jochum; (i) Abbado, with V. State Op. Ch.
** Decca Dig. **414 391-2**; *414 391-4* (3). De Larrocha, Berlin RSO, Chailly; (i) with Berlin R. Ch.

Steven Lubin uses four different reproduction fortepianos, each of them contemporary with a given work. Only in No. 4 does the performance seem to miniaturize Beethoven, partly a question of balance, and here the *Andante* dialogue is disappointing. The *Emperor*, with the same instrument, sounds far fuller, providing overall weight and the necessary flair to the opening flourishes. Lubin uses the extra clarity of the fortepiano very tellingly and, though speeds are on the brisk side, he is never extreme, and slow movements are allowed to breathe and find poetry and repose. Hogwood accompanies with freshness and resilience, and the recording is attractively vivid.

The digital set from Serkin, on Telarc, presents a generally satisfying set of performances. Technically the playing of the octogenarian is flawed – there is one amazing slip of finger in the second subject of the *First Concerto* which should not have been passed – but where in his late Mozart recordings for DG the lack of polish is distracting, here one consistently registers certainty and power, and there are frequent examples of those moments of magic and individual insight which are the mark of a live performance from a master, here caught in the recording studio. The accompaniments have comparable spontaneity and the sound is excellent.

In the Pollini set for DG, the last three concertos brought the unexpected but generally fruitful collaboration of this inspired but temperamental pianist with the veteran Boehm, and similarly in the first two concertos – recorded after Boehm's death – Jochum provides a sheet-anchor of tradition in accompaniments superbly judged. Pollini is sometimes wilful and rarely warm in expressiveness, but always fresh and spontaneously communicative. As a set this hardly compares with the finest but is a characterful reminder of a highly individual pianist.

Brendel's Chicago version was intended to prove how much more effective live recording is than studio performance, but the results – recorded at Orchestra Hall, Chicago – belie that. Anything Brendel does has mastery and distinction but, compared with his earlier studio recording of the concertos with Haitink and the Concertgebouw, this sounds self-conscious, less rather than more spontaneous-sounding. He did after all know that the tape was rolling, and that in itself must have affected the performances. The recorded sound gives a good sense of presence but is badly balanced, and loud applause at the end of each concerto is most intrusive.

Schnabel's performances fall into a special category. The concertos were recorded in 1932–3, save for the *B flat*, which dates from 1935; the solo pieces come from 1938 and some were unpublished. His playing has such enormous character that it transcends the limitations of sound that are inevitable at this period. The orchestral playing is occasionally lacking the finesse that we take for granted nowadays, but Schnabel's impulsive, searching and poetic playing offers special rewards. Not everything is equally successful: there is some roughness in the first movement of No. 3, but there are some marvellously spirited touches. The CD transfers are crystal clear and very little of the 78 r.p.m. hiss is apparent. However, for modern ears some adjustment is necessary to the dry orchestral texture, especially for the listener beginning with No. 1, where there is no bloom on the strings; the *Emperor*, however, sounds surprisingly well. Such is the electricity of the playing that one soon forgets the primitive recording and succumbs to Schnabel's spell. The three CDs are available separately.

Alicia de Larrocha, with the Berlin Radio Symphony Orchestra playing freshly under Chailly, offers the five Beethoven piano concertos plus the *Choral fantasia* on three discs, in modern digital sound, but the readings are not consistently successful. The first two concertos are given delightful performances, lightly pointed, on a Mozartian scale; but Larrocha sounds less spontaneous in the later works, adopting a weightier manner if rather self-consciously. The *Emperor* is preferable to Nos 3 and 4, bright and alert in the first movement, but with too little sense of struggle. Full, vivid Decca recording.

It is a formidable technical achievement for a pianist to direct all five Beethoven piano concertos from the keyboard, but Daniel Barenboim's readings with the Berlin Philharmonic are strangely underpowered, lacking the sharpness and character of his earlier cycle made in collaboration with Otto Klemperer. The lack of bite is underlined by the muddy quality of the sound, thick and ill-defined.

Piano concerto No. 1 in C, Op. 15.
** Nimbus Dig. **NIM 5003** [id.]. Mary Verney, Hanover Band. – *Symphony No. 1.***

Piano concerto No. 1; 6 Bagatelles, Op. 26.
** Decca Dig. **411 900-2**; *411 900-4* [id.]. Ashkenazy, VPO, Mehta.

Piano concerto No. 1; Piano sonata No. 14 (*Moonlight*).
** RCA **RD 85674 [RCA 5674-2-RC]**. Rubinstein, Boston SO, Leinsdorf.

Piano concerto No. 1; Piano sonata No. 21 (*Waldstein*).
(M) (**) Vox **MWCD 7106** [id.]. Brendel, Stuttgart PO, Boettcher.

With the pairing of the first two piano concertos now firmly established on CD – see below – the alternatives offering the *C major* alone, whatever the couplings, do not seem very useful or competitive. Certainly Pollini's DG compact disc is put completely out of the running as it has no coupling whatsoever, and the performance, for all its refreshing clarity of articulation, is brisk rather than poetic, in spite of the presence of Jochum directing the VPO (DG Dig. **410 511-2**).

Ashkenazy's Decca issue offers the *6 Bagatelles*, which are attractively played if hardly substantial. The reading of the *Concerto* stays essentially within the brief of early Beethoven, the first movement agreeably light and relaxed, with a tactful accompaniment from Mehta, the slow movement thoughtful in an unmannered way. Good, bright, finely detailed digital recording on CD, though the cassette is brilliant to the point of fierceness.

Rubinstein gives a sparkling, totally spontaneous-sounding performance which conveys the joy rather than the stress of early Beethoven. There are no half-tones, with no dynamic much below *mezzo forte* (partly a question of recording and close balance), but the sense of presence is vividly conveyed on CD in bright sound to bring out the clarity of articulation. The *Moonlight sonata* is a valuable, if scarcely generous, coupling.

Mary Verney is a persuasive advocate of playing Beethoven on a fortepiano. Though speeds are fast in all three movements of the *Concerto*, there is a gentleness and charm about the performance, intensified by the small scale of the solo instrument. Even with period instruments, the problems of balance are considerable, not just between soloist and orchestra but within the band. With CD clarifying the warmly reverberant sound – recorded in St Giles', Cripplegate – the unexpected perspectives are attractive.

Brendel's highly spontaneous 1975 Philips recording with Haitink and the LPO is still available on an excellent mid-priced CD, one of the finest performances of his earlier cycle and far preferable to his digital remake – see below. The coupling is a splendid account of the *Second Concerto*, comparably spontaneous and fresh. This is preferable to the Vox Prima CD, which offers his late-1960s version, originally issued on a Turnabout LP. The performance is undoubtedly distinctive, with the measured tempi of the outer movements held together by the concentration of the solo playing, and the expansiveness of the *Largo* comparably sustained by its natural weight of expression. The long cadenza in the first movement is interestingly confected from two of the cadenzas by Beethoven himself. The snag lies in the playing and recording of the orchestra, with seedy string-tone now sounding thinner than ever. The coupling is the famous version of the *Waldstein sonata* from the same period, with Brendel's fresh straightforward control of the overall structure bringing one of the finest performances of this work ever recorded. However, the piano timbre is unflatteringly hard.

DG have also made a CD issue of Michelangeli's intensely disappointing, strangely metrical performance coupled with the *Piano sonata No. 4* which is curiously aloof and detached. A very disappointing record (**419 248-2**).

Piano concertos Nos 1–2.
*** CBS Dig. **MK 42177**; *IMT 42177* [id.]. Perahia, Concg. O, Haitink.
*** DG Dig. **415 682-4**; *415 682-4* [id.]. Argerich, Philh. O, Sinopoli.
(M) *** DG **419 856-2**; *419 856-4* [id.]. Kempff, BPO, Leitner.
(M) *** Ph. **420 882-2**; *420 882-4* [id.]. Brendel, LPO, Haitink.
(*) Ph. Dig. **422 066-2; *422 066-4* [id.]. Arrau, Dresden State O, C. Davis.
(M) ** Pickwick Dig. **PCD 854**. Ortiz, City of L. Sinfonia, Hickox.
*(*) Ph. Dig. **412 787-2** [id.]. Brendel, Chicago SO, Levine.

Murray Perahia's coupling of Nos 1 and 2 brings strong and thoughtful performances very characteristic of this pianist, which yet draw a sharp distinction between the two works. No. 2, the earlier, brings a near-Mozartian manner in the first movement, but then rightly a deep and measured account of the slow movement takes Beethoven into another world, hushed and intense, looking directly forward to the slow movement of the *Fourth Concerto. The First Concerto* finds Perahia taking a fully Beethovenian view from the start, bringing a weight to it which leads naturally to his choice of cadenza, the longest that Beethoven wrote, here given with dash and fantasy. In the finale, too, the cadenza brings special point, when Perahia records for the first time an extended version discovered only recently among the composer's sketches. Bernard Haitink proves a lively and sympathetic partner, with the Concertgebouw playing superbly. The recording sets the orchestra in a pleasingly warm acoustic, with the piano sound agreeable if a little dull. On CD there is separate cueing for the cadenzas. The chrome cassette cannot be recommended: the orchestra is clouded by excessive bass response, though the piano timbre is truthful.

The conjunction of Martha Argerich and Giuseppe Sinopoli in Beethoven produces performances which give off electric sparks, daring and volatile. Even before the pianist enters in No. 1, Sinopoli has the Philharmonia playing with lightness and resilience, heralding a carefree sense of unpredictability in Argerich's contribution, which in phrase after phrase brings highly individual pointing. Argerich is jaunty in allegros rather than lightweight – one might even ask for more *pianissimo* – and slow movements are songful, not solemn. Very distinctive and stimulating performances, given full, vivid – albeit not ideally balanced – sound in a rather reverberant acoustic. Tape collectors will find the chrome cassette is of DG's best quality, far better balanced than CBS's Perahia tape.

Kempff's coupling is second to none, and the digitally remastered recording sounds remarkably fresh and vivid. Kempff's sense of repose is notable in the *First Concerto*. The slow movement is in fact faster than in his earlier mono version, yet the very profundity of Kempff's sense of calm creates the illusion of something much slower. Leitner's contribution, too, is especially distinguished, and the memorable orchestral response throughout is at its finest in the slow movement. In the finale the playing sparkles joyously. Again in No. 2, Kempff's playing is unmistakable in every bar and Leitner's conducting is both strong and sympathetic. The balance between piano and orchestra is particularly natural.

As in the other performances of this new series with Sir Colin Davis, Arrau's is a weighty, measured view which many will not find as appropriate in these early concertos as in the *Emperor*. Sir Colin accompanies sympathetically, but the full Dresden sound adds to the expansive character of the music making.

Cristina Ortiz's coupling of the first two concertos brings fresh and direct performances, vividly recorded, with bright and full piano sound. Speeds are unexceptionable, the manner undistracting, though the first movement of No. 2 is taken very briskly. At bargain price, this digital CD makes a fair recommendation, though these readings in their very lack of idiosyncrasy do not have the magnetism of the very finest accounts.

It is a paradox that, so far from sounding more spontaneous in his live recording of the *First Piano concerto* with Levine, Brendel appears more self-conscious and mannered, and Levine also makes matters worse in the first movement with phrases over-lovingly held back. The slow movement is much slower than in Brendel's 1979 studio recording and the finale less crisp. In this and much else, the penalties rather than the benefits of live recording are emphasized. The *Second* brings a similar reading with comparable flaws: a mannered first movement, a second movement (complete with groans from the soloist) less spacious than in Brendel's studio performance, and a finale sounding slightly rushed; imperfectly focused recording, not well balanced. The mastery of Brendel is never in doubt, but too much is stacked against it, not least the deafening applause at the opening and close, and this is not recommended. The earlier, analogue recordings with Haitink and the LPO are far preferable; the sound is excellent.

Piano concerto No. 2 in B flat, Op. 19.

(*) Telarc Dig. **CD 80064 [id.]. Serkin, Boston SO, Ozawa – *Concerto No. 4.***(*)

(*) Decca Dig. **411 901-2; *411 901-4* [id.]. Ashkenazy, VPO, Mehta – *Concerto No. 4.***(*)

** DG **413 445-2** [id.]. Pollini, VPO, Jochum – *Concerto No. 4.***

The natural gravitas of Serkin's view of Beethoven's earliest piano concerto – presaging last-period gravity at the end of the *Adagio* – is lightened by the humour of the playing, the inescapable sense of a great musician approaching the music afresh, spontaneously and without a hint of routine. Excellent support from Ozawa and full, vivid recording.

Ashkenazy's Vienna account of the *Second Piano concerto* is at once restrained and sparkling, thoughtful in the amazingly prophetic quasi-recitative which closes the slow movement, yet keeping the whole work well within an apt scale for early Beethoven. Excellent recording, bright and atmospheric, with a clean matching tape.

Pollini's version, taken from a live performance is one of the more attractive of his Beethoven concertos series. But though it is well coupled on CD, it cannot match its finest rivals.

Piano concertos Nos 2–3.
(*) RCA **RD 85675 [**RCA 5675-2-RC**]. Rubinstein, Boston SO, Leinsdorf.

Rubinstein's readings in both No. 2 and No. 3 (recorded in 1967 and 1965 respectively), much more than the rest of his Beethoven cycle, reflect his mastery as a Chopin interpreter. The rubato may be subtle but often is not very Beethovenian, and some may find it mannered. But the sparkle and spontaneity of Rubinstein's playing are vividly conveyed in bright, forward recording, made cleaner on CD, even as the close balance of the soloist is made the more apparent.

Piano concertos Nos 2; 4.
(*) HMV Dig. **CDC7 49230-2. Zacharias, Dresden State O, Vonk.

With consistently clean, rhythmic playing, Christian Zacharias gives fresh, bright performances of both Nos 2 and 4, beautifully recorded. As with Wilhelm Kempff, the brightness and clarity go with concentration, to make the slow movements of both concertos deeply thoughtful, not nearly as lightweight as they might otherwise seem. Zacharias does not have as keen a sense of fantasy as Kempff (or, among his contemporaries, Perahia), but his dedicated directness never runs the risk of seeming mannered. The weight and richness of the orchestral sound equally rebut any feeling of excessive lightness, though Vonk does not quite match the Mozartian elegance of his soloist in No. 2.

Piano concertos No. 2; 5 (Emperor), Op. 73.
(M) **(*) Decca **417 703-2** [id.]. Ashkenazy, Chicago SO, Solti.

In both concertos the partnership of Ashkenazy and Solti works well, with the vivid orchestral articulation matched by the responsive solo playing. The slow movement of No. 2 is strikingly beautiful and its hushed close creates a memorable feeling of serenity before the sparkling finale. The *Emperor* is an excitingly dramatic performance on the largest possible scale, yet one which is consistently imbued with poetry. Alongside the *Fourth Concerto*, this represents the peak of achievement of the analogue Chicago cycle. The remastered recording is brilliantly vivid, the piano clear and believably focused, but the orchestral textures are leaner than the originals, and some may like a more ample sound in the *Emperor*. But this is the only serious reservation about a coupling that is excellent value at mid-price.

Piano concerto No. 3 in C min., Op. 37.
(*) Telarc Dig. **CD 80063 [id.]. Serkin, Boston SO, Ozawa – *Choral fantasia.***(*)
(M) **(*) HMV **CDM7 69013-2**; *EG 769013-4* [id.]. Sviatoslav Richter, Philh. O, Muti – MOZART: *Piano Concerto No. 22.***(*)
** DG **413 446-2** [id.]. Pollini, VPO, Boehm – *Piano sonata No. 31.***(*)

Piano concerto No. 3. Andante favori, WoO 57; Für Elise, WoO 50.
(*) Decca Dig. **411 902-2; *411 902-4* [id.]. Ashkenazy, VPO, Mehta.

All the performances in Ashkenazy's Vienna series with Mehta are more relaxed than in his earlier Chicago set with Solti, but the first movement of the *Third Piano concerto* brings the most striking contrast of all, noticeably slower and less forceful. The result remains compelling, because it sounds so spontaneous and with fewer distracting agogic hesitations than before. Even Beethoven's big cadenza is presented relaxedly, not as a firework display. The slow movement is more easily lyrical than before, the finale lighter, more sparkling and with more charm than Ashkenazy usually allows himself. The two fill-ups come from much earlier sessions with less bright sound. The concerto, like the others in the series, has excellent sound, atmospheric as well as brilliant, but the coupling is both ungenerous and slight, although both pieces are played persuasively. The tape is brighter than the CD.

Serkin's Telarc version of the *Third Concerto* comes with the substantial bonus of the *Choral fantasia* as coupling. Though the octogenarian soloist's playing lacks some of its old fire, and the *Adagio* – taken relatively fast – is a little casual, the mastery of Serkin's conception is not in doubt, with his combination of ruggedness and flights of poetry, not least in the G minor and F minor passages at the beginning of the first-movement development. Though piano tone is a little twangy, the recording is outstandingly vivid and full.

Richter's 1978 version may be controversial – like its Mozart coupling – but clearly a master is at the keyboard and Muti draws a sympathetic accompaniment from the Philharmonia players. The performance is consciously wayward, essentially lyrical, but it has undoubted authority, and the remastered recording sounds first class, firmer and clearer than the original within a believable concert-hall ambience. The coupling brings a generous overall playing time of 72′.

The concentration of the playing and the single-minded clarity of Pollini's reading are matched by Boehm's strong, clear-minded accompaniment, but the performance is on the sober side for a youthful concerto that should sparkle more than it does here. On CD, the closeness of piano balance is more apparent than on LP, even though there are obvious gains in clarity. Unlike the original LP, the CD offers a sizeable bonus in the Op. 110 *Piano sonata*, an eloquent performance of considerable authority, which is (like the concerto) transferred impressively from an analogue original.

Piano concertos Nos 3–4.
*** CBS Dig. **MK 39814**; *IMT 39814* [id.]. Murray Perahia, Concg. O, Haitink.
(M) *** DG **419 467-2**; *419 467-4* [id.]. Kempff, BPO, Leitner.
(M) **(*) Ph. **420 861-2**; *420 861-4* [id.]. Brendel, LPO, Haitink.
(M) **(*) Decca **417 740-2**; *417 601-4* [id.]. Ashkenazy, Chicago SO, Solti.
*(*) Ph. Dig. **412 788-2** [id.]. Brendel, Chicago SO, Levine.

(i) *Piano concertos Nos 3–4; Piano sonata No. 21 in C (Waldstein), Op. 53.*
(B) *** DG Walkman *419 086-4* [id.]. Wilhelm Kempff, (i) with BPO, Leitner.

Perahia gives readings that are at once intensely poetic and individual, but also strong. In many ways he gives reminders of Wilhelm Kempff, a supreme Beethovenian of his time, with pointing and shading of passage-work that consistently convey the magic of the moment caught on the wing. As with Kempff, the diamond clarity and the touches of poetry may suggest for some an approach not rugged enough for Beethoven; but with Haitink and the Concertgebouw giving firmly sympathetic support, power is conveyed through sharpness of contrast, helped by fine, spacious and open recorded sound. Also as with Kempff, the magic never diminishes, with thoughtfully lyrical slow movements and delectably sparkling finales that are in no way mannered. The cassette with its extra bass resonance brings a loss of focus compared with the CD.

The return of the Kempff/Leitner performances on DG Galleria brings an outstanding mid-priced recommendation. The digital remastering has perceptibly clarified the sound without loss of bloom. In the *C minor Concerto* Kempff's approach is relatively measured, somewhat serious in mood; but in its unforced way, happily lyrical, brightly sparkling in articulation, it is refreshingly spontaneous. Kempff may characteristically adopt a flowing speed for the slow movement, but this natural thoughtfulness gives it the necessary gravity and intensity. Again, in the *Fourth Concerto* Kempff's delicacy of fingerwork and his shading of tone colour are as effervescent as ever, and the fine control of the conductor ensures the unity of the reading. In both concertos the recording of the orchestra is bright and resonant, the piano tone warm as well as clear. These performances are also available on a bargain-priced Walkman tape, offering the *Waldstein sonata* as a generous bonus.

Brendel's coupling, taken from his earlier analogue cycle with Haitink, is much preferable to his newer digital CD. In No. 3 there is an easy, relaxed account of the first movement, spontaneous-sounding, with the timpani raps of the coda even more measured and mysterious than usual. If the other two movements are less tense, with the finale thrown off in a mercurial manner, this adds up to a strong, persuasive performance. No. 4 brings a contrastingly strong, even tough reading, not immaculate as one might expect on detail, but producing an almost impressionistic thrust of urgency in the first movement. The slow movement is rapt in its simplicity, and the finale is treated almost flippantly, with some slips of ensemble which suggest the immediacy of live music-making, rather than the extra care of the studio. The remastered sound is impressively firm and realistic.

The Ashkenazy/Solti combination also brings playing full of character. The fierce intensity of the orchestral tuttis of the outer movements of the *C minor* may be counted controversial, emphasized by the brightly lit recording (with a touch of fierceness on the strings in the cassette transfer; the CD is smoother). But the strength of the playing is in no doubt, and the slow movement is finely done, the contrasts stronger than usual. A more relaxed atmosphere pervades the *G major*, one of the finest performances of the cycle; here the contrast between the personalities of soloist and conductor bring new insights to this masterly score, especially in the famous interplay of the *Andante*, where Solti's gruff boldness contrasts so tellingly with Ashkenazy's melting response. The 1973 recording is here admirably lively, full and convincingly balanced, and the CD transfer produces a particularly attractive piano image.

Brendel's newer digital CD coupling of Nos 3 and 4 is subject to all the reservations made concerning the complete cycle. Though Brendel's mastery and highly individual imagination are never in doubt, live performances are here, if anything, less spontaneous-sounding and more self-conscious than his earlier studio recordings. The audience noises, odd balances and intrusive applause are also obvious penalties.

(i) *Piano concerto No. 3;* (ii) *Violin concerto.*
(***) RCA mono **RD 85756 [RCA 5756-2-RC]**. (i) Rubinstein; (ii) Heifetz, NBC SO, Toscanini.

While both Rubinstein and Heifetz went on to re-record these works in stereo (Heifetz's account of the *Violin concerto* with Munch being particularly successful – see below), these earlier mono versions made during the war, in 1944 and 1940 respectively, have a legendary status because of the Toscanini partnership. This proves less fruitful with Heifetz than with Rubinstein. The notorious boxy acoustic of NBC's Studio 8-H means that the opening orchestral tutti is fierce and confined, and overall it is Heifetz's glowing lyricism and purity of spirit in the slow movement that make this account memorable. Toscanini's clear-sighted and certainly dramatic accompaniment sounds its best at lower dynamic levels. The *C minor Piano concerto*, however, triumphs over all its technical limitations; while Heifetz is certainly given a truthful presence, Rubinstein's crystalline articulation is most believably and vividly projected, and the joy of the first movement, particularly the buoyant development section played with much refinement by all concerned, comes through the limited sound-picture to grab and hold the listener's attention. The *Largo* is beautifully done and the finale has fine lightness and sparkle. The interest of the performances is increased by the soloists' choice of cadenzas. In the first movement, Heifetz adapts a cadenza by Leopold Auer, and then in the rest of the work makes his own versions of those by Joachim; Rubinstein uses Beethoven's cadenzas as edited by Busoni, but he too does some ingenious editing. There is some surface rustle still present from the 78 r.p.m. source, but it is not distracting; neither is the studio audience, who are commendably quiet during Rubinstein's performance until their vociferous response at the end which is wholly deserved.

Piano concerto No. 4 in G, Op. 58.
(*) Telarc Dig. **CD 80064 [id.]. Serkin, Boston SO, Ozawa – *Concerto No. 2.***(*)
(*) Decca Dig. **411 902-2; *411 902-4* [id.]. Ashkenazy, VPO, Mehta – *Concerto No. 2.***(*)
** DG **413 445-2** [id.]. Pollini, VPO, Boehm – *Concerto No. 2.***

Piano concerto No. 4; 32 Variations in C min., WoO 80.
** Ph. Dig. **416 144-2**; *416 144-4* [id.]. Arrau, Dresden State O, C. Davis.

Serkin in his eighties may lack some of the brio which made his earlier recordings of the *Fourth Piano concerto* so memorable, but his concentration and sense of spontaneity are as powerful as ever. Though strength is the keynote of his view in the outer movements, and the compression of the slow movement finds him at his most intense, the detailed poetry comes as the magic of the moment, a studio performance that captures the essence of what a live account should be. Excellent recording.

The relaxation and sense of spontaneity which mark Ashkenazy's Vienna cycle bring a performance of the *Fourth* which may lack something in heroic drive, but which in its relative lightness never loses concentration and brings a captivating sparkle to the finale. Though this may not be as powerful as Ashkenazy's earlier Chicago recording with Solti, it is fresher and more natural, with fewer expressive hesitations. Excellent recording to match the rest of the series, with a bright, clean cassette transfer.

There is an aristocratic feeling about Pollini's account, with classical poise and poetic sensitivity delicately balanced. Boehm is a faithful accompanist, but the end result is somewhat chilly; both Ashkenazy and Serkin are more spontaneously communicative. The CD has been successfully remastered from an analogue original.

Claudio Arrau has always taken a weighty view of Beethoven's *Fourth Concerto*, adopting speeds slower than usual. Here, in his eighties, his latest performance on record brings speeds slower than ever, and for many, despite countless individual touches and excellent playing from Sir Colin Davis and the Dresden orchestra, the sluggishness will hamper enjoyment. Beethoven's brilliant set of variations on a theme so compact they really become a passacaglia makes an attractive, if ungenerous filler, a piece often underrated, until a pianist like Arrau treats it with the spark of genius. Bass-heavy recording adds to the ponderous impression of the concerto, and this also makes the cassette sound muddy and opaque.

Piano concertos Nos 4 and 5 (Emperor).
(*) RCA **RD 85676 [**RCA 5676-2-RC**]. Rubinstein, Boston SO, Leinsdorf.

It makes a particularly generous coupling to have Beethoven's two last and greatest piano concertos on a single disc; characteristically, Rubinstein gives brilliant, spontaneous-sounding performances of both works. In the gentle opening solo of No. 4 the manner is easy and confidential, with no hush or sense of great arguments impending. The exchanges of the slow movement are cleanly and sharply contrasted, with no inner intensity but with keen, bright persuasion. The finale is wonderfully volatile with rhythms neatly pointed. In the *Emperor*, though passagework is a little sketchy and the slow movement, at a fast speed, becomes a bright untroubled interlude, Rubinstein's totally individual freshness is winning from first to last. As in the rest of the series, the 1960s recordings are bright and sharply focused, with the piano given close balance.

Piano concertos Nos 4 and 5 (Emperor), Op. 73; Piano sonatas Nos 14 (Moonlight), Op. 27/2; 19, Op. 49/1.
(B) *** HMV *TCC2-POR 154594-9*. Gieseking, Philh. O, Galliera.

These Gieseking stereo recordings from the late 1950s of the *G major* and *Emperor concertos* are here issued for the first time, in EMI's 'Portrait of the Artist' series on one double-length tape. The sound is astonishingly good, and Gieseking's incandescently bright timbre is captured truthfully, while the orchestra is full-bodied and well detailed. The performances are admirably fresh and imbued with classical feeling. Gieseking's playing is appealingly spontaneous and, with such impressive recording, admirers of this artist will not be disappointed, although the two *Sonatas* are rather cool. Each concerto is complete on one cassette side, with a sonata used as a balance.

Piano concerto No. 5 in E flat (Emperor), Op. 73.
*** Ph. Dig. **416 215-2**; *416 215-4* [id.]. Arrau, Dresden State O, Sir Colin Davis.
*** CBS Dig. **MK 42330**; *IMT 42330* [id.]. Perahia, Concg. O, Haitink.
*** Telarc Dig. **CD 80065** [id.]. Serkin, Boston SO, Ozawa.
(*) Decca Dig. **400 050-2 [id.]. Lupu, Israel PO, Mehta.
*(**) Decca Dig. **411 903-2** [id.]. Ashkenazy, VPO, Mehta.
** DG **413 447-2** [id.]. Pollini, VPO, Boehm.
** RCA Dig. **RD 85854 [RCD1 5854]**. Ax, RPO, Previn.
*(*) Ph. Dig. **412 789-2** [id.]. Brendel, Chicago SO, Levine – *Piano sonata No. 31*.**(*)

Piano concerto No. 5 (Emperor); Piano sonatas Nos 6; 20; 22 & 25.
(M) **(*) DG *419 468-4* [id.]. Kempff, BPO, Leitner.

Piano concerto No. 5 (Emperor); Piano sonata No. 7 in D, Op. 10/3.
(M) (**) EMI mono **CDH7 61005-2**. Edwin Fischer, Philh. O, Furtwängler.

Piano concerto No. 5 (Emperor); Piano sonata No. 32 in C min., Op. 111.
(M) *** DG **419 468-2** [id.]. Kempff, BPO, Leitner.

Piano concerto No. 5 (Emperor); (i) *Choral fantasia, Op. 80.*
(M) **(*) Ph. **420 347-2**; *420 347-4* [id.]. Brendel, LPO, Haitink, (i) with Alldis Ch.

The *Emperor* is well served on compact disc, and choice between Arrau, Perahia, Serkin and Kempff will be a matter of personal inclination, among those versions at the top of the list. Many will still count Kempff finest of all, even though the digital remastering has not been able to prevent the early-1960s recording from showing its age in the orchestral sound.

The wonder is that Arrau, for long an inhibited artist in the studio, should in his newest *Emperor* recording, made when he was over eighty, sound so carefree. There are technical flaws, and the digital recording is rather resonant in bass, but with Sir Colin Davis and the Dresden State Orchestra as electrifying partners, the voltage is even higher than in his earlier versions of the mid-1960s. One would expect Arrau in his eighties to become more reflective, but the opposite is the case. The slow movement flows more freely, less hushed and poised than before, while the finale at a relaxed speed is joyful in its jaunty rhythms. Intensely individual, the very opposite of routine, this is from first to last a performance which reflects new searching by a deeply thinking musician. This is a thrillingly expansive *Emperor* which will give much satisfaction. There is an excellent chrome cassette, full and wide-ranging.

Perahia's account of the *Emperor*, strong and thoughtful yet with characteristic touches of poetry, rounds off an outstanding cycle of the Beethoven concertos. The approach is spacious, and with Bernard Haitink and the Concertgebouw Orchestra firm, responsive partners, each movement immediately takes wing, though a touch of bass-heaviness in the recording needs correcting, even on CD. On the cassette, the extra degree of resonance brings muddiness and moments of congestion in orchestral fortissimos, though the piano timbre emerges relatively unscathed.

Kempff's version remains very desirable. Although it is not on an epic scale, it has power in plenty and excitement, too. As ever Kempff's range of tone-colour is extraordinarily wide, from the merest half-tone as though the fingers were barely brushing the keys to the crisp impact of a dry fortissimo. Leitner's orchestral contribution is of high quality and the Berlin orchestral playing has vigour and warmth. Some reservations need to be made about the sound of the digitally remastered CD. The bass is somewhat over-resonant and the orchestral tuttis are slightly woolly; the piano timbre is natural, but the slight lack of firmness in the orchestral focus is a drawback though it does not seriously detract from the music making. The cassette has an even more emphatic bass resonance. As can be seen, the couplings for the tape and CD are different but almost equally desirable. The earlier *Sonatas* are refreshingly imaginative; Opus 111 is undoubtedly a great performance.

With extraordinarily vivid recording, Serkin's Telarc *Emperor* is very satisfying. The great pianist is almost as commanding as ever, with fire and brilliance in plenty in the outer movements; yet there is also a degree of relaxation, of conscious enjoyment, that increases the degree of communication. The hushed expressive pianism that provides the lyrical contrast in the first movement is matched by the poised refinement of the *Adagio*; the finale is vigorously joyful. Ozawa's accompaniment is first class.

Lupu's version was the first to be issued on compact disc and the clarity of detail is impressive. The upper range is over-bright but the orchestral layout is convincing, and if the piano image seems a trifle near it gives a commanding presence to the solo playing. Lupu gives a performance which, without lacking strength, brings thoughtfulness and poetry even to the magnificence of the first movement, with classical proportions made clear. The slow movement has delicacy and fantasy, the finale easy exhilaration, though neither conductor nor orchestra quite match the soloist's distinction.

Philips offer two different Brendel versions on CD; the earlier (1977) account with Haitink is much superior in every respect to the later Chicago recording. The sound is beautifully balanced with a wide range and warmth, and the piano timbre is outstandingly natural in both formats and infinitely more successful than in the digital version. It goes without saying that there is much to admire from the artistic point of view, too. The reading is spaciously conceived and the phrasing has no lack of eloquence. Yet there is also a studied quality about the music making, particularly in the first movement, that prevents this from being at the top of the list. One has only to turn to the coupling, a splendid performance of the *Choral fantasia*, to have the difference highlighted by the electrifying solo playing at the very opening, where Brendel has a long solo cadenza. However, at mid-price this issue remains very good value, with the recording projecting equally well on CD and tape.

Though Ashkenazy's whole series with Mehta is easy and relaxed, only in the finale of the *Emperor* does that approach bring a slackening of tension to reduce the impact of the reading. The spaciousness of the first movement combined with clarity of texture is most persuasive, and so is the unusually gentle account of the slow movement. Excellent sound, warm and brilliant.

On cassette the sound is very bright, especially the upper strings. The mid-priced cassette of Ashkenazy's earlier Chicago recording with Solti is also very brilliantly transferred; indeed the strings are made to sound somewhat fierce and ill-focused at fortissimo level. This is a less generous issue than the comparable CD (see above) as the couplings are the *Overtures Coriolan* and *Egmont* (Decca *417 284-4*).

The clarity of Pollini's vision in his dedicated reading is never in doubt, and if at times his playing verges on the chilly, the strong and wise accompaniment of Boehm and the Vienna Philharmonic provides compensation. The slow movement is elegant, lacking the depth which the finest versions give it, and the finale is urgent and energetic rather than joyful. The analogue recording is acceptably transferred to CD but, by the standards of later issues, the quality is comparatively muzzy. The piano image is brilliant but close.

Edwin Fischer's reading of the *Emperor* partnered by Furtwängler is a classic performance, and it makes a valuable addition to EMI's mid-price Références series, particularly when Fischer's equally inspired reading of the *D major Sonata* comes as a generous makeweight. The snag is that, though the piano sound is good for its early period, the orchestra is given less body than in most Philharmonia recordings of the early 1950s.

Emanuel Ax gives a thoughtful rather than a forceful reading of the *Emperor*, sympathetically supported by Previn and the RPO. The relaxed quality in his playing makes this a less bitingly compelling version than many, with the first movement less of a contest than it can be; while the flowing speed for the slow movement and the scherzando quality in the finale make it less weighty than usual, powerful as Ax's articulation is. Unexceptionable recording, rather thin on piano tone.

In Brendel's 'live' Chicago recording, the CD emphasizes the snags, including the wild applause at the end. At the start there is a sudden switch-on of 'atmosphere', almost like tape-hiss starting; though in this more than in the earlier concertos Brendel's command and individuality come over powerfully, the relative constriction of the sound is distracting, with the piano aggressively clear. The *Sonata*, Op. 110, makes a generous fill-up; however, those wanting Brendel's performance of the *Emperor* would do better to stay with his earlier analogue version with Haitink.

DG have also reissued on CD Michelangeli's *Emperor* with Giulini, but like the account of the *First Concerto* from the same artists it is casual and uninvolving and the recording is harsh (**419 249-2**).

(i) *Piano concerto No. 5 (Emperor);* (ii) *Violin concerto, Op. 61;* (iii) *Fidelio: overture, Op. 72b.*
(B) *** DG Walkman *413 145-4.* (i) Eschenbach, Boston SO, Ozawa; (ii) Schneiderhan, BPO, Jochum; (iii) Dresden State O, Boehm.

Eschenbach gives a deeply satisfying interpretation of the *Emperor*, helped by the equally youthful urgency of his accompanist, Ozawa. With thoughtfulness, power and bravura nicely balanced, this interpretation is very impressive, if not quite as strong as Arrau's account. The high-level transfer conquers the reverberant acoustic; although detail is not as sharp as in some versions, the sound has fine weight and richness, with the piano timbre appropriately firm and bold. The recording dates from 1974, whereas the coupling – sounding hardly less full-bodied – is from 1962. Schneiderhan's stereo version of the *Violin concerto* is among the greatest recordings of this work: the serene spiritual beauty of the slow movement, and the playing of the second subject in particular, have never been surpassed on record; the orchestra under Jochum provides a background tapestry of breadth and dignity. It is a noble reading with an innate sense of classicism, yet the first movement offers wonderful lyrical intensity. As an added point of interest, Schneiderhan uses cadenzas that were provided for the transcription of the work for piano and orchestra. The first-movement cadenza is impressive in scale and adds a solo part for the timpani. This makes a very real bargain for tape collectors.

Violin concerto in D, Op. 61.
*** HMV Dig. **CDC7 47002-2**; *TCC-ASD 4059* [Ang. *4XS 37471*]. Perlman, Philh. O, Giulini.
*** Denon Dig. **C37 7508** [id.]. Kantorow, Netherlands C O, Ros-Marba.
*** DG **413 818-2** [id.]. Mutter, BPO, Karajan.
(*) RCA **RD 85402 [**RCD1 4502**]. Heifetz, Boston SO, Munch – BRAHMS: *Concerto.****
(***) HMV mono **CDC7 47119-2** [id.]. Menuhin, Philh. O, Furtwängler – MENDELSSOHN: *Concerto.*(***)
(M) **(*) RCA Dig. **GD 86536**; *GK 86536* [**RCA 6536-2-RG**]. Ughi, LSO, Sawallisch – MENDELSSOHN: *Concerto.***(*)
** Decca Dig. **400 048-2** [id.]. Kyung Wha Chung, VPO, Kondrashin.
(M) *(*) HMV **CDM7 69001-2** [id.]; *EG 769001-4.* Menuhin, New Philh. O, Klemperer.

Violin concerto; Romances Nos 1–2, Opp. 40 & 50.
(M) *** Ph. **420 348-2**; *420 348-4* [id.]. Grumiaux, Concg. O, C. Davis or New Philh. O, De Waart.
*** Ph. **416 418-2** [id.]. Szeryng, Concg. O, Haitink.
* DG Dig. **423 064-2**; *423 064-4* [id.]. Mintz, Philh. O, Sinopoli.

Perlman's outstanding HMV digital recording of Beethoven's *Violin concerto* must be counted among the great recordings of this work. Perlman's is the most commanding of readings. The violin emerges in the first movement almost imperceptibly, rising gently from the orchestra, but there and throughout the performance the element of slight understatement, the refusal to adopt too romantically expressive a style, makes for a compelling strength, perfectly matched by Giulini's thoughtful, direct accompaniment. Steadiness of pulse is a hallmark of this version, but there is never a feeling of rigidity, and the lyrical power of the music making is a vital element. The beautiful slow movement has a quality of gentle rapture, almost matching Schneiderhan's sense of stillness and serenity in his recording of 1953; and the finale, joyfully and exuberantly fast, is charged with the fullest excitement. The digital recording is satisfyingly full and spacious, yet admirably clear, with a good matching cassette. The CD adds extra presence and refines detail, although emphasizing the forward balance of the soloist.

Kantorow, who has also recorded a very successful set of the Mozart concertos for Denon, follows a performing tradition in the Beethoven *Violin concerto* whose most distinguished recent advocate was Wolfgang Schneiderhan. Kantorow's playing has a comparable incandescent classical lyricism and unforced naturalness of line and phrasing, and his reading takes its place alongside the very finest recorded versions. There are many moments of great beauty, not least the hushed reprise of the main theme at the end of the first-movement cadenza. The slow movement too is very moving in its gentle sustained intensity, while the finale is nimble in articulation, yet with lyrical feeling still very much to the fore. The use of a chamber-sized accompanying group enhances the classical scale of the performance, with Ros-Marba providing an understanding if relaxed supporting role. The orchestral wind playing is particularly fine and the principal bassoon must receive special mention. The recording is first class, very well balanced in a spacious acoustic framework which never clouds detail, while the background silence of the CD gives the soloist a very tangible presence.

Grumiaux recorded the Beethoven *Violin concerto* twice for Philips in stereo, the first occasion in the late 1960s with Galliera in London, and again in the mid-1970s with Sir Colin Davis in Amsterdam. The balance of advantage between the two versions – both among the finest ever made – is impossible to resolve. Both are imbued throughout with a spirit of classical serenity; both offer a superb account of the slow movement, and if there the partnership with Galliera seemed even more imaginatively spontaneous, the later version which is now reissued is still very beautiful, and the Concertgebouw recording is fuller and richer, even if there is not absolute clarity. Indeed the slightly diffuse orchestral tuttis seem to add to the atmospheric feeling, as in all the best analogue recordings. With fine accounts of the *Romances* (where the recording is more vivid and clear) offered as a bonus, this makes a splendid mid-priced recommendation in both CD and cassette formats. The digital remastering has been wholly beneficial.

The slow basic tempi of Anne-Sophie Mutter's beautiful reading on DG were her own choice, she claims, and certainly not forced on her by her superstar conductor. The first two movements have rarely, if ever, been more expansively presented on record, but the purity of the solo playing and the concentration of the whole performance make the result intensely convincing. The finale is relaxed too, but is well pointed, at a fair tempo, and presents the necessary contrast. Good atmospheric recording against the warm acoustic of the Philharmonie Hall in Berlin. On CD, the closeness of balance is emphasized, but the digital transfer of an analogue original brings attractively warm sound, with more bloom on it than is usual in the Philharmonie.

Szeryng's 1974 recording with Haitink brings a superb balance between lyricism and power. The orchestral introduction is immediately riveting in its breadth and sense of scale, and throughout the first movement Szeryng's playing has great beauty. His use of the Joachim cadenza is an added attraction. The slow movement blossoms with a richly drawn line, the glorious second subject phrased with great intensity; after this emotional climax, the link into the finale is managed with a fine sense of spontaneity. The dance-like mood which follows completes an interpretation that is as satisfying in its overall shape as in its control of mood and detail. The recording is full and resonant – inner orchestral definition is not always absolutely sharp – but the ambience is attractively warm, and the solo violin beautifully caught. Fine performances of the *Romances* (recorded two years earlier) are offered as a bonus.

Heifetz's unique coupling of the Beethoven and Brahms *Concertos* on a single disc is only possible because of his consistent refusal to linger. RCA's digital transfer of a recording originally made in the very earliest days of stereo is astonishingly vivid on CD, with a fine sense of realism and presence, and the soloist only a little closer than is natural. The extra immediacy of CD reinforces the supreme mastery of a performance which may adopt fast speeds but never sounds rushed, finding time for individuality and imagination in every phrase. For some listeners, the comparative lack of serenity in the first movement (though not in the *Larghetto*) will be a drawback, but the drama of the reading is unforgettable. Heifetz's unique timbre is marvellously captured; the assured aristocracy of the playing confounds criticism.

Recorded only months before the conductor's death, Menuhin's version with Furtwängler is a classic which emerges with extraordinary freshness in its new CD format. The bond between the wrongly reviled conductor and his Jewish champion brought an extra intensity to a natural musical alliance between two inspirational artists, here both at their peak. Rarely if ever has the Beethoven *Violin concerto* been recorded with such sweetness and tenderness, yet with firm underlying strength. With its generous coupling, it is a compact disc which defies the years. One hardly registers that this is mono recording.

Ughi's version has first-class digital recording, realistic and very well balanced: this mid-priced coupling with a strikingly fine performance of the Mendelssohn *Concerto* (also digitally recorded) was one of the most impressive early issues in RCA's attractively presented Papillon series. The performance of the Beethoven is first rate, fresh and unaffected, marked by consistent purity of tone in every register. If the last degree of imagination, of the kind which creates special magic in the slow movement, is missing here, nevertheless this remains well worth considering for those with limited budgets.

Miss Chung gives a measured and thoughtful reading which lacks the compulsion one would have predicted. That is largely due to the often prosaic conducting of Kondrashin. There is poetry in individual moments – the minor-key episode of the finale, for example, which alone justifies the unusually slow tempo – but with too little of the soloist's natural electricity conveyed and none of her volatile imagination, it must not be counted her final statement on a masterpiece. The digital recording is outstanding on the compact disc which is wonderfully transparent and real. The clarity and presence – and the silent background – are a joy and the balance is most natural.

Menuhin's 1966 recording with Klemperer is disappointing. The two artists do not bring out the best in each other and there is no feeling of incandescence. Moreover the soloist's timbre is often not very ingratiating, and the remastered recording makes it sound thinner still, alongside the orchestral violins which are without bloom.

Shlomo Mintz's version of the Beethoven is a serious disappointment from a young virtuoso lined up as a leading star. After a noble account of the tutti from Sinopoli, the whole performance goes flabby, thanks largely to Mintz's constant lagging behind the beat. With depressingly slow speeds he makes heavy weather of all three movements and at times the intonation is tentative. The sound is good, and the fill-up is apt, but little more can be said in favour.

Among other available versions, Francescatti's 1961 CBS account with Walter **(MK 42018)** now seems uncompetitive at full price while, among mid-priced cassettes, performances by Iona Brown, honest, clean-cut and always sympathetic but in the last resort not distinctive (Decca *417 280-4*) and Ferras with Karajan (DG *419 052-4*) must be regretfully passed over. Kremer's Philips CD with Marriner **(410 549-2)** is put out of court by his eccentric use of the Schnittke cadenza with its facile avant-garde effects.

Triple concerto for violin, cello and piano in C, Op. 56.
*** Capriccio Dig. **10 150**; *CC 27 148* [id.]. Funke, Timm, Rösel, Dresden PO, Kegel – *Choral fantasia.****
(B) *** CfP Dig. *CFP 41 4495-4*. Zimmermann, Cohen, Manz, ECO, Saraste.
(*) Chan. Dig. **CHAN 8409; *ABTD 1146* [id.]. Laredo, Robinson, Kalischstein, ECO, Gibson.

Triple concerto, Op. 56; Overtures: Coriolan; Egmont; Fidelio.
(*) DG **415 276 [id.]. Mutter, Zeltser, Yo-Yo Ma, BPO, Karajan.

Triple concerto, Op. 56; Romances for violin and orchestra Nos 1 in G, Op. 40; 2 in F, Op. 50.
*** HMV Dig. **CDC7 747427-2** [id.]; *EL 270079-4* [Ang. *4DS 38289*]. Hoelscher, Schiff, Zacharias, Leipzig GO, Masur.
* RCA Dig. **RD 71125** (*Romance 1* only). Verhey, Harnoy, Lechner, Brabant O, Marturet.

(i) *Triple concerto, Op. 56; Variations on 'Ich bin der Schneider Kakadu', Op. 121a.*
*** Ph. **420 231-2** [id.]. Beaux Arts Trio; (i) LPO, Haitink.

(i) *Triple concerto, Op. 56; Piano sonata No. 17 in D min. (Tempest), Op. 31/2.*
(M) **(*) HMV **CDM7 69032-2** [id.]. David Oistrakh, Rostropovich, Sviatoslav Richter, (i) BPO, Karajan.

Led by the cellist, Heinrich Schiff – a balance of responsibility suggested by Beethoven's own priorities in this work – the soloists in Masur's version make a characterful but finely integrated trio. Their rhythmic flair prompts Masur in turn to give one of his most sparkling Beethoven performances on record, and even the opening tutti is better sprung than those of their principal rivals. The long span of the first movement is firmly held together, the brief slow movement has inner intensity without being overweighted, while the finale is ideally clean and light. The sound is both full and detailed, far preferable to Karajan's DG. The two *Romances* are persuasively done and make a generous fill-up, with the most engaging orchestral detail in the accompaniment. There is a first-class cassette – one of EMI's best, firmly focused.

The star-studded cast on the other HMV recording is a breathtaking line-up, and to have Karajan as well seems almost too good to be true. The results are predictably arresting, with

Beethoven's priorities among the soloists well preserved in the extra dominance of Rostropovich over his colleagues. This is warm, expansive music-making that confirms even more clearly than before the strength of the piece. The three Soviet soloists revel in the multiplicity of ideas, with Richter in the sparse piano part providing a tautening influence. The resonant recording suffers from loss of focus in some climaxes, but this is not too serious. Richter's powerful reading of Beethoven's *D minor Sonata* makes a good coupling.

As an alternative, the choice of the world's most distinguished piano trio is a natural casting for this great but wayward concerto. If the Beaux Arts cellist, Bernard Greenhouse, lacks the full, vibrant character of a Rostropovich in his first entries on each theme, he is more clearly co-ordinated with his colleagues, and consistently the joy of this performance – with the soloists sharply focused in front of the orchestra – is to relish the interplay between the instruments. The result adds up to a really satisfying structure instead of a series of separate and memorable solo passages. Haitink's splendid direction helps too, with powerful tuttis and fine rhythmic pointing in the polacca rhythms of the finale. The engineers have found the problems of balance impossible to resolve, with the orchestra damped down during the solo passages, but the sound nevertheless has the beauty and refinement of the best Philips analogue offerings and the CD transfer enhances the overall clarity. The *Variations* make a refreshing encore piece.

In the East German performance the three soloists, Christian Funke, Jürnjacob Timm and Peter Rösel, play rather as a team in the outer movements, but in the slow movement their personalities blossom, particularly that of the fine cellist, while in the finale there is a striking lightness of articulation and a lively rhythmic emphasis from the conductor, Herbert Kegel. The recording is realistically balanced, with the soloists life size and the orchestra set back in a concert-hall acoustic that gives plenty of orchestral weight. While other versions may offer stronger projection up front, this performance has plenty of energy and momentum and also an outstanding coupling, a most successful version of the *Choral fantasia*. The cassette (though technically impressive) is not recommended. At the turnover, before the finale, the music fades out and then retracts a few bars on side two.

On Classics for Pleasure, with first-rate modern digital recording and with Robert Cohen leading an excellent team of prize-winning young soloists (his solo in the slow movement is superb), this makes an outstanding bargain version, keenly competitive with almost any full-priced issue, if not always as elegantly pointed as some. Jukka-Pekka Saraste and the ECO provide a lively, understanding accompaniment and the performance has splendid spontaneity throughout, with the finale sparkling in its sense of occasion. The recording is exceptionally well balanced, with most of the problems solved: the soloists forward, but not exaggeratedly so, and the orchestral backing given fine impact within the convincing acoustics of London's Henry Wood Hall. The high-level cassette transfer is very successful.

For their CD issue, DG have added three overtures as a reasonably generous makeweight, while the detail of the analogue recording has been sharpened, but the point is emphasized that after Karajan's formidable crescendo, within his very positive opening tutti, the soloists seem rather small-scale. But there are benefits from the unity brought by the conductor when each of the young players has a positive contribution to make, no less effectively when the recording balance for once in this work does not unduly favour the solo instruments. Yo-Yo Ma's playing is not immaculate, and he does not dominate each thematic statement, but the urgency, spontaneity and – in the slow movement – the depth of expressiveness make for an enjoyable version, well recorded.

The Chandos version with three young American soloists is exceptionally well recorded, with problems of balance solved better than usual. The playing is immaculate, and Sharon Robinson, the cellist, takes the lead with pure tone and fine intonation, though both her partners are by nature more forceful artists. Without a fill-up, the *Concerto* on its own is poor value, particularly on CD, but for a clean-cut, often refreshing view, beautifully recorded, no one will be disappointed with this. As usual with Chandos, the cassette, too, is in the demonstration class.

Also available on tape is the 1961 Fricsay recording, still sounding well, if somewhat dated now. The three soloists, Schneiderhan, Starker and Geza Anda, play well together and the performance has breadth and a convincing grasp of structure. Only in the first movement does one sense a slight want of spontaneity. In DG's Walkman series, coupled with Brahms's *Double concerto* and Mozart's *Violin concerto No. 3*, this is generous value (*415 332-4*).

The RCA version is disappointing in every way, with a seriously flawed, often sluggish performance, recorded in dull sound. For all the much-advertised qualities of Ofra Harnoy as a cellist, her playing here is not secure enough for the central role in the work, with intonation often suspect. Nor do the other two young performers make a good match.

The Creatures of Prometheus: Overture and ballet music, Op. 43 (complete).
*** DG Dig. **419 608-2**; *419 608-4* [id.]. Orpheus CO.

The *Prometheus Overture* is well enough known, with its opening discord very similar to that of the *First Symphony*; while the finale to Beethoven's early ballet provided a theme which resounded momentously later in the finale of the *Eroica symphony*, as well as in the *Eroica variations* for piano, Op. 35. As this splendid recording demonstrates, there is much else to admire in the dozen episodes in between, often anticipating later, greater works in sudden flashes, with moods varying widely from tragedy to country-dance felicity. The very talented conductorless orchestra plays most stylishly, helped by bright, clean recording. On the otherwise good chrome cassette the bass resonance brings a slight loss of sharpness of focus.

12 German Dances, WoO 8; 12 Minuets, WoO 7.
** HM **HMC 901017** [id.]. Bella Musica of Vienna Ens., Dittrich.

The CD by the Bella Musica of Vienna Ensemble offers all the advantages of the medium: truthful reproduction and excellent presence within a warm ambience. But the playing has the nonchalance of a background café group and, although it is in good style, it does not readily hold the attention.

March for wind sextet, WoO 29; Military marches, WoO 18–21; 24; Ecossaise, WoO 22.
** DG **419 624-2** [id.]. BPO Wind, Priem-Bergrath – *Egmont***(*); *Wellington's victory.***

This seems a strange coupling for *Egmont*; the performances are routine ones though well played. The wind march and the *Ecossaise* bring variety, although one or two of the military pieces are quite attractive, notably the *March in F*, WoO 19. The 1969 recording, made in the Jesus-Christus Kirche, Berlin (a curious venue) is not very sharply defined.

OVERTURES

The Creatures of Prometheus: Overture and ballet music: Nos 5, Adagio; 16, Finale, Op. 43. Overtures: King Stephen, Op. 117; Leonora No. 1, Op. 138; Leonora No. 2, Op. 72a; Leonora No. 3, Op. 72b.
(M) **(*) HMV *ED 290401-4* [Ang. *4AE 34441*]. Philh. or New Philh. O, Klemperer.

This tape generously collects together some major performances of Beethoven's overtures, though curiously *Fidelio* is omitted. The approach to the three *Leonoras* – as one expects with Klemperer – uses measured tempi to bring out the architectural strength. Such is the conductor's control over tension, however, that no unbiased listener could find the results dull or heavy, even if one must turn elsewhere for the full drama of the opera house. Klemperer invests the extra items from the *Prometheus* ballet with an unexpected nobility of contour (if at the expense of their terpsichorean feeling), and the comparatively slight *King Stephen* is given strength. The remastered recording is clear, with textures less ample than the originals. The cassette, transferred at the highest level, is bright and clean but with the strings a little lacking in body.

Overtures: Consecration of the house, Op. 124; Coriolan, Op. 62; Fidelio, Op. 72c; Leonora Nos 1–3, Opp. 138; 72a; 72b.
(*) HMV **CDC7 47190-2 [id.]. Philh. O, Klemperer.

This seems a more satisfyingly arranged collection than Klemperer's cassette (see above) which also includes the three *Leonora overtures*. Here *Fidelio* is properly added, a performance more serious than usual, and *Consecration of the house*, a magnificent account, perhaps the finest ever recorded. The CD transfers are remarkably fresh. The three *Leonora overtures* (1964) are more forwardly balanced and the effect is vividly dramatic. The ear immediately notices the more recessed perspective at the opening of *Fidelio* (1962) and, because of this, the earlier recordings, *Consecration* (1960) and *Coriolan* (1959), do not sound more dated. Indeed, they are evidence of the excellence of Walter Legge's judgement in the early days of stereo.

Overtures: Coriolan, Op. 62; The Creatures of Prometheus, Op. 43; Egmont, Op. 84; Fidelio, Op. 72c; Leonora No. 3, Op. 72b.
** HMV Dig. **CDC7 47086-2** [id.]. LPO, Tennstedt.

Fidelio is the most successful performance here, with an exciting closing section, but *Egmont* has a lower voltage. Although the approach is crisply dramatic, the slightly distanced trumpet call in *Leonora No. 3* produces little frisson of anticipation; and generally, although the orchestral playing is alert and polished, there is nothing to resonate in the memory. The CD is well balanced, clear and bright, but slightly lacking in ambient atmosphere.

Overtures: Coriolan, Op. 62; Creatures of Prometheus, Op. 43; Egmont, Op. 84; Leonora No. 1, Op. 138; Leonora No. 3, Op. 72b; The Ruins of Athens, Op. 113.
*** CBS Dig. **MK 42103**; *IMT 42103* [id.]. Bav. RSO, Sir Colin Davis.

This collection is very well recorded – the sound is spacious and beautiful, full yet refined, and has a remarkably wide dynamic range. In *Leonora No. 3* the dynamic contrast is electrifying and adds to the drama of the distanced trumpet calls. Both here and in *Leonora No. 1*, Sir Colin Davis secures playing of distinction from the Bavarian orchestra; and the lighter pieces, *The Ruins of Athens* (which opens the concert engagingly) and *Creatures of Prometheus*, are played with obvious enjoyment and flair. *Egmont* is weighty, and in *Coriolan* Davis's broad tempo brings a hint of heaviness. It was a pity *Leonora No. 2* was omitted in favour of these two, but this remains a distinguished collection. The resonant bass response adds weight on CD, but brings an unwanted emphasis on cassette where the treble response is less telling.

Romances for violin and orchestra Nos 1 in G, Op. 40; 2 in F, Op. 50.
*** Ph. Dig. **420 168-2**; *420 168-4* [id.]. Zukerman, St Paul CO – DVOŘÁK: *Romance*; SCHUBERT: *Konzertstücke* etc.***
(B) *** DG Walkman *413 844-4* [id.]. D. Oistrakh, RPO, Goossens – BRAHMS: *Violin concerto* **(*) (with BRUCH: *Concerto No. 1***).

Beethoven's two *Romances* could hardly be played more winningly than they are within this attractively chosen collection of short concert pieces for violin and orchestra. Zukerman's phrasing is warm and elegant, yet his playing does not stray outside the romantic boundaries of the period; in short, this is quite admirable, with naturally balanced recording in a pleasing acoustic, to give the music making plenty of ambient atmosphere. The two Beethoven pieces are separated and used as opener and centrepiece of the concert. A disc which is more than the sum of its parts with a first-class matching cassette.

David Oistrakh's performances of the Beethoven *Romances* are of high quality and are well recorded. If the other works on this generous Walkman tape are attractive, this is excellent value. The Bruch *Concerto* (Yong Uck Kim) is a very acceptable performance.

Symphonies Nos 1–9; Overtures: Consecration of the house; Coriolan; Egmont (with incidental music); *Fidelio. Grosse Fuge.*
(M) **(*) HMV *EX 290379-9* (6). Soloists, Philh. Ch. and O, Klemperer.

Symphonies Nos 1–9; Overtures: Coriolan; Egmont; Fidelio; Leonora No. 3.
** DG Dig. **415 066-2**; *415 066-4* (6) [id.]. Soloists, V. Singverein, BPO, Karajan.
(M) ** Ph. **416 274-2** (6) [id.]. Leipzig GO, Masur (with soloists and chorus).

Symphonies Nos. 1–9; Overture Egmont.
** Ph. Dig. **416 822-2**; *416 822-4* (6) [id.]. Soloists, Ch., Concg. O, Haitink.

It should have been pure gain having Karajan recording a cycle of the Beethoven symphonies with new technical developments in mind, in the shape of digital recording, CD and video. Instead, the sound seems to have been affected by the need to have a video version recorded at the same sessions. The gain is that these performances have keener spontaneity, the loss that they often lack the brilliant, knife-edged precision of ensemble one has come to regard as normal with Karajan: the opening of No. 1 brings an obvious example. Similarly in sound, the recording engineers seem not to have been so careful in their balancing. Though there is relatively little homing-in of microphones to spotlight individual detail, the sound too often grows thick and congested in big fortissimo tuttis. However, with the 1977 recordings now issued on individual mid-priced Galleria CDs, the attractions of this digital box are much reduced, even if interpretatively with speeds generally a little less extreme, there are a number of movements which sound more persuasive than before.

The separate discs in Klemperer's Philharmonia cycle, collected in a box, make up a set which, for all its flaws (see the separate reviews), has a weight and compulsion beyond all but the finest rivals. The overtures, like the symphonies, in their magisterial way have the Klemperer imprint firmly implanted. The six-tape layout is exceptionally generous, the quality enhanced, the new transfers clean.

Although it is probably not as satisfying all round as Klemperer's set, Kurt Masur's Beethoven cycle with the Leipzig Gewandhaus Orchestra has a very great deal to recommend it. In sheer naturalness of utterance, unforced expressiveness and the superlatively disciplined response of the orchestral playing, the Gewandhaus set has a good deal to offer. The first two symphonies are attractively fresh, with the slow movement of the *Second* memorable. The *Eroica* is uncommonly fine, particularly its nobly paced slow movement which is totally free from excessive emphasis in expression. In the *Fourth Symphony* Masur is particularly successful, and the Gewandhaus Orchestra respond with marvellously alert playing. In the slow movement Masur brings great imagination and poetry to his reading; the homogeneous, cultured orchestral sound of the Gewandhaus Orchestra and its rhythmic resilience and vitality are in themselves a source of pleasure. The digital remastering now places the nine symphonies and four overtures on six compact discs. The sound is considerably livelier than the originals, and on CD the violins above the stave are very brightly lit, though not edgy. The Masur set wears well and is eminently sound and reliable; at times it is very much more than that.

Bernard Haitink marked the end of his reign as Music Director of the Concertgebouw with a new Beethoven cycle. The readings are characteristically strong and sensitive, unsensational but taut and dramatic. The big disappointment is the recorded sound, which regularly gives an edge, even a thinness, to the glorious Concertgebouw string ensemble. Both on recording and on performance, Haitink's 1976 cycle with the LPO – long deleted – remains preferable.

Symphonies Nos 1, 4, 6 (Pastoral) & 7. Overtures: Creatures of Prometheus; Leonora No. 1.
(***) HMV mono *EX 290930-9* (2). BBC SO, Toscanini.

This collection of Toscanini's Beethoven recordings made with the BBC Symphony Orchestra in the years before the Second World War helps, more than many of his later recordings, to explain his supremacy among conductors of his day. The tension and electricity of Toscanini in Beethoven comes out in each of the symphonies, but unlike many of his later New York recordings these are rarely over-tense. The *Fourth Symphony* in particular is superbly done, while the *Seventh Symphony* comes in a recording made live in the old Queen's Hall in 1935 and never issued before. The reason was that, within months, RCA recorded him in the same symphony with the New York Philharmonic; but it is the BBC performance which springs the dance rhythms of the first movement the more infectiously. The sound is inevitably limited but generally well balanced and less harsh than in most of Toscanini's New York recordings. The cassettes are well engineered and the balance is very satisfactory; only in the string fortissimos of the outer movements of the *Pastoral* does the violin timbre above the stave become seriously lacking in body; elsewhere the bite compensates for any loss of bloom.

Symphony No. 1 in C, Op. 21.
(*) Ph. Dig. **416 329-2 [id.]. O of the 18th Century, Brüggen – MOZART: *Symphony No. 40.***(*)
** Nimbus Dig. **NIM 5003**. Hanover Band, Huggett – *Piano concerto No. 1.***

Symphonies Nos 1 in C; 2 in D, Op. 36.
*** CBS **MK 42009** [id.]. Columbia S O, Walter.
(*) O-L Dig. **414 338-2; *414 338-4* [id.]. AAM, Hogwood.
** DG Dig. **415 505-2**; *415 505-4* [id.]. BPO, Karajan.

With his talented band of 45 players, Frans Brüggen directs an individual and compelling reading of Beethoven's *First*, which gains interpretatively from being recorded live. This will appeal to many who do not normally enjoy authentic performance, and has a degree of warmth and expressiveness not often associated with recordings on period instruments. One snag is that recording balances are not ideal, and the timpani booms away very loudly.

The coupling of the *First Symphony* with the *First Piano concerto* adds point to the Hanover Band's Nimbus issue of Beethoven on period instruments. With Monica Huggett directing from the leader's desk, the reading is less distinctive than that of the *Concerto* but, with rhythms fast, light and resilient, it has many of the same qualities, and the distinctive sound is comparably attractive, even if its relatively soft focus will not please everyone.

Bruno Walter's set of Beethoven symphonies on CBS dates from the beginning of the 1960s, and the recordings have been remastered with striking success: the ambient warmth brings an attractive richness without blurring detail, and the upper string timbre remains fresh and lively. In the *First Symphony* Walter achieves a happy medium between the eighteenth-century quality of Karajan's analogue versions and the turgidity of Klemperer. The most controversial point about his interpretation of the *Second Symphony* is the slow movement which is taken very slowly indeed, with plenty of rubato. But the rich warmth of the recording makes the effect very involving. For the rest, the speeds are well chosen, with a fairly gentle allegro in the finale which allows the tick-tock accompaniment to the second subject to have a delightful lift to it. On technical grounds this reissue can stand alongside most of the more recent competition and the remaining hiss is not disturbing.

In his coupling of the first two Beethoven symphonies, Hogwood makes a promising start for his projected cycle of all nine using period instruments and authentic-sized forces. Though these performances do not have quite the exhilaration of his Haydn recordings, they avoid the over-abrasive manners of some of his Mozart symphony recordings. Some may want more positive, individual readings of this music; however, with sensible speeds, often fast but not gabbled, and with clean, finely balanced recording bringing out the freshness and transparency of authentic textures, the results are undistractingly attractive. The cassette is brightly lit and the upper range is more abrasive than on disc, especially in No. 2.

Karajan's new digital Beethoven series brings some surprisingly slack ensemble in the recording of the first two symphonies. The performances are relaxed in good ways too, with Karajan's flair and control of rhythm never leading to breathless speeds. Not unexpectedly, there are moments when detail is perceptively revealed, but the heavy reverberation of the recording makes the result arguably too weighty for these works and pianissimos are rarely gentle enough. The 1977 versions are now available on CD, differently coupled – see below – and, quite apart from costing less, they are more satisfying, both as performances and as recordings. There is not a great deal to choose between the quality of the newer digital CD and its equivalent cassette.

Symphonies Nos 1 & 3 (Eroica).
(***) RCA **RD 87197** [**RCD1 7197**]. NBC SO, Toscanini.

In the *Eroica* above all, the unparalleled high voltage of Toscanini's conducting brought consistent illumination, as is masterfully shown in this transfer of his Carnegie Hall performance of 1949. Here the extra screwing up of tension that marked his Beethoven conducting in his last years never gets in the way of natural, intense communication. Though the allegros are characteristically fast, his approach – as ever – to the great *Funeral march* was spacious, and the agony of the close of that movement, with the disintegration of the main theme, has rarely if ever been so movingly caught on record, even though the sound does not allow a true pianissimo. The digital transfer makes the harsh original NBC recording reasonably acceptable, though as in other Toscanini CDs some attempt should have been made to eliminate the low hum. The hum is marginally more intrusive on the 1951 recording of the *First Symphony* that comes as a very generous fill-up. There Toscanini's electrification process at times makes the result brittle, but this is still one of the most exciting accounts of the work on record, exuberant in its intensity, if with little joy.

Symphonies Nos 1 in C, Op. 21; 4 in B flat, Op. 60.
(***) HMV mono **CDC7 47409** [id.]. VPO, Furtwängler.
(B) **(*) DG Walkman *419 085-4* [id.]. VPO, Boehm – MOZART: *Symphony No. 39.***(*)
** ASV *ZCALH 968*. N. Sinf., Hickox.

Symphonies Nos 1 in C, Op. 21; 4 in B flat, Op. 60; Overture: Coriolan, Op. 62.
(M) **(*) HMV *ED 290270-4* [Ang. *4AE 34423*]. Philh. O, Klemperer.

Symphonies Nos 1 in C, Op. 21; 4 in B flat, Op. 60; Egmont overture.
(M) *** DG **419 048-2**; *419 048-4* [id.]. BPO, Karajan.

Karajan's 1977 series of Beethoven symphonies has been digitally remastered and reissued at mid-price. In almost all respects, without consideration of price, they are superior to the newer digital recordings. Certainly the sound is preferable, more realistically balanced, clear yet still weighty. No. 1 is just as exciting, polished and elegant as in the very first stereo version of 1962; in No. 4 the balance is closer, exposing every flicker of tremolando. Yet the body and ambience of the recording combine to give a realistic presence, and overall this is very impressive. If anything, Karajan conveys more weight and strength than before and there is a wider range of dynamic than in the later digital version. Only the extremely fast tempo for the finale marks a controversial development, but even there the brilliance and excitement are never in doubt. This is a particularly satisfying coupling, and there is an excellent equivalent chrome tape. The bonus of the *Egmont overture* is a real one, the performance has electricity and the recording plenty of amplitude as well as clarity.

The cassette coupling of Klemperer's digitally remastered versions matches one of the very finest of the set, the *Fourth*, with one of the less attractive, when the *First Symphony* is made to sound too heavy in the first and third movements. Even so, the concentration of the conductor and his characterful consistency are never in doubt. With an overture too, the coupling is as generous as the others in the series, with sound equally agreeable, remarkably fresh for its age. Readers will note that the tapes of this Klemperer series in the medium-price range cost about a third the price of the differently coupled CDs.

EMI's digital transfers of Furtwängler's recordings of the early 1950s are among the best historic issues on CD, and the *First* and *Fourth symphonies*, recorded in late 1952, are excellent examples. The performances are easy and amiable, with relaxed speeds freely moulded. What they demonstrate very clearly is that – whatever the legendary slackness of Furtwängler's beat – his rhythmic control was masterly in its light, crisp resilience. Slow movements here have a Mozartian elegance without losing their Beethovenian strength, and articulation in fast movements has crystal clarity.

Boehm's recordings come from his Vienna cycle of the early 1970s, centrally satisfying readings, smoothly recorded, though with a good deal of resonance in the lower range. What these mature readings may lack is the sort of sharp idiosyncrasy which makes for dramatic memorability. So the first movement of the *C major Symphony* is spacious and mellow (the effect emphasized by the richly upholstered sound). The *Andante* is beautifully played, and the remaining movements have both character and vitality although there is comparatively little extrovert excitement. In the *Fourth*, Boehm's reading notes the kinship with the *Pastoral symphony*. The *Allegro vivace* is relatively easy-going, but with big, satisfying contrasts; the slow movement is warmly lyrical, and the last two movements bounce along joyfully. If Boehm misses some of the tensions, there is no lack of strength or weight.

Hickox's coupling of Nos 1 and 4 is a good example of performances using a chamber orchestra, though the warm acoustic of Trinity Hall, Newcastle, where the recordings were made, gives a result hardly smaller-sounding than from a full-scale symphony orchestra. Hickox's view is unaffected and direct, lacking a little in refinement and dramatic tension. The very lack of idiosyncrasy makes for easy listening, but there are more compelling versions than this.

Symphonies Nos 1 in C; 5 in C min., Op. 67.
(**) HMV Dig. **CDC7 47447-2** [id.]; *EL 270449-4* [Ang. *4DS 38331*]. Phd. O, Muti.

Muti's coupling of Nos 1 and 5 brings characteristically taut and urgent readings of both symphonies with early Beethoven treated just as earnestly as if it were from the middle period. The Philadelphia Orchestra plays with the new brilliance instilled by Muti; sadly, however, the recording is among the harshest from this source, edgy and aggressive without much body and with ill-defined focus. The tape is restricted and bass-heavy.

Symphonies Nos 1 in C; 7 in A, Op. 92.
*** DG **419 434-2** [id] VPO, Bernstein.
(*) HMV **CDC7 47184-2 [id.]. Philh. O, Klemperer.

The recoupling for CD of the *Seventh*, one of the outstanding successes of Bernstein's Vienna cycle, with the *First* makes an attractive issue. In the first movement of the *Seventh* the lilting rhythms are sprung with delightful point, making one welcome the observance of the exposition repeat, while the *Allegretto* is finely detailed at a flowing speed without dragging. In the last two movements the adrenalin flows in a vintage Bernstein manner. One almost regrets the lack of applause. The recording is among the brightest of the series. In No. 1 the allegros are fast but not hectic, the slow introductions and slow movements carefully moulded but not mannered. In that work the live recording is not ideally clear, but very acceptable.

Klemperer's accounts of the *First* and *Seventh* are among the more controversial of his stereo cycle. The slow speeds and heavyweight manner in both works – in principle not apt for No. 1, while undermining the dance-like element in No. 7 – will for many get in the way of enjoyment. That said, the compulsion of Klemperer in Beethoven remains strong, with rhythmic pointing consistently preventing stagnation. The recordings (1958 and 1961 respectively) are full and vivid, if not quite among the best of the series.

Symphonies Nos 1; 8 in F, Op. 93.
(M) ** PRT **PVCD 8373** [id.]. Hallé O, Barbirolli.

(i) *Symphonies Nos 1 & 8;* (ii) *Creatures of Prometheus: Overture.*
** Delos **D/CD 3013** [id.]. (i) LAPO, (ii) LSO; Gerard Schwarz.

Barbirolli's PRT disc stands the test of time. It dates from the Hallé's centenary year, 1958, and the digital remastering has brought respectable sound-quality, clear and full and not too thin in the matter of string timbre. There is of course some background hiss but it is not a problem. Barbirolli's stylish, pointed way with Beethoven can stand against more famous interpretations. The outer movements of the *First Symphony* have elegance, but a sense of humour too, and the slow movement is most poetically phrased. Only the scherzo, with some less than perfect discipline, falls short. The *Eighth* is infectiously enjoyable, with sharp pointing and a springy step in the first movement. The speed for the *Allegretto* is conventional, but nicely shaped. The Hallé strings are less than immaculate in the minuet but make amends in the beautifully feathered opening of the finale, which is taken exhilaratingly fast. Those who remember this great conductor nostalgically might care to try this, at budget price.

Schwarz's coupling on Delos brings exceptionally clean and transparent recording, allowing inner lines to be heard in a way one associates more with authentic performance. In both these symphonies – the two least weighty of the whole cycle – such a chamber view is apt enough. As to performance, the *Eighth* is admirably alert, the *First* not quite so tense, lacking bite and at times sounding a little pedantic. The overture, recorded in quite a different, more ample acoustic, brings a limp start to the disc.

Symphonies Nos 2 in D; 4 in B flat, Op. 60.
*** HMV **CDC7 47185-2** [id.]. Philh. O, Klemperer.

Symphonies Nos 2 in D; 5 in C min., Op. 67.
(M) **(*) HMV *ED 290252-4* [Ang. *4AE 34425*]. Philh. O, Klemperer.
** DG Dig. **423 590-2**; *423 590-4* [id.]. VPO, Abbado.

Symphonies Nos 2 in D, Op. 36; 7 in A, Op. 92.
(M) *** DG **419 050-2**; *419 050-4* [id.]. BPO, Karajan.
(**(*)) RCA **RD 87198** [**RCD1 7198**]. NBC SO, Toscanini.

As with Karajan's coupling of Nos 1 and 4, the digitally remastered versions of the 1977 recordings of the *D* and *A major Symphonies* are remarkably successful, the sound vivid and clear, yet with plenty of body. In No. 2 the manner is a degree weightier than in the earlier, 1962 version, but with firm lines giving the necessary strength. The tempo for the slow movement, as with No. 1, is less controversial than before; the recording, now clearer in its newest format, brings close-up effects which are less believable. The *Seventh* is tense and exciting, with the conductor emphasizing the work's dramatic rather than its dance-like qualities. The slow introduction, taken at a fastish tempo, is tough rather than monumental, and the main *Allegro* is fresh and bright, and not very lilting in its 6/8 rhythm, though it is more pointed here than in the earlier (1962) version. The *Allegretto* is this time a little weightier, but consistency with the earlier reading is the point to emphasize. The chrome cassette makes an excellent alternative to the CD.

The different couplings for CD emphasize the consistency of Klemperer's approach to Beethoven, with both the *Second* and *Fourth* symphonies sounding the more powerful through weighty treatment, and the former looking forward, even more clearly than usual, to the later symphonies, rather than back to the eighteenth century. Only in the finale is the result rather too gruff. The *Fourth* brings one of the most compelling performances of all, with Klemperer's measured but consistently sprung pulse allowing for persuasive lyricism alongside power. Exposition repeats are observed in the first movements of both symphonies. The sound on CD is fresh yet full.

The stereo version of the *Fifth* is plainly less electric than Klemperer's earlier mono version but, with exposition repeats again observed in both the outer movements, the epic magnificence of this most concentrated of Beethoven's symphonies is tellingly brought out, with resilient rhythms lightening speeds that are slower than usual. Welcoming freshening of well-balanced 1960 sound in the new tape transfer.

Abbado couples a weighty, spacious reading of the *Fifth* – where the speed for the *Andante* is dangerously slow – with an account of No. 2 which convincingly marries together eighteenth-century elegance and Beethovenian weight, as in the first movement where a rather classical view of the slow introduction leads into a strong urgent *allegro*. The massiveness of the work, dwarfed only in relation to its successor, the *Eroica*, is underlined by the observance of all repeats. The sound in both symphonies is rather too thick, with inner textures often cloudy, but the sense of weight and presence compensates for that. A fair recommendation if this is the coupling you fancy. The cassette is not recommended: the quality is too muffled.

Though the NBC recordings remain defiantly harsh, with strings like tearing cloth, and Toscanini's approach is taut to the point of pain, the commanding intensity of his conducting is never in doubt. Speeds are generally fast in both symphonies, making it hard for the NBC violins to articulate the 6/8 galloping rhythms in the first movement of the *Seventh*, and making the slow movements of both symphonies less elegant than with most conductors; but the sheer drive is irresistible. For anyone looking for an example of Toscanini's art, this would not be the first choice, but with its generous coupling it is a valuable example none the less. As on the other NBC recordings of this vintage, there is a low hum which has not been eliminated.

Symphonies Nos 2 in D; 8 in F, Op. 93.
*** HMV Dig. **CDC7 47698-2** [id.]; *EL 270563-4*. L. Classical Players, Norrington.

Norrington's coupling of Nos 2 and 8 was the first of a projected Beethoven cycle using period instruments. Norrington's own London Classical Players are an authentic group with a distinctive sound, sweeter and truer in the string section than most, generally easier on non-specialist ears. Though the recording is warmly reverberant, Norrington secures admirably transparent textures, with the braying of the natural, valveless horns adding an apt tang and with the authentic small-size timpani adding military bite. Norrington's great interpretative point is to follow as closely as possible Beethoven's own very fast, often seemingly impossible, metronome markings. In both symphonies the results are exhilarating, never merely breathless, bringing far more than proof of an academic theory. Formidable as the scholarship is, the important point is the freshness and imagination of the communication. The iron-oxide cassette alternative to the CD is fully acceptable.

Symphony No. 3 in E flat (Eroica), Op. 55.
*** Ph. Dig. **410 044-2** [id.]. ASMF, Marriner.
(M) *** Ph. **420 853-2** [id.] (with rehearsal). Concg. O, Monteux.
(***) Decca mono **414 626-2**; *414 626-4* [id.]. VPO, Erich Kleiber.
*** Decca **417 235-2**; *417 235-4* [id.]. AAM, Hogwood.
(**(*)) HMV mono **CDC7 47410-2** [id.]. VPO, Furtwängler.
** HMV **CDC7 47594-2** [id.]. N. German RSO, Wand.

Symphony No. 3 (Eroica); Overture: Coriolan, Op. 62.
(*) CBS **MK 42010 [id.]. Columbia SO, Walter.
** DG Dig. **419 597-2**; *419 597-4* [id.]. VPO, Abbado.

Symphony No. 3 (Eroica); Overtures: Coriolan; Egmont.
(*) Decca **417 556-2 [id.]. Chicago SO, Solti.

Symphony No. 3 (Eroica); Egmont overture.
(*) DG Dig. **415 506-2; *415 506-4* [id.]. BPO, Karajan.
** DG **413 778-2** [id.]. VPO, Bernstein.

Symphony No. 3 (Eroica); Grosse Fuge, Op. 133.
*** HMV **CDC7 47186-2** [id.]; *ED 290271-4* [Ang. *4AE 34424*]. Philh. O, Klemperer.

Symphony No. 3 in E flat (Eroica); Overture: Leonora No. 3.
(M) **(*) DG **419 049-2**; *419 049-4* [id.]. BPO, Karajan.

The digital remastering of Klemperer's spacious 1961 version reinforces its magnificence, keenly concentrated to sustain speeds slower than in his earlier mono account. The stoically intense reading of the *Funeral march* is among the most impressive on record, and only in the coda to the finale does the slow tempo bring some slackening. The reissue includes the stereo version of the *Grosse Fuge*, dating from 1957, now available for the first time, and the sound is first rate, vivid and well balanced with the CD more natural on top. The excellent high-level cassette, however, is clear and clean.

Sir Neville Marriner's version is in every way outstanding, for although the Academy may use fewer strings, the impression is of weight and strength, ample for Beethoven's mighty inspiration, coupled with a rare transparency of texture and extraordinary resilience of rhythm. The dance-rhythms of the fast movements are brought out captivatingly with sforzandos made clean and sharp to have one applying to the *Eroica* Wagner's famous remark about the *Seventh*, 'the apotheosis of the dance'. The *Funeral march* may emerge as less grave and dark than it can be, but Marriner's unforced directness is most compelling. The recorded sound is among the best ever in a Beethoven symphony.

The gain in Karajan's latest digital version of the *Eroica* over his previous recordings lies most of all in the *Funeral march*, very spacious and intense, with dynamic contrasts intensified, even compared with his 1977 version. Here, and even more noticeably in the allegros, the playing is marginally less polished than before, lacking something of the knife-edged bite associated with Karajan. As with others in the series, the oddly balanced recording grows congested in big tuttis. Nevertheless, the power and concentration make it an epic reading, fully matching the scale of the argument, with tempi in the outer movements more relaxed and spacious than in the 1977 version. The sound in *Egmont*, given an urgently dramatic reading, is marginally more agreeable. CD and cassette are fairly closely matched.

Monteux's 1962 *Eroica* comes up electrically fresh, direct and intense. The disc is the more cherishable for including 15′ of rehearsal (in French), with the voice of the 87-year-old maestro sounding astonishingly young.

Erich Kleiber's Vienna Philharmonic record of the *Eroica* was made in 1955 but not issued until 1959 because the woodwind balance was imperfect and the horns also rather backward. That said, few apologies need be made for this CD. Decca have rightly returned to the mono master and ignored the stereo transcription issued on their Eclipse label at the beginning of the 1970s. The quality is vivid and the spacious acoustics of the Musikvereinsaal spread the sound and help to cushion the noticeably thin violins above the stave. The performance is in every way outstanding – even more wonderfully intense and dramatic than his earlier, Concertgebouw version, and it includes the repeat of the exposition in the first movement to make the whole structure more powerfully monumental. The electricity of the performance is maintained throughout, with the *Funeral march* deeply felt, the mood lightened in the scherzo, the finale making an apotheosis. The musical notes appear to derive from the French LP issue and are not translated very felicitously.

The challenge of the *Eroica* sparks off a performance from Hogwood which brings out all the finest qualities of his period-instrument players. The sharpness of attack and the clarity of rhythms and textures makes for an unusually refreshing account of the first movement. Speeds are fast there and elsewhere, but not breathlessly so. Though the great *Funeral march*, at a flowing andante rather than an adagio, lacks the meditative weight that we expect in traditional performances, nevertheless its darkness is strongly established, with contrasts just as clearly marked. The recording is fresh and full to match. There is an excellent cassette.

It is a pleasure to turn from other accounts of this symphony and hear as beautiful and sympathetic a performance as Walter's. He is not monumental in the different ways of Klemperer and, before him, Toscanini; but this interpretation has all the ripeness of the best of Walter's work with the Vienna Philharmonic Orchestra between the wars. The digitally remastered recording has all the amplitude one needs for such a reading: its expansive qualities bring rich horns as well as full-bodied strings. The disc opens with a superb account of the *Coriolan overture*, spacious, warm and dramatic, and the sound-balance is especially telling, even if here (as throughout) there is a small residue of background noise.

Furtwängler also has a broad, spacious view of the *Eroica*, demonstrating throughout his uncanny magnetism. Equally one can register just why, in an age when Toscanini was counted supreme by many, this seemed unacceptably slack. In all four movements speeds are very much on the slow side, and are subtly varied. In the first three movements that is unfailingly illuminating, but when it comes to the exaggeratedly slow statement of the first variation theme in the finale (the bass of the *Prometheus* theme) the result fails to carry conviction, a personal concept that might have worked in concert but not really on record. It is a marginal flaw in a superb example of Furtwängler's art.

Not everyone will identify readily with the fiery intensity of fast tempi in the outer movements of Karajan's 1977 performance, now reissued, digitally remastered, on Galleria. Contrasts are heightened with, if anything, a more intense account of the *Funeral march* than in earlier recordings. A point to consider is the absence of the exposition repeat in the first movement; but this is among the most polished as well as the most dramatic accounts available. An exciting performance of *Leonora No. 3* makes a very generous bonus. The sound, although it has ample fullness and weight, is better defined than the newer digital version. There is a first-class cassette.

Solti's *Eroica* is one of the finest performances from his complete analogue set of the mid-1970s. The digital remastering has brought leaner string textures and less amplitude in the bass, but the more brilliant treble does not become fierce under pressure. The power and weight of the reading are undiminished, the performance strong and positive with the very slow speed for the *Funeral march* sustained by an electric degree of tension which is naturally resolved in the sparkling scherzo and the vigorously lyrical finale. The overtures too are firm and dramatic, but this CD now seems overpriced.

Bernstein's 1980 Vienna Philharmonic recording of the *Eroica* brings a degree of disappointment compared with his earlier (1966) CBS record which was electrically intense. There is less incandescence in the first movement and a hard, clattering sound for the opening chords, which is emphasized in the digital remastering for CD. The first-movement exposition repeat is still observed and this is undoubtedly a strong and dramatic reading with a dedicated account of the *Funeral march*. This emerges as more clearly a march than before, yet very measured indeed, but its intensity is enhanced by the presence of an audience. The CD offers the *Egmont overture* as a bonus item, but the shallowness of the recording comes out more clearly than on the original LP.

Wand in the *Eroica* presents an honest, direct view that will please his many admirers, even if it lacks the full revelatory strength which marks his finest work. Neither the playing nor the recording is ideally clean.

Abbado with the Vienna Philharmonic presents an account of the *Eroica* which, for all the beauty of the playing, recorded live, lacks dramatic tension. Even in the first two movements it stands as a predominantly happy work. Its general absence of idiosyncrasy and the safe speeds may for some make it an agreeable version to live with. On CD the sound is pleasantly spacious, more than usually capturing the fine acoustics of the Musikvereinsaal in Vienna, but the cassette is rather bass-heavy.

Giulini's refined and individual reading, with its almost eccentrically measured view of the first movement, is among other CD versions which no longer seem really competitive (DG **410 028-2**); these include also a fresh but very plain account by Dohnányi with the Cleveland Orchestra well recorded by Telarc (**CD 80090**). EMI have reissued Sanderling's digital version on CD, a performance marked by its rugged honesty and plain unhurried speeds. The exposition repeat is included and the *Egmont overture* comes as a bonus; but, even though it is offered at mid-price, this will not command the interest of many collectors (HMV **CDM7 69201-2**).

Symphonies Nos 4 in B flat, Op. 60; 5 in C min., Op. 67.
(M) *** Pickwick Dig. **PCD 869**. LSO, Wyn Morris.
*** O-L Dig. **417 615-2**; *417 615-4* [id.]. AAM, Hogwood.
(*) CBS **MK 42011 [id.]. Columbia SO, Walter.
(M) **(*) Decca *417 602-4*. Chicago SO, Solti.

Wyn Morris's coupling of Nos 4 and 5 makes a first-rate budget recommendation. He generally adopts speeds close to those of Karajan and, though he cannot match that master in sharpness of focus or pointed intensity, his urgency goes with fine, biting strength, helped by some first-rate playing from the LSO. These are readings which, more than most, convey the varying tensions of a live performance, and one suspects the studio recordings were done in long takes. The sound is bright and slightly abrasive, but with enough body to sustain that. The weight of the readings is enhanced by the observance of all repeats. A bargain.

Hogwood's generous coupling of Nos 4 and 5 brings fresh, lively readings which, with generally fast speeds, present excellent versions for anyone wanting performances on period instruments. Dramatic contrasts are strongly marked with no feeling of miniaturization, and the clarity of textures is admirable, with natural horns in particular braying out superbly. Even the very fast tempo for the finale of No. 4 is exhilarating rather than breathless when violin articulation of semiquavers is so light and clean. Vivid sound, set in a believable acoustic. There is a good tape.

Bruno Walter's reading of the *Fourth* is splendid, the finest achievement of his whole cycle. There is intensity and a feeling of natural vigour which makes itself felt in every bar. The first movement may not have quite the monumental weight that Klemperer gives it, but it is livelier. The slow movement gives Walter the perfect opportunity to coax a genuinely singing tone from his violins as only he knows how; and the finale allows the wind department its measure of brilliance. All aspects of this symphony – so much more varied than we have realized – are welded together here and show what depths it really contains. The recording is full, yet clear, sweet-toned with a firm bass. Here as in the *Fifth* the sound-balance is richer and more satisfying than in many modern recordings. In Walter's reading of the *Fifth*, the first movement is taken very fast, yet it lacks the kind of nervous tension that distinguishes Carlos Kleiber's famous version. The middle two movements are contrastingly slow. In the *Andante* (more like *adagio*) there is a glowing, natural warmth, but the scherzo at this speed is too gentle. The finale, taken at a spacious, natural pace, is joyous and sympathetic, but again fails to convey the ultimate in tension. The digital remastering for CD has left behind a residue of pre-Dolby background hiss, but it is not too distracting.

Solti gives an unashamedly large-scale reading of the *Fourth*, vigorous and even exuberant, but not strong on charm: it is not one to make you love the work as representing Beethoven in restrained mood. With Solti the *Fourth* clearly points forward to the *Seventh Symphony*, which in structure it strikingly resembles on such points as the slow introduction and the extra sections in the scherzo. The Chicago playing is flawless, with a highly polished violin tone sustaining the poised beauty of the *Adagio*. The finale has superb vitality, but one wishes that the playing smiled more readily. The coupling with the *Fifth* is apt, for this too is a big, bold reading, tense but not neurotic, with a warm and expansive slow movement, a surprisingly measured view of the scherzo and a really joyful account of the finale. The digital remastering has somewhat lightened the textures of the rather beefy recording, but the sound is still full-bodied and bright on top. The cassette transfer is excellently managed.

Sanderling's Philharmonia digital coupling of the same two symphonies, reissued together at mid-price, might also be considered, both performances showing him a powerful and direct interpreter of Beethoven, lacking a little in rhythmic subtlety, almost too plain. The orchestral playing is very fine and the recording bold and clear (HMV **CDM7 69202-2**). Carlos Kleiber's Orfeo CD with the Bavarian State Orchestra offers a live performance of the No. 4 with plenty of electricity; but only the *Egmont overture* for coupling this seems poor value (**C 100841A**).

Symphonies Nos 4 in B flat; 7 in A, Op. 92.
** DG Dig. **415 121-2**; *415 121-4* [id.]. BPO, Karajan.

Karajan's digital coupling of the *Fourth* and *Seventh* symphonies comes from his most recent series of Beethoven symphony recordings. The impression is of more spontaneous, less meticulous performances than in his previous versions of these works, presumably recorded this time with longer takes. The bravura is most compelling, and there is no doubt about the command of Karajan's never-routine view of Beethoven – but too much is lost. The slow movement of the *Fourth* is fresh, sweet and beautifully moulded but is never hushed; and the *Allegretto* of No. 7, taken characteristically fast, is so smooth that the dactylic rhythm at the start is almost unidentifiable. Recording, not as detailed or analytical as usual, is undistracting.

Symphonies Nos 4 in B flat; 8 in F (trans. Liszt)
*** Tel. Dig. **ZK8 43419** [id.]. Cyprien Katsaris (piano).

Simply astonishing! The opening of the finale of the *Eighth Symphony* is an extraordinary feat of articulation. Apart from his dazzling technique, Katsaris has enormous musicianship, a great range of colour and a real sense of scale. The acoustic in which he is recorded is not ideal but it does not inhibit him from producing an altogether remarkable clarity of texture. There is plenty of Beethovenian vehemence and dramatic fire, but the approach is fresh. It is as if one is encountering this music for the first time.

Symphony No. 5 in C min., Op. 67.
(***) DG Dig. **410 028-2** [id.]. LAPO, Giulini.
(***) DG **415 861-2** [id.]. LAPO, Carlos Kleiber.

Symphony No. 5; Creatures of Prometheus: overture.
(**) Nimbus Dig. **NIM 5007**. Hanover Band, Huggett.

Symphony No. 5; Overture Leonora No. 3.
(***) Decca **400 060-2** [id.]. Philh. O, Ashkenazy.

Symphonies Nos 5; 6 in F (Pastoral), Op. 68.
(M) *** DG **423 203-2**; *423 203-4* [id.]. BPO, Karajan.
(*) DG Dig. **413 932-2 [id.]. BPO, Karajan.
(**) Decca mono **417 637-2** [id.]. Concg. O, Erich Kleiber.

Symphonies Nos 5–6 (Pastoral); Overture: Egmont.
(B) *** DG Walkman *413 144-4* [id.]. VPO, Boehm.

Symphonies Nos 5; 7 in A, Op. 92.
(*) Ph. Dig. **420 540-2 [id.]. Concg. O, Haitink.

Symphonies Nos 5; 8 in F, Op. 93.
(*) HMV **CDC7 47187-2 [id.]. Philh. O, Klemperer.

Symphonies Nos 5; 8 in F, Op. 93; Fidelio: overture.
(M) *** DG **419 051-2**; *419 051-4* [id.]. BPO, Karajan.
** DG **419 435-2** [id.]. VPO, Bernstein.

Those issues which offer the *Fifth Symphony* either alone or with just an overture as fill-up on premium-priced CD now seem uneconomic. Giulini certainly has the advantage of excellent digital sound and his performance possesses majesty in abundance and conveys the power and vision of this inexhaustible work, but DG need to withdraw this, add some more music and perhaps bring the price down, too. Carlos Kleiber's electrifying *Fifth* similarly needs coupling, perhaps to his version of the *Seventh* if the combined playing time allows this. It remains an exceptional performance: the graduation of dynamics from the hushed pianissimo at the close of the scherzo to the weight of the great opening statement of the finale has not been heard on disc with such overwhelming effect since Toscanini. Ashkenazy's is a vivid and urgent reading, notable for its rich Kingsway Hall recording. Well-adjusted speeds here (the *Andante* on the slow side, the finale on the fast side), with joyful exuberance a fair substitute for grandeur. The overture, also fast, finds Ashkenazy at his freshest, but overall this is short measure.

One therefore turns for a 'best buy' to the mid-priced pairing of Karajan's 1977 performances of Nos 5 and 8, with the digital remastering still allowing massively full textures for both works, without loss of clarity. Karajan's *Fifth* is magnificent in every way, tough and urgently incisive, with fast tempi bringing weight as well as excitement but no unwanted blatancy, even in the finale. The recording has a satisfyingly wide dynamic range. The coupling of an electrically intense performance of the *Eighth* plus the *Fidelio overture* is certainly generous. The earlier (1962) coupling of Nos 5 and 6 is just as generous. Here the *Fifth* is, if anything, even more intense, and more spacious in the *Andante*, with blazing horns in the finale. The *Pastoral* is a brisk lightweight performance, marred only by the absence of the repeat in the Scherzo.

The alternative digital versions of the *Fifth* and *Sixth* present characteristically strong and incisive readings, recorded in longer takes than previously. The sound may not be so cleanly focused as in his earlier Berlin versions, but the feeling of spontaneous performance is most compelling, so that the typically fast speed for the first movement of the *Pastoral* no longer sounds too tense. However, with Karajan's approach the power of No. 5 is more effective than the atmospheric poetry of No. 6.

Boehm's Walkman coupling is generous in offering the *Egmont* overture as well as the *Fifth* and *Sixth Symphonies* on a single cassette. Boehm's account of the *Fifth* may not be the most powerful available, but the excellent playing and recording, rich and weighty in the bass as well as lively on top, make it a good version to live with. It pairs naturally with Boehm's splendid account of the *Pastoral* (see below) in its display of positive feeling and absence of neurosis. The chrome-tape transfers of both works are very successful; in offering nearly 90′ of music, this tape is a bargain in every sense of the word.

On tape, Klemperer's *Fifth* is coupled with No. 2 (see above) and the *Eighth* with No. 7. For once the CD coupling is less generous although, as with the others in the series, CD brings a cleaner, more natural sound on top, notably in violin tone.

Haitink's more generous coupling of Nos 5 and 7 brings strong, unmannered readings of both works, well played and warmly if not brilliantly recorded. It is easy to underestimate Haitink in Beethoven, and this first issue in a projected new Beethoven cycle with the Concertgebouw promises to outshine his earlier, generally underprized, series with the LPO. There are minor differences this time, as in the marginally longer pause between the two sequential statements of the fate-knocking-at-the-door motif in the *Fifth*, and in the markedly less hectic speed for the finale of the *Seventh*. Also unlike last time, he observes the exposition repeat in the *Seventh*. As before, he does so too in the first movement of the *Fifth* but not in the finale. The sound is rich and generally spacious, though it lacks transparency in tuttis. An excellent recommendation if you fancy this coupling.

The reissue of Bernstein's analogue versions of Nos. 5 and 8 at premium price, even if the *Fidelio overture* is also included, makes this seem uncompetitive alongside Karajan's Galleria disc. The performance of the *Fifth* is impressive. Though it lacks the Toscanini-like tensions of Bernstein's New York performance which came earlier in his career, the warmth and conviction are most persuasive, with the finale blazing in triumph. The recording, made live, is ample but lacks presence, with some harshness on top and a heavy bass. This is not helpful in the *Eighth*; otherwise, a genial and individual reading.

The Hanover Band's recording on period instruments of the *Fifth Symphony* is its most successful yet. Balances at first seem strange with such gentle string tone, sharply focused (unlike some of the wind), but the extra clarity and pointedness of Beethoven on this scale is most refreshing. Speeds are all unexceptionable, not at all hurried as in many authentic performances of other music. Warm reverberation gives a pleasant bloom to the ensemble, but with brass made to sound washy. However, with Hogwood's version now available coupled to No. 4, this Nimbus CD cannot be recommended as a serious alternative for those tempted by 'authentic' Beethoven.

It is good that Erich Kleiber's majestic performances of Beethoven's *Fifth* and *Sixth* symphonies are again available. They are both profoundly classical readings, taut but never hard-driven, and leave the listener feeling that tempi and phrasing are exactly right – indeed such is their conviction that one feels this is the only possible way of playing these masterpieces. In both, the image is brighter and firmer though, as you might expect, there is still some coarseness in tutti. But there is a price to pay for the silent background, namely a loss of warmth and bloom, particularly on the strings. Incidentally, it would seem that the recordings were made in 1953 – not 1952 as listed on the sleeve or 1949 as given on the French Decca LP transfer of No. 5.

Among other stereo versions still available, those looking for an inexpensive tape might consider Maazel's Berlin Philharmonic recording which goes back to as early as 1961. Considering this, the sound isn't too dated and the warm playing of the great German orchestra tempers the conductor's impetuosity in a hard-driven, exciting perfomance, lacking something in dignity in the finale. The unexpected coupling is Mendelssohn's *Reformation symphony* (DG Focus *419 643-4*).

Symphony No. 6 in F (Pastoral), Op. 68.
*** Decca Dig. **410 003-2** [id.]; *KSXDC 7578* [Lon. *5LDR 71078*]. Philh. O, Ashkenazy.
(M) *** DG **413 721-2** (2) [id.]. VPO, Boehm – *Symphony No. 9.****
(*) Delos **D/CD 3017 [id.]. New York 'Y' CO, Schwarz.
(**) HMV mono **CDC7 47121** [id.]. VPO, Furtwängler.
(M) (*(*)) HMV mono *ED 290666-4*. VPO, Furtwängler (with BRAHMS: *Variations*(*(*))).

Symphony No. 6 (Pastoral); Overture: The Consecration of the house.
(*) Ph. Dig. **416 385-2; *416 385-4* [id]. ASMF, Marriner.

Symphony No. 6 (Pastoral); Overture: The Consecration of the house; (i) *Egmont: Overture; Die Trommel geruhet; Freudvoll und leidvoll; Klarchens Tod, Op. 84.*
(M) *** HMV *ED 290253-4* [Ang. *4AE 34426*]. Philh. O, Klemperer; (i) with Birgit Nilsson.

Symphony No. 6 (Pastoral); Overture: Creatures of Prometheus; (i) *Egmont: Overture and incidental music* (as above).
*** HMV **CDC7 47188-2** [id.]. Philh. O, Klemperer; (i) with Birgit Nilsson.

Symphony No. 6 (Pastoral); Overtures: Coriolan; Creatures of Prometheus; Ruins of Athens.
** DG **415 833-2**; *415 833-4* [id.]. BPO, Karajan.

Symphony No. 6 (Pastoral), Op. 68; Overture: Leonora No. 2, Op. 72a.
*** CBS **MK 42012** [id.]. Columbia SO, Walter.

Symphony No. 6 (Pastoral); Overture: Leonora No. 3.
** DG **413 779-2** [id.]. VPO, Bernstein.

Symphony No. 6 (Pastoral); (ii) *Calm sea and prosperous voyage* (cantata), *Op. 112;* (i, ii) *Choral fantasia.*
** DG Dig. **419 779-2**; *419 779-4* [id.]. (i) Pollini; (ii) V State Op. Ch.; VPO, Abbado.

Beethoven's much-loved *Pastoral symphony* is very well served in all price ranges – on CD and tape. Boehm's famous 1972 recording has been remastered, and on CD the fact that it was recorded a decade and a half ago is convincingly disguised. However, Klemperer's idyllic, deeply satisfying performance (to which we awarded a Rosette in our first *Penguin Stereo Record Guide*) is beginning to sound its age. It dates from 1958, and originally the string tone was not recorded as sweetly as Boehm's. Although refreshed by digital remastering, the upper range is noticeably a little thin; nevertheless, with its generous and worthwhile bonuses, it should be seriously considered by all collectors, especially as the matching tape is competitively priced. But the greater range and naturalness of Ashkenazy's Decca recording places it at the top of the list, even if the interpretation has less individuality than Klemperer's or Walter's and is somewhat more urbane than Boehm's conception.

Ashkenazy's is essentially a genial reading, almost totally unmannered. But the performance has a beguiling warmth and it communicates readily. With generally spacious tempi, the feeling of lyrical ease and repose is most captivating, thanks to the response of the Philharmonia players and the richness of the recording, made in the Kingsway Hall. After a *Storm* that is civilized rather than frightening, the performance is crowned by a radiant account of the *Shepherds' thanksgiving*. The sound, with its fairly reverberant acoustic, is particularly impressive on compact disc, but the chrome cassette too is of demonstration quality. On tape, there is slightly less edge on the strings, yet no loss of detail and the balance suits the music making admirably.

Boehm's recording is available in a choice of formats. On CD, it is coupled with an outstanding version of Beethoven's *Choral symphony*; moreover, the pair of compact discs is offered at less than full price. The remastering has brought a softer focus to the upper strings, while the bass remains expansively resonant and full. There is glowing woodwind detail and the beauty of the sound overall is enhanced. Background noise has all but disappeared. On tape it is available coupled to Boehm's *Fifth* on a bargain-priced Walkman issue (see above). The reading of the *Pastoral* has a natural, unforced beauty, and is very well played (with strings, woodwind and horns beautifully integrated). In the first movement Boehm observes the exposition repeat (not many versions do); although the dynamic contrasts are never underplayed and the phrasing is affectionate, there is a feeling of inevitable rightness about Boehm's approach, no sense of an interpreter imposing his will. Only the slow movement with its even stressing raises any reservation, and that is very slight.

Bruno Walter was always famous for his interpretation of the *Pastoral symphony*. It was the only Beethoven symphony he recorded twice in the 78 r.p.m. era (although his second version with the Philadelphia Orchestra was disappointing). The present version dates from the beginning of the 1960s and, like his recording of the *Fourth Symphony*, it represents the peak of his Indian summer in the American recording studios. The whole performance glows, and the gentle warmth of phrasing is comparable with Klemperer's famous version. The slow movement is taken slightly fast, but there is no sense of hurry, and the tempo of the *Peasants' merrymaking* is less controversial than Klemperer's. It is an affectionate and completely integrated performance from a master who thought and lived the work all his life. The sound is beautifully balanced, with sweet strings and clear, glowing woodwind, and the bass response is firm and full. The quality is very slightly shallower in the *Overture Leonora No. 2* which opens the disc, but this splendid performance shows Walter at his most dramatically spontaneous, and it is superbly played.

The digital remastering has left a small residue of background hiss, but it is never distracting. The sound is more transparent than Boehm's, with no less bloom, and Walter's CD has the advantage of being available separately.

Klemperer's account of the *Pastoral*, one of the very finest of all his records, prompted a legendary incident with the great recording producer, Walter Legge, when he queried the slow speed for the scherzo. 'You will get used to it,' the conductor drawled back; he even added insult to injury by picking up the phone to the control room five minutes later with the question: 'Have you got used to it yet, Walter?' That movement may in principle be eccentrically slow but, with superbly dancing rhythms, it could not be more bucolic and it falls naturally into place within the reading as a whole. The exquisitely phrased slow movement and the final *Shepherds' hymn* bring peaks of beauty, made the more intense by the fine new digital transfer, reinforcing the clarity and fine balance of the original sound, with violin tone amazingly fresh and clean for 1958. The ruggedness of Klemperer is well suited to the *Consecration of the house overture* which on tape precedes the symphony. The *Egmont* music follows it, an unusual but valuable coupling with Nilsson in her prime, unexpectedly but effectively cast in the two simple songs, the first made to sound almost Mahlerian. The CD offers the *Creatures of Prometheus overture* instead of *Consecration of the house*, but retains the *Egmont* coupling. As usual, there is added refinement, and the *Symphony* gains much from the background quiet.

Marriner's view of the *Pastoral* is genial, with a relaxed account of the first movement leading to an unusually spacious account of the *Scene by the brook*, and with the *Shepherds' thanksgiving* mingling joy and elegance. There are more powerful and individual performances but, beautifully played and recorded, it is a happy reading, well coupled – if not generously – with the still under-appreciated *Consecration of the house overture*. On cassette the sound is warm and full but the resonant bass tends slightly to outbalance the treble.

Although Schwarz uses a relatively small group of players, they are recorded in a warmly reverberant acoustic so that textures are glowingly full. His pacing of the first movement is very brisk (even with exposition repeat it takes only 10′ 10″), but the lightness of the articulation prevents any sense of breathlessness. By contrast, the *Shepherds' hymn* is quite relaxed, with the feeling of serenity pleasingly maintained. After the climax, which is well prepared, there is an engaging simplicity in the coda itself. The central movements are more conventional: the brook flows easily and the robust vitality of the peasants gives way to an impressive but not cataclysmic thunderstorm. Although the tempo for the first movement takes a bit of getting used to, overall this performance has a great deal of character; the beauty of the string playing is enhanced by the richness of the recording, with the distanced balance providing a convincing overall picture, even if inner definition is never sharp.

Karajan's 1977 performance brought a more congenial reading than his earlier, excessively tense 1962 recording with the same orchestra. It is fresh, alert, consistent with the rest of the cycle, a good dramatic version, with polished playing, and recording which is wide-ranging but suffering from the odd balances which mark the 1977 cycle. The digitally remastered Galleria issue adds three overtures from 1970: *Coriolan* comes before the symphony and the others follow on after. The sound is fuller in these earlier recordings, but in the *Symphony* there is still plenty of bloom and weight, as well as more refined detail. CD and chrome cassette are very similar in sound-quality.

Abbado's reading of the *Pastoral* is unexceptionable, slowish and easy-going in the first movement, fresh but unmagical in the slow movement and finding full inspiration only in the finale. It is not helped by dull, rather thick sound. The issue is chiefly valuable for the very generous fill-ups, rare choral works, both of which benefit from live recording in the spontaneous intensity conveyed, so essential in works variable in inspiration. Pollini in the big opening solo of the *Choral fantasia*, in effect a Beethoven improvisation written down, is at his most magnetic, as he is through the whole performance. Though still not ideal, the sound on CD in the two fill-ups is fuller and brighter than in the symphony. The cassette is generally muffled-sounding and is not recommended.

Bernstein's reading has plenty of character and, with its combination of joy and serenity, is persuasive, even if the performance fails to bite in the *Storm* sequence. But the inevitable inconsistencies of live recording – even with discreet editing between performances – come out on CD in the discrepancy between the symphony and the overture, with *Leonora No. 3* – recorded earlier, in 1978 – treated to fuller, more agreeable sound than the *Pastoral*.

As digitally transferred to CD, the sound of the Vienna Philharmonic under Furtwängler is reasonably fresh and full, with plenty of detail but occasional oddities of balance. The reading is a very personal one, with eccentrically slow speeds in the first two movements which, unlike those of Klemperer, sound wayward, when the style is additionally so flexible. The quirks would no doubt have sounded more natural in a live Furtwängler performance.

Recorded live during the Second World War in 1943, Furtwängler's earlier version of the *Pastoral* suffers from poor sound. The spaciousness of his view is still very compelling, as it also is in the Brahms *Haydn variations* used for coupling, also recorded in 1943.

Also reissued at mid-price on cassette comes Haitink's analogue LPO version coupled with *Leonora No. 3*. With tempi on the fast side, but never hectically so, in its unobtrusive way this is a consistently enjoyable reading (Ph. *420 000-4*).

Symphony No. 6 (*Pastoral*) (trans. Liszt).
** Tel. **ZK 8.42781** [id.]. Cyprien Katsaris (piano).

Katsaris, using an instrument with the ideal combination of weight and clarity, makes an excellent exponent of Liszt's transcription of the *Pastoral symphony*, direct and fresh, if not especially illuminating interpretatively. The recording is rather resonant.

Symphonies Nos 6 in F (*Pastoral*)*; 8 in F, Op. 93.*
*** HMV Dig. **CDC7 47459-2** [id.]; *EL 270476-4* [Ang. *4DS 38286*]. LPO, Tennstedt.

Tennstedt's fresh, alert and imaginative performance of the *Pastoral* comes in a generous coupling with the *Eighth*, given an equally enjoyable reading in which the second movement *Allegretto* at a fast speed is made into a scherzo while the Minuet is spaciously lyrical. In the *Pastoral*, the slow movement brings a finely moulded performance from Tennstedt, a dramatic account of the *Storm* and a radiant reading of the finale. Well-balanced, unobtrusive recording. If the coupling is suitable, this is well worth considering. There is a good cassette, though here the bass is rather over-resonant in the *Eighth*.

Symphony No. 7 in A, Op. 92.
(**(*)) DG **415 862-2** [id.]. VPO, Carlos Kleiber.

Symphony No. 7 in A; Overture: The Consecration of the house.
(*) HMV **CDC7 47815; *EL 270544-4*. Dresden State O, Tate.

Symphony No. 7 in A; Overtures: Coriolan; Egmont.
(*) Decca Dig. **411 941-2; *411 941-4* [id.]. Philh. O, Ashkenazy.

Symphony No. 7; Overture: The Creatures of Prometheus.
(M) *** HMV **CDM7 69183-2** [id.]; *ED 291341-4*. Philh. O, Klemperer.

Symphonies Nos 7 in A; 8 in F, Op. 93.
*** DG Dig. **423 364-2**; *423 364-4* [id.]. VPO, Abbado.
(M) **(*) HMV *ED 290328-4* [Ang. *4AE 34427*]. Philh. O, Klemperer.
** CBS **MK 42013** [id.]. Columbia SO, Walter.

Once again strong reservations have to be expressed about the CDs offering only a single symphony, without coupling, which have become uncompetitive at premium price in the current marketplace. Carlos Kleiber's DG version dates back to 1976, but the digital remastering has improved the sound and this is an incisively dramatic reading, marked with sharp dynamic contrasts and thrustful rhythms. Like his father, Kleiber maintains the pizzicato for the strings on the final brief phrase of the *Allegretto*, a curious effect.

Of those compact discs which include overtures as makeweights, Ashkenazy's Philharmonia performance takes pride of place. This is a warmly spontaneous, generally direct reading, taken steadily at unexaggerated speeds, and the result is glowingly convincing, thanks to fine playing and recording that sets new standards in this work, full and spacious yet warmly co-ordinated. The CD is distinctly preferable to the lively if slightly less refined cassette, with the bass more crisply focused. After a grave, simple account of the slow introduction, the allegro at first sounds deceptively relaxed in pastoral mood, until the dramatic urgency of the movement takes over, its dance rhythms nicely lifted. The finale is a shade slower than usual, but effectively so. The two coupled overtures are contrasted: *Coriolan* is given a weighty reading at a measured speed, while *Egmont*, equally dramatic, is on the fast side.

Klemperer's 1955 recording of the *Seventh* is among his very finest Beethoven interpretations on disc, and it sounds all the more vivid and full of presence in the stereo version, issued for the first time. Speeds are consistently faster, the tension more electric, with phrasing more subtly moulded, than in the later Philharmonia version. Though the later recording carries extra weight with its wider range, the 1955 sound is very acceptable, with good inner detail. The 1959 *Prometheus* was similarly omitted from the earlier Klemperer edition. Though it is not a generous makeweight, the disc comes very competitively at mid-price in the EMI Studio series.

Tate's is an exceptionally weighty reading of the *Seventh*, marked by speeds consistently slower than usual. In the first movement his powerful account of the slow introduction leads to a spacious reading of the main allegro, made the weightier with exposition repeat observed. The lightness and spring of the dotted 6/8 rhythms in lightly scored passages is set dramatically against the power of the tuttis. The scherzo too is beautifully sprung at a genuine presto with a marked slowing for the Trios, while Tate again adopts an easy allegro in the finale, allowing clean articulation by the violins, even though the reverberant recording does not allow the fullest clarity. The thickness of texture (particularly noticeable on tape) is increased by the recessing and lack of focus on horns. Though Tate's allegros are not as measured as those of Klemperer, there is something of the same weight in the interpretation. Where his reading is controversial is in the *Allegretto*. There the speed is even slower than in Klemperer's 1962 version, and even Tate finds it hard to keep the rhythm from sounding stodgy, despite refined playing by the strings and solo wind. The overture – also the subject of great Klemperer performances – makes a powerful makeweight, not so ungenerous when, with all repeats observed, Tate's performance of the symphony lasts over 46 minutes.

After a disappointing start to his Beethoven cycle, tackling first the most taxing of the symphonies, Nos 3 and 9, Abbado presents a superb coupling of Nos 7 and 8, electrifying, incandescent performances, fresh and rhythmic. The *Seventh* has always been a favourite symphony with Abbado, and the main allegro of the first movement is beautifully judged at a fastish speed, which is yet made resilient. Similarly, the finale blazes fearlessly but never becomes a gabble and, though the live recording is not ideally clear on inner detail, the sound is full and atmospheric, as it also is in the *Eighth* which, with such weight, is instantly established as more than a little symphony. As in the *Seventh*, speeds are beautifully judged, and the tensions of a live occasion are vividly conveyed, as they were not in the first issues of the series.

The digital remastering of Klemperer's stereo versions of the *Seventh* and *Eighth* symphonies offers an outstandingly generous coupling with well-balanced sound (from 1961 and 1958 respectively), made remarkably fresh in the new tape transfer. Although in No. 7 that incandescence which marked his superb earlier mono recording with the Philharmonia is missing, the power and concentration at broad speeds still make for a memorable performance. In No. 8 Klemperer's weighty approach is tempered by delightfully well-sprung rhythms.

Walter's *Seventh* has a comparatively slow first-movement allegro, but he had rehearsed his players well in the tricky dotted 6/8 rhythm and the result dances convincingly, even if the movement seems to lumber somewhat. The *Allegretto* also seems heavier than usual (partly because of the rich, weighty recording). It is rather mannered, with *marcato* emphases on most of the down beats, but the important point is that genuine tension is created with the illusion of an actual performance. The scherzo is also rather wayward: after a slow start, Walter suddenly livens up the middle with a faster pace, and this speed-change occurs in each repetition of the scherzo section. The Trio also takes its time, but in contrast the finale goes with a splendid lift to the playing and very brilliant horns and trumpets in the exciting coda. The coupled *Eighth* has similarly slow speeds, especially in the inner movements. The first goes well enough, but after that the pacing hampers the sustaining of any high degree of intensity. The reading is of course interesting and sympathetic, but there is a lack of grace, as though the players were not strongly involved; and the finale, though revealing many points with unusual clarity, has a tendency to dullness. The sound is full and well balanced, but – as in the rest of the series – the digital remastering has not been able to remove all the background noise.

Symphony No. 7 in A (trans. Liszt).

(*) Tel. Dig. **ZK8.43113 [id.]. Cyprien Katsaris (with SCHUMANN: *Exercises on Beethoven's Seventh Symphony***).

(*) Nimbus **NIM 5013 [id.]. Ronald Smith (with BACH/BUSONI: *Chaconne****).

Cyprien Katsaris does wonders in translating Liszt's transcription into orchestral terms. His is very clean, precise playing, often powerful, with textures commendably clear and with generally steady, unexceptionable tempi. He observes the exposition repeat in the first movement. The

Schumann Exercises make an apt if hardly inspiring fill-up, based on the main theme of the symphony's *Allegretto*. But the symphony is another matter, providing an unexpectedly illuminating listening experience, although for some reason Katsaris does not repeat the Trio in the scherzo. The sound is excellent.

Ronald Smith, much more than Katsaris, turns the Liszt transcription into a pianistic essay, treating the music with more expressive freedom, often more seductively. He is daring in the Presto scherzo, then unexpectedly light and easy in the finale, with an attractive spring in the rhythm. The performance is not technically flawless but here, and even more in the superb Bach–Busoni transcription, he consistently plays with virtuosic flair. The reverberant recording is pleasantly atmospheric, but not every note is clear.

Symphony No. 8 in F, Op. 93.
(*) Telarc Dig. **CD 80090 [id.]. Cleveland O, Dohnányi SCHUBERT. *Symphony No. 8.***

Symphony No. 8 in F; Overtures: Coriolan; Fidelio; Leonora No. 3.
(*) DG Dig. **415 507-2; *415 507-4* [id.]. BPO, Karajan.

Karajan's more relaxed view of the *Eighth* (compared with his 1977 Berlin version) is almost always pure gain. The second subject of the first movement, for example, is eased in more persuasively, while the second-movement *Allegretto* is made happily lyrical at a markedly slower speed than before. Nevertheless, Karajan's is a massive view of what has often been dubbed Beethoven's 'little symphony', taking it well into the powerful world of the nineteenth century, with fierceness part of the mixture in the outer movements. The three overtures are made massively Olympian too, with *Coriolan* especially impressive. The recording is marginally brighter and clearer than in most of the series, though there is still some congestion in fortissimos, and the cassette sounds rather opaque in tuttis.

Dohnányi, with the Cleveland Orchestra of which he is now principal conductor, is more successful in No. 8 than he is in the more challenging *Eroica*. This is a lively, resilient performance, exceptionally well played. The recording is not as bright as one expects from this source, but is acceptable. The coupling – once adopted in a classic Beecham record – could be, for some, an extra attraction.

Symphonies Nos 8; 9 (Choral).
(*) CBS Dig. **M2K 39711; *12T 39711* [id.]. Murphy, C. Watkinson, O'Neill, Howell, Tallis Ch., ECO, Tilson Thomas.

Though Tilson Thomas's version with the English Chamber Orchestra falls short of greatness, it makes a fine culmination to his Beethoven cycle with this orchestra, what one might think of as the first of a new generation of *Ninths*: on a modest scale but not using period instruments. Only in the slow movement does the slight thinness of violin sound betray the size of orchestra, but elsewhere the clarity of textural detail reinforces the freshness of the reading, direct in the first movement, relaxed in the scherzo, easy rather than weighty in the slow movement. The choral finale brings some fast speeds, but with a fine quartet of soloists and excellent singing from the small professonal choir the result is exhilarating. Tilson Thomas's view of the *Eighth* is clean, crisp and dramatic in the outer movements, with the modest scale again used to illuminate textures. Tape collectors will find that the cassettes are very well transferred, losing only a little bite at the top and thus making the strings sound slightly more expansive in the slow movement.

Symphony No. 9 in D min. (Choral), Op. 125.
(M) *** DG **415 832-2**; *415 832-4* [id.]. Tomowa-Sintow, Baltsa, Schreier, Van Dam, V. Singverein, BPO, Karajan.

(M) *** DG **423 204-2**; *423 204-4* [id.]. Janowitz, Rössl-Majdan, Kmentt, Berry, V. Singverein, BPO, Karajan.

(M) *** DG **413 721-2** (2) [id.]. Norman, Fassbaender, Domingo, Berry, Concert Singers of V. State Op., VPO, Boehm – *Symphony No. 6.****

(***) RCA mono **RD 85936 [RCA 5936-2]**. Farrell, Merriman, Peerce, Scott, Robert Shaw Chorale, NBC SO, Toscanini.

*** Decca Dig. **417 800-2**; *417 800-4* [id.]. Norman, Runkel, Schunk, Sotin, Chicago Ch. & SO, Solti.

(M) *** Ph. **420 701-2** [id.]. Tomowa-Sintow, Burmeister, Schreier, Adam, Leipzig R. Ch. & GO, Masur.

(*) HMV Dig. **CDC7 49221-2 [id.]; *EL 749221-4*. Kenny, Walker, Power, Salomaa, L. Schutz Ch., L. Classical Players, Norrington.

(*) DG Dig. **410 987-2 [id.]. Perry, Baltsa, Cole, Van Dam, V. Singverein, BPO, Karajan.

(*) Ph. Dig. **416 353-2 [id.]. Donath, Schmidt, König, Estes, Bav. R. Ch. and SO, Sir C. Davis.

(*) Telarc Dig. **CD 80120 [id.]. Vaness, Taylor, Jerusalem, Lloyd, Cleveland Ch. and O. Dohnányi.

(***) HMV mono **CDC7 47081-2** [id.]. Schwarzkopf, Höngen, Hopf, Edelmann, Bayreuth Fest. Ch. and O, Furtwängler.

** Ph. Dig. **410 036-2** [id.]. Janet Price, Finnila, Laubenthal, Rintzler, Concg. Ch. and O, Haitink.

** HMV **CDC7 47189-2** [id.]. Lövberg, Ludwig, Kmentt, Hotter, Philh. Ch. and O, Klemperer.

** HMV Dig. **CDC7 47741-2** [id.]; *EL 169595-4*. Wiens, Hartwig, Lewis, Hermann, Hamburg State Op. Ch., N. German R. Ch. & SO, Wand.

** Ph. **416 884-2** [id.]. Napier, Reynolds, Brilioth, Ridderbusch, Amb. S., New Philh. O, Ozawa.

*(*) DG Dig. **419 598-2**; *419 598-4* [id.]. Běnačková, Lippovšek, Winberg, Prey, V. State Op. Concert Assoc. Ch., VPO, Abbado.

Symphony No. 9 (Choral); Overture: Fidelio.

(M) ** HMV *ED 290272-4* [Ang. *4AE 34428*]. Lövberg, Ludwig, Kmentt, Hotter, Philh. Ch. and O. Klemperer.

There is a clear first choice among recordings of Beethoven's *Choral symphony* and it has the double advantage of being not only the finest available version but also the least expensive. Of the three stereo recordings Karajan has made of the *Ninth*, his 1977 account is the most inspired in its insight, above all in the *Adagio*, where Karajan conveys spiritual intensity at a slower tempo than in his earlier 1962 version and more searchingly than in the later digital recording, where the effect is more lyrical in its beauty. In the finale, the concluding eruption has an animal excitement rarely heard from this highly controlled conductor. The soloists make an excellent team, with contralto, tenor and bass all finer than their predecessors and the soprano markedly more secure than her successor in 1985. The sound has tingling projection and drama and there is an outstanding cassette. Though Karajan's 1962 version is less hushed and serene in the slow movement, the finale blazes even more intensely, with Janowitz's contribution radiant in its purity. This reflected the Berlin sessions when it rounded off a cycle, recorded over two weeks.

Just a few months before he died, Karl Boehm made his final statement on the work in this resplendent digital set. With generally slow tempi, his reading is spacious and powerful – the first movement even has a certain stoic quality – and in its broad concept it has much in common with Klemperer's version. Yet overall there is a transcending sense of a great occasion; the concentration is unfailing, reaching its peak in the glorious finale, where ruggedness and strength well over into inspiration, and that in spite of a pacing often highly individual, notably in the drum-and-fife march, which is much more serious in feeling than usual. But with an outburst of joy in the closing pages, the listener is left in no doubt that this recording was the culmination of a long and distinguished career. With a fine, characterful team of soloists and a freshly incisive chorus formed from singers of the Vienna State Opera, this is strongly recommendable; its issue on CD, appropriately coupled to another outstanding Beethoven recording of the *Pastoral Symphony*, is very welcome indeed, especially as the pair of CDs are offered at a reduced price, and the clarity of the sound is enhanced.

At a period when Toscanini was widely counted the top conductor of the world, his version of the *Ninth*, which appeared in the early 1950s, was awaited as no other. It proved just as apocalyptic in its vision as had been expected; and the immediacy and sense of presence are shattering, with the clarity and bite of the Shaw Chorale – a relatively compact band of mainly professional singers – adding to the impact. The clarity and precision of the excellent quartet of soloists also put many later versions to shame, and the style is more flexibly expressive than in most later Beethoven performances from this conductor; not hushed but warm and intense. The amazing thing is how little apology has to be made for the recording itself. Originally counted too dry to convey the score's full grandeur, the remastering reveals the underlying Carnegie Hall ambience, and although the forward balance never allows a true pianissimo, even in the slow movement, the drama and bite of the music making create their own range of dynamic. With fully acceptable string-tone and clear recording of the voices, this can be enjoyed alongside the more modern versions, and it is a good deal more compelling than most of them.

Sir Georg Solti, fifteen years after his first recording of Beethoven's *Ninth* with the Chicago orchestra, returned to the *Choral symphony* in celebration of his seventy-fifth birthday. The spaciousness of his reading, with unusually slow basic speeds in the first and third movements, has remained constant, with basic tempi even a fraction slower than before. The biting drama of the first movement and the resonant lyricism of the third are as intense as ever, though lines are now sculpted a shade more carefully. The choral finale is exuberant, with fine solo singing led by the dominant Jessye Norman. It is a pity that with rather backward balance the glowing contribution of the Chicago Symphony Chorus is not more sharply focused; otherwise, the sound is of excellent Chicago vintage, bright and full. The cassette does not match the CD in clarity.

Masur's Leipzig *Ninth* comes from his complete set of the mid-1970s. It is a spacious, well-proportioned and noble account, more conventional in its speeds than Solti and less weighty, yet in the excellent digital remastering the choral sound is fuller and more immediate than with the Decca recording, and the extra clarity extends to the other movements. At mid-price it can be considered alongside Karajan's Galleria version, although that has more drama, even if the balance is less natural. There is a very good tape equivalent.

Roger Norrington in his projected cycle of the Beethoven symphonies using period techniques took the bull by the horns in tackling the *Ninth* early in the series. He recorded it immediately after public rehearsals and a live performance which came as part of the 'Beethoven Experience' at the Queen Elizabeth Hall. Much of the sharp intensity and exhilaration of that event comes over on the finished disc, with most of Norrington's contentions over observing Beethoven's fast metronome markings validated in the success of the performance; so period violins cope very readily with the scampering demi-semiquavers of the first movement even at Norrington's speed, the scherzo is not unduly rushed, and the finale is chiefly surprising for the recitatives being taken *a tempo*, with some later speeds on the slow side rather than fast. What has to remain controversial is the slow movement which, at tempi far swifter than we are used to, becomes a sweet interlude rather than a meditation, far shorter than the other movements. It remains intensely refreshing. A more serious snag is the contribution of the male soloists. Petteri Salomaa's tremulous, aspirated singing on the command '*Nicht diese Töne*' is painful, while Patrick Power's plaintive tenor timbre goes with a very slow pace for the drum-and-fife march passage. Nevertheless, the impact of the whole performance is considerable, with reverberant recording still allowing the bite of timpani and valveless horns to cut through the texture. In no sense, except in the number of performers involved, is this a small-scale performance, rather an intensely refreshing view of a supreme masterpiece.

The high point of Karajan's most recent version of the *Ninth* is the sublime slow movement, here exceptionally sweet and true, with the lyricism all the more persuasive in a performance recorded in a complete take. The power and dynamism of the first two movements are striking too, but the choral finale is flawed above all by the singing of the soprano, Janet Perry, far too thin of tone and unreliable. The sound of the choir has plenty of body but is rather ill defined. As in the others in the series, CD helps to clarify recording which is less analytical than that usually given to Karajan.

Sir Colin Davis's easy manner makes for a relaxed view of the *Ninth*, one which underplays the apocalyptic power but which at a lower voltage presents a strong and enjoyable performance. The first movement – at a Furtwängler speed – is spacious but not overwhelming, lyrical with minor-key tensions underplayed, warm not tragic. The scherzo is light and lilting (with the long second repeat observed), and the slow movement has Elysian sweetness, though violin tone is not always ideally pure. In the choral finale, the drum-and-fife passage with tenor is easy and jaunty to contrast with the rough tones of the soloist, Klaus König. By contrast, the 6/4 *Allegro energico* is exceptionally fast and very exciting, helped by incandescent choral sound. Naturally balanced recording, with the soloists not sharply focused.

Starting on tremolos exceptionally precise in their definition of triplet rhythm, Dohnányi gives a crisp and direct reading which in its brisk, plain manner is consistently satisfying in the first two movements as well as in the choral sections of the finale which are thrillingly done, with an excellent chorus and quartet of soloists. Jerusalem sings the big tenor solo superbly with 6/8 rhythms made to skip infectiously. Before that, in the finale speeds are hectic, with the quasi-recitatives rattled off mercilessly and the quotations from previous movements sounding perfunctory. The slow movement inspires refined playing from the Cleveland Orchestra, but there is no mystery. The manner is chilly if not the sound, which is warmly atmospheric with fair reverberation.

It is thrilling to have a CD transfer of the historic recording made at the re-opening of the Festspielhaus in Bayreuth in 1951. The chorus may sound washy in the distance, almost as though placed at the bottom of the Rhine, and the lack of perspective in the mono sound is brought out the more on CD (along with audience noises), but the extra clarity and freshness impressively enhance a reading without parallel. The spacious, lovingly moulded account of the slow movement is among Furtwängler's finest achievements on record and, with an excellent quartet of soloists, the finale crowns a great performance.

Haitink's digital recording was made at a live concert in the Concertgebouw, but one would not know that; there are few if any signs of an audience, and – disappointingly – the performance rather fails to convey the feeling of an occasion, lacking a little in tension, even in comparison with Haitink's earlier studio version with the LPO. The reading, as before, is satisfyingly unidiosyncratic, direct and honest; but with this work one needs more. Happily, the clarity and precision of CD give a bite missing in the early LP and tape formats. But other CD versions convey more of the work's greatness.

Klemperer's digitally remastered tape goes one better by avoiding a turnover break in the slow movement and adding as a bonus his characteristically strong, serious version of the *Egmont overture*. The sound is amazingly good for its period (1958), with the finale fresher and better balanced than many recent recordings. However, Klemperer's weighty vision is marred by a disappointing quartet of soloists; and the slow speeds for the first two movements – the scherzo seems to go on for ever – come to sound ponderous. Yet the refined, flowing account of the slow movement is Klemperer at his finest. The CD omits the overture but offers compensating extra refinement, with the choral sound in the finale given astonishing presence and tangibility.

Günter Wand's is a rugged interpretation, thrustful and not always very refined. The very opening brings no mystery whatever, with the orchestra recorded close and made thicker through bass-heaviness. The scherzo is wild in its jollity; the drum-and-fife episode of the finale is free and easy, adding to an almost operatic feeling. The ruggedness extends to the slow movement, with the violins of the North German Radio Orchestra not always ideally sweet. At times ensemble is rough, and soloists and chorus are not ideally well drilled; but admirers of Wand's direct manner will not be disappointed. There is a good, well-balanced cassette.

Recorded in 1974, Ozawa's version with the New Philharmonia is fresh and direct, lacking something in dramatic tension, but sounding all the brighter and cleaner on CD, well transferred. The ease and confidence make this a youthful-sounding reading, helped in the choral finale (taken rather briskly) by the bright, clear singing of chorus and soloists.

It is sad that in his Beethoven cycle, recorded live wth the Vienna Philharmonic, Abbado gives such a surprisingly tentative account of the *Ninth* – at least in the first three movements. At generally slow speeds, much of the reading sounds too cautious, as though the conductor is self-consciously looking over his shoulder at great predecessors like Furtwängler. The phrasing often comes to sound self-conscious, too. The choral finale works better than the rest, thanks to some good solo and choral singing, but with variable sound – the chorus ill focused – this is not competitive.

Bernstein's reading of the *Ninth* makes a fine culmination to the complete cycle he recorded with the Vienna Philharmonic, and the electricity of a live concert performance comes over well, though (thanks to an indifferent transfer to CD) not as well as it should. Textures are not always clear and the sound has an edge which is often unpleasant, with the bass boomy at times. When DG has itself brought out finer versions, this full-price issue is hardly a front-runner (DG **410 859-2**).

It is sad too that Jochum's fine, rugged reading of the *Ninth* has been poorly transferred to CD. At a low level the sound is dried out, yet also lacks inner clarity. Even at mid-price it becomes a doubtful recommendation, despite the inspiration of the performance (HMV **CDM7 69030-2**).

Of the many other versions available, Bruno Walter's 1959 recording (CBS **MK 42014**) and Maazel's more recent New York performance (CBS **MK 76999**) must regretfully be set aside. The former suffers from a low level of tension, with the choral finale failing to rise to the occasion, while the latter is urgent to the point of aggressiveness. Reiner's 1962 Chicago reading has been reissued on an RCA mid-priced CD (**GD 86532**), but its merits do not add up to anything very compelling. It fails to come alive as a genuine performance should, even though chorus and soloists are very good in the finale. Solti's first stereo recording for Decca, also made in Chicago a decade later, has been economically reissued on tape, but the high level of the new transfer has brought fierce strings and an edginess and loss of focus to the soprano line of the chorus in the finale (Decca *417 486-4*). Schmidt-Isserstedt's Vienna recording with its starry solo group (Sutherland, Horne, King, Talvela), which served us so well in the late 1960s, has also been spoilt in its remastering for issue in Decca's low-priced Weekend series: the body of the recording has become dehydrated and the upper range is shrill (Decca *417 675-4*). Those with limited budgets, however, are admirably served by Karajan's Galleria cassette on DG.

Symphony No. 9 in D min. (Choral), Op. 125 (trans. Liszt).
(*) Tel. Dig. **ZK8 42956 [id.]. Cyprien Katsaris (piano).

Liszt made no attempt to create pianistically 'effective' arrangements, yet in his transcription of the *Ninth Symphony* he conveys so much of the character of an orchestra storming the heavens. Initially, one's thoughts turn to the pianistic melodramas of the silent movies, but one is soon drawn into the symphonic argument. Cyprien Katsaris's performance is nothing short of a *tour de force*: his virtuosity is altogether remarkable and there is a demonic Beethovenian vehemence and drive. He must have as many hands as an octopus has tentacles, for his ability to convey the teeming activity of the finale, to bring various strands to the foreground and then disappear into the mêlée, is astonishing. In its CD form, the image is firm in focus, but there must be a minor reservation on account of the sound: the piano is closely observed in a reverberant acoustic ambience and listeners may at times be disturbed by its somewhat jangly quality. The chrome tape is excellently managed, with the resonance offering no problems.

Wellington's victory (Battle symphony), Op. 91
** DG **419 624-2** [id.]. BPO, Karajan – *Egmont***(*); *Marches.***
** Telarc Dig. **CD 80079** [id.]. Cincinnati SO, Kunzel – LISZT: *Hunnenschlacht.***
** CBS **CD 37252** [id.]. VPO, Maazel – TCHAIKOVSKY: *1812.**(*)

Karajan's version is very well played, and the digital remastering adds presence to the opening assembly to left and right; but there is no sense of occasion and the battle-sounds are not entirely convincing, with the resonant acoustics of the Berlin Jesus-Christus-Kirche bringing atmosphere but not helping to focus the spectacle. However, Karajan's *Egmont* coupling is much more worth while than the alternatives offered by his competitors.

With a characteristically natural overall sound-balance, Kunzel's Telarc recording is technically the most sophisticated presentation of Beethoven's 'Battle' Symphony on record, though the real musketry and cannon featured in the recording sound curiously like a fireworks display. The performance is musically conceived and well played, but has no special individuality.

Maazel's version on CBS has more flair than Kunzel's and the CBS special effects are realistically interpolated. On compact disc, detail is clarified, but the drawback to this issue is the coupling, which is harshly recorded.

CHAMBER MUSIC

Cello sonatas Nos 1–5, Op. 5/1–2; Op. 69; Op. 102/1–2.
*** Decca Dig. **417 628-2**; *417 628-4*. Lynn Harrell, Vladimir Ashkenazy.
*** Ph. **412 256-2**; (M) *412 256-4* [id.]. Mstislav Rostropovich, Sviatoslav Richter.
*** CBS Dig. **M2K 42446** (2) [id.]. Yo-Yo Ma, Emanuel Ax.
(M) *** DG *413 520-4* [id.]. Wilhelm Kempff, Pierre Fournier.
(M) *** HMV *EM 291133-5* (2). Paul Tortelier, Eric Heidsiek.

Cello sonatas Nos 1 in F; 2 in G min., Op. 5/1–2.
(*) CBS **CD 37251; *40-37251* [id.]. Yo-Yo Ma, Emanuel Ax.
** HM **HMC 901179** [id.]. Christophe Coin, Patrick Cohen.

Cello sonatas Nos 3 in A, Op. 69; 5 in D, Op. 102/2.
*** CBS Dig. **MK 39024**; *IMT 39024* [id.]. Yo-Yo Ma, Emanuel Ax.
(B) *** CfP *CFP 41 4494-4* [*4RL 32060*]. Jacqueline Du Pré, Stephen Bishop-Kovacevich.

Cello sonata No. 3 in A; 7 Variations on Bei Männern (from Mozart's *Die Zauberflöte*), *WoO46; 12 Variations on See the conqu'ring hero comes* (from Handel's *Judas Maccabaeus*), *WoO45.*
** HM **HMC 901180** [id.]. Christophe Coin, Patrick Cohen.

Cello sonata No. 4 in C, Op. 102/1; 7 Variations on Bei Männern, WoO46; 12 Variations on See the conqu'ring hero comes, WoO45.
*** CBS Dig. **MK 42121**; *IMT 42121* [id.]. Yo-Yo Ma, Emanuel Ax.

Lynn Harrell and Vladimir Ashkenazy have the advantage of superb recording: they are sensibly balanced, neither instrument being too prominent or too reticent. The acoustic is open but the sound well focused. Artistically, too, these performances are in the first league – they are unfailingly sensitive and alert, well thought-out and yet seemingly spontaneous. Lynn Harrell on Decca is less extreme in his use of dynamics than Yo-Yo Ma on CBS, but his phrasing is every bit as alive, and comparison between Ashkenazy and Emanuel Ax is to the former's advantage. Without forgetting the strong claims of the classic Rostropovich–Richter account or the aristocratic Fournier–Kempff partnership, both of them special, the Harrell–Ashkenazy will be a first recommendation for many collectors interested in first-class sound.

Made in the early 1960s, the classic Philips performances by two of the instrumental giants of the day have withstood the test of time astonishingly well and sound remarkably fresh in this compact disc transfer. Apart from the usual gains in continuity and freedom from background, there is so much greater presence and realism. The *Sonata*, Op. 5, No. 1, and the two *Sonatas*, Op. 102, are accommodated on the first disc and the remaining two on the second. There are good tapes, but the sound is less fresh and transparent and the analogue source more obvious. The tapes are offered at mid-price.

By including the *Variations* the CBS set by Yo-Yo Ma and Emanuel Ax was originally less economical in layout, stretching to three CDs or tapes (available separately). But this has now been economically reissued on a pair of CDs. There are also balance problems in the coupling of the two Op. 5 *Sonatas*, where the piano often masks the refined lines that Yo-Yo Ma draws. Though the artists have the benefit of truthful digital recording in every other respect, here the dominance of the piano is an irritant. In Opp. 69 and 102, No. 2, the internal balance is much better judged, as it is in the third issue which includes Op. 102, No. 1, and the *Variations* which are most persuasively played, to make a most enjoyable concert. The balance difficulties cannot be blamed entirely on the engineers, for Emanuel Ax often produces a big, wide-ranging tone which must have posed problems, when related to the more introvert style of the cellist. Yo-Yo Ma plays with extraordinary sensitivity and imagination, even if there are times when one might think his pianissimo a bit overdone. Emanuel Ax's playing has vibrant personality and sure musical instincts. Both artists are heard at their most searching in the slow movements of the C major and D major works. None of these reservations should seriously deter collectors, for there are many individual beauties here and so much that is felicitous that Ax's moments of exuberance need not prove unduly worrying. The sound-quality is well focused and truthful and has great presence on CD.

The partnership of Fournier and Kempff was joined in the mid-1960s when their performances were recorded at live festival performances. The Paris audience is not seriously intrusive, and though the balances are not ideal the compulsion of the playing is such as to make the listener less critical than usual. The recording has been remastered and sounds remarkably fresh. Kempff can always be relied on, in his inspirational way, to produce memorable results; here, the clarity of his style balances perfectly with the relatively delicate timbre of Fournier's cello. These are performances marked by light, clear textures and rippling scale work, even in the slow introductions, which are taken relatively fast. Some of the weight found by Rostropovich and Richter is missing, but there is a mercurial quality here which is attractive in a different way.

The Tortelier set with Eric Heidsiek dates from the early 1970s and has the advantage of more modern and perhaps slightly better sound than the earlier Philips and DG sets; on the other hand, the iron-oxide tapes, though naturally balanced, do lose a little in upper range. The performances are distinguished and make a useful mid-priced alternative, as the style is bolder than the way of Fournier and Kempff, and less chimerical, too; indeed Tortelier and Heidsiek are nearer to Rostropovich and Richter, although they have their own insights.

The Du Pré/Bishop-Kovacevich recordings come from 1966, the year after Jacqueline had made her definitive record of the Elgar *Concerto*. Comparing this Beethoven coupling with rival versions, one cannot help noting the extra expressive urgency which marks the interpretations and makes them intensely vivid. The very opening of the *D major Sonata* underlines an unbuttoned quality in Beethoven's writing and when, after the hushed intensity of the slow introduction of Op. 69, the music launches into the allegro, both artists soar away fearlessly. More remarkable still is the range of expressiveness in the slow movement of Op. 102/2. Du Pré's tone ranges from full-blooded fortissimo to the mere whisper of a half-tone, and with Beethoven providing the indication *Adagio con molto sentimento* it is completely fitting that these artists allow the freest range of expressive rubato. There may be one or two technical faults, but rarely have artists so young plumbed such depths of expression on record. With excellent recording, this is an obvious bargain though on tape the focus of sound is perceptibly sharper on side one (Op. 69).

Harmonia Mundi offer us the sonatas with a difference: Christophe Coin and Patrick Cohen play period instruments (the hammerflügel is a Walter, an instrument that Mozart himself liked). The performances might be expected to rectify the imbalance one finds between the cello and the modern piano which can all too often drown the cellist. Of course, the cello plays an obbligato role anyway, but the problems of balance are not wholly solved. The cello line certainly registers but the thin-toned instrument sounds less persuasive than many instruments of that period. The playing of both artists is full of imagination and temperament, even if they seem at times a little 'self-aware'. However, this approach is nothing if not stimulating: both artists obviously deserve the high esteem in which they are held in early-music circles.

Clarinet trio in B flat, Op. 11.

*** HMV Dig. **CDC7 47683-2** [id.]. Sabine Meyer, Schiff, Buchbinder – BRAHMS: *Clarinet trio*.***

*** Decca **414 576-2** [id.]. Peter Schmidl, New V. Octet (members) – *Septet*.***

(*) Tel. **ZA8 48262 (2) [id.]. Benny Goodman, Berkshire Qt – BRAHMS: *Quintet*; *Trio*; WEBER: *Quintet*.**(*)

*(*) Mer. **CDE 84122**; *KE 84122*. Elin Eban, Israel Piano Trio (members) – BRAHMS: *Clarinet trio*.*(*)

The EMI digital version of the *Clarinet trio* has striking presence and clarity, and in its CD format produces a remarkably lifelike impression. Sabine Meyer is the highly accomplished clarinettist whom Karajan appointed to the Berlin Philharmonic amid much controversy some five years ago, and this recording was made not long after. She is a very impressive player and is well supported by Schiff and Buchbinder. This can be recommended with confidence.

The New Vienna Octet also makes a better case for the Op. 11 *Trio* than most previous rivals. The playing is wonderfully alert and has both sparkle and warmth. Taken on artistic merit alone, this is second to none, but the coupling brings an added inducement. The 1981 analogue recording is admirably balanced and has transferred smoothly and realistically to CD.

It is not surprising that Benny Goodman is at home in the repertoire gathered together in Telefunken's two-disc compilation of major chamber works, for he was classically trained before being seduced by ragtime, to which his talents, a first-class technique and a dominating timbre, were admirably suited. He certainly dominates in this characterful, well-paced performance, displaying a light rhythmic touch in the first movement, and he brings enticing bravura to the theme and variations of the finale. His colleagues support him spontaneously, although the string playing is a little pale and the recording, though truthful, somewhat two-dimensional.

An unsatisfactory balance spoils what is a musically satisfying account of the *Clarinet trio* from Elin Eban and members of the Israel Piano Trio. The cellist is rather backwardly placed and, though this does not seem quite as pronounced as in the Brahms with which it is coupled, it is still a great pity. The playing is full of life, and highly sensitive, too.

Horn sonata in F, Op. 17.

(*) Ph. Dig. **416 816-2 [id.]. Hermann Baumann, Leonard Hokanson (with Recital of works for horn and piano.**(*)).

Beethoven's *Horn sonata* is an early work, first performed in 1800. The horn writing has none of

Mozart's felicity and the bravura passages are inclined to sound clumsy. The closing *Rondo alla Polacca* is by far the best movement and Baumann, who is suitably bold throughout, makes the most of its liveliness. He is well partnered by Leonard Hokanson but the recording balance and the resonant acoustic, which slightly clouds the keyboard articulation, tend to make the piano part sound merely an accompaniment. Most of the other music in this recital is very slight.

Piano trios Nos 1–9; 10 (Variations on an original theme in E flat); 11 (Variations on 'Ich bin der Schneider Kakadu'); Allegretto in E flat, Hess 48.
*** HMV Dig. **CDS7 47466-8** [Ang. **CDCD 47455**]; *EX 290834-5* (4). Ashkenazy, Perlman, Harrell.
(M) **(*) DG **415 879-2** (3) (*Nos 1–3 & 5–7* only) [id.]. Kempff, Szeryng, Fournier.
** Chan. Dig. **CHAN 8352/5**; *DBTD 4004* (4) (without *Nos 4* and *Allegretto*) [id.]. Borodin Trio.
* Tel. Dig. **ZK8 43156** (*Nos 1–2*); **ZK8 43157** (*Nos 3–4*); **ZK 43197** (*Nos 5–6*) [id.]. V. Haydn Trio.

Piano trios Nos 1 in E flat; 2 in G, Op. 1/1–2.
*** Hyp. Dig. **CDA 66197**; *KA 66197* [id.]. L. Fortepiano Trio.
*** Sup. Dig. **C37 7490** [id.]. Suk Trio.

Piano trio No. 5 in D (Ghost), Op. 70/1.
(M) *** Ph. **420 716-2**; *420 716-4* [id.]. Beaux Arts Trio – SCHUBERT: *Trout quintet.***

Piano trios Nos 5 in D (Ghost); 6 in E flat, Op. 70/1–2.
** Sup. Dig. **C37 7284** [id.]. Suk Trio.

Piano trio No. 7 in B flat (Archduke), Op. 97.
(B) **(*) DG Walkman *415 333-4*. Kempff, Szeryng, Fournier – SCHUBERT: *Quartets Nos 12 & 14.***(*).

Piano trio No. 7 (Archduke), Op. 97; Variations on 'Ich bin der Schneider Kakadu', Op. 121a.
* Novalis Dig. **150 008-2**; *150 088-4* [id.]. Oppitz, Sitkovetsky, Geringas.

Piano trio No. 7 (Archduke); 9 in B flat, WoO 39.
*** HMV Dig. **CDC7 47010-2** [id.]. Ashkenazy, Perlman, Harrell.

Piano trios Nos 8 in E flat, WoO 38; 9 in B flat, WoO 39; 14 Variations on an original theme in E flat, Op. 44; Variations on 'Ich bin der Schneider Kakadu'.
*** Sup. Dig. **C37 7562** [id.]. Suk Trio.

Ashkenazy, Perlman and Harrell lead the field in this repertoire. Their four CDs comprise all of Beethoven's output for the piano trio. They also include the various additional works for the medium, the *Kakadu variations*, the isolated movements with WoO suffixes (works without opus numbers) and the early *Allegretto in E flat*, which most ensembles omit from their complete surveys. The recordings have been made over a period of five years and at various locations, but the sound is consistently fresher, warmer, more richly detailed and more present than with most other rivals. The playing is unfailingly perceptive and full of those musical insights that make one want to return to the set. No one investing in this set is likely to be disappointed,whether on the excellent CDs or the well-managed cassettes. On tape, although iron-oxide stock is used, involving some loss of range and presence, the resulting mellowness compensates agreeably for the less sharply defined imagery. The layout is good – only the *Archduke* involves a turnover break – and the documentation is excellent. The *Archduke*, coupled with *No. 9 in B flat*, is available on CD separately, and the striking clarity, presence and naturalness of the recording makes it a favoured selection for those wanting this favourite work on a single disc.

The Kempff–Szeryng–Fournier team recorded their survey of the Beethoven *Trios* in the early 1970s, and the DG engineers have been outstandingly successful in transferring them to the new medium. Few would be able to guess their early provenance. DG have squeezed the six major trios on to three mid-priced CDs but have sacrificed the additional works and variations. However, these are performances of distinction and well worth adding to any collection, given the excellence of the sound-quality. Wilhelm Kempff is an unfailingly interesting artist, and both Henryk Szeryng and that aristocrat of cellists, Pierre Fournier, are in impressive form throughout. Their crystalline reading of the *Archduke* is available separately, sounding well on a bargain Walkman tape coupled with Schubert.

The fine Supraphon performances were recorded in the House of Artists in Prague in 1983, and the reverberant acoustic and forward balance lend liveliness to the sound without there being any loss of detail. The playing is sparkling, that of the pianist, Josef Hala, being particularly felicitous. The Suk players also seem to have the knack of finding just the right tempi and do not rush either of the finales. The exposition repeats in the first movements are observed; however, for some reason the coupling of the Opus 70 *Trios* is given a closer balance and a slightly less open sound than the other two CDs in the set, and the effect is less natural; whereas on the third CD with *Trios Nos 8* and *9* and the *Variations* (a generous programme) the sound is very good indeed, articulate and transparent. These are all very enjoyable and inspiriting performances and thoroughly recommendable.

At present the London Fortepiano Trio have the field to themselves in the realm of 'authentic' performances. Monica Huggett is one of the leading violinists in the early-music field and, to judge from her playing here, her partner, Linda Nicholson, is hardly less expert. She plays with considerable virtuosity, particularly in the finales, which are taken at high speed and to considerable effect. The use of a fortepiano serves to enhance clarity of texture in this particular repertoire, and readers should make an effort to sample what one assumes will be a complete cycle. The performances also sound well in their cassette format.

Like Ashkenazy, Perlman and Harrell on EMI, the Borodins take four discs and offer the complete repertoire, save for the *B flat*, Op. 11 (the transcription of the *Clarinet trio*), and the little *Allegretto in E flat*. They are truthfully recorded in a warm if somewhat resonant acoustic, which matches their expansive style. They play with characteristic authority and panache, but their (broadly speaking) romantic approach will not be to all tastes. They are artists of generous feeling and their performances do have a higher emotional temperature than those of some rivals. Their playing is enormously vital but the odd rubati might strike some readers as mannered on repeated hearings. The chrome cassettes are of Chandos's highest quality, offering the players greater presence than the competing HMV tapes; however, the extra resonance of the Chandos recording is a disadvantage – more so on tape than on CD – and, generally speaking, the HMV cassettes are just as agreeable to listen to, and perhaps more so.

On Philips the Beaux Arts Trio couple the *Ghost trio* with an enjoyable version of Schubert's *Trout quintet*. The *Ghost* comes off marvellously and sounds very fresh, and the 1979 recording has responded well to digital remastering; the sound is firm, clear and truthfully balanced. The *Trout*, however, is rather less successful; the violinist Isidore Cohen's timbre is made to sound thinner and edgier than it is.

Another *Archduke* comes from Oppitz, Sitkovetsky and Geringas, but, for all the distinction of these players, it is by no means a front runner. Judged by the highest standards this does not have special claims – indeed their account of the slow movement is routine. Nor is the recording in the first bracket: the piano is rather closer than is ideal and less full-bodied than some rivals. *Vin ordinaire*.

The Vienna Haydn Trio is undoubtedly an accomplished ensemble and for the most part they give good, enjoyable performances, although the slow movement of the *Ghost trio* is too fast for comfort, and occasionally there is an element of blandness, as in the fluent account of the *C minor Trio*. Although Heinz Medjimorec is a first-class pianist, given the stiff opposition these records (available separately) must be regarded as also-rans. Not all repeats are observed (though, oddly, they are included in the first movement of Opus 11), yet there would have been plenty of room for more of them as playing times are not particularly generous. The recording, though bright and warm, is far from ideal so far as balance is concerned, with the piano tending to dominate the aural picture.

Piano and wind quintet in E flat, Op. 16.

*** CBS Dig. **MK 42099**; *IMT 42099* [id.]. Perahia, members of ECO – MOZART: *Quintet.****

*** Decca Dig. **414 291-2**; *414 291-4* [id.]. Lupu, De Vries, Pieterson, Zarzo, Pollard – MOZART: *Quintet.****

(*) Ph. Dig. **420 182-2; *420 182-4* [id.]. Brendel, Holliger, Brunner, Baumann, Thunemann – MOZART: *Quintet.****

** CRD **CRD 3367**; *CRDC 4067* [id.]. Ian Brown, Nash Ens. – MOZART: *Quintet.***

*(*) Telarc Dig. **CD 80114** [id.]. Previn, V. Wind Soloists – MOZART: *Quintet.*(*)*

*(*) DG Dig. **419 785-2**; *419 785-4* [id.]. Levine, Vienna/Berlin Ens. – MOZART: *Quintet.*(*)*

The view that Beethoven's *Piano and wind quintet* is less interesting than its Mozartian predecessor (which plainly inspired it) is almost confounded by Perahia's CBS version, recorded at The Maltings, Snape, with Neil Black (oboe), Thea King (clarinet), Tony Halstead (horn) and Graham Sheen (bassoon). The first movement is given more weight than usual, with a satisfying culmination. In the *Andante*, Perahia's playing is wonderfully poetic and serene and the wind soloists are admirably responsive. The pacing of the finale is ideally judged; and with the recording most realistically balanced, this issue can be recommended with all enthusiasm.

Radu Lupu and his colleagues also give a glorious account of the Beethoven *Quintet* and, while it would not necessarily weaken allegiance to Perahia and members of the ECO on CBS, it can certainly be recommended alongside it. The acoustic of the Kleine Zaal of the Amsterdam Concertgebouw is made to sound more spacious than that of Snape, and the balance achieved by the Decca engineers is very natural and true to life. There is plenty of space round the wind. Lupu's playing has sparkle and freshness, and the first movement has real elegance and – when required – wit. The wind offer beautifully blended and cultured playing, so suave that at times it seems almost bland. Still, this is a glorious performance and superbly recorded. Cassette collectors will find the sound of the Decca chrome tape more open than the competing CBS version.

Brendel and his colleagues are hardly less impressive in the Beethoven than they are in the Mozart coupling. The quality of the recording is remarkably clean and fresh and, generally speaking, the sound is well in the demonstration bracket. There are moments in the first movement (bars 112–26 and the corresponding section in the restatement) where Brendel sounds a little didactic (his staccati are almost spiky), as opposed to Lupu who makes this light and witty. But this is a most satisfying account and one that will rightly delight admirers of these artists. The Philips chrome cassette is first class in every way, beautifully balanced and technically more impressive than either the Decca or CBS alternatives.

The Nash version is now nine years old; however, the sound remains very fresh in these excellent CD transfers, which are eminently clean and firm. Ian Brown is a first-class pianist and some will prefer his more self-effacing approach to that of, say, Brendel. Good though they are, the Nash do not challenge or displace the top recommendations.

Previn is at his finest in the slow movement which he opens most persuasively; throughout, his wind colleagues emphasize the work's robust character, however, and the playing fails to sparkle as it might, although the finale goes well enough. Ensemble is good, if not immaculate; the recording, made in a rather resonant acoustic but naturally balanced, is faithful.

DG's account with James Levine and the Ensemble Wien–Berlin was recorded at Salzburg. There are many good things here – as there are, indeed, in the Mozart – though the balance tends to be rather too close, the overall sound is bright and forward. Levine is far from unimaginative or insensitive – on the contrary, he is a very fine pianist; despite the eminence of the artists, who include Karl Leister and Günter Högner, there is not quite the same finish that one encounters in the CBS and Decca sets.

Septet in E flat, Op. 20.
*** Decca **414 576-2** [id.]. New V. Octet (members) – *Clarinet trio.****
(M) *** Decca **421 093-2** [id.]. V. Octet (members) – MENDELSSOHN: *Octet.***(*)

The earlier recording of Beethoven's *Septet* by the older Vienna Octet held sway in the analogue stereo catalogue for more than two decades. In 1981 Decca replaced it with a more modern recording, also analogue, but of the highest quality. Like the earlier ensemble, the New Vienna Octet consists of the first desks of the VPO. This later version has all the elegance of the earlier one, but also conveys a sparkle and a sense of enjoyment that are thoroughly exhilarating. In terms of spirit and exuberance it is altogether special. Both CD transfers are very successful.

String quartets Nos 1–16; Grosse Fugue, Op. 133.
*** Valois **V 4401** (*Nos 1 & 5*); **V 4402** (*Nos 2–4*); **V 4403** (*Nos 6–7*); **V 4404** (*Nos 8–9*); **V 4405** (*Nos 10 & 12*); **V 4406** (*Nos 11 & 15*); **V 4407** (*Nos 13 & Grosse Fugue*); **V 4408** (*Nos 14 & 16*) [id.]. Végh Qt.
(M)**(*) DG **423 473-2** (7) [id.]. Amadeus Qt.

The Végh performances were recorded in the mid-1970s. On CD they are quite economically laid out on eight discs, available separately. Throughout the cycle, articulation is imaginative and alert; there is remarkably rhythmic grasp and flexibility and a subtle range of tone colour. These performances have been rightly hailed for their simplicity and depth. Intonation may not always be absolutely immaculate, but flaws are few and trivial when one considers the wisdom and experience the Végh communicate. In short they are in a different league from most of their rivals: there is no cultivation of surface polish though there is both elegance and finesse. Above all, there is no attempt to glamorize the sound. They observe all the first-movement exposition repeats, which is why they don't fit the Op. 18 set on two records. As an instance, in Op. 18, No. 1 they hit on the perfect tempo right at the beginning, and they find more depth in the slow movement than anyone else on record, even the Busch Quartet. Of course there are other fine versions too (most notably the Lindsay Quartet on ASV), but the Végh bring very special insights to this music; their playing is deep and searching, and when listening to them you are conscious only of Beethoven's voice. The CD transfers are successful in producing an altogether cleaner image and a slightly firmer focus than the original analogue LPs, although the imbalance towards the cello remains. The recording is less transparent and lifelike than the Alban Berg on EMI, but superior to the Talich on Calliope. However, it is the humanity and insight of this set that counts.

The Amadeus are at their best in the Op. 18 quartets, where their mastery and polish are heard to good advantage. In the middle-period and late quartets their sumptuous tone and refinement of balance are always in evidence, but they do not always penetrate very far beneath the surface. Norbert Brainin's vibrato often sounds disturbing and a shade self-regarding, and the readings, particularly of the late quartets, no longer sound freshly experienced as they did when this ensemble was first before the public. There is some superb quartet playing in this cycle, but there are more searching accounts of the late quartets to be found. The recording, from the beginning of the 1960s, is fresh and lifelike and the set is economically priced on seven CDs, but the Végh Quartet are worth the extra cost.

String quartets Nos 1–6, Op. 18/1–6.
*** HMV Dig. **CDS7 47127-8** [Ang. **CDC 47126**] (3). Alban Berg Qt.
(*) Cal. **CAL 9633/4 [id.]. Talich Qt.
** DG Dig. **410 971-2** (3) [id.]. Melos Qt.

String quartets Nos 1 in F; 2 in G, Op. 18/1–2.
(*) HM **HMC 901222; *HMC40 1222* [id.]. Brandis Qt.

The Alban Berg undoubtedly offer a polish and tonal finesse that put them in a class of their own. The affectation noted in their set of the *Rasumovskys* (the tendency to exaggerate dynamic extremes) is less obtrusive here, and the overall sense of style is so sure that few will be disappointed. For the time being, CD collectors are unlikely to do better than this. The playing is immaculate and the sound has all the usual advantages of the new medium, excellent definition, presence and body. The CDs are also being made available separately (**CDC7 47127/8/9-2**).

The Talich offer all six Op. 18 *Quartets* on two CDs and enjoy a distinct economic advantage over their compact disc rivals. Their performances have the merit of directness and simplicity of utterance; as music making there is a refreshing naturalness about this approach. Sometimes they are inclined to be a little measured and wanting in urgency, notably in Nos 1 and 4, while the conversation-like exchanges of the first movement of No. 2 could do with more wit and lightness of touch. The slow movement of No. 1, the greatest single movement in all six, is less deeply felt than one expects, but if there is some prose in this set there is no want of poetry either. First-movement exposition repeats are preserved except in Nos 1 and 6. The Calliope recording is very clean and present, if a trifle dry.

The performances by the Melos Quartet offer a refined blend, impeccable intonation and superb ensemble. However, admiration rather than unalloyed pleasure is one's final reaction. Speeds are on the fast side, and too often this group does not convey a sufficient sense of pleasure in the courtly exchanges that take place among the four instruments, while at times their playing has an aggressive edge. There are of course some very good things in the set, and there is no question as to the finesse and mastery of the playing or the vividness of the recording, but the Melos do not displace the Alban Berg on HMV.

The Brandis Quartet can more than hold their own with their current rivals. Tempi are well chosen, there is an enviable unanimity of ensemble and no lack of polish. The slow movement of the *F major* does not obliterate memories of the greatest performances of the past but, generally speaking, no one investing in these well-recorded performances need fear disappointment.

String quartets Nos 5 in A, Op. 18/5; 7 in F (Rasumovsky), Op. 59/1.
** Delos Dig. **D/CD 3033** [id.]. Orford Qt.

The Orford Quartet are Canadian and have been together for more than twenty years, as long as the Melos Quartet of Stuttgart. Their playing is rather high-powered and at times hard driven, and their approach to tempi on the fast side. Their sforzandi are at times rather aggressive. However, their account of Opus 18, No. 5, shows them at their best, and they are clearly recorded.

String quartets Nos 7–9 (Rasumovsky Nos 1–3), Op. 59/1–3; 10 in E flat (Harp), Op. 74; 11 in F min., Op. 95.
*** ASV *ZCLHB 307* (3) [id.]. Lindsay Qt.
(*) HMV Dig. **CDS7 47131-8 [Ang. **CDC 47130**] (3). Alban Berg Qt.

String quartets Nos 7–9; 10–11; Quartet in F (after *Piano sonata No. 9 in E, Op. 14/1*).
** DG **415 342-2**; *415 342-4* (3) [id.]. Melos Qt.

String quartet No. 7 in F (Rasumovsky No. 1), Op. 59/1.
*** ASV Dig. **CDDCA 553** [id.]. Lindsay Qt.
(*) HMV **CDC7 47131-2 [id.]. Alban Berg Qt.

String quartets Nos 8 in E min.; 9 in C (Rasumovsky Nos 2–3), Op. 59/2–3.
*** ASV Dig. **CDDCA 554** [id.]. Lindsay Qt.

String quartets Nos 7, Op. 59/1; 10 (Harp), Op. 74.
*** Cal. **CAL 9636** [id.]. Talich Qt.

String quartets Nos 8, Op. 59/2; 11 in F min., Op. 95.
(*) HMV **CDC7 47132-2 [id.]. Alban Berg Qt.
*(*) Delos Dig. **D/CD 3034** [id.]. Orford Qt.

String quartets Nos 8, Op. 59/2; 13 in B flat, Op. 130.
*** Cal. **CAL 9637** [id.]. Talich Qt.

String quartets Nos 9, Op. 59/3; 10 (Harp), Op. 74.
(*) HMV **CDC7 47133-2 [id.]. Alban Berg Qt.
*(*) Delos Dig. **D/CD 3035** [id.]. Orford Qt.

String quartets Nos 9, Op. 59/3; 14 in C sharp min., Op. 131.
*** Cal. **CAL 9638** [id.]. Talich Qt.

The Lindsay set contains performances of real stature; and though they are not unrivalled in some of their insights, among modern recordings they are not often surpassed. The *F major*, Op. 59/1, available separately on CD, is very impressive indeed. This is the most masterly account to have appeared for many decades, with exactly the right feeling and pace, inwardness and effortlessness. This version brings the listener closer to Beethoven than any of its rivals. Again, in each movement of the *E minor*, Op. 59/2, the Lindsays find the *tempo giusto* and all that they do as a result has the ring of complete conviction. The opening of Op. 59/3 has real mystery and awe, and how splendidly they convey the pent-up torrent of energy released in the fugal onrush of the *Allegro molto*. These quartets are coupled together on CD. The two remaining quartets in the tape box, Opp. 74 and 95, are not new; they were recorded in 1979 and are highly competitive. As a recording, this set is comparable with most of its competitors and superior to many; artistically, it can hold its own with the best.

The Talich have an impressive technical address, no less formidable than any of their current rivals, and they win our confidence by the essentially private character of their performances. One feels a privileged eavesdropper on an intimate discourse rather than a concert-hall listener waiting for another jet-setting, over-projecting ensemble. There is a real understanding of what this music is about. The recordings, which seemed a bit bottom-heavy when they first appeared, are more firmly defined and better focused than on LP and, while the sound is not in the demonstration class, the instruments are well placed and the timbre truthful – in fact, one quickly forgets about it and loses oneself in the music. Each of these three CDs offers exceptionally good value, containing over 70′ of music.

Unlike their Op. 18 set, the Alban Berg recordings cannot be welcomed without certain reservations. Generally they favour rather brisk tempi in first movements, which they dispatch with exemplary polish and accuracy of intonation. The slow movement of Op. 59/1 is free from excessive point-making, and throughout this quartet and its companions there is much perceptive music-making. However, there is a distinct tendency to exaggerate dynamic extremes. The introduction to Op. 59/3 suffers in this respect and the results sound self-conscious. In the first movements of Op. 59/2 and Op. 95 the brilliance of the attack almost draws attention to itself and perhaps the recording quality, which is closely balanced, gives it a slightly more aggressive quality than it really has. The HMV recordings have great presence and immediacy (some ears might feel too much) but there is no doubt as to the realism of the recorded sound. The three CDs are also being made available separately.

The Melos Quartet of Stuttgart adopt a generally sound approach and eschew unnecessary interpretative eccentricities. Dynamic nuances and other markings are scrupulously observed. But far too many of the finales are too fast, as they were in their Op. 18 set, and the Melos players are by no means as searching or humane as the Lindsays in Op. 59/1 – the first movement is terribly rushed. Although they perhaps offer performances of the others that are as finely played as any, the impression is of superb quartet playing rather than of great Beethoven. As a novelty, they include Beethoven's own transcription of the *Sonata*, Op. 14, No. 1, which is not otherwise available. The recording is strikingly real and the chrome cassettes are only marginally less impressive than the CDs.

The Orford Quartet are technically immaculate and can hold their own with any ensemble in the world, but theirs is very public music-making: one is not left with the impression of four players who have got together for pleasure. Generally speaking, the recordings are very clean and well detailed, though all are on the dry side. Although the balance-sheet is far from all negative and there is much to enjoy, it would not be possible to recommend them in preference to the Lindsay or the Talich.

String quartets Nos 11 in F min., Op. 95; 12 in E flat, Op. 127; Grosse Fuge, Op. 133.
*** Cal. **CAL 9635** [id.]. Talich Qt.

String quartets Nos 15 in A min., Op. 132; 16 in F, Op. 135.
*** Cal. **CAL 9639** [id.]. Talich Qt.

Having Opp. 132 and 135 on one disc is quite a bargain, especially so, given the quality of the performances. These penetrating accounts can hold their own with the very finest, and the quality of the recorded sound – though not spectacular in any way – is more than acceptable. Indeed in the new format it is eminently clean and well focused though not as warm or as alive as in some of the most recent rivals.

String quartets Nos 12 in E flat, Op. 127; 13 in B flat, Op. 130; 14 in C sharp min., Op. 131; 15 in A min., Op. 132; 16 in F, Op. 135; Grosse Fuge in B flat, Op. 133.
*** ASV **DCS 403**; *ZCLIIB 403* (4) [id.]. Lindsay Qt.
(*) Ph. **416 638-2 (4). Italian Qt.
(*) DG Dig. **415 676-2; *415 676-4* (3) [id.]. Melos Qt.
(*) HMV Dig. **CDS7 47135-8; *EX 270114-9* (**4**/3) [Ang. **CDC 47134**; *4DC 3973*]. Alban Berg Qt.

The Lindsays get far closer to the essence of this great music than most of their rivals. They have the benefit of very well-balanced recording (better than the Végh and the Talich which are both a little bottom-heavy – see above); the sound of the ASV set is more present on CD and cassette alike. They seem to find tempi that somehow strike the listener as completely right and which enable them to convey so much both of the letter and of the spirit of the music. They bring much rich musical characterization and musical strength, while there is some wonderfully rapt playing in slow movements, notably Op. 127. Everywhere the listener is carried along by the character of the playing. One relatively minor point: in the *molto adagio* middle section of the *Heiliger Dankegesang*, the leader eschews vibrato while his colleagues do not; yet tone is often beautifully matched elsewhere. On tape the Lindsays omit the alternative finale of Op. 130, but this is restored as an additional movement in the CD set. Taken overall, these are among the very finest versions to have been made in recent years.

The merits of the Italian Quartet's performances are considerable. The sonority that they produce is beautifully blended and splendidly focused, and yet their prime concern is with truth not beauty. Generally speaking, they give each musical point plenty of time to register. These accounts withstand the test of time and, although the recordings were made in the late 1960s, they still sound good. The transfers to compact disc have been well effected, though the gain in clarity also entails a slight loss of warmth in the middle register. Now they do not sound as sumptuous as some modern quartet recordings, and one is bound to reflect that their reissue on four premium-priced CDs is not strikingly competitive when the newer Melos set is on three. However, for many these searching and thoughtful interpretations may prove ultimately more satisfying than the more extrovert Melos approach.

The Melos Quartet seem more naturally attuned to the late quartets than the early or middle-period works. They are strong and positive in fast movements, deeply expressive in slow ones, although here the playing is not always as hushed as it might be. Overall these are warmly satisfying readings, and the players are particularly impressive in their powerful reading of the *Grosse Fuge*. Though speeds are not excessively fast, all six works are fitted on to three CDs and, with vividly immediate sound on CDs and cassettes alike, they are excellent value, although the bright lighting emphasizes that these are essentially 'public' performances that project, rather than private ones that are overheard. A small but important final point: the pauses between movements are often too short (only three seconds between the second movement of Op. 132 and the *Heiliger Dankegesang*).

Some listeners may find the sheer polish of the Alban Berg Quartet gets in the way, for this can be an encumbrance: late Beethoven is beautified at its peril. Others dig deeper into the soul of this music – the Lindsays do – and this tells in movements like the *Heiliger Dankegesang* of Op. 132 or the *Cavatina* of Op. 130. The CDs have greater clarity of focus, particularly at the bottom end of the spectrum, and a distinct gain in presence, yet there are excellent cassettes. The new medium does full justice to the magnificently burnished tone that the Alban Berg command and the perfection of blend they so consistently achieve. No single version of the late quartets can give us the complete truth, and no set is more magnificently played and recorded, yet, at the same time, it is difficult to suppress the feeling that others convey even more of the stature and depth of these great and profound works. The CDs are also being made available separately (**CDC7 47135/6/7/8-2**).

String quartets Nos 12 in E flat, Op. 127; 16 in F, Op. 135.
(*) HMV **CDC7 47135-2 [id.]. Alban Berg Qt.
** Tel. Dig. **ZK8 43207** [id.]. Vermeer Qt.
*(*) Ph. Dig. **420 926-2**; *420 926-4* [id.]. Guarneri Qt.

String quartet No. 13 in B flat, Op. 130; Grosse Fuge, Op. 133.
** Tel. Dig. **ZK8 42982** [id.]. Vermeer Qt.

The Vermeer are among the very finest of the current American quartets and their account of Op. 127 is in many ways a strong one. Certainly, as quartet playing goes, this is difficult to fault: ensemble is splendid and phrasing is articulate and intelligent. Perhaps there is not enough inwardness of feeling (what the Germans call *Innigkeit*) in the *Adagio*, and the middle section of the scherzo is a bit aggressive and too fast. Their Op. 135, however, is very impressive; tempi seem natural and the slow movement has no lack of depth. In Opus 130, while they give a perceptive and technically impeccable account of the first movement, they are perhaps a shade didactic – and this applies even more to the finale, which is a little too measured. The *Alla tedesca* movement and the *Cavatina*, on the other hand, may seem a shade fast for some tastes. A good performance all the same, and on both discs the recording is clean and well focused with a musical balance, even if the acoustic is on the dry side.

Superb playing, too, from the Guarneri Quartet, perhaps America's most prestigious ensemble. They are recorded in a warm acoustic and the sound is more satisfying than most current rivals. Theirs are very much public performances, oratory rather than more private exchanges. It is all very high-powered, and their expressive vehemence grows tiring. So does the mannerism in the finale where the players lean on one phrase each time it recurs. They dig deeply into the opening chords of Op. 127 and produce a rich yet slightly rough hewn sonority. There is impressive unanimity and a sumptuous tonal blend, but it is all a little glamorized.

Impressive though they are in some ways, they do not begin to match the very best in terms of humanity.

String quartet No. 13 in B flat, Op. 130; Grosse Fuge, Op. 133.
*** Decca Dig. **411 943-2** [id.]. Fitzwilliam Qt.
(*) HMV **CDC7 47136-2 [id.]. Alban Berg Qt.

String quartet No. 14 in C sharp minor, Op. 131.
(*) HMV **CDC7 47137-2 [id.]. Alban Berg Qt.

String quartet No. 15 in A min., Op. 132.
(*) Decca Dig. **411 643-2 [id.]. Fitzwilliam Qt.
(*) HMV **CDC7 47138-2 [id.]. Alban Berg Qt.

The Fitzwilliam Quartet offer performances of bold contrasts. In Op. 130 their characteristically wide dynamic and tonal range bring a sublime account of the fifth-movement *Cavatina*, here taken at a genuine *Adagio* with the marking *sotto voce* made breathtaking. At a steady pulse and with restrained phrasing the result completely avoids sentimentality; equally in the *Grosse Fuge*, given as the first option of the two finales Beethoven wrote, the unusually measured speeds bring a hushed contrast in the *meno mosso* sections that makes the bravura allegros the more dramatically intense. Similarly in Op. 132 the Fitzwilliams build a formidable structure round the central *Heiliger Dankegesang*, a genuine *molto adagio* with an exceptionally slow speed, superbly sustained and with the most hushed pianissimos. The extremes of the first movement equally are contrasted against the relaxation of the other movements, whether of ebullient joy or of songfulness. The recording balance is a little close to counter the resonance of Kingsway Hall, where the disc was recorded, but there is no doubting the realism and immediacy. However, with no coupling, many may turn to other versions which offer more generous measure. An alternative version by the Brandis Quartet is let down by the *Heiliger Dankegesang*, where the playing is curiously detached so that there is no sense of mystery or awe; otherwise, the performance is well paced and thoughtful, and the recording is lifelike and not overlit. However, it is difficult to recommend a performance in which the work's emotional core is relatively ineffective (HM **HMC 401221**).

String quartet No. 14 in C sharp min., Op. 131 (arr. for string orchestra)*; Overtures: Coriolan; Creatures of Prometheus; King Stephen.*
** DG **419 439-2** [id.]. VPO, Bernstein.

Bernstein is not the first to perform late Beethoven quartets in this fashion: Toscanini recorded two movements of Op. 135, and Mitropoulos conducted Op. 131 in the 1940s, a performance which Bernstein attended and now emulates. Obviously the added weight and the different colour that the full strings offer make for losses as well as gains; the intimacy of private feeling becomes transformed into the outpouring of public sentiment. There is no doubt as to the commitment and depth of feeling that Bernstein brings to this performance, dedicated to the memory of his wife; nor are there doubts as to the quality of the response he evokes from the Vienna Philharmonic strings. This is not a record about which we are in agreement: many collectors would never play it more than once. What we can agree about is that, if this is to be done at all, it could not be given more eloquent advocacy than it is here. The recording has excellent range and clarity.

String trios Nos 2 in G; 3 in D; 4 in C min., Op. 9/1–3.
*** Unicorn Dig. **DKPCD 9042**; *DKPC 9042* (*Nos 3 & 4 only*) [id.]. Cummings Trio.

The cassette offers the *D major* and *C minor Trios* only, while the CD manages to accommodate all three trios at 72 minutes. The playing is quite first class; fully prepared but never overcultivated, full of life but always thoughtful and perceptive. We were well served in this repertoire during the late 1960s by the Italian String Trio and the Grumiaux Trio. These are not only the finest since then – they can more than hold their own against them. This is real chamber-music playing. The *G major* is of particular interest, as its scherzo includes a newly discovered second trio. The recording is in the demonstration class in both media, but the omission of Op. 9/1 on the cassette, which could easily have included it at the expense of a little more tape, is inexplicable.

Violin sonatas Nos 1–10.
(M) *** DG **415 874-2** (3) [id.]. Yehudi Menuhin, Wilhelm Kempff.
*** CRD Dig. *CRDCD 4115/7* [id.]. Erich Gruenberg, David Wilde.
(*) CBS Dig. **M2K 39680;*12T 39680* (*Nos 1–4 & 9*); **M2K 39681**; *12T 39681* (*Nos 5–8 & 10*) [id.]. Isaac Stern, Eugene Istomin.
(*) Ph. **412 570-2 (4) [id.]. David Oistrakh, Lev Oborin.

Inspirational artists of genius, Menuhin and Kempff met together in London in June 1970 to record this cycle of the Beethoven *Violin sonatas* in Conway Hall. There, day after day, during perfect weather, they proceeded to enjoy themselves, generally letting the inspiration of the moment lead them to their joint interpretation rather than preparing meticulously ahead. Though these are not always the most immaculate performances on disc, they consistently reflect the joy and sense of wonder of pianist and violinist alike, often relaxed in tempo but magnetic from first to last. Menuhin at his own Gstaad Festival would with Kempff give just such inspired performances. The brightness of the CD transfer at times gives too much edge to the violin tone, but these vintage recordings still sound well, with the rippling articulation of Kempff a constant delight. Being issued at mid-price, they also enjoy the advantage of economy.

On CRD, Erich Gruenberg and David Wilde can hold their own with distinguished rivals. Their performances have sparkle and freshness; they are very attentive to minutiae of nuance and dynamics without for one moment losing their grasp of the overall architecture. Gruenberg produces a good tone, too; both he and his intelligent partner have the benefit of excellent recording that conveys the sense of a real concert-hall experience. These readings have a spontaneity and vitality that will not disappoint cassette collectors. They are on three separate double-length chrome tapes, each at normal premium price. The only snag is that this means the *Kreutzer* has to break between sides to accommodate the four works allotted to the final cassette. The quality of the transfers is outstandingly real and vivid.

Isaac Stern and Eugene Istomin also make an inspirational partnership, obviously striking sparks off each other in performances that are brimming with zest and vitality. The *Spring sonata* is more intense than some versions, but in the most involving way; the *C minor*, Op. 30/2, has similar electricity, and the *Kreutzer* is splendid. The recording has great presence – some might feel the balance is too close, but it suits this highly projected style of music making. These are first-class cassettes. The set is packaged in two halves each of a pair of CDs or tapes.

The Philips set was made in the early 1960s and sounds a trifle plummier than is usual nowadays. There is not a great deal of air round each of the instruments, though the recording is not dry. There is a relaxed, almost effortless quality and lyricism about these performances that is winning. Oistrakh's tone is warm and lines are finely drawn; there is admirable rapport throughout between the two partners. Some critics found these accounts a little bland when they first appeared, but dipping into them again, while they would not necessarily be a first choice in every sonata, there is a selfless, musicianly quality that cannot fail to win over the listener. Other versions have more electricity or have gone deeper, but few are as natural. It is good to have them with the advantage of continuity and a silent background, and in such good transfers.

Violin sonatas Nos 1 in D; 2 in A; 3 in E flat, Op. 12/1–3.
*** DG Dig. **415 138-2** [id.]. Gidon Kremer, Martha Argerich.
*** Decca **417 573-2** [id.]. Itzhak Perlman, Vladimir Ashkenazy.

The partnership of Kremer and Argerich, two inspirational artists, works superbly in the first three sonatas. Each sparks the other into individual, but never wilful, expression, with the to-and-fro exchanges typical of early Beethoven consistently delightful. Argerich is marginally the more dominant, but from the challenging opening of No. 1 onwards the sense of two individual musicians enjoying a new experience is irresistible. Argerich feared that she might sound self-conscious in Beethoven when pinned down on record, but she need not have worried. The CD gives a keen sense of presence.

Decca are sensibly regrouping the Perlman/Ashkenazy set for CD reissue. Their musicianship and vitality are matched by a poise and elegance that give consistent pleasure. The lilting opening *Allegro vivace* of the *A major* is infectious, while the *E flat Sonata* has exemplary warmth and naturalness; tempi are excellently judged and articulation could hardly be more alive. The recording balance remains exemplary between the two instruments, but the digital remastering has added a degree of edge to the image, particularly striking at the opening of the *First Sonata*. The piano timbre is strikingly real and well focused. This yields first place – just – to the Kremer/Argerich CD, which has the advantage of modern digital recording.

Violin sonata Nos 4 in A min., Op. 23; 5 in F (Spring), Op. 24.
(*) DG Dig. **419 787-2; *419 787-4* [id.]. Gidon Kremer, Martha Argerich.

The ungenerous coupling of Op. 23 and the *Spring sonata* yet brings characteristically compelling and individual readings from Kremer and Argerich, an inspired and characterful – if at times wilful – duo. In all but one movement, but that arguably the most important, they match their earlier issue of the three Op. 12 *Sonatas* in sparkle and imagination, giving a new and refreshing view of these early works. Where their individuality goes over the edge into mannerism is in the first movement of the *Spring*, where Kremer's refusal to keep a steady tempo, even within phrases, sounds fussy and uncomfortable. A memorable issue none the less, very well recorded on both CD and tape.

Violin sonatas Nos 4 in A min., Op. 23; 6 in A; 8 in G, Op. 30/1 & 3.
*** Decca **417 574-2** [id.]. Itzhak Perlman, Vladimir Ashkenazy.

A further outstanding recoupling from the Perlman/Ashkenazy series: Nos 4 and 8 come from 1976 and No. 6 was one of the last to be recorded, in 1977. It is well up to the standard of the rest. Discernment is matched by spontaneity and throughout everything is sparkling and alert; the manner is youthful, the style classical. The digital remastering is highly successful: the sound gives both violin and piano admirable presence and reality.

Violin sonatas Nos 5 in F (Spring), Op. 24; 9 in A (Kreutzer), Op. 47.
(M) *** HMV **CDM7 69021-2**; *EG 769021-4*. Pinchas Zukerman, Daniel Barenboim.
*** Decca **410 554-2** [id.]. Itzhak Perlman, Vladimir Ashkenazy.
(B) *** DG Walkman *415 615-4* [id.]. Yehudi Menuhin, Wilhelm Kempff – BRAHMS: *Violin sonata No. 2.****
(B) *** CfP *TC-CFP 4520*. Yehudi Menuhin, Hephzibah Menuhin.
(*) HMV Dig. **CDC7 47353-2 [id.]. Yehudi Menuhin, Jeremy Menuhin.
** Ph. **412 255-2** [id.]. David Oistrakh, Lev Oborin.
(M) ** Pickwick Dig. **PCD 833**. Lorraine McAslan, John Blakeley.

Zukerman and Barenboim's coupling of the two favourites among Beethoven's *Violin sonatas*, taken from their 1973 cycle, brings disarmingly spontaneous-sounding performances. Zukerman, challenged by his Beethovenian partner, has rarely sounded more inspired on record, in performances that are both strong and poetic. The CD transfers bring warm, natural sound that hardly betrays its age. An excellent issue, made the more desirable on EMI's mid-price Studio label. There is a very good chrome cassette.

On Decca an obvious recoupling from the Perlman/Ashkenazy series. The manner has a youthful freshness, yet the style is classical. The dynamism is there but never becomes too extrovert, and the music unfolds naturally and spontaneously. The recording quality is excellent and has transferred smoothly to CD, though the EMI transfer of the Zukerman/Barenboim recordings is even more impressive.

The Walkman tape offers a recoupling from the Menuhin/Kempff recordings of the early 1970s. Their reading of the *Spring sonata* has the magic which characterizes the whole cycle, and the performance of the *Kreutzer* is also unique. In many ways it is not as immaculate as earlier accounts, but the spontaneous imagination of the playing, the challenge between great artists on the same wavelength, is consistently present. The recording too is admirably 'live'.

In 1959, while still at the peak of his form, Yehudi Menuhin recorded inspirational accounts of these two sonatas with his sister, Hephzibah. The warmth and nobility of the phrasing is striking; this is music making of refreshing spontaneity: the wonderful flow of the opening pastoral melody of the *Spring sonata*, the sustained tension of the *Adagio* of the same work, or the beautiful closing pages of the variations in the *Kreutzer*. With excellent sound, the CfP tape makes a fine bargain. Then in 1986 Menuhin repeated the formula, in digital stereo, this time with his son, Jeremy, who plays remarkably well – if not quite matching Hephzibah in the slow movement of the *Kreutzer*. Menuhin's timbre is less rounded now and his technique less refined, but the nobility of line is still apparent, and the spontaneity and family chemistry are as potent as ever. The *Kreutzer* finale is joyfully spirited. Excellent recording in a resonant acoustic.

Philips have paired these two most popular sonatas from the 1962 Oistrakh/Oborin recordings for those who do not want to invest in the complete set. The first movement of the *Spring sonata* could perhaps have had more sparkle, but there is musicianship here, and a selfless quality that is most appealing. Oistrakh's is playing of the old school, leisurely and civilized, and in sheer character and zest must yield to Perlman and Ashkenazy on Decca, Zukerman and Barenboim on HMV.

Lorraine McAslan has established herself as one of the most talented of young British violinists, but this recording of Beethoven finds her sounding too cautious, with intonation not always quite immaculate. The digital recording is admirable, but on another mid-priced CD Zukerman and Barenboim are far preferable. A further alternative, at full price, on RCA by Ughi and Sawallisch, offering satisfying if rather plain readings, also now seems uncompetitive, in spite of well-balanced digital recording **(RD 70430)**.

Violin sonatas Nos 7 in C min., Op. 30/1; 10 in G, Op. 96.
*** Decca **411 948-2** [id.]. Itzhak Perlman, Vladimir Ashkenazy.

These performances emanate from the 1977 set and have been digitally remastered and re-coupled. The sound is improved, firmer and fresher than ever; no phrase is unimaginatively handled, and the playing of these artists is masterly. Technically this is one of the most impressive of the series: the sound has depth as well as presence, without added edge on the violin timbre.

Violin sonatas Nos 8 in G, Op. 30/3; 9 in A (Kreutzer), Op. 47.
(*) Amon Ra **CDSAR 16 [id.]. Ralph Holmes, Richard Burnett.

Ralph Holmes recorded these two Beethoven sonatas not long before he died. They reveal his art at its freshest and most alert in a period performance, accompanied by Richard Burnett on a sweet-toned Graf fortepiano of around 1820. Inevitably Holmes's Stradivarius overtops the fortepiano but, with recording realistically set in a helpful but intimate acoustic, the textures are admirably clear. The twanginess of the instrument is only distracting in sustained melodic passages, and Burnett's clean articulation is as much a delight as Holmes's strong and imaginative phrasing.

(Wind) *Octet in E flat, Op. 103; Quintet in E flat for oboe, 3 horns & bassoon; Rondino in E flat for wind octet, WoO 25; Sextet in E flat, Op. 71.*
*** ASV Dig. **CDCOE 807**; *ZCCOE 807* [id.]. Wind Soloists of COE.

Octet in E flat, Op. 103; Rondino in E flat, WoO 25; Sextet in E flat, Op. 71.
(*) Amon Ra Dig. **CDSAR 26; *CSAR 26* [id.]. Classical Winds.

The wind soloists of the Chamber Orchestra of Europe give strong and stylish performances of this collection of Beethoven's wind music, marked by some outstanding solo work, notably from the first oboe, Douglas Boyd. Despite the high opus numbers, these are early works. Aptly, the young COE players point rhythms elegantly, but with their strong contrasts of mood and dynamic they make the music genuinely Beethovenian, not Mozartian. With the little *Rondino* included alongside Opus 103, as well as the three-movement *Quintet*, it makes a generous collection, recorded in warm but clear sound with good presence. The chrome cassette, too, is of high quality, naturally balanced and real.

Using period instruments, Classical Winds give bright, sometimes abrasive performances of Beethoven's two major wind works, including the *Rondino* not as a separate work but as the fourth movement of Opus 103 immediately before the finale, citing interesting evidence for that incorporation. It is not just the relative clumsiness of the instruments that occasionally brings a stodginess of rhythm, with absence of light and shade. Generally these are fresh, lively performances very well recorded, not as stylish or persuasive as those from the COE soloists using modern instruments, but warmly recommendable to anyone who prefers period style at a lower pitch.

Piano sonatas Nos 1–32; Andante favori in F, G.170.
(*) Ph. **412 575-2 (11) [id.]. Alfred Brendel.

Piano sonatas Nos 1–15.
(*) DG Dig. **413 759-2 (6) [id.]. Daniel Barenboim.

Piano sonatas Nos 16–32.
(*) DG Dig. **413 766-2 (6) [id.]. Daniel Barenboim.

With eleven hours of music on eleven CDs, the Brendel cycle makes full use of the extra convenience of the new medium, not just in playing-length, but in ease of use, when any movement can be selected more readily than was ever the case with LP. The new format actually encourages more listening, and though the CD transfers bring out the discrepancies between different recordings made between 1970 and 1977, tape-hiss is minimal and the sound good with plenty of percussive bite. As to the performances, though they lack some of the fighting spontaneity of the young Brendel many years ago on Turnabout, they have a dark, thoughtful, deeply satisfying quality that consistently gives pleasure.

Spontaneity and electricity, extremes of expression in dynamic, tempo and phrasing as well as mood, mark Barenboim's DG cycle, as they did his much earlier one for HMV. Some of his more extreme readings – such as the sleep-walking tempo for the finale of the *Waldstein* – have been modified to fall short of provocation or eccentricity. This time spontaneity is even more evident, though that means he has a tendency at times to rush his fences, particularly in the early sonatas, giving a hint of breathlessness to already fast speeds. That is exceptional, and so is the hint of technical stress. The first movement of the *Appassionata* is given with all his old flair, even more a vehicle for display thanks to dramatic extremes of light and dark. Conversely, the second and third movements are now plainer and simpler. The plainness in the first movement of the *Moonlight* is disappointing, however, less poetic, with little veiled tone; but the light, flowing finale of the *Tempest*, Op. 31 No. 2, is now more magically Mendelssohnian than ever. All three movements of the *Waldstein* this time are more lyrical, and that applies in the late sonatas too, not just in slow movements but equally strikingly in the great fugal movements, where inner parts are brought out more clearly and warmly. Only in the final Adagio variations of Op. 111 does a hint of self-consciousness develop, thanks to agogic hesitations at a tempo even slower than before. The lyrical opening movement of Op. 101 in A is delectably done, flowing and simple. The role of such a cycle as this is not to set Barenboim's readings as though in amber, fixed for ever, but to act more nearly as a living document of a performer at a particular point in his career. The sound is warm and spacious, much more consistent than before. The CD transfers – taking the sonatas in consecutive order but on one more CD than Brendel's rival set – come in two separate boxes.

Piano sonatas Nos 1 in F min., Op. 2/1; 22 in F, Op. 54; 23 (Appassionata).
(*) Nimbus Dig. **NI 5050 [id.]. Bernard Roberts.

Piano sonatas Nos 2 in A, Op. 2/2; 24 in F sharp, Op. 78; 28 in A, Op. 101.
(*) Nimbus Dig. **NI 5051 [id.]. Bernard Roberts.

Piano sonatas Nos 3 in C, Op. 2/3; 19 in G min., Op. 49/1; 21 in C (Waldstein).
(*) Nimbus Dig. **NI 5052 [id.]. Bernard Roberts.

Piano sonatas Nos 4 in E flat, Op. 7; 10 in G, Op. 14/2; 26 (Les Adieux).
(*) Nimbus Dig. **NI 5053 [id.]. Bernard Roberts.

Piano sonatas Nos 5 in C min.; 6 in F; 7 in D, Op. 10/1–3.
(*) Nimbus Dig. **NI 5054 [id.]. Bernard Roberts.

Piano sonatas Nos 11 in B flat, Op. 22; 15 (Pastoral); 20 in G, Op. 49/2.
(*) Nimbus Dig. **NI 5055 [id.]. Bernard Roberts.

Bernard Roberts's series for Nimbus makes up his second complete sonata cycle for that company. The first set was in analogue sound, recorded by the direct-to-disc method, an amazing achievement when no editing whatever was possible. The performances had an inspired directness, with few if any distracting idiosyncrasies but with fine concentration. Roberts's return to the Nimbus studios brings performances of comparable directness and intensity. The sound on CD is even more vivid, a full-bodied recording well focused in a helpful but fairly intimate setting, while Roberts in his performances is a degree freer in his expression, having in the meanwhile given a number of Beethoven cycles in concert. Again these are undistracting readings, reflecting Roberts's dedication as a chamber-music pianist intent on presenting the composer's argument as clearly as possible, not drawing attention to himself. Unlike the earlier cycle, this one is appearing on separate discs, most of them presenting a varied range of sonatas, early, middle and late. That allows one to appreciate the pianist's consistency, when his treatment has an element of toughness even in the early sonatas, and the mature sonatas are marked by rugged power, with Roberts's virtuosity given full rein, as in the finale of the *Appassionata.* That favourite comes on the first disc of the series, coupled with the very first sonata of all and the little Op. 54. The second, third and fourth discs similarly lead in well-balanced programmes to one of the great middle or late sonatas. The fifth disc groups together the three Op. 10 sonatas, including the magnificent *D major*, Op. 10, No. 3, and the sixth has two of the most inspired of the early sonatas, Op. 22 and Op. 28 (*Pastoral*) as well as the sonatina-like Op. 49, No. 2. In sound, this is the finest Beethoven sonata-cycle yet on CD.

Piano sonatas Nos 2 in A, Op. 2/2; 4 in E flat, Op. 7.
*** DG Dig. **415 481-2** [id.]. Emil Gilels.

Gilels's magisterial Beethoven sonatas are one of the glories of the catalogue, and his leonine strength was tempered by a delicacy and poetry that few matched and none have surpassed. What marked Gilels off from other pianists was not just his aristocratic polish (Richter and Firkusny have that as well) or his commanding virtuosity, which in his case was a vehicle for deep musical insights, but his very special and totally individual tonal world. His accounts of the *A major Sonata* and the *E flat*, Op. 7, are as masterly as one expects and silence criticism. The recording is clear and well lit in the DG fashion, and does not perhaps do the fullest justice to the sound he produced in the concert hall; but, given such playing, there is no need to withhold the strongest recommendation. On CD, the piano image is very tangible.

Piano sonatas Nos 3 in C, Op. 2/3; 8 in C min. (Pathétique).
** Ph. Dig. **420 153-2**; *420 153-4* [id.]. Claudio Arrau.

These sonatas were recorded in 1986 when Arrau was eighty-three. Unlike the recent records of the Beethoven concertos, which sound fresh and youthful, they are a little wanting in the colour and vitality that distinguished his earlier cycle. The opening of Op. 2/3 is just a little stiff; the slow movement, on the other hand, is full of repose and thoughtfulness. Both performances are beautifully recorded; admirers of this great artist will want his latest thoughts – and the disc is worth considering for the sake of the slow movement of Op. 2/3. The chrome cassette transfer is faithful.

Piano sonatas Nos 3 in C, Op. 2/3; 21 (Waldstein), Op. 109.
** HMV Dig. **CDC7 47886-2**. Maria Tipo (piano).

There is much to enjoy in these musical performances by the Italian pianist and teacher, Maria Tipo. She has capable and sensitive fingers, a keen musical imagination and much warmth. There are moments of self-indulgence in the first movement of Op. 109 and, though there are more searching accounts of the variations, she produces consistent beauty of sound. There is much both to admire and to like in the first movement of the *Waldstein*; but it does perhaps lack a sense of scale: her slow movement is not searching enough (and is just a shade too fast), while the finale is rather wayward. Good performances that perhaps fall short of stature but which are far from inconsiderable, and which are very decently recorded.

Piano sonatas Nos 4 in E flat, Op. 7; 7 in D, Op. 10/3.
** Ph. Dig. **420 820-2**; *420 820-4* [id.]. Claudio Arrau.

While it is obvious that the great Chilean pianist is not in his youthful prime (the opening movement of Op. 7 is undervitalized), there are still special insights. The slow movements of both sonatas have wonderful repose and warmth, and the beauty of sonority that has always been a feature of his art remains. The recording is exemplary in timbre, but the instrument is a shade too forward by comparison with Op. 2, No. 3. There is a good tape.

Piano sonatas Nos 5 in C min.; 6 in F; 7 in D, Op. 10/1–3.
*** Decca **417 662-2** [id.]. Vladimir Ashkenazy (piano).

Ashkenazy's Op. 10 have sensibly been grouped together for reissue, and in their digitally remastered form the piano image is very real and tangible. Ashkenazy gives characteristically thoughtful and alert performances. Tempi are not always conventional – that of the finale of Op. 10/2 is questionably fast – but Ashkenazy's freshness of manner silences criticism and the account of the *D major*, Op. 10/3, is masterly. With such excellent sound this is an outstanding issue.

Piano sonatas Nos 5 in C min., Op. 10/1; 10 in G, Op. 14/2; 19 in G min.; 20 in G, Op. 49/1–2.
*** DG Dig. **419 172-2** [id.]. Emil Gilels.

Gilels manages to make one believe that his is exactly the *tempo giusto* even when one feels tempted to question the very deliberate speed he adopts in the slow movement of the *C minor*, Op. 10, No. 1. He can even almost convince one in what at first seems (and is) an eccentricity: the explosive opening to the second group of the first movement, a staccato sforzando sustained on the middle pedal. This really disturbs the balance of the phrase. However, such is his magic that, while under his spell, doubts are silenced. He is in any event never less than illuminating and he is well recorded, too.

Piano sonatas Nos 5 in C min., Op. 10/1; 32 in C min., Op. 111.
** Ph. Dig. **420 154-2**; *420 154-4* [id.]. Claudio Arrau.

This is Arrau's third account of Op. 111 and has many of the insights one would expect from this great artist – and some of the odd quirks too. There is some loss of the youthful power, and he stretches the expansive phrase just before the trill leading into the main allegro. Things almost come to a standstill as he moves into E flat in the exposition – but he somehow succeeds in persuading you that they should! He still produces much (but, alas, not all) of the tonal sound that made his art so distinctive. His earlier record of the companion *C minor Sonata*, Op. 10, No. 1, was more fleet-fingered and fresh. The new recording is natural and truthful and has good presence; the tape is good too but a little bass-orientated.

Piano sonata Nos 7 in D, Op. 10/3; 18 in E flat, Op. 31/3; 15 Variations and fugue on a theme from Prometheus (Eroica variations), Op. 35.
*** DG **423 135-2** [id.]. Emil Gilels.

Gilels's account of the *Eroica variations* is second to none and superior to most: in short, it is masterly – and is very well recorded into the bargain. In the *D major Sonata* he is hardly less impressive, though there are odd mannerisms: the slight hesitation at the beginning of the second group of the first movement is one. Op. 31, No. 3 is distinguished, too, though the recording acoustic is somewhat drier than that of its companions. The disc is the equivalent of three LP sides accommodated on one CD, so it represents good value for money. The CD transfer does not represent a spectacular improvement over the excellently recorded black discs, though there is slightly greater range at the extremes of the dynamic spectrum.

Piano sonatas Nos 7 in D, Op. 10/3; 23 in F min. (Appassionata), Op. 57.
*** CBS Dig. **MK 39344**; *IMT 39344* [id.]. Murray Perahia.

Perahia is more than just a fine Mozart interpreter, as this remarkable record shows. Intense, vibrant playing in the *D major Sonata* with great range of colour and depth of thought. The slow movement is a model of sensitivity and keyboard colour, and Perahia's *Appassionata* is a performance of comparable stature. These are among the few interpretations to have appeared in recent years that can be recommended alongside Gilels. The recorded sound is truthful and present. There is a good tape, though not as firmly focused as the CD.

Piano sonatas Nos 8 (Pathétique); 13; 14 (Moonlight).
(*) DG Dig. **400 036-2 [id.]. Emil Gilels.

Piano sonatas Nos 8 in C min. (Pathétique], Op. 13; 14 in C sharp min. (Moonlight), Op. 27/2; 15 in D (Pastoral), Op. 28; 17 in D min. (Tempest), Op. 31/2.
(B) **(*) DG Dig. *419 826-4* [id.]. Emil Gilels (piano).

Gilels is served by good sound and, as always, his performances leave the overriding impression of wisdom. Yet this compact disc, coupling the two Op. 27 sonatas and the *Pathétique*, does not quite rank among his very best (such as the *Waldstein* and Op. 101). The opening movement of the *Moonlight* is wonderfully serene, and there are many felicities. But the first movement of the *E flat Sonata* is strangely reserved (the wonderful change to C major so subtly illuminated by Schnabel goes relatively unremarked here), as if Gilels feared the charge of self-indulgence or out-of-period sentiment. However, such are the strengths of this playing that few will quarrel with the magnificence of his conceptions of all three pieces. The digital recording is very lifelike on the compact disc: the background silence benefits the opening of the *Moonlight* very strikingly. This would have earned a technical accolade, were not the balance so close (which brings hardness on fortissimos), but even so the presence of the piano is remarkable. Readers will note that two of these performances are also available on a truthfully engineered chrome Pocket Music tape which also includes the *Pastoral* and *Tempest sonatas*, see below. The value is obvious, with four named sonatas offered at a fraction of the cost of the two equivalent compact discs, so that listeners will feel able to accept the close balance. The transfer level is high.

Piano sonatas Nos 8 (Pathétique); 14 (Moonlight); 15 (Pastoral); 24 in F sharp, Op. 78.
(M) *** DG **415 834-2**; *415 834-4* [id.]. Wilhelm Kempff.

Piano sonatas Nos 8 (Pathétique); 14 (Moonlight); 15 (Pastoral); 23 (Appassionata); 26 (Les Adieux).
(B) *** DG Walkman *413 435-4* [id.]. Wilhelm Kempff.

Piano sonatas Nos 8 (Pathétique), 14 (Moonlight); 17 in D min. (Tempest), Op. 31/2; 21 in C (Waldstein), Op. 53; 23 in F min. (Appassionata). Op. 57; 26 in E flat (Les Adieux), Op. 81a.
(M) *** DG *414 519-4* (2) [id.]. Wilhelm Kempff.

Piano sonatas Nos 8 (Pathétique); 14 (Moonlight); 21 (Waldstein); 26 (Les Adieux).
(B) **(*) HMV *TCC2-POR 54285*. Daniel Barenboim.

Kempff's masterly recordings show so well his ability to rethink Beethoven's music within the recording studio. Everything he does has his individual stamp, and above all he never fails to convey the deep intensity of a master in communion with Beethoven. The Walkman collection of five favourite named sonatas is an obvious bargain, yet the two-cassette set offers also the *Waldstein*, one of Kempff's most magical performances. However, the *Waldstein* is also available on Walkman, coupled with the *Third* and *Fourth Piano Concertos* (see above). The Galleria collection of four sonatas has been digitally remastered and the piano quality has undoubtedly gained in firmness.

Barenboim's performances, taken from his earlier HMV cycle, combine impetuosity with a confident control of line. There is a rhapsodic feel to his approach which is often very convincing. In his hands *Les Adieux* is made to sound much stronger than usual, but the *Waldstein* is more controversial in its choice of excessively slow tempi in the outer movements. The sound is full and clear.

Piano sonatas Nos 8 (Pathétique); 14 (Moonlight); 23 (Appassionata).
*** Decca **410 260-2** [id.]. Vladimir Ashkenazy.

*** HMV **CDC7 47345-2** [id.]; (M) *EG 290857-4* [Ang. *4AE 34414*]. Daniel Barenboim.
*** Ph. **411 470-2** [id.]. Alfred Brendel.
(*) DG Dig. **419 602-2; *419 602-4* [id.]. Daniel Barenboim.

For those wanting a compact disc of the three most popular named sonatas, Ashkenazy's readings will be found very satisfactory. The *Pathétique* is perhaps slightly understated for so ebulliently youthful a work, with the finale unusually gentle; nevertheless the performance conveys the underlying power. The *Moonlight* is generally successful, and the *Appassionata* is admirable. He is well served by the engineers and the analogue recordings are very well transferred to CD. However, the *Moonlight* and the *Appassionata* are also available at mid-price – see below.

Barenboim's HMV triptych comes from his complete set recorded in the late 1960s and it is altogether preferable, even on grounds of recording, to his later digital DG record where, although the *Appassionata* has real panache, the *Moonlight* is disappointing. The HMV performances consistently show the sort of inspiration he can display. The first movement of the *Pathétique*, for example, taken rather fast, has a natural wildness about it but, like the rhapsodic approach to the first movement of the *Appassionata*, is very compelling; again the slow speed for the central variations of the *Appassionata* brings a simple natural intensity of the kind which illuminates the opening of the *Moonlight sonata*. The piano sound is first class, with excellent presence and sonority, and one wishes this CD had been issued on EMI's mid-priced Studio label; as it is, the equally excellent cassette seems a much better investment at about a third of the price of the compact disc. It has some background noise certainly, but the CD is not absolutely silent.

Brendel's performances, too, are undoubtedly impressive, the *Moonlight* beautifully played, the others strong and thoughtful, yet not lacking power. The sound is full-bodied and clear, although plainly from an analogue source.

Piano sonata No. 11 in B flat, Op. 22; Kurfürsten sonatas: in E flat; in F min., WoO 47/1 & 2.
*** DG Dig. **419 173-2** [id.]. Emil Gilels.

Gilels couples the *B flat Sonata*, Op. 22, with the insubstantial *Kurfürsten sonatas* written for the Elector (Kurfürsten) of Cologne, composed when Beethoven was a boy of thirteen. They are not important pieces, but the great Russian pianist makes much of them. His Op. 22 is one of the finest in the catalogue, with a marvellously eloquent slow movement.

Piano sonatas Nos 13 in E flat, Op. 27/1; 15 (Pastoral); 21 (Waldstein).
*** DG Dig. **423 577-2** [id.]. Daniel Barenboim.

This triptych shows Barenboim at his best, with the lyrical flow in both the *Waldstein* and the *Pastoral* as evident as the undoubted spontaneity of the music making. Good recording.

Piano sonatas Nos 14 (Moonlight); 21 (Waldstein); 23 (Appassionata).
(M) *** Decca **417 732-2** [id.]. Vladimir Ashkenazy.

Piano sonatas Nos 14 (Moonlight); 21 (Waldstein); 26 (Les Adieux), Op. 81a.
(M) *** Decca *417 667-4* [id.]. Vladimir Ashkenazy.

An excellent mid-priced grouping of three popular sonatas. The opening of the *Moonlight* is thoughtful and poised. In this work the 1979 recording seems a little dry in its remastered form; in both the *Waldstein* and the *Appassionata* the piano's middle range is warmer in timbre. But all three recordings are given fine presence on CD. The *Waldstein* (1975) is splendidly structured and the *Appassionata* (1973) superb, although those who feel strongly about matters of tempo may well find Ashkenazy a little too free in the first movement. The cassette offers *Les Adieux* instead of the *Appassionata*, another fine performance. This costs less than the CD and is very well engineered, with the piano image most naturally projected.

Piano sonatas Nos 15 in D (Pastoral), Op. 28; 17 in D min. (Tempest), Op. 31/2.
(*) DG Dig. **419 161-2 [id.]. Emil Gilels.

This is a recoupling for CD, but in both recordings the DG engineers elect for a very close balance. It is as if one is observing the instrument from the vantage point of the keyboard itself, or at least very near it. Although the CD sounds slightly mellower than the original LP, the percussive qualities remain. The *Pastoral* is a strange performance – a laboured, almost hectoring first movement, very deliberate in tempo and character, with little sense of flow and only occasional glimpses of the wisdom and humanity one associates with this great artist. The *Tempest sonata*, Op. 31, No. 2, is another matter; this performance has excited universal acclaim, and rightly so. Readers will note that these same performances are also on a bargain Pocket Music tape coupled with Gilels's *Moonlight* and *Pathétique* recordings – see above. The cost of the tape is about a sixth of the combined price of the two CDs!

Piano sonatas Nos 16 in G; 17 in D min. (Tempest); 18 in E flat, Op. 31/1–3.
*** Decca **417 663-2** [id.]. Vladimir Ashkenazy (piano).

The CD grouping of the Op. 31 sonatas is highly successful. The *D minor* and *E flat Sonatas* were recorded in Kingsway Hall and the timbre is slightly softer grained than the *G major*, made in All Saint's Church, Petersham; but in all three cases the digital remastering has brought sound of the highest quality, with the image believable and not too forward. The performances are among the best of Ashkenazy's Beethoven cycle. He brings concentration of mind, together with a spontaneity of feeling. The command of keyboard colour is, as always, impressive and, in terms of both dramatic tension and the sense of architecture, these are thoroughly satisfying performances. The recordings date from 1976/7.

Piano sonatas Nos 17 in D min., Op. 31/2; 18 in E flat, Op. 31/3.
(*) Ph. **420 088-2 [id.]. Clara Haskil.

Clara Haskil recorded these performances in Switzerland in 1960, not long before her death, and they are wonderfully musical and authoritative performances. The studio in which they were recorded is obviously rather small and the sound less well-ventilated than is desirable. As a result, the piano is just a little forward in focus, but this does not prevent Haskil's fine pianissimo (in the recitative that prefaces the restatement of the first movement of Op. 31/2) registering effectively. Distinguished music-making.

Piano sonatas Nos 17 in D min., Op. 31/2; 18 in E flat, Op. 31/3; 26 in E flat (Les Adieux).
*** CBS Dig. **MK 42319**; *IMT 42319* [id.]. Murray Perahia.

Wonderfully concentrated performances which leave no doubt (not that by now there is any) that Perahia is as great an interpreter of Beethoven as he is of Mozart and Schubert. The *D minor*, Op. 31, No. 2, is magisterial in its control and command of poetic feeling: the finest since Solomon. There has been criticism of the recording, that it does not do full justice to Perahia's magical pianissimo tone, but this is only partly justified, though the *E flat Sonata* (*Les Adieux*), with its more distant placing and warmer acoustic, is undoubtedly finer. All these readings have the blend of authority, finesse and poetry that distinguish this great artist at his best. There is a good tape, although it is more restricted in upper range than the CD.

Piano sonatas Nos 17 in D min.; 29 (Hammerklavier), Op. 106.
(M) *** DG **419 857-2**; *419 857-4* [id.]. Wilhelm Kempff.

Kempff's *Hammerklavier* is relatively controversial but, both here and in the *Tempest sonata*, he has revelations to offer. The *Hammerklavier* performance is discussed below with his accounts of other late sonatas. The present Galleria issue has been remastered, and the sound is clean and clear.

Piano sonatas Nos 19–20, Op. 49/1–2; 21 (Waldstein); 23 (Appassionata); 26 (Les Adieux).
(B) *** DG Dig. *423 257-4* [id.]. Daniel Barenboim.

These performances all come from Barenboim's newest digital series, and at bargain price this Pocket Music tape is excellent value. The *Waldstein* has less controversial tempi than in his earlier HMV account, while the *Appassionata* has plenty of drama and panache. Good sound, clear and realistic.

Piano sonatas Nos 21 in C (Waldstein); 23 in F min. (Appassionata), Op. 57; 26 in E flat (Les Adieux), Op. 81a.
❀ *** DG **419 162-2** [id.]. Emil Gilels.
*** HMV Dig. **CDC7 49330-2** [id.]. Melvyn Tan (fortepiano).
(M) *** DG **419 053-2**; *419 053-4* [id.]. Wilhelm Kempff.

This recoupling for CD offers three of Gilels's finest analogue recordings dating from 1972-5. The piano is believably present, but much less closely observed than in his later digital recordings, to great advantage. The *Waldstein* sounds particularly well and only a hint of hardness creeps into fortissimos in Opp. 57 and 81a. The account of the *Appassionata* has previously been hailed by us as among the finest ever made, and much the same must be said of the *Waldstein*. It has a technical perfection denied even to Schnabel, and though in the slow movement Schnabel found special depths, Gilels is hardly less searching and profound. Moreover, Gilels's fastidiously sensitive yet commanding *Les Adieux* is also one of the most impressive ever committed to disc. These are all performances to relish, to study and to keep for special occasions.

Melvyn Tan offers a CD for those who are unconverted to the fortepiano and find its exponents tame. Tan, who hails from Singapore, has a strong musical personality and attacks his instrument with tremendous spirit and flair; every phrase lives and he is not afraid to present the widest dynamic spectrum and expressive range. In all three sonatas he exhibits consummate artistry and real temperament and fire. Nor is there any want of poetic feeling. He plays on a copy by Derek Adlam of a Streicher (1814), an instrument for which Beethoven himself expressed a strong preference. The EMI recording is excellent: in short, an outstanding issue.

Kempff's individuality in Beethoven is again established here. The *Appassionata* is characteristically clear, classically straight in the same way that the *Waldstein* is cooler and fresher than usual with a wonderful classical purity in the rippling quavers. *Les Adieux*, like the *Appassionata*, may be less weightily dramatic than in other readings, but the concentration is irresistible. The digital remastering has brought clean sound to match, perhaps not ideally sonorous, but with the piano image given believable presence, although on CD there is an added hardness on *fortissimos*.

Piano sonatas Nos 21 in C (Waldstein); Op. 53; 26 in E flat (Les Adieux), Op. 81a; 27 in E min., Op 90.
*** Decca **414 630-2** [id.]. Vladimir Ashkenazy.

Taking a broadly lyrical view, Ashkenazy gives a deeply satisfying reading of the *Waldstein sonata*. His degree of restraint and his occasional hesitations intensify his thoughtful approach, while never interrupting the broader span of argument. *Les Adieux* brings a vehement first movement and memorable concentration, while the account of the *E minor Sonata*, Op. 90, is masterly. The analogue recordings are first class and sound full, firm and clear in their CD transfer. There is slight variation in quality between the three works, with No. 27 in E minor (recorded in 1981, whereas the other two date from 1975) slightly fuller in timbre. Readers will note that Ashkenazy's *Waldstein* is also available on mid-priced CD (coupled with the *Moonlight* and the *Appassionata*) – see above.

Piano sonata No. 23 in F min. (*Appassionata*), *Op. 57.*
(M) *** RCA **GD 86518**; *GK 86518* [**RCA 6518-2-RG**]. Sviatoslav Richter – BRAHMS: *Piano concerto No. 2.****

Richter's thrilling 1960 *Appassionata* is a superb example of a studio recording sounding like a live performance, with the wide dynamic range bringing out both the drama and passion of this boldly contrasted sonata. Yet Richter's *piano* and *mezzo forte* playing is no less telling; the sonorous colour of the *Andante* is memorable; and the reading is deeply thoughtful as well as compellingly brilliant. This is clear from the overall control of the first movement after its deliberation at the opening. Some might feel that Richter goes over the top in the coda of the finale but the fervour is unmistakable, and this is an undeniably great interpretation. The recording brings out the percussive qualities of Richter's playing and the hardness of timbre, at times, is perhaps not entirely the fault of the engineers. But the remastering has made the most of the possibilities of the master-tape. The coupling of an equally memorable account of Brahms's *Second Concerto* makes this a mid-priced CD difficult to resist.

Piano sonatas Nos 24 in F sharp, Op. 78; 29 in B flat (*Hammerklavier*), *Op. 106.*
(*) Ph. **412 723-2; *412 723-4* [id.]. Alfred Brendel.

Piano sonatas Nos 26 (*Les Adieux*); *29 in B flat* (*Hammerklavier*), *Op. 106.*
(M) **(*) Ph. *412 918-4*. Alfred Brendel.

Piano sonata No. 29 (*Hammerklavier*).
*** DG Dig. **410 527-2** [id.]. Emil Gilels.

Gilels's *Hammerklavier* is a performance of supreme integrity, Olympian, titanic, subtle, imperious, one of the finest accounts ever recorded. Speeds for the outer movements are surprisingly spacious and relaxed, with clarity of texture and refinement of detail brought out. Yet the concentration brings the most powerful impact – not just in those movements but in all four. The recording is close and bright and harder than ideal: hearing Gilels play the work in London in 1984 left one in no doubt that there is more to the sound he produced in real life than the overlit quality the DG engineers have achieved.

Brendel's 1972 LP recording of the *Hammerklavier* for Philips came early in his re-recording of the whole Beethoven sonata cycle, and there are still signs of a self-consciousness which make it less powerful than his earlier recording for Vox [Turnabout 34392]. Yet, thanks to fine recording, he conveys a deep, hushed concentration in the slow movement. Though this may not be quite worthy of a pianist who has become one of the great visionary Beethovenians of our time, it remains a fine version, more attractively coupled than on its first issue, with *Les Adieux*. The full-bodied cassette is of Philips's best quality.

The CD coupling of the *Hammerklavier* and Opus 78 comes not from Brendel's complete sonata cycle but from a live recording made at the Queen Elizabeth Hall in London a decade later. Though there is greater urgency and dramatic tension in the allegro movements, the great *Adagio* of the *Hammerklavier*, intense as it is, lacks the spacious sublimity of the earlier version, taken even more slowly. The audience make their presence felt only between movements and the recording, especially on CD, is very believable. The atmospheric ambience of the hall is well caught and the piano image is not too forward. There is an excellent chrome cassette.

Piano sonatas Nos 28 in A, Op. 101; 29 (Hammerklavier); 30 in E, Op. 109; 31 in A flat, Op. 110; 32 in C min., Op. 111.
*** Decca **417 150-2** (2) [id.]. Vladimir Ashkenazy.
(M) *** DG *419 102-4* (2) [id.]. Wilhelm Kempff.
(*) DG **419 199-2 (2) [id.]. Maurizio Pollini.

Distinguished performances on Decca, as one would expect, and an impressive sense of repose in the slow movement of Op. 109, while the account of No. 28 is searching and masterly. This was Ashkenazy's second recording of the *Hammerklavier*, the performance fresher, more spontaneous than the earlier version, but the total experience is less than monumental. The last two sonatas are played with a depth and spontaneity which put them among the finest available. In the slow movement of Op. 111 Ashkenazy matches the concentration of the slowest possible speed which marks out the reading of his friend Barenboim, but there is an extra detachment. If anything, the interpretation of Op. 110 is even more remarkable, consistently revealing. The analogue recordings date from between 1974 and 1982, and the remastering is very successful indeed. The sound-quality is very natural and the balance excellent, and background noise is virtually banished.

Kempff's *Hammerklavier* performance represents his interpretative approach to Beethoven at its most extreme and therefore controversial. Here his preference for measured allegros and fastish andantes gives a different weighting to movements from the usual, but in each the concentration of the playing is inescapable. If the slow movement flows more quickly than is common, there is a thoughtfulness of utterance which gives it profundity, while in the finale Kempff's clarity of fingerwork brings a new freshness that lacks nothing in excitement. The reading of Op. 109 sets the style for Kempff's other performances of the late sonatas, intense in its control of structure but with a feeling of rhapsodic freedom too, of new visions emerging. The second movement of Op. 110 is not as fast as it might be, but the result is cleaner for that, and in typical Kempff style the great *Arietta* of Op. 111 is taken at a flowing tempo, not nearly so slowly as with many a recorded rival. These are all great performances; and the remastered recording is clean and firm.

Pollini's set (which on LP originally included No. 27) won the 1977 *Gramophone* Critics' award for instrumental music, and it contains playing of the highest order of mastery. Joan Chissell spoke of the 'noble purity' of these performances, and that telling phrase aptly sums them up, if also hinting perhaps at a missing dimension, which the CD transfer seems to emphasize. The sound has great presence but on the first disc there is hardness to the timbre in Opus 101 which becomes almost brittle in the fortissimos of the *Hammerklavier* with an adverse effect on the music making. Pollini's *Hammerklavier* is undoubtedly eloquent and so is Op. 111 which has a peerless authority and power. However, the slow movement of Op. 110 may be a trifle fast for some tastes, and in the A major work Gilels has greater poetry and humanity. The second disc brings a close balance to Opp. 109 and 110 but the recordings seem fractionally mellower, although a touch of hardness comes back in Op. 111.

Piano sonatas Nos 30 in E, Op. 109; 31 in A flat, Op. 110.
*** DG Dig. **419 174-2** [id.]. Emil Gilels.

The opening movement of Op. 110 is enormously spacious and its breadth of vision (and tempo) can only be called Olympian. Few pianists had so refined a tonal palette or distinctive a sound-world as did Gilels, though in this respect he is austere and restrained, not seducing us with irrelevant tonal beauties. Both sonatas are given performances of stature that seek out their profoundest truths. Even when Gilels storms the greatest heights in the closing fugue of

Op. 110, no fortissimo ever sounds percussive or strained. In any pantheon these performances rank alongside Schnabel, Solomon and, in recent years, Stephen Bishop-Kovacevich. DG seem to have found a more truthful sound than they did for his *Moonlight* and *Pathétique* which, though realistic, were very closely balanced.

Piano sonata No. 31 in A flat, Op. 110.
(*) DG **413 446-2 [id.]. Maurizio Pollini – *Piano concerto No. 3.***
(*) Ph. **412 789-2 [id.]. Alfred Brendel – *Piano concerto No. 5.**(*)

Both Pollini's and Brendel's performances are fill-ups for less successful concerto recordings. The Pollini account originates from his earlier set of the late sonatas in which his sober manners are more apt than in the concerto. Purity is the keynote here, rather than mystery or meditation. A good CD transfer from an analogue original.

Having the *Sonata*, Op. 110, as fill up to the *Emperor concerto* is generous. Brendel's account comes from a 1975 analogue recording made in the studio, and is much preferable to the live recording for the concerto, with mellow but realistic piano sound and little perceptible tape-hiss. The thoughtfulness of the reading is most compelling.

Piano sonatas Nos 31 in A flat, Op. 110; 32 in C min., Op. 111.
(*) DG Dig. **423 371-2 [id.]. Daniel Barenboim.

Though Barenboim's readings of the last two sonatas – taken from his DG cycle of all 32 – are not as spaciously spontaneous-sounding as they were in his earlier series for EMI, they make a splendid coupling, deeply thoughtful and strongly expressed.

Piano sonata No. 32, Op. 111.
(*) DG Dig. **410 520-2 [id.]. Ivo Pogorelich – SCHUMANN: *Études symphoniques* etc.*(*)

Ivo Pogorelich produces consistent beauty of tone throughout the sonata, and his account of this masterpiece contains many felicities. It is imposing piano playing and impressive music-making. At times he seems to view Beethoven through Lisztian eyes, but there is much that is powerful here. Pogorelich has a strong personality and will provoke equally strong reactions. There are self-indulgent touches here and there, but also moments of illumination. The compact disc is admirably clear and realistically balanced, but the clarity of the recording and its background silence tend to emphasize the slightly dry bass quality.

Miscellaneous piano music

6 Bagatelles, Op. 126; 6 Ecossaises, WoO 83; Für Elise, WoO 59; 15 Variations and fugue on a theme from Prometheus (Eroica variations), Op. 35.
*** Ph. **412 227-2**; *412 227-4* [id.]. Alfred Brendel.

Brendel may lack some of the sheer bravura of his own early playing in this collection of shorter pieces, but his consistent thoughtfulness and imagination bring out the truly Beethovenian qualities of even the most trivial pieces. The *Eroica variations*, not as flamboyant as with some, plainly point to the magnificence of their culminating development in the *Eroica* finale. Excellent recording, with the CD outstandingly realistic. The cassette is good too, but lacks the extra degree of presence of the compact disc.

Bagatelles, Op. 26; Polonaise in C, Op. 89; Variations and fugue on a theme from Prometheus (Eroica variations), Op. 35.
*** Nimbus Dig. **NIM 5017** [id.]. Bernard Roberts.

Bernard Roberts gives a characteristically fresh and forthright reading of the *Eroica variations*, recorded in exceptionally vivid sound. He may not have quite the dash of Brendel, but the crispness and clarity of his playing are most refreshing. The shorter pieces bring performances even more intense, with the *Bagatelles* for all their brevity given last-period intensity.

33 Variations on a Waltz by Diabelli, Op. 120.
(*) Ph. **416 295-2; *416 295-4* [id.]. Claudio Arrau.

Arrau in his eighties demonstrates formidable virtuosity in tackling this Everest of the keyboard, even if at times the strain shows. What matters is the concentration of his playing, his ability to hold the whole massive structure together, whatever the problems of detail, full of new insights. The sound is very immediate, perhaps too much so for such a work, with a touch of bass-heaviness, emphasized on the cassette, which consequently is less clear and less realistic.

VOCAL MUSIC

An die ferne Geliebte, Op. 98. Lieder: *Adelaide; L'amant impaziente; Es war einmal ein König; In questa tomba oscura; Maigesang; Zartliche Liebe.*
(*) DG **415 189-2 [id.]. Dietrich Fischer-Dieskau, Joerg Demus – BRAHMS: *Lieder.***(*)

Recorded in 1966, Fischer-Dieskau's DG Beethoven selection finds him at his vocal peak, and though Demus's accompaniment is not as imaginative as the singer received in other versions of these songs, Fischer-Dieskau's individuality is as positive as ever, with detail touched in as with no one else. The coupling with the Brahms is very generous, adding up to over seventy minutes of music, with transfers hardly betraying the age of the recording.

An die ferne Geliebte, Op. 98. Lieder: *Adelaide; Andenken; An die Hoffnung; Aus Goethes Faust (Song of the flea); Busslied; Ich liebe dich; Der Kuss; Mailied; Neue Liebe; Resignation; Der Wachtelschlag; Der Zufriedene.*
(*) Amon Ra **CDSAR 15. Ian Partridge, Richard Burnett.

Partridge, accompanied on an 1800 fortepiano, gives delightful performances of a wide-ranging and generous collection of Beethoven songs, including the song-cycle *An die ferne Geliebte*. The honeyed tones of Partridge's tenor and his finely detailed feeling for words come over well – particularly suited to such soaring lyrical songs as *Adelaide* and *An die Hoffnung*. The twangy fortepiano is recorded much more dully.

Choral fantasia in C, Op. 80.
*** Capriccio Dig. **10 150**; *CC 27 148* [id.]. Rösel, Leipzig R Ch., Dresden PO, Kegel – *Triple concerto.****
(*) Telarc Dig. **CD 80063 [id.]. Serkin, Boston Ch. & SO, Ozawa – *Piano concerto No. 3.***(*)

With four excellent vocal soloists from the chorus and a splendid contribution from the pianist, Peter Rösel, Hubert Kegel shapes a highly convincing account of Beethoven's *Choral fantasia*, clearly looking ahead to the *Choral symphony* in the closing pages, with the chorus making a thrilling climax. The recording is first rate, very well balanced and vivid in both formats.

As a fill-up for Serkin's version of the *Third Piano concerto*, the *Choral fantasia* is most welcome, even though the long opening solo lacks something in brio, the necessary evocation of Beethoven himself improvising. But Ozawa draws committed performances from chorus and orchestra, though vocal balances are odd, with the chorus close and the soloists rather distant in a reverberant acoustic.

The famous Brendel/Haitink version from the late 1970s is available on CD coupled with the *Emperor Concerto* (see above).

Christus am Ölberge, Op. 85.
(*) HM **HMC 905181; *HMC 40 5181* [id.]. Pick-Hieronimi, Anderson, Von Halem, Ch. & O Nat. de Lyon, Baudo.

With Beethoven depicting Christ (James Anderson, tenor) as another Florestan, it is appropriate that Monica Pick-Hieronimi, a singer of some power, should bring Leonore-like qualities to her role as Seraph. This oratorio is a stronger and more interesting work than has often been thought. Baudo directs an energetic and lively account of it which, if lacking the utmost refinement of detail, generates urgency and breadth in the fine closing section. The chorus sings vividly and the Lyon orchestra is committed too in a recording which projects well and is convincingly balanced. There is an excellent matching cassette.

Egmont: Overture and incidental music, Op. 84.
(*) DG **419 624-2 [id.]. Janowitz, Schellow, BPO, Karajan – *Wellington's Victory; Marches.***

Karajan's abridged recording of *Egmont* dates from 1969 and was originally part of DG's Beethoven Edition. There is no lack of drama and Gundula Janowitz sings the two Lieder impressively; Erich Schellow's narration is reduced to a single melodrama before the finale. The sound is clear and vivid but ideally needs more sonority. The couplings too are uninspiring.

Folksong arrangements: Again my love; Bonnie laddie; The deserter; Helpless woman; Judy lovely; March Megan; Oh! who, my dear Dermot, The parting kiss, The sweetest lad was Jamie.
*** HMV Dig. **CDC7 47420-2** [id.]; *EL 270323-4* [Ang. *4DS 37352*]. Robert White, Sanders, Peskanov, Rosen, Wilson – WEBER: *Folksong arrangements.****

Robert White follows up the success of his earlier RCA disc of Beethoven settings of folksongs with another delightful and often unusual collection. Beethoven may not even have seen the words – the publisher George Thomson often fitted new words to old tunes – but the charm and imagination of each one are delightful. In *Helpless woman* we even have a Beethoven setting of a Robert Burns poem. White's heady tenor and sharply expressive delivery are ideally suited to this music, and he is warmly accompanied by his instrumental ensemble. Warm recording, but with no lack of presence.

(i) *Mass in C, Op. 86; Meeresstille und glückliche Fahrt (Calm sea and a prosperous voyage), Op. 112.*
(*) Decca Dig. **417 563-2; *417 563-4* [id.]. (i) Dunn, Zimmermann, Beccaria, Krause; Berlin RIAS Chamber Ch. & RSO, Chailly.

Beethoven's *Mass in C* has been consistently underrated. It was designed as a successor to the late great Haydn masses, like them being commissioned for the Princess Esterházy's name-day. The present performance is on the right expansive scale; the singing of the Berlin RIAS Chorus has vigour and exuberance, yet conveys the full range of emotions expressed in the *Kyrie* and *Sanctus*. The solo team are also very good although the tenor, Bruno Beccaria, is too histrionically operatic in style. The recording has the widest dynamic range, and this adds drama to the fine performance of the rare cantata which is used as an encore (it is comparatively short, just over 8′). The balance favours the singers rather than the orchestra, but the recording overall is admirably vivid and there is an excellent tape.

Missa solemnis in D, Op. 123.
*** DG **413 780-2**; *3370 029* (2) [id.]. Moser, Schwarz, Kollo, Moll, Netherlands Ch., Concg. O, Bernstein.
(M) *** HMV **CMS7 69246-2** (2) [id.]; *EX 769246-4*. Janowitz, Baltsa, Schreier, Van Dam, V. Singverein, Philh. O, Karajan.
(*) DG Dig. **419 166-2; *419 166-4* (2) [id.]. Cuberli, Schmidt, Cole, Van Dam, V. Singverein, BPO, Karajan.

Bernstein's DG version with the Concertgebouw was edited together from tapes of two live performances, and the result has a spiritual intensity matched by very few rivals. Edda Moser is not an ideal soprano soloist, but the others are outstanding, and the *Benedictus* is made angelically beautiful by the radiant playing of the Concertgebouw concertmaster, Hermann Krebbers. The recording is a little light in bass, but outstandingly clear as well as atmospheric. The CD clarifies the sound still further, and there is also a good tape set. A firm primary recommendation for Beethoven's choral masterpiece in both formats.

Karajan's earlier EMI version is notably more dedicated and dramatic than his DG digital recording. Though the resonance obscures some detail, the urgency of Karajan's view here is most compelling. There is no feeling that he is skating over the surface of a spiritual experience, and the solo team are excellent. Digitally remastered at mid-price, this makes a fine alternative to Bernstein. There are excellent chrome tapes.

On DG Karajan conducts a powerful reading marked by vivid and forward recording for orchestra and soloists, less satisfactory in rather cloudy choral sound. This was one of Karajan's recordings made in conjunction with a video film, and that brings both gains and losses. The sense of spontaneity, of a massive structure built dramatically with contrasts underlined, makes for extra magnetism, but there are flaws of ensemble and at least one serious flaw of intonation in the singing of Lella Cuberli, otherwise a full, sweet-toned soprano. There is an excellent equivalent chrome-tape set, which matches the CDs closely in quality and is also provided with the CD booklet. But on balance Karajan's earlier Berlin recording for EMI brought a performance even more satisfying, and on CD Bernstein's Concertgebouw performance is more deeply spiritual, generally preferable with sound more spacious and better detailed.

OPERA

Fidelio (complete).
(M) *** HMV **CMS7 69290-2** (2) [id.]; *EX 769290-4*. Dernesch, Vickers, Ridderbusch, Van Dam, Kelemen, German Op. Ch., BPO, Karajan.
*** DG **419 436-2**; (M) *413 288-4* (2) [id.]. Janowitz, Kollo, Sotin, Jungwirth, Fischer-Dieskau, Popp, V. State Op. Ch., VPO, Bernstein.
** Decca **410 227-2** (2) [id.]. Behrens, Hofmann, Sotin, Adam, Ghazarian, Kuebler, Howell, Chicago Ch. & SO, Solti.
*(*) Eurodisc **610 093** (3) [id.]. Altmeyer, Jerusalem, Meven, Wohlers, Adam, Nimsgern, Leipzig & Berlin R. Ch., Leipzig GO, Masur.

Karajan's splendid 1971 recording has been remastered and reissued on a pair of mid-priced CDs, to challenge even the famous Klemperer set which is still awaited on CD. Comparison between Karajan's strong and heroic reading and Klemperer's version is fascinating. Both have very similar merits, underlining the symphonic character of the work with their weight of utterance. Both may miss some of the sparkle of the opening scene, but it is better that seriousness should enter too early than too late. Since seriousness is the keynote, it is rather surprising to find Karajan using bass and baritone soloists lighter than usual. Both the Rocco (Ridderbusch) and the Don Fernando (Van Dam) lack something in resonance in their lower range. Yet they sing dramatically and intelligently, and there is the advantage that the Pizarro of Zoltan Kelemen sounds the more biting and powerful as a result – a fine performance. Jon Vickers as Florestan is if anything even finer than he was for Klemperer; and though Helga Dernesch as Leonore does not have quite the clear-focused mastery of Christa Ludwig in the Klemperer set, this is still a glorious, thrilling performance, outshining lesser rivals than Ludwig. The orchestral playing is superb. There are very good chrome tapes.

Bernstein, as one would expect, directs a reading of *Fidelio* full of dramatic flair. The recording was made in conjunction with live performances by the same cast at the Vienna State Opera, and the atmosphere in the domestic scenes at the start might almost come from a predecessor of the stage musical (compliment intended), with Lucia Popp as Marzelline particularly enchanting. The spoken dialogue is splendidly produced too. The Canon Quartet in Act I has warmth and humanity rather than monumental qualities; and though Bernstein later rises splendidly to the high drama of Act II (the confrontation with Pizarro in the Quartet is as exciting as in Klemperer's classic reading), it remains a drama on a human scale. Gundula Janowitz sings most beautifully as Leonore, shading her phrases in the long opening section of the *Abscheulicher*, coping superbly with the intricacies of the *Allegro* and falling short only at the very end, in a less than triumphant pay-off. Kollo as Florestan is intelligent and musicianly but indulges in too many intrusive aitches, and there is some coarseness of tone. Hans Sotin as Pizarro sings with superb projection, and the size of voice makes up for its not sounding villainous. Manfred Jungwirth makes an engaging Rocco, though his singing is not always perfectly steady. Fischer-Dieskau – once an incomparable Pizarro – here makes a noble Don Fernando in the final scene. On CD the quality of solo singing and the imagination of Bernstein's interpretation make it a strong contender. The digital transfer of an analogue recording is very vivid, even if slight discrepancies of balance come out the more sharply. There are also very good chrome cassettes, which are offered at mid-price, costing about a third as much as the CDs.

Solti's set was the first-ever digital recording of an opera. The sound is full, clean and vividly atmospheric, matched by the conductor's urgent and intense direction. With fine choral singing the ensembles are excellent, but the solo singing is too flawed for comfort. Hildegard Behrens seems ungainly in the great *Abscheulicher*, the voice sounding less beautiful than usual; and both Peter Hofmann as Florestan and Theo Adam as Pizarro too often produce harsh unattractive tone. The compact discs can be recommended strongly for their sound quality, with balances fresh and clear, but in all other respects Bernstein's set is far superior.

Masur's is a solidly reliable reading that fails to rise to the spiritual challenge of *Fidelio*. The orchestra's playing and the choral singing are excellent, recorded vividly if with little atmosphere, and there is some first-rate solo singing, not least from Siegfried Jerusalem as Florestan. Jeannine Altmeyer makes an unmemorable Leonore, and on three CDs the set is extravagantly laid out.

Bellini, Vincenzo (1801–35)

I Capuleti ed i Montecchi (complete).

(*) HMV **CDS7 47388-8 [Ang. **CDCB 47387**] (2). Baltsa, Gruberova, Howell, Raffanti, Tomlinson, ROHCG Ch. and O, Muti.

Muti's set was recorded live at a series of performances at Covent Garden when the production was new, in March 1984. With the Royal Opera House a difficult venue for recording, the sound is hard and close, far less agreeable and well balanced than in the previous EMI version of this opera, recorded in the studio with Beverley Sills and Dame Janet Baker, and now deleted. On the later version, Agnes Baltsa makes a passionately expressive Romeo and Edita Gruberova a Juliet who is not just brilliant in coloratura but sweet and tender, too. It is an unlikely but very successful matching of a Zerbinetta with a Carmen, but it is the masterful conducting of Muti that, more than anything, makes one tolerant of the indifferent sound. If (for good reasons) he has often been considered something of a sprinter in opera, here he is superb with the pacing, balancing fast and incisive choruses against passages of warmth, relaxation and repose. That mastery is especially striking at the end of Act I, when the five principals sing a hushed quintet in which Romeo and Juliet musically reveal their understanding, singing sweetly in thirds. With excellent contributions from the refined tenor, Dano Raffanti (Tebaldo), Gwynne Howell and John Tomlinson, it is a performance to blow the cobwebs off an opera that – even in the earlier recording – seemed one of Bellini's less compelling pieces.

Norma (complete).
(*) Decca Dig. **414 476-2; *414 476-4* (3) [id.]. Sutherland, Pavarotti, Caballé, Ramey, Welsh Nat. Op. Ch. & O, Bonynge.
(***) HMV mono **CDS7 47304-8** [**CDCB 47303**]; (M) *EX 290066-5* (3). Callas, Filippeschi, Stignani, Rossi-Lemeni, La Scala, Milan, Ch. and O, Serafin.
(M) ** RCA **GD 86502** (3) [**RCA 6502-2-RG**]. Caballé, Domingo, Cossotto, Raimondi, Amb. Op. Ch., LPO, Cillario.

It was an amazing achievement for Dame Joan Sutherland, fifty-eight when her second Norma recording was made, to give so commanding a performance of this most taxing of Bellini roles at so late a stage in her career. Few other sopranos could even have attempted it, but, with signs of age undisguisable, it is an amazing achievement considering, not absolute. There are some advantages in the extra weight of voice, and the beat which has latterly developed is at its minimum. The coloratura is still remarkably flexible, but the ornamentation in the great melody of *Casta diva* is flicked off a little too lightly to sound quite secure, and in the cabaletta the tone is masked, not as sparklingly fresh as it used to be. The remarkable conjunction of Sutherland with Pavarotti and Caballé does not always work easily. Though Pavarotti is in some ways the set's greatest strength, easily expressive yet powerful as Pollione, Caballé as Adalgisa seems determined to outdo Sutherland in mooning manner, cooing self-indulgently. The advantage in relation to Sutherland is that, with a lighter voice, she is more convincingly a younger sister, and the extra challenge of the duet, *Mira o Norma*, makes for thrilling results. Equally, in the big Act II Trio the three principals effectively and excitingly sink their stylistic differences. Bonynge, as in the earlier Sutherland recording (which would still make a first choice if it were to appear on CD), paces Bellini well, and the Welsh National Opera Orchestra and Chorus respond most sympathetically. Full, brilliant, well-balanced recording. Unlike the Callas set, which makes the traditional cuts, this is complete.

Though the flatness of the 1954 mono recording is emphasized by the precision of CD, the sense of presence gives wonderful intensity to one of Callas's most powerful performances, recorded at the very peak of her powers, before the upper register acquired its distracting wobble. Balance of soloists is close, and the chorus could hardly be dimmer, but as a perfect re-creation of a classic, irreplaceable recording this is one of the jewels of the CD catalogue. This must not of course be confused with the later stereo recording which Callas made, also with Serafin; for not only is Callas in much fresher, firmer voice with electric intensity in every phrase, the casting of the veteran, Ebe Stignani, as Adalgisa gives Callas a worthily characterful partner in the sisters' duets. Filippeschi is disappointing by comparison, thin-toned and at times strained, and Rossi-Lemeni is not well treated by the microphone either. The tapes cost much less, and the transfer is well managed; however, the accompanying booklet is hardly sophisticated, with a microscopic typeface.

Montserrat Caballé's recording of *Norma*, made in 1972, on paper has an exceptionally strong cast, and there are many vocal delights; but it fails to add up to the sum of its parts.

Reissued in RCA's mid-price CD opera series, it makes a fair enough bargain, particularly for devotees of Caballé. She characteristically exploits a wide range of dynamic, so that the opening of *Casta diva* is very gentle, sweet and reflective, with delicate ornamentation, later expanding strongly and easily – maybe too easily when, even at this key point, the singing does not sound deeply involved, though the cabaletta to the aria is fierily positive. The extremes in the Norma/Adalgisa duet, *Mira o Norma*, bring exaggeratedly drawn-out phrasing in the main part and no delicacy at all in the cabaletta. Cossotto sings strongly at all points, but with diction poor it is a generalized performance. Placido Domingo makes a fine heroic Pollione, but the voice is really too robust for Bellini. The diction is excellent, with intelligent illumination of words, but the duet with Adalgisa finds him growing coarser by association. Cillario's conducting is intelligent but a little underpowered. With recording that still sounds well, this might be worth considering at the price, but hardly matches the finest versions.

I Puritani (complete).

*** Decca **417 588-2** (3). Sutherland, Pavarotti, Ghiaurov, Luccardi, Caminada, Cappuccilli, ROHCG Ch. & O, Bonynge.

(***) HMV mono **CDC7 47308-8** [Ang. **CDCB 47308**]; (M) *EX 290874-5* (3). Callas, di Stefano, Panerei, Rossi-Lemeni, La Scala, Milan, Ch. & O, Serafin.

Ten years after her first recording of *I Puritani*, made in Florence, Dame Joan Sutherland returned to this limpidly lyrical music. 'Opera must make people weep, shudder, die through the singing,' wrote Bellini to his librettist, and this sharply committed performance – much crisper of ensemble than the earlier one, with Bonynge this time adopting a more urgently expressive style – breathes life into what can seem a rather limp story about Cavaliers and Roundheads. Where the earlier set was recorded when Sutherland had adopted a soft-grained style, with consonants largely eliminated and a tendency to lag behind the beat, this time her singing is fresher and brighter. The lovely aria *Qui la voce* is no longer a wordless melisma, and though the great showpiece *Son vergin vezzosa* is now taken dangerously fast, the extra bite and tautness are exhilarating. Pavarotti, possessor of the most radiantly beautiful of tenor voices, shows himself a remarkable Bellini stylist, rarely if ever coarsening a legato line, unlike so many of his Italian colleagues. Ghiaurov and Cappuccilli make up an impressive cast, and the only disappointing contributor is Anita Caminada in the small role of Enrichetta – Queen Henrietta Maria in disguise. Vivid, atmospheric recording enhanced and given added presence by the digital remastering.

Those who complain that this opera represents Bellini at his dramatically least compelling should certainly hear Callas. In 1953, when she made the recording, her voice was already afflicted with hardness on top with some unsteadiness, and for sheer beauty of sound Sutherland is consistently preferable. But Callas, once heard, is unforgettable, for the compulsion of her singing is irresistible. None of the other soloists is ideally stylish, though most of the singing is acceptable. As can be heard at the very opening, the upper range of the sound is restricted, though later the recording opens up and the solo voices project vividly.

La Sonnambula (complete).

*** Decca Dig. **417 424-2** (2) [id.]. Sutherland, Pavarotti, Della Jones, Ghiaurov, L. Op. Ch., Nat. PO, Bonynge.

(***) HMV mono **CDS7 47378-8** [**CDCB 47377**]; *EX 290043-5* (2). Callas, Monti, Cossotto, Zaccaria, Ratti, La Scala, Milan, Ch. and O, Votto.

As Joan Sutherland said, when she decided to record *La Sonnambula* again in her fifties, there was no question of her trying to be kittenish. As Richard Bonynge has pointed out, the original Amina was also the original Norma, and the extra weight of the voice – still not sounding at all old – suits the music if not the character. The result is a performance even more affecting and more stylish than her earlier version, generally purer and more forthright, if with diction still clouded at times. The challenge of singing opposite Pavarotti adds to the bite of the performance, crisply and resiliently controlled by Bonynge. The star tenor may be stylistically coarser than Nicola Monti on Sutherland's earlier set, but the beauty and size of the voice help to focus the whole performance more positively, not least in such ensembles as the finale of Act I. The rest of the cast is vocally strong too, and the early digital recording comes up very vividly on CD, with excellent separation of voices and orchestra. Like the earlier LPs, the CD set has on its box a delightful, not-quite-serious portrait of Sutherland as the Sonnambula by Michael Stennett.

Substantially cut, the Callas version was recorded in mono in 1957, yet it gives a vivid picture of the diva at the peak of her powers. By temperament she may not have related closely to Bellini's heroine, but the village girl's simple devotion through all trials is touchingly caught, most of all in the recitatives. The recording has transferred remarkably well to CD. There is a fair amount of atmosphere, and both orchestra and chorus are well caught. Nicola Monti makes a strong rather than a subtle contribution but blends well with Callas in the duets; and Fiorenza Cossotto is a good Teresa. Callas admirers will find this enjoyable as an overall performance.

'Great arias' from: *Norma; I Puritani; La Sonnambula.*
*** Decca *417 176-4* [id.]. Maria Chiara, Luciano Pavarotti, Joan Sutherland – DONIZETTI: *Arias.****

Decca are good at tape anthologies, and this starry collection of Bellini and Donizetti makes a splendid entertainment. Maria Chiara's ravishing account of *Vien, diletto* from *I Puritani* is matched by Joan Sutherland's breathtaking *Ah! non giunge* from her earlier, 1970, *La Sonnambula,* while Pavarotti is at his most resonant in *A te, o cara,* also from *Puritani.* The transfers are excellently vivid, and the coupled Donizetti selection is hardly less tempting.

Benjamin, George (born 1960)

(i) *Ringed by the flat horizon.* (ii) *At first light. A Mind of winter.*
*** Nimbus Dig. **NI 5075** [id.]. (i) BBC SO, Elder; (ii) Penelope Walmsley-Clark, L. Sinf., composer.

George Benjamin, favourite pupil of Messiaen and the most naturally talented young British composer of his generation, is here well represented by works from early in his career, written around the age of twenty, full of natural flair, amazingly accomplished in their expression. *Ringed by the flat horizon* is a 20-minute orchestral piece that conceals the detailed complexity of its argument in warmly expressive, evocative use of the orchestra, with the big climax masterfully built. *At first light* and *A Mind of winter* (the latter the winner of the Koussevitzky International Record Award in 1987) both date from a year or so later. *A Mind of winter* is a 9-minute setting of *The Snowman* by Wallace Stevens, beautifully sung by the soprano Penelope Walmsley-Clark, with Benjamin himself conducting the London Sinfonietta. It has been aptly described as a winter equivalent of Debussy's *L'après-midi d'un faune.* Sound of great warmth and refinement to match the music.

Berg, Alban (1885–1935)

(i) *Chamber concerto for piano, violin and wind ensemble;* (ii) *Violin concerto.*
** CBS *MT 42139* [id.]. Isaac Stern, with (i) Peter Serkin, LSO members, Abbado; (ii) NYPO, Bernstein.

The CBS issue conveniently couples Berg's two concertante works with violin, featuring Isaac

Stern in both. The yoking, however, is uneven, when these are recordings made 24 years apart. The 1962 recording of the *Violin concerto* underlines the coarser side of the performance, in which Stern takes a red-blooded romantic view of the work, as does Bernstein, with finer points skated over. There is coarseness in the *Chamber concerto* too, when the recording balance is aggressively close. Though this is a virtuoso performance, the interplay of instrumentalists is less subtle than it might be, with Stern's violin for once placed rather backwardly in relation to the wind players. The digital sound is very immediate and the tape is clear and vivid in both works. No doubt this coupling will appear on CD in due course.

Violin concerto.
*** DG **413 725-2** [id.]. Itzhak Perlman, Boston SO, Ozawa – STRAVINSKY: *Concerto.****
*** Decca Dig. **411 804-2**; *411 804-4* [id.]. Kyung Wha Chung, Chicago SO, Solti – BARTÓK: *Concerto.****

Violin concerto; 3 Orchestral pieces, Op. 6.
(*) Ph. **412 523-2 [id.]. Gidon Kremer, Bav. RSO, Sir Colin Davis.
(*) CBS Dig. **MK 39741 (id.]. Zukerman, LSO or BBC SO, Boulez.

As far as the musical public is concerned, Berg has always been seen, rightly or wrongly, as the acceptable face of dodecaphony, the human side of the tone-row, though it is only the *Violin concerto* that has made real inroads into the concert repertory. Even so, it is remarkable that the CD catalogue already offers four different versions of this work.

Perlman's performance is totally commanding. The effortless precision of the playing goes with great warmth of expression, so that the usual impression of 'wrong-note Romanticism' gives way to total purposefulness. The Boston orchestra accompanies superbly and, though the balance favours the soloist, the recording is excellent. It has been convincingly remastered for CD, although the resonance of the Boston acoustic and the backward balance for the orchestra mean that detail is inevitably less sharp than in either the Decca or Philips alternative.

Perlman may be tougher, more purposeful in his performance of the Berg *Concerto*, but he does not excel Chung in tenderness and poetry. Played like this, it makes an excellent coupling for the Bartók on the reverse, another two-movement concerto. Despite the official two-movement layout, the Decca CD thoughtfully provides bands for the two sections in each. The violin is placed well in front of the orchestra, but not aggressively so. The recording is brilliant in the Chicago manner, but more spacious than some from this source.

Kremer's performance of the *Concerto* is more problematic, for it too is often intensely felt and enormously accomplished. However, there is an element of narcissism here, and Kremer often stresses the music's self-pity. The solo posturing at bars 43–57 of the second movement is unappealing and so is the withdrawn, nasal tone of the chorale. Besides providing an admirable accompaniment for the *Concerto*, the Bavarian Radio Orchestra give a fine account of themselves in the Op. 6 *Pieces*, and Sir Colin makes much of their refined textures and powerful atmosphere. This is a really compelling performance. The Philips recording is of altogether remarkable clarity and definition, completely truthful, while in the *Concerto* the balance between violin and orchestra is perfectly judged. In this respect it far surpasses Perlman's. In its combination of clarity, atmosphere and ambient warmth this CD is in the demonstration class.

Zukerman's strong, urgent playing and virtuoso flair make his a robust rather than a subtle or poetic reading. The elegiac quality is missing. The power of his playing is reinforced by the very close balancing of the soloist, allowing him no range below mezzo-forte and with the orchestra heard through a haze of violin tone. The toughness of the performance is matched by Boulez's accompaniment. His account of the Opus 6 *Pieces* is strong and positive too, but again the recording is questionable, with the occasional solo passages excessively forward.

Lyric Suite (3 movements).
*** HMV Dig. **CDC7 47923-2**; *EL 169588-4*. Junge Deutsche Philharmonie CO, Gülke – SCHOENBERG: *String quartet No. 2*; WEBERN: *5 Pieces, Op. 5*.***
*** DG **423 132-2** [id.]. BPO, Karajan – SCHOENBERG: *Pelleas*.***

In 1928, at the request of his publisher, Berg transcribed three of the six movements of his *Lyric Suite* for full string orchestra. They have been recorded in the past (by Karajan and Boulez, among others) but scarcely with the same intensity that distinguishes this account. The recording is transparent yet full-bodied and the playing has an enthusiasm, eloquence and commitment that are quite special. The cassette too is first class in every way.

Karajan's purification gives wonderful clarity to these often complex pieces, with expressive confidence bringing out the romantic overtones. The recording is beautiful and refined and this is an outstandingly played alternative view of these pieces; but Gülke's version has greater vitality.

3 Pieces for orchestra, Op. 6.
*** DG Dig. **419 781-2** [id.]. BPO, Levine – SCHOENBERG; WEBERN: *Pieces*.***

In one of his first recordings with the Berlin Philharmonic, Levine gives a powerful, warmly emotional reading of Berg's Opus 6, well coupled with other masterpieces representing the composer's two colleagues of the Second Viennese School, similarly in the full flush of early maturity. Written several years after the Schoenberg and Webern pieces, the Berg set is broader and more conventionally structured, but just as imaginative. Levine is particularly impressive in the big build-up of the third and last piece, the *March*, though there as elsewhere odd emphasis of individual lines is intrusive in an otherwise full and vivid recording.

Lulu (with orchestration of Act III completed by Friedrich Cerha).
*** DG **415 489-2** (3) [id.]. Stratas, Minton, Schwarz, Mazura, Blankenheim, Riegel, Tear, Paris Op. O, Boulez.

The full three-act structure of Berg's *Lulu*, first unveiled by Boulez in his Paris Opéra production and here treated to studio recording, was a revelation with few parallels. The third Act, musically even stronger than the first two and dramatically essential in making sense of the stylized plan based on a palindrome, transforms the opera. Although it ends with a lurid portrayal of Jack the Ripper's murder of Lulu – here recorded with hair-raising vividness – the nastiness of the subject is put in context, made more acceptable artistically. The very end of the opera, with Yvonne Minton singing the Countess Geschwitz's lament, is most moving, though Lulu remains to the last a repulsive heroine. Teresa Stratas's bright, clear soprano is well recorded, and there is hardly a weak link in the cast. Altogether this is a historic issue, presenting an intensely involving performance of a work which in some ways is more lyrically approachable than *Wozzeck*. The CD version brings a number of advantages over the LP, not just in the extra clarity and immediacy of sound but in the layout on three discs instead of four, one per Act. That means the multilingual spoken commentaries are omitted; but a note by Boulez and Friedrich Cerha's commentary on his completion are included with the libretto.

Bergman, Erik (born 1911)

Bim bam bum; Fåglarna; Hathor Suite; Nox.
*** Chan. Dig. **CHAN 8478**; *ABTD 1189* [id.]. Walmsley-Clark, Varcoe, Potter, New London Chamber Ch., Endymion Ens., James Wood.

The Finnish composer, Erik Bergman, is best known for his *Aubade for orchestra*, an atmospheric evocation of dawn over the Bosphorus. He is at his best and most characteristic in writing for voices; the four works on this issue offer ample evidence of his individuality and resource. *Nox* (1970) is a setting of four poems on the theme of Night, while for *Bim bam bum* (1976) he turns to Morgenstern, whose gallows-songs inspired earlier works. *Fåglarna* (*The Birds*) is earlier (1962) but is no less resourceful in its use of choral colour; and the *Hathor Suite* is based on ancient Egyptian cult texts dedicated to the goddess Hat-hor. All four are well performed and recorded, and the record forms an invaluable introduction to a highly imaginative and sensitive artistic personality.

Berio, Luciano (born 1925)

Eindrucke; Sinfonia.
*** Erato Dig. **ECD 88151**; *MCE 75198* [id.]. Pasquier, New Swingle Singers, O Nat. de France, Boulez.

It was in 1969 that Berio's *Sinfonia*, written for the New York Philharmonic, made a far wider impact on the music world than is common with an avant-garde composer. The colour and energy of his writing, his wit (not least in the vocal commentary for the Swingle – now the New Swingle – Singers) make for a piece that is both memorable and attractive. His own CBS recording, made in New York at the time, had a deserved success, but it omitted the fifth movement, which within months he had added to the original four. Boulez records the complete work for the first time in this fine Erato version, and that substantial finale proves essential to an appreciation of the whole piece, when with its reminiscences it sums up what has gone before. *Eindrucke*, written between 1973 and 1974, is another powerful work, much more compressed, bare and uncompromising in its layering of strings and wind. Boulez draws vivid performances of both from his French players, and the recording is colourful to match, though vocal balances sometimes sound contrived.

A-Ronne.
*** HMV Dig. *EL 270452-4*. Electric Phoenix – CAGE: *Hymns and variations.****

The brilliantly disciplined singers of Electric Phoenix bring out all the wit and fun in Berio's *A-Ronne* in a virtuoso performance, with its play on noises, words and part-words. It is Berio's gift to write with poise and point in a relatively trivial work, always communicating vividly. The original five-part version is used instead of the eight part expansion previously recorded. The sound, exceptionally vivid and full of presence in its LP format, is acceptable but less sharply focused in its tape format.

Berlioz, Hector (1803–69)

(i) *Harold in Italy, Op. 16; Overture: Le Carnaval romain, Op. 9.*
*** DG Dig. **415 109-2**; *415 109-4* [id.]. (i) Christ; BPO, Maazel.

(i) *Harold in Italy; Overture: Le Carnaval romain, Op. 9; La Damnation de Faust: Rákóczy march. Roméo et Juliette: Queen Mab scherzo.*
(***) RCA mono **RD 85755** [**RCA 5755-2**]. (i) Cooley; NBC SO, Toscanini.

(i) *Harold in Italy;* (ii) *Tristia:* (*Méditation religieuse; La mort d'Ophélie; Marche funèbre pour la dernière scène de Hamlet*), *Op. 18; Les Troyens à Carthage: Prelude to Act II.*
*** Ph. **416 431-2** [id.]. (i) Imai; (ii) Alldis Ch.; LSO, C. Davis.

The Philips account offers splendid value and is the equivalent of three sides of an LP. In addition to a noble account of *Harold* in which Nobuko Imai is on top form, this CD offers the *Tristia* which includes the haunting *Funeral march for the last scene of Hamlet* given with chorus, as well as the *Prelude* to the second Act of *Les Troyens*. The sound is completely natural and realistic, and has impressive transparency and detail. The recordings emanate from the 1970s but still lead the field. A first recommendation.

Maazel's *Harold* was recorded at a public performance at the Philharmonie, Berlin, in April 1984 and is the first new recording of Berlioz's masterpiece to appear since the late 1970s. It is undoubtedly very fine; the structure is well held together, and there is a well-paced sense of forward movement in all four movements and no lack of poetic feeling. Maazel secures a nicely judged internal balance, there is some imaginative phrasing and he invariably finds the *tempo giusto*. Wolfram Christ is an eloquent and dignified protagonist. Maazel's fill-up deserves special mention: in his hands the overture, *Le Carnaval romain*, has exhilaration and momentum, as well as an infectious sparkle. The DG recording is marvellously clean and vivid. Incidentally, readers preferring the cassette format can be assured that the differences between it and the LP are minimal. But CD offers the usual advantages of the new medium over the old.

All but one of Toscanini's performances were recorded in Carnegie Hall in the early 1950s: only the *Rákóczy march* comes from the notorious Studio 8-H. The *Roman carnival overture* is very high voltage and so, of course, is the famous recording of *Harold*. There is in fact not a great deal to choose between this and the pioneering Koussevitzky version, for Carlton Cooley is an excellent soloist. The demonic fires glow with equal intensity in both versions of the *Orgy of the Brigands* – perhaps the *Pilgrims' march* is just a shade hard driven. The *Queen Mab scherzo* is absolutely magical and wonderfully delicate. The RCA engineers have accomplished much in the transfer to the new medium but, even with the most advanced techniques of digital remastering, there is a limit to what can be achieved here, and the sound calls for tolerance, particularly in the *Rákóczy march*, but the excitement of the performances still comes across the intervening decades.

Overtures: Béatrice et Bénédict; Le Carnaval romain, Op. 9; Le Corsaire, Op. 21; Rob Roy; Le Roi Lear, Op. 4.
(*) Chan. Dig. **CHAN 8316; *ABTD 1067* [id.]. SNO, Gibson.

Rob Roy is the rarity of Sir Alexander Gibson's Berlioz collection. It adds an aptly Scottish tinge to the record, even when traditional melodies – *Scots wha hae* at the opening – are given distinctly Berliozian twists. It is if anything even wilder than the other pieces, and with its anticipations of *Harold in Italy* finds Gibson and the SNO at their most dashingly committed. *King Lear*, another rarity, also comes out most dramatically, and though *Béatrice et Bénédict* is not quite so polished, the playing is generally excellent. With first-rate digital recording, outstanding on CD, this can be generally recommended. The chrome tape is strikingly vivid but lacks something in the middle range.

Overtures: Le Carnaval romain, Op. 9; Le Corsaire, Op. 21; Les Francs Juges, Op. 3; Le Roi Lear, Op. 4; Waverley, Op. 26.
(*) Ph. **416 430-2. LSO, C. Davis.

Sir Colin Davis's collection of overtures dates from the mid-1960s and, while the CD transfer has freshened the recording, the original balance was not ideal, although the woodwind detail remains well integrated. This is music which ideally calls for modern digital sounds; in spite of this, Sir Colin's collection can hold its own, even though some will feel it should be in the CD mid-price bracket. The playing undoubtedly has fire and brilliance, *Les Francs Juges* is exhilarating and the performance of *King Lear* is outstanding, challenging comparison with Beecham.

Overture: Le Carnaval romain, Op. 9.
(M) *** EMI Dig. **CD-EMX 9511**; *TC-EMX 2108*. Royal Liverpool PO, Litton – SAINT-SAËNS: *Symphony No. 3*.**(*)

Andrew Litton keeps the Royal Liverpool Philharmonic Orchestra on their toes in their brilliant and exciting account of a famous orchestral showpiece. The resonant acoustics of Liverpool Cathedral, which offer some problems in the coupled Saint-Saëns *Symphony*, suit the Berlioz, bringing a resplendent sonority to the brass and making the thrilling final chord a moment to relish as the reverberation ebbs away naturally. The cassette transfer, too, is very well managed, retaining the breadth and vividness yet mellowing the brightness in the upper strings caused by the necessarily close microphone layout.

Romance, rêverie et caprice, Op. 8.
*** DG Dig. **400 032-2** [id.]. Perlman, O de Paris, Barenboim – LALO: *Symphonie espagnole*.***

Berlioz's short concertante work for violin and orchestra uses material originally intended for *Benvenuto Cellini*. Perlman's ripely romantic approach to the *Rêverie* brings out the individuality of the melody, and with a sympathetic accompaniment from Barenboim the work as a whole is given considerable substance. First-rate digital recording.

Symphonie fantastique, Op. 14.
*** Ph. **411 425-2** [id.]; *416 659-4*. Concg. O, C. Davis.
(M) **(*) HMV **CDM7 69002-2** [id.]; *EG 769002-4*. O Nat. de France, Bernstein.
(*) HMV Dig. **CDC7 47278-2 [id.]; *EL 270235-4* [Ang. *4DS 38210*]. Phd. O, Muti.
(*) DG **415 325-2 [id.]. BPO, Karajan.
(*) DG Dig. **410 895-2 [id.]. Chicago SO, Abbado.
(B) **(*) DG Dig. *419 827-4*. Chicago SO, Abbado – MUSSORGSKY: *Pictures*.**(*)
(*) Decca Dig. **414 203-2; *414 203-4* [id.]. Montreal SO, Dutoit.
(*) Erato Dig. **ECD 88028 [id.]. O Nat. de France, Conlon.
(M) *(*) Pickwick Dig. **PCD 870**. LSO, Richard Williams.

(i) *Symphonie fantastique;* (ii) *Overtures: Le Carnaval romain, Op. 9; Le Corsaire, Op. 21.*
(*) ASV Dig. **CDDCA 590; *ZCDCA 590* [id.]. RPO, Bátiz.
(M) **(*) RCA **GD 86720**; *GK 86720* [**RCA-6720-2RG**]. Boston SO, (i) Prêtre; (ii) Munch.

(i) *Symphonie fantastique;* (ii) *Overture: Le Corsaire;* (ii; iii) *Les Troyens: Royal hunt and storm.*
(*) HMV **CDC7 47863-2 [id.]. (i) French Nat. RO; (ii) RPO; (iii) Beecham Ch. Soc., Beecham.

Sir Colin Davis's 1974 Concertgebouw recording – his first with that orchestra – remains a primary recommendation. The Philips recording was always a fine one, but the digital remastering for CD has been outstandingly successful and there is a very striking improvement in the firmness of focus, while detail is clearer – much more so than in Abbado's Chicago digital version. If this does not quite match Dutoit, for instance, in brilliance and definition, the overall balance is very satisfying and the reading itself is paramount. Sir Colin recorded the work earlier with the LSO, and that proved a stepping-stone for a performance which has much in common with the earlier account, except that the Concertgebouw performance has far more life and colour. The slow movement, superbly played, is more atmospheric than before, and with CD the crude side-break of the original LP format (which, incredibly, still remains on the recently reissued tape) is eliminated. The two final movements are very exciting, with a fine rhythmic spring given to the *March to the scaffold* and the finale gripping to the last bar.

Beecham's account still enjoys classic status, though it is now over twenty-five years old. While the *March to the scaffold* is ominously deliberate, the performance has a demonic intensity that is immediately compelling. Gounod wrote that 'with Berlioz, all impressions, all sensations – whether joyful or sad – are expressed in extremes to the point of delirium', and Beecham brought to this score all the fire and temperament, all the magic and affection, in his armoury. He drew from the French National Radio Orchestra playing of great rhythmic subtlety; the Waltz has never sounded more elegant. This is an indispensable record. Unfortunately the transfer to CD has produced a less than ideal sound-picture with thin, sometimes fizzy upper strings and an intermittent hum. The recording is much fuller in the tinglingly atmospheric *Royal hunt and storm* and the classic account of the *Corsaire* overture.

Bernstein directs a brilliant and understanding performance which captures more than most the wild, volatile quality of Berlioz's inspiration. Sir Colin Davis may give a clearer idea of the logic of the piece, but Bernstein (unlike Davis, omitting the exposition repeat) has even more urgency, and his reading culminates in superb accounts of the *March to the scaffold* and the *Witches' sabbath*, full of rhythmic swagger and natural flair. However, the remastering of the late 1970s analogue recording gives slight over-emphasis to the brilliance with its tendency to shrillness in the upper strings. Some weight has been lost at the bass end, too, but the warm resonance of the recording retains the body of the orchestral sound. There is a successful chrome tape, not as bright as the CD on top, but well balanced.

The balance of fierceness against romantic warmth in Muti's own personality works particularly well in this symphony, so that he holds the thread of argument together firmly without ever underplaying excitement. The sound is among the best which Muti has had in Philadelphia – full in range, if not always ideally clear in texture – but cannot equal Dutoit on Decca in realism or fidelity of balance. There is a good, though not outstandingly refined, XDR tape.

Karajan's reading is highly individual in its control of tempo in the first movement, but the Berlin Philharmonic are fully equal to his quixotic pacing, and the effect is certainly compelling. In the slow movement, the intensity of pianissimo playing is enhanced by the beautiful orchestral sound; this analogue recording from 1975 has a much more attractive ambience than many of Karajan's later digital records. The Waltz has characteristic panache and the spacious yet immensely dramatic finale sends the adrenalin racing. Here the recording is very vivid throughout and it brings out every nuance of the Berlin orchestra's subtle tone-colours. Unlike Sir Colin Davis, however, Karajan does not observe the first-movement repeat, and there is no doubt that Davis's structural control and overall pacing are more convincing.

Abbado brings the right dreamy atmosphere and feverish intensity to this score and the playing of the Chicago Symphony Orchestra has all the polish and finesse one could expect. There is much poetic feeling, the slow movement is outstandingly fine, and he observes the exposition repeat in the first movement (also in the *March to the scaffold*). The DG recording is rich in texture but the balance is less than ideal. The effect is recessed and, while the background silence of the CD allows the magical pianissimo playing in the slow movement to register effectively, the resonance sometimes clouds finer points of detail. Abbado's version is also available on a bargain DG Pocket Music chrome tape, where the high level of the transfer has brightened the sound and brought a degree more immediacy, though there is some loss of richness at the lower end of the spectrum. But with a brilliant version of the Mussorgsky *Pictures* offered as coupling the value is obvious.

Bátiz also has the advantage of a first-class modern digital recording, brilliant yet full-bodied and very well balanced. As always in the recording studio, he brings the score vividly to life, and his consistent warmth and intensity are highly persuasive. Points of detail may be less subtle than with Davis or Beecham, but one has the feeling here of live music-making, and the two overtures are equally strong and spontaneous.

The spectacular wide-ranging recorded sound is the first point to note with the Dutoit version, the fullest yet on CD, with excellent detail and a rich ambience, too. The performance is more controversial, if only because Dutoit tends to prefer speeds slower than usual, and in direct comparison that sometimes makes him seem less exciting than his finest rivals. Yet by keeping the pulse steady, he adds to structural strength while never limiting expressive warmth in lyrical passages or the crisp lifting of rhythm in allegros. Though the *Dies irae* passage of the finale may seem rather stolid next to a faster, more frenetic reading, the power is most impressive. On the chrome cassette – a state-of-the-art Decca transfer – the recording quality is outstandingly fine, strikingly vivid but with a glowing bloom on the overall sound-picture.

Prêtre's early stereo recording, like Beecham's, suffers from thin overlit violins, but the Boston ambience brings weight and the sound is otherwise resonantly full, with exciting projection for the brass. It is a highly volatile performance but, while Prêtre dashes away capriciously soon after the opening, his sense of neurosis is convincing and the ebb and flow of the first movement are convincingly handled. The Waltz is warmly elegant, with a blaze of orchestral bravura at the end. The heart of the interpretation lies in the beautiful slow movement, spacious and poised but with a burst of high drama at the 'recitativo' climactic interchange between wind and strings. The *March to the scaffold* has a jaunty sense of melodrama, and the finale combines an element of the grotesque with high adrenalin flow. An individual and involving account. With the two overtures, recorded earlier in 1958, the upper range becomes shrill, although the recording undoubtedly makes the strongest impact. These famous performances come from Munch's outstanding LP collection (which also included an unforgettable *Royal hunt and storm*). They have great panache and excitement. At mid-price one can accept the need to cut back the treble, and enjoy the music making for its exuberance.

James Conlon is convincingly volatile in the first movement, and his reading has a fine sense of spontaneity. The Waltz is engagingly *galant*, yet the element of neurosis is present and rises to the surface in a dazzlingly effective accelerando at its close. The slow movement brings beautifully serene playing from the strings, with textures radiant. The *March to the scaffold* has a jaunty air, and the exuberant finale is less overtly satanic than in some hands. The fairly close balance gives more detail and projection than with Abbado, but the overall effect lacks the ambient beauty of the Decca recording. Even so, this is a very enjoyable account, impetuously sensitive to the work's charismatic mood changes.

While a modern digital CD at mid price would be a welcome addition to the catalogue, Richard Williams's Pickwick version is disappointingly underpowered, only springing fully to life in the closing pages of the finale. Elsewhere the playing of the LSO is polished and well detailed, but lacks adrenalin and bite, and the slightly distanced recording does not help to give the music making an immediate impact.

Of other available versions, Maazel's Telarc disc offers resplendent sound and the performance is naturally expressive in a spontaneous-sounding way, without losing precision of ensemble, but this rather plain account cannot quite compete with the finest rivals (**CD 80076**). Mehta too offers a fresh, direct but not especially illuminating reading with the NYPO, but while his Decca recording also has demonstration potential, the performance overall is stronger on extrovert brilliance than on poetic feeling (**400 046-2**). Solti's Chicago version – reissued on a mid-price CD coupled with the *Francs Juges* overture – is no more successful, in spite of extremely vivid sound. Hardly a semiquaver is out of place, but the spirit of the music eludes the conductor (Decca **417 705-2**). Other versions by Barenboim and Maazel (for CBS) and Munch (for EMI) must also go to the very bottom of the list.

(i) *Symphonie fantastique;* (ii) *Le Corsaire: overture; La Damnation de Faust: Danse de follets. Les Troyens: Trojan march;* (iii) *Royal hunt and storm.*

(B) *** EMI *TCC2-POR 290115-9.* (i) French Nat. RO; (ii) RPO; (iii) with Beecham Choral Society, Beecham.

Apart from Beecham's outstanding performance of the *Symphonie fantastique*, this reissue in

EMI's 'Portrait of the Artist' series also includes other outstanding Beecham recordings, notably the *Royal hunt and storm*, which sound uniquely atmospheric in his hands. All the recordings come up well on this double-length tape which is an unquestionable bargain, and here the strings sound fuller than on CD.

VOCAL MUSIC

La damnation de Faust, Op. 24.

*** Ph. **416 395-2** (2) [id.]. Veasey, Gedda, Bastin, Amb. S., Wandsworth School Boys' Ch., LSO Ch., LSO, C. Davis.

*** Decca Dig. **414 680-2** (2) [id.]. Riegel, Von Stade, Van Dam, King, Chicago Ch. & SO, Solti.

The Philips set first appeared in 1974 and offered quite outstanding sound for its time. Both Gedda as Faust and Bastin as Mephistopheles are impressive, and the response of the orchestra and chorus is never less than intelligent and, in the quieter passages, highly sensitive. The LSO plays marvellously for Davis and the recording perspective is outstandingly natural and realistic. On CD its vividness is focused all the sharper. The subtlety and fantasy of Davis's reading are finely matched. The only snag is the tape-hiss, but that is easily ignored.

Solti's performance, searingly dramatic, is given stunning digital sound to make the ride to Hell supremely exciting. But with Von Stade singing tenderly, this is a warmly expressive performance too; and the *Hungarian march* has rarely had such sparkle and swagger. CD brings out the full range of the recording, with the bass drum, for example, clearly in focus. The extra brightness matches the extrovert quality of the performance, less subtle than Davis's.

La Damnation de Faust: highlights.

(*) Decca Dig. **410 181-2 [id.] (from above recording, cond. Solti).

Starting with the *Hungarian march* in spectacular wide-ranging sound, Solti's CD of highlights may give only a limited idea of the complete work, but the selection is intelligently made and there are warmly expressive moments, too. Certainly the recording on CD is immediate and vivid.

L'enfance du Christ, Op. 25.

*** Ph. **416 949-2** (2) [id.]. Baker, Tappy, Langridge, Allen, Herincx, Rouleau, Bastin, Alldis Ch., LSO, C. Davis.

*** Erato Dig. **ECD 75333** (2) [id.]. Von Otter, Rolfe-Johnson, Van Dam, Cachemaille, Bastin, Monteverdi Ch., Lyons Op. O, Gardiner.

(*) ASV Dig. **CDDCD 452 (2); *ZCDDD 452* [id.]. Kimm, Rolfe-Johnson, Luxon, Van Allan, Alldis Ch., ECO, Ledger.

Davis characteristically directs a fresh and refined reading for Philips of one of Berlioz's most directly appealing works. The beautifully balanced recording intensifies the colour and atmosphere of the writing, so that for example the *Nocturnal march* in the first part is wonderfully mysterious. There is a fine complement of soloists, and though Eric Tappy's tone as narrator is not always sweet, his sense of style is immaculate. Others are not always quite so idiomatic, but Dame Janet Baker and Thomas Allen, as ever, both sing beautifully. The refinement of the recording is all the more impressive on CD. More than in most works, one relishes the absence of background except for an almost imperceptible analogue hiss.

John Eliot Gardiner has the advantage of fine modern recording made in the Church of Sainte-Madeleine, Pérouges, very well balanced, but with the resonance bringing warm atmosphere rather than great clarity. He has some fine soloists, too; some will prefer Anthony Rolfe-Johnson's mellow narration to Eric Tappy's rather more characterful but less melliflous contribution on the Davis set. Anne-Sophie von Otter's Mary is outstanding, sung with rapt simplicity. The others are more mixed in appeal, although Giles Cachemaille is a very impressive Joseph. Gardiner often – though not always – adopts brisker tempi than Davis, and his vibrancy brings a new dimension to some of the music. But generally Davis's choice of pacing is even more apt – he has a special feeling for this work, born of long experience (he has recorded it previously for Argo), notably so in the *Shepherd's chorus*, where he moves the music on more firmly than Gardiner.

Ledger's version is taken from the soundtrack of a television film first shown in 1985. The sound is first rate, full and vivid, and if the violins in the orchestra sound a little undernourished, no doubt that is an accurate image. The team of soloists has no weak link, but the singing is a shade lacking in character compared with the Davis set. Philip Ledger as a fine choral conductor guides his forces freshly and intelligently, presenting music and story simply and effectively, but with less idiomatic flair than Davis. The alternative tape version offers the work complete on a single extended-length cassette, the sound clear and well balanced, with natural projection of the solo voices and refined choral sound. There is, however, no translation of the text.

(i) *La Mort de Cléopâtre;* (ii) *Les Nuits d'été, Op. 7* (see also below).
*** DG Dig. **410 966-2** [id.]. (i) Jessye Norman. (ii) Kiri Te Kanawa, O de Paris, Barenboim.

The coupling of Jessye Norman in the scena and Dame Kiri Te Kanawa in the song-cycle makes for one of the most ravishing of Berlioz records, with each singer at her very finest. Norman has natural nobility and command as the Egyptian queen in this dramatic scena while Te Kanawa encompasses the challenge of different moods and register in *Les Nuits d'été* more completely and affectingly than any singer on record in recent years, more so than Norman in her beautiful but rather bland recording with Davis. Excellent DG recording for Barenboim and first-rate playing from the Paris Orchestra. The CD adds to the sense of presence and realism of both singers, intensifying the warmth and compulsion of the performances.

Les Nuits d'été (song cycle), *Op. 7* (see also above).
(*) Ph. **412 493-2 [id.]. Jessye Norman, LSO, Sir Colin Davis – RAVEL: *Shéhérezade.***(*)
** Telarc Dig. **CD 80084** [id.]. Elly Ameling, Atlanta SO, Shaw – FAURÉ: *Pelléas et Mélisande.***
*(*) Ph. Dig. **416 807-2**; *416 807-4* [id.]. Baltsa, LSO, Tate – WAGNER: *Wesendonk Lieder.**(*)

Jessye Norman is in fine voice here but does not get fully inside this most magical of orchestral song-cycles. There is no lack of voluptuousness, but the word-meanings are less subtly registered than in the finest rival versions. Davis's tempi too are sometimes over-deliberate. The CD transfer of a 1979 analogue recording has been well done, with extra presence of voice and orchestra, but cannot match the finest.

Very realistically recorded in a relatively intimate acoustic, Elly Ameling's version concentrates on pure beauty. Emotionally the performance is restrained, cautious even, with crisp, calculated, rather reticent playing from the orchestra.

Tough, abrasive and provocative, Agnes Baltsa gives strongly characterized readings of Berlioz's evocative songs that challenge the ear but completely miss the sensuous beauty. The only way that Baltsa finds to soften her tone is to sit on the flat side of the note, but the voice is so precise that the flatness is always obtrusive. Excellent accompaniment and recording,

Other versions by Hildegard Behrens and Frederica von Stade are similarly disappointing. Behrens has too cumbersome a voice for the opening *Villanelle* (Decca **411 895-2**), while Von Stade, always intelligent and naturally musical, yet sounds less spontaneous than usual (CBS **MK 39098**). Admirers of Régine Crespin and Ansermet will be glad to know that their analogue Decca version is again available on tape (*417 228-4*). Crespin's sheer richness of tone and a style which has an operatic basis do not prevent her from bringing out the subtlety of Berlioz's writing. *La spectre de la rose* is particularly successful, given an operatic sense of drama, while

Ansermet provides a brilliant accompaniment. The sound too is strikingly vivid and wide-ranging.

Requiem mass (Grande messe des morts), Op. 5.

(*) HMV **CDS7 47540-8 (2) [Ang. **CDCB 47540**]. Keith Lewis, N. & S. Cologne R. Choirs, Cologne RSO, Bertini.

** Telarc Dig. **CD 80109** (2) [id.]. Aler, Atlanta Ch. & SO, Robert Shaw – BOITO: *Mefistofele: Prologue;* VERDI: *Te Deum.***

(i) *Requiem mass; Symphonie fantastique.*

*(**) RCA **RD 86210** (2) [**RCA 6210-2-RC**]. (i) Simoneau, New England Conservatory Ch., Brass bands; Boston SO, Munch.

(i) *Requiem mass;* (ii) *Symphonie funèbre et triomphale, Op. 15.*

(*) Ph. **416 283-2 (2) [id.]. (i) Dowd, Wandsworth School Boys' Ch., LSO Ch.; (ii) John Alldis Ch.; LSO, Sir Colin Davis.

Sir Colin Davis's recording of the *Requiem* and the *Symphonie funèbre* both date back to 1970, so the CD coupling is logical and quite generous. For the recording of the *Requiem* Philips went to Westminster Cathedral, which should have been atmospheric enough, but then the engineers managed to produce a sound which minimizes the massiveness of forces in anything but the loudest fortissimos, thanks to the closeness of the microphones. In many passages one can hear individual voices in the choir. Once that is said, the performance is impressive, if not ideally expansive. In the *Rex tremendae* for example, Davis's clean taut account is less than tremendous, while the *Lacrymosa* is concise – even angular – in its precision. The large-scale brass sound is formidably caught and the choral fortissimos are glorious, helped by the fresh cutting edge of the Wandsworth School Boys' Choir. It was Davis's idea, not Berlioz's, to have boys included, but it is entirely in character. The LSO provides finely incisive accompaniment, and there is no doubt that the CD remastering has added to the overall impact and tangibility, in spite of the balance.

The *Symphonie funèbre et triomphale* is a fascinating product of Berlioz's eccentric genius, designed as it was to be performed not just in the open air but on the march. The *Funeral march* itself provides the most haunting music, but it needs more persuasive handling than Sir Colin's if it is not to outstay its welcome. The apotheosis too can be made to sound more effective than this.

Munch's Boston version was recorded as early as 1959 and is an astonishing technical achievement for its time. The four brass groups make a bold effect within the resonant Boston acoustics and the big climaxes of the *Dies irae* and the *Tuba mirum*, though not perfectly focused, are still thrilling. Munch's overall direction has a fine lyrical flow; he brings powerful expressive feeling to the *Lacrymosa*, where the chorus is at its finest. The *Sanctus* – where Leopold Simoneau, with headily beautiful tone, does full justice to the tenor solo – is particularly moving. Here the quiet effects of shimmering strings are almost as memorable as the crashing chords of the *Tuba mirum*. Berlioz's trick of orchestration, using low notes on the trombones with a trio of flutes high above, which he features in the *Hostias* and elsewhere, is a strange and ethereal sound in Munch's hands. All in all, this is a most distinguished set and it is a great pity that it is offered in harness with an unsatisfactory version of the *Symphonie fantastique*. Although well recorded (in 1954), this is far from compelling. There are erratic speed-changes in the first movement, yet a low level of tension and seldom a convincing sense of spontaneity.

Bertini's version of the *Requiem*, colourful and dramatic too, was recorded live by engineers of West German Radio (WDR) in the Cathedral of Altenberg. The sound is vividly atmospheric, wider in range than Davis's 1970 Philips, but inevitably less clear on many details. Bertini's style is more consciously expressive than Davis's, with brass in the outbursts of *Tuba mirum* more rounded and opulent, less abrasive. Ensemble is not flawless, but this will please anyone who looks for atmosphere above all in this massive work.

Robert Shaw directs a fresh and straightforward reading of Berlioz's monumental score with attractively clean and well-disciplined choral singing. The Telarc recording, though not ideally clear in the massive fortissimos which bring some clouding, has a better sense of presence on instruments than on voices, with the massive forces contained in a pleasant but not at all ample acoustic. Male voices in the choir lack bite in exposed passages. More seriously, what the performance misses is grandeur and a sense of occasion, such as is found on earlier recordings by Davis, Bernstein or Previn. So the *Tuba mirum* lacks weight and dramatic bite, for all the power of fortissimo; fresh and bright though the choral sound is in *Rex tremendae*, with strands well defined, the impression is not powerful enough. John Aler makes an excellent tenor soloist in the *Sanctus*, but the following *Hosanna* is pedestrian. The CD version was the first to arrive in the catalogue and brings exceptionally generous makeweights in the substantial Verdi and Boito items.

Roméo et Juliette, Op. 17.
*** DG **423 068-2** (2) [id.]. Hamari, Dupouy, Van Dam, New England Conservatory Ch., Boston SO, Ozawa – TCHAIKOVSKY: *Romeo and Juliet.****
*** Ph. **416 962-2** (2) [id.]. Kern, Tear, Shirley-Quirk, Alldis Ch., LSO Ch. & O, C. Davis.
** HMV Dig. **CDC7 47437-8** [Ang. **CDCB 47437**] (2); *EX 270445-5*. Norman, Aler, Estes, Westminster Ch., Phd. O, Muti.

(i) *Roméo et Juliette, Op. 17. Symphonie funèbre et triomphale, Op. 15.*
*** Decca **417 302-2**; *417 302-4* (2) [id.]. (i) Quivar, Cupido, Krause, Tudor Singers, Montreal Ch. & SO, Dutoit.

Dutoit's is a masterly, heart-warming reading of Berlioz's curious mixture of symphony, cantata and opera, superbly recorded in richly atmospheric sound, with a triumphantly successful account of the *Symphonie funèbre et triomphale* as a generous coupling. Dutoit consistently brings out the romantic lyrical warmth of the work – not least in the great orchestral love-scene – while giving Berlioz's instrumentation all the refinement and subtlety it needs. When that is coupled with brilliant choral singing, incisive and atmospheric, it is an unassailable mixture. Though the mezzo, Florence Quivar, is less steady than she should be, the other soloists are first rate, Alberto Cupido witty in his scherzetto, Tom Krause aptly firm and resonant. In the *Symphonie funèbre*, Dutoit is at his most uninhibited, brilliantly skirting the very edge of vulgarity in this outgoing ceremonial piece. The Decca cassettes are splendidly fresh and clear, revealing delicacy of texture as well as fine sonority.

Ozawa's 1976 recording has been remastered successfully for CD; the sound is more refined in detail, yet the ambient atmosphere remains and though the chorus is not sharply focused the Boston acoustics are pleasing in other ways. If not quite as strong in personality as Dutoit's Decca performance, Ozawa's reading is both warm and dramatic. His spontaneity helps to unify the early fragmentary passages; the party music has swagger and the great love-scene – source of inspiration for Wagner in *Tristan* – is convincingly built over the longest span, with a tempo not too expansive. With a fine team of soloists, this produces a warmer effect than the rather more severe manner of Davis. The coupling of Tchaikovsky's *Romeo and Juliet* is appropriate enough; it is a first-class performance but will involve most collectors in duplication.

Sir Colin Davis – it hardly needs saying – has a rare sympathy with this score and secures playing of great vitality and atmosphere from the LSO. His soloists are excellent too, and so is the chorus. The 1968 recording still sounds excellent; it is natural in tone and balance, and the CDs bring added presence. But with no coupling this is less competitive, especially compared with Dutoit.

Despite the starry line-up of soloists, Muti's version is disappointing after Dutoit's. This is partly a question of recording, relatively thick and ill focused, but also a matter of interpretation, less idiomatic and fanciful, whatever the brilliance of the Philadelphia playing. It is good to hear Jessye Norman in the lovely *Strophes*, but the weight of voice and the personality hardly match the incidental quality of that sequence.

Te Deum, Op. 22.
*** DG Dig. **410 696-2** [id.]. Araiza, LSO Ch., LPO Ch., Woburn Singers, Boys' Ch., European Community Youth O, Abbado.
*** Ph. **416 660-2**; (M) *416 660-4* [id.]. Tagliavini, Wandsworth School Boys' Ch. LSO Ch. & O, N. Kynaston (organ), C. Davis.

The newest DG recording from Abbado is very impressive. The sound is wide-ranging with striking dynamic contrasts and a much greater sense of presence than its predecessors. Artistically, too, it is of considerable merit: Abbado brings great tonal refinement and dignity to this performance, and the spacious sound helps. Francisco Araiza is altogether first class and has eloquence as well as tonal beauty to commend him. The choirs are responsive as are the young players Abbado has assembled. Memories of Beecham in mono and Colin Davis on the Philips label are not banished, however; Sir Colin has a natural feeling for the pace of this work and his reading is perhaps the more moving. In some respects Abbado's version is superior (certainly as far as the soloist is concerned) and collectors acquiring it are unlikely to be disappointed. On compact disc the quality is very impressive, bringing extra gain in definition and spatial feeling.

Sir Colin Davis's 1969 Philips recording has been successfully remastered. Davis conveys massiveness without pomposity, drama without unwanted excesses of emotion, and his massed forces with the LSO respond superbly. The expansive choral climaxes and Nicolas Kynaston's fine organ contribution are impressively contained and while the CD has the technical edge, the chrome tape sounds excellent too and costs very much less.

OPERA

Béatrice et Bénédict (complete).
*** Ph. **416 952-2** (2). Baker, Tear, Eda-Pierre, Allen, Lloyd, Van Allan, Watts, Alldis Ch., LSO, C. Davis.

Well produced for records, with a smattering of French dialogue between numbers, *Béatrice et Bénédict* here reveals itself as less an opera than a dramatic symphony, one of the important Berlioz works (like *Romeo and Juliet*) which refuse to fit in a conventional category. The score presents not just witty and brilliant music for the hero and heroine (Dame Janet Baker and Robert Tear at their most pointed) but sensuously beautiful passages such as the duet for Hero and Ursula at the end of Act I and the trio they later share with Beatrice, both incidental to the drama but very important for the musical structure. First-rate solo and choral singing, brilliant playing, while the CD transfer – like the others in Davis's Berlioz series – brings out the exceptionally high quality of the Philips engineering, with sound refined and clear in texture, bright and fresh, even if minimal hiss betrays an analogue source.

Les Troyens, Parts 1 & 2 (complete).
❀ *** Ph. **416 432-2** (4) [id.]. Veasey, Vickers, Lindholm, Glossop, Soyer, Partridge, Wandsworth School Boys' Ch., ROHCG Ch. & O, C. Davis.

The complete recording of Berlioz's great epic opera was an achievement to outshine all other centenary offerings to this composer, indeed to outshine almost all other recording projects whatever. Davis had long preparation for the task, both in his concert performances and in his direction of the Covent Garden production, on which this recording is firmly based. The result is that, even more than in most of his other Berlioz recordings, he conveys the high dramatic tension of the music. Throughout this long and apparently disjointed score Davis compels the listener to concentrate, to appreciate its epic logic. His tempi are generally faster than in the theatre, and the result is exhilarating with no hint of rush. Only in the great love scene of *O nuit d'ivresse* would one have welcomed the more expansive hand of a Beecham. It is interesting too to find Davis pursuing his direct, dramatic line even in Dido's death scene at the end. Veasey on any count, even next to Dame Janet Baker, makes a splendid Dido, single-minded rather than seductive, singing always with fine heroic strength. Of the rest, Berit Lindholm as Cassandra, in the first half of the opera, is the only soloist who falls short – the voice is not quite steady – but otherwise one cannot imagine a more effective cast, with Vickers as a ringing Aeneas. The Covent Garden Chorus and Orchestra excel themselves in virtuoso singing and playing, while CD brings out the superb quality of sound all the more vividly, and the new format brings even more advantages than usual. Quite apart from the ease with which one can index any section of this epic structure, the Acts are arranged on the four discs with no break within any Act. Acts II and III come together on the second disc, with the other Acts on a disc apiece.

Les Troyens à Carthage: ballet music.
** Decca Dig. **411 898-2** [id.]. Nat. PO, Bonynge – LECOCQ: *Mam'zelle Angot;* WEBER: *Invitation to the dance.****

Berlioz's ballet music sounds insubstantial heard away from its source. Although it has characteristic fingerprints it does not show its composer at his finest. It is very well played here and the brightly lit recording is vivid.

Berners, Lord (Gerald) (1883–1950)

The Triumph of Neptune (suite); Fantaisie espagnole; Fugue in C minor; Nicholas Nickleby (film music); Trois morçeaux.
*** HMV Dig. **CDC7 47668-2**; *EL 270501-4.* Royal Liverpool PO, Wordsworth.

The Triumph of Neptune has not been available since the days of Beecham, who recorded it twice. Barry Wordsworth has put us in his debt by restoring it to the catalogue and giving it in a more complete form. While memories of Beecham remain undimmed (in his hands *Cloudland* and *The Frozen Forest* had a very special character and elegance that sparkled through all the surface noise), Wordsworth captures the character of this music remarkably well. Moreover we have other enjoyable (and valuable) repertoire; the *Trois morçeaux* and the *Fantaisie espagnole* are new to the catalogue. They date from 1918 and are Gallic in inspiration and sympathy, as their titles suggest, and attractively imaginative. Some commentators have drawn parallels with Satie: both were renowned eccentrics, both had an irreverent sense of humour, but Satie's vein of melancholy went deeper and his awareness of pain was more acute. The recording is good without being in the demonstration class; detail is well defined and there is plenty of body. The cassette, unfortunately, lacks range in the treble and the bass tends to boom. Chrome rather than iron-oxide stock was needed here. But on CD this is well worth exploring.

Bernstein, Leonard (born 1918)

Candide: overture.
*** DG Dig. **413 324-2**; *3302 083* [id.]. LAPO, Bernstein – BARBER: *Adagio;* COPLAND: *Appalachian spring;* SCHUMAN: *American festival overture.****

Bernstein's *Candide overture* is one of the most dazzlingly brilliant of the century, and the composer directs it in this live recording with tremendous flair, his speed a fraction slower than in his New York studio recording for CBS. One item in an outstanding collection of American music, brilliantly recorded in both formats.

Candide: overture; Divertimento for orchestra; Mass: Simple song. On the Town: 3 Dances. West Side story: selection. *Wonderful Town:* selection.
** Ph. Dig. **416 360-2** [id.]. Boston Pops O, John Williams.

John Williams conducts the Boston Pops Orchestra in brash performances of popular Bernstein pieces, recorded in bold sound to match. The *Divertimento*, which he wrote for the Boston Symphony Orchestra's centenary, with its eight little squibs of movements makes an apt item, and the only disappointment comes in the rather anonymous selections from *West Side story* and *Wonderful Town.*

(i) *Candide: overture;* (ii) *Divertimento; On the Town: 3 Dance episodes. On the Waterfront* (Symphonic suite); (i) *West Side story: Symphonic dances.*
(*) DG Dig. **423 198-2 [id.]. (i) LAPO, (ii) Israel PO, composer.

This collection is entitled 'The best of Bernstein' which may not be strictly true, but certainly some of the best of him is here, from the vivacious overture to the marvellous tunes encapsulated in the *Symphonic dances* from *West Side story*. Although a good deal more generous (73′) than the companion CD collection, the Pocket Music tape (which omits the overture) is more generous still, and costs a third as much – see below.

Candide: overture; Facsimile (choreographic essay)*; Fancy free* (ballet)*; On the Town* (*3 Dance episodes*).
(*) HMV **CDC7 47522-2 [id.]; *EL 270510-4* [Ang. *4DS 37358*]. St Louis SO, Slatkin.

Though Slatkin cannot quite match Bernstein himself in the flair he brings to his jazzier inspirations, this is an attractive and generous collection. Next to Bernstein, Slatkin sounds a little metrical at times, but it is a marginal shortcoming, and he directs a beautiful, refined reading of the extended choreographic essay, *Facsimile*. As a gimmick, the song 'Big Stuff' before *Fancy Free* is recorded in simulation of a juke-box, complete with 78 r.p.m. surface-hiss and a blues singer with very heavy vibrato. The sound otherwise is full rather than brilliant, set in a helpful, believable acoustic. The cassette, however, lacks bite in the treble, with the bass over-emphasized.

Candide: overture; On the Town: 3 Dance episodes; On the Waterfront (*Symphonic suite*) *West Side story: Symphonic dances.*
* CBS **MK 42263** [id.]. NYPO, composer.

This collection comes from Bernstein recordings made at the beginning of the 1960s and although the NYPO is in cracking form – the bravura of the *Candide overture*, taken breath-takingly fast, is highly infectious – and the vitality of the rhythms in the excerpts from *West Side story* and *On the Town* is undeniable, the expressive side of these scores comes over less tellingly because of the sound. The digital remastering produces a very bright upper range and no warmth in the middle. As Bernstein has re-recorded all this music, the documentary value of this anthology is limited and it is overpriced.

Divertimento for orchestra.
** Hung. **HCD 12631-2** [id.]. Bav. RSO, composer – BARTÓK: *Music for strings, percussion and celesta.***

Divertimento for orchestra; (i) *Halil* (*Nocturne*)*;* (ii) *3 Meditations from Mass; On the Town* (*3 Dance episodes*).
(*) DG **415 966-2 [id.]. (i) Rampal; (ii) Rostropovich; Israel PO, composer.

This DG compact disc has been compiled from two separate LPs of shorter works. At just under an hour of music, the measure is generous enough, but the selection could easily have included one or more other pieces. Early Bernstein is well represented in the colourful and vigorous dances from *On the Town*, one of the most memorable of all musical films, while the other three works show the later Bernstein sharply sparked off by specific commissions. The *Divertimento*, easily and cheekily moving from one idiom to another, is often jokey, but amiably so. The two concertante pieces, *Halil* for flute and strings and the *Meditations* for cello and orchestra, both beautifully reflect the individual poetry of the two artists for whom they were written and who perform masterfully here. The aggressive digital sound of the original recording bites even more on CD, with a brilliant top and spectacular bass leaving the middle light. With Bernstein, such sound does little harm.

The Hungaroton recording is much fuller, indeed there is more beef than refinement both in the performance – recorded live at a concert in Budapest – and in the recording. However, the composer/conductor's flair is well projected by the orchestra, notably when Bernstein uses his favourite seven-in-a-bar rhythms. Brahms's *Hungarian dance No. 6* makes a lively encore.

(i) *Divertimento for orchestra;* (ii) *3 Meditations from Mass, Musical toast; On the Town: 3 Dance episodes; On the Waterfront* (Symphonic suite)*;* (iii) *West Side story: Symphonic dances.*
(B) *** DG Dig. *419 828-4* [id.]. (i) Israel PO; (ii) Rostropovich; (iii) LAPO, composer.

This well-engineered DG chrome Pocket Music tape makes an excellent introduction to Bernstein's music, showing the consistency of his inspiration, whether in music for film, musical theatre or the concert hall. The lyrical power of the score for *On the Waterfront* is the counterpart to its aggressive force, matching the similar interplay of emotions in the microcosm of *West Side story. Times Square*, the last of the three episodes from *On the Town*, readily demonstrates the composer's catchy melodic and rhythmic facility, and the same quality prevents the *Musical toast* to André Kostelanetz (with the musician's name carolled by the orchestra) from being just an occasional piece. The *Three Meditations* are comparatively serious yet strikingly imaginative in design, and just as enjoyable as the witty orchestral *Divertimento*. The sound throughout is vividly clear, if a little dry in the bass.

Prelude, fugue and riffs.
(***) CBS **MK 42227**; *MT 42227*. Goodman, Columbia Jazz Combo, composer – COPLAND: *Clarinet concerto;* STRAVINSKY: *Ebony concerto;* BARTÓK: *Contrasts,* GOULD: *Derivations.*(***)
*** CBS *MPT 39768*. Goodman, Columbia Jazz Combo, composer – BRUBECK: *Dialogues;* STRAVINSKY: *Ebony concerto; Ragtime; Preludium; Tango.****

Bernstein's exuberant, sometimes wild, yet structured *Prelude, fugue and riffs* fits equally well within these two CBS collections of jazz-inspired pieces in this vintage performance, directed by the composer. It sounds exceptionally vivid on CD, but both tapes are well enough transferred, although they have less life in the upper range.

Symphonies Nos 1 (*Jeremiah*)*;* (i) *2* (*The age of anxiety*) for piano and orchestra.
*** DG **415 964-2** [id.]. Israel PO, composer; (i) with Lukas Foss.

Bernstein's musical invention is always memorable, if at times a little too facile to match the ambitiousness of his symphonic aim; but the compelling confidence of his writing speaks of a genius stretching himself to the limit. The *Jeremiah symphony* dates from Bernstein's early twenties and ends with a moving passage from Lamentations for the mezzo soloist. As its title suggests, the *Second Symphony* was inspired by the poem of W. H. Auden, with the various movements directly reflecting dramatic passages from it, though no words are set in this work for orchestra alone. These performances with the Israel Philharmonic are not always quite as polished or forceful as those Bernstein recorded earlier in New York, but with excellent recording they never fail to reflect the warmth of Bernstein's writing. In No. 2 the concertante piano part is admirably played by Lukas Foss, and in both works the remastering for CD has brought vivid sound, clear and well balanced.

Piano music: *2 Anniversaries; 4 Anniversaries; 5 Anniversaries; 7 Anniversaries; Moby diptych; Song without words; Touches;* Arr. of COPLAND: *El salón México.*
(**) Pro Arte **CCD 109** [id.]. James Tocco.

James Tocco won the 1973 Munich Piano Competition and has made a reputation for himself as an exponent of modern American music. This record collects on to one disc Bernstein's complete output for piano, together with his transcription for one piano of Copland's *El salón México*. Apart from the *Seven Anniversaries*, a beautiful set of pieces which Bernstein himself recorded for RCA, these are all new to the catalogue. Nearly all these miniatures are of high quality and are very sensitively played by James Tocco. Bernstein has used some of the material elsewhere in his output: the *Five Anniversaries*, for example, found their way into the *Serenade for violin, strings and percussion*. Unfortunately the recording does not do him justice: the instrument sounds imperfectly tuned and the acoustic in which it is recorded is too small. Nevertheless, in the absence of any rival, this must carry a cautious recommendation.

Chichester Psalms.
*** ASV Dig. **CDRPO 8004**; *ZCRPO 8004* [id.]. Aled Jones, LSO Ch. RPO, Hickox – FAURÉ: *Requiem.****

Chichester Psalms (reduced score).
*** Hyp. Dig. **CDA 66219**; *KA 66219* [id.]. Martelli, Corydon Singers, Masters, Kettel, Trotter; Best – BARBER: *Agnus Dei;* COPLAND: *In the beginning* etc.***

Bernstein's *Chichester Psalms* were commissioned for the 1965 Chichester Festival during a period when the composer was reassessing his musical life and relating his output to a background of what he saw as 'serial strictures' and 'a dearth of romance'. This he revealed in an article in the *New York Times*, in which he expressed his feelings about his new musical child:

> These psalms are a simple and modest affair,
> Tonal and tuneful and somewhat square,
> Certain to sicken a stout John Cager,
> With tonics and triads in E flat major.

As might be expected, the work makes an instant communication and responds to familiarity too, especially in Richard Hickox's fresh and colourful reading, with Aled Jones making an ethereal contribution to the setting of the 23rd Psalm. As a bonus for a fresh and sympathetic account of the Fauré *Requiem*, this can be recommended strongly. The recorded sound is firm and well focused.

Martin Best uses the composer's alternative reduced orchestration which omits the three trumpets and three trombones specified in the original commission, and settles for a single harp (instead of a pair), organ, and percussion, spectacularly played here by Gary Kettel. There is no musical loss, but instead a subtle change of character and an increase in intimacy. The treble soloist, Dominic Martelli, cannot match Aled Jones, but his chaste contribution is persuasive and the choir scales down its pianissimos to accommodate him, with elegiac effect. Indeed the singing of the Corydon Singers is first rate, rising well to the catchy 7/4 rhythms in Psalm 100. Excellent sound, with the acoustic of St Jude-on-the-Hill, Hampstead, creating the right atmosphere, particularly in the serene closing verse from Psalm 133.

(i) *Songfest* (cycle of American poems); (ii) *Chichester Psalms*.
*** DG **415 965-2** [id.]. (i) Dale Elias, Williams, Rosenhein, Reardon, Gramm, Nat. SO of Washington; (ii) Soloist from V. Boys' Ch., V. Jeunesse Ch., Israel PO; composer.

Songfest, one of Bernstein's most richly varied works, is a sequence of poems which ingeniously uses all six singers solo and in various combinations. Not only the plan but the writing too is ingenious, one song using strict serialism in the most approachable, idiomatically American way. Characteristically, Bernstein often chooses controversial words to set, and by his personal fervour welds a very disparate group of pieces together into a warmly satisfying whole, comparable with Britten's *Serenade*, *Nocturne* or *Spring symphony*. The coupling with the *Chichester Psalms* is new for CD. The latter was recorded live in 1977. One might have slight reservations over the treble soloist from the Vienna Boys' Choir, but otherwise the performance is first class, with the music's warmth and vigour compellingly projected. This makes a fine pairing with the near-definitive account of the *Songfest* which is superbly sung by all the participating artists. CD adds to the feeling of immediacy in both works.

Songs: La bonne cuisine (French and English versions); *I hate music* (cycle); *2 Love songs; Piccola serenata; Silhouette; So pretty; Mass: A simple song; I go on. Candide: It must be so; Candide's lament. 1600 Pennsylvania Ave: Take care of this house. Peter Pan: My house; Peter Pan; Who am I; Never-Never Land.*
*** Etcetera Dig. **KTC 1037** [id.]. Roberta Alexander, Tan Crone.

Trivial as most of these songs are – no fewer than 27 of them – they make a delightful collection, consistently bearing witness to Bernstein's flair for a snappy idea as well as his tunefulness. There is a charming artlessness about the four songs he wrote for a 1950 production of *Peter Pan* with Jean Arthur and Boris Karloff; even earlier is the cycle of five *Kid songs*, *I hate music*, first performed by Jennie Tourel in 1943. It is good to have the haunting number from the unsuccessful bicentennial musical, *1600 Pennsylvania Avenue*, not to mention the two songs from the brilliant Voltaire-based *Candide*. Roberta Alexander's rich, warm voice and winning personality are well supported by Tan Crone at the piano. The recording is lifelike and undistracting.

THEATRE MUSIC

Candide (revised 1982 version).
*** New World Dig. **NWCD 340/1** [id.]. John Lankston, David Eisler, Erie Mills, Scott Reeve, Joyce Castle, NY City Op. Ch. & O, Mauceri.

John Mauceri in this issue from New World Records conducts what is described as the 'Opera House Version 1982' of Bernstein's musical based on Voltaire. For that, Mauceri himself edited together a text incorporating as much as possible of the material that had been written for the piece at its various revivals from the first production in 1956 onwards. Whatever the demands of the Broadway stage, the result on record makes a splendid, fizzing entertainment, necessarily episodic but held together by the electricity of Mauceri's direction and the singing of a cast that nicely bridges the demands of opera and musical. Some of the numbers quoted in the brilliant overture, like *The best of all possible worlds* and *Oh, happy we*, are a particular delight. The recording is aptly bright and clear, with voices placed in firm focus well in front of the orchestra.

A Quiet place (complete).
*** DG Dig. **419 761-2** (2) [id.]. Wendy White, Chester Ludgin, Beverly Morgan, John Brandstetter, Peter Kazaras, Vocal Ens., Austrian RSO, composer.

Soon after writing his one-act opera, *Trouble in Tahiti*, in 1951, Leonard Bernstein started thinking about the characters involved – a suburban American couple – and wondering how they might have developed. Thirty years later he finally got around to following up their story in a full-scale opera. That is the concept behind *A Quiet place*, which in flashbacks in Act II incorporates the 1951 score, with its popular style set in relief against the more serious idiom adopted for the main body of the opera. The opening Act is sharply conceived, set in a funeral parlour. The wife from *Trouble in Tahiti* (its exotic title taken from a film) has just died in a car crash, and for the first time in years the family is reunited, along with an assortment of relatives and friends, all sharply characterized. Sadly, those characters never reappear; the central figures of the family (father, daughter, gay son and lover who has been passed on to the daughter in a *ménage à trois*) quickly seem to have come not from a grand opera but from a soap opera. Bernstein's score is full of thoughtful and warmly expressive music, but nothing quite matches the sharp, tongue-in-cheek jazz-influenced invention of *Trouble in Tahiti*. It does not help that all three Acts end reflectively on a dying fall. Admirers of Bernstein will find much to interest them in the recording, which was made at the time of the first performance of the definitive version in Vienna, with an excellent cast of American singers, and with the Austrian Radio orchestra responding splendidly on its first visit to the Vienna State Opera. With each CD containing over 74 minutes of music, a long work is neatly contained on two discs merely. Considering the problems of live recording of opera, the sound is excellent, remarkably well balanced.

West Side story: complete recording; *On the Waterfront* (Symphonic suite).
❀ *** DG Dig. **415 253-2** (2) [id.]. Te Kanawa, Carreras, Troyanos, Horne, Ollman, Ch. and O, composer.

West Side story (only).
** DG Dig. *415 253-4* (2) [id.]. As above, cond. composer.

Bernstein's recording of the complete score of his most popular work – the first time he had ever conducted the complete musical himself – takes a frankly operatic approach in its casting, but the result is highly successful, for the great vocal melodies are worthy of voices of the highest calibre. Dame Kiri Te Kanawa may not be a soprano who would ever be cast as Maria on stage, but even in the kittenish number, *I feel pretty*, the magnificence of the voice adds a dimension, when the girlishly coy lines of each stanza, sparklingly done, explode with vitality for the pay-off phrase. José Carreras, the only Spanish-speaking member of the cast, but ironically the one in the story who has to be a real American guy, may be apparently miscast, but the beauty of such songs as *Maria* or *Tonight*, or even a sharp number like *Something's coming*, with floated pianissimos and subtly graded crescendos, has one admiring the score the more. Tatiana Troyanos, herself brought up on the West Side, spans the stylistic dichotomy to perfection in a superb portrayal of Anita, switching readily from full operatic beauty to a New York snarl and back, and Kurt Ollman as Riff equally finds a nice balance between the styles of opera and the musical. The clever production makes the best of both musical worlds, with Bernstein's son and daughter speaking the dialogue most affectingly. If patently more mature voices take over when the music begins, one readily adjusts when the singing itself so gloriously captures the spirit of the piece. Bernstein conducts a superb instrumental group of musicians 'from on and off Broadway', and they are recorded with a bite and immediacy that is captivating, whether in the warm, sentimental songs or, above all, in the fizzing syncopated numbers, sounding even more original when precisely played and balanced as here. On CD, the power of the music is greatly enhanced by the spectacularly wide dynamic range of the recording (the chrome cassettes are more restricted and, though they sound well, there is much less bite). With a relatively dry acoustic keeping the sound-picture within an apt scale but without losing bloom, the two humorous ensembles, *America* for girls, and *Gee, Officer Krupke* for the boys, are given tremendous vitality and projection, with the chorus (and the exuberant orchestral percussion) adding colour most winningly. On CD only, the two-disc set includes, besides the musical, the vivid *Symphonic suite*, which was arranged from Bernstein's film music for the Marlon Brando film, *On the Waterfront*, written about the same period.

West Side story: highlights.
*** DG Dig. **415 963-2**; *415 963-4* [id.] (from above recording, cond. composer).

By cutting the dialogue, all the main numbers are included here, presented as vividly as on the complete set, and with just over 53′ of music included this is very good value. But the moving *Tonight* loses much without the spoken interchanges between the lovers, although the 'mock marriage' sequence is included in *One hand, one heart*, as is the introductory interchange which sets the scene for *Gee, Officer Krupke*. As with the complete set, the cassette has less presence and bite and does not begin to match the CD.

West Side story: Symphonic dances.
*** DG Dig. **410 025-2**; *3302 082* [id.]. LAPO, composer: GERSHWIN: *Rhapsody in blue* etc.**(*)
(B) *** DG Walkman *413 851-4* [id.]. San Francisco SO, Ozawa – GERSHWIN: *American in Paris* etc.**(*)
(*) DG **419 625-2 [id.]. San Francisco SO, Ozawa – GERSHWIN: *An American in Paris***(*); RUSSO: *Street music.***

Bernstein, recorded live, is at his most persuasive conducting a highly idiomatic account of the orchestral confection devised from his most successful musical. It may not be quite so crisp of ensemble as his earlier New York version, but it has more spirit, with the players contributing the necessary shouts in the *Mambo* representing a street fight. Vivid if close-up sound, with the compact disc showing no marked difference from the standard LP and tape issues, although the resonance is controlled more cleanly.

Ozawa's performance is highly seductive, with an approach which is both vivid and warm, yet conceals any sentimentality. The 1973 recording has responded well to its digital remastering: the rich ambience remains and the focus is almost always clean. But this should have been reissued at mid-price. One attraction is the separate cueing of the nine sections, each titled. The performance is additionally issued on a Walkman tape. The sound is excellent in this format and the couplings are generous.

West Side story: suite (arr. Eric Crees).
** Decca Dig. **417 354-2**; *417 354-4* [id.]. Philip Jones Brass Ens. – WEILL: *Little Threepenny music.***

Eric Crees has made his selection from the full score, rather than using Bernstein's own excerpts in the *Symphonic dances*, but the transcription of this music for brass is of doubtful advantage, even though the playing is expert and the recording brilliantly present – some ears might think too much so.

Bertrand, Anthoine de (1540–81)

Amours de Ronsard, Book 1; *Amoirs de Cassandre*: excerpts.
** HM Dig. **HMC 901147** [id.]. Clément Janequin Ens.

Anthoine de Bertrand was born in the Auvergne and died in Toulouse in 1581. His settings of the First Book of Ronsard's *Amours* appeared in 1576, twenty-five years after they had first appeared in print and had come to occupy a dominant position in the history of the French chanson. The interest Bertrand took in chromaticism and enharmonic procedures is known to historians rather than to the non-specialist listener. However, the chansons recorded here by the Clément Janequin Ensemble show him to be, if not a great master, at least a composer of feeling and considerable resource. *Mon Dieu, mon Dieu que ma maistresse est belle* (No. 10 on the CD) is a touching and memorable piece. The fourteen chansons recorded here are interspersed with four short pieces by the French lutenist and composer, Guillaume de Morlaye, active in the 1550s. The performances are excellent throughout, as one would expect from this distinguished group; and Claude Debôves makes out a good case for the rather anonymous Morlaye pieces. Good performances and admirable recording makes this a worthwhile (if not, perhaps, indispensable) addition to the catalogue.

Berwald, Franz (1797–1868)

Symphonies Nos 1 in G min. (*Sérieuse*)*; 2 in D* (*Capricieuse*)*; 3 in C* (*Singulière*)*; 4 in E flat.*
*** DG Dig. **415 502-2**; *415 502-4* [id.]. Gothenburg SO, Järvi.

Franz Berwald has neither the range nor the stature of a Sibelius, but he is incontestably the leading Scandinavian symphonist of the first half of the nineteenth century. His first four symphonies receive a distinguished and auspicious CD début. The present set of recordings outclasses the previous Björlin versions on HMV and almost all previous rivals. First, the orchestral playing has abundant spirit and energy: this is music that is wholly in the life-stream of the Gothenburg orchestra; and secondly, the excellent acoustic of the Gothenburg Hall shows the scores to great advantage. Neeme Järvi sets generally brisk tempi, yet the pacing feels right; if the account of the *Capricieuse* seems mercurial, it is exhilarating and fresh. Although this is not the finest of Berwald's symphonies, Järvi almost convinces us that it is. Even if the slow movement is taken too fast, its distinctive eloquence is not lost. The same could be said for the *Singulière* – and indeed the others in the set, which are given a similar bracing treatment. The sound, particularly on CD, is altogether superb, with every detail coming through with great clarity, and this can be strongly recommended. The chrome tapes are not quite as wide-ranging at the top, but are satisfyingly balanced.

Grand septet in B flat.
*** CRD *CRDC 4044*. Nash Ens. – HUMMEL: *Septet.****

Berwald's only *Septet* is a work of genuine quality and deserves a secure place in the repertory instead of on its periphery. It dates from 1828 and is for the same forces as the Beethoven and Kreutzer *Septets*; the invention is lively and the ideas have charm. It is eminently well played by the Nash Ensemble and finely recorded. The cassette (as is usual with CRD) is an altogether excellent transfer.

String quartet in G min.
*** CRD *CRDC 4061*. Chilingirian Qt (with WIKMANSON: *Quartet****).

Berwald composed four quartets: two in 1849 after the symphonies, and two in his mid-twenties. The *G minor Quartet* and a companion in B flat which has not survived, date from

1818. This work did not appear in print until the 1940s, when the parts of the middle movements were discovered during stocktaking at the Royal Swedish Academy of Music. It is, as one would expect from an accomplished violinist, a remarkably assured piece, and the first movement is full of modulatory audacities. If the thematic substance has not the same quality of inspiration as in Arriaga's quartet, it is still both characterful and appealing. The trio of the scherzo has a touching charm that is almost Schubertian, though it is impossible that Berwald could have been aware of his great contemporary. This is a highly interesting and often bold quartet, and the Chilingirian players give a well-shaped and sensitive account of it. They are truthfully recorded, and the coupling – another Swedish quartet – enhances the attractions of this issue. The cassette transfer is outstandingly fresh and clear. Strongly recommended.

Biber, Heinrich (1644–1704)

Balletae a 4; Battaglia, Sonata 1 a 8; 2 a 8; 3 a 5; Sonata a 6; Sonata a 7.
(M) *** Tel. **ZS8 43779** [id.]. VCM, Harnoncourt.

An altogether delightful record. All the works here were composed by Biber for the Archbishop of Olmutz's virtuoso orchestra and were later included in the collection, *Sonatae tam aris quam aulis.* The music is inventive and high-spirited, and has great appeal. The *Battaglia* (subtitled *The Dissolute revelling of Musketeers, March, Battle and laments of the wounded imitated with Airs and dedicated to Bacchus*) is particularly vivid and entertaining, with dissonances worthy of Milhaud. The inventive *Sonata a 8* for strings and the groups of clarini are hardly less rewarding. Lively performances, recorded in 1971 but still sounding fresh.

Sonatas Nos 1–6.
*(*) Chan. Dig. **CHAN 8448/9**; *DBTD 2009* (2). Cantilena, Adrian Shepherd – MUFFAT: *Concerti grossi.**(*)

These sonatas come from *Fidicinium sacro-profanum*, which Biber published in 1683; they are, perhaps, technically less advanced than the celebrated *Rosenkranz* sonatas. These ensemble sonatas are beautifully wrought pieces whose eloquence is well conveyed by these players. They are at their best in the slow movements, which are performed with a convincing feeling for atmosphere; in the faster ones, ensemble could be more unanimous and articulation cleaner. Nevertheless a worthwhile issue and very well recorded.

(i) *Missa Sancti Henrici; Sonatae tam aris quam aulis servientes.*
(*) EMI **CDC7 49034-2. Regensburger Domspatzen, (i) Coll. Aur.

Little is known of the provenance of the *Missa Sancti Henrici*, though the Henry of the title is probably Henry II of the Holy Roman Empire. It is a late work, preserved in a copy from 1701 in the Benedictine monastery at Kremsmunster. Elements of the old polyphonic and the new homophonic style are alternated in an ingenious and resourceful fashion. Two of the sonatas from the 1676 collection, on which Harnoncourt draws for his record listed above, serve as fill-ups. The performances are eminently musical, perhaps ultimately a little under-energized.

Bizet, Georges (1838–75)

L'Arlésienne (incidental music)*: suites Nos 1–2.*
*** HMV **CDC7 47794-2** [id.]. RPO, Beecham – *Symphony.****

L'Arlésienne: suites Nos 1–2; Carmen: suites Nos 1–2.
** Ph. **412 464-2** [id.]. LSO, Marriner.

L'Arlésienne: suites Nos 1–2; Carmen: suite No. 1; suite No. 2: excerpts.
(B) *** DG Walkman *413 422-4* [id.]. LSO, Abbado (with CHABRIER: *España*; DUKAS: *L'apprenti sorcier*; RIMSKY-KORSAKOV: *Capriccio espagnol* **(*)).

L'Arlésienne: suites Nos 1–2; Carmen: suite No. 1.
(M) *** DG **423 472-2** [id.]. LSO, Abbado.
(*) DG Dig. **415 106-2 [id.]. BPO, Karajan.
(B) **(*) DG Dig. *419 829-4* [id.]. BPO, Karajan – OFFENBACH: *Overtures.***(*)
(M) **(*) DG *419 469-4* [id.]. BPO, Karajan – OFFENBACH: *Barcarolle* etc.**(*)

Carmen: suites Nos 1–2.
** Telarc Dig. **CD 80048** [id.]. St Louis SO, Slatkin – GRIEG: Peer Gynt.**(*)

All recordings of Bizet's enchanting incidental music for *L'Arlésienne* are overshadowed by Beecham's magical set dating from 1957. Miraculously, even though it was in the early days of stereo, the EMI engineers captured the RPO within an attractive ambient bloom, and also achieved realistic detail so that today the recording sounds astonishingly full and vivid. Besides the beauty and unique character of the wind solos, Beecham's deliciously sprightly *Minuet* and his affectingly gentle sense of nostalgia in the *Adagietto* (both from the first suite) are as irresistibly persuasive as the swaggering brilliance of the closing *Farandole* of the second.

Karajan, too, secures marvellous playing from the Berlin Philharmonic Orchestra, but he is less naturally at home in this repertoire, and tempi are not always ideally apt (notably the *Pastorale* and *Intermezzo* from the second suite) and he sounds too languid at times. The modern digital recording has the widest possible range of dynamic, but the effect sometimes seems rather inflated in tuttis. The *Carmen* suite, taken from his complete opera recording of 1983, is vividly played throughout – Karajan is at his best here. These recordings are also available on a bargain-priced Pocket Music tape, coupled with Offenbach overtures. The sound is excellent and the cost a tiny fraction of that of the two equivalent CDs. Karajan's earlier (1971) analogue recordings (on DG Galleria *419 469-4*) are in some ways slightly more spontaneous than the later set, but the Galleria coupling – also Offenbach – is more modest.

Those looking for a bargain can also turn to the CD or to the Walkman tape of the 1981 Abbado performances. On tape his account of the *Carmen* suite is supplemented with two extra items, well played by the Hague Philharmonic Orchestra under Willem van Otterloo. The other highlight of this tape is Lorin Maazel's famous 1960 recording of Rimsky-Korsakov's *Capriccio espagnol*, lustrously played by the Berlin Philharmonic Orchestra in sparkling form, and there are also lively accounts of *L'apprenti sorcier* (Fiedler and the Boston Pops) and Chabrier's *España*, in a spirited performance by the Warsaw Philharmonic Orchestra under Jerzy Semkow. Among recent couplings of *L'Arlésienne* and *Carmen*, Abbado's recording undoubtedly stands out. The orchestral playing is characteristically refined, the wind solos cultured and eloquent, especially in *L'Arlésienne*, where the pacing of the music is nicely judged. A vibrant accelerando at the end of the *Farandole* only serves to emphasize the obvious spontaneity of the music making. There is warmth too, of course, and in the opening *Prélude* of the *Carmen suite* plenty of spirit. With vivid and truthful recording, this is very attractive if the couplings are suitable, for the tape transfers are well managed. The CD sounds even better.

Marriner's collection is exceptionally generous, offering eleven items from *Carmen* and both *L'Arlésienne suites*, missing out only the *Intermezzo* from the latter. But the musical characterization is sometimes lacking in flair and, indeed, brio; in spite of fine LSO playing and warm natural (1979) analogue recording, this must take second place to Karajan, let alone Beecham.

The Telarc digital recording of the *Carmen suites* combines glitter with a natural perspective and the playing is good if not distinctive. Audiophiles will undoubtedly respond to the range and vividness of the sound, complete with an over-prominent bass drum, a Telarc early digital trademark. Other versions of *L'Arlésienne*, conducted by Ozawa paired with *Carmen* on HMV (**CDC7 47064-2**) and with *Jeux d'enfants* recorded by Fournet in Tokyo (Denon **C37 7802**), remain uncompetitive.

Symphony in C.

(M) *** Decca **417 734-2**; *417 734-4* [id.]. ASMF, Marriner – PROKOFIEV: *Symphony No. 1;* STRAVINSKY: *Pulcinella.****

*** HMV **CDC7 47794-2** [id.]. French Nat. R. O, Beecham – *L'Arlésienne.****

Symphony in C; Jeux d'enfants: suite

*** Ph. **416 437-2** [id.]. Concg. O, Haitink – DEBUSSY: *Danses sacrée et profane.****

Symphony in C; Carmen: extended suite.

** Eurodisc **610 521** [id.]. Bamberg SO, Prêtre.

It would be easy to be happy with any of the top three recordings of Bizet's engagingly youthful *Symphony*. Beecham's version from the beginning of the 1960s above all brings out its spring-like qualities. The playing of the French orchestra is not quite as polished as that of Marriner's group or the Concertgebouw, but Beecham's panache more than compensates and the slow movement is delightfully songful, even if there is a moment of suspect intonation at its opening and close. The remastered sound is rather fuller in the bass than the balance Decca have now contrived for Marriner, and is bright on top, without glare.

Marriner's performance is played with all the polish and elegance characteristic of the vintage ASMF records of the early 1970s; the slow movement has a delectable oboe solo and the finale is irrepressibly gay and high-spirited. The recording, originally rather reverberant, is now much drier, the bass less expansive, not entirely to advantage, but at mid-price and with highly desirable couplings, this remains excellent value. There is a splendid chrome cassette.

The warmest, most pleasing sound comes from Haitink's sunny 1979 Concertgebouw performance. His reading obviously takes into account the Amsterdam acoustics for it is essentially spacious, although the finale does not lack vivacity. The serene slow movement is particularly eloquent, with a beautiful oboe solo. *Jeux d'enfants* is also delectably played; here, the recording is demonstration-worthy in its sparkling detail. The unexpected Debussy coupling also sounds beautiful.

After this, Prêtre's version for Eurodisc, well played as it is, must with regret be passed over, unless the particular coupling is essential.

OPERA

Carmen (complete)

*** DG Dig. **410 088-2**; *3382 025* (3) [id.]. Baltsa, Carreras, Van Dam, Ricciarelli, Barbaux, Paris Op. Ch., Schoenberg Boys' Ch., BPO, Karajan.

(*) Decca **414 489-2 (2) [id.]. Troyanos, Domingo, Van Dam, Te Kanawa, John Alldis Ch., LPO, Solti.

(*) DG **419 636-2 (3) [id.]. Berganza, Domingo, Cotrubas, Milnes, Amb. S., LSO, Abbado.

(*) HMV **CDC7 49240-2 (3) [Ang. **CDCB 49240**]. De los Angeles, Gedda, Blanc, Micheau, Fr. R. Ch. and O, Petits Chanteurs de Versailles, Beecham.

** Erato Dig. **ECD 880373** (3) [id.]. Migenes Johnson, Domingo, Raimondi, Esham, Watson, French R. Ch. & Children's Ch., O Nat. de France, Maazel.

** HMV **CDS7 47313-8** (3) [Ang. **CDC 47312**]. Callas, Gedda, Massard, René Duclos Ch., Children's Ch., Paris Nat. Op. O, Prêtre.

On CD, Karajan's newest DG set of *Carmen* makes a clear first choice among currently available versions, with the performance combining affection with high tension and high polish. Where in his earlier RCA version he used the old text with added recitatives, here he uses the Oeser edition with its extra passages and spoken dialogue; this may account in part for the differences of approach, more intimate in the presentation of the drama, less extreme over certain controversial tempi. In Carreras he has a Don José, lyrical and generally sweet-toned, who is far from a conventional hero-figure, more the anti-hero, an ordinary man caught up in tragic love. The *Flower song* is exquisitely beautiful in its half-tones. The Micaela of Katia Ricciarelli is similarly scaled down, with the big dramatic voice kept in check. José van Dam – also the Escamillo for Solti – is incisive and virile, the public hero-figure, which leaves Agnes Baltsa as a vividly compelling Carmen, tough and vibrant yet musically precise and commanding. Where on stage (as at Covent Garden) Baltsa tends to exaggerate the characterization, here Karajan encourages her to be positively larger than life but still a believable figure, with tenderness under the surface. In her brief exchanges with Escamillo before the final scene, you are made to believe in her love for the bullfighter. As for Karajan, he draws richly resonant playing from the Berlin Philharmonic, sparkling and swaggering in the bullfight music but delicate and poetic too. The digital recording is bright and atmospheric, if not always ideally balanced. The spoken dialogue distractingly sounds like the soundtrack of a French film. The compact discs bring benefit in extra clarity, but also bring out more noticeably the degree of close-up aggressiveness in the recording, with a tendency to bass-lightness. The cassette transfer is refined and truthful, but the upper range is less telling, and the focus is softer than the CD quality.

By the side of the digital Karajan recording, the Solti discs sound less strikingly brilliant than they seemed on first appearance. But this Decca performance, apart from offering a satisfactory solution to the vexed question of text, is remarkable for its new illumination of characters whom everyone thinks they know inside out. Tatiana Troyanos is quite simply the subtlest Carmen on record. The blatant sexuality which is so often accepted as the essential ingredient in Carmen's character is here replaced by a far more insidious fascination, for there is a degree of vulnerability in this heroine. You can understand why she falls in love and then out again. Escamillo too is more readily sympathetic, not just the flashy matador who steals the hero's girl, in some ways the custodian of rationality, whereas Don José is revealed as weak rather than just a victim. Troyanos's singing is delicately seductive too, with no hint of vulgarity, while the others make up the most consistent singing cast on record to date. Solti, like Karajan, uses spoken dialogue and a modification of the Oeser edition, deciding in each individual instance whether to accept amendments to Bizet's first thoughts. Fine as other versions are of a much-recorded opera, this dramatic and sensitive account from Solti holds its place among recommended versions, but though the CD transfer brings out the generally excellent balances of the original analogue recording, it exaggerates the bass to make the sound boomy. The voices retain their fine realism and bloom, but orchestral textures are heavier and less clear than they should be, unless controls are adjusted.

Superbly disciplined, Abbado's performance nails its colours to the mast at the very start in a breathtakingly fast account of the opening prelude. Through the four Acts there are other examples of idiosyncratic tempi, but the whole entertainment hangs together with keen compulsion, reflecting the fact that these same performers – Sherrill Milnes as Escamillo excepted – took part in the Edinburgh Festival production directly associated with this recording project. Conductor and orchestra can take a large share of credit for the performance's success, for though the singing is never less than enjoyable, it is on the whole less characterful than on some rival sets. Teresa Berganza is a seductive if somewhat unsmiling Carmen – not without sensuality, and producing consistently beautiful tone, but lacking some of the flair which makes for a three-dimensional portrait. If you want a restrained and thoughtful view, then Tatiana Troyanos in Solti's set (see above), also opposite the admirably consistent Placido Domingo, is preferable. Ileana Cotrubas as Micaela is not always as sweetly steady as she can be; Milnes makes a heroic matador. The spoken dialogue is excellently produced, and the sound is vivid and immediate, with the CDs hardly betraying the fact that the sessions took place in different studios (in London as well as Edinburgh).

Beecham's approach to Bizet's well-worn score is no less fresh and revealing. His speeds are not always conventional but they always *sound* right. And unlike so many strong-willed conductors in opera Beecham allows his singers room to breathe and to expand their characterizations. It seems he specially chose De los Angeles to be his Carmen although she had never sung the part on the stage before making the recording. He conceived the *femme fatale* not as the usual glad-eyed character, but as someone far more subtly seductive, winning her admirers not so much by direct assault and high voltage as by genuine charm and real femininity. De los Angeles suits this conception perfectly: her characterization of Carmen is absolutely bewitching, and when in the Quintet scene she says *Je suis amoureuse* one believes her absolutely. Naturally the other singers are not nearly so dominant as this, but they make admirable foils; Gedda is pleasantly light-voiced as ever, Janine Micheau is a sweet Micaela, and Ernest Blanc makes an attractive Escamillo. The stereo recording does not add to things in the way that the best Decca opera recordings do, and there seems to have been little attempt at stage production, but in the CD transfer the sound is certainly brilliant, and the recording does not too greatly show its age.

The glory of Maazel's Erato version is the Don José of Placido Domingo, freer and more spontaneously expressive than in his two previous recordings, not least in the lovely account of the *Flower song*. Julia Migenes Johnson is a fresh-toned Carmen, often exaggerating detail but presenting a vibrant, sexy character as she does in Francesco Rossi's brilliantly atmospheric film. Ruggero Raimondi sings cleanly and strongly as Escamillo, but Faith Esham is a shrill, thin-toned Micaela, vocally quite out of character. Maazel's conducting is bright and dramatic, if not always tender enough. The recording is clean, well balanced and natural, and very well reproduced on CD, less brilliant than Karajan's DG but arguably the best yet in the new medium. A recommendable set for those who have enjoyed the film.

Though in so many ways the vibrant, flashing-eyed personality of Maria Callas was ideally suited to the role of Carmen, her complete recording – unlike two separate aria recordings she made earlier – is disappointing. One principal trouble is that the performance, apart from her, is so slipshod, lacking a taut dramatic rein, with slack ensemble from singers and orchestra alike. The moment the heroine enters, the tension rises, but by Callas standards this is a performance rough-hewn, strong and characterful but lacking the full imaginative detail of her finest work. 'Callas is Carmen', said EMI's original advertisements, but in fact very clearly Callas remains Callas. The CD transfer clarifies textures but brings out the limitations of the Paris recording.

Bernstein's 1973 New York recording of the 1875 original version is not yet available on CD but the mid-priced tapes are quite well transferred and Marilyn Horne's vivid characterization of the heroine's role is impressive (DG *413 279-4*). However, those looking for bargain tapes for the car should try the Classics for Pleasure set, offered in a chunky plastic box. Frühbeck de Burgos also chooses the 1875 version; if his Carmen, Grace Bumbry, is not as individual as some in this role, she still sings vibrantly, and Jon Vickers provides a memorable *Flower song*. The performance has plenty of zest – the *Danse Bohème* notably so – and the sound is vivid (*CFPD 41 4454-5*).

Carmen: highlights.

*** DG Dig. **413 322-2**; *413 322-4* [id.] (from above recording with Baltsa, Carreras, cond. Karajan).

(*) Erato Dig. **ECD 88041 [id.] (from above recording with Migenes Johnson, Domingo, cond. Maazel).

Good representative selections from both sets, with recording to match. The Erato CD will seem, for many, a better way of remembering the film than the complete set. It includes most of the key numbers and the sound is strikingly refined and clear. A generous selection from Solti's set is available on an excellent mid-priced cassette in Decca's Opera Gala series (*417 172-4*).

Carmen (ballet): suite (arr. and scored for strings & percussion by Rodion Shchedrin).
(M) **(*) Olympia Dig. **OCD 108** [id.]. Moscow Virtuoso CO, Armenian State Ch. Ens. & Percussion Ens., Spivakov – SHCHEDRIN: *Frescoes of Dionysius*.**
(*) HMV **CDC7 47198-2 [id.]. LACO, Schwarz.

Rodion Shchedrin's free adaptation of Bizet's *Carmen* music uses Bizet's tunes, complete with harmony, and reworks them into a new tapestry using only strings and percussion (including vibraphone). There is a degree of fragmentation and alterations of timing (not time signatures) to effect some dramatic surprises. The whole thing is brilliantly done and wears surprisingly well. Shchedrin's answer to the obvious question is disarming. 'The image of Carmen has become so well known,' he writes. 'I think that a Carmen without Bizet will always tend to disappoint people. Our memory is too firmly attached to the musical images of the opera. That's why I decided to write a transcription.' The playing of the Moscow Virtuoso group justifies its name; Vladimir Spivakov, having created considerable tension at the pianissimo Introduction, maintains the electricity throughout an exciting performance. He is helped by the concert-hall acoustics of the brilliant digital recording; however, the brightness of the upper strings does bring a degree of harshness in the vivid climax of the *Flower song*. Here the HMV recording made in Los Angeles is warmer and richer, though not more passionate.

Schwarz is more relaxed and smiling throughout, helped by his smoother, more expansive recorded sound. But the bite and drama which make the Russian recording so compulsive are missed at times, and Spivakov is wittier in the *Changing of the Guard* sequence. Schwarz makes for easier and more beguiling listening, but the transient bite of the Russian sound, notably of the side-drum snares, is more arresting. Spivakov also has an interesting if not essential coupling, and is cheaper.

Jeux d'enfants, Op. 22.
*** Ph. Dig. **420 159-2**; *420 159-4* [id.]. Katia & Marielle Labèque – FAURÉ: *Dolly*; RAVEL: *Ma Mère l'Oye*.***

Bizet's enchanting evocation of *Children's games* is not otherwise available on CD except in the less complete orchestral transcription which Haitink has recorded. Even were others to appear, it would not be easy to surpass the Labèque sisters. They characterize Bizet's wonderfully inventive cycle of twelve pieces with vitality, great wit and delicacy of feeling and touch. Superb recording in the best Philips tradition. The cassette, too, is admirably truthful. There is incidentally a complete survey of Bizet's two-handed piano music on Chant du Monde by Par Setrak, but the playing is not persuasive, nor does the recording enjoy the advantage of a sympathetic acoustic.

La jolie fille de Perth (complete).
*** HMV Dig. **CDS7 47559-8**; *EX 270285-9* (2). Anderson, Kraus, Quilico, Van Dam, Zimmermann, Bacquier, Ch. and New PO of R. France, Prêtre.

Based on Scott's *Fair Maid of Perth*, the plot of Bizet's opera is as improbable as many others of the Romantic period, yet it inspired Bizet to one delectable number after another, not just the famous *Serenade* for the tenor hero, Henry Smith. Even that *Serenade* has generally been done in a corrupt version with two parallel verses; in the original score, faithfully reproduced on this fine first recording, the restatement of the melody in the second verse is developed dramatically.

Some of the other numbers – not just arias but choruses too, including some of the finest – were either modified or cut entirely. One of the many delights of the piece lies in relating it to Bizet's supreme masterpiece of eight years later. Here, as in *Carmen*, you have a principal gypsy role for mezzo soprano contrasted against a purer-toned soprano heroine; but this time it is the soprano who is the deliberately provocative one, leaving Henry Smith almost as wounded as Don José in *Carmen*. Unlike *Carmen*, however, this piece ends happily, with the crazed heroine delivering a Lucia-like mad song (coloratura delightfully done by June Anderson) before shocked into sanity for the final curtain. As the hero, Alfredo Kraus sings stylishly – even if at times the voice shows its age. Gino Quilico is superb as the predatory Duke of Rothsay; José van Dam as the apprentice Ralph is aptly lugubrious in his drunken song, and the veteran Gabriel Bacquier makes a delightfully bluff figure of the heroine's father. Margarita Zimmermann (not always well treated by the microphone) as Mab, queen of the gypsies, makes an equivocal role convincing. Georges Prêtre's conducting is warm and understanding, even if ensemble is not always ideally crisp. Full, warm recording to match which sounds most attractive in its more present CD format, though very pleasing on tape also.

Blake, Howard (born 1938)

Clarinet concerto.
*** Hyp. Dig. **CDA 66215**; *KA 66215* [id.]. Thea King, ECO, composer – LUTOSLAWSKI: *Dance preludes*; SEIBER: *Concertino.****

Howard Blake wrote the music for *The Snowman*, a children's story that was an enormous success on TV, video and record. Here he turns his unostentatious lyrical invention to the concert hall, and produces a comparatively slight but endearing *Clarinet concerto*, which is played here with great sympathy by Thea King who commissioned the work. With its neo-classical feeling, it is improvisatory and reflective in its basic style, but produces plenty of energy in the finale with its whiff of Walton. Both couplings are extremely attractive; admirers of the clarinet and of Miss King will find this a most rewarding collection. It is extremely vividly recorded on CD – there is almost a sense of over-presence; the state-of-the-art chrome cassette, however, seems ideal in all respects.

Bliss, Arthur (1891–1975)

(i) *Adam Zero* (ballet): *suite; Checkmate* (ballet): *suite;* (ii) *Meditations on a theme of John Blow.*
*** HMV **CDC7 47712-2**; (M) *ED 291213-4*. (i) Royal Liverpool PO, (ii) CBSO; Handley.

Checkmate was Arthur Bliss's first ballet score and was composed for the Royal Ballet's first visit to Paris in 1937. The idea of a ballet based on chess, with all its opportunities for symbolism and heraldic splendour, appealed to Bliss, and the score he produced remains one of his most inventive creations. The HMV CD, following the precedent the composer himself set in compiling an orchestral suite, omits the main body of the action preceding the final checkmate. The *Adam Zero* music is more extensively represented and much of its invention seems empty nowadays. Yet Vernon Handley makes out the strongest case for both scores and secures playing of great spirit from the Liverpool orchestra. Admirers of Bliss's music need not hesitate here and though *Adam Zero* may not show his muse at its most fertile, there are still good things in it. By far the most substantial and worth while of these three works is *Meditations on a theme of John Blow*, which is Bliss's counterpart to Vaughan Williams's *Tallis fantasia*, though it also has some reminders of *Job*. Using a noble string melody from Blow's setting of Psalm 23, Bliss develops a set of six rhapsodical variations (unfortunately not banded separately on the CD), alternating tranquil and troubled moods, with some dramatic intrusions which the composer attributed to 'the presence of lurking evil'. The work ends with an Interlude, *Through the valley of the shadow of death*, leading to a triumphant finale, *In the House of the Lord*. This, rightly, comes first on the programme and, as the radiant opening immediately demonstrates, shows Handley at his inspirational best, securing the most dedicated playing from the Birmingham orchestra. All this music was recorded within reverberant acoustics; the CD remastering has not been able to add real bite to the ballet suites without creating artificiality, while the more powerful climaxes of the *Meditations* have not the tangibility one would expect with a digital recording; but the full ambient atmosphere, which is so important in this work, is fully retained. There is nearly 74′ of music overall. The tape is offered at mid-price, so costs far less than the CD, but the latter has better definition; however, the cassette quality is fully acceptable and is well balanced.

A Colour symphony; Checkmate (ballet): *suite*.
*** Chan. Dig. **CHAN 8503**; *ABTD 1213* [id.]. Ulster O, Handley.

Bliss's *Colour symphony* has not been committed to disc since the composer's own recording in the mid-1950s. The work itself comes from the early 1920s, and its dissonance raised conservative English eyebrows at the time, though its romantic lineage is obvious. Of course, alongside such of his contemporaries as Stravinsky, Schoenberg and Bartók, Bliss's rhetoric seems mild and his dissonances pale. Given the fact that it was Bliss's first major orchestral score, it shows great expertise and feeling for sonority. Each of its movements evokes the heraldic symbolism of four colours – purple, red, blue and green – and the quality of his invention and imagination is fresh. Vernon Handley plays with complete authority and evident enthusiasm; the *Checkmate* ballet is less of a rarity on record and is given with equal success. Chandos has an enviable reputation for the quality of its engineering and this issue is one of their very best, of demonstration standard on chrome cassette in its own right, as well as on CD.

Things to come (film music): *extended suite* (arr. Palmer).
(*) HMV *ED 291053-4*. RPO, Groves – WALTON: *Capriccio burlesco* etc.(*)

Things to come is given in an extended form, admirably assembled by Christopher Palmer, who has also scored the opening *Prologue*, since the full score and parts do not survive. This work dates more than the *Symphony*, and its style is at times somewhat eclectic. But its invention is always attractive, and the splendid *March* offers what is perhaps the single most memorable idea to come from the pen of its composer. Sir Charles Groves and the RPO are splendid advocates, and the HMV engineers lavish on it their richest and most natural sound. Unfortunately, the use of iron-oxide stock means that the cassette produces a blunted upper range and we must hope a CD is in the offing.

Clarinet quintet.
*** Chan. Dig. *ABTD 1078* [id.]. Hilton, Lindsay Qt – BAX: *Clarinet sonata*** (with VAUGHAN WILLIAMS: *Studies****).

The *Clarinet quintet*, composed in the early 1930s, is arguably Bliss's masterpiece; the present performance is a worthy successor to the 1963 recording by Gervase de Peyer and members of the Melos Ensemble. These artists have the measure of its autumnal melancholy; the recording is natural and well focused, and the chrome cassette is of the highest quality.

String quartets Nos 1 in B flat; 2 in F min.
*** Hyp. **CDA 66178** [id.]. Delmé Qt.

The Bliss *Quartets* make a most welcome addition to the CD catalogue. Bliss's first essay in the quartet medium comes from 1914 but was suppressed – as indeed was a second, composed in California in 1923. The two quartets he acknowledged were both much later works, No. 1 dating from 1940 and its successor from 1950. These performances by the Delmé Quartet are not only thoroughly committed but enormously persuasive and can be recommended even to readers not normally sympathetic to this composer. Both are fine pieces: the *First* is a work of strong character, finely proportioned and not dissimilar in quality of inspiration to the *Music for strings*, written a few years earlier. Bliss regarded the *Second* as his finest chamber work, and the Delmé certainly do it justice. We found the Hyperion recording first rate in its LP format, but on CD it has the extra definition and presence one has grown to expect from silver disc. Strongly recommended.

VOCAL MUSIC

Lie strewn the white flocks.
*** Hyp. **CDA 66175**; *KA 66175* [id.]. Shirley Minty, Judith Pierce (flute), Holst Singers & O, Hilary Davan Wetton – BRITTEN: *Gloriana: Choral dances*; HOLST: *Choral hymns from Rig Veda.****

Bliss's *Pastoral* may be severely classical in its inspiration, from Pan and the world of shepherds and shepherdesses, but its warm and natural expressiveness makes it one of Bliss's most immediately appealing works. It is given a winning performance by the Holst Singers and Orchestra, with the choral sections (the greater part of the work) aptly modest in scale but powerful in impact. With glowing sound and very attractive works for coupling, this is an outstanding issue, the more impressive on CD, but the cassette, too, is first class.

Bloch, Ernest (1880–1959)

Schelomo: Hebrew rhapsody (for cello & orchestra).
*** HMV **CDC7 49307-2** [id.]. Rostropovich, O. Nat. de France, Bernstein – SCHUMANN: *Cello concerto.**(*)
(*) Decca Dig. **414 162-2; *414 162-4* [id.]. Harrell, Concg. O, Haitink – SHOSTAKOVICH: *Cello concerto No. 1.***(*)

Schelomo; Voice in the wilderness.
(M) *** Decca *414 166-4* [id.]. Starker, Israel PO, Mehta.

With the exception of the Elgar *Concerto*, *Schelomo* is arguably the greatest and most eloquent work for cello and orchestra of the first decades of this century. Its colours are intoxicatingly vivid and its atmosphere strong. Bloch originally conceived the score for voice and orchestra but was unsure which language to use for the passages in *Ecclesiastes* that inspired him, and was eventually persuaded to cast it for cello. *Schelomo* calls for a large, though by no means outsize, orchestra including celeste and two harps. Lynn Harrell and Haitink capture much of its rhapsodic intensity, its vision of Solomon's earthly power and the sumptuous riches of his court, though some of its magic eludes them. The excellence of the playing and the clarity and definition of the recording earn it a fairly strong recommendation, even if the coupling is not exceptionally generous.

However, by the side of the Rostropovich version, even Harrell and Haitink sound a bit wan. The collaboration of the great Russian cellist with Leonard Bernstein is a triumph. The rich expressiveness of both artists – with the French orchestra also persuaded into passionately committed playing – blends superbly, so that the rhapsodic flow conveys total concentration, from the deeply meditative opening phrases (*con somma espressione*) onwards. The recording is full to match, but spotlights the soloist. It is a great pity that the Schumann on the reverse is not nearly so successful.

The Starker performances, reissued in the London Enterprise series, come from 1970, a vintage period for Decca analogue recording, and the sound is first rate and very well balanced. The chrome tape is extremely vivid, with transparent textures and a wide range. The *Voice in the wilderness*, a symphonic poem with cello obbligato, is diffuse in layout but has its imaginative moments. *Schelomo* is the more disciplined work. It is finely played by Starker, and Mehta proves sympathetic in both works, even if the last degree of passionate intensity is missing.

Blomdahl, Karl-Birger (1916–68)

Aniara (complete).
*** Cap. **CAP 22016:1/2** [id.]. Noel, Anderberg, Saeden, Arvidson, Haugan, Swedish R. Ch. and SO, Westerberg.

The action of the opera *Aniara* is placed in the remote future when interplanetary travel is almost commonplace. *Aniara* is a space-ship bound for Mars with some 8,000 people on board who are escaping from the poisoned, radio-active atmosphere of the Earth. Soon, the *Aniara* is thrown off course by a shower of meteorites, and her passengers are panic-stricken to learn that they are doomed to travel for ever into inter-galactic space. The years of travel and the immensities of space take their toll: various sects emerge; the ship's evil master, Chefone, establishes a tyranny over the passengers. Ultimately, one by one they perish, until the only survivor, the woman pilot, remains to dance her sad and lonely swan song. There is no doubt that Blomdahl possessed a sophisticated aural imagination and a vital sensibility. What he does lack is real thematic vitality: it is not just a matter of good tunes – most contemporary operas suffer a similar handicap – but the fact that the lines lack both real direction and interest and the stamp of a commanding personal idiom. *Aniara* adds up to a good deal less than the sum of its parts: there is good craftsmanship rather than white-hot inspiration, and expertise rather than mastery. This persuasive and totally committed account by this wonderful cast certainly shows it to best advantage. The recording is in the demonstration class, with remarkable range and altogether superb definition.

Boccherini, Luigi (1743–1805)

Cello concertos Nos 1 in E flat, G. 474; 7 in G, 480; 9 in B flat, G. 482.
(*) HMV Dig. **CDC7 49083-2; *EL 270630-4* [id.]. Möller, Linde Consort, Linde.

The Linde Consort, renowned for their Baroque repertoire, now venture equally authentically into the *galant* world of Boccherini. Here we have the original version of the *B flat Concerto*, played freshly, if without strong individuality, by the excellent Wouter Möller. The orchestral group (4.2.2.1, with 2 oboes, 2 hand horns and harpsichord) plainly seeks a chamber style, but the resonant acoustic amplifies the effect of both the forwardly placed soloist and the accompanying group. Möller plays the fine slow movement of G. 482 with restrained *espressivo*, and throughout his articulation in allegros is neatly rhythmic. Linde provides polished accompaniments, and intonation (so important when there is only the merest hint of vibrato) is excellent: the finale of the *B flat Concerto* has an attractively easy pacing. The other works are hardly less successful, and the *G major* (No. 7) brings out the very best in the performers, with articulate, resilient strings in the outer movements and Möller comparatively intense in the *Adagio*. There is a good chrome cassette, but the CD is sharper in detail.

Cello concerto No. 2 in D, G. 479.

(B) *** DG Walkman *415 330-4* [id.]. Rostropovich, Zurich Coll. Mus., Sacher – HAYDN**; DVOŘÁK: *Cello concertos.****

*(*) Chan. Dig. *ABTD 1145* [id.]. Turovsky, I Musici di Montréal – VIVALDI: *Concertos.**(*)

This is among the most worthwhile of DG's series of bargain-priced double-length Walkman tapes, for it includes a superb account of the Dvořák *Cello concerto* partnering Fournier and Szell. Fournier's account of the Haydn is less memorable, perhaps; but Rostropovich in Boccherini also offers a highly individual musical experience. Although essentially a performance in the grand manner (with Rostropovich providing his own cadenzas), the music making has tremendous vitality, with extremely lively outer movements to balance the eloquence of the *Adagio*. The forceful nature of the performance is short on charm and so perhaps a little out of character for an essentially elegant composer like Boccherini; but Rostropovich is so compelling that reservations are swept aside. He is given an alert accompaniment by Sacher, and the recording has fine body and presence. The chrome tape has excellent range and detail.

Turovsky displays a paler personality and his account is acceptable rather than distinguished, although the recording is good, if not up to Chandos's very best efforts.

Cello concerto No. 9 in B flat, G. 482 (original version).

** Chan. Dig. **CHAN 8470**; *ABTD 1181* [id.]. Turovsky, I Musici di Montréal – J. C. BACH: *Cello concerto* etc.**

The famous *B flat Concerto* cannot be as popular as one imagines, for its representation on compact disc remains modest. Yuli Turovsky, who directs as well as plays, has elegance and warmth, and gets an alert response from the orchestra. Tiny insecurities of intonation make one wonder whether it is always wise to combine both functions, but they are not serious enough to inhibit a recommendation. The recording is truthful and well balanced, and the tape sound is good if a shade diffuse.

Cello concerto in B flat (arr. Grützmacher).

*** CBS **MK 39964**; *IMT 39964* [id.]. Yo-Yo Ma, St Paul CO, Zukerman – J. C. BACH: *Sinfonia concertante* etc.**(*)

(*) HMV **CDC7 47840-2 [id.]. Jacqueline du Pré, ECO, Barenboim – HAYDN: *Concerto in D.****

** Denon Dig. **C37 7023** [id.]. Fujiwara, Netherlands CO, Inoue – HAYDN: *Concerto in D.***

Like Jacqueline du Pré before him, Yo-Yo Ma chooses the Grützmacher version of the Boccherini *Concerto*, romantically derived from three different Boccherini works, but highly effective in its own right. He plays it with taste and finesse, not wearing his heart on his sleeve as obviously as du Pré, but with his warm, if refined, timbre and style not missing the romanticism. The recording is first class.

It is surprising that Jacqueline du Pré chose to do the completely unauthentic Grützmacher version of this concerto, but, as she said herself, 'The slow movement is so beautiful', much more beautiful in fact than the one Boccherini provided. Working for the first time in the recording studio with her husband, Daniel Barenboim, du Pré was inspired to some really heart-warming playing, broadly romantic in style, but then that is what Grützmacher plainly asks for. Perhaps occasionally, by musical instinct, interpreting musicians know better than scholars. The 1967 recording has retained much of its fullness and atmosphere, and the solo cello has good presence, but the orchestral sound is rather less well focused than the Haydn coupling. An endearing performance none the less.

Mari Fujiwara plays with eloquent phrasing, much musical intelligence and beauty of tone; were the orchestral playing under Michi Inoue of equal quality, this would deserve a whole-hearted recommendation. The recording is faithful and well balanced, and it is a pity that the orchestral contribution is not as distinguished.

Keyboard concerto in E flat.
** HMV Dig. **CDC7 47527-2**. Selheim, Coll. Aur., Maier – FIELD: *Rondo*; SCHOBERT: *Concerto*.**

This is an attributed work, but the fortepiano writing has certain Boccherinian characteristics so it may perhaps be authentic. The performance is quite stylish, but does not make a great deal of the theme and variations which ends the piece. The overall effect is cool, aided by the clean, clear recording.

Symphonies: in D; in C, Op. 12/3; in D min., Op. 12/4; in B flat, Op. 35/6; in D min., Op. 37/3; in A, Op. 37/4.
** Chan. Dig. **CHAN 8414-5**; *DBTD 3005* (3) [id.]. Cantilena, Adrian Shepherd.

In all, Boccherini composed twenty symphonies, seven of which are included in this set. Three of the four collections he published, Op. 12 (1771), Op. 35 (1782) and Op. 37 (1786–7), are represented here. The earliest symphony in this set dates from Boccherini's years in Lucca and served as an overture to an extended cantata of 1765; all the others come from the time he spent in Madrid in the service of the Spanish royal family. The *D minor*, Op. 12, No. 4, is the celebrated *La casa del diavalo*, whose finale is based on the chaconne of Gluck's *Don Juan* ballet. Adrian Shepherd and his Cantilena have the measure of this music's grace and gentleness, and are scrupulous in observing repeats. These are sympathetic rather than high-powered performances and will give considerable pleasure, though lacking the last ounce of finish. But there is no want of feeling for this unjustly neglected repertoire and the symphonies are well recorded.

Symphonies: in D min. (*La casa del diavolo*), *Op. 12/4; in A, Op. 12/6; in A, Op. 21/6.*
*** Hyp. Dig. **CDA 66236**; *KA 66236* [id.]. L. Fest. O, Ross Pople.

Ross Pople's record duplicates only one work included in the more ambitious Chandos collection, *La casa del diavolo*, Op. 12/4; in his account the demons are certainly let loose in the finale with the most frantically energetic playing from the strings. Elsewhere the performances are the soul of elegance; in the sunny *A major*, Op. 12/6, where the flutes add a helping of cream to the strawberries, the finesse of the playing gives much pleasure in itself. This is the most ambitious work included here and shows its composer at his most beguiling, even if in the opening movement, as Stanley Sadie aptly commented in *Gramophone*, 'he says nothing twice if he can get away with it four times'. The other A major symphony is also good-tempered and inventive, and altogether this well-played collection can be given the warmest welcome. The mellow acoustics of Watford Town Hall are used to grace the music, and the recording is naturally balanced. Yet textures are transparent and lines are clean, showing how well these symphonies can sound without using period instruments. There is an excellent cassette.

6 Duets, G. 76 (from *String quartets G. 195–200*); *Fandango* (from *String quintet in D, G. 341*).
*(*) HM Dig. **HMC 901233** [id.]. William Christie, Christophe Rousset (harpsichords).

These are transcriptions for two harpsichords of string quartets – or rather *quartettinos* (they are in two movements, hence the diminutive) – composed by Boccherini in 1778 and published three years later as his Op. 32. The manuscript which survives in the Sächsische Landesbibliotek in Dresden would appear to have been made at the end of that century by an unknown hand. They sound less idiomatic in this instrumental format than the *Fandango*, an arrangement of a movement from the *Quintettino for strings*, Op. 40/2, written in 1788. Boccherini himself transcribed it for guitar and quartet ten years later (see below). It certainly works more successfully in this medium than the other quartets. The playing is lively but closely balanced, and recorded at a high level so that the overall effect is somewhat unremitting.

Guitar quintets Nos 4 in D (Fandango); 5 in D; 6 in G, G. 448/50.
*** Ph. **420 385-2** [id.]. Pepe Romero, ASMF Chamber Ens.

The *D major* and *G major Quintets*, G. 449–50, are arrangements of other works made for the benefit of the Marquis of Benavent. Their music is eminently agreeable, but possesses no darker undercurrents. The work subtitled *Fandango* produces a sudden burst of Spanish fireworks in the finale complete with rattling castanets. All three performances are spontaneous and have plenty of warmth, and this makes excellent late-evening background listening. The digital remastering of the 1978/9 originals brings a fine sense of reality and presence, though the sharpening of definition within a fairly resonant acoustic has made the string focus seem just a little fuzzy.

String quartets: in E flat, Op. 6/30 in G (La tiranna spagnola), Op. 44/4.
** Denon Dig. **CO 1029** [id.]. Nuovo Qt – VERDI: *Quartet.***

The Nuovo Quartet, founded in 1983, includes as violist Carlo Chiarappa, who served 32 years with the Quartetto Italiano. They play expertly together, their ensemble is precise, and they give Boccherini's music the finesse it needs. But the approach lacks the ability to charm. They take the opening *Largo* of the *E flat Quartet* very seriously and the result is rather sombre, while the finale of Op. 44/4, a Minuet, has poise but little conveyed enjoyment. At times they seem too intense. This repertoire is of considerable interest and the Denon recording is strikingly truthful and present, but there is more to this music than the Nuovo players discover.

Boismortier, Joseph (1689–1775)

Bassoon sonatas, Op. L/1, 2, 4 & 5; Op. 26/4.
*** Gallo **CD 367**; *47-367* [id.]. Kim Walker, Darryl Nixon, Clena Stein.

Kim Walker, the personable and gifted young bassoonist, born in Chicago but Swiss-trained, here joins that growing group of feminine woodwind executants (alongside Emma Johnson, Thea King and Michala Petri) who have star quality. Her warm timbre and elegant phrasing give consistent pleasure in these tunefully inventive *Sonatas* of Boismortier, with their brief, forcefully characterized movements and distinct flavour, sometimes with a hint of Handel, as in the *D minor Sonata*, Op. L/4, with its very vocal opening cantilena. These are essentially miniature dance suites for bassoon and continuo, with a profusion of engaging *Allemandes*, *Gigs* and *gavottes*. Excellent recording, with a very good tape, although the close balance of the bassoon makes the accompanying continuo sound very discreet, and also tends to reduce the dynamic light and shade. But this is a most attractive collection – although the overall playing time of about 34′ is distinctly ungenerous, and the less expensive tape is consequently recommended.

Boito, Arrigo (1842–1918)

Mefistofele (complete).
(*) Decca Dig. **410 175-2 [id.]. Ghiaurov, Pavarotti, Freni, Caballé, L. Op. Ch., Trinity Boys' Ch., Nat. PO, Fabritiis.
** HMV **CDS7 49522-2** (3) [*CDCB 49522*]. Treigle, Domingo, Caballé, Amb. Op. Ch., Wandsworth School Boys' Ch., LSO, Rudel.

Boito's *Mefistofele* is a strange episodic work to come from the hand of the master-librettist of Verdi's *Otello* and *Falstaff*, but it has many fine movements. The modern digital recording given to the Fabritiis set brings obvious benefits in the extra weight of brass and percussion – most importantly in the heavenly prologue. With the principal soloists all at their best – Pavarotti most seductive in *Dai campi, dai prati*, Freni finely imaginative on detail, Caballé consistently sweet and mellifluous as Elena, Ghiaurov strongly characterful if showing some signs of strain – this is a highly recommendable set, though Fabritiis in his last recording lacks a little in energy, and the chorus is placed rather distantly.

On the mid-1970s HMV set, Caballé assumed the principal role of Margherita; though she missed some of the dark intensity that made Tebaldi's earlier Decca account so moving, particularly in *L'altra notte* (where she also lacks the feeling for detail shown by Freni), she is nevertheless in very good voice. Norman Treigle made the part of Mefistofele his own at the New York City Opera and makes a strong contribution. Though he is not as characterful as Ghiaurov, the Faust/Margherita duet is beautifully done. Placido Domingo as Faust is his usual stylish, confident self, and Rudel conducts with considerable warmth. The sound, however, even in its remastered form, cannot compare with the spectacular Tebaldi Decca set, particularly in the Prologue.

Mefistofele: Prologue.
** Telarc Dig. **CD 80109** [id.]. John Cheek, Young Singers of Callanwolde, Atlanta Ch. and SO, Shaw – BERLIOZ: *Requiem*; VERDI: *Te Deum*.**

Along with Verdi's *Te Deum*, the whole of the *Prologue* from *Mefistofele* makes a generous and attractive fill-up to the CD version of the Telarc Berlioz *Requiem*. Despite some excellent choral singing, finely disciplined, the performance remains obstinately earth-bound, though the heavenly choirs are more convincing than their infernal counterparts, which lack demonry. Fine, clear recording, with massed forces all precisely placed.

Nerone (complete).
(*) Hung. Dig. **HCD 12487/9-2 [id.]. Nagy, Tokody, Dene, Miller, Takács, Gregor, Hungarian R. and TV Ch., Hungarian State Op. O, Queler.

Eve Queler conducts a powerful and atmospheric performance of Boito's massive, uncompleted opera. It occupied the composer for the last fifty years of his life, and though (not surprisingly) it hardly matches his earlier *Mefistofele* in freshness and variety and presents an unsatisfyingly episodic plot, there are dozens of marvellous ideas, starting with the strikingly original opening, sliding in like *Aida* updated. Later too the piece is full of prayers and ceremonial music, all of it richly colourful and superbly performed by the company of the Hungarian State Opera whose soloists are far less afflicted with Slavonic wobbles than is common in Eastern Europe. Notable in the cast are Ilona Tokody as the heroine, Klara Takács, Lajos Miller as the Christian leader, and Janos Nagy as a disconcertingly engaging Nero, a tenor role. The recording is of outstanding quality, with the atmospheric perspectives demanded by the score most realistically conveyed.

Borodin, Alexander (1833–87)

Symphonies Nos 1 and 3.
** Chant du Monde **LDC 278 781**. USSR Ac. SO, Svetlanov.

Symphony No. 2 in B min.; In the Steppes of central Asia; (i) *Prince Igor: Polovtsian dances.*
(*) Chant du Monde **LDC 278 272 [id.]. USSR Ac. SO; (i) and Ch.; Svetlanov.

Symphony No. 2 in B min.; Prince Igor: Overture; Polovtsian dances.
(M) *** ASV Dig. **CDQS 6018** [id.]; *ZCQS 6018* [id.]. Mexico State SO, Bátiz.

Svetlanov gives vivid and well-characterized readings of the Borodin symphonies which may not be the most subtle performances but none the less have plenty of spirit as well as acceptable recording to commend them. His accounts are the first Borodin symphonies to reach CD. Glazunov completed the first two movements of the *Third*, relying on his memory of Borodin's performances on the piano, aided by sketches; whatever their authorship, the results are highly attractive. Svetlanov gives a convincing account both of it and of the little-heard *First Symphony*, though there could perhaps be more refinement at times, notably in the scherzo. The sound is very acceptable, without being in any way outstanding. On the second of the two CDs the *Polovtsian dances* make a vivid and exciting bonus. The recording dates from 1966.

Bátiz's bright, modern digital recording certainly makes a vivid impression and the performances are extremely spirited. The first movement is taken very fast and reminds us of Martinon's famous version with the LSO (now deleted). The slow movement is undoubtedly eloquent, with a fine horn solo, but in the vivacious scherzo (and again later in the *Prince Igor overture*) one is made to realize that the Mexican State orchestra, though impressively rehearsed, cannot match the finest European orchestras in virtuosity and finesse. Even so, Bátiz has the gift of bringing music alive in the recording studio, and this applies to the *Overture* also (though at times he drives rather hard). The *Polovtsian dances* are without a chorus and the effect is slightly shrill, but the energy of the performance is arresting. This is issued in the budget range and is excellent value.

String quartets Nos 1 in A; 2 in D.
*** HMV **CDC7 47795-2** [id.]. Borodin Qt

String quartet No. 2 in D.
(M) *** Olympia Dig. **OCD 138** [id.]. Borodin Qt – TANEYEV: *Quintet.****
* Denon Dig. **C37 7814** [id.]. Prague Qt – PROKOFIEV: *Quartet No. 2.**

The HMV performances from the eponymous Borodin Quartet are admirable in all respects. They are completely effortless and idiomatic; indeed, so total is their sense of identification with these scores that one is scarcely conscious of the intervention of the interpreter. The quality achieved by the Melodiya engineers has fine clarity; this is enhanced in the CD transfer, and the focus of the first violin line is firmer than before. But the ambient warmth remains, although the sound is perhaps just a shade harder than on the original analogue LP. The recording dates from 1980.

On Olympia, the alternative version from the Borodin Quartet is equally masterly. The performance is virtually indistinguishable in quality from their HMV version and they are beautifully recorded. The Olympia CD has a price advantage, and the Taneiev *Quintet* is certainly well worth investigating.

The Prague ensemble recorded their account in Tokyo in 1977 and, to be frank, theirs is no match for the Borodin Quartet. It seems to begin promisingly but rhythms are heavy, and the dynamic range is by no means as wide. Nor do they possess the delicacy or the inner vitality or imagination of their celebrated rivals, though they are well recorded.

The famous *Nocturne* from the *Second Quartet* is included as a bonus on the Philips coupling of Dvořák's *American quartet* and Schubert's *Death and the Maiden* by the Italian Quartet (**420 876-2**; *420 876-4*), a mid-priced bargain.

Prince Igor: Overture; Polovtsian dances.
(M) *** Decca *417 689-4* [id.]. LSO, Solti – GLINKA: *Russlan overture*; MUSSORGSKY: *Night on the bare mountain* etc.***
*** Telarc Dig. **CD 80039**. Atlanta Ch. and SO, Shaw – STRAVINSKY: *Firebird suite.***(*)

Prince Igor: Polovtsian dances.
*** HMV **CDC7 47717** [id.]; (M) *ED 291180-4.* Beecham Choral Soc., RPO, Beecham – RIMSKY-KORSAKOV: *Scheherazade.****
(M) *** DG **419 063-2**; *419 063-4* [id.]. BPO, Karajan – RIMSKY-KORSAKOV: *Scheherazade.****
(M) *** HMV **CDM7 69041-2** [id.]. Philh. O, Karajan – GOUNOD: *Faust ballet****; OFFENBACH: *Gaîté parisienne***(*); PONCHIELLI: *Dance of the hours.****
** Decca **414 124-2** [id.]. Lausanne R. Ch. and Children's Ch., SRO, Ansermet – RIMSKY-KORSAKOV: *Scheherazade.***

Beecham's 1957 recording of the *Polovtsian dances*, made in EMI's Abbey Road studios, sweeps the board, even though it omits the percussion-led opening *Dance of the Polovtsi Maidens.* Beecham draws an almost Russian fervour from his choristers who sing with enormous enthusiasm, and the orchestral playing creates a comparable excitement, building to a tremendous climax. The recorded sound is little short of astonishing in its fullness, vividness and clarity. There is a very good cassette, which costs much less than the CD, but the latter is well worth every penny.

Karajan's Berlin Philharmonic version does include the introductory section missing on the Beecham record (so does Solti) and his account has great flair and excitement too, though not a chorus. It is linked to another very impressive version of *Scheherazade* and has a distinct price advantage. The alternative Philharmonia account comes from 1960 but hardly shows its age – the recording sounds full as well as brilliant. The Philharmonia wind playing is a pleasure in itself, and there is plenty of dash and excitement at the end.

Solti's account was originally issued in 1967. It is part of an outstanding collection of Russian music which includes charismatic Mussorgsky and a breathtaking version of Glinka's *Russlan and Ludmilla overture.* Reissued on tape in Decca's bargain Weekend series, it is well worth its modest cost, even if the new transfer is artificially brightened, for the basic recording has plenty of body and colour. His version of the *Polovtsian dances* is also among the finest ever recorded, with good choral singing – even if the chorus takes a little longer to warm up than Sir Thomas's group. The *Overture* too has fine dash, with the LSO players consistently on their toes.

It would be churlish not to give the remarkable Telarc digital recording of the *Polovtsian dances* a full recommendation. The choral singing is less clearly focused in the lyrical sections of the score than at climaxes, but the singers undoubtedly rise to the occasion. The entry of the bass drum is riveting and the closing section very exciting. The vivid sound balance is equally impressive in the *Overture*, and if the Atlanta orchestra does not possess the body of string timbre to make the very most of the sweeping second subject, the playing has vitality and spontaneity in its favour. Robert Shaw's overall direction is thoroughly musical.

Ansermet's performance is a reliably good one, though the tension tends to sag in the passages where the choir – which is not outstanding – is expected to carry the music with only slight support from the orchestra. The end goes well.

Bottesini, Giovanni (1821–89)

Music for double-bass: *Capriccio bravura; Fantasia on Beatrice di Tenda; Grande allegro di concerto; Introduzione e gavotta; Romanza drammatica.*
** ASV *ZCALH 939.* Martin, Halstead.

The mechanical limitations of the double-bass mean that harmonics performed with scientific accuracy are out of tune. Thomas Martin is a superb virtuoso of the instrument, who relishes these display pieces, but some of the high melodies are oddly painful. A curiosity issue with first-rate sound and excellent accompaniment from Anthony Halstead, better known as a fine horn-player. The cassette is well balanced, but the upper range is slightly restricted.

Gran duo concertante for violin, double-bass and orchestra; Gran concerto in F sharp min. for double-bass; Andante sostenuto for strings; Duetto for clarinet and double-bass.
(*) ASV Dig. **CDDCA 563; *ZCDCZA 563* [id.]. Garcia, Martin, Emma Johnson, ECO, Andrew Litton.

The ASV recording combines the *Gran duo concertante* with another *Duo for clarinet and double bass* which Emma Johnson ensures has plenty of personality. The *Andante sostenuto for strings* is pleasant enough, but the *Double-bass concerto* fails to convince. Thomas Martin makes an essentially lyrical approach, whereas a gruffer manner might have given greater projection; musically, however, he is responsive and his technique and intonation are remarkable to produce such an easy style. To be frank, none of this amiable music is very distinctive. The recording is excellent, well balanced and truthful, and there is a good cassette. There is an alternative recording of the *Gran duo concertante* on Philips, coupled with Mendelssohn's early *Concerto for violin and piano*, a curious pairing (**420 272-2**; *420 272-4*). The performances are good and so is the recording, but those interested in the Bottesini will find the ASV issue more worth while.

Boughton, Rutland (1878–1960)

The Immortal hour (opera): complete.
*** Hyp. Dig. **CDA 66101/2** [id.]. Kennedy, Dawson, Wilson-Johnson, Davies, Geoffrey Mitchell Ch., ECO, Melville.

This gently lyrical evocation of Celtic twilight hit London by storm in the 1920s and early 1930s, with four extended runs. There is far more to it than the still-celebrated *Faery song*, which hauntingly is heard first at the end of Act I, sung by a chorus in the distance. Analysed closely, much of it may seem like Vaughan Williams and water, but this fine performance conducted by a lifelong Boughton devotee brings out the hypnotic quality which had 1920s music-lovers attending performances many times over. The simple tunefulness goes with a fine feeling for atmosphere. The excellent cast of young singers includes the Ferrier prizewinner, Anne Dawson, as the heroine Princess Etain and Maldwyn Davies headily beautiful in the main tenor rendering of the *Faery song*. Warm, reverberant recording, undoubtedly enhanced in its CD format.

Boyce, William (1710–79)

Concerti grossi: in B flat; in B min.; in E min.; Overture in F.
*** Chan. *ABT 1005*. Cantilena, Shepherd.

Though these *Concerti grossi* have not quite the consistent originality which makes the Boyce symphonies so refreshing, the energy of the writing – splendidly conveyed in these performances – is recognizably the same, with fugal passages that turn in unexpected directions. The overture which complements these three *Concerti grossi* (all that Boyce completed) was written for the *New Year's Ode* in 1762, a French overture with fugue. Good recording; the high-level cassette transfer is full and natural.

12 Overtures.
**(*) Chan. *DBT 2002* (2). Cantilena, Shepherd.

The eight Boyce symphonies have been recorded many times, but this collection, put together ten years later in 1770 though including at least one work from as early as 1745, has much of comparable vigour. Unfortunately the first overture is not one of the best, but each has its attractions, and those which bring out the brass are most exciting. In 1770 Boyce, already deaf, was regarded as old-fashioned and was never given a proper hearing with this music. Cantilena's performances are not always as crisp and vigorous as they might be, but they certainly convey enough of the freshness of Boyce's inspiration; the recording, though oddly balanced, is convincingly atmospheric. On cassette the sound was originally much brighter (to the point of fierceness) on the first tape than on the second, which is better balanced without loss of vividness. However, this imbalance may have been corrected by now.

Symphonies Nos 1–8.
*** DG Dig. **419 631-2** [id.]. E. Concert, Pinnock.
*** Argo **417 824-2** [id.]. ASMF, Marriner.
*** CRD **CRD 3356**; *CRD 4056* [id.]. Bournemouth Sinf., Ronald Thomas.

Pinnock's disc of the Boyce *Symphonies* is a delight, the first recording to use period instruments. It wears its scholarship very easily and in so doing brings not only lively, resilient playing but fresh revelation in the treatment of the *vivace* movements, which are normally taken faster than is authentic, when that marking in eighteenth-century England did not have its modern connotation of speed. Nicely scaled recording, bright but atmospheric.

Marriner also treats these superb examples of English baroque to exhilarating performances, with the rhythmic subtleties in both fast music and slow guaranteed to enchant. The recording was made in 1978 at St John's, Smith Square, and it has plenty of ambience, while the digital remastering ensures brighter lighting to the upper strings in a beneficial way. The listener now experiences more of the bite one would expect from an authentic version, yet the expressive style of modern instruments and the absence of bulges in the phrasing bring an approach that should satisfy most ears. It is a pity that there is no indexing – there is only a single cue for each symphony.

Thomas's tempi are often brisker than those adopted by Marriner, and certainly swifter-paced than Pinnock's 'new look'. But even against such strong competition as this, the buoyant playing still gives much pleasure by its sheer vitality. The CD is impressively remastered. With the orchestra placed at a believable distance – though the harpsichord fails to make a strong impression – the balance is truthful and detail is enhanced. The cassette too is first rate.

Brahms, Johannes (1833–97)

Piano concertos Nos 1–2; Fantasias, Op. 116.
*** DG **419 158-2** (2); (M) (without *Fantasias*) *413 229-4* (2). Gilels, BPO, Jochum.

In the Brahms *Piano concertos*, the performances from the early 1970s by Gilels with Jochum still dominate the catalogue. Gilels brings a combination of magisterial strength and a warmth, humanity and depth that are altogether inspiring. Jochum is a superb accompanist. The recording is resonant and does not focus the piano in truthful proportion to the orchestra, but the digital remastering has improved definition and the sound is full in an appropriately Brahmsian way. The CDs also offer the *Fantasias*, Op. 116, where Gilels displays artistry of an order that silences criticism; the excellent chrome cassettes offer the concertos alone, but by way of compensation are in the mid-price range.

Piano concerto No. 1 in D min., Op. 15.
*** Ph. Dig. **420 071-2**; *420 071-4* [id.]. Brendel, BPO, Abbado.
*** Decca Dig. **410 009-2** [id.]. Ashkenazy, Concg. O, Haitink.
(M) **(*) EMI *EMX 41 2085-4* [Ang. Sera. *4XG 60411*]. Barenboim, New Philh. O, Barbirolli.
(*) RCA **RD 85668 [**RCA 5668-2-RC**]. Rubinstein, Chicago SO, Reiner.

(*) Ph. **420 702-2; *420 702-4* [id.]. Arrau, Concg. O, Haitink.
** DG Dig. **413 472-2** [id.]. Zimerman, VPO, Bernstein.
(B) ** DG Dig. *419 831-4*. Zimerman, VPO, Bernstein (with SCHUMANN: *Concerto***).
*(*) RCA Dig. **RD 84962** [**RCD1 4962**]. Ax, Chicago S O, Levine.
(M) *(*) DG **419 470-2**; *419 470-4* [id.]. Pollini, VPO, Boehm.

(i) *Piano concerto No. 1; Variations on a theme of Haydn* (*St Anthony chorale*).
(***) Decca mono **421 143-2** [id.]. Curzon; Concg. O, Van Beinum.

Piano concerto No. 1; Intermezzi: in E flat, Op. 117/1; in C, Op. 119/3.
*** Decca **417 641-2** [id.]. Clifford Curzon, LSO, Szell.

Alfred Brendel's 1987 version of Brahms's *First Piano concerto* brings one of his very finest concerto performances on record. He produces a consistently beautiful sound and balances the combative and lyrical elements of the work with well nigh perfect judgement. With Claudio Abbado and the Berlin Philharmonic as understanding partners, he completely shakes off the inhibitions that have sometimes seemed to beset him in the studio – or even when he has consciously planned a live recording – and the result is both strong and spontaneous. His control of Brahmsian rubato is masterly, when it is easily flexible but totally unexaggerated, and the basic tempi are well and steadily set. The first movement has youthful urgency combined with mature weight, the slow movement is raptly intense, and the finale, at a daringly fast speed, is exhilarating. The balance is not too forward and, though the Berlin recording is not ideally transparent (this is particularly noticeable on the chrome tape), the effect is warmly satisfying.

Clifford Curzon's 1962 recording, produced by John Culshaw in Kingsway Hall, returns to the catalogue, carefully remastered by the Decca engineers. The original fierceness in the strings, especially in the powerful opening tutti, has been convincingly smoothed without too much loss of range. The overall sound seems fuller on some reproducers than on others, but the piano tone is consistently good. Curzon has the full measure of Brahms's keyboard style and penetrates both the reflective inner world of the slow movement and the abundantly vital and massive opening movement. The piano balance is most satisfying. As a bonus for the reissue, Decca have added two beautifully played *Intermezzi*, recorded in the Vienna Sofiensaal – although here the restriction of the upper range of the piano timbre, with the elimination of background, is the more noticeable.

Ashkenazy gives a commanding and magisterial account of the solo part that is full of poetic imagination. All the different facets of the score – its combative energy, its strength and tenderness – are fully delineated. In the slow movement the atmosphere is not quite as rapt or hushed as in the Zimerman version; taken as a whole, however, the performance is very impressive indeed and there is superlative playing from the Concertgebouw Orchestra. The recording is enormously vivid, though the balance may worry some collectors. The forward placing of the soloist gives the lower and middle registers of the piano a disproportionate amount of aural space, and one or two octaves appear not to be absolutely true.

The partnership of Barenboim and Barbirolli, when they made their recording in 1968, was an inspirational one. The playing is heroic and marvellously spacious, yet the performance is sustained by its intensity of concentration, especially in the pianissimo passages of the slow movement. The recording is realistic and well balanced, although the cassette is slightly restricted in the upper range. We must hope that this is down for later reissue on CD.

Rubinstein's Chicago recording was made in stereo as early as 1954 and the sound remains remarkably good, thanks to the sympathetic Chicago acoustics. This is a poetic and essentially lyrical reading, impulsive and avoiding Brahmsian stodginess – though it is by no means without power, for Reiner's control of the orchestra, volatile and imaginative, has a spacious strength. The only snag is the forward balance of the piano which means that, as in Rubinstein's

RCA version of the *Second Concerto*, a real pianissimo fails to register, although the recording attractively brings out the brightness of Rubinstein's tone. This is a fine memento of a great artist, not the most profound version but a consistently enjoyable one.

Arrau's reading has vision and power and, though there are some characteristic agogic distortions that will not convince all listeners, he is majestic and eloquent. There is never an ugly sonority even in the moments of the greatest vehemence. By the side of Curzon he seems idiosyncratic but, given the excellence of the digitally remastered recording and the warmth of Haitink's support, this is well worth considering in the medium-price range. The chrome tape is very good but the resonant bass needs adjusting.

Clifford Curzon's early mono version, recorded with the Concertgebouw in 1953, makes a welcome reappearance as one of the Dutch orchestra's centenary celebration issues, and the coupling with Eduard van Beinum's 1952 version of the Brahms *Haydn variations* is both welcome and generous. Though it cannot quite match Curzon's later version with Szell in its poetic intensity and breadth (the timing alone of the slow movement underlines the contrast between the two performances with Szell much more spacious, lasting three minutes longer), it still finds the pianist at his freshest and most individual, bitingly spontaneous in the first movement, warmly lyrical in the slow movement and concentrated in the finale, even if not quite as sparkling as in the later version. The mono sound, obviously limited, adjusts easily to the ear.

Krystian Zimerman's remarkable partnership with Bernstein brings the most spacious reading, in which slow speeds are pursued steadily with rapt concentration. Undoubtedly Zimerman is allowed to dominate the performance, but although the slow movement is lovingly played the generous use of rubato in the first movement is not entirely convincing and there is a tendency to lay greater store by beauty of detail than coherence of structure. Nevertheless the CD has impressive presence. Admirers of these artists will note, however, that this performance is available on a bargain-priced Pocket Music tape, generously coupled with the Schumann *Piano concerto*. The high transfer level is of sophisticated quality, the sound-balance somewhat brighter than on the CD. The tape turnover comes before the last movement.

Emanuel Ax gives a thoughtful and intelligent reading in which his reticence is contrasted with the extrovert boldness of conductor and orchestra. The meditation of the slow movement is played with moving simplicity. The recording acoustic is helpfully reverberant, with good balance between piano and orchestra, but there is a distracting edge on high violins and some lack of inner clarity in tuttis.

With Pollini there is always much to admire, not least the masterly pianism. But he brings little spontaneity or tenderness to this concerto and this performance in no way matches his admired account of the *Second*. This is uncommitted and wanting in passion. Good recording.

There is also, on Olympia, a memento of the 1986 Tchaikovsky Piano Competition, with a performance from the winner, Barry Douglas. The recording, made at a Moscow concert, is acceptable (though there is a microphone bump in the opening tutti). Douglas gives a muscular and often thoughtful reading: there is some fine pianissimo tone, even if his fortissimo is occasionally over-assertive. But with sluggish orchestral playing at the opening and opaque orchestral textures, this fails to be really competitive, even at a reduced price (**OCD 137**).

Arrau's 1961 version with Giulini has also been reissued at mid-price (HMV **CDC7 69177-2**). Never fiery, it is essentially a relaxed, graceful performance, but with a big climax in the slow movement. On the whole the later Philips CD is preferable.

Piano concerto No. 2 in B flat, Op. 83.

(M) *** RCA **GD 86518**; *GK 86518* [RCA **6518-2-RG**; *6518-4*]. Sviatoslav Richter, Chicago SO, Leinsdorf – BEETHOVEN: *Piano sonata No. 23.****

(M) *** DG **419 471-2**; *419 471-4* [id.]. Pollini, VPO, Abbado.

(B) *** DG Walkman *419 087-4* [id.]. Gilels, BPO, Jochum – SCHUMANN: *Concerto.****

**(*) DG Dig. *415 359-2* [id.]. Zimerman, VPO, Bernstein.
(M) **(*) EMI *TC-EMX 2110* [Ang. Sera. *4XG 60412*]. Barenboim, New Philh. O, Barbirolli.
(M) **(*) Ph. *416 238-4* [id.]. Arrau, Concg. O, Haitink.
** Decca Dig. **410 199-2** [id.]. Ashkenazy, VPO, Haitink.
(M) ** Decca **417 710-2** [id.]; *417 710-4*. Ashkenazy, LSO, Mehta.
*(*) Decca **414 142-2** [id.]; (B) *417 682-4*. Backhaus, VPO, Boehm.

Piano concerto No. 2; Intermezzi: in E min., Op. 116/5; in B flat min., Op. 117/2; Rhapsody in G min., Op. 79/2.
*** RCA **RD 85671**. Rubinstein, RCA SO, Josef Krips.

Brahms's *Second Piano concerto* is remarkably well represented on CD at mid-price. To make the 1960 Richter version even more attractive, RCA have added his powerful reading of Beethoven's *Appassionata sonata*. The performance of the concerto has all the intensity of a live occasion and finds Richter in splendid form. It is a wayward account, mannered in places, but the basic structure is always kept in sight; there is impressive weight and authority as well as a warm Brahmsian lyrical feeling. It is far more spontaneous and dashing than Richter's later recording with Maazel and the Orchestre de Paris for EMI, or indeed Zimerman's more recent digital version; Richter's reading catches fire and, with the recording enhanced by the digital remastering – there is slight loss in the upper range but the piano timbre is fuller and the Chicago acoustics ensure that the orchestral texture is full-bodied and atmospheric – this is highly recommendable.

Pollini's 1977 recording makes a good alternative choice, also at mid-price, and there is an excellent matching chrome tape. Pollini's account is powerful, in many ways more classical in feeling than Gilels's or Richter's. He has the measure of the work's scale and breadth and is given first-rate support by the Vienna Philharmonic under Abbado. This is among the most impressive versions in the catalogue; there is unfailing perception here and detail is never invested with excessive significance at the expense of the overall view. The remastered sound has a Brahmsian body and warmth, although the upper range is not as open as a digital recording would be.

Rubinstein's scintillating and very involving performance was recorded at the Manhattan Center, New York City, in 1958. In many respects the remastered recording sounds splendid, but the piano, for all its vivid realism, is almost in one's lap; the close balance means that a true pianissimo is never registered, even though the playing of soloist and orchestra alike obviously seeks the widest range of dynamic. Rubinstein was at his peak, and his technical mastery brings a charismatic response to the changing moods of the first movement, while the finale is a delight with its deftness of articulation and rippling lyricism. Rubinstein was lucky to have Josef Krips as his collaborator, for he brings a Viennese touch to the orchestra and matches Rubinstein's spontaneity. This is a reading which emphasizes the bright and luminous aspects of the work and is all the more refreshing for that, even if other accounts have more gravitas and weight. The three substantial encores are well chosen to make a miniature (15-minute) solo recital after the concerto; once again, the sound is realistic and the playing distinguished.

For tape collectors there is a marvellous bargain Walkman where Gilels's performance is coupled with Wilhelm Kempff's 1974 recording of the Schumann *Concerto*, which is no less desirable. In the Brahms, the partnership of Gilels and Jochum produces music making of rare distinction; if the resonant recording has some want of sharpness of focus, the spacious acoustic and rich piano timbre seem well suited to this massive concerto.

The Bernstein/Zimerman account is eccentric to an extreme; indeed the tempo of the opening movement reaches the composer's *Allegro non troppo* marking only at the orchestral tutti. Throughout the performance there is a constant ebb and flow in the music's momentum, and while music making of this calibre, which combines charismatic brilliance with both power and grandeur, could be marvellously stimulating at a live concert, the self-conscious nature of the reading is likely to prove more worrying with the repetition possible on the gramophone. While the mastery of both soloist and conductor is never in doubt, and the recording is spacious and wide-ranging with the forwardly balanced piano very tangible on CD, this record must be approached with a degree of caution.

Barenboim's account with Barbirolli is also controversial. It is another highly individual view, with slow tempi, which enables Barbirolli to draw much loving playing from the New Philharmonia. If the first two movements are grandly heroic (with the lyrical passages merging naturally into the slow basic tempi), the slow movement has something of the awed intensity one finds in the middle movement of the *First Concerto*. Yet, with its glowing spontaneity, it is a performance to love, once the spacious conception has registered successfully. The recording has been freshened, with only slight loss of body.

Arrau's account of the concerto is competitive at medium price. There are one or two idiosyncratic touches (bars 89–91 in the first movement) and some detail is underlined expressively in this artist's characteristic way; but the playing has a splendid combination of aristocratic finesse and warmth of feeling, and Haitink and the Concertgebouw Orchestra give excellent support. The engineers strike the right balance between the piano and orchestra, and the orchestral texture is better focused and cleaner than in the earlier Arrau recording. Although this is not a first choice, it must figure high on the list and should not be missed by admirers of the great Chilean pianist. As with the *First Concerto*, the cassette has been remastered and given quite a high transfer level, so that the sound is full and vivid, with a bold, natural piano image, if not quite so clear overall as the companion tape of the *First Concerto*. No doubt this recording will appear on mid-priced CD in due course.

What is surprising about the two Ashkenazy versions is not only how alike they are, in spite of very different conductors, but that both suffer from lack of electricity. The new digital version with Haitink is given sound of striking presence, and the partnership brings a conception that is thoughtful in detail, but without a strong forward impulse. Speeds are cautious and the style of the lyrical episodes of the second movement is overtly expressive. The slow movement is very beautiful, and the finale offers the proper contrast; in the last resort, however, this is disappointing. The earlier version, with Mehta, was recorded in conjunction with a live performance at the Festival Hall, the sessions taking place (at Kingsway Hall) immediately after the concert. That being so, it is the more remarkable to find that the chief shortcoming of the account is lack of tension. With much beautiful detail and some very poetic playing from Ashkenazy, the performance still fails to come alive as it should, and throughout one is left uninvolved. The recording quality is excellent and the remastering has tamed the originally somewhat edgy strings; now they sound full and sweet. There is a lack of transparency compared with the later digital version, but plenty of atmosphere and bloom.

Admirers of Backhaus will be glad to have his late 1960s Decca recording, available both on CD and on an inexpensive Weekend tape, sounding fresh and clear with only slight loss of body. Whether or not one responds to his sober and unsmiling performance, there is no question of either its magisterial grandeur or his massive technique. There is undoubtedly a certain marmoreal splendour here and also first-class orchestral playing under Boehm; but in the finale there is too little real affection or sense of joy.

Like the companion version of No. 1, the Arrau/Giulini recording from the early 1960s has its merits. However, the performance suffers from one or two mannerisms which are unappealing and there is some lack of overall spontaneity (HMV **CDM7 69178-2**).

Alas, the Gilels/Reiner partnership of 1959, an early staple of the stereo catalogue, has been spoilt in its CD remastering by shrill orchestral sound and a clattery piano image; it cannot possibly be recommended (RCA **RD 85405 [RCD1 5406]**).

Violin concerto in D, Op. 77.
(M) *** Ph. **420 703-2**; *420 703-4* [id.]. Grumiaux, New Philh. O, C. Davis – BRUCH: *Concerto No. 1.***(*)
*** RCA **RD 85402** [**RCD1 5402**]. Heifetz, Chicago SO, Reiner – BEETHOVEN: *Concerto.***(*)
*** DG Dig. **400 064-2**; *3302 032* [id.]. Mutter, BPO, Karajan.
(M) (***) EMI mono **CDH7 61011-2** [id.]. Ginette Neveu, Philh. O, Issay Debrowen – SIBELIUS: *Concerto.*(***)
(M) **(*) HMV **CDM7 69034-2** [id.]. David Oistrakh, French Nat. R. O, Klemperer.
(M) **(*) CBS **MYK 42609.** Stern, Phd. O, Ormandy.
(*) CBS [MK 42257**]. Stern, Phd. O, Ormandy – DVOŘÁK: *Concerto.***(*)
(*) HMV **CDC7 47166-2 [id.]. Perlman, Chicago SO, Giulini.
(*) Decca **411 677-2. Belkin, LSO, Ivan Fischer.
(B) **(*) DG Walkman *413 844-4* [id.]. Ferras, BPO, Karajan – BEETHOVEN: *Romances**** (also with BRUCH: *Violin concerto No. 1***).
(M) ** Olympia Dig. **OCD 102** [id.]. Tretyakov, USSR RSO, Fedoseyev – SCHUMANN: *Cello concerto.***(*)

(i) *Violin concerto;* (ii) *Variations on a theme of Haydn;* (ii; iii) *Alto rhapsody, Op. 53.*
(M) *(**) RCA **GD 86716**; *GK 86716* [**RCA 6716-2-RG**]. (i) Szeryng, LSO, Monteux; (ii) Phd. O, Ormandy; (iii) with Verrett and Temple University Ch.

(i) *Violin concerto;* (ii) *Violin sonata No. 2 in A, Op. 100.*
(M) ** DG *415 838-4* [id.]. Zukerman; (i) O de Paris, Barenboim; (ii) Barenboim (piano).

Violin concerto; (i) *Double concerto for violin, cello and orchestra, Op. 102.*
(B) * DG Dig. *419 832-4*. Kremer; (i) with Maisky, VPO, Bernstein.

Grumiaux's performance of the Brahms *Concerto*, it goes without saying, is full of insight and lyrical eloquence, and Sir Colin Davis lends his soloist the most sympathetic support. His introduction to the first movement has striking breadth. Grumiaux is a wonderful player; at mid-price, coupled with the Max Bruch *G minor Concerto* (a work with which Grumiaux, with his essentially classical style, has slightly less natural affinity), this excellent CD could well be first choice for many readers, particularly in view of the excellence of the remastered Philips sound, which is firm, detailed and refined, with believable presence, and a warm ambience.

Heifetz's 78 r.p.m. gramophone performances were always something of an occasion, and his compact disc début in the Brahms *Concerto* is certainly cause for celebration. Like the Beethoven on the reverse, the CD transfer of this dazzling performance makes vivid and fresh what on LP was originally a rather harsh Chicago recording, more aggressive than the Boston sound in the Beethoven. With the CD, the excellent qualities of RCA's Chicago balance for Reiner come out in full, giving a fine three-dimensional focus to display this high-powered partnership at its most formidable. The speeds for all three movements may be fast, but Heifetz's ease and detailed imagination make them more than just dazzling. Genuine allegros in the outer movements give a totally refreshing slant on a work often regarded as more lyrical than urgently dramatic, while the central *Andante*, at a flowing speed, is delectably songful. Anyone who wants to hear this great virtuoso, counted to be the master of masters, at his very peak cannot do better than obtain this superb CD. The two concertos together play for rather longer than 72 minutes and therefore just fit within the possible time-span.

Anne-Sophie Mutter, early in her career, provided a performance of the Brahms *Concerto* as commanding as any, matching fiery bravura with a glowing expressive quality, in a reading that is freshly spontaneous in every bar. In many ways her playing combines the unforced lyrical feeling of Krebbers (whose highly recommendable version is currently out of the catalogue) with the flair and individuality of Perlman. There is a lightness of touch, a gentleness in the slow movement that is highly appealing, while in the finale the incisiveness of the solo playing is well displayed by the clear (yet not clinical) digital recording. Needless to say, Karajan's accompaniment is strong in personality and the Berlin Philharmonic play beautifully, but he is by no means the dominant musical personality; the performance represents a genuine musical partnership between youthful inspiration and eager experience. The recording is given vivid presence on compact disc, although its clarity emphasizes the close balance of the soloist, and there is a touch of fierceness in the orchestral upper range in tuttis. The chrome cassette is smoother.

Unlike her classic reading of the Sibelius concerto, Ginette Neveu's other concerto recording, of the Brahms, also made in London not long before she was so tragically killed in an air-crash, has been long neglected. It is a magnificent performance, urgently electric, remarkable not just for the sweetness of tone and pinpoint intonation but for the precision and clarity of even the most formidable passages of double-stopping. This is a reading as remarkable for its toughness and power as for the warmth and poetry one would expect from an outstanding woman virtuoso. Though dynamic contrasts are limited, the transfer from the original 78s brings satisfyingly full-bodied sound, surprisingly good on detail. Coupled with the Sibelius on a mid-price Références disc, it makes an outstanding bargain.

The conjunction of two such positive artists as Oistrakh and Klemperer make for a reading characterful to the point of idiosyncrasy, monumental and strong rather than sweetly lyrical; the opening of the first movement has a feeling of engulfing power. The slow movement is particularly fine, and the French oboist plays beautifully. Oistrakh sounds superbly poised and confident, and in the finale, if the tempo is a shade deliberate, the total effect is one of clear gain. The 1961 recording is quite full and clear, but the CD transfer has brought, along with a bright treble, an element of steeliness to the solo violin timbre.

Stern's 1959 recording, with Ormandy, made when he was at the peak of his career, is undoubtedly a great performance, which in the USA has been issued on compact disc, coupled with the Dvořák *Concerto*. For the UK mid-priced CD issue which is uncoupled, the orchestral sound has been clarified but has lost some of its body. Yet the solo playing still emerges as ripely full-blooded, and Ormandy contributes a wonderfully positive Brahmsian warmth to a reading that carries the listener forward in its expressive spontaneity and fire. It is undoubtedly a performance which one can return to again and again with increasing satisfaction. The musical rewards of this account are slightly undermined by an artificially forward balance which highlights the soloist. Nevertheless, this must be numbered among the very finest of all available recorded performances, with the inspiration of the occasion caught on the wing.

A distinguished account of the solo part from Perlman, finely supported by Giulini and the Chicago Symphony Orchestra, a reading of darker hue than is customary, with a thoughtful, searching slow movement rather than the autumnal rhapsody which it so often becomes. Giulini could be tauter, perhaps, in the first movement, but the songful playing of Perlman always holds the listener. The recording places the soloist rather too forward, and the orchestral detail could be more transparent. Admirers of Perlman, however, need not hesitate; granted a certain want of impetus in the first movement, this is an impressive and convincing performance.

Szeryng's recording, made in 1958, dominated the early stereo catalogue. The playing combines East European brilliance and bite with a warmth and expressiveness recalling southern climates. Brahms had something of these opposites in his personality: his concerto has its bleak, powerful moments and it also contains much that is intense and sunlit. Szeryng lives up to these changing moods, and if there is any lack of depth this is compensated for by the sparkle of the playing. The recording is immensely vivid, with the violin in a spotlight, the digital remastering very brightly lit, bringing a degree of rawness to the solo timbre from the close microphones, while the orchestral focus is not always clean. But the power of this music making comes through the years and the listener cannot fail to be involved in this heartfelt performance, when the soloist is so well served by Monteux and the LSO. Ormandy's account of the *Haydn variations* is agreeable, very much less tense, and his Brahmsian warmth is even more effective in the *Alto rhapsody* which is dominated by Shirley Verrett's resonant performance, with her powerful lower register ringing out against the male voices of the choir.

Boris Belkin's performance with the LSO and Ivan Fischer has been given one of Decca's best recordings. On CD it is especially impressive and a strong contender on technical grounds. The performance is direct and spontaneous. The tempo of the first movement is measured and spacious (especially alongside Heifetz), but the reading is deeply felt and makes a strong impression. This is far more than a routine performance, without being of real stature but, fine though it is, it is outclassed by several other versions.

Much depends on one's attitude to Ferras's tone colour whether the Ferras/Karajan Walkman version is a good recommendation or not. DG have placed him close to the microphone so that the smallness of tone that in the concert hall is disappointing is certainly not evident here. Moreover, there is a jewelled accuracy about the playing that is most appealing, and Karajan conducts vividly. The recording is of good quality and the high-level transfer is of striking liveliness.

Zukerman is rightly famed for his sweetness of tone, and his general approach can often seem a little bland by comparison with the greatest artists. This is a well-conceived reading that has finish and facility yet ultimately leaves the listener untouched by any feeling that he is in contact with great music. Zukerman is exposed to a close balance, but this does not mask the Orchestre de Paris under Barenboim, who give excellent support and receive a well-detailed recording in spite of the unrealistic perspective. The sound of the solo violin is even more present in digitally remastered format, as is the coupled *Violin sonata*, a generous bonus.

The Russian version by Viktor Tretyakov is in many ways a fine performance, with a commanding, eloquent soloist who is placed rather too near the microphone, so that the bright digital recording brings a spiky edge to the upper tessitura under pressure. The orchestra, too, is given a lightness in the bass which robs the sonority of Brahmsian warmth, even though the playing is often eloquent. The oboe soloist, however, presses on at the opening of the *Adagio* and thus loses the combination of serenity and melancholy that can make this episode so telling. Overall, the performance does not lack impetus and spontaneity.

Kremer's version is powerful in attack, but favours consistently fast speeds: his second movement is hardly a true *Adagio*. Bernstein, who accompanies him with the VPO, is much broader than the soloist, who tries to move things on; ultimately Kremer is too narcissistic and idiosyncratic to carry a firm recommendation (DG **410 029-2**). As can be seen, this performance is also available at bargain price on a DG Pocket Music tape, coupled to another (more attractive) version of the *Double concerto*. However, the very bright tape transfer loses some of the body of the *Violin concerto* and emphasizes the forward balance of the *Double concerto*.

Double concerto for violin and cello in A min., Op. 102.
(*) CBS **MK 42024 [id.]. Francescatti, Fournier, Columbia SO, Bruno Walter – SCHUMANN: *Piano concerto*.**(*)
(M) **(*) HMV *EG 270268-4*. Menuhin, Tortelier, LPO, Berglund.

Double concerto; Tragic overture.
*** DG Dig. **410 603-2**; *410 603-4* [id.]. Mutter, Meneses, BPO, Karajan.

The Brahms *Double concerto* has been lucky in its recordings since the earliest days of stereo, as records conducted by Galliera, Fricsay and Bruno Walter readily demonstrate. Now the era of the digital compact disc produces a version which sets new standards. With two young soloists Karajan conducts an outstandingly spacious and strong performance. If from Antonio Meneses the opening cello cadenza seems to lack something in urgency and command, that is a deceptive start for, from then on, the concentration and power of the piece are built up superbly. As in her commanding performance of the Brahms *Violin concerto* – also with Karajan and the Berlin

Philharmonic – Anne-Sophie Mutter conveys a natural authority comparable to Karajan's own, and the precision and clarity of Meneses' cello as recorded make an excellent match. (The chrome cassette is equally clear.) The central slow movement in its spacious way has a wonderful Brahmsian glow, and all these qualities come out the more vividly in the CD version, though the relatively close balance of the soloists – particularly the cellist – is more evident, too.

Bruno Walter's recording with Francescatti and Fournier dates from 1959 and the compact disc represents another astonishing example of digital remastering which enhances the original to extraordinary effect, with solo instruments most tangible and orchestral detail consistently vivid within an attractively warm ambience. The timbre of the violins is particularly agreeable. As the commanding opening shows, Fournier is magnificent and, if one can adjust to Francescatti's rather intense vibrato (caught more flatteringly here than in the Beethoven *Violin concerto*), this can stand among the most satisfying of available versions. Walter draws playing of great warmth from the Columbia orchestra and oversees the reading as a whole with his customary humanity, yet tuttis are thrillingly expansive and vital. With an unexpected but rewarding coupling and 62 minutes of music, this is excellent value when the music making has such distinction.

The version by Menuhin and Tortelier presents two outstandingly warm and individual soloists against the background of strong accompaniment, steadily paced. As in the earlier recording, the soloists are placed well forward, but this time the result is more genial as well as big and positive. The challenge between two volatile, inspirational artists brings the best out of both of them, with the slow movement sweet and relaxed and the finale slower than usual but nicely lilting and crisply pointed. Excellent, full recording, debatable only on the question of the forwardness of the soloists.

We have always enjoyed the Schneiderhan/Starker/Fricsay version of the *Double concerto* ever since it first came out on a ten-inch LP in the early 1960s. It still sounds fresh and quite full, although again the two soloists are rather forwardly placed. Fricsay shapes the work splendidly; coupled with a comparable version of Beethoven's *Triple concerto*, this makes a fair bargain on a DG Walkman cassette which also includes Mozart (*415 332-4*). Also on DG is a performance by Kremer and Maisky, recorded at live concerts in the Vienna Musikvereinsaal in 1981–2, but this suffers from a want of real momentum in the first two movements and is not really competitive on CD (**410 031-2**). It is also available on a bargain-priced Pocket Music tape, coupled with Kremer's similarly narcissistic account of the *Violin concerto* (see above).

Hungarian dances Nos 1–21 (complete).
*** Ph. Dig. **411 426-2** [id.]. Leipzig GO, Masur.
*** DG Dig. **410 615-2** [id.]. VPO, Abbado.

In Nos 5 and 6 Masur uses Parlow's scoring instead of Martin Schmelling (as preferred by Abbado) and in Nos 7 and 8 he opts for Schollum rather than Hans Gál. Masur is just a shade more relaxed and smiling and the timbre of the strings is generally richer and warmer than that achieved by the DG engineers in Vienna. Abbado has great sparkle and lightness, but the Leipzig orchestra is hardly less dazzling than the Viennese. The Philips issue has the finer sound.

Hungarian dances Nos 1, 5–7, 12–13, 19, 21.
(B) *** Decca *417 696-4*. VPO, Reiner – DVOŘÁK: *Slavonic dances*.***

Reiner's collection was a favourite record of the late John Culshaw, and the recording (from the beginning of the 1960s) wears its years lightly. Reiner indulges himself in rubato and effects of his own (witness No. 12); but the affection of the music making is obvious, and the sound balances brilliance with ambient warmth. Now reissued on a bargain-priced Weekend tape, this excellent combination of the charms of Brahms and Dvořák will surely be ideal for the car.

Serenade No. 1 in D, Op. 11.
(*) DG Dig. **410 654-2 [id.]. BPO, Abbado.
(*) RCA Dig. **RD 86247 [**RCA 6247-2**]. St Louis SO, Slatkin.

Neither of these alternative versions of Brahms's delightful *Serenade* is ideal, and neither CD is especially generous in playing time. Abbado's performance is a fine one, vital, imaginative and sensitive, but the digital recording is rather dry and lacking in bloom, though clear enough in its CD format.

Leonard Slatkin gives a very well-paced and tautly conceived performance of the *Serenade* on RCA which is pleasingly free from mannerisms. Slatkin manages to find the right tempi and gets an excellent response from the St Louis orchestra. This is a straightforward reading, but with no want of personality. The recording is perfectly good without being in the demonstration bracket: the acoustic is far from dry, yet could do with a little more warmth.

Serenade No. 2 in A, Op. 16 – see below under *Symphony No. 3*.

Symphonies Nos 1–4; Academic festival overture; Tragic overture.
(M) **(*) Decca **421 074-2** (4) [id.]. Chicago SO, Solti.

Sir Georg Solti's Chicago cycle of the four symphonies in a mid-price box makes a satisfying, individual set. He came to the Brahms symphonies relatively late in his recording career, when his earlier urgency had given way to a mellower approach. These are all spacious rather than impetuous readings, marked by beautifully refined, poised playing by the Chicago orchestra, notably the strings. Even at slow speeds, tension and electricity remain at times – as in No. 1 – not always relaxed enough in lyricism. No. 2 is powerful and weighty, broad and noble, and a big-scale view of No. 3, with the second movement more an *Adagio* than an *Andante*, reinforces the epic power of the very opening. No. 4 is similarly powerful, though (against Solti's general tendency) the first movement is fast and direct, with the cellos in the first movement outstandingly rich. The recording is warmly atmospheric with a weighty – at times over-weighty – bass, clarified a degree on CD.

Symphony No. 1 in C min., Op. 68.
*** DG Dig. **423 141-2**; *423 141-4* [id.]. BPO, Karajan.
(*) CBS **MK 42020 [id.]. Columbia SO, Bruno Walter.
(*) HMV Dig. **CDC7 47824-2 [id.]. N. German RSO, Wand.
(*) Decca **414 458-2 [id.]. Chicago SO, Solti.
** ASV Dig. **CDDCA 531**; *ZCDCA 531* [id.]. Royal Liverpool PO, Janowski.
** DG Dig. **410 023-2** [id.]. LAPO, Giulini.
** Tel. Dig. **ZK8 43479** [id.]. Cleveland O, Dohnányi.
** HMV **CDC7 47029-2** [id.]. LPO, Tennstedt.

Symphony No. 1; Tragic overture.
(M) ** Decca **417 729-2** [id.]. VPO, Karajan.

Symphony No. 1; Variations on a theme of Haydn, Op. 56a.
(***) DG mono **415 662-2** [id.]. BPO, Furtwängler.

Karajan in his 1987 recording draws a typically powerful and dramatic performance from the Berlin Philharmonic. It is beautifully played and sounds warmer and more spontaneous than some of his previous accounts. The sound is full and weighty to match on CD, but where Karajan in the concert hall clarifies heavy textures, here the recording is thick and generalized in tuttis. It is comfortable enough overall but could be better defined. Characteristically Karajan does not observe the first-movement exposition repeat; with any reservations about that and the relative lack of inner clarity, this still takes its place at the top of the list of recommendations. At the opening, the cassette is heavy in bass, and it is generally thick in texture, though bright on top, even if the string sound is not over-refined.

Walter's first two movements have a white-hot intensity that shows this conductor at his very finest. The first movement combines the best of all possible worlds. It is as magisterial and dramatic as Klemperer's famous record (no doubt to appear on CD in due course) – less forceful at the opening, perhaps, but with great underlying tension – and at the same time by adhering to a fairly consistent speed (barely any rallentando for the second part of the second subject) it conveys the architecture of the movement strongly. The second movement too is most impressive, warm with natural, unforced phrasing. But then comes a slight change. The third movement begins with a less than ravishing clarinet solo and, though the 6/8 section is lively enough, the playing is not as crisp as in the first two movements and there is not quite the same feeling of spontaneity. Things are back to normal in the last movement, however, though some might find the big string tune too slow. How beautiful the remastered recording makes the strings sound here, though; and later the brass is comparably sonorous. The coda is slower than in Walter's two earlier versions. The 1960 recording is full and well balanced; as sound, this is preferable to many more recent versions.

The CD of Furtwängler conducting Brahms's *First Symphony* features a live radio recording made in February 1952, only two weeks after the Vienna performance also issued on disc (by EMI on LP). Despite a limited recording which becomes ill focused in heavy tuttis, the weight and grandeur of Furtwängler's reading, as well as its spontaneous poetry, come out magnificently. After the richness of the first movement, the slow movement is spacious and loving, and though characteristically in the finale Furtwängler moulds the tempo freely, he conceals the gear-changes far more cunningly than most, ending with a thrilling coda, where booming timpani adds to the excitement. The *Variations*, given a similarly weighty and personal reading, make a generous fill-up, a radio recording made in June 1950 with rather different characteristics, brighter, less fuzzy, but with the audience far more obtrusive. This was one of the finest of DG's issues for the Furtwängler centenary.

Wand's is an individual and refreshing reading, which explains his belated recognition as a thinker among conductors, the opposite of a showman. In the first movement, like Toscanini, Wand brings fierce intensity to the slow introduction by choosing an unusually fast speed, then leading naturally by modular pacing into the main allegro. The extra unity is clear. There is comparable dramatic intensity in the finale, though the choice of a tempo for the main marching melody, far slower than the rest, brings uncomfortable changes of gear. With a sense of spontaneity as in a live performance, the individuality of the reading is most convincing, helped by fresh recording which on CD brings a touch of fierceness on violin tone.

With the Chicago orchestra's playing as refined as any on record, Solti here directs a performance both spacious and purposeful, with the first movement given modular consistency between sections by a single pulse preserved as far as possible. Some will want more relaxation, for the tension and electricity remain here even when tempi are expansive. The recording is both atmospheric and clear. However, on CD there is excessive bass resonance to cut back; otherwise, the original analogue sound is freshened.

Janowski's plain yet sympathetic reading is greatly enhanced on CD, which is full bodied, clearly detailed and well balanced. The added fullness is much more flattering to the orchestral timbres and makes a very satisfying sound overall. Janowski, unlike most, does observe the exposition repeat in the first movement.

Giulini takes a spacious view of the *First*, consistently choosing speeds slower than usual. Generally his keen control of rhythm means that slowness does not deteriorate into heaviness, but the speed for the big C major theme in the finale is so slow that it sounds self-conscious, not *Allegro ma non troppo* at all. As a result, that movement loses its concentration, even with

Giulini's magnetic control. It remains a noble, serene view of a heroic symphony, beautifully played and well recorded. The compact disc is strikingly free and clear.

Dohnányi in the *First* gives a strong, direct reading, beautifully controlled and finely textured, but lacking a little in the tensions of live communication. The Telefunken recording is rich as well as being naturally balanced, well detailed and full of presence. However, while this may be agreeable to live with, there are more distinctive versions available.

Karajan's 1960 version with the Vienna Philharmonic comes out powerfully in its CD transfer, with its moments of underlined expressiveness set in place. The recording is still quite full for its age, with a firm, clear bass, but with high violins acquiring an unnatural edge above forte, which makes the very opening the least impressive passage. Only in the slow movement is the moulding of phrase distracting. The rest is strong and dramatic. At mid-price with a good coupling, this could please more than just the Karajan devotees.

As a recording, Tennstedt's EMI account is among the very finest; the CD version has well-defined detail and impressive body and presence. The LPO strings, however, are less sumptuous in tone and less sophisticated in colour than some rival accounts and, if sheer beauty of orchestral sound is a first consideration, this will probably not be a good first choice. Tennstedt's reading is plain and unadorned and has something of Klemperer's integrity and directness. It is an honest and sober account rather than an inspired one, but the excellence of the recorded sound may well prove a considerable compensation for some listeners.

An alternative performance from Bernstein with the VPO now seems too idiosyncratic, particularly in the finale, for serious recommendation. Though Bernstein's electricity makes the results compelling, this is hardly a version for constant repetition (DG **410 081-2**).

(i) *Symphonies Nos 1;* (ii) *4 in E min., Op. 98.*
(B) *** DG Walkman *413 424-4* [id.]. (i) BPO, (ii) VPO, Boehm.

Boehm's set of Brahms symphonies, issued in excellent transfers on a pair of chrome tapes, at bargain price, make one of the outstanding bargains in the Walkman catalogue. Anyone learning their Brahms from these performances cannot go far wrong. Boehm's Berlin Philharmonic version of the *First* comes from the early 1960s (he recorded it again later, rather less successfully, with the VPO). It is a centrally recommendable version, with tempi that are steady rather than volatile; but with polished playing from the Berliners, the performance is undoubtedly effective, and the well-balanced recording emerges here to excellent effect.

Symphony No. 2 in D, Op. 73.
(M) *** HMV **CDM7 69227-2** [id.]. Philh. O, Karajan – SCHUBERT: *Symphony No. 8.****
(*) HMV Dig. **CDC7 47871-2 [id.]. N. German RSO, Wand.
** DG Dig. **400 066-2** [id.]. LAPO, Giulini.

Symphony No. 2; Academic festival overture, Op. 80.
(*) CBS **MK 42021 [id.]. Columbia SO, Bruno Walter.
** DG Dig. **410 082-2** [id.]. VPO, Bernstein.

Symphony No. 2; Tragic overture, Op. 81.
(*) Decca **414 487-2 [id.]. Chicago SO, Solti.
(M) ** Pickwick Dig. **PCD 857.** Hallé O, Skrowaczewski.
*(*) ASV Dig. **CDDCA 547**; *ZCDCA 547* [id.]. Royal Liverpool PO, Janowski.

Symphony No. 2; Variations on a theme of Haydn, Op. 56a.
*** DG Dig. **423 142-2**; *423 142-4* [id.]. BPO, Karajan.

In his 1987 Brahms series, Karajan's reading of the *Second Symphony* suffers less than the *First* from the thick, undifferentiated recording, when textures in this later work tend to be lighter. It is a magnificent reading, even warmer and more glowing than his previous versions as well as more spontaneous-sounding, with consistently fine playing from the Berlin Philharmonic who approach with striking freshness a symphony which they must have played countless times. As in the *First Symphony*, Karajan omits the first-movement exposition repeat, but compensates with an appealing performance of the *Haydn variations*. Like the disc, the cassette sounds much better than that for the *First Symphony*. The sound is agreeably full and well focused; the detail in Karajan's spirited account of the *Variations* is particularly vivid.

Walter's performance is wonderfully sympathetic, far more affectionate than his earlier mono version with the New York Philharmonic. The performance has an inevitability, a rightness which makes it hard to concentrate on the interpretation as such, so cogent is the musical argument. As though to balance the romanticism of his approach on detail, Walter – as in the *First Symphony* – keeps his basic speeds surprisingly constant: in the first movement he refuses to accelerate the strong soaring melody towards the end of the second subject, yet little of the passion is lost in consequence. In the finale, too, Walter refuses to be hurried (or, for that matter, to be slowed down by such markings as *tranquillo*) and the measured general tempo succeeds in creating a most satisfying whole. It is a masterly conception overall and one very easy to live with. The CD opens with a vigorous and yet expansive account of the *Academic festival overture*, sumptuously recorded; when the *Symphony* begins, the ear notices that in the remastering there is some loss in the lower middle and bass, which is less richly resonant than in the *First Symphony*. But the bloom remains and it is only when the strings soar loudly above the stave that one feels need of rather more support at the bottom end. This is a marginal point; on the plus side, detail is remarkably clear, and the middle string timbre is always fresh and warm, an important point in this symphony.

Gunter Wand's version of No. 2 is the pick of his Brahms series, a characteristically glowing and steady reading recorded with a richness and bloom missing in the companion issues. Wand's unsensational approach exactly matches this sunniest of the symphonies. Its lyricism is made to flow freely, and the slow movement is robust, its melancholy underplayed. The third movement is light and fresh, the finale warm and exhilarating. However, on CD it makes very short measure, particularly when Wand does not observe the exposition repeat.

Karajan's 1957 account with the Philharmonia, very generously coupled at medium price, must also be seriously considered. The performance unfolds with an unforced naturalness that is warmly compelling. The first movement is agreeably spacious and the horn solo (bars 455–77) is hauntingly poetic, more so than his later Berlin Philharmonic versions. Yet for all the relaxed atmosphere, the grip that all his Berlin accounts have shown is strongly evident here. The slight blemishes (intonation between wind and strings at the beginning of the development, and a tape join later on) are not too important. The recording has less range than modern accounts and is somewhat unrefined at both ends of the spectrum, but it is beautifully balanced, and the substantial Schubert coupling is no less distinguished.

A powerful, weighty performance from Solti, its lyrical feeling passionately expressed in richly upholstered textures. The reading displays a broad nobility, but the charm and delicately gracious qualities of the music are much less a part of Solti's view. Yet the lyric power of the playing is hard to resist, especially when the recording is so full-blooded and brilliant. Solti includes the first-movement exposition repeat and offers a splendidly committed account of the *Tragic overture* as a bonus. On CD, the heavy bass has to be tamed if boominess is not to spoil the otherwise pleasing analogue sound, as digitally remastered.

With beautifully open and transparent sound, not thick in an old-fashioned Brahmsian way, Skrowaczewski and the Hallé Orchestra give a measured and restrained reading, unsensational, fresh and thoughtful. The opening may seem sleepy, but Skrowaczewski's broad speeds and patient manner build up increasingly as the movement progresses. The *Adagio* is plain but warm, the third movement gentle and unmannered, and the restrained finale leads to a coda in which the brass is rich but not blatant. With exposition repeat observed and a generous fill-up, plus excellent digital recording, luminous to match the performance, it is a fair mid-priced recommendation.

In his live recording, Bernstein directs a warm and expansive account of the *Second*, notably less free and idiosyncratic than the others in the series, yet comparably rhythmic and equally spontaneous-sounding. Good recording, considering the limitations at a live concert. The compact disc sounds well.

The restraint which made Giulini's recording of Beethoven's *Eroica symphony*, with the same orchestra so individual yet so compelling is evident in Brahms, too. The result is less immediately magnetic, particularly in the first movement, but the recording is both vivid and fresh in its CD format.

Janowski's plain style is least convincing in this most lyrical of symphonies, with rhythms tending to sound too rigid, whether in his metrical view of the slow movement or the rather charmless account of the third. The overture is much more successful and the recording is considerably enhanced on CD.

(i) *Symphonies Nos 2–3;* (ii) *Academic festival overture.*
(B) **(*) DG Walkman *415 334-4*. (i) VPO, Boehm; (ii) BPO, Abbado.

Boehm's readings of the two middle symphonies will seem to most Brahmsians more idiosyncratic than those of Nos 1 and 4, though the conductor himself might have pointed out that he learnt his Brahms interpretations from the composer's friend, Eusebius Mandyczewski. His approach to the *Second Symphony* is certainly volatile in the first movement, with the *Adagio* very expansive indeed. But here the conductor's moulded style rivets the attention and one quickly accepts the extra spaciousness. After a gracefully phrased *Allegretto*, the finale is strong. The *Third Symphony* is very broadly conceived, the reins held comparatively slackly throughout until the finale, where the increased momentum creates a sense of apotheosis. The recordings date from 1976 and sound well, with the Vienna strings given more body than in the original LP issue of No. 2. The excellent account of the *Academic festival overture* by Abbado makes a generous bonus for a chrome cassette already offered at bargain price.

Symphony No. 3 in F, Op. 90.
** HMV Dig. **CDC7 47872-2** [id.]. N. German RSO, Wand.
(M) ** Decca **417 744-2** [id.]. VPO, Karajan – DVOŘÁK: *Symphony No. 8*.**(*)

Symphony No. 3; Academic festival overture.
(*) Decca **414 488-2 [id.]. Chicago SO, Solti.

(i) *Symphony No. 3 in F, Op. 90;* (ii) *Serenade No. 2 in A, Op. 16; Academic festival overture.*
(M) *** HMV **CDM7 69203-2** [id.]. (i) LSO; (ii) LPO, Sir Adrian Boult.

Symphony No. 3; Variations on a theme of Haydn.
*** CBS **MK 42022** [id.]. Columbia SO, Bruno Walter.

Bruno Walter's *Third* is highly recommendable both as a performance and as a recording. His pacing is admirable and the vigour and sense of joy which imbues the opening of the first movement (exposition repeat included) dominates throughout, with the second subject eased in with wonderful naturalness. The central movements provide contrast, though with an intense middle section in II. There is beautifully phrased string and horn playing in the *Poco Allegretto*. The finale goes splendidly, the secondary theme given characteristic breadth and dignity, and the softening of mood for the coda sounding structurally inevitable. The CD transfer brings soaring upper strings, excellent detail with glowing woodwind, and a supporting weight. The account of the *Variations* is relaxed and smiling, with deft and affectionate detail, moving forward to a majestic restatement of the chorale. The recording is clear and spacious.

If there are slight reservations about the sound – which isn't ideally open, although there is no lack of Brahmsian warmth – Boult's mid-priced CD, offering 74′ 42″ of Brahms, is a formidable bargain. The 1971 performance of the *Third Symphony* has great dignity and spaciousness. Boult captures the autumnal feeling of the slow movement with great success, after including the exposition repeat in the first. It is essentially a mellow performance, keenly lyrical in feeling, but the LSO play with great enthusiasm and fire, so the music making exudes vitality. In the finale Sir Adrian indulges in his only eccentricity, a sudden spurt at bar 70 and at the corresponding passage later in the movement. After an expansive account of the *Academic festival overture*, the *Serenade in A major* is again glowingly lyrical. Tempi are not always conventional, but Boult's simplicity is disarming and engaging enough to blunt any criticism of detail. At the very opening of the symphony the bass resonance seems not quite natural, but the balance is good and, throughout, the upper strings have weight and bloom. There is a cassette, but it is impossibly bass-heavy and the resonance overwhelms the treble.

Solti takes a big-scale view of the *Third*, by far the shortest of the Brahms symphonies. The epically grand opening, Solti seems to say, demands an equivalent status for the rest; and the result, lacking a little in Brahmsian idiosyncrasy, is most compelling. Solti's Brahms should not be underestimated and, with strikingly rich sound, this gives much satisfaction. However, as in the others of the cycle, there is too much bass emphasis on the CD transfer, although this can be tamed.

The HMV Wand version has much in its favour, except for its short measure: it is difficult to recommend a premium-priced CD of the Brahms *Third* when no fill-up is included, even though in this (though not in the other Brahms symphonies) Wand observes the exposition repeat. Wand's wise way with Brahms, strong and easy and steadily paced, works beautifully here, bringing out the autumnal moods, ending with a sober view of the finale. The sound is inclined to be edgy on top, which underlines the reedy twang of the Hamburg woodwind – rather rough in the slow movement – while the horn is none too secure in his solo in the third movement.

Karajan's Decca recording from the early 1960s is not without substance in its remastered format, but the strings are fierce, the upper range exaggerated. He takes the opening expansively, which makes it surprising when he omits the exposition repeat and the movement is left rather short. Even though the third movement is slow, the shortness of the work overall leaves room for Dvořák's *Eighth Symphony*, a vintage performance but one also suffering from very bright lighting in its CD incarnation, which is not an advantage in this particular symphony.

Bernstein's account of the *Third* was recorded live like the others in the series but, with speeds in the first three movements so slow as to sound sluggish, it lacks the very quality of flow one hopes to find in a concert performance. The result is disappointingly self-conscious, and only the finale at an aptly fast speed brings Bernstein's usual incisiveness (DG **410 083-2**).

Symphonies Nos 3–4.
(B) ** DG Dig. *419 830-4* [id.]. VPO, Bernstein.

Bernstein's digital VPO recordings of the *Third* and *Fourth Symphonies* are conveniently coupled on a bargain-priced DG Pocket Music chrome cassette. While the *Third* is unsatisfactory, the *Fourth* is highly successful, so this may be counted fair value.

Symphony No. 4 in E min., Op. 98.
(*) DG Dig. **400 037-2 [id.]. VPO, Carlos Kleiber.
(M) **(*) HMV **CDM7 69228-2** [id.]. Philh. O, Karajan – LISZT: *Les Préludes.****
(*) Decca **414 563-2 [id.]. Chicago SO, Solti.

(*) Tel. Dig. **ZK8 43678 [id.]. Cleveland O, Dohnányi.
** HMV Dig. **CDC 169530-2**. N. German RSO, Wand.

Symphony No. 4; Academic festival overture.
** ASV Dig. **CDDCA 533**; *ZCDCA 533* [id.]. Royal Liverpool PO, Janowski.

Symphony No. 4; Tragic overture.
*** CBS **MK 42023** [id.]. Columbia SO, Bruno Walter.
*** DG Dig. **410 084-2** [id.]. VPO, Bernstein.

Symphony No. 4; Tragic overture: Variations on a theme of Haydn.
*** DG **423 205-2**; *423 205-4* [id.]. BPO, Karajan.

Walter's opening is simple, even gentle, and the pervading lyricism is immediately apparent; yet power and authority are underlying. The conductor's refusal to linger by a wayside always painted in gently glowing colours adds strength and impetus, building up to an exciting coda, the unanimity and cutting edge of the strings bringing a cumulative effect. A beautifully moulded slow movement, intense at its central climax, is balanced by a vivacious exhilarating scherzo. The finale has an underlying impetus so that Walter is able to relax for the slow middle section. Walter's account of the *Tragic overture*, with its characteristic breadth, opens the record powerfully, so that the mellow opening of the *Symphony* is the more striking. The CD brings full, well-balanced sound in an attractively spacious ambience, with glowing wind detail. The upper strings – as throughout this 1960 series – have not always quite the body of the finest modern recordings, but their freshness and the absence of edge, combined with the natural ambient warmth in the middle range, is appealing, and there is a full resonance in the bass.

Karajan's 1964 version has been reissued, aptly and very generously coupled with both the *Tragic overture* and the *Haydn variations*. The performance is richer and more relaxed than the Philharmonia account, more spacious in all four movements, yet the passacaglia has splendid grip in Karajan's hands and so too does the slow movement. The recording also is firmer and more wide-ranging.

Bernstein's Vienna version of Brahms's *Fourth*, recorded live, is exhilaratingly dramatic in fast music, while the slow movement brings richly resonant playing from the Vienna strings, not least in the great cello melody at bar 41, which with its moulded rubato comes to sound surprisingly like Elgar. This is the finest of Bernstein's Vienna cycle and with good sound is well worth considering. Like the others in the set, the compact disc gains in clarity, definition and range and gives the orchestra fine presence.

Any record from Carlos Kleiber is an event, and his is a performance of real stature. Everything is shaped with the attention to detail one would expect from this great conductor. Apart from one moment of expressive emphasis at bar 44 in the first movement, his reading is completely free from eccentricity. A gripping and compelling performance. With the more critical medium of CD, the limitations of the early digital recording, less clean and detailed than it might be, are more exposed. The strings above the stave sound a little shrill and glassy, while at the other end of the spectrum there is a want of opulence in the bass.

Karajan's glowing HMV performance almost holds its own with his later mid-1960s Berlin version. The keynote of the performance is its complete naturalness; the symphony unfolds at an unforced pace and possesses a glowing eloquence that is unfailingly impressive. The sound is remarkably good, given that it is over thirty years old. The range is not as wide as in a modern record, but the balance was excellently judged and the remastering is very successful. The Philharmonia play marvellously for Karajan, and with its Liszt bonus this is a bargain.

The *Fourth* was the first of Solti's Brahms cycle to be recorded. The most distinctive point about the reading, after a very direct, fast and steady first movement, is that the *Andante moderato* of the second movement is very slow indeed, more an *Adagio*. It is not just that it starts slowly, as in some other versions; Solti characteristically maintains that speed with complete concentration. Not everyone will like the result, but it is unfailingly pure and strong, not only in the slow movement but throughout. The playing of the Chicago orchestra is magnificent – note the cellos in the second subject of the first movement, and the articulation of the anapaestic rhythms in the scherzo – and the recording is full and precise. However, on CD the very resonant bass needs cutting well back.

Janowski's is a refreshingly direct reading. Speeds are unexceptionable, with the second-movement *Andante* slower than usual. The recording has been greatly enhanced in its CD format with added body and presence, and the weight of the final passacaglia is now properly established. The coda of the symphony (like the overture which follows) brings real excitement.

Beautifully recorded in full and well-detailed sound, Dohnányi's version of the *Fourth* brings a strong and finely controlled reading, lacking only occasionally in a flow of adrenalin. The slow movement is hushed and thoughtful, the third clear and fresh in its crisp articulation, while the weight of the finale is well caught – even if it is not thrust home at the close as sharply as it might be. An enjoyable version then, but one that does not quite measure up to the finest available.

Wand's reading of No. 4 initially seems understated. At a fastish speed the first movement is melancholy rather than tragic, while the slow movement, similarly steady and flowing, makes no warm expansion for the big melody of the counter-subject. The third movement in jollity has plenty of light and shade, and the finale is rather brisk and tough, with the great flute passage in the passacaglia tender but not drawn out. It is quite a strong reading, but marred by recording that is less than ideally clear even on CD, with edgy violins, as in Nos 1 and 3 in Wand's series. (As we go to press, this issue has been withdrawn and is likely to reappear with a new catalogue number.)

CHAMBER MUSIC

Cello sonatas Nos 1 in E min., Op. 38; 2 in F, Op. 99.
*** DG Dig. **410 510-2**; *3302 073* [id.]. Mstislav Rostropovich, Rudolf Serkin.
*** Decca **414 558-2**. Lynn Harrell, Vladimir Ashkenazy.
*** Hyp. Dig. **CDA 66159**; *KA 66159* [id.]. Steven Isserlis, Peter Evans.
(*) RCA Dig. **RD 87022 [RCA 1-7022]. Yo-Yo Ma, Emanuel Ax.
** RCA Dig. **RD 71255**. Ofra Harnoy, William Aide.

The partnership of the wild, inspirational Russian cellist, and the veteran Brahmsian pianist is a challenging one. It proves an outstanding success, with inspiration mutually enhanced, whether in the lyricism of Op. 38 or the heroic energy of Op. 99. Good if close recording.

Harrell and Ashkenazy give almost ideal performances of the two Brahms *Cello Sonatas*, strong and passionate as well as poetic. However, although they are naturally recorded and well balanced, the acoustic is resonant and the imagery lacks the last degree of sharpness of focus. This is far less distracting with the clarification brought by CD, making the result attractively atmospheric.

Isserlis is one of a talented generation of young cellists, not just a fine technician but an able communicator. Using gut strings – which he always prefers – he produces an exceptionally warm tone, here nicely balanced in the recording against the strong and sensitive playing of his regular piano partner. In every way this perceptive and well-detailed reading stands in competition with the finest. The heroic power of the opening of the *F major* is presented with all the projection – if at less sheer volume – that Brahms himself would have expected. Warm, unaggressive Hyperion sound.

Distinguished performances come from Yo-Yo Ma and Emanuel Ax. Their partnership favours the piano, for Ax sometimes produces too thick a sound in climaxes and Ma is, as always, sensitive and smaller in tone. Theirs is an essentially romantic view, and some might find the first movement of the *E minor Sonata* rather too wayward. They are certainly more measured in their tempi than almost any of their rivals. Yo-Yo Ma's pianissimos occasionally draw attention to themselves, though the grace and tenderness of his playing is not in question. The claims of these readings reside in their refined lyricism rather than their muscularity, and these artists have splendid rapport. The RCA recording is very truthful and admirers of this great cellist need not hesitate.

Ofra Harnoy and William Aide are sensitive interpreters, but they stress the more inward qualities of this music rather than its physicality and momentum. Generally speaking, these readings are well paced except, perhaps, the *Adagio* of the *F major* which is too leisurely. Here (and elsewhere in the performances) one feels the need for a stronger interpretative profile and bigger sound.

Clarinet sonatas Nos 1 in F min., 2 in E flat, Op. 120/1–2.
*** Chan. Dig. **CHAN 8562**; *ABTD 1265* [id.]. Gervase de Peyer, Gwendolyn Prior.
(*) Hyp. Dig. **CDA 66202; *KA 66202* [id.]. Thea King, Clifford Benson.

Superb performances from Gervase de Peyer and Gwendolyn Prior, commanding, aristocratic, warm and full of subtleties of colour and detail. The recording too is outstandingly realistic in both media.

Thea King and Clifford Benson give finely paced, warm and musicianly accounts of both works. Even if it is possible to imagine readings of greater intensity, the performances will give pleasure on all counts, and the recording is well balanced and truthful. The chrome cassette, too, is notably vivid and realistic.

Clarinet quintet in B min., Op. 15.
(M) *** Pickwick Dig. **PCD 883.** Keith Puddy, Delmé Qt – DVOŘÁK: *Quartet No. 12.* ***
(M) **(*) Decca **417 643-2** [id.]. Boskovsky, V. Octet (members) – BAERMANN: *Adagio*; MOZART: *Quintet.***(*)
(*) CRD Dig. **CRD 3445; *CRDC 4145* [id.]. Michael Collins, Nash Ens. – MOZART: *Clarinet quintet.***(*)

(i) *Clarinet quintet in B min., Op. 115;* (ii) *Clarinet trio in A min., Op. 114.*
*** Hyp. **CDA 66107**; *KA 66107* [id.]. King, (i) Gabrieli Qt; (ii) Georgian, Benson (piano).
(*) Tel. **ZA8 48262 (?) [id.]. Benny Goodman, Berkshire Qt. (members) – BEETHOVEN: *Trio*; WEBER: *Quintet.***(*)

Clarinet trio in A min., Op. 114.
*** HMV Dig. **CDC7 47683-2** [id.]. Meyer, Schiff, Buchbinder – BEETHOVEN: *Clarinet trio.****
*(*) Mer. Dig. **CDE 84122**; *KE 84122* [id.]. Eban, Israel Piano Trio (members) – BEETHOVEN: *Clarinet trio.**(*)

(i) *Clarinet trio in A min., Op. 114;* (ii) *Horn trio in E flat, Op. 40.*
(*) Decca Dig. **410 114-2. (i) Schmidl, (ii) Hogner; András Schiff, members of the New Vienna Octet.

Thea King and the Gabrieli Quartet give a radiantly beautiful performance of the *Clarinet quintet*, as fine as any put on record, and generously provide the ideal coupling in Brahm's other ensemble work for clarinet. Expressive and spontaneous-sounding, with natural ebb and flow of tension as in a live performance, this reading very surely resolves the perennial interpretative problem, when even the fast music is as much lyrical as dramatic. Not only does Thea King produce heavenly pianissimos, above all in the slow movement, she plays with exceptional bite and point in such a passage as the central Hungarian section in that movement. The *Trio*, a gentler work, brings a less positive performance – but still a most sensitive one. The recording of the strings is on the bright side, very vivid and real. There is an excellent cassette.

Keith Puddy's warm tone is well suited to Brahms and, with spacious speeds in all four movements, this is a consistently sympathetic reading; the recording is equally fine, vivid and full. Excellent value.

Boskovsky's is a rich-toned, relaxed account; the first movement could be tauter and the slow movement is on the gentle side; but with generous couplings and good sound, this is certainly attractive.

Michael Collins plays beautifully on CRD and the recording is most naturally balanced. There is much to admire here, not least the well-integrated textures and the lovely, gentle solo timbre in the slow movement. But overall the music making seems too unassertive, as if coming under Brahms's spell, an agreeable languor affecting the vitality of the performance, and contrasts are not strong enough to bring out all the mood changes in which the work abounds. It is attractive playing, nevertheless, and the sound is first class, with an excellent matching chrome cassette.

Benny Goodman made his recordings in his seventies towards the end of his career – the recording date is given as 1985 – and he displays an easy familiarity with the music and idiom, suggesting that while he was making jazz in public he was still playing the classics for his own pleasure. With good support from the Berkshire group he gives strong, affectionate accounts of both works. The different character of each is well caught, and it is a pity that the studio recording, though truthful, is a little dry; the string playing, too, could be more expansive.

Sabine Meyer, whose controversial appointment to the ranks of the Berlin Philharmonic caused much ill-feeling between Karajan and the orchestra, joins forces with Heinrich Schiff and Rudolf Buchbinder to produce a memorable account of the *Trio*. As sound it is strikingly fresh in the CD format, producing a remarkably lifelike impression and vivid presence.

With members of the New Vienna Octet joining András Schiff on Decca, the *Clarinet trio* is given a delightful performance, relaxed and warm, with a glowing account of the slow movement and Viennese lilt in the scherzo. The *Horn trio* has less urgency, though dramatic contrasts of dynamic are strongly brought out. Schiff's incisive playing is brightly caught on the full and realistic digital recording.

On Meridian, Eli Eban's playing is most musical and the performance would give much musical satisfaction were it not for a very backward cello balance – surprisingly, given the quality of the sound in every other respect. The excellent cellist is really very reticent, and this does inhibit unqualified pleasure.

Karl Leister's Orfeo version of the *Quintet* is most disappointing, lacking lustre compared with the distinguished Berlin Philharmonic clarinettist's earlier DG recording (**C 068831**).

(i) *Clarinet quintet, Op. 115;* (ii) *Piano quintet, Op. 34; String quintets Nos 1–2, Opp. 88 & 111; String sextets Nos 1–2, Opp. 18 & 36.*
(M) **(*) DG **419 875-2** (3) [id.]. (i) Leister; (ii) Eschenbach; augmented Amadeus Qt.

These performances derive from a fifteen-LP set of Brahms chamber music, first issued in 1969. This mid-priced CD box is remarkably generous and the merits of assembling four relatively little-played but inspired works alongside two better-known ones are obvious. Moreover the convenience of CD with its many points of access and the newly minted freshness of the transfers add to the attractiveness. The playing is consistently polished and tempi are well chosen. Karl Leister plays with considerable sensitivity in the *Clarinet quintet*, while in the *Piano quintet* Christoph Eschenbach gives a powerful account of the piano part. Perhaps it is at times over-projected, but the performance has no want of life. Elsewhere the element of suaveness which at times enters the Amadeus contribution seems minimized by the immediacy of the sound, and there is much to enjoy and to satisfy here.

Horn trio in E flat, Op. 40 (see also above).
*** Decca **414 128-2** [id.]. Tuckwell, Perlman, Ashkenazy – FRANCK: *Violin sonata.****

A superb performance of Brahms's marvellous *Horn trio* from Tuckwell, Perlman and Ashkenazy. They realize to the full the music's passionate impulse, and the performance moves forward from the gentle opening, through the sparkling scherzo (a typical Brahmsian inspiration, broad in manner as well as vivacious, with a heart-warming trio) and the more introspective but still outgiving *Adagio* to the gay, spirited finale. The recording is worthy of the playing, although the engineers in their care not to out-balance the violin with the horn have placed the horn rather backwardly. They should have trusted Brahms: he knew what he was doing when he invented this unusual but highly effective combination. The relatively early recording date (1969) means that one must expect, even on CD, an essentially analogue sound-picture, atmospheric, rather than sharp in detail. But certainly the naturalness is enhanced when there is so little background noise.

Piano quartet No. 1 in G min., Op. 25.
*** CBS Dig. **MK 42361**; *MT 42361* [id.]. Murray Perahia, Amadeus Qt (members).

Piano quartets Nos 1 in G min.; 3 in C min., Op. 60.
*** Virgin Dig. **VC 790709-2;** *VC 790709-4* [id.]. Domus.

This Perahia version of the *G minor Piano quartet* has an expressive power and eloquence that silence criticism. The sound has both warmth and presence in its CD format and this is arguably the finest account of the work since Gilels recorded it with the same string group. However, Domus offer not only the *G minor Quartet* but also the *C minor*, and they give marvellously spontaneous accounts of both works, urgent and full of warmth, yet with no lack of subtlety. The full, vivid recording (not quite as wide-ranging on tape as on CD) can be recommended strongly.

Piano quartet No. 2 in A, Op. 26.
(**) Ph. Dig. **420 158-2**; *420 158-4* [id.]. Sviatoslav Richter, Borodin Qt (members).

Richter's recording of the radiant *A major Piano quartet* with members of the Borodin Quartet almost has to be ruled out of court on grounds of sound. The performance derives from a concert given at the Grange du Meslay in Tours before an exemplary but (one imagines) numerous audience, in an ungenerous acoustic: the sound is very dry. The balance is close with the piano, and the string instruments have no warmth or sonority. There is nothing wrong with the distinguished performance whatever and the dead acoustic may not worry all listeners. The cassette is smoothly transferred.

Piano quartet No. 1 in G min., Op. 25 (orch. Schoenberg).
*** HMV Dig. **CDS7 47301-8** (2) [id.]. CBSO, Rattle – MAHLER: *Symphony No. 10.****
** MMG **MCD 10018** [id.]. Baltimore SO, Comissiona.

Schoenberg's orchestral transcription of the Brahms *Piano quartet* was a labour of love and sprang from his dissatisfaction with the concert performances he heard in which the pianist was all too dominant. It has excited much – and distinguished – admiration, and it obviously enjoys Simon Rattle's devotion and commitment. Schoenberg went so far as to call it Brahms's fifth symphony and was at pains to redistribute the piano writing with all the skill at his command. The use of a xylophone in the finale strikes some listeners as bizarre, but it is the thickness of some passages that seems surprising, given Schoenberg's mastery of the orchestra. However, these are doubtless matters of opinion; the playing of the Birmingham orchestra for Rattle is so inspiriting that many doubts are silenced. Readers who want this transcription can rest assured that this performance is first class and the EMI recording natural and wide-ranging. On CD, the transcription forms a generous bonus for Rattle's account of Mahler's *Tenth Symphony*.

A persuasive performance from the Baltimore orchestra under Comissiona, particularly by the strings, and a warm acoustic which produces an admirably Brahmsian sound. However, by present-day standards this is distinctly short measure (just over 40 minutes).

Piano quintet in F min., Op. 34.
*** Ph. **412 608-2** [id.]. André Previn, Musikverein Qt.
(*) DG **419 673-2 [id.]. Pollini, Italian Qt.

(i) *Piano quintet in F min., Op. 34. Ballade, Op. 104; Fantasias, Op. 116/3, 4 & 7.*
*(*) RCA Dig. **RD 86673**; *RK 86673* [RCA **6673-2-RC**; *6673-4-RC*]. Barry Douglas; (i) Tokyo Qt.

André Previn recorded this work before with the Yale Quartet for HMV, but his new account with the much-admired Musikverein (the old Küchl) Quartet is far superior in every way. It is also much better recorded than its chief modern rival (Pollini and the Quartetto Italiano on DG) and the balance between pianist and quartet is very well judged. The work is beautifully shaped; the only reservation that might worry some collectors is the rather sweet vibrato of the leader, Rainer Küchl. However, this is generally a safe recommendation and a first choice in this work on CD. The playing has fine vigour, warmth and spontaneity.

There is some electrifying and commanding playing from Pollini, and the Italian Quartet is eloquent too. The balance, however, is very much in the pianist's favour; he dominates the texture rather more than is desirable, and occasionally masks the lower strings. There are minor agogic exaggerations, but neither these nor the other reservations need necessarily put off prospective purchasers. The CD has opened up the sound somewhat, but at fortissimo levels the piano and strings could ideally be better separated.

With the exception of a vigorous account of the scherzo, Barry Douglas's version with the Tokyo Quartet is a disappointment, low in tension and often slack in ensemble, with the slow movement dragging stodgily. The solo pieces are welcome as a fill-up but hardly make the issue recommendable. The recording is well balanced in both media.

Piano trio No. 1 in B, Op. 8.
*** HMV Dig. **CDC7 47681-2** [id.]. Zacharias, Hoelscher, Schiff.

Piano trios Nos 1 in B, Op. 8; 2 in C, Op. 87; 3 in C min., Op. 101; 4 in A, Op. posth.
*** Ph. Dig. **416 838-2**; *416 838-4* (2) [id.]. Beaux Arts Trio.

Piano trios Nos 1–3.
*** Chan. Dig. **CHAN 8334/5**; *DBTD 2005* (2) [id.]. Borodin Trio.

Piano trios Nos 1–2.
(*) RCA **RD 86260 [**RCA 6260-2**]. Rubinstein, Szeryng, Fournier.

Piano trios Nos 1 in B, Op. 8; 3 in C min., Op. 101.
*** CRD **CRDC 3432**; *CRDC 4132* [id.]. Israel Piano Trio.

Piano trio No. 2 in C, Op. 87.
*** CRD **CRD 3433**; *CRDC 4133* [id.]. Israel Piano Trio – SCHUMANN: *Piano trio No. 1*.**(*)

Ulf Hoelscher, Christian Zacharias and Heinrich Schiff give a finely poised and thoroughly idiomatic account of the Brahms *B minor Piano trio*. Their recording is not of the most recent provenance (1982) but it is of the best quality. Great care has been expended over problems of balance both by the artists and by the recording team. The playing is altogether excellent and can hold its own in most exalted company. The CD offers short measure, but there is no doubt about the distinction of this issue. However, most readers will be looking for a complete set of the *Trios*, or at least a coupling of two of them, and the alternatives are more satisfactory in this respect.

The Beaux Arts recorded the Brahms *Trios* (including the posthumously published *A major*) in the late 1960s, and those performances have worn well. They were taut in the outer movements, lyrical in the slow movements, with eminently serviceable recordings, though constricted in acoustic. The new digital recordings are made in La Chaux-de-Fonds, Switzerland, and also bring one close to the artists, the bottom end of the piano being larger than life, at times strikingly so (in Op. 87, particularly the third variation of the slow movement). The playing, however, is always highly vital and sensitive. There is a splendid, finely projected sense of line and the delicate, sensitive playing of Menahem Pressler is always a delight. There are excellent chrome cassettes. Although the claims of the Borodin Trio are considerable, they do not offer the posthumous *Trio* which gives the Beaux Arts' set a distinct advantage.

The Borodin Trio give most musical and sensitive accounts of the three trios that convey the sense of music making in the home. Theirs are not high-powered performances in the manner of the Israel Piano Trio and they are accorded strikingly natural recording. There is strength when it is called for, lightness of touch and a sense of repose. They are not always perfectly in tune (the opening of the slow movement of Op. 8 is an example – and there are suspicions elsewhere) and this might well prove tiresome on repetition. However, the odd imperfections should not stand in the way of a recommendation on compact disc. The sound is extremely lifelike and present. The chrome cassettes have no lack of body and range and reproduce the piano tone most beautifully, but there is some fizziness at the very top.

The Israel Piano Trio give powerful accounts of all three *Trios*. They are recorded with great clarity and presence by the CRD team and play with sparkle and lightness of touch in the scherzo of Op. 8, and real sensitivity and inwardness of feeling in the slow movement. In the first movements they tend towards 'public' rather than chamber performances, the pianist at times sounding as if he is tackling a concerto, but they have no lack of eloquence or feeling. They give a fine muscular account of the opening of the *C major Trio*, though they tend to pull back somewhat self-indulgently for the second group. Throughout, however, the intensity is such that they always hold one's attention. They are very different in style from the Borodins, and their intonation is very accurate. As chamber-music making, the Chandos performances are less high-powered and in some ways more sympathetic, but the Israel group show a Brahmsian feel and their playing is commanding and spontaneous. The CDs offer fine presence and tangibility. The cassettes too are first class, and the firm focus and rich textures of the CRD tapes are preferable to the Chandos alternatives, though on CD the Chandos recording more than holds its own. However, Chandos only offer the three *Trios*, while CRD offer a substantial Schumann makeweight.

Rubinstein, Szeryng and Fournier went to Geneva one summer in the mid-1970s to record a series of chamber-music discs, including a complete set of the Brahms *Piano trios*. The first two of these have now been reissued and show a spontaneous conviction in the performances that many will find attractive. The ensemble is less crisp than that of the Beaux Arts Trio and the concentration is less keen than that of the Israeli players, but the individuality of each of these artists, of whom Rubinstein is the clear leader, is still most persuasive. The recording is rather closely observed, particularly Szeryng's violin, and the sound could ideally have more ambient warmth.

String quartets Nos 1 in C min.; 2 in A min., Op. 51/1–2.
*** Chan. Dig. **CHAN 8562**; *ABTD 1264* [id.]. Gabrieli Qt.
*(*) Tel. **ZK8 43115** [id.]. Alban Berg Qt.

Richly recorded in an agreeably expansive ambience, the Gabrielis give warm, eloquent performances of both the Op. 51 *Quartets*, deeply felt and full-textured without being heavy; the *Romanze* of Op. 51, No. 1, is delightfully songful. There are both tenderness and subtlety here, and the sound is first class in both media.

The Alban Berg Quartet play Brahms with their usual musical intelligence and offer a sophisticated blend of timbre, and immaculate ensemble. The playing has many subtleties, but the necessary Brahmsian warmth is missing. The 1978 analogue recording has good presence but is inclined to produce shrillness when the violin timbre reaches above the stave in fortissimo. There is much to admire here in the playing itself, but this is not really satisfying.

String sextet No. 1 in B flat, Op. 18.
*** CRD *CRDC 4034* [id.]. Augmented Alberni Qt – SCHUBERT: *String quartet No. 12* (*Quartettsatz*).***

Brahms-lovers who normally fight shy of his chamber music are urged to try this work (scored for two violins, two violas and two cellos) with its richly orchestral textures. The second-movement theme and variations is immediately attractive, while the *Ländler*-like trio of the scherzo will surely find a ready response in any lover of Viennese-style melody. In short this is a most rewarding piece, especially when it is played as eloquently as it is here, with a ripely blended recording to match the warmth of the playing. At times one might feel that a degree more fire would be welcome, but the performance does not lack spontaneity. The tape transfer is immaculate and beautifully balanced. No doubt this will arrive on CD in duc coursc.

String sextet No. 2 in G, Op. 36.
*** CRD **CRD 3346**; *CRDC 4046*. Augmented Alberni Qt – BRUCKNER: *Intermezzo and trio*.***

A splendid account of the *Second String sextet* to match the excellence of the *First* by this same group. Both works have proved elusive in the recording studio, but now we have thoroughly recommendable versions. The playing is splendidly alive and succeeds in matching expressive feeling with vigour. The finale is especially spirited. On CD the sound is full-blooded, with a fresh, bright, clean treble, and there is an excellent matching cassette.

Viola sonatas Nos 1 in F min., 2 in E flat, Op. 120/1 & 2.
(*) Chan. Dig. **CHAN 8550; *ABTD 1256* [id.]. Imai, Vignoles – SCHUMANN: *Märchenbilder*.**(*)

Nobuko Imai is an almost peerless violist and it is difficult to find a flaw in her accounts of the two Op. 120 *Sonatas* with Roger Vignoles. She brings great warmth and a splendid feeling for line to these fine works, and has altogether excellent support from her partner. The reverberant acoustic does not show the piano to good advantage but, apart from that, this is an impressive issue.

Violin sonatas Nos 1 in G, Op. 78; 2 in A, Op. 100; 3 in D min., Op. 108.
*** HMV Dig. **CDC7 47403-2** [id.]. Itzhak Perlman, Vladimir Ashkenazy.
*** DG **415 989-2** [id.]. Pinchas Zukerman, Daniel Barenboim.
(M) **(*) Decca **421 092-2** [id.]. Josef Suk, Julius Katchen.
(*) Chan. Dig. **CHAN 8517; *ABTD 1227* [id.]. Lydia Mordkovitch, Gerhard Oppitz.
** Novalis Dig. **150 019-2**; *150 019-4* [id.]. Dmitri Sitkovetsky, Bella Davidovich.

Perlman and Ashkenazy bring out the trouble-free happiness of these lyrical inspirations, even in the *D minor Sonata* where the melody which opens the second-movement *Adagio* finds Perlman broad and warm, weighty yet avoiding underlying tensions. In their sureness and flawless confidence at generally spacious speeds, these are performances which carry you along cocooned in rich sound.

Zukerman and Barenboim in partnership are inspired to take an expansive view of Brahms. They relish the lyricism, so that the result is songful, not inflated. These are spontaneous-sounding performances that in the tenderness of transitions or the pull of rubato in a melody catch the inspiration of the moment. Recorded in 1975, the sound is ripe and warm to match, less subtle than on some digital versions, but with more presence than most. The CD format with the three sonatas on a single disc is more convenient than previous multi-disc issues. Compared with Perlman and Ashkenazy, the manner is warmer and more spontaneous, less self-conscious – if at times less refined. But either of these two CDs will give much pleasure.

Suk's personal blend of romanticism and the classical tradition is warmly attractive but small in scale. These are intimate performances and, in their way, very enjoyable, since the remastered 1967 recording remains smoothly realistic, with only a hint of rawness on top.

Lydia Mordkovitch is an artist of quality, and her imaginative and subtle phrasing are a source of admiration. Both she and Gerhard Oppitz give an authoritative and perceptive account of all three *Sonatas*, which would carry a higher recommendation, were it not for the over-reverberant sound.

Dmitri Sitkovetsky and Bella Davidovitch are a highly musical partnership and give pleasingly lyrical performances, relaxed rather than strong. All three *Sonatas* are decently played, although Op. 78 is somewhat too leisured. The recording is truthful and the acoustic is pleasing, but this would not be a first choice. On tape, which is of high technical quality, Op. 100 is omitted!

Violin sonata No. 2 in A, Op. 100.
(B) *** DG Walkman *415 615-4* [id.]. Christian Ferras, Pierre Barbizet – BEETHOVEN: *Violin sonatas 5 & 9.****

This intimately lyrical performance of the *A major Sonata* is most enjoyable. It is placed on side one of the Walkman cassette, immediately following the Menuhin/Kempff version of Beethoven's *Spring sonata*, and acts as an excellent foil to it. The recording is truthful and the transfers excellent.

PIANO MUSIC

4 Ballades, Op. 10 (see also below).
*** DG Dig. **400 043-2** [id.]. Michelangeli – SCHUBERT: *Sonata No. 4.***

4 Ballades, Op. 10; 8 Pieces, Op. 76; Scherzo in E flat, Op. 4.
*** Ph. Dig. **411 103-2** [id.]. Stephen Bishop-Kovacevich.

4 Ballades; 2 Rhapsodies, Op. 79; Waltzes, Op. 39.
*(*) CBS Dig. **CD 37800** [id.]. Glenn Gould.

4 Ballades; Variations and fugue on a theme by Handel, Op. 24; Variations on a theme by Paganini (Books 1 & 2), Op. 35.
** Decca **417 644-2** [id.]. Julius Katchen.

Michelangeli plays an instrument made in the 1910s that produces a wonderfully blended tone and a fine mellow sonority. The *Ballades* are given a performance of the greatest distinction and without the slightly aloof quality that at times disturbs his readings. Gilels had the greater insight and inwardness, perhaps, but there is no doubt that this is very fine playing, and it is superbly recorded. The compact disc is very impressive and approaches demonstration standard.

We know from his (now-deleted) accounts of the concertos that Bishop-Kovacevich is a distinguished Brahmsian. His fine performances of both the *Ballades* and the Op. 76 *Klavierstücke* have both fire and tenderness, and are most truthfully recorded. The Philips engineers seem to be particularly fortunate with the piano, and this record is no exception. The CD is wonderfully realistic and has the utmost presence. One hopes that Philips will encourage this artist to go on to record the complete piano music.

Julius Katchen is unexpectedly successful in the *Ballades*: his style is not coaxing, yet this is most distinguished playing, full of character, the colouring often subtle. The *Handel variations* are attractively spontaneous and strong, and it is in the two books of the *Paganini* set that his playing is least illuminating. For all their pyrotechnical display, they remain less compelling than the other performances on this generous CD (67′ 12″). The sound is firm and clear throughout, undoubtedly truthful in bringing out the percussive qualities of Katchen's articulation, but not lacking warmth of sonority: the *Ballades* sound well.

Glenn Gould seems reluctant to let the *D minor Ballade* speak for itself and indulges in much exaggeration, lingering over cadences and losing any sense of natural movement. He has many insights of interest to offer but, overall, his view is too idiosyncratic to be widely recommended, and certainly not as an only version. The sound is dry and shallow, which is presumably what this artist liked, since his name is billed as co-producer.

8 Capriccii & Intermezzi, Op. 76; 7 Fantasias, Op. 116; 3 Intermezzi, Op. 117; 6 Pieces, Op. 118; 4 Pieces, Op. 119.
(M) *** HMV Dig. *EM 291178-5* (2). Dimitri Alexeev.

7 Fantasias, Op. 116; 3 Intermezzi, Op. 117; 6 Pieces, Op. 118; 4 Pieces, Op. 119.
** HMV Dig. **CDC7 47556-2**. Mikhail Rudy.

7 Fantasias, Op. 116; 3 Intermezzi, Op. 117; 4 Pieces, Op. 119.
*** Ph. **411 137-2** [id.]. Stephen Bishop-Kovacevich.

3 Intermezzi, Op. 117; 6 Pieces, Op. 118; 4 Pieces, Op. 119; 2 Rhapsodies, Op. 79.
*** Decca **417 599-2**. Radu Lupu.

6 Pieces, Op. 118; 2 Rhapsodies, Op. 79; 12 Waltzes, Op. 39.
*** Ph. Dig. **420 750-2** [id.]. Stephen Bishop-Kovacevich.

Alexeev's collection comes from 1976 and 1979, and was warmly welcomed at the time – and rightly so. His playing has an autumnal warmth and a ruminative, rhapsodic feeling that is wholly appropriate to this repertoire. He brings the right kind of tenderness and insight to the quieter pieces. Those who have been troubled by his excessive *martellato* in recent years will find nothing over-projected here. The recording is very natural and truthful. At lower mid-price, this tape-set is very competitive, even considering the distinction of some of the current rivals. The piano timbre is rich, slightly bass-orientated, but eminently suitable for Brahms.

Also from HMV comes a well-filled compact disc at 72 minutes, offering all of Brahms's late piano works in expressive performances by Mikhail Rudy. Judging from this record, he is for the most part a thoroughly idiomatic Brahmsian even if occasional doubts surface, as in the *Intermezzi*, Opp. 116/5 and 117/3, which are slow and curiously stilted. Yet it is a pity to single out the shortcomings when there is much beautiful playing. The recording is rather closely balanced in the somewhat unglamorous acoustic of the Salle Blanqui, Paris, and lacks the space and warmth of his finest rivals.

The pair of discs from Stephen Bishop-Kovacevich can receive the strongest recommendation. He finds the fullest range of emotional contrast in the Op. 116 *Fantasias*, but is at his finest in the Op. 117 *Intermezzi* and four *Klavierstücke*, Op. 119, which contain some of Brahms's most beautiful lyrical inspirations for the keyboard. The *Allegro risoluto* of the final *Rhapsodie* of Op. 119, which ends the first recital, has splendid flair and presence. The companion disc offers playing of comparable distinction. The playing is not only thoughtful but full of the sharpest contrasts. Even the gentle inspiration of the much-loved set of *Waltzes*, Op. 39 has him using the fullest range of dynamic and expression. The result is most compelling, both here and in the later, more demanding pieces. Both CDs offer fine piano tone, well caught by the engineers.

Radu Lupu's late Brahms is quite outstanding in every way; moreover his Decca CD is very generous (70′ 56″ overall). The analogue recordings date from 1971 (Op. 79/1 and Op. 117) and 1978 (Op. 79/2; Opp. 118–19), and the CD transfer has brought greater emphasis on the middle and lower sonorities in the earlier recordings. The quality of the recorded sound is otherwise wide in range and the piano image very tangible, and Lupu's warmth and delicacy of colouring are most truthfully conveyed. He brings to this repertoire both concentration and depth of feeling. There is great intensity and inwardness when these qualities are required and a keyboard mastery that is second to none. This is undoubtedly one of the most rewarding Brahms recitals currently before the public, and no connoisseur of this repertoire should overlook it.

Hungarian dances Nos 1–21.
** Ph. **416 459-2** [id.]. Katia and Marielle Labèque.

The Labèque sisters give a superb demonstration of their precision of ensemble in an almost immaculate account of these vigorous and colourful dances. But the expressive freedom and range of rubato are extreme to the point where the result sounds unspontaneous and mannered. This is better than rigidity in this music, but affection must always be heard to come from the heart. First-rate sound.

Hungarian dances Nos 1–21 (for piano duet); *Waltzes Nos 1–16, Op. 39.*
** HMV **CDC7 47642-2**; (M) *EG 290830-4*. Michel Béroff & Jean-Philippe Collard.

Béroff and Collard are crisp and unlingering in a characteristically French way: these are sparkling performances which are freshly convincing rather than charming. Some Brahmsians may prefer a more relaxed approach, but the urgency of these brilliant young French pianists is infectious. The 1973/4 recording is bright and clearly chiselled, a fraction hard, but there is warmth of timbre too. The *Waltzes* have been added for the CD issue (63′), and here the sound is much more clattery on top, although the sparkle of the playing is beguiling. Surprisingly, the actual recording date is later (1979/80) and the recording venue is the same – the Paris Salle Wagram.

Intermezzos, Op. 76/3, 4, 6, 7; Op. 116/2, 4, 5, 6; Op. 117/1–3; Op. 118/1, 2, 4, 6; Op. 119/1–3.
(*) Chan. **CHAN 8467; *ABTD 1177* [id.]. Luba Edlina.

Only one (Op. 117) of these sets of Brahms piano pieces is complete; otherwise, Luba Edlina singles out all the movements called intermezzi in his output except for the fourth movement of the Op. 5 *Sonata*. The resultant record, of course, misses the contrast that the complete sets have. The playing of Luba Edlina (the pianist of the Borodin Trio) has great warmth and a ruminative lyricism, and Chandos provide recording of excellent quality. The chrome cassette is extremely vivid and realistic. However, it would be perverse to direct collectors who are starting a CD library to this anthology in preference to the more comprehensive surveys discussed above.

Piano sonatas Nos. 1 in C, Op. 1; 2 in F sharp min., Op. 2; 3 in F min., Op 5; 4 Ballades, Op. 10; Scherzo in E flat, Op 4.
(*) **DG 423 401-2 (2) [id.]. Krystian Zimerman.

Krystian Zimerman's account of the lesser-known *C major Sonata* is powerful and concentrated. He brings to this music qualities of mind and spirit of the kind that ensures that the listener's attention is concentrated exclusively on Brahms and not on Zimerman. Those who have hitherto regarded this sonata, with its echoes of the *Hammerklavier*, as an uninteresting piece should lose no time in hearing this performance. The work emerges with altogether fresh urgency and expressive power. His version of the *F minor*, Op. 5, is also particularly commanding and is worthy to stand alongside the great performances of the past. There is leonine power, tempered with poetic feeling. There is no want of tenderness as well as strength in the Op. 10 *Ballades*, while the recording sound is very good, although in adding presence the digital remastering has brought a degree of hardness to the upper range at higher dynamic levels.

Piano sonata No. 3 in F min., Op. 5.
(*) Hung. Dig. **HCD 12601 [id.]. Zoltán Kocsis.
(*) ASV *ZCALH 948* [id.]. Shura Cherkassky – SCHUBERT: *Sonata No. 13.*(*)

Piano sonata No. 3; 4 Ballades, Op. 10; Intermezzo, Op. 116/6; Romance, Op. 118/5.
** RCA **RD 85672** [**RCA 5672-2-RC**]. Artur Rubinstein.

Piano sonata No. 3; Theme and variations in D min. (from *String sextet, Op. 18*).
*** Decca Dig. **417 122-2**. Radu Lupu.

Noble, dignified and spacious are the adjectives that spring to mind when listening to Lupu's Op. 5. He does not, perhaps, have the youthful ardour of Kocsis or the communicative qualities of Krystian Zimerman's account (which DG will surely make available on CD during the lifetime of this book). At times in the first movement one feels the need for a greater sense of forward movement: Lupu's view is inward, ruminative and always beautifully rounded. The *Variations* are at present only otherwise available in Zimerman's DG version. The recording is most realistic, the piano set slightly back, the timbre fully coloured, and the focus natural.

Kocsis gives an ardent account of the *F sharp minor Sonata*. Though this is not quite in the same flight either artistically or technically as his Debussy CD on Philips, it still has much to recommend it. His performance is spacious and expansive, and there is no lack of warmth. The slow tempo (an *adagio* rather than *andante*) he adopts in the second and fourth movements may worry some listeners – though this is not quite as disturbing as the small agogic exaggerations in which he indulges. The last few bars of the exposition of the first movement are pulled out of shape and the music comes to a virtual standstill at bar 24 of the second. Yet what wonderful points he makes elsewhere: never have those forward-looking harmonies in the *Intermezzo* (bars 19–23) sounded more Debussian, and he brings an almost nightmarish intensity to the gaunt, powerfully charged opening. For all one's reservations, this is playing of great imagination and artistry, and the recording is eminently truthful.

Cherkassky's recording was made in 1968 at a recital in London's Queen Elizabeth Hall with an unusually unobtrusive audience whose presence is disclosed only by the final applause. The performance is a magnificent one and shows a warmth and wisdom that resound in the memory. The *Andante* has wonderful inwardness and imagination, and only the fourth movement, *Rückblick*, lets it down with some eccentricities of rubato and a terribly slow tempo. There is an insecure moment in the first movement but, all in all, this performance has such eloquence and humanity that criticism is disarmed. The sound is very truthful, like a well-balanced broadcast, but is not as full-bodied as the most recent Decca or Philips studio recordings, and the tape judders very slightly at bar 38 of the *Andante* of the *F minor Sonata*. Strongly recommended all the same, particularly in view of the bonus in the form of the Schubert *A major Sonata*. The cassette transfer has plenty of life, but the upper range of the piano timbre is somewhat shallow in fortissimos.

Rubinstein's impulsive way with Brahms, though arresting at the opening of the *Sonata*, is not always convincing. His comparatively fast pacing of the second and fourth movements means that he does not entirely catch the feeling of reverie in the *Andante*, suggested by Brahms's quotation from Stenau: *'The eve is falling . . . the moonbeams rise'*, and in the finale the entry of the chorale-like secondary theme is almost thrown away by the forward momentum. The rather hard, unexpansive 1959 recording does not help the music. The sound is appreciably fuller in the rest of the programme, recorded in Rome in 1970, although the balance remains close and the acoustic cool. The *Ballades* are given a totally unsentimental approach and there are times when one feels the playing is somewhat shorn of mystery: one misses the extremes of both tension and repose. Nevertheless this is still music making to reckon with, remarkably youthful in spirit and full of personality, even if it does not really match the poetry of some others of the Brahms/Rubinstein records, the *Second Concerto*, for instance, where the finale is an absolute delight.

Variations and fugue on a theme by Handel in B flat, Op. 24; Variations on a theme by Paganini, Op. 35; Variations on a theme by Schumann in F sharp min., Op. 9; Variations on an original theme in D; Variations on a Hungarian song in D, Op. 21/1–2.
(M) **(*) DG Dig. *419 353-4* (2). Tamás Vásáry.

Tamas Vasary's set of *Variations* is conveniently packaged on a pair of chrome tapes in a DG 'flap pack'. The 1983 digital recording is of excellent quality and the box is good value at mid price. Vásáry displays less gravitas than some pianists; his readings are lighter in mood and texture, although he can be boldly authoritative, as in the fugue of the *Handel variations*. The character of the playing of each of these works obviously seeks to carry through some of the style of the theme into the rest of the music; Handel brings clean classical articulation, although the lyrical moments are not dry; Paganini often brings a chimerical feeling, and the Schumann set is lyrically romantic. The *Variations* on Brahms's own theme, Op. 21, No. 1, is perhaps the least successful performance but the *Variations on a Hungarian song* suit Vásáry's lighter style very well. All in all this is an enjoyable if unpredictable set.

Variations on a theme of Haydn, Op. 56a (arr. for piano duet).
*** CBS Dig. **MK 42625**; *IMT 42625* [id.]. Murray Perahia, Sir Georg Solti – BARTÓK: *Sonata for 2 pianos and percussion.****

It seems likely that Brahms wrote out his *Variations* in piano score (for two pianos, four hands) before completing the orchestration. Murray Perahia and Solti bring out the fullest possible colouring in their performance, so that one hardly misses the orchestra. Highly spontaneous music-making which gives great pleasure, and very well recorded too.

ORGAN MUSIC

11 Chorale preludes, Op. 22; Choral prelude and fugue on 'O Traurigkeit, O Herzeleid'; Fugue in A flat min.; Preludes and fugues: in A min.; G min.
*** CRD Dig. *CRDC 4104*. Nicholas Danby.

Danby gives restrained, clean-cut readings of this collection of Brahms's complete organ works, refreshingly at home both in the early and amiable *Preludes and fugues* – piano style not completely translated – and in the very late *Eleven chorale preludes* from the period of the *Four Serious Songs*. The sound of the Farm Street organ, beautifully recorded, is incisive rather than warm. The chrome tape is impressively faithful and well balanced, the focus nearly always clean.

VOCAL MUSIC

Lieder: *Abendregen; Alte Liebe; Feldensamkeit; Immer leiser wird mein Schlummer; Der Jäger; Liebestreu; Mädchenfluch; Mädchenlied; Das Mädchen spricht; Meine Liebe is grün; Regenlied; Salome; Der Schmied; Sommerabend; Therese; Der Tod, das ist die kühle Nachte; Von ewiger Liebe; Vor dem Fenster; Wir wandelten.*
*** Orfeo **C 058831A** [id.]. Margaret Price, James Lockhart.

Margaret Price gives a delightful Brahms recital; sensitively supported by James Lockhart, she sings radiantly, with the voice ideally suited to the soaring lines of many of these songs, finely coloured over the changes of mood in a song such as *Alte Liebe*. Clean, bright recording.

Lieder: *Alte Liebe; Auf dem Kirchhofe; Feldeinsamkeit; Nachklang; O wusst' ich doch; Verzagen. Vier ernste Gesänge* (*4 Serious Songs*), *Op. 21.*
(*) DG **415 189-2 [id.]. Dietrich Fischer-Dieskau, Joerg Demus – BEETHOVEN: *Lieder.***(*)

Recorded in the late 1960s, Fischer-Dieskau's Brahms selection on CD brings consistently imaginative singing. His darkness and intensity in the *Four Serious Songs* are hardly matched in the relatively lightweight accompaniments from Demus – placed at a disadvantage by the recording balance; this is, however, an attractive choice of repertoire and, with excellent transfers presenting an ageing recording in the best possible light, the disc can be warmly recommended, particularly when the measure of music (over 70 minutes) is so generous.

(i) *Alto rhapsody, Op. 53;* (ii; iii) *German requiem, Op. 45; Nänie, Op. 82;* (iv) *Rinaldo, Op. 50; Song of destiny, Op. 54; Song of the Fates, Op. 89;* (iii) *Song of triumph, Op. 55.*
*** DG Dig. **419 737-2** (3) [id.]. (i) Fassbaender; (ii) Popp; (iii) Wolfgang Brendel; (iv) Kollo; Prague P. Ch., Czech PO, Sinopoli.

(i) *Alto rhapsody; German requiem, Op. 45.*
(B) *** DG Dig. *419 833-4* [id.] (from above recordings, cond. Sinopoli).

Sinopoli's box of the choral music with orchestra for DG's *Brahms edition* brings performances both challenging and controversial which – particularly in the rare works – are a revelation. The *German requiem* is given a performance of extremes, generally very measured but consistently positive and dramatically contrasted in mood and colour. Brigitte Fassbaender makes a strong, noble soloist in the *Alto rhapsody*, but it is the other works which command first attention in such a collection, not least the one generally dismissed as mere occasional music, the *Triumphlied* of 1870 which, Elgar-like, had Brahms doing his patriotic bit. Sinopoli, helped by incandescent singing from the Czech choir, gives it Handelian exhilaration. There is freshness and excitement too in the other rare works, with Sinopoli lightening rhythms and textures. In *Rinaldo* for example – the nearest that Brahms came to writing an opera – Sinopoli moulds the sequence of numbers dramatically. René Kollo is the near-operatic soloist. The recording of the whole box, made in Prague, is warm and sympathetic with the orchestra incisively close and the chorus atmospherically behind. With greater clarity and a natural focus on CD, the effect is very real and tangible; the dark colouring of *Denn alles Fleisch*, the second section of the *German requiem*, is particularly telling, while the fervour of the chorus in *Rinaldo* is given extra bite and projection. Technically as well as musically this is a highly stimulating set, offered on three CDs against the original four LPs, with excellent internal access (there are twelve separate cues for *Rinaldo*).

Sinopoli's performances of the *German requiem* and the *Alto rhapsody* have also been issued together on a single bargain-priced Pocket Music tape. The transfers are of DG's highest quality, and the wide dynamic range of the recording is captured with fine body and good clarity, with the climaxes of the *Requiem* opening up effectively. The choral focus is equally impressive in the noble apotheosis of the *Alto rhapsody*, Brigitte Fassbaender's voice riding over the male voices splendidly. This is remarkable value and much the most economical way of obtaining this repertoire.

Alto rhapsody, Op. 53.
*** HMV **CDC7 47854-2** [id.]. Dame Janet Baker, John Alldis Ch., LPO, Boult – R. STRAUSS: *Lieder***(*); WAGNER: *Wesendonk Lieder.****

(i) *Alto rhapsody, Op. 53; Funeral ode, Op. 13; Nänie, Op. 82; Song of the Fates, Op. 89.*
(*) HM Orfeo **C 025821A [id.]. (i) Alfreda Hodgson; Bav. R. Ch. and SO, Haitink.

Alto rhapsody Op. 53; Song of destiny (Schicksalslied), Op. 54.
** CBS **MK 42025** [id.]. Mildred Miller, Occidental College Concert Ch., Columbia SO, Walter – MAHLER: *Lieder eines fahrenden Gesellen.***

Dame Janet Baker's devoted performance of the *Alto rhapsody* with Sir Adrian Boult (originally a fill-up to the *Second Symphony*) is well recoupled in a mixed recital with the *Wesendonck Lieder* of Wagner and four Strauss songs. The Brahms remains meditative, even though the tempo is unlingering, and the manner totally unindulgent. The warm recording, from the beginning of the 1970s, has responded well to digital remastering which has brought greater presence, yet retained the fullness.

Alfreda Hodgson and Bernard Haitink make a good partnership in the *Alto rhapsody*. Both respond to the work with an element of restraint, but there is also eloquence; though there is some lack of warmth, a natural response to the words brings dramatic articulation, too. The other works combine refinement with moments of fervour in much the same way, and there is some splendid singing from the Bavarian choir, especially in the *Funeral ode*. The 1981 analogue recording was made within a resonant acoustic, with the chorus and orchestra slightly backward in a concert-hall setting. Not everything is crystal clear, but the overall impression suits the music admirably and gives a convincing sense of realism.

Mildred Miller is a fresh rather than inspirational soloist in the *Alto rhapsody*, and in spite of coaching from Walter (who had decided views on the interpretation of this fine work) she gives a somewhat strait-laced account of the opening pages. The *Song of destiny* is very satisfactory, however, and displays the capability of the chorus to good effect. The CD transfers are well managed, with the orchestral detail in the *Rhapsody*, and the fine choral singing in both works, showing that Walter's directing hand has a special contribution to make.

Lieder: *Die Botschaft.* (i) *2 Songs with viola, Op. 91 (Gestillte Sehnsucht; Geistliches Wiegenlied). Immer leiser; Die Mainacht; Meine Liebe ist grün; O komme holde Sommernacht; Ständchen; Therese; Der Tod das ist die kühle Nachte; Von ewiger Liebe; Wie Melodien zieht es mir.*
** Ph. **416 439-2** [id.]. Jessye Norman, Geoffrey Parsons, with (i) von Wrochem.

The scale and tonal range of Jessye Norman's voice are ideal for many of these songs, but in some of them there is a studied quality which makes the result a little too static. That is particularly so in the most ambitious of the songs. *Von ewiger Liebe*, which mistakenly is put first. Nevertheless, there is much distinguished singing and playing here, and it is superbly recorded. The CD remastering adds presence and the effect is most realistic.

Lieder: *Dein blaues Auge hält; Dort in den Weiden; Immer leiser wird mein Schlummer; Klage I & II; Liebestreu; Des Liebsten Schwur; Das Mädchen; Das Mädchen spricht; Regenlied; Romanzen und Lieder, Op. 84; Salome; Sapphische Ode, Op. 94/4; Der Schmied;* (i) *2 Songs with viola, Op. 91; Therese; Vom Strande; Wie Melodien zieht es; Zigeunerlieder, Op. 103.*
*** DG Dig. **413 311-2** [id.]. Jessye Norman, Daniel Barenboim; (i) Wolfram Christ.

Jessye Norman is at her finest in this delightful and strongly contrasted selection from DG's Lieder box in the Brahms Edition. For the compact disc equivalent of an earlier digital LP, the two *Songs with viola* have been added to make a highlight of the new recital, plus four other songs not previously included. The task of recording a complete set of women's songs seems in this instance to have added to the warmth and sense of spontaneity of both singer and pianist in the studio, while Wolfram Christ makes a distinguished contribution to Op. 91. The heroic scale of *Der Schmied* is superb, as is the open simplicity of the *Zigeunerlieder*, while the gentler songs find the gloriously ample voice exquisitely scaled down. The recording is wonderfully vivid, giving the artists a tangible presence. This is one of the finest Lieder collections in the CD catalogue.

Deutsche Volkslieder (*German folksong settings*).
*** HMV **CDS7 49088-8** (2) [id.]. Elisabeth Schwarzkopf, Dietrich Fischer-Dieskau, Gerald Moore.

This collection of German folksongs, published only three years before Brahms's death in 1897, represents the love of a lifetime. Particularly during his last years, when the creative springs ran less generously, he loved to set the folksongs he had collected over the years – usually with straight, undistracting accompaniment, but almost always with some hint of genuine Brahms. Having so many short songs sung consecutively may seem too much of a good thing, but few singers in the world today could match Schwarzkopf and Fischer-Dieskau in their musical imagination and depth of understanding. It may well be wisest to dip into the collection, which one can do readily with CD, but there are few folksong collections of any nation that can rival this in breadth of expression. The fact that the great classical masters tended to base their idiom on German folk-style should not prevent us from appreciating it as the voice of the country people. Gerald Moore proved the ideal accompanist, and the recording quality is vivid, with some enchanting conversation-pieces between the two soloists.

German requiem, Op. 45.
*** Tel. Dig. **ZL8 43335** (2); *CY4 43335* [id.]. M. Price, Ramey, Amb. S., RPO, Previn.
*** HMV **CDC7 47238-2** [id.]. Schwarzkopf, Fischer-Dieskau, Philh. Ch. & O, Klemperer.
(*) DG Dig. **410 521-2; *410 521-4* [id.]. Hendricks, Van Dam, V. Singverein, VPO, Karajan – BRUCKNER: *Te Deum.***
(M) **(*) HMV **CDM7 69229-2** [id.]. Tomowa-Sintow, Van Dam, V. Singverein, BPO, Karajan.
(*) RCA Dig. **RD 85003 [RD-1 5003]. Battle, Hagegard, Chicago Ch. & SO, Levine.
** Telarc Dig. **CD 80092** [id.]. Augér, Stilwell, Atlanta Ch. & SO, Shaw.

(i) *German requiem;* (ii) *Alto rhapsody. Song of destiny* (*Schicksalslied*), *Op. 54.*
** HMV Dig. **CDS7 47414-8** [Ang. **CDCB 47414**]; *EX 270313-5* (2) [Ang. *4DS 3983*]. (i) Norman, Hynninen; (ii) Meier; LPO Ch., LPO, Tennstedt.

German requiem; Song of destiny, Op. 54.
(*) Ph. Dig. **411 436-2 [id.]. Janowitz, Krause, V. State Op. Ch., VPO, Haitink.

German requiem; Variations on a theme of Haydn, Op. 56a.
** Decca **414 627-2** [id.]. Te Kanawa, Weikl, Chicago Ch. & SO, Solti.

Previn may not often be thought of as a Brahmsian, but in the concert hall he has given many revealing accounts of the *German requiem*. Here he commits his spacious, dedicated reading to disc, with radiant singing from the chorus. It is the seeming simplicity of his approach, with measured speeds held steadily, that so movingly conveys an innocence in the often square writing, both in the powerful opening choruses and in the simple, songful *Wie lieblich*. The great fugatos are then powerfully presented. Both soloists are outstanding, Margaret Price golden-toned, Samuel Ramey incisively dark. The recording is warmly set against a helpful church acoustic with the chorus slightly distanced. The only snag is that at 76 minutes the set comes on two CDs, though at a special price. It is also available, however, on a single tape.

Measured and monumental, Klemperer's performance would clearly have roused Bernard Shaw's Wagnerian derision, but, as so often, Klemperer's four-square honesty defies pre-conceived doubts. The speeds are consistently slow – too slow in the vivace of the sixth movement, where Death has little sting – but, with dynamic contrasts underlined, the result is uniquely powerful. The solo singing is superb, and the Philharmonia singers were at the peak of their form. The CD transfer is excellent, with voices and instruments placed in a realistic sound-spectrum. The breadth of Klemperer's view does not prevent the whole from being fitted on a single disc.

The chorus of the Vienna Singverein sounds disappointingly opaque in Karajan's latest DG version of a work which he has now recorded four times, but that is the only serious shortcoming of a reading which persuasively brings out the warmth of Brahms's writing, not merely its devotional or monumental qualities. The performance is not quite so polished as previous versions, but the sense of spontaneity is all the keener, and the soloists provide characterful contributions, even if the rapid vibrato of Barbara Hendricks detracts from a feeling of innocence in *Ihr habt nun Traurigkeit*. The relative closeness of the orchestra in the recording balance adds to the feeling of constriction in the sound. The cassettes are well managed, but the CDs have extra definition, although this serves to emphasize the faults of balance.

The reissue of Karajan's 1977 EMI set on a mid-priced CD offers considerable competition to the later digital version. The chorus is both full and clearly focused, and soloists and orchestral detail are vividly projected. Indeed the most striking difference between this and the DG set lies in the choral sound, bigger and closer, with sharp dramatic contrasts. As a reading it is characteristically smooth and moulded, a complete contrast to Klemperer's four-square account. The soloists are both excellent: Tomowa-Sintow sings with a rich tone-colour, while José van Dam is equally expressive with firm tone. The remastering is certainly a success and this is competitively priced.

Haitink chooses very slow tempi in the *German requiem*. There is a rapt quality in this glowing performance that creates an atmosphere of simple dedication; at slow speed *Denn alles Fleisch* (*All flesh is grass*) is made the more relentless when, with total concentration, textures are so sharply clarified. The digital recording offers beautiful sound and, with outstanding soloists – Gundula Janowitz notably pure and poised – this is very persuasive. The fill-up is the rarely recorded *Schicksalslied* (*Song of destiny*), which is most welcome and is admirably sung and played. On CD, with extra clarity and natural bass response, the warm and atmospheric qualities of the recording are all the more impressive.

Levine's version starts with two assets: it is contained complete on a single CD of over 70 minutes' length, and Margaret Hillis's celebrated Chicago Symphony Chorus is probably the finest in America. In addition, the two soloists both prove excellent, Kathleen Battle pure and sweetly vulnerable-sounding, Hagegard clear-cut and firm. Nor does Levine race the music to get it down to CD length. The outer movements of the seven may be faster than usual so that the first is hardly meditative, but there is no sense of haste. More serious is Levine's choice of an exceptionally slow speed for the second movement, *Denn alles Fleisch*, even slower than Haitink's and, unlike his, sounding rhythmically stodgy if undeniably powerful in impact. Levine may not be the most illuminating conductor in this work, and the recording is not ideal – with inner textures growing cloudy in tuttis – but it will give much pleasure.

Even more strikingly than in his set of the Brahms symphonies, Solti here favours very expansive tempi, smooth lines and refined textures. There is much that is beautiful, even if the result overall is not as involving as it might be. Dame Kiri Te Kanawa sings radiantly, but Bernd Weikl with his rather gritty baritone is not ideal. Fine recording, glowing and clear.

Tennstedt's is an unusually spacious view of the *Requiem*, with speeds slower than on any rival version. His dedication generally sustains them well, with a reverential manner always alert, never becoming merely monumental, though the choir's ensemble is not always perfect. Jorma Hynninen proves an excellent soloist. What does sound monumental rather than moving is Jessye Norman's solo, *Ihr habt nun Traurigkeit*, though the golden tone is glorious. Waltraud Meier is a strong rather than a beautiful soloist in the *Alto rhapsody*. The *Schicksalslied* is also given a spacious, strong performance, with the London Philharmonic Choir singing dedicatedly. On CD generally fine, spacious recording, which has also transferred to tape without blurring.

Robert Shaw's experience as a leading choirmaster – working with his Chorale for Toscanini during the maestro's last years – makes for some exceptionally fresh and well-disciplined singing. The superb definition of the Telarc recording – more successful here than in the parallel recording of the Berlioz *Requiem* – brings even Brahms's murkiest passages into the light of day; and the firmness and clarity of the organ pedal at the very start demonstrates the quality of the engineers' work, though in places the very weight of the bass might be counted too heavy, even though it brings no boominess or distortion. This means that even in murmured choral pianissimos there is nothing hazy, but the very plainness underlines a limitation in the interpretation. For all its freshness and innocence, it does not convey the sense of occasion or detailed imagination of Karajan or – to take another single-disc version – Levine on RCA, which is notably more individual. Good solo singing, with Arleen Augér superbly silvery and true in *Ihr habt nun Traurigkeit*.

The best point about Sawallisch's Orfeo version is the noble singing of Thomas Allen as baritone soloist. Margaret Price also sings powerfully in her one solo but misses the innocent purity of expression needed. The rest is disappointing, often too slow and heavy, and the recording brings thin violin tone and choral sound that tends to overload (**CO 39101A**).

Liebeslieder waltzes, Op. 52; New Liebeslieder waltzes, Op. 65; 3 Quartets, Op. 64.
*** DG Dig. **423 133-2** [id.]. Mathis, Fassbaender, Schreier, Fischer-Dieskau; Engel and Sawallisch (pianos).

For its *Brahms edition* DG assembled these characterful yet well-matched voices. The result brought one of the most successful recordings yet of the two seductive but surprisingly difficult sets of *Liebeslieder waltzes*. The CD has fine realism and presence.

Brian, Havergal (1876–1972)

Symphonies Nos 7 in C; 31. The Tinker's wedding: comedy overture.
*** HMV Dig. **CDC7 49558-2**; *EL 749558-4*. Royal Liverpool PO, Mackerras.

Mackerras and the Royal Liverpool Philharmonic, in this recording made in association with the Havergal Brian Society, contribute the most valuable record of his music to date. The choice of symphonies from the thirty-two he completed is a shrewd one, bringing together the last of the expansive works, No. 7, completed in 1948, allying Brian's earlier style with the often elliptical manners of his later, more concentrated work, and the penultimate symphony of the whole series, written just twenty years later, after an amazing eruption of creative activity. The brilliant comedy overture, *The Tinker's wedding*, more conventional in its material and manner, yet still at times unpredictable, provides an attractive makeweight. Starting with a martial fanfare, the *Seventh Symphony* was inspired not by war but by the city of Strasbourg and its cathedral. The moderately paced second movement also features tolling bells and fanfare, and it is the third movement, the longest of the four, combining slow movement and scherzo which brings weightier argument, before the finale again revolves round the bell sounds and fanfares characteristic of the work. No. 31 in a single movement, starting with a jolly idea which with its jingling might have Christmas overtones, yet brings a characteristic example of Brian's later compressed style, relying on elaborate counterpoint. The unconverted may still have doubts whether Brian's music has quite the cohesion and musical strength it obviously aims at, but this collection presents him and his achievement more effectively than any other disc. Beautifully played and vividly recorded, it can be recommended to anyone fascinated by an extraordinary, offbeat composer. There is a very good chrome tape, although the lower range here is rather less cleanly focused than on the CD.

Symphonies Nos 8 in B flat min.; 9 in A min.
(M) *** HMV *ED 290869-4*. Royal Liverpool PO, Groves.

It is astonishing that Havergal Brian's music has been so shamefully neglected by the recording companies in favour of avant-garde scores of much more dubious merit. But this enterprising coupling from HMV undoubtedly deserves support. Groves gives a splendid account of the *Ninth*, a work of undoubted power and atmosphere. No. 8 is a rather more complex and enigmatic piece, and the performance is marginally less assured. There is fine orchestral playing throughout and the coupling merits the strongest recommendation, for the music's harmonic language is not too 'difficult' for anyone who enjoys Mahler to come to terms with. The recording is first-class and the cassette is well balanced, although, using iron-oxide stock, it lacks the ultimate range.

Bridge, Frank (1879–1941)

Cherry ripe; Enter Spring (rhapsody); Lament; The Sea (suite); Summer (tone-poem).
(M) *** HMV *EG 290868-4*. Royal Liverpool PO, Groves.

This fine collection spans the whole range of Frank Bridge's orchestral output from early to late. Writing in the early years of the century, the composer confidently produced a magnificent seascape in the wake of Debussy, *The Sea*; but already by 1914 his responses were subtler, more original. *Summer*, written in that fateful year, was free of the conventional pastoral moods of what has been called the 'cowpat' school, while in the last and greatest of Bridge's tone-poems, *Enter Spring*, he was responding to still wider musical horizons in experimentation that matches that of European contemporaries. Groves's warm advocacy adds to the impressiveness. First-rate recording with the tape transfer well managed, clear but with plenty of body and warmth.

Elegy for cello and piano.
*** ASV *ZCACA 1001*. Lloyd Webber, McCabe – BRITTEN: *Suite****; IRELAND: *Sonata*.**(*)

Though written as early as 1911, the *Elegy*, darkly poignant, points forward to the sparer, more austere style of later Bridge. It is good to have this important miniature included on this richly varied tape. The performance is deeply committed, though the recording balance strongly favours the cello. The cassette transfer is of excellent quality.

Enter spring (rhapsody); (i) Oration (Concerto elegiaco).
*** Pearl **SHECD 9601** [id.]. (i) Baillie; Cologne RSO, Carewe.

Oration (*Concerto elegiaco*).
*** HMV Dig. **CDC7 49716-2**; *EL 749716-4*. Isserlis, City of L. Sinfonia, Hickox – BRITTEN: *Cello symphony*.***

Completed in 1930, *Oration* is in effect a massive cello concerto in nine linked sections lasting a full half hour. It is an elegiac work which, like Bridge's ambitious *Piano sonata* of 1924, reflects the composer's continuing desolation over the deaths of so many of his friends in the First World War. As in the *Sonata*, Bridge's idea of writing an elegiac work made for the opposite of comfortable consolation. In its often gritty textures and dark concentration it is fundamentally angry music, stylistically amazing – like other late Bridge – for a British composer to have been writing at the time.

Though Isserlis is not always as passionate as Julian Lloyd Webber was on the earlier Lyrita version, his focus is sharper, and with Hickox he brings out the originality of the writing all the more cleanly. It is fascinating to find some passages anticipating the more abrasive side of Britten, and specifically the *Cello symphony* with which this is coupled. There is a first-class chrome tape.

Alexander Baillie is certainly no less eloquent than Steven Isserlis in Bridge's fine concertante work, at times wearing his heart unashamedly on his sleeve, at others more thoughtfully reticent. John Carewe matches his rhapsodic approach and secures wholly idiomatic playing from the fine Cologne orchestra, both here and in a splendidly fluid account of the expansive tone-poem, *Enter spring*, which is wholly spontaneous and generates considerable power. The studio recording is vivid and wide-ranging and is by no means second best compared with its EMI competitor (made at Abbey Road). Choice may be dictated by coupling; admirers of Frank Bridge will not want to be without this fine modern version of *Enter spring*.

2 Entr'actes: Rosemary; Canzonetta. Heart's ease. 3 Lyrics for piano: No. 1, Heart's ease (orch. Cornford). *Norse legend;* (i) *Suite for cello and orchestra* (*Morning song; Elegie; Scherzo*) arr. & orch. Cornford. *Threads* (incidental music)*: 2 Intermezzi. 3 Vignettes de danse. The turtle's retort* (one-step) orch. Wetherell.
*** Pearl **SHECD 9600** [id.]. (i) Lowri Blake; Chelsea Op. Group O, Howard Williams.

Like the more ambitious coupling of *Enter spring* and *Oration*, this Pearl collection, showing the composer relaxing, was financed by the Frank Bridge Trust. Those who enjoy Elgar's lighter music will surely find much to delight them in this diverse and very tuneful collection, even if a number of the items are arrangements by other hands. The *Norse legend* is quite brief; then comes the Elgarian *Rosemary*; but the *Suite for cello and orchestra* (arranged from music for cello and piano) is by no means insubstantial and it has a sympathetic, rich-toned soloist in Lowri Blake. The incidental music for *Threads* brings more nostalgia, the first piece elegiac and the second an atmospheric waltz, somewhat reminiscent of Geoffrey Toye. *Heart's ease* has a delicious oriental delicacy and the *Three Vignettes* celebrate a combined alpine and Mediterranean holiday, taken in 1925, and recall three lady friends, obviously of very contrasting dispositions. *The turtle's retort* ends the concert in good rhythmic spirits and Eric Wetherell's scoring is nicely judged. Altogether this is a most entertaining concert that is more than the sum of its constituents. The Chelsea orchestra are a semi-professional group, but no apologies need be made for their response or their ensemble, and Howard Williams directs with spontaneous warmth and an apt sense of pacing. The recording is first rate, with plenty of colour and ambient warmth.

The Sea (suite).
*** Chan. Dig. **CHAN 8473**; *ABTD 1184* [id.]. Ulster O, Handley – BAX: *On the sea-shore;* BRITTEN: *Sea interludes*.***

Bridge's suite, *The Sea*, was a work which Benjamin Britten heard as a boy at the Norwich Festival in 1924. It impressed him so deeply that before long it led to his taking composition lessons with the older composer. Completed in 1911, it is an inspired example of Bridge's ability to use a relatively traditional idiom in a totally original way, a British counterpart to Debussy's *La mer*, far more than just scene-painting. It receives a brilliant and deeply sympathetic performance from Handley and the Ulster Orchestra, recorded with a fullness and vividness to make this a demonstration disc. The chrome tape is comparably fine.

Suite for strings.

*** Chan. Dig. **CHAN 8390**; *ABTD 1112* [id.]. ECO, Garforth – IRELAND: *Downland suite; Holy Boy; Elegiac meditations.****

*** Nimbus Dig. **NI 5068** [id.]. E. String O, Boughton – BUTTERWORTH: *Banks of green willow; Idylls; Shropshire lad;* PARRY: *Lady Radnor's suite.****

Suite for strings; Summer; There is a willow grows aslant a brook.

*** Chan. **CHAN 8373**; (M) *CBT 1018* [id.]. Bournemouth Sinf., Del Mar – BANTOCK: *Pierrot of the minute;* BUTTERWORTH: *Banks of green willow.****

The Bournemouth recording comes from 1979 and was subsequently digitally remastered. *Summer*, written in 1914 just before the outbreak of the First World War, is one of Bridge's most evocative and imaginative scores, and it is beautifully played by the Bournemouth Sinfonietta under Norman Del Mar. The same images of nature permeate the miniature tone-poem, *There is a willow grows aslant a brook*, written in 1927. Both are inspired pieces and they are sensitively played. The *Suite for strings* is somewhat earlier (1909–10). Its third movement, a *Nocturne*, is lovely. The CD transfer is excellent and one can relish its fine definition and presence. There is also a very good (mid-price) cassette.

The ECO also play well for David Garforth in the *Suite for strings*, which can no longer be called neglected. Which version one buys will now depend on the chosen coupling. This performance, though not scrupulous in observing the composer's metronome markings, is extremely committed; it is certainly excellently recorded, with great clarity and presence. The slow movement in particular is played with great eloquence. The disc does not score high marks on playing time – it runs for under 50 minutes – but it scores on every other point. The chrome cassette, too, is one of Chandos's finest, clear, full and truthful in timbre.

The Nimbus collection is more generous and is certainly well chosen. Here Bridge's *Suite* again receives a lively and responsive performance, from William Boughton and his excellent Birmingham-based orchestra, treated to ample, sumptuously atmospheric recording, more resonant than its competitors.

There is a willow grows aslant a brook.

(*) HMV Dig. **CDC7 47945-2; *EL 270592-4*. ECO, Jeffrey Tate – BUTTERWORTH: *Banks of green willow; Idylls***(*); BAX: *3 Pieces****; MOERAN: *Lonely waters* etc.***

Bridge's Impression for small orchestra, *There is a willow grows aslant a brook*, is a masterpiece of evocation that yet completely avoids English cliché, bringing many indications of the composer's later development. It makes a welcome item in Tate's English collection, beautifully if not quite magically done in warm, refined sound.

Cello sonata.

*** Chan. Dig. **CHAN 8499**; *ABTD 1209* [id.]. Raphael & Peter Wallfisch – BAX: *Rhapsodic ballad;* DELIUS: Sonata; WALTON: Passacaglia.***

*** Max Sound *MSCB 20/21* (Dolby B); *MSCC 20/21* (Dolby C). Caroline Dale, Keith Swallow – DELIUS: *Sonata***; PROKOFIEV; MARTINŮ: *Variations.****

Frank Bridge planned his *Cello sonata* in 1913 but it did not reach fruition until 1917. It is a powerful and original work, which Rostropovich and Britten served to reintroduce into the repertoire. At first sight it seems to bear all the imprints of the English pastoral school with its pastel colourings and gentle discursive lines, but there is no lack of fibre here and a pervasive sense that the pre-war Edwardian world was gone beyond recall. It is a distinctive world that Bridge evokes and one to which Raphael Wallfisch and his father, Peter, are completely attuned. There is a sense of scale about their reading which is impressive, and they are beautifully recorded, with a first-class equivalent tape.

Caroline Dale was the winner of the BBC's first Young Musician of the Year competition and, in an excellent partnership with the sensitive Keith Swallow, she too gives a wholly responsive account of the *Sonata*. This is part of a high-quality chrome tape (offered in alternative Dolby B and Dolby C configurations) which plays for over 80 minutes and includes fine performances of music by Martinů and Prokofiev, and a slightly less convincing version of the Delius *Sonata*.

Piano trio No. 2
*** Chan. Dig. **CHAN 8495**; *ABTD 1205* [id.]. Borodin Trio – BAX: *Piano trio*.***

Frank Bridge's *Second Piano trio* of 1928 is one of his most exploratory scores – and indeed one of the most original in English chamber music. The extraordinary piano writing is very forward-looking and later served as a model for Britten. The playing of the Borodin Trio is very distinguished and, given such advocacy and the excellence of the Chandos recording, let us hope that this will win new friends for this music. The chrome-cassette transfer is first class.

String quartet No. 2 in G min.; An Irish melody; Christmas dance; Londonderry air; 2 Old English songs (Sally in our ally; Cherry ripe); Sir Roger de Coverley.
*** Chan. Dig. *ABTD 1073* [id.]. Delmé Qt.

As more of Bridge's works are recorded, so his stature seems to grow greater. The *String quartet No. 2* develops on the formula of the *Phantasie quartet*, bringing together a sequence of movements thematically linked, each of which has a wide range of moods and tempi, phantasy-style. Not one of the three is strictly a slow movement, but the result is yet beautifully balanced and meticulously worked with memorable material to produce a satisfying and original structure. Though by 1915 disillusion had not set in to sour and darken Bridge's range of expression, his idiom here is quite distinctive, and it is good to have this generally first-rate performance, beautifully recorded on chrome tape which approaches demonstration quality and has fine range without an exaggerated treble response. The very enjoyable coupling offers five of his finely crafted and original pieces, based on folk tunes.

Britten, Benjamin (1913–76)

An American overture, Op. 27; Occasional overture, Op. 38; Sinfonia da Requiem. Op. 20; Suite on English folk tunes: A time there was, Op. 90.
*** HMV Dig. **CDC7 47343-2** [id.]; *EL 270263-4*. CBSO, Rattle.

Although concentrating on early works, this collection spans Britten's composing career. Both the *Sinfonia da Requiem* (1940) and the *American overture* (1941), with its attractive whiff of Copland, belong to the composer's wartime residence in the USA. The *Occasional overture* (1946) with its brilliant orchestral command was commissioned by the BBC for the opening of the Third Programme. The *Suite on English folk tunes* was not completed until 1974, although one movement, the quirky *Hankin Booby* – for wind and drums – dates from 1966, another commission, this time for the opening of the Queen Elizabeth Hall. While the most ambitious piece is the *Sinfonia da Requiem*, written after the death of Britten's parents, the *Folk tunes suite* is a good deal more diverse in mood than one might expect, with the eloquent last movement, *Lord Melbourne*, with its beautiful cor anglais evocation, the longest and most memorable. The whole programme is splendidly played by the City of Birmingham orchestra under Rattle, whose passionate view of the *Sinfonia da Requiem* is unashamedly extrovert, yet finding subtle detail too. The recording is admirably vivid and clear, especially in its CD format; the cassette is one of EMI's best and is very well balanced, but the compact disc has an extra dimension of presence.

Piano concerto, Op. 13.
** Chan. *ABT 1061* [id.]. Lin, Melbourne SO, John Hopkins – COPLAND: *Piano concerto.***(*)

(i) *Piano concerto, Op. 13;* (ii) *Violin concerto, Op. 15.*
(M) *** Decca *417 308-4*. (i) Sviatoslav Richter; (ii) Lubotsky, ECO, composer.

Violin concerto in D min., Op. 15.
(M) *** HMV *ED 290353-4*. Ida Haendel, Bournemouth SO, Berglund – WALTON: *Concerto.****

Both these works come from early in Britten's career, but as the Decca performances amply confirm, there is nothing immature or superficial about them. Richter is incomparable in interpreting the *Piano concerto*, not only the thoughtful introspective moments but the Liszt-like bravura passages (many of them surprising from this composer). The *Violin concerto* is constructed in three movements, but the manner and idiom are subtler. With its highly original violin sonorities it makes a splendid vehicle for another Soviet artist, the young violinist Mark Lubotsky. Recorded in The Maltings, the playing of the ECO under the composer's direction matches the inspiration of the soloists. The 1971 recording sounds splendid on this reissued Decca London Enterprise tape.

Gillian Lin provides a useful alternative to Richter's classic recording. Miss Lin cannot match the Soviet master in detailed imagination, but from her sharp attack on the opening motif onwards she gives a strong and satisfying reading, well accompanied by Hopkins and the Melbourne orchestra. The recorded sound is wide-ranging and well balanced on this lively cassette. It makes a fair alternative if you need the Copland coupling.

Miss Haendel's ravishing playing places Britten's *Violin concerto* firmly in the European tradition. She brings much panache and brilliance to the music, as well as great expressive warmth. This is a reading very much in the grand manner, and it finds Paavo Berglund in excellent form. His support is sensitive in matters of detail and full of atmosphere. The recording is most realistic, with a spacious perspective and warm string tone that is positively Mediterranean in feeling. The soloist is balanced a little close, but generally the security of her technique can stand up to such a revealing spotlight. The tape transfer is very successful in catching the full bloom of the violin timbre and managing the resonant orchestral acoustic without problems.

Matinées musicales, Op. 25; Soirées musicales, Op. 9.
*** Decca Dig. **410 139-2**. Nat. PO, Bonynge – ROSSINI: *La Boutique fantasque.****

Matinées musicales; Soirées musicales; Variations on a theme of Frank Bridge.
(M) *** EMI *TC-EMX 2111*. ECO, Gibson.

Britten wrote his *Soirées musicales* for a GPO film-score in the 1930s; the *Matinées* followed in 1941 and were intended as straight ballet music. Both are wittily if rather sparsely scored, deriving their musical content directly from Rossini, though Britten (like Respighi before him) brings the music into the twentieth century by his style of orchestration. Bonynge's versions are brightly played and extremely vividly recorded in the Decca manner, and on the compact disc the sparkle in the upper range and the vivid orchestral detail are very striking indeed. The balance is forward but there is no lack of ambience.

The ECO play very well for Alexander Gibson and, apart from giving a characterful account of the *Variations*, the charm and high spirits of Britten's two sets of *Musicales* are splendidly conveyed. The strikingly realistic recording – the strings especially full and vivid in the *Frank Bridge variations* – has transferred well to cassette, with the resonance having only a minor effect on the upper range, which remains acceptably focused.

Men of goodwill; The young person's guide to the orchestra, Op. 34; Peter Grimes: 4 Sea interludes.
(*) HMV Dig. **CDC7 49300-2 [id.]. Minnesota O, Marriner.

The brief orchestral piece, *Men of goodwill*, a set of variations on *God rest ye merry gentlemen*, was constructed from music which Britten wrote in 1947 for a BBC radio feature. It is a slight but attractive piece. The Minnesota performances of the well-known music are a little stiff but enjoyable enough. First-rate digital sound, clean and clear. The balance is fairly close and the ambient effect of Orchestra Hall, Minneapolis, is not allowed to cloud any of the textures. The *Peter Grimes interludes*, however, are not wanting in atmosphere. There is no internal cueing provided for the different instrumental sections of *The young person's guide*.

Prelude and fugue for 18 solo strings, Op. 29; Reflections on a song of Dowland; Simple symphony, Op. 4; Variations on a theme of Frank Bridge, Op. 10.
(*) Nimbus Dig. **NIM 5025 [id.]. Roger Best, E. String O, William Boughton.

Prelude and fugue for 18 solo strings, Op. 29; Simple symphony, Op. 4; Variations on a theme of Frank Bridge, Op. 10.
*** ASV Dig. **CDDCA 591**; *ZCDCA 591* [id.]. Northern Sinfonia, Hickox.
(*) Chan. **CHAN 8376; (M) *CBT 1018* [id.]. Bournemouth Sinf., Ronald Thomas.

Among these three collections of Britten's string music, the ASV issue is notable for an outstandingly fine account of the *Frank Bridge variations*, which stands up well alongside the composer's own version. Hickox's reading encompasses the widest range of emotion and style from the genial, exuberant bravura of the *Moto perpetuo* to the powerful intensity of the *Funeral march* and the hauntingly atmospheric, ethereal passage before the final bars. The earlier parodies have a wittily light touch; throughout, the string playing is committedly responsive, combining polish with eloquence, the rich sonorities resonating powerfully in the glowing ambience of All Saints Quayside Church, Newcastle. The reverberation also recalls Britten's own famous account of the *Simple symphony*, made in The Maltings, even if Hickox does not quite match the composer's rhythmic bounce in the *Playful pizzicato*. His approach is less lighthearted than Britten's, with a strong as well as *Boisterous bourrée* and a strain of *nobilmente* in the *Sentimental sarabande*. The *Prelude and fugue* is comparably eloquent, although here the playing is marginally less assured. The recording is first class, with the bright upper range well supported by the firm bass. The chrome cassette is very impressive too.

Though comparisons with Britten's own recordings of these three string works inevitably reveal felicities that are missing here, the Chandos coupling is also most attractive, the performances have a natural expressive warmth which is most engaging and, not least, the recording has a ripeness and resonance which are most satisfying, particularly in the bass registers, especially telling in the *Variations* in their CD format. The cassette too is extremely successful.

Warmly recorded in the Great Hall at Birmingham University, Boughton's collection of

Britten pieces brings sympathetic and lively performances not just of the popular *Variations* and *Simple symphony* but of the relative rarities, the ingenious *Prelude and fugue* written for the Boyd Neel String Orchestra (like the *Variations*) and the *Dowland reflections*. There is not a great deal to choose between these two collections, though the Nimbus disc has the advantage of a digital master and a completely silent background.

(i) *Simple symphony, Op. 4; Variations on a theme of Frank Bridge, Op. 10;* (ii) *The Young person's guide to the orchestra* (*Variations and fugue on a theme of Purcell*), *Op. 34.*
*** Decca **417 509-2**; (M) *417 509-4*. (i) ECO, (ii) LSO; composer.

These recordings come from 1964 (*The Young person's guide*), 1967 (the *Variations*) and 1969 (the *Simple symphony*), but the enhancement of the sound, with very tangible strings and great clarity and presence overall on the CD, is remarkable; some ears, however, might decide that the violins are *too* brightly lit, and they will be happy with the chrome tape, which is also of a demonstration standard, but is mellower on top – and, of course, costs much less. Britten takes a very brisk view of his *Young person's guide*, so brisk that even the LSO players cannot always quite match him. But every bar has a vigour which makes the music sound more youthful than usual, and the headlong, uninhibited account of the final fugue (trombones as vulgar as you like) is an absolute joy. In the *Frank Bridge variations* Britten goes more for half-tones and he achieves an almost circumspect coolness in the waltz-parody of the *Romance*; in the Viennese waltz section later, he is again subtly atmospheric; and in the *Funeral march* he is relatively solemn, showing here that for all the lighthearted mood of the opening sections of the work, this is music to be taken seriously. The *Simple symphony* makes a splendid foil, with its charm and high spirits; no one else has found quite the infectious bounce in the *Playful pizzicato* that the composer does, aided by the glowing resonance of The Maltings where the recording was made.

Symphony for cello and orchestra, Op. 68.
*** HMV Dig. **CDC7 49716-2**; *EL 749716-4*. Isserlis, City of L. Sinfonia, Hickox – BRIDGE: *Oration.****

(i) *Symphony for cello and orchestra, Op. 68; Death in Venice: suite, Op. 88* (arr. Bedford).
*** Chan. Dig. **CHAN 8363**; *ABTD 1126* [id.]. (i) Wallfisch; ECO, Bedford.

(i) *Symphony for cello and orchestra, Op. 68; Prelude and fugue, Op. 29; Sinfonia da requiem, Op. 20.*
(M) *** Decca *417 312-4*. (i) Rostropovich; ECO or New Philh. O, composer.

The restoration of the composer's own recordings of the *Cello symphony* and the *Sinfonia da requiem* (both made in 1964) is most welcome, particularly as the cassette sound is first class, extremely vivid and clear, with pianissimos registering admirably. The *Prelude and fugue* (from 1977) makes a worthwhile bonus on this highly recommendable mid-priced London Enterprise reissue. Both performances are definitive, and in particular Rostropovich's account of the *Cello symphony* is everything one could ask for. It is a marvellous piece, very much a new landscape in Britten's world.

With a comparison ready to hand, it is the more remarkable how closely Wallfisch – in collaboration with the conductor who carried on the Aldeburgh tradition when Britten ceased to conduct – manages to match the earlier version. If Wallfisch's tone is not so resonant as Rostropovich's the slight help from the recording balance gives it all the power needed, and there is a case for preferring Wallfisch's rather more direct approach to the craggily fragmentary first movement. Sounding less improvisatory than Rostropovich, he and Bedford give a more consistent sense of purpose, and the weight and range of the brilliant and full Chandos recording quality add to the impact. If in the brief central scherzo Wallfisch does not achieve the lightness and fantasy of the dedicatee, the differences are minimal. Equally, the power and purpose of the finale are formidable, with Bedford's direction even more spacious than the composer's, the effect emphasized by the Chandos ambience, spacious and warm. Steuart Bedford's encapsulation of Britten's last opera into this rich and colourful suite makes a splendid coupling. It brings together most of the richest and most atmospheric passages from an outstandingly intense and moving work which has never enjoyed the currency of his earlier stage masterpieces. The sequence of movements exactly follows the dramatic order in the opera, but by happy chance the result makes an exceptionally cogent and well-integrated musical structure in a continuous movement. Even so, it is a pity that the CD does not have bands between the separate sections. Otherwise performances and recording can hardly be faulted, and in its compact disc format the clarity and definition are outstanding. The chrome cassette sounds splendid too, with the *Death in Venice suite* especially well projected.

Steven Isserlis provides a valuable alternative both to Rostropovich, inspirer of the *Cello symphony* and the soloist in the first recording, and to Raphael Wallfisch on Chandos. With speeds generally a little slower, Isserlis is not quite as taut and electric as his rivals, partly because the recording does not present the solo instrument quite so cleanly. It remains a powerful, dramatic performance, highly recommendable if the Bridge coupling is preferred. The chrome cassette transfer is well managed, though the bass resonance of the solo cello is somewhat emphasized.

The Young person's guide to the orchestra (*Variations and fugue on a theme of Purcell*), *Op. 34*.
(M) *** HMV *TC-ESD 7114* (without narration). Royal Liverpool PO, Groves – PROKOFIEV: *Peter*; SAINT-SAËNS: *Carnival*.***
** RCA **RD 82743 [RCD1 2743]** (without narration). Phd. O, Ormandy – PROKOFIEV: *Peter*.**

The Young person's guide to the orchestra; Gloriana: Courtly dances (*suite*).
(*) Telarc Dig. **CD 80126 [id.] (without narration). RPO, Previn – PROKOFIEV: *Peter*.***

The composer's own version – discussed above – tends to upstage all newcomers in its uninhibited brilliance, but those looking for an inexpensive yet completely recommendable tape will find that Groves's Liverpool recording from the late 1970s has been imaginatively and generously recoupled (at medium prices) with excellent versions of *Peter and the Wolf* and the *Carnival of the Animals*, making a superb anthology for children of all ages. Groves's performance of the *Variations* is lively and genial; if it lacks the last degree of finesse, it has both high spirits and a fine sense of pace. The trumpet variation displays splendid bravura, and the flute and clarinet variations too are engagingly extrovert. The recording is first class, vividly colourful and full-bodied, with an outstandingly brilliant cassette transfer.

Unlike Previn's earlier EMI version, in which he gave a spoken narration, the Telarc disc brings a straight performance, rather relaxed compared with the composer's own, too well-behaved at times (as in the percussion section) but ending with a fizzing account of the finale. The *Gloriana dances*, a rarity on record, done with great flair, make a welcome filler. The CD has only four tracks but plentiful index points for the different variations and movements.

Ormandy's CD derives from a 1978 analogue master. The performance is straightforward and very well played. It has no special individuality except, perhaps, for the clarinets, whose contribution is attractively genial. The digital remastering emphasizes the brilliance of the sound. There is a touch of shrillness in the upper strings and no supporting weight in the bass. The brass and percussion add a touch of spectacle, but there is nothing distinctive here and this CD is overpriced.

CHAMBER MUSIC

(i) *Suite for harp, Op. 83;* (ii) *2 Insect pieces, for oboe & piano; 6 Metamorphoses after Ovid* (for oboe solo), *Op. 49.*
*** Mer. **CDE 84119**; *KE 77119* [id.]. (i) Osian Ellis; (ii) Sarah Watkins; Ledger – *Tit for Tat* etc.***.

It was for Osian Ellis that Britten wrote the *Harp suite*, which sounds surprisingly unlike any other harp music at all. Ellis remains the ideal performer. A younger artist, the oboist Sarah Watkins, gives biting and intense performances of the unaccompanied *Metamorphoses*, as well as the two early *Insect pieces*, with Philip Ledger – a long-time Aldeburgh associate – at the piano. The sound is full and immediate, set convincingly in a small but helpful hall. This is part of a cleverly planned recital which includes *Tit for Tat* and six folksong arrangements with their original harp accompaniments (see below).

String quartets Nos 1–3; String quartet in D; Quartettino; Alla marcia, 3 Divertimenti; Rhapsody (all for string quartet); (i) *Elegy for solo viola;* (ii) *Phantasy for oboe & string trio; Phantasy in F min. for string quintet.*
*** HMV Dig. *EX 270502-5* (3). Endellion Qt (augmented); (i) Garfield Jackson; (ii) with Douglas Boyd.

In addition to the three mature *Quartets*, which are familiar to collectors, this set brings a number of early works that are completely new: the early *Rhapsody* (1929), the *Quartettino* (1930), an *Elegy* for viola, a *Phantasy Quintet* for strings, and the *Three Divertimenti* (1933). In fact the only omissions are the very first three quartets composed before Britten began his studies with Frank Bridge. Also offered is the *Quartet in D* (1931) which the composer published in the last year of his life. This survey affords an invaluable insight into the young Britten, and is of importance, not merely in showing us 'the father to the man', but as a rewarding musical experience in its own right. In the last few years, the Endellions have established themselves as one of the finest quartets in the country, and their playing is as responsive and intelligent as one could possibly wish for. There are three cassettes which are, of course, not much more expensive than just one of the CDs. On tape, the frequency ceiling is lower than on the compact discs, but the balance is good and the strings have life as well as a natural fullness and bloom. Cassette collectors will note that the Alberni versions of the three *String quartets* remain available separately on a pair of excellent CRD tapes. No. 1 is coupled with the Shostakovich *Piano quintet* (*CRDC 4051*), and Nos 2 and 3 are together (*CRD 4095*). These performances are a degree less refined than those by the Endellion Quartet, but the playing is from the heart, vividly recorded and strongly characterized.

String quartet No. 1, Op. 25a; Alla marcia; 3 Divertimenti; (i) *Phantasy for oboe and string trio, Op. 2.*
*** HMV Dig. **CDC7 47695-2**. Endellion Qt, (i) Douglas Boyd.

String quartets Nos 2 and 3.
*** HMV Dig. **CDC7 47696-2**. Endellion Qt.

On the first disc here we have Britten's first published quartet, written in 1941 in response to a commission from Elizabeth Sprague Coolidge; the three *Divertimenti* from 1936, which derive from a suite of contrasting character movements entitled *Alla quartetto serioso* written three years earlier; and the eloquent *Oboe Phantasy quartet*. Britten may have looked back self-deprecatingly on his early work ('Here was no early Mozart, I'm afraid'), but listening again to this Op. 2 one is taken aback by the sheer fertility of his invention and the abundance of his imagination. The *Alla marcia* followed a year afterwards and resurfaced in 1939 in 'Parade' in

Les illuminations. In every way the performances and recordings are exemplary, while on the companion CD the performances of the *Second* and *Third Quartets* can match the much (and rightly) admired pioneering accounts by the Zorian and Amadeus groups.

String quartet No. 3, Op. 94.
*** ASV Dig. **CDDCA 608;** *ZCDCA 608* [id.]. Lindsay Qt – TIPPETT – *Quartet No. 4*.***

The Lindsay performance, unusually if aptly coupled with Tippett's late quartet, brings the most expansive and deeply expressive reading on record. The commitment of the performers makes the final slow movement all the more affecting, baring the inner heart of Britten's rarefied inspiration. The ASV recording is vivid, with fine presence; but extraneous sounds are intrusive at times – heavy breathing, snapping of strings on finger-board etc. There is a good cassette.

(i) *Elegy for solo viola; Phantasy in F min. for string quintet; Rhapsody; Quartettino; String quartet in D.*
*** HMV Dig. **CDC7 47694-2**. Endellion Qt; (i) Garfield Jackson.

The *Elegy for viola*, Britten's own instrument, was one of the last pieces Britten wrote before taking up his scholarship at the Royal College of Music in London in 1930. The remarkable three-movement *Quartettino* is at times almost Berg-like and shows how exploratory were his musical instincts and how keenly he responded to the stimulus of Frank Bridge. (As John Evans puts it in his notes, 'Here is the Bridge of the *Third Quartet* (1926) and more besides!') Britten reworked the 1931 *D major Quartet* when he was convalescing after open-heart surgery towards the end of his life. Originally Bridge had complained that its counterpoint was too vocal, but there is much that is characteristic in this fluent and well-crafted piece. Excellent playing from the Endellions and altogether first-class sound; on CD there is that greater definition and range which give the illusion of presence.

Suites for unaccompanied cello Nos 1, Op. 72; 2, Op. 80.
(M) *** Decca *417 309-4*. Rostropovich.

This is rough, gritty music in Britten's latterday manner. It is characteristic of him that, not content with tackling the almost insoluble problem of writing for solo cello in a single work, he wrote a sequel. The *First Suite*, with its clean-cut genre pieces, remains the more strikingly memorable of the two; but Rostropovich gives such an inspired account of the *Second* that its even grittier manner reveals more and more with repetition on record. Fine 1969 recording; superlative performances, and a first-class tape transfer.

Suite for unaccompanied cello No. 3, Op. 87.
*** ASV *ZCACA 1001*. Lloyd Webber – BRIDGE: *Elegy****; IRELAND: *Sonata*.**(*)

The *Third Suite* which Britten also wrote for Rostropovich may be less ambitious in plan than its predecessors, but in such a performance as Julian Lloyd Webber's the very directness and lyrical approachability in the sharply characterized sequence of pieces – *Marcia*, *Canto*, *Barcarolla*, *Dialogo*, *Fuga* etc. – make for the extra emotional impact. With Lloyd Webber the climax of the extended final *Passacaglia* is extraordinarily powerful, and all through he brings out what might be described as the schizophrenic side of the work, the play between registers high and low. These sharp contrasts are used not just to imply full orchestral textures but to interweave opposing ideas as the movements merge. The recording is full and warm; the cassette balance is wholly natural (although the level could have been a little higher).

VOCAL MUSIC

(i) *A Birthday Hansel, Op. 92;* (ii) *Holy sonnets of John Donne, Op. 35;* (iii) *Nocturne, Op. 60.*
(M) *** Decca *417 310-4.* Peter Pears; (i) Osian Ellis; (ii) composer (piano); (iii) LSO, composer.

A Birthday Hansel was written to celebrate the seventy-fifth birthday of the Queen Mother. The music has a tangy angularity to match the character of Burns's words, but it has charm, too, and atmosphere, with Osian Ellis, the great Welsh harp player, bringing extra inspiration. This was recorded in 1976, whereas *The holy sonnets of John Donne* were earlier (1969) and this shows in a touch of hardness on the sound of the tape transfer. But this performance sets a definitive standard for what was in some ways the deepest of the many sets of songs written for Peter Pears. The voice is amazingly even, coping with both the dramatic outbursts and the lyrical soaring which in fine contrast put this among the richest of modern song-cycles. The tape transfer throughout is clear and vivid. On CD the *Nocturne* is differently coupled – see below.

A Birthday Hansel, Op. 92: Afton Water; My Hoggie; Wee Willie; The winter. A Charm of Lullabies. Folksong arrangements: *The ash grove; Come you not from Newcastle?; How sweet the answer; The last rose of summer; The minstrel boy; O can ye sew cushions; O Waly Waly; Quand j'étais chez mon père; The trees they grow so high.*
(*) HM Dig. **KTC 1046; *XTC 1046* [id.]. Yvonne Kenny, Carolyn Watkinson, Tan Crone.

Yvonne Kenny's collection of Britten songs usefully brings together two of his rarer cycles, and a generous collection of folksongs. When Britten's songs are more regularly associated with the male voice, it is refreshing to have not only the *Charm of Lullabies*, originally written for the mezzo-soprano Nancy Evans, but Colin Matthews' neat arrangement of four songs from the cycle, *A Birthday Hansel*, originally written for tenor and harp. As well as transcribing the harp part for piano – easy enough – Matthews has added endings to each song, when in the original they were linked, and in a different order. Yvonne Kenny's voice, with vibrato sometimes obtrusive, is not ideally suited to recording; but these are sensitive and intelligent performances, well recorded.

A boy was born, Op. 3; Festival Te Deum, Op. 32; Rejoice in the Lamb, Op. 30; A Wedding anthem, Op. 46.
*** Hyp. **CDA 66126**; *KA 66126* [id.]. Corydon Singers, Westminster Cathedral Ch., Best; Trotter (organ).

Britten's brilliant set of choral variations, atmospheric and strikingly varied in character, was completed when he was only nineteen, a masterly work here beautifully performed and recorded, and generously coupled with a group of other small Britten choral works. All of them are sharply inspired, usually to match the requirements of particular occasions, as for example the *Wedding anthem* written for the wedding of Lord Harewood and Marion Stein, and never recorded before. *Rejoice in the Lamb* is the most masterly of the pieces, poignantly matching the pain as well as the innocence of the words of the mad poet, Christopher Smart. The refinement and tonal range of the choirs could hardly be more impressive, and the recording is refined and atmospheric to match.

The Burning fiery furnace (2nd Parable), Op. 77.
(M) *** Decca *414 663-4.* Pears, Tear, Drake, Shirley-Quirk, Ch. & O of E. Opera Group, composer & Viola Tunnard.

Britten's conception of the church parable, so highly individual with its ritual elements (the audience turned into a medieval congregation), yet allows the widest variety of construction and expression. The story of *Burning fiery furnace* is obviously dramatic in the operatic sense, with vivid scenes like the Entrance of Nebuchadnezzar, the Raising of the Idol, and the putting of the three Israelites into the furnace. Britten is as imaginative as ever in his settings, and one must mention also the marvellous central interlude where the instrumentalists process round the church, which is stunningly well conveyed by the recording. The performers, both singers and players, are the same hand-picked cast that participated in the first performance at Orford Parish Church, where this record was made. This is another example of the way Decca served Britten in providing definitive versions of his major scores for the guidance of all future performers, as well as for our enjoyment at home. The tape transfer is remarkably lively and vivid, and we must hope Decca plan to issue the two companion works in this suitably named London Enterprise series.

A Ceremony of carols; Deus in adjutorium meum; Hymn of St Columba; Hymn to the Virgin; Jubilate Deo in E flat; Missa brevis, Op. 63.
*** Hyp. Dig. **CDA 66220**; *KA 66220* [id.]. Westminster Cathedral Ch., David Hill; (i) with S. Williams; J. O'Donnell (organ).

It was for the trebles of Westminster Cathedral Choir – when directed by George Malcolm – that Britten wrote his *Missa brevis*. Under David Hill, the present choir shows brilliantly how well standards have been kept up, not least in the treble section. Particularly impressive is the boys' singing in the *Ceremony of carols*, where the ensemble is superb, the solo work amazingly mature, and the range of tonal colouring a delight. Along with the other rarer pieces, this is an outstanding collection beautifully and atmospherically recorded, the more vivid in CD, but sounding excellent on the chrome tape, too.

(i) *A Ceremony of carols, Op. 28; Hymn to St Cecilia, Op. 17;* (ii) *Jubilate Deo;* (i) *Missa brevis, Op. 63;* (ii; iii) *Rejoice in the Lamb, Op. 30; Te Deum in C.*
*** HMV **CDC7 47709**; (M) *ED 291185-4*. King's College, Cambridge, Ch., (i) Willcocks with Ellis; (ii) Ledger with James Bowman, D. Corkhill, J. Lancelot.

Britten liked an earthily boyish tone among trebles, and the King's trebles under Willcocks may have less edge in the *Ceremony of carols* than some of their rivals, while the *Missa brevis* can certainly benefit from throatier sound. Yet these Willcocks performances, made towards the end of his stay at Cambridge, are dramatic as well as beautiful, and well recorded, too. To make a particularly generous concert, HMV have added performances taken from Philip Ledger's first record as director of the choir. He scored a notable first in using a new version of the cantata, *Rejoice in the Lamb*, with timpani and percussion added to the original organ part. The differences are minor but they add to the weight and drama of this haunting setting of the words of Christopher Smart. The biting climaxes are sung with passionate incisiveness, while James Bowman is in his element in the delightful passage which tells you that 'the mouse is a creature of great personal valour'. The *Te Deum* setting and the *Jubilate* make an additional bonus and are no less well sung and recorded. The mid-priced cassette is generally well transferred; the atmospheric King's acoustic does not offer too many problems, though the focus is superior on CD and the organ accompaniments (and percussion) are better defined. There are 71 minutes of music included here.

Folksong arrangements: *The ash grove; Avenging and bright; La belle est au jardin d'amour; The bonny Earl o'Moray; The brisk young widow; Ca' the yowes; Come you not from Newcastle?; Early one morning; How sweet the answer; The last rose of summer; The minstrel boy; The miller of Dee; Oft in the stilly night; The plough boy; Le roi s'en va-t' en chasse; Sweet Polly Oliver; O Waly, Waly.*
(M) *** Decca *411 802-4*. Peter Pears, Benjamin Britten.

Folksong arrangements: *The ash grove; La belle est au jardin d'amour; The bonny Earl o'Moray; The brisk young widow; Ca' the yowes; Come you not from Newcastle?; The foggy, foggy dew; The Lincolnshire poacher; Little Sir William; The minstrel boy; O can ye sew cushions; Oliver Cromwell; O Waly, Waly; The plough boy; Quand j'étais chez mon père; Le roi s'en va-t' en chasse; The Sally Gardens; Sweet Polly Oliver; The trees they grow so high.*
(M) *** HMV *ED 290352-4*. Robert Tear, Philip Ledger.

Folksong arrangements: *The ash grove; La belle est au jardin d'amour; Come you not from Newcastle?; Dear harp of my country; Early one morning; Fileuse; How sweet the answer; The last rose of summer; Little Sir William; O can ye sew cushions; Oft in the stilly night; Oliver Cromwell; O Waly, Waly; The plough boy; Quand j'étais chez mon père; Sweet Polly Oliver; There's none to soothe; The trees they grow so high; Voce le printemps.*
** HMV Dig. **CDC7 49510-2**; *EL 749510-4*. Sarah Brightman, Geoffrey Parsons.

The reissue of the Pears/Britten collection reminds us of the *Punch* jingle:

There's no need for Pears
To give himself airs;
He has them written
By Benjamin Britten.

We must be grateful for such bounty. *Earl o'Moray* has almost too much Britten, and the accompaniment for *Early one morning* is unnecessarily clever and almost distracting. But others are delightful, especially *The ash grove* and the French song about the king going hunting. The recording is admirably faithful.

Close as Robert Tear's interpretations are to those of Peter Pears, he has a sparkle of his own, helped by resilient accompaniment from Philip Ledger. In any case, some of these songs are unavailable in Pears' versions, and the record is a delight on its own account. *Oliver Cromwell* is among the most delectable of pay-off songs ever written. Fine recording.

Sarah Brightman, a charming if slight-toned soprano in the music that her husband, Andrew Lloyd-Webber, has written for her, is disappointing in these Britten folksongs, trying too hard to inject expression, often at speeds manifestly too slow (as in the first item, *Early one morning*), regularly missing the carefree sparkle. Geoffrey Parsons does his best to compensate: one hopes Miss Brightman's next such venture will prove less inhibited. The recording has fine presence on CD and chrome cassette alike.

(i) *The Heart of the matter. 3 Early songs; 3 realisations of Henry Purcell. The children and Sir Nameless; Dawtries's devotion; The gully; If it's ever spring again; Night covers up; Not even summer yet; The oxen; To lie flat on the back.*
*** HMV Dig. **CDC7 49257-2**; *EL 270653-4*. Neil Mackie, Roger Vignoles, (i) with Pears (nar.), Tuckwell.

Neil Mackie's headily beautiful tenor, light, free and unstrained, is ideally suited both to the microphone and to the demands of Britten songs originally written with Peter Pears in mind. It is a more obviously beautiful voice than Pears', lacking perhaps an abrasive quality, but Sir Peter recognized the kinship. Together with Mackie, he gave a broadcast performance in 1985 of the main work here, *The Heart of the matter*. That is a sequence of songs, readings and horn fanfares to texts by Edith Sitwell, centring round Britten's *Canticle No. 3, Still falls the rain*, written the year before the sequence was first performed in 1956. Sir Peter died before the project to make an EMI recording could be achieved, but the BBC allowed Sir Peter's spoken narrations to be inserted in the finished recording. The *Canticle* with sequence of six verses and variations and its horn obbligato provides the major musical argument, but the sequence round it with three songs previously unrecorded heightens its impact, particularly when Barry Tuckwell and Roger Vignoles provide such powerful support for Mackie. The coupling is a collection of rare, mostly unpublished tenor songs, fragments from the master's workbench. Songs to words by Hardy and Soutar were the 'leftovers' from song-cycles, the Soutar items more memorable than most of *A Birthday Hansel*, from which they were omitted. Three boyhood songs, Auden settings to texts inspired by Britten himself, and Purcell arrangements make up a fascinating survey of Britten as song-writer, even if no masterpiece is thrown up. Warm, atmospheric recording with the voice set back, not spotlit.

(i) *6 Hölderlin fragments, Op. 61;* (ii) *Phaedra, Op. 93;* (iii) *The poet's echo, Op. 75;* (iv) *Songs and proverbs of William Blake, Op. 74.*
*** Decca *417 313-4.* (i) Pears, composer; (ii) Dame Janet Baker, ECO, Steuart Bedford; (iii) Vishnevskaya, Rostropovich; (iv) Fischer-Dieskau, composer.

A marvellously generous and rewarding anthology. Perhaps the highlight is *Phaedra*, which Britten wrote at the end of his life for Dame Janet Baker. Setting words from Robert Lowell's fine translation of Racine's play, the composer encapsulated the character of the tragic heroine, and provided vocal writing which brings out every facet of her glorious voice, sounding wonderfully fresh when the recording was made in 1977. *The poet's echo* – Britten's setting of Pushkin poems in the original Russian – were written as a personal tribute to Vishnevskaya and her versatile cellist/pianist husband, and these miniatures have all the composer's characteristic crispness of image. Vishnevskaya's voice, with its Slavonic unevenness, is not the most suited in controlling the subtle line of such delicate songs, but with the help of Rostropovich the (1969) performance is committed and atmospheric. The Blake cycle was also specially written for the artist who sings here. It is an intense setting of visionary words and, following Britten's latterday pattern, it presents fewer moments of sweetness or relaxation. Fischer-Dieskau's performance is ideal, with the composer accompanying, re-creating his inspiration. The six *Hölderlin fragments* stand rather apart from Britten's other songs, reflecting a highly individual response to the German language and the sensitive word-painting of Hölderlin. They may not be as striking as Britten's English songs, but with Pears and the composer to interpret them they make a highly original impression. The high-level tape gives a vivid presence throughout. The sound is at its finest in *Phaedra*, but brings a touch of shrillness to Vishnevskaya and hardens the voice at climaxes.

(i) *Les Illuminations* (song cycle), *Op. 18;* (ii) *Phaedra, Op. 93;* French folksong arrangements: *La belle est au jardin d'amour; Eho! Eho!; Fileuse; Quand j'étais chez mon père; Le roi s'en va-t'en chasse.*
*** Dig. **CDC7 49259-2**; *EL 270654-4* [id.]. (i) Jill Gomez; (ii) Felicity Palmer; Endymion Ens., Whitfield.

Sir Peter Pears was such a dominant interpreter of Britten's vocal music that the original inspiration of the orchestral cycle, *Les Illuminations*, using a soprano has rather been forgotten. Though Heather Harper recorded a fine performance, Jill Gomez, ably backed by John Whitfield and the Endymion Ensemble, is far more seductively sensuous, with the soloist bringing out a gorgeous feminine beauty, matching the exotic quality of the Baudelaire poems. Felicity Palmer, contrasting strongly, gives strong, intense performances both of the late dramatic cantata, *Phaedra* (tougher and less tender than the dedicatee, Janet Baker) and of the five French folksong arrangements not previously recorded in this colourful orchestral form. Vivid, well-balanced recording on CD, with a first-class matching chrome tape.

(i) *Les Illuminations* (song cycle), *Op. 18;* (ii) *Serenade for tenor, horn and strings, Op. 18;* (iii) *Nocturne.*

*** Decca **417 153-2** [id.]. Peter Pears, (i; ii) ECO; (ii) with Barry Tuckwell; (iii) wind soloists, LSO strings; composer.

Peter Pears' voice is so ideally suited to this music, his insight into word-meaning as well as phrase-shaping so masterly, that for once one can use the adjective 'definitive'. With dedicated accompaniments under the composer's direction, *Les Illuminations* and the *Serenade* (with its superbly played horn obbligato by Barry Tuckwell), which both come from the mid-1960s, make a perfect coupling. For the CD release, Decca have added the recording of the *Nocturne* from 1960. In this wide-ranging cycle on the subject of night and sleep, Britten chose from a diverse selection of poems – by Coleridge, Tennyson, Wordsworth, Wilfred Owen and Keats, finishing with a Shakespeare sonnet. It is a work full – as so much of Britten's output is – of memorable moments. One thinks of the 'breathing' motif on the strings which links the different songs, the brilliant dialogue for flute and clarinet in the Keats setting, and above all the towering climax of the Wordsworth excerpt. Each song has a different obbligato instrument (with the ensemble unified for the final Shakespeare song), and each instrument gives the song it is associated with its own individual character. Pears as always is the ideal interpreter, the composer a most efficient conductor, and the fiendishly difficult obbligato parts are played superbly. The recording is brilliant and clear, with just the right degree of atmosphere. An alternative well-transferred cassette issue (*417 311-4*) omits the *Nocturne*, but this is included on a companion cassette, also at mid price – see above.

(i) *Serenade for tenor, horn and strings, Op. 31; 7 Sonnets of Michelangelo, Op. 22;* (ii) *Winter words, Op. 52.*

(***) Decca mono *417 183-4*. Peter Pears; (i) Dennis Brain (horn), Boyd Neel String O, composer; (ii) composer (piano).

The historic first recording of Britten's *Serenade*, made in 1945, may suffer from dry, boxy sound, but in many ways it has never been matched since. Peter Pears was then in fresher, more agile voice than in his later recordings, and the immediacy of a totally inspired work, still new, comes over the more urgently. The playing of Dennis Brain, for whom the obbligato part was written, adds to the character and vividness of the performance. The recordings of the other two song-cycles date from 1954, radiant performances, particularly of the highly atmospheric *Winter words*, then new. Sadly, Pears and Britten never made another commercial recording of either cycle.

Songs and proverbs of William Blake, Op. 74, Tit for Tat, 3 Early songs: Beware that I'd ne'er been married; Epitaph; The clerk. Folksong arrangements: *Bonny at morn; I was lonely; Lemady; Lord! I married me a wife!; O Waly, Waly; The Sally Gardens; She's like the swallow; Sweet Polly Oliver.*

(*) Chan. Dig. **CHAN 8514; *ABTD 1224* [id.]. Benjamin Luxon, David Williamson.

Benjamin Luxon, long associated with early performances of Britten's church parables at the Aldeburgh Festival, yet breaks out of the regular Britten mould in his imaginatively planned song-recital. His lusty baritone gives an abrasive edge whether to early song, folksong settings or the Blake cycle originally written for Dietrich Fischer-Dieskau. Only rarely does he become too emphatic – as in his overpointing of the three very early boyhood songs – and the *Tit for Tat* cycle of De la Mare settings written a few years later, teenage inventions, are bitingly powerful. The Blake cycle is commandingly done, despite some signs of strain, and the most valuable items of all are the five very late folksong settings – originally with harp accompaniment – which Britten wrote in the very last year of his life, ending with the most touching, the hauntingly melancholy *She's like the swallow*. Excellent, sensitive accompaniment and first-rate recording, on chrome tape as well as CD.

Spring symphony, Op. 44; Peter Grimes: 4 Sea interludes.
*** HMV **CDC7 47667-2** [id.]; (M) *ED 291047-4*. Armstrong, Baker, Tear, St Clement Dane's School Boys' Ch., LSO Ch., LSO, Previn.

(i) *Spring symphony; Simple symphony for strings.*
(M) *** Decca *410 171-4*. (i) Vyvyan, Proctor, Pears, Wandsworth School Boys' Ch., Ch. and O of ROHCG; (ii) ECO; composer.

In 1961 Decca took advantage of a BBC performance with the same forces to obtain a recording of unusual brilliance and strength. If the title 'Symphony' is misleading – the work is much more an anthology akin to the *Serenade* and the *Nocturne* – Britten again shows by the subtlest of balancing that unity and cohesion are not just a matter of formal patterns. The four parts do come to have the coherence of balanced movements. But it is the freshness of Britten's imagination in dozens of moments that makes this work as memorable as it is joyous. Who but Britten would have dared use so unexpected an effect as boys whistling? Who but he would have introduced a triumphant C major *Sumer is icumen in* at the end, the boys' voices ringing out over everything else? Here of course a recording helps enormously. Thanks to the Decca engineers one hears more than is usually possible in a live performance. Jennifer Vyvyan and Peter Pears are both outstanding, and Britten shows that no conductor is more vital in his music than he himself. The reissue couples the work to Britten's joyful account of his delightful *Simple symphony* with the rich Maltings acoustic making the *Playful pizzicato* resonate gloriously as in no other version. The chrome cassette is of high quality.

Just as Sir Colin Davis's interpretation of *Peter Grimes* provided a strikingly new view of a work of which the composer seemed the natural interpreter, so André Previn's reading of the *Spring symphony* is valuably distinctive. Like Britten, Previn makes this above all a work of exultation, a genuine celebration of spring; but here more than in Britten's recording the kernel of what the work has to say comes out in the longest of the solo settings, using Auden's poem *Out on the lawn I lie in bed.* With Dame Janet Baker as soloist it rises above the lazily atmospheric mood of the opening to evoke the threat of war and darkness. Perhaps surprisingly, it is Britten who generally adopts faster tempi and a sharper rhythmic style, whereas Previn is generally the more atmospheric and mysterious, grading the climaxes and shading the tones over longer spans. He also takes more care over pointing Britten's pay-offs, often with the help of Robert Tear's sense of timing, as at the very end on *I cease*. The *Four Sea interludes*, which make a generous bonus, are presented in their concert form with tailored endings. Previn springs the bouncing rhythms of the second interlude – the picture of Sunday morning in the Borough – even more infectiously than the composer himelf in his complete recording of the opera. Both recordings were among EMI's finest of the analogue era and they have responded well to digital remastering. Some of the original sumptuousness at the bass end has been exchanged for a marginal improvement in the *Spring symphony*. There is an extremely vivid cassette which costs considerably less than the CD.

(i) *Tit for Tat:* (ii) Folksong arrangements: *Bird scarer's song; Bonny at morn; David of the White Rock; Lemady; Lord! I married me a wife; She's like a swallow.*
*** Mer. **CDE 84119**; *KE 84119* [id.]. Shirley-Quirk; (i) Ledger; (ii) Ellis – *Suite for harp* etc.***

This Meridian collection celebrates a nicely varied group of works which Britten wrote for friends to perform at the Aldeburgh Festival. John Shirley-Quirk was the baritone who first sang the cycle, *Tit for Tat*, with the composer at the piano, and he is still unrivalled in the sharp yet subtle way he brings out the irony in these boyhood settings of De la Mare poems. It is good too to have him singing the six late folk-settings with harp accompaniment which Britten originally wrote for Peter Pears, much more distinctive in these original versions than with piano accompaniment, here played by Osian Ellis, for whom they were written. The recording is naturally balanced and immediate.

War Requiem, Op. 66.

*** Decca **414 383-2** [id.]; *K 27 K 22* [Lon. *OSA5-1255*]. Vishnevskaya, Pears, Fischer-Dieskau, Bach Ch., LSO Ch. Highgate School Ch., Melos Ens., LSO, composer.

*** HMV Dig. **CDS7 47034-8** [id.]. Söderström, Tear, Allen, Trebles of Christ Church Cathedral Ch., Oxford, CBSO Ch., CBSO, Rattle.

The vivid realism of Britten's own 1963 recording of the *War requiem*, one of the outstanding achievements of the whole analogue stereo era, comes over the more strikingly in the CD transfer, with uncannily precise placing and balancing of the many different voices and instruments, and John Culshaw's contribution as producer is all the more apparent. Britten pointed the contrast between the full choir and orchestra in the settings of the *Requiem* and the tenor, baritone and chamber orchestra in the intervening settings of the Wilfred Owen poems. But what a recording can do that is impossible in a cathedral or concert hall is to modify the acoustic for each, and this has been done most sensitively and effectively by the Decca engineers. The Owen settings strike one more sharply than the Latin settings, but gradually as the work progresses the process of integration is accomplished, and the way the soloists' cries of *Let us sleep now* fade into the final chorus is almost unbearably moving on record as in performance. The recorded performance comes near to the ideal, but it is a pity that Britten insisted on Vishnevskaya for the soprano solos. Having a Russian singer was emotionally right, but musically Heather Harper would have been so much better still. The digital remastering for CD, as with *Peter Grimes*, brings added textural refinement and makes the recording sound newly minted; it also reveals a degree of background hiss, that is, surprisingly, less noticeable on the cassettes, which are almost comparably vivid.

The HMV recording for Rattle, much closer in its perspectives and wider in frequency range but not more realistic than Britten's own set, is all the more immediate on CD, and with a fully digital recording there is no problem over background noise. The most striking difference between Rattle's interpretation and that of Britten himself lies in the relationship between the settings of Owen's poems and the setting of the liturgy in Latin. With Söderström a far more warmly expressive soloist than the oracular Vishnevskaya, the human emotions behind the Latin text come out strongly with less distancing than from the composer. One registers the more clearly the meaning of the Latin. Tear and Allen are fine soloists, though at times balanced too forwardly. If Tear does not always match the subtlety of Pears on the original recording, Allen sounds more idiomatic than Fischer-Dieskau. Rattle's approach is warm, dedicated and dramatic, with fine choral singing (not least from the Christ Church Cathedral trebles). The dramatic orchestral contrasts are superbly brought out as in the blaze of trumpets on *Hosanna*. The various layers of perspective are impressively managed by the superb digital recording. Yet in its combination of imaginative flair with technical expertise, the Culshaw recording of two decades earlier is by no means surpassed by this new HMV venture, although the EMI set has the considerable digital advantage of a silent background.

OPERA

Gloriana: Choral dances.

*** Hyp. **CDA 66175**; *KA 66175* [id.]. Martyn Hill, Thelma Owen, Holst Singers & O, Hilary Davan Wetton – BLISS: *Lie strewn the white flocks;* HOLST: *Choral hymns from the Rig Veda.****

It is little short of a scandal that so great an opera as *Gloriana* still remains to be recorded complete. The composer's own choral suite, made up of unaccompanied choral dances linked by passages for solo tenor and harp, make a valuable if tantalizing sample, an excellent coupling for the equally attractive Bliss and Holst items. Excellent atmospheric recording, very well transferred to tape.

Peter Grimes (complete).

❀ *** Decca **414 577-2** [id.]. Pears, Claire Watson, Pease, Jean Watson, Nilsson, Brannigan, Evans, Ch. and O of ROHCG, composer.

The Decca recording of *Peter Grimes* was one of the first great achievements of the stereo era. Few opera recordings can claim to be so definitive, with Peter Pears, for whom it was written, in the name part, Owen Brannigan (another member of the original team) and a first-rate cast. One was a little apprehensive about Claire Watson as Ellen Orford, a part which Joan Cross made her own, but in the event Miss Watson gives a most sympathetic performance, and her voice records beautifully. Another member of the cast from across the Atlantic, James Pease, as the understanding Captain Balstrode, is brilliantly incisive musically and dramatically; but beyond that it becomes increasingly unfair to single out individual performances. Britten conducts superbly and secures splendidly incisive playing, with the whole orchestra on its toes throughout. The recording, superbly atmospheric, has so many felicities that it would be hard to enumerate them, and the Decca engineers have done wonders in making up aurally for the lack of visual effects. Moreover, the digital remastering for CD miraculously has improved the sound still further. The striking overall bloom remains, yet solo voices and chorus are vividly clear and fully projected. Owen Brannigan sounds wonderfully ripe and present in the Prologue, while the orchestral sound is glorious. Some background noise remains, of course, but it is not really intrusive and, apart from that, one might think this a modern digital set. The 44 cues bring access to every item in the score. A marvellous sampler is provided by trying band 5 on the first disc; this brings the evocative *First Sea interlude*, glowing with atmosphere, the very slight edge on the upper strings adding to the sense of bleakness.

Peter Grimes: 4 Sea interludes and Passacaglia.

*** Chan. Dig. **CHAN 8473**; *ABTD 1184* [id.]. Ulster O, Handley – BAX: *On the Sea-shore;* BRIDGE: *The Sea.****

Britten, influenced deeply from boyhood by his teacher, Frank Bridge, similarly turned to the sea as subject. Born in Lowestoft and living most of his life a few miles south of Aldeburgh, Britten had the sea as neighbour all his life, and here – in a work first inspired in America during the Second World War by nostalgic thoughts of home – he created one of the most original seascapes in the whole of music, highly distinctive in its spareness. The suite is made up of four interludes, taken from an opera consistently rich in evocation, that with the *Passacaglia* make a finely balanced concert piece. Handley draws brilliant and responsive playing from the Ulster Orchestra in readings that fully capture the atmospheric beauty of the writing, helped by vivid recording of demonstration quality, the finest ever made of this music – and that applies to the chrome cassette as well as to the superb CD.

Brubeck, Howard (born 1916)

Dialogues for jazz combo and orchestra

*** CBS *MPT 39768*. Brubeck Qt, NYPO, Bernstein – BERNSTEIN: *Prelude, fugue and riffs;* STRAVINSKY: *Ebony concerto* etc.***

Howard Brubeck's *Dialogue* was written in 1959 for the artists on this recording. Obviously improvisational in style, it is not over-ambitious and, with superb contributions from Dave Brubeck (piano) and the eloquent saxophone of Paul Desmond, is undoubtedly effective, making a comparatively romantic contrast with the more abrasive Bernstein and the cooler Stravinsky couplings. The sound on the tape is well balanced.

Bruch, Max (1838–1920)

Violin concerto No. 1 in G min., Op. 26.

(M) *** Decca **417 707-2** [id.]. Kyung Wha Chung, RPO, Kempe – SAINT-SAËNS: *Havanaise;* TCHAIKOVSKY: *Concerto.****

(M) *** Pickwick Dig. **PCD 829** [**MCA MCAD 25934**]. Jaime Laredo, SCO – MENDELSSOHN: *Concerto.****

*** DG **419 629-2**. Shlomo Mintz, Chicago SO, Abbado (also with KREISLER: *Caprice viennoise; Liebeslied; Liebesfreud*) – MENDELSSOHN: *Concerto.***(*)

*** DG Dig. **400 031-2**; *3302 016* [id.]. Mutter, BPO, Karajan – MENDELSSOHN: *Concerto.****

(M) *** HMV **CDM7 69003-2** [id.]. Menuhin, Philh. O, Susskind – MENDELSSOHN: *Concerto.****

(*) Decca Dig. **421 145-2; *421 145-4* [id.]. Joshua Bell, ASMF, Marriner – MENDELSSOHN: *Concerto.***(*)

(*) Denon Dig. **C37 7123 [id.]. Kantorow, Netherlands CO, Ros-Marba – MENDELSSOHN: *Concerto.***(*)

(M) **(*) Ph. **420 703-2**; *420 703-4* [id.]. Grumiaux, New Philh. O, Wallberg – BRAHMS: *Concerto.***(*)

(B) ** Sup. **2SUP 0002**. Ishikawa, Brno State PO, Belohlavek – SIBELIUS: *Concerto.****

The much-loved Bruch *G minor Violin concerto* is one of those works which is exceptionally well served by mid-priced recordings; even so, Cho-Liang Lin's digital version for CBS, coupled with the *Scottish Fantasia* (see below), must be considered among the finest of all, while Heifetz's similar coupling, which offers Vieuxtemps as well, is by no means to be discounted in spite of the unnatural balance. Stern's version from the end of the 1960s is even more unrealistically balanced, with the soloist displaying more opulence of tone than the orchestra. But that remains one of the great recordings of the work, warmhearted and with a very moving account of the slow movement, which sustains the greatest possible intensity. Ormandy's accompaniment is first class and triumphs over the unrealistic balance. This is not currently available on CD in the UK, but in the USA comes paired with a powerful account of the Beethoven *Violin concerto* which demonstrates a comparably intense partnership with Bernstein and the NYPO (CBS **MK 42256**).

Even against all this formidable competition, the magic of Kyung Wha Chung, a spontaneously inspired violinist if ever there was one, comes over very beguilingly in her (mid-priced) Decca interpretation, while Kempe and the Royal Philharmonic give a sympathetic, if not always perfectly polished accompaniment, well caught in a glowing recording from the early 1970s which has responded well to its remastering. There may be more glossily perfect accounts of the concerto, but Chung goes straight to the heart, finding mystery and fantasy as well as more extrovert qualities.

Jaime Laredo with consistently fresh and sweet tone gives a delightfully direct reading, warmly expressive but never for a moment self-indulgent. His is a beautiful, reflective account of the slow movement. The orchestral ensemble is particularly impressive, when no conductor is involved. With first-rate modern digital recording – the background silence is particularly telling in this work – this is a bargain, a highlight of the Pickwick mid-priced catalogue.

Shlomo Mintz used the Bruch/Mendelssohn coupling for his recording début in 1981, and his account of the Bruch is exceptionally exciting and warm-blooded. The balance is flattering, but his forward placing means that dynamic shading is less evident than it might be; nevertheless Mintz certainly makes the listener hang on to every phrase and his playing is undoubtedly compelling. The vibrato is wide (one notices it at the pianissimo opening of the *Adagio*) but his approach is so distinctive and interesting that few listeners will not be fired. The Chicago Symphony Orchestra plays with great brilliance and enthusiasm, and Abbado's direction is most sympathetic. The vivid recording has transferred splendidly to CD; the presence and detail of the sound are more impressive than some digital discs, yet without edge. As an encore, after the two concertos, Mintz plays the three Kreisler lollipops with great flair, and here the violin image is even more present.

In Anne-Sophie Mutter's hands the concerto has an air of chaste sweetness, shedding much of its ripe, sensuous quality but retaining its romantic feeling. There is a delicacy and tenderness here which are very appealing and, although the tuttis have plenty of fire, Karajan sensitively scales down his accompaniment in the lyrical passages to match his soloist. There is no doubting the dedication and conviction of the solo playing or its natural spontaneity. The digital recording provides a natural balance and a vivid orchestral texture. Though not as rich in timbre as Mintz's performance this has a pervading freshness that gives much pleasure. While the compact disc does not bring the degree of improvement over the excellent tape that the finest examples of this new medium readily provide, the opening of the concerto obviously gains from the background silence.

Menuhin's performance has long held an honoured place in the catalogue. It was a work to which he made a particularly individual response, and he was in very good form when he made the disc (his playing is technically much more adroit than in his later version with Boult – available on HMV *EG 290491-4* [Angel *4AM 34742*]). The performance has a fine spontaneity, the work's improvisatory quality very much part of the interpretation, and there is no doubt about the poetry Menuhin finds in the slow movement, or the sparkle in the finale. The bright forward sound of the 1960 recording has transferred vividly to CD.

The performance by Decca's newest star soloist, 21-year-old Joshua Bell, who comes from Bloomington, Indiana, is very impressive. He demonstrates a flawless technique and plays with plenty of warmth and poetry, if missing something of the withdrawn, 'inner' quality of the slow movement. He is not helped by a very forward balance which places him in a spotlight at the expense of the orchestra, although Marriner's fine accompaniment is not entirely masked. The effect is to boost the romantic boldness of his playing, and many will respond to such powerful projection. This is certainly very enjoyable, but the uneven partnership between soloist and orchestra prevents the fullest recommendation.

Kantorow proves an excellent soloist in one of his first major concerto recordings, fully living up to the reputation he has acquired after winning a unique collection of international prizes. The tone is pure and, even with the double-stopping in the finale, not only incisive but sweet and smooth with no scratch. Though his natural artistry makes for expressive phrasing, his is a plainer, less individual view than some. The accompaniment is reliable if not inspired. The sound is first rate: technically, this is a most impressive CD of this coupling.

Grumiaux's version with Wallberg would not be counted a first choice; but as a coupling for an outstanding performance of the Brahms *Concerto* it offers a refreshingly different view, civilized, classical in its refinement, if slightly cool. Yet Grumiaux brings all his beauty of tone and expressive technique to this music making, and he is well accompanied and recorded.

Shizuka Ishikawa is technically very impressive and he plays with more extrovert ardour than Grumiaux, but the brightly lit remastering of the 1978 analogue recording tends to emphasize the lack of tenderness in the approach. However, this is coupled with a formidably fine account of the Sibelius *Concerto*. This CD is in the bargain range.

On HMV, Perlman's newest digital recording with Haitink must be counted a disappointment and is not helped by its harsh, early digital recording which gives an acid edge to the soloist's timbre (**CDC7 47074-2**). The performance is heavily expressive and not nearly as spontaneous as his earlier analogue recording with Previn, which we hope will soon reappear in EMI's mid-priced Studio CD series.

Violin concerto No. 1 in G min., Op. 26; Scottish fantasy, Op. 46.
⊛ *** CBS Dig. **MK 42315**; *IMT 42315* [id.]. Cho-Liang Lin, Chicago SO, Slatkin.
*** RCA **RD 86214** [**RCA 6214-2-RC**]. Heifetz, New SO of L, Sargent – VIEUXTEMPS: *Concerto No. 5.****

Cho-Liang Lin gives radiantly beautiful performances of Bruch's two most popular concertante works for violin, totally compelling in their combination of passion and purity, strength and dark, hushed intensity. Lin, unlike many of his rivals, uses the widest range of dynamic, down to a whisper of pianissimo, a point well realized in the Chicago recording, which in its natural balance is far finer than many from this source. A fraction less volatile than Kyung Wha Chung in her Decca LP coupling of these works but even more powerful in bravura, Lin is particularly imaginative and moving in the longer and lesser-known of the two works, the *Scottish fantasy*, which emerges as far more than a collection of Scottish melodies. There have been few accounts on record of the slow movement of the *G minor* that begin to match the raptness of Lin, most sensitively accompanied by Slatkin and the Chicago orchestra. There is an acceptable chrome cassette, but it does not match the CD in range.

Heifetz's recordings were first issued in 1963, but although his CD is generous in including also a brilliant account of the Vieuxtemps No. 5, the snag is the balance, which favours the soloist, if not to the exclusion of the orchestra, which remains fully in the picture. Heifetz plays with supreme assurance and the slow movement shows this fine artist in top romantic form. All lovers of great violin playing should at least hear this coupling, for Heifetz's panache and the subtlety of his bowing and colour bring a wonderful freshness to Bruch's charming Scottish whimsy. Sargent accompanies sympathetically, and it is noticeable that though the soloist is close, there is never any doubt that Heifetz can still produce a true *pianissimo*.

Kol Nidrei, Op. 47.
(*) Decca Dig. **410 144-2; *KSXDC 7608* [Lon. *LDR 5-71108*]. Harrell, Philh. O, Ashkenazy – DVOŘÁK: *Cello concerto.***(*)

This withdrawn, prayerful Bruch piece finds a natural response in Lynn Harrell whose musical personality is often comparatively reticent, and his account with Ashkenazy is both eloquent and atmospheric and certainly very well recorded, especially in its compact disc format. There is a good cassette, too.

Bruckner, Anton (1824–96)

Symphony No. 1 in C min.
*** Orfeo Dig. **C 145851A** [id.]. Bav. State O, Sawallisch.
** HMV **CDC7 47742-2** [id.]. Cologne RSO, Wand.

Symphonies Nos 1 in C min.; 5 in B flat.
(*) DG **415 985-2 (2) [id.]. BPO, Karajan.

As was the case with Bruckner's later symphonies, *No. 1 in C minor* underwent periodic retouching after its first performance in 1868, before he subjected it to a thorough revision in Vienna after the composition of the *Eighth Symphony*. Sawallisch's account is probably the best-sounding of the CDs before the public and his interpretation is impressive in its honesty and dignity. There is warmth and some beautiful playing from the fine Bavarian orchestra which is recorded in a spacious, yet not over-reverberant acoustic.

Günter Wand in his recording with his Cologne Radio orchestra uses the 1891 version of the *First Symphony* with its richer tonal palette. He makes out a very persuasive case for so doing, though some collectors may find the gear change when the second group comes in the first movement a little disruptive. The CD transfer produces a cleaner and more present aural image than the older LP version.

Karajan's versions of Nos 1 and 5 come yoked together, which saves a disc but may not suit all collectors. No. 1 is digital (1882) but the recording is brightly lit and not always ideally expansive at the bottom end. It is still an incisive and powerful reading of a work, which may come at the beginning of a massive symphony cycle but which is in no sense an immature piece, written as it was when the composer was already in his forties. Karajan, like Sawallisch, uses the revised Linz version and here as elsewhere shows a clear-headed concentration, making light of the problems of co-ordinating arguments which in lesser hands can seem rambling.

The *Fifth Symphony* has its first movement immediately following the finale of No. 1 on the first disc, and immediately the ear registers a greater resonant warmth in the (1977) analogue sound, for the recording generally is richer and more spacious than its digital companion: even though the remastering has lightened the bass somewhat and the brass is a shade fierce at fortissimo levels, the strings sound gloriously full in the *Adagio*. Karajan's reading is not just poised and polished; it is superbly structured on every level, clear on detail as well as on overall architecture. Here, as in his other Bruckner performances for DG, Karajan takes a patrician view of this great and individual symphonist; even if the slow movement lacks some of the simple dedication which makes Jochum's earlier reading with the same orchestra so compelling (hopefully to be issued on Galleria before too long), the result is undoubtedly satisfying. The playing of the Berlin Philharmonic is magnificent.

Symphony No. 2 in C min.
*** DG Dig. **415 988-2** [id.]. BPO, Karajan.
** HMV **CDC7 47743-2** [id.]. Cologne RSO, Wand.

Karajan's reading is not only powerful and polished, it is distinctive on matters both of tempi and of text. He modifies the Nowak edition by opening out some of the cuts, but by no means all. He starts reticently, only later expanding in grandeur. The scherzo at a fast speed is surprisingly lightweight, the finale relatively slow and spacious. It is a noble reading, not always helped by rather bright digital recording. However, the CD brings a firmer sound-image than the LP, with more weight at the bottom than some in this series, and the strings do not lack amplitude in the *Andante*.

Günter Wand's account on EMI is not to be dismissed lightly. His opening is rather matter-of-fact but the symphony as a whole is well shaped and, though it is not as awesome as the very finest before the public (currently the Karajan), it is not mannered. The acoustic has pleasing warmth and detail is clearly defined, though it is very much that of a broadcasting studio. Not a first choice, but satisfying all the same.

Symphony No. 3 in D min. (original 1873 version).
(*) Tel. Dig. **ZK8 42922 [id.]. Frankfurt RSO, Inbal.

There are in all three versions of the *Third Symphony*: the first completed on the last day of 1873, a second which Bruckner undertook immediately after the completion of the *Fifth Symphony* in 1877, and then, after that proved unsuccessful, he made a third in 1889. The 1873 is by far the longest version, running to nearly 66 minutes (the first movement alone is 24′), and for those who have either of the others it will make far more than a fascinating appendix. The playing of the Frankfurt Radio orchestra under Inbal is very respectable indeed, with a sensitive feeling for atmosphere and refined dynamic contrasts; the recording in its CD format is most acceptable without being top-drawer. This edition has never been recorded before, and the symphony can at last be heard in the form in which it was presented to Wagner.

Symphony No. 3 in D min.
*** DG Dig. **421 362-2** [id.]. BPO, Karajan.
(*) Decca Dig. **417 093-2 (id.]. Berlin RSO, Chailly.
** CBS Dig. *MK 39033* [id.]. Bav. RSO, Kubelik.
*(*) HMV **CDC7 47744-2** [id.]. Cologne RSO, Wand.

Karajan's account of the *Third Symphony* is very impressive indeed. He opts for the Nowak edition of 1888–9, as opposed to the fuller 1878 version favoured by such Bruckner authorities as Robert Simpson and the late Deryck Cooke. One is awe-struck by the eloquence and beauty of the orchestral playing and the command of architecture that Karajan shows. His digital recording is spacious and refined. Karajan achieves a sense of majesty in the opening movement and an other-worldliness and spirituality in the slow movement that cannot fail to move the listener. In the CD format, the usual gains can be noted and few readers are likely to be disappointed. At the same time, fine though it is, this is not a state-of-the-art recording and it is not as transparent or detailed as, say, Chailly's Bruckner *Seventh* on Decca.

Vividly recorded and beautifully played, Chailly's version of No. 3 – using the 1889 text as Karajan does – has admirable qualities, but by the standards of the finest Bruckner recordings it is undercharacterized. This is a broad, spacious view of the works, not unlike Karajan's; but Karajan himself consistently demonstrates his natural mastery in a reading that glows the more intensely, the more spontaneously.

Kubelik uses the fuller 1878 edition (edited by Fritz Oeser) but compensates with brisk tempi in the outer movements, especially the finale. Although the performance has an attractive freshness, it is – like his Mahler – essentially lightweight, though with an eloquent slow movement. The bright, clear recording emphasizes that impression, although the resonance brings the odd moment when clarity of focus slips, even on CD.

Wand's account of the *Third* is far from pedestrian, but it is not the most inspired of his cycle; though it is truthfully recorded and well played by the Cologne Radio Symphony Orchestra, it would not be a first recommendation.

Those primarily interested in the second (1878) version of the score will find an acceptable 1964 tape from Haitink and the Concertgebouw Orchestra on Philips (*416 859-4*). The reading is a bit sober and the bright sound somewhat dry, but there is fine orchestral playing here and the text is fuller than Nowak's, while the architecture is seen to good advantage.

Symphony No. 4 in E flat (*Romantic*) (original 1874 version).
(*) Tel. Dig. **ZK8 42921 [id.]. Frankfurt RSO, Inbal.

Like the *Third*, there are three versions of the *Romantic symphony*, and no one has recorded the original before. The score of this version of No. 4 was first published in the mid-1970s; even to a listener who knows but is not steeped in the definitive version, the differences will be striking. They are most obvious in the scherzo, a completely different and more fiery movement, but there were also extensive changes elsewhere. The opening of the finale is also totally different. Inbal's performance is more than adequate – indeed he has a genuine feeling for the Bruckner idiom and pays scrupulous attention to dynamic refinements. The recording is well detailed though the climaxes almost (but not quite) reach congestion. An indispensable and fascinating issue.

Symphony No. 4 in E flat (*Romantic*).
*** DG **415 277-2** [id.]. BPO, Karajan.

*** HMV **CDC7 47745-2** [id.]. Cologne RSO, Wand.
(M) **(*) HMV **CDM7 69006-2** [id.].; *EG 769006-4* [Ang. *4AM 34735*]. BPO, Karajan.
(*) Decca Dig. **410 550-2 [id.]. Chicago SO, Solti.
(*) CBS **MK 42035 [id.]. Columbia SO, Walter.
(M) **(*) EMI *TC-EMX 2102*. BPO, Tennstedt.
(*) HMV Dig. **CDC7 47352-2 [id.]. BPO, Muti.
(*) Denon Dig. **C37 7126 [id.]. Dresden State O, Blomstedt.
** Decca **411 581-2** [id.]. VPO, Boehm.
*(*) Ph. Dig. **412 735-2**; *412 735-4* [id.]. VPO, Haitink.

Karajan's opening has more beauty and a greater feeling of mystery than almost anyone else on CD. As in his earlier EMI record, Karajan brings a keen sense of forward movement to this music as well as showing a firm grip on its architecture. His slow movement is magnificent and is much brisker than either Boehm or Blomstedt. The DG analogue recording lacks the transparency and detail of the Decca or the bloom of the Dresden, but there is no doubt that this is a performance of considerable stature.

No. 4 is also one of the best in Günter Wand's cycle: he holds the score together extremely well and produces distinguished playing from the Cologne Radio orchestra which has an unforced and natural eloquence. The recording dates from 1978 and sounds very fresh and realistic. This is musically a very satisfying account and can be recommended alongside the finest.

Karajan's 1972 recording has now been reissued at mid price, on both CD and tape. This earlier reading has undoubted electricity and combines simplicity and strength. The playing of the Berlin Philharmonic is very fine. The snag is the considerable resonance which has led to a degree of harshness appearing in the tuttis with the added brilliance of the digital remastering. Brass sounds are brazen and although the effect is physically exciting, the advantage of the added atmosphere is offset by the lack of internal clarity of focus in the noisier climaxes. Pianissimos are relatively diffuse. The (more expansive) DG performance is tauter and more crisply disciplined, while keeping all the qualities of strength and mystery.

As a Brucknerian, Solti can hardly be faulted, choosing admirable tempi, keeping concentration taut through the longest paragraphs, and presenting the architecture of the work in total clarity. Raptness is there too, and only the relative lack of Brucknerian idiosyncrasy will disappoint those who prefer a more loving, personal approach. Like Blomstedt and Boehm, Solti prefers the Nowak edition with the opening motif brought back on the horns at the end of the finale. The compact disc immediately establishes its advantage at the atmospheric opening horn call over shimmering strings, the more magnetizing when heard against silence. Yet the slightly artificial brightness of the sound-picture is more apparent, too; this is not a mellow, cultured aural tapestry that one expects, for instance, from the Concertgebouw. Those who like plenty of brilliance from their Bruckner, however, will find Solti's version meets these needs admirably.

Although not quite as impressive as his Bruckner *Ninth*, Bruno Walter's 1960 recording is transformed by its CD remastering, with textures clearer, strings full and brass sonorous. It is not quite as rich as the Blomstedt Dresden recording on Denon, but is still pretty impressive, and the superbly played 'hunting horn' scherzo is wonderfully vivid. Walter makes his recording orchestra sound remarkably European in style and timbre. The reading is characteristically spacious. Walter's special feeling for Bruckner means that he can relax over long musical paragraphs and retain his control of the structure, while the playing has fine atmosphere and no want of mystery.

Tennstedt's digital recording was originally issued on a pair of LPs; now it can be had economically on a well-managed mid-priced tape, sounding clear and full, though there is some blare on the final climax. This is a reading that combines concentration and a degree of ruggedness, less moulded than Karajan. Here plainness goes with pure beauty and natural strength in the first two movements; the scherzo is correspondingly urgent, the finale resplendent. One or two modifications apart, the Haas edition is used. With modern sounds this makes a compelling budget tape version.

With warm, slightly distanced sound, the sensuous beauty of the Berlin Philharmonic string section has rarely been caught so beautifully in recent recordings. Muti as a Brucknerian has a fine feeling for climax, building over the longest span, and his flexible phrase-shaping of Brucknerian melody, very different from traditional rugged treatment, reflects a vocal style of expressiveness. With that extra warmth and high dramatic contrasts, Muti takes Bruckner further south than usual. For those fancying such treatment, this is an excellent version – but it will not suit everyone.

Blomstedt, like Boehm, opts for the Nowak edition, and the spacious and resonant acoustic in which his version is recorded lends it a pleasing sense of atmosphere. The dynamic range is wide and this performance has a certain ardour and conviction that impress. The slow movement has more feeling and poetry than one normally associates with this conductor, and the sumptuous tone produced by the Dresden orchestra is a joy in itself. This is less bright and analytical than Solti's, for instance, but it is a beautiful sound and it suits Bruckner; many will prefer it to the greater detail of the Decca. The performance has much to recommend it and is both eloquent and dignified.

Boehm's record was made in 1974 and the sound in the CD format is very 'present' indeed – the gain is incontestable. The performance is based on the Nowak edition and is finely shaped with the benefit of beautiful orchestral playing. There was always a sobriety about Boehm and he was occasionally *kapellmeister*-ish. Good though this is, it would be idle to pretend that this reading is as fresh and inspired as Walter or Karajan.

Haitink's new Vienna version has no want of authority and has predictably fine orchestral playing and a well-defined Philips recording to commend it (on tape as well as CD). It falls short of the highest inspiration that this conductor can command and, although there are many moments of eloquence and splendour, there is ultimately more prose than poetry.

Symphony No. 5 in B flat (see also under *Symphony No. 1*).
* HMV **CDC7 47746-2** [id.]. Cologne RSO, Wand.

There are good things in Wand's account of the *Fifth* – though the first movement is not one of them. Here the changes of gear are not convincing: they are really quite disruptive. The slow movement, on the other hand, is very eloquent; the finale gives the brass their head and the acoustic does not fully accommodate the climaxes. Far from a first recommendation, then.

Symphony No. 6 in A.
*** Orfeo Dig. **C 024821** [id.]. Bav. State O, Sawallisch.
(*) DG **419 194-2 [id.]. BPO, Karajan.
(*) Decca **417 389-2 [id.]. Chicago SO, Solti.
* HMV **CDC7 47747-2** [id.]. Cologne RSO, Wand.

Sawallisch's account of the *Sixth Symphony* is beautifully shaped, spacious yet never portentous or inflated. Tempi – never too slow but never hurried – are beautifully judged, and the Bavarian State Orchestra respond splendidly to his direction. The acoustic has plenty of warmth but is not too reverberant, and the recording, criticized by some in its CD format as being over-bright, sounds excellent, though it needs to be played at a slightly lower than usual level. This is one of the finest versions of this symphony now before the public – and probably the best since Jochum's 1966 version with the Bavarian Radio orchestra.

Karajan is not as commanding as usual in his Bruckner recordings. It is still a compelling performance, tonally very beautiful and with a glowing account of the slow movement that keeps it in proportion – not quite the match of the sublime slow movements of Nos 8 and 9. The transfer of the 1980 analogue recording is well enough managed, although the bright upper range is more noticeable than the lower, which might ideally have been more expansive.

Solti offers a strong, rhetorical reading, powerfully convincing in the outer movements and helped by playing and recording of outstanding quality. Where he is less persuasive is in the slow movement, which fails to flow quite as it should; the expressiveness does not sound truly spontaneous. The analogue recording emerges vividly enough in its CD format.

Strange that a conductor with such obvious feeling for Bruckner should produce such disparate results as does Günter Wand. His account of the *Sixth* is far less convincing than his *Fourth* or *Seventh*, and the actual quality of the orchestral playing, particularly in the scherzo, is less than distinguished – which is putting it politely. With such performances as Sawallisch and Karajan on the market, this need not detain readers.

Symphony No. 7 in E.
*** Decca Dig. **414 290-2** [id.]. Berlin RSO, Chailly.
*** Ph. **420 805-2** [id.]. Concg. O, Haitink.
*** DG **419 195-2** [id.]. BPO, Karajan.
*** Denon Dig. **C37 7286** [id.]. Dresden State O, Blomstedt.
(M) *** HMV *EG 290858-4*. BPO, Karajan.
(*) HMV **CDC7 47748-2 [id.]. Cologne RSO, Wand.
(*) DG Dig. **419 627-2; *419 627-4* [id.]. VPO, Giulini.
(M) ** DG **419 858-2**; *419 858-4* [id.]. VPO, Boehm.
** Decca Dig. **417 631-2**; *417 631-4* [id.]. Chicago SO, Solti.
*(*) CBS **M2K 42036** (2) [id.]. Columbia SO, Bruno Walter – WAGNER: *Siegfried idyll.***(*)

Bruckner's *Seventh*, understandably a great favourite with the musical public, is exceptionally well represented on CD and one could gain great satisfaction from any of the first half-dozen CDs listed above. While Karajan and Haitink both give of their finest in this work, Chailly's account, with its superb Decca digital recording, also ranks among the best available. He obtains some excellent playing from the Berlin Radio Symphony Orchestra and, though he may not attain the warmth and, indeed, the spirituality of Karajan and Jochum, his is a committed performance, and the apparent lack of weight soon proves deceptive. He has a considerable command of the work's architecture and controls its sonorities expertly. The recording, made in the Jesus-Christus-Kirche, Berlin, is outstanding in every way. It is splendidly balanced, having realistic string tone, with a nice bloom and a natural perspective. Warm, full tone throughout all the departments of the orchestra, yet a clean and refined sound which is especially impressive on CD.

Both the Haitink and Karajan CDs offer analogue recordings from the late 1970s, but the Philips remastering is conspicuously the more successful. The recording is wide in range and refined in detail, yet retains much of the ambient warmth of the Concertgebouw, while the climax of the radiantly textured slow movement is resplendently capped with its cymbal clash. Haitink's reading is more searching than his earlier version made in the 1960s. The first movement is considerably slower and gains in mystery and atmosphere, and the *Adagio* expands in vision, too. Yet there is nothing studied here: both movements grow with an unforced naturalness that is deeply impressive, and there is an altogether richer world of feeling. The Concertgebouw play with their accustomed breadth of tone and marvellously blended ensemble – the closing section of the *Adagio* is wonderfully serene.

Like Bruckner's *Fourth*, Karajan recorded the *Seventh* for HMV five years before his DG version, and both have now resurfaced simultaneously. The earlier reading showed a superb feeling for the work's architecture, and the playing of the Berlin Philharmonic was gorgeous.

The recording had striking resonance and amplitude, and its expansive climaxes have been successfully encompassed on an excellent (inexpensive) tape which offers the long slow movement without a break on the first side. In the newer DG versions, Karajan draws enormously compelling playing from the same orchestra and this performance shows even greater power and nobility. This is undoubtedly a great performance, and the recording was one of the best in Karajan's analogue series, with rich strings and sonorous yet biting brass. The digital remastering, however, is not quite as successful in freshening the sound as is Haitink's Philips CD.

A well-shaped account of the *Seventh* comes from Herbert Blomstedt and the Staatskapelle, Dresden. It is not quite as moving as his version of the *Fourth*, but it is still very fine, and the beautiful playing of the Dresden orchestra and the expansive acoustic of the Lukaskirche are strong points in its favour. The recording is finely balanced, the strings having a natural warmth and the orchestra being placed in well-judged perspective. The reading is totally dedicated and Blomstedt has both strength and imagination to commend him. It has rather more gravitas than the Chailly version, and many will prefer it on this count.

Wand's recording of the *Seventh* is one of the finest in his cycle with the Cologne Radio Symphony Orchestra. It is consistently well shaped without the disruptive gear-changes that disfigured his *Fifth* and with much finer and more disciplined orchestral playing. The Cologne orchestra may not, perhaps, be the equal of the Berlin Philharmonic or the Staatskapelle, Dresden, but they play with ardour and conviction. Wand, incidentally, eschews the famous cymbal clash in the slow movement, which is given a reading of great dignity.

Giulini secures playing of the utmost refinement from the Vienna Philharmonic and shapes each paragraph lovingly – indeed, at times some might think too lovingly: the Vienna strings are occasionally prone to be a little too sweet. All the same, here are some wonderful things and music making of a real and affecting eloquence. The only major reservation to be made concerns a want of a consistent forward movement. The DG recording has splendid warmth and does justice to the sumptuous sounds that the Vienna orchestra produce. The balance and perspective are natural. There is a very good cassette, where the layout avoids a slow-movement break.

Boehm's *Seventh* was originally issued in harness with the *Eighth*, but is now reissued on a Galleria CD and tape. It goes without saying that the playing of the Vienna Philharmonic is of the highest order, but the performance taken as a whole is plain to the point of being dour. There is a fine sense of architecture and the music is firmly held together, but Boehm's phrasing is often prosaic and lacking in magic. The recording is admirably vivid and clear but the tape, unnecessarily, has a turnover break in the slow movement.

Solti takes an extraordinarily spacious view, and the Chicago orchestra respond to his affectionate concern over every detail of the score with playing of great refinement and produce climaxes of considerable weight and power. But this very relaxed approach means that the outer movements are lacking in ultimate grip, and the scherzo is comparatively lightweight. The sublime *Adagio* is drawn out to an inordinate extent and, while the textures created by the orchestra have great beauty, many listeners will find Solti's indulgence verging on lassitude. The total playing time of the first two movements (46′ 38″) means that the cassette has a turnover break in the middle of the slow movement and cannot be recommended. Its sound balance lacks the upper range of the CD and there is more weight in the middle and bass. The CD has characteristic Chicago brightness, but with a realistic amplitude and depth.

Walter's reading suffers from the basic fault of concentrating on detail at the expense of structure. The outer movements bring many illuminating touches and the final climax of the first is imposingly built, but overall the tension is loosely held. In the *Adagio*, which is kept moving fairly convincingly, the climax is disappointing, and made the more so by the absence of the famous cymbal clash, as Walter uses the original text. The 1963 recording has been opened up in its remastering for CD and sounds fuller and more spacious than the original LPs; but the layout on two discs, even though Wagner's *Siegfried idyll* is included, is unacceptably uneconomic.

Symphony No. 7 in E; (i) *Te Deum.*
(B) *** DG Walkman *419 391-4* [id.]. (i) Stader, Sieglinde Wagner, Haefliger, Lagger, Berlin Op. Ch.; BPO, Jochum – WAGNER: *Parsifal: Good Friday music.****

Jochum's approach to the *Seventh* is entirely characteristic, with a relaxed manner and generally slow tempi in all four movements. But the concentration is never in doubt; such a passage as the transition into the second subject in the slow movement is indicative of the magic that this conductor distils in this marvellous score. The Walkman layout avoids a slow-movement break; it offers also Jochum's eloquent account of the *Te Deum*, with excellent soloists and superbly loving orchestral support from the Berliners. The sound of these recordings from the 1960s (the symphony dates from 1967) is rich and spacious and the tape has no problems with the expansive climaxes. With Jochum's inspirational account of the *Good Friday music* from Wagner's *Parsifal* also included, this is a bargain and a half!

Symphony No. 8 in C min. (first 1887 version).
(*) Tel. Dig. **ZL8 48218 (2) [id.]. Frankfurt RSO, Inbal.

Inbal has strong Brucknerian instincts and although the Frankfurt Radio Orchestra is not thought of as being in the first bracket, it produces more than acceptable results. There are considerable divergences here from the versions we know, and readers will undoubtedly derive much fascination from comparing them. The recording is very good and, like its companions (Nos 3 and 4), this is mandatory listening for all Brucknerians.

Symphony No. 8 in C min.
*** DG **419 196-2** (2) [id.]. BPO, Karajan – WAGNER: *Siegfried idyll.****
*** Ph. Dig. **412 465-2** (2) [id.]. Concg. O, Haitink – WAGNER: *Siegfried idyll.****
(*) DG Dig. **415 124-2; *415 124-4* (2) [id.]. VPO, Giulini.
(*) HMV **CDS7 47749-8 (2) [id.]. Cologne RSO, Wand.

Karajan does not have the advantage of a digital recording, but his 1976 analogue set had striking richness and refinement of texture and it has transferred to CD with impressive clarity, the Berlin Philharmonic string timbre very real and tangible. The performance is majestic, massive in scale, yet immaculate in detail, the reading both noble and searching. Karajan recorded the work earlier (in 1958) for EMI, and that had amazingly good sound: when it is reissued on CD at budget price, it should offer formidable competition. But meanwhile the DG version is made the more attractive by the inclusion of Karajan's glorious account of Wagner's *Siegfried idyll*, which also sounds full and fresh in the remastered form.

Haitink's is a noble reading of this massive symphony, using the extended Haas edition. Never one to force the pace, Haitink's degree of restraint will please those who find Karajan too powerfully concentrated. The spaciousness of the slow movement brings a rare clarity and refinement; the tempo is relentlessly steady, even slower than Karajan's. On compact disc, the resonant Concertgebouw ambience has all the more atmospheric bloom, as well as fine detail, an aptly beautiful sound. Moreover, Haitink's fine performance of Wagner's *Siegfried idyll* is offered as a considerable bonus.

Giulini's account of Bruckner's *Eighth Symphony* has stature and will be eagerly sought out by his many admirers. He elects to use the Nowak edition, which may worry some collectors and incline them to opt for Haitink, Karajan or Wand who all opt for the Haas. If these considerations do not worry you, the Giulini will be a strong contender, for he is a conductor of vision, and the Vienna orchestra give him wonderful support. This reading has undoubted spirituality and power, and the DG recording is spacious and clean. However, the absence of any coupling limits the fullest recommendation.

Another impressive *Eighth* comes from Günter Wand and the Cologne Radio forces. It was recorded (most truthfully) in the late 1970s in a warm and spacious studio, and he gives a reading of natural and unaffected eloquence, well paced and finely structured. One quibble: both Wand and Giulini spread the symphony over two discs. Haitink and Karajan offer a fill-up, and it would have been sensible for Wand to give us, say, Bruckner's *G minor Overture*, which is not yet available in the new format.

Symphony No. 9 in D min. (1896 original version).
** Tel. Dig. **ZK8 43302** [id.]. Frankfurt RSO, Inbal.

Eliahu Inbal has demonstrated his strong feeling for Bruckner in the pioneering accounts of the *Third, Fourth* and *Eighth Symphonies* he has given us in recent years and which are now making their way on to CD; his performance of the *Ninth* with the Frankfurt Radio orchestra is far from negligible, even though it may not be a performance of the highest stature. The playing is often very fine and Inbal is scrupulously attentive to detail; however, there is not the sense of scale that is to be found in the finest of his rivals.

Symphony No. 9 in D min.
❀ *** CBS **MK 42037** [id.]. Columbia SO, Bruno Walter.
*** DG **419 083-2** [id.]. BPO, Karajan.
*** Ph. Dig. **410 039-2** [id.]. Concg. O, Haitink.
*** Decca Dig. **417 295-2**; *417 295-4* [id.]. Chicago SO, Solti.
** HMV **CDC7 47751-2** [id.]. Cologne RSO, Wand.

There are four outstanding versions of Bruckner's *Ninth*, each offering a contrastingly different view. Two (Haitink's and Solti's) are digital, but the analogue alternatives are well transferred, especially the remastering by CBS of Bruno Walter's 1959 recording which is a superb achievement. This was one of the most beautiful results of Walter's Indian summer in the CBS studio, and now the results are immeasurably enhanced, with a blend of rich, clear strings and splendidly sonorous brass. Walter's mellow, persuasive reading leads one on through the leisurely paragraphs so that the logic and coherence seem obvious where other performances can sound aimless. Perhaps the scherzo is not vigorous enough to provide the fullest contrast though the sound here has ample bite – yet it exactly fits the overall conception. The final slow movement has a nobility which makes one glad that Bruckner never completed the intended finale. After this, anything would have been an anticlimax.

DG have understandably chosen Karajan's later (1977) recording for CD remastering, but we trust that the superlative earlier version from the late 1960s will appear in due course on mid-priced Galleria. Even in a competitive field this glorious first stereo account stands out, to be ranked alongside Walter. In his later reading Karajan clearly wanted to convey a tougher, more majestic impression, and the interpretation concentrates on strength and impact. As before, however, the playing of the Berlin Philharmonic is both technically immaculate and dedicated. The recording balance is closer than before but the digital transfer is not without ambient atmosphere and is truthful in matters of orchestral timbre.

The extremely measured speed of the first movement in Haitink's pure and dedicated reading may be taken as a deciding factor; he underlines the elegiac mood. Though the great dynamic contrasts are superbly and fearlessly caught, this is not as thrustful an interpretation as Solti's or Karajan's. The spaciousness of the sound against an ambient Concertgebouw acoustic gives a degree of distancing which matches the interpretation. On CD, the absence of background and the bite of fortissimos are specially impressive, as well as the clarity and refinement of light textures.

Wand's recording of the *Ninth Symphony* has much to recommend it, though the strings of the Cologne Radio Symphony Orchestra do not possess the opulence of the Berlin Philharmonic or the Concertgebouw. Tempi are sensible and the performance is finely shaped. The recording, which dates from 1979, is faithful and well balanced without being in the demonstration category. A dignified account of some breadth and nobility.

Solti's is a large-scale reading of the *Ninth*, spacious in its view. The brilliance and concentration of the Chicago orchestra's playing are matched by the wide-ranging Decca sound. There is no question of Solti rushing the argument. He gives the music full time to breathe, but the tension is unrelenting, making the big climaxes thrillingly powerful, as in the outbursts in the long last movement. Others may be more deeply meditative – Walter for one – but the power of Solti and the brilliance of the playing and the recording are formidable.

Intermezzo and trio for string quintet.
*** CRD **CRD 3346**; *CRDC 4046* [id.]. Augmented Alberni Qt – BRAHMS: *Sextet No. 2.****

Bruckner wrote this attractive *Intermezzo and trio* as an alternative movement for the scherzo of his *Quintet in F major*, which was considered 'too difficult'. Following on after the vigorous finale of the Brahms *Sextet* the autumnal feeling of the Bruckner with its lighter (but still rich) textures makes a most pleasing encore. The recording is excellent and the CD transfer is freshly vivid.

VOCAL MUSIC

(i) *2 Aequale for three trombones;* (ii) *Libera me; Mass No. 2 in E min.*
** Hyp. Dig. **CDA 66177**; *KA 66177* [id.]. (i) Sheen, Brenner, Brown; (ii) Corydon Singers, ECO Wind Ensemble, Matthew Best.

The CD begins with the first of the two *Aequale*, written in 1847 when Bruckner was twenty-three, and sandwiched between them comes the *Libera me* for choir and three trombones composed some years later. The acoustic is a spacious one which naturally shows the music to best advantage, and the balance suitably distant. Indeed, some may find the aural image a little diffuse and wanting in real focus. Matthew Best gives a caring and sensitively shaped account of the *Mass* and gets a wide dynamic range from the Corydon Singers. Though they rise to the expressive demands of the piece, they are not as well blended or by any means as secure-toned as the forces used by Jochum and Karl Forster in their recordings from the 1960s.

(i) *Masses Nos 1 in D min.; 2 in E min.; 3 in F min.;* Motets: *Afferentur regi; Ave Maria; Christus factus est pro nobis; Ecce sacerdos magnus; Locus iste; Os justi; Pange lingua; Tota pulchra es, Maria; Vexilla regis; Virga Jesse.* (ii) *Psalm 150; Te Deum.*
(M) **(*) DG **423 127-2** (4) [id.]. (i) Soloists, Bav. R. Ch. & SO; (ii) Soloists, Ch. of German Op., Berlin, BPO; Jochum.

Bruckner's choral music, like the symphonies, spans his musical career, though the *Masses* are far less well known, and these recordings, made over a decade (1963–72), had only a limited catalogue life in their original LP formats. Now Brucknerians have an excellent chance to get to know this unjustly neglected music, in highly sympathetic and dedicated performances from one of the composer's most understanding and eloquent advocates. The *D minor* and *E minor Masses* are early, dating from 1864 and 1866 respectively (and are concurrent with the *Sym-*

phonies Nos 0 and *1*); the *F minor* was written in 1867/8 and the composer revised all three in 1876. The glorious *Te Deum* was conceived in 1881 (the time of the *Sixth Symphony*) and the powerful setting of *Psalm 150* appeared a decade later. The ten motets included here were also written over a fairly long time span and are among Bruckner's most beautiful music; they are superbly sung and are among Jochum's most distinguished recordings. With excellent soloists, including Maria Stader, Edith Mathis, Ernst Haefliger, Kim Borg and Karl Ridderbusch, the performances of the large-scale works have fine eloquence and admirable breadth and humanity, and no lack of drama, although other accounts – of the *Te Deum*, for instance – have had more blazing intensity. But that is not Jochum's way, and the concentration of these performances is never in doubt, with much magic distilled, notably in the early *D minor Mass*, a noble and moving account. The original recordings tended to be distanced; in making the sound more present and clear, the CD remastering has lost some of the atmospheric fullness, although the effect is undoubtedly fresher and brighter, if not always absolutely clean on top. The motets are particularly successful, and available newer CD versions cannot match the warmth and refinement of Jochum's splendid Bavarian Radio Chorus.

Motets: *Afferentur regi; Ave Maria; Christus factus est; Ecce sacerdos magnus; Inveni David; Locus iste; Os justi medititur; Pange lingua; Tota pulchra es; Vexilla regis; Virga Jesse.*
(*) Hyp. **CDA 66062; *KA 66062* [id.]. Salmon, Corydon Singers, Best; Trotter (organ).

A much more resonant acoustic setting than the one which DG provided for Jochum in the late 1960s: his erred on the side of dryness but it takes precedence over this record. The Corydon Singers under Matthew Best are not quite as well blended or as homogeneous in tone as were the Bavarian Radio Chorus, but Best's direction is often imaginative and he achieves a wide tonal range. The motets span the best part of Bruckner's creative life; given their devotional character, though, they are best heard two or three at a time rather than at one sitting. The chrome cassette is well transferred and makes a viable alternative to the CD.

Requiem in D min.; Psalms 112 and 114.
(*) Hyp. **CDA 66245; *KA 66245* [id.]. Rodgers, Denley, Maldwyn Davies, George, Corydon Singers, ECO, Best; T. Trotter (organ).

Following up his two previous Bruckner discs with the Corydon Singers, Andrew Best here tackles the very early setting of the *Requiem* which Bruckner wrote at the age of twenty-five, often gauche in the string-writing, but with a number of pointers to the future, notably in the *Benedictus*. The quality of the writing in the Psalm settings also varies; but with fine, strong performances from singers and players alike, including an excellent team of soloists, this is well worth investigating by Brucknerians. First-rate recording, although on tape the resonance brings some loss of focus.

Te Deum.
** DG Dig. **410 521-2**; *410 521-4* (2) [id.]. Perry, Müller-Molinari, Winbergh, Malta, V. Singverein, VPO, Karajan – BRAHMS: *German requiem.**(*)*

With Janet Perry a shrill soprano soloist, and with the big choral tuttis constricted in sound, the Bruckner *Te Deum* makes a disappointing fill-up for Karajan's latest version of the Brahms *Requiem*, though the majesty of his vision is never in doubt.

Buller, John (born 1927)

The Theatre of Memory; (i) *Proenca.*
*** Unicorn Dig. *DKPC 9045* [id.]. BBC SO, Mark Elder; (i) with Sarah and Timothy Walker.

Written for the BBC Symphony Orchestra to play at the Proms in 1981, its Golden Jubilee year, *The Theatre of Memory* ingeniously takes the sixteenth-century concept, based on an actual theatre created for King Francis I of France, which harked back in its use and layout to Greek concepts of drama. Buller echoes this both in the layout of the players – with seven soloists coming forward in turn as principal actors in front of formalized 'chorus' groups – and in the argument, the full plan and even the rhythmic detail. Much of the wildness which lends such attractiveness to *Proenca* is missing in this much more controlled work, but in its strong lines, clear structure and memorable landmarks it is another fine example of Buller's belated flowering, a musician who really found himself as a composer only in his fifties. It is much to Buller's credit that he so completely ignores fashions and trends in his use of an adventurous but approachable idiom. Though the invention is not so distinctive, there is something of the flavour of the latterday Tippett, stretching concepts to the limit. Mark Elder, who conducted these same performers at the Proms, here draws a passionately committed account from the BBC orchestra, vividly recorded. The tape – of outstanding quality – has the additional advantage of containing double measure (71′ 40″), not only *The Theatre of Memory* but the other big Buller work recorded by Unicorn, *Proenca.*

Burgon, Geoffrey (born 1941)

At the round earth's imagined corners; But have been found again; Laudate Dominum; Magnificat; Nunc dimittis; A prayer to the Trinity; Short mass; This world; Two hymns to Mary.
(*) Hyp. Dig. **CDA 66123; *KA 66123* [id.]. Chichester Cathedral Ch., Alan Thurlow.

Thanks to being used in a popular BBC television serial, John le Carré's *Tinker, tailor, soldier, spy*, Burgon's *Nunc dimittis* became temporarily a top hit with its haunting tune. Here it is well matched with the *Magnificat* that Burgon later wrote to complement it and a series of his shorter choral pieces, all of them revealing his flair for immediate, direct communication, and well performed here. First-rate recording, with an equally impressive matching cassette.

Bush, Alan (born 1900)

Variations, nocturne and finale on an old English sea song.
(M) (**) PRT **PVCD 8372**. David Wilde, RPO, Snashall – DELIUS: *Double concerto.***(*)

This reissue from 1966 is welcome if only as a comparatively lightweight and palatable adjunct for the magnificent Delius concerto with which it is coupled. The opening variations have a bright charm, but both the nocturne and finale go on for too long. Excellent playing from David Wilde, who is most truthfully recorded, though the orchestral sound is rather restricted. Although this is not expensive, the presentation is inadequate, with no information whatsoever about the music. Also, on our copy, the very opening bar was attenuated.

Bush, Geoffrey (born 1920)

Air and Round-O for wind quintet; Dialogue for oboe and piano; Quintet for wind; Trio for oboe, bassoon & piano.
*** Chan. Dig. *ABTD 1196* [id.]. ECO Wind Ens., composer (piano).

Always inventive, catching the ear at once, far more than just a fine craftsman, Geoffrey Bush is a composer who deserves to have much more of his music recorded. This attractive collection neatly brings together a group of his works for wind, with two of them, involving piano, featuring the composer himself: the *Dialogue for oboe and piano* of 1960 and the *Trio for oboe, bassoon and piano* of 1952. The other pieces are for a standard wind quintet, with the big *Quintet* of 1962 ranging ambitiously wide in its emotions. Ideal performances from superb ECO ensemble with first-class sound within a nicely resonant acoustic which doesn't blur detail. The cassette labelling, however, reverses the content of the two sides.

Busoni, Ferruccio (1866–1924)

Divertimento for flute and orchestra, Op. 52.
*** Ph. Dig. **412 728-2** [id.]. Nicolet, Leipzig GO, Masur – NIELSEN; REINECKE: *Concertos.****

Busoni's highly individual *Divertimento*, with its bitter-sweet mixture of wit and lyricism, is in three brief linked movements. The whole piece plays for only 9′ 19″, but the engaging quirkiness of the invention and diversity of mood are nicely controlled within an appealingly concise structure. The performance here is first rate, always responsive and freshly spontaneous, with the gentle but dark melancholy of the *Andante* acting as a foil to the spirited outer sections. There is an element of the unexpected in this score which is especially enticing. The recording is beautifully balanced on CD.

Sarabande und cortège (Doktor Faust), Op. 51.
❀ (M) *** HMV *ED 291172-4*. RPO, Revenaugh – SCHMIDT: *Variations*; LUTOSLAWSKI: *Symphonic variations.**** ❀

While he was working on his last and greatest opera, *Doktor Faust*, Busoni made these two orchestral studies using ideas he intended for the opera. The *Sarabande* and *Cortège* instantly draw one into his imaginative world: this music has a powerful sense of mystery and a quiet and haunting depth. These two fragments take 20 minutes and are coupled with other repertoire of equally exceptional interest. Performances are excellent, the digitally remastered recordings first rate and the price is extraordinarily competitive. Recommended with all possible enthusiasm.

3 Album Leaves; An die Jugend; Ballet scene No. 4, Op. 33a; Chamber fantasy on Bizet's Carmen; Chorale prelude on a fragment by Bach; Ciaccona; 2 Dance pieces, Op. 30a; Elegies; Fantasia contrappuntistica; Fantasy after J. S. Bach; Indian diary, Book 1; Machiette mediaevali, Op. 33; Notturni; Nuit de Noel; Perpetuum mobile; Pieces, Op. 33b; 24 Preludes, Op. 37; Prelude & Etude in arpeggios; Preludio-Fantasia; Prologo; Racconti fantastici, Op. 12; 7 Short Pieces; Sonatinas 1–2; Sonatina ad usum infantis· Sonatina brevis: In signo Joannis Sebastiani Magni; Sonatina in diem navita is Christi MCMXVII; Sonatina super Carmen; Suite campestre, Op. 18; Toccata; Variations & fugue on Chopin's C minor Prelude (Op. 28/20), Op. 22; 10 Variations on a Chopin Prelude, Op. 22 (2nd version).
** Ph. Dig. **420 740-2** (6) [id.]. Geoffrey Douglas Madge.

An important and long-overdue undertaking: Busoni's representation on disc has been negligible. The *Carmen fantasia*, the *Elegies* and the *Ballet scene* represent the tip of an iceberg which now emerges to full view. Such is the scale of the undertaking that it deserves an unqualified welcome: six well-filled CDs, including so much that is technically demanding and forbidding (such as the *Fantasia contrappuntistica*). Busoni was one of the most transcendental pianists of all time and, as E. J. Dent put it when discussing his account of the *Hammerklavier*,

'Never for a moment, even in the most thundering passages or in the intricacies of the fugue, did he lose his unique beauty of tone quality.' Geoffrey Douglas Madge, an Australian pianist who teaches in The Hague, has a formidable rather than a transcendental technique. He produces less than beautiful tone in climaxes, where he tends to overpedal. Gratitude for this mammoth undertaking should be unstinting, for much of this repertoire is new to record, even if in the *Elegies*, for example, he does not outclass those who have recorded Busoni before and the piano sound is not up to the high standard we expect of Philips: it lacks transparency and tends to coarsen on climaxes. Busoni needs the most persuasive advocacy and beauty of sonority. However, this set is a must for those who care about this repertoire and, these shortcomings apart, must be given a warm welcome.

Butterworth, George (1885–1916)

The Banks of green willow.
*** Chan. **CHAN 8373**; (M) *CBT 1018* [id.]. Bournemouth Sinf., Del Mar – BANTOCK: *Pierrot of the minute*; BRIDGE: *Suite for strings* etc.***

The Banks of green willow; 2 English idylls.
(*) HMV Dig. **CDC7 47945-2; *EL 270592-4*. ECO, Jeffrey Tate – BAX: *3 Pieces****; BRIDGE: *There is a willow***(*); MOERAN: *Lonely water*; *Whythorne's shadow.****

The Banks of green willow; 2 English idylls; A Shropshire Lad.
*** Nimbus Dig. **NI 5068** [id.]. E. String O, Boughton – BRIDGE: *Suite*; PARRY: *Lady Radnor's suite.****

The four Butterworth pieces, done with tender simplicity in sumptuously atmospheric sound, provide the centrepiece for a Nimbus issue that has become one of that company's best-sellers. As in the Parry and Bridge items, Boughton secures from his Birmingham-based orchestra warm and refined playing in well-paced readings. In an ample acoustic, woodwind is placed rather behind the strings.

The Banks of green willow and the two *English idylls* also make attractive items in Tate's recital of English pieces, but it is a pity that *A Shropshire Lad* was not also included. The playing is refined and sensitive, but lacks something in magic, with slow speeds for the *Idylls* making them sound a little unspontaneous. Warm, full recording, with a good cassette.

On Chandos, Del Mar gives a glowingly persuasive performance of *The Banks of green willow*, which comes as part of another highly interesting programme of English music, devoted to Butterworth's somewhat older contemporaries, Bantock and Frank Bridge. The digital transfer of a 1979 analogue recording has the benefit of even greater clarity without loss of atmosphere. There is a first-class cassette which has the advantage of being in the mid-price range.

A Shropshire Lad.
(M) **(*) PRT **PVCD 8380**. Hallé O, Barbirolli – BAX: *Garden of Fand*; VAUGHAN WILLIAMS: *Symphony No. 8.***(*)

Butterworth's *Shropshire Lad* represents the English folksong school at its most captivatingly atmospheric. This is music that continues to wear well and lend itself to a variety of interpretative approaches. Barbirolli brings characteristic ardour to his wonderfully expressive performance, but the delicacy of Butterworth's genius is not missed. The mid-1960s recording sounds remarkably fresh in Michael Dutton's digital remastering: the sound has warmth and atmosphere and the body of the Hallé strings has not been lost. An indispensable reminder of the art of England's second greatest conductor (after Beecham).

Buxtehude, Diderik (*c.* 1637–1707)

Trio sonatas: in G; B flat and D min., Op. 1/2, 4 & 6, (BuxWV 253, 255 & 257); in D; G min., Op. 2/2–3, (BuxWV 260–1).
*** ASV/Gaudeamus **CDGAU 110**; *ZGGAU 110.* Trio Sonnerie.

The Trio Sonnerie consists of Monica Huggett (baroque violin), Sarah Cunningham (viola da gamba) and Mitzi Meyerson (harpsichord); they give us five of the trio sonatas Buxtehude published in the mid-1690s. Three come from his first book of seven (1694) and the remaining two from the second collection (1696). Make no mistake, this is music of real quality: its invention is fertile and distinguished by a lightness of touch and colour that is quite individual; the melodic lines are vivacious and engaging, and their virtuosity inspiriting. The Trio Sonnerie play this music with real enthusiasm and expertise, and their virtuosity is agreeably effortless and unostentatious. Most musical performances – and very well recorded, too. The chrome tape is also well managed, but not quite as sharply focused as the CD. But whichever format is chosen, this is highly recommended, especially to those who regard Buxtehude as merely a name in the musical history books.

Byrd, William (1543–1623)

Hughe Ashton's ground; Pavanes and galliards Nos 1 & 6; Sellinger's round.
** CBS *MPT 39552* [id.]. Glenn Gould (piano) (with GIBBONS: keyboard pieces**).

Not for purists, but certainly for pianists. Like Tureck, Glenn Gould possessed an altogether remarkable capacity for clarifying part-writing in contrapuntal keyboard scores and one cannot but admire the extraordinary flair he brings to this repertoire, all of which comes from *My Ladye Nevell's Booke*. Although the recording is neither new nor top-drawer, this issue is well worth investigating for the sake of Gould's artistry: it undoubtedly throws fresh light on this music. The dry recorded timbre means that the chrome tape is very clear and lucid.

Pavans and galliards (collection).
*** HM **HMC 901241/2**; *HMC 40.1241/2* [id.]. Davitt Moroney (harpsichord).

On the first of the two discs Davitt Moroney presents the sequence of nine pavans and galliards Byrd composed in the 1570s and '80s, which come from *My Ladye Nevell's Booke* (1591), and the second creates a second cycle of pieces on the same lines. He begins with the tenth pavan and galliard, *William Petre*, found at the end of the 1591 collection, and closes with the great 32-bar *Quadran*, a set of variations based on a famous Italian ostinato bass, the *Passamezzo moderno*. Between them, Davitt Moroney constructs a sequence of Byrd's finest late pavans, taking care to model it on the same lines of symmetry and contrast that distinguishes Byrd's own. Moroney contributes a thorough and scholarly note which sets out the thinking behind his compilation. The playing is totally committed and authoritative though a trifle didactic, for at times he seems to be somewhat lacking in the kind of sparkle his mentor, Thurston Dart, brought to the keyboard. His recording is made on an Italian instrument of 1677 at A = 415 in quarter-comma meantone tuning. It is very naturally recorded, though collectors will have to use a very low-level setting to get realistic results. This pair of CDs comprises half of Byrd's output in this field and is a most valuable contribution to the catalogue. Like the CDs, the chrome cassettes give exceptionally realistic sound, though again a low volume setting is required. The documentation is excellent.

Ave verum corpus; Christe qui lux es et dies; Laetentur coeli (motets)*; Lamentations; Masses for 3, 4 and 5 voices.*
** HMV Dig. **CDS7 49205-8**; *EX 270096-9* (2). Hilliard Ens., Paul Hillier.

Ave verum corpus; Defecit in dolore; Infelix ego; Masses for 3, 4 and 5 voices.
*** Gimell Dig. *ZCBYRD 345* [id.]. Tallis Scholars, Phillips.

Ave verum corpus; Masses for 3, 4 and 5 voices.
*** Gimell Dig. **CDGIM 345** [id.]. Tallis Scholars, Phillips.

Ave verum corpus; Great service: Magnificat and Nunc dimittis. Mass for five voices.
(M) *** Argo *414 366-4*. King's College Ch., Cambridge, Willcocks.

Mass for three voices; Mass for four voices.
(M) (***) Argo *411 723-4*. King's College Ch., Cambridge, Willcocks.

Mass for four voices; Mass for five voices.
(M) **(*) EMI Dig. **CD-EMX 9505**; *TC-EMX 2104*. St John's College Ch., Cambridge, Guest.

Peter Phillips's performances are altogether more ardent than those recorded by Argo at King's, and some might prefer the greater serenity of the latter. But Phillips is a master of this repertoire; undoubtedly these performances have more variety and great eloquence so that, when the drama is varied with a gentler mood, the contrast is the more striking. This enormously rewarding music lends itself to an imaginatively varied treatment, and certainly the sound made by the Scholars in Merton College Chapel is beautiful, both warm and fresh. The CD omits two of the motets and ends with a movingly simple account of the *Ave verum corpus*. The excellent cassette includes everything, so offers the best of all worlds.

In the Argo King's performances of the *Mass for five voices*, *Ave verum* and *Great service*, which were recorded in 1960, the style is more reticent, less forceful than in the famous coupling of the *Masses for three* and *four voices*, made three years later. These beautiful settings are sustained with an inevitability of phrasing and a control of sonority and dynamic that completely capture the music's spirit and emotional feeling. The recording of all this music is wonderfully clean and atmospheric, the acoustic perfectly judged so that the music seems to float in space yet retain its substance and clarity of focus. In the absence of compact disc this is well suited to cassette, with its freedom from extraneous noises. Unfortunately, the tape coupling the *Masses for three* and *four voices* is on iron-oxide stock, and the high-level transfer approaches saturation point and brings some loss of focus at peaks. The coupling of the *Mass for five voices* and music from the *Great service* uses chrome tape and the results are very impressive, with the resonant acoustic admirably caught.

There is no lack of enthusiasm in the performances of the Choir of St John's College, Cambridge, and they can at times be more persuasive than are professional groups, even if they do not have the same experience or maturity. The *Five-part Mass* fares best and is given with genuine fervour. The balance of the recording is rather closer than is usual in this venue though there is a reasonable glow round the singers. George Guest features rather more pronounced cadential ritardandi than are favoured in Early Music circles, but there is a sense of real music-making here. The CD is exceptionally realistic in its presence (though the sound is strikingly vivid and clear on tape also) but serves to emphasize the robust nature of the singing.

The Hilliard Ensemble, using one voice per part, present pure and detached readings, recorded in an intimate rather than an ecclesiastical acoustic. Arguably, these were works which when they were written in Elizabethan times would be sung in private recusant chapels rather than openly, but that situation itself argues a more involved response. The motets on the fourth side, sung in a very similar style, make a suitable complement. The recording is full yet clear, and in this respect the XDR cassettes match the compact discs reasonably closely, though the advantage of complete background silence for this music is paramount.

Cantiones sacrae: Aspice Domine; Domine secundum multitudinem; Domine tu iurasti; In resurrectione tua; Ne irascaris Domine; O quam gloriosum; Tristitia et anxiestas; Vide Domine afflictionem; Virgilate.
(*) CRD Dig. **CRD 3408; *CRDCD 4120* [id.]. New College, Oxford, Ch., Higginbottom.

Though the New College Choir under its choirmaster Edward Higginbottom does not sing with the variety of expression or dynamic which marks its finest Oxbridge rivals, it is impossible not to respond to the freshness of their music making. The robust, throaty style suggests a Latin feeling in its forthright vigour, and the directness of approach in these magnificent *cantiones sacrae* is most attractive, helped by recording which is vividly projected, yet at once richly atmospheric. While CD brings the usual obvious advantages, the cassette is very impressive, a demonstration of CRD's characteristically high standard of transfer.

Cantiones sacrae, Book 2: Circumdederunt me; Cunctis diebus; Domine, non sum dignus; Domine, salva nos; Fac sum servo tuo; Exsurge, Domine; Haec dicit Dominus; Haec dies; Laudibus in sanctis Dominum; Miserere mei, Deus; Tribulatio proxima est.
(*) CRD Dig. **CRD 3439; *CRDC 4139* [id.]. New College, Oxford, Ch., Higginbottom.

This record gives eleven of the twenty-one motets in the 1591 collection. The boys of the Choir of New College, Oxford, produce a fine-focused, well blended sound, and the performances under Edward Higginbottom are eminently well paced. This is Byrd's last collection of large-scale motets and, though one can imagine performances of greater finish, there is much to relish here. The cassette transfer is outstandingly fresh and clean and well up to the usual high CRD standard. The recording itself has rather more reverberance than one has encountered before in this venue.

The Great Service (with anthems).
*** Gimell Dig. **CDGIM 011**; *1585T-11* [id.]. Tallis Scholars, Phillips.
*** HMV Dig. **CDC7 47771-2**; *EL 270564-4*. King's College Ch., Cambridge, Cleobury; Richard Farnes (organ).

Peter Phillips and the Tallis Scholars give a lucid and sensitively shaped account of Byrd's *Great Service*. Theirs is a more intimate performance than one might expect to encounter in one of the great English cathedrals; they are fewer in number and thus achieve greater clarity of texture. Of course, the top lines are sung by women – excellently, too – and the firmer focus will not be seen as a disadvantage by many collectors. The recording is quite excellent: it is made in a church acoustic (the Church of St John, Hackney) and captures detail perfectly. It includes three other anthems, two of which (*O Lord make thy servant Elizabeth* and *Sing joyfully unto God our strength*) are included on the rival EMI disc. This CD will give great musical satisfaction, and so will the chrome cassette, which is of the highest quality and (helped by the smaller numbers and clearer acoustic) is more subtle in registering detail than the competing EMI tape.

Collectors wanting *The Great Service* in a cathedral acoustic will turn to the King's version, which is beautifully recorded on EMI. They have the advantages of boy trebles, a larger complement of singers who can offer more contrast between solo and full verses, and an organ accompaniment, which it probably had in the 1580s. Richard Farnes is the expert organist and his registration is eminently discreet, never clouding the vocal texture. Stephen Cleobury also sets the music in a more authentic liturgical background: he offers the *Kyrie* and puts the two canticles for *Evensong* into their context with anthems and responses. A rarity on record, the appearance of these *Great Service* issues was stimulated by the publication in 1982 of Craig Monson's scholarly edition and reconstruction of the work. At 65 minutes, this is excellent value, and there is a very good XRD iron-oxide tape.

Cabezón, Antonio de (1510–66)

Keyboard tablatures: excerpts (arr. Savall). CRECQUILLON (arr. Cabezón): *Un gay bergier; Pour un plaisir*. WILLAERT (arr. Cabezón): *Le fille quant Dieu me donne de quoy*.
*** HMV Dig. *EL 270385-4*. Hesperion XX, Jordi Savall.

Cabezón was Philip II's favourite court musician and he accompanied his king on his journeys to Italy, Germany and the Netherlands – and to London, where his virtuoso playing may well have served to inspire the flowering of English virginal music. He was one of the greatest contrapuntalists of his age. Jordi Savall's group of vihuela players produce some glorious sounds, as do the highly accomplished brass players here. Cabezón's output is preserved in the form of keyboard tablatures and they were intended for keyboard, harp or vihuela. The eighteen pieces recorded here are transcribed mainly for groups of vihuela de arco and brass, as well as two vihuela de mano. Their polyphonic inventiveness is heard to clear advantage in this form. In addition to the music of Cabezón himself, there are pieces by Crecquillon and Willaert. The recording does full justice to the remarkably beguiling sonorities of this ensemble. A most distinguished and rewarding issue, given a smooth well-balanced cassette presentation; we must hope the CD will arrive soon.

Cage, John (born 1912)

Hymns and variations (with BILLINGS: Hymns: *Heath; Old North*).
*** HMV Dig. *EL 270452-4*. Electric Phoenix – BERIO: *A-Ronne*.***

In *Hymns and variations* John Cage has taken the two Billings hymns also included in the programme and dreamed up a sequence based on them, poetic in its quiet simplicity. It is beautifully sung. Written in 1979, this gives a far clearer idea of Cage's experimental genius than most of his works. On tape the sonority of the Billings originals is effectively caught and the fragmented detail of Cage's variations is clear enough.

Sonatas and Interludes for prepared piano.
*** Denon Dig. **C37 7673** [id.]. Yuji Takahashi.

The dynamic Japanese pianist, Yuji Takahashi – pictured on the sleeve plucking the strings of his prepared piano – is a persuasive advocate of these early miniatures by Cage, pieces which show him very near to his fellow eccentric of a generation earlier, Eric Satie. The sixteen sonatas, each in binary form not very different from Scarlatti's, are – by Cage's standards – closely structured, and in their sequence are punctuated by four interludes, very similar in style. One can readily appreciate the attraction of an Eastern performer to this music with its pentatonic passages as well as its odd textures and unexpected sounds – induced by the insertion of bolts, screws, coins, etc., on most of the piano strings. Takahashi's commitment is reinforced by close, rather dry recording, apt for this music.

Campra, André (1660–1744)

Requiem Mass.

*** Erato **ECD 88186**; *MCE 71310* [id.]. Nelson, Harris, Orliac, Evans, Roberts, Monteverdi Ch., E. Bar. Soloists, Gardiner.

(*) HM **HMC 901251; *HMC40 1251* [id.]. Baudry, Zanetti, Benet, Elwes, Varcoe, Chapelle Royale Ch. & O, Herreweghe.

The music of André Campra, who came from Provence and had Italian blood, often possesses a genial lyricism that seems essentially Mediterranean. Although he is best-known now for *L'Europe galante* and other *opéras-ballets*, he wrote a large quantity of sacred music, psalm settings and motets. This *Requiem* is a lovely work, with luminous textures and often beguiling harmonies, and its neglect is difficult to understand. John Eliot Gardiner and his team of fine singers and players have clearly lavished much affection on this performance, and they bring to it intelligence and sensitivity. Campra is one of the most delightful composers of this period and this admirably recorded disc should go some way towards gaining him a rightful place in the repertoire. The radiance of the singing of the Monteverdi Choir is caught all the more vividly on CD, as well as the bloom on the voices of the excellent team of soloists, with the contrasted tenor timbres of the Frenchman Jean-Claude Orliac and of the Welsh singer, Wynford Evans, brought out the more sharply. The intimacy of the accompaniment in such a number as the *Agnus Dei*, with its delicate flute solo, is set nicely in scale, though in slow sections the strings of the English Baroque Soloists are edgier and more squeezy than they became after 1981, when this recording was made. There is an excellent cassette, full and very well focused – one of Erato's best tapes.

Herreweghe with refined solo and choral singing directs a fine performance of the beautiful *Requiem Mass* of Campra. It makes a good alternative to the more ardent and dramatic reading of John Eliot Gardiner on Erato for those who prefer a cooler approach to church music of 1700. The recording is refined to match the performance.

Canteloube, Marie-Joseph (1879–1957)

Chants d'Auvergne: Series 1–5.

*** HMV **CDC7 47970-2**; *EL 290802-4*. Victoria de los Angeles, LOP, Jacquillat.

It was Victoria de los Angeles who made the pioneering stereo recordings of the Auvergne arrangements (alongside Natania Davrath's justly admired Vanguard set which is available only in the USA [**VBD 2090**]). The warmth and sweetness of De los Angeles' tone when the recordings were made (1973 and 1975) matches the allure of Canteloube's settings. Now the twenty-four songs have been reissued, squeezed on to one CD and a matching tape (playing for over 70 minutes). In the lighter songs, the *Bourrées*, for instance, the singing combines sparkle with a natural feeling for the folk idiom, and there is the most engaging vocal colour in *Hé! beyla-z-y dau fé!* and *Tè, l'co tè!*; elsewhere, De los Angeles can be ravishing with her fine-spun vocal timbre, as in *La Delaïssádo* or the gentle *Lou Boussu*, while *Lou Coucut* speaks for itself. The accompaniments are highly sympathetic (fine wind solos at the opening of *Lo Calhé*) and the atmospheric recording is attractive too, although at times not ideally clear in focusing orchestral detail (*L'Antouèno* has rather washy strings). But these are quibbles: this is most enjoyable, and excellent value.

Chants d'Auvergne: L'Antouèno; Baïlèro; 3 Bourrées; Lou Boussu; Brezairola; Lou coucut; Chut, chut; La Delaïssádo; Lo Fïolairé; Jou l'pount d'o Mirabel; Malurous qu'o uno fenno; Passo pel prat; Pastourelle; Postouro, sé tu m'aymo; Tè, l'co tè.

❀ *** EMI Dig. **CD-EMX 9500**; (M) *EMX 41 2075-4* [Ang. *4AE 34471*]. Jill Gomez, Royal Liverpool PO, Handley.

Jill Gomez's selection of these increasingly popular songs, attractively presented on a mid-price label, makes for a memorably characterful record, which as well as bringing out the sensuous beauty of Canteloube's arrangements keeps reminding us, in the echoes of rustic band music, of the genuine folk base. Jill Gomez's voice could not be more apt, for the natural radiance and the range of tone-colour go with a strong feeling for words and feeling, helped by her intensive study of Provençal pronunciation. Vernon Handley's accompaniments have a directness as well as a warmth which supports the voice admirably, and the recording is outstandingly full and vivid. For sample, try the tender and gentle *La Delaïssádo*, just as beautiful as the well-known *Baïlèro*. The chirpy opening song, *L'aïo dè rotso* (*Spring water*) immediately demonstrates the added presence and tangibility of the CD, with the voice real and immediate, while orchestral detail is wonderfully clear against an attractive background ambience. A splendid bargain. There is a good cassette, but the compact disc is well worth its extra cost.

Chants d'Auvergne: L'Antouèno; Baïlèro; 3 Bourrées; 2 Bourrées; Brezairola; La Delaïssádo; Lo Fïolairé; Lou Boussu; Malurous qu'o uno fenno; La pastrouletta è lou chibalie; Passo pel prat; La pastoura als camps; Pastourelle.
*** Decca Dig. **410 004-2**; *KSXDC 7604* [Lon. *LDR 5-71104*]. Te Kanawa, ECO, Tate.

Dame Kiri Te Kanawa's recital has long been a favourite collection of Canteloube's lovely settings, with the warmly atmospheric Decca recording bringing an often languorous opulence to the music making. In such an atmosphere the quick songs lose a little in bite and *Baïlèro*, the most famous, is taken extremely slowly. With the sound so sumptuous, this hardly registers and the result remains compelling, thanks in great measure to sympathetic accompaniment from the ECO under Jeffrey Tate. Here one wallows in Canteloube's uninhibited treatment, worrying less about matters of authenticity, especially as the recording is so vivid (on tape as well as CD); yet both Jill Gomez and Victoria de los Angeles – who is much more robust in the famous *Baïlèro* – can produce ravishing results and at the same time exude greater vitality.

Chants d'Auvergne: L'Antouèno; Baïlèro; 3 Bourrées; 2 Bourrées; Brezairola; Lou coucut; Chut, chut; La Delaïssádo; Lo Fïolairé; Oï ayaï; Passo pel prat; Pour l'enfant; Tè, l'co, tè; Uno jionto postouro.
(*) CBS Dig. **CD 37299; *40-37299* [id.]. Frederica von Stade, RPO, Almeida.

Fine as Frederica von Stade's singing is, she is stylistically and temperamentally far less at home in Canteloube's lovely folksong settings than Victoria de los Angeles, Dame Kiri Te Kanawa or Jill Gomez in their different ways. Words are clear but, thanks in part to the more abrasive recording, the result is far less persuasively sensuous. The CD is clean and immediate but not as richly beautiful as the Decca, nor indeed as vividly atmospheric as Jill Gomez's EMI CD.

Chants d'Auvergne: Hé! beyla-z-y dau fé; Jou l'pount d'o Mirabel; Là-haut, sur le rocher; Lou boussu; Lou diziou bé; Malurous qu'o uno fenno; Obal din lo coumbèlo; La pastoura als camps; Pastorale; Pastourelle; La pastrouletta è lou chibalie; Postouro sé tu m'aymo; Quand z'eyro petitoune. Triptyque: Offrande à l'été; Lunair; Hymne dans l'aurore.
*** CBS Dig. **MK 37837**; *IMT 37837* [id.]. Frederica von Stade, RPO, Almeida.

Frederica von Stade's second collection not only has more charm and personal identification than the first but also includes Canteloube's haunting *Triptyque*, written in 1914. It is very much in the tradition of twentieth-century French song-cycles in its colourful expressionism, but also anticipates the orchestral style to be made famous by his folk settings. The second of the three,

Lunaire, is particularly evocative. This is its first recording in stereo. Von Stade's performance is eloquent and the recording suitably atmospheric, if not quite as sumptuous as the Decca sound for Kiri Te Kanawa. There is an excellent cassette.

Chants d'Auvergne, 4th and 5th series (complete).
(*) Decca **411 730-2 [id.]. Te Kanawa, ECO, Tate – VILLA-LOBOS: *Bachianas Brasileiras No. 5*.***

This second collection of Canteloube folksong arrangements from Kiri Te Kanawa, again with Jeffrey Tate providing richly beautiful accompaniments, fills in the gaps left in the first, and presents all remaining items in the five sets of the songs. They are not all as inspired as those in the earlier collection, and there is less variety, partly a question of Dame Kiri's preference for producing a continuous flow of sensuously beautiful sounds rather than giving a folk-like tang. The orchestral playing and the ripely atmospheric recording add to the richness of the mixture.

Carissimi, Giacomo (1605–74)

Jepthe. Judicium Salomonis (*The Judgement of Solomon*); *Jonas* (oratorios).
*** Mer. Dig. **CDE 84132**; *KE 77132* [id.]. Coxwell, Hemington Jones, Harvey, Ainsley, Gabrieli Cons. 8 Players, Paul McCreesh.

Although Carissimi was maestro di cappella at the Jesuit German College in Rome from 1629 to 1674 for which he composed much liturgical music, he is best known for his chamber oratorios – and in particular *Jepthe*. They were commissioned for the non-liturgical services held every Friday in Lent by the Archconfraternity of the Most Holy Crucifix, a brotherhood of educated noblemen. This present disc collects three of the best-known, all written before 1650, and each presenting a biblical episode. No opening sinfonia survives for *Jepthe* and the editor chooses to preface the oratorio with a Frescobaldi *Toccata*, which works well. *Jepthe* is affectingly presented in this well-prepared and intelligent performance, which is let down only by some vocal insecurities at the very top. The continuo part is imaginatively realized with some pleasing sonorities (organ, double harp, chitarrone, etc.). Despite some undoubted shortcomings, this is the most convincing account of the work since Gottfried Wolters' 1953 Archiv mono set.

Carlsson, Mark (born 1952)

Nightwings.
*** Crystal Dig. **CD 750** [id.]. Westwood Wind Quintet – BARBER: *Summer music*; LIGETI: *Bagatelles*; MATHIAS: *Quintet*.***

Mark Carlsson, who is now in his mid-thirties, lives in California and is a flautist and movement teacher as well as composer. In *Nightwings* the flute assumes the persona of a dreamer, the taped music may be perceived as a dream-world and the other four instruments appear as characters in a dream. The music is almost wholly diatonic and immediately accessible, but it is not an unimaginative conception. On this evidence it would be difficult to say whether there is a strong creative personality here: the idea is in some respects more interesting than the piece itself. Excellent playing and recording.

Carmina Burana (*c.* 1300)

Carmina Burana – songs from the original manuscript.
*** O-L Dig. **417 373-2** [id.]. New L. Cons., Pickett.

(*) HM **HMC 90335 [id.]. Clemencic Cons., René Clemencic.
(M) ** Tel. **ZS8 43775** [id.]. Studio der Fruhen Music, Thomas Binkley.

This was the collection on which Carl Orff drew for his popular cantata. The original manuscript of *Carmina Burana* came into the possession of the Court Library of Munich in 1803 after the secularization of the Bavarian monasteries. It comprises a vast collection of lyric pieces from many countries, mostly Latin, from the late eleventh to the thirteenth century. They acquired their name ('Songs of Beneditbeuren') from the monastery in which they were found. The manuscript assembles more than 200 pieces, organized according to subject-matter: love songs, moralizing and satirical songs, eating, drinking, gambling and religious texts. To quote Philip Pickett's note, 'in view of the lewd and offensive nature of part of the collection, it is miraculous that the manuscript survived at all'. The performances on this well-filled Oiseau-Lyre disc have the merit of excellent singing from Catherine Bott and Michael George, and sensitive playing from the instrumentalists under Pickett. The engineering is excellent and strikes a virtually ideal balance between voice and instruments. There is a pleasing acoustic ambience. It is a clear first choice, given the clarity and warmth of the sound.

René Clemencic's disc draws on a four-LP set of the *Carmina Burana* made in 1977. The performances have immense spirit and liveliness, and there is much character. It suffers slightly in comparison with its rivals from slightly over-reverberant sound, though this at times brings a gain in atmosphere. Of course, there are many ways of realizing these songs and the colour the Clemencic bring to this repertoire is undoubtedly appealing. However, most collectors will prefer the better-focused sound of its immediate rivals.

The Teldec CD includes twenty-one songs recorded in the mid-1960s and sounding remarkably clean and well focused. There is more of a studio atmosphere than in the livelier acoustics of Pickett and Clemencic. Thomas Binkley has the advantage of fine performers, including Grayston Burgess, Andrea von Ramm and Nigel Rogers, and his realization of these pieces is of unfailing interest. Good though it is, this is probably not a first choice now – and the present issue, though it has song texts, offers no background essay. It does, however, have the advantage of economy.

Carter, Elliott (born 1908)

(i) *Piano concerto; Variations for orchestra.*
*** New World **NWCD 347** [id.]. (i) Ursula Oppens; Cincinnati SO, Gielen.

The *Piano concerto* is a hard nut to crack: it is uncompromising and is far from immediately accessible. However, unlike much uncompromising contemporary music, one is left with the feeling that there is something of substance to access. The *Concerto* and the *Variations* date from two different stylistic periods; the *Variations* come from 1954–5 and reflect Carter's emergence from the rhetoric of the American tradition of Ives, Harris and Schuman and his absorption of the expressionism of Schoenberg, Varèse and so on. It is an inventive and fascinating work, splendidly played by these Cincinnati forces. The *Concerto* comes from the mid-1960s and is a densely argued piece, complex in its structure – exploring what the annotator calls, 'the tragic possibilities of an alienated texture on a visionary scale'. The work contrasts an isolated soloist (Ursula Oppens its heroine) whose character is 'free, fanciful and sensitive' with an orchestra that functions as a massive and mechanical ensemble, and with a concertino of seven instruments, surrounding the piano, who act as 'a well-meaning but impotent intermediary'. It is a strange work that seems at first impenetrable but which is undeniably powerful and disturbing. The recording was made at concert performances and is excellent.

Castelnuovo-Tedesco, Mario (1895–1968)

Guitar concerto in D, Op. 99.

*** Ph. Dig. **416 357-2**; *416 357-4* [id.]. Pepe Romero, ASMF, Marriner – RODRIGO: *Sones en la Giralda*; VILLA-LOBOS: *Concerto.****

(*) Decca Dig. **417 199-2; *417 199-4* [id.]. Fernández, ECO, Martinez – RODRIGO: *Concierto; Fantasia.***(*)

(B) **(*) CBS *MGT 39017*. John Williams, ECO, Groves – RODRIGO: *Concierto; Fantasia*; VILLA-LOBOS: *Concerto.****

Castelnuovo-Tedesco's innocently romantic *Concerto*, with its slow-movement melody that faintly recalls another even more famous tune, is splendidly played by Pepe Romero while Sir Neville Marriner's accompaniments are affectionate, polished and full of character. With a good balance, natural sound and tempting couplings, this will be hard to beat.

Eduardo Fernandez is also given warmly atmospheric recording on Decca, and his too is a highly agreeable performance, at its best in the ruminative *Andante*, which is perhaps even more improvisatory in feeling than Pepe Romero's account. Miguel Gomez Martinez provides amiable support with the ECO; but in the finale, which the composer marks *Ritmico e cavalleresco*, Marriner's articulation has a markedly greater degree of rhythmic bite, helped by the slightly clearer Philips recording. The Decca disc offers generous Rodrigo couplings, but the performances are less distinctive than the finest available.

John Williams's more recent version of the *Concerto* with Groves is more vividly recorded than his earlier account with Ormandy and the Philadelphia Orchestra, but that was fresher and had more pace. He is placed far forward here, so that it is not always possible to locate him in relation to his colleagues. But if the sound is synthetic as far as perspective is concerned, it is by no means unpleasing. These artists make the most of the slow movement's poetry and the *Concerto* has no lack of charm. The generous couplings and distinguished performances (about which there are few reservations) make this extended-length tape issue a real bargain, for the transfers are well managed.

Cavalli, Francesco (1602–76)

Xerse (complete).

*** HM HMC **901175/8** [id.]. René Jacobs, Nelson, Gall, Poulenard, Mellon, Feldman, Elwes, De Mey, Visse, Instrumental Ens., Jacobs.

Ombra mai fù, sings King Xerxes in the opening scene, addressing a plane tree, and most listeners will have a double-take, remembering first Handel's *Largo*, and then that Cavalli set the same libretto 84 years earlier than Handel, in 1654. Handel's *Serse* (note the difference of spelling) is a perky comedy, full of sparkling ideas, as the inspired English National Opera production made clear on stage; but Cavalli's opera, even longer but just as brisk in its action, can be presented just as winningly, as here in the first ever recording. Authentic performances of Cavalli have often sounded bald after Raymond Leppard's ripe renderings for Glyndebourne, but Jacob's presentation is piquant to match the plot, often genuinely funny, sustaining the enormous length very well. As well as directing his talented team, Jacobs sings the title role, only one of the four counter-tenors, nicely contrasted, who take the castrato roles. The fruity alto of Dominique Visse in a comic servant role is particularly striking, and among the women – some of them shrill at times – the outstanding singer, Agnès Mellon, takes the other servant role, singing delightfully in a tiny laughing song. Most of the text is set to fast-moving recitative, but Cavalli flexibly introduces charming and concise songs and the occasional duet. The three Acts of the opera are preceded by an allegorical prologue taken from *Il Ciro*, an opera Cavalli wrote at about the same time. Excellent sound which consistently allows the fresh, young voices of the principals to make every word plain. Notes and libretto are first rate.

Arias: *La Calisto: Ardo, sospiro è piango. La Didone: Cassandra's lament. L'Egisto: Clori's lament. L'Orimonte: Numi ciechi più di me. Scipione Africano: Non è, non è crudel. Xerse: La bellezza è un don fugace.*
(*) Erato Dig. **ECD 88100 [id.]. Frederica von Stade, Scottish CO, Leppard – MONTEVERDI: *Arias.***(*)

Frederica von Stade, in excellent voice, sings *Cassandra's lament* (which opens the group) with a dignified simplicity, and she finds a similar direct eloquence for Clori's lament, *Amor, che ti diè l'alti* from *L'Egisto*. The recital is well planned so that between them comes the delightful *La bellezza è un don fugace* (given attractively light articulation), and then follows *Numi ciechi più di me*, which – with a deliciously pointed accompaniment from Leppard and the Scottish Chamber strings – really sparkles. This is a most attractive programme, well balanced and recorded; the music itself is so appealing that one can forgive some lack of variety in timbre and dramatic presentation. Italian vocal texts are provided, without translations, and documentation is poor.

Cesti, Antonio (1623–69)

Orontea (opera): complete.
❀ *** HM *HM 40 1100/02* [id.]. Müller-Molinari, Cadelo, Poulenard, Feldman, Reinhart, Jacobs, James, Sarti, Bierbaum, Giacinta Instrumental Ens., Jacobs.

As performed here under the singer and musicologist, René Jacobs, this early Italian opera – written in various versions from 1656 onwards – emerges as far more than an interesting historical curiosity. Its vigour and colour and – perhaps most important of all – its infectious sense of humour in treating a conventional classical subject make it a delight even today. It was – after the operas of Monteverdi and Cavalli – the most popular Venetian opera of its day, and those who know Cavalli will recognize similar fingerprints. This performance using singers who both sing authentically and characterize strongly presents the piece very much as a dramatic entertainment, and the vividly immediate recording gives an excellent sense of presence in a small-scale domestic performance. Outstanding among the singers are Helga Müller-Molinari, David James, Gastoni Sarti and Jacobs himself. The cassettes, transferred at the highest level, are in the demonstration class.

Chabrier, Emmanuel (1841–94)

Bourrée fantastique; España; Gwendoline overture; Marche joyeuse; Le Roi malgré lui; Danse slave. Suite pastorale.
*** Erato Dig. **ECD 88018**; *MCE 75079* [id.]. Fr. Nat. PO, Jordan.

A sparkling collection which provided Chabrier's compact disc début. The playing is admirably spirited, even boisterous in the *Marche joyeuse*, and the melodramatic *Gwendoline overture* is relished with proper gusto. Perhaps Paray's account of the engaging *Suite pastorale* (on Mercury) was that bit more distinctive, but here the tempo of the third movement, *Sous bois*, is less controversial. *España* has infectious élan, yet rhythms are nicely relaxed so that the gaiety is never forced. The recording is generally first class, with the body and range of the CD especially telling. The balance of sound on tape is thinner, although there is no lack of liveliness.

OPERA

L'Étoile (complete).
❀ *** HMV Dig. **CDS7 47889-8** (2) [Pathé id.]. Alliot-Lugaz, Gautier, Bacquier, Raphanel, Damonte, Le Roux, David, Lyon Opéra Ch. and O, Gardiner.

This fizzing operetta is a winner. Musically a cross between *Carmen* and Gilbert and Sullivan, with plenty of Offenbach thrown in, the subtlety and refinement of Chabrier's score go well beyond the usual realm of operetta, and Gardiner directs a performance that from first to last makes the piece sparkle bewitchingly. Improbably, it was the poet Paul Verlaine who suggested the original idea to his friend, Chabrier, when he wrote some naughtily sado-masochistic Impalement Verses. As they emerge in the finished operetta, they are no more improper than the Mikado's song in G. & S., and the exotic plot about King Ouf I who enjoys the spectacle of a little capital punishment has plenty of Gilbertian twists. Central to the story, the star of *L'Étoile* is the pedlar, Lazuli, a breeches role, and Gardiner has been lucky to include in his company at the Lyon Opéra a soprano with just the personality, presence and voice to carry it off, Colette Alliot-Lugaz. Except for Gabriel Bacquier as the Astrologer, Sirocco, the others are not well known either, but all are first rate. The helpful French dialogue adds to the sparkle (just long enough to give the right flavour), and numbers such as the drunken duet between King and Astrologer are hilarious. Outstandingly good recording, especially tangible and vivid on CD with excellent access.

Chadwick, George (1854–1931)

Symphony No. 2, Op. 21.
*** New World Dig. **NWCD 339**; *NWMC 339* [id.]. Albany SO, Julius Hegyi – PARKER: *Northern Ballad.****

George Chadwick was a Bostonian who studied with Reinecke in Leipzig and Rheinberger in Munich before returning home to become the director of the New England Conservatoire. His *Second Symphony* (1883–6) breathes much the same air as Brahms and Dvořák; the scoring is beautifully clean and the ideas appealing, if perhaps wanting the distinctive stamp of an original. The scherzo had to be repeated at its first performance – independently of the whole symphony – when one critic noted that it 'positively winks at you'. It is quite delightful and not dissimilar to the scherzo of Svendsen's *First Symphony*. The symphony as a whole is cultivated, well crafted and civilized, rather than highly individual. In fact its slow movement carries numerous reminders of other composers, one phrase even recalling the slow movement of Mozart K.467. Very natural recorded sound and an excellent performance from these New England forces. An interesting disc.

Chaminade, Cécile (1857–1944)

Concertino for flute and orchestra, Op. 107.
(M) *** RCA *GK 85448* [*AGK1 5448*]. Galway, RPO, Dutoit – FAURÉ: *Fantaisie*; IBERT: *Concerto*; POULENC: *Sonata.****

The Chaminade *Concertino* undoubtedly has great charm. The principal theme of the first movement is of the kind that insinuates itself irresistibly into the subconscious, and the work has a delightful period atmosphere. It is splendidly played by James Galway, who is given excellent support by the RPO under Charles Dutoit. The recording, admirably spacious and finely detailed, has been digitally remastered since its last appearance, but on the chrome tape the quality is slightly edgy at the top (though tameable).

Charpentier, Marc-Antoine (1634–1704)

Concert à 4 (for viols), *H. 545; Musique de théâtre pour Circé et Andromède; Sonata à 8* (for 2 flutes & strings), *H. 548.*
(*) HM Dig. **HMC 901244; *HMC 40 1244* [id.]. London Baroque, Medlam.

The exploration of Marc-Antoine Charpentier's enormous output proceeds apace, and his representation in the record catalogues is at last becoming commensurate with the extent and quality of his music. Most non-specialist collectors associate him with sacred cantatas and oratorios, but he was hardly less prolific a composer of instrumental music – equally at home, as it were, in the *Comédie-Française* as he was at Sainte-Chapelle. Before Molière's death he wrote a substantial amount of incidental music for *Le Malade imaginaire*. His music for Thomas Corneille's *Circé* was written in 1675, and its companion for Pierre Corneille's *Andromède* followed seven years later. The pieces are most expertly played here by the members of London Baroque (though the string sound still does not entirely escape the faint suspicion that it has been marinaded in vinegar) and well reward investigation. As usual in recordings from this source, the sound is excellent.

Motets: *Alma Redemptoris; Amicus meus; Ave regina; Dialogus inter Magdalenam et Jesum; Egredimini filiae Sion; Elevations; O pretiosum; O vere, o bone, Magdalena lugens; Motet du saint sacrement; O vos omnes; Pour le passion de notre Seigneur* (2 settings)*; Salve regina; Solva vivebat in antris Magdalena lugens.*
*** HM **HMC 901149** [id.]. Concerto Vocale.

Half of the motets on this record are for solo voice and the others are duets. All were intended for liturgical use. Among the best and most moving things here are the *O vos omnes* and *Amicus meus* which are beautifully done. Another motet to note is *Magdalena lugens* in which Mary Magdalene laments Christ's death at the foot of the Cross. This Harmonia Mundi series continues to go from strength to strength and serves to establish Charpentier as a really major figure in French music. Expressive singing from Judith Nelson and René Jacobs, and excellent continuo support. Worth a strong recommendation.

Caecilia, virgo et martyr, H.397; De profundis, H.189.
** Erato Dig. **ECD 88163** [id.]. Degelin, Reyghere, Mols, James, Meens, Van Croonenborch, Ghent Madrigal Ch. & Cantabile, Musica Polyphonica, Devos.

Charpentier composed seven settings of the *De profundis* (Psalm 129 in the Roman Psalter), only one of which is part of the Requiem Mass; the others are in all probability separate pieces. The one recorded here is the most elaborate; it is lavishly scored (soloists, double-chorus, two orchestras, with flutes and continuo) and was composed in 1683 for the funeral of Louis XIV's first Queen, Marie-Thérèse. It is an impressive and moving piece which can only further enhance the growing recognition of Charpentier's stature. The performance is perhaps a little under-vitalized and some of the grandeur and power of this music seems to elude Devos, even though he uses considerable forces. *Caecilia, virgo et martyr*, fares better, though collectors will find some textual differences from William Christie's earlier record (see below).

Caecilia, virgo et martyr; Filius prodigus (oratorios)*; Magnificat.*
*** HM Dig. **HMC 90066** [id.]. Grenat, Benet, Laplenie, Reinhard, Studer, Les Arts Florissants, Christie.

As the sleeve-note puts it, these Latin oratorios or dramatic motets of Charpentier occupy 'an isolated, if elevated position in French seventeenth-century music'. The two works recorded here come from different periods of his life: *Caecilia, virgo et martyr* was composed for the Duchesse de Guise in 1675, when he wrote a number of works on the subject of St Cecilia; the second, on the theme of the Prodigal Son, dates from the later period when Charpentier was *maître de chapelle* at Saint Louis-le-Grand (1684–98), and is richer in expressive harmonies and poignant dissonances. The music could scarcely find more eloquent advocates than these artists under William Christie; its stature and nobility are fully conveyed here. Included on the CD is another setting of the *Magnificat*, different from that recorded by Devos – see above. It is a short piece for three voices and has an almost Purcellian flavour. One thing that will immediately strike the listener is the delicacy and finesse of the scoring. All this music is beautifully recorded; the present issues can be recommended with enthusiasm.

In navitatem Domini nostri Jésus Christi (canticum), H.414; Pastorale sur la naissance de notre Seigneur Jésus Christ, H.483.
*** HM **HMC 901082**. Les Arts Florissants Vocal & Instrumental Ens., Christie.

This CD appropriately re-couples two attractive works, both associated with Christmas and both composed for Marie de Lorraine, Duchesse de Guise, whose ensemble Charpentier directed until her death in 1688. This *Canticum* has much of the character of an oratorio (indeed, the word 'canticum' was loosely used to indicate both the motet and the oratorio) and affirms the composer's debt to his master, Carissimi. The invention has great appeal and variety. The *Pastorale* is not new to the gramophone, but this version supersedes its predecessor (in the edition of Guy Lambert) from which William Christie departs. The present issue offers music that was not included in the Guy Lambert edition which contained a different second part that had been intended for use at the Jesuit College in the Rue Saint-Antoine, Paris. It is a most rewarding piece, and the grace and charm of the writing continue to win one over to this eminently resourceful composer. This series, undertaken by William Christie, seems almost self-recommending, so high are the standards of performance and recording, and so fertile is Charpentier's imagination. The CD remastering is very successful; the only snag in the presentation is the minuscule print of the accompanying texts.

In navitatem Domini nostri Jésus Christ, H.416; Pastorale sur la naissance de notre Seigneur Jésus Christ.
*** HM **HMC 905130** [id.]. Les Arts Florissants Vocal & Instrumental Ens., Christie.

As with the companion disc above, both works here are based on the Christmas story and show contrasting sides of Charpentier's stylistic personality. They are, of course, different settings. The cantata, *In navitatem*, is one of some 35 in this genre (the French call them *histoires sacrées*) he composed after returning from Rome: it is one of his grandest and dates from the late 1680s. It is a finely balanced edifice in two complementary halves, separated by an instrumental section, an eloquent evocation of the night. The little pastorale, written in the tradition of the ballet de cour or divertissement, was yet another piece written for performance in the salon of the Duchesse de Guise. This is enchanting music, elegantly played and excellently recorded.

Laudate Dominum; 3rd Magnificat; Te Deum.
** Erato Dig. **ECD 88027** [id.]. Degelin, Jansen, Nirouet, Caals, Widmer, Ghent Madrigal Ch. & Cantabile, Musica Polyphonica, Devos.

Many readers will know the *Te Deum* from the Eurovision fanfare. It has been recorded a number of times, but this account from Louis Devos is as good as, if not better than, any of its predecessors. The two companion pieces, the setting of *Laudate Dominum* and the present setting of the *Magnificat* (one of many), are also from the mid-1690s and are comparative rarities. The performances are very good indeed and the standard of the singing more acceptable than the recording, which balances the team of soloists rather forwardly while the recording is not perhaps state-of-the-art. Nevertheless, a recommendation, even if collectors embarking on a Charpentier collection on CD might start elsewhere.

Leçons de ténèbres.
*** HM **HMC 901005** [id.]. Jacobs, Nelson, Verkinderen, Kuijken, Christie, Junghänel.

Charpentier was an almost exact contemporary of Lully whom he outlived but whose shadow served to obscure him during his lifetime. These *Leçons de ténèbres* are eloquent and moving pieces, worthy of comparison with Purcell and more substantial musically than Couperin's later setting. Since the falsetto tradition was weak, it seems unlikely that any of the music was intended for male alto, a fact that the counter-tenor René Jacobs readily concedes in his notes. Yet his performance (like that of his colleagues) is so authentic in every respect that it is difficult to imagine it being surpassed. The pursuit of authenticity often produces inhibited phrasing and over-careful voice production, but here the results are a tribute to both musicianship and scholarship. The music has depth and these artists reveal its stature to fine effect. The recording is as distinguished as the performances.

Méditations pour le Carême; Le reniement de St Pierre.
*** HM Dig. **HMC 905151** [id.]. Les Arts Florissants, William Christie.

Le reniement de Saint Pierre is one of Charpentier's most inspired and expressive works and is again modelled on Carissimi. According to H. Wiley Hitchcock, the score dates from the 1670s and its text draws on the account in all four Gospels of St Peter's denial of Christ. The *Méditations pour le Carême* are a sequence of three-voice motets for Lent with continuo accompaniment (organ; theorbo and bass viol) that may not have quite the same imaginative or expressive resource but which are full of nobility and interest. The performances maintain the high standards of this ensemble, and the same compliment can be paid to the recording.

Miserere, H.219; Motets: pour la seconde fois que le Saint Sacrament vien au même reposoir, H.372; pour le Saint Sacrement au reposoir, H.346. Motet pour une longue offrande, H.434.
*** HM Dig. **HMC 901185** [id.], Mellon, Poulenard, Ledroit, Kendall, Kooy, Chapelle Royale, Herreweghe.

Charpentier's *Motet pour l'offertoire de la Messe rouge* was so called because it was performed at the ceremony that accompanied the annual reopening of the Parlement de Paris in mid-November, attended by magistrates in their scarlet robes. (He subsequently changed its title to *Motet pour une longue offrande*.) It was written during the last years of his life when in 1698 he had been appointed *Maître de musique des enfants* at Sainte-Chapelle. In fact it is one of his most splendid and eloquent works and finds the composer at the height of his powers. There are some poignant dissonances in the *Deus justus et patiens* section. The *Miserere*, the last of four settings Charpentier made of Psalm 50, was written for the Jesuit Church on Rue Saint-Antoine, whose ceremonies were particularly sumptuous. All four works on the disc are powerfully expressive and beautifully performed. The recording, made in collaboration with Radio France, is most expertly balanced.

Messe pour les Trépassés, H.2; Dies irae, H.12; Motet pour les Trépassés, H.311.
** Erato **ECD 88121** [id.]. Rosat, Smith, Schaer, Elwes, Serafim, Huttenlocher, Brodard, Gulbenkian Foundation O, Lisbon, Corboz.

The *Messe pour les Trépassés* (Mass for All Souls' Day) is scored for large forces, soloists, double-chorus and orchestra. In this account a *Dies irae* and a motet are inserted into its course. They were all recorded in 1972 and, for ears attuned to period-instrument performances, will sound distinctly old-fashioned. Readers who welcome the opportunity to hear this music on modern instruments, however, will find much to reward them. Corboz draws some lively singing from both soloists and choir, and the generous acoustic in which the recording was made serves to give a pleasing effect. The music itself dates from the 1670s, not long after Charpentier's return from Italy, and is both powerful and eloquent. The recorded sound, if not up to the best modern standards, is eminently acceptable.

OPERA

Actéon (complete).
*** HM **HMC 901095**; *HMC 40.1095* [id.]. Visse, Mellon, Laurens, Feldman, Paut, Les Arts Florissants Vocal & Instrumental Ens., Christie.

Actéon is a short work in six scenes; the exact date of its composition remains unknown. As in so many other works which Harmonia Mundi and Erato are now investigating, the sheer fecundity and, above all, quality of invention take one by surprise – though, by this time, one should take for granted Charpentier's extraordinarily rich imagination. Actéon is particularly well portrayed by Dominique Visse; his transformation in the fourth tableau and his feelings of horror are almost as effective as anything in nineteenth-century opera! William Christie has devoted such energy and scholarship to this composer that the authority of his direction ensures the success of this venture. Although scholarship is an important ingredient in this undertaking, musicianship and flair are even more important, and these are in welcome evidence. The other singers are first rate, in particular the Diane of Agnès Mellon. Alert playing and an altogether natural recording which is truthfully balanced and sounds splendidly fresh, as well as excellent presentation, make this a most desirable issue. The chrome cassette too is outstanding.

Medée (complete).
❀ *** HM **HMC 901139/41** [id.]. Feldman, Ragon, Mellon, Boulin, Bona, Cantor, Les Arts Florissants Ch. & O, Christie.

Few records of early Baroque opera communicate as vividly as this, winner in 1985 of the International record critics' award and the Early Music prize in the *Gramophone* record awards. Despite the classical convention of the libretto and a strictly authentic approach to the performance, Christie's account has a vitality and a sense of involvement which bring out the keen originality of Charpentier's writing, his implied emotional glosses on a formal subject. This was Charpentier's only tragédie-lyrique, and richly extends our knowledge of a long-neglected composer. Les Arts Florissants, in the stylishness of its playing on period instruments, matches any such group in the world, and the soloists are all first rate. Excellent recording.

Chausson, Ernest (1855–99)

Poème for violin and orchestra, Op. 25.
*** HMV **CDC7 47725-2** [id.]. Perlman, O de Paris, Martinon – RAVEL: *Tzigane;* SAINT-SAËNS: *Havanaise* etc.***
*** DG Dig. **423 063-2**; *423 063-4* [id.]. Perlman, NYPO, Mehta – RAVEL: *Tzigane;* SAINT-SAËNS: *Havanaise* etc.: SARASATE: *Carmen fantasy*.***
*** Decca **417 118-2** [id.]. Kyung Wha Chung, RPO, Dutoit – RAVEL: *Tzigane;* SAINT-SAËNS: *Havanaise* etc.***

(M) **(*) HMV Dig. **CDC7 47623-2** [id.]; (M) *TC-EMX 2100* [Ang. *4AM 34778*). Nigel Kennedy, LPO, Kamu – TCHAIKOVSKY: *Violin concerto*.**(*)

Chausson's beautiful *Poème* has been generously represented on records; Perlman's 1975 account with the Orchestra de Paris under the late Jean Martinon was to the 1970s what the youthful Menuhin's was to the 1930s or Grumiaux's was in the 1960s: it is a classic account by which newcomers are measured. What a glorious and inspired piece it is when played with such feeling! It comes on a particularly distinguished anthology which has a brilliant account of the *Tzigane* and the eternally fresh Saint-Saëns pieces so beloved of virtuosi, and of the public too, when played like this. The digital transfer exchanges some of the opulence of the original for a gain in presence (not that Perlman isn't near enough already) but still sounds full. Perlman's glorious tone is undiminished, even if now the ear perceives a slightly sharper outline to the timbre.

Perlman's 1987 digital version is also a very fine one and will disappoint nobody. The sound is immediate and refined in detail, while the balance of the soloist is very slightly less forward. The New York Philharmonic players are undoubtedly responsive under Mehta; yet Martinon displays a more subtle feeling for the atmosphere of the piece. At the opening of the HMV version, Perlman seems wholly caught in the spell of Chausson's music; he plays very beautifully in the later account but is a fraction more detached. Both soloist and conductor without question are helped by the warm resonance of the Salle Wagram, Paris, on HMV; the Manhattan Center, New York, is that bit cooler, although by no means dry. It is a small difference and in making a choice some readers will wish to bear in mind that the DG compact disc includes a stunning bonus performance of Sarasate's *Carmen fantasy*. The DG cassette is of good quality but has a marked reduction of presence and range compared with the CD.

Chung's performance of Chausson's beautiful *Poème* is deeply emotional; some may prefer a more restrained approach but, with committed accompaniment from the RPO and excellent recording, this makes an admirable foil for the virtuoso pieces with which it is coupled. The CD enhances the natural balance of the sound with its absence of background, and rearranges the programme order, with the Chausson coming between the two Saint-Saëns display pieces, and the concert ending with the Ravel *Tzigane*.

Nigel Kennedy's version of the *Poème*, unusually expansive and sensuous with ripe and powerful build-up of climaxes, comes as a welcome if not very generous coupling for his warmly romantic reading of the Tchaikovsky *Concerto*, recorded in similarly rich, full sound. There is a good tape.

Symphony in B flat min., Op. 20; Soir de Fête, Op. 32; The Tempest, Op. 18: 2 Scenes.
(*) Chan. Dig. **CHAN 8369; *ABTD 1135* [id.]. RTB SO, Serebrier.

Symphony in B flat, Op. 20; Viviane (symphonic poem), *Op. 9.*
(*) Erato Dig. **ECD 88169 [id.]. Basle SO, Jordan.

The Chandos recording is a co-production made in collaboration with RTB (Radio-Télévision Belge), and the sound is certainly natural. Serebrier succeeds in drawing playing of real conviction and some sensitivity from his players. He also offers the *Soir de Fête*, which Chausson wrote in the year before his death and had intended to revise, and which makes an excellent effect in this recording. In addition, the Chandos disc includes two dances from the incidental music which he composed for *The Tempest*, unlisted in most reference works on the composer. They are slight but attractive. The recording is very good indeed, without being in the demonstration class. The chrome cassette, too, is wide-ranging and brightly lit.

Armin Jordan and the Basle orchestra give a well-shaped account of the *Symphony* and are thoroughly atmospheric in the Wagnerian slow movement. The orchestral playing is responsive and the recording has an agreeable warmth, with plenty of space round the sound. Jordan is a fine (and much underrated) conductor with an obvious sympathy for this work, and he is thoroughly convincing in both the symphony and *Viviane*. This issue did not deserve its generally cool press reception and can be recommended alongside (but not in preference to) the Serebrier on Chandos.

Admirers of Ansermet may like to consider his 1967 recording which has been reissued on a well-transferred mid-priced London Enterprise tape, coupled with Magnard's *Symphony No. 3*. It is a warmly sympathetic performance and the brilliant sound is not too dated (Decca *417 636-4*).

CHAMBER MUSIC

Concert in D for piano, violin and string quartet, Op. 21; String quartet in C min., Op. 35 (comp. d'Indy).
*** HMV Dig. **CDC7 47548-2**; *EL 270381-4* [id.]. Collard, Dumay, Muir Qt.

Concert for piano, violin and string quartet, Op. 21.
*** Essex **CDS 6044**. Accardo, Canino, Levin, Batjer, Hoffman, Wiley – SAINT-SAENS: *Violin sonata No. 1.****
(*) CBS Dig. **MK 37814 [id.]. Perlman, Bolet, Juilliard Qt.

(i) *Concert for piano, violin and string quartet, Op. 21;* (ii) *Piece for cello and piano, Op. 39.*
** HM **HMC 901135**. (i) R. Pasquier, Daugareil, Simonot, B. Pasquier; (ii) Ridoux; (i; ii) Pennetier.

Since the pioneering records of Thibaud and Cortot, versions of the Chausson *Concert* for violin, piano and string quartet have hardly been thick on the ground. Ironically, things have improved to the extent that there have been four new recordings in recent years. EMI's recent version with Jean-Philippe Collard and Augustin Dumay unquestionably leads the field; indeed, it is unlikely to be surpassed. These artists are completely attuned to the sensibility of the period, and they bring an impressive authority to the work. Both Dumay and Collard are scrupulous in their observance of the dynamic markings, and there is an authenticity of feeling that is completely involving. The *C minor String quartet* that was left incomplete before Chausson's fatal bicycle ride, and to which Vincent d'Indy put the finishing touches, provides a splendid makeweight, and this is not otherwise available. The playing is effortless and unforced, and the recording is extremely vivid and lifelike. There is a well-balanced cassette, warm, full and clear, though the use of iron-oxide stock means that there is a loss of ultimate range at the top.

Salvatore Accardo and Bruno Canino and their four colleagues convey a sense of effortless music-making and of pleasure in making music in domestic surroundings. The quartet do not speak with the unanimity of outlook you find in the Muir, and the refined, aristocratic personality of Accardo dominates. Accardo is particularly songful in the third movement, light and delicate elsewhere. While it does not displace the Dumay–Collard version on EMI, which is more concentrated and powerful, it is a thoroughly enjoyable account, recorded in a warm acoustic.

Good though it is, the CBS version is not as natural in terms of recorded sound. The playing of both Itzhak Perlman and Jorge Bolet is highly sensitive but both they and the Juilliard Quartet are rather closely observed by the microphone. The Juilliards tend to overproject and seem reluctant to trust the natural eloquence of the music. Even so, there is much to admire in this performance but collectors will note that the *Concert* comes alone, without a coupling of any kind.

On Harmonia Mundi there is an added inducement in the form of the Op. 39 *Piece* for cello and piano, which is not included on either the LP or the cassette. But good though Régis Pasquier and Jean-Claude Pennetier are, the distinction of the EMI team does tell. The French account is by no means wanting in imagination, but it is less poetic; the HMV recording is in every way superior.

Piano quartet in A, Op. 30. Piano trio in G min., Op. 3.
** HM **HMC 901115** [id.]. Les Musiciens.

A well-filled and valuable issue that couples two rarities. The Op. 30 *Piano quartet* of 1896 is one of Chausson's finest works and reinforces the oft-quoted claim that he is the connecting link between Franck and Debussy (there are parallels between it and the Debussy *G minor Quartet*, composed three years earlier). Les Musiciens comprise the Pasquier Trio and Jean-Claude Pennetier, but they are recorded in a less than ample acoustic, and their performance is lacking the subtlety and colour one knows this ensemble can command. The effect both here and in the early *G minor Trio*, Op. 3, is somewhat monochrome. A pity, since this is enormously civilized music.

Piano trio in G min., Op. 3.
*** Ph. Dig. **411 141-2** [id.]. Beaux Arts Trio – RAVEL: *Trio in A min.****

The early *G minor Trio* will come as a pleasant surprise to most collectors, for its beauties far outweigh any weaknesses. There are many glimpses of the promise to come, and the invention is strong. The playing of the Beaux Arts Trio is superbly eloquent and the recording is very impressive on CD, even if the piano looms a little too large in the picture. A distinguished issue.

OPERA

Le roi Arthus (complete).
*** Erato Dig. **ECD 88213**; *MCE 75271* (3) [id.]. Zylis-Gara, Quilico, Winbergh, Massis, R. France Ch. & New PO, Jordan.

Chausson, like many of his French colleagues in the 1890s, was a dedicated Wagnerian, and in *Le roi Arthus*, based on the legend of King Arthur, he boldly produced a French Wagnerian epic to answer Bayreuth in its own language. Though completed ten years before the composer's tragic death – he was knocked off his bicycle and killed – it was never performed in his lifetime, and has long been dismissed as inflated and unoperatic. This first ever recording helps to right the balance, revealing *Le roi Arthus* as a powerful piece, full of overt Wagnerian echoes, which puts Arthur, Lancelot and Guinevere in a sequence of situations closely parallel to those of King Mark, Tristan and Isolde. The musical parallels are often bare-faced, and the result could easily have emerged as just a big Wagnerian pastiche, but the energy and exuberant lyricism of the piece give it a positive life of its own. The vigour and panache of the opening suggest *Tannhäuser* and *Valkyrie* rather than *Tristan*, while the forthright side of *Parsifal* lies behind the noble music for Arthur himself, a more virile figure than King Mark. The love duets in Tristan-style, of which there are several, have a way of growing ever more lusciously lyrical to bring them close to Massenet and Puccini. In this joint production from Radio France and Erato, Armin Jordan directs a warmly committed performance which brings out the full stature of the work, far more than just a radio recording translated. Gino Quilico in the name part sings magnificently, and the freshness and freedom of Gösta Winbergh's tone is very apt for Lancelot's music. Teresa Zylis-Gara, though not always ideally sweet-toned, is an appealing Guinevere, and the recorded sound is generally full and well balanced, a valuable addition to the catalogue, guaranteed to delight many more than specialists in French opera.

Chávez, Carlos (1899–1978)

Symphonies Nos 1; 2 (Sinfonia India); 3.
*** MMG Dig. **MCD 10002** [id.]. LSO, Mata.

Though several generations younger than Chávez, Eduardo Mata was a personal friend of the composer and studied these symphonies with him, when Chávez himself was earlier recording them for CBS. This coupling of the first three, the most approachable, including the colourful *Sinfonia India* (more a symphonic poem than a symphony), provides an attractive sample from the complete cycle, very well played and recorded.

Cherubini, Luigi (1760–1842)

Coronation mass for King Charles X; Marche religieuse.
*** HMV Dig. **CDC7 49302-2** [id.]. Philh. Ch. & O, Muti.

Beethoven's warm admiration for Cherubini has not prevented his music from falling into neglect. Berlioz, too, spoke with enthusiasm of this *Mass* – as well he might, for one can almost sense his voice in the beautiful opening pages. Born ten years earlier than Beethoven, Cherubini survived him for fifteen years. This *Mass* dates from 1825 and there are signs in the *Gloria* that Cherubini was influenced by both *Fidelio* and the *Ninth Symphony*, and in the *Incarnatus* and *Crucifixus* by the *Missa solemnis*. But Cherubini's church music has a character of its own, beautifully crafted, with moments of real inspiration, such as the closing bars of the *Kyrie*. Muti presents the music with an intensity to hide any limitations, and both chorus and orchestra respond superbly. He secures the widest dynamic refinements (some may feel his dynamic range too extreme) and the digital sound is bold and full, with ceremonial trumpets braying magnificently, particularly in the *Et Resurrexit*. There is an instrumental appendix in the form of a *Marche religieuse*, written for Charles X at communion, which Berlioz described as 'mystic expression in all its purity', and it is indeed a very fine piece. The EMI recording is excellent in every respect.

Requiem in D min.
*** HMV Dig. **CDC7 49301-2** [id.]. Amb. S., Philh. O, Muti.

The darkness of tone in the use of male voices in Cherubini's *D minor Requiem* goes with much solemn minor-key music (a little inflated by Beethovenian standards) and some striking anticipations of Verdi. In this fine, committed performance under Muti, the listener forgets the scarcity of really memorable melodies, and relishes the drama and the distinctive textures, particularly as the recording is outstandingly fine.

Medea.
*** Hung. **HCD 11904/5** [id.]. Sass, Luchetti, Kováts, Takács, Kalmár, Gregor, Hungarian Radio and TV Ch., Budapest SO, Gardelli.

Gardelli conducts a powerful performance of Cherubini's formidable opera, explaining very clearly why Beethoven so admired this composer. Written originally before *Fidelio*, it anticipates much that was to follow in the world of opera, not just with Beethoven or Weber, but even Berlioz. In our times, Maria Callas brought the piece back to life, but the recording she made at La Scala with limited sound gave only a partial idea of her dramatic dynamism, and her supporting cast was seriously flawed. This Hungarian set, originally made in 1978 but sounding very fresh and vivid on CD, shows off the formidable strengths of the Hungarian State Opera, and in particular the artistry of Sylvia Sass, who has rarely if ever sounded as impressive on disc as here, full and firm, the tone creamier than it has latterly become, unexaggerated in expression yet intensely dramatic. One hardly misses the extra individuality of a Callas in a consistently gripping performance, helped by fine support from the other principals, not to mention Gardelli and the orchestra. Kolos Kováts as Creon and Klára Takács as Neris are particularly fine, and Veriano Luchetti is stronger and more individual than he has generally been on disc. Well-balanced sound, cleanly transferred. The two CDs give exceptionally generous measure with 137 minutes of music.

Chopin, Frédéric (1810–49)

CONCERTANTE AND ORCHESTRAL MUSIC

Piano concertos Nos 1 in E min., Op. 11; 2 in F min., Op. 21.
*** DG **415 970-2** [id.]. Zimerman, LAPO, Giulini.
(*) RCA **RD 85612 [RCA 5612-2-RC]. Rubinstein, London New SO, Skrowaczewski or Symphony of the Air, Wallenstein.
** RCA **RD 85317 [RCD1 5317]**. Ax, Phd. O, Ormandy.

(i) *Piano concertos Nos 1;* (ii) *2; Piano sonatas Nos 2 in B flat min.* (*Funeral march*), *Op. 35; 3 in B min., Op. 56.*
(M) **(*) DG *413 235-4* (2) [id.]. Argerich, (i) LSO, Abbado; (ii) Washington Nat. SO, Rostropovich.

Piano concerto No. 1
(*) DG **415 061-2 [id.]. Argerich, LSO, Abbado – LISZT: *Concerto No. 1.***(*)

(i) *Piano concerto No. 1; Andante spianato et Grande polonaise brillante, Op. 22; Piano sonata No. 3 in B min., Op. 58; Mazurka in F sharp min., Op. 59/3; Prelude in C sharp min., Op. 45.*
(B) **(*) DG Walkman *419 089-4* [id.]. Argerich; (i) LSO, Abbado.

(i) *Piano concerto No. 1 in E min., Op. 11; Andante spianato et Grande polonaise, Op. 22; Waltz No. 1 in E flat* (*Grande valse brillante*), *Op. 18.*
(M) *** DG **419 054-2**; *419 054-4*. Krystian Zimerman, (i) Concg. O, Kondrashin.

Piano concerto No. 1; Ballade No. 1, Op. 23; Nocturnes Nos 4 & 5, Op. 15/1–2.
(M) *** HMV **CDM7 69004-2** [id.]; *EG 769004-4*. Pollini, Philh. O, Kletzki.

Piano concerto No. 1; Ballade No. 1 in G min., Op. 23; Nocturnes Nos 4 in F; 5 in F sharp, Op. 15/1 and 2; 7 in C sharp min.; 8 in D flat, Op. 27/1 and 2; Polonaises Nos 5 in F sharp min., Op. 44; 6 in A flat, Op. 53.
(B) *** HMV *TCC2-POR 54275*. Pollini, Philh. O, Kletzki.

(i) *Piano concerto No. 1; Barcarolle, Op. 60; Berceuse in D flat, Op. 57; Fantaisie in F min., Op. 49.*
** CBS **MK 42400** [id.]. Perahia; (i) NYPO, Mehta.

Piano concerto No. 1; Variations on Là ci darem, Op. 2.
(M) ** Ph. **420 706-2**; *420 706-4* [id.]. Arrau, LPO, Inbal.

Pollini's classic recording, made shortly after he won the Warsaw Prize in 1960 as a youth of eighteen, still remains the best available of the *E minor Concerto*, particularly now that the sound has been improved. This is playing of such total spontaneity, poetic feeling and refined judgement that criticism is silenced. It is so marvellously sparkling and the rubato so superbly judged that one forgets about the performers and thinks only of Chopin. This performance is now issued on a mid-priced CD in EMI's Studio series. The digital remastering has been generally successful. Orchestral texture is drier and clearer, with slight loss of bass, but there is better definition; the piano timbre is unimpaired. The additional items come from Pollini's first

HMV solo recital, and the playing is equally distinguished, the recording truthful. There is also a recommendable double-length cassette which includes the whole of that first recital alongside the *Concerto*; it is excellent value and well transferred, if without quite the clarity and presence of the CD.

The CD coupling of Zimerman's performances of the two Chopin *Concertos* with Giulini is also hard to beat. This is arguably the finest version of the *First Concerto* to have appeared in the 1970s and is worthy to stand alongside Pollini's classic account. Zimerman is fresh, poetic and individual in his approach; this is a sparkling, beautifully characterized reading. His reading of the *F minor Concerto* has also won much acclaim, and rightly so. Elegant, arisocratic, sparkling – all these epithets spring to mind; this has youthful spontaneity and at the same time a magisterial authority, combining sensibility with effortless pianism. Both recordings are cleanly detailed. While the balance favours the soloist too much, in this respect the *F minor* is an improvement on the *E minor*, although the piano is still made to sound marginally too close. This leads the field, without question.

Zimerman's alternative mid-price version of the *E minor Concerto* comes from a live performance at the Concertegbouw in 1979, recorded by Hilversum Radio, while its companions come from 1977 Polish recordings. Zimerman gives a characteristically authoritative and poised performance and seems to have established a particularly good rapport with Kondrashin. He is balanced rather forwardly, but not to quite the same extent as in his later record with Giulini in Los Angeles, and there is a little more spontaneity (particularly in the slow movement and finale) than in the studio account. The *Andante spianato* comes from the first LP record DG issued in 1977, while the *Waltz* comes from a Polish record made at the time of the 1975 Warsaw competition and is drier and less open in acoustic. Otherwise the sound is altogether excellent and in no way inferior to the later version. A strong three-star recommendation, particularly given its price.

Rubinstein's performances are no less welcome and, although there must be reservations, both musical and technical, there is much that is unforgettably magical in the solo playing. The *First Concerto* does not quite equal Pollini's account, partly because the (1961) recording does not allow the widest dynamic range and in Skrowaczewski's hands the opening orchestral tutti is a shade bland. But the acoustics of Walthamstow Assembly Hall provide a pleasing bloom on the music making; Rubinstein's shaping of the secondary theme of the first movement is memorable, and in the *Larghetto* his control of colour and rubato are inimitable. The (1958) recording of the *F minor* (despite the use of Carnegie Hall) is strangely confined: the close integration of the piano with the dry orchestral textures gives an impression of a studio rather than a concert hall. Yet again Rubinstein's contribution is an object lesson in the delicate playing of Chopin's poetic moments, with the florid decorations of the slow movement allowed to ripple away with such a natural rubato that they sound as if extemporized. As with nearly all the CD issues of Rubinstein's early recordings, the piano timbre is much fuller and and less twangy than it sounded on the original LPs; indeed in the *First Concerto* it is strikingly believable and natural.

Emanuel Ax is the only other artist to offer both concertos on the same CD. His account of the *F minor* has admirable taste and finesse though not quite the sense of character of his finest rivals. The RCA recording, too, is not quite top-drawer though it is perfectly acceptable. In the *E minor Concerto* Ax and Ormandy are rather better served by the engineers and he is fresh and full of character. Not a first choice, perhaps, in either concerto, but there is still a lot to admire here.

Martha Argerich's recording dates from 1969 and helped to establish her international reputation. The distinction of this partnership is immediately apparent in the opening orchestral ritornello with Abbado's flexible approach. Martha Argerich follows his lead and her affectionate phrasing provides some lovely playing, especially in the slow movement. Perhaps in the passage-work she is sometimes rather too intense, but this is far preferable to the rambling style we are sometimes offered. With excellent recording this is one of the most satisfactory versions available of this elusive concerto. The recording was originally of high quality, and it sounds remarkably fresh in its CD format. Definition is still good, and the ambient warmth of the analogue recording is preserved, although there is very slight recession of the image in pianissimo passages. There is very little background noise. However, there is an alternative Walkman tape, generously coupled with fine performances of the *B minor Sonata*, the *Andante spianato* plus two other pieces. This sounds extremely well and costs much less than the CD. Argerich's performance is also available within a medium-priced set of two chrome tapes, coupled with her rather less successful version of the *F minor Concerto* in which she is partnered by Rostropovich. It is a strong but not always very romantic performance. Although the slow movement has an eloquent climax, its full poetry does not emerge until the closing pages; the finale, though vivacious, is not really memorable. Also included in the package are the *B flat minor Sonata* (from 1975) and the *B minor* (from 1968). Both are fiery, impetuous and brilliant performances, with no want of poetic vision to commend them. They hold their own with many in the catalogue, though both have a highly-strung quality that will not be to all tastes. The sound in the *Concertos* is excellent; the solo piano timbre in the *Sonatas* is somewhat drier.

Perahia produces some wonderfully poetic playing, with an unforced naturalness and a sense of grace that one expects from an artist of his quality. But partnering him with Zubin Mehta, who sees the music from a more extrovert and essentially robust viewpoint, produced inevitable hazards. Orchestral tuttis are strong, even coarse grained and seem ill matched with the delicacy and flair of the soloist. Given better casting, Perahia should give us an account of this concerto second to none, but this is not it. The 1980 recording has transferred vividly to CD and the disc includes also three items from Perahia's 1985 solo recital – see below.

Arrau's playing is immaculately aristocratic but his rubato will not convince everyone. His expressive hesitations do not always grow naturally out of what has gone before and, for all its merits, this would not be a first choice, even at mid-price. The 1973 recording is of fine Philips quality, and the CD transfer retains a truthful timbre; even if the balance gives the soloist undue prominence, the illusion of presence is tangible and the orchestra is clear. The *Variations* makes an attractive bonus. There is a very good cassette.

Piano concerto No. 2 in F min., Op. 21.
(M) *** Decca **417 750-2** [id.]. Ashkenazy, LSO, Zinman – TCHAIKOVSKY: *Piano concerto No. 1.****
(*) CBS Dig. **MK 39153 [id.]. Cécile Licad, LPO, Previn – SAINT-SAËNS: *Concerto No. 2.***(*)
(M) **(*) ASV **CDQS 6003**; *ZCQS 6003* [id.]. Vásáry, N. Sinfonia – SCHUMANN: *Concerto.***(*)
** Decca Dig. **411 942-2** [id.]. András Schiff, Concg. O, Dorati – SCHUMANN: *Concerto.***
// Ph. **416 443-2** [id.]. Clara Haskil, LOP, Markevitch – FALLA: *Nights.***

Piano concerto No. 2; Andante spianato et Grande polonaise brillante, Op. 22; Krakowiak (rondo), Op. 14.
(M) ** Ph. **420 654-2**; *420 654-4* [id.]. Arrau, LPO, Inbal.

Piano concerto No. 2; Krakowiak (rondo), Op. 14.
** Ph. Dig. **410 042-2** [id.]. Davidovich, LSO, Marriner.

(i; ii) *Piano concerto No. 2 in E min.;* (iii) *3 Mazurkas, Op. 59;* (i) *Nocturnes Nos 1 in B flat min., Op. 9/1; 9 in B; 10 in A flat, Op. 32/1–2; in C sharp min., Op. posth.;* (iv) *Waltzes Nos 2, 4, 8–10, 11, 13–14.*
(B) *** DG Walkman *413 425-4* [id.]. (i) Vásáry; (ii) BPO, Kulka; (iii) Argerich; (iv) Zimerman.

Piano concerto No. 2; 3 Mazurkas, Op. 59; Polonaise-Fantaisie, Op. 61; Scherzo No. 2 in B flat min., Op. 31.
(M) ** DG **419 859-2**; *419 859-4* [id.]. Argerich, Washington Nat. SO, Rostropovich.

Ashkenazy's 1965 recording was originally paired with Bach in its LP format, but it has now been sensibly recoupled with a not especially flamboyant, but certainly satisfyingly perceptive account of the Tchaikovsky *B flat minor* for its mid-price Decca Ovation reissue. It is a distinguished performance. Ashkenazy's sophisticated use of light and shade in the opening movement, and the subtlety of phrasing and rubato, are a constant source of pleasure. The recitativo section in the *Larghetto*, which can often sound merely rhetorical, is here shaped with mastery, and there is a delectable lightness of touch in the finale. David Zinman and the players of the LSO are obviously in full rapport with their soloist, and the vintage 1960s recording has been most satisfactorily remastered.

The Walkman collection is excellent value. Tamás Vásáry's performance of the *Concerto* is one of his finest Chopin recordings and the 1964 sound remains first class. The balance is exceptionally convincing. The slow movement is played most beautifully, and in the other movements Kulka's direction of the orchestra has striking character and vigour. Side one is completed by four *Nocturnes* and side two includes a generous selection from Zimerman's distinguished set of the *Waltzes*, with performances as fine as any in the catalogue. It ends with Martha Argerich characteristically volatile in three *Mazurkas*. The transfers to chrome tape are first class throughout. A bargain.

Cécile Licad gives a very impressive account of the *F minor Concerto*: she has the appropriate combination of fire and delicacy. Comparisons with the most distinguished versions are not to her disadvantage; moreover, her sense of style earned her the imprimatur of the International Chopin competition in Warsaw, who chose this for their concerto record prize in 1985. She has excellent support from the LPO under Previn and the benefit of very natural recording, which sounds particularly refined on CD.

Vásáry's newest recording on ASV in which he not only plays but directs the Northern Sinfonia from the keyboard has the advantage of fresher and well-balanced sound, but the playing, while it has much delicacy and refinement, is not so boldly characterized nor as full of ardour and flair as was his earlier account – and there seems little case for his dividing his attentions between the keyboard and the orchestra whose contribution is pale by comparison with the Berliners. There are, however, lovely things and some highly sensitive touches, and the sound is well balanced and cleanly recorded; those looking for an inexpensive CD might well consider this, for the Schumann coupling is both poetic and strong. There is a chrome tape.

Intensely poetic and individual, Schiff's expressiveness has full room to breathe at generally spacious basic speeds. This is gentle Chopin, given an even softer focus by the recorded balance, with piano as well as orchestra placed at a distance against a warmly reverberant acoustic. However, the piano sound is rather boomy at the bottom and twangy at the top, while Concertgebouw ensemble is less crisp than usual.

Clara Haskil's recording dates from 1960 and last appeared, on a mid-priced LP, at the end of that decade. It is well recorded but overpriced on CD. The playing has undoubted freshness, but Clara Haskil gives the impression at times in the first movement that she is playing Mozart. While the *Larghetto* has genuine sensibility, this is not very competitive with Zimerman's CD offering outstanding performances of both concertos.

Bella Davidovich's is a very musical reading, and there is undoubted poetry in the slow movement. She is beautifully recorded and the compact disc offers a particularly natural sound-picture, warmly ambient, yet with excellent definition and detail. This is a pleasure to listen to, yet it must be admitted that the performance is somewhat undercharacterized. However, the attractions of this issue are increased by Davidovich's delightful account of the engaging *Krakowiak rondo*, sparkling and fresh, a very real bonus.

Argerich's recording with Rostropovich is discussed above; it is generously coupled at mid price, and well if dryly recorded, but this would not be a first choice.

Arrau's performance is not always convincingly spontaneous and his rubato will at times seem mannered. The LPO under Inbal give loyal support but, as in the companion CD of the *First Concerto*, the piano is forwardly balanced to dominate the proceedings, and this account is not one to kindle universal enthusiasm; although the couplings are more successful this is for Arrau specialists only. The cassette is acceptable but could be clearer in its orchestral focus.

Pogorelich was invited by DG to make his recording after winning the 1980 Warsaw Chopin competition and the result can certainly be described as charismatic. This is pianism of no mean order, but at the service of a wholly narcissistic sensibility: Chopin doesn't get too much of a look-in (DG **410 507-2**).

Les Sylphides (ballet; orch. Douglas).

(M) *** DG **423 215-2**; *423 215-4* [id.]. BPO, Karajan – DELIBES: *Coppélia*; OFFENBACH: *Gaîté parisienne*.***

(M) *** DG *413 981-4*. BPO, Karajan – DELIBES: *Coppélia suite*.***

(*) Capriccio Dig. **10 073. Berlin RSO, Fricke – DELIBES: *Coppélia*.***

(M) ** Decca *417 600-4* [id.]. Nat. PO, Bonynge – ROSSINI: *Boutique fantasque* **(*); WEBER: *Invitation to the dance*.**(*)

Karajan has the advantage of limpid and svelte playing from the Berlin Philharmonic Orchestra, and he evokes a delicacy of texture which consistently delights the ear. The woodwind solos are played gently and lovingly, and one can feel the conductor's touch on the phrasing. The upper register of the strings is bright, fresh and clearly focused, the recording is full and atmospheric, and this is one of Karajan's finest lighter issues. At medium price it is unbeatable, coupled on CD with not only *Coppélia* (although the suite is not complete) but also Offenbach's *Gaîté parisienne*. The chrome cassette is admirably managed, noticeably more vivid in the upper range. At the time of going to press, the earlier cassette is still listed in the DG catalogue.

The Berlin Radio Symphony Orchestra give the famous ballet its CD début and play it very well. If Fricke's phrasing and feeling for rubato is rather less subtle than Karajan's, the orchestral response is warm and fresh and the recording is splendid, bright yet full with an attractive ambient glow. As sound this is far superior to the older DG version – and the attractive Delibes coupling is more generous, too.

Bonynge's performance shows a genuine feeling for the dance rhythms of the music and the orchestral playing is polished and lively. The Decca tape transfer, too, is first class and the couplings are very generous. This is good value, but Karajan remains unsurpassed for those wanting a tape of this beautiful score.

Cello sonata in G min., Op. 65.

*** Claves **CD 50-703** [**CD 703**]. Claude Starck, Ricardo Requejo – GRIEG: *Cello sonata*.***

Cello sonata in G min., Op. 65; Introduction and polonaise brillante in C, Op. 3.

(M) *** DG *419 860-4* [id.]. Rostropovich, Argerich – SCHUMANN: *Adagio and allegro*.***

With such characterful artists as Rostropovich and Argerich challenging each other, this is a memorably warm and convincing account of the *Cello sonata*, Chopin's last published work, a piece which clicks into focus in such a performance. The contrasts of character between expressive cello and brilliant piano are also richly caught in the *Introduction and polonaise*, and the recording is warm to match. The digital remastering for the Galleria mid-priced reissue is most successful; the sound always refined, with a good balance, is now firmer and clearer. It reproduces most realistically in its chrome-tape format.

The *Cello sonata* never remains long in the catalogue but it is a finely wrought and rewarding piece, particularly when it is played as well as it is here by Claude Starck and Ricardo Requejo.

The performance is fluent and well characterized and, though the recording is not in the very highest flight, it is still eminently truthful; the playing has such authority and dedication that collectors need not hesitate, if the Grieg coupling is suitable.

SOLO PIANO MUSIC

Albumblatt in E; Allegro de concert, Op. 46; Barcarolle, Op. 60; Berceuse, Op. 57; Boléro, Op. 19; 2 Bourrées; Cantabile in B flat; Contredanse in G flat; 3 Écossaises, Op. 72/3; Fugue in A min.; Galop marquis; Largo in E flat; Marche funèbre, Op. 72/2; 3 Nouvelles Études; Rondos, Opp. 1, 5, 16 & 73; Sonata No. 1 in C min., Op. 4; Tarantelle, Op. 43; Variations brillantes, Op. 12; Variation No. 6 from Hexameron; Variations on a German National air; Variations (Souvenir de Paganini); (i) *Variations for piano duet.* (i) *Wiosna* from *Op. 74/2.*
*** Decca **421 035-2** (2) [id.]. Vladimir Ashkenazy; (i) with Vovka Ashkenazy.

Decca have reassembled here much of the less familiar music Ashkenazy included in his complete survey of Chopin's solo piano writing and which he recorded over a decade (1975–85). The original LPs, instead of adopting the usual generic approach, were compiled as a series of mixed programmes which had the benefit of musical contrast and also served to show something of Chopin's musical development. However, given the competition, it was inevitable that the major repertoire should be offered on CD in the more normal groupings. Many of the shorter pieces presented here are very early, the *Écossaises*, for instance, the *Rondos*, Opp. 1 and 5, and the ingenious *Variations on a German National air* (*Der Schweizerbub*). Here as elsewhere, Ashkenazy's playing is often magical, fresh and direct, full of touches of insight. But there are substantial works too, including the *Barcarolle* and *Berceuse*, both superbly done, as is the *Allegro de concert* (1832). The *D major Variations* in which Ashkenazy is joined by his son, come from before 1829 and the *C major Sonata*, still a rarity, from 1827. It is not deeply characteristic, but Ashkenazy makes out a more persuasive account for it than anyone who has recorded it so far. Some of the other miniatures derive from the period 1841–3, when Chopin's relationship with George Sand was at its height, notably the chromatic *Albumblatt*, the two *Bourrées*, the *Galop marquis* and the little *A minor Fugue*. The piano transcription of his song, *Wiosna*, is particularly fetching. Throughout, Ashkenazy's playing is authoritative and poetic, and the recordings are excellent. A number of venues were used, and while the ear registers the slight differences of balance and acoustics, the quality of the digital remastering offers consistent realism and presence.

Andante spianato et Grande polonaise brillante, Op. 22; Barcarolle in F sharp min., Op. 60; Berceuse in D flat, Op. 57; Bolero in C, Op. 19; Impromptus Nos 1–4; Fantaisie-impromptu, Op. 66; 3 Nouvelles études, Op. posth.; Tarantelle in A flat, Op. 43.
*** RCA **RD 89911** [**RCA 5617-2-RC**]. Artur Rubinstein.

In Chopin piano music generally Rubinstein has no superior. The *Andante spianato and Grande polonaise* is a curious but memorable piece that inspires him, and his clear and relaxed accounts of the *Impromptus* make most other interpretations sound forced by comparison. The magnificent *Barcarolle* and *Berceuse* contain some of Chopin's finest inspirations – and if the *Tarantelle* may appear musically less interesting and not very characteristic, in Rubinstein's hands it is a glorious piece, full of bravura. Throughout this generous recital the great pianist's way with Chopin is endlessly fascinating; as in the others of his series, the digital remastering has improved the timbre of the recording, at the same time adding presence.

Allegro de concert, Op. 45; Ballades Nos 1–4; Introduction & variations on Je vends des scapulaires, Op. 12.
*** CRD **CRD 3360**; *CRDC 4060*. Hamish Milne.

Ballades Nos 1–4; Cantabile in B flat; Contredanse in G flat; Feuille d'album in E; Fugue in A min.; Largo in E flat; Souvenie de Paganini in A.
**(*) CBS Dig. *IMT 42207*. Fou Ts'ong.

Ballades Nos 1–4; Impromptus Nos 1–3; Fantaisie-impromptu.
(*) Ph. Dig. **411 424-2 [id.]. Bella Davidovich.

Ballades Nos 1–4; Scherzi Nos 1–4.
*** RCA **RD 89651 [RCD1 7156]**. Artur Rubinstein.
*** Decca **417 474-2** [id.]. Vladimir Ashkenazy.

Ballades Nos 1–4; Scherzi Nos 1–4; Sonatas Nos 2–3.
*** RCA *RK 85460* (3) [*ARK3 5460*]. Artur Rubinstein.

Ballades Nos 1–4; Sonata No. 3 in B min., Op. 58.
(*) HMV Dig. **CDC7 47707-2; *EL 270585-4*. Cécile Ousset.

Rubinstein's readings are unique and the digital remastering has been highly successful. The piano timbre now has more warmth and colour in the middle register, and the slight loss of brightness in the treble must be counted an improvement. The layout on CD is generous, but the chrome tapes share much of the improvement in sound. The performances of the *Ballades* are a miracle of creative imagination. From the romantic splendour of the main theme of the *G minor* to the hushed half-tones of the tiny coda of the *F major*, Rubinstein is at his most inspired. The *Scherzi*, which gain most of all from the improved sound (they were originally very dry), are both powerful and charismatic. The readings of the *Sonatas* are unsurpassed.

Ashkenazy's performances of the *Ballades* and *Scherzi* are not reissues of his first set of recordings made in the 1960s, but are taken from his chronological recitals and were made quite recently. The second and third *Ballades* and the third *Scherzo* are analogue, but the ear hardly registers the difference in sound. The digital recordings are first class, with splendid presence, range and body; only in the *B minor Scherzo* is there a suspicion that the microphones were a little near, to emphasize the prodigious brilliance of Ashkenazy's right hand. The playing is full of poetry and flair, as the opening *G minor Ballade* readily demonstrates, while the *Ballade in A flat* has exceptional warmth and sonority. The *Scherzi* have characteristic panache and the whole programme is imbued with imaginative insights and a recital-like spontaneity.

Hamish Milne gives thoughtful and individual performances of the *Ballades*. They may initially sound understated, but in their freshness and concentration they prove poetic and compelling. Similarly he plays the two rarities with total conviction, suggesting that the *Allegro de concert* at least (originally a sketch for a third piano concerto) is most unjustly neglected. The recorded sound is first rate.

Fou Ts'ong's account of the four *Ballades* on CBS is a fine one and occupies a valued place in the catalogue. Moreover he plays the smaller pieces with a distinction and dedication that completely win one over. The recording is not quite top-drawer, wanting in bloom. All the same it is fully acceptable, and in the cassette format few would find cause to complain.

The unaffected sensitivity of Bella Davidovich's interpretations also gives much pleasure, and she is helped by the excellence of the Philips piano sound. Her performances of the three additional *Impromptus* also enhance the not inconsiderable attractions of this issue.

Cécile Ousset gives a strong, big-boned account of the *Sonata* which has the benefit of a marvellously vivid and realistic EMI recording, with an excellent matching tape. Some of the tenderness and poetry of the slow movement, notoriously difficult to bring off, eludes her though she brings warmth to it. There is more virtuosity than grace in the first movement and in the *Ballades* which complete this well-filled disc. In the latter she has a splendid panache but some ideas are presented in a matter-of-fact, rather direct fashion. Her playing has undoubted polish and spontaneous brilliance, but this issue is not a first recommendation in any of the *Ballades* or the *Sonata*. Other versions of *Ballades* and *Scherzi* are available, by Duchable, Katsaris and Gavrilov, but the field is dominated by the recordings of Rubinstein and Ashkenazy.

Barcarolle, Op. 60; Berceuse, Op. 57; Fantaisie in F min., Op. 49; Impromptu No. 1 in A flat, Op. 29; Impromptu No. 2 in F sharp, Op. 36; Impromptu No. 3 in G flat, Op. 51.
*** CBS Dig. **MK 39708**; *IMT 39708* [id.]. Murray Perahia.

Perahia confirms the impression made in his *Sonata* record and his account of the *Préludes* that he is a Chopin interpreter of the highest order. There is an impressive range of colour and an imposing sense of order. This is highly poetic playing and an indispensable acquisition for any Chopin collection. The CBS recording does him justice. There is an excellent cassette, losing only a little of the upper range of the CD.

Barcarolle in F sharp, Op. 60; Berceuse in D flat, Op. 57; Fantaisie in F. min., Op. 49; Nocturne No. 4 in F, Op. 15/1; Polonaise No. 4 in C min., Op. 40/2; Sonata No. 3 in B min., Op. 58.
(M) **(*) Pickwick Dig. **PCD 834**. John Ogdon.

John Ogdon's collection of favourite Chopin items presents a generous and attractive mid-price digital CD of fresh and thoughtful performances, not as electrifying as some he recorded earlier in his career but often bold and full of individual insights. His speeds for the slower pieces are at times daringly extreme, but he sustains them well, and the delicacy of much that he does is a delight, set in contrast to his natural strength in bravura. Bright, clear, realistic recording, giving the piano a powerful presence. The recital plays for 73′ 25″.

Barcarolle in F sharp, Op. 60; Berceuse in D flat, Op. 57; Fantasie in F min., Op. 49; Polonaise No. 7 (Polonaise-Fantaisie), Op. 61; Souvenir de Paganini in A; Variations brillantes Op. 12.
(M) **(*) EMI *TC-EMX 2117*. Daniel Barenboim.

Barenboim's recital dates from 1974. He is imaginative and persuasive not only in the great mature works which make up the bulk of this collection, but also in the two rarities, the *Souvenir de Paganini* and the *Variations*, both sparklingly performed. He rarely if ever fails to convey a sense of new discovery: his approach is never predictable, and this especially applies to the *Barcarolle* and *Berceuse*. Excellent analogue recording, with the upper range just a little dulled by the iron-oxide transfer.

Études, Op. 10/1–12; Op. 25/1–12; 3 Nouvelles études.
*** Chan. Dig. **CHAN 8482**; *ABTD 1194* [id.]. Louis Lortie.

Études, Op. 10, Nos 1–12; Op. 25, Nos 1–12.
*** HMV Dig. **CDC7 47452-2** [id.]; *EL 747452-4*. Andrei Gavrilov.
*** Decca **414 127-2** [id.]. Vladimir Ashkenazy.
*** DG **413 794-2** [id.]. Maurizio Pollini.
** Erato Dig. **ECD 88001** [id.]. François-René Duchable.
(M) *(*) Ph. **420 705-2**; *420 705-4*. Nikita Magaloff.

Andrei Gavrilov's performances bring an exuberant virtuosity that is impossible to resist, even if some of the tempi are breathtakingly fast, as in what Joan Chissell, in her excellent notes, describes as the 'spitfire velocity' of Op. 10/4 or the 'dancing triplets' of Op. 10/5 *in G flat*. Yet the sustained legato of the famous *No. 3 in E major* is lovely, and his poetic feeling, both here and in *No. 6 in E flat minor*, is indisputable. The impulsive bravura is often engulfing, so that one feels the need to take a breath on the soloist's behalf after the furious account of the

Revolutionary study, but this is prodigious playing, given a bold forward recording to match. There is an excellent cassette. With any reservations noted, the spontaneous brilliance and great technical command of Gavrilov's set give it the strongest claims, even if the three *Nouvelles Etudes* are not included.

Louis Lortie's set of the 24 *Études* can hold its own with the best and justifies the golden opinions this young Canadian pianist collected at the 1984 Leeds competition. His playing has a strong poetic feeling and an effortless virtuosity which should win him many admirers. He is beautifully recorded at The Maltings, Snape (whose acoustic occasionally clouds the texture), but collectors wanting a first-class account of these extraordinary pieces will find the youthful Lortie an admirable alternative to the familiar keyboard lions who have dominated the catalogues for so long; moreover the Chandos disc is the only CD also to include the three *Nouvelles Études* of 1839. The equivalent chrome tape is also first class, the sound highly realistic.

Ashkenazy's 1975 version sounds wonderfully vivid in its CD form and, although there is little to choose between his performances and those of Pollini, the warmer sound that Decca provide for Ashkenazy might well make this a first choice for many collectors. However, honours are very evenly divided between them.

Pollini's record also comes from 1975 and sounds splendidly fresh in its digitally remastered form. This is playing of much stature. These are vividly characterized accounts, masterly and with the sound eminently present and seeming freer than in its original LP form.

François-René Duchable proves the equal of his rivals technically and brings considerable finesse and polish to the *Études*. He is not perhaps quite as imaginative in the more inward pieces as his distinguished colleagues, but he is obviously an artist to reckon with, and is generally well recorded. This is very much more successful than his *Ballades*.

Nikita Magaloff on CD is well recorded and his Philips issue has the advantage of economy. These are eminently serviceable accounts, with felicitous touches that compel admiration, but they fall short of the distinction that Ashkenazy, Pollini and Lortie bring to this repertoire. The cassette is boldly transferred, but because of the resonance the image is not always absolutely clear cut.

Mazurkas Nos 1–51.
*** RCA **RD 85171** (2) [**RCA 5614-2-RC**]; *RK 85171* [CRK2-5171]. Artur Rubinstein.
*** Decca **417 584-2** (2) [id.]. Vladimir Ashkenazy.

Mazurkas Nos 1–49.
** HMV Dig. **CDS7 47932-8** (2). Dinorah Varsi.

The *Mazurkas* contain some of Chopin's most characteristic music. That they are often ignored by virtuoso pianists simply reflects the fact that as a rule they are less tricky technically, and concert pianists prefer to show off. Yet, as Rubinstein continually demonstrates, they contain some wonderfully pianistic ideas, none the worse for being expressed simply. At the one end you have certain *Mazurkas* which are first cousins to Chopin's *Polonaises*, and at the other end some that might almost be *Nocturnes*, while a lot in the middle could almost as readily have been included with the *Waltzes*. All are delightful, even if there is no need to linger very long over some of them. Rubinstein could never play in a dull way to save his life, and in his hands these fifty-one pieces are endlessly fascinating, though on occasion in such unpretentious music one would welcome a completely straight approach. As with the *Ballades* and *Scherzi*, the digital remastering has brought a piano timbre much more pleasing to European ears. The clarity of articulation is not dimmed, yet the quality is softer-grained than with the original LPs, slightly more so on the chrome cassettes (which are excellent) than on the pair of CDs.

Ashkenazy's recordings were made at different times between 1975 and 1985. His are finely articulated, aristocratic accounts and the sound is amazingly fresh and consistent, considering the time-span involved. He includes the posthumously published *Mazurkas* (the one dedicated to Emile Galliard and the so-called *Notre temps*). These are distinguished performances as far as complete sets are concerned, and the recording quality is more modern and more natural than that afforded to Rubinstein, with a believable presence.

Dinorah Varsi is a sound guide in this repertoire. She has both poetry and intensity, indeed a certain inflammable quality that is appealing. As in her set of the *Nocturnes*, she has recourse to an edition used by Chopin's pupil, Jane Stirling, and her interpretations are well thought out and fully characterized. Again as in her set of the *Nocturnes*, Dinorah Varsi includes only those *Mazurkas* with opus numbers, which puts her at a disadvantage compared with her rivals. Nor is the recording in the very first flight, though it is perfectly acceptable.

Fou Ts'ong is also currently recording the *Mazurkas* for CBS; so far the first thirteen have been released (*IMT 42207*). He brings great imagination to many of them (and in particular the *A minor*, Op. 17/4); though there are some occasional lapses and some inelegant forte tone, there is much to admire. The recording, however, is less than ideal; in the cassette format the treble sounds a little unnatural and there is a touch of shallowness.

Nocturnes Nos 1–19.
*** RCA **RD 89563** (2) [**RCA 5613-2-RC**]; (M) *GK 89836* (Nos 1–10); *89837* (Nos 11–19). Artur Rubinstein.
*(*) HMV Dig. **CDS7 47755-8** (2). Dinorah Varsi.

Nocturnes Nos 1–21.
*** Decca **414 564-2**; *414 564-4* (2) [id.]. Vladimir Ashkenazy.
*** Ph. **416 440-2**; *7699 088* (2) [id.]. Claudio Arrau.
(M) **(*) DG *419 368-4* (2). Tamás Vásáry.

Rubinstein in Chopin is a magician in matters of colour; again and again throughout these two discs, there are moments of perfection where the timing of a phrase exactly catches the mood and atmosphere of the composer's inspiration. His magical sense of nuance and the seeming inevitability of his rubato demonstrate a very special musical imagination in this repertoire. The recordings were the best he received in his Chopin series for RCA, and the quality is now finer still in these excellent CD transfers. There is no appreciable background noise. On tape these recordings are available at mid-price on two separate cassettes.

Ashkenazy's set includes the two posthumously published *Nocturnes*: the performances are all drawn from the fifteen-LP set he has recorded over the last decade. The disparity in dates seems not to have affected the consistency of sound that the Decca engineers have achieved. The playing is splendidly ruminative and atmospheric. As always, Ashkenazy is completely attuned to Chopin's unique sound-world, though occasionally some may feel that his tone is too big in fortissimo passages for these intimate pieces – as if he is playing in a large concert hall rather than in a late-night salon.

Arrau's approach clearly reflects his boyhood training in Germany, creating tonal warmth coupled with inner tensions of the kind one expects in Beethoven. In this he has something in common with Barenboim (see below). With the *Nocturnes* it can be apt to have an element of seriousness, and this is a very compelling cycle, full of poetry, the rubato showing an individual but very communicable sensibility. This is among Arrau's very finest Chopin recordings. It was made in the Amsterdam Concertgebouw in 1977/8; the analogue recording sounds wonderfully natural in its new CD format, though the rich, refined sound-balance also projects well on the excellent cassettes.

Those looking for an inexpensive complete set of *Nocturnes* on tape might well consider Tamás Vásáry's fine collection from the mid-1960s. The recording is excellent and the chrome transfers offer first-class quality, the piano timbre well focused but suitably mellow. The playing has undoubted freshness, character and insight, and Vásáry's flexibility in moulding a Chopin phrase to find its kernel of poetry is always apparent. His thoughtfulness of approach brings a fairly consistent mood of repose – though he can break out of this when the music demands it – so his performances are suitable for the late evening, even if they may at times seem a little introvert.

One point of interest about Dinorah Varsi's set on EMI is that she bases her edition on photocopies of an edition belonging to Chopin's pupil, Jane Stirling, which have some indications pencilled in by the composer himself. However, she omits the two *C minor Nocturnes*, both published posthumously, though she does include the *E minor*, Op. 72, No. 1, which was also published after Chopin's death. There is some sensitive playing but some moments of exaggeration as well, in terms of both dynamics and tempi. Moreover she is recorded in a drier acoustic than her rivals.

The 1980 Chopin prizewinner, the Vietnamese pianist, Dang Thai Son, has also recorded the *Nocturnes* in Japan (Victor **VDC 5019-30**); were these to become available in the lifetime of this book, they would rate very highly indeed. The playing is poetic and authoritative, and very well recorded too.

The *Nocturnes* are also available on two bargain-priced Supraphon CDs (**2SUP 0007** and **2SUP 0022**). Pavel Štěpán's performances are acceptable but not really distinguished and the CD transfer emphasizes the treble at the expense of the piano's middle and lower sonorities.

Nocturnes Nos 2 in E flat, Op. 9/2; 4 in F; 5 in F sharp; 6 in G min., Op. 15/1–3; 7 in C sharp min., Op. 27/1; 9 in B, Op. 32/1; 11 in G min.; 12 in G, Op. 37/1–2; 13 in C min.; 14 in F sharp min., Op. 48/1–2; 15 in F min., Op. 55/1; 18 in E, Op. 62/2; 19 in E min., Op. posth.
(*) DG Dig. **415 117-2 [id.]. Daniel Barenboim.

Barenboim's performances, taken from his complete set, are intense, thoughtful and poetic readings, the phrasing lovingly moulded, following rather in the mid-European tradition. Compared with Rubinstein, they lack a mercurial dimension, and the chosen selection tends to emphasize their repose. The sound is first class.

Polonaises Nos 1–7.
*** RCA **RD 89814** [RCA **5615-2**]; (M) *GK 89920* (Nos 1–6 only). Artur Rubinstein.
*** DG **413 795-2** [id.]. Maurizio Pollini.

Polonaises Nos 1–9.
(M) ** Ph. **420 704-2**; *420 704-4* [id.]. Adam Harasiewicz.

Artur Rubinstein has recorded these pieces more than once before, but his last attempt – recorded in Carnegie Hall – was as freshly individual as ever. Master pianist that he was, he seems actually to be rethinking and recreating each piece, even the hackneyed '*Military*' and *A flat* works, at the very moment of performance. Other performances may bring out different facets of the pieces, but none is likely to outshine Rubinstein's in easy majesty and natural sense of spontaneous phrasing. The equivalent mid-priced cassette omits No. 7, the *Polonaise-Fantaisie*.

Pollini offers playing of outstanding mastery as well as subtle poetry, and the DG engineers have made a decent job of the transfer. This is magisterial playing, in some ways more commanding than Rubinstein (and rather better recorded) though not more memorable.

Adam Harasiewicz's collection generously offers the first nine *Polonaises* including the *Polonaise-Fantaisie* in which he displays a thoughtful poetic feeling which is already apparent in the opening *C sharp minor* work, Op. 26/1. He is less commanding in the *'Military' Polonaise* although the *A flat* is attractively unaggressive. There is some glittering digital dexterity in *No. 8 in D minor*, and he is at his best both here and in the flexible account of *No. 9 in B flat*. The recording (from 1967–70) is bold and full, not as sharply focused as with Rubinstein and Pollini, but naturally balanced. There is a well-managed chrome tape. This is good value at mid-price with 67′ 45″ of music, although the playing is not really distinctive.

24 Preludes, Op. 28.
*** DG **413 796-2** [id.]. Maurizio Pollini.

24 Preludes, Op. 28; Barcarolle, Op. 60; Polonaise No. 4 in C min., Op. 40/2; Rondeau in E flat, Op. 16.
** Ph. **420 389-2** [id.]. Bella Davidovich.

24 Preludes, Op. 28; Preludes Nos 25, Op. 43; 26, Op. posth.
** HMV Dig. **CDC7 47662-2**; *EL 270494-4*. Dmitri Alexeev.

24 Preludes, Op. 28; Preludes Nos 25–26; Barcarolle, Op. 60; Polonaise No. 6 in A flat, Op. 53; Scherzo No. 2 in B flat min., Op. 31.
(M) **(*) DG **415 836-2**; *415 836-4* [id.]. Martha Argerich.

24 Preludes, Op. 28; Preludes Nos 25–26; Impromptu Nos 1–4; Fantaisie-impromptu, Op. 66.
*** Decca **417 476-2** [id.]. Vladimir Ashkenazy.

Ashkenazy's set of the *Preludes* was recorded in 1979 and the CD transfer is first class, with plenty of colour and body to the timbre as well as presence. The reading overall combines drama and power with finesse and much poetic delicacy when called for. The presence of the four *Impromptus* and the *Fantaisie-impromptu* makes this CD even more attractive. There is an aristocratic quality about these excellently recorded performances that is wholly Chopinesque.

Pollini's set, it goes without saying, is also highly distinguished. He has impeccable taste in handling rubato, the firmest sense of line and form and no trace of excess sentiment; the reading evinces an effortless and complete mastery. His recording is good; though the sound is not as natural and fresh as the Decca, the DG engineers have been very successful with the present transfer. However, the absence of later *Preludes* or of any other additional items is not in this issue's favour.

Martha Argerich's 1977 set of *Preludes* is generously supplemented on her Galleria reissue with other pieces recorded between 1961 and 1975. The *Preludes* show her at her finest, spontaneous and inspirational, though her moments of impetuosity may not appeal to all tastes. But her instinct is sure and the music making flows onwards compellingly, with many poetic individual touches. The other pieces are splendidly played and the *Scherzo* impressively demonstrates her technical command, if that were not already apparent from the *Preludes*. The digital remastering gives the piano image striking presence and the recording is resonant and full in timbre. But at fortissimo levels the timbre becomes hard in the CD format, and the chrome cassette is preferable.

There is a great deal to admire in Dmitri Alexeev's splendidly recorded set of the *Preludes*. In some of them he is second to none and he is rarely unilluminating. However, although he carries all before him much of the time, elsewhere he leaves one impressed but unmoved. *No. 17 in A flat*, for instance, is rather too understated, while there is some ugly fortissimo tone in the left hand in *No. 9 in E major*. There is much fine artistry here, but this is not a first choice.

Bella Davidovich is also extremely well recorded by the Philips engineers and she plays these pieces, and her bonus items, with no mean degree of accomplishment and personality, though she is not always scrupulous about dynamic nuances. In terms of musical characterization she is not the equal of Ashkenazy or Pollini.

24 Preludes, Op. 28; Sonata No. 2 in B flat min. (*Funeral march*), *Op. 35.*
(M) ** Pickwick Dig. **PCD 862** [id.]. Howard Shelley.

This is good value at mid-price, with very generous measure. There are no grumbles about Howard Shelley's playing – his virtuosity and sensitivity can be taken for granted. He gives eminently thoughtful and musicianly accounts both of the *Preludes* and of the *B flat minor Sonata*, but the recording is rather bottom-heavy and tubby, and ideally needs more room to expand.

Scherzos Nos 1–4; Fantaisie-impromptu, Op. 66. (See also above with *Ballades.*)
*** Ph. Dig. **412 610-2** [id.]. Claudio Arrau.

Arrau's last recording of the four *Scherzi* was in the 1950s; this new one was made in Munich, just after the artist's eightieth birthday. There is little sign of age, even if he would have produced a greater weight of sonority at the height of his prowess. However, these accounts are full of wise and thoughtful perceptions and remarkable pianism, recorded with great presence and clarity. The middle section of the *First Scherzo* may strike some collectors as unusually slow and a trifle mannered, but there are magical things elsewhere, notably in the *Fourth.* Arrau's fire may have lost some of its youthful charisma, but the gains in wisdom and delicacy of feeling are adequate compensation. The Philips engineers seem to produce piano quality of exceptional realism. However, this is short measure.

Sonata No. 2 in B flat min. (*Funeral march*), *Op. 35; Andante spianato et Grande Polonaise brillante, Op. 22; Ballade No. 3 in A flat, Op. 47; 4 Mazurkas, Op. 24; Variations brillantes, Op. 12.*
(M) **(*) Olympia **OCD 193** [id.]. Peter Katin.

Sonata No. 2 in B flat min. (*Funeral march*), *Op. 35; Andante spianato et Grande Polonaise brillante, Op. 22; Études, Op. 10/3–4; Nocturne No. 8 in D flat, Op. 27/2.*
(*) Mer. **ECD 84070; *KE 77070* [id.]. John Bingham.

Sonata No. 2 (*Funeral march*)*; Ballade No. 1 in G min., Op. 23; Barcarolle, Op. 60; Nocturnes: in F, F sharp, Op. 15/1–2; Scherzo No. 2 in B flat min., Op. 31.*
(M) *** Decca **417 729-2** [id.]. Vladimir Ashkenazy.

Ashkenazy's 1972 recording of the *Second Sonata* (plus the two *Nocturnes*) was made during a live recital at Essex University, and the concert was also filmed. Decca made sure that the sound suffered no loss from the circumstances; indeed the CD transfer is pleasingly natural: the piano has splendid resonance and realism, and now the applause has been edited out. The performance of the *Sonata* is of the highest distinction, of great power and eloquence, yet with the poetry fully realized – the playing of the middle section of the slow movement is exquisite. If the final *Presto* of the work is not absolutely immaculate, who will cavil, with music making of this quality? The two *Nocturnes*, recorded at the same time, have a comparable spontaneity; the rest of the programme, taken from records made at Decca's West Hampstead studios in 1964 and 1967, is also distinguished, particularly the *Barcarolle*. At mid-price this is excellent value, offering only a few seconds short of an hour of music.

John Bingham is a much underrated artist – he is surely among the finest of British pianists and has not received the recognition that is his due. His account of the *Sonata* is highly sensitive and most musicianly and if it lacks the sense of scale or range of rivals such as Ashkenazy or Rubinstein it has a special dimension of its own. He appears to withdraw into a completely different world in the trio section of the second movement and some may find him far too rhapsodic here – and in the first movement's second group. There is some most beautiful playing in the *Nocturne* and the two studies. The Meridian recording is not made in an ideal acoustic, but on tape the piano timbre is warm and pleasing. This playing is certainly full of individuality.

Pogorelich's self-aware reading of the *B flat minor Sonata* does not wear well. There is no doubting the masterly pianism nor the extraordinary feeling for colour, but on CD his interpretation seems more self-conscious than ever (DG **415 123-2**).

Sonatas Nos 2 in B flat min. (Funeral march), Op. 35; 3 in B min., Op. 58.
*** DG Dig. **415 362-2**; *415 362-4* [id.]. Maurizio Pollini.
(M) *** EMI Dig. **CD-EMX 9515**; *TC-EMX 2121*. Philip Fowke.
(*) Erato **ECD 88083 [id.]. François-René Duchable.

Sonatas Nos 2 (Funeral march); 3 in B min., Op. 58; Fantaisie in F min., Op. 49.
*** RCA **RD 89812 [RCA 5616-2-RC]**. Artur Rubinstein.
*** Decca **417 475-2** [id.]. Vladimir Ashkenazy.

Sonatas Nos 2 in B flat min. (Funeral march), Op. 35; 3 in B min., Op. 58; Scherzo No. 3 in C sharp min., Op. 39.
(M) **(*) DG **419 055-2**; *419 055-4* [id.]. Martha Argerich.

Sonata No. 3 in B min., Op. 58; Ballade No. 4 in F min., Op. 52; Barcarolle, Op. 60; Mazurkas, Op. 59/1–3; Polonaise-Fantaisie, Op. 61.
(M) **(*) Olympia **OCD 186** [id.]. Peter Katin.

Rubinstein's readings of the *Sonatas* are unsurpassed, with a poetic impulse that springs directly from the music and a control of rubato to bring many moments of magic, not least in the second group of the first movement of the *B flat minor Sonata* and later in the central section of the *Funeral march*. The sound is improved, too, though both Pollini and Ashkenazy gain in this respect.

Pollini's performances are enormously commanding; his mastery of mood and structure gives these much played *Sonatas* added stature. The slow movement of Op. 35 has tremendous drama and atmosphere, so that the contrast of the magical central section is all the more telling. Both works are played with great distinction, but while the CD gives plenty of presence, the balance is just a shade close, and the sound is good rather than special, as with many others of Pollini's DG records.

Philip Fowke, who in the past has displayed inhibitions in the recording studio, gives highly impressive readings of both *Sonatas*, wide-ranging in their expression, dramatic and poetic, as when he is playing live. He is perhaps at his finest in the *B minor Sonata*, the first movement freely rhapsodic in feeling, the *Largo* both thoughtful and intense. His formidable articulation in the scherzo is not quite matched in the finale of the *B flat minor Sonata*, but this too is a fine performance, the *Funeral march* gently solemn and the middle section touchingly nostalgic. The recording is admirably realistic and full in timbre and presence, with the warm acoustics of St Barnabas Church, Finchley, creating an agreeable background ambience without clouding detail. The cassette sounds much mellower than the CD and the presence is diminished by the use of iron-oxide stock.

Ashkenazy's *B flat minor Sonata* is the version released in 1981 in the context of his complete LP survey, not the fine 1972 University of Essex concert performance (see above). Both this and its companion are impressive, though not necessarily a first choice – if such there can be – in this field. There is a shade less tenderness and vision in the slow movement of the *B minor* than there is in some rival versions, though the *B flat minor* has wonderful panache. An authoritative account of the *F minor Fantasy* provides an excellent makeweight. The recordings still sound first class.

Duchable's readings are strongly impulsive and have character. His account of No. 3 is among the finest to have appeared in recent years, commandingly eloquent, with a memorable slow movement, rhapsodic in feeling, and a brilliantly articulated finale, exhilarating in its bravura. A similar sense of drama pervades the *B flat minor Sonata*, with its stormy first movement. The *Funeral march* is immediately commanding in its intensity, with the middle section elegiacally simple (much straighter than with Rubinstein). The return of the main theme is dramatic. The finale, by contrast, is under-articulated. Duchable is given a bold, full piano image. Some might find his reading of Op. 35 too intensely volatile – Rubinstein's performance has an aristocratic poise which is not part of Duchable's vocabulary – but his playing is commandingly spontaneous and has different insights to offer.

It is good to see the Chopin performances of Peter Katin restored to the catalogue; both these Olympia CDs bring beautiful sound, realistically balanced by the Norwegian team of producer and engineer, Arne-Peter Rognan and Arne Akselberg. The earlier recital (**OCD 186**) was recorded in Bristol, the second (**OCD 193**) at the Henie-Onstad Centre in Oslo with, if anything, even better results. Katin produces a consistently refined sonority throughout the dynamic range and there is much sensitivity and poetic feeling in the *Andante spianato* and *Mazurkas*. His is an essentially ruminative and private approach, and in both the *Ballades* and *Sonatas* one misses a sense of scale and the narrative grip one finds in Rubinstein and Ashkenazy. But there is so much that is felicitous and responsive here that this is of comparatively little account. Admirers of this fine artist need not hesitate.

Martha Argerich's recordings date from 1975 and 1968 respectively. Both are fiery, impetuous and brilliant performances, with no want of poetic vision to command them. They hold their own with many in the catalogue, though each has a highly strung quality that will not be to all tastes. The recording is vivid and clear, but a little dry.

Waltzes Nos 1–19.
*** HMV Dig. **CDC7 47501**; *EL 270289-4* [Ang. *4AE 34488*]. Dimitri Alexeev.
*** Decca **414 600-2**; *414 600-4* [id.]. Vladimir Ashkenazy.
** Ph. **412 890-2** [id.]. Zoltán Kocsis.

Waltzes Nos 1–14.
*** RCA **RD 89564** [**RCD1-5492**]; (M) *GK 89835*. Artur Rubinstein.
*** Ph. **400 025-2** [id.]. Claudio Arrau.
** Erato **ECD 88067** [id.]. Maria João Pires.

Waltzes Nos 1–14; Barcarolle, Op. 60; Mazurka in C sharp min., Op. 50/3; Nocturne in D flat, Op. 27/2.
❀ *** HMV **CDC7 47390-2** [id.]. Dinu Lipatti.

All current versions of the Chopin *Waltzes* – for all the brilliance and realism of their digital sound – tend to rest in the shadow of Lipatti's set. These classic performances were an obvious and urgent candidate for transfer to the new medium. They were recorded by Walter Legge in the rather dry acoustic of a Swiss Radio studio at Geneva in the last year of Lipatti's short life, and with each LP reincarnation they seem to have grown in wisdom and subtlety. Their appearance on CD, together with the *Barcarolle* and *Nocturne* recorded in 1947, cannot be too warmly welcomed and the transfer has been most successfully accomplished. The reputation of these meticulous performances is fully deserved.

Dimitri Alexeev's record of the *Waltzes* retains its high profile among modern recordings. In the new format it sounds excellent. Alexeev has personality, a genuinely aristocratic feeling and a natural sense of style. This music making is unforced and the varied moods of these pieces are always successfully projected. The greater definition and range of the CD enhances its claims, though there is also a good cassette.

Ashkenazy's recordings were made over the best part of a decade (1977–85) but, despite the time-span, the sound is expertly matched by the engineers. There is an impressive feeling for line throughout, an ability to make these *Waltzes* seem spontaneous and yet as carefully wrought as a tone-poem. Decca have also made them available in cassette format, and the chrome tape is bright and clean, with plenty of body.

When we first discussed the original LP of Rubinstein's performances, we spoke of their chiselled perfection, suggesting the metaphor of finely cut and polished diamonds, emphasized by the crystal-clear, rather hard quality of the RCA recording. The digital remastering has softened the edges of the sound image, and there is an illusion of added warmth. Rubinstein's pacing is always perceptive, his rubato subtle and his phrasing elegant, and now the playing seems less aloof, more directly communicative. The CD is a separate issue with a companion mid-priced cassette. On tape, the quality is slightly softer-grained but still very pleasing.

Arrau produces his own specially rich, rounded tone-colours and is accorded beautiful sound by the Philips engineers. These are performances of elegance and finesse, though there are, as always, moments when the great pianist invests detail with a heavier significance than some listeners may feel is justified. But these are readings of real personality and, however the individual collector may respond, they are searching and considered. The compact disc is very fine indeed, and there is virtually no appreciable background noise stemming from the analogue master.

Unlike many of her rivals, Maria João Pires does not include the posthumously published pieces. She has a real sense of style, good musical judgement and taste, along with an impeccable technique. Moreover, she is well recorded, and it is only rarely (in the *A minor*, Op. 34, No. 2) that she falls short of real poetic distinction. The Erato recording has fine realism and presence.

Zoltán Kocsis is full of fire and temperament but just a little too concerned to dazzle us with his superb technical prowess. Many of these are breathlessly fast and rushed, though there is no want of poetry in some of them. He includes five of the posthumous waltzes omitted by Arrau and Rubinstein. Kocsis is vividly – albeit too closely – recorded, but his playing is too eccentric and rushed to displace Alexeev and Ashkenazy.

RECITAL COLLECTIONS

Ballade No. 1 in G min., Op. 23; Barcarolle in F sharp, Op. 60; Fantasy in F min., Op. 49; Impromptus: in F sharp, Op. 36; in G flat, Op. 51; Nocturnes: in C sharp min., Op. 27/1; in D flat, Op. 34/1; Polonaise in A flat, Op. 53; Waltz in E flat, Op. 34/1.
(B) **(*) Castle Dig. **CICD 1010**. Craig Shepherd.

It is a pity that Craig Shepherd opens his recital with the *Fantasy in F minor*, as the rather deadpan performance is short on fantasy and is the least attractive item here. The *Barcarolle* flows much more readily and the *Ballade* satisfyingly combines flair and poetry. The *Impromptu in F sharp*, a memorable piece, is also finely done, and both *Nocturnes* show him at his best: the *D flat major*, perhaps the loveliest of the whole set, brings most sensitive nuancing and a fine control of colour and dynamic. It is the highlight of a generally enjoyable recital, very realistically recorded and offered at a reasonable price.

'Favourite Chopin': Ballade No. 1 in G min., Op. 23; Études, Op. 10/3, 4, 5 & 12 (Revolutionary); Mazurkas: in F min., Op. 7/3; A min., Op. 17/4; D flat, Op. 30/3; D, Op. 33/2; E min., Op. 41/2; F sharp min., Op. 59/3; Nocturne in F sharp min., Op. 55/1; Polonaises: in A, Op. 40/1; A flat, Op. 53; Prelude in B min., Op. 28/6; Scherzo No. 1 in B min., Op. 20; Waltzes: in A min., Op. 34/2; C sharp min., Op. 64/2.

(***) CBS **MK 42306** [id.]. Vladimir Horowitz.

The playing here is dazzling; its virtuosity is enormously refreshing and so often illumined by the sense of poetry and fine musical judgement that Horowitz abundantly commands that one is at a loss to single out individual items for specific admiration. Yet the recording seldom reflects any credit on the CBS engineers – and while one would like to say that the playing is so remarkable that reservations on this score are of secondary account, this, alas, is not so. The CD remastering emphasizes the lack of bloom and body to the piano sound which deprives the opening *Polonaise in A flat major* of its breadth. This comes from a studio session, but other items were recorded at public performances; the *C sharp minor Waltz* includes audience noises and is poorly focused, as are the excerpts from the 1966 Carnegie Hall recital, the *Ballade* and *Nocturne*. The general thinness of timbre makes the *A major Polonaise* sound aggressive, and it is a great pity that the CD transfer was not able to produce a more natural sound, or avoid the stridency which often occurs at levels above *mezzo forte*. The recital plays for 72′, but the ear needs a rest in the middle!

Ballade No. 1 in G min., Op. 23; Mazurkas Nos 19 in B min., 20 in D flat, Op. 30/2–3; 22 in G sharp min., 25 in B min., Op. 33/1 and 4; 34 in C, Op. 56/2; 43 in G min., 45 in A min., Op. 67/2 and 4; 46 in C; 47 in A min., 49 in F min., Op. 68/1–2 and 4; Prelude No. 25 in C sharp min., Op. 45; Scherzo No. 2 in B flat min., Op. 31.
(*) DG **413 449-2 [id.]. Arturo Benedetti Michelangeli.

Although this recital somehow does not quite add up as a whole, the performances are highly distinguished. Michelangeli's individuality comes out especially in the *Ballade*, a very free rhapsodic performance which nevertheless holds together by the very compulsion of the playing. Michelangeli's special brand of poetry is again felt in the *Mazurkas*, which show a wide range of mood and dynamic; and the *Scherzo* is extremely brilliant, yet without any suggestion of superficiality. The piano tone is real and lifelike, and has been most realistically transferred to CD.

'Favourite Chopin': Ballade No. 3 in A flat, Op. 47; Barcarolle in F sharp, Op. 60; Études, Op. 10, Nos. 3 in E (Tristesse); 5 in G flat (Black keys); 12 in C min. (Revolutionary); Op. 25, No. 11 in A min. (Winter wind); Nocturne in F min., Op. 55/1; Polonaise in A., Op. 40/1; Preludes: in D sharp (Raindrop), Op. 28/15; in C sharp min., Op. 45; Waltzes: in D flat; C sharp min., Op. 64/1 & 2.
(*) Decca **410 180-2; (M) *410 180-4* [id.]. Vladimir Ashkenazy.

Digitally remastered from recordings made between 1975 and 1982, the sound here is slightly variable, but has striking vividness and presence. The upper range is less soft-grained than on the original LPs, with the treble brightly lit and often producing an edge on top in fortissimos, notably in the *Revolutionary study* and the *Polonaise*, while the *Black keys study* is somewhat clattery. The background silence serves to enhance this effect. Yet the middle range is warm and the bass firm and resonant. As can be seen, the selection is generous (nearly an hour of music) and popular. Ashkenazy is shown at his most commanding, though perhaps the inclusion of more *Nocturnes* would have given a better-balanced picture of his special sensibilities in this repertoire. This recital has now been issued on a mid-priced tape, which sounds well and loses only a little of the presence of the CD; it costs about a third of the price. The slightly metallic quality in the treble remains.

Ballade No. 3 in A flat, Op. 47; Barcarolle in F sharp, Op. 60; Fantaisie in F min., Op. 49; Fantaisie-impromptu, Op. 66; Nocturnes Nos 2 in E flat, Op. 9/2; 5 in F sharp, Op. 15/2; Prelude in D flat, Op. 28/15; Waltzes Nos 7 in C sharp min., Op. 64/2; 9 in A flat, Op. 69/1.
(M) *** Ph. **420 655-2**; *420 655-4* [id.]. Claudio Arrau.

A fine recital showing both poetry and the thoughtful seriousness which distinguishes Arrau's Chopin, which is West rather than East European in spirit. The CD is admirably transferred, bringing the fullness of timbre and natural balance we expect of Philips; but the cassette, too, sounds extremely well.

'Favourite Chopin': Ballade No. 3 in A flat, Op. 47; Études: in G flat, Op. 10/5; A flat, Op. 25/1; G flat, Op. 25/9; Nocturnes Nos 10 in A flat, Op. 32/2; 15 in F min., Op. 55/1; Polonaise No. 6 in A flat, Op. 53; Preludes, Op. 28, Nos 6 in B min.; 20 in C min.; Scherzo No. 3 in C sharp min., Op. 39; Waltzes Nos 1 in E flat (*Grande valse brillante*), *Op. 18; 11 in G flat, Op. 70/1.*
(M) *** EMI *TC-EMX 41 2045-4*. Daniel Adni.

This collection was recorded in 1971 to provide a brilliant début for a young and talented artist who was only nineteen at the date of the recording. His sensibility in this repertoire is striking, and his musicianship is matched by the kind of effortless technique that is essential to give Chopin's music its line and flow. From the glitter and brilliance of the opening *Grande valse brillante* to the evocative yet expansive reading of the famous *'Sylphides' Nocturne in A flat major*, the tonal shading is matched by the spontaneity of the rubato. The whole of the first side of the tape is beautifully balanced to make a miniature recital, working towards a superb account of the *Scherzo in C sharp minor*. This is one of the freshest and most enjoyable Chopin collections available at any price; it is given most natural recorded sound, with sparkle and sonority in equal measure, though the level of the tape drops on side two (most noticeably in the closing *Polonaise*).

Ballade No. 4 in F minor, Op. 52; Études in C min., Op. 10/12; Op. 25/8; Polonaise in A flat, Op. 53; Grand valse brillante in F, Op. 34/3; 4 Mazurkas, Op. 33; Nocturne in F sharp min., Op. 15/2; Sonata No. 3 in B minor, Op. 58.
** DG Dig. **423 067-2** [id.]. Stanislav Bunin.

Stanislav Bunin, still in his early twenties, won the 1983 Marguerite Long Competition in Paris, when he was only sixteen, and the Warsaw Chopin Competition two years later. He is a player of some fire and temperament, and these recordings (made during the course of the Warsaw Competition) show his remarkable technical address and musicianship. He is less poet than virtuoso, less of an aristocrat than Krystian Zimerman and less lyrical than the 1980 Vietnamese prizewinner, Dang-Thai Son. His fingers are more than equal to the challenges of this repertoire and he has a strong sense of style – but he is rather self-aware, too. There are some unsuccessful things: he gabbles the *Grande valse brillante*, though it evokes much applause, and there is little tenderness in his shaping of the second group of the first movement of the *B minor Sonata*; by the high standards of the gramophone this is not competitive. But there is also playing of elegance and pianistic finesse here. The recording is balanced fairly close and does not perhaps do full justice to his dynamic range. There is a good cassette, but it has not quite the presence of the CD.

Impromptu in A flat, Op. 29; Largo in E flat, Op. posth.; Mazurkas: Op. 30/1–4; Op. 33/1–4; Nocturnes: Op. 32: Nos 1 in B; 2 in A flat; in C min., Op. posth.; Scherzo in B flat min., Op. 31; Variation No. 6 in E (from *Hexameron*)*; Waltz in F, Op. 34/3.*
*** Decca Dig. **410 122-2**; *410 122-4*. Vladimir Ashkenazy.

Volume Eight in Ashkenazy's historical series was the only recital to be issued on compact disc (apart from the separate anthology of 'favourite' items – see above). It is well up to the high standard of the series, both in sensibility and in recording, with a splendid chrome tape. The opening *Impromptu* is thrown off with a marvellous unaffected insouciance and the programme (which is concerned with music written in 1836–8) includes a memorably serene account of the

Sylphides nocturne, Op. 32/2. The playing is full of mercurial contrasts, the *B flat minor Scherzo* a fine example of Ashkenazy's current style combining bold drama with subtlety of inner feeling. The virtually unknown *Largo* is a rather solemn piece, but fits splendidly into a recital that is as well planned as it is expertly played. The CD itself is of the highest quality, and readers collecting this series need not hesitate.

Impromptu No. 3 in G flat, Op. 51; Nocturnes Nos 5 in F sharp min., Op. 15/2; 8 in D flat, Op. 27/2; 14 in F sharp min., Op. 48/2; Polonaise-fantaisie, Op. 61; Waltzes Nos 4 in F, Op. 3/3; 6 in D flat (Minute), Op. 64/1; 11 in G flat, Op. 70/1.
** RCA Dig. **RD 84437**. Peter Serkin.

Peter Serkin, unlike his famous father, Rudolf, has something of the reputation of a tearaway pianist; but here, in a well-chosen if hardly generous mixed bag of Chopin pieces, he gives sensitive and tasteful, almost classical readings, well recorded and believably transferred to CD.

VOCAL MUSIC

Songs: *The bridegroom; The double end; Enchantment; Handsome lad; I want what I have not; Leaves are falling; Lithuanian song; Melody; Merrymaking; The messenger; My darling; Out of my sight; Reverie; The ring; The sad river; Spring; The warrior; What she likes; The wish.*
*** Decca Dig. **414 204-2**; *414 204-4* [id.]. Elisabeth Söderström, Vladimir Ashkenazy.

The magical partnership of Elisabeth Söderström and Vladimir Ashkenazy, which has brought intense illumination to the songs of Rachmaninov, Tchaikovsky and Sibelius, is here just as revealing. Nothing establishes Chopin more clearly as a red-blooded Pole than these generally simple, unsophisticated songs with their plain folk melodies and sharp Slavonic rhythms. Söderström and Ashkenazy find an ideal balance, bringing out endless niceties of expression in pointing of word, phrase and rhythm, but keeping the essential freshness of inspiration. The excellent note of the late Martin Cooper points the listener to the special qualities of each of the nineteen songs which are here strongly contrasted. They build up to three of the most individual. *The bridegroom* with its dramatic picture of a lover finding his bride dead, the *Lithuanian song* with its innocent folk-style exchanges, and *Leaves are falling*, more extended than the rest, a Pole's response to the Russians' callous treatment of his country in 1830. Well-balanced sound, full of presence, with an excellent cassette.

Arrangements by Leopold Godowsky: *Études: Op. 10, Nos 1, 3, 5* (2 versions), *6–7; Op. 25, No. 1; Trois Nouvelles Études: No. 1, Op. posth.; Waltzes, Op. 64/1 and 3; p. 69/1; Op. 70/2–3; Op. 18* (concert paraphrase).
(M) ** Decca *414 544-4* [id.]. Jorge Bolet.

It seems remarkable today that anyone should want to try to 'improve' on Chopin, yet Leopold Godowsky (1870–1938) made transcriptions of a great deal of his music, elaborating the textures in such a way as to place the new versions beyond the reach of all but the bravest virtuosi. It must be said that these performances by Jorge Bolet show the most remarkable technical command of Godowsky's complexities, but what he fails to do is to convince the listener that the prodigious effort is really worth while. A degree more audacity of manner might have helped, but, brilliant as the playing is, one is not persuaded to enjoy oneself in spite of all preconceptions. The recording is of good quality and the transfer on this London Enterprise reissue is clear and full, if with a touch of hardness on top.

OTHER COLLECTIONS

Many of the recitals in Ashkenazy's chronological series still remain available on tape, but now that they have been reissued on CD in regrouped formats, they are likely to disappear. Among miscellaneous anthologies of popular repertoire there are several excellent tape collections available. The Decca Weekend issue of 'Favourite Pieces' has an artists' roster including Ivan Davis, Ilana Vered, Joseph Cooper, Magaloff, Katchen and Peter Katin (*417 690-4*); DG's Focus compilation features Cherkassky, Vásáry, Anda, Stefan Askenase and Sviatoslav Richter (*419 658-4*), while there is an excellent bargain-priced Classics for Pleasure recital of '*Masterpieces*' played by Daniel Adni, Malcuzynski, John Ogdon, Ohlsson and Pollini that is cunningly chosen to include many famous melodies and a nice combination of poetry and bravura (*CFP 41 4501-4*). Most generous of all, and very suitable for the car, is EMI's 'Miles of Music' double-length cassette called '*Late-night Chopin*'. This is especially valuable for centring on outstanding recordings Malcuzynski made for EMI in the early 1960s, playing with aristocratic grace and flair and very much in the grand manner. He is very well recorded. The rest of the programme includes sensitive performances from Daniel Adni, John Ogdon, Sylvia Kersenbaum and Moura Lympany. The sound is variable but always fully acceptable (HMV *TC2-MOM 290889-9*).

Cilea, Francesco (1866–1950)

Adriana Lecouvreur (complete).
(*) RCA Dig. **RD 71206 (2). Kabaivanska, Cupido, D'Orazi, Milcheva, Bulgarian Ch., TV & RSO, Arena.

Just as Hungaroton has produced some very enjoyable, well-recorded sets of Italian opera in Budapest, so Bulgarian Balkanton shows what Sofia can produce, with a cast assembled by Bulgarian Radio and Television. The digital sound is bright and clean, the direction by Maurizio Arena is brisk and lively, and most of the singing is very enjoyable. Some earlier recordings, no longer available, may be subtler and more refined, but this melodrama about a great actress caught up in an international intrigue benefits from this bold treatment. Raina Kabaivanska, Bulgarian born but long domiciled in Italy, makes a characterful, vibrant heroine. The recording exaggerates her vibrato only a little, and her performance is strongly presented from the first aria onwards, *Io son l'umile ancella*, the grand tune of which then proceeds to pervade the whole opera. Alberto Cupido sings capably as Maurizio, even if his rather unrounded tenor shows signs of strain under pressure. In some ways the most memorable singing comes from Alexandrina Milcheva as the Princesse de Bouillon, rival to Adriana for the love of Maurizio. She is a trumpet-toned Slavonic mezzo whose fire-eating style and keen projection strike home powerfully. One advantage of CD is that an opera which always took three LPs here comes on two discs only.

Cimarosa, Domenico (1749–1801)

Concertante in G for flute, oboe and orchestra.
*** Ph. Dig. **416 359-2**; [id.]. Nicolet, Holliger, ASMF, Sillito – SALIERI; STAMITZ: *Double concertos.****

Cimarosa's engaging *Concertante* is notably operatic in feeling. The music is not without substance, but the singing, lyrical secondary theme in the first movement and the interplay of flute and oboe in the *Largo* show a distinct vocal style. With such superb playing from Nicolet and Holliger, nicely turned accompaniments and first-rate recording this CD, with its attractive coupling, is most entertaining.

Oboe concerto in C min. (arr. Benjamin).
(M) *** **PRT PVCD 8374**. Rothwell, Pro Arte O, Barbirolli – ALBINONI; MARCELLO: *Concertos.****

This enchanting concerto was arranged by Arthur Benjamin from four single-movement keyboard sonatas. It sounds in no way manufactured and is one of the finest concertante works available for the oboe. The concerto is given a quite ideal performance and recording by Evelyn Rothwell and her husband. The pastoral opening theme is phrased exquisitely, and after the gentle allegro which follows, the beautiful flowing *Siciliana* is played with a wonderful combination of affection and style. The gently rollicking finale is again caught to perfection, with Sir John sensitive to his wife's mood in every bar. The recording is well judged in matters of balance and tone, and the CD transfer improves clarity and reduces background. As in the rest of this sparsely produced budget series there are no musical notes, and the overall playing time of the collection is only 38′. But this is a case where the quality of the music and of the music making is paramount.

Il Maestro di Capella.
*** Hung. Dig. **HCD 12573** [id.]. József Gregor, Boys of Schola Hungarica, Corelli CO, Pál – TELEMANN: *Der Schulmeister.****

Gregor's firm rich bass goes with a comparably strong personality and a striking ability to act the buffoon in this romp of an intermezzo with its comic conflict between the maestro di cappella and the orchestra. Plainly, Gregor's performance has benefited from stage experience. Though his comic style is on the broad side, his magnetism pulls the piece together very effectively, with Thomás Pál a responsive conductor. It is aptly if ungenerously coupled with the more heavily Germanic Telemann cantata. First-rate recording.

Clemens non Papa, Jacob (*c.* 1510/15–*c.* 1555/6)

Missa Pastores quidnam vidistis; Motets: *Pastores quidnam vidistis; Ego flos campi; Pater peccavi; Tribulationes civitatum.*
❀ *** Gimell Dig. **CDGIM 013**; *1585T-13* [id.]. Tallis Scholars, Peter Phillips.

This admirable disc serves as an introduction to the music of Jacob Clement or Clemens non Papa (who was jokingly known as Clemens-not-the-Pope, so as to distinguish him from either Pope Clement VII or the Flemish poet, Jacobus Papa). He was one of the later representatives of the Renaissance Flemish school, following on after Dufay, Ockeghem and Josquin, and is regarded as a somewhat conservative figure because of his complex imitative style of polyphony which, while carrying the meaning of the text musically, often obscures the actual words by its prolix interplay of melodic lines. But the beauty of line and richness of texture are full justification and in the masterly *Missa Pastores quidnam vidistis* Peter Phillips aids the listener by making clear breaks, between sections of the *Credo* for instance, before *Et incarnatus est de Spiritu Sancto* and again preceding *Et resurrexit tertia die*, with striking musical effect. Tempi are flexible and, while the overall momentum is convincingly controlled, Phillips heightens the tension by quickening the pace in the closing phrases of different parts of the Mass as in *Cum Sancto Spiritu* in the *Gloria* and in *Hosanna in excelsis* which acts as a 'coda' for the *Benedictus*. The programme opens with the parody motet associated with the Mass, which has a glorious eloquence, carried through, by full-throated singing in the *Kyrie*, to the Mass itself which follows on naturally. Of the other motets, *Pater peccavi*, solemnly rich-textured, is especially memorable, but the whole programme is designed to reveal to twentieth-century ears another name hitherto known only to scholars. He left us with much to be explored: he wrote 15 masses and some 233 motets! The recording has the imprint of the famous sound engineer from Classics for Pleasure, Mr Bear, and is uncannily real and superbly balanced in its CD format, though the chrome tape is also in the demonstration class. It was made in the ideal acoustics of the Church of St Peter and St Paul, Salle, Norfolk.

Clementi, Muzio (1752–1832)

Piano sonatas: in F min., Op. 13/6; in B flat, Op. 24/2; in F sharp min., Op. 25/5; in G, Op. 37/1.
*** Accent **ACC 67911D** [id.]. Jos van Immerseel.

Very fleet and brilliant performances from Jos van Immerseel, playing on an instrument made by Michael Rosenberger in 1795, recorded at Finchcocks in 1979 – and very well, too. As Horowitz showed us in the 1950s, Clementi is a very considerable composer and possessed a fertile imagination. The slow movements of these sonatas have some considerable expressive depth, and the outer ones are full of a brilliance that is well served by this eminently skilful and excellent artist.

Coates, Eric (1886–1958)

(i) *By a sleepy lagoon;* (ii) *Calling all workers* (march)*;* (iii) *Cinderella* (phantasy)*; From meadow to Mayfair: suite; London suite; London again suite;* (i) *The Merrymakers overture;* (iii) *Music everywhere* (march)*;* (iv) *Saxo-rhapsody* (i) *The three bears* (phantasy)*;* (ii) *The three Elizabeths* (*suite*)*;* (i) *The three men* (*suite*)*: Man from the Sea.* (iii) *Wood nymphs* (valsette).
(B) *** CfP *CFPD 4456-5* (2). (i) LSO, Mackerras; (ii) CBSO, Kilbey; (iii) Royal Liverpool PO, Groves; (iv) with Jack Brymer.

By a sleepy lagoon; Cinderella (phantasy)*; Dambusters march; From meadow to Mayfair: suite; London suite; London again suite; Saxo-rhapsody; The three bears* (phantasy)*; The three Elizabeths suite: Springtime in Angus.*
(B) ** EMI *TC2-MOM 154651-9*. Royal Liverpool PO, Groves.

On the whole, Groves proves a persuasive advocate, although occasionally his approach is slightly bland. Jack Brymer is the excellent soloist in the *Saxo-rhapsody*, and the other piece with a diluted jazz element, *Cinderella*, also goes with a swing. On tape the recording is smooth and pleasing, with the upper range a little restricted. In the car – at which the 'Miles of Music' series is directed – it makes an entertaining ninety minutes, though best heard in two separate parts.

However, the Classics for Pleasure collection, on a pair of tapes in a chunky box, is even more generous and includes, besides some very lively performances from Sir Charles Mackerras, several outstanding ones from the CBSO under Reginald Kilbey. He proves the ideal Coates conductor, with a real flair for catching the sparkle of Coates's leaping allegro figurations, notably in the first movement of *The three Elizabeths*, where also his shaping of the central slow movement – one of the composer's finest inspirations – has an affectionate grace. The marches are splendidly alive and vigorous. With good transfers, this is much the best Coates compilation currently available.

Cinderella; London suite; London again suite; The three bears.
(*) Ara. **Z 8036** [id.]. Royal Liverpool PO, Groves.

Groves's Coates recordings were originally made in EMI's often unsuccessful hi-fi-conscious

Studio Two sound-balance which provided an exaggerated brilliance at the expense of the bass response. On the Arabesque CD, the digital remastering has amplified this effect and though *Cinderella* triumphs over the sound by its sheer energy, elsewhere the orchestra seems emaciated, with its very bright, clear upper range unsupported by any weight from the lower strings.

Songs: *Always as I close my eyes; At sunset; Bird songs at eventide; Brown eyes I love; Dinder courtship; Doubt; Dreams of London; Green hills o'Somerset; Homeward to you; I heard you singing; I'm lonely; I pitch my lonely caravan; Little lady of the moon; Reuben Ranzo; Song of summer; A song remembered; Stonecracker John; Through all the ages; Today is ours.*
*** ASV Dig. **CDDCA 567**; *ZCDCA 567*. Brian Rayner Cook, Raphael Terroni.

Eric Coates, as well as writing skilful orchestral music, also produced fine Edwardian ballads, which in many instances transcended the limitations of the genre, with melodies of genuine refinement and imagination. Most date from earlier in his career, prior to the Second World War. Brian Rayner Cook, with his rich baritone beautifully controlled, is a superb advocate and makes a persuasive case for every one of the nineteen songs included in this recital. His immaculate diction is infectiously demonstrated in the opening *Reuben Ranzo* (a would-be sailor/tailor) in which he breezily recalls the spirited projection of another famous singer of this kind of repertoire in the early days of the gramophone, Peter Dawson. The recording is admirably clear and the cassette transfer very well managed.

Coleridge-Taylor, Samuel (1875–1912)

(i) *Hiawatha's wedding feast; The Bamboula* (rhapsodic dance).
*** HMV Dig. *EL 270145-4*. (i) Rolfe-Johnson, Bournemouth Ch.; Bournemouth SO, Alwyn.

(i) *Hiawatha's wedding feast;* (ii) *Petite suite de concert.*
(M) *** HMV **CDM7 69689-2**. (i) Lewis, Royal Choral Soc., Philh. O, Sargent; (ii) Philh. O, Weldon.

In its day *Hiawatha's wedding feast* blew a fresh breeze through a turgid British Victorian choral tradition; since then, the work has been kept alive in fairly frequent performances by amateur choral societies. The newest digital recording is first class in every way, and Kenneth Alwyn – who enters the recording studios too infrequently – secures a vigorous and committed contribution from his Bournemouth forces, with Anthony Rolfe-Johnson an excellent soloist in the famous *Onaway! Awake, beloved!* The music throughout is delightfully melodious and extremely well written for the voices, and this can be recommended strongly. *The Bamboula* makes an agreeable if inconsequential encore. The cassette transfer is well managed, but we need a CD. Instead, EMI have offered a CD reissue of Sir Malcolm Sargent's earlier recording. Here the somewhat over-heavy orchestration, which one notices at a live performance, is happily toned down by the remastering and this is a demonstration of how much a fine choir benefits from the ambience around it. Everything about this disc is a success, including of course Richard Lewis's stylish performance of *Onaway! Awake, Beloved!* For the reissue EMI have generously added a bonus in George Weldon's polished Philharmonia recording of the *Petite suite de concert*, a salon pastiche of great charm. The second movement (*Demande et response*) with its delicate string melody was once a popular 'hit' in long-gone Palm court days.

Copland, Aaron (born 1900)

Appalachian spring: ballet suite.
*** Decca **414 457-2**; *414 457-4* [id.]. Detroit SO, Dorati – STRAVINSKY: *Apollon musagète.****

*** DG Dig. **413 324-2**; *3302 083* [id.]. LAPO, Bernstein – BARBER: *Adagio*; BERNSTEIN: *Candide overture*; SCHUMAN: *American festival overture*.***

Appalachian spring (suite); Fanfare for the common man.
(M) *** Decca **417 716-2**; *417 716-4* [id.]. LAPO, Mehta – GERSHWIN: *American in Paris; Cuban overture; Rhapsody in blue*.**

Appalachian spring: ballet suite; Fanfare for the common man; Rodeo: 4 Dance episodes.
(*) Telarc **CD 80078 [id.]. Atlanta SO, Lane.

Appalachian spring: ballet suite; Short symphony.
*** Pro Arte Dig. **CCD 140** [id.]. St Paul CO, Russell Davies – IVES: *Symphony No. 3*.***

All the compact disc versions offer the orchestral suite. Dorati has the full measure of Copland's masterly score, creating a fine evocation at the opening and a feeling of serene acceptance at the close, while the affectionately witty portrayal of *The Revivalist and his flock* is presented with sparklingly precise rhythms and splendid string and woodwind detail. The *Solo dance of the Bride* is equally characterful; throughout, Dorati finds a balance between the nicely observed interplay of the human characters and the spacious and lonely grandeur of the Appalachian backcloth. The Decca recording is striking in its range and vividness and again confirms the excellence of the acoustic of the Old Orchestral Hall, Detroit. The cassette is splendid too, fairly close to the CD in its definition, although the latter has that extra touch of presence and tangibility that we have come to expect from the Decca engineers.

Bernstein's newest version was recorded at a live performance, and the conductor communicates his love of the score in a strong, yet richly lyrical reading. Some might feel that, carried away by the occasion, he pushes the climax of the variations on the haunting Shaker theme, *Simple gifts*, too hard, but the compulsion of the music making is obvious. The recording is close but not lacking atmosphere, and it sounds extremely vivid in both formats.

Mehta's performance is second to none: this is one of the most distinguished of several fine recordings he made for Decca in the late 1970s which also included the spectacular *Fanfare for the common man*. Here the digital remastering gives riveting presence to the percussion at the opening, without quite going over the top like the Telarc version. The sound is excellent in the ballet also, which is powerfully atmospheric: the bold, folksy characterization of *The Revivalist and his flock* is particularly striking, the work's climax is exhilarating and the closing pages movingly serene. The couplings are generous but less distinctive. There is an excellent chrome tape, although the CD has noticeably enhanced presence and detail, especially in the *Fanfare*.

The Telarc coupling is given recording of demonstration quality, naturally balanced and with glowing ambient warmth and vivid woodwind colouring. Lane's account of *Appalachian spring*, without missing the score's lyrical qualities, has an attractive feeling of the ballet theatre about it, with the strings lightly rhythmic. *Rodeo* too is not as bitingly dramatic and incisive as Bernstein's version (see below), but is more lyrical and atmospheric. The snag, however, is the extremely forward balance of the bass drum and tam tam at the opening of the *Fanfare for the common man*. The sheer force and amplitude of that simultaneous opening crash is unnerving. The level of transfer is extremely high; apart from making the listener jump (to say the least), if the volume control is set too high, one fears for the safety of the loudspeaker cones! This is more suitable for hi-fi demonstration than for the living-room.

Using a smaller ensemble than is usual, Russell Davies conducts fresh and immediate performances of both the *Short symphony* of 1933, one of several early works, and the well-known suite from *Appalachian spring*, which was originally conceived for chamber orchestra. The recording is bright and forward to match the performances. An excellent and recommendable anthology.

Appalachian spring: suite; Billy the Kid: suite; Danzón Cubano; Fanfare for the common man (from *Symphony No. 3*); *Rodeo: 4 Dance episodes; El Salón México.*
(B) *** CBS *40-79020*. NYPO, Bernstein.

This excellent double-length tape gathers together Bernstein's vintage recordings of Copland's most popular works, and it was a good idea to feature the famous *Fanfare* by using an extract from the *Third Symphony*. The playing of the New York orchestra, on peak form, is superb and the music making is full of electricity. The sound is slightly less sharply defined at the top than the LP originals, but that is not an aural disadvantage, for there is no lack of atmosphere. The only drawback is the lack of documentation, consisting solely of a list of titles on the front of the box.

Billy the Kid (complete ballet); *Rodeo* (complete ballet).
*** HMV Dig. **CDC7 47382-2** [id.]; *EL 270398-4* [Ang. *4DS 37357*]. St Louis SO, Slatkin.

Slatkin's record of two favourite Copland works is specially valuable for presenting the ballet scores complete. In practice this means the inclusion of a number of passages which Copland excised from his concert suites solely out of concern for length. So *Billy the Kid* here includes among other things a haunting slow romantic waltz based on the Mexican dance heard earlier, representing Billy finding refuge with his Mexican sweetheart, a charming passage. *Rodeo* also has substantially more music, including a piano interlude in *Saturday night waltz*. Slatkin conducts strong and colourful performances, very well recorded with plenty of detail as well as bloom on the sound. The atmospheric bite in Billy's gun-battle with its fortissimo timpani is very impressive. It is a pity, however, that the CD has only one track for the whole of *Billy the Kid*, 32 minutes of music, without any subdivisions. *Rodeo* has four tracks. The cassette offers acceptable sound in *Billy the Kid*, but in the *Rodeo* the transients are blunted more than is desirable for this kind of writing.

Ceremonial fanfare; John Henry (*A railroad ballad*); *Jubilee variations;* (i) *Lincoln portrait;* (ii) *Old American songs, set 1; An Outdoor overture; The Tender Land: The promise of living.*
*** Telarc Dig. **CD 80117** [id.]. Cincinnati Pops O, Kunzel; (i) with Katharine Hepburn (nar.); (ii) Sherrill Milnes.

Katharine Hepburn's remarkable delivery of Abraham Lincoln's words quite transcends any limitations in Copland's *Lincoln portrait* and makes it an undeniably moving experience. There is a burning inner fire flickering beneath her slightly tremulous vocal delivery which renders it extraordinarily powerful. Indeed she conveys genuine awe at the political magnificence of Lincoln's prose, and Kunzel, clearly inspired by the authority of her reading, punctuates the text with orchestral comments of singular power. When the closing statement is reached: 'government of the people, by the people, and *for* the people' (the emphasis is unmistakable), an almost biblical profundity is conveyed, such is the moral intensity of the delivery. Incidentally there is much fine orchestral writing in this piece before the narration begins, which Kunzel delivers eloquently. Altogether this is by far the finest playing we have heard from the talented Cincinnati orchestra: the shorter pieces are given splendid life, notably the refreshing *Outdoor overture* and the short set of variants on the ballad, *John Henry*, both vintage Copland. The brief *Jubilee variations* were part of a composite work, commissioned by Eugene Goossens, who provided the theme. This is the first recording. The *Ceremonial fanfare* is more nostalgic than the famous *Fanfare for the common man* and is certainly worth having on disc. Sherrill Milnes's highly infectious performance of the first set of *Old American songs* shows a spirited boisterousness that recalls Howard Keel in *Seven Brides for Seven Brothers* – the singing is naturally idiomatic and sensitive to the folksy inspiration. *The Promise of living* comes from the finale of

Act I of Copland's opera, *The Tender Land*: it is effectively placed to follow the *Lincoln portrait*. Altogether a collection that is more than the sum of its parts, given superlative Telarc recording, highly spectacular and realistic, yet with natural balance.

Clarinet concerto.

*** CBS **MK 42227**; *MT 42227* [id.]. Benny Goodman, Columbia SO, composer – BERNSTEIN: *Prelude, fugue and riffs*; GOULD: *Derivations*; STRAVINSKY: *Ebony concerto****; BARTÓK: *Contrasts*.(***)

*** ASV Dig. **CDDCA 568**; (M) *ZCDCA 568* [id.]. MacDonald, N. Sinfonia, Bedford – FINZI: *Concerto*; MOURANT: *Pied Piper*.***

*(*) Unicorn Dig. **DKPCD 9066**; *DKPC 9066* [id.]. Gray, RPO, Newstone – ARNOLD: *Concerto* **; LUTOSLAWSKI: *Dance preludes***; ROSSINI: *Variations*.*(*)

Benny Goodman gives a splendid account of the *Concerto* he commissioned in 1947, and the recording from the early 1960s sounds admirably fresh in remastered form – the slight astringency in the violin timbre suits the music. With the composer directing the accompaniment, this performance is eminently recommendable if the ingeniously assembled couplings are attractive. There is a good matching cassette, rather mellower in the upper range than the CD. Goodman's performance is also available on an alternative mid-priced cassette, coupled with the *Piano concerto*, with the composer as soloist, but in the latter work the sound is excessively thin (CBS *40-61837*).

George MacDonald, a Canadian clarinettist trained in Britain who was a founder member of the Northern Sinfonia, gives a virtuoso performance of the Copland *Clarinet concerto*, not quite as dramatic and full of flair as that of the dedicatee, Benny Goodman, but in many ways subtler in expression and particularly impressive in the long lyrical paragraphs of the first of the two movements. Well recorded, though with some distancing of the instruments, it makes an unusual and valuable coupling for the fine Finzi *Concerto*. The cassette transfer is of excellent quality, sharper in focus than the full-priced Goodman tape.

Gary Gray comes from Indiana and is principal clarinettist of the Los Angeles Chamber Orchestra. His performance is disappointing, curiously static in the opening section and lacking rhythmic sparkle in the finale. The recording is atmospheric and well balanced; our copy of the tape, transferred at a high level, had some discoloration in the upper partials of the clarinet timbre, but this is unlikely to be present in later batches.

Piano concerto.

(*) Chan. *ABT 1061*. Lin, Melbourne SO, John Hopkins – BRITTEN: *Piano concerto*.

Gillian Lin is undoubtedly successful in the Copland *Concerto*, bringing out the jazz element in this syncopated music. Copland uses that easily imitable idiom far more imaginatively than most of his American colleagues – which helps to explain the work's continuing success – and one would hardly appreciate from the idiom alone how this is a work (written in 1926) which represents the composer before he had attained full maturity. The cassette transfer is made at a lower level than the Britten coupling, and has slightly less immediacy; but it still sounds well.

Dance symphony; Danzón cubano; Fanfare for the common man; The Red Pony: suite.

(M) **(*) HMV *ED 270375-4*. Mexico City PO, Bátiz.

Copland's *Red Pony* suite, written for Lewis Milestone's film, is among his most endearing lighter scores. The composer summed up the film and thus the music as 'a series of vignettes concerning a teenage boy called Jody and his life in a Californian ranch setting'. The music's nostalgia is well caught by this excellent performance by the Mexico orchestra under Bátiz, the best recording they have yet made together. The playing is notable both for its understanding and for its excellent ensemble. The *Dance symphony* is derived from an unperformed ballet composed with Diaghilev in mind. It was devised to fit a bizarre scenario involving dancing corpses, coffins and a vampire called Grohg, but was stillborn; the music turned up in its present format in 1929. If the orchestral ensemble is less impressive here, the playing is again alert and committed, as it is in the *Danzón cubano*, where the orchestra catches the element of colourful vulgarity with nice flair. Excellent sound and a mid-priced format make this issue worth getting for *The Red Pony* alone. A very good high-level cassette, though our copy brought a momentary discoloration in the brass in the spectacular opening *Fanfare*.

Dance symphony; El salón México; Fanfare for the common man; Rodeo (ballet)*: 4 dance episodes.*
(*) Decca Dig. **414 273-2 [id.]. Detroit SO, Dorati.

There is a bright, extrovert brilliance about Dorati's attractive collection of Copland works, chosen for their immediate, cheerful, wide-open-spaces qualities. The playing demonstrates very clearly that orchestral virtuosity in the United States extends to orchestras other than the big five, and the digital recording has a clarity and impact that suit the music. The only reservation is that, rather surprisingly, Dorati's treatment of jazzy syncopations – an essential element in Copland of this vintage – is very literal, lacking the lift we think of as idiomatic. As usual, the transfer to CD brings added presence; as sound, this is very impressive.

El Salón México.
** HMV **CDC7 47716-2** [id.]. Utah SO, Abravanel – GROFÉ: *Grand Canyon suite.***

This is distinctly short measure for a full-priced CD; although there is plenty of local colour and lively rhythmic feeling projected by the Utah orchestra, this performance does not match Bernstein's (see above) for dynamism and precision. The CD transfer is vivid but sacrifices some of the opulence of the original analogue master.

Quiet city.
*** Argo **417 818-2**; *KZRC 845* [id.]. ASMF, Marriner – BARBER: *Adagio*; COWELL: *Hymn*; CRESTON: *Rumor*; IVES: *Symphony No. 3.****

Marriner's 1976 version is both poetic and evocative, and the playing of the trumpet and cor anglais soloists is of the highest order. The digital remastering has brought added clarity without loss of atmosphere. The excellent original cassette remains available.

Symphony No. 3.
(M) *** CBS *40-61869*. Philh. O, composer.

Symphony No. 3; Danzón Cubano; El Salón México.
*** HMV Dig. **CDC7 47606-2** [id.]. Dallas SO, Mata.

Symphony No. 3; Quiet city.
*** DG Dig. **419 170-2** [id.]. NYPO, Bernstein.

The composer's natural authority asserts itself in his fine performance with the Philharmonia, and if this account is less powerfully extrovert than Bernstein's, the freshness of communication still communicates readily, especially in the slow movement with its reflective calm. The mid-priced CBS tape is very well managed; even if the sound does not match the HMV Dallas recording in warmth and beauty of texture, it is certainly vivid and suitably expansive in the finale.

With Bernstein conducting Copland's *Third Symphony*, you appreciate more than with rival interpreters – even the composer himself (who has recorded it twice) – that this is one of the great symphonic statements of American music. He consciously exaggerates the rhetoric, leading up to the fantasy on the *Fanfare of the common man*, which opens the finale. In absolute terms he may be accused of going over the top, but recorded at live concerts the electricity of the performance is irresistible, a reflection not just of Bernstein's love of Copland, his one-time mentor, and of his music but of a reunion between Bernstein and the orchestra of which he was music-director for so long. The result is unfailingly magnetic, grabbing the ear in a way that rival versions rarely do. The recording, full-bodied and bright, brings too much spotlighting in the DG manner, but its brashness is apt for the performance. The hushed tranquillity of *Quiet city*, another of Copland's finest scores, is superbly caught by Bernstein in the valuable fill-up.

Eduardo Mata and the Dallas Symphony Orchestra give a powerful, unexaggerated reading. If Leonard Bernstein (in a work which he has rather made his own) underlines the eloquent rhetoric, the symphonic grandeur of Copland's argument, Mata follows far more closely what the composer has put in the score, not least his often-repeated instruction, 'with simple expression'. He trusts Copland's authority more, and the concentration and cohesiveness of the whole performance bear out his confidence, helped by full and well-balanced recording. The two extra items, Copland at his most attractive finding inspiration in Latin-American music, provide a valuable makeweight, with Mata, born in Mexico City, adding his own touches of authenticity. In these two shorter pieces the recording, always excellent, reaches demonstration standard in its combination of atmosphere and vividness of detail, within a concert-hall perspective.

Piano quartet.
** Pro Arte **CDD 120** [id.]. Frank Glazer, Cantilena Chamber Players – FOSS: *Round a common center*; WYNER: *Intermezzi.***

The *Piano quartet* of 1950 is one of Copland's most masterly and challenging works and is not otherwise available on CD, cassette or LP. It is an imaginative but at times austere score; it shows that Copland still had a keen interest in composing in 'an idiom that might be accessible only to cultivated listeners'. It receives an impressive performance from the Cantilena Chamber Players – though by the standards of, say, the best Philips chamber-music issues, the recording is what one might call synthetic and unventilated. However, it is more than adequate and the playing of these artists is both accomplished and dedicated.

Piano sonata; 4 Piano blues; Variations.
** Chan. *ABT 1104* [id.]. Gillian Lin.

Gillian Lin is a Singapore-born pianist who recorded the Copland and Britten concertos successfully some time ago. Her performances here are eminently acceptable, particularly in the *Four piano blues*; she also gives a good account of the *Sonata*, which is not otherwise available at present since the deletion of Leo Smit's authoritative account. These recordings were made in association with the Australian Broadcasting Commission and are truthful and well balanced.

VOCAL MUSIC

Canticle of freedom; (i) *Old American songs, sets 1 & 2;* 4 Motets: *Help us, O Lord; Thou, O Jehovah, abideth forever; Have mercy on us, O my Lord; Sing ye praises to our King.*
** CBS Dig. **MK 42140**; *IMT 42140* [id.]. Mormon Tabernacle Choir, (i) with Don Becker; Utah S O, Tilson Thomas.

The Mormon Tabernacle Choir bring a dimension of their own to everything they sing, and the devotional approach to the motets is very different from the clear-cut lines of Corydon Singers (see below). What is not helpful is the rather mushy, reverberant recording which clouds the diction, both here and in the choral versions of the *Old American songs*. Nevertheless the Mormons have a natural response to this music which is close to the feeling of the originals; the lovely *Simple gifts* (made famous by *Appalachian spring*), the resonantly committed *At the River*, the lighter *I bought me a cat* and the charming *Ring-a-ring-chaw* are highly effective. Don Becker's solo contributions are direct and pleasing. The 1955 *Canticle of freedom* has an eloquence here that would be more elusive with a professional choir without a religious background, and the orchestral introduction is vintage Copland. The documentation provides all the words, and excellent notes which tell us that the choral transcriptions were not made by the composer but jointly by Irving Fine and Raymond Wilding-White. The tape transfer seriously lacks focus in the choral texture – the resonance has blunted the upper range.

(i) *In the Beginning; Help us, O Lord; Have mercy on us, O my Lord; Sing ye praises to our King.*
*** Hyp. Dig. **CDA 66219**; *KA 66219* [id.]. (i) Catherine Denley; Corydon Singers, Best – BARBER: *Agnus Dei*; BERNSTEIN: *Chichester Psalms*.***

In the Beginning, a large-scale, fifteen-minute motet for unaccompanied chorus and soprano solo, written in 1947, makes a fascinating contrast with the Bernstein work, the *Chichester Psalms*, with which it is coupled. Where Bernstein, setting Hebrew words, works very much within a Jewish context even when writing for an Anglican cathedral, Copland, Jewish also, writes with clear Anglican overtones. The open harmonies and clean textures and lines are very characteristic of the composer at his most approachable, and the long span of the work is well structured with the help of the soprano soloist, here the fresh-toned Catherine Denley. The chorus is just as clear and alert in its singing, not just in the big motet but also in the three delightful little pieces which come as an appendix. The last is vigorous like a carol, but all three bring out Copland's deft use of voices. Vivid recording, full of presence, with a fine matching cassette.

Corelli, Arcangelo (1653–1713)

Concerti grossi, Op. 6/1–12.
*** HMV **CDS7 47919** (2) [Ang. **CDCB 47419**]. La Petite Bande, Kuijken.
*(*) Chan. Dig. **CHAN 8336/8**; *DBTD 3002* (3) [id.]. Cantilena, Shepherd.

Concerti grossi, Op. 6/5, 6, 7, 8 (Christmas concerto).
** Erato **ECD 88080** [id.]. Sol. Ven., Scimone.

Corelli's masterly Op. 6 concertos are rich in melodic invention and harmonic resource, and one wonders why they have been neglected for so long at a time when much lesser music of this period has been duplicated on record.

La Petite Bande offers an economical CD layout and first-class performances. Authentic instruments are used, but to excellent effect; the textures are more transparent as a result, and the playing is always expressive and musical. The recordings are made in a highly sympathetic acoustic, that of the Cedernsaal at Schloss Kirchheim, and are splendidly lifelike. These performances convey more of the nobility and grandeur of Corelli than the Chandos set and the CD remastering is first class in every way.

Although digitally recorded, with an excellent cassette equivalent, the Cantilena performances are not as polished, nor do they have the authentic feeling and nobility of the playing by La Petite Bande. The music making is genial enough, but at times a little rough-and-ready. Moreover the layout on three CDs and tapes is expensive.

I Solisti Veneti offer more polished accounts of the set than Cantilena on Chandos and are well enough recorded by the Erato engineers. They bring a robust vitality to some of the quicker movements – but are heavy-handed on occasion. On CD, the sound is fresh and full-bodied and the recorded image is very realistic; however, more transparency of texture and a lighter touch are needed in this repertoire, if modern stringed instruments are to be used.

Concerto grosso in G min. (*Christmas*), *Op. 6/8.*
** DG **415 301-2** [id.]. BPO, Karajan – ALBINONI: *Adagio***; VIVALDI: *Four seasons.***

This is a bonus for Karajan's 1973 set of Vivaldi's *Four seasons*. It is beautifully played, although the style is hardly authentic. The sound is acceptable, but this is not one of DG's most impressive examples of digital remastering.

Oboe concerto (arr. Barbirolli).
(M) (***) PRT **PVCD 8378**. Rothwell, Hallé O, Barbirolli – HAYDN: *Concerto*; PERGOLESI: *Concerto*.(***)

Barbirolli's concerto is cunningly arranged from a trio sonata, and in its new form it makes one of the most enchanting works in the oboe repertoire. The performance here is treasurable. The opening, with its beautiful Handelian theme, is shaped with perfect dignity, and the gracious, stately allegro that follows has a touch of gossamer from the soloist. The finale is no less delectable, and the clean, clear recording projects the music admirably. The CD derives from a mono master, as the stereo equivalent was found to be degraded; but the ear adjusts almost immediately, as there is plenty of ambience and the balance is truthful.

Trio sonatas, Op. 1/1, 3, 7, 9, 11, 12; Op. 2/4, 6, 9, 12.
*** DG Dig. **419 614-2** [id.]. E. Concert (members), Pinnock.

Trio sonatas, Op. 1/9, 10 & 12 (*Ciacona*)*; Op. 2/4; Op. 3/5; Op. 4/1; Violin sonata, Op. 5/3; Concerto grosso in B flat, Op. 6/5.*
(*) HMV Dig. **CDC7 49965-2; *EL 270600-4*. L. Baroque, Medlam.

Trio sonatas, Op. 1/9; Op. 2/4 & 12 (*Ciaconna*)*; Op. 3/12; Op. 4/3; Op. 5/3, 11 & 12* (*La Follia*).
*** Hyp. Dig. **CDA 66226**; *KA 66226* [id.]. Purcell Qt.

Of the ten sonatas on this DG Archiv CD, six are *sonate da chiesa* and four *sonate da camera*; the former are recorded, appropriately, with organ and cello (or archlute) continuo, and the latter with harpsichord and cello. Corelli is a composer more praised than played, and the quality of invention in these pieces underlines the injustice of their neglect. The players from the English Concert dispatch them with a virtuosity and panache that is inspiriting, and their evident enthusiasm for this music is infectious. This is a most impressive and rewarding issue, and excellently recorded into the bargain.

The London Baroque collection also mixes church and chamber sonatas, with an impeccable feeling for the style of the period and a continuo which includes archlute and organ, appropriately. Ornamentation is judicious and intonation is secure. Though not lacking vitality, the performances here are graceful and comparatively restrained, lighter in feeling and texture than Pinnock and his English Concert, and thus providing a genuine alternative approach. While the sheer vigour of the DG Archiv performances is refreshing, the more intimate manner of Charles Medlam and his excellent group is also enjoyable, although it is less telling in the *Concerto grosso* from Op. 6 which could ideally sound more robust. The HMV recording is admirably transparent and vivid in its CD format, slightly less clean in focus on the otherwise well-managed chrome tape.

The Hyperion disc is one of six designed to illustrate the widespread use in the eighteenth century of the famous *La Follia* theme; each is devoted to one composer (Scarlatti, Geminiani, Vivaldi, etc.). This record includes a varied collection of *sonate da chiesa* and *sonate da camera*, together with an arrangement in D major for viola da gamba of the *Sonata in E major*, Op. 5, No. 11. (Not that there is much point in mentioning keys, since these artists play at A = 392!) Excellent performances from all concerned and recording to match. The acoustic has warmth and resonance while the detail is admirably defined. A thoroughly enjoyable issue which deserves wide currency. There is a good equivalent cassette.

Violin sonatas, Op. 5/1, 3, 6, 11 and 12 (*La Follia*).
*** Accent Dig. **ACC 48433D** [id.]. Sigiswald & Wieland Kuijken, Robert Kohnen.

When authenticity of spirit goes hand in hand with fine musical feeling and accomplishment, the results can be impressive, as they undoubtedy are here. In *Sonatas 1, 3* and *6* Sigiswald Kuijken bases his ornamentation on those of the Roger edition, adding his own for *No. 11*. Indeed, in terms of liveliness and imagination, this eclipses the earlier version on Archiv from Melkus. The results are not only convincing in terms of sonority but draw one into the sensibility of the period. This is a thoroughly recommendable issue which deserves to reach a wider audience than early music specialists; the recording is natural and the musicianship refined and totally at the service of Corelli.

Couperin, François (1668–1733)

Concerts Royaux Nos 1 in G; 2 in D; 3 in A; 4 in E min.
*** ASV Gaudeamus **CDGAU 101** [id.]. Trio Sonnerie.
*(*) HM **HMC 901151** [id.]. Claire, See, Jaap ter Linden, Davitt Moroney.

The *Concerts Royaux*, composed for Louis XIV's diversion of a Sunday evening, were the first of Couperin's chamber works to appear in print. They were originally published as a supplement to his Third Book of harpsichord pieces, and were printed like keyboard music on two staves, some of the pieces having a 'contrepartie pour la viole' on a separate stave. 'At Court they were performed by Messieurs Duval, Philidor, Alarius and Dubois; I played the harpsichord,' wrote Couperin in the preface. They can be performed in a variety of forms (violin, flute, oboe, viol and bassoon) and in pre-war days they were played in rich chamber-orchestral transcriptions. The Trio Sonnerie give them in the most economical fashion (violin, viola da gamba and harpsichord). Monica Huggett's violin playing in particular is distinguished by subtlety of phrasing and keenness of musical response, and the contribution of all three musicians is unfailingly imaginative. Excellent recording.

Davitt Moroney and his colleagues opt for two flutes, bass viol and harpsichord in the *Concerts Royaux*. As a result, there is a certain uniformity of colour, and in addition their playing is just a little wanting in panache and vitality.

Pièces de clavecin (*Harpsichord suites*): *Orders 8 and 9*.
*** Denon Dig. **CO 1719** [id.]. Huguette Dreyfus (harpsichord).

Huguette Dreyfus would seem to be following the example of her mentor, Ruggiero Gerlin, who made the first complete recording of the Couperin *Ordres* on LP in the 1950s. For *Ordres 8* and *9* in her series she chooses an eighteenth-century instrument by Jacques Goerman, restored by Mercier-Ythier and tuned in accordance with Marpurg temperament (A = 415). Its colours are rather sombre and subdued, and Huguette Dreyfus plays with her customary authority and restraint. The *Eighth Ordre* includes the famous *Passacaille* that Landowska played with such panache and flair. Excellent balance and recording.

Pièces de clavecin (*Harpsichord suites*): *Ordres 11 and 13*.
*** Denon Dig. **C37 7070** [id.]. Huguette Dreyfus (harpsichord).

For *Ordres 11* and *13*. Huguette Dreyfus plays a Dowd and shows herself yet again to have great understanding of this style. Couperin has been called the 'Chopin of the harpsichord'; Mme Dreyfus certainly has the poetic sensibility and the grasp of rubato so necessary in the interpretation of his art. She is impeccably recorded – though to get a truthful aural picture of the instrument, readers would be well advised to play this at a very low-level setting.

Motets: *Domine salvum fac regem; Jacunda vox ecclesiae; Laetentur coeli; Lauda Sion salvatorem; Magnificat; O misterium ineffabile; Regina coeli; Tantum ergo sacramentum; Venite exultemus Domine; Victoria, Christo resurgenti*.
** HM **HMC 901150** [id.]. Feldman, Poulenard, Reinhart, Linden, Moroney.

This record explores unfamiliar ground: indeed, four of the items have only recently been discovered; the sole exception is the Easter motet, *Victoria, Christo resurgenti*, which has been recorded before. The consensus of informed opinion is that the *Tenebrae* represent Couperin's sacred music at its best, but there is much here that is well worth investigating, and the motets on this record cover a wider spectrum of feeling and range of expressive devices than might at first be imagined. The performances are eminently acceptable, with some particularly good singing from Jill Feldman; the recording is made in a spacious and warm acoustic. The CD represents a distinct gain over LP, from which it derives, in clarity of focus; there is no doubting that this is an issue of special interest to all lovers of French Baroque music.

Messe a l'usage ordinaire des paroisses.
*** HM **HMC 90714** [id.]. Michel Chapuis (organ of St Mazimin-en-Var).

Couperin was an organist all his working life, but the two Organ Masses which constitute his entire output for the instrument were composed in 1690 when he was twenty-two. The *Messe a l'usage ordinaire des paroisses pour les fêtes solonelles* was written for his own use at St Gervais and is the larger and more conventional of the two. Michel Chapuis uses the organ of St Mazimin-en-Var, completed in the 1770s by Jean-Esprit Isnard, a beautiful instrument that sounds excellent in this recording which – though not of recent provenance (it dates from 1967) – could well be, so vivid is its sound. The performance has all the scholarship, authority and style one would expect from this fine player.

Cowell, Henry (1897–1965)

Hymn and fuguing tune No. 10 for oboe and strings.
*** Argo **417 818-2**; *KZRC 845* [id.]. Nicklin, ASMF, Marriner – BARBER: *Adagio*; COPLAND: *Quiet City*; CRESTON: *Rumor*; IVES: *Symphony No. 3*.***

Henry Cowell attracted a good deal of attention in the 1920s with his iconoclastic piano music (it was he who invented 'tone clusters') and he was a prolific symphonist. He also wrote a pioneering study of Ives. This likeable *Hymn and fuguing tune* is well worth having and is expertly played and recorded here. The digital remastering has slightly clarified an already excellent recording. There is a first-class cassette.

Creston, Paul (born 1906)

A Rumor.
*** Argo **417 818-2**; *KZRC 845* [id.]. ASMF, Marriner – BARBER: *Adagio*; COPLAND: *Quiet City*; COWELL: *Hymn*; IVES: *Symphony No. 3.****

At one time Creston was represented in the catalogue by his *Second* and *Third Symphonies*, and his current neglect seems unjust. *A Rumor* is a thoroughly witty and engaging piece and is played here with plenty of character by the Academy under Sir Neville Marriner. It completes a thoroughly rewarding and approachable disc of twentieth-century American music that deserves the widest currency. The sound is first class on both the remastered CD and the original chrome tape.

Crusell, Bernhard (1775–1838)

Clarinet concertos Nos 1–3.
** BIS Dig. **CD 345** [id.]. Karl Leister, Lahti SO, Osmo Vänskä.

Clarinet concertos Nos 1 in E flat, Op. 1; 3 in E flat, Op. 11.
*** Hyp. **CDA 66055**; *KA 66055* [id.]. Thea King, LSO, Francis.

Crusell, born in Finland in 1775 but working in Stockholm most of his career, was himself a clarinettist. Most of the works, which on record and in the concert hall have latterly been infiltrating the repertory, include that instrument, and these delightful concertos are among the most impressive. The echoes are of Mozart, Weber and Rossini with a hint of Beethoven, and though the writing is demanding for the soloist, Crusell generally avoided cadenzas. Thea King with her beautiful liquid tone makes an outstanding soloist, well accompanied by Francis and the LSO. The recording is first class, with an attractive ambient effect, well caught on CD. The cassette is vivid and wide-ranging, to match.

With speeds consistently on the fast side, Karl Leister neatly fits all three Crusell clarinet concertos on to a single disc. As one would expect of Leister, for so long the principal clarinet in Karajan's Berlin Philharmonic, the performances are both sensitive and brilliant, with the fast speeds rarely seeming rushed, even though the Finnish players from the Lahti orchestra are sometimes stretched. Nevertheless, next to the ever-imaginative playing of Thea King on her Hyperion recordings, or the engaging Emma Johnson in No. 2, Leister is a little lacking in character and sense of fantasy or fun. Nor is the recorded sound ideal, with No. 2 (placed first on the disc) noticeably cleaner and more atmospheric than the other two.

Clarinet concerto No. 2 in F min., Op. 5.
❀ *** ASV Dig. **CDDCA 559**; *ZCDCA 559* [id.]. Emma Johnson, ECO, Groves – BAERMANN: *Adagio*; ROSSINI: *Intro., theme and variations*; WEBER: *Concertino.****
*** Hyp. **CDA 66088**; *KA 66088* [id.]. Thea King, LSO, Francis – WEBER: *Concerto No. 2.****

Emma Johnson chose Crusell's *Second Concerto* for the final of the BBC's 'Young Musician of the Year' contest in 1984. It made her a star, and in return she put Crusell's engagingly lightweight piece firmly on the map. Her delectably spontaneous performance is now caught on the wing, for she seems quite unintimidated by the recording studio and this recording sounds very like a live occasion. There is an element of daring in the music making, the sparkling virtuosity of the outer movements bringing a lilting bravura that has one relishing the sense of risks being taken and brought off with ease. The songful *Andante* is no less appealing; throughout, it is the imaginative individuality of the phrasing and the natural feeling for dynamic light and shade that make this performance special. Groves is a lively and sympathetic accompanist, and the balance is a natural one. There is a good tape, but the CD version has slightly sharper detail.

Thea King's wide range of tone-colour and her unfailing artistry make this so-called *Grand concerto,* dedicated to Alexander I of Russia, seem even finer than it is, with its Beethovenian first movement, its *Andante pastorale* slow movement in the warm key of D flat and its jaunty *Allegretto* finale. Not the obvious coupling for the better-known Weber concerto, but an attractive one. The digital recording is full and atmospheric with the soloist balanced forward. The CD, vividly clarifying a reverberant acoustic, is exceptionally realistic. There is also an outstandingly faithful cassette.

Introduction, theme and variations on a Swedish air.
*** ASV Dig. **CDDCA 585**; *ZCDCA 585* [id.]. Emma Johnson, ECO, Yan Pascal Tortelier – DEBUSSY: *Rapsodie*; TARTINI: *Concertino*; WEBER: *Concerto No. 1.****

Emma Johnson, a naturally inspirational artist, skates lightly over any banalities in Crusell's *Variations*, giving a carefree performance, often witty, youthfully daring. Well recorded in a helpful acoustic, it makes an attractive item in a mixed collection of concertante pieces which show contrasted sides of a winning young instrumentalist. The chrome cassette gives good quality.

Clarinet quartets Nos 1 in E flat, Op. 2; 2 in C min., Op. 4; 3 in D, Op. 7.
*** Hyp. *KA 66077*. Thea King, Allegri Qt (members).

These are captivatingly sunny works given superb performances, vivacious and warmly sympathetic. Thea King's tone is positively luscious, as recorded, and the sound is generally excellent, with a splendid high-level cassette transfer in the demonstration class.

Clarinet quintet in C min., Op. 4.
*** Orfeo **C 141861A** [id.]. Karl Leister, Pražák Qt – MOZART: *Clarinet quintet.***(*)

Crusell's brilliant *Clarinet quintet* makes an attractive and unusual coupling for Karl Leister's strong performance of the Mozart. Aptly, he plays this extrovert Scandinavian piece with dash and flair. One feels that he actually enjoys it – at this stage of his career – more than the Mozart masterpiece.

Divertimento in C, Op. 9.
*** Hyp. **CDA 66143** [id.]. Francis, Allegri Qt – KREUTZER: *Grand quintet*; REICHA: *Quintet.****

Crusell has become something of a light industry at Hyperion, who seem to be recording his complete works. (All three clarinet concertos and quartets enrich their enterprising list.) His music certainly has charm and grace, and the *Divertimento*, Op. 9, is no exception. It is available on the Finlandia label – hardly surprisingly since he was born in Finland – but no one wanting this slight but charming piece and its companions need look further than this nicely played and well-recorded account.

Danzi, Franz (1763–1826)

Horn concerto in E.
(M) **(*) Tel. **ZS8 43629** [id.]. Baumann, Concerto Amsterdam, Schröder – HAYDN; ROSETTI: *Concertos.***(*)

Danzi was born in Mannheim and worked in Munich, Stuttgart and Karlsruhe. His *Horn concerto* is a straightforward affair. The opening of the first movement is elegant, with flutes decorating the simple orchestration; the *Romance* is smoothly contoured, but the amiable closing Rondo is the most attractive section. Baumann plays the piece sympathetically and he is well accompanied. The remastered 1969 recording gives him an open rather than an opulent timbre and the violins are clearly rather than warmly projected.

Debussy, Claude (1862–1918)

Berceuse héroïque; La Boîte à joujoux (ballet)*; Children's corner suite* (both orch. Caplet)*; Images pour orchestre; Marche écossaise.*
(B) *** EMI *TCC2-POR 290112-9*. O Nat. de l'ORTF, Martinon.

A generous and welcome double-length tape taken from Jean Martinon's complete set of the orchestral music. Martinon draws some extremely fine playing from the ORTF orchestra, and these performances can hold their own with any in the catalogue. *La Boîte à joujoux* is not as delicately articulated or quite as atmospheric as was Ansermet's, though there is no doubt that this is the better orchestral playing. The recordings have transferred well to tape, with only slight loss in the extreme upper range; the *Images* sound particularly vivid. A bargain.

La Boîte à joujoux (orch. Caplet)*; 6 Épigraphes antiques* (orch. Ansermet)*; Sarabande* (orch. Ravel).
** Erato **ECD 88073** [id.]. Basle SO, Jordan.

Debussy's delightful ballet score about adventures in a children's box of toys has an entirely miniature flavour. Although the work was completed by the composer in 1913, five years before his death, he only sketched the orchestration, which was completed later by André Caplet. Ansermet's own recording for Decca (currently out of the catalogue) had a pellucid vividness, not quite matched by the Basle account, but Armin Jordan's is the only current version. It is serviceable, though not really distinguished by playing of the very first order. But it is well recorded, the performance is eminently respectable and thoroughly idiomatic and the coupling most attractive. Ansermet's orchestration of the *Six Épigraphes antiques* is highly effective and, in the absence of his own account, this is most welcome, as is Jordan's sympathetic account of Ravel's arrangement of the *Sarabande* from *Pour le piano*. In the absence of competition this is a worthwhile CD. The remastered recording (made in 1981 in a warm, ecclesiastical acoustic) sounds well.

Danse (*Tarantelle styrienne*)*; Sarabande* (orch. Ravel).
(*) Decca Dig. **417 611-2; *417 611-4* [id.]. Concg. O, Chailly – MUSSORGSKY: *Pictures***; RAVEL: *Boléro*.**(*)

Ravel's orchestrations of two Debussy piano pieces, the *Sarabande* from the suite, *Pour le piano*, and *Danse*, an arrangement of the early *Tarantelle styrienne*, make delightful and rare items in Chailly's disc demonstrating Ravel's genius as orchestrator. *Danse* readily outshines the original in fantasy; but in the *Sarabande* it is harder for a full orchestra to play with the subtlety of rubato that the stylized music seems to demand. Ripely brilliant recording.

Danses sacrée et profane.
*** Ph. **416 437-2** [id.]. Vera Badings, Concg. O, Haitink – BIZET: *Symphony* etc.***

A ravishingly beautiful account of Debussy's contrasting *Danses*, matching elegance and refinement with warmth. The sound is suitably warm and glowing, atmospheric rather than sharply defined.

(i) *Fantasy for piano and orchestra;* (ii) *Rhapsody for clarinet and orchestra;* (iii) *Rhapsody for saxophone and orchestra.*
*** Erato *MCE 71400*. Monte Carlo Op. O, Jordan, with (i) Queffélec, (ii) Morf, (iii) Delangle.

Not a well-filled but certainly a well-played and excellently recorded tape. The *Rhapsodies* for saxophone and clarinet respectively are underrated, though they have rarely been absent from the catalogue (even in pre-war days, when Piero Coppola recorded them). Here they receive eloquent performances, as also does the *Fantasy for piano and orchestra*. Not a strong work this, but in Anne Queffélec's hands it makes a good impression. The cassette transfer is full, clear and atmospheric.

Images (complete).
(B) *(*) DG Dig. *419 838-4* [id.]. O de Paris, Barenboim – RAVEL: *Boléro etc.***

Images, Jeux, Prélude à l'après-midi d'un faune; (i) *Rhapsody for clarinet and orchestra.*
(B) ** Sup. **2SUP 0023**. Czech PO, Baudo; (i) with André Boutard.

Images; Le Martyre de Saint Sébastien (symphonic fragments).
*** Ph. **420 392-2** [id.]. LSO, Monteux.

Images; Prélude à l'après-midi d'un faune.
*** HMV Dig. **CDC7 47001-2**. LSO, Previn.

Previn's account of *Images* was the first EMI digital record to appear, and understandably it was also included in the first release of HMV compact discs. Detail emerges clearly, yet there is no highlighting and no interference in the natural perspective one would expect to encounter in reality. Every colour and sonority, however subtle, registers; so vivid is the picture that there seems no intermediary between the musicians and the listener. Such is the clarity that this factor outweighs such reservations as one might have (it won both the *Gramophone* awards for the best sound and the best orchestral record of 1979). There is much to admire in Previn's performance, too. Dynamic nuances are carefully observed; there is much felicitous wind playing and no lack of intelligent and musical phrasing. By the side of some of Previn's rivals there does seem to be a want of atmosphere in *Gigues*. Nor is that last ounce of concentration and electricity that is the hallmark of a great performance present in the other movements, particularly *Rondes de printemps*. Previn himself has given us more atmospheric accounts of the *Prélude à l'après-midi d'un faune* than this, though none is more vividly captured by the engineers. The CD confirms the triumphant technical success, with the silent background enhancing the tangibility and refinement of the orchestral texture.

The restoration of Monteux's classic coupling to the catalogue is most welcome, and it makes a splendid addition to the Debussy discography, particularly as the remastered CD has fine immediacy and detail. Indeed one would hardly suspect that the recording dates from 1963, for the woodwind colouring is translucent and there is a fine sheen of sensuousness to the string tone (especially in *Le parfums de la nuit*). Monteux's performance of the *Images* was notable for its freshness and impetus (although this is achieved by the electricity of the playing rather than fast tempi). There is a vivid yet refined feeling for colour which is carried through into the orchestral sections from *Le Martyre* (in its fuller form a cantata written to a text by D'Annunzio). The delicacy of texture of Debussy's exquisite scoring is marvellously balanced by Monteux and he never lets the music become static. There is very little background noise, and our only real reservation is that this might more reasonably have been reissued in Philips's mid-priced Silverline series.

Baudo's performances of *Jeux*, the *Prélude* and *Rhapsody* were highly praised in their day: they date from 1967. The wide vibrato of the Czech Philharmonic flautist in the *Prélude*, which opens the concert, is a little disconcerting, but his phrasing is elegant; and the rest of the orchestra successfully catch the opening mood and the central climax flowers spontaneously. *Jeux* is equally well played and full of atmosphere, and André Boutard is an excellent soloist in the *Rhapsody*. The digital remastering is successful: there is greater inner clarity than originally, but no lack of atmosphere. *Images*, however, though with the advantage of more modern recording (1977) is less compelling, with detail projected somewhat at the expense of evocation. Though the orchestral playing is often responsive, *Les parfums de la nuit* do not float on the evening air as hauntingly as they might.

Barenboim's 1982 recording of *Images* is now coupled with music of Ravel on an impressively engineered bargain-priced Pocket Music tape. The sound is well balanced, atmospheric and vivid; Barenboim secures a good response from the Orchestra de Paris and there are many felicitous touches. However, there is nothing very special here: the performance remains serviceable rather than distinguished and there is an ultimate lack of real profile, which is in the last resort disappointing.

(i) *Images;* (ii) *La Mer.*
(M) *** DG **419 473-2**; *419 473-4* [id.]. (i) Boston SO, Tilson Thomas; (ii) LAPO, Giulini.

Michael Tilson Thomas's set of *Images* was made in the early 1970s and does not match the finest digital versions in terms of clarity, depth and range. It has two strong advantages, however. First, it is extremely well played and very atmospheric; it conveys the flavour of *Gigues* and the languor of the middle movement of *Ibéria* far more convincingly than most of its rivals, and the playing is fresher and more committed, too. Secondly, this is a mid-price issue. Moreover, the recording, though it must yield to the EMI sound-picture for Previn, is very good indeed. It is truthfully balanced, there is plenty of presence and body, and no want of detail in the new Galleria CD transfer, which has lost none of its warmth and atmosphere. The *Images* are particularly vivid and translucent. A bargain.

Giulini's DG version of *La Mer* is also very fine. During his tenure at Los Angeles he produced a sound from the orchestra that is infinitely cultured; the string texture is both rich and fine-textured, and the wind blend is homogeneous. There is much excitement here, as well as poetry. The way in which Giulini shapes the hushed D flat passage towards the end of *Dialogue du vent et de la mer* is quite magical, a model of the sensitivity that does not draw attention to itself. The sound is fully acceptable, though perhaps the balance is not quite natural. This does not displace the first DG Karajan or entirely banish memories of Giulini's earlier Philharmonia set, but it is highly competitive; those wanting this particular coupling need not hesitate. The cassette transfer is somewhat diffuse, not as vivid as the *Images*.

(i) *Images: Ibéria* (only)*; La Mer; Prélude à l'après-midi d'un faune.*
*** Ph. **416 444-2** [id.]. Concg. O, Haitink.

It is a pity that Philips decided to separate *Ibéria* from the complete *Images* for Haitink's CD issue (the recordings were made in the late 1970s), but this is still a first-class collection and the remastering is admirable, serving to demonstrate the naturalness and realism of the original balance. Haitink's response to the atmosphere of *Ibéria* is very personal: he is positive in his evocation of *Les parfums de la nuit* (less Latin in feeling than some versions), but the subtlety of the orchestral playing is constantly telling, no more so than at the magical opening of *Le matin d'un jour de fête*. Haitink's pacing of *La Mer* is comparable with Karajan's tempo in his 1964 recording. Both conductors pay close attention to dynamic gradations, and both secure playing of great sensitivity and virtuosity from their respective orchestras. *De l'aube à midi sur la mer* has real atmosphere in Haitink's hands. The *Jeux de vagues* is no less fresh; the *Dialogue du vent et de la mer* is both fast and exciting. An interesting point is that the brief fanfares that Debussy removed eight bars before fig. 60 are restored (as they were by Ansermet), but Haitink gives them no horns. (Karajan, who omitted them in the first DG version, restores them in his HMV record, but on trumpets.) The *Prélude à l'après-midi d'un faune* is atmospherically played too. The Philips recording is truthful and natural, with beautiful perspective and realistic colour, a marvellously refined sound.

(i) *Images: Ibéria.* (ii) *Nocturnes.*
*** HMV **CDC7 47423-2** [id.]. (i) French Nat. RO; (ii) LSO with women's chorus, Stokowski – RAVEL: *Alborada: Rapsodie.****

This is vintage Stokowski from the end of the 1950s and the early '60s. The warmly resonant recording prevents the sound from seeming too dated, although the relatively forward balance of the wind solos reduces the dynamic range. But the playing is so lustrous that reservations are banished: in *Ibéria* the sultry atmosphere of *Les parfums de la nuit* is as potent as are the fiery brilliance and bright primary colours of *Le matin d'un jour de fête*. The *Nocturnes* are superbly evocative: the string sound is characteristically imbued with sentient warmth, yet the translucent texture of *Nuages* has all the delicate refinement the ear could wish for, while in *Fêtes* the processional derives spontaneously out of a dreamlike reverie. Perhaps the choral singing in *Sirènes*, balmy as it is, is not ideally ethereal, but Stokowski's sensuous warmth is enveloping in the most agreeable way. The CD transfer is admirably done, but more cues or index points would have been appreciated. The Ravel coupling is equally fine.

Images: Ibéria. Prélude à l'après-midi d'un faune; (i) *La damoiselle élue.*
*** DG Dig. **423 103-2**; *423 103-4* [id.]. (i) Maria Ewing, Brigitte Balleys, LSO Ch.; LSO, Abbado.

The London Symphony Orchestra has rarely sounded as sensuously beautiful on record as in Abbado's Debussy collection, bringing together two favourite works, in coupling with the exotic early cantata inspired by Rossetti's Blessèd Damozel, *La damoiselle élue*. With a warm church resonance adding to the bloom not just of the orchestral sound but of the voices, the cantata brings the most distinctive performance, poised and spacious. Maria Ewing has never sounded sweeter on record, and Brigitte Balleys, a touch raw-toned on some notes, sings with attractive freshness. Languorous as the performance is, aptly so, it builds to formidably strong climaxes. The purely orchestral works bring more urgent, even impulsive performances, marked by a warmly persuasive rubato style. Though, with some homing-in of microphones in the reverberant recording, balances are not always quite natural, the ambient warmth of All Saints, Tooting, seems ideal for the music, orchestral as well as vocal, and the effect is very vivid and glowing, without loss of detail. There is a very good chrome tape, one of DG's best.

Jeux; La Mer; Prélude à l'après-midi d'un faune.
❀ (M) *** EMI Dig. **CD-EMX 9502**; *EMX 41 2090-4* [Ang. **CDM 62012**]. LPO, Baudo.
(M) **(*) CBS **MYK 42546**; *40-42546* [**MYK 37261**; *MYT 37261*]. New Philh. O, Boulez.

Serge Baudo's version of *La Mer* on the EMI Eminence label is first class, and can be ranked alongside the finest accounts now on disc. The beautifully natural and expertly balanced recording yields nothing to the sound Philips achieve for Haitink or EMI for Previn. The performance has more character than the latter and can hold its own against the former. The same may be said for Baudo's lovely account of *Prélude à l'après-midi d'un faune*, as atmospheric as any in the catalogue and more beautifully shaped than many. In the faster sections, *Jeux* is at times brisker than we are used to from Haitink, and well conveys the sense of the playfulness of the tennis match. Given its competitive price, many collectors will not feel the need to look further afield. The cassette is extremely well managed – the loss at the top is minimal, but the

CD is very much in the demonstration class (especially *Jeux*, which is wonderfully refined and transparent).

Boulez's *La Mer* is also very fine; we have perhaps underestimated it in the past, when it came in the shadow of Karajan's outstanding DG analogue version made at the same time (the mid-1960s). There is no doubt about the grip Boulez exerts on the proceedings, nor the excellence and electricity of the playing. *Jeux* too is persuasively given, and the control of rhythm and colour here has considerable subtlety. The *Prélude à l'après-midi d'un faune* lacks the last degree of atmosphere and poetry, although it is well shaped. The snag is the recording balance which, while acceptable in gramophone terms, is artificially contrived to spotlight detail, rather than place everything naturally within a concert-hall perspective. In *La Mer* the fortissimo strings are somewhat bleak, even if the digital remastering still allows the necessary ambient atmosphere. This would be tempting at mid-price, but it is outclassed both musically and technically by Baudo's collection.

Jeux; (i) *Nocturnes.*
*** Ph. **400 023-2** [id.]. Concg. O, Haitink, (i) with women's Ch. of Coll. Mus.

However overstocked the catalogue may be, there must always be a place for performances and recording of the quality of this Philips issue. The playing of the Concertgebouw Orchestra is of the highest order, and Haitink's *Jeux* easily matches any recent rivals. His reading is wonderfully expansive and sensitive to atmosphere, and *Jeux* undoubtedly scores over Boulez's much (and rightly) admired version from the more measured tempo and pensive approach that Haitink chooses. Competition is even stiffer in the *Nocturnes*, but this great orchestra and conductor hold their own. The cruel vocal line in *Sirènes* taxes the women of the Collegium Musicum Amstelodamense, but few versions are quite as beguiling and seductive as Haitink's. Add to this an equally admirable recorded quality, with transparent textures, splendidly defined detail and truthful perspective – in short, demonstration sound – and the result is very distinguished indeed. In its original LP format this received a twin *Gramophone* award, for the best orchestral and best engineered record of 1980. It is, of course, an analogue recording; but it has been digitally remastered for its compact disc issue, which brings just a little greater sense of concert-hall presence, with the bass also somewhat better defined.

La Mer.
(M) (**) HMV mono *EH 291345-4*. BBC SO, Toscanini – ELGAR: *Enigma variations*.(***)

La Mer; (i) *Nocturnes.*
*** HMV Dig. **CDC7 47028-2**; *TC-ASD 143632-4* [Ang. *4DS 37929*]. LSO, Previn; (i) with Amb. S.
(*) Ph. Dig. **411 433-2 [id.]. Boston SO, Sir Colin Davis; (i) with Tanglewood Fest. Ch.
** CBS Dig. **37832** [id.]. Philh. O, Tilson Thomas; (i) with Amb. S.

La Mer; (i) *Nocturnes. Prélude à l'après-midi d'un faune.*
* Decca Dig. **417 488-2**; *417 488-4* [id.]. Cleveland O, Ashkenazy; (i) with women's Ch.

La Mer: Prélude à l'après-midi d'un faune.
(M) *** DG **423 217-2**; *423 217-4* [id.]. BPO, Karajan – RAVEL: *Boléro*; *Daphnis et Chloe*.***
(M) **(*) HMV **CDM7 69007-2** [id.]; *EG 769007-4*. BPO, Karajan – RAVEL: *Boléro*.**(*)
** DG Dig. **413 589-2**; *413 589-4* [id.]. BPO, Karajan – RAVEL: *Daphnis*.**
(M) ** Decca *417 603-4* [id.]. Chicago SO, Solti – RAVEL: *Boléro*.**

After more than two decades, Karajan's 1964 DG account of *La Mer* is still very much in a class of its own. So strong is its evocative power that one feels one can almost see and smell the ocean. It enshrines the spirit of the work as effectively as it observes the letter, and the superb playing of the Berlin orchestra, for all its virtuosity and beauty of sound, is totally self-effacing.

The performance of the *Prélude à l'après-midi d'un faune* is no less outstanding, the cool perfection of the opening flute solo matched by ravishing string playing in the central section. For CD reissue, these performances are now coupled not only with his magical version of the *Second suite* from *Daphnis et Chloé*, but also with a gripping account of Ravel's *Boléro*.

Previn's *La Mer* is not quite as fine as Karajan's 1964 version, but it is a considerable achievement. His reading is more overtly passionate than Davis's; his ocean is clearly in the southern hemisphere, with Debussy's orchestral colours made to sound more vividly sunlit. The playing of the LSO is extremely impressive, particularly the ardour of the strings. There is less restraint and less subtlety than with Davis or Haitink, emphasized by the recording which has glittering detail and expands brilliantly at climaxes (though, even on CD, there is a slight loss of refinement at the very loudest peaks). The *Nocturnes* have even greater spontaneity. Some might feel that the *Sirènes* are too voluptuous (Davis's restraint is telling here), but this matches Previn's extrovert approach. The spectacular qualities of the EMI sound-picture certainly provide both works with a highly effective CD presentation, for, though definition is very clear, there is no lack of ambient atmosphere. The cassette is full-bodied and well defined.

Sir Colin Davis's *La Mer* is a great success, too. The waters that this reading evokes are colder and greyer than Previn's, and there is always the sense of tremendous power used with restraint. One critic was reminded of Sibelius here – and Sir Colin does grasp the essentials of both. The set of *Nocturnes* is also very fine. Some will be surprised at Sir Colin's measured approach to *Sirènes*, but it is a convincing one, marvellously sustained in both feeling and atmosphere. *Nuages* is hardly less concentrated in poetic feeling, slow and ethereal. This is a very different view of *Nocturnes* from that of Haitink and the Concertgebouw Orchestra, but it is no less valid and is sumptuously played and recorded. The snag is that the acoustics of the Boston Hall tend to blur inner detail; although the definition of the CD is better than that of the original LP, compared with Previn's HMV recording the effect is less than ideal, though the recording faithfully reflects the hall ambience (albeit without an audience).

Karajan's 1978 re-recording of *La Mer* for HMV may not have the supreme refinement of his earlier version – partly a question of the warmer, vaguer recording – but it has a comparable concentration, with the structure persuasively and inevitably built. At the very opening of the work the extremes of dynamic and tempo may seem exaggerated, and at times there is a suggestion of the pursuit of beauty of sound for its own sake, but there is never any doubt about the brilliance and virtuosity of the Berlin orchestra. The *Prélude* has an appropriate languor and poetry, and there is a persuasive warmth about this performance, beautifully moulded; but again the earlier version distilled greater atmosphere and magic. The digital remastering of the HMV recording has brightened the sound, but detail remains diffuse. The brighter treble, however, has brought a degree of fortissimo fierceness, especially in the final climax of the *Dialogue du vent et de la mer*, but this is not too serious.

Michael Tilson Thomas and the Philharmonia give highly sensitive and atmospheric performances of both scores, and it would be a pleasure to recommend them with enthusiasm. Unfortunately, the recording is not up to the much higher standards we have come to expect in the last few years from CBS, in that the engineers have elected for a clarity that negates all that impressionism stands for. Comparing this with Previn, Karajan or Haitink is rather like observing a landscape by Manet alongside a sharply focused photograph of the same scene. Artistically, however, there is a lot to admire.

Karajan's 1964 recording of *La Mer* for DG remains pre-eminent; his re-make for HMV was not quite so successful, and nor is the newest digital version. The orchestral playing is eminently satisfactory – and if one takes an individual excerpt from it, there seems to be no cause for complaint. But the sheer magic that informed the 1964 account is missing. The flautist in the *Prélude à l'après-midi d'un faune* has a very pronounced vibrato. The sound is clear and vivid, on cassette as well as CD.

In June 1935, when EMI recorded Toscanini and the BBC Symphony Orchestra in Elgar's *Enigma*, the engineers also took the opportunity to record *La Mer*, and the sense of occasion is similarly vivid. Unlike *Enigma*, however, this cannot quite compare with Toscanini's much later NBC recording which, with far crisper ensemble, bites harder. The BBC performance is important in demonstrating the warmth of Toscanini – the maestro singing away happily in places – but the playing is often rough and the recording, well handled by the engineers, is seriously marred by audience noises (there are some appalling coughs to disfigure the quiet opening section). The chrome tape is technically first class.

Whether or not influenced by the character of the Ravel coupling, Solti treats the evocative Debussy works as virtuoso showpieces. That works very well in the two fast movements of *La Mer* (helped by brightly analytical recording), but much of the poetry is lost in the opening movement, not to mention *L'après-midi*. The cassette sound is vivid and clear.

Decca also offer a digitally remastered collection from Ansermet. Technically the transfers are remarkable; *La Mer* dates from 1964, the *Nocturnes* and *Prélude à l'après-midi* from 1957; indeed *Fêtes* sounds amazing. These readings have undoubted electricity and Ansermet secures a rather individual sound from his orchestra, but this CD is overpriced (Decca **414 040-2**). Ansermet's accounts, however, show infinitely more grip than Ashkenazy's Cleveland versions of the same works, although the latter have the advantage of superb 1987 digital sound. Ashkenazy seems unable to get inside the music, tempi are often unconvincing and the beautiful *Prélude à l'après-midi d'un faune* lacks shape without a really strong central climax. Similarly, a collection by Leonard Slatkin, sumptuously if none too clearly recorded by Telarc (**CD 80071**) offering *La Mer*, the *Prélude* and the *Danses sacrée et profane*, fails to make a real impression: they are well played, but there is too little electricity here.

Nocturnes: (*Nuages; Fêtes; Sirènes*).
** DG **415 370-2** [id.]. New England Conservatory Ch., Boston SO, Abbado – RAVEL: *Daphnis suite No. 2; Pavane;* SCRIABIN: *Poème de l'extase.***

Abbado's 1970 recording of the *Nocturnes* has not been enhanced by its CD transfer. The DG engineers have sought to clarify the resonant Boston acoustic, and fortissimos are less comfortable than on the old analogue LP. Abbado's fastidious care for detail needed no artificial help, for it was combined with a keen feeling for atmosphere without losing sight of the music's structure. The playing of the Boston orchestra remains immensely polished, but some of the naturalness which this performance exuded has evaporated with this slight artificial boosting.

Prélude à l'après-midi d'un faune.
(M) ** Decca **417 704-2** [id.]. Chicago SO, Solti – RAVEL: *Boléro***; STRAVINSKY: *Rite of spring.****

On CD, Solti's version of *L'après-midi* is coupled with his powerful version of Stravinsky's *Rite of spring*, music to which he is more readily attuned.

Rhapsody for clarinet and orchestra.
*** ASV Dig. **CDDCA 585**; *ZCDCA 585* [id.]. Emma Johnson, ECO, Yan Pascal Tortelier – CRUSELL: *Introduction, theme & variations;* TARTINI: *Concertino;* WEBER: *Concerto No. 1.****

Debussy's lovely *First Rhapsody* so-called (he never wrote a second) brings out the most persuasive qualities in Emma Johnson's artistry. The range of expression with extreme contrasts of tone and dynamic makes this an exceptionally sensuous performance, yearningly poetic. In some ways it is the most remarkable performance in Emma Johnson's very attractive collection of concertante pieces, well recorded in a helpful acoustic. The chrome cassette also produces excellent quality.

COLLECTIONS

(i) *Danses sacrée et profane; La Mer; Nocturnes; Prélude à l'après-midi d'un faune; Rêverie* (arr. Smith); *Suite bergamasque: Clair de lune* (arr. Caillet).
(M) **(*) CBS *40-79023*. Phd. O, Ormandy; (i) with M. Costello.

A double-length cassette to show the Philadelphia Orchestra at the height of its powers during the Ormandy regime. The sound is remarkably good, with a slight smoothing at the top to mellow the excessively bright lighting from which CBS recordings of this orchestra have often suffered. Detail remains quite clear and the music making is vividly projected. The overall impression is one of languor, the *Nocturnes* especially atmospheric and *La Mer* evocative, though the last movement, the *Dialogue of the wind and the waves*, is as exciting as anyone could wish for, with superb unselfconscious bravura from all departments of the orchestra. With ninety minutes' music offered, this is excellent value and the arrangements at the end of the concert make attractive *bonnes-bouches*: they are beautifully played and warmly recorded. The documentation, however, is a disgrace, with just a list of titles at the front of the hinged plastic box.

La Boîte à joujoux: Valsette. Children's corner: The little shepherd. Danses sacrée et profane; Petite suite: Ballet. La petite nègre; Prélude: La fille aux cheveux de lin. Rêverie; Sonata for flute, viola and harp. Syrinx for solo flute.
(*) RCA Dig. **RD 87173; *RK 87173* [**RCD1-7173**; *HRE1-7173*]. Galway, Robles, Oppenheimer; COE, Galway.

An agreeable and well-recorded late-evening Debussy collection, mostly lightweight (although both the *Danses* and the *Sonata* add attractive ballast) and distinctly appealing when the artists concerned are of the calibre of Marisa Robles, Graham Oppenheimer and the excellent Chamber Orchestra of Europe. James Galway's performance of *Syrinx* is memorable, and the *Trio* is very fine too.

CHAMBER MUSIC

Cello sonata; Petite pièce for clarinet and piano; Première Rapsodie for clarinet and piano; Sonata for flute, viola and harp; Violin sonata; Syrinx for solo flute.
*** Chan. **CHAN 8385**; *ABT 1036* [id.]. Athena Ens.

This well-recorded set from 1981 scores in being generously filled. In addition to the three late sonatas and *Syrinx*, we are given the two clarinet pieces (the *Rapsodie* is better known in its orchestral form). The most ethereal of these pieces is the *Sonata for flute, viola and harp*, whose other-worldly quality is beautifully conveyed here; indeed, this version can hold its own with the best in the catalogue. In the case of the other sonatas, there are strong competitors (Kyung Wha Chung and Lupu in the *Violin sonata*, Rostropovich with Britten in the *Cello sonata*). The works for wind are especially successful in the cassette version, which sounds admirably fresh; the string pieces are slightly less immediate.

Cello sonata in D min.
*** Decca **417 833-2** [id.]. Rostropovich, Britten – SCHUBERT: *Arpeggione sonata***(*); SCHUMANN: *5 Stücke.****
** Denon Dig. **C37 7563** [id.]. Fujiwara, Rouvier – STRAVINSKY: *Suite italienne;* SHOSTAKOVICH: *Sonata.***
** ASV Dig. **ZCDCA 522** [id.]. Colin Carr, Francis Grier – FAURÉ: *Elégie* etc.; FRANCK: *Sonata.***

Like Debussy's other late chamber works, this is a concentrated piece, quirkily original, not least in the central *Serenade*, with its sharp pizzicatos imitating the guitar. It was one of the first of a planned cycle of six sonatas for various instruments, written, so Debussy emphasized, by a 'musicien français'. The classic version by Rostropovich and Britten, now restored to the catalogue at premium price on CD, has a clarity and point which suits the music perfectly. The recording is first class, and if the couplings are suitable, this holds its place as first choice.

Mari Fujiwara and Jacques Rouvier give an elegant and idiomatic account of the Debussy *Sonata*, with plenty of fire in the finale. It is not superior to some of its rivals, but is worth a recommendation in its own right. Well-balanced recording.

Colin Carr's account of this elusive work is one item on a tape of French cello music called 'The virtuoso cello', and he certainly lives up to the title in the sureness of his playing which allows the free fantasy of the central *Serenade*, with its strange pizzicatos, to come over with seeming spontaneity. Good recording, if rather dry in ambience.

Sonata for flute, viola and harp.
(M) *** Decca *414 063-4*. Ellis, Melos Ens. (members) – RAVEL: *Introduction and allegro;* ROPARTZ: *Prelude, marine and chansons;* ROUSSEL: *Serenade.****

This Oiseau-Lyre 1960s anthology of French chamber music is more than welcome back to the catalogue. The age of the recording hardly shows, and the tape is vividly transferred. Debussy's *Sonata*, one of a set of three written late in his career, needs just the kind of performance it receives here at the hands of three fine chamber music players, its ethereal atmosphere well caught. The couplings are hardly less desirable.

(*i*) *Cello sonata;* (ii) *Violin sonata.*
(*) Chan. Dig. **CHAN 8458; *ABTD 1170* [id.]. (i) Yuli Turovsky; (ii) Rostislav Dubinsky; Luba Edlina – RAVEL: *Piano trio.****

In the *Cello sonata*, Turovsky gives a well-delineated, powerful account, with Luba Edlina, less reticent, perhaps – and, some might feel, less refined in feeling – than some of the great performances of the past. There is a wide dynamic range and no lack of commitment. In the *Violin sonata*, Rostislav Dubinsky and Luba Edlina (his wife) are in excellent form, though at the risk of sounding glib; this is red-blooded Slavonic Debussy rather than the more ethereal, subtle playing of a Grumiaux. There is a first-class chrome cassette.

String quartet in G min.
*** DG **419 750-2** [id.]. Melos Qt – RAVEL: *Quartet.****
(M) *** Ph. **420 894-2**; *420 894-4* [id.]. Italian Qt – RAVEL: *Quartet.****
*** Denon Dig. **C37 7830** [id.]. Nuovo Qt – RAVEL: *Quartet.***(*)
(*) HMV Dig. **CDC7 47347-2 [id.]. Alban Berg Qt – RAVEL: *Quartet.***(*)
(*) Telarc Dig. **CD 80111 [id.]. Cleveland Qt – RAVEL: *Quartet.***(*)
// Hyp. Dig. **CDA 66207**; *KA 66207* [id.]. Fairfield Qt – RAVEL: *Quartet.**(*)
*(*) Nimbus Dig. **NI 5077** [id.]. Medici Qt – SHOSTAKOVICH: *Quartet No. 8.***
*(*) Ph. Dig. **411 050-2** [id.]. Orlando Qt – RAVEL: *Quartet.**(*)

The reputation of the Melos Quartet can only be enhanced by this outstanding coupling. The playing of the quartet is distinguished by perfect intonation and ensemble, scrupulous accuracy in the observance of dynamic markings, a natural sense of flow and great tonal beauty. It would be difficult to imagine a finer account of the Debussy than this; and though the Italian Quartet recording on Philips has long been a yardstick against which newcomers are measured, the

Melos have the advantage of excellent recorded sound, wider in range and sonority than the Philips; the balance is neither too forward nor too reticent, and is truthful in matters of perspective as well as of timbre. The transfer of the analogue recording to CD is eminently successful. The DG engineers have resisted the temptation to try and add artificial presence, and if the sound is less vivid than some of the digital versions, the balance is truthful and textures have body and warmth as well as clarity; the improvement on the original LP is real in every sense of the word.

It need hardly be said that the playing of the Italian Quartet is also outstanding. Perfectly judged ensemble, weight and tone make this a most satisfying alternative choice, and the recording engineers have produced a vivid and truthful sound-picture, with plenty of impact. For CD collectors, this is by no means a second-best alternative to the Melos issue and there is a considerable price advantage. There is also a very good cassette.

The Nuovo Quartet are very musical and there is a natural, unforced quality about their playing that is likeable. There are some moments of affectation and they pull the development section of the first movement around. The scherzo is marvellously delicate and a delight – and their slow movement, too, is appropriately thoughtful and inward-looking. Were the first movement as good as this, they would sweep the board. They blend very beautifully and the recording is well focused in an acoustic that has warmth and space. This is one of the best accounts overall and can be warmly recommended to those seeking a digital version of this coupling.

Technically the Alban Berg Quartet are in a class of their own, yet, strangely enough, one finishes listening to this with greater admiration than involvement. Not that they are in any way outside Debussy's world; rather, the performance beautifies the work and has little spontaneous feeling. It is superbly recorded but, for sheer musical pleasure, the Melos Quartet of Stuttgart on DG still remains a first choice.

The Cleveland remains one of the finest American quartets and their performance of the Debussy is among the finest in the current catalogue. It is all high voltage, with impressive attack, a rich sonority and splendid tone, a wide dynamic range and a keen sensitivity to the changing tempo indications. Some readers may feel that, like the Alban Berg, they use Debussy as a vehicle for their own superb quartet playing and that there is a certain loss of intimacy. However, there is certainly a lot to admire here, including the recording which has plenty of body and presence.

The Fairfield Quartet pay great attention to dynamic markings and they have a vital sense of spirit. They give a very sensitive account of the scherzo, even if something of the inwardness of the slow movement eludes them. The recording is well defined, but one is placed near the instruments and this forward balance lends immediacy but slightly weakens the sense of atmosphere for which they are striving. Recommendable but by no means a first choice. The chrome cassette has striking presence, with the upper range brightly lit.

The Medici Quartet give an account that is acceptable rather than exceptional on Nimbus. The dynamic range is not as wide nor the tonal blend as refined as, say, the Melos Quartet of Stuttgart or the Alban Berg, and the recording is a little on the dry side.

The Orlando Quartet is a superlative ensemble and they throw themselves into this work with complete dedication. They have a wide dynamic range, yet rarely does one feel that any detail is exaggerated and their tonal blend is magnificent. However, seven bars after fig. 1 comes a sudden drop in pitch and, later on (6 bars before 5), there is another discernible pitch change. The playing itself is so characterful elsewhere and so vividly recorded that one would want to report that these discrepancies are of no moment – but, alas, they are.

A further alternative by the Viotti Quartet on the Verany label (**PV 786 102**) offers not only the Ravel as coupling, but also the Fauré; unfortunately their playing is very rough and ready and lacks the refinement and sensitivity that this music calls for.

Violin sonata in G min.
(M) *** Ph. **420 777-2** [id.]. David Oistrakh, Frida Bauer – PROKOFIEV: *Mélodies;* RAVEL: *Sonata;* YSAŸE: *Sonata.****
DG Dig. **415 683–2**; *415 683–4* [id.]. Shlomo Mintz, Yefim Bronfman – FRANCK; RAVEL: *Sonatas.*

David Oistrakh produces a rich yet finespun line and conveys all the poetry and atmosphere of the score. Frida Bauer's imaginative response is no less keen. This is beautifully proportioned and well transferred to CD, and the couplings are no less appealing.

Shlomo Mintz and Yefim Bronfman give a performance of the *Violin sonata* that is difficult to fault and gives much pleasure. They can be recommended alongside, though not in preference to, Chung and Lupu who are not yet available on CD. They have the additional advantage of offering a fine account of the Ravel *Sonata* as coupling, as well as the Franck. This is undoubtedly a magnificent account and excellently recorded too, with an outstandingly truthful and well-balanced cassette to set alongside the CD.

PIANO DUET

6 Épigraphes antiques; Marche écossaise; La Mer; Petite suite.
* Claves Dig. **CD 50-8508**. Duo Crommelynck (piano, 4 hands).

Patrick Crommelynck and Taeko Kuwata offer one rarity, the piano-duet arrangement of *La Mer*, which is new to the catalogue – not that it works particularly well in that form: this sounds very monochrome. The performances are generally rather low-voltage and pedestrian, save possibly for the *Épigraphes antiques*.

SOLO PIANO MUSIC

Arabesques Nos 1–2; Ballade; Danse bohémienne; Hommage à Haydn; L'isle joyeuse; Masques; Suite bergamasque; Valse romantique.
*(*) Denon Dig. **C37 7734** [id.]. Jacques Rouvier (piano).

By comparison with Rouvier's *Préludes* and *Images*, this is something of a let-down. In the *Passepied* of the *Suite bergamasque* he is surprisingly prosaic, and the recording produces some hardness in forte passages in the *Ballade* and, indeed, throughout this recital. He is a cultured and imaginative player and there are some good things, but he is not as well served by the engineers here as on other discs in this cycle. One or two notes on the instrument need the attention of a tuner. His *Suite bergamasque* is no match for the Kocsis on Philips, and this is not especially generous measure at forty-seven minutes.

Arabesques Nos 1–2; Ballade; Images, Book 1; L'isle joyeuse; La plus que lente; Rêverie; Suite bergamasque.
*** Conifer Dig. **CDCF 148**; *MCFC 148* [id.]. Kathryn Stott.

After her extremely successful Fauré disc, Kathryn Stott repeats the formula with Debussy, assembling an admirable recital which spans Debussy's composing career from the earliest attractive miniatures, the *Deux Arabesques* of 1888 and the *Rêverie* and *Ballads* of 1890, through to *La plus que lente* (1910). She is unerringly sensitive to atmosphere – *Reflets dans l'eau* from the first book of *Images* is an evocative delight – and the *Suite bergamasque*, too, is strongly characterized. There is no lack of finesse and her impetuosity always sounds spontaneous. This is a very refreshing programme, given excellent realism and presence on both CD and tape, although on the cassette there is just a suspicion of hardness on top – the transfer level is high.

Arabesques Nos 1–2; Ballade; Images, Book 1: Reflets dans l'eau; Mouvement. Book 2: Poissons d'or. L'isle joyeuse; Préludes, Book 2: Feux d'artifice. Suite bergamasque.
(M) *** EMI *EMX 412055-4*. Daniel Adni.

This collection dates from 1972 and was a follow-up to a similarly successful Chopin recital which had served as Daniel Adni's gramophone début the previous year. It is outstanding in every way: this young Israeli pianist proves himself a Debussian of no mean order. His recital is well planned and offers playing that is as poetic in feeling as it is accomplished in technique. The HMV engineers have provided piano tone of satisfying realism, and tape collectors seeking this particular compilation need not hesitate.

Berceuse héroïque; Children's corner suite; Danse; D'un cahier d'esquisses; Mazurka; Morceau de concours; Nocturne; Le petit nègre; La plus que lente; Rêverie.
*** Denon Dig. **C37 7372** [id.]. Jacques Rouvier.

An enjoyable and interesting Debussy recital from Jacques Rouvier which has the advantage of very truthful recording. This serves as a very useful addition to the catalogue and can be thoroughly recommended.

Children's corner; Estampes; Pour le piano; Suite bergamasque.
(*) HMV **CDC7 47374-2**. Samson François.

During the 1960s Samson François enjoyed a tremendous vogue in France, which explains the reappearance of these rather unsympathetic performances on CD. Whatever his merits in other repertoire, he showed limited feeling for Debussy and there is scant regard for atmosphere or for the lowest dynamic nuances. Since these were recorded, France has produced some really outstanding Debussians – Pascal Rogé, Jean-Philippe Collard and Michel Béroff; their records must take precedence.

Children's corner; Images, Sets 1 & 2.
*** DG **414 372-2** [id.]. Michelangeli.

Michelangeli's CD is outstanding in this repertoire. It is a magical and beautifully recorded disc. Michelangeli has made few records, but this is one of his best. It is also among the most distinguished Debussy playing in the catalogue. The remastering of the 1971 recording has been wonderfully successful. Although just a trace of background noise remains, it is not disturbing, and the tangibility of the piano image is remarkable.

Estampes; Images I & II; Images oubliées (1894); Pour le piano.
*** Denon Dig. **CD 1411** [id.]. Jacques Rouvier.

Jacques Rouvier made a positive impression with his 1982 recording of the Second Book of *Préludes*, and this issue is hardly less successful. His is a generously filled disc including not only both sets of *Images* but the earlier set (1894), which appeared in print only in the 1970s. He is very well recorded, slightly more closely in the Stadsgehoolsaal in Leiden than in the excellent Harlem Concertgebouw in which the earlier disc was made. But there is plenty of atmosphere and space round the sound. His account of the *Cloche à travers les feuilles* has great poise and *Et la lune descend sur le temple qui fut* has wonderful atmosphere and repose. In the *Images oubliées* he is not quite as imaginative (or as outstandingly recorded) as Zoltán Kocsis on Philips, but all the same this is an impressive issue.

Estampes; Images I & II; Préludes, Book 1, No. 6, Des pas sur la neige.
❀ *** Vox **MCD 10003** [id.]. Ivan Moravec.

A most distinguished recital. Wonderfully poetic and atmospheric playing, as one might expect from this fine Czech pianist. Indeed this is one of the most satisfying Debussy recitals on the market. Although Moravec is not a 'celebrity' in the UK, his playing is every bit as fine as the better-known names who figure in the current catalogue. This is really rather special.

Estampes; Images oubliées (1894); Pour le piano; Suite bergamasque
*** Ph. Dig. **412 118-2** [id.]. Zoltán Kocsis.

An exceptionally well-played and intelligently planned recital from Zoltán Kocsis. He gives us *Pour le piano* together with its 1894 precursor, the *Images oubliées*, and adds the *Estampes*, whose last movement is also related to the third of the set, *'Quelques aspects de "Nous n'irons plus au bois" parcequ'il fait un temps insupportable'*. Beautifully alert playing in which every nuance is subtly graded. This is repertoire that benefits enormously from the totally silent background that compact disc can offer, and the Philips engineers have captured the piano with exceptional realism and fidelity. As one expects from Kocsis, the playing is enormously refined and imaginative.

Préludes, Books I & II (complete).
(M) ❀ *** EMI mono **CDH7 61004-2** [id.]. Walter Gieseking.

Préludes, Books I & II; Pour le piano; L'isle joyeuse.
* HMV Dig. **CDS7 47608-8**; *EX 270432-5* (2). Cécile Ousset.

In his day, Walter Gieseking was something of a legend as a Debussy interpreter and this superb CD transfer testifies to his magic. The recordings were made in EMI's Abbey Road Studio No. 3 in 1953; Geraint Jones produced the First Book and Walter Legge the Second. The sound is quite splendid, and the listener could well be forgiven for thinking this was modern stereo, such is the richness of sonority and the sense of presence. Background is almost vanquished; our copy produced some very slight noise near the opening, but for the most part this is simply not a problem. Gieseking penetrates the atmosphere of the *Préludes* more deeply than almost any other artist. This is playing of rare distinction and great evocative quality. Moreover the CD plays for nearly 70′ and is offered on EMI's mid-priced Référence label. The documentation is concerned solely with the artist and gives no information about the music save the titles and the cues.

Cécile Ousset brings impressive technical address but less sense of poetry to this repertoire. Her playing has no lack of brilliance – as in such pieces as *Feux d'artifice* or *Les Tierces alternées* – but she shows too little regard for Debussy's dynamic markings below *piano*. These are very big-boned, large-scale and often unatmospheric performances which do not begin to compete in sensitivity with the distinguished competition. The quality of the recording is excellent, but this issue is not really recommendable.

Préludes, Book 1; Estampes; Images, Book 1.
*** Ph. **420 393-2** [id.]. Claudio Arrau.

Préludes, Book 1.
(*) DG **413 450-2 [id.]. Arturo Benedetti Michelangeli.
(*) Denon Dig. **C37 7121 [id.]. Jacques Rouvier.

Arrau has been consistently underrated as a Debussy interpreter and his CDs of the *Préludes* confirm his stature in this repertoire. But good as his accounts of the two Books of *Préludes* are, arguably his performances of the *Estampes* and *Images* are even finer. The playing combines sensitivity and atmosphere with a warmth that sometimes eludes Michelangeli in his much (and rightly) admired Debussy records. In Arrau's hands the famous *Reflets dans l'eau* and *Jardins sous la pluie* are particularly vivid. The opening *Prélude*, the *Danseuses de Delphes*, is perhaps a little too stately; generally speaking, Arrau's tempi here are unhurried, but that is no bad thing. There are some beautifully coloured details and a fine sense of atmosphere. He produces a magnificently full sonority for *La cathédrale engloutie*. Here he is helped by the richness of timbre provided by the Philips engineers; indeed the piano in these 1978/9 analogue recordings has a consistent body and realism typical of this company's finest work.

It goes without saying that Michelangeli's account reveals the highest pianistic distinction; it is in many ways a wholly compelling and masterful reading of these miniature tone-poems, with hardly a note or dynamic out of place, and it can be confidently recommended. However, in its CD format, this playing seems even cooler and more aloof and, while one remains lost in admiration for Michelangeli's actual playing, it must be conceded that not all collectors will find his readings sympathetic.

Jacques Rouvier has to face formidable competition from Michelangeli – which he survives. His playing has atmosphere and elegance; though Michelangeli exhibits the greater keyboard control and (at times) evocation of character, Rouvier has greater warmth and a pleasing humanity. He is given an excellent recording, too.

Préludes, Book 2; Images, Book 2.
*** Ph. **420 394-2** [id.]. Claudio Arrau.

Préludes, Book 2.
(*) Denon Dig. **C37 7043 [id.]. Jacques Rouvier.

Arrau's account of Book 2 of the *Préludes* is an invaluable record – to be treasured alongside the classic accounts of Gieseking and Casadesus. At first, Arrau's approach in *Brouillards* and *Feuilles mortes* seems a bit too leisurely, but these pieces gain in atmosphere at this speed. It is difficult to imagine a more penetrating or revealing account of *Canopes*, whose other-worldly melancholy is fully conveyed. *Feux d'artifice*, too, is splendidly projected, while the humour of *Hommage à S. Pickwick* is nicely caught. In the second Book of *Images*, *Et la lune descend sur le temple que fut* is hauntinglyly atmospheric and, throughout, the Philips recording (1979) is particularly impressive – really vivid and lifelike, with a warmly resonant bass.

There is some beautiful playing from Jacques Rouvier, a rather steady but atmospheric and well-controlled *Brouillards* and a highly accomplished reading of *Les fées sont d'exquises danseuses*. The staccato and forte markings in *La puerto del vina* are a trifle exaggerated, but there are very few points with which one would quarrel. *La terrasse des audiences de clair de lune* is more measured than many interpreters on record, but it is marked *lent*, and Rouvier succeeds in shaping it with considerable mastery and makes the most of its different moods. All in all, this is most responsive playing and Rouvier is very well recorded.

VOCAL MUSIC

Mélodies: *Ariettes oubliées; Fêtes galantes; 5 poèmes de Charles Baudelaire.*
(*) HMV Dig. **CDC7 47888-2; *EL 270294-4*. Barbara Hendricks, Michel Béroff.

Barbara Hendricks has the advantage of superb accompaniments from Michel Béroff, full of colour and perceptive touches; yet he never overshadows the voice. There is much that is vocally beautiful here, although Barbara Hendricks does not always succeed in using her middle and lower register to produce the intimacy she seeks, and the microphones are not always kind to her. Words are clear and word meanings are conveyed with considerable artistry; both artists clearly have a feeling for this repertoire, but the end result is uneven.

Mélodies: *Beau soir; 3 Chansons de Bilitis; 3 Chansons de France; Les cloches; Fêtes galantes, Set 2; Mandoline.*
*** Unicorn **DKPCD 9035**; *DKPC 9035* [id.]. Sarah Walker, Roger Vignoles – ENESCU: *Chansons****; ROUSSEL: *Mélodies.***(*)

Sarah Walker's Debussy collection, three fine groups of songs plus three separate songs from much earlier (*Les cloches*, *Mandoline* and *Beau soir*), makes an outstandingly fine disc of French songs. With deeply sympathetic accompaniment from Roger Vignoles, Sarah Walker's positive and characterful personality comes over vividly, well tuned to the often elusive idiom. Excellent recording, with CD adding realism in the warm acoustic.

La damoiselle élue (see also above, under *Images*).
*** Ph. Dig. **410 043-2** [id.]. Ameling, Taylor, women's voices of San Francisco Symphony Ch., San Francisco SO, De Waart – DUPARC: *Songs;* RAVEL: *Shéhérazade.****

The purity of Elly Ameling's voice makes for a ravishingly beautiful account of Debussy's early cantata. Other versions have either been more sensuous or more brightly focused, but the gentleness of this is certainly apt for such a pre-Raphaelite vision. Radiant recording to match, which is enhanced by the compact disc. This has a remarkable translucent richness of texture, with the chorus slightly distanced yet naturally focused.

Coupled with a disappointing version of Berlioz's *Les nuits d'été*, von Stade's reading of *La damoiselle élue* is only marginally more recommendable, failing to create the necessary atmosphere. That is less due to von Stade's singing than to the unidiomatic narrator and the chorus (CBS **MK 39098**).

(i) *La damoiselle élue;* (ii) *L'enfant prodigue.*
*** Orfeo Dig. *M 012821A* [id.]. (i) Cotrubas, Maurice; (ii) Jessye Norman, Carreras, Fischer-Dieskau; Stuttgart R. Ch. & SO, Bertini.

Debussy's two early and evocative cantatas make an excellent and enjoyable coupling, particularly in performances as fine as these under Gary Bertini, recorded very beautifully. The earlier of the two, *L'enfant prodigue*, the work with which Debussy belatedly won the Prix de Rome at the third attempt, is here superbly characterized by the three soloists: Carreras as the prodigal son himself, rather too warmly Italianate for this music, but movingly expressive; Jessye Norman rich-toned yet graceful as the mother (the well-known *Air de Lia* superbly done); and Fischer-Dieskau as the forgiving father. *La damoiselle élue* is not nearly so rare, but Cotrubas gives a memorable reading, girlish and winning, pure and radiant. The chorus is rather too distant in the later cantata, but otherwise the sound is excellent.

OPERA

Pelléas et Mélisande (complete).
*** HMV **CDS7 49350-2** (3). Stilwell, Von Stade, Van Dam, Raimondi, Ch. of German Op., Berlin, BPO, Karajan.

Karajan's is a performance that sets Debussy's masterpiece as a natural successor to Wagner's *Tristan* rather than its antithesis. To that extent the interpretation is controversial, for this is essentially a rich and passionate performance with the orchestral tapestry at the centre and the singers providing a verbal obbligato. Debussy after all rests a high proportion of his argument on the many interludes between scenes; paradoxically, the result of this approach is more not less dramatic, for Karajan's concentration carries one in total involvement through a story that can seem inconsequential. The playing of the Berlin Philharmonic is both polished and deeply committed, and the cast comes near the ideal, with Frederica von Stade a tenderly affecting heroine and Richard Stilwell a youthful, upstanding hero set against the dark incisive Golaud of Van Dam. Few operas gain so much from CD as *Pelléas*, whether in absence of background noise, extra vividness of atmosphere and sense of presence or, in this instance, the layout with no side-breaks. The first and third discs each contain two Acts, with Act III contained on the much shorter middle disc. Voices are particularly vivid, with the orchestra, pleasantly mellow, set rather behind.

Delibes, Léo (1836–91)

Coppélia (ballet): complete.
(B) *** CfP *TC-CFPD 4712* (2). Paris Op. O, Mari.
*** Decca Dig. **414 502-2**; *414 502-4* (2) [id.]. Nat. PO, Bonynge.

Delibes wrote a marvellous score for *Coppélia*. There is never a dull bar, and the sparkling succession of tunes, orchestrated with consistent flair and imagination, provides a superb musical entertainment away from the theatre. The Classics for Pleasure set is in every way worthy of Delibes' masterpiece. The elegant and sensitive orchestral playing conjures up a marvellously theatrical atmosphere and the stage scene is readily created in the mind's eye. Mari uses ballet tempi throughout, yet there is never any loss of momentum and the long-breathed string phrasing is a source of continuous pleasure. The telling musical characterization, from the robust peasantry to the delicately pointed *Dance of the Automatons*, is vividly memorable. The recording is clear and balanced most effectively within a perfectly chosen acoustic, and this is one of the finest complete ballet recordings ever made. At CfP price it is a bargain of bargains.

Bonynge has recorded the ballet previously for Decca with the Suisse Romande Orchestra, but clearly the National Philharmonic with its personnel of expert British sessions musicians is able to bring a more polished and no less spirited ensemble, and the wind solos are a constant delight. The only slight drawback is the relatively modest number of violins which the clarity of the digital recording makes apparent. In moments like the delicious *Scène et valse de la poupée*, which Bonynge points very stylishly, the effect is Mozartian in its grace. But the full body of strings above the stave lacks something in amplitude and the fortissimos bring a digital emphasis on brilliance that is not wholly natural. Having said that, the recording in all other respects is praiseworthy, not only for its vividness of colour, but for the balance within a concert-hall acoustic (Walthamstow Assembly Hall). In the many colourful and elegantly scored interchanges for woodwind and strings the tangibility of the players is very striking. Bonynge has the full measure of the music, and the orchestra obviously enjoy it, too. With 31 cues, the CDs provide admirable access for anyone wanting to make up a personally chosen suite. The chrome cassettes offer less ready internal access, but some might prefer the sound which gives a softer focus to the violins and slightly fuller timbre, without losing the overall vividness of the recording.

Coppélia (ballet): suite.
*** Capriccio Dig. **10 073** [id.]. Berlin RSO, Fricke – CHOPIN: *Les Sylphides*.**
(M) *** DG **423 215-2**; *423 215-4* [id.]. BPO, Karajan – CHOPIN: *Les Sylphides*; OFFENBACH: *Gaîté parisienne*.***
(M) *** DG *413 981-4*. BPO, Karajan – CHOPIN: *Les Sylphides*.***

Although the playing of the Berlin Radio orchestra is not quite as cultured as that of the Berlin Philharmonic under Karajan, it is still very fine, and Fricke displays a lighter touch in the

Czárdás. He also includes more music, both at the opening and in the delectable *Music of the Automatons*, one of Delibes' most piquant and memorable inspirations. The Capriccio recording is first class, with sparkle and warmth and an attractive ambient effect.

Karajan secures some wonderfully elegant playing from the Berlin Philharmonic Orchestra, and generally his lightness of touch is sure. The *Valse de la poupée* is beautifully pointed and the variations which follow have a suave panache which is captivating. The *Czárdás*, however, is played very slowly and heavily, and its curiously studied tempo may spoil the tape for some. The recording is even better than on the reverse and can be made to sound very impressive. Only part of the suite is included on the CD, which is generously re-coupled not only with *Les Sylphides* but with Offenbach's *Gaîté parisienne* ballet suite. As we go to press the earlier cassette is still available and this offers the complete suite.

Lakmé (opera): complete.
** HMV **CDS7 49430-2** (2). Mesplé, Burles, Soyer, Millet, Paris Opéra-Comique Ch. & O, Lombard.

Lakmé: highlights.
** HMV **CDC7 47807-2**; (M) *EG 290160-4* (from above recording, cond. Lombard).

With the outstanding 1969 Decca/Sutherland set of *Lakmé* still awaited on CD, HMV have rushed in first with Alain Lombard's opéra-comique version from the beginning of the 1970s, the point being that a British Airways TV commercial has made the *Flower duet* a top classical pop. This is quite nicely sung here by Mady Mesplé and Danielle Millet and those who seek it on CD or tape would do better with the highlights issue than with the complete set, which is marred by the otherwise thin and wobbly, if idiomatic, singing of Mesplé in the title role. Charles Burles sings with a fair degree of charm as Gérard and Roger Soyer offers strong support as Nilakantha. Lombard conducts with understanding, and the recording is agreeable if rather reverberant.

Delius, Frederick (1862–1934)

Air and dance for string orchestra; Fennimore and Gerda: Intermezzo. Hassan: Intermezzo & Serenade (arr. Beecham). *Irmelin: Prelude. Koanga: La Calinda. On hearing the first cuckoo in spring; Sleigh ride; A song before sunrise; Summer evening* (ed. Beecham); *Summer night on the river.*
*** HMV Dig. **CDC7 47610-2**; *EL 270453-4*. N. Sinfonia, Richard Hickox.

Richard Hickox's Delius collection neatly brings together most of the shorter pieces in finely shaped, well-played readings, recorded in aptly atmospheric sound. Hickox's warm moulding of phrase goes with fine playing from the Northern Sinfonia. This is currently the best-recorded of the post-Beecham collections of this repertoire and has the digital advantage of an absolutely silent background. There is a good cassette, but it does not quite share that advantage.

Air and dance for string orchestra; On hearing the first cuckoo in spring; Summer evening; Summer night on the river.
*** Chan. **CHAN 8330**; *ABTD 1106* [id.]. LPO, Handley – VAUGHAN WILLIAMS: *Serenade* etc.***

Handley as an interpreter of Delius generally takes a more direct, less gently lingering view than is common, but here that refusal to sentimentalize – which can miss the more sweetly evocative qualities of the music – goes with the most subtle nuances in performance, fresh as well as beautiful and atmospheric. *Summer evening* is little more than a salon piece, but no less attractive for that. The tonal richness of the LPO's playing is well caught in the Chandos recording, which is all the more vividly real-sounding on CD. The chrome tape also reflects a high state of the art, refined in every respect.

American rhapsody (Appalachia); Norwegian suite (Folkeraadet: The Council of the people); Paa Vidderne (On the heights); Spring morning.
** Marco Polo **8.220452** [id.]. Slovak PO, Bratislava, John Hopkins.

A fascinating collection of early Delius, mostly uncharacteristic, but with pre-echoes of his later work. *Paa Vidderne*, the most substantial piece, was based on a poem by Ibsen and first performed in Oslo in 1891. It is rather melodramatic but has a distinct melodic interest. *Spring morning* (1890) is shorter and similarly picaresque in its orchestral effects, but the *Folkeraadet suite*, written for the comedy by the Norwegian playwright, Gunnar Heiberg, displays a sure orchestral touch and is most attractive in its diversity of invention. The *American rhapsody* is a concise version of *Appalachia* without the chorus, given here in its original 1896 format. John Hopkins brings a strong sympathy and understanding to this repertoire and secures a committed and flexible response from his Czech players in music which must have been wholly unknown to them. Ideally, a greater weight of string tone is needed in the two tone-poems, but the vivid recording projects well, and the interest of this programme is enough to offset any lack of refinement in the music making.

2 Aquarelles (arr. Fenby)*; Fennimore and Gerda: Intermezzo* (arr. Beecham)*; Hassan: Intermezzo & Serenade* (arr. Beecham)*; Irmelin: Prelude; Late swallows* (arr. Fenby); *On hearing the first cuckoo in spring; Song before sunrise; Summer night on the river.*
*** Chan. **CHAN 8372**; (M) *CBT 1017* [id.]. Bournemouth Sinf., Del Mar.

There are few finer interpreters of Delius today than Norman Del Mar, once a protégé of Beecham, and this nicely balanced collection of miniatures is among the most broadly recommendable of Delius collections available. The performances are warmly atmospheric and have a strong sense of line. Full recording to match, and a successful digital transfer, the sound fresh yet with an excellent overall bloom. The analogue master dates from 1977, but this is not very apparent in the sound quality. However, the reissue on tape is at mid-price and costs considerably less than the CD. The cassette transfer, made at the highest level, is splendidly managed.

2 Aquarelles; Fennimore and Gerda: Intermezzo. On hearing the first cuckoo in spring; Summer night on the river.
*** DG **419 748-2** [id.]. ECO, Barenboim – VAUGHAN WILLIAMS: *Lark ascending* etc.*;* WALTON: *Henry V.****

Barenboim's luxuriant performances have a gorgeous sensuousness – they are in the Barbirolli Italianate tradition rather than owing any allegiance to Beecham – and their warm, sleepy atmosphere should seduce many normally resistant to Delius's pastoralism. The couplings are no less enticing and the 1975 recording has retained its body and warmth in the digital remastering. Some might feel that this music making has almost a touch of decadence in its unalloyed appeal to the senses.

Brigg Fair; Dance rhapsody No. 2; Fennimore and Gerda: Intermezzo. Florida suite; Irmelin: Prelude; Marche-caprice; On hearing the first cuckoo in spring; Over the hills and far away; Sleigh ride; Song before sunrise; Summer evening; Summer night on the river; (i) *Songs of sunset.*

❀ *** HMV **CDS7 47509-8** [id.]; (M) *EM 290323-5*. RPO, Beecham; (i) with Forrester, Cameron, Beecham Choral Society.

Brigg Fair; Fennimore and Gerda: Intermezzo; Florida suite; Irmelin: Prelude; Marche-caprice; On hearing the first cuckoo in spring; Sleigh ride; Song before sunrise; Summer evening; Summer night on the river.
(B) *** HMV *TCC2-POR 154601-9*. RPO, Beecham.

We are now discovering that the best of Beecham's recordings, made at the end of the 1950s and in the early '60s were among the finest musical and technical achievements of the early stereo era. No doubt the great conductor's meticulous ear for subtlety of balance contributed much to this, but the EMI producers and engineers of the period (in the present instance Lawrance Collingwood and Christopher Parker) must also share the credit. The remastering of the complete stereo orchestral recordings of Delius's music, plus the choral *Songs of sunset* is something of a technological miracle, and it fully deserved *Gramophone* magazine's 1987 award for remastering 'historical' material. The result is far from historical in effect, for it brings Beecham's ravishing performances into our own time with an uncanny sense of realism and presence. Background noise is all but banished, and the delicacy of wind and string textures is something to marvel at. Beecham's fine-spun magic, his ability to lift a phrase, is apparent from the very opening of *Over the hills and far away*, which comes first, although *Brigg Fair* might have been a better opener as it shows Delius at his most inspired and Beecham's orchestra at their most incandescent. The shorter pieces bring superb wind solos, while the great conductor often conjures a hazy sentient warmth from the strings – as in *On hearing the first cuckoo in spring*, but more especially in *Summer night on the river* – which no other conductor has matched since. The *Sleigh ride* shows Beecham sparkling, and he is no less persuasive in the *Florida suite*, Delius's first orchestral work, strong in melodic appeal, if not characteristic. In the *Songs of sunset* the choral focus is soft-grained, but the words are surprisingly audible, and the backward balance of the soloists is made to sound natural against the rich orchestral textures. The music is also available on a pair of well-managed cassettes, offered at what almost amounts to bargain price, but, good as the transfers are, the CDs are more than worth their extra cost and are generously full. For those not wanting the *Songs of sunset*, the alternative double-length tape in EMI's 'Portrait of the Artist' series can be recommended, although it lacks proper back-up documentation. The CDs have the best documentation of all, including a booklet in which Lyndon Jenkins describes the relationship between the composer and his great interpreter. The gramophone offers here music making which is every bit as rewarding as the finest live performances.

Cello concerto.
*** RCA **RD 70800**; *RK 70800*. Lloyd Webber, Philh. O, Handley – HOLST: *Invocation;* VAUGHAN WILLIAMS: *Fantasia*.***

Lloyd Webber is inside the idiom and plays the *Concerto* – not one of Delius's strongest works perhaps, though it was the composer's own favourite among his four concertos – with total conviction. Its lyricism is beguiling enough but the *Concerto* proceeds in wayward fashion, and the soloist must play every note as if he believes in it ardently – and this Lloyd Webber and his partners do. Though he does not produce a big sound in the concert hall, the RCA balance is ideal and conveys an almost chamber-like quality at times, with great warmth and clarity. One of the strengths of this version, apart from its technical excellence, is the interest of the coupling, which brings a first recording of Holst's *Invocation*. There is a recommendable chrome cassette, the sound fresh yet atmospheric, but the CD is strikingly refined in texture; the slightly diffuse quality is very evocative and right for the music.

Violin concerto; Légende for violin and orchestra; Suite for violin and orchestra.
*** Unicorn Dig. **DKPCD 9040**; *DKPC 9040* [id.]. Ralph Holmes, RPO, Handley.

Shortly before his cruelly premature death, Ralph Holmes went to the studio and recorded this strong and beautiful performance of one of Delius's supreme masterpieces, the *Violin concerto*. Though the structure superficially may seem rhapsodic, it is in fact closely co-ordinated, as the late Deryck Cooke amply illustrated. Holmes and Handley, an ideal partnership, bring out the Delian warmth in their shaping of phrase and pointing of rhythm, while keeping firm control of the overall structure. The *Légende* – long forgotten in this orchestral form – and the early *Suite* make ideal couplings, played with equal understanding. Holmes's beautifully focused playing is nicely balanced against the wide span of the orchestra behind him in first-class digital recording, particularly impressive on CD. There is also an excellent tape.

Double concerto for violin and cello.
(M) **(*) PRT **PVCD 8372** [id.]. Raymond Cohen, Warburg, RPO, Del Mar – BUSH: *Variations*.(**)

Delius's *Double concerto* has been neglected (even Peter Warlock was somewhat scathing about it), but it proves to be one of the most cogently argued of Delius's longer works, using – like the *Violin concerto*, written at about the same time during the First World War – an extended one-movement form with confidence and a real sense of logic. The cellist, Gerald Warburg (a member of an American banking family as well as a talented player), helped finance the recording in the mid 1960s. Although the performance is far from immaculate, it has a red-blooded committedness that is far more important in such music. The balance is remarkably good, and Norman Del Mar draws playing from the RPO of which Beecham might have been proud. It is a most affecting performance and the remastered 1966 recording, although limited, is vivid and yet smoothly integrated, to produce a seamless Delian flow of sound, with the solo instruments retaining their body of timbre. The one blot in this issue is the total absence of documentation about the music.

Florida suite; North Country sketches.
*** Chan. Dig. **CHAN 8413**; *ABTD 1150* [id.]. Ulster O, Handley.

Having taken over Sir Adrian Boult's mantle in recording the works of Elgar, Vernon Handley here turns back to Delius to evoke the spirit of Sir Thomas Beecham. In the delicacy of the orchestral playing (the muted Ulster strings create some exquisite textures) and the easy rhapsodic freedom of the melodic lines, this is music making in the Beecham mould, but of course the readings are Handley's own. His choice of tempi is always apt and it is fascinating that in the *North Country sketches* which evoke the seasons in the Yorkshire moors a Debussian influence is revealed. The delicious tune we know as *La Calinda* appears in the first movement of the *Florida suite*; elsewhere, the local influences absorbed by the young composer in America bring parallels with Dvořák. But Handley's refined approach clearly links the work with later masterpieces. The recording is superbly balanced within the very suitable acoustics of the Ulster Hall; one's only real criticism is the lack of sumptuous weight to the violins when they have an eloquent musical line in the *Florida suite*; but otherwise tuttis are superbly expansive. The chrome tape represents the highest state of the art but the CD gains in presence and definition.

Life's Dance; North Country sketches; Song of summer.
(M) **(*) HMV *ED 290026-4*. RPO, Groves.

This attractive Delius tape contains a virtually unknown piece, *Lebenstanz*, or *Life's dance*, which was written in the 1890s immediately before the tone-poem *Paris*. It presents a fascinating contrast, beginning with an urgency not always associated with this composer. *Song of summer*, a typically evocative piece, comes from the other end of Delius's career; it was conceived just before he lost his sight and was subsequently dictated to his amanuensis, Eric Fenby. The *North Country sketches*, depicting with Delian impressionism the seasons of the year, make an apt coupling. Groves is a sensitive interpreter, even if he rarely matches the irresistible persuasiveness of a Beecham. The balance is vivid and warm, almost too close in sound to do justice to such delicately atmospheric music. However, the recordings have transferred particularly successfully to cassette.

(i) *Dance rhapsody No. 1; Eventyr; Paris, the song of a great city;* (ii) *Song of summer;* (iii) *Cynara;* (iv) *Sea drift.*
(B) **(*) HMV *TCC2-POR 54295.* (i) Royal Liverpool PO, (ii) RPO; Groves, with (iii) Shirley-Quirk; (iv) Noble, Royal Liverpool PO.

For any conductor attempting to interpret Delius today, the first thing is to try to forget the ghost of Sir Thomas Beecham and to produce spontaneous-sounding performances that may or may not correspond to his. Groves does just this in the magnificent picture in sound, *Paris*, as well as in the shorter works. The tempi are less extreme than Beecham's but refreshingly persuasive. *Cynara* (1907) is a setting of Dowson. John Shirley-Quirk does the solo part impressively and the performance of this work is very fine. *Sea drift* is by comparison disappointingly matter-of-fact, failing to convey the surge of inspiration that so exactly matches the evocative colours of Walt Whitman's poem about the seagull, a solitary guest from Alabama. However, taken as a whole this 'Portrait of the Artist' double-length cassette certainly shows Groves as a persuasive Delian, and none of the performances are otherwise available, except *A Song of summer* (see above). The recording is generally excellent.

Cello sonata.
*** Chan. Dig. **CHAN 8499**; *ABTD 1209* [id.]. Raphael & Peter Wallfisch – BAX: *Rhapsodic ballad;* BRIDGE: *Cello sonata;* WALTON: *Passacaglia.****
** Max Sound *MSCB 20/21*; *MSCC 20/21.* Caroline Dale, Keith Swallow – BRIDGE; PROKOFIEV: *Sonatas;* MARTINŮ: *Variations.****

The Delius *Sonata* is an exact contemporary of the Bridge with which it is coupled. It is a less concentrated, more discursive piece, but there is, as always with Delius, a highly personal atmosphere, and these Chandos performers give as strong and sympathetic an account of it as is to be found. They are also excellently recorded, although the sound on cassette is slightly more diffuse than the CD.

Caroline Dale's account of the Delius *Sonata* is slightly less convincing than the other performances on this generous 83′ chrome tape. The work dates from 1919 and its flowing, endlessly lyrical lines bring a less than ripe response from the cellist, although this effect is partly contributed to by a balance which favours Keith Swallow's much more positive performance. However, the rest of the music in this recital is very successful and the Delius performance is by no means inconsequential.

String quartet.
*** ASV Dig. *ZCDCA 526* [id.]. Brodsky Qt – ELGAR: *Quartet.****

The young members of the Brodsky Quartet in their first commercial recording give a richly expressive performance of Delius's *String quartet* of 1916 with its evocative slow movement, *Late swallows.* In this music the ebb and flow of tension and a natural feeling for persuasive but unexaggerated rubato is vital; with fine ensemble but seeming spontaneity, the Brodsky players consistently produce that. First-rate recording, and an excellent cassette.

VOCAL AND CHORAL MUSIC

(i) *An Arabesque; Dance rhapsody No. 2; Fennimore and Gerda: Intermezzo;* (i; ii) *Songs of sunset.*
*** Unicorn Dig. **DKPCD 9063**; *DKPC 9063* [id.]. (i) Thomas Allen; (ii) Sarah Walker; Amb. S.; RPO, Fenby.

It is good that Eric Fenby, without whose help for the blind and paralysed composer the late Delius works would never have existed, makes an ardent and persuasive interpreter, particularly in neglected music like this that needs positive advocacy. The present collection follows up Fenby's earlier two-disc set for Unicorn (see below), and brings equally warm, well-sung and well-played performances, atmospherically recorded. What emerges as a Delius masterpiece, absurdly little known, is *An Arabesque*, a 15-minute work for baritone, mixed chorus and orchestra, setting a Pan-worship poem (in English translation) of the Norwegian poet and biologist, Jens Peter Jacobsen. Maybe the vague and even misleading title with its indefinite article has hindered appreciation. The emotional thrust of the opening sequence, superbly sung by Thomas Allen and with passionate singing from the chorus too, subsides into characteristic Delian reflectiveness, but with a distinction and sense of purpose to put it among the composer's finest works – which is where Fenby says he himself places it. The *Songs of sunset* also bring ravishing sounds, with Sarah Walker as deeply expressive as Allen. The *Dance rhapsody No. 2* gives the lie to the idea of Delius as an unrhythmic composer, crisply sprung in this performance, while the sensuousness of the *Fennimore and Gerda Intermezzo* returns us to gorgeously characteristic orchestral textures. Warm, full sound, yet refined and transparent on CD, with the chrome cassette also offering a state-of-the-art transfer.

2 Aquarelles. (i) *Caprice & elegy. Fantastic dance; Irmelin: Prelude; Koanga: La Calinda; A Song of Summer.* (ii) *Cynara* (ii; iii) *Idyll.* (iv) *A Late Lark.* (v) *Songs of Farewell.*
*** Unicorn Dig. **DKPCD 9008/9** [id.]. Fenby, with (i) Lloyd Webber; (ii) Allen; (iii) Lott; (iv) Rolfe Johnson; (v) Amb. S.; RPO.

Eric Fenby draws loving, dedicated performances from the RPO. *A Song of Summer* is the finest of the works which Fenby took down from the dictation of the blind, paralysed and irascible composer, but the *Songs of Farewell* (to words of Whitman) and the love scene entitled *Idyll*, rescued from an abortive opera project, are most beautiful too, with Felicity Lott and Thomas Allen especially impressive in the *Idyll*. These major works, like such trifles as the *Fantastic dance* (dedicated to Fenby), were based on earlier sketches, while other items here were arranged by Fenby with the composer's approval. The *Irmelin Prelude*, for example, took material from the opera at a time when it seemed it would never receive a full performance. Christopher Palmer's notes on the pieces are deeply sympathetic as well as informative, making this two-disc issue essential for anyone interested in Delius. The transfer to CD is expertly managed, with Delius's comparatively thick choral textures here sounding fresh and almost transparent. The digital recording was an early one but this shows only in a slight lack of sumptuousness in the orchestral fortissimos; otherwise the balance is outstandingly fine.

Hassan (incidental music).
(M) **(*) HMV *ED 291186-4*. Hill, Rayner Cook, Ch., Bournemouth Sinf., Handley.

Although the recording in its immediacy lacks atmosphere, Handley secures clean-cut, enjoyable performances of all the pieces Delius wrote for Flecker's play *Hassan* (including a choral version of the famous *Serenade*). Both playing and singing are first rate and though memories of Beecham's briefer selection from the incidental music are rarely if ever effaced, this is a most valuable issue for Delians. The tape transfer is smooth and well balanced.

Idyll (*Once I passed through a populous city*); (i) *Requiem*.
(M) **(*) HMV *ED 290027-4*. Harper, Shirley-Quirk, RPO, Meredith Davies, (i) with Royal Choral Society.

The reissue of this 1968 recording is particularly welcome since it couples two Delius rarities. The *Requiem* is not only new to the gramophone, but until recently had remained unperformed since the 1920s. It was written during the First World War, and Delius's well-known atheism as well as his disillusion with life did not find a responsive echo at the first performance; indeed, the work was written off. Though it is not an austere work, it is far sparer than most other Delius works of the period, and much of it is rewarding, particularly in as fine a performance as this. The *Idyll* is much earlier, or at least its material is. The music, though uneven in inspiration, is often extremely impressive, and readers need have no reservations about either performance or recording. This is a good XDR cassette, with the upper range of the chorus not too seriously cushioned.

English songs: *I-Brasil; So white, so soft; To daffodils*. French songs: *Avant que tu ne t'en ailles; Chanson d'automne; Le ciel est pardessus le toit; La lune blanche; Il pleure dans mon cœur*. Scandinavian songs: *Autumn; In the garden of the Seraglio; Irmelin rose; Let springtime come; Silken shoes; Twilight fancies; The violet; Young Venevil*.
*** Unicorn Dig. *DKPC 9022* [id.]. Lott, Sarah Walker, Rolfe Johnson, Fenby.

This collection of English, French and Scandinavian songs – almost all of them slow and dreamy – provides a charming sidelight on Delius's art. Apart from the early *Twilight fancies*, they are little known, but all reflect the composer's sympathy for words. Except for three in German, the Scandinavian songs are sung in English. The three soloists all sing most understandingly, warmly supported by Eric Fenby's piano accompaniments. Excellent recording.

Song of the high hills; Songs: *The bird's story; Le ciel est pardessus le toit; I-Brasil; Il pleure dans mon cœur; Let springtime come; La lune blanche; To daffodils; Twilight fancies; Wine roses*.
❀ *** Unicorn Dig. **DKPCD 9029**; *DKPC 9029* [id.]. Lott, Sarah Walker, Rolfe Johnson, Amb. S., RPO, Fenby.

Even among Delius issues, this stands out as one of the most ravishingly beautiful of all. Eric Fenby, as a young man the composer's amanuensis and a lifelong advocate, draws a richly atmospheric performance from Beecham's old orchestra in one of the most ambitious and beautiful, yet neglected, of Delius's choral works. Inspired by the hills of Norway, Delius evocatively conveys the still, chill atmosphere above the snow-line by episodes for wordless chorus, here finely balanced. The coupling of Delius songs in beautiful, virtually unknown orchestral arrangements is ideally chosen, with all three soloists both characterful and understanding.

OPERA

Irmelin (complete).
(*) BBC Dig. **CD 3002 (2). Hannan, Rippon, Mitchinson, Rayner Cook, BBC Singers & Concert O, Del Mar.

'The best first opera by any composer,' said Sir Thomas Beecham of *Irmelin*, and this recording, conducted by one of Beecham's most individual and inspired pupils, goes a long way towards confirming that. The piece – a strange amalgam of *Parsifal*, *Turandot* and *Pelléas et Mélisande* (those last two operas postdating this) – is dramatically flawed, with Rolf the Robber hardly a convincing figure, but the love music here for Irmelin and Nils is among the most sensuously beautiful that Delius ever wrote. Though the plot disconcertingly prevents the two meeting until Act III, each continually dreams of an ideal of love, finally found. That draws from Delius his warmest writing, as is well known from the so-called *Prelude* which the composer confected, with the help of Eric Fenby, from salient motifs in the then unperformed opera. The soaring arc of the main love-motif hauntingly recurs in every conceivable transformation, finally returning as the lovers depart, unconcerned, into the sunset, fast and rhythmic with orchestral jingles adding a trimming of silver. Outstanding in the cast is Eilene Hannan in the name part, singing radiantly. Sally Bradshaw sings sweetly as the heavenly Voice in the Air, the messenger to Irmelin that her ideal of a prince is on his way. It is a pity that, for all the power of his singing, John Mitchinson does not sound younger as the hero, Nils, and a darker voice is needed for Rolf than Brian Rayner Cook's light baritone; but with Del Mar drawing warmly committed playing from the BBC Concert Orchestra (not quite sumptuous enough in the string section) this is a richly enjoyable set, beautifully balanced and recorded. The set is now issued on a pair of CDs against the original three LPs, but the libretto has no cue indications, which is a distinct drawback to internal access.

(i) *The Magic Fountain;* (ii) *Margot La Rouge.*
(*) BBC **CD 3004X [Ara. **Z 6546**] (2). (i) Mitchinson, Pring, Welshby, Anglas, Thomas, BBC Singers; (ii) McDonall, Woollam, Donelly, Andrew, Jackson; BBC Concert O, Del Mar.

The generous coupling of these two Delius operas on a pair of CDs, playing for 140 minutes, is certainly welcome, and the BBC recordings have transferred well to the new format. The presentation and documentation, however, leave much to be desired. Cues are limited and they are not indicated on the librettos; with the French text in use in *Margot la Rouge*, it would have been more sensible to place the English translation alongside it, rather than separately.

In the passionately committed reading of *The Magic Fountain* – taken direct from Del Mar's world première performance given on Radio 3 in November 1977 – the work emerges as arguably the most consistently inspired of Delius's operas. Writing in the 1890s, Delius was influenced in his plot by *Tristan*: the heroine's hatred of the hero – a Spanish nobleman searching for the Fountain of Eternal Youth – turns to passionate love. The pity is that Delius's dramatic sense let him down. There is much beautiful atmospheric writing – particularly for the chorus – and although none of these soloists is perfect and the sound-effects are sometimes intrusive, this is a most valuable and enjoyable set, cleanly recorded.

The gestation of *Margot la Rouge* was a curious one. That Delius of all composers opted to write an opera using a Grand Guignol melodramatic story may seem odd, until you discover that he was simply abiding by the rules of an Italian competition he entered. He rejected the piece but, in the last years of his life with Eric Fenby, rearranged some of the love music to words by Walt Whitman and so produced the *Idyll*. The full score of the opera was subsequently mislaid; using a piano score made by Ravel (the story gets odder) Fenby reconstructed the whole piece, and that was also given its world première on BBC Radio 3 (in October 1981). With warmly committed, highly atmospheric playing under Del Mar and with a strong if not ideally characterful cast, it makes an important addition to the Delius canon. The theatrical action music is effective but unoriginal. The real Delius lies in the love music alone. Beautifully balanced recording.

A Village Romeo and Juliet (complete).
(M) ** HMV *EM 290404-5* (2). Luxon, Mangin, Tear, Harwood, Shirley-Quirk, John Alldis Ch., RPO, Meredith Davies.

There are some wonderfully sensuous moments in this highly characteristic opera of Delius, written at the turn of the century. The famous *Walk to the Paradise Garden* with its passionate orchestral climax (superbly performed here) is the most memorable passage, but the music of the Dark Fiddler and much of the music for the two ill-starred lovers is intensely expressive. Unfortunately there is too little mystery in Meredith Davies's performance. He fails to persuade one to listen on when Delius's inspiration lets him run on dangerously long. Nevertheless there is some excellent singing and playing, and first-rate recording. The reissue is reasonably priced, so this is well worth exploring. The tapes are satisfactory but the sound is less transparent than is ideal and the upper range is somewhat restricted, though the balance is good.

Devienne, François (1759–1803)

Bassoon quartets (for bassoon, violin, viola and cello), *Op. 73*.
*** Gallo *47-472* [id.]. Kim Walker, Eric Pritchard, Paul Yarbrough, Sandy Wilson.

Kim Walker, the Chicago-born, Swiss-trained young bassoonist, brings the full charm of her musical personality to bear on these slight but amiable *Quartets*. The music is tuneful and eclectically inventive – a bit like Boccherini, but with Mozartian derivations, too. The *Grazioso con variazioni*, which forms the last movement of *No. 2 in F*, and the *Adagio cantabile* of *No. 1 in D* both bring reminders of the Mozart horn concertos in their melodic contour. Most remarkable, however, in the first movement of No. 2 is a section from the strings which uses an idea which appears in Beethoven's *Horn sonata* (1800). The style of the playing is infectious as well as elegant: the finale of No. 1 is delightful. The recording was made in Holy Trinity Church, New York, and the balance is rather too close (though eminently truthful) which robs the playing of its full range of dynamic and prevents a real *piano* registering from the soloist. But with any reservations this is still an entertaining collection.

Dickinson, Peter (born 1934)

(i) *Organ concerto;* (ii) *Piano concerto.*
*** HMV Dig. **CDC7 47584-2**; *EL 270439-4*. (i) Jennifer Bate; (ii) Howard Shelley, BBC SO, Atherton.

Peter Dickinson in these two colourful concertos displays his gift for communicating immediately and directly, contrasting serious and popular influences. The *Piano concerto* is the more ambitious and the more variably successful. The one extended movement in its various sections – mainly slow – layers material in contrasted styles, setting ragtime and blues ideas in a serious frame. The *Organ concerto* is even more dramatic in its use of contrasting textures, with the solo instrument set against the orchestra rather than grafted on to it. Again the structure is ingenious, and the writing – with the celeste playing an important part – colourful. The wide-ranging and atmospheric recording underlines the impact of the orchestration, particularly on CD. But the XDR iron-oxide cassette is very well managed, with good detail and both solo instruments realistically caught.

4 Blues; Blue rose; Concerto rag; Extravagances; Hymn-tune rag; Quartet rag; A red, red rose; So, we'll go no more a roving; Stevie's tunes; Wild rose rag.
(*) Conifer Dig. **CDCF 154; *MCFRA 134* [id.]. Meriel Dickinson, Peter Dickinson.

Dickinson's eclectic style and ingenious mind are well illustrated in this collection of miniatures, with musical references and allusions adding to the point of the pieces. As in his *Piano* and *Organ concertos*, his love of American popular music provides a basic element. With the composer accompanying his sister, Meriel, in the songs, it makes an entertaining disc, with clear sound, just a little dry on piano tone. There is an excellent tape.

Dohnányi, Ernst von (1877–1960)

(i) *Suite in F sharp min., Op. 19;* (ii) *Variations on a nursery tune, Op. 25.*
(M) (***) HMV *ED 291275-4.* (i) RPO, Sargent; (ii) composer, RPO, Boult.

Variations on a nursery tune (for piano and orchestra), Op. 25.
(*) Decca Dig. **417 294-2; *417 294-4* [id.]. Schiff, Chicago SO, Solti – TCHAIKOVSKY: *Piano concerto No. 1.***

When he recorded his famous *Nursery tune variations* in 1956 Dohnányi was nearly eighty, but his playing is extraordinarily vital and characterful. The producer of this recording was Lawrance Collingwood, under whose baton Dohnányi recorded these same variations before the war. Naturally, the later performance is not quite as dazzling as it was when he was younger, but he is still amazingly witty and sprightly. Sir Adrian gets splendid playing from the RPO and the recording, which appears in stereo for the first time, is in the demonstration category. Sargent's account of the delightful *F sharp minor Suite* is slightly later (1961) and also comes up well. What a marvellously resourceful piece this is, inventive, expertly scored and full of charm! It should be as popular as the *Variations*, yet it is not otherwise available at present. EMI should give top priority to issuing this on CD. Meanwhile we have to report that the cassette transfer is unacceptably lacking in upper range, which robs the sound of vitality and sparkle – a disastrous example of this company's misguided use of iron-oxide stock for strictly commercial reasons. So until a CD arrives, only the LP – which is spectacularly successful in its clarity, transparency and body – can be recommended (ED 291275-1).

Solti dominates the Decca performance and his vehemence in the orchestral introduction sounds as if he is trying to consign the pianist to the flames of the burning Valhalla. But this points up the contrast with the piquant piano entry, and although later Solti's lyrical climaxes have a certain pungency there are moments of wit too, and Schiff's neat, crisp articulation makes a sparkling foil for the more aggressive orchestral response. Certainly the recording is spectacular, especially on CD, but this account is not strong on charm, even if it is undoubtedly compulsive.

Donizetti, Gaetano (1797–1848)

Il Barcaiolo; Cor anglais concertino in G; Oboe sonata in F; (Piano) *Waltz in C* (with PASCULLI: *Concerto on themes from La Favorita; Fantasia on Poliuto.* LISZT: *Réminsciences de Lucia di Lammermoor*).
*** Mer. **CDE 84147**; *KE 77147* [id.]. Jeremy Polmear, Diana Ambache.

This collection, entitled 'The other Donizetti', shows an essentially lightweight side to the composer, but is given some substance by the stylish elegance of Jeremy Polmear's playing. The *Sonata in F* is an agreeable piece with a fluent *Andante* and a catchy finale, and the vignette, *Il Barcaiolo*, is even more engaging. The *Cor anglais concertino* centres on a set of variations which are not unlike the fantasias on themes from his operas by Pasculli. However, these demand the utmost bravura from the soloist. The *La Favorita concerto* has a finale marked *Allegro velocissimo* which speaks for itself, and in the *Poliuto fantasia* Jeremy Polmear is made to sound like one of Rimsky-Korsakov's bumble-bees set loose in the Italian sunshine. Diana Ambache proves a sympathetic partner and gives a suitably flamboyant account of Liszt's famous *Lucia paraphrase*. The recording, made in Eltham College, London, is a shade too reverberant here, though the resonance is more agreeable in the duos. The artists are well balanced and are afforded striking naturalness and presence. Much of this concert is relatively trivial, but it is never treated as such by its advocates.

String quartet No. 13 in A.
*** CRD *CRDC 4066* [id.]. Alberni Qt – PUCCINI: *Crisantemi;* VERDI: *Quartet.****

This, the thirteenth of nearly twenty quartets which Donizetti wrote in his early twenties, is an endearing work with a scherzo echoing that in Beethoven's *Eroica* and with many twists of argument that are attractively unpredictable. It is well coupled here with other works for string quartet by Italian opera composers, all in strong, committed performances and well recorded. The cassette transfer has plenty of character with good body and detail, although the treble is brighter and has more edge than in the couplings

Miserere in D min.
** Hung. **HCD 12147-2** [id.]. Pászthy, Bende, Slovak Ch. and PO, Maklári.

From the solemn opening you would not readily recognize this *Miserere* as the work of Donizetti. That opening chorus and the final one too, *Tunc acceptabis*, bring a consciously weighty manner. This was a piece – a setting of Psalm 50 in the Vulgate numbering (No. 51 in the Authorized Version) – which Donizetti wrote at the age of twenty-three, soon after graduating. Other movements are less ambitious, with one or two jolly secular touches to give a hint of the opera-composer to come. The text of the work was reassembled by Istvan Mariassy from source material in various Italian libraries and, in a fresh and unpretentious performance, makes an attractive rarity on disc. The clarinet obbligato in the second number is rather raw, but the horn in the fifth is splendid, and both the soprano Julia Pászthy and the baritone Zsolt Bende sing with fresh, clear tone, though at times challenged by the technical difficulties. The 1980 analogue recording comes up very freshly in the digital transfer to CD.

OPERA

Anna Bolena (complete).
*** Decca Dig. **421 096-2**; *421 096-4* (3) [id.]. Sutherland, Ramey, Hadley, Mentzer, Welsh Nat. Op. Ch. & O, Bonynge.

In this 1987 recording of *Anna Bolena*, Sutherland crowns her long recording career with a commanding performance. Dazzling as ever in coloratura, above all exuberant in the defiant final cabaletta, she poignantly conveys the tragedy of the wronged queen's fate with rare weight and gravity. Ramey as the king is outstanding in a fine, consistent cast. Excellent recording.

Il Campanello (complete).
*** CBS Dig. **MK 38450** [id.]. Baltsa, Dara, Casoni, Romero, Gaifa, V. State Op. Ch., VSO, Bertini.

A modern recording of this sparkling one-act piece on something like the same story which Donizetti developed later in *Don Pasquale* is very welcome. The principals all catch a nice balance between musical precision and playing for laughs, generally preferring to rely on vocal acting. Enzo Dara as the Apothecary, Don Annibale, and Angelo Romero as the wag, Enrico, are delightful in their patter duet, and Agnes Baltsa is a formidable but sparkling Serafina. Gary Bertini is a sympathetic conductor who paces things well, and the secco recitatives – taking up rather a large proportion of the disc – are well accompanied on the fortepiano. Generally well-balanced recording, given even greater immediacy in its CD format.

Don Pasquale (complete).
*** HMV Dig. **CDS7 47068-2** (2) [Ang. **CDCB 47068**]. Bruscantini, Freni, Nucci, Winbergh, Amb. Op. Ch., Philh. O, Muti.

Muti's is an outstanding set of Donizetti's most brilliant comic opera. With sparkle and spring on the one hand and easily flexible lyricism on the other, this is a delectably idiomatic-sounding reading, one which consistently captures the fun of the piece. It helps that three of the four principals are Italians. Freni is a natural in the role of Norina, both sweet and bright-eyed in characterization, excellent in coloratura. The buffo baritones, the veteran Bruscantini as Pasquale and the darker-toned Leo Nucci as Dr Malatesta, steer a nice course between vocal comedy and purely musical values. They sound exhilarated, not stressed, by Muti's challenging speeds for the patter numbers. On the lyrical side, Muti is helped by the beautifully poised and shaded singing of Gösta Winbergh, honey-toned and stylish as Ernesto. Responsive and polished playing from the Philharmonia and excellent studio sound.

Don Pasquale: highlights.
** Hung. Dig. **HCD 12610**. Gregor, Kalmar, Hungarian R. & TV Ch., Hungarian State O, Ivan Fischer.

As many Hungaroton releases have witnessed, opera is thriving in Budapest. Ivan Fischer conducts an energetic and well-drilled team in a generous collection of highlights which brings particularly enjoyable singing from the bass, Jozsef Gregor, in the name part and from Istvan Gati as Malatesta, both clear and agile. The soprano, Magda Kalmar, and the tenor, Janos Bandi, are less stylish but are reliable enough. What is missing – largely thanks to the conductor – is lightness and the sparkle of comedy. The relative heaviness is underlined by the recording which brings out the voices well but makes the orchestra sound woolly.

L'Elisir d'amore (complete).
*** Decca **414 461-2** (2) [id.]; *K 154 K32* [Lon. *OSA-5 13101*]. Sutherland, Pavarotti, Cossa, Malas, Amb. S., ECO, Bonynge.
(*) Eurodisc **601 097 (3). Popp, Dvorsky, Weikl, Nesterenko, Munich R. Ch. & O, Wallberg.
*(*) Ph. Dig. **412 714-2** (2) [id.]. Ricciarelli, Carreras, Nucci, Trimarchi, Rigacci, Turin R. Ch. & O, Scimone.
DG Dig. **423 076-2**; *423 076-4* (2) [id.]. Bonney, Winbergh, Weikl, Panerai, Maggio Musicale Fiorentino Ch. & O, Ferro.

Joan Sutherland's comic talents in a Donizetti role came out delectably in her performances on stage and on record of *La Fille du régiment*. Here she repeats that success, making Adina a more substantial figure than usual, full-throatedly serious at times, at others jolly like the rumbustious Marie. Malibran, the first interpreter of the role, was furious that the part was not bigger, and got her husband to write an extra aria. Richard Bonynge found a copy of the piano score, had it orchestrated, and included it here, a jolly and brilliant waltz song. Though that involves missing out the cabaletta *Il mio fugor dimentica*, the text of this frothy piece is otherwise unusually complete, and in the key role of Nemorino Luciano Pavarotti proves ideal, vividly portraying the wounded innocent. Spiro Malas is a superb Dulcamara, while Dominic Cossa is a younger-sounding Belcore, more of a genuine lover than usual. Bonynge points the skipping rhythms delectably, and the recording is sparkling to match. The CD transfer brings out the fullness, brilliance and clean focus of the 1971 sound, which has more presence than many modern digital recordings.

Wallberg conducts a lightly sprung performance of Donizetti's sparkling comic opera, well recorded and marked by a charming performance of the role of Adina from Lucia Popp, comparably bright-eyed, with delicious detail both verbal and musical. Nesterenko makes a splendidly resonant Dr Dulcamara with more comic sparkle than you would expect from a great Russian bass. Dvorsky and Weikl, both sensitive artists, sound much less idiomatic, with Dvorsky's tight tenor growing harsh under pressure, not at all Italianate, and Weikl failing similarly to give necessary roundness to the role of Belcore. Like other sets recorded in association with Bavarian Radio, the sound is excellent, naturally balanced with voices never spotlit. Though this does not displace the Sutherland/Pavarotti/Bonynge set on Decca, it makes a viable alternative, especially for admirers of Lucia Popp.

Scimone's set is disappointing. In a gentle way he is an understanding interpreter of Donizetti; but with recording that lacks presence, the chorus and orchestra's sound is slack next to rivals on record, and none of the soloists is on top form, with even Carreras in rougher voice than usual, trying to compensate by overpointing. Leo Nucci too as Belcore produces less smooth tone than normal, and Domenico Trimarchi as Dulcamara, fine buffo that he is, sounds too wobbly for comfort on record. Katia Ricciarelli gives a sensitive performance, but this is not a natural role for her and, unlike Sutherland, she does not translate it to her own needs.

It is surprising to find such a scholar of the period as Gabriele Ferro conducting so charmlessly in the DG set. It is a coarse reading from conductor, orchestra and soloists alike, with pianissimos very few and far between. Gösta Winbergh sets the pattern with an unrelievedly loud and unsympathetic account of Nemorino's first aria, *Quanto e bella* – nothing shy or tentative about this. As for *Una furtiva lagrima* in Act II, at an unrelieved forte, it has no charm or tenderness at all, and one is amazed that this is the singer who made an appealing Ernesto in the Muti set of *Don Pasquale* for EMI. Barbara Bonney has her moments of sweetness as Adina, but with a hint of flutter in the voice the sound does not record well, and she shows little charm or delicacy. Bernd Weikl's un-Italianate voice makes his portrait of Sergeant Belcore unconvincing, and among the principals it is the veteran Rolando Panerai as the quack, Dulcamara, who is by far the most stylish. When on his entry he cries out *Udite, udite, o rustici*, the simple phrase at once establishes a different degree of communication, though even he rarely sings softer than forte, perhaps a reflection of the recording as well as of the unsympathetic conducting. Voices in a relatively dry theatre acoustic (the Teatro Verdi in Florence) are balanced well forward. It is odd that a recording of this of all Donizetti operas should convey so little sparkle or sense of comedy.

La Fille du régiment (complete).
*** Decca **414 520-2** (2) [id.]; *K 23 K 22* [Lon. *OSA-5 1273*]. Sutherland, Pavarotti, Sinclair, Malas, Coates, ROHCG Ch. & O, Bonynge.

Recorded at a vintage period in Decca history, Joan Sutherland's set of *La Fille du Régiment* – she dominates it from first to last, even in competition with the young Pavarotti – comes out with tingling freshness and immediacy in the CD transfer. It was with this cast that the piece was revived at Covent Garden, and Sutherland immediately showed how naturally she takes to the role of tomboy. Marie is a *vivandière* in the army of Napoleon, and the jolly, almost Gilbertian, plot involves her translation back to a noble background from which as an infant she was lost. This original French version favoured by Richard Bonynge is fuller than the Italian revision and, with a cast that at the time of the recording sessions was also appearing in the theatre, the performance could hardly achieve higher spirits with keener assurance. Sutherland is in turn brilliantly comic and pathetically affecting, and no better sampler of the whole set need be suggested than part of the last scene, where Marie is reunited with her army friends (including the hero). Pavarotti makes an engaging hero, Monica Sinclair a formidable Countess, and even if the French accents are often suspect it is a small price to pay for such a brilliant, happy opera set, a fizzing performance of a delightful Donizetti romp that can be confidently recommended for both comedy and fine singing. Recorded in Kingsway Hall, the sound has wonderful presence and clarity of focus. The CD format is all the more convenient, but irritatingly Tonio's celebrated 'High-C's' solo in the finale of Act I is not banded separately, or even indicated in the libretto. (It comes half way through band 13 of the first disc.) The chrome cassettes are also of Decca's best quality, bright and sparkling, yet offering warmth and bloom.

Lucia di Lammermoor (complete).

*** Decca **410 193-2** (2) [id.]; *K2 L22* [Lon. *OSA-5 13103*]. Sutherland, Pavarotti, Milnes, Ghiaurov, Ryland Davies, Tourangeau, ROHCG Ch. & O, Bonynge.

(*) HMV **CDS7 47440-8 (2) [id.].; (M) *EX 290876-5* [Ang. *4AV 34066*]. Callas, Tagliavini, Cappuccilli, Ladysz, Philh. Ch. & O, Serafin.

(M) ** RCA **CD 86504** (2) [**6504-2-RG**]. Moffo, Bergonzi, Sereni, Flagello, RCA Italiana Op. Ch. & O, Prêtre.

It was hardly surprising that Decca re-recorded Sutherland twice in the role with which she is inseparably associated. Though some of the girlish freshness of voice which marked the 1961 recording disappeared in the 1971 set, the detailed understanding was intensified, and the mooning manner, which in 1961 was just emerging, was counteracted. No one today outshines Sutherland in this opera; and rightly for this recording she insisted on doing the whole of the Mad scene in a single session, making sure it was consistent from beginning to end. Power is there as well as delicacy, and the rest of the cast is first rate. Pavarotti, through much of the opera not as sensitive as he can be, proves magnificent in his final scene. The sound-quality is superb, though choral interjections are not always forward enough. In this set, unlike the earlier one, the text is absolutely complete. The analogue recording is greatly enhanced by the compact disc remastering, with balance and focus outstandingly firm and real. The silent background is particularly valuable in the pauses and silences of the Mad scene, the opera's powerful climax.

The Callas stereo version was recorded in Kingsway Hall in 1959, at the very same time that Serafin was conducting this opera at Covent Garden for the newly emergent Joan Sutherland. The sound is very good for its period and comes over the more freshly on CD, with little trouble over reproducing edgy top notes from Callas. Her flashing-eyed interpretation of the role of Lucia remains unique, though the voice has its unsteady moments to mar enjoyment. One instance is at the end of the Act I duet with Edgardo, where Callas on the final phrase moves sharpwards and Tagliavini – here past his best – flatwards. Serafin's conducting is a model of perception. The score has the cuts which used to be conventional in the theatre. The cassettes, which are quite well managed, are offered at mid price.

Prêtre's version, recorded in 1965 with Anna Moffo as the heroine, has been reissued in RCA's series of operas on mid-price CDs. It makes a fair bargain, when the total playing time of over two and a quarter hours is squeezed on to merely two discs. Though the male principals – notably Carlo Bergonzi – sing stylishly, Moffo, for all the sweetness of her voice, adopts a performing style far more appropriate to Puccini than to Donizetti. The sound is good for its period.

Arias from: *Don Pasquale; Don Sebastiano; Il Duca d'Alba; L'elisir d'amore; La Favorita; La Fille du régiment; Lucia di Lammermoor; Maria Stuarda.*

*** Decca **417 638-2** [id.]. Luciano Pavarotti with various orchestras & conductors.

A cleverly chosen compilation of Pavarotti recordings of Donizetti from various sources – not just complete sets but previous recital discs. It is an asset that Pavarotti so readily encompasses both comic and tragic. It is good to have one or two rarities along with the favourite numbers, including Tonio's celebrated 'High-C's' solo from the Act I finale of *La Fille du régiment*. Sound from different sources is well co-ordinated. This collection demonstrates clearly that Pavarotti is at his very finest in this repertoire.

'Great arias' from: *L'elisir d'amore; La Fille du régiment; Lucia di Lammermoor; Lucrezia Borgia.*
(M) *** Decca *417 176-4* [id.]. Joan Sutherland, Marilyn Horne, Luciano Pavarotti, Giuseppe di Stefano – BELLINI: *Arias.****

One of the most rewarding and generous tape collections in Decca's Opera Gala series, this centres round Joan Sutherland's famous and unsurpassed 1959 version of the Mad scene from *Lucia di Lammermoor*, but includes also Marilyn Horne's stunning account of *Il segreto per esser felice* from *Lucrezia Borgia* – a collector's item if ever there was one. As if challenged to show what he could do, Pavarotti obliges with his exhilarating display of vocal fireworks in *Pour mon âme* from *La Fille du régiment*, while Giuseppe di Stefano provides a moment of melting bel canto in *Una furtiva lagrima* from *L'elisir d'amore*. Excellent, vivid transfers offering slight problems only in the Mad scene, where there is some momentary peaking on high notes. The Bellini coupling is hardly less tempting.

Dowland, John (1563–1626)

Lachrimae, or Seaven teares.
*** BIS Dig. **CD 315** [id.]. Dowland Consort, Jakob Lindberg.

The full title of Dowland's publication is *Lachrimae, or Seaven Teares figured in Seaven Passionate Pavans with divers other Pavans, Galliards, and Almands set forth for the Lute, Viols or Violins, in five parts.* Jakob Lindberg and his consort of viols give a highly persuasive account of Dowland's masterpiece. The texture is always clean and the lute clearly present. Unlike Thurston Dart's LP from the 1950s, Lindberg groups the first seven pavans together (as did Anthony Rooley), making a case for them to be thought of as an entity. They are followed by a further fourteen pieces: three more pavans, nine galliards and two almands, all of them dedicated to a particular individual. (Diana Poulton's authoritative note includes a brief biographical sketch of each dedicatee.) The recording is made in the pleasing acoustic of Wik Castle, near Uppsala, and needs to be reproduced at a low-level setting. Beautiful playing, expertly recorded.

There is an enormous amount of Dowland's instrumental, keyboard and vocal music listed in the major LP catalogues; we hope the success of what little is already transferred to CD will encourage the major companies to make more available in this format.

Lute music: *Almaine; Dowland's first galliard; Earl of Derby, his galliard; Earl of Essex, his galliard; Farewell (fancy); Forlorne hope (fancy); Frog galliard; Lachrimae antiquae; Lachrimae verae; Lady Rich, her galliard; Lord d'Lisle, his galliard; Melancholie galliard; Mrs Vaux's gigge; My Lady Hunsdon's puffe; My Lord Willoughby's welcome home; Piper's pavan; Resolution; Semper Dowland, Semper dolens; The Shoemaker's wide* [*a toy*]*; Sir Henry Gifford, his almaine.*
*** RCA **RD 89977**. Julian Bream (lute).

Compiled from two LPs recorded in the late 1960s and late 1970s (with no great differences between their sound) this CD recital demonstrates the skill and innate musical sympathies of the most gifted British lutenist. Julian Bream captures the melancholy (the piece entitled *Semper Dowland, semper dolens* is certainly autobiographical) and the eloquence of these endlessly imaginative miniatures. He produces an astonishing range of colour from the lute: each phrase shows distinction, nothing is in the least routine. The CD gives Bream the most realistic presence, though care should be exercised with the volume control – a lower-level setting is advisable for a truthful image. The internal access provided by the cueing is ideal: who would not want to sample pieces with names like *Mrs Vaux's gigge* or *My Lady Hunsdon's puffe*?

Dufay, Guillaume (*c.* 1400–1474)

Missa l'homme armé. Motets: *Al a redemptoris mater; Ecclesiae militantis; Nuper rosarum flores; O Sancte Sebastiane; Salve flos Tuscae gentis.*
*** HMV Dig. **CDC7 47628-3**; *EL 270426-4.* Hilliard Ens., Paul Hillier.

It is exciting to find early choral music like this, performed with such freshness and vigour as well as refinement, by the Hilliard Ensemble. The extraordinary inventiveness of this fifteenth-century French composer is sharply presented in the big cyclic Mass using the popular melody, *L'homme armé*, as its basis. The approach is dramatic, but scholarly too, with fresh, clear voices well caught by the recording. The Mass is a late work of Dufay, so that the coupling of much earlier motets provides a pointful survey of the whole span of his achievement. The pleasantly atmospheric ambience of the recording suits the music without ever undermining detail. While the CD has obvious advantages, the cassette, too, is very well managed – the sound is full-bodied yet clearly defined.

Dukas, Paul (1865–1935)

L'apprenti sorcier (*The sorcerer's apprentice*).
*** DG Dig. **419 617-2**; *419 617-4* [id.]. BPO, Levine – SAINT-SAËNS: *Symphony No. 3.****
*** RCA **RD 86205 [RCA 6205-2-RC**]. NBC O, Toscanini – (with Concert: *Light classics*(***)).
(*) RCA Dig. **RCD 14439 [RCD1 4439]; (M) *GK 84439.* Dallas SO, Mata (with Concert***).

It was Stokowski and Walt Disney in *Fantasia* who made Dukas's masterpiece a world favourite orchestral showpiece. Astonishingly, since Stokowski's 78 r.p.m. version (on three sides with appallingly inconvenient musical breaks), there has been no recording entirely worthy of one of the finest (and most succinct) of all orchestral musical fairy-tales. Levine chooses a faster basic tempo than Stokowski, though not as fast as Toscanini (who managed with only two 78 sides), but achieves a deft, light and rhythmic touch to make this a real orchestral scherzo. Yet the climax is thrilling, helped by superb playing from the Berlin Philharmonic; in the gentle 'epilogue' the picture of a crestfallen Mickey Mouse handing the broom back to his master comes readily into the mind's eye. The sound is suitably expansive and its clarity reveals the brilliance of Dukas's scoring. The cassette is excellent, but the CD has an amplitude and sparkle which is especially telling.

Toscanini's overall timing is 10′ 09″. He creates memorably translucent textures at the opening and then sets off with great dash at the entry of the main theme. The effect is undoubtedly exhilarating, and the Studio 8-H recording (clear and clean, if not ideally resonant), has been most satisfactorily remastered from an excellent 1950 mono LP, so that the sound quality is fully acceptable. The performance is unique.

Mata's performance comes from an outstanding early RCA compact disc which was one of the first demonstration records of the CD era. The orchestral balance set back naturally within the attractive Dallas concert-hall ambience, remains very impressive, even if detail is less sharp than on some digital recordings. The performance of Dukas's justly famous orchestral scherzo is spirited and affectionately characterized, with a nicely paced forward momentum. There is little sense of calamity at the climax, but this fits in with Mata's genial conception. The well-transferred cassette is offered at mid-price.

L'apprenti sorcier; La Péri; Polyeucte.
* H M Forlane **UCD 16545**; *UMK 6545* [id.]. Bordeaux-Aquitaine O, Benzi.

The best thing on this record is *La Péri*, given with its splendid opening fanfare. The other performances are really rather lacklustre, and that of *L'apprenti sorcier* is not competitive. Roberto Benzi and the Bordeaux-Aquitaine Orchestra are no match for rivals which have appeared over the last decade or so.

Symphony in C; La Péri (*poème dansée*).
(*) Erato Dig. **ECD 88089; *MCE 75175* [id.]. SRO, Jordan.

This was the first account of either the Dukas *Symphony* or *La Péri* to reach CD. Armin Jordan offers good value and the Suisse Romande Orchestra play very well for him. Jordan's reading has musical conviction, and he is equally sensitive to atmosphere in *La Péri*. The Erato recording is eminently satisfactory and can be recommended to readers wanting this coupling. On the high-level tape, the sound is clear and vivid, but rather dry and hard on top.

Duparc, Henri (1848–1933)

Chanson triste; L'Invitation du voyage.
*** Ph. Dig. **410 043-2** [id.]. Ameling, San Francisco SO, De Waart – DEBUSSY: *La damoiselle élue;* RAVEL: *Shéhérazade.****

L'Invitation au voyage gains from being orchestrated, with Ameling's pure and lovely voice warmly supported. *Chanson triste* is beautifully sung too, but it sounds slightly overblown with orchestral rather than piano accompaniment. An apt, unusual coupling for the two bigger works, beautifully recorded. The splendid compact disc shows these performances off to fine advantage: it is wonderfully atmospheric, with a natural balance for the voice and a beguilingly rich orchestral texture.

Mélodies: *Au pays où se fait la guerre; Chanson triste; L'invitation au voyage; Le manoir de Rosamonde; Phidylé; Testament; La vie intérieure.*
** HMV Dig. **CDC7 47111-2** [id.].; *EL 270135-4* [Ang. *4DS 38061*]. Kiri Te Kanawa, Belgian Nat. Op. O, Pritchard – RAVEL: *Shéhérazade.***

Dame Kiri often produces a most beautiful sound and is excellently supported by Sir John Pritchard and the Belgian Opera Orchestra; for all this, however, she is not wholly successful in terms of characterization. The EMI recording is very well balanced and her admirers may want to sample this, but she is not at her best here.

Dupré, Marcel (1886–1971)

Symphony in G minor for organ and orchestra, Op. 25.
*** Telarc Dig. **CD 80136** [id.]. Michael Murray, RPO, Ling – RHEINBERGER: *Organ concerto No. 1.****

If you enjoy Saint-Saën's *Organ symphony* you'll probably enjoy this. The organ's contribution is greater, though it is not a concerto. It is a genial, extrovert piece, consistently inventive if not as memorably tuneful as its predecessor. It was premiered at a London Promenade Concert and is dedicated to Sir Henry Wood, so it is appropriate that the massive Albert Hall organ should be used for this recording, which has all the spectacle one associates with Telarc in this kind of repertoire. The performance has warmth, spontaneity and plenty of flair, and the finer detail of the score emerges as well as its physical excitement. Michael Murray was a pupil of Dupré and his interpretation has obvious authority.

Chorale and fugue, Op. 57; 3 Esquisses, Op. 41; Preludes and fugues: in B; G min., Op. 7/1 & 3;

Le tombeau de Titelouse; Te lucis ante terminum; Placare Christe servulis, Op. 38/6 & 16; Variations sur un vieux Noël, Op. 20.
*** Hyp. Dig. **CDA 66205**; *KA 66205* [id.]. John Scott (St Paul's Cathedral organ).

An outstandingly successful recital, more spontaneous and convincing than many of the composer's own recordings in the past. Dupré's music is revealed as reliably inventive and with an atmosphere and palette all its own; not just the *Noël variations*, but many of the shorter pieces have a strong personality. John Scott is a splendid advocate and the St Paul's Cathedral organ is unexpectedly successful in this repertoire. The reverberation does bring some clouding of detail, but the swirling sounds are always pleasing to the ear, and details focus well at lower dynamic levels. There is a very good cassette, but the CD adds the ultimate presence.

Duruflé, Maurice (born 1902)

Requiem; Danse lente, Op. 6/2
*** CBS *40-76633*. Te Kanawa, Nimsgern, Amb. S., Desborough School Ch., New Philh. O, Andrew Davis.

(i) *Requiem, Op. 9;* (ii) *4 Motets, Op. 10.*
*** Erato Dig. **ECD 88132** [id.]. (i) Berganza, Van Dam, Colonne Ch. & O; (ii) Jean Sourisse, Philippe Corboz (organ); (i; ii) Audite Nova Vocal Ens., cond. Michel Corboz.

Requiem, Op. 9 (3rd version)*; 4 Motets, Op. 10.*
*** Hyp. Dig. **CDA 66191;** *KA 66191* [id.]. Ann Murray, Thomas Allen, Corydon Singers, ECO, Best; Trotter (organ).

Those who have sometimes regretted that the lovely Fauré *Requiem* remains unique in the output of that master of delicate inspiration should investigate this comparably evocative *Requiem* of Duruflé. The composer wrote it in 1947, overtly basing its layout and even the cut of its themes on the Fauré masterpiece. The result is far more than just an imitation, for (as it seems in innocence) Duruflé's inspiration is passionately committed. Andrew Davis directs a warm and atmospheric reading, using the full orchestral version with its richer colourings. Kiri Te Kanawa sings radiantly in the *Pié Jésu*, and the darkness of Siegmund Nimsgern's voice is well caught. In such a performance Duruflé establishes his claims for individuality even in the face of Fauré's comparable setting. The fill-up is welcome too; and the recording is excellent. The chrome-cassette transfer is well managed, but we hope CBS have plans to issue this on CD too.

Using the chamber-accompanied version with strings, harp and trumpet – a halfway house between the full orchestral score and plain organ accompaniment – Best conducts a deeply expressive and sensitive performance of Duruflé's lovely setting of the *Requiem*. With two superb soloists and an outstandingly refined chorus, it makes an excellent recommendation, well coupled with motets, done with similar freshness, clarity and feeling for tonal contrast. The recording is attractively atmospheric, but more clearly focused than the Corboz/Erato CD. The Hyperion chrome tape is slightly more diffuse, but very well transferred.

Corboz conducts a warmly idiomatic reading. He uses the full orchestral version; the slight haziness of the sound, merging textures richly, adds to the sense of mystery, where the very clarity of Andrew Davis on CBS might be counted a disadvantage. However, the Hyperion version strikes a happy medium in this respect. The Erato soloists are excellent, but even on CD the lack of internal focus remains apparent.

Dusik, Jan Ladislav (1760–1812)

Sonata in F min. (*L'Invocation*), *Op. 77; 12 Études mélodiques, Op. 16; Rondo* (*Les Adieux*).
** Sup. **CO 1853** [id.]. Jan Panenka.

Dusik is one of the most interesting of Beethoven's contemporaries and the *F minor Sonata*, Op. 77, is one of his most powerful contributions to the genre. Panenka plays this and the other pieces on a fortepiano by Graff with tremendous spirit and gusto. He shapes phrases with an imagination and fire that will pleasantly surprise those who imagine early-music performances to be bloodless. There are two snags: the acoustic is resonant, which makes the instrument sound unnecessarily clattery, and at 45 minutes it offers short measure. Artistically, however, it is first class.

Dutilleux, Henri (born 1916)

L'Arbre des Songes (*Violin concerto*).
*** CBS Dig. **MK 42449**; *IMT 42449* [id.]. Stern, O Nat. de France, Maazel – MAXWELL DAVIES: *Violin concerto.****

Dutilleux's *Violin concerto*, written for Isaac Stern, is a beautiful work that makes an excellent coupling for the Maxwell Davies concerto, also written for Stern and first heard in 1986. Dutilleux, always the perfect craftsman and consistently writing with refinement, yet shows – as with Walton in this country – how taut self-discipline can go with natural expressive warmth. There are passages in this tightly knit structure of seven linked sections which sound very like Walton updated; and the underlying romantic fervour finds Stern playing with warm commitment, strongly accompanied by Maazel and the Orchestre National. First-rate recording.

Cello concerto (*Tout un monde lointain*).
*** HMV **CDC7 49304-2** [id.]. Rostropovich, O de Paris, Baudo – LUTOSLAWSKI: *Cello concerto.****

Dutilleux's *Cello concerto* (whose subtitle translates as 'A whole distant world') is a most imaginative and colourful score which exerts an immediate appeal and sustains it over many hearings. Rostropovich plays it with enormous virtuosity and feeling, and the Orchestre de Paris under Serge Baudo gives splendid support. This record won the composer the 1976 Koussevitzky Award, and the 1975 recording is immensely vivid, with Rostropovich looming larger than life but given great presence.

Symphony No. 1; Timbres, espace, mouvement.
❀ *** HM Dig. **HMC 905159**; *HMC 40.5159* [id.]. O Nat. de Lyon, Serge Baudo.

For a modern French symphony, Dutilleux's *First* has done well on record; this is the fourth version to appear – and also the best. Written in 1950 when he was in his early thirties, it still reveals an admiration for such figures as Bartók, Roussel, Messiaen and, above all, Honegger; but these disparate influences are assimilated and the sound-world he evokes is very much his own. There is a mercurial intelligence and a vivid imagination at work, and the orchestral textures are luminous and iridescent. What is particularly impressive is its sense of forward movement: you feel that the music is taking you somewhere. If you enjoy the Bartók or Lutoslawski *Concertos for orchestra*, you will respond to this marvellous piece. *Timbres, espace, mouvement* is a more recent work, dating from 1978, the result of a commission from Rostropovich and the Washington orchestra. Judging from this disc, it is obvious that the Orchestra National de Lyon need not fear comparison with the great Paris orchestras, even if the upper strings do not have quite the same lustre or bloom; and Serge Baudo is an authoritative interpreter of this composer. The engineering is superb: there is plenty of space round the various instruments, and the balance is thoroughly realistic.

Piano sonata.
(*) Archduke Dig. **DARC 2; *MARC 2* [id.]. Donna Amato (piano) – BALAKIREV: *Sonata.***(*)

The Dutilleux *Sonata* enjoys classic status in France. It is an inventive and exuberant piece dating from 1947, three years before the *First Symphony*. It has been absent from the catalogue since John Ogdon recorded it in the early 1970s. The *Sonata* has an almost symphonic breadth and sense of scale; it is tonal – the first movement is in F sharp minor and its centrepiece, a *Lied*, is finely wrought and original, and skilfully linked to the final chorale and variations. Donna Amato, a young American pianist, gives a totally committed and persuasive account of it, and the recording, though not in the demonstration class, is very truthful; given the interest and rarity of the coupling, this is a most desirable issue. The cassette is first class.

Dvořák, Antonin (1841–1904)

Overtures: Carnaval, Op. 92; In Nature's realm, Op. 91; Othello, Op. 93. Scherzo capriccioso, Op. 66.
*** Chan. Dig. **CHAN 8453**; *ABTD 1163* [id.]. Ulster O, Handley.

In what one hopes may be the first of a series of Dvořák symphonic poems, Vernon Handley – in his premier recording with the Ulster Orchestra, of which he is now Musical Director – couples a brilliant and beguiling account of the *Scherzo capriccioso* with the three linked *Overtures*, Opp. 91–3. Dvořák wrote this triptych immediately before his first visit to America in 1892. Until now, Opp. 91 and 93 have tended to be eclipsed by the just public acclaim for the *Carnaval overture*. Handley's superb performances put the three works in perspective. The opening of *Othello* is particularly beautiful, with the Ulster strings radiantly serene; later, Handley minimizes the melodrama, yet, with a fine overall grip, provides plenty of excitement. The idyllic *In Nature's realm* immediately introduces the linking motif which is most memorable when magically taken up by the cor anglais in the mysterious central episode of *Carnaval*. Handley does not seek breathless brilliance in this piece but brings breadth as well as excitement, ensuring that his excellent players can articulate cleanly without being rushed off their feet. In the *Scherzo capriccioso* his subtly lilting treatment of the lyrical secondary theme on the strings gives special pleasure. A splendid issue, superbly recorded in the attractive ambience of Ulster Hall, Belfast. The CD has striking realism and presence; the chrome cassette is full and clear, but not quite so wide-ranging at the top.

Cello concerto in B min., Op. 104.
*** DG **413 819-2** [id.]. Rostropovich, BPO, Karajan – TCHAIKOVSKY: *Rococo variations.****
(M) *** RCA **GD 86531**; *GK 86531* [**6531-2-RG**]. Harrell, LSO, Levine – SCHUBERT: *Arpeggione sonata.****
(B) *** DG Walkman *415 330-4* [id.]. Fournier, BPO, Szell – BOCCHERINI***; HAYDN: *Cello concertos.***
(*) HMV **CDC7 47614-2. Jacqueline du Pré, Chicago S O, Barenboim – HAYDN: *Concerto in C.****
(*) Ph. **412 880-2 [id.]. Heinrich Schiff, Concg. O, C. Davis – ELGAR: *Concerto.***(*)
(*) Decca Dig. **410 144-2; *KSXDC 7608* [id.]. Harrell, Philh. O, Ashkenazy – BRUCH: *Kol Nidrei.***(*)
** Erato Dig. **ECD 88224**; *MCE 75282* [id.]. Rostropovich, Boston S O, Ozawa (with TCHAIKOVSKY: *Rococo variations***).

Cello concerto; Silent woods, Op. 68.
*** CBS Dig. **MK 42206**; *IMT 42206* [id.]. Yo-Yo Ma, BPO, Maazel.
(*) BIS **CD 245 [id.]. Helmerson, Gothenburg S O, Järvi.

The collaboration of Rostropovich and Karajan in Dvořák's *Cello concerto* makes a superb version, warm as well as refined in reflection of the finest qualities in each of the two principals. If Rostropovich can sometimes sound self-indulgent in this most romantic of cello concertos, the degree of control provided by the conductor gives a firm yet supple base, and there have been few recorded accounts so deeply satisfying. The result is unashamedly romantic, with many moments of dalliance, but the concentration is never in doubt. Splendid playing by the Berliners, and a bonus in the shape of Tchaikovsky's glorious *Rococo variations*. The analogue recording dates from 1969 and its warm resonance does not lend itself to much clarifying in its new CD format. However, the original sound was both rich and refined, and that effect is certainly enhanced when the background is considerably reduced.

The partnership of the passionately extrovert Maazel – witness his spaciously powerful orchestral introduction – and the more withdrawn artistry of Yo-Yo Ma is unexpectedly successful in Dvořák's gorgeous concerto, providing a real challenge to the Rostropovich/Karajan partnership, with the advantage of modern digital recording, at once vivid and atmospheric. Ma's rapt concentration and refined control of colour bring at times an elegiac dimension to the reading, and Maazel accompanies with understanding and great sensitivity, fining down the orchestral textures so that he never masks his often gentle soloist, yet providing exuberant contrast in orchestral fortissimos. If Ma's playing is characteristically subtle, it is never narcissistic: sometimes there is but a thread of tone, but it is a magical thread. The CBS recording, made in the Philharmonie, could hardly be more different from the results the DG engineers usually achieve for Karajan. The orchestra is set back within a warmly resonant concert-hall ambience which lends its bloom to the overall sound-picture – the solo cello is most skilfully balanced – and ensures that the pianissimo detail of the *Adagio* registers naturally. The twilight evocation of *Silent woods* is equally well caught. There is a good tape, but the CD has greater range and presence.

In Lynn Harrell's first RCA recording, made in the mid-1970s, his collaboration with James Levine proved a powerful and sympathetic one. After an unusually positive account of the opening tutti, with an unashamed slowing for the horn solo which directly anticipates the soloist's treatment of the second subject, Harrell at once establishes power and incisiveness. Richly satisfying accounts of the first and second movements culminate in a reading of the finale which proves the most distinctive of all. The main body of the movement is finely integrated, but it is the *andante* epilogue which brings the most memorable playing, very expansive but not at all sentimental, with a wonderful sense of repose. The recording is bright and full and has been most successfully remastered for CD. The tape is also a very good buy. Both are in their respective mid-price ranges, with Levine exchanging the rostrum for the keyboard for the Schubert coupling.

Fournier's reading has a sweep of conception and richness of tone and phrasing which carry the melodic lines along with exactly the mixture of nobility and tension that the work demands. Fournier can relax and beguile the ear in the lyrical passages and yet catch the listener up in his exuberance in the exciting finale. The phrasing in the slow movement is ravishing, and the interpretation as a whole balances beautifully. DG's recording is forward and vivid, with a broad, warm tone for the soloist. It dates from 1962 and sounds newly minted on this Walkman chrome-tape transfer. With couplings of Haydn (Fournier stylish but less impressively accompanied) and Rostropovich's larger-than-life version of Boccherini, this is another fine DG bargain.

Jacqueline du Pré's reading conveys the spontaneous passion which marked her playing in public. There are more immaculate performances available, but for du Pré's many admirers this performance will be impossible to resist. The pity is that the recording is badly balanced, the cello too forward, while the trumpet solo at the end of the first movement is too backward. Nevertheless it is an interpretation which captures very vividly the urgent flair of both husband and wife, soloist and conductor. The CD coupling of the lesser-known Haydn *C major Concerto* is both distinguished and generous.

We have been inclined to underrate Schiff's reading in previous editions. It may not be full-bloodedly romantic in the way of Rostropovich and Harrell, but it has an unexaggerated vein of poetry more akin to Yo Yo Ma, and its range of emotion is satisfying on a smaller scale. It sounds extremely well in its CD transfer and, with a generous and successful Elgar coupling, is well worth considering.

Frans Helmerson is a young Swedish cellist who caused a stir in London some years ago when he replaced Rostropovich in this concerto. His version with Neeme Järvi and the Gothenburg orchestra faces – and survives – stiff competition in the CD catalogue from Rostropovich and others. Helmerson may not have the outsize personality of Rostropovich but he plays with eloquence and feeling, and the orchestra provide exemplary support. Although the Rostropovich/Karajan version remains a clear first choice, this makes a fine alternative.

Lynn Harrell's newest recording of the Dvořák *Concerto* for Decca is a little disappointing and does not match his earlier RCA version, with the LSO under James Levine. Here again the finale is the most successful, but the performance, though still impressive in its strength and detail, generally lacks the spontaneous power and incisiveness of the RCA account. The Decca digital sound is richly vivid (though forwardly balanced) and the compact disc, as usual, adds refinement of detail. The effect is more realistic than Rostropovich's much older recording, but Harrell's performance has less emotional weight.

Rostropovich's most recent digital recording, with Ozawa, is a great disappointment, and it doesn't even sound as well as the DG version made some two decades earlier. Rostropovich is as ever poetic, but the flames burn less brightly in Boston; Ozawa's accompaniment is respectful, rather than stimulating his soloist to flights of inspiration as did Karajan.

Piano concerto in G min., Op. 33.

*** HMV **CDC7 47967-2**; (M) *EG 291286-4*. Sviatoslav Richter, Bav. State O, Carlos Kleiber – SCHUBERT: *Wanderer Fantasia*.***

** Mobile Fidelity **MFCD 814** [Vox Prima **MWCD 7114**]. Firkusny, St Louis S O, Susskind.

Dvořák's *Piano concerto* comes from a vintage period which also saw the completion of the *F major Symphony*. The quality of the inspiration falls below that of the *Violin concerto*, but it still has many striking beauties, notably in the fine slow movement which has never before sounded so moving as it does in Richter's hands. Much has been made of the concerto's pianistic deficiencies, but Richter plays the solo part in its original form (and not the more pianistically 'effective' revision by Wilém Kurz which is published in the Complete Edition), and his judgement is triumphantly vindicated. This is the most persuasive and masterly account of the work ever committed to disc; its ideas emerge with an engaging freshness and warmth, while the greater simplicity of Dvořák's own keyboard writing proves in Richter's hands to be more telling and profound. Carlos Kleiber secures excellent results from the Bavarian orchestra, and the 1977 recording has clarity and good definition to recommend it, although the digital remastering for CD has produced an over-bright and relatively unrefined sound for the violins in their upper-range fortissimos. Most systems will be able to deal with this, however: one needs the aural equivalent of dark glasses, and although the piano timbre in the coupled *Wanderer Fantasia* of Schubert is also rather hard, we see no reason to withhold the fullest recommendation, such is the distinction of the performances. There is a good cassette, with the more restricted upper range smoothing the orchestral sound on top.

Rudolf Firkusny, who studied with Wilém Kurz and has consistently championed this concerto, has previously played a *mélange* of the Kurz and the original. In this, his third recording, he returns to the original, which he speaks of as 'far purer than any subsequent version and more truly characteristic of the young Dvořák'. His recording, made at about the same time as Richter's, is authoritative and aristocratic. His first movement is slightly tauter and more urgent than Richter's account, and the recording has both immediacy and body. Moreover the St Louis orchestra rise to the occasion and give a very fine account of themselves. A distinguished performance, but it is needlessly handicapped by short playing time (less than 37 minutes).

Violin concerto in A min., Op. 53; Romance in F min., Op. 11.
*** HMV **CDC7 47168-2** [id.]. Perlman, LPO, Barenboim.
*** DG Dig. **419 618-2**; *419 618-4* (without *Romance*) [id.]. Mintz, BPO, Levine – SIBELIUS: *Concerto.***(*)

Perlman and Barenboim still sound pretty marvellous and show all the warmth and virtuosity one could desire. This CD also has the eloquent and touching *F minor Romance*. Perlman is absolutely superb in both pieces: the digital remastering undoubtedly clarifies and cleans the texture, though there is a less glowing aura about the sound above the stave. In its day as an LP this was the first recommendation in this wonderful concerto – and it remains so now.

There is some pretty dazzling playing from Schlomo Mintz, whose virtuosity is effortless and his intonation astonishingly true. A performance of this lovely and much underrated concerto without freshness and innocence is a non-starter – and Mintz brings both qualities to the work. The Berlin orchestra under James Levine are at their excellent best and the DG engineers produce a very well-balanced and opulent recording (made in the Jesus-Christus Kirche rather than the Philharmonie itself). There is good rapport between soloist and conductor, and the performance has the sense of joy and relaxation that this radiant score needs. The digital sound is warmer and more natural in its upper range than the remastered HMV recording; those tempted by Mintz's more generous Sibelius coupling will not be disappointed on technical grounds, and there is an excellent matching cassette.

In the USA, Isaac Stern's recording has been reissued, generously recoupled with the Brahms *Concerto*. The performance is not lacking in power and eloquence, but it is less natural in feeling than its competitors and the recording is much less convincingly balanced [CBS **MK 42257**].

Czech suite, Op. 39; Nocturne for strings in B, Op. 40; Polka for Prague students in B flat, Op. 53a; Polonaise in E flat; Prague waltzes.
*** Decca Dig. **414 370-2** [id.]. Detroit SO, Dorati.

A collection of Dvořák rarities exhilaratingly performed and brilliantly recorded. The *Czech suite* can sometimes outstay its welcome, but certainly not here. The other items too have the brightness and freshness that mark out the Dvořák *Slavonic dances*, especially the *Polka* and *Polonaise*. The most charming piece of all is the set of *Waltzes* written for balls in Prague – Viennese music with a Czech accent – while the lovely *Nocturne* with its subtle drone bass makes an apt filler. The recording has an attractive warmth and bloom to balance its brightness; this is the more striking on CD, which also emphasizes a momentary excess of resonance contributed by the bass drum to the *Polonaise*.

In Nature's realm, overture, Op. 91.
(*) Ph. Dig. **420 607-2; *420 607-4* (2) [id.]. Concg. O, Dorati – SMETANA: *Má Vlast.***(*)

An ungenerous coupling for *Má Vlast* (there is no reason why the complete triptych, Opp. 91–3, could not have been offered). Dorati's performance is excitingly direct and very well played and recorded.

Romance, Op. 11.
*** Ph. Dig. **420 168-2**; *420 168-4* [id.]. Zukerman, St Paul CO – BEETHOVEN: *Romances*; SCHUBERT: *Konzertstücke* etc.***

Dvořák's *Romance* dates from 1876; its beguiling main theme comes from an unpublished string quartet. Zukerman gives it a simple, heartwarming performance within a most attractive concert of short pieces for violin and orchestra, and he is beautifully recorded: the delightful opening and closing sections are glowingly atmospheric.

Serenade for strings in E, Op. 22.
*** DG Dig. **400 038-2** [id.]. BPO, Karajan – TCHAIKOVSKY: *String serenade*.***
(B) *** DG Dig. *423 258-4* [id.]. BPO, Karajan – TCHAIKOVSKY: *String serenade***(*); R. STRAUSS: *Metamorphosen*.***
(*) Ph. Dig. **422 031-2; *422 031-4* [id.]. Bav. RSO, C. Davis – TCHAIKOVSKY: *String serenade*.**(*)
(M) **(*) Ph. **420 883-2**; *420 883-4*. ECO, Leppard – TCHAIKOVSKY: *String serenade*.**(*)
(M) ** Decca **417 736-2**; *417 736-4* [id.]. ASMF, Marriner – TCHAIKOVSKY: *String serenade***(*) (with Sibelius: *Valse triste*.***)

Serenade for strings in E; Serenade for wind in D min., Op. 44.
*** ASV Dig. **CDCOE 801**; *ZCCOE 801* [id.]. COE, Alexander Schneider.
*** Ph. **400 020-2** [id.]. ASMF, Marriner.
*** Decca Dig. **417 452-2**; *417 452-4* [id.]. LPO, Hogwood.
*(*) Chan. Dig. **CHAN 8459**; *ABTD 1172* [id.]. Philh. O, Christopher Warren-Green.

Serenade for strings; String sextet in A, Op. 48.
** Novalis Dig. **150 011-2**; *150 011-4* [id.]. Camerata Bern, Füri.

The young players of the Chamber Orchestra of Europe give winningly warm and fresh performances of Dvořák's *Serenades*. The distinction of the wind soloists in this fine orchestra has been demonstrated many times on disc, and the *Wind serenade* brings a particularly distinguished performance. The clarinettist, Richard Hosford, gives an inspired account of his solo in the slow movement, where Schneider's sophisticated rubato is made to seem naturally expressive and idiomatic, not at all mannered. Schneider's approach in the *String serenade* is equally romantic and no less persuasive, with slow speeds and expressive phrasing – extreme in the *Larghetto* – always seeming natural, and with the COE string players producing beautifully refined playing, vividly caught in the ASV recording, particularly on CD. The freshness and vividness of sound as well as the natural affection of the performances make this a first choice for this apt and attractive coupling.

Both Sir Neville Marriner's recordings of Dvořák's *String serenade* are now available on CD. The earlier (Argo) version is coupled with the Tchaikovsky, and also (on this mid-priced Decca Ovation reissue) includes Sibelius's *Valse triste* as a lollipop encore. With its rather mannered opening, it was not numbered among Marriner's vintage ASMF performances. It dates from 1970 and the originally excellent recording has suffered from its digital remastering – the violin timbre now sounds excessively thin on CD – although the sparer textures tend to make the effect of the reading seem rather less indulgent; the playing itself is first rate. The later (Philips) performance is far preferable, more direct without loss of warmth, with speeds ideally chosen and refined, yet spontaneous-sounding and consistently resilient string playing. It still remains very competitive, although the Philips recording is not quite as transparent as the newer ASV. But the Academy in the *Wind serenade* is comparably stylish, with beautifully sprung rhythms and the recording most vivid. With a rich, firm bass to balance the brightness of the treble, there is a fine sense of immediacy set against a rather drier acoustic.

A fresh, bright and spring-like account of both works from Hogwood and the LPO in clean, slightly recessed sound. Textually this version of the *String serenade* is unique on record when it uses the original score, newly published, in which two sections, one of 34 bars in the scherzo and the second of 79 bars in the finale, are now included which are missing in the normal printed edition. Though these performances are not quite as winning or rhythmically subtle as Marriner's Philips coupling, they are still very enjoyable, and the inclusion of the extra material brings added interest.

Karajan's digital version of the *String serenade* is given a recording of striking finesse. The brilliance is tempered on the compact disc, which is transferred at a marginally lower level than the Tchaikovsky coupling. The recording has plenty of atmosphere and a very wide dynamic range, plus a slight tendency for the image to recede at pianissimo level. Karajan's approach is warmly affectionate in the opening movement and there is greater expressive weight than with Marriner, with the colouring darker. Yet the playing is both sympathetic and very polished; though the focus is slightly more diffuse and less firm in the bass than the Tchaikovsky coupling, many will feel that the softer delineation suits the music. Karajan's fine performance is also available on a bargain DG Pocket Music tape, splendidly transferred – the sound has excellent range but its body and warmth are equally striking – coupled not only with the Tchaikovsky *Serenade* but also with Strauss's *Metamorphosen*. The value offered, for a fraction of the cost of the CD, is astonishing.

Sir Colin Davis in his version with the Bavarian Radio Symphony Orchestra gives a heavyweight performance, marked by speeds on the slow side, particularly in the first movement. With the Bavarian string sound rich and silky and a well-upholstered bass, it is warmly enjoyable, with the dance rhythms subtly sprung, but it misses some of the spring-like freshness of the work's inspiration.

The reissue on CD and tape of Leppard's fine Philips ECO recording from the late 1970s is also welcome at mid-price; even though the remastering has taken away a little of the bloom on the violins above the stave, the effect is much less severe than on the Marriner/Decca reissue. Leppard is more robust than Marriner and the tempi of his allegros have a strong momentum, but the natural flexibility of the playing prevents the brisk manner from losing its resilience. The finale is strikingly fresh and invigorating. The tape is blander than the CD.

By comparison, Christopher Warren-Green's rather languorous approach verges dangerously near sentimentality, and despite glowing sound and fine playing from the Philharmonia strings and wind alike, neither *Serenade* is as effectively characterized as the competition. A further DG issue of the same coupling by the Orpheus Chamber Orchestra is also sadly lacking in bite: the limp opening of the *String serenade* is most disconcerting **(415 364-2)**.

The Camerata Bern number fourteen string players in all, two fewer than the strings of the Orpheus Chamber Orchestra. Naturally they have a less full-bodied sonority than their rivals and there is nothing high-powered about them; indeed their playing is agreeably unforced and very musical. They are recorded in the Berne Radio studios, whose acoustic has a shade less warmth than that of the Orpheus. The disc is worth considering particularly for the sake of the endearing *A major Sextet* which is a beautiful piece and not otherwise available in the CD format. It was written only three years after its more familiar companion.

Another CD (on Delos) from the Los Angeles Chamber Orchestra under Gerard Schwarz is made relatively uncompetitive by ungenerous couplings. Moreover the account of the *String serenade*, though accomplished, is emotionally cool and lacking charm **(D/CD 3011)**.

Serenade for wind, Op. 44.

*** CRD *CRDC 4110* [id.]. Nash Ens. – KROMMER: *Octet-Partita*.***

(*) HM Orfeo Dig. **C 051831A [id.]. Munich Wind Ac., Brezina – GOUNOD: *Petite symphonie*.**(*)

The Nash Ensemble can hold their own with the competition in the *D minor Serenade*, and their special claim tends to be the coupling, a Krommer rarity that is well worth hearing. The CRD version of the Dvořák is very well recorded (the chrome cassette is the best available of this work) and the playing is very fine indeed, robust yet sensitive to colour, and admirably spirited.

The sumptuously weighty ensemble of Munich players at the opening of Dvořák's first movement sets the scene for a performance that is essentially robust, yet very well played. The *Andante*, slightly selfconscious in its spaciousness, yet ideally needs a lighter touch, but the very entertaining scherzo is quite bucolic in its deft and spirited articulation. The finale goes well, too. The recording (made in St Stephen's Church, Munich) is amply textured throughout, yet detail is not clouded and there is individuality and character in the solo playing. The CD brings fine presence, but is short on playing time – there would have been plenty of room for another piece alongside the Gounod coupling.

Slavonic dances Nos 1–16, Opp. 46 and 72.
(M) *** DG **419 056-2**; *419 056-4* [id.]. Bav. RSO, Kubelik.
(M) **(*) Decca Dig. **411 749-2** [id.]. RPO, Dorati.
(*) Sup. Dig. **C37 7491 [id.]. Czech PO, Neumann.
(*) Chan. Dig. **CHAN 8406; *ABTD 1143* [id.]. SNO, Järvi.

Slavonic dances Nos 1–16; Slavonic rhapsodies Nos 1–3.
(*) Ph. Dig. **416 623/4–2; *416 368-4* (2) [id.]. Leipzig GO, Masur.

Kubelik's *Slavonic dances* are long admired; the recording dates from 1975 and is of excellent quality. Now at last, for the digitally remastered Galleria reissue, DG have managed to fit them on to one CD. The orchestral playing is first rate and the performances are infectiously full of flair. Kubelik is a natural Dvořákian and his feeling for the subtlety and rubato of this music is always attractive, especially so in the second set, where Dvořák's ideas are often particularly imaginative. The sound (as with other DG Bavarian recordings made at this time) is a little dry in the bass, but the middle response is full and there is no shrillness on top. There is an excellent tape. A bargain in either format.

Dorati's set has now been reissued on a mid-price Decca Ovation CD. His performances have characteristic brio, the RPO response is warmly lyrical when necessary, and the woodwind playing gives much pleasure. Sparkle is the keynote and there is no lack of spontaneity. The Kingsway Hall venue with its natural resonance seems to have offered more problems than usual, and on CD the louder tuttis are not as sweet in the upper range of the strings as one would expect. However, the digital sound is generally superior to Kubelik's DG alternative.

Masur's performances are also highly sympathetic and very well played. Moreover the Philips sound is much fuller than the DG recording for Kubelik, although the Leipzig auditorium brings some clouding of focus. However, the layout, with the *Dances* split over a pair of CDs, is uneconomical; although the three *Slavonic rhapsodies* make a substantial bonus, their invention is less succinct and No. 3 (which Beecham favoured) is probably the finest. The two CDs are available separately; the tapes are together in a box.

Of the other issues in single-CD format, Neumann's Supraphon set, recorded in the House of Artists, Prague, is a marginal first choice. The *Dances* are very well played, with much felicitous detail from the Czech orchestra, who clearly have not grown tired of this engaging music. The recording is clear and naturally balanced, with no artificial digital brightness; it is also a little dry at the lower end, a truthful reflection of the acoustics of the recording site. But the alert vivacity of the music making is winning. One of the advantages of CD is that one can readily make one's own selection, rather than having them always in numerical sequence.

The Chandos CD also has the advantage of offering all sixteen *Slavonic dances* on a single disc; moreover, Järvi has the measure of this repertoire and he secures brilliant and responsive playing from the SNO. The recording, made in the SNO Centre, Glasgow, has the orchestra set back in an acoustic of believable depth, but the upper strings are brightly lit and fortissimos bring some loss of body and a degree of hardness on top, so that after a while the ear tends to tire. Unusually for Chandos, there is a noticeable loss of upper range in the treble on the chrome cassette; the sound is richer but has lost some of its sparkle.

Slavonic dances, Op. 46/1–5.
(B) *** DG Walkman *413 159-4* [id.]. Bav. RSO, Kubelik – LISZT: *Hungarian rhapsodies* etc.; SMETANA: *Má Vlast* excerpts.***

Slavonic dances Nos 1, 3, 8, 9–10.
(M) *** Decca *417 696-4*. VPO, Reiner – BRAHMS: *Hungarian dances.****

The performances on the Walkman cassette are part of an attractive compilation of popular Slavonic music (with Kubelik again conducting Smetana and Karajan in Liszt). Kubelik's accounts of the five *Slavonic dances* from Op. 46 offer polished, sparkling orchestral playing and very good sound.

Reiner's way with Dvořák's dance music is indulgent but has plenty of sparkle, and the Vienna Philharmonic are clearly enjoying themselves; any reservations about the conductor's idiosyncrasies are soon forgotten in the pleasure of listening to such colourful music so vivaciously and spontaneously played. This is a much reissued compilation and now reappears in a good transfer on Decca's new tape-only Weekend series.

Symphonies Nos 1–9; Overture Carnaval; Scherzo capriccioso; The Wood Dove, Op. 110.
(M) **(*) DG **423 120-2** (6). BPO, Kubelik.

Kubelik's set originally appeared on LP in the early 1970s as part of DG's Symphony edition. It has much to recommend it: first and foremost the glorious playing of the Berlin Philharmonic and the natural warmth that Kubelik brings to his music making. He seems less convinced by the earliest symphonies than Kertesz on Decca and in No. 3 he sounds almost routine by the side of the Decca recording (not yet issued on CD). In spite of some idiosyncratic but not unidiomatic touches, however, he achieves glowing performances of Nos 6–9 (even if No. 6 is without the refreshingly imaginative new look given to it by Järvi on Chandos). At mid-price this remains a desirable set and holds the field until the first two symphonies appear separately. The bonus items are all well played and recorded and are equally idiomatic.

Symphony No. 3 in E flat, Op. 10.
** Sup. Dig. **C37 7668** [id.]. Czech PO, Neumann.

Symphony No. 3 in E flat, Op. 10; Carnaval overture, Op. 92; Symphonic variations, Op. 78.
*** Chan. Dig. **CHAN 8575**; *ABTD 1270* [id.]. SNO, Järvi.

This was the first of Dvořák's symphonies to show the full exuberance of his genius. When he wrote it in 1873 – eight years after the first two – he was very much under the influence of Wagner, but nowhere do the Wagnerian ideas really conceal the essential Dvořák. Even the unashamed crib from *Lohengrin* in the middle section (D flat major) of the slow movement has a Dvořákian freshness. This long slow movement is in any case the weakest of the three, but the outer movements are both delightful and need no apology whatever. The very opening of the symphony with its 6/8 rhythm and rising-scale motifs can hardly miss, and the dotted rhythms of the second subject are equally engaging. Järvi directs a characteristically warm and persuasive reading, not ideally sharp of rhythm in the first movement – in this respect Kertesz's Decca account, still awaited on CD, has a defter touch – but totally sympathetic. His account of the *Adagio* blossoms and the finale effectively combines energy with weight. The recording is well up to the standards of the house and the fill-ups are particularly generous, with an exhilarating performance of *Carnaval* followed by a strongly characterized set of variations, with a rich, lyrical emphasis. There is a first-class chrome cassette.

Neumann's directness of manner in Dvořák is more successful in this work than in some other of the early symphonies. The steady forward momentum of the first movement is attractive and the simple presentation of the second subject is helped by the fine orchestral playing. Again in the *Adagio* the flowing tempo is effective, with the restrained eloquence from the orchestra maintaining the tension consistently. After the climax, the delicate woodwind detail is nicely balanced by elegant string espressivo, with ardour never too overt to create a feeling of melodrama. This is left for the finale, which is thrustful, a trifle square but with crisp rhythms and excellent ensemble preventing heaviness. The recording is full and well detailed, if without the colour and glow of the finest Western CDs. Without a filler, however, the CD is poor value as it plays for only 38 minutes.

Symphony No. 4 in D min., Op. 13.
*(*) Sup. Dig. **C37 7442** [id.]. Czech PO, Neumann.

Symphony No. 4 in D min., Op. 13; The Golden spinning wheel, Op. 109.
(*) Decca **417 596-2 [id.]. LSO, Kertesz.

Compared with the exuberant symphonies which flank it on either side in the Dvořák canon, this is a disappointment. The opening theme – a fanfare-like idea – is not as characterful as one expects, but then the second subject soars aloft in triple time. The slow movement begins with so close a crib from the *Pilgrims' Music* in *Tannhäuser* one wonders how Dvořák had the face to write it, but the variations which follow are attractive, and the scherzo has a delightful lolloping theme, which unfortunately gives way to a horribly blatant march trio with far too many cymbal crashes in it. The finale, despite rhythmic monotony, has at least one highly characteristic and attractive episode. And, whatever the shortcomings of the work, there is much that is memorable. Kertesz gives a good dramatic performance, and the reissue of his 1966 recording is welcome, though the digital remastering has added only marginally to the clarity of the sound. In the fine performance of *The Golden spinning wheel*, which makes a generous coupling, there is a distinct loss of bloom, and the violins sound noticeably thinner above the stave. This would have been more competitive in Decca's mid-priced Ovation series. The cassette of the analogue master remains available (it offers *In Nature's realm* instead of *The Golden spinning wheel*) and, although the focus is less sharp, so is the cost (*KJBC 113*).

The symphony needs more coaxing than Neumann gives it. He is not helped by the rather stark acoustic of the Supraphon recording, which gives faithful detail without much overall bloom. The reading has plenty of thrust in the first movement, with the pacing in this new CD version distinctly faster than in his 1975 analogue account (the exposition repeat omitted on both occasions). The *Andante sostenuto* refuses to blossom and the Wagnerian quotation is curiously unexpansive. The most successful movement is the scherzo, and Neumann emphasizes its Lisztian associations without too much bombast. Overall, the dryness of the string timbre reduces the appeal of this issue, though the orchestral playing has plenty of character.

Symphony No. 5 in F; My home, overture, Op. 62; Hussite overture, Op. 67.
(*) Decca **417 597-2 [id.]. LSO, Kertesz.

Symphony No. 5 in F, Op. 75; The Water Goblin, Op. 107.
❀ *** Chan. Dig. **CHAN 8552**; *ABTD 1258* [id.]. SNO, Järvi.

Dvořák's *F major Symphony* used to be called the *Pastoral*, but although it shares Beethoven's key and uses the flute a great deal (a Dvořákian characteristic) the nickname is not specially apt. What initially strikes one are the echoes of Wagner – forest murmurs (Bohemian ones) in the opening pages, a direct lift from *Siegfried's Rhine Journey* in the second theme and so on – but by the time he wrote the work, 1875, Dvořák's individuality as a musician was well established, and the composer's signature is in effect written on every bar. The slow movement is as beautiful as any in the symphonies, the scherzo is a gloriously bouncing piece with themes squandered generously, and the finale, though long, is intensely original in structure and argument.

Neeme Järvi and the Scottish National Orchestra present the pastoral opening with an airy beauty never matched on record before. The reverberant Chandos recording adds to the open-air feeling of this shimmering nature music, adding warmth too to the robust ideas which quickly follow. Järvi is most effective in moulding the structure, subtly varying tempo between sections to smooth over the often abrupt links. His persuasiveness in the slow movement, relaxed but never sentimental, brings radiant playing from the SNO, and though in the last two movements ensemble is not quite as crisp as earlier, Czech dance-rhythms are sprung most infectiously leading to an exhilarating close to the whole work, simulating the excitement of a live performance. The fill-up is unusual and colourful, a piece based on a gruesome little fairy-story full of sharp dramatic contrasts. Wagnerian echoes in the water music are most atmospherically brought out. It is a highly rewarding piece and a substantial bonus when the advocacy is so strong. As usual with Chandos, there is a first-class cassette, which approaches demonstration standard in the vivid orchestral effects of the symphonic poem.

Kertesz's performance is straight and direct, certainly dramatic, with tempi well chosen to allow for infectious rhythmic pointing. The LSO playing has the freshness of new discovery, for this work was hardly ever played in the concert hall when the Decca record was made in the mid-1960s. But there is no doubt that Järvi's Scottish performance is freer and rather more imaginative. The Decca recording sounds well in its remastered format; it is brighter, although the overall gain is not striking. The two couplings are less substantial than Järvi's tone-poem, but attractive enough. This issue is still available on cassette (without the patriotic *Hussite overture*), sounding well and costing far less (*KJBC 114*). There is also a Supraphon CD by the Czech Philharmonic under Neumann but, with no couplings, it is uncompetitive (**C37 7377**).

Symphony No. 6 in D, Op. 60; The Noon Witch, Op. 108.
*** Chan. Dig. **CHAN 8530**; *ABTD 1240* [id.]. SNO, Järvi.

Symphony No. 6 in D, Op. 60; Symphonic variations, Op. 78.
*** Decca **417 598-2** [id.]. LSO, Kertesz.

Järvi and the Scottish National Orchestra give a wonderfully sympathetic reading of Dvořák's *Sixth*, bringing out its Brahmsian warmth, underlining the direct links with Brahms's *Second Symphony*, notably at the start of the first and fourth movements. The big grandioso sunburst when the first theme opens out is superbly presented, with Järvi moulding the tempo naturally without mannerism. The bloom on the Chandos sound adds to the lyrical warmth and sweetness of the slow movement, ripely and relaxedly done but without self-indulgence. The *Furiant*, rhythmically sprung like a jolly dance, leads to a finale taken challengingly fast but with lifted rhythms too, and with sharp contrasts of mood. In the fill-up, Järvi brings out the programmatic story-telling of the piece, with tremolo strings breathtakingly delicate on the entry of the witch. Both on CD and chrome cassette the recording is in the demonstration bracket.

As in the others of his series, Kertesz's mid-1960s recordings gave us fresh insight into these vividly inspired works. His reading of the *Sixth* is one of the most characteristic, direct, literal and dramatic, with consistently responsive playing from the LSO. The *Symphonic variations* is also extremely successful – little performed – it is one of Dvořák's finest orchestral works. With lively, bright sound (especially in the *Variations*, recorded later, at the beginning of the 1970s) this is the most attractive of his Decca reissues, alongside the *New World symphony*.

Neumann and the Czech Philharmonic are let down by a severe, lustreless recording which prevents any projection of Brahmsian amiable feeling, though the fierceness of the tuttis certainly gives brilliance to the *Furiant* scherzo. There is no coupling and this is uncompetitive in all respects (Sup. **C37 7242**).

Symphonies Nos 7–9 (New World).
*** Decca Dig. **421 082-2** (2) [id.]. Cleveland O, Dohnányi.
(*) Ph. Dig. **412 542-2 (2) [id.]. Minnesota O, Marriner.

By placing the last three symphonies on a pair of CDs, Decca in effect offer these splendid Dohnányi performances at 'mid-price', so perhaps it seems churlish to complain that with Nos 7 and 8 coupled on the first disc (72′ 48″) there was room on the second – which offers only the *New World*, and without the first-movement exposition repeat, (39′ 63″) for the *Scherzo capriccioso* (originally coupled with No. 8). Nevertheless these are all among the finest available CD versions – see below – and with top-drawer Decca sound this is an excellent way of acquiring these works as economically as possible on compact disc.

Marriner's Philips set offers comparable value, and his recordings are not at present available separately on CD. Admirers of this conductor will find nothing to complain of on technical grounds; his is an enjoyably successful triptych; but in general the Dohnányi Decca set is to be preferred. Marriner's approach to Dvořák is mellow and warm-hearted, helped by the attractively rich textures of the Philips recording, with its agreeable ambient glow. Some might feel that the *Seventh* is a little too easy-going and lacking in drama, the account of the *New World*, too, introduces a strong element of nostalgia, both at the opening and in the beautifully played *Largo*. But the scherzo is thus made to sound more contrasted than usual, vivacious and light-hearted. The outer movements are fresh and strong without being heavy, though there is a slightly self-conscious element in the phrasing of the famous second subject of the first movement. The *Eighth* is the finest performance of the three, its sunny qualities most appealing. This should be issued separately on CD, for Marriner's smiling lyricism is very persuasive and the finale very much breathes the air of the *Slavonic dances*, with fine rhythmic bite and no pomposity whatsoever.

Symphony No. 7 in D min., Op. 70.
*** Decca Dig. **417 564-2**; *417 564-4* [id.]. Cleveland O, Dohnányi.
(*) Sup. **C37 7067 [id.]. Czech PO, Neumann.
** DG Dig. **410 997-2** [id.]. VPO, Maazel.
*(*) RCA Dig. **RD 85427** [**RCD1 5427**]. Chicago SO, Levine.

Symphony No. 7, Op. 70; The Golden spinning wheel, Op. 109.
*** Chan. Dig. **CHAN 8501**; *ABTD 1211* [id.]. SNO, Järvi.

We have long praised Carlos Païta's outstanding, inspirational version of Dvořák's *D minor Symphony*, a reading of striking lyrical ardour, matching excitement with warmth. This music making has the kind of spontaneity one experiences only at the most memorable of live performances, helped by a natural concert-hall balance and the strikingly wide dynamic range of the CD format. However, Païta has his own label; this record has become increasingly difficult (and expensive) to obtain, and at the time of going to press is only intermittently available (Lodia **LOD-CD 782**).

Of the other versions, Dohnányi's fine Decca Cleveland performance stands out, although the CD is distinctly short measure (36′), and it is better approached in conjunction with the two other late symphonies, offered complete on a pair of CDs – see above. The performance, if not quite as gripping as Païta's, is still an extremely fine one. Tempi are all aptly judged, and while the work's Brahmsian inheritance is acknowledged in the slow movement, the lighter Dvořákian lyrical flavour is dominant, notably in the nicely sprung scherzo, liltingly articulated and rhythmically infectious. The outer movements are strong, with the exciting climaxes demonstrating the commitment and vigour of the orchestral playing and never sounding forced. All in all this is very satisfying, and the Decca recording is first rate, brilliant yet with a convincing concert-hall ambience. There is an excellent cassette.

Järvi's Chandos version was the first to be issued in his complete cycle and, to be honest, it is just a little plain-spun, without quite the degree of imaginative freedom that illuminates the *Fifth* and (particularly) the *Sixth Symphonies*. He secures playing of considerable lyrical ardour from his excellent SNO players, but the articulation of the scherzo misses out that engaging 'comma' which is an essential part of the presentation of the main idea (a moment of sheer delight in the Païta account and almost equally felicitous with Dohnányi). However, it would be wrong to make too much of this; the lyrical feel of Järvi's Dvořák suggests a genuine affinity with this composer and the outer movements combine eloquence with excitement. Moreover the Chandos issue offers a very substantial bonus in including one of Dvořák's most memorable symphonic poems, much beloved of Sir Thomas Beecham. Järvi's account is less magical than his, but it still has plenty of drama and atmosphere. The CD brings a fine bloom to a warmly resonant orchestral sound-image, the middle strings are full and the woodwind have an agreeable glowing colour, although the bass is rather less firm than with Decca in Cleveland and the overall focus slightly less sharply defined. The cassette is excellently managed in all respects.

Neumann is much more successful in his CD of the *Seventh* than in the earlier symphonies. The reading has a positive character, but is less histrionic than Païta's. There is fine, often superb playing from the Czech Philharmonic, with the most engaging response from the woodwind to the first movement's second subject. The slow movement is eloquent, the scherzo winningly light and vivacious in a specially Czech way, and the finale steady and strong. The recording has less ambient glow than Dohnányi's or Järvi's and a fairly sharp focus, with orchestral timbres not lacking colour, and the overall balance realistic.

Maazel's reluctance to relax in Dvořákian happiness and innocence produces a powerful incisive performance, with the slow movement spacious and refined, though the bright DG recording fails to place the orchestra against any defined acoustic, making fortissimos rather aggressive.

Using modern digital techniques, the Chicago engineers seem unable to capture the acoustic of Symphony Hall, Chicago, with the bloom and naturalness they achieved in the earliest days of analogue stereo. Levine's virile account of the *D minor Symphony* is hampered by a sound-balance that makes tuttis seem aggressive (particularly the slow-movement climax) and the upper strings thin and febrile. The reading is direct and well played, but lacks charm: the sparkle of the scherzo is there, but Levine's inflection of the main idea is less affectionately subtle than Païta's.

(i) *Symphonies Nos 7 in D min., Op. 70; 8 in G, Op. 88;* (ii) *Slavonic dances Nos 9, 10 and 15, Op. 72/1, 2 and 7.*
(B) *** DG Walkman *419 088-4* [id.]. (i) BPO; (ii) Bav. RSO; Kubelik.

This is one of the very finest Walkman bargains, and is worth obtaining even if it involves duplication. The recordings sound admirably fresh, full yet well detailed, the ambience attractive. Kubelik gives a glowing performance of the *Seventh*, one of Dvořák's richest inspirations. His approach is essentially expressive, but his romanticism never obscures the overall structural plan and there is no lack of vitality and sparkle. The account of the *Eighth* is a shade straighter, without personal idiosyncrasy, except for a minor indulgence for the phrasing of the lovely string theme in the trio of the scherzo. Throughout both works the playing of the Berlin Philharmonic Orchestra is most responsive, with the polish of the playing adding refinement. The orchestral balance in the *G major Symphony* is particularly well judged. The recordings come from 1971 and 1966 respectively and sound in no way dated; nor do the beguilingly shaped *Slavonic dances*, from 1975, with the Bavarian orchestra on top form. They are used as encores following the close of each symphony.

Symphony No. 8 in G, Op. 88.
*** CBS **MK 42038** [id.]. Columbia SO, Bruno Walter – WAGNER: *Parsifal* excerpts.***
(*) Sup. Dig. **C37 7073 [id.]. Czech PO, Neumann.
(M) **(*) Decca **417 744-2** [id.]. VPO, Karajan – BRAHMS: *Symphony No. 3.***
** DG Dig. **415 971-2**; *415 971-4* [id.]. VPO, Karajan.

(i) *Symphony No. 8 in G, Op. 88;* (ii) *Carnaval overture, Op. 92.*
(M) **(*) ASV Dig. **CDQS 6006**; *ZCQS 6006* [id.]. (i) Royal Liverpool PO; (ii) LPO; Bátiz.

(i) *Symphony No. 8 in G, Op. 88;* (ii) *Czech suite, Op. 39.*
(M) *** Ph. *420 298-4* [id.]. (i) Concg. O, C. Davis; (ii) ECO, Mackerras.

Symphony No. 8 in G, Op. 88; Nocturne for strings, Op. 40.
(*) Chan. Dig. **CHAN 8323; *ABTD 1105* [id.]. LPO, Handley.

Symphony No. 8 in G, Op. 88; Scherzo capriccioso, Op. 66.
*** Decca Dig. **414 422-2**; *414 422-4* [id.]. Cleveland O, Dohnányi.

Walter's famous account of Dvořák's *Eighth* was one of the last he made (in 1962) during his CBS Indian summer just before he died. It has been in and out of the catalogue ever since. As with many of its companions in this CBS series, the improvement on CD is astonishing. The sound was always warm and full, but now is more naturally clear, the focus of all sections of the orchestra firmer with upper strings sweet (if with slightly less upper range than one would expect in a modern digital recording) and the violas, cellos and basses expansively resonant. It is a strong yet superbly lyrical reading; but the overall lyricism never takes the place of virility and Walter's mellowness is most effective in the *Adagio*. His pacing is uncontroversial until the finale, which is steadier than usual, more symphonic, although never heavy. With its inspired coupling of the *Prelude and Good Friday music* from *Parsifal*, this issue, like its *New World* companion, ranks high in the CBS legacy.

Rather like Kondrashin's splendid VPO version of the *New World*, Dohnányi's Decca Cleveland CD of the *Eighth* makes one hear it with new ears. Within the acoustics of the Masonic Hall, the Decca engineers have created a striking impression of realism. The layout of the orchestra is convincingly natural, the internal definition achieved without any kind of digital edge. The various string groups, notably cellos and basses, are particularly firm, the woodwind, like the violins, given a fine bloom; and the brass, horns, trumpets and trombones, which are set back, still make a spectacular effect, as do the timpani. The performance is attractively alive and spontaneous, although it includes a few self-conscious nudgings here and there. But the playing of the Cleveland Orchestra is so responsive that the overall impression is of freshness, and in the coda there is the kind of interpretative freedom that can come off at a concert, but less often on record. Here it makes an exhilarating culmination. The coupling with the *Scherzo capriccioso* is apt, when the performance finds an affinity with the *Symphony* in bringing out the Slavonic dance sparkle, and moulding the lyrical secondary theme with comparable affectionate flair. There is an excellent cassette.

Sir Colin Davis's reading has characteristic directness, and his performance balances an engagingly zestful exuberance in the outer movements with a beautifully played and eloquent *Adagio* and a lightly pointed scherzo. Here the Concertgebouw strings have a delightful lyrical freshness in the trio, and there is a spontaneous burst of high spirits in the coda. Mackerras gives a lively performance of the *Czech suite* and this makes a good bonus, even if the music making is not as distinctive as in the *Symphony*. Here the ECO recording is strikingly clear; in the main work the sound is full and vivid, though the Amsterdam acoustics bring a degree of clouding to the lower range. But at mid-price this tape is highly recommendable.

Neumann's *Eighth* is by far the finest of his cycle. The firm momentum established at the opening does not produce any loss of expansive warmth, and the vigour is maintained throughout. The *Adagio* is particularly fine, with a feeling of creative spontaneity at the improvisatory central point of the movement, before the main theme returns on the woodwind against those delightful horn chugs, with elegant string decoration. The scherzo is vivacious, with a rustic Czech flavour from the woodwind in the trio; and the exciting finale rounds the performance off, the closing section especially vivid. Although there is a degree of blatancy from the Czech brass, the sound is otherwise excellent, convincingly balanced and realistic, with the woodwind colouring well conveyed. However, with no coupling, this is short measure.

With exceptionally full and brilliant sound, Handley's Chandos version – originally part of a Beecham tribute box – makes a strong, fresh impact. The manner is direct with the opening relatively straight, not eased in. Though some will miss a measure of charm, the life and spontaneity of the reading are most winning, with the CD brightly vivid and with good inner clarity. The *Nocturne* makes a most agreeable bonus and is beautifully played. There is an excellent chrome cassette, of Chandos's usual high standard.

Karajan's 1965 Decca version of Dvorak's *Eighth* has far more charisma than his most recent digital version with the same orchestra. In the mid-1960s the VPO produced their very best playing for him, full of vigour, and they gave the impression of enjoying every bar of the music. There are moments of indulgence from Karajan in the scherzo, but this too stems from affection and, overall, this is a most winning performance, blending polish and spontaneity. The vintage analogue recording was full and fresh and well detailed; the digital remastering has brightened the strings above the stave to the point of fierceness in fortissimos and further clarified textures to no real advantage, as some of the amplitude has been lost. However, the ambience retains most of the body to the middle strings and, when the upper range is tamed, the effect remains vivid. The Brahms coupling, however, sounds distinctly thinner.

An excellent budget CD comes from Bátiz with consistently spirited playing from the Royal Liverpool Philharmonic Orchestra. The reading is direct, responsive and structurally sound and enjoyable in its easy spontaneity. The digital recording is vivid, yet does not lack warmth, although there is a touch of fierceness on climaxes. The overture is slightly less successful, but this is certainly good value. There is a very good chrome cassette.

On DG Karajan gives a characteristically big-scale reading of Dvořák's *Eighth*, well detailed but lacking a little in spontaneity. The recording with its close-up spotlighting of individual solos does not help. Lacking a coupling, it is not very competitive with a number of other modern versions, which are also better recorded. The clear sound-image has transferred well to cassette.

Symphonies Nos 8; 9 (New World).
(M) HMV *EG 291070-4*. BPO, Karajan.

Symphonies Nos 8; 9 (New World); Carnaval overture.
(B) ** DG Dig. *419 845-4* [id.]. VPO, Maazel.

Maazel's Pocket Music chrome-tape coupling is exceptionally generous and the transfers are of high quality. This costs a fraction of the two equivalent CDs (**415 205-2** and **410 032-2** respectively). But although the *Eighth* opens well it is a fierce performance, lacking the glow of warmth one associates with this work. Despite excellent incisive playing the hardness of the reading is underlined by the recording balance, which favours a bright treble against a rather light bass. Though the trumpet fanfare heralding the start of the finale is wonderfully vivid, the sound lacks something in body. The *New World* is similarly high-powered, incisive to the point of fierceness. It is superbly played and has moments of affection, most striking in the poised and pure account of the slow movement. On tape as well as CD the sound is very bright, lending a touch of aggressiveness to fortissimos, while the bass is lightened in the high-level tape transfer. The account of the overture is extremely brilliant.

Karajan's coupling of his EMI Berlin Philharmonic recordings of the late 1970s is potentially attractive. The *New World* comes off splendidly (see below) and although the *Eighth* is less spontaneously successful than his previous account (recorded a decade earlier for Decca), it is warm and very well played. However, the EMI iron-oxide tape transfer is little short of a disaster, with heavy bass resonance clouding the overall sound-picture.

Symphony No. 9 in E min. (*From the New World*), *Op. 95.*
*** Decca Dig. **400 047-2** [id.]; (M) *417 267-4* (with *Slavonic dances Nos 1, 3 & 8*) VPO, Kondrashin.
*** Decca Dig. **414 421-2**; *414 421-4* [id.]. Cleveland O, Dohnányi.
*** CBS **MK 42039** [id.]. Columbia SO, Bruno Walter.
(M) *** HMV **CDM7 69005-2** [id.]; *EG 769005-4*. BPO, Karajan – SMETANA: *Vltava.****
(M) *** DG **423 384-2** [id.]. BPO, Fricsay – LISZT: *Les Préludes***(*); SMETANA: *Vltava.****
(*) HMV **CDC7 47071-2 [id.]. BPO, Tennstedt.
** DG Dig. **415 509-2** [id.]. VPO, Karajan – SMETANA: *Vltava.***
** Decca Dig. **410 116-2** [id.]. Chicago SO, Solti.

Symphony No. 9 (*New World*); *Carnaval overture, Op. 92.*
(M) *(*) Pickwick Dig. **PCD 851**. LSO, Barry Tuckwell.

Symphony No. 9 (*New World*); *Carnaval overture; Humoresque* (arr. Foster).
(M) **(*) RCA **GD 86530**; *GK 86530* [**6530-2-RG**] Boston Pops O, Fiedler – ENESCU: *Rumanian rhapsody.***(*)

Symphony No. 9 (*New World*); *Carnaval overture; Scherzo capriccioso.*
(M) *** Decca **417 724-2** [id.]. LSO, Kertesz.

Symphony No. 9 (*New World*); *Slavonic dances Nos 1, 3 & 7, Op. 46/1, 3 & 7; 10 & 16, Op. 72/2 & 8.*
(M) *** DG **423 206-2**; *423 206-4* [id.]. BPO, Karajan.

Symphony No. 9 (*New World*); *My home overture, Op. 62.*
*** Chan. Dig. **CHAN 8510**; *ABTD 1220* [id.]. SNO, Järvi.

(i) *Symphony No. 9* (*New World*); (ii) *Symphonic variations.*
(B) *** CfP Dig. **CD-CFP 9006**; *TC-CFP 4382* (without *Variations*). LPO, Macal.
(M) *** DG *415 837-4* [id.] (i) BPO; (ii) Bav. RSO; Kubelik.
(M) **(*) Ph. **420 349-2**; *420 349-4* [id.]. (i) Concg. O; (ii) LSO; C. Davis.

(i) *Symphony No. 9* (*New World*); (ii) *Scherzo capriccioso, Op. 66;* (iii) *Serenade for strings in E, Op. 22.*
(B) *** DG Walkman *413 147-4*. (i) BPO; (ii) Bav. RSO; (iii) ECO; Kubelik.

The *New World* is the best served by the gramophone of any Romantic symphony. As can be seen from the list above, there are strong recommendations in each price range on both CD and cassette. Most offer a fill-up of some kind; but those collectors content with the symphony alone, and seeking the finest sound-quality, will probably choose between Dohnányi and Kondrashin, both on Decca, although Zdenek Macal's digital Classics for Pleasure CD is also extremely fine; with his performance second to none, this is a real bargain. Järvi's Chandos version is well up to the standards of the house (and has the *My home* overture as a bonus) but here the very lack of idiosyncrasy in an otherwise satisfyingly spacious performance may be counted a disadvantage by some.

Dohnányi's version, superbly played and recorded like the companion recordings of Nos 7 and 8, should by rights be a first recommendation, but it falls down by the lack of observance of the first-movement exposition repeat. But that can hardly be said to put it entirely out of court for many other famous conductors (including Karajan) fail to observe it, and Dohnányi shapes his account of the first movement accordingly. That said, there is much to praise in this grippingly spontaneous performance, generally direct and unmannered but glowing with warmth. In the first movement Dohnányi, without any stiffness, allows himself relatively little easing of tempo for the second and third subjects while the great cor anglais melody in the *Largo* and the big clarinet solo in the finale are both richly done, with the ripe and very well-balanced Decca recording adding to their opulence. The sound is spectacularly full and rich. The cassette too is one of Decca's best.

Kondrashin's Vienna performance *does* include the exposition repeat; its impact remains quite remarkable, although it was one of Decca's earliest CDs. Recorded in the Sofiensaal, the range of the sound is equalled by its depth. The ambient effect of the hall prevents a clinical effect, yet every detail of Dvořák's orchestration is revealed within a highly convincing perspective. Other performances may show a higher level of tension, but there is a natural spontaneity here, the cor anglais solo in the *Largo* is easy and songful, and the finale is especially satisfying with the wide dynamic range adding drama and the refinement and transparency of the texture noticeably effective as the composer recalls ideas from earlier movements. This performance is also available on an inexpensive tape which includes three *Slavonic dances*. Here the sound is good (especially the *Dances*), but the CD is in an altogether different class.

There is a comparable appealing directness in the way the music unfolds in Macal's CfP version, and again the digital recording, in its CD format, is strikingly believable in its natural balance, with body as well as brilliance and excellent definition. It is an outstanding performance, fresh, sparkling and incisively dramatic, and beautifully played. Even making no allowance for price, it stands at, or near, the top of a long list. Macal as a Czech takes a fresh and unsentimental view, with speeds far steadier than usual in the first movement. His inclusion of the repeat balances the structure convincingly. With idiomatic insights there is no feeling of rigidity, with the beauty of the slow movement purified, the scherzo crisp and energetic, set against pastoral freshness in the episodes, and the finale again strong and direct, bringing a ravishing clarinet solo. The *Symphonic variations*, which acts as coupling, is less distinctive, but well characterized. The analogue recording has been faithfully transferred. The cassette omits the *Variations*.

The sheer beauty of the playing as well as the high drama of the reading put Järvi's Chandos version also high on the list. The opening introduction establishes the spaciousness of his view, with lyrical, persuasive phrasing and a very slow speed. It becomes nature music, hardly ominous at all, leading into an allegro which starts relaxedly, but then develops in big dramatic contrasts. The expansiveness is underlined, when the exposition repeat is observed. The *Largo* too is exceptionally spacious, with the cor anglais player taxed to the limit, but effectively supported over ravishingly beautiful string playing. The scherzo is lilting rather than fierce, and the finale is bold and swaggering. *My home* overture is also given an exuberant performance, bringing out the lilt of dance rhythms.

Among earlier analogue accounts Kertesz's LSO version stands out. It remains one of the finest performances ever committed to record, with a most exciting first movement (exposition repeat included), in which the introduction of the second subject group is eased in with considerable subtlety; the *Largo* brings playing of hushed intensity to make one hear the music with new ears. Tempi in the last two movements are perfectly judged. This Ovation reissue offers also Kertesz's exuberant *Carnaval overture* and his brilliant and lilting account of the *Scherzo capriccioso*, as attractive as any in the catalogue. At mid-price this is formidable value, but it must be said that the digital remastering has not been entirely beneficial. Although the sound does not lack body and detail is enhanced (the horns are especially tangible), the fortissimo strings above the stave now have a hint of aggressiveness and the bass seems marginally lighter.

Bruno Walter's version dates from 1960 and was originally one of the first completely successful stereo recordings of this work. However, the CBS engineers have now resisted the temptation to 'enhance' the sound, which has a warm ambient resonance without clouding of detail, and the violins are fresh and sweet. There is some remaining background hiss but it is not troublesome. Walter's is not a conventional reading, but it is one to fall in love with. Its recognizably Viennese roots lead to a more relaxed view of the outer movements than usual. Nevertheless, as so often with Walter, there is underlying tension to knit the structure together; the *Largo* is radiant and the scherzo lilting. The spacious finale finds dignity without pomposity and the result is more involving and satisfying than some other rivals which have more surface excitement.

Karajan's 1964 DG recording held a strong place in the catalogue for two decades. For many readers it may prove the most attractive of his three currently available readings on CD, and it is certainly preferable to his digital version. It has a powerful lyrical feeling and an exciting build-up of power in the outer movements. The *Largo* is most beautifully played, and Karajan's element of detachment lets the orchestra speak for itself, which it does, gloriously. The rustic qualities of the scherzo are affectionately brought out, and altogether this is very rewarding. The recording is now very bright and open. The virtuoso performances of the *Slavonic dances*, used as a fill-up, are made to sound very brilliant indeed.

Karajan's 1977 *New World* for HMV has the advantage of an excellent and substantial coupling, a very successful account of Smetana's *Vltava*. The performance of the *Symphony* is robust and spontaneous-sounding, but refined too, and the cor anglais solo of the *Largo* is fresh, at a nicely flowing tempo. The digital remastering has brightened the sound and given it excellent projection but, as usual with EMI's remastered analogue recordings of this period, the bass is drier and the overall effect slightly less atmospheric than the original. This remains competitive at mid-price, even though the first-movement exposition repeat is omitted. It is altogether preferable to Karajan's newer DG digital recording which is less precise in definition, with an element of edginess on strings and brass. The VPO playing too is less refined than the earlier, Berlin Philharmonic account.

Kubelik's marvellously fresh account of the *New World*, recorded in the early 1970s, has now been reissued on DG's Galleria mid-priced label in digitally remastered form, which has brought a firmer bass and slightly clearer detail. The coupling is a sympathetic reading of the *Symphonic variations* with much felicitous detail from the Bavarian orchestra. The performance of the *Symphony* is certainly among the finest. The hushed opening immediately creates a tension which is to be sustained throughout, and the *Largo* has a compelling lyrical beauty, with playing of great radiance from the Berlin Philharmonic. After a scherzo of striking character and a finale of comparable urgency, Kubelik then relaxes magically, when the composer recalls earlier themes as in a reverie. This performance is also available in its original unremastered analogue incarnation on a self-recommending Walkman chrome tape with even more generous couplings. Kubelik's accounts of the *Scherzo capriccioso* and *String serenade* have a comparable freshness. The *Scherzo* is attractively spirited and colourful, while the account of the *Serenade* is beautifully lyrical, yet strong in impulse. The playing of the ECO here is attractively polished as well as resilient. The recording is brightly lit and, like the *Symphony*, somewhat dry in the bass, but the chrome-tape transfers are of DG's finest quality. The *Symphony* is offered without a break.

Ferenc Fricsay was one of the stars of the DG catalogue during the time of mono LPs, although his recording career continued into the stereo era. The *New World* dates from 1960 and the reading is characteristic of his approach to nineteenth-century repertoire. The style is somewhat old-fashioned, unashamedly romantic, including an affectionate and considerable *ritardando* at the entry of the first movement's secondary theme. The Berlin Philharmonic, on top form, are highly responsive and everything sounds completely spontaneous. The *Largo* is most beautiful and the finale is splendid, with a very exciting coda. What makes this disc especially attractive is the inclusion of Fricsay's electrifying accounts of *Les Préludes* and *Vltava*, where the river seems in full flood. The recording is generally brilliant in the digital remastering, although there is a degree of stridency in the fortissimo passages.

Tennstedt's is a warm, romantic reading, freely expressive at generally spacious speeds, very much in the German rather than the Czech tradition. Though he fails to observe the important exposition repeat in the first movement, the symphonic weight of the work is powerfully conveyed with full, forward recording and outstanding playing from the Berlin Philharmonic, not least the soloists. The natural, easy warmth of the famous cor anglais solo at the start of the slow movement has a pure felicity that it would be hard to match. The CD adds clarity to the rich, full recording; however, it also adds a degree of shrillness on the treble in fortissimos.

Now reissued at mid-price, Sir Colin Davis's 1979 Philips version continues to hold its place near the top of the analogue list. It is completely free from egotistic eccentricity; the music is allowed to unfold in the most natural way, its drama vividly projected, and with beautiful orchestral playing throughout this is very satisfying. For some listeners Davis's very directness may have its drawbacks. The cor anglais solo in the slow movement has an appealing simplicity, yet the effect is not very resilient, and later, when the horns echo the theme at the end of the opening section, the impression is positive rather than seductively nostalgic. The CD transfer is well managed, rich and full-bodied, though inner detail is not sharply defined, and the Amsterdam acoustic does bring some minor clouding in the bass. The coupling, a first-class performance of the *Symphonic variations* – one of Dvořák's finest works, much underrated by the public – is very welcome and sounds fresh.

Arthur Fiedler's performance was recorded in 1959 and the sound is most naturally balanced and vivid, characteristic of RCA's early stereo techniques. The performance too, if not individually distinctive, is satisfying in its direct simplicity, with responsive playing from every section of the orchestra, no interpretative eccentricities, and an attractively relaxed feeling, as if all the players were enjoying the music. Significantly, Fiedler observes the first-movement exposition repeat, by no means an automatic procedure in the late 1950s, and his feeling for the work's structure is well conveyed. The dashing account of the *Carnaval overture* comes from 1964 and here the recording brightens and is slightly less natural in the matter of string timbre. After the very welcome Enesco *Rhapsody*, Fiedler provides an agreeable lollipop encore, Stephen Foster's outrageous arrangement of the *Humoresque*, intertwined with his own *Swanee River*. Anyone coming upon this mid-priced CD (or tape) and purchasing it on impulse should be well pleased with the value for money.

Solti's is a characteristically fierce reading, somewhat larger than life, recorded with rather aggressive brilliance, impressive but not too sympathetic. The CD, vivid though it is, does not match Kondrashin's version in beauty of texture and refinement of detail.

Barry Tuckwell's *New World* is well played and sensibly paced, with the elegiac *Largo* by far the most memorable movement. The scherzo is sprightly, but otherwise this reading is seriously undercharacterized and simply doesn't generate enough electricity to be competitive, in spite of first-class modern digital recording.

Other recordings of this work abound, both on CD and tape, but none that need detain us here, apart from a Decca Weekend tape of Kertesz's vibrant earlier Vienna Philharmonic performance (coupled with an exciting *Vltava*) which, though not ideally balanced – the timpani are too close – still comes over very compellingly (*417 678-4*). Kubelik's splendid Berlin Philharmonic performance is also available in yet a further permutation on DG's Focus label, coupled with the first four *Slavonic dances* (*419 645-4*). The recording has been remastered (compared with the Walkman) and sounds slightly cleaner, though the improvement is marginal. Both these tapes are in their respective companies' lowest price ranges.

CHAMBER AND INSTRUMENTAL MUSIC

Piano quartet No. 2 in E flat, Op. 87.
(*) RCA **RD 86256 [RCA **6256-2-RC**]. Rubinstein, Guarneri Qt – FAURÉ: *Piano quartet No. 1.***(*)

Rubinstein's recording was made in December 1970 and in its LP format was originally issued without a coupling. Now it has Fauré, recorded at the same time and showing a comparable warmth and felicity. The sound itself is enhanced and is now fuller than originally – though not especially transparent – and the close balance prevents a real pianissimo. Nevertheless this is infectious music-making and there is much to enjoy. The players observe the exposition repeat and this has a generous playing time (66′).

Piano quintets: in A, Op. 5; in A, Op. 81.
** Ph. Dig. **412 429-2**; *412 429-4* [id.]. Sviatoslav Richter, Borodin Qt.

The early *Quintet* comes from about 1872 when Dvořák was just over thirty and beginning to outgrow some of the worst excesses of his infatuation with Wagner. Later he revised it, not long before composing the famous Op. 81 *Quintet*. It is good to have it for the first time, even if it is by no means fully characteristic. Richter's recording was made at a public concert, this time in Prague at the 1982 Festival. The public is eminently well behaved, but the recording does tend to give excessive prominence to the pianist, and the Borodin Quartet do not have the tonal opulence and bloom which they possess in reality. The performance itself is a good one, though some may be worried by moments of waywardness in the onward flow of tempi; however, in general this is not as fine as Curzon's classic 1963 recording with the VPO Quartet (which we hope may soon appear on CD) or Stephen Bishop's excellent version, recorded in Berlin (Ph. *7310 571*), which is coupled with a neglected masterpiece, the Op. 97 *String quintet*, and which is an excellent tape but is likely to be withdrawn soon.

Piano quintet in A, Op. 81.
*(*) Sup. Dig. **COS 1329** [id.]. Panenka, Smetana Qt – SCHUMANN: *Piano quintet.**(*)

(i) *Piano quintet in A, Op. 81; String quartet No. 12 in F (American), Op. 96.*
* Denon Dig. **C37 7338** [id.]. (i) Josef Hála; Smetana Qt.

Jan Panenka and the Smetana Quartet were recorded in the House of Artists in Prague with indifferent success. Panenka's playing is most musical, but the recording acoustic does not do full justice to the Quartet, who are not perhaps what they were some years ago. The violins sound distinctly wiry and edgy. This can be tamed, but the piano suffers a little from the reverberant acoustic.

The coupling of the *A major Piano quintet* with Dvořák's most famous string quartet is an attractive idea, and it is surprising that it has not been offered before. In the event, however, these performances by the Smetana Quartet, with Josef Hála the pianist in Op. 81, are very disappointing. They were recorded live, and the balance produces a wan sound-picture, which is unflattering to the leader, Jiři Novák. The sense of urgency which one expects from live music-making is not apparent here and, with textures often meagre, the expressive side of the playing is under-projected. Allegros are spirited and the artists clearly appreciate the inherent dance rhythms, but the lack of ambient warmth robs the music of necessary body.

Piano trios Nos 1–4; 4 Romantic pieces (for violin & piano), *Op. 78; Romance in G min.* (for cello & piano), *Op. 94.*
**(*) CRD *CRDC 4086/8* [id.]. Cohen Trio.

Piano trios Nos 1 in B flat, Op. 21; 2 in G min., Op. 26.
(*) Sup. **COS 1409 [id.]. Suk Trio.

Piano trio No. 3 in F min., Op. 65.
*** Chan. Dig. **CHAN 8320**; *ABTD 1107* [id.]. Borodin Trio.

Piano trios No. 3 in F min., Op. 65; 4 in E min. (*Dumky*), *Op. 90.*
*** Sup. **COS 1410** [id.]. Suk Trio.

Piano trio No. 4 in E min. (*Dumky*), *Op. 90.*
*** Chan. Dig. **CHAN 8445**; *ABTD 1157* [id.]. Borodin Trio – SMETANA: *Piano trio.****
(*) Ph. Dig. **416 297-2; *416 297-4* [id.]. Beaux Arts Trio – MENDELSSOHN: *Piano trio No. 1.***(*)
(*) Sup. **C37 7057 [id.]. Suk Trio – SUK: *Elegy.***(*)

The Suk Trio bring a special authority to this music (after all, Josef Suk can trace his ancestry back to the composer himself), and their readings have the benefit of concentration and intellectual grip. They hold the architecture of each movement together most impressively and also play with considerable emotional eloquence. The recordings date from 1977 and are clean, vivid and well balanced. The first two *Trios* have transferred rather less successfully to CD than Nos 3 and 4: there is a thinness on the violin timbre which was not noticeable on the original analogue LPs. The coupling of Op. 65 and the *Dumky*, however, has been very well managed, the sound a little dry but eminently truthful. The alternative coupling of the *Dumky* with Suk's *Elegy* is similarly successful, but this CD offers much less generous measure.

The Cohen is a family trio, so opportunities for rehearsal should be unlimited. Their set also adds Opp. 78 and 94, which the rival account does not include, but this means spreading to three tapes. The playing is always thoroughly musical, though not quite as masterly as that of the Suk Trio. The recording is very good, and collectors are unlikely to find much here to disappoint them. The cassettes are each available separately and offer faithful transfers, although one notices slightly greater presence on the second sides of *CRDC 4086* and *4087* than the first. On *CRDC 4088*, which couples the *Dumky trio* with Opp. 75 and 94, the level is higher and this cassette is demonstrably more vivid.

Dvořák's *F minor Trio* comes from the same period as the *D minor Symphony* and finds him at his most consistently Brahmsian. It is powerful in structure, but as Alex Robertson puts it in his *Master Musicians* monograph, 'the shape of the themes, the writing of the piano and the general feeling of the music "continually do cry" Brahms'. The playing of the Borodin Trio is little short of superb: they have great warmth and fire, such imperfections as there are arising from the natural spontaneity of a live performance, for one feels this is what it must have been, with few if any retakes. Rotislav Dubinsky is slightly under the note at the opening of the second group of the first movement; the pianist, Luba Edlina, is balanced rather forward. The wide-ranging Chandos recording has transferred with impressive presence to CD; the chrome tape too is very realistic, though there is a hint of edge on the violin timbre.

Those unfamiliar with Dvořák's marvellous *E minor Piano trio* might think the sobriquet 'Dumky' indicates some kind of national dance. It is in fact the plural of the Russian word, *dumka* (a term also found in both Poland and Czechoslovakia), which can be broadly translated as a lament. Musically, it implies alternating slow and fast movements, with brightness lightening the melancholy. Dvořák's six-movement *Trio* follows this pattern, with contrasting sequences inherent in the structure of each. It is the spontaneous flexibility of approach to the constant mood changes that makes the splendid Borodin performance so involving, as well as the glorious playing from each of the three soloists. The recording is naturally balanced and the illusion of a live occasion is striking. Highly recommended in both formats, for the cassette is extremely well managed.

The Beaux Arts have recorded the *Dumky* twice before in stereo, once for Philips and more recently for Pearl. The latest performance is rather more assertive than the earlier approach and, although not lacking dramatic contrast and refinement of detail (Menahem Pressler's playing always gives pleasure), has a degree less spontaneity than before. The new digital recording has striking realism and presence, but again the acoustic of the earlier record produced a more intimate sound. But for those who like high drama this new version should be very satisfactory. The cassette is in the demonstration bracket.

4 Romantic pieces, Op. 75; Sonatina in G for violin and piano, Op. 100.
*** HMV Dig. **CDC7 47399-2** [id.]. *EL 270183-4.* Itzhak Perlman, Samuel Sanders – SMETANA: *From my homeland.****

Though this may not be good value in terms of playing time (40 minutes), in every other respect it is. The *Sonatina* is an enchanting piece and so, for that matter, are the *Four Romantic pieces*: both are beautifully played and well recorded, save for the imbalance between the celebrated violinist and the more recessed pianist. There is a very good cassette, fresh and well balanced, perhaps because it is slightly weighted towards the left.

String quartet No. 10 in E flat, Op. 51.
*(*) Tel. Dig. **ZK8 43105** [id.]. Vermeer Qt – VERDI: *Quartet.***

String quartets Nos 10 in E flat; Op. 51; 14 in A flat, Op. 105.
* Denon Dig. **C37 7235**. Kocian Qt.

The *E flat Quartet* comes from the period of the *Violin concerto*, when Dvořák was in his late thirties, and the wonderful *A flat Quartet* was written in 1896 after his return from Prague. They are lovely works but are given curiously lacklustre readings by the Kocian Quartet, and the recording is not particularly spacious or distinguished. The Vermeer Quartet on Teldec have greater tonal bloom and play with finesse and more refined ensemble, but they too are recorded in a small studio and the CD rather brings out its dryness.

String quartets Nos 11 in C, Op. 61; 12 in F (American), Op. 96.
(***) Calliope **CAL 9617** [id.]. Talich Qt.

The *C major Quartet* is a rarity and not Dvořák at his greatest, but it is far from negligible. Those wanting this work have no alternative on CD at present and there is fine playing and recording to recommend this performance. The more familiar *F major Quartet* is well shaped: the players seem just a shade self-conscious at times – the second group of the first movement is somewhat coy – but on the whole this performance has great warmth and sweetness of tone. There is, however, a snag: two bars before fig. 3, the music skips half a beat; this editing error was not present on the original LP.

String quartet No. 12 in F (American), Op. 96.
(M) *** Pickwick Dig. **PCD 883**. Delmé Qt – BRAHMS: *Clarinet quintet.****
*** Ph. Dig. **420 803-2**; *420 803-4* [id.]. Guarneri Qt – SMETANA: *String quartet No. 1.****
*** Ph. **420 396-2** [id.]. Orlando Qt – MENDELSSOHN: *String quartet No. 1.****
(M) *** Ph. **420 876-2**; *420 876-4* [id.]. Italian Qt – SCHUBERT: *String quartet No.14**** (also with BORODIN: *Nocturne****).

String quartets Nos 12 (American); 13 in G, Op. 106.
* Denon Dig. **C37 7234** [id.]. Kocian Qt.

String quartets Nos 12 (American); 14 in A flat, Op. 105.
(M) *** HMV *EG 291029-4*. Smetana Qt.
*(*) Sup. Dig. **C37 7565** [id.]. Panocha Qt.

String quartet No. 12 (American); Cypresses.
*** DG Dig. **419 601-2**; *419 601-4* [id.]. Hagen Qt – KODÁLY: *Quartet No. 2*.***

String quartet No. 12 (American); (i) *String quintet in G, Op. 77.*
*(*) Ara. Dig. **Z 6558**; *ABCQ 6558* [id.]. Portland Qt; (i) with Gary Karr.

The *American quartet* is now particularly well served on CD, and choice here will be dictated by the most suitable coupling. The Delmé Quartet on a superbly recorded Pickwick disc at mid-price give a winningly spontaneous-sounding performance, marked by unusually sweet matching of timbre between the players, which brings out the total joyfulness of Dvořák's American inspiration. The exuberant finale in particular has its rhythms sprung with delectable lightness, leading to an exhilarating close. The unusual coupling, a similarly warm reading of the Brahms *Clarinet quintet*, is both attractive and generous.

The Guarneri performance is warmly romantic; the articulation of the lovely secondary theme of the first movement is particularly affectionate, and both here and in the *Largo sostenuto* one notices the rich cello line of David Soyer, within a responsive texture of finely blended lyricism. Of course there is plenty of life too, and the dance-like finale has an agreeable rhythmic lightness. The recording is full in timbre and most natural in balance and presence. The cassette is very good, but slightly middle- and bass-orientated.

The Hagen Quartet make an uncommonly beautiful sound and their account of this masterly score is very persuasive indeed. Their playing is superbly polished, though their pursuit of tonal beauty has struck some people as approaching the self-conscious. However, their playing is so musical and so satisfying that few will fail to respond. In the finale, for example, they are marvellously spirited, and they play the enchanting *Cypresses*, which Dvořák transcribed from the eponymous song-cycle, with great tenderness. The recording is altogether superb, very present and full-bodied. The chrome cassette, too, is in the demonstration class.

The digital remastering of the 1980 Orlando recording brings very striking presence and immediacy; it emphasizes that their approach, while still romantic, has more drama than the Guarneri account. But again the slow movement is beautifully played and the finale has the most sparkling articulation and dash. With such realistic sound, this ranks among the very best versions of the *Quartet*, with the finely balanced and well-blended tone, excellent musical judgement and great sensitivity.

An outstanding account from the Italian Quartet, notable for its spontaneous, unforced naturalness. It was splendidly recorded by the Philips engineers in 1968 and still sounds most realistic, warm and full in texture as well as clearly defined. This version is second to none and is made more enticing in this reissue by the inclusion of the famous *Nocturne* from Borodin's *Second Quartet*, which comes as an encore at the very end of the CD. (The Schubert coupling is placed first.) There is a good tape, full and smooth, but not quite as clear as the compact disc.

The HMV coupling dates from 1967 and the performances from the Smetana Quartet are first class in every way: there is a splendid freshness, spontaneity and musicality distinguishing this playing, and the recording is well balanced and truthful. In his invaluable *Master Musicians* book, Alec Robertson expressed reservations about the length of the finale of the *A flat Quartet*, which the Smetana Quartet evidently share, since they make a cut (11 bars after fig. 11 to four bars after fig. 12). Tape collectors will find this a good bargain, as the transfer is crisp, clear and realistic.

On Supraphon, the Panocha Quartet are balanced closely and, though their timbres are truthfully caught, one would have liked more space round the instruments. Their expressive playing is not unresponsive, yet the end effect is rather dry. The light articulation in the scherzo and finale of the *American quartet* is attractive, while the lively account of the second movement of Op. 105 (which Dvořák marked *molto vivace*) is spirited without being aggressive. The CD's presence is in no doubt, but a warmer ambience would have added to the effect of this music making.

The Kocian Quartet couple Op. 96 with the late *G major Quartet*. The performances of both this and the *F major* are good but fall short of distinction, and the recording is made in the same unflattering acoustic as their Opp. 51 and 105. This does not represent a serious challenge to the best versions.

On Arabesque, Op. 96 receives an acceptable but not particularly distinguished performance. The *G major String quintet*, Op. 18 (which Simrock published as Op. 77), originally had five movements but the slow movement that separated the scherzo from the first movement was dropped for publication, and Dvořák refashioned it as the glorious *Notturno for strings*, Op. 40. The Portland include the earlier version, which lends undoubted interest to their disc: earlier LP recordings have mostly confined themselves to the published edition. Gary Karr has a distinguished solo career on the double-bass, and the engineers encourage him to continue it here, for he is far too prominent and the violist too reticent. Not a strong contender.

Slavonic dances Nos 1–16, Opp. 46 & 72.
(*) Ara. Dig. **Z 6559; *ABQC 6559* [id.]. Artur Balsam, Gena Raps (piano, four hands).
(*) Hyp. Dig. **CDA 66204; *KA 66204* [id.]. Peter Noke, Helen Krizos (piano, four hands).

Generally fine performances from Artur Balsam and Gena Raps, who respond to the music in a spirit of relaxed enjoyment, yet do not miss its brio. The recording too is well balanced in a pleasing acoustic.

Peter Noke and Helen Krizos often play with more dash but some of the more reflective moments are less sensitively observed here although their impetuous verve is undoubtedly exhilarating at times. The Hyperion recording is more resonant and, coupled to a fairly close microphone placing, the effect is less convincing although there is no lack of focus and brightness to the sound on CD; the cassette has rather more problems with the reverberation.

VOCAL AND CHORAL MUSIC

Te Deum, Op. 103; Psalm 149, Op. 79; Heirs of the White Mountain, Op. 30.
(*) Sup. **C37 7230 [id.]. Beňačkova-Čápová, Souček, Prague Philharmonic Ch., Czech PO, Neumann.

Dvořák's exuberant setting of the *Te Deum* was written to be performed at the celebration of the 400th anniversary of Columbus's discovery of America, and the composer conducted its première in October 1892 in New York. It makes a powerful impression in this eloquent Czech performance, with choral singing of inspired fervour and a fine solo contribution from Gabriela Beňačkova-Čápová, movingly serene in the *Sanctus*. Her colleague, Jaroslav Souček, is less distinctive, a little wobbly, if not seriously so. The sound has a wide dynamic range and the layout of chorus and orchestra is convincingly real, although detail is less refined than it would be in a Western recording. Neumann's eloquent direction and the fine playing of the Czech Philharmonic ensure that the music grips the listener throughout. The other two works are less distinguished but are sung with such conviction that the listener cannot fail to respond. This is one of Neumann's finest Dvořák records.

OPERA

Rusalka (complete).
*** Sup. Dig. **C37 7201/3** [id.]. Beňačková-Čápová, Novak, Soukupová, Ochman, Drobkova, Prague Ch. & Czech PO, Neumann.

Dvořák's fairy-tale opera is given a magical performance by Neumann and his Czech forces, helped by full, brilliant and atmospheric recording which, while giving prominence to the voices, brings out the beauty and refinement of Dvořák's orchestration. Written right at the end of the composer's career in his ripest maturity but with Wagnerian influences at work, the piece has a unique flavour; where on stage it can seem too long for its material (though not in the highly imaginative version staged by the English National Opera at London's Coliseum), it works beautifully on record. The title role is superbly taken by Gabriela Beňačková-Čápová. The voice is creamy in tone, characterfully Slavonic without disagreeable hooting or wobbling, and the famous *Invocation to the Moon* is enchanting. Vera Soukupová as the Witch is just as characterfully Slavonic in a lower register, though not so even; while Wieslaw Ochman sings with fine, clean, heroic tone as the Prince, with timbre made distinctive by tight vibrato. Richard Novak brings out some of the Alberich-like overtones as the Watersprite, though the voice is not always steady. The banding on compact disc is both generous and helpful.

Dyson, George (1883–1964)

At the Tabard Inn: overture; (ii) *In honour of the City;* (i; ii) *Sweet Thames run softly.*
*** Unicorn Dig. **DKPCD 9048**; *DKPC 9048*. RPO with (i) Stephen Roberts; (ii) Royal College of Music Chamber Ch., Willcocks.

There could hardly be a better introduction to Sir George Dyson's music than this collection, with two vigorously sung choral works preceded by the overture based upon themes from his best-known work, *The Canterbury Pilgrims*. This orchestral piece is not very succinctly constructed, but its tunes are personable and the scoring vivid. *In honour of the City*, Dyson's setting of William Dunbar, appeared in 1928, nine years before Walton's version of the same text; but Dyson, unlike Walton, uses a modern translation of Dunbar's Chaucerian English and to fine, direct effect. Dyson, who came from the West Riding of Yorkshire, loved the good things of life, and he clearly loved London too, for the third work here shows him at his most spontaneous. *Sweet Thames run softly* has words by Spenser taken from his *Prothalamion*, celebrating a famous marriage of 1596 when the two young daughters of the Earl of Worcester sailed up the Thames as far as the Temple. The score is full of imaginative touches with a pair of virginal flutes to represent the brides-to-be. The piece has a fine climax, sung here with fervour; the music itself (a late work, written when the composer was in his seventies) draws on the wells of both Elgar and Vaughan Williams, but has a freshness and ardour of its own. With Stephen Roberts an excellent baritone soloist in the more ambitious cantata, these performances, full of life and warmth, could hardly be bettered; and the recording is first class. There is a good matching chrome cassette, of Unicorn's usual high standard, even though, because of the resonance, it is not transferred at the highest level.

Benedicte; Benedictus; Evening services in D; Hail, universal Lord; Live forever, glorious Lord; Te Deum; Valour. (i) (Organ) *Prelude; Postlude; Psalm-tune prelude* (*I was glad*)*; Voluntary of praise.* (with HOWELLS: *Dyson's delight*).
*** Unicorn Dig. **DKPCD 9065**; *DKPC 9065*. St Catherine's College, Cambridge, Ch., Owen Rees; (i) Owen Rees (organ).

Sir George Dyson's career was based on his love for and wish to continue the great tradition of English church music. 'If a man would live again the musical history of a thousand years,' he wrote, 'let him sit in the choir of a cathedral and listen.' It was a limited view but a deeply sincere one, and this programme of freshly conceived music demonstrates his own ability to perpetuate his musical inheritance. The writing may not always be strikingly individual, but every so often its invention soars. There are some well-made organ pieces too (plus an admiring contribution from Herbert Howells based on two themes from Dyson's *Canterbury Pilgrims*), but it is the vocal music that is the more memorable. It is all sung with striking freshness by choristers who, young as some of them may be, seem to have its inflexions in their very being. Excellent recording too, in a properly spacious acoustic, though the words come over well. Even so, there is an excellent leaflet, provided with both CD and tape, setting them out and giving much useful information about the composer and his music, a model of its kind.

Elgar, Edward (1857–1934)

Adieu (arr. Geehl). *Beau Brummel: Minuet. Sospiri, Op. 70. The Spanish Lady: Burlesco. The Starlight Express: Waltz. Sursum corda, Op. 11.*
(*) Chan. **CHAN 8432; (M) *CBT 1004*. Bournemouth Sinf., Hurst – VAUGHAN WILLIAMS: *Collection*.**(*)

A collection of delightful Elgar rarities. Most unexpected is the *Sursum corda* for organ, brass, strings and timpani (no woodwind), an occasional piece written for a royal visit to Worcester in 1894, which has real *nobilmente* depth. The *Burlesco*, a fragment from the unfinished Elgar opera, is delightfully done, and each one of these items has its charms. Well coupled with rare Vaughan Williams, warmly performed and atmospherically recorded. The CD transfer demonstrates the excellence of the 1975 master; a little lack of amplitude in the violins above the stave is the only suggestion that this is not a recent recording. The cassette, at medium price, sounds excellent, and costs a great deal less than the CD.

3 Bavarian dances, Op. 27. Caractacus, Op. 35: Woodland interludes. Chanson de matin; Chanson de nuit, Op. 15/1 and 2. Contrasts, Op. 10/3. Dream children, Op. 43. Falstaff, Op. 68: 2 Interludes. Salut d'amour. Sérénade lyrique. (i) *Soliloquy for oboe* (orch. Jacob).
*** Chan. **CHAN 8371**; (M) *CBT 1016*. Bournemouth Sinf., Del Mar, (i) with Goossens.

The real treasure in this superb collection of Elgar miniatures is the *Soliloquy* which Elgar wrote right at the end of his life for Leon Goossens. It was the only movement completed of a projected suite, a wayward improvisatory piece which yet has a character of its own. Here the dedicatee plays it with his long-recognizable tone-colour and feeling for phrase in an orchestration by Gordon Jacob. Most of the other pieces are well known, but they come up with new warmth and commitment in splendid performances under Del Mar. The (originally RCA) recording is of high quality, full and vivid, and it has now been digitally remastered with great success to make a first-class CD. The cassette offers very good sound and considerable economy too.

3 Bavarian dances, Op. 27; Caractacus, Op. 35: Triumphal march. The Light of Life, Op. 29: Meditation. Polonia, Op. 76; Wand of Youth suites Nos 1 & 2, Op. 1a–b.
(M) *** HMV **CDM7 69207-2**; *ED 291129-4*. LPO, Boult.

Sir Adrian's outstanding performances of the *Wand of Youth suites* catch both the innocence and the intimacy of this music, which is very much part of Elgar's personal world. The fragile charm of the delicate scoring is well realized and there is plenty of schoolboy gusto for the rollicking *Wild Bear* (only playfully wild, of course). The orchestral playing is first rate and carries through the conductor's obvious affection to the listener. The 1968 recording is of vintage EMI quality and has adapted splendidly to CD remastering, even if the roisterous scoring for the *Wild Bear* portrait becomes a little noisy because of the resonance. The string tone retains the warmth and bloom of the analogue original. As can be seen, this issue (available also on a quite pleasing tape) duplicates two interesting items included on the bargain CfP collection below, recorded in 1975. Altogether this makes a highly recommendable reissue in EMI's mid-priced Studio series. The total playing time is 74′.

Caractacus, Op. 35: Triumphal march. Carillon, Op. 75. Dream Children, Op. 43/1 and 2. Elegy for strings, Op. 58. Grania and Diarmid, Op. 42: Funeral march. The Light of Life, Op. 29: Meditation. Polonia, Op. 76. Funeral march (Chopin, orch. Elgar).
(B) ** CfP *TC-CFP 4527*. LPO, Boult.

The main interest here is provided by two pieces Elgar wrote at the beginning of the First World War as a gesture to help refugees from Belgium and Poland. The *Carillon*, written for 'gallant little Belgium', is rather effective and one can imagine its success at the time; the *Polonia* has character too, and both show the composer's flair for flag-waving orchestral sounds. The rest of the programme, although it displays a good sprinkling of Elgarian fingerprints, is uneven in quality and does not seem to fire Sir Adrian to his more persuasive advocacy. Even the *Dream Children* seem on the cool side, although some will undoubtedly like the restraint which Boult provides. The orchestration of Chopin's *Funeral march* is moderately effective. The sound is full-bodied, but the iron-oxide tape is not ideal for the transients in the *Caractacus march*, and *Polonia* sounds too thick in texture; there is no lack of bloom elsewhere.

Caractacus: Interlude. Carissima; Chanson de matin; Chanson de nuit, Op. 15/1–2; Contrasts (The Gavotte, AD 1700–AD 1900), Op. 10/3; Dream children, Op. 43/1–2; Falstaff: 2 Interludes. May song; Mazurka, Op. 10/1; Mina; Rosemary (That's for remembrance); Salut d'amour, Op. 12; Serenade lyrique; Serenade mauresque, Op. 10/2.
*** HMV Dig. *EL 270493-4*. N. Sinfonia, Hickox.

Although much of this programme is slight, it has great charm, and Richard Hickox's performances are both affectionate and sensitive, helped by fine recording. The *Falstaff* interlude and the *Caractacus* excerpt slot nicely in among the regular pieces. The cassette is well transferred; although the sound is slightly diffuse, its atmosphere suits the music. But the silent background of a CD would be ideal for these often gently scored pieces.

Caractacus: Triumphal march. Coronation march, Op. 65; Crown of India suite, Op. 66; Grania and Diarmid, Op. 42: Funeral march. Imperial march, Op. 32; The Light of Life, Op. 29: Meditation. Nursery suite; Severn suite, Op. 87.
(B) **(*) HMV *TCC2-POR 154590-9*. Royal Liverpool PO, Groves.

It is good to have these performances by Sir Charles Groves – recorded while he was principal conductor of the Royal Liverpool Philharmonic Orchestra – restored to the catalogue. This is all music that he understands warmly, and the results give much pleasure. One does not have to be an imperialist to enjoy any of the occasional pieces, and it is interesting to find the patriotic music coming up fresher than the little interlude from *The Light of Life*, beautiful as that is. The *Triumphal march* from *Caractacus* makes one want to try the complete recording of this major cantata; it is played with fine swagger. Both the *Nursery suite* (written for the Princesses Elizabeth and Margaret Rose) and the orchestral version of the *Severn suite* (written for a brass band contest) come from Elgar's very last period when his inspiration came in flashes rather than as a sustained searchlight. The completely neglected *Funeral march* was written in 1901 for a play by W. B. Yeats and George Moore; it is a splendid piece. The collection is gathered together on one of EMI's 'Portrait of the Artist' double-length tapes. The sound is of generally good quality, lacking the last degree of brilliance on top, but otherwise well balanced. The documentation, however, is poor, offering no information about the music except titles.

(i) *Carillon; Le Drapeau belge;* (ii) *Fringes of the Fleet. Polonia* (symphonic prelude), *Op. 76;* (i; iii) *Une voix dans le désert, Op. 77.*
* Pearl **SHCD 9602** [id.]. (i) Richard Pasco; (ii) Kenyon, Godward, Theobald, Watson; (iii) Teresa Cahill; Rutland Sinfonia, Barry Collett.

The orchestral versions of *Carillon* and the symphonic prelude, *Polonia*, have been successfully recorded by Boult and the LPO. The present disc is notable mainly for its documentary value, as it includes the melodramatic narrations, not only for the (1914) *Carillon* but also *Le Drapeau belge*, written in 1916. This found less favour with the public as by then war fever had abated, after the horrors of the Somme and Verdun. *Un voix dans le désert* is the most telling of these three hybrid compositions, as its centrepiece is a song, looking forward hopefully to spring, framed by the sombre spoken verse reflecting wartime reality. The words of all three were written by a Belgian, Emile Cammaerts, and translated into English by his wife. It is vivid doggerel, spoken here in a highly theatrical way by Richard Pasco. Teresa Cahill is sympathetic in the song, but none of these works, heard in their original formats, is likely to enhance the composer's reputation. *Fringes of the Fleet* is a setting of four Kipling poems and Elgar described them as being 'in broad saltwater style'. Although written within a wartime atmosphere, they have a potential, not fully realized here, as not one of the four baritones who participate is a strongly individual personality, and the effect is rather wan. The Rutland Sinfonia is a semi-professional group and although they are very committed and Barry Collett is a sympathetic Elgarian, the playing is barely adequate for a gramophone record, acceptable perhaps in the accompaniments, but much less satisfactory in the fairly long *Polonia* (14′ 29″) in which the composer quotes not only from the Polish National Hymn, but also from the *Fantaisie Polonaise* of Paderewski – to whom the piece is dedicated – and Chopin's *G minor Nocturne*, Op. 37/1. The sound is good, but this collection has a very limited appeal.

Chanson de matin, Op. 15/2; Chanson de nuit, Op. 15/1; Elegy, Op. 58; Introduction and allegro, Op. 47; Serenade in E min., Op. 20; The Spanish Lady (suite).
(*) Nimbus **NIM 5008 [id.]. E. String O, William Boughton.

Boughton conducts warm, sympathetic performances of an attractive selection of shorter Elgar works – including the suite drawn from his unfinished opera, *The Spanish Lady*. The reverberant recording is less crisply detailed than is ideal – like the actual playing – but, with the clarification of CD, presents a pleasingly natural ensemble.

Chanson de matin; Chanson de nuit (arr. Fraser)*; Elegy for strings, Op. 58; Introduction and allegro for strings, Op. 47; Mazurka, Op. 10/1; Salut d'amour* (arr. Fraser)*; Serenade for strings in E min., Op. 20.*
(*) Ara. Dig. **Z 6563; *ABQC 6563* [id.]. ECO, Sir Yehudi Menuhin.

Sir Yehudi Menuhin on the Arabesque disc couples Elgar's three substantial string pieces, the *Introduction and allegro*, the *Serenade* and the *Elegy*, with string arrangements of favourite trifles as well as the *Mazurka*. Well played, it makes an attractive collection, with the solo quartet in the *Introduction and allegro* particularly sensitive and with warm, atmospheric recording. Even if neither this piece nor the *Serenade* are quite as strongly characterized as the Barbirolli versions, the recording is obviously more modern. There is an excellent tape.

Cockaigne overture; Crown of India suite, Op. 66; Pomp and circumstance marches Nos 1–5, Op. 39.
*** Chan. **CHAN 8429**; (M) *CBT 1012.* SNO, Gibson.

Overtures: Cockaigne; Froissart; In the South. Overture in D min. (arr. from Handel: *Chandos anthem No. 2*).
*** Chan. Dig. **CHAN 8309**; *ABTD 1077* [id.]. SNO, Gibson.

(i) *Cockaigne overture;* (ii) *Introduction and allegro for strings, Op. 47;* (i) *Variations on an original theme* (*Enigma*), *Op. 47.*
(M) *** HMV *TC-ESD 7169.* (i) Philh. O, (ii) London Sinfonia and Allegri Qt; Barbirolli.

(i) *Cockaigne overture, Op. 40; Pomp and circumstance marches Nos 1–5;* (ii) *Variations on an original theme* (*Enigma*), *Op. 36.*
(M) **(*) Decca **417 719-2**; *417 456-4* (without *Cockaigne*). (i) LPO; (ii) Chicago SO; Solti.

Elgar's picture of London in *Cockaigne* is of course an Edwardian one, but little of the scenery has changed; the military bands and the Salvation Army are still there, and if the lovers in the park today are more uninhibited, they should not be disappointed with Barbirolli's warmth in their music. Indeed Barbirolli, himself a Londoner, paints a memorably vivid picture. HMV's splendid recording does Elgar's richly painted canvas real justice, and the whole piece moves forward with a sweep worthy of the then greatest city in the world. Barbirolli's reading of the *Enigma variations* is no less satisfying. It has both richness and warmth, and is superbly played and recorded and, especially in the variations where the strings are given their head, the music could have no more eloquent advocate. To make this mid-priced Greensleeve cassette irresistible, EMI have made room for Barbirolli's inspired performance of the *Introduction and allegro for strings*, recorded with the London Sinfonia and Allegri Quartet. Here Barbirolli's passionate lyricism, plus exceptionally fine string playing, provides a quite outstanding version of Elgar's masterly string work. The EMI stereo is of vintage quality. As we go to press, Barbirolli's *Enigma* is announced on mid-priced CD, coupled with *Falstaff* (HMV **CDM7 69185-2**).

On the earlier (1978) Chandos SNO collection Sir Alexander Gibson directs vigorously sympathetic performances of an attractive programme, well recorded. *Cockaigne* is attractively spirited, and although the Scottish orchestra misses something of the music's opulence, this is undoubtedly very enjoyable. The *Pomp and circumstance marches* are taken at a spanking pace, but with no lack of swagger, and there is a strong feeling of pageantry too. The music has great forward thrust, and the recording acoustic is suitably reverberant. In the *Crown of India suite* Gibson is consistently imaginative in attention to detail, and the playing of the Scottish orchestra here is warmly sensitive. In all this music the CD transfer of the 1978 analogue recording is first rate in every way. There is also a very good cassette in the mid-price range.

Gibson's later Chandos collection is given a brilliantly truthful digital recording. The Scottish orchestra makes a vividly cohesive sound, although again the strings are just a little lacking in richness of timbre. The picture of London is full of bustle and pageantry, with bold brass and flashing percussion, and the closing pages have striking impact. *In the South* has strong impetus, and Gibson's directness serves *Froissart* and the Handel arrangement equally well. The CD is very impressive, the treble smooth and the overall effect extremely vivid, with greater tangibility and body to the sound than the cassette, although this is of high quality.

Solti's *Cockaigne* is sharply dramatic and exciting; his view of the *Marches* is both vigorous and refined, with sharp pointing in the outer sections, spaciousness in the great melodies. The result is both striking and satisfying. In the *Marches* the CD remastering brings vivid sound with full-bodied strings; *Cockaigne* is somewhat brighter, especially in the brass, and there is a touch of glare. In the *Enigma variations* there are ample cues to give access to each portrait. Although the opening is affectionately Elgarian, with Solti the work becomes essentially a dazzling showpiece. Though *Dorabella* is suitably dainty, otherwise the charm of the work is given short measure, but the structure emerges the more sharply. The fast variations are taken at breakneck speed, with the Chicago orchestra challenged to supreme virtuosity. *Nimrod* opens elegiacally but, with a basic tempo faster than usual, Solti allows himself to get faster and faster still, although there is a broadening at the end. This won't be to all tastes, but the brilliant recording suits the drama of the playing. The cassette omits *Cockaigne*; it is well transferred.

(i) *Cello concerto, Op. 85;* (ii) *Violin concerto, Op. 61; Chanson de matin; Chanson de nuit; Cockaigne overture; Introduction and allegro for strings; Pomp and circumstance march No. 1; Serenade for strings; Symphonies Nos 1–2; Variations on an original theme* (*Enigma*).
(M) ** HMV *EX 290617-5* (4). LPO, New Philh. O, LSO; Sir Adrian Boult; (i) Tortelier; (ii) Menuhin.

This box assembles the recordings Boult made between 1966 and 1977. The merits of these are already well known: the two symphonies, the *Enigma variations* and the *Introduction and allegro* are already available on compact disc, plus Tortelier's fine account of the *Cello concerto*. This makes an economical way of collecting these authoritative performances, but there are certain snags. The digital remastering has not been entirely beneficial. Detail is certainly clearer and the treble is brighter, but the violin timbre is thinner and, while the bass is full and firm, some of the middle range has been lost too. However, the main criticism concerns the tape layout. Among the large-scale works only the *Enigma* and the *Cello concerto* can be heard uninterrupted. Both symphonies and the *Violin concerto* involve turnover breaks which are quite unnecessary in this format. The back-up booklet is a photocopy and offers minuscule print.

Cello concerto in E min., Op. 85.
❀ *** HMV **CDC7 47329-2** [id.]; *TC-ASD 655*. Du Pré, LSO, Barbirolli – *Sea Pictures.**** ❀
*** CBS Dig. **MK 39541**; *IMT 39541* [id.]. Yo-Yo Ma, LSO, Previn – WALTON: *Cello concerto.****
(*) Ph. Dig. **412 880-2 [id.]. Heinrich Schiff, Dresden State O, Marriner – DVOŘÁK: *Cello concerto.**(*)*
/(*) Chan. Dig. **CHAN 8384**; *ABTD 1007* [id.]. Kirshbaum, SNO, Gibson – WALTON: *Cello concerto.*(*)*

(i) *Cello concerto; Elegy for strings, Op. 58; In the South, Op. 50.*
(B) *** CfP **CD-CFP 9003**; *TC-CFP 40342*. (i) Robert Cohen, LPO, Del Mar.

(i) *Cello concerto; Introduction and allegro for strings, Op. 47; In the South.*
(M) *** HMV **CDM7 69200-2**. (i) Tortelier; LPO, Boult.

(i) *Cello concerto; Variations on an original theme* (*Enigma*), *Op. 36.*
*** Ph. Dig. **416 354-2**; *416 354-4* [id.]. (i) Julian Lloyd Webber; RPO, Menuhin.

(i) *Cello concerto;* (ii) *Cockaigne overture; Variations on an original theme* (*Enigma*), *Op. 36.*
*** CBS **MK 76529**. (i) Du Pré, Phd. O; (ii) LPO; Barenboim.

It was in the Elgar *Cello concerto* that Jacqueline du Pré first won world recognition, and the HMV recording gives a wonderful idea of how so young a girl captured such attention and even persuaded the Americans to listen enraptured to Elgar. Du Pré was essentially a spontaneous artist, no two performances by her are exactly alike; wisely, Barbirolli at the recording sessions encouraged her above all to express emotion through the notes. The style is freely rhapsodic. The tempi, long-breathed in the first and third movements, are allowed still more elbow-room when du Pré's expressiveness requires it; in the slow movement, brief and concentrated, her inner intensity conveys a depth of espressivo rarely achieved by any cellist on record.

Brilliant virtuoso playing too in scherzo and finale. CD brings a subtle extra definition to heighten the excellent qualities of the 1965 recording, with the solo instrument firmly placed. In such a meditative work the absence of background is a special blessing. There is a good tape.

The Philips coupling of the *Cello concerto* and the *Enigma variations*, the two most popular of Elgar's big orchestral works, featuring two artists inseparably associated with Elgar's music, made the disc an immediate bestseller, and rightly so. These are both warmly expressive and unusually faithful readings, the more satisfying for fidelity to the score and the absence of exaggeration. The speeds – as in the flowing *Moderato* in the first movement of the *Concerto* – are never extreme, always well judged, and Lloyd Webber in his playing has never sounded warmer or more relaxed on record, well focused in the stereo spectrum. If the performance of the *Variations* is not always quite as polished as some, it is both well detailed and powerful in its natural expression, helped by warm and full recording. There is a very good tape, perhaps not quite as sharply defined as the CD.

Jacqueline du Pré's second recording of the Elgar *Cello concerto* was taken from live performances in Philadelphia in November 1970, and whatever the slight blemishes (questionable balances, some coughing) this is a superb picture of an artist in full flight. Here on CBS you have the romantic view of Elgar at its most compelling, and though some Elgarians will fairly enough prefer more restraint in this autumnal work, the mastery of du Pré lies not just in her total commitment from phrase to phrase but in the feeling for the whole. More than in any other account on record, even her own with Barbirolli, this one sets sights on the moment in the Epilogue where the slow-movement theme returns, the work's innermost sanctuary of repose. In the finale, at a cracking basic tempo, the ensemble is not flawless but, all through, the Philadelphia Orchestra plays with commanding virtuosity, and Daniel Barenboim is the most understanding of accompanists. Barenboim's view of *Enigma* is full of fantasy. Its most distinctive point is its concern for the miniature element. Without belittling the delicate variations, Barenboim both makes them sparkle and gives them emotional point, while the big variations have full weight, and the finale brings extra fierceness at a fast tempo. *Cockaigne* is comparably lively and colourful. The sound of the CBS transfer lacks something in body and amplitude.

In its rapt concentration Yo-Yo Ma's recording with Previn brings a version to set alongside the classic account of the young Jacqueline du Pré with Barbirolli. The dark, tear-laden quality of the work comes out from her performance as from no one else, yet Ma's concentration is just as keen, plus his sense of controlled spontaneity. The first movement is lighter, a shade more urgent, and in the scherzo he finds more fun, just as he finds extra sparkle in the main theme of the finale. The key movement with Ma, as it is with du Pré, is the *Adagio*, echoed later in the raptness of the slow epilogue, and there his range of dynamic is just as daringly wide with a thread of pianissimo at the innermost moment, poised in its intensity. Warm, fully detailed recording, finely balanced, with understanding conducting from Previn. It sounds even more refined on CD, and tape collectors will be glad to know that the chrome cassette is also first class.

Tortelier gives a noble and restrained performance, that is very moving and second to none in natural eloquence, if not wearing its heart on its sleeve. It is part of a particularly generous collection (74′ 14″) of outstanding Boult/Elgar performances which show this conductor in his prime. His committed accounts of the *Introduction and allegro* and *In the South*, which in its incisiveness is both dramatic and noble, are particularly satisfying, and no one played *Froissart* with greater flair and spontaneity. The vintage recordings derive from the early 1970s and have been remastered to great effect: definition is better yet the bloom and atmosphere remain and there is plenty of body to the tuttis. A bargain.

The Classics for Pleasure CD is also a good bargain. Robert Cohen's performance is firm and intense, with steady tempi, the colouring more positive, less autumnal than usual, relating the work more closely to the *Second Symphony*. Yet there is no lack of inner feeling. The ethereal half-tones at the close of the first movement are matched by the gently elegiac poignancy of the

Adagio. Del Mar's accompaniment is wholly sympathetic, underlining the soloist's approach. He also directs an exciting account of *In the South* (recorded in a single take), not quite as exhilarating as Silvestri's famous performance (currently out of the catalogue) but certainly spontaneous in effect. The *Elegy* makes an eloquent bonus. The recording is wide-ranging and well balanced, but shows Cohen's tone as bright and well focused rather than especially resonant in the bass. The CD transfer retains all the bloom of the original analogue master but with some sharpening of detail. There is a good tape, but the CD is worth its cost.

Schiff gives a warm, thoughtful account, at his most successful in the lovely slow movement and the epilogue, both played with soft, sweet tone. Other readings may convey more of the structural cohesion, but this lyrical view has its place. The sound is superb, to match the orchestra's richness. The elegiac atmosphere at the opening of the *Concerto* is especially persuasive. The coupling of the Dvořák *Concerto* is generous, if less appropriate than the couplings of Du Pré and Julian Lloyd Webber, and is also attractive, another refined performance which, like the Elgar, is easy to live with.

Kirshbaum, a fine cellist, is disappointing here. At the very start the great double-stopped chords are anything but commanding, not helped by recessed recording, and the whole performance sounds tentative rather than expressing spontaneity. Originally issued as an analogue disc, this was displaced by a digital version, which is crisper in outline but cannot cure the balance. The CD improves detail further, but the effect is marginal: this is not a commanding version.

Violin concerto in B min., Op. 61.
(🏵) *** EMI Dig. **CDC7 47210-2** [id.]; (M) *EMX 41 2058-4*. Nigel Kennedy, LPO, Handley.
** DG Dig. **413 312-2** [id.]. Itzhak Perlman, Chicago SO, Barenboim.

Kennedy's is a commanding reading, arguably even finer than the long line of versions with star international soloists from outside Britain. With Vernon Handley as guide, it is at once the most centrally Elgarian of all those on record in its warm expressiveness; equally, in its steady pacing it brings out more than is usual the clear parallels with the Beethoven and Brahms concertos. That is particularly striking in the first movement and, both there and in his urgent account of the allegro in the finale, Kennedy has learnt more than any recorded rival from the example of the *Concerto*'s first great interpreter, Albert Sammons. Yet the example of Yehudi Menuhin is also clear, not least in the sweetness and repose of the slow movement and in the deep meditation of the accompanied cadenza which comes as epilogue. The recording, with the soloist balanced more naturally than is usual, not spotlit, is outstandingly faithful and atmospheric. This made a worthy outright winner of the *Gramophone* Record Award, 1985. The mid-priced cassette is disappointing: the reverberation has produced a restriction of the upper range. The CD is well worth the extra cost.

Perlman's ease in tackling one of the most challenging violin concertos ever written brings an enjoyable performance, though he misses some of the darker, more intense elements in Elgar's inspiration. The solo instrument is forwardly balanced and the recording is bright and vivid rather than rich, lacking some of the amplitude one expects in the Elgar orchestral sound. The CD emphasizes the presence of the soloist but confirms the lack of expansiveness in the orchestra.

Elegy for strings, Op. 58; Introduction and allegro for strings, Op. 47; Serenade for strings in E min., Op. 58.
* DG Dig. **419 191-2**; *419 191-4* [id.]. Orpheus CO – VAUGHAN WILLIAMS: *Tallis fantasia* etc.*

Elegy for strings, Op. 58; Serenade for strings, Op. 20; Sospiri, Op. 70.
(*) HMV Dig. *EL 270146-4*. City of L. Sinfonia, Hickox – PARRY: *English suite* etc.(*)

Hickox draws beautifully refined string-playing from his City of London Sinfonia, notably in the three elegiac movements, the slow movement of the *Serenade* as well as the two separate pieces. An excellent coupling for the rare Parry items on the reverse, excellently recorded. On the XDR tape, textures are ample, but the upper range is very smooth and the overall effect is slightly bland.

The recordings by the Orpheus Chamber Orchestra are disappointing. Though their keen articulation tells in the *allegro* of Op. 47, the playing overall suggests a lack of experience in this repertoire; the sharply focused, vividly realistic recording of a string group that is plainly too few in number to be fully effective in this music also emphasizes the lack of ripeness in the readings.

Falstaff, Op. 68; Variations on an original theme (*Enigma*), *Op. 36.*
(*) Chan. **CHAN 8431; (M) *CBT 1029* [id.]. SNO, Gibson.
(*) HMV Dig. **CDC7 47416-2; *EL 270374-4.* LPO, Mackerras.

Sir Alexander Gibson's coupling of *Falstaff* and the *Enigma variations* is one of the very finest of the recordings he made for Brian Couzens (who was subsequently to found Chandos) in the late 1970s. *Falstaff* is particularly spontaneous; Gibson generates a strong forward momentum from the very opening bars, yet detail is consistently imaginative and the closing section is most touchingly played. Both here and in the *Enigma variations* the Scottish orchestra are in excellent form and play with character and commitment. Like the symphonic study, *Enigma* moves forward from variation to variation in a refreshingly direct manner, each portrait full of character, and without self-consciousness in its presentation; *Nimrod* has genuine eloquence, and the finale goes splendidly. The 1978 recording, made in Glasgow City Hall, has a natural perspective, and has been most successfully remastered for CD, though the (mid-priced) tape also sounds extremely well. The sound has some lack of opulence but is truthful in all other respects. However, although the separate variations are cued, there is no internal access to *Falstaff*, which is a considerable drawback.

With recorded sound far more reverberant than is common in EMI's recordings of Elgar, Mackerras's powerful readings of the composer's own favourite among his orchestral works, together with the most popular, are given a comfortable glow, while losing some inner clarity. The reading of *Falstaff* is superb, among the most electrically compelling put on disc, but *Enigma* is marred by mannered and self-conscious phrasing in the opening statement of the theme and first variation, as well as in *Nimrod.* However, with detail slightly sharper, these recordings sound extremely well in their CD format, and *Falstaff* is very generously indexed.

(i) *Introduction and allegro for strings, Op. 47; Serenade for strings, Op. 20;* (ii) *Elegy, Op. 58; Sospiri, Op. 70.*
*** HMV **CDC7 47537-2.** (i) Sinfonia of L. with Allegri Qt; (ii) New Philh. O, Barbirolli – VAUGHAN WILLIAMS: *Tallis fantasia* etc.***

Introduction and allegro for strings, Op. 47; Serenade for strings, Op. 20; Variations on an original theme (*Enigma*), *Op. 36.*
(M) **(*) EMI Dig. **CD-EMX 9503**; *EMX 2011-4* [Ang. *4AE 34432*]. LPO, Vernon Handley.

Barbirolli's inspirational coupling of the string music of Elgar and Vaughan Williams was made in 1963 and, both musically and technically, it was in every way outstanding. Barbirolli brings an Italianate ardour and warmth to this music without in any way robbing it of its Englishness; and the response of the string players, full-throated or subtle as the music demands, was matched by superb analogue recording, notable for its combination of clarity and ambient richness. For CD, the *Elegy*, like the *Serenade* showing Barbirolli in more gentle, beguiling mood, and the passionate

Sospiri, have been added for good measure. The CD transfer, however, while retaining the fullness and amplitude, seems more restricted on top and has lost some of the original bite.

Vernon Handley's generously full Eminence collection is given brilliantly wide-ranging digital sound (although the cassette has a more restricted treble response). In the string works, particularly the *Introduction and allegro*, the CD makes the emphasis of the upper range at the expense of the middle the more striking; one needs more amplitude here. The readings are in the Boult tradition and very well played. But Handley's strong personal identification with the music brings a consciously moulded style that tends at times to rob the *Enigma variations* of its forward impulse. The Elgarian ebb and flow of tension and dynamics are continually underlined in a highly expressive manner and, although he uncovers much imaginative detail, there is a consequent loss of spontaneity. The performances of the string works are more direct, although the *Larghetto* of the *Serenade* is also somewhat indulgent. Comparison with Barbirolli is not in Handley's favour, although his performances are full of insights.

Nursery suite; Wand of Youth suites Nos 1 and 2, Op. 1a and 1b.
*** Chan. Dig. **CHAN 8318**; *ABTD 1079* [id.]. Ulster O, Bryden Thomson.

An admirable coupling. The Ulster Orchestra plays most beautifully and the ambience of the recordings is well suited to the music's moments of gentle nostalgia. Although Boult's performances of the more robust items from the *Wand of Youth* brought marginally more exuberance, the playing in Ulster is attractively spirited; in the gentle pieces (the *Sun dance*, *Fairy pipers* and *Slumber dance*) which show the composer at his most magically evocative, the music making engagingly combines refinement and warmth. The *Nursery suite* is strikingly well characterized and with first class digital sound this is highly recommendable. Much of this music is delicately scored, and on CD it gains a great deal from the background silence and the refined detail at pianissimo level, while the dynamic range expands impressively when it needs to. There is just a hint of thinness in the upper string timbre, but this is more noticeable on the otherwise excellent chrome tape.

Serenade for strings in E min., Op. 20.
** ASV Dig. **CDDCA 518**; *ZCDCA 518* [id.]. ASMF, Marriner – TIPPETT: *Fantasia concertante***; VAUGHAN WILLIAMS: *Lark ascending* etc.**(*)

Sir Neville Marriner's recording of the *Serenade*, for ASV, offers well-defined and cleanly focused sound; perhaps it is just a little too 'present' and forward, though not unreasonably so. The performance adds nothing to his earlier recording on Argo, made in the late 1960s, which generated greater atmosphere; but that has still to reappear on CD, and the newer version can certainly be recommended if the couplings are suitable.

(i) *Pomp and circumstance marches Nos 1–5, Op. 39;* (ii) *Variations on an original theme* (*Enigma*), *Op. 36.*
*** Ph. Dig. **416 813-2**; *416 813-4* [id.]. RPO, André Previn.
*** HMV **CDC7 47206-2**. (i) LPO; (ii) LSO; Sir Adrian Boult.

When André Previn first recorded the *Enigma variations* with the LSO for EMI, there was a slight hint of inhibition, of being on best behaviour in a reading that was very straight. In his RPO version, Previn remains just as straight, but his extra ease gives the result more warmth and commitment, a performance rather in the Boult mould, noble and unexaggerated in *Nimrod*, very delicate in the *Romanza* and *Dorabella*, and particularly impressive in the surging accelerando of the final variation. The five *Pomp and circumstance marches* make an attractive coupling, not quite as flamboyant as some versions but beautifully sprung. The recording is warm and slightly recessed. The sound on tape is rich and well balanced too, but the transients are less telling than on CD.

Boult's *Enigma* comes from the beginning of the 1970s and, although the recording does not sound as ample as Previn's, it has been freshly transferred to CD. The reading shows this conductor's long experience of the work, with each variation growing naturally and seamlessly out of the music that has gone before. *Nimrod* in particular glows, superbly sustained. Perhaps the finale lacks the fire that Barbirolli gives to it, but it has undoubted strength and forms a satisfying culmination. Boult's approach to the *Pomp and circumstance marches* is brisk and direct, with an almost no-nonsense manner in places. There is not a hint of vulgarity and the freshness is most attractive, though it is a pity he omits the repeats in the Dvořák-like No. 2.

Monteux's famous *Enigma* from the beginning of the 1960s, coupled with a vigorous set of marches from Sir Arthur Bliss, still sounds fresh on a Decca Weekend tape, but the recording is dated and lacks ideal fullness (*417 878-4*).

Romance for cello and orchestra, Op. 62.
*** HMV Dig. **CDC7 47622-2**; *EL 270430-4*. Julian Lloyd Webber, LSO, Mackerras – HERBERT; SULLIVAN: *Concerto*.***

The Elgar *Romance*, written in full maturity between the two symphonies, is well enough known in its original form with bassoon solo; but Julian Lloyd Webber rescued what had long been forgotten, the composer's own version with cello, a delightful makeweight for the rare concertos by Sullivan and Victor Herbert, well played and recorded on CD. The resonance robs the cassette of inner clarity, and it is bass-heavy.

Serenade for strings in E min., Op. 20 (see also above).
(M) *** Pickwick Dig. **PCD 861**. Serenata of London – GRIEG: *Holberg suite*; MOZART: *Eine kleine Nachtmusik* etc.***

A particularly appealing account of Elgar's *Serenade*, with unforced tempi in the outer movements admirably catching its mood and atmosphere so that the elegiac *Larghetto*, beautifully and sensitively phrased, finds a natural place in the overall scheme. The Serenata of London is led rather than conducted by Barry Wilde; but this is a performance of undoubted personality, and it is recorded with remarkable realism and naturalness. With excellent couplings, this is an outstanding bargain.

Symphony No. 1 in A flat, Op. 55.
(B) *** CfP **CD-CFP 9018**; *TC-CFP 4541*. LPO, Vernon Handley.
*** Ph. Dig. **416 612-2**; *416 612-4* [id.]. RPO, André Previn.
** Chan. Dig. **CHAN 8541**; *ABTD* 1161 [id.]. LPO, Bryden Thomson.
(M) ** EMI *EMX 41 2084-4*. Philh. O, Barbirolli.

Symphony No. 1 in A flat, Op. 55; Chanson de matin; Chanson de nuit, Op. 15/1–2; Serenade for strings, Op. 20.
*** HMV **CDC7 47204-2** [id.]. LPO, Boult.

Vernon Handley directs a beautifully paced reading which can be counted in every way out-standing, even making no allowance for price. The LPO has performed this symphony many times before but never with more poise and refinement than here. It is in the slow movement above all that Handley scores, spacious and movingly expressive. With very good sound, well transferred to CD, this is a clear first choice.

Previn's version, first of a projected Elgar series, finds the conductor as idiomatic and understanding as he is in Walton and Vaughan Williams. His view of the first movement is spacious, with moulding of phrase and lifting of rhythm beautifully judged, to bring natural flexibility within a strongly controlled structure, steadier than usual in basic tempo. Previn's espressivo style tends towards accelerando rather than tenuto, towards fractional anticipation rather than hesitation, which makes for alert allegros and a slow movement that is warm but not self-indulgent. The syncopations of the scherzo/march theme have an almost jazzy swagger, and the reading is crowned by a flowing account of the finale. There Previn confirms his ability to point Elgarian climaxes with the necessary heart-tug, above all in the lovely passage where the main theme is augmented in minims on high violins, here achingly beautiful, neither too reticent nor too heavy-handed. The Philips sound is more refined than the typical Elgar sound from EMI, but there is no lack of richness or bite. Particularly on CD, it is outstandingly full and open, but the chrome cassette too is splendidly managed and is most satisfying in its excellent body, range and definition.

Boult clearly presents the *First Symphony* as a counterpart to the *Second*, with hints of reflective nostalgia amid the triumph. Until this final version, made when Sir Adrian was eighty-seven, his recordings of the *First* had been among his less riveting Elgar interpretations. But the HMV disc contains a radiantly beautiful performance, with no extreme tempi, richly spaced in the first movement, invigorating in the syncopated march rhythms of the scherzo, and similarly bouncing in the Brahmsian rhythms of the finale. Most clearly distinctive is the lovely slow movement, presented as a seamless flow of melody, faster, less 'inner' than with Previn, and above all glowing with untroubled sweetness. The CD remastering, as so often, is not all gain: the violin timbre is thinner and, although the brass is gloriously full, the sharpening of the image of the resonant 1977 recording has brought fortissimos that are less than clean. The choice of the lightweight *Chansons* as fillers is curious, but the 1973 *Serenade* is a more appropriate coupling, with Boult's simplicity bringing delicacy and tenderness, compared with Barbirolli's riper and more overtly romantic view. The sound is vivid, although it is thinner in the *Chansons* which are earlier (1968).

Bryden Thomson's view of the Elgar symphonies could hardly be more spacious, with speeds far slower than usual. In the *First* the outer movements are the ones that suffer, with the first movement allegro dragging seriously for all the beauty of the playing, and the finale leading to a ponderous account of the recapitulation and epilogue. The middle two movements are beautifully done, and though the reverberant recording obscures detail in big tuttis, the sound is warm and glowing. There is an excellent tape.

Barbirolli's 1963 recording still sounds well, not very dated, as the original recording had plenty of amplitude. It is a characteristically subjective reading, obviously deeply felt, but Barbirolli's tempi are controversial; apart from the very slow speed for the slow movement, there is a hint of heaviness in the first movement too, where after the march introduction the music should surge along. On the otherwise good cassette, the upper range is slightly restricted.

Symphony No. 2 in E flat, Op. 47.
(B) *** CfP **CD-CFP 9023**; *TC-CFP 4544*. LPO, Vernon Handley.
(*) HMV Dig. **CDC7 47299-2 [id.]; *EL 270147-4*. Philh. O, Haitink.
(M) ** EMI *EMX 41 2093-4*. Hallé O, Barbirolli.
*(*) Chan. Dig. **CHAN 8452**; *ABTD 1162* [id.]. LPO, Bryden Thomson.

Symphony No. 2 in E flat, Op. 47; Cockaigne overture, Op. 40.
*** HMV **CDC7 47205-2** [id.]. LPO, Boult.

Handley's is the most satisfying modern version of a work which has latterly been much recorded. It is broadly in the Boult mould, never forcing the pace (as Elgar himself did and, following him, Solti) but equally adopting tempi such as Sir Adrian preferred at the height of his career, rather more urgent, less elegiac. What Handley conveys superbly is the sense of Elgarian ebb and flow, building climaxes like a master and drawing excellent, spontaneous-sounding playing from the orchestra which more than any other has specialized in performing this symphony. The sound is warmly atmospheric and vividly conveys the added organ part in the bass just at the climax of the finale (eight bars after fig. 165 in the score) which Elgar himself suggested 'if available': a tummy-wobbling effect. This would be a first choice at full price, but as a bargain CD there are few records to match it. There is a very good cassette too.

For his fifth recording of the *Second Symphony* Sir Adrian Boult, incomparable Elgarian, drew from the LPO the most richly satisfying performance of all. Over the years Sir Adrian's view of the glorious nobility of the first movement had mellowed a degree. The tempo is a shade slower than before (and much slower than the composer's own in the great leaping 12/8 theme), but the pointing of climaxes is unrivalled. With Boult more than anyone else the architecture is clearly and strongly established, with tempo changes less exaggerated than usual. The peak comes in the great *Funeral march*, where the concentration of the performance is irresistible. The LPO strings play gloriously, with the great swooping violin phrases at the climaxes inspiring a frisson as in a live performance. The scherzo has lightness and delicacy, giving more room to breathe. In the finale, firm and strong, Boult cleverly conceals the repetitiveness of the main theme, and gives a radiant account of the lovely epilogue. With brilliant recording, this is a version to convert new listeners to a love of Elgar. The CD remastering has taken away some of the original opulence, but added to the vividness, notably in the central section of the scherzo where the drama is heightened. The disc opens with *Cockaigne*, an attractively direct performance, incisive and spirited, if not as ripe as Barbirolli's version. The remastering is particularly effective here: there is weight as well as a brighter upper range, although the violins sound thinner than on the original analogue LP.

Bernard Haitink gives Elgar's *Second Symphony* its CD début, and many Elgarians will want to make its acquaintance, even though the reading is controversial and the CD sound is just a little disappointing. There is no doubt that he produces some altogether wonderful playing from the Philharmonic Orchestra and also offers valuable and fresh insights. There are many details to relish and beauties to discover – but there are also many wayward touches that fail to convince entirely on repeated hearing. Basically it is a straight, measured view, far from idiomatically Elgarian but always illuminating and often refreshing. It is a reading which clearly relates Elgar to Richard Strauss on the one hand but, more unexpectedly and more significantly, to Bruckner on the other. The way that Haitink keeps his eye on the culminating moment of climax with slow, steady speeds brings a very Brucknerian feeling to much of this music, and the control of transition passages has Brucknerian raptness. Elgarians will miss some of the usual spring in the 12/8 compound time of the first movement; the digital recording, more analytical and less full-bodied than one expects of Elgar sound from this source, adds to the unexpectedness of the performance. But for many, if not for dedicated Elgarians, it will be a revelation in its strength and lack of self-indulgence. As so often, the CD emphasizes the character of the recording, and the ear notices the more readily that the sound of the strings (middle and upper) is not as expansively opulent as expected, especially bearing in mind that the balance engineer was Christopher Parker, who has few peers in this repertoire. There is a very good cassette.

Barbirolli's interpretation is a very personal one, deeply felt but with the pace of the music often excessively varied, sometimes coarsening effects which Elgar's score specifies very precisely and weakening the structure of the finale. The recording dates from the mid-1960s and the remastered sound on tape is fresh and clear but lacks something in ripeness of texture in the middle range.

It is an astonishing statistic that Bryden Thomson in this symphony takes almost a quarter of an hour longer than the composer himself in his original recordings. It is a tribute to the music that such spaciousness remains valid, with crispness of ensemble making up for lack of excitement. But in the finale Thomson's slowness at its most extreme becomes ponderous; though the opulent Chandos recording, more reverberant than most, gives a fine bloom to Elgar's rich textures, these textures are clouded in heavy tuttis. There is a faithful chrome cassette.

Variations on an original theme (Enigma), Op. 36.
(M) (***) HMV mono *EH 291345-4.* BBC SO, Toscanini – DEBUSSY: *La Mer.* (**)

(i) *Enigma variations;* (ii) *Pomp and circumstance marches Nos 1 and 3.*
(B) *** DG Walkman *413 852-4* [id.]. (i) LSO, Jochum; (ii) RPO, Del Mar – HOLST: *Planets.***(*)

Enigma variations; Crown of India: March of the Mogul Emperors; Pomp and circumstance marches Nos 1 and 2.
* DG Dig. **413 490-2** [id.]. BBC SO, Bernstein

The Walkman issue is an extraordinary bargain in combining Steinberg's exciting and sumptuously recorded complete set of the Holst *Planets* with Eugen Jochum's inspirational reading of *Enigma*, and – if that was not already remarkable value – adding as a bonus two of Del Mar's extremely spirited *Pomp and circumstance marches*. When Jochum recorded *Enigma* in 1975, he had not conducted it for several decades, but his thoughtful insight, in fresh study, produced an outstanding reading, consistently satisfying. The key to the whole work as Jochum sees it is *Nimrod*. Like others – including Elgar himself – Jochum sets a very slow *adagio* at the start, slower than the metronome marking in the score; unlike others, he maintains that measured tempo and, with the subtlest gradations, builds an even bigger, nobler climax than you find in *accelerando* readings. It is like a Bruckner slow movement in microcosm, around which revolve the other variations, all of them delicately detailed, with a natural feeling for Elgarian rubato. The finale has a degree of restraint in its nobility, no vulgarity whatever. The playing of the LSO and the recording match the strength and refinement of the performance. The chrome-tape transfer is not made at the highest level, but the sound does not seem to suffer.

Buried for half a century, Toscanini's HMV recording with the BBC Symphony Orchestra stemmed from the record company's attempt on his visit to London in 1935 to record the maestro live. The result – never approved by Toscanini himself, who obstinately refused to listen to the results – gives a vivid impression of him at his most passionate and committed. This freely expressive reading makes a fascinating contrast with his much later NBC orchestra recording, done live but in much more clinical conditions. Where the American orchestra plays the notes brilliantly but, as it seems, too literally, what is basically the same interpretation comes over with far more sense of fantasy, of idiomatic warmth and flair in the electric atmosphere of Queen's Hall. *Nimrod* may be preferable in the plainer, purer, more tautly controlled and slightly slower NBC reading, but for the rest the BBC performance is far more richly rewarding, helping to explain the idolization of Toscanini in the 1930s and after, ending with a dazzling account of the finale, which promptly inspires an eruption of joy and excitement from an audience suddenly freed from the British inhibitions of the time. This, one remembers, was just a year after Elgar's death. Though audience noises intrude, the sound – superbly mastered by Keith Hardwick – is astonishingly vivid on this chrome tape, especially for a transfer from 78 r.p.m., roughening at times as at the very end of the finale.

Bernstein's is quite the most perverse reading of *Enigma* ever recorded, and most listeners will fail to respond to its outrageous self-indulgence – not least in *Nimrod*, which is dragged out to almost unimaginable lengths. Though wilful, Bernstein is always passionate, and with good playing and recording he may attract those who want to hear a fresh view or who enjoyed the television programme made at the time of the recording. Best of all are the fill-ups, bold and swaggering. The CD is impressive in its presence; but few Elgarians are likely to find the performance of the main work the kind that they can live with.

CHAMBER AND INSTRUMENTAL MUSIC

Music for wind quintet: *Adagio cantabile* (*Mrs Winslow's soothing syrup*); *Andante con variazione* (*Evesham Andante*); *4 Dances; Harmony music Nos 1–5; 6 Promenades.*
(M) ** Chan. *CBT 1014-5* [id.]. Athena Ens.

As a budding musician, playing not only the violin but also the bassoon, Elgar wrote a quantity of brief, lightweight pieces in a traditional style for himself and four other wind-players to perform. He called it 'Shed Music'; though there are few real signs of the Elgar style to come, the energy and inventiveness are very winning, particularly when (as here) the pieces – often with comic names – are treated to bright and lively performances. Excellent recording, with the cassettes in the demonstration class.

Piano quintet in A min., Op. 84; String quartet in E min., Op. 83.
*** HMV Dig. **CDC7 47661-2**; *EL 270420-4*. Bernard Roberts, Chilingirian Qt.
(*) Mer. **ECD 84082; *KE 77082*. John Bingham, Medici Qt.

Bernard Roberts and the Chilingirian Quartet are well attuned to the Elgarian sensibility: they have dignity and restraint, and capture the all-pervading melancholy of the *Quintet*'s slow movement. In the *String quartet*, the Chilingirians are excellent, too, though they do not quite match the ardour of the Medicis; indeed some people have found them too low-voltage. However, they are excellently recorded in a warm acoustic and there is plenty of space around the aural image. An impressive and rewarding issue, with a good matching cassette.

John Bingham and the Medici Quartet play with a passionate dedication and bring almost a symphonic perspective to the *Piano quintet*. Some may find their account too intense and wanting in the reticence that is also an element in Elgar's make-up; yet there is no denying their ardour and commitment, particularly in the slow movement. They also give a fine and thoroughly considered account of the *Quartet*, and feel every measure. Again the slow movement is more extrovert in its expressive feeling than with the Chilingirians, and overall their reading is full of perceptive and thought-provoking touches. There will be many who will respond to the higher voltage. Unfortunately they are accorded an unsatisfactory balance: they are far too close in the *Quartet* (though less so in the *Quintet*) and, although the added immediacy is at one with the music making, it still remains difficult for a real *pp* to register, and as a result tone tends to harden somewhat on climaxes. The cassette, which is softer in grain and focus, minimizes these faults; it takes away some of the presence of the *Quartet* to advantage.

String quartet in E min., Op. 83.
*** Chan. Dig. **CHAN 8474**; *ABTD 1185*. Gabrieli Qt – WALTON: *Quartet*. ***
*** ASV Dig. *ZCDCA 526*. Brodsky Qt – DELIUS: *Quartet*.***

In the last couple of years we have had two accounts coupling the *Quartet* with the *Piano quintet*. Apart from its intrinsic excellence, the Gabrieli performance restores the Walton *Quartet* to circulation. The playing has a far-from-autumnal vitality and much eloquence; and the recording, made in the excellent acoustic of The Maltings, Snape, is up to the high standards one expects from this source, on cassette as well as CD.

The young players of the Brodsky Quartet take a weightier view than usual of the central, interlude-like slow movement of Elgar's still-neglected *Quartet* but, with the ease and warmth of their playing, amply justify it. The power of the outer movements, too, gives the lie to the idea of this as a lesser work than the two other chamber works, the *Piano quintet* and the *Violin sonata*, which Elgar also wrote at the very end of his creative career, not long before his wife died. First-rate recording in the cassette format; we hope a CD is in the pipeline.

Violin sonata in E min., Op. 82.
(*) ASV Dig. *ZCDCA 548* [id.]. McAslan, Blakely – WALTON: *Sonata*.(*)

Violin sonata in E min., Op. 82; Canto popolare; Chanson de matin; Chanson de nuit, Op. 15/1 & 2; Mot d'amour, Op. 13/1; Salut d'amour, Op. 12; Sospiri, Op. 70; 6 Easy pieces in the first position.
*** Chan. Dig. **CHAN 8380**; *ABTD 1099* [id.]. Nigel Kennedy, Peter Pettinger.

At the start of the *Sonata*, Kennedy establishes a concerto-like scale, which he then reinforces in a fiery, volatile reading of the first movement, rich and biting in its bravura. The elusive slow movement, *Romance*, inspired by a sinister clump of dead trees near Elgar's Sussex home, is sharply rhythmic in its weird Spanishry, while in the finale Kennedy colours the tone seductively. This is a warmer, more spontaneous-sounding performance than Hugh Bean's (earlier) purer, more detached account on HMV. As a coupling, Kennedy has a delightful collection of shorter pieces, not just *Salut d'amour* and *Chanson de matin* but such rare chips off the master's bench as the *Six very easy pieces in the first position*, written for a favourite niece who was learning the violin. Even in their simplicity Kennedy finds genuine Elgar, and he is matched beautifully throughout the record by his understanding piano partner, Peter Pettinger. The recording is excellent, most vivid and realistic in its CD version. The chrome cassette, too, is in the demonstration class.

Though Lorraine McAslan cannot match the virtuoso command and warmth of tone of Nigel Kennedy's Chandos recording of the *Sonata*, hers is an impressive and warm-hearted version, full of natural imagination, helped by the incisive playing of John Blakely. Good, forward recording which gives the violin tone less bloom than it might.

Organ sonata in G min., Op. 28
(*) ASV *ZCALH 958* [id.]. Jennifer Bate (Royal Albert Hall organ) – SCHUMANN: *Four sketches*.(*)

The Royal Albert Hall organ is just the instrument for Elgar's early *Sonata*, a richly enjoyable piece, full of characteristic ideas, not least the grand opening. Jennifer Bate plays with all the necessary flair, with her rubato only occasionally sounding unidiomatic, bringing out the dramatic contrasts of dynamic encouraged by this vast organ in its massive setting – emphasized by its special facility of causing the sound image to recede in quieter passages. The analogue recording provides good detail against the warm atmosphere which the cassette matches.

PIANO MUSIC

Adieu; Carissima; Chantant; Concert allegro; Dream children, Op. 43; Griffinesque; In Smyrna; May song; Minuet; Pastorale, Presto, Rosemary, Serenade; Skizze; Sonatina.
(*) Chan. Dig. **CHAN 8438; *ABTD 1164*. Peter Pettinger.

This record includes all of Elgar's piano music, from his earliest keyboard forays made when he was fifteen through to the *Sonatina* of 1931. Together with the transcriptions it runs all told to 70 minutes. Elgar did not have anywhere near the same feeling for the keyboard as so many of his contemporaries – and the earlier writing is both derivative and poorly laid out for the instrument. It has not established itself in the piano repertoire but, as Peter Pettinger shows, there are interesting things in this byway of English music (such as the *Skizze* and *In Smyrna*).

We get both the 1889 version of the *Sonatina* and its much later revision. Committed playing from this accomplished artist, and a pleasing recording too. There is fine presence on CD, but also an excellent matching cassette.

VOCAL AND CHORAL MUSIC

The Banner of St George, Op. 33; (i) *Great is the Lord* (*Psalm 48*), *Op. 67; Te Deum and Benedictus, Op. 34.*
*** HMV Dig. **CDC7 47658-2**; *EL 270555-4.* (i) Stephen Roberts; LSO Ch., N. Sinfonia, Hickox.

Written in 1897 with an eye on Queen Victoria's Diamond Jubilee, *The Banner of St George* suffers from its impossibly jingoistic words; but in telling the story of St George slaying the dragon and saving the Lady Sylene, Elgar is at his most colourful, with the battle sequence leading to beautifully tender farewell music (bringing one of Elgar's most yearningly memorable melodies) and a final rousing chorus. The three motets, written at the same period, bring 'Pomp and circumstance' into church and, like the cantata, stir the blood in Hickox's strong, unapologetic performances, richly recorded. The XDR cassette is acceptable, but a better focus could have been achieved with chrome stock.

The Black Knight (symphony for chorus and orchestra)*;* Part-songs: *Fly singing bird; The snow; Spanish serenade.*
*** HMV Dig. **CDC7 47511-2**; *EL 270157-4.* Liverpool PO Ch., Royal Liverpool PO, Groves.

The Black Knight was Elgar's first big choral work, written just after his marriage to Alice, the woman who effectively ensured that Elgar could, against the odds, become a great composer. The happiness and confidence of the writing is what comes over with winning freshness, even though the Elgarian must inevitably miss the deeper, darker, more melancholy overtones of his later, greater music. The subject, a tale of chivalry and a royal feast which brings disaster, is strikingly like that of Mahler's almost contemporary *Das klagende Lied*, but neurotic tensions are here far distant. Sir Charles Groves conducts a strong, fresh performance, not always perfectly polished in its ensemble but with bright, enthusiastic singing from the chorus. The three part-songs from the same period make an apt and attractive coupling. Clear, full recording; the CD copes admirably with the large forces. The tape transfer is quite well managed, with well-focused choral sound, but losing some of the extreme upper range.

Coronation ode, Op. 44.
*** HMV **CDC7 49381-2**; *EX 749381-4* (2). Lott, Hodgson, Morton, Roberts, Cambridge University Music Soc., King's College Ch., New Philh. O, Band of Royal Military School of Music, Ledger – *The Kingdom.****

(i) *Coronation ode, Op. 44; The Spirit of England, Op. 80.*
*** Chan. **CHAN 8430**; (M) *CBT 1013* [id.]. Cahill, SNO Ch. and O, Gibson; (i) with Anne Collins, Rolfe Johnson, Howell.

Elgar's *Coronation ode* is far more than a jingoistic occasional piece, though it was indeed the work which first featured *Land of hope and glory*. The most tender moment of all is reserved for the first faint flickerings of that second national anthem, introduced gently on the harp to clarinet accompaniment. All told, the work contains much Elgarian treasure.

Sir Alexander Gibson's coupling (66′ 50″) on Chandos is not only generous but is outstandingly successful in its CD format. The 1977 recordings were among the finest made by Brian Couzens in Gibson's Elgar series with the SNO. Gibson's performance combines fire and panache, and the recorded sound has an ideal Elgarian expansiveness, the choral tone rich and well focused, the orchestral brass given plenty of weight, and the overall perspective highly convincing.

Gibson is stirringly forthright in the *Coronation ode*, helped by excellent soloists, with Anne Collins movingly eloquent in her dignified restraint when she introduces the famous words of *Land of hope and glory* in the finale; and the choral entry which follows is truly glorious in its power and amplitude. *The Spirit of England*, a wartime cantata to words of Laurence Binyon, is in some ways even finer. The final setting of *For the fallen* rises well above the level of occasional music, at times even foreshadowing Britten's *War requiem*. Again the recording, with its combination of immediacy and ambience, is very effectively balanced. As usual with Chandos, there is a very good (mid-priced) tape, but here the CD is well worth its extra cost.

In the *Coronation ode* Ledger is superb in capturing the swagger and panache, flouting all thoughts of potentially bad taste. There is excellent singing and playing, although the male soloists do not quite match their female colleagues. The spectacular 1969 recording, made in King's College Chapel, with extra brass bands makes a splendid impact, with the resonant acoustics creating a jumbo *Land of hope and glory* at the close. The remastering, however, in attempting to clarify the sound-image, only makes the ear aware that detail cannot be sharp and the engineers might have done better to be content with a modest enhancement, the Chandos sound-image for Gibson is altogether firmer. Even so, the HMV version remains a compulsive listening experience, although the tape equivalent is rather bass-heavy.

The Dream of Gerontius, Op. 38.

*** HMV **CDS7 47208-8** (2). Helen Watts, Nicolai Gedda, Robert Lloyd, John Alldis Ch., LPO, Boult – *The Music Makers*.***

(*) HMV Dig. **CDS7 49549-2; *EX 749549-4* (2). Dame Janet Baker, John Mitchinson, John Shirley-Quirk, CBSO Ch. & O, Rattle.

(*) CRD **CRD 3326/7, *CRDC 4026/7* [id.]. Robert Tear, Alfreda Hodgson, Benjamin Luxon, SNO Ch. & O, Gibson.

Elgarians have been eagerly awaiting the transfer of Sir Adrian Boult's outstanding set of *The Dream of Gerontius* to CD. 'This is the best of me,' wrote Elgar on the score, and the comment could be applied equally to Sir Adrian's wonderfully glowing performance. Boult's total dedication is matched by a sense both of wonder and of drama. The spiritual feeling is intense, but the human qualities of the narrative are fully realized, and the glorious closing pages are so beautiful that Elgar's vision is made to become one of the most unforgettable moments in all musical literature. Boult's unexpected choice of Nicolai Gedda in the role of Gerontius brings a new dimension to this characterization, which is perfectly matched by Helen Watts as the Angel. The dialogues between the two have a natural spontaneity as Gerontius's questions and doubts find a response which is at once gently understanding and nobly authoritative. It is a fascinating vocal partnership, and it is matched by the commanding manner which Robert Lloyd finds for both his roles. The orchestral playing is always responsive and often, like the choral singing, very beautiful. The lovely wind playing at the opening of Part II is matched by the luminosity of tone of the choral pianissimos, while the dramatic passages bring splendid incisiveness and bold assurance from the singers. The fine 1976 analogue recording is extremely well balanced and has responded admirably to its CD remastering. There is slight loss of ambience, but the added clarity adds impact to the big choral climaxes and the magical opening and closing pages of Part II are not robbed of their atmosphere and sense of mystery. There is one misjudgement and it is a serious one. In order to make room for *The Music Makers*, a welcome enough bonus, Part I of *Gerontius* is broken at the end of the first disc, immediately before the Priest's dramatic *Proficiscere, anima Christiana*, a most unfortunate choice, robbing the listener of the surprise entry of the brass. Some may feel that the provision of the extra work compensates, but we do not – continuity is one of the possible virtues of the medium – and we have withdrawn the Rosette allotted to this recording in our last edition.

Although undoubtedly it has moments of great imaginative force, Simon Rattle's new digital recording is in the last resort a disappointment. The flamboyant operatic style of the performance is certainly not lacking in dynamism and there is much that is moving, but Rattle's control of the ebb and flow of tempo and tension is not always convincing. The most striking instance is in the famous *Praise to the holiest in the height*, where the chorus, while producing gloriously rich and luminous sounds, is pressed into an impetuous accelerando at the close, so that the climax is approached at breakneck speed, in complete contrast to the broad and heavily accented opening section. Similarly, the brief but profound orchestral interlude where the soul of Gerontius goes forward to meet his Maker is robbed of dignity by a sudden quickening of pace, so that the apocalyptic fortissimo chord conveys the bizarre impression that the Lord has smitten him down for his eagerness. John Mitchinson sings powerfully and dramatically in Part I and Rattle's accompaniment throbs with fervour; but the voice soon develops an uncomfortably wide vibrato under pressure, which is less congenial in Part II. Dame Janet Baker's assumption of the Angel's role is justly famous, but the close microphones are not kind to her high fortissimos; she comes into her own, however, at the work's valedictory close, helped by the rapturously lovely sounds made by chorus and orchestra alike. Rattle's view of heaven is more romantic than Boult's, but the ravishing textures he creates are wonderfully supportive, both here and in the earlier dialogue between soul and angel. John Shirley-Quirk's contribution is authoritative, eloquent and commanding, no more so than in the histrionic *Proficiscere, anima Christiana* where Rattle (not robbed, like Boult, of the element of surprise, by a break in continuity) heightens the effect by a magnetic pause before the stabbing brass chord. The *Go forth* chorus expands magnificently, while later, in Part II, the demons are given comparable bite and malignancy. The recording has the widest possible dynamic range (this is not a record for a small flat) and, with the solo voices recessed and pianissimos having a tendency to recede, it is difficult, though not impossible, to achieve a setting which is comfortable in the work's lyrical sections and yet not overwhelming at climaxes. The use of the Great Hall of Birmingham University has brought a wide reverberation but this is cushioned by the microphone placing. The effect, though not wholly natural, is certainly evocative, and the amplitude and weight of the climaxes are arresting. But Boult's masterly version with its seamless overall control and greater spirituality, especially at the close, is a more satisfying listening experience. Both HMV sets are generously cued in the CD formats, but neither booklet, in printing out the text, places the cues with the words, which would have been much more helpful.

Gibson's performance cannot quite compete with Boult's version. It is impressively spontaneous and very dramatic, as is immediately apparent in the strong contrasts of dynamic in the *Prelude*. When in his opening section Gerontius (Robert Tear) describes 'this strange innermost abandonment, this emptying out of each constituent', the orchestral response sends a shiver down the spine. The same sense of drama attends the demons (who are forthright rather than sinister), although here the brightness of the CD transfer verges on fierceness. The male soloists match Gibson's urgency, although there is no lack of repose in the dialogue between the Angel (sensitively portrayed by Alfreda Hodgson) and Gerontius at the opening of Part II. But Gibson does not manage to create the sense of unearthly stillness and quiet beauty that is so moving in Boult's marvellous performance. Equally the accelerando to the close of the *Praise to the holiest* section is not as intuitively calculated as in Britten's (deleted) version (which uncannily matches the composer's own performance, which Britten could not have heard, as it was not published when he made his Decca recording, not yet issued on CD). The closing pages with Gibson are sensitively done but are without the magical feeling of blissful infinity that Boult conjures up. The CRD recording is generally excellent. Like Rattle's HMV set, it has almost too wide a dynamic range: a volume setting where the gentler music is agreeably present is very loud indeed at fortissimo. The cueing is inadequate, with only 2 bands for Part I and 3 for Part II. The tapes are first class.

King Arthur: suite; (i) *The Starlight Express, Op. 78: suite.*
(*) Chan. **CHAN 8428; (M) *CBT 1001.* Bournemouth Sinf., Hurst, (i) with Glover, Lawrenson.

The *King Arthur suite* is put together from incidental music that Elgar wrote in 1923 – well after his creative urge had fallen away – for a pageant-like play by Laurence Binyon. Though not great at all, it is full of surging, enjoyable ideas and makes an interesting novelty on record. *The Starlight Express suite* is similarly taken from music Elgar wrote in the First World War for a children's play, very much from the same world as the *Wand of Youth suites*, with a song or two included. Though the singers here are not ideal interpreters, the enthusiasm of Hurst and the Sinfonietta is well conveyed, particularly in the *King Arthur suite*. The recording is atmospheric if rather over-reverberant, but the added firmness of the CD and its refinement of detail almost makes this an extra asset in proving a most evocative ambience for Elgar's music and projecting the voices of the very personable soloists, Cynthia Glover and John Lawrenson, vividly. Many Elgarians will find just about the right amount of music from these two works included here to make a well-balanced concert. The cassette lacks range (most noticeably in *King Arthur*) compared with the CD.

The Kingdom, Op. 51.
*** HMV **CDC7 49381-2**; *EX 749381-4* (2). Margaret Price, Minton, Young, Shirley-Quirk, LPO. Ch., LPO, Boult – *Coronation ode.****

Boult was devoted to this oratorio, identifying with its comparative reticence, openly preferring it even to *Gerontius*, and his dedication emerges clearly throughout a glorious performance. It has often been suggested that it is too static, but the Pentecost scene is intensely dramatic, and the richness of musical inspiration in the rest prevents any feeling of stagnation, certainly in a performance as inspired as this. The melody which Elgar wrote to represent the Holy Spirit is one of the noblest that even he created, and the soprano aria *The sun goeth down* (beautifully sung by Margaret Price) leads to a deeply affecting climax. The other soloists also sing splendidly, and the only reservation concerns the chorus, which is not quite as disciplined as it might be and sounds a little too backward for some of the massive effects which cap the power of the work. However, there is no doubt but that the strikingly successful remastering process has brought a gain in presence while retaining the quality of the 1977 original; here the freshening brings better definition without loss of body. The coupling of the *Coronation ode* is handy and certainly welcome, rather than particularly appropriate. There is good cueing to give internal access to both works. The chrome tapes also sound most impressive.

The Music Makers, Op. 69.
*** HMV **CDS7 47208-8** (2). Dame Janet Baker, LPO Ch., LPO, Boult – *Dream of Gerontius.****

The Music Makers, Op. 69; Sea pictures, Op. 37.
(*) HMV Dig. **CDC7 47674-2; *EL 270589-4.* Felicity Palmer, LSO Ch. & O, Hickox.

(i) *The Music Makers, Op. 69. 3 Bavarian dances, Op. 27; Chanson de matin; Chanson de nuit, Op. 15/1–2; The Wand of Youth suites Nos 1–2, Op. 1a–1b.*
(B) **(*) HMV *TCC 2 POR 54291.* (i) Dame Janet Baker, LPO Ch., LPO, Boult.

Elgar's long-neglected cantata sets the Shaughnessy poem of the same name. It was a mature work, written soon after the *Symphonies* and *Violin concerto*, and is full of warm, attractive writing for both voices and orchestra. But it is some measure of the musical material that the passages which stand out are those where Elgar used themes from his earlier works. If only the whole piece lived up to the uninhibited choral setting of the *Nimrod* variation from *Enigma*, it would be another Elgar masterpiece. As it is, there are enough moments of rich expansiveness to make it essential for any Elgarian to hear, particularly as understanding a performance as this. Dame Janet Baker sings with dedicated mastery, though unfortunately her example is not always matched by the comparatively dull-sounding choir. It was a happy idea to include *The Music Makers* in EMI's 'Portrait of the Artist' series and place it complete on one side of an extended-length tape. The sound is good, losing only a little of the upper range (the chorus has rather more bite on disc). But to couple this with much slighter music, however attractively performed, is more controversial. Even so, Boult's performances of the *Wand of Youth suites* are well worth having, for they capture both the innocence and the fragile charm of this music. The orchestral playing is first rate and the sound is fully acceptable, although this cassette, like the others in this series, offers no information whatsoever about the music, except titles and details of performers.

Hickox's generous coupling of *Sea pictures* and the big cantata, *The Music Makers*, brings strong, powerful performances, very individual in the song-cycle thanks to the urgent, tough singing of Felicity Palmer, very different from that of Dame Janet Baker, or Bernadette Greevy (see below), but just as characterful. Though Hickox in *The Music Makers* cannot quite match the finesse of Sir Adrian Boult's splendid recording (issued on CD as coupling for *The Dream of Gerontius*), it is a convincing, red-blooded reading, atmospherically recorded with voices well caught, but with reverberation masking some of the orchestral detail. There is a good cassette, offering rich sound and clearly projected voices; the extra resonance in the bass quite suits the music.

4 Partsongs, Op. 53; 5 Partsongs from the Greek anthology, Op. 45. Choral songs: *Christmas greeting; Death on the hills; Evening scene; The fountain; Fly, singing bird; Goodmorrow; Go, song of mine; The herald; How calmly the evening; Love's tempest; My love dwelt; Prince of sleep; Rapid stream; Reveille; Serenade; The shower; Snow; Spanish serenade; They are at rest; The wanderer; Weary wind of the West; When swallows fly; Woodland stream; Zut! zut! zut!*

*** Hyp. Dig. **CDA 66271/2**; *KA 66271/2* [id.]. Worcester Cathedral Ch.; Donald Hunt Singers, Hunt; K. Swallow, J. Ballard; R. Thurlby.

With Donald Hunt drawing bright, fresh singing from both the choirs he trains, Hyperion's complete collection of Elgar's choral songs is not merely valuable for filling in gaps but is also highly enjoyable in its own right. Though many of the partsongs, particularly the early ones, show Elgar at his most conventional, these offcuts from the master's workbench bring many delights and at least one extraordinarily original item in the last of the *Four Partsongs* Opus 53 of 1908, *Owls*. Set to words of Elgar himself, it is dedicated (in Latin) to his daughter Carice's pet rabbit, and presents a weirdly chromatic and pauseful piece, quite unlike the rest. The finest item is the last, in which both choirs join, the eight-part setting of *Cavalcanti* in translation by Rossetti, *Go, song of mine*. It is also fascinating to find Elgar in 1922, with all his major works completed, writing three charming songs for boys' voices to words by Charles Mackay, as refreshing as anything in the whole collection. He was plainly enjoying himself over such trifles. The last piece to be written, dating from 1929, is a setting of the Tudor poet, George Gascoigne, *Goodmorrow*. Designed for the choir of St George's Chapel, Windsor, it was first performed – with broadcast relay by new-fangled radio – in thanksgiving after the then king, George V, had recovered from serious illness. Atmospherically recorded – the secular singers rather more cleanly than the cathedral choir – it is a delightful collection for anyone fascinated by Elgar outside the big works. There are excellent equivalent cassettes, in a chunky box.

Scenes from the Saga of King Olaf, Op. 30.

❀ *** HMV Dig. **CDS7 47659-8**; *EX 270553-4* (2). Cahill, Langridge, Rayner Cook, LPO Ch., LPO, Handley.

This recording of *King Olaf*, issued in 1987, completed a cycle started by the composer himself. It is the last of Elgar's major works to be put on disc, and Vernon Handley, outstanding among today's Elgarians, makes it an appropriate landmark. The emotional thrust in Handley's reading confirms this as the very finest of the big works Elgar wrote before the *Enigma variations* in 1899. In its proportions it almost exactly anticipates *The Dream of Gerontius*, 90 minutes long with first half shorter than the second, while in its big choruses its style keeps anticipating the later masterpieces, equally reflecting the influence of Wagner's *Parsifal*. The wonder is that Elgar's inspiration rises high above the doggerel of the text (Longfellow, adapted by Harry Acworth), and though the episodic dramatic plan tails off towards the end, it is the opposite with Elgar's music, which grows even richer. Towards the end the charming 'gossip' chorus leads to the radiant pastoral duet between Olaf and Thyri, the third of his brides, followed by the exciting, dramatic chorus, *The Death of Olaf* (very Wagnerian), and finally an epilogue which transcends everything, building to a heart-tugging climax on the return of the 'Heroic Beauty' theme. Though strained at times by the high writing, Philip Langridge makes a fine, intelligent Olaf, Teresa Cahill sings with ravishing silver purity and Brian Rayner Cook brings out words with fine clarity; but it is the incandescent singing of the London Philharmonic Chorus that sets the seal on this superb set, ripely recorded, one of the finest in EMI's long Elgar history. The cassettes are well managed and fully acceptable, but the use of iron-oxide stock prevents ultimate fidelity, while the CDs are in the demonstration class.

Sea pictures (song cycle), *Op. 37*.
❀ *** HMV **CDC7 47329-2** [id.]; *TC-ASD 655*. Dame Janet Baker, LSO, Barbirolli – *Cello concerto*.*** ❀

(i) *Sea pictures, Op. 37; Pomp and circumstance marches Nos 1–5, Op. 39*.
(B) *** CfP **CD-CFP 9004**; *TC-CFP 40363*. (i) Bernadette Greevy; LPO, Handley.

Sea pictures hardly matches the mature inspiration of the *Cello concerto* with which it is coupled on HMV, but it is heartwarming here none the less. Like du Pré, Baker is an artist who has the power to convey on record the vividness of a live performance. With the help of Barbirolli she makes the cycle far more convincing than it usually seems, with words that are often trite clothed in music that seems to transform them. On CD, the voice is caught with extra bloom, and the beauty of Elgar's orchestration is enhanced by the subtle added definition.

Bernadette Greevy – in glorious voice – gives the performance of her recording career in an inspired partnership with Vernon Handley, whose accompaniments are no less memorable, with the LPO players finding a wonderful rapport with the voice. The singer's imaginative illumination of the words is a constant source of delight and her tenderness in the *Sea slumber song* and the delightfully idyllic *In haven* contrasts with the splendour of the big central and final songs, where Handley revels in the music's surging momentum. Here he uses a telling *ad lib.* organ part to underline the climaxes of each final stanza. The recording balance is excellent, although the CD suggests that the microphone was rather close to the voice, rich and clear against an orchestral background shimmering with atmospheric detail. The coupled *Marches* are exhilarating, and if Nos 2 and (especially) 3 strike some ears as too vigorously paced, comparison with the composer's own tempi reveals an authentic precedent. The sound is again rich and full-bodied, with the right degree of brilliance. There is a good cassette.

Scenes from the Bavarian Highlands, Op. 27 (original version).
*** Conifer Dig. **CDCF 142**; *MCFC 142* [id.]. CBSO Ch, Halsey; Richard Markham – HOLST: *Dirges & Hymeneal* etc.***

Scenes from the Bavarian Highlands, Op. 27 (orchestral version).

*** HMV **CDC7 49738-2**. Bournemouth Ch. & SO, Del Mar – VAUGHAN WILLIAMS: *In Windsor Forest; Towards the Unknown Region.****

The CBSO Chorus has appeared on many of the Birmingham orchestra's choral recordings, but its coupling of Elgar and Holst brought its first solo record. Three movements from this choral version of *Scenes from the Bavarian Highlands* were later to become the *Bavarian dances* for orchestra; but with piano accompaniment this original version is if anything even more charming, particularly when sung as freshly as by the Birmingham choir, vividly recorded. While the CD has extra sharpness of definition, the chrome cassette also handles the resonant acoustic well, to give a good focus.

The HMV recording uses the orchestral version of the score but, although the choral recording is agreeably full, balances are not always ideal, with the choral descant in the *Lullaby* outweighing the attractive orchestral detail. However, the performances are infectiously spirited, conveying warmth as well as vigour – Del Mar is a natural Elgarian. Moreover the HMV couplings of Vaughan Williams are more generous than the Holst offered on the Conifer CD.

Eller, Heino (1887–1970)

Dawn (tone poem); (i) *Elegia for harp & strings; 5 pieces for strings.*
*** Chan. Dig. **CHAN 8525**; *ABTD 1235* [id.]. (i) Pierce; SNO, Järvi – RAID: *Symphony No. 1.****

A most enterprising and rewarding issue. The *Elegy*, particularly, casts a strong spell. Heino Eller was an Estonian composer and teacher whose pupils included Eduard Tubin, Arvo Pärt and Kaljo Raid. He belongs, roughly speaking, to the same generation as Martinů and Prokofiev. He was really quite prolific – there are three symphonies, a violin concerto, five string quartets, and much else besides, all virtually unknown in the West. The earliest work is a tone-poem written at the end of the First World War which is frankly romantic – with touches of Grieg and early Sibelius as well as the Russian nationalists. (He studied with Shostakovich's teacher, Maximilian Steinberg.) The *Five Pieces for strings* of 1953 are transcriptions of earlier piano miniatures and have a wistful Grieg-like charm. The *Elegia for harp and strings* of 1931 strikes a deeper vein of feeling and has nobility and eloquence, tempered by quiet restraint; there is a beautiful dialogue involving solo viola and harp which is quite haunting. Excellent performances and recording, too. Strongly recommended. As Michelin would say, 'worth a special detour' – for the first-class chrome cassette as well as the CD.

Ellington, Edward Kennedy 'Duke' (1899–1974)

Mainly black (suite, arr. Kennedy).
*** HMV Dig. **CDC7 47621-2**; *EL 270538-4*. Nigel Kennedy, Alec Dankworth – BARTÓK: *Violin sonata.****

As a fascinating and surprisingly apt coupling for the Bartók *Solo Violin Sonata*, Nigel Kennedy gives an equally brilliant account of his own free arrangement of Duke Ellington's suite for big band, *Black, Brown and Beige*. With only a double-bass as partner, the haunting beauty of the melody in *Come Sunday* is all the more intense. In other movements the bass sharpens the impact of Kennedy's always vital playing. The sound is outstandingly vivid and full of presence on CD; the cassette is less sharply defined and present, but offers truthful timbre and balance.

Englund, Einar (born 1916)

Piano sonata No. 1; Sonatine in D; Introduction & Toccata; Pavane & Toccata; Prelude (Notturno); Gnome; Humoreski; Scherzino; What the hens tell.
** BIS Dig. **CD 277**. Eero Heinonen.

Einar Englund is Finnish though he lives on the Swedish island of Gotland where he was born. A composer in the classical mould, his music has a strong sense of line and purpose. His idiom is neo-classical, and much of the time there is a powerful sense of direction. The *Introduction and Toccata* makes an excellent beginning (there is quite a bit of Stravinsky in it) and the *Piano sonata* has a genuine sense of logic. The Finnish pianist, Eero Heinonen, is an excellent player; but the recording, though eminently acceptable, is just a little wanting in transparency.

Enescu, Georges (1881–1955)

Roumanian rhapsody No. 1.
(*) RCA Dig. **RCD 14439 [RCD1 4439]; (M) *GK 84439*. Dallas SO, Mata (with Concert**(*)).
(M) **(*) RCA **GD 86530**; *GK 86530* **[6530-2-RG]**. Boston Pops, Fiedler – DVOŘÁK: *Symphony No. 9.***(*)

For the general musical public, Georges Enescu seems fated to remain a one-work composer, like Paul Dukas with his *Sorcerer's apprentice*. Enescu's chimerical *First Roumanian rhapsody* combines a string of glowing folk-derived melodies with glittering scoring, to make it the finest genre piece of its kind in laminating East European gypsy influences under a bourgeois orchestral veneer. The Dallas performance, with the help of superbly lustrous digital sound, brings out all the colour and much of the sparkle, although Mata does not quite find the flair and exhilaration in the closing pages which distinguish the best analogue versions. But the RCA compact disc is truly demonstration-worthy in its natural vividness.

Fiedler's version has more dash than Mata's; this was music the conductor of the Boston Pops did uncommonly well, and the orchestral playing is first rate. The recording, however, is not so rich as the coupled Dvořák *New World symphony*, the violins lack something in body above the stave. But there is no edginess and plenty of sparkle and colour.

7 Chansons de Clément Marot.
*** Unicorn Dig. **DKPCD 9035**; *DKPC 9035* [id.]. Sarah Walker, Roger Vignoles – DEBUSSY: *Songs****; ROUSSEL: *Songs.***(*)

The set of Enescu songs, written in 1908, makes a rare, attractive and apt addition to Sarah Walker's recital of French song. As a Rumanian working largely in Paris, Enescu was thinking very much in a French idiom, charming and witty as well as sweetly romantic. Ideal accompaniments and excellent recording, particularly vivid on CD.

Erkel, Ferenc (1810–93)

Hunyadi László (opera): complete.
*** Hung. **HCD 12581/3** [id.]. Gulyás, Sass, Molnár, Dénes, Sólyom-Nagy, Gáti, Hungarian People's Army Male Ch., Hungarian State Op. Ch. and O, Kovács.

Hunyadi László is a patriotic piece which, in 1844 at its first performance, aroused the sort of nationalistic fervour in Hungary that Verdi inspired in Italy with *Nabucco*. The end of Act I even brings a rousing chorus, which, like *Va pensiero* in *Nabucco*, has all the qualities of a pop tune. Like the much later Erkel opera, *Bank ban*, *Hunyadi László* has never been out of the repertory in Hungary, and this live recording makes one understand why. Unlike its predecessor in the Hungaroton lists, it goes back to the original score instead of the corrupt reworking devised in the 1930s. Erkel's use of national music may not be as strikingly colourful as Smetana's in Czechoslovakia or Glinka's in Russia – both comparable figures – but the flavour is both distinctive and attractive, strongly illustrating a red-blooded story. Janos Kovács conducts with a vigour suggesting long experience of this work in the opera house. Denes Gulyás is a heroic, heady-toned hero, while Andras Molnár is equally effective as the villainous king, surprisingly another tenor role. Sylvia Sass is excellent as the hero's mother, in this version allowed to sing the beautiful prayer just before Laszlo's execution, excised from the earlier recording. First-rate sound. An excellent, unusual set, full of strong ideas, making easy listening.

Falla, Manuel de (1876–1946)

El amor brujo; The Three-cornered hat (ballet): complete.
⊛ *** Decca Dig. **410 008-2** [id.]; *KSXDC 7560* [Lon. *LDR 5- 71060*]. Boky, Tourangeau, Montreal SO, Dutoit.

(i; ii) *El amor brujo* (complete); (iii) *Nights in the gardens of Spain;* (ii) *The Three-cornered hat* (ballet): *suite.*
(*) HMV **CDM7 69037-2 [id.]. (i) De Los Angeles; (ii) Philh. O, Giulini; (iii) Soriano, Paris Conservatoire O, Frühbeck de Burgos.

(i) *El amor brujo* (complete); (ii) *Nights in the gardens of Spain; La vida breve: Interlude and dance.*
*** Chan. Dig. **CHAN 8457**; *ABTD 1169* [id.]. (i) Sarah Walker; (ii) Fingerhut, LSO, Simon.

(i) *El amor brujo* (complete); *The Three-cornered hat: suites 1 & 2.*
(B) ** CfP *TC-CFP 4512*. (i) De Los Angeles; Philh. O, Giulini.

El amor brujo: Ritual fire dance (only); *The Three-cornered hat* (ballet): complete.
(*) Ph. Dig. **411 046-2 [id.]. Von Stade, Pittsburgh SO, Previn.

The Three-cornered hat (ballet): complete; *La vida breve: Interlude and dance.*
** Decca **414 032-2** [id.]. Berganza, SRO, Ansermet.

Dutoit provides the ideal and very generous coupling of Falla's two popular and colourful ballets, each complete with vocal parts. Few more atmospheric records have ever been made and, particularly in the compact disc version, the very opening, with the mezzo-soprano slightly distanced, with castanets, cries of '*Olé!*' and insistent timpani, is immediately involving. Performances are not just colourful and brilliantly played, they have an idiomatic feeling in their degree of flexibility over phrasing and rhythm. The ideal instance comes in the tango-like seven-in-a-bar rhythms of the *Pantomime* section of *El amor brujo* which is lusciously seductive. The sound is among the most vivid ever, whatever the format, but the compact disc easily takes priority in its tangibility.

Previn's crisp and refreshing view of *The Three-cornered hat* provides a strong contrast with the sensuously beautiful Dutoit version. In its clarity and sharpness of rhythm it underlines the point that this Diaghilev ballet followed in the line of those of Stravinsky. The difference of approach is brought out at the very start, when von Stade's mezzo is presented very close, not distanced at all. Next to the Decca issue, the Philips fill-up is ungenerous, only a single item from *El amor brujo* instead of the whole ballet. Excellently clean-cut recording.

Ansermet aficionados will be glad to know that his rightly admired 1966 *El amor brujo*, which is meticulous in detail but has lots of character too, plus a potent gypsy-style vocal contribution from Marina de Gabarain, has been economically reissued, sounding remarkably fresh on a

Decca Weekend tape. The programme includes his distinguished 1963 *Boléro* plus the same composer's *Rapsodie espagnole* (1957), and an infectious account of Chabrier's *España*, altogether good value (*417 691-4*).

The coupling of the complete *El amor brujo* and *Nights in the gardens of Spain*, as offered by Chandos, is no less sensible than bringing the two ballets together, and may suit some collectors better. The brightly lit Chandos recording emphasizes the vigour of Geoffrey Simon's very vital account of the ballet, and Sarah Walker's powerful vocal contribution is another asset. Her vibrantly earthy singing brings an added dimension of flamenco drama at the outset, and her passionate contribution to the closing *Bells of the morning* is highly involving. Simon's account of the *Ritual fire dance* is comparably vivid. But in the more atmospheric sections of the score, Dutoit finds just a degree of extra subtlety which gives the Montreal performance its distinction. The Simon/Fingerhut version of *Nights in the gardens of Spain* also makes a strongly contrasted alternative to Alicia de Larrocha's much-praised reading (see below). Here the Chandos sound has a sharper focus than the Decca and the effect is more dramatic, with the soloist responding chimerically to the changes of mood, playing with brilliance and power, projecting a strong personality, yet not missing the music's delicacy. The softly focused Decca sound is undoubtedly more luminous, but the Chandos recording is certainly not without atmosphere, and the extrovert nature of the music making brings added excitement. The *Interlude* and *Dance* from *La vida breve* make a very attractive encore: overall, this compilation is highly recommendable, with a splendid matching tape.

Giulini's performances come from the mid-1960s – the original coupling is available on a quite well transferred bargain CfP tape – for the CD Soriano's excellent account of *Nights in the gardens of Spain* replaces some of the music from *The Three-cornered hat*, but the collection is still a very generous one. The Philharmonia playing is polished and responsive, and Giulini produces civilized and colourful performances. But the recording, though brightly coloured, has lost some of its bloom in the digital remastering (the textures of *Nights in the gardens of Spain*, too, are more leonine than on the 'Portrait of the Artist' tape anthology – see below), and in any case *El amor brujo* is not as red-blooded here as it is in the hands of either Dutoit or Geoffrey Simon.

In *The Three-cornered hat* the Suisse Romande Orchestra play with vigour and spirit for Ansermet: even the occasional roughness of detail seems appropriate, and there is no lack of vividness. Berganza is a characterful soloist. The coupling is not generous. With vintage Decca sound from the 1960s, this compact disc for all its added definition (and, because the recording is resonant, the gain is more marginal than usual) is surely over-priced and cannot possibly stand up to the competition from Dutoit on the same label.

Nights in the gardens of Spain.

*** Decca Dig. **410 289-2**; *410 289-4* [id.]. De Larrocha, LPO, Frühbeck de Burgos – TURINA: *Rapsodia Sinfónica**** (with ALBÉNIZ: *Rapsodia española****).

*** Erato Dig. **ECD 88255**; *MCE 75316* [id.]. Argerich, O de Paris, Barenboim – ALBÉNIZ: *Ibéria*.**

(B) **(*) DG Walkman *413 156-4* [id.]. Margrit Weber, Bav. RSO, Kubelik – RODRIGO: *Concierto serenata* etc.**

** Ph. **416 443-2** [id.]. Clara Haskil, LOP, Markevitch – CHOPIN: *Concerto No. 2*.**

(i) *Nights in the gardens of Spain; El amor brujo: Ritual fire dance.*

(*) RCA **RD 85666. Rubinstein; (i) Phd. O, Ormandy – FRANCK: *Symphonic variations*; SAINT-SAËNS: *Concerto No. 2*.**(*)

Alicia de Larrocha has recorded the work before for Decca, but her newest compact disc version – made in Walthamstow Town Hall – has the advantage of superb digital sound, rich and lustrous, with refined detail. The piano image, although admirably tangible and truthful in timbre, is well forward, yet this allows the listener to relish the freshness and brilliance of the soloist's articulation in the work's latter sections. Miss de Larrocha's playing has undoubted poetry and this beguiling and atmospheric performance makes for a very desirable issue indeed. There is a thoughtful, improvisatory quality about the reading (which has less thrust than Soriano's – see below) and the closing pages, consciously moulded, are particularly beautiful.

The volatile combination of the charismatic Martha Argerich and Daniel Barenboim creates consistent electricity in the exciting Erato version, recorded at a public performance. There is a degree of latitude here that would be impossible to bring off in a recording studio but, with the spur of communication from the audience, the ebb and flow of tension, with marked accelerandos at climaxes, involves the listener throughout. The recording itself is somewhat restricted but the lush orchestral textures serve as an admirable backcloth for Argerich's digital bravura, and much flamenco-style improvisatory feeling is engendered. The closing section provides a glowing apotheosis, almost Wagnerian in its breadth, but very telling when the whole performance has such spontaneity.

The DG recording is even more vivid, with the performers going all out to bring the utmost grip and excitement to the score. With Margrit Weber giving a brilliant account of the solo part, particularly in the latter movements, the effect is both sparkling and exhilarating. A little of the fragrant atmosphere is lost, particularly in the opening section (where de Larrocha is gentler), but the performance, with its strong sense of drama, is certainly not without evocative qualities. This generously full Walkman cassette is in the main devoted to the music of Rodrigo, and the three coupled recordings are of mixed appeal, but those wanting Rodrigo's *Concierto serenata* for harp should not be disappointed with the Falla. There is also an alternative coupling on DG's lower-mid-priced Focus label, where *Nights in the gardens of Spain* comes with an enjoyable East German version of Gershwin's *Rhapsody in blue* plus Rachmaninov's *Rhapsody on a theme of Paganini*. Good sound and good value, with the proviso that there is an awkward turnover before the final section of *Nights in the gardens of Spain*, surprising in a DG issue (*423 016-4*).

Rubinstein's version dates from 1970. His is an aristocratic reading, treating the work as a brilliantly coloured and mercurial concert piece, rather than a misty evocation, with flamenco rhythms glittering in the finale. Ormandy's accompaniment and the clear, rather dry RCA sound-picture match the soloist; there is no lack of subtlety here in musical matters, but more atmosphere and warmth would have been welcome. Nevertheless this is fine playing and the two encores which follow are even more arresting. Rubinstein appeared in a black-and-white Hollywood documentary during the 1940s, playing the *Ritual fire dance* dramatically, with his hands flying high above the keyboard in the repeated staccato notes. Even without the visual image, the power of this performance comes over strongly, while a similar sharpness of attack gives a piquantly abrasive quality to the *March* from the *Love of three oranges*.

There is no lack of atmosphere in Clara Haskil's account with Markevitch, and the 1960 recording still sounds fresh and vivid, if not very transparent. This version would seem to be mainly of interest to admirers of the pianist, although the performance is by no means to be dismissed. At the same price, however, one can have de Larrocha's beautiful Decca CD.

(i; ii) *Nights in the gardens of Spain;* (ii) *El amor brujo: Ritual fire dance*. (iii; iv) *The Three-cornered hat* (ballet): complete; (iii; v) *La vida breve:* excerpts.

(B) **(*) HMV *TCC2-POR 154591-9*. (i) Soriano, (ii) Paris Conservatoire O, (iii) De Los Angeles, (iv) Philh. O, (v) Higuero, Moreno, Ch., Nat. O of Spain; all cond. Frühbeck de Burgos.

An outstanding double-length tape collection, let down only by the total lack of provision of back-up documentation. It seems perverse to include a fascinating selection of excerpts from *La vida breve* and offer no information whatsoever about the scenario. Soriano gives a first-class account of the solo part in *Nights in the gardens of Spain* and Frühbeck de Burgos accompanies with a natural feeling for the subtleties of Falla's scoring. Apart from the opening '*Olés*' (which were recorded separately and dubbed on), the performance of the complete *Three-cornered hat* is highly recommendable, combining warmth with high spirits. Victoria De Los Angeles does not sound quite earthy enough, but she sings splendidly and the sound is consistently vivid. In the attractive *Vida breve* excerpts there is demonstration presence.

The Three-cornered hat (complete ballet)*; Homenajes; La vida breve: Prelude & dance.*
** Telarc Dig. **CD 80149** [id.]. (i) Florence Quivar; Cincinnati SO, Lopez-Cobos.

Telarc's recording is quite different from Decca's for Dutoit, with the proceedings cushioned by wider reverberation so that the opening of the ballet with its '*Olés!*' and castanets underlined by insistent timpani are much less sharply defined; elsewhere the warm ambience, with the orchestra set back in a concert-hall balance, is pleasingly atmospheric. But although the Cincinnati orchestra provides much felicitous detail (the violins in the *Grapes* sequence and the wit of the bassoon making fun of the Corregidor, for instance) this is overall a less distinctive and less dramatic reading than Dutoit's. The four *Homenajes* are not otherwise available and are impressively sombre, while the excerpts from *La vida breve* make an enjoyably contrasting end-piece. In the ballet, Florence Quivar's vocal contribution might with advantage have been earthier – it has more the feeling of the opera house than a gypsy encampment.

PIANO MUSIC

4 piezas españolas; Fantasia Baetica; El amor brujo: suite; The Three-cornered hat: 3 dances.
*** Decca **417 816-2** [id.]. Alicia de Larrocha.

This welcome and attractive issue fills an admirable place in the catalogue. It assembles the main piano music of Falla on one CD in exemplary performances and good recordings from 1974 which have transferred with pleasing naturalness to the new medium.

Fantasia Baetica.
** ASV *ZCALH 949* [id.]. Alma Petchersky (piano) – ALBÉNIZ: *Suite española***(*) (with GRANADOS: *Allegro di concierto***).

Falla's masterly *Fantasia Baetica* calls for more dramatic fire and projection than Alma Petchersky commands. But she is a musical and neat player, and the recording is far from unacceptable. The cassette is clear and well balanced.

Fauré, Gabriel (1845–1924)

(i) *Après un rêve; Dolly* (*suite*)*, Op. 56;* (i) *Élégie for cello & orchestra, Op. 24;* (iii) *Pavane, Op. 50;* (ii) *Pelléas et Mélisande* (incidental music)*: suite, Op. 80.*
** DG Dig. **423 089-2**; *423 089-4* [id.]. (i) Jules Erskine; (ii) Loraine Hunt; (iii) Tanglewood Fest. Ch.; Boston SO, Ozawa.

One might have expected Ozawa's characteristic reticence to be highly suitable for Fauré, but here the understatement perhaps goes a shade too far at times. *Pelléas et Mélisande* includes the rarely heard *Chanson de Mélisande*, sung simply and sweetly by Loraine Hunt; but neither she nor the eminently musical cello soloist in the two concertante pieces displays a strong individuality. The *Pavane* is almost certainly sung in French, though the words are inaudible, partly because of the Boston resonance; the choral embroidery however adds an agreeable touch of vitality to a rather solemn performance. The music making springs to life in the delectable opening movement of

Dolly – with its indelible associations with 'Listen with Mother' – and Ozawa's performance has the deftest touch throughout; the second movement, *Mi-a-ou* (fortunately not as onomatopoeic as it sounds), is delightful and the gay finale, *Le pas espagnole*, worthy of Sir Thomas himself; indeed this is the most attractive recorded account since Beecham's and, like the rest of the programme, it is very pleasingly recorded within a warm concert-hall ambience. The chrome cassette nevertheless has excellent definition and is quite as enjoyable as the CD.

(i) *Ballade for piano and orchestra, Op. 19;* (ii) *Berceuse for violin and orchestra, Op. 16; Caligula, Op. 52; Les Djinns* (orchestral version), *Op. 12;* (iii) *Élégie for cello and orchestra, Op. 24;* (i) *Fantaisie for piano and orchestra, Op. 111; Pénélope: Prélude.*

*** HMV **CDC7 47939-2** [id.]. (i) Collard; (ii) Yan-Pascal Tortelier; (iii) Paul Tortelier; Toulouse Capitole O, Plasson.

Masques et bergamasques (complete), *Op. 112; Pelléas et Mélisande* (incidental music), *Op. 80; Shylock, Op. 57.*

*** HMV **CDC7 47938-2** [id.]. Von Stade, Gedda, Bourbon Vocal Ens., Toulouse Capitole O, Plasson.

Although Fauré's most deeply characteristic thoughts are intimate rather than public, and his most natural outlets are the mélodie, chamber music and the piano, this set of his orchestral music nevertheless contains much that is highly rewarding. It includes the delightful *Masques et bergamasques* and the *Pelléas et Mélisande* and *Shylock* music, as well as such rarities as *Les Djinns* and *Caligula*. The Orchestre du Capitole de Toulouse may lack the finesse and bloom of the leading Parisian orchestras, but Michel Plasson gets an alert and spirited response and is blessed with very decent orchestral sound. He displays a genuine feeling for the Fauréan sensibility, and the fine-spun lyricism of the *Nocturne* from *Shylock* is well conveyed. The two works for piano and orchestra are particularly valuable; Jean-Philippe Collard gives a really distinguished account of both the early *Ballade* and the seldom-heard *Fantaisie*, Op. 111. This is a lovely set in every way, though the piano sound is a trifle hard (not the playing, of course). It contains many delights and cannot be too warmly recommended. Originally issued in a box of three LPs, the music has now been most satisfactorily remastered on to a pair of CDs, available separately, with good internal access.

Caligula, Op. 52; Les Djinns, Op. 12; Masques et bergamasques, Op. 112; Pavane, Op. 50; Pelléas et Mélisande, Op. 80; Pénélope: Prélude; Shylock, Op. 57.

(B) *** HMV *TCC2-POR 154596-9*. Bourbon Vocal Ens., Toulouse Capitole O, Plasson.

The collection also derives from the set of three LPs which included all Fauré's orchestral music. By omitting the concertante works, EMI have been able to transfer the rest of Plasson's Fauré anthology on to one double-length XDR ferric tape, which copes well with the warm resonance of the recording. Indeed the sound is consistently beautiful, catching voices as well as orchestra quite naturally and losing only a little of the upper range, although, with a slight drop in level, definition in the choral writing is slightly less clear on side two. Nevertheless this is highly rewarding music, and tape collectors should find this a worthwhile investment.

Élégie (for cello and orchestra), *Op. 24.*

*** Decca Dig. **414 387-2** [id.]. Harrell, Berlin RSO, Chailly – LALO: *Concerto*; SAINT-SAËNS: *Cello concerto No. 2.****

A most distinguished performance of Fauré's *Élégie*, played with eloquence and restraint by Lynn Harrell and admirably accompanied by Chailly. The recording is extremely fine, and especially believable in its CD format. Fauré was pupil and friend of Saint-Saëns, and the coupling with his little-known *Second Cello concerto* is most apt.

Fantaisie for flute and orchestra (arr. Galway).
(M) *** RCA *GK 85448* [*AGK1 5448*]. Galway, RPO, Dutoit – CHAMINADE: *Concertino*; IBERT: *Concerto*; POULENC: *Sonata*.***

James Galway's arrangement of a *Fantaisie for flute and piano* that Fauré composed in the late 1890s makes an appealing fill-up to an enterprising collection of concertante flute works impeccably played and finely recorded. There are two genuine flute concertos here (Ibert and Chaminade) and two arrangements, this and Lennox Berkeley's expert orchestration of Poulenc's *Flute sonata*. A well-transferred tape that will give great pleasure, if just a little top cut is applied to the sound-balance.

(i) *Fantaisie for flute and orchestra, Op. 79* (orch. Aubert); *Masques et bergamasques, Op. 112; Pavane, Op. 50; Pelléas et Mélisande: suite, Op. 80.*
** Argo Dig. **410 552-2** [id.]. (i) Bennett; ASMF, Marriner.

This ASMF Fauré recital certainly offers excellent sound; detail is well defined and there is excellent body. The recording is most impressive on the compact disc version. Were the performances in quite the same league, this would be an indispensable issue for all lovers of the French composer. Not that the playing is second-rate or routine, and William Bennett is most sensitive in the *Fantaisie*, but there could be greater freshness and charm.

Fantaisie for piano and orchestra, Op. 111.
*** Decca **417 583-2** [id.]. De Larrocha, LPO, Frühbeck de Burgos – FRANCK: *Symphonic variations* **(*); RAVEL: *Piano concertos*.***

The Fauré *Fantaisie* is a late work, aristocratic in style; it is to late Fauré what the *Ballade* is to his earlier period. Alicia de Larrocha is at one with its delicacy of feeling; this is an account of distinction and it is beautifully recorded, the sound at once warm and refined. The main items on this record are the Ravel *Piano concertos* and they are very successful, too. Even more generously, the CD includes also an account of the Franck *Symphonic variations* which has comparable delicacy, perhaps slightly less suitable for this romantically rather more robust work. But with over 73′ included, this is formidable value.

Pelléas et Mélisande: suite, Op. 80.
** Telarc Dig. **CD 80084** [id.]. Atlanta SO, Shaw – BERLIOZ: *Nuits d'été*.**

Splendidly recorded in clear, natural sound, Robert Shaw and the Atlanta orchestra give a refined, beautifully shaped performance of Fauré's tenderly atmospheric suite, but it makes an odd and rather ungenerous coupling for the similarly reticent account of the Berlioz song-cycle.

CHAMBER MUSIC

Cello sonatas Nos 1 in D min., Op. 109; 2 in G min., Op. 117; Élégie, Op. 24; Sicilienne, Op. 78.
(*) CRD **CRD 3316; *CRDC 4016* [id.]. Thomas Igloi, Clifford Benson.

Noble performances from the late Thomas Igloi and Clifford Benson that do full justice to these elusive and rewarding Fauré sonatas. Emile Vuillermoz's remark that Fauré 'concealed his harmonic learning where another composer would have advertised it' applies to all his music but particularly these late sonatas. Here is a master who never parades his artistry but leaves one to discover it oneself. His music will always elude those in search of quick returns and has corresponding rewards for those prepared to look below its surface. Igloi plays with fervour and eloquence within the restrained expressive limits of the music and the recording is clear, if not one of CRD's finest in terms of ambient effect.

Élégie, Op. 24; Papillon, Op. 77; Romance, Op. 69 (for cello and piano).
** ASV Dig. *ZCDCA 522* [id.]. Colin Carr, Francis Grier – DEBUSSY: *Sonata*; FRANCK: *Sonata*.**

These three Fauré pieces make an attractive coupling for the more substantial sonatas on Carr's record of French cello music. The *Romance* was originally written for cello and organ, while *Papillon* was designed expressly as a contrasting companion piece for the celebrated *Élégie*, light and Mendelssohnian. The digital recording is truthful, but the ambience is rather dry.

Piano quartet No. 1 in C min., Op. 15.
(*) RCA **RD 86256 [RCA 6256-2-RC]. Rubinstein, Guarneri Qt – DVOŘÁK: *Piano quartet No. 2.***(*)

Piano quartets Nos 1 in C min., Op. 15; 2 in G min., Op. 45.
❀ *** Hyp. **CDA 66166**; *KA 66166* [id.]. Domus.
*** CRD Dig. **CRD 3403**; *CRDC 4103* [id.]. Ian Brown, Nash Ens.

Lovely playing from all concerned in this immensely civilized music. Domus have the intimacy that this repertoire calls for, and their performance has the requisite lightness of touch and subtlety. Their nimble and sensitive pianist, Susan Tomes, can hold her own in the most exalted company (including Jean-Philippe Collard whose aristocratic accounts of these quartets both on record and in the concert hall resonate in the memory). This is really first-class chamber music playing, without any of the public concert-hall projection that is so prevalent nowadays. Their performances have just the right sense of scale and grasp of tempi. The recording is excellent, too, though the balance is a little close, but the sound is not airless. Some machines may cope less well than others with this; in any event, the playing is of such compelling quality that this qualification is of small account. The (iron-oxide) cassette is acceptable. Inner detail is less clearly defined than on CD, but is better on side two than on side one.

The Nash Ensemble on CRD appear to be recorded in a more open acoustic than the Domus on Hyperion and their performance is splendidly projected. Their readings are perhaps less inward and searching than the Hyperion team's, but they do not fall short of excellence, and the clarity and presence of the recording very much tell in its favour. The slow movement of the *G minor*, Op. 45, is played with particular eloquence and sensitivity, and the pianist, Ian Brown, is excellent throughout. A three-star issue then, in both formats, but the wonderfully responsive Domus performance has something special which gives it preference.

The RCA coupling was recorded in December 1970 and, like other Rubinstein reissues from this period, is affected by a rather close balance which prevents a real pianissimo. Otherwise the sound is truthful, well integrated rather than especially transparent. The performance is warm and spontaneous and readily conveys the players' highly musical response to this attractive music. Rubinstein's touch is especially felicitous in the scherzo.

Piano quintets Nos 1 in D min., Op. 89; 2 in C min., Op. 115.
*** Claves Dig. **CD 50-8603** [id.]. Quintetto Fauré di Roma.

These two quintets are much less popular than the two piano quartets and inhabit a more private world. This is immensely civilized music; the *Second Quintet* comes from 1921 and radiates a peaceful intensity. Norman Suckling spoke of Fauré's first movements as being 'vigorous without protestation, the finales joyous without effervescence' and the intervening andantes 'distilling an atmosphere of peaceful intensity where every vibration is significant without being insistent'. These artists have the measure of Fauré's subtle phrasing and his wonderfully plastic melodic lines, and their performances are hard to fault. The pianist is Maureen Jones, and the quartet are members of I Musici. The recording, made in a Swiss church, is warm and splendidly realistic. This music, once you get inside it, has a hypnotic effect and puts you completely under its spell.

Piano trio in D min., Op. 120; (i) *La bonne chanson, Op. 61.*
**(*) CRD *CRDC 4089* [id.]. Nash Ens., (i) with Sarah Walker.

The characterful warmth and vibrancy of Sarah Walker's voice, not to mention her positive artistry, come out strongly in this beautiful reading of Fauré's early settings of Verlaine, music both tender and ardent. The passion of the inspiration is underlined by the use of a long-neglected version of the cycle in which the composer expanded the accompaniment by adding string quartet and double-bass to the original piano. Members of the Nash Ensemble give dedicated performances both of that and of the late rarefied *Piano trio*, capturing both the elegance and the restrained concentration. The atmospheric recording is well up to CRD's high standard in chamber music; on cassette, however, there is a hint of edge on the voice in *La bonne chanson*, and in the *Piano trio* the resonance brings an inner focus that is slightly less than ideally sharp.

String quartet in E min., Op. 121.
Verany **PV 86102**. Viotti Qt (with DEBUSSY; RAVEL: *Quartets*).

Fauré's *String quartet* is one of the most demanding and rewarding works of his last years, and it deserves a performance of greater sympathy and accomplishment than the Viotti give it here. In no respect do they match earlier performances on LP. CD collectors should wait.

Violin sonata No. 1 in A, Op. 13.
** Chan. Dig. **CHAN 8417**; *ABTD 1151* [id.]. Lydia Mordkovitch, Gerhard Oppitz – R. STRAUSS: *Violin sonata.***(*)

Violin sonatas Nos 1 in A, Op. 13; 2 in E min., Op. 108.
(M) ❀ *** Ph. *412 397-4*. Arthur Grumiaux, Paul Crossley.
** DG Dig. **423 065-2**. Shlomo Mintz, Yefim Bronfman.

Four decades separate the two Fauré sonatas and they make a perfect coupling. The *First* is a richly melodious piece which, strangely enough, precedes the César Franck sonata by a dozen or so years, while the *E minor* was written in the same year as Debussy's (1917). They are immensely refined and rewarding pieces, with strange stylistic affinities and disparities: the second movement of the *E minor* actually uses a theme intended for a symphony that Fauré had discarded more than thirty years earlier. Although they have been coupled before, they have never been so beautifully played or recorded as on the Philips issue. Indeed, this is a model of its kind: there is perfect rapport between Grumiaux and Crossley, and both seem totally dedicated to and captivated by Fauré's muse. Moreover the two artists sound as if they are in the living-room; the acoustic is warm, lively and well balanced. Reissued on Philips's 'Musica da camera' at mid-price and immaculately transferred to cassette, this coupling is more desirable than ever. Fauré is not and never will be a popular composer, and it is doubtful whether this tape will survive the lifetime of this *Guide*; however, perhaps it is not too much to hope that a CD version will arrive – much more obscure repertoire is currently surviving in the new format.

Lydia Mordkovitch and Gerhard Oppitz give a sensitive account of the popular *A major Sonata* but they are not ideally matched: the balance tends to favour the pianist. Her other-worldly, disembodied pianissimo tone does not draw playing of comparable dynamic range and sensitivity from the pianist, though the acoustic (St Luke's Church, Chelsea) may have posed problems for him. All the same, the playing of both artists will still give a great deal of pleasure. The chrome cassette is transferred at the highest level and fortissimos have less refinement than usual from Chandos.

Splendid playing, too, from Shlomo Mintz who is also rather swamped by the pianist, Yefim Bronfman, at times. The acoustic of the Deutschlandfunk Sendesaal takes some getting used to – the piano, like many instruments in radio studios, sounds not in ideal condition and is a trifle jangly. No complaints about the pianist, though: his virtuosity and sensitivity is not in question, nor is the lyrical intensity of Mintz's playing.

Ballade in F sharp, Op. 19; Mazurka in B flat, Op. 32; 3 Songs without words, Op. 17; Valses caprices Nos 1–4.
*** CRD Dig. **CRD 3426**; *CRDC 4126* [id.]. Paul Crossley.

This was the last to be issued of Paul Crossley's five records and tapes of Fauré's solo piano music. The *Songs without words* are early, written in the composer's teens, yet already the Fauréan sensibility is present. Crossley's playing seems to have gone from strength to strength in his series, and he is especially good in the quirky *Valses caprices*, fully equal to their many subtleties and chimerical changes of moods. He is extremely well recorded too, on both CD and cassette.

Barcarolles Nos 1–13 (complete).
*** HMV **CDC7 47358-2** [id.]. Jean-Philippe Collard.
*** CRD **CRD 3422**; *CRDC 4122* [id.]. Paul Crossley.

The *Barcarolles* encompass the best part of Fauré's creative life; the first dates from the 1880s and the last, Op. 116, comes from 1921. Jean-Philippe Collard displays unerring judgement in this music and an instinctive feeling for its shifting moods and colours. The recordings were made in 1970 in the Salle Wagram, but the acoustic sounds confined. Collard's *ff* sounds more overpowering in this enclosed environment than it does in real life, but the playing is totally idiomatic. The level and balance change very slightly between the end of No. 6 and the beginning of No. 7 as they did on LP. The differences between the LP and CD formats are relatively marginal. This glorious and haunting music is played with such artistry that minor quibbles about recording quality should be put aside.

Paul Crossley is also a fine interpreter of the gentle yet powerful French master. He has a highly sensitive response to the subtleties of this repertoire and is fully equal to its shifting moods. The CRD version was made in the somewhat reverberant acoustic of Rosslyn Hill Chapel, and is more vivid than the 1971 EMI recording of Jean-Philippe Collard. Honours are pretty evenly divided between the two players; at times Collard appears the more subtle of the two, at others Crossley. Collard gauges the temper of *No. 7 in D minor* more naturally than his English rival, but elsewhere Crossley's aristocratic sensibility seems the more completely attuned to Fauré's world. Both will give pleasure and, if Collard's account is not displaced, the CRD is still a strong challenger. It has the advantage of an excellent chrome-tape equivalent which catches the full bloom of the piano timbre and loses only a fraction of the sharpness of focus.

Barcarolles Nos 1, 4–6; Impromptus 1–3; Nocturnes 1, 4, 6; 3 Romances sans paroles, Op. 17.
*** Conifer Dig. **CDCF 138**; *MCFC 138* [id.]. Kathryn Stott.

A lovely recital. Kathryn Stott produces not only a wide dynamic range but a rich and subtle variety of colours in this well-chosen Fauré anthology. She does not shrink from passion; indeed on occasion something of the understatement and reticence of this music almost eludes her. The *F sharp minor Barcarolle* is a case in point and steps outside the boundaries of the

Fauréan sensibility. But for the most part this is a most intelligently planned and boldly executed recital – a particularly enterprising choice for a début recital record. She has a strong artistic personality and has thought deeply and to good purpose about this wonderful music. She is excellently recorded: both the CD and the chrome cassette approach a demonstration standard of realism, and this fine recital would make a highly rewarding introduction for any newcomer to Fauré's piano music.

Dolly, Op. 56.
*** Ph. Dig. **420 159-2**; *420 159-4* [id.]. Katia and Marielle Labèque – BIZET: *Jeux d'enfants*; RAVEL: *Ma Mère l'Oye.****

Fauré's touching suite was written for Hélène Bardac, who was known as *Dolly* and whose mother was Debussy's second wife. The *Kitty waltz* was a gift for her fourth birthday. The Labèque sisters give a beautiful account of it, their playing distinguished by great sensitivity and delicacy. The recording is altogether first class, totally natural and very realistic in its CD format. The chrome tape too offers comparably beautiful and well-defined sound.

Impromptus Nos 1–5; 9 Préludes, Op. 103; Theme and variations in C sharp min., Op. 73.
*** CRD **CRD 3423**; *CRDC 4123* [id.]. Paul Crossley.

The *Theme and variations in C sharp minor* is one of Fauré's most immediately attractive works; Paul Crossley plays it with splendid sensitivity and panache, so this might be a good place to start for a collector wanting to explore Fauré's special pianistic world. The *Préludes* were written in a group within a comparatively brief period and yield much to a performer who responds instinctively to their changes of mood and colour. Crossley never forces the music, yet his purity of style is never chaste, and his concentration and sense of scale demonstrates his full understanding of this repertoire. The *Impromptus*, if generally more extrovert, are by no means easy to bring off, but the characterization here is highly sympathetic and strong. The recorded sound, too, is extremely well judged, with a most realistic piano image, nicely placed in relation to the listener. There is an excellent cassette.

Nocturnes (complete)*; Pièces brèves, Op. 84.*
(*) CRD **CRD 3406-7; *CRDC 4106-7.* [id.]. Paul Crossley.

Paul Crossley has great feeling for Fauré's piano music and penetrates its elusive world. It is good news that he has recorded it complete for CRD, for he has a great deal to say about it. The recording is rather closely balanced, albeit in an ample acoustic, but the result tends to emphasize a percussive element that one does not normally encounter in this artist's playing. The beautifully inward *F sharp minor Nocturne*, Op. 104, No. 1, almost loses the intimate private quality of which Crossley speaks in his excellent notes, and it is not the only one to do so. There is much understanding and finesse, however, and the *Pièces brèves* are a valuable fill-up. Tape collectors may well decide that the Crossley recordings are worth investigating, as the chrome transfers are first class.

Pavane, Op. 50 (with *Songs of the Auvergne* (arr. Goff Richards)*: À la campagne; Le baylère, L'eau de source; Une gente bergère; Là-bas dans le Limousin*).
** HMV Dig. **CDC7 47708-2**; *EL 270586-4.* King's Singers, Scottish CO, Carl Davis – SAINT-SAËNS: *Carnival.**

The King's Singers aptly include Fauré's own choral version of the *Pavane* in their collection '*À la Français*', but the optional choral parts are too prominent, made even less misty-sounding by having a male alto top line. They have included also some of the same *Songs of the Auvergne* made popular by Canteloube, but Goff Richards' arrangements are totally different, to fit the group's characteristic style, alternating between the pointed and the sentimental. So *Baïlero* becomes *Le Beylère*, just as sensuous in close harmony as in the more familiar soprano line. There is a good tape, but the sound is less cleanly focused than on the CD.

Requiem, Op. 48.
*** ASV Dig. **CDRPO 8004**; *ZCRPO 8004* [id.]. Aled Jones, Stephen Roberts, LSO Ch., RPO, Hickox – BERNSTEIN: *Chichester Psalms.****
(B) *** CfP *TC-CFP 40234* [Ang. **CDC 47836**]. De Los Angeles, Fischer-Dieskau, Brasseur Ch., Paris Conservatoire O, Cluytens.
(*) Ph. Dig. **412 743-2 [id.]. Popp, Estes, Leipzig R. Ch., Dresden State O, C. Davis.
(*) DG Dig. **419 243-2; *419 243-4* [id.]. Battle, Schmidt, Philh. Ch. & O, Giulini (with RAVEL: *Pavane***(*)).

Requiem; Pavane, Op. 50.
(M) *** HMV **CDM7 69038-2** [id.]. Sheila Armstrong, Fischer-Dieskau, Edinburgh Fest. Ch., O de Paris, Barenboim.

(i) *Requiem; Pavane;* (ii) *Pelléas et Mélisande (suite), Op. 80.*
(M) ** Ph. **420 707-2**; *420 707-4* [id.]. (i) Ameling, Kruysen, Netherlands R. Ch., Fournet; D. Chorzempa; Rotterdam PO, (i) Fournet; (ii) Zinman with J. Gomez.

Requiem, Op. 48; Cantique de Jean Racine, Op. 11.
*** Conifer Dig. **CDCFRA 122**; *MCFRA 122* [id.]. Ashton, Varcoe, Cambridge Singers, L. Sinfonia (members), Rutter.
(*) HMV Dig. **CDC 747317-2; *EL 270168-4* [Ang. *4DS 38252*]. Hendricks, Van Dam, Orfeon Donastiarra, Toulouse Capitole O, Plasson.

Rutter's Conifer disc, which won the choral prize in the *Gramophone* record awards, 1985, brings a revelation in returning to Fauré's original chamber instrumentation without violins and with a quartet of divided violas and cellos. Rightly, Rutter includes the two extra movements which Fauré added for a performance in 1893, along with two horns to augment the small ensemble. The result, in a fresh, understanding performance under Rutter with first-rate Cambridge singers, has extra intensity from the intimacy of ensemble and, far from seeming too small in scale, the periodic dynamic contrasts come out all the more sharply. The soloists are rightly presented as part of the ensemble, not as stars, the boyish-sounding soprano of Caroline Ashton very apt. The CD gives extra precision to an already well-balanced recording. The cassette is admirably clear and vivid on side one, but the transfer level rises on side two and vocal fortissimos lose their refinement of focus.

Richard Hickox opts for the regular full-scale text of the *Requiem*, yet at speeds rather faster than usual – no faster than those marked – he presents a fresh, easily flowing view, rather akin to John Rutter's using the original chamber scoring on his Conifer issue. Aled Jones sings very sweetly in *Pié Jesu*, but hardly deserves his inflated star-billing on the cover. Soloists are placed rather close, with the total sound firm and full. With its generous and equally successful coupling, this makes a strong alternative recommendation to the Conifer version. There is a good tape.

Barenboim's 1975 recording has been splendidly remastered for its reissue on HMV's mid-priced Studio series. The recording was always first class, rich and full-bodied, and now the choral sound is firmer and better focused without loss of atmosphere: the moment when the trumpets enter in the *Sanctus* at the cry '*Hosanna in excelsis!*' is vibrant indeed. The Edinburgh Festival Chorus is freshly responsive so that, although the sound is beefier than with Rutter, the effect is never heavy and the performance is given a strong dimension of drama. Yet there is splendidly pure singing from Sheila Armstrong, and her *Pié Jesu* is even more successful here than with De Los Angeles. Fischer Dieskau is not quite as mellifluous as in his earlier account with Cluytens, but brings a greater sense of drama. A first-rate CD, including a sensitive account of the *Pavane*, and well worth considering in the budget range.

The De Los Angeles/Fischer-Dieskau version made under the late André Cluytens in the early 1960s is still available on an excellent bargain-price tape in the UK and on a CD in the US. It has always been a good-sounding recording, with great expressive eloquence in its favour, even if the choir is not as fine as Barenboim's or Rutter's groups, and its claims on the collector's pocket are almost irresistible.

Sir Colin Davis also uses the familiar orchestral score and the Philips recording is very well balanced, with the chorus believably recessed in a glowing acoustic aura which does not cloud detail. The choral singing is both warm and refined, pianissimos serene, climaxes swelling out with a natural eloquence. Lucia Popp provides a touchingly gentle *Pié Jesu*, her innocence contrasting with Simon Estes' highly dramatic contribution, operatic in feeling and hardly apt in style. Nevertheless, overall this is a movingly expansive account, with the moulded choral line ever responsive to the text, and projecting strong expressive feeling in the *Sanctus* and *Libera me*. The closing *In paradisum* has lyrical warmth yet remains ethereal in atmosphere. However, this CD lasts a mere 40 minutes and now seems uncompetitive, given the alternatives available.

Michel Plasson's performance is even broader than Davis's in its basic conception, yet it is also more volatile. At the very opening Plasson's articulation is bolder, essentially dramatic; throughout the contrasts of dynamic are highlighted. The choir sing beautifully and, if some of the gentler moments seem rather withdrawn, climaxes are certainly powerful, as on the words '*Hosanna in excelsis*' in the *Sanctus* and in the transition from the *Agnus Dei* to the *Libera me*. Even the *In paradisum* has surges rising above its usually placid surface, although its loveliness is unimpaired. The sound is both fresh and atmospheric, with the acoustic setting admirably managed by the engineers. There is a bonus in the inclusion of the *Cantique*, an early work dating from 1885, to which Plasson and his choir bring passionate advocacy. But, of course, Rutter offers this too, and his account of the *Requiem* is even more refreshing.

Carlo Maria Giulini, with large-scale Philharmonia forces, adopts consistently slow speeds and a very reverential manner. That view usually makes the work too sentimental, but Giulini's care for detail in textures and his unexaggerated expressive style keep the result hushed and prayerful rather than sugary, with warm, atmospheric recording to match. Kathleen Battle sings with glowing warmth in *Pié Jesu*, sounding sumptuous but not really in style. With the *Requiem* lasting 42 minutes, the Ravel fill-up, done with similarly measured dedication, provides a minimal bonus. There is a good cassette, but the sound is a little misty at lower dynamic levels.

The Philips mid-priced Silverline reissue is most generous of all in the amount of music offered, but the Fournet account of the *Requiem*, while the singing of the Netherlands Radio Chorus is first class, in most other respects is rather cool, and the recording tends to make both soloists (who sing well enough) sound rather too close. However, the major coupling, David Zinman's highly refined and beautifully played account of the *Pelléas et Mélisande suite* is another matter. This is the finest modern version of this lovely score and far preferable to Ozawa's (see above). There is a pervasive tenderness and delicacy (the *Sicilienne* is memorable) and, to make the selection complete, Jill Gomez gives a ravishing account of Mélisande's song, *The three blind daughters*. The recording is in the demonstration bracket on CD and tape alike – and for that matter the 1975 recording of the *Requiem* has come up pretty well, too.

Ferguson, Howard (born 1908)

(i) *Concerto for piano and string orchestra, Op. 12;* (ii) *Amore langueo, Op. 18.*
*** HMV Dig. **CDC7 49627-2**; *EL 749627-4.* (i) Howard Shelley; (ii) Martyn Hill, LSO Ch., City of L. Sinfonia, Hickox – FINZI: *Eclogue.****

This makes a substantial addition to Howard Ferguson's representation on record and should bring the composer new friends. Ferguson was a fine pianist and his concerto has something in common with the lyrical feeling of John Ireland's comparable work. At first it sounds more like a concerto grosso, for there is a substantial opening ritornello for the strings; but the piano makes a major contribution to the memorable theme and variations which is the work's centrepiece. As with Ireland the finale is gay and melodically carefree. Howard Shelley's performance is admirable and Hickox secures highly sympathetic response from the City of London Sinfonia string section. *Amor langueo* is an extended cantata, lasting just over half an hour and is based on a fifteenth-century text. Although it is subtitled *Christ's complaint to Man* and concerns Christ's spiritual love for mankind, its imagery also explicitly draws distinctly erotic associations with romantic sexual passion. To the medieval mind, spiritual and secular love were not always seen as separate experiences. The setting, for tenor solo and semi chorus, with a strong contribution from Martyn Hill, brings a powerful response in the present performance, and Ferguson's music moves from the depiction of Christ's suffering on the Cross to the sometimes even playful atmosphere of lovers in the bedchamber with remarkable ease. An unusual and rewarding piece, recorded with great vividness on both CD and the excellent chrome-tape equivalent, but it is a pity that the separate sections of so big a work as *Amor langueo* are not individually cued on CD.

Ferlendis, Giuseppe (1755–1802)

Oboe concerto No. 1 in F.
(*) Ph. Dig. **420 179-2; *420 179-4* [id.]. Holliger, ASMF, Sillito – MOZART: *Concerto* etc.**(*)

Giuseppe Ferlendis was an oboist at the court of the Archbishop of Salzburg, and Mozart composed the *Concerto*, K. 313, expressly for him. Ferlendis's *Oboe concerto* was, for a time, also attributed to Mozart although it is difficult to see why: it is quite well put together, but the *Adagio* is brief (2′ 36″) and the level of invention by no means out of the ordinary. It thus makes a less than completely enticing coupling for Holliger's latest recording of Mozart's illustrious work, although it is impeccably played and well recorded.

Ferranti, Marco Aurelio Zani de (1801–78)

Exercice, Op. 50/14; Fantaisie variée sur le romance d'Otello (Assisa à piè), Op. 7; 4 Mélodies nocturnes originales, Op. 41a/1–4; Nocturne sur la dernière pensée de Weber, Op. 40; Ronde des fées, Op. 2.
❀ *** Chan. Dig. **CHAN 8512**; *ABTD 1222* [id.]. Simon Wynberg (guitar) – FERRER: *Collection.****

This is a real find and is recommended to all lovers of guitar music. Ferranti, now virtually forgotten, was a famous figure in his day, poet and Dante scholar as well as composer, and he numbered Rossini and Paganini among his admirers as a guitarist. Let Berlioz sum up the contemporary view of his prowess: 'It is truly impossible to imagine the effects Zani de Ferranti draws from that meagre instrument. With a Paganinian technique Zani combines a communicative sensibility and an ability to sing that few, as far as I know, have ever possessed before. He soothes you, magnetizes you; it should be added that he writes excellent music for the guitar and that, to a large degree, the charm of his compositions contributes to the spell over the listener.' Here Simon Wynberg casts a comparable spell. His playing fully enters the innocently compelling sound-world of the Bolognese composer; it is wholly spontaneous and has the most subtle control of light and shade. Both the Rossinian *Fantaisie* (10′ 35″) and the *Nocturne* which has little to do with Weber (9′ 16″) are fairly ambitious in scale, but seem not a whit too long; and the four brief *Mélodies nocturnes* have a winsome lightness, as indeed has the attractive *Ronde des fées*. Ferranti's invention is most appealing and this makes ideal music for late-evening reverie. The guitar is most realistically caught in a friendly acoustic; the cassette is admirable, but the added definition and the background silence of the CD give a very real illusion of presence.

Ferrer, José (1835–1916)

Belle (*Gavotte*); *La danse de naïades; L'étudiant de Salamanque* (*Tango*); *Vals.*
*** Chan. Dig. **CHAN 8512**; *ABTD 1222* [id.]. Simon Wynberg (guitar) – FERRANTI: *Collection.****❀

José Ferrer was born near Gerona but eventually became Professor of Guitar at Barcelona Conservatoire. He is a less substantial figure than Ferranti, but these four vignettes (each lasting two to three minutes) are almost as winning as that composer's music. They form a centrepiece in Simon Wynberg's excellent and enterprising recital which is most enjoyable. The Vals immediately catches the ear by its piquancy and the engaging tango, *L'étudiant de Salamanque*, has some effective fingerboard 'drumming' at its close. The recording has striking realism and presence, with an excellent matching tape.

Fiala, Josef (1754–1816)

Cor anglais concerto in E flat.
(M) *** Ph. *412 354-4.* Holliger, ECO, Leppard – J. C. BACH: *Oboe concerto;* HUMMEL: *Introduction and variations.****

Joseph Fiala was himself an oboe player and was admired by Mozart as a musician. His *Cor anglais concerto* is small in scale but most appealing, with an engaging *Adagio cantabile*, lasting under three minutes, and a spiritedly elegant finale. Holliger plays it beautifully and is attentively accompanied and well recorded. He provides his own cadenza for the first movement.

Fibich, Zdeněk (1850–1900)

Symphony No. 1 in F, Op. 17; The Tempest (symphonic poem), *Op. 46.*
** Sup. **CO 1091** [id.]. Brno State PO, Vronsky.

'Dvořák without the tunes' is generally the first response many listeners have to this agreeable composer. But he is a fine craftsman writing in a genial idiom, and his music gives undoubted pleasure. His first published symphony – there are two earlier examples, in E flat and G minor, written in his late teens – comes from his early thirties and is an attractive piece with appealing (if ultimately unmemorable) melodic ideas. The scherzo is an exhilarating piece and has a zest for life which is reminiscent of his great contemporaries. *The Tempest* is a later and less interesting work, full of stock-in-trade dramatic gestures. Good performances, but a rather indifferent recording with not enough space round the various instruments: tuttis need more room to expand. All the same, for all those who like Smetana and Dvořák, this is worth investigating.

(i) *Symphonies Nos 2 in E flat, Op. 38;* (ii) *3 in E min., Op. 53.*
(*) Sup. **CO 1256 [id.]. Brno State PO, (i) Waldhans; (ii) Bělohlávek.

Fibich's *Second Symphony* is the most often played and, though its melodic inspiration is not as spontaneous as that of Dvořák and Smetana, it has considerable appeal. The music proceeds at times in a somewhat predictable way, yet the *Adagio* is undoubtedly eloquent, and elsewhere the writing is congenial and, at its best, as in the scherzo, stirring and colourful. The Brno orchestra under Jiří Waldhans give a straightforward performance and the 1976 recording is clear with plenty of body and a convincing ambient effect, retained in the CD transfer, though the balance does not flatter the tone of the front desks. The *Third Symphony*, like the *Second*, dates from the last decade of the composer's life: indeed the *Third* was written only two years before his death. The invention is fresher than that of its predecessor and the scherzo with its catchy syncopations has great charm. Fibich at times suffers from a certain squareness, but this symphony is less vulnerable on this score. The performance, directed by Jiří Bělohlávek, is fresh and alive; the 1981 recording, made, like its companion, in the Stadion Hall, Brno, has a concert-hall balance and greater vividness, while being kinder to the excellent strings of the Brno orchestra. The conductor finds a Dvořákian affinity not only in the lyricism of the first movement but also in the central movements; the finale has fine impetus and vigour. This generous coupling (73′) should win Fibich new friends.

Field, John (1782–1837)

Rondo in A flat.
** HMV Dig. **CDC7 47527-2**. Selheim, Coll. Aur. – BOCCHERINI; SCHOBERT: *Concertos.***

Field's *Rondo* is agreeably entertaining, with considerable vigour of invention and a hint of the romanticism we find in his nocturnes. The performance (Eckert Selheim uses a fortepiano) is fully equal to the bravura of the florid treatment of the main theme. The sound is clear and tends to emphasize a lack of charm in the playing.

Finzi, Gerald (1901–56)

Clarinet concerto, Op. 31.
*** Hyp. **CDA 66001**; *KA 66001* [id.]. Thea King, Philh. O, Francis – STANFORD: *Concerto.****
*** ASV Dig. **CDDCA 568**; *ZCDCA 568* [id.]. MacDonald, N. Sinfonia, Bedford – COPLAND: *Concerto*; MOURANT: *Pied Piper.****

Finzi's *Clarinet concerto*, composed in 1948, is one of his finest works. If it lacks the contemplative qualities of the ambitious *Cello concerto*, its more extrovert character is no less compelling. The expressive intensity of the slow movement communicates immediately, and the joyous pastoral lyricism of the finale has sharp memorability. On the Hyperion label, Thea King (pupil of the dedicatee of the concerto, Frederick Thurston, who gave the first performance and advised the composer during composition) gives a definitive performance, strong and clean-cut.

Her characterful timbre, using little or no vibrato, is highly telling against a resonant orchestral backcloth. The accompaniment of the Philharmonia under Alun Francis is sympathetic, bringing out the amiability of the finale in fine contrast to the eloquent *Adagio*. Originally the orchestral recording lacked clarity of internal focus; this has been sharpened in the digital remastering. The strings now sound bright and athletic, with perhaps a hint of shrillness in the violins above the stave. The cassette is smoother, but no less vivid. With Stanford's even rarer concerto this makes a most attractive issue.

The alternative CD from ASV has the advantage of a digital master. The coupling of Finzi and Copland makes an unexpected but attractive mix, with the Canadian clarinettist (and founder-member of the Northern Sinfonia), George MacDonald, giving a brilliant and thoughtful performance, particularly impressive in the spacious, melismatic writing of the slow movement. The finale with its carefree 'travelling' theme could be more lightly handled. Refined recording, with the instruments set slightly at a distance. Again there is a first-class tape (the upper range strikingly clean in detail), and in either medium this makes a fine alternative for those preferring the Copland coupling.

(i) *Clarinet concerto; Love's labours lost: suite; Prelude for string orchestra; Romance for strings.*
*** Nimbus Dig. **NI 5101** [id.]. (i) Alan Hacker; E. String O, Boughton.

Many will welcome a third alternative account of the *Clarinet concerto*, from the highly responsive Alan Hacker, particularly as it is coupled with more of Finzi's music within a generous orchestral collection, playing for some 65′. Alan Hacker's reading is improvisatory in style, freely flexible in tempi with the slow movement at once introspective and rhapsodic. The interpretation finds a release from its essentially elegiac feeling in the songful exhilaration of the finale, with William Boughton's sensitive accompaniment following the changes of mood of his soloist most persuasively. The programme opens with a concert suite of incidental music originally written for a 1946 BBC production of Shakespeare's *Love's labours lost*, subsequently expanded for the 1952 Cheltenham Festival, and again in 1955 for an open-air production of the play. The music begins with attractive fanfares and a melody in the Bliss/Elgar/Walton tradition, and the rest of the suite, which lasts for nearly half an hour, is amiably atmospheric and pleasing in invention and in the colour of its scoring. The two string pieces are by no means slight, and have something in common with Grieg's *Elegiac melodies*, though the atmosphere is unquestionably English. They are played most expressively, and the *Romance* is particularly eloquent in William Boughton's hands. The recording, made in the Great Hall of Birmingham University, has the characteristic richness and ambient warmth we associate with Nimbus's fine series of recordings with this group; inner detail, if not sharp, is generally satisfactory, while the overall effect is most natural.

Eclogue for piano and string orchestra.
*** HMV Dig. **CDC7 49627-2**; *EL 749627-4*. Howard Shelley, City of L. Sinfonia, Hickox – FERGUSON: *Piano concerto* etc.***

This is the central movement of an uncompleted piano concerto which the composer decided could stand on its own. It was Howard Ferguson who edited the final manuscript and set the title, and it is appropriate that this essentially valedictory piece should be coupled with his own concerto. The mood is tranquil yet haunting, and the performance brings out all its serene lyricism. The recording is admirably realistic in both formats.

God is gone up; Lo, the full, final sacrifice; Magnificat.
*** HMV Dig. **CDC7 47663-2**; *EL 270440-4*. King's College, Cambridge, Ch., Cleobury; R. Farnes – BAX: *I sing of a maiden* etc.***

The three Finzi choral-pieces with organ accompaniment provide attractive contrasts to the unaccompanied Bax pieces on a beautifully planned disc which shows the King's Choir at its finest. Both the extended anthem, *Lo, the full, final sacrifice*, setting Richard Crashaw's version of an Aquinas hymn, and the *Magnificat* were commissioned works, the one for St Matthew's, Northampton, the other for Massachusetts; in their rich climaxes they bring out a dramatic side in Finzi along with his gentle beauty, splendidly conveyed by the King's Choir. The recording made in the Chapel is so nicely balanced that part-writing is clear even against the ample acoustic. The iron-oxide tape, however, brings a comparatively blurred focus.

Fiorillo, Federigo (1755– after 1823)

Violin concerto No. 1 in F.

*** Hyp. Dig. **CDA 66210**; *KA 66210* [id.]. Oprean, European Community CO, Faerber – VIOTTI: *Violin concerto No. 13.****

Fiorillo, an exact contemporary of Viotti, with whom he has much in common, was a violin virtuoso who travelled Europe and composed profusely. The present work is charmingly romantic; the *Larghetto* is not ambitious, but the finale is agreeably gay. Adelina Oprean, who won first prize in the London Carl Flesch competition in 1982 and has studied under Menuhin and Sandor Végh, is just the soloist for it. Her playing can only be described as quicksilver: her lightness of bow and firm, clean focus of timbre are most appealing. She is given a warm, polished accompaniment by this first-class chamber orchestra, conducted with vitality and understanding by Joerg Faerber. The recording, made in the attractive ambience of the London Henry Wood Hall, is eminently truthful and well balanced. There is a first-class tape. One's only complaint is that there was room here for a third concerto; the measure is not generous.

Foss, Lukas (born 1922)

Round a common center.

** Pro Arte Dig. **CDD 120** [id.]. Orson Welles, Elaine Bonazzi, Yehudi Menuhin, Cantilena Chamber Players – COPLAND: *Piano quartet*; WYNER: *Intermezzi.***

Round a common center was the outcome of a commission from the Cantilena Chamber Players (a piano quartet) for a new piece to be performed at the US Winter Olympics. The commission asked for optional parts for speaker and violin, as Menuhin was due to play with the group during the Olympics. And so Lukas Foss was confronted with the task of composing a piece that would make sense as a Piano quartet or a Piano quintet, with or without voice. Foss, appropriately enough, chose *The Runner*, a poem by Auden, and his work is tonal and highly resourceful. He calls it a work 'strictly for virtuosi' and it receives a thoroughly committed reading here on this recording, well, if rather forwardly, balanced and sympathetic. Not great music perhaps, but a compelling, thoughtful piece with strong atmosphere.

Fossa, François de (1775–?)

Guitar quartets, Op. 19/1–3.

*** Chan. *ABTD 1109* [id.]. Simon Wynberg, Gabrieli Qt (members).

The repertoire for the guitar is not extensive; these quartets by the French amateur, François de

Fossa, form a useful addition to it. He was born in France in 1775 but emigrated to Spain at the outbreak of the revolution, where he served with distinction as a civil servant and in the army. These quartets make a worthwhile alternative to those of Boccherini, whom de Fossa served as a copyist. These are interesting pieces, well worth reviving, and contain many individual touches. They are beautifully played by Simon Wynberg and the Gabrielis, and pleasingly recorded. Recommended.

Foulds, John (1880–1939)

String quartets Nos 9 (Quartetto intimo), Op. 89; 10 (Quartetto geniale), Op. 97. Aquarelles, Op. 32.
❀ *** Pearl **SHECD 9564** [id.]. Endellion Qt.

This superb first recording by the Endellion Quartet, one of the outstanding groups of its generation, brings an exciting discovery. John Foulds, born in Manchester, was early recognized for his serious work, not least by Hans Richter, conductor of the Hallé, but he later came to be known best for his light music. Then, withdrawing to India in the 1930s, he continued the impressive series of string quartets he had begun in his youth. The *Quartetto intimo*, written in 1931, is a powerful five-movement work in a distinctive idiom more advanced than that of Foulds' British contemporaries, with echoes of Scriabin and Bartók. Also on the disc is the one surviving movement of his tenth and last quartet, a dedicated hymn-like piece, as well as three slighter pieces which are earlier. Passionate performances and excellent recording, which is enhanced by the CD transfer. There is greater presence without loss of body, and the absence of background is especially telling in the two *Lento* from Op. 89 and Op. 97. A uniquely valuable issue.

Françaix, Jean (born 1912)

Piano concertino; Piano concerto.
(**) Ara. Dig. **Z 6541**; ***ABQC 7541* [id.]. Ian Hobson, Sinfonia da Camera – SAINT-SAËNS: *Piano concerto No. 2.**(*)

The charms of the Françaix *Concertino* with its four brief but delectable miniature movements are pretty irresistible, but in this instance they are not fully projected. Ian Hobson's playing is often dazzling, but the balance is synthetic and the orchestra has little substance. The effect is a little too unsmiling. On the CD submitted for review and a second copy tried elsewhere, the opening phrase of the *Concertino* is missing, although the equally engaging *Concerto* is unaffected. This has an appropriate gamin-like quality, but the acoustic is rather cramped. The sound is altogether smoother and more congenial on the cassette. Until the fault on the CD is rectified, this issue is obviously *hors de combat*.

Franck, César (1822–90)

Le chasseur maudit (The accursed huntsman): symphonic poem.
(*) RCA **RD 85750 [RCA **5750-2-RC**]. Boston SO, Munch – POULENC: *Organ concerto***(*); SAINT-SAËNS: *Symphony No. 3.****

Le chasseur maudit; Les Éolides; Psyché (orchestral sections only).
(*) Erato Dig. **ECD 88167 [id.]. Basle SO, Jordan.

These three underrated works by Franck get excellent performances from Armin Jordan. There is much fine musicianship in evidence in *Psyché*, and the playing of the Basle orchestra has delicacy and sensitivity. Jordan generates considerable excitement in *Le chasseur maudit*, one of Beecham's favourites; this is a worthy successor to his celebrated account, and both *Les Éolides* and the orchestral movements we are given from *Psyché* show real *tendresse*. The only thing lacking is real weight of sonority in the lower strings, but the intelligence of the playing makes up for this. Recommended.

Munch's performance of *Le chasseur maudit* is also vivid and exciting and comes as part of a generous compilation showing him in good form in repertoire for which he has a natural feeling. The present recording dates from 1962 and sounds quite spectacular, with plenty of fullness, if with a touch of inflation, provided by the warm acoustics of Symphony Hall, Boston. Franck's horn calls come over arrestingly. As an engaging extra, the CD offers four cued subtitles for the music, reminiscent of a Victorian lantern-slide show, notably the last two sections: '*The Curse*' and '*The demons' chase*'.

Symphonic variations for piano and orchestra.
(*) RCA **RD 85666. Rubinstein, NY Symphony of the Air, Wallenstein – FALLA: *Nights* etc.; SAINT-SAËNS: *Concerto No. 2*.**(*)
(*) Decca **417 583-2 [id.]. De Larrocha, LPO, Frühbeck de Burgos – FAURÉ: *Fantaisie*; RAVEL: *Piano concertos*.***

Rubinstein's recording of the *Symphonic variations* was the first to appear in stereo and remains one of the finest available recorded performances of it. There is refinement and charm, yet his bravura tautens the structure while his warmth and freedom prevent it from seeming hard or in any way aggressive. The sound is dry but its intimacy is attractive.

The Spanish interpreters, Alicia de Larrocha and Frühbeck de Burgos, give a reading that, more than usual, brings out the delicacy of the *Variations* while the pleasingly warm and atmospheric 1973 Decca recording adds to the romantic feeling. Both Rubinstein and Curzon display more charisma in this work, but De Larrocha is undoubtedly beguiling, and her couplings are even more recommendable and certainly generous: the CD plays for 73′.

Reminder. Clifford Curzon's 1960 Decca performance with the LSO under Boult has stood the test of time. It is an engagingly fresh reading without idiosyncrasy and can be recommended unreservedly in its present tape format, coupled with equally impressive accounts of the Grieg *Piano concerto* and the Litolff *Scherzo* (*KJBC 104*). We hope this may arrive as a Decca Ovation mid-priced CD during the lifetime of this book.

Symphony in D min.
(M) ❀ *(**) RCA *GK85261* [*AGK15261*]. Chicago SO, Monteux.
(***) Ph. mono **416 214-2** [id.]. Concg. O, Mengelberg – R. STRAUSS: *Don Juan*.(***)
(*) DG Dig. **400 070-2 [id.]. O Nat. de France, Bernstein (with SAINT-SAËNS: *Rouet d'Omphale****).
(*) Decca **417 287-2** [id.]. VPO, Furtwängler – SCHUMANN: *Symphony No. 1*.(**)

Symphony in D min.; Le chasseur maudit.
(*) HMV Dig. **CDC7 47849-2 [id.]. Phd. O, Muti.

Symphony in D min.; Psyché: Psyché et Eros.
*(*) DG Dig. **419 605-2**; *419 605-4* [id.]. BPO, Giulini.

Symphony in D min.; (i) *Symphonic variations.*
(M) **(*) HMV **CDM7 69008-2**; *EG 290853-4*. (i) Weissenberg; BPO, Karajan.
(*) Decca Dig. **417 487-2; *417 487-4* [id.]. (i) Bolet; Concg. O, Chailly.
** HMV Dig. **CDC7 47547-2** [id.]. (i) Collard; Capitole Toulouse O, Plasson.

Monteux's stereo recording of the Franck *Symphony* was made in Chicago in January 1961. It has been absent from the British catalogues for two decades, and during that period it has never been surpassed. Beecham's 1962 account is not quite its equal, nor are the Boult or Maazel versions from the same era, or indeed Karajan's – although all these are fine performances with insights of their own. Monteux exerts a unique grip on this highly charged Romantic symphony, and his control of the continuous ebb and flow of tempo and tension is masterly, so that any weaknesses of structure in the outer movements are disguised. His reading brings a sense of mystery at the very opening while the *Andante* becomes a centrepiece of elegiac delicacy. The splendid playing of the Chicago orchestra is ever responsive to the changes of mood: the fervour of the thrusting chromatic secondary tune of the first movement is matched by the dynamism of the transformation of the main theme of the *Andante* when it reappears in the finale, before the superbly prepared apotheosis of the coda. Reissued in RCA's 'Legendary Performances' series (the sobriquet for once fully justified), the sound has been digitally freshened, but the harshness in the brass remains, and the added clarification has brought a degree of edge to the upper range at climaxes which need taming if listening is to be comfortable. However, the Chicago ambience provides an underlying fullness and weight, and in Monteux's hands Franck's work takes its place naturally alongside the great Romantic symphonies. We hope that when this appears on CD the sound will be further improved.

Karajan's recording of the Franck *Symphony* dates from 1970 and marked the beginning of a relatively brief recording period with EMI, before he returned to DG. It is a large-scale performance, given strong projection by the CD remastering. Karajan's tempi are all on the slow side, but his control of rhythm prevents any feeling of sluggishness or heaviness. There is always energy underlying the performance, and by facing the obvious problems squarely Karajan avoids the perils. The impact of the recording, now sounding more brightly lit but with textures still full and bold, is considerable; there is potent atmosphere and the finale has both amplitude and plenty of bite. Weissenberg's account of the *Symphonic variations* has less distinction, but the poetry of the lyrical sections is not missed and Karajan ensures that the orchestral contribution is a strong one. Taken as a whole, this is spontaneous and enjoyable if not outstanding. The sound is full and clear, the balance favouring the orchestra slightly more than usual, but the pianist is realistically defined. There is a well-managed cassette.

Riccardo Chailly's performance of the *Symphony* is weighty and well considered. He pays scrupulous attention to dynamic shadings and nuances, and the overall effect, particularly in the first movement, is one of seriousness. In its way it is an impressive account, with first-class playing from the Concertgebouw Orchestra and no want of tonal refinement. Jorge Bolet brings a certain majesty and great clarity to the *Symphonic variations* without having quite the same delicacy as Rubinstein, De Larrocha or Collard. The sound is eminently satisfactory, and the balance on the whole well judged. Not perhaps a first choice, but certainly among the best. There is a very good tape, with the textures of the *Symphony* not too opulent, and the *Variations* very well balanced.

Bernstein conducts a warmly expressive performance which, thanks in part to a live recording, carries conviction in its flexible spontaneity. It has its moments of vulgarity, but that is part of the work. Next to Monteux, the very opening may sound sticky, and the central *Allegretto* is unusually slow and drawn out, while the return of the *Allegretto* in the finale brings a vulgar slowing; but the reservations are of less importance next to the glowing positive qualities of the performance. The recording is vivid and opulent, but with the brass apt to sound strident. The compact disc version brings out the qualities the more positively and is specially valuable for its absence of background in the *Allegretto* and the expanses of the slow introduction.

Plasson on EMI gives a very straightforward and unfussy account of the *Symphony* with his Orchestre du Capitole, Toulouse, which has conviction, though its dynamic range is less wide than some rivals. Yet though there is much more to admire than to criticize, when the last note dies away you are not left feeling that it is as great a work as it seems in the hands of Beecham or Monteux. The recording is a little opaque, certainly not top-drawer EMI. Jean-Philippe Collard's performance of the *Symphonic variations* is characteristically sensitive and full of imaginative colours. It is touched by distinction and deserves to be available in a different and perhaps more competitive coupling.

Muti's is a strongly committed but unsentimental reading. The cor anglais solo in the *Allegretto* is most beautiful and the finale is particularly refreshing in its directness. The fill-up is welcome, a vividly dramatic symphonic poem, strongly presented; but with Karajan's version at mid-price, this is not especially competitive, except for those seeking a digital master. The 1983 recording, robust and vivid, is certainly improved in its CD format, generally well integrated and among EMI's better Philadelphia records made in the 1980s.

Giulini and the Berlin Philharmonic – an unexpected combination in this work – take an extremely spacious view. With textures well upholstered, the first movement *allegro* at an extraordinarily slow speed sounds ponderous, and the scherzando element is completely missing in the contrasting passages of the central *Allegretto*, while the finale with its exhilarating main theme lacks energy. Though Giulini conducts with total dedication and the playing is superb, this is one of his less successful records.

Among the historical recordings, the Mengelberg stands out: it is one of the more desirable of the Mengelberg transfers to CD. In his hands, the *Symphony* is highly intense and dramatic and has one sitting on the edge of one's seat. The slow movement is very tautly held together and the playing of the incomparable Concertgebouw Orchestra incandescent. Whether one likes these interpretations or not, this is playing of the highest voltage whose current, thanks to the miracle of digital recording, triumphantly traverses four decades and glows with astonishing freshness. The sound is amazingly good, all things considered, and the Philips engineers have managed to secure excellent definition and detail.

Furtwängler's 1953 recording for Decca brings a characteristically heavyweight reading, rugged in its spacious but purposeful manner. It makes a fascinating historical document, presenting a great conductor in unexpected repertory; but the sound is restricted, with CD clarifying not just orchestral textures but distortions as well.

String quartet in D.
* Denon Dig. **C37 7806** [id.]. Prague Qt.

Franck's *Quartet* is highly ambitious in its scale: its almost orchestral textures and its complex use of cyclic form always seem on the point of bursting the seams of the intimate genre of the string quartet. Yet as a very late inspiration it contains some of the composer's most profound and most compelling thought. In every sense this is a work which seeks to take up the challenge presented by late Beethoven in a way that few nineteenth-century composers attempted, not even Brahms.

The present account by the Prague Quartet is inadequate. It dates from 1980 and, though played with confidence and conviction, is wanting in variety of colour and dynamic shading, and the actual sound is confined and unventilated. No doubt the outstanding Fitzwilliam version on Oiseau-Lyre will soon return to the catalogue in CD format.

Violin sonata in A.
*** DG Dig. **415 683-2**; *415 683-4* [id.]. Shlomo Mintz, Yefim Bronfman – RAVEL; DEBUSSY: *Sonatas.****
*** Ph. Dig. **416 157-2**; *416 157-4* [id.]. Pinchas Zukerman, Marc Neikrug – SAINT-SAËNS: *Sonata No. 1.****

*** Decca **414 128-2** [id.]. Itzhak Perlman, Vladimir Ashkenazy – BRAHMS: *Horn trio*.***
(*) Erato Dig. **ECD 88177; *MCE 75258* [id.]. Pierre Amoyal, Mikhail Rudy – GRIEG: *Sonata No. 3*.**(*)

On DG, Shlomo Mintz and Yefim Bronfman give a superbly confident account of the *Sonata*. It is impeccably played with wonderfully true intonation from the violinist and highly accomplished support from the pianist. They are splendidly recorded, too. This can rank alongside the several superb accounts to have appeared in recent years (notably Chung and Lupu on Decca). The matching chrome cassette is also outstandingly truthful.

A powerfully volatile performance from Zukerman and Marc Neikrug, with the central section attractively free. Throughout, the music making has the thrust and inspiration of a live recital and, with the recording in the demonstration class in its vivid realism and presence – on the splendid chrome cassette as well as the CD – this too can receive the strongest advocacy.

Although derived from a 1980 analogue master, readers who fancy the excellent Brahms coupling need have no hesitations about acquiring the recording by Perlman and Ashkenazy. The first movement catches the listener by the ears with its forward impulse, and the passionate commitment of the playing in no way swamps the work's lyrical flow. The CD transfer is admirably done and the analogue sound is enhanced, although the warmly atmospheric ambience means that there is not the sharpness of detail one would expect in a digital recording.

Pierre Amoyal and Mikhail Rudy are let down by inadequate recording. Amoyal's playing is masterly – as anyone who has heard him live will expect – purity of tone, intelligent phrasing and keen imagination are all in evidence. Unfortunately the engineers do not do justice to Mikhail Rudy's accompaniment: the piano is ill defined and wanting a realistic presence. Amoyal's playing is mostly glorious, and readers prepared to overlook the shortcomings of the recording will be rewarded by many musical insights.

Cello sonata in A (arr. of *Violin sonata*).
** ASV Dig. *ZCDCA 522* [id.]. Colin Carr, Francis Grier – DEBUSSY: *Sonata*; FAURÉ: *Élégie* etc.**

The Franck *Violin sonata* has come more and more to be performed and recorded in its optional cello version. Carr's recording, powerfully and warmly expressive, can be recommended to anyone wanting the Debussy and Fauré couplings. Clear, rather dry digital recording.

ORGAN MUSIC

Cantabile; Chorale No. 1; Fantaisie in C; Pièce héroïque; Prélude, fugue and variation.
**(*) Unicorn *DKPC 9013* [id.]. Jennifer Bate.

3 Chorales; Pastorale, Op. 19; Prélude, fugue et variation, Op. 18.
*** Argo Dig. **411 710-2** [id.]. Peter Hurford.

Chorale No. 2 in B min.; Fantaisie in C, Op. 16; Grande pièce symphonique, Op. 17.
(*) Unicorn Dig. **DKPCD 9014; *DKPC 9014* [id.]. Jennifer Bate.

Chorale No. 3 in A min.; Final in B flat, Op. 21; Pastorale, Op. 19; Prière in C sharp min., Op. 20.
** Unicorn Dig. **DKPCD 9030**; *DKPC 9030* [id.]. Jennifer Bate.

Peter Hurford is recorded on a Cavaillé-Coll at the Church of Saint-Sernin, Toulouse, and has the benefit not only of the right instrument but of the right engineers. His are masterly accounts of the three *Chorales* Franck composed in the last year of his life: these performances are beautifully shaped and grandly paced, and there is no real doubt that, among modern digital recordings, this leads the field in the compact disc format.

Jennifer Bate plays the Danion-Gonzalez organ at Beauvais Cathedral and is given the benefit of an excellent digital recording. The spacious acoustic contributes an excellent ambience to the aural image, and Miss Bate's brilliance is not in question. In general, however, Peter Hurford is musically more satisfying and every bit as well recorded. Nevertheless, the first of the Unicorn series offers fine accounts of the *Cantabile* and the *Pièce héroïque*, of which the latter seems rather well suited to the massive sounds which the Beauvais organ can command.

In the third volume of Jennifer Bate's survey (**DKPCD 9030**) the digital sound is as impressive as in earlier issues, and the fine organ at Beauvais Cathedral is shown to best advantage. She rushes the opening of the *A minor Chorale*, some of whose detail does not register in this acoustic at the speed, though the *Pastorale* and the *Prière* fare better. The cassette transfers are well managed throughout the series.

Fantaisie in A; Pastorale.
*** Telarc Dig. **CD 80096** [id.]. Michael Murray (organ of Symphony Hall, San Francisco) – JONGEN: *Symphonie concertante.****

Michael Murray plays these pieces very well and, although the San Francisco organ is not tailor-made for them, they are certainly effective as a fill-up for Jongen's engagingly spectacular *Symphonie concertante*. The Telarc recording is well up to standard.

VOCAL AND CHORAL MUSIC

Les Béatitudes.
(*) Erato Dig. **ECD 88217 (2) [id.]. Lebrun, Berbié, Stutzmann, Randall, Jeffes, Vanaud, Loup, Ottevaere, French R. Ch. & Nouvel PO, Jordan.

Les Béatitudes has been out of circulation for some years: the Schwann Musica Sacra version conducted by Jean Alain was made as long ago as 1962. The oratorio occupied Franck through the 1870s, but despite the revival of interest in his work in recent years, it has never really established itself. There is much writing of quality as one would expect, but also much that is pedestrian by the standards of the *Symphony*, the *Sonata* or *Psyché*. Also on such a canvas – the score runs to two hours – the invention is curiously deficient in character and in rhythmic variety. The recording was made at a live performance in Paris in 1985 and is sensitively shaped under the baton of Armin Jordan. The solo singers are more than adequate, the choral and orchestral contributions are also admirable, and the sound-picture is very natural.

Frescobaldi, Giralomo (1583–1643)

Canto partite sopra passacagli; Canzon terza della La Crivelli; Canzona terza; Capriccio sopra la bassa fiamenga; Partite 14 sopra l'aria della Romanesca; Toccatas 9 & 10.
(M) *** Tel. **ZS8 43774** [id.]. Bob van Asperen (harpsichord).

Frescobaldi was one of the most important Italian composers in the generation after Monteverdi. He was also a brilliant singer, a powerful organist and harpsichord player and an extraordinary improviser. The excellent Dutch harpsichordist conveys splendidly a feeling of the improvisatory style that Frescobaldi must have commanded in these fine performances. They concentrate on his style in four keyboard genres: the Canzone, the Capriccio, the Toccata and the Partita. Bob van Asperen uses a harpsichord made by Martin Skowroneck and modelled on an Italian instrument of the seventeenth century. The music is full of interesting chromatic touches. The recording, made in 1970, is very closely balanced; it needs to be replayed at about a third of your normal listening level if it is to sound remotely lifelike.

Gabrieli, Giovanni (1557–1612)

Canzon per sonar a 4; Canzoni Nos 4 a 6; 12 a 8; In ecclesiis; Jubilate Deo; O Jesu mi dulcissime; O magnum mysterium; Quem vidistis pastores?; Timor et tremor.
*** Argo Dig. **417 468-2**; *417 468-4* [id.]. King's College, Cambridge, Ch., P. Jones Brass Ens., Cleobury.

The widely resonant acoustics of King's College Chapel make an admirable alternative to St Marks for this repertoire and the Decca team (Chris Hazel and Simon Eadon) are to be congratulated on the success of Gabrieli's major CD début. Particularly in the festive motet, *In ecclesiis*, with its three choirs, plus organ and instrumental accompaniment, is the complex layout convincing and indeed thrilling (although here the trebles – not quite the strongest contingent this choir has ever fielded – can only just compete), but the Christmas motet, *Quem vidistis pastores?*, with its solo voices from the choir representing the shepherds, is also very well managed. Other highlights include the light and joyful *Jubilate Deo* and the highly atmospheric *O magnum mysterium*; while *Timor and tremor* is richly appealing in texture. The programme is given variety by the inclusion of canzoni sonorously played by the Philip Jones brass group. Altogether a fine achievement. There is a splendid chrome tape, but the CD is very much in the demonstration bracket.

Canzona. Sol sol la sol; Sonata pian' e forte. Angelus ad pastores; Audite principes; O magnum mysterium; Quem vidistis pastores; Salvator noster.
(M) *** Decca *417 883-4*. Monteverdi Ch., P. Jones Brass Ens., Gardiner (with MONTEVERDI and BASSANO: *Motets****).

This 1972 collection, originally entitled 'Christmas in Venice', is now allotted to a 'Weekend' on Decca's tape-reissue label. Although the engineering remains impressive, the original excellent documentation has now disappeared; but the performances – among the first to demonstrate John Eliot Gardiner's recording flair – remain compulsive, with the music all effectively edited by the conductor. The Philip Jones Brass add to the splendour of the occasion. The performance of *Quem vidistis pastores*, which is used to close side one, is particularly eloquent; but *Salvator noster*, written for three five-part choirs, is also memorable, rejoicing jubilantly in the birth of Christ. The rest of the concert includes equally fine music by Monteverdi and Giovanni Bassano.

Gade, Niels (1817–90)

Symphonies Nos 1 in C min. (On Sjøland's fair plains), Op. 5; 8 in B minor, Op. 47.
*** BIS Dig. **CD 339** [id.]. Stockholm Sinf., Järvi.

Mendelssohn conducted the première of Gade's *First Symphony* (1841–2) and his influence is all-pervasive. It is a charming piece and in the outer movements quotes a song Gade had composed a few years earlier in 1838. Thirty years separate it from his *Eighth* and last symphony, still much indebted to Mendelssohn. Despite this debt, there is still a sense of real mastery and a command of pace. The Stockholm Sinfonietta and Neeme Järvi give very fresh and lively performances, and the recording is natural and truthful.

Symphonies Nos 2 in E, Op. 10; 7 in F, Op. 45.
(*) BIS Dig. **CD 355 [id.]. Stockholm Sinf., Järvi.

The debt to Mendelssohn here is still enormous but the invention has fluency and charm. The ink was hardly dry on the *First* before Gade embarked on No. 2, which was a huge success when he conducted it in Leipzig in 1844. Schumann thought it 'reminiscent of Denmark's beautiful beechwoods'. It is very likeable and more spontaneous than the *Seventh*, written twenty years later in 1864–5, though this has a delightful scherzo. Splendid playing from the Stockholm Sinfonietta under Järvi, and good recording too.

Symphonies Nos 3 in A min., Op. 15; 4 in B flat, Op. 20.
*** BIS Dig. **CD 338** [id.]. Stockholm Sinf., Järvi.

Throughout Gade's life, Mendelssohn was the dominant influence and the key of No. 3 (1847) naturally prompts one's thoughts to turn to the *Scottish symphony*, composed only five years before. Yet there is great freshness and a seemingly effortless flow of ideas and pace, and with a fine sense of musical proportion. No. 4 (1850) was more generally admired in Gade's lifetime – by the great Bach scholar, Philipp Spitta, among others – but its companion here is the more winning. Like most of its companions in this series, it is beautifully played and recorded.

Symphonies Nos (i) *5 in D min., Op. 35; 6 in G min., Op. 32.*
*** BIS Dig. **CD 356** [id.]. Stockholm Sinf., Järvi; (i) with Roland Pöntinen.

In 1852 Gade married the daughter of the long-lived Danish composer, J. P. E. Hartmann (1805–1900). His engagement present was the charming *Spring fantasy* for voices, piano and orchestra, and his wedding present was the *Fifth Symphony*. This is a delightfully sunny piece which lifts one's spirits; its melodies are instantly memorable, and there is a lively concertante part for the piano, splendidly played by the young Roland Pöntinen. Delightful music which will give much pleasure. Sadly, his bride died three years later, though it would be difficult to discern any sense of this tragedy from the *Sixth Symphony* of 1857. It is rather more thickly scored and more academic. The recording is perhaps less transparent and open than others in the series but, given the charm of the *Fifth Symphony* and the persuasiveness of the performance, it must be warmly recommended.

Geminiani, Francesco (1687–1772)

Concerti grossi, Op. 2/5–7; Op. 3/3; Op. 7/2; in D min. (*after Corelli: Op. 5/12*)*: Theme & variations* (*La Follia*).
*** HMV Dig. **CDC7 47656-2**. La Petite Bande, Sigiswald Kuijken.

A more considerable and innovative figure than is generally supposed, the quality of invention in the Geminiani concertos recorded here rises high above the routine. There is considerable expressive depth in some of the slow movements, too. La Petite Bande is incomparably superior to many of the period-instrument ensembles; the string-tone is light and feathery, accents are never overemphatic, and there is a splendid sense of movement. Readers who are normally allergic to the vinegary offerings of some rivals will find this record a joy. It is beautifully recorded too. In short, this makes an admirable introduction to this underrated and genial composer.

6 Concerti grossi, Op. 3.
*** O-L **417 522-2** [id.]. AAM, Schröder; Hogwood.

Some of these concertos have been available in various anthologies, but this is the first complete set for some years, and it reveals the vigour and freshness of Geminiani's invention to admirable effect. Though Burney hailed Op. 3 as establishing Geminiani's character and placing him at the head of all the masters then living, it must be conceded that they are less inspired than Handel or the best of Vivaldi, though still melodious and resourceful. They are given performances of genuine quality by the Academy of Ancient Music under their Dutch leader, and readers normally resistant to the cult of authentic instruments can be reassured that there is no lack of vigour, body and breadth in these performances. They are also extremely well recorded (analogue, 1976), although the CD transfer notices some studio noise and there is a curious moment of background hum which comes up suddenly and disappears on track 8 (Op. 3/2).

German, Edward (1862–1936)

Welsh rhapsody.
(M) *** HMV **CDM7 69206-2**; *ED 290208-4*, SNO, Gibson – HARTY: *With the Wild Geese;* MACCUNN: *Land of Mountain and Flood;* SMYTH: *The Wreckers overture.****

Edward German's *Welsh rhapsody*, written for the Cardiff Festival of 1904, makes a colourful and exciting finale for this enterprising collection of genre British tone-pictures. German is content not to interfere with the traditional melodies he uses, relying on his orchestral skill to retain the listener's interest, in which he is very successful. The closing pages, based on *Men of Harlech*, are prepared in a Tchaikovskian manner to provide a rousing conclusion. This is a good example of a tune with an inbuilt eloquence that cannot be improved upon. The CD transfer is very well managed, though the ear perceives a slight limitation in the upper range. There is a very good cassette.

Merrie England (opera): complete (without dialogue).
(B) ** CfP *TC-CFPD 4710*. Bronhill, Sinclair, Kern, McAlpine, Glossop, Glynne, Williams Singers, O, Michael Collins.

Although all the singers here were in fact from the Sadler's Wells company this is not the Sadler's Wells production, but one conceived at EMI. The 1960 recording, which has a tendency to edginess, suggests a production team from the popular rather than the classical side of the company. However, the stereo has atmosphere and the cassette transfer tends to smooth off the vocal sound, though the focus is not absolutely clean. Taken as a whole, the score does not wear too well (much of it sounds like diluted Gilbert and Sullivan). But if the moments of coarseness in the libretto can be forgiven, there is much pleasing lyricism in German's music and one or two really outstanding tunes which will ensure that the score survives. Among the soloists Howell Glynne is splendid as King Neptune, and Monica Sinclair sings with her usual richness and makes *O peaceful England* more moving than usual. Patricia Kern's mezzo is firm and forward, while McAlpine as Sir Walter Raleigh sings with fine, ringing voice. The Rita Williams Singers are thoroughly professional even if just occasionally their style is suspect.

Gershwin, George (1898–1937)

An American in Paris.
(*) DG **419 625-2 [id.]. San Francisco SO, Ozawa – BERNSTEIN: *West Side Story: Symphonic dances***(*)*; RUSSO: *Street music.***

An American in Paris; (i) *Piano concerto in F.*
(*) ASV Dig. **CDRPO 8009; *ZCRPO 8009* [id.]. (i) Vakarelis; RPO, Henry Lewis.

An American in Paris: (i) *Piano concerto in F;* (ii) *Rhapsody in blue.*
*** HMV **CDC7 47161-2**; (M) *EG 290849-4* [id.]. André Previn with LSO.
(*) Ph. Dig. **412 611-2; *412 611-4* [id.]. André Previn with Pittsburgh SO.
(M) *** Ph. **420 492-2**; *420 492-4* [id.]. (i; ii) Werner Haas; Monte Carlo Op. O, De Waart.
(B) *** CfP **CFPD-9012**; *TC-CFP 4413-4*. (i; ii) Blumenthal; ECO, Steuart Bedford.
(B) **(*) DG Walkman *413 851-4* [id.]. San Francisco SO, Ozawa; (i) Szidon, LPO, Downes; (ii) Siegfried Stöckigt, Leipzig GO, Masur – BERNSTEIN: *West Side Story: Symphonic dances.****
*(*) Ara. Dig. **Z 6587**; *ABQC 6587* [id.]. (i; ii) David Golub; LSO, Mitch Miller.

An American in Paris; (i) *Piano concerto in F; Rhapsody in blue; Variations on 'I got rhythm'.*
(M) **(*) RCA **GD 86519;** *GK 86519* [**RCA 6519-2-RG**]. (i) Earl Wild; Boston Pops O, Fiedler.

An American in Paris; Cuban overture; Lullaby; (i) *Rhapsody in blue* (version for 2 pianos).
** Decca Dig. **417 326-2**; *417 326-4* [id.]. (i) Katia & Marielle Labèque; Cleveland O, Chailly.

An American in Paris; Cuban overture; Porgy & Bess: symphonic picture (arr. Bennett).
** RCA Dig. **RCD 14551** [**RCD1 4551**]; (M) *GK 84551*. Dallas SO, Mata.

An American in Paris; Cuban overture; (i) *Rhapsody in blue.*
(M) ** Decca **417 716-2**; *417 716-4* [id.]. (i) Ivan Davis; Cleveland O, Maazel – COPLAND: *Appalachian spring* etc.***

(i) *An American in Paris;* (ii) *Rhapsody in blue.*
❀ *** CBS **MK 42264** [id.]. (i) NYPO, Bernstein; (ii) Bernstein with Columbia SO – GROFÉ: *Grand Canyon suite.***
(*) Telarc Dig. **CD 80058 [id.]. Eugene List, Cincinnati SO, Kunzel.

Piano concerto in F; Rhapsody in blue; Second Rhapsody.
(*) MMG **MCD 10111 [id.]. Jeffrey Siegel, St Louis SO, Slatkin.

Rhapsody in blue; Prelude for piano No. 2.
(*) DG Dig. **410 025-2; *3302 082* [id.]. Bernstein with LAPO – BERNSTEIN: *West Side Story: Symphonic dances.****

With the arrival in 1987 of the fiftieth anniversary of Gershwin's death, the various permutations of *An American in Paris* and the ever fresh *Rhapsody in blue* proliferated to an extraordinary degree, with reissues vying with various new versions. Towering over them all is Bernstein's 1959 coupling recorded when (at the beginning of his forties) he was at the peak of his creativity, with *West Side story* only two years behind him. This record set the standard by which all subsequent pairings of these two works came to be judged. It still sounds astonishingly well as a recording; the CD has brought only enhancement and a decrease of background; the *Rhapsody* in particular has better piano-tone than CBS often provided in the 1970s, while the NYPO brass brings splendid weight and bite, and the strings show plenty of bloom. Bernstein's approach is inspirational, exceptionally flexible but completely spontaneous. Although the jazzy element is not masked, it is essentially a concert performance, fully justifying the expanded orchestration, masterly in every way, with much broader tempi than in the composer's piano-roll version, but quixotic in mood, rhythmically subtle and creating a life-enhancing surge of human warmth at the entry of the big central tune. The performance of *An American in Paris* is vividly characterized, brash and episodic; an unashamedly American view, with the great blues tune marvellously timed and phrased as only a great American orchestra can do it. Though the Grofé bonus is by no means indispensable, the Gershwin performances most certainly are.

André Previn has made two excellent records offering the obvious triptych of the *American in Paris*, *Concerto* and *Rhapsody* (where there are some textual abbreviations), and until now we have been more attracted to the later digital version on Philips. But the digital remastering of the HMV set, made over a decade earlier at the beginning of the 1970s, has brought an extraordinary enhancement of the recording itself and the way these earlier performances are projected. There is now much more sparkle, and the extra vividness comes without loss of body; indeed, in the *Concerto* the strings sound particularly full and fresh and the piano timbre clean and natural. The performance of the *Concerto* was always a fine one by any standards, but now the *Rhapsody* sounds more charismatic too. With a nostalgically rich presentation of the big tune and much affectionate detail from Previn at the piano, one senses many affinities with the famous Bernstein account. Maybe *An American in Paris* has more structural cohesion on Previn's Philips version, but the HMV performance is exuberantly volatile, and the entry of the great blues tune on the trumpet has a memorable rhythmic lift. There is a good bright tape, but it does not match the CD in refinement.

The Previn Philips performances have merits of their own, and it is only the excessive reverberation of the digital recording that brings any serious reservation. On CD the dynamic range is spectacularly wide and the cymbals overwhelmingly prominent (the percussion-led opening of the *Concerto* certainly commands attention). Brightness and imagination are the hallmarks, with Previn finding a skittish scherzando quality in his solo playing, both at the opening of the *Rhapsody* and in the first movement of the *Concerto* (which is again a memorable performance overall). There is obvious affection too, as in the big tune of the *Rhapsody* (warm yet never schmaltzy) and in the graceful orchestral phrasing of the lyrical secondary themes of the outer movements of the *Concerto*. The *Adagio* is nostalgically poetic, with the solo trumpet outstanding, as in the great blues tune of *An American in Paris*, while the Pittsburgh woodwind play beautifully throughout both works. Previn knits the structure of Gershwin's Paris evocation convincingly together, yet his touch remains light-hearted, and the jazzy 'nightclub' sequence has a splendid rhythmic exuberance. On the excellent chrome cassette, the dynamic contrast – though still wide – is slightly reduced and the enthusiastic cymbals are tempered by the smoother overall sound-picture which, nevertheless, retains its vividness.

Among the British and European compilations, the Philips collection from Monte Carlo stands out. This is contemporary with the first Previn version, dating from 1971/2. Again digital remastering has brought noticeable improvement in the sound which always had appealing body and warmth; now the treble is brighter but not edgier and, although the upper range is still not as wide as on more recent versions, there is no real feeling of restriction. The *Concerto* is particularly successful; its lyrical moments have a quality of nostalgia which is very attractive. Werner Haas is a volatile and sympathetic soloist, and his rhythmic verve is refreshing. Edo de Waart's *An American in Paris* is not only buoyant but glamorous, too – the big blues melody is highly seductive and, as with all the best accounts of this piece the episodic nature of the writing is hidden. There is a cultured, European flavour to this music making that does not detract from its vitality, and the jazz inflections are not missed, with plenty of verve in the *Rhapsody*. There is an excellent matching chrome cassette.

At bargain price and with first-rate recording Daniel Blumenthal, American prizewinner in the 1983 Leeds Piano Competition, gives performances of the two concertante pieces which convincingly combine Ravelian delicacy of articulation with genuine feeling for the jazz-based idiom. The syncopations are often naughtily pointed, to delightful effect, and Bedford and the ECO, unlikely accompanists as they may be, give warm and understanding support. *An American in Paris* is warmly done too but with less panache, the episodic nature of the piece undisguised. But for those wanting a cultured flavour in this music, this can be strongly recommended. The warmly resonant recording is only marginally clarified on CD and there is some bass emphasis (most noticeable in the *Concerto*).

The mid-priced RCA CD (with excellent matching tape) is particularly generous (70′) in including, besides the usual triptych, the *'I got rhythm' variations*, given plenty of rhythmic panache. Indeed these are essentially jazzy performances: Earl Wild's playing is full of energy and brio, and he inspires Arthur Fiedler to a similarly infectious response. In many ways these performances are as fine as any; if the *Rhapsody* has not the breadth of Bernstein's account, it is nearer the Paul Whiteman original and is rewarding in quite a different way. The outer movements of the *Concerto* are comparably volatile and the blues feeling of the slow movement is strong. At the end of *An American in Paris* Fiedler adds to the exuberance by bringing in a bevy of motor horns. The brightly remastered recording suits the music making, though the resonant Boston acoustics at times prevent absolute sharpness of focus: the spectacular percussion at the beginning of the *Concerto* should ideally sound cleaner.

The DG Walkman tape provides a mid-European slant on Gershwin, although the performance of the *Rhapsody* comes from further East, with the Leipzig Gewandhaus Orchestra under Masur providing a cultured accompaniment to the extremely lively account of the piano part by Siegfried Stöckigt. The jazzy flavour is enhanced by the blend of saxophone and string timbre in the big tune, which has an air of pre-1939 Berlin. The performance of the *Concerto* is even finer, with Robert Szidon treating the work as he would any other Romantic concerto; with rhythms superbly lithe and subtle tonal colouring, the result has both freshness and stature. The jazz idiom is seen here as an essential, but not overwhelmingly dominant, element. Downes and the LPO match the soloist in understanding and virtuosity. The softness of focus of Ozawa's account of *An American in Paris* fits in well with this more restrained approach to Gershwin's genius, especially as the sound throughout this chrome tape is full as well as vivid. The Bernstein coupling is no less attractive. Ozawa's *American in Paris* is also issued on CD, and this 1977 recording sounds well in digitally remastered form. It is easy to respond to such opulence, with the performers revealing the music's vivid tunefulness and rich scoring, but this is clearly overpriced and should have been reissued on DG's mid-priced label – the Russo coupling is far from indispensable.

Jeffrey Siegel's CD comes from a group of recordings he made for Vox in 1974. The performance of the *Rhapsody in blue* is among the finest, substantial yet full of those jazzy inflections which give the music its character and lift. The *Concerto* is a lightweight account, essentially lyrical but again very idiomatic, with the blues feeling in the slow movement obviously in the bones of the performers. The finale has plenty of zest. It was a pity that the *I got rhythm variations* was not chosen instead of the *Second Rhapsody*, but the performers do their best for the latter piece. The recording is sumptuous with a gorgeously resonant bass; the upper range has been slightly smoothed to remove the hiss, but the results are still very attractive.

Eugene List has also recorded the *Rhapsody in blue* for Turnabout. On that occasion he used the original scoring; on Telarc he is accompanied by a full symphony orchestra and very sumptuously recorded indeed, in a glowingly resonant acoustic. Some of the work's rhythmically abrasive qualities are submerged, but the pianist does not lose the skittish character of the work's scherzando section. The rich sound is ideal for those who like to wallow in the melodic richness of *An American in Paris*. The blues tune certainly sounds expansive and there is no real lack of vitality, although in both works the hi-fi conscious engineers have provided rather too much bass drum (a characteristic of Telarc CDs).

In his most recent recording for DG, Bernstein rather goes over the top with his jazzing of the solos in Gershwin. The encore too brings seductively swung rhythms, one of the three solo piano *Preludes*. Such rhythmic freedom was clearly the result of a live rather than a studio performance. The big melody in *Rhapsody in blue* is rather too heavily pointed for comfort (almost in the style of his reading of Elgar's *Nimrod*), but the effect of live recording is electric. The immediacy of the occasion is most compellingly projected on the compact disc, and there is also an excellent cassette, but this does not match Bernstein's inspired 1959 analogue coupling for CBS.

The performances by Janis Vakarelis and the RPO, strongly directed by Henry Lewis, have the advantage of a first-class digital recording, made in the Henry Wood Hall, London. The sound and balance are most realistic. The performance of the *Concerto* is spontaneously fresh, with the lyrical and rhythmic elements well contrasted and affectionately underlined: the blues theme in the slow movement produces an attractive, easy trumpet solo and an admirable response from the RPO woodwind. *An American in Paris* is vigorously done, though the fluent treatment of the blues tune lacks sentience; however, there is more first-class trumpet playing in the night-club sequence and the piece ends enthusiastically (though without motor horns), even if some of the accenting on the way lacks transatlantic rhythmic flair. But with only two works included this does not stand up well against the stiff competition. There is a very successful chrome cassette.

Chailly's Decca programme has characteristically spectacular Decca Cleveland recording, which gives vivid projection and colour to the dance rhythms of the *Cuban overture*, a warm glow to the strings in the *Lullaby* (a fine piece), and a brightly lit Parisian scene. The performance of *An American in Paris* is notable for its powerfully extrovert trumpet solo in the blues sequence, and Chailly's account is altogether invigorating. There seems no special reason, however, for preferring the two-piano version of the *Rhapsody*, and the Labèque duo make their account more controversial by adding their own improvisatory element (more decorative than substantial) to the piano parts. The playing, as in their earlier recording without orchestra, does not lack sparkle, but the performance is not entirely idiomatic.

Maazel's triptych dates from 1974. The performances of all three works are strikingly energetic (Ivan Davis both brilliant and sophisticated in the *Rhapsody*) and the boisterous account of the *Cuban overture* is immensely spirited, almost disguising its emptiness. But the big tune at the centre of the *Rhapsody* and the blues melody in *An American in Paris* (given an upbeat reading) have a lack of sensuous warmth which means that a dimension is missing in both works. The chrome tape is well managed, but the sound is somewhat more subdued than on the extremely lively CD.

Mata's performances are recorded in sumptuous digital sound and the compact disc offers gorgeously rich textures. But the conductor is not completely at home in this repertoire and the playing tends to lack vitality. The *Porgy and Bess symphonic picture* is the most successful piece here, but Dorati's CD is even finer – see below.

Mitch Miller travelled with Gershwin on a 1934 trans-American tour, playing oboe in a 55-piece orchestra conducted by Leo Reisman and Charles Previn (uncle of André), so this music has been in his bones throughout a distinguished musical career in popular music and frequently flirting with the classics. All the more disappointing, then, to record that his readings are unacceptably self-conscious and eccentric. The disc overall plays for 74 minutes; the first movement of the *Concerto*, for instance, takes 1½ minutes longer than Previn's Philips version, and the *Rhapsody in blue* 18′ 49″ against Bernstein's (CBS) 16′ 26″, which, even allowing for any minor textual changes, makes a difference. In the *Concerto* – although he has a responsive soloist and the strength of his personality carries the music making – he is very lyrically indulgent indeed, while the big climax of the blues tune in *An American in Paris* is held back, rhythmically grotesquely mannered against insistent drum-beats. The recording – made at EMI's Abbey Road Studios – has striking presence and realism, and the music making has undoubted spontaneity, but such mannerisms do not bear the scrutiny of repetition.

(i) *An American in Paris;* (ii) *Broadway overtures: Girl crazy; Funny face; Let 'em eat cake; Of thee I sing; Oh Kay!; Strike up the band.* (iii) *Rhapsody in blue* (original version).

(*) CBS **MK 42240 [id.]. (i) NYPO; (ii) Buffalo PO; (iii) George Gershwin (piano-roll), Columbia Jazz Band; Tilson Thomas.

(i; ii) *Rhapsody in blue;* (iii) *Overtures: Girl crazy; Strike up the band.* (iv) *But not for me* (medley);

Nice work if you can get it (medley)*;* Songs: *Do, do, do it again; Fascinatin' rhythm; Foggy day; I've got a crush on you; The man I love; Sweet and low-down; Porgy and Bess: excerpts.*
(B) **(*) CBS *MGT 39488*. (i) Composer (from 1925 piano-roll), (ii) Columbia Jazz Band; (iii) Buffalo PO; (iv) Sarah Vaughan; LAPO; cond. Tilson Thomas.

Rhapsody in blue; Second Rhapsody; Preludes for piano; Short story (1925); Violin piece; For Lily Pons (1933)*; Sleepless night* (1936)*; Promenade (Walking the dog).*
(*) CBS Dig. **MK 39699; *IMT 39699* [id.]. Michael Tilson Thomas (piano), LAPO.

Rhapsody in blue (original version)*; Who cares?* (ballet from Gershwin Songbook, arr. Hershy Kay)*;* Arr. of songs for piano: *Clap your hands; Do, do, do it again; Nobody but you; Swanee.*
(*) ASV Dig. **CDRPO 8008; *ZCRPO 8008*. Andrew Litton with RPO.

The remastered Tilson Thomas CD and the much cheaper CBS tape anthology centre on the famous 1976 recording of the *Rhapsody in blue*, which added to the piano-rolls of the composer's own performance of the piano part an exhilarating accompaniment (1920s style) by the Columbia Jazz Band, using the original Whiteman score. The result proved refreshingly controversial – there is one tutti which sounds like an old film speeded up. This has transferred admirably to CD, with added bite and presence. Tilson Thomas's direction of *An American in Paris* has comparable flair, but here the remastered recording lacks something in fullness and weight at the bottom to balance the brilliant upper range. The Broadway overtures are given expert and idiomatic performances, with the Buffalo Philharmonic clearly on their toes and enjoying themselves. Here the remastered sound is again bright, with good stereo definition and wide range; but the remastering has lost some of the body of the original analogue sound and is a little flat and two-dimensional: these scores call for vividness and affectionate detail (which they find here in plenty) but also, ideally, a degree more sumptuousness in the orchestral fortissimos.

The cassette also includes show-medleys and songs. The intercommunication between Miss Vaughan and her audience brings singing of consistently high voltage (*Fascinatin' rhythm* is a *tour de force*). Often – as in *Porgy and Bess* – one just gets snippets of songs, but the programme is more generous than the above listing would indicate, the medleys including a number of favourites. With very acceptable sound (although iron-oxide stock is used) this is thoroughly worth while, even if the documentation is inadequate.

Michael Tilson Thomas's newest Gershwin record supplements rather than displaces his earlier account of *Rhapsody in blue* accompanying the composer's 1924 piano-roll. There is no doubt that Tilson Thomas is an accomplished pianist, but there is not quite the same hell-for-leather excitement and zest for life that the earlier performance generated. Tilson Thomas has also taken the trouble to restudy the autographs of the *Second Rhapsody*, and the result of his researches brings us much closer to Gershwin's intentions. Even so, if it is not impertinent to dissent from the composer's own view, it is still far from being one of his best pieces. What is a real discovery, however, is *Sleepless night*, an altogether enchanting miniature, poignant and touching – and alone worth the price of the record. This and some of the other piano works that Tilson Thomas plays with such style are new to the catalogue. The *Violin piece* is previously unpublished, and Tilson Thomas in collaboration with Ira Gershwin has transcribed and expanded it. He gets very good results from the Los Angeles Philharmonic and is eminently well served by the CBS engineers. Strongly recommended. The CD is impressive in its presence, but the chrome tape, though fully acceptable, by its side sounds less sharply defined.

Andrew Litton follows in Michael Tilson Thomas's footsteps by adopting the original Whiteman score of the *Rhapsody in blue*. The performance is lively enough and thoughtful too, so it has some elements of the Bernstein approach, particularly in the improvisatory-like passage before the big tune arrives. When it does, its reedy textures emphasize the smaller, less inflated sound which Gershwin originally conceived, while earlier the brass tuttis have a jazzy exuberance, without the players sounding rushed off their feet. In its way, this is very enjoyable and far better recorded than the CBS version, but the rhythmic inflexions are clearly from this side of the Atlantic, and this applies even more strikingly to the (attractively) amiable performance of Hershy Kay's ballet-score adapted from Gershwin's own 'Song Book for Balanchine'. Litton then usefully plays as solo piano items the four remaining songs which Kay discarded, and very well too. There is an excellent cassette and this music is particularly attractive as background for a car journey.

Catfish Row (suite from *Porgy and Bess*).
*** Telarc Dig. **CD 80086** [id.]. Tritt, Cincinnati Pops O, Kunzel – GROFÉ: *Grand Canyon suite.****

Catfish Row (suite from *Porgy and Bess*); *Rhapsody in blue; Variations on 'I got rhythm'.*
* HMV Dig. **CDC7 47152-2** [id.]. Weissenberg, BPO, Ozawa.

Catfish Row was arranged by the composer after the initial failure of his opera and already existed when Fritz Reiner in 1941 commissioned Robert Russell Bennett's more sumptuous *Symphonic picture*, which uses much of the same material. But comparisons are not useful here; both scores are highly effective, if Gershwin's is the more subtle. It includes a brief piano solo, played with fine style by William Tritt in the highly sympathetic Telarc performance which is very well recorded and coupled to a highly spectacular *Grand Canyon suite* (with an optional ending including real Arizona thunder).

The Ozawa HMV CD, useful in its time, is now superseded. Neither pianist nor orchestra would suggest themselves for this repertoire, and Weissenberg sounds uncommitted in the *Rhapsody*, rather better in the *Variations*. In *Catfish Row* he is unidiomatic in the 'Jazzbo Brown' sequence.

Broadway music: *Damsel in Distress: Stiff upper lip* (*Funhouse dance sequence*). *Overtures: Girl crazy; Of thee I sing; Oh Kay!; Primrose; Tip-toes.*
(*) HMV Dig. **CDC7 47977-2 [id.]; *EL 270575-4* [Ang. *4D5 47977*]. New Princess Theatre O, John McGlinn.

John McGlinn has recorded his selections using the original scores and parts which came to light in a famous mid-1980s discovery. They were lying, forgotten treasure-trove, in the Warner Brothers music warehouse in Secaucus, New Jersey. The extended dance-sequence, *Stiff upper lip*, also draws on the RKO Studio archive; it comes from a 1937 movie, *A Damsel in Distress*, featuring Fred Astaire and has some good tunes. So has *Oh Kay!* (half a dozen) while *Girl crazy* offers the irresistible *I got rhythm*. Elsewhere, the famous melodies are more thinly spread, but the marvellous playing of the New York pick-up orchestra (gorgeous saxes and brass) has splendid pep. On CD the presence of the close-miked instruments brings edginess with a touch of shrillness on the strings, though the background ambience is voluptuous enough. There is only 42′ music overall so this is more recommendable in its excellent chrome-tape format, which is smoother on top, and ideal for a car journey.

Cuban overture. (i) *Second Rhapsody* (arr. McBride). *Porgy and Bess: Symphonic picture* (arr. Bennett).
** HMV Dig. **CDC7 47021-2** [id.]. LSO, Previn, (i) with Ortiz.

Gershwin's *Cuban overture* is rather long for its material, but the music has genuine vitality. Here Previn plays it with such gusto, and the digital recording is so infectiously brilliant, that one's reservations are almost swept aside. Similarly the *Second Rhapsody* cannot compare with the *Rhapsody in blue* for melodic appeal (Gershwin, like Hollywood, was not good at sequels);

but this performance is very persuasive. The highlight here is of course the brilliant arrangement by Robert Russell Bennett of themes from *Porgy and Bess*, which has established a separate identity of its own. At the opening one fears the performance is going to be too self-conscious (although one can understand Previn revelling in the gorgeous LSO playing – *Summertime* is ravishing). But the music soon takes wing and again the ear revels in the glittering sonics. However, Previn unaccountably makes two cuts, notably the long slow introduction, which is so effective in Dorati's hands, and also in the storm sequence which separates *I've got plenty of nothin'* and *Bess, you is my woman now*.

PIANO DUET

An American in Paris (original version).
** HMV Dig. **CDC7 47044-2** [id.]; *EJ 270122-4* [Ang. *4DS 38130*]. Katia & Marielle Labèque (pianos) – GRAINGER: *Fantasy*.**

The Labèque sisters here present the first recording of the composer's own two-piano score of his famous overture, in which several brief passages are included, later cut in the orchestral score. There is plenty of freshness and bite in the performance, if not much warmth. Recording to match, bright to the point of aggressiveness, and this clattery quality is unattractively accentuated on the tape.

Piano concerto in F; Rhapsody in blue (versions for 2 pianos).
** Ph. **400 022-2** [id.]. Katia & Marielle Labèque.

Both the *Rhapsody in blue* and the *Concerto* were originally sketched out on four staves, and the *Rhapsody* and two movements of the *Concerto* were first performed on two pianos. Katia and Marielle Labèque are a highly accomplished duo actively interested in jazz, and they play with flawless ensemble and superb attack. These are sparkling accounts and are vividly recorded. Anyone with an interest in this repertoire might consider this issue, although both works undoubtedly lose a good deal of colour without the orchestral contrast.

SOLO PIANO MUSIC

Impromptu in 2 keys; Jazzbo Brown blues (from *Porgy and Bess*)*; Merry Andrew; Promenade; Preludes 1–3; Three quarter blues; 2 Waltzes in C*. Arrangements of songs: *Clap yo' hands; Do it again; Do, do, do; Fascinatin' rhythm; I got rhythm; I'll build a stairway to paradise; Liza; The man I love; My one and only; Nobody but you; Oh, Lady be good; Somebody loves me; Strike up the band; Swanee; Sweet and low-down; 'S wonderful; That certain feeling; Who cares*. (With DONALDSON: *Rialto ripples*).
(M) **(*) HMV *ED 291347-4*. Richard Rodney Bennett.

Richard Rodney Bennett turns a composer's ear on Gershwin's piano music, including the latter's own arrangements of some of his most famous songs, and perhaps that is why the performances are not always fully idiomatic. Their rhythmic vigour is underpinned by considerable expressive conviction, yet the melodic exhilaration does not always come over, although there are undoubted insights. But such a comprehensive collection is welcome, especially as the recording – made in a resonant acoustic – is first class, with an excellent wide-ranging cassette transfer. The digital remastering is certainly successful: the piano image has fine presence.

VOCAL MUSIC

'Kiri sings Gershwin': Boy wanted; But not for me; By Strauss; Embraceable you; I got rhythm; Love is here to stay; Love walked in; Meadow serenade; The man I love; Nice work if you can get it; Somebody loves me; Someone to watch over me; Soon; Things are looking up. Porgy and Bess: Summertime.

(*) HMV Dig. **CDC7 47454-2 [id.]; *EL 270574-4* [Ang. *4DS 47454*]. Kiri Te Kanawa, New Theatre O, McGlinn (with Chorus).

It is not too far-fetched to regard Gershwin as a kind of twentieth-century Schubert. He had a supreme melodic gift and the finest of these songs often bring the kind of harmonic shift that creates musical magic. If it is less subtle than Schubert's magic, the use of the English language gives Gershwin's output a far wider currency than a Lieder composer could ever hope for. And it is not just the marvellous tunes that communicate. The lyrics (already bringing a nostalgia for the recent past and a far more cultivated age of popular music) have a bourgeois meaning, too; if there is sentiment, that is an important part of human nature. In short these songs are nearly all masterpieces, and it is good to have them presented with their original orchestrations, even if the packaging is too glossy, especially so in Dame Kiri's gorgeously sung *Summertime* from *Porgy and Bess* where the distanced heavenly chorus creates the purest kitsch. But most of the numbers are done in an upbeat style (quite different from the companion Hendricks recital – see below), which has the advantage of carrying the vocal introductions before the verse and preventing their sounding superfluous out of stage context. Dame Kiri is at her most relaxed and, with breezy accompaniments from John McGlinn and his excellent band, she gives constant pleasure as one marvellous tune follows another in a seeming flood. Ideally, there should be more variety of pacing: *The man I love* is thrown away at the beginning of side two at the chosen tempo. But for the most part the ear is seduced by the lovely sounds and the direct rhythmic style of the presentation, with the captivating *Meadow serenade* as effective as the witty semi-pastiche, *By Strauss*. The pop microphone techniques bring excessive sibilants in the CD format, but the chrome tape softens the upper range somewhat, without losing the vividness, and in many ways is preferable to the CD.

Songs: *But not for me; Embraceable you; I got rhythm; The man I love; Nice work if you can get it; Our love is here to stay; They can't take that away from me. Blue Monday: Has anyone seen Joe. Porgy and Bess: Summertime; I loves you, Porgy.*

(*) Ph. **416 460-2 [id.]. Barbara Hendricks, Katia & Marielle Labèque.

An obvious follow-up to the Labèque duo's LP of the *Concerto* and *Rhapsody in blue*. Here they are joined by Barbara Hendricks, an impressively gifted coloured singer who studied at the Juilliard School of Music and played Clara in Maazel's set of *Porgy and Bess*. She is at her finest in the operatic numbers (*I loves you, Porgy* is particularly eloquent), and the warm beauty of the voice gives much pleasure throughout the programme. The performances of the songs are lushly cultured, often indulgently slow (even the faster numbers lack something in vitality), and create a sophisticated Hollywoodian image of late-evening cocktails and cigarette smoke, low-cut silky dresses and dinner jackets. The piano arrangements are elaborate; the playing is elegantly zestful, not out of style, but giving the presentation a European veneer that in its way is very beguiling. The sound is first class and the stereo layout most realistic.

Let 'em Eat Cake; Of Thee I Sing (musicals).

*** CBS Dig. **M2K 42522**; *F2T 42522* [id.]. Jack Gilford, Larry Kert, Maureen McGovern, Paige O'Hara, David Garrison, NY Choral Artists, St Luke's O, Tilson Thomas.

Of Thee I Sing and *Let 'em Eat Cake* are the two satirical operettas that George Gershwin wrote in the early 1930s on a political theme, the one a sequel to the other. But where *Of Thee I Sing* had an impressive Broadway success, the sequel with its more bitter flavour – fascist dictatorship taking over in America – was a relative failure. Over the years the original orchestrations were lost. Those of *Of Thee I Sing* were rediscovered in 1984, and that has prompted not only this first fully authentic recording but a recording of *Let 'em Eat Cake* too, using splendid new orchestrations by Russell Warner. Though the aim is satirical in both works, the musical tone of voice has the easy tunefulness of typical Gershwin shows, with only the occasional hint of Kurt Weill to suggest a more international source of inspiration. What the British listener will immediately register is the powerful underlying influence of Gilbert and Sullivan, not just in the plot – with Gilbertian situations exploited – but in the music, with patter-songs and choral descants used in a very Sullivan-like way. Ira Gershwin, too, as lyric-writer ensured that numbers were linked together, making them more complex and more dependent on musical structure than most Broadway shows, genuine operettas in fact. As to musical inspiration, *Let 'em Eat Cake* proves just as memorable as the earlier piece, amply deserving this revival.

Though it is highly unlikely that either show could ever be successfully translated to the West End stage – or to anywhere outside the United States, when Presidential elections and the triviality of the candidates' campaigns are the theme – these two very well-filled discs are a delight, offering warm and energetic performances by excellent artists under Michael Tilson Thomas, not just a star conductor but a leading Gershwin scholar. Larry Kert's distinctive voice in the central role of President – later ex-President – Wintergreen may not please all ears, but both he and Maureen McGovern as his wife make a strong partnership, with Jack Gilford characterful as the Vice-Presidential candidate, Alexander Throttlebottom, and Paige O'Hara excellent as the interloping Diana in *Of Thee I Sing*. With the recording on the dry side and well forward – very apt for a musical – the words are crystal clear, not least from the splendidly disciplined chorus that, for much of the time, is protagonist. The well-produced booklets (one for each operetta) give full words – though, as with many CD sets, you need a magnifying glass to read them. The pair of chrome cassettes offers the documentation as a folded photo-copied insert leaflet – a disgraceful substitute from an international company! The transfers are acceptable but lose the essential sparkle at the top, particularly on the orchestra.

OPERA

Porgy and Bess (complete).

*** Decca **414 559-2** [id.]. White, Mitchell, Boatwright, Quivar, Hendricks, Clemmons, Thompson, Cleveland Ch., Children's Ch., Cleveland O, Maazel.

*** RCA **RD 82109** (3) [**RCD3 2109**]. Ray Albert, Dale, Andrew Smith, Shakesnider, Marschall, Children's Ch., Houston Grand Op. Ch. and O, DeMain.

If anyone was ever in doubt whether in *Porgy and Bess* Gershwin had really written an opera as opposed to a jumped-up musical, this superb recording with Cleveland forces conducted by Maazel establishes the work's formidable status beyond question. For one thing, Maazel includes the complete text, which was in fact cut even before the first stage presentation. Some half-hour of virtually unknown music, including many highly evocative passages and some striking choruses, reinforces the consistency of Gershwin's inspiration. It is not just a question of the big numbers presenting some of the most memorable melodies of the twentieth century, but of a grand dramatic design which triumphs superbly over the almost impossible conjunction of conventions – of opera and the American musical. With a cast that makes up an excellent team, there is no attempt to glamorize characters who are far from conventional, and the story is the more moving for that, with moments potentially embarrassing ('I's the only woman Porgy ever had,' says Bess to Crown in Act II) given genuine dramatic force à la Puccini. The vigour and colour are irresistible, and the recording is one of the most vivid that even Decca has produced. Willard White is a magnificent Porgy, dark of tone, while Leona Mitchell's vibrant Bess has a moving streak of vulnerability, and François Clemmons as Sportin' Life achieves the near-impossible by actually singing the role and making one forget Cab Calloway. But it is above all Maazel's triumph, a tremendous first complete recording with dazzling playing from the Cleveland Orchestra. The compact disc version is one of the most impressive transfers of an analogue original that Decca has yet issued, with the excellent balance and sense of presence intensified.

The distinction is readily drawn between Maazel's Cleveland performance and John DeMain's equally complete and authoritative account on RCA. Where Maazel easily and naturally demonstrates the operatic qualities of Gershwin's masterpiece, DeMain – with a cast which had a riotous success with the piece on Broadway and elsewhere in the United States – presents a performance clearly in the tradition of the Broadway musical. There is much to be said for both views, and it is worth noting that American listeners tend to prefer the less operatic manner of the RCA set. The casts are equally impressive vocally, with the RCA singers a degree more characterful. Donnie Ray Albert, as Porgy, uses his bass-like resonance impressively, though not everyone will like the suspicion of hamming, which works less well in a recording than on stage. That underlining of expressiveness is a characteristic of the performance, so that the climax of the key duet, *Bess, you is my woman now*, has a less natural, more stagey manner, producing, for some ears, less of a frisson than the more delicate Cleveland version. For others, the more robust Houston approach has a degree of dramatic immediacy, associated with the tradition of the American popular theatre, which is irresistible. This basic contrast will decide most listeners' approach, and although the RCA recording has not quite the Decca richness it is strikingly vivid and alive. The RCA CD transfer is not quite as sophisticated as the Decca, but it readily creates a theatrical atmosphere. The sound has plenty of bloom and excellent presence, within a believable acoustic setting – it is as if one were sitting in the middle stalls.

Porgy and Bess: highlights.
(*) RCA **RD 84680. Ray Albert, Dale, Andrew Smith, Shakesnider, Children's Ch., Houston Grand Op. Ch. and O, DeMain.
(*) Ph. Dig. **412 720-2; *412 720-4* [id.]. Estes, Alexander, Curry, Berlin R. Ch. and SO, Slatkin.

This highlights disc is taken from the robust and colourful, highly idiomatic complete recording made by RCA in the late 1970s. Donnie Ray Albert as Porgy has fine bass resonances but tends to underline expressiveness in a hammy way. That goes with the natural feeling in this performance for the tradition of the American musical, as distinct from grand opera. The recording gives fine projection to the voices, particularly on CD. There is an element of shrillness in the orchestral sound.

Slatkin's collection of highlights, opulently recorded, is totally geared to the glorious voices of Simon Estes and Roberta Alexander, both of them richer-toned than their opposite numbers in the complete sets. Naturally, each soloist sings numbers from several characters, not just hero (anti-hero?) and heroine. The rich darkness of Estes' voice is clearly operatic in style, but tough and incisive too, not just as Porgy but equally impressively as Sportin' Life in *It ain't necessarily so*. Only the Berlin Chorus lacks sharpness. Slatkin draws understanding playing from the orchestra, and the sound on CD is particularly rich. The chrome tape, too, is strikingly vivid and wide-ranging.

COLLECTIONS

(i) *An American in Paris;* (ii) *Rhapsody in blue* (original version)*;* (iii) *Manhattan:* Medley from Woody Allen film*;* (iv) *A foggy day* (arr. for guitar)*; Liza* (arr. for flute)*;* (v) *3 Preludes for piano;* (vi) *Embraceable you;* (vii) *Porgy & Bess: Overture* and (vii; viii) *Medley.*
(**) CBS **MK 42516**; *IMT 42516* [id.]. (i) NYPO, Bernstein; (ii) Composer (piano-roll), Columbia Jazz Band, Tilson Thomas; (iii) NYPO, Mehta; (iv) John Williams & Ens.; (v) Tilson Thomas; (vi) Cleo Laine; (vii) LAPO, Tilson Thomas; (viii) Sarah Vaughan & Trio.

A mixed bag of an anthology that cuts across other CDs. *An American in Paris* and *Rhapsody in blue* sound splendidly vivid here, as does *Liza* on Jean-Pierre Rampal's stylish flute, while Michael Tilson Thomas gives admirable accounts of the three piano *Preludes*. Cleo Laine's smoky version of *Embraceable you* is another asset, but the *Manhattan* medley and the *Porgy* overture are very shrill and the Sarah Vaughan items go impossibly over the top. They are already close-miked but on CD the digital remastering over-projects and hypes up the voice grotesquely. The presence is reduced on the cassette which is much smoother, but the orchestral shrillness remains.

But not for me (medley)*; Nice work if you can get it* (medley). Songs: *Do it again; Fascinatin' rhythm; A foggy day; I've got a crush on you; The man I love; My man's gone now; Sweet and low-down. Porgy and Bess: Overture and medley.*
*** CBS **MK 73650**. Sarah Vaughan and Trio; LAPO, Tilson Thomas.

This is live recording at its most impressive. The sound is vivid and one can readily forgive the beat in the voice and the occasional strident moment. The accompaniments are worthy of the occasion, with the orchestra under Tilson Thomas exciting in its own right. With any reservations about the soloist, not always at her best vocally, this remains a compelling musical experience.

'Fascinatin' Rampal': An American in Paris: excerpts*; Fascinatin' rhythm; A foggy day; I got rhythm; The man I love; Nice work if you can get it; 3 Preludes for piano; Someone to watch over me; Porgy and Bess: Bess, you is my woman; My man's gone; Summertime.*
(*) CBS **MK 39700 [id.]. Jean-Pierre Rampal, LAPO (members), Colombier.

Rampal is balanced closely and his rich timbre is seductively larger than life. Yet in the bright work he can display the lightest touch, and his stylish embroidery of *Fascinatin' rhythm* is most engaging, while *Nice work if you can get it* is attractively jaunty. His indulgently slow tempi in the lyrical tunes create a mood of languor, notably in *The man I love*, while *Summertime* is positively sultry. *An American in Paris* is a well-dovetailed potpourri of the main tunes from the piece, lasting about eight minutes, with the famous blues melody sounding unexpectedly elegant. The sophisticated accompaniments feature a small group of players from the Los Angeles Philharmonic, plus a synthesizer. The recording balance is essentially artificial within a warmly glowing acoustic. With the compact disc the presence of the accompanying group is extraordinarily tangible, and the ear revels in the cultured polish and sophistication of the playing. Yet one wishes that these fine musicians had been given more to do by the arranger, to provide greater variety of colour.

Gesualdo, Carlo (*c.* 1561–1613)

Ave, dulcissima Maria; Ave, regina coelorum; Maria mater gratiae; Precibus et meritus beatae Mariae (motets). *Tenebrae responsories for Holy Saturday.*
*** Gimell Dig. **CDGIM 015**; *1585T-15* [id.]. Tallis Scholars, Peter Phillips.

Gesualdo's *Tenebrae responsories* for Holy Saturday, *Sabbado Sancto*, are as uncannily forward-looking as is all the other rule-breaking sacred music that he wrote to be performed for his own delectation in the private chapel of his castle. The astonishing dissonances and chromaticisms may not be as extreme as in some of Gesualdo's secular music but, as elaborate as madrigals, they still have a sharp, refreshing impact on the modern ear which recognizes music leaping the centuries. The rule-breaking may often be perverse, but it is not wilfulness for its own sake. Rather it is akin to the uninhibited self-expression of today's composers, freed from academic rules, and similarly it communicates intensely when genuine emotion lies behind the inspiration. The Tallis Scholars give superb performances, finely finished and beautifully blended, with women's voices made to sound boyish, singing with freshness and bite to bring home the total originality of the writing with its awkward leaps and intervals. Beautifully recorded, this is another of the Tallis Scholars' ear-catching discs, powerful as well as polished. The chrome cassette is fully acceptable, but the transfer level is not especially high and the definition is better on the CD.

Gibbons, Orlando (1583–1625)

Anthems & Verse anthems: *Almighty and everlasting God; Hosanna to the Son of David; Lift up your heads; O Thou the central orb; See, see the word is incarnate; This is the record of John.* Canticles: *Short service: Magnificat & Nunc dimittis. 2nd Service; Magnificat & Nunc dimittis.* Hymnes & Songs of the church: *Come kiss with me those lips of thine; Now shall the praises of the Lord be sung; A song of joy unto the Lord. Organ fantasia: Fantasia for double organ; Voluntary.*

*** ASV Dig. **CDDCA 514**; *ZCDCA 514* [id.]. King's College Ch., Ledger; London Early Music Group; John Butt.

An invaluable first CD anthology of Gibbons that contains many of his greatest pieces. In a way this is a natural (and worthy) successor to the famous Gibbons record, made in the early 1960s with the same King's forces under David Willcocks and with Thurston Dart, which was one of the classics of its day. This accommodates more music, seventeen items in all, including superlative accounts of such masterpieces of the English repertoire as *This is the Record of John* and *Almighty and Everlasting God.* Not only are the performances touched with distinction, the recording too is in the highest flight. Strongly recommended. There is a good cassette.

Ginastera, Alberto (1916–83)

Guitar sonata, Op. 47.

*** Decca Dig. **414 616-2**; *414 616-4* [id.]. Eduardo Fernández – VILLA-LOBOS: *5 Preludes; 12 Études.****

The Ginastera *Sonata* comes relatively late in his career and was composed in 1976 for the Brazilian guitarist, Carlos Barbosa-Lima. Ginastera evokes the rhythms and sounds of different South American countries and uses a wide and imaginative range of colouristic devices. Eduardo Fernández rises to its virtuosic demands and produces sonorities of great refinement, beautifully captured in this excellent Decca recording. The cassette, too, has excellent presence and definition, but access is less convenient as the *Sonata* is placed partway through side one, following the five Villa-Lobos *Preludes*.

Giordano, Umberto (1867–1948)

Andrea Chénier (complete).

(*) Decca Dig. **410 117-2 (2) [id.]. Pavarotti, Caballé, Nucci, Kuhlmann, Welsh Nat. Op. Ch., Nat. PO, Chailly.

*(*) CBS Dig. **M2K 42369** (2) [id.]. Carreras, Marton, Zancanaro, Hungarian State R. & TV Ch., Hungarian State O, Patane.
* HMV **CDS7 49060-8** (2). Corelli, Sereni, Stella, Rome Opera Ch. & O, Santini.

The sound of the Decca set is so vivid and real, particularly on CD, that it often makes you start in surprise at the impact of fortissimos. Pavarotti may motor through the role of the poet-hero, singing with his usual fine diction but in a conventional barnstorming way; nevertheless, the red-blooded melodrama of the piece comes over powerfully, thanks to Chailly's sympathetic conducting, incisive but never exaggerated. Caballé, like Pavarotti, is not strong on characterization but produces beautiful sounds, while Leo Nucci makes a superbly dark-toned Gérard. Perhaps to compensate for the lack of characterization among the principals, a number of veterans have been brought in to do party turns; Hugues Cuénod as Fléville delightfully apt, Piero de Palma as the informer, Incredible, Christa Ludwig superb as Madelon, and Astrid Varnay well over the top caricaturing the Contessa di Coigny. Though this cannot replace the intermittently available RCA/Levine set with Domingo, Scotto and Milnes, it is a colourful substitute with its demonstration sound. The CD has the advantage of being on only two discs.

The CBS set, featuring the same soprano, tenor and conductor as in its other Giordano set from Hungary, *Fedora*, is disappointing. Eva Marton is less well cast here, with the vibrato often obtrusive and the scale of the voice too heavy. José Carreras sings with passion and involvement; but there are many signs of strain, as in the climax of the poet's outburst in the *Improvviso* of Act I; the voice at such points grows disappointingly grainy. Giorgio Zancanaro as Gérard sings cleanly, but without sinister weight he sounds too noble for the revolutionary leader. With the orchestra set behind the voices, Patane's direction sounds underpowered.

It is odd that EMI has resurrected for CD a 1964 set that was never quite competitive, despite the full-throated singing of Franco Corelli. Heard now, his performance in the old Italian style makes you realize how much more responsive the star tenors are today in this repertory. Antonietta Stella's voice never sounds quite under control and, though Mario Sereni sings with fine focus, he gives little idea of character. Santini also is uncharacterful in an opera that needs to be painted in bright colours.

Fedora (complete).
** CBS Dig. **M2K 42181**; *12T 42181* (2). Marton, Carreras, Martin, Kincses, Gregor, Hungarian R. & TV Ch. & O, Patane.

Fedora is mostly remembered for one ripely expansive tune, the hero's solo, *Amor ti vieta*, which arrives in Act II as suddenly as love itself, and then pervades the opera, one fine example of Giordano's stagecraft. There are other memorable ideas too, as well as many of the effects we associate with Puccini; but Giordano's piece, with its episodic libretto, is crude by comparison. Like *Tosca*, it was based on a Sardou play designed as a vehicle for Sarah Bernhardt; but in fact *Fedora* anticipated *Tosca* by two years and the influence, if anything, is the other way round.

Eva Marton as Fedora, Romanov princess, is more aptly cast than in the CBS set of *Andrea Chénier*, also conducted by Patane with José Carreras taking the role of hero. In a work that should sound sumptuous it is not a help that the voices are placed forwardly, with the orchestra distanced well behind. That balance exaggerates the vibrato in Marton's voice, but it is a strong, sympathetic performance; Carreras, too, responds warmly to the lyricism of the role of the hero, Loris, giving a satisfyingly forthright account of *Amor ti vieta*. The rest of the cast is unremarkable, and Patane's direction lacks bite, again partly a question of orchestral balance. This is a fair stop-gap, and a reissue of the 1970 Decca set with Magda Olivero and Mario del Monaco would be preferable.

Giuliani, Mauro (1781–1828)

Guitar concertos Nos 1 in A, Op. 30; 3 in F, Op. 70. Grand overture, Op. 61.
*** HMV Dig. **CDC7 47896-2** [id.]; (M) *TC-EMX 2125* (without *Overture*). Angel Romero, ECO, Leppard.

Guitar concertos Nos 1, Op. 30; 3, Op. 70.
*** Ph. **420 780-2** [id.]. Pepe Romero, ASMF, Marriner.

The HMV coupling must be first choice, because a digital master with its absolute background silence has great advantages in guitar music and the warm, clear recording has a most attractive ambience. Moreover there is the bonus of the *Grand overture*, Op. 61, while in Op. 30 Leppard restores some 100 bars representing the first movement's development section (about a third of the total length). Angel Romero plays the slow movement very engagingly and he is in top form in the *F major Concerto*, which is almost a mirror image of the *A major*, equally innocent and charming and no less tuneful (even if the Sicilian theme and variations which make up the slow movement are perhaps a trifle long). This was originally written for the Terz guitar, which is tuned a minor third higher than the standard instrument. Angel Romero plays it on a normal guitar with the pitch raised. On CD the HMV record is in the demonstration class. There is a good Eminence cassette, at mid-price, but it omits the *Grand overture* and, though it sounds well, the focus is less sharp and the background is not silent.

When Pepe Romero's account of Op. 30 was first issued in the mid-1970s we gave it a warm welcome, not just for the fine solo playing but for Marriner's splendid accompaniment which has a smiling quality that is difficult to resist. The finale is marvellously vivacious, the sparkling orchestral rhythms a constant joy, while in the first movement the shaping of the naïf contours of Giuliani's orchestral ritornello is deliciously elegant. For the CD reissue it has been recoupled with Op. 70, which is also most enjoyably played, although here Marriner's amiable approach to the finale is perhaps too rhythmically gentle. Nevertheless, with refined Philips sound this makes an agreeable alternative to the HMV disc.

Sonata for violin and guitar.
*** CBS **MK 34508** [id.]. Itzhak Perlman, John Williams – PAGANINI: *Cantabile* etc.***

Giuliani's *Sonata* is amiable enough but hardly substantial fare; but it is played with such artistry here that it appears better music than it is. The recording is in need of more ambience, but sound is invariably a matter of taste, and there is no reason to withhold a strong recommendation. The CD transfer is admirably managed.

Glass, Philip (born 1937)

Dance Pieces: Glasspieces; In the Upper Room: Dances Nos 1, 2, 5, 8 & 9.
*** CBS Dig. **MK 39539**; *FMT 39539* [id.]. Ens. dir. Michael Riesman.

These two ballet scores bring typical and easily attractive examples of Glass's minimalist technique. *Glasspieces* was choreographed by Jerome Robbins for the New York City Ballet and draws on earlier works, including the Funeral episode from *Akhnaten*, while *In the Upper Room* was written for the celebrated Twyla Tharp Dance Company. The scoring features woodwind, piano and strings, often heard in separate groups, plus voices, synthesizer and rhythm. Obviously the music aligns extraordinarily effectively with the stage images, with abstract formations and vividly coloured costumes bringing the kind of symbiosis that one finds in Stravinsky's *Les Noces*. Heard away from the stage, the music seems to have a subliminally hypnotic effect, even though rhythmic patterns often repeat themselves almost endlessly. It is a pity that the chrome cassette offers only a restricted upper range compared with the CD, as the tape medium is likely to have the widest appeal.

OPERA

Akhnaten (opera): complete.
*** CBS **M2K 42457** (2) [id.]. Esswood, Vargas, Liebermann, Hannula, Holzapfel, Hauptmann, Stuttgart State Op. Ch., Russell Davies.

Akhnaten, Glass's powerful third opera, is set in the time of Ancient Egypt; here the composer's minimalist ostinatos, proceeding uninterrupted in the accompaniment, represent time itself. Against this is set a historical parade of events; the construction and style are remorselessly ritualistic, yet there are some powerful sounds to bring a sense of drama, and the opera's haunting closing scene with its wordless melismas is like nothing else in music. The work was commissioned by the Stuttgart State Opera and both orchestra and chorus make superb contributions. Among the soloists, Paul Esswood in the title role is reserved, strong and statuesque; perhaps a more red-blooded approach would have been out of character – this is an opera of historical ghosts, and its life-flow lies in the hypnotic background provided by the orchestra. It offers a theatrical experience appealing to a far wider public than usual in the opera house, as the English National Opera production readily demonstrated.

Einstein on the beach (complete).
(***) CBS Dig. **M4K 38875** (4) [id.]. Childs, Johnson, Mann, Sutton, Ch., Zukovsky (violin), Philip Glass Ens., Riesman.

As the surreal title implies, *Einstein on the beach* is more dream than drama. In this, his first opera, Glass, a leader in the minimalist movement, translated his use of slowly shifting ostinatos on to a near-epic scale. In the original stage production, the impact of the piece was as much due to the work of the avant-garde director, Robert Wilson, as to Glass's music. The opera takes significant incidents in Einstein's life as the basis for the seven scenes in three Acts, framed by five 'Knee Plays'. Einstein's life – starting with the child watching the trains go by – is then linked with related visual images in a dream-like way, reflecting the second half of the title, *On the Beach*, a reference to Nevil Shute's novel with its theme of nuclear apocalypse. The hallucinatory staging exactly reflected the music, which on its own conveys little. Other works of Glass, including the operas, are more communicative on record than this. Dedicated performances and first-rate recording. The booklet gives copious illustrations of the stage production.

Satyagraha.
*** CBS Dig. **M3K 39672** [id.]. Perry, NY City Op. Ch. and O, Keene.

Like Glass's first opera, *Einstein on the beach*, this one takes scenes from the life of a great man as the basis of the 'plot' and sets them not in a narrative way but with hallucinatory music in Glass's characteristic repetitive style. The subject here is the early life of Mahatma Gandhi, pinpointing various incidents; and the text is a selection of verses from the Bhagavadgita, sung in the original Sanskrit and used as another strand in the complex repetitive web of sound. The result is undeniably powerful. With overtones of India Raga at the very start, Glass builds long crescendos with a relentlessness that may anaesthetize the mind but which have a purposeful aesthetic aim. Where much minimalist music in its shimmering repetitiveness becomes static, a good deal of this conveys energy as well as power, notably the moving scene at the start of Act II in which Gandhi, attacked in the streets of Durban, is protected by Mrs Alexander, wife of the superintendent of police. The writing for chorus is often physically thrilling, and individual characters emerge in only a shadowy way. The recording, using the device of overdubbing, is spectacular. Warning has to be given of potential damage to loudspeakers from some of the sounds.

Glazunov, Alexander (1865–1936)

Violin concerto in A min., Op. 82.
*** RCA **RD 87019** [**RCD1-7019**]. Heifetz, RCA SO, Hendl – PROKOFIEV; *Concerto No. 2*; SIBELIUS: *Violin concerto.****

Heifetz is incomparable here; his account is the strongest and most passionate (as well as the most perfectly played) in the catalogue. In his hands the *Concerto*'s sweetness is tempered with strength. It is altogether a captivating performance that completely absolves the work from any charge of synthetic sweetness. The RCA orchestra under Hendl gives splendid support, and although the 1963 recording is not beyond reproach, the disc is a must – as it includes also Heifetz's masterly account of the Sibelius *Concerto*. The Prokofiev too is glorious, though the recording is earlier (1959). The digital remastering has brought a bright but pleasingly clean new sound-image.

Cortège solennel, Op. 91; Finnish sketches, Op. 89; Overture No. 1 on 3 Greek themes; Poème épique; Spring, Op. 34; Triumphal march, Op. 40.
** Marco Polo Dig. **HK8 220309** [Rec. Int. **7001-2**]. Hong Kong PO, Schermerhorn.

This is generally a more successful collection than its companion from the same source. *Spring* is freshly picturesque, nicely scored and not too long. The *Overture on Greek themes*, one of them very engaging, is an early piece, written just after the *First Symphony*, and immediately shows the composer's orchestral flair, with pleasing changes of colour, if not a great deal besides. The other works are less distinctive: the *Cortège solennel* quotes *Ein feste Burg* as a last resort, and the *Triumphal march* makes a good deal of fuss about *John Brown's body*. The *Poème épique* is hardly epic but has its moments, though there are rather too many of them. The performances are committed and sympathetic: the Hong Kong Philharmonic do their best – which is a less sophisticated effort than we would expect further West. The sound is good.

From darkness to light, Op. 53; Karelian legend, Op. 99; March on a Russian theme, Op. 76; Oriental rhapsody, Op. 29.
*(*) Marco Polo **HK8 220444** [id.]. Hong Kong PO, Almeida.

The *March on a Russian theme* is agreeable, quite tuneful and colourfully scored. Glazunov's feeling for colour, and his undoubted orchestral skill, does not in the end save the other three pieces. They all have their moments, notably the *Oriental rhapsody*, which begins well; but all outstay their welcome, and the close of *From darkness to light* is bombastic. The Hong Kong orchestra under Almeida plays the music competently and certainly with spirit, and the record, made in Hong Kong Town Hall, is vivid, but these pieces need the coaxing of a Beecham to bring them to life.

Raymonda (ballet), *Op. 57:* extended excerpts from Acts I & II.
*** Chan. Dig. **CHAN 8447**; *ABTD 1159* [id.]. SNO, Järvi.

The Bolshoi Ballet brought a sumptuous and dazzlingly danced new production of *Raymonda* to Britain on their 1987 tour and readily demonstrated why Glazunov's music stays alive in the Soviet repertoire. Järvi shows himself well under its sensuous spell and produces glowingly rich string textures with his fine Scottish orchestra; the woodwind has a contrasting lightness of touch, but even the brass fanfares at the opening share the languor which pervades this very affectionate music-making. Järvi chooses some 56′ of music from the first two Acts, omitting entirely the Slavic/Hungarian Wedding Divertissement of the closing Act, and this contributes to the slight feeling of lassitude. But with rich Chandos recording this is a record for any balletomane to wallow in, even if a Russian performance would undoubtedly have more extrovert fire. There are 24 dividing bands, and it is a pity that they are not directly related to the fairly detailed synopsis.

Les ruses d'amour (ballet), *Op. 61* (complete).
(*) Marco Polo **8.220485 [id.]. Rumanian State O, Andreescu.

(i) *Les ruses d'amour* (ballet), *Op. 61;* (ii) *The Sea* (fantasy), *Op. 28;* (iii) *March on a Russian theme.*
(M) **(*) Olympia **OCD 141** [id.]. (i) USSR RSO, Ziuraitis; (ii) Provatorov; (iii) USSR Ministry of Defence O, Maltsiev.

Les ruses d'amour is new to the UK domestic catalogue. The analogue recording is one of Olympia's better CD transfers, with plenty of body along with its Russian brightness and colour. There are some 55 minutes of ballet music here, not unlike *Raymonda* though not perhaps quite as fine as *The Seasons*; but there is a charming peasant waltz, and the *Puppet dance* shows the composer's scoring at its most felicitous. The ballet – loosely based on Pushkin's *The Lady-Peasant* – opens with a highly agreeable miniature set of variations, a genre that suited Glazunov's talent very well. *The Sea* has undoubtedly effective pictorial content and is not too long for its material; the *March* is ingenuous. All are very well played, especially the main work which reveals Algis Ziuraitis as a deft exponent of his compatriot's music.

The Marco Polo CD offers the ballet alone. It is a modern digital recording and, as sound, rather fuller and more natural than the Russian disc, although the difference is not all that great. The Rumanian orchestra have the full measure of this attractive music, and Horia Andreescu gives a vital and affectionate performance, nicely paced. Some may prefer this, even if less music is offered and the price is more expensive.

The Seasons (ballet), *Op. 67; Concert waltzes Nos 1, Op. 47; 2, Op. 51.*
*** HMV **CDC7 47847-2** [id.]. Philh. O, Svetlanov.

The Seasons is an early work, first performed at St Petersburg in 1900, the choreography being by the famous Petipa. With colourful orchestration, a generous sprinkling of distinctive melody and, at the opening of *Autumn*, one of the most virile and memorable tunes Glazunov ever penned, the ballet surely deserves to return to the concert repertoire. Svetlanov's account is most beautifully played and recorded. His approach is engagingly affectionate; he caresses the lyrical melodies persuasively, so that if the big tune of the *Bacchanale* has slightly less thrust than usual it fits readily into the overall conception. The richly glowing HMV recording is outstanding in every way and the transfer to CD is entirely successful: detail is refined, but the full orchestral bloom is retained. The two charming *Concert waltzes* are played most gracefully with the lightest rhythmic touch, to make a pair of splendid encores.

Decca have also issued Ansermet's recording (from the late 1960s) of the same music on a London Enterprise tape, vividly transferred. But the playing lacks the warmth and refinement of the Philharmonia and this is now clearly superseded, even though it also includes an even earlier Ansermet version of *Stenka Razin* (*414 662-4*).

Stenka Razin (symphonic poem), *Op. 13.*
*** Chan. Dig. **CHAN 8479**; *ABTD 1191* [id.]. SNO, Järvi – RIMSKY-KORSAKOV: *Scheherazade.****

Stenka Razin has its moments of vulgarity – how otherwise with the *Song of the Volga Boatmen* a recurrent theme? – but it makes a generous and colourful makeweight for Järvi's fine version of *Scheherazade*. If anything, the performance of the Glazunov is even more committed, with the brassiness of much of the writing uninhibitedly brought out. The recording is splendid and the spacious Scottish acoustic is ideal for the music. The CD is pretty spectacular, but the chrome cassette, too, is in the demonstration class.

Symphonies Nos 1 in E, Op. 5; 5 in B flat, Op. 55.
(*) Orfeo Dig. **C 093101A [id.]. Bav. RSO, Järvi.

Symphonies Nos 1 in E, Op. 5; 7 in F, Op. 77.
(M) *** Olympia Dig. **OCD 100** [id.]. USSR Ministry of Culture (MoC) SO, Rozhdestvensky.

Glazunov composed his prodigious *First Symphony* in the early 1880s (it is not only remarkably accomplished but delightfully fresh) and the last in 1906 when he had just turned forty. In some ways, the symphonies chart a decline in the loss of natural musical innocence that makes Nos 1 and 2 so captivating and their command of resource so remarkable. However, Rozhdestvensky's persuasive advocacy enhances the appeal of all this music. Under his direction the *First Symphony* sounds even more mature, and the finale, given the lightest touch, is particularly effective. Its slow movement is eloquently shaped, as is that of the 'Pastoral' *Seventh*, with its dignified brass chorale and subsequent fugato. Throughout the woodwind playing has an agreeable lyrical lightness. The scherzos, always Glazunov's best movements, are a delight, helped by the sparkling ensemble of this fine new Soviet orchestra. The digital recording is also bright, full and vivid, matching the conductor's warmth in its resonance without coarsening the sound-picture. These are easily the finest available versions of these works currently available. With the Olympia CD playing over 70′, the value of this issue is obvious.

The playing of the Bavarian Radio Symphony Orchestra under Neeme Järvi is highly sympathetic and polished. The music is made to sound cogent and civilized, if perhaps a little bland at times. The Orfeo recording is naturally balanced and ample in texture but, like the performances, lacks something in glitter, although the scherzos remain highly effective. Overall the Russian performances project more vitality, although in their way Järvi's versions are certainly enjoyable.

Symphony No. 2 in F sharp min., Op. 16; Concert waltz No. 1, Op. 47.
(*) Orfeo Dig. **C 148101A [id.]. Bamberg SO, Järvi.

(i) *Symphony No. 2 in F sharp min., Op. 16; Romantic intermezzo, Op. 69; Stenka Razin, Op. 13.*
(M) **(*) Olympia Dig. **OCD 119** [id.]. (i) USSR MoC SO, Rozhdestvensky; USSR RSO, Dimitriedi.

The *Second Symphony* dates from 1886, only four years after the *First*, and is its equal in quality. The melodic material has an unmistakably Slavic feeling and, in Rozhdestvensky's hands, is played with enormous eloquence, with glowingly colourful woodwind solos from this splendid orchestra. The *Andante* is expansively passionate and the scherzo is captivating; if the finale is weaker, it is given plenty of vigour and purpose; indeed here the work becomes a major Russian symphony. The snag is the recording which, although it has a most attractive basic ambience, produces problems at fortissimo levels, where the brass bray fiercely and the violins above the stave lose a good deal of body and tend to shrillness. The performance is outstanding enough for one to tolerate this degree of digital edge. Both the *Romantic intermezzo*, which also generates considerable fervour, and *Stenka Razin*, which is very exciting indeed, especially in its vulgarly thrilling closing section, are analogue recordings and have considerably more body at climaxes; indeed they sound extremely vivid.

Järvi's Orfeo sound is altogether more comfortable, and the performance is more comfortable too; indeed the opening fanfare (somewhat piercing in the Russian version) is made to sound almost Schumannesque. However, within its boundaries, which are more inhibited than Rozhdestvensky's, this is a very good performance; the playing is eloquent and does not miss the Russian glamour of the slow movement; the scherzo is beautifully cultivated and undoubtedly fresh, although the finale sounds relatively lame without the added histrionics. The recording is full-bodied and naturally balanced, but could do with just a bit more brilliance. Even so, the CD is very impressive, and many will prefer the orotund string textures of the slow movement to the much thinner Russian sound. The *Concert waltz* makes an attractive encore.

Symphony No. 3 in D, Op. 33; Poème lyrique, Op. 12; Solemn procession.
(M) **(*) Olympia Dig. **OCD 120** [id.]. USSR MoC SO, Rozhdestvensky.

The *Third Symphony* dates from 1890. Its excellent scherzo – the scoring of the outer sections is particularly felicitous – is its best movement, but all four movements – save possibly the finale, which is rather too long for its material (14′ 29″ in Rozhdestvensky's performance) – show him in good form. The very opening, with its gently throbbing woodwind chords, has a Mendelssohnian lightness of touch, but when the brazen Russian trombones enter, they take the music into a distinctly Slavic world and the Russian-ness of the lyricism soon asserts itself. The *Lyric poem*, written three years before the symphony, is a fine, expansive, romantic piece which suffers in the Soviet performance at its climax (like the *Andante* of the *Symphony*) from the braying coarseness of the brass and the lack of amplitude in the recorded string tone. Otherwise, the playing of the USSR Ministry of Culture Symphony Orchestra is well up to the excellent standard of this series (particularly in the scherzo of the *Symphony*), with notably fine woodwind solos. Rozhdestvensky directs committedly powerful and vital readings of both works and is especially good in the *Solemn procession* (1907), which is more optimistic than the title suggests. It is an agreeable mixture of derivations from Rimsky and Borodin and has a distinct melodic appeal, though again the rather papery sound of the violins above the stave and the edgy brass of the recording are a drawback.

Symphonies Nos 4 in E flat, Op. 48; 5 in B flat, Op. 55.
(M) *** Olympia Dig. **OCD 101** [id.]. USSR MoC SO, Rozhdestvensky.

Symphonies Nos 4 in E flat, Op. 48; 7 in F, Op. 77.
(*) Orfeo **C 148201A [id.]. Bamberg SO, Järvi.

Glazunov's *Fourth* is one of the least recorded, yet it is a charming and well-composed symphony, full of good things and distinctly Russian in outlook, and held together structurally by a theme which Glazunov uses in all three movements. The *Fifth* is much better known and has a particularly fine slow movement, which reveals even greater depths than hitherto suspected in Rozhdestvensky's fervent Russian performance. This also gives great pleasure by the colour and beauty of the woodwind playing, so effective in the scherzos of both works – always the most effective movement in any Glazunov symphony. The string playing too confirms the Ministry of Culture State Symphony as currently the finest Soviet orchestra. The recording is extremely vivid, among the best in this revelatory series of recordings which undoubtedly give the strongest advocacy to Glazunov's music.

The *Seventh* has understandably been dubbed the 'Pastoral'. With its key of F and some engaging woodwind writing, notably for the oboe in the first movement, it has much to attract the listener. The *Andante* is undoubtedly eloquent in Järvi's performance and the scherzo, marked *giocoso*, is well up to form. The finale has plenty of bustle, even if here it sounds rather long. The sound, as in the rest of Järvi's series, is full and naturally balanced, lacking something in spectacle.

Symphony No. 6 in C min., Op. 58; Scènes de ballet, Op. 52.
(M) **(*) Olympia Dig. **OCD 104** [id.]. USSR MoC SO or RSO, Rozhdestvensky.

Glazunov's *Sixth* was well received at its première; Rimsky-Korsakov praised it profusely, but it is nevertheless one of the weaker works in the set. It has an *Intermezzo* (*Allegretto*) in the place of a scherzo, pleasing but not memorable, and a finale ominously marked *Andante maestoso*, bold enough in Rozhdestvensky's hands but inflated and a trifle pompous too. The first movement opens atmospherically, but the Theme and variations which form the slow movement is undoubtedly the most pleasingly inventive section. Rozhdestvensky directs the work with the kind of thrust and conviction to make the very most of it, and is suitably affectionate in the variations. Here, however, the brass chorale is a bit fierce as recorded, and the upper string sound could ideally be more glamorous. The *Scènes de ballet* is analogue: the recording is still very bright, but has slightly more depth. It is characteristic of the composer's favourite genre, assured and often tuneful, with the piquantly scored *Marionettes* and the *Scherzino* given quite delicious colouring. The Olympia CD is generous, playing for 70′.

(i) *Symphony No. 8 in E flat, Op. 83; Ballade, Op. 78; Slavonic festival, Op. 26.*
(M) *** Olympia Dig. **OCD 130** [id.]. (i) USSR MoC SO, Rozhdestvensky; USSR RSO, Dimitriedi.

Symphony No. 8 in E flat, Op. 83; Overture solonnelle, Op. 73; Wedding procession, Op. 21.
(*) Orfeo **C 093201A [id.]. Bav. RSO, Järvi.

The *Eighth* is Glazunov's last complete symphony (there is a one-movement torso of the *Ninth*) dating from the middle of the first decade of this century. It is a very considerable, well-constructed piece. Like the *Seventh* it deserves to be more popular. Rozhdestvensky's performance provides the most powerful advocacy, particularly in the fine first movement and the expansively eloquent *Mesto*. The scherzo is less charming, more purposive than is usual in a Glazunov symphony; it is splendidly played, and in the finale the brass chorale is without the blatancy one tends to expect from a Russian performance. Indeed this is one of Glazunov's most convincing finales, with an attractive lyrical strain. The two bonuses are well worth having. The *Ballade* contrasts expressively intense writing for the strings (played with great fervour) with a brass interlude, where again the Russian playing is colourful rather than edgy. The *Slavonic festival* is a most engaging piece, a kaleidoscope of vigorous dance-themes and sparkling orchestration – Glazunov at his best. It is based on the finale of his *Third String quartet*, but is obviously much more effective in its orchestral dress. The recording throughout is more agreeable than many in Rozhdestvensky's cycle, not lacking vividness but fuller and better balanced. This is a good place to start on an exploration of this surprisingly rewarding repertoire. The CD offers 69′ 31″.

As in the rest of his series, Järvi and the Bavarian players give the piece a cultivated, polished performance, not lacking commitment and vigour, and certainly with plenty of colour in the scherzo, but bringing to the music a Schumannesque quality at times. This is partly contributed by the warm, cushioned orchestral sound which needs a touch more glitter to bring out the full Russian character of the writing. Nevertheless the performance is thoroughly musical and undoubtedly enjoyable, with spaciousness to some extent compensating for passion.

String quartet No. 1 in D, Op. 1.
(M) *** Olympia **OCD 157** [id.]. Shostakovich Qt – TCHAIKOVSKY: *Trio.* **(*)

Glazunov's *First quartet* is extraordinarily assured and inventive. It dates from the year after the *First Symphony*, when its composer was eighteen. With a genuinely eloquent *Andante* – beautifully played here – and an accomplished scherzo, the piece ends appealingly with a moderately paced and tuneful finale. The performance is superb: the immaculate ensemble of the Shostakovich Quartet is matched by their warmth and body of tone. One could not imagine a better account. The recording, made in 1974, is well balanced and immediate.

Piano sonatas Nos 1 in B flat min., Op. 74; 2 in E min., Op. 75; Grand concert waltz in E flat, Op. 41.
(*) Pearl **SHECD 9538 [id.]. Leslie Howard.

Both of Glazunov's piano sonatas date from 1901 and neither is otherwise available. Though not as distinctively personal as Rachmaninov's, which are a few years later, nor as impressively wrought as Balakirev's superb essay in this form, the Glazunov sonatas are well worth investigating, particularly in performances as committed and as well recorded as these. Leslie Howard is a devoted champion of neglected composers and his fine technique and fluent fingers make out a strong case for both pieces, and for the slighter concert waltz that serves as fill-up. Howard does not always make the most of the poetry here and is not always consistent in observing dynamic nuances, but there is more to praise than to criticize. Admirers of Glazunov's art should investigate this issue which sounds extremely impressive in its CD format. The analogue recording is most realistically transferred; the piano is given a natural presence and its middle range is full in timbre.

Glière, Reinhold (1875–1956)

The Red Poppy (ballet)*: suite.*
(M) *(*) Olympia **OCD 202**. Bolshoi Theatre O, Yuri Fayer (with KNIPPER: *Symphony No. 4*).

By far the best part of Glière's *Red Poppy* ballet suite (33′ 53″) is the *Russian sailors' dance*, which lasts for just over three minutes. The rest is pretty empty stuff, at its most personable when featuring cliché interjections of the pentatonic scale. It is all vividly played here, given a bright, slightly shallow 1963 Russian analogue recording. The Glière ballet is coupled to a Soviet patriotic symphony by Lev Knipper (1898–1974) ominously subtitled *'Poem of the Komsomol Fighter'*. It is for soloists, chorus and orchestra and is more a cantata, drawing heavily for its material on the most famous of Russian folksongs which is delivered with ever increasing fervour.

Symphony No. 1, Op. 8; The Sirens, Op. 33.
*(*) Marco Polo Dig. **HK8 220349**. Slovak PO, Gunzenhauser.

Best known for his mammoth *Ilya Mourametz symphony* and the ballet, *The Red Poppy*, Glière has fallen from the repertoire nowadays. The *First Symphony* is a somewhat derivative piece, coming from a composer in his mid-twenties. The idiom draws heavily on Tchaikovsky and Borodin, though the ideas are not in themselves distinguished. *The Sirens* is somewhat later (1908), predating *Ilya Mourametz* and with some of the Scriabinesque *art nouveau* spirit of that symphony. The recorded sound is no more than acceptable: the acoustic is inclined to be dryish and this tells, particularly in the rather lacklustre upper strings which need more bloom. A curiosity worth hearing once, rather than a high-priority recommendation.

Glinka, Mikhail (1805–57)

Russlan and Ludmilla: overture.
(M) *** Decca *417 689-4*. LSO, Solti – BORODIN: *Prince Igor*: excerpts; MUSSORGSKY: *Khovanshchina: Prelude* etc.***

(M) *** Decca **417 723-2** [id.]. LSO, Solti – MUSSORGSKY: *Night****; TCHAIKOVSKY: *Symphony No. 5.**(*)

(*) Andante **CDACD 85702 [Var./Sara. **VCD 42708**]. LSO, Tjeknavorian – RIMSKY-KORSAKOV: *Scheherazade.***(*)

It is reported that, at the opening of the St Petersburg Conservatoire, Tchaikovsky dashed inside as soon as the doors were opened and played Glinka's *Russlan and Ludmilla overture* from memory on the piano, to ensure that it was the first music to be heard in the new building. It certainly represents one of the earliest examples of what we now know as characteristic Russian orchestral music, with its energy and sparkle and vivid feeling for the orchestral palette. It is doubtful whether Tchaikovsky played the overture as fast as Solti. His spanking pace has the LSO on the very tips of their toes: a bravura performance, superbly articulated, which is irresistible. The performance is available on a Decca budget Weekend tape with basically vivid sound, though the upper range is artificially bright, and also on a less attractive CD, coupled with Solti's hard-driven, unexpansive account of Tchaikovsky's *Fifth Symphony*.

Tjeknavorian's account is also a lively one and makes a good, well-recorded filler for his CD of Rimsky-Korsakov's *Scheherazade*.

Grand sextet in E flat.

*** Hyp. **CDA 66163**; *KA 66163* [id.]. Capricorn – RIMSKY-KORSAKOV: *Quintet.****

Glinka's *Sextet* dates from 1832 while he was still in Italy, where he came into contact with Mendelssohn, Bellini and Donizetti. It is not very individual but is very fluently written. The invention is rather engaging, particularly when played with such aplomb as it is here. The contribution of the pianist, Julian Jacobson, is brilliantly nimble and felicitous. The recording has an attractive ambience and, if the balance places the piano rather backwardly for a resonant acoustic, the CD provides good detail and overall presence. There is also an excellent cassette.

Trio pathétique in D min.

*** Chan. Dig. **CHAN 8477**; *ABTD 1188* [id.]. Borodin Trio – ARENSKY: *Piano trio.****

Glinka began his *Trio* in Italy in 1832, towards the end of his three-year stay in the country where he succumbed to increasing bouts of depression and homesickness. It was originally written for clarinet, bassoon and fortepiano – and was recorded for this medium ten years ago; it was hearing a clarinet quintet by the Finnish virtuoso, Bernhard Crusell, that had kindled his interest in music. The work itself is prefaced by a superscription; 'Je n'ai connu l'amour que par les peines qu'il cause' (I have known love only through the misery it causes). David Brown does not speak very highly of it in his study of Glinka – and indeed it is no masterpiece – but the Borodins play it for all their worth and almost persuade one that it is. As we have come to expect from this source, the recording is vivid and has excellent presence. The chrome-tape transfer is smooth and realistic in Chandos's best manner.

Gluck, Christoph (1714–87)

Alceste (complete).

** Orfeo Dig. **C 027823F** (3) [id.]. Jessye Norman, Gedda, Krause, Nimsgern, Weikl, Bav. R. Ch. and SO, Baudo.

The French version of *Alceste*, quite different from the Italian, was for many years seriously in need of a complete recording; it was a great pity that the opportunity was not taken of recording Dame Janet Baker in the Covent Garden production conducted by Sir Charles Mackerras. However, this very well-cast set makes a valuable substitute, with Jessye Norman commanding in the title role, producing gloriously varied tone in every register. What is rather lacking – even from her performance – is a fire-eating quality such as made Dame Janet's performance so memorable and which comes out to hair-raising effect in Callas's recording of *Divinités du Styx*. Here it is beautiful but relatively tame. That is mainly the fault of the conductor, who makes Gluck's score sound comfortable rather than tense. The other protagonist is in effect the chorus, generally singing well but recorded rather distantly to reduce dramatic impact. The other principals sing stylishly; however, as a set, this does not quite rebut the idea that in Gluck 'beautiful' means 'boring'. Good, well-focused sound from Bavarian Radio engineers.

La Cinesi (*The Chinese woman*).
*** HMV **CDC7 47752-2**; *EL 169575-4*. Poulenard, Banditelli, Sofie von Otter, De Mey, Schola Cantorum Basiliensis, Jacobs.

Gluck's hour-long opera-serenade, written in 1754 for a palace entertainment given by Prince Joseph Friedrich of Saxe-Hildburghausen, provides a fascinating view of the composer's lighter side. In the comedy here, one can even detect anticipations of Mozart, though with recitative taking up an undue proportion of the whole – including one solid span, near the beginning, of over ten minutes – Gluck's timing hardly compares. The chinoiserie of the story was reflected at that first performance in elaborate Chinese costumes, a novelty at the time; more importantly for us, Gluck, rather like Mozart in *Entführung*, uses jangling and tinkling percussion instruments in the overture to indicate an exotic setting. Otherwise the formal attitudes in Metastasio's libretto – written some twenty years before Gluck set it – are pure eighteenth century.

René Jacobs, a distinguished singer himself, directs a fresh, lively and understanding performance, marked by good singing from all four soloists, notably Anne-Sophie von Otter and Guy de Mey. There is an aria for each of the soloists and, typical of the genre, they come together for a final quartet. First-rate playing and excellent sound. The iron-oxide cassette, however, has a very restricted range and cannot compare with the CD.

Iphigénie en Tauride (complete).
❀ *** Ph. Dig. **416 148-2**; *416 148-4* (2) [id.]. Montague, Aler, Thomas Allen, Argenta, Massis, Monteverdi Ch., Lyon Op. O, Eliot Gardiner.
* Orfeo **CO 52832H** (2). Lorengar, Bonisolli, Groenroos, Fischer-Dieskau, Bav. R. Ch. & SO, Gardelli.

Gardiner's electrifying reading of *Iphigénie en Tauride*, based on the team he has built up at the Lyon Opera House, is a revelation. Anyone who has found Gluck operas boring should hear this dramatically paced performance of an opera that is compact and concentrated in its telling of a classical story, departing strongly from the *opera seria* tradition which Gluck inherited, even while it contains some of the composer's loveliest melodies. Far more than usual, one can here understand how such advocates of romantic opera as Berlioz and Wagner were excited by this culminating example of Gluck's reformism, with its speed and fluidity and breaking-down of formal structures. Gardiner, who made his Covent Garden début in 1973 conducting this opera, is an urgent advocate, bringing out the full range of expression from first to last. He leads from the overture into the storm music with *Otello*-like intensity and, though his Lyon orchestra does not use period instruments, its clarity and resilience and, where necessary, grace and delicacy are admirable.

The cast is first rate. Though Diana Montague in the name part does not attempt a grand romantic characterization such as a conventional prima donna might have given, she sings with admirable bite and freshness, making the lovely solo *O malheureuse Iphigénie* pure and tender. Thomas Allen is an outstanding Oreste, characterizing strongly – as in his fury aria – but singing with classical precision. John Aler is a similarly strong and stylish singer, taking the tenor role of Pylade, with some fine singers from Gardiner's regular team impressive in other roles. The recording is bright and full, with the balance favouring voices but not inappropriately so. There are splendid cassettes, too.

The brief contribution of Fischer-Dieskau in the unsympathetic role of Thoas underlines by contrast the serious disappointment of the alternative Orfeo set as a whole. His imagination and life provide quite a different perspective on the music from the rest, and Pilar Lorengar as recorded sounds so tremulous and uneven as the heroine that it is wearing to listen to. Bonisolli produces fine heroic tone but sings unimaginatively, and Walton Groenroos is gritty-toned as Oreste. This is a total disappointment, despite the good recorded sound.

Orfeo ed Euridice (complete).

(*) Ariola **302588. Lucia Popp, Lipovsek, Kaufman, Munich R. O, Hager.

** Accent **ACC 48223/4D** (2). Jacobs, Kweksilber, Falewicz, Ghent Coll. Vocale, La Petite Bande, Kuijken.

With the finest LP sets yet to be transferred to CD, Hager's Munich version, recorded in 1986 in full and atmospheric if slightly distanced sound, brings a good, enjoyable middle-of-the-road performance. Marjana Lipovsek has a beautiful, rich mezzo inclined to fruitiness, which yet in this breeches role is well able to characterize Orfeo strongly and positively. So *Che farò* is warm and direct in its expressiveness, with Lipovsek avoiding distracting mannerism both here and in recitative. Lucia Popp makes a delightful Euridice and Julie Kaufman, though less distinctive, is fresh and bright as Amor. The chorus is on the heavyweight side for Gluck, but that adds to the power of the performance which uses the 1762 Vienna version of the score, though with instrumental numbers added from the Paris version.

With period instruments and counter tenor in the title role, Kuijken's set – using the original Italian version of 1762 – provides a fair alternative for those looking for an 'authentic' performance. Jacobs is especially impressive as Orfeo; however, exceptionally *Che farò*, taken very slowly, is disappointing, and not everyone will like his ornamentation. Marjanne Kweksilber makes an appealing Eurydice; but generally, with authentic style sounding a degree self-conscious, the whole performance lacks a necessary degree of involvement. This is *Orfeo* coolly dissected. Good recording.

There is also a Philips set of highlights from this opera, unevenly sung and unimaginatively conducted, which cannot be recommended (**410 729-2**).

Paride ed Elena (opera): complete.

(*) Orfeo Dig. **C 118842** (3) [id.]. Cotrubas, Bonisolli, Greenberg, Fontana, Tedards, Jelosits, Schoenberg Ch., Austrian R. Ch. & SO, Zagrosek.

Paride ed Elena, dating from 1770, fell between early and late operatic styles in Gluck's output. Though it contains many beautiful numbers, such as Paris's Serenade in Act III, it was never a success even in the composer's lifetime; nowadays it presents formidable problems of presentation which this performance with its highly anachronistic style does little to solve. The central objection is to the casting of Franco Bonisolli in the role of Paris, originally designed for a high soprano castrato. To transfer what was intended to be eerily penetrating and exotic to the tones of a lusty modern Verdi tenor with little or no idea of classical style and regularly attacking notes from below, is to undermine the whole project. Ileana Cotrubas, a delightful, stylish soprano as a rule, here sounds dispirited, and the balance in favour of the voices brings out the vocal faults all the more. Zagrosek's conducting is efficient, and the choral singing solidly effective, but the lack of authentic style prevents anything more than a recommendation for interest.

Godowsky, Leopold (1870–1938)

18 Studies on Chopin Études.
** Ara. Dig. **Z 6537**; *ABQC 7537* [id.]. Ian Hobson.

Godowsky composed these extraordinary studies between 1900 and 1914; Professor Frank Cooper describes them graphically thus: 'notes slip and slide above, through and below the melodies and textures of Chopin's originals, while harmonies are intensified, made iridescent and rhythms compounded to the point of diffusion . . . at times, the music seems impressionistic; at others surrealistic'. They are bizarre inventions and at times highly disconcerting. Ian Hobson takes their difficulties in his stride, but these pieces call for transcendental keyboard powers and must be tossed off with enormous aplomb and dazzling virtuosity. Hobson has formidable technique but he communicates comparatively little sense of abandon or joy; he is distinctly short on charm. Jorge Bolet has recorded a more widely ranging collection of Godowsky's Chopin arrangements (see under CHOPIN, p. 308) but he, too, is not entirely convincing.

Goldmark, Karl (1830–1915)

Violin concerto No. 1 in A min., Op. 28.
*** HMV **CDC7 47846-2** [id.]. Perlman, Pittsburgh SO, Previn – KORNGOLD: *Violin concerto.****

Like the *Rustic Wedding symphony* this, the first of Goldmark's two violin concertos, maintains a peripheral position in the catalogue. It is a pleasing and warm-hearted concerto in the Romantic tradition that deserves to be better known. It could not be more beautifully played than by Itzhak Perlman, whose effortless virtuosity and lyrical poise challenge even Milstein's aristocratic record of the late 1950s (now deleted). The latter was better balanced, for the EMI engineers have placed Perlman very much in the foreground – so much so that orchestral detail does not always register as it should. The sound-quality is fresher in the newer recording, and Previn accompanies sympathetically. This is very charming and likeable music, and Perlman plays it most winningly. The CD transfer is clear and refined, losing perhaps a little of the warmth of the analogue master. The new coupling, however, is more appropriate as well as more generous.

Overtures: Der gefesselte Prometheus, Op. 38; Im Frühling, Op. 36; In Italien, Op. 49; Sakuntala, Op. 13.
(*) Hung. Dig. **HCD 12552 [id.]. Budapest PO, Korodi.

The overtures recorded here are expertly crafted and, in the case of *Im Frühling*, have good inventive ideas and no mean charm. Two of them, *Sakuntala* and *Der gefesselte Prometheus*, are longer than one would expect and, indeed, rather outstay their welcome. The playing of the Budapest orchestra under Andreas Korodi is very good; so, too, is the recording which has considerable depth.

Symphony No. 2 in E flat, Op. 35; Penthesilea Overture, Op. 31.
* Marco Polo **HK8 220417** [id.]. Rhenish SO, Halasz.

The *Second Symphony* comes from the 1880s when Goldmark was at the height of his fame. The indebtedness to the Mendelssohn–Schumann–Brahms line is obvious, but there are charming moments. Goldmark had a lyrical facility that compensates for his lack of symphonic breadth. Neither the *Symphony* nor its companion is a masterpiece; nor is the playing under Michael Halasz particularly distinguished. This has more curiosity value than artistic importance. The recording is like the music and the performances, acceptable rather than distinctive.

Die Königin von Saba (opera).
(*) Hung. **HCD 12179/82 [id.]. Nagy, Gregor, Kincses, Jerusalem, Miller, Takács, Hungarian State Op. Ch. and O, Fischer.

Goldmark's most successful works came within a relatively short span in his career, of which this long opera is the most ambitious product. With the Queen of Sheba representing evil and the lovely Sulamit representing good, its theme links directly with that of Wagner's *Tannhäuser*, but in style Goldmark rather recalls Mendelssohn and Gounod, with a touch of Meyerbeer. In the tenor role of Asad, Siegfried Jerusalem gives a magnificent performance, not least in his aria *Magische Töne*. Klára Takács is dramatic and characterful as the Queen of Sheba, but on top the voice is often raw. Sándor Nagy is an impressive Solomon, and Adam Fischer, one of the talented family of conductors, draws lively performances from everyone. The recording is very acceptable, but even on CD there are many details which do not emerge as vividly as they might. The documentation, too, is poorly reduced and shortened, in no way comparable with the splendid booklet offered with the original LP set.

Gottschalk, Louis (1829–69)

Grande fantaisie triomphale sur l'Hymne Nationale Brésilien, Op. 69 (arr. Hazel).
*** Decca Dig. **414 348-2**; *414 348-4* [id.]. Ortiz, RPO, Atzmon – ADDINSELL: *Warsaw concerto*; LITOLFF: *Scherzo*; RACHMANINOV: *Concerto No. 2*.***

Gottschalk's *Grand fantasia* has naïvety and a touch of vulgarity, too, but the performers here give it an account which nicely combines flair and a certain elegance, and the result is a distinct success. The balance, within a resonant acoustic, places the piano backwardly; some might feel that there is a lack of glitter, but the CD emphasizes the naturalness, and the ambience is agreeably flattering.

Piano pieces: *Le Bananier* (chanson nègre); *The Banjo* (Grotesque fantaisie); *The Dying Poet* (méditation); *Grand scherzo*; *Le Mancenillier* (sérénade); *Manchega* (Étude de concert); *O ma charmante* (caprice); *Souvenirs d'Andalousie; Souvenir de Porto Rico; Suis moi; Tournament galop.*
(M) *** Decca *414 438-4* [id.]. Ivan Davis.

Ivan Davis's collection of Gottschalk pieces is irresistible, for he is a fun pianist who warmly relishes – with just a hint of tongue-in-cheek – a consciously sentimental piece like *The Dying Poet*, and whose rhythmic pointing in *The Banjo* has fine wit. The result is that the composer's genuine imagination comes through far more keenly than in over-solemn performances. The recording is excellent, especially brilliant and immediate in its tape format.

Gould, Morton (born 1913)

Derivations for clarinet and band.
*** CBS **MK 42227**; *MT 42227* [id.]. Benny Goodman, Columbia Jazz Combo, composer – BARTÓK: *Contrasts*; BERNSTEIN: *Prelude, fugue and riffs*; COPLAND: *Concerto*; STRAVINSKY: *Ebony concerto*.(***)

Gould's *Derivations* is in Gershwinesque mould, seeking to bridge the gap between popular music and the concert hall. The first-movement *Warm-up* is well managed, but the central *Contrapuntal blues* and (especially) the *Rag* are the most memorable of these four miniatures. Benny Goodman is in his element and the accompaniment under the composer is suitably improvisatory in feeling. Very good sound, with the chrome cassette rather less vivid than the CD.

Gounod, Charles (1818–93)

Petite symphonie for wind in B flat.
(*) HM Orfeo Dig. **C 051831A [id.]. Munich Wind Ac., Brezina – DVOŘÁK: *Wind serenade.***(*)

The playing of the Munich Academy is first class: they have an impressive overall blend and the solo contributions have plenty of individuality. The finale is especially engaging and the scherzo is deft. In the first two movements the musicians' geographical location is felt in the style, which is less vital and fresh than the famous Netherlands version under Edo de Waart which we hope may reappear on a mid-priced CD during the lifetime of this book. The Orfeo recording, made in a Munich church, is very believable, and the music itself is a delight.

Messe solennelle de Saint Cécile.
*** HMV Dig. **CDC 747094-2** [id.]; *EL 270134-4* [Ang. *4DS 38145*]. Hendricks, Dale, Lafont, Ch. and Nouvel O Philharmonique of R. France, Prêtre.

Gounod's *Messe solennelle*, with its blatant march setting of the *Credo* and sugar-sweet choral writing, may not be for sensitive souls, but Prêtre here directs an almost ideal performance, vividly recorded, to delight anyone not averse to Victorian manners. Prêtre's subtle rhythmic control and sensitive shaping of phrase minimize the vulgarity and bring out the genuine dramatic contrasts of the piece, with glowing singing from the choir as well as the three soloists: Barbara Hendricks aptly sensuous-sounding, Laurence Dale confirming in his first major recording the high promise of his stage and concert performances, and Jean-Philippe Lafont a clear, idiomatic baritone. In the wide-ranging recording, the organ-tone comes out most impressively, especially on CD. There is a good tape.

Faust (complete).
(*) Ph. Dig. **420 164-2; *420 164-4* (3) [id.]. Te Kanawa, Araiza, Nesterenko, Bav. R. Ch. and SO, C. Davis.
** HMV **CDS7 47493-8** (3) [id.]. Freni, Domingo, Thomas Allen, Ghiaurov, Paris Op. Ch. & O, Prêtre.

Sir Colin Davis, with his German orchestra and with no French singer among his principals, gives a performance which from the very measured account of the opening onwards relates back to the weight of Goethe as much as to French opera. As in his other recordings of French opera – notably another Goethe inspiration, Massenet's *Werther* – he removes the varnish of sentimentality. It may not always be idiomatic but, with fine singing from most of the principals, it is a refreshing version. Dame Kiri, more than you might expect, makes a light and innocent-sounding Marguerite, with the *Jewel Song* made to sparkle in youthful eagerness leaping off from a perfect trill. Evgeni Nesterenko as Mephistopheles is a fine saturnine tempter; Andreas Schmidt as Valentin sings cleanly and tastefully in a rather German way; while Pamela Coburn as Siebel is sweet and boyish. The big snag is the Faust of Francisco Araiza, a disappointing hero with the voice, as recorded, gritty in tone and frequently strained. He underlines the simple melody of *Salut, demeure*, for example, far too heavily, not helped by a syrupy violin solo. The sound is first rate, with the voices cleanly focused and well balanced against the orchestra, giving a fine sense of presence. The chrome cassettes are superbly managed too, very much representing the state of the art and, as they are documented with the CD booklet and cost considerably less, many may feel that they represent a very sensible way to approach this flawed but certainly enjoyable performance.

Though Prêtre working with a French orchestra has claims to a more idiomatic approach than most of his current rivals, the playing is relatively coarse and lacking in intensity. Among the soloists Placido Domingo produces golden tone, rich and heroic, even if the characterization is rather anonymous. Thomas Allen makes an outstanding Valentin, both firm and imaginative, but Mirella Freni too often sounds strained, and Nicolai Ghiaurov is less rich and resonant than he was in his earlier Decca recording under Richard Bonynge. The 1979 recording is full and warm, and the CD transfer is laid out most conveniently on the three CDs, with very generous banding.

Faust: ballet music (suite).
(M) *** HMV **CDM7 69041-2** [id.]. Philh. O, Karajan – BORODIN: *Polovtsian dances****; OFFENBACH: *Gaîté parisienne***(*); PONCHIELLI: *Dance of the Hours.****
(*) Decca Dig. **411 708-2 [id.]; *411 708-4*. Montreal SO, Dutoit – OFFENBACH: *Gaîté parisienne.***(*)

Karajan's 1960 recording offers elegant, sparkling playing from the Philharmonia at their peak and, if *Les Troyennes* are languorously gracious, the closing *Danse de Phryne* has contrasting gusto. The sound is pleasingly full as well as bright.

Gounod's attractive suite is warmly and elegantly played by the Montreal orchestra under Dutoit, although the conductor's touch is not as light as one would have expected. The CD sounds first rate, however, and there is an excellent chrome cassette.

Roméo et Juliette (complete).
*** HMV Dig. **CDS7 47365-8** (3) [id.]. Alfredo Kraus, Malfitano, Van Dam, Quilico, Midi-Pyrenées Regional Ch., Capitole Toulouse Ch. and O, Plasson.

The Plasson set, well sung and vividly recorded, makes an excellent choice for an opera that has been unlucky on record. Kraus may no longer be youthful-sounding in the role of Roméo, but the range and finesse of expression are captivating, while Malfitano proves a delectably sweet and girlish Juliette. Excellent contributions too from Gino Quilico and José van Dam, beautifully set against ripely sympathetic playing from the Capitole orchestra, and atmospherically recorded. Plasson's setting of scenes is most persuasive, whether in the love music or the big ensembles. The fairly resonant recording has produced improved focus and firmer outlines than on the original LPs, and there is slightly greater body to the sound. The documentation and cueing are good, although track 5 of the second disc includes more music than the booklet suggests.

Grainger, Percy (1882–1961)

Blithe bells (Free ramble on a theme by Bach: Sheep may safely graze): Country gardens; Green bushes (Passacaglia); Handel in the Strand; Mock morris; Molly on the shore; My Robin is to the greenwood gone; Shepherd's hey; Spoon River; Walking tune; Youthful rapture; Youthful suite; Rustic dance, Eastern intermezzo.
*** Chan. **CHAN 8377**; (M) *CBT 1022* [id.]. Bournemouth Sinf., Montgomery.

Montgomery's anthology of Grainger's music stands out for the sparkling and sympathetic playing of the Bournemouth Sinfonietta and an engaging choice of programme. Among the expressive pieces, the arrangement of *My Robin is to the greenwood gone* is highly attractive, but the cello solo in *Youthful rapture* is perhaps less effective. The passacaglia on *Green bushes* is characteristically repetitive, yet the diversity in the inner parts show Grainger's decorative imagination in full flight. Favourites such as *Country gardens*, *Shepherds hey*, *Molly on the shore* and *Handel in the Strand* all sound as fresh as paint, and among the novelties the *Rustic dance* and *Eastern intermezzo* (in musical style a cross between Eric Coates and Edward German) have undoubted period charm. The recording is first class in both media.

Fantasy on George Gershwin's Porgy and Bess.
** HMV Dig. **CDC7 47044-2** [id.]; *EJ 270122-4* [Ang. *4DS 38130*]. Katia & Marielle Labèque (pianos) – GERSHWIN: *American in Paris.***

The Labèque sisters in their tough way bring out the strong dramatic contrasts of Grainger's two-piano arrangement of passages from *Porgy and Bess*, a piece more obviously pianistic than the composer's own two-piano version of the overture on the reverse. A fair coupling, recorded with a brightness that threatens to become aggressive, with the tape even more clattery than the CD, the transfer level approaching saturation point.

Granados, Enrique (1867–1916)

Cuentos de la juventud, Op. 1: Dedicatoria. Spanish dances, Op. 37/4 & 5; Tonadillas al estilo antiguo: La Maja de Goya. Valses poéticos.
❀ *** RCA **RCD 14378** [RCD1 4378]. Julian Bream – ALBÉNIZ: *Collection.****❀

Like the Albéniz items with which these Granados pieces are coupled, these performances show Julian Bream at his most inspirational. The illusion of the guitar being in the room is especially electrifying in the middle section of the famous *Spanish dance No. 5*, when Bream achieves the most subtle pianissimo. Heard against the background silence, the effect is quite magical. But all the playing here is wonderfully spontaneous. This is one of the most impressive guitar recitals ever recorded.

Allegro de concierto; 6 escenas románticas; 6 peizas sobre cantos populares españoles.
*** Decca Dig. **410 288-2** [id.]. Alicia de Larrocha.

The spirited *Allegro de concierto*; the colourful and folk-orientated *Seis piezas*, and the more subtle, expressively ambitious *Escenas románticas* show the surprisingly wide range of Granados's piano music and Alicia de Larrocha's natural accord with his sound-world. She plays with consummate artistry and enviable technical fluency; her authority in this programme is matched by her ability to communicate. The recording is first class and has great presence and reality in its CD format.

Danzas españolas, Op. 37
*** Decca **414 557-2** [id.]. Alicia de Larrocha.

In this repertoire Alicia de Larrocha enjoys special authority; this fine Decca recording supersedes her earlier account on Erato. She has an aristocratic poise to which it is difficult not to respond, and plays with great flair and temperament. There have been other fine accounts, but this is undoubtedly the most desirable and best-recorded version in circulation. The transfer of the analogue master to CD has been very successful and the sound has enhanced presence.

Goyescas (complete).
*** Decca **411 958-2** [id.]. Alicia de Larrocha.

The Decca recording is most distinguished. Alicia de Larrocha brings special insights and sympathy to the *Goyescas*; her playing has the crisp articulation and rhythmic vitality that these pieces call for, and the overall impression could hardly be more idiomatic in flavour. These performances displace the alternative listing (Rajna on CRD), not least for the excellence of the recorded sound which is remarkably firm and secure.

Grieg, Edvard (1843–1907)

Piano concerto in A min., Op. 16.

*** Ph. **412 923-2**; (M) *412 923-4*. Bishop-Kovacevich, BBC SO, Sir Colin Davis – SCHUMANN: *Piano concerto.****

(*) HMV Dig. **CDC7 47611-2 [id.]; *EL 270184-4* [Ang. *4DS 38235*]. Ousset, LSO, Marriner – MENDELSSOHN: *Piano concerto No. 1.**(*)*

(M) **(*) Decca **417 728-2**; *414 432-4* [id.]. Radu Lupu, LSO, Previn – SCHUMANN: *Concerto.**(*)*

(M) *(**) Decca **417 676-2**; *417 676-4* [id.]. Curzon, LSO, Fjelstad – TCHAIKOVSKY: *Piano concerto No. 1.**(*)*

(M) ** DG **415 850-2**; *415 850-4* [id.]. Anda, BPO, Kubelik – SCHUMANN: *Concerto.***

*(*) DG Dig. **410 021-2** [id.]. Zimerman, BPO, Karajan – SCHUMANN: *Concerto.***

*(*) RCA **RD 85363** [**RCD1 5364**]. Rubinstein, O, Wallenstein – TCHAIKOVSKY: *Piano concerto No. 1.**(*)*

(M) * HMV **CDC7 47164-2** [id.]; *EG 290292-4*. Sviatoslav Richter, Monte Carlo Op. O, Von Matacic – SCHUMANN: *Concerto.**

* Erato Dig. **ECD 88164** [id.]. Duchable, Strasbourg PO, Guschlbauer – RACHMANINOV: *Piano concerto No. 2.*(*)*

* Decca Dig. **417 112-2**; *417 112-4* [id.]. Bolet, Berlin RSO, Chailly – SCHUMANN: *Concerto.*(*)*

(i) *Piano concerto in A min.;* (ii) *Peer Gynt suites Nos. 1–2.*

(B) ** DG Walkman *413 158-4* [id.]. (i) Anda, BPO, Kubelik; (ii) Bamberg SO, Richard Kraus – SIBELIUS: *Finlandia; Karelia; Valse triste.****

(ii) *Piano concerto in A min., Op. 16; Peer Gynt suites Nos. 1–2; Holberg suite, Op. 40.*

(B) *(*) DG Dig. *419 834-4* [id.]. (i) Zimerman; BPO, Karajan.

The freshness and imagination displayed in the coupling of the Grieg and Schumann *Concertos* by Stephen Bishop-Kovacevich and Sir Colin Davis offers a recording collaboration which – with the cassette at mid-price – continues to dominate the catalogue. Whether in the clarity of virtuoso fingerwork or the shading of half-tone, Bishop-Kovacevich is among the most illuminating of the many great pianists who have recorded the Grieg *Concerto*. He plays with bravura and refinement, the spontaneity of the music making bringing a sparkle throughout, to balance the underlying poetry. The 1972 recording has been most successfully freshened, and now there is an extremely vivid chrome tape too, one of Philips's finest. Readers will note that this excellent cassette costs only a third of the price of the CD, which is nevertheless very welcome.

Ousset's is a strong, dramatic reading, not lacking in warmth and poetry but, paradoxically, bringing out what we would generally think of as the masculine qualities of power and drive. The result, with excellent accompaniment recorded in very full sound, is always fresh and convincing. A good choice for anyone wanting this unusual coupling of the Mendelssohn *Concerto*, except that for CD, although the sound is full, firm and clear, the measure is rather short. There is also a good cassette.

Radu Lupu's performance is most enjoyable and this Decca Ovation CD has the advantage of economy. The analogue recording dates from 1974 and is bold and now even more brightly lit than it was originally, not entirely to advantage. But the performance is a fine one; there is both warmth and poetry in the slow movement; the hushed opening is particularly telling. There is a hint of calculation at the coda of the first movement, but the performance does not lack spontaneity and the orchestral contribution under Previn is a strong one. The Schumann coupling, however, is marginally less appealing.

The sensitivity of Clifford Curzon in the recording studio is never in doubt and his has been a favourite performance since it was first issued at the beginning of the 1960s. Curzon's approach is not as individual as Bishop-Kovacevich's – there is a suggestion of self-effacement – but the performance has strength and power, as well as freshness. No doubt this will arrive on CD in due course; meanwhile it is available on a budget Decca CD and tape, coupled with the Tchaikovsky No. 1. The piano timbre is still full and firm but, as usual with this series, the upper range is very bright and there is some loss of body in the orchestra.

Anda's account of the *Concerto* is more wayward than Curzon's, but it is strong in personality and has plenty of life. Kubelik's accompaniment is very good too and the early 1960s recording sounds fresh enough, although there is a touch of orchestral glare on the CD. On the alternative Walkman tape a full selection from *Peer Gynt* is offered, vividly played; but the recording here sounds a bit thin in the strings. The Sibelius couplings, however, are first rate with two of the performances conducted by Karajan.

Zimerman and Karajan do not seem an ideal partnership here. There are, of course, many things to admire from this remarkable young pianist, but neither concerto on this CD conveys the sense that these artists are enjoying themselves very much, and there is a certain want of freshness. Judged by the standards he has set himself, Zimerman is neither as illuminating nor, indeed, quite so sensitive as one would expect in this most gentle and poetic of scores. The recording is admirably full and brilliant in its CD format. On the alternative bargain-priced Pocket Music cassette it sounds even brighter and drier. But this is certainly generous, with the *Peer Gynt* and *Holberg suites* showing Karajan at his most charismatic; however, again there is a loss of body and the bass support is not ideally rich and resonant.

Rubinstein usually has something interesting to say about any major concerto; it is a great pity that his partner here, Alfred Wallenstein, shows little sensitivity or imagination in his handling of the light-textured but all-important orchestral contribution. Nevertheless, Rubinstein produces some marvellously poetic and aristocratic playing towards the end of the slow movement, and the finale is both commanding and exciting, even if the orchestral response is aggressive. The remastering has produced a bold, if shallow, piano image, but the orchestral sound remains brashly two-dimensional. The coupled Tchaikovsky *Concerto* is infinitely finer in all respects.

On HMV Richter is disconcertingly wilful, drawing out many passages self-indulgently – this is not a competitive version. Nor is the Duchable/Erato CD – a strong, charmless reading which misses Grieg's gentle poetry. The recording too is dry and lustreless.

Bolet shows little affinity with Grieg's delightful concerto. He seeks to give a spacious reading and the result is merely lethargic and heavy; even the first-movement cadenza drags. The recording is the best part of the affair – it is of Decca's finest quality.

2 Elegiac melodies, Op. 34; Holberg suite, Op. 40.
*(*) DG Dig. **423 060-2**; *423 060-4* [id.]. Orpheus CO – TCHAIKOVSKY: *Serenade.***

2 Elegiac melodies, Op. 34; Holberg suite, Op. 40; Lullaby, Op. 68/5; 2 Melodies, Op. 53; 2 Melodies, Op. 56.
(*) BIS **CD 147 [id.]. Norwegian CO, Tønnensen.

2 Elegiac melodies, Op. 34; Peer Gynt suite No. 1, Op. 46; Sigurd Jorsalfar suite, Op. 56; 4 Symphonic dances, Op. 64.
** Chan. Dig. **CHAN 8524**; *ABTD 1234* [id.]. Ulster O, Handley.

Holberg suite, Op. 40.
*** DG Dig. **400 034-2**; *3302 031* [id.]. BPO, Karajan – MOZART: *Eine kleine Nachtmusik;* PROKOFIEV: *Symphony No. 1.****
(M) *** Pickwick Dig. **PCD 861** [id.]. Serenata of London – ELGAR: *Serenade*; MOZART: *Eine kleine Nachtmusik.****

Holberg suite, Op. 40; 2 Lyric pieces: Evening in the mountains; At the cradle, Op. 68/5.
(*) Ph. Dig. **412 727-2; *412 727-4* [id.]. ASMF, Marriner – SIBELIUS: *Karelia*; *Swan.***

Karajan's performance of the *Holberg suite* is the finest currently available. The playing has a wonderful lightness and delicacy, with cultured phrasing not robbing the music of its immediacy. There are many subtleties of colour and texture revealed here by the clear yet sumptuous digital sound. The cassette is very successful, but it is the compact disc which presents this recording in the best light of all, with striking presence and detail, and a full, firm bass-line.

The performance by the Serenata of London is also first class in every way, spontaneous, naturally paced and played with considerable eloquence. The contrasts in the finale are nicely made, with plenty of sparkle in the dance theme, while the *Gavotte* shows agreeable poise. Both slow movements have a pleasingly restrained *espressivo*, yet no lack of essential warmth. The ensemble is led rather than conducted by Barry Wilde, and he asserts his personality much in the way Marriner did in the early days of the ASMF. The digital recording is most realistic and very naturally balanced. A bargain.

Otherwise the most attractive collection here is the BIS CD, which includes all of Grieg's music for strings, including the slight but attractive *Melodies*, Opp. 53 and 56, plus the charming *Lullaby*, Op. 68. The playing, if not really distinctive, is enjoyably fresh. These young players, fourteen in number, produce clean attack, vital rhythms and sensitive phrasing, and though a larger ensemble would have provided greater weight, the texture is eminently transparent. The recording was made in 1979 but sounds admirably present.

Sir Neville Marriner's performance of the *Holberg suite* is even more beautifully recorded than Karajan's, with more air round the string textures and a natural balance. However, his performance is less distinguished. Brisk tempi in the odd-numbered movements (with even a sense of hurry in the *Gavotte*) are not balanced by a comparable serenity in the *Sarabande* and *Air*, although the account of the latter is not without eloquence. The playing itself is fresh and committed, but the end result remains slightly disappointing. What makes this coupling worth considering is the pair of *Lyric pieces*. Each is highly evocative, with a memorable cor anglais solo from Barry Davis to create the atmosphere of an *Evening in the mountains*. The string group is strikingly tangible on CD, with the recessed balance adding to the realism, yet not obscuring detail. The high-level cassette transfer is strikingly successful.

Handley's collection with the excellent Ulster Orchestra is in the last resort disappointing. There are imaginative touches. He is good in the central *Symphonic dances*, bringing out the delicate *grazioso* of the second and the *giocoso* of the third, while the *Intermezzo* from *Sigurd Jorsalfar*, *'Borghild's dream'*, has a sense of fantasy. But elsewhere, and especially in the *Peer Gynt suite*, his touch is surprisingly heavy and the music making refuses to take off. Very good recording – although the cassette is less recommendable, with an emphasis on the middle and bass.

The Orpheus account of the *Holberg suite* shows characteristic finesse, polish and commitment too, but a lack of idiomatic feeling. The pacing is not as assured as the playing: the *Prelude* and *Gavotte* are a shade fast and the *Andante religioso* marking of the slow movement is taken a shade too literally. The finale is brilliantly spick and span. The *Elegiac melodies* are eloquent without touching the heart. The recording is excellent: the acoustics of the Performing Arts Centre of New York State University give the group both body and transparency.

There is also a tempting-looking Decca Weekend budget tape which offers the *Elegiac melodies* and *Holberg suite* under Willi Boskovsky and Karajan's VPO *Peer Gynt* excerpts (also available on CD – see below). But Boskovsky isn't really at home in this repertoire and the high-level transfer brings impossibly shrill string sound (*417 798-4*). Not recommended.

Lyric suite, Op. 54; Norwegian dances, Op. 35; Symphonic dances, Op. 64.
*** DG Dig. **419 431-2**; *419 431-4* [id.]. Gothenburg SO, Järvi.

Lyric suite, Op. 54; Norwegian dances, Op. 35; Peer Gynt: excerpts, Op. 23.
(B) *** CfP *CFP 41 4503-4*. Hallé O, Barbirolli.

Excellent playing from the Gothenburg orchestra under Neeme Järvi. These pieces never seem to lose their vernal freshness, and in such sympathetic hands they have a simplicity and directness that are most appealing. Järvi secures light and transparent textures and finely balanced sonorities throughout. His *Lyric suite* includes *Klokkeklang*, (Bell-ringing); taken rather slowly, it sounds far more atmospheric than in the piano version where it is placed last. Very fine, wide-ranging recording, which makes excellent use of the celebrated acoustic of this orchestra's hall. Strongly recommended on CD but not on cassette, where the wide reverberation has brought transfer problems, producing a compression of the upper range plus a poor focus in the middle and bass.

Cassette collectors should be well satisfied with Barbirolli's CfP tape which offers excellent recordings from the late 1960s and early 70s, sounding admirably lively and showing their age only in some loss of amplitude in the upper string timbre. There are many characteristic touches in these performances and great warmth throughout. Barbirolli's *Lyric suite* is second to none and the complete set of *Norwegian dances* also suits his temperament especially well. Incidentally, readers who already have recordings of the two *Peer Gynt suites* will be pleased to find that the present issue enterprisingly includes the *Overture*, *Dance of the Mountain King's Daughter* and the *Norwegian bridal procession*, yet does not duplicate the more familiar music.

(i) *Old Norwegian romance with variations, Op. 51;* (ii) *4 Norwegian dances, Op. 35; Peer Gynt suites Nos 1, Op. 46; 2, Op. 55.*
** Ph. **420 081-2** [id.]. (i) Philh. O; (ii) ECO, Leppard.

Leppard is at his finest in the *Old Norwegian romance with variations*, a comparatively extended work: his phrasing is subtle and he secures beautifully refined playing from the Philharmonia Orchestra, while the digital recording is of Philips' best. The other items are mid-1970s analogue recordings; here, while the refinement remains, there is at times a lack of vitality. There are more strongly characterized accounts of the *Peer Gynt suites* available, notably Karajan's.

INSTRUMENTAL MUSIC

Cello sonata in A min.
*** Claves **CD 50-703 [CD 703]**. Claude Starck, Ricardo Requejo – CHOPIN: *Cello sonata.****
(*) CRD *CRDC 4091*. Robert Cohen, Vignoles (with FRANCK: *Cello sonata*(*)).

The Grieg *Sonata* is gratefully written for both instruments: chronologically it comes between the *Second* and *Third Violin sonatas* and dates from 1883. Its slow movement is related to the *Homage march* from *Sigurd Jorsalfar* and the work undoubtedly enriches the cellist's relatively small repertoire. The Swiss cellist Claude Starck is a pupil of Fournier and a remarkably fine artist whose expressive intensity at both ends of the dynamic spectrum is of the kind that never calls attention to itself. Both he and his Spanish partner play with a superb and compelling artistry. (Fournier himself has re-recorded the work – the record was made while he was in his late seventies – but while there are moments when the old flair reasserts itself, the performance lacks technical assurance: Philips **412 962-2**.)

With his clean, incisive style Cohen gives a strong performance of the rarely heard Grieg *Sonata*, sensitively accompanied by Roger Vignoles. In the folk element Cohen might have adopted a more persuasive style, bringing out the charm of the music more; but certainly he sustains the sonata structures well. The last movement is one of Grieg's most expansive. The recording lacks a little in range at both ends, but presents the cello very convincingly. The cassette transfer is of CRD's usual high quality.

Violin sonata No. 3 in C min., Op. 45.
(*) Erato Dig. **ECD 88177; *MCE 75258* [id.]. Pierre Amoyal, Mikhail Rudy – FRANCK: *Sonata.***(*)

Pierre Amoyal takes the Grieg *Sonata* more seriously than do many violinists and makes no attempt to prettify it. His is a sober yet ardent account which does justice to its freshness and poetry. As in the case of its companion, Mikhail Rudy is ill served by the engineers and the piano is not well focused. But there is nothing wanting artistically.

PIANO MUSIC

Holberg suite, Op. 40; Lyric pieces from Opp. 12, 38, 43, 47, 54, 57, 68, 71; Norwegian dance No. 2, Op. 35; Peer Gynt: Morning.
(*) Tel. Dig. **ZK8.42925 [id.]. Cyprien Katsaris.

As a glance at the above listing will show, Cyprien Katsaris draws on a wider range of Grieg's piano music than does the classic and, indeed, indispensable Gilels recital, which is drawn exclusively from the *Lyric pieces* (DG **419 749-2**). Katsaris starts off with *Morning mood* from *Peer Gynt*; the rest of the recital, apart from the opening ten minutes, is devoted to the suite *From Holberg's time* and one of the *Norwegian dances*, Op. 35. He is moreover accorded quite outstanding recording quality; the piano sound is particularly realistic and 'present', with plenty of range and colour. He plays with character and combines both temperament and sensitivity, and is generally scrupulous in observing dynamic nuances. Of course, Gilels has poetic insights and an aristocratic finesse that are special; there are occasions here when this young artist is a shade impetuous, as in Op. 54, No. 3, or the middle section of *Home-sickness*, Op. 57, No. 6; but, for the most part, these are strong and idiomatic performances – perhaps too 'strong' in the *Holberg suite* where he is masterful and exuberant and where more finesse could be in order.

Lyric pieces: Op. 12/1; Op. 38/1; Op. 43/1–2; Op. 47/2–4; Op. 54/4–5; Op. 57/6; Op. 62/4 and 6; Op. 68/2, 3 and 5; Op. 71/1, 3 and 6–7.
❀ *** DG **419 749-2** [id.]. Emil Gilels.

A generous selection of Grieg's *Lyric pieces*, from the well-known *Papillon*, Op. 43/1, to the less often heard and highly poetic set Op. 71, written at the turn of the century. With Gilels we are in the presence of a great keyboard master whose characterization and control of colour and articulation are wholly remarkable. An altogether outstanding record in every way. The CD has brought a rather soft-focused piano sound, but the result is ideal for this repertoire.

VOCAL MUSIC

Peer Gynt (incidental music), Op. 23 (complete).
(M)*** Unicorn **CD 2003/4** [id.]. Carlson, Hanssen, Björköy, Hansli, Oslo PO Ch., LSO, Dreier.

Peer Gynt (incidental music), Op. 23 (complete)*; Sigurd Jorsalfar (incidental music), Op. 56* (complete).
*** DG Dig. **423 079-2**; *423 079-4* (2) [id.]. Bonney, Eklöf, Sandve, Malmberg, Holmgren; Foss, Maurstad, Stokke (speakers); Gösta Ohlin's Vocal Ens., Pro Musica C. Ch., Gothenburg SO, Järvi.

No single performance of *Peer Gynt* included all the music Grieg composed, and various changes, omissions and additions were made for the Copenhagen (1886) and Christiania (1892) productions. Neeme Järvi's record differs from its predecessor by Per Dreier in offering the Grieg Gesamtausgabe *Peer Gynt*, which bases itself primarily on the twenty-six pieces he included in the 1875 production rather than the final published score prepared after Grieg's death by Halvorsen. Until recently the original autograph of the 1875 was believed incomplete, but this well-documented record comes as close as possible to Grieg's declared wishes. Järvi's version also comes closer to the original by including spoken dialogue, as one would have expected in the theatre. The set has an additional advantage of the complete *Sigurd Jorsalfar* score which includes some splendid music. The performances by actors, singers (solo and choral) and orchestra alike are exceptionally vivid, with the warm Gothenberg ambience used to creative effect. The vibrant histrionics of the spoken words undoubtedly add to the drama; indeed there is an added dimension here, for the perspective of the recording has striking depth as well as breadth (the choral sounds are particularly lovely). These CDs are undoubtedly in the demonstration class, and the tapes (which include the excellent CD documentation) are pretty impressive too.

Those who prefer not to have the Norwegian spoken dialogue can rest content with the excellent Unicorn analogue set from the end of the 1970s, which sounds admirably fresh in its CD format, the sound untampered with in the transfer. Per Dreier achieves very spirited results from his soloists, the Oslo Philharmonic Chorus and our own LSO, with some especially beautiful playing from the woodwind; the recording is generally first class, with a natural perspective between soloists, chorus and orchestra. The Unicorn set (without *Sigurd Jorsalfar*) may be thought less generous, but it includes thirty-two numbers in all, including Robert Henrique's scoring of the *Three Norwegian dances*, following the revised version of the score Grieg prepared for the 1886 production in Copenhagen. Whichever version one chooses, this music, whether familiar or unfamiliar, continues to astonish by its freshness and inexhaustibility.

Peer Gynt: extended excerpts.
(*) HMV Dig. **CDC7 47003-2 [id.]. Popp, ASMF, Marriner.
*(*) Ph. Dig. **411 038-2** [id.]. Ameling, San Francisco SO, De Waart.

(i) *Peer Gynt:* extended excerpts; (ii) *Holberg suite, Op. 40.*
(M) **(*) Decca *417 283-4* [id.]. (i) RPO, Weller; (ii) Nat. PO, Boskovsky.

(i) *Peer Gynt:* extended excerpts; *Overture In Autumn, Op. 11; Symphonic dance No. 2.*
(M) *** HMV **CDM7 69039-2** [id.]. (i) Ilse Hollweg, Beecham Ch. Soc.; RPO, Beecham.

All the single-disc compilations from *Peer Gynt* rest under the shadow of Beecham's, which is not ideal as a recording (the choral contribution lacks polish and is rather too forwardly balanced), but which offers moments of magical delicacy in the orchestral playing. Beecham showed a very special feeling for this score, and to hear *Morning*, the gently textured *Anitra's dance*, or the eloquent portrayal of the *Death of Aase* under his baton is a uniquely rewarding experience. Ilse Hollweg too is an excellent soloist. The recording dates from 1957 and, like most other Beecham reissues, has been enhanced by the remastering process. The orchestral sound is full and warm, and if the choral image remains too robust, the fierceness has been tamed. In short this is not to be missed, particularly at mid-price. The most delectable of the *Symphonic dances*, very beautifully played, makes an ideal encore after *Solveig's lullaby*, affectingly sung by Hollweg. The final item, the *Overture In Autumn*, not one of Grieg's finest works, is most enjoyable when Sir Thomas is so affectionately persuasive. Again the (1956) recording is made to seem more expansive than in its old LP format, with a firmer bass, and glowing colour from the woodwind and horns.

No disrespect is intended in calling Sir Neville Marriner's account of *Peer Gynt* serviceable, for the performance and recording are of good quality, the acoustic is pleasant and the sound agreeably fresh. No grumbles here, then, save for the fact that Lucia Popp sings in German – but then, so did Ilse Hollweg for Beecham. At the same time, this is not a performance that attains real distinction or character and, in spite of the excellence of the engineering, it does not displace Beecham. The compact disc is freshly detailed and glowing, but the music making does not really lift off here.

De Waart directs a warmly sympathetic reading of the *Peer Gynt* music, less sharply focused than the rival Marriner version on HMV. It brings an advantage in that Ameling, a fine soloist, sings in Norwegian, where Popp uses German. The *Wedding march* is not included, but the brief unaccompanied choral piece, *Song of the church-goers*, is. Otherwise the selection follows the now expanded grouping of movements. Warm, full, not specially brilliant recording.

Weller's is a purely orchestral collection, very positively characterized and showing the RPO in excellent form. The 1979 Decca recording is almost in the demonstration class and has transferred very well to tape. Boskovsky's *Holberg suite* is well played, but his rhythmic flair is less apparent here than in his home repertory. The sound is good, more brilliant, less atmospheric than the coupling. But this is generous measure and offers a good cassette for the car.

Peer Gynt: suites Nos 1, Op. 46; 2, Op. 55.
*** DG Dig. **410 026-2** [id.]. BPO, Karajan – SIBELIUS: *Pelléas et Mélisande*.***
(M) *** DG **423 208-2**; *423 208-4* [id.]. BPO, Karajan – SIBELIUS: *Finlandia* etc.***
(M) * CBS **MYK 42543** [id.]. NYPO, Bernstein – SIBELIUS: *Finlandia* etc.*

Peer Gynt: suite No. 1; suite No. 2: Ingrid's lament; Solveig's song.
(M) *** Decca **417 722-2** [id.]. VPO, Karajan – TCHAIKOVSKY: *Romeo and Juliet**** (with R. STRAUSS: *Till Eulenspiegel****).

Peer Gynt: suite No. 1; suite No. 2: Ingrid's lament; Arab dance.
(*) Telarc Dig. **CD 80048 [id.]. St Louis SO, Slatkin – BIZET: *Carmen suites*.**(*)

Peer Gynt: suites Nos. 1 & 2; Holberg suite; Sigurd Jorsalfar: Homage march.
(M) *** DG *419 474-4* [id.]. BPO, Karajan.

Grieg's perennially fresh score is marvellously played in Karajan's latest recording, though there are small differences between this and his earlier DG version with the same orchestra: Anitra danced with greater allure though no less elegance in 1972 and there was greater simplicity and repose in *Aase's Death*. The expressive portamenti in the latter may not be to all tastes, but the silkiness of the Berlin strings disarms criticism. The new recording is one of the best to have emerged from the Berlin Philharmonic, and the compact disc is particularly striking for its combination of presence, body and detail. Karajan's earlier analogue set remains available, reissued both on a mid-priced CD with Sibelius's *Finlandia*, *Tapiola* and *Valse triste* and additionally on the mid-priced Galleria label, with an excellent tape transfer. The highly expressive performances were played with superlative skill and polish, and most listeners will be lost in admiration for the orchestral playing. The coupling is again different so that any reader preferring the *Holberg suite* will not be disappointed. This is the 1982 digital version, which sounds first class. There is a touch of fierceness on the *Sigurd Jorsalfar* climaxes, but otherwise the earlier performances are given excellent recording.

To offer a further choice, Decca have also reissued Karajan's Vienna recording of the *First Suite* plus two favourite items from the *Second*, which come from ten years earlier. The digital remastering is highly successful, the new sound-image is full and firm, for the original was oustanding in its day for its fullness and clarity. The couplings – vintage Karajan (Richard Strauss and Tchaikovsky) – are equally vivid and this is excellent value (61′) on Decca's mid-priced Ovation label.

The Telarc digital recording is impressively vivid and clear. The over-resonant bass drum which muddies the fortissimos of the coupled incidental music from Bizet's *Carmen* is not troublesome here (although the climax of *In the Hall of the Mountain King* is not absolutely clean). The orchestra playing is good (*Morning* is not so evocative as in the finest versions), and the overall balance is natural. *Anitra's dance* is played by the first desks of the strings, which gives an intimate, chamber-scale presentation that is not ineffective.

Bernstein's performances have undoubted charisma, although there are mannerisms too, notably in *Anitra's dance*. But these have no special historic interest, and the sound is restricted and unrealistic in its CD format.

(i) *Sigurd Jorsalfar, Op. 22: incidental music* (see also above under *Peer Gynt*); *Funeral march in memory of Rikard Nordraak* (orch. Halvorsen); (i) *The Mountain spell, Op. 32.*
*** Unicorn *KPC 8003* [id.]. (i) Kåre Björköy; Oslo Philharmonic Ch., LSO, Per Dreier.

Grieg composed his incidental music for *Sigurd Jorsalfar* (Sigurd the Crusader) in 1872 for a production of Björnson's historical drama in Christiania (as Oslo was then known), though neither he nor the dramatist was particularly satisfied with it. The score comprised five movements in all (three instrumental pieces and two songs), from which Grieg drew the familiar suite; but there were additional sections as well, which are unfamiliar even to most Grieg enthusiasts: indeed, the *Prelude*, the *Horn calls* from Act II and *The King's Ballad* are all new to record and, more importantly, so is the moving *Funeral march in memory of Nordraak* which is given here in Halvorsen's orchestral transcription. Even though it does not claim to be a first recording, *Den Bergtekne* (*The Mountain spell*) for baritone, strings and two horns is something of a rarity, too. *The Mountain spell* (or 'thrall', as it is sometimes translated) is somewhat later than *Sigurd Jorsalfar* and was one of Grieg's favourite pieces. It is based on a ballad from Landstad's collection that is familiar to us through Keats's poem 'La Belle Dame sans Merci', and Grieg spoke of it once as 'possibly one of the few good deeds of my life'. It is a song of great beauty, and is alone worth the price of the tape. The Oslo Philharmonic Choir give a spirited account of themselves, as do the LSO, who play sensitively for Per Dreier. Kåre Björköy is an excellent soloist with well-focused tone and is particularly impressive in *Den Bergtekne*. The recording is very good indeed: detail is well defined, the texture clean and well ventilated, and the perspective is agreeably natural. However, readers will note that Järvi's more recent digital recording of *Sigurd Jorsalfar*, which is on balance finer than Per Dreier's, is included with the complete DG set of *Peer Gynt*.

Grofé, Ferde (1892–1972)

Grand Canyon suite.
*** Decca Dig. **410 110-2** [id.]. Detroit SO, Dorati (with GERSHWIN: *Porgy and Bess****).
*** Telarc Dig. **CD 80086** [id.] (with additional *Cloudburst* including real thunder). Cincinnati Pops O, Kunzel – GERSHWIN: *Catfish Row.****
** HMV **CDC7 47716-2** [id.]. Utah SO, Abravanel – COPLAND: *El Salón Mexico.***

Antal Dorati has the advantage of superlative Decca recording, very much in the demonstration class, with stereophonically vivid detail. Yet the performance combines subtlety with spectacle, and on compact disc the naturalness of the orchestral sound-picture adds to the sense of spaciousness and tangibility. With its outstanding coupling of Robert Russell Bennett's *Symphonic picture* from *Porgy and Bess*, this version is very much in a class of its own.

The Cincinnati performance is also played with great commitment and fine pictorial splendour, although Dorati scores at *Sunrise*, where his powerful timpani strokes add to the power of the climax, while at the opening of *Sunset* the Detroit strings have greater body and richness. Yet the Cincinnati *On the trail* has fine rhythmic point and piquant colouring. What gives the Telarc CD its special edge is the inclusion of a second performance of *Cloudburst* as an appendix. Over a period of five years the Telarc engineers had been recording genuine thunderstorms in both Utah and Arizona, and an edited version of their most spectacular successes is laminated into the orchestral recording. The result is overwhelmingly thrilling, except that in the final thunderclap God quite upstages the orchestra, who are left trying frenziedly to match its amplitude in their closing peroration. A word of warning: the opening of this movement is deceptively gentle – so don't be fooled into setting the volume level too high. And if you live in a flat, make sure all the neighbours are out, or at least warn them what to expect.

The Utah orchestra under Abravanel also provide an attractive account of Grofé's picaresque score, making the most of its melodic content and finding plenty of colour and warmth in its pictorialism. *On the trail* is wittily and affectionately done, and in spite of rather primitive storm effects (especially by comparison with Telarc) *Cloudburst* is rather telling. The analogue recording has been effectively remastered, but this should have been reissued on EMI's mid-priced Studio label. With only *El Salón Mexico* offered as a coupling, it is ungenerous and expensive.

Handel, George Frideric (1685–1759)

Amaryllis: suite (arr. Beecham); *Music for the Royal Fireworks; Water music: suite* (both arr. Baines).
(*) ASV Dig. **CDRPO 8002; *ZRPO 8002* [id.]. RPO, Menuhin.

Sir Yehudi Menuhin on one of the first issues on the RPO's own label chose in his Handel selection to include a colourful suite arranged by Beecham, *Amaryllis*. Totally out of fashion nowadays, using clarinets and triangle, with at least one of the movements fabricated by Beecham himself, it proves a charming piece. Like the well-known *Fireworks* and *Water music*, the latter in an arrangement by Anthony Baines that claims to use a contemporary source for re-ordering the movements, it is warmly and vigorously done by Beecham's old orchestra, helped by full, well-balanced recording. With any reservations duly noted concerning style, this is persuasive music-making, with the Beecham arrangement particularly light and delectable. The very resonant sound has led to a relatively low-level tape which seems clouded in comparison with the CD.

Ballet music: Alcina: overture; Acts I and III: suites. Il pastor fido: suite; Terpsichore: suite.
*** Erato Dig. **ECD 88084** [id.]. E. Bar. Sol., Gardiner.

As so often in the history of staged dance music, Handel wrote his ballet music for a specific dancer, in this case Marie Sallé, and her special skills demanded a high proportion of lyrical music. Handel rose to the challenge: the expressive writing here is very appealing; so is the scoring with its felicitous use of recorders. John Eliot Gardiner is just the man for such a programme. He is not afraid to charm the ear, yet allegros are vigorous and rhythmically infectious. The bright and clean recorded sound adds to the sparkle, and the quality is first class. A delightful collection, and very tuneful too.

Concerto grosso in C (Alexander's Feast); Oboe concertos Nos 1–3; Sonata a 5 in B flat.
*** DG Dig. **415 291-2**; *415 291-4* [id.]. E. Concert, Pinnock.

Concerto grosso in C (Alexander's Feast); Oboe concertos Nos 1–2; Organ concerto in D min., Sonata a 5 in B flat.
(*) Tel. **ZK8 43050 [id.]. Schaeftlein, Tachezi, VCM, Harnoncourt.

Rhythms are sprightly and Pinnock's performance of the *Alexander's Feast concerto* is as good as any now available. It has both vitality and imagination, and the strong tone has clarity and body. (The wine has not turned to vinegar, as is so often the case with period string tone.) The *B flat Sonata* (HWV 288) is to all intents and purposes a concerto, and it is given with great sensitivity and taste by Simon Standage and his colleagues. David Reichenberg is the excellent soloist in the *Oboe concertos* (HWV 301, 302a, 287), the first of which is definitely Handel, while the authenticity of the others is less certain. Excellently balanced and truthful recording enhances the attractions of this issue on chrome tape, but particularly in the CD format. The only minor criticism is that the record could have been filled more generously.

There is nothing wrong with Harnoncourt's collection except that, dating from 1974, it might more sensibly have been reissued at mid-price. Jurg Schaeftlein is a fine oboist, but he omits the third concerto (HWV 287) in favour of Herbert Tachezi's spirited performance of a fairly attractive hybrid organ concerto based on a sonata from the first set of Telemann's *Tafelmusik*. Alice Harnoncourt is the third soloist in the *Sonata a 5*. Good performances, all well recorded and cleanly transferred to CD; but Pinnock's concert is generally preferable, not least because of the fine modern digital recording.

Concerti grossi, Op. 3/1–6.
*** DG **413 727-2**; *413 727-4* [id.]. E. Concert, Pinnock.
*** Ph. Dig. **411 482-2** [id.]. ASMF, Marriner.
(*) Hung. Dig. **HCD 12463-2. Liszt CO, Janos Rolla.
(M) **(*) EMI *EMX 41 2086-4*. Prague CO, Mackerras.

The six Op. 3 *Concertos* with their sequences of brief jewels of movements find Pinnock and the English Concert at their freshest and liveliest, with plenty of sparkle and little of the abrasiveness associated with 'authentic' performance. For a version on period instruments, this could hardly be better with its realistic, well-balanced sound. The playing has breadth as well as charm. While the CD is particularly striking in its presence, the chrome cassette too is a state-of-the-art issue.

In Sir Neville Marriner's latest version with the Academy, tempi tend to be a little brisk, but the results are inspiring and enjoyable. The playing is of the usual high standard that we take for granted from this ensemble, with the wind playing particularly distinguished. The continuo is divided between organ and harpsichord, though the latter is reticently balanced; otherwise, the recording is altogether excellent, clean and well detailed with an agreeable ambience. This should well suit CD collectors who are not 'authenticists'; textures are fuller here than on Pinnock's competing Archiv recording, and the CD quality is admirably fresh.

A third version from Hungaroton also uses modern instruments to good effect, in some ways striking a happy medium between Pinnock's 'authentic' leanness of texture and Marriner's briskness. The Hungaroton digital recording combines fullness with clarity, although the harpsichord continuo could make a stronger effect, not entirely a matter of balance; the organist in the sixth concerto is a more striking player.

The mid-priced EMI version is a modern recording (1980) and Mackerras draws good playing from the Prague orchestra. Not unexpectedly from this conductor, there is plenty of vitality, although the expressive side of the music is not neglected. The effect, with modern instruments, is comparatively robust, but with a lively tape transfer and plenty of immediacy this remains competitive for those not insisting on original instruments.

12 Concerti grossi, Op. 6/1–12.
❀ *** Ph. Dig. **410 048-2** (3) [id.]. ASMF, Iona Brown.
(*) DG Dig. **410 897-2; *410 897-4* (1–4); **410 898-2**; *410 898-4* (5–8); **410 899-2**; *410 899-4* (9–12) [id.]. E. Concert, Pinnock.
** ASV Dig. *ZCDCB 303* (3). Northern Sinf., Malcolm.

Handel's set of twelve *Concerti grossi*, Op. 6 – the high-water mark of Baroque orchestral music – has a distinguished recording history. The first successful complete set came in the early days of the mono LP era, on six 10″ discs (later transferred, less successfully, to three 12″), from Boyd Neel and his String Orchestra, and very fine it was. Others followed, notably from Menuhin, but it was Sir Neville Marriner's 1968 ASMF version, recorded under the guiding scholarship of Thurston Dart, which dominated the catalogue for over a decade and set the standards by which all others were judged. That has now been deleted but will no doubt reappear on mid-priced CD in due course.

The young Iona Brown participated at Marriner's late-1960s recording sessions. She was soloist (among others, for the solo roles were shared, Marriner himself taking part) in the *Concerto No. 10 in D minor*, and she obviously absorbed a great deal from the experience of working with Thurston Dart. Her new Philips performances have much in common with the earlier set; tempi are sometimes uncannily alike, notably in Handel's marvellously entertaining fugues. But such similarities are deceptive, for the new readings have many new insights to offer and Miss Brown – while always remaining entirely at the service of the composer – sets her own personality firmly on the proceedings. In the expressive music (and there are some memorable Handelian tunes here) she is freer, warmer and more spacious. Where allegros are differently paced, they are often slightly slower, yet the superbly crisp articulation and the rhythmic resilience of the playing always bring added sparkle. On recording grounds, the Philips set gains considerably: the sound is fuller and (on CD especially) fresher and more transparent. The contrast between the solo group and the ripieno (already extremely effective in Marriner's Decca balance) is even more tangible. This can be recommended strongly in both media, for the chrome cassettes also represent the highest state of the art.

In his pursuit of authentic performance on original instruments, Pinnock finds a fair compromise between severe principle and sweetened practice. This set of Handel's most ambitious series of concertos, like Pinnock's set of Bach's *Brandenburgs*, adopts positive speeds which both give exhilaration and thrust to the fast movements (notably in the fugal writing) and provide an expressive feeling to slow movements. For all its 'authenticity', this is never unresponsive music-making, with fine solo playing set against an attractively atmospheric acoustic. Ornamentation is often elaborate – but never at the expense of line. However, these are performances to admire and to sample, but hardly to warm to. If listened through, the sharp-edged sound eventually tends to tire the ear and there is little sense of grandeur and few hints of tonally expansive beauty. It is difficult to believe that Handel's generation did not expect greater richness of texture in works of this kind. The recording is first class in both media, and each of the three cassettes and CDs is available separately.

George Malcolm's set uses a full complement of modern string players: the playing is polished and alert, but essentially expressive in style, heard at its best in the full-bodied opening of *Concerto No. 7*, with a genial fugato following. The best known, No. 5, is also strongly characterized and gives much pleasure, while throughout Malcolm conveys his own warmth for this endlessly inventive music. But, as in his earlier analogue ASV set of Op. 3, although the playing is always spirited, in the faster movements rhythms are sometimes jogging rather than sprightly. The recording, made in All Saints Church, Gosforth, is generally well balanced and agreeably realistic, although the harpsichord continuo might have been clearer.

Harnoncourt's set on Telefunken is too eccentric to be really competitive. The recording is beautifully clear, but this serves only to point up Harnoncourt's insistence on continual dynamic change between phrases (and often within a phrase) which gives the music a curious feeling of restlessness. The famous melody of No. 12, fast and jaunty, is almost unrecognizable, and elsewhere Harnoncourt and his Vienna Concentus Musicus miss much of the breadth and vision of Handel's masterpiece (**ZB8 35603**).

Concerto grosso in C (Alexander's Feast); Harp concerto, Op. 4/5; Concerto for lute and harp in B flat, Op. 4/6; Rodrigo: suite.
(M) *** Decca *414 052-4* [id.]. Ellis, Dupré, L. Philomusica, Granville Jones.

These recordings come from the earliest days of stereo (1959/60) but sound astonishingly undated. The *Rodrigo suite* has been added to fill out the original Oiseau-Lyre issue. They are wholly delightful performances and the recording is beautifully balanced. The cassette is splendidly managed.

Concerti a due cori: Nos 1 in B flat; 2 in F; 3 in F.
* O-L Dig. **411 721-2** [id.]. AAM, Hogwood.

Tolerance is at times stretched by early music groups, even the most distinguished. The sounds produced by this band might have given pleasure to period ears – though in as hedonistic an age as the eighteenth century, this is doubtful – but they don't always to ours. Even by the standards of period-instrument groups, the noise is pretty vinegary and miserable, and there is some less-than-perfect ensemble. Of course there are some good things but, generally speaking, this record is only recommended *faute de mieux*. The quality of the recorded sound has razor-edged clarity to match the Academy's strings.

Guitar concerto in F (arr. from *Organ concerto, Op. 4/5*).
** CBS **MK 39560**; *IMT 39560* [id.]. Williams, ASMF, Sillito – BACH and MARCELLO: *Concertos.***

This concerto originated as a recorder sonata (Op. 1/11), but is best known in Handel's later version for organ and strings. In this further transcription the music is much less effective, and the use of modern string instruments does not help the balance. John Williams plays with his usual musicianship, but overall this cannot be said to be a great success.

Organ concertos, Op. 4/1 6; Op. 7/1–6; Second set: Nos 1 in F; 2 in A; Arnold edition: Nos 1 in D min.; 2 in F.
*** Erato Dig. **ECD 881363** (3) [id.]. Ton Koopman, Amsterdam Bar. O.

Organ concertos, Op. 4/1–6; Op. 7/1–6.
(M) **(*) Tel. **ZB8 35282** (3) [id.]. Herbert Techezi, VCM, Harnoncourt.

Organ concertos, Op. 4/1–6; in F (Cuckoo and the nightingale), HWV 295; in A, HWV 296; Sonata in D min. (Il trionfo del tempo a del disinganno, HWV 46a.
*** Decca Dig. **414 604-2**; *414 604-4* (2) [id.]. Peter Hurford, Concg. CO, Rifkin.

Organ concertos, Op. 4/1–6; in A, HWV 296.
*** DG Dig. **413 465-2**; *413 465-4* (2) [id.]. Simon Preston, E. Concert, Pinnock.

Organ concertos, Op. 7/1–6; in F (Cuckoo and the nightingale); in D min., HWV 304.
*** DG Dig. **413 468-2**; *413 468-4* (2) [id.]. Simon Preston, E. Concert, Pinnock.

Organ concertos, Op. 7/1–6; in D min., HWV 304; in F, HWV 305 & Appendix.
*** Decca Dig. **417 560-2**; *417 560-4* (2) [id.]. Peter Hurford, Concg. CO, Rifkin.

Ton Koopman offers the complete sets of Opus 4 and Opus 7 plus four other *Concertos* on three CDs and rather sweeps the board, especially compared with Simon Preston's two packages which offer less music and involve an extra disc. In any case, Ton Koopman's recordings are generally preferable both as performances and as recordings. The playing has wonderful life and warmth, tempi are always aptly judged and, although original instruments are used, this is authenticity with a kindly presence, for the warm acoustic ambience of St Bartholomew's Church, Beek-Ubbergen, Holland, gives the orchestra a glowingly vivid coloration, and the string timbre is particularly attractive. So is the organ itself, which is just right for the music. Ton Koopman plays imaginatively throughout; no single movement sounds tired, while characterization is strong. The orchestral fugues emerge with genial clarity. Koopman directs the accompanying group from the keyboard, and the interplay between soloist and ripieno is a delight. The balance could hardly be better.

Simon Preston's set of the Handel *Organ concertos* comes in two separate packages. In the first, containing the six Op. 4 works, plus the *A major* (the old No. 14), though the balance of the solo instrument is not ideal, the playing of both Preston and the English Concert is admirably fresh and lively. Ursula Holliger is outstanding on a baroque harp in Op. 4, No. 6, and she creates some delicious sounds; however, it seems perverse not to include the organ version of this work, with the harp arrangement already available on other records. The second of the two boxes, containing the six Op. 7 works, plus the *'Cuckoo and the nightingale'* and the old *No. 15 in D minor*, was recorded on the organ at St John's, Armitage, in Staffordshire, and is even more attractive, not only for the extra delight of the works but for the warmth and assurance of the playing, which comes near the ideal for an 'authentic' performance. These are all recordings which positively invite re-hearing, with full, clear sound, all the fresher on CD, but sounding splendid, too, on the excellent chrome tapes.

Peter Hurford's Decca set also comes in two separate boxes, with extra works included, which is why a pair of CDs is needed in each case. The organ of the Bethlehemkerk, Papendrecht, Holland, has attractively fresh, bright registrations, particularly suited to the Op. 4 set, which are generally preferable to Preston's versions. Allegros are jaunty yet have substance too; slow movements have just the right degree of expressive weight. Ornamentation is well judged and the string playing is sprightly, polished and affectionate, a splendid example of modern instruments sounding just right in Baroque repertoire. The highly engaging *Cuckoo and the nightingale concerto* is particularly successful – here Hurford interpolates a Telemann movement instead of improvising, as the composer would have done. The *Sonata* is also attractive and, with splendid recording, fresh and yet not lacking weight where needed, this is very enjoyable indeed. The sound is in the demonstration bracket, on the excellent chrome tapes as well as the CDs. The Op. 7 set is presented in much the same way and has comparable sparkle, but the effect (especially of the first four concertos) seems rather lightweight compared with Simon Preston's Archiv alternatives. The latter's use of the Armitage organ brings added warmth and rather more breadth to the playing; and he and Pinnock were clearly inspired to music making of the utmost spontaneity. This remains the preferred version, in spite of Peter Hurford's considerable bonuses, which include a useful appendix. The F major work, HWV 305, was partly based on the first of Handel's *Concerti a due cori*; three additional movements from the latter, not used in Handel's five-movement organ concerto, are included as a bonus: the final allegro is a real lollipop, with some spectacular horn playing. The well-documented booklet lists the various movements (by Telemann, Avison and Stanley, as well as Handel) which Hurford interpolates throughout the set in the place of Handel's *ad libs*. As in the companion box, the sound is absolutely first class in both formats.

Herbert Tachezi concentrates on the twelve concertos which make up Opp. 4 and 7, which he offers complete. We are told in the accompanying booklet that the ornamentation in these performances was essentially spontaneous and even varied from take to take. This may have made Harnoncourt and his accompanying group over-cautious, for they sometimes seem unadventurous, even square. The overall scale of the music making is relatively modest, creating an agreeable chamber-music atmosphere. However, at times one feels that the more robust and grander qualities of Handel's inspiration are played down. Tachezi's registration and decorative flourishes give consistent cause for pleasure; his organ is a splendid instrument and obviously well chosen for this repertoire. It makes a strong contrast with the 'authentic' string group, which at times produce a rather sombre colouring. Their rhythmic pointing can sometimes be agreeably lively too. The recording (originally issued on LP in 1977) sounds admirable in its CD format, the Teldec transfers characteristically fresh and clean. The box is offered at upper mid-price.

Organ concertos, Op. 4/1 & 2; Op. 7/1 & 2.
(M) ** Tel. **ZS8 43628** [id.]. Karl Richter with CO.

Organ concertos, Op. 4/3 & 4; Op. 7/3 & 4.
(M) *** Tel. **ZS8 43770** [id.]. Karl Richter with CO.

Organ concertos, Op. 4/5 & 6; Op. 7/5 & 6.
(M) *** Tel. **ZS8 44007** [id.]. Karl Richter with CO.

Organ concertos, Op. 4/1 & 4; Op. 7/1; in F (Cuckoo and the nightingale).
(*) DG Dig. **419 634-2; *419 643-4* [id.]. Simon Preston, E. Concert, Pinnock.

These Teldec recordings come from a complete set which Karl Richter recorded in 1959 and which was originally issued in the UK by Decca, first at full price and later on the Ace of Diamonds label. The sound is surprisingly undated and the performances have the merit of exactly the right kind of organ (St Mark's, Munich) and a small, flexible orchestral group which Richter directs from the keyboard. The element of extemporization is a limited feature, at first, especially in Op. 4; but later, in Op. 7, organ *ad libs* are effectively included. Throughout, the playing is attractively buoyant; the full sound of the strings, contrasted with imaginative registration, makes this series increasingly attractive. The first disc (**ZS8 43628**) is enjoyable enough, but the second (**ZS8 43770**) is a most winning collection, offering four of Handel's very best works. The spirited solo contribution is matched by the strong personality of the orchestral group. The expressive string playing of the opening of Op. 4 No. 3 is matched by the vigour at the beginning of Op. 7 No. 3, with its *Hallelujahs*, and in the same work there is a vivacious minuet. The slow movement of Op. 4 No. 4 has an appropriately solemn sobriety, and the *Adagio* opening of Op. 7 No. 4 again offers a warm *espressivo* with the following *Allegro* appropriately jolly. Anyone looking for a single CD from which to sample these ever-inventive works could not do better than this. The third issue (**ZS8 44007**) is also comparably successful, and anyone collecting this series should find the overall value first class.

On DG Archiv, a useful sampler of the Preston/Pinnock recordings, although the choice of works is arbitrary.

Overtures: Agrippina; Alceste; Il pastor fido; Samson; Saul (Acts I & II); Teseo.
*** DG Dig. **419 219-2**; *419 219-4* [id.]. E. Concert, Pinnock.

Trevor Pinnock directs vigorous, exhilarating performances of these Handel overtures, most of them hardly known at all but full of highly original ideas, even in the most formally structured pieces. The *Grande Entrée* to *Alceste* is a fine maestoso movement in the French style, introducing a masque. Three other items come from operas and two from oratorios, all freshly and cleanly recorded to match the lively performances. Generous measure, too, at over an hour.

Music for the Royal Fireworks (original wind scoring).
*** Telarc Dig. **CD 80038** [id.]. Cleveland Symphonic Winds, Fennell – HOLST: *Military band suites.****❀

Music for the Royal Fireworks; Concerti a due cori Nos 1 and 2.
(*) Ph. Dig. **411 122-2 [id.]. E. Bar. Soloists, Gardiner.

Music for the Royal Fireworks; Concerti a due cori Nos 2 and 3.
*** DG Dig. **415 129-2**; *415 129-4* [id.]. E. Concert, Pinnock.

Music for the Royal Fireworks; Concerto a due cori No. 2 in F; Concerto No. 1 in F.
** HMV Dig. **CDC7 49026-2**. Cappella Coloniensis, Linde.

Music for the Royal Fireworks; (i) *Oboe concerto in G min.; Acis and Galatea: Sinfonia; Alexander's Feast: Overture.*
** ASV Dig. **CDDCA 521**; *ZCDCA 521*. Scottish CO, Gibson; (i) with Miller.

Music for the Royal Fireworks; Water music (complete).
*** Argo **414 596-2**; *KZRC 697* [id.]. ASMF, Marriner.
(M) **(*) Decca Dig. **417-743-2**; *417 273-4* [id.]. SCO, Münchinger.

Music for the Royal Fireworks; Water music: Suite in F.
*** O-L Dig. **400 059-2** [id.]. AAM, Hogwood.
(M) ** DG **419 861-2**; *419 861-4* [id.]. BPO, Kubelik.

Music for the Royal Fireworks; Water music; extended suite.
(M) *** Ph. **420 354-2**; *420 354-4* [id.]. ECO, Leppard.

Music for the Royal Fireworks; Water music: Suite in F; Solomon: Arrival of the Queen of Sheba.
** RCA Dig. **RD 85364**. COE, Galway.

Music for the Royal Fireworks: suite; Water music: suite (arr. Harty and Szell); *The Faithful Shepherd: Minuet* (ed. Beecham); *Xerxes: Largo* (arr. Reinhardt).
(M) *** Decca *417 694-4*. LSO, Szell.

(i) *Music for the Royal Fireworks; Water music* (both complete); (ii) *Harp concerto, Op. 4/6;* (iii) *Messiah: Sinfonia.*
(B) ** DG Walkman *413 148-4*. (i) BPO, Kubelik; (ii) Zabaleta, Kuentz CO, Kuentz; (iii) LPO, Karl Richter.

In 1959, Mackerras made an historic recording of Handel's *Fireworks music* with an enormous band of wind, including twenty-six oboes. That record is not yet available on CD. In 1978, in Severance Hall, Cleveland, Ohio, Frederick Fennell gathered together the wind and brass from the Cleveland Symphony Orchestra and recorded a new performance to demonstrate spectacularly what fine playing and digital sound could do for Handel's open-air score. Not all the sound is massive, of course: there is some refreshingly nimble articulation in the *Bourrée*. But in the *Overture*, *La Réjouissance* and the closing section of the *Minuet*, the effect is remarkable. The record also includes an inflated account of Bach's *Fantasia in G*, but that is not an asset. The performance of the Handel represents one of the first great successes of digital recording, and the reading itself has genuine grandeur. The overall sound-balance tends to favour the brass (and the drums), but few will grumble when the result is as overwhelming as it is on the compact disc, with the sharpness of focus matched by the presence and amplitude of the sound-image.

Pinnock does not attempt to compete with the outdoor performances, complete with added effects, except in spirit. He uses four flutes (for *La Paix*), three each of horns, trumpets, oboes and bassoons, and twenty-odd string players. The playing has tremendous spirit and zest, and for those wanting a period-instrument version this is not only the safest but the best recommendation. The DG recording is among the finest Archiv has given us, sounding excellent on CD, although on the chrome cassette the focus slips just a little in some of the more spectacular moments in the *Fireworks music*.

For collectors wanting a coupling of the *Royal Fireworks* and *Water music* in first-class performances, but insisting neither on the original score in the former nor on the use of baroque instruments in the latter, the 1972 Argo issue by the Academy of St Martin-in-the-Fields remains an obvious choice. Marriner directs a sparkling account of the complete *Water music*. All the well-loved movements we once knew only in the Harty suite come out refreshed, and the rest is similarly stylish. Scholars may argue that textures are too thick, but for many listeners the sounds which reach the ears have a welcome freedom from acerbity. It is a substantial advantage that the compact disc (for the transfer is very successful) – unlike most of its rivals – also includes the complete *Fireworks music*. There Marriner's interpretation is more obviously controversial, for he deliberately avoids a weighty manner, even at the magisterial opening of the overture. But with full, resonant recording, Sir Neville's generous coupling makes sound sense; and while other, more modern recordings may be more clearly defined, the digitally remastered Argo recording still sounds both full and fresh.

Münchinger's similar coupling has first-class 1982 digital recording: the effect is vivid and well focused. His style is a compromise between authenticity and the German tradition. In the complete *Water music*, he uses recorders most effectively; the balance, helped by Decca's very transparent sound, is often attractively lightweight. If occasionally tempi seem a shade on the slow side, there is much to enjoy, both here and in the *Fireworks music*, where the clarity reveals some shifts of perspective in the *Overture* and *Bourrée*. Some other versions of this music are more buoyant, but Münchinger is consistently sympathetic and never dull. With the additional advantage of economy, this is well worth considering. The tape transfer, too, is first class.

Alexander Gibson and the Scottish Chamber Orchestra are accorded a more consistent perspective than Münchinger, though the texture is more transparent in the Decca. However, the ASV recording has a better-defined bass and there is no lack of brilliance. The performance is thoroughly straightforward, fairly consistent in matters of double-dotting and generally stylish, but does not offer a serious challenge to the top recommendations. Sound, reliable playing without attaining real distinction – but musical and enjoyable throughout. Whereas Münchinger offers the complete *Water Music* (and at mid-price), Gibson gives us a sinfonia and an overture, plus an *Oboe concerto* finely played by Robin Miller. Gibson gives solid support and no more than routine accounts of the remaining pieces. There is a good cassette, but with a less vivid upper range than the CD.

Those looking for 'authenticity' plus a coupling with the *Water music* can turn to the Academy of Ancient Music on Oiseau-Lyre who offer the Suite in F (with many familiar numbers) taken from Hogwood's complete set, which is not yet issued on CD. In the *Fireworks music* the Academy certainly make a vivid impact (if not creating the feeling of grandeur offered by Fennell on Telarc). The added clarity of the compact disc does emphasize some faults in balance; nevertheless, Hogwood's version can be counted among the best available and has lively rhythms and keen articulation. Hogwood gives a strong impression of the score, even if no attempt is made to reproduce the forces heard in 1749. In the *Water music*, the timbres of the original instruments are consistently attractive, with vibrato-less string-tone never squeezed too painfully.

If original instruments (or their copies) are not essential, then Leppard's mid-priced Philips reissue offers an excellent alternative. The remastering is very successful (on tape as well as CD) and the resonance of the sound in the *Fireworks music* matches the broad and spectacular reading, while the substantial extract from Leppard's complete *Water music* recording has comparable flair, combining rhythmic resilience with an apt feeling for ceremony.

Many readers will, like us, have a nostalgic feeling for the Handel–Harty suites from which earlier generations got to know these two marvellous scores. George Szell and the LSO offer a highly recommendable coupling of them on a Decca lower-mid-priced issue with Handel's *Largo* and the *Minuet* from Beecham's *Faithful Shepherd suite* thrown in for good measure. The orchestral playing throughout is quite outstanding, and the strings are wonderfully expressive in the slower pieces. The horns excel, and the crisp new Decca re-transfer makes for a good bargain. The cassette is vividly realistic, and is in every way preferable to Previn's CD of the same arrangements (Ph. **411 047-2**) which sounds too comfortable and well stuffed.

John Eliot Gardiner secures an excellent response from his players and, as one would expect from this conductor, rhythms are alive and well articulated, and phrasing is always musical. Tempi are a bit on the fast side: there are the usual string bulges favoured by period-instrument groups and wind intonation is good, though not always impeccable. The Philips recording is in the best traditions of the house. Fine though this is, it does not displace Hogwood and the Academy of Ancient Music, or Pinnock and the English Concert on Archiv.

Linde and the Cappella Coloniensis give an eminently well-characterized account of the *Fireworks music*, and are well worth recommendation. There is some expert horn playing, but the performances are not as lean-textured or athletic as Pinnock's English Concert, and rhythms, particularly in the two *Concertos* (HWV 333 and 335b) are somewhat sluggish. The HMV digital recording is very well balanced and, though this is not a first choice, it is an eminently acceptable issue.

Kubelik's full orchestral version of the two suites makes an agreeable DG Galleria mid-priced CD and cassette; but it is outclassed by his Walkman tape which offers the complete *Water music*. This too has been freshly remastered and combines a sense of grandeur with liveliness. It is splendidly played, as is the *Fireworks music*, where the focus of the sound is slightly less clean. Zabaleta's approach to the *Harp concerto* is a trifle cool but eminently musical and the sound-balance is excellent. At bargain price this Walkman tape is certainly good value.

James Galway obtains polished and extremely spirited playing from the Chamber Orchestra of Europe. The sound is brightly vivid and the effect at times almost has an 'authentic' abrasiveness, created by sharp rhythms rather than spare textures. There is a good deal of fast music here, and the famous *Allegro* (the familiar opening movement of the old Harty suite) has surely never been paced more briskly on record. The result is invigorating but in the end a little wearing, especially as, in the closing encore, the *Queen of Sheba* comes in at a gallop.

Music for the Royal Fireworks; Water music: suite in F (both arr. Howarth)*; The Harmonious blacksmith* (arr. Dodgson). *Berenice: Minuet. Occasional oratorio: March. Solomon: Arrival of the Queen of Sheba. Xerxes: Largo* (arr. Archibald or Hazell).
*** Decca Dig. **411 930 2** [id.] Philip Jones Brass Ens., Howarth.

This is a fun concert played with true Baroque spirit, combining polish with bravura, and spectacularly recorded. The *Arrival of the Queen of Sheba* initially needs a mental adjustment, but is disconcertingly vivid in its very different costume, while *The Harmonious blacksmith* stands at his anvil in similarly bold relief. In the *Berenice Minuet* and the famous *Largo*, the sentiment of the bandstand is handsomely avoided, though the playing is warmly expressive, but it is the fast pieces with their intricately exhilarating detail that catch the ear. The sound is certainly spectacular in its CD format.

Water music: Suites Nos 1–3 (complete).
*** DG Dig. **410 525-2**; *410 525-4* [id.]. E. Concert, Pinnock.
*** ASV Dig. **CDDCA 520**; *ZCDCA 520* [id.]. ECO, Malcolm.
(*) Erato **ECD 88005 [id.]. E. Bar. Soloists, Gardiner.
(*) HMV Dig. **CDC7 47145-2 [id.]. BPO, Muti.
(*) Chan. Dig. **CHAN 8382; *ABTD 1136* [id.]. Scottish CO, Gibson.
(*) Ph. **416 447-2 [id.]. ASMF, Marriner.
(M) **(*) Delos Dig. **D/CD 3010** [id.]. LAPO, Schwarz.
(*) HMV Dig. **CDC7 47401-2 [id.]. Linde Cons., Linde.
(M) ** Pickwick Dig. **PCD 826**. City of L. Sinfonia, Hickox.
(B) ** CfP **CD-CFP 9002**; *TC-CFP 40092*. Virtuosi of England, Davison.
(B) *(*) Cirrus Dig. **CIDC 1009**. L. Mozart Players, Jane Glover.

Handel's consistently inspired *Water music*, which divides naturally into three suites, is very well represented in the current catalogue. For those wanting a performance on original instruments, Pinnock's version on DG Archiv is very enticing. Speeds are consistently well chosen and are generally uncontroversial. One test is the famous *Air*, which here remains an engagingly gentle piece. The recording is beautifully balanced and clear, but with bloom on the sound to balance the CD presence. The chrome cassette is good too, but when the brass enter on side two the focus of the tape transfer slips a little.

Those whose taste does not extend to 'authentic' string textures should be well satisfied with George Malcolm's splendid digital recording for ASV. The playing is first class, articulation is deft and detail admirable. Decoration is nicely judged and the alertness of the music making, combined with full, vivid sound, makes a strong impact. There is a sense of delight in the music which makes this version especially appealing. There is a good chrome tape but, though the transfer is made at a high level, some of the upper range is lost; the CD, however, has striking clarity and presence, though the acoustic is warm.

Among other performances on period instruments, Gardiner's is one of the more idiosyncratic, but its very oddities reflect a strong musical personality directing the performance with individuality. Some of his speeds are questionable – often slower than usual – but the life and sense of spontaneity in the performance are very winning, with excellent ensemble and balances. Strangely, he puts the *Overture* second in his scheme; but he has the bright solution, when Handel indicates 'three times' (first on strings, then on wind, finally all together), of doing each half separately, three times over, where normally, in effect, you get everything repeated six times in a movement such as the *Bourrée*. Almost everything he does has charm in it, and the Erato recording is first rate.

As might be imagined, the playing of the Berlin Philharmonic Orchestra under Muti is of the highest calibre, polished and elegant. In the *Overture* of the first suite, a small instrumental group is featured as a neat counterpoint to the main ripieno; throughout, there is a strong emphasis on contrast, with instrumental solos often treated in a concertante manner. In the famous *Air*, some might feel that the element of light and shade is over-stressed, but the playing is very responsive and the strings generally display a light touch. The horns, however, are almost aggressive in their spirited vigour in the famous fanfare tune. With a full yet clear sound-picture, especially vivid on CD, this is easy to enjoy.

Sir Alexander Gibson, like Muti, uses modern instruments. The Scottish Chamber Orchestra, competing directly against the Berlin Philharmonic, emerges with its head held high, not only in its sense of style and polish but also by the vigour and sparkle of the playing. Gibson's pacing of the allegros is brisk and he points the rhythms with infectious zest. There is fine lyrical playing too, notably from the principal oboe, while the horns are robust without being quite as emphatic as their counterparts in Berlin. The combination of energy and warmth comes as a welcome relief after prolonged exposure to period instruments. The ample acoustic of the Glasgow City Hall is attractive and, with excellent overall balance, the sound-image is very believable, especially on CD which has splendid clarity and firmness of definition. The chrome tape is impressive, too, well up to the usual high Chandos standard. Neither here nor in Muti's version does the harpsichord make a strong impression – but that is inevitable in a recording of this kind. In all, this is a very likeable performance which could well be a first choice for many readers.

The Philips account of the *Water music* brings Sir Neville Marriner's second complete recording – and characteristically he has taken the trouble to correct several tiny textual points read wrongly before. The playing too is even finer, helped by full-ranging, refined recording. For anyone wanting a version on a convincing scale, yet using modern instruments, this is recommendable. It dates from 1980, but offers Philips's finest analogue sound quality. However, given the competition, this now seems over-priced. The music making, for all its commitment and polish, has not quite the degree of individuality of Pinnock or Malcolm.

The Los Angeles performance under Gerard Schwarz is hardly less enjoyable, its character more athletic, with playing that is both polished and sprightly. It has an attractive freshness of spirit, yet is without the abrasiveness of early-instrumental timbres. In the second movement of the first suite the oboe soloist takes an extra degree of rhythmic freedom, yet still plays very stylishly. The sound is first class; the horns are crisp and in the *D major suite*, which is placed second, the trumpets are bright and gleaming. The clear detail does not prevent an overall ambient warmth.

Using period instruments, the Linde Consort provides a gentler, more intimate alternative to the outstanding versions of Pinnock and Gardiner. The ensemble is not always so polished, but the easy warmth of the playing is most attractive, not least in the G major movements for flute, recorder, bassoon and strings which Linde (himself the flute- and recorder-player) turns into a separate suite after the groups in F major and D major. First-rate sound back up bright but unabrasive performances.

Those seeking a budget-priced CD should on the whole be well satisfied with Hickox who secures excellent playing from the City of London Sinfonia and, using modern instruments, follows the Chrysander edition, including all nineteen movements. Good ensemble, stylish solo playing and realistically vivid digital recording combine to make this excellent value; although there is not quite the sparkle of Sir Alexander Gibson or the individuality of the Los Angeles account under Schwarz, this is still very enjoyable.

The essentially robust Davison version dates from 1975 and offers bright analogue sound which has remastered with considerable presence, perhaps too much, for the close balance means a reduction of dynamic contrast. The playing is polished and vigorous – the horn roulades are especially good – but the effect is somewhat anonymous. However, this is preferable to Jane Glover's digital alternative on the Cirrus label. Here the music is seriously under-characterized and there is a feeling of a routine run-through. Clearly this talented musician has not fully mastered the art of bringing a Handel performance fully to life in the recording studio.

Other CDs by Malgoire (on CBS) and Teldec's reissue of Harnoncourt's 1979 recording (both 'authentic' in style) are uncompetitive, given the considerable competition.

CHAMBER MUSIC

Flute sonatas, Op. 1/1a; in D; in A min., E min., and B min. (*Halle Nos 1–3*).
*** Ph. Dig. **412 606-2** [id.]. Bennett, Kraemer, Vigay.

These *Sonatas* were recorded in 1981 (the LP and cassette are now withdrawn). William Bennett's compact disc comprises the three *Halle sonatas* and two others: one from the Op. 1 set and the other a more recent discovery from a Brussels manuscript. Bennett uses a modern flute very persuasively, and Nicholas Kraemer and Denis Vigay provide admirable support. The CD transfer is altogether first class and brings to the aural image added freshness and presence.

Oboe sonatas (for oboe and continuo), *Op. 1/5 and 8; in B flat, HWV 357; Sinfonia in B flat for 2 violins and continuo, HWV 338; Trio sonatas: in E min. for 2 flutes, HWV 395; in F for 2 recorders, HWV 405.*
*** Ph. Dig. **412 598-2** [id.]. ASMF Chamber Ens.

Marvellously accomplished performances of the three oboe sonatas (Op. 1, Nos 5 and 8, and the *B flat Sonata*, HWV 357) from Neil Black and the Academy team. Michala Petri and Elisabeth Selin shine in the *F major Sonata* (HWV 405); and the *B flat Sonata for two violins* (HWV 338) finds hardly less persuasive advocacy from Kenneth Sillito and Malcolm Latchem. William Bennett and Trevor Wye give a refreshing account of the *E minor* (HWV 395); and all receive excellent continuo support. No reservations whatsoever here about either the performance or the recording quality, which is among Philips's best.

Recorder sonatas, Op. 1/2, 4, 7; 9 in D min. (originally for flute), *11; in B flat; Oboe sonatas, Op. 1/8; in B flat; in F* (alternative of *Op. 1/5*)*; Trio sonata in F for 2 recorders and continuo; Flute sonata in D, HWV 378.*
**(*) CRD Dig. *CRDC 4077/8* [id.]. L'Ecole d'Orphée.

Recorder sonatas, Op. 1/2, 4, 7, 9 and 11; in B flat.
*** Ph. Dig. **412 602-2** [id.]. Petri, Malcolm, Vigay, Sheen.
*** CRD Dig. **CRD 3412** [id.]. L'Ecole d'Orfée.

Michala Petri plays with her accustomed virtuosity and flair, and it would be difficult to imagine her performances being improved upon. She has the advantage of excellent rapport with her continuo players, and the Philips engineers have produced a natural and spacious sound that is particularly impressive in this compact disc format.

The CRD performances have already won much acclaim. There is some elegant and finished playing from the two recorder players, Philip Pickett and Rachel Becket. David Reichenberg deserves special mention for his contribution in the three *Oboe sonatas* on side four; and there are, as usual with this artist, some beguiling sounds from Stephen Preston. At times (the very opening of the *G minor Recorder sonata*, Op. 1) there is a slight air of inhibition or caution, but in faster movements there is genuine panache and a real sense of style. The *Flute sonata in D*, HWV 378, is a recent discovery and was formerly attributed to Johann Sigismund Weiss (1690–1737): it has already been recorded by William Bennett. In any event, this represents a positive advance over the earlier volumes in this series. The chrome cassettes are well engineered, but the transfer is very high and seems to be approaching saturation point in the *Oboe sonatas*. On CD the *Recorder sonatas* are grouped together and the sound is strikingly refined and realistic; this makes a rewarding alternative to Petri for those preferring 'authentic' timbres.

Trio sonatas, Op. 2/1–6; Sonatas for 2 violins: in F, HWV 392; in G min., HWV 393.
*** Ph. Dig. **412 595-2** [id.]. ASMF Chamber Ens.

Trio sonatas, Op. 5/1–7; Sonatas for 2 violins: in E, HWV 394; in C, HWV 403.
*** Ph. Dig. **412 599-2** (2) [id.]. ASMF Chamber Ens.

This is most musical playing and is beautifully recorded. This makes an admirable change from the period instruments favoured by L'Ecole d'Orphée (see below). The performances from Michala Petri, William Bennett, Kenneth Sillito, Malcolm Latchem and others are wonderfully accomplished and have a refreshing vigour and warmth. In these sonatas, Handel's invention seems inexhaustible and it is difficult to imagine readers not responding to them. The compact discs are excellent in every way.

Trio sonatas, Op. 2/1–2 and 4; in D, HWV 385; in G min., HWV 393; in E min., HWV 395.
*(*) HMV Dig. **CDS7 49201-8** (2) [id.]. Linde Cons. – BACH: *Trio sonatas.**(*)

For all their undoubted accomplishments, the Linde Consort are not wholly persuasive here, though they are very well recorded. They number some expert players among their ranks, including Han de Vries and Christopher Hogwood; surprisingly, however, the performances generally speaking are wanting in the flair and freshness one associates with their names.

Trio sonatas (for flute and violin), *Op. 2/1;* (for violins), *Op. 2/3; Op. 5/2 & 4; Violin sonata in A, Op. 1/3; Sonata for 2 violins in G min., HWV 393.*
*** DG Arc. Dig. **415 497-2** [id.]. E. Concert, Pinnock.

This playing is wonderfully alive and fresh, and also excellently recorded. Rhythms are vital, and the playing of the two violinists (Simon Standage and Micaela Comberti) has panache and style – as, for that matter, have the other contributors. The flautist, Lisa Beznosiuk, is particularly expert and imaginative in the *B minor Sonata*, Op. 2, No. 1; the whole enterprise gives pleasure and stimulus and can be recommended even to those normally unresponsive to period instruments or copies. On CD the recording has excellent ambience and warmth.

Trio sonatas, Op. 2/3–4 & 5; Sonata in F; Rigaudon in D min., Bourrée in G min., March in G.
*(*) Denon **C37 7026** [id.]. Holliger, Bourgue, Thunemann, Christiane Jaccottet, Nagashima.

Not to be confused with the recording Heinz Holliger, Maurice Bourgue and Christiane Jaccottet made for Philips (9500 766 – now deleted). Needless to say, we have expert and lively performances from this distinguished team with what the notes endearingly describe as Christiane Jaccottet 'harpsichord and improvised of basso continuo'! The three dance movements came to light only after the war, when Karl Haas found them in the British Museum and the Fitzwilliam in Cambridge, plus the *F major Sonata*, which is not genuine Handel. The recordings have the merit of clarity, but are made in a relatively small studio whose dryness diminishes the pleasure given by these fine players. A strictly qualified recommendation.

Trio sonatas, Op. 5/1–7.
**(*) CRD *CRDC 4079-80* [id.]. L'Ecole d'Orphée.

Those wanting baroque instruments in this repertoire will find the recordings by L'Ecole d'Orphée are well up to the high standard set by their series. As before, they are closely recorded, but the focus is firm and clean on the excellent chrome cassettes. The playing is expert and intonation is secure, with incisive articulation and lively tempi ensuring that the music is always vivid. The sound is undoubtedly astringent, and there is less geniality than in the Philips versions, but the approach is certainly committed and these performances are very good of their kind.

Viola da gamba sonata in G min., HWV 364b.
*** Decca Dig. **417 646-2**; *417 646-4* (2) [id.]. Lynn Harrell, Igor Kipnis (harpsichord) – BACH: *Viola da gamba sonatas.****

Handel's *Sonata* is another version of Op. 1 No. 6, but the layout is similar to the Bach works with which it is coupled, and in this fine performance and realistic recording it makes an enjoyable bonus to Harrell's Bach set.

Sinfonia (*Trio sonata*) *in B flat for 2 violins & continuo, HWV 338; Trio sonata in C for 2 violins & continuo, HWV 403; Trio sonata for 2 flutes & continuo in E min., HWV 395; Suite for 2 clarinets & horn in D, HWV 424.*
** CRD Dig. *CRDC 4082* [id.]. L'Ecole d'Orphée.

(i) *Violin sonatas: in D min.* (original version of *Op. 1/1*), *HWV 359a: in A, Op. 1/3, HWV 361; in G min., Op. 1/6, HWV 364a; in D, HWV 371; Movement in C min. for violin & continuo, HWV 408; Allegro in C min. for violin & continuo, HWV 412;* (ii) *Recorder sonata in G, HWV 358.*
** CRD Dig. *CRDC 4081* [id.]. (i) Holloway; (ii) Pickett, L'Ecole d'Orphée.

L'Ecole d'Orphée are much admired in Early Music circles and there is no want of style or dedication in these performances. The recording is less close and less unflattering than some of the earlier issues in this series. On its own terms, John Holloway's playing of the *D major Sonata* is accomplished and in excellent style, though it is best to put past recordings out of one's mind. There is none of the breadth of tone and nobility of spirit of a Szymon Goldberg; the thin sonority will give little pleasure to those who set store by beauty of sound. However, it is only fair to say that this series has enjoyed distinguished advocacy, and readers who have admired earlier issues in the series need not hesitate.

Violin sonatas, Op. 1/3, 6, 10, 12, 13–15; in D min., HWV 359a; in D min., HWV 367a; Fantasia in A, HWV 406.
*** Ph. Dig. **412 603-2** (2) [id.]. Iona Brown, Nicholas Kraemer, Denis Vigay.

Violin sonatas, Op. 1/3, 6, 10, 12–14, in D min., HWV 359a.
** Hung. Dig. **HCD 12657** [id.]. György Pauk, Mária Frank, János Sebestyén.

Violin sonatas, Op. 1/3, 12, 13 & 15.
*(*) Denon Dig. **C37 7053** [id.]. Suk, Ruzickova.

The Philips performances derive from a highly praised LP set of Handel's sonatas for various instruments, now withdrawn. In their compact disc format they sound pleasingly fresh. Iona Brown plays with vigour and spirit, and there is a welcome robustness about this music making; many will find it a relief to turn to the modern violin after the Gillette-like strains of the Baroque variety.

Offering over an hour of music, the Hungaroton CD is generous; the playing is lively and stylish, with a nice feeling for Handel's lyricism in slow movements – the *Affettuoso* which opens Op. 1 No. 13 is a good example. The digital recording, however, is not ideally balanced, the focus of the cello and harpsichord is subservient to the violin which is forward and brightly lit, with a hint of digital edge on the timbre.

Sturdy if old-fashioned performances by Josef Suk, full of warmth and vitality, though he does not blend ideally with Zuzana Ruzickova's harpsichord. Unfortunately, the recording is not ideal and the acoustic is rather cramped. While the CD catalogue can boast such beautifully recorded alternatives as those of Iona Brown on Philips, this has little chance, in spite of Suk's artistry.

KEYBOARD MUSIC

Chaconne in G, HWV 435; Suites Nos 3 in D min.; 4 in E min.; 13 in B flat; 14 in G.
** DG Dig. **410 656-2** [id.]. Trevor Pinnock (harpsichord).

Suites Nos 1 in A; 6 in F sharp min.; 7 in G min.; 10 in D min.; 11 in D min.
(M) **(*) HMV *EG 290847-4*. Andrei Gavrilov (piano).

Suites Nos 2 in F; 3 in D min.; 5 in E; 6 in F sharp min.; 7 in G min.
(*) HM **HMC 90447 [id.]. Kenneth Gilbert (harpsichord).

Suites Nos 2 in F; 3 in D min.; 9 in C min.; 14 in G; 16 in G min.
(M) *** HMV *EG 290848-4*. Sviatoslav Richter (piano).

Suite No. 5 in E (includes *The Harmonious blacksmith*).
*** Decca Dig. **417 372-2**; *417 372-4* [id.]. Alicia de Larrocha (piano) – BACH/BUSONI: *Chaconne*; MOZART: *Fantasy; Sonata No. 14.****

Like Couperin and Rameau, Handel is rarely heard on the piano these days, so the prominence of this instrument in these selections is particularly welcome. The recordings by Gavrilov and Richter derive from the 1979 Touraine Festival and were recorded at the Château de Marcilly-sur-Maulne. They were originally part of a four-LP box, and the separate issue of these two budget-priced cassettes is most welcome. It is a joy to hear this repertoire on the more modern keyboard instrument with its variety of tone colour, when the music making is of this order.

Occasionally the tempi are a shade extreme in the slower movements (some of Gavrilov's sarabandes are funereal), but the sheer refinement, combined with the finesse of the playing, of both artists is a joy in itself. For too long, pianists have felt intimidated by the Early Music lobby and have refrained from trespassing on this territory. The piano sound is good, the tapes are cleanly transferred and the audience noise mostly unobtrusive.

The Harmonia Mundi CD is compiled from Kenneth Gilbert's set of all eight harpsichord suites (HM 447/8). Gilbert is a scholar as well as a distinguished player. He uses a copy of a Taskin harpsichord by Bédard. Gilbert observes most first-half repeats but not the second, and he is as imaginative in the handling of decoration and ornamentation as one would expect. If one were to quibble, it would be merely that some grandeur, some larger-than-life vitality, is missing; but so much else is here that there is no cause for qualifying the recommendation. The recording is much better balanced and more natural than recent rivals.

We praised Trevor Pinnock's recital in its original LP format for its panache. However, although the playing has undoubted flair and imagination, the CD is transferred at a thunderous level and is altogether overpowering. The added presence emphasizes the closeness of balance, and the result is of a fairly uniform *forte*. The result conveys expertise in plenty but rather less in the way of enjoyment, and we must register disappointment at this degree of over-projection.

Alicia de Larrocha's recital – a most distinguished one – was recorded with great realism in the Henry Wood Hall. She gives a robust and vital account of the best known of Handel's *Suites*, with its famous variations, and again fully justifies the use of the piano for this repertoire. Her performance may not banish memories of Richter (strangely, his Touraine performance was not chosen for inclusion in the HMV reissue) but is thoroughly enjoyable in its own right. There is plenty of warmth and the recording is splendidly realistic.

VOCAL AND CHORAL MUSIC

Acis and Galatea (masque).

*** DG **423 406-2** (2) [id.]. Burrowes, Rolfe Johnson, Martyn Hill, Willard White, E. Bar. Soloists, Gardiner.

(M) *** Argo *414 310-4*. Sutherland, Pears, Galliver, Brannigan, St Anthony Singers, Philomus. O, Boult; Dart (harpsichord).

Acis and Galatea was written in the early 1730s for the Duke of Chandos (who also commissioned the *Chandos anthems* – see below) and included such famous numbers as *O ruddier than the cherry* and *Love in her eyes sits playing*. In this 1978 recording, freshly and brightly remastered for CD, some of John Eliot Gardiner's tempi are idiosyncratic (some too fast, some too slow), but the scale of the performance, using original instruments, is beautifully judged to simulate domestic conditions as they might have been at the first performance at Canons, the Duke's country house, with the vocal soloists banding together for the choruses. The acoustic is rather dry, the balance fairly close, but the soloists are consistently sweet of tone, although the singing is less individually characterful than in some previous versions. Willard White is a fine Polyphemus, but his *O ruddier than the cherry* has not quite the degree of genial gusto that Owen Brannigan brings to it. The authentic sounds of the English Baroque Soloists are finely controlled so as not to offend unprepared ears too blatantly, and the vibrato-less string timbre is clear and clean without being abrasive. A thoroughly rewarding pair of CDs.

Boult provided the début stereo recording of Handel's masque (originally issued in 1960 on the Oiseau-Lyre label). The starry cast obviously relish the high level of Handel's inspiration; Joan Sutherland, in fresh, youthful voice, makes a splendid Galatea, sparkling in the florid passages, warmly sympathetic in the lyrical music. Peter Pears, too, is at his finest and, although David Galliver is less striking, his contribution is still a good one; while Owen Brannigan was surely born to play Polyphemus, the genial one-eyed giant. We are given the opportunity to enjoy his splendid account of *O ruddier than the cherry* (where he makes a positive virtue of intrusive aspirates) on two occasions, for it is included as an appendix, in Handel's alternative version with treble recorder. Anyone hearing it who can resist a smile must be stony-hearted indeed. Boult's sympathetic direction ensures that the music making has a lift throughout; the recording sounds as vivid as ever, although the remastering has made the upper orchestral range sound thinner than it did, and this is most noticeable on the high-level chrome cassette. But the voices are given fine presence and the handy layout of the single extended-length tape (with full documentation) seems an ideal way of acquiring the piece. One wonders what Handel would have made of the suggestion that one day a performance of his masque could be carried comfortably in a jacket pocket.

(i) *Aci, Galatea e Polifemo*. (ii) *Recorder sonatas in F; C & G* (trans. to *F*).
*** HM Dig. **HMC 901253/4**; *HMC 40.1253/4* [id.]. (i) Kirkby, C. Watkinson, Thomas, L. Bar., Medlam; (ii) Michel Piquet, John Toll.

Harmonia Mundi UK must be congratulated on coming up with a long-neglected Handelian jewel. *Aci, Galatea e Polifemo* proves to be quite a different work from the always popular English masque, *Acis and Galatea*, with only one item even partially borrowed. Written eight years earlier, in 1708 during Handel's Neapolitan period, it is an Italian serenata, in effect a one-act opera full of delightful brief numbers, far more flexible in scale and layout than later full-scale Italian operas. Charles Medlam directs London Baroque in a beautifully sprung performance with three excellent soloists, the brightly characterful Emma Kirkby as Aci, Carolyn Watkinson in the lower-pitched role of Galatea (often – a little confusingly – sounding like a male alto), and David Thomas coping manfully with the impossibly wide range of Polifemo's part. The three recorder sonatas are comparably delightful, a welcome makeweight – though neither the box nor the booklet mentions that the third of them has accompaniment not on the harpsichord but on the theorbo lute. Excellent sound, full of presence.

Ah, che pur troppo è vero; Mi palpita il cor. Duets: *A miravi io son intento; Beato in ver chi può; Conservate, raddioppiate; Fronda leggiera e mobile; Langue, geme e sospira; No, di voi non vuo fidarni; Se tu non lasci amore; Sono liete, fortunate; Tanti strali al sen; Troppo cruda* (cantatas).
*** Hung, Dig. **HCD 12564-5**; *MK 12564/5* [id.]. Zádori, Esswood; Falvay, Németh, Ella (cello, flute and harpsichord).

The two vocal soloists, the clear-voiced soprano Maria Zádori and the counter-tenor Paul Esswood, sing delightfully throughout this generous collection of very rare Handel duet cantatas, most of them charmers. Seven of them date from his Italian period in 1710, three more from thirty years later, and two solo ones are of unknown date. This is music aiming to delight an aristocratic audience, and it succeeds amply when the singing is so sweet and accomplished and the coloratura so brilliantly turned. Excellent recording, particularly on CD. The chrome cassettes are also in the demonstration bracket, the voices most naturally focused and the accompaniment sounding very refined, with the harpsichord particularly realistic.

Alexander's Feast (with *Concerto grosso in F, Op. 3/4b*).
(M) ** Tel. **ZA8.35671** (2) [id.]. Palmer, Rolfe-Johnson, Roberts, Stockholm Bach Ch., VCM, Harnoncourt.

Reissued on CD as part of Telefunken's Handel Edition, Harnoncourt's 1978 recording of *Alexander's Feast* is variably successful. The team of soloists is first rate, with Felicity Palmer,

Anthony Rolfe-Johnson and Stephen Roberts all very stylish, even if Roberts is too light of voice for the magnificent *Revenge, Timotheus cries*. The Stockholm choir is consistently lively, a splendid ensemble. The Concentus Musicus of Vienna play with excellent precision, but the edginess of authentic performance of this vintage is often disconcerting and not always well served by the variable recording. It also seems perverse to include the *Concerto grosso*, Op. 3/4b, as a fill-up rather than the obvious choice of the concerto which carries the name of the vocal work, and which was almost certainly played at its first performance.

L'Allegro, il penseroso, il moderato.
*** Erato **ECD 880752** (2). Kwella, McLaughlin, Jennifer Smith, Ginn, Davies, Hill, Varcoe, Monteverdi Ch., E. Bar. Soloists, Gardiner.

Taking Milton as his starting point, Handel illustrated in music the contrasts of mood and character between the cheerful and the thoughtful. Then, prompted by his librettist, Charles Jennens, he added compromise in *Il moderato*, the moderate man. The final chorus may fall a little short of the rest (Jennens's words cannot have provided much inspiration), but otherwise the sequence of brief numbers is a delight, particularly in a performance as exhilarating as this, with excellent soloists, choir and orchestra. The recording is first rate.

Italian cantatas: *Alpestre monte; Mi palpita il cor; Tra le fiamme; Tu fedel? Tu costante?*
*** O-L Dig. **414 473-2**; *414 473-4* [id.]. Emma Kirkby, AAM, Hogwood.

Emma Kirkby's bright, pure voice is perfectly suited to these brilliant but generally lightweight inspirations of the young Handel's Italian period. The four cantatas chosen, all for solo voice with modest instrumental forces, are nicely contrasted, with the personality of the original singer by implication identified with *Tu fedel*, a spirited sequence of little arias rejecting a lover. Even 'a heart full of cares' in *Mi palpita il cor* inspires Handel to a pastorally charming aria, with a delectable oboe obbligato rather than anything weighty, and even those limited cares quickly disperse. Light-hearted and sparkling performances to match. With generous cues, to give access to the many little arias and recitatives, the CD is particularly easy to use. The chrome-tape transfer is beautifully fresh and clear – in the demonstration class – and this is one of Emma Kirkby's finest recitals.

Aminta e Fillide (cantata).
*** Hyp. **CDA 66118**; *KA 66118* [id.]. Fisher, Kwella, L. Handel O, Darlow.

This was one of the longer cantatas which Handel composed during his years of work and self-education in Italy, learning above all how to write most effectively for the voice. Written for two voices and strings, it presents a simple encounter in the pastoral tradition over a span of ten brief arias which, together with recitatives and final duet, last almost an hour. The music is as charming and undemanding for the listener as it is taxing for the soloists. This lively performance, beautifully recorded with two nicely contrasted singers (who arguably should be cast the other way round with Fisher more boyish, Kwella brighter), delightfully blows the cobwebs off a Handel work till now totally neglected. The CD is all the fresher in its sound.

Apollo e Dafne (cantata).
(*) HM **HMC 905157; *HMC 40.5157* [id.]. Judith Nelson, David Thomas; Hayes, San Francisco Bar. O, McGegan.

Apollo e Dafne is one of Handel's most delightful cantatas, with at least two strikingly memorable numbers, a lovely siciliano for Dafne with oboe obbligato and an aria for Apollo, *Come rosa in su la spina* with unison violins and a solo cello. Both soloists are first rate, and Nicholas

McGegan is a lively Handelian, though the playing of the orchestra could be more polished and the sound more firmly focused.

Athalia (oratorio).
*** O-L Dig. **417 126-2**; *417 126-4* (2) [id.]. Sutherland, Kirkby, Bowman, Aled Jones, Rolfe-Johnson, David Thomas, New College, Oxford, Ch., AAM, Hogwood.

It is quite a landmark for the Early Music Movement having Dame Joan Sutherland in an authentic performance of a Handel oratorio. As Queen Athalia, an apostate Baal-worshipper who comes to no good, she sings boldly with a richness and vibrancy to contrast superbly with the pure silver of the Movement's favourite soprano, Emma Kirkby, not to mention the celestial treble of the transient star, Aled Jones, in the role of the boy-king, Joas. That casting (with Dame Joan a fine Handelian but from a different tradition – not everyone will respond to her wide vibrato) is perfectly designed to set the Queen aptly apart from the good Israelite characters led by the Priest, Joad (James Bowman in a castrato role), and Josabeth (Kirkby). The libretto may be feeble compared with the great Racine tragedy on which it is loosely based, but Handel's characterizations are strong and come out the more effectively here. So where the Israelite solos regularly lead into choruses (representing the support of the people), the Queen's solos – notably her superb anger aria of Act II, brilliantly done – keep her apart. Emma Kirkby's jewelled ornamentation is brilliant too, and Aled Jones's singing – despite a few moments of caution – is ethereally beautiful, if only a little more remarkable than that of the three trebles from the Christ Church Choir who do the little trios for Three Virgins at the end of Act II. Christopher Hogwood with the Academy brings out the speed and variety of the score that has been described as Handel's first great English oratorio. Just over two hours long, it fits neatly on to two CDs and tapes with Act I on the first, Acts II and III on the second. The recording is bright and clean, giving sharp focus to voices and instruments alike. The cassettes are admirably managed – the transfer sophisticated and lively to match the CDs in all but the last bit of presence and range – and are documented with the excellent CD booklet.

Duets: *Beato in ver; Langue, geme; Tanti strali.* Cantatas: *Parti, l'idolo mio; Sento là che ristretto.*
*** HM **HMC 901004** [id.]. Judith Nelson, René Jacobs, W. Christie, K. Jünghanel.

These Handel duets – two of them very early from his Italian period – and the two cantatas – more substantial works – contain some delightful music, Handel at his most charming. With outstanding solo singing from both Judith Nelson and René Jacobs, they are given very stylish performances, cleanly recorded.

Brockes Passion.
(*) Hung. Dig. **HCD 12734/6-2 [id.]. Klietmann, Gáti, Zádori, Minter & soloists, Halle Stadtsingechor, Capella Savaria, McGegan.

At some date during his London period, Handel turned back to setting a relatively crude Passion text by Barthold Brockes (that was also set by other composers, including Telemann). It prompted a piece of some thirty or so arias, two duets and a trio, most of them brief but full of superb ideas, many of which Handel raided for his later oratorios. Thus, the deeply moving duet between Christ and the Virgin Mary just before the *Crucifixion* later became the duet for Esther and King Ahasuerus in *Esther*. Generally, this degree of depth – worthy to be compared with Bach's Passion music – is missing, but there is still much to enjoy. Nicholas McGegan with the excellent Capella Savaria using period instruments directs a lively, refreshing account of the piece that easily outshines previous versions. The team of soloists has no weak link, with Martin Klietmann outstanding as the Evangelist and another fine tenor, Guy de Mey, singing the roles of Faithful Soul and Peter most sensitively. Istvan Gáti as Jesus and Drew Minter as Judas are both excellent, and the only comparative reservation concerns the singing of the chorus, fresh but less polished than the rest. The Hungaroton recording is bright and well focused, with a fine sense of presence.

(i) *Cecilia vogi un sguardo* (cantata); *Silete venti* (motet).
*** DG Dig. **419 736-2** [id.]. Jennifer Smith, Elwes, E. Concert, Pinnock.

These two fine cantatas come from a later period than most of Handel's Italian-language works in this genre. Both reveal him at his most effervescent, a quality superbly caught in these performances with excellent singing and playing, most striking from Jennifer Smith whose coloratura has never been more brilliantly displayed on record. Excellent recording.

Chandos anthems: As pants the hart; The Lord is my light.
(M) *** Argo *414 294-4*. Cantelo, Partridge, King's College Ch., ASMF, Willcocks.

Handel wrote eleven anthems for his patron, the Duke of Chandos, to be performed at Canons, his country house near Edgware. Reflecting the period, they have grandeur but a direct unpretentiousness as well, and the elements of Italianate elaboration and German fugal complexity are married in them with an assurance that only Handel could achieve. These two, Nos 6 and 10, provide an attractive tape with all Teutonic pomposity avoided and the freshness of inspiration underlined. No. 6 includes a lovely Adagio chorus and beautiful soprano aria, while No. 10 is remarkable for some magnificent fugal writing. Excellent 1968 recording and a vivid transfer – very lively.

Chandos anthems: In the Lord put I my trust; I will magnify Thee.
(M) *** Argo *414 449-4*. Friend, Langridge, King's College Ch., ASMF, Willcocks.

Here are two more of Handel's anthems (these are Nos 2 and 5) written for the Duke of Chandos, attractive for their freshness of inspiration, their economical vocal writing for small forces producing agreeably resilient textures. The choral singing here is well up to the King's standard, and the solo contributions have plenty of character; Philip Langridge is notable for his eloquence and simplicity of approach. With characteristically fine Argo recording, in the best King's tradition, this can be enthusiastically recommended.

Chandos anthems: Let God arise; O Praise the Lord with one consent.
(M) *** Argo *411 980-4* [id.]. Vaughan, Young, Forbes Robinson, King's College Ch., ASMF, Willcocks.

The instrumentation here is simple, including only oboe and bassoon besides strings and continuo, and the choral writing effectively uses a small group of singers. The freshness of the idiom is delightful. The opening line of *O Praise the Lord with one consent* fits very nicely to the hymn tune we know as *O God our help in ages past*, but Handel only helps himself to this first line of the hymn and weaves his own music therefrom. This is an especially pleasing cantata with more than one reminder of *Messiah* (only the idiom less grandiose), and in this and its companion, *Let God arise*, the writing for the soloists is rewarding too. This latter work is marginally more conventional in style but redeems itself with a wonderfully imaginative chorus to the words *Praised be the Lord.* Excellent singing and recording from soloists and chorus alike, and a stylish accompaniment, all beautifully recorded, make this a most desirable tape for all Handelians. The transfer is first class in every way, strikingly fresh and clear, with the King's acoustic offering no problems.

Coronation anthems (*1, Zadok the Priest; 2, The King shall rejoice; 3, My heart is inditing; 4, Let Thy hand be strengthened*).
*** DG Arc. Dig. **410 030-2** [id.]. Westminster Abbey Ch., E. Concert, Preston; Pinnock (organ).
(M) **(*) Argo *414 073-4* [id.]. King's College Ch., ECO, Willcocks.

Coronation anthems (complete); *Judas Maccabaeus; See the conqu'ring hero comes; March; Sing unto God.*
*** Ph. Dig. **412 733-2**; *412 733-4* [id.]. ASMF Ch., ASMF, Marriner.

The extra weight of the Academy of St Martin-in-the-Fields Chorus compared with the Pinnock version seems appropriate for the splendour of music intended for the pomp of royal ceremonial occasions, and the commanding choral entry in *Zadok the Priest* is gloriously rich in amplitude, without in any way lacking incisiveness. Throughout, the Academy Chorus set a perfect balance between expressive eloquence and fervour, and in *My heart is inditing* the four soloists (Joan Rodgers, Catherine Denley, Anthony Rolfe-Johnson and Robert Dean) create a stylish contrast, acting as a solo quartet in sequence with the ripieno of the main vocal group. The instrumental accompaniments are fresh and glowing, and those who can enjoy modern violin timbre in Baroque repertoire will find that the radiant orchestra sounds created by the Academy add much to the colour of the overall presentation. Sir Neville Marriner's direction is full of imaginative detail, and the Philips recording, with its wide dynamic range, is admirably balanced and excitingly realistic in its CD format. The chrome tape is very good too, but its upper focus is less sharp. The excerpts from *Solomon* are a delightful bonus with *See the conqu'ring hero* making an engaging change of mood after the closing section of the *Fourth Coronation anthem. Sing unto God* ends the concert with a final burst of exhilaration.

Those who prefer sparer, more 'authentic' textures can turn to Pinnock, where, although the overall effect is less grand, the element of contrast is even more telling. It is thrilling on the Archiv disc, after the lightness and clarity of the introduction to *Zadok the Priest*, to have the choir enter with such bite and impact, most strikingly in the compact disc version which underlines the freshness and immediacy. Though the Westminster Abbey Choir is not large, the recording gives ample sense of power, and the use of original instruments gives plenty of character to the accompaniments. An exhilarating version.

On Argo, fine performances, brilliantly recorded, except in the matter of balance, and that is a problem inherent in the choral singing itself. This is stylish enough, but the kind of sound the choir makes is rather too light-textured for these large-scale ceremonial pieces. The result is that the orchestra tends to overwhelm the vocal sound, even though the engineering minimizes this as much as possible. However, even with reservations there is much to enjoy here, and the remastered 1963 recording is particularly successful in its tape format, the sound vivid and full-bodied and not clouded by the acoustic.

Dettingen Te Deum; Dettingen anthem.
*** DG Arc. Dig. **410 647-2** [id.]. Westminster Abbey Ch., E. Concert, Preston.

The *Dettingen Te Deum* was written to celebrate a famous victory during the War of the Austrian Succession. It is splendidly typical work and continually reminds the listener of *Messiah*, written the previous year. Arias and choruses alike are full of attractive invention, and one has the suspicion that Handel is knowingly capitalizing on the familiarity of his oratorio in almost plagiarizing himself. For the listener, nevertheless, the result is highly rewarding, particularly as the florid Baroque scoring, with liberal use of trumpets, gives so much pleasure in itself. Preston's new Archiv performance (with original instruments) from the English Concert makes an ideal recommendation, with its splendid singing, crisp but strong (Stephen Varcoe does the two brief airs beautifully), excellent recording and a generous, apt coupling. This setting of *The King shall rejoice* should not be confused with the *Coronation anthem* of that name. It is less inspired, but has a magnificent double fugue for finale. The recording is first class although, even on CD, the Westminster Abbey reverberation prevents a sharp choral focus.

Dixit Dominus; Zadok the Priest.
*** Erato **ECD 88072**. Palmer, Marshall, Brett, Messana, Morton, Thomson, Wilson-Johnson, Monteverdi Ch. and O, Gardiner.

Handel's *Dixit Dominus* dates from 1707 and was completed during his prolonged stay in Italy from 1706 to 1710. It divides into eight sections, and the setting, while showing signs of Handel's mature style in embryo, reflects also the Baroque tradition of contrasts between small and large groups. The writing is extremely florid and requires bravura from soloists and chorus alike. John Eliot Gardiner catches all its brilliance and directs an exhilarating performance, marked by strongly accented, sharply incisive singing from the choir and outstanding solo contributions. In high contrast with the dramatic choruses, the duet for two sopranos, *De torrente*, here beautifully sung by Felicity Palmer and Margaret Marshall, is languorously expressive, but stylishly so. Other soloists match that, and the analogue recording is first rate, proving ideal for CD remastering.

Esther (complete).
(*) O-L Dig. **414 423-2; *414 423-4* (2) [id.]. Kwella, Rolfe-Johnson, Partridge, Thomas, Kirkby, Elliott, Westminster Cathedral Boys' Ch., Ch. and AAM, Hogwood.

Hogwood presents *Esther*, Handel's first oratorio written in English, in a vigorous authentic performance. He has opted for the original 1718 score with its six compact scenes as being more sharply dramatic than the 1732 expansion, and he consistently brings out the composer's theatrical flair. Handel made this an oratorio rather than an opera only because biblical subjects were banned on the London stage at the time. Hogwood's rather abrasive brand of authenticity goes well with the bright, full recorded sound which unfortunately exaggerates the choir's sibilants. The Academy's own small chorus is joined by the clear, bright trebles of Westminster Cathedral Choir, and they all sing very well (except that the elaborate passagework is far too heavily aspirated, at times almost as though the singers are laughing). The vigour of the performance is unaffected and the team of soloists is strong and consistent, with Patrizia Kwella distinctive and purposeful in the name-part. The cassettes are bright and clear, to match the CD version, with the astringency of the upper range very slightly underlined by the high-level tape transfer.

9 German arias; Violin sonata in F, Op. 1/12.
(*) HMV Dig. **CDC7 49256-2 [CDC 47400]. Emma Kirkby, London Baroque.

Handel's *Nine German arias* were published only in 1921 (they were omitted from Chrysander) and the accompaniment remains instrumentally conjectural. The present version will please authenticists, though timbres are meagre and the playing not strong on charm. However, the London Baroque have hit on a good idea for providing variety by interspersing the four movements of the *F major Violin sonata* in between the songs. They are beautifully sung, and the characteristic artless innocence of Emma Kirkby's style catches the spirit of Brockes' poems which, if pantheistic in subject matter, are religious in feeling.

(i) *Israel in Egypt* (oratorio); *The Ways of Zion* (*funeral anthem*).
(*) Erato **ECD 88182 (2) [id.]. (i) Knibbs, Clarkson, Elliot, Varcoe, Monteverdi Ch. & O, Gardiner.

The choral brilliance of Gardiner's version of *Israel in Egypt* shines the more brightly in the clarity of CD. This was one of his earliest big Handel recordings, and though the solo singing shared between principals in the chorus is variable, the choruses are what matter in this work, making up a high proportion of its length, and the teamwork involved brings tingling excitement. It is good to have the moving funeral anthem as an extra item on CD. No doubt Simon Preston's version on Argo will reappear on CD, and perhaps the DG Mackerras account also. Both have superior solo contributions; but Gardiner's chorus remains the finest of the three.

Jephtha.

(M) *** Argo *414 183-4* (3). Rolfe-Johnson, Margaret Marshall, Hodgson, Esswood, Keyte, Kirkby, Ch. and ASMF, Marriner.

** Tel. **ZB8 35499** (3) [id.]. Hollweg, Gale, Linos, Esswood, Thomaschke, Sima, Mozart Boys' Ch., Schoenberg Ch., VCM, Harnoncourt.

Jephtha, the last oratorio that Handel completed, is a strange and not always very moral tale. With the threat of blindness on him, the composer was forced to break off from writing for several months, but that threat seems only to have added to the urgency of inspiration; and Marriner's performance, helped by the bright tones of trebles in the choruses, is refreshing from first to last, well sprung but direct in style. The soloists are excellent, with Emma Kirkby nicely distanced in the role of the Angel, her clean vibrato-less voice made the more ethereal. It is a very long oratorio, but in this performance it hardly seems so, with such beautiful numbers as Jephtha's *Waft her, angels* given a finely poised performance by Rolfe-Johnson. The recording is first rate, and the cassette transfer has a fine sparkle, with lively presence and detail.

Harnoncourt's pursuit of extra authenticity, with an orchestra using original instruments, will make his version an automatic choice for many; for the general listener, however, it has its snags, not just in the acid timbres of the strings. Harnoncourt takes a more operatic view of the work than Marriner on the rival version which appeared simultaneously, but he mars the impact of that by too frequently adopting a mannered style of phrasing. The soloists too are on balance far less impressive than those on the Marriner version. The recording acoustic, typically clean, is less helpful in its relative dryness next to the rival set. With a very full text this makes a long haul, although the CD format is on three discs against four LPs of the original issue.

Messiah (complete).

*** Ph. Dig. **411 041-2**; *7654 107* (3) [id.]. Marshall, Robbin, Rolfe-Johnson, Brett, Hale, Shirley-Quirk, Monteverdi Ch., E. Bar. Soloists, Gardiner.

*** Hyp. Dig. **CDA 66251/2**; (M) *KA 66251/2* [id.]. Lynne Dawson, Denley, Maldwyn Davies, Michael George, The Sixteen Ch. & O, Christophers.

*** Decca Dig. **414 396-2**; *414 396-4* (2) [id.]. Te Kanawa, Gjevang, Keith Lewis, Howell, Chicago Ch. & SO, Solti.

(M) *** Ph. **420 865-2** (2); *7699 009* (3) [id.]. Harper, Watts, Wakefield, Shirley-Quirk, LSO Ch., LSO, C. Davis.

(*) HMV **CDS7 49027-2 (2) [Ang. **CDCB 49027**]. Battle, Quivar, Aler, Ramey, Toronto Mendelssohn Ch. & SO, Andrew Davis.

(*) O-L **411 858-2; *K 189 K33* [id.]. Nelson, Kirkby, Watkinson, Elliott, Thomas, Christ Church Cathedral Ch., Oxford, AAM, Hogwood.

(*) Erato **ECD 880503; *MCE 751303* (3). Kweksilber, Bowman, Elliott, Reinhardt, The Sixteen, Amsterdam Bar. O, Koopman.

** Ph. Dig. **412 538-2**; *412 538-4* (3) [id.]. Margaret Price, Schwarz, Burrows, Estes, Bav. R. Ch. and SO, C. Davis.

The digital recording of *Messiah* directed by John Eliot Gardiner was the first to be issued on compact discs and it took the freshening process started by Sir Colin Davis and Sir Charles Mackerras in the mid-1960s a stage further. The momentum set off by these two famous recordings was continued by Marriner and Hogwood, both of whom attempted to re-create specific early performances and leave behind for ever the Victorian tradition of massive choral forces, exemplified by the Royal Choral Society and the famous Huddersfield Choir, directed in their halcyon days by Sir Malcolm Sargent. However, Gardiner's approach is not re-creative but essentially practical, with variants from the expected text rather the exception; thus the duet version of *He shall feed his flock* and the *Pastoral symphony* (with squeezed accents from the strings preventing the line from sounding too mellifluous) are both included. He chooses bright-toned sopranos instead of boys for the chorus, on the grounds that a mature adult approach is essential, and conversely he uses, very affectingly, a solo treble to sing *There were shepherds abiding*. Speeds are usually even faster and lighter than Hogwood's (or Sir Colin Davis's) and the rhythmic buoyancy in the choruses is very striking. There is drama and boldness, too. *Why do the nations* and *The trumpet shall sound* (both sung with great authority) have seldom come over more strongly. Perhaps most dramatic of all is the moment when, after a deceptively sedate opening, the *Amen chorus* suddenly bursts into full flood after the brief and gentle melisma from the violins, helped by the wide dynamic range of the recording. The soloists are all first class, with the soprano Margaret Marshall finest of all, especially in *I know that my Redeemer liveth* (tastefully decorated). There are times when one craves for more expansive qualities; the baroque string sound, though not as aggressively thin as it is under Hogwood, still can give cause for doubts. Yet there are some wonderful highlights, not least Margaret Marshall's angelic version of *Rejoice greatly*, skipping along in compound time. The set is rather extravagantly presented on three discs and cassettes, but with each of the three parts complete and separate. The CDs bring most items individually cued. The sound is outstandingly beautiful, fresh and natural, with some of the edge lifted from the baroque violins, so that, while the bite remains, there is beauty of texture too. Solo voices sound remarkably tangible, and the choral sound is wonderfully refined.

Harry Christophers' brilliant and stylish choir, The Sixteen, made a memorable contribution to the Erato set of *Messiah* directed by Ton Koopman; but in December 1986, Christophers himself conducted a series of four live performances at St John's, Smith Square, in London, which – suitably edited with no extraneous noises intruding – have resulted in an even fresher, more appealing performance, one of the most attractive ever on disc. The scale is compact – with three extra sopranos added to the regular sixteen singers – but the bloom on the sound of chorus and instruments alike gives them brightness and clean projection with no sense of miniaturization. Very distinctively for any latter-day recording, let alone one using period instruments, Christophers consistently adopts speeds more relaxed than those we have grown used to in modern performances. For anyone who has found in recent recordings that Handel has been made too tense, even breathless, this provides a superb answer, fresh, clear and resilient, with alto lines in the chorus taken by male singers. A counter-tenor, David James, is also used for the *Refiner's fire*, very effectively adopting Handel's higher option, but *He was despised* is rightly given to the contralto, Catherine Denley, warm and grave at a very measured tempo. The team of five soloists is at least as fine as that on any rival set, with the tenor, Maldwyn Davies, and the bass, Michael George, both excellent on an apt scale, and with the soprano, Lynne Dawson, singing with silvery purity to delight traditionalists and authenticists alike. The compound-time version of *Rejoice greatly* has seldom sounded sweeter, measured but fresh and unsentimental. The band of thirteen strings sounds as clean and fresh as the choir, avoiding disagreeable abrasiveness, while the trumpets and woodwind cut through dramatically. Even the *Hallelujah chorus* – always a big test in a small-scale performance – works well, with Christophers in his chosen scale, through dramatic timpani and trumpets conveying necessary weight. The sound has all the bloom one associates with St John's recordings, but – thanks to the dampening effect of an audience – no clouding from reverberation. The set comes on two compact discs, with the splendidly transferred pair of chrome cassettes coming near to matching the outstanding quality of the CDs. The tapes are offered at a special reduced price.

Surprisingly, Sir Georg Solti had never conducted *Messiah* before this recording, but he inspires the most vitally exciting reading on record. The Chicago Symphony Orchestra and Chorus respond to some challengingly fast but never breathless speeds, showing what lessons can be learnt from authentic performance in clarity and crispness. Yet the joyful power of *Hallelujah* and the *Amen chorus* is overwhelming. Dame Kiri Te Kanawa matches anyone on record in beauty of tone and detailed expressiveness, while the other soloists are first rate too, even if Anne Gjevang has rather too fruity a timbre. Brilliant, full sound on the splendid cassettes, but with even greater tangibility, breadth and clarity on the CDs. The layout on two cassettes and compact discs is attractive value, although those looking for economy will probably turn to the Colin Davis reissue.

The earlier Philips recording has not lost its impact and sounds brightly lit and fresh in its digitally remastered format. The fast speeds chosen by Sir Colin for the choruses set a new precedent, and the fine professional body he uses (unnamed) copes with every technical difficulty with ease. Textures are beautifully clear and, thanks to Davis, the rhythmic bounce of such choruses as *For unto us* is really infectious. Even *Hallelujah* loses little and gains much from being performed by a chorus of this size. Excellent singing from all four soloists, particularly Helen Watts who, following early precedent, is given *For He is like a refiner's fire* to sing, instead of the bass, and produces a glorious chest register. The performance is absolutely complete and now, fitted on to a pair of mid-priced CDs, it is a real bargain.

Andrew Davis's 1987 performance, recorded in the admirably spacious acoustics of the Centre in the Square, Kitchener, Ontario, seeks to step back a little in time to a recently traditional style of performance, 'swimming against the tide' as the conductor puts it in his accompanying notes. He also reminds us that the first performance using really large forces (including a chorus of 275) dates from as early as 1784 at the Handel Commemoration, twenty-five years after the composer's death; and he suggests, with some justice, that Handel loved grand effects and would have welcomed the larger forces. Nevertheless his performance follows current practice in using judicious decoration in *da capo* arias, and his tempi for choruses are lively, even though he uses a large amateur group. They are well trained and generally cope well with the demands placed on them, although their articulation is strained by the vigorous *Let us break their bonds asunder*. Surprisingly *Hallelujah*, joyful as it is, doesn't sound much more weighty than under Sir Colin Davis, until the end – when Beecham would have enjoyed the closing cadence, replete with organ and drums. The organ also adds to the grandeur in the apotheosis-like *Worthy is the Lamb*. A modern orchestra is used, but fined down for the simpler arias; with all this added weight, *For unto us* and *All we like sheep* remain attractively resilient. The special strength of the set lies in the soloists, a team without weakness. Kathleen Battle's sweet purity of timbre in *How beautiful are the feet* suggests a boy treble, yet *I know that my Redeemer liveth* has mature expressive feeling, though still radiantly simple. Florence Quivar's *He was despised* is comparably eloquent without being overladen with emotion; and the two combine for the engaging duet version of *He shall feed his flock*. Both male singers display a sense of drama. John Aler's *Thou shalt break them* is particularly telling, while Samuel Ramey's *Behold I tell you a mystery* leading to *The trumpet shall sound* is superbly strong and resonant. Overall the sound is first class, full, clear and believably balanced, and those who enjoy a more traditional approach to Handel's masterpiece will find a great deal to enjoy here.

By aiming at re-creating an authentic version – based meticulously on material from the Foundling Hospital, reproducing a performance of 1754 – Christopher Hogwood has managed to have the best of both worlds, punctilious but consistently vigorous and refreshing and never falling into dull routine. The trebles of Christ Church are superb, and though the soloists cannot match the tonal beauty of the finest of their rivals on other sets, the consistency of the whole conception makes for most satisfying results. As to the text, it generally follows what we are used to, but there are such oddities as *But who may abide* transposed for a soprano and a shortened version of the *Pastoral symphony*. The recording is superb, clear and free to match the performance, and the CD transfer is exceptionally successful, adding to the presence and immediacy within the resonant Christ Church acoustics. The cassettes too are very well managed.

With a small choir, an authentic baroque orchestra and clear-toned, lightweight soloists, Koopman's version provides an intimate view of what is usually presented in grandeur. The ease and relaxation of the approach, not at all abrasive in the way common with authentic performance, are attractive, helped by excellent recording which gives a fine sense of presence – but, inevitably, essential elements in Handel's vision are missing.

Sir Colin Davis's new digitally recorded set has some of the same electricity which made his classic 1967 recording with the LSO so refreshing, with fuller and richer sound on tape, and very impressive on CD. But there are notable snags. Hanna Schwarz, outstanding in the opera house, here sings painfully under the note with some ugly swooping, far less in style than her 1967 predecessor, Helen Watts. Other soloists are first rate, Margaret Price strong and pure and Simon Estes very distinctive with his clear, dark tone. The chorus is lively too, but the Bavarian Radio orchestra is a degree too smooth. This performance is far less well sprung rhythmically than Davis's earlier account, and so fails to convey the same freshness.

Harnoncourt's version was compiled from two public concerts in Stockholm in 1982 with ill-balanced sound that puts the choir at a distance, making it sound even fuller than it is. With the exception of Elizabeth Gale, the soloists are poor, and Harnoncourt's direction lacks vigour. No competitor for other 'authentic' versions (**ZB8.35617**).

Messiah: highlights.
*** Ph. Dig. **412 267-2**, *412 267-4* [id.] (from above set, cond. Gardiner).
*** Decca Dig. **417 449-2**; *417 449-4* [id.] (from above set, cond. Solti).
*** O-L Dig. **440 086-2** [id.] (from above set, cond. Hogwood).
(M) *** HMV **CDM7 69040-2** [id.]. Harwood, Janet Baker, Esswood, Tear, Herinx, Amb. S., ECO, Mackerras.
(B) **(*) CfP **CD-CFP 9007**. Morison, Marjorie Thomas, R. Lewis, Milligan, Huddersfield Ch. Soc., Royal Liverpool PO, Sargent.
(M) **(*) Pickwick Dig. **PCD 803** [MCA **MCAD 25852**]. Lott, Finnie, Winslade, Herford, Scottish Philharmonic Singers, Scottish SO, Malcolm.
(M) **(*) Decca **417 735-2** [id.]. Ameling, Reynolds, Langridge, Howell, Ch. & ASMF, Marriner.
(M) **(*) ASV Dig. **CDQS 6001**. Kwella, Cable, Kendal, Drew, Jackson, Winchester Cathedral Ch., L. Handel O, Neary.
(M) **(*) Decca **417 879-2**; *417 879-4*. Sutherland, Bumbry, McKellar, Ward, LSO Ch. & O, Boult.

As can be seen, the choice of *Messiah* highlights ranges widely, obviously tempting those who already have a complete set to sample one of the others. Gardiner's collection reigns supreme with the single caveat that *The trumpet shall sound* is missing. The *Amen* chorus is included, however, and rounds off a satisfying musical experience. There is a very good cassette, but the final chorus demonstrates the extra presence and realism of the new medium.

Solti's single disc and tape selection is undoubtedly generous, including all the key numbers and much else besides. The sound is thrillingly vivid and full. There is in addition a selection including all the important choruses (Decca **421 059-2**; *421 059-4*), but this has a much more limited appeal.

The digitally remastered compact disc of highlights from the Hogwood recording was issued before the complete set, and acts as an excellent sampler for it. There is just a little blurring at the top, caused by the resonance; but soloists and chorus alike (and of course the sharp-edged strings) are vividly projected against a virtually silent background. Listeners may immediately judge their reactions from the opening *Comfort ye* with its florid decorations. The solo singing is always fresh, David Thomas's *The trumpet shall sound* giving a robust reminder of an enduring style of presentation of this justly famous item. The recording is excellent.

Sir Charles Mackerras's 1967 HMV recording was a landmark in its day, with the adoption of Handel's previously forgotten alternative versions of arias. Dame Janet Baker was outstanding in a fine team of soloists and, with robust choruses from the Ambrosian Singers, this makes a clear mid-priced recommendation on CD. (There is a tape, too – *EMX 41 2070-4* – of good quality but a more restricted upper range.)

The great and pleasant surprise among the bargain selections is the Classics for Pleasure CD of highlights from Sir Malcolm Sargent's 1959 recording. This offers an amazing improvement in sound. The eloquent singing of the Huddersfield Chorus perpetuates a tradition, only recently supplanted by the authentic lobby and about to be renewed by a new large-scale recording which should appear during the lifetime of this book. Meanwhile Sargent's CD restores his reputation in this repertoire – his pacing is sure and spontaneous throughout, whether or not one agrees with it. There is some splendid solo singing, notably from Elsie Morison and Richard Lewis, and Marjorie Thomas's *He was despised* is very moving in its simplicity and vocal warmth. The choruses emerge vigorously from under the cloud of the old analogue master, with the words audible and the heaviness dissipated. The effect is not as clean as a new digital recording, and there are one or two extraneous noises, but no one will be disappointed with *Hallelujah* (the Victorians knew what they were about when they expanded Handel's chamber chorus into something more grandiloquent – this is worth standing up for) and the closing *Amen* has a powerful sense of apotheosis.

Beautifully sung by excellent soloists (especially Felicity Lott) and choir, the Pickwick issue makes another good mid-priced CD, very naturally and beautifully recorded in warmly atmospheric sound, though the performance at times could be livelier.

A highlights disc is probably the best way to sample the Marriner performance (which attempts to re-create the work's London premier of 1743) with its fresh sound and splendid solo and choral singing. The selection is generous. The same comment might apply to Boult's 1961 version, where Sutherland alone pays any attention to the question of whether or not to use ornamentation in the repeats of the *da capo* arias. However, this CD and tape are inexpensive and well engineered; it is supplemented by a further cassette which selects the choruses only, a very strong feature of Boult's set (Decca *411 841-4*).

Brightly if reverberantly recorded in Winchester Cathedral, Martin Neary's collection of excerpts gives a pleasant reminder of the work of one of our finest cathedral choirs. In its authentic manner Neary's style is rather too clipped to convey deep involvement, but the freshness is attractive, with some very good solo singing.

Ode for St Cecilia's Day.

*** DG Dig. **419 220-2**; *419 220-4* [id.]. Lott, Rolfe-Johnson, Ch. & E. Concert, Pinnock.
*** ASV Dig. **CDDCA 512**; *ZCDCA 512* [id.]. Gomez, Tear, King's College Ch., ECO, Ledger.
(*) Tel. **ZK8 42349 [id.]. Palmer, Rolfe-Johnson, Stockholm Bach Ch., VCM, Harnoncourt.

Trevor Pinnock's account of Handel's magnificent setting of Dryden's *Ode* comes near the ideal for a performance using period instruments. Not only is it crisp and lively, it has deep tenderness too, as in the lovely soprano aria, *The complaining flute*, with Lisa Beznosiuk playing the flute obbligato most delicately in support of Felicity Lott's clear singing. Anthony Rolfe-Johnson gives a robust yet stylish account of *The trumpet's loud clangour*, and the choir is excellent, very crisp of ensemble. Full, clear recording with voices vivid and immediate. There is a first-class tape.

Those seeking a version with modern instruments will find Ledger's ASV version a splendid alternative. With superb soloists – Jill Gomez radiantly beautiful and Robert Tear dramatically riveting in his call to arms, *The trumpet's loud clangour* – this delightful music emerges with an admirable combination of freshness and weight. Ledger uses an all-male chorus; the style of the performance is totally convincing without being self-consciously authentic. The recording is first rate, rich, vivid and clear, with good definition and great presence in the CD format. The cassette is good, too, if not quite so sharp in its upper focus.

Harnoncourt's Teldec version of the *Ode*, originally recorded in 1979, comes up well in its digital transfer to CD. It is only slightly less recommendable than Trevor Pinnock's Archiv version, though the non-British choir, for all its fluency, sounds less comfortable than its rival and sings rather less crisply. Anthony Rolfe-Johnson is excellent on both versions, while Felicity Palmer as soprano sings most characterfully. One special point in favour of Harnoncourt is his own striking cello playing in the beautiful setting of Dryden's second stanza, *What Passion cannot Musick raise and quell!* However, this might have been more fully competitive if it had been reissued on Teldec's new mid-priced CD label.

La Resurrezione.

*** O-L Dig. **421 132-2** (2) [id.]. Kirkby, Kwella, C. Watkinson, Partridge, Thomas, AAM, Hogwood.

In 1708, halfway through his four-year stay in Italy, the young Handel wrote this refreshingly dramatic oratorio. With opera as such prohibited in Rome, it served as a kind of substitute, and though it does not have the great choral music which is so much the central element of later Handel oratorios, it is a fine and many-faceted piece. Hogwood directs a clean-cut, vigorous performance with an excellent cast of singers highly skilled in the authentic performance of Baroque music. Emma Kirkby is at her most brilliant in the coloratura for the Angel, Patrizia Kwella sings movingly as Mary Magdalene and Carolyn Watkinson as Cleophas adopts an almost counter-tenor-like tone. Ian Partridge's tenor has a heady lightness as St John, and though David Thomas's Lucifer could have more weight, he too sings stylishly. Excellent recording, well balanced and natural in all respects, with an attractive ambient bloom.

Saul.

** Tel. **ZA8 35687** (2) [id.]. Fischer-Dieskau, Rolfe-Johnson, Esswood, Varady, V. State Op. Ch., VCM, Harnoncourt.

Harnoncourt's version was recorded live at the Handel tercentenary celebrations in Vienna in 1985 and, whatever the advantages of period performance, the extraneous noises of coughs and creaks, together with the odd slip of execution, seriously reduce its merits. Dietrich Fischer-Dieskau in the name-part is most characterful, but his expressive style is very heavy for Handel, particularly in the recitatives. It is still for the most part a rich and noble performance, and Julia Varady, though not quite idiomatic, is individual too, with tone cleanly focused. The English members of the cast sing stylishly, notably Anthony Rolfe-Johnson as Jonathan and Paul Esswood as David. Elizabeth Gale's bright soprano is not always sweetly caught by the microphones, but it is a sympathetic performance. Harnoncourt's direction is lively, but he misses much of the grandeur of the work, and some of the cuts he makes are damaging. The Vienna State Opera Concert Choir are responsive, but they never quite sound at home coping with English words. This is a fair stop-gap, at a period when there is no competition; but as an alternative, even with modern instruments and a large amateur chorus, Sir Charles Mackerras's 1973 version for DG Archiv is preferable on almost every count, and we hope this will shortly reappear on CD.

Solomon (complete).

❀ *** Ph. Dig. **412 612-2** (2); *412 612-4* (3) [id]. C. Watkinson, Argenta, Hendricks, Rolfe-Johnson, Monteverdi Ch., E. Bar. Soloists, Gardiner.

This is among the very finest of all Handel oratorio recordings, triumphant proof that authentic performance can be the opposite of dry, detached and inexpressive; and the theatrical flair of the piece in its three sharply differentiated Acts is consistently brought out. With panache, Gardiner shows how authentic-sized forces can convey Handelian grandeur even with clean-focused textures and fast speeds that will have the older traditionalists jumping up in alarm. *Swell the full chorus*, they all sing at the end of Act II, after Solomon's Judgement, and with trumpets and timpani you could hardly imagine anything more joyful, a dance movement translated. The choruses and even more magnificent double-choruses stand as cornerstones of a structure which may have less of a story-line than some other Handel oratorios – the Judgement apart – but which Gardiner shows has consistent human warmth. Thus in Act I, the relationship of Solomon and his Queen is delightfully presented, ending with the ravishing Nightingale chorus, *May no rash intruder*, while the Act III scenes between Solomon and the Queen of Sheba, necessarily more formal, are given extra warmth by having in that role a singer who is sensuous in tone, Barbara Hendricks. She is one of the five excellent women principals, all strongly contrasted with one another. Carolyn Watkinson's pure mezzo, at times like a male alto, is very apt for Solomon himself (only after Handel's death did baritones capture it), while Nancy Argenta is clear and sweet as his Queen. In the Judgement scene Joan Rodgers is outstandingly warm and characterful as the First Harlot, but the overriding glory of the set is the radiant singing of Gardiner's Monteverdi Choir. Its clean, crisp articulation matches the brilliant playing of the English Baroque Soloists, regularly challenged by Gardiner's fast speeds as in the *Arrival of the Queen of Sheba*. One big advantage from some judicious cutting of 'dead wood' is that the whole work, at 2 hours 20 minutes, is squeezed on to two CDs merely, and the sound is superb, coping thrillingly with the problems of the double choruses. There are three chrome cassettes, undoubtedly impressive in sound, but the compact discs are even finer.

The Triumph of time and truth.
*** Hyp. **CDA 66071/2** [id.]. Fisher, Kirkby, Brett, Partridge, Varcoe, L. Handel Ch. and O, Darlow.

This is officially Handel's very last oratorio, dating from 1757, an allegory on the subject suggested by the title. Almost all the material in fact dates from much earlier, much of it from an Italian treatment of the same subject which Handel wrote for Rome in 1707. Darlow's performance with the London Handel Choir and Orchestra using original instruments has an attractive bluffness. This is broader and rougher than the authentic recordings by John Eliot Gardiner which are now such a feature of the Handel repertory, but it is hardly less enjoyable. The soloists all seem to have been chosen for the clarity of their pitching – Emma Kirkby, Gillian Fisher, Charles Brett and Stephen Varcoe, with the honey-toned Ian Partridge singing even more beautifully than the others, but with a timbre too pure quite to characterize 'Pleasure'. Good atmospheric recording; through the chorus is a little distant, the increase in overall immediacy which has come with the CD transfer makes this less striking.

Utretcht Te Deum.
*(*) Tel. Dig. **ZK8.42955** [id.]. Palmer, Lipovsek, Langridge, Vienna Boys' Ch., Schoenberg Ch., VCM, Harnoncourt – BACH: *Magnificat.**

Utrecht Te Deum and Jubilate.
*** O-L **414 413-2** [id.]. Nelson, Kirkby, Brett, Elliot, Covey-Crump, Thomas, Ch. of Christ Church Cathedral, Oxford, AAM, Preston.

Handel wrote the Utrecht pieces just before coming to London, intending them as a sample of his work. Using authentic instruments and an all-male choir with trebles, Preston directs a performance which is not merely scholarly but characteristically alert and vigorous, particularly impressive in the superb *Gloria* with its massive eight-part chords. With a team of soloists regularly associated with the Academy of Ancient Music, this CD can be confidently recommended: the remastering from the original analogue recording is very successful.

Handel's magnificent *Utretcht Te Deum* makes a generous coupling for Bach's *Magnificat*, and in a relatively intimate acoustic Harnoncourt sometimes presents allegros briskly and lightly – but, as in the *Magnificat*, that is the exception. The characterful solo singing – the murky-sounding contralto apart – marries oddly with slow, heavy speeds and leaden rhythms, and the chorus, efficient enough, lacks brightness and rhythmic spring. Dryish recording.

OPERAS

Alcina (complete).

*** HMV Dig. **CDS7 49771-2**; *EX 270388-5* (4). Augér, Della Jones, Kuhlmann, Harrhy, Kwella, Maldwyn Davies, Tomlinson, Opera Stage Ch., City of L. Bar. Sinfonia, Hickox.

Richard Hickox's superb recording of one of Handel's greatest operas, the text complete, was based on a staged production at the Spitalfields and Cheltenham festivals, later taken to Los Angeles. That stage experience adds dramatic sharpness to what – for all the beauty of individual numbers – can seem a very long sequence of *da capo* arias. Hickox underlines the contrasts of mood and speed, conveying the full range of emotion. It would be hard to devise a septet of Handelian singers more stylish than the soloists here. Though the American, Arleen Augér, may not have the weight of Joan Sutherland (who in a much-edited text sang the title role both at Covent Garden and on record), she is just as brilliant and pure-toned, singing warmly in the great expansive arias. Even next to her, Della Jones stands out in the breeches role of Ruggiero, with an extraordinary range of memorable arias, bold as well as tender. Eiddwen Harrhy as Morgana is just as brilliant in the aria, *Tornami a vagheggiar*, usually 'borrowed' by Alcina, while Kathleen Kuhlmann, Patrizia Kwella, Maldwyn Davies and John Tomlinson all sing with a clarity and beauty to make the music sparkle. As for the text, it is even more complete than any known performance ever, when it includes as appendices two charming items that Handel cut even at the première. There are few Handel opera recordings to match this, with warm, spacious sound, recorded at EMI's Abbey Road studio. The tape transfer is generally well managed and is kind to the solo voices; however, the resonance does bring some problems, notably in the final chorus which is slightly congested.

Alessandro (complete).

(*) HMV **CDS7 47910-8 (3). Jacobs, Boulin, Poulenard, Nirouret, Varcoe, Guy de Mey, La Petite Bande, Kuijken.

Sigiswald Kuijken directs his team of period-performance specialists in an urgently refreshing, at times sharply abrasive reading of one of Handel's key operas, the first in which he wrote roles for the rival prima donnas, Faustina and Cuzzoni, not to mention the celebrated castrato, Senesino. As a high counter-tenor, René Jacobs copes brilliantly with the taxing Senesino role of Alexander himself. His singing is astonishingly free and agile, if too heavily aspirated. Among the others, Isabelle Poulenard at her best sounds a little like a French Emma Kirkby, though the production is not quite so pure and at times comes over more edgily. The others make a fine, consistent team, the more effective when the recording so vividly conveys a sense of presence with sharply defined directional focus.

Atalanta (complete).

*** Hung. Dig. **HCD 12612/4** [id.]. Farkas, Bartfai-Barta, Lax, Bandi, Gregor, Polgar, Savaria Vocal Ens. and Capella, McGegan.

It is welcome to find Hungary producing – with the help of a British conductor and continuo-player, Nicholas McGegan – so stylish an authentic performance of a Handel opera on period instruments. The fresh precision of the string playing of the Capella Savaria demonstrates – even without the help of vibrato – what Hungarian string quartets have been proving for generations, a superfine ability to match and blend. Though it is odd that a Communist country should have lighted on an opera expressly written to celebrate a royal occasion (the wedding of Frederick, Prince of Wales, whose long-standing animosity towards Handel promptly evaporated) it proves an excellent choice, crammed with dozens of sparkling light-hearted numbers with no lull in the inspiration, the opposite of weighty Handel. Led by the bright-toned Katarin Farkas in the name-part, the singers cope stylishly, and the absence of Slavonic wobbles confirms the subtle difference of Magyar voices; Joszef Gregor with his firm, dark bass is just as much in style, for example, as he regularly is in Verdi. First-rate recording.

Hercules (complete).

*** DG Dig. **423 137-2** (3) [id.]. Tomlinson, Sarah Walker, Rolfe-Johnson, Jennifer Smith, Denley, Savidge, Monteverdi Ch., E. Bar. Soloists, Gardiner.

Though the English libretto has its unintentional humour (the jealous Dejanira tells her husband Hercules to *'Resign thy club'*, meaning his knobkerrie not the Athenaeum), this is a great opera. Gardiner's generally brisk performance using authentic forces may at times lack Handelian grandeur in the big choruses, but it superbly conveys the vigour of the writing, its natural drama. Writing in English, Handel concentrated on direct and involving human emotions more than he generally did when setting classical subjects in Italian. Numbers are compact and memorable, and the fire of this performance is typified by the singing of Sarah Walker as Dejanira in her finest recording yet. John Tomlinson makes an excellent, dark-toned Hercules with florid passages well defined except for very occasional sliding. Youthful voices consistently help in the clarity of the attack – Jennifer Smith as Iole, Catherine Denley as Lichas, Anthony Rolfe-Johnson as Hyllus and Peter Savidge as the Priest of Jupiter. Refined playing and outstanding recording quality, with the CDs bringing a gripping immediacy and realistic projection to this admirably alive music-making.

Julius Caesar (complete, in English).

*** HMV Dig. *EX 270232-5* (3). Dame Janet Baker, Masterson, Sarah Walker, Della Jones, Bowman, Tomlinson, E. Nat. Op. Ch. and O, Mackerras.

Julius Caesar, particularly in English translation, as in this set based on the ENO stage production at the Coliseum, really does bear out what specialists have long claimed concerning Handel's powers of characterization in opera. With Mackerras's lively and sensitive conducting, this is vivid and dramatically involving in a way rare with Handel opera on record. Dame Janet, in glorious voice and drawing on the widest range of expressive tone-colours, shatters the old idea that this alto-castrato role should be transposed down an octave and given to a baritone. Valerie Masterson makes a charming and seductive Cleopatra, fresh and girlish, though the voice is caught a little too brightly for caressing such radiant melodies as those for *V'adoro pupille* (*Lamenting, complaining*) and *Piangero* (*Flow my tears*). Sarah Walker sings with powerful intensity as Pompey's widow; James Bowman is a characterful counter-tenor Ptolemy and John Tomlinson a firm, resonant Achillas, the other nasty character. The ravishing accompaniments to the two big Cleopatra arias amply justify the use by the excellent English National Opera Orchestra of modern, not period, instruments. The full, vivid studio sound makes this one of the very finest of the invaluable series of ENO opera recordings in English sponsored by the Peter Moores Foundation. No doubt a CD version will arrive before too long.

Rodelinda (complete).
** Decca Dig. **414 667-2**; *414 667-4* (2) [id.]. Sutherland, Nafé, Rayam, Buchanan, Tourangeau, Ramey, Welsh Nat. Op. O, Bonynge.

Rodelinda is an opera which, in 1959 during the Handel bicentenary celebrations, was given by the Handel Opera Society in London with the newly emergent Joan Sutherland dazzling in the name-part. It is the greatest of pities that that historic rendering was not recorded at once. Here in the late 1980s she finally tackled the role on record and, quite apart from the style now seeming dated, much more romantic than has become acceptable in this age of 'authentic' performance, Dame Joan's voice has developed a beat which obscures its beauty in slow numbers. Not only that, the slow speeds go with a rhythmic slackness and over-affectionate expressive style that undermine the classical purity. Even so, the flexibility of this still-glorious voice is thrilling in the fast arias, and one welcomes an opera in which the protagonist has so many important numbers. Scholars will also argue over the aptness of ornamentation as Richard Bonynge has devised it, though that will trouble the non-specialist listener less. Outstanding among the others is Isabel Nafé as Bertarido, the main castrato role. Her account of the best-known aria in the opera, *Dove sei?* (known in translation as *Art thou troubled?*) is most beautiful, firm and even. Curtis Rayam, in one of the earliest of tenor parts, copes confidently with the role of the usurper, Grimoaldo, and Samuel Ramey's dark bass is similarly effective in the villain's role of Garibaldo. Isobel Buchanan sings freshly, but is not at her sweetest, while Huguette Tourangeau is most disappointing, far too wobbly for Handel. The playing of the Welsh National Opera Orchestra is vigorous but not always polished; and the recording, though full and bright, has the voices too close. The cassettes are of a high standard, lively and wide-ranging; the very present recording has undoubtedly aided the clarity of the transfer. The layout, however, on four sides, prevents a division into separate Acts tailored to side-ends. The CD booklet is provided as documentation.

Tamerlano (complete).
*** Erato Dig. **ECD 88220**; *MCE 88220* (3) [id.]. Ragin, Robson, Argenta, Chance, Findlay, Schirrer, E. Bar. Soloists, Gardiner.

Recorded at a live concert performance for West German Radio, immediately after a staging in Lyons and Gottingen, John Eliot Gardiner's Erato set of *Tamerlano* presents a strikingly dramatic and immediate experience. One has no doubt whatever that this is one of Handel's most masterly operas. The pacing of numbers and of the recitative is beautifully thought out, and with a singing cast notable for clean, precise voices the result is electrifying, the more so when, more than usual, in this opera Handel wrote ensemble numbers as well as solo arias, most of them crisp and compact. Leading the cast are two outstanding counter-tenors whose encounters provide some of the most exciting moments: Michael Chance as Andronicus, firm and clear, Derek Ragin in the name-part equally agile and more distinctive of timbre, with a rich, warm tone that avoids womanliness. Nigel Robson in the tenor role of Bajazet conveys the necessary gravity, not least in the difficult, highly original G minor aria before suicide; and Nancy Argenta sings with starry purity as Asteria. The only serious snag is the dryness of the sound, which makes voices and instruments sound more aggressive than they usually do in Gardiner's recordings with the English Baroque Soloists. Even that flaw might be thought to add to the dramatic impact and it means that the cassettes (which are documented with the CD booklet) are also strikingly clear and vivid. This set now supersedes Malgoire's CBS version, with René Jacobs and Mieke van der Sluis outstanding among a generally good band of soloists (*13T 37893*).

COLLECTIONS

'Celebrated arias': (i) *Acis and Galatea: I rage . . . O ruddier than the cherry*. (ii) *Alcina: Tiranna gelosia . . . Tornami a vagheggiar;* (iii) *Verdi prati; Sta nell'Ircana.* (iv) *Atalanta: Care selve*. (v) *Ezio: Se en bell'ardire. Giulio Cesare:* (ii) *Da tempeste il legno;* (iii) *Piangero la sorte mia*. (vi) *Rinaldo: Lascia ch'io pianga*. (vii) *Rodelinda: Dove sei? Semele: Iris hence away;* (viii) *Where'er you walk;* (ix) *Leave me radiant light*. (x) *Serse: Ombra mai fù*.

(M) *** Decca *417 536-6* [id.]. (i) Luxon; (ii) Sutherland; (iii) Berganza; (iv) Pavarotti; (v) Forbes Robinson; (vi) Greevy; (vii) Horne; (viii) McKellar; (ix) G. Evans; (x) Tebaldi.

A starry tape anthology from Decca's 'Opera Gala' series that is self-recommending. It starts with a minor disadvantage in that the opening *Tiranna gelosia* from *Alcina*, an early recording showing Sutherland in dazzling form, has some peaking on loud high notes; but the rest of the transfers are vivid, yet without this problem; and the programme is irresistible. Marilyn Horne's *Dove sei?* (*Art thou troubled?*) has a ravishing pianissimo at the opening, and Bernadette Greevy's *Lascia ch'io pianga* is equally lovely. Tebaldi is chosen to sing the famous *Largo* (*Ombra mai fù*); Berganza and Luxon (a sparkling *O ruddier than the cherry*) are hardly less distinguished, while Kenneth McKellar reminds us of his warm Handelian legato in a fine account of *Where'er you walk*, when he upstages Pavarotti's *Care selve*. A splendid bargain, overall.

Arias: *Alexander's Feast: The Prince, unable to conceal his pain; Softly sweet in Lydian measures. Atalanta: Care selve. Giulio Cesare: Piangero. Messiah: Rejoice greatly; He shall feed his flock. Rinaldo: Lascia ch'io pianga. Samson: Let the bright Seraphim.*

(*) Delos Dig. **D/CD 3026 [id.]. Arleen Augér, Mostly Mozart O, Schwarz – BACH: Arias.**(*)

Arleen Augér's bright, clean, flexible soprano is even more naturally suited to these Handel arias than to the Bach items with which they are coupled. The delicacy with which she tackles the most elaborate divisions and points the words is a delight, and the main snag is that the orchestral accompaniment, recorded rather too close, is coarse, though the sound is bright and clear.

Arias: *Judas Maccabaeus: Father of heaven. Messiah: O Thou that tellest; He was despised. Samson: Return O God of Hosts.*

❀ (***) Decca mono **414 723-2**; stereo *414 623-4*. Kathleen Ferrier, LPO, Boult – BACH: *Arias*.(***)

Kathleen Ferrier had a unique feeling for Handel; these performances are unforgettable for their communicative intensity and nobility of timbre and line. She receives highly sympathetic accompaniments from Boult, another natural Handelian. While (here more than in the Bach coupling) there may be some who will prefer the more richly upholstered stereo orchestral sound of the cassette with its fuller upper string timbre, there is no doubt that the direct derivation of the CD from the original mono master-tape gives the voice greater freshness and realism. John Culshaw who produced the 1952 LP described this performance of *He was despised* as having 'a beauty and simplicity that I cannot think has been, or will be, surpassed'. On CD the deeply moving closing bars, when the orchestra drops away to leave the voice momentarily unaccompanied in the words 'He was despised . . . rejected', has an uncanny presence. There is, of course, pre-Dolby background noise, but in no way does it detract from the illusion of reality.

Opera arias: *Agrippina: Bel piacere. Orlando: Fammi combattere. Partenope: Funbondo spira il*

vento. Rinaldo: Or la tromba; Cara sposa; Venti turbini; Cor ingrato; Lascia ch'io pianga. Serse: Frondi tenere; Ombra mai fù.
(*) Erato Dig. **ECD 88034; *MCE 75047*. Marilyn Horne, Sol. Ven., Scimone.

Horne gives virtuoso performances of a wide-ranging collection of Handel arias. The flexibility of her voice in scales and trills and ornaments of every kind remains formidable, and the power is extraordinary down to the tangy chest register. The voice is spotlit against a reverberant acoustic. Purists may question some of the ornamentation, but voice-fanciers will not worry. The recording sounds well in both media.

Hanson, Howard (1896–1981)

Symphony No. 2 (Romantic), Op. 30.
*** HMV Dig. **CDC7 47850-2** [id.]. St Louis SO, Slatkin – BARBER: *Violin concerto*.***

Howard Hanson wrote his splendid *Second Symphony* for the fiftieth anniversary of the Boston Symphony Orchestra in 1931. The *Romantic* subtitle is wholly appropriate, for the music is very much in a post-Rachmaninov vein, though there is a strong transatlantic flavour to the lyricism. Apart from the memorable opening motif which finds its way into all three movements, the melody of the *Andante* is justly renowned in America where it has been used as theme music for TV. The symphony was also interpolated into the background score for the science-fiction movie, *Alien*. Such incidental use in no way detracts from the appeal of the symphony itself which, if harmonically not breaking any new ground, is structurally sound, imaginatively laid out and by no means lightweight. The composer himself has recorded it on LP with great ardour for Mercury, but Slatkin's performance is a very satisfying one too, responding to the expressive nostalgia of the slow movement and bringing an exhilarating attack to the finale – there are only three movements. The coupling with Barber's *Violin concerto* is apt, another ripely romantic twentieth-century work which is genuinely inspired. The rich atmospheric recording, beautifully balanced and rich in its washes of string tone, is a pleasure in itself.

Harris, Roy (1898–1979)

Symphony No. 3 in one movement.
*** DG Dig. **419 780-2** [id.]. NYPO, Bernstein – SCHUMANN: *Symphony No. 3*.***

Roy Harris's *Third* is the archetypal American Symphony. It is full of powerful sweeping paragraphs, yet at the same time it is taut and intense. There is a real sense of the wide open spaces, of the abundant energy and independent nature of the American pioneers, and an instinctive feeling for form. The music moves forward relentlessly from the very opening bars until the massive eloquence of its coda. Its compelling feeling of purpose and the rugged sense of line betoken a *real* symphonist. Like Samuel Barber's *First*, it is a one-movement work, but it is more convincingly held together, far less episodic, grander and more deeply original. It enjoyed an enormous vogue in the 1940s, thanks to the advocacy of Koussevitzky, who was Bernstein's mentor. This new record may not have the same high tension as the Koussevitzky, for (as in his earlier reading) Bernstein gives a keenly felt but essentially softer-grained account of the work. There is no lack of punch or weight, but the ends of some paragraphs are carefully rounded. However, this is a great symphony – splendidly played and well recorded.

Harty, Hamilton (1879–1941)

(i) *Piano concerto in B min.;* (ii) *In Ireland* (*Fantasy for flute, harp and orchestra*); *With the wild geese.*
*** Chan. Dig. **CHAN 8321**; *ABTD 1084* [id.]. (i) Binns, (ii) Fleming, Kelly; Ulster O, Thomson.

This is the most engaging of the records issued so far in this enterprising series which is uncovering the art of a minor but rewarding talent. The *Piano concerto*, written in 1922, has strong Rachmaninovian influences (there are indelible associations with that composer's *Second Concerto* in both slow movement and finale). But the melodic freshness remains individual and in this highly sympathetic performance the work's magnetism increases with familiarity, in spite of moments of rhetoric. The *In Ireland fantasy* is full of delightful Irish melodic whimsy, especially appealing when the playing is so winning. Melodrama enters the scene in the symphonic poem, *With the wild geese*, but its Irishry asserts itself immediately in the opening theme. Again a splendid performance and on CD a high standard of digital sound. On the excellent chrome tape a slightly lower transfer level in the *Concerto* softens the edge on the upper strings very appropriately.

Violin concerto in D; Variations on a Dublin air.
*** Chan. **CHAN 8386**; *ABT 1044* [id.]. Ralph Holmes, Ulster O, Thomson.

The *Violin concerto* is an early work and comes from 1908; it was written for Szigeti, who gave the first performance. Though it has no strongly individual idiom, the invention is fresh and often touched with genuine poetry. Ralph Holmes gives a thoroughly committed account of the solo part and is well supported by an augmented Ulster Orchestra under Bryden Thomson. The *Variations* are less impressive though thoroughly enjoyable, and readers who imagine that the orchestral playing will be indifferent (this was the début record of this provincial orchestra) will be pleasantly surprised. These are accomplished and well-recorded performances, the analogue masters successfully transferred to CD. The tape transfers are well balanced, but lack the last degree of range and sparkle in the treble.

An Irish symphony; A Comedy overture.
*** Chan. Dig. **CHAN 8314**; *ABTD 1027* [id.]. Ulster O, Thomson.

The *Irish symphony* dates from 1904 and arose from a competition for a suite or symphony based on traditional Irish airs, inspired by the first Dublin performance of Dvořák's *New World symphony*, 'founded upon negro melodies'! Harty's symphony won great acclaim for its excellent scoring and good craftsmanship. He revised it twice, and though it lays no claim to being a work of exceptional individuality, it is an attractive and well-wrought piece of light music. The scherzo is particularly engaging. It is extremely well played by the Ulster Orchestra under Bryden Thomson, and the overture is also successful and enjoyable. The recording is absolutely first class in every respect and sounds splendid in its CD format. The cassette is marginally less wide-ranging than the disc, but still yields excellent results.

With the wild geese (symphonic poem).
(M) *** HMV **CDM7 69206-2**; *ED 290208-4*. SNO, Gibson – GERMAN: *Welsh rhapsody*; MACCUNN: *Land of Mountain and Flood*; SMYTH: *The Wreckers overture*.***

With the wild geese, written in 1910 for the Cardiff Festival, is a melodramatic piece about the Irish soldiers fighting on the French side in the Battle of Fontenoy. The ingredients – a gay Irish theme and a call to arms among them – are effectively deployed; although the music does not reveal a strong individual personality, it is carried by a romantic sweep which is well exploited here. The 1968 recording, always vivid, sounds well in its digital remastering for CD. There is also a very good tape.

VOCAL MUSIC

The Children of Lir; Ode to a nightingale.
*** Chan. Dig. **CHAN 8387**; *ABTD 1051* [id.]. Harper, Ulster O, Thomson.

These two fine works span the full breadth of Harty's composing career. His setting of Keats' *Ode to a nightingale* written in 1907 reflects a time when a British (or Irish) composer could tackle boldly a grand setting of a poetic masterpiece almost too familiar. It says much for Harty's inspiration that the result is so richly convincing, a piece written for his future wife, the soprano, Agnes Nicholls. The other work, directly Irish in its inspiration, evocative in an almost Sibelian way, dates from 1939 and uses the soprano in wordless melisma, here beautifully sung by Heather Harper. The performances are excellent, warmly committed and superbly recorded, especially in their CD format. The cassette transfer of the symphonic poem on side one is made at only a modest level and lacks something in immediacy; the *Ode* is more effectively managed, with a good vocal presence and natural balance.

Haug, Halvor (born 1952)

Symphony No. 1; Silence for strings; Sinfonietta.
*** Aurora Dig. **ARCD 1910**. LSO, Per Dreier.

Halvor Haug is a Norwegian now in his mid-thirties and a most impressive talent. After studies in Oslo and at the Sibelius Academy in Helsinki, he spent some time in London in the late 1970s with Robert Simpson. He establishes an immediate feeling of his own identity; there is no mistaking its sense of place or the individuality of its world. The most important work on this disc is the powerful *First Symphony* (1982), which has great concentration of atmosphere and an almost Sibelian breadth, and a brooding intensity that calls Shostakovich to mind. Yet Haug is very much his own man. His early *Silence for strings* (1977) is a most imaginative piece, an evocation of tranquillity and a study in subtly changing textures. A fine *Sinfonietta* (1983) completes this introduction to Haug's music, which is superbly played and recorded.

Haydn, Josef (1732–1809)

6 Allemandes, Hob IX/12; 5 Contredanses: Minuet and Quadrille, Hob IX/24 and 29; 8 Gypsy dances, Hob IX/28; Ländler from The Seasons; Minuetti di ballo Nos 1–6, Hob IX/4; Notturni for 2 flutes and 2 horns, Hob II/D5.
*(*) HM Dig. **HMC 901057**. Bella Musica of Vienna Ens., Dittrich.

Although the music here is uneven, there is much of interest, not least the *Nocturnes* for flutes and horns and the first of the *Minuetti di ballo*, also attractively featuring flutes. The *Zingarese* survive only in a version for harpsichord, but Michael Dittrich has scored them traditionally, for a small group using a cymbalom; and one of the most appealing numbers is a solo for that characterful instrument, played very gently, and the more effective for the background silence of CD. However, in many of the pieces for the main group the dry acoustic and close microphones are unflattering to the violin timbre. It is not clear whether the players use 'original instruments', but the vinegar in the treble gives that impression, and robs the music making of a good deal of its charm.

Cello concerto in C, Hob VIIb/1.
*** HMV **CDC7 47614-2**. Jacqueline du Pré, ECO, Barenboim – DVOŘÁK: *Concerto.***(*)

Cello concertos in C and D, Hob VIIb/1–2.
*** O-L Dig. **414 615-2** [id.]. Christophe Coin, AAM, Hogwood.
(*) CBS **MK 36674 [id.]. Yo-Yo Ma, ECO, Garcia.
(M) **(*) HMV **CDM7 69009-2** [id.]; *EG 769009-4*. Lynn Harrell, ASMF, Marriner.
(*) HMV **CDC7 49305-2 [id.]. Rostropovich, ASMF.
** RCA Dig. **RD 70943**. Ofra Harnoy, Toronto CO, Robinson.

Cello concertos in C, Hob VIIb/1; in D, Hob VIIb/4.
(*) Ph. Dig. **412 793-2 [id.]. Julian Lloyd Webber with ECO.

Cello concerto in D, Hob VIIb/2.
*** HMV **CDC7 47840-2** [id.]. Jacqueline du Pré, LSO, Barbirolli – BOCCHERINI: *Concerto.***(*)
** Denon Dig. **C37 7023** [id.]. Fujiwara, Netherlands CO, Inoue – BOCCHERINI: *Concerto.***
(B) ** DG Walkman *415 330-4* [id.]. Fournier, Lucerne Fest. O, Baumgartner – DVOŘÁK; BOCCHERINI: *Concertos.****

Cello concertos in C and D, Hob VIIb/1–2; in G (arr. of *Violin concerto, Hob VIIa/4*).
(*) DG Dig. **419 786-2; *419 786-4* [id.]. Mischa Maisky, COE.

The discovery of Haydn's early *C major Cello concerto* in Prague in the early 1960s provided a marvellous addition to the limited cello repertory. For some, this concerto is even more attractive than the well-known D major work that for a time was fathered on Anton Kraft instead of Haydn. For those wanting the two concertos paired together, the young French soloist, Christophe Coin, provides a ready answer. He is a superb soloist and, provided the listener has no reservations about the use of original instruments, Hogwood's accompaniments are equally impressive. The style is not aggressively abrasive but gives extra clarity and point to the music, not least in the breathtakingly brilliant account of the finale of the *C major Concerto*. Certainly no fresher or more vital performance of these two works has been put on disc, although Coin's own cadenzas – undoubtedly stylish – are on the long side. Excellent sound.

Yo-Yo Ma provides an attractive alternative to Coin's reading of the two Haydn *Concertos*, both of them works of the sharpest imagination. Ma's approach is more restrained in expression, not as strongly moulded as Coin's in the lyrical slow movements, a degree more detached. Ma's refinement of approach has its own rewards, though some may prefer a bolder approach to music firmly belonging to the classical eighteenth century. Apart from one or two odd points of balance, the recording is clean and full and it has been transferred impressively on CD.

Harrell, rather after the manner of Rostropovich, seeks to turn these elegant concertos into big virtuoso pieces. The result is strong and impressive, helped by Marriner's beautifully played accompaniments, although touches of over-romantic expressiveness tend to intrude. Cadenzas are distractingly and unstylishly long. The remastered recording is vivid but not absolutely clean in focus; the chrome cassette has a lower frequency ceiling than the CD but sounds pleasant enough.

Mischa Maisky gives beautifully cultured readings of both concertos, which he also directs himself. He has much warmth and refinement, though his tempi are generally a bit too fast. For all his splendour of tone and his accomplishment, he rarely catches the listener by surprise; at the same time, there is nothing routine about his playing or direction. He adds a bonus in the shape of an arrangement of the *G major Violin concerto*. However, this is hardly likely to sway collectors one way or the other – and again it is fast. The recordings, made in the Vienna Konzerthaus, have admirable body and presence, and detail is well placed. Marvellous playing but not a first choice.

Ofra Harnoy is a young Israeli-born Canadian of great talent and promise. There is a commendable spirit in her approach to the two Haydn *Concertos*: at times her tempi are a bit on the fast side (the finale of the *C major*) and she is not always as subtle in matters of phrasing as some of her more established rivals (particularly Yo-Yo Ma). All the same, in spite of the superficial brilliance, there is much to admire here; and she is well supported by the Toronto Chamber Orchestra and the engineers, who produce a natural and well-judged balance. Not a first choice in this repertoire, but a record that augurs well for her future.

Lloyd Webber couples the *C major Concerto* with yet another newly discovered *Concerto in D*. This was originally published in a spurious 'improved' version by Grützmacher. The 'original edition' resurfaced in East Germany in 1948 and is claimed as authentic Haydn. This seems doubtful; although it is a substantial piece, it is of uneven appeal. Lloyd Webber's approach to both concertos is strong and committed, but rather heavy – he tends to overphrase. This is emphasized by a forward balance that makes the cello almost outweigh the orchestra. This larger-than-life impression is not the image this artist presents in the concert hall. In all other respects the recording is very good.

With Barbirolli to partner her, Jacqueline du Pré's performance of the best-known *D major Concerto* is warmly expressive. Though purists may object, the conviction and flair of the playing are extraordinarily compelling, and the romantic feeling is matched by an attractively full, well-balanced recording which belies its age (1969) in the splendid compact disc transfer. The cello is given a realistic presence, yet the orchestral backing has a wide range of dynamic, and Barbirolli scales his accompaniment to match the inspirational approach of his young soloist.

Rostropovich's earlier recording of the *C major Concerto* with Britten was brilliant enough but, at even faster speeds in the outer movements, his virtuosity in the reissued HMV performance is even more astonishing. With fuller, more modern and intimate recording, this has some claims on the collector, especially as it is aptly coupled with the *D major Concerto*; but quite apart from the extra haste (which brings its moments of breathless phrasing) Rostropovich's style has acquired a degree of self-indulgence in the warmth of expressiveness, and this is reflected in the accompaniment, which he also directed.

Mari Fujiwara is a player of considerable quality, and collectors allergic to authentic-instrument recordings might like to consider this. The orchestral contribution under Michi Inoue, though not distinguished, is perfectly acceptable and the soloist is splendid. So, too, is the recording. But the Denon CD, for all the fidelity of its digital sound, has not quite the individuality and warmth of Du Pré's record of the same coupling.

Fournier plays with style and polish; if Baumgartner's accompaniment is relatively unimaginative, the 1968 recording sounds better here than it has on some previous presentations. The Boccherini and Dvořák couplings are very attractive, and this Walkman chrome tape is certainly good value.

Du Pré's record of the *C major Concerto* was the first she made with her husband, Daniel Barenboim, and she gives a performance of characteristic warmth and intensity. Her style, as in the D major work, is sometimes romantic in a way that, strictly speaking, is inappropriate in this music – yet when the very power of her personality is strongly conveyed, even through rhythmic distortions, and Barenboim ensures that the orchestra follows every nuance, one can but marvel. This is the sort of performance that defies cold analysis. The recording is given extra life in the CD transfer, and the new coupling of the Dvořák *Concerto* is romantically appropriate.

(i) *Cello concerto in D;* (ii) *Trumpet concerto in E flat;* (iii) *Violin concerto in C.*
(*) CBS Dig. **MK 39310; *IMT 39310* [id.]. (i) Yo-Yo Ma, ECO, Garcia; (ii) Marsalis, Nat. PO, Leppard; (iii) Lin, Minnesota O, Marriner.

All these performances are still available with their original couplings and are discussed above and below. The CBS recording has excellent clarity and its presence is very striking on CD. The chrome cassette is generally softer in focus, the sound fuller.

Flute concerto in D, Hob VIIf/D1. Flute & oboe concertos (arr. from *Lira concertos* Nos 1, 2, 3–5), *Hob VIIh/1, 2, 3–5*; *Oboe concerto in C, Hob VIIg/C1.*
(*) CBS Dig. **M2K 39772 (2) [id.]. Rampal, Pierlot, Liszt CO, Rolla.

The *Flute and oboe concertos* are arrangements of Haydn's *Lira concertos*, commissioned by Ferdinand IV of Naples, written for a curious (now obsolete) instrument which was a cross between a hurdy-gurdy and a mechanical violoncello. The music Haydn composed for this (or rather two of them, for it was played in duet with a chamber group) is most attractive and worth reviving. In the 1960s Vox Turnabout issued an LP, containing some of these works and employing a modern electronic lira which enabled one musician to play both the duet parts. Here flute and oboe are effectively substituted; the only real complaint about these fresh, alert performances, briskly paced, is that the balance is rather close, reducing the opportunities for light and shade. Needless to say, Jean-Pierre Rampal and Pierre Pierlot are expert soloists and the latter's bright, rather pointed timbre makes a good foil for the flute, yet blends well with it; in the solo *Oboe concerto*, however, the tone could ideally be warmer. Rolla offers characteristically polished accompaniments and the orchestral sound is clear and vivid.

Horn concerto No. 1 in D, Hob VII/d3.
(M) **(*) Tel. **ZS8 43629** [id.]. Baumann, Concerto Amsterdam – DANZI; ROSETTI: *Concertos.***(*)

Horn concertos Nos 1 in D, Hob VII/d3; 2 in D, Hob VIII/d4.
*** Tel. Dig. **ZK8 42960** [id.]. Clevenger, Liszt CO, Rolla – M. HAYDN: *Concertino.****
(M) *** HMV *ED 290302-4* [Ang. *4AM 34720*]. Tuckwell, ECO – M. HAYDN: *Concertino.****

(i) *Horn concertos Nos 1–2;* (ii) *Trumpet concerto in E flat;* (i) *Divertimento a 3 in E flat.*
(*) Nimbus **NIM 5010 [id.]. (i) Thompson; (ii) Wallace; Philh. O, Warren-Green.

Dale Clevenger, principal horn with the Chicago Symphony, gives superb accounts of the two *Horn concertos* attributed to Haydn (the second is of doubtful lineage). He is especially good in the slow movements, a little solemn in the *First*, but eloquently so, with the *Adagio* of its companion given an air of gentle melancholy. This is a movement that can seem too long, but not here. The dotted main theme of the first movement, nicely pointed, is most engaging, and the performance projects a galant charm of the kind we associate with Hummel. The accompaniments are supportive, polished and elegant. These performances have fine spirit and spontaneity and on CD the Telefunken recording, made in a nicely judged and warm acoustic, is in the demonstration class: when Clevenger plays his solo cadenzas the tangibility of his presence is remarkable, yet the combination with the orchestra is hardly less convincing.

In his interesting notes for the Nimbus CD, Michael Thompson suggests that Haydn wrote his *First* and *Second Concertos* for his first and second horn players, Thaddäus Steinmüller and Carl Franz. Yet both works explore the widest range, and it was the *Divertimento*, an attractive bonus, that exploited Steinmüller's ability to slip easily into the stratosphere of the horn register. Thompson manages it too, with aplomb, and he gives bold, confident accounts of the two concertos, with a sprinkling of decoration. Christopher Warren-Green paces the slow movement of No. 1 only fractionally slower than Rolla, but his withdrawn, elegiac mood has a valedictory feeling. In contrast, the opening movement of the *Second Concerto* is slightly faster, but the orchestral playing is less precise (not helped by the reverberation) and the effect of the Clevenger performance is jauntier. John Wallace's trumpet timbre is strikingly brilliant, as recorded, and his playing in the *Trumpet concerto* is full of personality. He too likes to decorate and there are some attractive surprises in the finale. Again the pacing of the *Andante* is measured, but Wallace sustains the slower speed with nicely expressive phrasing. The recording was made in the resonant ambience of All Saints, Tooting, but the CD provides good definition under the circumstances, even if the harpsichord tends to get lost. This is very agreeable of its kind and, with 57′ of music, is better value than any of its competitors.

Barry Tuckwell has recorded these concertos before for Argo. For HMV he shares the same Michael Haydn work chosen by Clevenger. Needless to say, his playing is first class, with the solo line of the *First Concerto* memorably eloquent. The orchestral support is crisp and classical in feeling; the phrasing has less finesse than on the Argo disc (under Marriner) but is neat and musical. The sound is good, and this makes an admirable mid-priced recommendation on cassette.

Baumann's 1969 account has crisp clean classical lines, emphasized by the rather dry sound of the remastered recording which gives a bold, open horn timbre and unexpansive string timbre. The *Adagio* is rather sombre here (it has some splendidly resonating low notes from the soloist) but the finale is spirited enough.

(i) *Horn concerto No. 1 in D, Hob VII/d3;* (ii) *Organ concerto No. 1 in C, Hob XVIII/1;* (iii) *Trumpet concerto in E flat, Hob VIIe/1.*

(*) O-L Dig. **417 610-2; *417 610-4* [id.]. (i) Timothy Brown; (ii) Christopher Hogwood; (iii) Friedmann Immer, AAM, Hogwood.

An admirable collection aimed direct at authenticists. Timothy Brown plays the *Horn concerto* personably, using a valveless instrument, and he 'stops' the missing notes convincingly. It is an attractive account in its eighteenth-century scale. Hogwood plays the *Organ concerto* with elegance and spirit on a chamber organ, which produces piquant and colourful registration and there is no lack of expressive feeling in the engaging central *Largo*. But the real novelty here is a performance of the *Trumpet concerto* on the instrument for which it was written, a keyed *Klappentrompete* (lovely word). Immer's intonation and execution are very impressive, and the sounds have a character all their own. But if one listens to Hardenberger, André, Schwarz and others playing this marvellous work, one cannot help but reflect that Haydn would have been delighted with the soaring melisma and glittering bravura possible on the modern instrument.

Oboe concerto in C, Hob VIIg/C1.

(M) (***) PRT mono **PVCD 8378** [id.]. Evelyn Rothwell, Hallé O, Barbirolli – CORELLI; PERGOLESI: *Oboe concertos.*(***)

(i) *Oboe concerto in C, Hob VIIg/C1;* (ii) *Trumpet concerto in E flat, Hob VIIe/1.*

(M) *** DG *423 011-4*. (i) Lothar Koch; (ii) Maurice André, Munich CO, Stadlmair – M. HAYDN: *Trumpet concerto.****

Haydn's *Oboe concerto* is of doubtful authenticity, but in this account played by Evelyn Rothwell, deftly accompanied by her husband, Haydn surely would not have minded the attribution. The orchestra is given a very positive classicism by Barbirolli's firmness and in the opening movement his wife's delicacy makes a delightful foil for the masculine orchestral presentation. The slow movement, too, is well brought off, and it is only in the finale that a bolder line from the soloist might have been more effective. The 1958 recording is resonant and its agreeable ambience disguises the fact that this is taken from a mono master.

Koch's manner is slightly more square, but he too is a fine player and his poised style in the finale is particularly effective. He is well accompanied. André's account of the *Trumpet concerto* is second to none, the line of the lovely *Andante* beautifully managed and the finale full of easy bravura and crisp tonguing. Again the accompaniment is sympathetic, and the very good sound makes this tape a real bargain.

Organ concertos, Hob XVIII/1, 2, 5, 7, 8 and 10.
*** Ph. **416 452-2** (2) [id.]. Koopman, Amsterdam Bar. O.

Ton Koopman has chosen the organ of St Bartholomew at Beek-Ubbergen near Nijmegen which is reproduced to vivid effect in this excellently engineered pair of discs. The sonorities blend perfectly with those of the Amsterdam Baroque Orchestra and the performances have great personality and spirit. This is not great music but, played like this, it affords much stimulus and pleasure. Readers who fear the acerbities of 'authenticity' will find the astringency here is not overdone, for the acoustic is warm as well as clear and the transfer to CD has retained the ambient bloom, enhancing clarity without adding edge. Slow movements have the right expressive feeling and bulges in the melodic line are minimal and unobtrusive.

Piano concertos: in G; in D, Hob XVIII/4 & 11.
** HMV **CDC7 49324-2** [id.]. (M) *EG 290855-4.* Michelangeli, Zurich CO, De Stoutz.

Curiously detached playing from Michelangeli diminishes the appeal of this reissue. The great pianist adds to the range of the keyboard and thickens various chords. The piano timbre could be more natural and, despite the contribution of the Zurich orchestra under Edmond de Stoutz, this version cannot be accounted an unreserved success. The digital remastering of the 1975 recording has freshened the sound but the hardness on top makes the piano articulation sound rather forceful.

Trumpet concerto in E flat.
❀ *** Ph. Dig. **420 203-2**; *420 203-4* [id.]. Håkan Hardenberger, ASMF, Marriner – HERTEL***; HUMMEL*** ❀; STAMITZ: *Concertos.****
*** Delos Dig. **D/CD 3001** [id.]. Schwarz, New York 'Y' CO – HUMMEL: *Concerto.****
*** CBS **CD 37846** [id.]. Marsalis, Nat. PO, Leppard – HUMMEL; *Concerto**** (with L. MOZART: *Concerto****).
** DG Dig. **415 104-2** [id.]. Herseth, Chicago SO, Abbado – MOZART: *Concertos for Bassoon; Horn; Oboe.***

Haydn's most famous concerto is very well served on compact disc and tape. Michael Thompson's brilliant and characterful account on Nimbus should not be forgotten, nor should Maurice André's (see above and in the Concerts section) while Friedmann Immer gives an impressive performance on the instrument for which the work was actually written – see above. But the anthology of four trumpet concertos played with enormous dash and aplomb by the Swedish trumpeter Håkan Hardenberger, which includes also a superlative account of the Hummel played in its original key, rises pretty effortlessly to the top of the list; and the only possible reservation about this vividly recorded CD is that the acoustic in which the orchestra is set is a shade over-reverberant. The trumpet, however, placed well forward, is right in the room with the listener and its physical presence is highly involving. Hardenberger's playing of the noble line of the *Andante* is no less telling than his fireworks in the finale, and with Marriner providing warm, elegant and polished accompaniments throughout, this is probably the finest single collection of trumpet concertos in the present catalogue. There is an equally outstanding chrome cassette.

George Schwarz's account on Delos is hardly less memorable, but the Delos CD now seems distinctly short measure, although the Hummel coupling is equally desirable. Indeed, Schwarz's stylish command, richly gleaming timbre and easy bravura are impossible to resist, and in the lovely *Andante* he adds a little decoration to the melody, played with a warm, serene elegance. The finale combines wit and sparkle. The recording is attractively reverberant without inflating the lively accompaniment which Schwarz himself directs (easier for a trumpeter to do than a keyboard player), with the CD giving the soloist tangible presence.

Marsalis is splendid too, his bravura no less spectacular, with the finale a *tour de force*, yet never aggressive in its brilliance. He is cooler than Schwarz in the slow movement, and this element of reserve perhaps stems from an anxiety not to carry over too much freedom from the jazz world with which he had hitherto been more familiar. This record became a best-seller in America and led to his recording a captivating follow-up anthology of Baroque trumpet music in partnership with Edita Gruberová (see Recitals below). Certainly his way with Haydn is eminently stylish, as is Leppard's lively and polished accompaniment. The CBS recording is faithful and the CD gives a very vivid projection, although the orchestral sound is slightly artificial in its immediacy.

Adolph Herseth's performance is characterful and thoroughly musical. It is part of a generous collection of wind and brass concertos (the remaining three by Mozart), recorded by principals from the Chicago Symphony Orchestra. There is no lack of accomplishment here; Abbado's accompaniment is predictably refined and the DG recording is excellent. However, unless the couplings are especially suitable, this must be regarded as an also-ran.

Violin concerto in C, Hob VIIa/1.

*** Tel Dig. **ZK8 42917** [id.]. Zehetmair, Liszt CO – M. HAYDN: *Violin concerto.***(*)

(*) Ph. **412 718-2 [id.]. Van Keulen, Netherlands CO, Ros-Marba – MOZART: *Violin concerto No. 2.***(*)

** CBS Dig. **CD 37796** [id.]. Lin, Minnesota O, Marriner – VIEUXTEMPS: *Concerto No. 5.***(*)

Haydn's *C major Violin concerto* is given a superb performance by the young Hungarian violinist, Thomas Zehetmair, stylish, strong and resilient. He also directs the accompaniments which are alert and spirited in outer movements and responsive in the lovely *Adagio*. On his bow this central movement has a touching lyrical serenity, essentially classical in spirit, yet expressively beautiful in timbre. The recording is first class, with the soloist given the most realistic presence on CD, yet with no sense that the microphones were placed too near. The orchestra is truthfully balanced within an attractively resonant acoustic.

Isabelle van Keulen was the European 'Young Musician of the Year' in 1984 when aged only eighteen; she gave an impressive account of herself in the Vieuxtemps *Fifth Concerto*. She is hardly less sweet-toned or persuasive here in the *C major* Haydn. She is particularly good in the slow movement, whch shows her guilelessly lyrical phrasing to be as imaginative as her bowing is impeccable. The accompanying of the Netherlands orchestra under Antoni Ros-Marba is not, however, particularly distinguished. The recording is in the excellent traditions of the house, well balanced and truthful. The compact disc offers the usual gain in clarity and presence. The only grumble is that, at roughly 40′ overall, it offers short measure.

Cho-Liang Lin's performance has more strength and drive than Miss Van Keulen's and is not wanting in character, but it is lacking in charm, notably in the slow movement. Moreover, the CBS coupling seems ill-considered, although the recording is impressive. It is made in a drier acoustic than the Philips and the balance is forward; but on CD every detail is clear and the solo image is very believable, with Lin's full timbre displayed to advantage. He plays the Vieuxtemps coupling with considerable flair.

Violin concerto in G, Hob VIIa/4.

(*) Sup. Dig. **C37 7571 [id.]. Josef Suk, Suk CO, Vlach – VAŇHAL: *Concerto.***(*)

Haydn's three violin concertos are all early works, written for Luigi Tomasini. The *G major* is less memorable than the *C major* (Hob VIIa/1), but Suk's advocacy is persuasive. He is forwardly balanced, but his image is truthful and the playing is warm yet classical in spirit and has plenty of vitality in the outer movements. He is well accompanied, with the orchestra effectively alert and crisply rhythmic in the finale. The background ambience is well judged, and the sound is full-bodied. With only 38′ 11″ offered here, this CD is not, however, very generous.

Sinfonia concertante in B flat, Hob I/105.
(*) ASV Dig. **CDDCA 580; *ZCDCA 580*. L. Fest. O, Ross Pople – MOZART: *Sinfonia concertante, K.297b.***(*)

Sinfonia concertante in B flat; Symphony No. 94 in G (Surprise).
(*) DG Dig. **413 233-2; *413 233-4* [id.]. VPO, Bernstein.

Sinfonia concertante in B flat; Symphony No. 96 in D (Miracle).
*** DG Dig. **423 105-2**; *423 105-4* [id.]. COE, Abbado.

Abbado conducts the Chamber Orchestra of Europe in winning performances of both works, lively and sparkling in a way to remind you of the prize-winning recording he made with this same young orchestra of the Rossini rarity, *Il viaggio a Reims*. With outstanding solo contributions – the violinist and cellist just as stylish as their wind colleagues who have already appeared as soloists on several records – this issue of the *Sinfonia concertante* even outshines other excellent versions from Vienna and London with more mature soloists. These relative youngsters respond more readily to one another's expressive nuances, sounding more spontaneous. The symphony too brings some brilliant playing, with the oboe and bassoon (presumably Douglas Boyd and Matthew Wilkie again) very persuasive in their solos, capturing the fun of Haydn's inspiration without any hint of undue haste or breathlessness. Abbado has rarely made a record as happy as this and there is an excellent equivalent tape.

Bernstein chooses the *Surprise symphony* for his coupling, and it is a characteristically lively performance. The Vienna sound as recorded is rather fat, with textures thicker than usual, on disc and cassette alike, but that does not deter Bernstein from adopting challengingly fast speeds in the finales of both works, with his flair superbly illustrated in the alternations of orchestral flourish and violin solo which open that of the *Sinfonia concertante*. The slow movements are taken relaxedly, with the *Andante* of the *Sinfonia concertante* beautifully done over accompaniment figures that are elegantly lifted. Bernstein is never more winning than in Haydn; and this disc brings splendid examples, edited as usual from live recordings.

Directing the players from the solo cello, Ross Pople draws a strong and alert rather than an elegant performance from his London Festival Orchestra, well recorded in bright, firmly focused sound. Though the solo playing is not always ideally refined, there is a winning sense of musicians acting out a drama, at speeds that are comfortable, never exaggerated. The coupling of Mozart's wind *Sinfonia concertante*, also with four soloists, is very apt and attractive.

SYMPHONIES

Symphonies Nos 6 in D (Le Matin); 7 in C (Le Midi); 8 in G (Le Soir).
*** DG Dig. **423 098-2**; *423 098-4* [id.]. E. Concert, Pinnock.
*** Ph. Dig. **411 441-2** [id.]. ASMF, Marriner.

These were almost certainly the first works that Haydn composed on taking up his appointment as Kapellmeister to the Esterhazys and it seems very likely that their highly imaginative content and frequent use of instrumental solos was designed as much to stimulate the interest of his players as to make a grand effect on his employer. Everyone was given the opportunity to shine, from the leader, Luigi Tomasini (who was able to sound almost like an opera prima donna in the slow movement of *Le Midi*) through the woodwind to the horns and lower strings. Pinnock's players clearly relish their opportunities here and take them with strong personality. Once the flute starts on the happy allegro theme of *Le Matin*, with Lisa Beznosiuk phrasing magically, one cannot imagine anyone resisting, and even the vibrato-less string solos are given a strong character of their own. The performances are polished and refined, yet highly spirited, with infectious allegros and expressive feeling. The size of the string group (4; 4; 2; 2; 1) is made to seem expansive by the warm acoustics of the Henry Wood Hall and there is certainly weight here, yet essentially this is bracing musical experience with the genius of these early works fully displayed. There is a technically excellent cassette, but the turnover is made in the middle of the slow movement of No. 7, after the *Recitativo* section, even though the spare (and silent) length of tape that follows suggests that the rest of the movement could have been accommodated without difficulty, by adding on a few more inches.

Those wanting an account on modern instruments should not be disappointed with Marriner's (1982) alternative. The ASMF is nothing if not a band of soloists and there is plenty of character throughout this set, the best of its kind for some years, fresh and polished and very well balanced and recorded, though the harpsichord is only just distinguishable.

Symphonies Nos 22 in E flat (Philosopher), 24 in D, 30 in C (Alleluja).
*(*) Chan. Dig. **CHAN 8505**; *ABTD 1215* [id.]. Cantilena, Adrian Shepherd.

The Philosopher is not a success; the brisk tempo robs the opening of its breadth and dignity, and the minuet and Trio is pedestrian. Nos 24 and 30 are generally more successful, with better-judged tempi and rather more polish. All these symphonies come from the mid-1760s and display characteristic musical resource. As usual from Chandos, the sound is fresh and truthful on CD, though on tape the resonance has reduced the bite and the string quality is a little flabby.

Symphonies Nos 26 in D min. (Lamentatione); 41 in C; 43 in E flat (Mercury), 44 in E min. (Trauer); 48 in C (Maria Theresa); 52 in C min. Overture: Le Pescatrici.
**(*) CBS Dig. *13T 39040* (3) [id.]. L'Estro Armonico, Solomons.

Derek Solomons' project, to record the complete Haydn symphonies in chronological as opposed to (Breitkopf and Härtel) numerical order, here reaches the dark period of the *Sturm und Drang* symphonies, six remarkable works, not just the named ones but the powerful No. 52 in C minor and the C major, No. 41. Solomons keeps his ensemble of period instruments very small, with six violins but only one each of the other string instruments. Recorded in the pleasingly atmospheric acoustic of St Barnabas Church, Woodside Park, the sense of lively, intimate music-making is delightful. The ensemble is not always as polished as in some authentic performances, but for the general listener the important point is that Solomons has modified his earlier approach to slow movements, which no longer have the squeezing, bulging style sometimes favoured by the 'authentic' movement. So the haunting slow movement of No. 44 (the *Trauer* or *Mourning symphony* – the one which Haydn wanted played at his own funeral) has a silky gentleness. As before, the intimacy of ensemble never prevents allegros from having the necessary bite and vigour. Not everyone will welcome such generous observance of repeats, but this makes a desirable series, the more stylish now that the players, with no sense of routine, have settled down to their marathon task. The chrome cassettes are lavishly packaged; however, in spite of quite a high transfer level, the resonance clouds the upper range and the strings lack bite. No doubt the CDs will arrive in due course.

Symphonies Nos 35 in B flat; 38 in C (Echo); 39 in G min.; 49 in F min. (La Passione); 58 in F; 59 in A (Fire).
(*) CBS Dig. **M2K 37861 (2) [id.]. L'Estro Armonico, Solomons.

Like Derek Solomons' other Haydn recordings in this stimulating series, this set from 1766–8 is recorded in chronological order. The style (using original instruments and a small band) is fresh and lively, though ensemble is not always immaculate and not everyone will like the 'squeeze' style of slow movements with vibrato virtually eliminated. On their intimate scale these make an attractive alternative to versions using modern instruments, though the playing is less appealing than Pinnock's Archiv set of Nos 6, 7 and 8. The sound on CD is admirably fresh and clear.

Symphonies Nos 42 in D; 45 in F sharp min. (Farewell); 46 in B; 47 in G; 51 in B flat; 65 in A.
(*) CBS Dig. **M3K 39685 (3). L'Estro Armonico, Solomons.

This second volume of *Sturm und Drang* symphonies in Solomons' series centres round the musical marvel of No. 45 in the rare key (for Haydn's time) of F sharp minor. The picturesque story of the departing players in the finale tends to obscure the work's status as one of the most powerful of this rare, dark series of symphonies, not to mention the sheer originality (practical motives apart) of that amazing close. The other works in the box make a richly varied collection, all treated to Solomons' alert manner with no hint of routine in the playing. In virtuosity and stylishness, this series gains ground as it progresses, and few reservations need be made if you fancy authentic performances using period instruments on a scale Haydn himself employed at Esterháza: six violins and one each of the other string instruments. Special mention must be made of the brilliant horn playing of Anthony Halstead, astonishing in the high horn melody of the slow movement of No. 51. Excellent recording, full of presence on CD.

Symphonies Nos 43 in E flat (Mercury); 44 in E min. (Trauer); 49 in F min. (La Passione).
** Chan. Dig. **CHAN 8541**; *ABTD 1249* [id.]. Cantilena, Adrian Shepherd.

Symphony No. 44 in E min. (Trauer).
(M) *** Pickwick Dig. **PCD 820**. O of St John's, Smith Square, Lubbock – MOZART: *Symphony No. 40.***(*)

Symphonies Nos 44 in E min. (Trauer); 45 in F sharp min. [Farewell); 49 in F min. (La Passione).
(*) Erato Dig. **ECD 88173; *MCE 75255* [id.]. Amsterdam Bar. O, Koopman.

Symphonies Nos 44 in E min. (Trauer); 77 in B flat.
*** DG Dig. **415 365-2** [id.]. Orpheus CO.

Symphonies Nos 45 in F sharp min.; 81 in G.
*** DG Dig. **423 376-2** [id.]. Orpheus CO.

Symphonies Nos 48 in C (Maria Theresia); 49 in F min. (La Passione).
*** DG Dig. **419 607-2**; *419 607-4* [id.]. Orpheus CO.

Symphony No. 49 in F minor (La Passione).
(M) **(*) Pickwick Dig. **PCD 819**. O of St John's, Smith Square, Lubbock – SCHUBERT: *Symphony No. 5.***

Two of the symphonies (44 and 49) offered by Adrian Shepherd's Cantilena come from the so-called *Sturm und Drang* set. This group captures their spirit effectively – particularly in the so-called *Trauer* or 'Mourning' *symphony* in which tempi are well judged and the textures admirably clean. *La Passione* is committed enough, though the actual playing is less accomplished than in some rivals (notably the Orpheus Chamber Orchestra). The *E flat Symphony* (*Mercury*) is slightly less successful and is a bit matter-of-fact. Again the sound quality is clean and pleasing and the balance generally well handled, on the excellent chrome cassette as well as the CD.

The Orchestra of St John's are on their toes throughout their splendidly committed account of the *Trauersymphonie*. Outer movements are alert and vivacious – the finale has striking buoyancy and spring – and there is some lovely espressivo playing in the beautiful *Adagio* slow movement which brings out the forward looking qualities of the writing. The recording too is in the demonstration class, the St John's ambience producing particularly fresh and natural violin timbre and a warm overall bloom, without blurring of detail. Although the coupled Mozart performance is less distinctive, this is worth considering on Pickwick's mid-priced CD label.

There is no want of vitality or imagination in the performances on Erato, though not everything comes off. In the *Farewell*, Koopman uses 6 violins and 2 violas, the minimum Haydn had at Esterháza – insufficient to hold their own against the horns and wind. For the most part, however, the lightness of articulation is admirable and so, too, is the clarity of texture achieved here. Intonation is not always flawless but, generally, what is right about the spirit of these performances outweighs any reservations about the letter. Good, well-focused recording.

The Orpheus Chamber Orchestra is a conductorless group of twenty-six players from New York City who have been playing together since 1972. They certainly seem to be of one mind in No. 44, which they give with great freshness and spirit. All the players are expert, and so keenly do they listen to each other that they blend, almost as if they had a fine conductor in front of them. They capture the urgency of feeling of the *Trauersymphonie*, and No. 77 is given with a lightness of touch and infectious high spirits. Its humour and vivacity are beautifully realized, and the DG engineers provide excellent recording, too. Strongly recommended; as sound, this CD is especially believable.

The Orpheus group are at their very finest in their coupling of the *Farewell symphony* and *No. 81 in G*, a splendid work which comes first on the CD. The opening is rhythmically strong but the players catch the charming touch of melancholy which underlies the first movement's second group most appealingly, while the bassoon solo that lies at the centre of the Minuet is equally characterful. In the *Farewell symphony*, the tenderly refined *espressivo* of the strings in the *Adagio* is most beautiful, while the departing players in the finale present their solos with personable finesse. Both performances are imbued with vitality and have many touches of detail, which shows the most careful preparation and teamwork, for the result is highly spontaneous. The sound is first class. There is no better version of No. 45 in the catalogue and this is strongly recommendable.

The *Maria Theresia symphony* is a splendidly festive piece and is comparably served here by this excellent conductorless ensemble. They take its first movement very briskly – perhaps a shade too much so. The two horns playing at pitch, rather than an octave lower, give a particularly bright colouring; the Orpheus also omit the trumpets and drums which are of dubious authenticity. *La Passione* makes an excellent foil and these players capture the dark *Sturm und Drang* introspection of the piece. They have superb ensemble and attack throughout, and the excellence of their playing is matched by recording of keen presence and clarity, on both CD and the excellent chrome tape where the quality is robust, yet refined in detail.

John Lubbock's version of Haydn's *La Passione* is not quite as convincing as his fine account of No. 44. With the opening *Adagio* overtly expressive and the allegros boldly assertive in their fast, crisp articulation, this is certainly responsive playing, but there is at times a sense of over-characterization of an already powerfully contrasted work. The recording is first class.

Symphonies Nos 50 in C; 54 in C; 55 in E flat (*Schoolmaster*); *56 in C; 57 in D; 64 in A*.
*** CBS Dig. *M3T 42111* (3) [id.]. L'Estro Armonico, Solomons.

Though this group of symphonies is described on the box as *Sturm und Drang*, that biting style was beginning to mellow with Haydn in these six works. Written between 1766 and 1776, they centre round the undoubted masterpiece in this group, No. 55, nicknamed (but not by Haydn) *The Schoolmaster*, with the *Adagio* contrasting the two sides of the man, pedagogue and lover. The other movements are most original too, but in none of the six works is there any falling off of inspiration. Haydn, more than ever one feels, was incapable of being boring. Derek Solomons and his L'Estro Armonico go from strength to strength in their Haydn project, consistently responding to the freshness of the music, with the very small string section producing textures exceptionally light and clear, even for authentic performances. The two virtuoso horn-players, Anthony Halstead and Christian Rutherford, deserve special mention. Warm but intimate sound, with good presence. The chrome tapes are very well transferred, and for once the resonance seems to offer few problems. As usual in this series, the tape packaging is handsome and well documented.

Symphonies Nos 59 in A (Fire); 100 in G (Military); 101 in D (Clock).
(M) *** Ph. **420 866-2**; *420 866-4* [id.]. ASMF, Marriner.

This is just the way earlier analogue recordings of Haydn symphonies should be grouped for CD reissue, with a shorter earlier work (the *Fire symphony* plays for about 16′) joined to a pair of late works. These recordings derive from the mid-1970s and the performances are very satisfactory. The *Clock* is vital and intelligent, the playing of the Academy very spruce and elegant. There is perhaps not quite the depth of character that informs Sir Colin Davis's performances of this repertoire, but they do display finesse, and the readings are never superficial in expressive terms. The ambient warmth of the original recording has not disappeared in the digital remastering which improves immediacy and definition without loss of bloom. The chrome cassette has a fair degree of bass resonance and (as so often on tape) the 'military' effects in the *G major Symphony* bring a degree of muddle at this point. The CD is admirably focused.

Symphonies Nos 60 in C (Il Distratto); 63 in C (La Roxelane); 66 in B flat; 67 in F; 68 in B flat; 69 in C (Loudon), first version.
**(*) CBS Dig. *M3T 42157* (3) [id.]. L'Estro Armonico, Solomons.

The C minor *Presto* of the six-movement *Symphony No. 60 (Il Distratto)* looks back to *Sturm und Drang* tensions; but otherwise this group of symphonies again has Haydn in less tense mood, revelling in expanded orchestration, with trumpets and timpani more prominent than before. That very symphony stems from incidental music he wrote for a play, as does *Symphony No. 63 (La Roxelane)*. These are works where Haydn was increasingly echoing the folk melodies of central Europe, and, working at Esterháza, that seemed only natural. The intimacy of performances aiming to reproduce what was heard at Prince Esterházy's palace is again beautifully caught by Derek Solomons and his group. So far from the massive project becoming a routine exercise, this fifth volume of the series to be issued has the players more stylish and refined than before, lively and sympathetic, and with the expressiveness of slow movements aptly brought out. The tapes are again very well packaged and documented and the transfers generally acceptable, though there are some problems: the bass is over-resonant at times, notably in the finale of No. 69, and there is a tendency for the fortissimo horns to blur. At times the ear notices that the upper range is somewhat limited, as in No. 67. We hope this set will arrive shortly on CD.

Symphonies Nos 68 in B flat; 100 in G (Military).
** Tel Dig. **ZK8 43301** [id.]. Concg. O, Harnoncourt.

Harnoncourt's coupling of Nos 68 and 100 is unusual but apt, for both works are characterized by sharp, vivid effects such as he relished in his highly individual reading of Mozart's *Entführung*. Taken at a measured speed, the slow movement of the *Military* erupts weightily in its martial music, anticipating the Napoleonic Wars, while in the *Adagio cantabile* slow movement of No. 68 Harnoncourt similarly jabs home the curious *forte staccato* semiquavers which punctuate the main theme. This is a tough, weighty view of Haydn that deliberately rejects charm but refuses to be dismissed, though most listeners will prefer versions that take more account of the composer's sense of humour. There is a curious idiosyncrasy in the Trio of the second-movement minuet in No. 68, when Harnoncourt takes it – without any evident justification – at double speed. Currently this is the only separate version of this symphony. The sound is full, fresh and bright, clouding just a little in heavy tuttis.

Symphonies Nos 82 in C (The Bear); 83 in G min. (The Hen); 84 in E flat; 85 in B flat (La Reine); 86 in D; 87 in A (Paris symphonies).
** DG Dig. **419 741-2** (3) [id.]. BPO, Karajan.

Karajan's set is big-band Haydn with a vengeance; but of course the orchestra of the *Concert de la Loge Olympique* for which Haydn wrote these symphonies was a large band, consisting of forty violins and no fewer than ten double-basses. It goes without saying that the quality of the orchestral playing is superb, and Karajan is meticulous in observing repeats and in his attention to detail. There is no trace of self-indulgence or mannerisms. However, these are rather heavy-handed accounts, closer to Imperial Berlin than to Paris; generally speaking, the slow movements are kept moving but the minuets are very slow indeed, full of pomp and majesty – and, at times, too grand. In spite of the clean if slightly cool digital recordings, which have splendid presence, these performances are too charmless and wanting in grace to be wholeheartedly recommended. On CD the sound, if a trifle dry, is realistically balanced and has excellent presence.

Symphonies Nos 82 in C (The Bear); 83 in G min. (The Hen).
*** Ph. Dig. **420 688-2**; *420 688-4* [id.]. Concg. O, C. Davis.

These splendid performances very much perpetuate the spirit of Sir Thomas Beecham's Haydn in their combination of humanity and elegance and a lively communication of the music's joy. Rhythms are crisp and allegros are energetic without a suspicion of hurry, while slow movements are full of grace. Tempi always seem just right, especially in the minuets which some conductors find elusive. The playing is full of character: the hen clucks in picaresque reality in the second subject of the first movement of No. 83 and the solo flute trips daintily later in the Trio of the minuet. Sir Colin Davis has made no finer record than this, and the Philips engineers capture the seductive Concertgebouw string-textures more transparently than ever, without loss of warmth and weight.

Symphonies Nos 86 in D; 87 in A.
(*) Ph. **412 888-2 [id.]. ASMF, Marriner.

Marriner's LP and tape set of the six Haydn *Paris symphonies* (now withdrawn) was distinguished by excellent ensemble and keen articulation. Nos 86 and 87 are digital recordings (the remainder being analogue) and have now been issued separately on CD. It is possible to imagine performances of greater character and personality than these (slow movements do bring a hint of blandness), but they have a certain charm and are, generally speaking, lively and musical. Moreover, they sound admirably vivid in their CD format.

Symphony No. 88 in G.
(***) DG mono **415 661-2** [id.]. BPO, Furtwängler – SCHUMANN: *Symphony No. 4; Manfred.* (***)

Symphonies Nos 88 in G; 92 in G (Oxford).
(*) DG Dig. **413 777-2 [id.]. VPO, Bernstein.

Furtwängler's coupling of Haydn's *Symphony No. 88* with Schumann's *Fourth* is deservedly one of his most famous records and can be universally recommended, even to those collectors who usually find his interpretations too idiosyncratic. Here the beauty of his shaping of the main theme of the slow movement is totally disarming and the detail of the finale, lightly sprung and vivacious, is a constant pleasure. The Berlin Philharmonic plays marvellously well for him and the 1951 recording, made in the attractive ambience of the Jesus Christ Church, West Berlin, needs no apology. It is digitally remastered and sounds admirably fresh, yet has body too.

A warmly glowing account of both symphonies from Bernstein with the full strings of the Vienna orchestra and a richly upholstered recording. This is the kind of humane uncleaned-up Haydn one would have encountered in the pre-war era – not perhaps to all tastes nowadays. Bernstein observes the repeat of the development and restatement in the first movement of No. 88 and gives a romantic and really rather beautiful account of the *Largo*. Both performances emanate from concerts at the Musikvereinsaal, but the audiences are inaudible. An unqualified recommendation on CD to admirers of Bernstein, but this will not enjoy universal approval.

Symphonies Nos 88 in G; 104 in D (*London*).
*** CRD **CRD 3370**; *CRDC 4070* (id.]. Bournemouth Sinf., Ronald Thomas.

Symphonies Nos 88 in G; 100 in G (*Military*).
*(*) CBS **MK 42047** [id.]. Columbia SO, Bruno Walter.

A much-admired CRD coupling which has received wide acclaim both for the quality of the performances and for the sound. Although the orchestra is smaller than the Concertgebouw or LPO, the playing has great freshness and vitality; indeed it is the urgency of musical feeling that Ronald Thomas conveys which makes up for the last ounce of finesse. They are uncommonly dramatic in the slow movement of No. 88 and bring great zest and eloquence to the rest of the symphony too. In No. 104 they are not always as perceptive as Sir Colin Davis, but this brightly recorded coupling can be recommended alongside his version. The CD is vividly transferred – one might almost think this was a digital recording – and there is a first-class cassette.

On CBS the warm, naturally balanced recording belies its age, but the readings are disappointingly lacking in vitality, and the effect is rather one of a rehearsal than of a live performance. The glorious *Largo* of No. 88 drags, and the slow tempi of the *Military symphony* also bring heaviness. The finales of both works are the most successful movements. The focus of the CD transfer is not absolutely sharp, but the richness of the sound is attractive, even if its amplitude does not help to lighten the music making. The recording was made in 1961.

Symphonies Nos 90 in C; 93 in D.
(*) Ph. Dig. **422 022-2; *422 022-2* [id.]. O of 18th Century, Frans Brüggen.

As in his recordings of Mozart symphonies, Brüggen's approach to Haydn brings contradictions of style. The openings of both works are large-scale and portentous, generating an almost Beethovenian atmosphere, to contrast with the restrained 'authentic' string style in the *Largo cantabile* of No. 93. The performances have plenty of life and vigour and both finales are snappily rhythmic. The resonant acoustic increases the feeling of size, but the focus of the dynamically expansive tuttis is not absolutely clean.

Symphonies Nos 91 in E flat; 92 in G (*Oxford*).
*** Ph. Dig. **410 390-2** [id.]. Concg. O, C. Davis.

The *Oxford* and its immediate predecessor in the canon, No. 91 in E flat, are here given performances that are refreshingly crisp and full of musical life. It would be a sad day if Haydn were to be heard only on period instruments, for the sheer joy, vitality and, above all, sanity that these performances radiate is inspiriting and heart-warming. Excellent recorded sound, especially impressive on CD.

Symphonies Nos (i) *92 in G* (*Oxford*); (ii) *100 in G* (*Military*); *101 in D* (*Clock*).
(B) **(*) DG Walkman *415 329-4* [id.]. (i) VPO, Boehm; (ii) LPO, Jochum.

On this Walkman tape Boehm conducts the *Oxford symphony* and he secures finely disciplined playing from the VPO. The recording too is excellent, but there is something rather unsmiling about Boehm's Haydn that inhibits a whole-hearted response. Jochum's performances are another matter. He too is well recorded and inspires the LPO to fresh, polished performances that do not miss the genial side of Haydn. The performance of the finale of the *Military symphony* is very good indeed and, throughout, the *Clock* is alert and sparkling. The sound, from the early 1970s, is naturally balanced and has transferred admirably in its tape format.

Symphonies Nos 93 in D; 94 (Surprise); 96 (Miracle).
*** Ph. Dig. **412 871-2** [id.]. Concg. O, C. Davis.

Finely paced and splendidly recorded in clean but warm digital sound, Sir Colin Davis's performances top the present lists for those listeners not requiring period instruments. They have something of the spirit of Beecham about them, and the playing of the Amsterdam Concertgebouw Orchestra cannot be faulted in any department. To the original LP coupling of Nos 93 and 94 the *Miracle* has been added, a refreshing and substantial bonus. Do not look to this CD for sharply defined inner detail, rather a very well-balanced overall perspective that gives a convincing illusion of the concert hall.

Symphonies Nos 93 in D; 99 in E flat.
❀ *** Decca Dig. **417 620-2**; *417 620-4* [id.]. LPO, Solti.

The first three couplings in Solti's Haydn series (Nos 94 and 100, 96 and 101, and 102 and 103) all seemed to generate underlying tensions not wholly congenial to the spirit of Haydn; but this pairing of Nos 93 and 99, two favourites of Sir Thomas Beecham, brings no such problems. The atmosphere is sunny and civilized; there is no lack of brilliance – indeed the LPO are consistently on their toes – but the music making is infectious rather than hard driven. The string phrasing is as graceful as the woodwind articulation is light and felicitous, and pacing is wholly sympathetic. The lovely slow movement of No. 93 has both delicacy and gravitas and that of No. 99 is serenely spacious. The minuets are shown to have quite different characters, but both finales sparkle in the happiest manner. The sound on CD is very much in the demonstration class in its transparency, warmth and naturalness, and the cassette is hardly less impressive.

Symphonies Nos 94 in G (Surprise); 96 in D (Miracle).
*** O-L Dig. **414 330-2**, *414 330-4* [id.]. AAM, Hogwood.

Even more than in his compact disc of the *Military* and *London symphonies* (see below), Hogwood's coupling of the *Miracle* and *Surprise* brings striking revelations in the changes in texture and balance brought about by the use of original instruments. Moreover, the playing itself is superb: polished, feeling, and full of imaginative detail. The oboe solo in the Trio of the third movement of the *Miracle symphony* is a delight, and the sparkle in the finale with its crisp articulation and spirited pacing is matched by the elegance given to the engaging second subject of the first movement. The acid bottle has been abandoned by the strings, who play expressively, without squeezing the timbre unmercifully. The account of No. 94 is particularly dramatic and in the *Andante* there is not just the one 'surprise' (and that pretty impressive, with the contrast afforded by gentle strings at the opening) but two more *forte* chords to follow at the beginning of each subsequent phrase – a most telling device. The presence of Hogwood's fortepiano can also be subtly felt here, and later the wind solos are full of character. The minuet is fast, but this follows naturally after the drama of the slow movement, while the finale makes a light-hearted culmination. With superb recording, full yet transparent, this can be strongly recommended in both media, for while the CD has the usual advantages, the chrome cassette represents the highest state of the art. An issue to make converts to the creed of authenticity.

Symphonies Nos 94 in G (Surprise); 96 in D (Miracle); 100 in G (Military).
(M) *** Decca **417 718-2**; *417 718-4* [id.]. Philh. Hungarica, Dorati.

These three symphonies, collected from Dorati's historic complete Haydn cycle, make a delightful group on a mid-price CD on the Ovation label. Allegros are well sprung, with phrasing elegant and the wind playing a special delight. The only controversial speed comes in the *Andante* of the *Surprise*, much faster than usual, but the freshness of the joke is the more sharply presented. Dorati's flair comes out in the bold reading of the military section of the slow movement of No. 100, and though the digital transfer (on CD) exaggerates the brightness of upper frequencies, the warm acoustic of the hall in Marl, West Germany, where the recordings were done makes the result very acceptable. The chrome cassette has all the vividness and colour of the CD but – as so often – smooths the upper range just a little and takes the shrillness off the violins above the stave.

Symphonies Nos 94 in G (Surprise); 100 in G (Military).
** Decca Dig. **411 897-2** [id.]. LPO, Solti.

The Decca recording is altogether superb, more analytical and transparent than most rivals currently on the scene. Solti stresses the brilliance and fire of the outer movements, which are a bit hard driven, but there is no lack of vitality or *joie de vivre*. The recording approaches demonstration standard and should really have three stars, but the performance will not be to all tastes.

Symphonies Nos 94 in G (Surprise); 101 in D (Clock).
(*) DG Dig. **410 869-2 [id.]. BPO, Karajan.

Symphonies Nos 94 in G (Surprise); 101 in D (Clock); 104 in D (London).
(B) **(*) DG Dig. *419 846-4* [id.]. BPO, Karajan.

Karajan's Pocket Music tape is generous and very reasonably priced; it seems a better buy than the CD which offers only two symphonies for three times the cost. The emphasis of the performances is on breadth rather than geniality and charm, though No. 94 is not without humour. The sound made by the Berliners is always impressive, though the tape transfer is drier than the CD, and after the turnover (which comes at the central point of the *Clock*) the level rises and the sound brightens, so that *fortissimos* in the finale and in the *London symphony* are not without a touch of fierceness.

Symphonies Nos 94 in G (Surprise); 103 in E flat (Drum Roll); 104 in D (London).
(B) *** DG Walkman *413 424-4* [id.]. LPO, Jochum.

Like Jochum's companion Walkman coupling (see above), these performances derive from the complete set of *London symphonies* DG released in 1973, the *Surprise* having appeared the previous year as a trailer. The playing is elegant yet fresh, allegros marvellously crisp, slow movements warm and humane. This is among the musically most satisfying accounts of No. 104 in the catalogue; throughout, the recording is of DG's best analogue quality. A bargain.

Symphonies Nos 95 in C min; 104 in D (London).
*** Decca Dig. **417 330-2**; *417 330-4* [id.]. LPO, Solti.

Like the companion pairing of Nos 93 and 99, Solti's LPO coupling of the little-known but splendid *No. 95 in C minor* and the *London symphony* is altogether superb. At every point Sir Georg seems to find the right pacing, and the LPO playing – smiling and elegant, yet full of bubbling vitality – is a constant joy. No. 95 has a striking sense of cohesion and purpose, and there is no finer version of No. 104. Solti uses a full body of strings and all the resources of modern wind instruments with the greatest possible finesse, yet the spontaneity of the music and the music making is paramount. Top-drawer Decca sound (the record was made in the attractive acoustics of London's Henry Wood Hall) makes this an exceptionally natural-sounding CD, and there is a first-class chrome cassette.

Symphonies Nos 96 in D (Miracle); 100 in G (Military).
(*) DG Dig. **410 975-2 [id.]. BPO, Karajan.

Symphonies Nos 96 in D (Miracle); 101 in D (Clock).
** Decca Dig. **417 521-2** [id.]. LPO, Solti.

DG have recoupled these two symphonies for compact disc. They certainly sound splendid in this form, with impressive body and range. As big-band Haydn goes, Karajan has much to recommend him; however, though these performances have grandeur and dignity, they lack the lightness of touch and humour of Sir Colin Davis on Philips. The minuet of No. 100 is heavy-handed, almost Prussian.

Solti gives brilliant performances, rather too taut to convey much of Haydn's charm. With wide-ranging digital sound to match, they can be recommended for demonstration rather than for relaxed listening.

Symphonies Nos 100 in G (Military); 103 in E flat (Drum Roll).
*** HMV Dig. **CDC7 47650-2** [id.]; *EL 270514-4*. ECO, Jeffrey Tate.

Symphonies Nos 101 in D (Clock); 103 in E flat (Drum Roll).
(B) *** CfP *TC-CFP 4530*. RPO, Beecham.

Consistently Tate chooses speeds that allow the wit and sparkle of Haydn's writing to come out naturally, as in the second subject of the first movement of the *Military* or in the joyful lilt of the 6/8 rhythms of the first movement allegro in the *Drum Roll*. Tate's speeds bring out Haydn's humour far more than anything faster and fiercer would do. In the slow movement of the *Drum Roll*, Tate omits second-half repeats in the variations, but it is a long movement which, at a typically broad speed, balances the rest better as he does it. And always, with his slow speeds, crisp articulation ensures that the music sounds light and springy, never too heavy. Warm, well-balanced sound.

Beecham's coupling is self-recommending at bargain price (it would still be if it cost far more). He does not use authentic texts – he was a law unto himself in such matters – but the spirit of Haydn is ever present – just listen to the delicious way he handles the tick-tock of the *Clock symphony*, especially at its reprise. These works have rarely sounded as captivating and glowing as they do in his hands. The sound is full with a pleasingly resonant bass, although the cassette has lost a little of the upper range.

Symphonies Nos 100 in G (Military); 104 in D (London).
** Ph. **411 449-2** [id.]. Concg. O, C. Davis.
*** O-L Dig. **411 833-2**; *411 833-4* [id.]. AAM, Hogwood.

Sir Colin Davis's coupling has genuine stature and can be recommended without reservation of any kind. It has better claims than most current rivals: the performances have breadth and dignity, yet are full of sparkle and character. The playing of the Concertgebouw Orchestra is as sensitive as it is brilliant, and Davis is unfailingly penetrating. The performances also benefit from excellent recorded sound, with fine clarity and definition. There is warmth and humanity here, and in either work collectors need look no further. The 1977 analogue recording has responded readily to digital remastering.

Those looking for performances on period instruments will find Hogwood's accounts are uncommonly good ones and offer much better playing than was the case in some of his Mozart cycle. The wind execution is highly accomplished and the strings well blended and in tune. The change in the balance in the orchestral texture is often quite striking, particularly where the bassoon cuts through the lower strings. The 'Turkish' percussion instruments in the *Military symphony* are most effectively placed, and the performances are not only vital but also splendidly paced. The recording has clarity and presence, in its compact disc form very much so. An altogether impressive issue. There is a very good chrome cassette, with the detail well handled and only slightly less well focused than on the disc.

Symphonies Nos 100 in G (*Military*)*; 104 in D* (*London*) (arr. Salomon for flute, string quartet and fortepiano).
*** HMV Dig. **CDC7 49169-2** [id.]; *EL 270631-4*. Linde Cons., Linde.
*** O-L *414 434-4* [id.]. Beznosiuk, Salomon Qt, Hogwood.

These engaging and ingenious arrangements were made by Salomon (long before the age of the gramophone) to enjoy Haydn's invention domestically. It is remarkable how much of the music's colour is caught in these sprightly, polished and by no means lightweight accounts. The sharp, clear and transparent sound enables detail to register consistently and the spirited music-making cannot help but give pleasure, even though the 'authentic' style is slightly astringent.

However, Hans-Martin Linde also uses period instruments, but with a sunnier countenance than the Oiseau-Lyre versions. His leader, Herbert Hoever, is not afraid of a touch of vibrato, and with Linde's own nimble contribution on the flute as beguiling as the overall style is relaxed and infectious, these performances are even more enjoyable. There is an added warmth which in no way detracts from the freshness, and the players' delight in the music itself is well conveyed. The recording is first class, the acoustic bringing an attractive bloom, the effect less abrasive than with Hogwood. There is an excellent chrome tape.

Symphonies Nos 101 in D (*Clock*)*; 104 in D* (*London*).
(*) Erato Dig. **ECD 88079 [id.]. Scottish CO, Leppard.

Eminently sane, likeable performances from Raymond Leppard and the Scottish Chamber Orchestra. These artists convey a pleasure in what they are doing, and that is more than half the battle. They bring not only geniality and high spirits to these symphonies, but also grace and considerable poetic feeling. The recording is agreeably natural and as fresh and warm as the performances themselves. A very useful chamber-sized alternative to the larger orchestras favoured in this repertoire by DG, Decca and Philips.

Symphonies Nos 102 in B flat; 103 in E flat (*Drum Roll*).
** Decca Dig. **414 673-2** [id.]. LPO, Solti.

The beauty and refinement of the playing of the LPO under Solti are admirable, but the tensions – with even the lovely *Adagio* of No. 102 failing quite to relax – speak of the twentieth rather than the eighteenth century. Excellent recording.

Symphonies Nos 102 in B flat; 104 in D (*London*).
*** HMV Dig. **CDC7 47462-2** [id.]; *EL 270451-4*. ECO, Jeffrey Tate.

Tate's coupling of two of Haydn's most inspired symphonies, No. 104, the very last, with No. 102, with its soaringly lyrical slow movement and exhilarating outer movements, makes an outstanding disc. His speeds are a fraction broader than is common today, but that allows him to point the humour and wit the more winningly, with rhythms consistently crisp and resilient. The *Adagio* of No. 102, the most radiant of Haydn's slow movements, is an exception, Tate there preferring a flowing speed which keeps the melody the more airborne. Warm, well-balanced recording. The CD has the extra convenience that slow introductions and first-movement allegros are separately banded. There is also a perfectly satisfactory cassette.

Symphonies Nos 103 in E flat (Drum Roll); 104 in D (London).
*** DG Dig. **410 517-2**; *410 517-4* [id.]. BPO, Karajan.
(**) Tel. Dig. **ZK8 43752** [id.]. Concg. O, Harnoncourt.

Karajan recorded these symphonies with the Vienna Philharmonic Orchestra for Decca at the beginning of the 1960s. In the newer Berlin coupling, the first movement of No. 104 has greater weight and dignity, with altogether splendid string playing from the Berlin Philharmonic. As in his earlier Vienna account, Karajan observes the exposition repeat and refrains from any interpretative self-indulgence. The minuet and Trio is marginally even faster than on the earlier record. No. 103 has comparable gravitas: there is an undeniable breadth and grandeur here, as well as magnificent orchestral playing. The recording, too, is undoubtedly impressive.

Like his coupling of No. 68 with the *Military symphony*, Harnoncourt's record has some bizarre eccentricities. He opens the *Drum Roll* not with a roll but with a timpani fanfare, and no explanation is given for this in the accompanying notes. The performances are undoubtedly forward-looking. Pacing is fast and the minuet of No. 104, strongly accented, almost becomes a scherzo. This is music making of a powerful persuasion, very well played and recorded, but it cannot receive a general recommendation.

Symphony No. 104 in D (London).
(M) **(*) DG Dig. **423 210-2**; *423 210-4* [id.]. BPO, Karajan – MOZART: *Symphony No. 41.****

The coupling of Haydn's *London symphony* with Mozart's *Jupiter* at mid-price was one of the issues made to celebrate Karajan's eightieth birthday in April 1988.

CHAMBER MUSIC

Baryton trios Nos 71 in A; 96 in B min.; 113 in D; 126 in C.
*** Gaudeamus **CDGAU 109**; *ZCGAU 109* [id.]. John Hsu, Miller, Arico.

Baryton trios Nos 87 in A min.; 97 in D (Fatto per la felicissima nascita de S:ai:S Principe Estorhazi); 101 in C; 111 in G.
*** Gaudeamus **CDGAU 104**; *ZCGAU 104* [id.]. John Hsu, Miller, Arico.

Prince Esterházy was particularly fond of the baryton, whose delicate sonorities much appealed to him. He was a keen amateur player himself, and during his years at Eisenstadt Haydn composed 126 trios for his delectation. As John Hsu puts it on the sleeve, 'the baryton is a kind of viola da gamba with a broadened neck, behind which is a harp . . . the metal harp-strings are exposed within the open-box-like back of the neck so that they may be plucked by the thumb of the left hand'. These are most beguiling performances which have subtlety and finesse. Natural and well-balanced recorded sound. The second collection is no less desirable than the first, with a good cassette equivalent.

Divertimenti (Cassations): in G, Hob II/1; in G, Hob II/G1; in C (Birthday), Hob II/11; in F, Hob II/20.
(*) HMV Dig. **CDC7 47941-2; *EL 270588-4*. Linde Consort, Linde.

Haydn's *Cassations* and *Divertimenti* have not the finesse of the best works of Mozart, but they have plenty of imaginative touches, particularly in their instrumentation. Two of those offered here are fairly ambitious (Hob II, Nos G1 and 20) scored for nonet (including a pair each of oboes and horns); the remaining two, written around 1765, are scored for a sextet (including flute and oboe), often used with charm and effectively demonstrating the special timbres of the early instruments played here. Overall the performances have plenty of character, although in the hands of, say, the ASMF they would undoubtedly be more winning still. The recording, made in a fairly reverberant acoustic, has a quite large-scale effect, but the result is not unstylish. The chrome cassette is vivid, if somewhat less sharply focused than the disc.

Flute trios, Hob IV, Nos 1 in C; 2 in G; 3 in G; 4 in G (London). Divertimentos, Hob IV, Nos 7 in G; 11 in D.
*** CBS Dig. **MK 37786** [id.]. Rampal, Stern, Rostropovich.

Eminently winning performances of some charming if minor pieces of Haydn's London years, as well as some earlier *Divertimenti.* These players convey a sense of enjoyment and pleasure, and the recording is perfectly acceptable. On compact disc there is that extra degree of tangibility, so attractive with small instrumental groups.

String quartets: in E flat, Op. 1/0; Nos 43 in D min., Op. 42; 83 in B flat, Op. 103.
(*) Mer. **ECD 88117; *KE 74117* [id.]. English Qt.

This disc explores off-the-beaten-track and rarely played Haydn: the first of the *Quartets*, in E flat (left out of the Op. 1 set), and the very last, Op. 103, composed more than half a century later and which Haydn left incomplete. The *D minor*, Op. 42 of 1785, the most rewarding of the three, is also relatively neglected in the concert hall. The Op. 1, 'No. 0', is no masterpiece but has distinct charm, particularly when it is as well played as it is here. These fine players rise to all the challenges posed by this music, and the recorded sound is eminently truthful. There would have been room for another *Quartet* on this disc, which offers rather short measure at 43′. However, at the time of writing there are no alternative recordings of any of these works on CD.

String quartets Nos 17 in F (Serenade), Op. 3/5; 76 in D min. (Fifths); 77 in C (Emperor), Op. 76/2–3.
* Denon Dig. **C 37 7094**. Berlin Philh. Qt.

These performances are by the Philharmonia Quartet of Berlin, a relatively new ensemble whose first violin is leader of the Radio orchestra, and two of his colleagues come from the Philharmonic. Put alongside the finest now before the record-buying public, these accounts are serviceable rather than distinguished. Neither in vitality nor in musical imagination can they be said to match the finest versions from the LP analogue era.

String quartets Nos 37–42, Op. 33/1–6.
*** Hung. **HCD 11887/8-2** [id.]. Tátrai Qt.

The Tátrai present the Op. 33 *Quartets* in the original order: *No. 5 in G, 2 in E flat (The Joke)*, and *1 in B minor* on the first disc; *No. 3 in C, 6 in D* and *4 in B flat* on the second. The order usually observed by groups such as the Wellers who have recorded them in the past is not Haydn's but that of the first Paris publisher, Sieber. The Tátrai recording comes from 1979 and maintains the generally high standard of the cycle; in other words, the playing is unfailingly musical and intelligent, and the recording eminently acceptable. There is no current alternative, though it can be only a matter of time before the Lindsays record them.

String quartets Nos 50–56 (The Seven Last Words of our Saviour on the cross), Op. 51.
(*) Ph. Dig. **412 878-2 [id.]. Kremer, Rabus, Causse, Iwasaki.
** RCA **RD 86254** [**RCA 6254-2-RC**]. Guarneri Qt.

The Aeolian Quartet version on Decca (currently out of the catalogue) interspersed readings by Peter Pears between each of the movements, which enhances the impact of this work. This Philips account presents the seven movements without a break, as have all the preceding versions. Musically this does not displace the Aeolian, either as a performance or as a recording; but it is a useful addition to the catalogue. Moreover, the CD brings sound of remarkable realism, recorded within a most attractive ambience.

The RCA recording is given a closer balance and, although the Guarneri Quartet play quite eloquently, there is less light and shade and generally the Philips version is preferable.

String quartets Nos 57 in G; 58 in C; 59 in E, Op. 54/1–3.
*** ASV Dig. **CDDCA 582**; *ZCDCA 582* [id.]. Lindsay Qt.

This is a relatively neglected set, though the second, the *C major* (placed last on this recording), is a profound and searching masterpiece. Like the three of Op. 55 and the six of Op. 64, they were written for Johann Tost, one of the principal players in the Esterházy orchestra, and the *G major* gives a taste of the high-flying violin writing that distinguishes the set. The playing of the Lindsay Quartet is splendidly poised and vital, and the recording is very fine indeed in its CD format. The cassette is good too, though not so refined in the upper range: there is a degree of edge on the first violin.

String quartets Nos 69 in B flat; 70 in D; 71 in E flat, Op. 71/1–3; 72 in C; 73 in F; 74 in G min. (Reiter), Op. 74/1–3 (Apponyi Quartets).
*** Hung. **HCD 12246/7-2** [id.]. Tátrai Qt.

Hungaroton have chosen to issue these performances by the Tátrai Quartet, rather than commission new ones from their expert younger ensembles such as the Eder or the Takács – a wise decision, since these are civilized, selfless readings that never deflect the listener's attention away from Haydn's inexhaustible invention. The Apponyi Quartets (so named because their 'onlie begetter' was Count Antal Apponyi, and composed between the two visits Haydn made to London) are among the composer's finest – the best known is the *G minor*, Op. 74, No. 3, nicknamed *The Rider*. They could not be better served than they are here, with sound eminently natural and warm.

String quartets Nos 69 in B flat; 70 in D, Op. 71/1–2.
*** Hyp. **CDA 66095** [id.]. Salomon Qt.

String quartets Nos 71 in E flat, Op. 71/3; 72 in C, Op. 74/1.
*** Hyp. **CDA 66098** [id.]. Salomon Qt.

String quartets Nos 73 in F; 74 in G min., Op. 74/2–3.
*** Hyp. **CDA 66124** [id.]. Salomon Qt.

The Opp. 71 and 74 *Quartets* belong to the same period as the first set of *Salomon symphonies* (1791–2) and are grander and more 'public' then any of their predecessors. The appropriately named Salomon Quartet use period instruments. They are vibrato-less but vibrant; the sonorities, far from being nasal and unpleasing, are clean and transparent. There is imagination and vitality here, and the Hyperion recording is splendidly truthful. Its clarity is further enhanced in the CD transfers.

String quartets Nos 75 in G; 76 in D min. (*Fifths*)*; 77 in C* (*Emperor*)*; 78 in B flat* (*Sunrise*)*; 79 in D; 80 in E flat, Op. 76/1–6.*
*** Hung. mono **HCD 12812/3-2** [id.]. Tátrai Qt.
(M) **(*) DG **415 867-2** (2) [id.]. Amadeus Qt.

The Tátrai's classic set of the *Erdödy Quartets* is more than twenty years old and was always much admired. They have something of the humanity and wisdom that the Busch brought to the Beethoven quartets. These performances are unforced and natural, as intimate as if they were playing for pleasure, and as authoritative as one could hope for. The splendours of this set are as inexhaustible as those of the Beaux Arts set of the *Trios*. What will surprise many collectors is the quality of the mono sound, which is in many ways more congenial than some more recent records. A very strong recommendation on all counts – artistic and technical.

The Amadeus performances are certainly polished but by the side of the Tátrai, relatively mannered. Norbert Brainin's vibrato is a little tiresome on occasion; but, generally speaking, there is much to reward the listener here; the recordings are vivid and they have enhanced realism and presence in their new CD format. They are also offered at mid-price. But the Tátrai mono set is the one to buy, irrespective of cost.

String quartets Nos 76 in D min. (*Fifths*)*; 77 in C* (*Emperor*)*; 78 in B flat* (*Sunrise*)*, Op. 76/2–4.*
*** Tel Dig. **ZK8 43110** [id.]. Eder Qt.

The Eder is a Hungarian quartet who have only recently begun to make a name for themselves on records, even though public appearances have met with acclaim. The players command a refined and beautiful tone, with generally excellent ensemble and polish. These are elegant performances that are unlikely to disappoint even the most demanding listener, save perhaps in the finale of the *Emperor*, which they take a little too quickly. They are unfailingly thoughtful players whose internal balance and tonal blend are practically flawless. The recording is altogether excellent on CD.

String quartet No. 77 in C (*Emperor*)*, Op. 76/3.*
** DG Dig. **410 866-2** [id.]. Amadeus Qt – MOZART: *Quartet No. 17.***

Although the recording is obviously more modern, this newest version of the *Emperor* by the Amadeus Quartet is not an improvement on the older 1964 version (no longer available). The playing is expert, but there is an element of routine here, and the overall impression is of a lack of communicative warmth. The recording has great presence on the compact disc, but also a touch of edginess.

String quartets Nos 78 in B flat (*Sunrise*)*; 80 in E flat, Op. 76/4 & 6.*
*** Ph. Dig. **410 053-2** [id.]. Orlando Qt.

One of the best Haydn quartet records currently available. The playing has eloquence, vitality and warmth; there is a keen sense of rhythm and phrases breathe with refreshing naturalness. Philips have given this fine ensemble first-rate recorded sound. The coupling had the distinction of being the first Haydn chamber music to be issued on compact disc. The naturalness is enhanced; there is striking body and realism to the sound image, especially in Op. 74, No. 6, which is very slightly smoother on top than its companion. What a wonderful work it is!

KEYBOARD MUSIC

Piano sonatas, Hob XVI/20; 32; 34; 37; 40; 42; 48–52; Adagio in F, Hob XVII/9; Andante with variations in F min., Hob XVII/6; Fantasia in C, Hob XVII/4.
*** Ph. **416 643-2** (4). Alfred Brendel.

This collection offers some of the best Haydn playing on record – and some of the best Brendel, too. There are eleven sonatas in all, together with the *F minor Variations* and the *C major Fantasia* (or *Capriccio*). They have been recorded over a number of years and are splendidly characterized and superbly recorded. The first is analogue, the remainder digital.

Piano sonatas Nos 36 in C min., Hob XVI/20; 43 in C, Hob XVI/48; 46 in C, Hob XVI/50.
*** Denon Dig. **C37 7801** [id.]. András Schiff.

Those who do not respond to Brendel's strong keyboard personality and find his Haydn a shade self-conscious should consider this disc. Schiff plays with an extraordinary refinement and delicacy; he is resourceful, and highly imaginative in his use of tone colour; his phrasing and articulation are a constant source of pleasure. Superb in every way and beautifully recorded, too.

Piano sonatas Nos 47 in B min., Hob XVI/32; 53 in E min., Hob XVI/34; 56 in D, Hob XVI/42; Adagio in F, Hob XVII/9; Fantasia in C, Hob XVII/4.
*** Ph. Dig. **412 228-2**; *412 228-4* [id.]. Alfred Brendel.

Haydn's keyboard sonatas have been consistently underrated and need a powerful musical mind to do them justice. These performances are marvellously held together, self-aware at times, as many great performances are, but inspiriting and always governed by the highest intelligence. The *B minor Sonata* has a *Sturm und Drang* urgency, and Brendel's account has vitality and character. Moreover, the recording is splendidly realistic, particularly in the compact disc format. The two shorter pieces are a delight. The chrome tape is realistically balanced but lacks ultimate refinement in the extreme upper range, which robs the image of the presence and reality of the CD.

Piano sonatas Nos 50 in D, Hob XVI/37; 54 in G, Hob XVI/40; 55 in B flat, Hob XVI/41; Adagio in F, Hob XVII/9.
*** Mer. **ECD 84083** [id.]. Julia Cload.

Julia Cload was a protégée of the late Hans Keller, who declares on the sleeve that there is not 'a single second-hand shape among her phrasings, a single symptom of standardization'. Be that as it may, her playing is fresh, characterful and intelligent, and will give considerable pleasure. She has the advantage of very truthful recorded sound.

Piano sonatas Nos 50 in D, Hob XVI/37; 54 in G, Hob XVI/40; 62 in E flat Hob XVI/52; Andante with variations in F min., Hob XVII/6.
*** Ph. Dig. **416 365-2**; *416 365-4* [id.]. Alfred Brendel.

Brendel at his finest, and Philips, too: he is splendidly recorded. The playing has a jewelled precision – not perhaps to all tastes (some will find it too self-aware). However, its intelligence and artistry will win over most collectors. The CD is amazingly present and lifelike. It is included in the four-disc compilation (see above), but those who have collected the earlier discs individually will be glad of its separate availability. The equivalent chrome cassette is beautifully focused, the piano image most believable and natural.

Piano sonatas Nos 58 in C, Hob XVI/48; 60 in C, Hob XVI/60; 61 in D, Hob XVI/51.
*** Ph. Dig. **411 045-2** [id.]. Alfred Brendel.

Brendel plays magnetically in these three mature and original works. He uses crisp, bright articulation which keeps the piano sound in scale, but in such movements as the opening *Andante con espressione* of No. 58 (Hob XVI/48) he conveys a Beethovenian intensity without overweighting the music with emotion. Rightly in the large-scale *allegro* of No. 60 Brendel takes repeats of both halves. The piano sound is among the most vivid ever, wonderfully real-sounding on compact disc with its silent background.

VOCAL MUSIC

The Creation (*Die Schöpfung*).
(M) *** DG *410 951-4* (2) [id.]. Janowitz, Ludwig, Wunderlich, Krenn, Fischer-Dieskau, Berry, V. Singverein, BPO, Karajan.
*** DG Dig. **419 765-2**; *419 765-4* (2) [id.]. Blegen, Popp, Moser, Ollmann, Moll, Bav. R. Ch. & SO, Bernstein.
*** Ph. **416 449-2** [id.]. Mathis, Fischer-Dieskau, Baldin, Ch. & ASMF, Marriner.
(*) DG Dig. **410 718-2 (2) [id.]. Mathis, Araiza, Van Dam, V. Singverein, VPO, Karajan.
(*) Accent **ACC 58228/9D [id.]. Laki, Mackie, Huttenlocher, Ghent Coll. Vocale, La Petite Band, Kuijken.
(B) **(*) CfP *CFPD 41 444-5* (2). Donath, Tear, Van Dam, Philh. Ch. & O. Frühbeck de Burgos.
** Tel. Dig. **ZA8 35722** (2) [id.]. Gruberová, Protschka, Holl, Schoenberg Ch., VSO, Harnoncourt.

The Creation is very well served on CD, but it is significant that the finest version of all comes from the pre-CD era. Karajan's 1969 set remains unsurpassed. Available very inexpensively indeed on a pair of chrome cassettes of high quality, this is a clear first choice in spite of two small cuts (in Nos 30 and 32). Here Karajan produces one of his most rapt choral performances. His concentration on refinement and polish might in principle seem out of place in a work which tells of religious faith in the most direct of terms. In fact the result is outstanding. The combination of the Berlin Philharmonic at its most intense and the great Viennese choir makes for a performance that is not only polished but warm and dramatically strong, too. The soloists are an extraordinarily fine team, more consistent in quality than those on any rival version. This was one of the last recordings made by the incomparable Fritz Wunderlich, and fortunately his magnificent contribution extended to all the arias, leaving Werner Krenn to fill in the gaps of recitative left unrecorded. The recording quality has a warm glow of atmosphere round it.

Bernstein's version, recorded at a live performance in Munich, makes a highly enjoyable CD alternative. It uses a relatively large chorus, encouraging him to adopt rather slow speeds at times. What matters is the joy conveyed in the story-telling, with the finely disciplined chorus and orchestra producing incandescent tone, blazing away in the big set-numbers, and the performance is compulsive from the very opening bars. At a very relaxed speed *The Heavens are telling* (*Die Himmel erzahlen*) becomes majestic rather than urgent, but the joy is still intense. Bernstein's set also brings the advantage that five soloists are used instead of three, with the parts of Adam and Eve sung by nicely contrasted singers. So the charming, golden-toned Lucia Popp is a warmly human Eve, to contrast with the more silvery and ethereal Gabriel of Judith Blegen; and Kurt Ollmann as Adam is lighter and less magisterial than his angelic counterpart, Kurt Moll as Raphael who, with his dark bass tone, produces the most memorable singing of all. Bernstein's tenor, Thomas Moser, combines a lyrical enough quality with heroic weight, confirming this as an unusually persuasive version, well recorded in atmospheric sound. The chrome cassettes are first class and have the CD booklet for documentation.

Marriner's version makes an excellent choice if you fancy the work on a relatively intimate scale. With generally fast tempi Marriner draws consistently lithe and resilient playing and singing from his St Martin's team. There is no lack of weight in the result. The great cry of *Licht* on a fortissimo C major chord when God creates light is overwhelming. You might even count Dietrich Fischer-Dieskau in the baritone role as too weighty, recorded rather close, but his inflexion of every word is intensely revealing. The soprano is Edith Mathis, very sweet of tone if not always quite as steady as some of her rivals on record, with *Nun beut die Flur* (*With verdure clad*) very light and pretty. The one notable snag is that Aldo Baldin's tenor is not well focused by the microphones. Otherwise the 1980 analogue recording is first rate and the CD transfer, while adding refinement, has not lost the warmth; indeed the bass resonance is quite strong.

Karajan's later recording is taken from a live performance given at the Salzburg Festival in 1982. Not surprisingly, it cannot match the perfection of the earlier one either in musical ensemble or in recording balance, but there are many compensations, for there is greater warmth in the later version. For example 'the flexible tiger' (*der gelenkige Tiger*) bounces along more engagingly in Uriel's recitative, with Van Dam's bass firm and beautiful; and the choruses brim with joy at speeds generally a degree more relaxed. Edith Mathis cannot match her predecessor, Gundula Janowitz, in ethereal purity, but she gives a sweeter-toned performance than she did for Marriner on Philips, though the close balancing of voices is hardly flattering to any of the soloists. The sense of presence is what matters, and this is a fine memento of a powerful, glowing occasion, caught in wide-ranging digital sound. The compact discs offer a tangible presence – but also give greater emphasis to the faults of balance. The choral focus too is less than ideal.

Recorded live at the Liège Festival in Belgium in 1982, Kuijken's version is admirably fresh, with period instruments adding a tang without sounding too aggressive. That is so, even though the top emphasis in the recording (brought out the more on CD) adds an edge to violins as well as to voices that is not quite natural, with sibilants exaggerated. The brightness and immediacy of the sound also means that performance noises are exceptionally clear, as though one were on stage with the performers. But the consistently clean tones of the soloists and the precision of the small chorus, coupled with Kuijken's happy choice of speeds and unfailing stylishness, will not disappoint anyone who fancies an 'authentic' performance. The aria we know as *With verdure clad* is particularly beautiful, relaxed in tempo and with the soprano Krzystina Laki singing with heavenly purity. Neil Mackie sings the tenor solos with heady clarity, and Philippe Huttenlocher makes an asset of a less heavyweight approach than usual.

Rafael Frühbeck de Burgos directs a genial performance, recorded with richness and immediacy. Though the early Karajan version has even crisper ensemble in both chorus and orchestra, the easier pacing of Frühbeck provides an alternative which at bargain price remains very good value. The soloists are all excellent, and though Helen Donath is not as pure-toned as Janowitz on DG, with a hint of flutter in the voice, she is wonderfully agile in ornamentation, as in the bird-like quality she gives to the aria *On mighty pens*. The chorus might gain from a rather more forward balance. The cassette transfer is clear and vivid.

Harnoncourt's version with the Vienna Symphony Orchestra was recorded live. It follows the first printed edition of 1800, using the same size of forces as in performances of that date, with a gentle fortepiano replacing harpsichord in recitatives. Compared with the finest versions the ensemble is on the rough side, and the singing of the male soloists is often rough, too. The tenor, Josef Protschka, shouts Uriel's first entry, but settles down after that; while by far the most distinguished singing of the set comes from Edita Gruberová, dazzling and imaginative, with slightly backward balance helping to eliminate the touch of hardness that the microphone often brings out in her voice. The sound otherwise is full and clear.

Mass No. 3 in C (*Missa Cellensis*): *Missa Sanctae Caeciliae.*

*** O-L Dig. **417 125-2**; *417 125-4* [id.]. Nelson, Cable, Hill, Thomas, Ch. of Christ Church Cathedral, AAM, Preston.

The *Missa Cellensis* (also known as the *Missa Sanctae Caecilliae*) is Haydn's longest setting of the liturgy; the *Gloria* alone (in seven cantata-like movements) lasts nearly half an hour. Preston directs an excellent performance with fine contributions from choir and soloists, set against a warmly reverberant acoustic. Reissued on a single CD and tape (which plays for well over an hour) this makes a valuable addition to the catalogue to supplement the Argo series of Masses. The cassette is admirably vivid and well focused but the CD brings a very positive advantage in the extra clarity and sense of presence.

Masses Nos 5 in B flat: (i) *Missa brevis Sancti Joanna de Deo* (*Little organ Mass*)*;* (ii) *11 in B flat* (*Schöpfungmesse*).
(M) *** Argo *417 307-4* [id.]. Cantelo, Watts, (i) J. Smith, J. Scott (organ); (ii) Tear, Forbes Robinson; St John's College, Cambridge, Ch., ASMF, Guest.

This admirable reissue generously combines two performances taken from a distinguished series of Argo analogue recordings which continue to dominate the catalogue in this repertoire. The *Little organ Mass* dates from 1775 and contains much fine invention. The *Schöpfungmesse* or *Creation Mass* was the last but one of the magnificent series that Haydn wrote yearly in his retirement for his patron, Prince Esterházy. George Guest draws fresh, direct performances from his own St John's College Choir and a first-rate band of professionals. Excellent solo singing, notably from Robert Tear in the lovely *Incarnatus est* from the later Mass, while the orchestral support is first class. The remastering of these recordings (the *Little organ Mass* dating from 1978, the *Creation Mass* earlier, 1969, but not sounding its age) is outstandingly successful; the cassette has fine range and clarity, yet plenty of body and atmosphere.

Masses Nos (i) *6 in C* (*Missa Cellensis*)*: Mariazeller Mass;* (ii) *8 in B flat* (*Heiligmesse*)*: Missa Sancti Bernardi von Offida.*
(M) *** Argo *417 306-4* [id.]. (i) J. Smith, Watts, Tear, Luxon; (ii) Cantelo, Minty, Partridge, Keyte; St John's College, Cambridge, Ch., ASMF, Guest.

H. C. Robbins Landon called the *Mariazeller Mass* of 1782 'the most perfect large-scale work Haydn achieved' in this particular period; and in this well-sung and admirably direct recording (from 1978) one can hear why. Its coupling with the later *Heiligmesse* is particularly apt. This is one of the most human and direct in its appeal of all Haydn's Masses. Its combination of symphonic means and simple vocal style underlines its effectiveness. Haydn started writing this Mass in the first year after his return from London, at about the time he wrote the *Paukenmesse*, but it was not completed until later, and was finally dedicated to the memory of St Bernard of Offida, newly canonized by Pope Pius VI barely a century after his death. The name *Heiligmesse* derives from the church song on which Haydn based the *Sanctus*. Among the special points of interest in the work are the slow introduction to the *Kyrie*, very like the introductions to Haydn's late symphonies, and the subdued *Agnus Dei* in the (for the time) extraordinary key of B flat minor. Like the other records in this series this is very well engineered and splendidly performed. The solo singing is good if not always equally distinguished, and the choral response is excellent. The recording was made a decade earlier (1967) than the coupling, but the remastering has been highly successful and the tape transfer offers Decca's best standard – the choral tone is full and incisive and the balance with soloists and orchestra excellent.

Mass No. 7 in C (*Missa in tempore belli*)*: Paukenmesse.*
(M) *** Argo *417 163-4* [id.]. Cantelo, Watts, Tear, McDaniel, St John's College, Cambridge, Ch., ASMF, Guest – M. HAYDN: *Salve regina.****
** HMV Dig. **CDC7 47425-2** [id.]; *EL 270413-4* [Ang. *4DS 37988*]. Marshall, C. Watkinson, Lewis, Hall, Leipzig R. Ch., Dresden State O, Marriner.
*(*) Ph. Dig. **412 734-2** [id.]. Blegen, Fassbaender, Ahnsjö, Sotin, Bav. R. Ch. & SO, Bernstein.

The *Paukenmesse* (or *Mass in time of war*) was written in 1796 for the name-day of Princess Esterházy, when Austria was still at war with Napoleon. It derives its German nickname from the drum roll suggesting gunfire at the point where the *Agnus Dei* gives way to the *Dona nobis pacem*. This was the last of the much-admired Argo series and was recorded in 1970; and the performance is well up to standard. With the St John's College Choir, George Guest provides a clean, brightly recorded account with excellent soloists (though April Cantelo might have been sweeter-toned). That said, this is a wholly recommendable performance, still the finest available, and it offers a splendid bonus in the beautiful *Salve regina* by Haydn's brother, Michael. The tape transfer is vivid and clear.

Neville Marriner's is an eminently lively account, though he tends towards more extreme tempi than those of George Guest on his celebrated Argo version. The latter's 1970 recording is still the one to have, and we hope that Decca will transfer it to the new medium.

Bernstein's rhythmic flair and feeling for dramatic contrast put him among the most compelling of Haydn conductors, as revealed in the fast numbers here. However, with muffled recording which inflates the scale of the performance, with dangerously romantic treatment of slow sections, such as the introduction to the bass's *Qui tollis*, and with rough singing from the bass soloist (Hans Sotin well below form), the good qualities are quite cancelled out.

Mass No. 9 in D min. (Nelson): Missa in augustiis.

(M) *** Argo *417 469-4* [id.]. Stahlman, Watts, Wilfred Brown, Krause, King's College, Cambridge, Ch., LSO, Willcocks.

(*) Ph. Dig. **416358-2; *416 358-4* [id.]. Hendricks, Lipovsek, Araiza, Meven, Bav. R. Ch. & SO, C. Davis.

(*) Argo Dig. **414 464-2 [id.]. Bonney, Howells, Rolfe-Johnson, Roberts, LSO Ch., City of L. Sinfonia, Hickox.

** HMV Dig. **CDC7 47424-2** [id.]; *EL 270412-4*. Marshall, C. Watkinson, Lewis, Holl, Leipzig R. Ch., Dresden State O, Marriner.

*(*) Claves **CD 50-8108** [id.]. Graf, Piller, Haefliger, Stämpfli, Bern Ch. & CO, Dähler.

Mass No. 9 in D min. (Nelson); Te Deum in C, Hob XXIIIc/2.

*** DG Dig. **423 097-2**; *423 097-4* [id.]. Lott, C. Watkinson, Maldwyn Davies, Wilson-Johnson, Ch. & E. Concert, Pinnock.

The *Nelson Mass*, the third and most memorable of the six masterpieces that Haydn wrote after he had retired from day-to-day musical duties, yet each year producing a work to celebrate the name-day of Princess Esterházy, brings a superb first choral offering from Trevor Pinnock and the English Concert. Using a larger band of strings than in his highly successful recordings of Baroque instrumental music, Pinnock conducts an authentic performance guaranteed to win converts to the idea of period instruments. He brings home the high drama of Haydn's autumnal inspiration not just with the extra bite and clarity always associated with period performance but with natural weight and dedication too. The extraordinary instrumentation at the very start, with organ replacing wind, and horns and trumpets made all the more prominent, has never sounded more menacing. With incandescent singing from the chorus and fine matching from excellent soloists (Felicity Lott in exceptionally sweet voice), the exuberance of the *Gloria* is then brought home all the more by contrast. Misplaced accents, almost jazzy, add to the joyful exhilaration. Similarly exuberant syncopations mark the magnificent setting of the *Te Deum*, which comes as a very valuable makeweight. This was written at the same period, in Haydn's old age, but without soloists, setting the text with almost Stravinskian concision while still conveying grandeur. The inspiration of such music leaps forward from the eighteenth century all the more excitingly in an authentic performance such as this. Excellent full-blooded sound, with good definition. The chrome cassette is also a state-of-the-art transfer, so collectors in either medium are equally well served as there is excellent documentation in both formats.

The 1962 Argo recording continues to hold its place at the top of the list. Its impact is still breathtaking, and tape collectors should be well satisfied with the way the transfer accommodates the many exciting and very loud climaxes within the ample King's acoustic. The solo singing is uniformly good: Sylvia Stahlman negotiates her florid music with great skill; and Sir David Willcocks maintains quite remarkable tension throughout.

From Sir Colin Davis a fine, broadly landscaped performance in the grand manner, with good singing from soloists and chorus alike. Pacing is appreciably more relaxed than Pinnock's version in the *Kyrie* and *Gloria*, though not elsewhere; but there is never any sense of lethargy, and even if this does not banish memories of the King's/Willcocks version, made with smaller forces, it is satisfying in a quite different way. The Philips recording is very natural and well balanced on CD; the tape is well transferred, but the resonant Bavarian acoustic means there is less bite here than on either the DG Archiv or Decca cassettes.

Hickox conducts a lively, well-sung reading of the most celebrated of Haydn's late Masses, most impressive in the vigorous, outward-going music which – with Haydn – makes up the greater part of the service. What is disappointing is the recessed sound of the choir, with inner parts less well defined than they should be. The soloists are good but, as recorded, Barbara Bonney's soprano has a thinness along with the purity. Enjoyable as this is, it falls short of the superb Argo version of twenty years earlier from Sir David Willcocks and King's College Choir, which is preferable even in its better-focused, more atmospheric sound.

Marriner's is a perfectly acceptable performance, with good soloists and fine singing from the Leipzig Radio Choir. The Dresden acoustic is fairly ample, but it does not prevent internal clarity (except on the iron-oxide cassette where the choral sound is plushy). There are moments of considerable vigour, but overall the effect is essentially cultured, weighty and just a shade bland.

The Swiss performance on the Claves label lacks the necessary vigour for Haydn's most celebrated Mass, and the recording balance, with the soloists very close and the rest too far away, rules it out still further, with technical flaws the more apparent in the CD version.

Mass No. 10 in B flat (*Theresienmesse*).
(M) *** Argo *417 162-4* [id.]. Spoorenberg, Greevy, Mitchinson, Krause, St John's College Ch., ASMF, Guest.

The *Theresa Mass* followed on a year after the *Nelson Mass*, the best known of the six magnificent settings of the Mass which Haydn wrote for his patron, Prince Esterházy, after his return from London. It may be less famous, but the inspiration is hardly less memorable, and Haydn's balancing of chorus against soloists, contrapuntal writing set against chordal passages, was never more masterly than here. George Guest injects tremendous vigour into the music (as in the *Harmoniemesse* there is a 'military' conclusion in the *Dona nobis pacem*), and the St John's Choir shows itself a ready match for the more famous choir at King's College. Good solo singing and brilliant, vivid recording, made in 1965, which sounds splendid in the new transfer, clear and full, with naturally projected soloists.

Mass No. 12 in B flat (*Harmoniemesse*).
(*) Hung. Dig. **HCD 12360 [id.]. Tokody, Takács, Gulyas, Gregor, Slovak Philh. O and Ch., Ferencsik.

(i) *Mass No. 12 in B flat* (*Harmoniemesse*); (ii) *Salve regina in G min.*
*** Argo *417 305-4* [id.]. (i) Spoorenberg, Watts, Young, Rouleau, St John's College, Cambridge, Ch., ASMF, Guest; (ii) Augér, Hodgson, Rolfe-Johnson, Howell, L. Chamber Ch., Argo CO, Heltay.

The *Harmoniemesse* was the last of the six Masses, all of them masterpieces, that Haydn wrote after his return from London. In 1802, when he wrote it, the Esterházy orchestra was at its most expansive, and Haydn typically took advantage of the extra wind instruments available. He was already over seventy when he started writing it, but the freshness and originality of the writing are as striking as anything in the earlier works. In particular the last section of the Mass brings a wonderfully memorable passage, when from a gentle setting of the *Agnus Dei* Haydn bursts out with fanfares into a vigorous, even aggressive *Dona nobis pacem*. The performance matches the fine quality of George Guest's other recordings with the St John's Choir and Academy of St Martin's. The quartet of soloists is strong, with Helen Watts in particular singing magnificently. The *Salve regina* is an early work but is striking in its depth of feeling. It is given here with full chorus, although solo voices were originally intended; the weight of the piece is better conveyed in this way, especially when Heltay's performance is so committed. This is a relatively recent recording (1980) whereas the Mass dates from 1967, but both are effectively remastered and sound is most realistic, with excellent body as well as clarity to the choral tone.

With four of Hungary's outstanding singers as soloists (all increasingly well known on record), Ferencsik conducts for a recording of Haydn's last, masterly setting of the Mass, designed to celebrate the conductor's seventy-fifth birthday. The age of the conductor may have influenced his choice of speeds, generally on the slow side, and the weight of sound from the relatively large choir brings some lack of clarity, if no lack of vigour. The Argo LP version may be more buoyant, but Ferencsik gains in such a passage as the *Gratias* in the *Gloria*. The pure originality of the writing, with Haydn determined not simply to repeat himself in words he had set so often, is consistently brought out – as in the minor-key switch on *Et resurrexit* and the light, molto allegro *Benedictus*, not to mention the explosive triumph of the final *Dona nobis pacem*. It was almost as though the old man was challenging himself at those points to do the impossible. Excellent digital recording.

The Seasons (in German).
*** Ph. Dig. **411 428-2** (2) [id.]. Mathis, Jerusalem, Fischer-Dieskau, Ch. & ASMF, Marriner.
(*) Tel. Dig. **ZA8 35741 (2) [id.]. Blasi, Protschka, Holl, Schoenberg Ch., VSO, Harnoncourt.
(M) **(*) HMV **CMS7 69224-2** [id.]; *EX 769224-4* (2) [id.]. Janowitz, Hollweg, Berry, Ch. of German Op., BPO, Karajan.

The Seasons: highlights.
(M) **(*) HMV **CDM7 69010-2** [id.]; *EG 769010-4* [Ang. *4AM 34732*] from above recording, cond. Karajan.

Sir Neville Marriner followed up the success of his resilient recording of *The Creation* with this superbly joyful performance of Haydn's last oratorio, effervescent with the optimism of old age. Edith Mathis and Dietrich Fischer-Dieskau are as stylish and characterful as one would expect, pointing the words as narrative. The tenor too is magnificent: Siegfried Jerusalem is both heroic of timbre and yet delicate enough for Haydn's most elegant and genial passages. The chorus and orchestra, of authentic size, add to the freshness. The recording, made in St John's, Smith Square, is warmly reverberant without losing detail. The transfer to CD brings two discs which are handsomely presented with a pair of booklets (including full texts). The CD virtually transforms the sound, with added definition for both chorus and soloists, with cues for every individual item, and a total playing time of nearly two hours and a quarter. Highly recommended.

Harnoncourt's version is characteristically vibrant and his dramatization of the elements strong, with Robert Holl making a memorable contribution in *Winter*. On the other hand,

Protschka's style is lighter than that of Siegfried Jerusalem with his honeyed elegance and heroic ring. Angela Maria Blasi has a sweet, small timbre and is consistently persuasive. The Arnold Schoenberg Choir sing with fine bite and fervour and are especially invigorating in the harvest celebrations of *Autumn*. Throughout the work detail is perceptively observed and Harnoncourt brings his usual powerful rhythmic feeling to the music making – accents are more readily stressed here than with Marriner, and the narrative flow is vividly maintained. The Teldec recording is excellent, with good balance and realistic projection, and if there is less charm than under Marriner – who captures the work's innocent pictorialism with pleasing naturalness – there is certainly no lack of drama.

Karajan's 1973 recording of *The Seasons* offers a fine, polished performance of Haydn's mellow last oratorio which is often very dramatic too. The characterization is vivid, and in Karajan's hands the exciting Hunting chorus of Autumn (*Hört! Hört! Hört das laute Getön*) with its lusty horns anticipates *Der Freischütz*. The remastered sound is drier than the original but is vividly wide in dynamic range. Choruses are still a little opaque, but the soloists are all well caught and are on good form; and the overall balance is satisfactory. However, Marriner displays a lighter, more human touch here; those drawn to Karajan might try the generous (53′) highlights CD or the very successful equivalent cassette which costs even less.

Stabat Mater.

(M) *** Argo *417 471-4* [id.]. Augér, Hodgson, Rolfe-Johnson, Howell, L. Chamber Ch., Argo CO, Heltay.

(*) Erato Dig. **ECD 88033; *MCE 75025* [id.]. Armstrong, Murray, Hill, Huttenlocher, Lausanne Vocal Ens. & CO, Corboz.

Haydn's *Stabat Mater*, one of his first major masterpieces, showing him at full stretch, was written in his early years at Esterháza. Scored for strings with oboes, the work is far bigger in aim than that scale might suggest, and some of the choruses include harmonic progressions which in their emotional overtones suggest music of a much later period. Until recently, both in the recording studio and in the concert hall, the work has been scandalously neglected, and it is good that Heltay's reading conveys its essential greatness, helped by admirable soloists and atmospheric recording. The original issue comprised a pair of LPs, but now the work has been fitted on to a single mid-priced cassette, giving first-class sound, clean and vivid; no doubt a CD will follow in due course.

The Erato version offers brisker speeds; but, with an excellent quartet of soloists, fine choral singing of the kind we have come to expect from the Lausanne choir, and first-rate digital recording, it makes a most recommendable alternative, even if Heltay's Argo account brings a more devotional manner, without loss of vitality. There is an excellent cassette of the Erato performance, coping with the resonance with very little loss of refinement in the upper range. Even so, other considerations apart, the Argo tape has a price advantage.

Te Deum in C, Hob XXIIIc/2.

(M) **(*) RCA **GD 86535**; *GK 86535*. V. Boys' Ch., Chorus Viennensis, VCO, Gillesberger – MOZART: *Requiem mass; Ave verum.***(*)

A fine, vigorous account of the *Te Deum* by these Viennese forces, very vividly recorded, coupled to a not inconsiderable account of Mozart's *Requiem*. At mid-price it is excellent value.

COLLECTIONS

English songs: *Content; Despair; Fidelity; The lady's looking glass; Mermaid's song; O tuneful voice; Pastoral song; Piercing eyes; Pleasing pain; Recollection; Sailor's song; She never told her love; Spirit's song; Sympathy; The wanderer*. Folksong settings: *Cupido; Eine sehr gewöhnliche Geschichte; Der erste Kuss; Pensi a me si fido amante; Das strickende Mädchen; Un tello umil.*
*** Ph. **420 217-2** [id.]. Elly Ameling, Joerg Demus.

This very attractive recital is compiled from a three-LP set of Haydn's English songs and folksong settings, recorded in 1980, offering repertoire to display the artless charm of Elly Ameling to perfection. The songs are simple but often touching. The celebrated ones like *The Sailor's Song* (with its improbable refrain of 'hurly-burly') and *The Mermaid's Song* are well matched by many others, equally rewarding, some with clear anticipations of nineteenth-century Lieder. Joerg Demus is a brightly sympathetic accompanist. Elly Ameling's singing has a mixture of charm and purity that is most engaging: she is totally unaffected. The recording has been admirably transferred to CD and is sparkling and fresh. At 70′ the playing time is most generous.

Ein' Magd ein' Dienerin (cantilena); *Miseri noi, misera patria!* (cantata). Interpolation arias: *Chi vive amante* (for BIANCHI: *Alessandro nell' Indie*). *La moglie quando è buona* (for CIMAROSA: *Giannina è Bernadone*). *Il meglio mio carettere* (for CIMAROSA: *L'Impresario in Angustie*). *Ah, crudel! poi chè la brami* (for GAZZANIGA: *La Vendemmia*). *Sono Alcina* (for GAZZANIGA: *L'isola di Alcina*). *Son pietosa* (for pasticcio by Naumann).
*** Erato Dig. **ECD 88011** [id.]. Teresa Berganza, Scottish CO, Leppard.

Most of the items on this delightful recital disc are 'insertion' arias which Haydn wrote for productions of other composers' operas at Esterháza in the years between 1780 and 1790. They are generally short and tuneful, boasting of the singers' constancy in love or whatever, and Berganza with brilliant accompaniment sings them with delicious sparkle. The most substantial item is *Miseri noi, misera patria*, darker and more deeply expressive; and there, too, Berganza rises superbly to the challenge. Excellent Erato recording, most successfully transferred to compact disc, where both the voice and the accompanying group sound vivid within a natural perspective. Recommended.

Haydn, Michael (1737–1806)

Concertino for horn and orchestra in D.
*** Tel. Dig. **ZK8 42960** [id.]. Clevenger, Liszt CO, Rolla – J. HAYDN: *Horn concertos.****
(M) *** HMV *ED 290302-4* [Ang. *4AM 34720*]. Tuckwell, ECO – J. HAYDN: *Horn concertos.****

Michael Haydn's *Concertino* is in the form of a French overture, beginning with a slow movement, followed by a fast one, and closing with a minuet and Trio in which the soloist is featured in only the middle section. The music itself is attractive; the second-movement allegro is played with fine style by Dale Clevenger, whose articulation is a joy in itself. Rolla and his orchestra clearly enjoy themselves in the minuet, which they play with elegance and warmth and, in the absence of the soloist, the unnamed continuo player embroiders the texture gently and effectively. The recording, like the coupled concertos by Josef Haydn, is very realistic indeed, especially during the solo cadenzas which Dale Clevenger provides for the first two movements. An outstanding coupling.

Needless to say, Barry Tuckwell also plays the *Concertino* brilliantly and stylishly. The HMV recording is a modern one (1979) and sounds very well on tape. An excellent mid-priced recommendation.

Trumpet concerto in D.
(M) *** DG *423 011-4* [id.]. André, Munich CO, Stadlmair – J. HAYDN: *Trumpet; Oboe concertos.****

Michael Haydn's *Trumpet concerto* is not quite as memorable as his brother's famous work, but it is a fine piece nevertheless, and Maurice André plays it with style and finesse. He is sympathetically accompanied, and this inexpensive tape, with vivid, clean sound, is well worth considering.

Violin concerto in B flat.
(*) Tel Dig. **ZK8 42917 [id.]. Zehetmair, Liszt CO – J. HAYDN: *Violin concerto.****

A *Violin concerto* from Michael Haydn (written in 1760) makes an enterprising coupling for the better-known work by his brother, Josef. It is not melodically as memorable as Josef's but is a fine piece, with a lively first movement, rather briskly paced here, and a central *Adagio* of some depth. The finale is the weakest part, though not lacking in spirit. The performance with Thomas Zehetmair combining roles of soloist and conductor is strongly characterized and very well recorded. One's only reservation concerns a tendency for the phrasing – notably in the slow movement – to have squeezed emphases, so that the melodic line swells out dynamically, though this is not an alternative to the use of vibrato, as in 'authentic' performances.

Symphonies: in E flat, P. 1; in A, P. 6; in D, P. 11; in C, P. 12.
(*) Tel. **ZK8 43188 [id.]. Liszt CO, Rolla.

Michael Haydn may not have had the abundant genius of his brother, Josef, but as a composer he could be inspired, as these lively, well-recorded performances of four of his symphonies show. P. 11 *in D*, written in Salzburg in 1774, is quite well known, but the other three have only recently been reconstructed by scholars working in Budapest; they contain at least one supremely beautiful inspiration: the elegiac *Andante* in A minor for strings with solo oboe from P. 12 *in C*. Apart from some braying East European horn tone, the playing is admirable.

Symphonies: in D min., P. 20; in D, P. 42; in F, P. 32.
(M) **(*) Vox **MWCD 7124 [MCD 10026]**. Bournemouth Sinf., Farberman.

These three symphonies are notable for their helter-skelter finales (marked *presto scherzando* or *vivace*) which have tremendous energy, well generated by Farberman and his Bournemouth players. The slow movement of P. 42 is also particularly fine, reminiscent of Josef, and in the *Adagio* of P. 32 Michael introduces a long, piquant solo for the bassoon. The performances are well made and sympathetic, exhilaratingly athletic in the allegros; but they lack the final degree of flexibility and imagination in the expressive writing. The sound is excellent, fresh and immediate, although the harpsichord tinkles away in the background only just audibly. Worth exploring, in spite of the reservations mentioned, even if in P. 20 the conductor adds a timpani part which is not in the autograph score.

Divertimenti: in C, P. 98; in C, P. 115.
*** Denon Dig. **C37 7119** [id.]. Holliger, Salvatore Qt – J. C. BACH: *Oboe quartet*; MOZART: Adagio.***

Josef Haydn's brother is seriously neglected on record. Both these *Divertimenti* contain captivating and original inspirations. The longer of the two, P. 98, has a fizzing first movement and a joyful *Presto* finale, while P. 115 brings unexpected timbres. Well coupled and vividly recorded.

Salve regina.
(M) *** Argo *417 163-4* [id.]. St John's College Ch., Guest – J. HAYDN: *Mass No. 7.****

This lovely unaccompanied motet makes an unexpected and welcome fill-up for the fine Argo version of the *Paukenmesse*. The recording was made in 1973 and the sound is first class.

Hebden, John (18th century)

6 Concertos for strings (ed. Wood).
(*) Chan. Dig. **CHAN 8339; *ABTD 1082* [id.]. Cantilena, Shepherd.

Little is known about John Hebden except that he was a Yorkshire composer who also played the cello and bassoon. These concertos are his only known works, apart from some flute sonatas. Although they are slightly uneven, at best the invention is impressive. The concertos usually feature two solo violins and are well constructed to offer plenty of contrast. The performances here are accomplished, without the last degree of polish but full of vitality. The recording is clear and well balanced and given good presence on compact disc; the chrome tape is wide-ranging but has a touch of edginess on top.

Herbert, Victor (1859–1924)

Cello concerto No. 2, Op. 30.
*** HMV Dig. **CDC7 47622-2** [id.]; *EL 270430-4*. Julian Lloyd Webber, LSO, Mackerras – ELGAR: *Romance*; SULLIVAN: *Concerto.****

Victor Herbert, long remembered for such successful operettas as *Naughty Marietta*, early in his career was one of the most distinguished cellists of his time, principal in the orchestra of the Metropolitan Opera before establishing himself as composer and conductor. Dvořák is said to have been inspired to write his *Cello concerto* after hearing this work of Herbert's, given first in New York in 1894. Certainly the opening is magnificent, grandly symphonic, and the *Lento tranquillo* gently nostalgic; if the rest rather fails to live up to the promise of its beginning, it is still a formidable piece, beautifully written for the instrument. Julian Lloyd Webber proves a persuasive advocate, making this an apt and attractive coupling for the rare Sullivan and Elgar. On CD the recording is excellent, but the cassette is middle- and bass-orientated, with a limited upper range.

Herrmann, Bernard (1911–75)

Film scores: *Citizen Kane: suite. The Devil and Daniel Webster: Sleigh-ride; Swing your partners. Jane Eyre: selection. Jason and the Argonauts: suite. The Snows of Kilimanjaro: Interlude; Memory waltz.*
(M) *** Decca *417 852-4* [id.]. LPO or Nat. PO, composer.

Hitchcock film scores: Marnie: excerpts. *North by Northwest: Overture. A Portrait of Hitch* (from *The Trouble with Harry*). *Psycho* (A narrative for orchestra). *Vertigo: Prelude; The nightmare; Scène d'amour.*
(M) *** Decca *417 847-4* [id.]. LPO, composer.

Bernard Herrmann, whose highly inventive and brilliantly scored film music stands up remarkably well away from the visual images, was given his chance by Orson Welles in *Citizen Kane*. The first of these two valuable anthologies opens with the vivacious overture for that film and includes three other vignettes. The other excerpts show Herrmann's vivid imagination constantly at work and also his strong lyrical flair, as in the music for *Jane Eyre*. The most spectacular scoring comes in the brief suite from *Jason and the Argonauts*, illustrating Jason's meeting with Talos; while the *Interlude* and *Memory waltz* from *The Snows of Kilimanjaro* are hauntingly nostalgic. The highlight of the Hitchcock selection is undoubtedly the chilling 'murder in the shower' sequence from *Psycho*, with its highly original, blood-curdling whoops from the violins above the stave; but the music for *Vertigo* and *North by Northwest* also has strong individual atmosphere, while *A Portrait of Hitch* shows the composer in wittily light-hearted form. Herrmann was not always an effective conductor of other people's music, but he was second to none in his own, and the playing here is polished, powerfully vivid and always spontaneous. The recordings, nearly all made in 1969/70, originate from Phase Four masters (a hi-fi-orientated recording system of the analogue stereo era, designed to overcome losses between master tape and finished pressing). They offer most vivid sound on these well-engineered and inexpensive chrome tapes; it is only a pity that the production department decided to spend their available cash on glossy liner-leaflets (admittedly quite effective) rather than on documentation – which is non-existent, apart from titles.

Hérold, Ferdinand (1791–1833)

La Fille mal gardée (ballet, arr. Lanchbery): complete.
*** Decca Dig. *410 190-4* (2) [id.]. O of ROHCG, Lanchbery.

La Fille mal gardée: extended excerpts.
❀ *** HMV Dig. **CDC7 49403-2**. Royal Liverpool PO, Wordsworth.

John Lanchbery's earlier record of extracts from this fizzingly comic and totally delightful ballet has been a treasured item in the catalogue for many years. Here, with sound of spectacularly high fidelity, he conducts an equally seductive account of the full score with the orchestra which plays it for ballet performances. The comic *Clog dance* for the widow Simone (a male dancer in drag) must be among the most famous of all ballet numbers outside Tchaikovsky, and there is much else of comparable delight. The Decca tapes are brilliantly transferred.

However, many may feel that two cassettes for this lightweight score is too much of a good thing; they are well served by Barry Wordsworth's scintillating account of a generous extended selection from the ballet on CD, including all the important sequences. With playing from the Royal Liverpool Philharmonic Orchestra that combines refinement and delicacy with wit and humour, this is also highly recommendable, with the HMV recording in the demonstration bracket.

Hertel, Johann (1727–89)

Trumpet concerto in D.
*** Ph. Dig. **420 203-2**; *420 203-4* [id.]. Hardenberger, ASMF, Marriner – HAYDN *** ❀; HUMMEL *** ❀; STAMITZ: *Concertos*.***

Johann Hertel's *Trumpet concerto* is typical of many works of the same kind written in the Baroque era, with a highly placed solo line, a touch of melancholy in the *Largo* and plenty of opportunities for crisp tonguing in the finale. Håkan Hardenberger clearly relishes every bar and plays with great flair. He is stylishly accompanied and vividly recorded, though the acoustic is a shade resonant. The cassette, like the CD, sounds splendid.

Hildegard of Bingen (1098–1179)

Hymns and sequences: *Ave generosa; Columba aspexit; O Ecclesia; O Euchari; O Jerusalem; O ignis spiritus; O presul vere civitatis; O viridissima virga.*
*** Hyp. **CDA 66039**; *KA 66039* [id.]. Gothic Voices, Muskett, White, Page.

Abbess Hildegard of Bingen was one of the great mystics of her age and both Popes Gregory IX and Innocent IV proposed her canonization. From 1141 onwards she was Abbess of the Benedictine order at Disibodenberg near Bingen, twenty-five miles south-west of Mainz. She was a naturalist, playwright and poetess as well as composer, and corresponded with many of the leading figures of the age, popes, emperors, kings, archbishops and so on. Her series of visions, *Scivias*, occupied her for the best part of a decade (1141–51); this record draws on her collection of music and poetry, the *Symphonia armonie celestium revelationum* – 'the symphony of the harmony of celestial revelations'. These hymns and sequences, most expertly performed and recorded, have excited much acclaim – and rightly so. A lovely CD. The cassette is of the highest quality, too, with good range and presence. The original LP won the *Gramophone* Early Music award for 1983.

Hindemith, Paul (1895–1963)

Concert music for strings and brass, Op. 50; (i) *Horn concerto; Nobilissima visione (suite); Symphony in B flat for concert band.*
(M) *** HMV *EH 291173-4*. (i) Dennis Brain; Philh. O, composer.

Concert music for strings and brass; Symphonic metamorphoses on themes of Weber.
*** HMC **CDC 47615-2**. Phd. O, Ormandy.

Recorded in 1956, Hindemith's own performances with the Philharmonia Orchestra of four of his most characteristic works come out with astonishing vividness in this digital transfer of thirty years later; indeed the sheer bloom of the sound and the naturalness of the balance suggest that it could have been made in the 1970s. The *Horn concerto* – distinctly laid out in two fast movements followed by a longer, more formal slow movement as summary – is dazzlingly played by its original performer, Dennis Brain. That has been available in stereo before this latest issue, but it is a revelation to have the other three works, notably the fine ballet score, *Nobilissima visione*. Though there is much in his output that is manufactured and arid, *Nobilissima visione*, the work he composed in the 1930s on the theme of St Francis, shows Hindemith at his most inspired. The slow movement has a grave beauty that is quite haunting and its eloquence here should touch even those who regard him as normally outside their reach. There is also dignity and nobility in its splendid opening, and the composer proves a most persuasive interpreter of his own music, drawing refined and committed performances and finding wit in the *Symphony for concert band*. These 73 minutes of music make an ideal introduction to Hindemith's orchestral writing, and tape collectors can rest assured that the transfers are well managed throughout.

It is a pity that Hindemith's own collection clashes with Ormandy's coupling on CD, for this was one of the very finest records the latter made (at the end of the 1970s) during the last years of his tenure with the Philadelphia Orchestra. They give a superb performance of the *Concert music for strings and brass*, bringing opulent tone and virtuosity to this rewarding score. The *Symphonic metamorphoses on themes of Weber* is more generously represented on record; although these artists play with splendid panache and brilliance, the humour of the second movement is perhaps less effectively realized in their hands than it is in Abbado's performance – see below. In every other respect this is first class, and the CD transfer of the recording does full justice to the quality of sound this orchestra produces. The slightly monochrome effect of Hindemith's scoring is most faithfully caught in the *Symphonic metamorphoses* (originally conceived as a ballet for Massine, but hastily withdrawn when the composer discovered that Salvador Dali was to provide the decor).

Horn concerto (see also above).
(***) HMV **CDC7 47834-2** [id.]. Brain, Philh. O, composer – R. STRAUSS: *Horn concertos*.(***)

This CD has been produced by Angel, the American offshoot of EMI International. The transfer is acceptable, but certainly not superior to the sound offered on the cassette described above, which is a far better way of obtaining Dennis Brain's illustrious account of the *Horn concerto*. The remastering of the Richard Strauss couplings for CD has been inexpertly managed, with uningratiatingly thin orchestral textures. The CD documentation, too, is unsatisfactory.

(i) *The Four temperaments; Nobilissima visione.*
(*) Delos Dig. **D/CD 1006 [id.]. (i) Carole Rosenberger; RPO, James de Preist.

The Four temperaments, a set of variations on a three-part theme for piano and strings of 1940, is one of Hindemith's finest and most immediate works. Carole Rosenberger takes a broader approach than did Lukas Foss in his pioneering record with the Zimbler Sinfonietta and, generally speaking, gives a formidable reading of this inventive and resourceful score. James de Preist also secures responsive playing from the RPO strings and gives a sober, well-shaped account of the *Nobilissima visione* suite, doing justice to its grave nobility. The recording is natural and well balanced but could be more transparent, particularly at the top end of the spectrum.

(i) *Violin concerto;* (ii) *Symphonic metamorphoses on themes of Weber.*
(M) *** Decca *414 437-4* [id.]. (i) David Oistrakh; (i; ii) LSO; (i) composer; (ii) Abbado.

David Oistrakh's inspired 1963 recording of Hindemith's *Concerto* had a revelatory quality, turning what had hitherto seemed a somewhat dry work into an expansive lyrical utterance. The composer's own direction of the orchestral accompaniment has a matching passion, with the soloist providing many moments when the ear is ravished by the beauty of the phrasing and inflexion. Originally rather incongruously coupled with the *Scottish fantasia* of Max Bruch, the new pairing with the *Symphonic metamorphoses on themes of Weber* makes for one of the most enterprising of Decca's mid-priced London Enterprise series. Abbado's account of the latter work is no less outstanding. It is a relief to find here a conductor content to follow the composer's own dynamic markings and who does not succumb to the temptation to score interpretative points at the music's expense. The stopped notes on the horns at the beginning of the finale, for example, are marked *piano* and are played here so that they add a barely perceptible touch of colour to the texture. The Decca engineers balance this so musically that this effect is preserved. This admittedly unimportant touch is symptomatic of the subtlety of the conductor's approach in a performance that in every respect is of the highest quality. The tape transfer is strikingly successful, thrillingly vivid and admirably clear. The *Concerto* sounds particularly realistic.

Mathis der Maler.
(M) *** HMV **CDM7 69242-2** [id.]. BPO, Karajan – BARTÓK: *Music for strings, percussion and celesta.***(*)
(*) Chan. **CHAN 8533; *ABTD 1243* [id.]. LSO, Horenstein – R. STRAUSS: *Death and transfiguration.***

Karajan's 1960 account of the *Mathis symphony* is beautifully spacious and among the very finest versions of the work ever made. Karajan succeeds in producing a more refined and transparent texture than we are accustomed to, and both dynamic nuances and details of phrasing are attentively followed without creating a sense of beautification. The first two movements in particular are fresh and atmospheric, and the opening of the finale is wonderfully dramatic. The recording is atmospheric too and has more body than the original LP. However, the performance is so fine – and certainly the best on the market at the time of writing – that the recommendation must be unqualified.

Horenstein's account of *Mathis der Maler* was the last record he made, and it has the merit of breadth and weight. The recording, originally issued by Unicorn, has been remastered satisfactorily and there is a very good tape; but this issue is overpriced in both formats: there are a number of stunning accounts of Richard Strauss's *Death and transfiguration* which eclipse Horenstein's. His admirers none the less will probably want this reissue.

Organ sonatas Nos 1–3 (with DISTLER: *4 Spielstücke, Op. 18/1*; KROPFREITER: *Toccata francese*).
*** Argo Dig. **417 159-2**; *417 159-4* [id.]. Peter Hurford (organ of Ratzeburg Cathedral).

Hindemith's cunning craftsmanship was well applied in his three *Organ sonatas*, works which, without making excessive demands on the player, exploit the instrument to maximum effect. They are given with attractively tangy attack by Peter Hurford on the Ratzeburg Cathedral organ, which he earlier used for some of his Bach recordings. The Distler pieces and the Kropfreiter *Toccata* are not of the same quality, but find Hurford similarly convincing.

When lilacs last in the dooryard bloom'd.
*** Telarc Dig. **CD 80132** [id.]. DeGaetani, Stone, Atlanta Ch. & SO, Robert Shaw.
** Orfeo Dig. **C 112851A** [id.]. Fassbaender, Fischer-Dieskau, V. State Op. Ch., VSO, Sawallisch.

Robert Shaw's record carries special authority, since it was he who commissioned Hindemith to compose this 'Requiem for those we loved' at the end of the 1939–45 war. It is one of the composer's most deeply felt works and one of his best; as a recently naturalized US citizen, he liked to think of it as one of the high points of the new American music. Hindemith took Whitman's poem in memory of Lincoln and fashioned from it a requiem that is both non-liturgical and highly varied – not just recitatives and arias, but marches, passacaglias and fugue. Robert Shaw gives a performance of great intensity and variety of colour and nuance. Both his soloists are excellent, and there is both weight and subtlety in the orchestral contribution. Splendid recording.

The Orfeo record comes from a performance given at the Grosse Musikvereinsaal in Vienna in 1983. It has illustrious soloists and a good chorus, and Sawallisch is sympathetic and imaginative. There are minor imperfections of the kind that can occur on a live occasion, but these in themselves are of small account; more important is the quality of the choral sound, which is by no means as well defined as in the rival version by Robert Shaw.

Hoffmeister, Franz (1754–1812)

Flute concertos: in D; in G.
(M) **(*) ASV **CDQS 6012**; *ZCQS 6012* [id.]. Dingfelder, ECO, Mackerras; Leonard – C. P. E. BACH: *Concerto*.**(*)

Franz Hoffmeister, a Viennese music publisher, is best remembered for his association with Mozart's K.499 *String quartet*, but he wrote a great deal of music himself. His two *Flute concertos* are elegantly inventive if not distinctive. They are well recorded and make pleasant late-evening listening. Sandwiched between them on this CD is a far greater work by C. P. E. Bach; by the side of this highly imaginative writing, they sound doubly innocuous. The performances are sprightly and polished, and the accompaniments have plenty of spirit. The sound is brightly lit, but not excessively so.

Holst, Gustav (1874–1934)

(i) *Beni Mora (oriental suite), Op. 29/1;* (ii) *Brook Green suite;* (iii) *Egdon Heath, Op. 47; The Perfect Fool: ballet suite, Op. 39;* (iv) *St Paul's suite, Op. 29/2;* (v) *Festival Te Deum;* (vi) *Psalm 86.*

*** HMV **CDC7 49784-2.** (i) BBC SO, Sargent; (ii) ECO, Bedford; (iii) LSO, Previn; (iv) RPO, Sargent; (v) LSO Ch., St Paul's Cathedral choristers, LPO, Groves; (vi) Partridge, Purcell Singers, ECO, Imogen Holst.

An admirable and generous anthology recorded during the 1960s and 1970s. All the performances are good ones and many are distinctive. *Beni Mora*, an attractively exotic piece that vividly shows Holst's flair for orchestration, is well played here under Sir Malcolm Sargent, while the account of the *St Paul's suite* is equally accomplished, full of verve and character. The *Brook Green suite* from Steuart Bedford is also lively and spontaneous. Previn gives a darkly intense performance of *Egdon Heath*, illuminatingly different from Boult's earlier version which was much more coolly detached. The rip-roaring ballet music from *The Perfect Fool* presents a colourful contrast. The *Short Festival Te Deum* comes from 1919; it takes only a little over four minutes and is an 'occasional' piece, less original than the *Hymn of Jesus*, written in the same year. The setting of Psalm 86, with its expressive tenor part sung beautifully by Ian Partridge, is also included in this bountiful compilation and is very well recorded; the success of this performance owes much to the inspired direction of the composer's daughter. The CD transfers are all well managed, and this compilation is indispensable for any true Holstian.

Invocation for cello and orchestra, Op. 19/2.

*** RCA **RD 70800**; *RK 70800.* Lloyd Webber, Philh. O, Handley – DELIUS: *Concerto;* VAUGHAN WILLIAMS: *Folksongs fantasia.****

Holst's *Invocation for cello and orchestra* comes from 1911 and pre-dates *The Planets.* Indeed, in her book on her father, Imogen Holst spoke of it as 'trying out some of the ideas for the texture of Venus'. It is a highly attractive and lyrical piece well worth reviving, and a valuable addition to the growing Holst discography. Both the performance and recording are of admirable quality. The CD brings increased vividness, yet is strikingly refined, and there is an excellent cassette. Recommended.

Military band suites Nos 1–2.

❀ *** Telarc Dig. **CD 80038** [id.]. Cleveland Symphonic Winds, Fennell – HANDEL: *Royal Fireworks music.****

Holst's two *Military band suites* contain some magnificent music – much underrated because of the medium – and they have been lucky on records. Frederick Fennell's famous Mercury recording, made at the beginning of the 1960s, is remembered nostalgically by many collectors and was a landmark in its day. His new versions have more gravitas though no less *joie de vivre.* They are magnificent, and the recording is truly superb – digital technique used in a quite overwhelmingly exciting way. Perhaps there is too much bass drum, but no one is going to grumble when the result is so telling. The *Chaconne* of the *First Suite* makes a quite marvellous effect here. The playing of the Cleveland wind group is of the highest quality, smoothly blended and full in slow movements, vigorous and alert and with strongly rhythmic articulation in fast ones. To be reproduced properly, the compact disc version needs amplifier and speakers that can easily handle the wide amplitude and range of the sound; then the result offers a most remarkable demonstration of spectacular sound reproduction that should convince even the most hardened sceptic as to the full possibilities of this new format.

Suites for military band Nos 1–2. Hammersmith: Prelude & scherzo, Op. 52.
(M) *** ASV **CDQS 6021**; *ZCQS 6021* [id.]. L. Wind O, Denis Wick – VAUGHAN WILLIAMS: *English folksong suite* etc.***

The two Holst *Military band suites* make an exhilarating listening experience when they are played as brilliantly and with such obvious pleasure as by this group of wind soloists drawn from the LSO. The performances have great spontaneity even if they are essentially lightweight, especially when compared with the Fennell versions. *Hammersmith*, however, is well worth having on CD, although the approach is freshly direct rather than seeking to evoke atmosphere. The sound is first class and the Vaughan Williams couplings are no less successful; this reissue is very competitively priced.

The Planets (suite), Op. 32.
*** Decca Dig. **417 553-2**; *417 553-4* [id.]. Montreal Ch. & SO, Dutoit.
*** HMV **CDC7 47160-2** [id.]; (M) *EG 290850-4*. Amb. S., LSO, Previn.
(M) *** HMV **CDM7 69045-2** [id.]. LPO, Boult (with G. Mitchell Ch.).
(M) *** Decca **417 709-2** [id.]. V. State Op. Ch., VPO, Karajan.
(*) DG Dig. **400 028-2; *3302 019* [id.]. Berlin Ch. & BPO, Karajan.
(M) **(*) DG **419 475-2**; *419 475-4* [id.]. Boston Ch. & SO, Steinberg – LIGETI: *Lux aeterna*.***
(B) **(*) DG Walkman *413 852-4* [id.]. Boston Ch. & SO, Steinberg – ELGAR: *Enigma variations*.***
(M) **(*) RCA *GK 85207*. Phd. Ch. & O, Ormandy.
(*) Telarc Dig. **CD 80133 [id]. RPO with Ch., Previn.
(M) **(*) EMI Dig. **CD-EMX 9513**; *TC-EMX 2106*. Amb. S., Philh. O, Rattle.
(*) Decca **414 567-2 [id.]. LPO & Ch., Solti.
(*) Chan. Dig. **CHAN 8302; *ABTD 1010* [id.]. SNO & Ch., Gibson.
M **(*) CBS **MYK 42545** [**MYK 37226**]. NYPO & Ch., Bernstein.
** Ph. Dig. **420 177-2**; *420 177-4* [id.]. Boston Pops O & Ch., John Williams.
** HMV Dig. **CDC7 47417-2**; *EL 270429-4*. Toronto SO & Children's Ch., A. Davis.
(M) ** Decca *417 677-4*. LAPO & Master Chorale, Mehta.
(**) HMV mono *ED 290725-4*. BBC SO & Ch., Boult (with ELGAR: *String serenade* (**)).

Charles Dutoit in many of his finest Montreal records has deliberately challenged his orchestra to the limit, preparing meticulously beforehand but then making the actual recording on a very taxing schedule, if in very congenial conditions, in the lovely country church of Saint-Eustache. Before this recording of *The Planets*, the orchestra had not played Holst's brilliant showpiece for many years; but Dutoit's natural feeling for mood, rhythm and colour, so effectively used in his records of Ravel, here results in an outstandingly successful version, both rich and brilliant, and recorded with an opulence to outshine all rivals. It is remarkable that, whether in the relentless build-up of *Mars*, the lyricism of *Venus*, the rich exuberance of *Jupiter* or in much else, Dutoit and his Canadian players sound so idiomatic. The final account of *Saturn* is chillingly atmospheric. This marvellously recorded disc is a clear first choice on CD, but the tape is comparatively disappointing: the wide amplitude and warm resonance blur the sound at times, noticeably in *Mars* and *Jupiter*.

Previn's remastered EMI analogue version of 1974 remains highly desirable. Though it does not have quite the range of a digital recording, the focus is firm and the realistic perspective gives an admirable illusion of depth. Strings are full-bodied and brass sounds are sonorous and thrilling, while the slowly graduated diminuendo into silence of the offstage chorus at the end of *Neptune* is wonderfully atmospheric. Previn's interpretation is an outstandingly attractive one, with many of Holst's subtleties of orchestral detail telling with greater point than on many other versions. The performance is basically traditional, yet has an appealing freshness. There is also a good cassette, but it is not as refined as the CD, especially in *Mars*.

It was Sir Adrian Boult who, over sixty years ago, first 'made *The Planets* shine', as the composer put it, and in his ninetieth year he recorded it for the last time. It sets the seal on a magnificent Indian summer in the recording studio, a performance at once intense and beautifully played, spacious and dramatic, rapt and pointed. If the opening of *Mars* – noticeably slower than in Boult's previous recordings – suggests a slackening, the opposite proves true: that movement gains greater weight at a slower tempo. *Mercury* has lift and clarity, not just rushing brilliance, and it is striking that in Holst's syncopations – as in the introduction to *Jupiter* – Boult allows himself a jaunty, even jazzy freedom which adds an infectious sparkle. The great melody of *Jupiter* is calculatedly less resonant and more flowing than previously but is more moving, and *Uranus* as well as *Jupiter* has its measure of jollity, with the lolloping 6/8 rhythms delectably pointed. The spacious slow movements are finely poised and the recording has gained presence and definition with its digital remastering, and yet not lost its body and atmosphere. At mid-price, this could well be a first choice for many.

Still very competitive indeed is Karajan's earlier Decca version which, even though it is (amazingly) over twenty-five years old, still sounds remarkably vivid with its brilliantly remastered recording, now more precise in detail but retaining its atmospheric analogue sound-picture. Now reissued on Decca's mid-priced Ovation label, this holds its place near the top of the list on most counts. It was here we first heard Karajan's transformation of a work we had tended to think of as essentially English into an international score. There are many individual touches, from the whining Wagnerian tubas of *Mars*, *Venus* representing ardour rather than mysticism, the gossamer textures of *Mercury*, and the strongly characterized *Saturn* and *Venus*, with splendid playing from the Vienna brass, now given more bite. The upper range of the strings, however, has a touch of fierceness at higher dynamic levels.

Karajan's later digital CD (for DG) is undoubtedly spectacularly wide-ranging. Indeed, the dynamic contrast is something to be marvelled at; the opening of *Mars* has remarkable bite, while the marvellously sustained pianissimo playing of the Berlin Philharmonic Orchestra – as in *Venus* and the closing pages of *Saturn* – is the more telling against a background of silence. But the 'digital edge' on the treble detracts from the overall beauty of the orchestra in fortissimos, and *Jupiter* ideally needs a riper body of tone. The bass is less resonant than in some digital recordings from this source, so that the organ pedals at the end of *Saturn* come through more positively in the old Sargent recording from the earliest days of stereo. However, one should not make too much of this. The chrome cassette is very impressive, and it would be perverse to suggest that the compact disc does not add to the impact and refinement of detail. Moreover, it is a thrilling performance that makes one hear Holst's brilliant suite with new ears. With the Berlin Philharmonic in peak form, Karajan improves even on the performance he recorded two decades earlier with the Vienna Philharmonic, modifying his reading to make it more idiomatic; for example, in *Jupiter* the syncopated opening now erupts with joy and the big melody has a natural flow and nobility. *Venus* has sensuous string phrasing, *Mercury* and *Uranus* have beautiful springing in the triplet rhythms, and the climax of that last movement brings an amazing glissando on the organ, made clear by the thirty-two-channel recording.

Recorded in 1971, Steinberg's Boston set of *Planets* was another outstanding version from a vintage analogue period. This has now been remastered for its Galleria CD reissue and sounds brighter and sharper in outline, and with some loss of opulence (though slightly less on the equivalent cassette). It remains one of the most exciting and involving versions, and DG have had the happy inspiration to offer Ligeti's *Lux aeterna* as an encore. With its associations with the film *2001*, this has the kind of mysticism one can readily associate with the infinity of space, and it makes an apt coupling.

Steinberg's performance is also available in its original analogue format as a fine bargain in DG's Walkman series, placed uninterrupted on one side of a double-length chrome tape and coupled with Jochum's inspirational account of *Enigma*, plus a dash of *Pomp and circumstance* to balance out the side-lengths. Steinberg draws sumptuous playing from the Boston Symphony, and he is helped by reverberant recording that makes this a feast of sound. Anyone who wants to wallow in the opulence and colour of this extrovert work will certainly be delighted – the more so, one suspects, when Steinberg departs in certain respects from British convention. *Mars* in particular is intensely exciting. At his fast tempo he may get to his fortissimos a little early, but rarely has the piece sounded so menacing on record. The testing point for most will no doubt be *Jupiter*, and here Steinberg the excellent Elgarian comes to the fore, giving a wonderful nobilmente swagger. The tape transfer faithfully captures the richly vivid qualities of the recording, even though the resonance has brought a lower than usual level.

Ormandy's RCA recording has also been digitally remastered very effectively and will no doubt shortly appear on CD. It was one of the finest records he made in the last few years before he retired as the principal conductor of the Philadelphia Orchestra. The playing has great electricity, and it is a pity that the recording is so brilliant (the orchestra does not sound like this in the flesh). Even so, this is a highly compelling reading, and the sound gives added edge to the ferocity of *Mars*, balanced by an eloquently peaceful *Venus* with rapt, translucent textures. Ormandy paces the central tune of *Jupiter* slowly and deliberately. (This seems almost to be an American tradition; transatlantic performances of Vaughan Williams's arrangement of *Greensleeves* show a similar gravity.) The performance is at its finest in *Uranus* (with crisply vigorous brass articulation) and the restrained melancholy of *Saturn*, deeply felt and somehow personal in its communication. *Neptune* too is beautifully tapered off at the close. The recording sounds exceptionally clear and its super-brilliance responds quite well to the controls, without loss of the undoubtedly vivid detail.

André Previn's Telarc version broadly preserves the magnificent concept of *The Planets* contained in his superb EMI account with the LSO; however, with sound that is wide-ranging and atmospheric but slightly diffused, and with a rather more relaxed approach to some of the movements, it lacks the final bite which made the earlier record so compelling. It remains an excellent version for anyone wanting fine modern sound – but Dutoit offers that in abundance, and his is a more sharply characterized performance.

For Simon Rattle, HMV's digital recording provides wonderfully atmospheric sound at the very opening (the col legno tapping at the start of *Mars*) and the very close of *Neptune* (the fading chords in endless alternation from the offstage women's chorus). The quality in *Venus* and *Mercury* is also beautiful, clear and translucent. Otherwise it is not as distinctive a version as one might have expected from this leading young conductor; it is sensibly paced but neither so polished nor so bitingly committed as Karajan, Previn or Boult or, for that matter, Ormandy, who is at his finest on his Philadelphia record. The CD undoubtedly produces a more sharply defined sound-picture than the tape (or indeed the original LP), but it seems to have less warmth.

The Decca recording for Solti's Chicago version is extremely brilliant, with *Mars* given a vivid cutting edge at the fastest possible tempo. Solti's pacing is exhilarating to the point of fierceness in the vigorous movements; undoubtedly his direct manner is refreshing, the rhythms clipped and precise, sometimes at the expense of resilience. His directness in *Jupiter* (with the trumpets coming through splendidly) is certainly riveting, the big tune taken literally rather than affectionately. In *Saturn* the spareness of texture is finely sustained and the tempo is slow, the detail precise; while in *Neptune* the coolness is even more striking when the pianissimos are achieved with such a high degree of tension. The analogue recording has remarkable clarity and detail, and Solti's clear-headed intensity undoubtedly brings refreshing new insights to this multi-faceted score, even if some will prefer a more atmospheric viewpoint. The CD gives the orchestra great presence, but the digital remastering has brought an edge to the brightness of the upper range, and the performance is often made to sound too tense in the wrong way.

Gibson's version with the Scottish National Orchestra had the distinction of being the first set of *Planets* to be recorded digitally. The reading is characteristically direct and certainly well played. Other versions have greater individuality and are more involving, but there is no doubt that the Chandos recording has fine bite and presence (slightly too much so in *Neptune*, with the chorus too positive and unethereal) and excellent detail, although even on the compact disc there are moments when one would have expected a greater degree of transparency. The CD format also has a marginal element of fierceness in *Mars* but gains at the lower dynamic levels from the absence of any kind of background interference. With sound this vivid, the impact of such a colourful score is enhanced – but undoubtedly Previn's analogue version brings a richer overall sound (notably in *Jupiter*) and more delicacy of texture in *Venus* and *Neptune*. The cassette is well managed but is less wide-ranging in the treble.

Bernstein, like Ormandy, suffers from a characteristically over-brilliant transatlantic sound-balance, and is also rather dry in the bass. Like Ormandy's, the performance is charismatic, with moments of striking individuality. The choral singing in *Neptune* is most refined and the closing diminuendo very beautiful.

John Williams starts off by taking *Mars* very fast so that, although it is exciting, it loses its sinister aspect. The rest of the performance is genially attractive and well played, but generally lacks the individuality of the finest versions. The exception is *Uranus*, which is very gripping and spectacular, although the mystic chorus in *Neptune*, after producing an impressive pianissimo entry, seem less than ideally firm. The resonant Boston acoustics bring plenty of warmth and bloom, if less sharpness of internal detail, though there is an impressive bass drum in *Uranus*.

Andrew Davis recorded *The Planets* with the Toronto orchestra as the first of a series for EMI, taking the players to a new and more helpful venue outside the city. Alas for good intentions, the results do not quite match those achieved in very similar circumstances by the Toronto orchestra's direct rival in Montreal. Though full and firm, the sound is not as open or as atmospheric as that on the finest versions (as, for example, Dutoit's Decca) and Davis's taut control of the music, with fast speeds in *Mars* and *Saturn* diminishing the relentlessness of the argument, makes the result sound just a little inhibited. It is a good, beefy account – but in so strong a field there are many finer versions.

When it was first issued in 1971, the Los Angeles Decca recording set a new standard for sonic splendour in a work which has since the days of 78s put the recording engineers on their mettle. The power and impact of *Mars* are still impressive; and the brass and timpani in *Uranus* have fine body and bite. In short this was vintage Decca analogue sound (though the remastered cassette is a little disappointing, not quite as refined as the original in the upper range). There are also reservations about the performance which has not the individuality of those of Karajan, Boult, Previn or even Steinberg.

There are also versions by Ozawa (Ph. **416 456-2**) and Maazel (CBS **CD 37429**), but in a crowded marketplace they are uncompetitive.

Sir Adrian Boult's 1945 recording of *The Planets* was a landmark of the period for its sound. Even forty years later, a new transfer is impressive, vividly capturing the quality not just of Boult's understanding direction – never fresher than here – but of the fine orchestra that Boult had created. Eight years earlier, before the Second World War, it was if anything in even finer shape for the Elgar *Introduction and allegro*, and again the sound is amazing for its age. However, this tape is essentially of historical interest; Boult has since recorded both works in greatly improved sound.

(i) *The Planets; Egdon Heath; The Perfect Fool: suite.*
(B) **(*) HMV *TCC2-POR 54290*. LSO, Previn, (i) with Amb. S. – VAUGHAN WILLIAMS: *Fantasia on Greensleeves***(*) (with BUTTERWORTH: *The Banks of green willow***(*)).

Previn's fine version of *The Planets*, as on the HMV CD above, is here offered without interruption on one side of EMI's 'Portrait of the Artist' cassette but with an attractive anthology of English music on the other. Previn's account of *Egdon Heath* is darkly intense, and the rip-roaring ballet music from *The Perfect Fool* presents a colourful contrast. Butterworth's idyll and the Vaughan Williams *Greensleeves fantasia* add a suitably pastoral dimension to an attractive programme. The sound is good, but the CD of *The Planets* has a more sparkling upper range.

Air and variations; 3 Pieces for oboe & string quartet, Op. 2.
*** Chan. Dig. **CHAN 8392**; *ABTD 1114* [id.]. Francis, English Qt – BAX: *Quintet*: MOERAN: *Fantasy quartet*: JACOB: *Quartet*.***

The material here derives from an early work from Holst's student days. It was revised in 1910 when the *Air and variations* (restored here as an introduction) was omitted. The three pieces are engagingly folksy, consisting of a sprightly little *March*, a gentle *Minuet* with a good tune, and a *Scherzo*. Performances are first class and so is the recording. There is an excellent chrome tape.

VOCAL MUSIC

Choral hymns from the Rig Veda (Groups 1–4), H. 97–100; 2 Eastern pictures for women's voices and harp, H. 112; Hymn to Dionysus, Op. 31/2.
(*) Unicorn Dig. **DKPCD 9046; *DKPC 9046* [id.]. Royal College of Music Chamber Ch., RPO, Willcocks; Ellis.

The *Choral hymns from the Rig Veda* show Holst writing with deep understanding for voices, devising textures, refined, very distinctively his, to match atmospherically exotic texts. Sir David Willcocks's collection, using the choir of the college where he was Principal for many years, is the most complete yet assembled on disc. Though performances are not always ideally polished, the warmth and thrust of the music are beautifully caught. The *Hymn to Dionysus*, setting words from the *Bacchae* of Euripides in Gilbert Murray's translation, a rarity anticipating Holst's *Choral symphony*, makes a welcome and substantial fill-up along with the two little *Eastern pictures*. Beautifully clean and atmospheric recording, with a very good matching cassette.

(i) *Choral hymns from the Rig Veda (Group 2), H. 98; Hymn of Jesus, Op. 37; Ode to Death, Op. 38;* (ii) *The wandering scholar* (opera, ed. Britten and I. Holst) complete.
*** HMV **CDC7 49409-2**. (i) LSO Ch., St Paul's Ch., LPO, Groves; (ii) Burrowes, Tear, Rippon, Langdon, E. Op. Group, ECO, Bedford.

This extremely generous CD (71′ 42″) offers an indispensable collection of mostly little-known Holst. The recording of *The Hymn of Jesus* is on the whole finer than Boult's older Decca account which has served collectors well over the years. Sir Charles Groves brings great sympathy and conviction to this beautiful and moving score whose visionary quality has never paled. The *Ode to Death* is from the same period, written in memory of Holst's friends killed in the 1914–18 war. A setting of Whitman, it must be accounted one of Holst's most inspired and haunting works, comparable in quality with the *Choral fantasia*. The second group of the *Rig Veda hymns* are less of a novelty: they were written in the immediate wake of Holst's Algerian visit of 1909 which also produced *Beni Mora*. They are on familiar Holstian lines, though they make considerable demands on these singers. The one-act comic opera, *The wandering scholar*, works delightfully on stage, but on record its galumphing humour is less than sparkling. It is a very late work, which the composer himself never saw produced, and the score required an amount of intelligent editing before it was given modern performances. Whatever one's response to the comedy, the musical inspiration has the sharp originality and economy one associates with Holst's last period, a fascinating score. The recordings all come from the mid-1970s and were of very high quality, but the CD is something of a revelation in opening up the choral sound, while still retaining the atmosphere and bloom of the analogue originals. The words of the soloists in *The wandering scholar* are also clear. An outstanding reissue in every way.

Choral hymns from the Rig Veda (Group 3) H. 99, Op. 26/3.
*** Hyp.**CDA 66175**; *KA 66175* [id.]. Holst Singers & O; Davan Wetton; T. Owen – BLISS: *Lie strewn the white flocks;* BRITTEN: *Gloriana: Choral dances.****

The third group of *Choral hymns from the Rig Veda*, for women's voices with harp accompaniment, is the best known. Like the whole series it reveals Holst in his Sanskritic period at his most distinctively inspired. In this responsive performance, it makes an excellent coupling for the attractive Bliss and Britten items, atmospherically recorded.

(i) *Choral symphony, Op. 41;* (ii) *Choral fantasia, Op. 51.*
*** HMV **CDC7 49638-2**. (i) Palmer, LPO Ch., LPO, Boult; (ii) Baker, Partridge, Purcell Singers, ECO, Imogen Holst; R. Downes (organ).

In the *Choral symphony*, though the Keats poems give a faded aura to this ambitious work, Boult and his performers demonstrate the beauty and imagination of the writing. Holst even manages to set the *Ode on a Grecian Urn* without aesthetic problems; and until the finale the writing is always taut and intensely individual. The finale is altogether looser-limbed, but Boult in this totally unsentimental performance manages to draw it together. As samplers, try the strange *Prelude* with its monotone mutterings or the seven-in-a-bar energy of the *Bacchanal*. A fine and unjustly neglected work, superbly performed. The 1974 recording remains richly atmospheric in its CD format, with the opening pianissimos of the *Prelude* and second movement enhanced by the background quiet. Many will feel that the mistiness of the sound suits the music, although the *Scherzo* could ideally be more sharply focused. Holst's *Choral fantasia* – a setting of words written by Robert Bridges in commemoration of Purcell – was one of his later works, and probably the unusual combination of performers has prevented more frequent performances. It is not an easy work to grasp, and Holst's extremes of dynamic tend to hinder rather than help. But it is well worth getting to know. Dame Janet Baker once again shows her supreme quality as a recording artist. The success of the performance owes much to the inspired direction of the composer's daughter, Imogen Holst. The recording dates from 1964 – yet, though not lacking ambient colour and warmth, it is clearer than the coupling (indeed the organ pedals are only too clear). If not as open in sound as the companion Holst collection including the *Hymn of Jesus* – see above – still there is no lack of projection and vividness, and the bloom of the analogue original remains untarnished.

Dirge and Hymeneal, H. 124; 2 Motets, H. 159/60; 5 Part-songs, H. 61.
*** Conifer Dig. **CDCF 142**; *MCFC 142* [id.]. CBSO Ch., Halsey, R. Markham (piano) – ELGAR: *Scenes from the Bavarian Highlands.****

It is fascinating to find among these Holst part-songs the original musical idea that he used later in the *Saturn* movement of *The Planets* suite, with the piano accompaniment pivoting back and forth. That is from the *Dirge and Hymeneal*, withdrawn when *The Planets* appeared and never recorded before. The other items – all unaccompanied – bring writing just as hauntingly beautiful and original, not least the most demanding and ambitious of the items, the motet *The evening watch*, in eight parts, slow and hushed throughout. Beautiful, refined performances, atmospherically recorded. There is a good cassette.

(i) *Savitri* (complete); (ii) *Dream city* (song cycle, orch. Matthews).
(*) Hyp. Dig. **CDA 66099 [id.]. (i) Langridge, Varcoe, Palmer, Hickox Singers; (ii) Kwella; City of L. Sinf., Hickox.

There are few chamber operas so beautifully scaled as Holst's *Savitri*. The simple story is taken from a Sanskrit source – Savitri, a woodcutter's wife, cleverly outwits Death, who has come to take her husband – and Holst with beautiful feeling for atmosphere sets it in the most restrained way. With light texture and many slow tempi, it is a work which can fall apart in an uncommitted performance, but the Hyperion version makes an excellent alternative to Imogen Holst's earlier recording with Dame Janet Baker, bringing the positive advantage of fine digital recording. Felicity Palmer is more earthy, more vulnerable as Savitri, her grainy mezzo well caught. Philip Langridge and Stephen Varcoe both sing sensitively with fresh, clear tone, though their timbres are rather similar. Hickox is a thoughtful conductor both in the opera and in the orchestral song-cycle arranged by Colin Matthews (with Imogen Holst's approval) from Holst's settings of Humbert Wolfe poems. Patrizia Kwella's soprano at times catches the microphone rather shrilly.

Honegger, Arthur (1892–1955)

Concerto da camera.
** None. **CD 79018** [id.]. Shostac, Vogel, LACO, Schwarz – R. STRAUSS: *Duet concertino.***

Honegger's *Concerto da camera* for flute, cor anglais and strings comes from 1949. It is a work of immediate charm and strong appeal, and is as civilized and atmospheric as the *Fourth Symphony*. Good though not distinguished playing and recording.

Symphony No. 1; Pastorale d'été; 3 Symphonic movements: Pacific 231; Rugby; No. 3.
*** Erato Dig. **ECD 88171** [id.]. Bav. RSO, Dutoit.

Honegger's *First Symphony* is a highly stimulating and rewarding piece: its level of energy is characteristic of the later symphonies, and the slow movement has a dignity and eloquence that foreshadow the corresponding movements of the *Second* and *Third*. Charles Dutoit gets an excellent response from the Bavarian Radio Symphony Orchestra who produce a splendidly cultured sound and particularly beautiful phrasing in the slow movement. The couplings are generous. Dutoit gives an atmospheric and sympathetic account of the *Pastorale d'été* and offers also the *Three Symphonic movements*, of which *Pacific 231* with its robust and vigorous portrait of a railway engine is by far the best known. All three are well done, although *Rugby* may be a little genteel by comparison with Bernstein's CBS version; but the playing and recording are more than adequate compensation.

Symphonies Nos 2 & 3 (Symphonie liturgique).
(M) ❀ *** DG **423 242-2** [id.]. BPO, Karajan.

On its first appearance we greeted this as a first recommendation for both works and as 'an altogether marvellous record'. There is no reason to modify this view about the CD reissue: it includes arguably the finest versions of any Honegger works ever put on record. It is difficult to imagine any newcomer challenging either symphony in terms of performance; certainly none of the commercial recordings to have appeared since the 1940s, when the two symphonies were written, matches them, though Munch's two accounts of the *Second* and Mravinsky's *Liturgique* are very impressive. The Berlin strings in No. 2 have extraordinary sensitivity and expressive power, and Karajan conveys the sombre wartime atmosphere to perfection. At the same time, there is astonishing refinement of texture in the *Liturgique*, whose slow movement has never sounded more magical. The recording was always one of DG's best and this transfer brings to life more detail and greater body and range. A great record, completely in a class of its own.

Symphonies Nos 2; 4 (Deliciae Basiliensis).
(*) Erato Dig. **ECD 88178 [id.]. Bav. RSO, Dutoit.

Dutoit has the advantage of excellent recording. The perspective is completely natural and there is plenty of air around the various instruments, while detail is clean and well focused. He gets very cultured string playing from the Bavarian Radio orchestra in the dark, introspective *Symphony for strings*, and his performance is thoroughly meticulous in its observance of detail. But it is just a shade deficient in vitality and drive. The *Deliciae Basiliensis* also has rather measured tempi. However, this beautifully recorded performance is superior to Ansermet's and serves to rekindle enthusiasm for a much underrated work whose sunny countenance and keen nostalgia bring unfailing delight.

Symphonies Nos 3 (Liturgique); 4 (Deliciae Basiliensis).
(M) ** Decca *414 435-4* [id.]. SRO, Ansermet.

The *Fourth Symphony*, written for Paul Sacher and the Basle Chamber Orchestra (hence its title), is a charming work, full of character and invention, and probably the most relaxed, unpretentious and successful of the cycle. Quite frankly, the playing here does not do full justice to its lightness and wit; the orchestra is neither as alert nor as sensitive in its phrasing as one could wish. However, the 1969 Decca recording is extremely fine. The cassette, available for the first time, is precise and vivid in its orchestral detail, yet the ambient effect remains very convincing.

Symphonies Nos 3 (Symphonie liturgique); 5 (Di tre re).
** Erato **ECD 88045** [id.]. Bav. RSO, Dutoit.

The playing of the Bavarian Radio orchestra is alert and disciplined, and Dutoit gives thoroughly idiomatic accounts of both. In the *Fifth*, Dutoit does not galvanize his orchestra into playing of such volcanic fire and vitality as Serge Baudo secured from the Czech Philharmonic on Supraphon within his complete set of the five symphonies. Of course, the Erato recording is fresher and more detailed than the Supraphon, but in the *Liturgique* it is only marginally better than the DG, and the performance is not in the same street.

String quartets Nos 1–3.
*** Erato Dig. *MCE 75101* [id.]. Geneva Qt.

Only the *Second* of Honegger's three quartets has been available before in the UK (on Supraphon), and though the *First* was recorded way back in the days of shellac, no LP has ever collected all three. Harry Halbreich's excellent note reminds us that Honegger was himself attached to these works, in particular to the *First*. Its textures are dense and the lines chromatic and, as Honegger himself put it: 'It has its faults, its longueurs, but I recognize myself in it as in a mirror.' There is no doubting its seriousness of purpose or that of its two successors, which are less thick in texture and are notable for the dignity and interest of their slow movements. The excellent Quatuor de Genève were formed in 1966 and come from the Suisse Romande Orchestra. They play with total commitment and good sonority, and they are no less expertly recorded in a warm acoustic. Recommended.

Christmas cantata (*Cantate de Noël*).
*** HMV Dig. **CDC7 49559-2**; *EL 749559-4*. Sweeney, Waynflete Singers, Winchester Cathedral Ch., ECO, Neary – POULENC: *Mass; Motets.****
** Sup. Dig. **CO 1090** [id.]. Zitek, Kuhn Children's Ch., Czech PO, Pešek – POULENC: *Stabat Mater.***

At last a recording of Honegger's charming *Cantate de Noël* to do it full justice. Ansermet's mid-1960s account has served us well for the last two decades but this new EMI version is incomparably superior in every way. It was Honegger's last completed work and deserves to be more popular at the festive season outside France. The CD is impressively wide-ranging and well defined. The chrome cassette, transferred at a high level, has some loss of refinement at the loudest climaxes but certainly sounds vivid.

The only alternative comes from Supraphon, though it is differently coupled. However, the reverberant acoustic of the House of Artists in Prague poses problems and the choral sound is inclined to be opaque. Generally speaking the *Cantata* is decently sung and well played by these Czech forces under Libor Pešek, but ultimately it is a serviceable rather than a distinguished record.

Horovitz, Joseph (born 1926)

Alice in Wonderland (ballet) complete.
*** Max Sound Dig. Dolby B: *MSCB 1*; Dolby C: *MSCC 1*. Northern Sinfonia, composer.

Horovitz wrote the score for Anton Dolin Festival Ballet's production of *Alice in Wonderland* in 1953. The music itself is amiable and elegant, nicely scored and surely ideal for its purpose. Its invention is melodious in an easygoing way, with one quite memorable idea to represent Alice. The performance by the Northern Sinfonia under the composer is first rate, responsive, polished and spontaneous, while the kindly acoustics of Leeds Grammar School, where the recording was made, are suitably flattering. There is even a choice in the matter of cassette formats, with both Dolby B and Dolby C available, ordered by different catalogue numbers. The Dolby C transfer has a marginally cleaner treble response and slightly less hiss, but both cassettes have admirable presentation. Horovitz's music may be slight, but it is very agreeable. The recording is published independently by a small Yorkshire firm called Max Sound.

Hovhaness, Alan (born 1911)

(i) *Armenian rhapsody No. 1;* (ii) *Prayer of St Gregory;* (iii) *Symphony No. 11* (*All men are brothers*)*;* (i; iv) *Tzaikerk* (*Evening song*) *for flute, violin, strings & timpani.*
** Crystal **CD 801** [id.]. (i) Crystal CO, Ernest Gold with (ii) Stevens; (iv) Shapiro, Shanley; (iii) RPO, composer.

The *Symphony* is of little real substance. It is rather like film music, atmospheric and well scored, but wanting in distinctive personality or any sense of real movement. Nor is there too much to the companion pieces which try – and eventually exhaust – one's patience. Repetitive, modal doodling, spectacularly uninventive! The recording dates from 1970 and is worth two stars.

(i) *Artik concerto for horn and strings, Op. 78;* (ii) *Symphony No. 9* (*St Vartan*), *Op. 180.*
*** Crystal **CD 802** [id.]. (i) Meir Romin, Israel PO strings, David Amos; (ii) Nat. PO of London, composer.

The *Saint Vartan symphony* 'looms as one of Hovhaness' true masterpieces . . . a highly coloured, intensely emotional work . . . teeming with extraordinary invention and originality', claims the sleeve. Not so; indeed, anything but! There is little or no evidence of mastery, and precious little invention. Both works are static and wanting in rhythmic variety; the mysticism of the symphony borders on the unctuous and its pursuit of simplicity is unremitting. The three stars are to indicate good performances and excellent recording.

Symphony No. 24 (*Majnun symphony*), *Op. 273.*
*** Crystal **CD 803** [id.]. Hill, Wilbraham, Sax, John Alldis Ch., Nat. PO of London, composer.

The *Majnun symphony* was composed in 1973 in response to a commission from the International Center for Arid and Semi-arid Land Studies for Focus on the Arts Series at Texas Technical University. Unlikely though it may seem, we are not making this up – and arid is certainly the word for this musically uneventful and naïve composition. It is scored for tenor solo, mixed chorus, solo trumpet, solo violin and strings, and takes 48 minutes. It draws for its inspiration on *Salaman and Absal* by the Persian poet, Jami, and tells of the love of Majnun for Layla. For those bold enough to sample this for themselves, the recording, made in 1974, is eminently satisfactory.

Howells, Herbert (1892–1983)

Collegium Regale; St Paul's service.
(M) *** Argo *414 646-4* [id.]. King's College, Cambridge, Ch., Willcocks; Andrew Davis (organ) (with VAUGHAN WILLIAMS: *Songs****).

The outstanding item in these reissued 1967 Argo performances of Howells's music is the setting of Anglican morning and evening services he wrote for this very choir of King's College, Cambridge (hence the title *Collegium Regale*). Few settings of Matins and Evensong rival it in the sensitivity and aptness of word treatment, and the *Gloria* is almost unequalled in Anglican church music for the exuberance and intensity of joy it conveys. Not that the King's Choir quite launch into the music as one knows from live performances in the past they can do. Even so, it is good to have this music so well performed, and the St Paul's setting of Evensong (more obviously influenced by the French impressionists) is welcome on record too, not to mention the other less well-known items. Excellent recording on the impressive high-level cassette.

Requiem.
*** Hyp. **CDA 66076**; *KA 66076* [id.]. Corydon Singers, Best – VAUGHAN WILLIAMS: *Mass*; *Te Deum.****

Howells's *Requiem* was composed in the immediate aftermath of his son's death, and some of its material was reworked in the *Hymnus Paradisi.* In some ways this piece, which he released for publication only three years before his death, is more concentrated and direct than the *Hymnus*, its language shorn of any artifice. This is a most moving piece and one of the crowns of English church music. The Corydon Singers sing with conviction and eloquence, and the recording, made in a spacious acoustic, serves them and the composer well.

Hummel, Johann (1778–1837)

Piano concertos: in A min., Op. 85; B min., Op. 89.
*** Chan. Dig. **CHAN 8505**; *ABTD 1217* [id.]. Stephen Hough, ECO, Bryden Thomson.

Hummel has always occupied a somewhat peripheral position in the catalogue, though he was obviously a musician of remarkable powers. The *A minor* is his most often-heard piano concerto, albeit in a broadcasting context rather than in the concert hall (though it has been recorded commercially, by Artur Balsam and Martin Galling among others). Never better, however, than by Stephen Hough on this Chandos disc. The coda of the *A minor Concerto* is quite stunning; it is not only his dazzling virtuosity that carries all before it but also the delicacy and refinement of colour he produces. The *B minor*, Op. 89, is more of a rarity, and is given with the same blend of virtuosity and poetic feeling which Hough brought to its companion. Of course, neither attains the quality of inspiration of the Chopin concertos, but they are far from inferior to Mendelssohn's and Weber's essays in this genre. Stephen Hough is given expert support by Bryden Thomson and the ECO – and the recording is first class, no less so on tape than on disc.

Trumpet concerto in E.
❀ *** Ph. Dig. **420 203-2**; *420 203-4* [id.]. Hardenberger, ASMF, Marriner – HAYDN ***❀; HERTEL***; STAMITZ: *Concertos.****

Trumpet concerto in E flat.
*** Delos Dig. **D/CD 3001** [id.]. Schwarz, New York 'Y' CO – HAYDN: *Concerto.****
*** CBS **CD 37846** [id.]. Marsalis, Nat. PO, Leppard – HAYDN: *Concerto**** (with L. MOZART: *Concerto*).
** Erato Dig. **ECD 88007**; *MCE 75026* [id.]. André, Paris O Ens., Wallez – NERUDA; TELEMANN: *Concertos.***

Hummel's *Trumpet concerto* is usually heard in the familiar brass key of E flat, but the brilliant Swedish trumpeter, Håkan Hardenberger, uses the key of E which makes it sound brighter and bolder than usual (though the marvellously assured playing makes a considerable contribution to this). Neither he nor Marriner miss the genial lilt inherent in the dotted theme of the first movement, yet this seductive element is set off by the brassy masculinity of the actual timbre. The slow-movement cantilena soars beautifully over its jogging pizzicato accompaniment, and the finale captivates the ear with its high spirits and easy bravura; Hardenberger's crisp tonguing and tight trills are of the kind to make you smile with pleasure. This is the finest version of the piece in the catalogue, for Marriner's accompaniment is polished and sympathetic. The recording projects the vibrant trumpet image forward with great presence, and the only slight complaint is that the orchestral recording is a shade too reverberant. There is an excellent tape that seems to find no transfer problems in the resonance.

Both Schwarz and Marsalis give fine accounts of Hummel's *Concerto*, but neither player quite catches its full galant charm. In matters of bravura, however, neither can be faulted; on Schwarz's lips the slow movement's melodic line is nobly contoured. Both artists relish the sparkling finale. If Marsalis is more reserved in the slow movement, he has the advantage of very fine accompaniment from Leppard, and the CBS record includes a substantial extra work. Both CDs give their respective soloists striking presence; the CBS orchestral sound is relatively dry by comparison with the more flatteringly resonant New York acoustic. Schwarz directs his own accompaniments very ably.

Needless to say, Maurice André is also an expert player; but Wallez's direction of the first movement is square and the genial jauntiness of its character is lost.

Introduction, theme and variations in F minor/major.
(M) *** Ph. *412 354-4*. Holliger, ECO, Leppard – J. C. BACH: *Oboe concerto*; FIALA: *Cor anglais concerto.****

This is most appealing music, especially when played with such elegant virtuosity. Holliger holds the attention, whether in the ingenuous lyrical writing or the delicacy of his bravura; and with the accompaniment attractively scored, Leppard's contribution is equally enjoyable. Excellent recording.

Grand military septet in C, Op. 114.
*** CRD *CRDC 4090* [id.]. Nash Ens. – KREUTZER: *Septet.****

Hummel's *Military septet* is not really as grand as its name implies. It features a trumpet, certainly, but that makes a major contribution only in the third movement, although in the first its fanfare-like interjections do bring in a somewhat refined reminder of the work's title. The invention throughout is ingenuous but attractive, particularly in such a delightfully spontaneous account as is provided by the Nash Ensemble. There is sparkle and warmth, and the playing itself has beguiling elegance. The recording is superb and the balance of the trumpet part (very nicely played by James Watson) is most felicitous. Highly recommended, especially in view of the apt coupling.

Septet in D min., Op. 74.
*** CRD *CRDC 4044*. Nash Ens. – BERWALD: *Septet.****

Septet in D min., Op. 74; Piano quintet in E flat, Op. 87.
*** Decca *417 635-4* [id.]. Lamar Crowson, Melos Ens. of L.

Hummel's *Septet* is an enchanting and inventive work with a virtuoso piano part, expertly dispatched here by Clifford Benson. The *Septet* is full of vitality, and its scherzo in particular has enormous charm and individuality. A fine performance and excellent recording make this a desirable issue, particularly in view of the enterprising coupling, which is not otherwise available. The cassette is up to the usual high standard of CRD chamber-music tapes: the sound has warmth and bloom, with good detail.

The alternative Decca London Enterprise tape is a straight reissue of a famous Oiseau-Lyre record of the mid-1960s. These two most engaging works both show the composer at his most melodically fecund and his musical craftsmanship at its most apt. One can see here how Hummel charmed nineteenth-century audiences into regarding him as a greater composer than he was, for his facility and skill at shaping and balancing a movement can be impressive. It is the ideas themselves (as in all music) that make or break the structure, and here they are entirely appropriate to music designed in the first instance to entertain. This these works certainly do in such spontaneous and polished performances, and the high-level cassette transfer certainly projects the music making vividly.

Violin sonatas: in E flat, Op. 5/3; in D, Op. 50; Nocturne, Op. 99.
*** Amon Ra **CD-SAR 12** [id.]. Ralph Holmes, Richard Burnett.

It is important to set the volume control exactly right – not too loud – and then one can get a most realistic effect from this forward but well-balanced recording. Ralph Holmes's violin timbre is bright and the Graf fortepiano under the fingers of Richard Burnett has plenty of colour and does not sound clattery. The *D major Sonata*, which comes first, is a very striking work with hints of early Beethoven, but the *D flat Sonata*, written a decade and a half earlier in 1798, has a memorably eloquent slow movement which shows Ralph Holmes at his finest. Throughout, this is a felicitous and understanding partnership; Richard Burnett has a chance to catch the ear in the finale of the *D major Sonata* when he uses the quaintly rasping cembalo device (without letting it outstay its welcome). *The Nocturne* is an extended piece (nearly 16′) in variation form and it is a pity that the CD, while banding the movements of the two sonatas, does not provide more internal cues. A thoroughly worthwhile issue, 'authentic' in the most convincing way, which shows this engaging composer at his most assured and inventive.

Piano sonatas: Nos 1 in C, Op. 2/3; 6 in D, Op. 106.
** Ara. Dig. **Z 6564**; *ABQC 6564* [id.]. Ian Hobson.

Piano sonatas: Nos 2 in E flat, Op. 13; 5 in F sharp min., Op. 81.
** Ara. Dig. **Z 6565**; *ABQC 6565* [id.]. Ian Hobson.

Piano sonatas: Nos 3 in F min., Op. 20; 4 in C, Op. 38.
** Ara Dig. **Z 6566**; *ABQC 6566* [id.]. Ian Hobson.

As Frank Cooper reminds us in his excellent note, Hummel succeeded Haydn at Esterháza and preceded Liszt at Weimar; he counted Goethe and Beethoven among his friends, Mozart and Haydn among his teachers and Mendelssohn among his pupils. The first of his six *Piano sonatas* was composed in 1792 when he was fourteen, and the last more than thirty years later in 1824. As one might expect from hearing the award-winning record of the two *Concertos*, these are enormously fluent works, close to Clementi at the early end of his career and to Weber in the brilliant finale of No. 4. They are not innovative in style but they have undoubted charm. Though the music offers great expressive depths to explore, it is always accomplished and well crafted, the product of fine intelligence. Ian Hobson, a former Leeds prizewinner, plays with enormous facility and clarity of articulation. The recordings are alive and present, though the instrument goes out of tune in the slow movement of No. 4. Of the six, this and the *F sharp minor Sonata* (No. 5) make a good starting point. There are admirably faithful cassettes.

Humperdinck, Engelbert (1854–1921)

Hansel and Gretel.
(M) *** HMV **CMS7 69293-2** (2) [id.]; *EX 769293-4*. Schwarzkopf, Grümmer, Metternich, Ilsovay, Schürhoff, Felbermayer, Children's Ch., Philh. O, Karajan.
(*) Decca **421 111-2 (2) [id.]. Fassbaender, Popp, Berry, Hamari, Schlemm, Burrowes, Gruberova, V. Boys' Ch., VPO, Solti.
* Tel. Dig. **ZA8 35074** (2) [id.]. Springer, Hoff, Adam, Schröter, Schreier, Dresden Kreuzchor & State O, Suitner.

Karajan's classic 1950s set of Humperdinck's children's opera, with Schwarzkopf and Grümmer peerless in the name-parts, is enchanting; this was an instance where everything in the recording went right. The original mono LP set was already extremely atmospheric. One notices that the main image stays centrally situated between the speakers, but in all other respects the sound has as much clarity and warmth as rival recordings made in the 1970s. There is much to delight here; the smaller parts are beautifully done and Else Schürhoff's Witch is memorable. The snag is that the digital remastering has brought a curious orchestral bass emphasis, noticeable in the Overture and elsewhere, but notably in the *Witch's ride*. This is acceptable on CD but not on the cassettes, which are very boomy at times.

Solti with the Vienna Philharmonic directs a strong, spectacular version, emphasizing the Wagnerian associations of the score. It is well sung – both principals are engaging – but just a little short on charm. The solo singing is not as steady in tone as on the EMI set, and the lack of geniality in the atmosphere is a drawback in a work of this nature. Needless to say, Solti does the *Witch's ride* excitingly, and the VPO are encouraged to play with consistent fervour throughout. Edita Gruberova is an excellent Dew Fairy and Walter Berry is first rate as Peter. Anny Schlemm's Witch is a very strong characterization indeed and there are some imaginative touches of stereo production associated with *Hocus pocus* and her other moments of magic. The recording is even more vivid in its CD transfer, but its sense of spectacle does not erase one's memories of the Karajan version.

Suitner conducts a bright, direct reading of this fairy-tale opera, cleanly and forwardly recorded. There is little or no magic in the atmosphere, whether in the sound or the performance, and the often unsteady Gretel of Renate Hoff is most unconvincing. The Hänsel of Ingeborg Springer is much more effective; of the women singers, Gisela Schröter as the children's mother is the most characterful. The role of the Witch is taken by a tenor, Peter Schreier. That device is dramatically unconvincing with so distinctively male a voice, but at least it avoids the usually exaggerated whining delivery which women singers generally assume in this role.

Ibert, Jacques (1890–1962)

Bacchanale; Bostoniana; Divertissement; Louisville concerto; Symphonie marine.
(*) HMV **CDC7 49261-2; (M) *ED 291344-4*. CBSO. Frémaux.

An enterprising reissue from the mid-1970s; but, truth to tell, for the most part the performances and recording are better than the music itself. The *Louisville concerto* – more a concerto grosso – is agreeable and the *Symphonie marine* has some good atmospheric effects, but much of this writing seems over-extended in relation to its invention. The *Divertissement* is a different matter, showing this often charming composer at his most wittily exuberant. It is played with gusto and enthusiasm, and the digital remastering has brought a better focus to the recording, which was originally too reverberant. While the CD offers the best sound, the tape is well managed and provides a more economical way to sample this second-line repertoire.

Flute concerto.
(M) *** RCA *GK 85448* [*AGK1 5448*]. Galway, RPO, Dutoit – CHAMINADE: *Concertino*; FAURÉ: *Fantaisie*; POULENC: *Sonata*.***

Ibert's high-spirited and inventive *Concerto* deserves the widest currency; it is full of charm and lyrical appeal, particularly when it is as well performed as it is here by James Galway and the RPO under Charles Dutoit. Moreover, it has the distinct advantage of highly attractive couplings. It will be difficult to supersede this version, which enjoys a clear, spacious recording which has been digitally remastered. The cassette quality has a degree of edge on the flute timbre and the strings, but it is not difficult to smooth.

d'India, Sigismondo (*c.* 1582–*c.* 1630)

Amico hai vint'io; Diana (Questo dardo, quest' arco); Misera me (Lamento d'Olympia); Piangono al pianger mio; Sfere fermate; Torna il sereno zefiro.
*** Hyp. **CDA 66106** [id.]. Emma Kirkby, Anthony Rooley (chitarone) – MONTEVERDI: *Lamento d'Olympia* etc.***

All these pieces are rarities. They are also of very great interest. Sigismondo d'India's setting of the *Lamento d'Olympia* makes a striking contrast to Monteverdi's on the other side, and is hardly less fine. This is an affecting and beautiful piece and so are its companions, particularly when they are as superbly sung and sensitively accompanied as they are here. A very worthwhile CD début.

Indian music

Ragas: Gara; Hameer; Mohan Kauns (Homage to Mahatma Gandhi). Talas: Farodast; Tintal. Improvisation on the theme of Rokudan.
(B) *** DG Walkman *415 621-4* [id.]. Ravi Shankar (sitar), Alla Rakha (tabla), Prodyot Sen (bass tanpura), Sunil Kumar Banerjee (treble tanpura), Mrs Jiban (2, 3), Mrs Widya (2–4) (tanpuras), Susumu Miyashita (koto), Horzan Tyamamoto (shakuhachi).

This recording comes outside our terms of reference, but undoubtedly Indian music has a fascination for many Western listeners, and its sounds, textures and tensions cannot fail to communicate when the performances are as authentic and committed as they are here. The recording gives the instrumentalists good presence and this is an inexpensive way of making a first exploration. It is a great pity that no proper documentation or background information is provided, to help the listener find his or her way about.

d'Indy, Vincent (1851–1931)

Diptyque méditerranéan; Poème des rivages (symphonic suite).
**(*) HMV Dig. *EL 270335-4*. Monte Carlo PO, Prêtre.

Neither work represents d'Indy at his most consistently inspired but there are still good things. As Martin Cooper put it in his study of French music, 'in the *Poème des rivages* [d'Indy] distilled the last drops of that honey he had gathered so assiduously in the garden of Franck'. The comparison often made between the *Diptyque* and the glorious *Jour d'été à la montagne* is not flattering. But the *Soleil matinal* of the *Diptyque* has that blend of the Wagner of *Parsifal* and a quality of conservative impressionism that d'Indy made so much his own after the turn of the century. There are considerable beauties in this piece and in the *Poème* and, though the recording is not top-drawer, this is still worth investigating, despite some unequalness of inspiration. The cassette is well transferred, clear and with plenty of atmosphere and warmth, although the massed violin timbre is a little thin. We assume a CD will appear in due course.

Symphonie sur un chant montagnard français (Symphonie cévenole).
*** Conifer Dig. **CDFC 146**; *MCFC 146*. Michel Block, Berne SO, Peter Maag – MARTINŮ: *Rhapsody-Concerto*.***

Vincent d'Indy's most famous work, the *Symphony on a French mountain air*, subtitled *Symphonie cévenole*, is neither a symphony nor really a concertante work, for although the piano part employs a wide range of keyboard devices, it eschews virtuosity and assumes rather an obbligato role. Michel Block won Rubinstein's acclaim at Warsaw coinciding with Pollini's rise to prominence. A sensitive and intelligent player, he gives a sympathetic account of this strange but, in his hands, appealing work. The recording is well balanced, the piano slightly but not unrealistically forward, and the perspective is natural: it could perhaps open out more at climaxes and the very top of the piano is less transparent than is ideal. However, at present there is no alternative and, even were one to appear, few would regret investing in this thoroughly recommendable issue. The chrome cassette is first class in all respects, truthful in timbre and balance.

Ippolitov-Ivanov, Mikhail (1859–1935)

Caucasian sketches (suite), *Op. 10.*
(M)** Olympia **OCD 107** [id.]. USSR RSO, Fedoseyev – ARENSKY: *Piano concerto* etc.**

The *Caucasian sketches* are justly famed for a single number, the *Procession of the Sardar*, much loved on bandstands and, in the past, on seaside piers. The other three items rely mainly on atmosphere for their appeal, and their orientalism is more redolent of the *Desert song* than of a convincing folk-idiom. Nevertheless the picaresque writing is effectively presented here, and the recording is fully acceptable.

Ireland, John (1879–1962)

Piano concerto in E flat.
*** Unicorn **DKPCD 9056**; *DKPC 9056* [id.]. Tozer, Melbourne SO, Measham – RUBBRA: *Violin concerto.****

Piano concerto in E flat; Legend for piano and orchestra; Mai-Dun (symphonic rhapsody).
*** Chan. Dig. **CHAN 8461**; *ABTD 1174* [id.]. Parkin, LPO, Thomson.

John Ireland's only *Piano concerto* has recently come back into favour and can now sometimes be heard in the concert hall as well as on records. Its previous neglect is undeserved. Its distinctive melodic inspiration throughout all three movements and its poetic lyricism are in the best traditions of the finest English music. Eric Parkin recorded the *Concerto* with Sir Adrian Boult for Lyrita in the 1960s: his is a splendidly refreshing and sparkling performance and benefits from excellent support from Bryden Thomson and the LPO. They are no less impressive in *Mai-Dun* and the beautiful *Legend for piano and orchestra.* Obviously those with a keener interest in John Ireland will gravitate to this Chandos issue, particularly in view of the wonderfully present and detailed recording and the excellent equivalent chrome cassette. The somewhat greater transparency of the texture tells very much in favour of this CD, though the attraction of the Rubbra *Violin concerto* on the competing Unicorn issue will sway some collectors, for it is a work of considerable substance.

Geoffrey Tozer also gives a characterful account of Ireland's lyrical and often whimsical *Concerto*. It wears well and its charms have not faded in the half-century or more since it was composed. Tozer conveys the poetic feel of the slow movement and, though he takes a rather measured tempo in the finale, the music loses none of its freshness. The recording is a little studio-bound, and a slightly more open acoustic would have been preferable – but too much should not be made of this. Doubtless the coupling will decide matters for most collectors but, as far as the *Concerto* itself is concerned, Tozer is a safe choice, and the chrome cassette can be recommended alongside the CD.

A Downland suite; Elegiac meditation; The Holy Boy.
*** Chan. Dig. **CHAN 8390**; *ABTD 1112* [id.]. ECO, David Garforth – BRIDGE: *Suite for strings.****

When he is played as well as he is here, one is tempted to call Ireland one of the finest and most individual of English composers of his day. David Garforth and the ECO play with total conviction and seem wholly attuned to Ireland's sensibility. *A Downland suite* was originally written for brass band, and in 1941 Ireland began to make a version for strings. As was the case with the *Comedy overture* for brass band which he rewrote in 1936, he completely reconceived it. However, his reworking was interrupted by the German invasion of the Channel Islands and he never resumed work on it. The present version was finished and put into shape by Geoffrey Bush, who also transcribed the *Elegiac meditation*. The recording is first class, clear and naturally balanced; the chrome cassette offers a slightly softer-grained string mixture, but its diffuse warmth especially suits the lovely miniature, *The Holy Boy*.

Cello sonata.
(*) ASV *ZCACA 1001*. Lloyd Webber, McCabe – BRIDGE: *Elegy*; BRITTEN: *Suite.**

The *Cello sonata* is among Ireland's most richly inspired works, a broad-spanning piece in which ambitious, darkly intense outer movements frame one of his most beautiful slow movements. Julian Lloyd Webber, who has long been a passionate advocate of the work, here conveys its full expressive power. The piano is placed at a distance, but perhaps that is apt for a work in which the cello should be presented in full strength. The cassette is of good quality, though the resonance means that the focus is not absolutely sharp.

Ives, Charles (1874–1954)

Symphonies Nos 1 in D min; 2.
(M) **(*) Decca *414 661-4*. LAPO, Mehta.

Ives's engaging *First Symphony*, a student work much influenced by Dvořák and Tchaikovsky but still with touches of individuality, is given a first-class performance by Mehta. The pity is that he makes a substantial cut in the finale to make it 'more compact and convincing', and one is inevitably suspicious of such claims. The performance of the *Second*, a more uneven work, is also highly committed and very well played. Both recordings stem from the 1970s and are extremely vivid, though the high level of the present tape transfer has brought a dryness to the bass, with the upper strings less than ideally expansive.

Symphony No. 3 (The Camp meeting).
*** Argo **417 818-2**; *KZRC 845* [id.]. ASMF, Marriner – BARBER: *Adagio*; COPLAND: *Quiet City*; COWELL: *Hymn*; CRESTON: *Rumor*.***
*** Pro Arte Dig. **CCD 140** [id.]. St Paul CO, Russell Davies – COPLAND: *Appalachian spring* etc.***

Symphony No. 3 (The Camp meeting); (i) *Orchestral set No. 2.*
*** CBS Dig. **MK 37823**; *IMT 37823* [id.]. Concg. O, Tilson Thomas; (i) with Concg. Ch.

Tilson Thomas's version of Ives's most approachable symphony is the first to use the new critical edition, prepared with reference to newly available Ives manuscripts. Thanks to that and to Tilson Thomas's clear, incisive manner, it avoids any hint of blandness; the *Second Orchestral set*, with its three substantial atmosphere pieces, brings performances of a sharpness to back up the characteristically wordy titles – *An elegy to our forefathers*, *The rockstrewn hills join in the people's outdoor meeting* and *From Hanover Square North at the end of a tragic day the voice of the people again arose*. That last and most vivid of the pieces was written in 1915 as a direct response to the sinking of the *Lusitania*. First-rate recording to match the fine performances, especially refined and atmospheric on CD, but also sounding well on tape.

Russell Davies does not use the new edition of Ives's score; nevertheless, he gives a fine account of this gentlest of Ives's symphonies, with its overtones of hymn singing and revivalist meetings. It makes a good coupling for the fine Copland works on the reverse. Though the forward, relatively intimate acoustic may not evoke a church atmosphere at all, the beauty of the piece still comes over strongly.

Marriner's account is first rate in every way. It does not have the advantage of a digital master, but the 1976 analogue recording has slightly sharper detail in this remastered format. The performance has plenty of conviction; moreover it comes as part of an anthology that is of unusual interest and merit. There is an excellent cassette.

Symphony No. 4.
(*) Chan. Dig. **CHAN 8397; *ABTD 1118* [id.]. John Alldis Ch., LPO, Serebrier.

Ives's *Fourth Symphony*, scored for an immense orchestra, was not finally brought to the light of performance until long after the composer's death, when Stokowski and the All American Symphony Orchestra gave it in New York some half-century after it was written. American critics predictably greeted it as a masterpiece, and if it is hardly that (even by Ives's standards) it has a marvellous array of musical squibs and caprices that never let the listener go. The *Allegretto* second movement (not so much a scherzo as a bare-faced comedy) is another of Ives's mixed-up brass-band pieces, but for all the ingenuity and breathlessness of so many tunes being mixed together (with *Columbia, gem of the ocean* triumphing as usual) it does not quite match the best of the genre. The plain truth seems to be that Ives's most intense inspirations came when he limited himself to a single piece; though he was a big enough man to encompass symphony-length, it was difficult for him to fit the pieces together. Even so, no Ives enthusiast should miss this preposterous work. Stokowski's recording is currently not available in the UK.

José Serebrier acted as subsidiary conductor for Stokowski when he conducted the world première of this audacious and complex work in New York. In this English performance he somehow manages to find his way through multi-layered textures which have deliberately conflicting rhythms. The players respond loyally, and the movement representing *Chaos* is particularly colourful and dramatic in its sharp contrasts of dynamic, brutal but somehow poetic. *Order* is represented by a fugue, and the finale brings an apotheosis, a vivid, gripping work, but maybe not as great as some American commentators originally thought. For the record collector at least, it provides a store-house of fantastic orchestral sound, in a recording as vivid as this, particularly in its CD format. The chrome tape is impressive, too, though in the more spectacular moments the resonance brings a slight reduction in the sharpness of focus.

Songs: *Autumn; Berceuse; The cage; Charlie Rutlage; Down East; Dreams; Evening; The greatest man; The Housatonic at Stockbridge; Immortality; Like a sick eagle; Maple leaves; Memories: 1, 2, 3; On the counter; Romanzo di Central Park; The see'r; Serenity; The side-show; Slow march; Slugging a vampire; Songs my mother taught me; Spring song; The things our fathers loved; Tom sails away; Two little flowers.*
*** Etcetera Dig. **KTC 1020** [id.]. Roberta Alexander, Tan Crone.

Roberta Alexander presents her excellent and illuminating choice of Ives songs – many of them otherwise unavailable on record – in chronological order, starting with one written when Ives was only fourteen, *Slow march*, already predicting developments ahead. Sweet nostalgic songs predominate, but the singer punctuates them with leaner, sharper inspirations. Her manner is not always quite tough enough in those, but this is characterful singing from an exceptionally rich and attractive voice. Tan Crone is the understanding accompanist, and the recording is first rate.

Jacob, Gordon (1895–1987)

Oboe quartet.
*** Chan. Dig. **CHAN 8392**; *ABTD 1114* [id.]. Francis, English Qt – BAX: *Quintet*; HOLST: *Air and variations* etc.; MOERAN: *Fantasy quartet*.***

Gordon Jacob's four-movement *Oboe quartet* is the slightest of the four works included in this admirable anthology, but is none the less very welcome. It is well crafted and entertaining, particularly the vivacious final Rondo. The performance could hardly be bettered, and the recording is excellent too, highly effective in both media.

Janáček, Leoš (1854–1928)

(i) *Capriccio for piano left hand, and wind instruments; Sonata 1.x.1905.*
*(*) Hyp. *KA 66167* [id.]. Papadopoulos, (i) with RPO – STRAVINSKY: *Concerto for piano and winds.**(*)

Marios Papadopoulos is a young Cypriot-born pianist who has made quite a name for himself as a soloist. He gives a ruminative, thoughtful account of the *Sonata* to which few will fail to respond. The *Capriccio for piano left hand*, which Papadopoulos directs from the keyboard, is not so successful. The performance is less well held together and not quite incisive enough; memories of Firkusny are not effaced. The piano, recorded in Rosslyn Hill Chapel, is occasionally swamped by the brass and has an unpleasing twang. The cassette is acceptable, but the resonance tends to blunt the focus.

(i) *Danube symphony; Idyll for strings.*
(*) Sup. Dig. **CO 1150 [id.]. (i) Jonasova; Janáček PO, Trhlik.

Readers who have not heard of the *Danube symphony* need not reproach themselves. After the successful performances of *Kátya Kabanová* in Bratislava in 1922, Janáček conceived the idea of a four-movement symphony in celebration of the Danube. It occupied him during the period 1923–8 and was left incomplete on his death. His student, Oswald Chlubna (transliterated back from the Japanese notes as Frubna), put it into performing shape; and it was first performed in 1948 by the Brno Radio Orchestra. This account restores the high-flying soprano part Janáček originally intended in the scherzo movement. It is a shortish work of some 17 minutes' duration, full of characteristically quirky touches. It is no lost masterpiece and is more rhapsodic than symphonic in character, but as always with Janáček there are wonderfully imaginative moments. The playing is committed, though the strings of the Ostrava orchestra could have greater warmth and sonority. (Not that it is vitally important, but the notes are riddled with errors and misprints: they tell us that Janáček was 'found' of the lovely old 'twon' (Bratislava)!) The *Idyll* is nicely played under Otakar Trhlik: here the recording is perfectly acceptable though not outstanding.

Idyll for strings; Lachian dances.
** Erato Dig. **ECD 88095** [id.]. Rotterdam PO, Conlon.

(i) *Idyll for strings;* (ii) *Mládi for wind sextet.*
(*) None. Dig. **CD 79033 [id.]. (i) LACO, Schwarz; (ii) Los Angeles Wind Ens.

Mládi.
(*) DG Dig. **415 668-2 [id.]. Orpheus CO – BARTÓK: *Divertimento* etc.**(*)

Mládi (*Youth*) is a work of Janáček's old age and the *Idyll*, for strings, a product of his youth. The latter, written in 1878 when he was in his early twenties, springs from the tradition of Dvořák, though its thematic material lacks the spontaneity and freshness of that master. It is very persuasively played by the Los Angeles Chamber Orchestra, under Gerard Schwarz, and they are sensitive to dynamic nuances and shape phrases with imagination; the sound is very lifelike and clean. The wind players of the Los Angeles Chamber Orchestra play marvellously and with altogether superb ensemble and blend. They show sensitivity, too, in the *Andante sostenuto* (particularly from fig. 6 onwards), though they are not helped by the recording balance. They are placed very forward, though the acoustic is warm and the detail remarkably clean.

On the DG version, the coupling is more generous than that offered by Schwarz, the playing is excellent and the recording very realistic. Tempi may at times seem brisker by comparison with some past performances on record, but the music is never made to seem hurried. This makes a fine alternative for those preferring the pairing with Bartók.

Idyll and the *Lachian dances*, both being early works, make a logical coupling; though neither is vintage Janáček, they have no want of appeal. James Conlon gets very good playing from the Rotterdam orchestra, but neither performance has quite the spirit and character one finds from native artists. These are capable and eminently well-recorded accounts that give pleasure.

Sinfonietta.
*** HMV Dig. **CDC7 47504-2** [id.]. Philh. O, Rattle – *Glagolitic mass.****
** HMV **CDC7 47837-2** [id.]. Chicago SO, Ozawa – BARTÓK: *Concerto for orchestra.***

Sinfonietta; Taras Bulba (*rhapsody*).
*** Decca Dig. **410 138-2**; *KSXDC 7519* [Lon. *LDR5-71021*]. VPO, Mackerras.
*** HMV Dig. **CDC7 47048-2** [id]. Philh. O, Rattle.
*** Sup. Dig. **C37 7056** [id.]. Czech PO, Neumann.

Mackerras's coupling comes as a superb supplement to his Janáček opera recordings with the Vienna Philharmonic. The massed brass of the *Sinfonietta* has tremendous bite and brilliance as well as characteristic Viennese ripeness, thanks to a spectacular digital recording. *Taras Bulba* too is given more weight and body than is usual, the often savage dance rhythms presented with great energy. The cassette has comparable brilliance and range, although on some machines the upper range is fierce and needs taming. The compact disc thrillingly combines tangibility and presence with atmosphere, and increases the sense of a natural perspective.

Simon Rattle and the Philharmonia give impressive performances that can hold their own with most rivals and will provide a fine CD alternative to Mackerras and the Vienna Philharmonic on Decca. Rattle gets an altogether first-class response from the orchestra and truthful recorded sound from the EMI engineers. The only quibble as far as recording is concerned (the excessively distant and pianissimo organ at bar 22 of *Taras Bulba*) still holds good in the compact disc format. The rival Decca recording is a hi-fi spectacular, with rather forward placing and a hint of aggression; many collectors may find the EMI sound more pleasing. The Decca has greater clarity and presence in its favour, as well as Mackerras's authority in this repertoire. However, Rattle's alternative coupling with the *Glagolitic mass* is very attractive indeed and will be first choice for many collectors.

Neumann's recording with the Czech Philharmonic is also eminently recommendable. This conductor is often dull, but these performances have a distinctive flavour. The textures are marvellously transparent and light, and the Czech players have just the right colour and internal blend. Moreover, Neumann keeps a firm grip on the proceedings without ever seeming in the least inflexible. The recording is set back rather more than the current rivals, with some loss of immediacy but not of truthfulness. Those looking for the highest-fi and maximum impact will gravitate towards the Mackerras on Decca or Simon Rattle on HMV; but Neumann and the Czechs are a viable alternative, and some will actually prefer them for their complete naturalness.

The Chicago Symphony Orchestra play brilliantly under Ozawa, but the recording dates from the beginning of the 1970s and the CD transfer has failed to open up the brass fortissimos convincingly, and elsewhere the sound lacks depth. This reissue is overpriced.

String quartets Nos 1 (*Kreutzer sonata*); *2* (*Intimate pages*).
*** Sup. **C37 7545** [id.]. Smetana Qt.
** Sup. Dig. **CO 1130** [id.]. Smetana Qt.

The Smetana Quartet offer two versions of the Janáček *Quartets*. The first is analogue and was made in 1976. These are splendidly authoritative and intense accounts that can hold their own with distinguished earlier issues on LP by the Gabrielis and Medicis. The aural image is boldly defined and very realistic, though perhaps a richer sound could have been achieved.

The later coupling was made in 1979 at a live concert in the Dvořák Hall. The playing has intensity and attack though there are occasional moments of roughness. The audience is admirably quiet, but the recording is somewhat forwardly balanced and could be richer tonally.

VOCAL MUSIC

Amarus (cantata).
*** Sup. Dig. **C37 7735** [id.]. Němečková, Vodička, Zítek, Czech Philharmonic Ch. and O, Mackerras – MARTINŮ; *Field mass.****

Amarus is relatively early, coming from 1897, well before *Jenůfa*. It is a powerfully written piece whose individuality was acknowledged by Dvořák, to whom Janáček sent the score. It is full of atmosphere and has a real sense of movement. The choral writing is powerful and the orchestration skilful and imaginative. The performance is a fine one; the recording is excellent on CD, which enjoys the usual advantages of the medium, greater range and body; the only minor grumble is that the soloists are a little too closely balanced. But this is strongly recommended and supersedes the earlier version by Vaclav Neumann on all counts.

The Diary of one who disappeared (song cycle).
(*) Sup. Dig. **C37 7541** [id.]. Soukupová, Gedda, Prague R. Female Chamber Ch., Josef Páleníček (piano).

Janáček's haunting song-cycle is not otherwise represented in the current compact disc catalogue, but this 1985 account from Nicolai Gedda and Czech artists cannot be recommended. The voice is now sadly showing strain and has lost its vocal bloom, particularly at the top end of the register. Indeed, tonally there is none of the quality and lustre one recalls from the days of LP. The recorded sound is wonderfully clear and the contributions of the chorus and the pianist, Josef Páleníček, are admirable.

Glagolitic mass.
*** HMV Dig. **CDC7 47504-2** [id.]. Palmer, Gunson, Mitchinson, King, CBSO & Ch., Rattle – *Sinfonietta.****
*** Sup. **C37 7448** [id.]. Söderström, Drobková, Livora, Novák, Prague Philharmonic Ch., Czech PO, Mackerras.

Written when Janáček was over seventy, this is one of his most important and most exciting works, full of those strikingly fresh uses of sound that make his music so distinctive. The opening instrumental movement has much in common with the opening fanfare of the *Sinfonietta*, and all the other movements reveal an original approach to the church service. The text is taken from native Croatian variations of the Latin text, but its vitality bespeaks a folk inspiration. Rattle's performance, aptly paired with the *Sinfonietta*, is strong and vividly dramatic, with the Birmingham performers lending themselves to Slavonic passion. The recording is first class. An outstanding coupling. Mackerras's new Czech version has the power and authority characteristic of his Janáček series. He secures superb singing, of great fervour and expressive eloquence, from the Czech choir; and the Czech Philharmonic Orchestra give an inspired accompaniment, whether in the rasping brass introduction or in the gentler pages at the opening of the *Sanctus*. The soloists too make a strong, if not always refined, team (the balance places them forwardly) and are obviously caught up in the excitement of the occasion. The recording, made in the House of Artists, Prague, has the right degree of resonance, although the sound is a little raw at times – but this only adds to the Slavonic bite. The layout is spacious, the overall perspective convincing.

OPERA

The Cunning little vixen (complete); *Cunning little vixen* (suite, arr. Talich).
*** Decca Dig. **417 129-2** (2) [id.]. Popp, Randová, Jedlická, V. State Op. Ch., Bratislava Children's Ch., VPO, Mackerras.

Mackerras's thrusting, red-blooded reading is spectacularly supported by a digital recording of outstanding demonstration quality. His determination to make the piece more than quaint is helped by the Viennese warmth of playing. That Janáček deliberately added the death of the vixen to the original story points very much in the direction of such a strong, purposeful approach. The inspired choice of Lucia Popp as the vixen provides charm in exactly the right measure, a Czech-born singer who delights in the fascinating complexity of the vixen's character: sparkling and coquettish, spiteful as well as passionate. The supporting cast is first rate, too. Talich's splendidly arranged orchestral suite is offered as a bonus in a fine new recording.

Suites: The Cunning little vixen; Fate; From the House of the Dead.
** Sup. Dig. **C37 7303** [id.]. Czech PO, Jílek.

Most Janáček lovers will want to have these operas undiluted, whether on CD or cassette. However, those allergic to singers may welcome these transcriptions, which are eminently well played by the Czech Philharmonic under Frantisek Jílek. *The Cunning little vixen* suite is not the unforgettable Talich arrangement, which the great conductor recorded in the early 1950s, but concentrates on the interludes and on parts of the last Act, while the excerpts from *Osud* come mainly from the third act. Not even *From the House of the Dead* loses much of its eloquence in this transcription. The Supraphon recording is of generally high quality.

Jenůfa (complete).
❀ *** Decca Dig. **414 483-2** (2) [id.].Söderström, Ochman, Dvorský, Randová, Popp, V. State Op. Ch., VPO, Mackerras.

This is the warmest and most lyrical of Janáček's operas, and it inspires a performance from Mackerras and his team which is both deeply sympathetic and strongly dramatic. After Mackerras's previous Janáček sets, it was natural to choose Elisabeth Söderström for the name-part. Mature as she is, she creates a touching portrait of the girl caught in a family tragedy. Where this set scores substantially over previous ones is in the security and firmness of the voices, with no Slavonic wobblers. The two rival tenors, Peter Dvorský and Wieslav Ochman as the half-brothers Steva and Laca, are both superb; but dominating the whole drama is the Kostelnitchka of Eva Randová. For the first time on record one can register the beauty as well as the power of the writing for this equivocal central figure. Some may resist the idea that she should be made so sympathetic, but particularly on record the drama is made stronger and more involving. The layout on CD uses two discs only, which give great clarity and fine definition to the warm, wide-ranging Vienna recording, the voices caught with special vividness.

Jolivet, André (1905–74)

(i) *Concertino for trumpet, piano and strings; Trumpet concerto.*
*** CBS Dig. **MK 42096**; *IMT 42096* [id.]. Wynton Marsalis, (i) Craig Shepherd, Philh. O, Salonen – TOMASI: *Concerto.****

As crossover music goes, this is rather successful, with the brilliant musicianship, dizzy bravura and natural idiomatic feeling of Wynton Marsalis tailor-made for this repertoire. There is not a great deal for Craig Shepherd to do in the duet concertino, but he does it well enough. This is certainly a flamboyant piece – but the solo concerto is the finer work, with the Latin-American dance-rhythms fully laminated to the music itself. The nocturnal *Grave* is particularly evocative. With vividly garish scoring, the livelier moments have an almost bizarre rhythmic exhilaration, especially when the solo playing is so uninhibited yet perfectly in control. The recording is not especially clear, but this does not seem to matter too much, though some ears will detect background hum at times. The cassette has its documentation provided on an additional folded leaflet, lightly printed in a minuscule typeface, but the transfers are technically satisfactory. The CD offers poor value at only 35′.

Jongen, Joseph (1873–1953)

Symphonie concertante, Op. 18.
*** Telarc Dig. **CD 80096** [id.]. Murray, San Francisco SO, De Waart – FRANCK: *Fantaisie* etc.***

Jongen's harmonic idiom is not adventurous (the *Symphonie concertante* was written in 1926); but it is a very well crafted piece, amiably eclectic in derivation and skilfully written for the medium. Anyone who likes the Saint-Saëns *Third Symphony* should enjoy this. Even if the music is on a lower level of inspiration, the passionate *Lento misterioso* and hugely spectacular closing *Toccata* make a favourable impression at first hearing and wear surprisingly well afterwards. The performance here is undoubtedly persuasive in its verve and commitment, and (as we know from his Bach records) Michael Murray has all the necessary technique to carry off Jongen's hyperbole with the required panache. He receives excellent support from Edo de Waart and the San Francisco Symphony Orchestra. The huge Ruffatti organ seems custom-built for the occasion and Telarc's engineers obviously had the time of their lives, capturing all the spectacular effects with their usual aplomb. A demonstration disc indeed.

Joplin, Scott (1868–1917)

Rags (arr. Perlman): *Bethena; The Easy Winners; Elite syncopations; The Entertainer; Magnetic rag; Pineapple rag; Ragtime dance; Solace; The strenuous life; Sugar cane rag.*
*** HMV **CDC7 47170-2** [id.]. Perlman, Previn.

Perlman and Previn letting their hair down present a winning combination in a whole sequence of Joplin's most naggingly haunting rags. This is very much Previn's country, and his rhythmic zest infects his brilliant partner. The naturally balanced 1975 sound is enhanced by the freshness of the CD transfer, and though the focus is not quite as sharp as one would expect in a more modern digital recording, the violin image is pleasingly without edge.

Josephs, Wilfred (born 1927)

Concerto for brass.
(M) *** Trax Dig. **TRXCD 114**; *MCFC 114* [id.]. L. Collegiate Brass, Stobart – LLOYD: *Symphony No. 10.****

Josephs' *Concerto* is an engaging set of variations (twenty-five in all) which, after an opening cornet flourish, sets off genially with its catchy theme. It is a slight work, but the invention is ingenious and entertaining, and the climax is a bizarre Sousa-esque march. With superbly clear, resonant brass recording and fine playing, this makes a very useful coupling for George Lloyd's more ambitious *Tenth Symphony*. There is a first-class cassette.

Requiem, Op. 39.
*** Unicorn Dig. *DKPC 9032* [id.]. Dawe, De Almeida, Adelaide Qt, Adelaide Ch. and SO, Measham.

It was this *Requiem* for baritone, chorus, string quintet and orchestra that first put Wilfred Josephs on the musical map, when in 1963 it won first prize in the city of Milan's first Composers' Competition, judged by a jury chaired by the conductor, Victor de Sabata. Subsequently it had more striking success in the United States than in Britain – where Josephs was regarded, unfairly, with suspicion by the musical establishment – and Carlo Maria Giulini, who conducted it in Chicago, pronounced it the most important work by a living composer. Even if that is an exaggeration, it is a piece well deserving of a recording; this one from Australia, conducted with keen commitment by a talented British musician, presents a very convincing account. Writing at exactly the same time as when Britten was composing his *War Requiem*, Josephs simultaneously had the idea of presenting the message of mourning on different levels. So, in commemoration of the Jewish dead of the Second World War, he frames a full choral setting of passages from the Kaddish, the lament for the dead, with darkly intense, mainly slow movements for string quintet alone. Stylistically, he makes a distinction between the Mahlerian anguish of the quintet movements and the plainer idiom of the choruses. It may be a dauntingly gloomy work, but the dedication of the performance, very well recorded, brings out the expressive warmth as well as the intensity of the inspiration, confidently matching an ambitious theme. The chrome cassette is of high quality, and this is music that needs to be heard without intrusive background noises.

Josquin des Prés (*c.* 1450–1521)

Motets: *Absolom, fili mi; Ave Maria, gratia plena; De profundis clamavi; In te Domine speravi per trovar pietà; Veni, Sanctus Spiritus;* Chansons: *La déploration de la mort de Johannes Ockeghem; El grillo; En l'ombre d'ung buissonet au matinet; Je me complains; Je ne me puis tenir d'aimer; Mille regretz; Petite camusette; Scaramella va alla guerra; Scaramella va la galla.*
*** HMV Dig. **CDC7 49209-2** [id.]. Hilliard Ens.

Josquin spent much of his life in Italy, first as a singer in the choir of Milan Cathedral and subsequently in the service of the Sforza family. Although Josquin research has become something of a light industry (to judge from the 1976 Congress in New York devoted to him), little of his vast output has reached the wider musical public and still less has been recorded. As Paul Hillier points out in his notes, 'in the carnival songs and frottole we encounter a native Italian style which composers such as Isaac and Josquin may have ennobled but which in turn had its own influence on this music. This fusion of learned polyphony and tuneful rhythmic gaiety laid the foundations of the Italian madrigal.' The chansons recorded here have both variety of colour and lightness of touch, while the motets are sung with dignity and feeling by the Hilliard Ensemble. Indeed, these performances will kindle the enthusiasm of the uninitiated as will few others. The recording is expertly balanced and eminently truthful.

Motets: *Ave Maria, gratia plena; Ave, nobilissima creatura; Miserere mei, Deus; O bone et dulcissime Jesu; Salve regina; Stabat mater dolorosa; Usquequo, Domine, oblivisceris me.*
*** HM Dig. **HMC 901243** [id.]. Chapelle Royale Ch., Herreweghe.

A valuable Josquin anthology from Philippe Herreweghe and the Choir of the Chapelle Royale which gives us the *Miserere* so much admired by the doyen of Josquin scholars, Edward Lowinsky. The Chapelle Royale comprise some nineteen singers, but they still produce a clean, well-focused sound and benefit from excellent recorded sound. Their account of the expressive *Stabat mater* sounds thicker-textured than the New College forces under Edward Higginbottom, but there is a refreshing sense of commitment and strong feeling. They are well served by the recording engineers.

Antiphons, Motets and Sequences: *Inviolata; Praeter rerum serium; Salve regina; Stabat mater dolorosa; Veni, sancte spiritus; Virgo prudentissima; Virgo salutiferi.*
*** Mer. **ECD 84093** [id.]. New College, Oxford, Ch., Higginbottom.

Having suffered some neglect in the past few years, it is good to see Josquin's representation suddenly and dramatically increased. The Meridian anthology collects some of Josquin's most masterly and eloquent motets in performances of predictable excellence by Edward Higginbottom and the Choir of New College, Oxford. Higginbottom does not shrink from expressive feeling and at the same time secures both purity of tone and clarity of texture. The *Stabat mater*, one of Josquin's most powerful compositions, is mandatory listening. An admirable introduction to Josquin, and an essential acquisition for those who care about this master.

Missa – L'homme armé super voces musicales.
*** DG Arc. **415 293-2** [id.]. Pro Cantione Antiqua, Bruno Turner – OCKEGHEM: *Missa pro defunctis.****

This *Mass* on the *L'homme armé* theme is both one of the most celebrated of all Mass settings based on this secular melody and at the same time one of Josquin's most masterly and admired works. It was written in the late 1480s or early '90s and is called *super voces musicales* to distinguish it from his *Missa L'homme armé in sexti toni* (in the sixth mode). In this *Mass*, the cantus firmus appears on all the natural degrees of the hexachord C–A, while the overall tonality remains Dorian. Jeremy Noble recorded its companion in 1973, and one hopes that it will not languish in oblivion, for it too deserves to be reissued. His edition is used in the present (1977) performance, which must be numbered among the very finest accounts not only of a Josquin but of any Renaissance Mass to have appeared on record. On CD, the transparency of each strand in the vocal texture is wonderfully clear and the singers are astonishingly present. An outstanding issue.

Missa Pange lingua.
*** HM Dig. **HMC 901239** [id.]. Clément Janequin Ens.

Missa Pange lingua; Missa La sol fa re mi.
*** Gimell Dig. **CDGIM 009**; *1585T-09* [id.]. Tallis Scholars, Peter Phillips.

The *Missa Pange lingua* is generally thought of as Josquin's masterpiece and is well served on record at present. The Gimell recording has collected superlatives on all counts and was voted record of the year in the *Gramophone* magazine's 1987 awards. The Tallis Scholars have made a considerable name for themselves in the past decade, mostly in music by Byrd, Palestrina and, of course, Tallis. Josquin, a great master of an earlier period, finds them in equally good form. The tone they produce is perfectly blended, each line being firmly defined and yet beautifully integrated into the whole sound-picture. Their recording, made in the Chapel of Merton College, Oxford, is first class, the best of the *Missa Pange lingua* and the first of the ingenious *Missa La sol fa re mi*. Not to be missed. As usual with this label, the chrome tape is a state-of-the-art transfer, and loses very little of the definition and clarity of the compact disc.

The Clément Janequin Ensemble is among the very finest groups now before the public, and their performance of this Mass can hardly be flawed. They use eight singers but also make considerable use of solo voices. The Mass is interspersed with chant appropriate to the Feast of Corpus Christi sung by the Organum Ensemble under Marcel Peres. Although this naturally enhances its atmosphere on first or second hearing, it does, of course, increase its length. CD players can be programmed to omit some or all of these bands – but, even so, it puts rival versions at something of an advantage when they can accommodate another Mass. The Tallis Singers offer a rarity in the shape of the *Missa La sol fa re mi.*

Kabalevsky, Dmitri (born 1904)

Cello concerto No. 1 in G min.
*** CBS Dig. **CD 37840** [id.]. Yo-Yo Ma, Phd. O, Ormandy – SHOSTAKOVICH: *Cello concerto No. 1.****

Both of Kabalevsky's cello concertos have been recorded before, though neither with such persuasive force as Yo-Yo Ma brings to the *First*. This is an amiable piece to which great depth of feeling is quite alien. It opens very much in the manner of Prokofiev and Myaskovsky, and is well crafted and pleasing. The excellence of the performance is matched by a fine recording. However, the CD, one of CBS's very best, adds considerably to the refinement and presence of the sound, and its vividness is such as to seem to add stature to the music itself.

Violin concerto in C, Op. 48.
(**) Chant du Monde mono **LDC 278883** [id.]. David Oistrakh, USSR Nat O, composer – KHACHATURIAN: *Violin concerto.**** ❀

Kabalevsky's gay, extrovert *Concerto* dates from 1948. If its style is essentially old-fashioned, the work is spontaneous and tuneful. It has been recorded in stereo by Zukerman for CBS and no doubt his excellent account will appear on CD in due course. David Oistrakh was not its dedicatee, but his advocacy helped to make it known in the West. His 1955 mono recording is in most ways definitive, with the composer helping to make the delightfully atmospheric slow movement quite memorable. Oistrakh's clean articulation and sparkle in the finale are also outstanding – and it is a pity that so much allowance has to be made for the 1955 mono recording, which is papery, with a shrill solo image and whistly orchestral strings. At a modest volume level, with a top cut, it is listenable, however, and the playing itself is highly rewarding.

Kálmán, Emmerich (1882–1953)

Countess Maritza: highlights (in English).
*** That's Entertainment **CDTER 1051**; *ZCTER 1051.* Hill-Smith, Remedios, Barber, Livingstone, Tudor Davies, Moyle, New Sadler's Wells Op. Ch. and O, Wordsworth.

The label, 'That's Entertainment', has brought out an enterprising series of recordings of stage musicals. Here it adds a recording based on the New Sadler's Wells production (in English) of Kálmán's operetta. Voices are fresh, playing and conducting are lively and the recording excellent. Much recommended for those who prefer their operetta in English, for the CD has fine presence.

Ketèlbey, Albert (1875–1959)

Bank holiday; Bells across the meadow; The clock and the Dresden figures; Dance of the merry mascots; In a Chinese temple garden; In a monastery garden; In a Persian market; In the mystic land of Egypt; Sanctuary of the heart; With honour crowned.
** Ph. Dig. **400 011-2** [id.]. Reeves, Dale, Amb. Ch., L. Prom. O, Faris.

Bells across the meadow; Chal Romano (*Gypsy lad*); *The Clock and the Dresden figures; In a Chinese temple garden; In a monastery garden; In a Persian market; In the moonlight; In the mystic land of Egypt; Sanctuary of the heart.*
*** HMV **CDC7 47806-2** [id.]. Midgley, Temperley, Amb. S., Pearson (piano), Philh. O, Lanchbery.

A splendid collection in every way. John Lanchbery plainly has a very soft spot for Ketèlbey's tuneful music (and there are some very good tunes here), and he uses every possible resource to ensure that when the composer demands spectacle he gets it. *In the mystic land of Egypt*, for instance, uses soloist and chorus in canon in the principal tune (and very fetching too). *The Clock and the Dresden figures* is deliciously done, with Leslie Pearson playing the concertante piano part in scintillating fashion. In the *Monastery garden* the distant monks are realistically distant, in *Sanctuary of the heart* there is no mistaking that the heart is worn firmly on the sleeve. The orchestral playing throughout is not only polished but warmhearted – the middle section of *Bells across the meadow*, which has a delightful melodic contour, is played most tenderly and loses any hint of vulgarity. Yet when vulgarity is called for it is not shirked – only it's a stylish kind of vulgarity! The *Chal Romano* has an unexpectedly vigorous melodic impulse, reminding the listener of Eric Coates. The recording is excellent, full and brilliant and it has transferred to CD with striking presence and warmth. Noël Coward's famous quote (from *Private Lives*) comes readily to mind here: 'Extraordinary how potent cheap music is.'

The alternative Philips collection is effective enough. The enterprise is in proper scale, not too overblown, and the contributions of Michael Reeves, Laurence Dale and the Ambrosian chorus cannot be faulted. But Lanchbery displays far more flair and the HMV recording is more vivid.

Khachaturian, Aram (1903–78)

Piano concerto in D flat.
(M) *** PRT **PVCD 8376** [id.]. Mindru Katz, LPO, Boult – PROKOFIEV: *Piano concerto No. 1.***(*)

(i) *Piano concerto in D flat; Gayaneh* (ballet) *suite; Masquerade: suite.*
(*) Chan. Dig. **CHAN 8542; *ABTD 1250* [id.]. (i) Orbelian, SNO, Järvi.

(i) *Piano concerto in D flat; Sonatina; Toccata.*
** ASV Dig. **CDDCA 589**; *ZCDCA 589* [id.]. Portugheis; (i) LSO, Tjeknavorian.

Mindru Katz gives a really gripping performance of this colourful work which can too easily sound garrulous and inflated. He and Boult have a firm grasp on the first movement, yet the breadth is impressive too, and the bravura (and there is much opportunity for it) does not turn the affair into a mere display of pianistic fireworks. The impetus springs entirely from the music and Boult's flexibility of tempo is wholly spontaneous. The slow movement is hauntingly atmospheric, even if the flexitone is not used as confidently here as on later versions. The 1959 recording is a fine example of early stereo: the piano timbre is bold and tangible, and the orchestral sound is full, with its analogue ambience adding to the weight without blurring; the balance is most convincing. At mid-price, coupled with an excellent Prokofiev No. 1, this is a clear first choice.

Of course the Chandos recording is splendid technically, well up to the standards of the house. Recorded in the SNO Centre, Glasgow, the acoustic is warm and expansive. Constantin Orbelian, an Armenian by birth, plays brilliantly and Järvi achieves much attractive lyrical detail. He scores in the slow movement by making the most of the curious whistly overtones of the flexitone, used with greater aplomb here than in the Boult version. The bass clarinet, too, drools sinuously at the end. Overall it is a spacious account, and though the finale has plenty of gusto, the music making seems just a shade too easy-going in the first movement. The couplings, sumptuously played, are both generous and appealing, especially *Masquerade* – an attractively romantic account of this rather engaging music. Four famous numbers are included from *Gayaneh*, among the finest music Khachaturian ever wrote, and they are played with considerable panache.

Alberto Portugheis's timing for the first movement of the concerto is 15′ 05″ against Orbelian's 14′ 11″, and the effect is to make the music sound rambling. The rest of the performance goes well (again the flexitone is used with confidence, to good effect) and the recording is admirably vivid. But the couplings are ungenerous: the *Sonatina* is an insubstantial piece and the more memorable *Toccata* is merely a spirited encore.

Violin concerto in D min.

❀ *** Chant du Monde **LDC 278883**. David Oistrakh, USSR RSO, composer – KABALEVSKY: *Violin concerto*.(**)

(*) HMV Dig. **CDC7 47087-2 [id.]. Perlman, Israel PO, Mehta – TCHAIKOVSKY: *Méditation*.***

Khachaturian's splendid *Violin concerto*, wonderfully vital and tuneful and very Russian (albeit Armenian-Russian), and the original score for *Gayaneh*, both of which date from the early 1940s, are undoubtedly his finest works. David Oistrakh, for whom the concerto was written, gave the work its première, and is its dedicatee. He is peerless in its performance, not only in projecting its very Russian bravura, but also in his melting phrasing and timbre in the sinuous secondary theme of the first movement, which returns in the finale, and in the equally haunting melody of the *Andante*. Indeed this quite marvellous performance is unlikely ever to be surpassed. It has all the spontaneity of a live occasion. The composer, clearly inspired by the expressive response of his soloist, creates a rapt degree of tension in the slow movement and affectionately caresses the Armenian colour and detail in the very atmospheric orchestral accompaniment. The finale has an irresistible exhilaration, and the return of the big tune on the G string is heart-warming. The digital remastering makes the very most of the excellent (1970) Russian recording which is warm and very well balanced, especially in its relationship of soloist with orchestra. The acoustic is resonant in the right way – there is bloom but no muddiness or fierceness. This must be listed among the all too few great stereo recordings in which the music's composer has been able to participate.

Perlman's performance sparkles too – indeed it is superb in every way, lyrically persuasive in the *Andante* and displaying great fervour and rhythmic energy in the finale. He is well accompanied by Mehta (who nevertheless does not match the composer's feeling for detail); were the Oistrakh version not available, this would be a ready choice. However, on CD one's ear is drawn to the very forward balance of the soloist, his timbre truthful and clearly focused. Orchestral detail is certainly tangible, but the generally bright lighting becomes rather fierce at the opening tutti of the finale – the comparatively dry Israeli acoustic does not provide an ideal bloom on the music making.

Flute concerto (arr. Rampal/Galway)*; Gayaneh: Sabre dance. Masquerade: Waltz. Spartacus: Adagio of Spartacus and Phrygia.*

*** RCA Dig. **RD 87010**. Galway, RPO, Myung-Whun Chung.

Khachaturian's *Flute concerto* is a transcription of the *Violin concerto* made by Jean-Pierre Rampal, with the composer's blessing. Galway has prepared his own edition of the solo part 'which goes even further in its attempts to adapt the solo line to the characteristics of the flute'. He has the advantage of a modern digital recording, but the resonant acoustic of Watford Town Hall tends to coarsen the orchestral tuttis very slightly, especially the big fortissimo flare-up towards the end of the slow movement, which is fierce – and especially so in the CD format. Needless to say, the solo playing is peerless. Galway's special gift is to make a transcription sound as if it was actually written for the flute; his radiant timbre in the engaging lyrical secondary theme of the first movement is matched by the dreamy languor of the sinuously beautiful *Andante*. In the finale, even Galway cannot match the effect Oistrakh makes with his violin, but the ready bravura is sparklingly infectious. As encores, he offers three of Khachaturian's most famous melodies. They are marvellously played, with the *Sabre dance* elegant rather than boisterously noisy.

Gayaneh (ballet): original score: highlights.
(***) RCA **RD 70952** [id.]. Nat. PO, Tjeknavorian.

Gayaneh (ballet): *suite.*
(B) **(*) DG Walkman *413 155-4* [id.]. Leningrad PO, Rozhdestvensky – RIMSKY-KORSAKOV: *Scheherazade*; STRAVINSKY: *Firebird suite*.**(*)

Gayaneh (ballet): *suite; Spartacus* (ballet): *suite.*
(*) HMV Dig. **CDC7 47348-2 [id.]. RPO, Temirkanov.
(M) **(*) Decca **417 737-2**; *417 737-4* [id.]. VPO, composer – PROKOFIEV: *Romeo and Juliet*.***

Loris Tjeknavorian made a pretty definitive recording of Khachaturian's *Gayaneh* in 1977. He used the original score, not the inflated revised version which the composer was persuaded to produce to accompany a completely new 'classical' story-line for the Bolshoi. The RCA highlights disc, which plays for a generous 71′, includes the kernel of the score and offers at least a dozen numbers with strong melodic and rhythmic appeal and apt scoring. The performance is first class, with polished and alive orchestral playing directed by the sympathetic Tjeknavorian, himself an Armenian by birth. Unfortunately, the CD transfer produces artificially brightened sound which is very wearing to listen to – for there is much that is noisy. While the gentler numbers still sound beautiful (notably the *Lullaby* and Gayaneh's *Adagio*) and the ambient effect retains the middle warmth, the bass is light, which emphasizes the brightly lit treble. Of course the *Lesginka* and *Sabre dance* emerge with great gusto and impact, but the record's producers seem obsessed with the commercial appeal of the latter piece, and the lion's share of the meagre documentation is devoted to its unnecessary advocacy.

A new digital recording of excerpts from both *Gayaneh* and the more uneven *Spartacus* was therefore overdue; the HMV CD, also brightly lit and vivid, but not unacceptably so, if a little studio-ish in acoustic, is most welcome. Temirkanov opens *Gayaneh* with the boisterous but engaging *Gopak*, rather than the *Sabre dance* (which follows on soon enough); in the nine items from this ballet and the slightly shorter selection from *Spartacus* musical characterization is strong, rhythms are well sprung and the lyrical music is treated with contrasting tenderness. The RPO respond with playing that is both alert and polished. In the famous *Adagio* from *Spartacus* Temirkanov refuses to go over the top – the composer's own recording is more passionate – but the element of slight reserve is not unattractive.

The composer's own selection on Decca was recorded in 1962 and offers five items from *Gayaneh* and four from *Spartacus*, coupled to an intelligent selection from Maazel's complete Cleveland set of Prokofiev's *Romeo and Juliet*, dating from a decade later. Khachaturian achieves a brilliant response from the VPO and everything is most vivid, notably the famous *Adagio* from *Spartacus* which is both expansive and passionate. Because of the success of the BBC TV series, *The Onedin Line*, the analogue LP from which these recordings derive was a bestseller for a long period. It was very well recorded and balanced, and it is a pity that the Decca remastering process has brought everything into such strong focus; the presence of the sound certainly makes an impact, but the massed violins now have an added edge and boldness of attack, at the expense of their richness of timbre. The equivalent cassette has much more warmth and amplitude, and many will prefer it.

There is also a 1977 EMI recording of the same coupling by the same artists on an Eminence tape (*TC-EMX 2119*) which sounds more romantically sumptuous, although the definition is less clean. The items included are not identical to those on the Decca issue, but this could be first choice if it is issued on CD. At present it is ungenerous, with no coupling.

No one does the *Sabre dance* like the Russians, and with Rozhdestvensky it makes a sensational opening, exploding into the room at the end of Stravinsky's *Firebird suite*. The performance overall combines excitement with panache, and the original drawback of a rather fierce recording has been met here by the slight attenuation of the upper range of the chrome-tape transfer. But the sound remains vivid.

Symphony No. 2 in C minor.
(M) **(*) Decca *414 169-4* [id.]. VPO, composer.

This was a propaganda piece, written during the war when the composer was evacuated from Moscow. Khachaturian lays the Armenian colour on very thickly but, unlike the splendid *Violin concerto* of two years earlier, this does not develop into a coherent argument, let alone a genuinely symphonic one. The musical value is roughly in inverse proportion to the noise made, and it is a very loud score indeed. The performance is very fine and the magnificent quality of the 1962 recording deserves better material. The first-class chrome cassette cannot be faulted on technical grounds.

Knussen, Oliver (born 1952)

(i; ii) *Symphony No. 2 for soprano and orchestra, Op. 7;* (iii) *Symphony No. 3, Op. 18;* (ii) *Coursing for chamber orchestra, Op. 17; Ophelia dances, Book 1, Op. 13;* (iv) *Cantata for oboe and string trio, Op. 15;* (v) *Trumpets for soprano and 3 clarinets, Op. 12.*
*** Unicorn Dig. *DKPC 9027* [id.]. (i) Elaine Barry; (ii) London Sinf., composer; (iii) Philh. O, Tilson Thomas; (iv) Gareth Hulse, Nash Ens.; (v) Linda Hirst, Collins, Pillinger, Mitchell.

Oliver Knussen attracted attention with his *Symphony No. 1*, written when he was only sixteen and first performed by the LSO with the boy composer conducting. The *Second Symphony* followed when he was nineteen and is in the form of a song-cycle involving the fantasy of a sleeper with nightmarish dreams and her awakening into reality. It is a highly imaginative conception, realized with remarkable confidence. The *Third Symphony* was finished in 1979 and is dedicated to Michael Tilson Thomas, who conducted its first performance at a Prom the same year. Its idiom is accessible; its sound-world, like the rest of the music here, is distinctive and reflects an alive, vivid musical mind at work. The language itself seems to have grown from Messiaen – and even perhaps from Britten and Henze – yet its accents are personal. It is a short 15-minute piece in one movement. The *Ophelia dances* are related to the symphony and are no less inventive and rewarding. In the Trakl setting of *Trumpets*, nothing is quite predictable and the verbal and musical imagery is characteristically individual. *Coursing* is another short piece for small orchestra, producing a burst of energy which is then allowed to evaporate slowly. The *Cantata* is both energetically improvisatory and lyrically rhapsodic. All the performances are expert, splendidly committed and alive, and the recordings are luminously clear yet within an agreeable resonance. This state-of-the-art chrome cassette offers the contents of 1½ LPs and makes a quite admirable introduction to the composer. It is not for faint-hearts, but those who like to explore will find some fascinating sounds here, reproduced with the utmost fidelity.

Where the Wild Things are (complete).
*** Unicorn Dig. **DKPCD 9044**; *DKPC 9044* [id.]. Rosemary Hardy, Mary King, Herrington, Richardson, Rhys-Williams, Gallacher, L. Sinf., composer.

In a closely argued score, yet which communicates immediately and vividly, Oliver Knussen has devised a one-act opera that beautifully matches the grotesque fantasy of Maurice Sendak's children's book of the same name, with its gigantic monsters or Wild Things which prove to have hearts of gold, and make the naughty boy, Max, their king. On stage at Glyndebourne and elsewhere, the fun and ingenuity of Sendak's own designs and costumes tended to distract attention from the score's detailed concentration, but the record compensates here, while still presenting the piece with the bite and energy of a live performance. It helped that the sessions took place immediately after a series of stage performances. The final rumpus music, which Knussen managed to complete only after the rest, here feels like the culmination intended. Rosemary Hardy makes a superb Max, not just accurate but giving a convincing portrait of the naughty child with little or no archness. Mary King sings warmly in the small part of the Mother. The CD is particularly convenient to use, with no fewer than 26 separate bands. Any particular passage is promptly spotted, in a work of such detail, so that it feels far longer than 40 minutes. The brilliant recording vividly conveys a sense of presence and space with the excellent chrome cassette closely matched.

Kodály, Zoltán (1882–1967)

(i) *Concerto for orchestra;* (ii) *Háry János: suite.*
** Hung. **HCD 12190** [id.]. (i) Hungarian State O; (ii) Budapest PO, Ferencsik.

Ferencsik conducts the Budapest Philharmonic in a delightfully pointed and witty account of the *Háry János suite*, bringing out the narrative points in this brilliant sequence of characterful numbers. Rhythms are light and well sprung, ensemble crisp, and recording generally excellent. The *Concerto for orchestra*, an attractive coupling, is given a far less satisfactory performance and recording. Made in 1980, it is too reverberant to allow the detailed textures of this showpiece work to emerge, with much lost in a background haze.

Dances of Galánta.
*** Ph. **416 378-2** [id.]. Concg. O, Zinman – BARTÓK: *Concerto for 2 Pianos, percussion & celesta.****

Dances of Galánta; Dances of Marosszék; Variations on a Hungarian folksong (*Peacock*).
(*) Hung. Dig. **HCD 12252 [id.]. Budapest SO, Lehel.

Lehel conducts warmly idiomatic readings of three of Kodály's most colourful and approachable orchestral works, lacking only the last degree of virtuoso brilliance. The bright, immediate recorded sound makes up for that lack, with the instruments well defined within a helpful but hardly reverberant acoustic.

David Zinman offers an attractively vivid performance of the *Dances of Galánta.* Although this is not a very generous coupling for the Bartók *Concerto*, the recording is very much in the demonstration class. Philips experimentally used simple microphone techniques and the result brings an uncanny sense of presence and realism, indeed of sitting in the concert hall.

Variations on a Hungarian folksong (*The Peacock*); (i) *Psalmus hungaricus.*
** Hung. **HCD 11392-2** [id.]. (i) Simandy, Hungarian R. & TV Children's Ch., Budapest Ch.; Hungarian State O, Dorati.

It makes an attractive coupling having on this disc two of the strongest and most colourful of Kodály's larger works. For all the colour and richness of the orchestration, the *Peacock variations* are disarmingly direct in their development of a Hungarian folktune, covering a wide range of moods. The performance here, from one of Hungary's most distinguished orchestras, is warmly committed, very well recorded if with rather heavy bass and some spotlighting of individual solos. The *Psalmus hungaricus* fares much less well. The choral singing is first rate, but the singers are far too distantly placed, leaving centre-stage to the tenor soloist, whose wobbly contributions are a sore trial, when they make up the greater part of the work. Dorati, as ever, is at his most sympathetic in this Hungarian music.

(Unaccompanied) *Cello sonata, Op. 8;* (i) *Duo, Op. 7.*
(*) Chan. Dig. **CHAN 8427; *ABTD 1102* [id.]. Yuri Turovsky, (i) with Eleonora Turovsky.

Kodaly's solo *Cello sonata* was made famous by a justly admired mono recording by Janos Starker; no one has ever surpassed it on record, and its virtuosity and intensity are stunning. Yuri Turovsky plays with considerable intensity and understands the work's rhapsodical nature. He is given striking body and presence by the recording, which on tape becomes a little bass-orientated. The *Duo* is another fine work, and with Eleonora Turovsky taking the lead this performance is even more compellingly spontaneous. The recording is very well balanced.

String quartets Nos 1 and 2.
(*) Hung. Dig. **HCD 12362 [id.]. Kodály Qt.

String quartet No. 2, Op. 10.
*** DG Dig. **419 601-2**; *419 601-4* [id.]. Hagen Qt – DVOŘÁK: *String quartet No. 12* etc.***

The two Kodály *Quartets* have been completely overshadowed by Bartók, but they deserve more than the toe-hold on the repertoire that they enjoy at present. The two performances from this eponymous quartet make an excellent coupling, warmly committed and spontaneous. Though the playing is not as refined as from the most polished Hungarian quartet groups, the natural understanding brings out the sharply contrasted character of the two works very convincingly. Much the more ambitious and more passionate is the *First*, Kodály's Op. 2, written in 1909; in its luxuriant span it inhabits very much the same world as Bartók's *First Quartet* of the same period, yearningly lyrical but bitingly dramatic too, with its characteristic folk element. The *Second Quartet* of 1918 is altogether simpler and less intense, a delightful, compact piece, which reveals Kodály's own character more clearly, very different from that of his close colleague. Excellent, immediate recording.

The Hagen give a marvellously committed and beautifully controlled performance of the *Second* – indeed as quartet playing it would be difficult to surpass. They might strike some collectors as almost too polished – Hungarian peasants in their best Sunday suits, rather than in everyday attire – but, in range of dynamic response and sheer beauty of sound, this is thrilling playing and welcome advocacy of a neglected but masterly piece. The recording is well balanced and admirably present; the chrome cassette, too, is in the demonstration bracket, quite remarkably realistic.

Budávari Te Deum; Missa brevis.
*** Hung. **HCD 11397-2** [id.]. Andor, Ekert, Makkay, Mohácsi, Szirmay, Réti, Gregor, Hungarian R. & TV Ch., Budapest SO, Ferencsik.

The *Budávari Te Deum*, celebrating the 250th anniversary of the recapture of the castle of Buda from the Turks, is predictably nationalist in feeling. The *Missa brevis* is given in the 1950 orchestral form (not the organ version, often used) and is also one of Kodály's strongest works, almost comparable in stature to the *Psalmus hungaricus*. The performances first appeared on record in the early 1970s but sound remarkably fresh in their CD incarnation. The singing is accurate and sensitive, and the playing of the Budapest orchestra under Ferencsik absolutely first class.

Háry János (musical numbers only).
(*) Hung. **HCD 12837/8-2 [id.]. Sólyom-Nagy, Takács, Sudlik, Póka, Mésozöly, Gregor, Palcsó, Hungarian R. & TV Children's Ch., Hungarian State Op. Ch. and O, Ferencsik.

When originally issued on LP, this Hungarian recording of the complete *Háry János* included a full hour of spoken dialogue in Hungarian. For the CD transfer the dialogue has been cut out, which means there is no dramatic continuity; but when Kodály's score is so colourful – not just in the movements of the well-known suite but in many other numbers too – the piece becomes a rich chocolate-box of delights. Ferencsik's performance with Hungarian singers and players is committedly idiomatic, with strong singing, not always ideally well characterized but very stylish, from some of the most distinguished principals of the Budapest Opera. The CD transfer gives extra clarity and a sense of presence to the original recording.

Háry János: suite.
*** HMV Dig. **CDC7 47109-2** [id.]. LPO, Tennstedt – PROKOFIEV: *Lieutenant Kijé.****

Tennstedt might seem an unlikely conductor for Kodály's sharply characterized folk-based score, but his performance has sympathy as well as power and brilliance, drawing out the romantic warmth of the *Intermezzo*. Digital sound of the fullest, richest EMI vintage.

(i) *Hymn of Zrínyi; Jesus and the traders; The aged; Norwegian girls; Too late; Ode to Liszt.*
** Hung. Dig. **HCD 12352-2** [id.]. (i) Lajos Miller, Hungarian Radio–TV Ch., Ferencsik.

The longest work here is the *Hymn of Zrínyi* for baritone and *a cappella* choir, an ambitious ballad nearly 20 minutes in duration. The singing is first class throughout the set, but the recording, made presumably in the studio, could do with a richer acoustic. There are some beautiful pieces here, foremost among them *Too late*, to words of Endre Ady. The CD offers translations but no notes on the music itself.

Kokkonen, Joonas (born 1921)

Requiem.
** Finlandia Dig. **FACD 353** [id.]. Vihavainen, Hynninen, Academic Ch., Helsinki PO, Söderblom.

As his symphonies and the opera, *The Last Temptations*, show, Joonas Kokkonen is a composer of considerable substance. His music is expertly fashioned and its speech is completely direct and accessible. The *Requiem* was written in 1981 to commemorate his wife, Maija, who had died two years earlier. It is less polyphonic in texture than some of his earlier music and relies predominantly on harmonic effect. It has something of the immediacy of the *Chichester Psalms* of Bernstein. Some of the recurring simple harmonic sleights-of-hand are a bit cloying: it is not a long work, a little shorter in fact than the Duruflé. The soloists are excellent and the choral and orchestral forces under Ulf Söderblom give a committed account of the score, though the choral tone is not always perfectly focused. The recording is very natural and lifelike, but the CD offers short measure.

Korngold, Erich (1897–1957)

Violin concerto in D, Op. 35.
*** HMV **CDC7 47846-2** [id.]. Perlman, Pittsburgh SO, Previn – GOLDMARK: *Concerto.****

Korngold's film scores have largely disappeared from the UK catalogue, although American readers are better served and the British may be able to obtain some of them as special imports. The *Symphony* has gone too (for the moment) on both sides of the Atlantic – which is a great pity as Kempe's Munich recording is first class and his performance could hardly be more persuasive. We are left with the *Violin concerto* which largely draws its material from the film scores. It was written for Huberman, but was a favourite of Heifetz's. He gave the first performance, and one would have thought that his recording would remain forever the supreme interpretation. It has to be played as if it is a masterpiece and with consummate virtuosity if it is to carry conviction. Perlman, dashing and romantic, with more of a sense of fun than the older maestro, gives such a superlative account, and though he is placed too close to the microphone, the recording overall is vivid, with Previn and the Pittsburgh orchestra warmly committed in their accompaniment. Although it is pure kitsch, there is something endearing about this piece and it deserves a place in the catalogue, if only to remind us of the calibre of this famous Hollywood musician. It is also marvellous violin music. No doubt Heifetz's unique recording will appear on CD in due course, but in the meantime this generously and appropriately coupled disc can be recommended. The remastered sound has gained in presence, but lost a little amplitude and warmth.

Kreisler, Fritz (1875–1972)

Caprice Viennoise, Op. 2; La Chasse (Caprice in the style of Cartier); Liebesfreud; Liebeslied; Preghiera in the style of Martini; Romance, Op. 4; Schön Rosmarin; Tempo di minuetto in the style of Pugnani. Arrangements: DVOŘÁK: *Slavonic dance No. 2 in E min., Op. 46/2; Songs my mother taught me, Op. 55/4;* PAGANINI: *Moto perpetuo, Op. 11.* TARTINI: *Fugue in A.* RACHMANINOV: *Marguerite (Daisies), Op. 38/3.* GLUCK: *Mélodie.* GÄRTNER: *Viennese melody.* CHOPIN: *Mazurka in A min., Op. 67/4.*
*** HMV Dig. **CDC7 47467-2** [id.]; *EL 270477-4* [id.]. Itzhak Perlman, Samuel Sanders.

Perlman has made a series of analogue recordings for EMI of Fritz Kreisler's *morceaux de concert*, including also his compositions in the style of others, and actual arrangements. If Kreisler's own music is lightweight it is never trivial and much of it is very entertaining, as it was meant to be. No doubt some of this earlier material will be reissued on CD in due course, but meanwhile Perlman's first digital recital is well chosen to include examples of the three genres, not missing out the favourites like *Caprice viennoise* and *Liebeslied*, played with affection as well as flair. Paganini's *Moto perpetuo* shows Perlman in dazzling form, while he plays the pastiche items, like the *Minuet in the style of Pugnani*, with elegant simplicity. The partnership with Samuel Sanders is striking in the arrangements, where the interplay often has the intimacy of equals rather than that of star soloist and accompanist. The balance places Perlman forward, but the piano is well in the picture. The CD offers realistic presence, but the chrome tape is very lively too, if not quite as refined on top.

Those wanting a fuller selection on cassette can turn to Oscar Shumsky's three collections on ASV, also played with masterly virtuoso flair. Volume 1 (*ZCALH 947*) is called 'Viennese and in the style of' and presents many of Kreisler's more popular trifles; Volume 2 offers 'Dvořák/Kreisler and original music' (*ZCALH 951*), and Shumsky's third tape includes rather more ambitious pieces – arrangements of genuine eighteenth-century material, including the only readily available version of Tartini's *Devil's trill sonata* (*ZCALH 959*).

String quartet in A min., Op. 2.
** Ara. Dig. **Z 6521** [id.]. Portland Quartet – R. STRAUSS: *Quartet.**(*)

Kreisler's *String quartet* dates from 1919 and he recorded it two decades later on 78 r.p.m. discs. Since then it has been undeservedly forgotten. It is constructed with great skill and has considerable melodic appeal, with one quite haunting idea, somewhat Ravelian in feeling, that recurs to close the finale. The overall mood is nostalgic and only in the Scherzo is there any hint of the style of the composer's shorter genre pieces. The Portland performance is sympathetic and thoroughly accomplished, and it is a pity that the recording, though truthful, is closely balanced with a rather dry acoustic: this music needs more room to expand.

Kreutzer, Conradin (1780–1849)

Septet in E flat, Op. 62.
*** CRD *CRDC 4090* [id.]. Nash Ens. – HUMMEL: *Military septet.****

Kreutzer's *Septet* is a delightful work, and it is given a thoroughly engaging performance here by the Nash Ensemble, whose playing is as lyrically elegant as it is full of refined detail. The care of the players over the use of dynamic graduation is matched by the warmth of their phrasing. The Hummel coupling too is most apt, as both works date from the same period (around 1830). The recording is first class in every way, beautifully balanced, and the demonstration-worthy cassette is well up to CRD's usual high standard.

Kreutzer, Rodolphe (1766–1831)

Grand quintet in C.
*** Hyp. **CDA 66143** [id.]. Sarah Francis (oboe), Allegri Qt – CRUSELL: *Divertimento*; REICHA: *Quintet.****

This is the Kreutzer of the Beethoven sonata – not to be confused with Conradin, whose *Grand septet* is available on a splendid CRD tape (see above). The *Grand quintet* is thought to date from the 1790s; it is a rather bland but far from unpleasing piece when it is played as beautifully as it is here. The CD has fine presence.

Krommer, Franz (Kramar, František) (1759–1831)

Clarinet concertos: in E flat, Op. 36; in E min., Op. 86; (i) *Double clarinet concerto in E flat, Op. 35.*
(*) Claves Dig. **CD 50-8602 [id.]. Friedli; (i) Pay, ECO, Pay.

Apart from being one of the most interesting of Beethoven's contemporaries, Krommer was very prolific, with more than 300 works to his credit. Although his music plumbs no great depths, it is delightfully fresh and vital. Both the solo concertos here are fine works, tuneful and full of character. Op. 36 is an outgoing piece, with a fine expressive *Adagio* and a lilting, genial finale, in which Thomas Friedli is in his element. Op. 86 is rather more serious, with even a sombre touch to the *Adagio*, but the clouds clear away in the Rondo. Friedli's tone is full and luscious in both works. Anthony Pay directs spirited accompaniments and then joins him on the first desk in the *Double concerto*, which has a grand opening and even a hint of melodrama as the slow movement unfolds. The finale again lightens the mood deliciously with the closely woven interplay, in which the two parts are written throughout, becoming jocular. The only fault with the solo playing is a relative lack of dynamic light and shade, but the shared enjoyment of the duo is readily conveyed, especially in the bouncing last movement, which is infectious. The recording might ideally be more transparent, but it is full and pleasing and well balanced.

Flute concerto in G, Op. 30; Flute and oboe concertino, Op. 65; Oboe concerto in F, Op. 52.
(*) Claves Dig. **CD 50-8203 [id.]. Graf, Holliger, ECO.

Krommer's harmonic sense was highly developed, as in the slow movement of the Op. 52 *Oboe concerto*; it is these unpredictable felicities that lend his work its charm. This issue does not duplicate any of the currently available Krommer. Peter-Lukas Graf is the flautist and directs the performance of the *Oboe concerto*, while in the *Concerto for flute* Heinz Holliger returns the compliment for him. The playing is expert, though the recording is not in the first flight: the soloists are a little too forward and there is a need for greater transparency, even on CD.

Octet-Partita in E flat, Op. 79.
*** CRD *CRDC 4110* [id.]. Nash Ens. – DVOŘÁK: *Serenade.****

The Nash Ensemble give an excellent and lively account of this attractive Krommer piece. It is not great music but it is highly agreeable, and the Nash readily demonstrate its charm in a direct way for which the bright recording is admirably suited.

Lalo, Edouard (1823–92)

Cello concerto in D min.
*** CBS Dig. **MK 35848** [id.]. Yo-Yo Ma, O Nat. de France, Maazel – SAINT-SAËNS: *Concerto No. 1.****
*** Decca Dig. **414 387-2** [id.]. Harrell, Berlin RSO, Chailly – FAURÉ: *Elégie*; SAINT-SAËNS: *Cello concerto No. 2.****
*** RCA *RK 70798* [*ARK1-4665*]. Lloyd Webber, LPO, Lopez-Cobos – RODRIGO: *Concierto.****
(B) *** DG Walkman *423 290-4* [id.]. Schiff, New Philh. O, Mackerras – SAINT-SAËNS: *Concerto No. 1*; SCHUMANN: *Concerto*; TCHAIKOVSKY: *Rococo variations.****

Yo-Yo Ma is an artist who eschews overstatement, and his account of the Lalo *Concerto* must rank as the finest now available. It has great sensitivity, beauty of tone and expressive feeling to commend it, and indeed it makes the work seem better than in fact it is. Moreover, Maazel and the Orchestre National de France give understanding support, matching the sensitivity of the soloist. The quality of the recorded sound is excellent, beautifully balanced and spacious, yet with detail admirably refined in its CD format.

Lynn Harrell's Decca account was recorded within the attractive acoustic of the Jesus Christ Church, Berlin (the venue of many of Furtwängler's successful mono LPs of the 1950s). The orchestra is given vivid colour and presence. Chailly's accompaniment is attractively bold, more assertive than Maazel's for Yo-Yo Ma. Lynn Harrell's performance is an extremely fine one, perhaps less subtle but no less ardent than Ma's, and certainly no less convincing. While the playing remains refined in polish and detail, there is a yearning intensity in the *Intermezzo*, while the outer movements combine spontaneity and vigour. The cello image is very tangible on CD (though, like Yo-Yo Ma's, it is modest in scale) and, while the orchestra creates a dramatic contrast, the balance remains totally believable. Harrell's couplings are more generous than Ma's, including not only the attractive and virtually unknown *Second Concerto* of Saint-Saëns, but also a splendid account of Fauré's *Elégie*.

No complaints about Julian Lloyd Webber's account of the Lalo *Concerto*. It is played with style and feeling. The performance does not quite match that of Yo-Yo Ma on CBS, while Harrell has a finer recording, although the RCA is perfectly satisfactory, if less rich. But many may choose the attractive Rodrigo coupling, one of that composer's most endearing recent works. The first-class chrome cassette is strikingly refined in detail.

The DG Walkman tape is a marvellous bargain in offering Heinrich Schiff's début recording, an account which is as fresh and enthusiastic as it is polished. Moreover it is given in harness with not only his version of the Saint-Saëns No. 1 but also fine Rostropovich performances of the Schumann *Concerto* and the Tchaikovsky *Rococo variations*. The chrome transfers are of high quality.

Symphonie espagnole, Op. 21.

*** DG Dig. **400 032-2** [id.]. Perlman, O de Paris, Barenboim – BERLIOZ: *Romance*.***

(B) *** DG Dig. *423 261-4* [id.]. Perlman, O de Paris, Barenboim – SAINT-SAËNS: *Violin concerto No. 3*; WIENIAWSKI: *Concerto No. 2*.***

*** Decca Dig. **411 952-3** [id.]. Kyung-Wha Chung, Montreal SO, Dutoit – SAINT-SAËNS: *Concerto No. 1*.***

(*) HMV Dig. **CDC7 47318-2 [id.]. Mutter, O Nat. de France, Ozawa – SARASATE: *Zigeunerweisen*.**(*)

(M) *(*) RCA **GD 86520**; *GK 86520*. Perlman, LSO, Previn – RAVEL: *Tzigane*; SIBELIUS: *Violin concerto*.**(*)

Lalo's brilliant five-movement distillation of Spanish sunshine is well served here. While the compact disc version of Perlman's newest DG digital recording shows no marked improvement on the LP (if anything it emphasizes the degree of digital edge), the sound remains both vivid and refined. The very opening sets the style of the reading, with a strongly articulated orchestral introduction from Barenboim that combines rhythmic buoyancy with expressive flair. The lyrical material is handled with great sympathy, and the richness and colour of Perlman's tone are never more telling than in the slow movement, which opens tenderly but develops a compelling expressive ripeness. The brilliance of the scherzo is matched by the dancing sparkle of the finale. The recording is extremely lively and the forward balance of the soloist does not obscure orchestral detail. As can be seen above, this recording is also available on a bargain-priced Pocket Music tape, much more generously coupled with Saint-Saens and Wieniawski.

Kyung-Wha Chung has the advantage of a first-class Decca digital recording (the CD technically preferable to either the DG or EMI alternatives), with a highly effective, natural balance. Hers is an athletic, incisive account, at its most individual in the captivatingly lightweight finale, with an element almost of fantasy. For some ears, the lack of sumptuousness of style as well as timbre may be a drawback; Miss Chung does not have quite the panache of Perlman. But Charles Dutoit's accompaniment is first class and the orchestral characterization is strong throughout.

Anne-Sophie Mutter's account is second to none, with its dazzling display of bravura, the first movement immediately commanding. The scherzo has an engaging element of fantasy; the finale is scintillating. Many will find the delicacy of her phrasing in the second subject of the first movement refreshing, with its absence of schmaltz, although Perlman is more sinuously beguiling here. Similarly, the opening of the slow movement is especially imaginative, with Ozawa's strong orchestral statement answered by the soloist with gentle, touching serenity. Both in the *Intermezzo* and *Andante* there is solo playing of passionate eloquence, the timbre richly expansive. While the orchestral detail is good, the balance projects the violin well to the front and the slightly-too-close microphones add a touch of shrillness to the upper range; a degree of digital edge affects the orchestra, too; on CD, the orchestral violins sound thin above the stave.

Perlman's RCA issue, which is coupled with Ravel and Sibelius, looks a bargain; certainly Perlman plays the work brilliantly, sparkling in the bravura and relishing the expressive melodies without over-indulging them. He is ably supported by Previn; but the snag is the recording balance which places the violin much too far forward. The digital remastering casts a fierce aural spotlight on the soloist, thinning the timbre and providing added projection at the orchestra's expense. Accompanying detail is sometimes all but masked. Previn ensures that the tuttis have plenty of impact, but the harshness on the violin tone also affects the orchestral sound, which lacks bloom.

Langgaard, Rued (1893–1952)

(i) *Symphony No. 10* (*Yon dwelling of thunder*); (ii) *Symphony No. 14* (*The Morning*).
** Danacord **DACOCD 302** [id.]. Danish RSO, (i) Schmidt; (ii) Schonwandt.

This coupling marks Langgaard's début on CD. He was something of an outsider in Danish music and has been compared with such figures as Ives and Havergal Brian. Although his roots were firmly in the nineteenth century, his musical language is not wholly consistent. His music is not highly personal – but, at the same time, it must be admitted that the two works recorded here are not quite like anything else. Moments of real vision rub shoulders with music of mind-boggling banality. No. 10 was finished in 1945, and Langgard had already reached No. 14 only two years later. Both are offered in live recordings from the Danish Radio. They are well balanced, have plenty of colour and a wide range.

Lassus, Orlandus (*c.* 1530–94)

Motets and Chansons: *Cum natus esset; In monte Oliveti; Stabat Mater; Bon jour mon coeur* (two versions)*; Fleur de quinze ans; J'ayme la pierre precieuse; Margot labourez les vignes; La nuict froide et sombre; Pour courir en poste a la ville; Susanne ung jour* (two versions).
*** HMV Dig. **CDC7 49210-2** [id.]. Hilliard Ens., Hillier.

One side is devoted to motets, the other to chansons; both are sung one voice to a part. The tonal blend is as perfect as is usual with this ensemble, intonation is extraordinarily accurate, and there is no vibrato. The sacred pieces, and in particular the setting of the *Stabat Mater* which opens the first side, are most impressive. In some of the chansons, there is a discreet lute accompaniment to lend variety. Of the chansons, *La nuict froide et sombre* is quite magical and given with great feeling and colour. A useful addition to the Lassus discography and beautifully recorded.

Missa Pro defunctis a 4.
** Hyp. Dig. **CDA 66066** [id.]. Pro Cantione Antiqua, Mark Brown.

The Pro Cantione Antiqua sing this four-part *Requiem* one voice to a part and the gain in clarity of texture is offset by a loss of grandeur and majesty. The singers are impressive for all that, and the *Requiem* is interspersed with plainchant from the Office for the Dead. The recording, made in the warm acoustic of St John's Church, Hackney, places the singers rather close to the listener, which again helps clarity but reduces the sense of mystery. The four singers blend well and intonation is generally true.

7 Penitential Psalms.
*** HMV Dig. **CDS7 49211-8**; *EX 270424-5* (2). Hilliard Ens., Kees Boeke Cons., Hillier.

The Lassus *Penitential Psalms* are one of the masterpieces of the Renaissance and few works of this period compare with them in magnificence and splendour – or indeed depth. Ambros, writing in the 1860s, called them one of 'those very great monuments of art, over which the stream of time flows powerfully while it bears away lesser things . . . their expression is altogether profoundly and powerfully enthralling, it is awe-inspiring but also elevating and wondrously consoling'. Lassus wrote them in 1559–60 for his patron, Duke Albrecht V of Bavaria, who held them in such high esteem that they were reserved for his ear alone. The sumptuous frontispiece of the manuscript depicts Duke Albrecht listening to Lassus's Hofkapelle where both the vocal and the instrumental forces were much larger than the ten voices and seven instrumentalists employed by Hilliard and Kees Boeke on this recording. Nevertheless they have the measure of the restraint, breadth and dignity of this music, and the recording itself, made in Jesus College, Cambridge, is present and truthful. The cassettes are admirably faithful, too.

Leclair, Jean-Marie (1697–1764)

Scylla et Glaucus (opera): complete.
⊛ *** Erato Dig. **ECD 75339(3)** [id.]. Donna Brown, Crook, Mellon, Yakar, Monteverdi Ch., E. Bar. Soloists, Gardiner.

A younger contemporary of Rameau, Jean-Marie Leclair regrettably wrote only this one opera. First heard at the Paris Opéra in 1746, it follows the formal pattern of the tragédie lyrique laid down by Lully and developed by Rameau, involving an allegorical prologue and five Acts. The style is more direct, less elaborate than Rameau's, and the speed with which the brief numbers follow each other – some arias as brief as a minute long – give the piece a freshness which easily sustains its length of nearly three hours.

In 1979 John Eliot Gardiner was responsible for the first performance (at St John's, Smith Square, London) anywhere in modern times, followed by a broadcast. Here with a different cast of principals in a production sponsored by Lyon Opera, of which he is music director, Gardiner crowns that achievement, demonstrating this to be one of the neglected masterpieces of late French baroque, every bit as worthy to be remembered as Rameau's operas. Quite apart from Gardiner's characteristically electrifying direction, the playing and singing can hardly be faulted. Donna Brown makes a sweet-toned Scylla, who yet rises to the extra challenge of her longer numbers. Howard Crook is superb in the tenor role of Glaucus, headily beautiful, never strained by the highest tessitura; while Rachel Yakar characterizes the malevolent role of the sorceress, Circe, without ever transgressing the bounds of classical stylishness. With all these singers, ornamentation becomes a natural point of expression, never clumsy or forced, and the recording, made in St Giles, Cripplegate, is brightly atmospheric, full and clear.

Lecocq, Alexandre (1832–1918)

Mam'zelle Angot (ballet, arr. Gordon Jacob).
*** Decca Dig. **411 898-2** [id.]. Nat. PO, Bonynge – BERLIOZ: *Les Troyens: ballet***; WEBER: *Invitation to the dance.****

La Fille de Madame Angot was a highly successful operetta of the 1870s. The ballet originated for Massine's post-Diaghilev company and was first danced in New York in 1943. It found its definitive form, however, in a later Sadler's Wells production, also choreographed by Massine. The narrative line follows the story of the operetta, and much of the music is also drawn from that source; however, Gordon Jacob includes excerpts from other music by Lecocq. It is a gay, vivacious score with plenty of engaging tunes, prettily orchestrated in the modern French style. There are flavours from other composers too, from Adam to Sullivan, with Offenbach's influence strongly felt in the final carnival scene. Bonynge offers the first recording of the complete score, and its 39 minutes are consistently entertaining when the orchestral playing has such polish and wit. The Kingsway Hall recording is closely observed: the CD brings sharp detail and tangibility, especially at lower dynamic levels. Some ears may find the violin timbre a shade over-bright.

Lehár, Franz (1870–1948)

Waltzes: *Eva; Gold and silver; Gypsy love. The Count of Luxembourg: Luxembourg. Giuditta: Where the lark sings. The Merry Widow: Ballsirenen.*
(*) HMV Dig. **CDC7 47020-2 [id.]. Johann Strauss O of Vienna, Boskovsky.

Gold and silver was Lehár's waltz masterpiece; the others are his arrangements, using melodies from the operettas. They are ravishingly tuneful; given such warmly affectionate performances and a recording which is sumptuous and has sparkling detail, this is easy to enjoy. Lehár's scoring is often imaginative, but in the last resort one misses the voices. The CD is first class in every way.

The Count of Luxembourg (highlights, in English).
*** That's Entertainment **CDTER 1050**; *ZCTER 1050*. Hill-Smith, Jenkins, Tierney, Nicoll, Richard, New Sadler's Wells Op. Ch. and O, Wordsworth.

Like its companion disc of selections from Kálmán's *Countess Maritza*, this record from That's Entertainment presents lively and fresh performances from the cast of the New Sadler's Wells Opera production. Particularly in the general absence of records of operetta in English, this is very welcome. Bright digital sound, which is given plenty of presence on CD.

The Land of Smiles (*Das Land des Lächelns;* complete in German).
*** HMV Dig. **CDS7 47604-8** (2). Jerusalem, Donath, Lindner, Finke, Hirte, Bav. R. Ch., Munich RO, Boskovsky.

The Land of Smiles is a strange piece, a revamped version of an operetta, *The Yellow Jacket*, which was a failure in 1923. In 1929 its mixture of Eastern and Western values (with the principal tenor a Chinese prince) proved a great success, thanks in good measure to the tailoring of that central role to the needs of Richard Tauber, who promptly made the song *Dein ist mein ganzes Herz* an enormously popular signature-tune of his own. Siegfried Jerusalem, who plays Sou-Chong here, has nothing like the same charm as Tauber, but it is a strong and sympathetic reading, lacking only a vein of implied tragedy, the wistfulness behind the smile. Helen Donath sings sweetly as his beloved Lisa, and the whole ensemble is admirably controlled in a colourful performance, warmly recorded, by Willi Boskovsky. The CD adds extra clarity and an enhanced presence to the sound.

The Merry Widow (*Die lustige Witwe;* complete in German).
❀ *** HMV **CDS7 47178-8** [Ang. **CDC 47177**] (2). Schwarzkopf, Gedda, Waechter, Steffek, Knapp, Equiluz, Philh. Ch. and O, Matacic.
(*) Denon Dig. **C37 7384/5** [id.]. Irosch, Minich, Prikopa, Koller, Karczykowski, Huemer, Ruzicka, V. Volksoper Ch. and O, Bibl.

Matacic provides a magical set, guaranteed to send shivers of delight through any listener with its vivid sense of atmosphere and superb musicianship. It is one of Walter Legge's masterpieces as a recording manager. He had directed the earlier *Merry Widow* set, also with his wife Elisabeth Schwarzkopf as Hanna, and realized how difficult it would be to outshine it. But outshine it he did, creating a sense of theatre that is almost without rival in gramophone literature. If the Decca approach to opera has always been to conceive it in terms of a new medium, Legge went to the opposite view and produced something that is almost more theatrical than the theatre itself. No other opera record more vividly conveys the feeling of expectancy before the curtain rises than the preludes to each Act here. The CD opens up the sound yet retains the full bloom, and the theatrical presence and atmosphere are something to marvel at. The layout is less than ideal, however, and only two bands are provided on each CD, though there is generous indexing.

Recorded live in a stage performance given in Tokyo in 1982, the Vienna Volksoper version is easily idiomatic, but lacks the polish and finesse to make Lehár's charming operetta sparkle. With singing generally too rough to give much pleasure on record (shrill from the women, strained and wobbly from the men), the result is jolly but coarse. The recorded sound does not help, thin in the middle, lacking body. Banding is limited to beginnings of Acts, which is the more irritating when there is so much spoken dialogue to wade through.

The Merry Widow: highlights.
*(*) DG **415 524-2** [id.]. Harwood, Stratas, Kollo, Hollweg, Keleman, Grobe, Krenn, German Op. Berlin Ch., BPO, Karajan.

'Brahms's *Requiem* performed to the tunes of Lehár' was how one wit described the Karajan version of *The Merry Widow*, with its carefully measured tempi and absence of sparkle. Though Elizabeth Harwood is an appealing Widow, she seems relatively colourless beside Schwarzkopf. This CD selection of highlights is generous, some 68 minutes, and all the important numbers are included. The reverberant recording has been dried out a little, but this means that the choral focus is not always quite clean, although the solo voices have plenty of presence. There is a synopsis but no libretto.

Der Zarewitsch (complete).
*** Eurodisc **610 137** (2). Kollo, Popp, Rebroff, Orth, Hobarth, Bav. R. Ch., Munich R. O, Wallberg.

Wallberg conducts a delightful and idiomatic performance of one of Lehár's later, more ambitious operettas which consciously extends the normal limits of the genre, and designedly provided a vehicle for the ever-charming Richard Tauber, the supreme operetta tenor of his day. René Kollo may not have the finesse of a Tauber, but he sings with a freshness and absence of mannerism that bring out the melodic beauty. Lucia Popp as the heroine, Sonya, sings ravishingly, and there is no weak link in the cast elsewhere. With two extra numbers given to the Grand Duke (Ivan Rebroff), both taken from Lehár's *Wo die Lerche singt*, sides are generously long, and the speed of the entertainment comes over all the more refreshingly in the excellent CD transfer. No text is given, only notes in German.

Leoncavallo, Ruggiero (1858–1919)

I Pagliacci (complete).
*** DG **419 257-2** (3) [id.]. Carlyle, Bergonzi, Benelli, Taddei, Panerai, La Scala, Milan, Ch. & O, Karajan – MASCAGNI: *Cavalleria Rusticana*.***
(***) HMV **CDS7 47981-8** [Ang. **CDCC 47981**] (3); (M) *EX 291269-5*. Callas, Di Stefano, Gobbi, La Scala, Milan, Ch. & O, Serafin – MASCAGNI: *Cavalleria Rusticana*.(***)
*(*) Ph. **411 484-2** (2). Stratas, Domingo, Pons, Rinaldi, La Scala, Milan, Ch. & O, Prêtre.

The Italian opera traditionalists may jib at Karajan's treatment of Leoncavallo's melodrama – and for that matter its companion piece. He does nothing less than refine them, with long-breathed, expansive tempi and the minimum exaggeration. One would expect such a process to take the guts out of the drama, but with Karajan – as in *Carmen*, *Tosca*, *Aida*, etc. – the result is superb. One is made to hear the beauty of the music first and foremost, and that somehow makes one understand the drama more. Passions are no longer torn to tatters, Italian-style – and Karajan's choice of soloists was clearly aimed to help that – but the passions are still there; and rarely if ever on record has the La Scala Orchestra played with such beautiful feeling for tone-colour. Bergonzi is among the most sensitive of Italian tenors of heroic quality, and it is good to have Joan Carlyle doing a major operatic role on record, touching if often rather cool. Taddei is magnificently strong, and Benelli and Panerai could hardly be bettered in the roles of Beppe and Silvio. The opulence of Karajan's performance is well served by the extra clarification given on CD, with voices more sharply defined. As a filler, DG provides a splendid set of performances of operatic intermezzi from *Manon Lescaut*, *Suor Angelica*, Schmidt's *Notre*

Dame, Giordano's *Fedora*, Cilea's *Adriana Lecouvreur*, Wolf-Ferrari's *Jewels of the Madonna*, Mascagni's *L'amico Fritz*, plus the *Meditation* from *Thaïs* (with Michel Schwalbé), and the *Prelude* to Act III of *La Traviata*.

It is thrilling to hear *Pagliacci* starting with the Prologue sung so vividly by Tito Gobbi. The bite of the voice and its distinctive timbres are unique. Di Stefano, too, is at his finest, but the performance inevitably centres on Callas. She never attempted the role of Nedda on the stage, and the flashing-eyed characterization is never conventional. There are many points at which she finds extra intensity, extra meaning, so that the performance is worth hearing for her alone. Serafin's direction is strong and direct. The mono recording is dry, like the others made at La Scala, with voices placed well forward but with choral detail blurred (if not unacceptably so), a balance underlined in the clarity and definition of CD. The tapes sound well, too, and are offered at mid-price.

The Prêtre version is taken from the soundtrack of Zeffirelli's film of the opera, and is principally remarkable for the large-scale heroic performance, superbly sung, of Placido Domingo as Canio. Singing of this calibre makes nonsense of the allegation that he fails to characterize his roles individually. Much of the rest is less recommendable. Juan Pons sings the Prologue impressively and exploits his fine baritone as Tonio; but Teresa Stratas and Alberto Rinaldi (Silvio) both suffer from uneven vocal production, with Stratas's earthy timbres going raw under pressure. The CD transfer manages to place the opera complete on a single disc, although the extra clarity and presence serve only to underline the vocal flaws.

Liadov, Anatol (1855–1914)

Polonaise, Op. 49.
(*) HMV Dig. **CDC7 47505-2 [id.]. CBSO, Järvi – BALAKIREV: *Symphony No. 1.****

Liadov has much enchanting music to his credit – *The enchanted lake* and *Kikimora*, to name the two most obvious pieces. His *Polonaise*, Op. 49, which precedes the Balakirev *Symphony* sounds like an amiable and not-too-distant relative of the *Polonaise* from *Eugene Onegin*. It is a rather feeble makeweight for an impressive symphony.

Ligeti, György (born 1923)

Bagatelles.
*** Crystal **CD 750** [id.]. Westwood Wind Quintet – CARLSSON: *Nightwings*; MATHIAS: *Quintet*; BARBER: *Summer music.****

Ligeti's folk-inspired *Bagatelles* were originally written for piano and in 1953 arranged by the composer for wind quintet. They are highly inventive and very attractive; and they are played with dazzling flair and unanimity of ensemble by this American group.

Lux aeterna.
(M) *** DG **419 475-2**; *419 475-4* [id.]. N. German R. Ch., Helmut Franz – HOLST: *The Planets.***(*)

What seems an unexpected coupling for a performance of Holst's *Planets* is linked by the film *2001* in which this choral piece took an honoured place, fascinating the unlikeliest listeners with its evocative clouds of vocal sound. Performance and recording are first class.

Liszt, Franz (1811–86)

Ce qu'on entend sur la montagne (*Bergsymphonie*), *G. 95.*
(*) ASV Dig. **CDDCA 586; *ZCDCA 586* [id.]. LSO, Yondani Butt – TCHAIKOVSKY: *The Tempest.***(*)

Ce qu'on entend sur la montagne is the first of Liszt's symphonic poems and the longest (28′). It suffers not only from formal weakness but also from a lack of really interesting material, the most memorable idea being a chorale known as 'The Song of the Anchorites' which appears in the brass at the centre of the work. The programme (based on ideas from a poem by Victor Hugo) concerns the conflict between Nature and Humanity. The treatment is unashamedly melodramatic, yet the piece has some very effective passages, even if there is a violin solo which hovers dangerously near sentimentality. Yondani Butt's fine performance skirts such dangers: he gives the work with much conviction, and the LSO respond with some powerful and expressive playing. The recording is appropriately spectacular, with a wide dynamic range on CD. The chrome cassette is acceptable, but the sound is much more restricted. The coupling, an early symphonic poem of Tchaikovsky, more inspired music, is very appropriate.

Piano concerto No. 1 in E flat, G. 124.
*** HMV **CDC7 47221-2** [id.]. Ousset, CBSO. Rattle – SAINT-SAËNS: *Concerto No. 2.****
(*) RCA **RD 86244 [RCA 6255-2-RC]. Rubinstein, RCA SO, Wallenstein – SCHUMANN: *Concerto* etc.**
(*) DG **415 061-2 [id.]. Argerich, LSO, Abbado – CHOPIN: *Concerto No. 1.***(*)

For those seeking the *First Concerto* alone Cécile Ousset's is a magical performance, sparklingly individual, full of spontaneity. The scherzando movement and the final *Allegro marziale* have wit and humour, with Ousset making light of the technical difficulties. Rattle equally draws exciting and warmly expressive playing from the CBSO and the recording is first rate, save for the forward balance of the soloist, who seems to be in a slightly different acoustic. But those looking for a red-blooded modern recording should be well satisfied with this.

Rubinstein's performance too is quite splendid, full of panache, with an aristocratic command and glittering digital dexterity. Wallenstein accompanies with gusto and the whole affair is like a live performance, gathering pace and excitement to give the finale fine dash and excitement. Astonishingly, the recording dates from 1956, yet it is bold and full-bodied, and the Carnegie Hall acoustics bring a fine resonance and bloom. The usual snag of the absence of any real pianissimo is less serious in an extrovert work like this, although it does affect the Schumann coupling.

By the side of Rubinstein, Martha Argerich seems much less flamboyant. Hers is a clear, direct, even fastidious approach. She plays the *Larghetto* meltingly, and there is an excellent partnership with Abbado, who also seeks refinement without reducing the underlying tension. The CD remastering of the 1969 recording is extremely successful, the sound hardly dated at all.

Piano concertos Nos 1 in E flat, G. 124; 2 in A, G. 125.
*** Ph. **412 006-2**; (M) *412 006-4* [id.]. Sviatoslav Richter, LSO, Kondrashin.

Piano concertos Nos 1–2; Hungarian fantasia, G. 123.
** Erato Dig. **ECD 88035** [id.]. Duchable, LPO, Conlon.

Piano concertos Nos 1–2; Années de pèlerinages, Supplement: Venezia e Napoli, G. 162.
(M) *** DG **415 839-2**; *415 839-4* [id.]. Lazar Berman, VSO, Giulini.

Piano concertos Nos 1–2; 3 Études de concert, G. 144.
*** Ph. **416 461-2** [id.]. Arrau, LSO, Sir Colin Davis.

Piano concertos Nos 1 and 2; Étude transcendante d'après Paganini, G. 140/2.
(B) **(*) DG Walkman *413 850-4* [id.]. Vásáry, Bamberg SO, Prohaska (with RACHMANINOV: *Piano concerto No. 2* etc.**).

Among the couplings of both Liszt *Concertos*, Richter's 1962 recordings sweep the board. They are particularly distinguished, not only by the power and feeling of Richter's own playing and the obvious rapport between conductor and soloist, but also because of a similar and striking communication between Richter and the orchestra. The orchestral playing throughout is of the very highest order and achieves a remarkably poetic response when orchestral soloists are called on to share a melody with the piano. The recording, which is perhaps slightly below the finest modern standard, has been vividly remastered; this is the second time it has reappeared on cassette at medium price. While the compact disc offers a marginal improvement in quality, the sound on the tape is very well managed, too – and it costs about a third the price of the CD.

Lazar Berman has the advantage of Giulini's sensitive and masterly accompaniment with the Vienna Symphony, and even if you feel that these scores hold no surprises for you, try to hear his record. Berman's playing is consistently poetic and he illuminates detail in a way that has the power to touch the listener. Some of his rapt, quiet tone would probably not register without the tactful assistance of the DG engineers, who enable all the detail to 'tell', but the balance is most musical and well judged. A very thoughtful account of No. 1 and a poetic reading of the *A major* make this a most desirable record. Giulini keeps a strong grip on the proceedings and secures an excellent response from his players. These performances do not eclipse Richter's but they are among the best currently available. The Galleria reissue has been digitally remastered with great success and the sound is rich and firm. On CD the *Second Concerto* is most generously cued. The *Concertos* were recorded in 1966 and, to make the Galleria issue even more desirable, DG have added the three pieces which make up the *Années de pèlerinages Supplement*, with *Gondoliera* and the *Canzone* following the *First Concerto*, and *Tarantella* used as a final encore piece. There is more magnificent piano playing here, and this is a bargain in every sense of the word.

Claudio Arrau made a stunning record of the *E flat Concerto* with Ormandy and the Philadelphia Orchestra in the 1950s, and this new account, made in his mid-seventies, is scarcely less fine. Even though some of the youthful abandon is tamed, Arrau's virtuosity is transcendent. There is a greater breadth in No. 1 here than in the earlier version, and there are many thoughtful touches throughout. This artist's Indian summer shows no loss of fire, and he brings plenty of panache to the *A major Concerto*. This does not displace Lazar Berman or, of course, Richter among the top recommendations but takes its place beside them. First-class sound. Curiously, the remastering for CD has resulted in a very reticent triangle in the scherzo of the *First Concerto*; in fact one has to listen very carefully to hear it at all. The CD adds Arrau's 1976 recordings of the three *Concert studies*, G. 144, of which the last, *Un sospiro*, has been a favourite since the days of 78s.

The generously coupled Walkman tape offers three concertos, plus solo items, and – while Vásáry's version of the Rachmaninov *C minor* is less impressive than his Liszt – this is still a bargain. His recording of Liszt's *E flat Concerto* still sounds very well indeed; the performance is distinguished by considerable subtlety and refinement, yet with no loss of impact, even if there is little barnstorming. His approach to the *A major*, too, is thoughtful and sensitive. The accompaniments under Prohaska are sympathetic, and the 1960 sound remains vivid, clear and full.

Duchable's performances are flamboyantly extrovert, and the bold, forwardly balanced piano helps to underline that effect. The orchestra makes a strong impression, however, and Conlon matches his soloist with firm and vigorous accompaniments. On CD the *Second Concerto* comes first and is made to sound more melodramatic than usual. In both works, while the lyrical episodes do not lack expressive feeling, they are without the melting spontaneity of the famous Richter versions. The dash and brilliance of the playing best suit the *Hungarian fantasia*. Certainly on CD the sound has plenty of presence.

Dante symphony, G. 109.
*** Hung. **HCD 11918-2** [id.]. Kincses, Hungarian R. & TV Ch., Budapest SO, Lehel.
** Erato Dig. **ECD 88162** [id.]. Helmond Concert Ch., Rotterdam PO, Conlon.

(i) *Dante symphony; Mephisto waltz No. 2; Les Préludes; Tasso, lamento e trionfo.*
(B) **(*) HMV *TCC2-POR 54292.* (i) Arndt, St Thomas's Ch., Leipzig; Leipzig GO, Masur.

Lehel's account is second to none and better than most previous versions. Veronika Kincses is a fine singer, and Lehel gives a strongly characterized performance with well-focused singing and fiery, intense orchestral playing. The Hungaroton recording has plenty of detail and presence, and the acoustic is agreeably warm. Like Lopez-Cobos before him, Lehel offers the *Magnificat* ending, which comes off splendidly in his hands.

The double-length iron-oxide tape, in EMI's 'Portrait of the Artist' series, offers a selection from Masur's distinguished integral recording of all Liszt's orchestral music. (A further compilation, on both mid-priced CD and cassette, which overlaps with this, is discussed below.) The *Dante symphony* is complete on one side without a break, and Masur proves as persuasive an advocate as any on record in this repertoire. The sound matches the original recordings in catching the rich sonorities of the Leipzig lower strings and the dark, perfectly blended woodwind timbre. The tape transfer is well detailed and convincingly balanced, but loses a little of the original sparkle on top.

Conlon's performance is atmospheric but a little lacking in charisma and grip: the Inferno sequence has more impact in Masur's hands, although the advantages of CD and a well-balanced digital recording cannot be disputed, and the Rotterdam account is well played and sung.

2 Episodes from Lenau's Faust: Der nächtliche Zug; Mephisto waltz No. 1 (Der Tanz in der Dorfschenke); 2 Legends, G. 354; Les Préludes, G. 97.
(*) Erato Dig. **ECD 88235 [id.]. Rotterdam PO, Conlon.

If this Liszt anthology falls short of the highest distinction, it is still impressive and enjoyable. James Conlon gives us the original orchestration of the *St Francis Legends* plus the rarely heard and highly imaginative *Der nächtliche Zug*. Conlon secures responsive playing from the Rotterdam orchestra, and the engineering is excellent without being in any way spectacular. There is a good, full-bodied and well-balanced sound-picture.

Fantasia on Hungarian folk tunes, G. 123.
(M) **(*) HMV *EG 290615-4*. Katsaris, Phd. O, Ormandy – BARBER: *Adagio*; R. STRAUSS: *Also sprach Zarathustra.***(*)

Katsaris plays the *Hungarian fantasia* with undoubted flair and brilliance and Ormandy accompanies persuasively. The engineers obviously chose a balance to make the piano glitter, and the result is somewhat twangy, but otherwise the sound is full and wide-ranging.

Fantasia on Hungarian folk tunes, G. 123; Malédiction, G. 121; Totentanz, G. 126 (all for piano and orchestra).
*** Decca Dig. **414 079-2** [id.]. Bolet, LSO, Ivan Fischer.

Bolet is the masterful soloist in a splendid triptych of concertante works, the second of which – using strings alone – is unjustly neglected. Bolet's performance, sensitive as well as brilliant, should do much to rectify that, and the accounts of the two well-known works, persuasive enough to paper over any structural cracks, bring out all of Bolet's characteristic bravura.

Excellent accompaniments from the LSO under an understanding Hungarian conductor, and recording of demonstration quality, particularly impressive on CD.

(i) *Fantasia on Hungarian folk tunes, G. 123. Hungarian rhapsodies, G. 359/2, 4 & 5; Mazeppa, G. 100; Mephisto waltz No. 1; Les Préludes, G. 97; Tasso, lamento e trionfo, G. 96.*
❀ *** DG **415 967-2** (2). (i) Shura Cherkassky; BPO, Karajan.

(i) *Fantasia on Hungarian folk tunes. Hungarian rhapsodies, G. 359/2 & 5; Mephisto waltz No. 1, G. 359.*
(M) *** DG *419 862-4* [id.]. (i) Cherkassky, BPO, Karajan.

For the CD collection, DG have added to the orchestral works, recorded by Karajan over the years, Shura Cherkassky's glittering 1961 recording of the *Hungarian fantasia.* It is an affectionate performance with some engaging touches from the orchestra, though the pianist is dominant and his playing is superbly assured. Here as elsewhere the remastering for CD has improved the range and body of the sound impressively, with firm detail throughout the orchestra. The cellos and basses sound marvellous in the *Fifth Rhapsody* and *Tasso*, and even the brashness of *Les Préludes* is a little tempered. The quiet background for the coda of *Mazeppa* adds to the frisson-creating effect of the distanced brass. *Mazeppa* is a great performance, superbly thrilling and atmospheric. A superb achievement, showing Karajan and his Berlin orchestra at their finest. The Galleria reissue offers a popular grouping centred on the *Hungarian fantasia.* Here the sound on cassette is slightly less sharply focused than on CD.

(i) *Fantasia on Hungarian folk tunes;* (ii) *Hungarian rhapsodies, G. 359/2, 4 & 6* (*Pest Carnival*); (iii) *Rákóczy march.*
** Hung. Dig. **HCD 12721-2** [id.]. (i) Jenö Jando, Hungarian State O, Ferencsik, (ii) Szeged SO, Pál, (iii) Németh.

The three *Hungarian rhapsodies* are well enough played by the Szeged orchestra under Támas Pál, and there is no lack of paprika in the proceedings. Jenö Jando is rather closely balanced in the recording with the late János Ferencsik and the Hungarian State Orchestra, and sounds pretty thunderous at times. There is fine body and the sound is particularly rich and firmly defined in the bass. But this is not an outstanding issue in any way.

A Faust symphony, G. 108.
*** HMV **CDC7 49260-2** [id.]; (M) *ED 291342-4*. Alexander Young, Beecham Ch. Soc., RPO, Beecham.
*** HMV Dig. **CDC7 49062-2** [id.]. Winberg, Westminster Ch. College Male Ch., Phd. O, Muti.
*** Erato Dig. **ECD 880682** [id.]. John Aler, Slovak Philharmonic Ch., Rotterdam PO, Conlon.
(*) Decca Dig. **417 399-2; *417 399-4* [id.]. Jerusalem, Chicago Ch. & SO, Solti.
(*) Hung. **HCD 12022-2 [id.]. Korondy, Hungarian Army Ch. & State O, Ferencsik.

Sir Thomas Beecham's classic 1959 recording, well transferred to CD, shows this instinctive Lisztian at his most illuminatingly persuasive. His control of speed is masterly, spacious and eloquent in the first two movements without dragging, brilliant and urgent in the finale without any hint of breathlessness. Though in the transfer string-tone is limited in body, balances are very convincing, and the sound is unlikely to disappoint anyone wanting to enjoy a uniquely warm and understanding reading of an equivocal piece, hard to interpret. On tape the violins are shrill above the stave and, even though this costs much less, the CD is far preferable.

Those looking for a modern digital recording will probably turn to Muti. As an ardent Tchaikovskian, he shows a natural sympathy for a piece which can readily seem overlong, and he finds obvious affinities in the music with the style of the Russian master. Some might feel that he is too overtly melodramatic in the finale, yet his pacing of the first movement is admirable, finding tenderness as well as red-blooded excitement. In the *Gretchen* movement he conjures the most delicately atmospheric playing from the orchestra and throughout he is helped by the ambience of the Old Met. in Philadelphia which seems especially suitable for this score. The digital recording is brilliant yet full-bodied, and without glare.

James Conlon also gives an extremely satisfying account on Erato. The Rotterdam orchestral playing is very alive and committed and the choral finale comes off splendidly. Overall there are less histrionics than with Muti, particularly in the last movement, but the performance has much sensitivity and plenty of weight. The Erato sound-balance is strikingly realistic in the CD format.

It was after hearing Beecham's classic recording that Sir Georg Solti was persuaded to tackle Liszt's great *Faust* triptych, a work which – surprisingly, for a musician born in Hungary – he had not till then studied. It is a spacious, brilliant reading, marked by superb playing from the Chicago orchestra. The bright Decca recording underlines the fierce element in Solti's reading, removing some of its warmth. There are more tender versions of the portrait of Gretchen but none so expansive in its purity, while the Mephistophelean finale brings the most impressive playing of the set, with Solti's fierceness chiming naturally with the movement's demoniac quality. The recording is typical of Decca's work in Chicago, very brilliant but lacking the depth of focus which would set the brightness in context.

With the relatively brisk speeds Ferencsik directs a very idiomatic reading of Liszt's three portraits, lacking a little in weight and dramatic tension, but ending with a biting and brilliant account of the scherzando music representing Mephistopheles. The Hungarian players are on their mettle there, and are very well recorded.

Hungarian rhapsodies Nos 1–6, G. 359.
** Ph. Dig. **412 724-2**; *412 724-4* [id.]. Leipzig GO, Masur.
(M) ** HMV **CDM7 69011-2** [id.]; *EG 769011-4*. Philh. Hungarica or LPO, Boskovsky.

Neither Masur nor Boskovsky seem to be able to let their hair down sufficiently to respond to the chimerical nature of Hungarian gypsy music which (however cosmopolitanized) was the basis of Liszt's inspiration. The mercurial element – those sudden changes of mood which are the essential idiomatic feature – needs a greater show of temperament, a sense of almost going over the top. Masur secures sophisticated playing, polished and responsive, from the splendid Leipzig orchestra, and he has the advantage of digital recording, although the Leipzig resonance prevents ideal clarity (especially with the cimbalom in No. 3). There is some graceful and elegant string playing – the interplay between violins and flute in No. 4 is most engaging – and the performances have spontaneity, but one wants a more extrovert flair and a stronger flow of adrenalin. There is a good tape.

Boskovsky's recordings come from 1977/8 and are also well played. No. 3 comes off rather well, with the gypsy element better managed. The remastered EMI recording is drier and clearer than the Philips, the bass response slightly attenuated. This collection has a price advantage and is certainly enjoyable. The chrome cassette is more restricted in upper range than the CD but sounds quite agreeable.

Hungarian rhapsodies Nos 2 and 4; Les Préludes, G. 97.
(B) *** DG Walkman *413 159-4* [id.]. BPO, Karajan – DVOŘÁK: *Slavonic dances*; SMETANA: *Vltava* etc.***

Karajan is completely at home in this repertoire. He goes over the top in *Les Préludes*, not helped by a top-heavy recording balance which manages to make even the Berlin Philharmonic sound brash; but in the rest of the music here he secures marvellous playing and fine characterization. The approach to the *Hungarian rhapsodies* is somewhat urbane, yet there is plenty of sparkle. On the excellently engineered Walkman tape, three most popular works are featured as part of a well-organized anthology of Slavonic music.

Hunnenschlacht (symphonic poem), *G. 105.*
** Telarc Dig. **CD 80079** [id.]. Cincinnati SO, Kunzel – BEETHOVEN: *Wellington's victory.***

A direct, unsubtle performance of a rarely recorded piece, not one of Liszt's finest works in the genre. The Telarc sound, however, is highly spectacular with the organ interpolation adding to the expansiveness of texture. Those wanting the *'Battle' symphony* of Beethoven won't be disappointed with this, although the CD is rather short measure.

Orpheus, G. 98; Mazeppa, G. 100; Les Préludes, G. 97; Tasso, lamento e trionfo, G. 96.
(M) ** HMV **CDM7 69022-2** [id.]; *EG 769022-4.* Leipzig GO, Masur.

Orpheus, G. 98; Les Préludes, G. 97; Tasso, lamento e trionfo, G. 96.
** Hung. Dig. **HCD 12446-2** [id.]. Hungarian State O, Ferencsik.

Les Préludes, G. 97.
(M) *** HMV **CDM7 69228-2** [id.]. Philh. O, Karajan – BRAHMS: *Symphony No. 4.***(*)
(M) **(*) DG **423 384-2** [id.]. BPO, Fricsay – DVOŘÁK: *Symphony No. 9;* SMETANA: *Vltava.****
** HMV Dig. **CDC7 47022-2** [id.]. Phd. O, Muti – RAVEL: *Boléro;* TCHAIKOVSKY: *1812.**

(i) *Les Préludes;* (ii) *Mephisto waltz No. 1, G. 110/1;* (i) *Prometheus, G. 99;* (ii) *Tasso, lamento e trionfo, G. 96.*
(***) Decca **417 513-2** [id.]. (i) LPO; (ii) O de Paris, Solti.

Masur offers one more work than Ferencsik in this generous helping from his complete recording of Liszt's orchestral music, issued by EMI in two 4-LP boxes (now deleted). The four works gathered here play for just over an hour and, although the digital remastering has robbed the sound of some of its rich sonority in the lower strings, the brightness of the new sound-balance has a different kind of appeal. Masur is not altogether at home in the melodrama of *Les Préludes* and *Mazeppa* – although the latter is excitingly done, if without the panache of Karajan (see above). He breezes through *Orpheus* at record speed, and misses the endearing gentleness that Beecham brought to it in the early 1960s. Nevertheless these performances are all strongly characterized and extremely well played. There is a good chrome cassette, with the sound-balance rather fuller if less transparent than the CD. *Orpheus* and *Tasso* on side two sound especially well.

Janos Ferencsik is a sympathetic Lisztian; he gives a refined account of *Orpheus* and actually makes *Les Préludes* sound restrained. The image is well focused and has plenty of body, particularly at the bottom end of the register.

Solti's collection derives from two different analogue records of the mid-1970s. He secures playing of the highest quality from the Orchestre de Paris; *Tasso*, in particular, is a reading of great power and atmosphere. He is characteristically brash in *Les Préludes*, but the *Mephisto waltz* has splendid charisma. The drawback here is the digital remastering which has brought coarseness and edgy brass to an analogue recording which was originally outstandingly good and didn't call for any 'enhancing'.

Karajan's 1958 *Les Préludes* found much favour in its day, as well it should. It still sounds thrilling now, and demonstrates the fine musical judgement of the original balance engineers. Musically, this is the equal of any modern version.

Fricsay has exactly the right temperament for *Les Préludes.* His performance is highly romantic – the detail of the pastoral interlude is delightful – yet the performance has enormous conviction and ardour and generates great excitement without vulgarity. The recording, made in the Jesus Christus Church, Berlin, was originally outstanding, but the 'drying-out' effect of the digital remastering has rather coarsened the sound. One can obtain this also on a mid-priced

Focus tape, coupled with Smetana, as on CD, and also with some Tchaikovsky; this reproduces more smoothly and is also much less expensive (DG *419 656-4*).

Muti's *Les Préludes* is suitably exuberant and the Philadelphia Orchestra are on top form. The recording, however, is far from ideal in the matter of sonority, suggesting that – as so often in this piece – the engineers were striving for brilliance above all. The Ravel and Tchaikovsky couplings sound even less congenial.

PIANO MUSIC

Albumblatt in waltz form, G. 166; Bagatelle without tonality, G. 216a; Caprice-valses Nos 1 & 2, G. 214; Ländler in A flat, G. 211; Mephisto waltzes nos 1–3, G. 514–5 and 216; Valse impromptu, G. 213; 4 Valses oubliées, G. 215.
*** Hyp. Dig. **CDA 66201**; *KA 66201* [id.]. Leslie Howard.

On his excellent Hyperion disc Leslie Howard collects all of Liszt's original piano pieces that might be described as waltzes. Fascinatingly, he includes a fourth *Valse oubliée* that he himself has notionally completed from material long buried. This is not a collection to match the waltzes of Chopin in consistency, but rather one to illustrate the variety and range of expression possible in the genre. Howard, on the cool side as a recording artist, gives clean, fresh, dramatic performances, very well recorded, on tape as well as CD.

Années de pèlerinage, 1st Year (Switzerland), G. 160.
*** Decca Dig. **410 160-2**; *410 160-4* [id.]. Jorge Bolet.
*** DG Dig. **415 670-2**; *415 670-4* [id.]. Daniel Barenboim.

Années de pèlerinage, 1st Year (Switzerland); Concert paraphrase on Wagner's Isoldens Liebestod, G. 447.
*(*) Ph. Dig. **420 202-2**; *420 202-4* [id.]. Alfred Brendel.

Winner of the instrumental prize in the *Gramophone* awards 1985, this recording of the Swiss pieces from the *Années de pèlerinage* represents Bolet at his very peak, in some ways even transcending his masterly achievement in earlier discs in the series, with playing of magical delicacy as well as formidable power. So *Au bord d'une source* brings playing limpid in its evocative beauty. The piano sound is outstandingly fine, set against a helpful atmosphere, and there is a very good cassette; the compact disc, however, gains greatly from its complete background silence.

Barenboim's set is also distinguished, rather warmer in pianistic colour and romantic feeling. Some ears find Bolet's playing a trifle cool in its sonorities, for all his grip and powerful command. Barenboim's approach is freer, more improvisatory at times (though Bolet's poetic mastery in the closing two pieces is undeniable). The DG recording projects an image of striking fullness, yet still not lacking brilliance.

Brendel made some of his first conquests in the recording studio in this repertoire and his 1959 survey of the first book of the *Années de pèlerinage* was among the finest. This newcomer has many impressive moments but also some ugly fortissimi that are not wholly the responsibility of the engineers. Brendel plays the First Book *segue*, without pauses, and, although there is some atmospheric playing in the set, the moments of magic are relatively few.

Années de pèlerinage, 2nd Year (Italy), G. 161 (complete).
*** Decca Dig. **410 161-2**; *410 161-4* [id.]. Jorge Bolet.
(M) *** Ph. *412 364-4*. Alfred Brendel.
*(*) Ph. Dig. **420 169-2**; *420 169-4* [id.]. Alfred Brendel.

The pianistic colourings in this fine instalment in Bolet's Liszt series are magically caught here, whether in the brilliant sunlight of *Sposalizio* or the visionary gloom of *Il penseroso*. The *Dante sonata* brings a darkly intense performance, fresh and original and deeply satisfying. The piano sound is brilliant but not clangorous. On cassette, the wide range is impressively caught, but the focus is slightly less sharp than on CD.

Brendel's earlier performances are also of superlative quality. This was outstanding among Liszt records in the analogue era: not only is the playing highly poetic and brilliant but the 1973 recording offers Philips's most realistic quality, which sounds admirable in its cassette format.

The later version is not its equal. There is some ugly percussive tone here and little sense of atmosphere. Of course Brendel is always to be heard with respect, but this playing is out of scale and over-projected.

Années de pèlerinage, 2nd Year, G. 161; Après une lecture du Dante (Dante sonata); 6 Chants polonais (Chopin), G. 480; Harmonies poétiques et religieuses, G. 173; Funérailles.
*** Ph. Dig. **411 055-2** [id.]. Claudio Arrau.

This is very distinguished playing, astonishing for an artist then approaching his eightieth birthday. The *Dante sonata* is wonderfully commanding: it has a magisterial grandeur; and *Funérailles* is hardly less impressive. The transcriptions of Chopin songs are done with great charm and subtlety, too. The recording quality is totally realistic and splendidly focused – among the best recordings of the instrument we have had in the last few years. The compact disc attains near-perfection by adding a reliably silent background.

Années de pèlerinage, 2nd Year, G. 161: Après une lecture du Dante. Concert paraphrases on Gounod's Faust, G. 407; Verdi's Rigoletto, G. 434; 6 Consolations, G. 172.
** Denon Dig. **C37 7332** [id.]. Jean-Yves Thibaudet.

Jean-Yves Thibaudet is a young French pianist of considerable prowess who has many prizes to his credit, including the French Radio prize which he won in 1977 when he was only fifteen. He has a formidable technique which enables him to bestride the hurdles of the Faust paraphrase a little more readily than he encompasses the simplicity of the *Consolations*. He plays with plenty of brilliance and dramatic fire in the *Dante sonata* and is obviously an artist to watch. His recording, made in Japan, is splendidly vivid and truthful; no reader attracted by this programme need hesitate on this score. Dezsö Ránki recorded the *Dante sonata* for Denon in the 1970s when he was about the same age (see below), and the Hungarian's greater artistic maturity, freedom and excitement tell.

Années de pèlerinage, 2nd Year, G. 161: Après une lecture du Dante (Dante sonata); Concert paraphrase on Wagner's Isoldens Liebestod, G. 447.
(*) RCA Dig. **RD 85931; *RK 85931*. Barry Douglas – MUSSORGSKY: *Pictures*.**(*)

There is plenty of colour and fire in Barry Douglas's performances which are an encore for an impressive account of Mussorgsky's *Pictures at an exhibition*. The *Wagner paraphrase* is particularly strong and involving. Good full piano tone, on both CD and a faithful equivalent chrome tape.

Années de pèlerinage, 2nd Year, G. 161: Sonetti del Petrarca Nos 47, 104 & 123; Supplement, Venezia e Napoli: Gondoliera, G. 162; Consolation No. 3, G. 172; Études de concert, G. 144, No. 3 in D flat. Impromptu, G. 191; Liebestraum No. 3, G. 541.
*** CRD *CRDC 4108* [id.]. Paul Crossley.

Very fine performances of wide range and keen sensitivity from Paul Crossley, who has the measure of this repertoire. He is on the whole well recorded and, though the piano is at times closely observed, the sense of over-presence is mellowed by the otherwise very faithful tape transfer. Crossley's playing is thoughtful and poetic, and this is a most persuasive recital.

Années de pèlerinage, Book 2. Supplement: Venezia e Napoli (*Gondoliera; Canzone; Tarantella*), *G. 162; 3rd Year: Les jeux d'eau à la Villa d'Este, G. 163/4; Ballade No. 2 in B min., G. 171; Harmonies poétiques et religieuses: Bénédiction de Dieu dans la solitude, G. 173/3.*
*** Decca Dig. **411 803-2**; *411 803-4* [id.]. Jorge Bolet.

Even in Bolet's prize-winning Liszt series, this sixth volume stands out for its performances, both brilliant and dedicated, of a group of the most colourful and popular pieces, 'a dazzling pendant to Liszt's Italian *Années de pèlerinage*', as the sleeve-note describes them, and also of two of the weightiest, the *Bénédiction* and the *Ballade*, both spaciously conceived and far too little known. As he progresses in his series, so Bolet seems even more at ease in the studio; the concentration of the long pieces, as well as the magically sparkling textures of the sunny Italian pieces, is masterfully conveyed. Vivid and full piano recording. It has the usual added tangibility in its CD format, but the chrome tape too is another Decca issue to represent the highest state of the art.

Années de pèlerinage, 3rd Year (*Italy*), *G. 163* (complete).
*** Ph. Dig. **420 174-2**; *420 174-4* [id.]. Zoltán Kocsis.

Zoltán Kocsis gives the most compelling account of these sombre and imaginative pieces; apart from beautiful pianism, he also manages to convey their character without exaggeration. He has impeccable technical control and can convey the dark power of the music without recourse to percussive tone. He is splendidly recorded by the Philips engineers. Lisztians need not hesitate.

Années de pèlerinage, 3rd Year: Les jeux d'eau à la Villa d'Este. Études d'exécution transcendante, G. 139: Chasse-neige, Riccordanza. Gaudeamus igitur: Legend No. 1: St Francis of Paulo walking on the water, G. 175; Mephisto waltz No. 1; Soirées de Vienne, G. 457.
* HMV **CDC7 47562-2** [id.]. György Cziffra.

A disappointing recital with none of the effortless panache and virtuosity with which Cziffra dazzled listeners in the 1950s. There is little of the old delicacy and magic in evidence on this record, in fact the playing is often rather laboured. Cziffra is not helped by the shallow quality of the sound.

Années de pèlerinage, 3rd Year: Tarantella. Harmonies poétiques et religieuses: Pensées des morts; Bénédiction de Dieu dans la solitude, G. 153; Legend: St Francis of Assisi preaching to the birds, G. 175. Mephisto waltz No. 1, G. 514; Rapsodie espagnole, G. 254.
*** Virgin Dig. **VC 790700-2**; *VC 790700-4* [id.]. Stephen Hough.

Stephen Hough's imaginatively planned Liszt recital in the Virgin Classics label is outstanding in every way. The choice of items is both illuminating and attractive, with substantial rarities like the two *Harmonies poétiques et religieuses* (*Pensées des morts* and *Bénédiction*) included alongside popular favourites like the *Mephisto Waltz No. 1* and *St Francis preaching to the birds*. That last item is magically poetic in its re-creation of birdsong, while in the *Tarantella* Hough gives an inspired performance, combining power and searing virtuosity with delicate poetry and keen wit. Full, vivid recording. This amply confirms what Hough's prizewinning record of Hummel concertos for Chandos suggested, that he is a natural, magnetic communicator in the recording studio. The chrome cassette is disappointing – the sound is full, but the resonance has meant a fairly low transfer level and the upper range is restricted.

Années de pèlerinage, 3rd Year, G. 163: Sursum corda. Harmonies poétiques et religieuses: Invocations, G. 173. Vexilla regis prodeunt, G. 185; Weihnachtsbaum: Abendglocken (Evening bells), G. 186.
** Ph. Dig. **420 156-2**; *420 156-4* [id.]. Alfred Brendel – MUSSORGSKY: *Pictures.***

Brendel always has something to say in Liszt, but the playing here, except in the evocative *Evening bells*, which is charmingly done, lacks something of the incandescence that made his earlier recordings so memorable. The recording is good, but the coupled Mussorgsky is not among the finest available versions.

Concert paraphrases of Schubert Lieder: *Auf den Wasser zu singen; Aufenthalt; Erlkönig; Die Forelle; Horch, horch die Lerch; Lebe wohl!; Der Lindenbaum; Lob der Tränen; Der Müller und der Bach; Die Post; Das Wandern; Wohin.*
*** Decca Dig. **414 575-2** [id.]. Jorge Bolet.

Superb virtuosity from Bolet in these display arrangements of Schubert. He is not just a wizard but a feeling musician, though here he sometimes misses a feeling of fun. First-rate recording, with the CD adding the usual extra sense of presence, and gaining from the silent background.

Concert paraphrase of Verdi's: *Rigoletto, G. 434; Études d'exécution transcendante d'après Paganini: La Campanella, G. 140/6. Harmonies poétiques et religieuses: Funérailles, G. 173/7. Hungarian rhapsody No. 12, G. 244; Liebestraum No. 3, G. 541/3. Mephisto waltz No. 1, G. 514.*
*** Decca Dig. **410 257-2** [id.]. Jorge Bolet.

Bolet's is a superb collection of Liszt items, the first to be recorded of his current series. The playing is magnetic, not just because of virtuosity thrown off with ease (as here in the *Rigoletto* paraphrase) but because of an element of joy conveyed, even in the demonic vigour of the *Mephisto waltz No. 1.* The relentless thrust of *Funérailles* is beautifully contrasted against the honeyed warmth of the famous *Liebestraum No. 3* and the sparkle of *La Campanella*. Even with the most hackneyed pieces, Bolet – superbly recorded – conveys complete freshness. The compact disc is thrillingly realistic in its spectacular sense of presence.

Concert paraphrases of Wagner: *Der fliegende Höllander: Spinning chorus; Ballade, G. 440; Lohengrin: Elsa's dream and Lohengrin's rebuke, G. 446; Rienzi: Fantasia on themes from Rienzi, G. 439; Tannhäuser: Entry of the guests, G. 443; Tristan and Isolde: Isoldens Liebestod, G. 447.*
(*) DG Dig. **415 957-2 (id.]. Daniel Barenboim.

Zoltán Kocsis has recorded an outstanding selection of this repertoire for Philips, including some fine transcriptions of his own. We hope this may appear on CD. Barenboim's recital overlaps with Kocsis's in offering the *Liebestod* from *Tristan*, but in every other respect the discs are complementary. Liszt transcribed four passages from *Lohengrin*, and their choice does not coincide. The sound of the DG recording has been enhanced by the CD transfer and is now most realistic. If Barenboim lacks the youthful ardour of the young Hungarian and his response to the *Flying Dutchman* episodes is (by his standards at any rate) relatively routine, there are many good things, too, notably the *Liebestod* itself and the excerpts from *Lohengrin*.

3 Concert studies, G. 144; 2 Concert studies, G. 145; 6 Consolations, G. 172; Réminiscences de Don Juan (Mozart), G. 418.
*** Decca **417 523-2** [id.]. Jorge Bolet.

This was one of Jorge Bolet's first recitals for Decca, dating from 1979, to which have been added the *Consolations* (1985) for the CD reissue. In the *Concert studies* the combination of virtuoso precision and seeming spontaneity is most compelling, and the record is particularly valuable for including a splendid account of the *Don Juan* paraphrase, a piece which is neglected on record. The *Consolations* show Bolet at his most romantically imaginative, and indeed this disc includes two of Liszt's most popular pieces, the *Third Consolation* (a dreamy meditation on the opening of Chopin's *D flat Nocturne*, Op. 27/2) and the *Concert study* in the same key, better known as *Un sospiro*. Bolet plays them most beautifully.

Études d'exécution transcendante, G. 139 (complete).
(M) *** HMV **CDM7 69111-2** [id.]. György Cziffra.
*** Ph. **416 458-2** [id.]. Claudio Arrau.
(*) Decca Dig. **414 601-2; *414 601-4* [id.]. Jorge Bolet.

György Cziffra's set of the *Études d'exécution transcendante* has a deservedly legendary status, although hitherto it has been available only in mono LP format. It was recorded in 1959 when Cziffra was at the height of his powers; the playing is highly volatile and charismatic and shows enormous technical command. The clean, light articulation in *Wild Jagd* and the glitter of *Feux-follets* contrast with the delicate rubato and fine sensibility of *Ricordanza*, while *Appassionata* and *Vision* display the fullest romantic power. The recording is not distinguished, the upper range somewhat restricted, and there is at times a bass orientation; but the panache of the playing triumphs over the early stereo technology.

Arrau made this recording in 1977 and it was a formidable achievement for an artist in his seventies. Arrau plays always with great panache and musical insight, which more than compensate for the occasional smudginess of the recorded sound. On record Cziffra brings greater obvious virtuosity to these pieces, but is of course a much younger man. Arrau's playing is most masterly and poetic, and the recording, if too reverberant, is admirably truthful, and the CD transfer adds to the feeling of tangibility.

In the *Transcendental studies* Jorge Bolet in his Liszt series gives powerful performances of the bravura pieces, massive and sure rather than exciting, contrasting them against such poetic studies as *Paysage* (No. 3) and *Harmonies du soir* (No. 11). If you are looking principally for pianistic fireworks, Bolet is a little disappointing, lacking a little in demonry, but as a searching interpreter of the composer and his musical argument he has few rivals. The Decca recording presents big-scale piano sound to match the performances.

Etudes d'exécution transcendante d'après Paganini Nos 1–6, G. 140; Années de pèlerinage, 1st Year (Switzerland): Au lac de Wallenstadt, G. 160/2; 2nd Year (Italy): Il Penseroso, G. 160/2; 3rd Year: Les jeux d'eau à la Villa d'Este, G. 163/4. Hungarian rhapsody No. 13 in A min., G. 244/13.
(*) HMV Dig. **CDC7 47380-2 [id.]. André Watts.

André Watts gives sensitively conceived, well-paced accounts of these pieces in which his virtuosity, though it can be taken for granted, does not dominate at the expense of sensibility. Watts made his début some years ago on CBS but his translation to EMI brings better sound. There are some minuscule miscalculations which the artist, believing in the importance of truth and of the kind of playing one encounters in the concert hall, does not correct. These performances have no lack of spontaneity, and the recording is very acceptable.

Hungarian rhapsodies Nos 1–19, G. 244.
** Ph. Dig. **416 463-2** [id.]. Misha Dichter.

Hungarian rhapsodies Nos 1–19, G. 244; Rapsodie espagnole, G. 254.
(M) *** DG *419 362-4* (2) [id.]. Roberto Szidon.

Hungarian rhapsodies Nos 2; 5 (Héroide élégiaque); 9 (Carnival in Pest); 14; 15 (Rákóczy march); 19.
(M) *** DG *423 019-4* (from above). Szidon.

Hungarian rhapsodies Nos 2; 6; 9 (Carnival in Pest); 12–14; 15 (Rákóczy march).
*** HMV **CDC7 47370-2** [id.]. György Cziffra.

Roberto Szidon offers Liszt playing of the highest order, and recording quality to match. Szidon won acclaim some years ago with a début record (Prokofiev *Sixth Sonata*, Scriabin No. 4 and Rachmaninov No. 2), and his 1973 set of the complete *Hungarian rhapsodies* more than fulfilled the promise shown in his very first record. He has flair and panache, genuine keyboard command and, when required, great delicacy of tone. Those not wanting the complete set can safely invest in the shorter selection. All six pieces included are of high musical quality, and the playing readily demonstrates Szidon's finely judged rubato, boldness of line, and sure sense of style. The recording is first class, and the tape transfers (both on the complete set, issued in one of DG's 'flap-packs', and on the selection at lower mid-price on the Focus label) are most realistic.

Misha Dichter's account of the *Hungarian rhapsodies* is in many ways very impressive, and he has little difficulty in meeting their formidable technical demands. He is also recorded with extraordinary definition and realism, but the playing is curiously wanting in colour and temperament. In this respect he is no match for Szidon.

Cziffra's performances are dazzling. They are full of those excitingly chimerical spurts of rubato that immediately evoke the unreasonably fierce passions of gypsy music. The high degree of neurosis in the playing, with hardly two consecutive phrases at an even tempo, makes even Szidon (who has the full measure of the music) seem staid. Cziffra, with glittering rhythmic and digital dexterity, sets every bar of the music on fire. Some might find him too impulsive for comfort, but the *Rákóczy march* is a *tour de force* and his command of the keyboard is masterly. The recording, made in the Salle Wagram, Paris, in 1974/5, is a little dry, but otherwise truthful.

Liebesträume Nos 1–3, G. 541.
*** DG **415 118-2** [id.]. Daniel Barenboim – MENDELSSOHN: *Songs without words****; SCHUBERT: *6 Moments musicaux.***

This is a recoupling from three different analogue LP sources. These famous Liszt pieces come from 1981 and are most naturally recorded. Barenboim plays them with unaffected simplicity and he is equally at home in Mendelssohn's *Songs without words*. The Schubert pieces are slightly more self-conscious but, taken as a whole, this is a rewarding CD.

Mephisto waltzes Nos 1–4, G. 514–6 & 696; Mephisto polka, G. 217; Bagatelle without tonality, G. 216a; Harmonies poétiques: Bénédiction de Dieu dans la Solitude, G. 173.
(*) Tel. **ZK8 42829 [id.]. Cyprien Katsaris.

Cyprien Katsaris possesses an astonishing technique – indeed, as collectors of the Liszt/Beethoven symphony transcriptions will know, he has few peers in this respect. Dazzling though his playing is, this record is not unflawed: there are some mannered touches in the *First Mephisto waltz*; the instrument itself is not always perfectly tuned and is too closely observed by the engineers. However, his playing is never lacking in imagination or musical insight and should undoubtedly be heard by Lisztians. Both the *Bagatelle sans tonalité* and the *Bénédiction* are beautifully concentrated in atmosphere.

Piano sonata in B min., G. 178.
(*) RCA **RD 85673 [RCA 5673-2RC]. Artur Rubinstein – BACH: *Chaconne* (with FRANCK: *Prelude, chorale & fugue****).

Piano sonata; Années de pèlerinage, 2nd Year, G. 161: Il Penseroso; 3rd Year, G. 162: Les jeux d'eau à la Villa d'Este. Hungarian rhapsody No. 15 (Rákóczy march), G. 244; Mephisto waltz No. 1, G. 514.
❀ *** Olympia Dig. **OCD 172** [id.]. Mikhail Pletnev.

Piano sonata; Années de pèlerinage, 2nd Year, G. 161: Sonetti del Petrarca Nos 47, 104 & 123; Après une lecture du Dante (Dante sonata).
** Delos **D/CD 3022** [id.]. John Browning.

Piano sonata in B min.; Années de pèlerinage, 2nd Year, G. 161: Après une lecture du Dante (Dante sonata). Mephisto waltz No. 1, G. 514.
*** Denon Dig. **C37 7547** [id.]. Dezsö Ránki.

Piano sonata; Bagatelle without tonality, G. 216; Concert study in D flat (Un Sospiro), G. 144/3; Étude d'exécution transcendante No. 10, G. 139; En rêve, G. 207; Nuages gris, G. 199; Schlaflos, Frage und Antwort, G. 203; Valse oubliée No. 1, G. 215/1.
(*) HMV Dig. **CDC7 47381-2 [id.]. André Watts.

Piano sonata; Berceuse, G. 174; Concert study: Gnomenreigen, G. 145/2; Liebestraum No. 3, G. 541; Valse oubliée No. 1, G. 215/1.
(M) *** Decca *411 727-4*. Clifford Curzon.

Piano sonata; 3 Concert studies, G. 144.
*** Chan. Dig. **CHAN 8458**; *ABTD 1123* [id.]. Louis Lortie.

Piano sonata; Études d'exécution transcendante, Nos 1–2, 3 (La Campanella), 4–6, G. 140.
*** HMV Dig. **CDC7 47514-2** [id.]. Cécile Ousset.

Piano sonata; Grand galop chromatique, G. 219; Liebesträume Nos 1–3; Valse impromptu, G. 213.
*** Decca Dig. **410 115-2**; *410 115-4*. Jorge Bolet.

Piano sonata; 2 Légendes (St Francis of Assisi preaching to the birds; St Francis of Paulo walking on the water), G. 175; Harmonies poétiques et religieuses: Bénédiction de Dieu dans la Solitude, G. 173/3.
** Erato Dig. **ECD 88091** [id.]. François-René Duchable.

Piano sonata; 2 Légendes, G. 175; La lugubre gondola, Nos 1 and 2, G. 200.
*** Ph. Dig. **410 040-2** [id.]. Alfred Brendel.

The permutations of the Liszt *Sonata* on CD are now pretty formidable, but most Lisztians will surely need more than one version. They will not want to be without Brendel's famous record, nor perhaps Curzon's tape, but the most exciting new recording to have appeared recently has come from Russia. Like rare French vintages, the Russians keep the best for themselves: until a year or so ago Mikhail Pletnev's visits to the West had been few. The winner of the 1978 Tchaikovsky competition, he has a commanding musical authority, exceptional even among such laureates, a highly distinctive timbre and an amazing dynamic range and variety of colour. His technique is transcendental and can be compared only with the young Horowitz, and there is a refinement and poetry that are hardly less remarkable. He dispatches the *Sonata* with an awesome brilliance and sense of drama, and his *Mephisto Waltz* is altogether thrilling. While the recording does not do full justice to his highly personal sound-world, it is eminently satisfactory. A most exciting disc.

Brendel's latest account of the *Sonata* has received wide acclaim; the critics of *Gramophone* magazine voted it the piano record of 1983. It is certainly a more subtle and concentrated account than his earlier version made in the mid-1960s – brilliant though that was – and must be numbered among the very best now available. There is a wider range of colour and tonal nuance, yet the undoubted firmness of grip does not seem achieved at the expense of any spontaneity. There have been many outstanding versions of this work in the past; this certainly ranks with them, among other reasons because of the striking excellence of the engineering, for it is amazingly well recorded. On compact disc, the presence of the recording is enhanced by the absence of any intrusive noise, yet there is a feeling of ambience; although the balance is close, the effect is very realistic.

Curzon shows an innate understanding of the *Sonata*'s cyclic form, so that the significance of the principal theme is brought out subtly in relation to the music's structural development. There are only a few performances to compare with this and none superior, and Decca's 1963 recording matches the playing in its excellence. The shorter pieces too are imaginatively played. With an excellent tape transfer, this is superb value at mid-price.

Louis Lortie was the young Canadian pianist whose account of the Beethoven *G major Concerto* made so strong an impression at the 1984 Leeds competition. He gives almost as commanding a performance of the Liszt *Sonata* as any in the catalogue; its virtuosity can be taken for granted and, though he does not have the extraordinary intensity and feeling for drama of Pletnev, he has a keen awareness of its structure and a Chopinesque finesse that win one over. The Chandos recording is made at The Maltings, Snape, and, though a shade too reverberant, is altogether natural. As usual from Chandos, there is a good tape, a shade bass-orientated.

The power, imagination and concentration of Bolet are excellently brought out in his fine account of the *Sonata*. With the famous *Liebestraum* (as well as its two companions) also most beautifully done, not to mention the amazing *Grand galop*, this is one of the most widely appealing of Bolet's outstanding Liszt series. Excellent recording, especially on CD, but the cassette too is first class.

Dezsö Ránki's performances come from 1975 and his anthology was one of the very earliest digital recordings to be made. His account of the *Dante sonata* is very impressive indeed, with real fire and a masterly control of dramatic pace. The *Mephisto waltz* and the *Sonata* are hardly less powerful in the hands of the young Hungarian master; indeed, the latter can hold its own with almost any of its rivals. The Denon recording is absolutely first class and has admirable clarity, body and presence. This is one of the best Liszt recital programmes currently available.

Cécile Ousset enjoys an enviable reputation in the UK, and her following is unlikely to be disappointed with this Liszt recital. There is something of that hard steely tone in the first of the studies which does not enjoy universal appeal, but there is no denying that she has a formidable musical personality. Her account of the *B minor Sonata* is one of the finest now before the public; it is a thoroughly integrated view of this piece, played with extraordinary flair and forward drive. It is very impressive indeed and will appeal even to those who normally do not number themselves among her admirers. The recording is little short of superb, and has plenty of space and presence.

On CD, Rubinstein's performance of the *Sonata* functions as a bonus for his outstanding coupling of the Bach/Busoni *Chaconne* and Franck's *Prelude, chorale and fugue* which appeared together on LP. The *Sonata* was recorded five years earlier, in 1965, and there is some hardness of timbre in fortissimos. But at *piano* and *mezzo forte* levels (and there is a wider range of dynamic here than on some Rubinstein records) the tone is subtly coloured and Rubinstein's mercurial approach to the music is wonderfully spontaneous, bringing an astonishing fire and brilliance for a pianist of his age and considerable poetry to the more thoughtful moments.

André Watts's performance of the *Sonata* has not the sheer dramatic power or concentration of such artists as Brendel, Bolet or Pletnev, but it is still very fine and can be thoroughly recommended, albeit not as a first choice in a wide field. The other works are also well done and have undoubted spontaneity; even if there are a few details one could cavil at, overall this is undoubtedly distinguished Liszt playing. The recording is good.

John Browning's Liszt recital offers good measure at 71′ 45″ and his performances are predictably brilliant. He gives us the last four of the Italian book of the *Années de pèlerinage* and the *B minor Sonata*. The only other pianist to couple the *Dante sonata* and the *B minor* together is Dezsö Ránki. Although Ránki's Denon recording is well over ten years old, it is not inferior, and artistically he gives the more satisfying performances. Browning, who gave us such inspired Ravel in the 1960s, has a searching intelligence and refined musicianship, but there are some disruptive agogic touches and he does not observe scrupulously all of Liszt's dynamic markings; Bolet, Brendel and Ránki do. Of course, there are many impressive and brilliant things here, though Browning's forte tone does at times harden a little.

François-René Duchable also gives a dashing account of the *B minor Sonata*; in terms of virtuosity, he is in the highest bracket. In a way, he allows his virtuosity to run away with him and dazzles rather than illuminates. Others have a greater musical impact, though this fine French pianist is often poetic, particularly in the third of the *Harmonies poétiques et religieuses*. The Erato recording is not as warm as the best of Philips (Brendel), Decca (Bolet) or HMV (Ousset).

ORGAN MUSIC

Fantasia and fugue on 'Ad nos, ad salutarem undam', G. 259.
(*) DG Dig. **415 139-2 [id.]. Simon Preston (organ of Westminster Abbey) – REUBKE: *Sonata on the 94th Psalm.****

Fantasia and fugue on 'Ad nos, ad salutarem undam'; Prelude and fugue on the name BACH, G. 260; Variations on Bach's 'Weinen, Klagen, Sorgen, Zagen', G. 673.
*** Pierre Verany Dig. **PV 783041** [id.]. Chantal de Zeeuw (organ of Aix-en-Provence Cathedral).

An impressive compact disc début. Mlle Chantal de Zeeuw plays Liszt's ripely romantic evocations of classical forms with striking flair and the resonant acoustic of Aix Cathedral helps to make a spectacular effect. The microphones are close enough to capture the organ's action noise, but the overall sound-picture remains convincing.

The organ in Westminster Abbey has a quite different character from the instrument in Aix, and the recording seeks an essentially atmospheric effect in an acoustic which prevents sharpness of detail. As in his previous analogue recording for Argo, Preston concentrates on colour (often dark-hued) and vivid contrasts, rather than extrovert excitement, although his playing is undoubtedly powerful. Those preferring the Reubke coupling will find that this sounds very impressive on CD, as long as one is willing to accept the blurred focus provided by the ambience of Westminster Abbey.

VOCAL MUSIC

Christus (oratorio), *G. 3.*
(*) Erato Dig. **ECD 88231 [id.]. Valente, Lipovšek, Lindroos, Krause, Slovak Philharmonic Ch., Rotterdam PO, Conlon.

Liszt's *Christus* is less an oratorio than an episodic sequence of contrasted pieces, many of them very beautiful, inspired by the person of Christ. It is not part of the scheme to personify Christ even in the way that Bach does in the Passions, but to intersperse devotional hymns – such as *The Three Kings* or the carol-like *O filii et filiae* – between atmospheric scene-paintings such as *The Beatitudes* or *The miracle depicting Christ walking on the waters.*

James Conlon and his Rotterdam forces give a dedicated reading, full of warmth and understanding. The liveliness of the acoustic and the distancing of the sound may obscure some detail, but this is an account, recorded at a live concert, which brings out the beauties and expressiveness of the writing to the full. Tiny mishaps, inevitable in a live performance, are not likely to undermine enjoyment.

Lieder: *Comment, disaient-ils; Die drei Zigeuner; Ein Fichtenbaum steht einsam; Enfant, si j'étais roi; Es muss ein Wunderbares sein; Oh, quand je dors; S'il est un charmant gazon; Über allen Gipfeln ist Ruh; Vergiftet sind meine Lieder.*
*** DG Dig. **419 238-2** [id.]. Brigitte Fassbaender, Irwin Gage – R. STRAUSS: *Lieder.****

Coupled with an equally characterful collection of Strauss songs, Brigitte Fassbaender's Liszt selection richly deserved to win the Solo Vocal prize in the *Gramophone* awards in 1987. This is singing which in its control of detail, both in word and in note, as well as in its beauty and range of expression is totally commanding. There are few women lieder singers in any generation who can match this in power and intensity, with each song searchingly characterized. Fassbaender proves just as much at home in the four Victor Hugo settings in French as in the German songs. Sensitive accompaniment, well-placed recording.

Lieder: *Es muss ein Wunderbares sein; Es war ein König in Thule; Die Fischerstochter; Freudvoll und leidvoll* (2 settings)*; Ich liebe dich; Ihr Glocken von Marling; I'vidi in terra angelici; Jeanne d'Arc au Bûcher; Jugendglück; Die Loreley; Mignons Lied; O lieb, so lang du lieben kannst; La perla; Wo weilt er.*
*** DG Dig. **419 240-2**; *419 240-4* [id.]. Hildegard Behrens, Cord Garben.

Hildegard Behrens with her dramatic soprano brings out the Wagnerian element in these Liszt songs, most strikingly of all in the three substantial scenas which are the most valuable rarities on the disc, late pieces from the 1870s. This piano version of *Joan of Arc at the stake* followed the original orchestral one, but in its austerity it is just as haunting. In the more lyrical songs Behrens (more than usual on record) keeps the voice well under control, and the accompaniment is unfailingly sensitive, helped by well-balanced recording. There is an excellent cassette.

Lieder: *Es muss ein Wunderbares sein; Freudvoll und leidvoll* (3 settings)*; Gestorben war ich; Hohe Liebe; Kling leise; Die Loreley; Mignons Lied; O lieb, so lang du lieben kannst; 3 Sonnette di Petrarca; Die stille Wasserrose; La tombe et la rose; Über allen Gipfeln ist Ruh; Wie singt die Lerche schön.*
(*) Tel. Dig. **ZK8 43342 [id.]. Margaret Price, Cyprien Katsaris.

Margaret Price's Liszt recital brings superbly poised singing of a fascinating collection of songs, including the original soprano versions of the *Petrarch sonnets*, better known in their later baritone versions and, even more, the final piano transcriptions. It is also good to have all three versions of *Freudvoll und leidvoll*, all winningly done. The most substantial item is the solo arrangement of Goethe's *Über allen Gipfeln*, a dramatic scena arranged from a choral piece, again beautifully done. Dramatic bite may not be Price's strongest suit, even in *Die Loreley*, but these songs glow the more expressively from such subtly shaded treatment. Though the recording acoustic is on the dry side (not helpful to the piano), the voice keeps its creamy beauty.

Hungarian Coronation mass, G. 11.
*** Hung. **HCD 12148-2** [id.]. Kincses, Takács, Gulyás, Polgár, Hungarian R. & TV Ch., Budapest SO, Lehel.

Written for the coronation of Franz Josef I as King of Hungary, this setting of the Mass, completed in a month, shows Liszt at his most direct, freely indulging his sympathy with a wide range of sources: operatic (with even a touch of Wagner's *Lohengrin*), Hungarian (in the *Sanctus*), plainchant and, with the *Graduale*, added later, bringing in Lisztian chromaticism. Sung here with dedication by excellent Hungarian forces under Gyorgy Lehel, its plain homophonic textures – with the soloists generally used together as a quartet – make a strong impact, and the reverberant recording allows plenty of detail to be heard against an apt church acoustic.

The Legend of St Elisabeth, G. 2.
*** Hung. Dig. **HCD 12694/6-2** [id.]. Marton, Kováts, Farkas, Solyom-Nagy, Gregor, Gáti, Budapest Ch., Hungarian Army Male Ch., Children's Ch., Hungarian State O, Joó.

Though uneven in inspiration, Liszt's oratorio on *The Legend of St Elisabeth* contains some of his finest religious music in its span of six tableaux. On one level it may be regarded as a choral symphony, on another as a religious opera in which diatonic writing is seemingly intended to reflect the purity of the subject; but a performance as committed as this, with fine singing and playing, well recorded, makes one forget such equivocal points. Arpad Joó drives the work hard, but never to undermine the expressiveness of chorus and soloists, with Eva Marton as Elisabeth more firmly controlled than she has sometimes been in opera, and with no weak link in the rest of the team of principals.

Missa solemnis, G. 9.
(*) Hung. **HCD 11861-2 [id.]. Kincses, Takács, Korondy, Gregor, Hungarian R. & TV Ch., Budapest SO, Ferencsik.

This ambitious setting of the Mass is sometimes called the *Gran Mass* after the place, Gran (later Esztergom), where it was first given at the consecration of the new cathedral in 1855. It is one of Liszt's finest choral inspirations, full of powerful, dramatic ideas, with thematic links between movements that make it stylistically more consistent than most. Ferencsik's recording, made in the mid-1970s, brings a spacious, powerful performance, well played and sung, with four of Hungary's most distinguished singers as soloists. The analogue recording is not ideal, and the problems of balance created by a reverberant church acoustic are brought out the more in the digital transfer of the original analogue sound on CD. But this remains far more than a stop-gap and is a noble account of a masterly choral work.

Via Crucis, G. 53.
*** Ph. Dig. **416 649-2** [id.]. Netherlands Chamber Ch., De Leeuw (piano).

This rarely heard work was written late in Liszt's career (1878/9). Its atmosphere is spare and austere. Short dramatic choruses are punctuated by imaginative keyboard solos which, as Reinbert de Leeuw shows, are highly effective played on the piano, although, when the choir is being accompanied, the use of the piano is less telling than the more usual organ with its ability to sustain. The baldness of the writing does not imply a lack of beauty or imaginative use of harmony, and the spacious simplicity of the presentation here, with very fine singing from the Netherlands, is agreeably serene. The recording is first class.

OPERA

Don Sanche (complete).
(*) Hung. Dig. **HCD 12744/5-2 [id.]. Garino, Hamari, Gáti, Farkas, Hungarian R. & TV Ch., Hungarian State Op. O, Támas Pál.

At the age of thirteen, well before Beethoven died, the child prodigy, Liszt, sought to demonstrate in this fairy-tale opera that he was a composer as well as a pianist. *Don Sanche or the Castle of Love*, first given in Paris in 1825, was the boy's first essay at a stage work; it was totally forgotten for a century and a half until it was revived (in Britain) in 1977. The piece tells of a magic castle of love ruled over by a sinister magician, and how the knight, Don Sanche, finally wins the love of the disdainful Elzire. The only really Lisztian quality is the way the boy composer lights on instruments relatively exotic at the time, loading piccolos and trombones on to writing which suggests Weber or Rossini with dashes of Haydn, Schubert or even an occasional watered-down echo of Beethoven's *Fidelio*. The pity is that, after a promising start, the 90-minute one-acter tails off, with invention growing thinner and thinner, suggesting that childish enthusiasm for an improbable subject waned, and he wanted to get it over with.

Támas Pál conducts a lively performance, with some stylish singing from the lyric tenor, Gerard Garino, in the name-part. Other principals are variable, including Julia Hamari as the hard-hearted heroine; as long as you keep firmly in mind that this is the work of a thirteen-year-old, however, it will give much pleasure. The sound is bright and close.

Litolff, Henri (1818–91)

Concerto symphonique No. 4, Op. 102: Scherzo.

*** Ph. Dig. **411 123-2**; *411 123-4* [id.]. Misha Dichter, Philh. O, Marriner (with Concert of concertante music ***).

*** Decca Dig. **414 348-2**; *414 348-4* [id.]. Cristina Ortiz, RPO, Atzmon – ADDINSELL: *Warsaw concerto*; GOTTSCHALK: *Grand fantaisie*; RACHMANINOV: *Concerto No. 2*.***

Litolff's delicious *Scherzo*, famous since the days of 78 r.p.m. discs, receives its compact disc début from Misha Dichter, who gives it a scintillating account, played at a sparklingly brisk tempo. Marriner accompanies sympathetically and the recording is excellent in both media.

Cristina Ortiz's version has less extrovert brilliance but an agreeable elegance. The intimacy of this account is emphasized by the balance which places the piano within the orchestral group, making the gentle central section especially effective. The pianism is assured in its delicacy and, with excellent – if reverberant – sound, this can be recommended alongside Dichter. The Decca couplings are more substantial and the CD is impressively natural.

Loewe, Frederick (born 1904)

My Fair Lady (musical).

*** Decca Dig. **421 200-2**; *MFLC 1* [id.]. Kiri Te Kanawa, Jeremy Irons, John Gielgud, Warren Mitchell, Jerry Hadley, London Voices, LSO, Mauceri.

Hoping to follow the great success of Bernstein's recording of *West Side Story*, Decca set up a starry cast to make a brand-new digital version of Loewe's splendid music. Alas, it did not work out quite as planned, and the issue was not the hoped-for best-seller, perhaps because of Kiri Te Kanawa's difficulty with Eliza's cockney persona. Although she sings *I could have danced all night* ravishingly, memories of Julie Andrews are not banished; and Jeremy Irons, who gives a forceful portrayal of Higgins, does not match Rex Harrison's elegant timing, especially in his first early mono recording. Clearly this is a studio production. Having said that, it is a joy to hear the music presented with such vigour and sophistication. Warren Mitchell's Doolittle is endearingly crusty and Jerry Hadley sings *On the street where you live* very engagingly. One realizes just how many good tunes there are. If the original cast is forgotten, the interplay between the characters here works very well, and with spirited direction from John Mauceri this is a first-class entertainment, with the recording giving depth as well as presence.

Lloyd, George (born 1913)

Symphonies Nos 2 and 9.
*** Conifer Dig. **CDCF 139**; *MCFC 139* [id.]. BBC PO, composer.

The remarkable current interest in George Lloyd has been created by the gramophone, rather than the concert hall, aided by the BBC and recently helped by fine performances from the Manchester-based BBC Philharmonic Orchestra, which the composer is known to admire. The continuing success of his immediately communicative music stems partly from the frustration of an intelligent musical public, looking for contemporary works with which they can identify and unable to come to terms with the musical barbed wire which is so often on offer. George Lloyd does not seek to scale Olympian heights but he feels an affinity with Dvořák (both composers share a love of the flute in their scoring); 'we need more Dvořáks today' is his view, and who would disagree?

Lloyd's *Second Symphony* dates from 1933, but he revised it in 1982. It was first performed by the BBC Philharmonic in 1986, who then went on to record it for Conifer. Like the *Ninth*, with which it is coupled, it is a lightweight, extrovert piece, conventional in form and construction, though in the finale the composer flirts briefly with polytonality, an experiment he did not repeat. The *Ninth* (1969) is similarly easygoing; the *Largo* is rather fine, but its expressive weight is in scale, and the finale, 'a merry-go-round that keeps going round and round', has an appropriate energetic brilliance. Throughout both works the invention is attractive, and in these definitive performances, extremely well recorded, the composer's advocacy is very persuasive. There is a first-class chrome cassette.

Symphony No. 7.
*** Conifer Dig. **CDFC 143**; *MCFC 143* [id.]. BBC PO, composer.

The *Seventh Symphony* is on a larger scale than most of Lloyd's earlier works. It is a programme symphony, using the ancient Greek legend of Proserpine. 'There's another dimension somewhere – the Greeks understood this,' Lloyd comments enigmatically. The slow movement is particularly fine, an extended soliloquy of considerable expressive power, based on a quotation from Swinburne:

> Pale beyond porch and portal,
> Crowned with calm leaves she stands
> Who gathers all things mortal
> With cold immortal hands . . .

The last and longest movement (there are only three), is concerned with 'the desperate side of our lives – "Dead dreams that the snows have shaken, Wild leaves that the winds have taken",' yet, as is characteristic with Lloyd, the darkness is muted; nevertheless the resolution at the end is curiously satisfying. Again he proves an admirable exponent of his own music and has expressed satisfaction with the ebb and flow of the *Lento* ('it needs an awful lot of rubato') on this record. The recording is splendid and there is an excellent equivalent chrome cassette.

Symphony No. 10 (November journeys).
(M) *** Trax Dig. **TRXCD 114**; *TRXC 114* [id.]. L. Collegiate Brass, Stobart – JOSEPHS: *Concerto for brass.****

To write a full-scale and genuinely symphonic canvas for brass is a considerable achievement; it plays for just under 30 minutes. The bitter-sweet lyricism of the first movement is most attractive (the use of the piccolo-trumpet a piquant added colouring), but the linear writing is more complex than usual in a work for brass. In the finale a glowing *cantando* melody warms the spirit, to contrast with the basic *Energico*. The performance by the London Collegiate Brass is expert – the *Calma* slow movement is quite haunting, no doubt reflecting the composer's series of visits to English cathedrals which are the reason for the subtitle. The recording is in the demonstration class, with an excellent equivalent chrome tape.

Symphony No. 11.
*** Conifer Dig. **CDCF 144**; *MCFC 144* [id.]. Albany SO, composer.

Having been neglected for so long, George Lloyd has celebrated the renewal of interest in his work with a burst of septuagenarian creativity. Completed in 1985, this *Eleventh Symphony* was commissioned by the Albany Symphony Orchestra; in its five substantial movements it proves a more outward-going work than some of his earlier symphonies. The urgently dynamic first movement is described by the composer as being 'all fire and violence', but any anger in the music quickly evaporates, and it conveys rather a mood of exuberance, with very full orchestral forces unleashed. The second movement, *Lento*, is a songful interlude; the third, a dance, leads to the fourth, a funeral march that for all its drumbeat rhythms is not really mournful. The finale (like the first movement, more substantial than the middle movements) starts with cheerful carolling trumpets, and sets the seal on Lloyd's basic message of optimism. With the orchestra for which the work was commissioned, Lloyd conducts a powerful performance, very well played, demonstrating just how high American standards are, even in orchestras outside the top ranks. The recording was made in the Music Hall of Troy Savings Bank near Albany, which proves to have acoustics that have something in common with the Concertgebouw; it is spectacularly sumptuous and wide-ranging. There is a faithful cassette, but it does not quite match the CD, which is a real demonstration disc.

Lloyd Webber, Andrew (born 1948)

Variations.
(*) Ph. Dig. **420 342-2; *420 342-4* [id.]. Julian Lloyd Webber, LPO, Maazel – William LLOYD WEBBER: *Aurora.****
(*) MCA **DCML 1816. Julian Lloyd Webber, Airey, Argent, Hiseman, Mole, More, Thompson, composer.

This fascinating hybrid work inhabits the world of 'pop' music of the late 1970s yet draws inspiration from the classical mainstream of variations on Paganini's ubiquitous theme, which has inspired so many diverse compositions over the past century and a half. Andrew Lloyd Webber's piece began life as a comparatively short 20-minute work, composed with his brother's brilliant cello-playing very much in mind. It was then expanded to the format here recorded by MCA, about half an hour, and has since been blown up to even greater proportions for its orchestral version, scored by David Cullen. The vulgarity of the ambience of its 'pop' sections will exasperate many listeners, yet its sheer vitality cannot be ignored and the lyrical variations, featuring the flute and solo cello, are genuinely memorable. Although the earlier account sits more comfortably between the world of 'pop' and concert hall, the MCA recording does not match the Philips digital sound and most readers will probably identify more readily with the orchestral expansion. Julian Lloyd Webber makes a distinguished contribution to both recordings and obviously keeps a brotherly eye on the latter version, ably directed by Maazel who has been so successful with his recording of the *Requiem*.

Requiem.
*** HMV Dig. **CDC7 47146-2** [id.]; *EL 270242-4* [Ang. *4DS 38218*]. Brightman, Domingo, Miles-Kingston, Drew, Winchester Cathedral Ch., ECO, Maazel; J. Lancelot (organ).

Let no one be put off by the media hype that surrounded the first performances of this serious essay by a popular composer. This *Requiem* may be derivative at many points, with echoes of Carl Orff – not to mention the *Requiems* of both Verdi and Fauré – but, with Maazel conducting a performance of characteristic intensity, it certainly has a life of its own. The *Pié Jesu* – which rose to the top of the pop-singles at a time when the LP was listed in the pop-album charts – is a model of bridge-building, a melody beautiful and individual by any standard, which yet has all the catchiness of one of Lloyd Webber's tunes in a musical. Plainly the high, bright voice of Sarah Brightman (Mrs Lloyd Webber) was the direct inspiration, and the beauty of her singing certainly earns her this place alongside Placido Domingo contributing in a role rather less prominent. Radiant sounds from the Winchester Cathedral Choir, not least the principal treble, Paul Miles-Kingston. Above all, this is music to which one returns with increasing appreciation and pleasure. The CD gives extra presence and clarity to the excellent sound, while the cassette too is outstandingly successful, though the tape back-up documentation is a disgrace.

Tell me on a Sunday (song cycle).
*** Polydor **833 447-2**; *POLDC 5031*. Marti Webb, LPO, Rabinowitz.

This inspired song cycle by Andrew Lloyd Webber with splendid lyrics by Don Black chronicles a disastrous series of love affairs of an English girl living in America. The theme of the songs is both nostalgic and life-enhancing, for the heroine gradually comes to terms with her failures and it is she who makes the final break. The music itself is memorable. One thinks of the lovely curving contour of *It's not the end of the world*, the steamy *Sheldon Bloom*, the witty tunefulness of *Capped teeth and Caesar salad*, with its repeated pay-off line 'Have a nice day', the sparklingly happy *I'm very you* (the lyrics of these songs sometimes recalling Cole Porter) and above all the haunting title melody. The performance by Marti Webb (for whom the cycle was written) cannot be praised too highly. She is splendidly accompanied by Harry Rabinowitz and members of the LPO, and there is much fine solo playing. The recording is very good on CD and tape alike, and the only small snag is that the opening number, *Take that look off your face*, was stridently heated up to secure its entry into the charts as a hit single.

The Phantom of the Opera (complete).
*** Polydor **831 273-2** [id.]; *PODVC 9* (2). Michael Crawford, Sarah Brightman, Steve Barton, Ch. & O of original London cast, Michael Read.

The Phantom of the Opera: highlights.
*** Polydor **831 563-2**; *POLHC 33* (from above recording).

The worldwide success of *The Phantom of the Opera* means that the recording of the score needs no advocacy from us. It can be said however that there are more good tunes in it than the ubiquitous *Music of the night*, and the chromatic *Phantom theme* is the real stuff of melodrama. As the anti-hero of the piece was a neglected composer, Lloyd Webber needed to write some pastiche opera for him, and this he does very skilfully. The vividly recorded highlights will be the best way to approach this score, but the complete set is also surprisingly compulsive. Extraordinarily, there are no internal cues on the CDs.

Lloyd Webber, William (1914–82)

Aurora (tone poem).
*** Ph. Dig. **420 342-2**; *420 342-4* [id.]. LPO, Maazel – Andrew LLOYD WEBBER: *Variations*.**(*)

The world fame of Andrew Lloyd Webber has led to an interest in his father, who is shown here as a talented composer in his own right, if one without the individuality of his son. *Aurora*, a gentle evocation of the Roman goddess of Dawn, Youth and Beauty, is very well played and recorded. It is coupled with Andrew's more positively inspired, but often more vulgar *Variations*.

(i) *Missa Sanctae Mariae Magdalenae;* (ii) Arias: *The Divine compassion: Thou art the King. The Saviour: The King of Love. 5 Songs.* (iii; iv) *In the half light* (*soliloquy*); *Air varié* (after Franck); (iv) *6 Piano pieces.*
*** ASV Dig. **CDDCA 584**; *ZCDCA 584* [id.]. (i) Richard Hickox Singers, Hickox; I. Watson (organ); (ii) J. Graham Hall; P. Ledger; (ii) Julian Lloyd Webber; (iv) John Lill.

William Lloyd Webber, father of two talented sons (Andrew the composer of hit musicals and Julian the cellist), was a distinguished academic, a virtuoso organist and a composer who in a few beautifully crafted works laid bare his heart in pure romanticism. In his varied collection, the *Missa Santae Mariae Magdalenae* is both the last and the most ambitious of his works, strong and characterful, building up to moments of drama, as when the organ enters for the first time, not in the opening *Kyrie* but suddenly and unexpectedly in the *Gloria* which follows, to thrilling effect. John Lill is a persuasive advocate of the *Six Piano pieces*, varied in mood and sometimes quirky, and accompanies Julian Lloyd Webber in the two cello pieces, written – as though with foresight of his son's career – just as his second son was born. Graham Hall, accompanied by Philip Ledger, completes the recital with beautiful performances of a group of songs and arias, no more remarkable than many works by talented academics, but well worth hearing. Recording, made in a north London church, is warm and undistracting. There is a very satisfactory cassette.

Locatelli, Pietro (1695–1764)

Flute sonatas, Op. 2/2, 6, 7 & 10.
*** Ph. Dig. **416 613-2**; *416 613-4* [id.]. Hazelzet, Koopman, Van der Meer.

Born in Bergamo, Locatelli was a pupil of Corelli in Rome before settling in Amsterdam in the late 1720s. These *Sonatas* come from his set of twelve, Op. 2, and were published in 1732. They are fine pieces which show his developing style to excellent effect. The set was sufficiently admired in its day to sell out and be reprinted, and a generous melodic fertility can be heard in the four recorded here. The performances could hardly be more sympathetic and stylish, while the recording itself, dating from 1980, is very truthful and immediate.

Lully, Jean-Baptiste (1632–87)

Atys (opera): complete.
*** HM Dig. **HMC 901257/9**; *HMC40 1257/9*. Guy de Mey, Mellon, Laurens, Gardeil, Semellaz, Rime, Arts Florissants Ch. & O, Christie.

Harmonia Mundi's valuable set of *Atys* brings the first ever complete recording of a Lully opera to be issued commercially. Like Charpentier's *Medée*, earlier recorded for Harmonia Mundi by William Christie and Les Arts Florissants, this authentic performance demonstrates from first to last that French opera of this early period need not seem stiff and boring. Consistently Christie and his excellent team give life and dramatic speed to the performance, so much so that, though this five-act piece lasts nearly three hours, one keeps thinking of Purcell's almost contemporary masterpiece on quite a different – miniature – scale, *Dido and Aeneas*. Invention is only intermittently on a Purcellian level, but there are many memorable numbers, not least those in the sleep interlude of Act III. Outstanding in the cast are the high tenor, Guy de Mey, in the name-part and Agnes Mellon as the nymph, Sangaride, with whom he falls in love. The three well-filled discs are very conveniently laid out, with the Prologue and Act I on the first, and the other two each containing two Acts complete. The equivalent cassettes are first class, too.

Lutoslawski, Witold (born 1913)

Cello concerto.
*** HMV **CDC7 49304-2** [id.]. Rostropovich, O de Paris, composer – DUTILLEUX: *Cello concerto.****

(i) *Cello concerto;* (ii) *Concerto for oboe, harp and chamber orchestra;* (iii) *Dance preludes.*
*** Ph. Dig. **416 817-2**; *416 817-4* [id.]. (i) Schiff; (ii) H. and U. Holliger; (iii) Brunner; Bav. RSO, composer.

The *Cello concerto* was written in response to a commission by Rostropovich, who made a memorable disc of it in 1975. This has now been reissued on CD, sounding extremely vivid. As in some other Lutoslawski pieces, there are aleatory elements in the score, though these are carefully controlled. The sonorities are fascinating, and heard to good advantage on the HMV CD. The soloist is rather forward, but in every other respect the recording is extremely realistic. Rostropovich is in his element and gives a superb account of the solo role, and the composer's direction of the accompaniment is grippingly authoritative.

Heinrich Schiff is hardly less impressive and, like his predecessor, has the advantage of the composer's direction and a Philips recording of exceptional clarity and refinement. The *Concerto for oboe, harp and chamber orchestra* is a later piece, written in 1980 for the Holligers, who are its expert advocates here; it mingles charm, irony and intelligence in equal measure. The *Dance preludes* are much earlier (1953) but were subsequently scored for orchestra (1955) and later for nine instruments (1959). They are more folk-like in idiom and speech, and are attractively presented here by Eduard Brunner. Lutoslawski himself gets splendid playing from the Bavarian Radio Symphony Orchestra and readers knowing, say, the *Concerto for orchestra* and wanting to explore a cross-section of this composer's music should find this a rewarding issue. The recording is excellent, and the chrome cassette is also well balanced, with very good detail.

Concerto for oboe, harp and chamber orchestra.
*** MMG Dig. **MCD 10006** [id.]. H. and U. Holliger, Cincinnati SO, Gielen – R. STRAUSS: *Oboe concerto.***(*)

Lutoslawski's *Concerto for oboe and harp* is also available within a more sensibly chosen collection of concertante music. But this 1984 début CD from the same soloists is also very attractive, even though the measure is short. The bright clean digital recording brings a strong projection to the furious opening bursts of string tone (like a hive of buzzing bees) with its florid and crisply articulated oboe response; and it is equally effective in the fascinating pizzicatos from harp and strings of the central *Dolente* and the bizarre finale, marked *Marciale e grotesco.* The performance is gripping in its spontaneity and atmosphere, and the slightly astringent orchestral texture suits the music admirably. The coupling may be thought less appropriate until one discovers that, like the Lutoslawski, it was commissioned and first performed by Paul Sacher's Zurich Collegium Musicum. An early issue, the CD has no internal cues, except to divide the two works.

Dance preludes (for clarinet and orchestra).
*** Hyp. Dig. **CDA 66215**; *KA 66215* [id.]. Thea King, ECO, Litton – BLAKE: *Clarinet concerto;* SEIBER: *Concertino.****

** Unicorn Dig. **DKPCD 9066**; *DKPC 9066* [id.]. Gary Gray, RPO, Newstone – ARNOLD: *Concerto***; COPLAND: *Concerto*; ROSSINI: *Variations*.*(*)

Lutoslawski's five folk-based vignettes are a delight in the hands of Thea King and Andrew Litton, who give sharply characterized performances thrown into bold relief by the bright, clear recording. With equally attractive couplings, this CD is more than the sum of its parts, and so is the cassette, which is in the demonstration bracket.

Gary Gray and Newstone offer the strongest contrasts in Lutoslawski's suite of five miniatures, although perhaps the two slow pieces are excessively sombre. Good atmospheric recording on CD, although on our copy of the cassette there was very slight discoloration in the upper partials of the clarinet timbre: this may not apply to later batches. Unfortunately, the couplings are less recommendable, including an underpowered account of Copland's *Concerto*.

Symphony No. 3; (i) *Les espaces du sommeil.*

*** CBS Dig. **M2K 42271** (2). (i) Shirley-Quirk; LAPO, Salonen – MESSIAEN: *Turangalîla symphony*.**(*)

*** CBS *IMT 42203* (recording as above) cond. Salonen.

*** Ph. Dig. **416 387-2**; *416 387-4* [id.]. (i) Fischer-Dieskau; BPO, composer.

Esa-Pekka Salonen jumped in ahead of even the composer himself in recording Lutoslawski's *Third Symphony*, one of that composer's strongest and most communicative works. Even next to Lutoslawski's own interpretation, Salonen's brings an extra revelation. This is a deeply committed, even passionate account of a work which may be rigorous in its argument but which is essentially dramatic in one massive, continuous span. In *Les espaces du sommeil*, setting a surreal poem by Robert Desnos, Salonen also presents a different slant from the composer himself, making it – with the help of John Shirley-Quirk as an understanding soloist – much more evocative and sensuous. This is certainly the disc for anyone not already committed to liking Lutoslawski's music, bringing red-blooded and persuasive performances that blossom in full and well-balanced sound.

Lutoslawski's *Third Symphony*, powerfully argued over a 35-minute span, is given an authoritative reading by the composer himself conducting the Berlin Philharmonic. The performance of *Les espaces du sommeil* too might be counted definitive with the composer joined by the dedicatee, the baritone Dietrich Fischer-Dieskau. Treated to refined, finely analytical recording, these are superb, sharply focused performances, but in warmth and thrust of communication they finally yield to those of Esa-Pekka Salonen on his CBS version. On CD as on the excellent matching cassette this Philips issue is limited to the two Lutoslawski works, where on CD Salonen's rival CBS version comes in coupling with Messiaen's *Turangalîla* in a two-disc set.

Postlude No. 1; Symphonic variations.

❀ (M) *** HMV *ED 291172-4*. Polish RSO, composer – FRANZ SCHMIDT: *Variations on a Hussar's Song*; BUSONI: *Sarabande and Cortège* (*Doktor Faust*).*** ❀

Lutoslawski's *Symphonic variations* is an early work, first performed in 1939, a year fateful for Poland. The mantle of Szymanowski, who had died only two years earlier, can still be discerned: indeed the work has the poignant and ecstatic atmosphere that one finds in that master. Lutoslawski's short *Postlude No. 1* was written twenty years later and sounds very different but no less atmospheric on this excellently transferred cassette, exceptional value for it also gives us Busoni's haunting *Sarabande and Cortège* and Franz Schmidt's glorious *Variations on a Hussar's Song*.

Variations on a theme of Paganini.
*** Ph. Dig. **411 034-2** [id.]. Argerich, Freire – RACHMANINOV: *Suite No. 2*; RAVEL: *La valse*.***

Lutoslawski's *Variations* for piano duo date from 1941; they are exhilarating and played with great virtuosity by Martha Argerich and Nelson Freire. The recording is very realistic and natural. The compact disc makes more obvious the rather reverberant acoustic of the recording location.

MacCunn, Hamish (1868–1916)

Overture: Land of the Mountain and the Flood.
(M) *** HMV **CDM7 69206-2** [id.]; *ED 290208-4*. SNO, Gibson – HARTY: *With the wild geese*; GERMAN: *Welsh rhapsody*; SMYTH: *The Wreckers: overture*.***

This imaginative anthology, entitled 'Music of four countries', was first issued in the late 1960s. MacCunn's descriptive overture has since become famous by its use on TV. It is no masterpiece, but it has a memorable tune, is attractively atmospheric and is effectively constructed. Sir Alexander Gibson's performance is quite outstanding in its combination of warmth, colour and drama, and the recording is excellent. The CD remastering has improved definition marginally but retained the atmosphere. The cassette too sounds very well.

MacDowell, Edward (1861–1908)

Piano concertos Nos 1 in A min., Op. 15; 2 in D min., Op. 23.
❀ *** Archduke Dig. **DARC 1**; *MARC 1* [id.]. Donna Amato, LPO, Paul Freeman.

MacDowell's two *Piano concertos* were written in the early 1880s when the composer was in his twenties. The *First* is marginally the lesser of the two. Liszt's influence is strong (MacDowell studied with him) and there is plenty of dash, but the melodic content, though very pleasing, is slightly less memorable than in the *Second*, which has been recorded before, by both Van Cliburn and Szidon. It is a delightful piece, fresh and tuneful, redolent of Mendelssohn and Saint-Saëns. Donna Amato's scintillating performance is entirely winning, and she is equally persuasive in the *A minor*, which Liszt himself played. The present performance has the kind of virtuoso flair one would have expected of him; and the LPO accompany with enthusiasm, creating an engagingly serene atmosphere for the gentle *Andante tranquillo*. This music needs polish and elegance as well as fire, and Paul Freeman's accompaniments supply all three. The recording, made in All Saints, Tooting, has the right resonance for the Lisztian spectacle and agreeable ambient warmth for the music's lyrical side. A highly rewarding coupling in all respects, with an admirable chrome cassette equivalent.

Machaut, Guillaume (1300–77)

Messe de Nostre Dame.
(*) HMV Dig. **CDC7 47949-2 [id.]. Taverner Ch. and Cons., Parrott.

Andrew Parrott's version of this great work sets it in the context of a plainsong liturgy, thus greatly enhancing its effect. The (deleted) Grayson Burgess version used no instruments and interspersed organ music between the Mass sections. This HMV issue is splendidly recorded and there are many beauties, some of them obscured by Parrott's decision to transpose the work down a fourth, thus darkening its texture, which reduces internal clarity. However, the sound of the CD brings a most realistic impression.

Magnard, Albéric (1865–1914)

Symphony No. 3 in B flat min., Op. 11.
(M) **(*) Decca *417 636-4.* SRO, Ansermet – CHAUSSON: *Symphony.***(*)

It is indeed good news that moves are afoot to record all the Magnard symphonies in France, and that the revival of this composer's fortunes is at last gathering pace. The present recording dates from 1968 – though it still sounds excellent in this new tape transfer. It has an inspired opening: there is a certain austerity about the wind writing that is quite original and an eloquence that makes his long neglect puzzling. The scherzo is inventive, and the third movement, *Pastoral*, is marvellously sustained. Let us hope that the coming year brings us this work in an up-to-date version on compact disc; but this London Enterprise reissue is sufficiently well played and recorded to be far more than just a stop-gap. A fairly strong recommendation.

Symphony No. 4 in C sharp min., Op. 21; Chant funèbre, Op. 9.
*** HMV **CDC7 47373-2** [id.]. Toulouse Capitole O, Plasson.

The *Fourth Symphony* dates from 1913, the year before the composer's death, and is a welcome addition to the catalogue. It has an impressive intellectual power. Like his countryman Guy-Ropartz, with whom he is often paired, Magnard is grievously neglected even in his home country; as is the case with the *Third Symphony*, his music is well crafted and there is no shortage of ideas. For all the appearance of academicism there is a quiet and distinctive personality here, and dignity too. The fill-up, the *Chant funèbre*, is an earlier work that has a vein of genuine eloquence. The Toulouse Capitole Orchestra under Michel Plasson play this music as if they believe in every note, as indeed they should, and the recording is sonorous and well defined. This was the first of his works to appear on CD, and it is a very good one.

Guercoeur (opera) complete.
*** HMV **CDS7 49193-8** (3). Behrens, Van Dam, Denize, Lakes, Orféon Donostiarra, Toulouse Capitole O, Plasson.

Following up the success of his prizewinning record of Magnard's *Fourth Symphony*, Plasson here presents with similar warmth and conviction the large-scale opera on an ambitious theme that occupied the composer over his early thirties from 1897 to 1901. Acts I and III are set in Heaven, where Vérité (Truth) rules. Guercoeur, the hero, saviour of his people in a medieval city-state, has died, and in Act I pleads to be allowed to return to earth. Act II on earth finds him disillusioned that his friend, Heurtal, having become the lover of his wife, Giselle, plans to use his power to restore the dictatorship. Though Act III brings a beautiful, inspired ensemble towards the end, inevitably the return to Heaven in disillusionment makes a downbeat conclusion. With its distant echoes of Wagner's *Tristan*, its warm lyricism and superbly crafted writing, it makes a fine offering on record, almost as rich and distinctive as Magnard's symphonies. It echoes specific passages in Wagner less than Chausson's *Le roi Arthus*, the other fine French opera of the period now restored through recording; but Magnard's lyricism is almost too rich, so regularly heightened that the key moments stand out too little.

José van Dam makes a magnificent hero, the ideal singer for the role with his firm, finely shaded baritone. Hildegard Behrens makes a similarly powerful Vérité. Though some of the soprano singing among the attendant spirits in Heaven is edgily French, the casting is generally strong, with Gary Lakes a ringing Heurtal and Nadine Denize a sweet-toned Giselle. A rich rarity, warmly recorded.

Mahler, Gustav (1860–1911)

Symphony No. 1 in D (Titan).
(M) *** Decca **417 701-2**; *417 275-4* [id.]. LSO, Solti.
*** RCA **RD 80894** [**RCD1 0894**]. LSO, Levine.
*** Decca Dig. **411 731-2** [id.]. Chicago SO, Solti.
*** CBS Dig. **MK 42141**; *IMT 42141* [id.]. VPO, Maazel.
(*) HMV Dig. **CDC7 47032-2. Phd. O, Muti.
(*) CBS **MK 42031 [id.]. Columbia SO, Walter.
(*) Denon Dig. **C37 7537 [id.]. Frankfurt RSO, Inbal.
** Ph. **420 080-2** [id.]. Concg. O, Haitink.
** HMV **CDC7 47884-2** [id.]. LPO, Tennstedt.
(M)*(*) CBS **MK 42194** [id.]. NYPO, Bernstein.

Symphony No. 1 (with Blumine).
** HMV Dig. **CDC7 49044-2** [id.]. Israel PO, Mehta.

Symphony No. 1 in D min.; (i) *Lieder eines fahrenden Gesellen.*
(*) Virgin Dig. **790703-2; *VC 790703-4* [id.]. (i) Murray; RPO, Litton.

Symphony No. 1; (i) *5 Rückert Lieder.*
(B) **(*) DG Dig. *419 835-4* [id.]. Chicago SO, Abbado; (i) with Hanna Schwarz.

Among a wide choice, first preference lies between Solti's remastered LSO recording, which also has a price advantage to supplement its artistic claims, and Levine on RCA. Those who want a modern digital version should be happy with Solti's later Chicago record, or with Maazel on CBS.

The London Symphony Orchestra play Mahler's *First* like no other orchestra. They catch the magical writing at the opening with a singular evocative quality, at least partly related to the peculiarly characteristic blend of wind timbres. Solti gives the orchestra its full head and coaxes some magnificent playing from the brass in the finale, and throughout wonderfully warm string tone. His tendency to drive hard is felt only in the second movement, which is pressed a little too much, although he relaxes beautifully in the central section. Specially memorable is the poignancy of the introduction of the *Frère Jacques* theme in the slow movement, and the exultant brilliance of the closing pages. The remastering for CD has improved definition without losing the recording's bloom. There is an excellent cassette.

Like Solti, James Levine has the LSO for this symphony, and arguably he draws from it the most exciting playing of all. It is a reading of high contrasts, with extremes of tempo and dynamic brought out with total conviction. In that emphasis on drama, Levine is at times less beguiling than Solti, but the result is just as convincing. The brilliant 1975 recording is noticeably more modern, with greater amplitude than Solti's, made a decade earlier; even so, partly because of the balance, the LSO violins are warmer and fuller in the earlier Decca version.

Because of the excellence of the 1964 LSO version, which has been a prime choice for many years, it was hard for Solti and the Decca engineers to match his earlier achievement, even with exceptionally high-powered playing from the Chicago orchestra and brilliant, crystal-clear digital recording. Particularly on CD, that very clarity takes away some of the atmospheric magic – the feeling of mists dispersing in the slow introduction, for example – but charm and playfulness in this *Wunderhorn* work emerge delightfully; one of the happiest of Solti's records, tinglingly fresh, with perfectly chosen speeds.

With superb playing and refined recording, Maazel's account of the *First* has the Viennese glow which marks out his CBS series and notably the *Fourth*. Though there are other versions which point detail more sharply, this performance has a ripeness and an easy lyricism that put it among the most sympathetic readings in a very long list. The sound too is full and atmospheric as well as brilliant.

Muti's version was the first recording made by the Philadelphia Orchestra in a new venue; though the sound does not have the sharpness of definition of Solti's Decca CD, this gives an excellent idea of the richness of timbre typical of this orchestra. Muti, like other conductors prone to fierceness, manages to relax most persuasively for the gentler *Wunderhorn* inventions, contrasted sharply against extrovert outbursts, with rhythms crisply pointed and solo playing exceptionally fine.

Bruno Walter's 1961 record sounds splendid in its CD format. The compellingly atmospheric opening is magnetic, heard against the almost silent background, and Walter is at his most charismatic here. While the recording's range is obviously more limited than more recent versions, the balance and ambient warmth are entirely satisfying, emphasizing the Viennese character of the reading, with the final apotheosis drawn out spaciously and given added breadth and impact. The orchestral playing throughout is first class; other conductors have whipped up more animal excitement in the finale, but that is not Walter's way.

Edited together from a couple of live performances, Inbal's Frankfurt version may not be as polished or high-powered as the finest from top international orchestras, but it has an easy-going charm which, coupled to recording that puts fine bloom on the sound, will please many. The happy expansiveness and gentle manners of the first three movements then lead to a powerful and urgent reading of the finale which is more tautly held together than usual. One point of detail: the CD has no fewer than 22 bands for the four movements, making it particularly easy to find any passage.

Vividly recorded in bright and clear rather than atmospheric sound, Andrew Litton's record, one of the initial Virgin Classics releases, has the advantage of being the first version to include the most apt (and generous) of couplings, the *Lieder eines fahrenden Gesellen*, the song-cycle that provided material for the symphony. Litton's way with Mahler is fresh and generally direct, with well-chosen speeds, but the playing of the RPO strings is not always quite polished or taut enough. Ann Murray's mezzo, characterful and boyish in tone, yet catches the microphone rawly at times. There is a good chrome cassette which, transferred at only a modest level, loses some of the recording's brightness but compensates with added warmth and a somewhat more diffuse and agreeably atmospheric overall effect. The spectacular effects of the finale are less cleanly caught, however.

By rights, Abbado's reading should be among the first choices, for it is pure and superbly refined and consistently well paced. But the opening is a little slow in springing to life, and overall he misses some of the natural tension of a performance that should communicate as in a live concert. In the *Wunderhorn* inspirations of the first two movements the music smiles too rarely, although the funeral march of the slow movement is wonderfully hushed, more spontaneous-sounding than the rest. This is available on CD (**400 033-2**) but the Pocket Music tape version would seem a more economical way of sampling this performance, particularly as it includes Hanna Schwarz's glorious account of the *5 Rückert Lieder*, which Abbado accompanies superbly. The sound of the high-level tape transfer is bright and clean, but drier and slightly less expansive than the CD, which is fuller at the lower end of the spectrum.

If Haitink's version from the early 1970s had been reissued on Philips's mid-priced Silverline label it would have been more competitive. The reading is thoughtfully idiomatic in this conductor's unexaggerated Mahler style and, if it lacks something in drama, it has a refined recording to match, which sounds well in its remastered format.

Tennstedt's manner in Mahler is somewhat severe, with textures fresh and neat and the style of phrasing generally less moulded than we have come to expect. This concentration on precision and directness means that when the conductor does indulge in rubato or speed changes it does not sound quite consistent and comes as a surprise, as in the big string melody of the finale. Most

Mahlerians will prefer a more felt performance than this. The full, clear recording is first class.

Mehta's version with the Israel Philharmonic brings a hybrid – the regular four-movement version in its revised instrumentation, into which is inserted the lyrical *Blumine* movement from the original version, which Mahler later excised. On CD you can easily programme the work without including *Blumine*, and Mehta's reading of the whole work, though not the most individual or illuminating, is satisfyingly warm and direct, helped by very full, forward recording, among the best made in the difficult acoustic of the Mann Auditorium.

Though the voltage of Bernstein's reading is high, the age of the recording (from the late 1960s) and the occasional self-indulgence in the interpretation (as in the trio of the Ländler) make it uncompetitive.

Symphony No. 2 in C min. (*Resurrection*).

❀ *** HMV **CDS7 47962-8** [Ang. **CDCB 47962**]; *EX 270598-5* (2). Augér, J. Baker, CBSO Ch., CBSO, Rattle.
*** Decca Dig. **410 202-2** (2) [id.]. Buchanan, Zakai, Chicago SO Ch. & SO, Solti.
*** CBS **M2K 42032** (2) [id.]. Cundari, Forrester, Westminster Ch., NYPO, Walter.
*** Decca **414 538-2** (2) [id.]. Cotrubas, Ludwig, V. State Op. Ch., VPO, Mehta.
(*) HMV Dig. **CDS7 47041-8 [Ang. **CDC 47040**] (2). Mathis, Soffel, LPO Ch., LPO, Tennstedt.
(*) DG Dig. **423 395-2; *423 395-4* (2) [id.]. Hendricks, Ludwig, Westminster Ch., NYPO, Bernstein.
** CBS Dig. **M2K 38667** (2) [id.]. Marton, Norman, VPO, Maazel.
** Telarc. Dig. **CD 80081/2** [id.]. Battle, Forrester, St Louis Ch. & SO, Slatkin.
** Ph. Dig. **420 824-2**; *420 824-4* (2) [id.]. Te Kanawa, Horne, Tanglewood Fest. Ch., Boston SO, Ozawa
*(*) Denon Dig. **C37 7603/4** [id.]. Donath, Soffel, Frankfurt R. Ch. & SO, Inbal.
(B) * Sup. **2SUP 0020**. Randova, Benachova-Capova, Czech Ch. & PO, Neumann.

(i) *Symphony No. 2* (*Resurrection*); (ii) *Kindertotenlieder*.

(M) ** CBS **M2K 42195** (2) [id.]. (i) Armstrong, J. Baker, Edinburgh Fest. Ch., LSO; (ii) J. Baker, Israel PO; Bernstein.

(i) *Symphony No. 2* (*Resurrection*); (ii) *Des Knaben Wunderhorn*.

*(*) Ph. **420 234-2** 2 [id.] (i) Ameling, Heynis, Netherlands R. Ch.; (ii) J. Norman, Shirley-Quirk; Concg. O, Haitink.

(i) *Symphony No. 2* (*Recurrection*); (ii) *Lieder eines fahrenden Gesellen*; (iii) *Lieder und Gesänge* (*aus der Jugendzeit*): excerpts.

*** DG Dig. **415 959-2**; *415 959-4* (2) [id.]. (i) Fassbaender, Plowright, Philh. Ch.; (ii) Fassbaender; (iii) Weikl; Philh. O, Sinopoli.

Simon Rattle's reading of Mahler's *Second* is among the very finest records he has yet made, superlative in the breadth and vividness of its sound and with a spacious reading which in its natural intensity unerringly sustains generally slow, steady speeds to underline the epic grandeur of Mahler's vision. This comes closer than almost any rival version to creating the illusion of a live performance, its tensions and its drama, while building on the palpable advantage of well-balanced studio sound. There are points of detail that may be controversial – the rallentando on the final flourish in the first movement, for example, already taken at a dangerously slow basic speed – but Rattle here establishes himself as not merely a good but a great Mahlerian with a strongly individual view, controlling tensions masterfully over the broadest span. The playing of the CBSO is inspired, matching that of the most distinguished international rivals and out-shining others in sheer commitment. The choral singing, beautifully balanced, is incandescent, while the heart-felt singing of the soloists, Arleen Augér and Dame Janet Baker, is equally distinguished and characterful. Recorded in Watford Town Hall instead of the orchestra's usual

Birmingham venue, the sound is full and clear even in the heavyweight textures of the finale, with a crisper sense of presence than in most of Rattle's choral recordings. The chrome cassettes too are of EMI's very finest quality, and tape collectors need not hesitate.

Sinopoli's version of the *Resurrection*, tough and intense, incisively presenting a distinctive vision of this massive work, brings the additional advantage that the two CDs also include two Mahler song-cycles: the *Lieder eines fahrenden Gesellen*, beautifully sung by Brigitte Fassbaender, and the *Songs of Youth 'aus der Jugendzeit'*, skilfully orchestrated by Harold Byrns, well sung by Bernd Weikl, bringing extra anticipations of the mature *Des Knaben Wunderhorn* songs. Characteristically, in the symphony Sinopoli has meticulous concern for detail, at times drawing attention to individual shaping of phrase, as in the second subject of the first movement. In this he still conveys consistently the irresistible purposefulness of Mahler's writing, fierce at high dramatic moments and intense too, rarely relaxed, in moments of meditation, with *Urlicht* beautifully sung with warmth and purity by Fassbaender. The recorded sound, though not quite as full and vivid as that for Rattle, is among the most brilliant of any in this work. Rosalind Plowright is a pure and fresh soprano soloist, contrasting well with the equally firm, earthier-toned mezzo of Fassbaender. There are first-class equivalent chrome cassettes.

In digital sound of extraordinary power Solti has re-recorded with the Chicago orchestra this symphony which with the LSO was one of the finest achievements of his earlier Mahler series. Differences of interpretation are on points of detail merely, with a lighter, more elegant rendering of the minuet-rhythms of the second movement. Though the digital recording is not always as well balanced as the earlier analogue (Isobel Buchanan and Mira Zakai are too close, for example), the weight of fortissimo in the final hymn, not to mention the Judgement Day brass, is breathtaking. Interpretatively too, the outer movements are as fiercely intense as before. The compact discs with their extra precision make the brilliant sound of the Chicago orchestra even more immediate. In the last movement, the first cellist's groan before his solo – made more evident on CD – may worry some listeners.

Like Walter's other Mahler recordings, the 1958 CBS set of the *Resurrection symphony* is among the gramophone's indispensable classics. In the first movement there is a restraint and in the second a gracefulness which provides a strong contrast with a conductor like Solti. The recording, one of the last Walter made in New York before his series with the Columbia Symphony Orchestra, was remarkably good for its period and the dynamic range is surprisingly wide. In remastering for CD, the CBS engineers have sought to remove as much as possible of the pre-Dolby background noise, and the treble response is noticeably limited, with the attractively warm ambience tending to smooth internal definition. But the glowing resonance of the sound brings an evocative haze to the score's more atmospheric moments, and in the finale the balance with the voices gives the music making an ethereal resonance. If the choral focus is less than ideally sharp, the performance makes a profound impression, with the closing section thrillingly expansive.

Zubin Mehta sounds a different conductor, not at all like his Los Angeles self, when he is drawing so sympathetic a Mahler performance as this from the Vienna Philharmonic. The refinement of the playing puts this among the finest versions of the symphony. At the very start Mehta's fast tempo brings resilience, not aggressiveness, and the *espressivo* lyricism is equally persuasive. The second movement has *grazioso* delicacy, and though the third movement begins with the sharpest possible timpani strokes, there is no hint of brutality, and the *Wunderhorn* rhythms have a delightful lilt. After that comes *Urlicht*, *pianissimo* in D flat after the scherzo's final cadence in C minor, and Christa Ludwig is in superb form. The enormous span of the finale brings clarity as well as magnificence, with fine placing of soloists and chorus and glorious atmosphere in such moments as the evocation of birdsong over distant horns, as heavenly a moment as Mahler ever conceived. The 1975 analogue recording has responded extremely well to its digital remastering, retaining its fullness and clarity; indeed definition is sharper and cleaner.

Tennstedt's is a dedicated performance, not quite as well played as the finest, conveying Mahlerian certainties in the light of day and underplaying neurotic tensions. The recording on CD is impressively full and clear, though naturally balanced.

The big advantage of Bernstein's DG version over his previous CBS recording with the LSO lies in the quality of sound. Recorded live in Avery Fisher Hall, New York, the engineers have to a remarkable degree overcome the acoustic problems of that hall, presenting a weighty and wide-ranging sound, set against a warm reverberation (superimposed?) not associated with that venue. The expansion for the choral finale is well handled, and it is there in the urgency of the final chorus that Bernstein's interpretation gains over his previous one, recorded in the studio, a shade more intense. Otherwise, like earlier recordings in Bernstein's DG series, the live performance shows the conductor more self-indulgent than before, as well as more expansive, often overlaying Mahler's simplest and most tender melodies with forced expressiveness – even if, as ever, the voltage is high. Unlike the CBS version, the DG has no coupling, but the break between discs is less damaging, after the second movement.

Bernstein made a memorable television film concurrently with recording this symphony in Ely Cathedral. The CBS set with the LSO is valuable in recalling that idiosyncratic performance with its superb contributions from the two soloists, not to mention the chorus and orchestra, but the recording is far too badly balanced for the discs to be recommended generally. Though CD cannot radically alter faults in that original recording, even exaggerating odd balances, the extra clarity gives this vivid performance an extra immediacy. The live recording, made in Israel, of *Kindertotenlieder* with Dame Janet Baker, one of the soloists in the symphony, brings a valuable fill-up.

With full recording, clear and atmospheric, and no lack of presence, Maazel's Vienna version brings impressively weighty accounts of the vocal passages in the last part of the symphony, the vision of Judgement Day. But even there, Maazel's preference for a very steady pulse, varied hardly at all by rubato and tenuto, married to exceptionally slow speeds, undermines the keen intensity of the performance. Rhythmically the first movement becomes leaden and, paradoxically with the orchestra, the Vienna element in Mahler is minimized.

Superbly recorded, with even the weightiest and most complex textures at once well detailed and well coordinated, and with fine, polished playing from the St Louis orchestra, Slatkin's Telarc set yet lacks the sense of occasion essential in this work. The tension and weight needed in the first movement, for example, are not fully conveyed, and though the easy manners are attractive in their relative plainness, one really needs higher voltage. That higher voltage immediately makes itself felt when Maureen Forrester – a mezzo often chosen by Bruno Walter and a great stylist in Mahler – enters in the hushed opening of the fourth movement, *Urlicht*. In an instant, one can appreciate what has been missing; Kathleen Battle's contributions as the soprano soloist similarly bring an extra concentration. The engineers excel themselves in the great Judgement Day finale with even the organ textures clear, but the chorus's *pianissimo* entry is recorded so low that it is barely audible.

Ozawa's version, well performed and recorded, has suffered seriously from appearing simultaneously with Simon Rattle's visionary account. By comparison – or even not by comparison – it seems lightweight and even detached. Choral singing is good, and both soloists have characterful voices, but neither sounds very involved, with Horne's vibrato too prominent.

Haitink's late-1960s version has been reissued at full price, with an attractive and generous coupling of Jessye Norman's and John Shirley-Quirk's *Das Knaben Wunderhorn*. The results in the song-cycle are refined and satisfying, but the symphony, although well played and sung, lacks the sense of occasion that this work ideally needs.

Inbal is a stylish and sympathetic Mahlerian, but the digital recording exposes both the limitations of the Frankfurt orchestra and detailed imprecisions of ensemble. The first movement lacks weight, and the rising violin theme of the second subject sounds thin, not sweet; while the second movement, taken at a very slow speed, brings a painstaking manner which undermines the scherzando quality. Doris Soffel, the same mezzo soloist as on Tennstedt's EMI recording, again sings characterfully in *Urlicht*; distractingly, in the finale the two soloists are placed far closer than the chorus and orchestra. That brings out all the more the sense of a less-than-monumental occasion, not helped by imperfect ensemble. Recording good, but not as clear as in the best rival versions.

As the underpowered and loosely articulated opening shows, Neumann is not a born Mahler interpreter, and this uneven Supraphon performance tends towards melodrama, although the choral finale is lacking in real tension. The Slavonic style of the soloists is not an advantage, and although orchestral playing is good and the recording fully acceptable the only notable feature of this Supraphon issue is its low cost.

Symphony No. 3 in D min.
*** DG Dig. **410 715-2** (2) [id.]. J. Norman, V. State Op. Ch., V. Boys' Ch., VPO, Abbado.
*** RCA **RD 81757 [RCD2 1757]**. Horne, Ellyn Children's Ch., Chicago Ch. & SO, Levine.
*** HMV Dig. **CDS7 47405-8** (2) [Ang. **CDCB 45405**]. Wenkel, Southend Boys' Ch., LPO Ch., LPO, Tennstedt.
(*) Decca Dig. **414 268-2 (2) [id.]. Dernesch, Glen Ellyn Children's Ch., Chicago Ch. & SO, Solti.
(*) Denon Dig. **C37 7828/9 [id.]. Soffel, Limburger, Domsingknaben, Frankfurter Kantorei, Frankfurt RSO, Inbal.
** HMV Dig. **CDS7 47568-8** (2) [id.]. Killebrew, Coll. Josephinum Boys' Ch., Bav. & W. German R. Ch., Cologne RSO, Bertini.
** CBS Dig. **M2K 42403** (2) [id.]. Baltsa, V. Boys' Ch., V. State Op. Ch., VPO, Maazel.

(i) *Symphony No. 3* (ii) *Das klagende Lied.*
(*) Ph. **420 791-2 (2) [id.]. (i) Forrester, Netherlands R. Ch., St Willibrord Boys' Ch.; (ii) Harper, Procter, Hollweg, Netherlands R. Ch.; Concg. O, Haitink.

(i) *Symphony No. 3;* (ii) *4 Rückert Lieder; 7 Lieder und Gesänge* (*aus der Jugendzeit*).
(M) **(*) CBS **M2K 42196** (2) [id.]. (i) Lipton, Schola Cantorum Ch., Boys' Ch., NYPO, Bernstein; (ii) Fischer-Dieskau; Bernstein (piano).

With sound of spectacular range, Abbado's performance is sharply defined and deeply dedicated. The range of expression, the often wild mixture of elements in this work, is conveyed with extraordinary intensity, not least in the fine contributions of Jessye Norman and the two choirs. The recording has great presence and detail on CD.

James Levine directs a superbly rhythmic account of the *Third Symphony*, with splendidly judged tempi which allow extra swagger (most important in the first movement), more lilt and a fine sense of atmosphere. The choral contributions, too, are outstanding. In the radiant finale Levine's tempo is daringly slow, but he sustains it superbly, though in that movement the recording has some congestion at climaxes; otherwise the 1977 sound is nicely rounded, with the posthorn beautifully balanced in the third movement. On CD, refinement is enhanced by the virtually silent background: this is plainly not a digital recording, but it represents the highest analogue standards.

Tennstedt too gives an eloquent reading, spaciousness underlined with measured tempi. With Ortrun Wenkel a fine soloist and the Southend boys adding lusty freshness to the bell music in the fifth movement, the HMV performance with its noble finale is very impressive, and it is splendidly recorded.

In Solti's earlier series of Mahler recordings for Decca with the LSO the *Third Symphony* brought disappointment, notably in the brassy and extrovert account of the last movement. In his Chicago version that movement is transformed, hushed and intense, deeply concentrated, building up superbly even though the hastening is a shade excessive towards the end. The other movements have brilliance, freshness and clarity, with Helga Dernesch a fine if rather detached soloist. Solti remains a bold Mahler interpreter, missing some of the *Wunderhorn* fun. The virtuoso playing of the Chicago orchestra is brilliantly caught by the wide-ranging recording, though the posthorn of the third movement is placed unatmospherically close; such a fault of balance is all the more striking on the otherwise very impressive CDs.

In a work that can seem over-inflated Haitink's straightforwardness as a Mahlerian makes for a deeply satisfying performance. Though in the first movement his rather fast speed allows for less lift in the rhythm than, say, Bernstein's, he captures to perfection the fresh, wide-eyed simplicity of the second movement and the carol-like quality of the fifth movement, *Bell song*. Best of all is the wonderfully simple and intense reading of the long concluding slow movement, which here is given an inner intensity that puts it very close to the comparable movement of Mahler's *Ninth*. Haitink's soloists are excellent, the playing of the Concertgebouw is refined and dedicated. For CD the *Symphony* has been recoupled to *Das klagende Lied*, a much earlier recording, but one of high quality, although the performance is not ideal, lacking urgency and a sense of imaginative imagery. Both works emerge the fresher from their digital remastering, the sound refined but remaining full-bodied, though the lack of a true pianissimo is a notable drawback in the radiant, immaculately played account of the slow finale, which crowns the performance of the *Symphony*.

Bernstein's reading of the *Third*, one of the first to be recorded in his Mahler cycle, remains one of the most satisfying, strong and passionate with few of the stylistic exaggerations that sometimes overlay his interpretations. His style in the final slow movement is more heavily expressive than Haitink's, but some will prefer a more extrovert way. The recording copes well with the heavy textures, though next to the finest versions it is somewhat coarse. However, it has emerged vividly in its digital remastering and the CD format provides a particularly generous coupling for what is Mahler's longest symphony.

Eliahu Inbal in his Frankfurt version for Denon takes a spacious view, well sustained by very fine playing from the orchestra. This marked the point in the joint project between Denon and Hesse Radio where the intensive planning of a whole Mahler cycle within a two-year span began to deliver extra intensity in the finished results as recorded. The slow speeds are sustained easily and naturally, with the *Wunderhorn* element brought out more prominently than usual. The sound, as in the rest of the series, is excellent in its natural balances; but there are readings which convey the grandeur of Mahler's vision more powerfully.

Recorded in warm, spacious sound, with the chorus particularly fresh and vivid in the fifth-movement *Bell song*, there are many fine qualities in Bertini's Cologne version, but it finally lacks the weight and intensity that the work's scale demands, and ensemble is not always quite crisp enough, though tonal matching is outstanding. Bertini is at his most effective in his spacious account of the slow finale. Full, atmospheric recording.

As in his other Mahler symphony recordings with the Vienna Philharmonic, Lorin Maazel draws beautiful, refined playing from the orchestra; however, at a time when a spacious approach in this symphony has become the norm, he outdoes others in his insistence on slow speeds until the very measured gait for the finale comes to sound self-conscious, lacking a natural forward pulse. The recording is refined and undistractingly balanced, but there are other, more compelling versions, more vividly recorded.

Symphony No. 4 in G.

*** CBS Dig. **MK 39072** [id.]. Kathleen Battle, VPO, Maazel.
*** Denon Dig. **C37 7952** [id.]. Helen Donath, Frankfurt RSO, Inbal.
*** DG **415 323-2**; (M) *419 863-4* [id.]. Edith Mathis, BPO, Karajan.

*** Decca Dig. **410 188-2** [id.]. Kiri Te Kanawa, Chicago SO, Solti.
*** Ph. Dig. **412 119-2** [id.]. Roberta Alexander, Concg. O, Haitink.
*** HMV Dig. **CDC7 47024-2** [id.]. Lucia Popp, LPO, Tennstedt.
*** RCA **RD 80895** [**RCD1 0895**]. Judith Blegen, Chicago SO, Levine.
(M) ** Ph. **420 350-4**; *420 354-4* [id.]. Elly Ameling, Concg. O, Haitink.
** DG **413 454-2** [id.]. Frederica von Stade, VPO, Abbado.
(M) *(*) Decca **417 745-2** [id.]. Sylvia Stahlman, Concg. O, Solti.
(M) * CBS **MK 42197** [id.]. Reri Grist, NYPO, Bernstein.

As in the days of analogue stereo, Mahler's engagingly relaxed *Fourth Symphony* is extremely well served on CD. At the top of the list are Inbal's delightful and superbly recorded Frankfurt version and Maazel's VPO recording, unexpectedly the most completely successful issue so far in his cycle. The superbly refined and warmly atmospheric recording enhances a performance that – unlike other Mahler from this conductor – reflects the Viennese qualities of the work while still conveying structural strength, above all in the beautiful, wide-ranging slow movement played with great inner intensity. Kathleen Battle with her radiant soprano brings aptly child-like overtones to the *Wunderhorn* solo in the finale, until the final stanza is given with rapt intimacy to match Maazel's whole reading.

Inbal's version of the *Fourth* marked an engineering triumph for the engineers in his fine Frankfurt series. With a rather smaller orchestra than in the other symphonies, they were able to rely entirely on the source drawn from single-point placing of microphones. (They always prefer to use primary source, but in the other symphonies, to varying degrees, it has had to be married with the alternative multi-miked circuit.) The result is outstandingly fresh and natural, matching a delightful performance of the *Symphony*, the tone of which is set by the easy, happy and relaxed manner of the opening. There is a pastoral element in Inbal's approach all through, reflecting the *Wunderhorn* basis, and even the spacious slow movement is easily songful rather than ethereal. Helen Donath brings boyish Hansel-like timbre to her solo in the finale.

With playing of incomparable refinement – no feeling of rusticity here – Karajan directs a performance of compelling poise and purity, not least in the slow movement, with its pulse very steady indeed, most remarkably at the very end. Karajan's view of the finale is gentle, wistful, almost ruminative, with the final stanzas very slow and legato, beautifully so when Edith Mathis's poised singing of the solo is finely matched. Not that this quest for refinement means that joy has in any way been lost in the performance; with glowing sound, it is a worthy companion to Karajan's other Mahler recordings, effectively transferred to CD. The tape is at mid-price and is technically first class.

Solti's digital version gives the lie to the idea of his always being fierce and unrelaxed. This sunniest of the Mahler symphonies receives a delightfully fresh and bright reading, beautifully paced and superbly played. The recording is bright, full and immediate in the Decca Chicago manner, without inflating the interpretation. Dame Kiri Te Kanawa sings beautifully in the child-heaven finale.

With outstandingly refined playing from the Concertgebouw superlatively recorded, Haitink's reading has a fresh innocence that is most winning. Thus the lovely *Adagio*, rather than conveying the deepest meditation, presents an ecstatic, songful musing in the long paragraphs of the main theme, and Roberta Alexander makes a perceptive choice of soloist for such a reading, both fresh and creamy of tone.

Tennstedt conducts a strong, spacious reading which yet conveys an innocence entirely in keeping with this most endearing of the Mahler symphonies. He makes the argument seamless in his easy transitions of speed, yet never deliberately adopts a coaxing, charming manner; in that, he is followed most beautifully by Lucia Popp, the pure-toned soloist in the finale. The peak of the work, as Tennstedt presents it, lies in the long slow movement, here taken very slowly and intensely. The recording is among EMI's finest, full and well balanced.

James Levine, a thoughtful yet warmly committed Mahlerian, mature beyond his years, draws a superlative performance from the Chicago orchestra, one which bears comparison with the finest versions, bringing out not merely the charm but the deeper emotions too. The subtlety of his control of tempo, so vital in Mahler, is superbly demonstrated and, though he may not quite match the nobility of Szell's famous analogue CBS version in the great slow movement, he has the advantage of more modern (1975) recording. Blegen makes a fresh, attractive soloist.

Haitink's earlier version is predictably well played and the recording has come up very well indeed on the mid-priced CD reissue (though the tape is rather bass-heavy). The performance is sober, but it has an attractive simplicity, and Elly Ameling matches Haitink's approach in her serene contribution to the finale. Although it lacks drama, this is an easy version to live with.

After his superb performance of the Mahler *Second* with the Chicago orchestra, Abbado's recording of the *Fourth* is disappointing, above all in the selfconsciously expressive reading of the slow movement. There is much beauty of detail, but the Vienna Philharmonic has played and been recorded better than this.

Solti's early stereo recording with the Concertgebouw is also disappointing. The recording is well balanced and vivid, but Solti's grip on the first movement is both wilful and uncertain. The finale is the most successful movement, and here Sylvia Stahlman sings charmingly.

Bernstein's version, dating from 1971, brings another erratic reading, less controlled than his finest Mahler performances and not really competitive in quality of sound.

Symphony No. 5 in C sharp min.
(M) ❀ *** HMV **CDM7 69186-2**. New Philh. O, Barbirolli.
*** DG **415 096-2** (2) [id.]. BPO, Karajan – *Kindertotenlieder.****
*** DG Dig. **415 476-2**; *415 476-4* [id.]. Philh. O, Sinopoli.
*** Denon Dig. **CO 1088** [id.]. Frankfurt RSO, Inbal.
(*) Ph. **416 469-2 [id.]. Concg. O, Haitink.
(*) Decca **413 321-2 [id.]. Chicago SO, Solti.
(*) RCA **RD 89570 [**RCD1 5453**]. Phd. O, Levine.
** CBS Dig. **MK 42310** [id.]. VPO, Maazel.
(M) *(*) Decca **417 730-2**; *414 467-4* [id.]. LAPO, Mehta.
*(*) CBS **MK 42198** [id.]. NYPO, Bernstein.
(B) (*) Sup. **2SUP 0021**. Czech PO, Neumann.

Symphony No. 5; Symphony No. 10: Adagio.
*** HMV **CDS7 47104-8** [Ang. **CDC 47103**] (2). LPO, Tennstedt.

While Karajan's recording may be a first choice for Mahler's *Fifth*, its expensive layout, involving a pair of CDs, must be counted a drawback, even if Christa Ludwig's warm singing in the *Kindertotenlieder* is a worthwhile fill-up. Karajan's characteristic emphasis on polish and refinement goes with sharpness of focus. His is among the most beautiful and the most intense versions available, starting with an account of the first movement which brings more biting funeral-march rhythms than any rival. Resplendent recording, rich and refined.

Barbirolli's famous 1969 version has been digitally remastered on to one mid-priced CD. On any count it is one of the greatest, most warmly affecting performances ever committed to record, expansive yet concentrated in feeling. A classic version and a fine bargain.

Sinopoli's version, the first of his Mahler series with the Philharmonia Orchestra, draws the sharpest distinction between the dark tragedy of the first two movements and the relaxed *Wunderhorn* feeling of the rest. Thus, the opening *Funeral march* is tough and biting, expressive but moulded less than one associates with this conductor; here, as later, Sinopoli seems intent on not overloading the big melodies with excessive emotion. This comes out the more clearly in the central movements, where relaxation is the keynote, often with a pastoral atmosphere. The third-movement Ländler has the happiest of lilts, but leads finally to a frenetic coda, before the celebrated *Adagietto* brings a tenderly wistful reading, songful and basically happy, not tragic. If that seems understated and gentle compared to forcefully high-powered readings, it fits the more clearly with a *Wunderhorn* mood which returns in full joy in the finale, starting with a magical evocation of the Austrian countryside. Warmly atmospheric recording, not lacking brilliance, but – even on CD – not always ideally clear on detail. Both CD and tape share the advantage of being complete on two sides. The cassette, which is of a high technical standard, divides up the work conveniently so that the *Adagietto* opens side two.

Tennstedt takes a ripe and measured view of this symphony; though his account of the lovely *Adagietto* lacks the fullest tenderness (starting with an intrusive balance for the harp), this is an outstanding performance, thoughtful on the one hand, warm and expressive on the other. The first movement of the *Tenth Symphony* makes an acceptable fill-up; the recording, not quite as detailed as in this conductor's later digital Mahler recordings with the LPO, is warm and full to match the performance. The sound is enhanced on CD.

As in his accounts of the earlier Mahler symphonies, Inbal brings out the *Wunderhorn* element in the *Fifth* very convincingly. That applies to all five movements. He may not be as exciting as some rivals, but, with superb playing and beautifully balanced sound, full and atmospheric, it is an exceptionally sympathetic reading. The second and third movements, unusually relaxed, lead to an account of the *Adagietto* that is the opposite of portentous, warmly songful yet hushed and sweet, while the finale conveys the happiness of pastoral ideas leading logically to a joyful, triumphant close.

Those who resist Sinopoli's toughness and Karajan's refinement will probably find the ideal alternative in Haitink's fresh and direct reading, with finely judged tempi, unexaggerated observance of Mahler markings, and refined playing from the Concertgebouw. The famous *Adagietto* is relatively cool, but its beauty is as intense as ever. Good, well-balanced Philips recording which, as usual, has responded well to digital remastering.

Solti's recording has also been digitally remastered on to a single CD; the 1971 analogue sound now has sharper detail without losing too much body. The opening *Funeral march* sets the tone of Solti's reading. At a tempo faster than usual, it is wistful rather than deeply tragic, even though the dynamic contrasts are superbly pointed and the string tone could hardly be more resonant. In the pivotal *Adagietto*, Solti secures intensely beautiful playing, but the result lacks the 'inner' quality one finds so abundantly in Karajan's interpretation.

Apart from a self-consciously slow account of the celebrated *Adagietto*, Levine directs a deeply perceptive and compelling performance, one that brings out the glories of the Philadelphia Orchestra. The other movements are beautifully paced, and the remastering for CD is vivid without losing its body and becoming fierce.

Maazel's Vienna version, like others in his CBS series, is marked by fine playing and warmly sympathetic recording, but its fluctuations of speed come to sound wayward, particularly in the first two movements. Though he takes a flowing view of the *Adagietto*, this is a performance which, for all its qualities, fails to hang together.

Brilliant as the recording is of Mehta's Los Angeles version, and the playing too, it misses the natural warmth of expression that the same conductor found in his reading of No. 2 with the Vienna Philharmonic. Most impressive is the virtuoso scherzo, but in their different ways the opening *Funeral march* and the beautiful *Adagietto* both lack the inner quality which is essential if the faster movements are to be aptly framed. The brilliance of the finale is exaggerated by Mehta's very fast tempo, missing the *Wunderhorn* overtones of this most optimistic of Mahler's conclusions.

Bernstein's reading is remarkable for the delicate beauty and intensity of the fourth-movement

Adagietto. This was the piece that Bernstein conducted at the funeral of his friend, President Kennedy, and for some time in the United States that made this recording a best-seller. The other movements are not so compelling, and the age of the recording, despite a good CD transfer, makes it recommendable only with reservations.

As his recording of the *Resurrection symphony* demonstrates, Vaclav Neumann is not really at home in Mahler: he turns drama into melodrama with his sporadic bursts of orchestral passion, and the famous *Adagietto* lacks any kind of magic. The recording is serviceable but this cannot be recommended, even at its low price.

Symphony No. 6 in A min.
*** DG **415 099-2** (2) [id.]. BPO, Karajan – *5 Rückert Lieder.***(*)
(*) HMV Dig. **CDC7 47050-8 [Ang. **CDC 47049**] (2). LPO, Tennstedt.
(*) Decca **414 674-2 (2) [id.]. Chicago SO, Solti – *Lieder eines fahrenden Gesellen.****
** Denon Dig. **CO 1327/8** [id.]. Frankfurt RSO, Inbal.

(i) *Symphonies Nos 6 in A min;* (ii) *8 in E flat.*
(M) ** CBS **M3K 42199** (3) [id.]. (i) NYPO; (ii) Soloists, Ch., LSO, Bernstein.

Symphony No. 6; Symphony No. 10: Adagio.
*** DG Dig. **423 082-2**; *423 082-4* (2) [id.]. Philh. O, Sinopoli.

Symphony No. 6; (i) *Lieder eines fahrenden Gesellen.*
(*) Ph. **420 138-2 (2) [id.]. Concg. O, Haitink; (i) with Hermann Prey.

With superlative playing from the Berlin Philharmonic, Karajan's reading of the *Sixth* is a revelation, above all in the slow movement which here becomes far more than a lyrical interlude. With this *Andante moderato* made to flower in poignant melancholy, and with a simpler lyrical style than Karajan usually adopts, it emerges as one of the greatest of Mahler's slow movements and the whole balance of the symphony is altered. Though the outer movements firmly stamp this as the darkest of the Mahler symphonies, in Karajan's reading their sharp focus – with contrasts of light and shade heightened – makes them both compelling and refreshing. Significantly, in his care for tonal colouring Karajan brings out a number of overtones related to Wagner's *Ring*. The superb DG recording, with its wide dynamics, adds enormously to the impact. It is further enhanced in the remastering for compact disc; Christa Ludwig's set of the *Five Rückert Songs* has been added as a bonus.

Sinopoli's version of the *Sixth* presents a strongly individual view, outstandingly convincing in the first two movements which, tough and urgent, are given rhythmic elbow room, but sounding less purposeful in the last two movements, both taken notably slower than usual. In the first movement his control of light and shade, along with the swaggering gait of the march rhythm, has a power comparable with that of Karajan, but without his clipped militaristic fierceness. In the second-movement scherzo Sinopoli finds a haunted quality. With brass whooping and sprung rhythms, it conveys an even more sinister fantasy than with Karajan. The slow movement, taken very slowly indeed, with agogic hesitations peppered over the phrasing, lacks the warm flow of Karajan, refined as it is. That movement, like the finale, finds the right tensions after opening self-consciously, and overall the breadth of vision makes this one of the most compellingly individual versions of all. The *Adagio* from the *Tenth Symphony* makes a generous fill-up, but Sinopoli's very slow reading, with detail heavily underlined, takes away the dark purposefulness of the argument. The recording of both works is among DG's fullest and most brilliant, matching the vividness and realism of Karajan's DG sound with extra range from a fully digital recording. The cassettes are also of DG's highest quality.

Tennstedt's reading is characteristically strong, finding more warmth than usual even in this dark symphony. Thus, the third-movement *Andante* is open and songlike, almost Schubertian in its sweetness, though there is never any question of Tennstedt taking a sentimental view of Mahler. His expressiveness tends towards conveying joy rather than Mahlerian neurosis and, for some, that may make it too comfortable a reading. Karajan has more power and bite; his scale is bigger and bolder, the Berlin playing more brilliant. Naturally, in his digital recording Tennstedt gains from extra range in the recording of the famous hammer-blows of fate in the finale. The sound is full and the acoustic warm; the CD has added extra refinement of detail.

Solti draws stunning playing from the Chicago orchestra. This was his first recording with them after he took up his post as principal conductor, and, as he himself said, it represented a love-affair at first sight. The electric excitement of the playing confirms this; with brilliant, immediate but atmospheric recording, Solti's rather extrovert approach to Mahler is here at its most impressive. His fast tempi may mean that he misses some of the deeper emotions but – with an outstandingly successful performance of the *Wayfaring Lad* cycle on the fourth side (Yvonne Minton a splendid soloist) – this is a very convincing and attractive set. On CD the immediacy of the sound is the more striking, although the ambient effect tempers the brightness.

Haitink, like Bernstein and Solti, takes a fast tempo for the first movement, but the performance is marked by refinement rather than fire, helped by well-balanced Philips recording. The whole performance reflects Haitink's thoughtful, unsensational approach to the composer, a characteristically satisfying reading. The 1969 recording sounds well in its new format, although violin timbre is a little dry. There is noticeably more warmth in the 1970 set of *Lieder eines fahrenden Gesellen*, which Hermann Prey sings most beautifully.

Inbal's account of the *Sixth* is one of the disappointments of his Frankfurt series. Whether or not intending to relate it to the earlier *Wunderhorn* symphonies, he takes a relatively relaxed view, so even the first movement emerges as too easy-going, lacking tension; though his brand of Mahlerian songfulness brings moments of freshness and insight, the power of the work is diminished. It does not help that the recording, refined like others in the series, presents the orchestra at a distance.

Bernstein's account of the *Sixth* stands out among other fine Mahler recordings he has made. One can argue that tempi are inclined to be too fast – particularly in the first movement, which no longer sounds like a funeral march – but here, even more than usual, the searing intensity of a Bernstein performance comes over, helped by the vivid recording. The *Eighth*, recorded in Walthamstow Town Hall, is a comparably fine performance, with incisive singing from the Leeds Festival Chorus, strongly stiffened with professionals. The unfortunate point, undermining much of Bernstein's achievement, is the closeness of the sound, which the CD remastering is unable to do anything about. A flawed package, but the electricity of the conductor still makes the results very compelling.

Symphony No. 7 in E min.

*** DG Dig. **413 773-2**; *413 773-4* (2) [id.]. Chicago SO, Abbado.
*** Denon Dig. **CO 1553/4** [id.]. Frankfurt RSO, Inbal.
*** Decca **414 675-2** (2) [id.]. Chicago SO, Solti – *Des Knaben Wunderhorn*: excerpts.***
*** DG Dig. **419 211-2**; *419 211-4* (2) [id.]. NYPO, Bernstein.
(*) Ph. Dig. **410 398-2 (2) [id.]. Concg. O, Haitink.
** RCA **RCD 84581 [RCD2 4581]** (2). Chicago SO, Levine.
** HMV Dig. **CDS7 47879-8** (2). LPO, Tennstedt.

Abbado's command of Mahlerian characterization has never been more tellingly displayed than in this most problematic of the symphonies; even in the loosely bound finale, which might unkindly be described as ramshackle in structure, Abbado unerringly draws the threads together, while contrasting each section with the next in clear distinction. The contrasts in the earlier movements, too, are superbly brought out, with the central interludes made ideally atmospheric, as in the eeriness of the scherzo and the haunting tenderness of the second *Nachtmusik*. The precision and polish of the Chicago orchestra go with total commitment, and the recording is one of the finest DG has made with this orchestra. The CD version, besides having a degree more tangibility and presence, is generously banded within movements. There is an excellent chrome tape equivalent.

Inbal's account of the *Seventh* is one of the high points of his Mahler series, masterfully paced, relaxed and lyrical where appropriate, but incorporating all the biting tensions that are missing in his version of the *Sixth*, the other dark, middle symphony. Inbal's easy, natural manner is particularly effective in the three middle movements, and the radiant beauty of the second *Nachtmusik*, taken at a flowing speed, has never sounded more Elysian, with its sweet violin melody and tinkling mandolin. Inbal, there as always, completely avoids sentimentality, and the easy purposefulness of the finale in its many sections brings a masterly example of his unforced, incisive control, ending exuberantly at full power. The recording is outstandingly fine in its vivid natural balances.

The sound of Solti's Decca issue is glorious, even riper and more brilliant than that of his two earlier Chicago recordings of Mahler and on CD much clearer. In interpretation, this is as successful as his fine account of the *Sixth Symphony*, extrovert in display but full of dark implications. The tempi tend to be challengingly fast – at the very opening, for example, and in the scherzo (where Solti is mercurial) and in the finale (where his energy carries shock-waves in its trail). The second *Nachtmusik* is enchantingly seductive and, throughout, the orchestra plays superlatively well. On balance this is even finer than the Haitink version. For the CD issue, Yvonne Minton's fine performance of four Lieder from *Des Knaben Wunderhorn* has been added. (They were originally coupled with the *Fifth Symphony*, now reissued on a single disc.)

Unlike his earlier CBS versions, Leonard Bernstein's Mahler series for DG was recorded at live performances. The *Seventh*, one of the first two issues, brought out the fine qualities, but also pointed to some of the latter-day dangers in the all-out Bernstein view. This is a riveting performance from first to last, ending with a searingly exciting account of the finale which triumphantly flouts the idea of this as a weak conclusion. It is a performance to send you off cheering, while the purposeful control of earlier movements also minimizes the obvious objections in principle to wilful exaggerations in phrasing and changes of tempo. This is Mahlerian expression at its most red-blooded, and with fine playing from the New York Philharmonic – marginally finer even than in his CBS version – it is a splendid example of Bernstein's flair in Mahler. The recording, fuller than in his much earlier CBS account, is yet a little harsh at times, next to the finest modern digital sound.

Beauty is the keynote of Haitink's newer, digitally recorded version of Mahler's *Seventh*. The superb playing of the Concertgebouw Orchestra is richly and amply caught; however, with spacious speeds to match, tensions have tended to ease since Haitink's earlier account; the vision of darkness is softened a degree. On CD, the wide dynamic range is very telling, with detail clarified.

With a broad, warmly expressive account of the first movement and a riotously extrovert one of the finale, Levine's reading has many of the fine qualities of his other Mahler recordings but, with recording balances at times odd and some rhythmic self-indulgence, it cannot match the finest.

Tennstedt's spacious view has something of the ruggedness that made the controversial old Klemperer reading so characterful, more convincing in the power of the outer movements than in the more delicate atmosphere of the three middle movements. Unfortunately the early (1981) digital recording sounds harsh next to the finest versions of the work, but those who follow Tennstedt in Mahler will not be seriously disappointed.

Symphonies Nos 7; 9; 10: Adagio.
(M) **(*) CBS **M3K 42200** (3) [id.]. NYPO, Bernstein.

The CD transfers of Nos 7, 9 and the *Adagio* of No. 10 come together in a well-devised box of three CDs, with the sound still very acceptable. In the *Ninth* this CBS New York version is far preferable to DG's recent one with the same orchestra, with the great expanse of the slow finale so much more tautly presented, less self-indulgently slow. In the *Seventh* Bernstein draws a performance of characteristic intensity and beauty from the New York Philharmonic. His love of the music is evident in every bar and the orchestral playing is superb. Similarly in the *Adagio* from the *Tenth*, the passionate commitment of his performance is hard to resist, with contrasts underlined between the sharpness of the *Andante* passages and the free expressiveness of the main *Adagio*.

Symphony No. 8 (Symphony of 1000).
❀ *** HMV Dig. **CDS7 47625-8** (2) [Ang. **CDCB 47625**]. Connell, Wiens, Lott, Schmidt, Denize, Versalle, Hynninen, Sotin, Tiffin School Boys' Ch., LPO Ch., LPO, Tennstedt.
*** Decca **414 493-2** (2) [id.]; *KCET2 7006*. Harper, Popp, Augér, Minton, Watts, Kollo, Shirley-Quirk, Talvela, V. Boys' Ch., V. State Op. Ch. & Singverein, Chicago SO, Solti.
*** Denon Dig. **CO 1564/5** (2) [id.]. Robinson, Cahill, Heichele, Budai, Henschel, Riegel, Prey, Stamm, Bav. N., S. & W. German R. Choirs, RIAS Chamber Ch., Limburg Cathedral Ch., Hesse Radio Children's Ch., Frankfurt RSO, Inbal.
** Ph. Dig. **410 607-2** (2) [id.]. Robinson, Blegen, Sasson, Quivar, Myers, Riegel, Luxon, Howell, Tanglewood Fest. Ch., Boston Boys' Ch., Boston SO, Ozawa.
(M) ** DG **419 433-2** [id.]. Arroyo, Spoorenberg, Hamari, Mathis, Procter, Grobe, Fischer-Dieskau, Crass, Bav. N. & W. German R. Choirs, Regensburg Ch., Bav. RSO, Kubelik.

(i) *Symphony No. 8; Symphony No. 10: Adagio.*
** Ph. **420 543 2** (2) [id.]. (i) Cotrubas, Harper, Van Borkh, Finnila, Dieleman, Cochran, Prey, Sotin, Amsterdam Choirs; Concg. O, Haitink.

Tennstedt's magnificent account of the *Eighth*, the last of his Mahler series to be recorded, long delayed through problems of casting, marks a superb culmination, the finest of his whole cycle. Though it does not always have the searing intensity that marks Solti's overwhelming Decca version, Tennstedt's broader, grander view makes at least as powerful an impact, and with the extra range and richness of the modern EMI recording, coping superbly with even the heaviest textures, it will for most listeners be even more satisfying. Not the least impressive point about the recording is the firm, opulent sound of the Westminster Cathedral organ, dubbed on afterwards but sounding all the better focused for that. Next to this EMI recording, the 1972 Decca sound, for all its vividness, with solo voices made more immediate, sounds a little rough, underlining the fierceness. That said, the contrasting approaches of Tennstedt and Solti make them equally cherishable in their illumination of Mahler. It is the urgency and dynamism of Solti which make his reading irresistible, ending in an earth-shattering account of the closing hymn. Tennstedt, both there and elsewhere, finds more light and shade. The lyricism of the opening *Veni creator spiritus* comes out affectingly alongside the grandeur, while the hushed pianissimo at the start of the final *Alles vergangliche* in the second movement leads from deep meditation to total ecstasy in the closing pages. Tennstedt's soloists, though a strong, characterful team, are not as consistent as Solti's. Even Felicity Lott as Mater Gloriosa is less pure-toned than she has sometimes been, but her solo is the more moving for being ethereally balanced. The great glory of the set is the singing of the London Philharmonic Choir, assisted by Tiffin School Boys' Choir. The chorus may be rather smaller than in live performance, but diction and clarity are aided, with no loss of power. This is a work which for many Mahlerians brings nagging doubts; but Tennstedt – like Solti, only more thoughtfully – confirms from first to last his own deep conviction that it is a masterpiece. This was a worthy winner in the orchestral category of the 1987 *Gramophone* Awards. The HMV cassette, unfortunately, is unsatisfactory technically; Solti's Decca tape, however, is very impressive indeed.

Inbal, like others recording complete Mahler symphony cycles, left the *Symphony of a Thousand* to the last. The difference with him was that in the collaboration between Denon and Hesse Radio, the whole project was completed in a two-year period. The exhilaration of this culminating performance, recorded (like earlier ones) at sessions linked to live performances, comes over vividly. Even with a very large chorus, the sound is superbly detailed as well as full and atmospheric. *Veni creator spiritus* is wonderfully fresh and eager, but the clarity of detail does at times reveal fractional imprecision of ensemble. The refinement of sound gives extra intensity to the meditations of the great second movement, and Inbal's fast speed for the closing hymn makes it all the fresher and more purposeful, exuberant in joy. The team of soloists is a strong one but, like Tennstedt's octet, cannot match Solti's in consistency. The sound, naturally balanced, with as little tampering as possible – not for Denon the overdubbing of an alien organ – is extremely fine, not as spectacular as Tennstedt's but deeply satisfying in its warmth and beauty.

Though the Philips digital recording is very good indeed, Ozawa's Boston reading of the *Symphony of a Thousand* rather lacks the weight and intensity of its finest rivals. It is a performance which has one thinking back to earlier Mahler of *Wunderhorn* vintage rather than accepting the epic scale. There is much beautiful singing and playing, recorded in a mellow acoustic, but this work needs a greater sense of occasion. On CD the refinement and beauty of the recording are particularly striking in the work's closing section.

Haitink's version, characteristically thoughtful and direct, also lacks the biting intensity needed to convey the work's epic purpose to the full. The solo singing has its blemishes, but on CD the recording, originally rather dull and limited, has come up very freshly, with balances cleanly registered. It also has the advantage of including a substantial fill-up in a superb account of the *Adagio* from the *Tenth Symphony*. There, Haitink in the broad expanses of the movement draws dedicated, concentrated and refined playing from the Concertgebouw, a performance all the more moving for its degree of reticence.

Even in this massive symphony Kubelik concentrates on refinement, and the recording engineers match him faithfully. The result is crisp and clear but largely unexciting, giving little idea of a live occasion. Generally good solo singing. Kubelik's fastish speeds – giving the whole work a timing of just under 75 minutes – have allowed the DG transfer engineers to make this the first single-disc version of the *Eighth*, a substantial advantage. The sound is crisp, clean and bright.

Symphony No. 9 in D min.
*** DG Dig. **410 726-2** (2) [id.]. BPO, Karajan.
*** HMV **CDS7 47113-8** (2) [Ang. **CDC 47112**]. LPO, Tennstedt.
*** CBS **M2K 42033** (2) [id.]. Columbia SO, Bruno Walter.
(*) Decca Dig. **410 012-2 (2) [id.]. Chicago SO, Solti.
** RCA **RD 83461** (2). Phd. O, Levine.
*(*) DG Dig. **419 208-2**; *419 208-4* (2) [id.]. Concg. O, Bernstein.

Symphony No. 9; Symphony No. 10: Adagio.
*** Denon Dig. **CO 1566/7** [id.]. Frankfurt RSO, Inbal.
(*) CBS Dig. **M2K 39721 (2) [id.]. VPO, Maazel.

Symphony No. 9; (i) *Kindertotenlieder.*
*** Ph. **416 466-2** (2) [id.]. Concg. O, Haitink; (i) with Hermann Prey.

Karajan recorded Mahler's *Ninth* twice within a space of two years, and both performances transcended his earlier Mahler. The combination of richness and concentration in the outer movements makes for a reading of the deepest intensity, and in the middle movements point and humour are found, as well as refinement and polish. For his later version he added a new dimension of glowing optimism in the finale, rejecting any Mahlerian death-wish. It is this newer performance which appears on CD, recorded at live performances in Berlin and making it a supreme achievement. Despite the problems of live recording, the sound is bright and full, if somewhat close.

Haitink is at his very finest in Mahler's *Ninth*, and the last movement, with its slow expanses of melody, reveals a unique concentration. Unlike almost all other conductors he maintains his intensely slow tempo from beginning to end. This is a great performance, beautifully recorded, and with the earlier movements superbly performed – the first movement a little restrained, the second pointed at exactly the right speed, and the third gloriously extrovert and brilliant – this will be for many Mahlerians a first recommendation. The CD transfer freshens the 1969 recording, which still sounds highly impressive in its body and natural focus. Hermann Prey's early 1970s version of the *Kindertotenlieder* is added, a fresh, intelligent account, yet lacking something in imagination and intensity of expression.

Inbal's version brings the most refined, most subtly shaded recording of the *Ninth*. In the great expanses of the slow outer movements the actual sound helps to convey a hushed intensity, where with most rivals *pianissimos* tend to become *mezzo fortes*. Inbal's reading may not have the epic power or the sweeping breadth of Karajan, but his simple dedication brings a performance just as concentrated in its way, simulating the varying tensions of a live performance. The second-movement Ländler brings peasant overtones in the rasping woodwind; the third movement is finely pointed, emphasizing its joyfulness; and the simple gravity of the finale, easily lyrical in the big melodies, leads to a wonderfully hushed culmination, not tragic as with Karajan, but in its rapt ecstasy looking forward to the close, on murmurs of *'Ewig'*, of *Das Lied von der Erde*. As a logical fill-up, the *Adagio* from the *Tenth Symphony* brings a similarly natural and warm reading. The sound in both works is excellent in its natural balances, a fine example of the Denon engineers' work. Through the whole series the CD transfers, unlike most rivals, have provided copious index-points within the separate tracks devoted to whole movements, a considerable convenience.

Tennstedt directs a performance of warmth and distinction, underlining nobility rather than any neurotic tension, so that the outer movements, spaciously drawn, have architectural grandeur. The second movement is gently done, and the third, crisp and alert, lacks just a little in adrenalin. The playing is excellent and the recording full, sharper in focus and better detailed on CD.

Walter's performance – recorded in 1961 during his retirement in California – lacks mystery at the very start, but through the long first movement Walter unerringly builds up a consistent structure, controlling tempo more closely than most rivals, preferring a steady approach. The middle two movements similarly are sharply focused rather than genial, and the finale, lacking hushed pianissimos, is tough and stoically strong. A fine performance, not at all the reading one would have predicted from Walter. The CD transfer, like the others in this fine series, is full and well balanced, if lacking ultimate range, although background noise has been minimized and the sound is still impressive.

Clear and certain from the first hushed murmur of the opening movement, Solti in his newest Chicago version – in forward and full digital sound – presents the power of the piece with total conviction. What he lacks in the outer movements is a sense of mystery; he is also short of charm in the central movements, which should present a necessary contrast. His earlier LSO reading was much warmer and more spontaneous-sounding, with recording balanced more naturally, and was outstanding for its time. The compact disc version brings considerable advantage in the absence of background, but with the sound so clearly focused there is even less feeling of mystery, and the lateral spread seems a fraction narrower. The range is formidable.

Maazel's superbly controlled Vienna version brings the obvious advantage of having a generous fill-up, a comparably powerful reading of the opening *Adagio* of the *Tenth*. Maazel may not have quite the gravity and masterful control of tension that mark the very finest versions – Karajan's, for example – but with glorious playing from the Vienna strings and with unexaggerated speeds it is hard to fault Maazel on any point. He steers a masterly course between the perils of being either too plain or too mannered. Though some may miss an element of temperament, this is one of the more satisfying in his Mahler series, and is extremely well recorded. On CD, however, the spectacular sound quality with the widest range of dynamic does bring a feeling in the climaxes that the microphones were very near the orchestra.

Levine's RCA version brings a positive, confident performance, beautifully played, with little of tragedy in it. It has one of the most dazzling accounts ever recorded of the *Rondo Burleske*, but in the outer movements the close balance of the recording, and its relative coarseness, completely undermine any atmosphere of hushed intensity.

Bernstein's DG version, recorded live with the Concertgebouw, presents a surprising – and largely unwelcome – contrast with his earlier CBS account of the *Ninth*. In the outer movements his basic speeds are so slow that they lose necessary impulse, even with his magnetic control. By the end of the final *Adagio*, very slow indeed and heavily underlined, it feels as though the work will never end. The middle movements are characterized by Bernstein's brand of grotesquerie, but even there in the *Rondo Burleske* he rushes the music to its close, to undermine the virtuosity of even the Concertgebouw players. Otherwise there is some beautifully refined playing; but with sound less than DG's finest, this can be recommended only to those devotedly following Bernstein's new DG series.

Symphony No. 10 in F sharp (*Unfinished*) (revised performing edition by Deryck Cooke)
*** HMV Dig. **CDS7 47301-8** [Ang. **CDCB 47300**] (2). Bournemouth SO, Rattle – BRAHMS/SCHOENBERG: *Piano quartet*.***
(*) RCA Dig. **RD 84553 [**RCD2 4553**] (2). Phil. O, Levine.
(*) Decca Dig. **421 182-2; *421 182-4* (2) [id.]. Berlin RSO, Chailly – SCHOENBERG: *Verklaerte Nacht*.**

With digital recording of outstanding quality, Simon Rattle's vivid and compelling reading of the Cooke performing edition has one convinced more than ever that a remarkable revelation of Mahler's intentions was achieved in this painstaking reconstruction. To Cooke's final thoughts Rattle has added one or two detailed amendments; the finale in particular, starting with its cataclysmic hammer-blows and growing tuba line, is a deeply moving experience, ending not in neurotic resignation but in open optimism. In the middle movements, too, Rattle, youthfully dynamic, has fresh revelations to make. The Bournemouth orchestra plays with dedication, marred only by the occasional lack of fullness in the strings. On the CDs, a generous filler has been added in Schoenberg's orchestration of Brahms's *Piano quartet No. 1 in G minor*.

Levine's complete Mahler symphony cycle will be the first to include the full five-movement version of the *Tenth Symphony*. The performance typically reveals Levine as a thoughtful and searching Mahlerian; the spacious account of the first movement is splendid, with refined Philadelphia string tone; however, the recording, digital or not, does not always do justice to the high violins which lack something in bloom, not least in the epilogue to the finale. The sound lacks a little in bass, too. These faults of balance remain on the CDs, although the sound overall is more refined and the silent background adds to the poignancy of the finale. However, although the playing is more polished than that of the Bournemouth orchestra on the rival HMV version, as a rule Levine is less intense, relaxing well in the jolly second movement, for example, but not quite conveying the same range of emotion as the work develops.

Chailly's Decca version is superbly recorded, and his grasp of the musical structure is keen.

The Berlin Radio orchestra is highly responsive, yet the internal tension of the music making is without the high voltage of Rattle's version and, indeed, Levine's. There is much to admire here, but in the last resort this is a less compulsive musical experience than those offered by its competitors, and the coupled *Verklaerte Nacht* is also rather cool.

LIEDER AND SONG-CYCLES

Kindertotenlieder.
*** DG **415 096-2** (2) [id.]. Christa Ludwig, BPO, Karajan – *Symphony No. 5.****

Kindertotenlieder; Lieder eines fahrenden Gesellen.
** Decca **414 624-2** [id.]. Kirsten Flagstad, VPO, Boult – WAGNER: *Wesendonk Lieder.****

(i) *Kindertotenlieder; Lieder eines fahrenden Gesellen;* (ii) *5 Rückert Lieder.*
*** HMV **CDC7 47793-2** [id.]. Dame Janet Baker, (i) Hallé O; (ii) New Philh. O, Barbirolli.

Kindertotenlieder; 5 Rückert Lieder.
(M) **(*) DG *419 476-4* [id.]. Christa Ludwig, BPO, Karajan.

5 Rückert Lieder.
(*) DG **415 099-2 (2) [id.]. Christa Ludwig, BPO, Karajan – *Symphony No. 6.****

Dame Janet Baker's collaboration with Barbirolli represents the affectionate approach to Mahler at its warmest. The Hallé strings are not quite as fine as the New Philharmonia in the *Rückert Lieder*, but this generous recoupling brings results that are still intensely beautiful, full of breathtaking moments. The spontaneous feeling of soloist and conductor for this music comes over as in a live performance, and though a baritone like Fischer-Dieskau can give a stronger idea of these appealing cycles, this brings out the tenderness to a unique degree. The remastering has freshened the sound, but the ambient warmth of the original recording has not been lost. An indispensable CD.

Christa Ludwig's singing is very characterful too, if not as magical as Baker's. The *Rückert Lieder* are fine positive performances (they were originally coupled to Karajan's extravagant two-LP layout of *Das Lied von der Erde*). It is the distinction and refinement of the orchestral playing and conducting that make this Galleria reissue valuable, although the microphone conveys some unevenness in the voice. The transfer is clear and clean.

Flagstad sings masterfully in these two most appealing of Mahler's orchestral cycles, but she was unable to relax into the deeper, more intimate expressiveness that the works really require. The voice is magnificent, the approach always firmly musical (helped by Sir Adrian's splendid accompaniment), but this recording is recommendable for the singer rather than for the way the music is presented. The coupled *Wesendonck Lieder*, however, offers repertoire far more suited to her special artistry. The recording (late-1950s vintage) re-emerges with remarkable freshness.

(i) *Kindertotenlieder;* (ii) *Lieder eines fahrenden Gesellen;* (i) *4 Rückert Lieder* (*Um Mitternacht; Ich atmet' einen linden Duft; Blicke mir nicht in die Lieder; Ich bin der Welt*).
*** DG **415 191-2** [id.]. Dietrich Fischer-Dieskau, (i) BPO, Boehm; (ii) Bav. RSO, Kubelik.

As one of the Fischer-Dieskau series that DG issued to celebrate the great baritone's sixtieth birthday, this CD of his Mahler performances makes an attractive collection, drawing on more than one LP to make up generous measure. Only four of the *Rückert Lieder* are included (*Liebst du um Schönheit* being essentially a woman's song), but otherwise this conveniently gathers Mahler's shorter and most popular orchestral cycles in performances that bring out the fullest range of expression in Fischer-Dieskau at a period when his voice was at its peak. The CD transfer gives freshness and immediacy to both the 1964 recording with Boehm and the 1970 recording with Kubelik.

Das klagende Lied (complete).
*** HMV Dig. **CDC 747089-2** [id.]; *EL 270136-4* [Ang. *4DS 38159*]. Döse, Hodgson, Tear, Rea, CBSO and Ch., Rattle.

Das klagende Lied (published version).
(M) *** Nimbus **NI 5085** [id.]. Anna Reynolds, Zylis-Gara, Kaposy, Amb. S., New Philh. O, Wyn Morris.

The electricity of Simon Rattle as a recording conductor has rarely been more strikingly illustrated than in this fine recording of *Das klagende Lied*, complete with the dramatically necessary first part which Mahler came to discard. This is an amazing piece for a twenty-year-old to write, one which contains so much that is typical of the mature Mahler, not least the sense of drama and colour, and drawing on large-scale forces. Pierre Boulez was the first to record the work complete, a clean-cut and dramatic version that has been intermittently available from CBS. Like Boulez, Rattle brings out the astonishing originality but adds urgency, colour and warmth, not to mention deeper and more meditative qualities. So the final section, *Wedding Piece*, after starting with superb swagger in the celebration music, is gripping in the minstrel's sinister narration and ends in the darkest concentration on a mezzo-soprano solo, beautifully sung by Alfreda Hodgson. It adds to the attractiveness of this version that on CD the whole cantata is on a single disc in vivid sound, thin only in the off-stage party music. The ensemble of the CBSO has a little roughness, but the bite and commitment could not be more convincing.

The reissue of Wyn Morris's 1967 Delysé recording, carefully remastered on Nimbus, is most welcome. These are committed, idiomatic performances with fine solo singing, and the recording is as atmospheric as ever with the off-stage band at the wedding celebrations more vividly caught than on Rattle's version. This is excellent value on a mid price label.

Des Knaben Wunderhorn.
(M) **(*) Nimbus **NI 5084** [id.]. Dame Janet Baker, Sir Geraint Evans, LPO, Morris.
** HMV **CDC7 49045-2** [id.]; *EL 270619-4*. Lucia Popp, Bernd Weikl, LPO, Tennstedt.

Dame Janet and Sir Geraint recorded Mahler's cycle in 1966 for Delysé, long before they had both received the Queen's accolade. This was also Wyn Morris's first major essay in the recording studio; though he secures crisp playing from the LPO, the orchestral phrasing could ideally show more affection and be less metrical in charming songs that need some coaxing. Dame Janet, in particular, turns her phrases with characteristic imagination, and her flexibility is not always matched by the orchestra. Baker could hardly be more ideally cast, but Sir Geraint is more variable. He points the humour of the song about the cuckoo and the donkey with typical charm, but sometimes the voice does not sound perfectly focused. That may partly be attributed to the recording which, although vivid and warmly atmospheric, is not always sharply defined, as at the very opening with its resonance in the bass.

Tennstedt's version, very forwardly recorded, is disappointing, too unrelenting as a performance and with flawed singing. Bernd Weikl's gruff baritone, never sweet on record, is here used at times in a forced, almost cabaret style more fitting for Kurt Weill. Popp, though more aptly characterful, pointing the Laendler rhythms of the lighter songs charmingly, is not helped either by the close balance. However, this does produce an excellent and clearly transferred chrome tape.

Des Knaben Wunderhorn: excerpts (*Das irdische Leben; Verlor'ne Müh; Wo die schönen Trompeten blasen; Rheinlegendchen*).
(*) Decca **414 675-2 (2) [id.]. Minton, Chicago SO, Solti – *Symphony No. 7*.***

Yvonne Minton, a singer whom Solti encouraged enormously in her career at Covent Garden, makes a splendid soloist in these colourful songs from *Des Knaben Wunderhorn*. They were originally coupled with the *Fifth Symphony* but now make an attractive bonus for the CD issue of the *Seventh*.

Lieder eines fahrenden Gesellen (see also above, under *Symphony No. 6*).
*** Decca **414 674-2** (2) [id.]. Minton, Chicago SO, Solti – *Symphony No. 6***(*)
** CBS **MK 42025** [id.]. Mildred Miller, Columbia SO, Walter – BRAHMS: *Alto rhapsody* etc.**

Yvonne Minton's performance of the *Wayfaring Lad* cycle is outstandingly successful, and very well recorded too.

Mildred Miller sings well enough, although her vocal production is at times a little restricted and instead of long, resonant phrases the listener sometimes receives an impression of short-term musical thought. Yet Walter keeps the performance dramatically alive and there is superb orchestral detail, most vividly brought out by the excellent CD transfer, which is atmospheric and refined. The tangibility of both voice and orchestra is striking and the balance is first class.

Lieder eines fahrenden Gesellen; Lieder und Gesänge (aus der Jugendzeit); Im Lenz; Winterlied.
❀ *** Hyp. **CDA 66100** [id.]. Dame Janet Baker, Geoffrey Parsons.

Dame Janet presents a superb collection of Mahler's early songs with piano, including two written in 1880 and never recorded before, *Im Lenz* and *Winterlied*; also the piano version of the *Wayfaring Lad* songs in a text prepared by Colin Matthews from Mahler's final thoughts, as contained in the orchestral version. The performances are radiant and deeply understanding from both singer and pianist, well caught in atmospheric recording. A heart-warming record.

Das Lied von der Erde.
(M) *** Ph. *412 927-4*. J. Baker, J. King, Concg. O, Haitink.
(M) *** DG **419 058-2**; *419 058-4* [id.]. Ludwig, Kollo, BPO, Karajan.
*** DG Dig. **413 459-2** [id.]. Fassbaender, Araiza, BPO, Giulini.
*** HMV **CDC7 47231-2** [id.]. Ludwig, Wunderlich, New Philh. O and Philh. O, Klemperer.
*** Decca **414 066-2** [id.]. Minton, Kollo, Chicago SO, Solti.
(M) **(*) CBS **MK 42034** [id.]. Mildred Miller, Haefliger, NYPO, Walter.
(**) Decca mono **414 194-2**; *414 194-4*. Ferrier, Patzak, VPO, Walter.
*(*) Ph. Dig. **411 474-2** [id.]. Norman, Vickers, LSO, Sir Colin Davis.

Dame Janet Baker's outstanding version continues to dominate the field; indeed, the combination of this most deeply committed of Mahler singers with Haitink, the most thoughtfully dedicated of Mahler conductors, produces radiantly beautiful and moving results, helped by refined and atmospheric recording. If usually these songs reflect a degree of oriental reticence, Dame Janet more clearly relates them to Mahler's other great orchestral songs, so complete is the sense of involvement, with the conductor matching his soloist's mood. The concentration over the long final *Abschied* has never been surpassed on record (almost all of it was recorded in a single take). Haitink opens the cycle impressively with an account of the first tenor song that subtly confirms its symphonic shape, less free in tempo than usual but presenting unusually strong contrasts between the main stanzas and the tender refrain, *Dunkel ist das Leben*. James King cannot match his solo partner, often failing to create fantasy, but his singing is intelligent and sympathetic. The balance with the tenor is realistic, but Dame Janet's voice is brought a shade closer; for this mid-priced reissue the sound has been brightened and made more vivid, at the expense of some of the original bloom and warmth. Yet the closing pages remain tellingly atmospheric. The chrome cassette is of high quality, but we urgently need this on CD.

If Haitink presents *Das Lied* as a great symphonic masterpiece (Mahler himself called it a symphony, but for superstitious reasons failed to number it), Karajan presents it as the most seductive sequence of atmospheric songs. It may seem strange that so central a conductor generally avoided Mahler until late in his career, but the result here is everything one could have hoped for, combining Karajan's characteristic refinement and polish with a deep sense of melancholy. The balancing of textures, the weaving of separate strands into a transparent tapestry, has never been so flawlessly achieved on record as here. Karajan's way of presenting Mahler's orchestration in the subtlest tones rather than in full colours is arguably more apt. In any case what matters is that here, along with his characteristic refinement, Karajan conveys the ebb and flow of tension as in a live performance. He is helped enormously by the soloists, both of whom have recorded this work several times, but never more richly than here. Originally issued as a two-record set, the recording has been successfully remastered and reappears on one mid-priced Galleria CD or tape. The sound is more sharply defined, and some of the ambient effect has gone, but the quality is admirably vivid and does not lack a basic warmth.

Giulini conducts a characteristically restrained and refined reading. With Araiza a heady-toned tenor rather than a powerful one, the line *Dunkel ist das Leben* in the first song becomes unusually tender and gentle, with rapture and wistfulness keynote emotions. In the second song, Fassbaender gives lightness and poignancy to the line *Mein Herz ist müde* rather than dark tragedy; and even the final *Abschied* is rapt rather than tragic, following the text of the poem. Not that Giulini fails to convey the breadth and intensity of Mahler's magnificent concept; and the playing of the Berlin Philharmonic could hardly be more beautiful. Warmer, more refined and more atmospheric recording than this orchestra has lately been receiving.

Klemperer's way with Mahler is at its most individual in *Das Lied von der Erde* – and that will enthral some, as it must infuriate others. True, there is less case for Klempereran nobility in so evocative and orient-inspired a piece as *Das Lied* than there is in the symphonies; if the ear is open, however, Klemperer's preference for slow tempi and his refusal to languish reveal qualities far removed from the heaviness his detractors deplore. With slower speeds, the three tenor songs seem initially to lose some of their sparkle and humour; however, thanks to superb expressive singing by the late Fritz Wunderlich – one of the most memorable examples of his artistry on record – and thanks also to pointing of rhythm by Klemperer himself, subtle but always clear, the comparative slowness will hardly worry anyone intent on hearing the music afresh, as Klemperer intends. As for the mezzo songs, Christa Ludwig sings them with a remarkable depth of expressiveness; in particular, the final *Abschied* has the intensity of a great occasion. Excellent digitally remastered recording (1967 vintage), apart from a forward woodwind balance, sounding most impressive on CD.

In breadth of sound and precision of texture, few versions can match Solti's with the Chicago orchestra, helped by brilliant but refined 1972 recording. As an interpretation, it may lose something in mystery because of this very precision, but Solti's concentration, in a consciously less romantic style than normal, is highly compelling, above all in the final *Abschied*: slower than usual and in the final section bringing an unusually close observance of Mahler's *pianissimo* markings. Minton exactly matches Solti's style, consistently at her most perceptive and sensitive, while Kollo presents Heldentenor strength, combined with sensitivity. The recording has no need to give the tenor an unnaturally close balance, and the result is the more exciting, with the background quiet of the CD making everything seem more tangible.

Though Bruno Walter's New York version does not have the tear-laden quality in the final *Abschied* that made his earlier Vienna account (in mono) with Kathleen Ferrier unique, that is its only serious shortcoming. Haefliger sparkles with imagination and Miller is a warm and appealing mezzo soloist, lacking only the last depth of feeling you find in a Ferrier; and the maestro himself has rarely sounded so happy on record, even in Mahler. The remastered recording has been considerably improved for CD and now sounds both warm and vivid.

It is a joy to have the voice of Kathleen Ferrier so vividly caught on CD – not to mention that of the characterful Patzak – in Bruno Walter's classic Vienna recording for Decca. It is also an enormous advantage having silent background with minimum tape-hiss, to be able to appreciate the radiance of the performance, not least in the ecstatic closing pages and the final murmurs of '*Ewig*'. The sad thing is that the violin tone, by being given extra top, in high loud passages has acquired a very unattractive edge, not at all like the Vienna violins, and this makes for uncomfortable listening.

Sir Colin Davis rarely if ever recorded Mahler before his London reading of *Das Lied von der Erde*. Despite beautifully refined playing, the result is stiff and unpersuasive, lacking in tension. Vickers strains uncomfortably in the first song, gritty of tone, with no attempt at a *pianissimo* for *Dunkel ist das Leben*. Jessye Norman, as ever, is magnificent, deeply and naturally expressive, quite the finest element in the reading. Full and refined recording.

Manzoni, Giacomo (born 1932)

Masse: Omaggio a Edgard Varèse.
*** DG Dig. **423 307-2** [id.]. Pollini, BPO, Sinopoli – SCHOENBERG: *Chamber symphony*.***

Manzoni might be broadly classed as a follower of Luigi Nono, a teacher and critic as well as a composer. *Masse* has nothing to do with church liturgy, but refers to measures or quantities, and in its tribute to Varèse follows up a science-based mode of thought which proves surprisingly dramatic and colourful. Only the piano solo has much in the way of melodic interest, and Pollini exploits it all he can, not least in the elaborate cadenza-like passages. Sinopoli too in his first major recording already revealed the feeling for texture and dynamic which has since made his conducting so memorable.

Marais, Marin (1656–1728)

La Gamme en forme de petit opéra; Sonata à la marésienne.
*** HM **HMC 901105** [id.]. L. Baroque.

This is something of a curiosity. Published in 1723, *La Gamme* is a string of short character-pieces for violin, viole de gambe and harpsichord that takes its inspiration from the ascending and descending figures of the scale. Although it is *en forme de petit opéra*, its layout is totally instrumental and the varied pieces and dramatic shifts of character doubtless inspire the title. It plays without a break of any kind – unlike, say, the sets of character-pieces one encounters in the Couperin *Ordres* – and its continuity is enlivened by much variety of invention and resource. The *Sonata à la marésienne* is less unusual in character but it, too, has variety and character. The London Baroque is an excellent group, and they are well recorded too. The transfer to the new medium has been wholly successful.

Marcello, Alessandro (1669–1750)

Oboe concerto in C minor (arr. Bonelli).
(M) *** PRT **PVCD 8374** [id.]. Rothwell, Pro Arte O, Barbirolli – ALBINONI; CIMAROSA: *Concertos*.***

Sir John's subtlety in matters of light and shade within an orchestral phrase brings the music immediately alive and at the same time prevents the rather jolly opening tune from sounding square. There is a beautiful *Adagio* and a gay finale, both showing the soloist on top form, and the well-balanced recording adds to one's pleasure. The remastering for CD has been most successful, but no musical notes are provided.

Marcello, Benedetto (1686–1739)

Guitar concerto in C min. (arr. Williams).
** CBS **MK 39560**; *IMT 39560* [id.]. Williams, ASMF, Sillito – BACH; HANDEL: *Concertos.***

Like the other arrangements on this disc, the change of solo instrument (in this instance the original was for oboe) is not an improvement, and although Williams is impressive in the *Adagio*, this collection will direct its main appeal to guitar enthusiasts and admirers of the soloist. The sound is good, with the chrome tape not as sharply defined as the CD.

Martin, Frank (1890–1974)

Piano concertos Nos 1–2; Ballade.
** Claves Dig. **CD 50-8509** [id.]. Antonioli, Turin PO, Viotti.

Frank Martin was already in his early forties by the time he came to write his *First Concerto*, and it bears many of the fingerprints one recognizes from such mature works as the *Petite symphonie concertante* and the *Concerto for seven wind instruments*. It is a rewarding discovery, and in some ways a more characteristic and poetic work than its successor, written in the late 1960s. The sustained pedal notes of the opening, the purposeful sense of movement which betrays an affinity with the thinking we find in the slow movements of the Honegger symphonies, and the pale, haunting instrumental colourings evoke Martin's own special world. Indeed it possesses the stronger atmosphere of the two, though the slow movements of both are marvellous, the product of a keen and refined sensibility and a subtle musical intelligence. Jean-François Antonioli is an impressive player: he is entirely inside the idiom and dispatches the solo parts with expertise. The conductor, too, has obvious sympathy with this music and offers him sensitive support. However, the unglamorous acoustic in which the recordings were made does not help either of them, and the balance gives a somewhat artificial aural perspective, with the piano very much up front. The Turin orchestra is adequate rather than distinguished: there are some sensitive contributions from the wind and brass, but the strings are not of comparable quality.

Petite symphonie concertante.
(*) Chan. *ABT 1060* [id.]. Sydney SO, Otterloo (with DEBUSSY: *Danses*; RAVEL: *Introduction and allegro*).

Frank Martin's *Petite symphonie concertante* is arguably his masterpiece, and its highly resourceful contrast of sonorities makes it particularly appealing. It is a searching, inventive and often profound work, though inevitably it causes problems of balance between the three concertante instruments and the double strings. These were solved in its pioneering mono record under Ansermet, but they seem to have eluded recording engineers fairly consistently in the stereo era. The soloists are a bit forward in this Chandos version, but not unreasonably so, and the performance is atmospheric and committed, capturing much of the work's subtle contrasts and pale colouring. The strings of the Sydney Symphony Orchestra are a little wanting in bloom but this is, *faute de mieux*, the only version currently available and the work is as haunting as it is masterly. The successful cassette transfer lacks only the last degree of upper range.

Martinů, Bohuslav (1890–1959)

La Bagarre; Half-time; Intermezzo; The Rick; Thunderbolt.
*** Sup. **CO 1669** [id.]. Brno State O, Vronsky.

La Bagarre and *Half-time* are early evocations, the latter a Honeggerian depiction of a roisterous half-time at a football match that musically doesn't amount to a great deal. The three later works are much more interesting – *Intermezzo* is linked to the *Fourth Symphony* – and the collection as a whole will be of great interest to Martinů addicts, if perhaps not essential for other collectors. All the performances are alive and full of character, and the recording is vividly immediate.

Rhapsody-Concerto for viola and orchestra.
*** Conifer Dig. **CDFC 146**; *MCFC 146* [id.]. Golani, Berne SO, Maag – D'INDY: *Symphonie sur un chant montagnard français.****

This is not quite a viola concerto: though there are the elements of dialogue and display we associate with the genre, it is primarily gentle and reflective. It comes from 1952, a year before the *Sixth Symphony*, which it foreshadows, particularly in the second of its two movements. The *Rhapsody* is free in its formal layout, and the quieter episodes of the *Adagio* have an impressive inner repose. The violist Rivka Golani plays with a gloriously warm tone and much musical insight, and the whole performance is agreeably natural: there is nothing high-powered or overdriven. As admirers of Peter Maag will expect, this is a selfless performance of the old school that allows this music to speak for itself and penetrates deeper under the surface. The sound is that of a very fine broadcast rather than a seat in a concert hall, but detail is kept in an excellent and believable perspective. Very strongly recommended. The chrome cassette is first class in all respects, naturally balanced and truthful.

Symphonies Nos 1–4.
*** BIS Dig. **CD 362-3** [id.]. Bamberg SO, Järvi.

Martinů did not turn to the symphony until he settled in America during the war, after which he composed one a year for five years – a *Sixth* followed in the early 1950s. Martinů always draws a highly individual sound from his orchestra and secures great clarity, even when the score abounds in octave doublings. He often thickens his textures in this way, yet, when played with the delicacy these artists produce, they sound beautifully transparent. On hearing the *First*, Virgil Thomson wrote, 'the shining sounds of it sing as well as shine', and there is no doubt this music is luminous and life-loving. The *Fourth* is the most popular and is coupled with the more highly charged and intensely felt *Third*. It is probably best to start with them, but few, having done so, will be able to resist their companions. The thrilling recording is in the demonstration class yet sounds completely natural, and the performances under Neeme Järvi are totally persuasive and have a spontaneous feel for the music's pulse.

Cello sonatas Nos 1–3.
*** Sup. **CO 1718** [id.]. Josef Churcho, Josef Hála.

The *Cello sonatas* were written over a period of thirteen years between 1939 and 1952, the first in Paris, the second in the USA, and the superb third work partly in France, partly in America. The *First Sonata* is a fine piece, but the *Second* is more than that, with the energetic flow of the outer movements balanced by the essentially serene yet romantic beauty of the central *Largo*. The *Third Sonata*, however, is one of those totally memorable works that, once heard, is never forgotten, from the eloquent opening *Poco Andante*, through the *Moderato* to the haunting *Andante* and the rhythmically individual finale. There is the eloquence of Dvořák in the melodic invention, although Martinů is always his own man. The performances are outstandingly committed and spontaneous. The recording is truthful and well balanced, a shade studio-ish and close, but realistic. A most welcome addition to the Martinů discography that is of wide appeal – the *Third Sonata* should be in the standard repertoire.

Nonet; Trio in F for flute, cello and piano; La Revue de cuisine.
*** Hyp. **CDA 66084** [id.]. Dartington Ens.

A delightful record. None of these pieces is otherwise available on CD or cassette and all of them receive first-class performances and superb recording. The sound has space, warmth, perspective and definition. *La Revue de cuisine* is very much of its decade and the *Charleston* is most engaging, even if not all the others are Martinů at his most characteristic or inventive. The *Trio,* written after a bout of depression in 1944, is as fresh and inventive as his very best work and is deliciously played, and its *Andante* deserves to be singled out for special mention: it is a most beautiful movement. The *Nonet*, for string trio plus double-bass, flute, clarinet, oboe, horn and bassoon, was finished five months before his death and is as life-enhancing as the *Sinfonietta giocosa* of 1940, also composed when he was in penury and danger. An indispensable issue for lovers of Martinů's music.

(i) *Piano quintet No. 2;* (ii) *3 Madrigals for violin & viola.*
*** Sup. **CO 2049** [id.]. (i) Páleníček, Smetana Qt; (ii) Jiří Novák, Milan Škampa.

Martinů's *Second Piano quintet* was written in New York in 1944. While clearly in direct line from Dvořák's *Quintet*, its originality and freshness are entirely characteristic of the composer's finest work. The radiance of texture is striking, with the violin line often lying high, while the shifting rhythms and harmonies over the purposeful basic pulse of the allegros are balanced by the lyrical intensity of the *Adagio* and the deeply expressive *Largo*, which opens and later returns to the finale. The Czech performance combines vitality with spontaneity; the recording is well balanced if a little close. The *3 Madrigals* (1947) also have a complexity of texture and polyphony to suggest at times to the ear that two players alone cannot be creating such rich sounds. Yet they do and the shimmering central *Poco Andante* makes a fine centrepiece. Again the recording is very vivid and immediate. These are both major additions to the Martinů repertoire.

Variations on a theme of Rossini; Variations on a Slovak folksong.
*** Max Sound *MSCB 20/21; MSCC 20/21.* Caroline Dale, Keith Swallow – BRIDGE; PROKOFIEV: *Sonatas****; DELIUS: *Sonata.***

A pair of unfamiliar but entertaining lightweight works from a master who clearly identifies with his source material. If the extension of the Slovak folksong has the most imaginative treatment, the *Rossini variations* are not wanting in fun and spirit. The performances are splendid, with both performers clearly stimulated by the music's ardour and bravura. Excellent sound on a chrome tape offering 83′ music, which is available in alternative Dolby B or Dolby C formats.

Field mass.
*** Sup. Dig. **C37 7735** [id.]. Zítek, Czech Philharmonic Ch. and O, Mackerras – JANÁČEK: *Amarus.****

Martinů's *Field mass* is full of delightful and original sonorities, and this persuasive account under Mackerras shows it in the best possible light. The *Field mass* was intended for performance in the open air and is scored for the unusual combination of baritone, male chorus, wind instruments, percussion, harmonium and a piano, as well as a triangle and a number of bells. The resultant sounds are as fresh and individual as one could imagine, and so is Martinů's invention. The *Mass* was written in France in 1939 in the dark days of the war, yet it retains a life-enhancing quality and a sense of faith that is moving. It is very impressively performed by the Czech forces under Sir Charles Mackerras, and the recording is quite outstanding.

Mascagni, Pietro (1863–1945)

L'Amico Fritz (complete).

*** HMV **CDS7 47905-8** (2) [Ang. **CDCB 47905**]. Pavarotti, Freni, Sardinero, ROHCG Ch. and O, Gavazzeni.

The haunting *Cherry duet* from this opera whets the appetite for more, and it is good to hear so rare and charming a piece, one that is not likely to enter the repertory of our British opera houses. Even so, enthusiasm has to be tempered a little, because no other number in the opera approaches the famous duet in its memorability. The libretto too is delicate to the point of feebleness. This performance could be more refined, though Freni and Pavarotti are most attractive artists and this was recorded in 1969 when they were both at their freshest. The Covent Garden Orchestra responds loyally; the recording is clear and atmospheric, and it has transferred very successfully to CD. While the dramatic conception is at the opposite end of the scale from *Cavalleria Rusticana*, one is easily beguiled by the music's charm, and the Puccinian influences are by no means a disadvantage.

Cavalleria Rusticana (complete).

*** RCA **RD 83091**; *RK 13091* [*CRK1 3091*]. Scotto, Domingo, Elivira, Isola Jones, Amb. Op. Ch., Nat. PO, Levine.

*** DG **419 257-2** (3) [id.]. Cossotto, Bergonzi, Guelfi, Ch. & O of La Scala, Milan, Karajan – LEONCAVALLO: *I Pagliacci**** (also with collection of *Operatic intermezzi****).

(***) HMV mono **CDS7 47981-8** [Ang. **CDCC 47981**]; (M) *EX 291269-5* (3). Callas, Di Stefano, Panerai, Ch. & O of La Scala, Milan, Serafin – LEONCAVALLO: *I Pagliacci.*(***)

(M) (***) RCA mono **GD 86510** [**RCA 6510-2-RG**]. Milanov, Bjoerling, Merrill, Robert Shaw Chorale, RCA O, Cellini.

*(*) Ph. **416 137-2** [id.]. Obraztsova, Domingo, Bruson, Barbieri, La Scala, Milan, Ch. & O, Prêtre.

(i) *Cavalleria Rusticana* (complete). *Guglielmo Ratcliffe: Intermezzo. Iris: Introduction and Hymn to the sun. Le Maschere: Overture.*

(B) ** EMI *TCC2-POR 290111-9* (i) De los Angeles, Corelli, Sereni, Lazzarini; Rome Opera Ch. & O, Santini.

There is far more to recommend about the RCA issue than the fact that it is available on a single CD (libretto included) or cassette. On balance, in performance it stands as the best current recommendation, with Domingo giving a heroic account of the role of Turiddu, full of defiance. Scotto, strongly characterful too, though not always perfectly steady on top, gives one of her finest performances of recent years, and James Levine directs with a splendid sense of pacing, by no means faster than his rivals (except the leisurely Karajan), and drawing red-blooded playing from the National Philharmonic. The recording is very good, strikingly present in its CD format, and the cassette transfer is first class, one of RCA's very best.

Karajan's direction of the other half of the inevitable partnership matches that of *Pagliacci*. He pays Mascagni the tribute of taking his markings literally, so that well-worn melodies come out with new purity and freshness, and the singers have been chosen to match that. Cossotto quite as much as Bergonzi keeps a pure, firm line that is all too rare in this much-abused music. Together they show that much of the vulgarity lies in interpretations rather than in Mascagni's inspiration. Not that there is any lack of dramatic bite (except marginally, because of the recording balance in some of the chorus work). The CD transfer cannot rectify the balance, but voices are generally more sharply defined, while the spacious opulence is retained. Karajan's fine performances of various opera-interludes make a welcome filler on the three-CD set.

Though on stage Maria Callas sang Santuzza in *Cav.* only as a young teenager, she gives a totally distinctive characterization, rarely if ever matched for intensity on record. Dating from the mid-1950s, these performances reveal the diva in her finest voice, with edginess and unevenness of production at a minimum and with vocal colouring at its most characterful. The singing of the other principals is hardly less dramatic and Panerai, here at the beginning of his long career, is in firm, well-projected voice. This powerful team is superbly controlled by Serafin, a master at pacing this music, giving it full power while minimizing vulgarity. However, with Callas providing the central focus, the performance seems to centre round the aria, *Voi lo sapete*, wonderfully dark and intense, and one soon adjusts to the fact that the restricted range means that the opera's opening choruses sound rather mushy; the solo voices, however, are vividly projected on both CD and the very acceptable mid-priced cassettes.

On a single mid-price CD in the Victor Opera series, RCA offers a vintage version recorded in New York in mono in the early 1950s with soloists from the Met. The sound is surprisingly full and vivid for its age, but none of the documentation gives any clue to the date of recording. Though Zinka Milanov starts disappointingly in the *Easter hymn*, the conjunction of three of the outstanding Met. principals of the period brings a warmly satisfying performance. Admirers of Milanov will not want to miss her beautiful singing of *Voi lo sapete*, and in the duet Merrill's dark, firm timbre is thrilling. Bjoerling brings a good measure of musical and tonal subtlety to the role of Turiddu, normally belted out, while Cellini's conducting minimizes the vulgarity of the piece.

On the EMI tape – very reasonably priced – an essentially lyrical performance. If the bitterness of Mascagni's drama is not a first consideration, this beautifully sung and warmly recorded set certainly gives scope for soaring Italianate singing of rich, memorable melodies. The three bonus items too are worth having. The sound is smooth, a little lacking in upper range but well balanced.

Taken from the soundtrack of a Unitel television film (like the companion version of *Pag.*) the Prêtre set can be recommended to those who want a reminder of the film, and maybe also to those who want to hear Domingo in ringing voice; but otherwise the flaws rule it out as a serious contender. Obraztsova's massive and distinctive mezzo is certainly characterful but hardly apt for the role, with its obtrusively edgy and uneven sounds. One or two moments are memorable – for example, the agonized utterance of the curse *A te la mala Pasqua*, not fire-eating at all – but she, like some of the others, equally unsteady, looked better than they all sound. Fedora Barbieri, a veteran of veterans among mezzos, makes a token appearance as Mamma Lucia. The recording is full and atmospheric with the sound-effects needed for television. The single-disc CD format brings a libretto in a slipcase.

Massenet, Jules (1842–1912)

Manon (ballet) complete (arr. Lucas).
*** Decca Dig. **414 585-2**; *414 585-4* (2) [id.]. ROHCG O, Bonynge.

The *Manon* ballet is a full-length work in three acts drawn from no fewer than thirteen of Massenet's operas (plus sundry other oratorios, songs and instrumental pieces), carefully leaving out Massenet's own operatic setting of this same story. This confection of Massenet lollipops – with the famous *Elégie* returning as an *idée fixe* – is the work of Leighton Lucas; with characteristically lively and colourful playing from the Covent Garden Orchestra under Richard Bonynge, it makes a delightful issue, the more attractive when, as with other Bonynge recordings of ballet, the Decca engineers deliver sound of spectacular quality.

Werther (complete).
*** Ph. **416 654-2** (2) [id.]. Carreras, Von Stade, Allen, Buchanan, Lloyd, Children's Ch., O of ROHCG, C. Davis.

Sir Colin Davis has rarely directed a more sensitive or more warmly expressive performance on record than his account of *Werther*. The magic of sound hits the listener from the opening prelude onwards, and the refined recording, coupled with a superbly cast performance based on a stage production at Covent Garden, makes for consistent compulsion. Frederica von Stade makes an enchanting Charlotte, outshining all current rivals on record, both strong and tender, conveying the understanding but vulnerable character of Goethe's heroine. Carreras may not be quite so clearly superior to all rivals, but he uses a naturally beautiful voice freshly and sensitively. Others in the cast, such as Thomas Allen as Charlotte's husband Albert and Isobel Buchanan as Sophie, her sister, are excellent, too. The CD transfer on to a pair of discs has been highly successful, with a single serious reservation: the break between the two compact discs is badly placed in the middle of a key scene between Werther and Charlotte, just before *Ah! qu'il est loin ce jour!* Otherwise this is one of the very finest French opera sets yet issued in the new medium.

Mathias, William (born 1934)

Lux aeterna, Op. 88.
*** Chan. Dig. *ABTD 1115* [id.]. Felicity Lott, Cable, Penelope Walker, Bach Ch., St George's Chapel Ch., Windsor, LSO, Willcocks; J. Scott (organ).

The influence of Benjamin Britten is strong in this multi-layered choral work, but the energy and sureness of effect make it far more than derivative, an attractively approachable and colourful piece, full of memorable ideas. Just as Britten in the *War Requiem* contrasted different planes of expression with Latin liturgy set against Wilfred Owen poems, so Mathias contrasts the full choir singing Latin against the boys' choir singing carol-like Marian anthems, and in turn against the three soloists, who sing three arias and a trio to the mystical poems of St John of the Cross. In the last section all three planes come together when the chorus chants the prayer *Lux aeterna*, and the boys sing the hymn, *Ave maris stella*, leaving the soloists alone at the end in a moving conclusion. There are choral and instrumental effects here which directly echo examples in Tippett and Messiaen, as well as Britten; but the confidence of the writing and of this excellent recorded performance reveal lessons well learnt. Outstanding recording, beautifully and atmospherically balanced.

Wind quintet.
*** Crystal **CD 750** [id.]. Westwood Wind Quintet – CARLSSON: *Nightwings*; LIGETI: *Bagatelles*; BARBER: *Summer music.****

William Mathias composed his accessible and high-spirited *Quintet* during his late twenties for the Cheltenham Festival. Of the five movements the scherzo is particularly felicitous and there is a rather beautiful *Elegy*. The playing of the Westwood Wind Quintet is highly expert and committed, though the recording is a little less transparent than in the Barber or Ligeti pieces with which it is coupled (it was made a year or so earlier than they). However, it is still very good indeed.

Matthews, Colin (born 1946)

(i) *Cello concerto;* (ii) *Sonata No. 5* (*Landscape*).
*** Unicorn Dig. *DKPC 9053* [id.]. (i) Baillie, L. Sinfonia; (ii) Berlin RSO; Carewe.

Colin Matthews' *Sonata No. 5*, subtitled *Landscape*, is one of the most powerful and ambitious orchestral works to have been written by a British composer of the younger generation, in effect a large-scale symphony in a single movement, richly and evocatively scored. In its concentration over a broad span it rises well above mere atmospheric associations of dark into light (the composer's broad theme), presenting a natural logic which the ear can appreciate even before the brain can analyse it. This is a formidable achievement, and though the Berlin live performance conducted by John Carewe is not as strong or committed as that which the BBC broadcast earlier, this is a splendid celebration of a fast-growing talent. The *Cello concerto* too is an impressive piece, again confidently argued on a broad scale. It is a pity with this of all instruments that Matthews does not allow himself a warmer lyricism; but with Alexander Baillie brilliantly bringing out the power of the declamatory writing and intensifying the underlying darkness of the piece, this too emerges as a fine, ambitious work, warm in its emotions. On this tape it is as well recorded as it is dedicatedly played.

Maw, Nicholas (born 1935)

(i) *La vita nuova* (for soprano and chamber ens.); (ii) *The Voice of Love*.
*** Chan. *ABT 1037*. (i) Christie, Nash Ens.; (ii) Walker, Vignoles.

These two song-cycles represent Maw's work at different periods of his career, yet both give warm evidence of his exceptional sensitivity towards the voice. To works specially written by the poet Peter Porter, *The Voice of Love* tells of the love affair of a seventeenth-century authoress, surrounding romantic emotion with colour and point in a rather Britten-like way. Sarah Walker, accompanied by the pianist Roger Vignoles, characterizes superbly. Nan Christie in the more recent cycle – setting Italian Renaissance love-lyrics – is less sweetly caught; but here too the natural expressiveness of Maw's writing comes over most persuasively, helped by first-rate recording. The tape transfer is excellent.

Maxwell Davies, Peter (born 1934)

The Bairns of Brugh; (i) *Image, reflection, shadow. Runes from the Holy Island.*
*** Unicorn *DKPC 9033* [id.]. (i) Knowles (cimbalom); Fires of London, composer.

Image, reflection, shadow is the major work in this collection, some 36 minutes long; it is evocative, like most of Maxwell Davies's Orkney pieces, of the impact of nature, not of storm or stress but of the play of light. It brings some of his happiest inspirations, with melody and thematic development more important than in most of his music. The third movement is particularly beautiful, developing on a meditative melody at the start into a dancing allegro and a cadenza for the cimbalom, an instrument that colours the chamber texture of the work consistently. The two shorter pieces make a valuable fill-up, *The Bairns of Brugh* a tender lament (viola over marimba) and *Runes* a group of brief epigrams. First-rate performances and recording.

Violin concerto.
*** CBS Dig. **MK 42449**; *IMT 42449* [id.]. Stern, RPO, Previn: DUTILLEUX: *L'Arbre des songes.****

Maxwell Davies wrote this massive *Violin concerto* (over half an hour long) specifically with Isaac Stern in mind, to a commission from the RPO to celebrate its fortieth anniversary. There are parallels here with the Walton *Violin concerto* of over forty years earlier. The composer was inspired to draw on a more warmly lyrical side such as he has rarely displayed. Davies claims to have been influenced by his favourite violin concerto, Mendelssohn's, but there is little of

Mendelssohnian lightness and fantasy here; for all its beauties, this is a work which has a tendency to middle-aged spread, not nearly as taut in expression as the Walton or, for that matter, the fine Dutilleux concerto, also first heard in 1986, with which it is coupled. Stern seems less involved here than in that other work, though this coupling makes a strong, meaty issue for anyone wanting to investigate the recent development of these characterful composers. There is a good tape.

Sinfonia; Sinfonia concertante.
*** Unicorn Dig. *DKPCD 9058* [id.]. Scottish CO, composer.

In his *Sinfonia* of 1962 Peter Maxwell Davies took as his inspirational starting point Monteverdi's *Vespers* of 1610. Except perhaps in the simple, grave beauty of the second of the four movements, where the analogy is directly with *Pulchra es* from the *Vespers*, it is not a kinship which will readily strike the listener, but the dedication in this music, beautifully played by the Scottish Chamber Orchestra under the composer, is plain from first to last. The *Sinfonia concertante* of twenty years later, as the title implies, is a much more extrovert piece for strings plus solo wind quintet and timpani. The balance of movements broadly follows a conventional plan, but in idiom this is hardly at all neo-classical, and more than usual the composer evokes romantic images, as in the lovely close of the first movement. Virtuoso playing from the Scottish principals, not least the horn. Well-balanced recording.

Sinfonia accademica; (i) *Into the Labyrinth.*
*** Unicorn Dig. *DKPC 9038* [id.]. (i) Neil Mackie; Scottish CO, composer.

These two works, both written in 1983 but well contrasted, are fine examples of Maxwell Davies's recent output, inspired by the sights and sounds of Orkney where he has made his home, away from urban civilization. *Into the Labyrinth* (just over half an hour long), in five movements, might be regarded more as a song-symphony than as a cantata. The words by the Orcadian poet (and the composer's regular collaborator), George Mackay Brown, are a prose-poem inspired by the physical impact of Orkney, with the second movement a hymn of praise to fire, wind, earth and water, and the fourth – after a brief orchestral interlude in the third – bringing the centrepiece of the work, comprising almost half the total length, an intense meditation. The fine Scottish tenor, Neil Mackie, gives a superb performance, confirming this as one of Maxwell Davies's most beautiful and moving inspirations. The *Sinfonia accademica*, written for Edinburgh University, provides a strong and attractive contrast with its lively, extrovert outer movements and a central slow movement which again evokes the atmosphere of Orkney. Strong, intense performances under the composer, helped by first-rate recording. The cassette is first class in every way.

Symphony No. 3.
*** PRT BBC Dig. **CD 560**. BBC PO, Edward Downes.

Within six months of the first performance in Manchester by these same performers, Peter Maxwell Davies's *Symphony*, written for the fiftieth anniversary of the BBC Philharmonic (formerly the BBC Northern Symphony Orchestra), appeared in this excellent recording on the BBC Artium label. It presents a powerful case for a work which, more concerned with lyricism than its predecessors, yet builds a structure just as powerful. Where in the *First Symphony* Maxwell Davies's direct inspiration came from Sibelius, here he has taken his cue from the *Ninth Symphony* of Mahler, with two lighter scherzando movements in the middle, and ending with a long *Lento* finale which calmly draws the many threads together to make a most satisfying conclusion. Downes coaxes playing from his Manchester orchestra of a commitment and brilliance to match any rival. Excellent recording.

(i) *Eight songs for a Mad King;* (ii) *Miss Donnithorne's maggot.*
*** Unicorn Dig. **DKPCD 9052** [id.]. (i) Julius Eastman; (ii) Mary Thomas; Fires of London, composer.

Eight songs for a Mad King, first heard in 1969, was a landmark in the composer's career. It was followed five years later by another chillingly explicit depiction of madness, *Miss Donnithorne's maggot*, to make this generous coupling particularly pointful. The *Songs for a Mad King* provide the more sharply powerful experience. In this unforgettable piece there are many levels of imagination at work: it is at once a re-creation of George III's madness, with the reciter/singer taking the role of the king; an example of inventive sing-speech with vocal harmonics and double notes part of the king's raving; a dramatic fantasy with flute, clarinet, violin and cello representing caged birds that the king tried to teach; a musical fantasy on tunes played by a mechanical organ which the king actually possessed and which survives today. It is harrowing in its expressionistic venom, playing on hidden nerves; but the power of inspiration, superbly conveyed in this performance with Julius Eastman as soloist and conducted by the composer, comes over vividly. The 1970 analogue recording is all the fresher and more immediate in the CD transfer. The performance of *Miss Donnithorne*, recorded in 1984, again with the composer conducting the Fires of London, is equally vivid, with Mary Thomas bringing out in her abrasive thrust and intensity the kinship with *Pierrot Lunaire*. Though sharp in expression, this is more diffuse than the *Mad King*, a celebration of the eccentric who provided Dickens with his model for Miss Havisham in *Great Expectations*. The digital recording is both vivid and immediate.

Vesalii icones.
*** Unicorn *UKC 7016*. Ward Clarke, Fires of London, composer.

Maxwell Davies has the great quality of presenting strikingly memorable visions, and this is certainly one, an extraordinary cello solo with comment from a chamber group. It was originally written to accompany a solo dancer in a fourteen-fold sequence, each dance based on one of the horrifying anatomical drawings of Vesalius (1543) and each representing one of the stations of the Cross. Characteristically Davies has moments not only of biting pain and tender compassion but of deliberate shock-tactics – notably when the risen Christ turns out to be Antichrist and is represented in a final jaunty foxtrot. This is difficult music, but the emotional landmarks are plain from the start, and that is a good sign of enduring quality. Jennifer Ward Clarke plays superbly, and so do the Fires of London, conducted by the composer. Excellent recording. The tape is admirably clear and vivid.

Mendelssohn, Felix (1809–47)

(i) *Piano concerto in A min.;* (ii) *Violin concerto in D min., Op. posth.*
*** Tel. Dig. **ZK8 42917** [id.]. (i) Katsaris; (ii) Zehetmair; Liszt CO, Rolla.

These two youthful concertos of Mendelssohn, both using string orchestra, make an apt coupling and receive from these fine Hungarian musicians lively, enjoyable performances. That of the *Violin concerto* is the more engaging in its lightness. Though the orchestral introduction to the slow movement, taken rather slowly, is too heavy, the imagination of the soloist then transforms the movement, while the outer movements are full of flair, fizzing energetically, particularly the Hungarian-dance finale, in which Hungarian musicians find a winning degree of wildness. The youthful *A minor Piano concerto* is an extended piece lasting over half an hour, far longer than the two numbered piano concertos, an amazing work for a thirteen-year-old, endlessly inventive.

Cyprien Katsaris gives it a fresh and strong reading, marked by delightfully crisp and clean articulation, lacking only the last degree of sparkle and charm. Splendid orchestral playing and first-rate recording.

Piano concerto No. 1 in G min., Op. 25.
(*) HMV Dig. **CDC7 47611-2 [id.]; *EL 270184-4* [Ang. *4DS 38235*]. Ousset, LSO, Marriner – GRIEG: *Concerto*.**(*)

Piano concertos Nos 1 in G min.; 2 in D min., Op. 40.
*** Decca Dig. **414 672** [id.]. András Schiff, Bav. RSO, Dutoit.

Piano concertos Nos 1–2; Capriccio brillant, Op. 22.
*** Tel. Dig. **ZK8 43681** [id.]. Katsaris, Leipzig GO, Masur.

(i) *Piano concertos Nos 1–2; Prelude and fugue, Op. 35/1; Rondo capriccioso, Op. 14; Variations sérieuses, Op. 54.*
*** CBS **MK 42401** [id.]. Murray Perahia; (i) ASMF, Marriner.

Mendelssohn's two *Piano concertos* are not in the class of the famous *Violin concerto in E minor*, but when played with discernment they are agreeably entertaining. Perahia's playing catches the Mendelssohnian spirit with admirable perception. There is sensibility and sparkle, the slow movements are shaped most beautifully and obviously the partnership with Marriner is very successful, for the Academy give a most sensitive backing. The recording is not distinguished – it could be more transparent; but it does not lack body, and the piano timbre is fully acceptable. Moreover this CBS issue offers three substantial bonuses from Perahia's admirable digital solo recital.

András Schiff plays marvellously, with great delicacy and fluency; his virtuosity is effortless and never pursued for the sake of personal display. There is plenty of poetic feeling, too. He is given excellent accompaniments by Dutoit and the Bavarian players, and the Decca recording is first class and especially vivid and transparent in its CD transfer. By the side of the CBS coupling, this is short measure, but the sound is far more realistic.

It is impossible not to respond to the robust vitality of Katsaris. He plays with enormous vigour in the outer movements and receives strong support from Masur. There is nothing heavy, yet the music is given more substance than usual, while the central slow movements bring a relaxed lyrical *espressivo* which provides admirable contrast. The sheer vigour and impetus of the finale of the *G minor* with its dashing roulades from Katsaris is exhilarating, although some may feel that all the allegros are pressed on a shade too hard. The *Capriccio brilliant* is done with comparable flair and the full, well-balanced recording has attractive ambience and sparkle.

Those wanting the better-known *G minor Concerto* will have nothing to grumble at technically in Cécile Ousset's HMV disc, with the piano bold and tangible and the orchestra fully in the picture. As in the Grieg on the reverse, Ousset gives a performance of power rather than of poetry, not always bringing out Mendelssohn's sparkle and charm but in her robust way establishing this as a bigger work than its length suggests. Strong accompaniment, very well recorded. An excellent choice for those who fancy the rare coupling. There is a very good cassette, firm and clear.

Violin concertos: in D min., Op. posth.; E min., Op. 64.
*(*) HMV **CDC7 47429-2** [id.]; *EL 270366-4*. Frank Peter Zimmermann, Berlin SO, Albrecht.

Though it makes an apt and attractive coupling to have Mendelssohn's great *E minor Violin concerto* coupled with his youthful essay in the genre, Zimmermann's disc has to be approached with caution. It is in the major work that he falls short. Not helped by a close balance which exaggerates the soloist's tonal idiosyncrasies, the violin sound has a distinct edge, with the melodic line often gulpingly uneven. The second subject then gives respite, but the slow movement is ungainly, and only in the finale does the playing sound happy and relaxed – though even there Zimmermann does not compare with the finest versions. Though in the youthful concerto the slow movement is delightfully persuasive, the outer movements fail to sparkle as they should. Apart from the distractingly close balance of the soloist, the sound is full and firm, and there is an excellent cassette in which the edginess is somewhat tamed.

Violin concerto in E min., Op. 64.
*** Decca Dig. **410 011-2** [id.]. Kyung-Wha Chung, Montreal SO, Dutoit – TCHAIKOVSKY: *Concerto.****
(M) *** DG **423 211-2;** *423 211-4* [id.]. Mutter, BPO, Karajan – MOZART: *Concerto No. 5.****
*** DG Dig. **400 031-2;** *3302 016* [id.]. Mutter, BPO, Karajan – BRUCH: *Concerto No. 1.****
*** CBS Dig. **MK 39007** [id.]. Cho-Liang Lin, Philh. O, Tilson Thomas – SAINT-SAËNS: *Concerto No. 3.****
(M) *** Pickwick Dig. **PCD 829** [MCA **MCAD 25934**]. Jaime Laredo, SCO – BRUCH: *Concerto No. 1.****
(M) *** HMV **CDM7 69003-2** [id.]; *EG 769003-4*. Menuhin, Philh. O, Kurtz – BRUCH: *Concerto No. 1.****
(M) *** DG **419 067-2;** *419 067-4* [id.]. Milstein, VPO, Abbado – TCHAIKOVSKY; *Concerto.****
(*) RCA **RD 85933 [**RCA 5933-2-RC**]. Heifetz, Boston SO, Munch – TCHAIKOVSKY: *Concerto; Sérénade mélancolique* etc.**(*)
(***) HMV mono **CDC7 47119-2** [id.]. Menuhin, BPO, Furtwängler – BEETHOVEN: *Concerto*(***).
(*) Decca Dig. **421 145-2; *421 145-4* [id.]. Joshua Bell, ASMF, Marriner – BRUCH: *Concerto No. 1.***(*)
(*) Denon Dig. **C37 7123 [id.]. Kantorow, Netherlands CO, Ros-Marba – BRUCH: *Concerto No. 1.***(*)
(M) **(*) Decca **417 687-2;** *417 687-4* [id.]. Ricci, Netherlands RPO, Fournet – TCHAIKOVSKY: *Concerto.***(*)
(M) **(*) RCA Dig. **GD 86536;** *GK 86536* [**RCA 6536-2-RG**]. Ughi, LSO, Prêtre – BEETHOVEN: *Concerto.***(*)
(*) DG **419 629-2 [id.]. Shlomo Mintz, Chicago SO, Abbado (also with KREISLER: *Caprice viennoise; Liebeslied; Liebesfreud*) – BRUCH: *Concerto No. 1.****

Violin concerto in E min.; Octet in E flat, Op. 20 (ed. Zukerman).
** Ph. Dig. **412 212-2** [id.]. Zukerman, St Paul CO.

Chung favours speeds faster than usual in all three movements, and the result is sparkling and happy with the lovely slow movement fresh and songful, not at all sentimental. With warmly sympathetic accompaniment from Dutoit and the Montreal orchestra, amply recorded, the result is one of Chung's happiest records. Some may find the helter-skelter of the finale a little too breathless, but the exhilaration of a tight challenge superbly taken is very hard to resist. This is almost the reading that Heifetz might have recorded with speeds similarly fast but with the manner far sweeter and more relaxed. The Tchaikovsky coupling is generous. The compact disc version emphasizes the closeness of the soloist but the result is very real.

Here even more than in her Bruch coupling, the freshness of Anne-Sophie Mutter's approach communicates vividly to the listener, creating the feeling of hearing the work anew. Her gentleness and radiant simplicity in the *Andante* are very appealing, and the closing pages have real magic, with Karajan catching the mood and scale in his accompaniment. Similarly, the second subject of the first movement has great charm, and the light, sparkling finale (again with the orchestral balance superbly managed) is a delight. This performance is available coupled with Mozart at mid-price, or in its original premium-priced CD format, paired with Bruch. Mutter is given a small-scale image, projected forward from the orchestral backcloth, but the orchestral layout itself does not have the luminous detail of the Decca recording, although the sound is both full and refined.

To judge from Cho-Liang Lin's account of the Mendelssohn *Concerto*, Yo-Yo Ma is not the only Chinese-American artist destined for greatness. His is a vibrant and keenly intelligent performance, breathtaking in its virtuosity, and always musical. Cho-Liang Lin also has the benefit of really excellent support from the Philharmonia Orchestra and Michael Tilson Thomas, and excellent CBS engineering. This is one of the best CD versions of the Mendelssohn on the market and is strongly recommended to those for whom the Saint-Saëns coupling is suitable, a comparably distinguished performance, full of flair. The compact disc has splendid presence and definition.

Laredo's version on a mid-price CD brings an attractively direct reading, fresh and alert but avoiding mannerism, marked by consistently sweet and true tone from the soloist. On record it makes a better general recommendation than more wilful versions from more celebrated soloists. The orchestral ensemble is amazingly good when you remember that the soloist himself is directing. The recording is vivid and clean.

Menuhin's 1960 recording has withstood the test of time. The restrained nobility of his phrasing of the famous principal melody of the slow movement has long been a hallmark of his reading; with Efrem Kurtz providing polished and sympathetic support, and the Philharmonia on their toes, this remains a first-rate coupling. The sound of the CD transfer is bright, with the soloist dominating, but the orchestral texture well detailed. The solo timbre is not edgy, and at mid-price this remains very competitive with a good tape equivalent.

Milstein's version comes from the early 1970s. His is a highly distinguished performance, very well accompanied. His account of the slow movement is more patrician than Menuhin's, and his slight reserve is projected by DG sound which is bright, clean and clear in its CD remastering; the cassette is slightly more expansive. But those attracted to a coupling with the Tchaikovsky *Concerto* should not be disappointed. However, this is also available on a Walkman tape within a particularly generous Mendelssohn collection – see below.

As one might expect, Heifetz gives a fabulous performance. His speeds are consistently fast, yet in the slow movement his flexible phrasing sounds so inevitable and easy, it is hard not to be convinced. The finale is a *tour de force*, light and sparkling, with every note in place. The recording has – like his comparable versions of the Beethoven and Brahms concertos – been successfully remastered digitally and the sound is smoother than before. The CD coupling includes Tchaikovsky's *Sérénade mélancolique*, as well as the *Concerto*.

Menuhin's unique gift for lyrical sweetness has never been more seductively presented on record than in his classic version of the Mendelssohn concerto with Furtwängler, recorded – like the Beethoven concerto with which it is coupled – only months before the conductor's death. The digital transfer is first rate, though not ideally clear. One hardly registers that this is a mono recording from the early 1950s.

Joshua Bell's flawless technique and easy virtuosity stand comparison even with that of Heifetz. Like that great violinist's RCA recording, Bell is given a very forward balance by the Decca engineers; but, also like Heifetz, Bell can still achieve a genuine *pianissimo* when he wants to, as at the lead into the first-movement cadenza which is a moment of magic. Overall, this is a boldly romantic reading, full of warmth and not without poetry, but with the *Andante*, taken slowly, in danger of becoming too measured and heavy. The finale is excitingly brilliant, and this remains a performance to be reckoned with; even so, the spotlight on the soloist, which all but masks Marriner's fine accompaniment, is a distinct drawback.

Jean-Jacques Kantorow gives a fresh, bright account with well-chosen speeds, excellently recorded. The restrained poetry will appeal to those who are not looking for a powerfully individual reading – though Kantorow, winner of many prizes, has easy, natural flair, and plays with flawlessly pure tone. Understanding, if not inspired, accompaniment.

Ricci's account with the Netherlands Radio Orchestra under Fournet has been reissued on a Decca CD and tape, in that company's lowest price range. It was originally recorded in Phase 4, so the balance places him well forward and reveals plenty of orchestral detail by the close microphoning of the woodwind. In the finale the listener's pleasure is enhanced by Fournet's precision in matching the solo line with the accompaniment, which adds considerable extra sparkle. The slow movement has a disarming simple eloquence, and the reading as a whole is undoubtedly distinguished. The vivid recording is equally lively on CD and the high-level cassette.

Ughi's version has been generously recoupled with the Beethoven *Concerto* on RCA's mid-priced Papillon label. If anything, the performance of the Mendelssohn is even finer. It is a fresh, totally unsentimental reading but both the slow movement and finale are very successful. Ughi lacks only the final individuality of artists like Mutter or Chung, but he is highly musical and he has the advantage of an excellent digital recording, clean and well balanced and set against a believable atmosphere. There is a very good cassette.

Mintz's version is powerfully conceived, less reticent than Mutter, less spontaneous than Chung. It is not quite the equal of the Bruch coupling, although Abbado gives fine support, as he does for Milstein. To make the reissue more competitive at full price, DG have added some *morceaux de concert* of Kreisler, which are most winningly played. The remastering brings excellent presence and a good balance.

Zukerman's performances, both of the *Concerto* – with the solo part technically impeccable – and of the *Octet*, are to some extent controversial, though undoubtedly fresh. The atmosphere of the *Concerto* with its simple lyricism is surprisingly classical, the chamber scale of the accompaniment playing down the work's romanticism. In the finale the focus is unusually clear, with superb articulation all round. The *Octet* is presented in Zukerman's own arrangement using varying numbers of strings, usually multiples in outer movements, but reserving the slow movement for eight soloists. The effect is attractive but adds nothing to Mendelssohn's original. The sound is truthful within a comparatively dry acoustic, with fine clarity on CD.

Among other recordings, Perlman's digital version with Haitink is disappointing, not nearly so fresh and spontaneous-sounding as his earlier analogue recording with Previn and badly balanced, with the soloist far too close and the orchestra thin (HMV **CDC7 47074-2**). Stern's newest digital recording must also be discounted for similar reasons. It is meagre of tone, and the close balance and clarity of the CD only make things worse (CBS **MK 37204**).

(i) *Violin concerto in E min., Op. 64;* (ii) *Symphony No. 4 in A (Italian), Op. 90;* (iii) *A Midsummer Night's Dream: Overture and incidental music.*

(B) *** DG Walkman *413 150-4.* (i) Milstein, VPO, Abbado; (ii) BPO, Maazel; (iii) Mathis, Boese, Bav. RSO with Ch., Kubelik.

This attractive compilation is one of the outstanding bargains in DG's Walkman series. Milstein's 1973 account of the *Violin concerto* is highly distinguished. With excellent recording and balance this is worthy to rank with the best, and it is greatly enhanced by the sensitivity of Abbado's accompaniment. Maazel's *Italian* offers a fast, hard-driven but joyous and beautifully articulated performance of the first movement and equal clarity and point in the vivacious finale. The central movements are well sustained, and altogether this is highly enjoyable, the recording resonantly full-timbred. Kubelik's fairly complete version of the incidental music for *A Midsummer Night's Dream* is no less enjoyable and the sound is first class here, too.

2 Concert pieces for clarinet, bassett horn and orchestra, Opp. 113–14.

*** HMV Dig. **CDC7 47233-2**; *EL 270220-4.* Sabine Meyer, Wolfgang Meyer, Württemberg CO, Jörg Faerber – BAERMANN: *Adagio*; WEBER: *Clarinet quintet.****

The Mendelssohn pieces are recorded in a slightly drier acoustic than the Baermann. They are arrangements either by Mendelssohn himself or by Baermann's son, Carl, of pieces originally written for clarinet, bassett horn and piano. They are high-spirited and delightful, and most expertly played by Sabine Meyer and her brother, Wolfgang.

Overtures: Calm sea and a prosperous voyage, Op. 27; Fair Melusina, Op. 32; The Hebrides (Fingal's Cave), Op. 21; A Midsummer Night's Dream, Op. 21; Ruy Blas, Op. 95; Trumpet overture, Op. 101; Overture for wind instruments, Op. 24.
*** DG Dig. **423 104-2** [id.]. LSO, Abbado.

Three of these performances were originally released with the symphonies in 1985; the rest are new. *Calm sea and a prosperous voyage* is especially evocative and All Saints, Tooting, was also a well-chosen venue for Abbado's stirring *Ruy Blas* with its resonant brass. The other overtures were recorded in St John's, Smith Square, Walthamstow Town Hall and EMI's Abbey Road Studio – yet, even on CD, the ear is not troubled by the changing acoustics. Neither the *Overture for wind* (1824) nor the (1826) *Trumpet overture* (more notable for furiously busy strings) are forgotten masterpieces. All the other pieces sound strikingly vivid and spontaneous in Abbado's hands, and the recording, wide in range and always with plenty of ambience, suits the music admirably. The overall timing is generous (73′ 54″).

Symphonies for string orchestra, Nos 2 in D; 3 in E min.; 5 in B flat; 6 in E flat.
(M) *** EMI *EMX 41 2092-4*. Polish CO, Maksymiuk.

Digitally recorded on a mid-price label, this collection of the boy Mendelssohn's early *String symphonies* (written when he was only twelve) is most invigorating. These earlier symphonies of the series of twelve may look to various models from Bach to Beethoven, but the boy keeps showing his individuality and, however imitative the style, the vitality of the invention still bursts through. The slow movement of the *Symphony No. 2*, for example, is a Bachian meditation that in its simple beauty matches later Mendelssohn. The Polish strings are set in a lively acoustic, giving exceptionally rich sound. This is a splendid tape – fresh, full and clear – and no doubt this programme will appear on CD during the lifetime of our book.

Symphonies for string orchestra Nos 4 in C min.; 9 in C; 12 in G.
(*) Mer. **CDE 84131; *KE 77131* [id.]. Guildhall String Ens.

It is a pity that the Meridian issue duplicates two works in Ross Pople's excellent Hyperion collection, and the playing of the London Festival Orchestra is rather more polished. Nevertheless the Guildhall group are very accomplished and if their ensemble in the Scherzo of No. 9 could be more sharply precise, they play the slow movement with an attractive elegiac feeling. The recording, made in the Church of St Edward the Confessor, Mottingham, Kent, is warm and natural, and detail is not clouded. *No. 4 in C minor* (which is offered here only) is certainly well up to the standard of the others in the set. The cassette transfer is first class. These are warmly spontaneous performances and very enjoyable in their own right: at times – as in the finale of No. 12 – they play with a lightness and grace that are very appealing.

Symphonies for string orchestra, Nos 9 in C min.; 10 in B min.; 12 in G min.
*** Hyp. **CDA 66196**; *KA 66196* [id.]. L. Fest. O, Ross Pople.

It is good fortune (or good planning) that Ross Pople's excellent collection does not duplicate any of the works on the EMI issue. He leads the London Festival Orchestra from the first desk and achieves performances that are as polished and spirited as they are lyrically responsive.

No. 9 has a particularly gracious slow movement following the drama of its opening, but No. 12 with its clear debt to Bach (the neatly articulated fugal writing gives much pleasure here) is the most impressive, and it too has a very fine slow movement. Excellent sound on both CD and the very well-managed cassette.

Symphonies Nos 1–5; Overtures: Fair Melusina, Op. 32; The Hebrides (Fingal's Cave), Op. 26; A Midsummer Night's Dream, Op. 21; Octet, Op. 20: Scherzo.

*** DG Dig. **415 353-2** (4) [id.]. LSO, Abbado (with Connell, Mattila, Blochwitz and LSO Ch. in *Symphony No. 2*).

Abbado's is a set to brush cobwebs off an attractive symphonic corner. He made his reputation as a Mendelssohn interpreter on record with an outstanding coupling of the two most popular symphonies, the *Scottish* and the *Italian*, fresh and athletic; it was an excellent idea to have him do a complete series with the same orchestra. If this time in the *Italian* the speed and exhilaration of the outer movements occasionally hint at breathlessness (some might feel that the pacing of the finale, like the allegro of the *Midsummer Night's Dream overture*, is too fast), there is pure gain in the more flowing speed for the pilgrim's march second movement. In the *Scottish* his view has changed relatively little, and the performance gains this time from having the exposition repeat observed in the first movement. Otherwise it is Abbado's gift in the lesser-known symphonies to have you forgetting any weaknesses of structure or thematic invention in the brightness and directness of his manner. Instead of overloading this music with sweetness and sentiment, as the Victorians came to do, he presents it more as it must have appeared at the very beginning, when on good evidence the composer himself was known to favour brisk, light allegros and crisp rhythms. So the youthful *First* has plenty of C minor bite. The toughness of the piece makes one marvel that Mendelssohn ever substituted the scherzo from the *Octet* for the third movement (as he did in London), but helpfully Abbado includes that extra scherzo, so that on CD, with a programming device, you can readily make the substitution yourself. Good, bright recording, though not ideally transparent.

Symphony No. 2 in B flat (Hymn of Praise), Op. 52.

*** DG Dig. **423 143-2**; *423 143-4* [id.]. Connell, Mattila, Blochwitz, LSO Ch., LSO, Abbado.
(*) Ph. **416 470-2 [id.]. Margaret Price, Sally Burgess, Jerusalem, LPO Ch. & O, Chailly.

Mendelssohn's *Hymn of Praise* was once a favourite work with Victorian choral societies, who often forgot to include the first three purely instrumental movements. Latterly it has been unduly neglected, because it so manifestly falls short of its great model, Beethoven's *Ninth Symphony*. As on Abbado's complete CD set of Mendelssohn symphonies, *The Hymn of Praise*, fitted on to a single CD and tape, brings very generous measure, only a few seconds under the maximum of 75 minutes. Abbado's view of the work, brushing aside all sentimentality, is both fresh and sympathetic, and though the recording is not ideally clear on inner detail the brightness reinforces the conductor's view. The chorus, well focused, is particularly impressive, and the operatic flavour of some of the solo work comes over well, notably *Watchman, what of the night?* The sweet-toned tenor, Hans-Peter Blochwitz, is outstanding among the soloists, and Elizabeth Connell brings weight as well as purity to the main soprano part. The cassette needs a high-level playback to make a full effect, but the choral focus is not as sharp as on CD.

One clear advantage of the Chailly version of *Hymn of Praise* lies in its outstanding trio of soloists, with Margaret Price soaring radiantly in *Lobe den Herrn, meine Seele* and the women of the London Philharmonic Choir matching her. Siegfried Jerusalem also sings gloriously, with tone both bright and sweet, not least in the duet with Price. The balance is realistic, so that Chailly's fresh and unaffected interpretation has its maximum impact, helped by fine playing and choral singing from London Philharmonic sources. However, although the 1980 analogue recording has been successfully remastered and the sound both of the soloists and of the orchestra is fresh and vivid, the chorus is less well focused than in the DG digital version, and words are not ideally clear.

Symphony No. 3 in A min. (*Scottish*); *Overture: The Hebrides* (*Fingal's Cave*).
(M) *** DG **419 477-2**; *419 477-4* [id.]. BPO, Karajan.
(B) *** DG Walkman *419 390-4* [id.]. BPO, Karajan – SCHUMANN: *Symphony No. 3.****
(*) Hung. Dig. **HCD 12660-2 [id.]. Hungarian State O, Ivan Fischer.

Symphony No. 3 (*Scottish*); *A Midsummer Night's Dream overture, Op. 21.*
*** DG Dig. **415 973-2** [id.]. LSO, Abbado.
** Orfeo Dig. **C 089841A** [id.]. Bav. RSO, C. Davis.

Symphonies Nos 3 (*Scottish*); *4* (*Italian*), *Op. 90.*
(M) *** ASV **CDQS 6004**; (B) *ZCQS 6004* [id.]. O of St John's, Lubbock.
(*) Argo **411 931-2; (M) Decca *417 684-4* [id.]. ASMF, Marriner.
** Ph. Dig. **420 211-2** [id.]. LPO, Bychkov.

Symphonies Nos 3 (*Scottish*); *4* (*Italian*); *Overture: The Hebrides* (*Fingal's Cave*).
(M) **(*) Decca **417 731-2**; *417 458-4* [id.]. VPO, Dohnányi.

Symphonies Nos 3 in A min. (*Scottish*); *5 in D* (*Reformation*).
(M) *** Ph. **420 884-2**; *420 884-4* [id.]. LPO, Haitink.

The permutations of the Mendelssohn symphonies on CD and tape seem almost endless, with much distinction in available performances. Most will opt for a pairing of the *Scottish* and *Italian symphonies*, where Lubbock's mid-priced coupling leads the field, but neither Haitink's nor Karajan's versions of the *Scottish* should be readily passed over.

Haitink's Philips recording of the *Scottish symphony* has been attractively remastered, the upper strings glowingly fresh and woodwind rich and luminous. Yet the sumptuous body of tone of the full orchestra does not bring clouded detail. Haitink sets a fast pace in the opening movement yet loses nothing of the music's lyrical power. There is a feeling of symphonic breadth too (helped by the resonant fullness of the recording), in spite of the omission of the exposition repeat. In the other three movements the warm ambience of the Philips recording is always telling, especially at the opening of the scherzo, and for the dancing violins in the finale. The final peroration sounds magnificent. Now linked to an almost equally fine version of the *Reformation symphony*, with the rich Concertgebouw acoustics especially effective in bringing out the rich brass writing, this makes a splendid mid-priced recommendation. There is a first-class tape.

Karajan's account, too, is very fine indeed. The performance contains some slight eccentricities of tempo: the opening of the symphony is rather measured, while the closing pages of the finale are taken with exuberant brilliance. But the orchestral playing is superb – the pianissimo articulation of the strings is a pleasure in itself and the conductor's warmth and direct eloquence, with no fussiness, is irresistible. The scherzo is marvellously done and becomes a highlight, while there is no doubt that Karajan's final coda has splendid buoyancy and power. With a characterful account of *Fingal's Cave* as coupling, this remains highly recommendable and the effectively remastered CD is well worth considering. Meanwhile tape collectors are offered another of DG's outstanding Walkman bargains, where the original analogue tape master of the symphony, glowingly full and fresh, is offered coupled with Karajan's superb account of Schumann's *Rhenish symphony* in equally expansive sound.

Of the other issues of the *Scottish symphony* alone, Abbado's account comes from his complete set (see above). It is admirably fresh, brightly recorded and also has the advantage of including the first-movement exposition repeat. The overture is briskly paced.

A beautifully played performance from Sir Colin Davis and the Bavarian orchestra, with the *Midsummer Night's Dream* music also impressive in its detail. The sound too is refined, but in the last resort this has not the sparkle of the finest analogue versions.

Helped by recorded sound that is exceptionally full and immediate, Fischer conducts strong and dramatic readings of both symphony and overture. Generally, the playing is fresh and alert rather than refined, with string sound not ideally sweet, but the clarity and precision of the scherzo are a delight and the close balance adds to the internal clarity as in the horn semiquavers, normally obscured. The slow movement is on the heavy side, at a relatively brisk speed, but in the main pacing is unexceptionable. The overture is spaciously done.

Lubbock's coupling of the *Scottish* and *Italian symphonies* makes an outstanding bargain issue, offering performances of delightful lightness and point, warmly and cleanly recorded. The string section may be of chamber size but, amplified by a warm acoustic, that adds to clarity without detracting from weight or drive. The first movement of the *Scottish* is taken rather fast but, as in the first movement of the *Italian* (complete with the important exposition repeat), the result sparkles, with rhythms exhilaratingly lifted. The slow movements are both on the slow side but flow easily with no suspicion of sentimentality, while the *Saltarello* finale, with the flute part delectably pointed, comes close to Mendelssohnian fairy music. In every way this matches or even outshines all rivals in this coupling. The tape is offered at bargain price yet has been splendidly remastered on chrome tape.

Dohnányi's mid-priced Decca reissue is particularly generous in offering both symphonies (the *Italian* one of Decca's very first digital recordings; the *Scottish* analogue but with outstanding sound quality), plus a rather slow and romantic account of *The Hebrides*, also digital. It is a refreshing account of the *Italian*, never pushed too hard, though the *Saltarello* is taken exhilaratingly fast. It is a pity that the first-movement exposition repeat is omitted, so one misses the extended lead-back passage. The *Scottish* too is fresh and alert, and the weighty recording helps to underline the stormy quality that Dohnányi aptly finds in the first movement, although in other movements this is a less characterful account than Lubbock's. Not all the woodwind playing is as elegant as that emanating from St John's, Smith Square. Yet those looking for outstanding recording quality at a reasonable price will not be disappointed here. The overture comes between the two main works. There is a first-class tape, also very competitively priced.

In Marriner's Argo performance, the *Adagio* of the *Scottish* is so spacious (arguably too much so, since the middle section grows heavy) that the finale had to be put on side two of the original LP. This means that the *Italian* is given without the exposition repeat and the twenty-bar lead-back. The performances are stylish and well sprung but have no special individuality. The use of a smaller-scaled ensemble brings a crisper, more transparent effect than usual. The recording is excellent, especially in the CD format. The tape is brightly transferred in Decca's Weekend series, but is by no means a first choice.

Bychkov does observe the exposition repeat in the first movement of the *Italian* but not in the *Scottish*. He gets good playing from the LPO but his reading is not free from point-making. Fast tempi tend to be hectic and slow movements too measured and laboured. There are good things all the same, and the recording is admirably truthful: nevertheless this is not a first recommendation. The tape is bass-heavy.

Among other versions, Solti offers high-powered, glossy readings, essentially unsympathetic, with little or no Mendelssohnian sparkle (Decca **414 665-2**); Klemperer is broad and expansive in the *Scottish symphony*, the approach almost Brahmsian, but his version of the *Italian* is altogether more convincing, in spite of slower tempi than usual. The performance sparkles and has an incandescence deriving from superb Philharmonia playing which makes it memorable. This is available on a good cassette (HMV *ED 290579-4*) and will no doubt appear on CD in due course.

Symphony No. 4 in A (Italian), Op. 90.
*** DG Dig. **410 862-2**; *410 862-4* [id.]. Philh. O, Sinopoli – SCHUBERT: *Symphony No. 8.*** ❀
(M) *** DG **415 848-2**; *415 848-4* [id.]. BPO, Karajan – SCHUBERT: *Symphony No. 8.****
(M) *** DG **423 209-2**; *423 209-4* [id.]. BPO, Karajan – SCHUMANN: *Symphony No. 1.****

Symphony No. 4 (Italian); Overtures: Fair Melusina, Op. 32; The Hebrides (Fingal's Cave), Op. 26; Son and stranger (Die Heimkehr aus der Fremde), Op. 89.
(M) *** Pickwick Dig. **PCD 824** [MCA **MCAD 25849**]. Berne SO, Peter Maag.

Symphonies Nos 4 (Italian); 5 (Reformation), Op. 107.
*** DG Dig. **415 974-2** [id.]. LSO, Abbado.
** Hung. Dig. **HCD 12414-2** [id.]. Hungarian State O, Ivan Fischer.
(B) (**) Sup. **2SUP 0010**. Czech PO, Delogu.

Symphony No. 4 (Italian); A Midsummer Night's Dream: Overture, Op. 21; Incidental music, Op. 61: Scherzo; Nocturne; Wedding march.
(M) *** Ph. **420 653-2**; *420 653-4* [id.]. Boston SO, C. Davis.

Symphony No. 5 in D (Reformation), Op. 107.
(M) **(*) DG **419 870-2**; *419 870-4* [id.]. BPO, Karajan – SCHUMANN: *Symphony No. 3.****
(B) **(*) DG Walkman *419 822-4* [id.]. BPO, Maazel – SCHUBERT: *Symphony No. 4*; SCHUMANN: *Symphony No. 4.**(*)*

Peter Maag, making a welcome return to the recording studio with his Berne orchestra, here offers a performance of the *Italian symphony*, plus an attractive group of overtures, which once more confirms him as a supreme Mendelssohnian. In the opening *Allegro vivace* of the symphony he gives a winningly relaxed performance. It is only fractionally slower than on most versions, but that much allows rushing triplets to be given a rhythmic spring, with passagework shaped pointfully. With fine ensemble from the Berne Symphony Orchestra – only marginally let down at times by the strings – the forward thrust is more compelling than with the taut, unyielding approach too often favoured today. Even more than usual, one welcomes the observance of the important exposition repeat with its long lead-back. The other movements are also beautifully paced, to allow fine rhythmic point and clear texturing. The final *Saltarello* bites hard but not viciously, again beautifully sprung. *The Hebrides* receives a spacious reading and the two rarer overtures are a delight too, particularly *Son and stranger*, which in Maag's hands conveys radiant happiness. At budget price, with well over an hour of music and with spacious, full and brilliant recording, it is a first-rate bargain.

Sinopoli's great gift is to illuminate almost every phrase afresh. His speeds tend to be extreme – fast in the first movement, but with diamond-bright detail, and on the slow side in the remaining three. Only in the heavily inflected account of the third movement is the result at all mannered but, with superb playing from the the Philharmonia and excellent Kingsway Hall recording, this rapt performance is most compelling. Like the disc, the chrome cassette is first class; but for refinement of detail, especially at lower dynamic levels, the compact disc is among the most impressive digital recordings to have come from DG. Interestingly, the engineers achieve here a brighter lighting for the upper strings than is usual in this venue.

Karajan's performance of the *Italian* is superbly polished and well paced. The reading is straighter than Sinopoli's, notably so in the third movement, though the effect of Karajan's slower pace is warm, never bland. There is a less striking sense of spontaneity in the central movements than in the outstanding Schubert coupling which Karajan recorded eight years earlier (in 1965). The recording of the *Italian* is very brightly lit in its remastered transfer and has lost some of its depth. Excellent value, whether on CD or the first-class tape. There is an alternative coupling on CD with Schumann's Symphony No. 1.

Abbado's coupling comes from his complete set, discussed above. Both performances are admirably fresh, though the pacing of the outer movements of the *Italian* is very brisk. But with fresh sound, this makes an easy first choice if you want both works together on CD.

On Philips, Sir Colin Davis provides a delightful Mendelssohn coupling, an exhilarating but never breathless account of the *Italian symphony* (complete with exposition repeat), coupled with the four most important items from the *Midsummer Night's Dream* music. Unlike so many versions of this symphony, this is not one which insists on brilliance at all costs, and the recording is warm and refined. One recognizes that the Philips engineers are working in Boston. Again there have been more delicate readings of the *Midsummer Night's Dream* pieces, but the ripeness of the Boston playing is most persuasive. The freshened 1976 recording offers a full yet lively orchestral balance. The cassette is also very successful, if a bit weighty in the bass.

With full and immediate sound as in the companion version of the *Scottish symphony*, Ivan Fischer's coupling of Nos 4 and 5 brings generally clean and direct readings of both symphonies, lacking only a degree of individuality, with rhythms sometimes too square.

On Supraphon, Delogu's attractively played performances – the *Italian* is strikingly vivacious and the first-movement exposition repeat is included – are spoiled by a digital remastering which brings shrill violins and too much emphasis on the treble so that the sound becomes tiring to the ear.

Like his companion account of the *Italian*, Karajan's performance of the *Reformation symphony*, though outstandingly well played, is just a shade wanting in spontaneity and sparkle. Everything is most beautifully shaped and finely phrased, though rhythms in the first movement are perhaps a little too heavily accented, with the result that there is a certain lack of forward momentum. The remastered recording has also lost some of the analogue bloom, and in the finale the famous chorale, *Ein' feste Burg*, has the brass less rounded than on the original LP. Karajan is at his most persuasive in the *Andante*, however, and this is still a thoroughly worthwhile coupling.

Maazel's 1961 recording of the *Reformation symphony* springs grippingly to life from the very opening bars. The Berlin Philharmonic brass is most commanding in the introduction, and this high level of tension continues throughout, supported by the most committed orchestral response. The finale is splendidly vigorous, with the great chorale ringing out resplendently. The recording is admirably spacious, but the resonance brings a focus that is less than ideally sharp – DG have used the analogue master for this Walkman transfer.

CHAMBER AND INSTRUMENTAL MUSIC

Octet in E flat, Op. 20.
(M) **(*) Decca **421 093-2** [id.]. Vienna Octet (members) – BEETHOVEN: *Septet*.***

(i) *Octet in E flat, Op. 20; String quartet No. 2 in A min., Op. 13.*
Telarc Dig. **CD 80142** [id.]. Cleveland Qt, (i) with Meliora Qt.

Octet in E flat, Op. 20; String quintet No. 2 in B flat, Op. 87.
*** Ph. **420 400-2** [id.]. ASMF Chamber Ens.

The ASMF made an earlier record of Mendelssohn's *Octet* for Argo in the late 1960s; this Philips successor comes from just over a decade later and is an improvement. The playing has greater sparkle and polish; the recorded sound is also superior and sounds extremely well in its CD format. Now there is room too for an important work of Mendelssohn's later life, the *Second Quintet*. This is an underrated piece and it too receives an elegant and poetic performance that will give much satisfaction.

The 1973 Vienna version of the *Octet* is highly competitive at mid-price, coupled with an equally attractive account of Beethoven's *Septet*. The playing is polished and spontaneous and the recording has re-emerged freshly in its CD format, although the upper register of the strings is not quite as cleanly focused as the Beethoven coupling.

The playing of the Cleveland Quartet (who use instruments once owned by Paganini) is undoubtedly impressive, but they suffer badly from an unpleasingly close balance. The sound is congested and strident, and the *Octet* is even worse. This is no challenge to the Academy of St Martin-in-the-Fields or the Vienna Octet.

Piano trio No. 1 in D min., Op. 49.
(*) Ph. Dig. **416 297-2; *416 297-4* [id.]. Beaux Arts Trio – DVOŘÁK: *Piano trio No. 4.***(*)

Piano trios Nos 1 in D min., Op. 49; 2 in C min., Op. 66.
(*) Chan. Dig. **CHAN 8404; *ABTD 1141* [id.]. Borodin Trio.

As with the Dvořák coupling, the Beaux Arts players have recorded the *D minor Trio* previously, both for Philips and most recently on a Pearl LP. The latest performance essays a rather larger scale but is slightly less spontaneous, particularly in the simple slow movement which has an attractive Mendelssohnian innocence, not entirely captured here. The first movement is emphatic in its drama and the effect can be rather over-forceful. The recording is appropriately full-bodied and present, and there is an excellent cassette.

The Borodin Trio are recorded in a very resonant acoustic and are rather forwardly balanced. They give superbly committed but somewhat overpointed readings – in other words, they are not content to let the music speak for itself but tend to underline the odd expressive detail. All the same, there is much musical pleasure here and although the Beaux Arts CD of the *D minor* is marginally to be preferred, there is no alternative version of the *C minor* at present.

String quartets: Nos 1 in E flat, Op. 12; 2 in A min., Op. 13; 3–5, Op. 44/1–3; 6 in F min., Op. 80; 4 Movements, Op. 81.
(M) ** DG **415 883-2** (3) [id.]. Melos Qt.

Mendelssohn's string quartets are not well served on record and the majority are at present unavailable except in this set by the Melos Quartet of Stuttgart. His first quartet was written as early as 1823, a year before the *C minor Symphony* (No. 1), but was probably not intended for publication, and the last was finished only a few months before his death. The present set has the merit of completeness and also has the advantage of good engineering. However, the performances succumb to the temptation to play far too quickly: the first movement of the *A minor* loses all charm as a result, and they undercharacterize many of the ideas, giving an overall impression of blandness. They do not observe exposition repeats in the first movements of Op. 44. There is more to these quartets than this brilliant ensemble finds; but, in the absence of any alternatives, this set is acceptable enough. It has been freshly remastered on to three mid-priced CDs, so now does not cost very much more than in its original four-LP format.

String quartet No. 1 in E flat, Op. 12.
*** Ph. **420 396-2** [id.]. Orlando Qt – DVOŘÁK: *String quartet No. 12.****

This was one of the first recordings from the Orlando Quartet, and their performance of Mendelssohn's *E flat Quartet* is one of the very best ever put on record. It is played with lightness of touch, delicacy of feeling and excellent ensemble. The original analogue recording was totally natural and lifelike; the CD transfer has added a touch of glare on the first violin, and the effect is almost too present. However, it responds to the controls and we see no reason to withhold a strong recommendation.

String quartets Nos 3 in D, 5 in E flat, Op. 44/1 & 3.
** Pearl **SHECD 9603** [id.]. Roth Qt.

In the Pearl recording, the Roth are rather on top of one, though not excessively so. In the first movement of the *D major* they are very alert and vital (occasionally a trifle aggressive), but there is plenty of sensitivity in the charming slow movement. They are not generally as accomplished as the Melos, but the latter are high-powered and rush outer movements off their feet. The Roth, though a bit rough-and-ready, still give pleasure.

Violin sonatas: in F min., Op. 4; in F (1838).
*** DG Dig. **419 244-2** [id.]. Shlomo Mintz, Paul Ostrovsky.

Mendelssohn was only fourteen when he composed the *F minor Sonata, Op. 4*, and it is not surprising that it is derivative. Beethoven's *Sonata Op. 31, No. 2*, served to influence its shape; but even so it is not wanting in individuality and is much more than a youthful exercise. The 1838 *Sonata* comes from Mendelssohn's productive Leipzig period but remained unpublished until Menuhin disinterred it in the 1950s. Its first movement looks forward to the *D major Cello sonata*, Op. 58, of 1843. The performances are beyond reproach; the playing of both artists is a model of sensitivity and intelligence, and the recording is absolutely first class. Strongly recommended.

PIANO MUSIC

Andante and rondo capriccioso in E min., Op. 14; Prelude and fugue in E minor/major, Op. 35/1; Sonata in E, Op. 6; Variations sérieuses in D min., Op. 53.
*** CBS Dig. **MK 37838** [id.]. Murray Perahia.

Readers seeking a single CD of Mendelssohn's piano music could hardly better this. Perahia is perfectly attuned to Mendelssohn's sensibility and it would be difficult to imagine these performances being surpassed. In Perahia's hands, the *Variations sérieuses* have tenderness yet tremendous strength, and neither the popular *Rondo capriccioso* nor the *Prelude and fugue* have sounded more fresh or committed on record. An essential issue for all who care about nineteenth-century piano music and who may have written off Mendelssohn's contribution to this medium. The quality of the CBS recording is very good indeed.

Étude in F min.; Preludes & 3 Études, Op. 104; 6 Preludes & fugues, Op. 35; Prelude & Fugue in E min.
(M) **(*) Nimbus **NI 5071** [id.]. Martin Jones.

Fantasy in F sharp min., Op. 28; 3 Fantaisies et caprices, Op. 16; Fantasy on 'The last rose of summer', Op. 15; Variations: in E flat, Op. 82; in B flat, Op. 83; Variations sérieuses in D min., Op. 53.
(M) **(*) Nimbus **NI 5072** [id.]. Martin Jones.

Sonatas: in E, Op. 6; in G min., Op. 105; in B flat, Op. 106; Kinderstücke, Op. 72.
(M) **(*) Nimbus **NI 5070**]id.]. Martin Jones.

In his collection of Mendelssohn piano music, Martin Jones provides a fascinating slant on the composer, particularly his youthful inspirations. In many ways the disc of sonatas – all three written when he was in his teens – is the most interesting of all, reflecting Mendelssohn's devotion to Beethoven and his sonatas. That the opening of Mendelssohn's Opus 6 for example – the only one to have been published in his lifetime – is a direct crib from the opening of Beethoven's *Opus 101 in A* detracts little from its intrinsic value and shows that the boy was already appreciating the later, more elusive side of that master, just as he did in his early string quartets. That the *B flat sonata*, like Beethoven's *Hammerklavier sonata* in the same key, is labelled Opus 106 might be taken as presumption, except that it was some nineteenth-century editor (or publisher) who devised that echo, not Mendelssohn himself who, aged eighteen, wrote a strong, well-argued work – but one very limited in scale next to the Beethoven. The *G minor*, Opus 105, is the earliest and least striking of the sonatas, but is still a remarkable achievement for a thirteen-year-old.

Just as the sonatas reflect Beethoven's influence, so the *Preludes and fugues* inevitably reflect his even deeper devotion to Bach, then still under-appreciated. The six *Preludes and fugues* were originally written over a period of ten years, and were brought together as a set only later. Even so, the style is positive and consistent, with sweet Mendelssohnian lyricism as well as dashing bravura marking the *Preludes*, and even the *Fugues*, of which the most extended is the *E minor* (*Andante espressivo*), bringing far more than Bachian echoes. The later *E minor Prelude and fugue* makes a complete contrast with its *Allegro energico* fugue. The sets of variations on the third disc – including the well-known *Variations sérieuses*, which has always remained in the repertory – were mostly written later in his career, examples of his high skill and love of the keyboard, rather than works of genius. The masterpiece here is the *F sharp minor Fantasy*, in effect a free, improvisatory sonata in three movements, highly original and with more Beethovenian touches.

Martin Jones is a excellent advocate, playing all these piano works dedicatedly and persuasively but without mannerism. The analogue recordings, made in the 1970s, come up very well in the CD transfers, with the atmosphere of a small hall realistically conveyed. This playing has not the distinction of Perahia, but it is fresh and spontaneously enjoyable.

Fantasia in F sharp min. (*Sonata écossaise*), *Op. 28; 3 Fantaisies et caprices, Op. 16; Rondo capriccioso in E, Op. 14; Sonata in E, Op. 6.*
(*) Chan. **CHAN 8326; *ABTD 1081* [id.]. Lydia Artymiw.

Lydia Artymiw is highly persuasive in the *Sonata* as she is in the other works, which are by no means inconsequential. The *Fantasia* is a considerable piece and the three movements which make up Op. 16 are delightful, as is the more famous *Rondo capriccioso*, which sparkles. This is an altogether excellent disc, very well recorded, although it must be said that, fine though Miss Artymiw's playing is, she does not match Perahia in quality of imagination or subtlety of dynamic gradation. His are the finer accounts of the Op. 6 *Sonata* and the *Rondo capriccioso* (see above).

Songs without words, Books 1–8 (complete).
(M) *** DG *419 105-4* (2) [id.]. Daniel Barenboim.
(*) Hyp. Dig. **CDA 66221/2; *KA 66221/2* [id.]. Livia Rev.

Barenboim is the ideal pianist for what were once regarded (for the most part wrongly) as faded Victorian trifles. Whether in the earlier, technically more difficult pieces or in the later simple inspirations, Barenboim conveys perfectly the sense of a composer relaxing. He himself seems to be rediscovering the music, regularly turning phrases with the imagination of a great artist, relishing the jewelled passage-work of many of the pieces in simple, easy virtuosity. Originally coupled on three discs with other music, the complete set is now available on a pair of mid-priced tapes, on which the sound is altogether excellent. With such fine recording quality, this is a set to charm any listener.

Livia Rev is a thoughtful, sensitive and aristocratic artist who has never really received her due on record. Her survey of the *Songs without words* has charm and warmth, and she does not try to make too much of these simple, unaffected pieces. She includes a hitherto unpublished piece, dated February 1844, that is in the Cracow Library. The set is handsomely presented and includes a thematic index to all the forty-nine pieces recorded here. The recording is warm and pleasing, rather close, but not lacking ambience; it is, however, somewhat bottom-heavy. Yet the slightly diffuse effect suits the style of the playing, and this can be recommended. The cassettes (in a chunky box) are well transferred and very well documented, although without the thematic index.

Songs without words: Op. 19/1, 2, 4, 5 & 6 (Venetian gondola song); Op. 30/3, 4, 5 & 6 (Venetian gondola song); Op. 38/1, 2 & 6; Op. 53/1, 2 & 3; Op. 62/1 & 6 (Spring song); Op. 67/4 (Spinning song) & 6; Op. 85/6; Op. 102/3 & 5.
(*) Decca Dig. **421 119–2; *421 119-4* [id.]. András Schiff.

András Schiff has already shown he is a sympathetic Mendelssohnian with his recording of the *Concertos*. He plays the *Songs without words* simply, coolly and directly, his style straighter than Livia Rev (some may feel that her gentle fluctuations of the melodic line bring greater warmth to this music). Schiff is particularly good with a flowing cantilena which he lets unfold without emphases, yet with unerring sensibility. The famous *Spring song* shows him at his finest. This is his penultimate item and he ends the recital neatly with the engaging Op. 102, No. 3. The recording is most natural and realistic, and the CD plays for just under an hour.

Songs without words, Op. 19/1; Op. 30/6; Op. 38/6; Op. 62/1 and 6; Spring song, Op. 62/6; Spinning song, Op. 67/4; Op. 67/5; Op. 102/6.
*** DG **415 118-2** [id.]. Daniel Barenboim – LISZT: *Liebesträume****; SCHUBERT: *Moments musicaux.***

An admirable selection from Barenboim's fine 1974 complete set of the *Songs without words*, coupled with Liszt and Schubert. The playing is fresh and imaginative, and the excellent recording has transferred most naturally to CD.

ORGAN MUSIC

Organ sonatas Nos 2 in C min.; 3 in A; 6 in D min., Op. 65/1–6. Preludes & fugues: in C min.; in G; in D min., Op. 37/1–3.
❀ *** Argo Dig. **414 420-2** [id.]. Peter Hurford (organ of Ratzeburg Cathedral).

Hurford's performances of Mendelssohn bring the same freshness of approach which made his Bach series so memorable. Indeed, the opening of the *Prelude and fugue in C minor* is given a Baroque exuberance, and he finds a similar identification in his magnificent account of the *Sixth Sonata*. Here Mendelssohn more than pays homage to Bach in his splendidly imaginative set of choral variations (and fugue) on *Vater unser* (Our Father). Throughout the recital the throaty reeds of the characterful Ratzeburg organ prevent any possible hint of blandness, yet in the *Andantes* – essentially songs without words for organ – the registration has engaging charm. The recording is superb, as the majestic opening of the *Third Sonata* immediately demonstrates, with the CD giving marvellous presence.

VOCAL MUSIC

Elijah (oratorio): complete (sung in German).
* Ph. **420 106-2** (2) [id.]. Ameling, Burmeister, Schreier, Adam, Leipzig R. Ch. & Gewandhaus O, Sawallisch.

Sawallisch's 1968 performance in German, lacking fervour, never very recommendable despite fine singing from Elly Ameling and Peter Schreier, seriously shows its age, and cannot be recommended. Theo Adam makes an unsteady Elijah. We assume that Frühbeck de Burgos's classic EMI set with Gwyneth Jones, Nicolai Gedda, Dame Janet Baker and (more controversially) Dietrich Fischer-Dieskau taking the part of the Prophet will appear on CD in due course.

(i) *Das erste Walpurgisnacht* (cantata), *Op. 60;* (ii) *A Midsummer Night's Dream: Overture, Op. 21 & incidental music, Op. 61.*
(M) *** Decca *417 882-4* [id.]. (i) Lilowa, Laubenthal, Krause, Sramek, V. Singverein, VPO, Dohnányi; (ii) Bork, Hodgson, Amb. S., New Philh. O, Frühbeck de Burgos.

As a boy, Mendelssohn became a favourite visitor of the poet Goethe, and later he repaid the affection in the setting of an early and rather strange Goethe poem about Druids and their conflict with early Christians, seen – perhaps unexpectedly – from the point of view of the Druids. It is an oddity, but one full of interest for the modern listener. Witches and Druids are angrily pursued by Christians on the Brocken; and, especially in the big tarantella-like chorus for the Druids, the invention is lively and enjoyable. Indeed some of the more dramatic moments suggest that, had he been given the right libretto, Mendelssohn might have made an opera composer. The performance under Dohnányi is fresh and vivid and the recording on this Decca Weekend tape is crisp and bright. Coupled with a fairly generous selection from the *Midsummer Night's Dream incidental music*, which is also very well played under Frühbeck de Burgos, this budget-priced reissue is well worth investigating.

A Midsummer Night's Dream: Overture, Op. 21; Incidental music, Op. 61.
*** HMV **CDC7 47163-2** [id.]. Watson, Wallis, Finchley Children's Music Group, LSO, Previn.
*** Ph. **411 106-2** [id.]. Augér, Murray, Amb. S., Philh. O, Marriner.
(M) *** DG **415 840-2**; *415 840-4* [id.]. Mathis, Boese, Bav. R. Ch. & SO, Kubelik – WEBER: *Overtures: Oberon; Der Freischütz.****
(*) HMV **CDC7 47230-2 [id.]; (M) *TC-SXLP 30196* [Ang. *4AE 34445*]. Harper, J. Baker, Philh. Ch. & O, Klemperer.
(*) Hung. Dig. **SLPD 12510 [id.]. Kalmar, Bokor, Jeunesses Musicales Girls' Ch., Hungarian State O, Adam Fischer.
** Ph. Dig. **420 161-2** [id.]. Lind, Cairns, V. Jeunesse Ch., VPO, Previn.
** RCA Dig. **RD 82084** [**RCD1 2084**]. Blegen, Von Stade, Mendelssohn Club Ch., Phd. O, Ormandy.

A Midsummer Night's Dream, Overture, Op. 21; Scherzo; You spotted snakes; Intermezzo; Nocturne; Wedding march; Finale.
** DG **415 137-2** [id.]. Blegen, Quivar, Chicago Ch. & SO, Levine – SCHUBERT: *Rosamunde.***

A Midsummer Night's Dream: Overture; Scherzo; Intermezzo; Nocturne; Wedding march. Overtures: Fair Melusina, Op. 32; The Hebrides (Fingal's Cave), Op. 26; Ruy Blas, Op. 95.
(*) Decca Dig. **417 541-2; *417 541-4* [id.]. Montreal SO, Dutoit.

On HMV, Previn offers a wonderfully refreshing account of the complete score; the veiled pianissimo of the violins at the beginning of the overture and the delicious woodwind detail in the *Scherzo* certainly bring Mendelssohn's fairies into the orchestra. Even the little melodramas which come between the main items sound spontaneous here, and the contribution of the soloists and chorus is first class. The *Nocturne* (taken slowly) is serenely romantic and the *Wedding march* resplendent. The recording is naturally balanced and has much refinement of detail. The CD brings the usual enhancement, with the fairy music in the *Overture* given a most delicate presence. A clear first choice.

Marriner's disc is complete except for the inconsequential melodramas which separate the main items. The *Overture*, taken briskly, has the lightest possible touch, with the most delicate articulation from the strings; the *Scherzo* too is engagingly infectious in its gentle bustle, and there is a complementary sense of joy and sparkle from soloists and chorus alike. The *Nocturne* is rather broadly romantic, yet the *Wedding march* sounds resplendent when the quality is so vivid. There is a brief cut at the end of the *Intermezzo* but, this apart, the Philips recording, warm as well as refined in detail, has much to recommend it; the CD brings the background silence we have come to expect.

Among reissues, that by the Bavarian Radio Orchestra takes pride of place. The playing and 1965 recording (equally clear and clean on CD and cassette, yet not lacking atmosphere) are both strikingly fresh. Even with the advantage of economy, however, this does not displace Previn, whose performance has extra imagination and sparkle (the *Nocturne*, too, is more romantic); but at medium price the DG version is still very attractive. Although Kubelik omits the melodramas, this makes room for an appropriate coupling of the two finest Weber overtures, both also associated with magic, and *Oberon* drawing an obvious parallel with Mendelssohn. They are marvellously played.

Klemperer's recording (which dates from 1960) was made when the Philharmonia was at its peak, and the orchestral playing is superb, the wind solos so nimble that even the *Scherzo*, taken slower than usual, has a light touch. The contribution of soloists (Heather Harper and Dame Janet Baker) and chorus is first class and the disc has the advantage of including the *Fairy march* and *Funeral march*. The quality is remarkably fresh and transparent, yet there is no lack of body. However, the excellent tape is offered at mid-price, and as this selection plays for only 49′ would seem to be the best buy.

The Hungaroton CD offers much lovely playing, and fine singing from the soloists too, although many will count it a disadvantage that the vocal numbers are sung in German (with translation provided). While the soft focus is attractively atmospheric, the resonant acoustic has to some extent subdued the sound, although the digital recording is full and natural. There is fine, delicate articulation from the woodwind and strings in the *Scherzo*, but the hint of vibrato on the horn solo of the *Nocturne* will not please all ears, although the playing is very responsive. Fischer includes the more important melodramas but omits Nos 2, 4, 6 and 10.

Previn's latest digital recording for Philips is also sung in German, though very engagingly so by the two soloists, Eva Lind and Christine Cairns. The highlight of the performance is the *Scherzo*, which is deliciously neat, but in the *Overture* the effect is more robust than in the earlier EMI version; although the VPO violins articulate delicately, there is more fairy magic in the earlier account. In Vienna the *Fairy march* and *Intermezzo* are agreeably spry, but the *Nocturne* sounds a shade self-conscious, while the Elysian string melody which comes at the end of the *Overture* and again in the finale has not quite the incandescence of the HMV recording. The melodramas are omitted, though Previn includes the music heard between Scenes 1 and 2, just before the finale. The Philips sound is more expansive, of course, notably in the *Wedding march*, but overall this is something of a disappointment.

So is Charles Dutoit's Decca recording of the orchestral suite. It is, however, marvellously recorded. The acoustics of Saint-Eustache in Montreal are ideal for the music, giving a wonderful bloom to the dancing strings of the *Overture* and a very convincing concert-hall illusion for the whole programme. The performances are admirably spirited; *Ruy Blas* comes off especially well, with its commanding brass opening ringing out superbly and the scurrying violins very vivid and tangible. The other highlight of the disc is the delightful *Fair Melusina*, a most affectionate portrait that recalls the felicity of Beecham. But the *Midsummer Night's Dream* selection is altogether more routine: the very brisk *Scherzo* conveys little charm, although the *Wedding march* is grand without being pompous.

Ormandy's version also uses the German translation of Shakespeare (which is of course what Mendelssohn originally set), so that *You spotted snakes* has a straight quaver rhythm when it becomes *Bunte Schlagen*. The Philadelphia Orchestra's playing is light and brilliant, if not quite as infectiously pointed as in some versions. Ormandy includes most of the extra melodramas, but not in the usual order. The 1978 recording is among RCA's best from this source and sounds quite fresh, if by no means outstanding, in its new format.

Instead of doing the *Midsummer Night's Dream* music absolutely complete, Levine offers the *Overture* and six main items (the *Scherzo, You spotted snakes, Intermezzo, Nocturne, Wedding march* and *Finale*), all well done and with excellent singing from soloists and chorus. This leaves room for three of Schubert's *Rosamunde* pieces. Recorded sound better than most from this source, vivid on CD.

On a Denon CD, Maag offers less music than Ormandy and, though he is better recorded (the Denon CD sounds impressive) and also uses the German text, otherwise the Japanese performance has less felicity, with unmemorable soloists. In the *Overture* there are some curious agogic pauses before certain emphatic chords, including some of Bottom's 'hee-haws'. The Japanese orchestral playing is meticulous rather than magical (**C37 7654**).

St Paul, Op. 36.

(*) Ph. **420 212-2; *420 212-4* (2). Janowitz, Lang, Blochwitz, Stier, Polster, Adam, Leipzig R. Ch. & Gewandhaus O, Masur.

In his oratorio, *St Paul* – in German, *Paulus* without mention of sainthood – Mendelssohn was harking back to the choral music of his adored Bach far more directly than in *Elijah*, echoing the Passions. Despite the ambitiousness of that aim, the result, though less consistently inspired than the more celebrated work, is full of strong and satisfying ideas, confidently expressed, well worthy of the composer of the *Italian symphony*. Like *Elijah* of ten years later, this was Mendelssohn's substitute for opera, and in youthful zest it erupts in great Handelian choruses amid the Bachian story-telling, in which the soprano joins the traditional tenor in the narration. What reduces the dramatic effectiveness is that Mendelssohn, ever the optimist, comes to his happy resolution far too quickly, with too little struggle involved.

Masur, always a persuasive interpreter of Mendelssohn, here directs a performance which, without inflating the piece or making it sanctimonious, conveys its natural gravity. Theo Adam is not always steady, but otherwise the team of soloists is exceptionally strong, and the chorus adds to the incandescence, although placed rather backwardly. The Leipzig recording is warm and atmospheric.

Psalms Nos 42: Wie der Hirsch schreit, Op. 42; 95: Kommt, lasst uns anbeten, Op. 46; 115: Nicht unserm Namen, Herr, Op. 31.

(*) Erato **ECD 88120 [id.]. Baumann, Silva, Brunner, Ihara, Blaser, Ramirez, Huttenlocher, Lisbon Gulbenkian Foundation Ch. and O, Corboz.

These performances appeared in the late 1970s on two different LPs (Psalms 42 and 95 on STU 71101, and 115 together with other pieces on STU 71123). The compact disc, which runs to 70 minutes, is able to accommodate all three – and very beautiful they are, too. They have been generally underrated by critics and scholars. The singers are mostly excellent, particularly Christiane Baumann in Nos 42 (*Wie der Hirsch schreit*) and 95 (*Kommt, lasst uns anbeten*); the only problem here is the vibrato of Pierre-André Blaser in Psalm 95 which will not enjoy universal appeal. Philippe Huttenlocher is however impressive in No. 115, and both the choral singing and the orchestral playing are of quality. The acoustic is warm and spacious, and the balance between the solo singers and the chorus and orchestra is excellently judged. The sound is not spectacular or in the demonstration category but, more important, it is musically satisfying.

Menotti, Gian-Carlo (born 1911)

Amahl and the Night Visitors (opera): complete.
*** That's Entertainment **CDTER 1124**; *ZCTER 1124*. Lorna Haywood, John Dobson, Curtis Watson, Christopher Painter, James Rainbird, ROHCG Ch. & O, David Syrus.

Recorded under the supervision of the composer himself, this Royal Opera House production of what was originally a television opera brings a fresh and highly dramatic performance, very well sung and marked by atmospheric digital sound of striking realism. With voices very firmly placed on (and off) a believable stage, it vividly succeeds in telling the sentimental little story of the cripple-boy who offers his crutch to the three Kings to take to the Infant Jesus. In the note accompanying the record, Menotti touchingly tells how the work came to be written: of his fascination with the story of the three Kings as a child in Italy (where they take on something of the role of Father Christmas); of his characterization of them in his mind then; and of his sudden inspiration many years later on seeing Bosch's 'Adoration of the Magi'. This helps to explain the extraordinary immediacy and effectiveness of the piece. The dramatic timing is masterly, beautifully brought out by the conductor, David Syrus, in this performance which – though recorded in the studio – followed a run of the staged production at Sadler's Wells Theatre. Central to the success of the performance is the astonishingly assured and sensitively musical singing of the boy treble, James Rainbird, as Amahl, purposefully effective even in the potentially embarrassing moments. Lorna Haywood sings warmly and strongly as the Mother, with a strong trio of Kings. The realism of the recording makes the chamber size of the string section sound thin at the start, but the playing is both warm and polished.

Mercadante, Saverio (1795–1870)

Clarinet concerto in B flat.
*** Claves **CD 50-813** [id.]. Friedli, SW German CO, Angerer – MOLTER; PLEYEL: *Concertos*.***

Mercadante's *Concerto* is the slightest of the three works played on this CD by Thomas Friedli, the excellent principal clarinettist of the Berne Symphony Orchestra. Its two movements consist of an *Allegro maestoso* and a *galant Andante with variations*. But the music is agreeably fluent and very well played by the soloist. An interesting collection of works, showing the development of the clarinet as a solo instrument.

Messiaen, Olivier (born 1908)

Turangalîla symphony.
(*) CBS Dig. **M2K 42271 (2) [id.]. Crossley, Murail, Philh. O, Salonen – LUTOSLAWSKI: *Symphony No. 3* etc.***

(i) *Turangalîla symphony;* (ii) *Quartet for the end of time.*
*** HMV Dig. **CDS7 47463-8** [id.]; *EX 270468-5* (2). (i) Donohoe, Murail, CBSO, Rattle; (ii) Gawriloff, Deinzer, Palm, Kontarsky.

Simon Rattle conducts a winning performance of *Turangalîla*, not only brilliant and dramatic but warmly atmospheric and persuasive. More than a sharply literal reading – such as Salonen's – this is an account which is going to win friends for Messiaen from those who have not previously been convinced. It is not just that his rendering of the love music is ripely sensuous: in his rhythmic control of the fast dramatic movements he is equally understanding, nudging the syncopations of the fifth movement, *Joie du sang des étoiles*, to bring out the exuberant jazz overtones. The recording is warm and richly co-ordinated while losing nothing in detail. Peter Donohoe and Tristan Murail play with comparable warmth and flair, rhythmically persuasive, and the orchestra responds superbly to the challenge of a virtuoso score, conveying a degree of commitment that suggests intensive preparation and repeated experience of live performance. Led by the pianist, Aloys Kontarsky, the German performance of the *Quartet for the end of time* is a strong one. Recorded in 1976, it provides a contrasted approach to Messiaen from Rattle's, when atmospheric warmth is only an incidental. Nevertheless it is most convincing, and makes an exceptionally generous and apt coupling on the two-disc set, bringing the total timing to 130 minutes. The chrome cassettes offer sophisticated transfers, with the *Symphony* and *Quartet* each complete on one tape. The CD documentation is provided.

Esa-Pekka Salonen directs a performance of Messiaen's masterpiece in sharp focus. Relatively, this is an account which minimizes the atmospheric beauty, the sensuousness, and underlines the points which look forward to later composers. This is emphasized by the close balance of the piano and ondes martenot, which stand out instead of emerging as part of the rich orchestral texture. So the passagework for piano, beautifully played by Paul Crossley, sounds angular in a very modern way rather than evoking birdsong. Tristan Murail on the ondes martenot also sounds very different here compared to Rattle's EMI version, sympathetic though his playing again is. Significantly, the syncopated rhythms of the energetic fifth movement are pressed home very literally, at a speed faster than usual, with little or no echo of jazz. The Philharmonia plays brilliantly and the recording underlines the sharp focus of the reading, while giving ample atmosphere. On CD but not tape (*I2T 42126*), Lutoslawski's *Third Symphony* and *Les espaces du sommeil* make a valuable if unrelated filler.

PIANO MUSIC

Cantéyodjaya; Fantaisie burlesque; 4 études de rythme; Rondeau.
*** Unicorn Dig. **DKPCD 9051**; *DKPC 9051* [id.]. Peter Hill.

Peter Hill, playing a Bösendorfer, is a sympathetic guide in this repertoire; he has a good feeling for atmosphere and makes out an excellent case for all these pieces, save perhaps for the somewhat repetitive *Fantaisie burlesque* of 1932, which outstays its welcome. The playing is consistently sensitive and has great finesse, and the *Cantéyodjaya* (1948) is particularly refined. The recording is unobtrusively natural and sounds well in both formats.

Catalogue d'oiseaux, Books 1–3.
*** Unicorn Dig. **DKPCD 9062**; *DKPC 9062* [id.]. Peter Hill.

These scores derive their inspiration from Messiaen's beloved birdsong. Little of the piano writing is conventional, but there is no question as to the composer's imaginative flair, and the music is vivid and colourful to match the plumage of the creatures which Messiaen depicts so strikingly. Yvonne Loriod has recorded this music for Supraphon on LP under the composer's supervision; but Peter Hill has the full measure of this repertoire, and he is most naturally recorded.

Préludes; Pièce pour le tombeau de Paul Dukas.
*** Unicorn Dig. *DKPC 9037* [id.]. Peter Hill.

The eight *Préludes* are early works written while Messiaen was studying composition at the Paris Conservatoire with Paul Dukas. Though there is a residual influence of Debussy, these *Préludes* still have a great deal of originality and are obviously the work of a strong personality. They are played with great sensitivity by Peter Hill, who is beautifully recorded in this chrome tape format, with the piano image completely truthful and very little background noise.

ORGAN MUSIC

Livre du Saint Sacrement.
*** Unicorn Dig. **DKPCD 9067/8**; *DKPC 9067/8* [id.]. Jennifer Bate (organ of Saint-Trinité, Paris).

What a sound! This is a quite spectacular recording and carries the composer's imprimatur. The *Livre du Saint Sacrement* was composed in 1984 and consists of eighteen movements of great intensity. Jennifer Bate makes an impressive and compelling case for these hypnotic pieces, and the recording is in the demonstration bracket. A most impressive and distinguished issue (although the work lasts for some two hours and is best taken in sections). There are excellent chrome tape equivalents, but the CDs are worth their extra cost.

La Nativité du Seigneur (9 meditations).
(*) Hyp. **CDA 66230; *KA 66230* [id.]. David Titterington (organ of Gloucester Cathedral).
(M) **(*) Decca *414 436-4* [id.]. Simon Preston (organ of Westminster Abbey).

La Nativité du Seigneur (9 meditations); *Le banquet céleste.*
❀ *** Unicorn Dig. **DKPCD 9005**; *DKPC 9005* [id.]. Jennifer Bate (organ of Beauvais Cathedral).

'C'est vraiment parfait!' said Messiaen after hearing Jennifer Bate's Unicorn recording of *La Nativité du Seigneur*, one of his most extended, most moving and most variedly beautiful works. The nine movements are each hypnotically compelling in their atmospheric commentaries on the Nativity story, never more so than when played by so naturally understanding an artist as Jennifer Bate on an ideally toned instrument. For the separate CD and cassette issue, *Le banquet céleste* has generously been added. It is among the earliest of Messiaen's works to have been published and among the best known, already an intense comment on the religious experience which has inspired all of the composer's organ music. The recording of the Beauvais Cathedral organ is of demonstration quality. The cassette too is first class.

David Titterington's Hyperion record is made on the organ of Gloucester Cathedral, from which he draws some highly impressive and idiomatic sounds. His playing is resourceful and intelligent, but not perhaps as totally convincing as that of Jennifer Bate, recorded at Beauvais.

Simon Preston is also a convinced advocate of this score and conveys its hypnotic power most successfully. The recording reproduces with great fidelity, although the organ and ambience of Westminster Abbey accommodate the music less readily than a French location. The high-level cassette gives the organ fine presence, although there is a touch of fierceness on fortissimos.

Miaskovsky, Nikolay (1881–1950)

(i) *Violin concerto, Op. 44;* (ii) *Symphony No. 22 in B min., Op. 54.*
(M) **(*) Olympia **OCD 134** [id.]. Grigori Feigin, USSR RSO, Dmitriev; (ii) USSR SO, Svetlanov.

It is good that Miaskovsky is at last coming into his own. A great figure in Russian musical life, he was the teacher of Kabalevsky, Khachaturian and Shebalin, among others, and the composer of twenty-seven symphonies and thirteen quartets. The *Violin concerto* comes from 1938 and is every bit as accessible as the Glazunov: indeed it would not be difficult to imagine 1905 as its date of composition; yet, in its old-fashioned way, it has a distinctive personality and a rich vein of lyricism. The ideas flow generously and the architecture is well held together; its slow movement in particular seems to look back nostalgically to a secure, genuinely happy world on whose passing the composer sadly muses. Miaskovsky touches a vein of nostalgia that is very much his own and there is a gentle melancholy that is very appealing. Grigori Feigin is the excellent soloist and plays with the right amount of warmth and virtuosity. The *Symphony* is a wartime work, composed when Miaskovsky was evacuated to the Caucasus in 1942; it is a more powerful and ambitious piece and far more substantial than its immediate neighbours. Neither recording is new; both were made in 1974.

(i) *Lyric concertino in G, Op. 32, No. 3;* (ii) *Symphony No. 3 in A min., Op. 15.*
(M) **(*) Olympia **OCD 177** [id.]. USSR SO; (i) Verbitzky, (ii) Svetlanov.

The *Third Symphony* is an epic, ambitious work, conceived in the grand manner and cast in two long movements. It was completed just before the outbreak of the First World War; its world is close to that of Glière's *Ilya Mourmetz symphony*. It is a dark, powerful piece, and Svetlanov is a persuasive advocate. The *Lyric concertino* comes from the late 1920s and is less satisfactorily recorded. The playing is a little less polished, too – which is a pity, as there are imaginative and original touches in the slow movement which show that Miaskovsky knew his French music.

(i; ii) *Serenade in E flat, Op. 32/1;* (iii; ii) *Sinfonietta in B min., Op. 32/2;* (iv) *Symphony No. 19 in E, Op. 46.*
(M) *(*) Olympia **OCD 105** [id.]. (i) USSR SO; (ii) Verbitzky; (iii) USSR Ac. SO; (iv) USSR Ministry of Defence O, Mikailov.

Not perhaps the best introduction to Miaskovsky. The slow movements of both the *Serenade* and the *Sinfonietta* have an appealing melancholy but they are indifferently played; the strings are undernourished. The *Nineteenth Symphony* was written in 1937 for the Red Army (Miaskovsky was a natural choice on account of his military background). It is a dignified piece; Miaskovsky subsequently transcribed the two middle movements for strings, but the outer movements are less eloquent. The *Symphony* is better played and recorded than its companions. This is recommended to the converted rather than the uninitiated.

(i) *Sinfonietta No. 2 in A min. for strings, Op. 68;* (ii) *Symphony No. 27 in C min., Op. 85.*
(M) ** Olympia **OCD 168** [id.]. USSR Ac. SO; (i) Verbitzky, (ii) Svetlanov.

The *Sinfonietta in A minor* is a late work composed in 1945–6, though the idiom is wholly nineteenth century – as, indeed, is *Symphony No. 27.* Unfortunately the recording is made in a dry, cramped acoustic which does not flatter the strings; they sound positively unpleasing. The *Symphony*, written in 1949, the year following the notorious Zhdanov Congress, is Miaskovsky's penultimate work, and is tuneful; its harmonic vocabulary scarcely embraces a chord that would be out of place in Borodin or Brahms – and the slow movement is particularly Brahmsian. It is an endearingly old-fashioned work, and is very much better played than the *Sinfonietta.* The recording, which dates from 1980, is made in a warm acoustic; the sound image is in excellent perspective, even if the balance will be too recessed for some tastes.

Symphonies Nos (i) *5 in D, Op. 18;* (ii) *11 in B flat, Op. 34.*
(M) **(*) Olympia **OCD 133** [id.]. (i) USSR SO, Ivanov; (ii) Moscow SO, Dudarova.

Although it was not performed until 1920, Miaskovsky worked on the *Fifth Symphony* while serving during the 1914–18 war; like, say, Vaughan Williams' *Pastoral symphony*, which evokes the wartime countryside of France, it gives little feeling of the horror of the times. Miaskovsky himself called it his 'quiet' symphony; it is also pastoral in feeling and more introspective than Glazunov. The *Eleventh* dates from 1931–2 and is also conservative in idiom, yet the language is unpredictable: there are even suggestions of Reger, and a distinctive melodic style is particularly evident in the finale. One American academic has spoken of Miaskovsky as a 'manipulator rather than a master of form' and, though there is substance in this charge, there is still much that is convincing here. The recording of the *Eleventh Symphony* comes from 1978, and the *Fifth* is probably earlier: if neither is in the first flight, they are eminently serviceable and a more than welcome addition to this composer's representation on record.

String quartets Nos 3 in D min., Op. 33/3; 10 in F, Op. 67/1; 13 in A min., Op. 86.
(M) **(*) Olympia **OCD 148** [id.]. Leningrad Taneiev Qt.

Both the *Third* and *Tenth Quartets* are revisions of earlier pieces: No. 3 was originally composed in 1910, at about the time of his *First Symphony*, and revised in 1930; while No. 10 (1907) was much more radically overhauled during the war years and was eventually finished in 1945. The *Thirteenth Quartet* is Miaskovsky's last work, one of fastidious craftsmanship and refined musicianship. It is a beautifully wrought score, in which ideas of great lyrical fervour flow abundantly. The Leningrad Taneiev Quartet, a first-class ensemble who play with dedication, take a more leisurely view of the first movement than did the Beethoven Quartet, who were closely associated with both Miaskovsky and Shostakovich. The recordings, though not of the very highest quality (there is quite a discrepancy in level between the end of No. 10 and the beginning of No. 13), are very acceptable indeed.

Milhaud, Darius (1892–1974)

Le bœuf sur le toit.
(*) Sup. Dig. **CO 1519 [id.]. Czech PO, Válek – POULENC: *Les Biches*; SATIE: *Parade.***(*)

Le bœuf sur le toit; La Création du monde; Saudades do Brazil Nos 7, 8, 9 & 11.
(*) HMV **CDC7 47845-2 [id.]. O Nat. de France, Bernstein.

Vladimír Válek's account of *Le bœuf sur le toit* is on the whole preferable to Bernstein's version, even if the American conductor has a more natural affinity with its rhythmic character. The Czech Philharmonic give a very spirited account of it, and the digital Supraphon recording is firmer and cleaner. Moreover the couplings, two equally attractive Diaghilev ballet scores, are also vivacious and well played.

The Mediterranean charm which characterizes Milhaud's best music comes over well in the *Saudades do Brazil*, which comes from the period when he served as Claudel's secretary in Rio de Janeiro, while the two ballet scores come from the 1920s. As one would expect, Bernstein finds this repertoire thoroughly congenial, though his performance of *La Création du monde* disappoints slightly: the French orchestra do not respond with the verve and virtuosity that the Boston orchestra gave Munch in the RCA recording (now deleted). Nor does *Le Bœuf sur le toit* have quite the sparkle and infectious gaiety that the music ideally demands. This is not to deny that these are good performances and well worth acquiring, although the recordings, made in 1978, have not entirely benefited from their digital remastering. The sharpening of the focus, within a fairly reverberant acoustic, has lost a little of the body in the sound, although it is lively enough and not edgy.

La Création du monde; Suite for clarinet, violin and piano; Scaramouche; Caramel mou; 3 Rag-caprices.
(*) Arabesque Dig. **Z 6569; *ABQC 6569* [id.]. Ian Hobson, Sinfonia da camera.

This is the chamber version of Milhaud's jazz-inspired ballet, not the orchestral arrangement he made later, which Bernstein, Válek and others have recorded. Ian Hobson and this Illinois group give a spirited account of the piece; if at times they are a trifle too well-bred and polite, they are very civilized too. In the other pieces they capture the warmth and spontaneity of this relaxed music, if not all of its charm. The acoustic is a shade dry, but not excessively so; it rather suits the gently atmospheric scoring at the opening of *La Création du monde*, and gives Ian

Hobson's attractively cool accounts of the *Modère* section of *Scaramouche* and the *Tendrement* from the *Rag-Caprices* the right kind of sonority. There is an excellent cassette.

Music for wind: *La Cheminée du Roi René, Op. 105; Divertissement en trois parties, Op. 399b; Pastorale, Op. 47; 2 Sketches, Op. 227b; Suite d'après Corrette, Op. 161b.*
**(*) Chan. *ABT 1012* [id.]. Athena Ens., McNicol.

Two of these pieces were derived from film music: *La Cheminée du Roi René* is based on a score Milhaud wote to *Cavalcade d'Amour*, set in the fifteenth century; and the *Divertissement* draws on material composed for a film on the life of Gauguin. The *Suite d'après Corrette* features music written for a Paris production of *Romeo and Juliet*, using themes by the eighteenth-century French master, Michel Corrette. Though none of this is first-class Milhaud, it is still full of pleasing and attractive ideas, and the general air of easy-going life-loving enjoyment is well conveyed by the alert playing of the Athena Ensemble. One's only quarrel with this issue is the somewhat close balance, which picks up the mechanism of the various keys, and does less than justice to the artists' pianissimo tone. However, this can be remedied a little by a lower level setting, and there is far too much to enjoy here to inhibit a recommendation. The cassette transfer is excellent.

Sonatina for clarinet and piano; Sonatina for flute and piano; Sonata for flute, oboe, clarinet and piano; Sonatina for oboe and piano.
*** Orfeo Dig. **CO 60831A** [id.]. Brunner, Nicolet, Holliger, Maisenberg.

The *Sonata* comes from 1918, the same period as the *Saudades do Brazil*, when Milhaud worked at the French Embassy in Rio de Janeiro. It is an ingenious and delightful piece, most expertly played on this record. The later *Sonatinas* have no less charm and polish, and are beautifully played and very naturally recorded. A strong recommendation for a very attractive concert.

String quartets Nos 1, Op. 5; 7 in B flat, Op. 87; 10, Op. 218; 16, Op. 303.
*** Cybella Dig. **CY 804** [id.]. Aquitaine National Qt.

It was Milhaud's declared ambition to compose eighteen string quartets, just one more than Beethoven, an achievement he had fulfilled by the 1950s. The *First Quartet* dates from 1912 and is a beautifully relaxed, sunny work, rather Debussian in feel (Milhaud as a young violist visited Debussy to play through the latter's *Sonata for flute, viola and harp* before its first performance, but was too shy to tell him he was a composer). The *Seventh* (1925) speaks Milhaud's familiar, distinctive language and was the first of the quartets to be recorded; its four short movements are delightful, full of melody and colour. The *Tenth* (1940), written on board ship during his wartime Atlantic crossing, was presented as a birthday present for Elizabeth Sprague Coolidge; the *Sixteenth* (1950) was a wedding anniversary present for his wife, and its first movement has great tenderness and warmth. The recordings are very good, though No. 1 appears to be recorded in a slightly drier acoustic than its companions. Individual movements in the quartets are not indexed. Incidentally, this is a new recording project for CD, not a transfer of the earlier LP set discussed in our last volume; moreover the newer recordings are made by a different and much finer ensemble, whose intonation is good and whose playing is more polished. The recording has both wider dynamic range and more spacious tonal spectrum.

String quartets Nos 5, Op. 64; 8, Op. 121; 11, Op. 232; 13, Op. 268.
*** Cybella Dig. **CY 805** [id.]. Aquitaine National Qt.

The *Fifth Quartet*, dedicated to Schoenberg, is not one of his most inspired and its textures are dense and overcrowded; the *Eighth*, on the other hand, has much to commend it, including a poignant slow movement. Nos 11 and 13 come from the 1940s; the former has a splendid pastoral third movement and a lively jazzy finale; the latter has overtones of Mexico in its finale and a beguiling and charming *Barcarolle*. As in the companion disc, the Aquitaine National Quartet play very well indeed, and both performance and recording are very good.

Suite française.
*** ASV *ZCALH 913*. L. Wind O, Wick (with GRAINGER: *Irish tune* etc.; POULENC: *Suite française* ***).

The *Suite française* is an enchanting piece, full of Mediterranean colour and an earthy vitality. It would be difficult to imagine a more idiomatic or spirited performance than this one, which has excellent balance and blend. Vivid recording. This is an extraordinarily appealing work and ought to be far more popular than it is. This is a first-class cassette.

Moeran, Ernest J. (1894–1950)

(i) *Cello concerto; Sinfonietta.*
*** Chan. Dig. **CHAN 8456**; *ABTD 1167* [id.]. (i) Raphael Wallfisch; Bournemouth Sinf., Del Mar.

The *Cello concerto* (1945) has been recorded before (by Moeran's widow, Peers Coetmore, with Boult), but this is incomparably finer in every respect. It is a pastoral, ruminative work with elegiac overtones, save in the rather folksy finale. Raphael Wallfisch brings an eloquence of tone and a masterly technical address to this neglected piece, and he receives responsive orchestral support from Norman Del Mar and the Bournemouth players. The well-crafted *Sinfonietta* (1944) was a BBC commission from the same period, and is among Moeran's most successful pieces: its invention is delightfully fresh, and there is that earthy, unpretentious musicality that makes Moeran so appealing a composer. The recording is a little on the reverberant side but well balanced and present. There is a very good tape, which copes well with the resonance.

(i) *Lonely waters. Whythorne's shadow.*
*** HMV Dig. **CDC7 47945-2** [id.]; *EL 270592-4*. ECO, Tate; (i) with Ann Murray BAX: *3 Pieces****; BUTTERWORTH: *Banks of green willow* etc.**(*); BRIDGE: *There is a willow.***(*)

The two Moeran pieces in Tate's English recital present a complete contrast with each other, the first atmospheric and impressionistic, the second reflecting the composer's interest in the Elizabethan madrigal. They are given finely judged, refined performances, warmly recorded. There is a good cassette.

Symphony in G min.; Overture for a masque.
*** Chan. Dig. **CHAN 8577**; *ABTD 1272* [id.]. Ulster O, Vernon Handley.

Moeran's superb *Symphony in G minor* was written between 1934 and 1937. It is in the best English tradition of symphonic writing and worthy to rank with the symphonies of Vaughan Williams and Walton, with which it has much in common. But for all the echoes of these composers (and Holst and Butterworth, too) it has a strong individual voice. There is no question of the quality of the invention throughout the lyrical sweep of the first two movements and in the rhythmically extrovert and genial scherzo. If the structure and atmosphere of the finale are unmistakably Sibelian, it makes a cogent and satisfying close to a very rewarding work.

Vernon Handley gives a bitingly powerful performance, helped by superb playing from the Ulster Orchestra, totally committed from first to last, rivalling any other players, even in London. With the brass cutting through rich textures with thrilling edge, the whole symphony carries more menace with it than in previous recordings, relating to both the dark nature-music of Sibelius and the pre-war period in which it was written. The English pastoral tradition, though clear, is less paramount than usual. The first movement, at an urgent speed, is made the more tautly symphonic and the slow movement, spaciously done, is the more atmospheric, while the scherzo is delectably light and relaxed. The finale, in its summing up, brings the most brilliant playing of all, with the powerful timpani ostinato vividly dramatic. The *Overture for a masque*, a brash, brassy piece in its fanfare opening and Waltonian cross-rhythms, makes an attractive and generous fill-up. The recording is superb, spacious and full, with a dramatic range of dynamic and the Ulster strings sounding exceptionally sweet. The cassette is disappointing – the resonance has brought a low transfer level, and the sound with its reduced upper frequency ceiling seriously lacks bite.

Fantasy quartet for oboe and strings.
*** Chan. Dig. **CHAN 8392**; *ABTD 1114* [id.]. Francis English Qt – BAX: *Quintet*; HOLST: *Air and variations* etc.; JACOB: *Quartet*.***

Moeran's folk-influenced *Fantasy quartet* is an attractively rhapsodic single-movement work, written in 1946 and dedicated, like the coupled Bax *Quintet*, to Leon Goossens, who gave its first performance. It is admirably played here, and the recording is excellent, well balanced too, with a splendid matching chrome cassette. This is part of a highly rewarding anthology of English music for oboe.

(i) *String quartet in A min.;* (ii) *Violin sonata in E min.*
*** Chan. Dig. **CHAN 8465**; *ABTD 1168* [id.]. (i) Melbourne Qt; (ii) Donald Scotts, John Talbot.

Both pieces are early works, written when Moeran was still in his twenties. The *String quartet in A minor* comes from 1921, and the *Violin sonata* was finished two years later. There is a strong folksong element in the *Quartet*, and some French influence too. It is not Moeran at his most distinctive or inspired, but these pieces are stronger than they have been given credit for. This is not music for those allergic to the English folksong school, but it certainly merits an occasional outing; this Chandos disc is worth investigating, particularly in view of the good performances and recording. There is a first-class chrome cassette, well up to Chandos standards of transfer.

Molter, Johann (1696–1765)

Clarinet concerto in D.
*** Claves **CD 50-813** [id.]. Friedli, SW German CO, Angerer – MERCADANTE; PLEYEL: *Concertos*.***

Molter's *Concerto* is for D clarinet and its high tessitura means that it is a piece readily appropriated by trumpeters of the calibre of Maurice André. Heard on a modern version of the instrument for which it was written, the timbre sounds uncannily like a soft-grained trumpet – and very effective, too, especially when the playing is both expert and sympathetic. It is very much a Baroque concerto (with flavours of Bach and Handel) and well worth having on CD. The accompaniment is good rather than outstanding, and though the CD gives the soloist good projection, and both he and the orchestra are heard within a pleasing ambience, orchestral detail is not ideally clear and the harpsichord contribution is only just audible. Nevertheless, this remains a most enjoyable collection, for the coupled works are equally interesting.

Monn, Georg Matthias (1717–50)

Cello concerto in D (arr. Schoenberg).
*** CBS Dig. **MK 39863** [id.]. Yo-Yo Ma, Boston SO, Ozawa – R. STRAUSS: *Don Quixote.* **(*)

As a fill-up to his *Don Quixote*, Yo-Yo Ma gives us an interesting rarity. In 1912 Guido Adler asked Schoenberg to edit a *Cello concerto* by Monn for publication in the *Denkmäler der Tonkunst in Oesterreich.* Two decades later, as a token of thanks for Casals' hospitality in inviting him to conduct the Barcelona Orchestra, Schoenberg made a free transcription for cello and orchestra of another Monn concerto, albeit for keyboard. His letter was at pains to stress that 'nowhere is it atonal'. In a sense it can be compared with Strauss's *Couperin suite*, though Schoenberg's scoring varies from a Regerian delicacy to altogether thicker sonorities. It is beautifully played and recorded.

Monteverdi, Claudio (1567–1643)

Ab aeterno ordinata sum; Confitebor tibi, Domine (3 settings)*; Deus tuorum militum sors et corona; Iste confessor Domini sacratus; Laudate Dominum, O omnes gentes; La Maddalena: Prologue: Su le penne de venti. Nisi Dominus aedificaverit domum.*
❀ *** Hyp. Dig. **CDA 66021**; *KA 66021* [id.]. Kirkby, Partridge, Thomas, Parley of Instruments.

There are few records of Monteverdi's solo vocal music as persuasive as this. The three totally contrasted settings of *Confitebor tibi* (Psalm 110) reveal an extraordinary range of expression, each one drawing out different aspects of word-meaning. Even the brief trio *Deus tuorum militum* has a haunting memorability – it could become to Monteverdi what *Jesu, joy of man's desiring* is to Bach – and the performances are outstanding, with the edge on Emma Kirkby's voice attractively presented in an aptly reverberant acoustic. The accompaniment makes a persuasive case for authentic performance on original instruments. The cassette (issued some time after the disc had become something of a best-seller in its field) gives the performers a natural presence and is very well balanced. The CD does not differ too greatly from the cassette; in fact, this sounds superb in both media.

Madrigals: *Addio Florida bella; Ahi com'a un vago sol; E così a poco a poco torno farfalla; Era l'anima mia; Luci serene e chiare; Mentre vaga Angioletta ogn' anima; Ninfa che scalza il piede; O mio bene, a mia vita; O Mirtillo, Mirtill'anima mia; Se pur destina; Taci, Armelin deh taci; T'amo mia vita; Troppa ben può questo tiranno amore.*
*** HM **HMC 901084** [id.]. Concerto Vocale.

A highly attractive collection of generally neglected items, briskly and stylishly performed. The most celebrated of the singers is the male alto, René Jacobs, a fine director as well as soloist. With continuo accompaniment – the common factor in this set, in which no *a cappella* madrigals are included – the contrasting of vocal timbres is superbly achieved. Excellent recording, well transferred to CD.

Madrigals, Book 4 (complete).
*** O-L Dig. **414 148-2**; *414 148-4* [id.]. Cons. of Musicke, Anthony Rooley.

Monteverdi's Fourth Book of madrigals, published in Venice in 1603, contains many of his most brilliant and taxing pieces in this genre, a dazzling collection that from the start demanded the virtuoso technique of professional singers. Under Anthony Rooley the fine, well-integrated singers of the Consort of Musicke give masterly performances which readily compass not only the vocal pitfalls but the deeper problems of conveying the intensity of emotions implied by both music and words. The flexibility and control of dramatic contrast, conveying consistent commitment, make this one of this group's finest records, helped by atmospheric but aptly intimate recording. The chrome cassette, too, is of a demonstration standard.

Madrigals from Books 7 and 8: *Amor che deggio far; Altri canti di Marte; Chiome d'oro; Gira il nemico insidioso; Hor ch'el ciel e la terra; Non havea Febo ancora – Lamento della ninfa; Perchè t'en fuggi o Fillide; Tirsi e Clori* (ballo concertato for 5 voices and instruments).
*** HM **HMC 901068** [id.]. Les Arts Florissants, Christie.

There are eight of Monteverdi's finest madrigals here, very well sung by this distinguished team. Many of them, like *Chiome d'oro* and *Hor ch'el ciel e la terra,* will be familiar to older collectors from the famous Nadia Boulanger set. The singing of this famous group is full of colour and feeling and, even if intonation is not absolutely flawless throughout, it is mostly excellent. Much to be preferred to the bloodless white tone favoured by some early music groups. Good recording.

Concerti spirituali: Audi caelum; Exsulta filia, Salve Regina. Madrigals: *Augellin che la voce al canto spieghi; Mentre vaga Angioletta; Ninfa che scalza il piede; O mio bene; Se vittorie si belle; Vaga su spina ascosa; Zefiro torna.*
** DG **415 295-2** [id.]. Nigel Rogers, Ian Partridge, Keyte, Ens. Jürgens.

All these recordings date from the early 1970s and are tenor duets with continuo support, with or without a bass. Nigel Rogers has great style and virtuosity – though there is a certain dryness about the vocal timbre that tires the ear. Ian Partridge and Christopher Keyte are no less skilled, but Jürgen Jürgens does opt for rather brisk tempi. A useful but not indispensable addition to the Monteverdi discography on CD. Good recorded sound.

Selva morale e spirituale: Beatus vir a 6; Confitebor tibi; Deus tuorum militum a 3; Dixit Dominus a 8; Domine a 3; Jubilet tota civitas; Laudate dominum a 5; Laudate pueri a 5; Magnificat a 8; Salve Regina a 3.
** HMV **CDC 747016-2** [id.]. Kirkby, Rogers, Covey-Crump, Thomas, Taverner Cons. Ch. and Players, Parrott.

There is some fine singing from Emma Kirkby and Nigel Rogers, and the recorded sound is very good. The performances really need more breadth and grandeur, and there is at times a somewhat bloodless quality about the singing of some of the pieces; but there is enough to admire, such as the attractive account of *Salve Regina* and the opening *Dixit Dominus.* The CD adds to the clarity and presence, but tends to emphasize minor faults of balance between instruments and voices, and suggests to the ear that a little more spaciousness in the acoustic would have given the music making (even with these comparatively small numbers) more amplitude. Even so, this collection is worth considering.

Lamento d'Olympia; Maladetto sia l'aspetto; Ohimè ch'io cado; Quel sdengosetto; Voglio di vita uscia.
*** Hyp. **CDA 66106** [id.]. Emma Kirkby, Anthony Rooley (chitarone) – D'INDIA: *Lamento d'Olympia* etc.***

A well-planned recital from Hyperion contrasts the two settings of *Lamento d'Olympia* by Monteverdi and his younger contemporary, Sigismondo d'India. The performances by Emma Kirkby, sensitively supported by Anthony Rooley, could hardly be surpassed and her admirers can be assured that this ranks among her best records. Its claims, apart from excellence, reside as much as anything else in the sheer interest of the pieces by Sigismondo d'India.

Canti amorosi: Mentre vaga Angioletta; Lamento della ninfa. Il combattimento di Tancredi e Clorinda. Ogni amante e guerrier.
(*) Tel Dig. **ZK8. 43054 [id.]. Hollweg, Schmidt, Palmer, Murray, Perry, Langridge, VCM, Harnoncourt.

Harnoncourt conducts sharply characterized readings of substantial items from Monteverdi's eighth Book of Madrigals plus two *Canti amorosi*. The substantial scena telling of the conflict of Tancredi and Clorinda is made sharply dramatic in a bald way. *Ogni amante e guerrier*, almost as extended, is treated with similar abrasiveness, made attractively fresh but lacking subtlety. The two *Canti amorosi* are treated quite differently, in a much warmer style, with the four sopranos of *Mentre vaga Angioletta* producing sensuous sounds. *Lamento della ninfa*, perhaps the most celebrated of all Monteverdi's madrigals, brings a luscious performance with the solo voice (Ann Murray) set evocatively at a slight distance behind the two tenors and a bass. On CD the recording is extremely vivid, with voices and intruments firmly and realistically placed. No translations are given, only the Italian text of *Tancredi e Clorinda*.

Missa de cappella a 4; Missa de cappella a 6 (In illo tempore); Motets: *Cantate domino a 6; Domine ne in furore a 6.*
*** Hyp. Dig. **CDA 66214**; *KA 66214* [id]. The 16, Harry Christophers; M. Phillips.

Two of Monteverdi's three surviving settings of the Mass make a splendid coupling, along with two magnificent motets, both of which (like the *Missa in illo tempore*) are in six parts. Harry Christophers draws superb singing from his brilliant choir, highly polished in ensemble but dramatic and deeply expressive too, suitably adapted for the different character of each Mass-setting, when the four-part Mass involves stricter, more consistent contrapuntal writing and the six-part, in what was then an advanced way, uses homophonic writing to underline key passages. In that the incisiveness and clarity of articulation of the Sixteen add enormously to the dramatic bite. Vivid, atmospheric recording, and a splendid cassette to match the excellent CD fairly closely.

Vespro della Beata Vergine (Vespers).
*** HMV Dig. **CDS7 47078-8** [Ang. **CDCB 47077**]; *EX 270129-5* [Ang. *4D2S 3963*] (2). Kirkby, Nigel Rogers, David Thomas, Taverner Ch., Cons. & Players, Canto Gregoriano, Parrott.
*** Decca **414 572-2** (2) [id.]. Gomez, Palmer, Bowman, Tear, Langridge, Shirley-Quirk, Rippon, Monteverdi Ch. & O, Salisbury Cathedral Boys' Ch., Jones Brass Ens., Murrow Recorder Cons., Gardiner.
(*) Tel. Dig. **ZA8 35710 (2) [id.]. Margaret Marshall, Palmer, Langridge, Equiluz, Korn, Tolz Boys' Ch., V. Hofburg Church Ch. Scholars, Schoenberg Ch., VCM, Harnoncourt.
** HM Dig. **HMC 901247/8** [id.]. Mellon, Laurens, Darras, Crook, Kendall, O'Beirne, Kooy, Thomas, Chapelle Royale, Coll. Vocale, Saqueboutiers de Toulouse, Herreweghe.
*(*) Erato **ECD 88024** (2) [id.]. Jennifer Smith, Michael Evans, Elwes, Huttenlocher, Brodard, Lausanne Vocal Ens. & Instrumental Ens., Corboz.

Though Andrew Parrott uses minimal forces, with generally one instrument and one voice per part, so putting the work on a chamber scale in a small church setting, its grandeur comes out superbly through its very intensity. Far more than usual with antiphons in Gregorian chant it becomes a liturgical celebration, so that the five non-liturgical compositions or concerti are added to the main Vesper setting as a rich glorification. They are brilliantly sung here by the virtuoso soloists, above all by Nigel Rogers, whose distinctive timbre may not suit every ear but who has an airy precision and flexibility to give expressive meaning to even the most taxing passages. Fine singing from Parrott's chosen groups of players and singers, and warm, atmospheric recording, with an ecclesiastical ambience which yet allows ample detail; this is particularly beautiful and clear on CD, which is made more convenient to use by the banding. The high-level tape transfer is also first class.

'The grand quasi-theatrical design of this spectacular work has always seemed compelling to me,' says John Eliot Gardiner, and his fine set presents the music very much in that light. The recording was made in 1974, before Gardiner had been won over entirely to the claims of the authentic school. Modern instruments are used and women's voices, but Gardiner's rhythms are so resilient that the result is more exhilarating as well as grander. The whole span of the thirteen movements sweeps you forward with a sense of complete unity. Singing and playing are exemplary, and the recording is one of Decca's most vividly atmospheric. The digital remastering for CD is superb, with relatively large forces presented and placed against a helpful, reverberant acoustic. The grandeur, drama and incisiveness of Gardiner's reading are formidably reinforced, making this in many ways a safer recommendation than the more 'authentic' approach of Parrott on HMV.

Harnoncourt's version, recorded live, gives a keen sense of occasion, with the grandeur of the piece linked to a consciously authentic approach. There is a ruggedness in the interpretation, entirely apt, which is lightened by the characterful refinement of the solo singing from an exceptionally strong team of soloists, not to mention the fine singing from all three choirs. Ample, atmospheric recording.

Herreweghe with his fine team of skilled period performers gives a low-key reading of the *Vespers*, despite ample contrast of scale between soloists and full choir. The church atmosphere of the recording – made at L'Abbaye-aux-Dames at Saintes – is enhanced by the use of plainsong, though the inclusion of women's instead of boys' voices undermines the impression of a liturgical performance. Soloists and chorus are good, but what is lacking is the final polish of ensemble and dramatic edge to give the necessary bite to the music. Gardiner, with a less authentic performance, presents the work with far more panache; among the more authentic readings, Parrott's intimate account is much more compelling than Herreweghe's. The recording is partly to blame, atmospheric but not fully detailed.

Corboz's version is reverential rather than dramatic, genial and smooth with little feeling of grandeur, despite the spacious church acoustic. Like Parrott on his EMI version, Corboz includes antiphons, freshly sung by the boys of Notre Dame de Sion, and the team of soloists is a strong one, but rhythms are pointed consistently less crisply than in the two main rival versions. The recording is full and atmospheric, though there are too few bands on the CDs.

OPERA AND OPERA-BALLET

Il ballo delle ingrate; Sestina: Lagrime d'amante al sepolcro dell'amata.
(*) HM Dig. **HMC 901108 [id.]. Les Arts Florissants, Christie.

William Christie directs refreshingly dramatic accounts of both *Il ballo delle ingrate* and the *Sestina.* His singers have been chosen for character and bite rather than for beauty of tone, and the final lament of *Il ballo* is spoilt by exaggerated plaintiveness, but (particularly in the *Sestina*) the boldness of Christie's interpretation makes for very compelling performances, beautifully recorded. The note on the CD version irritatingly omits details of the soloists.

Il Combattimento di Tancredi e Clorinda. L'Arianna: Lasciatemi Morire (*Ariadne's lament*) (with FARINA: *Sonata* (*La Desperata*). ROSSI: *Sonata sopra l'aria di Ruggiero.* FONTANA: *Sonata a tre violini.* MARINI: *Passacaglia a 4. Sonata sopra la Monica; Eco a tre violini.* BUONAMENTE: *Sonata a tre violini*).
(*) DG **415 296-2 [id.]. C. Watkinson, Rogers, Kwella, David Thomas, Col. Mus. Ant., Goebel.

Under Reinhard Goebel, the Cologne Musica Antiqua using original instruments has built up a formidable reputation on record, and these tasteful performances of two masterly Monteverdi settings, coupled with sonatas by Monteverdi's contemporaries, are welcome. Carolyn Watkinson's singing of the *Lament* is finely controlled and certainly dramatic. So too is the performance of the touching and powerfully imaginative narrative about the battle of Tancredi and Clorinda, which understandably moved the audience to tears at its première. The other pieces are of more mixed appeal. Highlights are Fontana's engaging *Sonata for three violins* and Marini's ingenious *Eco a tre violini*, which is performed here to great effect, with the imitations echoing into the distance. Elsewhere, the slightly spiky sounds produced by the string players, with the close microphones bringing a touch of edginess, may not appeal to all tastes. The transfers of the 1979 analogue recordings are impeccably managed. Full texts and notes are provided.

Ballet e balletti: *Orfeo: Lasciate i monti; Vieni imeneo; Ecco pur ch'a voi ritorno; Moresca. Tirsi e Clori: ballet. Scherzo musicali: Il ballo delle ingrate; De la belleza la dovute lodi; Volgendo il ciel.*
(*) Erato **ECD 88032 [id.]. Kwella, Rolfe-Johnson, Dale, Woodrow, Monteverdi Ch., E. Bar. Soloists, Gardiner.

This is in effect a Monteverdi sampler; while the mosaic from *Orfeo*, for instance, may not suit the specialist listener, it makes delightful listening when the singing is so fresh. The music from the famous *Il ballo delle ingrate* is very short (about 3½ minutes) and seems pointless out of context; but all the rest, notably the choral ballet from *Tirsi e Clori*, is most engaging with its changes of mood: sometimes dolorous, sometimes gay and spirited. Gardiner's direction, as always, is vivid and his pacing lively; there is much to titillate the ear in the spicy vocal and orchestral colouring. The balance is fairly close, but the overall perspective is well defined, within a warm acoustic. On CD this sounds especially well.

L'Incoronazione di Poppea.
(M) **(*) Tel. **ZC8 35247** (4) [id.]. Donath, Söderström, Berberian, Esswood, Luccardi, Gartner, Gaifa, Hansmann, Langridge, Equiluz, VCM, Harnoncourt.

Harnoncourt's recording of *L'Incoronazione di Poppea* has the dual advantages of being both complete and authentic. There are features of any performance of this great work which are bound to be conjectural, and here scholars may argue about the instrumentation used or the ornamentation (which matches it in elaboration). But there is no question that the dramatic power of the music comes across. Helen Donath is commanding as Poppea, and she is extremely well supported by Paul Esswood as Ottone and by Cathy Berberian, whose characterization of Ottavia is an imaginative one. Donath's singing has not the richness and dignity that Dame Janet Baker gives to this role, but she brings the character fully to life. Elisabeth Söderström has the almost impossible task of creating a heroic image in the role of Nero, written for a high castrato, but her performance is excellent, even if she fails wholly to submerge her femininity. Harnoncourt brings plenty of vitality to the performance as a whole, and his instrumental group provides beautiful if arguably over-decorative accompaniments. As with almost all Harnoncourt's analogue recordings, the excellent focus of the 1975 original master has lent itself to a highly successful CD transfer, very vivid and clear and with good ambience. The layout on four CDs may seem extravagant, but there is about four hours of music here, and at least the set is offered at a reduced price.

Orfeo (opera): complete.
*** DG Dig. **419 250-2**; *419 250-4* (2) [id.]. Rolfe-Johnson, Baird, Lynne Dawson, Von Otter, Argenta, Robson, Monteverdi Ch., E. Bar. Soloists, Gardiner.

*** HMV Dig. **CDS7 47142-8** [Ang. **CDCB 47141**]; *EX 270131-5* [Ang. *4D2X 3954*] (2). Nigel Rogers, Kwella, Kirkby, Jennifer Smith, Varcoe, David Thomas, Chiaroscuro, L. Bar. Ens., L. Cornett & Sackbutt Ens., Rogers & Medlam.

(M) ** Tel. **ZA8 35020** (2) [id.]. Kozma, Hansmann, Katanosaka, Berberian, Rogers, Equiluz, Van Egmond, Villisech, Munich Capella Antiqua, VCM, Harnoncourt.

*(*) Erato **ECD 88133** (2) [id.]. Quilico, Carolyn Watkinson, Voutsinos, Tappy, Chapelle Royal Vocal Ens., Lyons Op. O, Corboz.

John Eliot Gardiner very effectively balances the often-conflicting demands of authentic performance – when this pioneering opera was originally presented intimately – and the obvious grandeur of the concept. The very atmospheric recording vividly conveys the impression of some hall in a prince's palace, much more likely as a venue than a small room, and lively enough to give bloom to the voices and to the colourful instrumentation. So the Monteverdi Choir, twenty-one strong, conveys, on the one hand, high tragedy to the full, yet sings the lighter commentary from nymphs and shepherds with astonishing crispness, often at top speed. However, Gardiner is strong on pacing. He does not simply race along in the way that authentic performance has tended to encourage but gives full and moving expansion to such key passages as the messenger's report of Euridice's death, sung with agonizing intensity by Anne-Sophie von Otter. It intensifies that narration that the singer is heard first from a distance, then gradually approaches. Lynne Dawson is also outstanding as the allegorical figure of Music in the Prologue, while Anthony Rolfe-Johnson shows his formidable versatility in the title role. Though rival tenors with smaller voices have been more flexible in the elaborate *fioriture* of the Act III aria, presenting it more urgently, it is an advantage having a fuller-bodied voice that can yet focus cleanly. This is a set to take you through the story with new involvement. Though editing is not always immaculate, the recording on CD is vivid and full of presence.

Nigel Rogers – who recorded the role of Orfeo ten years earlier for DG Archiv – in the EMI Reflexe version has the double function of singing the main part and acting as co-director. In the earlier recording under Kurt Jürgens, ample reverberation tended to inflate the performance but, this time in a drier acoustic, Rogers has modified his extraordinarily elaborate ornamentation in the hero's brilliant pleading aria before Charon, and makes the result all the freer and more wide-ranging in expression, with his distinctive fluttering timbre adding character. With the central singer directing the others, the concentration of the whole performance is all the greater, telling the story simply and graphically. The sound of thunder that fatefully makes Orpheus turn round as he leads Euridice back to earth is all the more dramatic for being drily percussive; and Euridice's plaint, beautifully sung by Patrizia Kwella, is the more affecting for being accompanied very simply on the lute. The other soloists make a good team, though Jennifer Smith as Proserpine, recorded close, is made to sound breathy. The brightness of the cornetti is a special delight, when otherwise the instrumentation used – largely left optional in the score – is modest. Excellent, immediate recording, at its finest on CD, but the cassettes too are outstanding. Transferred at the highest level they offer EMI's best quality.

In Harnoncourt's version, the ritornello of the Prologue might almost be by Stravinsky, so sharply do the sounds cut. He is an altogether more severe Monteverdian than Nigel Rogers. In compensation, the simple and straightforward dedication of this performance is most affecting, and the solo singing, if not generally very characterful, is clean and stylish. One exception to the general rule on characterfulness comes in the singing of Cathy Berberian as the Messenger. She is strikingly successful and, though slightly differing in style from the others, she sings as part of the team. Excellent restrained recording, as usual in Harnoncourt's remastered Telefunken CD series, projecting the performance even more vividly than on LP. The extra clarity and sharpness of focus – even in large-scale ensembles – add to the abrasiveness from the opening *Toccata* onwards, and the 1969 recording certainly sounds immediate, with voices very realistic.

Corboz's version was recorded as a by-product of a successful staging of the piece at the Aix-en-Provence Festival, and the approach is more conventionally operatic than in most current versions, with the baritone, Gino Quilico, singing the name-part in an almost verismo manner, so that *Possente spirito* is made lachrymose. Textures tend to be rich, opulent even, with sweet string-tone, and Corboz attempts, misguidedly, to exaggerate speeds in the dramatic interludes, ritornellos and sinfonias, but without making them sharp enough. The singing, solo and choral, is variably successful, with Carolyn Watkinson the most stylish as the Messenger, and Frangiskos Voutsinos the least effective in the two bass roles of Charon and Pluto. Ample recording, too reverberant for this music.

COLLECTIONS

Con che soavita; Lamento d'Arianna; Lettera amorosa; (i) *L'Incoronazione di Poppea: O reine infortune; Tu che dagli avi miei . . . Maestade, che prega; Addio Roma. Orfeo:* (ii) *Mira, de mira, Orfeo . . . In un fiorito prato.*
(M) *** Tel. **ZS8 43625** [id.]. Cathy Berberian, (i) with Esswood; (ii) Nigel Rogers, Kozma, Theuring; VCM, Harnoncourt.

This admirably planned anthology from 1975 would make an excellent introduction to the composer for a newcomer (alongside the Hyperion collection – **CDA 66021**, see above), yet will be equally satisfying for the experienced Monteverdian. Cathy Berberian gives a movingly eloquent account of the *Lamento d'Arianna* but is hardly less impressive in the excerpts from *L' Incoronazione di Poppea*, where she is supported by Paul Esswood. Here her account of *Addio Roma* is most involving. The recording has astonishing presence and plenty of ambience, and the mid-price adds to the appeal of this excellent CD.

Collection: *Et è pur dunque vero; Ohimè ch'io cado; L'Incoronazione di Poppea: Disprezzata regina; Addio Roma.*
(*) Erato Dig. **ECD 88100 [id.]. Frederica von Stade, SCO, Leppard – CAVALLI: *Arias.* **(*)

Frederica von Stade sings these Monteverdi songs and arias stylishly and freshly. She is at her best in the delightful *Et è pur dunque vero*, while at the opening of *Addio Roma*, with its dramatic short pauses, the colouring of her lower register is telling. Here Leppard's accompaniment increases the tension, and elsewhere he gives admirable support. The recording gives the voice a strong presence and the overall balance is very good, too. Other accounts of the two *Poppea* excerpts have shown greater expressive ardour; however, this recital, with its attractive Cavalli coupling, still gives much pleasure. It would have been even greater had translations of the Italian texts been provided; as it is, the documentation is poor.

Moscheles, Ignaz (1794–1870)

(i) *Double concerto for flute and oboe;* (ii) *Piano concerto No. 3 in G min. Bonbonnière musicale.*
*** Sup. **CO 1326** [id.]. (i) Valék, Mihule; (ii) Klánský; Dvořák CO, Pařík.

A distinguished musician and piano teacher – Mendelssohn was numbered among his pupils – Moscheles, who was born in Prague, spent twenty years at the London Royal Academy of Music (1825–45) and ended his career as a professor at Leipzig Conservatoire. This record makes an admirable introduction to his own music. His essentially classical style is tempered a little at times – the passagework in the *Piano concerto* is reminiscent of the Chopin. Ivan Klánský gives strong, attractive performances (helped by Pařík's polished accompaniment) both here and in the *Bonbonnière musicale*, an eight-movement suite, not at all trivial and often highly inventive. The pianism is full of energy and spirit, but can relax when necessary – *A la Espagnole*, the penultimate *bonbon*, is most affectionately played. The *Concerto for flute and oboe* is lighter in style, and its unexpected opening demonstrates that Moscheles could be unconventional – it is a most winning work, particularly the gay finale with its complex intertwining of the two solo instruments. Excellent recording throughout, with a realistic balance in the concerto; the piano is a bit close in the suite, but the image is eminently realistic.

Mourant, Walter (born 1910)

The Pied Piper.
*** ASV Dig. **CDDCA 568**; *ZCDCA 568* [id.]. MacDonald, Northern Sinfonia, Bedford – COPLAND: *Concerto*; FINZI: *Concerto*.***

Walter Mourant's *Pied Piper* is a catchy, unpretentious little piece for clarinet, strings and celeste, which in a gently syncopated style effectively contrasts 3/4 and 6/8 rhythms. It makes an attractive filler after the Copland *Concerto*.

Mozart, Leopold (1719–87)

Cassation in G: Toy symphony (attrib. Haydn). (i) *Trumpet concerto in D*.
*** Erato Dig. **ECD 88021**. (i) Touvron; Paillard CO, Paillard – MOZART: *Musical Joke*.***

One could hardly imagine this *Cassation* being done with more commitment from the effects department, while the music itself is elegantly played. The Minuet is particularly engaging, with its aviary of bird-sounds plus a vigorous contribution from the toy trumpet; and the finale, with its obbligato mêlée, is dispatched with an infectious sense of fun. After this, the more restrained approach to the excellent two-movement *Trumpet concerto* seems exactly right. The recording has plenty of presence and realism, with the balance very well judged, both for the solo trumpet and for the toy instruments in the *Cassation* – which are properly set back. An excellent CD début.

Cassation in G (*Toy symphony*).
(*) Ph. Dig. **416 386-2; *416 386-4* [id.]. ASMF, Marriner – MOZART: *Adagio and fugue*; *Eine kleine Nachtmusik*; PACHELBEL: *Canon and Gigue*.**(*)

With the toy instruments played for all they are worth and more, the additions to the *Toy symphony* make the strongest contrast with Sir Neville's characteristically elegant and refined performance. This is generally effective, though the raucousness of the grotesquely mismatched cuckoo-whistle is hard to take. A good item in an attractive mixed bag, treated to warm, well-balanced recording with an agreeable cassette equivalent.

Trumpet concerto in D.
*(*) Tel. Dig. **ZK8 43673** [id.]. Immer, VCM, Harnoncourt – MOZART: *Bassoon concerto* etc.*(*)

Leopold Mozart's *Trumpet concerto* is a pretty florid piece, and Friedemann Immer does not make a very good case for playing it on an 'authentic' keyed trumpet, which at times produces an unattractively strangulated tone. He is brightly accompanied. Strictly for authenticists only.

Mozart, Wolfgang Amadeus (1756–91)

Cassations Nos 1 in G, K.63; 2 in B flat, K.99; 3 (*Serenade*) *in D, K.100; March in D, K.62*.
(*) Erato Dig. **ECD 88101 [id.]. Paillard CO, Paillard.

The range and command of instrumental colour displayed by these three *Cassations*, written in

Salzburg in 1769 by the thirteen-year-old Mozart, are quite remarkable. Moreover, the delicate first *Andante* of K.99 is uncannily prophetic of a famous Trio in *Così fan tutte* both in mood and in its gentle string figurations. K.63 introduces a memorable *Adagio* cantilena featuring solo violin, and K.100 has two *Andantes*, of which the second – paced rather fast here – is also captivating. The performances are essentially orchestral in character and the slightly too resonant acoustic emphasizes this. But the CD ensures that detail is well caught, and while Paillard does not always show an instinctive feeling for exactly the right tempo, he secures committed and responsive playing throughout and his allegros are always alert. The music is what counts and the Erato CD (with 61 minutes of music) is most welcome. The *March* is associated with and used to introduce K.100; the other two works have brief introductory marches as opening movements.

Cassation No. 2 in B flat, K.99; Divertimento No. 2 in D, K.131.
*** Ph. Dig. **420 924-2**; *420 924-4* [id.]. ASFM, Marriner.

Beecham's performance (mono only) of the *Divertimento in D* remains firmly in the memory but, even by Beecham's standards, Marriner gives a fine performance. The Academy strings bring the soul of finesse to these performances, and with the horns adding an agreeably robust element (they are very tangible on CD) to K.131, there is sparkle as well as grace. Marriner's pacing in both works is apt and, except for those demanding 'authentic' vinegar, this unashamedly warm and elegant music-making will give much pleasure. There is a good tape, but the CD is better defined and more transparent.

(i) *Bassoon concerto in B flat, K.191;* (ii) *Clarinet concerto in A, K.622.*
(*) Claves Dig. **CD 50-8205 [id.]. (i) Thunemann; (ii) Friedli; Zurich CO, Stoutz.
(B) ** CfP *CFP 41 4484-4.* (i) Nakanishi; (ii) Andrew Marriner; L. Mozart Players, Glover.

(i) *Bassoon concerto;* (ii) *Clarinet concerto;* (iii) *Flute concerto No. 1 in G, K.313;* (iv) *Oboe concerto in C, K.314.*
(B) *** Ph. *412 903-4* [id.]. (i) Chapman; (ii) Brymer; (iii) Claude Monteux; (iv) Black; ASMF, Marriner.

(i) *Bassoon concerto;* (ii) *Clarinet concerto;* (iii) *Oboe concerto.*
(M) ** HMV **CDM7 69014-2** [id.]; *EG 769014-4.* (i) Piesk; (ii) Leister; (iii) Koch; BPO, Karajan.

(i) *Bassoon concerto;* (ii) *Clarinet concerto;* (iii) *Divertimento in B flat for wind, K. 186.*
(M) ** DG *419 480-4* [id.]. (i) Walt; (ii) H. Wright; Boston SO, Ozawa; (iii) VPO Wind Ens.

(i) *Bassoon concerto;* (ii) *Clarinet concerto. March in D, K.249; Thamos, King of Egypt, K.345; Entr'acte No. 2.*
*** HMV **CDC7 47864-2** [id.]. (i) Brooke; (ii) Brymer; RPO, Beecham.

The early HMV coupling of the *Bassoon* and *Clarinet concertos* is one of Beecham's most beguiling recordings. Both his soloists play with great character and beauty, and the accompaniment is wonderfully gracious. Beecham's tempi are affectionately leisurely in the *Clarinet concerto*, but there is magic in every bar and both performances have the spontaneity of a live occasion. Of the two lollipops chosen to complete the programme, the *Entr'acte* from *Thamos* is itself almost a miniature concerto, featuring the oboe, and this too is most winningly played. The 1959 recording in no way sounds its age and still leads the field.

An outstanding collection on Philips's 'On Tour' chrome tape. The performances of these concertos are among the finest available, and although the forward balance tends to make the soloists sound larger than life, the sound is otherwise realistic and eminently truthful in timbre. Michael Chapman plays with great spirit and verve and is stylishly supported. Jack Brymer's recording of the *Clarinet concerto* is the third he has made; in some ways it is his best, for he plays with deepened insight and feeling. The flute and oboe concertos are hardly less recommendable, and the tape transfers are admirably managed.

The performances on the Claves CD are also first class, fresh and direct, sensitive without affectionate lingering in the Beecham manner, but with slow movements nicely expressive, and plenty of vitality elsewhere. Both soloists are forwardly balanced and Klaus Thunemann's woody bassoon timbre has lots of character (although not all will take to his vibrato). The digital recording is bright, fresh and clean.

Though Karajan's smooth approach to Mozart dominates the Berlin performances, thickening textures, his triptych makes a generous coupling on a mid-price issue, with stylish playing from the distinguished wind principals of the Berlin Philharmonic. The recording is a degree too opulent, matching the readings. There is a good chrome tape.

The Boston performances from DG are thoroughly musical and beautifully recorded on disc and tape alike. The warm tone of the clarinet soloist is especially appealing. However, Ozawa's accompaniments, though well fashioned and neatly laid out, are rather matter-of-fact, and the overall effect is accomplished rather than inspired. The *Wind divertimento*, however, is a very real bonus.

Producing a beautifully even flow of warm tone, Andrew Marriner gives a distinguished performance of the *Clarinet concerto* which yet lacks a feeling of spontaneity, the forward thrust, the inspiration of the moment. It would be hard to find a more beautiful timbre in the slow movement, but nevertheless the effect remains placid. Nakanishi is a talented player who copes well with the technical problems of the *Bassoon concerto*, but he is more recessive still, and the orchestral playing adds to the feeling of a studio run-through rather than a live experience. However, at CfP's bargain price this tape is fairly attractive, but its smooth upper range and warm bass response slightly increase the feeling of blandness.

(i) *Bassoon concerto;* (ii) *Horn concerto No. 3 in E flat, K.447;* (iii) *Oboe concerto.*
** DG **415 104-2** [id.]. (i) Willard Elliot; (ii) Dale Clevenger; (iii) Ray Still; Chicago SO, Abbado – HAYDN: *Trumpet concerto.***

Anyone wanting this particular collection of Mozart concertos coupled with Haydn's *Trumpet concerto* should not be too disappointed, for the playing is expert, the recordings are truthful and well balanced and Abbado's accompaniments characteristically refined and elegant. However, while Ray Still's phrasing is nicely turned, and Willard Elliot plays a nimble bassoon, neither artist registers very strongly here as an instrumental personality, and even Dale Clevenger, who is so impressive in his Telefunken disc of Haydn's *Horn concertos*, proves less individual in Mozart, although his solo contribution is highly musical and technically effortless. The recordings sound their best on CD.

(i) *Bassoon concerto in B flat, K.191; Notturno for 4 orchestras, K.286; Serenade No. 6* (*Serenata notturna*), *K.239.*
*(*) Tel. Dig. **ZK8 43673** [id.]. (i) Milan Turkovic; VCM, Harnoncourt – L. MOZART: *Trumpet concerto.**(*)

By far the most attractive music-making here is from Milan Turkovic, who plays Mozart's *Bassoon concerto* convincingly and with considerable character on a Viennese Tauber seven-key bassoon which may be primitive but can be made to sound colourfully attractive. However, in the *Serenata notturna*, which opens the concert, Harnoncourt creates explosive fortissimos with his drums, together with plentiful accents. The *Notturno* is made to sound ungratefully harsh, and utterly fails to create the atmosphere of an evening serenade, and the antiphonal horn effects seem crude. Vivid recording.

Clarinet concerto in A; Andante in C, K.315/285 (trans. for clarinet).
** RCA **RD 89831**. Stoltzman, ECO, Schneider – WEBER: *Concerto No. 1*.**(*)

Richard Stoltzman's clean, clear clarinet tone makes his a distinctive reading, but one in which his tonal tautness seems to affect the interpretation, giving it an element of stiffness at times. Only in the finale does he open out more. The *Andante*, K.315, transcribed from the flute original, makes a welcome and unusual extra item.

(i) *Clarinet concerto;* (ii) *Flute and harp concerto in C, K.299*.
*** ASV Dig. **CDDCA 532**; *ZCDCA 532* [id.]. (i) Emma Johnson; (ii) Bennett, Ellis; ECO, Leppard.
(M) *** Pickwick Dig. **PCD 852** [MCA **MCAD 25965**]. (i) Campbell; (ii) Davies, Masters, City of L. Sinfonia, Hickox.
(*) DG **413 552-2 [id.]. (i) Prinz; (ii) Schulz, Zabaleta; VPO, Boehm.

(i) *Clarinet concerto;* (ii) *Flute concerto No. 1 in G, K.313;* (iii) *Flute and harp concerto*.
(B) *** DG Walkman *413 428-4* [id.]. (i) Prinz, VPO, Boehm; (ii) Linde, Munich CO, Stadlmair; (iii) Schulz, Zabeleta, VPO, Boehm.

Emma Johnson, the BBC's Young Musician of the Year in 1984 and an immediate and winning star on television through that competition, went on within months to record this performance in the studio. The result lacks some of the technical finesse of rival versions by more mature clarinettists, but it has a sense of spontaneity, of natural magnetism which traps the ear from first to last. There may be some rawness of tone in places, but that only adds to the range of expression, which breathes the air of a live performance, whether in the sparkle and flair of the outer movements or the inner intensity of the central slow movement, in which Emma Johnson plays magically in a delightfully embellished lead-back into the main theme. Leppard and the ECO are in bouncing form, as they are too for the *Flute and harp concerto* on the reverse, though there the two excellent soloists are somewhat on their best behaviour (not taking the risks that Emma Johnson does), until the last part of the finale sends Mozart bubbling up to heaven. First-rate recording, given the greater clarity on CD. There is a first-class cassette, too.

The Pickwick coupling of the *Clarinet concerto* and the *Flute and harp concerto* is an excellent recommendation, even making no allowance for the bargain price. David Campbell's agile and pointed performance of the clarinet work brings fastish speeds and a fresh, unmannered style in all three movements. Though some will prefer a weightier or more individual approach, and the reverberant recording tends not to differentiate the soloist sharply enough, his tonal shading is very beautiful, not least in the lovely lead-back to the main theme in the slow movement. The earlier flute and harp work is just as freshly and sympathetically done, with a direct, unmannered style sounding entirely spontaneous. Again the rather reverberant acoustic brings wide-ranging digital sound, not ideal in its detail or definition of the soloists but attractively warm.

Prinz's 1974 recording of the *Clarinet concerto* is available either on an immaculately transferred CD, coupled with the *Flute and harp concerto*, which seems short measure, or on an excellent Walkman tape (at less than a third the price of the compact disc). Here there is a bonus, in the form of Linde's impeccably played account of the *G major Flute concerto*. It has a touch of rigidity in the outer movements, but in the slow movement the playing is beautifully poised and the melody breathes in exactly the right way. Boehm's *Flute and harp concerto* comes from 1976 and the performance could hardly be bettered. The balance, as far as the relationship between soloists and orchestra is concerned, is expertly managed, and this is altogether refreshing. The sound throughout these recordings is excellent, except that Linde's 1966 *Flute concerto* shows its earlier date in the quality of the string timbre.

Another vintage coupling from ten years earlier is also offered on a well-transferred Decca Weekend tape. These performances under Münchinger, with Prinz, Tripp and Jellinek the soloists, remain very recommendable. The balance is well calculated and the playing shows refinement and beauty of tone and phrase. Münchinger provides most sensitive accompaniments (Decca *421 023-4*).

(i) *Clarinet concerto;* (ii) *Horn concertos Nos 1 in D, K.412; 4 in E flat, K.495.*
*** DG Dig. **423 377-2**; *423 377-4* [id.]. (i) Neidich; (ii) Jolley, Orpheus CO.

This seems an awkward coupling, but the performances are most enjoyable and their acquisition is well worth considering, even if it means duplication. Like Thea King, Charles Neidich chooses the basset clarinet and clearly relishes not only its range but also its colour. In the very spirited finale he produces some captivating lower tessitura, while in the *Adagio* he plays radiantly, after a bright, briskly paced first movement, essentially fresh and spring-like. At the reprise of the main theme in the second movement he drops to pianissimo and then decorates the lovely melody simply and affectionately; this leads to a glorious blossoming as the orchestra takes up the melody. The appropriately named David Jolley is equally personable in the *Horn concertos*. The Rondos are played with a winning flair and crisp articulation while, like his colleague, he can fine his tone down to a pianissimo with striking sensibility, and the slow movement of K.495 is particularly imaginative. A comparable use of light and shade elsewhere makes both performances distinctive, in the accompaniments as well as the solo playing. The recording is very realistic and well balanced, although the definition on the tape is less sharp than the CD.

(i) *Clarinet concerto in A, K.622;* (ii) *Oboe concerto in C, K.314.*
(*) O-L Dig. **414 399-2 [id.]. (i) Pay; (ii) Piguet, AAM, Hogwood.
(*) Ph. **416 483-2. (i) Brymer; (ii) Black, ASMF, Marriner.

Antony Pay's version makes a good alternative choice for anyone wanting to hear this masterpiece on period instruments. In this instance the original instruments include the soloist's basset clarinet, with its extra range allowing Mozart's original solo lines to be followed. Pay is a more restrained, less warm-toned player than his main rivals, with a relatively cool account of the beautiful slow movement; but that is apt for the stylistic aims of the performance. The French oboist, Michel Piguet, is an equally stylish soloist in the *Oboe concerto* on the reverse, providing not a generous coupling but an attractive one. Clean, well-balanced recording, particularly on CD.

The coupling of Jack Brymer's third recording of the *Clarinet concerto* with Marriner and Neil Black's fine version of the *Oboe concerto* is also available on a Philips 'On Tour' tape, offering two more concertos (see above) and costing about a third as much as this CD which, although well transferred, seems poor value by comparison.

(i) *Clarinet concerto;* (ii) *Clarinet quintet in A, K.581.*
*** Hyp. Dig. **CDA 66199**; *KA 66199* [id.]. Thea King, (i) ECO, Tate; (ii) Gabrieli Qt.
(M) **(*) Ph. **420 710-2**; *420 710-4* [id.]. Brymer, (i) LSO, C. Davis; (ii) Allegri Qt.
** RCA **RD 85275 [RCD1-5275]**. Benny Goodman, (i) Boston SO, Munch; (ii) (mono) Budapest Qt.

Thea King's coupling makes an outstanding choice in both media, bringing together winning performances of Mozart's two great clarinet masterpieces. Thea King's earlier recording of the *Quintet* for Saga was for many years a top choice; here she again steers an ideal course between classical stylishness and expressive warmth, with the slow movement becoming the emotional heart of the piece. The Gabrieli Quartet is equally responsive in its finely tuned playing. For the *Clarinet concerto* Thea King – like Antony Pay in his period-instrument recording for Oiseau-

Lyre – uses an authentically reconstructed basset clarinet such as Mozart wanted. Its extra range allows certain passages to be played as originally intended with octave jumps avoided. With Jeffrey Tate an inspired Mozartian, the performance – like that of the *Quintet* – is both stylish and expressive, with the finale given a captivating bucolic lilt. Excellent recording on CD, with the cassette also sounding extremely well, even though it uses iron-oxide stock.

Jack Brymer's second recording of the *Clarinet concerto* with Sir Colin Davis was made in 1965. It has a warm autumnal feeling, and its soft lyricism is appealing in the slow movement. It is full of the detail which marks all Brymer's playing, but there is not quite the magic of the earlier version with Beecham – see above – until a fast speed for the finale brings extra exhilaration, even next to the Beecham version. The *Quintet* is comparably warm and smiling, with a gently expressive *Larghetto* and a genial finale. This is certainly worth considering at mid-price in either format; the sound is bright and fresh.

Benny Goodman's Boston version of the *Clarinet concerto* from the 1950s here comes in coupling, not with the recording of the *Clarinet quintet* he made at the same period, but with his first flirtation with Mozart on record, a transfer of the 78 r.p.m. discs of 1938. Ever correct, Goodman in both performances is on the reticent side as a Mozart interpreter, but the cool purity of the slow movements is classically apt despite the lack of pianissimo, and in the finales his natural exuberance comes out winningly. The transfer of the 1938 recording is indifferent, and the performance with members of the Budapest Quartet no more stylish than Goodman's later one. It would have been preferable to have that original coupling.

Flute concertos Nos 1 in G; 2 in D, K.313–4.
(M) *** Pickwick Dig. **PCD 871**. Judith Hall, Philh. O, Peter Thomas.
(M) *** Pickwick **PCD 807**. Galway, New Irish Chamber Ens., Prieur.

Flute concertos 1–2; Andante in C for flute and orchestra, K.315.
*** Eurodisc **610 130**. Galway, Lucerne Fest. O, Baumgartner.
** Ph. **416 892-2**; (M) *416 244-4* [id.]. Nicolet, Concg. O, Zinman.
*(*) HMV Dig. **CDC7 47643-2** [id.]; *EL 279472-4*. Linde, Linde Cons.

Judith Hall produces a radiantly full timbre. Moreover she is a first-class Mozartian, as she demonstrates in her cadenzas as well in the line of the slow movements, phrased with a simple eloquence that is disarming. There is plenty of vitality in the allegros, and Peter Thomas provides polished, infectious accompaniments to match the solo playing. The *tempo di minuetto* finale of the *G major Concerto* is sheer delight, with the pointed yet gentle staccato of the soloist matched by the articulation of the orchestral strings. The balance is most realistic and the sound overall is in the demonstration bracket. It was a pity that Pickwick didn't run to including the *Andante*, K.315 – but, even so, this issue sweeps the board, irrespective of price.

Needless to say, Galway plays this music superbly and his Pickwick alternative is also a bargain, although he is certainly not preferable to Judith Hall. The accompaniments, ably directed by André Prieur, are reasonably polished and stylish, and the recording (although it gives a rather small sound to the violins) is excellent, clear and with good balance and perspective. It might be argued that Galway's vibrato is not entirely suited to these eighteenth-century works and that his cadenzas, too, are slightly anachronistic. But the star quality of his playing disarms criticism. The slow movement of the *First Concerto* is beautifully paced; the timbre and phrasing have exquisite delicacy, and the pointed articulation in the finale (nicely matched by the orchestra) is a delight. In No. 2 Galway again floats the melodic line of the first movement with gossamer lightness, and after another enchanting slow movement the finale sparkles joyously, with the orchestra once more on top form. The sound is crisp, fresh and well balanced.

Galway's Lucerne performances, issued on the Eurodisc label, derive from the RCA catalogue; they also can be recommended with no reservations whatsoever. This playing, too, has spontaneity, virtuosity, charm and refinement. Galway is well supported by the Lucerne orchestra and the sound is good, though the resonant acoustic means that orchestral detail is less sharply defined. The orchestral playing itself is slightly more refined, but not more spirited. The advantage of this compact disc is that it includes a bonus by way of the *Andante*, K.315. But it also costs more.

The Nicolet/Zinman couplings are available at mid-price on an excellent tape, so the CD seems expensive by comparison, although these are fairly new recordings. The performances are very positive, with the flute balanced well forward and dominating the proceedings, though David Zinman's accompaniments are alert and strong. Both finales are particularly attractive, briskly paced, and the solo playing throughout is expert and elegantly phrased. However, Galway displays a lighter touch generally and is to be preferred.

Hans-Martin Linde conducts, as well as playing the flute. The ensemble of little more than a dozen players is expert and the textures eminently well ventilated. Listening to period flutes, one understands something of Mozart's aversion to the instrument, for the sound though at first appealing is slightly watery. Ultimately this account is let down by a want of flair and exuberance; the general approach is just a little too inhibited to be a strong recommendation. Good recorded sound and well-judged balance. The cassette, however, has a rather misty focus and a bass emphasis.

(i) *Flute concerto No. 1 in G, K.313;* (ii) *Oboe concerto in C, K.314.*
(*) DG **413 737-2; (M) *419 865-4* [id.]. (i) Tripp, (ii) Turetschek; VPO, Boehm.

Highly musical performances, with Boehm in complete rapport with his soloists. But the 1975 sound shows its age a little in these CD transfers, with the string timbre more brightly lit than on the original LP. However, at premium-price this is ungenerous, and the fact that the coupling has appeared on an excellent mid-priced Galleria tape suggests that the CD may also be reissued too.

(i) *Flute and harp concerto in C, K.299. Flute concerto in G, K.622G* (arrangement of *Clarinet concerto*, ed. Galway).
(M) **(*) RCA *GK 89919* [*AGK1 5442*]. Galway, LSO, Mata, (i) with Robles.

The *Flute and harp concerto* has seldom sounded as lively in a recording as it does here, with an engaging element of fantasy in the music making, a radiant slow movement, and an irrepressibly spirited finale. Marisa Robles makes a characterful match for the ubiquitous Galway. The balance of the soloists is forward, but not unrealistically so. The *Flute concerto* arranged from Mozart's masterpiece for clarinet is more controversial; the key of G major as well as Galway's silvery flute timbre make for even lighter results than one might have anticipated. The scintillating finale is especially successful. The recording is admirably bright and clear, and full bodied, too.

(i) *Flute and harp concerto in C, K.299;* (ii) *Oboe concerto in C, K.314.*
(M) **(*) EMI Dig. **CD-EMX 9510**; *TC-EMX 2116* [Ang. **CDM 62027**]. (i) Snowden, Thomas; (ii) Hunt, LPO, Litton.

With distinguished principals from the LPO as soloists and with the young American, Andrew Litton, showing his flair as a recording conductor, the EMI Eminence issue makes an excellent bargain in whatever format, helped by first-rate digital recording. The performance of the *Flute and harp concerto* is the more winning. Where Gordon Hunt in the *Oboe concerto* seems less happy as a concerto soloist than he is in his consistently imaginative playing in the orchestra, the flautist Jonathan Snowden, in collaboration with Caryl Thomas on the harp, is both sparkling and sensitive, a natural soloist, regularly imaginative in his individual phrasing. There is an excellent cassette.

Horn concertos Nos 1 in D, K.412; 2–4 in E flat, K.417, 447 & 495.
(M) (***) EMI mono **CDH7 61013-2** [id.]. Dennis Brain, Philh. O, Karajan.
*** Decca Dig. **410 284-2** [id.]. Barry Tuckwell, ECO.
*** Tel. **ZK8 41272** [id.]. Hermann Baumann (hand-horn), VCM, Harnoncourt.
(M) *** DG **419 057-2**; *419 057-4* [id.]. Gerd Seifert, BPO, Karajan.
**(*) ASV Dig. *ZCCOE 805* [id.]. Jonathan Williams, COE, Schneider.
(*) Ph. Dig. **421 737-2 [id.]. Hermann Baumann, St Paul CO, Zukerman.
** DG **412 792-2** [id.]. Günter Högner, VPO, Boehm.

Horn concertos Nos 1–4; Concert rondo in E flat, K.371.
*** HMV Dig. **CDC7 47453-2** [id.]; *EL 250536-4*. Radovan Vlatkovic, ECO, Tate.
(M) *** Ph. **420 709-2**; *420 709-4* [id.]. Alan Civil, ASMF, Marriner.
(M) ** Pickwick Dig. **PCD 865**. Richard Watkins, City of L. Sinfonia, Hickox.
** Denon Dig. **C37 7432** [id.]. Zdeněk Tylšar, Prague CO.

Horn concertos Nos 1–4; Concert rondo, K.371; Fragment in E, K.494.
(*) CBS Dig. **MK 42324; *MT 42324* [id.]. Dale Clevenger, Liszt CO, Rolla.

Horn concertos Nos 1–4; Fragment in E, K.494a.
*** BBC Dig. **CD 600**; *ZCN 600*. Michael Thompson, BBC Scottish SO, Maksymiuk.
(M) *** Decca *417 872-4* [id.]. Barry Tuckwell, LSO, Maag.
(M) *(*) Nimbus Dig. **NI 5104** [id.]. Anthony Halstead (hand-horn), Hanover Band, Roy Goodwin.

(i) *Horn concertos Nos 1–4;* (ii) *Adagio and fugue in C min., K.546.*
(B) * Sup. **2SUP 0005**. (i) Milós Petr, Musica de Praga, Hlaváček; (ii) Czech CO, Vlach.

An extraordinary profusion of recordings of the four *Horn concertos*, most of them distinguished, reflects their current popularity as the public's favourite Mozart. For many years Dennis Brain's famous 1954 record with Karajan was EMI's best-selling classical LP, and all other versions rest in its shadow. Alas, in its CD format it is a somewhat diminished shadow, for the remastering has been mismanaged; in seeking to achieve greater presence and clarity, the engineers have produced emaciated, shrill violin tone. Fortunately the horn timbre – with full Kingsway Hall resonance – is unimpaired, but the orchestra has lost its bloom and some of its weight. Yet Boyd Neel's oft-quoted comment that Dennis was the finest Mozartian of his generation comes readily to mind as one listens to these performances which have a unique combination of poetry and exuberance of spirit. The glorious tone and phrasing – every note is alive – is life-enhancing in its warmth; the *espressivo* of the slow movements (especially the *Romanza* of No. 4, K.495) is matched by the joy of the Rondos, spirited, buoyant, infectious and smiling. Karajan's accompaniments, too, are a model of Mozartian good manners – there is none of the excessive smoothness that has marred some of his more recent concerto records – and the Philharmonia at their peak play wittily and elegantly. It is a pity the players are so unflattered by the sound (there was nothing wrong with Walter Legge's original analogue master), but the ear adjusts and this remains a unique recorded document.

Barry Tuckwell was the natural successor for the Brain mantle. His easy technique, smooth, warm tone and obvious musicianship command attention and give immediate pleasure. His earlier (1960) set stands up to more recent competition. It includes the *Fragment* from a fifth concerto in E which ends nostalgically where Mozart left it at bar 91. The solo playing is vigorous, spontaneous and lyrically exuberant, and Peter Maag's accompaniments are admirably crisp and nicely scaled, giving his soloist buoyant support. The vintage recording still sounds first rate on an inexpensive Decca Weekend tape, full, clear and very well balanced.

Tuckwell has re-recorded the four concertos digitally – without extra items – and in the new digital set he plays as well as ever and also directs the accompanying ECO, ensuring that the string phrasing echoes the horn in every detail. The orchestra provides crisp, polished and elegant accompaniments, to make a perfectly scaled backcloth for solo playing which again combines natural high spirits with a warmly expressive understanding of the Mozartian musical line. The recording is slightly drier than before but again is very well balanced, very realistic and present. However, this does not improve on the earlier set, which remains a bargain, particularly as it includes an extra, albeit quite short, item.

Among the newer digital versions, that of Michael Thompson is in every way outstanding and there are grounds for suggesting it as a clear front-runner. Thompson demonstrates that the generation following after Tuckwell has something new and fresh to say about these many-faceted works. On the BBC record, Thompson forms a splendid partnership with Jerzy Maksymiuk and the excellent BBC Scottish Symphony Orchestra, of which he became principal horn at the age of nineteen. Clearly, soloist and conductor strike sparks together. Michael Thompson's contribution has great zest. In the Rondo of No. 3, K.447, he infectiously adds an ad lib. roulade while his cadenzas have a comparable spontaneity. First movements are given with striking rhythmic character, slow movements are wonderfully warm with a touch of ardour in the phrasing which never goes too far. The Rondos are breezily good-humoured and, with vividly real recorded sound, this is irresistible.

Radovan Vlatkovic was born in Zagreb and is principal horn of the Berlin Radio Symphony Orchestra. His tone is very full, with the lower harmonics telling more resonantly than is characteristic of a British soloist; there is also the slightest hint of vibrato at times, but it is applied with great discretion and used mostly in the cadenzas. His performances are full of imaginative touches, and he has the perfect partner in Jeffrey Tate, who produces sparkling accompaniments. The strings dance in the allegros and provide gracious elegance in the lyrical music. The *Romanza* of K.447 is more deliberate than usual, but the soloist's flexibility prevents any heaviness, while the Rondos have the lightest rhythmic bounce throughout; the opening movement of No. 1, too, is particularly characterful. All-in-all, another outstanding set, most winningly different from the playing of the British generation. Moreover Vlatkovic includes the *Concert Rondo*, K.371, a substantial bonus. There is a pleasing tape.

For those seeking an authentic approach, Hermann Baumann's Teldec CD provides a stimulating recommendation. Baumann successfully uses the original hand-horn, without valves, for which the concertos were written, and the result is a *tour de force* of technical skill, not achieved at the expense of musical literacy or expressive content. Inevitably, this implies at least some alterations in timbre, as certain notes have to be 'stopped', with the hand in the bell of the instrument, if they are to be in tune. Baumann is not in the least intimidated by this problem; he plays throughout with consummate tonal smoothness and in a totally relaxed manner. He lets the listener hear the stopped effect only when he decides that the tonal change can be put to good artistic effect, as for instance in the Rondo of No. 2 or in his own cadenza for No. 3. Here – in the cadenza – he also uses horn chords (where several notes are produced simultaneously by resonating the instrument's harmonics), but as a complement to the music rather than as a gimmick. The slow movement of No. 3 has one of Mozart's richest melodies and its touch of chromaticism is managed with superb flexibility and smoothness, so that one can only wonder at Baumann's artistry and skill. In short, these are remarkably satisfying performances by any standards. Baumann's execution in the gay Rondos is a delight and his tone is particularly characterful. It is splendid to have such a successful representation of the horn timbre and technique that Mozart would have recognized, and which indeed all nineteenth-century composers would have expected. The 1974 recording has been digitally remastered for CD; while the horn is given added presence and tangibility, the brightness of the strings has brought some roughness of focus, as the original recording was mellow and reverberant. However, it is the astonishing horn playing that is the main interest here, and that is certainly well projected.

Alan Civil has recorded the concertos three times. The finest and freshest were made in 1967 with Kempe (EMI *TC-EMX 2004*) and offer a splendid cassette alternative to Tuckwell's Decca Weekend tape. Civil's most recent set was made in 1973 and includes the *Concert rondo*, an attractive extra piece which is seldom played in public. The recording is obviously more modern and the performances are highly enjoyable, with Sir Neville Marriner's polished and lively accompaniments giving pleasure in themselves. The balance has the effect of making the horn sound slightly larger than life, but on CD the warmly resonant sound, now remastered, has better detail than originally, and there is a very good tape.

Gerd Seifert has been principal horn of the Berlin Philharmonic since 1964, and his warm tone is familiar on many records. His approach to the Mozart concertos has an attractive, simple eloquence based on absolute technical mastery of his instrument. His phrasing and control of light and shade give particular pleasure and he shows here a special feeling for Mozart's lyrical flow, so that the slow movement of the *Second Concerto* and the first movement of the *Third* are memorable. His tone is velvety and warm, his articulation light and neat, and his nimbleness brings an effective lightness to the gay Rondos of the last three concertos and a more robust quality to No. 1. Karajan here almost matches his earlier accompaniments for Dennis Brain, and the orchestral playing is strong in character, although he never overwhelms his soloist. The 1969 recording has been effectively remastered; there is just a hint of over-brightness on the *forte* violins, but this adds to the sense of vitality without spoiling the elegance.

Dale Clevenger not only includes both the *Fragment* and the *Concert rondo* but adds to the interest of his disc by playing just the *First Concerto*, very expertly, on a hand-horn. The other works are played on a modern instrument, yet the timbre is not so very different. All the performances are assured and cultivated – the pointing of the Rondos gives especial pleasure and the accompaniments are rounded and responsive. But the overall effect is more anonymous than with some of his rivals, and though the recording is very good this would not be a first choice.

Nor would the collection of Jonathan Williams on ASV (not yet issued on CD) even though the accompaniments by the Chamber Orchestra of Europe are a delight in themselves, with polished, easily flexible phrasing. Jonathan Williams's timbre is lighter than that of most of his colleagues, but while his playing is hardly self-effacing, his personality does not project strongly except, perhaps, in the finales which are attractively crisp and neat. Undoubtedly Williams is a highly sympathetic Mozartian, but this collection will appeal most to those who enjoy horn tone which is very clearly focused without too much spread. There is a good cassette.

In his newest recording for Philips, Hermann Baumann uses a modern horn and he produces an agreeably broad and richly lyrical flow of sound. His articulation is especially attractive in the finales, which are robust and vigorous. There is no lack of expressive warmth here, but his use of light and shade is less subtle, less imaginative than with Civil or Tuckwell. The *Romanza* of K.495 is more melting in Civil's version. Baumann's most attractive performance is K.417, where the partnership with Zukerman is heard at its finest, with nicely pointed orchestral playing, genially echoed by the solo line. In the finale of K.412, Baumann again astonishes with a sumptuous series of horn chords as part of his cadenza. The recording is of Philips's best quality, warmly resonant, with the CD clarifying detail; this is certainly enjoyable, if not as fascinating as his earlier set using the Bohemian hand-horn.

Richard Watkins has the advantage of first-class modern digital recording on a mid-priced label. He is an expert player and his seamless line in the first movement of *Concerto No. 2*, K.417, which begins his record, shows a genuine Mozartian sensibility. But this easy lyrical flow does mean that slow movements are very limpid and relaxed and even the Rondos, articulated lightly, take wing more gently than usual. Hickox's accompaniments, on the other hand, are efficient and positive; the partnership works well in No. 3, with an attractively spontaneous interplay between horn and orchestra, the *Larghetto* slightly sombre and the finale fast and light. But generally there is a somewhat self-effacing quality to the solo performances which detracts from the music's projection.

Günter Högner plays with much character; no one will be disappointed with the DG issue, which is well recorded and has splendid accompaniments from the VPO under Boehm. However, this would not be a first choice in a very competitive field.

Zdeněk Tylšar is also a stylish Mozartian and he is given neat accompaniments by the Prague orchestra. He is very well recorded, within a rather warmer acoustic than Tuckwell's digital Decca set. The effect of the performances is definitely on a chamber scale; though the solo playing by no means lacks personality (his neat articulation gives special pleasure), other accounts are rather more vivid. Moreover, the touch of vibrato on the lyrical melodies, although applied musically and judiciously, will not appeal to all Western ears.

Anthony Halstead uses a natural, valveless horn in all four concertos and, like others before him, he demonstrates that with the use of stopped notes – here strong and buzzing – Mozart's chromatics can be encompassed securely on the hand-horn without valves. The sound he makes, however, is rather dull in timbre and the playing is seriously lacking in charm. The finales, played with considerable bravura, are certainly spirited; but the lyrical music fails to blossom, not helped by the strings of the Hanover Band which, though articulating neatly, offer the characteristically meagre sustained tone of 'authentic' performances. The rather resonant recording could be better focused.

The bargain-priced Supraphon issue dates from the 1970s and the digital remastering has brought artifically bright lighting to the violins, verging on shrillness. The soloist, Milós Petr, is an excellent artist, but he uses a vibrato which brings euphonium associations in slow movements, especially the *Romanza* of K.447. There is some very good orchestral playing here – the slow movement of K.417 has a striking touch of melancholy – but, with a curious fill-up (a rather solemn version of the *Adagio and fugue for strings*), this is not competitive.

Oboe concerto in C, K.314.
*** ASV Dig. **CDCOE 808**; *ZCCOE 808* [id.]. Douglas Boyd, COE, Berglund – R. STRAUSS: *Oboe concerto.****

Oboe concerto in C, K.314; Arias*: Ah se in ciel, benigne stelle, K.538; Sperai vicino il lido, K.368.*
(*) Ph. Dig. **420 179-2; *420 179-4* [id.]. Heinz Holliger, ASMF, Sillito – FERLENDIS: *Concerto.***(*)

The two most cherishable of oboe concertos by Mozart and Richard Strauss make a delightful, if hardly generous, coupling. Anyone wanting this combination will not be disappointed, when Douglas Boyd is strikingly imaginative in both works. Like his colleagues of the COE, in the Mozart this brilliant young player is never afraid to point the phrasing individually, spontaneously and without mannerism. Others may be purer in their classicism, but this is a very apt reading next to Strauss. Recorded in Henry Wood Hall, the sound is full and vivid. There is a first-rate cassette.

This is Holliger's third recording of Mozart's concerto: his timbre is creamier than ever in the lovely melisma of the *Adagio*, while the finale Minuet-Rondo has the most engaging rhythmic felicity. Holliger makes less of a case for the transposition of the arias. In terms of range and layout they adapt well enough but, without the words, they are much less interesting, and even Holliger's skill with timbre cannot compensate for the absence of vocal colour. The accompaniments are polished and stylish, but the acoustic is perhaps a shade too resonant, although Holliger is naturally balanced and most truthfully recorded. There is an excellent cassette.

Piano concertos (for piano and strings) after J. C. Bach, *K.107, Nos 1 in D; 2 in G; 3 in E flat.*
*** CBS Dig. **MK 39222** [id.]. Perahia, ECO – SCHRÖTER: *Piano concerto.****

Piano concertos: K.107/1–3; Nos 1–6, 8, 9, 11–27; Concert rondos Nos 1–2, K.382 and 386.
❀ *** CBS **M13K 42055** (13) [id.]. Perahia, ECO (with SCHRÖTER: *Concerto*).

Piano concertos Nos 5, 6, 8, 9, 11–27; (i) *Double piano concertos, K.242 and K.365; Concert rondos 1–2.*
(*) Ph. **412 856-2 (10) [id.]. Brendel, (i) Imogen Cooper, ASMF, Marriner.

Murray Perahia's cycle is the first complete set on compact disc. He not only includes the first four derived juvenile works but as an appendix (also available separately) the three concertos written some time between 1765 and 1772, when Mozart would have been nine and fifteen. They are arrangements he made of keyboard sonatas by J. C. Bach. They are slight pieces which can sound quite unremarkable, but Perahia plays them with all the subtlety and poetic feeling they can bear. The results are quite charming, and readers normally unresponsive to them should hear them, particularly *No. 3 in E flat*, in such persuasive hands. The complete set is a remarkable achievement and it is difficult to imagine its being surpassed. In terms of poetic insight and musical spontaneity the performances are in a class of their own. There is a wonderful singing line and at the same time a sensuousness that is always tempered by spirituality. Schnabel's famous dictum, that Beethoven wrote music that was better than it can ever be played, applies to all great music – and every bit as much to Mozart. It is a measure of Perahia's imagination and achievement that, after listening to him in this repertoire, one wonders whether in this case it is true. The CBS recordings have improved since the cycle started and the more recent are excellent – although generally the sound Decca have afforded Ashkenazy has greater bloom and a firmer focus. Wagner spoke of Mozart as 'a genius of light and love'; although there are darker sides to these concertos, one is often reminded of these words in studying this set.

Brendel's 'complete' box (which mixes the earlier analogue recordings with the ten he made digitally) does not include the four early concertos, K.37 and K.39–41, or the three based on J. C. Bach, K.107. The *Lodron concerto* and a handful of others (K.175, K.246, K.413, K.451 and the *Coronation*, K.537) are new; throughout, his thoughts are never less than penetrating. Where analogue recordings have been transferred to CD, the digital remastering has produced clean and successful results. The transfers are consistently of the very highest quality, as is the playing of the Academy of St Martin-in-the-Fields under Sir Neville Marriner.

Piano concertos Nos 1 in F, K.37; 2 in B flat, K.39; 3 in D, K.40; 4 in G, K.41.
*** CBS Dig. **MK 39225** [id.]. Murray Perahia, ECO.
*** HMV **CDC7 47987-2** [id.]. Daniel Barenboim, ECO.

The first four concertos which occupy the present issue date from the spring or summer of 1767, when Mozart was eleven. They draw for their thematic ideas on sonatas by Hermann Raupach, Leontzi Honauer, Schobert, Eckhard and Carl Philipp Emmanuel Bach. Of course, they are not the equal of any of his more mature concertos; however, played, as they are here, with such grace and affection, they make delightful listening. Throughout Murray Perahia's cycle with the ECO, the orchestral playing is imaginative and sensitive, and the CBS recordings are in the very first flight.

Barenboim, too, gives sensitive accounts of all four works. One of the more striking movements is the *Andante* of K.37 (probably based on Schobert), with its 'Scottish snap' rhythmic feature, which obviously caught the young composer's fancy and which is highly effective in Barenboim's hands. The 1975 recording has been most successfully remastered: the piano tone remains very natural and now the orchestral texture sounds fresher and more transparent.

Piano concertos Nos 5 in D, K.175; 6 in B flat, K.238.
(*) Ph. Dig. **416 366-2; *416 366-4* [id.]. Alfred Brendel, ASMF, Marriner.

Short measure perhaps at 43 minutes, but some lively playing from Brendel in these early works. He is brightly recorded, with a rather more forward piano in K.175 than in its companion. There is prose as well as poetry here, but admirers need not hesitate.

Piano concertos Nos 5 in D, K.175; 8 in C, K.246. Concert rondos Nos 1 in D, K.382; 2 in A, K.386.
*** DG Dig. **415 990-2**; *415 990-4* [id.]. Malcolm Bilson, E. Bar. Soloists, Gardiner.

Bilson's coupling of the two early, lightweight concertos with the two *Concert rondos* is apt and attractive, as ever demonstrating the advantages of period performance at their most telling. The *Rondo*, K.382, was intended as an alternative finale to K.175, when the original theme and variations movement can easily outstay its welcome. The modern CD listener can now programme Mozart's alternative version very easily, stylistically inconsistent though it may be. What comes out in these early concertos, perhaps even more pointedly than in later and more individual works, is the expressive tonal range possible on the fortepiano in even the simplest passage-work. Warm, well-balanced recording. There is a good chrome tape, although the resonance does mean that orchestral tuttis are rather less refined than on CD.

Piano concertos Nos 5 in D, K.175; 25 in C, K.503.
*** CBS Dig. **MK 37267** [id.]. Murray Perahia, ECO.

Murray Perahia never loses sight of the space and grandeur of the *C major*, K.503, and has the measure of its strength and scale, as well as displaying tenderness. Perahia invests the landscape with delicate and subtle colourings and there is a sparkle and poetry that is unfailingly affecting. The sheer refinement of keyboard sound is a joy in itself and never narcissistic; at only one point – the F major section of the finale (bar 163 onwards) – does the listener wonder whether Perahia and the wind players of the ECO caress the melodic line in a way that almost steps outside the sensibility of the period. A wonderful performance, however, and coupled with an account of the *D major*, K.175, which has an innocence and freshness that is completely persuasive. The recording is good without being as distinguished as the performance. On CD, the upper strings are a little fierce and not too cleanly focused.

Piano concertos Nos 6 in B flat, K.238; 13 in C, K.415.
*** CBS Dig. **MK 39223** [id.]. Murray Perahia, ECO.

Perahia brings a marvellous freshness and delicacy to the *B flat Concerto*, K.238, but it is in the *C major* that he is at his most sparkling and genial. There have been fine accounts from Haskil, Barenboim and, more recently, Ashkenazy; but in its sense of character and its subtle artistry this is a first recommendation, even if Ashkenazy's Decca recording is better balanced. Perahia's piano is rather more forward and the acoustic ambience less spacious. However, the CBS sound is still very good indeed.

Piano concertos Nos 8 in C (Lützow), K.246; 9 in E flat (Jeunehomme), K.271.
(*) Decca Dig. **414 543-2; *414 543-4* [id.]. Vladimir Ashkenazy, Philh. O.

Thoroughly musical performances from Ashkenazy and the Philharmonia, though some may find the slow movements a little too relaxed. K.271 is not as well held together as in Ashkenazy's delightful LP with Kertesz, made in 1966. However, the playing is still sunny, though with just a trace of 'automatic pilot'. It is less fresh than the Perahia version. Excellent recording on CD and also a particularly good cassette, fresh and wide-ranging.

Piano concertos Nos 8 in C, K.246; 22 in E flat, K.482.
*** CBS *40-76966* [*IMT 35869*]. Murray Perahia, ECO.

Murray Perahia's version of the great *E flat Concerto* is second to none. He has the measure of its scale, and yet every phrase is lovingly shaped too. Perahia is an artist who blends unusual qualities of spirit with wonderful sensuousness; not only does he draw magical sounds from the keyboard, he also inspires the wind players of the ECO, who invest the serenade-like episodes in the slow movement with great eloquence. This is a reading of real stature. It is well recorded, though there is not quite the range and depth that distinguished Perahia's slightly earlier coupling of K. 414 and K.595. The early *C major Concerto* is unfailingly fresh and elegant in his hands. The cassette, on chrome tape, is of good quality.

Piano concertos Nos 8 in C, K.246; 26 in D (Coronation), K.537.
*** Ph. Dig. **411 468-2**; *411 468-4*. Alfred Brendel, ASMF, Marriner.

Brendel's accounts of both concertos have the advantage of well-defined, clean digital recording. As always, his articulation and intelligence excite admiration: everything is well thought out and impressively realized. Only in the slow movement of the *Coronation concerto* does one feel a trace of didacticism. Recommended, though not in preference to the award-winning account from Perahia.

Piano concertos Nos 8 in C, K.246; 27 in B flat, K.595.
* DG Dig. **410 035-2** [id.]. Rudolf Serkin, LSO, Abbado.

Rudolf Serkin is an artist of keen musical intellect; older collectors will recall his K.449 with the Busch Chamber Players with both affection and admiration. This new cycle he is recording with Claudio Abbado and the LSO is not in that league. The opening of K.595 is very measured and spacious, and Serkin's contribution is wanting in the grace he once commanded. There are moments of inelegance (the theme of the slow movement is a case in point) and little real sparkle in the quicker movements. The orchestral playing is a little sluggish, too. The recording is excellent.

Piano concertos Nos 9 in E flat, K.271; 11 in F, K.413.
*** DG Dig. **410 905-2** [id.]. Malcolm Bilson, E. Bar. Soloists, Gardiner.

This was the first to be recorded of a projected complete series of the Mozart keyboard concertos, featuring original instruments and including a copy of Mozart's own concert piano. Malcolm Bilson may have made his reputation as an academic, but here he shows himself a lively and imaginative artist, well matched by the ever-effervescent and alert Gardiner. The recording on CD catches superbly the lightness and clarity of the textures, with the fortepiano sound not too twangy and with wind balances often revelatory. The darkness of the C minor slow movement of K.271 is eerily caught. The lightness of keyboard action encourages Bilson to choose fast allegros, but never at the expense of Mozart.

Piano concertos Nos 9 in E flat, K.271; 17 in G, K.453.
*(*) DG Dig. **415 206-2** [id.]. Rudolf Serkin, LSO, Abbado.

Serkin has a powerful musical mind – but his magisterial reputation should not obscure the fact that his playing is not as supple and refined as it once was. The second group of the first movement of the *G major Concerto*, K.453, is ungainly in presentation and there are other inelegances that diminish pleasure. There are no quarrels with the sound, however, which is very vivid and clear.

Piano concertos Nos 9 in E flat, K.271; 21 in C, K.467.
*** CBS **MK 34562** [id.]. Murray Perahia, ECO.
(B) ** CfP Dig. **CD-CFP 9016**; *TC-CFP 4531.* Stephen Hough, Hallé O, Bryden Thomson.

Perahia's performances date from the mid-1970s, but it would be difficult to fault or surpass them. Perahia's reading of K.271 is wonderfully refreshing, delicate with diamond-bright articulation, urgently youthful in its resilience. The famous *C major Concerto* is given a more variable, though still highly imaginative performance. If the first movement is given charm rather than strength, the opposite is true with the slow movement and finale. Faithful, well-balanced recording.

As in his prize-winning recording for Chandos of two Hummel concertos, Stephen Hough plays with fine freshness, point and clarity; but where in Hummel he gave the works a bigger stature than you might expect, here he tends to prettify two of Mozart's strongest concertos, minimizing their greatness. This delicate, Dresden-china treatment would have been more acceptable half a century ago, but it leaves out too much that is essential. Excellent playing and recording, a fair bargain at CfP price despite the limitations, with very good recording on tape as well as compact disc.

Piano concertos Nos 11 in F, K.413; 12 in A, K.414; 13 in C, K.415.
*** HMV **CDC7 49064-2** [id.]. Daniel Barenboim, ECO.

There is something very persuasive about Barenboim's performances of the earlier concertos, as they re-emerge on CD. The recordings were made over a period: No. 13 comes from 1967, the others from 1972–3; but all three sound very realistic in their CD format, with particularly attractive piano timbre and freshened orchestral sound. K.414 is presented with all his usual flair, but it is the *C major* which is especially memorable, given one of the finest performances of the series. It is full of life, imaginatively phrased, sparkling, thoroughly musical and beautifully shaped, with orchestral playing of the highest order.

Piano concertos Nos 11 in F, K.413; 12 in A, K.414; 14 in E flat, K.449.
*** CBS **MK 34543** [id.]. Murray Perahia, ECO.

Wonderful playing from Perahia and the ECO. The praises of these performances have been sung by us before: they date from the late 1970s and remain in a class of their own. When it first appeared, we thought the *F major*, K.413, the most impressive of Perahia's Mozart concerto records so far, its slow movement wonderfully inward; and the *E flat concerto*, K.449, is the best since Serkin's sparkling pre-war set with the Busch Chamber Players. CD enhances the realism and presence of the sound.

Piano concertos Nos 11 in F, K.413; 16 in D, K.451.
*** Ph. Dig. **415 488-2**; *415 488-4* [id.]. Alfred Brendel, ASMF, Marriner.

As always, Brendel's performances are distinguished by wonderful clarity of articulation: the ideas are always finely shaped without ever being overcharacterized, and the textures are clean and alive. Both recordings were made late in the cycle and are therefore digital; both are refreshing in sound and to the spirit. There is an excellent tape.

Piano concertos Nos 12 in A, K.414; 13 in C, K.415.
*** Decca Dig. **410 214-2** [id.]. Vladimir Ashkenazy, Philh. O.

Vladimir Ashkenazy's account of K.414 and 415 must be numbered among the most successful of his cycle. The *A major* is well served on CD, with splendid versions from Barenboim and Perahia, both of which will give pleasure. Ashkenazy's account admirably combines expressive feeling with sparkle and conveys real enjoyment: he is moreover fortunate in having the benefit of well-defined and transparent recording, superior to that given Perahia. The *C major* has equally strong claims and readers collecting the Ashkenazy survey will not be disappointed. The compact disc is particularly impressive. The piano is forwardly balanced, but the naturalness of timbre and the bloom on the overall sound-picture are such as to confound criticism. The slow movement of K.414 is given memorable depth when the quality is so beautiful and the ambience so attractive.

Piano concertos Nos 12 in A, K.414; 14 in E flat, K.449.
*** DG Dig. **413 463-2** [id.]. Malcolm Bilson, E Bar. Soloists, Gardiner.
(*) Chan. Dig. **CHAN 8455; *ABTD 1166* [id.]. Louis Lortie, I Musici di Montreal, Turovsky.

Malcolm Bilson's coupling of the *'Little A major'*, K.414, and the tough *Concerto in E flat*, K.449, amply confirms the wisdom of choosing him for the Archiv project of recording the Mozart concertos using a fortepiano. Though you might argue that authenticity would demand having no conductor, Gardiner and the English Baroque Soloists prove to be ideal accompanists, matching Bilson's expressiveness on the one hand while on the other relishing the very fast speeds he prefers in finales. The extra clarity of authentic instruments and the small scale here never prettify the music; rather, they make it seem all the stronger in its lean resilience. Excellent recording, fresh and clear.

One of the brilliant young talents highlighted by the 1984 Leeds Piano Competition, Louis Lortie gives sensitive accounts of both concertos, full of natural poetry and imagination. The Montreal players give stylish, resilient accompaniment, and the only questionable point is the reverberant recording, with Chandos's characteristically open acoustic less apt in Mozart than in Romantic music, making the ensemble sound bigger than it is.

Piano concertos Nos 12 in A, K.414; 15 in B flat, K.450.
*(*) Arabesque Dig. **Z 6552**; *ABQC 6552* [id.]. Steven Lubin, Mostly Mozart O.

Steven Lubin made his American recording of Nos 12 and 15 well before he embarked on the much bigger project of recording the Beethoven concertos with Christopher Hogwood. Here, one is much more conscious of the limitations of a fortepiano than in Malcolm Bilson's versions in his complete series with John Eliot Gardiner. That is so both in expressive and in tonal range, with rhythmic interest undermined by fast speeds. Bilson is much to be preferred, if you want period performances.

Piano concertos Nos 12 in A, K.414; 20 in D min., K.466.
*(*) DG Dig. **400 068-2** [id.]. Rudolf Serkin, LSO, Abbado.

Piano concertos Nos 12 in A, K.414; 21 in C, K.467; 27 in B flat, K.595.
(B) *(*) DG Dig. *419 837-4* [id.]. Rudolf Serkin, LSO, Abbado.

Serkin made some distinguished Mozart concerto records way back in the days of shellac; at the beginning of the 1980s he embarked on a new cycle as the eightieth year of his own life was fast approaching. It would be a pleasure to report on the *A major* with enthusiasm, but Serkin's playing is far from elegant and, though there are flashes of authority, the ends of phrases are not beautifully turned. Though his thoughtfulness as an artist is often clear, his passage-work in these performances is scrappy; indeed, the playing is distressingly prosaic with uneven scales. Refined accompaniments from Abbado – the opening of K.595 is measured and spacious – with an excellent response from the LSO, but even there the styles clash, for Serkin is wanting in the grace he once commanded. There are moments of inelegance (the theme of the slow movement is a case in point) and little real sparkle in quicker movements, where the orchestral playing tends to follow Serkin's lead. The recording is bright, clear and full, and this well-engineered chrome tape would seem the most economical way to sample this series. On CD, K.466 offers no real challenge to Perahia, Ashkenazy and Barenboim.

Piano concertos Nos 12 in A, K.414; 21 in C, K.467.
(M) **(*) Decca *417 685-4* [id.]. Radu Lupu, ECO, Segal.

There is much that is beautiful here, including really lovely sounds from the orchestra, and hushed playing from Radu Lupu in the slow movements of both concertos. The music making has life and sensibility, and both performances are very enjoyable. Even if No. 12 is not quite as sparkling as Ashkenazy's account, and there are even finer full-priced versions of K.467, this is excellent value in the mid-price range. The high-level Decca Weekend chrome cassette transfer, however, has brought a brightened treble response, and though the piano timbre is natural the violins are inclined to be fierce above the stave at higher dynamic levels.

Piano concertos Nos 12 in A, K.414; 23 in A, K.488.
(*) Hung. Dig. **HCD 12472 [id.]. Zoltan Kocsis, Liszt CO, Rolla.

Those wanting the two A major concertos could do worse than invest in the Hungaroton version from Zoltan Kocsis and the Liszt Chamber Orchestra. In the 'little' *A major Concerto*, K.414, Kocsis is marvellously sensitive and alert, and he is given excellent support by Janos Rolla. The small forces involved enhance the effect of intimacy, and Kocsis's participation in the orchestral ritornello is eminently discreet. As piano playing, this can hold its own with the best; the performance of K.488 is hardly less impressive. Kocsis is unfailingly vital and imaginative: he shapes the main theme of the second movement with all the finesse and subtlety of Barenboim on HMV, but without the slightest trace of self-indulgence. Unfortunately, the finale is completely rushed off its feet. The recording is a little wanting in opulence and bloom, yet even though it would not be a first choice, there is so much to delight the collector here that it must still have a fairly strong recommendation.

Piano concertos Nos 12 in A, K.414; 27 in B flat, K.595.
*** CBS *40-76731* [*MT 35828*]. Murray Perahia, ECO.

Murray Perahia has the capacity to make the piano breathe and to persuade the listener that the sound he produces is almost independent of any physical agency. Yet this spiritual dimension harmonizes with a flesh-and-blood intensity and strongly classical instincts. Both these performances have great sparkle and a sense of naturalness and rightness: listening to the finale of K.414, one feels it could not be taken at any other speed or phrased in any other way. In K.595, Perahia produces some wonderfully soft colourings and a luminous texture, yet at the same time he avoids underlining too strongly the sense of valediction that inevitably haunts this magical score. There is a sublime simplicity to the slow movement in these artists' hands – for the ECO too seem as inspired as the soloist-director. The cassette has a slightly restricted upper range, but with a bass cut the sound-balance is pleasing, and there is no muffling of the strings.

Piano concertos Nos 13 in C, K.415; 15 in B flat, K.450.
*** DG Dig. **413 464-2** [id.]. Malcolm Bilson, E. Bar. Soloists, Gardiner.

This third record in Bilson's projected complete series of Mozart piano concertos, using a fortepiano at low pitch in unequal temperament, completes the trilogy of works which Mozart wrote in the winter of 1782–3. Festive with trumpets, this last of the group makes a striking impact, despite the modest-sized forces (5, 4, 2, 2, 1 strings). Though Bilson opts for brisk allegros, which emerge with exceptional clarity, he and Gardiner relax well in the central andante and the two adagio episodes of the finale. K.450 brings woodwind to the fore, and the English Baroque players match their string colleagues in stylishness. The recording on CD, nicely balanced without spotlighting – there is a single crossover microphone over the conductor's head – is so vivid you can hear the clicking keys of the wind instruments.

Piano concertos Nos 14 in E flat, K.449; 18 in B flat, K.456.
*(*) Mer. **ECD 84086** [id.]. Diana Ambache, Ambache CO.

A capable, musical and very well-recorded coupling offering music making which would give some satisfaction in the concert hall but which does not compete with the finest records. Diana Ambache is a good rather than an inspired player and does not put a strong personal stamp on either work. She directs both performances from the keyboard; tempi are generally well chosen, but the orchestral playing falls short of real distinction.

Piano concertos Nos 14 in E flat, K.449; 26 in D (Coronation), K.537.
**(*) DG *419 649-4* [id.]. Tamás Vásáry, BPO.

Yet another pianist directing the orchestra from the keyboard. Tamás Vásáry is a fine Mozartian with exemplary taste and judgement, though ultimately these performances do not sparkle quite so much as the finest of their rivals. The *D major*, K.537, is the better of the two, and has grandeur as well as vitality. The quality of the recorded sound is very good indeed, and the transfer of this DG Focus tape reissue is clear and bright.

Piano concertos Nos 15 in B flat, K.450; 16 in D, K.451.
*** CBS Dig. **MK 37824** [id.]. Murray Perahia, ECO.
*** Decca **411 612-2** [id.]. Vladimir Ashkenazy, Philh. O.

These two concertos, written for subscription concerts in March 1774, make an apt and attractive coupling. Perahia's are superbly imaginative readings, full of seemingly spontaneous touches and turns of phrase very personal to him, which yet never sound mannered. This is as near to live music-making as a record can approach. Perahia's version of the *B flat Concerto* has all the sparkle, grace and intelligence one would expect to encounter from this artist; both these performances uphold the special claims this cycle has of being to the 1980s what Edwin Fischer's Mozart concerto records were to the 1930s – that is to say, very special indeed. The recording is absolutely first rate, intimate yet realistic and not dry, with the players continuously grouped round the pianist. Trumpets and timpani in K.451 come out the more sharply.

Needless to say, Ashkenazy's performances also show characteristic sensibility. He takes a more direct view, yet there are many imaginative touches: both slow movements are played very beautifully yet without a trace of narcissism, and the finales sparkle. There is some splendid wind playing from the Philharmonia and the result is consistently clean and refreshing, but rather less individual than Perahia. The Decca sound is first rate, especially on CD.

Piano concertos Nos 15 in B flat, K.450; 21 in C, K.467.
*** Ph. Dig. **400 018-2** [id.]. Alfred Brendel, ASMF, Marriner.

Brendel is fine in K.450 and hardly less so in its companion. The outer movements of K.467 are brisk, but tempo is not in itself a problem. Each detail of a phrase is meticulously articulated, every staccato and slur carefully observed in an almost didactic fashion. The finale sounds over-rehearsed, for some of the joy and high spirits are sacrificed in the sense of momentum.

However, it is curmudgeonly to dwell on reservations when there is so much to delight in these performances. The playing is very distinguished indeed, and so, too, is the recording. In CD form the sound is more present and it is admirably transparent, too.

Piano concertos Nos 15 in B flat, K.450; 22 in E flat, K.482.
* DG Dig. **415 488-2**; *415 488-4*. Rudolf Serkin, LSO, Abbado.

Of course there are felicities in the Serkin/Abbado account of the *B flat* and *E flat Concertos* – but not enough to leaven the heaviness. The DG recording is admirably clean and clear, but Serkin's playing gives little pleasure. No one listening to this would imagine that this was the same Serkin whose playing so captivated listeners to the old Busch Chamber Players' account of the *Brandenburg No. 5*. That sparkled with delight; this is hard work, with only the occasional glimmer of past glories.

Piano concertos Nos 16 in D, K.451; 17 in G, K.453.
*** DG Dig. **415 525-2**; *415 525-4* [id.]. Malcolm Bilson, E. Bar. Soloists, Gardiner.

Bilson's coupling of Nos 16 and 17 brings outstanding examples of his excellent Mozart series using a fortepiano. In K.451, the least popular of the 1784 concertos, the gains are more than usual, with textures so beautifully clarified and the relationship between keyboard and orchestra revealed on record more tellingly than it would be in concert, thanks to shrewd balancing. K.453, as ever, is a delight, with Bilson allowing himself a natural degree of expressiveness within the limits of classical taste. As in the rest of the series he uses apt ornamentation in the slow movements, in the *Andante* of K.451 adding discreetly to the decorations which Mozart himself wrote out for his sister. Warm, well-balanced recording. The cassette, too, is strikingly clear and real, a state-of-the-art transfer.

Piano concertos Nos 17 in G, K.453; 18 in B flat, K.456.
*** CBS **MK 42242** [id.]. Murray Perahia, ECO.
*(*) Decca Dig. **414 289-2** [id.]. András Schiff, Salzburg Mozarteum Camerata Academica, Végh.

The *G major Concerto* is one of the most magical of the Perahia cycle and is on no account to be missed. It is one of the few that can be mentioned in the same breath as the pre-war Edwin Fischer records with the Busch Chamber Players. The *B flat*, too, has the sparkle, grace and finesse that one expects from him. Even if you have other versions, you should still add this to your collection, for its insights are quite special. The CD transfer enhances definition and presence without any loss of the warmth of the original LP.

András Schiff and Sandor Végh are rather ruled out of court because of the excessive resonance of the acoustic, in which the soloist seems lost. Schiff and Végh opt for a rather leisurely tempo in the opening movement of the *G major*, and not every reader will care for the staccato-like Alberti bass to which at times Végh reduces the accompaniment of the opening theme. The ensemble includes such distinguished figures as Aurèle Nicolet, Heinz Holliger and Klaus Thunemann; but the sound is too unfocused to compete alongside the best now available.

Piano concertos Nos 17 in G, K.453; 21 in C, K.467.
*** Decca **411 947-2** [id.]. Vladimir Ashkenazy, Philh. O.

Ashkenazy's performances combine a refreshing spontaneity with an overall sense of proportion and balance. There is a fine sense of movement and yet nothing is hurried; detail is finely characterized, but nothing is fussy. Moreover, the recording is clear and lucid, with the balance between soloist and orchestra finely judged.

Piano concertos Nos 17 in G, K.453; 24 in C min., K.491.
** Ph. Dig. **412 524-2** [id.]. André Previn, VPO.

These are the same two concertos that Previn recorded earlier for EMI with Sir Adrian Boult conducting; in these Philips performances, however, with his favourite Mozartian orchestra, the co-ordination is keener, bringing a natural interplay between soloist and players. Previn is generally a brisk Mozartian, fresh and direct with the crispest rhythmic pointing. The sparkle in the music making prevents the result from seeming rushed, even if some listeners may find the result lacking in charm. Previn offers comparatively little variety of keyboard colour, and dynamics are rarely reduced below *mezzo forte*. Compared with such strong keyboard personalities as Ashkenazy and Perahia, this seems slightly wanting in character, even though spontaneity is not lacking. Both piano and orchestra are superbly recorded in warm Vienna sound.

Piano concertos Nos 17 in G, K.453; 26 in D (Coronation), K.537.
(*) HMV **CDC7 47968-2 [id.]. Daniel Barenboim, ECO.

The *G major Concerto* is phrased most musically and is full of life, but it may be spoilt for some by the unusually brisk tempo Barenboim adopts for the first movement. In some ways he recalls the pre-war Fischer Mozart concerto recordings, but comparison here is not to Barenboim's advantage, for Fischer succeeded in maintaining forward momentum without loss of poise or adopting too fast a tempo. However, Barenboim's account of the *Coronation concerto* must be counted one of the most successful on disc. Altogether this is a fine record, worth acquiring for the sake of the *D major* alone. The digital remastering is highly felicitous, adding presence without impairing the very natural recording of the piano and freshening the orchestral textures.

Piano concertos Nos 18 in B flat, K.456; 19 in F, K.459.
(*) DG Dig. **415 111-2 [id.]. Malcolm Bilson, E. Bar. Soloists, Gardiner.

The fourth of Malcolm Bilson's series brings an account of the *B flat Concerto* which is among the most attractive so far, with buoyantly spirited articulation in the outer movements, briskly paced but never sounding rushed, and the colour of the fortepiano made enticing in the *Andante*, by subtlety of inflexion and imaginative dynamic shading. The performance of *No. 19 in F* is rather more controversial. Gardiner's fast, crisp tempo in the first movement is initially disconcerting and, with the *Allegretto* marking for the second movement observed to the letter, there is less contrast than usual. But again the sparkle of the finale rounds off a reading that is consistent in its freshness and momentum. The clear, naturally balanced recording adds much to the pleasure of this series, especially telling on CD.

Piano concertos Nos 18 in B flat, K.456; 20 in D min., K.466.
** Decca Dig. **414 337-2**; *414 337-4* [id.]. Vladimir Ashkenazy, Philh. O.

Ashkenazy is just a shade wanting in spontaneity in K.456 and does not convey the sparkle and delight that so often distinguish his music making. The *D minor* is not perfunctory but it is not as distinguished as his earlier version with Schmidt-Isserstedt (see below). The Philharmonia sound rather well nourished and the piano looms rather larger in the aural picture than is usual from Decca. In K.466, Curzon or Perahia remain unchallenged.

Piano concertos Nos 18 in B flat, K.456; 24 in C min., K.491.
*(*) DG Dig. **423 062-2**; *423 062-4* [id.]. Rudolf Serkin, LSO, Abbado.

Serkin's performances are for aficionados only. His playing is short on finish and elegance, and this is not offset in the balance sheet by the interpretative insights that distinguished his pre-war Mozart records. Well recorded though it is on tape as well as disc, this playing is just too unsmiling to convey pleasure in K.456 and insufficiently searching in the great *C minor*.

Piano concertos Nos 19 in F, K.459; 22 in E flat, K.482.
*** Decca Dig. **410 140-2** [id.]. Alicia de Larrocha, VSO, Segal.

Alicia de Larrocha can hold her own against most of her rivals in terms of both scale and sensitivity, though her K.482 is perhaps not as completely integrated or as touching as the Perahia which has particularly eloquent playing from the ECO wind. She is on good form, too, in the *F major*; the Decca recording is beautifully transparent and clear, as well as being warmly resonant, which increases the tinge of romantic feeling in these performances. The sound on compact disc is particularly natural, with the upper range smooth yet well defined. Although the ear is drawn slightly to the forward balance of the woodwind, the piano image is most believable, the treble pellucid with no edge.

Piano concertos Nos 19 in F, K.459; 23 in A, K.488.
❀ *** CBS Dig. **MK 39064**; *IMT 39064* [id.]. Murray Perahia, ECO.
*** DG **413 793-2** [id.]. Maurizio Pollini, VPO, Boehm.

Murray Perahia gives highly characterful accounts of both concertos and a gently witty yet vital reading of the *F Major*, K.459. As always with this artist, there is a splendidly classical feeling allied to a keenly poetic sensibility. His account of K.488 has enormous delicacy and inner vitality, yet a serenity that puts it in a class of its own. There is however a robust quality about the finale and a fresh but controlled spontaneity. The slow movement has an elevation of spirit that reaffirms one's conviction that his version is one of the classics of the gramophone. Even in a series of such distinction, this performance stands out. On CD, the sound is particularly fresh and natural, but the chrome cassette has an excess of bass resonance.

The DG is also a distinguished record. Pollini is sparkling in the *F major*, and in the *A major* has a superbly poised, vibrant sense of line. Every phrase here seems to speak, and he is given excellent support from Boehm and the Vienna orchestra. There is no sense of haste in the outer movements; everything is admirably paced. Good, well-detailed and finely balanced analogue recording, which has transferred very well to CD, makes this one of the finest Mozart concerto records DG have given us. Among the K.488s, this must also be ranked very highly.

Piano concertos Nos 19 in F, K.459; 24 in C min., K.491.
*** Decca **414 433-2** [id.]. Vladimir Ashkenazy, Philh. O.

Ashkenazy's account of the *C minor Concerto* is a strong one and must be numbered among the very finest now on the market. He has the measure of the work's breadth and emotional power; his playing, while showing all the elegance and poise one could desire, never detracts from the coherence of the whole. His is a balanced view of the first movement which avoids investing it with excessive intensity yet never loses impact. He is every bit as sensitive as his most formidable rivals (Barenboim and Perahia) in the middle movement and highly characterful in the finale. The *F major Concerto* also comes off effectively; it is subtle and sparkling. Clean, well-focused recording and an orchestral response that does almost as much credit to the pianist as his solo contribution. The CD offers the usual advantages and the transfer of the analogue master cannot be faulted.

Piano concertos Nos 19 in F, K.459; 25 in C, K.503.
*(*) DG Dig. **410 989-2** [id.]. Rudolf Serkin, LSO, Abbado.

If Serkin's 1984 Mozart was as good as the pre-war vintage – or, for that matter, some of the recordings he made at Marlboro in the 1960s – this would be a most valuable coupling. There is much to admire, including a clear and well-focused recording, but he is no match for the current competition; the insights this distinguished Mozartian brings to these concertos do not compensate for the ungainly passage-work and other infelicities. His vocal melisma is also slightly distracting.

Piano concertos Nos 20 in D min., K.466; 21 in C, K.467.
❀ *** DG Dig. **419 609-2**; *419 609-4* [id.]. Malcolm Bilson, E. Bar. Soloists, Gardiner.
(M) *** DG **419 842-2**; *419 842-4* [id.]. Friedrich Gulda, VPO, Abbado.
(*) Ph. Dig. **416 381-2; *416 381-4* [id.]. Mitsuko Uchida, ECO, Tate.

Effective as Malcolm Bilson was in the earlier recordings in his projected Mozart cycle, concentrating on the earlier and smaller works, the real breakthrough, bringing even keener revelation, came with this coupling of two of the later and more expansive masterpieces. Here, even more than before, the benefits of period performance are striking in the way that, along with the extra transparency, the scale of the argument and its dramatic bite, far from being minimized, are actually reinforced. These are vital, electric performances, expressive within their own lights, neither rigid nor too taut in the way of some period Mozart, nor inappropriately romantic. This is a disc to recommend even to those who would not normally consider period performances of Mozart concertos, fully and vividly recorded with excellent balance between soloist and orchestra – better than you would readily get in the concert hall. A good tape, more sharply defined in K.466 than in K.467.

Gulda's record was first issued at about the same time as a TV programme showing Gulda and Abbado rehearsing and playing together. On television Gulda used a Bösendorfer piano (which he has favoured previously in the recording studio), and one suspects that this instrument was used here. The piano tone is clean, crisp and clear, with just a hint of the character of a fortepiano about it. The quality of the tone colour is admirably suited to these readings, which have an element of classical restraint yet at the same time are committed and have no lack of warmth. Abbado's introduction for the *C major Concerto* shows him immediately a first-class Mozartian, and the orchestral wind-playing is delightful. The famous slow-movement melody too is simply phrased, without excess romanticism, and the gay finale makes a perfect foil. The *D minor* is equally well proportioned and only marginally less memorable. The recording (from 1975) has been satisfactorily digitally remastered: there is added clarity and the bass is firmer; there is no loss of ambient bloom, but the upper strings are now very brightly lit. The excellent chrome tape tends to smooth the upper range somewhat, without loss of vividness.

Uchida's coupling of Nos 20 and 21 was the first in her projected series of concerto recordings, following up her stylish and sensitive accounts of the *Piano sonatas*. These are beautiful performances, guaranteed never to offend and most likely to delight, but on the highest level their degree of reticence – despite the superb orchestral work of the ECO under Tate – makes them less memorable than the very finest versions. Excellent sound, on tape as well as CD, though the cassette is rather boomy in the bass. Uchida was due to achieve more striking results in the second of the series, coupling Nos 22 and 23.

Piano concertos Nos 20–21; 24 in C min., K.491.
(B) *(*) HMV *TCC2-POR 54277*. Daniel Barenboim, ECO.

Barenboim's account of K.466 is among his finest Mozart recordings, and K.467 is also highly accomplished. The *C minor* is rather more controversial (see below). The layout of the three works on one extended-length cassette has the advantage of economy, but little else. The sound is generally good, although there is some loss of refinement in K.466 in the upper range of the orchestral tuttis; moreover, there is an irritating side-break after the first movement of K.467.

Piano concertos Nos (i) *20 in D min., K.466;* (ii) *24 in C min., K.491.*
(M) **(*) Decca **417 726-2** [id.]. Vladimir Ashkenazy, (i) LSO, Schmidt-Isserstedt; (ii) Philh. O.
(*) HMV **CDC7 49007-2 [id.]. Daniel Barenboim, ECO.
(*) Ph. **412 254-2 [id.]. Clara Haskil, LOP, Markevitch.
*(*) Ph. Dig. **420 823-2**; *420 823-4* [id.]. John Gibbons, O of 18th Century, Bruggen.

Piano concertos Nos 20 in D min., K.466; 24 in C min., K.491; Concerto rondo No. 1 in D, K.382.
(M) *** Ph. **420 867-2**; *420 867-4* [id.]. Alfred Brendel, ASMF, Marriner.

Brendel's account of the *D minor* originally appeared as a budget-priced sampler for his complete Philips set, coupled with K.488. The two minor concertos are superbly played and the analogue recording is of Philips's best. Perhaps the last ounce of tragic intensity is missing – both works are well represented and one is aware of the intense competition. However, at mid-price with the *D major Rondo* now included, there is nothing to inhibit a three-star recommendation. The cassette, however, is slightly opaque.

The mid-priced Decca reissue recouples recordings from 1968 and 1979. They sound quite different: the *D minor* very immediate and fresh; the *C minor*, more distantly balanced, with sound natural but more diffuse. The great *D minor Concerto* is conducted by Hans Schmidt-Isserstedt and it is a performance of some personality although perhaps a little too regulated in emotional temperature (the *Romance* is rather precise), yet it has no want of vividness and life. Ashkenazy's account of the *C minor* is a strong one and must be numbered among the finest. It has the measure of the work's breadth and emotional power and his playing, while displaying all the elegance and poise one could desire, never detracts from the coherence of the whole. His is a balanced view of the first movement which avoids investing it with excessive intensity, yet never loses impact. He is every bit as sensitive as his most formidable rivals (Perahia and Barenboim) in the middle movement and highly characterful in the finale. With good sound, this is something of a bargain; though some reservations remain about the *D minor*, it is preferable to the later digital version – see above.

Barenboim's performance of *No. 20 in D minor* was the first of his Mozart concerto series with the ECO, recorded in 1967, and his playing has all the sparkle and sensitivity one could ask for. The orchestral accompaniment is admirably alive and one's only serious reservation concerns the somewhat fast tempo he adopts in the finale. K.491 brings a more controversial performance; the very first entry of the piano shows to what a degree Barenboim wants to make it a romantic work. His conviction is unfailing, but some may find the first two movements too heavily dramatized for their taste, while the finale is compensatingly fast and hectic. The digital remastering matches the performance, with the sound vividly bright, the upper range not as natural as in others of this CD series. The effect is much the same in the *D minor*, although the piano timbre remains natural in both works.

Clara Haskil's recordings, made shortly before her death in 1960, were last available on LP in a seven-record set devoted to her Mozart; their reappearance on CD will give particular satisfaction to all her admirers. The poise she brought to Mozart and her effortless sense of style, with no straining after effect, are a source of wonder. Comparing the compact disc transfer with its last incarnation on LP, there is much greater body and clarity of detail – and, of course, greater range. The image is more firmly in focus. The orchestral sound from the Lamoureux Orchestra is certainly beefier than we are used to nowadays from the chamber forces favoured by artists such as Perahia and Ashkenazy, but the playing still remains rather special.

John Gibbons, playing a fortepiano with the Orchestra of the 18th Century, in a live recording, gives readings that are curiously inconsistent. Though the forces used are authentic, the performance-style is unduly heavy, even romantic. The sound is as vivid and well balanced as is possible in a live recording.

Piano concertos Nos 20 in D min., K.466; 27 in B flat, K.595.
*** CBS **MK 42241** [id.]. Murray Perahia, ECO.
*** Decca **417 288-2** [id.]. Clifford Curzon, ECO, Benjamin Britten.

Perahia's 1980 record of the *B flat Concerto* elicited a Rosette (as did Gilels's DG account) in earlier editions, and its qualities well withstand the test of time. He produces wonderfully soft colourings and a luminous texture, yet at the same time he avoids underlining too strongly the sense of valediction that inevitably haunts this magical score. The ECO sound as inspired as their director-soloist, and the CBS sound, always fresh-toned and well balanced, is enhanced by the firmer focus of CD. In the *D minor Concerto*, none of the darker, disturbing undercurrents go uncharted, but at the same time we remain within the sensibility of the period. Not, perhaps, the only way of looking at this work, but a wonderfully compelling one. An indispensable issue.

In September 1970 Sir Clifford Curzon went to The Maltings at Snape, and there with Benjamin Britten and the ECO recorded these two concertos. K.595, the last concerto of all, was always the Mozart work with which he was specially associated; and not surprisingly – when he was the most painfully self-critical and distrusting of recording artists – he wanted to do it again. Just before he died in September 1982, sessions had been organized to make such a recording (as they had on previous occasions), but anyone hearing this magical record, full of the glow and natural expressiveness which always went with Britten's conducting of Mozart, will recognize both performances as uniquely individual and illuminating, with Curzon at his very finest. The coupling was kept from issue until after Sir Clifford's death, but it sounds vivid and well balanced in its CD format. This record also elicited a Rosette in our last edition – and this is a coupling to consider alongside, rather than instead of, Perahia.

Piano concertos Nos 21 in C, K.467; 24 in C min., K.491.
(M) *** Pickwick Dig. **PCD 832**. Howard Shelley, City of L. Sinfonia.

Howard Shelley gives delightfully fresh and characterful readings of both the popular *C major* and the great *C minor* concertos, bringing out their strength and purposefulness as well as their poetry, never overblown or sentimental. His Pickwick disc makes an outstanding bargain, with accompaniment very well played and recorded.

Piano concertos Nos 21 in C, K.467; 23 in A, K.488.
*(*) DG Dig. **410 068-2** [id.]. Rudolf Serkin, LSO, Abbado.

It is sad that Serkin had to leave it until his eighties to attempt a full series of the Mozart concertos. Though his thoughtfulness as an artist is often clear, his playing is distressingly prosaic, with no dynamic less than *mezzo forte*, scrappy passage-work and uneven scales. Refined accompaniment from Abbado and the LSO, but even there the styles clash. There are stronger and more sensitive accounts of both concertos, though few that are better recorded. The compact disc is of first-class quality, even if it reveals some of the soloist's vocal additions.

Piano concertos Nos 21 in C, K.467; 27 in B flat, K.595.
(*) HMV **CDC7 47269-2 [id.]. Daniel Barenboim, ECO.

This is a straight CD reissue of Barenboim's original coupling, first issued early in 1969. There need be no reservations about this account of K.467, which is accomplished in every way. His version of K.595 will be more controversial. He indulges in great refinements of touch, and his reading of the slow movement particularly is overtly romantic. Finer versions of this are available, by Perahia, Curzon and, of course, Gilels.

Piano concerto No. 22 in E flat, K.482.
(M) **(*) HMV **CDM7 69013-2**; *EG 769013-4* [id.]. Sviatislav Richter, Philh. O, Muti – BEETHOVEN: *Concerto No. 3.***(*)

Richter's 1983 recording, like its Beethoven coupling, is both fascinating and controversial; it is well worth exploring at mid-price, particularly as the recording sounds very well indeed, with a firmer focus given to both piano and orchestra within the resonant acoustic than on the original LP. The resonance emphasizes the fact that this is big band Mozart, and Richter is clearly looking forward towards Beethoven, particularly in the slow movement. He plays with all the poise and authority one would expect, and there are numerous felicities. He uses cadenzas by Benjamin Britten. Muti draws lively and sympathetic support from the Philharmonia – though, following Richter's example, the finale is weighty, if not without rhythmic bounce.

Piano concertos Nos 22 in E flat, K. 482; 23 in A, K.488.
*** Ph. Dig. **420 187-2**; *420 187-4* [id.]. Mitsuko Uchida, ECO, Tate.
** HMV Dig. **CDC7 47428-2** [id.]; *EL 270367-4*. Christian Zacharias, Dresden State O, Zinman.

In balance, fidelity and sense of presence, few recordings of Mozart piano concertos can match Uchida's fine coupling of the late *E flat*, K.482, with its immediate successor, the beautiful *A major*. It makes a fascinating match, presenting illuminating contrasts rather than similarities, and Uchida's thoughtful manner, at times a little understated, is ideally set against outstanding playing from the ECO with its excellent wind soloists. Though there are more strongly characterized readings than these, there are few as unobtrusively satisfying. Collectors who have enjoyed her sonata recordings will find this music making equally agreeable in much the same way. There is a first-class chrome cassette.

From Christian Zacharias and the Dresden Staatskapelle under David Zinman we have good, intelligent playing that might well be highly recommendable, were not greater performances available. K.482 is neatly articulated, there is plenty of spirit and no lack of musicianship. (The cadenza – Zacharias's own, with wind interpolations – might not wear well, and his embellishments in the *Andante* of the *A major* may not be to all tastes.) He is sympathetically supported by the Dresden orchestra and very well recorded. However, as far as personality and imagination are concerned, he is not in the same league as Perahia or many others. The XDR iron-oxide tape sounds rather muddy and the orchestra is middle- and bass-orientated.

Piano concertos Nos 22 in E flat, K.482; 24 in C min., K.491.
*** CBS **MK 42242** [id.]. Murray Perahia, ECO.

There have been many fine recordings of the great *E flat Concerto*, but Perahia's is arguably the greatest since the pre-war Fischer version. Not only is his contribution inspired, but the wind players of the ECO are at their most eloquent in the slow movement. The *C minor Concerto* emerges as a truly Mozartian tragedy rather than the foreshadowing of Beethoven that some artists give us. Both recordings are improved in focus and definition in the CD transfer.

Piano concertos Nos 23 in A, K.488; 24 in C min., K.491.
(M) ❀ *** DG **423 885-2**; *423 885-4* [id.]. Kempff, Bamberg SO, Leitner.
(M) **(*) Decca *417 278-4* [id.]. Clifford Curzon, LSO, Kertesz.
(B) **(*) CfP Dig. *TC-CFP 4511*. Ian Hobson, ECO, Gibson.

Curzon's accounts of these two concertos are immaculate, and no connoisseur of the piano will fail to derive pleasure from them. Curzon has the advantage of sensitive support from both Kertesz and the Decca engineers, and only the absence of the last ounce of sparkle and spontaneity prevents this tape from being strongly recommendable. Kempff's outstanding performances of these concertos are uniquely poetic and inspired, and Leitner's accompaniments are comparably distinguished. The 1960 recording still sounds well, and this is strongly recommended on CD and cassette.

Ian Hobson, the fourth-prizewinner in the 1978 Leeds Piano Competition who then came back to win that international event three years later, is generally associated with virtuoso piano music, but here shows himself a stylish Mozartian, if a somewhat reticent one. These are clean, generally refreshing performances, remarkably free of mannerism and lacking only the last degree of individuality. Speeds are unexceptionable, the accompaniment admirable and the sound first rate, making this an excellent cassette bargain, clear and vivid. Hobson contributes his own tasteful cadenza for the first movement of K.491.

Piano concertos Nos 23 in A, K.488; 26 in D (Coronation), K.537.
** Tel. Dig. **ZK8.42970** [id.]. Friedrich Gulda, Concg. O, Harnoncourt.

Like Zoltan Kocsis in his Hungaroton recording of K.488 (see above), Friedrich Gulda discreetly participates in the orchestral ritornelli. The playing of the Concertgebouw Orchestra is careful in handling both balance and nuances, and Nikolaus Harnoncourt is particularly successful in conducting the *Coronation concerto*. Gulda gives an admirably unaffected and intelligent account of the *A major*, which is enjoyable – as, for that matter, is his reading of the *Coronation* – but it does not constitute a challenge to such rivals as Perahia or Brendel.

Piano concertos Nos 23 in A, K.488; 27 in B flat, K.595.
*** Decca Dig. **400 087-2** [id.]. Vladimir Ashkenazy, Philh. O.
(M) *** Ph. **420 487-2**; *420 487-4* [id.]. Alfred Brendel, ASMF, Marriner.

Ashkenazy is on his finest form in both concertos and gets excellent results from both the keyboard and the Philharmonia Orchestra. His *A Major* is beautifully judged, alive and fresh, yet warm – one of the most satisfying accounts yet recorded. No quarrels either with the *B flat*, which is as finely characterized as one would expect. The recording focuses closely on the piano, but nevertheless no orchestral detail is masked and the overall impression is very lifelike in the excellent CD format. Along with Brendel, Perahia and Gilels, this is one of the finest versions of the *B flat*.

On Philips, two of the best of Brendel's Mozart concertos. There is little to add to our comments in earlier editions. Both performances come from the early 1970s and sound wonderfully fresh in these digitally refurbished transfers. Allegiance to Gilels in K.595 remains strong. The Philips chrome tape, too, is first class in every way, vivid and well focused with a most realistic piano image.

Piano concerto No. 23 in A, K.488; Piano sonata No. 13 in B flat, K.333 (K.315c).
*** DG Dig. **423 287-2**; *423 287-4* [id.]. Vladimir Horowitz, La Scala, Milan, O, Giulini.

Playing of such strong personality from so great an artist is self-recommending. With both Horowitz and Arrau there are occasional reminders of the passage of time, but they are astonishingly few, and the artistry remains undiminished. The Busoni cadenza is an unusual (and far from unwelcome) feature of the concerto. As usual the piano is tuned within an inch of its life, and the slightly shallow sound of the instrument is not solely due to the engineers. This is very much Horowitz's record – and at times in the finale there is not too much of the orchestra, nor is there much sign of rapport between Horowitz and Giulini! Still, this is remarkable piano playing, quite unlike any other, and in the *Sonata* not free from affectation. In the concerto, the recording is synthetic and dryish; the *Sonata* is slightly less constricted but far from first rate. The cassette reflects the CD pretty faithfully.

Piano concerto Nos 24 in C min., K.491; 27 in B flat, K.595.
(*) HMV **CDC7 47432 [id.]; *EL 270415-4.* Christian Zacharias, N. German RSO, Wand.

There are many felicitous touches from Christian Zacharias and the NDR Orchestra under Wand, and there need be no complaints about the clarity of the recording. There is also a good cassette. Zacharias is being strongly promoted in Germany, and there is no doubting his musical accomplishment. He plays both concertos elegantly and thoughtfully, and he produces some refined dynamic shadings. In many ways these performances are more interesting than his accounts of K.482 and K.488 – not that they displace existing recommendations and in no way challenge Gilels in K.595 or Perahia in K.491.

Piano concertos Nos 25 in C, K.503; 26 in D (Coronation), K.537.
*** DG Dig. **423 119-2; 423 119-4** [id.]. Malcolm Bilson, E. Bar. Soloists, Gardiner.
*** Decca Dig. **411 810-2** [id.]. Vladimir Ashkenazy, Philh. O.
** HMV Dig. **CDC7 49226-2** [id.]; *EL 270646-4.* Christian Zacharias, Bav. RSO, Zinman.
** Tel. Dig. **ZK8 42970** [id.]. Friedrich Gulda, Concg. O, Harnoncourt.

Malcolm Bilson's coupling of the great *C major Concerto*, K.503, and the *Coronation concerto* brings home how powerful period performances of Mozart on a fortepiano can be. With Gardiner and the English Baroque Soloists also taking a dramatic view – biting down sharply on the repeated chords of the first movement – the magnificent scale of the work is formidably established. The *Coronation concerto*, which can seem merely decorative after the great works preceding it, is presented strongly as well as elegantly, with the authentic timpani cutting dramatically through the textures in the first movement. Full and spacious recording in a helpful acoustic.

Ashkenazy obviously sees K.503 as a 'big' concerto; his opening is on the grandest scale, emphasized by the weighty bass response of the recording. It is a strong reading, set in relief by the more delicate feeling of the *Andante*. Perahia establishes no less command but with a lighter orchestral texture, and his account is more imaginatively distinctive. However, Ashkenazy has much superior recording in every respect. Although the Philharmonia strings are brightly lit they are clearly focused and woodwind detail is glowing, while the piano timbre is most beautiful. In the *Coronation concerto* Ashkenazy's approach to the first movement is comparably magisterial, while he produces some exquisitely shaded playing in the *Larghetto*, with the final *Allegretto* hardly less refined. Again the Decca recording is of the highest quality on CD; Perahia – though less beautifully recorded – is even finer, but those wanting Ashkenazy's coupling should not be disappointed.

There is some very fine playing from the gifted young German pianist, Christian Zacharias, in both these concertos and he is eminently well supported by the Bavarian Radio Orchestra under David Zinman. Zacharias composed his own cadenzas, and they are in good taste and style. Although it is difficult to fault playing of such accomplishment (and no one wants to), there is something slightly prim and well-bred about these performances. The second group of the first movement of the *C major Concerto* is sensitively shaped – but how much more smiling it is in the Barenboim or Perahia accounts. There is much to admire, and the recording is excellent; in its own right it will give pleasure, but it is not a first choice.

With Harnoncourt drawing fresh-textured playing from the Concertgebouw, Gulda gives characterful, alert performances of both concertos. He is particularly successful in the decorative *Coronation concerto*, bringing flair to all three movements. The first movement of the great *C major*, however, is on the ponderous side at a slowish speed, while (like many others) Gulda treats the central *Adagio* as an *Andante*. In both works he makes continuo contributions to the tuttis, as well as letting out the occasional vocal comment.

Piano concertos Nos 25 in C, K.503; 27 in B flat, K.595.
(M) ** DG **419 479-2**; *419 479-4* [id.]. Friedrich Gulda, VPO, Abbado.

These performances come from the mid-1970s, and this coupling is not nearly as attractive as its companion offering Nos 20 and 21. Gulda is a strangely cool pianist at times, though he disciplines his responses splendidly, and there is no basic want of feeling or finesse as, for instance, in the second group of the first movement of K.503, although overall there is a lack of charm. There are felicitous moments elsewhere, but the account of K.595 does not compare with the finest available, in spite of very good playing from the Vienna Philharmonic. The digital transfer is bright and clear, but there is also a certain shallowness of sonority and want of bass.

Piano concerto No. 26 in D (Coronation), K.537; Concert rondos, Nos 1 in D, K.382; 2 in A, K.386.
*** CBS Dig. **MK 39224** [id.]. Murray Perahia, ECO.

Perahia's award-winning account of the *Coronation concerto* is a performance of stature. He succeeds in making the work mean more than do most of his rivals, and the dignity and breadth of his reading are matched in the slow movement by enormous delicacy and sensibility. This is a magical performance in which the level of inspiration runs high. The concerto is coupled with superb accounts of the two *Concert rondos*, K.382 and K.386, which incorporate for the first time on record the closing bars newly discovered by Professor Alan Tyson. The recording is naturally balanced within a fairly resonant ambience; on CD, detail is refined and the piano image very tangible.

Piano concerto No. 27 in B flat, K.595; (i) Double piano concerto in E flat, K.365.
❀ (M) *** DG **419 059-2**; *419 059-4* [id.]. Emil Gilels, VPO, Boehm, (i) with Elena Gilels.

Gilels playing Mozart is in a class of his own. His is supremely lyrical playing that evinces all the classical virtues. No detail is allowed to detract from the picture as a whole; the pace is totally unhurried and superbly controlled. There is no point-making by means of agogic distortion or sudden rapt pianissimo; all the points are made by means of articulation and tone, and each phrase is marvellously alive. The slow-movement theme, for example, is played with a simplicity that is not arch, as it is in some performances; nor is it over-refined in tone; the result gives added depth and spirituality. This is playing of the highest order of artistic integrity and poetic insight, while Boehm and the Vienna Philharmonic provide excellent support. The performance of the marvellous *Double concerto* is no less enjoyable. Its mood is comparatively serious, but this is not to suggest that the music's sunny qualities are not brought out, and the interplay of phrasing between the two soloists is beautifully conveyed by the recording without exaggerated separation. The quality both on CD and on tape is first class, and this is certainly one of the very finest Mozart piano concerto couplings in the catalogue. The digital remastering has been strikingly successful, refining detail yet not losing ambient warmth.

Double piano concerto in E flat, K.365; Triple piano concerto in F (Lodron), K.242 (arr. for 2 pianos).
*** Ph. **416 364-2** [id.]. Alfred Brendel, Imogen Cooper, ASMF, Marriner.
(M) **(*) EMI Dig. *TC-EMX 2124* [Ang. **CDC 47473**]. Christoph Eschenbach, Justus Frantz, Helmut Schmidt, LPO, Eschenbach.

Brendel chooses Mozart's own version of the so-called *Lodron triple concerto*, for two pianos, and couples it with the splendid *E flat Double concerto*. The playing is cultured and elegant, strikingly poised – particularly in K.242 – combining vigour with tonal refinement. Marriner's accompaniments are comparably polished and the Philips engineers afford the music making a most natural sound-balance in the CD format. The analogue recording of K.365 dates from 1977; K.242 is digital and was made in 1984.

Eschenbach's version of the *Double concerto* which he directs from the keyboard is the only one to include the clarinets, trumpets and timpani published in the orchestral material by Breitkopf & Härtel in 1881. These instruments were added for the Vienna performance of 1781, but there is some doubt as to their authenticity. Both Eschenbach and Frantz are lively and persuasive in the concerto, though comparison with the Gilels version on DG, coupled with K.595, is not to their advantage: that is a glorious record. In the *Triple concerto* the third pianist is Helmut Schmidt, at the time of the record Chancellor of West Germany, who makes a creditable showing. The digital recording is very good indeed in both formats, but the coupling does not displace Gilels in K.365. At the moment, this is available on CD only in the USA.

(i) *Triple harpsichord concerto in F, K.242; Harpsichord concertos* (after J. C. Bach) *K.107, Nos 1 in D; 3 in E flat.*
** Denon Dig. **C37 7600** [id.]. Huguette Dreyfus, (i) Baumont, Kiss; V. Capella Academica, Melkus.

There seems no special reason for preferring the so-called *Lodron triple concerto* on three harpsichords rather than on three fortepianos (or, indeed, pianos), but those attracted to the earlier keyboard instrument will find the present account well managed and well recorded. The two solo works, based on sonatas by J. C. Bach, are admirably suited to the harpsichord, and Huguette Dreyfus plays them sympathetically. The accompaniments are sound and the balance is very good.

Violin concertos Nos 1–5; Adagio in E, K.261; Rondos Nos 1–2, K.269 and 373.
(*) DG Dig. **419 184-2 (3) [id.]. Itzhak Perlman, VPO, Levine.

Perlman gives characteristically assured virtuoso readings of these concertos of Mozart's youth, which, with Levine as a fresh and undistracting Mozartian, bring exceptionally satisfying co-ordination of forces. The virtuoso approach sometimes involves a tendency to hurry, and the power is emphasized by the weight and immediacy of the recording. Warmth is here rather than charm; but Perlman's individual magic makes for magnetic results all through, not least in the intimate intensity of slow movements.

Violin concertos Nos 1 in B flat, K.207; 2 in D, K.211; 3 in G, K.216.
** Novalis **150 012-2**; *150 012-4*. Dmitri Sitkovetsky, ECO.

Violin concertos Nos 1 in B flat, K.207; 2 in D, K.211; Rondo No. 1 in B flat, K.269.
*** Denon Dig. **C37 7506** [id.]. Jean-Jacques Kantorow, Netherlands CO, Hager.

Violin concertos Nos 1 in B flat, K.207; 2 in D, K.211; 4 in D, K.218.
*** Ph. **416 632-2** [id.]. Arthur Grumiaux, LSO, C. Davis.

Violin concertos Nos 1 in B flat, K.207; 4 in D, K.218.
(*) HMV Dig. **CDC7 47431-2 [id.]; *EL 270414-4*. Frank Peter Zimmermann, Württemberg CO, Faerber.

Violin concerto No. 1; Adagio in E, K.261; Rondos Nos 1, K.269; 2, K.373.
*** DG Dig. **415 958-2**; *415 958-4* [id.]. Itzhak Perlman, VPO, Levine.

Violin concerto No. 1; (i) *Sinfonia concertante in E flat for violin, viola and orchestra, K.364.*
** DG Dig. **413 461-2** [id.]. Gidon Kremer; (i) Kashkashian; VPO, Harnoncourt.

Violin concerto No. 2 in D, K.211.
(*) Ph. Dig. **412 718-2 [id.]. Isabelle Van Keulen, Netherlands CO, Ros-Marba – HAYDN: *Concerto in C.***(*)

Violin concerto No. 2; Adagio in E, K.261; Rondos Nos 1, K.269; 2, K.373.
(*) HMV Dig. **CDC7 49227-2 [id.]. Frank Peter Zimmermann, Württemberg CO, Faerber.

Violin concerto No. 2; (i) *Sinfonia concertante for violin and viola in E flat, K.364.*
(*) Argo Dig. **411 613-2 [id.]. Iona Brown; (i) Suk; ASMF, Marriner.

Perlman's version of K.207 is first class in every way and, like the particularly graceful account of the *Adagio*, K.261, and the two engaging *Rondos*, comes from his 1986 complete set. Accompaniments are beautifully played and perfectly integrated in a recording which is ideally balanced and very truthful. The cassette has slightly less sharpness of definition, but is pleasingly smooth.

Kantorow's coupling makes an excellent start to his Mozart series. He is given alert, stylish accompaniments by Leopold Hager and the Netherlands Chamber Orchestra, and the recording is eminently realistic, with the balance of the soloist only a trifle too close. Kantorow's full personality emerges gradually in the first movement of K.207, although he plays strongly with a fine classical spirit. The *Adagio* is beautifully done, and the presto finale sparkles. The account of K.211 is splendid in all respects, with a warmth and serenity in the *Andante* balanced by the character of the first movement and the elegant vivacity of the finale. The *B flat Rondo* makes an excellent bonus. Kantorow plays his own cadenzas – and very good they are. Highly recommended.

Grumiaux's celebrated set of the Mozart concertos was made in 1962 (save for No. 2, which was recorded three years later) and has long – and rightly – enjoyed classic status. His tone has real nobility and purity, and there is an aristocratic quality that stands out in an age of excessive sweetness and vibrato. As one would expect with such a Mozartian as Sir Colin Davis, the LSO provide excellent support. Grumiaux plays his own cadenzas in all but the first movement of No. 4 (when he uses the Ysaye). The recordings sound remarkably fresh and belie their years.

Frank Peter Zimmermann is a highly talented young German whose earlier accounts of the *G major* and *A major Concertos* won golden opinions. Now he has completed the cycle most impressively; though his interpretations do not quite match those of Perlman, Grumiaux or, among recent comers, Cho-Liang Lin, no one investigating them will be disappointed. They are distinguished by fine musicianship and an effortless technical command. He uses cadenzas by Zukerman and Oistrakh in No. 2 and Joachim in No. 4. The recordings have agreeable warmth and freshness and are excellently balanced, and there is a very good cassette. Jörg Faerber is an excellent partner and gets extremely alive playing from the Württemberg orchestra.

Iona Brown's account of the *D major Concerto* is also a fine one, even more positively classical in spirit, with striking vitality in the outer movements. The Brown/Suk partnership works well in the *Sinfonia concertante*, but there is an element of restraint in the slow movement which does not quite blossom here in the different ways one experiences with Zukerman and Perlman (on DG) or Brainin and Schidlof (on Chandos) – see below. Nevertheless these are both fine performances; if the coupling is more suitable, there are no grounds for complaint about the sound, which is fresh and clear. The CD gives realistic projection, but the ambience is not as warming as on some Argo recordings.

Many readers will recall Isabelle van Keulen as the winner of the European Young Musician of the Year in 1984 when, aged only eighteen, she gave an impressive account of a Vieuxtemps concerto. She is hardly less persuasive in Mozart, though there is formidable competition from Iona Brown and the Academy of St Martin-in-the-Fields on Argo. The Philips recording is excellently balanced and very vivid, particularly in the compact disc format, but the playing of the Netherlands Chamber Orchestra under Antoni Ros-Marba is a little deficient in character and vitality, by the side of Marriner's Academy. The agreeably warm ambience is more flattering than the Argo acoustic.

Dmitri Sitkovetsky is a very natural player whose virtuosity is as striking as his musicianship. As well as playing, he also directs the ECO in performances that are unaffected in manner and impeccable in technique. At the same time there is perhaps less personality in evidence than in the case of some rivals (Perlman and Grumiaux, for instance) and though these are good performances they do not resonate in the memory or captivate the listener.

Neither of the Kremer performances is especially individual, though the playing is expert. For all the finesse of the soloist, the *B flat Concerto* is curiously uninvolving, and the digital recording is inclined to be fierce in the treble. There are much more rewarding accounts of the *Sinfonia concertante* available – see below.

Violin concertos Nos 2 in D, K.211; 3 in G, K.216.
(*) DG Dig. **415 482-2; *415 482-4* [id.]. Gidon Kremer, VPO, Harnoncourt.

Violin concertos Nos 2, K.211; 4 in D, K.218.
*** HMV Dig. **CDC7 47011-2** [id.]. Anne-Sophie Mutter, Philh. O, Muti.
*** DG Dig. **415 975-2**; *415 975-4* [id.]. Itzhak Perlman, VPO, Levine.

(i) *Violin concertos Nos 2; 5 (Turkish), K.219;* (ii) *Divertimento for string trio in E flat, K.563.*
(B) **(*) DG Walkman *423 289-2* [id.]. (i) Wolfgang Schneiderhan, BPO; (ii) Italian String Trio.

Anne-Sophie Mutter followed up her famous record of the *G Major*, K.216, and *A Major*, K.219, with Karajan on DG – see below – with the two D major concertos on HMV and a different orchestra and conductor. The results are hardly less successful. She is given very sensitive support from the Philharmonia under Muti. Her playing combines purity and classical feeling, delicacy and incisiveness, and is admirably expressive. Its freshness too is most appealing and she is a strong contender in a very competitive field. The HMV recording is very good indeed; on CD the images are sharply defined, but the balance is good.

Perlman's coupling, taken from his complete set with the Vienna Philharmonic and James Levine on DG, is second to none. There seems a total artistic rapport between soloist and orchestra; Perlman's virtuosity is effortless and charismatic, and the orchestral playing is glorious. Moreover the DG recording is well balanced with Perlman forward but not excessively so; the acoustic has warmth and the perspective is on the whole well judged. There is an extremely vivid cassette – a state-of-the-art transfer.

Harnoncourt is nothing if not inconsistent in his approach to Mozart. His opening movement of K.211 is brisk and clean, then the slow movement is purposefully moulded. In the *G major*, K.216, the first movement flows at just the right pace and then in the *Andante* a comma is placed to romanticize the climbing opening phrase of the main theme. With Kremer playing sweetly throughout, this is undoubtedly beguiling and both finales are attractively spirited, with some fine wind solos from the Viennese players. There is a liberal sprinkling of cadenzas; that in the first movement of the *G major* seems a shade long. The recording, made in the Musikverein, is pleasingly warm with the cassette focus markedly softer than the CD. With all its idiosyncrasies this is certainly enjoyable when the solo playing is so neat and assured.

Schneiderhan's performances come from a complete set, made with the Berlin Philharmonic Orchestra at the end of the 1960s. He plays with effortless mastery and a strong sense of classical proportion. The Berlin orchestra accompany well for him, though there is a slightly unsmiling quality at times. The Walkman tape transfers are very successful, smooth and vivid. The recording of the masterly *Divertimento for string trio* also sounds well in its tape format. The performance is remarkable for its accuracy of intonation. The Italian String Trio is a wonderfully polished group – in a sense too polished, for their trim, fast speeds reveal rather too little temperament. Even so, this is highly acceptable when it is so generously coupled.

Violin concerto No. 3 in G, K.216.
(B) ** DG Walkman *415 332-4* [id.]. Wolfgang Schneiderhan, BPO – BEETHOVEN: *Triple concerto*; BRAHMS: *Double concerto*.**

Violin concertos Nos 3, K.216; 4 in D, K.218.
(*) CBS **MK 42030 [id.]. Zino Francescatti, Columbia SO, Walter.

Violin concertos Nos 3, K.216; 4 in D, K.218; 5 in A (Turkish), K.219.
(B) ** CBS *40-39799*. Pinchas Zukerman, ECO, Barenboim.

Violin concertos Nos 3 in G, K.216; 5 in A (Turkish), K.219.
*** DG **415 327-2** [id.]. Anne-Sophie Mutter, BPO, Karajan.
*** HMV Dig. **CDC7 47426-2** [id.]. Frank Peter Zimmermann, Württemberg CO, Faerber.
(*) DG Dig. **410 020-2 [id.]. Itzhak Perlman, VPO, Levine.
(*) Ph. **412 250-2 [id.]. Arthur Grumiaux, LSO, C. Davis.
(*) Denon Dig. **C37 7504 [id.]. Jean-Jacques Kantorow, Netherlands CO, Hager.
(M) **(*) Decca *417 876-4*. Mayumi Fujikawa, RPO, Weller.
** BIS Dig. **CD 282** [id.]. Kim Sjøgren, Copenhagen Coll. Mus., Schønwandt.
*(*) CBS Dig. **CD 37290** [id.]. Pinchas Zukerman, St Paul CO.

Violin concertos Nos 3, K.216; 5 (Turkish); Adagio in E, K.261.
*** CBS Dig. **MK 42364**; *MT 42364* [id.]. Cho-Liang Lin, ECO, Leppard.

Lin's version of this favourite coupling brings a substantial makeweight in the *E major Adagio* which was the nineteen-year-old's first idea for a slow movement for K.219. The Salzburg concertmaster inexplicably found it 'too studied', and Mozart duly obliged with the bigger-scale movement that we know. The advantage on CD is that one can programme that concerto either way, and Lin's persuasive style brings out the tenderness of both slow movements. There is an element of youthful lightness running through these performances of both concertos, though there is no lack of bite and point either. Lin is full of fancy and imagination, apt for the music of a teenager, and only the first movement of K.216 brings a performance less fresh and sparkling on some details. Leppard and the ECO are the most responsive of partners, and the recording is first rate. There is a good tape, well balanced, though some of the upper range is lost.

Extraordinarily mature and accomplished playing from Anne-Sophie Mutter, who was a mere fourteen years of age when her recording was made. The instinctive mastery means that there is no hint of immaturity: the playing has polish, but fine artistry too and remarkable freshness. The lovely phrasing in the slow movements of both works is matched by an engaging spring in the first movement of K.219, with the 'Turkish' interlude in the finale also sparkling vividly. It goes without saying that she receives the most superb orchestral support from the Berlin Philharmonic. Karajan is at his most sympathetic and scales down the accompaniment to act as a perfect setting for his young soloist. The analogue recording is beautifully balanced, and on CD detail is enhanced and the imagery made firmer.

On their first appearance we found Zimmermann's highly intelligent performances thoughtful without being in the least self-conscious . . . alive in feeling, with finely spun tone and keenly articulated rhythms. The soloist was nineteen at the time of this recording and possesses a sensitive musical personality. On CD they sound every bit as fresh and appealing, and the playing of the Württemberg orchestra under Jörg Faerber is first rate. Not necessarily a first recommendation, but certainly among the first.

Francescatti's coupling of the *Third* and *Fourth* Mozart *Concertos* is probably his finest record, and in their remastered CD format these fine performances from 1959 are given a new lease of life. The playing is at times a little wayward, but Bruno Walter accompanies throughout with his usual warmth and insight and falls into line sympathetically with his soloist. Both slow movements are beautifully played, albeit with an intensity that barely stops short of Romanticism, and the changing moods of the finale in the *G major Concerto* are admirably contrasted. In some ways the *D major* suits Francescatti's opulent style of playing best of all, and there is a warm glow about the second subject of the first movement – a sinuous and enchanting tune – that almost reminds one of Kreisler, while in both works the cadenzas are made a most attractive feature. The whole atmosphere of this music making represents the pre-authentic approach to Mozart at its most rewarding. The sound is just right for the music, warm and full with no apologies for the ample orchestral textures.

With the violin balanced rather close, Perlman treats the two most popular of the Mozart violin concertos rather more as virtuoso showpieces than is common. For some the tone will be too sweet for Mozart, and though with sympathetic accompaniment these are both enjoyable performances, they have not quite the natural felicity that marks Perlman's finest work on record. Full digital recording which brings out the idiosyncrasy of the balance. This is noticeable on the compact disc, where one hears also that the woodwind is somewhat reticent. On the CD the sound is strikingly clear and clean, but there is just a touch of digital edge on top.

Grumiaux's classic accounts from the early 1960s still sound excellent. His playing is beautifully finished and intonation is impeccable. Sir Colin Davis gives spirited and sensitive support. However, with only the two concertos offered, this is short measure for a full-priced CD – it would be more competitive at mid-price.

Jean-Jacques Kantorow is a highly intelligent player and has obviously studied these scores with meticulous care. In his hands they come up very freshly indeed. Kantorow uses the Ysaye cadenzas, which are shorter. In a way his are the best thought-out of the present set, though in terms of personality and tonal beauty others are to be preferred.

Mayumi Fujikawa is a first-class artist. Her timbre may be small-scale, but it is silvery and sweet without cloying; this is very fine Mozart playing, with both slow movements showing a natural Mozartian sensibility. Excellent accompaniments, polished and alive, from Weller and the RPO, are supported by very good sound: this Decca Weekend tape is excellent value.

Kim Sjøgren is little known to collectors outside the Scandinavian countries but he is obviously a player to watch. His are very musical performances that are well worth considering – and well worth anyone's money. Schønwandt also gets good results from his Danish ensemble and for those bored with the big glamorous names, this could be a refreshing change.

Schneiderhan's is a finely wrought performance, strongly classical and well recorded for its period. He plays his own cadenzas and although there is a slight want of sparkle, and perhaps also the atmosphere is a shade cool, the reading is still thoroughly enjoyable. The Walkman tape is well engineered and offers generous couplings.

The CBS tape from Zukerman is in the same price-range as the DG Walkman and certainly offers good value for money as the sound is warm and pleasing. However, Barenboim's direction is at times very romantic. The slow movement of K.218 is played with an almost cloying warmth, and the finale, also taken slowly, is affectionate to the point of self-indulgence. The character of the *Turkish concerto* is markedly brighter and more extrovert.

In his later digital recording Zukerman directs as well as playing, His admirers will not be disappointed, though his sweet tone and effortless facility do not always engage one's sympathies. He languishes lovingly in the slow movements, particularly that of the *G major*, and is not always subtle in his projection of feeling. The St Paul's orchestra obviously consists of some fine players, and the CBS recording is very fine indeed. There is much to admire here, but this would not be a first choice. The cassette is smoothly transferred but the upper range is rather restricted.

Violin concerto No. 4 in D, K.218; Adagio in E, K.261; Rondos for violin and orchestra Nos 1 in B flat, K.269; 2 in C, K.373.
** CBS **MK 37839** [id.]. Pinchas Zukerman, St Paul CO.

Violin concerto No. 4; Adagio, K.261; Rondo No. 2, K.373; (i) *Concerto for violin and forte-piano, K. Anh. 56/315f* (fragment); (ii) *Sinfonia concertante in A, K. Anh. 104/320e* (fragment).

(*) Denon Dig. **C37 7505 [id.]. Jean-Jacques Kantorow, (i) Glen Wilson, (ii) Vladimir Mendelssohn, Mari Fujiwara; Netherlands CO, Hager.

Violin concertos (i) *Nos 4, K.218;* (ii) *5* (*Turkish*), *K.219.*

*** Nimbus Dig. **NIM 5009**. Oscar Shumsky, Scottish CO, Yan Pascal Tortelier.

(M) *** RCA *GK 85250* [*AGK1 5250*]. Jascha Heifetz, (i) New SO, Sargent; (ii) with CO.

(M) **(*) HMV **CDM7 69064-2** [id]. David Oistrakh, BPO.

** Novalis **150 007-2**; *150 007-4* [id.]. Dmitri Sitkovetsky, ECO.

Violin concerto No. 5 (*Turkish*), *K.219.*

(M) *** DG **423 211-2**; *423 211-4* [id.]. Anne-Sophie Mutter, BPO, Karajan – MENDELSSOHN: *Concerto.****

Shumsky's performances with the Scottish Chamber Orchestra have the advantage of being totally unaffected, natural and full of character. He seems to have an excellent rapport with Yan Pascal Tortelier who secures a very alive and thoroughly musical response from the Scottish Chamber Orchestra. They do not produce as sumptuous or as beautiful a sound as, say, the Vienna Philharmonic for Levine in Perlman's DG record of Nos 3 and 5, yet the results are every bit as enjoyable, because the players themselves convey enthusiasm and pleasure. The recording is nicely balanced.

Marvellously exhilarating Mozart from Heifetz. The *D major*, K.218, was recorded in London in 1962 with Sir Malcolm Sargent, who proved a most responsive partner. The sound is attractively full and, though the soloist is balanced forward, the orchestral detail is well in the picture. The *A major* was a studio recording made a year later; the acoustic is much drier. Heifetz directs the accompanying group himself, the only occasion he did so on record. Both performances are memorable, with the crystalline clarity of articulation and warm timbre of the soloist always at the service of the composer. The 'Turkish' interludes of the finale of K.218 are brought off with great élan and both slow movements have a superb line and much grace and subtlety of detail. The digital remastering is very successful: the sound is fresh, clear and has plenty of body. The tape transfer is beautifully clean in focus.

David Oistrakh's performances come from his complete set of 1972. The remastering has lightened the sound, and the orchestral violins, notably in K.218, now sound just a little papery above the stave; otherwise the full ambience offsets the drier bass response, and the touch of rhythmic heaviness in the accompaniments from the Berlin Philharmonic is less striking. The slow movement of K.219 is particularly fine, and so too is the finale. At mid-price this is more than acceptable.

Kantorow's account of the *D major Concerto* is well up to the standard of his fine Mozart series, with fresh, intelligent solo playing, essentially classical in spirit, and with an agreeable but not exaggerated warmth in the slow movement. The two shorter pieces are also splendidly done, the *Adagio*, K.261, particularly fine. There is undoubted interest in the inclusion of the two fragments, from an unfinished *Double concerto* and the *Sinfonia concertante*, featuring three soloists. However, they are disconcertingly short and break off abruptly. The recording is first class and very well balanced.

Zukerman's performance of the *Concerto* is unmannered and stylish, admirably direct in approach, although the *Andante* is taken rather slowly. The pacing of the last movement is also somewhat idiosyncratic. The shorter pieces are played with some flair, the *Adagio* most expressively. The accompaniments, which Zukerman also directs, are polished, the recording vivid and rather brightly lit. There is a touch of digital edge here.

Sitkovetsky's performances are highly musical and polished and well recorded, too. However, compared with those of most of his competitors they are a little lacking in flair.

Concertone in C for 2 violins and orchestra, K.190; Sinfonia concertante in E flat for violin, viola and orchestra, K.364.

❀ *** DG **415 486-2**; *415 486-4* [id.]. Perlman, Zukerman, Israel PO, Mehta.
*** Chan. Dig. **CHAN 8315**; *ABTD 1096* [id.]. Brainin, Schidlof, SNO, Gibson.
(*) Denon Dig. **C37 7507 [id.]. Kantorow, Olga Martinova, Vladimir Mendelssohn, Hans Meijer, Netherlands CO, Hager.

An obviously sensible coupling is well served on Chandos by excellent performances and sound of demonstration quality, made in the warmly flattering ambience of St Barnabas's Church in London. The responsive playing of Norbert Brainin and Peter Schidlof communicates readily, even if their expressive fervour does bring a degree of romanticism to the slow movement of the *Sinfonia concertante*, and their phrasing employs tenutos, at times rather indulgently. Yet there is no lack of vitality in outer movements, and Sir Alexander Gibson's accompaniments are stylish and strong. The *Concertone*, where Schidlof changes from viola to violin, is also very successful, with Neil Black making an elegant contribution in the concertante oboe role. This is a less inspired work but does not lack a sense of stature here. A most enjoyable issue, especially on CD, but sounding well on tape, the latter vivid but fractionally less refined.

The alternative DG version of the *Sinfonia concertante* was recorded in Tel Aviv at the Huberman Festival in December 1982. It is less successfully balanced, with the soloist a fraction too near the microphones and with orchestral detail not so clearly focused as on Chandos. This is slightly emphasized on CD, and many will find the quality on the admirable chrome cassette to be slightly smoother in its solo imagery, without loss of vividness. The performance is in a class of its own and is an example of 'live' recording at its most magnetic, with the inspiration of the occasion caught on the wing. On the bows of Perlman and Zukerman the slow movement has an unforgettable serenity and spiritual beauty. The two artists play as one, yet their timbres are marvellously contrasted, with the silvery image of the violin set against the dark, rich viola tone. After the elegiac close to the *Andante*, the joyful finale with its 'whoopsing' rhythms is a delight. Zubin Mehta is caught up in the music making and accompanies most sensitively, in the slow movement creating an almost ethereal pianissimo with his first violins. The *Concertone* is also splendidly done (with a fine oboe contribution from Chaim Jouval); the ear notices the improvement in the sound balance of the studio recording of this work. But the *Sinfonia concertante*, with the audience incredibly quiet, conveys an electricity rarely caught on record.

The second alternative, from Denon, offers performances which in character fall neatly between those offered on DG and Chandos. Kantorow forms an excellent partnership with Vladimir Mendelssohn in the *Sinfonia concertante*; in the *Concertone*, Olga Martinova, the violinist, and the fine oboist, Hans Meijer, distinguish themselves. In keeping with the style of Kantorow's concerto series, the playing is refined and classical in spirit. It has character and spontaneity, and the slow movement of the *Sinfonia concertante* does not stray outside the boundaries of Mozartian expressive feeling, while not lacking warmth. With recording which is naturally balanced and realistic (and in K.364 aurally more pleasing than on the DG), this Denon CD offers performances which give much pleasure in their freshness and natural responsiveness.

Divertimenti for strings Nos 1 in D; 2 in B flat; 3 in F, K.136–8; Serenade No. 6 in D (Serenata notturna). K.239.

*** Ph. Dig. **412 120-2** [id.]. I Musici.

Divertimenti for strings Nos 1–3, K.136–8; Serenades Nos 6 (Serenata notturna); 13 in G (Eine kleine Nachtmusik), K.525.
(M) **(*) Decca **417 741-2**; *417 460-4* [id.]. ASMF, Marriner.
(M) **(*) Ph. **420 712-2**; *420 712-4* [id.]. I Musici.
(M) ** DG **423 212-2**; *423 212-4*. BPO, Karajan.

(i) *Divertimenti for strings Nos 1, K.136, & 3, K.138; Serenade No. 6 (Serenata Notturna);* (ii) *Serenade No. 13 (Eine kleine Nachtmusik);* (iii) *Sinfonia concertante in E flat, K.297b.*
(B) **(*) DG Walkman *413 152-4* [id.]. (i) BPO, Karajan; (ii) VPO, Boehm; (iii) BPO, Boehm.

The three Salzburg *Divertimenti* date from early 1772, when Mozart was sixteen. They can be regarded as string quartets (and are indeed so listed in the *New Grove*), but more often than not are played by a fuller complement of strings, as they are here. The newest digital recording of them by I Musici is particularly successful, extremely vivid and clean, bringing the players before one's very eyes. Their earlier analogue recording from 1974, however, still sounds well in its mid-priced reissue which offers more music. The sound is not lacking presence in its re-mastered format, with a good tape. The playing is spirited and beautifully stylish. With the *Night music* added to the *Serenata notturna* as couplings, this is good value (K.525 is attractively done, if not quite as fine as I Musici's newest digital recording – see below). On cassette, the drums tend to boom a bit in the *Serenata notturna.*

The playing of the Academy in this repertoire comes from a vintage period and is marvellous, with Marriner's choice of tempi equally apt. The same warm stylishness distinguishes the *Serenata notturna,* while *Eine kleine Nachtmusik* is delightfully played. Versions of this most popular of Mozart's serenades which have such fresh, unaffected refinement are rare. However, the remastered recordings from the late 1960s and early 1970s are very brightly lit, with the violins noticeably thin above the stave in *Eine kleine Nachtmusik*; the touch of shrillness is less striking in the three *Divertimenti.* On tape the vividness remains, but the upper range is smoother and more comfortable.

Karajan's performances of the *String divertimenti* and the *Serenata notturna* are beautifully played and as such they prompt the liveliest admiration. At the same time there is a predictably suave elegance that seems to militate against spontaneity. Cultured and effortless readings, beautifully recorded and well balanced, they somehow leave one untouched. There is too much legato and not always a balancing sparkle. Boehm's contribution to this generous bargain-priced Walkman tape is another matter. His 1976 VPO version of Mozart's *Night music* is among the finest available, polished and spacious, with a neat, lightly pointed finale. The account of the *Sinfonia concertante* is of superlative quality, sounding amazingly idiomatic and well blended, with the balance between soloists and orchestra nicely managed. This is altogether refreshing. The chrome-tape transfers are first class, except in *Eine kleine Nachtmusik* where the upper range lacks the last degree of freshness, although the quality remains full and clear in detail.

On the alternative mid-priced CD, all three *String divertimenti* are offered and Karajan's *Eine kleine Nachtmusik* is substituted for Boehm's, showing his Mozartian manners at their most appealing. The string playing is very graceful and the delicacy in the finale matches the re-finement of the delightful middle section of the slow movement. The sound is good, although the late-1960s recording date of K.136/8 brings a certain thinness to the string timbre.

Divertimenti for strings Nos 1–2, K.136/7; Serenades Nos 6 (Serenata notturna), K.239; 13 (Eine kleine Nachtmusik), K.525.
*** Capriccio **10185** [id.]. Salzburg Mozarteum Camerata Academica, Végh.

This second offering in Végh's Salzburg series of Mozart's *Divertimenti* and *Serenades* brings not only an exceptionally popular and attractive group of works from early to late but delightfully bold, fresh and characterful performances, very well recorded. Only in the slow movement of *Eine kleine Nachtmusik*, taken rather slowly, is the playing a shade less refined. Curiously, Végh changes the regular order of movements in K.137, making it a conventional fast-slow-fast piece, though neither the label nor the note recognizes the change. In every way this outshines the rather disappointing first disc in the series (see below), and promises well for the rest of the project.

Divertimento for strings No. 1, K.136; A Musical Joke, K.522; Serenade No. 13 (Eine kleine Nachtmusik), K.525.
*** Ph. Dig. **412 269-2** [id.]. ASMF Chamber Ens.

Three popular Mozart pieces given with elegance and polish by the Academy Chamber players and recorded with complete fidelity and splendid definition by the Philips engineers. All three will give pleasure. Readers wanting this particular coupling need not hesitate on either artistic or technical grounds. The compact disc conveys an excellent sense of presence and realism.

Divertimento for strings No. 2 in B flat, K. 137; Divertimenti Nos 1 in E flat, K.113; 11 in D, K.251.
(*) Ph. **420 181-2; *420 181-4* [id.]. ASMF Chamber Ens.

The *E flat Divertimento*, K.113, for 2 clarinets, 2 horns and strings is an assured and inventive piece for a fifteen-year old; K.251 dates from five years later. It still uses horns and strings, but adds an elaborate oboe part, elegantly played here by Celia Nicklin. The *String divertimento*, played with considerable vitality – very much a Salzburg symphony – forms the centrepiece of an attractive concert. The playing throughout is polished and full of life, if perhaps a shade anonymous in its overall effect. The sound is extremely vivid, though the cassette is rather bass-heavy.

Divertimento for strings No. 2, K.137; Serenade No. 3 in D, K.185; March in D, K.189.
(*) Hung. Dig. **HCD 12861 [id.]. Liszt CO, János Rolla.

János Rolla directs strongly articulated performances and also takes the solo violin role in the *Serenade*. The playing is stylish and polished but rhythmically not as resilient as, say, the ASMF under Marriner in this repertoire. The music making has an agreeable directness, but rather less in the way of charm, and the *Andante grazioso* in K.185 could be more expansive. The recording is excellent, very vivid and with excellent presence and good definition within an acoustic that is warm without being too resonant.

Divertimento for strings No. 3 in F, K.138; Divertimento No. 17 in D, K.334.
** Capriccio **10153**; *CC 27157* [id.]. Salzburg Mozarteum Camerata Academica, Végh.

Végh directs his Salzburg players in bright, robust performances of these *Divertimenti*, recorded closely and vividly to show up roughnesses in the matching and blending. This first of a projected series of Mozart *Divertimentos* and *Serenades* is less recommendable than subsequent issues, when the composition of the Camerata – which changes every year – was less refined than later, and the performances rhythmically less resilient. In the splendid *Divertimento*, K.334, Végh disappointingly omits the exposition repeat in the first movement and both repeats in the lovely fourth-movement *Adagio*, but that allows him to include the delightful K.138, the third of the so-called Salzburg symphonies.

Divertimento for strings No. 3 in F, K.138; Serenade No. 13 (Eine kleine Nachtmusik), K.525.
*(*) Denon Dig. **C37 7178** [id.]. Lucerne Fest. Strings, Baumgartner – VIVALDI: *Concertos*.*(*)

These are well-articulated, musical performances, played with a fine degree of polish and most realistically recorded. Baumgartner's touch is just a little severe, however, and the slow movement of the *Night music*, though not ungracious, fails to smile as it can.

Divertimento No. 2 in D, K.131; Divertimento for wind No. 12 in E flat, K.252; Serenade No. 13 in G (Eine kleine Nachtmusik), K.525.
(*) DG Dig. **419 192-2; *419 192-4* [id.]. Orpheus CO.

The Orpheus group are at their finest in the *D major Divertimento*, famous in a Beecham mono version, but also recorded very successfully indeed by Marriner and his Academy (see above under *Cassations*). The Orpheus group play it with affection and spirit, and there is elegant phrasing from the strings and a strikingly buoyant contribution from the horns. The *Wind divertimento* is also most agreeable, but the famous *Night music* is rather lacking in charm with a very brisk opening movement, alert enough and very polished but somewhat unbending. The recording is excellent in both media, though the CD is fresher and more transparent.

(i) *Divertimenti Nos 10 in F, K.247; 11 in D, K.251;* (ii) *Sinfonia concertante for violin, viola and orchestra in E flat, K.364.*
(B) ** DG Walkman *419 388-4* [id.]. BPO, (i) Karajan; (ii) Boehm, with Thomas Brandis, Giusto Cappone.

Like Karajan's recordings of the *String divertimenti*, these larger-scale works offer cultured, effortless playing that is perhaps too agreeably smooth, though it is easy to admire. The recordings were made in 1967–8 and still sound well. If the *Sinfonia concertante* under Karl Boehm really requires more individual playing (especially in the slow movement) than Messrs Brandis and Cappone provide, the strong directing personality of the conductor keeps the music alive throughout. The sound on the Walkman tape is full and well balanced.

Divertimento No. 11 in D for oboe, 2 horns and string quartet, K.251.
** Ph. Dig. **412 618-2** [id.]. Holliger, Baumann, Gasciarrino, Orlando Qt, Guldemond – *Oboe quartet* etc.***

A disappointing performance of an attractive work. The playing itself is polished, alive and well integrated, as one might expect from this cast list, but the approach is rhythmically heavy at times – though the gentler movements come off well – not helped by the close balance. The sound is good.

Divertimenti Nos 11 in D, K.251; 14 in B flat, K.270; Serenade No. 6 in D (Serenata notturna). K.239.
*** DG Dig. **415 669-2** [id.]. Orpheus CO.

These are wholly admirable performances. Alert, crisply rhythmic allegros show consistent resilience, strong yet without a touch of heaviness, while slow movements are warmly phrased, with much finesse and imaginative use of light and shade. The minuet second movement of K.251 is particularly appealing in this respect, while the fourth movement, which is also a minuet but with three variations, has much engaging detail. The *Serenata notturna*, which can easily sound bland, has a fine sparkle here; while the *B flat Divertimento* with its scoring for 2 oboes, 2 horns and 2 bassoons makes an effective contrast. Here the oboe playing is particularly felicitous. This is another collection to confirm first impressions (from this group's début in Haydn and Rossini) that the Orpheus Chamber Orchestra is one of the world's finest, and perhaps to convince the listener that a conductor can be superfluous in certain repertoire. Impeccable in ensemble, this playing has no sense of anonymity of character or style. The recording, made in the Performing Arts Centre of New York State University at Purchase, is truthful but rather closely balanced. The sharply defined CD brings a touch of edginess to the violins above the stave.

Divertimento No. 15 in B flat, K.287; Divertimento for strings No. 3, K.138.
*** Ph. Dig. **412 740-2** [id.]. ASMF Chamber Ens.

The K.287 *Divertimento*, composed in Salzburg for the Countess Lodron, is a major six-movement piece, with an attractive theme with variations coming second and a central *Adagio*, led by the first violin, of considerable expressive intensity. The finale is witty and humorously based on a folksong ('The farmer's wife has lost the cat'). This piece was intended for solo instruments; the performance here, with a double bass and two horns added to a string quartet, is admirable and beautifully recorded. The *String divertimento* makes an agreeable filler, less substantial, perhaps, but with a warmly appealing slow movement.

Divertimento No. 17 in D, K.334; March in D, K.445.
*** Ph. Dig. **411 102-2** [id.]. ASMF Chamber Ens.

Divertimento No. 17, K.334; Divertimento for strings No. 1, K.136.
*** Denon Dig **C37 7080** [id.]. Augmented Berlin Philh. Qt.

Divertimento No. 17; Serenata notturna, K. 239.
** DG Dig. **423 375-2**; *423 375-4* [id.]. BPO, Karajan.

The engaging *D major Divertimento* with its famous Minuet has been frequently recorded in orchestral dress, but it is now more often given as a chamber version, as it is by the Academy. This is an expert performance with plenty of charm and a recording to match. In its compact disc format it is wonderfully lifelike and present.

On Denon, a hardly less successful account from the augmented Berlin Philharmonia Quartet. The music making has the integrated feeling of outstanding ensemble playing, achieved without a conductor. It is polished, spirited and full of warmth. The famous Minuet is just a shade indulgent, but in all other respects this is first class. The *String divertimento* is equally attractive and makes a more substantial encore than the *March*. With a particularly believable recording, this can be enthusiastically recommended alongside, though not in preference to, the ASMF version.

Karajan offers both works in full evening orchestral dress; the result, within a resonant acoustic, is opulent and gracious – with some marvellously polished playing from the Berlin violins – but, notably in the famous Minuet, is unashamedly indulgent. In the *Serenata notturna*, the timpani are backward and not too cleanly focused and this performance lacks real zest.

German dances, K.509/1–6; K.571/1–6; K.600/1–6; K.602/1–4; K.605/1–3; 3 Marches in D, K.189 and K.335/1–2.
(*) Ph. **416 484-2 [id.]. ASMF, Marriner.

Mozart wrote these dances in his capacity as Royal and Imperial Chamber Musician in Vienna, to which he was appointed in December 1787 (and was paid less than half as much as his predecessor, Gluck). They are hardly among his greatest music but contain much attractive invention and some individual touches like the use of the hurdy-gurdy in K.602, while in K.600/5 there is a 'canary' trio. The *Sleigh ride* of K.605 is justly famous. The performances here are spirited and nicely turned, but perhaps a shade heavy in rhythmic feeling at times, although the reverberant acoustic contributes to this effect. The playing itself is admirably warm and suitably elegant. The set of dances, K.571, are especially enjoyable and the closing number has a suitably neat coda. Excellent sound, warm and full.

6 German dances, K.571; Les petites riens: ballet music, K.299b; Serenade No. 13 (Eine kleine Nachtmusik), K.525.
*** Erato Dig. **ECD 88014** [id.]. Scottish CO, Leppard.

An excellent collection in every way. The performance of *Les petites riens* is delightful, spirited and polished, and the *German dances* are no less lively and elegant; the famous *Nachtmusik* is nicely proportioned and very well played. The sound is especially believable on CD, giving a tangible impression of the players sitting together out beyond the speakers.

Masonic funeral music, K.477; Overtures: Così fan tutte; The Impresario; Le Nozze di Figaro; Die Zauberflöte; Serenade No. 13 (Eine kleine Nachtmusik), K.525.
(*) CBS **MK 42029 [id.]. Columbia SO, Bruno Walter.

Walter conducts all this music with evident affection; even if some may feel that he is almost too loving at times, particularly in *Eine kleine Nachtmusik* (where there is a hint of indulgence in the *Andante* and a touch of heaviness in the Minuet), there is still something very special about this music making. His tempi in the overtures are unerringly apt (*Così* is a delight and the bassóons as well as the violins are made to dance in the fugue of *Die Zauberflöte*). The account of the *Masonic funeral music* is particularly fine. The recording is characteristic of this highly successful CBS series, warm and full, with an ample bass, but a remarkably fresh upper range, with sweet violins. The *Night music* dates from 1958 and the remainder of the programme from 1961.

A Musical Joke, K.522.
*** Erato Dig. **ECD 88021** [id.]. Paillard CO, Paillard – L. MOZART: *Cassation* etc.***

A Musical Joke, K.522; Serenade No. 13 in G (Eine kleine Nachtmusik], K.525.
*** DG **400 065-2** [id.]. Augmented Amadeus Qt.

Happily paired with a high-spirited version of Leopold Mozart's *Toy symphony*, Paillard's account of Mozart's fun piece makes the most of its outrageous jokes, with the horns in the opening movement boldly going wrong and the final discordant clash sounding positively cataclysmic; yet it takes into account the musical values, too. The *Adagio cantabile* is very graciously played and the finale (famous as a TV signature-tune) is articulated with infectious sparkle. The recording is excellent, the orchestral group being placed within a warm ambience which yet does not cloud inner detail. The overall effect may be less subtle than the Amadeus version, but the boisterous approach is not spoilt by clumsiness.

Eine kleine Nachtmusik has rarely sounded as refreshing and exhilarating as in this Amadeus chamber performance; the finale in particular is delectably resilient. The musical clowning in the *Musical Joke*, which can so often seem heavy and unfunny, is here given charm. The horn players, Gerd Seifert and Manfred Klier, are from the Berlin Philharmonic. The recording is first rate.

Notturno for four orchestras, K.286; Serenade No. 6 (Serenata notturna), K.239; Serenade No. 13 (Eine kleine Nachtmusik), K.525.
*** O-L Dig. **411 720-2** [id.]. AAM, Hogwood.

Eine kleine Nachtmusik is usually given in the four-movement form that survives. Christopher Hogwood follows Dart's earlier example by adding the missing minuet, though – unlike Dart, who transcribed a minuet from a piano sonata – Hogwood uses a minuet that Mozart composed in collaboration with his English pupil, Thomas Attwood. All the repeats in every movement save one are observed – which is perhaps too much of a good thing. The performance is given one instrument to a part and is sprightly and alive. The *Serenata notturna* and the *Notturno for four orchestras* are for larger forces and are given with considerable panache. This record should in fact be investigated by those not normally responsive to period instruments as the musical results are certainly thought-provoking. Technically, this is first class, with clean and well-defined recorded sound and great presence in the compact disc format.

Overtures: La Clemenza di Tito; Così fan tutte; Don Giovanni; Die Entführung aus dem Serail; Idomeneo; Lucio Silla; Le Nozze di Figaro; Der Schauspieldirektor; Die Zauberflöte.
*** HMV Dig. **CDC7 47014-2** [id.]. ASMF, Marriner.

Marriner's collection is strongly characterized, emphasizing the spirit of the opera house, offering plenty of drama in *Don Giovanni* and *Idomeneo* and a sense of spectacle with the percussion effects in *Die Entführung*. *Così fan tutte* and *Figaro* bring a lighter touch; throughout, the ASMF playing is characteristically spirited and stylish, with the string detail nicely clean and polished. The digital recording is bright and bold. The CD, however, softens the focus and the sound is more natural than on the original LP.

Serenade No. 3 in D, K.189.
(*) O-L Dig. **411 936-2 [id.]. Schröder, AAM, Hogwood.

Mozart's first large-scale *Serenade* dates from 1773 and is sometimes given the sobriquet *'Andretter'*, after the name of its commissioner, a Salzburg military official who needed music for his son's wedding. In this work Mozart established the feature of including a miniature violin concerto as part of the structure, though here its movements are interspersed with others. This presents the only drawback to the present recording, for Schröder's account of the solo role in the *Andante* is rather too straight and direct, although he offers more charm later on when he contributes to the Trio of the Minuet. The performance overall is brimming with vitality, the finales especially neat and infectious, and those who do not object to the astringency of 'original' string timbres in a piece essentially intended to divert will find that the diversity of Mozart's invention is fully characterized. The recording is first rate.

Serenade No. 4 in D (Colloredo), K.203; March in D, K.237.
** HMV **CDC7 47825-2.** Coll. Aur., Maier.

Serenade Nos 4 in D (Colloredo); 6 in D (Serenata notturna); March in D, K.237.
*** Ph. Dig. **420 201-2**; *420 201-4* [id.]. ASMF, Marriner.

The *Colloredo serenade*, named after Mozart's patron at Salzburg, is virtually a lightweight symphony with a miniature violin concerto as its centrepiece. The performance under Marriner is highly estimable, very much in the best traditions of the Academy, with Iona Brown making a distinguished and appealing contribution as soloist. The *Serenata notturna*, too, is first class, crisply rhythmic in the first movement with the drums cleanly focused. The recording, like the playing, is strikingly warm and fresh, and this record makes a very good case for performing this consistently engaging music on modern instruments, with elegance of style a keynote of the music making. There is a good tape.

The alternative account of K.203 from Franzjosef Maier and his Collegium Aureum is lively and spirited, a bit rough and ready perhaps – the solo violin is not terribly sensitive. An acceptable and decently recorded version, but unlikely to arouse enthusiasm.

Serenade No. 5 in D, K.204.
** HMV **CDC7 47832-2**. Coll. Aur., Maier.

Like its companion, the performance under Franzjosef Maier is enjoyable enough without attaining real distinction. Although, as we go to press, there is no rival, this state of affairs is bound to be soon remedied. In the meantime this is far from unacceptable and offers some good playing. The recording dates from the mid-1970s and has been successfully remastered for CD.

Serenades Nos 6 in D (Serenata notturna), K.239; 9 in D (Posthorn), K.320.
*** Novalis Dig. **150 013-2**; *150 013-4* [id.]. Bav. RSO, C. Davis.

Sir Colin Davis's account of the *Posthorn serenade* is second to none, and should be considered alongside the much-praised ASMF version under Marriner (see below). Davis secures consistently spirited and responsive playing from the Bavarian Radio Orchestra, not only from the strings but also from the woodwind in their concertante section. The posthorn soloist is also a very stylish player; his contribution is unusually refined, yet still tonally robust. With apt tempi and a fine sense of spontaneity throughout, this is very refreshing. The *Serenata notturna* is also well done, if without quite the sparkle of K.320 – here the backwardly balanced drums sound a shade too resonant, although this is more striking on the (otherwise excellent) tape than on the CD.

Serenades Nos 6 in D (Serenata notturna), K.239; 13 in G (Eine kleine Nachtmusik), K.525.
(M) *** Pickwick Dig. **PCD 861**. Serenata of London – ELGAR: *Serenade*; GRIEG: *Holberg suite*.***

The performance of the *Night music* by the Serenata of London is as fine as any available. There is not a suspicion of routine here; indeed the players, for all the excellence of their ensemble, give the impression of coming to the piece for the first time. Barry Wilde's pacing (he leads from the front desk) is admirably balanced over the four movements: the first is fresh but not hurried, the *Romance* has striking poise, and overall there is elegance as well as plenty of spirit. The *Serenata notturna* is perhaps not quite so inspired a work, but these excellent players make a good case for it and are agreeably sprightly whenever given the opportunity. The recording has striking naturalness and realism; with its excellent and generous couplings (the total playing time is 65′ 12″), this is an outstanding CD bargain.

Serenade No. 7 in D (Haffner), K.250; March in D, K.249.
*** Ph. Dig. **416 154-2** [id.]. I. Brown, ASMF, Marriner.
(M) *** Ph. *416 977-4* [id.]. Dresden State O, Edo de Waart.
** Tel. Dig. **ZK8 43062** [id.]. Zehetmair, Dresden State O, Harnoncourt.
(M) ** DG **419 866-2**; *419 866-4* [id.]. BPO, Boehm (without *March*).
(B) * Sup. **2SUP 006**. Suk, Prague CO, Hlaváček (without *March*).

A spacious, yet warm and polished account of the *Haffner serenade* from Marriner and his Academy players, with Iona Brown making a superb contribution in the concertante violin role. There is sparkle here as well as expressive grace. The Academy string tone is sweet and smooth, yet articulation is neat, with admirable rhythmic freshness in the outer movements. The recording is resonant, which increases the impression of a full orchestral performance rather than one on a chamber scale. As usual, the Philips engineers provide a natural sound-balance with rich, full textures, especially refined on CD.

Though not so well recorded as Marriner's, Edo de Waart's Dresden version is perhaps the only one that can be mentioned in the same breath (though no doubt Boskovsky's fine Decca account will re-emerge in due course). It has rhythmic poise, delightful spontaneity and warmth and can safely be recommended to tape collectors, although we hope it will arrive on CD before too long.

Like the *Posthorn serenade*, the *Haffner* enfolds a miniature violin concerto within its eight movements. As in his record of the former, Harnoncourt's soloist is Thomas Zehetmair, who gives a splendid account of himself. Harnoncourt offers an eminently spacious and expressive view of the piece, at times a little idiosyncratic. (He puts the brakes on the Trio sections of the Minuets of movements 3, 5 and 7, and the phrasing is mannered.) However, though the recording is very good, this does not displace older versions, particularly Edo de Waart on Philips, while on CD Marriner is first choice.

The Berlin Philharmonic play with such polish and vivacity, and articulation is so beautifully crisp, that one is inclined to accept Boehm's uncharacteristic lack of mellowness and his willingness to drive the allegros rather hard. Thomas Brandis is the excellent violin soloist, but at times there is more exhilaration here than charm. The freshened recording sounds just a little fierce at times in its remastered format and is not absolutely refined.

Libor Hlaváček has the advantage of good 1977 sound and Josef Suk to play Mozart's concertante violin solos. The Prague Chamber Orchestra provide good ensemble, too, but the performance overall is disappointingly square and rhythmically inflexible.

Serenade No. 9 in D (Posthorn); 2 Marches, K.335.
*** Ph. Dig. **412 725-2** [id.]. ASMF, Marriner.
*(*) Tel. Dig. **ZK8 43063** [id.]. Dresden State O, Harnoncourt.

Serenades Nos 9 in D (Posthorn); 13 (Eine kleine Nachtmusik), K.525.
(M) *** Decca **417 874-2**; *417 874-4* [id.]. V. Mozart Ens., Boskovsky.
(*) Telarc **CD 10108 [id.]. Prague CO, Mackerras.
(*) DG Dig. **410 085-2 [id.]. VPO, Levine.
(M) **(*) DG **415 843-2**; *415 843-4* [id.]. BPO or VPO, Boehm.

Mozart's *Posthorn serenade* is well served on compact disc, but there is a first choice, unless a coupling of the *Night music* is essential. Marriner's performance is spacious, cultured and marvellously played. The posthorn, which gives the work its sobriquet, plays only a minor (if effective) role in the Trio of the second Minuet. The work's kernel is its central movements which – in the place of the usual miniature violin concerto – feature concertante wind in four pairs. The Academy wind players make a compelling case for modern instruments here, as do the strings in the lovely *Andantino* which follows, where the mood darkens. The outer movements are both spirited and strong, the minuets lively and resilient. Michael Laird's contribution on the posthorn is characterful yet elegant. The two marches are used as 'entrance' and 'exit' music, the first, with its jaunty oboe solo, setting an infectious atmosphere for the main work which is to follow. The recording, in a fairly resonant acoustic, adds to the feeling of breadth without blurring detail. The sound is first class.

Bargain hunters should be well pleased with Decca's Weekend reissue of Boskovsky's performance with its natural musicality and sense of sparkle. The newest transfer is a little dry in the matter of string timbre, but there is plenty of bloom on the wind, detail is clean and the posthorn is tangible in its presence. The coupled *Night music* is one of the freshest and most attractive performances of this much-played work in any format, and the small string group is most realistically balanced and vividly projected. A bargain.

The Prague strings have great warmth and Mackerras gets vital results from his Czech forces. Rhythms are lightly sprung and the phrasing is natural in every way. The Telarc acoustic is warm and spacious with a wide dynamic range (some might feel it is too wide for this music), and most ears will find the effect more agreeable than the drier, brighter DG sound-balance. The performance of the *Posthorn serenade* here has slightly more character than Levine's, although in the *Night music* Levine's direct, elegant manner is in some ways more telling.

In the *Posthorn serenade* Levine's tempi are well judged, and the Vienna Philharmonic play with distinction. This performance is certainly among the best now available, and the coupling is no less persuasive. The recording is clean and well balanced, but with less warmth than the

Telarc. Indeed, there is a sharpness of outlines on the DG compact disc which suggests that the microphones were a shade too close to the musicians.

Harnoncourt's soloist is Thomas Zehetmair – and very good he is, too. The ample acoustic of Dresden helps to inflate the performances, which are quite unlike those we are used to from this conductor. Marriner on Philips is more straightforward, less overtly charming and yet more winning, and the recording is cleaner.

Boehm's 1971 Berlin Philharmonic recording of the *Posthorn serenade* sounds particularly fresh in its digitally remastered format which, with its bright and transparent, yet full textures, does not emphasize the fact that a large orchestral group is used. The playing is characteristically polished, warm and civilized. Incidentally, as well as naming the excellent posthorn soloist, the documentation reveals the principal flautist as James Galway and the fine oboist as Lothar Koch. *Eine kleine Nachtmusik* dates from 1976, and the Vienna orchestra are on top form. Boehm's reading is attractively polished and spacious with a neat, nicely pointed finale. The recording is brighter than it was, but retains its bloom. There is an excellent tape.

Serenade No. 10 in B flat for 13 wind instruments, K.361.
*** ASV Dig. **CDCOE 804**; *ZCCOE 804* [id.]. COE Wind Soloists, Schneider.
*** Ph. Dig. **412 726-2**; *412 726-4* [id.]. ASMF, Marriner.
(*) Accent **ACC 68642D [id.]. Octophorus, Kuijken.
(M) **(*) EMI Dig. **CD-EMX 9520**; *EMX 41 2059-4*. LPO Wind Ens.
(*) DG Dig. **423 061-2; *423 061-4* [id.]. Orpheus CO.
** HMV **CDC7 47818-2**. Coll. Aur. (members).
(**) Tel. **ZK8 42981** [id.]. V. Mozart Wind Ens., Harnoncourt.

Serenades Nos 10 in B flat, 11 in E flat, K.375.
(M) *** Ph. **420 711-2**; *420 711-4* [id.]. Netherlands Wind Ens., Edo de Waart.

The brilliant young soloists of the Chamber Orchestra of Europe, inspired by the conducting of Alexander Schneider, give an unusually positive, characterful reading, making most of the groups who play without a conductor sound pale and uncharacterful by comparison. Right at the start, the flourishes from the first clarinet are far more effective when played as here, not literally, but with Schneider leading them on to the first forte chord from the full ensemble. From then on the individual artistry of the players is just as winning as on the COE record of the two great *Serenades for wind octet*, K.375 and K.388. The only controversial point is that where the first *Adagio* – nowadays the most popular movement of all, thanks to the sound-track of the film, *Amadeus* – flows very persuasively rather faster than usual; the second *Adagio*, phrased subtly, sounds rather heavier than usual at a slower, more relaxed speed. The sound is exceptionally vivid and faithful and there is a good tape.

The Marriner version fits very stylishly in the Academy's series of Mozart wind works, characteristically refined in its ensemble, with matching of timbres and contrasts beautifully judged, both lively and graceful with rhythms well sprung and speeds well chosen, yet with nothing mannered about the result. Though a touch of idiosyncrasy might have added a more positive character and made it more memorable, this must stand among the very finest versions of a work which has become more popular than ever. Full, warm recording that yet allows good detail. The chrome cassette, too, is first class, clear, yet full.

The Netherlanders offers not only the *B flat Serenade* but also the *E flat*, K.375, a very substantial bonus. Their performances are fresh and alive, admirably sensitive both in feeling for line and in phrasing, but never lingering too lovingly over detail. The account of the famous *B flat Serenade* does not erase memories of Barenboim's HMV version (which we hope will appear on CD in due course) but, apart from the sheer quality of the playing, both works here are enhanced by the presence and sonority of the recording, which is beautifully balanced and combines rich homogeneity of timbre with crispness of focus. There is a considerable price advantage too. The cassette is also excellently managed, with K.375 sounding particularly vivid.

On period instruments Barthold Kuijken directs his talented team in an authentic performance that, as far as possible, gets the best of both worlds. Though the distinctive character of eighteenth-century instruments brings a sparer, lighter texture, as it should, the matching is never uncomfortably raw, with fine intonation. Speeds tend to be on the cautious side, which (with less dependable instruments than those of today) is fair enough, but the liveliness of the playing makes up for that. The recording adds to the clarity.

Outstanding playing from the wind ensemble of the London Philharmonic, richly blended, warmly phrased and full of character. The articulation and rhythmic feeling of the outer movements and the Theme and variations are particularly spontaneous; however, in the slower sections, notably the third-movement *Adagio*, one feels the need of a conductor's directing hand: there is some loss of character both here and, occasionally, elsewhere. Even so, with modern digital recording, attractively coloured by the ambience and refined in detail, this is good value at mid-price.

The Orpheus Chamber Orchestra, working as always without a conductor but in close democratic consultation, give a refined, finely detailed reading, which yet rather lacks the individual character of the finest versions. The first-movement allegro, for example, sounds just a little stiff, even breathless, though ensemble is splendid, and the slow movements are very smoothly done, with finely controlled dynamics. Good, full-toned recording in both edia.

Using period instruments, the Collegium Aureum is less successful than its direct rivals in blending the sound to suit the modern ear, and the very plain rhythmic style is a degree disappointing too, though the relaxed manner of the variation movement is most attractive.

Harnoncourt's Telefunken version is more controversial. The actual playing of the Vienna Mozart Wind Ensemble is exemplary and the wind blend beautifully. The opening is double-dotted as authorized in the *Neue Mozart Ausgabe*, but tempi will doubtless worry many collectors. The *allegro* of the first movement is far from *'molto'* – but that in itself would not disturb those familiar with, say, Furtwängler's classic account. What renders this version unacceptable are the grotesque tempi of the third movement (*Adagio*) and (even more so) of the second Minuet. The treatment of the C minor section in the *Romance* is also very heavy-handed. The recording itself is absolutely first class – and so, needless to say, is the playing. But this is emphatically not a safe recommendation.

Serenades Nos 11 in E flat, K.375; 12 in C min., K.388.
*** ASV Dig. **CDCOE 802**; *ZCCOE 802* [id.]. COE, Schneider.
(*) Hung. Dig. **HCD 12549 [id.]. Budapest Wind Ens., Berkes.
(*) O-L Dig. **417 249-2; *417 249-4* [id.]. Amadeus Winds.
** Mer. **CDE 84107** [id.]. Albion Ens.
** Tel. **ZK8 43097** [id.]. V. Mozart Wind Ens., Harnoncourt.
** Orfeo Dig. **C 134851A** [id.]. BPO Wind Ens.
** Chan. Dig. **CHAN 8407**; *ABTD 1144* [id.]. SNO Wind Ens., Jarvi.

The talented young wind players of the Chamber Orchestra of Europe had made an impressive recording of the Dvořák *Wind serenade* before they turned their attention to these two supreme examples of wind music. With Schneider as a wise and experienced guide, they give performances which combine brilliance and warmth with a feeling of spontaneity. Where some older rivals are either on the one hand mannered or too tautly disciplined on the other, here Schneider very persuasively encourages the individuality of particular soloists, so that the result is both natural and compelling. K.375 in particular is a delight, as genial as it is characterful, conveying the joy of the inspiration. K.388 might have been more menacing at the C minor opening, but the result is most persuasive, with excellent digital sound set against a warm but not confusing acoustic. There is an excellent cassette.

The dry acoustic of the Hungaroton recording emphasizes the extraordinary precision of ensemble that marks the work of this group. Yet for all that precision, the result lacks the sort of fizz, the sense of spontaneous communication, which has been so striking a quality in the group's live performances. The studio conditions seem to have muted individuality a little, to make the results a shade machine-like. Nevertheless, it presents a fine, clean view of Mozart, beautifully paced, with no suspicion of mannerism, and with dazzling technical accomplishment.

Anyone wanting a period performance of these two supreme *Serenades* for wind octet can safely have the Amadeus Winds version recommended to them. Though the timbre is not as raucous as one might expect from relatively primitive wind instruments – bringing mellow but characterful blending – the sounds are not easy on the modern ear. Where one has begun to expect speeds faster than usual in period performances, these are on the leisurely side, though well lifted both rhythmically and in phrasing. The speeds are a recognition of the players' technical problems, coping with less sophisticated mechanisms, a point noisily brought home in the clear, full recording with much clicking of keys. There is an excellent cassette.

The Albion Ensemble version of this ideal coupling brings fine performances, vividly recorded, lacking – except in the slow movements – the last degree of individuality and purposefulness that a conductor can bring. This recording will please those who value above all speeds on the slow side and superfine ensemble, with the individuality of the principal players – George Caird (first oboe), Andrew Marriner (first clarinet) and Michael Thompson (first horn) – blossoming delightfully in the slow movements.

Harnoncourt begins K.375 with an eccentrically slow tempo for the first movement, made to sound the more self-conscious by the agogic hesitations which also mar the slow movement. Though he regularly adopts a moulded style, he brings out the tonal contrasts between the instruments, never blending. Otherwise allegros are generally on the fast side, well pointed and with fine rhythmic flair; and the whole of K.388 is lively and colourful.

On Orfeo, elegantly turned performances, as one would expect from an ensemble which includes the clarinettist, Karl Leister, and the oboe of Hansjörg Schellenberger, who play their solos most imaginatively in the two slow movements. However, they are not quite as characterful or as spirited as the Chamber Orchestra of Europe on ASV, and accompaniment figures that are too metrical rob the music of resilience. Very good recording with plain, immediate sound.

The Chandos recording for the Scottish ensemble sets the players at a distance against a warm reverberation, not so much blunting the edge as lightening the effect. Passagework is delicate and neat, and these are enjoyable accounts, although ensemble is not as crisp as with most direct rivals. There is a characteristically faithful chrome cassette.

Serenade No. 13 in G (Eine kleine Nachtmusik), K.525.

*** Ph. Dig. **410 606-2** [id.]. I Musici (with concert of Baroque music***).

*** DG Dig. **400 034-2**; *3302 031* [id.]. BPO, Karajan – GRIEG: *Holberg suite*; PROKOFIEV: *Symphony No. 1.****

Serenade No. 13 (Eine kleine Nachtmusik); Adagio & fugue in C min., K.546.

(*) Ph. Dig. **416 386-2; *416 386-4* [id.]. ASMF, Marriner – L. MOZART: *Toy symphony;* PACHELBEL: *Canon & Gigue.***(*)

Recordings of Mozart's celebrated *Night music* are legion, coupled in various ways, including fine accounts by Karl Boehm, Raymond Leppard, Bruno Walter and not forgetting a particularly refreshing version from Boskovsky paired with the *Posthorn serenade*, only available on tape at present. It was Karajan who gave the work its digital début in an early compact disc entitled 'Digital concert'. Apart from a self-conscious and somewhat ponderous minuet, it is a very fine performance, the playing beautifully cultured, with finely shaped phrasing and well-sprung rhythms. The digital sound, well detailed and not without bloom, is a little sharp-edged.

First choice probably rests wth the new version from I Musici, who play the music with rare freshness, giving the listener the impression of hearing the work for the first time. The playing is consistently alert and sparkling, with the *Romanze* particularly engaging. The recording is beautifully balanced.

In his miscellaneous group of popular classical and Baroque pieces, Sir Neville gives a polished and elegant account of *Eine kleine Nachtmusik,* clearly designed to caress the ears of traditional listeners wearied by period performance. The second-movement *Romanze* is even more honeyed than usual on muted strings. Beautifully balanced recording, with a smooth matching cassette. The warmth of the sound is preferable to the much more astringent character of Marriner's earlier Argo version (coupled with the *Divertimenti for strings*) now digitally remastered on Decca's Ovation label, although that is a more vital performance. The *Adagio and fugue* makes a curious encore, played quite strongly but in no way distinctive.

Serenade No. 13 (Eine kleine Nachtmusik); Symphony No. 40 in G min., K.550.
(B) ** Castle Cirrus Dig. **CICD 1006** [id.]. LSO, Cleobury.

With the extremely brisk tempi in the outer movements of the symphony and in the opening allegro of the *Night music*, these are essentially bracing performances, with the LSO players rising brilliantly to the occasion. There is an opportunity for repose in the *Andante* of the symphony and the remaining three movements of the serenade are more relaxed; but this is essentially a bright, breezy approach to Mozart, with the fast pacing made acceptable by the overall feeling of spontaneity. The digital recording is excellent, well balanced and vivid.

Sinfonia concertante in E flat for oboe, clarinet, horn, bassoon and orchestra, K.297b.
(*) ASV Dig. **CDCOE 803; *ZCCOE 803* [id.]. COE, Schneider – BACH: *Double violin concerto*; VIVALDI: *Concerto, RV.556.***(*)
(*) ASV Dig. **CDDCA 580; *ZCDCA 580* [id.]. L. Fest. O, Ross Pople – HAYDN: *Sinfonia concertante.***(*)

The team of young wind soloists of the Chamber Orchestra of Europe is exceptional, and though their live recording of the *Sinfonia concertante* brings a performance less immaculate than we expect from them, it is a lively, stylish account with atmospheric if imperfectly balanced sound, not helped by audience noises.

Well coupled with the Haydn *Sinfonia concertante*, Ross Pople's version also brings a lively, alert performance, with speeds relaxed enough to allow a winning lift to rhythms, making it a genial, affectionate reading which yet never falls into sentimentality. Only in the finale is the result a little heavy, but the 6/8 coda becomes all the more playful. Alan Hacker's distinctive reedy clarinet tone provides an extra tang, and the way the soloists appear in turn as protagonists in the variation finale is delightfully done. The sound is bright, firm and well balanced.

(i) *Sinfonia concertante in E flat, K.297b;* (ii) *Horn quintet in E flat, K.407;* (iii) *Piano and wind quintet in E flat, K.452.*
(*) Decca Dig. **421 393-2 [id.]. (i) ECO, Tuckwell; (ii) Tuckwell, Gabrieli Qt; (iii) John Ogdon, Wickens, Hill, Tuckwell, Gatt.

These recordings derive from a 1984 boxed set containing a good deal of Mozartian repertoire in which the horn has a solo or participating role and, with 73′ overall, is generous measure. Tuckwell directs as well as providing the concertante horn part in the *Sinfonia concertante*, and it is an entirely beguiling performance, beautifully shaped and aptly paced. The *Adagio* has the lightest possible touch and a radiant grace, with the sparkling finale providing spirited contrast. The playing of the wind soloists is extremely fine, never more attractive than in the bubbling triplets which well up in the last movement from each of the woodwind in turn. This is the finest current recording of the normal, published version of the score. Tuckwell also leads the *Horn quintet* – very like a concerto with string quartet instead of orchestra – with characteristic sensibility and aplomb, and is at his most infectious in the finale. The contribution of the Gabrielis is rather severe; one would have liked the string playing to smile a bit more, but they are not helped by a rather close, grainy string timbre; more ambience would have helped here. The *Piano and wind quintet* is enjoyable but not distinctive. The outer movements are alert and briskly paced, but John Ogdon seems not entirely at ease in the *Larghetto*, which lacks the incandescence Perahia brings to it. The recording throughout has striking presence and clarity, and is especially well balanced in the *Sinfonia concertante*.

SYMPHONIES

Symphonies: in A min. (Odense); in G (Alte Lambach), K.45a; in D, K.167a.
*** O-L Dig. **417 234-2**; *417 234-4* [id.]. AAM, Schröder; Hogwood.

These three symphonies, all very early, come as a necessary supplement to Christopher Hogwood's formidable set of the complete Mozart symphonies on period instruments. The *A minor* is nicknamed *Odense* after the Danish town where a set of parts was found in 1983. The score matches an incipit in the Breitkopf manuscript catalogue, but on stylistic grounds it is almost certainly inauthentic, lively as it is. K.45a was originally excluded from the complete set, when the theory then extant was that it was by Leopold Mozart. In 1982 discovery of a manuscript proved it inauthentic, and this is the first recording of the *Alte Lambach* using the text as revised from that source. The third work has been pieced together from movements out of the seven-movement *Serenade in D*, K.185, fairly enough, when the other five Salzburg serenades also exist in symphony versions. The performances and recording beautifully match those of the series as a whole, making it a valuable appendix.

Symphonies: in A min. (Odense); Nos 1 in E flat, K.16; 4 in D, K.19; in F, K.19a.
**(*) Unicorn Dig. *DKPC 9039* [id.]. Odense SO, Vetö.

As it was in Odense that the lost *A minor Symphony* was discovered by the archivist, Gunnar Thygesen, the honour of giving the first performance went to the local orchestra, an excellent band, under its permanent conductor, the Hungarian Tamás Vetö. Even if it is not authentic, it is an engaging work in the *Sturm und Drang* manner and it is given a persuasive performance here, well coupled with an apt group of other early Mozart symphonies, all done with warmer tone than those in the Hogwood series. First-rate recording in this cassette format.

Symphonies Nos 1 in E flat, K.16; 4 in D, K.19; in F, K.19a; 5 in B flat, K.22; in D, K.32; 11 in D, K.73q; 13 in F, K.112; 44 in D, K.73e; 45 in D, K.73n; 46 in C, K.111; in D, K.111a; 47 in D, K.73m.
*** O-L **417 140-2** (2) [id.]. AAM, Schröder; Hogwood.

This Volume 1 of the Academy's monumental series of the complete Mozart symphonies authentically performed gathers together the works which the boy Mozart wrote on his foreign tours in England, Italy and the Netherlands. The earliest pieces here are the three London symphonies written in Chelsea in 1764, when Mozart was only 8½, obviously influenced by J. C. Bach, then an arbiter of musical fashion in London. K.19a was only recently rediscovered.

A little later come two symphonies written for The Hague, but most of the works were written for Italy, including the overture to the opera, *Mitridate*, written for Milan in 1770. With vigour and resilience in outer movements and no lack of charm in slow movements, this is among the most successful of an important and historic series, superbly recorded. Throughout, the performances are directed by Jaap Schröder, with Christopher Hogwood contributing the continuo from the harpsichord. The CD transfers are highly successful in every way, with the two discs encompassing material which filled three LPs, and offering excellent internal access in a way not possible on LP or tape.

Symphonies Nos 1, 4–6, 7a, 8–20, 42–7, 55; in C. K.208/102; in D, K.45, 111/120, 141a & 196/121; in G.
*** Ph. **416 471-2** (6) [id.]. ASMF, Marriner.

Marriner's survey has a splendid Mozartian vitality and seems to combine the best qualities of previous sets by Boehm on DG and Kehr on Turnabout. The Academy play with great style, warmth and polish; the Philips engineers, having responded with alive and vivid recording, offer admirable (analogue) transfers into the CD format. As with the set of later symphonies (see below), the layout is over six compact discs (offered for the price of five). These are altogether delightful records and can be strongly recommended.

Symphonies Nos 9 in C, K.73; 14 in A, K.114; 15 in G, K.124; 16 in C, K.128; 17 in G, K.129; in C, K.35; in D, K.38; in D, K.62a/K.100; (42) in F, K.75; in G, K.75b/K.110.
*** O-L **417 518-2** (2). AAM, Schröder; Hogwood.

The fourth volume to appear in the Academy of Ancient Music series deals with the earliest Salzburg symphonies (those that Mozart composed before 1770 were written in London). The work in D, K.62a, is also known and played as the *Serenade No. 1*, K.100. It is vitality and sharpness of articulation which dominate the reading here. In the later symphonies textures are sometimes thinned even further by the use of solo strings in sections of the music, which produces the feeling of a chamber ensemble, and seems a questionable practice. However, Schröder and his group are nothing if not consistent, and those collecting this series can be assured that this volume is as vigorous and dedicated as the others. The recording too is lively, although the acoustic at times seems somewhat over-resonant, especially in the earlier works. However, the CD transfers are admirably clean.

Symphonies Nos 18 in F, K.130; in D, K.141a; 19 in E flat, K.132; 20 in D, K.133; 21 in A, K.134; in D, K.135; 26 in E flat, K.161a; 27 in G, K.161b; 22 in C, K.162; 23 in D, K.162b; 24 in B flat, K.173dA.
*** O-L **417 592-2** (3) [id.]. AAM, Schröder; Hogwood.

This was the first box of the Academy of Ancient Music's issue of the complete recording of Mozart symphonies using authentic texts and original instruments; and very invigorating it proved. The series, meticulously planned under the guidance of the American Mozart scholar Neal Zaslaw, aims to reproduce as closely as possible the conditions of the first performances. It includes not just the symphonies in the regular numbered series but works which might have been compiled as symphonies (the overture to *Lucio Silla*, for example), and the variety of scale as well as of expression makes it a very refreshing collection, particularly as the style of performance, with its non-vibrato tang, sharply picks out detail of texture rather than moulding the sound together. The recording is excellent, and the CD transfers are bright and clean.

Symphonies Nos 21–41 (complete).
*** Ph. **415 954-2** (6) [id.]. ASMF, Marriner.

Marriner, following up the success of his splendid volume of the early symphonies, here presents the later works in comparably stylish, well-recorded performances. The layout, on six CDs, offers the symphonies in numerical sequence, with no single symphony divided between discs; the only exception to the ordering is No. 40, which is presented at the beginning of the second CD, immediately after the *'little' G minor* (No. 25). The transfers are of high quality; only in No. 40 and the *Haffner* (which date from 1970, nearly a decade before the rest) does a somewhat over-resonant bass betray the age of the originals. Perhaps when he reaches the *Jupiter*, Marriner fails to capture the full weight of Mozart's argument (exposition repeat not observed in the finale); but the wonder is that so many symphonies have been performed with no hint of routine.

Symphonies Nos 25 in G min., K.183; 26 in E flat, K.184; 27 in G, K.199.
(*) DG Dig. **419 234-2; *419 234-4* [id.]. VPO, Levine.

Levine's coupling of the *'little' G minor* and the two much less well-known symphonies that come next in the series makes a lively, attractive issue. There have been more characterful and distinctive readings of No. 25 than this; but the Levine formula of fast allegros, brilliantly played, and crisp slow movements, all marked by refined Viennese playing, certainly works well enough, helped by undistracting sound. The cassette is acceptable but could ideally be more transparent in texture.

Symphonies Nos 25 in G min., K.183; 28 in C, K.200; 29 in A, K.201; 30 in D, K.202; in D, K.203, 204 and 196/121.
*** O-L **417 841-2** (3) [id.]. AAM, Schröder, Hogwood.

With this second batch of Salzburg works the Academy of Ancient Music come to symphonies that have long been established in the regular modern repertory. It is a revelation to find that a symphony such as the *G minor* (No. 25) is not a 'little *G minor*' at all, for with repeats all observed (even those in the Minuet the second time round), it acquires extra weight; and in as lively and fresh a performance as this the extra length from repetition proves invigorating, never tedious. The *A major* – another 'big' symphony – also has a new incisiveness and clarity, without losing anything in rhythmic bounce; so too with the less well-known works. Though it is confusing not to have the regular numbers appended – particularly when the series is so liberally supplied with rarities – the notes by Neal Zaslaw add enormously to the excitement of new discovery. As in the other volumes, the recording is superb, and the CDs have added presence and transparency of texture with, of course, excellent internal access.

Symphonies Nos 25 in G min., K.183; 29 in A, K.201.
(*) O-L **414 631-2 [id.]. AAM, Schröder; Hogwood.

The combination of the Academy's versions of the *G minor* (with all repeats) and the *A major* makes a strongly characterized sampler of this famous series, but for all the vitality of the music making the spirit of Beecham is not very close in slow movements, while for some ears the razor-edged tuttis are not easy to accept.

Symphonies Nos 25 in G min., K.183; 40 in G min., K.550.
*** Erato Dig. **ECD 88078** [id.]. Scottish CO, Conlon.
*(*) Tel. Dig. **ZK8 42935** [id.]. Concg. O, Harnoncourt.

Conlon's coupling of the *G minor Symphonies* is well up to the standard of his two previous issues in his Mozart series. The first movement of K.183 is particularly arresting and the

Andante is beautifully played, serene in its sense of repose to make a striking contrast with the movements around it. The later symphony too is finely paced and well proportioned, spontaneous and alert. Those seeking a chamber scale yet wishing to avoid the astringencies and idiosyncrasies of the authentic style will find this very satisfying. Conlon's directness in no way prevents an imaginative approach to detail. Even the relatively relaxed speed for the first movement of No. 40 justifies itself in the crispness of rhythm and extra clarity. The sound is naturally balanced and clearly detailed within a convincing acoustic.

Harnoncourt secures fine playing from the Concertgebouw, but his coupling of the two *G minor Symphonies* (in itself not a good plan) is only variably successful, with some extreme speeds (as in the very brisk slow movement of No. 40) and an unsettled mood overall, hardly Mozartian. The sound on CD is bright and clear, with good presence.

Symphonies Nos 28 in C, K.200; 33 in B flat, K.319.
** DG Dig. **419 606-2**; *419 606-4* [id.]. VPO, Levine.

Though close in the numerical order, these two works, coupled in Levine's lively, reliable series, represent different Mozartian worlds, that of the teenager set against that of the already mature twenty-three-year-old, much more sophisticated in expression. The performances, with characteristically brisk allegros and no sluggishness in slow movements, are marked by beautiful Viennese string playing. Despite the lovely muted string-tone in the slow movement of K.200, it does rather outstay its welcome when, as here, all repeats are observed. In the Minuet of No. 33, Levine observes repeats in the *da capo*, as Hogwood does in his Oiseau-Lyre series.

Symphonies Nos 29 in A, K.201; 33 in B flat, K.319.
*** Ph. Dig. **412 736-2** [id.]. E. Bar. Soloists, Gardiner.

Although the opening is deceptively gentle, the first movement of John Eliot Gardiner's *A major Symphony* soon develops an athletic strength. Delicacy returns in the *Andante*, nicely proportioned and beautifully played. After a bright, crisp Minuet, the finale has plenty of energy and bite, without being hurried. The account of *No. 33 in B flat* is outstandingly successful, the outer movements a delight, full of rhythmic character, with the good humour of the first nicely caught, and the secondary theme of the finale lilting and gracious. The *Andante* brings some slight squeezing of phrases, but overall this is authenticity with a winning countenance and without the abrasiveness of the Academy of Ancient Music in this repertoire. The recording is fresh and immediate and very well balanced, its tangibility striking on CD.

Symphonies Nos 29 in A, K.201; 34 in C, K.338.
** DG Dig. **419 189-2**; *419 189-4* [id.]. VPO, Levine.

James Levine set out on his big project of recording all the Mozart symphonies with the Vienna Philharmonic, not with the early works nor with the later, more popular ones, but in the middle. In the coupling of Nos 29 and 34, two favourites in that group, he characteristically drives allegros hard, and draws polished, clean-toned playing from the Vienna strings in slow movements which are stylish but convey nothing deeper. Brilliant as the playing is, the feeling of breathlessness can be uncomfortable, as in the finale of No. 34. The finale of No. 29 on the other hand is exhilarating. Undistracting recording, rather close in focus, with a good cassette.

Symphonies Nos 29 in A, K.201; 35 in D (Haffner), K.385; Masonic funeral music, K.477.
(*) DG **413 734-2 [id.]. VPO, Boehm.

These performances, which first appeared not long before Boehm's death, are distinguished by finely groomed playing from the Vienna Philharmonic. The first movement of the *A major*

Symphony is on the slow side but there is some lovely expressive playing in the second. Boehm's unashamedly nineteenth-century approach may at times seem heavy; however, although the performances are weightier than his earlier complete set made with the Berlin Philharmonic, they have a relaxed quality and a glowing resonance which make them endearing, mature products of octogenarian wisdom. They may sometimes lack the drive of other performances, but they remain compelling. The *Masonic funeral music*, darkly characterful, makes a worthwhile filler. The 1981 recordings have been very well transferred to CD. Background noise is almost non-existent and the orchestral quality is warm, naturally balanced, yet tangible within its very attractive ambience.

Symphonies Nos 29 in A, K.201; 35 in D (Haffner), K.385; 40 in G min., K.550.
(M) **(*) Ph. **420 486-2**; *420 486-4* [id.]. ASMF, Marriner.

The original coupling here (to which a fine account of K.201 has been added) dates from 1970. Marriner uses original scorings of both works – minus flutes and clarinets in the *Haffner*, minus clarinets in No. 40. The readings are finely detailed but dynamic too, nicely scaled against warm recording, with a degree of excess bass resonance. But this is generous measure and all three performances are stylish and satisfying. No. 29 was recorded in 1979, but the sound matches up quite well; on tape it is split between the two sides.

Symphonies Nos 29 in A, K.201; 39 in E flat, K.543.
(*) DG Dig. **423 374-2; *423 374-4* [id.]. BPO, Karajan.
*(*) Tel. Dig. **ZK8 43017** [id.]. Concg. O, Harnoncourt.

Although this is very much big-band Mozart with full, weighty sound, it is easy to respond to the warmth of Karajan's approach to the *A major Symphony*. There is some radiant string playing from the Berlin orchestra – the sounds produced utterly different from the textures of Hogwood's Academy – and if the *E flat Symphony* has a degree of heaviness (like the Minuet of K.201), the strength of the reading is in no doubt and the woodwind detail of the finale is perceptively illuminated. The tape has a very ample bass response.

Although there is some fine orchestral playing, Harnoncourt's readings are unconvincing. Tempi are erratic: his pacing of the slow movement of No. 29 has little feeling of serenity or repose, and the Minuet of No. 39 is rushed, although the first movement of this symphony is well judged. The recorded sound is not always comfortable, resonant yet very bright, notably in No. 29.

Symphonies Nos 30 in D, K.202; 31 in D (Paris), K.297; 32 in G, K.318.
(*) DG Dig. **419 146-2; *419 146-4* [id.]. VPO, Levine.

This coupling of the *Paris symphony* with the single-movement No. 32 and its jokey little predecessor, No. 30, of several years earlier, was the first issue in Levine's Mozart cycle with the Vienna Philharmonic. Strong and stylish, with brisk, well-polished allegros, these performances lack a little in distinctiveness, and the recording is not as finely balanced as in later issues in the series; but it is a lively and attractive disc for those who fancy the coupling. The cassette is acceptable but not outstanding.

Symphonies Nos 31 in D (Paris), K.297; 33 in B flat, K.319; Andante, K.297.
(*) Tel. Dig. **ZK8 42817 [id.]. Concg. O, Harnoncourt.

Harnoncourt, when he stops conducting an orchestra of original instruments, may still favour speeds rather slower than usual, but the manner is relatively romantic in its expressiveness. This is the most successful of his Mozart records with the Concertgebouw, with beautiful, cleanly articulated playing. The alternative slow movements are given for the *Paris*, the second one much lighter in weight. In No. 33, Harnoncourt overdoes his slowness in the *Andante*, but adds to the breadth of the finale by giving the repeats of both halves. Very good recording. On compact disc, the strings are given a very tangible presence, woodwind is somewhat more forward than under live concert-hall conditions, yet the bright vividness and realism of the sound are most impressive.

Symphonies Nos 31 in D (Paris), K.297; 34 in C, K.338; 39 in E flat, K.543; 40 in G min., K.550.
(B) *** HMV *TCC2-POR 154598-9*. ECO, Barenboim.

This is the second, as issued, of Barenboim's groupings of Mozart symphonies, taken from recordings made in the late 1960s. The first is discussed below. Both make distinguished and useful additions to HMV's 'Portrait of the Artist' tape series. There are no disc equivalents. Here the *Paris symphony* is given an outstanding performance, the contrasts of mood in the first movement underlined and the finale taken at a hectic tempo that would have sounded breathless with players any less brilliant than the modest-sized ECO. No. 34 (a later recording, dating from 1972) also has a vivacious finale and the playing is equally impressive with its consistently imaginative phrasing. Barenboim's approach to No. 39 is warmly expressive, and some may well prefer it for just these qualities. The responsive phrasing from the strings, both here and in the *G minor Symphony*, is matched by wind playing in which the colour is well brought out. The performances are thoughtful, yet spacious, alive and exciting too. The scale is right, and the warm, smooth recording, perhaps a little lacking in ultimate range at the top, is generally well balanced (only in the *Paris* does the bass resonance become a fraction too insistent at times).

Symphonies Nos 31 in D (Paris), K.297; 35 in D (Haffner), K.385.
(*) Ph. Dig. **416 490-2; *416 490-4* [id.]. O of 18th Century, Brüggen.

In their period performances of Mozart, Brüggen and the Orchestra of the 18th Century could hardly provide a sharper contrast with the established recordings from the Academy of Ancient Music. With period instruments used, textures are comparably clean, but the emphasis is on sweetness and delicacy, with refined and distinctive blending. In phrasing and in expression generally, Brüggen as conductor moulds the music more subtly than would have been possible under the conditions of Mozart's day, making them rather mannered; but the delicacy of these performances will certainly attract many. On CD the sound is both warm and refined; the tape is excessively weighted in the bass.

Symphonies Nos 31 in D (Paris) (2 versions)*; 35 in D (Haffner), K.385* (2nd version)*; 38 in D (Prague), K.504; 39 in E flat, K.543; 40 in G min., K.550* (1st version)*; 41 in C (Jupiter).*
*** O-L Dig. **421 085-2** (3) [id.]. AAM, Schröder; Hogwood.

The last and greatest of Mozart symphonies fare well in the Academy's collected edition, for performances on original instruments bring sharpness and intensity to compensate for any lack of weight or resonance expected by modern ears. Outer movements are consistently refreshing and incisive, and though the lack of expressive freedom typical of slow movements in this series may be disappointing to some, the relative lightness comes to seem apt, even in the *Prague* and *Jupiter*. Only the slow movement of No. 40 disappoints in its rather prosaic manner. The *Paris symphony* is given two complete performances with alternative slow movements, both using more strings than the rest, as witnessed by the first Paris performances. Excellent recording, as in the whole series.

Symphonies Nos 31 in D (Paris); 35 in D (Haffner); 40 in G min., K.550; 41 in C (Jupiter).
(B) **(*) DG Walkman *413 151-4*. BPO, Boehm.
These recordings date from between 1960 and 1966 and come from Boehm's complete Berlin

cycle. The playing is first class, and the recordings sound well here. In the *G minor Symphony* Boehm's featuring of oboes in the place of clarinets (he uses Mozart's earlier version of the score) is hardly noticed, so mellifluous is the playing. This is excellent value at Walkman price, even if the later Vienna recordings (notably of Nos 40 and 41) have rather more character.

Symphonies Nos 31 in D (Paris), K.297; 36 in C (Linz), K.425.
(B) ** ASV *ZCABM 771* [id.]. LPO, Bátiz.

In the recording studio, Bátiz can almost invariably be relied upon to produce lively, spontaneous performances; here, his tempi are convincingly bright in allegros while the LPO are responsive in both slow movements. The recording is fresh and well balanced. A good, if not distinctive, bargain tape.

Symphonies Nos 31 in D (Paris), K.297; 40 in G min., K.550.
*** O-L **410 197-2** [id.]. AAM, Schröder; Hogwood.

A fine sampler from the complete Mozart symphony set by the Academy, with original instruments at their freshest and brightest in crisp, clear interpretations, with all possible repeats observed. The clarity and bite are made the cleaner and more immediate on compact disc.

Symphonies Nos 31 in D (Paris), K.297; 41 in C (Jupiter), K.551.
*** Erato Dig. **ECD 88029** [id.]. Scottish CO, Conlon.

This first of Conlon's Mozart symphony recordings for Erato brings an exceptionally fine account of the *Jupiter*, coupled with a fresh and resilient one of the *Paris symphony*. Conlon observes not only the exposition repeats in the outer movements but also the second-half repeat of the finale too, a positive gain with so weighty a movement. The sureness of focus of the orchestra, with the positioning of each instrument clearly defined within a believable acoustic, establishes the chamber scale very convincingly. As to Conlon's interpretations, the pacing cannot be faulted and the manner is never distractingly personal. The converse may be true: that the readings are not as distinctive as those from the finest rivals; for a sample, however, try the magically lilting account of the *Jupiter* Minuet. On CD the sound is even firmer and marginally more transparent.

Symphonies Nos 32 in G, K.318; 33 in B flat, K.319; 34 in C, K.338; 35 in D (Haffner), K.385; 36 in C (Linz), K.425; in C, K.213c/208; in D, K.248b/250 and 320.
*** O-L **421 104-2** (3) [id.]. AAM, Schröder; Hogwood.

This volume of the Academy of Ancient Music's collected edition of Mozart symphonies includes the works that Mozart wrote between 1775 and 1783, not just those in the regularly numbered series (Nos 32 to 36) but two other symphonies extracted from large-scale serenades (the *Haffner serenade* and the *Posthorn serenade*) as well as a short Italian-style *Sinfonia* taken from the overture to *Il Re pastore*. As before, using authentic performance style with all repeats observed, the readings are always fresh and illuminating, the speeds often brisk but never rushed, though some will prefer a more relaxed, less metrical style in slow movements. The recordings – with Hogwood's harpsichord presented clearly against the full ensemble (strings 9.8.4.3.2) – are superbly faithful to the aim of re-creating the sounds Mozart originally heard.

Symphonies Nos 32 in G, K.318; 35 in D (Haffner), K.385; 36 in C (Linz), K.425.
(M) *** DG *419 864-4* [id.]. BPO, Karajan.
*** Virgin Dig. **VC 790702-2**; *VC 790702-4* [id.]. Scottish CO, Saraste.

This is Karajan's big-band Mozart at its finest. These are beautifully played and vitally alert readings. There are details about which some may have reservations: the Minuet and Trio of the *Linz*, for instance, may seem too slow. But in general these are such finely proportioned performances that they rank among the very best. As recordings, they are alive yet smooth and strongly weighted in the bass.

Jukka-Pekka Saraste with the orchestra of which he is music director offers fresh, alert performances of these three symphonies, strong as well as elegant. More than most other versions on modern instruments they reflect the new lessons of period performance. These are more detached, less sostenuto performances than those of, for example, Jeffrey Tate and the ECO in these works and, with all repeats observed, make an excellent alternative. The recording, helpfully reverberant, yet gives lightness and transparency to textures, conveying an apt chamber scale. There is a good cassette but the sound is not as open and clearly defined as the CD.

Symphonies Nos 32, K.318; 35 (Haffner); 36 (Linz); 41 (Jupiter).
(B) *** HMV *TCC2-POR 54298.* ECO, Barenboim.

These Barenboim recordings were made towards the end of the 1960s and are not available in disc form. This extended-length ferric tape is of high quality, the sound full, clear and well balanced. Barenboim is at his finest in Mozart's last and longest symphony, where he rightly focuses attention on the finale. He observes the second-half repeat as well as the first, to give Mozart's complex fugal design a majesty comparable only with Beethoven, and that at a brisk, swashbuckling tempo. The rest of the symphony is interpreted with equal compulsion. The *Haffner* is also strongly vigorous, the first movement bold almost to the point of brusqueness. In the *Linz*, Barenboim obviously intends the full weight of the imposing introduction to be felt. When the allegro arrives it is gracious and alive and the impetus is nicely judged. The finale too is light-hearted and gay, to make a foil with the rather serious-minded *Andante*. The account of Mozart's *'Italian overture' symphony* is straightforward and spirited. With an authentic-sized orchestra playing very stylishly on modern instruments, this makes an attractive compilation.

Symphonies Nos 32 in G, K.318; 35 in D (Haffner), K.385; 39 in E flat, K.543.
*** HMV Dig. **CDC7 47327-2** [id.]; *EL 270253-4* [Ang. *4AE 34439*]. ECO, Tate.
*** ASV Dig. *ZCDCA 543* [id.]. ECO, Mackerras.

It is the gift of Jeffrey Tate to direct meticulously detailed readings of Mozart, full of stylish touches which never sound fussy or mannered, thanks to the natural electricity which he consistently reveals, whether in fast movements or slow. The phrasing of the first theme of the first-movement allegro in No. 39, for example, has the second and third beats meticulously slurred together, as marked, but the result remains fresh. As in his other late-symphony recordings, Tate is generous with repeats, and there is considerable gain from having both halves of the finale of No. 39 repeated, particularly when the ECO violins articulate so cleanly, more so than in most full orchestral versions. In the brief *Italian overture* of No. 32 and in the *Haffner*, Tate achieves comparable exhilaration at relatively spacious speeds, finding elegance on the one hand while bringing out dramatic contrasts on the other. Excellent sound, weighty but apt in scale. The high-level cassette is very brightly lit, especially on side one.

A decade after his series of Mozart symphony recordings for CfP, Sir Charles Mackerras began another series for ASV, of which this coupling of Nos 32, 35 and 39 was the first issue. With generally brisk speeds, the readings are attractively fresh and urgent. Mackerras rarely seeks to charm, but unfussily presents each movement with undistractingly direct manners. In places the fast speeds imperil ensemble a little, and the recording does not always capture the finest detail. These make excellent alternatives to the Tate coupling of the same symphonies, when the readings are so very distinct, with Tate regularly more spacious, more elegant and with marginally more polished playing from the same orchestra. The sound is bright and vivid on the high-level (iron-oxide) tape and cassette collectors should be well pleased with this coupling.

Symphonies Nos 32 in G, K.318; 36 in C (Linz), K.425; Lucio Silla: overture.
** Tel. **ZK8 43108** [id.]. Concg. O, Harnoncourt.

Harnoncourt's Mozart recordings with the Concertgebouw make a surprising contrast with his period performances, unusually weighty and even romantic in expression, though thoughtfully detailed. In the *Linz* he observes even more repeats than are marked in the regular scores, making it a much more expansive work than usual. It is apt to have the *Overture* to *Lucio Silla* set alongside the similarly structured *Symphony No. 32*, but the coupling is not generous. Weighty, full recording to match the performances.

Symphonies Nos 34 in C, K.338; 35 in D (Haffner), K.385.
*(*) Tel. Dig. **ZK8 42703** [id.]. Concg. O, Harnoncourt.

With bright, clear digital recording – quite different from the sound which Philips engineers get from this orchestra – the Harnoncourt coupling provides refreshing, directly dramatic performances of these two symphonies, marked by unforced tempi. Charm is somewhat missing, and the coupling provides rather short measure; but the immediacy of sound compels attention. On compact disc, however, although the sound-picture is vividly clear, there is a dryness in tuttis which borders on harshness. This is much less attractive than the companion CD coupling Nos 31 and 33.

Symphonies Nos 34 in C, K.338; 41 in C (Jupiter), K.551.
(*) O-L **411 658-2 [id.]. AAM, Schröder; Hogwood.

This separate issue from Hogwood's complete set of the Mozart symphonies has all the merits of the series, but the abrasiveness of the string sound will not suit those who are in any way resistant to the idea of a performance on period instruments. Slow movements lack tenderness and elegance, but the weight of expression of the *Jupiter* comes over well, with every single repeat observed. First-rate, clear-textured recording, bright and clean on CD.

Symphonies Nos 35 (Haffner); 36 (Linz); 38 (Prague); 39 in E flat; 40 in G min.; 41 (Jupiter).
*** DG Dig. **419 427-2**; *419 427-4* (3) [id.]. VPO, Bernstein.

Bernstein's recordings of Mozart's last and greatest symphonies were taken from live performances (between 1984 and 1986) and have all the added adrenalin that is expected (but not always achieved) in such circumstances. Besides the electricity, Bernstein's Mozart has breadth and style, too; only occasionally (as in No. 39) does a suspicion of self-consciousness mar the interpretation. Pacing is consistently well judged, except perhaps in finales, where the VPO are kept very much on their toes with speeds that are perilously brisk. For those not seeking the astringencies of 'authenticity', this is a fine modern set, with more vitality and charisma overall than the alternatives by Levine and Marriner, although the latter have their own merits. The sound is full and well balanced; the tapes somewhat weightier than the CDs, but not lacking freshness in the upper range. However, tape collectors will notice below that there is a bargain-priced Pocket Music tape which offers Nos 35, 40 and 41 together for a fraction of the cost of this box.

Symphonies Nos 35 in D (Haffner), K.385; 39 in E flat, K.543.
(*) CBS **MK 42026 [id.]. Columbia SO, Bruno Walter.

Walter gives a beautifully crisp, classical performance of the *Haffner*, a symphony whose brilliance at times belies its intensity. The slow movement and finale are outstanding in a reading where natural expressive warmth of phrasing is matched by alert, sparkling articulation. There is a breadth about his mature and reflective reading of K.543 which balances the music's inherent energy. The main theme of the first movement is nobly moulded and the remainder of the work reflects Walter's warmly human approach to Mozart. Pacing has a sense of inevitability in the way each movement relates to the others in Walter's overall conception. Fine playing and a wide-ranging recording, although the resonance and brightness on top bring a touch of fierceness to the high violins in fortissimos.

Symphonies Nos 35 (Haffner); 40 in G min., K.550; 41 in C (Jupiter), K. 551.
(B) *** DG Dig. *419 836-4* [id.]. VPO, Bernstein.
(M) *(*) HMV **CDM7 69012-2** [id.]; *EG 769012-4*. BPO, Karajan.

Symphonies Nos 35 (Haffner), K.385; 41 (Jupiter), K.551.
*** DG Dig. **415 305-2** [id.]. VPO, Bernstein.

The *Jupiter* brings one of the finest of all of Bernstein's Mozart recordings, edited together from live performances and exhilarating in its tensions. This is one of the very few recordings to observe the repeats in both halves of the finale, making it almost as long as the massive first movement; but Bernstein's electricity sustains that length, and one welcomes it for establishing the supreme power of the argument, the true crown to the whole of Mozart's symphonic output. Pacing cannot be faulted in all four movements, and the *Haffner* brings a similarly satisfying reading until the finale, when Bernstein in the heat of the moment breaks loose with a speed so fast that even the Vienna violins find it hard to articulate exactly. It remains exciting and, with recording on CD only slightly cloudy in heavy tuttis, far better than most taken from live performance; it makes an excellent recommendation, not as heavy in texture as most using regular symphony orchestras.

On the chrome Pocket Music tape, Bernstein's very sympathetic account of the *G minor* is added, to make a remarkable bargain. The vivid transfer gives an effect of brighter lighting than on CD and the bass is correspondingly drier, but the hall resonance prevents a loss of weight, although the treble may need a little softening on some reproducers.

HMV's mid-price Studio reissue offers comparable generosity; the sound, originally rather opaque on LP, has been freshened on CD. But Karajan's large-scale, over-smooth way with Mozart, not to mention the avoidance of exposition repeats, means that the disc can be considered only with caution. The tape is acceptable but has much of the opaque quality of the LP.

Symphonies Nos 35 in D (Haffner), K.385; 41 in C (Jupiter), K.551.
** HMV Dig. **CDC7 47466-2** [id.]; *EL 270401-4*. ASMF, Marriner.

With allegros on the brisk side, yet with rhythms well pointed and with immaculate, totally unmannered phrasing, Marriner's newest HMV digital coupling of the *Haffner* and the *Jupiter* will appeal to anyone preferring direct and unidiosyncratic Mozart. Crisp and polished as the playing is, some may find that the performances lack a little in both spontaneity and touches of individuality, next to the most magnetic readings; but, with excellent sound, forward and full but not aggressive, they make an agreeable choice in this coupling. There is a very good XDR tape, full-bodied and admirably clear.

Symphonies Nos 36 in C (Linz), K.425; 38 in D (Prague), K.504.
*** HMV Dig. **CDC7 47442-2** [id.]; *EL 270306-4* [Ang. *4AE 34468*]. ECO, Tate.
(*) DG Dig. **415 962-2; *415 962-4* [id.]. VPO, Bernstein.
(*) CBS **MK 42027 [id.]. Columbia SO, Bruno Walter.

Though the string playing of the ECO under Tate is less polished than that of some rivals (partly a question of the warm, forward recording which exposes detail very clearly), his coupling of the two late symphonies named after cities, *Linz* and *Prague*, is outstandingly successful in magnetizing the ear. These are very live-sounding performances translated to the studio, and Tate's ear for detail as well as his imagination in rethinking the music gives them wit as well as weight within a scale (woodwind balanced close) which never sounds too big or inflated. One detail to note is the way that – exceptionally – Tate brings out the extraordinary originality of instrumentation in the recapitulation of the central slow movement of the *Prague*, with the widest possible span between exposed flutes, oboes and bassoons (bar 105). That movement, with the repeat observed, is given extra weight, matching the enormous span of the first movement. The high-level chrome tape is very bright, the overall effect slightly less warm than the CD.

Bernstein's comparable coupling, taken from live performances, brings effervescent accounts of both Nos 36 and 38. Though speeds are dangerously fast in the finales, they are strong, stylish and characterful performances, beautifully played. In sound they cannot quite match the finest rivals, not least Tate and the ECO in this very coupling, and the scale is on the large side, but Bernstein is a consistently winning Mozartian. There is a vivid cassette.

Walter's (1960) account of the *Linz* is memorable in all respects. His thoroughness and attention to detail in an apparently straightforward score are balanced by the natural flow of the phrasing, with the slow movement particularly fine. The (1959) *Prague* is another of Walter's finest performances. He achieves just the right balance of tempi in the two sections of the first movement and draws from the *Andante* all the sweetness and lyrical power of which he is capable. The finale is brilliantly played, but the pace is never forced; if there are times when the tempo is slightly relaxed here and there, a careful listener will detect good musical reasons. The remastered recording is fresh and clear, with a strong, firm bass. It is not as full as we would expect today, and the violins are very brightly lit indeed above the stave, and lack body.

Symphonies Nos 36 in C (Linz); 39 in E flat, K.543.
(M) * Pickwick Dig. **PCD 877.** Scottish CO, Loughran.

Loughran's coupling of the *Linz* and No. 39, well recorded and offered in the budget price-range, brings disappointingly heavy performances, marked by generally slow speeds and unsprung rhythms. Only the finales of both works rise above that, but the ensemble is less polished than when this same orchestra has recorded Mozart with James Conlon for Erato.

Symphonies Nos 36 in C (Linz); 40 in G min., K.550.
*** HMV Dig. **CDC7 49073-2** [id.]; *EL 749073-4*. ASMF, Marriner.

Marriner's coupling of the *Linz* and No. 40 in his EMI series brings a keener sense of spontaneity, of conductor and players enjoying themselves, than his earlier issues. Brisk speeds and resilient rhythms go with subtle phrasing and refined ensemble, to make the disc a strong recommendation in this coupling. In No. 40 Marriner's view of the last two movements is markedly more dramatic, with crisper articulation and faster speeds, than in his earlier recording for Philips (see above), and this time in the slow movement he observes the first-half repeat. There is an excellent cassette.

Symphonies Nos 38 in D (Prague), K.504; 39 in E flat, K.543.
*** ASV Dig. **CDCOE 806**; *ZCCOE 806* [id.]. COE, Schneider.
(M) *** DG *419 478-4* [id.]. BPO, Karajan.
(*) HMV Dig. **CDC7 47334-2 [id.]; *EL 270308-4* [Ang. *4DS 38238*]. ASMF, Marriner.

(*) Erato Dig. **ECD 88093 [id.]. Scottish CO, Conlon.
(*) DG Dig. **423 086-2; *423 086-4* [id.]. VPO, Levine.
(*) DG **413 735-2 [id.]. VPO, Boehm.
(*) O-L Dig. **410 233-2 [id.]. AAM, Schröder; Hogwood.

Schneider's might be counted old-fashioned readings of both symphonies, with measured speeds both in allegros and in slow movements, marked by fine pointing and moulding. Though this is a chamber orchestra, defined as such in its title, the string band sounds larger than in some recent versions, and that is partly a question of the recording, set in a warm, helpful acoustic which brings out the sweetness of the COE violins and the bloom on the wind instruments. Schneider shows his allegiance to older fashion by not observing exposition repeats in the first movements or first halves of slow movements; but if all these qualities suggest heavy performances, that is not the end result, when the consistent rhythmic resilience of Schneider's direction and the superb playing of the COE lightens everything. As always with this orchestra, the solo wind playing is a delight.

Karajan's Galleria coupling makes a real mid-priced bargain. It is difficult to conceive of better big-band Mozart than these beautifully played readings, so aptly paced and shaped and given first-class, full-bodied analogue sound. In this particular coupling the music making throughout is resilient as well as strong. The tape transfer is splendidly managed.

Marriner's Academy pairing of Nos 38 and 39 was the first of a new Mozart series, bringing characteristically polished and stylish readings of both works in full and well-defined sound; the smoothness and polish of the string tone in the sweetly lyrical account of the slow movement of the *Prague* even suggest that that section has been reinforced. Outer movements are brisk, the style rather plain but well sprung and with no hint of overpointing or mannerism. These are strong, satisfying readings that will offend no one, even though – or perhaps because – they could be more positively characterful. There is a good tape, although the sound is rather thick-textured.

With outstandingly realistic and firmly defined sound, Conlon presents readings of both symphonies which in their cleanly established chamber scale are satisfyingly fresh and direct. Speeds are consistently well chosen, with rhythms well sprung and textures made transparent. It is true that with this approach on this scale the tragic *Don Giovanni* overtones of the *Prague* are minimized, and some may feel that Conlon's directness makes for an undercharacterized reading, but both symphonies are undistractingly satisfying in sound that on CD is exceptionally faithful.

Levine's coupling of the *Prague* and No. 39 brings characteristically brisk and athletic performances marked by superb playing from all sections of the Vienna Philharmonic. There is more life in these readings of better-known works than in the earlier issues in Levine's series, which dealt mostly with middle-period symphonies relatively little known. The speed is controversially brisk in the delectable Minuet of No. 39, but Levine's speeds have allowed every single repeat to be observed in both works – including the second halves of the finales. The sound is good on CD and cassette alike.

Boehm's versions, recorded when he had reached his mid-eighties, are sunnier and more genial than those he made as part of his complete Berlin Philharmonic series in the 1960s. Tempi are again spacious, but the results are less markedly magisterial. The glow of the performances is helped by the warm DG sound, which has transferred strikingly well to CD. Detail is less sharp than on digital alternatives, but the balance is truthful and the effect pleasingly natural. Admirers of Boehm interested in making a comparison with his Berlin versions of these same two symphonies will find the earlier performances inexpensively available on a DG Focus tape, digitally remastered and sounding much brighter than on the original analogue LP (DG *423 004-4*).

Those who prefer the acerbities of original instruments will find the Academy of Ancient Music coupling offers two splendid samples of this particular approach to the Mozart symphonies. The weight and scale of the *Prague* are the more keenly apparent in such a performance as this, with all repeats observed, even if Hogwood's and Schröder's determination not to overload slow movements with anachronistic expressiveness will disappoint some. Excellent, finely scaled recording in the CD format.

Symphonies Nos 38 in D (Prague), K.504; 41 in C (Jupiter), K.551.
(**) Tel. Dig. **ZL8 48219** (2) [id.]. Concg. O, Harnoncourt.

Harnoncourt's coupling was originally issued on two separate LPs, each at full-price, and although all repeats are included (even the *Prague* runs for 37′) the idea of offering these two symphonies on a *pair* of CDs seems extremely unrealistic. Harnoncourt turns out to be a much more romantic animal in Mozart. He secures superb playing from the Concertgebouw Orchestra, but the results in the *Jupiter* are on the heavy side, though the *Prague* is generally very successful.

Symphony No. 39 in E flat, K.543.
(B) **(*) DG Walkman *419 085-4* [id.]. BPO, Boehm – BEETHOVEN: *Symphonies Nos 1 and 4.***(*)

Boehm's 1966 recording of the *E flat Symphony* was one of the best of his earlier Berlin recordings, with effortlessly alert orchestral playing of great tonal beauty. The recording is warm and richly upholstered. This Walkman tape is much more generous in content and a third the price of Boehm's later Vienna coupling on CD (see above), but the Vienna performance has rather more grace and vitality.

Symphonies Nos 39 in E flat, K.543; 40 in G min., K.550.
(*) DG Dig. **413 776-2 [id.]. VPO, Bernstein.

Bernstein's coupling is inconsistent, with an electrifying account of No. 40, keen, individual and stylish, and a slacker, less convincing one of No. 39, recorded three years earlier. Though Bernstein's expressive manner is similar in the slow movements of both symphonies, the moulding of phrase sounds self-conscious in No. 39 – after a careless-sounding start to the movement – whereas it is totally convincing in No. 40. In the first movement of No. 39, the slow introduction is bitingly dramatic, but the relaxation for the main allegro loses necessary tension. It would be wrong to exaggerate the shortcomings of No. 39, when No. 40 is one of the finest versions available, keenly dramatic, with the finale delightfully airy and fresh. Considering the problems of making live recordings, the sound is first rate, lacking only the last degree of transparency in tuttis.

Symphonies Nos 39 in E flat, K.543; 41 in C (Jupiter), K.551.
*** Ph. Dig. **410 046-2** [id.]. Dresden State O, C. Davis.

Imaginative playing from the Staatskapelle, Dresden, under Sir Colin Davis, finely paced and beautifully balanced. Arguably the finest account of the *E flat Symphony* currently on the market – if one leaves Beecham and Bruno Walter out of the reckoning. Davis has recorded the *Jupiter* more than once, and this newcomer is all that one would expect: alert, sensitive, perceptive and played with vitality and finesse. Philips also provide very good recording. A self-recommending coupling.

Symphony No. 40 in G min., K.550.
(*) Ph. Dig. **416 329-2 [id.]. O of 18th Century, Brüggen – BEETHOVEN: *Symphony No. 1.***(*)
(M) **(*) Pickwick Dig. **PCD 820**. O of St John's, Smith Square, Lubbock – HAYDN: *Symphony No. 44.****

Using only marginally fewer players than in the Beethoven on the reverse, Brüggen's live recording using period instruments is more warmly communicative than most authentic performances, without losing the benefits of clarity and freshness. Speeds are on the fast side without being stiff or eccentric. Good atmospheric recording but with some exaggeration of bass.

Although not as distinctive as the attractive Haydn coupling, Lubbock's is a pleasingly relaxed account of Mozart's *G minor Symphony*, well played – the Minuet particularly deft – and nicely proportioned. The last ounce of character is missing from the slow movement, but the orchestra is responsive throughout, and the recording is in the demonstration class. Excellent value on Pickwick's mid-priced CD label.

Symphonies Nos 40 in G min., K.550; 41 in C (Jupiter), K.551.
*** HMV Dig. **CDC7 47147-2** [id.]; *EL 270154-4* [Ang. *4AE 34440*]. ECO, Tate.
*** CBS **MK 42028** [id.]. Columbia SO, Bruno Walter.
*** Telarc Dig. **CD 80139** [id.]. Prague CO, Mackerras.
*** DG **413 547-2** [id.]. VPO, Boehm.
(*) HMV **CDC7 47852-2 [id.]. Philh. O, Klemperer.
(*) O-L Dig. **417 557-2 [id.]. AAM, Schröder; Hogwood.
** Decca **414 334-2** [id.]. COE, Solti.
(M) ** Decca *417 695-4* [id.]. VPO, Karajan.
(M) ** Decca **417 727-2**; *417 727-4* [id.]. New Philh. O, Giulini.
*(*) DG **415 841-2**; *415 841-4* [id.]. LSO, Abbado.
*(*) RCA Dig. **RCD 14413 [RCD1 4413]**. Chicago SO, Levine.

In his project to record a series of the late Mozart symphonies with the ECO, Jeffrey Tate entered at the deep end with the last two symphonies, and succeeded superbly. For the general listener this account of the *Jupiter* makes an excellent first choice, with an apt scale which yet allows the grandeur of the work to come out. On the one hand it has the clarity of a chamber orchestra performance, but on the other, with trumpets and drums, its weight of expression never underplays the scale of the argument which originally prompted the unauthorized nickname. In both symphonies, exposition repeats are observed in outer movements, particularly important in the *Jupiter* finale, which with its miraculous fugal writing bears even greater argumentative weight than the first movement, a point firmly established by Tate. Those who like a very plain approach may find the elegant pointing in slow movements excessive, but Tate's keen imagination on detail, as well as over a broad span, consistently conveys the electricity of a live performance. The recording is well detailed, yet has pleasant reverberation, giving the necessary breadth; it is very impressive on CD. The XDR cassette transfer, made at the highest level with the sound wide-ranging and full, has a hint of harshness on the upper strings at fortissimo level.

This is one of Walter's most treasurable couplings, although the symphonies were originally differently paired: the *G minor* was recorded in 1959 and has some excess of bass resonance, most noticeably in the last two movements, while the *Jupiter* has warmth without undue resonance, with the weight of sound entirely appropriate. Here the ear notices a slight lowering of the upper frequency ceiling in the *Andante* in order to produce the background quiet. Both performances are spacious, and with the leisurely pacing of K.550 comes a characteristic humanity. In the first movement the tempo seems exactly right, while the *Andante* spells enchantment and the Minuet takes on an added measure of dignity. The refusal to hurry in the finale brings nicely observed detail. In the *Jupiter* neither the first-movement exposition nor the finale carry repeats, but Walter structures his interpretation accordingly and the reading has something of an Olympian quality. It makes a fitting peak to his cycle of late Mozart symphonies, a performance of indubitable greatness.

Sir Charles Mackerras's Prague coupling of Mozart's last two symphonies brings performances electrifying in their vitality. With generally fast speeds, so brisk that he is able to observe every single repeat and still not run over the 75-minute CD limit, he takes a fresh, direct view which, with superb playing from the Prague Chamber Orchestra, is also characterful. The speeds that might initially seem excessively fast are those for the Minuets, which – with fair scholarly authority – become crisp country dances, almost scherzos. Neither there, nor in any of the other movements, do the speeds sound breathless, largely thanks to delicate rhythmic pointing, with a spring always in the step. The definition of woodwind lines is immaculate, with string textures equally clear despite the warm acoustic, though the bassoon has a distinctly East European tone. On the question of repeats, the doubling in length of the slow movement of No. 40 makes it almost twice as long as the first movement, a dangerous proportion; though it is pure gain having both halves repeated in the magnificent finale of the *Jupiter*, the grandest as well as the most visionary of all Mozart's symphonic arguments.

Boehm recorded this same coupling earlier with the Berlin Philharmonic as part of his complete Mozart cycle (still available in brightly remastered format on an inexpensive DG Focus tape: *419 646-4*), but his Vienna versions, as well as being more vividly and immediately balanced, also present more alert, more spontaneous-sounding performances, with the octogenarian conductor sounding more youthful than before. Boehm takes a relatively measured view of the outer movements of No. 40, but the resilience of the playing rivets the attention and avoids any sort of squareness. Excellent recommendations for both symphonies, though in No. 41 the original single-sided LP format prevented the observance of exposition repeats which many count desirable in Mozart's most massive symphony. This is the only drawback to the CD transfer, which offers full, refined sound within a very attractive ambience.

Klemperer's weighty view of Nos 40 and 41 brings a fascinating reminder of his visionary intensity. However one may initially resist his solid view of the first movement of the *G minor*, the drama and bite of argument are most compelling. The majesty of the *Jupiter* has rarely been brought out more powerfully, yet ruggedness is consistently lightened by stylish pointing of rhythm and phrasing. With the 1960s sound wonderfully fresh and vivid on CD, it makes a splendid memento of his genius.

The separate issue of Nos 40 and 41 from Hogwood's collected edition makes a first-rate recommendation for those wanting period performances, brisk and light, but still conveying the drama of No. 40 and the majesty of the *Jupiter*.

The talented young players of the Chamber Orchestra of Europe, here recorded at the Alte Oper in Frankfurt, respond acutely to Solti's direction with finely disciplined ensemble, paradoxically producing an interpretation which in many places is uncharacteristic of the conductor, unforced and intimate rather than fiery. The middle movements of No. 40 are disappointing for opposite reasons, the *Andante* too self-consciously pointed, and the Minuet too heavy. The *Jupiter* is plainer and much more successful, brightly detailed and crisply articulated. Recording with plenty of bloom on the sound, as well as good detail.

Karajan's earlier (1963) Vienna recordings have been reissued yet again, freshly remastered on a Decca Weekend tape, and remain good value. In the *G minor* the exposition repeat is observed and every detail is beautifully in place, each phrase nicely shaped and in perspective. Slightly suave but beautifully articulate, this has genuine dramatic power although, like the *Jupiter*, which has strength and breadth as well as warmth (but no exposition repeat), one feels that the music making moves within carefully regulated emotional limits.

The Ovation reissue was Giulini's first recording for Decca with the New Philharmonia. They play well for him and the recording is full and detailed. However, the performances, although they offer beautifully polished playing, are curiously lacking in vitality, neither classically poised nor romantically charged. The new digital transfer is fresh, clean, but brightly lit.

Abbado directs generally immaculate but curiously faceless performances of Mozart's last symphonies. The *Jupiter* is marginally more convincing, but there are far better versions of this coupling, even though the remastered sound is well balanced and clear.

Levine's Chicago performances cannot be recommended with any enthusiasm. The *G minor* is matter-of-fact and wanting in real warmth; while the *Jupiter* is more than routine, it is less than distinguished, given the reputation of the orchestra and the musicianship and insight of this conductor. The recording, made in the Medinah Temple, Chicago, has no want of clarity and presence, but its claims cannot be pressed over rival performances.

Symphony No. 41 in C (Jupiter), K.551.
(M) *** DG **423 210-2**; *423 210-4* [id.]. BPO, Karajan – HAYDN: *Symphony No. 104.***(*)

Symphony No. 41 in C (Jupiter); Overture: La clemenza di Tito.
*(*) Ph. Dig. **420 241-2**; *420 241-4* [id.]. O of 18th Century, Brüggen.

Karajan's coupling with one of his strongest Haydn performances was issued – like countless other CDs – to celebrate his eightieth birthday. The Berlin Philharmonic plays superbly in the *Jupiter*, which has weight and power as well as surface elegance. The 1979 analogue sound has been effectively remastered; though, characteristically, Karajan is ungenerous in the matter of repeats, this is still a very fine performance. The Haydn coupling is digital.

Though Brüggen uses period instruments, and the strings play with little vibrato, his is fundamentally a romantic reading with unusually slow speeds. Although the refinement of the playing cannot be gainsaid, moulded more subtly than would ever have been possible in the eighteenth century without a conductor, the result tends to be sluggish, failing to find the necessary bite in moments of the most adventurous inspiration. Those who like a mixture of styles might consider this, if they can accept merely an overture as coupling. The cassette is thick and weighty in the bass and not ideally transparent.

CHAMBER MUSIC

Adagio in C for cor anglais, 2 violins & cello, K.580a.
*** Denon **C37 7119**. Holliger, Salvatore Qt – M. HAYDN: *Divertimenti*; J. C. BACH: *Quartet.****

Though the shortest of the four works on Holliger's charming disc, this Mozart fragment – reconstructed when Mozart left the solo cor anglais part complete but not the string parts – is in a world apart, deeply expressive. The lively performances of the undemanding works by J. C. Bach and Michael Haydn make an attractive coupling. Excellent performances and recording. Since making this recording for Denon, Holliger has made another for Philips, and this is coupled with, among other works, the *Oboe quartet*, K.370 – see below.

Adagio in C for cor anglais, 2 violins & cello, K.580a; Oboe quartet in F, K.370; Oboe quintet in C min., K.406.
(*) Claves Dig. **CD 50-8406 [id.]. Ingo Goritzki, Berne Qt (members).

This CD conveniently collects together Mozart's two major chamber works featuring the oboe, plus the haunting *Adagio* for cor anglais which Ingo Goritzki plays very sensitively, if not quite as memorably as Holliger. The *Oboe quartet*, too, is fresh and pleasing, but not as winning as some of the finest versions – see below. However, the interesting novelty is the *Quintet*, which derives from Mozart's own arrangement of the *Wind serenade*, K.388. The very opening suggests its origins and some might feel that it sounds best in its original format. The composer first reduced the eight parts to five to form the *String quintet*, K.516b, leaving the oboe part virtually unaltered, with the result that a double hybrid piece was left, and performers can choose between oboe and violin to lead the ensemble. Ingo Goritski makes a fairly convincing case for the choice of a broken consort and the performance is a good one, with the Berne players giving accomplished, if not highly imaginative, support. The recording is vivid and well balanced.

Clarinet quintet in A, K.581.
*** Denon Dig. **C37 7038** [id.]. Sabine Meyer, BPO Qt – WEBER: *Introduction, theme & variations.****
(*) Orfeo **C 141861A [id.]. Karl Leister, Prazak Qt – CRUSELL: *Clarinet quintet.****
(*) CRD Dig. **CRD 3445; *CRDC 4145* [id.]. Michael Collins, Nash Ens. – BRAHMS: *Clarinet quintet.***(*)
(M) ** (*) Decca **417 643-2** [id.]. Boskovsky, Vienna Octet (members) – BAERMANN: *Adagio*; BRAHMS: *Clarinet quintet.***(*)

Clarinet quintet in A, K.581; Clarinet quintet fragment in B flat, K.516c; (i) *Quintet fragment in F for clarinet in C, basset-horn and string trio, K.580b* (both completed by Duncan Druce).
*** Amon Ra/Saydisc **CD-SAR 17** [id.]. Alan Hacker, Salomon Qt, (i) with Lesley Schatzberger.

(i) *Clarinet quintet;* (ii) *Oboe quartet in F, K.370.*
(M) *** Pickwick Dig. **PCD 810**. (i) Puddy; (ii) Boyd, Gabrieli Qt.
(B) *** CfP *TC-CFP 40377.* (i) Andrew Marriner; (ii) Gordon Hunt, Chilingirian Qt.
(M) *** DG *423 018-4.* (i) Gervase de Peyer; (ii) Lothar Koch, Amadeus Qt.

Mozart's *Clarinet quintet* is understandably the most popular and most frequently performed of all his chamber works, and it is very well represented in all price-ranges. Leading the compact disc versions (alongside Thea King's outstanding coupling with the *Clarinet concerto* on Hyperion – see above) is a superb new recording by Alan Hacker with the Salomon Quartet, using original instruments. Those fearing that the warm lyricism of Mozart's scoring might be spoiled by spiky string textures will find their fears immediately quashed by the lovely sounds created in the opening bars which encapsulate the kernel of the music's radiantly nostalgic spirit. Anton Stadler, the clarinettist for whom the work was written, possessed a timbre which was described as 'so soft and lovely that nobody who has a heart can resist it'. Alan Hacker's gentle sound on his period instrument has a similar quality, displayed at its most ravishing in the *Larghetto*. He is matched by the strings, and especially by the leader, Simon Standage, who blends his tone luminously with the clarinet. Tempi are wonderfully apt throughout the performance, the first movement pressing onward without haste, the second leisurely and expansive, and the robust Minuet making a fine contrast. The rhythms of the finale are infectiously pointed and, following a passage of rhapsodic freedom from the soloist, there is a spirited closing dash. Hacker decorates the reprise of the *Larghetto* affectionately and adds embellishments elsewhere. His articulation in the second Trio of the Minuet is a delight; his chortling roulades in the last movement are no less engaging, the music's sense of joy fully projected. The recording balance is near perfect, the clarinet able to dominate or integrate with the strings at will; and the tangibility of the sound is remarkably realistic, with each of the stringed instruments clearly focused within a natural ambience. To add to the interest of this CD (which plays for over 60′), Alan Hacker includes a fragment from an earlier projected *Quintet*, probably written in 1787 (K.516c), and a similar sketch for a work featuring C clarinet and basset-horn with string trio, possibly dating from the same year as the famous *A major Quintet* (1789). Both are skilfully completed by Duncan Druce. The work in B flat has a memorable principal theme and its structure is nicely judged (8′ 38″); the piece including the basset-horn is also well worth having, although at 12′ 41″, it very nearly outstays its welcome.

Sabine Meyer was the young clarinettist whose appointment to the Berlin Philharmonic occasioned the open rift between Karajan and the orchestra that clouded their long relationship, in early 1983. Judging from this account of the Mozart, she is a most gifted player whose artistry is of a high order. She produces a full, rich and well-focused tone that is a delight to the ear, and she phrases with great musicianship and sensitivity. The performance is one of the best in the catalogue and is well recorded. The balance is well judged, if placing the listener rather forward. However, the effect is eminently realistic and there is no qualification on technical grounds to stand in the way of a three-star recommendation. On the compact disc, which is issued by Denon, the sound is remarkably refined and natural, although, of course, the forward balance remains. The only drawback to Ms Meyer's version is the coupling, which though agreeable is neither very substantial nor generous.

The medium-priced Pickwick CD brings a re-recording of the Mozart by artists who earlier did it for CfP. As before, the reading of the *Clarinet quintet* is clean and well paced, lacking the last degree of delicacy in the slow movement, but never less than stylish. The young oboist, Douglas Boyd, then gives an outstanding performance in the shorter, less demanding work, with the lilting finale delectably full of fun. The digital recording is vividly immediate and full of presence, with even the keys of the wind instruments often audible.

On cassette the best buy for this work would seem to be the bargain-priced CfP version recorded in 1981 by the young Andrew Marriner – son of Sir Neville – whose persuasive account is in the front rank, quite irrespective of price. It is coupled with an equally fine performance of the delightful *Oboe quartet* by Gordon Hunt, another young musician and principal oboe with the Philharmonia at the time of the recording. Marriner's playing in the *Quintet* is wonderfully flexible. It reaches its apex in the radiantly beautiful reading of the slow movement, although the finale is also engagingly characterized. The *Oboe quartet* is delectable too, with Hunt a highly musical and technically accomplished soloist. The Chilingirian players contribute most sympathetically to both works and the performances are much more generous in repeats than the competing DG Amadeus coupling. The CfP issue was recorded in the Wigmore Hall and the sound-balance is most believable.

The Amadeus coupling, of course, is splendid. Gervase de Peyer gives a warm, smiling account of the *Clarinet quintet*, with a sunny opening movement, a gently expressive *Larghetto* and a delightfully genial finale. The performance is matched by the refinement of Koch in the *Oboe quartet*. With creamy tone and wonderfully stylish phrasing he is superb. The Amadeus accompany with sensibility, and the recording is flawless. So is the cassette transfer, a demonstration tape. The recording dates from 1977 and this reissue on DG's Focus label costs only slightly more than the CfP issue.

With his warm, smooth tone, Karl Leister gives a strong, finely controlled performance which, in the occasional touch of self-consciousness in the phrasing, lacks a little in spontaneity and freshness. With good recording, it can certainly be recommended to those who fancy the fascinating coupling – the brilliant *Clarinet quintet* of Crusell.

Like their Brahms coupling, the Nash Ensemble give a warm, leisured account of Mozart's most famous chamber work, beguiling in its way, but a little lacking in vitality until the finale where, towards the end, there is a burst of bravura-tonguing from Michael Collins. In its way this is easy to enjoy and it is beautifully recorded on chrome tape as well as CD, but other versions have that bit more character.

Boskovsky's account from the mid-1960s is gracious and intimate, a little lacking in individuality, but enjoyable in its unforced way. The closing pages are given a real Viennese lilt. This is generously coupled with not only the Brahms *Quintet* but also Baermann's *Adagio*, once attributed to Wagner. The sound is excellent, well defined and sweet, to match the mellow approach.

Clarinet trio in E flat, K.498.

** CRD *CRDC 4111* [id.]. Anthony Pay, Nash Ens. (members) – SCHUMANN: *Fantasiestücke*; *Märchenerzählungen*.**(*)

Like their recording of the *Clarinet quintet*, the Nash Ensemble – even though the clarinet soloist is different – give a very relaxed and leisurely account of the *Trio*. It is well recorded and beguiling in its gentle way, but more vitality is ideally needed.

Divertimenti for 3 basset-horns Nos 1 in F; 3 in F; 6 in F (after arias from *Le Nozze di Figaro* & *Don Giovanni*), K.439b/1–3.
*(*) HMV Dig. **CDC7 47682-2** [id.]. Trio de Clarone.

These works are more usually heard on a trio of two clarinets plus bassoon, and while the original colouring has the element of novelty it can pall, especially when the playing is rather soft-grained and lacking a sense of fun. Moreover it seems very likely that the arrangements of arias from Mozart operas that form the sixth divertimento of the set were not made by the composer. In any case, they need presenting with far more flair to project properly. The sound itself is very realistic.

Divertimento in E flat for string trio, K.563.
*** CBS Dig. **MK 39561**; *MT 39561* [id.]. Kremer, Kashkashian, Yo-Yo Ma.
(*) Mer. **ECD 84079 [id.]. Cummings String Trio.

Divertimento in E flat for string trio, K.563; 3 Preludes & Fugues, K.404a.
*** Ph. **416 485-2** [id.]. Grumiaux, Janzer, Szabo.

Grumiaux has long been remarkable even among the most outstanding virtuosi of the day for his purity of intonation, and here he is joined by two players with a similarly refined and classical style. They may be an ad hoc group, but their unanimity is most striking, and Grumiaux's individual artistry gives the interpretation extra point. The hushed opening of the first-movement development – a visionary passage – is played with a magically intense half-tone, and the lilt of the finale is infectious from the very first bar. The title *Divertimento* is of course a monumental misnomer, for this is one of the richest of Mozart's last-period chamber works, far too rarely heard in the concert hall. The 1967 recording is exceptionally vivid, refined too, but the digital remastering has brightened the treble without a compensating emphasis in the lower range, and the texture is very much dominated by the solo violin. The three *Fugues* derive from Bach's *Well-tempered Clavier*, but they are prefaced by *Preludes* written by Mozart himself. The performances are direct, clear and purposeful, and here the balance is good.

Gidon Kremer, Kim Kashkashian and Yo-Yo Ma turn in an elegant and sweet-toned account on CBS and are excellently recorded. Indeed, the sound is fresh and beautifully realistic. There are many perceptive insights, particularly in the *Adagio* movement which is beautifully done; even if there are one or two narcissistic touches from Kremer (which one does not find on Grumiaux's recording), his playing is still most persuasive. This is the most satisfying account of the *Divertimento* to appear since Grumiaux on Philips and in terms of recorded sound is preferable, with an excellent cassette equivalent.

The Cummings String Trio also give a very fine account of the Mozart *Divertimento* which, in terms of musicianship, can well hold its own alongside more celebrated names. Accomplished though it is, this ensemble does not have quite the distinction and personality of the rival Kremer–Kashkashian–Ma (CBS) or Grumiaux Trio (Philips).

(i) *Duos for violin and viola Nos 1 in G, K.423; 2 in B flat, K.424;* (ii) *Piano trio in E flat (Kegelstatt), K.498.*
** DG Dig. **415 483-2**; *415 483-4* [id.]. (i) Gidon Kremer, Kim Kashkashian; (ii) with Valery Afanassiev.

Mozart wrote these *Duos* in 1783 for the Archduke of Salzburg. The original commission (which was for six) had gone to Michael Haydn, who was able to complete only four, and Mozart came to his rescue. They are substantial works in spite of their spare instrumentation and they contain much fine music. Kremer and Kashkashian play them skilfully, with good balance between the parts, although Kremer clearly dominates. But there is more to this music than these players find, and the music making grips the listener only fitfully. The *Kegelstatt trio* is another matter. Kegelstatt means skittle-alley, and this unlikely sobriquet suggests its composer as a player at the time of writing the piece! In fact this is an alternative version of the *Clarinet trio*, and the work is very effective in this form. It is given an attractively polished, elegant performance, and the players bring a Ländler-like lilt to the first movement. Excellent recording, very present and clear; the cassette too is in the demonstration class.

Flute quartets Nos 1 in D, K.285; 2 in G, K.285a; 3 in C, K.285b; 4 in A, K.298.
*** CBS Dig. **MK 42320**; *IMT 42320* [id.]. Rampal, Stern, Accardo, Rostropovich.
*** Accent **ACC 48225D.** Bernhard and Sigiswald Kuijken, Van Dael, Wieland Kuijken.
*(*) Denon Dig. **C37 7157** [id.]. Nicolet, Mozart String Trio.

It would be hard to think of a more starry quartet of players for this seemingly undemanding set of works. When, with the obvious exception of the lovely B minor *Adagio* of the principal work, K.285, the music is the opposite of weighty, it makes a perfect vehicle for musicians simply to relax over and enjoy themselves. The recording was made in a relatively dry studio, and the acoustic emphasizes the dominance of Rampal's flute in the ensemble, with the three superstar string players given little chance to shine distinctively except in the finale of K.285. A delectable record none the less. There is a very good cassette, though the transfer level drops slightly on side two.

Readers normally unresponsive to period instruments should hear these performances by Bernhard Kuijken, for they have both charm and vitality. Period instruments and the pedantic observance of the letter of performance practice – the trappings of a superficial authenticity – do not always go hand in hand with a comparable musical instinct. But these performances radiate pleasure and bring one close to this music. This record is rather special and cannot be too strongly recommended. The playing is exquisite and the engineering superb.

Nicolet plays stylishly and with both finesse and spirit to offer a reasonably recommendable CD version. But the accompanying Mozart String Trio is less subtle in matter of detail than either the CBS group or the Kuijken Ensemble. The sound is truthful and 'present', with Nicolet balanced forwardly. They are eminently serviceable performances – it would be unfair to call them routine – but at the same time they do not inspire great enthusiasm.

(i) *Horn quintet in E flat, K.407;* (i–iii) *A Musical Joke, K.522;* (iii) *Serenade No. 13* (*Eine kleine Nachtmusik*), *K.525.*
** Denon Dig. **C37 7229** [id.]. (i) Hauptmann; (ii) with Klier; Berlin Philh. Qt; (iii) with Güttler.

Norbert Hauptmann phrases fluently and musically in the *Horn quintet*, but he misses the wit of the finale, and the approach is rather serious: more obvious pleasure in this spontaneous music could have been communicated. The horn balance dominates the sound, and string detail is far less present and clear than it should be in a digital recording. *Eine kleine Nachtmusik* (where the Berlin Philharmonia Quartet is joined by Wolfgang Güttler, double bass) is a well-made, polished account, rather lacking individuality. It is much better balanced and well recorded. The *Musical Joke*, however, is stiff and its humour determinedly Germanic.

Oboe quartet in F, K.370; Adagio in C for cor anglais, 2 violins & cello, K.580a.
*** Ph. Dig. **412 618-2** [id.]. Holliger, Orlando Qt – *Divertimento 11.***

Holliger's performance has characteristic finesse and easy virtuosity; the Orlando support is first class and so is the Philips recording. The performance of the *Adagio* – a deeper, more expressive piece – is also eloquent, though not finer than Holliger's earlier version for Denon, differently coupled – see above. The *Divertimento* coupling here is less appealing.

Piano quartets Nos 1 in G min., K.478; 2 in E flat, K.493.
*** Ph. Dig. **410 391-2** [id.]. Beaux Arts Trio with Giuranna.
*** Decca Dig. **417 190-2**; *417 190-4* [id.]. Solti, Melos Qt.
(*) Amon Ra/Saydisc Dig. **CD-SAR 31; *CSAR 31* [id.]. Richard Burnett, Salomon Qt (members).
(M) ** Ph. **420 868-2**; *420 868-4* [id.]. Ingrid Haebler, Schwalbé, Cappone, Bortitzky.

These are splendidly alive and vitally sensitive accounts that exhilarate the listener, just as the Curzon–Amadeus set did in the early days of LP. The Beaux Arts play them not only *con amore* but with the freshness of a new discovery. Incidentally, both repeats are observed in the first movements, which is unusual on record. The usual high standards of Philips chamber music recording obtain here; in its CD format, the sound (particularly that of the piano) is exceptionally lifelike.

Sir Georg Solti as pianist proves an even more sparkling and individual Mozartian than he often is as a conductor. His performances of the two Mozart *Piano quartets*, masterpieces both, are magnetic in their spontaneous freshness, in the way that the pianist above all conveys the delight of new discovery, as in his individual pointing of rhythm and phrase. The balance favours the piano, but few will complain, when that underlines the individuality of these readings, vividly recorded. First-movement repeats are observed in both works. There is a very good tape, though the transfer level is not especially high.

With Richard Burnett and three players from the Salomon Quartet, one has the opportunity of hearing this music with much the same balance, dynamic range and clarity of texture as in Mozart's own day. They give very persuasive accounts of both works, though there is just a touch of reticence, as if they are inhibited by what they imagine to be the expressive constraints of the period. Not a first choice, perhaps, but eminently recommendable and well recorded.

Ingrid Haebler plays with elegance and grace and the Philips 1972 recording is first class, equally vivid on CD or cassette. Though not lacking character, this music making must yield to the Beaux Arts versions which have greater imaginative detail.

Piano quartet No. 1 in G min., K.478; Piano and wind quintet in E flat, K.452.
** Mer. **ECD 84115**; *KE 77115* [id.]. Diana Ambache, Ambache Chamber Ens.

Excellent recording, with a good matching tape, and very musicianly performances that would be thoroughly recommendable in a less crowded market. The wind players are all first class and Diana Ambache herself is sensitive and a good stylist. However, in terms of sheer imagination and poetry, they are outclassed by Perahia and Lupu. The slow movement of K.452 is just a little pedestrian, too.

Piano trios Nos 1 in B flat (Divertimento), K.254; 5 in C, K.548.
** Hyp. **CDA 66093** [id.]. London Fortepiano Trio.

Piano trios Nos 2 in G, K.496; 4 in E, K.542.
** Hyp. **CDA 66148** [id.]. London Fortepiano Trio.

Piano trios Nos 3 in B flat, K.502; 6 in G, K.564.
** Hyp. **CDA 66125** [id.]. London Fortepiano Trio.

For the specialist collector. Linda Nicholson plays a Schantz fortepiano of 1797 – and very well indeed; the string players may however pose problems for readers used to the more robust attack and articulation of modern performance practice. The muted sonorities and the tonal bulges and squeezes leave an initial impression of inhibition, but there is no doubt as to the refined musical intelligence and accomplishments of both artists. The recording is fairly well balanced, even if Linda Nicholson is just a little favoured at the expense of her two partners. The reason the performances take up three CDs is principally because the London Trio are very generous indeed in the matter of repeats. When the Beaux Arts set arrives on CD, as it surely must during the lifetime of this book, it should manage with a pair of discs and will almost certainly become our primary recommendation.

Piano and wind quintet in E flat, K.452.

*** CBS Dig. **MK 42099**; *IMT 42099* [id.]. Perahia, members of ECO – BEETHOVEN: *Quintet.****

*** Decca Dig. **414 291-2**; *414 291-4* [id.]. Lupu, De Vries, Pieterson, Zarzo, Pollard – BEETHOVEN: *Quintet.****

*** Ph. Dig. **420 182-2**; *420 182-4* [id.]. Brendel, Holliger, Brunner, Baumann, Thunemann – BEETHOVEN: *Quintet.***(*)

** CRD **CRD 3367**; *CRDC 4067* [id.]. Ian Brown, Nash Ens. – BEETHOVEN: *Quintet.***

*(*) Telarc Dig. **CD 80114** [id.]. Previn, V. Wind Soloists – BEETHOVEN: *Quintet.**(*)

*(*) DG Dig. **419 785-2**; *419 785-4* [id.]. Levine, Vienna/Berlin Ens. – BEETHOVEN: *Quintet.**(*)

An outstanding account of Mozart's delectable *Piano and wind quintet*, with Perahia's playing wonderfully refreshing in the *Andante* and a superb response from the four wind soloists, notably Neil Black's oboe contribution. The pacing throughout is perfectly judged, especially the finale which is nicely relaxed. Clearly all the players are enjoying this rewarding music, and they are well balanced, with the piano against the warm but never blurring acoustics of The Maltings, at Snape. The first-movement exposition repeat is observed and so is the first half of the *Larghetto*. Highly recommended.

Lupu and his Concertgebouw colleagues also have the advantage of excellent recording. There is plenty of space round the wind, a splendid sense of presence and a very realistic and lifelike balance. The engineers are particularly successful in capturing the piano. There is a refreshing sparkle from Lupu in the first movement and a sense of joy and spontaneity. The wind playing is beautifully blended and cultivated; at times (in the slow movement, for example) it is almost bland, but the performance as a whole gives such pleasure and delight that this is unlikely to disturb any except the most curmudgeonly. This excellent version deserves a strong recommendation alongside Perahia; tape collectors may count it a first choice as the Decca cassette has more range and freshness than the relatively restricted CBS tape.

Yet another fine account comes from Brendel and his distinguished companions on Philips. They convey an impressive concentration and strong personality; in the outer movements there is clarity and finesse, and in the slow movement no want of feeling. This is very different from its leading rivals but its intelligence and fire will surely win it many friends. Playing of strong personality and a certain didacticism, though one is at times aware of Brendel's slightly exaggerated staccato: his pianism is very different from that of Lupu or Perahia. The recording is again in the very first flight, with a sense of immediacy and a very natural balance among the five instruments. The chrome tape is in the demonstration class, striking in its clarity and realism.

The Nash version is some eight years old and their playing will give much pleasure in these excellent CD transfers, which have a splendidly firm focus and eminently good tonal body. Ian Brown is a first-class pianist and some will prefer his more self-effacing attitude to that of the more personal approach of a Brendel. Generally speaking though, given the stiff competition, the Nash is not a first recommendation. As with nearly all CRD issues, the equivalent cassette is of high quality.

Previn leads admirably throughout this performance of one of the most engaging of Mozart's chamber works, but the wind support is robust rather than refined. The opening of the slow movement brings elegant playing from the pianist and a rather heavy response from his colleagues. Previn articulates the engaging main theme of the finale most attractively and here the effect is very spirited. The resonant acoustic tends to spread the sound, in spite of the digital recording, although the balance is otherwise well managed.

DG's account with James Levine and the Ensemble Wien-Berlin (who include such eminent players as Karl Leister and Günter Högner) was recorded at Salzburg. The playing is eminently musical and with some felicitous touches, but there is much that is rough-and-ready. Some have complained of intrusive noises (intakes of breath and so on) but this in itself is unlikely to worry collectors. The recording is inclined to be a bit close, but the set falls short of the highest distinction.

String quartets Nos 1–23 (complete).
(M) *** Ph. **416 419-2** (8) [id.]. Italian Qt.

The Quartetto Italiano fit all twenty-three quartets of the Mozart cycle (as well as the original *Adagio* of the *G major*, K.157) on to eight CDs instead of the dozen or so LPs of the Complete Mozart Edition. The set is offered at mid-price and is well worth saving up for. There may have been more inspired accounts of some of these from individual quartets in the shellac and LP catalogues (the Pro Arte K.428 and the Netherlands Quartet's K.499), but one is unlikely to be able to assemble a more consistently satisfying overview of these great works, or one so beautifully played and recorded. There are still fine versions of individual quartets on the market but this set, begun in the 1960s, more than holds its own with them.

String quartets Nos 3 in G, K.156, 4 in C, K.157; 8 in F, K.168; 15 in D min., K.173.
*(*) None. Dig. **CD 79026** [id.]. Sequoia Qt.

These early quartets were composed when Mozart was sixteen and need the most elegant musical presentation. Predictably enough, the *D minor*, K.173, is the most impressive. The Sequoia Quartet give respectable enough accounts of these works, though they do not compare with the Quartetto Italiano on the Philips mid-price label; in terms of recorded sound, the Nonesuch issue is no match for the earlier Philips analogue sound-balance. However, the recordings by the Italian group are available only as a set of eight compact discs; the present issue stands unchallenged for those wanting these works in a separate format.

String quartets Nos 14–19 (*Haydn quartets*).
*** CRD *CRDC 4062/4* [id.]. Chilingirian Qt.
(M) ** DG **415 870-2** (3) [id.]. Melos Qt.

String quartets Nos 14 in G, K.387; 16 in E flat, K.428.
*** Hyp. Dig. **CDA 66188**; *KA 66188* [id.]. Salomon Qt.

String quartets Nos 15 in D min., K.421; 19 in C (Dissonance), K.465.
*** Hyp. Dig. **CDA 66170**; *KA 66170* [id.]. Salomon Qt.

String quartets Nos 17 in B flat (Hunt), K.458; 18 in A, K.464.
*** Hyp. Dig. **CDA 66234**; *KA 66234* [id.]. Salomon Qt.

The set of six quartets dedicated to Haydn contains a high proportion of Mozart's finest works in the genre, music which uncharacteristically he took (for him) a long time to complete, writing without the compulsion of a commission. The Chilingirian Quartet plays with unforced freshness and vitality, avoiding expressive mannerism but always conveying the impression of spontaneity, helped by the warm and vivid recording. International rivals in these works may at times have provided more poise and polish but none outshines the Chilingirians in direct conviction, and their matching of tone and intonation is second to none. Unlike most quartets they never sound superficial in the elegant but profound slow movements. The cassettes are each packaged separately and offer demonstration quality.

The Salomon Quartet has already given us some superb Haydn, and no one sampling their Mozart will be disappointed. It goes without saying that their playing is highly accomplished and has a real sense of style; they do not eschew vibrato, though their use of it is not liberal, and there is admirable clarity of texture and vitality of articulation. There is no want of subtlety or imagination in the slow movements. The recordings are admirably truthful and lifelike, and there are excellent cassettes. Those who seek 'authenticity' in Mozart's chamber music will not be disappointed here.

The Melos Quartet of Stuttgart do not wholly fulfil all the expectations one might legitimately harbour. Their musical judgement is sound and there is no want of tonal finesse or unanimity of approach. But phrasing is rather predictable, as if familiarity with these masterpieces has taken its toll of freshness of response. All the same, collectors requiring a complete mid-price package can rest assured that the playing is at a high level of accomplishment and that the transfers are successfully done: detail is well defined and well focused.

String quartets Nos 14 in G, K.387; 15 in D min., K.421.
*(*) Denon Dig. **C37 7228** [id.]. Kocian Qt.

Straightforward performances of both works, but there is nothing here to arouse great enthusiasm. They are really somewhat bland, without a wide range of colour or dynamics. Good recording.

String quartets Nos 14 in G, K.387; 21 in D, K.575 (Prussian No. 1).
** Tel. **ZK8 43122** [id.]. Alban Berg Qt.

These performances, digitally remastered for CD, date from the mid-1970s and are very fine indeed. The playing has style and character, and there is no attempt to beautify or glamorize the music. The disc loses a star only because it is just too reverberant for comfort.

String quartets Nos 15 in D min., K.421; 17 in B flat (Hunt), K.458.
*** Denon **C37 7003** [id.]. Smetana Qt.

These 1982 performances are both recorded in the House of Artists, Prague. The Smetana find just the right tempo for the first movement of the *D minor*, unhurried but forward-moving. *The Hunt*, which is placed first on the disc, is given a spirited performance and is rather more polished than most of its CD rivals. Not having enjoyed all of the Smetana Quartet's recent performances on this label, it is a pleasure to report with enthusiasm on these well-paced accounts.

String quartets Nos 16 in E flat, K.428; 17 in B flat (Hunt), K.458.
** Sup. Dig. **C37 7538** [id.]. Kocian Qt.

Good but not outstanding performances from this ensemble, formed in the early 1970s but little known outside Czechoslovakia. They are somewhat bland and do not penetrate deep below the surface in the sublime slow movement of the *E flat Quartet*, K.428. They are not wanting in sensitivity but they are prone to disruptive tempo changes (as in the Minuet and Trios of K.458, which sound unrelated) and these and other inconsistencies diminish the pleasure these performances give.

String quartet No. 17 (Hunt), K.458.
** DG Dig. **410 866-2** [id.]. Amadeus Qt – HAYDN: *Quartet No. 77.***

The Amadeus Quartet previously recorded this coupling with Haydn in the mid-1960s and it was one of their popular successes. It is, generally speaking, a most satisfying performance of the Mozart, well recorded, and it is still available on a Walkman tape, now recoupled with a fine account of Beethoven's *Ghost trio* (by Kempff, Szeryng and Fournier) and a less attractive version of Schubert's *Trout quintet* (DG *413 854-4*). The digital repetition of the original pairing with Haydn's *Emperor quartet* does not quite match the success of the older analogue version. There is a distinct absence of charm. Moreover, although the CD sound has striking presence, it is a little edgy in the treble.

String quartets Nos 17 in B flat (Hunt), K.458; 19 in C (Dissonance), K.465.
❀ *** Tel. **ZK8 43055** [id.]. Alban Berg Qt.

The Alban Berg Quartet recorded the *Hunt* in 1979 and it is still possibly the finest account on the market. It has much greater polish and freshness even than the Quartetto Italiano, the Melos or the Amadeus, and well withstands all the competition that has come since. The *Dissonance* is of similar vintage, though it never appeared in the UK at the time. It, too, is first class with a wonderfully expressive account of the slow movement. Although dynamic gradations are steep, there is no sense of exaggeration – on the contrary, there is only a sense of total dedication about these wholly excellent performances, which are recommended with enthusiasm. No reservations about the transfers.

String quartets Nos 18 in A, K.464; 19 in C (Dissonance), K.465.
(M) *** HMV **CDM7 69102-2** [id.]; *EG 291028-4*. Smetana Qt.
* Denon Dig. **C37 7721** [id.]. Kocian Qt.

The vintage analogue coupling from the Smetana Quartet is excellent in every way. The playing has impetus and feeling, finesse and vitality, and the sound is well balanced, full and clear in both formats. Excellent value at mid-price.

The performances from the Kocian Quartet do not substantially alter the somewhat pale impression given earlier in their Mozart cycle. There is little sense of mystery in the opening bars of K.465, and little feeling in the slow movement. The recording itself is excellent, truthful and clean, but does not materially affect the overall lack of enthusiasm this issue engenders.

String quartet No. 19 in C (Dissonance), K.465.
(*) HMV Dig. **CDC7 47439-2 [id.]; *EL 270447-4*. Alban Berg Qt – SCHUMANN: *Piano quintet.***(*)

A fine-grained and beautifully played account of the *Dissonance* from the Alban Berg Quartet, captured at a public concert in Carnegie Hall. There are some obtrusive audience noises in the slow movement, but there is much to be said for the warmth and charm of this performance and, it must be added, for the excellence of the recording. There is also a most satisfactory cassette, well balanced, full and clear.

String quartets Nos 20 in D (Hoffmeister), K.499; 21 in D, K.575; 22 in B flat, K.589; 23 in F, K.590 (Prussian Nos 1–3).
*** CRD **CRD 3427/8**; *CRDC 4127/8* [id.]. Chilingirian Qt.

The Chilingirian Quartet give very natural, unforced, well-played and sweet-toned accounts of the last four *Quartets* and they are extremely well recorded. Though perhaps not as highly polished as were the Melos on DG – though there is not a great deal in it – there is far more musical interest and liveliness here. They are very well recorded too, with cleanly focused lines and a warm, pleasing ambience; indeed in this respect these two discs are second to none. The cassettes, too, are in the demonstration bracket, the sound fresh and full, well focused and transferred without edge.

String quartets Nos 21 in D, K.575; 22 in B flat (Prussian), K.589.
*** Ph. Dig. **412 121-2** [id.]. Orlando Qt.

This Orlando recording comes from 1983 (before their change of personnel) and must be numbered among their most successful. Their account of the *B flat major*, K.589, is wonderfully unhurried and this generally relaxed approach extends to its companions – which makes a pleasant change from the high-powered and 'public' style of quartet playing which is now the norm. The same naturalness is to be found in the *D major*, K.575, which is placed second. The recording is spacious, yet with excellent definition and fine detail.

String quartets Nos 22 in B flat, K.589; 23 in F (Prussian), K.590.
*** Tel. **ZK8 42042** [id.]. Alban Berg Qt.
*** DG Dig. **423 108-2**; *423 108-4* [id.]. Hagen Qt.

These performances come from the 1970s, when the Alban Berg Quartet were extraordinarily fresh, spontaneous and vital. They had not at that time become 'beautifiers of the classics' and although there was no want of elegance, it never detracts from the naturalness of their playing. Their accounts of both Quartets would be difficult to fault. There is an honesty and directness, enhanced by polish and finesse, that make this very special. The sound is very good indeed.

The Hagen Quartet has been criticized in some quarters for its self-conscious charm, pursuit of beauty and over-cultivated tone; nevertheless it is difficult to resist such perfection of ensemble and refinement of blend. Slow movements in particular do not dig deep, but they have an elegance and homogeneity of tone that are remarkable and, at the present time, possibly unsurpassed. The DG recording does justice to their tonal finesse and subtlety. There is more to Mozart than they find, but what they achieve still excites the keenest admiration.

String quintets Nos 1–6.
*** Ph. **416 486-2** (3). Grumiaux Trio with Gerecz, Lesueur.

No reservations about the Grumiaux ensemble's survey of the *String quintets*: immensely civilized and admirably conceived readings. Throughout the set the vitality and sensitivity of this team are striking, and in general this eclipses all other recent accounts. The remastering of the 1973 recordings for CD is astonishingly successful. There is added presence – the tangibility of solo playing is remarkable – and the overall blend remains natural.

String quintets Nos 1 in B flat, K.174; 5 in D, K.593.
** Sup. Dig. **C37 7075** [id.]. Smetana Qt with Suk.

Vigorous performances, recorded in Japan in 1983. The sound is forward but perfectly acceptable. The Grumiaux set is still the more polished, particularly in K.174, but this is undoubtedly enjoyable.

String quintets Nos 2 in C min., K.406; 6 in E flat, K.614.
(*) Denon **C37 7179 [id.]. Smetana Qt with Suk.

The *C minor Quintet*, K.406, is of course an arrangement of the *Serenade for wind octet*, K.388, which Mozart made in 1787; the *E flat Quintet*, K.614, is his last important chamber work, written in the year of his death. The Smetana Quartet and Josef Suk give extremely fine accounts of both works, though they do not quite have the same lightness of touch as the Grumiaux series. They are accorded very realistic sound; the disc, a co-production with Nippon Columbia, Tokyo, can be warmly recommended, though not in preference to Grumiaux.

String quintets Nos 3 in C, K.515; 4 in G min., K.516.
** DG Dig. **419 773-2** [id.]. Melos Qt with Franz Beyer.
*(*) Hung. Dig. **HCD 12656-2** [id.]. Takács Qt with Dénes Koromzay.

The Mozart *Quintets* are not as generously represented on CD as the great *Quartets*; the Melos Quartet and their second violist, Franz Beyer, give a finely prepared and thoughtfully conceived account of both works. Tempi are well judged and phrasing thoroughly articulate, and the overall structure is well held together. But if they are sound, they are at the same time just a shade touched by routine; their dynamic range does not vary widely enough. Of single CDs, the only alternative is the Takács with Dénes Koromzay; the Melos are to be preferred on all counts, and the recording is much better. All the same, older collectors need not jettison treasured LPs of either work in favour of the Melos, good though it is.

The Takács are a young and gifted Hungarian quartet who came into prominence in the 1970s. Their recordings of the two great Mozart *Quintets* with Dénes Koromzay as second viola (though he plays first in the *C major*) have spontaneity and warmth, but there are drawbacks which inhibit a wholehearted recommendation. There could be a greater sensitivity to dynamic range, particularly at the *piano* end of the spectrum. There is some rough-and-ready intonation from Dénes Koromzay, too.

String quintets Nos 5 in D, K.593; 6 in E flat, K.614.
*(*) Hung. Dig. **HCD 12881-2** [id.]. Takács Qt with Dénes Koromzay.

Spirited rather than subtle performances. There is little variety of dynamic shadings; everything tends to be *mezzo forte* and there is little evidence of really quiet playing. They are well enough, if rather forwardly, recorded.

Violin sonatas Nos 17–28; 32–34; Sonatina in F, K.547; 12 Variations on La bergère Célimène, K.359; 6 Variations on Au bord d'une fontaine, K.360.
*** Ph. **416 902-2** (5) [id.]. Henryk Szeryng, Ingrid Haebler.

Violin sonatas Nos 17–28; 32–34; 6 Variations, K.360.
(*) Ph. **412 141-2 (4) [id.]. Arthur Grumiaux, Walter Klien.

Ingrid Haebler's Mozart has sometimes been disfigured by a certain primness and rectitude that qualified admiration for her purely pianistic skill. However, there is no hint of Dresden china in her playing of these sonatas: she brings an admirable vitality and robustness to her part. Her playing has sparkle and great spontaneity. Szeryng's contribution is altogether masterly, and all these performances find both partners in complete rapport. The analogue recordings from the mid-1970s provide striking realism and truthfulness, and they have been immaculately transferred to CD. The *Variations* included in the set are managed with charm; an extra set is included, plus the *Sonatina in F*, not offered by Klien and Grumiaux, which accounts for the need for five CDs. One feels, however, that a price reduction might have been offered.

The Grumiaux/Klien set runs to only four CDs. There is a great deal of sparkle and some refined musicianship in these performances, and pleasure remained undisturbed by the balance which, in the 1981 recordings, favours the violin. The later records from 1982 and 1983 are much better in this respect. It goes without saying that there is some distinguished playing in this set, even if the players are not quite so completely attuned as were Grumiaux and Haskil.

Some may be troubled by the occasional portamento but, for the most part, this can only give pleasure. Walter Klien is always an intelligent partner and the results in the slow movements of the later sonatas are invariably moving.

Violin sonatas Nos 17 in C, K.296; 22 in A, K.305; 23 in D, K.306.
*** DG Dig. **415 102-2** [id.]. Itzhak Perlman, Daniel Barenboim.

These three sonatas are the first of what Alfred Einstein described as Mozart's concertante sonatas; even here, however, the piano is dominant, a point reflected in the fact that, for all Perlman's individuality, it is Barenboim who leads. This is playing of a genial spontaneity that conveys the joy of the moment with countless felicitous details. Three sonatas on a full disc is far from generous measure for a compact disc, but the recording is undistractingly good, with the violin balanced less forwardly than is usual with Perlman, to everyone's advantage.

Violin sonatas Nos 18–21, K.301–4.
*** DG Dig. **410 896-2** [id.]. Itzhak Perlman, Daniel Barenboim.

Some very distinguished playing here from Perlman and Barenboim, with fine teamwork and alert and vital phrasing. The recording, too, is extremely lifelike (it will perhaps be too forward for some tastes) but it is amazingly clean and vivid in its CD form.

Violin sonatas Nos 18 in G, K.301; 19 in G, K.302; 21 in E min., K.304; 24 in F., K.376; 26 in B flat, K.378.
*** Ph. mono **412 253-2** [id.]. Arthur Grumiaux, Clara Haskil.

Violin sonatas Nos 32 in B flat, K.454; 34 in A, K.526.
*** Ph. mono **416 478-2** [id.]. Arthur Grumiaux, Clara Haskil.

These sonatas come from the box of seven LPs devoted to Clara Haskil which appeared two or three years ago and from which the *D minor* (K.466) and *C minor* (K.491) *Piano concertos* with Markevitch are taken (see above). This was a celebrated partnership and these classic accounts, which have excited much admiration over the years (and which will doubtless continue so to do), have been transferred excellently. Mozartians should not hesitate. The original mono recordings come from the late 1950s, yet the sound is remarkably vivid and true and background noise has been virtually vanquished. The performances represent the musical yardstick by which all later versions were judged. Highly recommended.

Violin sonatas Nos 24 in F, K.376; 25 in F, K.377; 12 Variations on La bergère Célimène, K.359; 6 Variations on Hélas, j'ai perdu mon amant, K.360.
*** DG Dig. **419 215-2**; *419 215-4* [id.]. Itzhak Perlman, Daniel Barenboim.

Itzhak Perlman and Daniel Barenboim are taking their time over recording the Mozart *Violin sonatas*, and evidently enjoy the project the more. Though some speeds are on the fast side, these performances are characterized most winningly. The contrast between the first movements of the sonatas – the one charming, the other brilliantly energetic – is strongly established in performances which make no apology, firmly presenting both as major Mozart. The two sets of variations, too, with their sharp changes of mood emerge as stronger than is generally supposed. First-rate recording, with a splendid cassette equivalent.

SOLO PIANO MUSIC

Adagio in B min., K.540; Allegros: in B flat, K.3; in C, K.9a; Fantasia in D min., K.397; Gigue in G, K.574; Klavierstücke in F, K.33b; Minuets, K.2; K.5; K.61g/2; K.355; Minuet and trio in G, K.1; Rondos: in D, K.485; in A min., K.511.
*** HMV **CDC7 47384-2** [id.]; *EL 270382-4*. Daniel Barenboim.

Barenboim's collection of shorter pieces makes an attractive and valuable supplement to his complete set of the Mozart *Sonatas*, also for EMI. The choice ranges effectively from childhood works like the little *Minuet and Trio*, K.1, to the two masterly minor-key pieces, in which the foretastes of romanticism are underlined by Barenboim. Editing is not always immaculate, but the piano sound is very natural and believable, with an outstandingly good tape to match the CD closely. There is some fine music here and all of it played with striking freshness to make a most enjoyable recital for the late evening.

Fantasy in C min., K.475; Piano sonata No. 14 in C min., K.457.
*** Decca Dig. **417 372-2**; *417 372-4* [id.]. Alicia de Larrocha – HANDEL: *Suite No. 5*; BACH/BUSONI: *Chaconne*.***

Alicia de Larrocha is recorded in Henry Wood Hall and the sound is outstandingly realistic in the best Decca tradition. She gives a finely balanced account of the *Fantasy* and *Sonata*, touched throughout with distinction. This can be warmly recommended not only to her admirers but to those who do not always respond to her art.

Fantasia in D min., K.397; Piano sonatas Nos 3 in B flat, K.281; 8 in A min., K.310; 6 Variations in F on Paisiello's 'Salve tu, Domine' from the opera *I filosofi immaginari, K.398*.
*(**) DG **413 997-2** [id.]. Emil Gilels.

This was recorded at a public recital in 1970; instead of imparting an extra degree of life and spontaneity to the playing, however, one is given the feeling of studied care by the pianist to ensure technical accuracy. Gilels's articulation is very precise and crystal clear, an effect accentuated by the recording, which is very cleanly focused, but also hard and dry. The result conveys strong intellectual control but little lightness or sparkle. Of course everything Gilels did was distinctive, but the two *Sonatas* are extremely serious-minded and not everyone will enjoy them. The most successful piece here is the *Fantasia in D minor*, which is freer in feeling.

Piano sonatas Nos 1–18 (complete)*; Fantasia in C min., K.475.*
*** HMV **CDS7 47336-8** (6) [Ang. **CDCF 47335**]. Daniel Barenboim.

We are exceptionally well served in this repertoire, with highly distinguished complete sets by Mitsuko Uchida and András Schiff. Barenboim, while keeping his playing well within scale in its crisp articulation, refuses to adopt the Dresden china approach to Mozart's *Sonatas*. Even the little *C major*, K.545, designed for a young player, has its element of toughness, minimizing its 'eighteenth-century drawing-room' associations. Though – with the exception of the two minor-key sonatas – these are relatively unambitious works, Barenboim's voyage of discovery brings out their consistent freshness, with the orchestral implications of some of the allegros strongly established. The recording, with a pleasant ambience round the piano sound, confirms the apt scale.

Piano sonatas Nos 1 in C, K.279; 14 in C min., K.457; 17 in D, K.576.
*** Ph. Dig. **412 617-2**; *412 617-4* [id.]. Mitsuko Uchida.

Piano sonatas Nos 2 in F, K.280; 3 in B flat, K.281; 4 in E flat, K.282; 5 in G, K.283.
*** Ph. Dig. **420 186-2**; *420 186-4* [id.]. Mitsuko Uchida.

Piano sonatas Nos 6 in D, K.284; 16 in B flat, K.570; Rondo in D, K.485.
*** Ph. Dig. **420 185-2**; *420 185-4* [id.]. Mitsuko Uchida.

Piano sonatas Nos 7 in C, K.309; 8 in A min., K.310; 9 in D, K.311.
*** Ph. Dig. **412 741-2**; *412 741-4* [id.]. Mitsuko Uchida.

Piano sonatas Nos 10 in C, K.330; 13 in B flat, K.333; Adagio in B min., K.450; Eine kleine Gigue in G, K.574.
*** Ph. Dig. **412 616-2**; *412 616-4* [id.]. Mitsuko Uchida.

Piano sonatas Nos 11 in A, K.331; 12 in F, K.332; Fantasia in D min., K.397.
*** Ph. Dig. **412 123-2**; *412 123-4* [id.]. Mitsuko Uchida.

Piano sonatas: in F, K.533/494; No. 15 in C, K.545; Rondo in A min., K.511.
*** Ph. Dig. **412 122-2**; *412 122-4* [id.]. Mitsuko Uchida.

Mitsuko Uchida's set of the Mozart *Sonatas* has won much glowing praise and the Philips engineeers frequent laurels for the naturalness of the recording, over the four years in which the individual records have been issued. This is playing of consistently fine sense and sound musicianship. There is no trace of pianistic narcissism but every indication that this will come to be regarded as a classic series to set alongside those of Gieseking and, more recently, András Schiff. Every phrase is beautifully placed, every detail registers, and the early sonatas are as revealing as the late ones. The *Adagio* which opens *No. 4 in E flat*, K.282, is wonderfully serene while the *Andante* which forms the centrepiece of *No. 5*, K.283, is equally captivating. Indeed the slow movements generally bring the kind of sensibility we associate with Perahia in the concertos. The shorter pieces, too, are beautifully played: the marvellous *B minor Adagio*, K.450, is given an appropriately searching reading. As for the *Rondo in A minor*, K.511, Mitsuko Uchida delivers a reading that is so haunting and subtle that one can hardly rest until one replays it, while her realization of the closing bars of the *D minor Fantasia* combine exquisite musical taste and refinement of judgement. Throughout, allegros are unerringly paced and impeccably stylish; each movement and each work is seen as a whole, yet detail is consistently illuminated. The piano recording is completely realistic, slightly distanced in a believable ambience. The cassettes are first class too, the sound slightly softer-grained, but not lacking body and clarity; however, the CDs offer the ultimate in presence.

Piano sonatas Nos 1 in C, K.279; 4 in E flat, K.282; 12 in F, K.332; 16 in B flat, K.570.
*** Decca **421 110-2** [id.]. András Schiff.

Piano sonatas Nos 2 in F, K.280; 5 in G, K.283; 6 in D, K.284; 10 in C, K.330.
*** Decca **421 109-2** [id.]. András Schiff.

Piano sonatas Nos 3 in B flat, K.281; 7 in C, K.309; 9 in D, K.311; 18 in F: (Allegro, Andante & Rondo), K.533/494.
*** Decca **417 572-2** [id.]. András Schiff.

Piano sonatas Nos 8 in A min., K.310; 11 in A, K.331; 17 in D, K.576.
*** Decca **417 571-2** [id.]. András Schiff.

Piano sonatas Nos 13 in B flat, K.333; 14 in C min., K.457; 15 in C, K.545; Fantasia in C min., K.475.
*** Decca **417 149-2** [id.]. András Schiff.

The survey of the Mozart *Sonatas* by András Schiff was recorded as a set in 1980. They are in no way inferior to the recordings of Uchida (or indeed Barenboim), if rather different in their individual character. Schiff, without exceeding the essential Mozartian sensibility, takes a somewhat more romantic and forward-looking view of the music. His fingerwork is precise, yet mellow, and his sense of colour consistently excites admiration. He is slightly prone to self-indulgence in the handling of some phrases, but such is the inherent freshness and spontaneity of his playing that one accepts the idiosyncrasies as a natural product of live performance, for that is the impression he gives, even though these are studio recordings. The piano is set just a little further back than in the Philips/Uchida recordings, and the acoustic is marginally more open, which suits his slightly more expansive manner. The realism of the piano image is very striking, and there is only a faint remnant of analogue background noise remaining. This is a fine achievement and these records are very satisfying. Moreover by laying out the *Sonatas* (usually with a balance struck between early, and middle and later works) Decca have managed to get four sonatas on to three of the CDs, and thus the whole set is more economically presented than with major rivals.

Piano sonatas Nos 1 in C, K.279; 2 in F, K.280; 3 in B flat, K.281; 4 in E flat, K.282; 5 in G, K.283.
(*) Denon Dig. **C37 7386 [id.]. Maria Joao Pires.

Piano sonatas Nos 6 in D, K.284; 7 in C, K.309; 8 in A min., K.310; Rondo in D, K.485.
(*) Denon Dig. **C37 7387 [id.]. Maria Joao Pires.

Piano sonatas Nos 9 in D, K.311; 10 in C, K.330; 11 in A, K.331; Rondo in A min., K.511.
(*) Denon Dig. **C37 7388 [id.]. Maria Joao Pires.

Maria Joao Pires is a good Mozartian – a stylist with a clean articulation and admirable technical address. These performances on Denon were recorded in the mid-1970s in Tokyo and show consistent intelligence and refinement, as did the Mozart concertos she recorded in the 1970s in Lisbon. Those sonatas to reach us of her complete cycle make a useful alternative to the Uchida, though the recording is not as rich-toned or full-bodied as the Philips. She is refreshingly unmannered and, though not quite as well recorded, her set (or what we have so far heard of it) is to be preferred to the Zacharias on HMV.

Piano sonatas Nos 1 in C, K.279; 12 in F, K.332; 17 in B flat, K.570.
** HMV Dig. **CDC7 47680-2** [id]. Christian Zacharias.

Piano sonatas Nos 4 in E flat, K.282; 6 in D, K.284; 14 in C min., K.457.
** HMV Dig. **CDC7 47038-2** [id.]. Christian Zacharias.

Piano sonatas Nos 5 in G, K.283; 13 in B flat, K.333; 15 in C, K.545.
** HMV Dig. **CDC7 47680-2** [id.]. Christian Zacharias.

There are some pleasing things here: this gifted artist is an intelligent, cultured player with an immaculate technique and he is difficult to fault in terms of taste. At times he seems a little prim – as in the first movement of the *C major*, K.279 – but he finds humour here and is very alive. In the slow movement of the late *B flat Sonata*, K.570, he tends to be a little mannered and the finale is deliciously neat – yet he reinforces some accents in a wilful and self-conscious manner. The very last chords are a shade arch. He takes all the repeats in the *G major Sonata*, K.283, and makes much out of it. In the *B flat Sonata*, K.333, he is in rather too much of a hurry and, although there is a sense of momentum, there are few subtleties of colour or dynamic nuance. In the slow movement – and this goes for the famous *C major Sonata* (K.545), too – he is a shade too self-aware. Again he takes all the repeats, including the second part, which is perhaps too much of a good thing. The sound is very good indeed and nicely balanced.

Piano sonatas Nos 4 in E flat, K.282; 5 in G, K.283; 15 in C, K.545.
*** Ph. Dig. **416 830-2**; *416 830-4* [id.]. Claudio Arrau.

An unusually thoughtful reading of the opening *Adagio* of K.282, distinguished by the warm, rich-toned sound that Arrau has made so much his own. There are occasional touches here and in the Minuet that are a bit idiosyncratic, and he surely invests the slow movement of the *C major Sonata* with too much reverence and feeling. On the whole, however, this is a lovely record, with particularly realistic piano sound. There is a very good cassette, too.

Piano sonatas Nos 4 in E flat, K.282; 10 in C, K.330; 11 in A, K.331; 12 in F, K.332.
*** Decca **417 817-2** [id.]. Alicia de Larrocha.

Alicia de Larrocha's recordings come from the mid-1970s and are anything but bloodless. This is playing of strong musical character, which we much liked on its first appearance – and still do. There is an attractive balance between warmth and poise, but her elegance never approaches preciosity. There is always a keen sensibility in control and truth is never sacrificed to surface beauty. The Decca recording is in the first flight, clean, present and realistic. These are four of Mozart's very finest sonatas and the coupling is generous.

Piano sonatas Nos 6 in D, K.284; 14 in C min., K.457; Fantasia in C min., K.475.
(*) Erato Dig. **ECD 88082 [id.]. Maria Joao Pires.

Maria Joao Pires is a gifted Mozartian who is making an excellent reputation for herself. She is a sensitive and intelligent player, who is well recorded here, too, but after this record she moved over to Denon.

Piano sonatas Nos 8 in A min., K.310; 14 in C min., K.457.
(**) Ph. Dig. **412 525-2** [id.]. Alfred Brendel.

The pianism is masterly, as one would expect from this great artist, but both performances strike one as the product of excessive ratiocination. There is no want of inner life, the texture is wonderfully clean and finely balanced, but the listener is all too aware of the mental preparation that has gone into it. The first movement of the *A minor* has immaculate control but is more than a little schoolmasterly, particularly in the development. The staccato markings in the slow movement are dreadfully exaggerated, by the side of Lipatti's 1950 record or, among modern pianists, Ashkenazy; and the movement as a whole is unsmiling and strangely wanting in repose. Any great artist who is widely acclaimed is always under pressure from within to renew his vision, to explore new dimensions of his familiar repertoire; and the result is often to focus unnatural attention on detail. In an article in the *New York Review of Books*, Brendel speaks of his conviction that the first movement of the *A minor* is orchestral; for all that, he seems intent on refusing to seduce us by beauty of sound. Self-conscious playing, immaculately recorded.

Piano sonatas Nos 10 in C, K.330; 11 in A, K.331; 13 in B flat, K.333; 15 in C, K.545.
* Ph. **420 251-2** [id.]. Ingrid Haebler.

Haebler's performances appeared in the Complete Mozart Edition and were recorded in the period from the late 1960s to early '70s. These accounts represent the Dresden china school of Mozart playing and though they are immaculate – and, in their way, beautiful – they display more 'sensibility' than engagement, and their bloodless pallor ultimately fails to hold one's attention.

Piano sonatas Nos 12 in F, K.332; 13 in B flat, K.333.
(*) Ph. Dig. **416 829-2; *416 829-4* [id.]. Claudio Arrau.

As always, the great Chilean pianist produces sound of much beauty and, though there are some signs of frailty, they are few. The slow movement of the *F major* has some slight expressive hesitations here and there that will not be to all tastes, but there is still much to admire. At times there is a certain pallor; his timbre is not quite as rich and fresh in colour as it was in his prime, but there is wisdom too. It is well worth hearing. The Philips engineers produce a very real and present sound and there is a good cassette, though it is not as open at the top as the CD.

Piano sonatas Nos 16 in B flat, K.570; 17 in D, K.576; Adagio in B min., K.540.
*(**) Ph. Dig. **411 136-2** [id.]. Claudio Arrau.

Arrau's Mozart is the product of enormous thought and a lifetime's wisdom. Yet these readings are highly personal – some would say idiosyncratic. He brings greater sonority and weight to them than do most artists, and his K.570 is powerful and compelling, much bigger in conception than that of most rivals. There are also some unusual agogic touches. Indeed, these accounts are so personal that they call for a specialist rather than a general recommendation, for admirers of this great pianist first, rather than to those starting out building a Mozart sonata collection. The recording is first class.

Double piano sonata in D, K.448.
*** CBS **MK 39511**; *IMT 39511* [id.]. Murray Perahia, Radu Lupu – SCHUBERT: *Fantasia in D min.****

The partnership of two such individual artists as Perahia and Lupu produces magical results, particularly when it was set up in the context of the Aldeburgh Festival, playing at The Maltings concert hall, where this Mozart *Sonata*, like the Schubert *Fantasia*, was recorded live. With Perahia taking the primo part, his brightness and individual way of illuminating even the simplest passagework dominate the performance, challenging the more inward Lupu into comparably inspired playing. Pleasantly ambient recording, beautifully caught on CD. The chrome cassette is 'plummier' in the middle range and less fresh on top.

VOCAL MUSIC

Lieder: *Abendempfindung; Ah, spiegarti, o Dio; Als Luise; Die Alte; An Chloë; Dans un bois solitaire; Im Frühlingsanfange; Das Lied der Trennung; Un moto di gioia; Oiseaux, si tous les ans; Ridente la calma; Sei du mein Trost; Das Traumbild; Das Veilchen; Die Verschweignung; Der Zauberer; Die Zufriedenheit.*
(*) Etcetera **KTC 1039 [id.]. Roberta Alexander, Glen Wilson.

Well accompanied on the fortepiano, Roberta Alexander gives a fresh and stylish account of these seventeen Mozart songs. Enterprisingly, they include a couple of rarities, *Im Frühlingsanfange* and *Die Alte*, though the latter is too crudely characterized. The singer's full, rounded tone is well caught in the recording, which gives a vivid sense of presence on an intimate scale.

Lieder: *Abendempfindung; Als Luise die Briefe; An Chloë; Im Frühlingsanfange; Das Kinderspiel; Die kleine Spinnerin; Oiseaux, si tous les ans; Ridente la calma; Sehnsucht nach dem Frühlinge; Der Zauberer; Die Zufriedenheit.*
*** HMV **CDC7 47326-2** [id]. Elisabeth Schwarzkopf, Walter Gieseking – SCHUBERT: *Lieder.**** ❀

As an extra coupling for Schwarzkopf's peerless Schubert record with Fischer come eleven of the Mozart songs which with comparable magic she recorded at the same (mid-1950s) period with Gieseking. Generous as this CD is, with sound clarified and the voice vividly caught, it is sad that three of the collection were left out, including Mozart's most famous song of all, *Das Veilchen*. But we should be thankful for what we do have, as here, when great artists at their most perceptive work together.

Concert arias: *Ah! lo previdi . . . Ah, t'invola, K.272; Bella mia fiamma . . . Resta oh cara, K.528; Chi sa, K.582; Nehmt meinen Dank, ihr holden Gönner, K.383; Non più . . . Non temer, K.490; Oh temerario Arbace! . . . Per quel paterno amplesso, K.79/K.73d; Vado, ma dove?, K.583.*
*** Decca **411 713-2** [id.]. Kiri Te Kanawa, V. CO, György Fischer.

Kiri Te Kanawa's set of Mozart's concert arias for soprano makes a beautiful and often brilliant recital. Items range from one of the very earliest arias, *Oh temerario Arbace*, already memorably lyrical, to the late *Vado, ma dove*, here sung for its beauty rather than for its drama. Atmospheric, wide-ranging recording, which has transferred well to CD.

Concert arias: *Ah! lo previdi, K.272; Ch'io mi scordi di te, K.506; Misera, dove son, K.369. Idomeneo: Padre germani addio! Lucio Silla: Frai pensier più funesti di morte. Le Nozze di Figaro: Dove sono. Die Zauberflöte: Ach, ich fühls.*
(*) HMV Dig. **CDC7 47122-2 [id.]. Barbara Hendricks, ECO, Tate.

Barbara Hendricks with her distinctive, characterful soprano tackles a challenging range of arias, including the most demanding of the concert arias, *Ch'io mi scordi di te*, interestingly done with violin instead of the usual piano obbligato, a valid alternative. Though with her flickering vibrato the voice is not always ideally suited to individual items, the warmth and intensity are very compelling, helped by strong and stylish accompaniment. Excellent sound.

Concert arias: *Alma grande e nobil core, K.578; Ch'io mi scordi di te, K.506; Vado, ma dove?, K.583*. Arias: *Don Giovanni: Ah fuggi il traditor; In quali eccessi . . . Mi tradi quell'alma ingrata; Batti, batti, o bel Masetto; Vedrai, carino; Crudele . . . Non mi dir. Idomeneo: Zeffiretti lusinghieri. Le Nozze di Figaro: Porgi amor; È Susanna non vien! . . . Dove sono; Non so più; Voi che sapete; Giunse alfin il momento . . . Deh vieni non tardar.*
*** HMV **CDC7 47950-2** [id.]. Elisabeth Schwarzkopf, LSO, Szell; Philh. O, Giulini; A. Brendel.

This generous collection of Mozart arias brings together Schwarzkopf performances recorded over the full span of her recording career, from 1952, when she made a recital recording with John Pritchard, to 1968, when with George Szell and the LSO she recorded Mozart concert arias as coupling for Strauss orchestral lieder. From 1959 come the Countess's arias from *Figaro* and Donna Elvira's arias from *Giovanni*, both taken from the complete sets, conducted by Giulini. Most effectively the recordings are presented in reverse chronological order, taking you from the Marschallin figure of the late years presenting display arias with immaculate style and deep thoughtfulness (and with Alfred Brendel commanding in the piano obbligato of *Ch'io mi scordi di te*), back to the radiant portraits of the Countess and Elvira, patrician in confidence with the voice still at its freshest; finally the delightful early characterizations of Cherubino as well as Susanna, of Ilia in *Idomeneo*, of Zerlina and – most strikingly, if unexpectedly – of Donna Anna in *Don Giovanni*. That last group is a *tour de force* for a singer still in her mid-twenties, but one which highlights the better-known recordings of the later years, filling in the portrait of a Mozartian with few equals. The CD transfers consistently bring out the beauty and tonal range of the voice with new clarity.

Concert arias: *Un bacio di mani, K.541; Ich möchte wohl der Kaiser sein, K.539*. Arias: *Così fan tutte: Donne mie la fate a tante. Don Giovanni; Metà di voi quà vadano; Deh, vieni alla finestra; Finch'han dal vino. Le Nozze di Figaro: Non più andrai; Bravo signor padrone . . . Se vuol ballare; Hai gia vinta la causa . . . Vedrò, mentre io sospiro; Tutto e isposto . . . Aprite un po' quegl'occhi. Zaïde: Nur mutig mein Herze. Die Zauberflöte: Der Vogelfänger bin ich ja; Ein Mädchen oder Weibchen.*
*** HMV Dig. **CDC7 47508-2** [id.]. Thomas Allen, Scottish CO, Armstrong.

There have been few recitals of Mozart baritone arias to match Thomas Allen's, stylish vocally with firm, characterful tone and with an engaging range of characterization. To the predictable favourite arias from the operas, Allen effectively adds the little concert aria, *Un bacio di mano*, which provided Mozart with a theme for the *Jupiter symphony*, and the swaggering song about the Kaiser. Excellent accompaniment and recording.

Concert arias: *Basta vincesti . . . Ah non lasciarmi, K.486a; Ch'io mi scordi . . . Non temer, amato bene, K.490; Exsultate, jubilate, K.165; Misera! dove son . . . Ah! non son io che parlo, K.369; Un moto di gioia, K.579; Vorrei spiegarvi, oh Dio, K.418. Il re pastore: L'amerò, sarò constante.*
** HMV Dig. **CDC7 47355-2** [id.]; *EL 270406-4*. Kathleen Battle, RPO, Previn.

Kathleen Battle offers an attractive collection of Mozart arias, but the performances sparkle less than on her best and most characterful records, with the sound relatively cloudy, not bright enough for Mozart. Significantly, the one opera aria, *L'amerò*, works better in its ethereal purity; within their limits, these are tasteful enough performances.

Concert arias: *Il burbero di buon cuore: Chi sà. Vado, ma dove, K.583. Exsultate, jubilate, K.165.* Arias: *La Clemenza di Tito: Parto, parto. Idomeneo: Ch'io mi scordi . . . Non temer, amato bene. Le Nozze di Figaro: Al desio di chi t'adore; Un moto di gioia mi sento.*
*** Erato **ECD 88090** [id.]. Dame Janet Baker, Scottish CO, Leppard.

In a Mozart programme which extends well beyond the normal mezzo-soprano repertory, Dame Janet Baker sings with all her usual warmth, intensity and stylishness, hardly if at all stretched by often high tessitura. The biggest challenge is the most taxing of all Mozart's concert arias, *Ch'io mi scordi di te*, with Leppard a brilliant exponent of the difficult piano obbligato part. There Dame Janet, so far from being daunted by the technical problems, uses them to intensify her detailed rendering of words. The two *Figaro* items are alternative arias for Susanna, both of them delightful. Sesto's aria from *Clemenza di Tito* presents another challenge, magnificently taken, as does the early cantata, *Exsultate, jubilate*, with its famous *Alleluia*. The other two arias were written for Louise Villeneuve – Dorabella to be – as an enrichment for her part in an opera by Soler, more delightful rarities. Excellent sound and warmly sympathetic accompaniment.

Ave verum corpus, K.618; Exsultate, jubilate, K.165; Kyrie in D minor, K.341; Vesperae solennes de confessore in C, K.339.
(*) Ph. **412 873-2 [id.]. Te Kanawa, Bainbridge, Ryland Davies, Howell, LSO Ch., LSO, Sir Colin Davis.

This disc could hardly present a more delightful collection of Mozart choral music, ranging from the early soprano cantata *Exsultate, jubilate*, with its famous setting of *Alleluia*, to the equally popular *Ave verum*. Kiri Te Kanawa is the brilliant soloist in the cantata, and her radiant account of the lovely *Laudate Dominum* is one of the highspots of the *Solemn vespers*. That work, with its dramatic choruses, is among the most inspired of Mozart's Salzburg period, and here it is given a fine responsive performance. The 1971 recording has been remastered for the CD issue; the original was very resonant and the choral sound is not ideally focused, though the Philips engineers were right not to try and clarify the sound artificially. The balance is otherwise truthful and the ear soon adjusts to the slightly cloudy ambience. Dame Kiri's voice is freshly caught.

(i; ii) *Ave verum corpus, K.618;* (iii; iv) *Exsultate, jubilate, K.165; Masses Nos* (i; ii; iii; v) *10 in C (Missa brevis): Spatzenmesse, K.220;* (ii; iii; vi) *16 in C (Coronation), K.317.*
(M) *** DG **419 060-2**; *419 060-4* [id.]. (i) Regensburg Cathedral Ch.; (ii) Bav. RSO, Kubelik; (iii) Edith Mathis; (iv) Dresden State O, Klee; (v) Troyanos, Laubenthal, Engen; (vi) Procter, Grobe, Shirley-Quirk, Bav. R. Ch.

Kubelik draws a fine, vivid performance of the *Coronation mass* from his Bavarian forces and is no less impressive in the earlier *Missa brevis*, with excellent soloists in both works. Then Edith Mathis gives a first-class account of the *Exsultate, jubilate* as an encore. All these recordings come from 1973 and the digital remastering is entirely beneficial, freshening the sound, sharpening the choral focus and losing none of the ambient warmth. The concert (just under an hour in total) ends with Bernard Klee directing a serenely gentle account of the *Ave verum corpus* (recorded in 1979). A splendid mid-priced bargain which is more than the sum of its parts. However, the *Coronation mass* is also available on a bargain-priced Walkman cassette (see below), complete with the *Requiem mass*.

(i; ii) *Ave verum corpus;* (ii; iii; iv) *Mass No. 16 in C* (*Coronation*), *K.317;* (iii; v) *Requiem mass, K.626;* (vi; i; ii) *Vesperae solennes de confessore, K.339; Laudate Dominum.*
(B) *** Ph. *416 225-4* [id.]. (i) LSO Ch.; (ii) LSO; (iii) John Alldis Ch.; (iv) Donath, Knight, Davies, Dean; (v) Donath, Minton, Davies, Nienstedt, BBC SO; (vi) Te Kanawa; all cond. C. Davis.

One of the very finest (if not *the* finest) of the various collections in Philips's bargain 'On Tour' tape series. The transfers are first rate and demonstrate the best features of the original recordings, which date from between 1967 and 1972. Sir Colin Davis's account of the *Coronation mass* is strong and intense and he has excellent soloists; the *Requiem*, with a smaller choir, is more intimate and here the soloists are more variable, yet this is still a satisfying version in its less ambitious way. The *Ave verum* and Kiri Te Kanawa's *Laudate Dominum* are discussed above. A bargain.

Exsultate, jubilate, K.165 (Salzburg version); Motets: *Ergo interest, K.143; Regina coeli* (2 settings), *K.108, K.127.*
*** O-L Dig. **411 832-2** [id.]. Emma Kirkby, Westminster Cathedral Boys' Ch., AAM Ch. and O, Hogwood.

The boyish, bell-like tones of Emma Kirkby are perfectly suited to the most famous of Mozart's early cantatas, *Exsultate, jubilate*, culminating in a dazzling account of *Alleluia*. With accompaniment on period instruments, that is aptly coupled with far rarer but equally fascinating examples of Mozart's early genius, superbly recorded. A most refreshing collection and sounding very well indeed on CD, giving the singer a most realistic presence.

(i) *Exsultate, jubilate, K.165;* (ii) *Litaniae Lauretanae in D, K.195; Mass No. 16 in C* (*Coronation*), *K.317.*
(M) **(*) Argo *417 472-4* [id.]. (i) Erna Spoorenberg; (ii) Cotrubas, Watts, Tear, Shirley-Quirk, Oxford Schola Cantorum; (i; ii) ASMF, Marriner.

It is good to have this fine 1972 coupling of two of Mozart's appealing early choral works back in the catalogue. The solo work is outstandingly good (notably the singing of the soprano Ileana Cotrubas) and the Academy provides the most sensitive, stylish accompaniment. On the reissued tape the choral focus, while not ideally sharp, is fully acceptable. The concert opens with Erna Spoorenberg's radiant 1967 recording of *Exsultate, jubilate*.

Masses Nos 10 in C (*Spatzenmesse*), *K.220; 16 in C* (*Coronation*), *K.317. Inter natos mulierum in G, K.72.*
(*) Ph. Dig. **411 139-2 [id.]. Jelosits, Eder, V. Boys' Ch., VSO, Harrer.

This coupling of the two C major masses that Mozart wrote as part of his duties in Salzburg will please those who prefer performances authentically using an all-male band of singers – if with a modern orchestra. The *Spatzenmesse* (Sparrow Mass) owes its nickname to the chirping of violins in the *Pleni sunt coeli*, a setting even more compressed than most. The *Coronation mass* is the most famous of the period, well sung and played, with the two named soloists joined by two lusty boy singers, making a well-matched quartet. A fair recommendation for those who fancy the coupling, but there are more distinctive versions of K.317. Atmospheric recording, generally well balanced.

Masses Nos 12 in C (Spaur), K.258; 14 in C (Missa longa), K.262.
(*) Ph. Dig. **412 232-2 [id.]. Shirai, Schiml, Ude, Polster, Leipzig R. Ch., Dresden PO, Kegel.

Kegel with his brilliant Leipzig Radio Chorus conducts attractive performances of two of Mozart's rarer settings of the mass, with Mitsuko Shirai outstanding among the soloists. Neither Mass reveals Mozart at his most inspired, but the *Spaurmesse*, much the shorter of the two, is the more consistent, the *Missa longa* the one with sharper contrasts. The recording is good, but places the singers too far in front of the orchestra.

Masses Nos 16 in C (Coronation), K.317; 17 (Missa solemnis), K.337.
(*) Argo Dig. **411 904-2. Margaret Marshall, Murray, Covey-Crump, Wilson-Johnson, King's College Ch., ECO, Cleobury.

Stephen Cleobury, inheritor of the King's choral tradition, imaginatively couples the well-known *Coronation mass* with the very last of the fifteen settings that Mozart wrote for Salzburg, a work just as inspired, with a similar anticipation of the Countess's music for *Figaro* in the *Agnus Dei* (reminding us of *Dove sono* in K.317, of *Porgi amor* in K.337). Though rhythmically this is not as lively as the finest versions of K.317, the coupling can be warmly recommended, with its excellent soloists and fresh choral singing all beautifully recorded.

Mass No. 16 in C (Coronation), K.317; Vesperae solennes de confessore in C, K.339.
(M) **(*) HMV **CDC7 69023-2** [id.]; *EG 769023-4*. Moser, Hamari, Gedda, Fischer-Dieskau, Bav. R. Ch. and SO, Jochum.

The digital remastering has greatly improved the sound of Jochum's fine 1977 performance of the *Coronation mass*, with its splendid choral response and eloquently spacious conception. Having the *Vespers* for coupling is particularly attractive; if Edda Moser is hardly the ideal choice for the heavenly *Laudate Dominum*, she sings simply and effectively. But, as in the Mass, it is the contribution of the chorus that is memorable and, with the resonance under control by the engineers, the effect is very stirring. This is one of the best of EMI's 1970's mid-priced reissues on CD.

(i) *Mass No. 16 in C (Coronation), K.317;* (ii) *Requiem mass in D min., K.626.*
(B) **(*) DG Walkman *419 084-4* [id.]. (i) Mathis, Procter, Grobe, Shirley-Quirk, Bav. R. Ch. and SO, Kubelik; (ii) Mathis, Hamari, Ochman, Ridderbusch, V. State Op. Ch., VPO, Boehm.

A characteristically generous Walkman coupling, with good sound throughout. Both recordings were made in the early 1970s. Kubelik draws a fine, mellow-toned performance of the *Coronation mass* from his Bavarian forces, lacking something in exuberance, but still alive and well sung. Boehm's account of the *Requiem* is also spacious but has more power, and the majesty of the closing *Agnus Dei* is very involving. This is also available in CD (see below), but the recording loses little in its chrome tape transfer and is strikingly well balanced; moreover, in this format it costs less than a third as much, and offers more music.

Mass No. 18 in C min. (*Great*), *K.427*.

*** Ph. Dig. **420 210-2**; *420 210-4* [id.]. McNair, Montague, Rolfe Johnson, Hauptmann, Monteverdi Ch., E. Bar. Soloists, Gardiner.
*** DG Dig. **400 067-2** [id.]. Hendricks, Perry, Schreier, Luxon, V. Singverein, BPO, Karajan.
(*) HMV **CDC7 47385-2 [id.]. Cotrubas, Te Kanawa, Krenn, Sotin, Alldis Ch., New Philh. O, Leppard.
(*) Tel Dig. **ZK8 43120 [id.]. Láki, Dénes, Equiluz, Holl, V. State Op. Ch. Soc., VCM, Harnoncourt.
(M) *(*) EMI Dig. **CD-EMX 9516**; *TC-EMX 2120*. Wiens, Lott, Dale, Lloyd, LPO Ch. & O, Welser-Möst.

John Eliot Gardiner, using period instruments, gives an outstandingly fresh performance of high dramatic contrasts, marked by excellent solo singing – both the sopranos pure and bright-toned and Anthony Rolfe Johnson in outstandingly sweet voice. Gardiner has modified the reconstruction of Alois Schmitt published in 1901, correcting some of his misreadings in the *Credo* and rewriting the string parts of *Et incarnatus* in a style closer to Mozart's – to beautiful effect, if at a relaxed speed, slower than many authenticists would allow. With the recording giving an ample scale without inflation, this can be warmly recommended to more than those simply wanting a period performance.

Karajan gives Handelian splendour to this greatest of Mozart's choral works, and though the scale is large, the beauty and intensity are hard to resist, for this, unlike much of Karajan's Mozart, is strongly rhythmic, not smoothed over. Solo singing is first rate, particularly that of Barbara Hendricks, the dreamy beauty of her voice ravishingly caught. Though woodwind is rather backward, the sound is both rich and vivid, and the compact disc is even more impressively realistic, though, as the opening shows, the internal balance is not always completely consistent. On the CD the thirteen movements are all separately banded.

Raymond Leppard uses the Robbins Landon edition, rejecting the accretions which were formerly used to turn this incomplete torso of a work into a full setting of the liturgy. He uses a modest-sized professional choir and his manner is relatively affectionate, which many will prefer, even in this dark work. The sopranos are the light-givers here, and the partnership of Ileana Cotrubas and Kiri Te Kanawa is radiantly beautiful. Fine, full, clear recording, more naturally balanced than Karajan's digital version, but the digital remastering has brought just a hint of shrillness to the choral fortissimos of this 1974 recording.

Harnoncourt's version, using period instruments, is strongly characterized, with authentic performance used not to smooth away dramatic contrasts but to enhance them. The emphatic rhythmic style in both slow and fast passages will not please everyone, but with a well-chosen quartet of soloists and responsive choral singing this fills an obvious gap. Reverberant recording is not always helpful to detail.

It was enterprising of EMI to give the young Austrian conductor, Franz Welser-Möst, his first chance to shine on record. He had already made his mark with the LPO, taking over a European tour at the last minute; but here the results lack the tension which distinguishes a recorded performance from a run-through, and Edith Wiens is a disappointing first soprano, with Felicity Lott also below her radiant best. Full, modern digital recording, with an excellent cassette.

Requiem mass (*No. 19*) *in D min., K. 626*.

*** DG Dig. **419 610-2**; *419 610-4* [id.]. Tomowa-Sintow, Muller-Molinari, Cole, Burchuladze, V. Singverein, VPO, Karajan.
*** Ph. Dig. **411 420-2** [id.]. Margaret Price, Schmidt, Araiza, Adam, Leipzig R. Ch., Dresden State O, Schreier.
(M) *** DG *419 867-4* [id.]. Tomowa-Sintow, Baltsa, Krenn, Van Dam, V. Singverein, BPO, Karajan.
(M) **(*) Ph. **420 353-2**; *420 353-4* [id.]. Donath, Minton, Ryland Davies, Nienstedt, Alldis Ch., BBC SO, C. Davis.

(M) ** Decca **417 746-2**; *417 133-4* [id.]. Cotrubas, Watts, Tear, Shirley-Quirk, Ch. & ASMF, Marriner.
(M) ** DG **413 553-2** [id.]. Mathis, Hamari, Ochman, Ridderbusch, V. State Op. Ch., VPO, Boehm.
(M) *(*) DG **423 213-2**; *423 213-4* [id.]. Lipp, Rössl-Majdan, Dermota, Berry, V. Singverein, BPO, Karajan.
*(*) Tel. Dig. **ZK8 42756** [id.]. Yakar, Wenkel, Equiluz, Holl, V. State Op. Ch., VCM, Harnoncourt.
*(*) HMV Dig. **CDC7 47342-2** [id.]. Battle, Murray, Rendall, Salminen, Ch. & O de Paris, Barenboim.
*(*) Telarc Dig. **CD 80128** [id.]. Augér, Ziegler, Hadley, Krause, Atlanta Ch. & SO, Shaw.

Requiem mass, K.626; Ave verum corpus, K.618.
(M) **(*) RCA **GD 86535**; *GK 86535* [**RCA 6535-2-RG**]. Equiluz, Eder, Vienna Boys' Ch., V. State Op. Ch. & O, Gillesberger; or VSO, Froschauer – HAYDN: *Te Deum.***(*)
(*) HMV Dig. **CDC7 49640-2 [id.]; *EL 749640-4*. Pace, Meier, Lopardo, Morris, Swedish R. Ch., Stockholm Chamber Ch., BPO, Muti.

Requiem mass, K.626; Kyrie in D min., K.341.
*** Ph. Dig. **420 197-2**; *420 197-4* [id.]. Bonney, Von Otter, Blochwitz, White, Monteverdi Ch., E. Bar. Soloists, Gardiner.

John Eliot Gardiner with characteristic panache gives a bitingly intense reading, opting for the traditional course of using the Süssmayr completion but favouring period instruments at lower pitch. The result is one of the most powerful performances ever, for while the lighter sound of the period orchestra makes for greater transparency, the weight and bite are formidable. In particular the heavy brass and the distinctively dark tones of basset horns give the piece an even more lugubrious character than usual, totally apt. The soloists are an outstanding quartet, well matched but characterfully contrasted too, and the choral singing is as bright and luminous as one expects of Gardiner's Monteverdi Choir. The superb *Kyrie in D minor* makes a very welcome and generous fill-up, to seal a firm recommendation. The cassette too is first class.

Karajan's newest digital version is a large-scale reading, but one that is white-hot with intensity and energy, not at all ponderous – even to ears now attuned to period performance. The power and bite of the rhythm are consistently exciting, not smooth in the manner usually associated with Karajan's Mozart; if anything, speeds are a fraction brisker than they were in his earlier (1976) recording. The solo quartet is first rate, though Tomowa-Sintow is not quite as fresh as she was in the earlier version, and Helga Muller-Molinari is on the fruity side for Mozart. Vinson Cole, stretched at times, yet sings very beautifully, and so does Paata Burchuladze with his tangily distinctive Slavonic bass tone. The close balance adds to the excitement, though the sound, both choral and orchestral, lacks transparency. There is an excellent matching cassette.

Peter Schreier's is a forthright reading of Mozart's valedictory choral work, bringing strong dramatic contrasts and marked by superb choral singing and a consistently elegant and finely balanced accompaniment. The recording is exceptionally well balanced and the orchestral detail emerges with natural clarity. The singing of Margaret Price in the soprano part is finer than any yet heard on record, and the others make a first-rate team, if individually more variable. Only in the *Kyrie* and the final *Cum sanctis tuis* does the German habit of using the intrusive aitch intrude. Altogether this is most satisfying.

Unlike his earlier recording (see below), Karajan's 1976 version is outstandingly fine, deeply committed. The toughness of Karajan's approach is established from the start with incisive playing and clean-focused singing from the chorus, not too large and set a little behind. The fine quartet of soloists too is beautifully blended, and through everything – whatever the creative source, Süssmayr or Mozart – the conductor superbly establishes a sense of unity. The reading has its moments of romantic expressiveness, but nothing is smoothed over, and with superbly vivid recording such a passage as the *Dies irae* has exceptional freshness and intensity. The remastered recording sounds first class in its chrome cassette format.

The surprise version is Gillesberger's, on an excellent mid-priced RCA CD and tape. Using treble and alto soloists from the Vienna Boys' Choir, who sing with confidence and no little eloquence, this performance also has the advantage of a dedicated contribution from Kurt Equiluz. Gillesberger's pacing is well judged and the effect is as fresh as it is strong and direct. The 1982 recording is excellent, vivid, yet full, and the result is powerful but not too heavy. Moreover this CD has a substantial bonus in offering also a highly dramatic account of Haydn's *Te Deum*, plus Mozart's *Ave verum*, very well sung, used as an interlude between the two main works. There is almost 65′ of music here, and, with such committed response from all concerned, this is certainly recommendable.

Davis with a smaller choir gives a more intimate performance than is common, and with his natural sense of style he finds much beauty of detail. In principle the performance should have given the sort of 'new look' to the Mozart *Requiem* that was such a striking success in Handel's *Messiah*, but Davis does not provide the same sort of 'bite' that in performances on this scale should compensate for sheer massiveness of tone. The BBC Symphony Orchestra is in good form and the soloists – although varying in quality – keep up a laudably high standard. Anyone wanting a version on this scale need not hesitate, but this is plainly not the definitive version. The recording is good but not ideally sharp in focus, although it is fully acceptable in CD; the chrome cassette, transferred at a fairly low level, is bass-heavy.

Muti's is a large-scale, essentially weighty reading. Although he uses fine Swedish choral groups, who sing with much spirit and incisiveness at times, notably in the *Confutatis*, the overall impression is of breadth. The soloists make a fair team, although the men are more impressive than the women. The digital recording is impressively full-bodied and does not lack clarity, while the basic ambience is warm, the Philharmonie acoustics sounding quite different here from the effect the DG engineers usually achieve for Karajan. The *Ave verum*, sung with rich espressivo but not romanticized, makes an enjoyable encore. There is a first-class chrome tape, full and well focused.

Marriner, who can usually be relied on to produce vigorous and sympathetic performances on record, generates less electricity than usual in the *Requiem*. It is interesting to have a version which uses the Beyer Edition and a text which aims at removing the faults of Süssmayr's completion, amending points in the harmony and instrumentation; but few will register any significant differences except in such points as the extension of the *Osanna*. Solo singing is good, but the chorus could be more alert. The remastered sound is brightly lit, with a very good tape.

Boehm's is a spacious and solemn view of the work, with good solo singing and fine choral and orchestral response. It is not as dramatic a reading as Schreier's, though it is immensely polished in every way. The recording dates from 1972 and sounds well in its new format; however, this is not as satisfying as the Schreier Philips CD. It is also available, sounding extremely well, on a Walkman chrome tape (see above), coupled with the *Coronation mass* at a fraction of the price of the CD.

Karajan's earlier (1962) reading, now reissued on CD, took a suave view of the work. The chief objection to this version is that detail tends to be sacrificed in favour of warmth and atmosphere. The solo quartet are wonderfully blended, a rare occurrence in this work above all, and though the chorus lacks firmness of line they are helped out by the spirited playing of the Berlin Philharmonic. However, the sound is nothing special and both the newest digital version and the 1976 analogue recording on Galleria are greatly preferable.

Harnoncourt's distinctive view of Mozart – heavier than you would expect from one so wedded to authenticity – is here negated by the washiness of the recording of voices. The chorus might have been performing in a swimming bath, and though ambience adds some glamour to the solo voices, a good team, it is disconcertingly inconsistent to have an orchestra of original instruments in all its clarity set against vocal sound so vague. The compact disc only serves to emphasize the flabbiness of the choral focus.

Since he recorded it earlier for EMI with an even more distinguished quartet of soloists, Barenboim's view of the Mozart *Requiem* has broadened and become more obviously romantic in manner. Set in a reverberant church acoustic, this is really too weighty for Mozart, a good performance but not one to compete with the finest. Even on CD, the sound is not especially clear.

Though Robert Shaw's quartet of soloists is second to none and the choir has been very well trained, the Telarc version lacks tension and bite and the recording, by the high standards of this company, is rather dim. Not competitive with the finest versions.

Requiem mass (*No. 19*) *in D min.* (edited Maunder).
(*) O-L Dig. **411 712-2 [id.]. Emma Kirkby, Watkinson, Rolfe-Johnson, David Thomas, Westminster Cathedral Boys' Ch., AAM Ch. and O, Hogwood.

Hogwood's version is strictly incomparable with any other, using as it does the edition of Richard Maunder, which aims to eliminate Süssmayr's contribution to the version of Mozart's unfinished masterpiece that has held sway for two centuries. So the *Lacrimosa* is completely different, after the opening eight bars, and concludes with an elaborate *Amen*, for which Mozart's own sketches were recently discovered. The *Sanctus, Osanna* and *Benedictus* are completely omitted as being by Süssmayr and not Mozart. This textual clean-out goes with authentic performance of Hogwood's customary abrasiveness, very fresh and lively to underline the impact of novelty, and to divide Mozartian opinion. With fine solo singing from four specialists in Baroque performance and bright choral sound, brilliantly recorded, it can be recommended to those who welcome a new look in Mozart. The CD has the usual advantages.

Thamos, King of Egypt (incidental music), *K.345.*
(*) Tel. Dig. **ZK8 42702. Perry, Mühle, Van Alterna, Thomaschke, Van der Kemp, Netherlands Chamber Ch., Concg. O, Harnoncourt.

Harnoncourt directs a spirited account of the *Thamos* incidental music, now thought to date from rather later than originally estimated and here made to seem strong and mature in incisive, sharply articulated performances. Playing is excellent, and though chorus and soloists are rather backwardly placed in a reverberant acoustic, the singing is enjoyable too.

OPERA

Bastien und Bastienne (complete). Lieder: *Kom liebe Zither, komm; Die Zufriedenheit.*
*** Ph. Dig. **420 163-2**; *420 163-4* [id.]. Soloists from Vienna Boys' Ch., VSO, Harrer.

Mozart's second opera, written at the age of twelve, is a German Singspiel so simple in style that often, as here, it is performed by boy trebles instead of the soprano, tenor and bass originally intended. Members of the Vienna Boys' Choir give a refreshingly direct performance under Uwe Christian Harrer, missing little of the piece's charm, though a recording with adult singers would still be welcome. The two songs with mandolin accompaniment, also sung by one of the trebles, make an attractive fill-up. First-rate sound on CD; the cassette loses some of the sparkle because of the resonance, although the sound is pleasingly smooth.

La Clemenza di Tito (complete).
*** Ph. **420 097-2** (2) [id.]. Dame Janet Baker, Minton, Burrows, Von Stade, Popp, Lloyd, ROHCG Ch. and O, Sir Colin Davis.

It was a revelation, even to dedicated Mozartians, to find in the 1970s Covent Garden production that *La Clemenza di Tito* had so much to offer. Sir Colin Davis's superb set, among the finest of his many Mozart recordings, sums up the achievement of the stage production and adds still more, for, above all, the performance of Dame Janet Baker in the key role of Vitellia has deepened and intensified. Not only is her singing formidably brilliant, with every roulade and exposed leap flawlessly attacked; she actually makes one believe in the emotional development of an impossible character, one who develops from villainy to virtue with the scantiest preparation. Whereas earlier Dame Janet found the evil hard to convey on stage, here the venom as well as the transformation are commandingly convincing. The two other mezzo-sopranos, Minton as Sesto and Von Stade in the small role of Annio, are superb too, while Stuart Burrows has rarely if ever sung so stylishly on a recording as here; he makes the forgiving emperor a rounded and sympathetic character, not just a bore. The recitatives add to the compulsion of the drama – here they are far more than mere formal links – while Davis's swaggering manner in the pageant music heightens the genuine feeling conveyed in much of the rest, transforming what used to be dismissed as a dry *opera seria*. Excellent recording, which gains in brightness and immediacy in its CD format. This brings not only excellent internal access but a new layout on two discs as against the original three LPs.

Così fan tutte.

[M] ❀ *** HMV **CMS7 69330-2** (3). Schwarzkopf, Ludwig, Steffek, Kraus, Taddei, Berry, Philh. Ch. & O, Boehm.

*** HMV Dig. **CDS7 47727-8** [id.]; *EX 270540-5* (3). Vaness, Ziegler, Watson, Aler, Duesing, Desderi, Glyndebourne Ch., LPO, Haitink.

*** Ph. **416 633-2** (3) [id.]. Caballé, Dame Janet Baker, Cotrubas, Gedda, Ganzarolli, Van Allan ROHCG Ch. & O, C. Davis.

(*) O-L Dig. **414 316-2 (3) [id.]. Yakar, Resick, Nafe, Winberg, Krause, Feller, Drottningholm Court Theatre Ch. & O, Östman.

With speeds often more measured than usual – the very opposite of those in the first CD version, under Arnold Östman – Haitink's EMI version yet consistently conveys the geniality and sparkle of live performances at Glyndebourne. Haitink has rarely sounded quite so relaxed on record. As in his prize-winning version of *Don Giovanni*, similarly based on a Peter Hall production at Glyndebourne, the excellent teamwork, consistently conveying humour, makes up for a cast-list rather less starry than that on some rival versions. This is above all a sunny performance, sailing happily over any serious shoals beneath Da Ponte's comedy. Claudio Desderi as Alfonso more than anyone among the singers helps to establish that Glyndebourne atmosphere, with recitatives superbly timed and coloured. They are consistently made to sound as natural as ordinary conversation, with the variety of pace compensating for any tendency to slowness in the set numbers. If Carol Vaness and Delores Ziegler are rather too alike in timbre to be distinguished easily, the relationship becomes all the more sisterly when, quite apart from the similarity, they respond so beautifully to each other. John Aler makes a headily unstrained Ferrando, beautifully free in the upper register; and two Glyndebourne regulars, Lilian Watson and Dale Duesing, make up a strong team. The digital recording gives fine bloom and an impressive dynamic range to voices and orchestra alike. The XDR cassettes are well managed.

Colin Davis has rarely if ever made a more captivating record than his magical set of *Così fan tutte*. His energy and sparkle are here set against inspired and characterful singing from the three women soloists, with Montserrat Caballé and Janet Baker proving a winning partnership, each challenging and abetting the other all the time. Cotrubas equally is a vivid Despina, never merely arch. The men too make a strong team. Though Gedda has moments of rough tone, his account of *Un aura amorosa* is honeyed and delicate, and though Ganzarolli falls short in one of his prominent arias, it is a spirited, incisive performance, while Richard van Allan here naturally assumes the status of an international recording artist with flair and imagination. Sparkling recitative (complete) and recording which has you riveted by the play of the action. The transfer to CD has brought an even greater sense of presence and the set is generously cued.

Arnold Östman has established a formidable reputation conducting authentic performances of Mozart in the beautiful little court opera house at Drottningholm, near Stockholm. Except that soloists of international standing have been introduced – an aptly fresh-voiced team, stylishly Mozartian – this recording aims to reproduce one of the most successful of his productions. The point initially to marvel at is the hectic speed of almost every number. The wonder is that with light-toned period instruments and with singers sufficiently agile, the anticipated gabble does not take place, and Östman refreshingly establishes a valid new view. Few Mozartians would want to hear *Così fan tutte* like this all the time, but with no weak link in the cast and with the drama vividly presented, it can be recommended to those who enjoy authentic performance and to all who are prepared to listen afresh. With ample cueing, the CD is particularly convenient to use, and the sound is even clearer and more immediate, but Mozartians are warned that those seeking the charm and humane geniality that Haitink and Davis find in this work will discover that Östman's set is less ingratiating, though it remains compulsive listening throughout.

First choice remains with Boehm's classic set, reissued on three mid-priced CDs, with its glorious solo singing, headed by the incomparable Fiordiligi of Schwarzkopf and the equally moving Dorabella of Christa Ludwig, a superb memento of Walter Legge's recording genius. It still stands any comparison with other recordings made before or since.

Don Giovanni (complete).

*** HMV **CDS7 47260-8** (3) [Ang. **CDCC 47260**]. Waechter, Schwarzkopf, Sutherland, Alva, Frick, Sciutti, Taddei, Philh. Ch. & O, Giulini.

*** HMV Dig. **CDS7 47037-8** (3) [Ang. **CDCC 47036**]. Thomas Allen, Vaness, Ewing, Gale, Van Allan, Keith Lewis, Glyndebourne Ch., LPO, Haitink.

*** DG Dig. **419 179-2**; *419 179-4* (3) [id.]. Ramey, Tomowa-Sintow, Baltsa, Battle, Winbergh, Furlanetto, Malta, Burchuladze, German Op. Ch., Berlin, BPO, Karajan.

*** Ph. **416 406-2** (3) [id.]. Wixell, Arroyo, Te Kanawa, Freni, Burrows, Ganzarolli, ROHCG Ch. & O, C. Davis.

(M) *** Decca *411 626-4* (3) [id.]. Siepi, Gueden, Della Casa, Danco, Corena, V. State Op. Ch., VPO, Josef Krips.

(*) CBS **M3K 35192 (3) [id.]. Raimondi, Moser, Te Kanawa, Berganza, Riegel, Van Dam, Paris Op. Ch. & O, Maazel.

(M) **(*) DG *413 282-4* (2) [id.]. Milnes, Tomowa-Sintow, Zylis-Gara, Mathis, Schreier, Berry, V. State Op. Ch., VPO, Boehm.

The return of the classic Giulini HMV set, lovingly remastered to bring out even more vividly the excellence of Walter Legge's original sound-balance, sets the standard by which all other recordings have come to be judged. Not only is the singing cast more consistent than any other; the direction of Giulini and the playing of the vintage Philharmonia Orchestra give this performance an athletic vigour which carries all before it. The whole production owes so much to the work of Walter Legge, uncredited in the original issue but the prime mover behind this and so many other Phiharmonia issues. Legge's wife, Elisabeth Schwarzkopf, as Elvira, emerges as a dominant figure to give a distinctive but totally apt slant to this endlessly invigorating drama. No wilting sufferer this, but the most formidable of women, who flies at the Don with such cries as *Perfido mostro!* unforgettably sung. The young Sutherland may be relatively reticent as Anna, but with such technical ease and consistent beauty of tone, she makes a superb foil.

Taddei is a delightful Leporello, and each member of the cast – including the young Cappuccilli as Masetto – combines fine singing with keen dramatic sense. Recitatives are scintillating, and only the occasional exaggerated snarl from the Don of Eberhard Waechter mars the superb vocal standards. Even that goes well with his fresh and youthful portrait of the central character.

Haitink's set superbly captures the flavour of Sir Peter Hall's memorable production at Glyndebourne, not least in the inspired teamwork. The only major change from the production on stage is that Maria Ewing (Lady Hall) comes in as Elvira, vibrant and characterful, not ideally pure-toned but contrasting characterfully with the powerful Donna Anna of Carol Vaness and the innocent-sounding Zerlina of Elizabeth Gale. Keith Lewis is a sweet-toned Ottavio, but it is Thomas Allen as Giovanni who – apart from Haitink – dominates the set, a swaggering Don full of charm and with a touch of nobility when, defiant to the end, he is dragged to hell – a spine-chilling moment as recorded here. Rarely has the Champagne aria been so beautifully sung, with each note articulated – and that also reflects Haitink's flawless control of pacing, not always conventional but always thoughtful and convincing. Excellent playing from the LPO – well practised in the Glyndebourne pit – and warm, full recording, far more agreeable than the actual sound in the dry auditorium at Glyndebourne. The CD with its ample cueing brings extra convenience as well as even cleaner sound.

With the presence of all the singers demanded at all sessions – something unheard-of elsewhere in the recording world – Karajan achieved an unusually spontaneous result, by deciding only at the very last minute on each day just which passages he would record. Though ensemble was at times imperilled by that free-and-easy approach, and the final scene of Giovanni's descent to Hell goes off the boil a little, the end result has fitting intensity and power, with a cast of eight highly distinctive principals. This is a performance of extremes, not as smooth as much of Karajan's earlier Mozart. Though the very opening is extraordinarily slow and massive, the rest of the performance is just as remarkable for fast, exhilarating speeds as for slow. Though in the pacing of recitatives Karajan was plainly thinking of a big auditorium, having Jeffrey Tate as continuo player helps to keep them moving and to bring out word-meaning. The starry line-up of soloists is a distinctive one, with all four bass-baritone roles taken by singers who have played Giovanni himself. Samuel Ramey is the one chosen for the title role, a noble rather than a menacing Giovanni, consistently clear and firm. Ferruccio Furlanetto's beautiful timbre as Leporello may not be contrasted quite enough, but both his style of singing – with sing-speech allowed into recitative – and his extrovert acting provide the necessary variation. The dark, firm bass of Paata Burchuladze as the Commendatore is thrillingly incisive, and Alexander Malta makes a bluff, mature Masetto, sharply contrasted with the fresh, sweet and innocently provocative Zerlina of Kathleen Battle. Anna Tomowa-Sintow has rarely if ever sung so animatedly on record as here in the role of Donna Anna, with *Or sai chi l'onore* showing her as a fire-eating obsessive, even while the tone remains beautiful. She is well matched by the virile Ottavio of Gösta Winbergh, unusually positive for a character who can seem limp. Most individual of all is the Donna Elvira of Agnes Baltsa. The venom and bite of her mezzo timbre go with a touch of vulnerability, so that even when – as in *Mi tradi* – ensemble falls apart, the result is memorable. Recording and editing are erratic, but the result is full and vivid.

The final test of a recording of this most searching of operas is whether it adds up to more than the sum of its parts. Colin Davis's certainly does, with a singing cast that has fewer shortcomings than almost any other on disc and much positive strength. For once one can listen untroubled by vocal blemishes. Martina Arroyo controls her massive dramatic voice more completely than one would think possible, and she is strongly and imaginatively contrasted with the sweetly expressive Elvira of Kiri Te Kanawa and the sparkling Zerlina of Freni. As in the Davis *Figaro*, Ingvar Wixell and Wladimiro Ganzarolli make a formidable master/servant team with excellent vocal acting, while Stuart Burrows sings gloriously as Don Ottavio, and Richard

Van Allan is a characterful Masetto. Davis draws a fresh and immediate performance from his team, riveting from beginning to end, and the recording, now better defined and more vivid than before, is still refined in the recognizable Philips manner.

Krips's recording of this most challenging opera has kept its place as a mid-priced version which is consistently satisfying, with a cast of all-round quality headed by the dark-toned Don of Cesare Siepi. The women are not ideal, but they form an excellent team, never overfaced by the music, generally characterful, and with timbres well contrasted. To balance Siepi's darkness, the Leporello of Corena is even more saturnine, and their dramatic teamwork is brought to a superb climax in the final scene – quite the finest spine-tingling performance of that scene ever recorded. The 1955 recording – genuine stereo – still sounds remarkably well and this makes a real bargain for tape collectors.

Whatever the inhibitions and influences of preparing his CBS recording as a soundtrack for the Losey film of *Don Giovanni*, Lorin Maazel directs a strong and urgent performance, generally very well sung. An obvious strength is the line-up of three unusually firm-toned basses: José van Dam a saturnine Leporello, not comic but with much finely detailed expression; Malcolm King a darkly intense Masetto, and Ruggero Raimondi a heroic Giovanni, not always attacking notes cleanly but on balance one of the very finest on record in this role. Among the women Kiri Te Kanawa is outstanding, a radiant Elvira; Teresa Berganza as a mezzo Zerlina generally copes well with the high tessitura; and though Edda Moser starts with some fearsome squawks at her first entry, the dramatic scale is certainly impressive and she rises to the challenge of the big arias. Unfortunately the recording, made in a Paris church, has the voices close against background reverberation and this is something the remastering for CD has not been able substantially to alter.

Recorded in 1977 at a sequence of live performances in the Kleines Festspielhaus at Salzburg, Karl Boehm's second recording of this opera has an engaging vigour. The tempi are sometimes on the slow side, but the concentration is unfailing, and the whole reading centres round an assumption of the role of the Don which is richly heroic and far more sympathetic in characterization than is common. Sherrill Milnes sings with a richness and commitment which match his swaggering stage presence. Anna Tomowa-Sintow as Donna Anna is generally creamy-toned, only occasionally betraying a flutter, while Teresa Zylis-Gara as Elvira controls her warm voice with delicacy. These are stylish performances without being deeply memorable. Edith Mathis sings with her usual intelligence, but the tone is not always perfectly focused. Firm reliable performances from the men. Unlike Boehm's Salzburg *Così fan tutte*, where the ensembles were distractingly ragged, this live *Giovanni* presents a strong and consistently enjoyable experience distinct from that on any other set. The recording – favouring the voices but amazingly good under the conditions – is especially vivid in the culminating scene. This set has one savouring the unique flavour of Mozart opera in Salzburg with remarkable realism and with few distractions. The cassette transfer does not tailor acts to side-ends and the use of a pair of tapes (charged as for three, but at medium-price) has no advantage except extra continuity. There is an agreeable bloom on the voices, but the overall focus is not absolutely sharp.

Don Giovanni: highlights.

*** DG Dig. **419 635-2**; *419 635-4* [id.] (from above recording, cond. Karajan).

(M) **(*) HMV **CDM7 69055-2** [id.]. Ghiaurov, Watson, Freni, Ludwig, Gedda, Berry, New Philh. Ch. & O, Klemperer.

A particularly generous selection from Karajan's digital set, most of the favourite items included and all the principals given a chance to shine, in solos, duets and ensembles, The selection opens with the Overture and closes with the powerful final scene. There is a good matching chrome tape, although the resonance does bring slight clouding to the upper range.

With two other CD versions dominating the complete recordings, it was understandable that EMI should choose to issue first a selection of highlights from their Klemperer set. Ghiaurov as the Don and Berry as Leporello make a marvellous pair, and among the women Ludwig is a strong and convincing Elivira, Freni a sweet-toned but rather unsmiling Zerlina. Most of the slow tempi which Klemperer adopts, far from flagging, add a welcome spaciousness to the music.

Die Entführung aus dem Serail (complete).

*** Tel. Dig. **ZB8 35673** (3) [id.]. Kenny, Watson, Schreier, Gamlich, Salminen, Zurich Op. Ch. & Mozart O, Harnoncourt.

(*) Decca Dig. **417 402-2; *417 402-4* (2) [id.]. Gruberova, Battle, Winbergh, Zednik, Talvela, V. State Op. Ch., VPO, Solti.

** Ph. **416 479-2** (2) [id.]. Eda-Pierre, Burrowes, Burrows, Tear, Lloyd, Jurgens, Alldis Ch., ASMF, C. Davis.

Based on a celebrated stage production in Zurich with these same forces, Harnoncourt's version establishes its uniqueness at the very start of the overture, tougher and more abrasive than any previous recording. What Harnoncourt contends is that Mozart wanted more primitive sounds than we are used to in his Turkish music, with the jingle of cymbals, Turkish drums and the like more than living up to the nickname 'kitchen department', with the stove itself seemingly included. It is not a comfortable sound, compounded by Harnoncourt's often fast allegros, racing singers and players off their feet. Another source of extra abrasiveness is the use of a raw-sounding flageolet instead of a piccolo. Once you get used to the sound, however, the result is refreshing and lively, with the whole performance reflecting the fine rapport built up in stage performance. Slow passages are often warmly expressive, but the stylishness of the soloists prevents them from seeming excessively romantic, as in Schreier's charming singing of *O wie ängstlich* in Act I. The other men are excellent, too: Wilfried Gamlich both bright and sweet of tone, Matti Salminen outstandingly characterful as an Osmin who, as well as singing with firm dark tone, points the words with fine menace. Yvonne Kenny as Constanze and Lilian Watson as Blonde sound on the shrill side – partly a question of microphones – but they sing with such style and point that one quickly accepts that. *Martern aller Arten* prompts the most brilliant coloratura from Kenny, with the coda including some extra bars, now authorized by scholarship, but doubtfully effective, one of the many textual niceties of the set. Good, clean, dryish recording.

Though Solti's speeds are disconcertingly fast at times – as in Pedrillo and Osmin's drinking duet, *Vivat Bacchus* – and the manner is consequently often too tense to be comic, the performance is magnetic overall, with the big ensembles and choruses electric in their clean, sharp focus. Gruberova makes a brilliant Constanze, but the edge on the voice is not always comfortable. Exciting as *Martern aller Arten* is, with a fire-snorting coda and some beautiful shading for contrast (surprising with so bright a voice), the edge on the voice is underlined by the recording. She is more appealing elsewhere. Gösta Winbergh makes an ardent, young-sounding Belmonte, Kathleen Battle a seductive, minxish Blonde and Heinz Zednik a delightfully light and characterful Pedrillo, with Martti Talvela magnificently lugubrious as Osmin. With brilliant recording this makes a fresh and compelling reading, but not one likely to make you smile often. The chrome cassettes are in the demonstration class, sparkling and vivid; the CD booklet provides documentation. No attempt is made to tailor acts to side-ends, however, which is unusual for Decca.

Sir Colin Davis, using a smaller orchestra, the St Martin's Academy, than he usually has in his Mozart opera recordings, produces a fresh and direct account, well but not outstandingly sung. There are no performances here which have one remembering individuality of phrase, and even so characterful a singer as Robert Tear does not sound quite mellifluous enough in the role of Pedrillo, while Robert Lloyd as Osmin is outshone by a number of his rivals, especially the incomparable Gottlob Frick in the deleted Beecham set. Crisp as the ensembles are, Davis's reading rather lacks the lightness and sparkle, the feeling of comedy before our eyes, which makes Boehm's DG set – overdue for issue on CD – so memorable.

Idomeneo (complete).

*** Decca Dig. **411 805-2**; *411 805-4* (3) [id.]. Pavarotti, Baltsa, Popp, Gruberova, Nucci, V. State Op. Ch., VPO, Pritchard.

(M) **(*) Tel. **ZB8 35547** (3) [id.]. Hollweg, Schmidt, Yakar, Palmer, Zurich Op. O, Harnoncourt.

** Ph. **420 130-2** (3) [id.]. Rinaldi, Shirley, Ryland Davies, Tear, Tinsley, BBC Ch. & SO, C. Davis.

More than any previous recorded performance, the Decca version conducted by Sir John Pritchard – who did the first ever recording of the opera with a Glyndebourne cast over thirty years ago – centres round the tenor taking the name-part. It is not just that Pavarotti has the natural magnetism of the superstar, but that he is the only tenor at all among the principal soloists. Not only is the role of Idamante given to a mezzo instead of a tenor – preferable, with what was originally a castrato role – but that of the High Priest, Arbace, with his two arias is taken by a baritone, Leo Nucci. The wonder is that though Pavarotti reveals imagination in every phrase, using a wide range of tone colours, the result remains well within the parameters of Mozartian style. By any reckoning this is not only the most heroic and the most beautiful but also the best controlled performance of this demanding role that we have on record. Casting Baltsa as Idamante makes for characterful results, tougher and less fruity than her direct rivals. Lucia Popp as Ilia tends to underline expression too much, but it is a charming, girlish portrait. Gruberova makes a thrilling Elettra, totally in command of the divisions, as few sopranos are; owing to bright Decca sound, the projection of her voice is a little edgy at times. As to Pritchard, he has relaxed a little since his Glyndebourne days – this is a bigger view than before – and (with text unusually complete) more than current rivals brings light and shade to the piece. There are splendidly vivid cassettes (with the CD documentation).

Using a text very close to that of the Munich première of Mozart's great *opera seria*, and with the role of Idamante given to a soprano instead of being transposed down to tenor register, Harnoncourt presents a distinctive and refreshing view, one which in principle is preferable to general modern practice. The vocal cast is good, with Hollweg a clear-toned, strong Idomeneo, and no weak link. Felicity Palmer finds the necessary contrasts of expression as Elettra. On LP, the voices were sometimes given an unpleasant edge, but, with the CD remastering, the sound is transformed and the edginess smoothed without loss of presence. It is surprising that, in an account which aims at authenticity, appoggiature are so rarely used. This is hardly a performance to warm to, but it is refreshing and alive.

It is the greatest pity that Sir Colin Davis was not allowed a more impressive singing cast for this, his first complete Mozart opera recording. His direction is never less than fresh and stylish, and the orchestra responds with vitality, but the singers when taxed with their important arias lack the polish and refinement one needs in recorded Mozart. It is good to welcome Pauline Tinsley on to record, but even for the part of Elettra the voice has an uncomfortable edge. George Shirley as Idomeneo and Ryland Davies as Idamante are well contrasted in timbre, but Sir John Pritchard's solution of having a woman in the castrato role of Idamante is preferable for reasons of vocal texture. Margherita Rinaldi makes a sweet-voiced Ilia. The Philips recording is acceptable but not outstanding.

Le nozze di Figaro (complete).

*** Decca Dig. **410 150-2** (3). Te Kanawa, Popp, Von Stade, Ramey, Allen, Moll, LPO & Ch., Solti.

*** DG **415 520-2** (3) [id.]. Janowitz, Mathis, Troyanos, Fischer-Dieskau, Prey, Lagger, German Op. Ch. & O, Boehm.

(M) *** Decca *417 315-4* (2) [id.]. Gueden, Danco, Della Casa, Dickie, Poell, Corena, Siepi, V. State Op. Ch., VPO, Erich Kleiber.

(*) HMV Dig. **CDS7 49753-2; *EX 749753-4* (3). Lott, Desderi, Rolandi, Stilwell, Esham, Korn, Glyndebourne Ch., LPO, Haitink.

** Ph. Dig. **416 870-2**; *416 870-4* (3) [id.]. Popp, Hendricks, Baltsa, Van Dam, Raimondi, Amb. Op. Ch., ASMF, Marriner.

** Decca **421 125-2** (3) [id.]. Cotrubas, Tomowa-Sintow, Von Stade, Van Dam, Krause, V. State Op. Ch., VPO, Karajan.

** HMV Dig. **CDS7 47978-8** [Ang. **CDCC 47978**] (3); *EX 270576-5*. Margaret Price, Battle, Murray, Allen, Hynninen, Rydl, V. State Op. Ch., VPO, Muti.

Le nozze di Figaro: highlights.

*** Decca Dig. **417 395-2** [id.] (from above recording, cond. Solti).

It is important not to judge Solti's effervescent new version of *Figaro* by a first reaction to the overture. It is one of the fastest on record (matching Karajan in the 'egg-timer' race). Elsewhere Solti opts for a fair proportion of extreme speeds, slow as well as fast, but they rarely if ever intrude on the quintessential happiness of the entertainment. Rejecting the idea of a bass Figaro, Solti has chosen in Samuel Ramey a firm-toned baritone, a virile figure. He is less a comedian than a lover, superby matched to the most enchanting of Susannas today, Lucia Popp, who gives a sparkling and radiant performance to match the Pamina she sang in Haitink's recording of Zauberflöte. Thomas Allen's Count is magnificent too, tough in tone and characterization but always beautiful on the ear. Kurt Moll as Dr Bartolo sings an unforgettable *La vendetta* with triplets very fast and agile 'on the breath', while Robert Tear far outshines his own achievement as the Basilio of Sir Colin Davis's amiable recording. Frederica von Stade, as in the Karajan set, is a most attractive Cherubino, even if *Voi che sapete* is too slow; but crowning all is the Countess of Kiri Te Kanawa, challenged by Solti's spacious tempi in the two big arias, but producing ravishing tone, flawless phrasing and elegant ornamentation throughout. With superb, vivid recording this now makes a clear first choice for a much-recorded opera.

Boehm's earlier version of *Figaro* was once available on the cheap Fontana Special label, but unlike that sprightly performance this newer one gives a complete text, with Marcellina's and Basilio's Act IV arias included. This is among the most consistently assured performances available. The women all sing most beautifully, with Janowitz's Countess, Mathis's Susanna and Troyanos's Cherubino all ravishing the ear in contrasted ways. Prey is an intelligent if not very jolly-sounding Figaro, and Fischer-Dieskau gives his dark, sharply defined reading of the Count's role. All told, a great success, with fine playing and recording, enhanced on CD.

Kleiber's famous set was one of Decca's Mozart bicentenary recordings of the mid-1950s. It remains an outstanding bargain at mid-price, an attractively strong performance with much fine singing. Few if any sets have since matched its constant stylishness. Gueden's Susanna might be criticized but her golden tones are certainly characterful, while Danco and Della Casa are both at their finest. A dark-toned Figaro in Siepi brings added contrast and if the pace of the recitatives is rather slow, this is not inconsistent within the context of Kleiber's overall approach. The recording still sounds remarkably well in its tape format.

As in his other Glyndebourne recordings, Haitink's approach is relaxed and mellow. Where in *Così* the results were sunny, here in *Figaro* there is at times a lack of sparkle. There is much lovely singing and fine ensemble from a strong team, yet one which does not quite match the casting of the Solti set. In particular Felicity Lott, although she sings *Dove sono* with melting simplicity, does not quite match the Countess of Kiri Te Kanawa.

After his sparkling set of the other Figaro opera, Rossini's *Barbiere di Siviglia*, Sir Neville Marriner this time in Mozart falls down on his dramatic timing, and the result fails to lift. As an instance, the delicious duet between Susanna and the Count at the beginning of Act III, *Crudel! perche finora*, is made lugubrious thanks to Raimondi, who is then superbly well focused in his big aria. Though Lucia Popp gives a deeply felt performance as the Countess, the strain on the voice tends to imperil the legato. Barbara Hendricks makes an attractively girlish Susanna and Van Dam a formidable Figaro, though one inclined to be too emphatic, not comic; even *Non più andrai* is too heavy. The final disappointment of the set is Marriner's failure to convey the necessary sense of resolution in the closing scene, with little or no poignancy conveyed. Despite the excellent recording in both formats, this could not be a first choice.

With Karajan the speed and smoothness of the overture establish the character of the whole performance. Too much is passed over with a deftness which quickly makes the result bland, despite superb singing and playing. Only Frederica von Stade as Cherubino establishes the sort of individuality of expression that is the very stuff of operatic drama; she alone emerges as a rounded character. With a bloom on the sound and added presence in the CD transfer, the performance is a joy to the ear but is likely to leave any Mozartian unsatisfied.

The Muti set of *Figaro* with the Vienna Philharmonic is disappointing for the cloudiness of focus in the recording, and the singing from a starry line-up of soloists is very variable. Margaret Price is a powerful, firm Countess, not quite as nobly distinctive as she might be, and Kathleen Battle is a sparkling Susanna. Commanding as Thomas Allen is as Figaro, this is not a comic figure, dark rather, and less than winning, more a Count translated. Hynninen is relatively uncharacterful as the Count and Ann Murray makes an edgy Cherubino. Muti's timing, often too fast, conveys little feeling for the comedy. There are well-managed cassettes.

Der Schauspieldirektor (*The Impresario;* opera): complete.
*** DG **419 566-2** (3) [id.]. Grist, Augér, Schreier, Moll, Dresden State O, Boehm – *Die Zauberflöte*.**(*)

This performance of *Der Schauspieldirektor* is without dialogue, so that it is short enough to make a fill-up for Boehm's *Zauberflöte*. Reri Grist's bravura as Madame Herz is impressive, and Arleen Augér is pleasingly fresh and stylish here. The tenor and bass make only minor contributions, but Boehm's guiding hand keeps the music alive from the first bar to the last.

Die Zauberflöte (complete).
*** HMV Dig. **CDS7 47951-8** (3) [Ang. **CDCC 47951**]. Popp, Gruberova, Lindner, Jerusalem, Brendel, Bracht, Zednik, Bav. R. Ch. & SO, Haitink.
*** DG Dig. **410 967-2** (3) [id.]. Mathis, Ott, Perry, Araiza, Hornik, Van Dam, German Op. Ch., Berlin, BPO, Karajan.
(*) DG **419 566-2 (3) [id.]. Lear, Peters, Otto, Wunderlich, Fischer-Dieskau, Hotter, Crass, Berlin RIAS Chamber Ch., BPO, Boehm – *Der Schauspieldirektor*.***
(*) Decca **414 568-2 (3) [id.]. Lorengar, Deutekom, Burrows, Fischer-Dieskau, Prey, Talvela, V. State Op. Ch., VPO, Solti.
(M) ** RCA **GD 86511** (3) [**RCA 6511-2-RG**]. Geszty, Donath, Schreier, Adam, Leib, Leipzig R. Ch., Dresden State O, Suitner.
*(*) Ph. Dig. **411 459-2** (3) [id.]. Margaret Price, Serra, Schreier, Moll, Melbye, Venuti, Tear, Dresden Kreuzchor, Leipzig R. Ch., Dresden State O, C. Davis.
*(*) HMV **CDS7 47827-8** (2). Rothenberger, Moser, Miljakovic, Schreier, Moll, Berry, Adam, Bav. State Ch. & O, Sawallisch.

Haitink in his first ever opera recording directs a rich and spacious account of *Zauberflöte*, superbly recorded in spectacularly wide-ranging digital sound. There is a sterling honesty in Haitink's approach to every number. With speeds generally a shade slower than usual, the point of the playing and the consistent quality of the singing present this as a Mozart masterpiece that is weighty as well as sparkling. The dialogue – not too much of it, nicely produced and with sound effects adding to the vividness – frames a presentation that has been carefully thought through. Popp makes the most tenderly affecting of Paminas (as she did in the Salzburg production) and Gruberova has never sounded more spontaneous in her brilliance than here as Queen of the Night: she is both agile and powerful. Jerusalem makes an outstanding Tamino, both heroic and sweetly Mozartian; and though neither Wolfgang Brendel as Papageno nor Bracht as Sarastro is as characterful as their finest rivals, their personalities project strongly and the youthful freshness of their singing is most attractive. The Bavarian chorus too is splendid, and the recording's perspectives featuring the chorus are extraordinarily effective, particularly in the superb Act I finale. Some readers will certainly prefer Karajan's more urgent, more volatile Berlin version, but the gravitas of Haitink's approach does not miss the work's elements of drama and charm, though nothing is trivialized.

Zauberflöte has also inspired Karajan to one of his freshest, most rhythmic Mozart performances, spontaneous-sounding to the point where vigour is preferred to immaculate precision in ensembles. The digital recording is not always perfectly balanced, but the sound is outstandingly fresh and clear. The CDs add presence and refine detail but also underline the variable balances. There are numbers where the tempi are dangerously slow (Tamino's *Dies Bildnis*, both of Sarastro's arias and Pamina's *Ach, ich fühl's*), but Karajan's concentration helps him to avoid mannerism completely. The choice of soloists may seem idiosyncratic, and in principle one would want a darker-toned Sarastro than José van Dam, but the clarity of focus and the fine control, not to mention the slow tempi, give the necessary weight to his arias. Francisco Araiza and Gottfried Hornik make impressive contributions, both concealing any inexperience. Karin Ott has a relatively weighty voice for the Queen of the Night, but in his tempi Karajan is most considerate to her; and the Pamina of Edith Mathis has many beautiful moments, her word-pointing always intelligent.

One of the glories of Boehm's DG set is the singing of Fritz Wunderlich as Tamino, a wonderful memorial to a singer much missed. Passages that normally seem merely incidental come alive, thanks to his beautiful intense singing. Fischer-Dieskau, with characteristic word-pointing, makes a sparkling Papageno on record (he is too big of frame, he says, to do the role on stage) and Franz Crass is a satisfyingly straightforward Sarastro. The team of women is well below this standard – Lear taxed cruelly in *Ach, ich fühl's,* Peters shrill in the upper register (although the effect is exciting), and the Three Ladies do not blend well – but the direction of Boehm is superb, light and lyrical, but weighty where necessary to make a glowing, compelling experience. Fine recording, enhanced in the CD set, which has also found room for Boehm's admirable account of *Der Schauspieldirektor*, a very considerable bonus.

If one is looking for Mozartian charm in this most monumental of Mozart's operas, then plainly Solti's reading must be rejected. It is tough, strong and brilliant, and it is arguable that in this opera those are the required qualities above all; but even so the absence of charm has a cumulative effect. The drama may be consistently vital, but ultimately the full variety of Mozart's inspiration is not achieved. On the male side the cast is very strong indeed, with Stuart Burrows assuming his international mantle easily with stylish and rich-toned singing. Martti Talvela and Fischer-Dieskau as Sarastro and the Speaker respectively provide a stronger contrast than usual, each superb in his way, and Hermann Prey rounds out the character of Papageno with intelligent pointing of words. The cast of women is less consistent. Pilar Lorengar's Pamina is sweetly attractive as long as your ear is not worried by her obtrusive vibrato, while Cristina Deutekom's Queen of the Night is technically impressive, though marred by a curious warbling quality in the coloratura, almost like an intrusive 'w' where you sometimes have the intrusive 'h'. The Three Ladies make a strong team (Yvonne Minton in the middle), and it was a good idea to give the parts of the Three Boys to genuine trebles. The brilliant and lively 1971 recording has been transferred to CD with the utmost vividness and there are ample cues to provide internal access to the opera. However, the adjective we originally applied to the LP libretto (sumptuous) hardly applies to the CD booklet. The coloured illustrations have reduced effectively to the smaller size, but the libretto itself is in small type, and not very bold.

In Suitner's Dresden version the sound is full and forward, the reading plain but generally lively, to make it a fair bargain recommendation at mid-price in the Victor Opera series. The cast has one notable flaw in the Sarastro of Theo Adam, unsteady if not as wobbly as he sometimes is; and the Papageno of Gunther Leib is undercharacterized; but Peter Schreier is at his finest as Tamino, generally outshining his other recorded accounts, and Helen Donath is a lovely, girlish-sounding Pamina and Sylvia Geszty a satisfyingly rich-toned Queen of the Night. Oddly, no one is credited with singing the Speaker or the Two Armed Men.

The last of Sir Colin Davis's recordings of Mozart's major operas, and the only one made outside Britain, is also the least successful. With speeds often slower than usual and the manner heavier, it is a performance of little sparkle or charm, one which seems intent on bringing out serious, symbolic meanings. Thus, although Margaret Price produces a glorious flow of rich, creamy tone, she conveys little of the necessary vulnerability of Pamina in her plight. Luciana Serra sings capably but at times with shrill tone and not always with complete security; while Peter Schreier is in uncharacteristically gritty voice as Tamino, and Mikael Melbye as Papageno is ill-suited to recording, when the microphone exaggerates the throatiness and unevenness of his production. The greatest vocal glory of the set is the magnificent, firm and rich singing of Kurt Moll as Sarastro. The recording is excellent.

Transferred to CD on only two discs instead of three, Sawallisch's Munich set of the early 1970s in effect makes a bargain version, to be recommended only with marked reservations. The sound is thin – far thinner than that of the RCA Dresden set of the same period – and though Sawallisch is a thoughtful Mozartian, the cast is flawed. The outstanding performance comes from Kurt Moll as Sarastro, and Walter Berry is a delightful Papageno. But even Peter Schreier sounds strained as Tamino, with bloom lacking on the voice, not nearly as fresh as on the RCA set. Edda Moser is a strong Queen of the Night but on the fruity side, and Anneliese Rothenberger is disturbingly fluttery as Pamina.

Die Zauberflote: highlights.

*** HMV Dig. **CDC7 47008-2** [id.] (from above recording, cond. Haitink).

*** DG Dig. **415 287-2** [id.] (from above recording, cond. Karajan).

(M) *** HMV **CDM7 69056-2** [id.]. Popp, Janowitz, Putz, Gedda, Berry, Frick, Philh. Ch. & O, Klemperer.

(*) Decca **421 302-2 [id.] (from above set, cond. Solti).

** RCA Dig. **RCD 14621 [RCD1 4621]**. Donat, Cotrubas, Kales, Tappy, Talvela, Boesch, V. State Op. Ch., VPO, Levine.

Haitink's disc makes a good sampler with the Papageno/Papagena music well represented to make a contrast with the lyrical arias and the drama of the Queen of the Night. Both the Karajan and Solti selections similarly display the characteristics of the complete sets from which they are taken. The Karajan disc concentrates on the major arias, and very impressive it is.

With the Klemperer set not yet issued on CD, the highlights are especially welcome at mid-price, given a bright, vivid transfer. The selection is well balanced and fairly generous, although it is a pity it does not include the passage most characteristic of Klemperer with the Armed Men. However, it does include the ensemble *Hm, hm, hm* between Papageno, Tamino and the Three Ladies, with Schwarzkopf, Ludwig and Höffgen at their very finest. The chief glory of the set vocally is the singing of the women; Gedda's Tamino and Frick's Sarastro are by comparison disappointing. But this makes a good sampler of a performance which, while distinctly massive, manages to find sparkle and humour too.

The RCA highlights CD offers fifteen excerpts and has a certain charm in detailing each in a lurid English translation; thus the Queen of the Night's second aria (*Die Hölle Rache*) is given as 'The vengeance of Hell boils in my heart'. It is variably sung. Zdzislawa Donat's contribution is one of the few outstanding performances here, alongside Cotrubas's Pamina – her aria *Ach, ich fühl's* is equally fine. Neither artist is named on the insert leaflet; however, this does provide a synopsis of 'The Plot'. There is nothing special about the CD sound, apart from the background silence. However, the dialogue which weighed down the complete LP set is omitted here.

Opera Recitals

Arias: *La Clemenza di Tito: Non più di fiori vaghe catene. Così fan tutte: Come scoglio. Don Giovanni: In quali eccessi . . . Mi tradi quell'alma ingrata. Crudele? non mi dir bell' idol mio. Die Entführung aus dem Serail: Welcher Kummer . . . Traurigkeit ward mir zum Lose. Idomeneo: Solitudini amiche . . . Zeffiretti lusinghiere. Le Nozze di Figaro: Voi che sapete; Giunse al fin il momento . . . Deh vieni; Porgi amor. Il re pastore: L'amerò, sarò costante.*
** HMV Dig. **CDC7 47019-2** [id.]. Lucia Popp, Munich R. O, Slatkin.

Lucia Popp was perhaps mistaken at this stage in her career to have attempted to assume such a wide variety of Mozartian roles within a single recital. She is an enchanting Susanna – *Deh vieni* is the highlight of the disc – but while her portrayal of Cherubino (*Voi che sapete*) is fresh and light, her characterization of the Countess (*Porgi amor*) lacks maturity of feeling. The *Don Giovanni* excerpts although impressive both musically and technically are made to sound almost like concert arias, and *Come scoglio* lacks fire. The recording is generally flattering, with the CD adding presence.

Arias: *La Clemenza di Tito: S'altro che lagrime. Così fan tutte: Ei parte . . . Sen . . . Per pieta. La finta giardiniera: Crudeli fermate . . . Ah dal pianto. Idomeneo: Se il padre perdei. Lucio Silla: Pupille amate. Il re pastore: L'amerò, sarò costante. Zaïde: Ruhe sanft, mein holdes Leben. Die Zauberflöte: Ach ich fühl's es ist verschwunden.*
*** Ph. Dig. **411 148-2** [id.]. Kiri Te Kanawa, LSO, C. Davis.

Kiri Te Kanawa's is one of the loveliest collections of Mozart arias on record, with the voice at its most ravishing and pure. One might object that Dame Kiri concentrates on soulful arias, ignoring more vigorous ones, but with stylish accompaniment and clear, atmospheric recording, beauty dominates all.

Muffat, Georg (1653–1704)

Concerti grossi: in A (Cor Vigilans); E min. (Delirium amoris); G (Propitia Sydera); Suites Nos 3 in D min. (Graditudo); 4 in B flat (Impatientia); 7 in G (Costantia).
*(*) Chan. Dig. **CHAN 8448/9**; *DBTD 2009* (2) [id.]. Cantilena, Shepherd – BIBER: *Sonatas.**(*)

Muffat is one of the most interesting figures of the Baroque period; his work was much influenced by Lully, with whom he studied. The concertos recorded here, on the other hand, owe much to Corelli and the Italian school. They come from a set of twelve called *Ausserlesene Instrumental-Music* (1701) and the suites from *Florilegium primum* (1695): Cantilena under Adrian Shepherd offer us three examples from each collection. This is not only interesting but also attractive music, and Chandos earn gratitude for their enterprise in committing it to disc. However, the performances are at times a little rough-and-ready in matters of ensemble, and this somewhat diminishes the value of this excellently recorded set.

Muldowney, Dominic (born 1952)

(i) *Piano concerto;* (ii) *Saxophone concerto.*
*** HMV Dig. **CDC7 49715-2**; *EL 749715-4*. (i) Peter Donohoe, BBC SO, Mark Elder; (ii) John Harle, L. Sinf. Masson.

Dominic Muldowney, born in 1952 and music director at the National Theatre since 1976, has latterly become a composer laudably concerned with direct communication to a wide range of listeners. These two colourful and dramatic concertos are excellent examples of his more recent style, far more approachable than his earlier work. His *Piano concerto* is a formidable work in a continuous half-hour span of many different sections. It uses Bachian forms, along with tough Bachian piano figuration, to move kaleidoscopically in a kind of musical collage of references to different genres, including jazz and the popular waltz. With Peter Donohoe giving one of his finest performances on record, and with colourful playing from the BBC Symphony Orchestra under Mark Elder, the piece emerges powerfully, with occasional gruff echoes of Hindemith. The *Saxophone concerto* (written for the outstanding young virtuoso of the instrument, John Harle, who plays it on the record) is a more compact, strongly characterized work in three movements, each throwing up a grateful number of warm, easy tunes without any sense of compromise or incongruity. Warm, well-balanced recording, and a very good chrome cassette.

Mundy, William (*c.* 1529–*c.* 1591)

Vox Patris caelestis.
*** Gimell **CDGIM 339** [id.]. Tallis Scholars, Phillips – ALLEGRI: *Miserere*; PALESTRINA: *Missa Papae Marcelli.****

Mundy's *Vox Patris caelestis* was written during the short reign of Queen Mary (1553–8). While it is almost exactly contemporary with Palestrina's *Missa Papae Marcelli*, its florid, passionate polyphone is very different from that of the Italian composer. This is emphasized by Peter Phillips's eloquent performance, which presses the music onwards to reach exultant climax in the closing stanza with the words *'Veni, veni, veni, caelesti gloria coronaberis'*. The work is structured in nine sections in groups of three, the last of each group being climactic and featuring the whole choir, with solo embroidery. Yet the music flows continuously, like a great river, and the complex vocal writing creates the most spectacular effects, with the trebles soaring up and shining out over the underlying cantilena. The imaginative force of the writing is never in doubt, and the Tallis Scholars give an account which balances linear clarity with considerable power. The recording is first class and the digital remastering for CD further improves the focus, adding firmness of outline and detail. The effect is wonderfully involving: this work is comparable with Tallis's famous motet, *Spem in alium*, in its power; it suggests that William Mundy's music deserves further exploration.

Mussorgsky, Modest (1839–81)

The Capture of Kars (march). *St John's Night on the Bare Mountain. Scherzo in B flat. Khovanshchina: Prelude to Act I;* (i) *Introduction to Act IV. The Destruction of Sennacherib.* (i; ii) *Joshua.* (i) *Oedipus in Athens: Temple chorus. Salammbô; Priestesses' chorus.*
*** RCA *GK 70405* [*ARK1 3988*]. LSO, Abbado, with (i) LSO Ch., (ii) Zehava Gal.

To commemorate the centenary of Mussorgsky's death Abbado and the LSO came up with this attractive and revealing anthology of shorter pieces. Some of the orchestral items are well enough known, but it is good to have so vital an account of the original version of *Night on the bare mountain*, different in all but its basic material from the Rimsky-Korsakov arrangement. Best of all are the four choral pieces; even when they are early and untypical (*Oedipus in Athens*, for example) they are immediately attractive, and they include such evocative pieces as the *Chorus of Priestesses* (intoning over a pedal bass) from a projected opera on Flaubert's novel. The chorus is rather recessed, but not inappropriately so, and the orchestra is given refined recording. The high-level cassette transfer is one of RCA's best.

Night on the bare mountain; Khovanshchina: Prelude (both arr. Rimsky-Korsakov).
(M) *** Decca *417 689-4* [id.]. LSO, Solti – BORODIN: *Prince Igor: Overture & Polovtsian dances*; GLINKA: *Russlan overture*.***

Night on the bare mountain (arr. Rimsky-Korsakov).
(M) *** Decca **417 723-2** [id.]. LSO, Solti – GLINKA: *Russlan overture* ***; TCHAIKOVSKY: *Symphony No. 5*.*(*)
(M) *** DG *419 873-4* [id.]. Chicago SO, Barenboim – RIMSKY-KORSAKOV: *Capriccio espagnol*; *Russian Easter festival overture*; TCHAIKOVSKY: *Marche slave*.***

Solti's *Night on the bare mountain* can stand up to all competition in its vintage 1967 recording with its fine amplitude and great brilliance. On the Decca Weekend tape the couplings are superbly done – the Glinka overture is electrifying – and this remains one of Solti's finest analogue collections. The CD is coupled with an unrecommendable performance of Tchaikovsky's *Fifth Symphony*, but the tape also offers the highly atmospheric *Khovanshchina Prelude*, which is beautifully played.

Barenboim's account of *Night on the bare mountain* is telling in a different way. In place of Solti's urgency, Barenboim's approach is spacious, weighty and very powerful. The wide amplitude of the Chicago recording adds to the sense of spectacle and breadth and the coupled Rimsky-Korsakov *Russian Easter festival* is no less memorable for its rich colouring. The superb playing of the Chicago orchestra is telling throughout this very successful concert, admirably remastered.

Night on the bare mountain; Khovanshchina: Prelude (both arr. Rimsky-Korsakov); *Pictures at an exhibition* (orch. Ravel).
(*) Decca Dig. **417 299-2; *417 299-4* [id.]. Montreal SO, Dutoit – RIMSKY-KORSAKOV: *Russian Easter festival overture*.**(*)

Dutoit's concert opens rather coolly. The *Khovanshchina prelude*, with its haunting evocation of dawn over the Moscow River, has sounded more magical in other hands. *A Night on the bare mountain* is strong and biting, but again the adrenalin does not flow as grippingly as in, say, Solti's version. Dutoit's *Pictures* have each movement strongly characterized and there is a sense of fun in the scherzando movements. But overall this is less involving than with Karajan. It is characteristic of Dutoit that, weighty as his account of *The Great Gate of Kiev* is, he keeps its sense of line clearly in mind at a measured speed. The brilliant, atmospheric recording is not as sumptuous as some other versions, but is naturally balanced with the bloom characteristic of the Montreal sound. The Rimsky-Korsakov overture comes after the other two shorter Mussorgsky pieces, the *Pictures*, with their more refined Ravel orchestration, coming as a climax.

Night on the bare mountain (arr. Rimsky-Korsakov); *Pictures at an exhibition* (orch. Ravel).
*** Telarc Dig. **CD 80042** [id.]. Cleveland O, Maazel.
(B) *** DG Walkman *413 153-4*. Boston Pops O, Fiedler; Chicago SO, Giulini – TCHAIKOVSKY: *1812* etc.**(*)

Night on the bare mountain; Pictures at an exhibition: Khovanshchina: Prelude.
** Decca **413 139-2** [id.]. SRO, Ansermet.

All current versions of this coupling rest under the shadow of the magnificently recorded Telarc disc, one of the first great successes of the early digital era. The quality of the recording is apparent at the very opening of *Night on the bare mountain* in the richly sonorous presentation of the deep brass and the sparkling yet unexaggerated percussion. With the Cleveland Orchestra on top form, the *Pictures* are strongly characterized; this may not be the subtlest reading available, but each of Mussorgsky's cameos comes vividly to life. The opening trumpets are more robust than in the Philadelphia version (see below), and *The old castle* is particularly evocative. The chattering children in the Tuileries are matched in presence by the delightfully pointed portrayal of the cheeping chicks, and if the ox-wagon (*Bydlo*) develops a climax potent enough to suggest a juggernaut, the similarly sumptuous brass in the *Catacombs* sequence cannot be counted as in any way overdramatized. After a vibrantly rhythmic *Baba-Yaga*, strong in fantastic menace, the closing *Great Gate of Kiev* is overwhelmingly spacious in conception and quite riveting as sheer sound. On compact disc, the background silence enhances the realism, although detail is not as sharply outlined as in the Karajan, Solti, Ansermet or Abbado CDs – see below. With the Cleveland set, the ear is conscious of the warm, glowing ambience of Severance Hall, although often individual wind solos have a luminous realism. The record's producer, Robert Woods, and the sound engineer, Jack Renner, continue their love affair with the bass drum, which is occasionally allowed to dominate the orchestral texture. But it is the richness and amplitude of the brass which make the work's final climax unforgettable. The programme notes provided with the CD are fully adequate, but a simple list of titles would have been useful; moreover, the *Pictures* are not separately banded. However, within the technical information supplied is the laudable claim that 'it is Telarc's philosophy to employ additional microphones *only* when the size of the performing forces is greater than can be accommodated appropriately by the basic three'. This recording impressively bears out the success of Telarc's refusal to embrace close multi-microphone techniques, much beloved in Europe at present, and which often produce the most unnatural effects.

It is interesting that Giulini's very successful account of the *Pictures* should use the Chicago orchestra, thus repeating Reiner's success of the early days of stereo. The modern recording, however, is noticeably more refined and detailed, with brilliant percussive effects (a superb bass drum in *The hut on fowl's legs*). With superlative orchestral playing and strong characterization, this is highly recommendable; the tape transfer is generally of excellent quality. It is here paired with an excitingly volatile account of *Night on the bare mountain*, directed by Fiedler. Both sound well on this bargain-price Walkman tape, generously coupled with Tchaikovsky.

Ansermet's compact disc is an astonishing technical achievement. His set of the *Pictures* dates from 1959, but in this digitally remastered format the ear would never guess that the recording was not quite modern – it sounds far more vivid than Sir Colin Davis's 1981 digital version. The performance itself takes a little while to warm up, but Ansermet's fastidious ear for detail is telling in the later portraits, with *The hut on fowl's legs* unforgettably sharp in characterization. *Night on the bare mountain* and the *Khovanshchina Prelude* come from the mid-1960s, and the former can stand alongside any of the modern versions. In the *Prelude* the translucent clarity of the sound reveals some less-than-perfect wind intonation, but Rimksy's marvellous scoring (especially in the closing section) still creates a magical effect. It is a pity that this record is over-priced, but aficionados will still want to consider it. There is uncannily little background noise.

Sir Colin Davis's coupling was the first digital recording from Philips (issued early in 1981) and proved technically a disappointment. Davis's performances are strangely short on brilliance.

The speeds are often on the slow side, which makes the music sound under-characterized and tame rather than weighty. (Ph. **411 473-2**).

(i) *Night on the bare mountain* (arr. Rimsky-Korsakov); *Pictures at an exhibition* (arr. Funtek). (ii) *Songs and dances of death* (arr. Aho).
*** BIS Dig. **CD 325** [id.]. (i) Finnish RSO, (i) Leif Segerstam; (ii) Järvi, with Talvela.

Like Abbado's anthology (on tape) above, this fascinating CD should not be missed by any true Mussorgskian. We have had various orchestrations of the *Pictures* besides Ravel's, as diverse in emphasis as those by Ashkenazy (see below) and Stokowski; this one by Leo Funtek – made in the same year as Ravel's (1922) – is especially fascinating for the way the different uses of colour change the character of some of Victor Hartman's paintings, as seen through the twice-filtered vision of Mussorgsky and his arranger. There are many subtle alterations and some very striking ones: the use of a cor anglais in *The old castle*, for instance, or the soft-grained wind scoring which makes the portrait of *Samuel Goldenberg and Schmuyle* more sympathetic, if also blander. The performances by the Finnish Radio Orchestra under Leif Segerstam both of this and of the familiar Rimsky *Night on the bare mountain* (Stokowski's own specially individual version of this is available in a superb miscellaneous concert of his transcriptions – brilliantly played by the Cincinnati orchestra – see Concerts section, below) are very spontaneously presented and very well recorded. The extra item is no less valuable, an intense, darkly Russian account of the *Songs and dances of death* from Martti Talvela with the orchestral accompaniment plangently scored by Kalevi Aho. The excellent documentation gives a full analysis of the orchestral detail in both major works.

Pictures at an exhibition (orch. Ravel).
(M) *** DG **423 214-2**; *423 214-4* [id.]. BPO, Karajan – STRAVINSKY: *Rite of spring*.***
*** DG Dig. **410 033-2** [id.]. LSO, Abbado – RAVEL: *La valse*.**(*)
*** HMV Dig. **CDC7 47099-2** [id.]. Phd. O, Muti – STRAVINSKY: *Firebird suite*.***
(M) *** Decca Dig. **417 754-2** [id.]. Chicago SO, Solti – BARTÓK: *Concerto for orchestra*.***
(M) *** DG **415 844-2**; *415 844-4* [id.]. Chicago SO, Giulini – RAVEL: *Ma mère l'Oye*; *Rapsodie espagnole*.***
(*) DG Dig. **413 588-2; *413-588-4* [id.]. BPO, Karajan – RAVEL: *Boléro*; *Rapsodie espagnole*.***
(B) **(*) DG Dig. *419 827-4* [id.]. LSO, Abbado – BERLIOZ: *Symphonie fantastique*.**(*)
** Decca Dig. **417 611-2**; *417 611-4* [id.]. Concg. O, Chailly – DEBUSSY: *Danse*; *Sarabande*; RAVEL: *Boléro*.**(*)
*(*) Ph. Dig. **416 296-2**; *416 296-4* [id.]. VPO, Previn – RAVEL: *La valse*.**

Among the many fine versions of Mussorgsky's *Pictures* on CD, not forgetting Maazel's spectacularly recorded Telarc disc (see above), Karajan's 1966 record stands out. It is undoubtedly a great performance, tingling with electricity from the opening Promenade to the spaciously conceived finale, *The Great Gate of Kiev*, which has real splendour. Other high points are the ominously powerful climax of *Bydlo* as the Polish ox-wagon lumbers into view very weightily, and the venomously pungent bite of the brass – expansively recorded – in the sinister *Catacombs* sequence, which is given a bizarre majesty. As with many of Karajan's finest records, one has the feeling that he has rethought the score, here very much in terms of a Straussian symphonic poem, for the Promenades, with tempi subtly varied and sometimes slower than usual, are well integrated into the overall structure. Detail is consistently pointed with the greatest imagination, not only in the lighter moments, but for instance in *The hut on fowl's legs*, where the tuba articulation is sharp and rhythmically buoyant. Throughout, the glorious orchestral playing, and especially the brass sonorities, ensnare the ear; even when Karajan is relatively restrained, as in the nostalgic melancholy of *The old castle*, the underlying tension remains. The remastered analogue recording still sounds pretty marvellous; even if it does not quite match the Abbado CD in dynamic range or, indeed, Karajan's newest digital version, it is little short of demonstration standard and is very well balanced, apart from an odd spot of bass resonance.

Karajan's 1987 record is also very impressive, very similar in many ways to the earlier account, again with superb Berlin Philharmonic playing and the weight of the climaxes contrasting with the wit of the *Tuileries* and the exhilaration of *The Market at Limoges*. Where the newest version is a shade disappointing, compared with the old, is in the finale. Here Karajan is as spacious as before but, from the beginning, is a little slack when he fails to detach the massive chords, and the culminating apotheosis falls a little short in physical excitement. The digital sound is very wide-ranging, if the sense of presence is less keen than his 1960s recording, with positioning less sharply defined. Yet in added weight and the silent background the new recording obviously brings benefits. There is a good tape.

Abbado takes a straighter, more direct view of Mussorgsky's fanciful series of pictures than usual, less consciously expressive, relying above all on instrumental virtuosity and the dazzling tonal contrasts of Ravel's orchestration. He is helped by the translucent and naturally balanced digital recording; indeed, the sound is first class, making great impact at climaxes yet also extremely refined, as in the delicate portrayal of the unhatched chicks. Abbado's speeds tend to be extreme, with both this and *Tuileries* taken very fast and light, while *Bydlo* and *The Great Gate of Kiev* are slow and weighty. Both readily demonstrate the recording's wide dynamic range. The fullness and clarity are especially impressive in the compact disc version which, although not as sumptuous as the famous Telarc disc, is among the finest of DG's issues in the new format. The digital effect is brilliant and sharply defined, but not so aggressive in the way that the Decca sound is for Solti's Chicago version. Abbado's version is also available on a DG chrome tape in the bargain-priced Pocket Music series, generously coupled with his excellent Chicago account of Berlioz's *Symphonie fantastique*. The tape transfer is brilliantly clear, but the high level brings an even more brightly lit upper range so that in the climaxes of *The Great Gate of Kiev* the ear is drawn to a slight imbalance at the bass end of the spectrum, which could ideally offer more expansive support.

Muti's reading is second to none. Any comparison is only with the finest previous versions (Toscanini, Koussevitzky, Karajan); given the excellence of its recorded sound, it more than holds its own. Moreover, it was one of the first records to do justice to the Philadelphia sound (although the balance is forward and perhaps not all listeners will respond to the brass timbres at the opening). But it is a far richer and more full-blooded quality than we have been used to in the 1960s and '70s from this source. The lower strings in *Samuel Goldenberg and Schmuyle* have extraordinary body and presence, and *Baba-Yaga* has an unsurpassed virtuosity and attack, as well as being of a high standard as a recording. Putting the LP and CD versions side by side, there is no doubt that the new format offers the greater range and firmness of texture. The coupling is no less thrilling. This can be recommended even to those readers who have not always responded to later records from this conductor.

Solti's performance is fiercely brilliant rather than atmospheric or evocative. He treats Ravel's orchestration as a virtuoso challenge, and with larger-than-life digital recording it undoubtedly has demonstration qualities. On CD the orchestral clarity has an almost X-ray precision, and the transparency of texture, given the forward balance, provides quite startling clarity. Now very generously recoupled at mid-price with Solti's outstanding version of Bartók's *Concerto for orchestra*, it makes a formidable bargain.

Giulini's 1976 Chicago recording had always been among the front runners. He is generally more relaxed and often more wayward than Karajan, but this is still a splendid performance and the finale generates more tension than Karajan's most recent digital version, though it is not as overpowering as the earlier analogue recording. What makes the Giulini very attractive is the generous Ravel couplings which show him at his finest. His Mussorgsky is also available on a Walkman tape – see above – and sounds pretty good in that format too, but the Galleria cassette of the Mussorgsky/Ravel coupling is even better defined.

Chailly's brilliant Concertgebouw recording – one of his first discs with the orchestra of which he has been appointed music director – takes an unusually metrical view of the score. That means that the Promenade links sound square and plodding, while the final *Great Gate of Kiev*, at a very slow and steady speed, is shattering in the wrong way as well as the right one. But the light, brilliant numbers are delightfully done and, as part of a fascinating group of works demonstrating the genius of Ravel as orchestrator, the disc has its place. Ripely brilliant, the Decca recording has spectacular range. There is a good if not outstanding cassette.

Previn's Philips version was recorded during live performances in Vienna. Obviously the Philips engineers had problems with the acoustics of the Musikvereinsaal, as the bass is noticeably resonant and inner definition is far from sharp. Otherwise the balance is truthful; but the performance, though not lacking spontaneity, is not disinctive, and there is a lack of the kind of grip which makes Karajan's version so unforgettable.

(i) *Pictures at an exhibition* (orch. Ravel); (ii) *Pictures at an exhibition* (original piano version).
(M) *** Ph. **420 708-2**; *420 708-4* [id.]. Rotterdam PO, Edo de Waart; (ii) Misha Dichter.

Those seeking the natural pairing of the original piano version of Mussorgsky's *Pictures* with Ravel's orchestration will hardly better this mid-priced Philips CD or tape. The Rotterdam orchestra play splendidly throughout, and Edo de Waart's performance has a natural, spontaneous momentum, with each picture aptly characterized and the final climax admirably paced and excitingly powerful. The 1975 recording is rather resonant, but detail comes through well enough. The weight in the bass (rather more noticeable in the cassette format) emphasizes the strong contribution from the drums in *Baba-Yaga* and the closing section. The surprise here, however, is Misha Dichter's outstanding performance of the original piano score, among the finest on record. The recording dates from 1974 and is of Philips's best quality: its sonority adds to the colour Dichter commands throughout the work. Every separate picture is telling and he perceptively varies the mood of each Promenade to provide an appropriate link. After a riveting account of *Baba-Yaga*, demonstrating great keyboard flair, the closing *Great Gate of Kiev* is overwhelmingly powerful. Dichter often seems a reticent pianist in the recording studio, but not here – Mussorgsky's spectacular finale has seldom sounded more gripping.

Pictures at an exhibition: (i) orch. Ashkenazy; (ii) original piano version.
(*) Decca Dig. **414 386-2 [id.]. (i) Philh. O, Ashkenazy; (ii) Ashkenazy (piano).

A side-by-side comparison between Mussorgsky's original piano score and the orchestral version is always instructive; but here the orchestration is Ashkenazy's own, which he made after finding dissatisfaction with Ravel's transcription, 'guided by the deeper undercurrents of this predominantly dark-coloured piece'. His arrangement concentrates on a broader orchestral tapestry – helped by the richness of the Kingsway Hall acoustic – and he does not attempt to match Ravel in subtlety of detail or precision of effect. The character of the pictures is not always very individual, although Ashkenazy finds plenty of Russian feeling in the music itself. The recording is brightly opulent rather than glittering. Ashkenazy's digital solo account of the *Pictures* does not differ in its broad essentials from his earlier, analogue recording. It is distinguished by spontaneity and poetic feeling but lacks something of the extrovert flair with which pianists like Richter or Berman can make one forget all about the orchestra. The piano focus is clear with fine presence, if not quite natural in balance.

Pictures at an exhibition (original piano version).
(M) (***) Ph. mono **420 774-2** [id.]. Sviatoslav Richter with *Recital*.(***)

(*) HMV Dig. **CDC7 49262-2 [id.]. Cécile Ousset – RAVEL: *Gaspard*.***
(*) RCA Dig. **RD 85931; *RK 85931*. Barry Douglas – LISZT: *Dante sonata* etc.**(*)
** Ph. Dig. **420 156-2**; *420 156-4* [id.]. Alfred Brendel – LISZT: *Collection*.**
(M) *(*) Pickwick Dig. **PCD 818**. Geoffrey Saba – STRAVINSKY: *Petrushka*.*

The Philips reissue offers Sviatoslav Richter's 1958 Sofia recital. The mono recording has been remastered using this company's NoNoise digital background reduction system but alas this cannot suppress the audience's bronchial afflictions, and a troublesome tape roar also remains. Nevertheless, the magnetism of Richter's playing comes over and his enormously wide dynamic range brings a riveting final climax, even if, with the piano backwardly positioned, some of the pianissimo playing is not too cleanly focused. Besides the Mussorgsky, the recital offers a generous programme (74′ overall) including Schubert *Impromptus* and a *Moment musical*, the Chopin *Etude in E*, Op. 10, No. 3, two Liszt *Valses oubliées* and excerpts from the *Transcendental studies*, all readily demonstrating the Richter magic in spite of indifferent sound.

The French pianist Cécile Ousset gives a commanding account of the *Pictures*, and hers is the finest of the modern digital records – indeed, she is extremely well recorded – the sound is most believable on CD. Her playing is ever responsive to the changing moods and colour of the music and is convincingly spontaneous. Hers is a big-boned and powerful reading and she is very impressive in the closing section. However, Misha Dichter's analogue version, coupled with the orchestral *Pictures* – see above – is even finer, even if the Philips recording has not quite the presence of the HMV CD.

Barry Douglas plays with fine impetus and much vividness of characterization, though he can also be thoughtful, as in *The old castle*. RCA's piano timbre is fully filled out, as well as being 'present', and allows Douglas plenty of weight in the finale. This is powerfully conceived but not electrifying in the manner of a Richter.

Brendel's performance has its own imaginative touches and some fine moments: the *Ballet of the Unhatched Chicks* is delightfully articulated, and both the *Bydlo* and *Baba-Yaga* are powerful, the latter coming after a darkly evocative *Catacombs/Cum mortuis* sequence. Brendel keeps the music moving, but effectively varies the style of the Promenades. The closing pages, however, need to sound more unbuttoned: Brendel is weighty, but fails to enthral the listener. The recording is faithful.

Geoffrey Saba, too, is given a fine modern digital recording, but he plays the *Pictures* like a suite of piano pieces and his rubato is very free. *The Ballet of the Unhatched Chicks* is rhythmically impetuous; *Bydlo*, however, sounds effectively solid and cumbersome with its strong accents. The finale is very broad and certainly not overwhelming. There is much that is musical here but, given the competition, this is not really a front runner, in spite of its reasonable price.

Pictures at an exhibition (original piano version). *Au village; En Crimée; Impromptu passionné; Méditation; Scherzo; Un larmé.*
* Denon Dig. **C37 7177** [id.]. Jacques Rouvier.

A disappointing alternative of Mussorgsky's original version. The piano is very closely balanced and its percussive character emphasized. The individual pictures are made to sound like boldly drawn cartoons. The six miniatures offered as a fill-up are more relaxed in feeling, but again the sound is unflattering.

Pictures at an exhibition (original version). *Children's playroom; Crimea: Gorzuf and Ayudaga; Ensign* (*Polka*)*; First punishment; Impromptu passione; On the Southern Coast of the Crimea: Canoes; Reminiscences of Childhood; Seamstress; Tears.*
(M) *(*) Olympia **OCD 117** [id.]. Viktoria Postnikova.

Viktoria Postnikova opens vibrantly and her playing throughout has undoubted character. But she is prone to inappropriate rubato in music that needs to flow, unimpeded by personal idiosyncrasy. Even so, there is much to impress the listener here – the boldly articulated *Bydlo* makes a strong impression – until *The Great Gate of Kiev*. This begins well enough but then the tension steadily sags through the rising and descending octaves and repeated chords (admittedly rather clumsy pianistic devices, but which can be effective in the right hands) until by the final climax she has slowed the pace of the music unmercifully and lost her grip on the listener. The rest of her programme (some 26′ – the disc plays for 72′ 24″ overall) is rare repertoire; but the performances, especially the lighter pieces, are lacking in charm; the polka, *Ensign*, again demonstrates her rather wilful rubato. The piano is realistically recorded and has excellent presence.

VOCAL MUSIC

Songs: *The classicist; Forgotten; The he-goat; Sadly rustled the leaves; Song of the flea; Sunless; Thou didst not know me.*
(*) DG Dig. **419 239-2 [id.]. Paata Burchuladze, Ludmilla Ivanova – RACHMANINOV: *Songs.***(*)

Paata Burchuladze's magnificent bass presents these Mussorgsky songs with a rare precision, richness and power, even if as yet he fails to project their full character in detailed expression. Nevertheless he manages a resonant laugh at the end of *The Flea*. First-rate sound.

OPERA

Boris Godunov (original version; complete).
(*) Ph. **412 281-2 (3) [id.]. Vedernikov, Arkhipova, Koroleva, Shkolnikova, Sokolov. USSR TV and R. Ch. and SO, Fedoseyev.

Fedoseyev conducts a powerful performance of Mussorgsky's masterpiece in its original scoring, using the composer's own 1872 revision, as near an 'authentic' solution as one can get with a problematic score that never reached definitive form. Some may miss the brilliance of the Rimsky-Korsakov revision, which still generally holds sway in the opera house and did so for a generation on record; but the earthy strength of the score comes over superbly, far more bitingly than it did in EMI's disappointing version recorded in Poland, now deleted. Ideally for records, one needs a firmer singer than the mature Vedernikov as Boris, but this is a searingly intense performance which rises commandingly to the big dramatic moments, conveying the Tsar's neurotic tensions chillingly. Arkhipova is also too mature for the role of Marina, but equally her musical imagination is most convincing. The rest of the cast is a mixed bag, with some magnificent Russian basses but a few disappointing contributions, as from the whining tenor, Vladislav Piavko, as the Pretender. Though the recording was made over a period of years, the sound is full and satisfying, if not always ideally balanced.

Boris Godunov (arr. Rimsky-Korsakov).
*** Decca **411 862-2** (3) [id.]. Ghiaurov, Vishnevskaya, Spiess, Maslennikov, Talvela, V. Boys' Ch., Sofia R. Ch., V. State Op. Ch., VPO, Karajan.
** HMV **CDS7 43997-8** (3). Christoff, Lear, Lanigen, Ouzousov, Alexieva, Sofia Nat. Op. Ch., Paris Conservatoire O, Cluytens.

The EMI set is chiefly valuable for the resonant contribution of Boris Christoff, for a generation unmatched in the role of Boris. Here he takes the part not only of the Tsar but of Pimen and Varlaam too, relishing the contrast of those other, highly characterful bass roles. It is good that this glorious voice is so vividly caught on CD, but sadly the overall performance under Cluytens does not quite add up to the sum of its parts, as the earlier mono recording with Christoff did.

If Ghiaurov in the title role lacks some of the dramatic intensity of Christoff on the HMV set, Karajan's superbly controlled Decca version, technically outstanding, comes far nearer than previous recordings to conveying the rugged greatness of Mussorgsky's masterpiece. Only the Coronation scene lacks something of the weight and momentum one ideally wants. This makes a clear first choice on CD, even if Vishnevskaya is far less appealing than the lovely non-Slavonic Marina of Evelyn Lear on HMV.

Mysliveček, Josef (1737–81)

Violin concertos in C; E.
*(*) Sup. Dig. **C37 7285** [id.]. Ishikawa, Dvořák CO, Pešek.

Violin concertos in D; F.
** Sup. Dig. **C37 7429** [id.]. Ishikawa, Dvořák CO, Pešek.

Josef Mysliveček was Czech, but spent much of his life in Italy where many of his operas were produced. The four *Violin concertos* offered on this pair of CDs are slight in musical substance but are, for all that, pleasing examples of the genre at a transitional stage from the Baroque to the Classical period. Mozart heard and admired him and praised his sonatas. 'They will no doubt delight everyone: they are easy to memorize and very effective when played with proper precision.' The same applies here, as these concertos are played with great sweetness of tone and flawless technical command by the young Japanese violinist, Shizuka Ishikawa, who has lived in Czechoslovakia since her student years, she is given adequate support by the Dvořák Chamber Orchestra under Libor Pešek. These concertos have some original and interesting touches – though no one in their right mind would play them in preference to Mozart; these have the manner of Mozart but no depth whatever. The recording, made in the highly resonant House of Artists, Prague, is good rather than outstanding. Supraphon miss a trick in being bound by the LP layout; instead of accommodating three of the concertos on one compact disc, they give us only two in each case, which together last under 40′. Needless to say, the improvement in definition and transparency of detail is very marked – but only the most dedicated enthusiast will be willing to invest so considerable an outlay for such lightweight music.

Neruda, Jan (1708–c. 1780)

Trumpet concerto in E flat.
** Erato Dig. **ECD 88007** [id.]. André, Paris Ens., Wallez – HUMMEL; TELEMANN: *Concertos.***

The *Trumpet concerto* by the Czech composer, Jan Neruda, is flexible of line and exploits the possibilities of its solo instrument in a conventional way, without producing music that is in any way memorable. Maurice André gives an expert performance and is well enough accompanied. The digital recording is good without being especially vivid.

Nielsen, Carl (1865–1931)

(i) *Clarinet concerto, Op. 57;* (ii) *Symphony No. 3* (*Sinfonia espansiva*). *Maskarade overture.*
*** BIS Dig. **CD 321** [id.]. (i) Ole Schill; (ii) Pia Raanoja, Knut Skram; Gothenburg SO, Myung-Whun Chung.

This is an ideal record with which to start building a library of Nielsen's orchestral music, for it contains a relatively early overture, a symphony of his full maturity and one of his most mysterious late works, the *Clarinet concerto*, music which really sounds as if it comes from another planet. The *Third Symphony* (*Sinfonia espansiva*) is an exhilarating and life-enhancing work which dates from roughly the same time as the *Fourth Symphony* of Sibelius, from whose bleak introspection it is far removed. It radiates a confidence and well-being soon to be shattered by the First World War. The young Korean conductor seems as completely steeped in the Nielsen tradition as is his fine Swedish orchestra. He secures playing of great fire and enthusiasm from the Gothenburgers, and has vision and breadth – and at the same time no want of momentum. Two soloists are called for in the pastoral slow movement singing a wordless vocalise, and their contribution is admirable. Myung-Whun Chung also gives a high-spirited and sparkling account of the *Overture* to Nielsen's comic opera, *Maskarade*. As for the *Concerto*, Ole Schill brings brilliance and insight to what is one of the most disturbing and masterly of all modern concertos. The BIS recording is marvellous, even by the high standards of this small company.

Flute concerto.
*** Ph. Dig. **412 728-2** [id.]. Nicolet, Leipzig GO, Masur – BUSONI: *Divertimento*; REINECKE: *Concerto.****

Nielsen's *Flute concerto* is a late work, written at about the same time as Sibelius's *Tapiola* – and moreover in the same country, Italy. It is a wonderfully subtle and affecting piece whose light spirits hide a vein of keen poetic feeling. Aurèle Nicolet's performance is first rate in every way fully catching the work's rhapsodic, indeed chimerical mood changes; he is given splendid support by the fine Leipzig orchestra under Masur. Moreover, the Philips recording is ideally balanced so that the various dialogues between the soloist and the orchestral woodwind are interchanged within a most believable perspective. The sound itself is beautiful, within an attractive ambience which does not blur detail. This can be strongly recommended.

(i) *Flute concerto;* (ii) *Wind quintet, Op. 43; The Mother* (incidental music)*:* (iii) *The fog is lifting;* (iv) *The children are playing; Faith and hope.* (v) *2 Fantasias, Op. 2* (arr. Galway).
*(*) RCA Dig. **RD 86359**; *RK 86539* [**RCA 6359-2-RC**]. Galway; (i) Danish RSO; (ii) Danish Wind Ens.; (iii) Sioned Williams (harp); (iv) Brian Hawkins (viola); (v) P. Moll (piano).

A good account of the *Concerto*, though it does not displace Aurèle Nicolet and the Leipzig Gewandhaus Orchestra on Philips. The orchestral playing, though eminently spirited, is no match for it in terms of finesse and polish. Nielsen composed the *Wind quintet* in 1922 as a kind of relaxation after his exertions on the *Fifth Symphony*. It is one of the most refreshing works in the repertory and has the fragrance and earthiness of the early morning. The main problem in this performance is the tendency to iron out dynamic extremes: the rather forward balance doesn't help matters and the larger-than-life balance hardly enhances its effect. Galway also gives us his arrangements of the early *Fantasies*, Op. 2, for oboe, which do not sit well on any other instrument. Philip Moll plays beautifully in Op. 2, but the sound itself is not ideal, thanks to the poorly focused balance. Galway's very sweet vibrato is not to all tastes, and collectors should wait until something better comes along. The chrome cassette is well engineered and matches the CD fairly closely.

(i) *Violin concerto, Op. 33; Symphony No. 5, Op. 50.*
*** BIS Dig. **CD 370** [id.]. (i) Dong-Suk Kang, Gothenburg SO, Myung-Whun Chung.

An impressive achievement on all counts. Dong-Suk Kang is more than equal to the technical demands of this concerto and is fully attuned to the Nordic sensibility. He brings tenderness and refinement of feeling to the searching slow movement and great panache and virtuosity to the rest. This is as fine a performance as this unjustly neglected concerto has ever received on record – including the authoritative Telmanyi account. Who would have forecast at the time of the

Nielsen renaissance in the 1950s that, thirty years on, two Korean artists would have produced such completely idiomatic results? The *Fifth Symphony* is hardly less successful and is certainly the best-recorded version now before the public. Myung-Whun Chung has a natural feeling for Nielsen's language and the first movement has real breadth. He misses the disembodied, other-worldly quality that Jensen used to get at fig. 67 in the second movement – but enough of nostalgia, this is still superb and an effective challenge to Ole Schmidt.

(i) *Symphony No. 1 in G minor, Op. 7;* (ii) *Little Suite, Op. 1.*
*(*) CBS Dig. **MK 42321**; *IMT 42321* [id.]. (i) Swedish RSO, Salonen; (ii) New Stockholm CO.

Extreme tempi make Salonen's version uncompetitive. Esa-Pekka Salonen starts this most genial of symphonies rather briskly. Tempi are consistently fast throughout, save in the *Andante* where he is very slow. The trouble is that once the basic relationship between the tempo of the movements is disturbed it is harder to convey any sense of organic coherence. The various parts do not seem to relate to the whole, and the listener does not sense a deeply held point of view behind this reading, such as this young artist has evinced in other repertoire. The finale is particularly breathless. The Swedish Radio Orchestra acquit themselves well, and the playing of the New Stockholm Chamber Orchestra in the delightful *Suite* for strings is very fine indeed. The recording is acceptable, but not in the first flight. Textures could be more transparent and there is relatively little sense of front-to-back perspective.

Symphonies Nos 1–6.
(*) Unicorn **UKCD 2000/2 [id.]. Gomez, Rayner Cook (in No. 3), LSO, Schmidt.

These are performances that are ablaze with life, warmth and a sense of discovery; they served us well in the 1970s. The recordings were always a bit rough, but the digital remastering represents an undoubted (though not spectacular) improvement, for the texture still remains coarse in tuttis. However, the brass is less garish and better integrated into the overall aural picture. In the last three symphonies Ole Schmidt is a sure and penetrating guide, and to their number must now be added *The Four Temperaments* (No. 2). Whatever quibbles one might have (Schmidt may be a little too fervent in the slow movement of the *First Symphony* for some tastes), his readings have an authentic ring to them, and Schmidt has real feeling for this glorious music. They obviously represent good value – though readers who are collecting the Gothenburg set on BIS have the advantage of much finer recording and orchestral playing that radiates enthusiasm born of a long Nielsen tradition.

Symphony No. 2 (*The Four Temperaments*); *Aladdin suite, Op. 34.*
*** BIS **CD 247** [id.]. Gothenburg SO, Myung-Whun Chung.

Myung-Whun Chung has a real feeling for this repertoire and his account of the *Second Symphony* is very fine. The Gothenburg Symphony Orchestra proves an enthusiastic and responsive body of players; Chung, who studied with Sixten Ehrling at the Juilliard, does not put a foot wrong. The recording is impressive, too, and can be recommended with enthusiasm. The Gothenburg orchestra plan to record all of Nielsen's output – as well as the complete Sibelius and a complete Stenhammar – and what has been issued so far suggests this will be a very distinguished set.

Symphony No. 4 (*Inextinguishable*), *Op. 29.*
*** DG Dig. **413 313-2** [id.]. BPO, Karajan.

Symphony No. 4 (*Inextinguishable*); *Helios overture, Op. 17.*
* CBS Dig. **MK 42093**. Swedish RSO, Salonen.

Symphony No. 4 (Inextinguishable); Pan and Syrinx, Op. 49.
(*) HMV Dig. **CDC7 47503-2 [id.]. CBSO, Rattle.

By far the best performance of Nielsen's *Fourth* ever recorded comes from Karajan. The orchestral playing is altogether incomparable and there is both vision and majesty in the reading. The strings play with passionate intensity at the opening of the third movement, and there is a thrilling sense of commitment throughout. The wind playing sounds a little over-civilized by comparison with the pioneering record from Launy Gröndahl and the Danish State Radio Orchestra, made in the early 1950s – but what exquisitely blended, subtle playing this is. It is excellently recorded, too; there is a distinct gain in presence and realism in the CD format.

Simon Rattle has the measure of this work and it is an undeniably powerful performance. The very opening has a splendid breadth and grandeur. The gain in weight is at the loss of a certain incandescence, though the Birmingham orchestra play with splendid intensity and conviction. The HMV recording is very present and detailed; moreover, it has the advantage of a makeweight in the form of *Pan and Syrinx*. This has, of course, been recorded by Blomstedt and, before him, by Ormandy, but Simon Rattle's version is vastly superior to either; it has great delicacy of texture and feeling for atmosphere. *Pan and Syrinx* is among the most refined and inspired of Nielsen's works, and it is unlikely that this account will be bettered in the immediate future.

There is no doubt that Esa-Pekka Salonen gets an excellent sonority from the Swedish Radio Symphony Orchestra and that the CBS and Swedish Radio engineers, working in the Berwald Hall in Stockholm, produce a very natural and well-balanced sound, with both clarity and space. Nor is there any question that this young Finnish conductor is a real musical personality, with an ear for orchestral balance, who in the fullness of time will become a conductor of stature. However, his account of this marvellous symphony simply will not do. The opening has a genuine sweep that promises well – but then disaster suddenly strikes, with a disruptive application of the brakes immediately after the second subject group. There is a further destructive pull-back at the end of this A major section, and the result is insupportably inflated and egocentric. The second movement is well done, though woodwind intonation is far from impeccable. The slow movement, too, nearly collapses at one point. This is a pity since there is so much else that is right about this performance, in particular the authentic atmosphere that is evoked. The playing is totally committed, and the climax, with the famous dialogue between the two timpani, is vividly exciting. However, the eccentricities prove as irksome on repetition as they do on first hearing.

Symphonies Nos 4 (Inextinguishable), Op. 29; 5, Op. 50; Helios overture, Op. 17; Saga-drøm, Op. 39.
(B) **(*) HMV *TCC2-POR 154593-9*. Danish RSO, Blomstedt.

Tape collectors should find this double-length 'Portrait of the Artist' cassette worth acquiring. Each symphony is complete on one side, with one of the two shorter works as a filler. The sound is full and brilliant. Blomstedt's version of the *Fourth* is excellent with some fine wind playing from the Danish orchestra. In the *Fifth* Myung-Whun Chung is to be preferred (see above), but with two major works offered for the price of one, this is good value.

CHAMBER MUSIC

Canto serioso; Fantasias for oboe and piano, Op. 2; The Mother (incidental music), *Op. 41; Serenata in vano; Wind quintet, Op. 43.*
** Chan. *ABT 1003* [id.]. Athena Ens.

A most useful tape which collects Nielsen's output for wind instruments in chamber form. The Athena Ensemble give a thoroughly lively account of the *Wind quintet*; they earn gratitude for observing the exposition repeat in the first movement but none for ignoring some of the dynamic markings! The ostinato figure at letter D in the first movement is marked *pp* but does not really sound it here, though the close balance does not help matters. The balance is rather more disturbing in the *Serenata in vano*, where the clarinet is in your lap; and similar points could be made about the other pieces. But none of them except *The Mother* is otherwise available and all are beautiful; they are also very well played. The cassette transfer is of good quality, smooth and refined.

Complete piano music: *Chaconne; Dream of merry Christmas; Festival prelude; Humoresque bagatelles; Piano music for young and old; Piece in C; 3 Pieces; 5 Pieces; Suite; Symphonic suite; Theme and variations.*
** Hyp. Dig. **CDA 66231/2** [id.]. Mina Miller.

Nielsen's keyboard music is the most important to come from Scandinavia since Grieg – and works like the *Suite*, Op. 45, and the *Three Pieces*, Op. 59, go a good deal deeper than the Norwegian master. Mina Miller is an American academic who has edited the new Hansen Edition of the Complete Piano Music. It is enterprising of Hyperion to fill an important gap in the catalogue now that the classic account of Arne Skiold Rasmussen is no longer available. Ms Miller knows what this music is about and, for the most part, conveys her intentions capably. Put alongside a great pianist, her playing is lacking real keyboard authority (hardly surprising, given her academic background) but even if she is not impeccable pianistically, she makes up for it in terms of musical understanding.

VOCAL MUSIC

(i) *Springtime in Fünen. Aladdin suite, Op. 34.*
*** Unicorn Dig. **DKPCD 9054**; *DKPC 9054* [id.]. (i) Ingo Nielsen, Von Binzer, Klint, Lille Muko University Ch., St Klemens Children's Ch.; Odense SO, Veto.

Springtime in Fünen is one of those enchanting pieces to which everyone responds when they hear it, yet which is hardly ever performed outside Denmark. It is wonderfully fresh and has strong melodic appeal. There is no CD alternative but, even if there were, it is difficult to think of this account being greatly improved on. The *Aladdin* orchestral suite is well played by the Odense orchestra. This disc is a little short on playing time – but no matter, it is well worth its cost and will give many hours of delight. The cassette is very well managed too, and tape collectors can acquire it with confidence.

Nono, Luigi (born 1924)

Fragmente: Stille, an Diotima.
** DG Dig. **415 513-2** [id.]. LaSalle Qt.

If anyone can convert the listener to the music of Luigi Nono, it is the LaSalle Quartet, for whom he wrote this taxing, endlessly pauseful work in two substantial movements of nearly 20 minutes each. The price-conscious collector might well complain not only of the short overall length but of the high proportion of silence on the disc. But the intensity of the playing will help the uncommitted listener to concentrate on intentionally weighty expression in which late Beethoven was an inspiration – not that one would readily recognize it. Full, immediate recording.

Novák, Vítézslav (1870–1949)

Slovak suite, Op. 32; South Bohemian suite, Op. 64.
(*) Sup. Dig. **CO 1743 [id.]. Czech PO, Vajnar.

What a heavenly score the *Slovak suite* is! *Two in love*, its fourth movement – if more widely propagated – could well become as popular as any piece of music you care to think of. Much of the score is as appealing as Dvořák: *In Church*, the opening movement, has something in common with Mozart's *Ave verum corpus*, althogh more obviously romantic, and the closing *At night* is beguilingly atmospheric. The *South Bohemian suite* is not quite so consistently inventive and though the opening *Pastorale* has a delightful atmosphere, at 10′ 30″ it is a shade long, as is the patrol-like *Once upon a time* (*The march of the Taborites*). František Vajnar secures highly sympathetic performances of both works from the great Czech orchestra and is quite touching in the *Epilogue* to Op. 64, *Good health, my native land*. The *Slovak suite*, recorded in 1984, is well balanced and has plenty of ambience; in the *South Bohemian suite* (recorded a few months earlier, in December 1983) the microphone placing seems slightly less judicious, though in the same hall, the House of Artists, Prague, for the violins have a 'digital' brightness above the stave and are lacking in body. But this is still a disc to try, if for Op. 32 alone.

Ockeghem, Johannes (*c.* 1410–97)

Requiem (*Missa pro defunctis*).
*** DG **415 293-2** [id.]. Pro Cantione Antiqua, Hamburger Bläserkreis für alte Musik, Turner – JOSQUIN DES PRÉS: *Missa – L'homme armé*.***

Requiem (*Missa pro defunctis*); *Missa Mi-Mi* (*Missa quarti toni*).
(*) HMV Dig. **CDC7 49213-2 [id.]. Hilliard Ens., Hillier.

Ockeghem's *Missa pro defunctis* is the first surviving polyphonic *Requiem*. The *Missa Mi-Mi* is his most widely performed Mass and survives in three different sources in the Vatican Library; in one it is called *Missa Quarti Toni* and in another *My-My*, which is assumed to derive from the short motif that appears in the bass section at the beginning of each main section and consists of a descending fifth. These HMV performances have the expertise, secure intonation, blend and ensemble that one expects from these singers, and the music itself has an austere and affecting simplicity. Although it has had a qualified welcome from specialists in this field, and despite a certain blandness, it would be curmudgeonly not to welcome such generally persuasive accounts of both works. They make an eminently serviceable introduction to the sacred music of this composer and are very well recorded, too.

The DG Archiv version of the *Missa pro defunctis* was originally recorded in Hamburg in 1973. The Pro Cantione Antiqua was unmatched at this period (with such artists as James Bowman and Paul Esswood as their counter-tenors, this is hardly suprising), and Bruno Turner's direction has both scholarly rectitude and musical eloquence to commend it. They do not cultivate the white, somewhat virginal and vibrato-less tone favoured by Early Music groups in the 1980s. For most of the *Requiem* (though not in the Josquin with which it is coupled), the lines are at times doubled by the excellent Hamburger Bläserkreis für alte Musik. It is an eminently welcome addition to the compact disc catalogue and is more involving than the alternative Hilliard version on HMV.

Offenbach, Jacques (1819–80)

Cello concerto.
*** RCA **RD 71003**. Ofra Harnoy, Cincinnati SO, Kunzel – SAINT-SAËNS: *Concerto No. 1*; TCHAIKOVSKY: *Rococo variations.****

Offenbach's *Cello concerto* is a delight, with all the effervescence and tunefulness of his operettas. It is played with verve and brio and a full range of colour by Ofra Harnoy and did much to establish her reputation, while the accompaniment from Kunzel and his Cincinnati players is just as lively and sympathetic. The CD has fine presence; this is worth having, even for collectors who already have one or more of the couplings, for these are just as refreshing. Excellent recording throughout. (The cassette (*RK 71004*) cannot be recommended as it omits the Tchaikovsky.)

Gaîté parisienne (ballet, arr. Rosenthal): complete.
*** Ph. Dig. **411 039-2** [id.]. Pittsburgh SO, Previn.
(*) Decca Dig. **411 708-2; *411 708-4*. Montreal SO, Dutoit – GOUNOD: *Faust: ballet music.***(*)

Previn's disc is first choice. He realizes that tempi can remain relaxed, and the music's natural high spirits will still bubble to the surface. The orchestral playing is both spirited and elegant, with Previn obviously relishing the score's delightful detail. The rhythmic spring is captivating, as is the gentle lilt in the *Barcarolle*, Ländler and Waltz movements (from *La Belle Hélène*, for instance). The fizzing effervescence does not prevent a minor sense of gravitas when necessary, and this is mirrored by the Philips sound-balance which has substance as well as atmosphere and brilliance. Perhaps the tuba thumping away in the bass is a shade too present, but it increases one's desire to smile through this engagingly happy music. The CD sounds splendid.

Dutoit has the advantage of sound that is brighter and has rather more projection than Previn's Philips disc, though the acoustic is resonant and detail is no clearer. But the recording is undoubtedly out of Decca's top drawer. He opens the music racily and there are many admirable touches, yet as the ballet proceeds there is a hint of blandness in the lyrical moments, and the *Barcarolle* is somewhat disappointing. Some might like the extra feeling of breadth Dutoit generates, but Previn catches the spirit of the score more naturally. The Decca record has the advantage of including also the *Faust* ballet music, warmly and elegantly played, but here also Dutoit's touch is a shade heavy. The feeling in both works is redolent of the concert hall rather than the ballet theatre, and this effect is enhanced on the excellent CD. The chrome cassette is also very successful.

Gaîté parisienne (ballet, arr. Rosenthal): extended excerpts.
(M) *** DG **423 215-2**; *423 215-4* [id.]. BPO, Karajan – CHOPIN: *Les Sylphides*; DELIBES: *Coppélia*: Suite excerpts.***
(M) **(*) HMV **CDM7 69041-2** [id.]. Philh. O, Karajan – BORODIN: *Polovtsian dances*; GOUNOD: *Faust ballet*; PONCHIELLI: *Dance of the hours.****

Karajan's selection is generous. On the DG disc, only Nos 3–5, 7 and 19–21 are omitted. The remastering of the 1972 recording is highly successful. Textures have been lightened to advantage and the effect is to increase the raciness of the music making, while its polish and sparkle are even more striking. There is characteristic elegance in the *Barcarolle*, and boisterous high spirits in the *Can-can*. On the whole this is preferable to the 1958 Philharmonia version. The London orchestra also plays with great brilliance, the players obviously revelling in the bravura, but the remastered sound is a little dry (the piccolo sometimes adds a touch of shrillness) and the bass response is unexpansive, save (fortunately) in the *Barcarolle*, where the Philharmonia strings are warm and gracious. However, the couplings are highly attractive and even more generous (73′ 18″) than the DG (71′ 39″), where the *Coppélia* suite has been cut back unnecessarily.

Overtures: *Barbe-Bleue; La Belle Hélène; Les deux Aveugles; La Fille du tambour major; La Grande-Duchesse de Gérolstein; Orphée aux enfers (Orpheus in the Underworld); La Périchole; La Vie parisienne.*
*** Ph. Dig. **411 476-2** [id.]. Philh. O, Marriner.

Overtures: *La Belle Hélène; Bluebeard; La Grande-Duchesse de Gérolstein; Orpheus in the Underworld; Vert-vert. Barcarolle* from *Contes d'Hoffmann.*
(*) DG Dig. **400 044-2 [id.]. BPO, Karajan.
(B) **(*) DG Dig. *419 829-4* [id.]. BPO, Karajan – BIZET: *L'Arlésienne*; *Carmen* **(*).

Other hands besides Offenbach's helped to shape his overtures. Most are on a pot-pourri basis, but the tunes and scoring are so engagingly witty as to confound criticism. *La Belle Hélène* is well constructed by Haensch, and the delightful waltz tune is given a reprise before the end. Karajan's performances racily evoke the theatre pit, and the brilliance is extrovert almost to the point of fierceness. But the Berlin playing is very polished and, with so much to entice the ear, this cannot fail to be entertaining. The demonstration item is *Vert-vert*, which is irresistibly tuneful and vivacious. The digital recording is extremely vivid but the compact disc emphasizes the dryness of the orchestral sound; the effect is rather clinical, with the strings lacking bloom. The DG Pocket Music tape is very generously coupled at bargain-price with both *L'Arlésienne* suites and the *Carmen* suite of Bizet. The dryness remains on the tape transfer, but this is undoubtedly excellent value.

Where Karajan in his Offenbach collection tends to use inflated versions of these operetta overtures by hands other than the composer's, Marriner prefers something nearer to the original scale, even though *Orpheus*, *Belle Hélène* and *La Périchole* are not originals. This music suits the sprightly, rhythmic style of Marriner splendidly, and the Philharmonia responds with polished playing, very well recorded. The CD sparkles attractively.

Overture: *Orpheus in the Underworld; Contes d'Hoffman: Barcarolle.*
(M) **(*) DG *419 469-4* [id.]. BPO, Karajan – BIZET: *L'Arlésienne; Carmen suites.* **(*)

These performances are first class and sound extremely well, but this Galleria issue cannot compare in generosity with the Pocket Music tape above. The coupling is with Karajan's earlier (1971) analogue Bizet recordings, which are in some ways fresher than the digital re-make.

La Belle Hélène (complete).
*** HMV **CDS7 47157-8** [Ang. **CDCB 47156**] (2). Norman, Alliot-Lugaz, Aler, Burles, Bacquier, Lafont, Capitole Toulouse Ch. and O, Plasson.

The casting of Jessye Norman in the name-part of *La Belle Hélène* may seem too heavyweight, but the way that the great soprano can lighten her magisterial voice with all the flexibility and sparkle the music calls for is a constant delight, and her magnetism is irresistible. John Aler, another American opera-singer who readily translates to the style of French operetta, makes a heady-toned Paris, coping superbly with the high tessitura in the famous Judgement couplets and elsewhere. The rest of the cast is strong too, not forgetting Colette Alliot-Lugaz as Oreste, who had such dazzling success in the central role of Chabrier's *L'étoile* in John Eliot Gardiner's brilliant recording. Michel Plasson here produces similarly fizzing results, with excellent ensemble from the choir and orchestra of the Capitole. Excellent recording, less reverberant than in some other discs from this source, and especially lively and present in its CD format. Indeed, with the compact discs it is very important not to set the volume level too high or the spoken dialogue will seem unrealistically close.

Les Contes d'Hoffmann (*The Tales of Hoffmann*): complete.

❀ *** Decca **417 363-2** (2) [id.]. Sutherland, Domingo, Tourangeau, Bacquier, R. Suisse Romande and Lausanne Pro Arte Ch., SRO, Bonynge.

The sparkling CD transfer (with the layout reduced from three LPs to a pair of compact discs, each playing for over 70′) makes Offenbach's inspired score sound even more refreshing, with the immediacy of the action even more striking, and the acoustics of Victoria Hall, Geneva, adding fullness and warmth to the vividness. Joan Sutherland gives a virtuoso performance in four heroine roles, not only as Olympia, Giulietta and Antonia but as Stella in the Epilogue, which in this version – very close to that originally prepared by Tom Hammond for the English National Opera – is given greater weight by the inclusion of the ensemble previously inserted into the Venice scene as a septet, a magnificent climax. Bonynge opts for spoken dialogue, and puts the Antonia scene last, as being the more substantial. His direction is unfailingly sympathetic, while Sutherland is impressive in each role, notably as the doll Olympia and in the pathos of the Antonia scene. As Giulietta she hardly sounds like a *femme fatale*, but still produces beautiful singing. Domingo gives one of his finest performances on record, and so does Gabriel Bacquier. It is a memorable set, in every way, much more than the sum of its parts. One's only real criticism concerns the cueing, which could be more generous in Acts II and III.

Orphée aux enfers (*Orpheus in the Underworld;* 1874 version).

*** HMV **CDS7 49647-2** (2). Sénéchal, Mesplé, Rhodes Burles, Berbié, Petits Chanteurs à la Croix Potencée, Toulouse Capitole Ch. and O, Plasson.

Plasson recorded his fizzing performance – the first complete set in French for thirty years – in time for the Offenbach centenary. He used the far fuller four-act text of 1874 instead of the two-act version of 1858, so adding such delectable rarities as the sparkling *Rondo* of Mercury and the *Policemen's chorus*. Mady Mesplé as usual has her shrill moments, but the rest of the cast is excellent, and Plasson's pacing of the score is exemplary. The recording is brightly atmospheric and the leavening of music with spoken dialogue just enough.

Orpheus in the Underworld: abridged version of Sadler's Wells production (in English).

(B) **(*) CfP *TC-CFP 4539*. Bronhill, Shilling, Miller, Weaving, Steele, Nisbett, Thurlow, Crofoot, Sadler's Wells Op. Ch. and O, Faris.

With a single reservation only, this is highly recommendable. Without visual help the recording manages to convey the high spirits and genuine gaiety of the piece, plus – and this is an achievement for a non-Parisian company – the sense of French poise and precision. June Bronhill in the *Concerto duet* is infectiously provocative about her poor suitor's music. One's only complaint is that Alan Crofoot's King of the Boeotians is needlessly cruel vocally. The sound is full and brilliant, with plenty of atmosphere, and there is no doubt that this reissue of a vintage recording dating from 1960 is very successful. The cassette transfer, made at a high level, is well managed.

Orpheus in the Underworld: highlights of English National Opera production (in English).

(*) That's Entertainment Dig. **CDTER 1134; *ZCTER 1134*. Kale, Watson, Angas, Squires, Bottone, Pope, Belcourt, Styx, Burgess, E. Nat. Op. Ch. & O, Mark Elder.

The English National Opera production, lively and provocative with its grotesque scenery and costumes in political cartoon style by Gerald Scarfe, has spawned a comparably lively collection of highlights, enterprisingly recorded by That's Entertainment Records. It starts not with the conventional overture but with a prelude, over which the invented character, Public Opinion, delivers a moral in unmistakable imitation of the Prime Minister. From then on, the whole entertainment depends a lot for its fun on the racy new adaptation and translation by Snoo Wilson and the ENO producer, David Pountney. It will delight all those who enjoyed the original show at the Coliseum; but Offenbach devotees should be warned: there is little of Parisian elegance in this version and plenty of good knockabout British fun, brilliantly conveyed by the whole company. For this kind of performance one really needs a video, when even Bonaventura Bottone's hilariously camp portrait of a prancing Mercury is not nearly so much fun when simply heard and not seen. Bright, vivid recording to match the performance.

La Périchole (complete).
(*) HMV Dig. **CDS7 47362-8 [Ang. **CDCB 47361**] (2). Berganza, Carreras, Bacquier, Sénéchal, Trempont, Delange, Toulouse Capitole Ch. and O, Plasson.

A good modern recording of this delightful piece was badly needed, and in many ways this fills the bill, for though the sound (as usual in Toulouse) is over-reverberant, the CD remastering has sharpened the impact and ensemble work is excellent, with diction surprisingly clear against full orchestral sound. The incidental roles are superbly taken, but it is odd that Spaniards were chosen for the two principal roles. José Carreras uses his always lovely tenor to fine effect but is often unidiomatic, while Teresa Berganza – who should have made the central character into a vibrant figure, as Régine Crespin used to – is surprisingly heavy and unsparkling. The CD disc-break is well placed between acts, but cueing might have been more generous.

La Vie parisienne (complete).
*** HMV **CDS7 47154-8** (2) [Ang. **CDCB 47154**]. Crespin, Mesplé, Masson, Sénéchal, Ch. and O of Capitole, Toulouse, Plasson.

Hardly less effervescent than the parallel version of *Orpheus in the Underworld*, also conducted by Michel Plasson for HMV, *La Vie parisienne* is a scintillating example of Offenbach's work, an inconsequential farce around the heady days of the International Exhibition in Paris. Though the HMV recording is not quite as consistent as the one of *Orphée aux enfers*, the performance and presentation sparkle every bit as brilliantly, with the spoken dialogue for once a special attraction. Régine Crespin in a smaller role is just as commanding, and though the cast lacks the excellent Vanzo and Massard, the style is captivatingly authentic. The CD transfer is vivid, without loss of ambient atmosphere.

Orff, Carl (1895–1982)

Carmina Burana.
*** HMV **CDC7 47411-2** [id.]; (M) *EG 291066-4* [Ang. *4AM 34770*]. Armstrong, English, Allen, St Clement Danes Grammar School Boys' Ch., LSO Ch., LSO, Previn.
(M) *** Decca **417 714-2** [id.]. Burrows, Devos, Shirley-Quirk, Brighton Fest. Ch., Southend Boys' Ch., RPO, Dorati.
(M) *** Pickwick Dig. **PCD 855** [MCA **MCAD 25964**]. Walmsley-Clark, Graham-Hall, Maxwell, Southend Boys' Ch., LSO Ch., LSO, Hickox.
(M) *** RCA **GD 86533**; *GK 85533* [RCA **6533-2-RG**]. Mandac, Kolk, Milnes, New England Conservatory Ch. & Children's Ch., Boston SO, Ozawa.
(*) RCA Dig. **RCD 14550 [**RCD1 4550**]. Hendricks, Aler, Hagegard, St Paul's Cathedral Boys' Ch., LSO Ch. & O, Mata.
(*) HMV **CDC7 47100-2 [id.]. Augér, Summers, Van Kesteren, Southend Boys' Ch., Philh. Ch. & O, Muti.
(B) **(*) DG Walkman *413 160-4* [id.]. Janowitz, Stolze, Fischer-Dieskau, Schöneberger Boys' Ch., German Op. Ch. & O, Jochum – STRAVINSKY: *Rite of spring*.**(*)
(M) **(*) Ph. **420 713-2**; *420 713-4* [id.]. Casapietra, Hiestermann, Stryczek, Dresden Boys' Ch., Leipzig R. Ch. & SO, Kegel.

(M) (***) HMV **CDM7 69060-2** [id.]. Popp, Unger, Wolansky, Noble, New Philh. Ch., Wandsworth School Boys' Ch., New Philh. O, Frühbeck de Burgos.

** Decca Dig. **411 702-2** [id.]. Greenberg, Bowman, Roberts, Berlin R. Ch. & SO, Chailly.

** DG Dig. **415 136-2** [id.]. Anderson, Creech, Weikl, Glen Ellyn Children's Ch., Chicago Ch. & SO, Levine.

** Telarc Dig. **CD 80056** [id.]. Blegen, William Brown, Hagegard, Atlanta Ch. & SO, Shaw.

(B) *(*) CfP **CD-CFP 9005**; *TC-CFP 4381*. Armstrong, Rayner-Cook, Peter Hall, Hallé Ch., Manchester Grammar School Ch., Hallé O, Maurice Handford.

Previn's 1975 analogue version, vividly recorded, still leads the available recorded performances of Orff's most popular work. It is strong on humour and rhythmic point. The chorus sings vigorously, the men often using an aptly rough tone, and if there is at times a lack of absolute precision, the resilience of Previn's rhythms, finely sprung, brings out a strain not just of geniality but of real wit. This is a performance which swaggers along and makes you smile. The recording captures the antiphonal effects impressively, better even in the orchestra than in the chorus. Among the soloists, Thomas Allen's contribution is one of the glories of the music making, and in their lesser roles the soprano and tenor are equally stylish. The digital remastering is wholly successful. The choral bite is enhanced, yet the recording retains its full amplitude. The background hiss has been minimized and is only really apparent in the quieter vocal solos in the latter part of the work. Twenty-five points of access are provided (essential in this quite complex setting) and there are full notes and a translation – which one cannot take for granted these days. A triumphant success.

There are three first-class medium-price versions, one digital and two from excellent analogue masters. Dorati's 1976 version was originally recorded in Decca's hi-fi-conscious Phase 4 system, and the balance is rather close, but the Kingsway Hall ambience helps to spread the sound and the dynamic range is surprisingly wide. The chorus are given plenty of body and impact in the highly successful CD remastering. It is a characteristically vibrant account; Dorati's speeds are generally brisk and the effect is exhilaratingly good-humoured, with the conductor showing a fine rhythmic sense. The characterization of the soloists is less sensuous than in some versions, but John Shirley-Quirk's account of the Abbot's song is very dramatic, with the chorus joining in enthusiastically. Because of Dorati's thrust this is more consistently gripping than Hickox's otherwise first-rate Pickwick account and, if there are moments when the overall ensemble is less than perfectly polished, the feeling of a live performance is engendered throughout, even though this is a studio recording. No translation is provided and the synopsis is cursory, which earns Decca a black mark.

Richard Hickox, on his brilliantly recorded Pickwick CD, like Previn uses the combined LSO forces, but adds the Southend Boys' Choir who make sure we know they understand all about sexual abandon – their 'Oh, oh, oh, I am bursting all over' is a joy. Penelope Walmsley-Clark, too, makes a rapturous contribution: her delicious song of uncertainty (between modesty and desire) is most tender (with alluring flutes to point the words) and her account of the girl in the red dress is equally delectable. The other soloists are good but less individual. The performance takes a little while to warm up (Hickox's tempi tend to be more relaxed than Dorati's), but the chorus rises marvellously to climaxes and is resplendent in the *Ave formosissima*, while the sharp articulation of consonants when the singers hiss out the words of *O Fortuna* in the closing section is also a highlight. The vivid orchestral detail revealed by the bright digital sound adds an extra dimension, with bass drum and percussive transients very telling, while the LPO brass, trumpets and horns especially, playing superbly are brilliantly projected. The documentation provides a vernacular narrative for each band but no translation.

Ozawa's account is one of his very finest records. His rhythmic touch is never too heavy, and this strong, incisive performance brings out the bold simplicity of the score with tingling immediacy, rather than dwelling on its subtlety of colour. The soloists, too, are all characterful, especially Sherrill Milnes, whose fine *Omnia sol temperat* immediately reveals a distinctive voice. The tenor, Stanley Kolk, sounds a little constrained with his *Roast Swan*, but otherwise the solo singing is always responsive. Overall this is a highly effective account and the blaze of inspiration of Orff's masterpiece comes over to the listener in the most direct way, when the sound is so well projected, yet without any unnatural edge. The snag is the absence of a translation or of any kind of documentation, except a listing of the twenty-five cued sections.

Mata's alternative full-priced RCA version is also most convincing as an overall performance and it also offers first-class sound. It is a volatile reading, not as metrical in its rhythms as most; this means that at times the LSO Chorus is not as clean in ensemble as it is for Previn. The choristers of St Paul's Cathedral sing with perfect purity but are perhaps not boyish enough; though the soloists are first rate (with John Aler coping splendidly, in high refined tones, with the Roast Swan episode). The compact disc has fine warmth of atmosphere and no lack in the lower range. *Pianissimo* choral detail is not sharply defined, but in all other respects the sound is superb, the background silence adding a great deal, especially when the tension is not as consistently high as in some versions.

The digital remastering of Muti's 1980 analogue recording is disappointing. The LP was remarkable for bringing out the fullest weight of bass (timpani and bass drum most spectacular at the opening) but had a balancing brilliance. This seems less obvious on the compact disc, although the orchestra is affected less than the chorus and soloists, who seem to have lost a degree of immediacy. Muti's is a reading which underlines the dramatic contrasts, both of dynamic and of tempo, so the nagging ostinatos are as a rule pressed on at breakneck speed; the result, if at times a little breathless, is always exhilarating. The soloists are first rate: Arleen Augér is wonderfully reposeful in *In trutina* and Jonathan Summers in his first major recording characterizes well. The Philharmonia Chorus is not quite at its most polished, but the Southend Boys are outstandingly fine. This is a performance which may lose something in wit and jollity but is as full of excitement as any available.

The DG production under Jochum is also highly distinguished, and some might well acquire it for Fischer-Dieskau's contribution. His singing is refined but not too much so, and his first solo, *Omnia sol temperat*, and later *Dies, nox et omnia* are both very beautiful, with the kind of tonal shading that a great Lieder singer can bring. Perhaps *Estuans interius* needs a heavier voice, but Fischer-Dieskau is suitably gruff in the Abbot's song – so much so that for the moment the voice is unrecognizable. Gerhard Stolze too is very stylsh in his falsetto *Song of the roast swan*. The soprano, Gundula Janowitz, finds a quiet dignity for her contribution and this is finely done. The chorus are best when the music blazes, and the closing scene is moulded by Jochum with a wonderful control, almost Klemperian in its restrained power. The snag is that in the quieter music the choral contribution is less immediate. The recording is currently available admirably transferred on to chrome stock and in this format it sounds first class. The Stravinsky coupling is rather less successful because of a resonant acoustic, but this remains very good value, even if there is no supporting translation or detailed analysis. The alternative mid-priced CD is without the Stravinsky ballet (**423 886-2**).

On Philips, Herbert Kegel secures very fine singing from the superb Leipzig choir, but the lightness of his touch produces some lack of tension in places, in spite of the variety of colour he finds in Orff's score. The very opening of the work, for instance, lacks the last degree of exuberance, and there is certainly a lack of electricity in the closing section of *Cour d'amour*. The soloists make a good team, and project well, notably the tenor, Horst Hiestermann. The 1974 recording is of high quality, both natural and vivid in its CD format, but the tape is transferred at too low a level and the choral sound is blunted.

Had the CD remastering been more successful, the (New) Philharmonia version conducted by Rafael Frühbeck de Bürgos would have been near the top of the list, but it seems as though the

EMI transfer engineers, having failed to enhance Muti's version in its CD format, have tried too hard with this one, and the result is unpleasantly edgy, with the treble response sounding fierce and artificial. This is a great pity for Frühbeck de Burgos gives the kind of performance of *Carmina Burana* which is ideal for gramophone listening. Where Ozawa favours a straightforward approach, with plenty of impact in the climaxes, it is in the more lyrical pages that Burgos scores with his much greater imagination and obvious affection. This is not to suggest that the Philharmonia account has any lack of vitality. Indeed the sheer gusto of the singing is the more remarkable when one considers the precision from both singers and orchestra alike. The brass too bring out the rhythmic pungency, which is such a dominating feature of the work, with splendid life and point. Lucia Popp's soprano solo *Amor volat* is really ravishing, and Gerhard Unger, the tenor, brings a Lieder-like sensitivity to his lovely singing of his very florid solo in the tavern scene. The documentation, too, is admirable (especially when this is offered at mid-price) with extensive notes and a full translation.

Using the Jesus-Christuskirche (a far more sympathetic Berlin venue for recording than the Philharmonie), Chailly's Decca performance brings outstandingly full and brilliant recording, particularly impressive on CD. The performance is strong and dramatic in a direct, clean-cut way, with fast allegros relatively unpointed and lacking in detail. Chailly compensates in his expressive treatment of the gentle moments, as in the final section, *The Court of Love*, in which Sylvia Greenberg's light, bright soprano has a girlish, innocent quality. James Bowman, for all his imagination, misses some of the comedy of the tenor role when, as a counter-tenor, he is singing falsetto all the time, instead of simply as a tenor's strainful expedient, which is what Orff intended. Stephen Roberts, another excellent singer, is also miscast, too gritty and too thin of tone for the baritone role.

Levine's Chicago account is enjoyable enough; on CD, the recording is spectacular, with greatly enhanced detail. Even so, the Chicago Chorus match neither Previn's group in their lusty projection of joyous vigour, nor Muti's Philharmonia Chorus in weight. The Chicago soloists are less distinctive, too – though Bernd Weikl's Abbot's drinking song is a highlight. Philip Creech's portrayal of the Roast Swan is less comfortable, but no doubt the roughness is part of the characterization. Levine makes a good deal of the atmosphere of the score and obviously responds to the earthy sentiment of the love poems; he is certainly expansive in the work's latter sections.

Telarc characteristically present exceptionally full and brilliant sound, though hardly more so than the analogue sound given to Previn on HMV. Like Muti, Robert Shaw (for some years Toscanini's choirmaster) prefers speeds on the fast side, though his manner is more metrical. In *The Court of Love* one wants more persuasive treatment, though the choral singing – recorded rather close in analytical sound – is superb. The soloists are good, but the Atlanta boys cannot quite match their rivals on most European versions. The compact disc issue is on two sides (as against three for the original LP set), but the recorded sound is unflattering to the soloists – notably the baritone, Håkan Hagegard – although the choral and orchestral sound is certainly spectacular.

The CfP version is a modern recording, notable for its excellent soloists, with Sheila Armstrong coming close to matching her supremely lovely performance for Previn. The men of the Hallé Choir provide some rough singing at times, but the women are much better, and the performance gathers energy and incisiveness as it proceeds, although there is some fall-off in tension at the very end. The CD transfer is effectively managed.

Osborne, Nigel (born 1948)

(i) *Concerto for flute and chamber orchestra;* (ii) *Remembering Esenin* (for cello and piano); (iii) *I am Goya;* (iv) *The sickle.*

*** Unicorn *DKPC 9031* [id.]. (i) Dobing; (ii) Kitt, Hill; (iii) Varcoe; (iv) Manning; with City of London Sinfonia, Hickox.

This well-chosen group of four works gives an excellent musical portrait of a composer of the middle generation, whose habitual language may be thorny and complex, but whose feeling for energy and colour and at times expressive warmth give even the unprepared listener the necessary landmarks. The two vocal works, setting Russian poems by Esenin and Voznesensky, are the more immediately striking, with Jane Manning superb in *The sickle*, the Esenin setting, and Stephen Varcoe equally intelligent in *I am Goya*. The work of lament for Esenin uses both cello and piano very originally; the *Flute concerto*, with Duke Dobing a brilliant soloist, is the lightest and most approachable of the pieces, with Hickox drawing committed playing from the City of London Sinfonia. Excellent recording.

Pachelbel, Johann (1653–1706)

Canon in D.

(M) *** Decca **417 712-2**; *417 266-4* [id.]. Stuttgart CO, Münchinger – ALBINONI: *Adagio****; VIVALDI: *Four Seasons*.**(*)

Canon and Gigue.

(*) Ph. Dig. **416 386-2; *416 386-4* [id.]. ASMF, Marriner – MOZART: *Serenade: Eine kleine Nachtmusik*; L. MOZART: *Toy symphony*.**(*)

(M) ** DG *419 488-4* [id.]. BPO, Karajan – ALBINONI: *Adagio*; VIVALDI: *Four Seasons*.**

Pachelbel's *Canon* is indelible in its tuneful simplicity: it is justly famous. There are many versions of it, usually included with other popular Baroquiana. Münchinger's is as good as any; if you want something more opulent and rather less stylish, Karajan's sumptuous version will serve, although the couplings are not among the most successful examples of DG's digital remastering. Those requiring something more abrasive might choose the Academy of Ancient Music (see Concerts – O-L **410 553-2**); Karajan also offers a sombre digital version, more refined than his earlier one, in which he again incorporates the lighter but less memorable *Gigue* (DG **413 309-2**). Marriner turns the two pieces into a ternary structure by oddly repeating the *Canon* again after the *Gigue*, a tiny concession to the short measure on his CD. Warm, well-balanced recording and a smooth tape.

Paganini, Niccolò (1782–1840)

Violin concerto No. 1 in D, Op. 6.

❀ *** HMV **CDC7 47101-2** [id.]; (M) *EG 291285-4*. Itzhak Perlman, RPO, Foster – SARASATE: *Carmen fantasy*.*** ❀

Itzhak Perlman demonstrates a fabulously clean and assured technique. His execution of the fiendish upper harmonics in which Paganini delighted is almost uniquely smooth, and with the help of the EMI engineers, who have placed the microphones in exactly the right place, he produces a gleamingly rich tone, free from all scratchiness. The orchestra is splendidly recorded and balanced too, and Lawrence Foster matches the soloist's warmth with an alive and buoyant orchestral accompaniment. Provided one does not feel strongly about Perlman's traditional cuts, there has been no better record of the *D major Concerto*, and when it is played with this kind of panache the effect is irresistible. The Sarasate *Carmen fantasy* offered as a bonus is quite stunning. Though this sounded well enough on LP, the CD enhances the presence of the recording and emphasizes the success of the original sound-balance (analogue – 1972) which is far more believable and natural than many of Perlman's more recent digital recordings, where the soloist is often unnaturally spotlit. The cassette is acceptable but rather resonant in the bass.

Violin concertos Nos 1 in D, Op. 6; 2 in B min. (*La Campanella*), *Op. 7.*
*** DG **415 278-2** [id.]. Accardo, LPO, Dutoit.
** HMV **CDC7 47088-2** [id.]. Menuhin, RPO, Erede.

Violin concertos Nos 1–2; Le Streghe (*Witches' dance*); *4 Caprices, Op. 1.*
(B) *** DG Walkman *413 848-4* [id.]. Accardo, LPO, Dutoit.

Violin concertos Nos 2 in B min. (*La Campanella*), *Op. 7; 4 in D min.*
(M) *** DG *419 482-4* [id.]. Accardo, LPO, Dutoit.

Violin concertos Nos 3 in E; 4 in D min.
*** DG **423 270-2** [id.]. Accardo, LPO, Dutoit.

Violin concerto No. 5 in A min.; Maestosa sonata sentimentale; La primavera in A.
*** DG **423 578-2** [id.]. Accardo, LPO, Dutoit.

Paganini's concertos can too often seem sensationally boring, or the scratchy upper tessitura can assault rather than titillate the ear. But, as Perlman has shown in the *First Concerto* – see above – when the recording balance is well managed and the playing and musicianship first class, they can be very entertaining. Accardo, like Perlman, has a formidable technique, marvellously true intonation and impeccably good taste and style; it is a blend of all these that makes these performances so satisfying and enjoyable. The recordings are taken from the complete set he made in the mid to late 1960s. He is beautifully accompanied by the LPO under Dutoit and the sound is very good. The concertos are obviously shown in their best light in the CD format, although the transfers seem to have generated some excess of bass resonance; however, DG's alternative Walkman tape costs a fraction of the price of the compact disc and offers more music. The recording's resonance has meant that DG's tape transfer is rather lower than usual, but the image has not lost its immediacy. Apart from the witchery of *Le Streghe*, Accardo includes also four *Caprices*, including the most famous, on which the multitude of variations are based. A real bargain for all cassette collectors. The Galleria tape offers a different coupling for No. 2 from the CD, so clashes with the Walkman, but it may suit some collectors better and sounds well. Of the coupling with the *Fifth Concerto*, *La primavera* is a late work; ideas from Haydn turn up in the *Maestosa sonata sentimentale*. The solo playing here is stunning.

Menuhin's performances have plenty of attack, although the accompaniments have rather less life and fire. But characterful though these readings are – and Menuhin can be very rewarding in the lyrical music – one feels that fiery bravura is not really Menuhin's *métier*, and his timbre sometimes sounds undernourished in the stratospheric reaches of the solo part. The clarity of the CD transfer and the close balance of the soloist do not really help matters.

Violin and guitar: *Cantabile; Centone di sonate No. 1 in A; Sonata in E min., Op. 3/6; Sonata concertata in A.*
*** CBS **MK 34508** [id.]. Itzhak Perlman, John Williams – GIULIANI: *Sonata.****

Superb playing from both Perlman and John Williams ensures the listener's attention throughout this slight but very agreeable music. With a good balance, the music making here gives much pleasure, and this is generally a distinguished disc. The CD transfer too is well managed, giving fine presence to these excellent artists.

Quartets Op. 4, Nos 1 in A min; 2 in C; 3 in A; for guitar, violin, viola and cello.
** HMV Dig. **CDC7 47739-2**. Sonja Prunnbauer, Rainer Kussmaul, Ulrich Koch, Marcel Cervera.

Of the fifteen quartets Paganini composed with guitar, those of Opp. 4 and 5 were written for amateurs, and they can hardly be said to be works of great substance or depth. The guitar writing is relatively undemanding and not particularly interesting. They receive elegant and accomplished performances and are very well recorded.

24 Caprices, Op. 1.
*** HMV **CDC7 47171-2** [id.]. Itzhak Perlman.
(*) DG Dig. **415 043-2 [id.]. Shlomo Mintz.

These two dozen *Caprices* probably represent the peak of violinistic difficulty, even though more than a century has gone by since their composition, and many new works continue to exploit the extraordinary range of effects possible on one four-stringed instrument. Perlman's playing is flawless, wonderfully assured and polished, yet not lacking imaginative feeling. Moreover, such is the magnetism of his playing that the ear is led on spontaneously from one variation to the next, even though with CD it is possible to programme any given selection from the set. The 1972 recording is extremely natural and the transfer to CD brings a very convincing illusion of realism, without the microphones seeming too near the violin.

Shlomo Mintz is often dazzling, as are most of the violinists who have recorded these astonishing pieces. There are many breathtaking things to admire, and plenty of colour and life in the set as a whole. He is recorded with admirable clarity and definition in good digital sound, though the overall effect is not as warm as Perlman's HMV record which is, if anything, more dazzling. There are times (*No. 17 in E flat* is an example) when one could wish that he had not been in quite so much of a hurry, for the characterization would gain as a result. On the other hand, others such as the *F major, No. 22*, could hardly be improved upon. The CD emphasizes the closeness of the balance at the expense of the surrounding ambience.

Paisiello, Giovanni (1740–1816)

Il barbiere di Siviglia (opera): complete.
*** Hung. Dig. **HCD 12525/6-2** [id.]. Laki, Gulyás, Gregor, Gati, Sólyom-Nagy, Hungarian State O, Adam Fischer.

Paisiello's *Barbiere di Siviglia* may for many generations have been remembered only as the forerunner of Rossini's masterpiece of a Beaumarchais adaptation, but latterly stage revivals have helped to explain why, before Rossini, the opera was such a success. The libretto may be much more of a muddle than the one Rossini used, over-complicated and with untidy ends, and the musical inspiration may too often be short-winded, but the invention is full of vitality, and that is captivatingly reflected in this Hungarian performance under Ivan Fischer. On Hungaroton opera sets one has come to recognize the sterling strength of the stars of the Budapest Opera, and this brings another excellent example of their teamwork and consistency. József Gregor, for example, is a vividly characterful Bartolo, a role more important here than in Rossini, while István Gati is a strong, robust Figaro. Krisztina Laki is a brilliant Rosina and Dénes Gulyás a clean, stylish Almaviva, relishing his Don Alonso imitation. Full, vivid recording.

Palestrina, Giovanni Pierluigi di (1525–94)

Canticum Canticorum; 8 Madrigali spirituali.
** HMV Dig. **CDS7 49010-8**; *EX 270319-5* (2). Hilliard Ens., Paul Hillier.

The twenty-nine motets Palestrina based on the *Canticum Canticorum* (*Song of Songs*) include some of his most inspired writing; all are for five voices. Into these impassioned texts with their strongly erotic overtones, Palestrina poured music of great feeling, remarkable beauty and finish of workmanship. *The Song of Songs* has always been regarded as a symbolic illustration of 'the happy union of Christ and His Spouse', the spouse being the Church, more especially the happiest part of it, namely perfect souls, every one of which is His beloved. The earlier LP of it by Michael Howard and the Cantores in Ecclesia (Oiseau Lyre) adopted a frankly expressive and sensuous approach, which is far removed from that of the Hilliard Ensemble. These are beautifully shaped performances, with refined tonal blend and perfect intonation, but they are more remote and ultimately rather cool in emotional temperature. The second CD includes eight Petrarch settings from the First Book of Madrigals. Excellent recording.

Missa brevis; Missa Nasce la gioia mia (with PRIMAVERA: Madrigal: *Nasce la gioia mia*).
*** Gimell Dig. **CDGIM 008**; *1585-T-08* [id.]. Tallis Scholars, Phillips.

There have been plenty of records of the *Missa brevis* (though this version by the Tallis Scholars under Peter Phillips has nothing to fear from comparison with any of them), but none of the *Missa Nasce la gioia mia*. Like the *Missa Nigra sum*, this was included in the 1590 Book of Masses and is a parody Mass, modelled on the madrigal, *Nasce la gioia mia* by Giovan Leonardo Primavera, who was born in Naples in 1540. The Tallis Scholars and Peter Phillips give an expressive, finely shaped account of the Mass, which they preface by the madrigal itself. A most rewarding disc: no grumbles about the recording; and the cassette is first class, too.

Missa Hodie Christus natus est. Motets: *Ave Maria; Canita tuba; Hodie Christus natus est; Jubilate Deo, O magnum mysterium; Tui sunt caeli.*
(M) *** EMI *TC-EMX 2098*. King's College, Cambridge, Ch., Ledger.

Philip Ledger directs colourful, dramatic readings of both Palestrina's magnificent eight-part Mass and the six motets, including the one directly related to the Mass. With the two choirs set in contrast and cross-rhythms sharply brought out, the joyfulness of Palestrina's inspiration is irresistibly conveyed, atmospherically set in the characteristically resonant chapel acoustic.

Missa Nigra sum (with motets on *Nigra sum* by LHERITIER; VICTORIA; DE SILVA).
*** Gimell Dig. **CDGIM 003**; *1585-T-03* [id.]. Tallis Scholars, Phillips.

Palestrina's *Missa Nigra sum* was published in 1590 but composed much earlier. It is a parody Mass, based on a motet by Jean Lheritier (*c.* 1480–1552), a French disciple of Josquin, and followers its model quite closely. Its text comes from the *Song of Solomon* ('I am black but comely, O ye daughters of Jerusalem: therefore has the king loved me, and brought me into his chambers'). Palestrina composed fifty-three parody Masses in all, more than half of which were modelled on other composers. On this record, the plainchant and the Lheritier motet precede Palestrina's Mass, plus motets by Victoria and Andreas de Silva, a relatively little-known Flemish singer and composer who served in the Papal chapel and later in Mantua. The music is inspiring and the performances exemplary. This is a most beautiful record and the acoustic of Merton College, Oxford, is ideal. The chrome cassette too is in the demonstration bracket.

Missa Papae Marcelli.
*** Gimell **CDGIM 339** [id.]. Tallis Scholars, Phillips – ALLEGRI: *Miserere*; MUNDY: *Vox Patris caelestis.****

Missa Papae Marcelli; Stabat Mater.
(M) *** Pickwick **PCD 863**. Pro Cantione Antiqua, Mark Brown.

Missa Papae Marcelli; Tu es Petrus (motet).
*** DG **415 517-2**; *415 517-4* [id.]. Westminster Abbey Ch., Preston (with ANERIO: *Venite ad me omnes*; NANINO: *Haec dies*; GIOVANNELLI: *Jubilate Deo**** – ALLEGRI: *Miserere.***(*)

Palestrina's *Missa Papae Marcelli* has a famous historical reputation for its influence on decisions made at the Council of Trent. The Catholic hierarchy had become concerned that the elaborate counterpoint of much church music, and the interpolation of non-liturgical texts, was obscuring the ritual purpose of the Mass itself. Palestrina's work, with its syllabic style and clear text, supposedly demonstrated that great music need not cover the religious message, and so influenced the decision not to ban polyphony altogether. If the story is apocryphal, there is no doubt that Palestrina's settings satisfied the authorities, while the quality of his music, and the memorability of the *Missa Papae Marcelli* in particular, are equally certain. With its apparent simplicity of line and serene beauty which disguises an underlying emotional power, it is not a work which lends itself readily to performers with an Anglican background. The account by the Westminster Abbey Choristers, however, transcends any such stylistic limitations. It is a performance of great fervour, married to fine discipline, rich in timbre, eloquent both at climaxes and at moments of serenity. The singing is equally fine in the hardly less distinctive motet, *Tu es Petrus*, also in six voices, written in 1573. Felice Anerio, Giovanni Bernardino Nanino and Ruggiero Giovannelli represent the following generation of composers in straddling the end of the sixteenth and beginning of the seventeenth century. Their contributions to this collection are well worth having, particularly Giovannelli's *Jubilate Deo* which makes a splendid closing item. The digital recording is first class. All Saint's, Tooting, was used, rather than the Abbey, and the acoustics are both intimate and expansive, while detail is beautifully caught, especially against the background silence of CD.

Pro Cantione Antiqua on the mid-price Pickwick label bring not only an outstandingly fresh and alert account of Palestrina's most celebrated Mass but one which involves keen scholarship. With an all-male choir and no boy-trebles, with one voice per part, this chamber choir yet sings with power and resonance against a warm and helpful church acoustic. The authentic atmosphere is enhanced by the inclusion of relevant plainchants between the sections of the Mass. The magnificent eight-part *Stabat Mater* also receives a powerful performance, warm and resonant.

The Gimell alternative is an analogue recording from 1980, but the digital remastering produces extremely fine sound, firm, richly blended and not lacking internal detail. The acoustics of Merton College, Oxford, are admirably suited to this music; while the recording sounds its best on CD. The singing has eloquence, purity of tone, and a simplicity of line which is consistently well controlled. The contrasts between serenity and power are striking, and this can be considered alongside the Preston version. Both the Allegri and Mundy couplings are outstandingly successful.

Motet and Mass – Tu es Petrus.
(*) Argo Dig. **410 149-2 [id.]. King's College Ch., Cleobury – VICTORIA: *O quam gloriosum.***(*)

Fine performances, positively shaped, with plenty of tonal weight and a natural flowing eloquence, with the blend secure, the voices given extra presence on CD. The King's style adapts well to this repertoire without achieving an entirely Latin feeling. But Palestrina's six-part *Mass* still projects impressively.

Panufnik, Andrzej (born 1914)

(i) *Metasinfonia;* (ii) *Universal prayer.*
*** Unicorn *DKPC 9049* [id.]. (i) J. Bate, LSO, composer; (ii) Cantelo, Watts, Mitchinson, Stalman, Watkins, Korchinska, Bonifacio, Kynaston, Halsey Singers, Stokowski.

Panufnik's music has been scandalously neglected even in Britain, his adopted country. Stokowski's urgent advocacy now allows us to hear on record this ambitious and ingenious setting of words by Alexander Pope, 'a prayer to the God of all religions'. Panufnik takes the thirteen stanzas of the poem and frames them in twenty-seven sections laid out with the symmetry of an Italian garden. There is a diagram on the sleeve explaining the elaborate contrasts and relationships, but once the basic approach has been grasped it is not all that difficult. Soloists (alone or in various combinations), chorus (singing the note B in more ranges of tone and expression than one would have thought possible) and instrumentalists are introduced in varying patterns. The cumulative experience is certainly arresting, even though the sectionalizing tends to hold up the flow. With the sort of intensity one always expects in a Stokowski performance (he later recorded it for television too) this is well worth hearing. The recording dates from 1970 and sounds very impressive. For this reissue it has been coupled to the composer's own 1985 recording of the *Metasinfonia*, another piece laid out on a consciously symmetrical plan, for structure and balance clearly mean as much to the composer as content. This is not for a moment to suggest that this is dry, unemotional music – indeed it is powerfully evocative and, like the *Universal prayer*, its sounds are highly individual, with the complex concertante organ part – played with unostentatious virtuosity by Jennifer Bate – winding its way through the texture hypnotically. The balance is excellent and the recording, like the vocal work, has been very well transferred to tape.

Parker, Horatio (1863–1910)

A Northern ballad.
*** New World Dig. **NWCD 339**; *NWMC 339* [id.]. Albany SO, Julius Hegyi – CHADWICK: *Symphony No. 2.****

Horatio Parker was a pupil of Chadwick, his first in fact. He, too, studied with Rheinberger in Munich before returning to teach at Yale. His *Northern ballad* of 1899 was an enormous success in its day and calls both Dvořák and Grieg to mind. It has remained unpublished and unperformed in recent times. Excellent playing and recording. An interesting disc.

Parry, Hubert (1848–1918)

An English suite; Lady Radnor's suite.
(*) HMV Dig. *EL 270146-4.* City of L. Sinfonia, Hickox – ELGAR: *Elegy* etc.(*)

On HMV, Parry's two elegant and beautifully crafted suites make an unusual and very apt coupling for the Elgar string music on the reverse. The combination of straightforward, warm expression with hints of melancholy below the surface is very Elgarian. Both suites were written later than the Elgar *Serenade*, with *An English suite* published only after the composer's death. The Bach tributes in *Lady Radnor's suite* are surface-deep; the slow minuet for muted strings is particularly beautiful. Refined playing and first-rate recording. On the XDR cassette, textures are rich and pleasing, but inner definition is less sharply defined and there is an element of blandness.

Lady Radnor's suite.
*** Nimbus Dig. **NI 5068** [id.]. E. String O, Boughton – BRIDGE: *Suite*; BUTTERWORTH: *Banks of Green Willow; Idylls; Shropshire lad.****

Parry's charming set of pastiche dances, now given an extra period charm through their Victorian flavour, makes an attractive item in an excellent and generous English collection, one of Nimbus's bestsellers. Warm, atmospheric recording, with refined playing set against an ample acoustic.

Symphony No. 5 in B min.; Symphonic variations; Elegy to Johannes Brahms; (i) *Blest Pair of Sirens.*
*** HMV **CDC7 49022-2**; (M) *ED 291274-4*. LPO, Boult, (i) with LPO Ch.

This was the last record made by Sir Adrian Boult, whose recording career was longer than that of any important rival. The *Fifth Symphony*, the last that Parry wrote, is broadly Brahmsian in style but with the four movements linked in a Lisztian cyclic manner; the slow movement is particularly beautiful. Equally impressive is the *Elegy*, not merely an occasional piece but a full-scale symphonic movement which builds to a powerful climax. The sharply inventive *Symphonic variations* – also recorded by Boult for an earlier Lyrita disc – fills out the Parry portrait. Recording and performances are exemplary, a fitting coda to Sir Adrian's recording career. To make the CD even more representative, it is good to welcome so enjoyably professional a motet as Parry's *Blest Pair of Sirens*. Much of the once-popular music by Parry and his contemporaries is unacceptably inflated, but certainly not this. The performance by the London Philharmonic Choir should be more incisive, but it still conveys much of the right atmosphere. Throughout, the digital remastering has been wholly beneficial. Textures are better defined and the strings sound fresher than originally, while the ambient bloom remains. By comparison, the tape is opaque and the chorus in the motet ill-focused.

Songs of farewell.
*** Conifer Dig. **CDCF 155**; *MCFC 155* [id.]. Trinity College, Cambridge, Ch., Richard Marlow – STANFORD: *Magnificat* etc.***

Parry's *Songs of Farewell* were written towards the end of his life, when the ominous approach and start of the First World War coincided for Parry with a period of growing personal unhappiness and isolation. The set of six represents his art at its deepest, beautiful inspirations that have been shockingly neglected on disc, even the relatively well-known setting of Henry Vaughan, *My soul, there is a country*. Finest and most searching of the set is the Donne setting, *At the round earth's imagined corners*, with its rich harmonies poignantly intense and beautiful, deeply emotional behind its poised perfection. Richard Marlow with his splendid Trinity Choir, using fresh women's voices for the upper lines instead of trebles (unlike its Cambridge rivals), directs thoughtful, committed performances which capture both the beauty and the emotion. This Parry collection is very well recorded and well coupled with the Stanford items, more contained though just as beautifully written for voices. There is a very good chrome tape.

Patterson, Paul (born 1947)

Concerto for orchestra; Europhony; Missa brevis.
*** HMV Dig. **CDC7 49258-2**; *EL 270606-4*. LPO Ch., LPO, Owain Arwel Hughes.

Like the other important recording of Patterson's music from Geoffrey Simon and the RPO, this disc offers representative examples of his recent work, much more approachable in idiom than his earlier music. The gem of the collection is the *Missa brevis*, using a seemingly simple style boldly and freshly. It must be as grateful for the singers as it is for the listener, with moments of pure poetry as in the *Benedictus*. The two orchestral pieces, though less individual, are colourful and immediately attractive. Their openness of idiom conceals the ingenuity of their construction, with *Europhony* clearly developing on variation form. Vigorous performances and wide-ranging recording. The chrome cassette, too, is one of EMI's very best, brilliant and cleanly focused, yet with excellent body to match the very good definition.

(i) *Mass of the sea, Op. 47; Sinfonia for strings, Op. 46.*
*** ASV Dig. **CDRPO 8006**; *ZCRPO 8006* [id.]. (i) Brighton Fest. Ch., RPO, Geoffrey Simon.

Paul Patterson's *Mass of the sea* is a warmly and immediately communicative choral piece on a large scale, written for the Gloucester Three Choirs Festival of 1983. Patterson's scheme was to frame the four main sections of the Mass – omitting the *Credo* – with apt quotations from the Bible on the subject of the sea, starting with Genesis in the *Kyrie* movement and 'darkness on the face of the deep', and ending with Revelation and 'there was no more sea' in the *Agnus Dei* movement. After the *Gloria*, where you would expect the *Credo*, Patterson has a dramatic movement on the Flood leading through storm (and God's wrath at corruption on earth) to salvation with a 'bow in the sky to save mankind'. The interspersing of English words and the Latin liturgy obviously relates the piece to Britten's *War Requiem*, and one can detect the occasional musical echo of Britten. Patterson's is a broadly eclectic style, which yet is so bold and inventive that echoes of other composers hardly matter. With warmly committed playing and singing under Geoffrey Simon, the *Mass* makes a powerful impact, a welcome addition to the other better-known choral works on the RPO label. The *Sinfonia for strings*, rather more abrasive in idiom with its echoes of Bartók, also makes a welcome addition to the catalogue, deftly written with neat pay-offs in each movement. The recording is very well balanced and has atmosphere and realistically defined detail. In this respect the chrome cassette is not as clear as the CD but otherwise sounds well.

Penderecki, Krysztof (born 1933)

Canticum canticorum Salomonis; De natura sonoris No. 1; The Dream of Jacob; Threnody to the Victims of Hiroshima.
*** HMV **CDC7 49316-2**. Polish R. National SO, composer.

The longest work on this nicely varied record of Penderecki's music is the setting of a text from the *Song of Solomon* for large orchestra and sixteen solo voices. Whether or not the ultimate impression from this glitteringly sonorous music is of sensuality, it represents the familiar brand of individual effect-making, deeply sincere but diffuse of argument. The other shorter pieces will probably have a more lasting impact. The beautiful and touching *Threnody* for 53 strings (1959–61) originally made the composer's name internationally and is here given a magnificent performance. *De natura sonoris No. 1* is more obviously brilliant in its use of orchestral contrasts, and the brief *Dream of Jacob* of 1974 is as inventive as the rest but sparer and more cogent. A co-production between EMI and Polish Radio, this sets high standards technically and musically.

(i) *St Luke Passion;* (ii) *Magnificat.*
*** HMV **CDC7 49313-2**. (i) Woytowicz, Hiolski, Ladysz, Bartsch (speaker), Tölz Boys' Ch., Cologne R. Ch. and SO, Czyz. (ii) Soloists, Boys' Ch., Polish R. Ch. of Krakow, Polish Nat. RSO, composer.

The *St Luke Passion*, written between 1963 and 1965, is the key work in Penderecki's career, the one which firmly launched him as an international figure. Taking a broadly Bachian view of setting the Passion, Penderecki with great virtuosity uses an enormously wide spectrum of choral and orchestral effects. The result is powerfully dramatic in a way which communicates directly to audiences unused to hearing advanced music. That drama is splendidly conveyed in this recording under the direction of the conductor who has specialized in Penderecki's music. Ensemble and solo singing are admirable, and so is the recording. The generous coupling for CD is the *Magnificat*; the dark intensity of Penderecki's setting of its twelve verses, its expansiveness and richness of effect put it firmly among the most strikingly individual choral works that this Polish composer has produced in the last two decades. That a composer working in a communist country should produce Christian music of such obvious commitment in an idiom which has nothing of Soviet realism in it should no longer surprise anyone, and this fine performance, superbly recorded as a co-production of EMI and Polish Radio, can be warmly recommended to the adventurous. One may question the cogency of argument in this generally slow-moving span – is it effect-making for its own sake? – but the sense of purpose is clear.

Pergolesi, Giovanni (1710–36)

Oboe concerto (arr. Barbirolli).
(M) (***) PRT **PVCD 8378** [id.]. Rothwell, Hallé O, Barbirolli – CORELLI: *Concerto****; HAYDN: *Concerto* (***).

Miss Rothwell's neat, feminine style suits this work to perfection. This is a Barbirolli arrangement using tunes from sonatas, a song and the *Stabat Mater*; but the whole is so felicitously put together that no one could guess it was not conceived in this form. The predominant mood is pastoral, with a slow opening leading to a gracious *Allegro* with an *Andantino* intervening before the gentle finale. The performance characterizes the music perfectly. The sound is full and quite well balanced, and is certainly fresh. The engineers have been forced to use a mono master tape as the source of this issue since the early stereo master has become degraded over the years. However, the natural resonance of the recording means that the ear hardly notices that this is not a stereo image.

Stabat Mater.
*** DG **415 103-2** [id.]. Margaret Marshall, Valentini Terrani, LSO, Abbado.
** Hung. **HCD 12201** [id.]. Kalmar, Hamari, Hungarian R. and TV Ch., Liszt CO, Gardelli.

Abbado's account brings greater intensity and ardour to this piece than any rival, and he secures marvellously alive playing from the LSO – this without diminishing religious sentiment. Margaret Marshall is an impressive singer; her contribution combines fervour with an attractive variety of colour, while Lucia Valentini Terrani – who was also on Scimone's Erato version – is an excellent foil. The DG recording has warmth and good presence and the perspective is thoroughly acceptable. This is now a clear first choice.

Gardelli conducts a sweet, smooth and well-mannered performance of a work that might be counted too sweet already. The soloists Magda Kalmar and Julia Hamari are both aptly pure-toned, but the concentration on smoothness allows few words to emerge. However, the use of a women's chorus does add greater variety of texture to the score, even if the singing here, though well drilled, lacks bite. The 1981 analogue recording has been transferred well, but unless the choral contribution is vital, Abbado's version has greater character and is preferable.

La serva padrona (opera) complete recording (includes alternative ending and insertion arias).
*** Hung. **HCD 12846-2** [id.]. Katalin Farkas, József Gregor, Capella Savaria, Németh.

Lasting just an hour and involving only two voices, *La serva padrona* is ideally suited to disc, and on this Hungaroton issue receives a delightful, sparkling performance well sung by two of the most characterful singers we have come to know from Budapest recordings and with the excellent period-performance group, Capella Savaria. Jószef Gregor sings with splendid buffo stylishness, while Katalin Farkas, as Serpina the maid, brings out the fun of the writing, with the shrewishness of the character kept in check. Bright, clean recording.

Pleyel, Ignaz (1757–1831)

Clarinet concerto in C.
*** Claves **CD 50-813** [id.]. Friedli, SW German CO, Angerer – MERCADANTE; MOLTER: *Concertos.****

Pleyel's *Concerto* is written for C clarinet. Thomas Friedli uses a modern instrument and it does not sound greatly different from the familiar B flat clarinet. Pleyel's *Concerto* is obviously post-Mozart and his debt to that master is obvious. The work is engagingly inventive throughout, with the finale especially attractive (it has a striking secondary theme), and it is altogether a well-made piece. Friedli plays it skilfully and sympathetically and gets good if not outstanding support from Angerer. The CD gives good presence to the soloist, but orchestral detail is a little clouded by the resonance. Nevertheless, in the interest of the repertoire one can make allowance for this, for the overall sound is very pleasing.

Ponchielli, Amilcare (1834–86)

La Gioconda (complete).
*** Decca Dig. **414 349-2** (3) [id.]. Caballé, Baltsa, Pavarotti, Milnes, Hodgson, L. Op. Ch., Nat. PO, Bartoletti.
*** HMV **CDS7 49518-2** [Ang. **CDCC 49518**] (3); *EX 749518-4* (2). Callas, Cossotto, Ferraro, Vinco, Cappuccilli, Companeez, La Scala, Milan, Ch. & O, Votto.

The colourfully atmospheric melodrama of this opera gives the Decca engineers the chance to produce a digital blockbuster, one of the most vivid opera recordings yet made, with CD enhancing the presence of both voices and orchestra to involve the listener strongly. The casting could hardly be bettered, with Caballé just a little overstressed in the title role but producing glorious sounds. Pavarotti, for long immaculate in the aria *Cielo e mar*, here expands into the complete role with equally impressive control and heroic tone. Commanding performances too from Milnes as Barnaba, Ghiaurov as Alvise and Baltsa as Laura, firm and intense all three. Bartoletti proves a vigorous and understanding conductor, presenting the blood and thunder with total commitment but finding the right charm in the most famous passage, the *Dance of the hours*.

Maria Callas gave one of her most vibrant, most compelling, most totally inspired performances on record in the title role of *La Gioconda*, with flaws very much subdued. The challenge she presented to those around her is reflected in the soloists – Cossotto and Cappuccilli both at the very beginning of distinguished careers – as well as the distinctive tenor Ferraro and the conductor Votto, who has never done anything finer on record. The recording still sounds well, though it dates from 1959. The remastering increases the vocal presence yet retains the bloom. The cassette transfer is fairly successful, the solo voices and choral detail heard within an atmospheric perspective and the result is less sharply defined than the CDs. The layout, on four sides, against three compact discs, brings less suitable side-breaks. The tapes include the CD booklet/libretto.

La Gioconda: Dance of the Hours.
(M) *** HMV **CDM7 69041-2** [id.]. Philh. O, Karajan – BORODIN: *Polovtsian dances****; OFFENBACH: *Gaîté parisienne***(*); GOUNOD: *Faust ballet.****

Ponchielli's miniature romantic ballet is much more familiar than the opera from which it derives, helped by the bizarre animation of Walt Disney's *Fantasia* with its parody of all that is balletic, featuring coy hippos and tu-tued elephants. The imaginative charm of the music is most engaging when presented with such elegance and spirit and the Philharmonia players obviously relish this attractive succession of tunes, glowingly scored. The 1960 recording, with its pleasingly full ambience, hardly sounds dated at all. Besides the listed couplings, this generous anthology also includes four minutes of Verdi's ballet from Act II of *Aïda*, equally vividly played and recorded. Karajan's later DG recording of the *Dance of the hours* is also available in a mid-priced Galleria collection of opera intermezzi and ballet music (DG **415 856-2**); there is a superbly recorded digital version in a similar collection on Philips, beguilingly played by the Dresden State Orchestra under Varviso (**412 236-2**).

Poulenc, Francis (1899–1963)

Aubade (Concerto choréographique); Piano concerto in C sharp min.; (i) *Double piano concerto in D min.*
*** Erato Dig. **ECD 88140** [id.]. Duchable; (i) Collard; Rotterdam PO, Conlon.
** HMV **CDC7 47369-2** [id.]. Tacchino, Paris Conservatoire O, Prêtre; (i) with Ringeissen, Monte Carlo PO, Prêtre.

The *Aubade* is an exhilarating work of great charm. It dates from the late 1920s and is a send-up of Mozart, Stravinsky, etc., though few would detect any stylistic development between it and its companion, the *Piano concerto* of 1949. The latter has a most beguiling opening theme and evokes the faded charms of Paris in the '30s. The skittish *Double concerto* is infectiously jolly. One could never mistake the tone of voice intended. Erato offer excellent value in providing three works on one CD. The 1985 recording is of altogether excellent quality, with splendid presence and a wide range, especially at the bottom end of the spectrum. The performances of the two solo works by François-René Duchable and the Rotterdam orchestra have a certain panache and flair that are most winning. The *Double concerto* too captures all the wit and charm of the Poulenc score, with the 'mock Mozart' slow movement particularly elegant. The balance is almost perfectly judged. Perhaps in the solo works Duchable is a shade too prominent, but not sufficiently so to disturb a strong recommendation.

On EMI the performance of the *Aubade* is nicely pointed, and the *Concerto* too receives a finely poised and brilliantly executed performance. However, the *Double concerto*, where Gabriel Tacchino is joined by Bernard Ringeissen, is disappointing, with the result brash and hard-driven. It was a great pity that EMI didn't choose the composer's own version of this work with Jacques Fevrier. Poulenc may have been only an amateur pianist, but his interpretation (with partner) had an agreeable lightness of touch, bringing out all the humour.

(i) *Les Biches* (ballet; complete). *L'Éventail de Jeanne: Pastourelle. La Guirlande de Campra: Matelot provençale. Variations sur le nom de Marguerite Long: Bucolique.*
(M) *** EMI *TC-EMX 2107*. Philh. O, Prêtre, (i) with Amb. S.

Georges Prêtre recorded *Les Biches* in the 1960s but not in its complete form or with the choral additions that Poulenc made optional when he came to rework the score. The title is untranslatable: it means 'female deer' and is also a term of endearment. Noel Goodwin's sleeve-note defines the *biches* as 'young girls on the verge of adventure in an atmosphere of wantonness;

which you would sense if you are corrupted, but which an innocent would not be conscious of'. The music is a delight, and so too are the captivating fill-ups here: a gravely touching tribute to Marguerite Long, which comes close to the Satie of the *Gymnopédies*, and the charming *Pastourelle* from *L'Éventail de Jeanne*. High-spirited, fresh, elegant playing and sumptuous recorded sound enhance the claims of this issue. The strings have wonderful freshness and bloom, and there is no lack of presence. The iron-oxide cassette too is of acceptable quality, though not as impressive as the original full-priced tape, which used chrome. We hope this is high on EMI's list for a compact disc version.

Les Biches (ballet): suite.
(*) Sup. Dig. **CO 1519 [id.]. Czech PO, Válek – MILHAUD: *Le bœuf sur le toit*; SATIE: *Parade.***(*)

The suite from *Les Biches* includes all the key numbers; in this spirited and well-played account by the Czech Philharmonic under Vladimír Válek it sounds attractively fresh. Válek's pacing is generally brisk, but he does not miss the music's elegance. The recording is brightly vivid but with a good ambient effect. The couplings are well chosen and are brightly done.

(i) *Les Biches* (ballet suite); (ii) *Concerto for organ, strings and timpani;* (iii) *Deux Marches et un intermède; Les Mariés de la Tour Eiffel; La Baigneuse de Trouville; Discours du Général; Sinfonietta; Suite française d'après Claude Gervaise.*
(B) *** HMV *TCC2-POR 54289*. (i) Paris Conservatoire O; (ii) Duruflé, French Nat. R. O; (iii) O de Paris; Prêtre.

A splendid representation for Georges Prêtre in this tape-only issue in the 'Portrait of the Artist' series, one of the most imaginatively programmed of any double-length cassette of its kind. All the music is attractive; the little-known *Sinfonietta* has much in common with Prokofiev's *Classical symphony*, while the scoring of the *Suite française* is attractively quirky. All the performances are good ones, notably the *Organ concerto*. The ambience for *Les Biches* is somewhat over-resonant but, throughout, the tape transfer is of high quality; this compilation is not to be missed, even if it means duplicating the ballet suite with Prêtre's later complete version of *Les Biches*.

(i) *Concert champêtre for harpsichord and orchestra;* (ii) *Concerto in G min. for organ, strings and timpani.*
*** Erato Dig. **ECD 88141** [id.]. (i) Koopman; (ii) Alain; Rotterdam PO, Conlon.

The *Organ concerto* has never come off better in the recording studio than on this Erato recording, made in Rotterdam's concert hall, the Doelen, with its excellent Flentrop organ. Marie-Claire Alain is fully equal to the many changes of mood, and her treatment of the *Allegro giocoso* racily catches the music's rhythmic humour. The balance is very well managed and the CD is in the demonstration bracket in this work. The *Concert champêtre* always offers problems of balance, as it is scored for a full orchestra, but the exaggerated contrast was clearly intended by the composer. Here the orchestral tapestry sounds very imposing indeed, against which the harpsichord seems almost insignificant. Those who like such a strong contrast will not be disappointed, for the performance is most perceptive, with a particularly elegant and sparkling finale. James Conlon provides admirable accompaniments.

Organ concerto in G min. (for organ, strings and timpani).
(M) *** Decca **417 725-2**; *417 605-4* [id.]. George Malcolm, ASMF, Iona Brown – SAINT-SAËNS: *Symphony No. 3.***(*)
(*) RCA **RD 85750 [**RCA 5750-2-RC**]. Zamkochian, Boston SO, Munch – FRANCK: *Le chasseur maudit***(*); SAINT-SAËNS: *Symphony No. 3.****

Poulenc wrote his endearing and inventive *Organ concerto* just before the Second World War. It is in one continuous movement, divided into seven contrasting sections, the last of which has a devotional quality very apt for its time. Stylistically there is much, probably conscious, imitation of Bach, and Poulenc balances his difficult forces with great skill. The remastered 1979 Argo recording, reissued on Decca Ovation, is a triumphant success. On CD the sound is very good indeed, and George Malcolm gives an exemplary account, his pacing consistently apt and with the changing moods nicely caught, from the gay *Allegro giocoso* to the elegiac closing *Largo*. The playing of the Academy is splendidly crisp and vital. The focus of the cassette is not quite as clean as the excellent CD, but otherwise the sound is bright and well projected.

Munch's Boston recording dates from 1960 and is an excellent example of early RCA stereo; although the Boston acoustics bring slight clouding, the sound is full and hardly dated, with the strings notably warm. Munch has the full measure of the music: his account is essentially genial and relaxed, but not lacking inner vitality; he and his soloist, Berj Zamkochian, find a touching nostalgia in the closing section. Unfortunately the CD provides no internal cueing or indexing.

(i) *Organ concerto in G min.;* (ii) *Gloria in G;* (iii) *4 Motets pour un temps de pénitence.*
(*) HMV **CDC7 47723-2 [id.]. (i) Maurice Duruflé; (ii) Rosanna Carteri, R.T.F. Ch.; both with French Nat. R. & TV O; (iii) René Duclos Ch.; Prêtre.

The *Organ concerto* receives a spirited performance from Duruflé although, as the opening chord shows, the digital remastering of the early 1960s recording has brought a slight loss of body and refinement in the interests of greater presence and definition. The *Gloria*, one of Poulenc's last works, has an arresting theatrical quality as well as many touching moments. Poulenc could move from Stravinskian high spirits to a much deeper vein of feeling with astonishing sureness of touch. The soprano solo, *Domine Deus*, is especially beautiful and the Italianate production of Rosanna Carteri's tone suits its slightly Verdian character, though her style is slightly reserved. In every other respect the performance is exemplary and – since it was recorded in the presence of the composer – presumably authoritative. Again, the new transfer has lost something of the original expansiveness, but the choral sound is undoubtedly clearer. The unaccompanied motets are among Poulenc's finest vocal music; the second, *Vinea mea electa*, has a cool memorability which is particularly well caught here, with the brightness of the choral timbre enhanced by the clean definition.

Piano concerto in C sharp minor.
(*) HMV Dig. **CDC7 47224-2 [id.]. Cécile Ousset, Bournemouth SO, Barshai – PROKOFIEV: *Concerto No. 3.***(*)

Ousset gives a good performance of the *Concerto*, but she is just a little lacking in charm; nor does Barshai display an ideal lightness of touch for this delicious score. The recording, however, is extremely good with the CD in the demonstration bracket.

Sonata for flute and orchestra (orch. Berkeley).
(M) *** RCA *GK 85448* [*AGK1 5448*]. Galway, RPO, Dutoit – CHAMINADE: *Concertino;* FAURÉ: *Fantaisie;* IBERT: *Concerto.****

Poulenc's *Flute sonata*, composed in the mid-1950s towards the end of his life, deserves to be widely popular, so beguiling is its delightful opening theme. Yet so far it remains relatively neglected in the British catalogue (though not in the American one) and this is the only version currently available. Let us hope that Sir Lennox Berkeley's delightful arrangement and James Galway's persuasive advocacy will bring it to a larger public. The performance is elegant and polished and the orchestration highly successful. The recording is admirably spacious and well detailed and the tape transfer is clear and clean although, with a rise of level on the second side, the upper range is given a cutting edge in the treble.

Sextet for piano, flute, oboe, clarinet, bassoon and horn. Clarinet sonata; Flute sonata; Oboe sonata; Villanelle for piccolo and piano.
** Erato Dig. **ECD 88044** [id.]. Chamber Music Society of Lincoln Center.

The resonant acoustic of St Bartholomew's Episcopal Church of White Plains, New York, is less than ideal for this programme, although the balance is faithful within the limitations of the blurring acoustic. In the *Sextet* the playing is boisterously spirited and the humour of the second-movement *Divertissement* is not lost on the performers. The three solo sonatas are very well done, with Gervase de Peyer especially memorable in the *Romanza* of the *Clarinet sonata*. The flautist, Paula Robinson (her instrument sounding somewhat larger than life), gives an engaging account of the piece for flute and also provides an attractive encore at the end with the *Villanelle* which takes a mere 1′ 40″.

Capriccio; Élégie; L'embarquement pour Cythère; Sonata for piano, four hands; Sonata for two pianos.
*** Chan. Dig. **CHAN 8519**; *ABTD 1229* [id.]. Seta Tanyel, Jeremy Brown.

Delightful and brilliant playing that is not to be missed. These two artists have a very close rapport and dispatch this repertoire with both character and sensitivity. They are ebullient and high-spirited when required and also uncover a deeper vein of feeling in the *Élégie*, written for the niece of the Princess de Polignac, and the *Sonata for two pianos*. The Chandos recording is excellent, very vivid and present, not only on the CD but also on the first-class chrome tape.

Improvisations Nos 1–3; 6–8; 12–13; 15; Mouvements perpétuels; 3 Novelettes; Pastourelle; 3 Pièces; Les soirées de Nazelles; Valse.
❀ *** Decca Dig. **417 438-2**; *417 438-4* [id.]. Pascal Rogé.

Pascal Rogé has never enjoyed the exposure or promotion he deserves. Nor, for that matter, has Poulenc's piano music; Ciccolini's LP was its only representation for some time. If you don't know this repertoire (and even if you do), the music will take you by surprise; it is full of unexpected touches and is all teeming with character. Rogé is a far more persuasive exponent of it than any previous pianist on record. The music is absolutely enchanting, full of delight and wisdom; the playing is imaginative and inspiriting, and the recording superb. There is a good chrome tape, but the piano image is not quite as free and clean as the CD (because of the resonance).

VOCAL MUSIC

(i) *Le Bal masqué; Le Bestiaire. Sextet for piano & wind; Trio for piano, oboe & bassoon.*
*** CRD Dig. **CRD 3437**; *CRDC 4137* [id.]. (i) Thomas Allen; Nash Ens., Lionel Friend.

An enchanting disc of some of Poulenc's most attractive music that cannot fail to lift the most downcast of spirits. Thomas Allen is in excellent voice and gives a splendid account of both *Le Bal masqué* and *Le Bestiaire*. The Nash play both the *Trio* and the *Sextet* with superb zest and character. The wit of this playing and the enormous resource, good humour and charm of Poulenc's music are well served by a recording of exemplary quality and definition. Not to be missed.

(i; ii) *Le Bal masqué (cantate profane); Le Bestiaire (ou Cortège d'Orphée);* (iii) *Gloria;* (iv) *4 motets pour le temps de pénitence;* (ii; iv; v) *Stabat Mater.*

(B) ** HMV *TCC2-POR 154597-9*. (i) Benoît; Maryse Charpentier (piano); (ii) Paris Conservatoire O; (iii) Carteri, Fr. Nat. R. & TV Ch. and O; (iv) René Duclos Ch.; (v) Crespin; all cond. Prêtre.

A thoroughly worthwhile tape-only anthology, let down by inadequate documentation (only music titles and performers' names are indicated) and the use of iron-oxide instead of chrome tape, plus variable transfer levels. The choral sound in the *Stabat Mater* on side one is not transparent and the recording has less than ideal definition. The *Motets* which follow are rather more effectively projected and *Le Bestiare*, admirably presented by Jean-Christophe Benoît, has more presence. Side two with an outstanding version of the *Gloria* – recorded in the presence of the composer – is more vivid; and the forward balance of *Le Bal masqué* with its witty accompaniment, offering an obvious musical similarity to Ravel's *L'Enfant et les sortilèges*, comes off best of all in terms of clarity and liveliness.

(i) *La dame de Monte-Carlo*. (ii) *Airs chantés; A sa guitare; C; Ce doux petit visage; Les Chemins de l'amour; La courte paille; Fiançailles pour rire; Métamorphoses; Nous voulons une petite sœur; 3 Poèmes de Louise de Vilmorin.*
** HMV Dig. **CDC7 47550-2**; *EL 270296-4*. Mady Mesplé, (i) Monte Carlo PO, Prêtre; (ii) Gabriel Tacchino.

As an operetta star, Mady Mesplé gives finely detailed, if often over-bright, accounts of these songs, ranging from the *Airs chantés* of 1927–8 to the very late *La courte paille* of 1960 and *La dame de Monte-Carlo* of a year later. Some of the deeper emotions of such songs as *C* evaporate under Mesplé's relentless voice; but with perfect diction bringing out the subtleties of the words, this is a valuable collection, idiomatically accompanied and well recorded. The tape transfer, too, is excellent, clean and fresh and kind to the voice.

Gloria (see also above, under *Organ Concerto*).
*(*) Telarc Dig. **CD 80105** [id.]. McNair, Atlanta Ch. SO, Shaw – STRAVINSKY: *Symphony of psalms.**(*)*

Helped by brilliant and well-balanced recording, Robert Shaw conducts a brightly sung and finely disciplined performance, yet which misses both the electricity and the necessary lightness of Poulenc's vision. Sylvia McNair is a disappointingly unsteady soloist.

Mass in G; 4 Motets pour le temps de Noël.
*** HMV Dig. **CDC7 49559-2** [id.]; *EL 749559-4*. Mark Harris, Winchester Cathedral Ch., ECO, Neary – HONEGGER: *Christmas cantata.****

The *G major Mass* was written in 1937 and dedicated to the memory of Poulenc's father. The shadow of Stravinsky hovers over the score and it is rather more self-conscious than his later choral pieces, certainly more so than the delightful *Quatre Motets pour le temps de Noël*. Martin Neary gets excellent results from the Winchester Cathedral Choir and his fine treble, Mark Harris. The HMV recording is also first rate with well-defined detail and firm definition. The chrome cassette offers good sound, but definition is less clean.

Stabat Mater.
** Sup. Dig. **CO 1090** [id.]. Gabriela Beňácková-Capová, Vaclav Zítek, Kuhn Children's Ch., Czech PO, Pešek – HONEGGER: *Christmas cantata.***

Stabat Mater; Litanies à la vierge noire; Salve regina.
*** HM Dig. **HMC 905149** [id.]. Lagrange, Lyon Nat. Ch. and O, Baudo.

Apart from an LP by Frémaux, Poulenc's *Stabat Mater* has not been recorded for almost two decades; this excellent account on Harmonia Mundi fills the gap with some measure of distinction. The recording is well detailed and made in a good acoustic. Serge Baudo is perhaps a more sympathetic interpreter of this lovely score than was Prêtre in his earlier record, and gets more out of it. He certainly makes the most of expressive and dynamic nuances; he shapes the work with fine feeling and gets good singing from the Lyons Chorus. Michèle Lagrange may not efface memories of Régine Crespin on Prêtre's 1964 version (still available on cassette), but she has a good voice and is an eminently expressive soloist. The coupling differs from its rival and offers the short *Salve Regina* and the *Litanies à la vierge noire*, an earlier and somewhat more severe work, written on the death of the composer, Ferroud. A welcome and worthwhile issue.

The recording of the *Stabat Mater*, made in 1983 by Czech forces under Libor Pešek, is dramatic and powerful. It is handicapped by the excessive reverberance of the House of Artists but there is plenty of impact in the louder sections, and the singing is generally better focused than in the Honegger cantata with which it is paired. Good singing and spirited playing outweigh the drawbacks of the acoustic, but this issue does not displace Baudo on Harmonia Mundi.

OPERA

La voix humaine (complete).
** Chan. Dig. **CHAN 8331** [id.]. Carole Farley, Adelaide SO, Serebrier.

This virtuoso monodrama, just one woman and a telephone, is ideally suited to a record if, as here, the full text is provided. Where on stage few singers can project the French words with ideal clarity to make every detail apparent, both the brightness of Carole Farley's soprano and the recording balance present the whole scena in vivid close-up. Ms Farley's French is clear but not quite idiomatic-sounding, and that rather applies to the playing of the Adelaide orchestra, crisply disciplined and sharply concentrated as it is. The result has little of French finesse. The fifteen bands of the CD are very helpful in finding one's way about the piece.

Praetorius, Michael (1571–1621)

Dances from Terpsichore (extended suite).
*** Decca Dig. **414 633-2**; *414 633-4* [id.]. New L. Cons., Philip Pickett.

Dances from Terpsichore (Suite de ballets; Suite de voltes). (i) Motets: *Eulogodia Sionia: Resonet in laudibus; Musae Sionae: Allein Gott in der Höh sei Ehr; Aus tiefer Not schrei ich zu dir; Christus der uns selig macht; Gott der Vater wohn uns bei; Polyhymnia Caduceatrix: Erhalt uns, Herr, bei deinem Wort.*
(M) *** HMV **CDM7 69024-2**; *EG 769024-4* [Ang. *4AM 34728*]. Early Music Cons. of L., Munrow, (i) with boys of the Cathedral and Abbey Church of St Alban.

One of the great pioneers of the 'authentic' re-creation of early music, David Munrow was never one to put scholarly or theoretical considerations before his main purpose, which was to bring the music fully to life and, at the same time, imaginatively to stimulate the ear of the listener. This record, made in 1973, is one of his most successful achievements. It is especially welcome in this mid-priced reissue, well documented on CD. The cassette, however, needed chrome stock to cope with the resonance of the recording; as it is, the sound lacks sharpness of focus in this format, although the CD is excellent in all respects. *Terpsichore* is a huge collection of some three hundred dance tunes used by the French-court dance bands of Henri IV. They were enthusiastically assembled by the German composer Michael Praetorius, who also harmonized them and arranged them in four to six parts. Moreover, he left plenty of advice as to their manner of performance, although he would not have expected any set instrumentation – that would depend on the availability of musicians. Any selection is therefore as arbitrary in the choice of items as it is conjectural in the matter of their orchestration. David Munrow's instrumentation is imaginatively done (the third item, a *Bourrée* played by four racketts – a cross between a shawm and comb-and-paper in sound – is fascinating). The collection is a delightful one, the motets on side two reminding one very much of Giovanni Gabrieli.

Philip Pickett's is the most substantial collection yet to have been recorded from Praetorius's dances. His instrumentation (based on the illustrations which act as an appendix to the maestro's second volume of *Syntagma Musicum* of 1619) is sometimes less exuberant than that of David Munrow before him; but many will like the refinement of his approach, with small instrumental groups, lute pieces and even what seems like an early xylophone! The music is divided into two sections (on each side of the tape, though continuous on the CD) and there are some attractively robust brass finales (sackbuts and trumpets) for each group. The use of original instruments is entirely beneficial in this repertoire; the recording is splendid, especially lively on CD, but sounding excellent on the chrome tape too, even if in tuttis the focus is marginally less sharp.

Christmas music: *Polyhymnia caduceatrix et panegyrica Nos 9–10, 12 & 17. Puericinium Nos 2, 4 & 5. Musae Sionae VI, No. 53: Es ist ein Ros' entsprungen. Terpsichore: Dances Nos 1; 283–5; 310.*

*** Hyp. Dig. **CDA 66200**; *KA 66200* [id.]. Westminster Cathedral Ch., Parley of Instruments, David Hill.

The sheer size of Praetorius's output, like that of Lassus, is so daunting that one feels one needs an extra life to explore it. Praetorius was much influenced by the polychoral style of the Gabrielis; these pieces from the *Polyhymnia caduceatrix et panegyrica* and the *Puericinium*, which come from the last years of his life, reflect this interest. The music is simple in style and readily accessible, and its performance on this atmospheric Hyperion record is both spirited and sensitive.

Christmas music: Polyhymnia caduceatrix et panegyrica Nos 10, Wie schön leuchtet der Morgenstern; 12, Puer natus in Bethlehem; 21, Wachet auf, ruft uns die Stimme; 34, In dulci jubilo.

*** HMV Dig. **CDC7 47633-2** [id.]; *EL 270428-4*. Taverner Cons., Ch. & Players, Parrott – SCHÜTZ: *Christmas oratorio.****

This is the finest collection of Praetorius's vocal music in the current catalogue. The closing setting of *In dulci jubilo*, richly scored for five choirs and with the brass providing thrilling contrast and support for the voices, has great splendour; Parrott brings an exhilarating dash to the closing improvised ritornello for the trumpets. Before that comes the lovely, if less ambitious *Wie schön leuchtet der Morgenstern*, where the opening shows how effectively Tessa Bonner and Emily Van Evera take the place of boy trebles. Some might think such a substitution of female voices unauthentic, but the result is to combine a serene purity of timbre with maturity of line. Both *Wachet auf* and *Puer natus in Bethlehem*, which come first, are on a comparatively large scale, their combination of block sonorities and florid decorative effects the very essence of Renaissance style. The recording is splendidly balanced, with voices and brass blending and intertwining within an ample acoustic which brings weight and resonance without clouding. The chrome cassette copes amazingly well with the amplitude, but the CD is in the demonstration class. The coupled Schütz *Christmas oratorio* is no less fine.

Prokofiev, Serge (1891–1953)

Boris Godunov, Op. 70 bis: Fountain Scene; Polonaise. Dreams, Op. 6. Eugene Onegin, Op. 71: Minuet, Polka, Mazurka. 2 Pushkin waltzes, Op. 120. Romeo and Juliet (ballet)*: suite No. 2, Op. 64.*
*** Chan. Dig. **CHAN 8472**; *ABTD 1183* [id.]. SNO, Järvi.

This is a kind of appendix to Järvi's Prokofiev series. The main work, of course is the second suite from *Romeo and Juliet*. It is vastly superior to either Muti (EMI) or Rostropovich (DG): it has sensitivity, abundant atmosphere, a sense of the theatre (which Muti's hard-driven account lacked), and is refreshingly unmannered. In terms of characterization, this is difficult to fault. Of the rarities, *Dreams* is atmospheric, if derivative, with a fair amount of Debussy and early Scriabin – to whom it is dedicated. In 1937, Prokofiev wrote extensive scores for Meyerhold's *Boris Godunov* and for a production of *Eugene Onegin*. Much of the music was eventually re-used in other works, but the *Two Pushkin waltzes*, Op. 120, are rather engaging lighter pieces commissioned in 1949 by Moscow Radio. All this music is well worth having and the performances are predictably expert. The range is wide, the balance finely judged and detail is in exactly the right perspective. There is a good chrome tape, although the relatively low transfer level means that the focus is somewhat diffuse.

Chout (The Buffoon): ballet, Op. 21.
(M) *** Olympia Dig. **OCD 126** [id.]. USSR Ministry of Culture SO, Rozhdestvensky.

Chout comes from Prokofiev's time in Paris and was the first of his ballets that Diaghilev actually staged. Although he had commissioned *Ala et Lolly* (better known as the *Scythian suite*), Diaghilev didn't like it enough to put it on. He did however commission *Chout*, a wonderfully imaginative score, full of colour and resource. Diaghilev never revived the ballet after 1922 and Prokofiev made a concert suite of twelve numbers, which both Susskind and Rozhdestvensky recorded. This is the first CD to give us the complete score and runs to just under an hour. Rozhdestvensky gives a very lively account of the ballet and gets good playing from his youthful Moscow orchestra. The recording is as vivid as the music; indeed some may find it a little overbright at the top. A most rewarding issue and strongly recommended.

Cinderella (ballet; complete), *Op. 87.*
*** Decca Dig. **410 162-2** (2) [id.]. Cleveland O, Ashkenazy.

Prokofiev's enchanting score had been neglected during the analogue stereo era until 1983 saw two new sets arrive, both by artists who are completely inside the idiom; honours were very evenly divided between the two. EMI have for the moment decided not to issue Previn's set complete; instead, they have selected a generous compilation of highlights – see below. Compact disc collectors wanting the complete ballet can safely invest in Ashkenazy without fear of disappointment. Some dances come off better in one version than in the other, and there is an element of swings and roundabouts in assessing them. Detail is more closely scrutinized by the Decca engineers; Ashkenazy gets excellent results from the Cleveland Orchestra. There are many imaginative touches in this score – as magical indeed as the story itself – and the level of invention is astonishingly high. On CD, the wonderful definition noticeable on the LPs is enhanced and the bright, vivid image is given striking projection.

Cinderella (ballet): highlights.
*** HMV Dig. **CDC7 47969-2** [id.]. LSO, Previn.
(*) RCA Dig. **RD 85321 [RCD1 5321]. St Louis SO, Slatkin.

Previn's set of highlights is extremely generous, following the narrative line through, with nine excerpts from each of the three acts. There is 71′ of music and, with the LSO playing very well indeed and digital recording from EMI which approaches demonstration standard in its vividness and colour, this will be hard to beat.

Slatkin's disc is listed as a 'suite', but the twenty numbers (from the fifty of the complete score) follow the ballet's action comprehensively. There is an excellent note by Richard Freed placing the music in its historical perspective in relation to other settings of the *Cinderella* story. Within the flattering St Louis acoustic, the orchestra is naturally balanced and the sound is vividly spectacular. The upper range is brightly lit but the CD has marginal added amplitude and bloom so that, while the violins above the stave at *fortissimo* are brilliant, there is no edginess. The orchestral playing is sympathetic, polished and committed; the wide dynamic range of the recording produces a riveting climax towards the end of the ballet when, at midnight, the stereoscopically ticking clock dominates the orchestra dramatically. Slatkin then creates an attractively serene contrast with the closing *Amoroso*. Earlier in the work, Slatkin's characterization is just a little tame, and the detail and rhythmic feeling of the music making has, at times, an element of blandness. Previn's disc is preferable and offers more music.

Cinderella (ballet)*: suites Nos 1 & 2, Op. 107–8:* excerpts. (i) *Peter and the wolf, Op. 67.*
*** Chan. Dig. **CHAN 8511**; *ABTD 1221* [id.]. (i) Lina Prokofiev; SNO, Järvi.

With Madame Lina Prokofiev, the composer's first wife, in her eighties giving a disarmingly grandmotherly account of the narration, Järvi's Prokofiev series here offers an exceptionally characterful version of *Peter and the wolf*. In time-length it is very slow, but the magnetism of Madame Prokofiev, with many memorable lines delivered in her tangily Franco-Russian accent, makes up for that leisurely manner with beautiful, persuasive playing from the Scottish National Orchestra. The very first mention of the wolf brings an unforgettable snarl, which most children will relish. Järvi's compilation of eight movements from the two *Cinderella suites* has even more persuasive playing from the orchestra, with the sensuousness of much of the writing brought out. Warmly atmospheric recording with the narration realistically balanced. There is a good cassette, though the orchestral focus in *Cinderella* could be sharper.

Piano concertos Nos 1 in D flat, Op. 10; 4 in B flat for left hand, Op. 53; 5 in G, Op. 55.
(M) *** HMV *EG 290851-4*. Béroff, Leipzig GO, Masur.

Piano concertos Nos 2 in G min., Op. 16; 3 in C, Op. 26.
(M) *** HMV *EG 290261-4* [*4AM 34705*]. Béroff, Leipzig GO, Masur.

A thoroughly satisfying mid-priced set. Michel Béroff plays masterfully: he is a pianist of genuine insight where Prokofiev is concerned, and Masur gives him excellent support. Béroff is free from some of the agogic mannerisms that distinguish Ashkenazy in the slow movement of the *Third*, and he has great poetry. The balance is good; although the overall sound-picture is not wholly natural, it is certainly vivid, and the timbre of the piano is sympathetically captured. Tape collectors will find this pair of cassettes excellent value.

Piano concerto No. 1 in D flat, Op. 10.
(M) **(*) PRT **PVCD 8376** [id.]. Mindru Katz, LPO, Boult – KHACHATURIAN: *Piano concerto.****

(i) *Piano concerto No. 1 in D flat, Op. 10. Romeo and Juliet* (ballet)*: suite, Op. 75* (arr. composer). *Suggestion diabolique.*
(M) *** HMV *EG 290326-4* [*4AM 34715*]. Gavrilov; (i) LSO, Rattle.

Piano concerto No. 1 in D flat; Piano sonata No. 5 in C, Op. 38.
*** ASV Dig. *ZCDCA 555* [id.]. Osorio, RPO, Bátiz – RAVEL: *Left-hand concerto* etc.***

A dazzling account of the *First Concerto* from the young Soviet pianist Andrei Gavrilov, who replaced Richter at Salzburg in 1975 and has astonished audiences wherever he has appeared. This version is second to none for virtuosity and for sensitivity: it is no exaggeration to say that this exhilarating account is the equal of any we have ever heard and superior to most. Apart from its brilliance, this performance scores on all other fronts, too; Simon Rattle provides excellent orchestral support and the EMI engineers offer vivid recording. The original coupling was the *Scene and dance of the young girls* from *Romeo and Juliet*, plus Ravel's *Left-hand Piano concerto* and *Pavane*. Now one needs to acquire an extra record to get the Ravel *Concerto*. In its place, Gavrilov's selection from the composer's piano arrangement of *Romeo and Juliet* has been expanded (and these pieces, even in their monochrome form, sound abundantly characterful in his hands), while the *Suggestion diabolique* makes a – by no means lightweight – encore after the *Concerto*. On cassette, the reverberation brings slight blunting of the transients, but otherwise the sound is good. At mid-price, this remains first-class value and will, no doubt, appear on a Studio CD in due course.

Jorge-Fredrico Osorio is a gifted Mexican player whose excellently recorded account of the Prokofiev *Concerto* challenges the EMI Gavrilov coupling with *Romeo and Juliet*, now at mid-price. However, ASV offer us generous and interesting fill-ups in the form of the Prokofiev *Fifth Sonata* which Osorio does in its post-war revised form. It is an interesting piece from the 1920s and a welcome addition to the catalogue. Osorio copes splendidly with the *Concerto* and is not as percussive a pianist as Gavrilov. Readers wanting this coupling need not fear that this is second best. It may be less dazzling but is not less perceptive.

A sparkling performance from Katz, and those wanting his coupled version of the Khachaturian (the finest in the catalogue) will find this spontaneously enjoyable. The recording dates from 1959 but has been expertly remastered: the piano tone is bold and clear and the balance is excellent. The orchestral playing is very good, if not as polished as that of the soloist. The overall effect is of sophisticated brilliance, with underlying warmth to prevent any sense of artificiality.

Piano concerto No. 3 in C, Op. 26.

*** DG **415 062-2** [id.]. Argerich, BPO, Abbado – TCHAIKOVSKY: *Piano concerto No. 1*.***

*** Decca **411 969-2** [id.]. Ashkenazy, LSO, Previn – BARTÓK: *Concerto No. 3*.**(*)

(*) HMV Dig. **CDC7 47224-2 [id.]. Ousset, Bournemouth SO, Barshai – POULENC: *Piano concerto*.**(*)

** Telarc Dig. **CD 80124** [id.]. Jon Parker, RPO, Previn – TCHAIKOVSKY: *Piano concerto No. 1*.*(*)

Martha Argerich made her outstanding record of the Prokofiev *Third Concerto* in 1968, while still in her twenties, and this record helped to establish her international reputation as one of the most vital and positive of women pianists. There is nothing ladylike about the playing, but it displays countless indications of feminine perception and subtlety. The *C major Concerto* was once regarded as tough music but here receives a sensuous performance, and Abbado's direction underlines that from the very first, with a warmly romantic account of the ethereal opening phrases on the high violins. When it comes to the second subject the lightness of Argerich's pointing has a delightfully infectious quality, and surprisingly a likeness emerges with the Ravel *G major Concerto*, which was written more than a decade later. This is a much more individual performance of the Prokofiev than almost any other available and brings its own special insights. The recording remains excellent, though there is less presence and immediacy than with the Ashkenazy CD, and a certain amount of the original tape hiss remains for keen ears to spot. Argerich's coupling is one of the finest versions of the Tchaikovsky *B flat Concerto* yet issued on CD; with nearly 63 minutes' music offered, this is fair value.

Ashkenazy's account of the *Third Concerto* is keen-edged and crisply articulated, and he is very sympathetically supported by Previn and the LSO. One's only reservation concerns the slow movement: Ashkenazy's entry immediately after the theme is uncharacteristically mannered. Yet his virtuosity remains thrilling and this is still a fine performance. The Prokofiev was recorded six years earlier than the Bartók coupling, yet the sound in the compact disc transfer is clearer and more transparent, if with a touch of thinness on violin tone.

Cécile Ousset has the advantage of fine modern digital recording, exceptionally vivid and clear, but the performance, expert though it is, wants the dash and sparkle that such artists as Argerich and Ashkenazy bring to it. Tempi are just that bit slower than Prokofiev's own in his pioneering recording, and Barshai's direction sounds slightly sluggish.

The Telarc recording is rich and well balanced, noticeably fuller than the DG sound for Argerich. Jon Kimura Parker plays the outer movements with considerable vigour, and he and Previn are at their most imaginatively communicative in the slow-movement variations. This is enjoyable enough but is in no way distinctive, and the Tchaikovsky coupling fails to take off.

Piano concerto No. 5 in G, Op. 55.
*** DG **415 119-2** [id.]. Sviatoslav Richter, Warsaw PO, Witold Rowicki – RACHMANINOV: *Piano concerto No. 2.****

Richter's account of the *Fifth Piano concerto* is a classic. It was recorded in 1959, yet the sound of this excellent CD transfer belies the age of the original in its clarity, detail and vividness of colour. In any event it cannot be too strongly recommended to all admirers of Richter, Prokofiev and great piano playing. The coupling has also been very successfully remastered.

Violin concertos Nos 1 in D, Op. 19; 2 in G min., Op. 63.
*** DG Dig. **410 524-2** [id.]. Mintz, Chicago SO, Abbado.
*** HMV Dig. **CDC7 47025-2** [id.]. Perlman, BBC SO, Rozhdestvensky.

Prokofiev's two *Violin concertos* are eminently well served in the present catalogue. Mintz's performances are as fine as any; he phrases with imagination and individuality – the opening of the *G minor* is memorably poetic – and if he does not display quite the overwhelming sense of authority of Perlman, there is an attractive combination of freshness and lyrical finesse. He has the advantage of Abbado's sensitive and finely judged accompaniments. Abbado has a special feeling for Prokofiev's sound-world, and here there is much subtlety of colour and dynamic nuance, yet the music's vitality is undiminished. In short this partnership casts the strongest spell on the listener and, with recording which is both refined and full, and a realistic – if still somewhat forward – balance for the soloist, this must receive the strongest advocacy. The compact disc is in the demonstration league, one of the most impressive to come from DG, adding to the presence and range of the sound-picture without over emphasis.

Perlman's performances bring virtuosity of such strength and command that one is reminded of the supremacy of Heifetz. Though the HMV sound has warmth and plenty of bloom, the balance of the soloist is unnaturally close, which has the effect of obscuring important melodic ideas in the orchestra behind mere passagework from the soloist, as in the second subject of the *First Concerto*'s finale, and this is even more apparent on CD. Nevertheless, in their slightly detached way these performances are impossible to resist: one is left in no doubt that both works are among the finest violin concertos written this century. Apart from the balance, the recording is very fine.

Violin concerto No. 2 in G min., Op. 63.
(M) *** RCA **RD 87019 [RCD1 7019]**. Heifetz, Boston SO, Munch – GLAZUNOV; SIBELIUS: *Concerto.****

Heifetz made the first recording of this work in the 1930s under Koussevitzky. His newer (1959) version uses the same Boston orchestra and Munch proves a worthy successor to the Russian conductor. In the *arioso*-like slow movement, Heifetz chooses a faster speed than is usual, but there is nothing unresponsive about his playing, for his expressive rubato has an unfailing inevitability. In the spiky finale he is superb, and indeed his playing is glorious throughout. The recording is serviceable merely, though it has been made firmer in the current remastering. But no one is going to be prevented from enjoying this ethereal performance because the technical quality is dated. This is available on CD, coupled with both the Sibelius and the Glazunov *Concertos* – treasure trove indeed.

Lieutenant Kijé (incidental music), *Op. 60: suite.*
*** HMV Dig. **CDC7 47109-2** [id.]. LPO, Tennstedt – KODÁLY: *Háry János.****

Prokofiev's colourful suite drawn from film music makes the perfect coupling for Kodály's *Háry János*, similarly brilliant and with a comparable vein of irony. Tennstedt's reading, in repertory with which he is not usually associated, is aptly brilliant and colourful, with rhythms strongly marked. Excellent recording, especially vivid and present in its CD format.

Lieutenant Kijé (suite), *Op. 60, Love of Three Oranges* (suite).
*** RCA Dig. **RD 85168 [RCD1 5168]**. Dallas SO, Mata – STRAVINSKY: *Suites.****

Lieutenant Kijé (suite); *Love of Three Oranges* (suite); *Symphony No. 1 in D* (*Classical*).
(*) CBS Dig. **MK 39557 [id.]. O Nat. de France, Maazel.

There are no finer performances of these two colourful suites available than on Mata's RCA Dallas versions, and the Stravinsky coupling is equally attractive. At the opening of *Kijé* the distanced cornet solo immediately creates a mood of nostalgia. The orchestral playing, both here and in the suite from *Love of Three Oranges*, is vividly coloured and full of character, and the ambience of the Dallas auditorium adds bloom and atmosphere. The CD is bright and sharp in definition and the music making is of the highest order; Mata shows an instinctive rapport with both these scores.

After a brilliant account of the *Classical symphony*, well played and brightly lit, Maazel gives exceptionally dramatic and strongly characterized accounts of Prokofiev's two colourful suites. Though he does not miss the romantic colouring of *Love of Three Oranges* or the nostalgia of *Kijé*, it is the pungency of the rhythms and the sharp pointing of detail that register most strongly, helped by the resonant acoustic which adds an effective degree of edge to Prokofiev's bolder scoring. Inner detail registers vividly at all dynamic levels; while Maazel is clearly seeking a strong projection rather than refinement, the committed orchestral response is exhilarating.

Lieutenant Kijé (suite); *Romeo and Juliet:* excerpts; *Symphony No. 1 in D* (*Classical*); (i) *Alexander Nevsky* (cantata), *Op. 78.*
(B) *** HMV *TCC2-POR 54278*. LSO, Previn, (i) with Reynolds, LSO Ch.

EMI could hardly have chosen better to represent Previn in their 'Portrait of the Artist' double-length tape series. The performances of the *Kijé suite* and the *Classical symphony* are among the finest available. *Alexander Nevsky* is currently not available in disc format and here it is presented without a break on one side of the cassette. All the weight, bite and colour of the score are captured; though the timbre of the singers' voices may not suggest Russians, they cope very confidently with the Russian text; and Previn's dynamic manner ensures that the great *Battle on the ice* scene is powerfully effective. Anna Reynolds sings the lovely lament for the dead most affectingly. The transfers are sophisticated throughout, the sound vivid with excellent range and a good choral focus.

On the Dnieper (*ballet*), *Op. 51; Le pas d'acier* (*ballet*), *Op. 41.*
*** Olympia Dig. **OCD 103** [id.]. USSR Ministry of Culture SO, Rozhdestvensky.

First recordings of both scores: *Le pas d'acier* (*The step of steel* or *The steel trot*), Prokofiev's third ballet (1927), and *On the Dnieper* (1930), both written in Paris. Earlier records of *Le pas d'acier* by Albert Coates and Rozhdestvensky have been of the suite; this gives us the newly published complete score. It is full of vitality and (apart from one or two numbers) highly attractive, very much in the *ballet mécanique* style: *On the Dnieper* is a lyrical work not dissimilar to *The Prodigal Son.* Colourful performances and recordings. Lovers of Prokofiev's ballets should not miss this welcome addition to the discography: neither is top-drawer Prokofiev – but second-rank Prokofiev is better than most twentieth-century composers at their best.

Peter and the wolf, Op. 67 (see also above, under *Cinderella*).
*** Telarc Dig. **CD 80126** [id.]. André Previn, RPO, Previn – BRITTEN: *Young person's guide* etc.**(*)
*** Ph. Dig. **412 559-2**; *412 559-4* [**412 556-2**, with Dudley Moore]. Terry Wogan, Boston Pops O, John Williams – TCHAIKOVSKY: *Nutcracker suite.****
*** DG **415 351-2** [id.]. Hermione Gingold, VPO, Boehm – SAINT-SAËNS: *Carnival.****
(M) *** ASV **CDQS 6017**; (B) *ZCQS 6017* [id.]. Angela Rippon, RPO, Hughes – SAINT-SAËNS: *Carnival.****
(M) *** HMV *TS-ESD 7114* [Ang. *4XG 60172*]. Michael Flanders, Philh. O, Kurtz – BRITTEN: *Young person's guide*; SAINT-SAËNS: *Carnival.****
** HMV Dig. **CDC7 47067-2** [id.]. Itzhak Perlman, Israel PO, Mehta – SAINT-SAËNS: *Carnival.***
** RCA **RD 82743** [**RCD1 2743**]. David Bowie, Phd. O, Ormandy – BRITTEN: *Young person's guide.***

André Previn's Telarc version, lightly pointed, lively, colourful and perfectly timed, has the enormous advantage of the conductor's own delightfully informal narration. In its direct communication to a child of any age it brings new and often amusing inflexions to freshen words that easily sound stale. The arrival of the wolf is marvellously sinister, yet in telling of the swallowing of the duck Previn keeps just a touch of avuncular kindness behind the horror, most delicately done. Vivid recording, with the voice balanced well against the orchestra without too much discrepancy.

Terry Wogan's amiably fresh narration is a great success. Any listener expecting a degree of archness or too much Irish whimsy will soon be disarmed by the spontaneity of the story telling and the way the added asides point the gentle irony of the tale and the involvement of its characters. The little bird shrugs its shoulders ('not an easy thing for a bird to do'); the hunters – against the thundering kettledrums – 'shoot at everything that moves' while, at the end, after Peter has caught the wolf without their aid, Wogan comments characteristically, 'I don't think the hunters liked Peter.' Perhaps the camped-up voice of Grandfather sounds a shade self-conscious, but the humour of the grumpy old man is nicely caught. This is one of the most endearing versions of the tale since Sir Ralph Richardson's classic Decca performance with Sir Malcolm Sargent. John Williams provides the most imaginative orchestral backing, full of atmosphere and with marvellous detail, so that one hears Prokofiev's miraculous score as if for the first time. The entry of the wolf is particularly telling, and he is certainly portrayed as the villain of the piece. By contrast, the wolf's capture has a deliciously light touch, with the final procession then played very grandly indeed. One small editing criticism: in the introductory section, which is agreeably less stilted than usual, the frequent repetition of the word 'tune' is not very felicitous; but this is a small point, not likely to worry younger listeners. The recording is superb, with the nicely resonant Boston acoustic bringing an attractive overall bloom (reminding one of Decca's very first mono LP, made in the Kingsway Hall, by John Culshaw with Frank Phillips and the LPO under Malko). The CD emphasizes the difference in acoustic between the separate recordings of voice and orchestra, but this is not a disadvantage for, within his cleaner ambience, Terry Wogan is able to use a *sotto voce* technique, even a whisper, to great effect. The chrome cassette is first class, though the level of transfer is a little low. In the American edition, Dudley Moore replaces Terry Wogan as narrator.

On DG, Hermione Gingold's narration is certainly memorable and the orchestral playing under Boehm is of a superlative standard. Some might find Miss Gingold a trifle too camp in her presentation of the text (which was amended and embellished by Edward Greenfield, so comment on our part is perhaps inappropriate). However, it is difficult to resist the strength of Miss Gingold's personality and her obvious identification with the events of the tale. Boehm gives a straightforward accompaniment, but is attentive to every detail, and the performance is beautifully characterized. The 1976 orchestral recording was considered to be of demonstration standard in its day; it is remarkably transparent and truthful. The voice itself is a little larger than life, but has such presence and such a well-judged background ambience that one cannot quibble.

Angela Rippon narrates with charm yet is never in the least coy; indeed she is thoroughly involved in the tale and thus involves the listener too. The accompaniment is equally spirited, with excellent orchestral playing, and the recording is splendidly clear, yet not lacking atmosphere. On CD this makes an excellent mid-priced recommendation; the well-engineered cassette is in the bargain range.

For tape collectors, the HMV Greensleeve issue is perhaps even more attractive in offering the excellent 1959 Michael Flanders recording of *Peter and the wolf* together with Saint-Saëns's *Carnival of the Animals*, plus a characterful account, under Sir Charles Groves, of Britten's *Young person's guide to the orchestra*. Michael Flanders adds a touch or two of his own to the introduction and narration, and, as might be expected, he brings the action splendidly alive. The pace of the accompaniment under Kurtz is attractively vibrant, and the Philharmonia are first rate. The recording is crisply vivid.

Itzhak Perlman makes Prokofiev's story very much part of his own culture; Peter's grandfather, an engaging character, is obviously Jewish as well as Russian. The whole presentation has a sense of transatlantic hyperbole and, in his involvement with the drama, Perlman nearly goes over the top, with the episode of the duck being swallowed very dramatic indeed. Some will also resist the rather schmaltzy opening with its 'gorgeous oboe' and the 'three mean horns' representing the wolf. Yet one succumbs to the strong personality of the story telling, and Mehta, who opens the proceedings a little cosily, is soon caught up in the action. The recording is clear and close, notably so on CD.

David Bowie's narration has undoubted presence and individuality. He makes a few additions to the text and colours his voice effectively for the different characters. He has the face to ask, 'Are you sitting comfortably?' before he begins; on the whole, the narration seems aimed at a younger age-group. The manner is direct and slightly dead-pan, but definitely attractive. Ormandy accompanies imaginatively and the orchestral players enter fully into the spirit of the tale. The recording is generally excellent (David Bowie's voice is very close, but admirably real), and the remastering for CD produces clear and clean sound, if not the ambient glow of the Philips version.

Romeo and Juliet (ballet), *Op. 64* (complete).
*** HMV **CDS7 49012-8** (2) [id.]. LSO, Previn.
*** Decca **417 510-2** (2) [id.]. Cleveland O, Maazel.
*** DG **423 268-20**; *423 268-4* (2) [id.]. Boston SO, Ozawa.
(B) **(*) CfP *CFPD 41 4452-5* (2). Bolshoi Theatre O, Zuraitis.

Almost simultaneously in 1973 two outstanding versions of Prokofiev's complete *Romeo and Juliet* ballet appeared, strongly contrasted to provide a clear choice on grounds of interpretation and recording. Previn and the LSO made their recording in conjunction with live performances at the Royal Festival Hall, and the result reflects the humour and warmth which went with those live occasions. Previn's pointing of rhythm is consciously seductive, whether in fast jaunty numbers or the soaring lyricism of the love-music. The recording quality is warm and immediate to match. Maazel by contrast will please those who believe that this score should above all be bitingly incisive. The rhythms are more consciously metrical, the tempi generally faster, and the precision of ensemble of the Cleveland Orchestra is little short of miraculous. The recording is one of Decca's most spectacular, searingly detailed but atmospheric too. Both sets have been strikingly successful in their CD transfers and are generously cued – the Previn set has fifty-one access points – and the synopsis admirably relates the stage action to each separate band. Both are now contained on a pair of CDs as against the original three-LP layout.

Ozawa has the advantage of outstanding modern digital recording, with the warm Boston acoustics ensuring a spacious ambience. Immediately at the opening one notices Ozawa's special balletic feeling in the elegance of the string phrasing and the light rhythmic felicity. Yet he can rise to the work's drama and in the love-music his ardour is compulsive. At times, one feels, the characterization has less affectionate individuality than Previn's, whose tempi are always so apt, and the element of pungency which Maazel brings to the score is almost entirely missing in Boston. But this music making is very easy to enjoy and the actual playing is very fine indeed, full of atmosphere and bringing out new facets of Prokofiev's masterpiece. There are excellent cassettes, but the superb CDs have that bit sharper focus and greater presence.

Though Zuraitis's version takes only two cassettes, he includes an important supplement in addition to the usual complete ballet score. Having studied the original manuscript material, he adds three movements finally omitted in the ballet, the *Nurse and Mercutio* (using familiar material), a sharply grotesque *Moorish dance* and a so-called *Letter scene* which provides a sketch for what eight years later became the scherzo of the *Fifth Symphony*. Zuraitis has scored this last with reference to the symphony. The performance generally may lack something in rhythmic flair and orchestral refinement compared with those of Previn and Maazel, but in its direct way it is warm and committed, with digital sound of colour and power, not always perfectly balanced. The chrome cassettes are of high quality and are well laid out, with Acts tailored to side-ends. A bargain.

Romeo and Juliet (ballet)*: suite.*

(M) *** Decca **417 737-2**; *417 737-4* [id.]. Cleveland O, Maazel – KHACHATURIAN: *Gayaneh*; *Spartacus.***(*)

An intelligently chosen selection of six pieces (including *Juliet as a young girl*, the *Balcony scene* and *The last farewell*) makes a generous coupling for Decca's Khachaturian ballet scores. The sound is vivid on CD, slightly more soft-grained on cassette.

Romeo and Juliet: suites Nos 1–2, Op. 64a/b.

(*) DG Dig. **410 519-2 [id.]. Nat. SO of Washington, Rostropovich.

(B) **(*) DG *419 840-4* [id.]. Nat. SO of Washington, Rostropovich – SHOSTAKOVICH: *Symphony No. 5.***

*(*) HMV Dig. **CDC7 47004-2** [id.]. Phd. O, Muti.

Rostropovich gives a carefully prepared account, thoroughly attentive to details of dynamic markings and phrasing, but symphonic rather than balletic in approach. At no time does the listener feel tempted to spring into dance. Nevertheless the effect is atmospheric in a non-theatrical way, and to some ears the feeling of listening almost to an extended tone-poem is most rewarding, though to others the effect of Rostropovich's approach is ponderous at times. To be fair, some movements give no cause for complaint. Friar Lawrence is even enhanced by the slower tempo, and the *Dance* (No. 4 of the *Second Suite*) has no want of momentum or of lightness of touch. The recording is clean, with sharply focused detail; it makes a thrilling impact on the compact disc, which is far more successful than Muti's, where the glossily brilliant sound tends to weary the ear. However, this recording is also available on a splendidly engineered Pocket Music tape, offered at bargain price and paired with Rostropovich's equally individual (and powerful) version of Shostakovich's *Fifth Symphony*.

Muti gives us the *First Suite* as published, and then in the *Second* he omits the *Dance* that forms the fourth number and the penultimate *Dance of the girls with lilies*. There is very impressive virtuoso playing from the Philadelphia Orchestra, and a full-blooded digital recording. There are some magical moments, such as the opening of the *Romeo and Juliet* movement of the *First Suite* but, for the most part, the performance is overdriven. Had Muti relaxed a little, the gain in atmosphere and charm would have been enormous. Other versions bring one closer to the heart of this wonderful score; Muti leaves us admiring but unmoved. On CD the sharpness of detail and the 'digital edge' on the upper strings in fortissimo increase the feeling of aggressiveness.

Romeo and Juliet: Suites Nos 1 and 2: excerpts.
❀ *** Telarc Dig. **CD 80089** [id.]. Cleveland O, Yoel Levi.
(B) *** DG Walkman *413 430-4* [id.]. San Francisco SO, Ozawa – TCHAIKOVSKY: *Sleeping Beauty; Swan Lake*.**(*)

Levi offers by far the finest single disc of excerpts from Prokofiev's masterpiece, to provide a fitting legacy of his four-year term as resident conductor at Cleveland, 1980–84. The recording, made at Severance Hall in 1983, combines the spectacular and natural qualities we associate with Telarc in this venue: the strings sumptuous, the brass given a thrilling sonority and bite, and luminous woodwind detail registering within a believable overall balance. Levi draws wonderfully eloquent playing from his orchestra, its virtuosity always at the service of the music. He seems to have a special affinity with Prokofiev's score, for pacing is unerringly apt and characterization is strong. The high drama of the very opening is matched later by the power and thrust of the *Death of Tybalt*. There are some wonderfully serene moments, too, as in the ethereal introduction of the flute melody in the first piece (*Montagues and Capulets*), and the delicacy of the string playing in *Romeo at Juliet's tomb* – which explores the widest expressive range – is touching. The quicker movements have an engaging feeling of the dance and the light, graceful articulation in *The child Juliet* is a delight. Levi draws on both suites but intersperses the movements to create contrast and make dramatic sense. His telling portrayal of *Friar Lawrence* (violas and bassoons) is affectionately sombre; but the highlights of the performance are the *Romeo and Juliet love scene* (Suite 1, No. 6) and *Romeo at Juliet's before parting* (Suite 2, No. 5), bringing playing of great intensity, with a ravishing response from the Cleveland strings leading on from passionate yearning to a sense of real ecstasy.

This is also one of Ozawa's finest recordings. He draws warmly committed playing from the San Francisco orchestra, helped by vividly rich recording and this shorter selection from Prokofiev's ballet is well chosen. In his coupled excerpts from *Swan Lake* the music making is at a lower voltage, but Rostropovich's companion suite from the *Sleeping Beauty* is marvellous. At Walkman price, with excellent transfers, this is good value.

Romeo and Juliet: suite No. 3, Op. 101; (i) *Sinfonia concertante in E min., Op. 125*.
*** Chan. Dig. **CHAN 8508**; *ABTD 1218* [id.]. (i) Raphael Wallfisch; SNO, Järvi.

This splendid Chandos issue is the first account of the Prokofiev *Sinfonia concertante* to appear for some years and fills an important gap in the catalogue. In 1947 Prokofiev heard the young Rostropovich play his *Cello concerto* and decided that it needed drastic revision. The *Sinfonia concertante* was the new work that arose from the ashes of the old; even so, some element of uncertainty must have persisted in Prokofiev's mind, since he did not reject or disown the earlier concerto but described the new piece as 'a reworking' of the material of the first, 'made in collaboration with Mstislav Rostropovich'. Indeed, far from disowning it, he had doubts at one point in the *Sinfonia concertante* itself: the published score even provides an alternative episode in the middle of the finale, to which recourse is rarely made. Wallfisch has the measure of the leisurely first movement and gives a thoroughly committed account of the Scherzo and the Theme and Variations that follow, and Neeme Järvi lends him every support. It is inevitable that the cello should be given a little help by the microphone (as is the case in the previous versions) but it does seem a shade too forward. The fill-up, the third suite from *Romeo and Juliet*, is an excellent makeweight.

Romeo and Juliet: excerpts*; Symphony No. 1 in D (Classical), Op. 25.*
*(*) Decca Dig. **410 200-2** [id.]. Chicago SO, Solti.

Solti compiles a selection of his own from *Romeo and Juliet.* He is wholly unmannered and secures a brilliant response from the Chicago orchestra. The outer movements of the *Symphony* could do with more spontaneity and sparkle; the slow movement, however, has an occasional moment of charm. As far as the sound is concerned, there is spectacular presence and impact, a wide dynamic range and maximum detail. Alas, there is little distance to lend enchantment and many collectors will find everything fiercely overlit, especially on CD. Neither work comes anywhere near the top of the recommended list.

Scythian suite, Op. 20.
*** DG **410 598-2** [id.]. Chicago SO, Abbado – BARTÓK: *Miraculous Mandarin* etc.***

When it was first issued in 1978, Abbado's account of the *Scythian suite* was the best to have appeared for many years. It has drive and fire; if it displays less savagery than some previous versions, the Chicago orchestra have no want of power and Abbado achieves most refined colouring in the atmospheric *Night* movement. The enhancement of the CD remastering is striking: the focus is firmer, yet there is no loss of warmth and body.

Symphony No. 1 in D (Classical), Op. 25.
*** Decca **417 734-2**; *417 734-4* [id.]. ASMF, Marriner – BIZET: *Symphony*; STRAVINSKY: *Pulcinella.****
*** DG Dig. **400 034-2;** *3302 031* [id.]. BPO, Karajan – GRIEG: *Holberg suite*; MOZART: *Serenade: Eine kleine Nachtmusik.****
*** Delos Dig. **D/CD 3021** [id.]. LACO, Schwarz – SHOSTAKOVICH: *Piano concerto No. 1* **(*); STRAVINSKY: *Soldier's tale suite.****

Marriner's famous recording has been effectively remastered and sounds very fresh; although there has been some loss of bass response, the ambient warmth ensures that the sound retains its body and bloom. Marriner's tempi are comparatively relaxed, but the ASMF are in sparkling form and play beautifully in the slow movement. Detail is stylishly pointed (the bassoon solo in the first movement is a joy) and the finale is vivacious, yet elegant too. There is a splendid cassette.

Karajan's performance is predictably brilliant, the playing beautifully polished, with grace and eloquence distinguishing the slow movement. The outer movements are wanting in charm alongside Marriner. The recording is bright and clearly detailed, though the balance is not quite natural. The compact disc has the upper strings very brightly lit, with a touch of digital edge, but the ambience is attractive. This is also available at mid-price, coupled with Karajan's superb version of the *Fifth Symphony*.

Schwarz's version, if not quite as brilliant as Karajan's, is a nicely paced performance, the slow movement particularly pleasing in its relaxed lyricism and the finale sparkling with high spirits. It is very well played; the orchestra is naturally balanced within a fairly resonant acoustic which provides plenty of air round the instruments. The couplings are unusual and attractive.

Symphonies Nos 1 in D (*Classical*); *4 in C, Op. 112* (revised 1947 version).
*** Chan. Dig. **CHAN 8400**; *ABTD 1137* [id.]. SNO, Järvi.

Unlike the *Third*, the *Fourth Symphony* does not have quite the same independence, and its balletic origins are obvious, both in terms of the melodic substance and in its organization. Prokofiev himself recognized this and drastically revised the score later in life. The extent of this overhaul, made immediately after the completion of the *Sixth Symphony*, can be gauged by the fact that the 1930 version takes 23′ 08″ and the revision 37′ 12″. The first two movements are much expanded; indeed, in playing time the first is doubled, and the *Andante* is half as long again. The orchestration is richer; among other things, a piano, which Prokofiev had used in the *Fifth* and *Sixth Symphonies*, is added. Not all of Prokofiev's afterthoughts are improvements, but Järvi succeeds in making out a more eloquent case for the revision than many of his predecessors. He also gives an exhilarating account of the *Classical symphony*, one of the best on record. The slow movement has real *douceur* and the finale is wonderfully high-spirited. On CD, the recording has fine range and immediacy, but in the *Fourth Symphony* the upper range is a little fierce in some of the more forceful climaxes. The splendid chrome cassette, which is also extraordinarily vivid, seems slightly smoother, yet there is no sense of loss of range or detail.

Symphonies Nos 1 in D (*Classical*), *Op. 25; 5 in B flat, Op. 100.*
*** Ph. Dig. **420 172-2**; *420 172-4* [id.]. LAPO, Previn.
(M) *** DG **423 216-2;** *423 216-4* [id.]. BPO, Karajan.

Previn's version of the *Fifth* is an almost unqualified success; indeed it is one of the finest records he has made in recent years. In the first movement the pacing seems exactly right: everything flows so naturally and speaks effectively. The Scherzo is not as high voltage as some rivals, but Previn still brings it off well; and in the slow movement he gets playing of genuine eloquence from the Los Angeles orchestra. He also gives an excellent account of the perennially fresh *Classical symphony*. The recording is beautifully natural with impressive detail, range and body. This must rank among the finest available of both works in the CD format, and the chrome tape also offers excellent sound.

Karajan's 1979 recording of the *Fifth* is in a class of its own. The playing has wonderful tonal sophistication and Karajan judges tempi to perfection so that proportions seem quite perfect. The Berlin Philharmonic are at the height of their form; in their hands the Scherzo is a *tour de force*. The recording has an excellent perspective and allows all the subtleties of orchestral detail to register; however, the digital remastering has brightened the upper range, while the bass response is drier. Although the basic ambient effect remains, there is a fierceness on top at fortissimo level which was not present on the old analogue master. Nevertheless this remains among the most distinguished *Fifths* ever recorded, and is coupled with Karajan's 1982 digital recording of the *Classical symphony*, which is discussed above.

Symphonies Nos 1 (*Classical*); *7 in C sharp min., Op. 131; Lieutenant Kijé* (*suite*), *Op. 60.*
*** HMV **CDC7 47855-2** [id.]; (M) *EG 290298-4* [Ang. *4AM 34711*]. LSO, Previn.

Symphonies Nos 1 (*Classical*); *7, Op. 131; Love of 3 oranges* (opera): *suite.*
(B) *** CfP *TC-CFP 4523*. Philh. O, Malko.

In both symphonies (a popular coupling since the earliest days of LP) Previn is highly successful. He produces much inner vitality and warmth, and the EMI engineers provide a strikingly integrated sound. The *Classical symphony* is more successful here than in Previn's earlier version on RCA. It is genuinely sunlit and vivacious. Previn is obviously persuaded of the merits of the underrated and often beguiling *Seventh Symphony*. As a substantial bonus, Previn's colourful, swaggering performance of the *Lieutenant Kijé suite* has been added, yet the recording retains its full vividness and sparkle. The digital remastering has improved freshness and detail and there is only a very marginal loss of bloom in the upper range. The tape is very good too, although there are slight problems with the bass drum in both *Kijé* and the *Seventh Symphony*.

Malko's performances were recorded in 1955, and the accounts of the two symphonies were the first stereo EMI ever made. (They did not appear at the time.) All the performances are quite excellent, and the *Seventh Symphony*, of which Malko conducted the UK première, is freshly conceived and finely shaped. What is so stunning is the range and refinement of the recording: the excellence of the balance and the body of the sound are remarkable. No less satisfying is the suite from *Love of Three Oranges*, an additional bonus making this outstanding value.

Symphony No. 2 in D min., Op. 40; Romeo and Juliet (ballet)*: suite No. 1, Op. 64.*
(*) Chan. Dig. **CHAN 8368; *ABTD 1134* [id.]. SNO, Järvi.

The *Second Symphony* reflects the iconoclastic temper of the early 1920s; the violence and dissonance of its first movement betray Prokofiev's avowed intention of writing a work 'made of iron and steel'. It is obvious that Prokofiev was trying to compete with Mossolov and the *style mécanique* of Honegger in *Horace Victorieux* in orchestral violence, even if the unremitting and sustained *fortissimo* writing is at times self-defeating. In its formal layout (but in no other respect), the symphony resembles Beethoven's Op. 111, with two movements, the second of which is a set of variations. It is this movement that more than compensates for the excesses of its companion. It is rich in fantasy and some of the variations are wonderfully atmospheric. Neeme Järvi produces altogether excellent results from the Scottish National Orchestra and has great bite and character; indeed, he has a real flair for this composer. The Chandos recording in its CD form is impressively detailed and vivid. The *Romeo and Juliet suite* comes off well; the SNO play with real character, though the quality of the strings at the opening of the Madrigal is not luxurious. On the chrome cassette, the sound in the *Symphony*, though vivid, is also rather fierce, but in *Romeo and Juliet* a slight drop in the level brings a mellower balance, entirely to advantage.

Symphonies Nos 3 in C min., Op. 44; 4 in C, Op. 47 (original 1930 version)
*** Chan. Dig. **CHAN 8401**; *ABTD 1138* [id.]. SNO, Järvi.

Neeme Järvi's account of the *Third* is extremely successful. He is particularly successful in the *Andante*, which derives from the last act of the opera, *The Fiery Angel*, and succeeds in conveying its sense of magic and mystery. The opening idea is austere but lyrical, and the music to which it gives rise is extraordinarily rich in fantasy and clothed in an orchestral texture of great refinement and delicacy. In the Scherzo, said to have been inspired by the finale of Chopin's *B flat minor Sonata*, he secures a very good response from the SNO strings. If one had made the acquaintance of the expanded version first, the original of the *Fourth Symphony* would possibly seem more like a ballet suite than a symphony: its insufficient tonal contrast tells. Neither version has the degree of organic cohesion or symphonic drama of Nos 5 and 6, but both have delightful and characteristic ideas. The scherzo, drawn from the music for the Temptress in *The Prodigal Son* ballet, is particularly felicitous. The chrome tape is first class.

Symphonies Nos 4 in C, Op. 47; 7 in C sharp min., Op. 131.
* Erato Dig. **ECD 75322** [id.]. O Nat. de France, Rostropovich.

The playing of the Orchestre National is first class and the recording has impressive body and range, but Rostropovich is terribly heavy-handed. He is over-emphatic and very laboured; one longs for a lighter touch throughout. Incidentally, Rostropovich adopts the first finale-ending and not the perky variant. Although the 1930 version of the *Fourth Symphony* is much tauter than the 1947 revision, it certainly doesn't seem so here. The opening is very relaxed and the slow movement interminable. Normally this symphony takes about 22 or 23 minutes: on this record, in Rostropovich's hands it runs to over 28.

Symphony No. 5 in B flat, Op. 100.
*** Chan. Dig. **CHAN 8576**; *ABTD 1271* [id.]. Leningrad PO, Jansons.
(*) CBS Dig. **CD 35877. Israel PO, Bernstein.
(*) RCA Dig. **RD 85035 [**RCD1 5035**]. St Louis SO, Slatkin.

Symphony No. 5 in B flat, Op. 100; Dreams, Op. 6.
*** Decca Dig. **417 314-2**; *417 314-4* [id.]. Concg. O, Ashkenazy.

Symphony No. 5 in B flat, Op. 100; Waltz suite, Op. 110.
*** Chan. Dig. **CHAN 85450**; *ABTD 1160* [id.]. SNO, Järvi.

Mariss Jansons's reading with the Leningrad Philharmonic was recorded at a live concert in Dublin and it conveys tremendous excitement; it marks the orchestra's return to the recording catalogue after a long absence. Needless to say, the playing is pretty high voltage with firm, rich string tone, particularly from the lower strings, and distinctive wind timbre. The wind is not quite as refined as with Western orchestras but it is good to hear Prokofiev's writing in vivid primary colours. Jansons goes for brisk tempi – and in the slow movement he really is too fast. The movement lacks breadth, and in the closing measures there is insufficient poetry. The Scherzo is dazzling and so, too, is the finale, which is again fast and overdriven. An exhilarating and exciting performance, eminently well recorded too. For special occasions rather than everyday use perhaps, but strongly recommended – alongside but not in preference to Previn's, like Karajan's version, coupled to No. 1.

Järvi's credentials in this repertoire are well established and his direction unhurried, fluent and authoritative. His feeling for the music is unfailingly natural. Although Karajan's version remains in a class of its own, for those seeking a modern digital recording on CD Järvi would be a good choice. The three *Waltzes* which derive from various sources are all elegantly played. The Chandos recording is set just a shade further back than some of its companions in the series, making a little more of the hall's ambience. Yet at the same time every detail is clear, and the upper range is more telling than in either the RCA or CBS rivals. There is an excellent chrome cassette.

Ashkenazy's Decca record has two factors in its favour: the quite superb playing of the Concertgebouw Orchestra and a splendidly vivid recording, with every strand in the texture audible yet in the right perspective. It has marvellous presence and range. The fill-up is *Dreams*, composed in 1910 while Prokofiev was still a student. It is an atmospheric piece, indebted to Debussy and early Scriabin.

It would be easy to underestimate Bernstein's version. Edited from live performances, it is a consistently powerful reading, but with the romantic expressiveness underlined. Bernstein is superb at building climaxes and the playing has great concentration, but for some ears there is too much emotional weight. The recording is bold and full, with a strong, firm bass line in its CD format.

Slatkin's account is superbly recorded. On CD, the sound has a very wide dynamic range, and the acoustic glow of the hall does not prevent detail from emerging vividly. Slatkin's performance has an attractive freshness, and its directness is appealing, especially when the orchestral playing is both polished and responsive (though no match for Karajan's Berliners in the Scherzo). But it would be idle to pretend that Slatkin's reading – for all its volatile freedom – has the power of Bernstein's, nor is it as imaginative. The climax of the slow movement is greatly helped by the expansive RCA recording, but there is more grip in the Israel account. Even so, its lyrical innocence is certainly engaging, when the recording is so warmly flattering.

Symphony No. 6 in E flat min., Op. 111; Scythian suite, Op. 20.
*(*) Ph. Dig. **420 934-2**; *420 934-4* [id.]. LAPO, Previn.

Symphony No. 6 in E flat min., Op. 111. Waltz Suite, Op. 110, Nos 1, 5 and 6.
*** Chan. Dig. **CHAN 8359**; *ABTD 1122* [id.]. SNO, Järvi.

Though it lags far behind the *Fifth* in popularity, the *Sixth Symphony* goes much deeper than any of its companions; indeed, it is perhaps the greatest of the Prokofiev cycle. Neeme Järvi has an instinctive grasp and deep understanding of this symphony; he shapes its detail as skilfully as he does its architecture as a whole. The various climaxes are expertly built and related to one another, and the whole structure is held together in a way that recalls the most distinguished precedents. At times, however, one longs for greater sonority from the strings, who sound distinctly lean at the top and wanting in body and weight in the middle and lower registers, even in quieter passages. This may seem churlish when in all other respects the orchestra rises so magnificently to the challenges of this score and is obviously playing with such commitment. These artists have the measure of its tragic poignancy more than almost any of their predecessors on record. A word about the balance: it has the distinct merit of sounding well blended and in good perspective, at whatever dynamic level you choose to play it. If you want the impact of a forward place in the hall, a high-level setting does not disturb the effect of overall naturalness and warmth. The bass is particularly rich, finely detailed and powerful. There is a first-class matching chrome cassette. The fill-up, as its title implies, is a set of waltzes, drawn and adapted from various stage works: Nos 1 and 6 come from *Cinderella* and No. 5 from *War and Peace*.

Previn's record of the *Sixth Symphony* is a disappointment, all the more so since it is a remarkable recording, and he has a long-proven affinity with this composer. Indeed, this is without question state-of-the-art sound. It deserves the highest technical accolade and is wonderfully natural in every respect. Unfortunately Previn's excellently prepared performance is wanting in tension throughout, and in the *Scythian suite*, too. In spite of the fabulous sound, this does not displace the Järvi account on Chandos, which has greater intensity and personality. There is great refinement of texture and colour, but by comparison with earlier performances it is curiously low voltage.

Symphony No. 7 in C sharp min., Op. 131; Sinfonietta in A, Op. 5/48.
*** Chan. Dig. **CHAN 8442**; *ABTD 1154* [id.]. SNO, Järvi.

Neeme Järvi's account of the *Seventh Symphony* is hardly less successful than the other issues in this cycle. He gets very good playing from the SNO and has the full measure of this repertoire. Earlier recordings of the *Seventh* from Nicolai Malko, Rozhdestvensky and Previn have coupled it with the *Classical*, but Chandos are more enterprising, offering the early *Sinfonietta*. The Chandos digital recording has great range and, given the attractions of the coupling (what a sunny and charming piece it is!), must be a first choice. There is a superb chrome cassette, handling the wide dynamic range and resonant ambience with spectacular realism.

CHAMBER AND INSTRUMENTAL MUSIC

Cello sonata in C, Op. 119.

*** Chan. Dig. **CHAN 8340**; *ABTD 1072* [id.]. Yuli Turovsky. Luba Edlina – SHOSTAKOVICH: *Sonata.****

*** Max Sound *MSCB 20/21*; *MSCC 20/21*. Caroline Dale, Keith Swallow – BRIDGE: *Sonata****; DELIUS: *Sonata* **; MARTINŮ: *Variations.****

Yuli Turovsky and Luba Edlina are both members of the Borodin Trio; they are eloquent advocates of this *Sonata*, which is a late work dating from 1949 not currently available in any alternative form. Rostropovich and Richter recorded it in the days of mono LP, but its subsequent appearances on record have been few. A finely wrought and rewarding score, it deserves greater popularity, and this excellent performance and recording should make it new friends. The balance is particularly lifelike on CD. The chrome cassette has fine presence, but the high-level transfer brings a rather dry timbre to the cello's upper range.

The performance by Caroline Dale and Keith Swallow is also first rate: the playing has fervour and a strong and spontaneous impulse, and the recording is very well balanced. Tape collectors should certainly consider this generous anthology, available in both Dolby B and Dolby C configurations.

5 Mélodies (for violin & piano), *Op. 35.*

(M) *** Ph. **420 777-2** [id.]. David Oistrakh, Frida Bauer – DEBUSSY; RAVEL; YSAŸE: *Sonatas.****

These five pieces are rarities – surprisingly so, considering their appeal. They are inventive and charming, at times passionate, at others delectably intimate. Wonderful playing from Oistrakh and Frida Bauer, and the excellent recording is given new presence on CD without degradation of the timbre, using the computerized NoNoise system virtually to eliminate background. There is just a hint of shrillness on violin fortissimos above the stave; otherwise this is in the demonstration class.

String quartet No. 2 in F, Op. 92.

* Denon Dig. **C37 7814** [id.]. Prague Qt – BORODIN: *Quartet No. 2.**

In August 1941, two months after Hitler invaded the Soviet Union, Prokofiev, along with other Soviet composers, was evacuated to the northern Caucasus. Here he continued his labours on the opera, *War and Peace*, and made a study of the musical folklore of Kabarda. The outcome was this work, which he described as 'an attempt at the combination of one of the least-known varieties of folksong with the most classical form of the quartet'. He set to work on it in November and the piano score was ready within a month. It was first performed in Moscow in September 1942 by the Beethoven Quartet.

The Prague Quartet, alas, play with dogged rhythmic determination and a barely relieved forte and in the slow movement one longs for the poetic feeling this wonderful score calls for.

Violin sonatas Nos 1 in F min., Op. 80; 2 in D, Op. 94a.

*** Chan. Dig. **CHAN 8398**; *ABTD 1132* [id.]. Mordkovitch, Oppitz.

Lydia Mordkovitch and Gerhard Oppitz are the first artists to offer the two Prokofiev *Sonatas* on CD; though their accounts do not displace earlier versions by Oistrakh and Richter or Perlman and Ashkenazy from the memory, neither is readily available at the time of writing; in any case, the new performances make a worthy successor. They are both thoughtful readings with vital contributions from both partners. They have the measure of the darker, more searching side of the *F minor*, and are hardly less excellent in the companion. They also have the benefit of well-balanced Chandos recording. Both artists bring insights of their own to this music that make these performances well worth having. Tape collectors will find that the sound on the chrome cassette has good presence and realism, and that the slightly spiky quality on top – notably in No. 1 – is easily smoothed.

Piano sonata No. 3 in A min., Op. 28. 10 Pieces from Romeo and Juliet, Op. 75.
(*) Ph. Dig. **412 742-2**; *412 742-4* [id.]. Bella Davidovich – SCRIABIN: *Sonata No. 2* etc.(*)

No grumbles about the playing: Bella Davidovich, a first prize winner at Warsaw in 1949, is, as one might expect, no mean interpreter of Prokofiev – but alas, this record will not do. There is no space round the instrument at all: fortissimos are thunderous, the acoustic small and the microphones very closely placed – the octave below middle C is horribly near and the bass thick and tubby. An ugly sound, unusual for a piano recording from this source. The *Romeo and Juliet* transcription made in 1985, three years later than the rest of the record, is only a bit better. Not recommended.

Piano sonata No. 6 in A, Op. 82.
❀ *** DG Dig. **413 363-2** [id.]. Pogorelich – RAVEL: *Gaspard de la nuit.****

Pogorelich's performance of the *Sixth Sonata* is quite simply dazzling; indeed, it is by far the best version of it ever put on record and arguably the finest performance of a Prokofiev sonata since Horowitz's hair-raising account of the *Seventh.* It is certainly Pogorelich's most brilliant record so far and can be recommended with the utmost enthusiasm in its CD format.

Piano sonata No. 7 in B flat, Op. 83.
*** DG **419 202-2** [id.]. Maurizio Pollini – Recital.***

This is a great performance, well in the Horowitz or Richter category. It is part of a generous CD of twentieth-century music which combines the content of two LPs, although many readers who respond to Prokofiev and Pollini's outstanding account of Stravinsky's *Three movements from Petrushka* may find the accompanying works of Boulez and Webern less to their tastes, fine as the performances are.

Alexander Nevsky (cantata), *Op. 78.*
(*) Mobile Fidelity Dig. **MFCD 808 [id.]. Claudine Carlson, St Louis Ch. & SO, Slatkin.
** Decca Dig. **410 164-2** [id.]. Arkhipova, Cleveland Ch. & O, Chailly.

(i) *Alexander Nevsky, Op. 78; Lieutenant Kijé* (suite), *Op. 60.*
*** DG **419 603-2** [id.]. (i) Elena Obraztsova, LSO Ch.; LSO, Abbado.
** Telarc Dig. **CD 80143** [id.]. (i) Christine Cairns, LA Master Chorale, LAPO, Previn.

(i) *Alexander Nevsky, Op. 78; Scythian suite, Op. 20.*
*** Chan. Dig. **CHAN 8584**; *ABTD 1275* [id.]. (i) Linda Finnie, SNO Ch.; SNO, Järvi.

(i) *Alexander Nevsky, Op. 78;* (ii) *Seven, they are seven* (cantata), *Op. 30; Festival song* (*Zdravitsa*), *Op. 85.*
(*) Chant du Monde **LDC 278389 [id.]. (i) Avdeyeva RSFSR Russian Ch., USSR SO, Svetlanov; (ii) Elnikov, Ch., Moscow R. O, Rozhdestvensky.

Choice for this surprisingly well-represented work is essentially between Järvi and Abbado, although Svetlanov's version has especially compelling Russian qualities. Previn's newest Telarc recording does not quite match his earlier HMV account in bite and intensity: that is still available on tape only – see above, under *Lieutenant Kijé*.

Järvi has the advantage of superb Chandos digital recording; the expansive acoustics of Caird

Hall, Dundee, where the record was made, add an extra atmospheric dimension. The bitter chill of the Russian winter can be felt in the orchestra at the very opening and the melancholy of the choral entry has real Slavic feeling; later in their call to 'Arise, ye Russian people' there is an authentic good-humoured peasant robustness. With Järvi the climactic point is the enormously spectacular *Battle on the ice*, with the recording giving great pungency to the bizarre orchestral effects and the choral shouts riveting in their force and fervour. Linda Finnie sings the final lament eloquently and Järvi's apotheosis is very affecting, but at the close Obraztsova and Abbado create an even graver valedictory feeling which is unforgettable. Both are, nevertheless, outstandingly fine performances and choice between them may well be helped by the coupling. Järvi chooses the ballet *Ala and Lolly*, which was written originally for Diaghilev but was never performed, and subsequently became the *Scythian suite*. Its motoric rhythms are characteristic of the composer at his most aggressive, but the lyrical music is even more rewarding. There is an excellent Chandos cassette.

With playing and singing of great refinement as well as of power and intensity, Abbado's performance is one of the finest he has ever recorded with the LSO. One might argue that a rougher style is needed in what was originally film music, but the seriousness underlying the work is hardly in doubt when it culminates in so deeply moving a tragic inspiration as the lament after the battle (here very beautifully sung by Obraztsova) and when the battle itself is so fine an example of orchestral virtuosity. The chorus is as incisive as the orchestra. The digital remastering of the 1980 recording has been all gain and the sound is very impressive indeed, with great weight and impact and excellent balance. *Lieutenant Kijé* (1978) also sounds splendid and Abbado gets both warm and wonderfully clean playing from the Chicago orchestra.

Svetlanov's is a vigorous, earthy performance, given fine bite and presence in the remastering for CD, which gains enormously from the authentic sounds of a Russian chorus. The recording is not refined but has plenty of weight and body; though the ensemble does not match that of the best performances from the West, the urgency of the inspiration is most compelling, and the *Battle on the ice* sequence has a splendid cutting edge. What makes this CD doubly attractive is the inclusion of two important bonuses. *Seven, they are seven* is one of Prokofiev's most adventurous and original scores. It consists of a series of contrasting episodes in which the mood changes from venomous violence to mysteriously sombre evocation, with undertones of an ageless ritual. The effect is hallucinatory and immensely involving when the performance is so powerful. By contrast, the *Festival song* (*Zdravitsa*) is radiantly life-enhancing. By setting folk-texts from the various provinces, Prokofiev achieves an energetic kaleidoscope of peasant life, with a beautiful Ukrainian lullaby providing radiant contrast. The fervour of the performance is remarkable; and the CD brings a sharp focus to the singers, without loss of body.

The Mobile Fidelity recording is clearly aimed at audiophiles, but the balance is natural and believable. The sound is immensely spectacular and the *Battle on the ice* climax is quite overwhelming in its intensity, projection and amplitude. This CD with its very wide dynamic range is certainly not suitable for a small flat. At the opening Slatkin is spaciously evocative and he misses the chilling effect which Järvi captures; nevertheless his chorus sings eloquently and if overall this hastn't quite the grip of Järvi or Abbado, there is a very moving account of the *Lament* from Claudine Carlson, comparable with Obraztsova in its depth of elegiac feeling. Overall this is undoubtedly satisfying and may be a first choice for those with an elaborate reproducing system, for whom spectacle is a high priority.

The Telarc recording is spectacular too and the breadth of amplitude gives the chorus impressive weight in the closing section, *Alexander's entry into Pskov*. But Christine Cairns, although she sings sensitively, has not the depth which her finer competitors display in the *Lament*, and Previn does not find the exuberance and bite which made his earlier, LSO recording for EMI so outstanding. The suite from *Lieutenant Kijé* which acts as coupling is most attractively done, and here the Telarc engineers produce top-drawer recording to match the warmth of the orchestral playing.

Chailly has the advantage of full-blooded Decca digital sound, and its richness adds to the emotional weight of the opening sections. The *Battle on the ice* is characteristically impulsive and, with Irina Arkhipova touchingly expressive in her elegiac aria, Chailly finds an effective exuberance in the work's closing pages. The recording is not always ideally clear on detail, even on CD, although it is not short on spectacle and the chorus projects well, but this is not strongly competitive.

5 Poems of Anna Akhmatova, Op. 27; 2 Poems, Op. 9; 5 Poems of Konstantin Balmont, Op. 36; 3 Romances, Op. 73.
(*) Chan. Dig. **CHAN 8509; *ABTD 1219* [id.]. Carole Farley, Arkady Aronov.

Rare and valuable repertoire. Prokofiev wrote relatively few songs (no more than about forty, excluding folksong arrangements) yet his contribution to the genre, though small in quantity, was not negligible in quality. The two songs of Op. 9 are vaguely impressionist in feeling, though the first is the more imaginative. Otherwise the piano writing in these songs is thoroughly personal, nowhere more so than in the Op. 36 Balmont settings. The songs are powerful and full of resourceful and imaginative touches. The Akhmatova settings, Op. 27 (1916), reflect something of the romanticism of Scriabin, but there is some French influence (particularly Ravel) and Stravinsky. In any event they are quite beautiful. The *Three Romances*, Op. 73, to words of Pushkin, written at the time of the Pushkin centenary (1936) are full of the wry harmonic sleights of hand that are so characteristic of his musical speech. The American soprano, Carole Farley, responds to the different moods and character of the poems and encompasses a rather wide range of colour and tone, although at times her voice is rather edgy and uneven in timbre. She observes dynamic markings scrupulously. The accompanying of Arkady Aronov is highly sensitive and perceptive; his playing is a joy throughout. The recording is completely truthful.

Puccini, Giacomo (1858–1924)

Capriccio sinfonico; Crisantemi; Minuets Nos 1–3; Preludio sinfonico; Edgar: Preludes, Acts I and III. Manon Lescaut: Intermezzo, Act III. Le Villi: Prelude; La Tregenda (Act II).
*** Decca Dig. **410 007-2** [id.]. Berlin RSO, Chailly.

In a highly attractive collection of Puccinian juvenilia and rarities, Chailly draws opulent and atmospheric playing from the Berlin Radio Symphony Orchestra, helped by outstandingly rich and full recording. The compact disc is of demonstration quality. The *Capriccio sinfonico* of 1876 brings the first characteristically Puccinian idea in what later became the opening Bohemian motif of *La Bohème*. There are other identifiable fingerprints here, even if the big melodies suggest Mascagni rather than full-blown Puccini. *Crisantemi* (with the original string quartet scoring expanded for full string orchestra) provided material for *Manon Lescaut* as did the three little *Minuets*, pastiche eighteenth-century music.

Crisantemi for string quartet.
*** CRD *CRDC 4066* [id.]. Alberni Qt – DONIZETTI: *Quartet No. 13*; VERDI: *Quartet.****

Puccini's brief essay in writing for string quartet dates from the late 1880s. It is given a warm, finely controlled performance by the Alberni Quartet and makes a valuable makeweight for the two full-scale quartets by fellow opera-composers. The cassette transfer is of demonstration quality, admirably vivid and clear.

(i) *Crisantemi; Minuets 1–3; Quartet in A min.: Allegro moderato; Scherzo in A min.;* (ii) *Foglio*

d'album; Piccolo tango; (iii; ii) *Avanti Urania; E l'uccellino; Inno a Diana; Menti all'avviso; Morire?; Salve regina; Sole e amore; Storiella d'amore; Terra e mare.*
*** Etcetera **KTC 1050**. (i) Raphael Qt; (ii) Tan Crone; (iii) Roberta Alexander.

This is an essential disc for Puccini-fanciers out to investigate the rare non-operatic corners of the master's *œuvre*. These chips off the work-bench, both early and mature, revealingly illuminate what we know of him. It is fascinating to find among early, rather untypical songs like *Storiella d'amore* and *Menti all'avviso* a charming little song, *Sole e amore*, written jokingly for a journal, 'Paganini', in 1888, which provided, bar for bar, the main idea of the Act III quartet in *La Bohème* of eight years later. Puccini's melodic flair comes out in such a song as *E l'uccellino*, written in Neapolitan style, and there is a rousing homophonic hymn for his fellow-huntsmen in *Inno a Diana*, while *Avanti Urania!* improbably was written to celebrate the launching of a titled friend's steam-yacht. The two piano pieces are simple album-leaves; among the six quartet pieces, *Crisantemi* is already well known for providing material for Act IV of *Manon Lescaut*. The rest are student pieces, including a delightful fragment of a Scherzo. Performances are good, though Roberta Alexander's soprano is not ideally Italianate. The recorded sound is vivid and immediate against a lively hall ambience.

Messa di Gloria.
*** Erato Dig. **ECD 88022** [id.]. Carreras, Prey, Amb. S., Philh. O, Scimone.

Puccini's *Messa di Gloria*, completed when he was only twenty, some 15 years before his first fully successful opera, has a vigour and memorability to put it within hailing distance (but no more) of the masterpiece which plainly inspired it, Verdi's *Requiem*, first given only six years earlier. The bold secularity of some of the ideas, as for example the brassy march for the *Gloria* itself, is very much in the Italian tradition, perilously skirting the edge of vulgarity. Scimone and a fine team are brisker and lighter than their predecessors on record, yet effectively bring out the red-bloodedness of the writing. José Carreras turns the big solo in the *Gratias* into the first genuine Puccini aria. His sweetness and imagination are not quite matched by the baritone, Hermann Prey, who is given less to do than usual, when the choral baritones take on the yearning melody of *Crucifixus*. Excellent, atmospheric sound.

OPERA MUSIC

La Bohème (complete).
*** HMV mono **CDS7 47235-8** (2). De los Angeles, Bjoerling, Merrill, Reardon, Tozzi, Amara, RCA Victor Ch. & O, Beecham.
*** Decca **421 049-2** (2) [id.]. Freni, Pavarotti, Harwood, Panerai, Ghiaurov, German Op. Ch., Berlin, BPO, Karajan.
(*) RCA **RD 80371 [**RCD2 0371**]. Caballé, Domingo, Milnes, Sardinero, Raimondi, Blegen, Alldis Ch., Wandsworth School Boys' Ch., LPO, Solti.
(*) Decca **411 868-2 (2) [id.]. Tebaldi, Bergonzi, Bastianini, Siepi, Corena, D'Angelo, St Cecilia Ac. Ch. & O, Rome, Serafin.
(***) HMV mono **CDS7 47475-8** (2) [id.]; (M) *EX 290923-5*. Callas, Di Stefano, Moffo, Panerai, Zaccaria, La Scala, Milan, Ch. & O, Votto.
** Erato Dig. **ECD 75450** (2) [id.]. Hendricks, Carreras, Quilico, Blasi, Davia, Ch. & O Nat. de France, Conlon.
(B) ** HMV *TCC2-POR 1545999*. Freni, Gedda, Adani, Sereni, Rome Op. Ch. & O, Schippers.
(B) ** CfP *TC-CFPD 4708*. Scotto, Kraus, Milnes, Neblett, Plishka, Manuguerra, Trinity Boys' Ch., Amb. Op. Ch., Nat. PO, Levine.
(M) ** RCA **GD 83969** (2); [**RCA-3969-2-RG**]. Moffo, Costa, Tucker, Merrill, Tozzi, Rome Opera Ch. & O, Leinsdorf.

** Ph. **416 492-2** (2) [id.]. Ricciarelli, Carreras, Wixell, Putnam, Hagegard, ROHCG Ch. & O, C. Davis.

Beecham recorded his classic interpretation of *Bohème* in 1956 in sessions in New York that were arranged at the last minute. It was a gamble getting it completed, but the result was incandescent, a unique performance with two favourite singers, Victoria de los Angeles and Jussi Bjoerling, challenged to their utmost in loving, expansive singing. Its magic is vividly caught on CD, triumphing over any limitations in the mono sound. The voices are far better treated than the orchestra, which is rather thinner-sounding than it has been on LP, though as ever the benefits of silent background are very welcome in so warmly atmospheric a reading. With such a performance one hardly notices the recording, but those who want fine modern stereo can turn readily to Karajan.

The rich sensuousness of Karajan's highly atmospheric reading is all the more vivid on CD, with the clean placing of voices enhancing the performance's dramatic warmth. He too takes a characteristically spacious view of *Bohème*, but there is an electric intensity which holds the whole score together as in a live performance – a reflection no doubt of the speed with which the recording was made, long takes the rule. Karajan unerringly points the climaxes with full force, highlighting them against prevailing pianissimos. Pavarotti is an inspired Rodolfo, with comic flair and expressive passion, while Freni is just as seductive a Mimi as she was in the Schippers set ten years earlier. Elizabeth Harwood is a charming Musetta, even if her voice is not as sharply contrasted with Freni's as it might be. Fine singing throughout the set. The reverberant Berlin acoustic is glowing and brilliant in superb Decca recording.

The glory of Solti's set of *Bohème* is the singing of Montserrat Caballé as Mimi, an intensely characterful and imaginative reading which makes you listen with new intensity to every phrase, the voice at its most radiant. Domingo is unfortunately not at his most inspired. *Che gelida manina* is relatively coarse, though here as elsewhere he produces glorious heroic tone, and never falls into vulgarity. The rest of the team is strong, but Solti's tense interpretation of a work he had never conducted in the opera house does not quite let the full flexibility of the music have its place or the full warmth of romanticism. However, the RCA recording – disappointing on LP – acquires extra brightness and clarity in the digital transfer to CD, to give extra point and sparkle to the performance.

The earlier Decca set with Tebaldi and Bergonzi was technically an outstanding recording in its day. Vocally the performance achieves a consistently high standard, Tebaldi as Mimi the most affecting: she offers some superbly controlled singing, but the individuality of the heroine is not as indelibly conveyed as with De los Angeles, Freni or Caballé. Carlo Bergonzi is a fine Rodolfo; Bastianini and Siepi are both superb as Marcello and Colline, and even the small parts of Benoit and Alcindoro (as usual taken by a single artist) have the benefit of Corena's magnificent voice. The veteran Serafin was more vital here than on some of his records. The recording, now nearly thirty years old, has its vividness and sense of stage perspective enhanced on CD, with minimal residue tape hiss, though the age of the master shows in the string timbre above the stave.

Callas, flashing-eyed and formidable, may seem even less suited to the role of Mimi than to that of Butterfly, but characteristically her insights make for a vibrantly involving performance. The set is worth getting for Act III alone, where the predicament of Mimi has never been more heartrendingly conveyed in the recording studio. Though Giuseppe di Stefano is not the subtlest of Rodolfos, he is in excellent voice here, and Moffo and Panerai make a strong partnership as the second pair of lovers. Votto occasionally coarsens Puccini's score – as in the crude crescendo in the closing bars of Act III – but he directs with energy. The comparatively restricted dynamic range means that the singers appear to be 'front stage', but there is no lack of light and shade in Act II. The orchestra sounds full and warm, and the voices are clearly and vividly caught, the more so on CD, though the mono sound cannot match in its perspectives the range of the best stereo versions. The cassettes are offered at mid-price but are poorly documented, and here the recording sounds even more restricted.

Following up the big box-office success of its *Carmen* film, with its attendant recording used for the sound-track, Erato presents an equivalent recording of *Bohème* for its Luigi Comencini film of the opera. It is a characterful reading, fluently conducted by James Conlon, though with sticky, over-exaggerated passages that may have been influenced by the two principal singers. José Carreras, making his last recording before his serious illness, gives a far freer, more varied and detailed account of Rodolfo's part then he did for Sir Colin Davis on the Philips set. There are moments of strain in *Che gelida manina* but a resonantly rich conclusion, which is reinforced by the close placing of the voice. Barbara Hendricks makes a provocative Mimi, at times minx-like, vulnerable but not in any way an innocent. Much of her singing is seductive to match the character, but with her the closeness of balance brings out any unevenness in the production, with some ungainly portamento, as in *Sì, mi chiamano Mimì*. Through the closeness of recording there is a hint of breathiness, as there also is with the Musetta of Angela Maria Blasi, a singer who might easily have been chosen as Mimi, warm and appealing but not really contrasted enough with Hendricks. Gino Quilico makes a magnificent, dark-toned Marcello, but the other two Bohemians are undistinctive, and Federico Davia's Benoit takes aged grotesquerie to the limit. With the orchestral sound set back and lacking a little in body, the recording has an edge that to a degree detracts from realism and presence.

HMV have reissued the Schippers 1964 *Bohème* on a single extended-length tape. The use of iron-oxide stock, even with the XDR monitoring system, means that the upper range is not quite as sharply focused as on the discs (which are still available in the USA), but the resonant acoustic is attractive and there is no lack of vividness. The presentation includes a plot summary instead of a libretto, but with the four Acts pairing neatly between the two sides (with only two seconds difference in their combined timing) the layout is convenient and this is a bargain. Freni's characterization of Mimi is so enchanting that it is worth ignoring some of the less perfect elements. The engineers placed Freni rather close to the microphone, which makes it hard for her to sound tentative in her first scene, but the beauty of the voice is what one remembers, and from there to the end her performance is conceived as a whole, leading to a supremely moving account of the death scene. Nicolai Gedda's Rodolfo is not rounded in the traditional Italian way but there is never any doubt about his ability to project a really grand manner of his own. Thomas Schippers' conducting starts as though this is going to be a hard-driven, unrelenting performance, but quickly after the horse-play he shows his genuinely Italianate sense of pause, giving the singers plenty of time to breathe and allowing the music to expand.

At a comparable price on CfP comes the 1980 HMV set, conducted by James Levine. Alfredo Kraus's relatively light tenor sets the pattern at the very start for a performance that is strong on comedy. One registers the exchanges more sharply than usual on record, and though Kraus (no longer as sweet of timbre as he was) tends to over-point in the big arias, it is a stylish performance. Scotto – who first recorded the role of Mimi for DG in 1962 – is not flatteringly recorded here, for the rawness and unevenness which affect her voice at the top of the stave are distracting, marring an affectionate portrait. Milnes makes a powerful Marcello and Neblett a strong Musetta, a natural Minnie in *Fanciulla* transformed into a soubrette. Levine, brilliant in the comic writing of Acts I and IV, sounds less at home in the big melodies. The recording has plenty of warmth and atmosphere, and its resonance has not blunted the tape transfer too much: the voices ride naturally over the rich orchestral texture.

The main recommendation for Leinsdorf's version from the 1960s is that it comes at mid-price in RCA's Victor CD Opera Series. Moffo is an affecting Mimi, Mary Costa a characterful Musetta, while Merrill and Tozzi provide strong support. Tucker gives a positive characterization as Rodolfo, though as ever he has lachrymose moments. Sadly, Leinsdorf's rigid direction, with speed fluctuations observed by instruction and never with natural expression, sets the singers against a deadpan, unsparkling accompaniment. Dated but acceptable recording.

The CD transfer in its clarity and sharp focus underlines the unidiomatic quality of Davis's reading, with un-Italianate singers like Ingvar Wixell and Ashley Putnam in key roles. As in *Tosca*, Sir Colin Davis here takes a direct view of Puccini, presenting the score very straight, with no exaggerations. The result is refreshing but rather lacks wit and sparkle; pauses and hesitations are curtailed. Ricciarelli's is the finest performance vocally, and Davis allows her more freedom than the others. *Sì, mi chiamano Mimì* is full of fine detail and most affecting. Carreras gives a good generalized performance, wanting in detail and in intensity and rather failing to rise to the big moments. Wixell makes an unidiomatic Marcello, rather lacking in fun, and Robert Lloyd's bass sounds lightweight as Colline. Ashley Putnam makes a charming Musetta, but at full price this is not really a competitive set.

La Bohème: scenes and arias.
(*) Decca **421 301-2; *417 335-4* [id.] (from above recording with Tebaldi and Bergonzi, cond. Serafin).

Most collectors will surely want a reminder of this vintage set with Tebaldi and Bergonzi at the height of their powers. The selection is well made, and the disc and tape are competitively priced.

La Fanciulla del West (*The Girl of the Golden West;* complete).
(M) *** DG **419 640-2** (2) [id.]. Neblett, Domingo, Milnes, Howell, ROHCG Ch. and O, Mehta.

Like *Madama Butterfly*, '*The Girl*', as Puccini called it in his correspondence, was based on a play by the American David Belasco. The composer wrote the work with all his usual care for detailed planning, both of libretto and of music. In idiom the music marks the halfway stage between *Butterfly* and *Turandot*.

DG took the opportunity of recording the opera when Covent Garden was staging a spectacular production in 1977. With one exception the cast remained the same as in the theatre and, as so often in such associated projects, the cohesion of the performance in the recording is enormously intensified. The result is magnificent, underlining the point that – whatever doubts may remain over the subject, with its weeping goldminers – Puccini's score is masterly, culminating in a happy ending which brings one of the most telling emotional coups that he ever achieved. Mehta's manner – as he makes clear at the very start – is on the brisk side, not just in the cakewalk rhythms but even in refusing to let the first great melody, the nostalgic *Che faranno i viecchi miei*, linger into sentimentality. Mehta's tautness then consistently makes up for intrinsic dramatic weaknesses (as, for example, the delayed entries of both heroine and hero in Act I). Sherrill Milnes as Jack Rance was the newcomer to the cast for the recording, and he makes the villain into far more than a small-town Scarpia, giving nobility and understanding to the first-Act *arioso*. Domingo, as in the theatre, sings heroically, disappointing only in his reluctance to produce soft tone in the great aria *Ch'ella mi creda*. The rest of the Covent Garden team is excellent, not least Gwynne Howell as the minstrel who sings *Che faranno i viecchi miei*; but the crowning glory of a masterly set is the singing of Carol Neblett as the Girl of the Golden West herself, gloriously rich and true and with formidable attack on the exposed high notes. Full, atmospheric recording to match, essential in an opera full of evocative offstage effects. The CD transfer captures the fullness and boldness of the original DG recording, but the slight drying-out process of the digital sound adds some stridency in tuttis, readily acceptable with so strong a performance.

Gianni Schicchi (complete).
*** Ariola-Eurodisc Dig. **258404** [id.]. Panerai, Donath, Seiffert, Munich R. O, Patané.
(*) Hung. Dig. **HCD 12541 [id.]. Melis, Kalmar, Gulya, Hungarian State Op. O, Ferencsik.

Like the parallel version of *Il Tabarro*, the first of the three *Trittico* one-acters, the Ariola Eurodisc record of *Gianni Schicchi* brings a co-production with Bavarian Radio, and the recording is similarly vivid and well balanced. Again Patané conducts a colourful and vigorous performance, very well drilled in ensembles, even when speeds are dangerously fast, and with the voices nicely spaced to allow the elaborate details of the plot to be appreciated by ear alone. Central to the performance's success is the vintage Schicchi of Rolando Panerai, still rich and firm. He confidently characterizes the Florentine trickster in every phrase, building a superb portrait, finely timed. Peter Seiffert as Rinuccio gives a dashing performance, consistently clean and firm of tone, making light of the high tessitura, and rising splendidly to the challenge of the big central aria. Helen Donath would have sounded even sweeter a few years ago, but she gives a tender, appealing portrait of Lauretta, pretty and demure in *O mio babbino caro*. Though Italian voices are in the minority, it is a confident team. Like *Il Tabarro*, the single disc comes in a double jewel-case and sadly, like that companion issue, has only two tracks, the second starting immediately after, not before, *O mio babbino caro*. Why will record companies not wake up to the necessary facilities of CD?

Ferencsik conducts all-Hungarian forces in an energetic and well-drilled account of Puccini's comic masterpiece, which makes up for some unidiomatic rigidity with red-blooded commitment. The singing is variable, with the incidental characters including some East European wobblers. György Melis is not always perfectly steady, but his is a fine, characterful reading, strongly projected; though Magda Kalmar sounds too mature for the girlish Lauretta, the tone is attractively warm and finely controlled, as is Denes Gulya's tenor in the role of Rinuccio. It is a pity that the CD has no banding whatever.

Madama Butterfly (complete).
*** Decca **417 577-2** (3) [id.]. Freni, Ludwig, Pavarotti, Kerns, V. State Op. Ch., VPO, Karajan.
(*) Decca **411 634-2; (M) *411 634-4* (2) [id.]. Tebaldi, Bergonzi, Cossotto, Sordello, St Cecilia Ac. Ch. & O, Serafin.
(*) HMV **CDS7 49575-2 (2) [id.]; (B) CfP *CFPD 41 4446-5*. De los Angeles, Bjoerling, Pirazzini, Sereni, Rome Op. Ch. & O, Santini.
(*) CBS **M2K 35181 (2) [id.]. Scotto, Domingo, Knight, Wixell, Amb. Op. Ch., Philh. O, Maazel.
(***) HMV mono **CDS7 47959-8** [id.]; (M) *EX 291265-5* (2). Callas, Gedda, Borriello, Danieli, La Scala, Milan, Ch. & O, Karajan.
** RCA **RD 86160** [**RCA 6160-2-RC**]. Leontyne Price, Tucker, Elias, Maero, RCA Italiana Ch. & O, Leinsdorf.
** Hung. **HCD 12256-7** [id.]. Kincses, Dvorský, Takács, Miller, Hungarian State Op. Ch. & O, Patané.

The sensuousness of Karajan's gloriously rich reading comes out all the more ravishingly on CD. Though the set is extravagantly laid out on three discs instead of two for most of the rival sets – slow speeds partly responsible – there is the clear advantage that each act is complete on a single disc. Karajan inspires singers and orchestra to a radiant performance which brings out all the beauty and intensity of Puccini's score, sweet but not sentimental, powerfully dramatic but not vulgar. He pays the composer the compliment of presenting each climax with precise dynamics, fortissimos surprisingly rare but those few presented with cracking impact. Freni is an enchanting Butterfly, consistently growing in stature from the young girl to the victim of tragedy, sweeter of voice than any rival on record. Pavarotti is an intensely imaginative Pinkerton, actually inspiring understanding for this thoughtless character, while Christia Ludwig is a splendid Suzuki. The recording is one of Decca's most resplendent, with the Vienna strings producing glowing tone.

Serafin's sensitive and beautifully paced reading is on two discs merely and is even cheaper in its excellent tape format. Tebaldi is at her most radiant. Though she was never the most deft of Butterflies dramatically (she never actually sang the role on stage before recording it), her singing is consistently rich and beautiful, breathtakingly so in passages such as the one in Act I where she tells Pinkerton she has changed her religion. The excellence of Decca engineering in 1958 is amply proved in the CD transfer, with one serious exception. The very opening with its absence of bass brings a disagreeably shrill and thin sound, promptly corrected once the orchestration grows fuller, with voices very precisely and realistically placed. Each of the two CDs has over 70 minutes of music and is generously banded.

In the late 1950s and early 1960s, Victoria de los Angeles was also memorable in the role of Butterfly, and her 1960 recording displays her art at its most endearing, her range of golden tone-colour lovingly exploited, with the voice well recorded for the period, though rather close. Opposite her, Jussi Bjoerling was making one of his very last recordings, and though he shows few special insights, he produces a flow of rich tone to compare with that of the heroine. Mario Sereni is a full-voiced Sharpless, but Miriam Pirazzini is a disappointingly wobbly Suzuki; while Santini is a reliable, generally rather square and unimaginative conductor who rarely gets in the way. With recording quality freshened, this fine set is most welcome either on a pair of CDs or, still sounding bright and clear, in its bargain-priced cassette format (offered in a chunky box with a synopsis rather than a libretto).

Maazel's CBS version brings the advantage on CD that a relatively modern recording is transferred on to two discs instead of three; but the digital transfer, in underlining the clarity and incisiveness of Maazel's reading, makes it sound even less persuasively natural, all too tautly controlled. Scotto, who assumes the title role, had recorded the opera previously with Barbirolli, but the late CBS version brought nothing but benefit. The voice – always inclined to spread a little on top at climaxes – had acquired extra richness and was recorded with a warmer tonal bloom. In perception too Scotto's singing is far deeper, most strikingly in Butterfly's *Un bel dì*, where the narrative leads to special intensity on the words *Chiamerà Butterfly dalla lontana*. Maazel is warmly expressive without losing his architectural sense; he has not quite the imaginative individuality of a Karajan or a Barbirolli, but this is both powerful and unsentimental, with a fine feeling for Puccini's subtle orchestration. Other contributors are incidental, even Placido Domingo, who sings heroically as Pinkerton but arguably makes him too genuine a character for such a cad. Wixell's voice is not ideally rounded as Sharpless, but he sings most sensitively, and Gillian Knight makes an expressive Suzuki. Among the others Malcolm King as the Bonze is outstanding in a good team.

The idea of the flashing-eyed Maria Callas playing the role of the fifteen-year-old Butterfly may not sound convincing, and certainly this performance will not satisfy those who insist that Puccini's heroine is a totally sweet and innocent character. But Callas's view, aided by superbly imaginative and spacious conducting from Karajan, gives extra dimension to the Puccinian little woman, and with some keenly intelligent singing too from Gedda as Pinkerton (a less caddish and more thoughtful character than usual) this is a set which has a special compulsion. The performance projects the more vividly on CD, even though the lack of stereo in so atmospheric an opera is a serious disadvantage. Yet the powerful combination of Callas and Karajan – each challenging the other both in expressive imagination and in discipline – makes a powerful effect on the listener; unlike Karajan's later and more sumptuous Decca version with Freni, this one is fitted on to two CDs only. The cassettes are acceptable, but the sound is more confined than on the discs.

Leontyne Price was in glorious voice when, in July 1962, she recorded this opera under Erich Leinsdorf. This is a weighty portrait of Butterfly, with Price's gloriously rich, creamy tone seamlessly controlled, even if occasionally she indulges in unwanted portamenti. The obvious snag is that some of the vocal acting sounds too crude for Puccini's little woman, and Tucker is at times similarly coarse as Pinkerton. Added to that, what puts the set finally out of court is Leinsdorf's extraordinarily metrical and unresilient conducting, and with that rigidity comes a straitjacketing of emotion. At full price it is not really competitive, though on two discs with the break in Act II well placed immediately after *Un bel dì*, the layout is both convenient and economical.

Recorded in 1981 in analogue sound, vividly remastered for CD, the Hungaroton set presents a warm, idiomatically conducted reading with dramatically convincing performances from the principals. Peter Dvorský's clear, fresh tenor takes well to recording; he gives an attractively lyrical performance as Pinkerton, sweet and concerned rather than an ardent lover in Act I. He remains a recessive character next to the Butterfly of Veronika Kincses who emerges as an attractively girlish figure with facial expression made clear in every phrase. For all the natural vibrancy there is no suspicion of a wobble, and it is only when the voice is pressed in the upper register that the tone hardens in vocal as well as dramatic terms from girlish tones through increasing warmth and on to growing maturity in Act II. Sadly, the least attractive singing comes in the final suicide aria, but Patené's commitment carries one over that. Lajos Miller makes a young-sounding Sharpless, pleasing of tone, while Klara Takács is a fruity, positive Suzuki and József Gregor a firmly resonant Bonze, impressive in the curse.

Madama Butterfly: highlights.
(*) Decca **417 733-2 [id.] (from above recording with Tebaldi and Bergonzi, cond. Serafin).

Like the companion disc of excerpts from *La Bohème*, this includes the key scenes including the *Love duet*, *Flower duet* and finale, and although at 51 minutes it is not especially generous, it still makes a superb reminder of the magnetism of the Tebaldi/Bergonzi partnership. The sound is rich in ambience and the dated upper string timbre is seldom distracting, for the voices are vividly caught.

Manon Lescaut (complete).
*** DG Dig. **413 893-2** (2) [id.]. Freni, Domingo, Bruson, ROHCG Ch., Philh. O, Sinopoli.
(M) (***) HMV mono **CDS7 47393-8**; (M) *EX 290041-5* (2). Callas, Di Stefano, Fioravanti, La Scala, Milan, Ch. and O, Serafin.
** HMV **CDS7 47736-8** (2) [id.]; (M) *EX 291175-5*. Caballé, Domingo, Sardinero, Mangin, Tear, Amb. Op. Ch., New Philh. O, Bartoletti.

After years of neglect from the record companies, Sinopoli's brilliant version of Puccini's first fully successful opera provides in almost every way the answer most Puccinians have been waiting for. With his concern for detail, his love of high dramatic contrasts, and the clear pointing of changes of mood, along with sharp control of tension, the plan of each Act is presented with new precision, reflecting the composer's own careful crafting. This is also the most sensuous-sounding reading on record, thanks also to the fine playing of the Philharmonia, taking over in what is in most respects a recording of the Covent Garden production. Plainly the chorus has benefited from having also worked with Sinopoli in the opera house, and Placido Domingo's portrait of Des Grieux is here far subtler and more detailed, with finer contrasts of tone and dynamic, than in his earlier EMI recording opposite Caballé. The nicely shaded legato of *Donna non vidi mai* in Act I contrasts with an Othello-like outburst on *No, no pazzo son*, making a shattering conclusion to Act III. Freni, taking the place of Kiri Te Kanawa in the stage production, proves an outstanding choice. Her girlish tones in Act I rebut any idea that she might be too mature. *In quelle trine morbide*, in Act II, retains freshness of tone with fine concern for word detail, while the long duet and aria of the last Act present a most moving culmination, not feeling like an epilogue. Freni and Sinopoli together bring a ravishing change of mood on the unexpected modulation from F minor to D flat on *Terra de pace* in that scene, a wonderful moment of stillness to heighten the impact of *Non voglio morir*. Of the others, a first-rate team, Renato Bruson nicely brings out the ironic side of Lescaut's character, and having Brigitte Fassbaender just to sing the madrigal adds to the feeling of luxury, as does John Tomlinson's darkly intense moment of drama as the ship's captain, bringing the happy resolution in Act III. The voices are more recessed than is common, but they are recorded with fine bloom, and the brilliance of the orchestral sound comes out particularly impressively on CD, which has the benefit of being on two discs, instead of three for LP.

The early La Scala mono set partnering Callas and Di Stefano has striking individuality and dramatic power. It is typical of Callas that she turns the final scene – which often seems an excrescence, a mere epilogue after the real drama – into the most compelling part of the opera. Serafin, who could be a lethargic recording conductor, is here electrifying, and Di Stefano too is inspired to one of his finest complete opera recordings. The cast-list even includes the young Fiorenza Cossotto, impressive as the singer in the Act II madrigal. The recording – still in mono, not a stereo transcription – minimizes the original boxiness and gives good detail. The CD transfer refines the boxiness a degree further than the LPs, but for once the new medium loses out when, unlike LP, a break is involved in Act II between the two discs, where LP had that Act complete on one side.

The EMI version conducted by Bartoletti is chiefly valuable for the beautiful performance of Montserrat Caballé as the heroine, one of her most affecting, with the voice alluringly beautiful. Her account of *In quelle trine morbide* is lightly flowing, while the big Act IV aria is strong and positive. Otherwise the set is disappointing, with Placido Domingo unflattered by the close acoustic, not nearly as perceptive as in his much later DG performance under Sinopoli. Bartoletti's conducting is also relatively coarse, with the very opening forced and breathless. The digital transfer on CD adds to the harsh glare of the 1972 analogue recording.

La Rondine (complete).
*** CBS Dig. **M2K 37852** [id.]. Te Kanawa, Domingo, Nicolesco, Rendall, Nucci, Watson, Knight, Amb. Op. Ch., LSO, Maazel.

Even more than usually, the gains in vividness and immediacy and the sense of the singers' presence is striking when comparing CD with LP in this fine CBS set. The precision of the vocal placing is determined with striking realism, so that the interplay between the characters is very tangible against the background silence. The orchestra too is beautifully caught, while off-stage effects are nicely managed. *La Rondine* was a product of the First World War, and though in subject nothing could be less grim than this frothy tale told in Viennese operetta-style, the background to its composition and production may have had their effect. It has never caught on, and a recording like this will almost certainly surprise anyone at the mastery of the piece, with a captivating string of catchy numbers. The story is based on a watered-down *Traviata* situation, culminating not in tragedy but in a sad-sweet in-between ending such as the Viennese (for whom it was written) loved. It is not just a question of Puccini taking Viennese waltzes as model but all kinds of other suitable dances such as tangos, foxtrots and two-steps. Not aggressively at all, for, as with so much that this most eclectic of composers 'cribbed', he commandeered them completely, to make the result utterly Puccinian. If there is a fault, it lies in the inability of the story to move the listener with any depth of feeling, but a recording does at least allow one to appreciate each tiny development with greater ease than in the theatre.

Maazel's is a strong, positive reading crowned by a superb, radiant Magda in Dame Kiri Te

Kanawa, mature yet glamorous. From the stratospheric phrases in *Il sogno di Doretta* which are headily beautiful, her performance has one spellbound. Domingo, by age too mature for the role of young hero, yet scales his voice down most effectively in the first two Acts, expanding in heroic warmth only in the final scene of dénouement. Sadly the second pair are far less convincing, when the voices of both Mariana Nicolesco and David Rendall take ill to the microphone. Others in the team are excellent, and though Maazel launches the very opening too aggressively, the rest is most sympathetically done, with fine playing from the LSO. One's only real criticism is the lack of access within the opera itself. Acts I and II are on the first disc, Act III on the second, but there are no cues to find individual arias.

Suor Angelica (complete).
(*) Hung. Dig. **HCD 12490 [id.]. Tokody, Poka, Barlay, Takacs, Hungarian State Op. Ch. and O, Gardelli.

Gardelli conducts a beautifully paced reading, marked by effective characterization from the Hungarian cast (suggesting stage experience) and vivid, lifelike digital sound. Ilona Tokody makes an attractively girlish-sounding Angelica, but above the stave her voice is shrill. The Zia Principessa of Eszter Poka is breathy and wobbly and not even formidable, the one unconvincing characterization.

Il Tabarro (complete).
(*) Ariola Eurodisc Dig. **258403 [id.]. Nimsgern, Tokody, Lamberti, Munich R. O, Patané.

Puccini's essay in Grand Guignol comes in a powerful performance from Munich forces under Patané, a co-production between Ariola Eurodisc and Bavarian Radio. Patané in his larger-than-life direction may at times run the risk of exaggerating the melodrama, but the result is richly enjoyable, less delicately atmospheric than it can be in its dark picture of the Seine under the bridges of Paris, but satisfyingly red-blooded. Ilona Tokody, already well known from Hungaroton opera sets, makes a powerful, strongly projected Giorgetta, somewhat showing up the relative weakness of the tenor, Giorgio Lamberti, as her lover, Luigi. His over-emphatic underlining mars his legato, but the main love duet comes over with gutsy strength. Siegmund Nimsgern makes a powerful Michele, a shade too explosive in the climactic final aria, but generally firm and clean in his projection, losing nothing in conviction by the un-Italianate timbre of the voice, rather making the character more sinister. The full and brilliant recording has voices set convincingly on a believable stage and well balanced against the orchestra. This first CD version fills an obvious gap, though it is a pity that the 51 minutes' span brings only two tracks, one for each scene, where separate indexing of sections should have been a high priority. The single disc comes with libretto in a double-disc jewel-box.

Tosca (complete).
❀ *** HMV **CDS7 47175-8** [id.]; *EX 290039-5* (2) [Ang. *4X2X 3508*]. Callas, Di Stefano, Gobbi, Calabrese, La Scala, Milan, Ch. and O, De Sabata.
*** DG **413 815-2** (2) [id.]. Ricciarelli, Carreras, Raimondi, Corena, German Op. Ch., BPO, Karajan.
*** Ph. **412 885-2** (2) [id.]. Caballé, Carreras, Wixell, ROHCG Ch. and O, C. Davis.
(*) Decca Dig. **414 597-2; *414 597-4* (2) [id.]. Te Kanawa, Aragall, Nucci, Welsh Nat. Opera Ch., Nat. PO, Solti.
(M) ** RCA **GD 84514** (2) [**RCA 4514-2-RG**]. Milanov, Bjoerling, Warren, Rome Opera Ch. & O, Leinsdorf.

There has never been a finer recorded performance of *Tosca* than Callas's first, with Victor de Sabata conducting and Tito Gobbi as Scarpia. One mentions the prima donna first because, in this of all roles, she was able to identify totally with the heroine and turn her into a great tragic figure, not merely the cipher of Sardou's original melodrama. Gobbi too makes the unbelievably villainous police chief into a genuinely three-dimensional character, and Di Stefano as the hero, Cavaradossi, was at his finest. The conducting of De Sabata is spaciously lyrical as well as sharply dramatic, and the recording (originally mono, here stereo transcription) is superbly balanced in Walter Legge's fine production. The CD remastering brings an extension of range at both ends of the spectrum, with a firm, full bass to balance the extra brightness and clarity in the treble. Though there is inevitably less spaciousness than in a real stereo recording, there is no lack of bloom even on the violins, and the voices are gloriously caught. Only in the big *Te Deum* scene at the end of Act I does the extra clarity reveal a hint of congestion, and this is minimal. One's only real complaint is the absence of comprehensive cueing throughout the set.

Karajan's alternative, superbly unified reading for DG presents *Tosca* as very grand opera indeed, melodrama at its most searingly powerful. For Karajan, the police chief, Scarpia, seems to be the central character, and his unexpected choice of singer, a full bass, Raimondi, helps to show why, for this is no small-time villain but a man who in full confidence has a vein of nobility in him – as in the *Te Deum* at the end of Act I or the closing passage of the big solo addressed to Tosca, *Già mi dicon venal*. Detailed illumination of words is most powerful, and Karajan's coaching is evident too in the contribution of Katia Ricciarelli – another singer who had not taken the role on stage before the recording. She is not the most individual of Toscas, but the beauty of singing is consistent, with *Vissi d'arte* outstanding at a very slow tempo indeed. Carreras is also subjected to slow Karajan tempi in his big arias and, though the recording brings out an unevenness in the voice (this is not as sweet a sound as in the performance he recorded with Sir Colin Davis for Philips), it is still a powerful, stylish one. The recording is rich and full, with the stage picture clearly established and the glorious orchestral textures beautifully caught. The CD transfer improves definition but also, and more importantly, increases the feeling of spaciousness, putting more air round the voices and adding bloom to the orchestral sound. The wide dynamic range, however, means that care has to be taken to select a playing level which strikes a compromise between general immediacy and containment of the expansive climaxes. There are 15 separate cues on the first CD, 16 on the second.

Pacing the music naturally and sympathetically, Sir Colin Davis proves a superb Puccinian, one who not only presents Puccini's drama with richness and force but gives the score the musical strength of a great symphony. Davis rarely if ever chooses idiosyncratic tempi, and his manner is relatively straight; but it remains a strong and understanding reading, as well as a refreshing one. In this the quality of the singing from a cast of unusual consistency plays an important part. Caballé may not be as sharply jealous a heroine as her keenest rivals, but with the purity of *Vissi d'arte* coming as a key element in her interpretation, she still presents Tosca as a formidable siren-figure ('*Mia sirena*' being Cavaradossi's expression of endearment). Carreras reinforces his reputation as a tenor of unusual artistry as well as of superb vocal powers. Though Wixell is not ideally well focused as Scarpia, not at all Italianate of tone, he presents a completely credible lover-figure, not just the lusting ogre of convention. The 1976 analogue recording is full as well as refined, bringing out the beauties of Puccini's scoring. It is given a strikingly successful CD transfer, with three-dimensional placing of voices. The overall effect is more consistent and certainly more spacious than on the remastered Karajan set – especially noticeable at the big choral climax at the end of Act I.

Sir Georg Solti's is a colourful and robust reading of Puccini's great melodrama, recorded in exceptionally vivid digital sound with a heroine who may not be a natural Tosca but who has magnetic star quality. Rarely has Solti phrased Italian melody so consistently *con amore*, his fiercer side subdued but with plenty of power when required. Even so, the timing is not always quite spontaneous-sounding, with transitions occasionally rushed. Scarpia's entry is presented with power but too little of the necessary menace. Nucci in that role sings strongly but not very characterfully. Aragall as Cavaradossi produces a glorious stream of heroic tone, vocally reliable from first to last, and the incidental characters are strongly cast too, with Spiro Malas giving an unusually resonant and firm account of the Sacristan's music, not at all doddery. But the principal *raison d'être* of the set must be the casting of Dame Kiri as the jealous opera-singer. Her admirers will – as with Aragall – relish the glorious stream of beautiful tone, but the jealous side of Tosca's character is rather muted. Her recognition of the fan shown to her by Scarpia. *E L'Attavanti!*, has no snarl of anger in it, even though she later conveys real pain in her half-tones, as Scarpia's poison begins to work. One distinctive point in the unusually vivid recording is that in the Prelude to Act III the bells have actually been recorded from churches and clocks, not conventionally in the orchestra, though that adds less atmosphere than you might expect. There are outstanding matching cassettes, of Decca's very finest quality, provided with the CD booklet for documentation.

At mid-price in RCA's Victor Opera Series, Leinsdorf's version makes a fair bargain, despite dated 1950s recording and the conductor's heavy style. Jussi Bjoerling was at the peak of his form as Cavaradossi; though Zinka Milanov was past her best and was sometimes stressed by the role, there is much beautiful singing here from a great soprano who recorded all too little. Leonard Warren was another characterful veteran, but the furry edge to his voice makes him a less-than-sinister Scarpia.

Tosca: highlights.
*** DG **423 113-2** [id.] (from above set with Ricciarelli and Carreras, cond. Karajan).

With the CD catalogue short of highlights discs of *Tosca*, this selection from Karajan's powerful, closely recorded Berlin version is welcome. The breadth of Karajan's direction is well represented in the longer excerpts – for example the opening of Act I up to the end of the love duet and Act III from *E lucevan le stelle* to the end of the opera. There is also Tosca's *Vissi d'arte*, but Scarpia's music is under-represented (the torture scene of Act II plus the duet with Tosca). That is a pity when Raimondi made such a distinctive Scarpia with his dark bass timbre. Bright vivid sound.

Turandot (complete).
*** Decca **414 274-2** (2) [id.]. Sutherland, Pavarotti, Caballé, Pears, Ghiaurov, Alldis Ch., Wandsworth School Boys' Ch., LPO, Mehta.
*** DG Dig. **410 096-2** (2) [id.]. Ricciarelli, Domingo, Hendricks, Raimondi, V. State Op. Ch., V. Boys' Ch., VPO, Karajan.
(***) HMV mono **CDS7 47971-8** (2) [id.]; (M) *EX 291267-5*. Callas, Fernandi, Schwarzkopf, Zaccaria, La Scala, Milan, Ch. & O, Serafin.
** CBS **M2K 39160** (2) [id.]. Marton, Carreras, Ricciarelli, Kerns, V. State Op. Ch. & O, Maazel.

On compact disc (two CDs, well banded, as opposed to three LPs) the Mehta set, in vividness, clarity and immediacy of sound, brings an astonishing tribute to Decca engineering in the early 1970s. In every way it outshines the later digital recordings of Karajan and Maazel, and the reading remains supreme. The role of Turandot, the icy princess, is not one that you would expect to be in Joan Sutherland's repertory, but here on record she gives an intensely revealing and appealing interpretation, making the character far more human and sympathetic than ever before. This is a character, armoured and unyielding in *In questa reggia*, whose final capitulation to love is a natural development, not an incomprehensible switch. Sutherland's singing is strong and beautiful, while Pavarotti gives a performance equally imaginative, beautiful in sound, strong on detail. To set Caballé against Sutherland was a daring idea, and it works superbly well; Pears as the Emperor is another imaginative choice. Mehta directs a gloriously rich and dramatic performance, superlatively recorded.

Karajan takes a characteristically spacious view of Puccini's last opera. His tempi are regularly slower than those in rival versions, yet his concentration is irresistible and he relishes the exotic colourings of the sound, just as he puts an unusual slant on the vocal colouring as well as the dramatic balance by his distinctive casting of the two contrasted heroines. Both the Liù of Barbara Hendricks and the Turandot of Katia Ricciarelli are more sensuously feminine than is usual. With her seductively golden tone, Hendricks is almost a sex-kitten, and one wonders how Calaf could ever have overlooked her. This is very different from the usual picture of a chaste slave-girl. Ricciarelli is a far more vulnerable figure than one expects of the icy princess, and the very fact that the part strains her beyond reasonable vocal limits adds to the dramatic point, even if it subtracts from the musical joys. By contrast, Placido Domingo is vocally superb, a commanding prince; and the rest of the cast presents star names even in small roles. The sound is full and brilliant, if at times rather close in the manner of DG engineers working in the Berlin Philharmonie. Ensemble is not always quite as flawless as one expects of Karajan with Berlin forces, though significantly the challenge of the manifestly less inspired completion of Alfano has him working at white heat. The compact discs bring added presence, although not all ears will find the balance completely satisfactory.

Having Maria Callas, the most flashing-eyed of sopranos, as Turandot is – on record at least – the most natural piece of casting. With her the icy princess is not just an implacable man-hater but a highly provocative female. One quickly reads something of Callas's own underlying vulnerability into such a portrait, its tensions, the element of brittleness. In the arioso from Alfano's completion, *Del primo pianto*, the chesty way she addresses Calaf as *Straniero!* in the opening phrase is unforgettable in its continuing threat. With her the character seems so much more believably complex than with others. It was sad that, except at the very beginning of her career, Callas felt unable to sing the role in the opera house, but this 1957 recording is far more valuable than any memory of the past, one of her most thrillingly magnetic performances on disc. It is made the more telling, when Schwarzkopf provides a comparably characterful and distinctive portrait as Liù, far more than a Puccinian 'little woman', sweet and wilting. Even more than usual one regrets that the confrontation between princess and slave is so brief. Schwarzkopf's meticulous observance of dynamic markings in Liù's arias reinforces their fine-spun Straussian quality. Next to such sopranos, it was unkind of Walter Legge as producer to choose so relatively uncharacterful a tenor as Eugenio Fernandi as Calaf, but his timbre is pleasing enough. By contrast, Serafin's masterly conducting exactly matches the characterfulness of Callas and Schwarzkopf, with colour, atmosphere and dramatic point all commandingly presented. The Ping, Pang and Pong episode of Act II has rarely sparkled so naturally. With such a vivid performance the 1957 mono sound will for many, if not most, opera-lovers hardly matter. The CD transfer makes it satisfyingly full-bodied, not boxy, even though the acoustic is rather dry, with solo voices balanced forward and with the choral sound tending to overload at climaxes. The cassettes cost far less but have a more restricted range, although Callas's voice is for the most part comfortably caught. The choral focus, however, is blunted.

Turandot brings the warmest and most sensuous performance in Maazel's Puccini series, thanks in good measure to its being a live recording, made in September 1983 at the Vienna State Opera House. Applause and stage noises are often distracting, and the clarity of CD tends to make one notice them the more. Recording balances are often odd, with Carreras – in fine voice – suffering in both directions, sometimes disconcertingly distant, at others far too close. Karajan's Turandot here becomes Liù, and the result is predictably heavyweight, though the beat in her voice is only rarely apparent. The strengths and shortcomings of Eva Marton as the icy princess come out at the very start of *In questa reggia*. The big, dramatic voice is well controlled, but there is too little variation of tone, dynamic or expression; she rarely shades her voice down. In the closing Act, during the Alfano completion, Marton's confidence and command grow impressively, with her heroic tone ever more thrilling. Recommendable to those who relish a live performance. Annoyingly, the CDs contain no bands within the Acts.

Le Villi: complete.
*** CBS **MK 76890** [**MK 36669**]. Scotto, Domingo, Nucci, Gobbi, Amb. Op. Ch., Nat. PO, Maazel.

Maazel directs a performance so commanding, with singing of outstanding quality, that one can at last assess Puccini's first opera on quite a new level. Its weaknesses have always been the feeble, oversimplified story and the cardboard characterization. With such concentration, and with musical qualities emphasized, the weaknesses are minimized, and the result is richly enjoyable. Puccini's melodies may be less distinctive here than they later became, but one can readily appreciate the impact they had on early audiences, not to mention Puccini's publisher-to-be, Giulio Ricordi. Scotto's voice tends to spread a little at the top of the stave, but like Domingo she gives a powerful performance, and Leo Nucci avoids false histrionics. A delightful bonus is Tito Gobbi's contribution reciting the verses which link the scenes; he is as characterful a reciter as he is a singer. The recording is one of CBS's best.

COLLECTIONS

Arias: *La Bohème: Quando m'en vo' soletta. Gianni Schicchi: O mio babbino caro. Madama Butterfly: Un bel dì. Manon Lescaut: In quelle trine morbide. La Rondine: Chi il bel sogno di Doretta. Tosca: Vissi d'arte. Le Villi: Se come voi piccina.*
*** CBS Dig. **CD 37298** [id.]. Kiri Te Kanawa, LPO, Pritchard – VERDI: Arias.***

The creamy beauty of Kiri Te Kanawa's voice is ideally suited to these seven lyrical arias – including rarities like the little waltz-like song from *Le Villi.* Expressive sweetness is more remarkable than characterization, but in such music, well recorded and sounding especially believable on CD, who would ask for more?

'Puccini heroines'; La Bohème: Sì, mi chiamano Mimì; Donde lieta uscì; Musetta's waltz song. Edgar: Addio, mio dolce amor. La Fanciulla del West: Laggiù nel Soledad. Gianni Schicchi: O mio babbino caro. Madama Butterfly: Bimba, bimba non piangere (Love duet, with Placido Domingo); *Un bel dì. Manon Lescaut: In quelle trine morbide; Sola, perduta, abbandonata. La Rondine: Ore dolci a divine. Tosca: Vissi d'arte. Turandot: In questa reggia. Le Villi: Se come voi piccina.*
*** RCA **RD 85999** [**RCA 5999-2-RC**]. Leontyne Price, New Philh. O or LSO, Downes; Santi.

With three extra items added to the original recital LP, this collection, running for 70′, is a formidable demonstration of the art of Leontyne Price at the very peak of her career, still marvellously subtle in control (the end of Tosca's *Vissi d'arte* for example), powerfully dramatic, yet able to point the *Rondine* aria with delicacy and charm. The Love duet from *Butterfly* in which she is joined by Domingo is particularly thrilling, and there is much else here to give pleasure. The remastering is extremely vivid and the voice is given fine bloom and presence. A Puccinian feast!

Arias: *La Bohème; Sì, mi chiamano Mimì; Donde lieta uscì. Gianni Schicchi: O mio babbino caro. Madama Butterfly: Un bel dì; Tu, tu piccolo Iddio. Manon Lescaut: In quelle trine morbide; Sola, perduta, abbandonata. La Rondine: Chi il bel sogno di Doretta. Tosca: Vissi d'arte. Turandot: Signore, ascolta!; Tu che di gel sei cinta. Le Villi: Se come voi piccina.*
*** HMV **CDC7 47841-2** [id.]. Montserrat Caballé, LSO, Mackerras.

Montserrat Caballé uses her rich, beautiful voice to glide over these great Puccinian melodies. The effect is ravishing, with lovely recorded sound to match the approach. This is one of the loveliest of all operatic recital discs and the comparative lack of sparkle is compensated for by the sheer beauty of the voice. The CD transfer is extremely successful, vivid yet retaining the full vocal bloom.

'Heroines': (i) *La Bohème: Musetta's waltz song;* (ii) *Sì, mi chiamano Mimì.* (iii) *Edgar: D'ogni dolor.* (i) *Gianni Schicchi: O mio babbino caro. Madama Butterfly: Un bel dì. Manon Lescaut: In quelle trine morbide;* (iii) *Sola, perduta, abbandonata.* (i) *La Rondine: Chi il bel sogno di Doretta.* (iii) *Suor Angelica: Senza mamma, o bimbo.* (i) *Tosca: Vissi d'arte.* (iv) *Turandot: Tu che di gel sei cinta* (Death of Liù); (v) *In questa reggia.* (i) *Le Villi: Se come voi piccina.*
(*) CBS **MK 39097 [id.]. (i) Kiri Te Kanawa; (ii) Ileana Cotrubas; (iii) Renata Scotto; (iv) Katia Ricciarelli; (v) Eva Marton; (iv; v) José Carreras.

The CBS compilation of Puccini 'heroines' neatly gathers together some fine performances out of its series of complete Puccini opera sets, plus other items such as the two *Bohème* arias taken from recitals. Vocally these are not always immaculate performances, but the quintet of sopranos represented is exceptionally characterful, contrasting strongly with one another, where Puccini recitals from a single soprano can lack variety. However, the layout does not make as much as possible of the interplay of different voices, as Kiri Te Kanawa's seven contributions are all placed together at the start of the collection. They come from her recital with Pritchard – see above – and have the character of concert performances. Ileana Cotrubas's assumption of Mimi has greater feeling of the opera house; other highlights include Katia Ricciarelli's *Death of Liù* and Renata Scotto's beautiful *Senza mamma* from *Suor Angelica*. The thrilling climax of *In questa reggia* (Eva Marton and José Carreras) is spoiled by a fade-out at the end, particularly unfortunate as it is the closing item. The CD gives the voices plenty of presence, but the variations in ambience and balance are made the more striking. There is also a very good cassette.

Arias from: *La Bohème; Gianni Schicchi; Madama Butterfly; Manon Lescaut; La Rondine; Suor Angelica; Tosca; Turandot; Le Villi.*
** CBS Dig. **MK 42167** [id.]. Eva Marton, Munich RSO, Patané.

Eva Marton's CBS recital covers a formidable range of fourteen Puccini arias, taking her well away from the big dramatic repertory which has generally been counted her forte. Surprisingly, she is at her most effective when totally unstressed in lyrical arias, regularly producing clear, creamy and beautifully scaled tone, as in Manon's *In quelle trine morbide* or in Mimi's two arias. What the microphone exposes too often is a forcing of tone and with it an ugly widening of vibrato when the voice is under pressure. Characterization is less varied than it might be, with *Turandot* – Marton's regular role – made more convincing than the rest. It is good to have the waltz-like aria from *Le Villi* and Magda's Act I aria from *La Rondine* included with the better-known arias. Warm, well-balanced recording.

Arias: *Manon Lescaut: Cortese damigella . . . Donna non vidi mai; Presto! In filia! . . . Guardate, pazzo son. Turandot: Non piangere Liù . . . Ah! Per l'ultima volta; Nessun dorma.*
*** DG Dig. **413 785-2** [id.]. Placido Domingo – VERDI: *Arias.****

These Puccini items, taken, like the Verdi, from earlier recordings made by Domingo for DG, make a fine heroic supplement, when he was challenged to some of his finest, most imaginative singing by Sinopoli and Karajan. The sound is consistently vivid.

Purcell, Henry (1659–95)

Abdelazer: suite. Bonduca: suite. The Gordian knot unty'd: suite. Timon of Athens: Overture; Curtain tune. The Virtuous wife: suite. Chacony in G min.
(*) Hyp. Dig. **CDA 66212; *KA 66212* [id.]. Parley of Instruments, Peter Holman.

Not a record to be played at one sitting. No relief is offered from instrumental timbres and few of the dance movements last much more than a minute. However, the performances are stylish and sensitive, all one-to-a-part as might well have been the case in some theatres of Purcell's day. The disc includes the newly discovered trumpet part for *Bonduca* which has not been recorded before. Excellent recording, as is invariably the case with Hyperion. The chrome tape is also of high quality.

Chacony in G min. Anthems: *Blow up the trumpet in Zion; My heart is inditing; O God, Thou art my God; O God, Thou hast cast us out; Rejoice in the Lord alway; Remember not, Lord, our offences.*
(M) *** Tel. **ZS8 43778** [id.]. King's College Ch., Willcocks; Leonhardt Cons., Leonhardt.

An outstanding reissue of a splendid 1970 concert which sounds as fresh as the day it was made in this expertly remastered format. The instrumental ensemble uses period instruments and playing style, but though the character of the sound is very distinctive it is not too abrasive. Not all the anthems have instrumental accompaniments but they are all very well sung, with the characteristic King's penchant for tonal breadth and beauty. Over the whole programme the music making happily blends scholarship and spontaneity. At mid-price, this is an excellent way to represent Purcell in a small (or large) collection.

Benedicte: O all ye works of the Lord. Coronation music for King James II: I was glad. Funeral music for Queen Mary: Man that is born of woman; In the midst of life; Thou knowest, Lord, the secrets of our hearts. Anthems: *Blow up the trumpet in Sion; Hear my prayer, O Lord; I will sing unto the Lord; Jubilate; Lord, how long wilt Thou be angry; O God, Thou art my God; O God, Thou hast cast us out; O Lord God of Hosts; Remember not, Lord, our offences; Save me, O God.*
*** Conifer Dig. **CDCF 152**; *MCFC 152* [id.]. Trinity College Ch., Cambridge, Marlow; Matthews; G. Jackson (organ).

A most successful record and a welcome addition to the catalogue. Richard Marlow gets good results from his singers; such expressive anthems as *Remember not, Lord, our offences* and *Hear my prayer, O Lord* are eloquently done and beautifully recorded. Dr Peter le Huray reminds us that all the music on this disc, apart from one anthem, was composed before Purcell was twenty-five. What an extraordinary achievement! Excellent performances from all concerned – not least the Conifer recording team, and the cassette too is a state-of-the-art transfer.

Come, ye Sons of Art; Funeral music for Queen Mary (1695).
*** Erato **ECD 88071** [id.]. Lott, Brett, Williams, Allen, Monteverdi Ch. and O, Equale Brass Ens., Gardiner.

Come, ye Sons of Art, the most celebrated of Purcell's birthday odes for Queen Mary, is splendidly coupled here with the unforgettable funeral music he wrote on the death of the same monarch. With the Monteverdi Choir at its most incisive and understanding the performances are exemplary, and the recording, though balanced in favour of the instruments, is clear and refined. Among the soloists Thomas Allen is outstanding, while the two counter-tenors give a charming performance of the duet, *Sound the trumpet*. The *Funeral music* includes the well-known *Solemn march* for trumpets and drums, a *Canzona* and simple anthem given at the funeral, and two of Purcell's most magnificent anthems setting the *Funeral sentences*.

Ode on St Cecilia's Day (*Hail! bright Cecilia*).
*** Erato Dig. **ECD 88046** [id.]. Jennifer Smith, Stafford, Gordon, Elliott, Varcoe, David Thomas, Monteverdi Ch., E. Bar. Soloists, Gardiner.

*** HMV Dig. **CDC7 47490-2** [id.]; *EL 270361-4*. Kirkby, Chance, Kevin Smith, Covey-Crump, Elliott, Grant, George, Thomas, Taverner Ch. & Players, Parrott.

Gardiner's characteristic vigour and alertness in Purcell come out superbly in this delightful record of the 1692 *St Cecilia Ode* – not as well known as some of the other odes he wrote, but a masterpiece. Soloists and chorus are outstanding even by Gardiner's high standards, and the recording excellent.

Though Parrott's EMI version lacks the exuberance of Gardiner's outstanding Erato issue, in a more reticent way it brings a performance full of incidental delights, particularly vocal ones from a brilliant array of no fewer than twelve solo singers, notably five excellent tenors. With pitch lower than usual, some numbers can be sung by tenors that normally require counter-tenors. Interestingly, Parrott includes the *Voluntary in D minor* for organ before the wonderful aria celebrating that instrument and St Cecilia's sponsorship of it, *O wondrous machine*. It holds up the flow, but at least on CD it can readily be omitted. Well-balanced recording, and a very good cassette.

Songs: *Ah! cruel nymph; As Amoret and Thirsis lay; The fatal hour; I lov'd fair Celia; Pious Celinda*. Elegies: *Upon the death of Mr Thomas Farmer; Upon the death of Queen Mary*. Arias: *Hail bright Cecilia: 'Tis Nature's voice. History of Dioclesian: Since from my dear Astrea's sight. History of King Richard II: Retir'd from any mortal's sight. Oedipus: Music for a while. Pausanias: Sweeter than roses.*
(*) Accent **ACC 57802D [id.]. René Jacobs, W. Kuijken, K. Jünghanel.

René Jacobs's distinctive counter-tenor is well suited to Purcell; with unusually wide range, he sings this selection, weighted in favour of solemn songs, very beautifully – if with too little feeling for variety of mood. The most ambitious song is the elegy on the death of Queen Mary to Latin words, a superb piece too little known. First-rate recording.

Songs: *Ah! How sweet it is to love; The earth trembled; An evening hymn; If music be the food of love; I'll sail upon the dog star; I see she flies me ev'rywhere; Let the night perish; Lord, what is man; Morning hymn; A new ground*. Arias: *Birthday ode for Queen Mary: Crown the altar. Bonduca: Oh! Lead me to some peaceful gloom. History of Dioclesian: Since from my dear Astrea's sight. The Indian Queen: I attempt from love's sickness to fly. The Mock marriage: Man that is for woman made. Oedipus: Music for a while. Pausanias: Sweeter than roses. The Rival sisters: Take not a woman's anger ill.*
*** ASV *ZCALH 963* [id.]. Ian Partridge, George Malcolm.

Appropriately titled 'Sweeter than Roses', this is a warmly sympathetic collection of favourite Purcell songs from a tenor whose honeyed tones are ideally suited to recording. The style smoother than we have come to expect latterly – this is a reissue of an earlier Enigma issue – but with ever-sensitive accompaniment from George Malcolm, who also contributes one brief solo, this is an excellent recommendation for those who resist the new style of authenticity. Atmospheric recording, with the voice well forward. The cassette is very faithful, with the voice caught in its presence and natural bloom and the harpsichord image believable and nicely focused.

Songs and airs: *Bess of Bedlam; Evening hymn; If music be the food of love; Lovely, lovely Albina; Not all my torments; Olinda in the shades unseen; The Plaint; O, Urge me no more; When first Amintas sued for a kiss*. Arias: *Birthday ode for Queen Mary: Crown the altar. The Fairy Queen: Hark! hark!; O, O let me weep; Ye gentle spirits of the air. The Indian Queen: I attempt from love's sickness to fly. Pausanias: Sweeter than roses. The Tempest: Dear pritty youths. Timon of Athens: The cares of lovers.*
*** O-L Dig. **417 123-2** [id.]. Emma Kirkby, Rooley, Hogwood.

The purity of Emma Kirkby's soprano – as delightful to some ears as it is disconcerting to others – suits this wide-ranging collection of Purcell songs splendidly, though you might argue for a bigger, warmer voice in the *Bess of Bedlam* song. The *Evening hymn* is radiantly done, and so are many of the less well-known airs which regularly bring new revelation. Excellent recording, if with the voice forward, given striking extra presence on CD.

Songs: *Come, let us drink; A health to the nut brown lass; If ever I more riches; I gave her cakes and I gave her ale; Laudate Ceciliam; The miller's daughter; Of all the instruments; Once, twice, thrice I Julia tried; Prithee ben't so sad and serious; Since time so kind to us does prove; Sir Walter enjoying his damsel; 'Tis women makes us love; Under this stone; Young John the gard'ner.*
*** HM **HMC 90242** [id.]. Deller Cons., Deller.

One section of this charming and stylish collection has a selection of Purcell's catches, some of them as lewd as rugby-club songs of today, others as refined as *Under this stone* – all of which the Deller Consort take in their stride. The final two pieces are extended items; *If ever I more riches*, a setting of Cowley, has some striking passages. The remastering for CD has greatly improved the sound, with voices fresh and first-rate recording of the instruments.

Songs: *The fatal hour comes on apace; Lord, what is man?; Love's power in my heart; More love or more disdain I crave; Now that the sun hath veiled his light; The Queen's Epicedium; Sleep, Adam, sleep; Thou wakeful shepherd; Who can behold Florella's charms.* Arias: *History of Dioclesian: Since from my dear Astrea's sight. Indian Queen: I attempt from love's sickness to fly. King Arthur: Fairest isle. Oedipus: Music for a while. Pausanias: Sweeter than roses. The Rival Sisters: Take not a woman's anger ill. Rule a wife and have a wife: There's not a swain.*
*** Etcetera Dig. **KTC 1013** [id.]. Andrew Dalton, Uittenbosch; Borstlap.

Andrew Dalton has an exceptionally beautiful counter-tenor voice, creamy even in its upper register to make the extended '*Hallelujahs*' of *Lord, what is man?* and *Now that the sun* even more heavenly than usual. One half has sacred songs, some of them less well known, the other secular, including various favourites. Many of them require transposition, but only in some of the soprano songs such as *Fairest isle* does that distract. A delightful disc, well recorded.

STAGE WORKS AND THEATRE MUSIC

Dido and Aeneas (complete).
*** Ph. Dig. **416 299-2**; *416 299-4* [id.]. Jessye Norman, McLaughlin, Kern, Allen, Power, ECO and Ch., Leppard.
*** Chan. Dig. **CHAN 8306**; *ABTD 1034* [id.]. Emma Kirkby, Nelson, Thomas, Taverner Ch. & Players, Parrott.
(M) (***) EMI mono **CDH7 61006-2** [id.]. Flagstad, Schwarzkopf, Hemsley, Mermaid Theatre Singers & O, Geraint Jones.
** HM **HMC 905173** [id.]. Laurens, Cantor, Feldman, Visse, Les Arts Florissants, Christie.
*(*) Tel. Dig. **ZK8 42919** [id.]. Yakar, Murray, Scharinger, Schmidt, Kostlinger, Gardow, Schoenberg Ch., VCM, Harnoncourt.

'Like *Tristan und Isolde* in a pint pot', says Raymond Leppard of *Dido and Aeneas*; here he provides crisply disciplined backing for the most magnificently expansive rendering of *Dido* since Kirsten Flagstad recorded it over thirty years ago. Authenticists should keep away, but Jessye Norman amply proves that this amazingly compressed setting of the epic *Aeneid* story has a dramatic depth and intensity to compare with Berlioz's setting – or, for that matter, with Wagner's *Tristan*. The opening phrase of *Ah Belinda* brings the most controversial moment, when Norman slows luxuriantly. But from then on the security and dark intensity of her singing make for a memorable performance, heightened in the recitatives by the equally commanding singing of Thomas Allen as Aeneas. The range of expression is very wide – with Jessye Norman producing an agonized whisper in the recitative just before Dido's *Lament* – but the unauthentic element must not be exaggerated. By most yardsticks this is finely poised and stylish singing, even if in the last resort Norman cannot match Dame Janet Baker in conveying the aching vulnerability of the love-lorn Dido. Marie McLaughlin is a pure-toned Belinda, Patrick Power a heady-toned Sailor, singing his song in a West Country accent, while Patricia Kern repeats her performance as the Sorceress, using conventionally sinister expression. The warm-toned counter-tenor, Derek Ragin, makes the Spirit Messenger into an eerie, other-worldly figure. Leppard's direction this time is a degree plainer and more direct than it was in his Erato version, again with some slow speeds for choruses. Excellent recording in both formats.

Andrew Parrott's concept of a performance on original instruments has one immediately thinking back to the atmosphere of Josias Priest's school for young ladies where Purcell's masterpiece was first given. The voices enhance that impression, not least Emma Kirkby's fresh, bright soprano, here recorded without too much edge but still very young-sounding. It is more questionable to have a soprano singing the tenor role of the Sailor in Act III; but anyone who fancies the idea of an authentic performance need not hesitate. The compact disc is exceptionally refined, the sound well focused, with analogue atmosphere yet with detail enhanced. The tape transfer, too, is fresh and clean, retaining the recording's bloom. There is just the faintest hint of peaking on one or two of Miss Kirkby's high notes.

Bernard Miles's inspiration in inviting Kirsten Flagstad to sing in Purcell's miniature epic at his original Mermaid Theatre in St John's Wood led in due course to this classic recording, in which Elisabeth Schwarzkopf added another characterful element, equally unexpected. In this excellent mid-price CD transfer on EMI's historic Références series the surprise is that, even in this age of period performance, this traditional account under Geraint Jones sounds fresh and lively still, not at all heavy. Though Flagstad's magnificent voice may in principle be too weighty for this music – one might point to the latter-day equivalent of Jessye Norman – she scales it down superbly in her noble reading, which brings beautiful shading and masterly control of breath and tone. Schwarzkopf is brightly characterful as Belinda, and though Thomas Hemsley is not ideally sweet-toned as Aeneas, he sings very intelligently. The mono sound, obviously limited, yet captures the voices vividly, and this above all is Flagstad's set.

A version of *Dido and Aeneas* such as the Harmonia Mundi issue with a predominantly French cast may seem an oddity but, with trifling exceptions, English accents are more than acceptable; William Christie, as in his recordings of other early operas, provides direction on an authentic chamber scale that makes the results both dramatic and intense. Particularly impressive – and an interesting idea for casting – is having the role of the Sorceress taken by the outstanding French counter-tenor, Dominique Visse. The shortcoming is that Guillemette Laurens makes a disappointing Dido, not strong or positive enough. First-rate recording.

Harnoncourt's idiosyncratic rhythmic style in Purcell, often in exaggerated marcato, as well as his extreme speeds in both directions, undermines the effectiveness of the whole performance, presenting the authentic view far less imaginatively than the Parrott set on Chandos. Ann Murray sings beautifully as Dido, but has to struggle against the funereal speed for the *Lament*. The chorus is excellent, and the other soloists consistently good, well trained in English but still distractingly foreign-sounding, even the heady-toned Sailor of Josef Köstlinger. Rachel Yakar is an agile Belinda, but she does not always blend well with Dido, and Trudeliese Schmidt a resonant, fire-eating Sorceress.

The Fairy Queen (complete).

*** DG Dig. **419 221-2** (2) [id.]. Harrhy, Jennifer Smith, Nelson, Priday, Penrose, Stafford, Evans,

Hill, Varcoe, Thomas, Monteverdi Ch., E. Bar. Soloists, Eliot Gardiner.

The Fairy Queen provides a classic example of a masterpiece, made non-viable by changed conditions, which happily records can help to keep alive, a score which is crammed with the finest Purcellian inspiration. Gardiner's performance is a delight from beginning to end, for though authenticity and completeness reign, scholarship is worn lightly and the result is consistently exhilarating, with no longueurs whatever. The fresh-toned soloists are first rate, while Gardiner's regular choir and orchestra excel themselves with Purcell's sense of fantasy brought out in each succeeding number. Performed like this, *The Fairy Queen* has a magic equivalent to *A Midsummer Night's Dream*, of which it usually seems so strange a distortion. Beautifully clear and well-balanced recording, sounding all the fresher on CD, with the silent background especially telling in the light-textured music. The layout places the first three Acts complete on disc one and the remaining two Acts on the second CD. There are over 60 access points.

The Indian Queen (incidental music; complete).
*** HM **HMC 90243** [id.]. Knibbs, Sheppard, Mark and Alfred Deller, Elliot, Bevan, Deller Singers, King's Musick, Deller.

Deller's group is at its liveliest and most characterful in *The Indian Queen. Ye twice ten hundred deities* is splendidly sung by Maurice Bevan; and the duet for male alto and tenor, *How happy are we* (with Deller himself joined by Paul Elliot), as well as the best-known item, the soprano's *I attempt from love's sickness to fly* (Honor Sheppard), are equally enjoyable.

King Arthur (complete).
*** Erato **ECD 880562** (2) [id.]. Jennifer Smith, Gillian Fischer, Priday, Ross, Stafford, Elliott, Varcoe, E. Bar. Soloists, Eliot Gardiner.

It is a tragedy that this magnificent work presents such difficulties of staging, not to mention textual problems, that it is unlikely to be given publicly as often as it deserves. Gardiner, with his combination of stylishness and electricity of the highest voltage, presents a performance on record which in almost every way provides the clear modern answer. *King Arthur* may be cumbersome on stage, but here its episodic nature matters hardly at all; one can simply relish the wealth of sharply inspired and colourful numbers. Gardiner's solutions to the textual problems carry complete conviction, as for example his placing of the superb *Chaconne in F* at the end instead of the start. Solo singing for the most part is excellent, with Stephen Varcoe outstanding among the men. As the Cold Genius he helps Gardiner to make the Frost scene far more effective than usual. He is also one of the trio that give a delightfully roistering account of *Harvest home. Fairest isle* is treated very gently after that, with Gill Ross, boyish of tone, reserved just for that number. Throughout, the chorus is characteristically fresh and vigorous, and the instrumentalists marry authentic technique to pure, unabrasive sounds beautifully. The recording vividly captures a performance in an aptly intimate but not dry acoustic, with the cueing of the CD making it very convenient to use.

Quilter, Roger (1877–1953)

Songs: *An old carol; Autumn evening; Barbara Allen; Drink to me only; Drooping wings; Go, lovely Rose; 5 Jacobean lyrics; The jolly miller; Love's philosophy; Now sleeps the crimson petal; Over the mountains; Slumber song; A song at parting; Three poor marriners; Three Shakespeare songs, Op. 6; To Julia; To wine and beauty; The walled-in garden.*
*** Hyp. Dig. *KA 66208* [id.]. David Wilson-Johnson, David O. Norris.

With Jessye Norman an enthusiastic advocate (before long on record, one hopes), the songs of

Roger Quilter are coming to be appreciated once more, not simply consigned to a lavender-scented cupboard. David Wilson-Johnson, most sympathetically accompanied by David Owen Norris, here on a single disc containing no fewer than twenty-nine songs enormously expands the range of his work available. He consistently demonstrates their sweetness, charm and point with stylish, refined singing, though some of these songs would benefit from a woman's voice. On this showing Quilter never surpassed his most popular song, the Shelley setting, *Love's philosophy*, surgingly delightful, full of open emotion uninhibitedly expressed. To hear all these at one sitting does point to limitations of range, but this is art-song of a precious kind which Wilson-Johnson with his accompanist warmly and exuberantly celebrates. Well-balanced recording.

Rachmaninov, Sergei (1873–1943)

Piano concertos Nos 1–4; Rhapsody on a theme of Paganini.
*** Chan. **CHAN 8521/2**; *DBTD 2011/2* [id.]. Earl Wild, RPO, Horenstein.
(**(*)) RCA mono **RD 86659 [RCA 6659-2-RC]** (*Nos 1, 4 & Rhapsody*); **RD 85997 [RCA 5997-2-RC]** (*Nos 2–3*). The composer, Phd. O, Ormandy or Stokowski.

The composer's own performances of his four concertos are very welcome on CD, although considerable allowance has to be made for the brittle sound in Nos 1 and 4 and particularly for No. 3, where the piano timbre is very hard indeed. These three are conducted by Ormandy: the recordings of the *First* and *Third Concertos* date from the winter of 1939–40, and No. 4 was recorded a year later. The *Second Concerto* and *Paganini rhapsody* are much earlier, 1929 and 1934 respectively, yet the sound is far superior – perhaps not surprisingly with Stokowski at the helm, for already at that period in his career he was taking great trouble over recording balances and microphone placings to produce richer string textures and a greater ambient effect. His success in the *Second Concerto* is striking, with the Philadelphia strings sounding full at the very opening and producing radiant timbre in the *Adagio*. The slow movement is also noticeable for the forward balance of the woodwind triplets which decorate the final reprise of the main tune, an effect less perceptible on many modern records and one which greatly enhances the melody. The *Rhapsody* is a marvellous performance; again Stokowski sees that the orchestral detail comes through splendidly, as well as ensuring that the famous eighteenth variation has great romantic panache. If the two Rachmaninov/Stokowski performances could be paired, they would make a very desirable record.

The Earl Wild set with Horenstein also originally derived from RCA. It was produced by Charles Gerhardt and recorded at the Kingsway Hall in 1965, to be issued subsequently in a subscription series through *Reader's Digest* magazine. The choice of soloist and conductor seemed controversial. Horenstein had a good reputation in the German classics and his musicianship was in no doubt, but to couple him to a young American virtuoso without a background of European music making was risky. In the event, however, they worked marvellously together, with Horenstein producing an unexpected degree of romantic ardour from the orchestra and both artists finding the natural feeling for the ebb and flow of phrases, so readily demonstrated in the composer's own performances, and which has now become a hallmark of Rachmaninovian interpretation. Earl Wild's technique is prodigious and sometimes (as in the first movement of the *Fourth Concerto* or at the end of the first movement of the *Third*) he almost lets it run away with him. This is not to suggest that the bravura is exhibitionistic for its own sake, and Wild's impetuosity is very involving. There is a strong personality at work, as is obvious at the climax of the first movement of the *Second Concerto* (which has more thrust than Rachmaninov's own version) and in the way the intensity is held at maximum in the closing pages of the slow movement of the same work, instead of relaxing as the music draws to its idyllic close. The finale goes splendidly, with great dash. What is surprising is how closely the interpretations here seem to be modelled on the composer's own versions – not slavishly, but in broad conception. This applies strikingly to the *First Concerto* and the *Rhapsody*. In the former Ormandy brings rather more romantic subtlety than Horenstein to the gentle secondary theme of the first movement and in the memorably lyrical idea of the finale (with his indulgent but irresistible nudge); in the eighteenth variation of the *Rhapsody*, Horenstein does not quite match Stokowski's flair, although in both instances his rather straighter approach is still idiomatically sensitive and helped by the rich body given to the strings by the Kingsway ambience. No. 3, a most successful and spontaneous performance, finds Wild and Horenstein more poised at the very opening than the composer and Ormandy, and the slow movement has great romantic expressive feeling. All in all, this is a first-class and very rewarding set and the sumptuousness of the sound belies the age of the recording; its sheer amplitude means that the tapes have had to be transferred at modest level and have a middle and bass emphasis, but the CDs are very believable indeed and the richness is exactly right for the music.

(i) *Piano concerto No. 1 in F sharp min., Op. 1;* (ii) *Rhapsody on a theme of Paganini, Op. 43.*
*** Decca Dig. **417 613-3**; *417 613-4* [id.]. Ashkenazy, (i) Concg. O; (ii) Philh. O, Haitink.

Piano concertos Nos 1; 2 in C min., Op. 18.
** Ph. Dig. **412 881-2**; *412 881-4* [id.]. Kocsis, San Francisco SO, De Waart.

This coupling finds Ashkenazy in excellent form. The *Paganini variations* are, if anything, even better than his earlier LP with Previn – and that is saying something! Haitink gets splendid sound from the Philharmonia in the *Variations* and Decca provides excellent recording. The *First Concerto* is no less impressive, and the Concertgebouw Orchestra under Haitink offer luxurious support. This is the best version of the coupling now on the market. There is a faithful chrome tape, although the transfer level could ideally have been a shade higher.

Zoltán Kocsis has fleet fingers and dashes through both concertos with remarkable panache and striking brilliance. But in No. 2 he gives the listener all too little time to savour incidental beauties or surrender to the melancholy of the slow movements. He is just a little too carried away with his own virtuosity and, although this is thrilling enough, it is not the whole story.

Piano concertos Nos 1 in F sharp min., Op. 1; 3 in D min., Op. 30.
(M) *** HMV **CDM7 69115-2** [id.]. Jean-Philippe Collard, Capitole Toulouse O, Plasson.

Jean-Philippe Collard's recordings of Nos 1 and 3 emanate from his 1977 LP box containing all the concertos and the *Rhapsody*. Artistically, his performance of No. 1 is impossible to fault; his playing is most exciting and his dazzling virtuosity second to none. Here is a performance that has one on the edge of one's seat. Its coupling is also very good, if not quite in the same class; at mid-price, this must be a strong recommendation. The recording is not of the very finest but is fully acceptable; there is some slight background that may worry a few listeners, but it will soon be forgotten by most.

Piano concerto No. 2 in C min., Op. 18.
*** RCA **RD 85912** [**RCA 5912-2-RC**]. Van Cliburn, Chicago SO, Reiner – TCHAIKOVSKY: *Concerto No. 1.****
*** DG **415 119-2** [id.]. Sviatoslav Richter, Warsaw PO, Wislocki – PROKOFIEV: *Concerto No. 5.****
*** Decca Dig. **414 348-2**; *414 348-4* [id.]. Ortiz, RPO, Atzmon – ADDINSELL: *Warsaw concerto*; LITOLFF: *Scherzo*; GOTTSCHALK: *Grande fantaisie.****
** Decca Dig. **421 181-2**; *421 181-4* [id.]. Bolet, Montreal SO, Dutoit – TCHAIKOVSKY: *Concerto No. 1.**(*)*
*(*) Erato Dig. **ECD 88164** [id.]. Duchable, Strasbourg PO, Guschlbauer – GRIEG: *Concerto.**

In April 1958 Van Cliburn, the twenty-three-year-old Texan pianist, came triumphantly home from winning the Tchaikovsky Competition in Moscow and captured the imagination of the American musical public with a sensational concert tour. At the same time he recorded both Rachmaninov's *Second* and *Third* and the Tchaikovsky *B flat minor concertos* with comparable success. With Reiner making a splendid partner, his account of the Rachmaninov *C minor* is second to none. The pacing of the first movement is comparatively measured, but the climax is unerringly placed, remaining relaxed yet enormously telling. The finale too does not seek to demonstrate runaway bravura but has sparkle and excitement, with the lyrical element heart-warming to match the very beautiful account of the central *Adagio*, full of poetry and romantic feeling. The recording is wonderfully rich, with the Chicago acoustic adding a glorious ambient glow, while the piano, though forwardly placed, has an unexpected body and fullness of timbre. In the finale the cymbals demonstrate an excellent upper range, and the enhancement of the digital remastering almost makes this seem as if it was made yesterday. Coupled with an equally splendid version of the Tchaikovsky *B flat minor*, albeit not so richly recorded, this coupling is a worldbeater.

The power and authority of Richter's performance of Rachmaninov's most popular piano concerto remain totally commanding; the digital remastering of the mid-1960s recording for CD has firmed up the orchestral image and increased the feeling of presence for the boldly realistic piano timbre. Richter has strong, even controversial ideas about speeds in this concerto. The long opening melody of the first movement is taken abnormally slowly, and it is only the sense of mastery which Richter conveys in every note which prevents one from complaining. One ends by admitting how convincing that speed can be in Richter's hands; away from the magic, however, one realizes that this is not quite the way Rachmaninov himself intended it. The slow movement too is spacious – with complete justification this time – and the opening of the finale lets the floodgates open the other way, for Richter chooses a hair-raisingly fast allegro, which has the Polish players scampering after him as fast as they are able. Richter does not, however, let himself be rushed in the great secondary melody, so this is a reading of vivid contrasts. The coupling is Richter's classic account of Prokofiev's *Fifth Concerto*, so this CD combines two of Richter's very finest performances for the gramophone.

Cristina Ortiz's account has the advantage of splendid Decca digital sound. Recorded in Walthamstow Assembly Hall, the piano is realistically distanced and, although the ambience is resonant, the orchestral layout is believable, with attractively rich string textures and an excitingly expansive dynamic range. The performance is warmly romantic, the first-movement climax satisfyingly expansive and the *Adagio* glowingly poetic, with the orchestral response under Atzmon matching the sensibility of the solo playing. A similarly successful partnership in the finale brings sparklingly nimble articulation from Ortiz and a fine expressive breadth from the strings in the famous lyrical melody. The CD offers a subtle extra degree of presence, although the reverberation means that detail is not always sharply registered.

Bolet's version is disappointing. The first movement has a fine climax, but the tension is allowed to ebb away before the end of the movement. The *Adagio*, helped by the glowing Montreal acoustics, is at its finest when Dutoit is in full command, as at the opening and close which are ravishingly romantic, with Bolet embroidering effectively. The finale is very measured and the effect becomes heavy rather than spacious, with the great lyrical melody sounding sluggish. The Decca recording is sumptuously spectacular, but with the Tchaikovsky coupling even less attractive, this is a non-starter.

Although not without moments of excitement and poetry in the *Adagio*, Duchable's account is not helped by a somewhat lustreless recording, clear rather than warm and glowing. It does not survive the considerable competition, and the Grieg coupling is even more disappointing.

Piano concerto No. 2 in C min.; 4 in G min., Op. 40.
(*) Decca Dig. **414 475-2; *414 475-2* [id.]. Ashkenazy, Concg. O, Haitink.
(M) ** DG **419 062-2**; *419 062-2* [id.]. Vásáry, LSO, Ahronovitch.

Unfortunately, in the *C minor Concerto* Ashkenazy's new account cannot quite match his hauntingly poetic earlier reading with Previn (see below). The opening theme is a touch ponderous this time, and elsewhere too the yearning passion of the work is rather muted, even in the lovely reprise of the main theme in the slow movement, which sounds much cooler than in the hands of Cristina Ortiz. Those reservations are relative; Ashkenazy gives a superb account of the *Fourth Concerto*, strong and dramatic and warmly passionate, with Haitink and the Concertgebouw establishing the work as more positively characterful than is often appreciated. As in Michelangeli's classic account of the 1950s, this becomes far more than a poor relation of the earlier concertos. Splendid Decca sound, with the Concertgebouw acoustics making a warmly resonant framework, yet with the CD ensuring refinement of detail. The cassette too is of high quality.

Vásáry's mid-priced coupling on DG is fair value. The partnership of the impetuous Ahronovitch and the more introvert pianist works well enough here. The first movement of the *C minor Concerto* has a fine climax, but after that the tension is lower and the languorous *Adagio* does not distil the degree of poetry which makes the Ashkenazy/Previn performance so beautiful. The opening movement of the *Fourth Concerto* has a strong forward thrust, but the lyrical relaxation brings a slowing of tempo. There is poetry in the slow movement, and the finale is brilliant, if with some lack of poise. The 1976/7 recording is extremely good, with an excellent balance, natural piano timbre and orchestral detail fuller and firmer in the digital remastering.

Piano concerto No. 2 in C min.; Rhapsody on a theme of Paganini, Op. 43.
(M) *** Decca **417 702-2** [id.]. Ashkenazy, LSO, Previn.
(B) *** CfP Dig. **CD-CFP 9017**; *TC-CFP 4383*. Tirimo, Philh. O, Levi.
*** HMV Dig. **CDC7 47223-2** [id.]; *EL 270103-4* [Ang. *4DS 38087*]. Ousset, CBSO, Rattle.
(M) **(*) Decca **417 880-2**; *417 880-4* [id.]. Katchen, LSO, Solti; or LPO, Boult.
(M) ** EMI Dig. **CD-EMX 9509**; *EMX 41 2083-4*. Fowke, RPO, Temirkanov.

Decca's recoupling of Ashkenazy's earlier recordings with Previn is a very desirable CD indeed. At mid-price it makes a clear first choice, except for those wanting the absolute background silence and the extra clarity of focus that digital recording brings, and the splendid Tirimo alternative serves in this respect. It is the warm lyricism of the playing on the Decca CD which is so compulsive. Ashkenazy's opening tempo, like Richter's, is slow, but the tension is finely graduated towards the great climax; and the gentle, introspective mood of the *Adagio* is very beautiful indeed. The finale is broad and spacious rather than electrically exciting, but the scintillating, unforced bravura provides all the sparkle necessary. The *Rhapsody* too is outstandingly successful, the opening variations exhilaratingly paced and the whole performance moving forward in a single sweep, with the eighteenth variation making a great romantic blossoming at the centre. The Kingsway Hall sound is rich and full-bodied in the best analogue sense; the digital remastering has retained all the bloom, especially in the slow movement of the concerto, perhaps the most beautiful on record (though Van Cliburn's is also outstanding). Detail is somewhat sharper in the *Rhapsody*; in the concerto, however, atmosphere rather than clarity is the predominating factor.

Concentrated and thoughtful, deeply expressive yet never self-indulgent, Tirimo is outstanding in both the *Concerto* and the *Rhapsody*, making this one of the most desirable versions of this favourite coupling, irrespective of price. Speeds for the outer movements of the *Concerto* are on the fast side, yet Tirimo's feeling for natural rubato makes them sound natural, never breathless, while the sweetness and repose of the middle movement are exemplary. The digital recording is full, clear and well balanced. An outstanding bargain on CD, with an excellent matching cassette.

Cécile Ousset gives powerful, red-blooded performances of both works in the grand manner, warmly supported by Simon Rattle and the CBSO. Her rubato may often be extreme, but it never sounds studied, always convincingly spontaneous, though the big melody of the eighteenth variation is on the heavyweight side. Ousset is second to none in urgency and excitement, brought out the more here by extreme range of dynamic, with the opening of the first two movements of the *Concerto* intensely hushed and poetic. The EMI recording copes well with that extreme range, the inner textures are clearer on CD than on the original LP and cassette.

Katchen's coupling comes from 1958/60 and, while the Decca recording remains clear and vivid, the sound is slightly dated in the upper range of the *Concerto*, though the violins sound admirably full in the *Rhapsody*. The piano timbre is excellent. Katchen's accounts of both works offer drama and excitement in plenty – the outer movements of the *Concerto* reach the highest pitch of excitement, with bravura very much to the fore. Solti makes an excellent partner here; and Boult sees that the *Rhapsody* is superbly shaped and has diversity and wit as well as romantic flair. The eighteenth variation has fine expansive ardour and the closing pages of the work gripping impetus. Bargain hunters should find this well worth trying in Decca's lower-mid-price Weekend series on both CD and cassette.

Philip Fowke gives tasteful, well-mannered performances, ultimately lacking the fire and bravura needed in both these display works. With good modern, digital recording and an excellent matching tape, it makes a generous bargain – but from the same source on the even cheaper CfP label is Martino Tirimo's excellent coupling of the same two works, also in first-rate digital sound and with more red-blooded performances.

Piano concerto No. 3 in D min., Op. 30.
*(**) RCA **RD 82633** [**RCD1 2633**]. Horowitz, NYPO, Ormandy.
(*) Decca Dig. **417 239-2; *417 239-4* [id.]. Ashkenazy, Concg. O, Haitink.
(*) Decca Dig. **417 671-2 [id.]; *KSXDC 7609*. Bolet, LSO, Fischer.
*(*) HMV Dig. **CDC7 47031-2** [id.]. Sgouros, BPO, Simonov.
*(*) HMV Dig. **CDC7 49049-2** [id.]; *EL 270623-4*. Gavrilov, Phd. O, Muti.

Piano concertos Nos 3; 4 in G, Op. 40.
*(**) Ph. Dig. **411 475-2** [id.]. Kocsis, San Francisco SO, De Waart.

(i) *Piano concerto No. 3;* (ii) *Rhapsody on a theme of Paganini, Op. 43.*
(M) **(*) RCA **GD 86524**; *GK 86524* [**RCA 6524-2-RG**]. (i) Ashkenazy, Phd. O, Ormandy; (ii) Pennario, Boston Pops O, Fiedler.

(i) *Piano concerto No. 3; Rhapsody on a theme of Paganini;* (ii) *The Isle of the Dead, Op. 29.*
(B) **(*) DG Walkman *419 392-4* [id.]. (i) Vásáry, LSO, Ahronovitch; (ii) BPO, Maazel.

Horowitz's legendary association with Rachmaninov's *D minor Concerto* daunted even the composer. Horowitz made it virtually his own property over half a century. Inevitably there are rosy memories of his first 78 r.p.m. recording with Albert Coates, but in most respects the mono LP, made in Carnegie Hall in May 1951 with Fritz Reiner, represents the highwater mark of his achievement. In January 1978 he was persuaded to re-record the work in stereo, again in Carnegie Hall, but this time at a live concert, with Ormandy drawing a committed and romantically expansive accompaniment from the New York Philharmonic Orchestra. Perhaps just a little of the old magic is missing in the solo playing but it remains prodigious, and Horowitz's insights are countless. The outer movements have undoubted electricity and there is a powerful climax to the *Adagio*, but it is the fascination of the detail that draws one back to this remarkable recorded document. Not all the playing is immaculate and there is some rhythmic eccentricity in the finale; but the communicative force of the reading is unquestionable. The snag is the recording, which was originally very dry and clinical, the piano timbre lacking bloom. For CD, the remastering has radically altered the sound-picture, considerably softening the focus, to bring a more romantic aura to the music making. The result is that at lower dynamic levels the image appears to recede, while the climaxes of the second and third movements expand very dramatically, with the rise in dynamic level immediately accompanied by a brighter, freer upper range. The effect is disconcerting – but one can adjust to it, and certainly the effect is more agreeable than the 'bare bones' of the original LP sound quality.

Ashkenazy has recorded this concerto four times; as a work, it seems to prove elusive for him. In his latest Decca recording he is beautifully recorded – the solo instrument is most realistically placed, it really does sound like this in the concert hall. At the same time there is some loss of presence, although much of this lies in the nature of the performance. Ashkenazy's interpretation has a great deal to commend it: there is unfailing sensitivity and musicianship, but one needs a greater sense of impact and focus – his very first recording with Fistoulari had more ardour and spontaneity. So too had his 1976 RCA version, recorded in Philadelphia with Eugene Ormandy. We were inclined to dismiss this in its old LP format because of the piano timbre, typical of transatlantic piano recordings of that period, which is hard and lacking richness. If one can adjust to this, then the mid-1970s performance has much to offer. It has great tension and the climax to the first movement has arresting breadth and power, with the simple reprise of the main theme that follows particularly moving. The rest of the interpretation has comparable charisma; and Ormandy, too, is at his finest. The coupling is a prodigiously brilliant account of the *Rhapsody* from Leonard Pennario and Fiedler which is certainly compulsive; the snag here is that the forward balance, coupled to the bright digital remastering, makes orchestral fortissimos sound shrill, notably the massed violins in the eighteenth variation. But with some control, and allowances for less than ideal technology, this CD is rewarding; and the tape, which smooths the top a bit, is even more so. The cassette of Ashkenazy's Decca performance is transferred at rather a low level and is full-bodied, but with a much more restricted upper range than the CD.

Bolet offers yet another alternative approach, bringing out the heroic side of this formidable concerto, and the recording of the piano – digitally bright to the point of clangorousness – underlines that. Again the cassette is smoother and richer, tempering the upper range attractively. In both formats Bolet's clarity of articulation and bravura are breathtaking and there is no lack of adrenalin, but some of the work's romantic tenderness is lost, with the orchestra tending to sound aggressive on CD.

Vásáry's Walkman tape is undoubtedly a bargain, as it also includes Maazel's fine version of *The Isle of the Dead* – see below. In the *Concerto* Vásáry uses the longer version of the first-movement cadenza; his playing is highly musical, clean and often gentle in style. The impetuous Ahronovitch offers some extremes of tempi; taken as a whole, however, this performance has both poetry and excitement (especially in the finale). The conductor's chimerical style is more obviously suited to the *Rhapsody*, with its opening faster than usual and with strong contrasts of tempo and mood between brilliant and lyrical variations. The sound is very good.

Zoltán Kocsis's recording with Edo de Waart and the San Francisco Symphony has had a bad press and, in so far as he rushes through the first movement, deservedly so. All the same, there is some very exciting playing here – and he earns one listener's thanks for opting for the shorter cadenza in the first movement. This he plays with electrifying brilliance. The *Fourth Concerto* is a good deal less rushed, though it is full of excitement and virtuosity, when this is required. Indeed, there is much thrilling playing here, but there are moments in both concertos when one feels Kocsis should perhaps rein in his fiery high spirits. The Philips recording places him rather far forward but there is no lack of orchestral detail and there is plenty of range.

Dmitri Sgouros possess an altogether remarkable technique – not only for his tender years but, one is tempted to say, for any age. It would be ungenerous not to give his first concerto recording a welcome, for much of the piano playing is pretty dazzling as such. But, however remarkable it may be for a boy of fifteen, the standards of the gramophone differ from those of the concert hall; much of the musical meaning seems to escape him and the bravura work often loses its meaning. Compare the main theme in the hands of a Rachmaninov or a Horowitz: it is evident that Sgouros is an artist of enormous facility and promise, rather than of fulfilment. He plays the second cadenza first recorded by Ashkenazy rather than the shorter one chosen by Rachmaninov himself. The recording itself is serviceable rather than distinguished. It is certainly not in the demonstration class, even in the compact disc format. The Berlin Philharmonic does not produce its characteristic rich strong sonority for Yuri Simonov. Not a front runner.

EMI issued a remarkable LP of Andrei Gavrilov's incandescent account of the *Third Concerto* at the time of the Tchaikovsky Competition, which was much (and rightly) acclaimed at the time. By its side this newcomer must be accounted a disappointment. It is what might be called idiosyncratic and by no means as authoritative or secure as his earlier account. Given the quality of the competition, this must unfortunately come well down the list. The recording is very good in both media.

Piano concerto No. 4 in G min., Op. 40.
❀ *** HMV **CDC7 49326-2** [id.]. Michelangeli, Philh. O, Gracis – RAVEL: *Piano concerto in G.**** ❀

As a performance this is one of the most brilliant piano records ever made. It puts the composer's own recorded performance quite in the shade and makes one wonder why the work has failed to achieve anything like the popularity of the earlier concertos. The fact that the slow movement has a theme which is a cross between *Three blind mice* and *Two lovely black eyes* – one reason given for its poor impact on the general public – in no way justifies neglect, for it is a very beautiful movement, set between two outer movements which have a brilliance that even Rachmaninov rarely achieved. Michelangeli's performance of the climax of the first movement has an agility coupled with sheer power which has one on the edge of one's seat. The recording does not quite match the superlative quality of the playing, but in the digital remastering has been made to sound more open, the piano tone clear and not hard. There is still an attractive ambience, although the massed violins above the stave could ideally have more body.

The Isle of the dead, Op. 29; The Rock, Op. 7.
(B) *** DG Dig. *419 841-4* [id.]. BPO, Maazel – TCHAIKOVSKY: *Symphony No. 6.***

It is good to have Maazel's powerful Berlin Philharmonic accounts of Rachmaninov's two symphonic poems in an economic format, separated from the symphonies with which they were originally coupled. At a fast speed Maazel's view of *The Isle of the Dead* is less sombre and brooding than usual, but the climaxes have real fervour and the result is intensely compelling. The recording is strikingly vivid and full on this splendid Pocket Music chrome tape. Even if Giulini's *Pathétique* is less memorable, this inexpensive issue is worth considering for the Rachmaninov alone.

The Isle of the dead, Op. 29; Symphonic dances, Op. 45.
*** Decca Dig. **410 124-2**; *410 124-4* [id.]. Concg. O, Ashkenazy.

The Isle of the dead, Op. 29; Symphonic dances, Op. 45; Aleko: Intermezzo & Women's dance. Vocalise, Op. 34/14.
(M) *** HMV **CDM7 69025-2** [id.]; EG *769025-4*. LSO, Previn.

Symphonic dances, Op. 45; Aleko: Intermezzo, Vocalise, Op. 34/14.
(*) DG Dig. **410 894-2 [id.]. BPO, Maazel.

Ashkenazy's is a superb coupling, rich and powerful in playing and interpretation. One here recognizes *The Isle of the Dead* as among the very finest of Rachmaninov's orchestral works, relentless in its ominous build-up, while at generally fast speeds the *Symphonic dances* have extra darkness and intensity too, suggesting no relaxation whatever at the end of Rachmaninov's career. The splendid recording, especially fine on CD, but also ample and brilliant on chrome cassette, highlights both the passion and the fine precision of the playing.

Previn's original full-priced issue (from 1976) offered the same coupling as Ashkenazy, but now it has been digitally remastered with great success and the vividly wide-ranging sound is highly spectacular, among EMI's most successful analogue reissues. The added clarity and sparkle have a balancing weight in the bass and the effect is very exciting. The addition of the *Aleko* excerpts, plus a fine lyrical account of the *Vocalise*, makes a generous mid-priced CD, playing for over 70′, which competes in every respect with Ashkenazy's digital alternative. There is a fine equivalent chrome tape.

Maazel's is a crisp, light-textured reading of the *Symphonic dances*. Brilliance is there in plenty, but full warmth of lyricism is lacking, as it is too in the *Vocalise*. Bright, spacious recording, among the best made in the Philharmonie in Berlin. On compact disc the detail and focus of the sound are the more striking and the precision of ensemble is given added freshness and projection. But Maazel comes into competition with Ashkenazy, who offers an equally fine (if fascinatingly different) reading of the *Symphonic dances*, plus a much more substantial coupling.

Rhapsody on a theme of Paganini, Op. 43.
(*) Ph. Dig. **410 052-2; *7337 164* [id.]. Davidovich, Concg. O, Järvi – SAINT-SAËNS: *Concerto No. 2.* **(*)

Bella Davidovich is given the benefit of natural and vivid recorded sound with genuine warmth and space round the various instruments. She plays with fleet-fingered fluency and no want of either brilliance or poetry, and Neeme Järvi gives excellent support. This is a likeable performance, but the characterization is romantically relaxed and other versions show deeper insights. The compact disc offers richly atmospheric quality, with the Concertgebouw acoustic bringing an ambient glow and flattering the piano timbre. The chrome cassette is rather middle- and bass-orientated.

(i) *Symphonic dances, Op. 45;* (ii) *The Bells, Op. 35.*
(M) **(*) Olympia Dig. **OCD 116** [id.]. (i) USSR RSO, Fedoseyev; (ii) Mikhailova, Larin, Bolshoi Theatre Ch., Moscow PO, Kitaenko.

The Russian performance of the *Symphonic dances* has less lyrical warmth than the Western versions, with the drier recording emphasizing the difference. Humour assumes a hint of irony. The rhythms are well pointed and the reading makes a most individual effect. The digital recording is vivid and well balanced. The use of a Russian choir and soloists from the Bolshoi also adds another dimension to *The Bells*. Both soloists are eloquent, and only a touch of wobble affects the soprano contribution; the chorus sings incisively and in the final *Lento lugubre* there is a striking combination of fervour and melancholy. Again the digital recording is very lively and clear, yet the ambience provides plenty of atmosphere.

Symphonies Nos 1–3; The Isle of the dead.
(*) DG Dig. **419 314-2 (3) [id.]. BPO, Maazel.

Symphonies Nos 1–3; Youth Symphony (1891).
(M) *** Decca Dig. **421 065-2** (3) [id.]. Concg. O, Ashkenazy.

Ashkenazy's set – offered at mid-price – can be given an unqualified recommendation. The performances, passionate and volatile, are intensely Russian; the only possible reservation concerns the slow movement of the *Second*, where the clarinet solo is less ripe than in some versions. Elsewhere there is drama, energy and drive, balanced by much delicacy of feeling, while the Concertgebouw strings produce great ardour for Rachmaninov's long-breathed melodies. The vivid Decca sound within the glowing Concertgebouw ambience is ideal for the music.

Maazel's set is also very impressive, and offers superb playing from the Berlin Philharmonic. However, the DG engineers secured a less sumptuous sound in the Berlin Philharmonie than their Decca colleagues, and this emphasizes Maazel's fiercer way with Rachmaninov's passionate impulse. The climaxes of the *Second Symphony* in particular would have been enhanced by a warmer middle and lower range. Maazel's readings are not to be dismissed: the *First Symphony* is particularly fine, with Rachmaninov's often thick orchestration beautifully transparent. The *Third* too is distinctive, unusually fierce and intense. The result is sharper and tougher than one expects, less obviously romantic, and the finale is made to sound rather like a Walton comedy overture at the start, brilliant and exciting, but at the end it lacks joyful exuberance. Exhilaration is the keynote throughout and there is an abundance of adrenalin, yet the lack of expansive romantic warmth is undoubtedly a drawback. Moreover, unlike the Decca set, this is at full price.

Symphony No. 1 in D min., Op. 13.
*** Decca Dig. **411 657-2** [id.]. Concg. O, Ashkenazy.

Ashkenazy's is an outstanding version, volatile and extreme in its tempi, with the Concertgebouw players responding in total conviction. In the first movement the cellos and basses articulate their comments on the first theme with phenomenal clarity. This was the last of Ashkenazy's Rachmaninov symphony series to be recorded and it is the most convincing of all. The digital recording is most beautiful, for the sound is full, atmospheric and brilliant. It is superb on CD. Though the weight of the opening of the finale is magnificent, the relentless hammering rhythms are presented vividly in scale, where they can easily seem oppressive. The Scherzo at a very fast speed has Mendelssohnian lightness, the flowing *Larghetto* is presented as a lyrical interlude.

Symphony No. 2 in E min., Op. 27.
(M) **(*) HMV **CDC7 47159-2** [id.]; *ED 290498-4* [Ang. *4AM 34740*]. LSO, Previn.
(*) Decca Dig. **400 081-2 [id.]; *KSXDC 7563* [Lon. *LDR-5 71063*]. Concg. O, Ashkenazy.
(*) Telarc Dig. **CD 80113 [id.]. RPO, Previn.
(*) Chan. Dig. **CHAN 8423; *ABTD 1021* [id.]. SNO, Gibson.
** HMV Dig. **CDC7 47062-2** [id.]. LAPO, Rattle.

Previn's 1973 recording of the *Second Symphony* has dominated the catalogue for over a decade. Its passionate intensity combines freshness with the boldest romantic feeling, yet the music's underlying melancholy is not glossed over. With vividly committed playing from the LSO and a glorious response from the strings, this remains a classic account, unlikely to be surpassed. Unfortunately, the digital remastering for this reissue produces a much drier sound-balance with the middle and bass response less expansive. The rich sumptuousness of the strings, so striking on the full-priced original LP, has been replaced by clean, full textures with noticeably reduced amplitude and ambient bloom. On CD, inner detail is undoubtedly fresher, and the orchestra generally has enhanced presence. The bass is firm. But the upper strings are thinner and there is a touch of shrillness in climaxes of the outer movements. In the *Adagio* the LSO violins are inspired to provide such body and intensity of timbre that climaxes still retain an impressive weight of tone. The tape is perhaps slightly more expansive.

Ashkenazy began his Rachmaninov series with the Concertgebouw on this most popular of the symphonies; though the result is most impressive, a performance of high contrasts, there are signs that the Dutch players had not fully adjusted to their guest conductor. In the *Adagio* third movement, the clarinet line is less smooth than in either of the Previn versions. Nevertheless, Ashkenazy's reading has a romantic urgency and drive that are missing from Previn's Telarc version, with the climaxes of the outer movements far more gripping. In the Scherzo too, the Amsterdam strings are tauter in ensemble; there is a vibrant impulse about the performance as a whole which is very Russian in its intensity. The Decca recording is full-bodied but with a degree of edge on the strings, and this extra bite suits Ashkenazy's approach; the CD has a balancing depth and richness. The chrome tape has all the fullness and bloom, yet softens the edge on top a little.

The greater feeling of spaciousness of Previn's 1985 Telarc recording is apparent at the very opening. The whole reading is more moderately paced than before, with long-breathed phrases moulded flexibly, with far less urgency and none of Ashkenazy's impetuosity (Ashkenazy's first movement is over two minutes shorter). Previn's *Adagio* is even more relaxed (17′ 17″ against Ashkenazy's 14′ 15″). This expansiveness is enhanced by the finely sustained playing of the RPO strings and the sumptuous Telarc recording with its luxuriant resonance. However, the comparative lack of drive in the Scherzo and the finale, with full reserves held back for the ultimate climax, emphasizes the reflective nature of the performance. With such superbly rich sound there are some ravishing moments, but in the last resort the lack of electricity – compared with the earlier LSO version – brings a degree of disappointment, and on CD Ashkenazy offers the more satisfying musical experience.

Gibson and the Scottish National Orchestra have the advantage of an excellent digital recording, made in the Henry Wood Hall in Glasgow. The brass sounds are thrilling, but the slightly recessed balance of the strings is a drawback and there is not the body of tone demonstrated by both the Telarc and Decca versions mentioned above. But this is a freshly spontaneous performance and overall the sound is admirably natural, even if it includes some strangely unrhythmic thuds at climaxes (apparently the conductor in his excitement stamping on the podium). The cassette transfer is clear and immediate, with crisply focused detail.

Rattle's first recording with the Los Angeles Philharmonic is also a disappointment. The problems of recording in the orchestra'a home, the Chandler Pavilion, have brought sound that is clear but lacks body in the string section, with violins made to sound emaciated. All this comes out the more clearly on CD. Rattle's performance also lacks urgency, with spacious speeds often without necessary tensions, particularly in the finale, which is unexciting compared with the finest rivals.

Symphony No. 3 in A min., Op. 14.
(M) *** HMV **CDM7 69564-2**; *EG 290859-4*. LSO, Previn – SHOSTAKOVICH: *Symphony No. 6.****
** Orfeo Dig. **CO 69831A** [id.]. Bamberg SO, Caetani.

Symphony No. 3, Youth Symphony (1891).
*** Decca Dig. **410 231-2** [id.]. Concg. O, Ashkenazy.

Ashkenazy's is a performance of extremes, volatile and passionate in a very Russian way. In the first movement the varying speeds are contrasted far more than usual, the allegros faster, the slow, lyrical passages (notably the great melody of the second subject) slower with copious rubato. The finale is fast and hectic to the point of wildness, but the Concertgebouw players respond superbly and the digital recording is full, rich and brilliant. The fragment of a projected symphony with its first subject plainly indebted to Tchaikovsky's *Fourth* – was written when Rachmaninov was only nineteen. It is an enjoyable and unusual makeweight. The glorious sound is even more impressive on compact disc.

Previn's HMV CD brings an outstanding performance; the digital remastering has had a less extreme effect here than in the *Second Symphony* and there is plenty of body alongside the sharpened detail, even if the amplitude has been reduced in the interest of greater clarity. There is much that is elusive in this highly original structure, and Previn conveys the purposefulness of the writing at every point, revelling in the richness, but clarifying textures. The LSO has rarely displayed its virtuosity more brilliantly in the recording studio, reflecting the fact that the sessions came immediately after a series of performances of the work in America. With its generous Shostakovich coupling, this is a bargain, and there is a very good cassette.

The Bambergers play very well for Oleg Caetani, and he shows a natural feeling for the Rachmaninov phraseology. The freely rhapsodic slow movement finds delicacy as well as rapture in the music; although overall the reading has less physical passion than the Decca version, it does not lack romantic feeling. The recording is excellent and very naturally balanced, but there is no fill-up; and this would not be a first choice.

CHAMBER AND INSTRUMENTAL MUSIC

Cello sonata in G min., Op. 19; Oriental dance, Op. 2/3; Prelude, Op. 2/1; Romance; Vocalise, Op. 34/14 (with ALTSCHULER: *Mélodie*).
*** Decca Dig. **414 340-2**; *414 340-4* [id.]. Lynn Harrell, Vladimir Ashkenazy.

Cello sonata in G min., Op. 19; Vocalise, Op. 34/14 (with DVOŘÁK: *Polonaise*; SIBELIUS: *Malinconia*).
(*) Ph. Dig. **412 732-2; *412 732-4* [id.]. Heinrich Schiff, Elisabeth Leonskaja.

Lynn Harrell and Vladimir Ashkenazy give an impassioned, full-throated account of the glorious *Cello sonata* and capture its melancholy perfectly. They are very well attuned to its sensibility and to the affecting charm of the smaller pieces. The Decca recording is in the high traditions of the house; the balance and perspective are completely natural. The Altschuler *Mélodie on a theme of Rachmaninov* makes a slight but agreeable encore. The tape is acceptable but less well defined than the CD.

Schiff's performance of the *Sonata* with Elisabeth Leonskaja may be less extrovert than the Harrell/Ashkenazy account, but it has a thoughtful, inward quality that draws the listener to it. Its nostalgia and melancholy are every bit as potent as in the rival version. In this of all sonatas, the piano is hardly less important than the cello, and Leonskaja is perhaps a less imaginative partner than Ashkenazy. Needless to say, the Philips recording is first class, but the Decca has the more logical and interesting coupling. The Sibelius *Malinconia*, an uncharacteristic piece, was written for the cellist, Georg Schneevoigt (better known as a conductor), and his wife, Sigrid. According to Erik Tawaststjerna, its ineffectiveness (particularly the piano part) owes much to the limitations of the Schneevoigt partnership. The Dvořák *Polonaise in A* comes from 1879, a year before the *Violin concerto* and the *Sixth Symphony*, and anticipates the finale of the *Quartet*, Op. 61, of two years later.

Trios élegiaques Nos 1 in G min., Op. 8; 2 in D min., Op. 9.
*** Chan. Dig. **CHAN 8431**; *ABTD 1101* [id.]. Borodin Trio.
*** Ph. Dig. **420 175-2;** *420 175-4* [id.]. Beaux Arts Trio.

The *G minor Trio* was composed when Rachmaninov was nineteen; its successor, the *D minor*, Op. 9, comes from the following year and was written in memory of Tchaikovsky. The first is a pensive one-movement piece lasting no more than a quarter of an hour, while Op. 9 is on a much larger scale, in three movements, the first alone lasting almost 20 minutes and the second not much less. They are both imbued with lyrical fervour and draw from the rich vein of melancholy so characteristic of Rachmaninov. The performances by the Borodin Trio are eloquent and masterly, and the recording is admirably balanced and has plenty of warmth. While the CD has the usual subtle gain in presence and definition, there is also a chrome cassette of the highest standard. The reverberant acoustic offers no transfer problems, the sound clear and realistic.

The Beaux Arts are more reticent than the Borodins. Whether you prefer the excellent Philips version to the Chandos will depend on whether you are drawn to understatement rather than its reverse. The Beaux Arts are less overtly intense and eloquent; they leave the music to speak for itself without ever being matter of fact. Their reading is lighter in colouring without being any the less deeply felt. It is difficult to make a clear choice: the Beaux Arts are splendidly aristocratic and have great refinement; the Borodins are full-blooded and ardent; either will give satisfaction. The Philips tape is transferred at rather a low level and is middle- and bass-orientated.

Études-tableaux, Op. 39, Nos 1–9; Variations on a theme of Corelli, Op. 42.
*** Decca Dig. **417 671-2**; *417 671-4* [id.]. Vladimir Ashkenazy.

Superb performances from Ashkenazy make this the most desirable of Rachmaninov issues. The *Corelli variations* is a rarity and a very fine work. The recording is first class.

Études-tableaux, Op. 33/5, 6 and 9; Op. 39/1–4, 7 and 9.
*** MMG Dig. **MCD 10031** [id.]. Sviatoslav Richter – TCHAIKOVSKY: *The Seasons*: excerpts.***

As might be expected, Richter gives marvellously authoritative and individual performances of the *Études-tableaux*, offering many insights and playing that is physically involving with its wide range of dynamic, yet at times with the timbre shaded right down. He chooses a selection from both Opp. 33 and 39 but makes up for the absent items by adding four of the most attractive of Tchaikovsky's *Seasons*, playing with comparable character. These begin the recital and are treated more intimately, so that when he opens the Rachmaninov group with Opus 33 No. 9, the change of mood is commanding. The recording stems from Melodiya but was engineered in Munich in April 1983. The sound is first class, with the piano very tangible.

24 Preludes (complete).
(M) ** Olympia **OCD 110 A/B** (2) [id.]. Peter Katin.

24 Preludes (complete)*; Piano sonata No. 2 in B flat min., Op. 36.*
*** Decca **414 417-2** (2). Vladimir Ashkenazy.

Considering his popularity and their quality, it is odd that Rachmaninov's *Preludes* have not been recorded complete more often. Ashkenazy's were the first to appear on CD, with the excellent recording further enhanced. There is superb flair and panache about this playing. As a bonus, the compact discs offer the *Second Piano sonata*, with Ashkenazy generally following the 1913 original score but with some variants. He plays with great virtuosity and feeling, and the result is a *tour de force*.

Katin too is splendidly recorded, and the bold, clear piano image itself lends a certain romantic splendour to these performances. Katin has the measure of the lyrical music and it is only in the pieces that make their full effect with sheer bravura that he is less than completely convincing.

Preludes: in C sharp min., Op. 3/2; Op. 23/1, 2, 4–6; Mélodie, Op. 3/3; Polichinelle, Op. 3/4; Variations on a theme of Corelli, Op. 42.
*** Conifer Dig. **CDCF 159**; *MCFC 159* [id.]. Kathryn Stott.

Kathryn Stott is one of the most gifted of the rising generation of British pianists and her playing on this Conifer recital will give undoubted satisfaction. She possesses a strong keyboard personality and a wide range of colour and dynamics; moreover she has a good feeling for Rachmaninov and gives well-considered accounts of all the pieces on this generously filled CD. It would be difficult to fault her sensitive performance of the *Corelli variations*; there is a strong rhythmic grip and her phrasing is keenly articulate. In the recording, one is fairly close to the piano, but not unreasonably so, and there is plenty of air round the instrument. There is a first-class cassette.

Piano sonatas Nos 1 in D min., Op. 28; 2 in B flat min., Op. 36 (revised 1931).
*** Hyp. *KA 66047* [id.]. Howard Shelley.

Like John Ogdon before him, Howard Shelley chooses the 1931 version of the *Sonata* and couples it with the relatively little-known *D minor Sonata*, Op. 28, which comes from 1907 and was written between the *Second Symphony* and *The Isle of the dead*. Shelley has plenty of sweep and grandeur and withstands comparison with the distinguished competition. He has something of the grand manner and an appealing freshness, ardour and, when required, tenderness. He is accorded an excellent balance by the engineers, which places the piano firmly in focus. The cassette transfer is first class.

Piano sonata No. 2 in B flat min., Op. 36 (original version)*; Fragments in A flat; Fughetta in F, Gavotte in D., Mélodie in E. Morceau de fantaisie in G min.; Nocturnes Nos 1–3; Oriental sketch in B flat; Piece in D min.; 4 Pieces; Prelude in E flat min.; Romance in F sharp min.; Song without words in D min.*
*** Hyp. **CDA 66198**; *KA 66198* [id.]. Howard Shelley.

Howard Shelley has already recorded the 1931 version of the *Second Sonata* for Hyperion, coupled on tape with the *First* (see above). He is an unfailingly musical and thoughtful player of sensitivity, intelligence and good taste. Most of the shorter pieces are early, and not all are Rachmaninov at his very greatest – but they are persuasively played, as is the *Sonata*; they have the merit of excellent recorded sound (although the cassette is less sharply defined than the CD). A valuable issue.

Suite No. 2, Op. 17.
*** Ph. Dig. **411 034-2** [id.]. Argerich, Freire – LUTOSLAWSKI: *Paganini variations*; RAVEL: *La valse.****

Argerich and Freire give a dazzling virtuoso account of the *Suite*, rushing the waltzes off their feet (the movement is marked *presto* but they play it *prestissimo*). They are fresh, idiomatic and thoughtful and their performance is thoroughly exhilarating. They are well recorded and can be recommended. The only drawback to the recording is the reverberation, which seems a trifle excessive, even for an expansively romantic score, and this is especially striking on the excellent compact disc.

Symphonic dances, Op. 45 (see also above under *The Isle of the dead*).
** DG Dig. **410 616-2** [id.]. Argerich, Economou – TCHAIKOVSKY: *Nutcracker suite.***

Argerich and Economou play with great temperament and everything is marvellously alive and well thought out. There is much sensitivity and a lively sense of enjoyment in evidence as well as (it goes without saying) great virtuosity, but the DG recording, although very acceptable, is rather dry.

Song transcriptions: *Dreams; Floods of spring; In the silent night; The little island; Midsummer eve; The Muse; O, cease thy singing; On the death of a linnet; Sorrow in springtime; To the children; Vocalise; Where beauty dwells.*
*** Dell'Arte **CD DBS 7001** [id.]. Earl Wild (piano).

Earl Wild is a pianist all too often taken for granted as a virtuoso pure and simple, rather than the great artist that he is. On this CD he plays twelve masterly transcriptions he has made of Rachmaninov songs, ranging from *In the silent night* from the Op. 4 set of 1890 to *Dreams* of Op. 38 (1916). Of course his virtuosity is dazzling – but so, too, is his refinement of colour and his musicianship. It is impossible not to give this recital three stars, though the recording is not of comparable distinction.

VOCAL MUSIC

Vespers, Op. 37.
(***) Chant du Monde **278 845** [id.]. Korkan, Ognevoi, RSFSR Ac. Russian Ch., Sveshnikov.

Rachmaninov's *Vespers* (1915) must be counted among his most profound and fascinating works. The fifteen movements are superbly written and are as dark, deeply affecting and richly sonorous as any Orthodox Church music. The performances can only be called superlative, and it will be a long time before they are superseded. The basses in particular have incredible richness (at one point they sing a low B flat) and the recording is in an appropriately resonant acoustic. The recording has plenty of atmosphere. The digital remastering produces very little background noise; but some of the liveliness of the original LP has been lost, and pianissimos tend to recede, though climaxes are expansive. The original CD (**278 552**) had the last three sections of the score omitted, but we are assured that the new number, listed above, will produce an untruncated version.

The Bells, Op. 35; 3 Russian songs, Op. 41.
*** Decca Dig. **414 455-2**; *414 455-4* [id.]. Troitskaya, Karczykowski, Krause, Concg. Ch. & O, Ashkenazy.

The Bells, Op. 35; Vocalise, Op. 34/14.
(*) Chan. Dig. **CHAN 8476; *ABTD 1187* [id.]. Murphy, Lewis, Wilson-Johnson, SNO Ch. & O, Järvi – TCHAIKOVSKY: *Romeo & Juliet duet* etc.***

Ashkenazy's volatile Russian style is eminently suitable for Rachmaninov's masterly cantata. After the magical silvery flutes at the opening, he certainly creates a vivid picture of 'sledges dashing in a row, their bells jingling'. His tenor soloist has just the right touch of temperament, and in the slow movement Natalia Troitskaya's contribution combines Slavonic feeling with freshness. The chorus respond readily to the black mood of the Scherzo and bring a melancholy intensity to the finale. The Decca recording is superb, wide in range, spacious and clear.

Järvi's recording was made in the Usher Hall, Edinburgh, and its expansive acoustics bring a glowing aura to Rachmaninov's woodwind scoring and give lustre and richness to the strings. The climaxes expand just as impressively as in the Decca set, and have great impact too, but detail is less clear and there is less bite. The three soloists all sing eloquently but without the Slavonic character of Ashkenazy's group. In short, magnificent as the sound is in Scotland, the Decca recording has an extra degree of intensity, especially in the vehemence of the Scherzo. Järvi's Tchaikovsky couplings are unique, but Ashkenazy's choice of the *Russian folksongs* seems more apt. The Decca chrome cassette is most successfully transferred, although it has not quite the range of the CD.

Songs: *All things pass by; At the gate of the holy abode; By the fresh grave; Christ is risen; Fate; Fragment from Musset; He took it all from me; In my soul; In the silence of the night; No; No Prophet; Were you hiccoughing?*
(*) Decca Dig. **419 239-2 [id.]. Paata Burchuladze, Ludmilla Ivanova – MUSSORGSKY: *Songs.***(*)

The natural gravity and intensity of these Rachmaninov songs comes over powerfully in fine, rich-toned performances from the remarkable Georgian bass with his uniquely firm and rich voice. Others may find deeper, more detailed expressiveness, but the musical satisfaction here is great, with the voice vividly caught by the recording.

Raid, Kaljo (born 1922)

Symphony No. 1 in C min.
*** Chan. Dig. **CHAN 8525**; *ABTD 1235* [id.]. SNO, Järvi – ELLER: *Dawn; Elegia* etc.***

Kaljo Raid fled to Sweden in 1944, but soon afterwards emigrated to the United States, where he took a degree in Divinity while continuing his musical studies with Ibert and Milhaud. Since 1954 he has been active as a Baptist priest in Canada, and for a time made a special study of medieval music. He has written in all manner of styles and is highly prolific. Raid's *First Symphony* of 1944 was written when he had just passed twenty-one and was still studying with Eller; it shows a genuine feel for form and a fine sense of proportion, even though the personality is not fully formed. Well worth hearing. Neeme Järvi gets very committed playing from the Scottish National Orchestra and the recording is warm and well detailed. There is an excellent tape.

Rameau, Jean Philippe (1683–1764)

Les Boréades: orchestral suite; Dardanus: orchestral suite.
*** Ph. Dig. **420 240-2**; *420 240-4* [id.]. O of 18th Century, Brüggen.

The orchestral suite from *Les Boréades* (1764), Rameau's last opera, occupies the larger part of the disc. The invention is full of resource and imagination and makes one wonder why this great composer is so underrated by the wider musical public. The playing of the Orchestra of the 18th Century under Frans Brüggen is spirited and sensitive and will provide delight even to those normally unresponsive to authentic instruments. Both suites are well played and can be recommended. Even more commendable is Gardiner's complete *Boréades* on Erato, and it can only be a matter of time before this appears on CD.

Dardanus: suite.
(*) Erato **ECD 88013 [id.]. E. Bar. Soloists, Gardiner.

John Eliot Gardiner offers a substantial selection from the orchestral music of both versions of Rameau's opera (the 1739 score and the score for the 1744 revival which involved radical rewriting of the last two Acts). There is plenty of variety here, from lightly scored dance music to the powerful closing *Chaconne*. Some of the music is slight and, out of context, does not make its full effect, but as a sampler this might tempt some listeners to try the whole work (available only on LP). The CD offers fine if not remarkable sound, with good presence but without the depth of perspective of the best recordings from this source.

Hippolyte et Aricie: orchestral suite.
*** HMV **CDC7 49133-2** [id.]. La Petite Bande, Kuijken.

There were three productions of *Hippolyte et Aricie* during Rameau's lifetime, in 1733, 1742 and 1757, for which various instrumental additions were made. This record collects virtually all the orchestral music from the three, in performances so lively and winning that the disc is irresistible. Sigiswald Kuijken gets delightful results from his ensemble; the melodic invention is fresh and its orchestral presentation ingenious. In every way an outstanding release – and not least in the quality of the sound.

Les Indes galantes: excerpts (harpsichord transcriptions).
*** HM **HMC 901028**; *40 1028*. Kenneth Gilbert.

These transcriptions are Rameau's own, made some time after the success scored by his first opera-ballet, *Les Indes galantes*, in 1735. He grouped a number of items into four suites or '*concerts*', and these included not only dance numbers and orchestral pieces but arias as well. Kenneth Gilbert, playing a fine instrument in contemporary tuning, reveals these miniatures as the subtle and refined studies they are. He could not be better served by the recording engineers, and the CD brings added presence and background quiet. The cassette is transferred at a very high level indeed and, while the quality is excellent, the image tends to be right on top of the listener unless care is exercised with the controls.

Pièces de clavecin: Suite (No. 1) in A minor; L'Agaçante; La Dauphine; L'Indiscrète; La Livri; La Pantomine: La Timide.
*** CRD **CRD 3320** [id.]. Trevor Pinnock.

For his second record of Rameau's harpsichord music (the first is listed below), Trevor Pinnock chose a more mellow instrument, making his stylish, crisply rhythmic performances even more attractive. The selection includes *La Dauphine*, the last keyboard piece that Rameau wrote, brilliantly performed. Excellent recording.

Harpsichord suites: in A min. (1728)*; in E min.* (1724).
*** CRD **CRD 3310** [id.]. Trevor Pinnock.

Harpsichord suites: in D min./ma (1724); in G ma/min. (1728).
*** CRD **CRD 3330** [id.]. Trevor Pinnock.

Excellent performances. Trevor Pinnock is restrained in the matter of ornamentation, but his direct manner is both eloquent and stylish. The harpsichord is of the French type and is well recorded.

Cantatas: *Les amants trahis; Aquilon et Orithie; Le berger fidèle; L'impatience.*
** Chant du Monde **LDC 278 774** [id.]. Poulenard, Elwes, Reinhart, Les Dominos.

Rameau's chamber cantatas are grievously neglected on record, and are relatively early works: he was in his forties and had not yet embarked on any of his operas. *L'impatience* and *Aquilon et Orithie* fare best, though these performances fall short of the ideal; the singing is mostly accomplished and in good style but the odd moment of doubtful intonation from the instrumental ensemble might have been corrected. Good, well-focused recording.

Grand motets: *In convertendo; Quam dilecta laboravi.*
*** HM **HM 90 1078** [id.]. Gari, Monnaliu, Ledroit, De Mey, Varcoe, Chapelle Royale Ch., Ghent Coll. Vocale, Herreweghe.

These two motets are among Rameau's finest works and come from the years preceding his first opera in 1733. The recordings are made in the Carmelite Church in Ghent which has a warm, reverberant acoustic, and the Ghent Collegium Vocale is stiffened by forces from La Chapelle Royale in Paris. They produce excellent results and the soloists are also very fine indeed. In his book on the composer, Girdlestone speaks of *In convertendo* as Rameau's greatest piece of church music, and this record makes out the most persuasive case for it. The instrumental ensemble includes several members of La Petite Bande and so its excellence can be almost taken for granted.

OPERA-BALLET AND OPERA

Anacréon (complete).
*** HM **HMC 90190** [id.]. Schirrer, Mellon, Feldman, Visse, Laplénie, Les Arts Florissants, Christie.

Rameau composed two works on the theme of the ancient Greek poet, Anacreon, famed for his devotion to Cupid and Bacchus! This is the second, originally designed as an *acte de ballet* to a libretto by P.-J. Bernard and composed in 1757. The music has charm, even if it is not Rameau at his most inventive; the performance is as authoritative and stylish as one would expect from William Christie's group. It is not essential Rameau, but readers with an interest in the period will want it – and it has moments of great appeal. The recording is admirable.

Castor et Pollux (complete).
(M) *** Tel. **ZB8 35048** (3) [id.]. Vandersteene, Souzay, Scovotti, Schele, Leanderson, Lerer, Villisech, Stockholm Chamber Ch., VCM, Harnoncourt.

Harnoncourt and his Viennese colleagues went to Stockholm to record this richly varied score, the second of Rameau's tragédies lyriques, telling the mythological story of Castor and Pollux, the heavenly twins, with many interludes for choral and balletic divertissements. Harnoncourt is a direct rather than a persuasive interpreter of old music. He brings edge rather than elegance to the music, underlining detail and contrasts of colour, with his refusal to smooth over lines in expressive legato. The result is fresh and immediate, helped by a strong singing cast. An invaluable recording of a masterpiece long neglected. Excellent clean recording, freshly re-mastered for CD.

Zoroastre (complete).
(*) HMV **CDS7 47916-8 (3) [id.]. Elwes, De Reyghere, Van Der Sluis, Nellon, Reinhart, Bona, Ghent Coll. Vocale, La Petite Bande, Kuijken.

Zoroastre was the last but one of Rameau's tragédies lyriques. It appeared 15 years before his final masterpiece, *Les Boréades*; but the original 1749 score was drastically revised to produce the text of 1756, recorded here. *Zoroastre* may not have quite the inspiration of *Les Boréades* in modifying once rigid conventions; but frequently, as in the monologue of the villain, Abramane, in Act III, Rameau was clearly taking a leaf out of Gluck's book in the dark originality of the instrumentation, here made transparent in finely detailed recording. Though Kuijken's characteristically gentle style with his excellent authentic group, La Petite Bande, fails to give the piece the bite and urgency that John Eliot Gardiner brings to *Les Boréades* in his Erato recording, it is a fine presentation of a long-neglected masterpiece, with crisp and stylish singing from the soloists, notably John Elwes in the name-part and Gregory Reinhart as Abramane. The Ghent Collegium Vocale, placed rather close, sings with vigour in the choruses, but the individual voices fail to blend. The five Acts (with Rameau here abandoning the old convention of an allegorical Prologue) are now offered on three CDs against the original set on four LPs.

Ravel, Maurice (1875–1937)

Alborada del gracioso; Une barque sur l'océan; Menuet antique; Pavane pour une infante défunte; La valse.
(*) DG **415 845-2; *415 845-4* [id.]. Boston SO, Ozawa.

Ozawa is at his finest in catching the atmosphere of *Une barque sur l'ocean*, and throughout this collection he secures admirable orchestral playing. If the last degree of character is missing, the 1975 recording is first class, beautifully balanced, with the hall ambience colouring the textures most naturally. There is an excellent cassette.

Alborada del gracioso; Boléro; Daphnis et Chloé (ballet)*: suite No. 2. Pavane pour une infante défunte; Rapsodie espagnole; La valse; Valses nobles et sentimentales.*
(B) **(*) CBS *MGT 39012.* Cleveland O and Ch.; NYPO, Boulez.

This double-length CBS cassette assembles Boulez's Ravel performances recorded in New York and Cleveland in the early 1970s, and they are very impressive. Detail is sensitively observed and both orchestras respond with splendid virtuosity to his direction. His *Rapsodie espagnole* is very well shaped; Boulez's Spain is brilliant and well lit. *Daphnis* too is beautifully done, and there is a sense of magic in the *Valses nobles et sentimentales.* The *Alborada* is superbly brilliant. The range is wide, though one could wish for more expansive textures on climaxes. The tape transfers are well managed at a high level and only the very last degree of refinement is missing. The very gentle drum taps at the opening of *Boléro*, however, are almost inaudible against the background noise not entirely removed by the Dolby pre-emphasis.

(i) *Alborada del gracioso;* (ii) *Boléro;* (i; iii) *Daphnis et Chloé: suite No. 2;* (i) *La valse.*
(M) ** CBS **MYK 42541**. (i) NYPO; (ii) O Nat. de France; (iii) Schola Cantorum; Bernstein.

These are works at which Bernstein excels. He has recorded *Boléro* three times and here secures a first-class response from the French orchestra. The NYPO gives a glittering acccount of the *Alborada*, and *La valse* has the expected panache. In the *Daphnis suite* (also superbly played, using the choral version of the score) the digital remastering has brought more body to recording which is elsewhere not without atmosphere, although brightly lit.

Alborada del gracioso; Boléro; Ma Mère l'Oye: suite; La valse.
** Erato Dig. **ECD 88159** [id.]. SRO, Jordan.

This is not an issue that need detain collectors unless the actual programme offered is essential. Armin Jordan secures good playing from the Suisse Romande Orchestra, but the performances have no special distinction. It is good to have *Boléro* beginning at a real pianissimo against a silent background and moving to a climax not heightened by artificially brilliant sound, as with Muti, but here the problem is the reverberation of the hall which, in spite of the excellent CD definition, still clouds the articulation of the *Alborada* and provides a degree of inflation to the textures of *La valse*. Its rhythms are affectionately inflected, but the rubato is a shade conventional. *Ma Mère l'Oye* is without the sense of gentle ecstasy that Dutoit finds, and *Le jardin féerique* makes a disappointing conclusion.

Alborada del gracioso; Boléro; Rapsodie espagnole.
(*) RCA Dig. **RCD 14438 [RCD1 4438]. Dallas SO, Mata.

Mata has helped to build the Dallas orchestra into a splendid band, and it gives impressive performances of these virtuoso showpieces. There are more distinguished accounts of each work, but the coupling is certainly recommendable, helped by digital recording of great range. *Boléro* develops from a whisper of pianissimo at the start to a formidably loud climax, though the detailed balancing is not always consistent. The compact disc is impressive, but this cannot compare with Dutoit's even finer (and more generous) collection – see below.

Alborada del gracioso; Boléro; Rapsodie espagnole; La valse.
*** Decca **410 010-2** [id.]; *KSXDC 7559* [Lon. *LDR5-71059*]. Montreal SO, Dutoit.

Even if you possess alternative versions of the works on this Decca record, you should consider this anthology, for it is a model of its kind. Not only is the playing of the Montreal orchestra under Charles Dutoit absolutely first class and thoroughly atmospheric, the recorded sound has a clarity, range and depth of perspective that are equally satisfying. This recording defines the state of the art and, apart from the sumptuous music-making, has impressive refinement and a most musically judged and natural balance. Outstanding on chrome tape, while the compact disc version has even greater immediacy and refinement of detail and texture.

Alborada del gracioso; Boléro; Rapsodie espagnole; La valse; Valses nobles et sentimentales.
** Decca **414 046-2** [id.]. SRO, Ansermet.

The offering is generous, but clearly this CD is overpriced when Dutoit's Montreal recordings of this repertoire are available, offering superior orchestral playing and more subtle sound. Yet Ansermet aficionados will be glad to discover how remarkably fine these recordings were, mostly from the early 1960s. Only the *Rapsodie* (1958) is dated by the thin string timbre in the *Prélude à la nuit*; yet in the other movements the vivid orchestral colours give pleasure and Ansermet's sense of detail is matched by the rhythmic energy of the playing. *Boléro* is a strikingly well-graduated performance, and the sound and range are enhanced as they are in the two waltz pieces. The *Valses nobles* are rather slow but have a certain sensuous allure, while *La valse* is excellent in its combination of poise and momentum. The resonance takes a little of the edge off the *Alborada*, which scintillates in the Dutoit version; generally, however, one can only register amazement at the overall fidelity of this digitally remastered analogue quality. There is minimal background noise.

Alborada del gracioso; Pavane pour une infante défunte; Rapsodie espagnole; Le tombeau de Couperin; Valses nobles et sentimentales.
(*) HMV **CDC7 47468-2 [id.]; *EL 270450-4*. RPO, Previn.

Opening with a provocatively languorous account of the *Valses nobles et sentimentales*, lazy of tempo and affectionately indulgent, Previn's whole collection is imbued with sentient warmth. It even pervades *Le tombeau de Couperin*, although with some delectable oboe playing; this retains its lightness of character and the *Forlane* is particularly beguiling. The *Rapsodie espagnole* is unashamedly sultry and the effect throughout is helped by the glowing EMI recording – made in EMI's No. 1 Studio at Abbey Road – and the committed response of the RPO, the players obviously revelling in Ravel's luxuriant textures. The mood of this concert may not be to all tastes, but of its kind it is distinctive. There is a good tape.

(i) *Alborada del gracioso;* (ii) *Rapsodie espagnole.*
*** HMV **CDC7 47423-2** [id.]. (i) French Nat. O; (ii) LSO, Stokowski – DEBUSSY: *Ibéria; Nocturnes.****

In Stokowski's hands the *Alborada* glitters, with rhythms exhilaratingly precise; while in the *Rapsodie espagnole* the old magician beguiles the ear with his liltingly sensuous accounts of the *Malagueña* and *Habañera* and then produces a brilliant burst of colour and incandescent energy in the *Feria*. The early stereo doesn't sound dated, except that the dynamic range of the *Alborada* is not as wide as we would expect today.

Boléro.
(M) **(*) HMV **CDM7 69007-2** [id.]; *EG 769007-4*. BPO, Karajan – DEBUSSY: *La mer* etc.**(*)
(*) Decca Dig. **417 611-2; *417 611-4* [id.]. Concg. O, Chailly – DEBUSSY: *Danse* **(*); MUSSORGSKY: *Pictures*.**
** Decca **417 704-2** [id.]. Chicago SO, Solti – DEBUSSY: *Prélude à l'après-midi d'un faune***; STRAVINSKY: *Rite of spring*.***
(M) ** Decca *417 603-4* [id.]. Chicago SO, Solti – DEBUSSY: *La mer* etc.**
* HMV **CDC7 47022-2** [id.]. Phd. O, Muti – LISZT: *Les Préludes***; TCHAIKOVSKY: *1812*.*

Karajan's digitally remastered 1978 version of *Boléro* has fine presence and a splendid forward impetus. The cassette is less recommendable, not as wide-ranging.

Chailly uses *Boléro* as the introduction to a collection demonstrating the genius of Ravel as orchestrator, leading to his transcriptions of Debussy and Mussorgsky. Chailly's view of *Boléro* is strictly metrical, light and classical at the start, increasingly relentless as the crescendo develops. Though this is not the most sympathetic of versions, it has all the brilliance you could want, both in the playing and in the recording, which has spectacular range.

Metrically vigorous, Solti builds up the nagging climax with superb relentlessness. Though it lacks seductive touches, the performance is poised, the recording brightly analytical. Couplings are different on tape and CD.

Muti sets a measured tempo and almost lingers in his expressive treatment of the opening statements of the theme. By the time the climax is in sight, however, the upper range has a harsh digital edge and the strings sound glassy; the final *fortissimo* is very fierce indeed.

Boléro; Daphnis et Chloé: suite No. 2.
*** DG **423 217-2;** *423 217-4* [id.]. BPO, Karajan – DEBUSSY: *La mer* etc.***

Karajan's 1964 *Boléro* is a very characteristic performance, marvellously controlled, hypnotic and gripping, with the Berlin Philharmonic at the top of its form. The 1965 *Daphnis et Chloé* suite is outstanding even among all the competition, one of the very best things Karajan has ever done for the gramophone. He has the advantage of the Berlin Philharmonic at their finest and it would be difficult to imagine better or more atmospheric playing. The CD has opened up the sound spectacularly although now there is a touch of glare.

Boléro; (i) *Daphnis et Chloé: suite No. 2; Pavane pour une infante défunte.*
*** HMV **CDC7 47162-2** [id.]. LSO, Previn.
*(*) Telarc Dig. **CD 80052** [id.]. St Louis SO, Slatkin, (i) with Ch.

Though an analogue recording, Previn's coupling of favourite Ravel pieces provides wonderfully rich, full and atmospheric sound for performances full of sparkle and flair. *Daphnis et Chloé* is sensuously beautiful (good augury for the complete recording of the ballet which Previn went on to make within months – see below), and *Boléro*, at a slow and very steady tempo rather like Karajan's, sounds splendidly relentless. On CD, the sound is spectacular, both brilliant and full, with detail enhanced. It must be counted a disadvantage, however, that there are no dividing bands within the *Daphnis et Chloé* suite. Moreover, the playing time at 41′ 15″ is distinctly ungenerous.

Slatkin directs capable performances of the Ravel showpieces, but they are lacking in rhythmic flair and the digital recording is, by Telarc standards, unspectacular, with a relatively limited range of dynamic.

Boléro; Daphnis et Chloé: suite No. 2; Pavane pour une infante défunte; Rapsodie espagnole.
(*) Ph. **416 495-2 [id.]. Concg. O, Haitink.
* HMV **CDC7 47356-2** [id.]. O de Paris, Munch.

Fine performances, distinguished by instinctive good judgement and taste. The playing of the Amsterdam orchestra is eminently polished and civilized, even if the heady intoxicating qualities of the music are missed. The *Rapsodie espagnole* lacks the last ounce of dash in the *Feria*, but the *Habañera* is lazily seductive when the orchestral playing is so sleek and refined. The remastered recordings are very impressive, improved in firmness of outline without loss of atmosphere or bloom.

Although Munch's CD offers one more piece than Previn's collection (see above), there is nothing to detain the listener here. The readings serve well enough, though they lack magnetism, but the orchestral playing is acceptable merely, with moments of suspect intonation; although the *Rapsodie* comes off quite well, Munch increases the pace of *Boléro*, albeit subtly. The analogue recording – from 1969 – has an element of harshness.

Boléro; Daphnis et Chloé: suite No. 2; Pavane pour une infante défunte; La valse.
(*) DG Dig. **400 061-2 [id.]. O de Paris, Barenboim.

Bolero; Pavane pour une infante défunte; La valse.
(B) ** DG Dig. *419 838-4* [id.]. O de Paris, Barenboim – DEBUSSY: *Images.**(*)

At a slow speed *Boléro* brings fine balancing and smooth solos. The *Pavane* and *La valse* too are both on the slow side, but the seductive phrasing makes them sound lusciously idiomatic. The *Daphnis* suite brings the most persuasive performance of all. The recorded sound is sumptuous to match, but it could have more air round it, qualities the more easily appreciated on compact disc. The Pocket Music tape includes three of these performances and is strikingly well transferred; however, the Debussy coupling is much less seductive.

Boléro; (i) *Daphnis et Chloé: suite No. 2; Pavane pour une infante défunte; La valse.*
*** Decca Dig. **414 406-2**; *414 406-4* [id.]. Montreal SO, Dutoit, (i) with chorus.

A further permutation of Dutoit's beautifully made Montreal recordings, warmly and translucently recorded at St Eustache. The *Daphnis et Chloé* suite is drawn from the highly praised complete set. If this programme is suitable, the performances and recordings cannot be bettered.

Boléro; Ma Mère l'Oye (complete)*; Pavane pour une infante défunte; Rapsodie espagnole.*
(*) DG Dig. **415 972-2; *415 972-4* [id.]. LSO, Abbado.

Abbado secures characteristically polished and refined playing from the LSO. There are some lovely gentle sounds in *Ma Mère l'Oye*, notably in the closing 'fair garden' sequence, but the conductor's fastidiousness is perhaps a shade cool. However, the sultry atmosphere of the *Rapsodie espagnole* is very evocative, the lazy rhythms of the *Habañera* contrasting well with the brilliance of the sparkling *Feria*. The *Pavane* has a grave, withdrawn melancholy. Only in *Boléro* is there any real idiosyncrasy – near the climax, Abbado makes a perceptible gear-change, pressing the tempo forward arbitrarily; his involvement is also conveyed by his vocal contributions in the closing pages. The recording, with its wide dynamic range, has fine focus and detail, yet plenty of ambience and warmth. There is an excellent matching tape.

Boléro; Ma Mère l'Oye: suite*; Pavane pour une infante défunte; Rapsodie espagnole; La valse.*
(M) *(*) RCA **GD 86522**; *GK 86522* [**RCA 6522-2-RG**]. Boston SO, Munch.

This is repertoire for which Munch was famous, but it does not show him at his best. *Boléro* is very flat until the climax and, although *Mother Goose* has its moments, there is an element of routine here too; the most impressive performance is the *Rapsodie*. *La valse* is rather coarsened by the Boston resonance; and in general the early stereo is not very refined.

Boléro; Ma Mère l'Oye: suite; *Pavane pour une infante défunte; La valse; Valses nobles et sentimentales.*
** HMV Dig. **CDC7 47648-2** [id.]; *EL 270535-4*. O du Capitole, Toulouse, Michel Plasson.

There are good things in Plasson's Ravel anthology with the Toulouse orchestra, but they are not good enough to see off the competition. There is some idiomatic playing in *Mother Goose* and the *Valses nobles*, and no lack of atmosphere in the reverberant acoustic. However, while these are eminently serviceable performances, they are not in any way memorable.

Boléro; Ma Mère l'Oye (ballet; complete)*; La valse.*
(M) **(*) **420 869-2**; *420 869-4* [id.]. LSO, Monteux.

Monteux's complete version of *Ma Mére l'Oye* is a poetic, unforced reading, given a naturally balanced sound. The 1964 recording has responded well to its digital remastering, retaining its warmth, while obtaining cleaner detail. On the Philips Silverline series at medium price, this can be recommended on disc, even though Monteux's reading of *Boléro* has a slight quickening of tempo in the closing pages. The cassette has slightly less transparency.

Boléro; Rapsodie espagnole.
*** DG Dig. **413 588-2**; *413 588-4* [id.]. BPO, Karajan – MUSSORGSKY: *Pictures*.**(*)

Karajan's latest versions of *Boléro* and *Rapsodie espagnole* – fill-ups for the Mussorgsky–Ravel *Pictures at an exhibition* – find the Berlin Philharmonic in characteristically brilliant form, recorded in very wide-ranging digital sound. Though the sense of presence may not be as keen as in his 1960s recording, with positioning less sharply defined, these are warm, spontaneous-sounding performances in which the thrust of *Boléro* and the sensuousness of the *Rapsodie* are conveyed with unerring power and magnetism.

Admirers of Ansermet may want to consider a well-transferred Decca Weekend tape which combines his fine 1963 *Boléro* and the early (1957) *Rapsodie espagnole*, coupled with Chabrier's *España*, plus the complete Falla *El amor brujo* ballet (*417 691-4*).

Piano concerto in G.
❀ *** HMV **CDC7 49326-2** [id.]. Michelangeli, Philh. O, Gracis – RACHMANINOV: *Concerto No. 4*.*** ❀

(i) *Piano concerto in G. Gaspard de la nuit; Sonatine.*
(M) *** DG **419 062-2**; *419 062-4* [id.]. Argerich, (i) BPO, Abbado.

There are some exceptionally distinguished accounts of Ravel's *Concerto* on record, but the first choice is clear. It was daring of Michelangeli to couple this neoclassical, jazz-influenced work with the sunset-glow of Rachmaninov's No. 4. In the event he plays both with superlative brilliance which yet has great sympathy for the tender moments. He achieves exactly the right compromise between inflating the Ravel work and preventing it from seeming 'little'. The opening whipcrack could have been more biting, but the orchestra generally plays with great vigour. The recording shows the same characteristics as that of the Rachmaninov but is if anything warmer. The exquisite playing in the slow movement (surely one of the most melting of all recordings of piano and orchestra) makes up for any deficiencies of dimensional balance.

The recording has been very successfully remastered and is of the highest quality, clear, with bold piano timbre and excellent orchestral detail.

Argerich's half-tones and clear fingerwork give the *G major Concerto* unusual delicacy, but its urgent virility – with jazz an important element – comes over the more forcefully by contrast. Other performances may have caught the uninhibited brilliance in the finale more fearlessly, but in the first movement few other versions can match Argerich's playing. The compromise between coolness and expressiveness in the slow minuet of the middle movement is tantalizingly sensual. Her *Gaspard de la nuit* abounds in character and colour, even if certain touches may disturb the perspective, and the *Sonatine* is a similarly telling performance. The remastered recordings (the concerto comes from 1967, the solo pieces from 1975) sound first class; the concerto balance is very successful and there is crisp detail, while the solo piano has fine presence and no want of colour.

Piano concerto in G; Piano concerto for the left hand.
*** Decca **417 583-2** [id.]. De Larrocha, LPO, Foster – FAURÉ: *Fantaisie****; FRANCK: *Symphonic variations.***(*)

(i) *Piano concerto in G; Piano concerto for the left hand. Une barque sur l'océan; L'éventail de Jeanne* (*Fanfare*)*; Menuet antique.*
(*) Decca Dig. **410 230-2; *KSXDC 7592* [Lon. *LDR5-71092*]. (i) Rogé; Montreal SO, Dutoit.

Piano concerto in G; Piano concerto for the left hand in D; Pavane pour une infante défunte; Jeux d'eau; (i) *La valse* (version for 2 pianos).
*** HMV **CDC7 47386-2** [id.]. Collard; (i) Béroff; O Nat. de France, Maazel.

Superbly vivid recording quality on HMV while Jean-Philippe Collard gives a meticulous, sparkling and refined account of the *G major Concerto* and a marvellously brilliant and poetic account of the *Left-hand concerto*. He brings great *tendresse* to the more reflective moments and there is real delicacy of feeling throughout. Maazel gives thoroughly sympathetic support, and the Orchestre National play superbly. In the *Left-hand concerto* Collard does not quite match the dash and swagger of Gavrilov's altogether dazzling account (see below), but he runs him pretty close. This is undoubtedly the best version of this coupling to have appeared for many years, and it will be difficult to surpass. The CD refines the recorded sound and adds three piano items (two solos and one duet): the *Pavane*, *Jeux d'eau* and *La valse*, all beautifully played.

Pascal Rogé brings both delicacy and sparkle to the *G major Concerto*, which he gives with his characteristic musical grace and fluency. He produces unfailing beauty of tone at every dynamic level – as indeed does Collard on HMV, who is more incisive in the outer movements. Rogé brings great poetry and tenderness to the slow movement, but in the *Left-hand concerto* he is a good deal less dynamic. There is a certain want of momentum here, even though there is much to admire in the way of pianistic finesse – and charm. The Decca recording offers excellent performances of three short orchestral pieces as a makeweight, which may tip the scales in its favour for some collectors.

Alicia de Larrocha's CD finds room not only for a superbly refined account of Fauré's *Fantaisie* but also a romantic version of Franck's *Symphonic variations*. The performances of the two concertos are very fine; given Decca's first-class (1974) sound, warmly atmospheric, yet with detail enhanced, this would seem a very good investment, if not a first choice. It plays for 73′.

(i) *Piano concerto for the left hand; Gaspard de la nuit; Pavane pour une infante défunte.*
(M) *** HMV **CDM7 69026-2** [id.]; *EG 769026-4*. Gavrilov; (i) LSO, Rattle.

(i) *Piano concerto for the left hand. Miroirs: Alborada del gracioso.*
*** ASV Dig. *ZCDCA 555* [id.]. Osorio, RPO, Bátiz – PROKOFIEV: *Piano concerto No. 1* etc.***

Gavrilov's recording of the *Left-hand concerto* is altogether dazzling. He plays with effortless virtuosity, brilliance and, when required, great sensitivity. This is at least the equal of any of the classic accounts either on 78s or LP. The *Pavane* is also very distinguished; apart from the strangely impulsive closing bars, this too is beautiful playing. This was originally coupled with Gavrilov's equally dazzling account of Prokofiev's *First Concerto*, but now *Gaspard de la nuit* is substituted, taken from a 1978 solo recital. The performance is not quite as distinctive as Ashkenazy's: both *Ondine* and *Le gibet* have an element of reserve. But *Scarbo* has superb dash, and the whole performance has impeccable style. The digital remastering is spectacular in its vividness. Perhaps the climaxes of the concerto are larger than life: they are very brightly lit, but the sound fits the extrovert bravura of the performance. The solo items have fine presence. The chrome cassette is well managed too.

Jorge-Fredrico Osorio's account of the *Left-hand concerto* can hold its own with the best, and it can certainly withstand comparison with the excellent Decca Rogé version on all counts. He gives a crisp and colourful performance of the *Alborada* also.

(i) *Piano concerto in G. Pavane pour une infante défunte; Ma Mère l'Oye* (complete)*; Le tombeau de Couperin; Valses nobles et sentimentales.*
(B) **(*) HMV *TCC2-POR 154600-9*. O de Paris, Martinon; (i) with Ciccolini.

These recordings are all taken from Martinon's 1975 (deleted) LP box and it is a pity that Ciccolini's version of the *Piano concerto* was included, as it is in no way distinctive. The rest of the programme, however, affords much pleasure; the slightly softened focus of the transfer suits Martinon's ravishingly beautiful account of *Ma Mère l'Oye*. *Le Tombeau de Couperin*, too, is one of the finest versions available, the orchestral playing refined, and with plenty of bloom on the recording.

Daphnis et Chloé (ballet; complete).
❀ *** Decca Dig. **400 055-2**; *KSXDC 7526* [Lon. *LDR 5-71028*]. Montreal SO and Ch., Dutoit.
*** CBS **MK 33523** [id.]. NYPO & Camarata Singers, Boulez.
*** HMV Dig. **CDC7 47123-2** [id.]. LSO & Ch., Previn.
(B) **(*) DG Walkman *415 336-4* [id.]. Boston SO. and Ch., Ozawa – STRAVINSKY: *Petrushka*.***
** DG Dig. **415 360-2** [id.]. V. State Op. Ch., VPO, Levine.

The compact disc of the Dutoit/Montreal *Daphnis et Chloé* immediately established itself as a demonstration disc *par excellence* in the new medium, from the opening *pianissimo* bringing a new dimension to sound recording. The sensation that a subtle veil is being withdrawn from the orchestral image persists throughout the performance, which is sumptuously evocative with Dutoit and his splendid orchestra creating the most ravishing textures. He adopts an idiomatic and flexible style, observing the minute indications of tempo change but making every slight variation sound totally spontaneous. The final *Danse générale* finds him adopting a dangerously fast tempo, but the Montreal players – combining French responsiveness with transatlantic polish – rise superbly to the challenge, with the choral punctuations at the end adding to the sense of frenzy. The digital recording is wonderfully luminous, with the chorus ideally balanced at an evocative half-distance. It is a pity that Decca do not provide cues to guide access to the main sections of the score. Tape collectors will be glad to know that the cassette, too, is in the demonstration class.

Boulez's account of *Daphnis* is also among the very finest now on the market. It has the essential ingredient without which any performance of the work must fall, namely a sense of ecstasy and enchantment, an ability to transport the listener into the enchanted landscape that this work inhabits with its wonder, its vivid colours and sense of innocence. The playing of the New York Philharmonic is beyond praise. Every detail is affectionately phrased; there is effortless virtuosity and brilliance, and despite some highlighting, which is unnecessary, the recording produces good quality, with wide-ranging and beautiful string tone. Boulez conceives *Daphnis* in one symphonic breath and yet pays sufficient attention to beauty of detail to convey the astonishing rapture and richness of imagination of this wonderful score. He does not displace Dutoit and he is not as well recorded as Previn, but other contenders are outclassed. The digital remastering has been highly successful. The CBS engineers have achieved greater transparency without losing depth and atmosphere. The opening emerges imperceptibly from the mists, yet the tingling excitement of the finale is admirably vivid. One must mention Julius Baker's flute playing, which is quite marvellous. Even though this analogue recording is over twenty years old it remains very competitive. Unlike the Dutoit and Previn CDs, which have little or no internal access, this CBS issue has 22 individual cues, and the accompanying synopsis relates the stage action in detail within each band.

With rhythm more important than atmosphere, Previn directs a very dramatic performance, clear-headed and fresh, an exciting alternative to the superlative Dutoit version. It is made all the more vivid in the excellent CD transfer, with textures sharply defined. It is regrettable that the opportunity was not taken to insert a full quota of bands, for the listener will obviously not always want to play the complete score from beginning to end.

Ozawa's 1975 *Daphnis* is not as distinctive as Dutoit's or Previn's, but it is superbly played; the flattering Boston acoustic adds to the glowing sense of rapture in *Daybreak*, while not blunting the sparkle of the finale. The tape transfer is particularly successful; as it is coupled with Dutoit's outstanding 1977 complete recording of *Petrushka*, this makes another fine Walkman bargain.

With ripe Viennese horns adding opulence to Ravel's rich textures and with recording that brings an uncomfortably wide dynamic range, Levine's reading could hardly be higher-powered, with superb playing from the Vienna Philharmonic. He has a natural feeling for Ravelian rubato, but what the reading consistently lacks is poetry, for in even the gentlest moments there is a want of evocative warmth. Despite the excessive contrasts between loud and soft and some hardness on violin tone, the recording is one of the most brilliant that DG engineers have made recently in Vienna.

(i) *Daphnis et Chloé* (ballet; complete). *Pavane pour une infante défunte; Rapsodie espagnole.*
(M) *** Decca *421 030-4* [id.]. LSO, Monteux, (i) with ROHCG Ch.

For many years and in several editions of this *Guide*, Pierre Monteux's complete *Daphnis et Chloé* held sway over all other versions and carried the Rosette which has more recently passed to Dutoit. Monteux conducted the first performance of *Daphnis et Chloé* in 1912; Decca's 1959 recording, a demonstration disc in its day, captured his poetic and subtly shaded reading in the most vivid colours within an agreeably warm ambience. The performance was one of the finest things Monteux did for the gramophone, and his version still sounds impressive in its current tape reissue, although the sound is just a little restricted in the upper range. As if this were not enough for a budget reissue, Decca have added his 1962 recording of the *Pavane*, wonderfully poised and played most beautifully, and the *Rapsodie espagnole*, in which Monteux achieves a balance and a contrast between the mood of quiet introspection for the opening and flashing brilliance for the *Feria*. The cassette plays for 73′.

Daphnis et Chloé (ballet)*: suites 1 & 2.*
*(*) ASV Dig. *ZCDCA 536* [id.]. LSO, Nowak – BARTÓK: *Dance suite.***(*)

The young Polish conductor, Grzegorz Nowak, making his début recording in two brilliant showpieces is far less successful here in Ravel than in the Bartók on the reverse. It is a worthy, undynamic account of richly atmospheric music, helped a little by fine recording. The excellent cassette makes a vivid impression.

Daphnis et Chloé: suites 1 & 2; Ma Mère l'Oye (complete ballet).
(M) *** Vox Prima **MWCD 7142** [id.]. Minnesota O, Skrowaczewski.

This Vox Prima CD offers another vintage coupling from the analogue era. The first *Daphnis* suite is absolutely magical in Skrowaczewski's hands and the orchestral sounds in *Ma Mère l'Oye* are equally lovely, full of a gentle rapture. In terms of sheer atmosphere and imaginative vitality, these performances can stand comparison with their most prestigious rivals. Though the Minnesota Orchestra may not be as superlative an ensemble as the Amsterdam Concertgebouw, there is absolutely nothing second-rate about its playing here; the beautifully balanced, wide-ranging recording has been subtly enhanced by the digital remastering: its sheen is unimpaired yet detail is that bit more tangible. Skrowaczewski conveys every subtlety of texture and colour, and he shapes phrases not only with the good taste that Haitink gives us in his Philips records, but with a genuine feel for the sensuous, sumptuous qualities of these scores. His *Ma Mère l'Oye* is complete, like Monteux's and Previn's, and stands comparison with either. Karajan is even finer in the second *Daphnis* suite, but this is still amazingly good; anyone seeking a coupling of these two scores need look no further.

(i) *Daphnis et Chloé: suites 1 & 2; Rapsodie espagnole; Le tombeau de Couperin.*
*(*) Erato Dig. **ECD 75311** [id.]. SRO, (i) with Ch., Jordan.

A disappointing collection. The highlight is *Le tombeau de Couperin*, which is nicely paced and gracious and offers some good oboe playing. There is a fine flautist too in *Daphnis*, but there is an element of routine here and the lazy sentience of the *Rapsodie* fails to take a real grip on the listener – the piece really springs to life only in the *Feria*. The recording is naturally balanced but diffuse.

Daphnis et Chloe: suite No. 2; Pavane pour une infante défunte.
** DG **415 370-2** [id.]. Boston SO, New England Conservatory Ch., Abbado – DEBUSSY: *Nocturnes*; SCRIABIN: *Poème de l'extase*.**
** DG Dig. **413 589-2**; *413 589-4* [id.]. BPO, Karajan – DEBUSSY: *Le mer* etc.**

Abbado's performance of the suite is characteristically refined. His feeling for the music's atmosphere is matched by care for detail. The performance is comparable with Karajan's 1965 versions; however, the remastering of the 1970 recording has not brought an improvement: there is added bite and the appearance of a wider dynamic range, but the effect is rather brash, unlike the original analogue master.

As in the case of *La mer*, this digital Karajan performance does not have the magic and sense of rapture and intoxication that informed Karajan's earlier Berlin account of the second *Daphnis* suite – surely one of the greatest performances of this glorious score ever committed to disc (see above). Good recording and quite a good cassette.

Ma Mère l'Oye (complete ballet).
*** Ph. Dig. **400 016-2** [id.]. Pittsburgh SO, Previn – SAINT-SAËNS: *Carnival of the Animals*.***

Ma Mère l'Oye (complete); *Rapsodie espagnole.*
(M) *** DG **415 844-2**; *415 844-4* [id.]. LAPO, Giulini – MUSSORGSKY: *Pictures*.***

Ma Mère l'Oye (complete); *Le tombeau de Couperin; Valses nobles et sentimentales.*
❀ *** Decca Dig. **410 254-2**; *410 254-4* [id.]. Montreal SO, Dutoit.

A few bars of this Decca record leave no doubt as to its quality. Charles Dutoit and the Montreal orchestra offer *Ma Mère l'Oye* complete, together with *Le tombeau de Couperin* and the *Valses nobles et sentimentales*, recorded, as have been its companions in the Decca Ravel series, in St Eustache, Montreal. This offers demonstration quality, transparent and refined, with the textures beautifully balanced and expertly placed. The CD is altogether outstanding: here is another instance where one could speak of the gauze being removed, for the CD has even more translucent detail, firmer focus and presence than the original LP – but both are superb. The performances too are wonderfully refined and sympathetic. *Ma Mère l'Oye* is ravishingly beautiful, its special combination of sensuousness and innocence perfectly caught. Tape collectors will find that the chrome cassette is hardly less sophisticated and desirable.

In Previn's version of the complete *Mother Goose* ballet, played and recorded with consummate refinement, the quality of innocence shines out. The temptation for any conductor is to make the music exotically sensuous in too sophisticated a way, but Previn keeps a freshness apt for nursery music. The recording is superb, with the Philips engineers refusing to spotlight individual instruments but presenting a texture of luminous clarity. Those qualities come out the more impressively on compact disc.

The Giulini Los Angeles performance conveys much of the sultry atmosphere of the *Rapsodie espagnole*. Indeed some details, such as the sensuous string responses to the cor anglais tune in the *Feria*, have not been so tenderly caressed since the intoxicating Reiner version of the early 1960s. The *Ma Mère l'Oye* suite is beautifully done too; though it is cooler, it is still beautiful. The CD transfer enhances detail and the cassette transfer is splendidly managed.

Tzigane for violin and orchestra.
*** HMV **CDC7 47725-2** [id.]. Itzhak Perlman, O de Paris, Martinon – CHAUSSON: *Poème*; SAINT-SAËNS: *Havanaise* etc.***
*** DG Dig. **423 063-2**; *423 063-4* [id.]. Itzhak Perlman, NYPO, Mehta – CHAUSSON: *Poème*; SAINT-SAËNS: *Havanaise* etc.; SARASATE: *Carmen fantasy*.***
*** Decca **417 118-2** [id.]. Kyung Wha Chung, RPO, Dutoit – CHAUSSON: *Poème*; SAINT-SAËNS: *Havanaise* etc.***
(M) **(*) RCA **GD 86520**; *GK 86520* [**RCA 6520-2-RG**]. Itzhak Perlman, LSO, Previn – LALO: *Symphonie espagnole*; SIBELIUS: *Violin concerto*.*(*)

Perlman's classic 1975 account of Ravel's *Tzigane* for EMI is marvellously played; the added projection of the CD puts the soloist believably at the end of the living-room. The opulence of his tone is undiminished by the remastering process and the orchestral sound retains its atmosphere, while gaining in clarity.

The later digital version is also very fine and the recording obviously more modern. The DG collection also includes a highly desirable extra Sarasate item. But the earlier performance has just that bit more charisma.

With its seemingly improvisatory solo introduction, *Tzigane* is a work which demands an inspirational artist, and Kyung Wha Chung is ideally cast, coupling this elusive piece with other concertante works too often neglected. Accompaniments and recordings are both excellent.

In his earliest stereo performance for RCA, Perlman is given an exaggeratedly close balance. Yet the performance is brilliantly involving and Previn accompanies imaginatively.

La valse.
(*) DG Dig. **410 033-2 [id.]. LSO, Abbado – MUSSORGSKY: *Pictures*.***
** Ph. Dig. **416 296-2**; *416 296-4* [id.]. VPO, Previn – MUSSORGSKY: *Pictures*.*(*)

Though detail is not as needle-sharp for this Ravel fill-up as for the Mussorgsky–Ravel *Pictures with which it is coupled, Abbado directs a fluent and incisive account, not quite ideally idiomatic* and lilting in its dance rhythms, but with a thrilling surge of adrenalin in its closing pages. The digital recording is outstanding on the compact disc, one of DG's best. The recording, however, has a shade too much resonance to be ideal, and this is even more obvious on CD.

Previn's rubato is less convincing than Abbado's but the piece is well played and recorded (the record was made with an audience present).

CHAMBER MUSIC

Introduction and allegro for harp, flute, clarinet and string quartet.

(M) *** Decca *414 063-4*. Osian Ellis, Melos Ens. – DEBUSSY: *Sonata*; GUY-ROPARTZ: *Prelude, marine and chansons*; ROUSSEL: *Serenade*.***

The beauty and subtlety of Ravel's sublime septet are marvellously realized by the 1962 Melos account, originally on Oiseau-Lyre and now reissued on Decca. The interpretation has great delicacy of feeling, and the recording, first class in its day, shows its age only slightly in the upper range, which has lost a little of its bloom in this remastered format. This is an excellent high-level tape.

Piano trio in A min.

*** Ph. Dig. **411 141-2** [id.]. Beaux Arts Trio – CHAUSSON: *Piano trio*.***

*** Chan. Dig. **CHAN 8458**; *ABTD 1170* [id.]. Borodin Trio – DEBUSSY: *Violin and Cello sonatas*.***

The most recent Beaux Arts account of the Ravel *Trio* is little short of inspired – as inspired as this music itself – and even finer than their earlier record of the late 1960s. The recording, too, is of high quality, even if the piano is rather forward and – if one is going to quibble – the bottom end of the instrument looms too large in the aural picture. But there is no doubt that this is a most distinguished chamber-music issue and must carry the strongest recommendation.

The Borodin Trio pair the Ravel with the two Debussy sonatas, which makes a logical and attractive coupling. They are excellently recorded and their playing has great warmth and is full of colour. Some may find them too hot-blooded by the side of the Beaux Arts, whose version is wonderfully poised and cultivated. However, though the latter must be a first choice, those wanting this particular coupling are unlikely to be disappointed. The Chandos cassette is in the demonstration class.

String quartet in F.

*** DG **419 750-2** [id.]. Melos Qt – DEBUSSY: *Quartet*.***

(M) *** Ph. **420 894-2** *420 894-4* [id.]. Italian Qt – DEBUSSY: *Quartet*.***

(*) Denon Dig. **C37 7830 [id.]. Nuovo Qt – DEBUSSY: *Quartet*.***

(*) HMV Dig. **CDC7 47347-2 [id.]. Alban Berg Qt – DEBUSSY: *Quartet*.**(*)

(*) Telarc Dig. **CD 80111 [id.]. Cleveland Qt – DEBUSSY: *Quartet*.**(*)

*(*) Hyp. Dig. **CDA 66207**; *KA 66207* [id.]. Fairfield Qt – DEBUSSY: *Quartet*.**

*(*) Ph. Dig. **411 050-2** [id.]. Orlando Qt – DEBUSSY: *Quartet*.*(*)

*(*) Nimbus Dig. **NI 5076** [id.]. Medici Qt – R. STRAUSS: *Capriccio: Sextet*.(*)

For many years the Italian Quartet held pride of place in this coupling. Their playing is perfect in ensemble, attack and beauty of tone and their performance remains highly recommendable, one of the most satisfying chamber-music records in the catalogue. Yet the new Melos account is even finer, and this group brings artistry of the very highest order to this magical score. Their slow movement offers the most refined and integrated quartet sound; in terms of internal balance and blend it would be difficult to surpass it, and the reading has great poetry. In both the Scherzo and finale the Melos players evince the highest virtuosity, and there is not the slightest trace of the prosaic phrasing that marred their Mozart D *minor Quartet*, K.421. They also have the advantage of superbly truthful recording, enhanced in the digital remastering. Highly imaginative playing touched with a complete identification with Ravel's sensibility. However, on mid-price CD the Italian Quartet will prove an admirable alternative and by no means second best. There is an excellent cassette too.

Denon's version with the Nuovo Quartet was recorded in the warm acoustic of the Villa di Poggio Reale, Rufina (Florence). A sympathetic and likeable account, it is by no means as immaculate as the finest now before the public (Alban Berg and Melos) but for the most part these players make a beautiful sound and show considerable feeling and sensitivity. There is an agreeably unforced quality about the way they let the music unfold. Very enjoyable, in spite of less than absolutely spot-on intonation, and very well recorded.

Superb, indeed incomparable playing from the Alban Berg Quartet, and splendidly rich and sonorous recording from the EMI engineers on compact disc. Yet while this is marvellously polished and has such excellence in terms of ensemble and tonal blend, there is a want of spontaneity that ultimately weighs against it. In a sense the Alban Berg beautify the work and, although Ravel's glorious *Quartet* must have polish, it must be a polish that enables one to forget the physical aspects of the music making and become totally immersed in the music itself.

The Cleveland on Telarc is a well-played version, not always fully observant of dynamic markings at the *pianissimo* end of the spectrum. Nor do the players fully convey the atmosphere and intimacy of the slow movement. All the same there is more that is right than is wrong in this highly accomplished and well-recorded account.

The Fairfield are less sensitive in this glorious *Quartet* than their reading of the Debussy would lead one to expect. There are good things, but they rather lack tenderness in the slow movement and are a little inclined to be rough-and-ready in the outer movements. Whereas they were scrupulous in their observance of dynamic markings in the Debussy, they neglect some *pianissimi* here. The recording has splendid presence but is just a bit too bright and forward to be ideal.

The Orlando Quartet are wonderfully passionate and possess glorious tone and ensemble. They press the Ravel to greater expressive extremes than do the Melos Quartet of Stuttgart; though the Orlando play with superb artistry and feeling, some will find the greater restraint of the Melos more telling, particularly in the slow movement. There is a sudden lurch in pitch in this movement, though it is not quite so ruinous as is the case in the Debussy on the reverse side.

Though not as polished as the Alban Berg or the Melos, the Medici give a genuinely felt account of the *Quartet* which can hold its head fairly high against the competition, both as a performance and as a recording, even if the balance is a bit forward. However, at less than 39′ playing time, this is distinctly uncompetitive.

A further version by the Viotti Quartet on Verany (**PV 786102**) which offers not only the Debussy but the Fauré *Quartet* as couplings must be ruled out of court. The playing is too unpolished and wanting in refinement to give lasting pleasure.

Violin sonata in G.

(M) *** Ph. **420 777-2** [id.]. David Oistrakh, Frida Bauer – DEBUSSY; YSAŸE: *Sonatas*; PROKOFIEV: *Melodies.****

*** DG Dig. **415 683-2**; *415 683-4* [id.]. Shlomo Mintz, Yefim Bronman – DEBUSSY; FRANCK: *Sonatas.****

Oistrakh's account of the Ravel *Sonata* is most beautiful and the interest of the couplings adds to its claims on the collector. The recording is remastered using Philips's newest NoNoise system: the sound is slightly brighter than the original but well balanced.

Shlomo Mintz and Yefim Bronman's account of the Ravel comes in harness with Franck and Debussy. Impeccable, highly polished playing, even if it is not so completely inside Ravel's world in the slow movement. The glorious sounds both artists produce is a source of unfailing delight. They are beautifully recorded too, with a superbly transferred cassette to match the CD pretty closely.

PIANO DUET

Ma Mère L'Oye.
*** Ph. Dig. **420 159-2**; *420 159-4* [id.]. Katia and Marielle Labèque – FAURÉ: *Dolly*; BIZET: *Jeux d'enfants.****

The Labèque sisters give an altogether delightful performance of Ravel's magical score, which he later orchestrated and expanded. They are somewhat slower than the metronome marking in the opening *Pavane de la Belle au bois dormant*, but in every other respect theirs is a meticulously prepared and fastidiously executed account. The recording could not be more realistic and present. The chrome tape, too, is first class in every way.

La valse.
*** Ph. Dig. **411 034-2** [id.]. Argerich, Freire – LUTOSLAWSKI: *Paganini variations*; RACHMANINOV: *Suite No. 2.****

The transcription is Ravel's own and was first heard in this form played by the composer himself and Alfredo Casella in Vienna in 1920. Indeed, the first idea of such a work came as early as 1906. This one is the only single issue of it. Brilliant, atmospheric playing and good recording.

SOLO PIANO MUSIC

À la manière de Borodin; À la manière de Chabrier; Gaspard de la nuit; Jeux d'eau; Menuet antique; Menuet sur le nom de Haydn; Miroirs; Pavane pour une infante défunte; Prélude; Sérénade grotesque; Sonatine; Le tombeau de Couperin; Valses nobles et sentimentales.
*** CRD Dig. **CRD 3383/4**; *CRDDC 4083–5* [id.]. Paul Crossley.

Paul Crossley is the only English pianist at present represented on record in the complete Ravel piano music. His is a fastidious musical personality, well attuned to Ravel's sensibility; his accounts of all these works are beautifully fashioned and can hold their own with the available competition. Crossley is aristocratic, with an admirable feeling for tone colour and line, and rarely mannered (the end of *Jeux d'eau* is an exception). His version of *Le tombeau de Couperin* has a classical refinement and delicacy that are refreshing. The CRD recording is very good indeed and this fine set deserves the warmest welcome. CRD merit congratulations in giving recognition to this much underrated player. The chrome cassettes are of high quality, softer-grained in the treble than is sometimes the case with CRD, which suits the music admirably, for definition is very good. But the CDs have extra realism and presence and, as the music is fitted on to two discs, they are especially attractive.

À la manière de Borodin; À la manière de Chabrier; Menuet antique; Prélude; Le tombeau de Couperin; Valses nobles et sentimentales.
(M) **(*) Nimbus **NIM 5011** [id.]. Vlado Perlemuter.

Gaspard de la nuit; Jeux d'eau; Miroirs; Pavane.
(M) **(*) Nimbus **NIM 5005** [id.]. Vlado Perlemuter.

Perlemuter, pupil and friend of Ravel himself, was asked by Nimbus to record the complete piano music, when he had reached his seventies. Though his technical command was not as complete as it had been, he gives delightful, deeply sympathetic readings; the sense of spontaneity is a joy. There may be Ravel recordings which bring more dazzling virtuoso displays, but none more persuasive. If the articulation in *Alborada del gracioso*, from *Miroirs*, is not as spectacular as from some younger pianists, the rhythmic vigour and alertness, the flair with which dance rhythms are presented, make this just as involving and exciting. The original three-LP set has here been transferred to two CDs, with the analogue sound freshened and clarified. Nimbus's preference for an ample room acoustic makes the result naturally atmospheric on CD, with light reverberation presenting a halo of sound.

Gaspard de la nuit.
*** DG Dig. **413 363-2** [id.]. Pogorelich – PROKOFIEV: *Sonata No. 6.**** ❀
*** HMV Dig. **CDC7 49262-2** [id.]. Cécile Ousset – MUSSORGSKY: *Pictures.***(*)

Pogorelich's *Gaspard* is out of the ordinary. In *Le gibet*, there is the self-conscious striving after effect that mars his Schumann *Études symphoniques* and attention soon wanders from the ends to the means. We are made conscious of the pianist's refinement of tone and colour first, and Ravel's poetic vision afterwards. But for all that, this is piano playing of astonishing quality and, despite the touches of narcissism, this is a performance to relish. His control of colour and nuance in *Scarbo* is dazzling and its eruptive cascades of energy and dramatic fire have one sitting on the edge of one's seat. The coupling. Prokofiev's *Sixth Sonata*, is quite simply stunning.

Cécile Ousset's version of *Gaspard* was greeted with much acclaim on its first appearance and is very fine indeed. Her *Scarbo* is particularly dazzling with all the electricity of a live concert performance, even if by comparison with Pogorelich she sounds uncontrolled. She is well recorded.

Gaspard de la nuit; Menuet sur le nom d'Haydn; Prélude; Sonatine; Valses nobles et sentimentales.
(*) Hung. Dig. **HCD 12317-2 [id.]. Dezsö Ránki.

On compact disc this fine Hungarian pianist faces formidable competition in *Gaspard* and the *Valses nobles* from Ashkenazy on Decca and, in the former, from Pogorelich on DG. Even so, Ránki acquits himself well and shows a keen sympathy for this repertoire. He is thoroughly attuned to the Gallic sensibility, and in the last of the *Valses nobles* – each is separately indexed on the CD – his playing has wonderful atmosphere and poignancy. Unfortunately, his recording is not quite as good as the sound given to his rivals – the piano is rather forward in a reverberant acoustic and does not altogether flatter him.

Gaspard de la nuit; Valses nobles et sentimentales; Pavane pour une infante défunte.
*** Decca Dig. **410 255-2** [id.]. Vladimir Ashkenazy.

Fresh from his nearly completed Chopin series and various triumphs on the podium, Vladimir Ashkenazy has now returned to Ravel. His earlier version of *Gaspard* (Decca SXL 6215) was in its day a yardstick by which others were judged, and is still pretty impressive. While there is no doubt as to the dazzling virtuosity and amazing control of colour and mood in Ivo Pogorelich's remarkable DG account, he is self-conscious, particularly in *Le gibet*, and his record is not for everyday listening. Ashkenazy's new account is hardly less impressive than the old and is in no way narcissistic. It does not altogether efface memories of the Argerich (see above), though there is not a great deal to choose between them. His *Valses nobles* are splendidly refined and aristocratic. The recording has marvellous range and is extremely vivid and open, but the slightly less bright sound of his earlier *Gaspard* is rather more pleasing. The newer issue offers somewhat short measure for CD.

Miroirs; Le tombeau de Couperin.
(*) BIS Dig. **CD 246. Yukie Nagai.

Yukie Nagai is a young Japanese pianist who has settled in Munich. She won the 1977 International Prize in Geneva and, as is the case with so many Oriental artists, obviously has a real feeling for French music. Her account of *Noctuelles* is marvellous refined, and her range of colour at the *piano* and *pianissimo* end of the range is particularly lovely. Her account of *Oiseaux tristes* is very slow and altogether magical in atmosphere, and she is hardly less impressive elsewhere. This is distinguished playing. The recording is good – though without being quite as wide-ranging as Bolet's Liszt records for Decca or Kocsis for Philips; it sounds as if it is made in a small studio, yet there is no lack of ambience.

VOCAL MUSIC

Mélodies: *Ballade de la Reine; Morte d'Aimer; Canzone italiana; Chanson du rouet; Chanson espagnole; Chanson française; Chanson hébraïque; Chansons madécasses; 5 mélodies populaires grecques; 2 épigrammes de Clément Marot; 2 mélodies hébraïques; Don Quichotte à Dulcinée; Un grand sommeil nuit; Les grands vents venus d'outremer; Histoires naturelles; Manteau de fleurs; Noël des jouets; Rêves; Ronsard à son âme; Sainte; Scottish song; Shéhérazade* (complete)*; Si morne!; Sur l'herbe; Tripatos; 3 poèmes de Stèphane Mallarmé; Vocalise en forme de Habañera.*
*** HMV Dig. **CDS7 47638-8** (2) [id.]. Norman, Mesplé, Lott, Berganza, Van Dam, Bacquier, Capitole Toulouse O or Paris CO, Plasson; Dalton Baldwin (piano).

With a composer whose expressive range in song-form (or mélodie) might have seemed limited, it is an excellent idea in the HMV set to have six strongly contrasted singers, each given an apt area to cover. So Teresa Berganza as well as singing *Shéhérazade* has two songs inspired by Spain, the *Vocalise in the form of an Habañera* and the *Chanson espagnole* from the set of five *Chants populaires*, each of which is allotted to a different singer. Felicity Lott's *Chanson écossaise* is a rarity, *Ye banks and braes* sung in a convincing Scots accent. For all the shallowness of Mady Mesplé's voice, it works well in the *Mélodies populaires grecques*, while Jessye Norman, rich-toned if not quite as characterful as usual, has the *Chansons madécasses* as well as lesser-known songs. It is the contribution of the two men that provides the sharpest illumination: José van Dam magnificently dark-toned in the *Don Quichotte* songs and the *Mélodies hébraïques* (making *Kaddish* thrillingly powerful in its agony of mourning), while Gabriel Bacquier twinkles in Figaro tones in the point songs. Excellent sound, and the pair of CDs particularly generous (136′) in offering the contents of three LPs.

(i) *Chansons madécasses;* (ii) *Don Quichotte à Dulcinée; 5 mélodies populaires grecques;* (iii) *3 poèmes de Stéphane Mallarmé;* (iv) *Shéhérazade.*
*** CBS Dig. **MK 39023** [id.]. (i) Norman, Ens. InterContemporain; (ii) José van Dam; (iii) Jill Gomez; (iv) Heather Harper; BBC SO, Boulez.

With four characterful and strongly contrasted soloists, Boulez's ceollection of Ravel's songs with orchestra (including arrangements) makes a delightful disc. This is an important supplement to the EMI set of Ravel's complete songs, when the *Don Quichotte* and the *Greek popular songs* (both with José van Dam as soloist) are rarely heard in this orchestral form. Van Dam may not be as relaxed as he is with piano on the HMV set, but the dark, firm voice is just as impressive. Excellent sound, with translations provided.

Shéhérazade (song cycle).
*** Ph. Dig. **410 043-2** [id.]. Elly Ameling, San Francisco SO, De Waart – DEBUSSY: *La damoiselle élue*; DUPARC: *Songs*.***
(*) Ph. **412 493-2 [id.]. Jessye Norman, LSO, C. Davis – BERLIOZ: *Nuits d'été*.**(*)
** HMV Dig. **CDC7 47111-2** [id.]; *EL 270135-4* [Ang. *4DS 38061*]. Dame Kiri Te Kanawa, Belgian Nat. Op. O, Pritchard – DUPARC: *Songs*.**
** Decca Dig. **411 895-2** [id.]. Hildegard Behrens, VSO, Travis – BERLIOZ: *Nuits d'été*.*(*)

Elly Ameling has a voice of innocence, pure of tone; however, when she sings Gershwin for example, she can colour it sensuously; and so it is here in Ravel's evocative song-cycle. Other versions may delve deeper into the exotic emotions behind the poems by 'Tristan Klingsor', but in its sweetness and beauty (enhanced by the orchestral playing and radiant recording) this has a place too, particularly when the coupling is apt and unusual. On the superb compact disc the effect is ravishing, the voice seemingly floating against a wonderfully luminous orchestral backcloth.

Jessye Norman seems more at home in Ravel's song-cycle than in the coupled account of the Berlioz, although she and Sir Colin Davis are languorous to the point of lethargy in *L'Indifférent*. With the voice very forward, the balance is less than ideal, though otherwise the sound is rich and atmospheric. Ameling, however, has special qualities to offer which Miss Norman does not match. The CD transfer enhances the presence of the recording while emphasizing the balance.

Unlike some of her colleagues, Dame Kiri elects to couple Ravel's glorious triptych with Duparc songs rather than the usual *Les Nuits d'été* favoured by Norman and Behrens. She is somewhat bland by comparison with her most formidable rivals, and despite good orchestral playing from the Belgian National Opera Orchestra under Sir John Pritchard and good EMI recording, this is not among the most memorable recorded versions of the cycle.

Behrens's version is rich-toned and evocative, with the weight of the voice adding to the impact – though the pure beauty of these songs has been more ravishingly caught in other versions. As in the disappointing account of the Berlioz on the reverse, the recording is outstandingly vivid and approaches demonstration standard.

Tape collectors may be glad to know that Régine Crespin's much-praised analogue recording with Ansermet is still available at mid-price as we go to print. Her style has distinct echoes of the opera house, but the sheer richness of her tone does not prevent this fine artist from being able to achieve the delicate languor demanded by an exquisite song like *The enchanted flute*. Ansermet accompanies superbly and the recording retains the atmospheric vividness characteristic of his vintage Decca issue (*417 228-4*).

OPERA

L'Enfant et les sortilèges.
*** HMV Dig. **CDC7 47169-2** [id.]. Wyner, Augér, Berbié, Langridge, Bastin, Amb. S., LSO, Previn.

Previn's dramatic and highly spontaneous reading of *L'Enfant* brings out the refreshing charm of a neglected masterpiece. Helped by a strong and stylish team of soloists, this makes superb entertainment. On CD, the precision and sense of presence of the digital recordings come out the more vividly, with subtle textures clarified and voices – including the odd shout – precisely placed. That precision goes well with Previn's performance, crisply rhythmic rather than atmospherically poetic. It is a pity that the 44-minute piece has only one band, divided only by index markings, unusable on many machines.

Reger, Max (1873–1916)

Ballet suite; Variations on a theme of Hiller, Op. 100.
*** Orfeo **C 090841** [id.]. Bav. RSO, C. Davis.

The *Hiller variations* (1907) is one of Reger's greatest works, full of wit, resource and, above all, delicacy. Each of the eleven variations takes the form of a more or less free fantasy, deriving from the carefree Hiller theme, and the work is enormously inventive. It culminates, as do so many Reger pieces, in a double fugue. The *Ballet suite* is a delightful piece, scored with great clarity and played, as is the *Hiller variations*, with charm and commitment. Sir Colin Davis emerges as a thoroughly echt-Reger conductor and the Bavarian orchestra is in excellent form; one can only hope that he will go on to record the heavenly *Mozart variations* and the Four Böcklin tone-poems. The recording is first rate, though we have one minor quibble: the individual variations are not indexed.

Chorale fantasia on Straf' mich nicht in deinem Zorn, Op. 40/2; Chorale preludes, Op. 67/4, 13, 28, 40, 48; Introduction, passacaglia & fugue in E min., Op. 127.
*** Hyp. Dig. **CDA 66223**; *KA 66223* [id.]. Graham Barber (organ of Limburg Cathedral).

An ideal disc to represent Reger's music in any collection. The longest and most important work here is the *Introduction, passacaglia and fugue*, which takes all of 28 minutes. It is bold in conception and vision, and is superbly played on this excellently engineered Hyperion disc by Graham Barber at the Klais organ of Limburg Cathedral, an instrument ideally suited to this repertoire. The five *Chorale preludes* give him an admirable opportunity to show the variety and richness of tone-colours of the instrument. The Hyperion recording captures the quality of the king of beasts marvellously on CD, but there is also a very good tape.

Lyrisches Andante.
*** Claves Dig. **D 8502** [id.]. Deutsche Kammerakademie Neuss, Goritzki – SCHOECK: *Cello concerto.****

Reger's *Lyrisches Andante* dates from his time in Wiesbaden (1893–8) and is a short, songful and gentle piece for strings. It is also known as 'Dream of Love' and should make many friends for this much misunderstood composer, particularly in this dedicated performance.

Reich, Steve (born 1936)

Eight lines; Vermont counterpoint.
*** HMV Dig. **CDC7 47331-2** [id.]; *EL 270291-4* [Ang. *4XS 37345*]. Solisti New York, Wilson – ADAMS: *Grand pianola music.****

Steve Reich's *Vermont counterpoint* is aurally fascinating, with its flute-dominated textures – Ransom Wilson here soloist as well as musical director – and the longer *Eight lines* is also ingeniously scored. But this is minimalist music with a vengeance, with the textural alterations relatively insignificant over a fairly long time-span, and the listener might be forgiven the impression that the recording is 'stuck in the groove'. Both performances are admirably fresh however, and the hypnotic effect of the music is undeniable. The recording is first class on CD. The XDR tape is also clear and vivid.

Variations for winds, strings & keyboard.
*** Ph. **412 214-2** [id.]. San Francisco SO, De Waart – ADAMS: *Shaker loops.****

Reich's *Variations*, written for the San Francisco orchestra in 1980, marked a new departure in the writing of this leading minimalist, using a large orchestral rather than a small chamber scale. The repetitions and ostinatos, which gradually get out of phase, are most skilfully used to produce a hypnotic kind of poetry, soothing rather than compelling. With the excellent Adams coupling and first-rate performance and recording, it can be warmly recommended to anyone wanting to sample minimalism. The CD does not add a great deal because of the resonant ambience, but the background silence increases the feeling of tension.

Reicha, Antonín (1770–1836)

Oboe quintet in F, Op. 107.
*** Hyp. **CDA 66143** [id.]. Sarah Francis, Allegri Qt – CRUSELL: *Divertimento*; KREUTZER: *Grand quintet.****

Born in the same year as Beethoven, Antonín Reicha was an enormously productive composer as well as a respected teacher whose pupils included Liszt and Berlioz. The *F major Quintet*, Op. 107, dates from the first half of the 1820s and is spectacularly unmemorable but always amiable. The present performance is of high quality and very well recorded.

Wind quintets: in E flat, Op. 88/2; in F, Op. 91/3.
*** Hyp. Dig. **CDA 66268**; *KA 66268* [id.]. Academia Wind Quintet of Prague.

Czech wind playing in Czech wind music has a deservedly high entertainment rating and the present performances are no exception. The music itself has great charm and geniality; it is ingenuous yet cultivated, with some delightful, smiling writing for the bassoon. The players are clearly enjoying themselves yet they play and blend expertly. Their sheer high spirits are difficult to resist. The sound too is admirable in both formats. Curiously, the *E flat Quintet* (like Devienne's *Second Bassoon quartet*) quotes quite positively the main theme of the first movement of Beethoven's *Horn sonata*.

Reinecke, Carl (1824–1910)

Flute concerto in D, Op. 283.
*** Ph. Dig. **412 728-2** [id.]. Nicolet, Leipzig GO, Masur – BUSONI: *Divertimento*; NIELSEN: *Concerto.****

Carl Reinecke was a great figure in Leipzig's musical life; for many years he was conductor of the Gewandhaus Orchestra and director of the Leipzig conservatoire. In his youth he served as pianist to the Danish court. His *Flute concerto* is a late work, as its vast opus number might indicate, written in 1908 when he was in his mid-eighties. It could have been written in the mid-1850s and is very much in the tradition of Mendelssohn; it has considerable charm and warmth as well as personality. The elegiac slow movement has real eloquence and is beautifully written; this *Concerto* will come as something of a discovery. Aurèle Nicolet plays it with effortless ease and is admirably supported by the Leipzig orchestra. The recording, made in a reverberant acoustic, is also excellent; even if the soloist is a shade too forward, the balance is well judged. Because of the resonance, the CD improves the definition only marginally.

Respighi, Ottorino (1879–1936)

Ancient airs and dances: suites Nos 1–3.
❀ *** Mercury **416 496-2** [id.]. Philh. Hungarica, Dorati.
(M) **(*) DG *419 868-4* [id.]. Boston SO, Ozawa.

Dorati's famous and very distinguished Mercury recording of the 1960s has been in and out of the British catalogue over the years and now returns in its excellently remastered CD format. The performance, one of the first recordings by this group of Hungarian expatriates based in Vienna, is of the utmost distinction. It combines brilliance with great sensitivity – the delicacy of articulation of the principal oboe is a special delight – to display a remarkable feeling for the colour and ambience of the Renaissance dances on which Respighi's three suites (the last for strings alone) are based. The refinement and warmth of the playing (and the sound) are very striking, particularly in the *Third suite*, and the touch of astringency which the digital remastering has added increases the piquancy. Dorati finds in this music a nobility and graciousness that make it obstinately memorable.

Ozawa is at his best in the *Second suite* where the luminous Boston wind playing combines with strong contrasts of dynamic and tempo to dramatic effect. Rhythmically very positive throughout, as so often his music making brings a feeling of ballet to the score. He is less memorable in the *Third suite*, but with brightly vivid sound this makes an enjoyable mid-price alternative for those not tempted to Marriner's tape collection – see below.

(i) *Ancient airs and dances: suites Nos 1–3;* (ii) *The Birds; 3 Botticelli pictures.*
(B) *** HMV *TCC2-POR 54276.* (i) LACO; (ii) ASMF, Marriner.

The Birds (suite); 3 Botticelli pictures.
*** HMV **CDC7 47844-2** [id.]. ASMF, Marriner.

An admirable compilation chosen to represent Sir Neville Marriner in HMV's 'Portrait of the Artist' double-length tape series. The account of the suite of dances is attractively light and gracious, offering an almost French elegance with pleasingly transparent textures. The performances of *The Birds* and the *Trittico Botticelliano* are no less delightful and beautifully recorded. The score for the *Botticelli pictures* is less well known and understandably so, for its inspiration is less assured; with presentation of this standard, however, the music is certainly enjoyable. The tape transfer is of high quality, with the sound pleasing; *The Birds* and the *Botticelliano* are notably warm and refined, yet there is excellent detail.

The separate CD of *The Birds* and *Botticelli pictures* is most successfully remastered – the sound is fresh and bright without too much loss of string sonority – but at 38′ this is poor value at premium price.

Ancient airs and dances: suite No. 3; The Birds (suite).
*** Ph. Dig. **420 485-2**; *420 485-4* [id.]. ASMF, Marriner – ROSSINI: *La Boutique fantasque.***(*)

Ancient airs and dances: suite No. 3; The Fountains of Rome; The Pines of Rome.
*** DG **413 822-2** [id.]. BPO, Karajan.

On CD, Karajan's highly polished, totally committed performances of the two most popular Roman pieces are well supplemented by the third suite of *Ancient airs and dances*, just as brilliantly done and with 1970s' analogue recording just as beautifully transferred, more impressive in sound than many more recent Karajan recordings. In the symphonic poems Karajan is in his element, and the playing of the Berlin Philharmonic is wonderfully refined. The evocation of atmosphere in the two middle sections of *The Pines of Rome* is unforgettable. A distanced and magically haunting trumpet solo is matched by the principal clarinet who is no less poetic. In *The Fountains* the tension is rather less tautly held, but the pictorial imagery is hardly less telling when the orchestral response is so magical.

Marriner gives a very beautiful account of the third suite of *Ancient airs and dances*, with gracious phrasing and luminous string textures. He catches both the music's noble melancholy and its moments of passionate feeling. The performance of *The Birds* is hardly less persuasive, the portrait of *The Dove* particularly tender, and there is much delicacy of texture elsewhere. The ASMF strings are wonderfully responsive and play as one. The sound is excellent too, in both media, though the CD has added presence and more refined detail. The coupling, however, is a curious choice, acting merely as a pleasant filler.

Belkis, Queen of Sheba: suite. Metamorphoseon modi XII.
*** Chan. Dig. **CHAN 8405**; *ABTD 1142* [id.]. Philh. O, Simon.

Geoffrey Simon follows up the success of his earlier Respighi recording (coupling *Church windows* and *Brazilian impressions*) with two even rarer pieces, one of which gives a surprising slant on a composer who often seems just an atmosphere man, a colourist rather than a musical arguer. The ballet-suite *Belkis, Queen of Sheba,* taken from a full-length ballet written in the early 1930s, is just what you would expect: a score that set the pattern for later Hollywood biblical film music; but *Metamorphoseon* is a taut and sympathetic set of variations. It has been ingeniously based on a medieval theme, and though a group of cadenza variations relaxes the tension of argument in the middle, the brilliance and variety of the writing have much in common with Elgar's *Enigma.* Superb playing from the Philharmonia, treated to one of the finest recordings that even Chandos has produced, outstanding in every way. This is very attractive music and the sound is certainly in the demonstration bracket in both media. The chrome cassette is quite astonishing.

The Birds; The Fountains of Rome; The Pines of Rome (symphonic poems).
** Ph. Dig. **411 419-2** [id.]. San Francisco SO, De Waart.

The Birds is an evocative and beautifully scored work; it makes a less usual coupling for Respighi's two finest symphonic poems associated with Rome. De Waart conducts brilliant and sympathetic performances, but an unnatural brilliance in the recording with unrealistic placing of instruments is underlined on the finest reproducers, not least in the compact disc version.

Brazilian impressions; Church windows (*Vetrate di chiesa*).
*** Chan. Dig. **CHAN 8317**; *ABTD 1098* [id.]. Philh. O, Simon.

Respighi's set of musical illustrations of church windows is not among his finest works (the second stained-glass portrait, representing St Michael, is the most memorable, with its extrovert colouring) but is well worth having when the recording is impressively spacious and colourful. Geoffrey Simon is sympathetic and he secures very fine playing from the Philharmonia. The superb digital recording and the useful coupling (which avoids duplication with Respighi's more famous works) will be an added incentive to collectors. On CD, the wide dynamic range and a striking depth of perspective create the most spectacular effects, and this is very much in the demonstration class. The chrome tape, too, has very good definition within the atmospheric acoustic.

Feste romane; The Fountains of Rome; The Pines of Rome (symphonic poems).
*** HMV Dig. **CDC7 47316-2** [id.]. Phd. O, Muti.
*** Decca Dig. **410 145-2**; *KSXDC 7591* [Lon. *LDR 5-71091*]. Montreal SO, Dutoit.
(M) *** DG **415 846-2**; *415 846-4* [id.]. Boston SO, Ozawa.

Muti gives warmly red-blooded performances of Respighi's Roman trilogy, captivatingly Italianate in their inflexions. With brilliant playing from the Philadelphia Orchestra and warmly atmospheric recording, far better than EMI engineers have generally been producing in Philadelphia, these are exceptional for their strength of characterization. Each scene is vividly dramatized, and the most impressive of the three is the most brazen of a brazen trio of works, *Feste romane*. Muti flouts the idea of vulgarity, and produces a reading that is well 'over the top', but all the more captivating for it. In the final orgiastic jubilation of *La Befana*, the jazzy jollity and outrageous intrusions of popular music are so exuberant they are enough to make you laugh. The CD version clarifies the reverberant recording very effectively, with individual soloists cleanly placed. Each of the four sections in each piece is separately banded.

Dutoit as in other brilliant and colourful pieces draws committed playing from his fine Montreal orchestra. Where many interpreters concentrate entirely on brilliance, Dutoit finds a vein of expressiveness too, which – for example in the opening sequence of *The Pines of Rome* – conveys the fun of children playing at the Villa Borghese. There have been more high-powered, even more polished performances on record, but none more persuasive. The recorded sound is superlative, most of all on compact disc, where the organ pedal sound is stunning. Cassette collectors too should be well satisfied, for the standard of tape transfer is remarkably fine.

Ozawa's 1979 record has been digitally remastered for its Galleria reissue and remains very competitive at mid-price, with an excellent matching chrome tape; however, while sharpening the focus and refining detail, the brighter treble has brought a hint of harshness to the loudest fortissimos.

OPERA

La Fiamma (complete).
*** Hung. Dig. **HCD 12591/3** [id.]. Tokody, Kelen, Takács, Sólyom-Nagy, Hungarian R. and TV Ch., Hungarian State O, Gardelli.

La Fiamma, a tale of witchcraft and the early church set in seventh-century Ravenna, might be described as Puccini updated – though the setting does also give Respighi plenty of opportunities to draw on his medievalist side, not just his love of exotic sounds. Richly atmospheric with choruses and ensembles both mysterious and savage, it makes a fine impact in this excellent first recording, idiomatically conducted by Lamberto Gardelli. The Hungarian cast is impressive, with Ilona Tokody producing Callas-like inflexions in the central role of Silvana, the young wife of the exarch, Basilio. She falls in love with her son-in-law, shocks her husband into falling down dead, and then cannot find tongue to deny a charge of witchcraft. Sándor Sólyom-Nagy is impressive as Basilio, Peter Kelen is aptly light-toned as the son-in-law, but it is the formidable Klára Takács as the interfering Eudossia who personifies the grit in the oyster, providing high melodrama. The playing is warmly committed and, apart from some distancing of the chorus, the sound is first rate, atmospheric but also precisely focused.

Reubke, Julius (1834–58)

Sonata in C min. on the 94th Psalm.
*** DG Dig. **415 139-2** [id.]. Simon Preston (organ of Westminster Abbey) – LISZT: *Fantasia and fugue on 'Ad nos salutarem'*.**(*)

Julius Reubke (son of an organ builder) studied under Liszt at Weimar and modelled his *Sonata* on Liszt's *Fantasia and fugue* (which is the appropriate coupling). He gave its première in 1857 and died the year after, only twenty-four years of age. His monothematic piece is powerfully conceived and ingeniously wrought; its three sections can be regarded either as separate movements or as different facets of a single structure. Simon Preston's performance is of the first rank and his playing is superbly recorded, with the CD adding a degree of extra definition. The acoustic of Westminster Abbey seems especially suited to the sombre *Adagio-Lento*, which is superbly eloquent in Preston's hands. In the outer sections the characteristic blurring created by the acoustics of the Abbey cannot be blamed on the engineers, but in the closing fugue Preston thrusts forward and the complex detail is welded into the texture. Here the CD comes into its own with its thrilling weight and projection.

Rezniček, Emil (1860–1945)

Symphony No. 4 in E min.
** Schwann **VMS 2091** [id.]. Philh. Hungarica, Gordon Wright.

Baron Emil Nikolaus von Rezniček is known to the wider musical public by one work only, his sparkling *Overture Donna Diana*. Most readers would not know that Rezniček had written one symphony – let alone four – and has to his credit a *Violin concerto*, four *String quartets*, a *Requiem* and no fewer than twelve operas. Rezniček was at first torn between the law and music; he went on to study in Leipzig with Reinecke and subsequently held conducting appointments at Mannheim, Prague, the Warsaw Opera and Komische Oper, Berlin. The *Symphony in F minor* dates from 1919, the year before he joined the staff of the Hochschule für Musik in Berlin, in which city he lived until his death in August 1945. We must regretfully part company with Hanspeter Krellman, who speaks of this symphony as 'in no sense a derivative work', for it is really little else. Its first movement is heavily indebted to Wagner and Bruckner, though there are occasional reminders of other composers, too, such as Dvořák and, in the slow movement, the *Trauermarsch auf den Tod eines Komödianten*, the *Eroica*, and in the Scherzo, Schubert. There are some individual touches, of course, and moments of dignity, even of nobility, but there is much that is portentous. Strangely enough, there is little real sense of mastery, and none of the melodic inventiveness or expert craftsmanship that distinguish *Donna Diana*. The playing of the Philharmonia Hungarica under George Wright is serviceable rather than distinguished, and much the same goes for the recording.

Rheinberger, Joseph (1839–1901)

Organ concerto No. 1 in F, Op. 137.
*** Telarc Dig. **CD 80136** [id.]. Michael Murray, RPO, Ling – DUPRÉ: *Symphony*.***

Rheinberger's *Concerto* is well made, its invention is attractive and it has suitable moments of spectacle that render it admirable for a coupling with the Dupré *Symphony*, with its use of the massive Albert Hall organ. The performance here is first rate, as is the large-scale Telarc digital recording. This is the sort of music Jack Renner's recording team do marvellously. A fine demonstration disc.

Rimsky-Korsakov, Nikolay (1844–1908)

Capriccio espagnol, Op. 34.
(B) *** DG Walkman *413 422-4* [id.]. BPO, Maazel – BIZET: *L'Arlésienne*; *Carmen*; DUKAS: *L'apprenti sorcier*; CHABRIER: *España*.**(*)

Maazel's 1960 recording of the *Capriccio espagnol* has never been surpassed. With gorgeous string and horn playing, and a debonair relaxed virtuosity in the *Scene e canto gitano* leading to breathtaking bravura in the closing section, every note in place, this is unforgettable. The remastering for the Walkman tape has smoothed the treble a little, but otherwise the sound remains vivid. With Claudio Abbado's splendid account of Bizet's *L'Arlésienne* and *Carmen* suites, this is worth acquiring, even if some duplication may be involved with the other items.

Capriccio espagnol; May night overture; Sadko, Op. 5; (i) *The Snow Maiden:* suite.
** Ph. Dig. **411 446-2** [id.]. Rotterdam PO, Zinman; (i) with Alexander and Ch.

Zinman secures some quite lustrous playing from his Rotterdam orchestra in the *Capriccio*, and he finds both atmosphere and colour in *Sadko* and the *May night overture*. But this is music that needs more than refined orchestral playing: there is a lack of charisma here, and the adrenalin begins to flow only at the very end of the Spanish piece. In the *Danse des oiseaux* (from *The Snow Maiden*) there is an effective vocal contribution. Even on compact disc, the recording, though naturally balanced, has no special presence, though it is full and pleasing.

Capriccio espagnol, Op. 34; Russian Easter festival overture, Op. 36.
(M) *** DG *419 873-4* [id.]. Chicago SO, Barenboim – MUSSORGSKY: *Night on the bare mountain*; TCHAIKOVSKY: *Marche slave*.***

After an arresting start to the *Capriccio espagnol*, Barenboim adopts a rather leisurely and indulgent pace in the variations, but the sumptuous recording brings vivid colouring; although this account has not quite the adrenalin of Maazel's, it is still very enjoyable. The *Russian Easter festival overture* is splendidly dramatic and full of warmth and atmosphere; the recording is very spectacular, with the percussion having a field day – the chrome tape just about accommodates the amplitude. This should sound marvellous on CD and may soon appear in that format.

Christmas eve (suite); Le Coq d'or: suite*; Legend of the invisible city of Kitezh:* suite*; May night:* overture*; Mlada:* suite*; The Snow Maiden:* suite*; The Tale of the Tsar Saltan:* suite.
*** Chan. Dig. **CHAN 8327-9**; *DBTD 3004* (3) [id.]. SNO, Järvi.

Much of the more memorable writing in Rimsky-Korsakov's fairy-tale operas is for orchestra alone, which the composer uses with enormous flair to create the background atmosphere for the exotic events of the narrative. There is an essential pantheism in Rimsky's art. The *Prelude* to *The invisible city of Kitezh* is described as a hymn to nature, while the delights of the *Christmas eve suite* (an independent work) include a magical evocation of the glittering stars against a snow-covered landscape and, later, a flight of comets. The plots, drawn on Gogol and Ostrovsky, are peopled by picaresque human characters. In *Le Coq d'or* the bumbling King Dodon has his counterpart in the alluring Queen Shemakha for whom Rimsky wrote one of his most sensuously languorous melodies, an idea – like so many here – of great memorability. Apart from the feast of good tunes, the composer's skilful and subtle deployment of the orchestral palette continually titillates the ear. Within the ideal resonance of their Glasgow home, Neeme Järvi draws the most seductive response from the SNO (who clearly relish the feline delicacy of Queen Shemakha's seduction of the King); he consistently creates orchestral textures which are diaphanously sinuous. Yet the robust moments, when the brass blazes or the horns ring out sumptuously, are caught just as delectably. The chrome tapes are in the demonstration class (slightly smooth in the treble but with an impressive range and amplitude), but the CDs have that extra degree of presence while the focus is that bit brighter and sharper. This Chandos set achieves new standards in this repertoire and the listener is assured that this is music that survives repetition uncommonly well.

Le Coq d'or: suite*; The Tale of Tsar Saltan:* suite.
** Ph. Dig. **411 435-2** [id.]. Rotterdam PO, Zinman.

While new digital recordings of this repertoire are welcome and the Rotterdam orchestra plays with appealing freshness, Zinman's approach seems over-refined; while there is no lack of colour, the sinuously sentient qualities of *Le Coq d'or* are minimized, and there is a lack of real sparkle elsewhere. On CD, the sound approaches demonstration standard. But Zinman's performances are much less enticing than Järvi's with the SNO, on Chandos.

Night on Mount Triglav; Pan Voyevoda: suite.
** Marco Polo **8220 438** [id.]. Slovak PO, Bystrik Režucha.

Two Rimskian curiosities, of distinct interest even if, in the end, not of lasting appeal. *Night on Mount Triglav* derives from a collaborative work that was stillborn. The music was written, alongside contributions from Cui, Borodin and Mussorgsky, for an opera, but Rimsky turned his discarded third act into a hybrid piece, part orchestral suite, part symphonic poem. Its world is very similar to that of *Le Coq d'or*, with even a chromatic clarinet theme to represent Queen Cleopatra, and before that a witches' sabbath. The instrumentation is characteristically exotic, but the invention is rather thin for a piece lasting over half an hour. The opera *Pan Voyevoda* has Chopin as its dedicatee, so not surprisingly the suite includes a good deal of Polish-style dance music and an amiable *Nocturne*. Again the orchestration is the most distinctive feature. The Slovak orchestra play both works with commitment and Bystrik Režucha makes the most of the atmospheric effects. The recording, too, is warmly resonant, without clouding.

Russian Easter festival overture, Op. 36.
(*) Decca Dig. **417 299-2; *417 299-4* [id.]. Montreal SO, Dutoit – MUSSORGSKY: *Pictures* etc.**(*)

Dutoit's version of the *Russian Easter festival overture* is strong, with a fine climax. The colourful Decca recording brings iridescent orchestral detail, but the music's romanticism does not blossom in the way it does in Barenboim's account (see above).

Scheherazade (symphonic suite), *Op. 35.*
❀ (M) *** HMV **CDC7 47717-2** [id.]; *ED 291180-4*. RPO, Beecham – BORODIN: *Polovtsian dances.****
*** Ph. **400 021-2** [id.]. Concg. O, Kondrashin.
*** Chan. Dig. **CHAN 8479**; *ABTD 1191* [id.]. SNO, Järvi – GLAZUNOV: *Stenka Razin.****
(M) *** DG **419 063-2**; *419 063-4* [id.]. BPO, Karajan – BORODIN: *Polovtsian dances.****
(M) *** RCA *GK 87018* [**RD CD1 7018** (with DEBUSSY: *La mer*)]. Chicago SO, Reiner.
(*) HMV Dig. **CDC7 47023-2 [id.]. Phd. O, Muti.
(*) Andante **CDACD 85702 [Var./Sar. **VCD 47208**]. LSO, Tjeknavorian – GLINKA: *Russlan overture.****
(*) Ph. Dig. **411 479-2 [id.]. VPO, Previn.
(B) **(*) DG Walkman *413 155-4* [id.]. Boston SO, Ozawa – STRAVINSKY: *Firebird suite*; KHACHATURIAN: *Gayaneh.***(*)
** Decca **414 124-2** [id.]. SRO, Ansermet – BORODIN: *Polovtsian dances.***
** DG **415 512-2** [id.]. BPO, Maazel.

Scheherazade; Capriccio espagnol.
(*) Decca Dig. **410 253-2; *410 253-4* [id.]. Montreal SO, Dutoit.

Scheherazade; The Tale of Tsar Saltan suite, Op. 56; The flight of the bumble bee.
(*) Decca Dig. **417 301-2; *417 301-4* [id.]. Philh. O, Ashkenazy.

Beecham's *Scheherazade* was recorded in London's Kingsway Hall in March 1957. It is a performance of extraordinary drama and charisma. Alongside the violin contribution of Stephen Staryk, all the solo playing has great distinction; in the second movement Beecham gives the woodwind complete metrical freedom (notably the bassoon), yet the electricity of the music making never for a moment flickers; later the brass fanfares have great flair and bite. The sumptuousness and glamour of the slow movement are very apparent, yet a sultry cultured refinement pervades the languor of the string phrasing. The finale has an explosive excitement, rising to an electrifying climax, which the dynamic range of the digital remastering frees from any restriction. Indeed the quality of the remastered recording is astonishing, with a firmer, fuller bass than before and the most natural detail. There is less body than in a modern recording, but the strings do not lack weight and the trombones and tuba have a blazing gusto in their sharp enunciation, especially in the finale. The coupled *Polovtsian dances* have comparable dash and excitement; undoubtedly, this marvellous CD (alongside Beecham's Delius) represents one of the greatest examples of his art on record. There is a very serviceable cassette, but it does not match the CD's range and sense of spectacle.

Kondrashin's version with the Concertgebouw Orchestra has the advantage of splendid modern analogue recorded sound, combining richness and sparkle within exactly the right degree of resonance. Here the personality of Hermann Krebbers (the orchestra's concertmaster) very much enters the picture, and his gently seductive portrayal of Scheherazade's narrative creates a strong influence on the overall interpretation. His exquisite playing, especially at the opening and close of the work, is cleverly used by Kondrashin to provide a foil for the expansively vibrant contribution of the orchestra as a whole. The first movement, after Krebber's tranquil introduction, develops a striking architectural sweep; the second is vivid with colour, the third beguilingly gracious, while in the finale, without taking unusually fast tempi, Kondrashin creates an irresistible forward impulse leading to a huge climax at the moment of the shipwreck. On CD, one notices that inner detail is marginally less sharp than it would be with a digital recording, but the analogue glow and naturalness more than compensate, and the richness of texture is just right for the music.

Järvi's version with the SNO may not be the most high-powered or weighty; nor is it as idiosyncratic as, for instance, the Beecham or Karajan versions; but, with the episodic argument strongly held together as in the telling of a story, it is most persuasive. The playing is no less fine than in versions from the most distinguished international orchestras, and the recorded sound is spectacular in the Chandos manner, spacious and refined. Indeed for those looking for a splendid modern digital version, this could well be first choice. The generous fill-up makes an added attraction with the playing, if anything, more committed – had the Rimsky-Korsakov that intangible extra degree of bite which Järvi gives to Glazunov, it would have been right at the top of the list alongside Beecham. The chrome cassette is well up to Chandos's high standards, wide-ranging and well detailed.

Karajan's 1967 recording is greatly enhanced in its CD format – one of the most successful examples of digital remastering yet to come from DG. The extra vividness brings more life and sparkle to the central movements, which are superbly played, and the brass fanfares in the second have a tingling immediacy. The added presence also increases the feeling of ardour from the glorious Berlin strings in the *Andante*, while the lovely horn solo at the close is made to sound particularly nostalgic. The outer movements have great vitality and thrust, and the bright percussion transients add to the feeling of zest. Yet Michel Schwalbé's sinuously luxuriant violin solos are still allowed to dominate the narrative. The fill-up is a sizzling account of the Borodin *Polovtsian dances*, with no chorus, but managing perfectly well without. There is a splendid tape, and at mid-price this is a real bargain in both formats.

Reiner's classic 1960 recording has been reissued on tape in the UK, but is available in the USA on CD (which we have not been able to sample) coupled with Debussy's *La Mer*. The remastered recording sounds remarkably sumptuous in its tape format, and the performance is given weight as well as dramatic force. The first movement has a strong forward impulse and the two central movements have beguiling colour, with Reiner's individual touches having something in common with Beecham's version, and sounding comparably spontaneous. The third movement is wonderfully languorous and the finale, brilliant and exciting, has a climax of resounding power and amplitude. The Chicago Hall ambience is very effective, making up in spaciousness for any lack of internal clarity.

In terms of playing time, Ashkenazy's Decca record is the most generous of all, offering besides the *Flight of the bumble bee* (which makes an amiable final encore) the dazzlingly scored *Tsar Saltan suite*, where Ashkenazy is in his element, and the Philharmonia players obviously relish the good tunes, sonorous brass writing and glittering effects. As it happens, the accompanying notes devote more space to the bonus items than to the main work! Here, with the orchestral balance set back naturally (in Walthamstow Assembly Hall) the violin solos, sweetly played by Christopher Warren-Green, are almost ethereal in their distancing. The recording has the widest dynamic range and Ashkenazy uses its full possibilities for drama, alternating the languorous string sequences of the first movement with powerful projection for the brass entries. The inner movements are fresh and full of colourful detail, but the relatively brisk pacing of the *Andante* loses some of the music's voluptuousness. The finale is racily exciting, but Ashkenazy pulls back to broaden the climax at the dramatic gong-clash, and this sounds not entirely spontaneous. The cassette lacks the ultimate range of the CD.

Muti's reading is colourful and dramatic in a larger-than-life way that sweeps one along. The bravura has one remembering that this was the orchestra which in the days of Stokowski made this a party-piece. The great string theme of the slow movement has all the voluptuousness one expects of Philadelphia strings in one of the best of HMV's latterday Philadelphia recordings, more spacious than usual, though not ideally balanced. There is a glare in the upper range to which not all ears will respond, even if the racy finale, with its exciting climax, carries all before it. The CD emphasizes the brightness of the treble, especially in climaxes; this digital emphasis is much less congenial than the Philips sound for Kondrashin.

Tjeknavorian's is an arresting performance and, with extremely brilliant and detailed recording, its sharpness of detail will certainly appeal to some ears. The overall sound-balance is bright rather than richly sumptuous, yet the bass response is strong and clear. Tjeknavorian paces the music briskly throughout: the first movement has a strong, passionate climax, and the slow movement has less repose than usual, sounding more elegant, less sensuous, its 6/8 rhythmic pattern readily apparent. The finale has a furious basic tempo, but the LSO players obviously revel in their virtuosity and the result is consistently exhilarating, with (for the most part) amazingly clear articulation. The climax has a brilliance to make the ears tingle, with a hint of fierceness in the recording itself.

Previn in his Vienna version opts for spacious speeds and a direct, unsentimental view of the fairy-tale suite. With his characteristic rhythmic flair and sumptuous playing from the Vienna Philharmonic, the result can be recommended to those wanting a more restrained reading than usual. Excellent, finely balanced sound with improved definition and presence on CD. But even on compact disc, in spite of the advantages of digital recording, this does not match Kondrashin in excitement and the recording is only marginally more effective.

Dutoit offers an exceptionally generous coupling; the recording is characteristic of the Montreal acoustic, full and warm with luminous detail. However, like Previn's, this is a relaxed, lyrical reading at speeds slower than usual; essentially an amiable view, lacking in virtuoso excitement. The *Capriccio espagnol* compensates to some extent for this shortcoming, again given a genial performance – though one not lacking in brilliance.

Ozawa's version is available on a Walkman cassette, making a bargain alternative if the couplings, Maazel's early stereo recording of the *Firebird suite* and Rozhdestvensky's *Gayaneh*, are suitable. It is an attractive performance, richly recorded. The first movement is strikingly spacious, building to a fine climax; if the last degree of vitality is missing from the central movements, the orchestral playing is warmly vivid. The finale is lively enough, if not earth-shaking in its excitement; the reading as a whole has plenty of colour and atmosphere, however, and it is certainly enjoyable. The chrome-tape transfer is sophisticated.

Ansermet's CD is of a historic reading of 1961; though the sound is impressive for its period, the rasp of the brass at the start and the occasional fuzz in heavy tuttis are revealed the more clearly as incipient distortion. As to the interpretation, Ansermet's skill as a ballet conductor comes out persuasively. The outer movements with their undoubted sparkle are the finest: the first is dramatic, and in the last the final climax makes a considerable impact. The music's sinuous qualities are not missed and every bar of the score is alive.

There is nothing to detain the collector in Maazel's DG version. The playing of the Berlin Philharmonic Orchestra is, of course, peerless, and in the slow movement they make some gorgeous sounds (though the acoustics of the Philharmonie are not entirely flattering on CD). But Maazel's reading is essentially spacious and the outer movements are wanting in electricity.

Among other recordings available only on tape, Haitink's 1974 LPO version stands out. Compared with Kondrashin, this shows its age just a little in string timbre, but in all other respects it is eminently truthful in sound and perspective. The playing of the LPO is both sensitive and alert, and Rodney Friend's violin solos are comparably subtle. Haitink's interpretation is wholly unaffected and totally fresh in impact, and the excitement rises spontaneously from the music making. When this is digitally remastered on CD, it should be very competitive (Philips *416 861-4*). Maazel's earlier Cleveland recording for Decca is reissued sounding dramatic and sumptuous on a mid-priced Decca tape, coupled with an enjoyable *Capriccio espagnol.* But the performance is relatively straight and lyrically direct; and Haitink is preferable, in spite of the extremely vivid and more modern Decca sound (*417 285-4*).

Symphonies Nos 1 in D min., Op. 1 (second version)*; 2* (*Antar*)*, Op. 9; 3 in C, Op. 32.*
** Chant du Monde **CD 278771/3** (2) [id.]. USSR Nat. O, Svetlanov.

Symphonies Nos 1 in E min., Op. 1; 3 in C, Op. 32.
(M)**(*) Olympia **OCD 158** [id.]. USSR Ac. SO, Svetlanov.

Symphony No. 3 in C, Op. 32; Skazka (*Fairy tale*)*, Op. 29.*
**(*) ASV Dig. *ZCDCA 538* [id.]. LSO, Butt.

Rimsky-Korsakov's *First Symphony* was sketched in 1860–61 but was not completed until 1865, only to be revised in its present format in the spring of 1884. So it falls between two stools, lacking the youthful spontaneity of, say, Bizet's *Symphony*, but without the mastery of maturity. Yet it has some good ideas and, not surprisingly, some effective orchestration. It has a sombre *Andante tranquillo*, which Svetlanov shapes impressively, and the finale is good-humoured and not too rhetorical. The *Second Symphony* is better known under its sub-title, *Antar*, a powerful precursor of *Scheherazade*. Its memorable themes and dramatic orchestral effects illustrate a story from mythology whose heroine (as characterized in Rimsky's sinuous descriptive orientalism) has a good deal in common with Queen Shemakha in *Le Coq d'or*. The *Third Symphony* is not one of the composer's strongest works but remains distinctly appealing, especially in Svetlanov's hands, where it becomes weightier and more symphonically commanding than in the ASV version under Yondani Butt. Its very opening has some delightful woodwind scoring and this makes a fine effect in Svetlanov's Olympia version which offers 70′ of music and a sensible coupling of Nos 1 and 3. Not surprisingly, the performances are very similar in both sets, with the *Andante* of No. 3 particularly eloquent in the Olympia version. The string playing has plenty of character and lyric fervour and the brass tend to bray a bit (and there is blare in the slow movements of both the Olympia and Chant du Monde versions). The bright sound is also common to both, and one could wish at times for a bit more amplitude in the massed strings, although the quality is clean and clear without being too edgy. There is a patch of distortion in the slow movement of the *First Symphony* in the Chant du Monde version.

The ASV recording of the LSO is altogether more sophisticated and Butt's performance, if lightweight, is also persuasive. In the *Andante*, with its characteristic sequential climaxes, Svetlanov is stronger; but overall Butt has a degree more charm. Moreover, he has the advantage of an interesting fill-up, *Skazka*, a somewhat Lisztian but highly inventive piece that has been out of the catalogue since Fistoulari's mono recording on Parlophone. With a good matching cassette, this can certainly be recommended as an alternative to the complete set, especially to those who already have *Antar*.

Symphony No. 2 (Antar), Op. 9.
*** Telarc **CD 80131** [id.]. Pittsburgh SO, Maazel – TCHAIKOVSKY: *Symphony No. 2.****

Lorin Maazel's first major recording of repertory works with the Pittsburgh orchestra, of which he was becoming music director, brought this welcome new version of Rimsky-Korsakov's *Antar symphony*, aptly and generously coupled with Tchaikovsky's *Little Russian*. Maazel's taut yet sympathetic reading holds together a work which, structurally at least, might more aptly be counted as a suite (as *Scheherazade* is) but which, with strong and colourful yet refined treatment like this, is fittingly regarded as belonging to Rimsky's symphonic canon. Excellent playing – notably in the finale, where the Pittsburgh woodwind excel themselves in delicacy – and brilliant, finely balanced recording.

Tsar Saltan, Op. 57: March.
*** Telarc Dig. **CD 80107** [id.]. RPO, Previn – TCHAIKOVSKY: *Symphony No. 5.****

The crisp, stylized *March* from *Tsar Saltan*, a fairy-tale piece, makes a delightful bonne-bouche, a welcome fill-up for Previn's fine account of the Tchaikovsky *Fifth Symphony*, equally well played and recorded.

Piano and wind quintet in B flat.
*** CRD *CRDC 4109* [id.]. Nash Ens. – ARENSKY: *Piano trio No. 1.****
*** Hyp. **CDA 66163**; *KA 66163* [id.]. Capricorn – GLINKA: *Grand Sextet.****

Rimsky-Korsakov's youthful *Quintet for piano, flute, clarinet, horn and bassoon* is a thoroughly diverting piece. In an earlier edition we described it as being like a garrulous but endearing friend whose loquacity is readily borne for the sake of his charm and good nature. The main theme of the finale is pretty brainless but singularly engaging, and the work as a whole leaves a festive impression. It has been out of the catalogue since the deletion of the Vienna Octet account on Decca, but the Nash Ensemble give a spirited and delightful account of it on CRD that can be warmly recommended for its dash, sparkle and clear, clean sound.

Capricorn is a young group, formed in the 1970s, who have been making a name for themselves in recent years. Their account of the Rimsky-Korsakov *Quintet* has great vivacity and is excellently recorded. There is not a great deal to choose between them and the Nash, though the excellence of the pianist, Julian Jacobson (formerly Dawson Lyall), should be noted: he contributes a rare sparkle to the proceedings. Personal requirements concerning the respective couplings may be safely left to decide matters. Both are rarities, and the Arensky is a delicious period piece.

Rodrigo, Joaquín (born 1902)

A la busca del más allá; (i) Concierto de Aranjuez; Zarabanda lejana, y Villancico.
(M) **(*) EMI Dig. *EMX 41 2068-4* [Ang. *4XS 37876*]. LSO, Bátiz; (i) with Moreno.

The *Zarabanda lejana* ('Distant sarabande') was Rodrigo's first work for guitar (1926), written in homage to Luis Milan. He later orchestrated it and added the *Villancico* to make a binary structure, the first part nobly elegiac, the second a gay dance movement, with a touch of harmonic astringency, but having something of the atmosphere of a carol. The symphonic poem, *A la busca del más allá* ('In search of the beyond') was written as recently as 1978 but, like all Rodrigo's music, its idiom is in no way avant-garde. It could easily be dismissed as film music without a film, yet it is evocative and powerfully scored and makes a curiously indelible impression. Bátiz plays it with strong commitment, as he does the earlier piece, and the vividly brilliant, forwardly balanced digital sound produces a considerable impact on the boldly transferred cassette. Unfortunately the performance of the ubiquitous *Concierto de Aranjuez*, although bright and sympathetic, is in no way outstanding, which reduces the attractiveness of this issue, even at mid-price. However, *A la busca* and *Zarabanda lejana* have been issued on CD, coupled with Falla's *Nights in the gardens of Spain* (in which Aldo Ciccolini is the soloist) and Turina's *Sinfonia Sevillana* (HMV **CDC7 49542-2**).

(i) *Concierto Andaluz;* (ii) *Concierto madrigal.*
*** Ph. **400 024-2** [id.]. (i) Los Romeros; (ii) P. and A. Romero, ASMF, Marriner.

Los Romeros and the Academy make the very most of the *Concierto Andaluz*, with infectious spirit in the outer sections and plenty of romantic atmosphere in the slow movement. The *Concierto madrigal* was also written for the Romero family; the performance here is definitive and beautifully recorded. Each of the twelve miniatures that make up this engaging work springs vividly to life. Sir Neville Marriner's contribution to both concertos has real distinction. The analogue recordings, originally first class, have responded most convincingly to digital remastering.

Concierto de Aranjuez (for guitar and orchestra).
(M) ** Pickwick Dig. **PCD 859**. Michael Conn, O of St John's, Smith Sq., Lubbock – ARNOLD: *Concerto.**(*)

Michael Conn's instrumental personality is rather anonymous, but he and Lubbock give a highly atmospheric yet touchingly simple account of the famous *Adagio*, which is not without its big passionate orchestral climax near the end. The vivid yet naturally balanced digital recording helps to project the outer movements, but the lack of a strong characterization from the soloist is a considerable drawback; even so, the finale goes rather well.

Concierto de Aranjuez; Fantasia para un gentilhombre.
(M) *** Decca Dig. **417 748-2**; *417 272-4* [id.]. Carlos Bonell, Montreal SO, Dutoit (with FALLA: *3-Cornered hat* ***).
*** CBS Dig. **CD 37848**; *IMT 37848* [id.]. John Williams, Philh. O, Frémaux.
*** Ph. **411 440-2** [id.]. Pepe Romero, ASMF, Marriner.
(B) *** CBS *MGT 39017*. Williams, ECO, Barenboim – CASTELNUOVO-TEDESCO: *Concerto* **(*); VILLA-LOBOS: *Concerto.****
(*) Decca Dig. **417 199-2; *417 199-4* [id.]. Eduardo Fernández, ECO, Martinez – CASTELNUOVO-TEDESCO: *Concerto.***(*)
(*) DG **413 349-2 [id.]. Narciso Yepes, Philh. O, Navarro.

(i) *Concierto de Aranjuez; Fantasia para un gentilhombre;* (ii) *Concierto serenata for harp and orchestra.*
(M) ** Ph. **420 714-2**; *420 714-4* [id.]. (i) Lagoya, (ii) Michel; Monte Carlo Op. O, Almeida.
(M) ** DG *419 483-4* [id.]. (i) Yepes, Spanish R. & TV O, Alonso; (ii) Zabaleta, Berlin RSO, Märzendorfer.
(B) ** DG Walkman *413 156-4* [id.]. (i) Yepes; (ii) Zabaleta (as above) – FALLA: *Nights.***(*)

(i) *Concierto de Aranjuez; Fantasia para un gentilhombre. En los trigales; Pastoral; Sonata à la espanola.*
(*) HMV Dig. **CDC7 49050-2 [id.]; *EL 270624-4*. Ernesto Bitetti; (i) Philh. O, Ros-Marba.

(i) *Concierto de Aranjuez; Fantasia para un gentilhombre. Elógio de guitarra.*
*** HMV **CDC7 47693-2** [id.]. Angel Romero, (i) LSO, Previn.

Having established a great success in the early days of CD with the Bonell/Dutoit coupling, Decca have made this issue even more attractive by adding a bonus of three dances from Falla's

Three-cornered hat (taken from Dutoit's complete set) and by placing the recording on their mid-priced Ovation label, where it makes a splendid bargain. But the reasons for the original success remain unaltered: an exceptionally clear and well-balanced digital recording (with an excellent tape equivalent) plus Bonell's imaginative and inspired account of the solo part, and the strong characterization of the orchestral accompaniments by Charles Dutoit and his excellent Montreal orchestra. In the *Concierto*, the series of vivid interjections by the orchestral wind soloists (cor anglais, bassoon and trumpet) is projected with the utmost personality and presence, and a feeling of freshness pervades every bar of the orchestral texture. Soloist and orchestra combine to give an outstandingly eloquent account of the famous slow movement, and the climax retains its clarity of texture. The finale has irresistible sparkle. In the *Fantasia*, the balance between warmly gracious lyricism and sprightly rhythmic resilience is no less engaging; here again, the orchestral solo playing makes a strong impression. This is a clear first choice for this coupling, especially on compact disc, where the ambient warmth counters the bright upper range.

John Williams's newest version of the *Concierto* (his third) also has the advantage of first-class digital recording. The balance is most believable, the soloist a little forward but with the guitar image admirably related to the orchestra, where inner detail is impressively clear. The acoustic, however, is a little dry compared with the Decca issue; this is emphasized on CD, which also suggests that the woodwind is a shade too forward. Nevertheless, this is technically superior to Williams's previous analogue partnership with Barenboim – see below – and the performance is even finer. The slow movement is wonderfully atmospheric, with the soloist's introspective yet inspirational mood anticipated and echoed by Frémaux, who secures most beautiful orchestral playing. The finale is light and sparkling with an element of fantasy and much delicacy of articulation in the accompaniment. The performance of the *Fantasia* is no less memorable. Its relaxed opening dialogue between soloist and orchestra is engagingly spontaneous and refined in feeling; later, when the music becomes more energetic, Frémaux brings out the Renaissance colours in the scoring most vividly. This is altogether a most winning coupling, not as extrovert as the Bonell/Dutoit partnership, but no less distinguished.

Pepe Romero's CD is digitally remastered from high-quality analogue recordings dating from 1979 and 1976 respectively. The performance of the *Concierto de Aranjuez* is as satisfying as any available, with a strong Spanish flavour and the musing poetry of the slow movement beautifully caught. The account of the *Fantasia* is warm and gracious, with the Academy contributing quite as much as the soloist to the appeal of the performance. The success of the CD transfer is remarkable; although inner detail is less sharply focused than on either the Bonell or Williams digital versions, it hardly matters, for the warm beauty of the analogue atmosphere emphasizes the Mediterranean feeling; indeed, many will like the softer-grained Philips quality. Background noise is virtually eradicated.

The Previn/Romero issue is undoubtedly very successful too. The recording sounds clearer in its remastered format; originally it was rather more atmospheric (but one must remember that the less expensive Decca version does not lack ambient effect). Angel Romero does not emerge as such a strong personality as John Williams, but the skill and sensibility of his playing are in no doubt, and Previn is obviously so delighted with the orchestral scores that he communicates his enthusiasm with loving care for detail. Thus, although the solo guitar is slightly larger than life in relation to the orchestra, Previn is still able to bring out the delightful woodwind chatter in the outer movements of the *Concierto*. The famous slow movement is very beautifully played indeed; the opening is especially memorable. The approach to the *Fantasia* is vividly direct, missing some of the essentially Spanish graciousness that marks the Marriner version (see above), but its infectious quality is more than enough compensation. However, this record would have been more competitive at mid-price. There is a short patch of less than perfectly focused *tutti* at the end of the slow movement.

Eduardo Fernandez gives an amiable account of Rodrigo's famous *Concierto*, attractively ruminative in the *Adagio* and with a cheerful finale. The *Fantasia* is also played with much warmth and affectionate detail and is even more characterful. The Decca recording is warmly atmospheric, with less bite than the Bonell/Dutoit versions, which are also more distinctive interpretations. However, the couplings are generous, with the Castelnuovo-Tedesco *Concerto* offered, besides the two Rodrigo works.

John Williams's second analogue recording of the *Concierto*, with Barenboim, made in 1975, is superior to his earlier version with Ormandy. The playing has marvellous point and spontaneity; the *Adagio* had rarely before been played with this degree of poetic feeling. There is a hint of rhythmic over-emphasis in the finale, but in general the performance is first class, and if the digital version on CD – see above – is even finer, this remains fully satisfying. The *Fantasia* too is impeccably played and thoroughly enjoyable, with Barenboim making the most of the vivid orchestral colouring. With an outstanding version of the Villa-Lobos *Concerto* and a very good one of the Castelnuovo-Tedesco, this is an unbeatable bargain in CBS's '90 Minute' tape series. The transfer level is high and the sound vivid, and it is generally preferable to the *tape* equivalent of the newest digital coupling of the two Rodrigo works.

The newest digital recording from EMI is attractive in combining Rodrigo's two favourite concertante guitar works with some worthwhile solo items which are very well played by Ernesto Bitetti; indeed the *Sonata a la española*, which ends this programme, was dedicated to him. He gives a rather introspective performance of it, but he is lively enough in the *Concierto*; the *Fantasia* is especially successful, with Ros-Marba and the Philharmonia providing a brilliantly coloured orchestral backing, full of bracing rhythmic vitality. There is an excellent chrome cassette.

Yepes' 1980 version of the *Concierto de Aranjuez* is an improvement on his recording of a decade earlier with the Spanish Radio and TV Orchestra – see below – mainly because of the superior accompaniment. Even here, however, there is a lack of vitality in the outer movements, although the poetic element of the *Adagio* is well managed. The performance of the *Fantasia*, too, has character and refinement, and in both works the analogue recording balance is clear and immediate. But Yepes comes into competition with more attractive versions in all price ranges and his coupling would not be a first choice. The CD transfer is in no way distinctive.

Philips have reissued on their mid-priced Silverline label Alexandre Lagoya's 1972 coupling of the *Concierto* and the *Fantasia*. Lagoya is a good player, but he does not always project strongly, except perhaps in the slow movement of the *Concierto*, which he plays with considerable feeling. The outer movements are agreeable, if not as sprightly as some versions. Nevertheless the digital remastering has given the recording added presence; we are now also offered an attractive account of the delectable *Concierto serenata* for harp, with Catherine Michel a splendid soloist and very good 1973 sound, well balanced, full and immediate.

A similar compilation from DG, also at mid-price, is rather less attractive. It offers Yepes' disappointing 1970 coupling of the two concertante works, with Odon Alonso not the most imaginative conductor (he is rhythmically rather stiff in the finale of the *Concierto*); although Yepes is at his finest in the *Adagio* and plays nobly in the *Fantasia* (which is generally more successful), the dry, studio-ish recording sounds even drier in its remastered format, on Galleria, while the *Concierto serenata*, played with much piquancy and charm by Zabaleta, is made to seem very sharply etched. As can be seen, these same recordings are also available on a Walkman tape, made from the original analogue master and sounding rather more atmospheric and without the brighter, sharper treble.

(i) *Concierto de Aranjuez; 3 Piezas españolas* (*Fandango; Passacaglia; Zapateado*); *Invocation and dance* (*Homage to Manuel de Falla*).
*** RCA Dig. **RD 84900 [RCD1 4900]**. Julian Bream, COE, Gardiner.

Bream's recording of the *Concierto* has a personality all its own. With outer movements offering strong dynamic contrasts and some pungent accents (from orchestra as well as soloist) the music's flamenco associations are underlined and the famous *Adagio* is played in a very free, improvisatory way, with some highly atmospheric wind solos in the orchestra. The whole presentation is immensely vivid, with the orchestration in the outer movements made to sparkle. The balance is more natural than usual, with the guitar set slightly back and heard in a convincing perspective with the orchestra. The only slight snag is that the resonance adds a touch of harshness to the emphatic orchestral tuttis. What makes this issue especially valuable, however, is the inclusion of the *Tres Piezas españolas*, of which the second, *Passacaglia*, is one of Rodrigo's finest shorter works. No less involving is his *Invocation* for Manuel de Falla, with both performances showing Bream at his most inspirationally spontaneous.

Concierto como un divertimento (for cello and orchestra).
*** RCA *RK 70798* [*ARK1 4665*]. Lloyd Webber, LPO, Lopez-Cobos – LALO: *Concerto.****

One suspects that Julian Lloyd Webber, in commissioning this new concerto, may not have known of the existence of the earlier *Concierto en modo galante* (written in 1949) as recorded by Robert Cohen, see below. If so, the gain is considerable, for the new work is delightful, and even more Spanish in feeling than the old. The style of writing is familiar, with a sinuously atmospheric *Adagio nostalgico* sandwiched between sparklingly inventive outer sections. The moto perpetuo finale has an engaging lyrical strain and the first movement, too, has a catchy main theme. It is all characteristically friendly music, and Lloyd Webber is obviously attuned to its spirit and completely equal to its technical demands. The sound is vividly transferred to the refined tape.

(i) *Concierto heróico* (for piano and orchestra); *5 piezas infantiles* (*5 Children's pieces*). *Soleriana: Pastoral; Passepied.*
**(*) HMV Dig. *EL 270397-4*. (i) Orsorio; PRO, Bátiz.

Rodrigo's *Piano concerto* was conceived in the early 1930s, but then set aside and the early sketches were lost; the present work dates from 1939. It has a programmatic content, with the four movements written 'under the signs of the Sword, the Spur, the Cross and the Laurel'. But heroism is not a quality one associates with Rodrigo's art; the first movement with its fanfare-like main theme soon becomes merely garrulous; the second outstays its welcome, and the best part is the *Largo* which, seeking a medieval ambience, is attractively atmospheric. The performers do their best for the piece and they are vividly recorded, but the best music here is the set of children's pieces, nicely conceived vignettes of some charm, while the two neo-classical evocations from *Soleriana* are also unostentatiously effective.

(i) *Concierto en modo galante;* (ii) *Concierto serenata;* (iii) *Musica para un jardin.*
❀ *** HMV Dig. **CDC7 47869-2** [id.]. (i) Robert Cohen, LSO; (ii) Nancy Allen, RPO; (iii) LSO, Bátiz.

The *Cello concerto in modo galante* dates from 1949; it is given a masterly performance by Robert Cohen: he combines elegance of phrasing with warm beauty of timbre (yet never too much tone) in the lovely yet delicate secondary theme (*in tempo di minuetto galante*) of the first movement and the no less haunting melody which dominates the *Adagietto*. His spirited articulation of the opening ostinato idea and the lively *Zapateado* rondo finale is matched by Bátiz. He secures playing which combines delicacy with temperament from the LSO who sound, both here and in the *Música para un jardin*, as if they had just returned from a holiday in the Spanish sunshine. In the *Concerto for harp*, Nancy Allen is a shade reticent – especially in the first-movement cadenza; but the clarity of the CD ensures that she does not become overwhelmed, and she consistently beguiles the ear by her gentleness, while Bátiz scales down his support to produce a successful partnership in this winning piece (the very opening with its cascade of trickling notes is wonderfully inviting). In both works the digital sound is translucently clear; indeed the balance in the *Cello concerto* is quite ideal. What makes the compact disc doubly attractive is the inclusion of one of Rodrigo's most imaginatively atmospheric orchestral works. *Música para un jardin* is a quartet of highly engaging cradle songs, scored with all the piquancy at the composer's command. Although the music is very much Rodrigo's own, the orchestration has influences from Françaix and even Messiaen, and the result is well summed up by John Duarte in the accompanying notes, describing the music as having 'a phantom-like quality; the subtle enchantment lies in its coolness, transparency and lyricism, spiced with a pleasant scattering of harmonic surprises'. The performance and recording fully capture the magic and earn the CD a rosette as an indispensable addition to the Rodrigo discography.

Concierto para una fiesta (for guitar and orchestra).
*** Ph. **411 133-2** [id.]. Pepe Romero, ASMF, Marriner – ROMERO: *Concierto de Málaga.***

Rodrigo's second solo guitar concerto dates from 1982 and was commissioned (in an excellent musical tradition that goes back to Mozart and before) by the McKay family of Fort Worth, Texas, for the social début of their two daughters. It had its first performance, with Pepe Romero the soloist, in March 1983. The recording followed soon after and has all the freshness of new discovery, with Romero playing with striking spontaneity and Marriner and his Academy providing an accompaniment that is characteristically polished as well as thoroughly committed. If Rodrigo does not quite repeat the success of the *Concierto de Aranjuez*, the first movement with its contrasting Valencian themes is highly engaging, and the *Andante calmo* has a hauntingly ruminative introspection, with its sombre main theme involving the dark-timbred cor anglais. The dance rhythms of the finale introduce an Andalusian *Sevillanas* as the principal idea, and the effect is unashamedly brash, in contrast to what has gone before. The recording is most natural and beautifully balanced.

Concierto pastoral (for flute and orchestra); *Fantasia para un gentilhombre* (arr. Galway for flute and orchestra).
*** RCA *GK 85446* [*AKL1 5446*]. Galway, Philh. O, Mata.

The *Concierto pastoral* was composed for James Galway in 1978. Its spikily brilliant introduction is far from pastoral in feeling, but the mood of the work soon settles down. At first hearing, the material seems thinner than usual, but Rodrigo's fragmented melodies and rhythmic ostinatos soon insinuate themselves into the listener's memory. The slow movement is especially effective, with a witty scherzando centrepiece framed by the *Adagio* outer sections. James Galway's performance is truly superlative, showing the utmost bravura and matching refinement. He is beautifully recorded, and the small accompanying chamber orchestra is well balanced. The arrangement of the *Fantasia* is a very free one, necessitating re-orchestration, exchanging clarinet and horn instrumentation for the original scoring for trumpet and piccolo. The solo part too has been rewritten and even extended, apparently with the composer's blessing. The result is, to be honest, not an improvement on the original. But Galway is very persuasive, even if there is a persistent feeling of inflation. No complaints about the tape transfer of the *Fantasia*; there is just a fractional loss of refinement in the *Concierto*, but it is of minor importance.

Sones en la Giralda.
*** Ph. Dig. **416 357-2**; *416 357-4* [id.]. Pepe Romero, ASMF, Marriner – CASTELNUOVO-TEDESCO; VILLA-LOBOS: *Concertos.****

La Giralda is the ancient tower of Seville Cathedral. Its character and its associations obviously stimulated Rodrigo's imagination so that the first of these two pieces is eerily atmospheric; then the clouds clear away and the finale sparkles with the flamenco dance rhythms of the *Sevillanas*. The work was conceived for harp and chamber orchestra; but Pepe Romero and Marriner show an immediate response to its evocation and spirit, and the result is memorable, helped by first-class recording.

Roman, Johan (1694–1758)

(i) *Violin concertos: in D min.; E flat; F min.; Sinfonias: in A; D and F.*
*** BIS Dig. **CD 284** [id.]. (i) Nils-Erik Sparf; Orpheus Chamber Ens.

Johan Helmich Roman, often called the 'Father of Swedish music', was a younger contemporary of Handel. He spent five years in England (1716–21) where he studied under Pepusch and acquired his love of the music of Handel, whom he met on a later visit. The best of his output is fully commensurate with Geminiani or Telemann, and there are often unpredictable quirks of line or harmony that make him most appealing. Ingmar Bengtsson, the authority on Roman, lists some thirty sinfonias in all, two of which (the *D major* and *E minor*) have been available on record at various times. None of the sinfonias here have appeared on disc before – and indeed only one (the *A major*) exists in print. Of the five violin concertos attributed to Roman, the three recorded here are classified by Bengtsson as 'probably authentic'. They are certainly attractive pieces, particularly in such persuasive hands as those of Nils-Erik Sparf and the Orpheus Chamber Ensemble (who are not to be confused with the distinguished American group, but are drawn from the Stockholm Philharmonic). Very stylish and accomplished performances that are scholarly in approach.

Romero, Celedonio (born 1918)

Concierto de Málaga (for guitar; orch. Torroba).
** Ph. **411 133-2** [id.]. Pepe Romero, ASMF, Marriner – RODRIGO: *Concierto para una fiesta*.***

Romero's *Concierto* originated as an *Andalusian suite* for solo guitar and was orchestrated by Moreno Torroba. Its material is slight and its structure more so; it will appeal most to those who like the passionate guitar-strumming effects of flamenco music, from which it is essentially derived. Pepe Romero creates a strong sense of involvement and is suitably atmospheric when called for, and the accompaniment is well managed. But this work is not on the level of its Rodrigo coupling.

Ropartz, Joseph Marie Guy (1864–1955)

Prelude, marine and chansons (for flute, violin, viola, cello and harp).
(M) *** Decca *414 063-4* [id.]. Ellis, Melos Ens. – DEBUSSY: *Sonata*; RAVEL: *Introduction and allegro*; ROUSSEL: *Serenade*.***

Guy-Ropartz's *Prelude, marine and chansons* makes a delightful bonus for a superb collection of French chamber music. The 1962 sound remains extremely full and vivid.

Symphony No. 3 (for soloists, chorus and orchestra).
*** HMV Dig. **CDC7 47558-2** [id.]; *EL 270348-4*. Pollet, Stutzmann, Dann, Vassar, Orfeon Donostiarra, Toulouse Capitole O, Plasson.

Like the Magnard symphonies, the *Third Symphony* of Ropartz has much nobility and there is a sense of scale and grandeur. It takes over 55′ and the composer himself apparently retained a lifelong affection for it. It dates from 1905; half a century later, Honegger had planned to put it on LP; alas, both musicians died that same year. There is much in the pantheistic vision of its opening pages which one cannot fail to respond to, and some felicitous harmonic invention. The fugato in the second movement is a little reminiscent of d'Indy, and it is with this sensibility rather than that of Debussy that this work has greatest affinity. There is a certain unrelieved thickness of texture, particularly in the finale, and for a work of these dimensions one feels the need for stronger dramatic contrast and variety of pace. However, there is a personality here, and all lovers of French music will find it rewarding. Even if the recording (and some of the solo singing) is not of the very highest order, the orchestral playing under Michel Plasson is thoroughly committed.

Rosetti, Antoni (1750–92)

Horn concertos: in E flat, K.3:39; in E, K.3:42; in E, K.3:44.
(M) *** EMI **CD-EMX 9514**; *TC-EMX 2095*. Barry Tuckwell, ECO.

Horn concerto in E, K.3:42.
(M) **(*) Tel. **ZS8 43629** [id.]. Baumann, Concerto Amsterdam – HAYDN; DANZI: *Concertos.***(*)

The Bohemian composer, born Franz Anton Rössler, who adopted an Italian version of his name, wrote prolifically for the horn; the present concertos are characteristic of the taxing melodic line he provides for the soloist, with high-ranging lyrical tessitura contrasting with very florid arpeggios. He was especially good at rondo finales, and the work which both Baumann and Tuckwell have recorded shows him at his melodically most exuberant. Tuckwell's style is agreeably robust and he is very well recorded. He directs his own accompaniments with polish and spirit.

Baumann's recording could do with a shade more warmth – the string tone is rather dry and the horn timbre open, but there is no lack of presence. But the EMI collection is well worth having for anyone who enjoys horn concertos, although the invention here is far more conventional than those of Mozart. The EMI CD has exceptional realism and presence; the cassette is good, too, but the upper range is more restricted.

Rossini, Gioacchino (1792–1868)

La Boutique fantasque (ballet, arr. Respighi); complete.
*** Decca Dig. **410 139-2** [id.]. Nat. PO, Bonynge – BRITTEN: *Matinées*; *Soirées.****
(M) **(*) Decca *417 600-4* [id.]. Nat. PO, Bonynge – CHOPIN: *Les Sylphides***; WEBER: *Invitation to the dance.***(*)

La Boutique fantasque: suite.
(*) Ph. Dig. **420 485-2; *420 485-4* [id.]. ASMF, Marriner – RESPIGHI: *Ancient airs*; *The Birds.****

Bonynge goes for sparkle and momentum above all in Respighi's brilliant and sumptuous rescoring of Rossini, a magical ballet if ever there was one. The Decca compact disc has great brilliance and the orchestral colours glitter and glow within the attractive resonance of Kingsway Hall, although there is a degree of digital edge on the treble. Bonynge's exuberance is certainly exhilarating when the sound is so spectacular. The Britten arrangements too are highly engaging, and the Decca CD plays for over an hour. The tape is less expensive, differently and perhaps more appropriately coupled. The sound is excellently balanced, though not as wide-ranging as the CD.

Marriner's suite is insubstantial, offering only about 20′ music, chosen rather arbitrarily. It is elegantly played and warmly recorded.

Introduction, theme and variations in C min. for clarinet and orchestra.
*** ASV Dig. **CDDCA 559**; *ZCDCA 559* [id.]. Emma Johnson, ECO, Groves – CRUSELL: *Concerto No. 2**** ❀; BAERMANN: *Adagio****; WEBER: *Concertino.****

On ASV, Sir Charles Groves immediately sets the atmosphere as for a Rossini opera aria, and this performance delectably combines wit with expressive freedom. As in all her recordings, Emma Johnson's lilting timbre and sensitive control of dynamic bring imaginative light and shade to the melodic line. Brilliance for its own sake is not the keynote, but her relaxed pacing is made to sound exactly right. Vivid recording, with a good matching tape.

Overtures: *Il Barbiere di Siviglia; La cambiale di matrimonio; L'inganno felice; L'Italiana in Algeri: La scala di seta; Il Signor Bruschino; Tancredi; Il Turco in Italia.*
❀ *** DG Dig. **415 363-2** [id.]. Orpheus CO.

The Orpheus Chamber Orchestra displays astonishing unanimity of style and ensemble in this splendid collection of Rossini overtures, played without a conductor. Not only is the crispness of string phrasing a joy, but the many stylish wind solos have an attractive degree of freedom, and one never senses any rigidity in allegros which are always joyfully sprung. *La scala di seta* is an especial delight, and the opening string cantilena of *Il Barbiere* is agreeably gracious. These are performances that in their refinement and apt chamber scale give increasing pleasure with familiarity. The DG recording is marvellously real and, when the perspective is so perfectly judged, the background silence gives the wind added tangibility. The string timbre is sweet and natural and entirely without edge in tuttis. A demonstration CD *par excellence* and one that displays admirable group musicianship put entirely at the service of the composer.

Overtures: *Il Barbiere di Siviglia; La cambiale di matrimonio; Otello; Semiramide; Le siège de Corinthe; Tancredi; Torvaldo e Dorliska.*
(*) Decca Dig. **414 407-2 [id.]. Nat. PO, Chailly.

This is Chailly's second collection of Rossini overtures; it shows a distinct improvement in offering cleaner ensemble and more polished detail, while retaining the high spirits and geniality of the first CD – see below. The novelties, *Otello* – played with great dash – and *Torvaldo e Dorliska*, with its witty interchanges between wind and strings, are among the highlights. *Semiramide* is also elegantly played and *The Barber* is nicely stylish. As before, detail is wonderfully clear in the music's gentler sections, but the vivid tuttis bring a touch of aggressiveness on the fortissimo strings. However, this can be tamed, and the performances are undoubtedly infectious.

Overtures: *Il Barbiere di Siviglia; La Cenerentola; La gazza ladra; L'Italiana in Algeri; La scala di seta; Semiramide; Il Signor Bruschino; William Tell.*
(M) (***) HMV **CDM7 69042-2** [id.]. Philh. O, Giulini.

Giulini's performances derive from two LP sources, recorded in 1961 and 1965. The performances offer characteristically refined Philharmonia playing, with Giulini's careful attention to detail balanced by a strong sense of drama; although these are not the most genial performances on record, they are strong in personality. The performance of *William Tell* is outstanding for the beauty of the cello playing at the opening and the affectionate detail of the pastoral section. There is generous measure here (nearly 71′) – it is a great pity that there must be the strongest reservations about the effect of the digital remastering, which brings the most aggressively fierce glare on the violins in fortissimo: the opening of *La scala di seta* is quite spoilt by the sound, which robs the music of all its elegance.

Overtures: *Il Barbiere di Siviglia; La Cenerentola; La gazza ladra; L'Italiana in Algeri; Otello; La scala di seta: Semiramide; William Tell.*
*** Ph. **412 893-2** [id.]. ASMF, Marriner.

These eight overtures, playing for about 70 minutes, are the best known, taken from Sir Neville Marriner's 'complete' survey, recorded in the late 1970s, which included two dozen in all. Original orchestrations are used and the performances are characteristically neat and polished. In the remastering for CD, while the sound remains beautifully natural and refined, there has been a fractional loss of transient sparkle in achieving a virtually silent background. However, the balance remains excellent; if the last degree of presence is missing, compared with DG's Orpheus recordings, this is still very enjoyable.

Overtures: *Il Barbiere di Siviglia; La Cenerentola; La gazza ladra; L'Italiana in Algeri; Le siège de Corinthe; Il Signor Bruschino.*
(M) *** DG **419 869-2**; *419 869-4* [id.]. LSO, Abbado.

Brilliant, sparkling playing, with splendid discipline, vibrant rhythms and finely articulated phrasing – altogether invigorating and bracing. There is perhaps an absence of outright geniality here, but these are superb performances and recorded with great fidelity, wide range and firm body. Whether the CD or the tape is chosen, this remains one of the very finest collections of Rossini overtures in the present catalogue, for the wit is spiced with a touch of acerbity, and the flavour is of a vintage dry champagne which retains its bloom, yet has a subtlety all its own.

Overtures: *Il Barbiere di Siviglia; La gazza ladra; Semiramide; William Tell.*
(*) DG **415 377-2 [id.]. BPO, Karajan – SUPPÉ: *Overtures.***(*)

Overtures: *Il Barbiere di Siviglia; La gazza ladra; L'Italiana in Algeri; La scala di seta.*
(M) **(*) DG **423 218-2**; *423 218-4* [id.]. BPO, Karajan – VERDI: *Overtures & Preludes.***(*)

These performances are all taken from Karajan's 1971 collection and offer orchestral playing of supreme polish and bravura. The recording is extremely realistic at *piano* and *mezzoforte* levels, with inner detail refined, but the digital remastering has made the treble sound fierce in tuttis and the focus is not always quite clean.

Overtures: *Il Barbiere di Siviglia; La scala di seta; Semiramide; Le siège de Corinthe; Il viaggio a Reims; William Tell.*
(*) HMV **CDC7 47118-2 [id.]; (M) *EG 290278-4* [Ang. *4AM 34707*]. Philh. O, Muti.

Muti, following the Rossini style of his great compatriot Toscanini, generally adopts fast tempi for these sparkling overtures. The performances are brilliant and thrustful, helped by large-scale recording, but at times they are just a little short on wit and delicacy. The CD version gives fine precision to the original 1980 analogue sound, with firm placing of instruments but some thickening of textures in tuttis. The cassette is in the mid-price range and costs less than half the price of the CD. The transfer is full-bodied and lively.

Overtures: *La gazza ladra; L'Italiana in Algeri; La scala di seta; Il Signor Bruschino; Il Turco in Italia; Il viaggio a Reims; William Tell.*
(*) Decca Dig. **400 049-2. Nat. PO, Chailly.

This was the first compact disc of Rossini overtures. The balance is truthful, with the orchestral layout very believable. Each of the solo woodwind is naturally placed within the overall perspective, the violins have a clean focus, with pianissimo detail given striking presence. There is a degree of digital edge on tuttis, but the bustle from the cellos is particularly engaging. The background silence is especially telling when Rossini's scoring is so light and felicitous, while the overall bloom afforded by the Kingsway Hall acoustic completes the concert-hall effect. The solo playing is fully worthy of such clear presentation: the cellos at the opening of *William Tell* and the principal oboe and horn in *The Italian Girl* and *Il Turco in Italia* (respectively) all demonstrate that this is an orchestra of London's finest musicians. The wind articulation in *La scala di seta* is admirably clean, although the bow tapping at the opening of *Il Signor Bruschino* is rather lazy. Just occasionally elsewhere the ensemble slips when the conductor, Riccardo Chailly, lets the exhilaration of the moment triumph over absolute discipline and poise. But if you want precision and virtuosity alone, go to Karajan; under Chailly the spirit of the music making conveys spontaneous enjoyment too, especially in *The Thieving Magpie* and the nicely paced account of *William Tell*. Incidentally, *Il viaggio a Reims* had no overture at its first performance, but one was put together later, drawing on the ballet music from *Le siège de Corinthe*.

(i) Overtures: *Il Barbiere di Siviglia; L'Italiana in Algeri; La scala di seta; Il Signor Bruschino; Tancredi; Il Turco in Italia.* (ii) *Sonatas for strings Nos 1 in G; 3 in C; 5 in E flat.*
(B) *** DG Dig. *423 260-4* [id.]. (i) Orpheus CO; (ii) Camerata Bern, Füri.

This exceedingly generous digital Pocket Music tape offers a programme taken from CDs praised above and below. The overtures have not quite the range at the top which makes the CD so free and present, but there are no complaints about the sound in the three *String sonatas*, all highly attractive.

String sonatas Nos 1 in G; 4 in B flat; 5 in E flat; 6 in D.
*** Tel. Dig. **ZK8 43099** [id.]. Liszt CO, Rolla.

String sonatas Nos 1 in G; 3 in C; 4 in B flat; 5 in E flat.
*** DG Dig. **413 310-2** [id.]. Bern Camerata, Füri.

These sonatas are the astonishing work of the twelve-year-old Rossini and are prodigious indeed. Although they were intended to be played one instrument to a part, with the composer himself as second violin, they are nearly always given by a small string ensemble.

The merits of the Liszt Chamber Orchestra and Janos Rolla who directs from the first desk are by now well known. They are hardly less virtuosic than the Camerata Bern under Thomas Füri, and have the advantage of very natural recorded sound. There have been many fine records of these enchanting pieces, and there is little to choose between this Hungarian performance and the best of its rivals. The CD offers the usual advantages.

The Bern performances have an elegance, virtuosity and sparkle that it is going to be very difficult to beat. The playing is pretty dazzling and they are accorded recording quality of the highest order. In its compact disc form the sound is particularly fresh and vividly focused; overall, the balance is very satisfying. This is a record that will give enormous pleasure.

Variations in C, Op. 109.
*(*) Unicorn Dig. **DKPCD 9066**; *DKPC 9066* [id.]. Gray, RPO, Newstone – ARNOLD: *Concerto***; COPLAND: *Concerto**(*)*; LUTOSLAWSKI: *Dance Preludes.***

Gary Gray plays Rossini's early set of *Variations* elegantly and with fine tone and polished phrasing. But his deliberate style misses a sense of fun. Good, atmospheric recording.

Petite messe solennelle.

*** Eurodisc **610 263** (2). Lovaas, Fassbaender, Schreier, Fischer-Dieskau, Münchner Vokalisten, Hirsch, Sawallisch (pianos), Baffalt (harmonium), Sawallisch.

*** HMV Dig. **CDS7 47482-8** (2) [id.]. Popp, Fassbaender, Gedda, Kavrakos, King's College, Cambridge, Ch., Katia and Marielle Labèque (pianos), Briggs (harmonium), Cleobury.

(i) *Petite messe solennelle;* (ii) *Mosè in Egitto: Preghiera.*

** Ph. Dig. **412 548-2** (2). (i) Ricciarelli, Zimmermann, Carreras, Ramey, Amb. S., Sheppard, Berkowitz (pianos), Nunn (harmonium); (ii) Anderson, Fisichella, Raimondi, Amb. Op. Ch., Philh. O; Scimone.

Rossini's *Petite messe solennelle* must be the most genial contribution to the church liturgy in the history of music. The description *Petite* does not refer to size, for the piece is comparable in length to Verdi's *Requiem*; rather it is the composer's modest evaluation of the work's 'significance'. But what a spontaneous and infectious piece of writing it is, bubbling over with characteristic melodic, harmonic and rhythmic invention. The composer never overreaches himself. 'I was born for *opera buffa*, as well Thou knowest,' Rossini writes touchingly on the score. 'Little skill, a little heart, and that is all. So be Thou blessed and admit me to paradise.' The Sawallisch performance would surely merit the granting of the composer's wish. The soloists are first rate, the contralto outstanding in the lovely *O salutaris* and *Agnus Dei*. Good choral singing, and fine imaginative playing from the two pianists. The – originally Ariola – recording, now available on Eurodisc, dates from the early 1970s and is of high quality.

Recorded, not in King's College Chapel – which would have been too reverberant for Rossini's original chamber textures – but in the Music Faculty at Cambridge, the EMI version provides a different and contrasted view from Sawallisch's. The use of the refined trebles of King's College Choir brings a timbre very different from what Rossini would have expected from boys' voices – but, arguably, close to what he would have wanted. That sound is hard to resist when the singing itself is so movingly eloquent. The work's underlying geniality is not obscured, but here there is an added dimension of devotional intensity from the chorus which, combined with outstanding singing from a fine quartet of soloists and beautifully matched playing from the Labèque sisters, makes for very satisfying results. The recording, too, attractively combines warmth with clarity.

Scimone conducts a sober performance of this highly attractive and original work, taking too much note of the adjective *solennelle*, instead of remembering that in effect this was yet another of what Rossini called his 'sins of old age'. Though the recording is clean and faithful with a pleasant bloom on it, the different tonal elements, including the highly distinctive sound of the harmonium, fail to coalesce, rather as the performance fails to add up to the sum of its parts. The team of soloists is strong, but even the stylish José Carreras sounds strained, and the accompanying instrumentalists sound dutiful rather than sympathetic. The fill-up, the *Preghiera* from Act III of *Mosè in Egitto*, with Ruggero Raimondi, Salvatore Fisichella and June Anderson as soloists, is taken from Scimone's earlier complete set of that opera, a brief but welcome makeweight.

Stabat Mater.

(*) DG Dig. **410 034-2 [id.]. Ricciarelli, Valentini-Terani, Gonzalez, Raimondi, Philh. Ch. and O, Giulini.

** HMV Dig. **CDC7 47402-2** [id.]. Malfitano, Baltsa, Gambill, Howell, Ch. and O of Maggio Musicale Fiorentino, Muti.

Rossini loses nothing of his natural jauntiness in setting a religious text, and generally conductors treat this music simply as an offshoot of Rossini opera. Giulini, however, takes a refined and dedicated view, one that lacks something in robust qualities. Some will feel that Rossini's broad, clean-cut tunes and strong rhythms should be presented more directly, but there is much here to enjoy in the singing of the chorus as well as of the soloists, though Ricciarelli is a times ungainly on top. This appeared simultaneously with Muti's Florence version for HMV, and it is a pity that the qualities of each could not have been shared. The DG version has much the more refined and atmospheric recording, and it has transferred exceptionally well to compact disc, the acoustics richly atmospheric, the ambience adding a great deal to the choral sound and giving the listener a convincing concert-hall effect, even though the balance of the soloists is well forward.

Muti's view of the *Stabat Mater* is a dramatic one, and it is sad that he did not record it with the Philharmonia (the orchestra for Giulini's DG version) or with the Vienna Philharmonic, with whom he gave a memorable reading at the 1983 Salzburg Festival. As it is, the Florence Festival forces are at times rough – notably the orchestra – and the singing at times unpolished, though the solo quartet is a fine one. Warm but rather unrefined recording.

OPERA

Il Barbiere di Siviglia (complete).

*** Ph. Dig. **411 058-2** (3) [id.]. Baltsa, Allen, Araiza, Trimarchi, Lloyd, Amb. Op. Ch., ASMF, Marriner.

*** HMV **CDS7 47634-8** (2) [Ang. **CDCB 47634**]; (M) *EX 291093-5*. Callas, Gobbi, Alva, Ollendorff, Philh. Ch. & O, Galliera.

(B) *** CfP *TC-CFPD 4704* (2). De Los Angeles, Alva, Cava, Wallace, Bruscantini, Glyndebourne Fest. Ch., RPO, Gui.

(M) *** RCA **GD 86505** (3) [**RCA 6505-2-RG**]. Roberta Peters, Valletti, Merrill, Corena, Tozzi, Met. Op. Ch. & O, Leinsdorf.

(*) DG **415 695-2 (2) [id.]. Berganza, Prey, Alva, Montarsolo, Amb. Ch., LSO, Abbado.

Il Barbiere di Siviglia: highlights.

*** Ph. Dig. **412 266-2**; *412 266-4* [id.] (from above set, cond. Marriner).

Il Barbiere has been a very successful opera on records and the newest version from Marriner is no exception to the rule. It was Sir Neville's first opera recording and he finds a rare sense of fun in Rossini's witty score. His characteristic polish and refinement – beautifully caught in the clear, finely balanced recording – never get in the way of urgent spontaneity, the sparkle of the moment. So for example in the big Act II quintet, when the wool is being pulled over Don Basilio's eyes, there is an ideal balance between musical precision and dramatic presentation. Thomas Allen as Figaro – far more than a *buffo* figure – and Agnes Baltsa as Rosina – tough and biting, too – manage to characterize strongly, even when coping with florid divisions, and though Araiza allows himself too many intrusive aitches, he easily outshines latterday rivals, sounding heroic, not at all the small-scale tenorino, but never coarse either. Fine singing too from Robert Lloyd as Basilio. On compact disc, the theatrical feeling and sense of atmosphere are enhanced, with the placing of the singers strikingly clear. There is extensive cueing of individual numbers.

The highlights are well chosen and admirably reflect the qualities of the complete set. While the CD has the usual gain in presence and immediacy, the chrome cassette is first class too, the sound particularly sparkling in the delightful Act II finale.

Gobbi and Callas were here at their most inspired, and with the recording quality nicely refurbished the HMV is an outstanding set, not absolutely complete in its text, but so crisp and sparkling it can be confidently recommended. Callas remains supreme as a minx-like Rosina, summing up the character superbly in *Una voce poco fa*. In the final ensemble, despite the usual reading of the score, Rosina's verse is rightly given premier place at the very end. Though this was not among the cleanest of Philharmonia opera recordings, the early stereo sound comes up very acceptably on a pair of CDs, clarified to a degree, presenting a uniquely characterful performance with new freshness and immediacy. The cassettes are offered at medium price and are smoothly transferred, lacking a little at the top, with tape two, at a slightly higher level, brighter than tape one. The slimline libretto has clear but very small print.

Tape collectors, however, should be very well satisfied with the De Los Angeles/Gui set which has been issued at bargain price on two cassettes in a chunky box, with synopsis instead of libretto. The transfer is kind to the voices and generally vivid. Victoria de los Angeles is as charming a Rosina as you will ever find: no viper this one, as she claims in *Una voce poco fa*. Musically it is an unforceful performance – Rossini's brilliant *fioriture* done lovingly, with no sense of fear or danger – and that matches the gently rib-nudging humour of what is otherwise a recording of the Glyndebourne production of the early 1960s. It does not fizz as much as other Glyndebourne Rossini on record, but with elaborate stage direction in the stereo production and with a characterful line-up of soloists, it is an endearing performance, which in its line is unmatched. The recording still sounds well.

In the Victor Opera Series, with a near-complete text and a performance consistently well sung, the Leinsdorf set from the late 1950s makes a good bargain CD version, though spread over three discs. Roberta Peters is a sparkling Rosina, a singer too little known in Europe, who here lives up to her high reputation at the Met., dazzling in coloratura elaborations in alt. Robert Merrill may not be a specially comic Figaro, but the vocal characterization is strong, with the glorious voice consistently firm and well focused. Valletti, Corena and Tozzi make up a formidable team, and Leinsdorf conducts with a lightness and relaxation rare for him on record. Good, clear sound of the period, set against a reverberant, helpful acoustic.

Abbado directs a clean and satisfying performance that lacks the last degree of sparkle. Berganza's interpretation of the role of Rosina remains very consistent with her earlier performance on Decca, but the Figaro here, Hermann Prey, is more reliable, and the playing and recording have an extra degree of polish. The text is not absolutely complete, but this means that the DG engineers have been able to fit the opera on to a pair of CDs. With fresh recorded sound and plenty of immediacy, this is certainly competitive; but Marriner has a stronger cast plus modern digital sound, and his version is more enjoyable on almost all counts.

La Cenerentola (complete).
** DG **415 698-2** (3) [id.]. Berganza, Alva, Montarsolo, Capecchi, Scottish Op. Ch., LSO, Abbado.

Unlike *The Barber*, *La Cenerentola* has not been lucky on record, and the DG set, although enjoyable, lacks the extrovert bravura and sparkle of an ideal performance. The atmosphere in places is almost of a concert version, with excellent balance between the participants, helped by the fine recording. The recitative in general has plenty of life, particularly when Dandini (Renato Capecchi) is involved. Berganza, agile in the coloratura, seems too mature, even matronly, for the fairy-tale role of Cinderella. Alva sings well enough but is somewhat self-conscious in the florid writing. Abbado, though hardly witty in his direction, inspires delicate playing throughout. The CD transfer of the 1972 analogue recording brings an admirable feeling of freshness, with plenty of presence for the voices and a good balance with the lively orchestral sound. Cueing is provided for all the major arias; the Act I finale, for instance, is given three access points.

La Donna del lago (complete).
*** CBS Dig. **M2K 39311** (2) [id.]. Ricciarelli, Valentini-Terrani, Gonzalez, Raffanti, Ramey, Prague Philharmonic Ch., COE, Pollini.

La Donna del lago – adapted with extreme freedom from Scott's *Lady of the Lake*, published not long before – may doubtfully be effective on stage, as the 1985 Covent Garden production suggested; on record, in a lively and understanding performance, it is a Rossini rarity to cherish. Philip Gossett, the Rossini scholar, has described it as 'by far the most romantic of Rossini's Italian operas and perhaps the most tuneful'. With Rossini echoing if not quoting the inflexions of Scottish folksong, whether in the Scottish snaps in the jolly choruses or the mooning melodies given to the heroine, it is certainly distinctive. Maurizio Pollini, forsaking the keyboard for the baton, draws a fizzing performance from the Chamber Orchestra of Europe, suggesting fascinating foretastes not just of Donizetti but of Verdi: of the *Anvil chorus* from *Il Trovatore* in the Act I March and of the trombone unisons of *La forza del destino* later in the finale. Though Pollini keeps his singers on a tight rein, there are three outstanding and characterful performances. Katia Ricciarelli in the title-role of Elena, Lady of the Lake, has rarely sung so stylishly on record, the voice creamy, with no suspicion of the unevenness which develops under pressure, and very agile in coloratura. Lucia Valentini-Terrani with her warm, dark mezzo is no less impressive in the travesti role of Elena's beloved, Malcolm; while Samuel Ramey as Elena's father, Douglas, makes you wish the role was far longer with his darkly incisive singing. Of the two principal tenors, Dalmacio Gonzalez, attractively light-toned, is the more stylish; but Dano Raffanti as Rodrigo Dhu copes with equal assurance with the often impossibly high tessitura. The recording, made at the end of a series of performances in the 1983 Rossini Festival in Pesaro, is clear and generally well balanced and given added immediacy in the new format which, as so often, is able to offer the opera complete on two discs as against the original three LPs.

Ermione.

*** Erato Dig. **ECD 75336** (2) [id.]. Gasdia, Zimmermann, Palacio, Merritt, Matteuzzi, Prague Philharmonic Ch., Monte Carlo PO, Scimone.

Ermione is the one Rossini opera never revived after its first production. First given in Naples in 1819, this *opera seria* is an adaptation of Racine's great tragedy, *Andromaque*; as the title suggests, it is slanted with Hermione at the centre and Andromaque (Andromaca in Italian) taking the subsidiary mezzo role. It begins very strikingly with an off-stage chorus, introduced in the slow section of the overture, singing a lament on the fall of Troy. The use of dramatic declamation, notably in the final scene of Act II, also gives due weight to the tragedy; however, not surprisingly, Rossini's natural sparkle keeps bursting through, often a little incongruously. The piece is interesting too for its structure, working away from the set aria towards more flexible treatment, allowing, for example, Oreste's cavatina in the third scene to have a duetting commentary from the principal tenor's companion, Pilade. That makes three important tenor roles in the opera, Pirro (Pyrrhus) and Pilade as well as Oreste, reflecting the abundance of tenors in the Naples opera at the time.

The formidable technical demands of the writing for tenor present the principal stumbling block for performance today. Though the three tenors in this Monte Carlo set from Erato are good by modern standards – Ernesto Palacio (Pirro), Chris Merritt (Oreste) and William Matteuzzi (Pilade) – they are uncomfortably strained by the high tessitura and the occasional stratospheric top notes. Cecilia Gasdia makes a powerful Ermione, not always even enough in her production but strong and agile; while Margarita Zimmermann makes a firm, rich Andromaca. Scimone, not always imaginative, yet directs a strong, well-paced performance. On this showing, *Ermione* certainly does not deserve the century and a half of neglect it has received, with brickbats even from Rossini specialists who should have known better. Rossini himself, asked to explain the poor audiences for *Ermione* in Naples, said it was written for posterity. Now at last, thanks to Erato, posterity can fully judge. The recording is rather dry on the voices, but the hint of boxiness is generally undistracting. The break between the two discs comes before the final scene of Act I.

L'Italiana in Algeri (complete).

*** Erato **ECD 88200** (2) [id.]. Horne, Palacio, Ramey, Trimarchi, Battle, Zaccaria, Prague Ch., Sol. Ven., Scimone.

*** CBS Dig. *M3T 39048* (3) [id.]. Valentini-Terrani, Ganzarolli, Araiza, Cologne R. Ch., Cappella Coloniensis, Ferro.

Scholarship as well as Rossinian zest have gone into Scimone's highly enjoyable version, beautifully played and recorded with as stylish a team of soloists as one can expect nowadays. The text is complete, the original orchestration has been restored (as in the comic duetting of piccolo and bassoon in the reprise in the overture) and alternative versions of certain arias are given as an appendix. Marilyn Horne makes a dazzling, positive Isabella, and Samuel Ramey is splendidly firm as Mustafa. Domenico Trimarchi is a delightful Taddeo and Ernesto Palacio an agile Lindoro, not coarse, though the recording docs not always catch his tenor timbre well. Nevertheless the sound is generally very good indeed, and the fullness and atmosphere come out the more vividly on CD.

Like the Erato set conducted by Claudio Scimone, this fine CBS version uses the critical edition of the score published by the Fondazione Rossini in Pesaro; it goes further towards authenticity in using period instruments including a fortepiano instead of harpsichord for the recitatives (well played by Georg Fischer). Though Ferro can at times be sluggish in slow music (even in the opening of the overture), he is generally a sparkling Rossinian, pacing well to allow a rhythmic lift to be married to crisp ensemble. The set also gains from forward and bright digital recording, more immediate than in previous sets, and the cast is at least as fine as in rival versions. Lucia Valentini-Terrani here gives her finest performance on record to date with her rich, firm voice superbly agile in coloratura. She may not be as tough and forceful as Marilyn Horne on the Erato set but, with a younger, sunnier voice, she is far more seductive, helped by greater consideration and imagination from the conductor. Francisco Araiza as Lindoro peppers the rapid passagework with intrusive aitches – but not too distractingly – and the strength of the voice makes the performance heroic with no suspicion of the twittering of a tenorino. Ganzarolli treats the role of the Bey, Mustafa, as a conventional *buffo* role, with a voice not ideally steady but full of character; the rest of the cast is strong, too. When this arrives on CD it will be strongly competitive; meanwhile the tapes are well transferred and lavishly packaged.

Maometto II (complete).

*** Ph. Dig. **412 148-2** (3) [id.]. Anderson, Zimmermann, Palacio, Ramey, Dale, Amb. Op. Ch., Philh. O, Scimone.

Claudio Scimone here repeats the success of his earlier set for Philips of *Mosé in Egitto*. But where he chose the most compressed of Rossini's three versions of that opera, here he chooses the most expansive early version of a work which the composer also radically revised for Paris as *Le siège de Corinthe*. There are cogent reasons for approving Scimone's preference in each instance. This account of *Maometto II* has Samuel Ramey magnificently focusing the whole story in his portrait of the Muslim invader in love with the heroine. The nobility of his singing makes Maometto's final self-sacrifice all the more convincing, even if the opera is made the less tense dramatically from having no villain. The other singing is less sharply characterized but is generally stylish, with Margarita Zimmermann in the travesti role of Calbo, June Anderson singing sweetly as Anna, not least in the lovely prayer which comes as an interlude in a massive Trio or Terzettone in Act I. Laurence Dale is excellent in two smaller roles, while Ernesto Palacio mars some fresh-toned singing with his intrusive aitches. Excellent recording, made the more attractive on CD. The well-chosen banding adds to one's enjoyment of an exceptionally long opera.

Mosè (complete recording of Paris version).
** Hung. **HCD 12290/2-2** [id.]. Gregor, Solyom, Nagy, Beganyi, Hamari, Kalmar, Hungarian R. & TV Ch., Hungarian State Op. O, Gardelli.

The Hungarian version of *Mosè*, using the Paris text of 1827 but translated back into Italian, has the merit of Gardelli's understanding conducting. Much of the singing is pleasing too, but when the far more vital 1819 text of *Mosè in Egitto* has been recorded on an excellent Philips set, this is hardly competitive. Act II, Scene iii is omitted. The Philips recording is almost certain to resurface on CD during the lifetime of this book. It is well cast with Ernesto Palaccio, June Anderson, Zehava Gal and Siegmund Nimsgern in the principal roles, and is vibrantly directed by Scimone.

Il Turco in Italia (abridged).
(***) HMV mono **CDS7 49344-2**; (M) *EX 749344-4* (2). Callas, Gedda, Rossi-Lemeni, Calabrese, Stabile, Ch. & O of La Scala, Milan, Gavazzeni.

Callas was at her peak when she recorded this rare Rossini opera in the mid-1950s. As ever, there are lumpy moments vocally, but she gives a sharply characterful performance as the capricious Fiorilla, married to an elderly, jealous husband and bored with it. Nicola Rossi-Lemeni as the Turk of the title is characterful too, but not the firmest of singers, and it is left to Nicolai Gedda as the young lover and Franco Calabrese as the jealous husband to match Callas in stylishness. It is good too to have the veteran Mariano Stabile singing the role of the Poet in search of a plot. Walter Legge's production has plainly added to the sparkle. On CD the original mono recording has been freshened and given a degree of bloom, despite the closeness of the voices. It is a vintage Callas issue, her first uniquely cherishable essay in operatic comedy. The chrome tapes are smoothly transferred and, apart from a degree of excess bass resonance at times, sound surprisingly vivid. They are offered at mid-price and packaged with the CD booklet.

Il viaggio a Reims (complete).
*** DG Dig. **415 498-2** (2) [id.]. Ricciarelli, Valentini-Terrani, Cuberli, Gasdia, Araiza, Gimenez, Nucci, Raimondi, Ramey, Dara, Prague Philharmonic Ch., COE, Abbado.

This fizzing piece of comic nonsense, which Rossini wrote as a gala piece for the coronation of Charles X in Paris, was painstakingly reconstructed and given its first modern performance at the 1984 Pesaro Festival. This recording was edited together from various performances which the DG engineers put on tape; the result is one of the most sparkling and totally successful live opera recordings available, with Claudio Abbado in particular freer and more spontaneous-sounding than he generally is on disc, relishing the sparkle of the comedy. The piece has virtually no story, with the journey to Rheims never actually taking place, only the prospect of it. The wait at the Golden Lily hotel at Plombières provides the opportunity for the ten star characters each to perform in turn: and one hardly wonders that after the first performances Rossini refused ever to allow a revival, on the grounds that no comparable cast could ever be assembled. Instead, he used some of the material in his delectable comic opera, *Le comte Ory*, and it is fascinating here to spot the numbers from it in their original form. Much else is delightful, and the line-up of soloists here could hardly be more impressive, with no weak link. Established stars like Lucia Valentini-Terrani, Katia Ricciarelli, Francisco Araiza, Samuel Ramey and Ruggero Raimondi, not to mention the *buffo* singers, Enzo Dara and Leo Nucci, hardly need commendation; in addition the set introduced two formidable newcomers in principal roles, Cecilia Gasdia as a self-important poetess (a nice parody of romantic manners) and, even finer, Lella Cuberli as a young fashion-crazed widow. The rich firmness and distinctive beauty of Cuberli's voice, coupled with amazing flexibility, proclaims a natural prima donna. Inconsequential as the sequence of virtuoso numbers may be, ensembles as well as arias, the inspiration never flags, and Abbado's brilliance and sympathy draw the musical threads compellingly together with the help of superb, totally committed playing from the young members of the Chamber Orchestra of Europe. The pair of CDs bring extra precision and clarity.

Guglielmo Tell (*William Tell:* complete).
*** Decca **417 154-2** (4) [id.]. Pavarotti, Freni, Milnes, Ghiaurov, Amb. Op. Ch., Nat. PO, Chailly.

Rossini wrote his massive opera about William Tell in French, and the first really complete recording (under Gardelli on HMV) used that language. But Chailly and his team here put forward a strong case for preferring Italian, with its open vowels, in music which glows with Italianate lyricism. Chailly's is a forceful reading, particularly strong in the many ensembles, and superbly recorded. Milnes makes a heroic Tell, always firm, and though Pavarotti has his moments of coarseness he sings the role of Arnoldo with glowing tone. Ghiaurov too is in splendid voice, while subsidiary characters are almost all well taken, with such a fine singer as John Tomlinson, for example, finely resonant as Melchthal. The women singers too are impressive, with Mirella Freni as the heroine Matilde providing dramatic strength as well as sweetness. The recording, made in 1978 and 1979, is one of the finest of Decca's late analogue vintage, and comes out spectacularly on CD. In the four-disc layout, Acts III and IV are each complete on the last two discs, so that – in complete contrast with the much-fragmented LP set – only the long Act I has any break. The *Pas de six*, included as a supplement in the LP set, is here banded into its proper place in Act I.

COLLECTION

L'assedio de Corinto: Avanziam . . . Non temer d'un basso affeto! . . . I destini tradir ogni speme Signormche tutto puio . . . Sei tu, che stendi, L'ora fatal s'appressa . . . Giusto ciel. La Donna del lago: Mura Felici; Tanti affetti. Otello: Assisa a pie d'un salice. Tancredi: Di tanti palpiti.
(M) ❀ *** Decca **421 306-2** [id.]. Marilyn Horne, Amb. Op. Ch., RPO, Henry Lewis.

Marilyn Horne's generously filled recital disc in Decca's mid-price Opera Gala series brings one of the most cherishable among all Rossini aria records ever issued. It is taken from two earlier LP discs, recorded when Horne was at the very zenith of her powers. The voice is in glorious condition, rich and firm throughout its spectacular range, and is consistently used with artistry and imagination, as well as brilliant virtuosity in coloratura. By any reckoning this is thrilling singing, the more valuable for mostly covering rarities – which, with Horne, make you wonder at their neglect. The sound is full and brilliant, hardly at all showing its age. Part of the recital was first reissued on a 'Grandi Voci' tape, omitting the *Otello* and *Tancredi* items (Decca *411 828-4*).

Roussel, Albert (1869–1937)

Bacchus et Ariane (complete ballet), *Op. 43; Le festin de l'araignée: symphonic fragments.*
*** HMV Dig. **CDC7 47376-2** [id.]. O Nat. de France, Prêtre.

Bacchus et Ariane is a relatively late score, composed in 1931, immediately after the *Third Symphony*. The ballet was originally choreographed by Lifar and had designs by Chirico but never captured the public imagination in quite the same way as *Le festin de l'araignée*. The music teems with life and is full of rhythmic vitality and richness of detail. It has perhaps less of the poetic feeling of *Le festin* but is nevertheless an exhilarating score. The recording, made in the generous acoustic of the Salle Wagram, is a shade too reverberant at times but no essential detail is masked. Georges Prêtre obtains an excellent response from the Orchestre National de France in both scores. This supersedes Martinon's albeit excellently balanced earlier version on Erato which merely contained the two suites (or acts) of the ballet and had no fill-up. The CD freshens detail a little, although the resonance means that the improvement is relatively limited. However, the background silence is certainly an asset in *The spider's feast*.

Symphonies Nos 1 in D min. (*Le Poème de la Forêt*), *Op. 7; 3 in G min., Op. 42.*
*** Erato Dig. **ECD 88225** [id.]. O Nat. de France, Dutoit.

The *First Symphony* belongs to the first decade of the present century, a particularly glorious one in French music which saw Debussy's *La mer*, Ravel's *Shéhérezade* and d'Indy's *Jour d'été à la montagne*, though Roussel is closer to d'Indy than Debussy, even if plenty of Debussian echoes resonate in his pages. It is subtitled *Le Poème de la forêt* and, unlike its successors, it is relatively loosely held together. The first movement, *Forêt d'hiver*, is a kind of prelude, though the winter would be gentle and warm to northern ears, and the closing bars have some of the balminess of a Mediterranean night. The *Third* is both Roussel's most concentrated and his best-known symphony. Dutoit gets first-class playing from the Orchestre National and the recording is excellent. The delicate colourings of *Le Poème de la forêt* are heard to great advantage on CD and there is altogether admirable range, body and definition.

Symphonies Nos 2 in B flat, Op. 23; 4 in A, Op. 53.
*** Erato Dig. **ECD 88226**. O Nat. de France, Dutoit.

The *Second Symphony* (1919–21) is the product of an abundantly resourceful musical mind and a richly stocked imagination, eminently well served by the finely developed feeling for craftsmanship Roussel had acquired from d'Indy. Indeed some of d'Indy's gravitas can be felt in the impressive, indeed thrilling, opening pages; this is a reading of great vitality. Dynamic and agogic markings are faithfully observed; but it is not just the letter but also the spirit of the score that is well served. The Erato engineers do full justice to the dark and richly detailed textures. The scoring has some of the opulence of the first two Bax symphonies, particularly in the lower wind, and in some of the work's brooding, atmospheric slow sections. While recordings of the *Third* come and go, the *Fourth Symphony* of 1934 has been relatively neglected: it is a delightful score and has Roussel's most infectiously engaging Scherzo. Again, in this and the captivating finale, Dutoit and the French National Orchestra are in excellent form. CD does particular justice to the opulence of Roussel's scoring and is particularly imposing in the definition of the bottom end of the register.

Symphony No. 3 in G min., Op. 42; Bacchus et Ariane: suite No. 2.
** Forlane Dig. **UCD 16529** [id.]. O de Bordeaux Aquitaine, Benzi.

On Forlane a useful coupling of Roussel's tautly written *Third Symphony* and parts of his imaginative score to *Bacchus et Ariane*. Benzi has the full measure of the *Symphony*. The outer movements have plenty of vigour and thrust, and the exciting climax of the *Adagio* is made the more telling by the expansive dynamic of the digital recording. The Scherzo has plenty of spirit and there is some attractively delicate woodwind articulation both here and in the joyously energetic finale. The ballet suite is not short on atmosphere, and again there is fine solo playing from the woodwind. The strings of the Bordeaux Aquitaine Orchestra lack body under pressure above the stave, but they play with fervour and, despite a degree of shrillness on top, the recording balance is convincing, with the orchestra set back within the resonant acoustic of the Church of Notre Dame, Bordeaux.

Serenade for flute, violin, viola, cello and harp, Op. 30.
(M) *** Decca *414 063-4*. Melos Ens. – RAVEL: *Introduction and allegro*; DEBUSSY: *Sonata*; GUY ROPARTZ: *Prelude, marine and chansons*.***

The Melos version has held its place in the catalogue for more than two decades. It is an inspired account and very well engineered, though beginning now to sound its age. It is part of a concert which includes an equally memorable account of Ravel's *Introduction and allegro*.

Songs: *Jazz dans la nuit; Mélodie, Op. 19/1: Light; 2 Mélodies, Op. 20; 2 Poèmes chinoises, Op. 35.*
(*) Unicorn **DKPCD 9035; *DKPC 9035* [id.]. Sarah Walker, Roger Vignoles – DEBUSSY; ENESCU: *Songs*.***

Sarah Walker may not plumb the full emotions of some of the deceptively deep songs in her Roussel group – *Light* for example – but the point and charm of *Jazz dans la nuit* are superbly caught, and the group makes an attractive and generous coupling for the Debussy and Enescu songs, all superbly recorded, with Vignoles a most sensitive accompanist.

Rubbra, Edmund (1901–86)

Violin concerto, Op. 103.
*** Unicorn Dig. **DKPCD 9056**; *DKPC 9056* [id.]. Carl Pini, Melbourne SO, Measham – IRELAND: *Piano concerto*.***

Edmund Rubbra's *Violin concerto* comes from 1959 and has never enjoyed the same following as the Ireland with which it is coupled. It has seriousness and depth; its beauties, particularly those of the slow movement, will come as no surprise to those who know the *Piano concerto* or the thoughtful *Improvisation for violin and orchestra*, written three years earlier. It is a matter of shame that the first recording of this work should not have been made in the UK, and no small debt of gratitude is owed to the Australian Broadcasting Corporation and Unicorn for enriching the catalogue now. If the centrepiece of the concerto is its reflective slow movement, the two outer movements are hardly less impressive. As always with this composer, the music unfolds with a seeming inevitability and naturalness and a strong sense of purpose. Carl Pini is the capable soloist; the Melbourne Orchestra under David Measham play with a conviction that more than compensates for the somewhat unventilated recording, which makes textures sound thicker than they in fact are. The matching cassette is of high quality.

Symphony No. 5 in B flat, Op. 63.
(*) Chan. *ABT 1018* [id.]. Melbourne SO, Schönzeler (with BLISS: *Checkmate*(*)).

Rubbra's *Fifth Symphony* is a noble work which grows naturally from the symphonic soil of Elgar and Sibelius. Although the Melbourne orchestra is not in the very first flight, they play this music for all they are worth, and the strings have a genuine intensity and lyrical fervour that compensate for the opaque effect of the octave doublings. The introduction is grander and more spacious here than in Barbirolli's pioneering record with the Hallé, made in the early 1950s, and the finale has splendid lightness of touch. More attention to refinement of nuance would have paid dividends in the slow movement, whose brooding melancholy does not quite emerge to full effect. Altogether, though, this is an imposing performance which reflects credit on all concerned.

The recording is well balanced and lifelike; on tape its sonority comes over effectively, but the ear perceives that the upper range is rather restricted.

Symphony No. 10 (Sinfonia da camera), Op. 145; Improvisations on virginal pieces by Giles Farnaby, Op. 50; A tribute to Vaughan Williams on his 70th birthday (Introduction and danza alla fuga), Op. 56.
*** Chan. **CHAN 8378**; (M) *CBT 1023* [id.]. Bournemouth Sinf., Schönzeler.

Rubbra's *Tenth Symphony* is for chamber orchestra and dates from 1975. It is a work of considerable substance whose language employs a received but distinctive vocabulary, consistent with the growth of Rubbra's musical personality. Nothing ever detracts from the musical argument and the gradual unfolding of the symphonic plan. It is a short one-movement work, whose opening has a Sibelian seriousness and a strong atmosphere that grip one immediately. It has moreover the advantage here of the convinced advocacy of the performers and a well-balanced recording. Schönzeler is scrupulously attentive to dynamic nuance and internal balance, while keeping a firm grip on the architecture as a whole. The 1977 recording has been impressively remastered. It has a warm acoustic and reproduces natural, well-placed orchestral tone. The upper range is crisply defined. The *Farnaby variations* is a pre-war work whose charm Schönzeler effectively uncovers, revealing its textures to best advantage. *Loath to depart*, the best-known movement, has gentleness and vision in this performance. Strongly recommended, especially on CD; though there is also an excellent cassette in the mid-price range.

Russo, William (born 1928)

Street music, Op. 65.
** DG **419 625-2** [id.]. Siegel, San Francisco SO, composer – GERSHWIN: *American in Paris*; BERNSTEIN: *West Side story: dances.***(*)

William Russo has been an assiduous advocate of mixing jazz and blues traditions with the symphony orchestra, and *Street music* has its attractive side. But despite Cork Siegel on harmonica, it is no more successful at achieving genuine integration than other pieces of its kind, and its half-hour span is far too long for the material it contains. Excellent 1977 recording, made the more vivid in this remastering; but this collection is overpriced.

Rutter, John (born 1943)

(i) *Brother Heinrich's Christmas;* Carols: *Candlelight carol; Deck the hall; I wonder as I wander; Jesus Child; Mary's lullaby; Shepherd's pipe carol; Star carol; The very best time of the year; We wish you a happy Christmas; The wild wood carol.*
*** Collegium Dig. *COLC 102* [id.]. (i) Brian Kay; Cambridge Singers, City of L. Sinfonia, composer.

Brother Heinrich's Christmas is a narrative with music, after the style of Prokofiev's *Peter and the wolf*. It is endearingly ingenuous and based on a legend which suggests that the famous carol *In dulci jubilo* was revealed in a visitation of angels on Christmas-night to a fourteenth-century Dominican monk, one Heinrich Suso, who fortunately wrote down what he heard. In Rutter's tale, Brother Heinrich has a (bassoon) donkey who – preposterously – is a member of the monastery choir and who saves the day by providing the final cadence for the carol which his friend and master cannot remember. Brian Kay is a good storyteller; with appropriate instrumental and choral illustrations, the result has great charm. The rest of the programme consists of Rutter carols, including arrangements (*I wonder as I wander* has an Appalachian source) with the special Rutter touch. The famous *Donkey carol* is not included, but *Mary's lullaby* and the *Shepherd's pipe carol* are, while the *Star carol* with its characteristic chattering flutes and *Jesus Child* with its happy syncopations are two more that are equally winning. Fine recording, clear and with plenty of atmosphere. We hope this will soon appear in CD format, but the tape would make a splendid Christmas gift.

(i) *Gloria;* (ii) Anthems: *All things bright and beautiful; For the beauty of the earth; A Gaelic blessing; God be in my head; The Lord bless you and keep you; The Lord is my Shepherd; O clap your hands; Open thou my eyes; Praise ye the Lord; A prayer of St Patrick.*
*** Collegium Dig. **COLCD 100**; *COLC 100* [id.]. Cambridge Singers, (i) Philip Jones Brass. Ens.; (ii) City of L. Sinfonia, composer.

John Rutter is one of those British composers who has quietly gone on composing traditional English church music without recourse to atonalism or barbed wire. He has a genuine gift of melody and his use of tonal harmony is individual and never bland. The resplendent *Gloria* was written as a concert work. It was commissioned by a Nebraska choir and the composer directed its US première in May 1974. It is a three-part piece, and Rutter uses his brass to splendid and often spectacular effect, which this marvellously real digital recording demonstrates admirably. It is music to which one responds at first hearing but which offers continuing rewards with familiarity. The anthems were written for various occasions over a period of some twelve years. They are diverse in style and feeling and, like the *Gloria*, have strong melodic appeal – the setting of *All things bright and beautiful* is delightfully spontaneous. It is difficult to imagine the music receiving more persuasive advocacy than under the composer, and the recording is first class in every respect. There is a good chrome tape, but the CD adds an extra dimension to the brass and organ in the *Gloria.*

(i) *Requiem; I will lift up mine eyes.*
*** Collegium Dig. **COLCD 103**; *COLC 103* [id.]. (i) Ashton, Dean; Cambridge Singers, City of L. Sinfonia, composer.

John Rutter's melodic gift, so well illustrated in his carols, is here used in the simplest and most direct way to create a small-scale *Requiem*, that is as beautiful and satisfying in its English way as the works of Fauré and Duruflé. It has a hauntingly memorable melodic fragment that fits easily to the work's title and which returns to dominate the serene closing *Lux aeterna*. The *Sanctus* has a pealing-bell effect (so like the carols) and the *Agnus Dei* is both intense and dramatic. The penultimate movement, a ripe setting of *The Lord's my shepherd*, with a lovely oboe obbligato, sounds almost like an anglicized Song of the Auvergne, while the delightful *Pié Jesu* – which Caroline Ashton sings with the purity of a boy treble – melodically is nearly as catchy as the similar movement in the Lloyd Webber *Requiem*; it makes one reflect that these two works would make a marvellous concert double bill. The performance is wonderfully warm and spontaneous, most beautifully recorded on both CD and the excellent chrome tape. *I will lift up mine eyes* makes a highly effective encore piece.

Saeverud, Harald (born 1897)

Symphony No. 9, Op. 45; Galdreslåtten, Op. 20; Kjempeviseslåtten, Op. 22a/5; Rondo amoroso, Op. 14/7.
*** Norwegian Composers **NCD 4913** [id.]. RPO, Per Dreier.

Saeverud is the doyen of Norwegian composers, now in his nineties, a figure unique in Norway; in terms of sheer personality and dry, laconic wit, he outstrips almost all his younger countrymen. This CD collects his *Ninth Symphony*, which comes frm the mid-1960s, with three better-known pieces. *Kjempeviseslåtten* (The Ballad of revolt) was prompted by his fury at the sight of Nazi barracks near Bergen and pays tribute to the heroes of the Norwegian resistance; it is dark, combative and inspiriting in character, and carries all before it with its insistent, unrelenting rhythms. The *Rondo amoroso* has a naïve, artless charm. The *Symphony* is rugged, craggy, full of imagination; it opens with a resourceful movement which combines sonata form and passacaglia; the mood of the *Andante* is powerfully concentrated; the waltz movement is splendidly tangy and characterful. There is, as always with Saeverud, a strong sense of the Norwegian landscape. Per Dreier gets lively and responsive playing from the RPO; and the recording is in the first flight, with admirable clarity and a realistic perspective.

Saint-Saëns, Camille (1835–1921)

Carnival of the animals.
*** Ph. Dig. **400 016-2** [id.]. Villa, Jennings, Pittsburgh SO, Previn – RAVEL: *Ma Mère l'Oye.****
(M) *** ASV **CDQS 6017;** (B) *ZCQS 6017* [id.]. Goldstone, Brown, RPO, Hughes – PROKOFIEV: *Peter.****
(M) *** HMV *TC-ESD 7114*. H. Menuhin, Simon, Philh. O, Kurtz – BRITTEN: *Young person's guide*; PROKOFIEV: *Peter.****

Carnival of the animals (with verses by Ogden Nash).
*** DG **415 351-2** [id.]. Hermione Gingold, Alfons & Aloys Kontarsky, VPO, Boehm – PROKOFIEV: *Peter.****
** HMV Dig. **CDC7 47067-2** [id.]. Perlman, Katia and Marielle Labèque, Israel PO, Mehta – PROKOFIEV: *Peter.***

Carnival of the animals (with additional songs by Carl Davis and Hiawyn Oram).
* HMV Dig. **CDC7 47708-2** [id.]; *EL 270586-4*. Shelley, McNamara, King's Singers, SCO, Carl Davis – FAURÉ: *Pavane & Auvergne folksongs.***

(i) *Carnival of the animals;* (ii) *Danse macabre, Op. 40; Phaéton, Op. 39; Le rouet d'Omphale, Op. 31.*
** Decca **414 460-2;** *414 460-4* [id.]. (i) Rogé, Ortiz, L. Sinf.; (ii) Philh. O, Dutoit.

(i) *Carnival of the animals;* (ii) *Septet in E flat for trumpet, strings & piano, Op. 65.*
** HMV **CDC7 47543-2** [id.]. (i) Béroff & Collard; (ii) André, Collard, with instrumental ens.

In the bargain range, the CfP tape (conducted by Sir Alexander Gibson with Peter Katin and Philip Fowke) of Saint-Saëns delightful zoological fantasy remains highly competitive for those not willing to go to a premium-priced issue (*TC-CFP 40086* – coupled with Ravel's *Ma Mère l'Oye* and Bizet's *Jeux d'enfants*). On CD, Previn's version makes a ready first choice, particularly when the coupling is outstanding and both are recorded in superbly rich and atmospheric sound. On some machines the bass resonance of the somewhat larger-than-life pianos may seem slightly excessive but, that apart, the quality has remarkable bloom. The music is played with infectious rhythmic spring and great refinement. It is a mark of the finesse of this performance – which has plenty of bite and vigour, as well as polish – that the great cello solo of *Le Cygne* is so naturally presented, with the engineers refusing to spotlight the soloist. The shading of half-tones in Anne Martindale Williams's exquisitely beautiful playing is made all the more tenderly affecting. Fine contributions too from the two pianists. The compact disc brings out all these qualities even more strikingly.

The two pianists on ASV play with point and style, and the accompaniment has both spirit and spontaneity. *The Swan* is perhaps a trifle self-effacing, but otherwise this is very enjoyable, the humour appreciated without being underlined. The recording is excellent, and this makes a good mid-priced CD recommendation, with the very acceptable cassette in the bargain range.

However, on tape HMV's Greensleeve reissue of Kurtz's splendid version from the end of the 1950s has even more generous couplings and offers some vintage solo contributions from members of the Philharmonia Orchestra. The recording too is first class, although, curiously, the definition is poor for the double-basses in their portrayal of *Tortoises*. Elsewhere orchestral detail is admirably firm and vivid, and *The Swan* is memorably serene. The two pianists are spirited, and Kurtz's direction is witty and attentive.

The Dutoit version, given a crisp, clean digital recording, is a sad disappointment. At almost every point the Previn Philips version is superior in detailed characterization and lightness of touch. Even the Pittsburgh pianists are wittier than their more famous rivals on Decca, and *The Swan* is played in a very-matter-of-fact way, whereas with Previn it is full of tenderness. Dutoit's couplings may sway the balance for some. They are analogue recordings but effectively remastered, and here Charles Dutoit shows himself an admirably sensitive exponent of this repertoire, revelling in the composer's craftsmanship and revealing much delightful detail. *Omphale's spinning wheel* and *Danse macabre* both show the composer at his most creatively imaginative. *Phaéton*, a favourite in the Victorian era, now sounds slightly dated, but remains attractively inventive. The Kingsway Hall recording has plenty of atmosphere and colour and is preferable to the very bright digital sound of the *Carnival*.

Not everyone will care for the inclusion of Ogden Nash's verses (Saint-Saëns's music stands up admirably without them), but those who do will find Miss Gingold's narration is splendidly performed – every inflexion of that superb voice is to be relished. Marvellous playing from the Kontarskys and the Vienna Philharmonic, and splendid 1976 analogue recording. The voice, the pianists, and the orchestra are all caught in perfect focus and natural sound.

Ogden Nash's often outrageous rhymes for Saint-Saëns's gently humorous masterpiece could have no more committed advocate than Perlman, and his diction and vocal inflexions combine clarity with nice timing. Too often, however, Nash's metaphor falls short of wit and such a dialogue – unlike the music – can lose its freshness. The performance overall is lively, with the Labèque duo in scintillating form, and with good support from Mehta. The acoustic is rather dry and the balance close, emphasized by the CD.

The HMV analogue coupling of the *Carnival* with the *Septet* is not an unalloyed success. The *Carnival* receives a bright-eyed chamber performance, recorded intimately within a comparatively dry acoustic (emphasized by the digital remastering). There is some good playing, but the lack of atmosphere is a drawback, and while there is sparkle there is little charm. The *Septet* is similarly unexpansive, although clear, and the curious instrumentation of trumpet, strings and piano does not seem to gel here, although the performance is lively enough.

Having the King's Singers present the *Carnival of the animals* in a choral framework is certainly individual, but whether the result is a success is questionable. Carl Davis's contribution as composer consists partly of choral recitative (a bit like Anglican chant in close harmony) and pretty little part-songs. The trouble is that Saint-Saëns more often than not has pre-empted the best and most obvious musical illustrations of each animal, as when Davis's braying for the donkey is no match for Saint-Saëns's hee-haws. The songs lead neatly and often ingeniously into each number; best of all is *Aquarium*, where Davis simply adds choral parts as descant over the original score. The snag here is that Hiawyn Oram's poem relates Saint-Saëns's innocent playful picture to modern drug-peddlers. Otherwise the targets are apt enough, though the poems are often unnecessarily obscure and always short on wit. Saint-Saëns is not helped by the balance of the recording, with the players set back well back behind the King's Singers.

(i) *Carnival of the animals;* (ii) *Piano concertos Nos 2 in G min., Op. 22; 4 in C min., Op. 44. 6 Études for the left hand only, Op. 135.*

(B) *** HMV *TCC2-POR 154595-9*. Ciccolini, with (i) Weissenberg and Prêtre; (ii) O de Paris, Baudo.

Tape collectors should be more than satisfied with this generous compilation, which offers very good sound. Ciccolini's performances of the two favourite *Concertos* are in every way distinguished; they combine elegance with spirit. No. 4 is especially fine. With the six *Études* thrown in as an attractive bonus (Saint-Saëns was a superb miniaturist), this is all most enjoyable.

Cello concerto No. 1 in A min., Op. 33.
*** CBS Dig. **MK 35848** [id.]. Yo-Yo Ma, O Nat. de France, Maazel – LALO: *Concerto.****
*** Decca Dig. **410 019-2** [id.]. Harrell, Cleveland O, Marriner – SCHUMANN: *Concerto.****
*** RCA Dig. **RD 71003.** Harnoy, Cincinnati SO, Kunzel – OFFENBACH: *Concerto*; TCHAIKOVSKY: *Rococo variations.****
(B) *** DG Walkman *423 290-4* [id.]. Schiff, New Philh. O, Mackerras – LALO: *Concerto*; SCHUMANN: *Concerto*; TCHAIKOVSKY: *Rococo variations.****

Yo-Yo Ma's performance of the Saint-Saëns *Concerto* is distinguished by fine sensitivity and beautiful tone. As in the Lalo, one is tempted to speak of him as being 'hypersensitive', so fine is his attention to light and shade; yet there is not a trace of posturing or affectation. The Orchestre National de France respond with playing of the highest quality throughout. Superb recorded sound which reflects great credit on the engineers, with added refinement and transparency of texture on CD.

Harrell's reading of the Saint-Saëns, altogether more extrovert than Yo-Yo Ma's, makes light of any idea that this composer always works on a small scale. The opening is positively epic, and the rest of the performance is just as compelling, with the minuet-like *Allegretto* crisply neoclassical. This coupling of Saint-Saëns and Schumann challenges comparison with the classic recording of Du Pré and Barenboim (now deleted), even if in warmth and commitment it cannot quite match that model. Recording is outstandingly, beautifully balanced, with the compact disc version particularly fine.

Ofra Harnoy's is also a first-rate account, the opening full of fervour and impulse, played with full tone, while later the timbre is beautifully fined down for the *Adagietto* minuet. The orchestral response is equally refined here; and this well-recorded account is in every way recommendable for its unexpected and attractive Offenbach coupling.

Schiff's Walkman tape is even more generous in offering three outstanding couplings at bargain price. This was his début recording and he gives as eloquent an account of this concerto as any on record. He sparks off an enthusiastic response from Mackerras and the orchestra and is excellently recorded. This deserves the strongest recommendation.

Cello concerto No. 2 in D min., Op. 119.
*** Decca Dig. **414 387-2** [id.]. Harrell, Berlin RSO, Chailly – LALO: *Concerto*; FAURÉ: *Elégie.****

Saint-Saëns wrote his *Cello Concerto No. 2* in 1902 when he was at the height of his powers. It has an attractive spontaneity and its ideas are memorable, notably the strongly rhythmic opening theme of the first movement – which returns to cap the finale – and the very engaging melody of the *Andante* (which is linked to the opening movement). At its close, Harrell refines his timbre to an exquisite half-tone and the effect is ravishing, with a gentle muted horn decoration. Chailly's accompaniment is sympathetic, polished and full of character; the attractive ambience of the Jesus Christ Church, Berlin, makes a convincing backcloth for the music making. On CD, the cello image is very tangible, and the balance is near perfect, while the orchestral sounds are glowing and vivid. A most welcome recording début; the work has not previously appeared in the British catalogue, although it has been available in France.

Piano concertos Nos 1–5.
*** Decca **417 351-2** (2) [id.]. Rogé, Philh. O, LPO or RPO, Dutoit.

Played as they are here, these concertos can exert a strong appeal: Pascal Rogé brings delicacy, virtuosity and sparkle to the piano part and he receives expert support from the various London orchestras under Dutoit. Altogether delicious playing and excellent piano sound from Decca, who secure a most realistic balance. In every respect, this set outclasses Aldo Ciccolini's survey of the early 1970s, good though that was. On CD the five *Concertos* are successfully accommodated on two discs and the digital remastering is wholly successful, retaining the bloom of the analogue originals, yet producing firmer detail and splendid piano sound.

Piano concertos Nos 1 in D, Op. 17; 2 in G min., Op. 22; 3 in E flat, Op. 29.
(M) *** HMV *EG 290571-4*. Ciccolini, O de Paris, Baudo.

There may be little development of style between the *First Concerto*, written when the composer was twenty-three, and the later works, but this is first-rate gramophone material. Beethoven, Bach and Mendelssohn all get their due in the *First Concerto*. The *Second* is already well known; only No. 3 falls short in its comparatively banal ideas – and even in that there is a hilarious finale which sounds like a Viennese operetta turned into a concerto. Ciccolini's performances are very enjoyable, and they are well recorded, too. The cassette is transferred at the highest level and the sound is projected with great vividness. There is about 81′ of music on this issue.

Piano concerto No. 2 in G min., Op. 22.
*** HMV Dig. **CDC7 47221-2** [id.]. Cécile Ousset, CBSO, Rattle – LISZT: *Concerto No. 1.****
(*) CBS Dig. **MK 39153 [id.]. Cécile Licad, LPO, Previn – CHOPIN: *Concerto No. 2.***(*)
(*) Ph. Dig. **410 052-2 [id.]; *7337 164*. Bella Davidovich, Concg. O, Järvi – RACHMANINOV: *Rhapsody on a theme of Paganini.***(*)
(*) RCA **RD 85666. Rubinstein, Phd. O, Ormandy – FRANCK: *Symphonic variations*; FALLA: *Nights* etc.**(*)
*(*) Chan. Dig. **CHAN 8546**; *ABTD 1254* [id.]. Israela Margalit, LPO, Thomson – SCHUMANN: *Concerto.**(*)
*(*) Arabesque **Z 6541**; *ABQC 7541* [id.]. Ian Hobson, Sinfonia da Camera of Illinois – FRANÇAIX: *Concertino; Concerto.*(**)

The most popular of Saint-Saëns's concertos has rarely received so winning a performance on record as Ousset's. The opening cadenza, so far from reflecting Bach-like qualities, is warm and urgent, genuinely romantic music, and the Scherzo, spikier than usual, brings dazzlingly clear articulation. This performance consistently conveys the flair and contrasted tensions of a live recording, though it was made in the studio. The recording favours the soloist but is rich and lively, with the CD bringing clean definition.

Cécile Licad and the LPO under Previn turn in an eminently satisfactory reading of the *G minor Concerto* that has the requisite delicacy in the Scherzo and seriousness elsewhere. It is a pleasing and persuasive performance of strong contrasts, with both power and thoughtfulness in the opening movement and a toccata-like brilliance of articulation in the finale. The recording is well balanced but a little diffuse, even in its CD format – although the centrally placed piano certainly dominates the proceedings.

Bella Davidovich also gives a most sympathetic account of the *G minor Concerto*; she has the advantage of excellent orchestral support from the Concertgebouw Orchestra. The recording is very natural and Davidovich draws most sympathetic tone-quality from the instrument, even if she lacks the brilliance that Licad brings to the Scherzo. This is warmly attractive music-making, but in the last resort it has less flair and life than Licad's version, although on compact disc the richly atmospheric sound is very persuasive.

Rubinstein, understandably, had a soft spot for the Saint-Saëns *Second Piano concerto*. He chose it for his début in Berlin in 1900 and he played it finally on his last TV show in 1979. He recorded it more than once in stereo; this version was made in 1970, and he is partnered by that most understanding of accompanists, Eugene Ormandy. His performance is by no means lightweight. He takes the first movement seriously and is particularly eloquent at its close; the Scherzo, obviously his favourite, scintillates with brilliance, and such is the power of his articulation that the toccata-like opening of the finale begins to sound like Prokofiev. Yet later he shows the lightest touch in the witty exchanges with the orchestral chorale, which Ormandy delivers most precisely. Rubinstein's secret is that, though he appears sometimes to be attacking the music, his phrasing is full of little fluctuations so that his playing never sounds stilted. The recording of the piano is rather dry, even hard at times, but the glitter seems just right for the centrepiece.

Israela Margalit's version of the *Concerto* has no want of abandon, but it lacks the aristocratic distinction that such rivals as Rubinstein and Rogé bring to it. The recording is somewhat resonant but the piano is rather forward in the aural picture. Her coupling, a rather idiosyncratic account of the Schumann, does not enhance the attractions of this issue. There is a faithful chrome tape.

Alas, the Sinfonia da Camera of Illinois is very 'camera' indeed and there is far too little string sonority; the cramped acoustic does not help, either. Ian Hobson's playing is very clean but wanting in the panache and flair of his current rivals such as Collard and Rogé. Disappointing.

Piano concertos Nos 2 in G min., Op. 22; 4 in C min., Op. 44.
*** HMV **CDC7 47816-2** [id.]; *EL 270552-4*. Jean-Philippe Collard, RPO, Previn.
** Erato Dig. **ECD 88002** [id.]. Duchable, Strasbourg PO, Lombard.

Jean-Philippe Collard brings authority and virtuosity to these two concertos, as well as impressive poetic feeling. His reading of the *G minor* has more refinement than Ousset and every bit as much brilliance. Apart from the sheer beauty of sound, he commands a wide dynamic range and a subtle tonal palette, and the Royal Philharmonic under Previn give him splendid support. He observes every dynamic nuance and brings panache and sensitivity in equal measure to these scores. Although allegiance to Pascal Rogé on Decca remains unshaken, Collard with his greater dynamic range and authority makes even more of this music. There is an excellent cassette.

The Erato pairing is less winning, even with the advantage of CD sophistication. The piano is forwardly balanced and Duchable's bold assertiveness in outer movements brings character of the wrong sort to music making which at times sounds aggressive. There is little charm; while the first movement of No. 2 is stronger than usual and the playing is never thoughtless or slipshod, this does not match the Collard version in character and flexibility of mood.

Piano concertos Nos 3 in E flat, Op. 29; 5 in F (Egyptian), Op. 103.
*** HMV Dig. **CDC7 49051-2** [id.]; *EL 270625-4*. Jean Philippe Collard, RPO, Previn.

The *Third Concerto* of 1869 is not the equal of its predecessor: its first movement is deficient in thematic variety, and the shadow of Liszt looms large. But there is much ingenuity in the piano writing, and it could hardly be heard to more persuasive effect than it is in Jean-Philippe Collard's hands. The *Fifth* is much better known, though it is not heard as often as Nos 2 or 4. Saint-Saëns travelled widely in the East, going as far afield as Ceylon, and he often wintered in Algeria. This concerto was composed on a visit to Egypt (hence its nickname) just over a quarter of a century later. The slow movement contains the most overtly exotic ideas, even though the exoticism does not run very deep. There is no doubting Saint-Saëns's skill in exploiting the genius of the piano to suggest Eastern sonorities. At one point Collard makes his instrument sound exactly like an Arab *qunan*, or zither. He plays throughout with superb control and finish, and Previn and the RPO are sensitive and sympathetic accompanists. This can be recommended alongside Pascal Rogé's complete Decca set: both artists offer cultured and elegant pianism, a wide range of colour and seemingly effortless virtuosity. There is, however, a greater transparency in the EMI recording and slightly greater detail in the middle, though the Decca still sounds refined and clean. There is a very good EMI cassette; though it is not quite as transparent as the CD, it is well balanced and vivid.

Violin concerto No. 1 in A, Op. 30.
*** Decca Dig. **411 952-2**. Kyung Wha Chung, Montreal SO, Dutoit – LALO: *Symphonie espagnole*.***

Saint-Saëns *First Violin concerto* is a miniature, playing for only eleven and a half minutes. It was written for Sarasate, and if it seems somewhat insubstantial, Kyung Wha Chung makes the most of the lyrical interludes and is fully equal to the energetic bravura of the outer sections. With a clear yet full-blooded digital recording and an excellent accompaniment from Charles Dutoit, this is persuasive. The CD, as in all Decca's Montreal recordings, refines detail and increases the feeling of natural presence.

Violin concerto No. 3 in B min., Op. 61.
*** CBS Dig. **MK 39007** [id.]. Cho-Liang Lin, Philh. O, Tilson Thomas – MENDELSSOHN: *Concerto*.***
*** DG Dig. **410 526-2** [id.]. Perlman, O de Paris, Barenboim – WIENIAWSKI: *Concerto No. 2*.***
(B) *** DG *423 261-4* [id.]. Perlman, O de Paris, Barenboim – WIENIAWSKI: *Concerto No. 2*; LALO: *Symphonie espagnole*.***

Cho-Liang Lin's account of the *B minor Concerto* with the Philharmonia Orchestra and Michael Tilson Thomas is exhilarating and thrilling; indeed, this is the kind of performance that prompts one to burst into applause. Bernard Shaw's famous remark about the Saint-Saëns *Concerto* as consisting of 'trivially pretty scraps of serenade music sandwiched between pages from the great masters' has always seemed almost on target, but Cho-Liang Lin manages to persuade one otherwise. He is given excellent recording from the CBS engineers and, in terms of both virtuosity and musicianship, his version is certainly second to none and is arguably the finest yet to have appeared. The CD format is admirably 'present'.

On DG, Perlman achieves a fine partnership with his friend Barenboim who provides a highly sympathetic accompaniment in a performance that is both tender and strong. They join together in finding an elegiac quality in the *Andantino*, while Perlman's verve and dash in the finale are dazzling. The forward balance is understandable in this work, but orchestral detail could at times be sharper. Tape collectors are offered a remarkable bargain in DG's Pocket Music cassette issue of the Perlman performance which offers not only the Wieniawski, as on CD, but also Lalo's *Symphonie espagnole*. The sound, if less transparent and wide-ranging than the CD, is still very good.

Havanaise, Op. 83; Introduction and rondo capriccioso, Op. 28.
*** HMV **CDC7 47725-2** [id.]. Itzhak Perlman, O de Paris, Martinon – CHAUSSON: *Poème*; RAVEL: *Tzigane*.***
*** DG Dig. **423 063-2**; *423 063-4* [id.]. Perlman, NYPO, Mehta – CHAUSSON: *Poème*; RAVEL: *Tzigane*; SARASATE: *Carmen fantasy*.***
*** Decca **417 118-2** [id.]. Kyung Wha Chung, RPO, Dutoit – CHAUSSON: *Poème*; RAVEL: *Tzigane*.***
(M) *** Decca **417 707-2** [id.] (*Havanaise* only). Chung, RPO, Dutoit – BRUCH: *Concerto No. 1*; TCHAIKOVSKY: *Concerto*.***

Perlman plays these Saint-Saëns warhorses with splendid panache and virtuosity; his tone and control of colour in the *Havanaise* are ravishing. The digital remastering brings Perlman's gorgeous fiddling right into the room, at the expense of a touch of aggressiveness when the orchestra lets rip; but the concert-hall ambience prevents this from being a problem.

Perlman's later, DG recordings are hardly less appealing. They have the advantage of an excellent digital sound-balance and the orchestral texture is fuller. Perhaps the early performances are a shade riper, but the closing pages of the *Havanaise* are particularly felicitous in the DG performance. The DG disc also includes the Sarasate *Carmen fantasy* as a winning extra item. There is a good tape; however, although the sound is well balanced, it lacks the sparkling presence of the CD.

On Decca the fireworks in two Saint-Saëns showpieces provide the necessary contrast for the more reflective works with which they are coupled. In both, Kyung Wha Chung shows rhythmic flair and a touch of the musical naughtiness that gives them their full charm. As in the other nicely matched pieces Dutoit accompanies most sympathetically, and the recording is excellent. As can be seen above, Chung's *Havanaise* is also available generously coupled to fine performances of the Max Bruch and Tchaikovsky concertos, a mid-priced bargain.

Symphony No. 2 in A min., Op. 55; Phaéton, Op. 39; Suite algérienne, Op. 60.
*** ASV Dig. **ZCDCA 599**; *ZCDCA 599* [id.]. LSO, Butt.

The *Second Symphony* is not as familiar as the *Third*; although it is rarely heard in the concert hall, it occasionally appears in broadcast programmes. It is full of excellent ideas, with a fugue delivered with characteristic aplomb in the first movement; the Scherzo is sparklingly concise and the similarly high-spirited *Tarantella* finale has something in common with Mendelssohn's *Italian symphony*. It is very well played here with the freshness of an orchestra discovering something unfamiliar and enjoying themselves; Yondani Butt's tempi are apt and he shapes the whole piece convincingly. He is equally persuasive in the picaresque *Suite algérienne*, the source of the justly famous *Marche militaire française*, and indeed in *Phaéton*, where the warmly atmospheric recording adds substance to this legend of the rash and inexpert youth seeking to drive the chariot of his father, the Sun, through the heavens. Catastrophe is narrowly averted when he veers towards the earth and Jupiter strikes him down with a thunderbolt. There is a good tape, though the resonance means that the focus is not as clean as on CD.

Symphony No. 3 in C min., Op. 78.
*** DG Dig. **419 617-2**; *419 617-4* [id.]. Simon Preston, BPO, Levine – DUKAS: *L'apprenti sorcier.****
*** ASV Dig. **CDDCA 524**; *ZCDCA 524* [id.]. Rawsthorne, LPO, Bátiz.
*** RCA **RD 85750** [**RCA 5750-2-RC**]. Zamkochian, Boston SO, Munch – POULENC: *Organ concerto*; FRANCK: *Le chasseur maudit.***(*)
/// Decca Dig. **410 201-2** [id.]. Hurford, Montreal SO, Dutoit.
(M) *** Pickwick Dig. **PCD 847** [**MCA MCAD 25933**]. Chorzempa, Berne SO, Maag.
*** Eurodisc **610 509.** Krapp, Bamberg SO, Eschenbach (with FRANCK: *Choral No. 3***).
(M) **(*) Decca **417 725-2**; *417 605-4* [id.]. Priest, LAPO, Mehta – POULENC: *Organ concerto.****
(M) **(*) EMI **CD-EMX 9511**; *TC-EMX 2108*. Tracey, Royal Liverpool PO, Litton – BERLIOZ: *Le Carnaval romain.****
*(*) Telarc Dig. **CD 80051** [id.]. Murray, Phd. O, Ormandy.
(B) * DG Dig. *419 839-4* [id.]. Cochereau, BPO, Karajan – WIDOR: *Symphony No. 5.****

(i) *Symphony No. 3*; (ii) *Danse macabre, Op. 40.*
(B) *** DG Walkman *413 424-4* [id.]. (i) Chicago SO; (ii) O de Paris, Barenboim (with FRANCK: *Symphony**(*)).

(i) *Symphony No. 3*; (ii) *Danse macabre; Le Déluge: Prélude, Op. 45; Samson et Dalila: Bacchanale.*
(M) *** DG **415 847-2**; *415 847-4* [id.]. (i) Litaize, Chicago SO, Barenboim; (ii) O de Paris, Barenboim.

Symphony No. 3; Phaéton, Op. 39; Le rouet d'Omphale, Op. 31.
*** HMV **CDC7 47477-2** [id.]; *EL 270499-4*. Lefebvre, O Nat. de France, Ozawa.

Saint-Saëns's *Organ symphony* has in recent years become a classical pop to rank as one of the great favourite gramophone works, alongside Dvořák's *New World symphony* and Vivaldi's *Four seasons*. It is extremely well served in all price ranges and in both formats, but pride of place must go to Levine's newest DG version. With the Berlin Philharmonic in cracking form, this is a grippingly dramatic reading, full of imaginative detail. The great thrust of the performance does not stem from fast pacing: rather it is the result of incisive articulation from players kept on their toes from the first note to the last. After the exhilarating fervour of the first movement, the *Poco Adagio*, with the organ subtly underpinning the string sonority, has a mood of sombre nobility, yet leading to a climax of great intensity. The Scherzo bursts upon the listener, full of exuberance from the Berliners, bows tight on strings, and in the engaging middle section the clarity of the digital recording allows the pianistic detail to register crisply. The thunderous organ entry in the finale makes a magnificent effect, and the tension is held at white heat throughout the movement with an unforgettably gutsy string entry about halfway through, echoed by resplendent brass. At the close Levine draws the threads together with a satisfying final quickening. With superb sound this issue is made the more attractive by having as its coupling quite the finest account of Dukas's *Sorcerer's apprentice* to have appeared since the advent of LP.

Ozawa's HMV disc is also generously – and perhaps even more appropriately – coupled with attractive performances of two of Saint-Saëns's most colourful symphonic poems, in which the conductor is in his element. The account of the *Symphony* is mellower than Levine's, with rich, atmospheric sound to match. His pacing of the first movement matches Levine's closely; but the articulation of the French orchestra has less bite, and the effect becomes more relaxed. The slow movement is certainly ripely romantic, but blander too. Ozawa's finale makes a splendidly opulent effect and undoubtedly, like the DG, the EMI CD is in the demonstration class, even if the overall effect is less overwhelming than with Levine, who undoubtedly produces greater dynamism. Yet Ozawa is very enjoyable and this performance certainly wears well.

Those looking for a bargain could hardly better Barenboim's inspirational 1976 version which dominated the catalogue for so long. The Galleria CD issue includes three attractive bonuses, including an exciting account of the *Bacchanale* from *Samson et Dalila*. The performance of the *Symphony* is a superlative one which glows with warmth from beginning to end. In the opening 6/8 section the galloping rhythms are irresistibly pointed, while the linked slow section has a poised stillness in its soaring lyricism which completely avoids any suspicion of sweetness or sentimentality. A brilliant account of the Scherzo leads into a magnificently energetic conclusion, with the Chicago orchestra excelling itself with radiant playing in every section. The sound has been digitally remastered and the effect is not wholly advantageous: while detail is sharper (most effectively so in the Scherzo) the massed violins above the stave sound thinner and the bass is drier. In the finale, the attempt to clarify the fairly resonant acoustic has lost some of the bloom, and the organ entry has a touch of hardness, while the bass focus is not necessarily cleaner. The inclusion of the extra items on the excellent equivalent Galleria tape means that there is a turnover in the symphony, immediately before the organ entry at the beginning of the finale (this does not, of course, apply to the CD), and tape collectors might prefer to choose the Walkman alternative which offers the symphony uninterrupted in a transfer made from the original analogue master, even if the coupled Franck *Symphony* is a much less attractive performance.

Munch's Boston recording dates from 1959 – a vintage year for RCA – and was one of his finest gramophone achievements. The recording sounds astonishingly well, another example of simple analogue techniques providing a most truthful sound-picture that is still spectacular today and does not sound dated – except that, in compressing the pre-Dolby background hiss, RCA have taken the edge off the treble response; in the resonance of Boston Symphony Hall, detail is foggy, especially in the Scherzo, where the piano figurations are ill-focused and the violins ideally need more bite. Having said that, the effect is gorgeously rich and sumptuous, so that the *Poco Adagio* has an enveloping warmth and in the finale there is a thrillingly sonorous contribution from the organist, Berj Zamkochian, whose powerful first entry is as arresting as any. The performance overall is very exciting, moving forward in a single sweep of great intensity – few other accounts maintain the momentum and electricity through the whole length of the last movement that Munch does, yet the feeling is always genial, never aggressively forced.

The other premium-priced CDs which offer the symphony without coupling now seem rather ungenerous. Bátiz's ASV version was the first digital success for this work, although originally the CD transfer had an unattractive digital edge. Now it has been remastered and sounds spectacularly ample, with the organ almost overwhelmingly resonant in the coda. Under an inspirational Bátiz, the orchestral playing is exhilarating in its energy and commitment while the *Poco Adagio* balances a noble elegiac feeling with romantic warmth. After the vivacious Scherzo, the entry of the organ in the finale is a breathtaking moment, and the sense of spectacle persists, bringing an unforgettable weight and grandeur to the closing pages. The cassette is successful too, losing only a fraction of the dynamic range. The tape, however, has to compete with Barenboim's Walkman.

Dutoit brings his usual gifts of freshness and a natural sympathy to Saint-Saëns's attractive score. There is a ready spontaneity here. The recording is very bright, with luminous detail, the strings given a thrilling brilliance above the stave. One notices a touch of digital edge, but there is a balancing weight. The reading effectively combines lyricism with passion. In the finale, Hurford's entry in the famous chorale melody is more pointed, less massive than usual, although Dutoit generates a genial feeling of gusto to compensate. With its wide range and bright lighting, this is a performance to leave one tingling, after Dutoit's final burst of adrenalin.

Those looking for a mid-priced digital recording should be well satisfied with Maag's extremely well-recorded Pickwick CD. This Berne performance has a Mendelssohnian freshness and the sprightly playing in the Scherzo draws an obvious affinity with that composer. The first movement has plenty of rhythmic lift and the *Poco Adagio* is eloquently elegiac, yet no one could be disappointed with the organ entry in the finale, which is certainly arresting, while the rippling delicacy of the piano figurations which follow is most engaging. The closing pages have a convincing feeling of apotheosis and, although this is not the weightiest reading available, it is an uncommonly enjoyable one in which the sound is bright, full and suitably resonant.

Eschenbach's Eurodisc reading has much in common with Munch's version, with its strong and consistent forward thrust. The slow section is expansively romantic, and the bite and vigour of the Scherzo offer a fine contrast before the organ entry makes the most grandiloquent effect. The excitement is well sustained to the end and the recording is resonantly spectacular. The coupling, however, will not satisfy everyone, although Edgar Krapp's account of Franck's *Third Choral* makes a strong impression.

Mehta's 1979 Los Angeles recording was highly regarded in the analogue-LP era and he draws a well-disciplined and exuberant response from all departments. The slow movement cantilena sings out vividly on the strings, helped by the brightened recording, and the finale has plenty of impact. The digital remastering produces a less sumptuous effect than on the original LP, and in the finale the focus of the more spectacular sounds is not absolutely clean; even so, this is very enjoyable and the tape too is impressive.

Litton's Liverpool recording on EMI Eminence offers a fair bargain version, although the long reverberation period of Liverpool Cathedral offers problems that are not entirely solved. The finale becomes a huge swimming bath of sound, especially in the closing bars where the echoing resonance brings a physical frisson. Litton cleverly times the music to take the acoustic overhang into account, with relatively steady tempi throughout, and his lyrical feel for the work, is attractive. But the balance and detail are achieved by close microphones; even though everything registers on CD (and surprisingly well on tape), one could not count this version a complete success.

Ormandy's Telarc performance is curiously lacking in vitality. It is not helped by the recessed, over-resonant recording in which the microphones place the organ in a forward, concerto-like position. Orchestral detail is poor and the piano contribution barely audible. In the finale, the closing climax is effectively balanced, but elsewhere the performance makes little real impact. On CD, the organ entry is spectacular and some may like the overall sumptuousness.

Karajan's recording (also available on CD – **400 063-2**) is one of DG's rare technical disasters. In an attempt to add spectacle to the finale, an artificial balance added an unattractively harsh edge to the organ timbre, making the overall sound uncomfortable. The Pocket Music tape conveys this only too readily, although the earlier movements are fully acceptable. The performance is notable for the conductor's very sombre approach to the *Poco Adagio*.

Other versions from Edo de Waart on Philips (**421 619-2**) and Janowski on Harmonia Mundi (**HMC 905197**) must be passed over; neither is sufficiently distinctive to survive the present competition.

Violin sonata No. 1 in D min., Op. 75.
*** Ph. Dig. **416 157-2**; *416 157-4* [id.]. Pinchas Zukerman, Marc Neikrug – FRANCK: *Sonata.****
*** Essex **CDS 6044** [id.]. Accardo, Canio – CHAUSSON: *Concert.****

Zukerman and Neikrug play Saint-Saëns's little-known *Sonata* with great sweep and virtuosity. The brilliant articulation of the captivating Scherzo is matched by the tremendous bravura of violinist and pianist alike in the thrilling fireworks of the finale. With superb recording, on CD and tape alike, this performance turns a relatively modest work into a seeming masterpiece.

The performance by Accardo and Canio is also marvellously played, selfless and dedicated. The recording too is very good, and this can be strongly recommended if the coupling is suitable.

Salieri, Antonio (1750–1825)

Double concerto in C for flute and oboe.
*** Ph. Dig. **416 359-2** [id.]. Nicolet, Holliger, ASMF, Sillito – CIMAROSA: *Concertante*; STAMITZ: *Double concerto.****

The film *Amadeus* has reawakened interest in Salieri's music. Certainly his *Concerto for flute and oboe* has great charm, with its chattering interplay in the outer movements and the elegant *Largo* bringing suitable contrast. It is superbly played by Nicolet and Holliger, and stylishly accompanied by Sillito. The recording is in the demonstration class on CD.

Falstaff (opera): complete.
*** Hung. Dig. **HCD 21789/91** [id.]. Gregor, Zempléni, Gulyás, Gáti, Pánczél, Csura, Vámossy, Salieri Chamber Ch. & O, Tamás Pál.

It is fascinating to find Salieri – unfairly traduced in the play and film, *Amadeus* – writing as lively a setting as this of Shakespeare's *Merry Wives of Windsor* almost a hundred years before

Verdi. First given in 1799, it is one of his many comic operas. Like Verdi, Salieri and his librettist ignore the Falstaff of the histories. They tell the story (minus the Anne and Fenton sub-plot and without Mistress Quickly) within the framework of the conventional two-act opera of the period. Dozens of little arias and duets are linked by brisk recitative leading to substantial finales to each Act, involving deftly handled comic interplay, and with the Act II finale bringing moments of tenderness and delicacy to nudge one forward towards Verdi. Though the opera is long, the speed is fast and furious, with the set numbers bringing many delights, as in the charming little duet, *La stessa, stessissima*, for the two wives reading their identical letters (Beethoven wrote variations on it), or Falstaff's first aria, swaggering and jolly, introduced by a fanfare motif, and a delightful laughter trio in Act II. None of the ideas, however charming or sparkling, is developed in the way one would expect in Mozart, but it is all great fun, particularly in a performance as lively and well sung as this. József Gregor is splendid in the name-part, with Dénes Gulyás equally stylish in the tenor role of Ford. Maria Zempléni as Mistress Ford and Eva Pánczél in the mezzo role of Mistress Slender (not Page) are both bright and lively. The eponymous chorus and orchestra also perform with vigour under Tamás Pál; the recording is brilliant, with a fine sense of presence. Enjoyment is greatly enhanced by the exceptionally generous CD banding of the discs.

Sallinen, Aulis (born 1935)

(i) *Cello concerto, Op. 44; Shadows* (*Prelude for Orchestra*), *Op. 52; Symphony No. 4, Op. 49.*
*** Finlandia Dig. **FACD 346** [id.]. (i) Arto Noras; Helsinki PO, Kamu.

All three works here are very effective and have immediate appeal. At first, as with much of Sallinen's music, one feels that the melodic ideas lack quality and the invention is wanting in substance. Yet so strong is the atmosphere that one always wants to return to the music, and it is not very long before new detail that at first hearing seemed insignificant comes to the surface. Perhaps the very accessibility of his musical language, with its overtones of Shostakovich, Puccini and Britten, is in itself deceptive. The *Fourth Symphony* is a three-movement work, but was composed, as it were backwards, the first movement on which Sallinen began work eventually becoming the finale. The middle movement is marked *Dona nobis pacem*; throughout the finale, bells colour the texture, as is often the case in his orchestral writing. In fact, the familiar fingerprints are to be found all over the score, and it is not long before one succumbs to its spell. *Shadows* is an effective short piece, related both thematically and in its atmosphere to his opera *The King goes north to France*. This is hardly surprising, since Sallinen composed it immediately after finishing the second act: its content reflects or 'shadows' the content of the opera. However, it is the *Cello concerto* of 1977 which is the most commanding piece here. It is oddly laid out, its long, expansive first moment taking almost twenty minutes and its companion only five. Yet the first, which is based on variation, never seems discursive, and Sallinen's ideas and his sound-world resonate in the mind. Arto Noras has its measure and plays with masterly eloquence. The performances under Okko Kamu are very impressive and the recording quite exemplary.

Sammartini, Giovanni Battista (1700–75)

Symphonies in D; G; String quintet in E.
*** HM **HMC 901245** [id.]. Ens. 145, Banchini – Giuseppe SAMMARTINI: *Concerti grossi* etc.***

Giovanni Battista was the younger of the two Sammartini brothers; he spent his whole life in Milan, where he was maestro di capella at the convent of Santa Maria Maddelena. (For a time in the 1730s Gluck studied with him.) On this record, the Ensemble 145, led by Chiara Banchini, offer two of his symphonies (he composed over eighty); although neither attains greatness, they have genuine appeal. Good recording.

Sammartini, Giuseppe (*c.* 1693–1750)

Concerti grossi Nos 6 & 8; (i) *Recorder concerto in F.*
*** HM **HMC 901245** [id.]. (i) Conrad Steinmann; Ens. 145, Banchini – Giovanni SAMMARTINI: *Symphonies* etc.***

A record that divides its attentions between the fratelli Sammartini. Giuseppe settled in England in the 1720s, becoming oboist at the Opera and eventually director of chamber music to the Prince of Wales. It is an excellent idea to contrast the different styles of these composers: Giuseppe influenced by the rather conservative English taste but a refined and inventive composer. The Ensemble 145 is a period-instrument group; they produce a firmly focused sound, even though the textures are light and the articulation lively. Excellent playing from Conrad Steinmann in the *Recorder concerto*.

Sarasate, Pablo (1844–1908)

Carmen fantasy, Op. 25.
❀ *** HMV **CDC7 47101-2** [id.]; (M) *EG 291285-4*. Itzhak Perlman, RPO, Foster – PAGANINI: *Concerto No. 1.****❀
*** DG Dig. **423 063-2**; *423 063-4* [id.]. Itzhak Perlman, NYPO, Mehta – CHAUSSON: *Poeme*; RAVEL: *Tzigane*; SAINT-SAËNS: *Havanaise* etc.***

This is the filler for Perlman's account of Paganini's *First Violin concerto*, but what a gorgeous filler. Sarasate's *Fantasy* is a selection of the most popular tunes from *Carmen*, with little attempt made to stitch the seams between them. Played like this, with superb panache, luscious tone and glorious recording, the piece almost upstages the concerto with which it is coupled. The recording balance is admirable; the truthfulness of the sound is the more apparent on CD, with the quality greatly to be preferred to many of Perlman's more recent digital records.

As can be seen, Perlman has re-recorded the work in a fine new digital version and it is generously coupled with other famous showpieces. The new performance is beyond criticism – but the earlier one is just that bit riper and more beguiling.

Zigeunerweisen (*Gypsy airs*). *Op. 21.*
(*) HMV Dig. **CDC7 47318-2. Mutter, O Nat. de France, Ozawa – LALO: *Symphonie espagnole.***(*)

A sparkling performance of Sarasate's gypsy potpourri from Anne-Sophie Mutter, given good support from Ozawa. There are some dazzling fireworks; but some may feel her playing in the famous principal lyrical melody too chaste; others will enjoy the total absence of schmaltz. The balance places the solo violin well forward, and the timbre is very brightly lit.

Satie, Erik (1866–1925)

Parade (ballet after Jean Cocteau).
(*) Sup. Dig. **CO 1519 [id.]. Czech PO, Valek – MILHAUD: *Le bœuf sur le toit*; POULENC: *Les Biches.***(*)

Parade was written for the Diaghilev company and reflects Satie's enthusiasm for the circus and its music. First comes a Chinese conjuror, followed by an American silent-film star whose various escapades are illustrated by the sounds of pistol shots and a typewriter, and finally there is a pair of acrobats. Satie's surrealist score is well presented here and the special effects come off well enough. The special attraction of this Supraphon issue is its appropriate couplings, another Diaghilev ballet plus Milhaud's engaging *Le bœuf sur le toit*.

Music for piano, 4 hands: *Aperçus désagréables; La belle excentrique; Cinéma; Trois Morceaux en forme de poire; Parade* (ballet).
** Denon **C37 7487** [id.]. Takahashi, Planès.

Satie's music for piano duet is not widely represented on disc, and this collection is a good introduction to it. In *La belle excentrique*, the pianists are joined by Juji Murai (clarinet) and Kuji Okasaki (bassoon), a particularly crazy touch. *Parade* in this somewhat monochrome format loses a little of its music-hall character but is none the less entertaining. Well-pointed performances from both artists, and satisfactory though not outstanding recording.

Avant-dernières pensées; (i) *La belle excentrique. Embryons desséchés*; *6 Gnossiennes*; *Groquis et agaceries d'un gros bonhomme en bois*; *3 Gymnopédies*; (i) *3 Morceaux en forme de poire*; *5 Nocturnes*; *Sonatine bureaucratique*; *Véritables préludes flasques* (*pour un chien*).
(*) HMV **CDC7 47474-2 [id.]. Aldo Ciccolini; (i) with Gabriel Tacchino (piano, 4 hands).

Aldo Ciccolino recorded these pieces on LP during the 1960s and he is completely in sympathy with their style. On this generously filled recital (it runs for 70′) he is joined by Gabriel Tacchino for the four-handed *Trois morceaux en forme de poire* and *La belle excentrique*. He is totally inside this music and makes the most of its (not particularly wide) contrasts of mood and atmosphere. The recorded sound is perfectly acceptable, though not as rich as those on Decca (Pascal Rogé) or BIS (Roland Pöntinen).

Avant-dernières pensées; (i) *Choses vues à droite et à gauche; Descriptions automatiques; Embryons desséchés; Préludes flasques* (*pour un chien*)*; Sonatine bureaucratique; Sports et divertissements; 3 Valses distinguées du précieux dégoûté; Véritables préludes flasques* (*pour un chien*).
** Denon Dig. **C37 7486** [id.]. Yuji Takahashi, (i) with Keiko Mizuno.

These recordings were made in 1979 and, like Yuji Takahashi's earlier recital (**C37 7485** – see below), suffer from a very dry recording acoustic, which may theoretically suit music of dry humour but does not beguile the ear. Takahashi's playing is certainly stylish, but some of this repertoire is already duplicated by Pascal Rogé, whose Decca recording is much more agreeable and flattering.

Avant-dernières pensées; Embryons desséchés; Fantaisie-Valse; 3 Gnossiennes; 3 Gymnopédies; Jack-in-the-Box; Je te veux; Le Piccadilly; Poudre d'or; Prélude en tapisserie; Sports et divertissements; Les trois valses distinguées du précieux dégoûté; Valse-ballet.
(M) ** **CD-EMX 9507**; *EMX 41 2071-4*. Angela Brownridge.

The fun of Satie is well represented in Angela Brownridge's collection. It is sensitively arranged as a programme to have *Gymnopédies* and *Gnossiennes* alternating with the lighter pieces echoing popular music. The playing is bright and stylish, sensitively reflecting the sharply changing moods and lacking only the last touches of poetry. A fair bargain on the Eminence label, with the reverberance of the recording clarified on CD.

Avant-dernières pensées; Embryons desséchés; 6 Gnossiennes; 3 Gymnopédies; Pièces froides; Sarabande No. 3; Sonatine bureaucratique; 3 Valses distinguées du précieux dégoûté; 3 véritables préludes flasques (pour un chien).
*** BIS Dig. **CD 317** [id.]. Roland Pöntinen.

Roland Pöntinen is a young Swedish pianist, still in his early twenties when this recording was made. He seems perfectly in tune with the Satiean world, and his playing is distinguished by great sensibility and tonal finesse. Moreover, in his recording the aural image has space round it and there is good definition and body. If he does not wholly displace Rogé on Decca, he offers keen and thoroughly recommendable competition.

Danses gothiques; 6 Gnossiennes; Petite ouverture à danser; Prélude de la porte héroïque du ciel.
(*) Ph. Dig. **412 243-2 [id.]. Reinbert de Leeuw.

This CD offers a not especially generous programme, taken from Reinbert de Leeuw's three-LP set concentrating on Satie's earlier music. He is a sensitive player and thoroughly attuned to Satie's sensibility. He takes the composer at his word by playing many of the pieces *très lente*; indeed, he overdoes this at times, though this impression may be caused by listening to too much slow music all at once. But if at times one feels the need for more movement (and, on occasion, for greater dynamic nuance), these are admirable performances, and any blame must lie partly with the producer of this CD in not seeking greater variety. There is no doubt that the playing creates and maintains a mood of poetic melancholy; this is helped by the beautiful recorded quality, so very effective on compact disc, when the piano image is so believable and the background is silent.

Embryons desséchés; 6 Gnossiennes; 3 Gymnopédies; Je te veux; Nocturne No. 4; Le Piccadilly; 4 Préludes flasques; Prélude en tapisserie; Sonatine bureaucratique; Vieux sequins et vieilles cuirasses.
*** Decca Dig. **410 220-2**; *410 220-4*. Pascal Rogé.

Pascal Rogé gave Satie's music its compact disc début in a fine recital which is splendidly caught by the microphone. Rogé has real feeling for this repertoire and conveys its bitter-sweet quality and its grave melancholy as well as he does its lighter qualities. He produces, as usual, consistent beauty of tone and this is well projected by the recording in both formats. This remains the primary recommendation on CD for this repertoire and there is a very good equivalent cassette.

Gnossiennes 1–3; Gymnopédies 1–3; Prélude de la porte héroïque du ciel; Je te veux; Nocturnes 1–5; Pièces froides: Airs à faire fuir 1–3; Danses de travers 1–3. Ragtime parade.
** Denon **C37 7485** [id.]. Yuji Takahashi.

Yuji Takahashi recorded these pieces in the mid-1970s and his strong rhythmic feeling and sense of style won him some considerable praise in the BBC's 'Record Review'. The snag is the forward balance and the cramped, dry acoustic of the Denon recording. If you can accept that (and the piano has undoubted presence), then there is much to admire here. But Pascal Rogé's softer contours and more sophisticated colouring, as recorded by Decca, sound much more sensuous.

Scarlatti, Alessandro (1660–1725)

Sinfonie di concerti grossi Nos 1–6.
*** Ph. Dig. **400 017-2** [id.]. Bennett, Lenore, Smith, Soustrot, Elhorst, I Musici.

These performances are taken from the complete set of twelve (originally issued on LP, now withdrawn). All are elegantly and stylishly played. All are scored for flute and strings; in No. 2 there is a trumpet as well, in No. 5 an oboe and in Nos 1 and 5 a second flute. No complaints about the performances, which are lively and attractive and eminently well recorded. The harpsichord is a little reticent, even on CD, but few will fail to derive pleasure from the music making here.

Madrigals: *Arsi un tempo; Cor mio deh non languire; Intenerite voi, la crime mia; Mori, mo dici; O morte; O selce, o tigre o ninfa; Sdegno la liamma estinse* (with LOTTI: Madrigals: *Inganni dell'umanita; Lamento di tre amanti; Moralita duenaperla; La vita caduca*).
*** HMV Dig. **CDC7 49189-2** [id.]. Consort of Music, Rooley.

The subtitle of this record is 'The Last Years of the Madrigal' and it offers seven rarities of Alessandro Scarlatti interspersed with four madrigals by his slightly younger contemporary, Antonio Lotti (1667–1740). It serves as a revealing rebuttal of the common belief that the polyphonic madrigal went into a rapid decline after Monteverdi. As Rooley points out, Scarlatti ingeniously combines all the techniques of the classical madrigal, such as imitative part-writing, word-painting and so on, with the newly developed features of the Baroque chamber cantata. The four Lotti madrigals are all early, coming from a 1705 collection dedicated to the Emperor Joseph I; they include the celebrated *La vita caduca*, which Bononcini passed off as his own composition in London! (His reputation never recovered after his deception was unmasked.) But this is more than just a recital of historical interest; it is a rewarding musical experience, excellently performed and beautifully recorded.

Scarlatti, Domenico (1685–1757)

Keyboard sonatas, Kk. 11, 14, 17, 87, 146, 204a, 204b, 205, 322, 323, 337, 338, 443, 444, 513.
(M) ** HMV **CDM7 68117-2** [id.]. Igor Kipnis (harpsichord & clavichord).

This collection (67′), put together by EMI's American label, Angel, is drawn from a pair of LPs not previously available here. Kipnis is a fine player, but his slight hesitations in the phrasing of the gentler sonatas is not always entirely convincing. He can be very commanding in the more forthright pieces, such as the two bold *G major Sonatas*, Kk. 14 and Kk. 337, and the three he plays on the clavichord (Kk. 87, 322 and 323) are among the most enjoyable performances: the intimacy of this miniature instrument brings out the best in him. The recording is faithful, though not to be played back at too high a level.

Keyboard sonatas, Kk. 24, 27, 30, 33, 69, 96, 141, 144, 146, 175, 259–60, 516–17, 544–5.
*** HMV **CDC7 49020-2** [id.]; *EL 270604-4*. Robert Woolley (harpsichord).

Robert Woolley plays a one-manual harpsichord by Michael Johnson, based on an anonymous Italian instrument of 1693. The sixteen sonatas he offers here are intelligently chosen and varied in mood. Woolley is both a thoughtful player and a very brilliant one, and his recital can more than hold its own with the current competition. By comparison with some of the great interpreters of the past – Landowska, Valenti or George Malcolm, say – he is a shade wanting in panache, and one often feels that he is being a little judicious. This is very good playing all the same, and many of the *Sonatas* are not duplicated on other recitals. The recording is thoroughly lifelike: the instrument is not too close nor is the level too high, as it is for Pinnock on Archiv. There is a good tape, comfortably transferred if without quite the presence and range of the CD.

Keyboard sonatas, Kk. 46, 87, 99, 124, 201, 204a, 490–92, 513, 520–21.
*** CRD **CRD 3368**; *CRDC 4068* [id.]. Trevor Pinnock (harpsichord).

No need to say much about this: the playing is first rate and the recording outstanding in its presence and clarity. There are few better anthologies of Scarlatti in the catalogue, and this has the advantage of including a half-dozen sonatas not otherwise available. The CD remastering is eminently successful and there is an excellent cassette.

Keyboard sonatas, Kk. 87, 104–5, 124:5, 244–5, 408–9, 420–21, 516–17, 544–5.
*** HMV Dig. **CDC7 47654-2** [id.]. Virginia Black (harpsichord).

Though less immaculate and polished than Trevor Pinnock's acclaimed CRD recital, this is an eminently satisfying addition to the Scarlatti CD discography. Virginia Black's recital (on a Dowd harpsichord) is planned with considerable imagination and her choice invariably favours less familiar sonatas. Her responses are keen and, although not every piece fares equally well, she brings sensitivity and skill to this repertoire. The recording is truthful.

Keyboard sonatas, Kk. 460–61, 478–9, 502, 516–17, 518 19, 529, 544–5, 546–7.
** DG Dig. **419 632-2** [id.]. Trevor Pinnock (harpsichord).

A rather overrated record. The playing is enormously fluent and brilliant, but it excites admiration rather than pleasure and does not wholly deserve its ecstatic press. Some of the sonatas seem a bit over-driven: the *D minor*, Kk. 516, is a case in point; where there is more rhythmic flexibility, as in its companion the *D major Sonata*, Kk. 479, the little hesitations sound more studied than spontaneous. Elsewhere, the *F major*, Kk. 518, for example, carries conviction; but the slightly relentless feel to the playing may be due to the recording, which reproduces at a thunderous level. To get a realistic playback level, the volume control has to be turned right down. There is genuine fire and sparkle in the *F minor*, Kk. 519, but the performances do not communicate the freshness or the quality of surprise at Scarlatti's teeming invention. However, critical acclaim has been unanimous and readers might well find they share it more than we did.

Stabat Mater.
*** Erato Dig. **ECD 88087** [id.]. Monteverdi Ch., E. Bar. Soloists, Gardiner – *Concert: 'Sacred choral music'.****

The *Stabat Mater* is an early work, written during Scarlatti's sojourn in Rome (1714–19) when he was maestro di capella at S. Giulia, and it shows him to be a considerable master of polyphony. It is extended in scale and taxing to the performers. This version from John Eliot Gardiner has nothing to fear from any comparison you might care to make: the singing is never less than excellent. The *Stabat Mater* has been written off by some critics as bland and wanting in individuality; though it falls off in interest towards the end, it still possesses eloquence and nobility – and it is far less bland than Pergolesi's setting. Gardiner's fine performance couples three motets of interest, by Cavalli, Gesualdo and Clément, which are also splendidly done. The recording is very good indeed, notably fresh in its CD format.

Schmidt, Franz (1874–1939)

Variations on a Hussar's song.
(M) ❀ *** HMV *ED 291172-4*. New Philh. O, Bauer – BUSONI: *Sarabande and cortège*; LUTOSLAWSKI: *Postlude*; *Symphonic variations.**** ❀

Apart from the four symphonies. the *Hussar variations* is Schmidt's only major piece for orchestra alone. It dates from 1931 and is obviously the product of a fertile and exuberant imagination with something of Strauss's confidence and Reger's delicacy. Hans Bauer and the

New Philharmonia Orchestra give a thoroughly persuasive account of the piece, and the recording is superb. The couplings make this a collection of quite exceptional interest and value which cannot be too strongly recommended. The cassette is excellently transferred.

Das Buch mit sieben Siegeln (*The Book with seven seals*): oratorio.
(*) Orpheus Dig. **C 143862H (2). Schreier, Holl, Greenberg, Watkinson, Moser, Rydl, V. State Op. Ch., Austrian RSO, Zagrosek.

There is a nobility about the best of Schmidt's music which is most sympathetic; though *Das Buch mit sieben Siegeln* is not quite the *chef d'oeuvre* that its Austrian admirers claim (the *Fourth Symphony* is surely his masterpiece), it has much music of substance and many moments of real inspiration. Peter Schreier's St John is one of the glories of this set, and there are fine contributions from some of the other soloists. However, it does not eclipse memories of Mitropoulos's set with Dermota, Hilde Guden and Wunderlich and the Vienna Philharmonic, made in 1959. This performance was recorded in the less appealing acoustic of the ORF studios and is wanting in the transparency that the score deserves. Detail is less vivid than it might be and the dynamic range is somewhat compressed, as in a broadcast; the engineers pull back at some climaxes. We are unlikely to get another version for a long time and this is more than acceptable.

Schnittke, Alfred (born 1934)

Violin sonata No. 1; Sonata in the olden style.
*** Chan. Dig. **CHAN 8343**; *ABTD 1089* [id.]. Dubinsky, Edlina – SHOSTAKOVICH: *Violin sonata.****

Schnittke is now over fifty and has achieved prominence as one of the leading Soviet composers of the middle generation. In the early 1950s he composed a number of relatively conventional works, including *Nagasaki* and *Songs of War and Peace*, but, after steeping himself in the idiom of Shostakovich and Prokofiev, he became attracted to the more exploratory musical idiom of the Western avant-garde who built their foundations on the Second Viennese School. The *First sonata* dates friom 1963 when he was still in his late twenties; it is a well-argued piece that seems to unify his awareness of the post-serial musical world with the tradition of Shostakovich. It is linked on this version with a pastiche of less interest, dating from 1977. Excellent playing from both artists and very good recording too. The chrome cassette almost matches the CD in presence and realism.

Cello sonata.
*** BIS Dig. **CD 336** [id.]. Thorleif Thedeen, Roland Pöntinen – STRAVINSKY: *Suite italienne*; SHOSTAKOVICH: *Sonata.****

The Schnittke *Sonata* dates from 1978 and is a powerfully expressive piece; its avant-garde surface enshrining a neo-romantic soul. Thorleif Thedeen is a young Swedish cellist who has won both the Casals Prize in Budapest and the Hammer–Rostropovich Prize in Los Angeles. He is a refined and intelligent player who gives a thoroughly committed account of this piece with his countryman, Roland Pöntinen.

Schobert, Johann (*c.* 1735–1767)

Keyboard concerto in G.
** HMV Dig. **CDC7 47527-2**. Selheim, Coll. Aur., Maier – BOCCHERINI: *Concerto*; FIELD: *Rondo.***

This is probably the most rewarding work of the three included here. The slow movement is distinctly engaging and, if the first movement is more conventional, the minuet finale is attractive too. With a good solo performance and well-integrated accompaniment in the 'authentic' style, this makes agreeable listening. The recording is fresh and clean.

Schoeck, Othmar (1886–1957)

Cello concerto, Op. 61.
*** Claves Dig. **D 8502** [id.]. Goritzki, Deutsche Kammerakadamie Neuss – REGER: *Lyrisches Andante.****

This is a forty-minute work, predominantly lyrical in character, and perhaps lacks immediate appeal. Yet its chamber-like scoring gives it a rather special private quality, and although it has its longueurs, its atmosphere is at times strong and haunting. The opening seems to strike vague echoes of Brahms and Elgar, but the slow movement is full of what the Germans call *Innigkeit*: it has a musing inwardness whose gentleness and melancholy almost recall Strauss's *Metamorphosen*. The opening bars of the finale are quite magical, coming as if from another world. No doubt there is an over-reliance on sequence; the material does not sustain its length and is encumbered by some routine writing. For all that, however, there are times when a quiet voice speaks – and one with powerful resonances. The performance by the soloist-conductor, Johannes Goritzki, and the Deutsche Kammerakademie Neuss is sensitive and totally dedicated, and the recording is very natural. As a fill-up, there is a short lyrical piece for strings by Reger, with whom Schoeck studied.

Schoenberg, Arnold (1874–1951)

Chamber symphony, Op. 9; Variations, Op. 31.
(M) **(*) Decca *414 440-4* [id.]. LAPO, Mehta.

It is good to have two Schoenberg masterpieces (one from early in his career and one from the very peak, arguably his finest instrumental work) coupled in brilliant performances from a virtuoso orchestra. It was, after all, to Los Angeles that Schoenberg moved to settle in his last years, and it would have gladdened him that his local Philharmonic Orchestra had achieved a degree of brilliance to match that of any other orchestra in America. The Op. 31 *Variations*, among the most taxing works Schoenberg ever wrote, somehow reveal their secrets, their unmistakable greatness, more clearly when the performances have such a sense of drive, born of long and patient rehearsal under a clear-headed conductor. The *First Chamber symphony* is also given a rich performance, arguably too fast at times, but full of understanding for the romantic emotions which underlie much of the writing. Brilliant 1969 recording, though the high-level tape (available for the first time) is shrill.

Chamber symphony No. 1, Op. 9.
*** DG Dig. **423 307-2** [id.]. BPO, Sinopoli – MANZONI: *Mass.****

A fine performance of Schoenberg's Op. 9 from Sinopoli. He links it positively back to the high romanticism of Richard Strauss, with the Berlin Philharmonic producing glorious sounds. Other versions may be more detailed but none are richer or more full-blooded. Full recording to match. The coupling may be a deterrent for many, though of its kind it is a fine and colourful work.

(i) *Piano concerto*: (ii) *Violin concerto.*
(*) Erato Dig. **ECD 88175 [id.]. (i) Peter Serkin; (ii) Pierre Amoyal; LSO, Boulez.

Schoenberg devotees often suggest that both these concertos from his American period, late in his career, present the most approachable road to appreciating the master. Both works consciously echo the world of the romantic concerto in twelve-note terms, but the thick textures very easily obscure the focus of the argument, making them sound like Brahms with the wrong notes. Boulez with his excellent soloists is a clarifier, choosing speeds on the measured side. In the *Violin concerto* Pierre Amoyal proves a warmly sympathetic soloist, conveying the full expressiveness of the lyrical writing without soupiness. Peter Serkin takes a more detached view and is less persuasive than Alfred Brendel on his earlier DG recording; but with first-rate sound, this apt coupling is highly recommendable.

Pelleas und Melisande, Op. 5.
*** DG **423 132-2** [id.]. BPO, Karajan. – BERG: *Lyric suite: 3 Pieces.****

The Straussian opulence of Schoenberg's early symphonic poem has never been as ravishingly presented as by Karajan and the Berlin Philharmonic in this superbly recorded version. The gorgeous tapestry of sound is both rich and full of refinement and detail, while the thrust of argument is powerfully conveyed in Karajan's radiant performance, well coupled with music of Berg.

5 Pieces for orchestra, Op. 16.
*** DG Dig. **419 781-2** [id.]. BPO, Levine – BERG: *3 Pieces*; WEBERN: *5 Pieces.****

The colour and power of Schoenberg's Opus 16 *Pieces*, marking a historic landmark in the development of the Second Viennese School, come over superbly in Levine's purposeful, concentrated reading. This is an interpretation designed – like those of the Berg and Webern pieces on the CD – to relate Schoenberg to his predecessors rather than to the future; but that will help, not hinder, the uncommitted listener looking for a representative collection of orchestral works by these key composers. Warm, full-toned recording, with some spotlighting.

Suite for strings in G; Verklaerte Nacht.
*** Erato Dig. **ECD 88211** [id.]. I Solisti Veneti, Scimone.

Claudio Scimone's coupling reveals this baroque specialist as an ardent Schoenbergian, bringing out the romantic warmth of *Verklaerte Nacht* in open Italianate lyricism, and equally presenting the *Suite for strings*, first product of Schoenberg's American years, less as a neoclassical exercise than as a vibrantly expressive example of his later style at its richest and most inventive. The string sextet version of *Verklaerte Nacht* is used. The recording, made in a Palladio villa, is warmly sympathetic.

Ode to Napoleon.
** DG Dig. **415 982-2** [id.]. Kenneth Griffiths, LaSalle Qt – WEBERN: *Quintet* etc.***

Written in 1942, the *Ode to Napoleon* sets the words of Byron in Schoenbergian *Sprechstimme* as a heartfelt protest against Nazi tyranny. With hatred at its core, it represents the composer at his most deeply committed, rebutting any idea of his music being merely intellectual. That bedrock of passion is strongly brought out in the playing of the pianist, Stefan Litwin, and the LaSalle Quartet; sadly, the declamation is harshly recorded in what sounds like another acoustic, a point made the more apparent on CD. Nevertheless, with Webern rarities for coupling, it makes an attractive recommendation.

Variations for orchestra, Op. 31; Verklaerte Nacht, Op. 4.
❀ *** DG **415 326-2** [id.]. BPO, Karajan.

Verklaerte Nacht, Op. 4.

*** Tel. **ZK8 43311**; *AZ4 43311* [id.]. Israel CO, Talmi – TCHAIKOVSKY: *Souvenir de Florence.****
(*) HMV **CDC7 47521-2 [id.]. Stokowski & SO – BARBER: *Adagio*; BARTÓK. *Music for strings, percussion & celesta.***(*)
(*) Decca Dig. **410 111-2 [id.]. ECO, Ashkenazy – WAGNER: *Siegfried idyll.****
** Decca Dig. **421 182-2**; *421 182-4* (2) [id.]. Berlin RSO, Chailly – MAHLER: *Symphony No. 10.***(*)

Karajan's version of *Verklaerte Nacht* is altogether magical and very much in a class of its own. There is a tremendous intensity and variety of tone and colour: the palette that the strings of the Berlin Philharmonic have at their command is altogether extraordinarily wide-ranging. Both these masterly performances are classics of the Karajan discography; their transfer to compact disc cannot be welcomed too strongly: the sound is firmer and more cleanly defined, and the increased range that the new medium offers enables both interpretations to be heard to even greater advantage than before.

Yoav Talmi and the Israel Chamber Orchestra play with great fervour and rich body of tone, yet delicacy too. They are given a superbly full but clear recording in an ideally warm acoustic. The conductor's flexibility of phrase and tempo adds to the passionately responsive appeal of this outstanding performance, coupled with an equally fine account of Tchaikovsky's *Souvenir de Florence*. The disc plays for well over an hour. There is an excellent tape, not quite as transparent in texture, but first class in all other respects.

As might be expected, Stokowski is in his element here, catching the diverse moods of the piece chimerically, the cool moonlight of the opening scene, the passionate, volatile climax, and the luxuriant radiance of the close. It is an outstanding performance in every way, and very well played. The recording comes from 1960 and the string textures are not as full-bodied as in a modern recording; but Stokowski's sound never lacks sensuous allure and the resonant acoustic helps to prevent this from sounding too dated. It might, however, have been more economically priced.

Ashkenazy conducts an outstandingly warm and lyrical reading, one which brings out the melodic richness of his highly atmospheric work, with passionate playing from the ECO. Full and brilliant recording. The compact disc brings an extra edge to the sound, not always quite comfortable on high violins.

Chailly's version is very well played and recorded, but is in no way distinctive.

String quartet No. 2 (arr. for string orchestra).

*** HMV Dig. **CDC7 47923-2** [id.]; *EL 169588-4*. Eva Csapo, Junge Deutsche Philharmonie CO, Gulke – BERG: *Lyric suite*; WEBERN: *5 Pieces.****

Schoenberg made this arrangement of his *Second quartet* some twenty years after its composition at the request of his publisher, Universal Edition. Again, as in its companions on this record, the playing of the strings of the Junge Deutsche Philharmonie is marvellously eloquent. Two of the movements (the *Litany* and the *Entrancement*) include a soprano part, admirably sung by Eva Csapo – who is perhaps not ideally balanced or focused here – but the performance is eminently persuasive and there is a powerful atmosphere and sense of commitment. There is a first-class cassette.

Gurrelieder.

*** Ph. **412 511-2** (2) [id.]. McCracken, Norman, Troyanos, Arnold, Scown, Tanglewood Fest. Ch., Boston SO, Ozawa.

Ozawa directs a gloriously opulent reading of Schoenberg's *Gurrelieder*, one which relates it firmly to the nineteenth century rather than pointing forward to Schoenberg's own later works. The playing of the Boston Symphony has both warmth and polish and is set against a resonant acoustic; among the soloists, Jessye Norman gives a performance of radiant beauty, at times reminding one of Flagstad in the burnished glory of her tone colours. As the wood-dove, Tatiana Troyanos sings most sensitively, though the vibrato is at times obtrusive; and James McCracken does better than most tenors at coping with a heroic vocal line without barking. Other versions have in some ways been more powerful – Boulez's, for one – but none is more sumptuously beautiful than this. The luxuriant textures are given a degree more transparency, with detail slightly clearer on CD.

Pierrot Lunaire, Op. 21.
*** Chan. *ABT 1046* [id.]. Jane Manning, Nash Ens., Rattle – WEBERN: *Concerto.****

Jane Manning is outstanding among singers who have tackled this most taxing of works, steering a masterful course between the twin perils of, on the one hand, actually singing and, on the other, simply speaking. As well as being beautifully controlled and far more accurate than is common, her sing-speech brings out the element of irony and darkly pointed wit that is an essential too often missed in this piece. In a 1977 recording originally made for the Open University, Rattle draws strong, committed performances from the members of the Nash Ensemble and, apart from some intermittently odd balances, the sound is excellent. The cassette contains an important fill-up in the late Webern piece, and the transfer offers a clear, atmospheric sound-picture.

OPERA

Moses und Aron.
*** Decca Dig. **414 264-2** (2) [id.]. Mazura, Langridge, Bonney, Haugland, Chicago Ch. and SO, Solti.

Recorded in conjunction with concert performances, working very much against the clock and with the whole opera completed in fourteen hours, Solti gives Schoenberg's masterly score a dynamism and warmth which set it firmly – if perhaps surprisingly – in the grand romantic tradition. This is no mere intellectual exercise or static oratorio, as it can seem, but a genuine drama. Solti instructed his performers to 'play and sing as if you were performing Brahms', and here *Moses und Aron* can almost be regarded as the opera which Brahms did not write – if with the 'wrong notes'. Particularly when two fine previous versions remain unavailable – Boulez on CBS, Gielen on Philips – Solti's broad romantic treatment presents a splendid alternative. This is a performance which in its greater variety of mood and pace underlines the drama, finds an element of fantasy and, in places – as in the *Golden Calf* episode – a sparkle such as you would never expect from Schoenberg. It is still not an easy work. The Moses of Franz Mazura may not be as specific in his sing-speech as was Gunter Reich in the two previous versions – far less sing than speech – but the characterization of an Old Testament patriarch is the more convincing. As Aaron, Philip Langridge is lighter and more lyrical, as well as more accurate, than his predecessor with Boulez, Richard Cassilly. Aage Haugland with his firm, dark bass makes his mark in the small role of the Priest; Barbara Bonney too is excellent as the Young Girl. Above all, the brilliant singing of the Chicago Symphony Chorus matches the playing of the orchestra in virtuosity. More than ever the question-mark concluding Act II makes a pointful close, with no feeling of a work unfinished. The brilliant recording shows little or no sign of the speed with which the project was completed, and the CD adds an even sharper focus.

Schröter, Johann (1752–88)

Piano concerto in C, Op. 3/3.
*** CBS Dig. **MK 39222** [id.]. Murray Perahia, ECO – MOZART: *Piano concertos Nos 1–3, K.107.****

Johann Samuel Schröter was born in Poland and was four years older than Mozart. He made his début in Leipzig in 1767 and then appeared in London at the Bach–Abel concerts; he eventually succeeded J. C. Bach as music master to the queen in 1782, six years before his death. (It was Schröter's widow for whom Haydn developed an attachment on his first visit to London.) He was a highly accomplished pianist, and this sparkling little concerto explains why he was so successful. Murray Perahia gives it all his care and attention without overloading it with sophistication. Delightful in every way, and beautifully recorded, it sounds particularly fresh and present in its CD form.

Schubert, Franz (1797–1828)

Konzertstücke in D, D.935; Polonaise in B flat, D.580; Rondo in A, D.438.
*** Ph. Dig. **420 168-2**; *420 168-4* [id.]. Zukerman, St Paul CO – BEETHOVEN: *Romances*; DVOŘÁK: *Romance.****

This was the nearest Schubert came to writing a violin concerto. None of this music is ambitious but it all has characteristic charm, especially when played so elegantly and affectionately and with such a sure sense of style. The engaging *Polonaise* is used separately as a foil between Beethoven and Dvořák, while the *Konzertstücke* and *Rondo* (both with slow introductions) are happily linked to round off a particularly satisfying collection of short concertante works for violin and orchestra. Zukerman is naturally balanced, and both he and his accompanying orchestral group are beautifully recorded.

Symphonies Nos 1–7; 8 (Unfinished); 9 (Great).
(*) DG **419 318-2 (4) [id.]. BPO, Boehm.

Boehm's recordings were made over a decade between 1963 and 1973. Throughout the Berlin Philharmonic plays with striking warmth and finesse. Boehm does not always smile as often as Schubert's music demands (especially by the side of Beecham in Nos 3 and 6), but he is always sympathetic. Certainly the Berlin wind are a joy to listen to in most of these symphonies, and in Nos 6, 8 and 9 Boehm is the best of Schubertians. It is only in the early symphonies that he does not quite capture the youthful sparkle of these delightful scores, although in its way No. 1 is brightly and elegantly done. The remastered sound is remarkably fine, fresher and clearer and without loss of bloom. But this set is over-priced.

Symphonies Nos 1–3; 4 (Tragic); 5–7; 8 (Unfinished); 9 in C (Great); 10 in D, D.936a; Symphonic fragments in D, D.615 and D.708a (completed and orch. Newbould).
*** Ph. Dig. **412 176-2** (6) [id.]. ASMF, Marriner.

Marriner's excellent set gathers together not only the eight symphonies of the regular canon but two more symphonies now 'realized', thanks to the work of Professor Brian Newbould of Hull University. For full measure, half a dozen fragments of other symphonic movements are also included, orchestrated by Professor Newbould. Those fragments include the four-movement outline of yet another symphony – Scherzo complete, other movements tantalizingly cut off in mid-flight. Though you can often appreciate what snags the young composer was finding in particular ideas, the authentic charm is consistently there. Newbould's No. 7 is based on a sketch which quickly lapsed into a single orchestral line, now devotedly filled out. That work proves less rewarding than 'No. 10', written in the last months of Schubert's life, well after the *Great C major*, which now appears to have been written a year or so earlier. This *Tenth*, in three movements, has a heavenly slow movement, with some bald Mahlerian overtones and a last movement that starts as a Scherzo and then satisfyingly ends as a finale.

Sir Neville's readings of the first six symphonies, recorded earlier, bring sparkling examples of the Academy's work at its finest, while the bigger challenges of the *Unfinished* (here completed with Schubert's Scherzo filled out and the *Rosamunde B minor Entr'acte* used as finale) and the *Great C major* are splendidly taken. These are fresh, direct readings, making up in rhythmic vitality for any lack of weight. The recordings, all digital, were made between 1981 and 1984; particularly on CD, they present consistent refinement and undistractingly good balance.

Symphonies Nos 1 in D, D.82; 2 in B flat, D.125.
** HMV Dig. **CDC7 47874-2** [id.]. Cologne RSO, Wand.

Günter Wand directs strong, honest performances of these two boyhood works which in close, immediate sound convey an apt scale. The Cologne strings may lack bloom – with violins very thin in the slow movement of No. 2 – but the natural way that Wand presents these sunny inspirations, bringing out the youthful energy, is consistently winning.

Symphonies Nos 2 in B flat, D.125; 8 in B min. (Unfinished), D.759.
** CBS Dig. **MK 39676** [id.]. BPO, Barenboim.

With fine playing from the Berlin Philharmonic, particularly brilliant in the perpetuum mobile finale of No. 2, in which the repeat is observed, Barenboim offers an unusual coupling for the *Unfinished.* It can be recommended with reservations to those who fancy the youthful work alongside the mature masterpiece, but the recording does not clarify textures sufficiently for No. 2, which becomes rather too inflated. Barenboim's approach to the *Unfinished* is fresh, yet thoughtfully expressive. Even with the added clarification of CD, the orchestral sound remains very weighty in the middle and bass registers.

Symphonies Nos 3 in D, D.200; 5 in B flat, D.485.
*(*) CBS Dig. **MK 39671** [id.]. BPO, Barenboim.

Barenboim's coupling of Nos 3 and 5 is well paced, finely detailed and beautifully played, but lacks the sense of spontaneity and rhythmic point to give these two delectable works their full charm. Too often they come to seem a little stodgy, not helped by the recording, which grows congested in tuttis.

Symphonies Nos 3 in D, D.200; 6 in D, D.589.
(*) HMV Dig. **CDC7 47875-2 [id.]. Cologne RSO, Wand.

Wand's coupling of Nos 3 and 6 brings exuberant performances of both works, vividly recorded to bring out the honest bluffness as well as the sunny joyfulness of both symphonies. That is specially true of the finales in each work, which find Schubert at his most effervescent and Wand drawing finely sprung, resilient playing from the Cologne orchestra – not the most refined in Germany, but one which vividly responds to the natural, spontaneous-sounding energy of the veteran conductor. The only controversial point is the very fast, though well-pointed, speed for the second-movement *Allegretto* of No. 3.

Symphonies Nos 3 in D, D.200; 8 in B min. (Unfinished), D.759.
(M) *** Pickwick Dig. **PCD 848** [MCA **MCAD 25954**]. City of L. Sinf., Hickox.
(*) Hung. **HCD 12616-2 [id.]. Budapest Fest. O, Ivan Fischer.
(*) DG Dig. **415 601-2 [id.]. VPO, Carlos Kleiber.

Hickox's coupling makes a first-rate bargain recommendation on the Pickwick label. These are fresh and direct readings, never putting a foot wrong, very well recorded, with a chamber orchestra sounding full and substantial. Others may find more individuality and charm, but the crisp resilience of the playing is consistently winning.

The Budapest Festival Orchestra, as on many Hungaroton issues, reveals itself as a finely matched band with an exceptionally fresh and responsive string section, here recorded rather immediately to give a pleasant chamber scale. Ivan Fischer draws bright, clean performances from the players, often at rather brisk speeds – to the point of breathlessness in the finale of No. 3 – with detached articulation that at times recalls period performance. Even though there are more searching accounts of the *Unfinished*, it is refreshing to have an intimate view so finely detailed and deeply thoughtful. First-rate recording, rather drier than some from this source.

Carlos Kleiber is a refreshingly unpredictable conductor; sometimes, however, his imagination goes too far towards quirkiness, and that is certainly so in the slow movement of No. 3, which is rattled through jauntily at breakneck speed. The effect is bizarre even for an *Allegretto*, if quite charming. The Minuet too becomes a full-blooded Scherzo, and there is little rest in the outer movements. The *Unfinished* brings a more compelling performance, but there is unease in the first movement, where first and second subjects are not fully co-ordinated, the contrasts sounding a little forced. The recording brings out the brass sharply, and is of pleasantly wide range. This is the more striking in the CD transfer.

Symphony No. 4 in C min. (Tragic), D.417.
(B) **(*) DG Walkman *419 822-4* [id.]. BPO, Boehm – MENDELSSOHN: *Symphony No. 5*; SCHUMANN: *Symphony No. 4* **(*)

A good (if, in the last analysis, not outstanding) version of the *Tragic* from Boehm, with splendid, disciplined playing from the Berlin Philharmonic, who are well if resonantly recorded. The couplings are all satisfactory and this is fair value at Walkman price.

Symphonies Nos 4 in C min. (Tragic), D.417; 5 in B flat, D.485.
*** Ph. Dig. **410 045-2** [id.]. ASMF, Marriner.

For the compact disc issue the sound remains warm and luminous, but the refinement of the presentation against the silent background makes the ear realize that the balance is not quite ideal in the relationship of wind and strings and the recording is not as clearly defined internally as one might expect, with the overall focus less sharp. Nevertheless, this remains a highly desirable issue.

Symphonies Nos 4 in C min. (Tragic); 8 in B min. (Unfinished).
*** HMV Dig. **CDC7 47876-2** [id.]. Cologne RSO, Wand.
*(*) Erato **ECD 88008** [id.]. Basle SO, Jordan.

Wand's is an inspired performance of the *Unfinished*, bringing out the sunny elements, but in a strong, bluff way contrasting that in both movements with Schubert's darker inspiration. Wand's account of No. 4, the *Tragic*, makes an apt coupling, for among the early symphonies in his complete cycle he gives it greater weight in keeping with the C minor intensity which prompted the work's title. The slow movement is on the fast side but easily lyrical, and the finale is electrically intense, helped by vivid, immediate recording. This is one of the very best issues in Wand's cycle.

Jordan's coupling is well played but the readings are not distinctive. The *Unfinished* lacks biting drama, nor does it have any special romantic feeling; while the *Tragic symphony* is undercharacterized until the finale, which suddenly springs to life. The recording is full and atmospheric but in no way special. A disappointing issue.

Symphony No. 5 in B flat, D.485.
(M) ** Pickwick Dig. **PCD 819** [MCA **MCAD 25845**]. O of St John's, Smith Square, Lubbock – HAYDN: *Symphony No. 49.***(*)

With tempi fractionally on the brisk side, Lubbock's pacing is nevertheless convincing; the playing is responsive, if not as polished as on Beecham's famous version. There is no want of character here and the recording is first class, but ultimately this is not a performance to resonate in the memory, though the slow movement has grace. Very good sound, and the price is competitive.

Symphonies Nos 5 in B flat, D.485; 8 in B min. (Unfinished), D.759.
*** Decca Dig. **414 371-2** [id]. VPO, Solti.
*** CBS **MK 42048** [id.]. Columbia SO or NYPO, Bruno Walter.
(M) **(*) HMV **CDM7 69016** [id.]. BPO, Karajan.

As with Solti's fresh, resilient and persuasive reading of the *Great C major* with the Vienna Philharmonic, his coupling of Nos 5 and 8 brings one of his most felicitous recordings. There have been more charming versions of No. 5 but few that so beautifully combine freshness with refined polish. The *Unfinished* has Solti adopting measured speeds but with his refined manner keeping total concentration. Excellent recording.

Bruno Walter brings special qualities of warmth and lyricism to the *Unfinished.* Affection, gentleness and humanity are the keynotes of this performance; while the first movement of the *Fifth* is rather measured, there is much loving attention to detail in the *Andante*. The 1961 recording emerges fresh and glowing in its CD format and, like the rest of the Walter series, completely belies its age. The sound is richly expansive as well as clear, and the CD is in every way satisfying.

Karajan's EMI coupling is taken from the complete cycle of Schubert symphonies which he recorded in the late 1970s. The performance of the *Unfinished* may lack the mystery and dark intensity of his DG recording of the work (see below), but both No. 5 and No. 8 here find Karajan at his freshest and least complicated. The mannered style which sometimes mars his Schubert is completely absent. With full, clear sound and superb playing, it makes a good mid-price coupling.

Symphonies Nos 5 in B flat, D.485; 9 in C (Great). Rosamunde: Ballet music No. 1, D.797.
(B) *** DG Walkman *419 389-4* [id.]. BPO, Boehm.

Boehm's version of No. 5 makes a perfect coupling for his *Great C major*: the first movement is wonderfully light and relaxed, the slow movement, though also relaxed, never seems to outstay its welcome, and in the last two movements the Berlin playing makes for power as well as lightness. Boehm's Berlin *Ninth* stands in the lyrical Furtwängler tradition. His modification of tempo in the various sections of the first movement is masterly in its finesse, often so subtle that it requires close attention to be spotted. In the slow movement the rhythmic spring to the repeated quavers is delectable. Nor is there any lack of drama in the performance, although in the finale, taken rather fast, the playing is slightly less gripping; even so, there is excitement in plenty. The recording is full and resonant.

Symphony No. 8 in B min. (Unfinished), D.759.
❀ *** DG Dig. **410 862-2**; *410 862-4* [id.]. Philh. O, Sinopoli – MENDELSSOHN: *Symphony No. 4.****
(M) *** DG **415 848-2**; *415 848-4* [id.]. BPO, Karajan – MENDELSSOHN: *Symphony No. 4.****
(M) *** HMV **CDM7 69227-2** [id.]. Philh. O, Karajan – BRAHMS: *Symphony No. 2.****
** Telarc Dig. **CD 80090** [id.]. Cleveland O, Dohnányi – BEETHOVEN: *Symphony No. 8.***(*)

Sinopoli here repeats a coupling made famous by Cantelli with the same orchestra (his World Records reissue, now withdrawn). Sinopoli secures the most ravishingly refined and beautiful playing; the orchestral blend, particularly of the woodwind and horns, is magical. It is a deeply concentrated reading of the *Unfinished*, bringing out much unexpected detail, with every phrase freshly turned in seamless spontaneity. The contrast, as Sinopoli sees it, is between the dark – yet never histrionic – tragedy of the first movement, relieved only partially by the lovely second subject, and the sunlight of the closing movement, giving an unforgettable, gentle radiance. The exposition repeat is observed, adding weight and substance. This takes its place among the recorded classics. The warmly atmospheric recording, made in Kingsway Hall, is very impressive and on CD the opening pages of each movement are wonderfully telling, with pianissimo orchestral tone projected against the silent background. The refinement of detail is matched by the drama inherent in the wide dynamic range. This is one of the finest compact discs yet to come from DG.

Karajan's 1966 recording of the *Unfinished* had a long catalogue life at full price and is now fully recommendable in the mid-range. Its merits of simplicity and directness are enhanced by the extraordinary polish of the orchestral playing, lighting up much that is often obscured. The first movement is extremely compelling in its atmosphere; the slow movement too brings tinglingly precise attack and a wonderful sense of drama. The recording was originally first rate; it sounds fresher still in remastered form. There is a splendid cassette.

Karajan's earlier *Unfinished* with the Philharmonia dates from the late 1950s. It is without any question a most beautiful account, and yet there is no attempt at beautification. The quality of the playing is remarkably fine and can hold its own against most of the mid-priced alternatives – and some of the full-price competition too. There is no question that this Karajan record belongs among the finest; given the coupling (Brahms's *Second Symphony*), this must be accounted an outstanding bargain.

If Dohnányi's reading lacks a little in poetry and magic, it presents a fresh and direct view, beautifully played. He omits the exposition repeat in the first movement. Like the Beethoven symphony on the reverse, this one is treated to a rather less bright recording than one expects from Telarc.

Symphony No. 8 in B min. (Unfinished); Rosamunde: Overture (Die Zauberharfe, D.644); Entr'actes Nos 1–3; Ballet music Nos 1 & 2; Shepherd's melody.
(M) *(*) Ph. **420 715-2**; *420 715-4* [id.]. Concg. O, Haitink.

Symphony No. 8 in B min. (Unfinished), D.759; Rosamunde: Overture (Die Zauberharfe, D.644); Ballet music Nos 1 and 2, D.797.
** Tel. Dig. **ZK8 43187** [id.]. VSO, Harnoncourt.

Harnoncourt takes a weighty view of the *Unfinished*, slow and rather solid in the first movement. The playing is commendably refined, but the full-ranging recording is not ideally clear. The performance of the *Rosamunde* music is more successful, strong and dramatic if lacking in charm.

Haitink's 1975 recording of the *Unfinished* is disappointingly dull. It is a bad sign when one does not welcome the exposition repeat in the first movement. The *Rosamunde* items are, however, very successful in their simplicity and natural sensitivity, although here the recording is not sharply defined.

Symphony No. 8 (Unfinished), D.759, including completed *Scherzo* and *Allegro* from *Rosamunde*, D.797 (arr. Newbould); *Symphonic fragments, D.708a* (completed and orch, Newbould).
*** Ph. **412 472-2** [id.]. ASMF, Marriner.

On CD the *Unfinished* from Marriner and the Academy – as it does in their boxed set – comes with a completion suggested by Professor Brian Newbould in which the Scherzo is filled out and the *B minor Entr'acte* from *Rosamunde* is used as finale; as makeweight, the CD has a generous offering in the four-movement outline of a complete *Symphony*, also in D, D.708a. All are immaculately done.

Symphony No. 8 (Unfinished), D.759; Rosamunde: Overture (Die Zauberharfe), D.644; Ballet music Nos 1 and 2; Entr'acte in B flat.
(*) Ph. Dig. **410 393-2 [id.]. Boston SO, C. Davis.

Symphony No. 8 (Unfinished), D.759; Rosamunde: Ballet music Nos 1 and 2.
(B) **(*) DG Walkman *413 157-4*. BPO, Boehm – SCHUMANN: *Symphony No. 1* etc.**(*)

Sir Colin Davis offers a strong, direct account of the *Unfinished*, the first movement taken briskly but beautifully played. The magic of the disc is concentrated on the second side where the refined, nicely sprung performances of the *Rosamunde* music are consistently refreshing. Warm Boston recording, made a degree clearer in the compact disc version.

Boehm conducts a glowing performance of the *Unfinished*, a splendid sampler of the Schubert cycle he recorded with the Berlin Philharmonic around 1960. The opening of the development in the first movement – always a key moment – gives the perfect example of Boehm magic. It is coupled with Kubelik's Schumann on the bargain-priced Walkman tape. Only two items from *Rosamunde* are included and, with a fairly long stretch of blank tape at the side-end, one wonders why the *Overture* could not have been added. The sound is excellent.

Symphony No. 9 in C (Great), D.944.
*** Virgin Dig. **VC 790708-2**; *VC 700708-4* [id.]. O of Age of Enlightenment, Mackerras.
*** Decca **400 082-2** [id.]. VPO, Solti.
(M) *** DG **419 484-2**; *419 484-4* [id.]. Dresden State O, Boehm.
(M) *** HMV **CDM7 69199-2** [id.]. LPO, Boult.
(*) HMV Dig. **CDC7 47478-2 [id.]; *EL 270500-4*. Dresden State O, Tate.
(*) CBS **MK 42049 [id.]. Columbia SO, Bruno Walter.
(*) DG Dig. **413 437-2 [id.]. Chicago SO, Levine.
** Denon Dig. **C37 7371** [id.]. Berlin State O, Suitner.
** Telarc Dig. **CD 80111** [id.]. Cleveland O, Dohnányi.
*(*) HMV Dig. **CDC7 47697-2** [id.]. VPO, Muti.
* CBS Dig. **MK 42316** [id.]. BPO, Barenboim.

Symphony No. 9 in C (Great); Symphonic fragments in D, D.615.
*** Ph. Dig. **412 474-2** [id.]. ASMF, Marriner.

Symphony No. 9 in C (Great); Rosamunde: overture (Die Zauberharfe), D.644.
(***) DG mono **413 660-2** [id.]. BPO, Furtwängler.

Symphony No. 9 in C (Great); Rosamunde: Overture; Entr'acte No. 2; Ballet No. 2.
(B) **(*) DG Dig. *423 262-4* [id.]. Chicago SO, Levine.

In the first recording to use period instruments, Sir Charles Mackerras and the Orchestra of the Age of Enlightenment on the Virgin Classics label give a winning performance, one that will delight both those who prefer conventional performance and devotees of the new authenticity. The characterful rasp and bite of period brass instruments and the crisp attack of timpani are much more striking than any thinness of string tone. It is a performance of outstanding freshness and resilience. Except in the first-movement allegro, speeds are on the fast side, with characteristically light, clean articulation, and with rhythms delectably sprung, making for extra clarity. With every single repeat observed, the heavenly length is joyfully as well as powerfully sustained, and the warm, atmospheric recording gives a fine sense of presence.

Sir George Solti is not the first conductor one thinks of as a Schubertian, but the *Great C major symphony* prompted him to one of the happiest and most glowing of all his many records, an outstanding version, beautifully paced and sprung in all four movements and superbly played and recorded. It has drama as well as lyrical feeling, but above all it has a natural sense of spontaneity and freshness, beautifully caught by the richly balanced recording, outstanding on compact disc. Here the slow movement in particular has wonderful refinement of detail so that one hears things missed even at a live performance, yet there is no sense that the added clarity is in any way unnatural. The silence which follows the central climax is breathtaking, and towards the end, when the melody is decorated by pizzicatos running through the orchestra, the feeling of presence is uncanny. Few of the first generation of CDs show more readily the advantages of the new technology than this, at the same time confirming the Vienna Sofiensaal as an ideal recording location.

Furtwängler gives the *Great C major* a glowing performance, if a highly individual one. The first movement brings an outstanding example of his wizardry, when he takes the recapitulation at quite a different speed from the exposition and still makes it sound convincing. In the *Andante*, his very slow tempo is yet made resilient by fine rhythmic pointing. The CD brings a sizeable bonus in *Rosamunde*, not as well recorded as the *Symphony*, the sound boxier, though clear enough; however, Furtwängler springs the main allegro with an attractive jauntiness. No apologies need be made for the sound in the *Symphony*. The mono recording dates from 1951 and, like Furtwängler's Haydn/Schumann coupling, was made in the Jesus Christ Church in West Berlin. The sound is fresh and very well balanced, with the dynamic range in the slow movement strikingly wide.

Taken from his collected edition of Schubert symphonies, Sir Neville Marriner's account of the *Great C major* makes up for any lack of weight with the fresh resilience of the playing, consistently well sprung. Though all repeats are observed, bringing the timing of the symphony to over an hour, an attractive fill-up is provided – as on the original six-disc set – in the little two-movement fragment, D.615, orchestrated by Brian Newbould. Written just after the *Sixth Symphony*, it consists of a slow introduction and first-movement exposition, plus a fragment of a sonata-rondo finale, which similarly breaks off. First-rate recording.

Boehm's Dresden performance was recorded live in January 1979, and presented marvellous evidence of his continuing energy in his mid-eighties. If anything, this is a more volatile performance than the glowing one included in his cycle of the Schubert symphonies, with a notable relaxation for the second subject in the first movement and extreme slowing before the end. The slow movement is fastish, with dotted rhythms crisply pointed and a marked slowing for the cello theme after the great dissonant climax. The Scherzo is sunny and lilting, the finale fierce and fast. It may not be quite as immaculate as the studio-recorded version, but it is equally a superb document of Boehm's mastery as a Schubertian, and the recording, though a little edgy on brass, has fine range. The tape is lively, too.

A splendidly wise and magisterial account from the doyen of British conductors. Sir Adrian's tendency to understate is evident in the slow movement, just as his feeling for the overall design is undiminished. The LPO respond with playing of high quality, and the EMI engineers have produced good results too. An eminently sound recommendation alongside Boehm's at mid-price.

Jeffrey Tate with the Dresden State Orchestra takes a rugged and spacious view, surprisingly echoing the four-square strength of Klemperer in this work. His rhythmic resilience, with dotted rhythms crisply sprung, consistently lightens what might otherwise seem heavy and over-emphatic. As with Klemperer and others, the choice of speeds on the slow side encourages a steadier pulse, with traditional, unmarked variations of tempo generally avoided. With all repeats observed, the ruggedness may be too much for some, when the finale for example is grimmer and less smiling than usual. Also the horn solo at the very start has rather wide vibrato. Otherwise the Dresden playing is characteristically refined and strong, given a pleasant bloom by the warm, helpful recording. There is a fair cassette.

Bruno Walter's 1959 CBS recording has been impressively enhanced on CD; the warm ambience of the sound – yet with no lack of rasp on the trombones – seems ideal for his very relaxed reading. The performance has less grip than Furtwängler's, while Solti shows greater spontaneity; but in the gentler passages there are many indications of Walter's mastery, not least in the lovely playing at the introduction of the second subject of the *Andante*. The mannered reading of the slow introduction gets the work off to a bad start, but the overall pacing of the outer movements has a firm momentum, and the closing section of each is very well managed. With much affectionate detail in the slow movement and an attractive Schubertian lilt to the Scherzo, there is much to admire, even if this never quite achieves the distinction of the conductor's earlier recordings of this symphony.

Levine conducts a refined performance, beautifully played and excellently recorded, especially on CD, which is commendably free from mannerism, yet may on that account seem under-characterized. He omits the exposition repeats in the outer movements (just as was universally done till recently). Conversely, all the repeats in the Scherzo are observed, which unbalances the structure. On the attractive Pocket Music tape, which costs far less than the CD, there is a miniature suite of music from *Rosamunde* as a bonus and the sound is excellent.

Recorded in East Berlin, Suitner's version brings a plain and direct reading, remarkable mainly for observing every single repeat, even the exposition in the finale, with the total time close on an hour. With the sound of the strings pleasantly recessed to give an agreeable bloom, the recording is faithful without being spectacular. The violins are not always consistent, sounding feeble in the Scherzo but cleanly resilient in the finale.

Dohnányi paces the first movement briskly and is not subtle enough to accommodate the second subject flexibly within his conception. The slow movement is beautifully played. In the Scherzo Dohnányi is less generous with repeats than Levine (and Suitner), and the overall effect of the reading is lightweight. The Telarc sound is warm and spacious but not brightly lit; the woodwind solos, though placed in believable perspective, lack vividness.

Muti's reading with the Vienna Philharmonic is bright and polished, finely detailed; but at no point does it lift in inspiration to convey Schubertian joy in the way that, for example, Solti's reading with the same orchestra consistently does. Speeds are generally well chosen, but the end of the first movement brings the sort of exaggerated series of rallentandos that one thought had been left behind years ago. The recording, while full ranging, is not one of EMI's cleanest.

Barenboim's reading in his Berlin series is disappointing, lacking the bite of spontaneity that always used to mark his records, at times – despite the refinement of the playing – even stodgy, notably in the slow movement. The trio is sluggish too, while the finale is rushed breathlessly, The recording, congested in tuttis, adds to the disappointment.

CHAMBER AND INSTRUMENTAL MUSIC

Arpeggione sonata, D.821 (arr. for cello).

*** Ph. Dig. **412 230-2** [id.]. Maisky, Argerich – SCHUMANN: *Fantasiestücke* etc.***

(M) *** RCA **GD 86531**; *GK 86531* [RCA **6531-2-RG**]. Lynn Harrell, James Levine – DVOŘÁK: *Cello concerto*.***

(*) Decca **417 833-2 [id.]. Rostropovich, Britten – DEBUSSY: *Sonata*; SCHUMANN: *5 Stücke*.***

The *Arpeggione* enjoyed too brief a life for it to have an extensive literature, and Schubert's *Sonata* is about the only work written for it that survives in the repertoire. To put it mildly, it is not one of Schubert's most substantial works; but even those who do not care for it should hear Mischa Maisky and Martha Argerich play it, for they make much more of it than any of their rivals. Their approach may be relaxed, but they bring much pleasure for their variety of colour and sensitivity. The Philips recording is in the very best traditions of the house.

Lynn Harrell's account of the *Arpeggione* with James Levine makes an excellent medium-priced choice. He is refreshingly unmannered and yet full of personality. Vital, sensitive playing excellently recorded, though the digitally remastered sound is rather light in bass.

Rostropovich gives a curiously self-indulgent interpretation of Schubert's slight but amiable *Arpeggione sonata*. The playing of both artists is eloquent and it is beautifully recorded, but it will not be to all tastes. However, the record is particularly valuable for the sake of the couplings. The remastered recording has fine body and presence.

Arpeggione sonata, D.821 (arr. in G min. for clarinet & piano).
*** Chan. Dig. **CHAN 8566**; *ABTD 1216* [id.]. Gervase de Peyer, Gwenneth Pryor – SCHUMANN: *Fantasiestücke*; *3 Romances*; WEBER: *Silvana variations*.***

So persuasive is the performance of Gervase de Peyer and Gwenneth Pryor that the listener is all but persuaded that the work was actually written for this combination. With rich timbre and affectionate phrasing, de Peyer brings out all its Schubertian charm. His many touches of colouristic detail are a delight, and with a most realistic recording in an agreeably resonant acoustic this makes delightful listening. There is an outstanding cassette too, very much a state-of-the-art transfer.

Arpeggione sonata in A min. (arr. for flute); *Introduction and variations on Trock'ne Blumen* from *Die schöne Müllerin; Schwanengesang: Ständchen, D.957/4.*
(*) RCA Dig. **RD 70421. James Galway, Phillip Moll.

This record is obviously addressed to Galway's many admirers. The *Arpeggione sonata* transcribes surprisingly well for the flute, and is played with skill and some charm by this partnership. The *Introduction and variations on Trock'ne Blumen* are designed for the medium and are as neatly played. Not an important issue, but those who enjoy Galway's music making will not be disappointed by this pleasing and well-recorded recital.

Octet in F, D.803.
*** Ph. **416 497-2** [id.]. ASMF Chamber Ens.
(*) DG Dig. **423 367-2 [id.]. Kremer, Van Keulen, Zimmermann, Geringas, Posch, Brunner, Vlatkovic, Thunemann.
(M) *(*) EMI Dig. *TC-EMX 2109*. Andrew Marriner, Warnock, Williams, Martin, Chilingirian Qt.

The Chamber Ensemble of the Academy of St Martin-in-the-Fields offer one of the very best versions of this endearing work. Everything is vital, yet polished and sensitive. The recording is beautifully balanced, and the performance has a warmth and freshness that justify the acclaim with which this issue was greeted when it was first issued in 1978. The analogue recording is smoothly realistic but lacks something in clarity of internal definition compared with a modern digital recording, although the compact disc transfer retains all the bloom of the original LP.

The DG version has the advantage of an excellent digital recording. The work was recorded during a series of live performances and the playing communicates strongly. The only snag is in the finale where the pacing tends to let the music seem too leisurely and there is not enough rhythmic lift in the playing to compensate. The ASMF group have a lighter touch here.

The bargain version on the Eminence label is very well recorded, with fine presence and plenty of bloom on all the instruments, but the performance lacks the charm and imaginative sparkle which this very long work calls for if its magic is to come over on record. This is more an accomplished run-through than a real performance. The tape transfer, however, is excellent.

Piano quintet in A (Trout), D.667.
*** Decca Dig. **411 975-2** [id.]. András Schiff, Hagen Qt.
*** Ph. **400 078-2** [id.]. Brendel, Cleveland Qt.
(*) HMV Dig. **CDC7 47009-2 [id.]. Sviatoslav Richter, Borodin Qt.
(M) ** CBS **MYK 42525** [**MYK 37234**]. Rudolf Serkin, Laredo, Naegele, Parnas, Levine.
(M) ** Ph. **420 716-2**; *420 716-4* [id.]. Beaux Arts Trio (augmented) – BEETHOVEN: *Piano trio No. 5 (Ghost).****
(B) ** DG Walkman *413 854-4* [id.]. Demus, Schubert Qt – BEETHOVEN: *Ghost trio* **; MOZART: *Hunt quartet.****
(B) *(*) Cirrus Dig. **CICD 1008**. Bingham, Wilde, Kennard, Robertson, Brittain.
* HMV Dig. **CDC7 47448-2** [id.]; *EL 270371-4*. Leonskaja, Alban Berg Qt (augmented).

(i) *Piano quintet in A (Trout)*; (ii) *String quartet No. 14 (Death and the Maiden).*
(M) **(*) Decca **417 459-2**; *417 459-4* [id.]. (i) Curzon, Vienna Octet (members); (ii) VPO Qt.

(i) *Piano quintet (Trout); String quartet No. 12 (Quartettsatz).*
(*) DG **413 453-2 [id.]. (i) Gilels; Amadeus Qt (augmented).

(i) *Piano quintet (Trout); Piano sonata No. 20 in A, D.959.*
(**) Arabesque mono **Z 6571** [id.]. Artur Schnabel, (i) Pro Arte Qt (augmented).

András Schiff with the talented young players of the Hagen Quartet – a family group from Austria of exceptional promise – gives a delectably fresh and youthful reading of the *Trout quintet*, full of the joys of spring, but one which is also remarkable for hushed concentration, as in the exceptionally dark and intense account of the opening of the first movement. Schiff, unlike many virtuosi, remains one of a team, emphatically not a soloist in front of accompanists; particularly on CD the recording balance confirms that, with the piano rather behind the strings but firmly placed. The Scherzo brings a light, quick and bouncing performance, and there is extra lightness too in the other middle movements. Unlike current rivals, this version observes the exposition repeat in the finale, and with such a joyful, brightly pointed performance one welcomes that.

The Brendel/Cleveland performance may lack something in traditional Viennese charm, but it has a compensating vigour and impetus, and the work's many changes of mood are encompassed with freshness and subtlety. The second-movement *Andante* is radiantly played, and the immensely spirited Scherzo has a most engagingly relaxed trio, with Brendel at his most persuasive. His special feeling for Schubert is apparent throughout: the deft pictorial imagery at the opening of the variations is delightful. The recording is well balanced and truthful. The compact disc is smooth and refined, but lacks something in upper range and sharpness of detail.

The Decca CD and tape which combine Clifford Curzon's 1958 recording of the *Trout* with the Vienna Philharmonic String Quartet's 1964 version of the *Death and the Maiden quartet* is an obvious CD pairing, with the overall timing of 71′ 22″ well within the limits of the format. The *Trout* is a classic performance, with a distinguished account of the piano part and splendidly stylish support from the Vienna players. Schubert's warm lyricism is caught with remarkable freshness. Some might find the brilliant Scherzo a little too fierce to match the rest of the performance, but such vigorous playing introduces an element of contrast at the centre of the interpretation and makes possible a disarmingly relaxed account of the last movement. The Vienna Philharmonic performance treats *Death and the Maiden* with comparable affection; the playing is peerless, Boskovsky, the leader, showing all his skill and musicianship in the variations. The team bring a genuinely Viennese quality to the Scherzo which is most fetching. The recordings have been carefully remastered; both have a pleasingly warm ambience and, in the *Trout*, the piano timbre is appealingly full in colour, but here the upper range is noticeably thin. The performance is so marvellously alive that the ear readily adjusts, and in the string quartet the upper range is fuller. The well-managed cassette retains the vividness but is smoother on top.

Richter dominates the HMV digital recording of the *Trout quintet*, not only in personality but in balance. Yet the performance has marvellous detail, with many felicities drawn to the attention that might have gone unnoticed in other accounts. The first movement is played very vibrantly indeed, and the second offers a complete contrast, gently lyrical. The variations have plenty of character; taken as a whole, this is very satisfying, even though other versions are better balanced and are stronger on Schubertian charm. The CD emphasizes the somewhat artificial balance but is certainly not lacking in projection. However, the upper string sound is thin and rather lacking substance.

Also among the full-price *Trouts* that have claims for consideration is the DG issue which includes an excellent account of the *Quartettsatz*. In the main work there is a masterly contribution from Gilels, and the Amadeus play with considerable freshness. The approach is very positive, not as sunny and springlike as in some versions, but rewarding in its seriousness of purpose. On CD, the 1976 analogue recording is enhanced in presence and the balance is convincing.

The performance led by Rudolf Serkin is undoubtedly distinguished with spontaneous if idiosyncratic playing from that master pianist. As a performance this remains a favourite; but in its digitally remastered format the recommendation must be muted because of the forward balance, with a jumbo-sized piano and the strings close and slightly shrill. The sound has plenty of underlying warmth and this is certainly vintage music-making, with Levine's double-bass resounding agreeably at the bottom.

The Beaux Arts *Trout* is a delightfully fresh performance. Every phrase is splendidly alive, there is no want of vitality and sensitivity, and the recording is basically well balanced. The snag is again the digital remastering which gives undue prominence to Isidore Cohen's violin, lighting it up brightly and thinning down the timbre. On the cassette, which is much smoother, this problem is minimized.

An agreeable if not distinctive performance on the Walkman tape, with Demus dominating, partly because the piano recording and balance are bold and forward and the string tone is thinner. There is – as befits the name of the string group – a real feeling for Schubert, and the performance has spontaneity. The first movement is especially arresting, and the *Theme and variations* are well shaped. The tape transfer is well managed; however, the Amadeus recording of the first movement of Mozart's *Hunt quartet* follows immediately after the end of the *Trout*, and their string timbre, fuller and firmer, emphasizes the relative lack of body of the Schubert recording. The other work included is Beethoven's *Ghost piano trio*.

Artur Schnabel's *Trout* was recorded in 1935 and will sound pretty faded to most listeners: the performance is totally straightforward and unencumbered by the slightest trace of sentimentality. The Pro Arte, one of the greatest quartets of the inter-war years, convey a refreshing sense of joy. Schnabel's magisterial account of the *A major Sonata*, made two years later, was one of the classics of the pre-war record scene and it is good to have it back. As always with Schnabel, this performance is not the last word in pianistic polish, but it is full of splendid insights.

John Bingham is as sensitive and perceptive as he is underrated, and his contribution to this Cirrus bargain-offer *Trout* is always deeply musical. Unfortunately the balance does not achieve a particularly convincing aural picture: the violin often seems reticent, and the overall performance, though full of musicianly touches, is wanting in stronger character.

EMI's record with Elisabeth Leonskaja, the Alban Berg Quartet and the ubiquitous Georg

Hörtnagel excited the highest expectations and, in the end, keenest disappointments. Despite the excellence of the recording and some incidental beauties, it remains a curiously uninvolving performance with routine gestures. There is little real freshness here and Leonskaja's playing is not rich in sensitivity or in variety of colour. Not the strong contender one would expect.

There is also an RCA CD version of the *Trout* by Emanuel Ax and the Guarneri Quartet, curiously coupled with an agreeable chamber-music version of Mozart's *Eine kleine Nachtmusik*. Ax is a thoughtful, intelligent pianist who on record too rarely projects his personality quite magnetically enough. That point is brought out here, when the balance rather favours the piano. Only recommendable at premium price if the coupling is especially suitable (RCA **RD 85167**).

Piano trio No. 1 in B flat, D.898; Notturno in E flat, D.897.
** Novalis Dig. **150 002-2**; *150 002-4* [id.]. Oppitz, Sitkovetsky, Geringas.

Piano trio No. 2 in E flat, D.929; Sonata in B flat, D.28.
** Novalis Dig. **150 003-2**; *150 003-4* [id.]. Oppitz, Sitkovetsky, Geringas.

Piano trios Nos 1–2; Notturno in E flat, D.897; Sonata in B flat, D.28.
** Ph. Dig. **412 620-2** (2) [id.]. Beaux Arts Trio.

Collectors who have the older Beaux Arts recordings of the Schubert *Trios* (or indeed the splendid Suk performance of the *B flat Trio* coupled with the *Notturno* on Supraphon) need look no further, for although this new set is much better recorded, the performances are not quite as fresh and spontaneous as the earlier issues.

The Novalis alternatives are not entirely the answer either. The recording is forwardly balanced, less natural-sounding than the Philips, and the piano timbre is very bright. The performances are highly musical and direct but they are less strong on charm. The music is given structural substance and the players are generous with repeats, but this music making seems objective rather than smiling. Sitkovetsky plays with fine tone and his phrasing has a natural classical line, but overall these performances are not wholly satisfying.

Piano trio No. 1 in B flat, D.898.
** Chan. Dig. **CHAN 8308**; *ABTD 1064* [id.]. Borodin Trio.
** CRD Dig. **CRD 3438**; *CRDC 4138* [id.]. Israel Piano Trio.

The Borodin Trio gives a warm and characterful interpretation, with natural expressiveness only occasionally overloaded with rubato. The impression is very much of a live performance, though in fact this is a studio recording marked by full and open sound. As the compact disc shows, the microphone balance is a little close, giving a slightly resiny focus to the strings. Otherwise there is fine presence and most realistic separation. This applies also to the chrome cassette, although here the upper range is slightly more abrasive.

The CRD version with the Israel Piano Trio does not materially affect current recommendations. It is all thoroughly musical: a broadly conceived and straightforward account, very well recorded in both media but offering no special illumination. No disrespect is intended by saying that playing of this order can be heard in any good concert hall anywhere in the world, Having heard and enjoyed it once, one would not rush to hear it again.

Piano trio No. 2 in E flat, D.929.
(*) Chan. Dig. **CHAN 8324; *ABTD 1045* [id.]. Borodin Trio.

Piano trio No. 2 in E flat; (i) *Fantasia in C, D.934.*
(M) (***) EMI mono **CDH7 61014-2** [id.]. (i) Rudolf Serkin, (ii) with A. and H. Busch.

On the EMI Référence CD by Rudolf Serkin, Adolf and Hermann Busch, the dated sound – the *Trio* from 1936 and the *Fantasy* made as long ago as 1931 – cannot dim these marvellous performances; one can only rejoice that they are again available for study by a younger generation of players and the musical nourishment of us all.

The Borodin Trio gives a strong and understanding performance of the *B flat Trio*, generally preferring spacious tempi. The outer movements are made the more resilient, and only in the Scherzo does the reading lack impetus. The speed for the slow movement is nicely chosen to allow a broad, steady pulse. The pianist is not always at her most subtle, but there is a sense of enjoyment here to which one responds. The compact disc is lifelike and present. The cassette is admirably clear and well balanced, though the sound seems drier in the treble.

String quartets Nos 1–15.
(M) **(*) DG **419 879-2** (6) [id.]. Melos Qt of Stuttgart.

Apart from the Endres (in an old Vox box), no other quartet has tackled a complete Schubert cycle, and the Melos put us in their debt by so doing. The early quartets have an altogether disarming grace and innocence, and some of their ideas are most touching. The Melos are an impressive body whose accounts of this repertoire are unmannered and on the whole sympathetic. They are let down by recording quality that is less than distinguished, but there is no other reason for qualifying enthusiasm for this valuable release. On CD the number of records is decreased by one and they are offered at medium price. The remastering, too, has brought added presence.

String quartets Nos 8 in B flat, D.112; 13 in A min., D.804.
*** ASV Dig. **CDDCA 593**; *ZCDCA 593* [id.]. Lindsay Qt.

In the glorious *A minor* the Lindsays lead the field. It would be difficult to fault their judgement so far as tempi and expression are concerned. Every phrase seems to arise naturally from what has gone before, and dynamics are always the result of musical thinking rather than cosmetic calculation. They are every bit as successful in their account of the *B flat Quartet* (D.112, or Op. 168 as it used to be called) and the recording team has done them much credit. The cassette offers smooth, pleasant sound, but ideally needed a somewhat higher level of transfer.

String quartets Nos. 9 in G min., D.173; 13 in A min., D.804.
(*) Tel. **ZK8 43341 [id.]. Alban Berg Qt.

The Alban Berg recorded this account of the *A minor* in 1975 and – in spite of the more generous coupling (the *Death and the Maiden*) offered in their more recent EMI version – this is to be preferred. It matches the latter in tonal finesse and perfection of ensemble and surpasses it in terms of spontaneity. The *G minor Quartet* is fine; on balance, both are better played here than by the Melos Quartet of Stuttgart, whose complete set is now available in the new medium.

String quartets Nos 10 in E flat, D.87; 12 in C min. (Quartettsatz), D.703; 13 in A min., D.804.
(*) DG Dig. **419 171-2; *419 171-4* [id.]. Hagen Qt.

The young Hagen Quartet, three of whose members are brothers and a sister, is of the highest quality, and their artistry has already brought them many prizes and a large public following: they possess a quite wonderful unanimity of ensemble and great tonal finesse. They also have a wide dynamic range and at the fortissimo end of the spectrum never make an ugly sound; nor, in the faster movements, do they ever cultivate virtuosity for its own sake. All the same there is more to Schubert than they find. Indeed, they come close to skating over the surface of the slow movement of the *A minor*, whose pathos they communicate only partially, and in the opening theme their gifted young leader seems a little too engrossed in his own beauty of phrasing and only just falls short of being narcissistic. One hopes they will not become the victims of their own tonal sophistication, because their musicianship is superb and as an ensemble they are second to none. There is a good cassette, but the CD has a sharper focus and greater transparency.

String quartets Nos 10 in E flat, D.87 (finale only); *14 in D min.* (*Death and the Maiden*), *D.810.*
** Sup. Dig. **C37 7546** [id.]. Smetana Qt.

The Supraphon version was recorded by the Smetana Quartet at a concert performance in Japan in November 1978, the finale of the early *E flat Quartet* being an encore. It is just a little disappointing: predictably, theirs is a good, straightforward performance but with less warmth and freshness than one expects from this illustrious ensemble. Nor is it as beautifully recorded as the finest rivals now on offer.

String quartet No. 12 in C min. (*Quartettsatz*), *D.703.*
*** CRD *CRDC 4034* [id.]. Alberni Qt – BRAHMS: *String sextet No. 1.****

A fresh and agreeably warm account of this fine single-movement work, originally intended as part of a full string quartet but finally left by Schubert to stand on its own. The coupling with the Brahms *Sextet* is appropriate, for it was Brahms who in 1870 arranged for the first publication of the *Quartettsatz*. The recording is first class, and the cassette transfer is of excellent quality; this can be highly recommended.

String quartets Nos 12 in C min. (*Quartettsatz*), *D.703; 14 in D min.* (*Death and the Maiden*), *D.810.*
*** Tel Dig. **ZK8 42868** [id.]. Vermeer Qt.
*** ASV Dig. **CDDCA 560**; *ZCDCA 560* [id.]. Lindsay Qt.
*** MMG Dig. **MCD 10004** [id.]. Tokyo Qt.
(*) DG Dig. **410 024-2 [id.]. Amadeus Qt.
(B) **(*) DG Walkman *415 333-4* [id.]. Amadeus Qt – BEETHOVEN: *Archduke trio.***(*)

String quartets Nos 13 in A min., D.804; 14 in D min. (*Death and the Maiden*), *D.810.*
(*) HMV Dig. **CDC7 47333-2 [id.]. Alban Berg Qt.

String quartet No. 14 in D min. (*Death and the Maiden*), *D.810.*
(M) *** Ph. **420 876-2**; *420 876-4* [id.]. Italian Qt – DVOŘÁK: *Quartet No. 12* *** (with BORODIN: *Nocturne* ***).
** Ph. Dig. **412 127-2** [id.]. Orlando Qt.

The Vermeer Quartet have thought deeply and to good effect about this *Quartet*, and are thoroughly scrupulous in observing both the spirit and the letter of the score. Indeed, there is nothing in the least routine about this reading: it has a splendid grasp of architecture – yet it is not over-intellectual, but conveys something of the grace of the slow movement. In every way – not least the recording quality – this is an impressive disc that can stand with the best. The reverberation of the very last chord of the finale is unfortunately cut short.

The Lindsays are now available on CD, and many listeners may count them first choice. Their intense, volatile account of the first movement of the *Death and the Maiden quartet*, urgently paced, played with considerable metrical freedom and the widest range of dynamic, is balanced by an equally imaginative and individual set of variations with a similar inspirational approach. The hushed opening for the presentation of the famous theme is deceptive, for the tune is made to expand eloquently before the variations begin, while the coda is equally subtle in preparation and realization. The finale has a winning bustle and energy; and the *Quartettsatz*, which acts as the usual filler, is unusually poetic and spontaneous in feeling. The recording is excellent on CD, but the (iron-oxide) tape transfer is less than ideal, with the high level bringing a touch of shrillness on the first side; side two is fuller and smoother, but with the upper range more restricted.

The Italian Quartet offer a fine mid-price CD, coupled with Dvořák and with the Borodin *Nocturne* thrown in for good measure. They bring great concentration and poetic feeling to this wonderful score, and they are free of the excessive point-making to be found in some rival versions. The sound of the reissue is first class on CD; the tape is smoother, less transparent and not as wide-ranging, but still sounds well.

The playing of the Tokyo Quartet is also first class. The performance has tension of the right kind in abundance, and phrasing is eloquent. The first movement has plenty of thrust and there is some imaginative characterization in the variations, while the finale has fine brio. With well-balanced, truthful recording this can be recommended alongside, though not in preference to, the Vermeer coupling.

The HMV issue offers very good value for money. The *Death and the Maiden quartet* usually occupies a whole disc with the *Quartettsatz* thrown in for good measure, but here we are offered two major quartets, marvellously played and truthfully recorded on one disc. In all, there is more than 70 minutes of music, and the only loss is the exposition repeat in the first movement of *Death and the Maiden*. The sleeve note gives no details of the 'original version' which the title billing claims, and it is difficult to determine in what significant way it differs textually from any other. The *A minor Quartet* is beautifully played, though the slow movement (with the theme of the *Rosamunde entr'acte*) is very fast indeed. All the same, even if the playing is breathtaking in terms of tonal blend, ensemble and intonation, one remains strangely unmoved, except perhaps in the minuet and trio of the *A minor*. The clear, clean recording is very brightly lit in its CD format with the sound certainly 'present', but also with a slightly aggressive feeling on fortissimos.

The 1983 Amadeus version of *Death and the Maiden* offers much to admire. The performance has a powerful momentum and though there is some rough playing from Brainin, there is relatively little sentimentality. The actual sound is not as pure as in their very first mono recording, when their blend was superb and the leader's vibrato unobtrusive. Good though it is, this does not displace the Italian Quartet. The compact disc brings impressive presence to the sound, but the balance seems a trifle close.

The Walkman cassette offers the earlier (1960) Amadeus stereo recording. The Quartet gives a wonderful impression of unity as regards the finer points of phrasing, for example at the very beginning of the variations in D.810. This is a worthwhile issue, even if this account of *Death and the Maiden* cannot match that of the Italians. The recording still sounds well, and the chrome-tape transfer is well managed.

The Orlando Quartet is superbly recorded on Philips. Their approach is impassioned, even a little rhetorical, with very pronounced dynamic extremes, and not wholly free from traces of affectation. There are exaggerated expressive touches (hushed pianissimos that draw attention to themselves) which might make this record irksome to replay. It robs Schubert of some of the grace and innocence that are central to his sensibility. It would be difficult to prefer this to the versions by the Vermeer, Lindsay or Italian Quartets. Without a coupling, this issue seems uncompetitive generally.

String quartets Nos 13; 14 (Death and the Maiden); 15.
(M) *** Nimbus **NIM 5048/9** [id.]. Chilingirian Qt.

In their two-disc set of the last three quartets, the Chilingirians give strongly committed, characterful and spontaneous-sounding readings, warmly recorded and full of presence. On the very reasonably priced Nimbus label, they make a most attractive recommendation.

(i) *String quartet No. 14* (*Death and the Maiden*), *D.810* (arr. Mahler; ed. David Matthews and Donald Mitchell). (ii) *Der Tod und das Mädchen.*
*** HMV Dig. **CDC7 47354-2** [id.]; *EL 270376-4*. (i) ECO, Tate; (ii) Ann Murray, Tate.

Never played complete in his lifetime, Mahler's string orchestra arrangement of *Death and the Maiden* makes a fascinating rarity. Only recently, Mahler's daughter noticed that her father's score of this Schubert quartet had virtually complete markings for playing it on a full string orchestra. It was known that he had actually conducted the slow movement in that form. David Matthews and Donald Mitchell then did the detailed work to compile the score used in this performance. In the event, the power and bite of dramatic moments are often intensified and, with his instrumental cunning, Mahler often intensifies Schubert's poetry, giving a haunted quality to the slow movement. Obviously, there are losses as well as gains in an orchestral performance where stresses are fewer. Jeffrey Tate directs the ECO in a satisfyingly dramatic reading. The original song makes an attractive prelude, intelligently sung by Ann Murray, but the disc provides short measure. The cassette offers agreeable sound-quality but the focus is less sharp than the CD.

String quartet No. 15 in G, D.887.
(M) *** HMV **CDC7 49082-2** [id.]. Alban Berg Qt.

In some ways, the Alban Berg players are the most dramatic and technically accomplished of all in this outstanding work. Indeed, they tend to overdramatize: pianissimos are the barest whisper and ensemble has razor-edge precision. They are marvellously recorded, however, and beautifully balanced; but it is the sense of over-projection that somehow disturbs the innocence of some passages. They do not observe the exposition repeat in the first movement. The analogue recording is exceptionally successful in its digital transfer – it has great presence and realism. But at 44′ it seems short measure.

String quintet in C, D.956.
*** ASV Dig. **CDDCA 537**; *ZCDCA 537* [id.]. Lindsay Qt with Douglas Cummings.
*** Decca Dig. **417 115-2** [id.]. Fitzwilliam Qt with Van Kampen.
*** HMV Dig. **CDC7 47018-2** [id.]. Alban Berg Qt with Heinrich Schiff.
*** CBS **MK 39134** [id.]. Cleveland Qt with Yo-Yo Ma.
(*) DG Dig. **419 611-2; *419 611-4* [id.]. Amadeus Qt with Robert Cohen.
(M) * DG **423 543-2** [id.]. Amadeus Qt with William Pleeth (with MOZART: *Adagio and fugue, K. 546* **).

String quintet in C, D.956; String quartet No. 12 (*Quartettsatz*).
(*) CRD **CRD 3310 [id.]. Alberni Qt with Thomas Ingloi.

The Lindsay version gives the impression that one is eavesdropping on music making in the intimacy of a private concert. Although there is plenty of vigour and power, there is nothing of the glamorized and beautified sonority that some great quartets give us. (The two cellos in the Lindsay version, incidentally, are both by the same maker, Francesco Rugeri of Cremona.) They observe the first-movement exposition repeat (as do the Fitzwilliam on Decca, but not so the Alban Berg), and the effortlessness of their approach does not preclude intellectual strength. The first movement surely refutes the notion that Schubert possessed an incomplete grasp of sonata form, an idea prompted by the alleged discursiveness of some of the sonatas. It is surely an amazing achievement, even by the exalted standards of Haydn, Mozart and Beethoven; and the Lindsays do it justice, as indeed they do the ethereal *Adagio*. Here they effectively convey the sense of it appearing motionless, suspended, as it were, between reality and dream, yet at the same time never allowing it to become static. The Lindsays may not enjoy quite the splendour or richness of the Alban Berg, nor in terms of tonal blend do they altogether match their homogeneity, but they have a compelling wisdom. Their reading must rank at the top and, for those who find the Alban Berg account 'too perfect', the Lindsays' will be an obvious first choice. The compact disc is well worth the extra outlay, for it has the additional presence, range and realism this medium offers. The cassette is of only moderate quality; it is inclined to be slightly shrill on top.

The Fitzwilliam Quartet with Van Kampen give a reading exceptionally faithful to Schubert's markings, yet one which, with freshness and seeming spontaneity, conveys the work's masterly power and impulse, too. They observe the exposition repeat in the first movement and play the second group with effortless elegance and lovely pianissimo tone. The melody is the more affecting in its simple tenderness when played, as here, exactly as the composer intended. The reading overall is deeply thoughtful, never exaggerated in expressiveness but naturally compelling. The great *Adagio* has a hushed intensity, played without affectation, and the last two movements are taken challengingly fast. Some might feel tempi are too brisk, yet the Scherzo is the more exhilarating when played presto as marked, and the finale keeps its spring to the very end. Just occasionally in this performance the leader is not absolutely dead in the centre of the note, though intonation is never a serious problem at any time. The recording is outstanding, superbly full and atmospheric. It has remarkable presence, and as usual the CD gives the group even greater tangibility, against the silent background.

Few ensembles offer timbre as full-bodied or richly burnished as that produced by the Alban Berg and Heinrich Schiff, whose recording has impressive sonority and bloom. Admirable though the Fitzwilliams are on Decca, the Alban Berg have the advantage of wonderfully homogeneous tone and, given the sheer polish and gorgeous sound that distinguish their playing, theirs must rank high among current recommendations. The performance is strongly projected and they have the advantage of excellent recording. However, unlike the Lindsays or the Fitzwilliams, they do not observe the first-movement exposition repeat.

The Cleveland Quartet and Yo-Yo Ma have won golden opinions for their account of the *Quintet* on CBS. They are scrupulous in observing dynamic markings (the second subject is both restrained and *pianissimo*) and they also score by making all repeats. Their performance has feeling and eloquence, as well as a commanding intellectual grip. Moreover, they are admirably recorded and thus present a strong challenge to both the Lindsays and the Fitzwilliam Quartet on Decca.

The Amadeus version with Robert Cohen was the last recording made by that unique quartet before the death of their viola-player, Peter Schidlof. It brings a typically warm and responsive reading, strongly characterized, emphatic even, not quite as refined in ensemble as in earlier Amadeus versions, but benefiting from full, forward digital sound, and with the exposition repeat observed. There is a clearly transferred cassette.

The Alberni and Thomas Igloi give an admirably unaffected and thoughtful account of the *Quintet*. The first movement is refreshingly straightforward and, like the Lindsays, they observe the exposition repeat; the slow movement has a natural simplicity of expression that is affecting. The recording has warmth and splendid definition, even if, by comparison with the Lindsays (ASV) or the Alban Berg (EMI), it has less depth and bloom. Not necessarily a first choice, but a safe one.

Regretfully, the earlier Amadeus version cannot receive a strong recommendation from us. Many find their playing so refined and perfect that this outweighs any reservations they harbour on points of interpretation. But not here. This performance of the *C major Quintet*, Schubert's sublimest utterance, is very mannered and superficial. The reissue includes an account of Mozart's *Adagio and fugue*, K.546, not available before.

MUSIC FOR PIANO DUET

Sonata in C (Grand Duo), D.812; Sonata in B flat (for piano, 4 hands), D.617.
** Hyp. Dig. **CDA 66217**; *KA 66217* [id.]. Peter Noke and Helen Krizos.

Peter Noke and Helen Krizos, a talented husband-and-wife team, give neat, crisply articulated performances of Schubert's duet music, but the *Grand Duo* – a massive inspiration that was once deduced to be the lost *Gastein symphony* – emerges at too small a scale. The performance is not tense enough, failing to measure up to the grandeur of the work's architecture, whatever the felicities of detail. The coupling is a generous one, with the little *B flat Sonata* of 1818, in three compact movements, making a welcome and attractive fill-up.

PIANO MUSIC

Allegretto in C min., D.915; Marche militaire No. 1 in D, D.733; Moments musicaux Nos 1–6, D.780; Piano sonata No. 17 in D, D.850.
(***) Arabesque mono **Z 6573** [id.]. Artur Schnabel.

(i) *Allegro in A min. (Lebensstürme), D.947; Andantino varié in B min., D.823. March in E, D.606; Marches militaires Nos 2 in G; 3 in E flat, D.733; Piano sonata No. 21 in B flat, D.960.*
(***) Arabesque mono **Z 6575** [id.]. Artur Schnabel; (i) with Karl-Ulrich Schnabel.

Our debt to Schnabel is often forgotten. Before he championed them in the inter-war years, the Schubert sonatas were rarely heard in the concert hall. His advocacy soon changed all that, and nowadays our catalogues are rich in duplications. His pioneering and magisterial accounts of the *D major* and *B flat Sonatas*, made in the late 1930s, are full of characteristic insights, though it must be admitted that later recordings of the *B flat* from Kempff and Curzon surpassed him technically. But as always with Schnabel there is imagination of a remarkable order, and both sonatas should be in any well-stocked library. These recordings are now fifty years old and it would be idle to pretend that later versions have not superseded them, but some of the playing Schnabel offers – in the slow movements of both sonatas – will never be less than special.

(i) *Divertissement à la Hongroise in G min., D.818. Marches: in G min.; B min., D.819/2–3.* (ii) Lieder: *Schwanengesang: Der Doppelgänger; Die Stadt. An die Laute; Der Erlkönig; Gruppe aus dem Tartarus; Der Kreuzzug; Der Musensohn.*
(**) Arabesque mono **Z 6574** [id.]. Artur Schnabel; with (i) Karl-Ulrich Schnabel; (ii) Therese Behr-Schnabel.

This is something of a family memento: the genial and touching *Divertissement à la Hongroise* is not at the moment otherwise on CD, though it cannot be long before EMI reissue the Eschenbach and Frantz version. It is a performance of characteristic warmth and humanity. The recordings of the songs, made in 1932, call for a good deal of tolerance, not only on technical grounds: Therese Behr-Schnabel is not a great singer, and the microphones maintain a discreet distance: she is often swamped by her husband from whose accompaniments lessons can still be learnt.

Fantasy in C (Grazer), D.605a; Piano sonata No. 18 in G, D.894.
**(*) Chan. Dig. *ABTD 1075* [id.]. Lydia Artymiw.

The *Grazer-Fantasy* is thought to date from 1817–18; it acquired its title simply because it was discovered in the 1960s among manuscripts once belonging to Schubert's friend, Huttenbrenner. Lydia Artymiw plays it with great expressive freedom and real feeling; she gives an equally romantic account of the *G major Sonata.* Here she is up against Lupu who recorded the work for Decca in the 1970s and has perhaps a stronger grip on its architecture. Nevertheless, this is a useful addition to the catalogue, and the Chandos engineering is quite superb, wide in dynamic range and truthful in timbre.

Fantasia in C (Wanderer), D.760.
*** HMV **CDC7 47967-2**; (M) *EG 291286-4*. Sviatoslav Richter – DVOŘÁK: *Piano concerto.****
*** CBS Dig. **MK 42124**; *IMT 42124* [id.]. Murray Perahia – SCHUMANN: *Fantasia in C.****
(M) *** Ph. **420 644-2**; *420 644-4* [id.]. Alfred Brendel – *Sonata No. 21.****
*** DG **419 672-2** [id.]. Maurizio Pollini – *Sonata No. 16.****
(*) Decca Dig. **417 327-2; *417 327-4* [id.]. Vladimir Ashkenazy – *Sonata No. 21.***(*)

The *Wanderer fantasia* is well served on CD. Richter's masterly account comes from as long ago as 1963 but still sounds well. It makes a superb bonus for his Dvořák *Piano concerto*. The piano timbre is a shade hard, though this is more striking on tape.

Murray Perahia's account of the *Wanderer* stands alongside the finest. In his hands it sounds as fresh as the day it was conceived, and its melodic lines speak with an ardour and subtlety that breathes new life into a score we all thought we knew too well. The recording is more than acceptable, even if it does not wholly convey the wide range of sonority and dynamics Perahia produces in the flesh.

Brendel's playing too is of a high order, and he is superbly recorded. This is coupled with what is perhaps Schubert's greatest *Sonata*, sometimes given a record to itself, or provided with only a small filler, so it is excellent value at mid-price. There is a very good tape.

Pollini's account is outstanding and, though he is not ideally recorded and the piano timbre is shallow, yet the playing shows remarkable insights. Moreover, the coupling is equally fine.

Ashkenazy's is a fine performance too, but let down by the clangorous quality of the recorded sound, acceptable here but not suitable for the great *B flat Sonata*.

Admirers of Wilhelm Kempff may be glad to know that his fine version is available on an inexpensive DG Focus tape, coupled with Beethoven's *Pathétique* and *Moonlight* sonatas. The recording is dry but acceptable (DG *419 657-4*).

Fantasia in C (Wanderer), D.760; Impromptus, D.899/3 & 4; Piano sonata No. 21 in B flat, D. 960.
❀ *** RCA **RD 86527** [**RCA 6527-2-RC**]. Artur Rubinstein.

This CD is among the very finest of all the Rubinstein reissues from the 1960s. He plays the *Wanderer fantasia* with sure magnificence. The extended structure needs a master to hold it together and, particularly in the variations section, Rubinstein is electrifying. He compels attention as though he is improvising the work himself, but even so avoids any sentimentality. The 1965 recording sounds surprisingly full, and it is even better in the two *Impromptus*, played with the most subtle shading of colour and delectable control of rubato, and in the superb account of the *Sonata*. Unaccountably, this has never been issued before, yet it shows Rubinstein as a magically persuasive Schubertian. The first movement is very relaxed (14′ 17″ as against Curzon's 13′ 18″) yet the effect is wonderfully luminous, and a similar inspired and ruminative spontaneity infuses the essentially gentle *Andante*. Then the articulation in the final two movements is a joy, light and crisp in the Scherzo, bolder but never heavy in the finale. Throughout, the great pianist conveys his love for the music, and the playing is wonderfully refined in detail. The sound is remarkably real, with fine presence and almost no shallowness.

Fantasia in D min., D.940.
*** CBS Dig. **MK 39511**; *IMT 39511* [id.]. Murray Perahia, Radu Lupu – MOZART: *Double piano sonata.****

Recorded live at The Maltings during the Aldeburgh Festival, the performance of Lupu and Perahia is full of haunting poetry, with each of these highly individual artists challenging the other in imagination. Where in the Mozart coupling Perahia plays primo, here it is the more recessive Lupu adding to the mellowness of this most inspired of all piano duet works, one of Schubert's supreme masterpieces. Warmly atmospheric recording, caught most naturally on CD, though the chrome tape is less fresh and rather middle-orientated.

Impromptus Nos 1–4, D.899; 5–8, D.935.
*** CBS Dig. **CD 37291** [id.]. Murray Perahia.
*** Ph. **411 040-2** [id.]. Alfred Brendel.
*** Decca Dig. **411 711-2** [id.]; *KSXDC 7594.* Radu Lupu.

Perahia's account of the *Impromptus* is very special indeed and hardly falls short of greatness. Directness of utterance and purity of spirit are of the essence here. As one critic has put it, Perahia's vision brings the impression of a tree opening out, whereas Brendel's suggests the moment of full bloom. The CBS recording is very good, truthful in timbre, with an increase in firmness on CD and added presence.

Brendel's complete set of *Impromptus* on Philips was previously split into two separate groups (each coupled with other music of Schubert). Now they are joined and the result is truly magical. The recording is very natural and rich, with a glowing middle range and fine sonority. It is difficult to imagine finer Schubert playing than this; to find more eloquence, more profound musical insights, one has to go back to Edwin Fischer – and even here comparison is not always to Brendel's disadvantage. The compact disc has been digitally remastered, but the piano image remains slightly diffuse.

Lupu's account of the *Impromptus* is of the same calibre as the Perahia and Brendel versions, and he is most beautifully recorded on CD. Indeed, in terms of natural sound this is the most believable image of the three. Lupu brings his own special insights to these pieces. Sometimes his rubato is almost Chopinesque in its delicacy; but the playing can also be robust and lyrically powerful. Perahia displays a fresher innocence; Brendel is more direct and wonderfully warm, but Lupu is compelling in his own way; and these performances yield much that is memorable. His musing, poetic romanticism in the *G flat Impromptu* (D.899/3) is wonderfully telling, when the piano timbre is so ravishingly caught by the engineers. The cassette too is superbly managed. Choice between the CBS, Philips and Decca versions is very difficult (we each have our own preferences) and the lack of a Rosette suggests that we might be inclined to award one to all three.

Impromptus Nos 1–4, D.899; Impromptus Nos 5–8, D.935; (i) *Rondo in A, D.951.*
(**) Arabesque mono **Z6572** [id.]. Artur Schnabel, (i) with Karl-Ulrich Schnabel.

Schnabel was in his late sixties when he recorded the *Impromptus* in 1950, only a year before his death. The *Rondo* comes from 1937 and was recorded by Fred Gaisberg. Desmond Shawe-Taylor and Edward Sackville-West's *Record Guide* of 1955 was rightly critical of his playing of the famous *E flat* (D.899, No. 2) which, apart from its technical shortcomings, also sounds curiously uninvolved. There are some beautiful things in the companion set but, generally speaking, this is not Schnabel at his greatest. The sound is frail, but the surface noise is barely audible except in the *Rondo*, in which he is joined by Karl-Ulrich.

Moments musicaux Nos 1–6, D.780.
(M) *** Decca *KJBC 145.* Clifford Curzon – *Piano sonata No. 17.****
** DG **415 118-2** [id.]. Daniel Barenboim – LISZT: *Liebesträume*; MENDELSSOHN: *Songs without words.****

Clifford Curzon gives superb performances of the *Moments musicaux*. These readings are among the most poetic now in the catalogue, and the recording throughout is exemplary.

In the *Moments musicaux* there is much to admire in Barenboim's performances. His mood is often thoughtful and intimate; at other times we are made a shade too aware of the interpreter's art, and there is an element of calculation that robs the impact of freshness. There are good things, of course, but this does not challenge Curzon. The recording is excellent and has fine presence in its CD format. The Liszt and Mendelssohn couplings show Barenboim at his finest.

Piano sonata No. 4 in A min., D.537.
** DG Dig. **400 043-2** [id.]. Michelangeli – BRAHMS: *Ballades.****

Piano sonatas Nos 4 in A min., D.537; 13 in A, D.664.
*(*) Ph. Dig. **410 605-2** [id]. Brendel.

Michelangeli's Schubert is less convincing that the Brahms coupling. He rushes the opening theme and rarely allows the simple ideas of the first movement to speak for themselves. Elsewhere his playing, though aristocratic and marvellously poised, is not free from artifice, and the natural eloquence of Schubert eludes him. Splendid recording which approaches demonstration standard on the compact disc.

Brendel's account of the *A minor Sonata* sounds a little didactic: the gears are changed to prepare the way for the second group, and this sounds unconvincing on the first hearing and more so on the repeat. He broadens, too, on the modulation to *F major* towards the end of the exposition, only to quicken the pulse in the development. The result is curiously inorganic. The *A major* is given with less simplicity and charm than one expects from this great artist. There are also some disruptive and studied agogic fluctuations which are not always convincing. Clear, well-focused recording, which sounds wonderfully natural in its compact disc format.

Piano sonatas Nos 4 in A min., D. 537; 21 in B flat, D.960.
(M) ** Olympia Dig. **OCD 188** [id.]. Peter Katin.

Peter Katin is very well recorded at Henry Wood Hall and he is unfailingly musical and sensitive in both pieces. He is occasionally wilful – he pulls back in the development section of the first movement of the *A minor*. His account of the great *B flat Sonata* opens beautifully, though there are some agogic mannerisms which might prove tiresome on repeated hearing. On the whole it is a good performance which offers many incidental beauties but is ultimately a little wanting in concentration. Some, perhaps, might be tempted to call it soft-centred – certainly the slow movement of the *B flat* does not hang together.

Piano sonata No. 13 in A, D.664.
(*) ASV *ZCALH 948* [id.]. Shura Cherkassky – BRAHMS: *Piano sonata No. 3.*(*)

The *A major Sonata* has great tenderness and poetry in Cherkassky's hands. Like the Brahms *F minor Sonata* with which it is coupled, the Schubert was recorded in 1968 at a recital in London's Queen Elizabeth Hall with an unusually rapt audience, as well they might be. There is a finger slip in the heavenly slow movement, as if to remind us that we are still on earth. In every way a performance of great artistic insight and real distinction. The sound is from a truthful and well-balanced broadcast, but not as good as the best modern studio recordings. The cassette transfer has plenty of life, but the upper range of the piano timbre is somewhat shallow in fortissimos.

Piano sonata No. 15 in C (Relique), D. 840.
*** Ph. **416 292-2** [id.]. Sviatoslav Richter.

Richter's approach to Schubert's unfinished *Sonata* is both dedicated and strong. He treats the opening movement very spaciously indeed, both in his slow pacing and in observing the exposition repeat, to extend it to 22½ minutes. The following *Andante* is comparably thoughtful. The recording was made at a live performance and captures the spontaneity of the occasion and the full range of the pianist's dynamic. Indeed, the sound is most realistic. With its aristrocratic assurance this is a very considerable account and it ends abruptly where the composer stopped, leaving the rest to the listener's imagination. The CD provides a remarkable feeling of presence (the balance is close) and, mercifully, the audience is unobtrusive. This recording is also available as a coupling with Peter Schreier's *Winterreise* – see below.

Piano sonata No. 16 in A min., D.845.
*** DG **419 672-2** [id.]. Maurizio Pollini – *Fantasia in C (Wanderer).****

This is piano playing of an altogether exceptional order. Pollini's account of the *A minor Sonata* is searching and profound. He is almost without rival in terms of sheer keyboard control, and his musical insight is of the same order. The piano sound as such could do with slightly more body, but, this apart, the recording is musically balanced and full of presence.

Piano sonatas Nos 16 in A min., D.845; 18 in G, D.894.
❀ *** Decca **417 640-2** [id.]. Radu Lupu.

Radu Lupu's version of the *A minor Sonata* of 1825 is searching and poetic throughout. He brings tenderness and classical disciplines to bear on this structure and his playing is musically satisfying in a very Schubertian way. The coupling is hardly less fine: Lupu's account of Schubert's great *Fantasy sonata* has a compulsion which reveals the artist at full stretch, a superb reading, relatively straight in its approach but full of glowing perception on points of detail; moreover, he observes the exposition repeat in the first movement. The analogue recordings date from 1975 and 1979 respectively and are of Decca's finest, with timbre of warm colour yet with an overall striking sense of presence. The disc plays for 74′.

Piano sonata No. 17 in D, D.850.
(M) *** Decca *KJBC 145*. Clifford Curzon – *Moments musicaux.****

The passage to savour first in the *Sonata* is the beginning of the last movement, an example of the Curzon magic at its most intense, for with a comparatively slow speed he gives the rhythm a gentle 'lift' which is most captivating. Some who know more forceful interpretations (Richter did a marvellous one) may find this too wayward, but Schubert surely thrives on some degree of coaxing. Curzon could hardly be more convincing – the spontaneous feeling of a live performance captured better than in many earlier discs. The Jubilee reissue is very generously coupled and the recording remains of Decca's finest analogue quality. The high-level cassette is bold and clear.

Piano sonatas Nos 19 in C min., D.958; 20 in A, D.959; 21 in B flat, D.960; Allegretto, D.915; Klavierstücke, D.946.
*** DG Dig. **419 229-2**; *419 229-4* (2) [id.]. Maurizio Pollini.

The three late sonatas and the glorious *Drei Klavierstücke* and the *C minor Allegretto*, D.915, all on two CDs and in completely masterful performances. Readers who have found the great Italian pianist curiously remote in recent years may be assured that he is back in form. In his hands these emerge as strongly structured and powerful sonatas, yet he is far from unresponsive to the voices from the other world to which these pieces resonate. Perhaps with his perfect pianism he does not always convey a sense of human vulnerability in the way that some of the greatest Schubert interpreters have. The sonatas were recorded at different venues (Salle Wagram in Paris, the Herkules-Saal, Munich, and the Grosser Saal of the Musikverein, Vienna); in the *A major*, for example, the sound is not always completely natural. However, this is playing of some distinction. The cassette transfers are highly sophisticated and the cassette box includes the CD documentation.

Piano sonata No. 20 in A, D.959; 3 Klavierstücke, D.946.
** Erato Dig. **ECD 88116** [id.]. Michel Dalberto.

A well-filled record, particularly as Michel Dalberto, the 1978 Leeds Prize-winner, shirks no repeats in either the *Sonata* or the *Klavierstücke*. His playing is accomplished and often refined, though the essentially romantic feeling at times seems insufficiently disciplined and concentrated. A good record, but no match for the very best.

Piano sonata No. 20 in A, D.959; 12 German dances, D.790.
** Ph. **411 477-2** [id.]. Alfred Brendel.

Brendel's late Schubert records are among his finest, but the *A major Sonata* suffers from rather more agogic changes than is desirable. Some listeners will find these interferences with the flow of the musical argument a little too much of a good thing. The coupling, however, is delightful and particularly beautifully played. The 1973 analogue recording is of Philips's best quality; it is enhanced on CD, where the dynamic range is made to seem even more dramatic than on the original LP, yet the timbre retains its colour and bloom.

Piano Sonata No. 20 in A, D.959; 6 Waltzes, D.365.
** Mer. **CDA 84103** [id.]. Paul Berkowitz.

Paul Berkowitz is a gifted Canadian pianist, now living and teaching in London. His account of the Schubert *A major Sonata* is eminently sound, well shaped and very musical; tempi are well chosen; nor is there any want of insight. If the field was less competitive, his record could be given a stronger recommendation, were it not for the fact that the recording is far from ideal: it does not really open out enough in louder passages and is a bit cramped.

Piano sonata No. 21 in B flat, D.960 (see also under *Fantasia* (*Wanderer*)).
(M) *** Ph. **420 644-2**; *420 644-4* [id.]. Alfred Brendel – *Wanderer fantasia.****
*** Hyp. Dig. **CDA 66004** [id.]. Stephen Bishop-Kovacevich.
(*) Decca Dig. **417 327-2; *417 327-4* [id.]. Vladimir Ashkenazy – *Wanderer fantasia.***(*)

Piano sonata No. 21 in B flat; Impromptu in A flat, D.935/2; 6 Moments musicaux, D.780.
❀ *** Decca **417 642-2** [id.]. Clifford Curzon.

Piano sonata No. 21 in B flat; Impromptus, D.899/2–3.
(*) Denon Dig. **C37 7488 [id.]. Dezsö Ránki.

Piano sonata No. 21 in B flat; Impromptus, D.899/3–4.
** Erato Dig. **ECD 88181** [id.]. Maria Joao Pires.

Curzon's is perhaps now the finest account of the *B flat Sonata* in the catalogue. Tempi are aptly judged, and everything is in fastidious taste. Detail is finely drawn but never emphasized at the expense of the architecture as a whole. It is beautifully recorded, and the piano sounds very truthful in timbre. For the reissue, the coupling has been extended to include the *Moments musicaux* and the disc plays for 70′. The digital remastering brings just a hint of hardness at fortissimo levels to a basically warm, full tone, and some slight background remains.

Brendel's performance too is as impressive and full of insight as one would expect. He is not unduly wayward, for his recording has room for the *Wanderer fantasy* as well, and he is supported by quite outstanding Philips sound. There is also a very good tape, and this is undoubtedly a genuine bargain.

Stephen Bishop-Kovacevich also gives one of the most eloquent accounts on record of this sublime sonata and one which is entirely free of expressive point making. It is an account which totally reconciles the demands of truth and the attainment of beauty. The first-movement exposition repeat is observed. The recording reproduces the piano timbre with the same complete naturalness that Bishop-Kovacevich brings to the sonata itself. However, without any couplings this seems short measure at premium price.

Ashkenazy plays with poetry and searching intensity in the ideal coupling of the great *B flat Sonata* and the *Wanderer Fantasy*. What seriously mars this issue is the clangy quality of the recording, much less sympathetic than the analogue sound for Brendel in his similar coupling for Philips.

Denon claim their CD as an early digital recording, but apologize for 'some minute noises' in the pianissimo music. These are hard to spot and the recording has the usual digital advantages of a most realistic presence and background quiet. The piano timbre has a bold outline (there is a not inappropriate hint of fortepiano tone at times, notably in the Scherzo), yet the bass has a full resonance, so important in the *B flat Sonata*. Dezsö Ránki was twenty-four when he made this record in 1975 and it is a performance impressive in its concentration. It must be counted controversial that Ránki begins with a very expansive pacing of the opening theme, far slower than his basic speed later, and he consistently returns to this slow tempo when the famous melody recurs. The effect is to make the first movement unusually volatile, but it is also spontaneous, and he has clearly thought deeply about this approach. The slow movement is intensely poetic, played with a lovely singing legato, and the middle section produces another bold contrast. With a nimbly articulated Scherzo and a finale which balances sparkle with strength, this is a very considerable reading, and it is matched by the two *Impromptus* which are beautifully played and nicely characterized.

Maria Joao Pires gives a characterful but often wilful reading, which will no doubt delight the many admirers of this sensitive Portuguese pianist. The disc is marred by the rather jangling piano tone.

VOCAL MUSIC

Lieder: *Abendbilder; An die Musik; An den Mond; Bertas Lied in der Nacht; Die Blumensprache; Erster Verlust; Frühlingssehnsucht; Der Knabe; Nachthymne; Schwestergruss; Sei mir gegrüsst; Die Sterne; Wiegenlied.*

*** Ph. Dig. **410 037-2** [id.]. Ameling, Baldwin.

Elly Ameling's is a fresh and enchanting collection of Schubert songs, starting with *An die Musik* and including other favourites like the *Cradle song* as well as lesser-known songs that admirably suit the lightness and sparkle of Ameling's voice. This was the first Lieder record to appear on compact disc, and it deserved an accolade, for the new medium with its absence of background enhances a recording already beautifully balanced. It gives astonishing sense of presence to the singer, with the bright top of the voice perfectly caught and the piano unusually truthful. Some ears, however, may notice that the microphone is just a little close.

Lieder: *Die Allmacht; An die Natur; Auf dem See; Auflösung; Erlkönig; Ganymed; Gretchen am Spinnrade; Der Musensohn; Rastlose Liebe; Suleika I; Der Tod und das Mädchen; Der Zwerg.*

*** Ph. Dig. **412 623-2** [id.]. Jessye Norman, Philip Moll.

It is remarkable that, with so magnificently large a voice, Jessye Norman manages to scale it down for the widest range of tone and expression in this beautifully chosen selection of Schubert songs. The characterization of the four contrasting voices in *Erlkönig* is powerfully effective, and the reticence which once marked Norman in Lieder has completely disappeared. The poignancy of *Gretchen am Spinnrade* is exquisitely touched in, building to a powerful climax; throughout, the breath control is a thing of wonder, not least in a surpassing account of *Ganymed*. Fine, sympathetic accompaniment from Philip Moll, and first-rate recording.

Lieder: *Am Bach; An den Tod; An die Entfernte; An die untergehende Sonne; Auf dem Wasser zu singen; Die Forelle; Fülle der Liebe; Ganymed; Die Götter Griechenlands; Im Abendrot; Im Frühling; Der Musensohn; Der Schiffer; Schwanengesang: Sehnsucht; Sprache der Liebe.*
*** Ph. Dig. **416 294-2**; *416 294-4* [id.]. Elly Ameling, Rudolf Jansen.

With Rudolf Jansen accompanying, Elly Ameling's 1987 Schubert recital brings many delights, even if the voice is not quite as fresh and agile as it is in her earlier collections, notably the 1973 one, now also transferred to CD. In compensation, in an attractively mixed programme of familiar and unfamiliar she is able to bring new depths to such a song as *An die Entfernte*. Her breath control remains immaculate – as in *Ganymed* – and she still brings delightful bounce to the ever-popular *Der Musensohn*. A generous measure of songs and first-rate recording.

Lieder: *An die Läute; An Sylvia; Der Blumenbrief; Du liebst mich nicht; Der Einsame; Im Abendrot; Die Liebe hat gelogen; Der Liebliche Stern; Das Mädchen; Die Männer sing méchant; Minnelied; Nacht und Traume; Rosamunde; Romance: Schlummerlied; Seligkeit; Die Sterne.*
*** Ph. **416 897-2** [id.]. Elly Ameling, Dalton Baldwin.

Elly Ameling's Schubert recital of 1973, sounding undated, brings a delightful selection of songs, showing off the diamond purity of the voice at its freshest and most girlish in an attractively arranged programme. The first half takes songs on the subject of night, the second on love in all its varied moods from joy to desolation. Baldwin's playing is most sensitive in support, and the analogue recording has been very well transferred to CD, though the measure remains short.

Lieder: *An die Musik; An Sylvia; Auf dem Wasser zu singen; Du bist die Ruh; Die Forelle; Frühlingsglaube; Gretchen am Spinnrade; Heidenröslein; Die junge Nonne; Litanei; Der Musensohn; Nacht und Träume; Rastlose Liebe; Der Tod und das Mädchen.*
*** HMV **CDC7 47861-2** [id.]. Dame Janet Baker, Geoffrey Parsons.

Take a poll of favourite Schubert songs, and a high proportion of these would be on the list. With a great singer treating each with loving, detailed care, the result is a charmer of a recital record. At the very start Dame Janet's strongly characterized reading of *Die Forelle* makes it a fun song, and similarly Parsons's naughty springing of the accompaniment of *An Sylvia* (echoed later by the singer) gives a twinkle to a song that can easily be treated too seriously. One also remembers the ravishing *subito piano* for the second stanza of *An die Musik* and the heart-felt expression of *Gretchen am Spinnrade*. The 1981 recording does not quite catch the voice at its most rounded and the digital remastering fails to achieve absolute sharpness of focus.

Lieder: *An die Musik; An Sylvia; Auf dem Wasser zu singen; Ganymed; Gretchen am Spinnrade; Im Frühling; Die junge Nonne; Das Lied im Grünen; Der Musensohn; Nachtviolen; Nähe des Geliebten; Wehmut.*
❀ *** HMV mono **CDC7 47326-2** [id.]. Elisabeth Schwarzkopf, Edwin Fischer – MOZART: *Lieder.****

At the very end of his career Edwin Fischer partnered Elisabeth Schwarzkopf near the beginning of hers, and the result was magical. The radiance of the voice, the control of line and tone (vibrato an important element, varied exquisitely) set this apart even among the finest Schubert recitals. The simplest of songs inspire intensely subtle expression from singer and pianist alike, and though Fischer's playing is not always perfectly tidy, he left few records as endearing as this. The mono sound has been freshened and the CD, with the voice beautifully caught, brings also as a generous coupling eleven of the fourteen songs from Schwarzkopf's Mozart collection with Gieseking, recorded three years later.

Lieder: *An die Nachtigall; An mein Klavier; Auf dem Wasser zu singen; Geheimnis;* (i) *Der Hirt auf dem Felsen; Im Abendrot; Ins stille Land; Liebhaben in allen Gestalten; Das Lied im Grünen; Die Mutter Erde; Romanze; Der Winterabend.*
*** HM Orfeo **C 001811 A** [id.]. Margaret Price, Sawallisch; (i) with H. Schöneberger.

Consistent beauty of tone, coupled with immaculately controlled line and admirably clear diction, makes Margaret Price's Schubert collection a fresh and rewarding experience. Right at the beginning of her recording career she made a similar recital record for CfP, but the performances on the Orfeo disc are even more assured and benefit from modern digital recording. Sawallisch as ever shows himself one of the outstanding accompanists of the time, readily translating from his usual role of conductor. The rather reverberant recording gives extra bloom to the voice.

Lieder: *An mein Herz; An Sylvia; Auf dem Wasser zu singen; Der Einsame; Fischerweise; Der Fluss; Die Forelle; Fülle der Liebe; Gretchen am Spinnrade; Die junge Nonne; Der Jüngling an der Quelle; Der Knabe; Die Rose; Der Schmetterling; Seligkeit; Der Wanderer an den Mond.*
*** HMV Dig. **CDC7 49633-2**. Lucia Popp, Irwin Gage.

The charm, sparkle and silvery beauty of voice displayed by Lucia Popp make hers an outstanding Schubert collection. The choice of songs is delightful, and not always predictable; though the voice momentarily loses some of its natural sweetness under pressure, this is memorably beautiful singing, most sympathetically accompanied. For sample, try *Der Jüngling an der Quelle*, hauntingly lovely.

Lieder: *An Sylvia; Der blinde Knabe; Du bist die Ruh'; Der Einsame; Die Forelle; Ganymed; Gretchen am Spinnrade; Im Frühling; Der König in Thule; Lied der Mignon; Der Musensohn; Nacht und Traüme; Rastlose Liebe; Suleika I & II; Der Wanderer an den Mond; Wanderers Nachtlied.*
(*) HMV Dig. **CDC7 47549-2 [id.]; *EL 270434-4*. Barbara Hendricks, Radu Lupu.

The duo of Barbara Hendricks and Radu Lupu makes a fascinating and characterful partnership in a delightful selection of Schubert songs, though some of these are far from conventional performances which will not please all lovers of Lieder, always beautiful if at times not well detailed. The bloom on the voice is caught well, with the singer's personality vividly conveyed – though, with such a distinguished accompanist, it is surprising that the piano is backwardly balanced.

Lieder: *Auflösung; Der Einsame; Gesänge des Harfners; Gruppe aus dem Tartarus; Herbst; Hippolits Lied; Im Abendrot; Nachtstück; Nacht und Träume; Über Wildemann; Der Wanderer; Der Wanderer an den Mond.*
*** Ph. Dig. **411 421-2** [id.]. Dietrich Fischer-Dieskau, Alfred Brendel.

The combination of Fischer-Dieskau and Brendel is particularly compelling in the dark or meditative songs which make up the majority of items here. A delicate song like *Der Einsame* loses something in lightness, but the intensity remains. A lifetime of experience in this repertoire brings a magical degree of communication from the great baritone, made the more immediate on compact disc, with the atmospheric recording naturally balanced.

Deutsche Messe with Epilogue (The Lord's prayer), D.872; Hymn to the Holy Ghost, D.964; Psalms Nos 23, D.706; 92, D.953; Salve Regina in F, D.379.
*** HMV **CDC7 47402-2** [id.]. Fischer-Dieskau, Capella Bavariae, Bav. R. Ch. and SO (members), Sawallisch.

Though this does not contain the most imaginative and original music from the first volume of Sawallisch's collection of Schubert's choral music, it is a pleasing selection, easy and undemanding and superbly sung and recorded. Some of the items, such as the setting of Psalm 23, have piano accompaniment by Sawallisch.

Masses Nos 4 in C, D.452; 5 in A flat, D.678.
(M) *** HMV **CDM7 69222-2** [id.]. Popp, Donath, Fassbaender, Araiza, Dallapozza, Fischer-Dieskau, Bav. R. Ch. & SO, Sawallisch.

This medium-priced reissue from Sawallisch's excellent choral series combines two settings of the Mass, including the finest (in A flat). The singing is outstanding from chorus and soloists alike, and the remastered recording has retained most of its fullness and gained in clarity and presence.

Rosamunde: Overture (Die Zauberharfe, D.644) and incidental music, D.797.
*** Ph. Dig. **412 432-2** [id.]. Ameling, Leipzig R. Ch., Leipzig GO, Masur.

Rosamunde: Overture (Die Zauberharfe, D.644); Entr'acte No. 3 in B flat; Ballet music No. 2 in G, D.797.
** DG Dig. **415 137-2** [id.]. Chicago SO, Levine – MENDELSSOHN: *Midsummer Night's Dream.***

Masur's fine new recording of the *Rosamunde Overture and incidental music* is a worthy replacement for Haitink's 1965 LP and tape which have dominated the catalogue for two decades. As with the Concertgebouw recording, the resonance of the Leipzig Gewandhaus seems over-reverberant for scoring designed for the theatre pit. Even on CD, the choral items are not very sharply focused and the bass is diffuse. Yet the ambient effect gives strings and woodwind a nice bloom and detail is not obscured. The superb Leipzig orchestra provides its usual cultured response to the music's drama as well as its lyricism – the second *Entr'acte* only just stops short of melodrama – and the innocent eloquence of Elly Ameling's contribution is matched by the direct vigour of the chorus of spirits, with affinities found with Mozart's *Die Zauberflöte* as well as with Weber.

From Levine, three favourite items from *Rosamunde*, all well – if not outstandingly – done, to provide a fair makeweight for a generous selection of *Midsummer Night's Dream* pieces.

Die schöne Müllerin (song cycle), *D.795.*
*** DG **415 186-2** [id.]. Dietrich Fischer-Dieskau, Gerald Moore.
(B) *** DG Walkman *423 291-4* [id.]. Fischer-Dieskau, Moore – SCHUMANN: *Dichterliebe.****
*** Capriccio Dig. **10 082**; *CC 27 089* [id.]. Josef Protschka, Helmut Deutsch.
*** Ph. **420 850-2** [id.]. Gérard Souzay, Dalton Baldwin.
*** HMV Dig. **CDC7 47947-2** [id.]; *EL 270573-4*. Olaf Bär, Geoffrey Parsons.
(*) DG Dig. **415 347-2 [id.]. Francisco Araiza, Irwin Gage.

With an excellent digital transfer to CD barely giving an indication of its analogue source back in 1972, Fischer-Dieskau's classic version remains among the very finest ever recorded. Though he had made several earlier recordings, this is no mere repeat of previous triumphs, combining as it does his developed sense of drama and story-telling, his mature feeling for detail and yet spontaneity too, helped by the searching accompaniment of Gerald Moore. It is a performance with premonitions of *Winterreise*. This recording is also available as an incredible Walkman cassette bargain, coupled with Schumann's *Dichterliebe*. The transfer is smooth and natural and the tape costs but a fraction of the price of the CD.

Born in Czechoslovakia, but working with the Cologne Opera, Josef Protschka is a remarkable tenor who, here in strongly characterized singing of Schubert's lovely cycle, gives an intensely virile, almost operatic reading which is made the more youthful-sounding in the original keys for high voice. As recorded, the voice, often beautiful with heroic timbres, sometimes acquires a hint of stridency, but the positive power and individuality of the performance make it consistently compelling, with all the anguish behind these songs intensely caught. The timbre of the Bösendorfer piano adds to the performance's distinctiveness, well recorded if rather reverberantly. The chrome tape is in the demonstration class, very clear and real; and readers are urged to try this as a highly rewarding alternative to the famous Fischer-Dieskau version, whether on CD or cassette.

Souzay made this recording in his prime in 1965; his lyrical style is beautifully suited to this most sunny of song-cycles. Fischer-Dieskau may find more drama in the poems, but Souzay's concentration on purely musical values makes for one of the most consistently attractive versions available, with the words never neglected and Dalton Baldwin giving one of his most imaginative performances on record. The Pears/Britten version (on Decca Jubilee *411 729-4*) has even more imaginative accompaniment, but Pears's voice is for once rather gritty. Fischer-Dieskau has Gerald Moore, of course; but on this occasion Baldwin provides an interesting alternative view. The sound belies the recording's age.

Olaf Bär, with Geoffrey Parsons an attentive partner, gives an attractively fresh, boyish-sounding reading of *Schöne Müllerin*. This may not have the dramatic variety of Fischer-Dieskau's strongly characterized readings but, with the songs following each other with hardly a break, it is one full of presence. The cassette is rather less well focused.

It says much for the versatility of the Spanish opera tenor, Francisco Araiza, that he gives such a stylish performance of *Die schöne Müllerin*, rarely if ever revealing that he is not a born German-speaker. There is youthful exuberance in the reading, coupled with a strong, heroic vocal tone which under pressure is, however, less sweet than this music really demands. Nevertheless the closing songs are particularly beautiful. Sensitive accompaniment from Irwin Gage and excellent recording. The CD thrusts the voice strikingly forward.

Schwanengesang (Lieder collection), *D.957*.
*** Ph. Dig. **411 051-2** [id.]. Dietrich Fischer-Dieskau, Alfred Brendel.
*** HMV **CDC7 49018-2** [id.]. Dietrich Fischer-Dieskau, Gerald Moore.
** Claves Dig. **CD 50-8506** [id.]. Ernst Haefliger, Joerg Dahler (fortepiano).

Schwanengesang (Lieder collection), *D.957;* Lieder: *An die Musik; An Sylvia; Die Forelle; Heidenröslein; Im Abendrot; Der Musensohn; Der Tod und das Mädchen.*
*** DG **415 188-2** [id.]. Dietrich Fischer-Dieskau, Gerald Moore.

Fischer-Dieskau's DG version with Moore, though recorded ten years before his CD with Brendel, brings excellent sound in the digital transfer, plus the positive advantages, first that the voice is fresher, and then that the disc also contains seven additional songs, all of them favourites. Taken from Fischer-Dieskau's monumental complete set of the Schubert songs, these performances represent a high-water mark in his recording of Schubert, and are all the more cherishable in the new medium.

Fischer-Dieskau's newest version (on Philips) offers deeply reflective performances, both from the singer and from his equally imaginative piano partner. His voice is not as fresh as on the earlier DG set but, particularly with the clarity and immediacy of compact disc, this is a beautiful, compelling record.

The HMV CD was recorded in the early 1960s and represents the second wave of Fischer-Dieskau's Schubert interpretations. Though the later DG version has greater thought and refinement, the direct power of expression here is superb too. Great performances which proclaim their greatness in every song, and good, lively recording which scarcely shows its age.

Haefliger's tenor is even drier than it was when he recorded *Winterreise* with the same pianist, playing a fortepiano as here. Again, taking his cue from the detached, clean style favoured by period instrumentalists, the singer gives very straight, restrained performances of these songs, hardly measuring up to their range of emotion. The voice is presented in a rather reverberant acoustic, not quite matched by the sound of the fortepiano.

Winterreise (song cycle), *D.911.*
*** DG **415 187-2** [id.]. Dietrich Fischer-Dieskau, Gerald Moore.
*** Ph. Dig. **411 463-2** [id.]; *411 463-4.* Dietrich Fischer-Dieskau, Alfred Brendel.
(M) *** Decca *417 473-4* [id.]. Peter Pears, Benjamin Britten.
(*) DG Dig. **423 366-2 [id.]. Christa Ludwig, James Levine.
(***) EMI mono **CDH7 61002-2** [id.]. Hans Hotter, Gerald Moore.
** Denon Dig. **C 37 7240** [id.]. Hermann Prey, Philippe Bianconi.
** Claves Dig. **CD 50-8008/9** (2) [id.]. Ernst Haefliger, Joerg Dahler.
*(*) BIS Dig. **CD 253/4** (1) [id.]. Martti Talvela, Ralf Gothoni.

Winterreise (song cycle), *D.911; Piano sonata No. 15 in C, D.840.*
*** Ph. Dig. **416 289-2** (2) [id.]. Peter Schreier, Sviatoslav Richter.

Taken from the collected recording of Schubert songs that Fischer-Dieskau made with Gerald Moore in the early 1970s, this DG version, now clarified and freshened in an excellent digital transfer to CD, is arguably the finest of his readings on record. At this period the voice was still at its freshest, yet the singer had deepened and intensified his understanding of this greatest of song-cycles to a degree where his finely detailed and thoughtful interpretation sounded totally spontaneous. Moore exactly matches the hushed concentration of the singer, consistently imaginative without drawing attention to himself with any waywardness. The single-CD format is an obvious benefit, with the enclosed leaflet containing lyrics and translation.

The collaboration of Dietrich Fischer-Dieskau with one of the great Schubert pianists today, Alfred Brendel, is an inspired one, bringing endless illumination in the interplay and challenge between singer and pianist, magnetic from first to last. This is the fifth recording of *Winterreise* that the singer has made, and any signs of wear on the voice are of minimal importance next to the keen involvement of the reading, reflecting a whole series of live concert performances the two artists gave. With incidental flaws, this may not be the definitive Fischer-Dieskau reading, but in many ways it is the deepest and most moving he has ever given, one which carries you on in seeming spontaneity, totally gripped by the plight of the sad traveller. The recording is excellent, vivid in its sense of face-to-face presence. The cassette, too, is of good quality though not as open as the disc.

Schubert's darkest song-cycle was in fact originally written for high not low voice, and quite apart from the intensity and subtlety of the Pears/Britten version it gains enormously from being at the right pitch throughout. When the message of these poems is so gloomy, a dark voice tends to underline the sombre aspect too oppressively, whereas the lightness of a tenor is even more affecting. That is particularly so in those songs where the wandering poet in his despair observes triviality – as in the picture of the hurdy-gurdy man in the last song of all. What is so striking about the Pears performance is its intensity. One continually has the sense of a live performance, and next to it even Fischer-Dieskau's beautifully wrought singing can sometimes sound too easy. As for Britten, he re-creates the music, sometimes with a fair freedom from Schubert's markings but always with scrupulous concern for the overall musical shaping and sense of atmosphere. The sprung rhythm of *Gefror'ne Tränen* is magical in creating the impression of frozen drops falling, and almost every song brings similar magic. In its original LP format (two discs) this carried a Rosette in earlier editions; now effectively remastered on to a single mid-priced cassette, it is a tape bargain to match Fischer-Dieskau's Walkman of *Die schöne Müllerin* and Schumann's *Dichterliebe*.

Recorded live at the newly restored Semper opera house in Dresden just after its reopening in February 1985, Schreier's is an inspired version, both outstandingly beautiful and profoundly searching in its expression, helped by magnetic, highly individual accompaniment from Richter, a master of Schubert. Speeds are not always conventional, indeed are sometimes extreme – but that only adds to the vivid communication which throughout conveys the inspiration of the moment. Rarely has the agonized intensity of the last two songs been so movingly caught on record, the more compellingly when the atmosphere of a live occasion is so realistically captured; it is a small price to pay that the winter audience makes so many bronchial contributions. A more serious snag is that the cycle – which can usually be contained on a single CD – spreads over on to a second, thanks to the slow speeds. Though the Schubert *Sonata* brings a comparably inspired performance from Richter (recorded live at Leverkusen in West Germany in December 1979), not everyone will want the coupling. Nevertheless, the two CDs provide generous measure at a total of 122′ playing time. The sound in the *Sonata* recording – though it has striking presence – is drier than the cycle, but is less troubled by audience noise.

Elena Gerhardt, supreme Lieder-singer of her generation, used to sing this greatest of song-cycles, normally reserved for a man's voice; but it took over half a century for the first recording using a woman's voice to appear, from Christa Ludwig. With James Levine a concentrated and often dramatic accompanist, consistently adding to the sense of spontaneous and immediate communication, Ludwig gives a warmly satisfying performance, making use of the mature richness of the voice rather than bringing any striking new insights. Though the different sections of *Frühlingstraum*, for example, are beautifully contrasted, the tonal range does not extend to a drained quality in the final songs. There the extra darkness of the piano in low keys is what adds most to the tragedy. Full, natural recording. A rival version promised by Brigitte Fassbaender might be worth waiting for.

Hans Hotter's 1954 recording of *Winterreise*, long regarded as a classic reading, brings an exceptionally dark, even sepulchral performance, lightened by the imagination of Gerald Moore's accompaniment. Hotter scales down his great Wagnerian baritone so that only occasionally is the tone gritty. His concern for detail brings many moments of illumination, but the lack of animation makes this an unrelievedly depressing view. The mono recording, clearly transferred, is on the dry side, but captures the voice vividly.

Prey's is a positive, intelligent reading which misses the meditative depth of this greatest of song-cycles. With often brisk speeds and light-of-day accompaniment, the tension of live communication is generally missing and the result sounds almost casual, though the final songs bring greater intensity. The sound is clean and faithful.

When he recorded this period performance of Schubert's great cycle with accompaniment on an 1820 fortepiano, Ernst Haefliger's tenor had grown thinner and drier than it used to be. In a way it suits the dry, clear tones of the instrument. He also adopts a more metrical and detached style of expression than is usual, equally reflecting period performance as it affects instruments.

The result is a cool performance, but one that has its distinctive character. The recording acoustic is rather hard, with the fortepiano less reverberantly caught.

Though Martti Talvela does wonders in lightening his big dark bass voice, making it surprisingly agile where necessary, it never sounds really comfortable, with the vibrato exaggerated in an ugly way. There is keen intensity in his reading, and the darkness in the cycle comes over well; but, with often prosaic accompaniment, poetry is lacking. The recording is very immediate, giving a striking vocal presence in the CD format, which is on a single disc (as against a pair of LPs).

Schuman, William (born 1910)

American festival overture.

*** DG Dig. **413 324-2**; *3302 083* [id.]. LAPO, Bernstein – BARBER: *Adagio;* BERNSTEIN: *Candide: Overture;* COPLAND: *Appalachian spring.****

Schuman's overture is the least known of the four representative American works making up this attractive disc. It is rather like a Walton comedy overture with an American accent, and is played here with tremendous panache. Close, bright and full recording on both disc and cassette, which are closely matched. Highly recommended – this collection is more than the sum of its parts.

Symphony No. 3.

*** DG Dig. **419 780-2** [id.]. NYPO, Bernstein – HARRIS: *Symphony No. 3****

The *Third* of William Schuman's ten symphonies is as much his visiting card as is the Harris with which it is coupled. It, too, has an authentic American feel to it: it certainly creates a sound-world all its own, but the world it evokes is more urban; there are bright, gleaming skyscrapers, streets teeming with activity, seedier areas with the 'smell of steaks in passageways'. The chorale movement is particularly evocative, full of nocturnal introspection and wholly original. Schuman is also one of the few modern composers to use fugue both individually and effectively. An impressive performance – not perhaps quite as powerful as earlier recordings by Ormandy and Bernstein himself, but superb all the same. The New York Philharmonic play with excellent discipline and are well recorded. Strongly recommended.

Schumann, Robert (1810–56)

Cello concerto in A min., Op. 129.

*** Decca Dig. **410 019-2** [id.]. Lynn Harrell, Cleveland O, Marriner – SAINT-SAËNS: *Concerto No. 1.****
(B) *** DG Walkman *423 290-4* [id.]. Rostropovich, Leningrad PO – LALO: *Concerto*; SAINT-SAËNS: *Concerto No. 1*; TCHAIKOVSKY: *Rococo variations.****
*(*) HMV **CDC7 49307-2** [id.]. Rostropovich, O Nat. de France, Bernstein – BLOCH: *Shelomo.****

The controversial point about Harrell's reading is that he expands the usual cadenza with a substantial sequence of his own. His is a big-scale reading, strong and sympathetic, made the more powerful by the superb accompaniment from the Cleveland Orchestra. The digital recording is outstandingly fine, with the compact disc version presenting a vividly realistic sound spectrum.

Rostropovich's DG performance is superbly made, introspective yet at the same time outgoing, with a peerless technique at the command of a rare artistic imagination. The sound is still vivid, and this Walkman tape compilation is an equally rare bargain.

Except in the finale, where energy triumphs, the collaboration of Rostropovich and Bernstein in Schumann sounds disappointingly self-conscious, quite unlike the Bloch performance on the reverse. Rostropovich is at his most self-indulgent, not least in the lovely slow section, which is pulled about wilfully at a very slow basic tempo. Bold recording, favouring the soloist.

Cello concerto in A min., Op. 129 (orch. Shostakovich).
(M) **(*) Olympia Dig. **OCD 102** [id.]. Lusanov, USSR MOC SO, Rozhdestvensky – BRAHMS: *Violin concerto.***

A fascinating version of Schumann's *Cello concerto*, re-orchestrated by Shostakovich to great effect. The performance of the soloist, Fedor Lusanov, is an uncommonly fine one, catching the work's melancholy and its nobility of line. Rozhdestvensky provides a splendid accompaniment but, as the Soviet writer of the liner-notes comments drily, 'It cannot be said that Shostakovich was successful in suppressing his own compositional characteristics', and in the finale the jaunty woodwind scoring, especially the flutes and piccolo, adds a touch of the bizarre. The result is very entertaining, but not entirely Schumann. With good digital recording (the cellist's timbre is clearly focused but lacks something in sonorous resonance) this remains a fine collector's item.

(i) *Cello concerto in A min., Op. 129*; (ii) *Konzertstück in F for four horns and orchestra, Op. 86*; (iii) *Concert allegro with Introduction in D min., for piano and orchestra, Op. 134.*
*** Erato Dig. **ECD 88212** [id.]. (i) Lodéon; (ii) Justafre, Gantiez, Barro, Courtois; (iii) Devoyon; French R. New PO, Guschlbauer.

A really worthwhile addition to the Schumann compact discography. None of these pieces is generously represented and all these performances more than hold their own against the competition. Frédéric Lodéon's version of the *Cello concerto* is wholly unaffected and natural; it is musical through and through. Its unforced eloquence is much more affecting than Maisky's: in Lodéon's hands there is restraint and intimacy of feeling. The orchestral playing under Theodor Guschlbauer is dedicated and the recording excellent. (The Nouvel Orchestre Philharmonique of the French Radio is emerging as a fine body and a worthy companion to their Orchestre National.) Their performance of the *Konzertstück in F major for four horns* has an engaging exuberance and spontaneity, and the soloists are excellent. So, too, is Pascal Devoyon in the rarely heard *Concert allegro with Introduction*, which dates from 1853 when Schumann was approaching insanity. There is splendid warmth and space, and the orchestral detail is agreeably transparent and expertly balanced, with soloists placed in just the right perspective.

(i) *Cello concerto in A min., Op. 129; Symphony No. 2 in C, Op. 61.*
** DG Dig. **419 190-2**; *419 190-4* [id.]. (i) Maisky; VPO, Bernstein.

The separate issue of Bernstein's version of Schumann's *Second* brings an unusual and attractive coupling with the *Cello concerto*. Both are live recordings which characteristically present each work rather larger than life, with heavily underlined expressiveness. Bernstein seems reluctant ever to let the music speak for itself; in the *Concerto*, that effects the eloquent, generous-toned soloist, who similarly has moments of self-indulgence. The digital sound, not ideally balanced, captures the extreme dynamic range of the performance very effectively.

Piano concerto in A min., Op. 54.
*** Ph. **412 923-2**; (M) *412 923-4* [id.]. Bishop-Kovacevich, BBC SO, C. Davis – GRIEG: *Concerto.****
*** Ph. **412 251-2** [id.]. Brendel, LSO, Abbado – WEBER: *Konzertstück.****
*** Decca **417 555-2** [id.]. Ashkenazy, LSO, Segal – TCHAIKOVSKY: *Concerto No. 1.****
(B) *** DG Walkman *419 087-4* [id.]. Kempff, Bav. RSO, Kubelik – BRAHMS: *Concerto No. 2.****
(*) CBS **MK 42024 [id.]. Istomin, Columbia SO, Bruno Walter – BRAHMS: *Double concerto.***(*)
(M) **(*) Decca **417 728-2**; *414 432-4* [id.]. Radu Lupu. LSO, Previn – GRIEG: *Concerto.***(*)
(M) **(*) ASV **CDQS 6003**; *ZCQS 6003* [id.]. Vásáry, N. Sinf. – CHOPIN: *Concerto No. 2.***(*)
(M) ** DG **415 850-2**; *415 850-4* [id.]. Anda, BPO, Kubelik – GRIEG: *Concerto.***
** RCA **RD 86255 [RCA 6255-2-RC]**. Rubinstein, Chicago SO, Giulini – LISZT: *Concerto No. 1.***(*)

** Decca Dig. **411 942-2** [id.]. Schiff, Concg. O, Dorati – CHOPIN: *Concerto No. 2.***
** DG Dig. **410 021-2** [id.]. Zimerman, BPO, Karajan – GRIEG: *Concerto.**(*)
*(*) Chan. Dig. **CHAN 8546**; *ABTD 1254* [id.]. Margalit, LPO, Thompson – SAINT-SAËNS: *Concerto No. 2.**(*)
*(*) Decca Dig. **417 112-2**; *417 112-4* [id.]. Bolet, Berlin RSO, Chailly – GRIEG: *Concerto.**
* HMV **CDC7 47164-2** [id.]; (M) *EG 290292-4* [id.]. Sviatoslav Richter, Monte Carlo Op. O, Von Matacic – GRIEG: *Concerto.**

This much-recorded favourite concerto has proved less successful than some comparable works in the recording studio. The fusing together of its disparate masculine and feminine Romantic elements has proved difficult, even for the finest artists. Thus our primary recommendation remains with the successful symbiosis of Stephen Bishop-Kovacevich and Sir Colin Davis who give an interpretation which is both fresh and poetic, unexaggerated but powerful in its directness and clarity. More than most, Bishop-Kovacevich shows the link between the central introspective slow movement and the comparable movement of Beethoven's *Fourth Concerto*, and the spring-like element of the outer movements is finely presented by orchestra and soloist alike. The sound has been admirably freshened for its mid-price reissue and the 1972 recording date is quite eclipsed. There is now also an outstanding chrome cassette, vivid and clear. The CD, of course, costs about three times as much as the cassette, but the sound is warm and beautiful, and naturally balanced.

Of recent accounts, Brendel's is easily the best; it is a thoroughly considered, yet fresh-sounding performance, with meticulous regard to detail. There is some measure of coolness, perhaps, in the slow movement, but on the whole this is a most distinguished reading. The orchestral playing under Abbado is good, and the occasional lapse in ensemble noted by some reviewers on its first appearance is not likely to worry anyone. The recorded sound is up to the usual high standards of the house and is especially fine on CD. Overall, this does not efface memories of the fresh and poetic account by Bishop-Kovacevich and Sir Colin Davis but remains an attractive alternative, if the coupling is suitable.

Ashkenazy's performance balances the demands of drama against poetry rather more in favour of the former than one might expect, but it is a refined reading as well as a powerful one, with the finale rather more spacious than usual. The recording from the late 1970s has been most successfully remastered. Those wanting a coupling with Tchaikovsky will find this a worthwhile record.

After a rather solid account of the opening chords of the concerto, Kempff proceeds characteristically to produce an unending stream of poetry. His tempi are generally leisurely, and he is richly supported by Kubelik and the Bavarian Radio Symphony Orchestra. The 1974 recording is full and resonant, with warm piano timbre. On this Walkman chrome tape, coupled with Gilels's masterly version of the Brahms *Second Concerto*, the bargain is obvious.

Istomin's distinguished performance, recorded in 1960, is unfamiliar in the UK. The reading attractively combines strength and poetry, with bold contrasts in the first movement, a nicely lyrical *Intermezzo* and a fluent, well-paced finale. Bruno Walter's directing personality is strong: there is a natural flow in the outer movements, with the tempo flexing easily to accommodate the dialogues between piano and woodwind, which are beautifully managed. The recording sounds remarkably fine in its digital remastering, the warm ambience preventing any feeling of aggressiveness being generated by the dramatic tuttis. The piano timbre is fuller in colour than one expects from CBS recordings of this period. Indeed, Istomin's contribution is most appealing and, while the orchestral texture is less transparent than one would expect in a more modern version, Walter ensures that detail registers to the fullest effect. If the coupling is suitable, this is excellent value, offering 62′ of music.

Lupu's performance with André Previn is also a fine one. The clean boldness of approach to the first movement is appealingly fresh, but the poetry is more unevenly apparent than with Bishop-Kovacevich. The end of the slow movement is less magical than it might be; in general, the balance between the work's expressive and dramatic elements is not managed with complete success. The digital CD transfer is especially telling in the quieter moments, but tuttis are less transparent than with a digital recording – although the sound overall is good; and there is a first-class cassette.

Támás Vásáry directing from the keyboard gives a characteristically refined and yet strong account of the concerto, free from eccentricity and thoroughly straightforward. Poetic, likeable and decently recorded, this is recommendable for those wanting this coupling but, taken on its own merits, it does not displace Bishop-Kovacevich. The recording is excellent.

Anda's performance is thoroughly musical and Schumannesque in feeling and, while it does not probe any depths, this account with good orchestral support is attractive. The remastered sound has brought a freshening, but there is no lack of body and the balance is good.

More than most of his 1960s recordings, Rubinstein's account of the Schumann *Concerto* suffers seriously from the absence of real pianissimos. The use of Chicago's Orchestra Hall has brought a warm orchestral sound and a pleasingly real piano image, but the forward balance means that everything, apart from the big orchestral tuttis, seems to continue at a pervading *mezzo forte*. There is much that is beautiful in Rubinstein's actual playing but, in his interchanges both with the wind soloists in the first movement and with the strings in the *Intermezzo*, there is little light and shade, and the gay little march theme across the beat, from the orchestra in the finale, is also too loud.

András Schiff's is an exceptionally gentle and lyrical reading, full of poetic insight. On CD, the recorded sound brings the same soft focus from distancing as in the Chopin on the reverse, but there is more bite of contrast both in Schiff's playing and in that of the Concertgebouw, giving necessary power to the work.

Zimerman gives a big-boned performance, bold rather than delicate. There is consummate pianism from this most aristocratic of young artists, and Karajan draws fine playing from the Berlin orchestra. The sound is full and brilliant, strikingly present in its CD format. However, there is an unyielding quality here in place of a natural romantic spontaneity, and this performance would not be a primary choice.

Israela Margalit brings no lack of warmth to the concerto but she is somewhat idiosyncratic. The central A flat section of the first movement is very measured and she is not averse to point-making by means of rubati. The recording is somewhat resonant but the piano is rather forward in the aural picture. This offers no serious challenge to the front-runners in the catalogue. There is a good cassette.

Jorge Bolet's Schumann is rather more successful than the Grieg on the reverse, but he does not show any true feeling for this repertoire. The performance is agreeably relaxed – the short central movement comes off best – but the interplay between wind soloists and pianist in the first movement seems disappointingly matter-of-fact and the finale tends towards heaviness. The recording is admirable.

Richter's HMV reading of the Schumann, like that of the Grieg on the reverse, is extraordinarily wayward. Though with this composer Richter can hardly help bringing occasional illumination, this remains on the whole a disappointing version. The recording is well balanced and the CD transfer is of good quality.

(i) *Piano concerto in A min., Op. 54; Symphony No. 3 in E flat* (*Rhenish*), *Op. 97*.
(*) DG Dig. **415 358-2 [id.]. (i) Justus Frantz; VPO, Bernstein.

Bernstein draws excellent playing from the Vienna Philharmonic on DG and, although there are some expressive indulgences, these are by no means as disruptive in the *Rhenish symphony* as some reviews have indicated. The performances derive from concerts given in 1984 in the Grossersaal of the Musikverein and have the electricity and immediacy of live music-making. There is some slight exaggeration in the fourth movement (said to be inspired by the sight of Cologne Cathedral), but there is no want of dignity and nobility. Justus Frantz's account of the *Piano concerto* does seem a little wanting in spontaneity and does not have quite the delicacy of feeling or subtlety of nuance that Bishop-Kovacevich commands. The recording is full-bodied yet clear. The concerto is also available coupled with Zimerman's account of the Brahms *First Concerto* (also with Bernstein) on a bargain-priced DG Pocket Music chrome tape of high quality, the sound brighter and somewhat drier in the bass than the CD (*419 831-4*).

Violin concerto in D min., Op. posth.
(*) HMV Dig. **CDC7 47110-2 [id]. Kremer, Philh. O., Muti – SIBELIUS: *Concerto.***

The Schumann *Violin concerto* has had a generally bad press since it resurfaced in 1937. Kulenkampff and Menuhin were among its earliest champions. Its vein of introspection seems to suit Gidon Kremer, who gives a generally sympathetic account of it and has very good support from the Philharmonia Orchestra under Riccardo Muti. It is not Schumann at his most consistently inspired, but there are good things in it, including a memorable second subject and a characteristic slow movement. The recording is full-bodied and vivid; while the CD, with its added firmness, slightly emphasizes the forward balance of the soloist (the violin timbre tangible), the integration with the orchestra is also more positive.

Symphony in G min. (Zwickauer); Symphony No. 2 in C, Op. 61.
** Capriccio Dig. **10094** [id.]. Stuttgart RSO, Marriner.

This record is of interest in including the *Zwickauer symphony*, named after the town where it received its first performance in 1832. Schumann then revised it and left a two-movement piece, the second combining *Andante* and *Allegretto*. The performances of this and the *Second Symphony* are agreeably light-hearted, but without the gravitas one expects from Schumann – at times one thinks more of Mendelssohn. The Stuttgart Radio Orchestra plays very well indeed, although there is a lack of drama and the mood is generally easy-going. The Capriccio recording is full and clear, with a good ambience, sounding rather like a broadcast.

Symphonies Nos 1 in B flat (Spring), Op. 38 (original 1841 version); 3 in E flat (Rhenish), Op. 97.
** Denon Dig. **CO 1516** [id.]. Berlin State O, Suitner.

Suitner offers the first recording of the original version of the *Spring symphony* (the score is kept in the Library of Congress). There are a number of minor changes (the most striking is at the opening where the fanfare of horns and trumpets is on the tonic B flat, rather than a third higher on D); in addition, the Scherzo has only a single trio, while at the beginning of the finale Schumann interpolates a rather engaging flute cadenza. The performance is a good one, relaxed rather than vibrant, but well played. In the *Rhenish*, however, there is a more noticeable lack of thrust and other versions are more consistently involving. The sound is naturally balanced – made in the Berlin Jesus Christus Kirche.

Symphony No. 1 in B flat (Spring), Op. 38.
(M) *** DG **423 209-2**; *423 209-4* [id.]. BPO, Karajan – MENDELSSOHN: *Symphony No. 4.****
(**) Decca mono **417 287-2** [id.]. VPO, Furtwängler – FRANCK: *Symphony.*(*)

Symphony No. 1 in B flat (Spring); Manfred overture, Op. 115.
(B) **(*) DG Walkman *413 157-4*. BPO, Kubelik – SCHUBERT: *Symphony No. 8* etc.**(*)

Symphony No. 1 in B flat (Spring); Manfred overture, Op. 115; Overture, scherzo and finale, Op. 52.
(*) Capriccio **CD 10 063. Stuttgart RSO, Marriner.

Symphonies Nos 1 in B flat (Spring); 2 in C, Op. 61.
(M) ** Vox Prima **MWCD 7116** [id.]. St Louis SO, Jerzy Semkow.

Symphonies Nos 1 in B flat (Spring); 3 in E flat (Rhenish), Op. 97.
*** ASV Dig. *ZCDCA 587* [id.]. Royal Liverpool PO, Janowski.

Symphonies Nos 1 in B flat (Spring); 4 in D min., Op. 120.
(M) *** DG *419 065-4* [id.]. BPO, Karajan.
(*) DG Dig. **415 274-2 [id.]. VPO, Bernstein.

Karajan's versions of the Schumann symphonies dominate all other modern recordings. His readings of both Nos 1 and 4 provide beautifully shaped performances, with orchestral playing of the highest distinction. He has a natural feeling for the ebb and flow of the music and his control of tempo is subtly varied to follow the musical line. No. 4 is especially fine: this can be classed alongside Furtwängler's famous record, with Karajan similarly inspirational, yet a shade more self-disciplined than his illustrious predecessor. The sound has been digitally remastered, ready for CD; it remains full but is sharper in focus and detail. The tape is first class.

Janowski's pairing of the *Spring* and *Rhenish symphonies* is particularly successful, coupling the finest performances from his complete Liverpool cycle. The pacing throughout both symphonies is most convincing, with a good deal of the inspirational pull that makes the Karajan readings so telling. The song-like lyricism of the *Larghetto* of the *First Symphony* is matched by the serenity of the slow movement of the *Third*, and both Scherzos are very strongly characterized. In the Cologne Cathedral evocation of the *Rhenish*, the Liverpool brass rise sonorously to the occasion and the recording is altogether first class, bright, clear and full, with a concert hall ambience.

Bernstein's VPO versions of Nos 1 and 4 have the extra voltage which comes with live music-making at its most compulsive; it is a pity that Bernstein, who displays a natural response to Schumann, seeks to impose personal idiosyncrasies on the performances less convincingly than Karajan and Furtwängler. Both symphonies have portentous openings, and tempi are not always consistently controlled. The first movement of the *Spring symphony* is pushed hard, while the outer movements of No. 4 are not allowed to move forward at a steady pulse. The big transitional climax before the finale of the *Fourth* is massively conceived, yet has not the spine-tingling sense of anticipation that Furtwängler generates at this point. Even so, with splendid orchestral playing and much engaging detail, there is a great deal to admire here; both slow movements have striking warmth and humanity, even if the phrasing at the opening of the *Romance* of No. 4 has an element of self-consciousness. The recording has an attractive ambience and is full and well balanced, with the woodwind attractively coloured.

Alongside Bernstein's performance, the bright directness of Marriner's reading of the *First Symphony* is the more striking, and there is certainly a spring-like freshness in the outer movements, with the finale sparkling in an almost Schubertian way. The string ensemble is first rate, with rhythms nicely sprung and the phrasing of the *Larghetto* agreeably songful. There is perhaps a lack of romantic weight, but throughout Sir Neville lets the music speak for itself and avoids interfering with the onward flow to register expressive emphases. The *Overture, scherzo and finale* is strongly characterized, again very well played, with the closing apotheosis lyrically powerful without melodrama. The *Manfred overture* too is eloquently done. Throughout, one's ear is drawn to the fine internal balance of the Stuttgart Radio Orchestra, with woodwind beautifully blended (the colouring of the second subject of the first movement of the *Symphony* is particularly telling), while the brass are firm and incisive, never blatant. The digital recording is first class within a kindly studio ambience that allows detail to register admirably, yet is not too dry.

Jerry Semkow's readings of Nos 1 and 2 have more urgency, but less polish and finesse than Marriner's Stuttgart performances. No. 2 has much fervour in the *Adagio*, and the closing *Allegro molto vivace* has plenty of bite. But in the last resort, these are not distinctive performances, especially alongside those of Karajan; and the recording, though it has been brightly remastered, is lively and well projected rather than expansive.

Kubelik's account of the *Spring symphony* dates from 1963 and the recording sounds well on this Walkman chrome tape. Both performances here have a sympathetic lyrical impulse; if the coupling is suitable, this should not disappoint, for the price is very competitive.

Furtwängler's brief dalliance with Decca brought in 1951 this poorly recorded but characteristically dedicated reading of Schumann's *Spring symphony*. Despite the very restricted sound, the incandescence of the performance consistently comes over, and though Furtwängler is typically free over tempo, varying and moulding, the purposefulness of this conducting is never in doubt. This may not match his incomparable reading of Schumann's *Fourth Symphony*, but it is welcome too, coupled with Furtwängler's less attractive, rugged, Germanic reading of the Franck *Symphony*.

Symphonies Nos 1 in B flat (Spring); 2 in C (arr. Mahler).
** BIS Dig. **CD 361** [id.]. Bergen PO, Ceccato.

For many decades it was fashionable to criticize Schumann's orchestration, whereas now we have evidence from Karajan and the Berlin Philharmonic that there is nothing much wrong with it that a great modern orchestra cannot put right. However, Mahler decided that he could improve on Schumann, and in these Bergen recordings his gentle and subtle pruning can at times be detected in a cleaner sound; however, the resonant ambience in which the recordings were made tends to cancel out some of the touchings-up. Certainly the brass opening of No. 2 sounds very clear and clean, but in the slow movement the woodwind remain virtually unaltered. Mahler also thought a little abbreviation would be judicious, and in this same work there is a big cut in the coda which reduces it from 196 bars to 118. The condensation is done with a composer's skill and would be difficult to detect without a score. The performances here are mellow and enjoyable, but hardly make out a case for Mahler's 'improvements'. This is mainly of curiosity value.

Symphony No. 2; Manfred overture.
(*) DG Dig. **410 863-2 [id]. VPO, Sinopoli.

Sinopoli's is a performance of extremes, consciously designed to reflect the composer's own mental torment. Even the lovely slow movement broods darkly rather than finding repose. The Vienna Philharmonic play with the necessary bite, with the recording providing some mellowness. On CD, the strings are given added bite and brilliance and wind detail is clarified, but the overall balance is not always completely convincing.

Symphonies Nos 2 in C; 4 in D min.
** ASV Dig. *ZCDCA 562* [id.]. Royal Liverpool PO, Janowski.

This is a less successful coupling than Janowski's companion recordings of Nos 1 and 3. No. 2 comes off better than No. 4, with some fine, expressive playing from the Liverpool strings in the *Adagio* and an exciting finale. There is no lack of freshness elsewhere. No. 4 is fast. Janowski does not relax enough to let the first movement's lyrical blossoming take the fullest effect. There is more poise in the *Romanze* (and some fine wind playing too) but the finale is pushed forward rather aggressively and the accelerandos at the end of both outer movements sound unspontaneous.

Symphony No. 3 in E flat (Rhenish), Op. 87.
(M) *** DG **419 870-2**; *419 870-4* [id.]. BPO, Karajan – MENDELSSOHN: *Symphony No. 5.***(*)
(B) *** DG Walkman *419 390-4* [id.]. BPO, Karajan – MENDELSSOHN: *Symphony No. 3.****

Symphony No. 3 in E flat (Rhenish); Manfred overture, Op. 115.
*** DG Dig. **400 062-2** [id.]. LAPO, Giulini.
(*) Ph. Dig. **411 104-2 [id.]. Concg. O, Haitink.

Symphonies Nos 3 in E flat (Rhenish); 4 in D min., Op. 120.
** Capriccio Dig. **10093** [id.]. Stuttgart RSO, Marriner.

Symphony No. 4 in D min., Op. 120.
(B) **(*) DG Walkman *419 822-4* [id.]. BPO, Kubelik – MENDELSSOHN: *Symphony No. 5*; SCHUBERT: *Symphony No. 4.***(*)

Symphony No. 4 in D min.; Manfred overture, Op. 115.
(***) DG mono **415 661-2** [id.]. BPO, Furtwängler – HAYDN: *Symphony No. 88.* (***)

Karajan's account of the *Rhenish* is one of the most impressive versions ever committed to disc, and certainly the finest currently available. The playing of the Berlin Philharmonic is beyond praise, and one's only reservation concerns the digital remastering. The ambient effect remains, but the bass is drier. On the outstandingly generous Walkman tape alternative the sound is richer and the coupling is Mendelssohn's *Scottish symphony.*

Despite the aristocratic qualities that distinguish his performances and the spirituality that is in evidence, Giulini can often obtrude by the very intensity of his search for perfection; as a result, while the sound he produces is of great beauty, he does not always allow the music to unfold effortlessly. This *Rhenish* is, however, completely free of interpretative exaggeration and its sheer musical vitality and nobility of spirit are beautifully conveyed. The Los Angeles players produce a very well-blended, warm and cultured sound that is a joy to listen to in itself. The recording is extremely fine, too, and is particularly impressive in its compact disc format.

Haitink's is a characteristically strong and direct reading, beautifully played with outstandingly resonant and rich brass – most important in this of all the Schumann symphonies. Speeds are finely chosen, with the slower movements nicely flowing. Good Concertgebouw sound, lacking a little in brilliance but allowing textures to be registered in fair detail.

Marriner's coupling of Nos 3 and 4 is well played and agreeable enough in its way, but the *Rhenish* is underpowered and the *Fourth* has a disappointing lack of urgency until the finale, which is attractively spirited. Compared with Karajan and, in No. 4, with Furtwängler, this is only half the story. The recording is good.

There is little doubt that Schumann's *Fourth Symphony* is one of Furtwängler's really great records. Even those who find this conductor's tampering with speeds too personal and wilful can hardly fail to be moved by the richness of his conception of this work. The appearance of the first movement's secondary theme is an unforgettable moment, while the *Romanze* is freshly spontaneous in its simplicity; but it is perhaps in the finale where the lack of a firm forward tempo is most striking – and equally (from the magnificently prepared 'Wagnerian' transition passage onwards) where the conductor is most successful in giving a sense of creation in the actual performance. There is superb playing from the Berlin Philharmonic, especially in the brass and strings. The recording has been remastered and the string timbre is clear rather than rich; but there is a supporting weight so that the ear readily adjusts, for the original 1953 mono recording (made in the Berlin Jesus Christus Church) was well balanced, with a fine ambience. *Manfred* – recorded in 1949 at a public performance – has rather less congenial sound, and the strings sound thinner. Moreover, there are audience noises to interrupt the rapt concentration of the closing pages. It is a characteristically Romantic reading, but convincingly controlled. With its splendid Haydn coupling, this is one Furtwängler CD to recommend without reservation to all readers.

Kubelik's account of the *Fourth* is beautifully played and well if slightly drily recorded. There is neither the drive of Karajan nor the imaginative force of Furtwängler, but the performance is direct in manner and certainly enjoyable. Generously coupled on this Walkman tape, it makes fair value.

CHAMBER AND INSTRUMENTAL MUSIC

Adagio and allegro in A flat, Op. 70.
*** BBC Dig. **CD 641**; *ZCN 641* [id.]. Michael Thompson, Catherine Dubois – R. STRAUSS: *Horn concertos.****
(M) *** DG *419 860-4* [id.]. Rostropovich, Argerich – CHOPIN: *Sonata* etc.***

The *Adagio and allegro* is awkwardly written for the horn; however, Michael Thompson surmounts its difficulties with ease and his excellent performance makes a suitable bonus for superb accounts of the Strauss *Horn concertos*.

Though this piece is generally given to the horn, it can as well be played on the cello, and Rostropovich makes a good case for this particular instrumentation, memorably expressive. The sound is excellent.

Fantasiestücke, Op. 73; Märchenerzählungen, Op. 132.
(*) CRD *CRDC 4111* [id.]. Anthony Pay, Nash Ens. (members) – MOZART: *Clarinet trio.*

Schumann's *Märchenerzählungen* (Fairy-tales) is late (1853) and is almost unique in being scored for the same combination as Mozart's *Trio for clarinet, viola and piano*. It makes an apt coupling for that work. The *Fantasiestücke* for clarinet and piano was written four years earlier, but both belong to the group of eight miscellaneous chamber works featuring various wind instruments, cello or horn. Both performances are sympathetic and spontaneous, easy-going perhaps, but welcome when the repertoire is rare. The recording is well balanced and truthful.

Fantasiestücke, Op. 73; 3 Romances, Op. 94.
*** Chan. Dig. **CHAN 8566**; *ABTD 1216* [id.]. Gervase de Peyer, Gwenneth Pryor – SCHUBERT: *Arpeggione sonata*; WEBER: *Silvana variations.****

The artistry of Gervase de Peyer is heard to splendid effect in these late works of Schumann. With warmth of tone and much subtlety of colour, he gives first-class performances and is well supported by Gwenneth Pryor. The recording is most realistic in both formats; in the *Fantasiestücke*, the effect is more voluptuous than in Anthony Pay's version.

Fantasiestücke, Op. 73; 5 Stücke in Volkston, Op. 102.
*** Ph. Dig. **412 230-2** [id.]. Maisky, Argerich – SCHUBERT: *Arpeggione sonata.****

Mischa Maisky and Martha Argerich give relaxed, leisurely accounts of these pieces that some collectors may find almost self-indulgent. Others will luxuriate in the refinement and sensitivity of this playing, coupled with an unusual and musically perceptive account of the *Arpeggione sonata*; an altogether outstanding Philips recording, especially tangible on CD.

Märchenbilder, Op. 113.
(*) Chan. Dig. **CHAN 8550; *ABTD 1256* [id.]. Imai, Vignoles – BRAHMS: *Viola sonatas.***(*)

The *Märchenbilder* are not the greatest Schumann but they have a good deal of charm. They come from 1851 and are pleasing miniatures; the third is particularly fine; they are persuasively played by Nobuko Imai and Roger Vignoles. The recording acoustic is not ideal, but this does not seriously detract from the value of this coupling, expecially as there is no alternative account of these pieces.

Piano quartet in E flat, Op. 47; (i) *Piano quintet in E flat, Op. 44.*
*** Ph. **420 791-2** [id.]. Beaux Arts Trio, Rhodes, (i) with Bettelheim.
(*) CRD **CRD 3324; *CRD 4024* [id.]. Rajna, members of the Alberni Qt.

The Beaux Arts Trio (with associates) give splendid performances of both these fine chamber works, which in 1842 showed the composer branching out from his great year of song. The vitality of inspiration is consistently brought out, whether in the *Quintet* or the relatively neglected *Quartet*, and with that goes the Beaux Arts' characteristic concern for fine ensemble and refined textures. The recording is beautifully clear and clean, if less atmospheric than before, but the digital remastering has improved detail.

Though not quite so flawlessly polished in their playing, Rajna and the Alberni give performances that are in their way as urgent and enjoyable as those on the Philips disc. The recording is brighter and crisper, which gives an extra (and not unlikeable) edge to the performances.

Piano quintet in E flat, Op. 44.
(*) HMV **CDC7 47439-2 [id.]; *EL 270447-4*. Philippe Entremont, Alban Berg Qt – MOZART: *String quartet No. 19.***(*)
*(*) Sup. Dig. **COS 1329** [id.]. Panenka, Smetana Qt – DVOŘÁK: *Piano quintet.**(*)

The record by Entremont and the Alban Berg Quartet emanates from a concert performance at Carnegie Hall, and the sparkle and spontaneity that distinguish the playing raise it far above the slightly remote, streamlined efficiency this ensemble can produce. The pianist, too, is more poetic and sensitive than is often the case. There is a price to pay in the form of audience noise (they burst into applause – quite rightly – after the third movement) and there is some coughing; but collectors interested in this coupling – another work at the same concert – should not allow this to deter them. The recording is lifelike and well integrated, although the XDR cassette is not as transparent as the disc.

On Supraphon the sound seems artificial, made in the House of Artists in Prague, and the playing of the Smetana Quartet not as refined as it was. Jan Panenka is superb, but the reverberant acoustic and rough-and-ready timbre from the Quartet does not make this a competitive version.

Piano trio No. 1 in D min., Op. 63.
(*) CRD **CRD 3433; *CRDC 4133* [id.]. Israel Piano Trio – BRAHMS: *Piano trio No. 2.***(*)

The *D minor Trio* dates from 1847 and is not otherwise represented on compact disc. The Israel Piano Trio give a powerfully projected account; the pianist is at times rather carried away, as if he were playing a Brahms concerto. The Scherzo is too emphatically – indeed, almost brutally – articulated and as akin to the world of Schumann as are the skyscrapers of Manhattan or Tel Aviv. There are, however, some sensitive and intelligent touches; and there is at present no CD alternative. The recording is first class and there is an extremely realistic cassette.

Funf Stücke (*5 Pieces*) *im Volkston* (for cello and piano).
(M) *** Decca **417 833-2** [id.]. Rostropovich, Britten – SCHUBERT **(*); DEBUSSY: *Sonatas.****

Though simpler than the Debussy sonata with which it is coupled, this is just as elusive a work. Rostropovich and Britten show that the simplicity is not so square and solid as it might seem at first, and that in the hands of masters these *Five Pieces in folk style* have a rare charm, particularly the last, with its irregular rhythm. Excellent recording on CD.

Violin sonatas Nos 1 in A min., Op. 105; 2 in D min., Op. 121.
*** DG Dig. **419 235-2**; *419 235-4* [id.]. Gidon Kremer, Martha Argerich.
(*) CBS Dig. **MK 42053 [id.]. Eva Graubin, Theodore Paraskivesco.

The *Violin sonatas* both date from 1851 and are among the finest of Schumann's later works. They were written before the illness that troubled his last years had taken a firm hold and are 'an oasis of freshness' in his last creative period. They have not been much favoured on LP but have received two recordings on CD since the appearance of our last volume. Kremer and Argerich lead the field: they are splendidly reflective and mercurial by turn and have the benefit of an excellent recording in both media.

Eva Graubin and Theodore Paraskivesco are hardly less impressive artistically and, particularly in the more ruminative slow movements, honours are evenly divided between them and their DG rivals. Unfortunately, although good, the recording is made in a smaller acoustic than is desirable (in the Studio La Clé d'Ut, in Paris) and is not ideally balanced – Paraskivesco rather dominates proceedings in the opening of the *D minor Sonata*. Graubin is splendid, however; despite these reservations, this account must be recommended.

PIANO MUSIC

Albumblätter, Op. 124, Kinderszenen, Op. 15; Waldszenen, Op. 82.
** Tel. Dig. **ZK8 43467** [id.]. Cyprien Katsaris.

The piano – as so often with Katsaris performances – is very close and sounds a shade synthetic compared with the best Philips or Decca recording. Katsaris is eminently successful in the *Albumblätter* – less so in *Kinderszenen* where, for all his poetic sense, he is a trifle mannered.

Arabeske in C, Op. 18; Études symphoniques, Op. 13.
*** DG Dig. **410 916-2** [id.]. Maurizio Pollini.

Pollini's account has a symphonic gravitas and concentration: it has the benefit of excellent recorded sound from DG. He includes the five additional variations that Schumann decided against including in either of the editions published during his lifetime, placing them as a group between the fifth and sixth variations. Pollini's is a most impressive record by any standards. The CD has fine presence.

Arabeske, Op. 18; Études symphoniques, Op. 13; Papillons, Op. 2.
*** Decca Dig. **414 474-2**; *414 474-4* [id.]. Vladimir Ashkenazy.

Impressive playing – and well recorded too. Ashkenazy's *Études symphoniques* have put on a little weight by comparison with his 1960s LP and have a breadth and splendour that is not entirely in tune with Schumann's sensibility.

The *Arabeske* is better served on CD than *Papillons* at present, but this account must be numbered among the most powerful. There is a good, full-bodied cassette.

Carnaval, Op. 9; Fantasia in C, Op. 17.
(*) Decca Dig. **417 401-2; *417 401-4* [id.]. Jorge Bolet.

Bolet's Schumann coupling of *Carnaval* and the *C major Fantasy* brings expansive readings, mellowed in maturity. The speeds on the slow side bring some heaviness. There is a lack of sparkle at times in the lighter pieces of *Carnaval*, but these are thoughtfully poetic as well as strong performances. The mellowness of the approach is counterbalanced by a recording that makes the piano a little clangy in fortissimos, though this is softened a little on the cassette.

Carnaval, Op. 9; Fantasiestücke, Op. 12; Romance, Op. 28/2; Waldszenen, Op. 82: The Prophet bird.
(*) RCA **RD 85667 [**RCA 5667-2-RC**]. Artur Rubinstein.

Rubinstein had a high reputation as a Schumann interpreter and this collection shows why. He brings the fullest spectrum of colours to bear on these most romantic and lyrical of Schumann's compositions, moving with artless ease from one mood to the next, always supremely sure of himself and always superbly in tune with the musical thought. Though the piano timbre is not as rich as the best recordings from Decca or EMI, there is a directness about the sound that helps captivate the attention and an immediacy about the disc as a whole, with its attractive encores, that puts it high on the list of RCA's CD reissues of this great pianist's repertoire.

Davidsbündlertänze, Op. 6; Fantasiestücke, Op. 12.
*** CBS *40-76202*. Murray Perahia.

Perahia has a magic touch, and his electric spontaneity is naturally caught in the studio. In works of Schumann which can splinter apart, this quality of concentration is enormously valuable, and the results could hardly be more powerfully convincing, despite recording quality which lacks something in bloom and refinement. The chrome cassette is very well managed, with good definition. The treble is smoothed a little to advantage, without loss of presence.

Davidsbündlertänze, Op. 6; Humoreske in B flat, Op. 20.
*** Chan. *ABT 1029* [id.]. Lydia Artymiw.

Lydia Artymiw attracted attention at the 1978 Leeds Piano Competition as a player of temperament and personality. Her finely delineated accounts of the *Davidsbündlertänze* and the *Humoreske* can both hold their own with the best now on the market. In both works Artymiw shows her finesse as a Schumann interpreter, drawing together music which in its very structure presents problems. Never exaggerating, she conveys consistent intensity as in a live concert. She is perhaps not as touching in the *Davidsbündlertänze* as Murray Perahia (see above), but she has the advantage of better recording. Her cleanly articulated playing has true artistry to recommend it alongside the naturally balanced sound image, very impressive on cassette.

Études symphoniques; Toccata, Op. 7.
*(*) DG Dig. **410 520-2** [id.]. Ivo Pogorelich – BEETHOVEN: *Piano sonata No. 32.***(*)

Pogorelich opens his performance of the *Études symphoniques* with a grotesquely self-conscious and studied presentation of the theme. This is pianism of the first order, but the listener's attention tends to be drawn from the music to the pianism, which is too wilful to be considered alongside Pollini's eloquent account (see above) or the fresh and ardent version by Murray Perahia. The recording is vivid and truthful, and has striking presence on compact disc.

Fantasia in C, Op. 17.
*** CBS Dig. **MK 42124**; *IMT 42124* [id.]. Murray Perahia – SCHUBERT: *Wanderer Fantasia.****

Murray Perahia has the measure of Schumann's sensibility as have few others. His account of the *C major Fantasy*, perhaps the most powerful and deeply felt of all Schumann's piano works, has few peers. It is a performance of vision and breadth, immaculate in its attention to detail and refinement of nuance. The recording is good, even if it does not wholly convey the wide range of sonority and dynamics Perahia produces in a concert performance.

Fantasia in C, Op. 17; Fantasiestücke, Op. 12.
*** Ph. Dig. **411 049-2** [id.]. Alfred Brendel.

Brendel's coupling is outstanding. As the very opening of the *Fantasiestücke* demonstrates, this is magically spontaneous playing, full of imaginative touches of colour, strong as well as poetic. The compact disc has a greater range and presence than the already impressive LP format. The actual sound is rather more forward than one would encounter in the recital room, but it serves Brendel well and truthfully conveys the depth of timbre.

Fantasia in C, Op. 17; Kreisleriana, Op. 16.
*** RCA **RD 86258 [RCA 6258-2-RC]**. Artur Rubinstein.

Rubinstein's account of the *Fantasia in C* is one of his finest Schumann performances on record. It is wonderfully subtle in its control of tempo and colour, and the poetry of the outer sections is quite magical, while the centrepiece is arrestingly bold. In spite of the close balance Rubinstein achieves exquisite gradations of tone; the recording, made in 1965, is among the best he received during this period. The CD opens with a hardly less compelling account of *Kreisleriana* in which the great pianist is at his most aristocratic. The impetuous opening is rather shallowly recorded, but the sound has plenty of fullness and colour at lower dynamic levels and the piano image has good presence.

Fantasia in C, Op. 17; Piano sonata No. 1 in F sharp min., Op. 11.
*** DG **423 134-2** [id.]. Maurizio Pollini.

This is among the most distinguished Schumann records in the catalogue. The *Fantasia* is as fine as Richter's now deleted version, and Pollini's playing throughout has a command and authority on the one hand and deep poetic feeling on the other that instantly capture the listener spellbound. The recording is good but not outstanding – it is rather hard in its digitally remastered form.

Kinderszenen (Scenes from childhood), Op. 15; Kreisleriana, Op. 16.
*(**) DG Dig. **410 653-2** [id.]. Martha Argerich.

There is no doubting the instinctive flair of Argerich's playing or her intuitive feeling for Schumann. However, she is let down by an unpleasingly close recording that diminishes pleasure somewhat.

4 Sketches, Op. 58.
(*) ASV *ZCALH 958* [id.]. Jennifer Bate (Royal Albert Hall organ) – ELGAR: *Sonata.*(*)

The *Four Sketches* were originally written for a piano with pedal attachment, and are here arranged for organ by E. Power Biggs. Each of the pieces is in 3/4 time, but the writing is attractively diverse. They are pleasant trifles, pleasing enough as a coupling for the fine Elgar performance on the reverse. Rich, atmospheric recording with fair detail, impressively transferred to tape.

Dichterliebe, Op. 48.
(B) *** DG Walkman *423 291-4* [id.]. Dietrich Fischer-Dieskau, Christoph Eschenbach – SCHUBERT: *Die schöne Müllerin.****

Dichterliebe (song-cycle), *Op. 48; Liederkreis* (song-cycle), *Op. 39; Myrthen Lieder, Op. 25.*
*** DG **415 190-2** [id.]. Dietrich Fischer-Dieskau, Christoph Eschenbach.

Fischer-Dieskau's Schumann recordings made with Christoph Eschenbach in the mid-1970s provide an attractive coupling of an outstandingly fine *Dichterliebe* (the voice still fresh) and the magnificent Op. 39 *Liederkreis*, made the more attractive on CD by the generous addition of seven of the *Myrthen* songs, making 39 items in all. Though a thoughtfully individual artist in his own right, Eschenbach here provides consistently sympathetic support for the singer. He is imaginative on detail without ever intruding distractingly. Very good sound for the period. As can be seen, the *Dichterliebe* is also available on an extremely generous Walkman tape.

Dichterliebe, Op. 48; Liederkreis, Op. 39.
*** Ph. Dig. **416 352-2**; *416 352-4* [id.]. Dietrich Fischer-Dieskau, Alfred Brendel.
*** HMV **CDC7 47397-2** [id.]; *EL 270364-4*. Olaf Bär, Geoffrey Parsons.

More than in his previous versions of Schumann's *Dichterliebe,* Fischer-Dieskau's latest one, done in inspired collaboration with Alfred Brendel, brings an angry, inconsolable reading, reflecting the absence of fulfilment in the poet's love. As in their other collaborations, singer and pianist present a fascinating interplay of expression, and it matters relatively little – though more than in, say, *Winterreise* – that Fischer-Dieskau's voice has more grit in it than before. The Op. 39 *Liederkreis* also brings inspired, spontaneous-sounding performances of these wonderfully varied songs, with the voice notably fresher. Excellent recording.

Olaf Bär made an impressive international recording début with this superb account of Schumann's two great song-cycles, finely detailed and full of insight, but relatively reticent in its expressive style. These are not such strongly characterized readings as those of Fischer-Dieskau; but in their fresher, more youthful manner they are outstandingly successful. Excellent recording, both on CD and on the clear, well-balanced tape.

Frauenliebe und Leben, Op. 42; Liederkreis, Op. 24; 3 Heine Lieder (*Abends am Strand; Lehn' deine Wang' an meine Wang'; Mein Wagen rollet langsam*). *Tragödie, Op. 64/3.*
*** DG Dig. **415 519-2** [id.]. Brigitte Fassbaender, Irwin Gage.

Positively characterized, with a wide range of expression and fine detail but little sense of vulnerability, Fassbaender's reading conceals the underlying sentimentality of the poems of *Frauenliebe*. There is little attempt to beautify the voice, though it is a fine, consistent instrument, for clear exposition of the words is the singer's prime aim. Passionate involvement also marks Fassbaender's singing of the Heine *Liederkreis*, of which there are surprisingly few recordings. The three songs of *Tragödie* and the three separate Heine settings make an important supplement. Irwin Gage is the understanding accompanist. The recording is well balanced, with fine presence.

Schütz, Heinrich (1585–1672)

Motets: *Auf dem Gebirge; Der Engel sprach; Exultavit cor meum; Fili mi Absalon; Heu mihi Domine; Hodie Christus natus est; Ich danke Dir, Herr; O quam tu pulchra es; Die Seele Christi, heilige mich; Selig sind die Todten.*
** ASV *ZCALH 960* [id.]. Pro Cantione Antiqua, Edgar Fleet.

An eminently useful and well-recorded anthology of Schütz motets that offers such masterpieces as *Fili mi Absalon* (for bass voice, five sackbuts, organ and violone continuo) and the glorious

Selig sind die Todten in well-thought-out and carefully prepared performances under Edgar Fleet. This first appeared in 1978 to a respectful rather than enthusiastic press, but these accounts have a dignity and warmth that make them well worth considering. Moreover, the cassette is splendidly managed, the sound rich and clear.

Christmas oratorio (*Weinachtshistorie*).
*** HMV Dig. **CDC7 47633-2** [id.]; *EL 270428-4*. Kirkby, Rogers, Thomas, Taverner Cons., Taverner Ch., Taverner Players, Parrott – PRAETORIUS: *Christmas motets*.***

The new EMI version of Schütz's *Christmas oratorio* has the advantage of three first-class soloists, all of whom are in excellent voice. One is soon gripped by the narrative and the beauty and simplicity of the line. There is no sense of austerity here, merely a sense of purity, with the atmosphere of the music beautifully captured by these forces under Andrew Parrott. Apart from a rather nasal edge on the violin tone, it is difficult to fault either this moving performance or the well-balanced and refined recording. There is an excellent chrome cassette.

Italian Madrigals, Book 1 (complete).
*** HMV **CDC7 47600-2** [id.]. Cons. of Musicke, Rooley.
*** HM **HMC 901162** [id.]. Concerto Vocale, René Jacobs.

Schütz's first and only Book of Italian Madrigals comes from his study years in Venice (1608–11) and reflects his encounter with the music of Giovanni Gabrieli and Monteverdi. As one would expect, Anthony Rooley's record with The Consort of Musicke has the advantage of impeccable intonation and blend, and the performances are all beautifully prepared and recorded.

The Concerto Vocale led by the counter-tenor, René Jacobs, are hardly less fine than their cross-Channel rivals, The Consort of Musicke. The latter are unaccompanied whereas the Concerto Vocale employ a theorbo which provides aural variety, and at times they offer a greater expressive and tonal range. They omit the very last of the madrigals, the eight-part *Vasto mar*, to which The Consort of Musicke do full justice on their disc.

Musikalische Exequiem; Psalm 136: Danket dem Herren, dem er ist freudlich.
*** HMV Dig. **CDC7 49225-2** [id.]. Nigel Rogers Vocal Ens., Basle Boys' Ch., Schola Cantorum Basiliensis, Linde.

Schütz's *Musikalische Exequiem* comes from 1635; it was written in response to a commission from Prince Heinrich Reuss for performance at his funeral, which the Prince planned in detail during his lifetime. The first part, subtitled 'Concert in the form of a burial Mass', is based on verses from the Bible and hymns which Reuss had ordered to be placed on his coffin; the second is the motet *Herr, wenn ich nur dich habe*, and the third the *Song of Simeon* from St Luke's Gospel, which was to be sung at the beginning of the burial. The present recording was made in 1979 and has been digitally remastered to excellent effect. The solo group of singers includes Jennifer Smith, Patrizia Kwella, James Bowman and Ian Partridge, as well as Nigel Rogers himself, and the instrumental team is hardly less distinguished. The fill-up, *Psalm 136* for two solo groups, chorus, and brass, comes from the *Psalms of David* (1619) and is an imposing piece in the Venetian style. A strong recommendation.

Psalms of David Nos 115; 128; 136; 150; Canzon: Un lob, mein Seel; Concerti: Lobe den Herren; Zion spricht; Jauchzet dem Herren; Motets: Ist nicht Ephraim; Die mit Tranen saen.
*(*) DG **415 297-2** [id.]. Regensburger Domspatzen, Hamburg Wind Ens., Ulsamer Coll., Schneidt.

The Psalms of David formed Schütz's first sacred work, published in 1619. There are twenty-six settings of Psalms plus two other biblical texts, written for single, double or triple chorus, with ad lib instrumental support. The last ten of these works are gathered together here, and in nine of them Schütz has indicated the required instrumentation. The performances here are more than adequate, quite well sung and played, although pacing tends to be brisk and the approach rather stiff. Unfortunately the 1972 recording is poorly focused: at the opening of Psalm 150 the impression is of 'fluff on the stylus', not an effect one expects from a digitally remastered CD.

St Matthew Passion.
*** HMV Dig. **CDC7 49200-2** [id.]. Hilliard Ens., Hillier.

Schütz's setting of the Passion Story, composed in 1666 when he was in his eighties, is exclusively vocal; its austerity extends to the absence not only of instrumental support but of any additional hymns or arias. Peter Pears's (now deleted) account with Roger Norrington's Heinrich Schütz Choir and John Shirley-Quirk as Jesus was recorded in the early 1970s; this new version from the Hilliard Ensemble and Paul Hillier, who takes the bass part of Jesus, makes an admirable successor. The solo parts are on the whole admirable and the restraint of Paul Elliot's Evangelist is impressive. The soloists double in the choral sections, which is less than ideal; in that respect, the Norrington version was to be preferred. In all others, however, there is no need to fault this excellently balanced and finely produced HMV version.

Der Schwanengesang (reconstructed by Wolfram Steude).
*** HMV Dig. **CDS7 49214-8** (2) [id.]. Hilliard Ens., Hannover Knabenchor, L. Bar., Hennig.

Schütz's *opus ultimum* is a setting of Psalm 119, the longest psalm in the psalter, which he divides into eleven sections. He finishes off this thirteen-part motet cycle with his final setting of Psalm 100, which he had originally composed in 1662, and the *Deutsches Magnificat*. Wolfram Steude's note recounts the history of the work, parts of which disappeared after Schütz's death; and his reconstruction of two of the vocal parts is obviously a labour of love. The project was undertaken in celebration of the European Music Year in 1985 and the recording a co-production with NDR (North German Radio). The performance is a completely dedicated one, with excellent singing from all concerned and good instrumental playing, and the conductor, Heinz Hennig, secures warm and responsive singing from his Hannover Knabenchor. The acoustic is spacious and warm, and the recording balance well focused. The sound is firm, clear and sonorous.

Scriabin, Alexander (1872–1915)

(i) *Piano concerto in F sharp min., Op. 20;* (ii) *Poème de l'extase, Op. 54;* (i) *Prometheus – The poem of fire, Op. 60.*
(M) *** Decca *417 252-4* [id.]. (i) Ashkenazy, LPO; (ii) Cleveland O; Maazel.

(i) *Piano concerto in F sharp min., Op. 20; Poème de l'extase, Op. 54; Rêverie, Op. 24.*
** Sup. Dig. **CO 2047** [id.]. (i) Garrick Ohlsson; Czech PO, Pešek.

This Decca London Enterprise reissue makes an admirable introduction to Scriabin's art and is a very distinguished recording in every respect. Ashkenazy plays the *Piano concerto* with great feeling and authority, and the Decca recording has both clarity and luminosity. Moreover Maazel accompanies most sympathetically throughout. *Prometheus* too is given a thoroughly poetic and committed reading by Maazel and the LPO, Ashkenazy coping with the virtuoso obbligato part with predictable distinction. Powerfully atmospheric and curiously hypnotic, the score reeks of Madame Blavatsky and Scriabin's wild mysticism, while abounding in the fanciful lines of *art nouveau*. Given such outstanding recording and performance, this makes a splendid starting point for any Scriabin collection. It was issued originally on 6 January 1972, the centenary of the composer's birth. For the reissue Decca have added Maazel's 1979 Cleveland recording of *Le Poème de l'extase*. This is a shade too efficient to be really convincing. The playing is often brilliant and the recording is very clear (the *Concerto* and *Prometheus* sound agreeably more diffuse) and the trumpets are rather forced and strident. But it can be regarded as a bonus for the other two works.

Garrick Ohlsson gives a splendidly romantic account of the *Piano concerto*, warmly and flexibly accompanied by Libor Pešek. Anyone coming in halfway through this work could be hard put to name its composer, when the playing is so seductive. Pešek has the full measure of the *Poème* also, and the Czech Philharmonic principal trumpet plays with memorable boldness. The snag is the rather close and somewhat dry recording, made at the House of Artists, Prague. This music needs a more expansive, evocative resonance for Scriabin's scoring to make its proper hypnotic effect.

Le Poème de l'extase, Op. 54.
(*) Erato Dig. **ECD 75360 [id.]. O de Paris, Barenboim – STRAVINSKY: *Rite of spring*.**(*)
** DG **415 370-2** [id.]. Boston SO, Abbado – DEBUSSY: *Nocturnes*; RAVEL: *Daphnis et Chloé; Pavane*.**

The *Poème de l'extase* is one of Scriabin's most successful works; this complex, opulent score needs an atmospheric recording to do justice to its lavish, self-intoxicating evocation, with its overtones of *art nouveau* and Theosophy. Its opening comes close to suggesting perfume and its originality is beyond question. On the whole the Erato recording meets these needs well enough, even if inner detail is not sharply defined. Barenboim's reading brings fine evidence of his work as music director of the Orchestre de Paris, in a ripely expressive, atmospheric reading. He emphasizes the piece's Wagnerian overtones, and Scriabin's debt to *Tristan* in particular. This is an orchestra which consistently produces warm, well-integrated textures, and that is stressed by the mellow, slightly recessed quality of the recording. Recommendable for those who fancy this unusual coupling, with the Stravinsky also acquiring a measure of mellowness.

Abbado's performance is superbly controlled, with the conductor's refinement acting as a brake on the blatancy of the score without destroying its impulse. The recording is atmospheric in the quiet opening pages but has a certain shrillness in the loudest moments which the digital remastering has emphasized, and the effect is inclined to be brash. The orchestra's principal trumpet uses a very striking vibrato in his dominating solos, which some ears may resist, but it fits the character of the music.

Symphony No. 1 in E, Op. 26.
*** HMV Dig. **CDC7 47349-2** [id.]. Toczyska, Myers, Westminster Ch., Phd. O, Muti.

Scriabin's *First Symphony* is a long, six-movement work dating from 1900, a highly rhapsodic score whose harmonic processes betray keyboard habits of mind, and whose lines are highly characteristic of *art nouveau*. It has been recorded before, by Svetlanov and Inbal; but neither commands the luxurious orchestral playing or the superb quality of the new EMI recording. Indeed, this inspired version eclipses all rivals and will be hard to beat. Muti brings great refinement of dynamic nuance and plasticity of phrasing to this score, showing its many beauties to the best possible advantage. It would be difficult to over-praise the sensitivity and polish of the Philadelphia wind or the sumptuous tone of the strings. The vocal contributions from Stefania Toczyska and Michael Myers in the last movement, a setting of Scriabin's own words, are also excellent. It is less overheated than the later symphonies and its lush pastures are brought wonderfully to life. This is undoubtedly one of Muti's best records in recent years and should acquire classic status. It sounds superb on CD.

Symphony No. 2 in C min., Op. 29; Rêverie, Op. 24.
*** Chan. Dig. **CHAN 8462**; *ABTD 1176* [id.]. SNO, Järvi.

Plenty of atmosphere here in Järvi's performance and a splendid orchestral response from his Scottish players. Although it is less amorphous than its predecessor, which has been so well recorded by Muti, the symphony needs the most fervent advocacy if the listener is to be persuaded. It occupied him throughout 1901 and, with its chromatic harmonies and sensuous and at times apparently directionless melodic lines, it could hardly be more characteristic of the *art nouveau* movement. It has enjoyed less exposure on record than its companions, and neither Semkow's nor Svetlanov's records lasted very long in the catalogue. This splendid account from Järvi, with its richly detailed Chandos recording, is likely to remain unchallenged for a long time. The chrome tape is well managed, although the resonance prevents detail from registering sharply.

Symphony No. 3 in C min. (Le divin poème), Op. 43.
*** BBC Dig. **CD 520**. BBC SO, Pritchard.
*** Etcetera **KTC 1027** [id.]. Concg. O, Kondrashin.

Scriabin's mammoth *Third Symphony* calls for vast forces: the scoring includes quadruple woodwind, eight horns (the BBC recording has nine), five trumpets, and so on. The work dates from 1903 and with its long, swirling lines is typical of the *art nouveau*. The commentator gives hostages to fortune by calling it 'one of the finest works of art created in its time or at any period in the history of music', but there is no doubt that it is original, both in layout and in substance. The BBC Symphony Orchestra play for Sir John Pritchard with commitment and give a thoroughly convincing account of this complex and at times inflated score. The recording, too, unravels the complexities of Scriabin's scoring with considerable success; the compact disc has great clarity and definition – and conveys an illusion of space. There is impressive range, particularly at the bottom end of the aural spectrum. Moreover, in so far as the symphony is played without a break, the CD has the obvious advantage of continuity.

Kondrashin and the Concertgebouw Orchestra recorded the *Third Symphony* at a public concert in 1976, and the performance has a certain authority and intensity that elude its rival. This, too, is well recorded – though not quite so well as the digital BBC version. Collectors for whom the clarity and definition of digital recording are a first priority should go for the BBC account, but others should note that honours are pretty well divided between the two versions, with Kondrashin's having a slight edge as an interpretation.

Preludes, Op. 11, Nos 2, 4–6, 8–14, 16, 18, 20, 22, 24; Op. 13, Nos 1–3; Op. 15, Nos 1 and 5; Op. 16, Nos 2 and 4. Prelude for the left hand in C sharp min., Op. 9/1; Étude in C sharp min., Op. 42/5. Piano sonata No. 4 in F sharp, Op. 30.
*** HMV Dig. **CDC7 47346-2** [id.]. Andrei Gavrilov.

Gavrilov does not give us any set of the *Preludes* or *Studies* complete but picks and chooses – which is no doubt ideal in a piano recital designed to show his sympathies, but less desirable from the point of view of a record collector. We have all the even-numbered *Preludes* of Op. 11, most of them exquisitely played, plus Nos 5, 9, 11 and 13, and a handful of preludes drawn arbitrarily from Opp. 9, 13, 15 and 16, one of the Op. 42 *Études* and the *Fourth Sonata*, Op. 30, which is about the finest account on record. At times the playing is impetuous and dynamics can be exaggerated: Op. 11, No. 20 begins *ff* when the marking is merely *mf*, and there are numerous such instances where a *piano* becomes *piano-pianissimo*. But playing of this order is still pretty remarkable, and imperfections – the odd ugly *ff* and a not particularly pleasing instrument – should be overlooked. The balance is not too close, yet the CD brings a tangible presence and the piano timbre is naturally caught.

Piano Sonatas Nos 1 in F, Op. 6; 6 in G, Op. 62; 8 in A, Op. 66; 4 Pieces, Op. 51.
*** Decca **414 353-2**; *414 353-4* [id.]. Vladimir Ashkenazy.

The *First Sonata* comes from 1892 and is a full-blown romantic piece in the received tradition, separated from its two companions on this disc by some twenty years. The last five sonatas were all written in 1911–13 and are all one-movement affairs. Scriabin never played the *Sixth Sonata* in public and regarded it with dread as 'nightmarish, murky, unclean and mischievous'. It is indeed extraordinarily intense and sinister, but there is a disturbed, maniacal quality about its successors too. The *Eighth*, the so-called *White Mass*, is hardly less remarkable and comes off marvellously. Scriabin has been well served on record in the past by such artists as Richter, Horowitz and Gilels; though there were fine things in Roberto Szidon's DG cycle some years ago, few modern pianists on record are more inside this music than Ashkenazy, who penetrates to the heart of its imaginative world. The recording is excellent (although the cassette quality is not as open as the CD) and we can only hope that it will not be too long before the remainder of the cycle is transferred to CD.

Piano sonata No. 2 in G sharp min., Op. 19. Mazurkas: in E min., Op. 25/3, in G flat and F sharp, Op. 40/1–2, Poèmes: in F sharp and D, Op. 32/1–2; Valse in F min., Op. 38.
(*) Ph. Dig. **412 742-2**; *412 742-4* [id.]. Bella Davidovich – PROKOFIEV: *Sonata No. 3*; *Romeo and Juliet*.(*)

Bella Davidovich gives an authoritative account of the *G sharp minor Sonata-Fantasy*, Op. 19 – as, indeed, she does in the other pieces. But the sound in the *Poèmes* is little short of amazing, close and ugly, with no space round the instrument at all. The fortissimos are thunderous and the acoustic is small. The octave below middle C is far too near and the bass is thick and tubby. A non-starter.

Seiber, Matyas (1905–60)

Clarinet concertino.
*** Hyp. Dig. **CDA 66215**; *KA 66215* [id.]. Thea King, ECO, Litton – BLAKE: *Concerto*; LUTOSLAWSKI: *Dance preludes*.***

Matyas Seiber's highly engaging *Concertino* was sketched during a train journey (before the days of seamless rails, in 1926) and certainly the opening *Toccata* has the jumpy rhythmic feeling of railway line joints and points. Yet the haunting slow movement has a touch of the ethereal, while the Scherzo has a witty jazz element. Thea King has the measure of the piece; she is well accompanied by Litton, and very well recorded on tape as well as CD. Recommended.

Sessions, Roger (1896–1985)

Symphony No. 4; Symphony No. 5; Rhapsody for orchestra.
*** New World Dig. **NWCD 345** [id.]. Columbus SO, Badea.

The symphonies of Roger Sessions have enjoyed a peripheral hold on the catalogue: in the past Nos 2, 3 and 8 have reached LP, as has the *Rhapsody* included on this CD. He shares with his tonal contemporary Walter Piston, who also composed eight symphonies, a highly developed sense of structure and an integrity that remained unshaken by changes of fashion. His musical language is dense and his logic is easier to sense than to follow. The performances by the Columbus Symphony Orchestra under Christian Badea appear well prepared, and there is no doubt as to their commitment and expertise. The sound ideally needs a larger acoustic, but every strand in the texture is well placed and there is no feeling of discomfort.

Shankar, Ravi (born 1920)

Sitar concerto; (i) *Morning love.*
(M) **(*) HMV **CDM7 69121-2** [id.]. Shankar, LSO, Previn, (i) with Jean-Pierre Rampal.

It would be easy to dismiss this concerto, since fairly evidently it is neither good Western music nor good Indian music. The idiom is sweet, arguably too sweet and unproblematic, but at least this is an attractive and painless conducted tour over the geographical layout of the Rága. It also prompts some brilliant music-making from Previn and the LSO, not to mention the composer himself, who launches into solos which he makes sound spontaneous in the authentic manner, however prepared they may actually be. In fact his playing has stiffened up compared with the original concert performance in January 1971. Provided one is not worried at having a 40-minute work with comparatively little meat in the way of good material, this provides a charming experience – ideal atmospheric background music. The additional item, a makeweight for the CD, features Jean-Pierre Rampal as an equally engaging soloist.

Shchedrin, Rodion (born 1933)

The Frescoes of Dionysius.
(M) ** Olympia Dig. **OCD 108** [id.]. Bolshoi Theatre Soloists' Ens., Lazarev – BIZET/SHCHEDRIN: *Carmen ballet.***(*)

A rather effective miniature, fairly static in feeling, owing something to minimalism in structure, inspired by the frescos of Ferapontov Monastery, near Kirilov. It is well played and recorded.

Lenin in the People's Heart.
(M) *(*) Olympia **OCD 204** [id.]. Zikina, Zizen, USSR R. Ch. SO, Rozhdestvensky – SHEBALIN: *Lenin symphony.**

Shchedrin's cantata dates from 1969 and is a resourceful and imaginative piece which richly displays his mastery of orchestral and vocal resource. It is not a work to which one would attach high priority, but it is certainly not without merit. The recording, though a little fierce, is far better than in the Shebalin coupling.

Shebalin, Dmitri (1902–63)

Dramatic symphony on Mayakovsky's Lenin.
(M) * Olympia **OCD 204** [id.]. Narrator, Soloists, Ch., USSR RSO, Gauk – SHCHEDRIN: *Lenin in the People's Heart.**(*)

Shebalin's *Symphony* was recorded in 1960 – and, alas, does not wear its years lightly. Nor does the score itself, an inflated piece with too many fugues chasing too little inspiration. There is a narrator and chorus – and the voices and brass are strident. The piece dates from 1931 and does not show this respected Soviet composer in the best light; indeed, parts of it are rather dreadful. Some of his quartets (we recall an impressive performance of No. 8) are worth making available, but this music is not for export.

Shostakovich, Dmitri (1906–75)

(i; ii; iii) *The Adventures of Korzinkina* (film music)*: suite, Op. 59;* (iv; ii) *Alone* (film music)*: suite, Op. 26;* (v) *La Comédie Humaine* (incidental music to Balzac), *Op. 37;* (i; ii) *Scherzos: in F sharp min., Op. 1; in E flat, Op. 7; Theme & variations in B flat, Op. 3;* (vi) *Spanish songs, Op. 100.*
(M) **(*) Olympia **OCD 194** [id.]. (i) USSR Ministry of Culture SO, (ii) Rozhdestvensky; (iii) with Ch. (iv) Soloists, Ens. of USSR Ac. SO; (v) Leningrad CO, Gurdzhi; (vi) Artur Eisen, A. Bogdanova.

None of the music on this record is familiar or without interest to admirers of this composer; indeed most of it appears for the first time. The first two pieces are wholly uncharacteristic. The Op. 1 *Scherzo* speaks with much the same voice as Glazunov or Liadov: it is a rather charming piece – as, for that matter, is the Op. 3 set of variations. The Op. 7 *Scherzo* is more characteristic – there is a prominent part for the piano and there is already evidence of Shostakovich's special kind of wit. The *Spanish songs* come from 1956 and are more substantial; they are splendidly sung by Artur Eisen. The film scores are from the '30s and uncover no masterpieces and nothing of the quality of his music for *Hamlet*, and some of the numbers are tiresome. Though the recordings were made during the 1980s and are not top-drawer, this disc is still well worth investigating.

Chamber symphony in C min. Op. 110a (arr. Barshai from *String quartet No. 8*)*; Symphony for strings, Op. 118a* (arr. Barshai from *String quartet No. 10*).
*** TRAX **TRXCD 110**; *TRXC 110* [id.]. Phoenix CO, Julian Bigg.

A moving record. The transcriptions for strings of the *Eighth* and *Tenth Quartets* were made by Rudolf Barshai and carry the composer's imprimatur. They lend the works even greater weight and emotional range. The performances have great intensity and feeling and are all held together by Julian Bigg; he secures a wide dynamic range, good phrasing and a robust attack when required. Though intonation is not a problem, the orchestra could be more finely tuned. The recording is made in a resonant acoustic and is well balanced. There is a good cassette.

Cello concerto No. 1 in E flat, Op. 107.
*** CBS Dig. **CD 37840** [id.]. Yo-Yo Ma, Phd. O, Ormandy – KABALEVSKY: *Cello concerto No. 1.****
*** Chan. Dig. **CHAN 8322**; *ABTD 1085* [id.]. Raphael Wallfisch, ECO, Geoffrey Simon – BARBER: *Cello concerto.****
(*) Decca Dig. **414 162-2; *414 162-4* [id.]. Lynn Harrell, Concg. O, Haitink – BLOCH: Schelomo.**(*)

Cello concertos Nos 1 in E flat, Op. 107; 2, Op. 126.
*** Ph. Dig. **412 526-2**; *412 526-4* [id.]. Heinrich Schiff, Bav. RSO, Maxim Shostakovich.

Yo-Yo Ma on CBS brings an ardent musical imagination to the *First Cello concerto*. He plays with an intensity that compels the listener and, as befits an artist who has been acclaimed as one of the greatest cellists now before the public, can hold his own with any competition, though the Philadelphia Orchestra play here at a slightly lower voltage than they did (also under Ormandy) a quarter of a century ago for Rostropovich. The CBS recording has ample presence and warmth, with the balance slightly favouring the soloist, but very well judged overall. The CD adds presence and refines detail.

Wallfisch's version on Chandos also has the advantage of an interesting coupling, the *Cello concerto* of Samuel Barber, a work of great freshness and charm. He handles the first movement splendidly, though there is not quite the same sense of momentum as in Yo-Yo Ma's account. However, Raphael Wallfisch gives a sensitive account of the slow movement and has thoughtful and responsive support from the ECO. The soloist is forward – but then so is Ma on CBS, and neither is unacceptably larger than life. The Chandos recording is outstandingly fine in both formats and, technically, the CD can more than hold its own alongside its rivals. The chrome tape has striking pianissimo detail.

The combination of Lynn Harrell, the Concertgebouw Orchestra and Bernard Haitink is pretty impressive, as one would expect, and the Decca engineers give them a wonderfully vivid recording. The collector wanting only the *First Concerto* will find little to disappoint him in this account. The orchestral playing of the Amsterdam orchestra is pretty flawless and the soloist is no less masterly. The playing of the solo horn, Julia van Leer-Studebaker, is also quite dazzling. Harrell and Haitink evoke a powerful atmosphere in the slow movement and are not wanting in excitement elsewhere. Doubtless the coupling will be the decisive factor in making a choice in this work: taken on its own, good though both performance and recording are, it would not be a first choice in the Shostakovich.

Heinrich Schiff on Philips is the only cellist so far to couple the two concertos. Schiff's superbly recorded account does not displace Yo-Yo Ma in the *First*, but it can hold its own, and interest inevitably centres on its companion. The *Second Concerto* comes between the *Thirteenth* and *Fourteenth Symphonies*, neither of which endeared Shostakovich to the Soviet Establishment. The concerto did not meet with the enthusiastic acclaim that had greeted No. 1; nor has it established itself in the repertory to anywhere near the same extent as its predecessor, perhaps because it offers fewer overt opportunities for display. It is a work of eloquence and beauty, inward in feeling and spare in its textures, rhapsodic, even fugitive in character, yet the sonorities have the asperity so characteristic of Shostakovich. A haunting piece, essentially lyrical, it is gently discursive, sadly whimsical at times and tinged with a smiling melancholy that hides deeper troubles. In both formats – and particularly on CD – the recording is enormously impressive. The chrome tape is exceptionally well managed too.

Piano concertos Nos 1–2; 3 Fantastic dances. Symphonies Nos 6 in B min., Op. 54; 11 in G min. (The Year 1905), Op. 103.
*** HMV **CDC7 47790-8** (2). Cristina Ortiz, Bournemouth SO, Berglund.

Cristina Ortiz gives fresh and attractive performances of both concertos, a degree under-characterized, but very well recorded and with a fine accompaniment from the Bournemouth orchestra. This music making is not as individual as some versions, but there is compensation in the EMI sound, and a small bonus in the *Three Fantastic dances*, which are played with splendid character. As we go to press, these performances are also available separately on a mid-priced tape (*ED 290210-4*).

Berglund gives new tragic depth to the *Sixth* and, with similar rugged concentration, demonstrates the massive power of the *Eleventh*, a work which, with its programme based on the abortive 1905 uprising in Russia, usually seems far too thin in material. Shostakovich's pessimism in both works is underlined, with hardly a glimmer of hope allowed. In the *Sixth*, the very measured tempo for the first movement, taken direct and with little *espressivo*, points the link with the comparable movement of the *Eighth Symphony*; the remaining two movements are made ruthlessly bitter by not being sprung as dance movements, as is more usual. No Soviet optimism here. In the *Eleventh* too, even more daringly, Berglund lets the music speak for itself, keeping the long opening *Adagio* at a very steady, slow tread, made compelling by the hushed concentration of the Bournemouth playing. With fine recording, Berglund's art has never been more powerfully conveyed on record. The two symphonies are also available separately on a bargain-priced 'Portrait of the Artist tape' – see below. On the well-transferred CDs (which play for 143′) the *Three Fantastic dances* come as a rather curious encore after the finale of the *Eleventh Symphony*.

Piano concerto No. 1 in C min., for piano, trumpet and strings, Op. 35.
(*) Delos Dig. **D/CD 3021 [id]. Rosenberger, Burns, LACO, Schwarz – PROKOFIEV: *Symphony No. 1*; STRAVINSKY: *Soldier's tale.****

There have been more witty accounts of the *First Concerto* than Rosenberger's, but the extra degree of gravitas in the first movement adds an unexpected depth to the music, and the *Lento* is beautifully played, with a fine expressive response from the strings of the Los Angeles Chamber Orchestra. The finale, taken fast, makes a brilliant contrast, though here the humorous vulgarity is not emphasized, though the trumpet playing has plenty of dash. The recording is resonant, the piano balanced more forwardly than would be ideal, but the CD certainly has splendid presence.

Piano concerto No. 2 in F, Op. 102; Symphony for strings in A flat, Op. 118a.
(*) Chan. Dig. **CHAN 8443; *ABTD 1155* [id.]. Dmitri Shostakovich, I Musici de Montreal, Montreal SO (members), Maxim Shostakovich.

Maxim Shostakovich, who gave the *Second Piano concerto* its première in 1957, on Chandos directs a performance in which his son is soloist, which ensures authenticity, and yet one must register a degree of disappointment. The outer movements are firm and crisply rhythmic, and the *Andante* avoids any suggestion of sentimentality. Its opening mood is elegiac, but the piano figurations, refusing to linger in any kind of romanticism, are a shade too straight, and the closing toccata is also somewhat anonymous in its very energetic progress. The *Symphony for strings* is certainly not lacking incisiveness in the account by I Musici de Montreal, although this does not seem an apt coupling for the *Concerto* and is rather more convincingly done by the Phoenix Chamber Orchestra – see above. The Montreal account is well, rather than outstandingly, played. The recording is impressively vivid in both works, although the acoustics of the Church of St Madeleine, Outremont, Montreal, are rather resonant for this music. This is most striking on the faithful chrome cassette.

Symphony No. 1 in F min., Op. 10; Festival overture, Op. 96.
** BBC Dig. **CD 637X**; *ZCN 637X* [id.]. BBC Welsh O, Jansons.

Symphonies Nos 1 in F, Op. 10; 6 in B min., Op. 54.
(*) Chan. Dig. **CHAN 8411; *ABTD 1148* [id.]. SNO, Järvi.

Symphonies Nos 1 in F min., Op. 10; 9 in E flat, Op. 70.
*** Decca Dig. **414 677-2** [id.]. LPO, Haitink.

Haitink's reading of the brilliant *First Symphony* may lack something in youthful high spirits (the finale does not sound quirky enough in the strange alternation of moods), but it is a strong, well-played performance none the less, and it is coupled with a superb account of No. 9, a symphony that has long been written off as trivial. Without inflation Haitink gives it a serious purpose, both in the poignancy of the waltz-like second movement and in the equivocal emotions of the outer movements, which here are not just superficially jolly, as they can so easily seem. The recording is outstandingly clean and brilliant, notably so on CD.

Järvi's account of the *First Symphony* is strikingly more volatile than Haitink's in the outer movements – there is no lack of quirkiness in the finale, while the *Largo* is intense and passionate. The *Sixth* has comparable intensity, with an element of starkness in the austerity of the first movement, even if the reading is not quite as powerful as Berglund's, while the SNO strings do not command the body of tone produced by the Concertgebouw players under Haitink. The Scherzo is skittish at first, but like the finale has no lack of pungent force. In both symphonies this is emphasized by the reverberant acoustics of Glasgow City Hall, bringing an element of brutality to climaxes (which are spectacularly expansive). This is less appropriate in the *First Symphony*. The CD underlines the wide dynamic range, affords striking presence to the wind soloists, but confirms the lack of amplitude in the massed strings. Yet these readings remain very convincing, and many will prefer Järvi's chimerical response to the changing moods of the *First Symphony* to Haitink's more serious manner. There is a very good chrome tape which copes remarkably well with the resonance.

Mariss Jansons' association with the BBC Welsh Orchestra as principal guest conductor inspired some outstanding playing, and the BBC Records issue presents formidable evidence of it in a characteristically intense and brilliant performance. The sound is full and natural, but a little recessed. The snag is that the disc offers such meagre playing time.

Symphonies Nos 2 (October Revolution), Op. 14; 3 (The First of May), Op. 20. The Age of gold (suite), Op. 22.
*** Decca Dig. **421 131-2** [id.]. LPO Ch. and O, Haitink.

Shostakovich was still in his early twenties when he composed these symphonies, neither of which shows him at his most inspired, even if the opening of the *Second Symphony* enjoyed a certain avant-garde interest in its day. Admirable performances and excellently balanced sound with great presence and body. Those collecting Haitink's cycle need not hesitate. The joky *Age of gold* suite makes an unexpected if attractive makeweight for the CD, recorded with comparable brilliance.

Symphony No. 5 in D min., Op. 47.
*** Decca Dig. **410 017-2** [id.]. Concg. O, Haitink.
*** HMV Dig. **CDC7 49181-2** [id.]; *EL 749181-4*. Oslo PO, Jansons.
*** Telarc Dig. **CD 80067** [id.]. Cleveland O, Maazel.
*** CBS **CD 35854** [id.]. NYPO, Bernstein.
(*) RCA **RD 85608 [RCA-5608-2-RC]. St Louis SO, Slatkin.
** DG Dig. **410 509-2** [id.]. Nat. SO of Washington, Rostropovich.
(B) ** DG Dig. *419 840-4* [id.]. Nat. SO of Washington, Rostropovich – PROKOFIEV: *Romeo and Juliet*.**(*)
* Ph. Dig. **420 069-2** [id.]. BPO, Bychkov.

Haitink is eminently straightforward and there are no disruptive changes in tempo. It comes as a breath of fresh air after the Rostropovich, and the playing of the Concertgebouw Orchestra and the contribution of the Decca engineers are beyond praise. There could perhaps be greater intensity of feeling in the slow movement, but, whatever small reservations one might have, it is at present a first recommendation artistically and well ahead in terms of sheer sound. The compact disc is superb. The presence, range and body of the sound is impressive, and the CD is one of the very best yet to appear.

Jansons' EMI version with the Oslo orchestra brings a tautly incisive, electrically intense reading, marked by speeds notably faster than usual that yet have the ring of authenticity. The development section in the first movement for example builds up bitingly into a thrilling climax, with the accelerando powerfully controlled, relating it to the war-inspired sections of the comparable movement of No. 8. As on the other Oslo Philharmonic records with Jansons, the orchestra plays with point and refinement, as well as power. There is an excellent tape.

Brilliant in performance, spectacular in recorded sound, like all of Maazel's Cleveland recordings for Telarc, this Shostakovich reading is also warm, with the Cleveland violins sweet and pure in the long-legged melody of the second subject in the first movement. Though Maazel is faster than is common in the exposition section, he allows himself less stringendo than usual in the build-up of the development. The other three movements are also on the fast side, with little feeling of Laendler rhythm in the Scherzo and a sweet rather than rarefied reading of the *Largo* slow movement. This fits neatly between the spacious but rather severe reading of Haitink and the boldly expressive Bernstein.

Recorded in Tokyo in 1979, when Bernstein and the New York Philharmonic were on tour there, the CBS version is the weightiest on record, partly because of the interpretation but also because of the digital sound, which is particularly rich in bass. Unashamedly Bernstein treats the work as a Romantic symphony. The very opening makes an impact rarely possible in the concert hall; then, exceptionally, in the cool and beautiful second-subject melody Bernstein takes a slightly detached view – though as soon as that same melody comes up for development, after the exposition, the result is altogether more warmly expressive. Yet the movement's central climax, with its emphasis on the deep brass, injects a powerful element of menace, and the coda communicates a strongly Russian melancholy – which is perhaps why the composer admired Bernstein above other American interpreters of his music. The *Allegretto* becomes a burlesque, but its Mahlerian roots are strongly conveyed. The slow movement is raptly beautiful (marvellously sustained pianissimo playing from the New York Philharmonic strings), and the finale is brilliant and extrovert, with the first part dazzlingly fast and the conclusion one of unalloyed triumph, with no hint of irony. On CD, the bass is made to sound full and rich and the slight distancing of the sound (compared with many CBS recordings) places the orchestra within a believable ambience. Even so, this does not match the quality of Haitink's Decca CD.

Leonard Slatkin has built the St Louis Symphony into a first-rate orchestra, and this fine, clear-headed reading of Shostakovich's *Fifth* is an outstanding example of his work. Speeds are sensibly chosen, with the architecture of each movement clearly established, and textures are clarified in a helpful acoustic. Without quite matching the finest versions in dramatic bite, it makes an admirable, undistractingly satisfying version.

Rostropovich's account is too idiosyncratic to be recommended without qualification. He secures a refined, cultured string-tone, capable of searing intensity and strength, and all sections of the orchestra play with excellent attack and ensemble. The opening is given with hushed *ppp* intensity (the marking is in fact *piano*) and all promises well until, as is so often the case with this great Russian musician, he disturbs the natural musical flow for the sake of expressive effect. The brakes are abruptly applied in the Scherzo (at fig. 56), just before the horn figure is repeated, and he pulls other phrases around, too. He wrings the last ounce of intensity out of the finale, which is undoubtedly imposing, but there is also a hectoring quality which is distinctly unappealing (like being lectured by Solzhenitsyn on the moral decline of the West). The recording is on the whole good, even if it is a multi-mike, somewhat synthetic balance; and the CD will impress all who hear it as strikingly 'present'. It is only when the Decca CD is put alongside it that its limitations strike the listener. This performance is also available eminently well transferred on a bargain-priced DG Pocket Music tape, coupled with Prokofiev.

Bychkov's is a disappointing version, lacking tension and self-indulgent in its expression. One would never recognize this as the Berlin Philharmonic.

Symphonies Nos 5 in D min., Op. 47; 9 in E flat, Op. 70.
(M) *** Olympia Dig. **OCD 113** [id.]. USSR MoC SO, Rozhdestvensky.

Rozhdestvensky's coupling of Nos 5 and 9 is exceptionally generous, and on the mid-price Olympia label these strong, spontaneous-sounding performances can be warmly recommended. The *Ninth* in particular suits Rozhdestvensky's personality ideally, with the element of wit and humour brilliantly presented, and with the darker, more emotional elements emerging strongly and committedly. The Ministry of Culture Orchestra, established only in recent years, demonstrates in that work that it is second to none in Moscow, though the playing is less polished in No. 5, where violin tone in the exposed passages is sometimes lacking fullness. Warm, vivid recording, with the players set fairly close against a reverberant acoustic. The disc plays for 72′ 40″.

Symphony No. 6 in B min., Op. 54.
(M) *** HMV **CDM7 69564-2**; *EG 290859-4*. LSO, Previn – RACHMANINOV: *Symphony No. 3.****

The opening slow movement of the *Sixth Symphony* is parallel to those of the *Fifth* and the *Eighth*, each among the composer's finest inspirations. Here Previn shows his deep understanding of Shostakovich in a powerfully drawn, unrelenting account of that massive structure, his slow tempo adding to the overall impact. After that the offhand wit of the central Scherzo comes over the more delicately at a slower tempo than usual, leaving the hectic finale to hammer home the deceptively joyful conclusion to the argument. Even at the end Previn effectively avoids bombast in the exuberance of joy. Excellent recording, impressively remastered, with a good cassette.

Symphonies Nos 6 in B min., Op. 54; 9 in E flat, Op. 70.
** DG Dig. **419 771-2**; *419 771-4* [id.]. VPO, Bernstein.

It is a measure of the extraordinary magnetism of Bernstein that he sustains his extremely slow speed for the first movement of No. 6 with such keen intensity. He is slow too in the Scherzo, but then rushes off headlong in the finale. It is a compelling reading, but one too idiosyncratic to be a first recommendation. In No. 9, Bernstein is far more convincing in the measured, intense music of the second and fourth movements rather than in the sharp, witty fast movements which, surprisingly, lack something in humour. The live recordings match the many others Bernstein has made at concerts in the Musikvereinsaal.

Symphonies Nos 6 in B min., Op. 54; 11 in G min. (1905), Op. 103.
*** HMV *TCC2-POR 54286*. Bournemouth SO, Berglund.

Symphonies Nos 6 in B min., Op. 54; 11 in G min. (1905), Op. 103; Overture on Russian and Kirghiz folk themes, Op. 115.
(*) Decca Dig. **411 939-2 (2) [id.]. Concg. O, Haitink.

Berglund's outstandingly generous CD coupling of the *Sixth* and *Eleventh Symphonies* together with the two *Piano concertos* is discussed above. The *Symphonies* are additionally available separately on tape in HMV's 'Portrait of the Artist' series. Although iron-oxide stock is used, there is only marginal loss of range, and the sound retains its weight and power and most of its bite. A bargain.

Haitink's pair of CDs includes merely the *Overture*, Op. 115, as a bonus. The performances of the *Symphonies* are characteristically refined and powerful. With superb playing from the Concertgebouw, particularly the strings, the textures have an extra transparency, helped also by the brilliant and atmospheric Decca recording in all three formats. Haitink's structural control, coupled with his calm, taut manner, also brings out the weight and power of the big slow movements which open both works; the *Largo* of No. 6 is particularly impressive, containing, as it does, the main symphonic meat of the work, anticipating the comparable movement of No. 8. Nevertheless, in comparison with the rival set coupling these same two works, from Berglund and the Bournemouth orchestra, Haitink seems almost detached, marginally lacking the concentrated tension of a genuine performance. Berglund's commitment makes the vast slow expanses of No. 11 even more compelling and moving.

Symphonies Nos 6 in B min., Op. 54; 12 in D min. (The Year 1917), Op. 112.
(M) *** Olympia Dig. **OCD 111** [id.]. USSR MoC SO, Rozhdestvensky.

Like others in Rozhdestvensky's Shostakovich series, the Olympia version provides (at 72′ 53″)

a very generous coupling. No. 6 is a work that the conductor responds to with exceptional warmth, giving weight and intensity to the magnificent opening slow movement and bringing out the spark of dark humour in the Scherzo and finale while giving them necessary bite and power. He is also most persuasive in the programmatic No. 12 with its picture of the events of the 1917 Revolution, bringing out the atmosphere and drama. Unfortunately the disc has the full span of the work, over 40 minutes of continuous music, with no separating bands for the different sections. First-rate playing from the Ministry of Culture Orchestra and full-bodied, warm recording.

Symphony No. 7 (Leningrad), Op. 60.
(*) HMV **CDC7 47651-2; (M) *EG 291135-4*. Bournemouth SO, Berglund.

Symphonies Nos 7 (Leningrad); 12 (The Year 1917), Op. 112.
*** Decca Dig. **412 392-2** (2). LPO or Concg. O, Haitink.

With his characteristic refinement and avoidance of bombast Haitink might not seem an apt conductor for the most publicized of Shostakovich's wartime symphonies, but in effect he transforms it, bringing out the nobility of many passages. One sees that the long first-movement *ostinato* – now revealed as having quite different implications from the descriptive programme suggested by the Soviet propaganda-machine in the war years – is almost an interlude in a work which otherwise in its deep seriousness challenges comparison with the other wartime symphony, the epic *Eighth*. The compact disc format includes also the *Twelfth Symphony* – a very generous coupling. Moreover, the pairing is particularly well designed in putting together two symphonies that have been seriously underestimated. The first compact disc contains the whole of No. 12, played without a break, as the composer wanted, followed by the long first movement of the *Leningrad*, some 72 minutes in all. The CD transfer brings the usual enhancement and greater sense of presence.

Berglund directs a doggedly powerful performance of a symphony of Shostakovich that has long been underestimated. Though Berglund is not always sensitive to the finer points of expressiveness, it is useful to have a good performance recorded with such vivid sound and offered uncoupled on a single CD.

Symphony No. 8 in C min., Op. 64.
*** Decca Dig. **411 616-2** [id.]. Concg. O, Haitink.

The *Eighth Symphony*, written in response to the sufferings of the Russian people during the Second World War, is one of Shostakovich's most powerful and intense creations, starting with a slow movement almost half an hour long, which emerges as not only emotionally involving but cogent in symphonic terms too. The sharp unpredictability of the remaining movements, alternately cajoling and battering the listener, shows Shostakovich at his most inspired.

Haitink characteristically presents a strongly architectural reading of this war-inspired symphony, at times direct to the point of severity. After the massive and sustained slow movement which opens the work, Haitink allows no lightness or relief in the Scherzo movements, and in his seriousness in the strangely lightweight finale (neither fast nor slow) he provides an unusually satisfying account of an equivocal, seemingly uncommitted movement. The playing of the Concertgebouw Orchestra is immaculate and the digital recording full, brilliant and clear. The compact disc has the usual virtues of added presence and definition, although it is marginally less impressive than the companion CD of the *Fifth Symphony*.

Symphony No. 10 in E min., Op. 93.
*** DG Dig. **413 361-2** [id.]. BPO, Karajan.
** HMV Dig. **CDC7 47350 2** [id.]; *EL 270315-4*. Philh. O, Rattle.

Already in his 1967 recording Karajan had shown that he had the measure of this symphony; this newer version is, if anything, even finer. In the first movement he distils an atmosphere as concentrated as before, bleak and unremitting, while in the *Allegro* the Berlin Philharmonic leave no doubts as to their peerless virtuosity. Everything is marvellously shaped and proportioned. The *allegro* section of the finale is taken up to speed (176 crotchets to the minute), faster than Mitropoulos and much faster than most other rivals. The digital sound is altogether excellent, and this must now rank as a first recommendation. It has greater intensity and grip than Haitink (the LPO's playing is not quite in the same league), and though Mitropoulos's pioneering account is still to be treasured, this 1982 Berlin version is marvellously powerful and gripping. The CD enjoys the usual advantages of greater range and presence.

Rattle's Philharmonia version is curiously wayward in the two big slow movements, first and third in the scheme. In the first, Rattle is exceptionally slow, and though in principle such a view might yield revelatory results, tension slips too readily. So too in the third movement. The Scherzo and energetic finale are much more successful. The recording does not help, with the strings sounding thin and lacking body. The cassette offers fuller but rather opaque sound.

Symphony No. 13 in B flat min. (*Babi-Yar*), *Op. 113.*
*** Decca Dig. **417 261-2** [id.]. Rintzler, Concg. Male Ch. and O, Haitink.
(*) Chan. Dig. **CHAN 8540; *ABTD 1248* [id.]. Storojev, CBSO, Kamu.

The often brutal directness of Haitink's way with Shostakovich works well in the *Thirteenth Symphony*, particularly in the long *Adagio* first movement, whose title, *Babi-Yar*, gives its name to the whole work. That first of five Yevtushenko settings boldly attacking anti-semitism in Russia sets the pattern for Haitink's severe view of the whole. The second movement, *Humour*, is made an unrelenting dance of death, missing something in irony; and the third movement, with its picture of women queueing in the snow outside a grocer's store, is less atmospheric than austere. Rintzler with his magnificent, resonant bass is musically superb but, matching Haitink, remains objective rather than dashingly characterful. The resolution of the final movement, with its pretty flutings surrounding a wry poem about Galileo and greatness, then works beautifully. Outstandingly brilliant and full sound, remarkable even for this series.

With a Russian bass soloist adding an extra touch of dark authenticity, Okku Kamu conducts a strong and sympathetic account of No. 13, well played and very well recorded. His degree of relaxation in the more pointed passages – such as the second movement, *Humour* – adds to the idiomatic feeling, though in weight and dark intensity he cannot always match Haitink, with a bass chorus rather light-toned.

(i) *Symphony No. 14, Op. 135;* (ii) *6 Poems of Marina Tsvetaeva, Op. 143a.*
*** Decca Dig. **417 514-2** [id.]. (i) Julia Varady, Fischer-Dieskau; (ii) Ortrun Wenkel; Concg. O, Haitink.

The *Fourteenth* is Shostakovich's most sombre and dark score, a setting of poems by Lorca, Apollinaire, Rilke, Brentano and Küchelbecker, all on the theme of death. It is similar in conception (though not in character) to Britten's *Nocturne* or *Spring symphony*, and is in fact dedicated to him. Earlier recordings under Barshai, Ormandy and Rostropovich have all been in Russian, but this version gives each poem in the original. This is a most powerful performance under Haitink, and the outstanding recording is well up to the standard of this fine Decca series. The song cycle, splendidly sung by Ortrun Wenkel, makes a fine bonus for the CD.

(i) *Symphony No. 15 in A, Op. 141;* (ii) *From Jewish Folk poetry* (song cycle), *Op. 79.*
❀ *** Decca **417 581-2** [id.]. (i) LPO; (ii) Söderström, Wenkel, Karcykowski, Concg. O, Haitink.

The *Fifteenth Symphony* was the second issue in Haitink's Shostakovich series and it brings a performance which is a revelation. Early readings of the composer's last symphony seemed to underline the quirky unpredictability of the work, with the collage of strange quotations – above all the *William Tell* gallop, which keeps recurring in the first movement – seemingly joky rather than profound. Haitink by contrast makes the first movement sound genuinely symphonic, bitingly urgent. He underlines the purity of the bare lines of the second movement; after the Wagner quotations which open the finale, his slow tempo for the main lyrical theme gives it heartaching tenderness, not the usual easy triviality. The playing of the LPO is excellent, with refined tone and superb attack, and the recording is both analytical and atmospheric. Although the textures are generally spare, the few heavy tuttis are difficult for the engineers, and Decca sound copes with them splendidly. The CD includes a splendidly sung version of *From Jewish Folk poetry*, settings which cover a wide range of emotions including tenderness, humour and even happiness as in the final song. Ryszard Karcykowski brings vibrant Slavonic feeling to the work, which with its wide variety of mood and colour has a scale to match the shorter symphonies.

CHAMBER AND INSTRUMENTAL MUSIC

Cello sonata in D min., Op. 40.
*** Chan. Dig. **CHAN 8340**; *ABTD 1072* [id.]. Turovsky, Edlina – PROKOFIEV: *Sonata.****
*** BIS Dig. **CD 336** [id.]. Thedeen, Pöntinen – SCHNITTKE: *Sonata.**** STRAVINSKY: *Suite italienne.****
** Denon Dig. **C37 7563** [id.]. Fujiwara, Rouvier – STRAVINSKY: *Suite italienne*; DEBUSSY: *Cello sonata.***

Yuli Turovsky and Luba Edlina play the *Cello sonata* with great panache and eloquence. At times, in the finale, they almost succumb to exaggeration in their handling of its humour – no understatement here. However, they are totally inside this music and the recording reproduces them truthfully. The record is also of particular value in restoring the Prokofiev *Sonata* to circulation after an absence of some years. The chrome cassette, made at the highest level, gives the artists great presence, but the balance gives slight exaggeration to the upper partials of the cello timbre. The CD is first class in every way.

The Swedish cellist, Thorleif Thedeen, is still in his mid-twenties but his account of the *Sonata* can hold its own with any in the catalogue. He has a real feeling for its structure and the vein of bitter melancholy under its ironic surface. Roland Pöntinen gives him excellent support and the BIS recording does justice to its glorious tone.

The coupling will probably decide matters for most readers as far as the Denon version is concerned. Fujiwara and Rouvier are quite brisk in the opening movement but slow up considerably for the second subject. Spirited though their playing is, they do not displace the Chandos CD by Turovsky and Edlina.

Piano quintet, Op. 57; Piano trio No. 2 in E min., Op. 67.
(*) Chan. Dig. **CHAN 8342; *ABTD 1088* [id.]. Borodin Trio, Zweig, Horner.
**(*) ASV *ZCALH 929* [id.]. Music Group of London.

(i) *Piano quintet, Op. 57; String quartets Nos 7 in F sharp min., Op. 108; 8 in C min., Op. 110.*
(*) HMV Dig. **CDC7 47507-2 [id.]. (i) Sviatoslav Richter; Borodin Qt.

Piano quintet, Op. 57; 2 Pieces for String quartet; (i) *7 Romances on poems of Aleksander Blok.*
*** Decca Dig. **411 940-2**; *411 940-4* [id.]. Ashkenazy; (i) Söderström; Fitzwilliam Qt.

Ashkenazy's account of the *Piano quintet* with the late lamented Fitzwilliam Quartet cannot be seriously faulted and withstands comparison with the illustrious Richter and Borodin Quartet version (HMV), not least on account of the quality of the recording. On the sleeve-note Alan George tells how in 1985 the State Copyright Agency in Moscow suddenly sent him the *Two Pieces* which had just come to light. The first is a poignant *Elegy*, more familiar as Katarina's aria at the end of Act I of the opera, *Lady Macbeth of Mtsensk*, and the second is none other than the *Polka* from *The Age of gold*. Both predate the *First quartet* by some seven years – and what strikes one is just how convincing they are in this medium. If you did not know the aria, it would be difficult to imagine the *Elegy* in any other form. The attractiveness of the issue is further enhanced by the *Seven Romances on Poems of Aleksander Blok* with Elisabeth Söderström, who sings these remarkable pieces with much feeling. The Decca recording is superb, and there is a first-class chrome cassette.

The Chandos and ASV issues bring together two of Shostakovich's most important chamber works. The Chandos version of the *Quintet* is bolder in character and more concentrated in feeling than any of the rival versions. There are one or two moments of vulnerable intonation but these are of little account, given the intensity of this playing. The Music Group of London show rather less panache but are still impressive, and in their hands the *Trio* is affectingly played. This is a particularly painful and anguished work, dedicated to the memory of a close friend, Ivan Sollertinsky, who died in the year of its composition. Excellent balance and good recording quality make this ASV tape an attractive proposition, although on performance alone the Chandos issue remains first choice. Here the sound is vivid, though the microphones are rather close and there is too much reverberation round the piano, an effect the more noticeable on CD. On tape, the presence is no less striking, although the string focus is not absolutely clean. The ASV tape is of good quality, and the resonance brings only very slight clouding to the piano focus.

A powerful performance by Richter and the Borodins of the *Piano quintet*, recorded at a public concert at the Moscow Conservatoire, and it goes without saying that the two *Quartets* are superbly played, too. Although the quality of the recorded sound is on the dry side in Nos 7 and 8, it is by no means as dry as some of the others in the complete set listed below. This coupling contains 70 minutes of music.

String quartets Nos 1 in C, Op. 49; 9 in E flat, Op. 117; 12 in D flat, Op. 133.
*** HMV **CDC7 49266-2** [id.]. Borodin Qt.

String quartets Nos 2 in A, Op. 68; 3 in F, Op. 73.
*** HMV **CDC7 49267-2** [id.]. Borodin Qt.

String quartets Nos 4 in D, Op. 83; 6 in G, Op. 101; 11 in F min., Op. 122.
*** HMV **CDC7 49268-2** [id.]. Borodin Qt.

String quartets Nos 5 in B flat, Op. 92; 15 in E flat min., Op. 144.
*** HMV **CDC7 49270-2** [id.]. Borodin Qt.

String quartets Nos 10 in A flat, Op. 118; 13 in B flat min., Op. 138; 14 in F sharp, Op. 142.
*** HMV **CDC7 49269-2** [id.]. Borodin Qt.

The Shostakovich quartets thread through his creative life like some inner odyssey and inhabit terrain of increasing spiritual desolation. This is the Borodin Quartet's second complete cycle and, incidentally, their third version of No. 8. Two of the performances derive from concerts. The audience is commendably attentive and their presence is only momentarily betrayed in the slow movement of No. 6. Whereas in the old LP format not all the quartets could be accommodated without side-breaks, on CD the continuity of each is unimpaired. The present set is made in a generally drier acoustic than its predecessors and the recordings from 1984, particularly

Nos 3 and 5, suffer in this respect. However, the ears quickly adjust and the performances can only be described as masterly. Indeed the sheer quality of the playing on this set is unlikely to be surpassed. The Borodins possess enormous refinement, an altogether sumptuous tone and a perfection of technical address that is almost in a class of its own – and what wonderful intonation! These and the Bartók six are the greatest quartet cycles produced in the present century and are mandatory listening.

String quartet No. 8, Op. 110.
(M) ** Nimbus Dig. **NI 5077** [id.]. Medici Qt – DEBUSSY: *String quartet in G min.**(*)

A good, well-played account of the *Eighth Quartet* on Nimbus coupled with a workmanlike performance of the Debussy. Good, but no match for the lamented Fitzwilliam performance on Decca, which we hope will reappear on CD within the lifetime of this book, let alone the Borodin Quartet on EMI.

Violin sonata, Op. 134.
*** Chan. Dig. **CHAN 8343**; *ABTD 1089* [id.]. Dubinsky, Edlina – SCHNITTKE: *Sonata No. 1* etc.***

Shostakovich composed his *Sonata* for Oistrakh's sixtieth birthday, and since his pioneering record, issued in the early 1970s, there have been versions by Kremer, Gavrilov and Lubotsky, also coupled with Schnittke, which all succumbed (like the Oistrakh/Richter version) to rapid deletion. The *Sonata* is a bitter and at times arid score, thought-provoking and, unusually in this composer, not totally convincing. Rostislav Dubinsky's account is undoubtedly eloquent, and Luba Edlina makes a fine partner. The recording is excellent too, with vivid presence, especially on CD, although it is balanced a shade closely. The Chandos chrome tape is clear and well focused and should provide a satisfying alternative in this medium.

Sibelius, Jean (1865–1957)

Academic march; Finlandia (arr. composer)*; Har du mod? Op. 31/2; March of the Finnish Jaeger Battalion, Op. 91/1;* (i) *The origin of fire, Op. 32; Sandels, Op. 28; Song of the Athenians, Op. 31/3.*
** **BIS CD 314** [id.]. (i) Sauli Tilikainen, Laulun Ystävät Male Ch., Gothenburg SO, Järvi.

The origin of fire is by far the most important work on the record. It has an early opus number but comes in fact from 1902, the period of the *Second Symphony*, though it seems closer to the darker world that was to come. Sauli Tilikainen is not quite as impressive as Hynninen on Berglund's record, but he is very good indeed, and the playing of the Gothenburg Symphony Orchestra under Neeme Järvi has plenty of feeling and atmosphere. None of the other pieces are essential Sibelius. *Sandels*, an improvisation for male chorus and orchestra, is another shortish piece, and not Sibelius at his strongest. The *Finnish Jaeger march* and the two pieces from Op. 31, *Har du mod?* ('Have you the courage?') and the *Song of the Athenians*, are all simple patriotic pieces and by Sibelius's exalted standards pretty insignificant. The *Academic march* (1919), written for a degree ceremony at Helsinki University, has a much stronger appeal. The singing of the Laulun Ystävät is good rather than outstanding, and the Gothenburg orchestra play with enthusiasm. Good recording in the best BIS traditions.

The Bard, Op. 64; The Dryad, Op. 45/1; En Saga, Op. 9; Finlandia, Op. 26; (i) *Luonnotar, Op. 70; Night ride and sunrise, Op. 55; The Oceanides, Op. 73; Pohjola's daughter, Op. 49; Tapiola, Op. 112; Varsäng* (*Spring song*)*, Op. 16.*
(*) Chan. **CHAN 8395/6; (M) *CBT 1027/8* [id.]. SNO, Gibson, (i) with Phyllis Bryn-Julson.

Sir Alexander Gibson's analogue recordings of the Sibelius tone-poems date from the late 1970s and were originally issued by RCA. The recordings have been digitally remastered with great success; the slightly distant sound-balance is admirably suited to the music, with the spacious acoustic of Glasgow City Hall generally flattering the orchestra and creating a suitable ambient atmosphere. Gibson's affinity with the Sibelius idiom is at its most convincing here, particularly in the more elusive pieces, like *The Bard* and *The Dryad*, although *En Saga*, which opens the collection, is also both evocative and shows an impressive overall grasp. Sometimes one would have welcomed a greater degree of dramatic intensity, and both *Pohjola's daughter* and *Tapiola* fall a little short in this respect, while *Night ride and sunrise* does not fully blossom until the closing section. Nevertheless there is much that is impressive here, and the fine playing and natural perspectives of the recording contribute a great deal to the music making in all formats. In *Luonnotar* the soprano voice is made to seem like another orchestral instrument; while there have been more histrionic versions, the singing is tonally beautiful, sensitive and well controlled. The excellent cassettes are at mid-price. However, on CD the recordings sound particularly fine: the strings are given a lovely freshness and bloom in *The Bard* and *The Dryad*, and have diaphanous delicacy of texture in *The Oceanides*. Although both ends of the sound spectrum are less sharply focused than in a true digital recording (most noticeable in *En Saga*) climaxes are made excitingly expansive, with the brass superbly sonorous: *Night ride and sunrise*, *Pohjola's daughter* and *Tapiola* are all enhanced.

Violin concerto in D, Op. 47.
*** RCA **RD 87019 [RCD1 7019]**. Heifetz, Chicago SO, Hendl – GLAZUNOV: *Concerto*; PROKOFIEV: *Concerto No. 2.****
*** Ph. Dig. **416 821-2**; *416 821-4* [id.]. Mullova, Boston SO, Ozawa – TCHAIKOVSKY: *Concerto.****
*** HMV **CDC7 47167-2** [id.]. Perlman, Pittsburgh SO, Previn – SINDING: *Suite.****
(M) (***) EMI mono **CDH7 61011-2** [id.]. Ginette Neveu, Philh. O, Susskind – BRAHMS: *Concerto.*(***)
(*) Erato **ECD 88109 [id.]. Amoyal, Philh. O, Dutoit – TCHAIKOVSKY: *Concerto.***(*)
(B) **(*) Sup. **2SUP 002**. Ishikawa, Brno State PO, Belohlavek – BRUCH: *Concerto No. 1.***
(*) DG Dig. **419 618-2; *419 618-4* [id.]. Mintz, BPO, Levine – DVOŘÁK: *Concerto.****
(*) PRT **CDPCD 14. Yaron, LPO, Soudant – TCHAIKOVSKY: *Concerto.***
** HMV Dig. **CDC7 47110-2** [id.]. Kremer, Phd. O, Muti – SCHUMANN: *Concerto.***(*)
(M) *(*) RCA **GD 86520**; *GK 86520* **[RCA 6520-2RG]**. Perlman, Boston SO, Leinsdorf – LALO: *Symphonie espagnole* *(*); RAVEL: *Tzigane.***(*)

(i) *Violin concerto; Finlandia, Op. 26; Tapiola, Op. 112.*
(*) DG **419 871-2; *419 871-4* [id.]. (i) Ferras; BPO, Karajan.

(i) *Violin concerto; Symphony No. 5 in E flat, Op. 82; Tapiola.*
(B) **(*) DG Walkman *415 619-4* [id.]. (i) Ferras, BPO, Karajan.

(i) *Violin concerto; Symphony No. 5 in E flat, Op. 82.*
*** HMV Dig. **CDC7 49717-2** [id.]; *EL 749717-4*. (i) Nigel Kennedy; CBSO, Rattle.

Heifetz's performance of the Sibelius *Concerto* with the Chicago Symphony Orchestra under Walter Hendl set the standard by which all other versions have come to be judged. It is also one of his finest recordings; in remastered form the sound is vivid, with the Chicago ambience making an apt setting for the finely focused violin line. The purity and luminous beauty of the violin tone at the opening put the seal on this as an interpretation of unusual depth, consummate technique and supreme artistry. Now coupled on CD with Heifetz's equally indispensable accounts of the Glazunov and Prokofiev *Second*, it is among this artist's most desirable discs.

There is some dryness added to the sound, which is very bright, but good results can be obtained by use of the controls.

Viktoria Mullova made the headlines some years ago by winning the Sibelius Competition and subsequently making a dramatic escape to the West. Her first commercial recording couples the Sibelius and Tchaikovsky *Concertos* and is a resounding success. In some of her concert appearances her Tchaikovsky has seemed very routine and uncaring, and her Sibelius rather cool. Not so her record with the Boston Symphony under Ozawa. Her account has a certain warmth, though it is mercifully free of the *zigeuner* element one so often encounters in performance. What the concerto needs above all else is finesse and a certain aristocratic feeling – without this, a performance fails. Mullova captures its magical element right from the very opening; the slow movement has a cool dignity that is impressive. The recording is excellent, though the cassette is very bass-orientated.

Itzhak Perlman first recorded this concerto in the mid-1960s with Leinsdorf and the Boston Symphony for RCA (see below). Here he plays the work as a full-blooded virtuoso showpiece, and the Pittsburgh orchestra under André Previn support him to the last man and woman. In the first movement his tempo is broader than that of Heifetz, and in the rest of the work he seems more expansive than he was in the earlier record. The new version takes 32′ 00″, whereas his Boston performance took 29′ 15″ (and fitted on one LP side). He is at his stunning best in the first cadenza and makes light of all the fiendish difficulties in which the solo part abounds. Perlman takes a conventional view of the slow movement, underlining its passion, and he gives us an exhilarating finale. The balance places Perlman rather forward. The sound is marvellously alive and thrilling, while the CD has the usual improvement in presence and definition, though the forward balance is even more apparent.

Ginette Neveu's reading of the Sibelius is a classic recording, a precious reminder of a great artist who died tragically young. Coupled with an outstanding version of the Brahms on a mid-price Références issue, with the mono sound satisfyingly full-bodied and well detailed, it is an issue not to be missed. The magnetism of Neveu in this, her first concerto recording, is inescapable from her opening phrase onwards, warmly expressive and dedicated, yet with no hint of mannerism. The note with the disc details the problems of the actual session, very limited in time; yet that challenge obviously added to the intensity and spontaneity of the finished recording. The finale is taken at a speed which is comfortable rather than exciting, but the extra spring of the thrumming dance-rhythms, superbly lifted, is ample compensation, providing a splendid culmination.

Nigel Kennedy's account of the *Violin concerto* is quite superbly balanced; the violin is in exactly the right perspective. He is the first English soloist to have tackled this work for many years and does so with considerable success. Throughout, his intonation is true and he takes the considerable technical hurdles of this concerto in his stride. There is a touch of the *zigeuner* throb in the slow movement (Kyung Wha Chung on Decca was incomparable here), but on the whole he plays with real spirit and panache. Of course the competition is horribly keen: Mullova is pure if cool, Neveu is nobler and more aristocratic, and Amoyal on Erato should not be forgotten – all of them differently coupled. Nevertheless this can be confidently recommended for the coupling with the *Fifth Symphony* is apt and generous.

It is amazing that Simon Rattle should already be making a second recording of the *Fifth* at the age of thirty-three! His new account is very fine indeed, generally speaking tauter and at times more intense than its predecessor, even if it does not entirely displace it. There is a powerful atmosphere and sense of space at the very opening and the bassoon lament in the development is marvellously hushed and mysterious. In the famous transition – notoriously difficult to bring off – he is faster on this occasion and not as finely controlled as in the Philharmonic reading. The slow movement is less spacious than the earlier one but still splendidly intense, and the ending could not be more sensitively or idiomatically handled. We are plunged too quickly into the finale which is tremendously exhilarating; the playing of the Birmingham orchestra is excellent throughout as, indeed, is the EMI recording, on the splendid chrome tape as well as the CD.

Admirers of Pierre Amoyal will not be surprised to learn that his interpretation can hold its own with most now available. He brings a splendid ardour, refined taste and great purity of tone to the concerto; and it goes without saying that he surmounts its many technical hurdles with aplomb. He is free from that slight suggestion of the *zigeuner* that disfigures some accounts and has greater spirituality than Kremer. The finale perhaps lacks the sheer excitement of Heifetz, whose pupil he was in the late 1960s; nevertheless it is good, and in the slow movement Amoyal has nobility and warmth. The recording is very natural, with a decent perspective and balance.

Shizuka Ishikawa's performance is technically very impressive indeed, and her playing combines passion with a clear, clean line. However, the brightly lit recording has touches of harshness in the orchestral tuttis, although otherwise the 1978 analogue recording is vividly transferred to CD. Even if the coupled Bruch is less successful, this is still a record to sample, for the performance of the Sibelius is among the finest on the market.

Christian Ferras's account of the *Violin concerto* is a very good one and is well recorded. Although he begins the work with a winningly golden tone, when he is under stress, at the end of the first movement and in the finale, his intonation and general security are less than impeccable. However, there is still much to enjoy, and Ferras again develops a rich romantic tone for the main tune of the slow movement. The couplings, also from the mid-1960s, are outstanding. *Tapiola* is a performance of great intensity and offers superlative playing. The 1964 recording of the *Fifth Symphony* is undoubtedly a great performance. The orchestral playing throughout is glorious and the effect is spacious and atmospheric. Karajan finds an engrossing sense of mystery in the development section of the first movement, and there is jubilation in the finale. The only snag is that the Walkman tape is transferred at the highest level and there is a degree of harshness in the climaxes of the symphony. The recording sounds freer and altogether more impressive in its CD format (coupled with the *Seventh Symphony* – see below), but this tape remains a formidable bargain. The alternative Galleria CD and cassette are less tempting.

Shlomo Mintz commands unstinted admiration in this concerto; his playing is dazzlingly brilliant and full of personality. Intonation is spot-on and there seem to be no technical hurdles he cannot surmount. But there is also something too high-powered and unrelieved about his intensity, and the playing often dazzles rather more than it illuminates. After a time one longs for more variety between intensity and repose, and a greater sense of space. The aristocratic quality of this work eludes him. He is slightly more forwardly balanced than in the coupling, though the recording is one of DG's best with plenty of space round the instruments. Not a first choice, perhaps, though in its way a *tour de force*. There is a very good cassette.

Yuval Yaron won the Sibelius Prize in Helsinki in 1975; the young Israeli violinist made this analogue recording in 1978. It is a more inward-looking reading than Perlman's, opening gently, and Yaron is persuasively poetic. The *Adagio* blossoms eloquently, with good support from Soudant who elsewhere is markedly less passionate than Previn or Muti, although the urgency of the solo playing is not inhibited. The analogue recording is atmospheric and naturally balanced, but not very vividly detailed. Overall, it is an account easy to enjoy but not distinctive enough to recommend as a first choice. Moreover, the Tchaikovsky coupling has rather less tension.

Kremer presents the *Concerto* essentially as a bravura showpiece and his is a vibrantly extrovert reading. While the recording balance places the soloist well forward, the orchestral texture has plenty of impact and good detail, and the fortissimo brass blaze out excitingly. There is undoubted poetry in the slow movement, and throughout Muti gives his soloist splendid support. However, their version does not displace Perlman nor, for that matter, the many other competitors listed above.

Perlman's earlier RCA recording suffers from over-bright sound (the orchestral tuttis now have an element of harshness) and a very close balance for the soloist. The *Concerto* is very finely played; but, in spite of attractive couplings and a reasonable price, Perlman's later HMV disc is far preferable.

En Saga, Op. 9; Finlandia, Op. 26; Legend: The Swan of Tuonela, Op. 22/2; Tapiola, Op. 112.
(M) **(*) HMV **CDM7 69017-2** [id.]; *EG 769017-4.* BPO, Karajan.

These recordings date from 1977. This was Karajan's third recording of *Tapiola* but his first of *En Saga*; where he is a brisk story-teller, more concerned with narrative than with atmosphere at the beginning; but the climax is very exciting and the *lento assai* section and the coda are quite magical. Here as in *Finlandia*, which is superbly played, the digital remastering gives a very brightly lit sound-picture, bringing a degree of harshness in the brass, stopping only just short of crudeness. *Tapiola* is broader and more expansive than the first DG version; at the storm section, the more spacious tempo is vindicated and again the climax is electrifying, although, with a loss of body and weight in the bass, the upper range tends to fierceness. But both are great performances and totally committed. *The Swan of Tuonela* is most persuasively done.

En Saga, Op. 9; Finlandia, Op. 26; Night ride and sunrise, Op. 55; Pohjola's daughter, Op. 49.
(M) *** Decca *417 697-4* [id.]. SRO, Horst Stein.

This Decca Weekend tape makes available again an exceptionally successful compilation from 1972, transferred with striking vividness and plenty of body and definition. These are distinguished and finely calculated performances offering some of the finest playing we have had from the Suisse Romande Orchestra in recent years. The performance here of *Finlandia* is exciting and sonorously recorded, but the achievement of the rest of the programmes makes one wish that something less ubiquitous had been included. Stein shows a gift for the special atmosphere of Sibelius. The highlight of the disc is an outstandingly exciting account of *En Saga*, with quite superb recording from Decca including the flamboyant use of the bass drum. *Night Ride and Sunrise* and *Pohjola's daughter* too are highly successful, although the broadening of the climax of the latter work does let the tension slip momentarily. But taken as a whole this is a fine cassette in every way and a real bargain.

En saga, Op. 9; Scènes historiques, Opp. 25; 66.
*** BIS Dig. **CD 295** [id.]. Gothenburg SO, Järvi.

Sir Alexander Gibson has also given us an outstanding set of the *Scènes historiques*, more interestingly coupled with *Rakastava* – see below. But his is an analogue recording, albeit a very good one; Järvi has the advantage of modern digital sound and the Gothenburg orchestra is fully inside the idiom of this music and plays very well indeed. Järvi's *En saga*, too, is exciting and well paced.

(i) *Finlandia, Op. 26;* (ii) *Karelia suite, Op. 11;* (i) *Kuolema: Valse triste, Op. 44.*
(B) *** DG Walkman *413 158-4* [id.]. (i) BPO, Karajan; (ii) Helsinki R. O, Kamu – GRIEG: *Piano concerto; Peer Gynt.***

Finlandia, Op. 26; Kuolema: Valse triste, Op. 44.
(M) *** DG **423 208-2**; *423 208-4* [id.]. BPO, Karajan – GRIEG: *Peer Gynt.****

These are familiar performances from the mid-1960s. *Valse triste* is played very slowly and in a somewhat mannered fashion. *Finlandia* is one of the finest accounts available, with eloquent playing from the Berliners, although on the CD one notices that the digital remastering has brightened the sound and that it has rather less body than originally, though it is still impressive, if rather less refined.

The bargain Walkman tape adds to the Karajan performances Kamu's splendid *Karelia suite*, as fine as any available, the outer movements atmospheric and exciting and the *Ballade* eloquently played, without idiosyncrasy. The sound is very good, too; Karajan's *Finlandia* has slightly more body here than on the compact disc. If the couplings are suitable (and Géza Anda's account of the Grieg *Piano concerto*, if not among the finest available, is certainly enjoyable), this is excellent value.

Finlandia; Karelia suite, Op. 11. Kuolema: Valse triste. Legends: Lemminkäinen's return, Op. 22/4; Pohjola's daughter, Op. 49.
(M) **(*) HMV **CDM7 69205-2** [id.]. Hallé O, Barbirolli.

Although the orchestral playing is not as polished as that of a virtuoso orchestra, it is enthusiastic and has the advantage of excellent recording. *Pohjola's daughter* is extremely impressive, spacious but no less exciting for all the slower tempi. *Lemminkäinen's return* is also a thrilling performance. Overall, a desirable introduction to Sibelius's smaller orchestral pieces, with admirable stereo definition. The original recording dates from the mid-1960s but has been effectively remastered digitally, and while the upper range is fresher in the CD format, there is no lack of body, with impressive brass, bright and sonorous.

Finlandia, Op. 26; Karelia suite, Op. 11; Kuolema: Valse triste, Op. 44; Legends: The Swan of Tuonela, Op. 22/2; Pohjola's daughter, Op. 49.
(B) ** Cirrus Dig. **CICD 1002**. LSO, Rozhdestvensky.

Rozhdestvensky's performances, very well played, are highly individual but often wayward in their control of the music's pulse. The opening of *Finlandia* is very grand and portentous, the overall conception spacious, but the ritenutos in *Valse triste* are rather indulgent. The central *Ballade* of the *Karelia suite* is very measured, though evocative, yet the *Alla marcia* has a fine climax. Rozhdestvensky is at his most convincingly poetic in the rhapsodic *Swan of Tuonela* (with a memorable solo from the cor anglais), and the opening and closing sections of *Pohjola's daughter* are also tellingly atmospheric, although again one misses a consistent forward momentum. The recording, made in EMI's No. 1 Studio, is impressively balanced to give a concert-hall effect, with a warm ambience. On CD, the slightly sharper focus makes plain, however, that this is a studio venue.

Finlandia; Kuolema: Valse triste; Legend: The Swan of Tuonela.
(M) * CBS **MYK 42543 [MYK 36718]**. NYPO, Bernstein – GRIEG: *Peer Gynt.**

Bernstein's account of *Finlandia* is brilliant and exciting; *The Swan of Tuonela*, too, is beautifully managed, with finesse as well as a fine sense of brooding atmosphere. Both this and the *Valse triste* are acceptably remastered; but in order to make the brash recording of *Finlandia* more comfortable, the upper frequencies have been restricted and there is a feeling of compression. There are other, much better CDs of this music.

Finlandia. Kuolema: Valse triste; Legends: The Swan of Tuonela; Lemminkäinen's return. Tapiola.
(*) HMV Dig. **CDC7 47484-2 [id.]. Philh. O, Berglund.

Berglund's Philharmonia performances of this collection of favourite Sibelius pieces do not entirely supersede his earlier Bournemouth readings, for not everyone will prefer the marginally slower speeds. The satisfying ruggedness remains, given both more impact (as in *Tapiola*) and

Haitink's pair of CDs includes merely the *Overture*, Op. 115, as a bonus.) by the full-ranging digital recording.

Finlandia, Op. 26; Kuolema: Valse triste, Op. 44; Legends: The Swan of Tuonela, Op. 22/2; Tapiola, Op. 112.
*** DG Dig. **413 755-2** [id.]. BPO, Karajan.

Karajan first recorded *Tapiola* with the Philharmonia Orchestra, then again in 1965 and 1977, on both occasions with the Berlin Philharmonic. This is his fourth and undoubtedly his greatest account of this score, for it has the full measure of its vision and power. Never has it sounded more mysterious or its dreams more savage, and the wood-sprites weaving their magic secrets come vividly to life. The great classic accounts from Kajanus, Koussevitzky and Beecham are all imaginative in their very different ways; however, while they may offer different insights, they are not superior to the new Karajan. Nor has the build-up to the storm ever struck such a chilling note of terror: an awesomely impressive musical landscape. *The Swan*, Karajan's third account on record, is powerful and atmospheric; and the remaining two pieces, *Valse triste* and *Finlandia*, reinforce the feeling that this Berlin/Karajan partnership has never been equalled, not even by Toscanini and the NBC Symphony Orchestra. As a recording, this does not surpass the Philharmonia version under Ashkenazy, coupled with the *Fourth Symphony* and *Luonnotar* on Decca, but it does not fall far short; the orchestral playing is, of course, really in a class of its own.

Karelia suite, Op. 11; Legend: The Swan of Tuonela, Op. 22/2.
** Ph. **412 727-2**; *412 727-4* [id.]. ASMF, Marriner – GRIEG: *Holberg suite; Lyric pieces.* **(*)

Marriner's performance of *Karelia* is curiously subdued (though on CD, against the background silence, the pianissimo opening of the *Intermezzo* is very telling) and the closing *Alla marcia* could be more exuberant. Even the central *Ballade* seems to lack momentum, though the cor anglais solo is beautifully played by Barry Griffiths, who is no less eloquent in *The Swan of Tuonela*. The recording is most naturally balanced.

4 Legends, Op. 22 (Lemminkäinen and the maidens of Saari; The Swan of Tuonela; Lemminkäinen in Tuonela; Lemminkäinen's return).
*** BIS Dig. **CD 294** [id.]. Gothenburg SO, Järvi.
*** HMV **CDC7 47612-2** [id.]. Phd. O, Ormandy.
*** Chan. **CHAN 8394**; (M) *CBT 1026* [id.]. SNO, Gibson.

Choice between the three current versions of the *Legends* is not straightforward. Ormandy's 1979 set is undoubtedly outstanding, and the analogue recording was one of the best of its period: it sounds well in its remastered format, but Järvi offers modern digital sound. As far as recording quality is concerned, the latter's issue is very fine, with splendid range and presence and a wonderfully truthful balance. How good it is to hear solo violins sounding so naturally life-size – and not larger than life! The bass drum sounds impressively realistic, too. Järvi gives a passionate and atmospheric account of the first *Legend*. One small reservation concerning internal balance comes in its closing paragraph, where the sustained chords on horns and trombone are obtrusively loud, thus masking the woodwind cries and robbing the coda of much of its atmosphere. Järvi's account of *The Swan of Tuonela* is altogether magical, one of the best in the catalogue. He takes a broader view of *Lemminkäinen in Tuonela* than many of his rivals and builds up an appropriately black and powerful atmosphere, showing the Gothenburg brass to excellent advantage. The slight disappointment is *Lemminkäinen's homeward journey* which, though exciting, hasn't the possessed, manic quality of Beecham's very first record, which sounded as if a thousand demons were in pursuit.

On Ormandy's disc in the first of the *Legends*, the wind are more closely observed than is ideal, and the sound would benefit from greater depth. Ormandy's account of the first *Legend* is not as spacious as Jensen's pioneering disc, but it is marvellously passionate. (These Maidens of Saari must have given Lemminkäinen quite a wild time!) Ormandy's *Swan of Tuonela* is among the very finest, full of atmosphere and poetry, and the third *Legend* is brooding and menacing. In *Lemminkäinen's Return*, he comes close to the famous hell-for-leather excitement generated in Beecham's old 78 set. Among CD versions, Ormandy's is by far the fleetest horse.

In many ways this is the finest Sibelius recording Gibson has given us. The recording – originally issued by RCA – dates from 1979 and the distanced balance is particularly suitable for these scores, especially as the digital remastering has refined inner detail. The Scottish orchestra play freshly and with much commitment. *The Swan of Tuonela* has a darkly brooding primeval quality, and there is an electric degree of tension in the third piece, *Lemminkäinen in Tuonela*. The two outer *Legends* have ardent rhythmic feeling, and altogether this is highly successful. The recorded sound is excellent in both formats. The CD is most impressive but the first-class cassette sounds very well indeed and is offered in the medium-price range.

Pelléas et Mélisande: suite.
*** DG Dig. **410 026-2** [id.]. BPO, Karajan – GRIEG: *Peer Gynt suites 1 & 2.****

At last a version of Sibelius's subtle and atmospheric score that can compare with the classic Beecham version, originally dating from 1957. Indeed in certain movements, *By the spring in the park* and the *Pastorale*, it not only matches Sir Thomas but almost surpasses him. The *Pastorale* is altogether magical, and there is plenty of mystery in the third movement, *At the seashore*, omitted from the Beecham set. Some may find the opening movement, *At the castle gate*, a little too imposing, but the fervour and eloquence of the playing should win over most listeners. The recording, particularly on compact disc, is very striking indeed, with great clarity and presence. Although Beecham's recording, when it appears on CD, will remain indispensable for most Sibelians, the Karajan must now be a prime recommendation.

Rakastava (suite). *Op. 14; Scènes historiques, Opp. 25, 66; Valse lyrique, Op. 96/1.*
*** Chan. **CHAN 8393**; (M) *CBT 1025* [id.]. SNO, Gibson.

Written for a patriotic pageant, the *Scènes historiques* are vintage Sibelius; some of them (the *Scena*, Op. 25, No. 2, and the *Love song*, Op. 66, No. 2) plumb real depths of feeling, while others, like *The Chase*, Op. 66, No. 1, have a sense of the sweep and grandeur of nature. In the *Love song* Gibson strikes the right blend of depth and reticence, while elsewhere he conveys a fine sense of controlled power. Convincing and eloquent performances that have a natural feeling for the music. Gibson's *Rakastava* is beautifully unforced and natural, save for the last movement, which is a shade too slow. The *Valse lyrique* is not good Sibelius, but everything else certainly is. Gibson plays this repertoire with real commitment. The recorded sound is excellent, with the relationships between the various sections of the orchestra very well judged. The digital remastering (the original dates from 1977) is very successful, with the orchestral layout, slightly distanced, most believable. As with the other issues in Gibson's series of Sibelius orchestral music, the excellent tape is offered at mid-price.

Symphonies Nos 1–7.
(M) *** Decca Dig. **421 069-2** (4) [id.]. Philh. O, Ashkenazy.

Symphonies Nos 1–7; En saga; Finlandia; Karelia suite; (i) *Luonnotar; Tapiola.*
(M) *** Decca Dig. *417 378-4* (4) [id]. Philh. O, Ashkenazy; (i) with E. Söderström.

Symphonies Nos 1–7; Finlandia; The Swan of Tuonela; Tapiola.
** Ph. **416 600-2** (4) [id.]. Boston SO, C. Davis.

Ashkenazy's Sibelius series makes a rich and strong, consistently enjoyable cycle. Ashkenazy by temperament brings out the expressive warmth, colour and drama of the composer rather than his Scandinavian chill, reflecting perhaps his Slavonic background. The recordings are full and rich as well as brilliant, most of them of demonstration quality, even though they date from the early digital period. On four CDs at mid-price, the set makes a most attractive recommendation. The equivalent chrome cassettes offer also four symphonic poems and the *Karelia suite* and are economically priced. The sound is rich and generally well detailed, though the CDs are undoubtedly superior in sonic terms. On tape the symphonies are placed back to back so that no turnover breaks are needed in the middle of works.

Davis's Boston set, well transferred from refined analogue original recordings, brings a degree more transparency to the warmly atmospheric sound. The performances are all most distinguished, not as colourful or dramatic as some, but both powerful and refined, and consistently satisfying, helped by finely polished playing. The four discs bring a valuable and generous makeweight in the three tone-poems; but, at full price, they are not very competitive when considered alongside the splendid Decca Ashkenazy set.

Symphony No. 1 in E min., Op. 39; Finlandia, Op. 26.
** BIS **CD 221**. Gothenburg SO, Järvi.

Symphony No. 1 in E min., Op. 39; Karelia suite, Op. 11.
*** Decca Dig. **414 534-2**; *414 534-4* [id.]. Philh. O, Ashkenazy.
(M) *** HMV Dig. **CDM7 69028-2** [id.]; *EG 769028-4*. BPO, Karajan.

Symphony No. 1 in E min., Op. 39; The Oceanides, Op. 73.
(*) HMV Dig. **CDC7 47515-2 [id.]. CBSO, Rattle.

Symphonies Nos 1 in E min., Op. 39; 6 in D min., Op. 104.
*** HMV Dig. **CDC7 49042-2** [id.]; *EL 749042-4*. Helsinki PO, Berglund.

Symphonies Nos 1 in E min., Op. 39; 7 in C, Op. 105.
*(*) Chan. Dig. **CHAN 8344**; *ABTD 1086* [id.]. SNO, Gibson.

As a recording, Ashkenazy on Decca is quite simply the best of all. It has superb detail and clarity of texture, and there is all the presence and body one could ask for. The bass-drum rolls are particularly realistic. Moreover, it is as successful artistically as it is in terms of recorded sound, and further evidence – if such be needed – of Ashkenazy's growing mastery as a conductor. It is well held together and finely shaped; it is every bit as committed as Simon Rattle's with the CBSO but free from the occasional mannerism that disfigures his account. Ashkenazy is exactly on target in the Scherzo (dotted minim = 104), fractionally faster than Karajan and much more so than Rattle, who is far too measured here. The resultant sense of momentum is exhilarating. The very opening of the work is strongly projected and boldly contrasted with the movement which grows out of it. Throughout, however, the sheer physical excitement that this score engenders is tempered by admirable control. Only at the end of the slow movement does one feel that Ashkenazy could perhaps have afforded greater emotional restraint. The playing of the Philharmonia Orchestra is of the very first order. The *Karelia* suite is very good too, the middle movement, *Ballade*, fresh and imaginative. As for the symphony, while allegiances to Karajan's earlier Berlin Philharmonic account remain, this Decca version must be the preferred recommendation.

The Tchaikovskian influence which the composer himself acknowledged is strong in the *First Symphony*, even though it speaks with distinctly northern rather than Slavonic accents. Karajan, a great Tchaikovsky interpreter, identifies with the work's inheritance; he does not view the early Sibelius through the eyes of the symphonist the composer was to become. But there is a sense of grandeur and vision here, and the opulence and virtuosity of the Berliners helps to project the heroic dimensions of Karajan's performance. The early digital recording (1981) is not top-drawer: the bass is overweighted; but the full upper strings sing out gloriously with the richest amplitude in the finale, which has an electrifying climax; the brass is comparably rich and resonant. However, in the outer movements of the *Karelia suite*, which Karajan paces quite deliberately, the extra weight at the bottom end of the spectrum is less of an advantage.

Berglund's *First* is a marked improvement on his earlier low-voltage account with the Bournemouth orchestra. Both the playing and the interpretation are impressive in their breadth and concentration, and both performances are untouched by routine. His *Sixth* is particularly fine, though the Scherzo may strike some listeners as too measured. But readers wanting this coupling need not hesitate. The Helsinki orchestra produces excellent sonority and the EMI engineering is first class. If neither of these performances is necessarily a first choice, at the same time one cannot go far wrong with either. There is an excellent chrome cassette, full-bodied and clearly defined, with good range.

Rattle can hold his own against most of the competition. In his hands, if the whole symphony was as fine as the first movement this would be a clear first recommendation. Rattle has a powerful grasp of both its structure and character, and elicits an enthusiastic response from his players. The slow movement is for the most part superb, with excellent playing from the wind and brass of the Birmingham orchestra; but he makes too much of the commas at the end of the movement, which are so exaggerated as to be disruptive. An effect that is successful in the concert hall can sound exaggerated on a record, and such is the case in this peroration. The Scherzo has splendid character but is a good deal slower than the marking; he also makes the *Lento* at letter H correspondingly – and unacceptably – slower, for Sibelius marks it *ma non troppo*. Sibelius composed *The Oceanides* in 1914 for his visit to America (incidentally, it is his only tone-poem not directly inspired by the *Kalevala*). The Oceanides were the nymphs who inhabited the waters of Homeric mythology, and the opening of the piece has an atmosphere that is altogether ethereal. Simon Rattle has its measure and conveys all its mystery and poetry. The refinements of dynamics are scrupulously observed, so that the differences between *pp* and *ppp* really tell, and serve to produce the right delicacy of colouring and transparency of texture. This is a subtle and masterly performance.

No one would pretend that the Gothenburg Symphony ranks alongside the great orchestras that have recorded this symphony (Vienna, Berlin, Boston, and the Philharmonia), but heaven forbid that this repertoire should be the sole preserve of the virtuoso orchestras. The Gothenburg strings are clean, well focused in tone, lean and lithe; the wind are well blended and the clarinet solo at the beginning is sensitively played; and there is an excellent sense of atmosphere. The first movement is finely shaped, and preparation for the return of the first group in the re-statement is handled with impressive power. The slow movement is restrained and all the more effective on this count; the *Symphony* on the whole, one or two touches apart, is commendably straightforward. Neeme Järvi pulls back and is overemphatic at one bar after letter F in the finale. Better characterized than Gibson and very well recorded.

On the generous Chandos coupling there is plenty of enthusiasm in the first movement of No. 1, and there is no doubt that Sir Alexander is an 'echt Sibelian' through and through. Moreover, the actual sound is first rate by any standards, extremely vivid and present. However, the pitch discrepancy at letter S in the first movement of the *First Symphony* is worrying. In the long run, the playing does fall short of real distinction. The excellence of the Chandos sound on CD cannot disguise the want of tension and power that troubles the *Seventh*. It would be perverse to recommend this performance in preference to its rivals currently in the lists; in the *Seventh Symphony* it cannot displace (even on sonic grounds) Ashkenazy and the Philharmonia – though it should in fairness be added that the Decca coupled with a powerful account of *Tapiola*, offers the shorter playing time.

Symphony No. 2 in D, Op. 43.
(*) Decca Dig. **410 206-2 [id.]. Philh. O, Ashkenazy.
(M) (***) Ph. **420 771-2** [id.]. Concg. O, Szell (with BEETHOVEN: *Symphony No. 5*).
(*) Chan. Dig. **CHAN 8303; *ABTD 1062* [id.]. SNO, Gibson.
* DG Dig. **419 772-2**; *419 772-4* [id.]. VPO, Bernstein.

Symphony No. 2 in D, Op. 43; Finlandia.
* Telarc Dig. **CD 80095** [id.]. Cleveland O, Levi.

Symphony No. 2; Finlandia; Kuolema: Valse triste; Legend: The Swan of Tuonela.
(*) Ph. **420 490-2; *420 490-4* [id.]. Boston SO, C. Davis.

Symphony No. 2; Kuolema, Op. 44: Scene with cranes.
(*) HMV Dig. **CDC7 47222-2 [id.]. CBSO, Rattle.

Symphony No. 2; Kuolema: Valse triste; Legend: The Swan of Tuonela; Pohjola's daughter.
(M) **(*) RCA **GD 86528**; *GK 86528* [**RCA 6528-2-RG**]. Phil. O, Ormandy.

Symphony No. 2 in D; Romance for strings in C, Op. 42.
*** BIS Dig. **CD 252** [id.]. Gothenburg SO, Järvi.

From BIS a thought-provoking and excellent-sounding issue with plenty of presence and body. Not only is it very interesting; it is often a powerful performance of much honesty and directness. Järvi is very brisk in the opening *Allegretto*: he is every bit as fast as Kajanus in his pioneering account of 1930 which enjoyed the composer's own imprimatur. This Gothenburg version has more sinew and fire than its rivals, and the orchestral playing is more responsive and disciplined than that of the SNO on Chandos. Throughout, Järvi has an unerring sense of purpose and direction and the momentum never slackens. Of course, there is not the same opulence as the Philharmonia under Ashkenazy on Decca, but the BIS performance is concentrated in feeling and thoroughly convincing. The *Romance for strings* is not otherwise available in the CD format.

We are divided in our response to the Ashkenazy version. There are no doubts about the quality of the recorded sound, which is superb. It is atmospheric, beautifully rounded in tone, and has splendid clarity, definition and depth. As for the performance, it is a passionate, volatile reading, in many ways a very Russian view of Sibelius, with Ashkenazy finding a clear affinity with the Tchaikovsky symphonies. At the very opening, the quick, flexible treatment of the repeated crotchet motif is urgent, not weighty or ominous as it can be. Ashkenazy's control of tension and atmosphere makes for the illusion of live performance in the building of each climax, and the rich digital sound (recorded in the ideal acoustic of the Kingsway Hall) adds powerfully to that impression. Yet some listeners may find it more difficult to respond positively to this reading; like R.L., they may feel the performance is wanting in firmness of grip, especially in the slow movement, with the dramatic pauses lacking spontaneity and unanimity of response.

Szell's marvellous account of the *Second Symphony* is splendidly taut and well held together, and its merits are well known: great tension and power. Unfortunately the digital remastering is no improvement over the LP. There is a firmer and deeper bass but the string sonority is drier. The sound seems to be cut off rather than dying away as it does on LP, and there is some loss of bloom. Hold on to your LP. (The CD coupling is a thrilling account of Beethoven's *Fifth*, but it sounds horribly aggressive and unpleasant in its remastered format.)

The *Second* is among the best of the Gibson cycle; it scores, thanks to the impressive clarity and impact of the recording. Sir Alexander has been a doughty champion of Sibelius ever since the early 1960s, and this version of the *Second* is honest and straightforward, free of bombast in the finale. Tempos are well judged and there is at no time any attempt to interpose the personality of the interpreter. The first movement is neither too taut nor too relaxed: it is well shaped and feels right. The strings do not possess the weight or richness of sonority of the Philharmonia, and the performance as a whole does not displace the first recommendations on CD. The cassette is first rate, full, vivid and clean, though side two (in the copy we sampled) is transferred at a lower level and needs a higher setting to make the maximum effect. The CD is impressive, and is extremely vivid.

The CBSO play with fervour and enthusiasm for Simon Rattle except, perhaps, in the first movement where the voltage is lower – particularly in the development, which is not easy to bring off and which can easily sound laboured. Rattle's is not the *Allegretto* of the pioneering Kajanus record, let alone Järvi's more recent CD version. Indeed, he is in fact slightly broader than Karajan in either of his recordings and the playing is less fine-grained. The slow movement is full-blooded and gutsy, convincing even when Rattle arrests the flow of the argument by underlining certain points. The Scherzo is bracing enough, though in the trio the oboe tune is caressed a little too much and is in danger of sounding sentimentalized. However, the transition to the finale is magnificent and Rattle finds the *tempo giusto* in this movement. The Birmingham strings, incidentally, produce a splendidly fervent unison here – and elsewhere in the *Symphony*. The recording is very alive, though the perspective needs greater depth and more air round the various orchestral sections. As a fill-up, Simon Rattle and the CBSO give an imaginative and poetic account of the *Scene with cranes* from the incidental music to *Kuolema*. A good record but not one that sweeps the board.

Sir Colin Davis gives a dignified and well-proportioned account that is free from any excesses or mannerisms. Although it has not the fervour of Szell, it has sensitivity and freshness in its favour. The sound is not as open at the top as is desirable and there is a certain tubbiness in the middle-to-bottom range (even more striking on cassette); there is both body and impact and the violins do not lack brightness. This is satisfying in its way. Of the couplings, *Finlandia* is expansive and *The Swan of Tuonela* has a powerful atmosphere.

Ormandy's mid-1970s account still makes a considerable impact and is marvellously played. However, the reading rarely sheds new light on this wonderful score. The overall impression is of a superbly disciplined response from the Philadelphians, well recorded, but wanting that extra degree of freshness and character to justify the exposure that repeated hearing will give it. Yet there is no doubt that the rich sweep of the Philadelphia strings in the big tune of the finale is very compulsive in its intensity. *Pohjola's daughter*, too, generates an exciting climax, while *The Swan of Tuonela* is darkly atmospheric. The digital remastering is vivid but not always absolutely refined, and the brass at the close of the *Symphony* has an element of coarseness.

Bernstein's last recording of this symphony was made in 1968 with the New York Philharmonic and had a great deal to commend it: generosity of feeling, intensity and dramatic fire. However, this new version with the Vienna Philharmonic is not the success one might have expected. The performance as a whole is insupportably inflated; his tendency to linger over cadential phrases undermines the music's sense of impetus. Bernstein dwells excessively on incidental moments of splendour and grandeur and he pulls the slow movement completely out of shape. The orchestral playing is impressive and the DG engineers produce a truthful and clean aural image. Bernstein is an artist of vision and a great Sibelian, but in this instance the very intensity of his feeling comes between us and the composer.

Levi's is a plainspun reading, essentially spacious, though with moments when he forces the pace. The Cleveland Orchestra play well for him, but the electricity sparks only fitfully, and overall the result fails to grip the listener. *Finlandia*, too, is unimpressive, although the rich Telarc sound (made in Cleveland's Masonic Auditorium) gives a fine body and bloom to strings and brass alike.

Symphony No. 3 in C, Op. 52; King Kristian II suite, Op. 27.
*** BIS Dig. **CD 228**. Gothenburg SO, Järvi.

Symphonies Nos 3 in C, Op. 52; 6 in D min., Op. 104.
*** Decca Dig. **414 267-2** [id.]. Philh. O, Ashkenazy.
** Chan. Dig. **CHAN 8389**; *ABTD 1097* [id.]. SNO, Gibson.

Symphonies Nos 3 in C, Op. 52; 7 in C, Op. 105.
*** EMI Dig. **CDC7 47450-2** [id.]; *EL270496-4.* CBSO, Rattle.

The two C major symphonies make a classic coupling: even in the early days of the gramophone, they kept company. Simon Rattle's account of the *Third* is vastly superior to his *First* and *Second.* He finds the *tempo giusto* throughout and is convincing not only in his pacing but also in his capacity to relate the parts to the whole. The slow movement is particularly fine; few have penetrated its landscape more completely since Kajanus. The withdrawn atmosphere in the section beginning at fig. 6 is wonderfully captured, and the movement throughout is magical. The way in which he gradually builds up the finale is masterly and sure of instinct. The recording, made in the Warwick Arts Centre, sounds very well balanced, natural in perspective and finely detailed. The *Seventh* is hardly less powerful and impressive: its opening is slow to unfold and has real vision. This is one of the finest *Sevenths* of recent years. Unfortunately the cassette is transferred on iron-oxide stock and the sound is rather opaque.

Vladimir Ashkenazy and the Philharmonia Orchestra give a first-class account of both the *Third* and *Sixth Symphonies.* In the first movement of the *Third,* Ashkenazy is a shade faster than the metronome marking, and so there is no want of forward momentum and thrust, either here or in the finale. The tempi and spirit of the *Andantino* are well judged, though the withdrawn passage in the slow movement (at fig. 6) could perhaps have more inwardness of feeling; Ashkenazy is not helped, however, by the balance, closer than ideal, which casts too bright a light on a landscape that should be shrouded in mystery. It is clear that Ashkenazy has great feeling for the *Sixth* and its architecture. There is no lack of that sense of communion with nature which lies at the heart of the slow movement or the sense of its power which emerges in the finale. He is a good deal broader than Karajan – though that performance has an altogether special atmosphere – and Ashkenazy lets every detail tell in the *Poco vivace* third movement. Indeed, this is possibly the most successful and technically impressive in the current Decca cycle, with the *Seventh* as a close runner-up. Early in the present century, Sibelius enjoyed the championship of another great Russian pianist-conductor, Alexander Siloti, in whose concerts the *Third Symphony* was heard as early as 1909. In Ashkenazy he has found a natural heir and a worthy successor.

Neeme Järvi's version of the *Third Symphony* comes as part of an ambitious series that he is undertaking with the Gothenburg Symphony Orchestra to record the complete orchestral output of Sibelius for BIS. Although Sir Alexander Gibson and he do not differ more than fractionally, there is more sense of the epic in Järvi's hands. There is, on the other hand, great excitement in the Gibson, and many may respond more positively to the sense of forward movement here. But in Gothenburg, the slow movement is first class and the much more leisurely tempo adopted here by the Estonian conductor is just right. Järvi's coupling is the incidental music to *King Christian II*; his account is splendidly committed throughout and free from the literalness that seems at times to distinguish this Finnish conductor. This is very beautifully played and recorded. Järvi's account of the *Third* can hold its own with any in the catalogue.

Sir Alexander Gibson and the Scottish National Orchestra last recorded the *Third Symphony* way back in the 1960s, coupling it with the *Seventh*, but this is his first recording of the *Sixth.* The SNO is in very good form, even though the 'cross-hatched' string writing in the slow movement of the *Sixth* does show their limitations. The first movement of the *Third* has real momentum. Gibson's tempo is a good deal brisker now than it was in his earlier recording, though the steadier pulse that he set in the 1960s is to be preferred. Yet the SNO play with genuine fire and enthusiasm and the recording is outstanding. The slow movement is another matter; here, Sir Alexander, as Anthony Collins before him, loses much of the inwardness and some of the fantasy of this enigmatic movement by pressing ahead too rapidly – and faster than the marking. Still, readers who are collecting the Gibson cycle will find there is more to admire than to cavil at. Both accounts are likeable; at the same time, it would be idle to pretend that as performances they displace Ashkenazy's coupling or, in the case of the *Sixth Symphony*, Karajan and the Berlin Philharmonic on DG, even if the Chandos recording is more vivid and better detailed. The cassette is hardly less impressive than the disc.

Symphony No. 4 in A min., Op. 63; Canzonetta, Op. 62/1; The Oceanides, Op. 73.
(*) BIS Dig. **CD 263 [id.]. Gothenburg SO, Järvi.

Symphony No. 4 in A min., Op. 63; Finlandia, Op. 26. (i) *Luonnotar, Op. 70.*
*** Decca Dig. **400 056-2** [id.]. Philh. O, Ashkenazy, (i) with Söderström.

Ashkenazy achieves great concentration of feeling in the *Fourth*. The brightness of the Philharmonia violins and the cleanness of attack add to the impact of this baldest of the Sibelius symphonies, and Ashkenazy's terracing of dynamic contrasts is superbly caught in the outstanding digital recording. Like his other Sibelius readings, this one has something of a dark Russian passion in it, but freshness always dominates over mere sensuousness; as ever, Ashkenazy conveys the spontaneity of live performance. There is splendid drama and intensity throughout, and this is a very impressive performance. The couplings add to the special attractions of this issue; *Finlandia* is made fresh again in a performance of passion and precision, and Elisabeth Söderström is on top form in *Luonnotar*, a symphonic poem with a voice (although some ears may find her wide vibrato and hard-edged tone not entirely sympathetic). The compact disc is splendid, with the silent background adding to the dramatic impact of the performance and the dynamic contrasts even more effective. The close balancing of certain instruments is more noticeable, but the Kingsway Hall acoustic is demonstrated as ideal for this score, with the brass both biting and sonorous. The voice of Söderström in *Luonnotar* is given extra immediacy.

The sound of the BIS recording is notably fresh and vivid, thanks to the celebrated acoustic of the Gothenburg Concert Hall and the expertise of the engineering. Neeme Järvi takes a very broad view of the first movement – and conveys much of its brooding quality. There is perhaps more introspection here, and less of the stoicism of Beecham or the granite-like density of Karajan's performance. The Scherzo has a splendid strength, even if Järvi allows the pace to slacken far too much towards the end. Both Järvi and Karajan portray the bleak yet otherworldly landscape of the slow movement to excellent effect, but the tension between phrases in the Karajan makes his the more powerful experience. In the finale Järvi opts for the tubular bells rather than the glockenspiel, which Sibelius wanted. As a fill-up, he gives us the *Canzonetta for strings*, Op. 62a, which derives from the music to *Kuolema*. It has great allure and charm and is beautifully played by the Gothenburg strings. *The Oceanides* is a very fine performance, too, though less subtle than Rattle's, particularly in its observance of dynamic nuances.

Symphonies Nos 4 in A min., Op. 63; 5 in E flat, Op. 82.
(M) *** HMV **CDM7 69244-2** [id.]. BPO, Karajan.

Symphonies Nos 4 in A min., Op. 63; 6 in D min., Op. 104.
✿ *** DG **415 107-2** [id.]. BPO, Karajan.
*** HMV Dig. **CDC7 47711-2** [id.]; *EL 747711-4*. CBSO, Rattle.

Symphonies Nos 4 in A min., Op. 63; 7 in C, Op. 105.
*** HMV Dig. **CDC7 47443-2** [id.]. Helsinki PO, Berglund.

Karajan's twenty-year-old recording of the *Fourth Symphony* is only marginally less powerful than Ashkenazy on Decca, and his performance is of real stature. Having found it too well groomed on first acquaintance in the mid-1960s, many collectors have come to discover its depths and to value its sense of mystery. Although one is bowled over by the Ashkenazy at first, it is the Karajan that has the greater concentration and tension. DG also offer his glorious account of the *Sixth Symphony* which remains almost unsurpassed among recent accounts. Among its predecessors, only the famous Beecham record offers more distinctive insights. Although this DG transfer does not quite have the range and body of the BIS and Decca versions, it sounds more vivid than on its earlier appearances and, like that of No. 4, the performance is a great one.

Simon Rattle's account of the *Fourth* with the Birmingham orchestra is one of the best to have appeared in recent years. He invokes a powerful atmosphere in its opening pages: one is completely transported to its dark landscape with its seemingly limitless horizons. The string tone is splendidly lean without being undernourished and achieves a sinisterly whispering pianissimo in the development. The slow movement is magical – not as fast as Beecham or as tautly held together as the Karajan – but very impressive in its own right. The finale is hardly less masterly: Rattle builds up most convincingly to the final climax and the enigmatic, almost resigned coda. His account of the *Sixth* is one of the very best. Gone are the days when this could be called the 'Cinderella' of the symphonies; all of the half-dozen or so versions now on CD have something to be said for them. In the slow movement Rattle does not have the tremendous grip that the Karajan version commands, or quite the concentration he achieves elsewhere – but make no mistake, this is still a *Sixth* to reckon with, and its closing bars are memorably eloquent. There is an excellent chrome cassette.

In some ways Karajan's re-recording of the *Fourth Symphony* for HMV must be counted controversial. He gives spacious – and highly atmospheric – accounts of the first and third movements, a good deal slower than his earlier DG version. He conveys eloquently the other-worldly quality of the landscape in the third movement. The first undoubtedly has great mystery and power. Again, in the HMV *Fifth* the opening movement is broader than the earlier, DG account, and he achieves a remarkable sense of its strength and majesty. The transition from the work's first section to the 'scherzo' is slightly more abrupt than in the 1965 recording; tempi generally in the work's first half are rather more extreme. The variety of tone colour and, above all, the weight of sonority that the Berlin Philharmonic have at their command is remarkable, and the bassoon lament in the development section finds the Berlin strings reduced to a mere whisper. Both the slow movement and finale are glorious and have real vision, and the recording is excellent. However, the digital remastering has brought drier, less opulent textures than in the original full-priced issues; there is now a degree of thinness on the string timbre above the stave, not apparent when the two symphonies were issued separately. In both works the earlier DG versions (each differently coupled) are even finer, but at mid-price this HMV disc offers formidable value, even if the CD brings a hint of stridency on the fortissimo brass.

Paavo Berglund has recorded both symphonies before: indeed, this is his third account of the *Fourth*, and it is legitimate to question the need for a newcomer. However, these are both performances of considerable stature; indeed, the *Seventh* is arguably one of the finest now before the public: it has a real nobility and breadth, and Berglund has the full measure of all the shifting changes of mood and colour. Moreover, the Helsinki orchestra play magnificently and seem to have a total rapport with him. The *Fourth* is hardly less imposing and has a stark grandeur that resonates in the mind. Both his earlier versions had a certain grim intensity but the slow movement in neither matches this newcomer in its brooding power and poetic feeling. It has a mystery that perhaps eludes him in the development of the first movement, though the opening is marvellous in his hands. There are one or two things worth noting: there is not a great deal of *vivace* in the second movement. (Ashkenazy gets the tempo of this movement absolutely right – and he, too, is spectacularly well recorded.) The finale is superb, even if some collectors may find the closing bars insufficiently cold and bleak. However, these are both excellent versions and must have strong claims on the collector.

Symphony No. 5 in E flat, Op. 82; Andante festivo; Karelia overture, Op. 10.
*(*) BIS **CD 222** [id.]. Gothenburg SO, Järvi.

Symphony No. 5; Night ride and sunrise, Op. 55.
*** HMV Dig. **CDC7 47006-2** [id.]. Philh. O, Rattle.

Symphony No. 5; Pohjola's daughter, Op. 49.
** CBS Dig. **MK 42366**; *MT 42366* [id.]. Philh. O, Salonen.

Symphony No. 5; En Saga.
*** Decca Dig. **410 016-2** [id.]. Philh. O, Ashkenazy.

Symphonies Nos 5 in E flat, Op. 82; 7 in C, Op. 105.
(*) DG **415 108-2 [id.]. BPO, Karajan.

Simon Rattle's record of the *Fifth Symphony* has collected numerous prizes in Europe – and deserves them all. Right from the very outset, one feels that he has found the *tempo giusto*. Ashkenazy conducting the same orchestra is fractionally more measured, and that slight difference is enough to affect the sense of flow. Moreover, one notices that the woodwind are better blended in the HMV version, whereas in the Decca the clarinets obtrude slightly. Rattle is scrupulous in observing every dynamic nuance to the letter and, one might add, spirit. What is particularly impressive is the control of the transition between the first section and the scherzo element of the first movement, where the listener is often made all too conscious of the changing of gears and releasing of levers. This relationship is ideally balanced and enables Rattle to convey detail in just the right perspective. There is a splendid sense of atmosphere in the development and a power unmatched in recent versions, save for the Karajan. The playing is superb, with the recording to match. *Night ride* is very good but not quite so outstanding; however, this is undoubtedly an exceptional *Fifth*. The CD gains in range, depth and presence. It is strikingly natural and vivid, one of the best compact discs to come from EMI.

Ashkenazy's performance is exceptionally well recorded, with fine, spacious and well-detailed digital sound. His reading is a thoroughly idiomatic one and disappoints only in terms of the balance of tempi between the two sections of the first movement. This is a fine rather than a great performance. Ashkenazy's *En Saga* is the best version of that work now in the catalogue; when one considers also the outstanding excellence of the recording, this issue will obviously have strong appeal. The compact disc must be listed among the best of Decca's earlier releases. The entry of the horns in the finale – perhaps the most impressive part of the performance – is especially telling; overall, the fullness of the sound is matched by its immediacy and warmth of atmosphere, with no trace of digital edginess, although the brass has bite as well as richness of sonority.

Such is the excellence of the classic Karajan DG *Fifth* that few listeners would guess its age. It is a great performance, and this 1964 version is indisputably the finest of the four he has made (two with the Philharmonia for Columbia and the 1977 Berlin account for HMV). Impressive though it is, his *Seventh* is not quite in the same class, and must yield both technically and even artistically to the Ashkenazy, which is very powerful and coupled with an impressive *Tapiola*. However, the virtues of the *Fifth* are well known and its appearance on compact disc more than welcome.

Neeme Järvi is broad and spacious in the first movement; indeed, he almost calls to mind the Tuxen account with the Danish Radio Orchestra from the early days of LP. There is, however, insufficient sense of mystery in the development movement, and the slow movement is a bit laboured. At the same time, it is a useful issue in that it also includes the *Andante festivo* (1922), a broad dignified piece for strings (the only work that Sibelius himself recorded), and the *Karelia overture*, not otherwise available at the time of writing. The Gothenburg orchestra has the advantage of a superb acoustic: it has both warmth and clarity.

Esa-Pekka Salonen's performance has much to recommended it, even if it is not an unqualified success. The young Finnish maestro has a sophisticated feeling for texture and colour but pays more attention to beauty of incident than to the overall coherence of the symphonic design. By far the most successful thing is the finale, which is well paced: it has breadth, spaciousness and nobility; there are also impressive things in the first movement – the hushed strings at the beginning of the development – and the massive build-up towards the transition, and the opening is very broad with a consequent gain in spaciousness and grandeur. However, the transition to the 'scherzo' section, a notoriously difficult passage to bring off, is not wholly convincing. He moves rapidly to a much quicker tempo, which might be acceptable were his opening section tauter and more concentrated in conception. The slow movement is very broad and the evocative wind writing over 'cross-hatch' *ppp* strings is quite magical – but then he spoils the string line (*poco largamente*) by sentimentalizing it. No complaints about the CBS recording, which is very good with a natural perspective and clarity, or his account of *Pohjola's daughter*, which has good atmosphere. However, not a first choice. The cassette is well managed.

Symphony No. 6 in D min., Op. 104, En Saga, Op. 9; Karelia suite, Op. 11; Kuolema: Valse triste.
*** HMV Dig. *EL 270407-4* [Ang. *4DS 37821*]. BPO, Karajan.

Symphony No. 6 in D min., Op. 104; Pelléas et Mélisande: suite, Op. 46.
(*) BIS Dig. **CD 237 [id.]. Gothenburg SO, Järvi.

The *Sixth* was the first of Sibelius's symphonies Karajan conducted half a century ago when it was still new music and, as a young conductor at Aachen, he was invited to Stockholm for concerts with the Swedish Radio Orchestra in the mid-1930s. He has recorded it twice before, with the Philharmonia in the 1950s and with the Berlin Philharmonic a decade later. This EMI version was made in 1981 and brings to life the other-worldly quality of this score: the long white nights of the northern summer and their 'fragile melancholy', that the slow movement (or, for that matter, the opening polyphony) conjures up. Even though this is a spacious account, we are never unaware of the sense of forward movement. Although this performance seems more spacious and more unhurried than the DG account recorded in 1967, each movement is in fact marginally quicker. In short, this is Karajan at his finest: not even Beecham made the closing pages sound more magical. This new recording is better than its predecessor, and the EMI team have achieved a more spacious acoustic ambience. The French critic, Marc Vignal, spoke of Sibelius as 'the aristocrat of symphonists', and this, surely, is the aristocrat of performances. It will doubtless appear on CD during the lifetime of this book. The fillers are all fine performances, recorded between 1977 (*En Saga*) and 1982. The tape transfers are well managed, though there is some excess bass resonance in *Karelia*.

The response of the Gothenburg orchestra to Järvi's direction is whole-hearted; one warms to the eloquence of the opening string polyphony and the impassioned finale. Järvi takes the main section very fast, much in the manner of the 1934 record by Schnéevoigt, who is headlong in this section. There are one or two overemphatic gestures in the closing paragraphs of the slow movement, but on the whole this is well thought out and often impressive. It can hold its own with most competition and can be recommended, albeit not in preference to the Karajan version, though it is better recorded. Both *Pelléas et Mélisande* and the *Symphony* are in the CD catalogue from Karajan, the former being altogether magical and likely to reign as the unchallenged classic for as long as did the celebrated Beecham version. Järvi produces a very atmospheric account of this score, in particular the brief but concentrated *By the sea*. Yet it would be idle to pretend that it can be preferred to the Berlin performance.

Symphony No. 7 in C, Op. 105; Canzonetta, Op. 62a; Kuolema: Valse triste; Scene with cranes, Op. 44. Night ride and sunrise, Op. 55; Valse romantique, Op. 62b.
*** BIS Dig. **CD 311** [id.]. Gothenburg SO, Järvi.

Symphony No. 7; Tapiola.
*** Decca Dig. **411 935-2** [id.]. Philh. O, Ashkenazy.

Magnificent sound and very impressive playing. Ashkenazy's accounts of both the *Symphony* and *Tapiola* have many insights; the Decca recording is of the very highest quality, with altogether splendid range and presence. Ashkenazy does not build up the *Symphony* quite as powerfully as Berglund, but he has the measure of its nobility. His *Tapiola* is atmospheric and keenly dramatic; the only quarrel one might have is with his frenetic storm, whose very speed diminishes its overall impact and detracts from the breadth and grandeur that otherwise distinguish this reading. Apart from these minor qualifications, there is much to admire – indeed, much that is thrilling – in these interpretations; in any event, it is difficult to imagine the recorded sound being surpassed for a long time to come. It is especially impressive on CD.

In the *Seventh Symphony*, Neeme Järvi and the Gothenburg orchestra call to mind the energy and concentration of the pioneering Koussevitzky records. Järvi is a sympathetic and authoritative guide in this terrain. Put alongside Rattle, they are worlds apart: to use an astronomical analogy, the Järvi is a white dwarf and the Rattle a red giant. The only disappointment is the final climax, which is perhaps less intense. However, it is a fine performance and the music to *Kuolema* is splendidly atmospheric: there is little to choose between Rattle and Järvi in the *Scene with cranes*. *Night ride* is strongly characterized and in some ways is more expansive than Rattle's (coupled with his Philharmonia account of the *Fifth*). The recording exhibits the usual characteristics of the Gothenburg Concert Hall and has plenty of body and presence.

String quartets: in A min. (1889); in B flat, Op. 4.
(*) Finlandia **FACD 345 [id.]. Sibelius Ac. Qt.

Voces intimae, the quartet he composed in Paris and London during 1908–9, is not Sibelius's only essay in the medium. Here, for the first time on record, are two early quartets, the *A minor*, written in 1889, his last year as a student, in Helsinki, and the *B flat*, composed the following year. Only the first violin part of the *A minor Quartet* was thought to survive, but a complete set of parts was recently discovered by Erik Tawaststjerna. There are many prophetic touches, as well as plenty of what Professor Tawaststjerna calls 'the fragile Nordic melancholy linked stylistically to Grieg'. It is interesting to see that the highly developed feeling for form we recognize from the mature Sibelius is already evident in these quartets. New ideas emerge at just the right moment (with the possible exception of the rather primitive fugal episode in the first movement of the *A minor*) and, given the fact that these are student works, the music is excellently paced. The playing of the Sibelius Academy Quartet is sympathetic and intelligent, very good rather than impeccable. The rather close balance of the recording does not do full justice to their dynamic range or tone colour and, despite the reverberant ambience, the sound does not really expand. Don't, however, be put off by this reservation; if the recording is not ideal, it is perfectly acceptable, and there is no doubt as to the commitment or expertise of the performances. An issue of great interest to all Sibelians.

VOCAL MUSIC

Kullervo Symphony, Op. 7.
** BIS Dig. **CD 313** [id.]. Mattila, Hynninen, Laulun Ystävät Male Ch., Gothenburg SO, Järvi.

(i) *Kullervo symphony, Op. 7; Scènes historiques: suite No. 1, Op. 25.*
(B) *** HMV *TCC2-POR 54287.* Bournemouth SO, Berglund, (i) with Kostia, Viitanen, Helsinki University Male Voice Ch.

Kullervo symphony, Op. 7; Oma maa (Our native land), Op. 92; The Origin of fire, Op. 32.
*** HMV Dig. **CDS7 47496-8** (2) [id.]. Naumanen, Hynninen, Estonian State Ac. Ch., Helsinki University Male Voice Ch., Helsinki University Ch., Helsinki PO, Berglund.

The *Kullervo symphony* is an ambitious five-movement work for two soloists, male-voice choir and orchestra, some seventy or so minutes long, which Sibelius wrote at the outset of his career in 1892. It brought him national fame and a commission from Kajanus that resulted in *En Saga*. After its first performance Sibelius withdrew the score and it was never performed in its entirety until 1958, a year after his death. It is revealed as an impressive work, full of original touches, particularly in its thoroughly characteristic opening. Naturally there are immaturities: the slow movement is overlong and overtly Tchaikovskian. What impresses, however, is the powerful vocal writing, and there are many exciting facets of Sibelius's early style to be found in this rewarding score.

Berglund's 1971 recording is available on tape, well transferred on a single bargain-priced 'Portrait of the Artist' double-length cassette. The first thing collectors will want to know is whether the new digital issue represents a decisive improvement on the old. Berglund's basic conception of the score remains unchanged, save for a somewhat steadier fourth movement; overall, there is a much greater lyrical intensity in the shaping of phrases and altogether greater fantasy in the treatment of detail. He digs deeper into the score and conveys more of its epic power and, above all, its poetry than he did in his earlier account. This reading makes more of dynamic contrast and grips one far more than did its predecessor; it is fresher and comes more from the heart. This recording also has the advantage of two very fine soloists. Eeva Liisa Naumanen and the incomparable Jorma Hynninen, while the male choirs from Helsinki University and from Estonia produce a splendidly firmly-focused and black tone-colour. The only area in which this does not represent a striking improvement is in the recording, which is in the same expert hands of Brian Culverhouse as before. Not that the new recording is anything but very fine – and, of course, there is the richer bass and range of digital recording – but the acoustic of the 1971 version (Guildhall, Southampton) definitely has greater warmth than the slightly drier Helsinki venue. Nevertheless the CDs bring greater definition and range and the inestimable advantage of background silence.

The newest issue also brings us two rarities: *Oma maa* (*Our native land*), written in 1918 between the *Fifth* and *Sixth Symphonies*, which has not been recorded before, and *Tulen synty*, Op. 32, otherwise known as *The Origin of fire* or *Ukko the Firemaker*. This comes from the period of the *Second Symphony* and was revised at the time the composer was working on the *Fourth*. *The Origin of fire* is a powerful piece; as Professor Erik Tawaststjerna puts it, it 'comes close to being one of Sibelius's masterpieces'. There is more in it that belongs closer to the darker world of the *Fourth Symphony* than to 1902. The solo part is marvellously sung here by Jorma Hynninen, while Berglund gives us a performance of great atmosphere and of brooding intensity. If one were asked to place *Our native land*, one's thoughts would turn more to the 1890s than to 1918, and it is certainly no match for its companion piece. The performance is a good one, though the sopranos of Helsinki University Choir are not quite as distinguished as the men.

On the face of it, Järvi offers quite a challenge: Paavo Berglund's recording labours at a considerable disadvantage, running to two discs; BIS accommodate the whole work on a single CD, no mean feat considering the wide dynamic range involved. Järvi is so fast that he almost robs the symphony of its epic character and its breadth. He allows himself no time to shape the main theme and, only a few bars in, he presses ahead still faster. 'Kullervo and his sister', the central movement, is the high point of this performance, thanks to the superb singing of Karita Mattila and Jorma Hynninen, who is, if anything, in finer voice than on the EMI set. If only the pace were less headlong, this would have been a first recommendation. The Gothenburg recording does justice to the large forces involved: the brass is marvellously rich and present as usual and the balance between the singers and orchestra excellently judged. But taken as a whole, either of the alternative HMV versions offers greater musical satisfaction.

Songs with orchestra: *Arioso; Autumn evening* (*Höstkväll*); *Come away, Death!* (*Kom nu hit Död*); *The diamond on the March snow* (*Diamanten på marssnön*); *The fool's song of the spider* (*Sången om korsspindeln*); *Luonnotar, Op. 70; On a balcony by the sea* (*På verandan vid havet*); *The Rapids-rider's brides* (*Koskenlaskian morsiammet*); *Serenade; Since then I have questioned no further* (*Se'n har jag ej frågat mera*); *Spring flies hastily* (*Våren flyktar hastigt*); *Sunrise* (*Soluppgång*).
*** BIS **CD 270** [id.]. Jorma Hynninen, Mari-Anne Häggander, Gothenburg SO, Panula.

This record collects all the songs that Sibelius originally composed for voice and orchestra, together with those for voice and piano that he himself subsequently orchestrated. The great find here is a newly discovered song of haunting beauty, *Serenade*, which begins the record. Not to put too fine a point on it, this is one of Sibelius's very greatest and most subtle songs. (It was recently discovered by Professor Erik Tawaststjerna.) The *Serenade* dates from 1895, the period of the *Lemminkäinen Legends*, and has the greatest delicacy and atmosphere: its whispering pizzicato strings are wonderfully suggestive. Jorma Hynninen is a fine interpreter of this repertoire, and it is strange that he has had such little exposure in this country. His singing can only be called glorious. Mari-Anne Häggander manages the demanding tessitura of *Arioso* and *Luonnotar* with much artistry, and her *Luonnotar* is certainly to be preferred to Söderström's. Her vibrato is minimal and her pitch dauntingly accurate. She succeeds beautifully, too, in achieving *pp* tone on the top B, towards the end of the piece. Jorma Panula proves a sensitive accompanist and secures fine playing from the Gothenburg orchestra. In any event, this is indispensable.

Songs: *Astray; Black roses; Come away, Death; Driftwood; In the field a maiden sings; King Christian II; The fool's song of the spider. Kullervo's lament; The maiden came from her lover's tryst; On a balcony by the sea; Pelléas et Mélisande: The three blind sisters; Sigh, sedges, sigh; Spring flies speedily; Swim, duck, swim!; To evening; Twelfth Night: 2 Songs. Was it a dream?; When that I was.*
*** HM *HMC 40 5142.* Jorma Hynninen, Ralf Gothoni.

Jorma Hynninen has altogether superb vocal artistry at his command; his powerful, finely focused voice always rings in the memory long after the turntable has come to rest; indeed, he is one of the finest Finnish singers now before the public. The recording, made as long ago as 1975 but not released in the UK until recently, is eminently well balanced, with the piano excellently placed. The performances are of a high order vocally and interpretatively, and Hynninen and his fine partner colour the words beautifully. The Shakespeare settings have wonderful atmosphere and are rightly given in Hagberg's Swedish translation: they do not fit the English at all.

The Maiden in the tower (opera). *Karelia suite, Op. 11.*
*** BIS Dig. **CD 250** [id.]. Häggander, Hynninen, Hagegård, Kruse, Gothenburg Ch. and SO, Järvi.

Sibelius abandoned his first operatic venture, *Veneen luominen* (*The building of the boat*) after visiting Bayreuth in 1894, only two years after *Kullervo*, though some of its material found its way into the *Lemminkäinen Legends*; indeed, the first version of *The Swan of Tuonela* originally served as its Prelude. Only two years later came the present work, which was performed in Helsinki in 1897 and never revived in the composer's lifetime. The feeble libretto has been blamed for the opera's failure, but this is only part of the problem. The plot itself does not rise above Victorian melodrama and the layout of the opera is scarcely convincing. It falls into eight short scenes and lasts no more than 35 minutes. Its short Prelude is not unappealing but does not promise great things – any more than the ensuing scene delivers them. But the orchestral interlude between the first two scenes brings us the real Sibelius, and the second scene is undoubtedly impressive; there are echoes of Wagner, such as we find in some of the great orchestral songs of the following decade, and the vocal line has the wide tessitura and dramatic flexibility of such masterpieces as *Höstkväll* and *Jubal*. All the same, Sibelius's refusal to permit its revival was perfectly understandable, for it lacks something we find in all his most characteristic music: quite simply, a sense of mastery. Yet even if it must be admitted that this is neither good opera nor good Sibelius, there is enough musical interest to warrant the attention of more than just the specialist collector. There are telling performances, too, from Mari-Anne Häggander and Jorma Hynninen and the Gothenburg orchestra. Neeme Järvi's account of the *Karelia suite* is certainly original, with its opening rather impressive in its strange way. It is difficult to imagine a more spacious account of the *Intermezzo*, which is too broad to make an effective contrast with the ensuing *Ballade*. Järvi's account of this movement is so slow that it sags. However, this is obviously a record that the Sibelian will want to investigate, and BIS have put us in their debt by making it.

Simpson, Robert (born 1921)

Symphonies Nos 6; 7.
*** Hyp. Dig. **CDA 66280**; *KA 66280* [id.]. Royal Liverpool PO, Handley.

The *Sixth* and *Seventh Symphonies* have two common features: both date from the same year and both are in one movement. Not surprisingly – since Robert Simpson has distinguished medical forebears and was originally intended for medicine – the *Sixth* is inspired by the idea of growth: the development of a musical structure from initial melodic cells in much the same way as life emerges from a single fertilized cell in nature. The *Seventh*, scored for the same chamber orchestral forces as his remarkable *Second Symphony* (1952–3), is hardly less powerful in its imaginative vision and sense of purpose. The opening, like so much else from this composer, betrays his keen astronomical interests. Both scores are bracingly Nordic in their inner landscape and exhilarating in aural experience. The playing of the Liverpool orchestra under Vernon Handley could hardly be bettered, and the recording is altogether first class in both media.

String quartets Nos 10 (For Peace); 11.
*** Hyp. Dig. **CDA 66225**; *KA 66225* [id.]. Coull Qt.

Robert Simpson's *Tenth* and *Eleventh quartets* form a pair. The subtitle *For Peace* of No. 10 refers to 'its generally pacific character' and aspires to define 'the condition of peace which excludes aggression but not strong feeling'. Though Simpson is an impressive symphonist and one would not be without any of these works, the string quartet enshrines the essential Simpson and the *Tenth* is among his very finest creations. Listening to this quartet is like hearing a quiet, cool voice of sanity that refreshes the troubled spirit after a long period in an alien, hostile world. The one-movement *Eleventh* draws on some of the inspiration of its predecessor. The composer himself is on record as being conscious of the influence of the Beethoven Op. 95, 'in which a fierce concentration of material makes room for later expansions'; it, too, is a work of enormous power and momentum. Excellent performances and recording. The cassette is one of Hyperion's best – most faithfully balanced.

Sinding, Christian (1856–1941)

Suite, Op. 10.
*** HMV **CDC7 47167-2** [id.]. Perlman, Pittsburgh SO, Previn – SIBELIUS: *Concerto.****

Heifetz recorded this dazzling piece in the 1950s, and it need only be said that Perlman's version is not inferior. Sinding's *A minor Suite* was originally composed in 1888 for violin and piano, and subsequently scored for double woodwind, two horns, strings and (in the finale) a harp. Its blend of archaism and fantasy sounds distinctively Scandinavian of the 1890s yet altogether fresh – and quite delightful. Such is the velocity of Perlman's first movement that one wonders whether the disc is playing at the right speed. Stunning virtuosity and excellent recording, which gains in immediacy in its CD format.

Piano sonata in B min., Op. 91; Alla marcia; Caprice; Capriccio; Con fuoco; Irrlicht; Marche grotesque; Mélodie; Pomposo; Rustles of spring; Serenade.
** Arabesque Dig. **Z 6578**; *ABQC 6578* [id.]. Jerome Lewenthal.

Sinding wrote more than 200 piano pieces (and 250 songs). His *Sonata* is a well-wrought composition, though its cascading arpeggios and ceaseless passagework sound dated. Three stars for Jerome Lewenthal's splendidly musical, sensitive and brilliant playing, which makes out a good case for the piece. The recording is made in what appcars to be a rather small acoustic, though the results are not unacceptable. However, there are one or two notes above the stave that are not perfectly in tune and one has to admit that, in spite of the fine advocacy, the music itself is not really first rate. There is an acceptable cassette.

Sinopoli, Giuseppe (born 1946)

Lou Salome (opera)*: suites Nos 1 and 2.*
*** DG Dig. **415 984-2** [id.]. Popp, Carreras, Stuttgart RSO, composer.

Giuseppe Sinopoli as composer writes in an approachable Bergian style, colourful and energetic by turns. You might know from the lyrical lines – not just for the voices – that this is an Italian composer. In this opera, first produced in Munich in 1981, the use of the orchestra is unfailingly imaginative. It follows the life and loves of the heroine of the title, Lou Salome, a real-life figure closely associated with such characters as the philosopher Nietzsche and the poet Rilke. The two suites are quite distinct. The first one after an atmospheric prelude, presents a big duet between Lou and her lover, Paul Ree; the second consists of a sequence of colourful genre pieces illustrating Lou's relationships with her partners. Under the composer's direction the performance is passionately committed, and the recording full and brilliant.

Smetana, Bedřich (1824–84)

Má Vlast (complete).
(*) Ph. Dig. **420 607-2; *420 607-4* (2) [id.]. Concg. O, Dorati – DVOŘÁK: *In Nature's realm.***(*)
(M) **(*) HMV *EG 290860-4.* Dresden State O, Berglund.
** Sup. Dig. **C37 7241** [id.]. Czech PO, Smetáček.
** Orfeo **C 115842H** (2) [id.]. Bav. RSO, Kubelik.

Má Vlast (complete). *The Bartered Bride: Overture and dances.*
*** DG Dig. **419 768-2**; *419 768-4* (2) [id.]. VPO, Levine.
(*) Tel. **ZA8 35672 (2) [id.]. Leipzig GO, Neumann.

There is a clear first choice here. Levine's performance of Smetana's often elusive cycle of symphonic poems is quite splendid, full of momentum and thrust, aptly paced, with much imaginative detail. The opening *Vyšehrad* immediately shows the impulse of the music making, yet it is warmly romantic too; while the two most famous pieces, *Vltava* and *From Bohemia's woods and fields*, are full of flair and most beautifully played. In *Tábor* (which has an arrestingly dramatic opening) and *Blaník* the VPO play with great vigour and commitment, and these patriotic pieces have both fervour and plenty of colour. *The Bartered Bride Overture* and *dances* which are used as makeweight are highly infectious: Levine offers the usual numbers plus the *Skočná*. The sound is full-bodied and vivid, with a wide amplitude and range, to give the music plenty of atmosphere. The chrome tapes are not quite as refined in focus as the CDs, because of the resonance, but still sound very well indeed.

Dorati's is also an extremely fine account of Smetana's cycle, avoiding most of the pitfalls with readings which combine vivid drama and orchestral playing of the finest quality. The music making has a high adrenalin level throughout, yet points of detail are not missed. The bold accents of the opening *Vyšehrad* may seem too highly stressed to ears used to a more mellow approach to this highly romantic opening piece, and *Vltava* similarly moves forward strongly. In *From Bohemia's woods and fields* the fugato for the strings is paced briskly but, because of the high level of tension, this also falls into place. In the closing *Blaník*, Dorati finds dignity rather than bombast and the pastoral episode is delightfully relaxed, with a fine rhythmic bounce to the march theme which then leads to the final peroration. The Philips sound is splendid, with a wide amplitude and a thrilling concert-hall presence. It is a pity, however, that the coupling is so ungenerous.

The Telefunken recording of *Má Vlast* dates from 1968 and runs to 81 minutes, just too long to fit on a single CD. But Neumann is on his best form and the Leipzig orchestra produce some superb playing for him. His is not the most dramatic reading, but *Vyšehrad*, with its evocative opening harp solo, is warmly romantic and both *Vltava* and *From Bohemia's woods and fields* bring much lovely detail, with glowing woodwind and a rich string sheen, although the violins remain very brightly lit. The music making has fine spontaneity throughout, and the recorded sound is first class in this digitally remastered form, with the Leipzig acoustic casting an agreeable ambient glow while never blurring detail. The *Bartered Bride* overture and dances are splendid, attractively combining spirit with polish. However the *Bartered Bride* items play for just under a quarter of an hour.

Berglund's 1979 *Má Vlast* has been digitally remastered from three sides to two, playing for 39′ 31″ and 38′ 02″ respectively. But such economy has not been achieved without some loss of range, and the recording now sounds slightly constricted in fortissimos. While it has not lost its bloom, it is a pity that originally superb sound has been degraded to ensure that the record remains competitive. On performance grounds the set has a great deal to commend it: the playing of the Dresden orchestra is magnificent. If *Vltava* is slightly undercharacterized, *Vyšehrad* is full of lyrical evocation and atmosphere, and *Tábor* and *Blaník* are jubilant rather than rhetorical, so that the very end of the cycle has a feeling of joyous release. At mid-price this is an obvious bargain, but because of the restricted sound it is less satisfying than Kubelik's DG recording.

Smetáček's approach is broad and spacious, seeking to emphasize the music's epic qualities rather than finding sharpness of characterization. There is certainly an absence of melodrama, and the closing pages of *Blanik* have a feeling of apotheosis. The orchestral playing is assured; the resonant ambience is warmly attractive, and the CD brings enhanced detail, with the brass brightened and percussive transients sharpened, while string timbres remain natural. In the last resort, this is not among the more memorable versions of Smetana's cycle. However, it does have the advantage of fitting on to a single CD, which makes it a much more economical proposition than the Telefunken set, even if *Vltava* and *From Bohemia's woods and fields* are far more imaginative under Neumann.

Kubelik's Orfeo set is put out of court by its layout on two CDs without coupling. It is well played and recorded and gives musical satisfaction, but is in no way distinctive. Kubelik's earlier (1971) version for DG is still available on tape as we go to press (*419 111-4* (2)), coupled with three symphonic poems. It is a far preferable performance with the Boston Symphony Orchestra and is well recorded, too. No doubt it will appear on CD during the lifetime of this book.

Má Vlast: Vltava.
(M) *** DG **423 384-2** [id.]. BPO, Fricsay – LISZT: *Les Préludes***(*); DVOŘÁK: *Symphony No. 9.****
(M) *** HMV **CDM7 69005-2** [id.]; *EG 769005-4.* BPO, Karajan – DVOŘÁK: *Symphony No. 9.****
** DG Dig. **415 509-2** [id.]. VPO, Karajan – DVOŘÁK: *Symphony No. 9.***

Fricsay's inspired account of *Vltava* is irresistible. The river sounds as if it is in full flood and moves towards its climax with a great onward flow. The village wedding sequence suggests that much wine has been flowing before the dance, yet later the moonlight flickers on the water with wonderful serenity, a lovely interlude. The remastered recording is very bright and vivid, giving extra fury to the St John's Rapids. This performance is also available on an excellent DG Focus tape, coupled with Liszt and Tchaikovsky (DG *419 656-4*).

As a fill-up for an excellent version of Dvořák's *New World symphony* Karajan's HMV account of Smetana's most popular piece is comparably vivid, sounding more robust in its digital remastering, but still expressively refined in detail and spontaneous-sounding.

Although Karajan's Vienna recording sounds a degree more expansive than the coupled *New World symphony*, there is also a bass emphasis that affects the overall naturalness. The performance is not without spontaneity, but it does not match Karajan's earlier analogue version made in Berlin nor his more recent digital Berlin Philharmonic account – see Concerts section below (DG **413 587-2**).

Má Vlast: Vltava; Vyšehrad.
(B) *** DG Walkman *413 159-4* [id.]. Bav. RSO, Kubelik – DVOŘÁK: *Slavonic dances*; LISZT: *Hungarian rhapsodies; Les Préludes.****

Part of a generally attractive collection of Slavonic music. Kubelik's excellent performances come from his complete set and are splendidly played and very well recorded, although the acoustic is slightly dry.

From my homeland (2 duets for violin and piano).
*** HMV Dig. **CDC7 47399-2** [id.]; *EL 270183-4.* Itzhak Perlman, Samuel Sanders – DVOŘÁK: *4 Romantic pieces*; *Sonatina.****

The two brilliant pieces, *From my homeland*, are the makeweight for the delightful Dvořák *Sonatina* and the *Four Romantic pieces*. Wonderful playing from Perlman and his less celebrated (and prominently balanced) partner. A pity that another work could not have been added to bring the playing time nearer an hour; this is short measure at 40 minutes. There is a good cassette.

Piano trio in G min., Op. 15.
*** Chan. Dig. **CHAN 8445**; *ABTD 1157* [id.]. Borodin Trio – DVOŘÁK: *Dumky trio.****

The composition of Smetana's only *Piano trio* is closely related to the death of the composer's four-year-old daughter from scarlet fever, which left him beside himself with grief. The writing of the *Trio* acted as a catharsis, so it is not surprising that it is a powerfully emotional work. Although it has an underlying melancholy, it is by no means immersed in gloom: there is serenity too, and the powerful finale ends with a sense of lyrical release. The writing gives fine expressive opportunities for both the violin and cello, which are taken up eloquently by Rostislav Dubinsky and Yuli Turovsky, and it need hardly be said that the pianist Luba Edlina is wonderfully sympathetic, too. In short, a superb account given a most realistic recording balance. Highly recommended in both media.

String quartet No. 1 in E min. (*From my life*).
*** Ph. Dig. **420 803-2**; *420 803-4* [id.]. Guarneri Qt – DVOŘÁK: *String quartet No. 12.****

As suggested by the subtitle, Smetana's *E minor Quartet* is autobiographical and its heart is in the glorious slow movement in which the composer recalls the happiness of his first love 'for the girl who later became my faithful wife'. The Guarneri performance of this movement is wonderfully warm, romantic without a trace of sentimentality, with some memorably rich playing from the cellist, David Soyer. The happiness of the second-movement *Polka* ('Reminiscences of youth') is nicely caught and in the finale the lightness of the opening is dramatically contrasted with the catastrophic onset of deafness, heralded by a high-pitched whistle on the first violin; the performance ends in a mood of touching elegiac reverie. The Philips recording is full-textured and most naturally balanced, with unexaggerated presence; the chrome cassette has a little excess of bass resonance, which can be cut back, and is otherwise very satisfying.

String quartets Nos 1 in E min. (*From my life*); *2 in D min.*
(*) Sup. Dig. **C37 7339. Smetana Qt.

These performances date from 1976. They are authoritative, idiomatic and fresh and, in their original mid-price LP format, warranted a strong recommendation. This compact disc transfer is at a much higher price, and whether it is worth the additional outlay will depend on individual priorities. There is an undoubted gain in background silence and a slight gain in definition when one puts the two together, but the sound could do with a little more warmth, and there is a certain glassiness above the stave. So far there is no alternative compact disc version of both quartets, but few performances are likely to be much better.

String quartet No. 1 (*From my life*) – orchestral version by George Szell. *The Bartered Bride: Overture and dances.*
*** Chan. Dig. **CHAN 8412**; *ABTD 1149* [id.]. LSO, Geoffrey Simon.

Geoffrey Simon, having already discovered and recorded some little-known Tchaikovsky, here turns his attention to George Szell's perceptive and effective orchestration of Smetana's finest autobiographical *Quartet*. The Czech feeling of his scoring is especially noticeable in the *Polka* (very successful here), but overall there is no doubt that the fuller textures add a dimension to the music, though inevitably there are losses as well as gains. The powerful advocacy of Simon and the excellent LSO playing, both here and in the sparkling excerpts from *The Bartered Bride*, provide a most rewarding coupling. The recording is well up to the usual high Chandos standards and there is a good tape, though the resonance takes some of the edge off the treble response, most noticeably in *The Bartered Bride*.

OPERA

The Bartered Bride (complete, in Czech).
*** Sup. Dig. **C37 7309/11** [id.]. Beňácková, Dvorský, Novák, Kopp, Jonášová, Czech Philharmonic Ch. and O, Košler.

The digital Supraphon set under Košler admirably supplies the need for a first-rate Czech version of this delightful comic opera. The recording acoustic may be rather reverberant for comedy, but the orchestral sound is warm and the voices are given good presence, while the performance sparkles from beginning to end with folk rhythms crisply enunciated in an infectiously idiomatic way. The cast is strong, headed by the characterful Gabriela Beňácková as Mařenka and one of the finest of today's Czech tenors, Peter Dvorský, as Jeník. Miroslav Kopp in the role of the ineffective Vašek sings powerfully too. As Kecal the marriage-broker, Richard Novák is not always steady, but his swaggering characterization is most persuasive. The CDs offer some of the best sound we have yet had from Supraphon, fresh and lively. The voices are placed well forward in relation to the orchestra, and there is occasionally just a hint of digital edge on the vocal peaks. But the effect overall has fine presence. The discs are generously banded. The libretto is of poor quality, badly printed in minuscule type, offering a choice of Czech, English and Japanese.

The Bartered Bride (complete): sung in German.
*** HMV **CDS7 49279-8** (2) [id.]. Lorengar, Wunderlich, Frick, Berlin RIAS Chamber Ch., Bamberg SO, Kempe.

The Bartered Bride: highlights (sung in German).
(M) *** HMV **CDM7 69094-2** [id.] (from above recording, cond. Kempe).

The Bartered Bride sung in German seems an unlikely candidate for a top recommendation, yet in the event this vivacious set is a remarkable success. This is an opera where the choruses form a basic platform on which the soloists can build their performances, and here they are sung with splendid lilt and gusto, Kempe's warm, guiding hand maintaining the lyrical flow perfectly. The discipline of the chorus and the lack of rigidity in the melodic line almost completely compensate for the absence of the idiomatic colouring that the Czech language can bring, and certainly the soloists here offer far more sophisticated singing than is likely from a Czech cast. Pilar Lorengar is most appealing as Mařenka and Fritz Wunderlich is on top form as Jeník. Gottlob Frick gives a strong, earthy characterization of Kecal, the marriage-broker. The whole production goes with a swing, and the high spirits do not drown the lyricism – Wunderlich and Lorengar see to that. The recording is bright and vivid, yet has plenty of depth. This is not an opera that calls for much 'production', but the entry of the comedians is particularly well managed.

For those buying the complete opera in Czech there is an admirable selection of highlights available at mid-price. The selection includes most of the key numbers and, playing for 70′, is a real bargain. Both here and in the complete set the digital remastering produces some occasional sibilance and thinness on top – but nothing to worry about, when the attractive ambience remains.

Libuše (complete).
(*) Sup. Dig. **C37 7438/40 [id.]. Beňačková-Čápová, Zítek, Švorc, Vodička, Prague Nat. Theatre Ch. and O, Košler.

Recorded live at the Prague National Theatre in 1983, this has many of the advantages of live recording, not least the communicated fervour of its nationalist aspirations, more convincing when shared with an audience. But this opera, written for the opening of the National Theatre of Prague in 1881, has a limited appeal for the non-Czech listener, with a plot essentially concerned with the Czech royal dynasty. The cast here is even stronger than that of the previous recording under Krombholc, with Gabriela Beňačková-Čápová as Libuše memorable in her prophetic aria in Act III, while Václav Zítek as Přemysl, her consort, provides an attractive lyrical interlude in Act II which, with its chorus of harvesters, has affinities with *The Bartered Bride*. In Act I there is some Slavonic wobbling, notably from Eva Děpoltová as Krasava, but generally the singing is as dramatic as the plot-line will allow. Košler directs committedly; with the stage perspectives well caught, an unintrusive audience, and no disturbing stage noises (the events being fairly static), the recording is very satisfactory. The libretto booklet is clear, even if the typeface is minuscule. But with only 16 cues provided to an opera playing for not far short of three hours, internal access is less than ideal. This issue is for the specialist, rather than the ordinary opera-lover.

Smyth, Ethel (1858–1944)

The Wreckers: overture.
(M) *** HMV **CDM7 69206-2** [id.]; *ED 290208-4*. SNO, Gibson – HARTY: *With the Wild Geese;* MACCUNN: *Land of Mountain and Flood;* GERMAN: *Welsh rhapsody.****

Ethel Smyth, one of the first emancipated English feminists, almost unbelievably managed to get all six of her operas produced during the time when the suffragette movement was gathering momentum. The best known is *The Wreckers* (first performed in England in 1909), and we must hope that one day the work will be revived. Meanwhile the *Overture* is a strong meaty piece, which shows the calibre of this remarkable woman's personality, for while the material itself is not memorable it is put together most compellingly and orchestrated with real flair. The story concerns the wrecking of ships by false signal lights on the Cornish coast. The recording is full, and the CD has refined detail marginally. There is also a good tape.

Soler, Vicente Martín y (1754–1806)

Canzonette: *Amor e gelosia; La costanza; L'innozenza; La mercede; La natura; La preghiera; La semplice; La volubile; Una cosa rara* (opera)*: Consola le pene mia vita; Dolce mi parve un di.*
*** Ph. Dig. **411 030-2** [id.]. Teresa Berganza, José Morenzo – SOR: *Seguidillas.***

Not to be confused with Antonio Soler, best known for his keyboard music, Vicente Martin y Soler in the generation immediately following was regarded as a rival of Mozart, who even quoted a bar or two of his in *Don Giovanni*. These songs and one aria are charming enough in their modest way, making a fair coupling for the more characterful Sor *Canzonette* on the reverse. Fine performances, well recorded.

Sor, Fernando (1778–1839)

Fantaisies, Opp. 7 and 30; Variations on a theme by Mozart, Op. 9.
(*) RCA Dig. **RD 84549 [RCD1 4549]. Julian Bream (guitar) – AGUADO: *Adagio* etc.**(*)

In his accompanying notes Julian Bream offers persuasive advocacy for the two Sor *Fantaisies*, declaring Op. 7 as his favourite work by this composer. They are both ambitious, each has a central set of variations, and Op. 7, with five sections, runs to 20′. Op. 30 has six sections, but is shorter at 13′ 44″. Where possible, Bream's approach is spacious and his deliberation – for all the variety and skill of the colouring – means that the listener is conscious of the music's length, although it is all agreeable enough, notably the catchily rhythmic *Allegretto* at the close of Op.

30. But as Bream also comments, the more concise Mozartian *Variations* remain Sor's most famous piece, 'and justifiably so', and the variety and flair of the playing demonstrate why. The studio recording, made in New York, is eminently truthful.

Fantaisies, Opp. 30 and 40 (*Variations on a favourite Scottish air*); *Fantaisie élégiaque, Op. 59. Fantaisie, Op. 7: Largo & Non tanto* (only); *Minuet & Andante from Op. 11; Sonata No. 2, Op. 25: Minuet; Allegro* (only). *Variations on a theme by Mozart, Op. 9.*
*** DG Dig. **419 247-2** [id.]. Göran Söllscher (guitar).

Sor often used the term *Fantaisie* to denote a theme and variations with an extended introduction. The most substantial (and moving) piece on this CD is the *Fantaisie élégiaque*, not a set of variations but an outpouring of grief on the death of Charlotte Beslay, a pianist much admired by Rossini. Playing of great polish and elegance from the Swedish guitarist, Göran Söllscher, on whom the mantle of Julian Bream and John Williams seems to have fallen. Excellent and truthful recording.

12 Seguidillas for voice and guitar; Andante (from *Divertimento, Op. 2/3*).
*** Ph. Dig. **411 030-2** [id.]. Teresa Berganza, José Morenzo – SOLER: *Canzonette*.***

Fernando Sor, best remembered for his guitar music, here provides a striking example of his equally characterful vocal style in twelve *Canzonette* which with their Spanish flavour admirably match the sharpness of the words. Berganza, well accompanied and well recorded, relishes their individuality.

Sousa, John Philip (1854–1932)

Marches: The Belle of Chicago; The Black Troop; The Crusader; El Capitan; The Fairest of the fair; The Gladiator; High school cadets; The Invincible Eagle; King Cotton; The Liberty Bell; Manhattan Beach; Semper fidelis; The Stars and Stripes forever; The Washington Post.
*** HMV Dig. **CDC7 47286-2** [id.]. H.M. Royal Marines Band, Hoskins.

Marches: Daughters of Texas; The Diplomat; From Maine to Oregon; The gallant Seventh; Golden Jubilee; Hail to the spirit of Liberty; Hands across the sea; Kansas Wildcats; The Legionnaires; Powhatan's daughter; Pride of the Wolverines; Royal Welsh Fusiliers; Sound off; The Thunderer.
*** HMV Dig. **CDC7 47669-2** [id.]; *EL 270152-4*. H.M. Royal Marines Band, Hoskins.

Marches: Solid men to the front; Beau Ideal; Charlatan; Flor de Sevilla; Glory of the Yankee Navy; Gridiron Club; Jack Tar; The Lambs; Marquette University; National game; New York Hippodrome; Nobles of the Mystic Shrine; Northern Pines; On the campus; Rifle Regiment.
*** HMV Dig. **CDC7 47940-2** [id.]; *EL 270587-4*. H.M. Royal Marines Band, Hoskins.

These are the most convincing performances of Sousa marches yet to appear from a British band. Lt. Col. Hoskins catches their breezy exuberance and his pacing is consistently well judged. While many of the favourites are included on the first CD, there is plenty of unfamiliar material here too, and while the music making still retains a sense that the performances emanate from this side of the Atlantic, the Royal Marines Band plays with style as well as enthusiasm. The digital recording is very much in the demonstration class (EMI have always known how to balance a military band effectively), and the result is stirringly realistic, with cymbal transients telling and the side-drum snares crisp without exaggeration. The tape transfers are only adequate: inner detail is far from sharp, though the sound is agreeable.

Marches: Bullets and bayonets; El Capitan; Glory of the Yankee Navy; Gridiron Club; Hands across the sea; High school cadets; Invincible Eagle; Kansas Wildcats; King Cotton; Liberty Bell; Manhattan Beach; National game; The Picadore; Pride of the Wolverines; Riders for the flag; The Rifle Regiment; Sabre and spurs; Sound off; The Stars and Stripes forever; The Thunderer; Washington Post; US Field Artillery.
*** Mercury/Ph. **416 147-2** [id.]. Eastman Wind Ens., Fennell.

Whereas the HMV recordings are modern, Fennell's collection derives from analogue recordings made in the early 1960s, a vintage Mercury era, and while detail is slightly clearer in the British performances, the Mercury sound remains demonstration-worthy. The performances have characteristic American pep, yet the natural exuberance never brings a lack of essential poise. In fact Fennell is a master of this repertoire and the Eastman Ensemble play with great flair. This CD, moreover, is more generous than any of the EMI offerings, including all the principal favourites and playing for over an hour. Sousa's music surely represents that life-assertive confidence in the power of human determination and vigour which helped to shape and is still shaping the New World, and its spirit is readily epitomized in this music making.

Spohr, Ludwig (1784–1859)

Clarinet concertos Nos 1 in C min., Op. 26; 4 in E min.
(*) Orfeo **C 088101A [id.]. Leister, Stuttgart RSO, Frühbeck de Burgos.

Clarinet concertos Nos 2 in E flat, Op. 57; 3 in F min.
(*) Orfeo **C 088201A [id.]. Leister, Stuttgart RSO, Frühbeck de Burgos.

The four *Clarinet concertos* of Spohr – the *Fourth* much grander than the other three – make up an attractive pair of discs, particularly when they are as beautifully played as by the long-time principal of the Berlin Philharmonic, Karl Leister. His smooth tone, the ease and agility with which he tackles virtuoso passagework and his ability to bring out the smiling quality of much of the inspiration make for delightful performances. The radio recording has relatively little stereo spread, but is undistractingly natural.

Symphonies Nos 6 in G (Historical), Op. 116; 9 in B min. (The Seasons), Op. 143.
** Orfeo **C 094841A** [id.]. Bav. RSO, Rickenbacher.

Spohr wrote ten symphonies, of which he subsequently discarded the first and the last. Nos 2–5, dating from between 1820 and 1837, show a personal voice. They were admired by Schumann and established the composer's symphonic reputation. No 6, written in 1839, reminds us of the Mikado's Gilbertian quip about 'Spohr interwoven with Bach and Beethoven'. The first movement sets a Baroque atmosphere, with fugal Bach contrasting genially with a Handelian pastoral style. Karl Rickenbacher has its full measure and the Bavarian orchestra play it most engagingly. The element of pastiche continues throughout, but the other movements are less successful, with the third utterly failing to evoke the energy of a Beethoven scherzo and producing watered-down Schumann instead. Indeed, Schumann's influence is also strong in the *Ninth Symphony*'s *Spring* movement (which comes second). The first, *Winter*, lacks strength of purpose, but the *Largo* of *Summer* is pleasingly warm, if a little bland. The finale, with its echoes of the hunt, is marked (like the finale of No. 6) *Allegro vivace*, and both movements suffer from Rickenbacher's easy-going manner. A more alert, vivacious approach might have brought these two symphonies more fully to life, although the playing of the Bavarian Radio Orchestra is always responsive and cultured, and the attractive ambience of the recording, sounding especially natural in its CD format, gives pleasure in itself. Despite reservations, this is a coupling of great interest, and we hope the earlier symphonies will follow in due course.

Nonet in F, Op. 31; Octet in E, Op. 32.
*** CRD *CRDC 4054* [id.]. Nash Ens.

Spohr's *Octet* is a work of great charm; the variations on Handel's *Harmonious blacksmith* which form one of the central movements offer that kind of naïveté which (when played stylishly) makes for delicious listening. The *Nonet* is also very attractive. Spohr's invention is again at its freshest and his propensity for chromaticism is held in reasonable check. Both works are very elegantly played here; the Nash Ensemble do not attempt to invest this music with more expressive feeling than it can bear. Quality throughout is natural and lifelike. This is civilized music, well worth having.

Piano and wind quintet in C min., Op. 52; Septet in A min., for flute, clarinet, horn, bassoon, violin, cello and piano, Op. 147.
*** CRD *CRDC 4099* [id.]. Ian Brown, Nash Ens.

The Nash Ensemble has made a speciality of recording rarities from the early nineteenth century, neglected more for the difficulty of assembling a particular grouping of instruments than for any lack of musical merit. These two pieces are among Spohr's most delightful, both the sparkling *Quintet* and the more substantial but still charmingly lighthearted *Septet*. Ian Brown at the piano leads the ensemble with flair and vigour and the recording quality is outstandingly vivid.

VOCAL MUSIC

Lieder: *An Mignon; 6 German Lieder, Op. 103; 6 Lieder, Op. 154; Lied beim Runetanz; Schlaflied; Scottische Lied; Vanitas!; Zigeuner Lied.*
*** Orfeo Dig. **C 103841A** [id.]. Julia Varady, Dietrich Fischer-Dieskau, Sitkovetsky, Schoneberger, Hartmut Holl.

The amiable inspiration of Spohr in his songs is delightfully presented in this collection from Dietrich Fischer-Dieskau and Julia Varady. It is characteristic of the composer that, even in his setting of *Erlkönig*, he jogs along rather than gallops, and fails to use the violin dramatically, just giving it an ordinary obbligato. The most attractive songs are the set sung by Varady with clarinet obbligato, but those sung by Fischer-Dieskau too are all highly enjoyable, as long as you do not compare them with the finest of the genre. Excellent recording.

Die letzten Dinge (*The Last Judgement*): oratorio.
*** Ph. Dig. **416 627-2**; *416 627-4* [id.]. Shirai, Lipovsek, Protschka, Hölle, Stuttgart Ch. & RSO, Kuhn.

The Last Judgement, first heard in 1826, was the most successful of Spohr's four oratorios. Though his picture of the Apocalypse was designed to please rather than to startle his listeners of the time, the 72-minute work contains many original ideas and ingenious argument. The gentle first half comes as an amiable preparation for the Judgement Day music in the second, launched in a vigorous Handelian chorus, followed by contemplation and rejoicing. The elaborate fugal writing is very skilled (Handel the main influence), but Beethoven, Cherubini and Mozart's *Zauberflöte* are also echoed in turn. Spohr's horror music too readily relies on conventional chromatic progressions, and the gently flowing tempi provide too little contrast; well performed, as here, this historical curiosity does prove well worth reviving. Among the soloists Mitsuko Shirai is outstanding, with Matthias Hölle also impressive as an imposing bass. Good, atmospheric recording.

Spontini, Gasparo (1774–1851)

Olympie (opera): complete.
(*) Orfeo Dig. **C 137862H (3) [id.]. Varady, Toczyska, Tagliavini, Fischer-Dieskau, Fortune, Berlin RIAS Chamber Ch., German Op. Male Ch., Berlin RSO, Albrecht.

Spontini's *Olympie*, based on an historical play by Voltaire about the daughter of Alexander the Great, had the misfortune to be superseded in popular fashion by Weber's *Der Freischütz* almost as soon as it appeared. Yet a modern revival shows that it looks forward in operatic history as well as back, presenting the story strongly and dramatically, with even the occasional hint of Berlioz, who himself admired the piece. The principal characters are Olympie, Alexander's daughter, and Statire, his widow, with rival suitors for Olympie's hand setting off the dramatic conflict: the tenor, Cassandre, as the goody and the baritone, Antigone, as the baddy. The writing is lively and committed and, despite flawed singing, so is this performance. Julia Varady is outstanding in the name-part, giving an almost ideal account of the role of heroine, but Stefania Toczyska is disappointingly unsteady as Statire and Franco Tagliavini is totally out of style as Cassandre. Even Dietrich Fischer-Dieskau is less consistent than usual, but his melodramatic presentation is nevertheless most effective. The text is cut to fit on to three CDs, but only scholars need worry.

Stainer, John (1840–1901)

The Crucifixion.
*** HMV Dig. **CDC7 47502-2** [id.]. Tear, Luxon, Westminster Singers, John Scott, Hickox.
(M) *** Argo *KCSP 267*. Lewis, Brannigan, St John's College, Cambridge, Ch., Brian Runnett, Guest.

The newest HMV digital recording of *The Crucifixion* differs from its predecessors in using mixed voices in the choir rather than the men and trebles of the Anglican tradition, well presented by the Argo Cambridge version, made two decades earlier, which is a vintage recording of the highest analogue quality. Stainer arranged further contrast by including five hymns in which the congregation are invited to join, and this device is used in both recordings. However, Hickox is freer in their treatment, which will be a plus point for some listeners, although the greater simplicity favoured by Guest is by no means a drawback. The devotional atmosphere of the contribution of the Westminster Singers is impressive and they rise well to the famous *Fling wide the gates, the Saviour waits* (even if this is not the happiest choice of rhyme). The organist, John Scott, makes a fine contribution here – as indeed he does elsewhere. Robert Tear and Benjamin Luxon are a well-matched pair of soloists, especially in their duet *So Thou liftest Thy divine petition*. But Richard Lewis and Owen Brannigan worked well together for Argo, with the effect rather more dramatic, and preference will be a matter of taste. The HMV recording sounds extremely vivid in its CD format. But the fine Argo version, which is available on tape, has a considerable price advantage.

Stamitz, Johann (1717–57)

Trumpet concerto in D (arr. Boustead).
*** Ph. Dig. **420 203-2**; *420 203-4* [id.]. Hardenberger, ASMF, Marriner – HAYDN; HUMMEL: *Concertos* *** ❀; HERTEL: *Concerto.****

This recently discovered concerto was written either by Stamitz or by a composer called J. G. Holzbogen. It has been realized by yet another musician, Alan Boustead. The writing lies consistently up in the instrument's stratosphere and includes some awkward leaps. It is quite inventive, however, notably the finale which is exhilarating on the lips of Håkan Hardenberger, who is also fully equal to its other technical problems. There is no lack of panache here and Marriner accompanies expertly. Good if reverberant recording, with the trumpet given great presence on CD. There is an excellent tape.

Stamitz, Karl (1745–1801)

Double concerto in G for flute, oboe and orchestra.
*** Ph. Dig. **416 359-2** [id.]. Nicolet, Holliger, ASMF, Sillito – CIMAROSA: *Concertante*; SALIERI: *Double concerto*.***

After greatly entertaining us with sparkling playing in Cimarosa and Salieri, Nicolet and Holliger complete their triptych with this elegant and well-crafted *Double concerto* which retains the interest throughout and has a rather good finale to round off the programme in fine style. As in the other works on this attractive CD, the recording is very real and immediate.

Stanford, Charles (1852–1924)

Clarinet concerto in A min., Op. 80.
*** Hyp. **CDA 66001**; *KA 66001*. King, Philh. O, Francis – FINZI: *Concerto*.***

This Hyperion issue offers a particularly attractive coupling of a masterpiece by Gerald Finzi and this lighter but highly engaging work by Stanford. He wrote his *Clarinet concerto* for Richard Mühlfeld, the artist who inspired the late clarinet works of Brahms, but it remained unpublished for nearly a century and was totally neglected. In three linked sections it shows Stanford characteristically fastidious in developing his ideas; the clarinet repertory is not so rich that such a well-written piece should be neglected, particularly as the final section throws aside inhibition and presents more sharply memorable themes in a warm, late-romantic manner. Thea King's crisp-toned playing is most stylish and the accompaniment thoroughly sympathetic. The recording is rather reverberant but otherwise attractively full and vivid; there is just a hint of edge on the upper strings in the CD transfer, but the clarinet timbre remains full. There is a very good cassette.

Symphony No. 3 in F min. (Irish), Op. 28; Irish rhapsody No. 5, Op. 147.
*** Chan. Dig. **CHAN 8545**; *ABTD 1253* [id.]. Ulster O, Handley.

This *Third* and most celebrated of the seven symphonies of Stanford is a rich and attractive work, none the worse for its obvious debts to Brahms. It was sheer bad luck that the *Irish symphony* appeared in 1887, only a year after Brahms's *Fourth*, for whether accidentally or not Stanford's slow movement has a close similarity in one of its themes to the main theme of Brahms's. The ideas are best when directly echoing Irish folk music, as in the middle two movements, a skippity jig of a Scherzo and a glowing slow movement framed by harp cadenzas; while the finale gives an attractive forward glance to Stanford's pupils, Holst and Vaughan Williams. The *Irish rhapsody No. 5* dates from 1917, some thirty years after the *Symphony*, reflecting perhaps in its martial vigour that wartime date. Even more characteristic are the warmly lyrical passages, passionately performed by Handley and his Ulster Orchestra, matching the thrust and commitment they bring also to the *Symphony*. This is even richer and more urgent that an earlier EMI issue of the *Irish symphony*, conducted by Norman Del Mar.

Symphony No. 5 in D (L'Allegro ed il Penseroso); Irish rhapsody No. 4 in A minor (The Fisherman of Loch Neagh and what he saw).
Chan. Dig. **CHAN 8581**; *ABTD 1277* [id.]. Ulster O, Handley.

Stanford's *Fifth Symphony* was written in 1894, when his status as Britain's leading composer – before Elgar's big success – still seemed secure. It is a warmly confident work, colourfully orchestrated and full of easy tunes, illustrating passages from Milton's *L'Allegro* and *Il Penseroso*. The brief solemn introduction in the minor key is a mere clearing-of-the-throat, before a jolly first-movement allegro in the major key. That leads to a charming, gentle pastoral movement in an easy Laendler rhythm. The last two movements more readily live up to Stanford's reputation as a Brahmsian, representing the *Penseroso* half of the work. A richly lyrical slow movement leads to a strongly argued finale, which in a broad sonata form, starting in the minor key, has elements of passacaglia – with an obvious nod towards Brahms's *Fourth*. Equally the slow epilogue brings reminders of Brahms's *Third*; but the ease and confidence of the writing makes it a winning work in a performance as committed and full of flair as this. The *Irish rhapsody*, dating from just before the First World War, is more distinctive of the composer, bringing together sharply contrasted, colourful and atmospheric Irish ideas under the title *The Fisherman of Loch Neagh and what he saw*. Excellent recording of the finest Chandos quality.

Magnificat in B flat, Op. 164; 3 Motets, Op. 38; Motet: Eternal Father, Op. 135.
*** Conifer Dig. **CDCF 155**; *MCFC 155* [id.]. Trinity College, Cambridge, Ch., Marlow – PARRY: *Songs of farewell.****

These fine Stanford motets and canticles, Anglican Church music at its most assured, make a welcome and attractive coupling for the moving and beautiful Parry choral songs. The *Three Motets*, early works, are settings of Latin hymns, *Eternal Father* is an elaborate setting of Robert Bridges; while the big-scale unaccompanied *Magnificat* for double choir makes a magnificent culmination. Immaculate performances and beautifully balanced, atmospheric recording. On chrome cassette the choral focus is slightly more diffuse but very acceptable.

Stanley, John (1712–86)

6 Organ concertos, Op. 10.
*** CRD **CRD 3409**; *CRDC 4065* [id.]. Gifford, N. Sinfonia.

John Stanley published these six concertos in 1775, towards the end of his long career as organist and composer. He gave the option of playing the solo part on the harpsichord or fortepiano, but this is essentially organ music, and these bouncing, vigorous performances, well recorded as they are on the splendid organ of Hexham Abbey, present them most persuasively. No. 4, with its darkly energetic C minor, is particularly fine. The recording is natural in timbre and very well balanced. The CD gives the attractive organ sounds added tangibility, although the 1979 recording stems from an analogue master. The only disappointment is the lack of bands for individual movements. There is a first-class cassette.

Stenhammar, Wilhelm (1871–1927)

Serenade, Op. 31 (with the *Reverenza* movement).
*** BIS Dig. **CD 310** [id.]. Gothenburg SO, Järvi.

The *Serenade for orchestra* is Stenhammar's masterpiece, his most magical work, but this version from the orchestra over whose fortunes the composer once presided differs from rival accounts. At its first performance in 1914, there were six movements. After the war Stenhammar returned to the score and removed the *Reverenza*, the movement which had been placed second, and revised the outer movements. In his BIS record, Neeme Järvi restores it to its original place. It is almost 7 minutes long and, although it is always thoroughly characteristic, it has some of the melancholy charm of Elgar, as well as an occasional reminder of Reger in its modulatory patterns and its delicacy of texture. Its presence enriches rather than diminishes the effect of the work as a whole. Glorious music, sensitively played and finely recorded.

Symphony No. 1 in F.
*** BIS Dig. **CD 219** [id.]. Gothenburg SO, Järvi.

The *First Symphony* was written in 1902–3, when Stenhammar was in his early thirties, but was withdrawn for revision after its first performance. Hans Richter programmed the new work with the Hallé Orchestra in Manchester, and so Stenhammar determined on a thorough reworking of the score. However, various commissions intervened and he never got around to it. (When he came to publish the *Second*, over a decade later, it was simply called *Symphony in G minor*.) It must therefore be stressed that this present work falls short of representing Stenhammar's final thoughts. The score betrays sympathies with such composers as Brahms, Bruckner, Berwald and, in the slow movement, even an affinity with Elgar. But there is plenty of originality in it. The recording has complete naturalness and truthfulness of timbre and perspective, and on CD there is additional presence and range, particularly at the bottom end of the register.

Symphony No. 2 in G min., Op. 34.
*** Cap. **CAP 21151** [id.]. Stockholm PO, Westerberg.

Symphony No. 2; Overture, Excelsior!, Op. 13.
*** **BIS CD 251** [id.]. Gothenburg SO, Järvi.

This is a marvellous symphony. It is an exact contemporary of Nielsen's *Fourth* and Sibelius's *Fifth* but resembles neither. It is direct in utterance; its ideas have splendid character and spirit; and there is a sense of forward movement, and the breadth and spaciousness of a symphonist with firm, secure roots. Stenhammar's classical sympathies lend his symphony strength; his feeling for nature gives it a distinctive sense of vision. Some of his music has a quality of reserve that masks his underlying warmth, but that is not the case here: the melodic invention is fresh and abundant, and the generosity of spirit it radiates is heart-warming. The Stockholm Philharmonic under Stig Westerberg play with conviction and eloquence; the strings have warmth and body, and they sing out as if they love playing this music. The wind are very fine too. The recording is vivid and full-blooded even by the digital standards of today: as sound, this record is absolutely first class, and in terms of musical interest its claims are scarcely less strong.

The acoustic of the Gothenburg Concert Hall is justly celebrated and enables the orchestra to be heard at its very best. They play with tremendous enthusiasm in *Excelsior!* and the CD produces sound of striking realism. This is a completely truthful and well-balanced recording that conveys to the listener exactly what it is like to be there. The Gothenburg Symphony was Stenhammar's own orchestra and it was with them that he gave the first performance of this glorious symphony in 1915. Neeme Järvi takes an altogether brisker view of the first movement than Westerberg (his overall timing is 42′ 37″ as opposed to the latter's 46′ 55″) but the playing is spirited and the recording very good indeed, though not quite as distinguished as on the Caprice rival. The special attraction of this issue, however, is the *Overture, Excelsior!* This dates from 1896, the period of the *Second Quartet*, and it was first given by Nikisch and the Berlin Philharmonic, no less. It is an opulent but inventive score in the spirit of Strauss and Elgar and is played with enormous zest. *Excelsior!* improves enormously on acquaintance and deserves to become a repertoire work.

String quartets Nos 1 in C, Op. 2; 2 in C min., Op. 14; 3 in F, Op. 18; 4 in A min., Op. 25; 5 in C (Serenade), Op. 29; 6 in D min., Op. 35.
*** Cap. **CAP 21337/9** [id.]. Fresk Qt; Copenhagen Qt; Gotland Qt.

Stenhammar was an active chamber musician as well as conductor and solo pianist, and it was his association with the Aulin Quartet which led to his interest in the quartet medium. The *First* (1894) shows him steeped in the chamber music of Beethoven and Brahms, though there is a brief reminder of the shadow of Grieg. It is a well-crafted work, its discourse civilized without being as yet personal. The *Second* is far more individual and one can detect the ardent voice of the real Stenhammar. By the *Third* and *Fourth*, arguably the greatest of the six, the influence of Brahms and Dvořák is fully assimilated and the composer thought highly enough of the latter to dedicate the work to Sibelius, who returned the compliment with his *Sixth Symphony*. The *Fourth* reflects that gentle melancholy which lies at the heart of Stenhammar's sensibility. The *Fifth* is the shortest, and Nielsen paid it the compliment of arranging it for full strings (and conducting it too). The *Sixth* comes from the war years when the composer was feeling 'worn out and deeply depressed' (as Dr Bo Wallner's copiously illustrated booklet, included with the set, tells us), though there is little evidence of this in the music. The Copenhagen Quartet play this marvellously. Those who admire, say, the quartets of Nielsen, Suk and Fauré will feel at home with this beautifully produced set. Performances are generally excellent, as indeed is the recording. These quartets are the product of a cultivated mind and a refined sensibility. It takes a little time to get to know them well, but their reticence is well worth overcoming.

(i) *The Song* (*Sången*) *Op. 44;* (ii) *Two sentimental romances, Op. 28;* (iii) *Ithaca, Op. 21.*
*** Cap. **CAP 21358** [id.]. (i) Sörenson, von Otter, Dahlberg, Wahlgren, State Ac. Ch., Adolf Fredrik Music School Children's Ch., (ii) Arve Tellefsen, (iii) Håkan Hagegård, Swedish RSO; (i) Blomstedt; (ii) Westerberg; (iii) Ingelbretsen.

The Song was commissioned in 1920 by the Swedish Academy of Music to mark its 150th anniversary and was Stenhammar's last important composition. Its performance in Gothenburg must have been quite an occasion: Stenhammar conducted *The Song* in the second half while Nielsen conducted his *Helios overture* and *Hymnus amoris* before the interval. The work's first half has been described as 'a great fantasy' and is Stenhammar at his best and most individual: the choral writing is imaginatively laid out and the contrapuntal ingenuity never seems contrived but always at the service of poetic ends. The second half is less individual, masterly in its way, a lively choral allegro in the style of Handel. The solo and choral singing is superb and the whole performance has the total commitment one might expect from these forces. The superbly engineered recording does them full justice. The *Two sentimental romances* have great charm and are very well played, and Hagegård is in fine voice in another rarity, *Ithaca*.

Sterndale Bennett, William (1816–75)

(i) *Piano concerto No. 4 in F min.; Symphony in G. min.*
*** Milton Keynes Music *MKM 861C* [id.]. (i) Malcolm Binns; Milton Keynes CO, Hilary Wetton.

Mendelssohn conducted the first performance (in 1839) of William Sterndale Bennett's *Fourth Piano concerto* in Leipzig. The work reflects Chopin (especially in the passagework in the first movement) rather more than Mendelssohn himself and is agreeable and well structured. Its lollipop slow movement is a winner and, given a little air coverage by the BBC, could well become a hit like the Litolff *Scherzo*, although its atmosphere is quite different. It is an engaging *Barcarolle*, and Sterndale Bennett's device of putting a cluster of piano filigree over a gentle pizzicato accompaniment was justly admired by the critics of the day. The *Symphony* is amiable, not unlike the Mendelssohn string symphonies, and the slow movement brings another engaging device of repeated overlapping woodwind notes. Overall it is very slight, but enjoyable enough. Both performances are uncommonly good ones. There is nothing whatsoever second rate about the Milton Keynes Chamber Orchestra; the string ensemble is spirited and clean and the wind playing is first class. Malcolm Binns is a persuasive advocate of the *Concerto*, and he has the full measure of the appealing slow movement, while Hilary Wetton paces both works admirably and clearly has much sympathy for them. This is not great music, but that *Barcarolle* is really rather indelible. The cassette quality is excellent, the resonant orchestral sound well focused and the piano given a timbre that is suitably bold and realistic, yet with plenty of sonority and colour.

Stockhausen, Karlheinz (born 1928)

Stimmung (1968).
*** Hyp. **CDA 66115** [id.]. Singcircle, Gregory Rose.

Gregory Rose with his talented vocal group directs an intensely beautiful account of Stockhausen's minimalist meditation on six notes. Expansively it spreads to a full 70 minutes, but it is the variety of effect and response within the sharply limited parameters which comes out in a performance as intense as this, making one concentrate. Though the unsympathetic listener might still find the result boring, this explains admirably how Stockhausen's musical personality can magnetize even with the simplest of formulae. Excellent recording.

Donnerstag aus Licht (exerpts); *Unsichtbare Chöre* (*Invisible choirs*).
*** DG Dig. **419 432-2** [id.]. Suzanne Stephens (clarinet), W. German R. Ch., Cologne, composer.

This record contains not the complete *Donnerstag aus Licht* – the first completed section of Stockhausen's massive projected heptalogy of operas – but just the background choruses for Acts I and III. They make a satisfying group, with Stockhausen at his most monumental in choruses which tell – with Hebrew texts – of Judgement Day and the joy of those who go to Paradise. In this the element of chant is important. This is very much music aimed to communicate directly, not to mystify, and the disc can be recommended to anyone wanting to investigate this key composer of today. The recording, originally taped as a layer to be inserted over live opera-house performances, brings impressive sound. On CD there is only a single track with no banding of sections.

Strauss, Johann, Snr (1804–49) Strauss, Johann, Jnr (1825–99) Strauss, Josef (1827–70) Strauss, Eduard (1835–1916)

(All music listed is by Johann Strauss Jnr unless otherwise stated)

'Favourites': Egyptischer Marsch; Persischer Marsch; Perpetuum mobile; Polkas: *Explosionen; Pizzicato* (with Josef); *Tritsch-Tratsch; Unter Donner und Blitz;* Waltzes: *Accelerationen; Künsterleben; Morgenblätter; Wiener Blut*. J. STRAUSS Snr: *Radetzky march*.
(M) *** Decca **417 747-2** [id.]. VPO, Boskovsky.

The recordings here come from various Boskovsky LPs made between 1958 and 1974. Yet the remastered sound is remarkably vivid in the best Decca manner, and only the massed violins at times hint that the source is not more modern. The sparkle and lilt of the playing give consistent pleasure – *Wiener Blut* is especially successful – and the programme is well planned to give plenty of variety. The disc plays for 65′ and can be recommended wholeheartedly. Apart from

Karajan's famous New Year Concert – see below – Strauss records don't come any better than this.

Egyptischer Marsch. Overtures: *Die Fledermaus*. *Der Zigeunerbaron; Perpetuum mobile*. Polkas: *Annen; Auf der Jagd; Pizzicato; Tritsch-Tratsch*. Waltzes: *An der schönen blauen Donau; Geschichten aus dem Wiener Wald; Kaiser; Rosen aus dem Süden; Wiener Blut*.
(B) **(*) DG Walkman *413 432-4* [id.]. Berlin R. O, Fricsay; BPO, Karajan; VPO, Boehm.

This Walkman tape juxtaposes the contrasting personalities of Ferenc Fricsay, Boehm and Karajan – all effective Johann Strauss exponents – in a generous collection of favourites. Fricsay's volatile temperament brings individuality to the *Blue Danube* and *Emperor* waltzes, and he is at his most charismatic in *Tales from the Vienna Woods* and in registering the changing moods of the *Fledermaus overture*. Boehm and Karajan are at their most exuberant in *Roses from the South* and *Vienna blood*, respectively, while the *Egyptian march* has striking panache in Karajan's hands. The recordings come from the 1960s, the earliest 1961; while the sound is variable, it does not seem obviously dated.

Egyptischer Marsch. Overture: *Der Zigeunerbaron*. *Perpetuum mobile*. Polkas: *Auf der Jagd; Pizzicato; Neue Pizzicato*. Waltzes: *An der schönen blauen Donau; Die Fledermaus; Frühlingsstimmen; Geschichten aus dem Wiener Wald; Kaiser; Rosen aus dem Süden; 1001 Nacht; Wiener Blut*.
(B) *** Decca *KMC2 9001*. VPO, Boskovsky.

An irresistible ninety-minute tape from Decca's vintage period of Strauss recordings in Vienna at the end of the 1960s. The sound is remarkably vivid and the performances leap out from the speakers to grab the listener with lilting *joie de vivre*. The spontaneity of the playing is a joy throughout; many later Strauss recordings cannot match this for the combination of polish and sparkle. Highly recommended to brighten up any motorway journey.

Egyptischer Marsch; Overture: *Der Zigeunerbaron;* Polkas: *Kreuzfidel; Leichtes Blut; Pizzicato* (with Josef)*; Unter Donner und Blitz;* Waltzes: *An der schönen blauen Donau; Geschichten aus dem Wiener Wald; Wiener Bonbons*.
** Tel. **ZK8 43337** [id.]. Concg. O, Harnoncourt.

Nikolaus Harnoncourt is not the first conductor to spring to mind in connection with a Strauss concert, but he shows in the *Gypsy Baron overture* that he has the full measure of the vivacity and character of the idiom, and he secures very polished and responsive playing from the Concertgebouw, with plenty of attack when needed. Elsewhere his care for detail sometimes seems to concentrate on the trees at the expense of the wood. The *Egyptian march* (complete with chorus) could have more verve, and the waltzes too are more easily flexible in other hands. A highlight is the very gentle *Pizzicato polka*. The sound is first class.

Kaiser Franz Josef Marsch. Polkas: *Annen; Auf der Jagd; Fata Morgana; Tritsch-Tratsch*. Waltzes: *An der schönen blauen Donau; Kaiser; Morgenblätter; Wiener Bonbons*. J. STRAUSS, Snr: *Cachucha Galop*. Josef STRAUSS: Polkas: *Moulinet; Ohne Sorgen*. *Aquarellen waltz*.
(*) Chan. Dig. **CHAN 8434; *ABTD 1039* [id.]. Johann Strauss O, leader Rothstein (violin).

The playing here is attractively spirited and infectious and the bright recording has plenty of bloom in its CD format. The strings have not the fullness and lustre of the VPO in Karajan's New Year Concert, but there is no lack of lilt in the waltzes, and the polkas go with an infectious swing; indeed the spontaneity of the music making is striking throughout.

Napoleon march. Perpetuum mobile. Die Fledermaus: Quadrille. Waltzes: *Geschichten aus dem Wiener Wald; Wiener Blut.* J. STRAUSS Snr: *Radetzky march.* Josef STRAUSS: Waltzes: *Delirien; Sphärenklänge.*
(*) DG Dig. **410 027-2 [id.]. BPO, Karajan.

This collection shows Karajan at his finest, with magically evocative openings to each of the four waltzes, and outstanding performances of *Sphärenklänge, Delirien* and (especially) *Wiener Blut. Perpetuum mobile* and the engaging *Fledermaus quadrille* make a piquant contrast. The brilliant digital recording is impressive. The compact disc, however, adds comparatively little but does emphasize detail, not entirely to advantage.

Persischer Marsch. Die Fledermaus: overture. Polkas: *Eljen a Magyar; Leichtes Blut; Unter Donner und Blitz.* Waltzes: *Accelerationen; An der schönen blauen Donau; Künstlerleben.*
(*) DG Dig. **400 026-2 [id.]. BPO, Karajan.

A superbly played selection. The virility and flair of the waltzes (especially *Künstlerleben*) are matched by the exuberance of the polkas, and the *Fledermaus overture* sparkles so vividly it sounds like a new discovery. This compact disc, however, sounds somewhat clinical in its added detail.

Persischer Marsch. Polkas: *Annen; Auf der Jagd; Pizzicato* (with Josef); *Unter Donner und Blitz.* Waltzes: *An den schönen blauen Donau; Geschichten aus dem Wiener Wald; Kaiser; Wiener Blut.* J. STRAUSS Snr: *Radetzky march.*
(M) *** DG *415 852-4* [id.]. BPO, Karajan.

These recordings are drawn from a pair of LPs, originally issued in 1967 and 1971. The digital remastering has brightened the sound, of the violins especially, but the resonant ambience means that the effect is warmer, with detail clear and less clinical than in the later recordings made in the Philharmonie. The offering is generous and many will like a selection that includes the three greatest waltzes. All the music is beautifully played; there are one or two indulgences (notably in *Wiener Blut*) but effective ones, when the results are still made to sound spontaneous, with the orchestra clearly enjoying their own spirited response.

'Weekend in Vienna': Persischer Marsch; Polkas: *Pizzicato* (with Josef); *Tritsch-Tratsch; Unter Donner und Blitz;* Waltzes: *An der schönen blauen Donau; Kaiser; Die Fledermaus; Geschichten aus dem Wiener Wald.* Josef STRAUSS: *Brennende Liebe.* J. STRAUSS Snr: *Radetzky march.*
(M) **(*) Decca *417 885-4* [id.]. VPO, Boskovsky.

A further permutation of Boskovsky performances, and an attractive one. The opening *Blue Danube* is particularly fine and if at times the focus of the cassette transfer slips a little, generally the sound is warm and vivid.

Marches: *Persischer; Russischer. Perpetuum mobile.* Polkas: *Annen; Explosionen; Unter Donner und Blitz.* Waltzes: *Accelerationen;* (i) *An der schönen blauen Donau; Morgenblätter.* Josef STRAUSS: Polka: *Feuerfest!* Waltzes: *Delirien; Sphärenklänge.*
*** Decca **411 932-2** [id.]. VPO, Boskovsky; (i) with V. State Op. Ch.

Digitally remastered from recordings made in the 1970s (the earliest from 1971, the last 1976 – though the ear registers very little difference in quality), the results are astonishingly successful, and this makes an excellent recommendation for compact disc collectors in this repertoire. There is a glorious ambient warmth; the upper range gives the cymbals the right metallic sparkle, yet the strings are naturally clear and lustrous. Detail is refined and the analogue warmth and ambient bloom are most beguiling. The novelty here is the inclusion of the Vienna State Opera Chorus in the original choral version of the *Blue Danube*. These are not the original words (which caused a political storm at the time), but new lyrics introduced in 1890. The effect is rather more robust than the version for the orchestra alone, but the performance has an infectious lilt, with the singers conveying their enjoyment. The rest of the programme is up to the highest Boskovsky standard; the Josef Strauss items are particularly successful, with the orchestra on top form. There is just about an hour of music here, the background is virtually silent, and the whole concert wonderfully spirited and life-enhancing.

Overtures: *Cagliostro in Wien; Das Spitzentuch der Königin.* Polkas: *Express; Grüss aus Österreich; Vom Donaustrande;* Waltzes: *Donauweibchen; Geschichten aus dem Wiener Wald; Wiener Frauen.* Josef STRAUSS: *Auf Ferienreisen* (polka); Eduard STRAUSS: Polkas: *Alpenrose; Reiselust; Unter der Enns.*
(*) HMV Dig. **CDC7 47449-2 [id.]; *EL 270409-4.* Johann Strauss O of V., Boskovsky.

Boskovsky's present concert explores much new ground and offers a number of items not previously available here. The quality of the music itself is also a little mixed. The performances, however, are fresh and idiomatic and the recording is excellent. But this is perhaps not an essential Strauss collection.

Overture: *Carneval in Rom';* Polkas: *Kreuzfide, Maskenzug;* Waltzes: *Carnevalsbilder; Carnevals-Botschafter; Du und Du; Kuss; Wein, Weib und Gesang.* Eduard STRAUSS: Polkas: *Ausser Rand und Band; Faschingsbrief; Mit Vergnügen; Wo man lacht und lebt.* Josef STRAUSS: *Masken-Polka.*
(*) HMV Dig. **CDC7 47719-2 [id.]; *EL 270405-4* [id.]. Johann Strauss O of V., Boskovsky.

Boskovsky here continues his exploration of unfamiliar repertoire, with a few favourite numbers such as the *Die Fledermaus waltz* (*Du und Du*) and *Wein, Weib und Gesang* thrown in. The latter, incidentally, has an abbreviated introduction. Eduard Strauss is again well represented with polkas, although it is in fact Josef's *Masken-Polka* that is the more memorable. The performances and recordings are well up to the standard of Boskovsky's present EMI series, although they do not recapture the magic of his VPO Decca recordings, made during the analogue era.

'The Spirit of Vienna': Eine Nacht in Venedig overture. Polkas: *Champagne; Eljen a Magyar; Im Krapfenwald; Neue Pizzicato.* Waltzes: *An der schönen blauen Donau; Geschichten aus dem Wiener Wald; Kaiser; Künstlerleben; Rosen aus dem Süden; Wiener Blut; Wo die Zitronen blüh'n.*
(B) ** HMV *TC2 MOM 102.* Johann Strauss O of V., Boskovsky.

The Boskovsky recordings offered on this 'Miles of Music' double-length tape date from the early 1970s. The performances are genial and stylish; there is no lack of lilt in the phrasing, and the control of rubato is effective. Yet the playing is less memorable and individual than on Boskovsky's Decca VPO tape (see above). With warm, agreeably resonant recording, the effect on the ear is pleasing, and this certainly makes entertaining and undistracting background entertainment for a long journey. At home, the reproduction lacks something in brilliance and detail, but still sounds very acceptable.

New Year concert. 1983. Overtures: *Eine Nacht in Venedig; Indigo und die vierdig Rauber.* Polkas: *Eljen a Magyar; Freikugeln; Wiener bonbons.* Waltzes: *Geschichten aus dem Wiener Wald; Wo die Zitronen blüh'n.* Josef STRAUSS: Polkas: *Aus der Ferne; Die Libelle; Vélocipède.*
** DG Dig. **410 516-2** [id.]. VPO, Maazel.

After the noisy applause at the opening, the warmly recessed orchestral image is most welcome.

The atmosphere is intimate and Maazel obviously seeks to beguile the ear rather than impress with energetic brilliance. But he goes to the opposite extreme, and both major waltzes are very mellow (although the indulgent opening piece, which gives the record its title, is certainly effective). The account of the *Night in Venice overture*, however, is noticeably self-conscious. In spite of the audience, the spontaneity of the occasion is only sporadically projected, although the orchestral playing is always assured. The recording is smooth without loss of detail, but this is not among the more memorable Strauss collections currently available.

Overtures: *Die Fledermaus; Der Zigeunerbaron;* Polkas: *Annen; Tritsch-Tratsch;* Waltzes: *An der schönen blauen Donau; Kaiser.*
(M) * HMV **CDM 769018-2** [id.]. BPO, Karajan.

Karajan's HMV collection from 1976 is disappointingly lethargic and indulgent. Even the two overtures, though splendidly played, are very mannered; only the *Tritsch-Tratsch polka* really springs to life. The *Annen polka* is stodgily phrased and a heavy, mannered rubato adds lethargy to the two famous waltzes. The ample, resonant sound-picture, at times bass-heavy (in spite of the digital remastering), does not help to provide resilience to the sumptuous orchestral textures.

'1987 New Year Concert in Vienna': Overture: *Die Fledermaus.* Polkas: *Annen; Pizzicato* (with Josef); *Unter Donner und Blitz; Vergnügungszug.* Waltzes: *An der schönen blauen Donau;* (i) *Frühlingsstimmen.* J. STRAUSS Snr: *Beliebte Annen* (polka)*; Radetzky march.* Josef STRAUSS: *Ohne Sorgen polka;* Waltzes: *Delirien; Sphärenklänge.*
❀*** DG Dig. **419 616-1**; *419 616-4* [id.]. VPO, Karajan; (i) with Kathleen Battle.

In preparation for this outstanding concert which was both recorded and televised, Karajan re-studied the scores of his favourite Strauss pieces; the result, he said afterwards, was to bring an overall renewal to his musical life beyond the scope of this particular repertoire. The concert itself produced music making of the utmost magic. With a minimum of gesture he coaxed the Viennese players into performances of the utmost warmth and freshness; familiar pieces sounded almost as if they were being played for the first time. The polkas are a delight and the two Josef Strauss waltzes were made to sound as distinctive as any by Johann. Kathleen Battle's contribution to *Voices of spring* brought wonderfully easy, smiling coloratura and much charm. *The Blue Danube* was, of course, an encore, and what an encore! It has never before been played so seductively on record, with the VPO, in Karajan's words, 'demonstrating that their feeling for waltz rhythms is absolutely unique'. In the closing *Radetzky march*, wonderfully crisp yet relaxed, Karajan kept the audience contribution completely in control merely by the slightest glance over his shoulder. The recording is superbly balanced and the acoustics of the Musikverein bring natural warmth to every department of the orchestra, but particularly to the strings. This indispensable collection makes an easy first choice among any Strauss compilations ever issued; it was an occasion when everything was right – and the only grumble is the almost unbelievable lack of accompanying documentation. The cassette is admirably transferred, but the compact disc has a very special sense of presence.

'New Year concert highlights': Die Fledermaus: Overture & Csardas. Der Zigeunerbaron: March. Perpetuum mobile. Polkas: *Chit-chat; Eljen a Magyar!; Pizzicato* (with Josef)*;* Waltzes: *An der schönen blauen Donau; Fruhlingsstimmen; Geschichten aus dem Wiener Wald; Kaiser; Rosen aus dem Suden; Wiener Blut.* Josef STRAUSS: *Delirien waltz.* J. STRAUSS Snr: *Radetzky march.*
(B) ** DG Dig. *419 844-4* [id.]. VPO, Maazel.

DG's excellently engineered Pocket Music tape draws on Maazel's Vienna New Year concerts from 1980–83. He did not take on Boskovsky's mantle very readily; for all the brilliance of the playing, the impression is one of energy rather than of charm. He can certainly shape the beginnings and ends of the waltzes elegantly, and the performances of the *Blue Danube* and *Tales from the Vienna Woods* are not without lilt; but elsewhere the feeling of the music making can seem too high-powered. The *Radetzky march*, for instance, for all the enthusiasm of the audience response, is tightly disciplined. The digital recording gives good presence – especially in the *Pizzicato polka* – but less atmosphere, and when the applause comes, one almost registers surprise. Some of these recordings are available on CD; but the cassette is far better value, and would liven up a car journey agreeably enough.

Der Zigeunerbaron overture. Polkas: *Annen; Auf der Jagd; Tritsch-Tratsch*. Waltzes: *Kaiser; Rosen aus dem Süden; Wein, Weib und Gesang*.
(*) DG Dig. **410 022-2 [id.]. BPO, Karajan.

This is less attractive than the companion Karajan collections (see above). After a refined introduction, the *Emperor* does not achieve the zest of some of the other waltzes; and although the playing is not without elegance, the noble contour of the principal melody is less potent here than in some versions. The polkas go well, and the overture is a highlight. The digital sound is full and brilliant. On compact disc, the wide dynamic range at the opening of the *Emperor* emphasizes the bright digital sheen on the upper strings. Detail is impressive, although ideally the recording could do with a little more warmth in the lower-middle range.

Perpetuum mobile; Polkas: *Annen; Auf der Jagd; Pizzicato* (with Josef); *Tritsch-Tratsch; Unter Donner und Blitz*. Waltzes: *An der schönen blauen Donau; Geschichten aus dem Wiener Wald; Kaiser; Wiener Blut*. Josef STRAUSS: *Delirien waltz*.
(M) **(*) DG **423 221-2**; *423 221-4* [id.]. BPO, Karajan.

Here is a further and very generous selection taken from the two analogue LPs made in 1967 and 1971 respectively. The performances have great flair and the playing of the Berlin Philharmonic has much ardour as well as subtlety, with the four great waltzes all finely done and the polkas wonderfully vivacious. Josef Strauss's *Delirien*, another Karajan favourite, goes especially well. But the remastering (as in many of these reissues on CD made for Karajan's eightieth birthday) has brought such brightness of lighting to the violins that the glare tends to over-project the music making, although the overall vividness and presence cannot be denied.

Perpetuum mobile; Polkas: *Champagne; Pizzicato* (with Josef); *Tritsch-Tratsch; Unter Donner und Blitz;* Waltzes: *An der schönen blauen Donau; Kaiser; Wiener Blut; Wo die Zitronen bluh'n*. J. STRAUSS Snr: *Radetzky march*.
(M) **(*) Pickwick Dig. **PCD 856** [**MCA MCAD 25967**]. LSO, Georgiadis.

John Georgiadis gives these performances plenty of lift. He is especially infectious in the polkas; but in the famous waltzes, although the phrasing is not without lilt, the extra magic of the best Viennese performances is missing. This is very spirited music-making given brilliant modern digital recording (the violins lacking something in sumptuousness above the stave) and there is no lack of either polish or affection. Many will count the concert (57′) enjoyably good value.

Polkas: *Auf der Jagd; Banditen (galop); Champagne; Pizzicato* (with Josef)*; Unter Donner und Blitz*. Waltzes: *An der schönen blauen Donau; Geschichten aus dem Wiener Wald*. J. STRAUSS Snr: *Radetzky march*. Josef STRAUSS: *Feuerfest polka*. Eduard STRAUSS: *Bahn Frei polka*.
* Telarc Dig. **CD 80098** [id.]. Cincinnati Pops O, Kunzel.

This collection is strictly for those who think the special effects are more important than the music. The accompanying booklet prints a warning in red letters cautioning the listener to 'read page 10 before playing!'. The *Explosions polka* then opens with a cannon shot across the bows which could offer problems to small speaker cones, and other items here are also used as an excuse for various bangs. At the end of the closing *Thunder and lightning polka* the final cannonade is left to echo in the distance. In the overall balance the orchestra is relegated to the background and, within the very resonant acoustic of Music Hall, Cincinnati, much detail is lost, so that the pianissimo plucks of the *Pizzicato polka* recede into inaudibility. Kunzel's performances are plainspun, occasionally rhythmically mannered (as in *Tales from the Vienna Woods*) and in no way memorable, although Josef Strauss's *Feuerfest polka* shows his approach at its most convincingly spectacular.

Polkas: *Czech; Pizzicato* (with Josef). Waltzes: *Kaiser; Rosen aus dem Süden; Sängerlust; Wiener Blut; Wiener Bonbons*. J. STRAUSS, Snr: *Radetzky march*. Josef STRAUSS: Polkas: *Feuerfest; Ohne Sorgen*.
(M) **(*) ASV **CDQS 6020**; *ZCQS 6020* [id.]. LSO, leader Georgiadis (violin).

Among the new generation of Strauss recordings led in the authentic style by violinist-conductor, this collection from John Georgiadis, a brilliant virtuoso in his own right, is easily the most successful. The LSO is on top form, and the rhythmic feel of the playing combines lilt with polished liveliness. There is delicacy (the *Czech polka* is enchanting) and boisterousness, as in the irresistible anvil effects in the *Feuerfest polka*. The closing *Radetzky march* is as rousing as anyone could wish, while the waltzes combine vitality and charm. With good recording in a suitably resonant acoustic, which tends to emphasize the bass, this is recommendable, especially at medium price. The cassette transfer is muffled and not really acceptable.

'Vienna première' (Volume II): *Pappacoda polka; Der lustige Kreig (quadrille); Klug Gretelein* (waltz). Josef STRAUSS: *Defilir marsch;* Polkas: *Farewell; For ever*. Eduard STRAUSS: *Weyprecht-Payer marsch;* Polkas: *Mädchenlaune; Saat und Ernte;* Waltzes: *Die Abonnenten; Blüthenkranz Johann Strauss'scher*. J. STRAUSS III (son of Eduard): *Schlau-Schlau polka*.
*** Chan. Dig. **CHAN 8527**; *LBTD 016*. Johann Strauss O of V., Rothstein, with M. Hill-Smith.

Volume I of *'Vienna première'* is a concert involving other composers besides the Strauss family; it was sponsored, like the present collection, by the Johann Strauss Society of Great Britain. This programme is admirably chosen to include unfamiliar music which deserves recording; indeed, both the *Klug Gretelein waltz*, which opens with some delectable scoring for woodwind and harp and has an idiomatic vocal contribution from Marilyn Hill-Smith, and *Die Abonnenten* (by Eduard) are very attractive waltzes. *Blüthenkranz Johann Strauss'scher*, as its title suggests, makes a pot-pourri of some of Johann's most famous melodies. The polkas are a consistent delight, played wonderfully infectiously; indeed, above all this is a cheerful concert, designed to raise the spirits; while the CD sounds sparkles, the tape, too, should prove a very pleasant companion for a car journey.

Waltzes: *Accelerationen; An der schönen blauen Donau; Frühlingsstimmen; Geschichten aus dem Wiener Wald; Kaiser; Künstlerleben; Wein, Weib und Gesang; Wiener Blut*.
** CfP Dig. **CD-CFP 9015**; *TC-CFP 4528*. Hallé O, Bryden Thomson.

These are polished, nicely turned and relaxed performances, with good detail and apt tempi. The music making is easy-going and enjoyable in its low-key way, and the recording is excellent. There is over 70′ of music here. But alongside the performances of Boskovsky with the VPO, or Karajan, the music is under-characterized.

Waltzes: *An der schönen blauen Donau; Frühlingsstimmen; Geschichten aus dem Wiener Wald; Kaiser; Künstlerleben; Rosen aus dem Süden; Wiener Blut.*
(*) HMV Dig. **CDC7 47052-2 [id.]. Johann Strauss O of V., Boskovsky.

This is Boskovsky's most impressive Strauss collection since his Decca era. From the very opening of the *Blue Danube* the playing balances an evocative Viennese warmth with vigour and sparkle. Each performance is freshly minted, rhythmic nuances are flexibly stylish and the spontaneity is enjoyably obvious. The digital sound is full and vivid. On CD, however, the string timbre has less bloom, and the resonant acoustic is emphasized. But the spirit of the dance is strikingly present throughout these enjoyable performances.

'Famous waltzes': An der schönen blauen. Donau; Fruhlingsstimmen; Geschichten aus dem Wiener Wald; Kaiser; Rosen aus dem Süden; 1001 Nacht; Wein, Weib und Gesang.
(M) **(*) Decca **417 706-2**; *417 279-4* [id.]. VPO, Boskovsky.

More vintage Boskovsky recordings for those wanting a collection of waltzes. As before, the strings massed above the stave show that the sources are not modern, but the Decca sound is basically vivid, with a pleasing ambience.

Die Fledermaus (opera): complete (gala performance).
(*) Decca **421 046-2 (2) [id.]. Gueden, Köth, Kmentt, Waechter, Berry, Zampieri (with guest artists: Nilsson, Tebaldi, Corena, Sutherland, Simionato, Welisch, Berganza, Leontyne Price), V. State Op. Ch., VPO, Karajan.

Die Fledermaus (complete).
(M) (***) HMV mono **CHS7 69531-2** (2) [id.]. Schwarzkopf, Streich, Gedda, Krebs, Kunz, Christ, Philh. Ch. & O, Karajan.
(B) **(*) CfP *TC-CFPD 4702* (2). Lipp, Scheyrer, Ludwig, Dermota, Terkal, Waechter, Berry, Philh. Ch. & O, Ackermann.
(*) HMV Dig. **CDC7 47480-8 [id.]; *EX 270472-5* (2). Popp, Lind, Domingo, Seiffert, Baltsa, Brendel, Bav. R.Ch., Munich Op. O, Domingo.
(*) DG **415 646-2 (2) [id.]. Varady, Popp, Kollo, Weikl, Prey, Rebroff, Bav. State Op. Ch. & O, Carlos Kleiber.
** Tel. Dig. **ZA8 35672** (2) [id.]. Gruberova, Bonney, Hollweg, Protschka, Kmentt, Lipovsek, Ch. & Concg. O, Harnoncourt.
* Denon Dig. **C37 7305/6** [id.]. Irosch, Holliday, Juster, Koller, Kmentt, Granzer, Karczykoski, Drahosch, Kraemmer, V. Volksoper Ch. & O, Binder.

If the catalogue has never been infested with Fledermice, that is a recognition of the quality of earlier sets, notably Karajan's 1955 version (originally issued on Columbia), produced by Walter Legge and now reissued on HMV. This recording has great freshness and clarity along with the polish which for many will make it a first favourite. Tempi at times are unconventional, both slow and fast, but the precision and point of the playing are magical and the singing is endlessly delightful. Schwarzkopf makes an enchanting Rosalinde, not just in the imagination and sparkle of her singing but also in the snatches of spoken dialogue (never too long) which leaven the entertainment. Needless to say she makes a gloriously commanding entry in the party scene, which is in every sense a highspot of Walter Legge's production. As Adèle, Rita Streich (like Schwarzkopf, a pupil of Maria Ivogün) produces her most dazzling coloratura; Gedda and Krebs are beautifully contrasted in their tenor tone, and Erich Kunz gives a vintage performance as Falke. The original mono, crisply focused, has been given a brighter edge but otherwise left unmolested.

The Karajan Decca version of 1960 was originally issued – with much blazing of publicity trumpets – as a so-called 'Gala performance', with various artists from the Decca roster appearing to do their turn at the 'cabaret' included in the Orlofsky ball sequence. This was a famous tradition of performances of *Die Fledermaus* at the New York Met, in the early years of this century. Now Decca have digitally remastered this original version with remarkable effect. The sound is sparklingly clear, although the ambience now seems rather less natural and the applause in the party scene somewhat too vociferous. The party pieces now have a vintage appeal and even Tebaldi's *Viljalied* (rather heavy in style) sets off nostalgia for an earlier era. There is a breathtaking display of coloratura from Joan Sutherland in *Il Bacio*, a Basque folksong sung with delicious simplicity by Teresa Berganza, and Leontyne Price is wonderfully at home in Gershwin's *Summertime*. But the most famous item is Simionato and Bastianini's *Anything you can do, I can do better*, sung with more punch than sophistication, but endearingly memorable, over a quarter of a century after it was recorded.

The performance of the opera itself has all the sparkle one could ask for. If anything, Karajan is even more brilliant than he was on the old Columbia mono issue, and the Decca recording is scintillating in its clarity. Where it does fall short, alas, is in the singing. Hilde Gueden is deliciously vivacious as Rosalinde, a beautifully projected interpretation, but vocally she is not perfect, and even her confidence has a drawback in showing how tentative Erika Köth is as Adèle, with her wavering vibrato. Indeed *Mein Herr Marquis* is well below the standard of the best recorded performances. Waldemar Kmentt has a tight, German-sounding tenor, and Giuseppe Zampieri as Alfred (a bright idea to have a genuine Italian for the part) is no more than adequate. The rest of the cast are very good, but even these few vocal shortcomings are enough to take some of the gilt off the gingerbread. It all depends on what you ask from *Fledermaus*; if it is gaiety and sparkle above everything, then with Karajan in control this is an excellent recommendation, and it certainly cannot be faulted on grounds of recording.

On a pair of CfP cassettes, offered in a chunky box with a synopsis rather than a libretto, comes another vintage *Fledermaus* from the same year as Karajan's set (1960). It makes a superb bargain, for the singing is consistently vivacious. Gerda Scheyrer's Rosalinde brings the only relative disappointment, for the voice is not ideally steady; but Wilma Lipp is a delicious Adèle and Christa Ludwig's Orlofsky is a real surprise, second only to Brigitte Fassbaender's assumption of a breeches role that is too often disappointing. Karl Terkal's Eisenstein and Anton Dermota's Alfred give much pleasure, and Erich Kunz's inebriated Frosch in the finale comes off even without a translation. Ackermann's direction has not the sparkle and subtlety of Karajan, but the final result is polished and with a real Viennese flavour. The sound has come up remarkably vividly – there is a nice combination of atmosphere and clarity. A splendid acquisition for the car (and for home listening, too).

It was not originally intended that Placido Domingo should sing the role of Alfred as well as conducting for the EMI recording of *Fledermaus*, but the tenor who had been originally engaged cancelled at the last minute, and Domingo agreed to do the double job, singing over accompaniments already recorded. The happiness of the occasion is reflected in a strong and amiable, rather than an idiomatically Viennese, performance. If Domingo's conducting lacks the distinction and individuality of some rivals, it is on the whole more satisfying for not drawing attention to itself in irritating mannerisms. Lucia Popp makes a delectable and provocative Rosalinde, and Seiffert a strong tenor Eisenstein, with Baltsa a superb, characterful Orlofsky. Eva Lind as Adèle sings girlishly, but the voice is not always steady or well focused. The rest of the cast has no weak link. With ensembles vigorous and urgent, this is a consistently warm and sympathetic account. More dialogue than usual is included – but, distractingly, it is recorded in a different, much less reverberant acoustic.

The glory of the DG set is the singing of the two principal women – Julia Varady and Lucia Popp magnificently characterful and stylish as mistress and servant – but much of the rest is controversial to say the least. Many will be delighted by the incisive style of Carlos Kleiber, deliberately rejecting many older conventions. Though he allows plenty of rhythmic flexibility, he is never easy-going, for in every rubato a first concern is for precision of ensemble; and that does not always allow the fun and sparkle of the score to emerge. But in its way the result is certainly refreshing, even electrically compelling, and the recording quality, both clear and atmospheric, is admirable. Hermann Prey makes a forthright Eisenstein, but René Kollo sounds lumberingly heavy as Alfred, and as for the falsetto Orlofsky of Ivan Rebroff, it has to be heard to be believed, unhealthily grotesque. For some ears this is so intrusive (as is the hearty German dialogue at times) as to make this set quite unacceptable for repeated listening.

Harnoncourt, with characteristic concern for scholarship in his version with the Concertgebouw Orchestra, presents the first recording to use a really full authentic text, as published in the new editions, including the complete ballet in Act II. The singing cast is very strong, with consistently fresh, clean voices, very well recorded in crisply focused sound, Harnoncourt's direction is unfailingly pointed too, with textures exceptionally clear, and the bright, incisive manner allows the necessary lightness. What nevertheless tends to be missing is the Viennese fizz and vivacity. Some of the aura of a scholarly approach seems to reduce the high spirits, though individual singers give deliciously characterized performances, notably Barbara Bonney as Adèle and Marjana Lipovsek as Orlofsky. Edita Gruberova, similarly characterful, reveals a different side to both her voice and her personality from what we have come to expect, weightier, more dramatic, but unfortunately with a beat beginning to develop in the lower and middle registers. Curiously, instead of spoken dialogue, separate bands are provided containing comment and narration. Non-German speakers can easily programme them out.

In June 1982, Denon engineers recorded their complete performance of *Fledermaus* on stage at the Sun Palace in Fukuoka during the Vienna Volksoper's visit. It is warm, idiomatic and involving, but there are even more snags than in most live recordings. The slabs of spoken dialogue in German sometimes last for four, five or even six minutes at a time, and hardly one of the principals matches in vocal standard what one expects in studio recordings of operetta. As a Viennese veteran, Waldemar Kmentt gives a vividly characterful portrait of Eisenstein, but the voice is painfully strained for much of the time, sometimes not even able to sustain a steady note. The other men are capable but often raw of tone, at times producing sing-speech. Mirjana Irosch as Rosalinde suffers from a pronounced vibrato, though the weight of voice is apt. Melanie Holliday is a tinkly Adèle in traditional mould; the voice is not always sweet enough, but she rises well to her big numbers. Dagmar Koller as Prince Orlofsky might be a parody of the traditional mezzo in this role, with Greta Garbo-like tones in her spoken dialogue erupting into a wobbly and fruity singing voice. Binder's brisk conducting is consistently sympathetic. The overture brings exceptionally vivid orchestral sound but, with the addition of stage microphones for the performance proper, the orchestra recedes. There is a great deal of clumping and banging about on stage, and the audience applauds at every conceivable moment. Using the discs is made much less convenient when there is no banding, or even indexing, except at the beginnings of Acts.

A Night in Venice (*Eine Nacht in Venedig*): complete.

(M) (***) HMV mono **CDH7 69530-2** [id.]. Schwarzkopf, Gedda, Kunz, Klein, Loose, Dönch, Philh. Ch. & O, Ackermann.

A Night in Venice was drastically revised by Erich Korngold many years after Strauss's death, and it is that version, further amended, which appears in this charming 'complete' recording, a superb example of Walter Legge's Philharmonia productions, honeyed and atmospheric. As a sampler, try the jaunty little waltz duet in Act I between Schwarzkopf as the heroine, Annina, and the baritone Erich Kunz as Caramello, normally a tenor role. Nicolai Gedda as the Duke then appropriates the most famous waltz song of all, the *Gondola song*; but with such a frothy production purism would be out of place. The digital remastering preserves the balance of the mono original admirably. The three LP sides have been fitted nicely on to a single CD. Like *Die*

Fledermaus, this is reissued at mid-price in EMI's 'Champagne operetta' series, and the sobriquet could not be more appropriate.

Wiener Blut (complete).

(M) (***) HMV mono **CDH7 69529-2** [id.]. Schwarzkopf, Gedda, Köth, Kunz, Loose, Dönch, Philh. Ch. & O, Ackermann.

*(*) Denon Dig. **C37 7430/1** [id.]. Martikke, Kales, Dallapozza, Dönch, V. Volksoper Ch. & O, Bibl.

To have Schwarzkopf at her most ravishing singing a waltz song based on the tune of *Morning Papers* is enough enticement for this superbly stylish performance of a piece which – with the composer a bored collaborator – was cobbled together from some of his finest ideas. The result may not be a great operetta, but in a recording it makes enchanting listening, with the waltz of the title made into the centrepiece. This Philharmonia version of the mid-1950s shows Walter Legge's flair as a producer at its most compelling, with Schwarzkopf matched by the regular team of Gedda and Kunz, and with Emmy Loose and Erika Köth in the secondary soprano roles. The original mono recording was beautifully balanced, and the facelift given here is most tactfully achieved.

This warmly idiomatic performance by the company of the Vienna Volksoper was recorded live in 1982 in Tokyo. Though the fun of the occasion comes over well, the performance is too flawed to give consistent pleasure, and the extended dialogue will please only fluent German speakers, though it is well acted. Both the principal women soloists are shrill of voice, Elisabeth Kales very edgy as the seductive dancer, Franzi, Siegrid Martikke fluttery as the Countess. Dallapozza as the Count gives the most accomplished performance, though even he overacts. Karl Dönch, veteran bass, also director of the Volksoper, makes a welcome appearance in the character role of the princely Prime Minister. The full text is given, together with translations in minuscule print, but no very relevant information about the operetta itself. There is no banding nor even any index points, except at the beginning of Acts. The recording is dry but realistic enough, not helpful to the singers.

Der Zigeunerbaron (*The Gipsy Baron*): complete.

(M) (***) HMV mono **CDH7 69526-2** (2) [id.]. Schwarzkopf, Gedda, Prey, Kunz, Köth, Sinclair, Philh. Ch. & O, Ackermann.

The Gipsy Baron has had a poor showing in the recording studio, which is particularly surprising because there are relatively few Strauss operettas, and by any standards this is outstanding. The plot (much praised in some quarters) is strangely offbeat, but the musical inspiration shows Strauss at his most effervescent, and this superb Philharmonia version from the mid-1950s has never been matched in its rich stylishness and polish. Schwarzkopf as the gipsy princess sings radiantly, not least in the heavenly Bullfinch duet (to the melody made famous by MGM as *One day when we were young*). Gedda, still youthful, sings with heady tone, and Erich Kunz as the rough pig-breeder gives a vintage echt-Viennese performance of the irresistible *Ja, das schreiben und das lesen*. The CD transcription from excellent mono originals gives fresh and truthful sound, particularly in the voices. A splendid further addition to EMI's 'Champagne operetta' series.

Strauss, Richard (1864–1949)

An Alpine symphony, Op. 64.

*** DG Dig. **400 039-2** [id.]. BPO, Karajan.

*** Ph. Dig. **416 156-2** [id.]. Concg. O, Haitink.

*** Decca **414 676-2** [id.]. Bav. RSO, Solti.

(M) *** Decca **417 717-2** [id.]. LAPO, Mehta.

An Alpine symphony, Op. 64; (i) *Songs with orchestra: Das Bächlein; Freundlich Vision; Meinem Kinde; Morgen!*
(*) Chan. Dig. **CHAN 8557; *ABTD 1263* [id.]. SNO, Järvi; (i) with Felicity Lott.

The *Alpine symphony* has all the rhetoric, confidence and opulence of the great Strauss tone-poems, but, judged by the finest of them, its melodic invention is less fresh and its gestures sometimes ring a hollow note. But there is much to relish and enjoy.

Karajan's account is recorded digitally, but orchestral detail is less analytical than in Solti's Decca version with the Bavarian Radio orchestra, which is fresher and more transparent and has not the slight edge to the upper strings that is a feature of the DG digital recording. But it would be wrong to give the impression that the DG sound is less than first class and, as a performance, the Karajan is in the highest flight. It is wonderfully spacious, beautifully shaped and played with the utmost virtuosity. This is certainly one of the finest accounts now available, though Kempe's version (see below) has more breadth and majesty and no less atmosphere. The compact disc increases the recording's presence and clarity and has a firmer, better-defined bass response.

Haitink's account on Philips is a splendid affair, a far more natural-sounding recording than the Karajan on DG, more spacious and less frenetic than Solti on Decca, and strongly characterized throughout. The offstage horns sound suitably exciting, the perspective is excellent, and there is plenty of atmosphere, particularly in the episode of the calm before the storm. Above all, the architecture of the work as a whole is impressively laid out and the orchestral playing is magnificent. This does not quite displace Karajan (or Kempe – see below), but it can hold its own with the best.

The Bavarian Radio Orchestra under Solti, recorded in the Herkulessaal in Munich, could hardly sound more opulent, with brass of striking richness. That warmth of sound and the superb quality of the 1980 analogue recording tend to counterbalance the generally fast tempi. Many of them are in principle too fast, but with such sympathetic and committed playing in such a setting, the results are warm rather than frenetic. The CD transfer is highly successful.

Those wanting a medium-priced version could hardly do better than turn to Mehta whose performance is among the best Strauss he has given us, and the vintage 1976 recording is outstandingly successful in combining range, atmosphere and body, with remarkable detail. It is more brightly lit in its digital transfer, but the Decca engineers let every strand of the texture tell without losing sight of the overall perspective. The effect remains spectacular.

Like most of his other Strauss recordings with the SNO, Järvi's version of *An Alpine symphony* brings a roundly enjoyable performance, ripely recorded in a helpfully reverberant acoustic, with a special bonus in the orchestral songs sung by Felicity Lott. Though the performance of the main work is not as electrically taut or crisp of ensemble as, say, Karajan's, tending to give too much too soon, it takes an exceptionally warm, genial view of the composer's mountain-climb and its incidents, characterizing the programme very vividly. Felicity Lott is at her finest in the four songs, gentle inspirations in which the sweet purity of her voice is never disturbed. The cassette is full and faithful.

An Alpine symphony; Ein Heldenleben.
(B) **(*) HMV *TCC-2 POR 54279*. Dresden State O, Kempe.

With no break in continuity in either work, this is one of the best-conceived issues in EMI's 'Portrait of the Artist' series; though the reverberant acoustic has brought minor problems, with transients not absolutely clean, in all other respects this is a success. The richness of tone provided by this splendid orchestra is captured in all its sumptuousness and both performances are glowing with life, under one of the most distinguished Straussians of our time.

Also sprach Zarathustra, Op. 30.
(*) Ph. Dig. **400 072-2 [id.]. Boston SO, Ozawa.
(*) CBS **CD 35888 [id.]. NYPO, Mehta.
(M) **(*) HMV *EG 290615-4* [Ang. **CDC 47636** (with BARBER: *Adagio*; SIBELIUS: *Legends*)]. Phd. O, Ormandy – BARBER: *Adagio*; LISZT: *Hungarian fantasia*.**(*)

Also sprach Zarathustra; Death and Transfiguration, Op. 24; Don Juan, Op. 20.
(M) *** Decca **417 720-2** [id.]. VPO, Karajan.

Also sprach Zarathustra; Death and Transfiguration; Till Eulenspiegel, Op. 28.
*** HMV **CDC7 47862-2** [id.]. Dresden State O, Kempe.

Also sprach Zarathustra; Don Juan, Op. 20.
*** DG Dig. **410 959-2** [id.]. BPO, Karajan.
(M) **(*) Ph. **420 521-2**; *420 521-4* [id.]. Concg. O, Haitink.

Also sprach Zarathustra; Don Juan; Till Eulenspiegel.
(*) Decca **414 043-2 [id.]. Chicago SO, Solti.

Also sprach Zarathustra; Don Juan; (i) *Lieder: Cäcile; Mütterandelei.*
** Chan. Dig. **CHAN 8538**; *ABTD 1246* [id.]. SNO, Järvi; (i) with Felicity Lott.

(i) *Also sprach Zarathustra*; (ii; iii) *Ein Heldenleben*; (iv; iii) *Till Eulenspiegel.*
(B) **(*) DG Walkman *413 431-4* [id.]. (i) Boston SO, Steinberg; (ii) VPO; (iv) BPO; (iii) Boehm.

Also sprach Zarathustra; Macbeth, Op. 23.
** Decca Dig. **410 146-2** [id.]. Detroit SO, Dorati.

Also sprach Zarathustra; Till Eulenspiegel; Salome: Salome's dance.
(M) *** DG **415 853-2**; *415 853-4* [id.]. BPO, Karajan.

The permutations of *Also sprach Zarathustra* are almost endless (Ormandy's Philadelphia version is available on CD in the USA differently coupled from the British tape); those early CDs which offer no couplings at all now seem uncompetitive. Even so, Ozawa's warmly persuasive version might be considered by audiophiles as it became one of the first demonstration records for the new medium, when the depth and unforced firmness of the organ pedal sound leading on to an extraordinary crescendo over the spectacular introduction gave clear indication of its extra potential. The solo strings are balanced rather close, but otherwise this is a wonderfully warm and natural sound, with both a natural bloom and fine inner clarity. Ozawa as a Strauss interpreter goes for seductive phrasing and warmth rather than high drama or nobility.

Karajan's 1974 DG version of *Also sprach Zarathustra* has now been reissued on CD at mid-price, coupled with his vividly characterized performance of *Till Eulenspiegel* plus his powerfully voluptuous account of *Salome's dance*. This account of *Also sprach* has long held sway and generally makes a strong recommendation. The Berlin Philharmonic plays with great fervour (the timpani strokes at the very opening are quite riveting) and creates characteristic body of tone in the strings, although the digital remastering has thrown a much brighter light on the violins, only just short of glare. The later (1984) version (coupled with an exciting account of *Don Juan*) has of course the advantage of the new digital technology and can offer greater dynamic range and presence, particularly at the extreme bass and treble. As a performance, this newest version will be very hard to beat and could well be first choice. The playing of the Berlin Philharmonic is as glorious as ever; its virtuosity can be taken for granted, along with its sumptuous tonal refinement, and in Strauss, of course, Karajan has no peer. As a recording it is very good indeed, though it does not offer the spectacular definition and transparency of detail of the Dorati CD version on Decca; but the playing, it goes without saying, is in a totally different league. Of course couplings come into it, and Dorati offers a rarity in the form of *Macbeth*.

The situation is further complicated by Decca's reissue at mid-price of Karajan's earlier Vienna performances of *Also sprach*, *Don Juan* and *Death and transfiguration*, dating from 1959/60 but impressively remastered. The sound of the Vienna orchestra is more leonine than that of the Berlin Philharmonic but does not lack either body or attack. Indeed the performances of both *Don Juan* and *Death and transfiguration* are among the very finest – the *Don* has great zest and passion. These accounts make up in flair and warmth for what they may slightly lack in polish compared with the later Berlin versions. *Also sprach Zarathustra*, produced by John Culshaw, had an enormously wide dynamic range; only now, some three decades after it was made, does the technology of CD permit its degree of contrast to register without difficulty. Even so, the slightly backward balance means that the *Joys and passions* section does not sound as sumptuous as on either of the DG recordings. But this Decca disc remains a fine recommendation in its own right.

Kempe's 1974 *Also sprach Zarathustra*, though powerful in its emotional thrust, is completely free of the sensationalism that marks so many newer performances. It is admirably paced and, while the Dresden orchestra may yield in virtuosity – though not much – to the Berlin Philharmonic under Karajan whose Galleria version was made in the same year, the HMV digital remastering retains the opulence of the Dresden acoustic and the orchestral sound has both body and bloom. Kempe's *Death and transfiguration* and *Till Eulenspiegel* are also marvellously characterized, and the Dresden Staatskapelle is hardly less refined an instrument than the Berlin Philharmonic. The rather mellow portrayal of *Till* is particularly attractive.

Haitink's 1974 *Also sprach Zarathustra* was often spoken of in the same breath as Karajan's, issued in the same year, and if the strings of the Berlin Philharmonic have greater rapture and lyrical intensity, there is no lack of ardour from the Concertgebouw players and the reading has breadth and nobility. Haitink's *Don Juan* too has a fine impetus. The snag is that the digital remastering, in attempting to clarify luxuriant textures, has lost some of the recording's inner focus, and some of the sumptuousness too.

Dorati's *Zarathustra* is well played but not so firmly held together as with Karajan and Kempe. *Macbeth* is a good rather than a distinctive account. It is an early work whose first version appeared in 1887 when Strauss was barely twenty-three; but the composer revised it at the instigation of von Bülow and it was completed in its definitive form after *Don Juan* – hence the later opus number.

Solti's performances come from analogue originals of the mid-1970s and the coupling is apt and generous. Solti is ripely expansive in *Also sprach Zarathustra* and throughout there is glorious playing from the Chicago orchestra in peak form. This is Solti at his strongest, with this most Germanic of American orchestras responding as to the manner born. The transfer to CD is impressive, even if the finest digital versions aerate the textures more.

On the Walkman tape, Steinberg's 1972 *Also sprach Zarathustra* is sumptuously recorded, with the orchestra slightly recessed within the warm Boston acoustic, which adds to the sentient feeling of what is essentially a lyrical account of considerable ardour. It has been well transferred to cassette. For *Ein Heldenleben* we are offered Boehm and the VPO; although the orchestral playing is first class, the reading lacks something in dash and fire. Boehm turns to the Berlin Philharmonic for his (1964) *Don Juan* which is exciting and vivid (glorious leaping strings and rich, thrusting horns).

Ormandy's *Also sprach Zarathustra* is superbly played, with its closing section especially fine. The sound seems fuller than the original LP issue, which was very brightly lit indeed, although on tape the famous opening is not entirely free of intermodulatory confusion. We have not sampled the American Angel CD.

Mehta's CBS account is predictably exciting and the recording is brilliantly clear and positive.

There is some superbly eloquent horn playing, and the forceful thrust of Mehta's reading brings undoubted exhilaration at climaxes; the appearance of the midnight bell at the apotheosis of the *Tanzlied* makes a spectacular effect, and the closing *Nachtwanderlied* is tenderly played. But Karajan finds more mysticism in the score than Mehta, and the bright sheen on the New York strings is less telling than the Berlin string timbre in the 'Yearning' and 'Passion' sequences.

Järvi's account of *Also sprach Zarathustra* is the least successful of his Strauss recordings for Chandos. The reverberant acoustic characteristic of the Caird Hall at Dundee here muddles the sound without giving it compensating richness. The organ pedal at the very opening is much too dominant, the timpani muffled beneath it. *Don Juan* is much better, both in sound and in performance, bluff rather than searingly brilliant. In the valuable song fill-ups, Felicity Lott is at her freshest in *Müttertandelei*, but the pressures of *Cäcilie* bring occasional roughness.

Le bourgeois gentilhomme: suite, Op. 60.
*** RCA Dig. **RD 85362**. Canadian Nat. Arts Centre O, Mata – WIRÉN: *Serenade.****

Strauss's delightful suite with its beguiling post-*Rosenkavalier* atmosphere is admirably suited to Mata's talents; he gives a persuasively warm and elegant account – the finest yet to have appeared on record. The orchestra is a chamber group led by Walter Prystawski whose playing of the violin obbligatos is wholly admirable. The recording ambience is perhaps a shade too resonant, but the effect is so pleasing, bathing the orchestra in a glowing ambient bloom, that criticism is disarmed. The CD refines detail and adds the advantage of background silence.

Le bougeois gentilhomme: suite, Op. 60; Metamorphosen for 23 solo strings.
*** HMV Dig. **CDC7 47992-2** [id.]; *EL 270614-4*. ECO, Jeffrey Tate.

Tate's ECO disc provides an unusual but attractive coupling of the much-neglected incidental music to *Le bourgeois gentilhomme* and the more frequently recorded late masterpiece, *Metamorphosen.* He is a warmly expansive Straussian, building *Metamorphosen* powerfully but not letting the sparkling suite get too heavy – quite a danger, when it is on the long side. Good EMI sound with plenty of bloom, although on cassette there is a lack of transparency.

Burleske, Op. 11; Parergon, Op. 73; Stimmungsbilder, Op. 9.
(*) Ara. Dig. **Z 6567; *ABQC 6567* [id.]. Ian Hobson, Philh. O, Del Mar.

(i) *Burleske in D min.; Sinfonia domestica, Op. 53.*
*** CBS **MK 42322**; *IMT 42322* [id.]. (i) Barenboim; BPO, Mehta.

Mehta's version of the *Sinfonia domestica* is generally speaking the best Strauss record he has given us for many years. (His recordings with the Los Angeles orchestra had no lack of brilliance but often a want of that character which marked his more distinguished rivals.) His account is the more relaxed and has greater warmth than Maazel (see below), and he certainly gets pretty sumptuous playing from the Berlin Philharmonic and has the advantage of very good sound. Of the two readings, this is the more humane with a greater sense of Wilhelmine Germany. As its fill-up, it has the *Burleske* for piano and orchestra, given with great brilliance and panache by Daniel Barenboim in a beautifully balanced recording. A highly recommendable disc. The cassette transfer is smooth but less sharply defined.

Ian Hobson's account of the *D minor Burleske* is less dazzling than Barenboim's and he takes fewer risks. Nevertheless, on its own terms it is eminently satisfactory, and he is well supported by Norman Del Mar and the Philharmonia, and is well recorded. Instead of the *Sinfonia domestica*, which comes on the Barenboim–Mehta record, we have the *Parergon* for left hand (on a theme from the early *Symphony*) that was composed for Paul Wittgenstein – again very well played. The Stimmungsbilder are early rather Schumannesque pieces written in 1884:

Hobson gives a rather touching account of *Träumerei*, and though one can imagine a performance of the *Intermezzo* with greater charm, there is still much to admire here. Decent recording, with an excellent matching cassette.

Horn concertos Nos 1 in E flat, Op. 11; 2 in E flat.

(***) HMV **CDC7 47834-2** [id.]. Dennis Brain, Philh. O, Sawallisch – HINDEMITH: *Horn concerto*.(***)

(*) Ph. Dig. **412 237-2 [id.]. Baumann, Leipzig GO, Masur.

(i) *Horn concertos Nos 1 in E flat, Op. 11; 2 in E flat;* (ii) *Andante for horn and piano.*

*** BBC Dig. **CD 641**; *ZCN 641* [id.]. Michael Thompson, (i) BBC PO, Downes; (ii) C. Dubois – SCHUMANN: *Adagio and allegro*.***

Dennis Brain made these concertos his own, and his superlative performances of them are most welcome on CD. But the digital remastering has brought an orchestral sound without much bloom, and though the horn timbre seems unimpaired by the relative dryness of the sound, Richard Strauss ideally needs richer orchestral textures.

Fortunately Michael Thompson has taken over Dennis Brain's mantle, and his performances are quite superlative in every way; Dennis would surely have been delighted to find such an assured successor. Edward Downes provides sumptuously responsive Straussian accompaniments and in the *Second Concerto* he and his soloist create a frisson of physical excitement in the opening and closing sections, with some exhilaratingly nimble articulation from the soloist in the coda. The simpler *First Concerto* is given with great character; when played with such panache it sounds nearly as good as Mozart. The orchestral recording is first rate and the balance excellent. The *Andante* is brief but makes a good encore when the soaring horn cantilena is so naturally eloquent.

Baumann is at his finest in the first movement of the *Second Concerto* (which comes first on the CD), where his glowing phrasing of the lyrical main theme is very engaging. His broad stream of tone and consummate technique bring much pleasure throughout both works, and the florid finale of the *Second Concerto* is articulated with enviable ease. But this easy-going quality also brings some relaxation of normal tensions. The bold contrasting episode at the centre of the slow movement of Op. 11 ideally needs a kind of *Don Juan*-like fervour to make its best effect, as Dennis Brain demonstrated. The soloist here is most truthfully caught, but the orchestra, slightly recessed in the reverberant Leipzig acoustic, loses some of its edge in the brilliant tuttis, while inner detail is not sharp. However, if you enjoy an essentially lyrical approach to these very tuneful concertos, this will be no disappointment, for the sound is consistently warm and flattering.

Oboe concerto in D.

*** ASV Dig. **CDCOE 808**; *ZCCOE 808* [id.]. Douglas Boyd, COE, Berglund – MOZART: *Oboe concerto*.***

(*) MMG Dig. **MCD 10006 [id.]. Holliger, Cincinnati SO, Gielen – LUTOSLAWSKI: *Oboe and harp concerto*.***

Douglas Boyd winningly brings out the happy glow of Strauss's inspiration of old age, and the ebb-and-flow of his expression with its delicate touching-in of the characteristic flourishes in the solo line sounds totally spontaneous. His warm oboe tone, less reedy than some, equally brings out the *Rosenkavalier* element in this lovely concerto. The coupling with Mozart may not be generous, but it is uniquely apt. With warm, well-balanced recording, the gentle contrast of romantic and classical in this work is delectably conveyed. There is a first-class cassette.

Holliger's Vox performance was recorded in 1984. He is never less than masterly, and this is a wholly engaging performance of one of Strauss's most glowing 'Indian summer' works. Gielen and the Cincinnati orchestra give a vivid accompaniment, wholly sympathetic to the soloist, and the only snag is that the recording of the orchestral violins is brightly lit, and the acoustic – so suitable for the Lutoslawski coupling – lacks ripeness, to increase the work's neo-classical character rather than bringing out its romanticism. Nevertheless Holliger's beguiling playing, especially in the *Andante*, goes a good way to restoring the balance, and this is still a most rewarding account, freshly spontaneous throughout. The measure, however, is short and there are no cues to give access to the work's individual movements.

Death and Transfiguration, Op. 24.
(*) HMV Dig. **CDC7 47013-2 [id.]. LPO, Tennstedt – *4 Last songs.****
** Chan. **CHAN 8533**; *ABTD 1243* [id.]. LSO, Horenstein – HINDEMITH: *Mathis der Maler.***(*)

Tennstedt's account of *Death and Transfiguration* is a direct yet impressively spacious performance, very well played and recorded, and the CD transfer is both full and clear.

Horenstein's account is spacious and the recorded sound, already vivid, is even more so in its digitally remastered format. However, competition is stiff and Horenstein would not displace Karajan or, indeed, Tennstedt. There is an excellent cassette.

Death and Transfiguration; Don Juan; (i) *Don Quixote, Op. 35.*
(B) *** DG Walkman *419 090-4* [id.]. (i) Fournier; BPO, Karajan.

Death and Transfiguration; Don Juan; Metamorphosen for 23 solo strings; Till Eulenspiegel; Salome: Dance of the seven veils.
(B) **(*) HMV *TCC2-POR 54296*. Philh. O, Klemperer.

Karajan's superlative analogue version of *Death and Transfiguration* can still be regarded as a showpiece, even among Karajan's earliest set of analogue Strauss recordings with the Berlin Philharmonic. Like *Don Juan* it dates from 1973; although, in its Walkman incarnation, textures are slightly leaner than in the latter piece, the sound is both vivid and refined in its detail. The thrilling account of *Don Juan*, played with stunning virtuosity, offers sound of striking fidelity in its Walkman transfer, with gloriously full violins above the stave and excellent overall clarity within an ambience that seems near ideal. In *Don Quixote*, Fournier's partnership with Karajan is outstanding. His portrayal of the Don has no less nobility than his previous rivals, and he brings great subtlety and (when required) repose to the part. The finale and Don Quixote's death are very moving in Fournier's hands, while Karajan's handling of orchestral detail is splendid. The 1963 recording has been remastered and sounds remarkably fresh and transparent, though the sound is less sumptuous than the Kempe/Tortelier Dresden version on HMV – see below.

This double-length tape in EMI's 'Portrait of the Artist' series admirably assembles Klemperer's Richard Strauss recordings in convenient form at a reasonable price. In his hands it is the *Metamorphosen* and *Death and Transfiguration* that excite the greatest admiration. With Klemperer the work for strings has a ripeness that exactly fits Strauss's last essay for orchestra, while *Death and Transfiguration* is invested with a nobility too rarely heard in this work. Not everyone will respond to Klemperer's spacious treatment of the other works. His account of *Salome's dance* is splendidly sensuous, but the ennobled *Till* lacks something in boisterous high spirits, and *Don Juan* is clearly seen as 'the idealist in search of perfect womanhood'. But with marvellous Philharmonia playing and a recording which still sounds sumptuous this collection is certainly not lacking in strength of characterization. The level of the tape transfers might have been higher (especially in *Metamorphosen*, where the cello line is not always very clear) but generally detail is good.

Death and Transfiguration; Don Juan; Till Eulenspiegel.
*** Ph. Dig. **411 442-2** [id.]. Concg. O, Haitink.

*** DG Dig. **410 518-2** [id.]. LSO, Abbado.
(*) CBS Dig. **CD 35826 [id.]. Cleveland O, Maazel.
(*) Decca Dig. **400 085-2 [id.]. Detroit SO, Dorati.
(M) **(*) EMI Dig. **CD-EMX 9501**; *EMX 41 2089-4*. LPO, Rickenbacher.

Death and Transfiguration; Don Juan; Till Eulenspiegel; Salome: Salome's dance.
(M) *** DG **423 222-2**; *423 222-4* [id.]. BPO, Karajan.

Among recent versions of this most popular coupling, Haitink's takes the palm. The Philips digital recording is less analytical than the sound pictures DG provide for Abbado or Decca for Dorati (which is exceptionally clear) but the ambient bloom of the Concertgebouw is admirably suited to Strauss's rich orchestral tapestries and detail is naturally defined. The CD enhances the overall effect, and the opening of *Death and Transfiguration* is particularly telling against the silent background. Haitink's performances are undoubtedly distinguished, superbly played, persuasively and subtly characterized. Even Karajan hardly displays more dash. He and the Berlin Philharmonic have a unique authority in this repertoire, but Haitink finds added nobility in *Death and Transfiguration*, while there is no lack of swagger in the characterizations of both the *Don* and *Till*. The easy brilliance of the orchestral playing is complemented by the natural spontaneity of Haitink's readings, seamless in the transition between narrative events, without loss of the music's picaresque or robust qualities. When the sound is so full and spacious as well as vivid this must receive the strongest recommendation.

The performances under Claudio Abbado have plenty of dash and their brilliance is tempered with sensitivity. Some may feel that *Don Juan* veers too much towards the exuberant showpiece and vehicle for display, but both this and *Till Eulenspiegel* must be numbered among the best available. Abbado's *Death and Transfiguration* is scarcely less impressive than Karajan's and has a marvellously spacious opening. The strings produce some splendidly silky tone and there is much sensitive wind playing too. Haitink and Karajan still reign supreme in this work, but Abbado runs them very close and he is equally well recorded, but, compared with the Philips Concertgebouw sound for Haitink, the DG upper range on CD is less smoothly natural.

Karajan's analogue recordings from the mid-1970s now resurface at mid-price and, even allowing for strides made in present-day digital recording, they are very competitive indeed. *Death and Transfiguration* has been superseded by Karajan's more recent version – see below – but here *Don Juan* has a degree of rapture not surpassed in the digital re-make. All three performances are winningly characterized and exhilarating in impulse, the orchestral playing in the highest class; and to make this reissue even more enticing, Karajan's voluptuous account of *Salome's dance* has been added. The only snag is the very bright lighting on the violins brought by the digital remastering (it nearly amounts to glare in *Don Juan*). But the ambient effect remains to give the overall sound plenty of atmosphere.

Maazel repeats a coupling made famous by George Szell at the peak of his era with the Cleveland Orchestra. Szell's performances had tremendous vitality and electricity. Maazel's approach is entirely different from Szell's. With superbly committed support from his players, he takes an extrovert view of *Death and Transfiguration*; the mortal struggle is frenzied enough, but there is comparatively little feeling of menace, and when the transformation comes, the opulent climax is endearingly rose-tinted. The portrayal of *Till* is warmly affectionate, but the reading is exhilaratingly paced and has excellent detail. *Don Juan* is made totally sympathetic, with Maazel relishing every moment. In the famous love scene, the oboe solo is glowingly sensuous; the final climax is ecstatic, the tempo broadened when the strings rapturously take up the great horn tune. On CD, the CBS digital sound is sumptuous, richly glowing, but does not lack clarity, and the brass has telling bite and sonority.

Dorati's Decca recording is also digital and its internal clarity is striking. Dorati's approach to *Death and Transfiguration* is more austere than Maazel's; there is plenty of atmosphere, a certain dignity in the struggle and a sense of foreboding before the release at the end, where the climax has real splendour (and a magnificent breadth of sound). Dorati's view of *Don Juan* is heroic, the sensuality played down by the sound-balance, brilliant rather than sumptuous. After a central love scene which is tenderly delicate, there is satiety and disillusion at the end. *Till* is essentially a picaresque portrait, not without humour and well paced, but a little lacking in affectionate involvement. On CD, the dazzling brilliance of detail and focus is even more telling.

On the mid-price Eminence label Karl Rickenbacher conducts sympathetic, unmannered readings of Strauss's three most popular symphonic poems in performances that are both well played and brilliantly recorded. They may not be quite as subtly expressive as the finest rivals, but on CD they have outstandingly good digital sound in their favour. The iron-oxide cassette is acceptable but cannot compare with the CD.

Death and Transfiguration; Metamorphosen for 23 solo strings.
❀ *** DG Dig. **410 892-2** [id.]. BPO, Karajan.

Karajan made the pioneering record of *Metamorphosen* with the Vienna Philharmonic in 1947 and brings a special authority to this valedictory work. His new digital account has even greater emotional urgency than the 1971 record he made with the Berlin Philharmonic and there is a marginally quicker pulse (in 1971 he took 27′ 30″ as opposed to 26′ 11″ in this 1983 version). The sound is fractionally more forward and cleaner (though some may find the richer ambience of the earlier analogue disc more appealing). The newer version, however, still sounds sumptuous and the account of *Death and Transfiguration* is quite electrifying. The recording balance is not as spectacular as Dorati's on Decca, nor as spacious as Tennstedt's on HMV (see above), but there is no lack of vividness, and the playing of the Berliners is in itself thrilling. It would be difficult to improve on this coupling by the greatest Strauss conductor of the day. The compact disc of the later recording is in a class of its own, bringing a marginally firmer image than the LP and greater range, while the background silence is especially telling in the *Metamorphosen*.

Divertimento after themes of Couperin, Op. 86; (i) *Capriccio* (*Interlude*)*; Der Rosenkavalier Waltzes.*
(M) *** Ph. mono **423 415-2** [id.]. Bamberg SO; (i) Bav. RSO; Clemens Krauss.

The *Divertimento*, based on harpsichord miniatures by Couperin, is a rarity and is not otherwise recorded. No later version can have quite the authority of this, since it was Krauss who gave its first performance as the ballet, *Verklungene Feste*, in 1941. He subsequently persuaded Strauss to expand it into this masterly and delightful eight-movement *Divertimento*. This Bamberg performance comes from a broadcast given in 1954, the year of Krauss's death; and the interlude from *Capriccio*, for which he provided the libretto as well as conducting its première, comes from a complete broadcast mounted by Bavarian Radio in 1953. (It leaves one longing to hear the complete performance.) As with the *Divertimento*, the digital remastering has removed a considerable layer of dirt from the LP without loss of warmth or ambience. A moving record.

Don Juan, Op. 20.
(***) Ph. mono **416 214-2** [id.]. Concg. O, Mengelberg – FRANCK: *Symphony*.(***)

Mengelberg gave many Strauss first performances, and this account of *Don Juan* penetrates to the very heart of its heroic fervour and its alternating virtuosity and tenderness. Listening to this performance leaves no doubt as to why the great German-born conductor exercised so strong a hold over audiences in the inter-war years. The Concertgebouw Orchestra has always been of legendary quality; its debt to Mengelberg, who guided its fortunes from 1895 until the end of the

Second World War, is obvious. Mengelberg achieves songful, powerfully shaped lines whose lyrical intensity and dramatic fire still strike home, even through the inevitably dated sound.

Don Juan; Ein Heldenleben, Op. 40.
*(**) RCA **RD 85408 [RCD1 5408]**. Chicago SO, Reiner.

Reiner's versions of both these Strauss showpieces are among the finest ever. *Don Juan* has a superbly thrilling climax where the great horn theme leaps out unforgettably. For its 1950s vintage the RCA early stereo of the time was outstanding. This generous coupling makes a valuable addition to the 'Legendary Performers' series, but in clarifying the rather muddy originals the digital transfer does not quite convey the full body of sound needed.

Don Quixote, Op. 35.
(*) CBS Dig. **MK 39863 [id.]. Yo-Yo Ma, Boston SO, Ozawa – MONN: *Cello concerto****

(i) *Don Quixote; Don Juan; Salome: Salome's dance.*
(M) *** HMV **CDM7 47865-2** [id.]. (i) Tortelier, Dresden State O, Kempe.

(i) *Don Quixote; Till Eulenspiegel.*
(M) **(*) DG Dig. **419 599-2**; *419 599-4* [id.]. Meneses, BPO, Karajan.

(i) *Don Quixote; Salome: Salome's dance.*
(*) Decca Dig. **417 184-2; *417 184-4* [id.]. Lynn Harrell, Cleveland O, Ashkenazy.

Kempe's 1973 performance of *Don Quixote* is one of the very finest available. The balance gives the cellist an exaggeratedly forward projection, so that the work is made to seem almost like a cello concerto at times, but Paul Tortelier's contribution is a very fine one; the overall orchestral balance combines warmth and body and the digital remastering has clarified detail. The other items are also superbly played; *Don Juan* is comparable with Karajan's reading and certainly does not come second best.

Yo-Yo Ma's portrait of the Don is masterly and, as always, he plays with impeccable taste and refined tone, though at times pianissimos are exaggerated and affectation comes dangerously close. Ozawa is a shade cautious in matters of characterization, as if he is determined not to be thought brash. Karajan's performance has more panache, and the opening theme is a shade more idiomatic in his hands. Although Ozawa pays scrupulous attention to detail (the encounter with the sheep is marvellously done), the very last ounce of Straussian braggadocio is wanting. The CBS recording has a lot going for it: tonally it is very natural and the balance between cello and orchestra is true to life. The orchestral texture is transparent and detail is excellent, though there is a trace of hardness evident when reproduced at a high level setting.

The sound Decca give Lynn Harrell and the Cleveland Orchestra under Ashkenazy is wonderfully transparent and finely balanced (with an excellent equivalent cassette). There is, perhaps, a trace of glare compared with more softly lit versions from the past (like the famous Krauss set) but, generally speaking, it is a splendidly wide-ranging and well-defined recording – and on this count among the best. Lynn Harrell gives a rich-toned and well-characterized interpretation of the Don, and is almost as eloquent as Yo-Yo Ma (and free from the slight touches of affectation, such as his exaggerated pianissimi at variation 5). There is some responsive playing from the Cleveland Orchestra under Ashkenazy, who is unaffected and direct. Nevertheless, this is not a great performance. The subtleties of phrasing you find in Kempe, Karajan, Clemens Krauss, Beecham or, of course, Strauss himself elude him. But he gets much else right! The *Dance of the seven veils* has an appealing allure in Ashkenazy's hands and makes a more attractive fill-up than the Schoenberg transcription of the Monn *Concerto* on CBS. All the same, not an ideal choice.

Nor, for that matter is the new Karajan with Antonio Meneses and Wolfram Christ. Both protagonists are excellent but neither the performance nor the recording is a patch on his earlier versions with Rostropovich (EMI) or the late Pierre Fournier. When either of these is transferred to CD, it will settle any problems about a first choice. The new DG recording is artificial – the perspective is far from natural and the sound in climaxes is hard. Karajan himself is more measured and, some might feel, guides the score with a heavier hand. He gets glorious playing from the Berlin Philharmonic. The *Till Eulenspiegel* is far less self-conscious and again beautifully played, though it is not noticeably superior as either a performance or a recording to his earlier version (see above, under *Death and Transfiguration*).

Duet concertino for clarinet, bassoon, strings and harp.
** None. Dig. **79018-2** [id.]. Shifrin, Munday, LACO, Schwarz – HONEGGER: *Concerto da camera.***

The Strauss work appeared within a year or two of the Honegger with which it is coupled, and so it is a late piece. It is very nicely played here, though the performance does not obliterate memories of the deleted Kempe version included in the Dresden Strauss complete concertos box on HMV, which had greater warmth both as a performance and as sound. The present issue is nevertheless a perfectly likeable account.

Ein Heldenleben, Op. 40.
*** Denon Dig. **C37 7561** [id.]. Dresden State O, Blomstedt.
(M) *** HMV **CDM7 69027-2** [id.]; *EG 769027-4*. BPO, Karajan.
(*) DG Dig **415 508-2 [id.]. BPO, Karajan.
(*) Decca Dig. **414 292-2 [id.]. Cleveland O, Ashkenazy.
(*) Ph. Dig. **400 073-2 [id.]. Boston SO, Ozawa.
** CBS **MK 76675** [id.]. Cleveland O, Maazel.

Ein Heldenleben, Op. 40; (i) *4 Last Songs.*
*** Chan. Dig. **CHAN 8518**; *ABTD 1228* [id.]. SNO, Järvi; (i) with Felicity Lott.

Among the many fine CDs of *Ein Heldenleben*, curiously, the Blomstedt disc with the Dresden Staatskapelle for Denon comes close to the sound we used to associate with DG in the analogue era, warm, with articulate detail, but great tonal homogeneity. Blomstedt shapes his performance with both authority and poetry. One can tell from the outset that this is the real thing, for there is a genuine heroic stride and a sense of dramatic excitement here, while the Dresden orchestra, which has a long Strauss tradition, creates glorious Straussian textures. The melodic lines always mean something (as indeed they do in the Karajan and Ashkenazy accounts), and the whole edifice is held together in a way that commands admiration. The violinist, Peter Mirring, is the finest of the players on the CD versions under review and worthy to be discussed alongside Michel Schwalbé in the earlier Karajan analogue version. The recording, though not as transparent as Ashkenazy's Decca, is warm and wide-ranging. The measure of a great Strauss conductor lies in his capacity to produce sumptuous, refined and well-balanced sonorities, to ensure that colours and expressive detail remain in the right perspective and, above all, to pace the score so that each climax registers at the right level. In these respects, Blomstedt's account is the most completely satisfying CD.

Karajan's 1975 HMV *Heldenleben* (which, like the analogue DG version, had Michel Schwalbé to play the violin solos) received an outstanding analogue recording from the EMI engineers. A little of its sumptuousness has been lost in the digital remastering in the interests of clarified detail, but the sound remains full. The performance shows a remarkable consistency of approach on Karajan's part and an equal virtuosity of technique on the part of the Berlin Philharmonic. The performance is outstanding; as a mid-priced reissue, this is very competitive.

Järvi's version brings the generous and valuable coupling of the *Four Last Songs*. His reading is very strongly characterized, warmly sympathetic from first to last without inflation, marked by powerfully thrustful playing from the SNO, lacking only the last degree of refinement in tone and ensemble. Any shortcoming on that score is counterbalanced by the richness and brilliance of the Chandos recording, beautifully and naturally balanced against a reverberant acoustic. The fill-up will tip the balance for many. Though there is a degree of reserve in the singer's performance, and the microphone catches an uncharacteristic roughness in Felicity Lott's voice when it is under pressure, this is a beautiful, moving account. The original order of the songs is restored, with *Beim Schlafengehen* first. There is a good tape, but the resonance tends to cloud detail somewhat.

Karajan's new *Heldenleben* is his third on records (and his second for DG), being separated from the first by no less than a quarter of a century. His reading of this score has tremendous sweep and all the authority and mastery we have come to expect – and, indeed, take for granted. Nor is the orchestral playing anything other than glorious – indeed, in terms of sheer virtuosity the Berlin players have never surpassed this. It is the architectural mastery, the sheer grip that Karajan exerts over the canvas as a whole that is so impressive, together with his tremendous command of the long-arched melodic line. There is also a dramatic fire and virtuosity that are quite electrifying. Leon Speirer gives a highly characterized account of the long solo cadenzas, with which some might quarrel, emphasizing the domineering and shrewish quality of Pauline; Michel Schwalbé in the 1959 Karajan set undoubtedly had the greater finesse and portrayed a more cultured Hero's Companion. Even with the advantage of CD, the recording falls a little short of the highest of present-day standards, though it has no want of firmness and body. The upper strings, however, are a little lacking in bloom and a shade congested.

The Decca version from Vladimir Ashkenazy and the Cleveland Orchestra is predictably the best recording *per se*. Of the CDs, the Decca has the greatest range and transparency of detail and the firmest definition. Ashkenazy gives a refreshing reading, with fast speeds the rule and a volatile element regularly dispelling any hint of pomposity. It has much to commend it, though something of the grandeur, the broad canvas and the sense of drama that the greatest Strauss conductors have found in it is missing. However, there is much more to admire than to deprecate, and it is, particularly in its compact disc form, the most impressive of recordings.

Ozawa's view of *Heldenleben* is free-flowing, lyrical and remarkably unpompous. He consistently brings out the joy of the virtuoso writing, and though the playing of the Boston orchestra is not quite as immaculate as in the companion version of *Zarathustra*, the richness and transparency are just as seductive, superbly caught by the Philips engineers. The compact disc version adds significantly to the sense of presence and reality.

Lorin Maazel is basically a perceptive and idiomatic Straussian, and it goes without saying that the playing of the Cleveland Orchestra is impressive under his direction – as it is, too, for Ashkenazy on Decca. Moreover, the breadth of his reading with its unhurried pace and thoroughly idiomatic feel is to be admired. But on CD the sound of the orchestra is cloaked in an opulent reverberation, the very opposite of an analytical recording. Even so, the overall effect is just a little unnatural, for the wind are not quite in perspective, and one remains aware of the multi-mike technique. Taken in isolation, the sound is far from unacceptable; but put alongside the best rival recordings, this lacks real transparency.

Metamorphosen for 23 solo strings.
(B) *** DG Dig. *423 258-4* [id.]. BPO, Karajan – DVOŘÁK***; TCHAIKOVSKY: *Serenades.***(*)

Karajan's outstanding digital version of the *Metamorphosen* (see above under *Death and Transfiguration*) is also available on a bargain-priced Pocket Music tape, coupled with Dvořák and Tchaikovsky *Serenades*. The sound is warm, full and clear.

Metamorphosen for 23 solo strings; Sonatine No. 1 in F for wind (From an invalid's workshop).
*** Ph. Dig. **420 160-2**; *420 160-4* [id.]. VPO, Previn.

André Previn's record with the Vienna Philharmonic is extremely successful. He seems to be completely attuned to the serene, darkly impassioned melancholy of this eloquent piece and he gets a glorious response from his players. The *Wind sonatine* is a relaxed and superbly wrought piece, written during the Second World War; in the persuasive hands of the Vienna wind, it is totally beguiling. The recording is first class in both media.

Symphonia domestica, Op. 53; Till Eulenspiegel. (i) Songs: *Die Heiligen drei Könige aus Morgenland; Zueignung.*
(*) Chan. Dig. **CHAN 8572; *ABTD 1267* [id.]. SNO, Järvi; (i) with Felicity Lott.

Symphonia domestica; Macbeth, Op. 20.
** DG Dig. **413 654-2** [id.]. VPO, Maazel.

Järvi's is a strongly characterized, good-natured account of the *Symphonia domestica*, not as refined in ensemble as some past rivals, but gutsy and committed to remove any coy self-consciousness from this extraordinarily inflated but delightful musical portrait of Strauss's family life. The cradle-song is delightfully tender, the *Adagio* finale is warm and passionate and the epilogue exuberant. The performance of *Till* brings out the joy of the work, too; and Felicity Lott's performance of two of Strauss's most delightful songs makes a generous coupling. Warm, rich recording to compensate for any occasional thinness in the SNO's violin tone.

Maazel's is a good if not very involving performance, but it is well coupled: the performance of *Macbeth* is highly polished and superbly played. The recording is excellent, but this is not really distinctive.

Symphony for wind in E flat (The happy workshop).
** Orfeo **C 004821A** [id.]. Munich Wind Ac., Sawallisch.

Strauss's *Wind symphony* is a late work, dating from 1944. The composer preferred to call it a sonata, and it was the publisher who decided on the title change. As suggested by the subtitle, it is essentially a genial piece, though the finale opens sombrely before the mood lightens. This comes off quite well, as does the nicely played *Andantino*, but the focus of the first movement is less sure and the music making often lacks a necessary smiling quality. The recording, though full and homogeneous in texture, does not display the inner clarity one would expect from a digital source; the CD is poor value, playing for only 38½′. There was certainly room here for another of Strauss's wind pieces.

String quartet in A, Op. 2.
*(*) Ara. Dig. **Z 6521** [id.]. Portland Qt – KREISLER: *Quartet.***

Strauss's *Quartet*, dating from 1879–80, is an impressive piece for a composer in his mid-teens. The structure is formal, with Mozartian elements, but there is a vigorous Scherzo and a rather solemn song without words as a slow movement. Apart from the musical confidence, there are no pre-echoes of things to come. It would have benefited from a warmer acoustic than Arabesque provide for the Portland Quartet. As it is, the dryness of timbre makes the music seem like a prodigiously gifted student's exercise, even though the playing is quite responsive.

Violin sonata in E flat, Op. 18.
(*) Chan. Dig. **CHAN 8417; *ABTD 1151* [id.]. Lydia Mordkovitch, Gerhard Oppitz – FAURÉ: *Sonata No. 1.***

Lydia Mordkovitch and Gerhard Oppitz give a compelling reading of the early Strauss *Sonata* to which they seem more attuned than in the coupled Fauré *Sonata*. The piano is still a little overpowering, though not closely balanced, but Oppitz certainly gives a fine account of his demanding role. Mordkovitch's playing has great refinement, and the only reservation one can make concerns this slight imbalance between the two players. The cassette is vivid but transferred at a very high level, approaching saturation point, which brings some edginess on the violin, while fortissimos are less than clean.

Piano sonata in B min., Op. 5; 5 Pieces, Op. 3.
*** CBS **CD 38659** [id.]. Glenn Gould.

This was Glenn Gould's last record, made in New York in September 1982. It is one of his finest, and many will be willing to accept the inevitable vocalise, for the interest of the repertoire and the mastery of the playing. The recording too is first rate, especially on CD, where the image is strikingly firm and believable. Strauss wrote the *Sonata* (his third) when he was sixteen, and its maturity and structural strength are remarkable. True, in the first movement, it quotes – freely and rather engagingly – from the first movement of Beethoven's *Fifth Symphony*, but the rest of the invention is fresh, if with no hints of the orchestral Strauss to come. The *Five Pieces*, from the same period, although very well wrought, are less distinctive, even if the opening *Andante* is most appealing. Gould characterizes them strongly, with superb articulation in the brilliant Scherzo, and the *Largo* played slowly and thoughtfully. All Straussians should try this, while admirers of Gould will find no better example of his recording skills.

VOCAL MUSIC

8 Lieder, Op. 10; 3 Liebeslieder (Songs of Roses) without opus number. Lieder: *Für fünfzehn Pfennige; Hat gesagt; Heimkehr; Leise Lieder; Leises Lied; Meinem Kinde; Schlagende Herzen; Schlechtes Wetter; Weissen Jasmin; Wiegenlied.*
*** HMV Dig. **CDC7 49318-2** [id.]. Lucia Popp, Wolfgang Sawallisch.

The bright-eyed charm, the ability to communicate word-meaning with vivid intensity, makes Popp's Strauss recital a delightful one, helped by accompaniment from Sawallisch that is comparably inspired, as in the dreamily beautiful accompaniment to *Die Georgine*. Including a number of less well-known songs as well as many favourites, it can be warmly recommended to aficionados and newcomers alike. The full, digital recording at times brings out an edge at the top of the voice, when it is under pressure, but otherwise the sweetness of the Popp sound adds to the delight.

5 Lieder, Op. 32; Gefunden; Heimkehr; Heimliche Aufforderung; Ich liebe dich; Morgen!; Die Nacht; Nichts; Ruhe, meine Seele!; Schlechtes Wetter; Schlichte Weissen, Op. 21/1–5; Ständchen; Traum durch die Dämmerung; Waldesfahrt; Winternacht.
*** DG Dig. **415 470-2** [id.]. Dietrich Fischer-Dieskau, Wolfgang Sawallisch.

A delightful collection, with the benefits of CD specially valuable in the hushed intimacy of Lieder-singing. The selection includes a fair proportion not only of the favourite Strauss songs but of Fischer-Dieskau's (and Sawallisch's) finest and most beautiful performances. First-rate sound.

Lieder: Allerseelen; Ach Lieb ich muss nun Scheiden; Befreit; Du meines Herzens Krönelein; Einerlei; Heimliche Aufforderung; Ich trage meine Minne; Kling!; Lob des Leidens; Malven; Mit deinen blauen Augen; Die Nacht; Schlechtes Wetter; Seitdem dein Aug; Ständchen; Stiller Gang; Traume durch die Dämmerung; Wie sollten wir geheim; Wir beide wollen springen; Zeltlose.
*** Ph. Dig. **416 298-2** [id.]. Jessye Norman, Geoffrey Parsons.

Jessye Norman's recital of Strauss brings heartfelt, deeply committed performances, at times larger than life, which satisfyingly exploit the unique glory of the voice. Quite apart from such deservedly popular songs as *Heimliche Aufforderung*, it is good to have such a rarity as Strauss's very last song, *Malven*, sung here far more compellingly than by Eva Marton on her CBS disc. Some of the songs bring extreme speeds in both directions, with expression underlined in slow songs and *Ständchen* given exhilarating virtuoso treatment at high speed. But the magnetism of the singer generally silences any reservations, and Geoffrey Parsons is the most understanding of accompanists, brilliant too. Good, natural recording.

Lieder: Allerseelen; All' mein Gedänken; Befreit; Cäcilie; Du meines Herzens Krönelein; Freundliche Vision; Heimliche Aufforderung; Ich schwebe; Kling!; Morgen; Die Nacht; Ruhe, meine Seele!; Seitdem dein Aug' in meines schaute; Ständchen; Wiegenlied; Winterweihe; Zueignung.
*** HMV Dig. **CDC7 47948-2** [id.]; *EL 270594-4*. Margaret Price, Wolfgang Sawallisch.

Margaret Price's Strauss recital brings a rich variety of mood, colour and expression, helped by exceptionally sensitive and imaginative accompaniments from Sawallisch. The evenness of her production, opening out gloriously in *Zueignung*, is typical, and so it is too in *Freundliche Vision*, well contrasted with the lightness of such a song as *All' mein Gedänken*. If maternal tenderness is missing in *Wiegenlied*, the beauty and precision with which Price follows every marking in the music is a delight, all done with seeming spontaneity. The recording captures the voice with fine bloom. There is a good cassette.

Allerseelen; Am Ufer; Aus den Liedern der Trauer; Heimkehr; Liebeshymnus; Lob des Leidens; Madrigal; Morgen; Die Nacht; Winternacht; Zueignung.
*** DG Dig. **419 238-2** [id.]. Brigitte Fassbaender, Irwin Gage – LISZT: *Lieder*.***

Coupled with an equally perceptive group of Liszt songs, Fassbaender's Strauss selection, winner of the *Gramophone* Solo Vocal Award for 1987, brings singing of exceptional command and intensity; always she communicates face to face, and the musical imagination – as in the very slow account of the popular *Morgen* – adds to the sharply specific quality she gives to each song. The voice is beautiful as recorded, but that beauty is only an incidental. Warmly understanding accompaniment; well-balanced recording.

Lieder: *Liebeshymnus; Muttertändelei; Das Rosenband; Ruhe, meine Seele.*
(*) HMV **CDC7 47854-2 [id.]. Dame Janet Baker, LPO, Boult – BRAHMS: *Alto rhapsody*; WAGNER: *Wesendonk Lieder*.***

In Strauss Lieder with piano accompaniment Dame Janet Baker has herself set supreme standards, while in the orchestral arrangements Schwarzkopf's records have been in a class on their own. These are beautiful performances, as one would expect, but for once Dame Janet sounds a little effortful, less naturally spontaneous. Even so, as a fine fill-up for a delightful coupling, the songs make a welcome group. Excellent recording, warmly transferred to CD.

Mädchenblumen, Op. 22; 3 Lieder, Op. 29; 4 Lieder, Op. 27; 8 Lieder aus letzte Blätter, Op. 10.
** Etcetera Dig. **KTC 1028** [id.]. Roberta Alexander, Ton Crone.

Although the Etcetera recording is too reverberant, the range and beauty of Roberta Alexander's voice come over well, particularly in the fuller and more dramatic songs, where her operatic experience is an obvious asset. Otherwise, by the standards of her finest rivals, these are readings rather lacking in perception and detail, with words not always clear. It makes a neat package, having four opus numbers of songs recorded complete; but the leaflet inconveniently puts English translations after the German, not alongside.

Four Last songs (*Vier letzte Lieder*).
*** HMV Dig. **CDC7 47013-2** [id.]. Lucia Popp, LPO, Tennstedt – *Death and Transfiguration.***(*)

Four Last songs; Lieder: *Das Bächlein; Freundliche Vision; Die heiligen drei Könige; Meinem Kinde; Morgen; Muttertändelei; Das Rosenband; Ruhe, meine Seele; Waldseligkeit; Wiegenlied; Winterweihe; Zueignung.*
❀ *** HMV **CDC7 47276-2** [id.]. Elisabeth Schwarzkopf, Berlin RSO, or LSO, Szell.

Four Last songs; Lieder: *Befreit; Morgen; Muttertändelei; Ruhe, meine Seele; Wiegenlied; Zueignung.*
(*) CBS **MK 76794 [id.]. Kiri Te Kanawa, LSO, Andrew Davis.

Four Last songs; Lieder: *Cäcilie; Meinem Kinde; Morgen; Ruhe, meine Seele; Wiegenlied; Zueignung.*
❀ *** Ph. Dig. **411 052-2** [id.]. Jessye Norman, Leipzig GO, Masur.

Strauss's publisher Ernest Roth says in the score of the *Four Last songs* that this was a farewell of 'serene confidence', which is exactly the mood Jessye Norman conveys. The power of her singing reminds one that the first ever interpreter (with Furtwängler and the Philharmonia Orchestra at the Royal Albert Hall in May 1950) was Kirsten Flagstad. The start of the second stanza of the third song, *Beim Schlafengehen*, brings one of the most thrilling vocal crescendos on record, expanding from a half-tone to a gloriously rich and rounded forte. In concern for word-detail Norman is outshone only by Schwarzkopf (unique in conveying the poignancy of old age), but both in the *Four Last songs* and in the orchestral songs on the reverse, the stylistic as well as the vocal command is irresistible, with *Cäcilie* given operatic strength. The radiance of the recording matches the interpretations, the more fully and immediately on compact disc.

For the CD version of Schwarzkopf's raptly beautiful recording of the *Four Last songs*, EMI has generously added not just the old coupling of Strauss orchestral songs but also the extra seven which she recorded three years later in 1969, also with George Szell conducting but with the LSO instead of the Berlin Radio Orchestra. There are few records in the catalogue which so magnetically capture the magic of a great performance, with the intensity of Schwarzkopf's singing in all its variety of tone and meaning perfectly matched by inspired playing. In the deep meditations of the *Four Last songs* it is especially valuable on compact disc to have background noise eliminated, with the precise balances of the original recording marking a high-water mark of the art of engineering.

Lucia Popp, too, gives a ravishingly beautiful performance of the *Four Last songs*. With the voice given an ethereal glow, naturally balanced in a warmly atmospheric digital recording, the radiance of texture is paramount. This is an orchestral performance rather than a deeply illuminating Lieder performance, and that matches the coupling, the early tone-poem on death which is quoted by the dying composer in the last of the songs. Tennstedt is a direct rather than a persuasive Straussian. The beauty of sound is unfailing; however, as the CD readily shows, the Philips recording for Jessye Norman has even more atmospheric warmth.

Dame Kiri Te Kanawa gives an open-hearted, warmly expressive reading of the *Four Last songs*. If she misses the sort of detail that Schwarzkopf uniquely brought, her commitment is never in doubt. Her tone is consistently beautiful, but might have seemed even more so if the voice had not been placed rather too close in relation to the orchestra. The orchestral arrangements of other songs make an excellent coupling (as a comparable selection does in the Schwarzkopf version); and Andrew Davis directs most sympathetically, if not with the sort of rapt dedication that Szell gave to Schwarzkopf.

(i) *Four Last songs*. (ii) *Arabella* (opera): excerpts. (i) *Capriccio* (opera): *closing scene*.
(M) (***) EMI mono **CDH7 61001-2** [id.]. Elisabeth Schwarzkopf, (i) Philh. O, Ackermann; (ii) Metternich, Gedda, Philh. O, Von Matacic.

As part of an exceptionally generous collection of classic mono recordings, Schwarzkopf's 1953 version of the *Four Last songs* comes on the mid-price Références label with both its original coupling, the closing scene from *Capriccio*, also recorded in 1953, and the four major excerpts from *Arabella* (over half an hour of music), which she recorded two years later. This is singing of supreme artistry. The *Four Last songs* are here less reflective, less sensuous, than in Schwarzkopf's later version with Szell, but the more flowing speeds and the extra tautness and freshness of voice bring equally illuminating performances. Fascinatingly, this separate account of the *Capriccio* scene is even more ravishing than the one in the complete set, also reissued on CD, and the sound is even fuller, astonishing for its period. In the *Arabella* excerpts von Matacic is a richly idiomatic conductor, with Metternich superb as Mandryka, though Anny Felbermeyer is a less distinguished Zdenka. Excellent transfers.

Four Last songs. Die heiligen drei Könige. Capriccio (opera): *Moonlight music and monologue* (closing scene).
(*) DG Dig. **419 188-2; *419 188-4* [id.]. Anna Tomowa-Sintow, BPO, Karajan.

Before he made this recording of the closing scene from *Capriccio* with Anna Tomowa-Sintow, Karajan, supreme Straussian, had never previously conducted Strauss's last opera. It is a ravishing performance from him and the Berlin Philharmonic, with one of his favourite sopranos responding warmly and sympathetically, if without the final touch of individual imagination that such inspired music cries out for. Similarly in the other late, great masterpiece, the *Four Last songs*, Tomowa-Sintow's lovely, creamy-toned singing tends – even less aptly – to take second place in the attention. The orchestral version of Strauss's nativity-story song makes an attractive if hardly generous extra item. Warm recording, lacking a little in sense of realism and presence. However, there is a very good matching cassette.

Four Last songs; (i) *Malven. Salome: Dance of the seven veils; Final scene. Die Liebe der Danae* (symphonic fragment).
** CBS Dig. **MK 42019** [id.]. Eva Marton, Toronto SO, Andrew Davis; or (i) A. Davis (piano).

Eva Marton's dramatic soprano is hardly comfortable in the *Four Last songs*, and the recording does not help, bringing out an unevenness in the production. She is far better suited to the closing scene from *Salome*, which is strong and dramatic. Marton's other item is a curiosity, a long-unpublished Strauss song, *Malven*, from the very end of his life. She sings it – in live performance – to Davis's piano accompaniment. The rare pot-pourri from *Die Liebe der Danae* and the dance from *Salome* make a useful coupling.

OPERA

Arabella (complete).
*** Decca Dig. **417 623-2**; *417 623-4* (3) [id.]. Te Kanawa, Fontana, Grundheber, Seiffert, Dernesch, Guttstein, ROHCG Ch. & O, Tate.

A new recording of *Arabella* has been long overdue, and Jeffrey Tate's set is most welcome, most beautifully played and recorded. If with Dame Kiri Te Kanawa in the name-part it might have turned into just another sweetmeat recording for the great soprano, to be classed with her golden discs of Broadway musicals, in fact it brings one of her very finest opera performances on record. She even outshines the most famous of recorded Arabellas, Lisa della Casa, not only in the firm beauty of her voice, but in the word-pointing and detailed characterization. It is a radiant portrait, languorously beautiful, and it is a pity that so unsuited a soprano as Gabriele Fontana should have been chosen as Zdenka next to her, sounding all the more shrill by contrast. Franz Grundheber makes a firm, virile Mandryka, Peter Seiffert a first-rate Matteo, while Helga Dernesch is outstandingly characterful as Arabella's mother. Though Tate's conducting is richly sympathetic, bringing out the sumptuousness of the score – helped by brilliant Decca recording – his speeds at times are dangerously slow, which might possibly worry established Straussians, if hardly anyone else. These are excellent cassettes.

Ariadne auf Naxos (complete).

(M) ⊛ (***) HMV mono **CMS7 69296-2** [id.]; *EX 769296-4* (2). Schwarzkopf, Schock, Rita Streich, Donch, Seefried, Cuenod, Philh. O, Karajan.

(*) DG Dig. **419 225-2; *419 225-4* (2) [id.]. Tomowa-Sintow, Battle, Baltsa, Lakes, Prey, VPO, Levine.

Karajan's 1954 recording of *Ariadne* brings a performance that even he has rarely matched on record. This classic recording, with a cast never likely to be equalled is all the more cherishable in this excellent CD transfer coming at mid-price on two discs instead of three. Though the absence of translation in the libretto, even at such a price, is a pity, the many index points on CD, cued to the synopsis, can be used almost as easily as a translation alongside the original German words. Elisabeth Schwarzkopf makes a radiant, deeply moving Ariadne, giving as bonus a delicious little portrait of the Prima Donna in the Prologue. Rita Streich was at her most dazzling in the coloratura of Zerbinetta's aria, and in partnership with the harlequinade characters sparkles dazzlingly. But it is Irmgard Seefried who gives perhaps the supreme performance of all as the Composer, exceptionally beautiful of tone, conveying a depth and intensity rarely if ever matched. Rudolf Schock is a fine Bacchus, strained less than most, and the team of theatrical characters includes such stars as Hugues Cuenod as the Dancing Master. The fine pacing and delectably pointed ensemble add to the impact of a uniquely perceptive Karajan interpretation. Though in mono and with the orchestral sound a little dry, the voices come out superbly, more vivid than ever they were in the days of LP.

James Levine conducts a spacious, sumptuously textured reading of *Ariadne* which almost makes you forget that it uses a chamber orchestra. As Ariadne herself, Tomowa-Sintow with her rich, dramatic soprano adds to the sense of grandeur and movingly brings out the vulnerability of the character. But ultimately she fails to create as fully rounded and detailed a character as her finest rivals, and the voice, as recorded, loses its bloom and creaminess under pressure, marring the big climaxes. Both Agnes Baltsa as the Composer and Kathleen Battle as Zerbinetta are excellent: the one tougher than most rivals with her mezzo-soprano ring, little troubled by the high tessitura, the other delectably vivacious, dazzling in coloratura, but equally finding the unexpected tenderness in the character, the underlying sadness clearly implied in the Prologue duet with the Composer. She brings home just why the boy is so enamoured. The *commedia dell'arte* characters and the attendant theatrical team are strongly taken by stalwarts of the Vienna State Opera, among them Kurt Rydl, Hermann Prey and Heinz Zednik, while the Heldentenor role of Bacchus, always hard to cast, is strongly taken by Gary Lakes, clear-toned and firm, at times pinched but never strained. On tape the voices and orchestra are smooth and natural, but the sound is bass- and middle-orientated, with some lack of definition at the top.

Capriccio (complete).

(***) HMV mono **CDS7 49014-8** (2) [id.]. Schwarzkopf, Waechter, Gedda, Fischer-Dieskau, Hotter, Ludwig, Moffo, Philh. O, Sawallisch.

In the role of the Countess in Strauss's last opera, Elisabeth Schwarzkopf has had no equals.

This recording, made in 1957 and 1958, brings a peerless performance from her, full of magical detail both in the pointing of words and in the presentation of the character in all its variety. That is in addition to the sheer beauty of the voice, poised and pure, shaded with immaculate control. For this recording, Schwarzkopf's husband, Walter Legge, as recording manager assembled a cast as starry as could ever be imagined. Not only are the other singers ideal choices in each instance, they form a wonderfully co-ordinated team, beautifully held together by Sawallisch's sensitive conducting. Even such a vignette role as that of the Italian soprano is taken by Anna Moffo. As a performance this is never likely to be superseded, and it comes as one of the most cherishable of operatic reissues on CD. The pity is that for technical reasons a stereo tape was never completed during the original sessions. The mono sound presents the voices with fine bloom and presence, but the digital transfer makes the orchestra a little dry and relatively backward by comparison.

Capriccio: closing scene; *Daphne:* closing scene.
*(*) Chan. Dig. **CHAN 8364**; *ABTD 1127* [id.]. Carole Farley, RTBF SO, Serebrier.

This couples two of the loveliest soprano passages from Strauss's later operas, potentially a magical coupling, but not when Carole Farley's voice is imperfectly controlled, too edgy and fluttery for this music. She is balanced close to make every word clear; the orchestral sound is vividly caught, though the fruity horn at the start of the *Capriccio* momentarily makes it sound like a brass band playing softly. Texts and translations are given. There is an excellent matching chrome cassette.

Capriccio: sextet for strings.
*(*) Nimbus Dig. **NI 5076** [id.]. Augmented Medici Qt – RAVEL: *Quartet*.*(*)

There is no alternative version for single strings of the *Sextet* that opens Strauss's last opera. This is a perfectly good one, though it is unlikely to weigh heavily enough in the balance to sway collectors in its favour, and this disc offers singularly ungenerous measure.

Elektra (complete).
*** Decca **417 345-2** (2) [id.]. Nilsson, Collier, Resnik, Stolze, Krause, V. State Op. Ch., VPO, Solti.
* HM Rodolphe **RPC 32420/21** [id.]. Vinzing, Rysanek, Forrester, Hiestermann, Norup, Schaer, French R. Ch., O Nat. de France, Perick.

The Decca set of *Elektra* was a *tour de force* of John Culshaw and his engineering team. Not everyone will approve of the superimposed sound-effects, but as in Wagner every one of them has justification in the score, and the end result is a magnificently vivid operatic experience created without the help of vision. Nilsson is almost incomparable in the name-part, with the hard side of Elektra's character brutally dominant. Only when – as in the recognition scene with Orestes – she tries to soften the naturally bright tone does she let out a suspect flat note or two. As a rule she is searingly accurate in approaching even the most formidable exposed top notes. One might draw a parallel with Solti's direction – sharply focused and brilliant in the savage music which predominates, but lacking the languorous warmth one really needs in the recognition scene, if only for contrast. Those who remember Beecham's old 78 r.p.m. set of the final scene may not be completely won over by Solti, but we are not likely to get a finer complete *Elektra* for a long time. The brilliance of the 1967 Decca recording is brought out the more in the digital transfer on CD, aptly so in this work. The fullness and clarity are amazing for the period.

The Harmonia Mundi set brings a live recording of a middling performance, well conducted but with too little dramatic bite, when with one exception the singing is undistinguished and sometimes poor, and words are often masked in the cloudy acoustic. The exception is the

Klytemnestra of the veteran contralto, Maureen Forrester, not always vocalized perfectly in the stress of the moment, but always projecting superbly a larger-than-life character. All the others, including Ute Vinzing as Elektra and Leonie Rysanek as Chrysothemis (sounding old now), suffer from varying degrees of unsteadiness.

Die Frau ohne Schatten (complete).
*** DG **415 472-2** (3) [id.]. Nilsson, Rysanek, Hesse, King, Berry, V. State Op. Ch. & O, Boehm.

Boehm's live recording of Strauss's most ambitious, most Wagnerian opera was edited together from two performances at the Vienna State Opera in October 1977, and provides a magnificent reminder of the conductor at his very finest. Though the Decca set of the mid-1950s – also conducted by Boehm in Vienna but recorded in the studio – still sounds amazingly well, with early stereo very well focused, the new one glows far more warmly. It is a performance to love rather than just to admire, with the opera-house acoustic handled persuasively by the engineers of Austrian Radio to give the solo voices plenty of bloom without losing precision. Inevitably, there are stage noises and the balance of the singers varies but this is outstanding among live recordings. The stage cuts are an irritation, but at least they allow the hour-long Acts to be accommodated each on a single CD. The cast is an excellent one, with Birgit Nilsson making the Dyer's Wife a truly Wagnerian character, richer as well as subtler than her Decca predecessor, Christel Goltz. As before, Leonie Rysanek sings the role of the other heroine, the Empress, musically almost as demanding; amazingly, if anything the voice has grown firmer and rounder between the mid-1950s and 1977. Barak the Dyer is sung by Walter Berry, not always as firmly Sachs-like as Paul Schoeffler was before, but searchingly expressive; and James King in the Heldentenor role of the Emperor is just as remarkable for his finely shaded pianissimo singing as for heroic moments, where he is occasionally strained. Until a full, uncut studio recording of this rich and grand if occasionally pretentious opera is recorded (one hopes one day with Solti, the keenest of advocates), this historic Boehm version stands as the most welcome of substitutes. On CD the perspectives are impressively caught at all levels of dynamic.

Die Frau ohne Schatten: symphonic fantasy; *Der Rosenkavalier:* concert suite (arr. Dorati).
** Decca Dig. **411 893-2** [id.]. Detroit SO, Dorati.

In his *Rosenkavalier* suite, Dorati has strung together most of the sweetest lollipops from the opera, keeping Strauss's orchestration but giving vocal lines to various instruments. The result may not appeal to the lover of the opera itself – particularly when Strauss's delicate final pay-off is substituted with a coarse return to the big waltz theme – but performance and recording are aptly opulent. Strauss's own symphonic fantasy on his biggest, most ambitious opera is artistically far more valuable, a piece compiled in his last years with nostalgia for some magnificent ideas. The digital recording is formidably impressive in its range and richness. The CD approaches the demonstration bracket.

Guntram (complete).
*** CBS Dig. **M2K 39737** (2) [id.]. Goldberg, Tokody, Sólomon-Nagy, Gati, Bándi, Hungarian Army Ch. & State O, Queler.

Strauss's very first opera suffers from an undramatic libretto written by the composer, a sloppy tale of knights-in-armour chivalry. Musically, however, the piece provides a marvellous musical wallow, with the young Strauss echoing *Don Juan* and other early symphonic poems in sumptuous orchestral writing. Even when he consciously adopts a Wagnerian stance, the music quickly turns sweet, often anticipating the more lyrical side of *Salome*. Heading the cast as the eponymous knight is Rainer Goldberg, on record the most reliable and open-toned of today's

Heldentenoren, only occasionally strained. Otherwise the cast is Hungarian, with Ilona Tokody strong and firm, if rarely beautiful, in the taxing role of the heroine, Freihild, originally written with Strauss's wife-to-be, Pauline, in mind. Warmly sympathetic conducting from Eve Queler. The recording acoustic too is attractively rich.

Intermezzo: 4 Symphonic interludes. Der Rosenkavalier: Waltz sequence. Salome: Dance of the 7 veils. Die Schweigsame Frau: excerpts.
** Tel. **ZK8 43446** [id.]. Bav. State O, Keiberth.

A collection that is interesting for its repertoire, notably the *Interludes* from *Intermezzo*, which stand up well, away from the opera, and the music from *Die Schweigsame Frau*. The performances are strong and well played and the 1966 recording still sounds well, though some background noise is perceptible. But this is over-priced.

Der Rosenkavalier (complete).
❀ *** HMV **CDS7 49354-8** [id.]; *EX 749354-4* (3). Schwarzkopf, Ludwig, Edelmann, Waechter, Philh. Ch. & O, Karajan.
(*) DG Dig. **413 163-2 (3) [id.]. Tomowa-Sintow, Baltsa, Moll, Perry, Hornik, VPO Ch. & O, Karajan.
(*) Decca **417 493-2 (3) [id.]. Crespin, Minton, Jungwirth, Donath, Wiener, V. State Op. Ch., VPO, Solti.
(*) CBS **M3K 42564 (3) [id.]. Ludwig, Gwyneth Jones, Berry, Popp, Gutstein, V. State Op. Ch., VPO, Bernstein.
*(*) Denon Dig. **C37 7482/4** [id.]. Pusar-Joric, Walther, Adam, Stejskal, Dresden State Op. Ch., Dresden State O, Vonk.

The glory of Karajan's 1956 version, one of the greatest of all opera recordings, shines out the more delectably on CD. Though the transfer in its very clarity exposes some flaws in the original sound, the sense of presence and the overall bloom are if anything more compelling than ever. As to the performance, it is in a class of its own, with the patrician refinement of Karajan's spacious reading combining with an emotional intensity that he has rarely equalled, even in Strauss, of whose music he remains a supreme interpreter. Matching that achievement is the incomparable portrait of the Marschallin from Schwarzkopf, bringing out detail as no one else can, yet equally presenting the breadth and richness of the character, a woman still young and attractive. Christa Ludwig with her firm, clear mezzo tone makes an ideal, ardent Octavian and Teresa Stich-Randall a radiant Sophie, with Otto Edelmann a winningly characterful Ochs, who yet sings every note clearly. These are first-class cassettes.

When Karajan re-recorded this opera in preparation for the 1983 Salzburg Festival with this same DG cast, inevitably he invited comparison with his own classic 1956 recording. The new set brings few positive advantages, not even in recorded sound: for all the extra range of the modern digital recording, the focus is surprisingly vague, with the orchestra balanced too far behind the soloists. One advantage there certainly is: the Vienna Philharmonic, having been brought up with a natural feeling for waltz rhythm, is a degree more idiomatic in providing a genuine Viennese lilt, if it is also at times less precise. The orchestral balance adds to the impression of relative lightness, and so does the casting. As successor to Schwarzkopf, Karajan chose one of his favourite sopranos, the Bulgarian, Anna Tomowa-Sintow; the refinement and detail in her performance present an intimate view of the Marschallin, often very beautiful indeed, but both the darker and more sensuous sides of the Marschallin are muted. *Da steht der Bub* she sings in the great Act III Trio, and the voice conveys pure maternal joy, hardly any regret for her own loss. The Baron Ochs of Kurt Moll, firm, dark and incisive, is outstanding, and Agnes Baltsa as Octavian makes the lad tough and determined, if not always sympathetic. Janet Perry's Sophie, charming and pretty on stage, is too white and twittery of tone to give much pleasure. For all the flaws, Karajan is once more presented as a supreme Straussian, even more daringly spacious than before (which will not please everyone). The benefits of CD in this opera are considerable, not only in the extra clarity of sound but in the way the new medium can contain Acts I, II and III on a single disc each, without a break.

The CD transfer of Solti's version is one of the more disappointing reissues from Decca. The brilliance of the original recording is exaggerated, with some of the compensating body in the sound removed, making the result too aggressive for this gloriously ripe score. Nevertheless it can be tamed and, like other CD versions, this one – which has an absolutely complete text without any statutory cuts – comes on three discs, one per Act. Crespin is here at her finest on record, with tone well focused; the slightly maternal maturity of her approach will for many appear ideal, but the range of expression, verbal and musical, in Schwarzkopf's interpretation stands unrivalled, one of the great performances of the gramophone. Manfred Jungwirth makes a firm and virile, if not always imaginative Ochs, Yvonne Minton a finely projected Octavian and Helen Donath a sweet-toned Sophie. Solti's direction is fittingly honeyed, with tempi even slower than Karajan's in the climactic moments. The one serious disappointment is that the great concluding *Trio* does not quite lift one to the tear-laden height one ideally wants.

Bernstein's CBS Vienna set commemorates a great theatrical occasion at the beginning of the 1970s when the Viennese were swept off their feet – much to their surprise – by the magic of the American conductor. His direction of this opera at the Vienna State Opera was an almost unparalleled success; his recorded version captures much of the ripeness in the fine, mature Marschallin of Christa Ludwig, which plainly owes much to the example of Schwarzkopf (for whom, on the EMI Karajan set, Ludwig was Octavian). Lucia Popp makes a charming Sophie and Walter Berry a strong, expressive Ochs, less limited in the lower register than one might expect. But Gwyneth Jones's Octavian, despite the occasional half-tone of exquisite beauty, has too many raw passages to be very appealing, a bad blot on the set. Bernstein follows traditional cuts. Surprisingly, when Decca engineers were responsible for the recording itself, the quality is more variable than one would expect, with vulgarly close horn balance.

The Denon set, recorded live at the opening of the reconstructed Semper Opera House in Dresden, also brings the obvious benefit of being on only three CDs, one per Act. Stage and audience noises are often obtrusive and the orchestra is balanced well behind the solo singers, but this can still be recommended to those who want a plain, generally brisk view, with plenty of atmosphere. Vonk's rather metrical manner affects even the waltzes, but the orchestral playing is superb, particularly from the horns. The Yugoslav soprano, Ana Pusar-Joric, has a warm, vibrant voice, and her fresh characterization brings delightful pointing of words; but too often she sits under notes, or slides up to them. Ute Walther is an attractively ardent Octavian and Margot Stejskal a thin-toned Sophie, shrill and fluttery at times. Theo Adam's characterful Ochs is marred by too much gritty, ill-focused tone.

Der Rosenkavalier: highlights.
(*) DG Dig. **415 284-2 [id.] (from above set with Tomowa-Sintow, cond. Karajan).

This highlights disc, taken from Karajan's re-recording of the complete opera, provides a generous sample of excerpts, incorporating most of the favourite passages, and includes the tenor aria, lightly sung by Vinson Cole. The richness and beauty of the score are hardly in doubt, but the flaws noted above are just as apparent.

Salome (complete).
*** Decca **414 414-2** (2) [id.]. Nilsson, Hoffman, Stolze, Kmentt, Waechter, VPO, Solti.
*** HMV **CDS7 49358-8** [id.]; *EX 749358-4* (2). Behrens, Bohme, Baltsa, Van Dam, VPO, Karajan.

Solti's recording of *Salome*, originally issued in 1962, was one of the most spectacular of the opera recordings produced by John Culshaw at the Sofiensaal in Vienna. It used what was called the Sonicstage technique – with the sound of Jokanaan's voice in the cistern recorded from another acoustic very precisely – and that sharpness of focus, coupled with opulence of texture, comes out with extraordinary brilliance in the digital transfer on CD. The additional absence of background makes the final scene, where Salome kisses the head of John the Baptist in delighted horror (*I have kissed thy mouth, Jokanaan!*), all the more spine-tingling, with a vivid close-up effect of the voice whispering almost in one's ear. Nilsson is splendid throughout; she is hard-edged as usual but, on that account, more convincingly wicked: the determination and depravity are latent in the girl's character from the start. Of this score Solti is a master. He has rarely sounded so abandoned in a recorded performance. The emotion swells up naturally even while the calculation of impact is most precise. Waechter makes a clear, young-sounding Jokanaan. Gerhardt Stolze portrays the unbalance of Herod with frightening conviction, and Grace Hoffman does all she can in the comparatively ungrateful part of Herodias. The CDs show Decca's technology at its most impressive, and the sound is extraordinarily vivid.

Recorded for EMI by Decca engineers in the Sofiensaal in Vienna, Karajan's sumptuously beautiful version faithfully recaptures the flair and splendour of the Salzburg product, which Karajan produced as well as conducted. It was daring of him when preparing both recording and stage production to choose for the role of heroine a singer then relatively unknown, but Hildegard Behrens is triumphantly successful, a singer who in the early scenes has one actively sympathizing with the girlish princess, and who keeps that sympathy and understanding to a stage where most sopranos have been transformed into raging harpies. The sensuous beauty of tone is ravishingly conveyed, but the recording – less analytical than the Decca set under Solti, also recorded in the Sofiensaal – is not always fair to her fine projection of sound, occasionally masking the voice. All the same, the feeling of a live performance has been well captured, and the rest of the cast is of the finest Salzburg standard. In particular José van Dam makes a gloriously noble Jokanaan, and in the early scenes his offstage voice from the cistern at once commands attention, underlining the direct diatonic strength of his music in contrast to the exoticry representing Salome and the court. Karajan – as so often in Strauss – is at his most commanding and sympathetic, with the orchestra, more forward than some will like, playing rapturously. This is a performance which, so far from making one recoil from perverted horrors, has one revelling in sensuousness. The smooth and warm recording for Karajan's version is clarified on CD. If it cannot match the vintage Decca in brilliance or atmospheric precision, it suits Karajan's ripe reading very well.

Stravinsky, Igor (1882–1971)

Apollo (*Apollon Musagète*): ballet (complete).
*** DG **415 979-2** [id.]. BPO, Karajan – *Rite of spring*.***
*** Decca Dig. **414 457-2**; *414 457-4* [id.]. Detroit SO, Dorati – COPLAND: *Appalachian spring*.***
(M) **(*) Nimbus Dig. **NI 5097** [id.]. E. String O, Boughton – TIPPETT: *Concerto for double string orchestra*.**(*)

Though Stravinsky tended to disparage Karajan's approach to his music as not being rugged enough, here is a work where Karajan's moulding of phrase and care for richness of string texture make for wonderful results. This neoclassical score is strong enough to stand such individual treatment, and the writing is consistently enhanced by the magnificent playing of the Berlin Philharmonic Orchestra. The recording dates from 1973 and sounds excellent in its CD format, if not quite as wide-ranging and 'present' as Dorati's newer digital version for Decca.

Although the playing of the Detroit orchestra cannot match the polish of the Berlin account under Karajan, Dorati's performance has an attractive vitality, while the variations of Terpsichore and Apollo are genially characterized and the splendid *Pas de deux* – one of Stravinsky's most memorable inspirations – is warmly played. The recording is first class, spacious and with strikingly realistic detail on the fine CD.

Boughton's version, unusually coupled with the Tippett *String concerto*, brings warm, responsive playing, lacking a little in refinement, with individual instruments often audible, but very sympathetically countering any idea that neoclassical Stravinsky of this vintage is chilly and reserved, thrustful rather. The very reverberant recording, made in the Great Hall of Birmingham University, adds a pleasant halo to the sound but obscures some detail. However, the record has a price advantage over its competitors.

Le baiser de la fée (ballet; complete). Tchaikovsky (arr. Stravinsky): *Sleeping Beauty: Bluebird pas de deux.*
*** Chan. **CHAN 8360**; *ABTD 1123* [id.]. SNO, Järvi.

Le baiser de la fée is a remarkable symbiosis of Tchaikovskian tuneful charm (as instanced by the unforgettable rhythmic theme for the horns, taken from a piano piece) and Stravinskian twentieth-century neoclassicism. Stravinsky was only occasionally a memorable tunesmith himself (Arthur Rubinstein once demonstrated in a TV interview how virtually all the famous melodies in the three great ballets are derived from Russian folk-themes). But he could illuminate and refine the invention of others more gifted in that respect, adding also a firm lamination of his own musical personality. The scoring here is a constant delight, much of it on a chamber-music scale; and its delicacy, wit and occasional pungency are fully appreciated by Järvi, who secures a wholly admirable response from his Scottish orchestra. The ambience seems exactly right, bringing out wind and brass colours vividly; the CD adds a degree of extra definition, alongside the background silence. The condensation of the scoring of the *Sleeping Beauty Pas de deux*, made for a wartime performance when only limited forces were available, also shows Stravinsky's orchestral individuality – he even introduces a piano.

Le baiser de la fée (Divertimento); (i) *Fanfare for a new theatre; Suites for orchestra: Nos 1 and 2; Octet;* (ii) *3 Pieces for clarinet solo.*
*** Decca Dig. **417 114-2** [id.]. L. Sinf., Chailly; (i) Watson; Archibald; (ii) Pay.

Ansermet made a famous mono LP (1951) of the four-movement *Divertimento*, which Stravinsky distilled from the complete ballet in 1934. The Swiss conductor re-recorded it later in stereo, but the second account proved rhythmically less taut and was not so well played. Chailly's version, admirably fresh, cannot be criticized on either of these counts. It is superbly played and Decca's recording is in the finest traditions of the house, especially in its CD format. After the gently nostalgic opening, Chailly's approach to the *Sinfonia* is dramatic and strong: clearly, he sees this movement in terms of the concert hall, rather than the ballet theatre. Stravinsky's dominance over the music is emphasized; later and especially in the Scherzo and *Pas de deux* the Tchaikovskian influences rise more readily to the surface. Chailly's pacing throughout is splendidly judged, rhythms are resilient – the pointing of the lighter rhythmic patterns is especially effective – and the espressivo playing is at once responsive and slightly cool, a most engaging combination. The rest of the programme is imaginatively chosen. The jagged *Fanfare*, written in 1964 for the opening of the State Theatre in New York's Lincoln Center, lasts a mere 0′ 43″; the three miniatures for solo clarinet are no less original and characteristic. They are splendidly played by Anthony Pay, who readily responds to taxing writing over the instrument's full range, with the bravura of the finale dispatched with an assured geniality. The two *Orchestral suites*, vivid orchestrations of *'Easy' pieces* for piano, provide a kaleidoscopic series of colourful vignettes. Unfortunately, on CD the individual movements are not banded. Finally, and very welcome indeed, the 1922 *Octet* is restored to the catalogue, a considerable piece for flute, clarinet, two bassoons – used to great effect – two trumpets, trombone and bass trombone. It is given a performance of infectious virtuosity, with individual bravura matched by polished ensemble and fine tonal blending. The second-movement *Theme and variations*, with its bizarre quotations of the *Dies irae*, is particularly memorable. Throughout the programme, the CD is very much in the demonstration class, with the tangibility and presence of the imagery enhanced by the background silence (the bass drum featured with rare subtlety). The overall bloom, without any clouding, again testifies to the ideal acoustic properties of London's Kingsway Hall.

Le Chant du rossignol (symphonic poem).
*** Decca Dig. **417 619-2**; *417 619-4* [id.]. Montreal SO, Dutoit – *Petrushka* etc.***
*** Erato **ECD 88107** [id.]. French Nat. O, Boulez – *Pulcinella*.**(*)
*** CBS **MK 42396** [id.]. NYPO, Boulez – *Firebird*.***
(*) Delos Dig. **D/CD 3051 [id.]. Seattle SO, Schwarz – *Firebird*.**(*)

Le Chant du rossignol (symphonic poem); *Fireworks, Op. 4*.
** Decca Dig. **414 078-2** [id.]. Berlin RSO, Chailly – *Symphony of Psalms*.**

Le Rossignol is an underrated Stravinsky opera; its derivative opening, with overtones of *Nuages*, and its Rimskian flavour have led to its virtues being undervalued. Among them is its extraordinarily rich fantasy and vividness of colouring; the symphonic poem that Stravinsky made from the material of this work deserves a more established place in the concert repertoire. Dutoit's account is full of colour and atmosphere and has the advantage of marvellous Montreal sound. The couplings too are particularly apt, and this is a very desirable disc in all respects.

Both Boulez performances are also masterly; the French National Orchestra on Erato capture detail vividly and have the advantage of a first-class 1982 recording. The New York account is, if anything, even better played, but the recording is earlier (1975). It was made in the Manhattan Center and combines magical evocation with vigour and bite. The delicate flute contribution of Julius Baker is notable but the orchestral wind solos generally respond to the score's Rimskian inheritance.

The Delos Schwarz recording has the most brilliantly etched detail, yet remains reasonably atmospheric. The extremely vivid and well-focused internal detail makes for the kind of record that will thrill audiophiles with equipment capable of making the most of its projection and clarity.

The score's exotic effects and glittering colours sound lustrously delicate in the ecclesiastical ambient glow of the Jesus Christus Church in West Berlin; but Chailly does not have this score in his bones and he tends to force the pace and overdramatize the music, instead of letting it blossom naturally. *Feux d'artifice* makes a curious encore, and the coupled *Symphony of Psalms* also suggests that this is not repertoire with which Chailly is naturally sympathetic, although the response of the Berlin Radio Symphony Orchestra is impressive throughout this collection.

Concerto for piano and winds.
*(*) Hyp. *KA 66167* [id.]. Marios Papadopoulos, RPO – JANÁČEK: *Capriccio for piano left hand; Sonata*.*(*)

Mario Papadopoulos is a young Cypriot-born pianist whose first record this is. He is obviously an accomplished player, though his view of the Stravinsky *Concerto*, which he directs from the keyboard, is perhaps a little too neat and not quite savage enough. The recording errs in the right direction as far as the balance between piano and wind is concerned, but there are times when the soloist seems a little too overwhelmed by the orchestral forces. The Hyperion tape lacks something in bite because of the resonance.

Concerto in E flat (Dumbarton Oaks); Pulcinella (suite); 8 Instrumental miniatures.
*** DG Dig. **419 628-2**; *419 628-4* [id.]. Orpheus CO.

Remarkably fine playing from this conductorless group. Their ensemble in the *Pulcinella suite* is better than that of most conducted orchestras, and the overall impression they convey is one of freshness and spontaneity. Much the same must be said of *Dumbarton Oaks*, which has great zest and brilliance. The DG recording is clean and lifelike and the perspective very natural. While this new disc does not eclipse memories of all rivals, it can more than hold its own with most competition, past and present. The chrome cassette too is a state-of-the-art transfer.

Ebony concerto.
*** CBS **MK 42227**; *MT 42227* [id.]. Benny Goodman, Columbia Jazz Ens., composer – COPLAND: *Concerto*; BARTÓK: *Contrasts*; BERNSTEIN: *Prelude, fugue and riffs*; GOULD: *Derivations.*(***)

(i; ii) *Ebony concerto;* (ii) *Preludium;* (iii) *Ragtime for 11 instruments;* (ii) *Tango.*
*** CBS *MPT 39768*. (i) Benny Goodman; (ii) Columbia Jazz Ens.; (iii) Columbia Chamber Ens.; all cond. composer – BERNSTEIN: *Prelude, fugue and riffs*; BRUBECK: *Dialogues.****

An appropriate grouping of Stravinsky's jazz-based works, from his first flurry of enthusiasm for the new ragtime flavour through to the *Ebony concerto*, written for Woody Herman in 1945. The sharp and pointed performances are well recorded and the tape transfer is well managed. The *Ebony concerto* is also available on CD, sounding strikingly vivid in an apt compilation centred on Benny Goodman's other comparable recordings.

Violin concerto in D.
*** DG **413 725-2** [id.]. Perlman, Boston SO, Ozawa – BERG: *Concerto.****

Perlman's precision, remarkable in both concertos on this disc, underlines the neoclassical element in the outer movements of the Stravinsky. The two *Aria* movements are more deeply felt and expressive, presenting the work as a major twentieth-century concerto. The balance favours the soloist, but no one will miss the commitment of the Boston orchestra's playing, vividly recorded. The CD subtly adds to the definition and presence of the recording.

Danses concertantes; Pulcinella (ballet)*: suite.*
*** Chan. Dig. **CHAN 8325**; *ABTD 1065* [id.]. ECO, Gibson.

Gibson and the ECO are very well recorded on Chandos and give highly enjoyable accounts of both works. The *Pulcinella* suite does not quite eclipse the Marriner on Argo (see below), but it is still very lively, and the *Danses concertantes* scores even over the composer's own in terms of charm and geniality. The CD is especially impressive in its firmness of detail. The chrome cassette is vivid and very bright on top; indeed, it may call for a little taming, especially in *Pulcinella*.

Complete ballets: *The Firebird; Petrushka; The Rite of spring.*
*** Decca **421 079-2** (2) [id.]. Detroit SO, Dorati.

Dorati's set of the three great Stravinsky ballets is economically laid out here (although at full price) on two CDs, with the *Firebird* on one and the remaining pair on the second. The Decca recording is consistently spectacular and realistic throughout. Dorati's version of *Petrushka* is based on the 1947 version, though at certain points Dorati reverts to the original 1911 scoring, in accordance with his recollections of a conversation he had with Stravinsky himself. *Petrushka* has always been a vehicle for the virtuosity of recording engineers, right from the early days of LP, when Decca put the famous first Ansermet mono LP on to the market. Dorati's version creates a comparable digital landmark. The sound is breathtakingly vivid and clean, yet remains naturally balanced and transparent. The performance does not always have the refinement of Abbado's, but it is immensely dramatic and also very telling in the scene where the frustrated Petrushka is confined to his cell. Dorati is at his finest in the final tableau, bringing out the robust Russian earthiness of the dancing peasants. The other two recordings are discussed below under their individual issues.

The Firebird (ballet) complete.
*** Ph. **400 074-2** [id.]. Concg. O, C. Davis.
*** Decca Dig. **410 109-2** [id.]. Detroit SO, Dorati.
*** CBS **MK 42396** [id.]. NYPO, Boulez – *Chant du rossignol.****
(*) Delos Dig. **D/CD 3051 [id.]. Seattle SO, Schwarz – *Chant du rossignol.***(*)
(*) Decca **414 141-2 [id.]. New Philh. O, Ansermet.
(*) HMV Dig. **CDC7 47017-2 [id.]. Boston SO, Ozawa.

The Firebird (ballet) complete; *Fireworks, Op. 4; Scherzo fantastique, Op. 3.*
*** Decca Dig. **414 409-2**; *414 409-4* [id.]. Montreal SO, Dutoit.

The Firebird (ballet) complete; *Fireworks; Scherzo fantastique; Scherzo à la Russe.*
*** CBS **MK 42432** [id.]. Columbia SO, composer.

Dutoit's version brings a characteristically colourful and atmospheric reading of Stravinsky's brilliant ballet score, ideally and generously coupled with the two early orchestral pieces which led Diaghilev to spot the young composer's talent. Thanks in part to Decca's sensuously beautiful Montreal recording (just as apparent on cassette as on the demonstration-standard CD), this is a reading that brings out the light and shade of the writing, so that even *Kaschei's dance* is not just a brilliant showpiece but part of the poetic and dramatic scheme. The pianissimos are of breathtaking delicacy – very vital in this work: the hushed introduction to the final scene with its lovely horn solo brings a sense of wonder. The fill-ups are sparklingly done, making this a clear first choice.

Stravinsky's own 1961 version of *Firebird* may lack the refinement of sound and the dynamic contrasts that mark the finest digital recordings, but it is of far more than documentary interest, when the composer so tellingly relates it to his later work, refusing to treat it as merely atmospheric. What he brings out more than others is the element of grotesque fantasy, the quality he was about to develop in *Petrushka*, while the tense violence with which he presents such a passage as *Kaschei's dance* clearly looks forward to *The Rite of spring*. That said, he encourages warmly expressive rubato to a surprising degree, with the line of the music always held firm. His two early and brilliant orchestral pieces make the ideal coupling – as they do in Dutoit's fine version – but in addition the jolly *Scherzo à la Russe* of 1944 comes as a bonus, done with infectious bounce.

With superb analogue sound, Sir Colin Davis directs a magically evocative account of the complete *Firebird* ballet, helped not just by the playing of the Concertgebouw Orchestra (the strings outstandingly fine) but by the ambience of the hall, which allows inner clarity, yet gives a bloom to the sound, open and spacious, superbly co-ordinated. The compact disc, digitally remastered, has sharpened up detail, somewhat at the expense of the magical analogue atmosphere. While there is more depth and bite, it is not all gain; although the brass has greater presence, the high violins sound less natural. Background noise has been virtually eliminated.

Dorati's Detroit version has the benefit of spectacular digital recording. The clarity and definition of dark, hushed passages is amazing, with the contra-bassoon finely focused, never sounding woolly or obscure, while string tremolos down to the merest whisper are uncannily precise. There is plenty of space round woodwind solos, and only the concertmaster's violin is spotlit. The performance is very precise, too; though Dorati's reading has changed little from his previous versions with London orchestras, there is just a little more caution. Individual solos are not so characterful and *Kaschei's dance* lacks just a degree in excitement, but overall this is a strong and beautiful reading, even if the Mercury LP account, an electrifying example of 1960s analogue engineering, is not entirely superseded. The somewhat literal quality of the Decca performance, lacking a touch of magic and intensity, is brought out the more on CD, though the vividness and impact of the sound are most impressive.

Boulez gives a highly coloured reading, and one which is very dramatic too. The 1975 recording is balanced relatively forward, yet is glowingly vivid in its highly successful remastered format. The playing is first class: the music making has considerable magnetism, and its element of warmth is balanced by the malignancy when Kaschei makes his entrance. The coupling is an outstanding account of *Le Chant du rossignol.*

The Delos version brings brilliant, exceptionally clean ensemble from the Seattle Symphony, showing its paces impressively under its music director, Gerard Schwarz. Next to Dutoit for example, this performance lacks a little in atmosphere and warmth, but it is a very viable issue, if the attractive coupling is what you prefer. The recording is brilliant and strikingly sophisticated in its detail. It has a demonstration potential in its clarity that is impressive in itself.

Ansermet's New Philharmonia version offers more polished playing than the performance he recorded earlier with his own Suisse Romande Orchestra, but generally the interpretations were amazingly consistent, with the principal difference lying in the extra flexibility of the London players. The firmness and precision of the sound with a vividly realistic (Kingsway Hall) acoustic make the 1968 recording very impressive in its CD transfer, even today. The brilliance sometimes brings a touch of hardness, and the growling basses at the start are not as sharply defined as they are in Dorati's digital recording, but the sense of presence is startling.

Ozawa's Boston version is more refined than his Paris record, also for HMV; but with the extra precision has come a degree of detachment, chill even. *Kaschei's dance* is less an orchestral showpiece than a delicate tapestry, relatively light and transparent, with dance rhythms well sprung and the bite of fortissimo reserved for sforzando chords. The CD brings satisfying weight to the brass. Nevertheless, as a recording this is less brilliant than Ansermet's, let alone Dorati's; and Sir Colin Davis remains a preferable choice on grounds of interpretation, while the Philips analogue sound is in many ways as impressive as the digital balance the EMI engineers give Ozawa.

The Firebird: suite (1919 version).
*** HMV **CDC7 47099-2** [id.]. Phd. O, Muti – MUSSORGSKY: *Pictures.****
(*) Telarc Dig. **CD 80039 [id.]. Atlanta SO, Shaw – BORODIN: *Prince Igor excerpts.****
(B) **(*) DG Walkman *413 155-4* [id.]. Berlin RSO, Maazel – KHACHATURIAN: *Gayaneh*; RIMSKY-KORSAKOV: *Scheherazade.***(*)

Muti gets excellent playing from the Philadelphia Orchestra and, though their response is admirably disciplined, they are not quite as overdriven as in some of the later records Muti has made in Philadelphia. Indeed, there is delicacy and poetry in the *Dance of the princesses* and the *Berceuse* in *Firebird*, and the colours of this score are heard in full splendour. There is no doubt that the new format offers the greater range and firmness. A welcome issue which can be recommended even to those readers who do not always respond to some of the later records from this conductor.

The *Firebird suite* has been recorded by the finest orchestras in the world; excellent as is the Atlanta Symphony, it would not claim to be of their number. Nevertheless Robert Shaw, the thoroughly musical conductor, achieves an atmospheric and vivid reading of Stravinsky's famous suite. The *Round dance of the princesses* is played very gently to maximize the shock of the entry of Kaschei. The very wide dynamic range of the digital recording achieves the most dramatic impact both here and in the closing pages of the finale. With its spectacular coupling this issue is designed to appeal to those wanting to show off their reproducer.

Maazel's reading of the *Firebird suite* has an enjoyable éclat and he has the advantage of the most beautiful woodwind playing; indeed the Berlin Radio Orchestra is consistently on top form. The recording dates from 1960 and tended to betray its age by the sound of the massed upper strings. However, in the present transfer the DG engineers have smoothed off the upper partials and in consequence the recording, although still impressive, has lost some of its bite.

The Firebird: suite (1919); *Petrushka:* complete (1947 score).
(M) *(**) CBS **MYK 42540**; *40-42540*. NYPO, Bernstein.

Bernstein's performance of *Petrushka* is one of the most involved and warm-hearted ever recorded. Even more than the composer himself, or Ansermet (whose sense of humour was pointedly stirred in this of all Stravinsky's music), Bernstein goes to the emotional heart of the score, without violating Stravinsky's expressed markings except in a couple of minor instances. The panoply of the fair music, the inbred hysteria of the puppet's rage, and above all the tragedy of his death are here conveyed with unrivalled intensity and with splendidly vivid recording. *Firebird* is warmly done, if without quite the same superb precision. The digital remastering has smoothed the treble, taking some of the aggressive edge off the recording as well as removing the background; however, the engineers let the top back in for the fierce climax of *Kaschei's dance* in *The Firebird.* The four separate tableaux of Petrushka are cued, but not the individual sections of the *Firebird suite.*

The Firebird: suite (1919 version); *Pulcinella* (ballet; rev. 1947 version)*: suite.*
* DG Dig. **415 127-2** [id.]. Israel PO, Bernstein.

Bernstein's version of Stravinsky's *Firebird* and *Pulcinella* with the Israel Philharmonic proves something of a disappointment. The dryness of the acoustic is all too evident at the end of the opening *Sinfonia* of *Pulcinella*, though less disturbing in *Firebird.* Like his *Petrushka*, the performances are neither as well executed nor as fully characterized as his earlier, highly atmospheric accounts with the New York Philharmonic. The Israel Philharmonic is not in the same league, and the strings in the *Tarantella* of the *Pulcinella suite* sound pretty scrappy and lack-lustre.

The Firebird suite (1910 version)*; The Rite of spring.*
(M) ** Nimbus Dig. **NI 5087** [id.]. LSO, Rozhdestvensky.

Though it is well coupled with the 1910 *Firebird suite* (the one that gives the first part of the ballet only, ending with *Kaschei's dance*) and comes at mid-price, Rozhdestvensky's Nimbus version merits only a qualified recommendation. *The Rite* is given a rugged, broad reading at generally slow speeds, convincingly spontaneous-sounding but lacking full bite in often slack ensemble. The digital recording is full and atmospheric.

The Firebird suite (1919 version)*; The Rite of spring.*
(M) *** DG **415 854-2**; *415 854-4* [id.]. LSO, Abbado.

Abbado's *Firebird suite* is a performance of great vitality and sensitivity; the conductor's feeling for colour and atmosphere is everywhere and the CD transfer loses nothing of the evocation of the analogue original. There is a degree of detachment in Abbado's reading of *The Rite of spring*; but on points of detail it is meticulous, and an orchestra whose members have sometimes claimed they could play this score without a conductor revels in the security given by the conductor's direction. There is a hypnotically atmospheric feeling at the opening of Part Two, emphasizing the contrast with the brutal music which follows. The drama is heightened by the wide dynamic range of the recording, and the effect is forceful without ever becoming ugly.

Jeu de cartes (ballet)*; Symphony in 3 movements.*
(*) Erato **ECD 88249 [id.]. Rotterdam PO, Conlon.

A first-class performance of the *Symphony in three movements* comes from James Conlon and his excellent Dutch forces. Everything is full of life and the orchestral playing in *Jeu de cartes* is crisp and athletic and full of wit. Good recording, though the solo violins and harp in the middle movement of the *Symphony* are reticently balanced. The performance of the *Symphony* does not displace Dutoit (see below) and it should be noted that the CD offers only 44′ playing time.

Petrushka (ballet; 1911 score) complete.
(*) DG Dig. **400 042-2 [id.]. LSO, Abbado.
(B) *** DG Walkman *415 336-4* [id.]. LSO, Dutoit – RAVEL: *Daphnis et Chloé.***(*)

Petrushka (1911 score)*; 4 Études.*
*** Decca Dig. **417 619-2**; *417 619-4* [id.]. Montreal SO, Dutoit – *Chant du rossignol.****

Petrushka (1947 score)*; Circus polka; Fireworks, Op. 4.*
(*) ASV Dig. **CDDCA 542 [id.]. RPO, Bátiz.

Petrushka (1947 score; complete)*; Scènes de ballet.*
** DG Dig. **410 996-2** [id.]. Israel PO, Bernstein.

Petrushka (1947 score)*; Scherzo à la russe.*
** CBS **CD 37271** [id.]. Philh. O, Tilson Thomas.

Dutoit in his Montreal version, benefiting from superb, atmospheric but well-detailed sound, on tape as well as CD, gives a sparkling performance that brings out the light and shade of *Petrushka*, its poetry and its rhythmic effervescence. The fun of the fair is lightly rather than robustly conveyed, and with it the underlying tenderness. As in other brilliant showpieces, the refinement of Montreal pianissimos adds to the atmospheric thrill, but there is no lack of either power or bite in this subtle telling of the story. There are only four separate tracks, dividing the four tableaux. The coupling of *Le Chant du rossignol* and the *Four Studies* is both generous and apt (the one evocative, the other sharply colourful) dating from the period soon after *Petrushka.*

Abbado's version of the 1911 *Petrushka* has the advantage of extremely spectacular digital sound, even though it is not quite as overwhelming sonically as Decca's for Dorati. The performance is strongly characterized, and the LSO play marvellously. Abbado combines refinement and a powerful sense of dramatic atmosphere (he is especially sympathetic in the central tableaux) with a kaleidoscopic brilliance. The recording has impressive range and colour. The compact disc emphasizes the virtues of the recording by its clarity and silent background, but there is a degree of digital edge on the upper strings which is certainly not entirely natural. Moreover the DG CD is ungenerous, without any fill-ups.

For a bargain tape version the Walkman is unbeatable. Charles Dutoit first recorded *Petrushka* for DG in 1977, before he had become a star conductor on the Decca roster. Interestingly, it was made almost impromptu: a planned opera recording fell through, and sessions were hastily re-allotted with little advance planning. The result is triumphantly spontaneous in its own right, with rhythms that are incisive yet beautifully buoyant, and a degree of expressiveness in the orchestral playing that subtly underlines the dramatic atmosphere, and is especially magical in the Third Tableau. The final section too is strongly coloured, so that the gentle closing pages make a touching contrast to the gaiety of the early part of the scene. The recording is rich and atmospheric, the only fault of balance being the prominence of the concertante piano soloist, Tamás Vásáry. In its Walkman chrome-tape format detail is less than sharply etched but the combination of drama and evocation is most satisfying. Coupled with an excellent complete *Daphnis and Chloé* under Ozawa, this is formidable value.

With bright, forward, well-detailed recording, the Bátiz issue brings a performance of comparatively little sparkle or charm more emphatic than usual, but therefore looking forward illuminatingly to the *Rite of spring*. The crispness of ensemble, the resilence of rhythms and the distinction of much of the solo work (notably the first flute) lightens what could have been too heavy, with some speeds slower than usual. The two lightweight fill-ups are certainly too heavily done, but are worth having as makeweights.

Sonic limitations qualified the enthusiasm with which Bernstein's version of *Le Sacre* could be greeted; his *Petrushka* was recorded in the same unglamorous acoustic of the Mann Auditorium, Tel Aviv. However, the results are by no means as unpleasing, though still too dry and unventilated. Bernstein coaxes some highly responsive playing from the Israel Philharmonic and secures much pleasing string tone – not always to be found from this body. Perhaps this *Petrushka* is not as touching as his earlier New York account made in the 1960s, surely one of the most vital and sensitively characterized versions of the work, but it is still vividly projected and keenly felt. Moreover, this record is particularly welcome for its coupling, the *Scènes de ballet* of 1944 which the Israeli orchestra play with something approaching elegance. This is a charming and underrated piece, not otherwise available at present. The CD draws the ear to the acoustic dryness of the recording, but the upper range is clear and clean and not edgy.

Michael Tilson Thomas can hold his own with the available competition artistically. He shows a keen imaginative insight and much poetic feeling in *Petrushka* and his reading has the merit of freshness. However, in its CD format it still sounds over-resonant, lacking the transparency and well-integrated balance of some of its rivals. The *Scherzo à la russe* is a much less generous fill-up than Bernstein's but it is played with much character.

Petrushka (1911 version)*; The Rite of spring.*
(M) *** Ph. **420 491-2**; *420 491-4* [id.]. LPO, Haitink.
(M) *(*) RCA **GD 86529** [**RCA 6529-2-RG**]. Boston SO, Monteux.

Petrushka (1947 version)*; The Rite of spring.*
❀ *** CBS **MK 42433** [id.]. Columbia SO, composer.
*** Ph. **416 498-2** [id.]. Concg. O, C. Davis.
(*) HMV Dig. **CDC7 47408-2 [id.]. Phd. O, Muti.

Stravinsky's own 1960 recordings of his two greatest ballets make a uniquely revelatory coupling; the only regret must be that CBS have not found room on a very well-filled disc for the spoken supplement which on the original LP of *The Rite* had the composer in his thick Russian-English making a moving commentary, ending: 'I am the vessel through which *Le sacre* passed.' It is not the same having the words just printed. That said, Stravinsky's own 1960 reading has never been surpassed as an interpretation of *The Rite*. Over and over again, one finds passages which in their balancing and pacing (generally fast) give extra thrust and resilience, as well as extra light and shade. The whole performance is magnetic, with the argument and tension superbly held together; that is so, despite the obvious limitations of a 1960 recording. The digital transfer may be on the bright side, and there is some slight background noise, but brass and percussion have thrilling impact, sharply terraced and positioned in the stereo spectrum. The 1960 recording of *Petrushka* has generally been underrated; it may lack something in lightness and sparkle on the one hand, and poetry on the other – largely a question of recording balance – but the composer presents a very convincing case for a basically fierce approach, full of malevolent grotesquerie; it is as though he has a malicious smile on his face. Even though the result may be relentless, the frenetic element is tellingly made to reflect the pathetic neurosis of the puppet-figure at the centre of the story. The digital remastering has brought coarser sound than in *The Rite*, for the original analogue LP was much less clear on detail; this lack of clarity remains, but the CD is easy enough to listen to. Interestingly, the term 'Columbia Symphony Orchestra' denotes two quite different groups of players: while *Petrushka* was recorded in Los Angeles, *The Rite of spring* with its greater magnetism was done in New York.

Haitink's 1974 *Petrushka* has been remastered with great success. There is a sense of expansion of the dynamic range and the performance is given added projection. It is a very involving account, with detail imaginatively delineated. The rhythmic feeling is strong, especially in the Second Tableau and finale, where the fairground bustle is vivid. The LPO wind playing is especially fine; the recording's firm definition and the well-proportioned and truthful aural perspective make it a joy to listen to. The natural, unforced quality of Haitink's *Rite* brings real compulsion. More than most – except in a few slow speeds – he convincingly echoes the example of the composer himself. Other versions may hammer the listener more powerfully, thrust him or her along more forcefully; but the bite and precision of the playing here is most impressive. Though some analogue hiss is detectable, the CD transfer of this exceptionally generous coupling brings cleanly balanced textures and a vivid sense of presence. There is also a strikingly successful tape.

Sir Colin Davis's Philips version of the 1947 score combines brilliant and rich recording with a performance which to an exceptional degree makes a positive case for the 1947 score over the original. The recording has some curious and not always perfectly balanced spotlighting of instruments (most unexpected from Philips), but it reveals details of the rich texture that are normally obscured. From first to last Davis makes it clear that he regards this as fun music, drawing brilliantly precise playing from the Concertgebouw and rarely if ever forcing the pace, though always maintaining necessary excitement. The piano solo starts a little cautiously in the Russian dance, but that is an exception in an unusually positive reading. Davis also has his idiosyncrasies in *The Rite of spring* (one of them is his strange hold-up on the last chord), but generally he takes an unusually direct view, and the result is strong, forthright and powerful. Some will prefer a more obviously involving reading, but with the opulent sound of the Concertgebouw Orchestra richly recorded the physical impact of this version is still irresistible. Its richness and body are well transferred to CD; but this is at premium price, and one remembers that Haitink's similar coupling is at mid-price.

Muti secures playing of stunning virtuosity from the Philadelphians in *Petrushka* and, while their response is breathtaking, his reading can best be described as breathless. There is unremitting drive here, with the *Danse russe* taken at breakneck speed and everything far too regimented. The recording has splendid impact and clarity, but there is too little tenderness and magic in this overdriven account. The compact disc is extremely brilliant, but though the sound has 'hi-fi' vividness, there is an aggressive sharpness of focus to the sound-picture which emphasizes Muti's forcefulness. Similarly Muti's *Rite of spring* offers a performance of Stravinsky's barbaric masterpiece which is aggressively brutal yet presents the violence with red-blooded conviction. Muti generally favours speeds a shade faster than usual, and arguably the opening bassoon solo is not quite flexible enough, for metrical precision is a key element all through. There are signs that Muti has studied the last of Stravinsky's own recordings of *The Rite* (by far the most convincing of the three he made), and it is good to have the amendment to the horn part sanctioned in it in the *Sacrificial dance* (two bars before fig. 75). The recording, not always as analytically clear as some rivals, is strikingly bold and dramatic, with brass and percussion exceptionally vividly caught. The effect is very exciting, without being fierce.

While it is worthwhile to have a CD of *The Rite of spring* from Monteux, who conducted its première, the RCA transfer is much less successful technically than Haitink's or indeed the composer's own. The mid-1960s recordings are given a shrill cutting-edge which is none too comfortable, while *Petrushka* is clouded by the Boston reverberation. The performances have undoubted flair and are very well played, but the sound here precludes a strong recommendation.

Petrushka (1947 version)*; Symphony in 3 movements.*
*** HMV Dig. **CDC7 49053-2** [id.]; *EL 749053-4.* CBSO, Rattle.
(M) ** Nimbus Dig. **NI 5088** [id.]. LSO, Rozhdestvensky.

Using the revised, 1947 scoring, Rattle gives a reading which brings out powerfully the sturdy jollity of the ballet, contrasting it with the poignancy of the puppet's own feelings. There is a robust exuberance about the approach, full of fun, colourful and dramatic in its evocation of the fairground. The full and brilliant recording is beefy in the middle and bass, but Rattle and his players benefit in clarity from the 1947 scoring, finely detailed to bring out many points that are normally obscured. The *Symphony in three movements*, done with comparable power, colour and robustness, makes an unusual but attractive coupling. Rattle with his jazz training brings out the syncopations and pop references with great panache.

With the same coupling as Simon Rattle's fine EMI version, Rozhdestvensky and the LSO on Nimbus cannot match their Birmingham colleagues in point and bite; too often the result is not just rugged but rough, lacking in tension. With full, atmospheric digital recording, the issue comes at mid-price.

Pulcinella (ballet) complete.
(*) Erato **ECD 88107 [id.]. Murray, Rolfe Johnson, Estes, Ensemble Intercontemporain, Boulez – *Le Chant du rossignol.****

(i) *Pulcinella* (ballet) complete*; Suites Nos 1 & 2* (for orchestra).
(M) *** EMI Dig. *TC-EMX 2126* [id.]. (i) Kenny, Tear, Lloyd, ASMF, Marriner.

Pulcinella (ballet) *suite.*
(M) *** Decca **417 734-2**; *417 734-4* [id.]. ASMF, Marriner – BIZET; PROKOFIEV: *Symphonies.****

The playing of the Academy of St Martin-in-the-Fields is very fine indeed, and they are accorded a natural balance with plenty of air round the instruments and no want of depth. The voices are a bit forward, but the singing is good enough for that not to matter. The EMI digital recording is mellow and richly detailed. Some might feel that a more astringent bouquet is called for in this music, but Marriner's approach brings out the geniality; the fine, often witty playing of the Academy is no less beguiling in the delectably scored orchestral *Suites* which are given as a coupling. No doubt this will appear on CD in due course; meanwhile the iron-oxide cassette is smooth, warm and clear, though lacking a little in bite at the top.

Boulez also secures some superb playing from the Ensemble Intercontemporain, and his singers are first class in every way. His is a fine performance too, but his pacing is more extreme than Marriner's, with contrasts between movements almost overcharacterized. However, some may like the periodic added edge, and the Erato recording has been excellently transferred to CD.

Those wanting merely the orchestral suite can rest content with Marriner's vintage (originally Argo, now Decca) version, one of the first recordings by which the Academy, known for many years as an outstanding recording team in Baroque music, spread its wings in the music of the twentieth century. The results are superb and the sound of the digitally remastered CD has all the bite one could ask for. It remains a demonstration disc with its sharp separation of instruments, particularly the trombones against double basses in the *Vivo.* Coupled with marvellous performances of the Prokofiev (*Classical*) and Bizet symphonies, it is a real bargain in both CD and tape formats.

The Rite of spring (complete ballet) (see also above, under *Petrushka*).
(M) *** DG **423 214-2**; *423 214-4* [id.]. BPO, Karajan – MUSSORGSKY: *Pictures.****
*** DG **415 979-2** [id.]. BPO, Karajan – *Apollo.****
*** Decca Dig. **400 084-2** [id.]. Detroit SO, Dorati.
(M) *** Decca **417 704-2** [id.]. Chicago SO, Solti – DEBUSSY: *Prélude à l'après-midi*: RAVEL: *Boléro.***
(*) Telarc Dig. **CD 80054 [id.]. Cleveland O, Maazel.
(*) Erato Dig. **ECD 75360 [id.]. O de Paris, Barenboim – SCRIABIN: *Poème de l'extase.***(*)
(B) **(*) DG Walkman *413 160-4* [id.]. Boston SO, Tilson Thomas – ORFF: *Carmina Burana.****
** DG Dig. **410 508-2** [id.]. Israel PO, Bernstein.

The Rite of spring; Circus polka; Fireworks; Greeting prelude: Happy birthday.
(M) *** EMI Dig. **CD-EMX 9517**; *TC-EMX 2128*. LPO, Mackerras.

The Rite of spring; 4 Norwegian moods.
(*) Decca Dig. **417 325-2; *417 325-4* [id.]. Cleveland O, Chailly.

The Rite of spring; Symphonies of wind instruments.
** Decca Dig. **414 202-2** [id.]. Montreal SO, Dutoit.

The days when *The Rite of spring* could be offered on a premium-priced CD without coupling are now behind us, and several recordings listed here can be counted competititve only if the interpretations are of special interest, while we have already discussed above a variety of couplings with the other major ballets, notably the composer's own recording.

Both of Karajan's DG stereo recordings are now available on CD and make a fascinating comparison. The earlier, 1966 version (now offered at mid-price, coupled with Mussorgsky's *Pictures*) came in for much snide criticism from the composer, who described one passage as being a *'tempo di hoochie-koochie'*, and doubted whether Berlin Philharmonic traditions could encompass music from so different a discipline. Yet listening to the vibrant sounds coming from the remastered CD (an exceptionally successful transfer) one cannot fully accept the composer's response. Certainly the playing of the Berlin Philharmonic is marvellously polished and civilized, yet it is not without bite or excitement, and the lack of malignancy serves to increase the feeling of symphonic strength, while the beauty of the sound created in the lyrical sections brings a potent nostalgia. Indeed for some ears this account, lacking the aggressive brutality of some versions (Solti and Muti, for instance), may be much more rewarding to live with. Nevertheless, in his 1977 version (coupled with *Apollo*), tougher, more urgent, less mannered, Karajan goes a long way towards rebutting Stravinsky's complaints, and the result is superb, perhaps more civilized than some versions; but Karajan is at his finest: persuasive still but never obtrusively so, and above all powerfully dramatic. The analogue recording has neither the bite of the Muti version nor the presence of Dorati's, but its spaciously rich sound has no lack of impact.

In terms of recorded sound, Dorati's *Rite* with the Detroit orchestra scores over almost all its rivals. This has stunning clarity and presence, exceptionally lifelike and vivid sound, and the denser textures emerge more cleanly than ever before. It is a very good performance too, almost but not quite in the same league as those of Karajan and Muti, generating plenty of excitement. The only let-down is the final *Sacrificial dance*, which needs greater abandon and higher voltage. The Detroit strings too are not as sumptuous as those of the Berlin orchestra and sound distinctly undernourished in places. Yet too much should not be made of this. Although Dorati does not match the atmosphere of his finest rivals, the performance is so vivid that it belongs among the very best – for those primarily concerned with recorded sound, it will probably be a first choice in its compact disc format. However, the most economical way to approach it is in the two-disc CD set of all three major ballets – see above.

Solti's is a powerful, unrelenting account of Stravinsky's revolutionary score, with virtuoso playing from the Chicago orchestra and recording that demonstrates with breathtaking clarity the precision of inner detail. Some of the gentler half-tones of the score are presented rather glaringly, but this view of the work is magnificently consistent, showing Solti at his most tautly dramatic. It is extremely vivid, and highly spectacular too. At mid-price this is competitive, although the couplings are rather less magnetic.

Mackerras's version is also at mid-price on the Eminence label and brings a powerful, often spacious performance, recorded in opulent and finely textured, if slightly distanced sound. The very opening with its bassoon solo finds Mackerras steadier, less volatile than most, then contrasting the introduction with an urgent, crisply detailed view of the chugging first allegro. The weight of the recording adds powerfully to the dramatic impact, though it is a pity that timpani are backward and less sharply focused than they might be. The playing of the LPO is strong and exuberant too, though not quite as crisp as it was in its earlier recording under Haitink (now also on mid-price CD, much more generously coupled with *Petrushka*). Though short measure, the three little orchestral trifles are done by Mackerras with delectable point and wit.

With speeds faster than usual – markedly so in Part Two – Chailly's taut and urgent reading brings one of Decca's sound spectaculars. The bass drum, so important in this work, leaps out with a power, precision and resonance to startle the listener. It may not be the easiest version to live with, and the fast speeds in Part Two provide less contrast than usual before the onslaught of the final *Sacrificial dance*, but anyone wanting the unpretentious little *Norwegian moods* as coupling – or, for that matter, to startle friends with the *Rite* – will be well pleased. Irritatingly, CD bands are not provided between the different sections of the *Rite*, but only for the two halves.

The sound on the Cleveland Orchestra version conducted by Lorin Maazel is also pretty spectacular. Indeed, it is superior in terms of balance to that of the Detroit version when the two CD versions are juxtaposed. However, there are a number of sensation-seeking effects such as excessive ritardandi in the *Rondes printanières* so as to exaggerate the trombone glissandi (fig. 53) which are vulgar. Compare, too, the opening of the second part in this version with that of Karajan, and one is in a totally different world.

Barenboim's version with the Orchestre de Paris brings a strongly committed performance that is warmly expressive and atmospheric rather than bitingly dramatic. That approach makes it the more apt as a coupling for the opulent Scriabin work. The recording is warm and well integrated, if slightly recessed.

Michael Tilson Thomas's reading is dramatic enough but warmly expressive too, missing some of the music's bite. The amply reverberant acoustic emphasizes his approach but, with fine playing from the Boston orchestra and the advantage of continuity, this Walkman tape is well worth considering, as it also contains Jochum's outstanding account of Orff's *Carmina Burana*, which has the composer's imprimatur.

Dutoit's Montreal CD offers sumptuous, finely detailed sound with a realistic balance and plenty of presence and body and, of course, a marvellous dynamic range. This compact disc will, no doubt, be widely demonstrated for its sonic splendours. The playing of the Montreal Symphony Orchestra is first rate in every department: the strings are rich in sonority, the wind playing flawless, and phrasing throughout is sensitive. Yet Dutoit has little of that blazing intensity which one finds in the composer's own 1960 record, while if the Dutoit account is put alongside Karajan at the opening of the *Sacrifice*, the greater atmosphere of the latter is immediately apparent. In short, this Montreal version is outstanding as a recording, but the performance falls short of the highest voltage. The fill-up, the *Symphonies of wind instruments*, the work Stravinsky composed in 1920 in memory of Debussy, is given a very effective and crisp performance by the excellent Montreal wind.

Stravinsky hailed Bernstein's earlier record of *The Rite* with the New York Philharmonic with an amazed 'Wow!' Now, a quarter of a century later, he has re-recorded the score with the Israel orchestra. Unfortunately the recording is made in a dry acoustic ambience (at the Mann Auditorium, Tel Aviv) and though there is no lack of clarity, there is a loss of atmosphere. Each strand in the texture is clearly audible and the dynamic perspective is perfectly judged, but the overall result sounds synthetic. The same criticism could be applied to the Dorati version on Decca, but there is a much livelier acoustic in which to operate. In its CD format, the clarity of Bernstein's version is quite stunning but the dryness of the acoustic is even more striking. The strings of the Israel orchestra are not in the same league as those of the NYPO nor, for that matter, are some of the wind.

The Soldier's Tale (complete).
(M) *** Nimbus Dig. **NIM 5063** [id.]. Christopher Lee, Scottish CO, Lionel Friend.

With the actor Christopher Lee both acting as narrator and taking the individual parts, the Nimbus issue brings an attractively strong and robust reading, lacking the last degree of refinement but with some superb solo playing – from the violinist, for example. The recording is vivid and full of presence, with the speaking voice related to instruments far better than is usual. For a version in English, it makes an excellent bargain.

The Soldier's tale: suite.
*** Delos Dig. **D/CD 3021** [id.]. LACO, Schwarz – PROKOFIEV; *Symphony No. 1****; SHOSTAKOVICH: *Piano concerto No. 1.***(*)

This made a splendid CD début for a work which is surprisingly little recorded. The acoustic is ideal for the music and the sound is wonderfully realistic and present. The performance makes a nice balance between pungency and the underlying lyricism; there is some splendid solo playing from Paul Shure (violin) and the superb trumpeter, Tony Plog, whose easy virtuosity and fine timbre add much to the music's appeal. Recommended, especially as the couplings are imaginative.

Suites Nos 1 and 2 for small orchestra.
*** RCA Dig. **RD 85168 [RCD1 5168]**. Dallas SO, Mata – PROKOFIEV: *Lieutenant Kijé* etc.***

Arranged by the composer from piano duets – 'Easy pieces' that are not so easy – these eight witty orchestral miniatures are a delight. They are played with marvellous finesse and point, and superbly recorded. Here the slight extra edge given by the CD is entirely apt, and the recording has presence and vividness.

Symphony in E flat, Op. 1; Symphony in C; Symphony in 3 movements; Ode (*Elegiacal chant in 3 parts*).
*** Chan. Dig. **CHAN 8345/6**; *DBTD 2004* (2). SNO, Gibson.

Even compared with the composer's own performances, this collection by the Scottish National Orchestra – in excellent form – under Sir Alexander Gibson stands up well. The vividness of the digital recording makes up for any slight lack of sparkle, and while the *Symphonies for wind instruments* might have seemed a more obvious makeweight for the three major works, it is good to have the *Ode* in memory of Natalia Koussevitzky, which has an extrovert, rustic scherzo section framed by short elegies. On CD, the bloom on the instruments in the amply atmospheric Glasgow acoustic is the more realistically caught. The sound is first class, with the reverberation rarely if ever obscuring detail. The cassettes are of generally good quality but use iron-oxide stock, and on side four (in the *Symphony in three movements*) the upper woodwind partials are not as clean as on CD. The accompanying leaflet, too, is poorly produced.

Symphony in E flat, Op. 1; Scherzo fantastique, Op. 3.
*** Decca Dig. **414 456-2**; *414 456-4* [id.]. Detroit SO, Dorati.

Stravinsky composed his *Symphony in E flat* in his early twenties (1905–7), and it was first performed by the St Petersburg Court Orchestra (which became the Leningrad Philharmonic). Ansermet conducted a revised version of it in 1914, after which it languished in obscurity until Stravinsky himself recorded it in the 1960s. It is written in the received post-nationalist tradition and has rarely been better served on record than it is here. It has an appropriate and attractive makeweight in the form of the *Scherzo fantastique*. Dorati gets an excellent response from the Detroit Symphony Orchestra and the Decca recording is in the high traditions of the house. The cassette transfer is also admirably managed.

Symphony in C; Symphony in 3 movements.
*** Decca Dig. **414 272-3** [id.]. SRO, Dutoit.
** DG Dig. **415 128-2** [id.]. Israel PO, Bernstein.
*(*) Ph. Dig. **416 985-2**; *416 985-4* [id.]. Bav. RSO, C. Davis.

Although the Suisse Romande Orchestra is not in the very first rank, it is in much better shape than when it last recorded these symphonies in the 1960s for Ansermet. The brilliant recording it now receives from the Decca team and the alert direction of Charles Dutoit make this a very winning coupling. These are both exhilarating pieces and Dutoit punches home their virile high spirits and clean-limbed athleticism. The sound is first class, even if the woodwind may strike one at times as just a shade forward. No matter, this is a splendid issue and unlikely to be superseded for a while. The fullness of the Geneva recording (made in the Victoria Hall) is the more impressive on CD, when the bass register is so firmly and cleanly caught, and the spaciousness of the acoustic brings clarity without aggressiveness.

While they may not be the last word in elegance and finish, Bernstein's performances have spirit. The orchestra is in good form and in the *Symphony in three movements* they play with freshness and immediacy. Although both performances have plenty of character, that of the *Symphony in C* is lightweight and at times (in the first movement particularly) there is the air of the ballet theatre, which also emerges in the lighter sections of the companion piece. Those who regard these as essentially sharp-edged works may find the orchestra's rhythmic attack not biting enough, particularly when Bernstein's speeds are often relatively slow. The recorded sound is not top-drawer, but at least it is present and vivid. But the Tel Aviv acoustic is dry and unflattering alongside Decca's Dutoit coupling, and this is still the version to have.

Davis's version of both works is a heavyweight one, inappropriately Germanic in its middle-aged spread, disappointingly lacking in the point and bite of his earlier Stravinsky records, and not helped by well-upholstered recording in both media.

CHAMBER AND INSTRUMENTAL MUSIC

Divertimento (from Le baiser de la fée); Duo concertante; Suite italienne.
*** CBS Dig. **MK 42101**; *IMT 42101* [id.]. Cho-Liang Lin, André-Michel Schub.
** HMV **CDC7 49322-2** [id.]. Itzhak Perlman, Bruno Canino.

The *Italian suite* was arranged from the Pergolesi-based ballet, *Pulcinella*, while the *Duo concertante* was written after the *Violin concerto* and for the same artist, Samuel Dushkin. The *Divertimento* is arranged from movements of the Tchaikovsky-derived ballet, *The fairy's kiss*. A special point of interest about the CBS record is that Cho-Liang Lin plays on the Stradivarius once owned by the dedicatee. Stravinsky toured with Dushkin in the early 1930s, including the *Suite italienne* and the *Divertimento* in his concert programmes. (He recorded not only the *Violin concerto* but the *Duo concertante* for Columbia with him.) Cho-Liang Lin's performance radiates rhythmic vitality and he plays with impeccable intonation and panache. Indeed he seems to capture something of the style of Dushkin's own playing and is expertly partnered by André-Michel Schub. A most stimulating issue, well served by the truthful CBS recording. There is an excellent tape.

Needless to say, Perlman also plays all this music with warmth and understanding, and his achievement in the *Duo concertante*, which has often seemed a dry work, is particularly remarkable. Bruno Canino makes a sympathetic partner and the 1976 recording, originally excellent, has been clearly and cleanly transferred to CD, the sound more strongly etched than the softer focus of the CBS recording.

Suite italienne.
*** BIS Dig. **CD 336** [id.]. Thorleif Thedeen, Roland Pöntinen – SCHNITTKE: *Sonata*; SHOSTAKOVICH: *Sonata*.***
** Denon Dig. **C37 7563** [id.]. Fujiwara, Rouvier – DEBUSSY: *Cello sonata*; SHOSTAKOVICH: *Cello sonata*.**

Stravinsky made several transcriptions of movements from *Pulcinella*, including the *Suite italienne* for violin and piano. This was arranged in 1932 with the aid of Piatigorsky and, with the exception of the first movement which is a little too sober, Mari Fujiwara and Jacques Rouvier give a very characterful account of these engaging pieces. However, the performances by Thorleif Thedeen and Roland Pöntinen, Swedish artists both in their mid-twenties, are even more felicitous and spontaneous, and they are afforded strikingly natural recording.

PIANO MUSIC

Concerto for 2 solo pianos; Petrushka (ballet): arr. for 2 pianos.
*** Ph. Dig. **420 822-2** [id.]. Katia and Marielle Labèque.

Although there have been a number of memorable versions of the *Petrushka* transcription for one piano by Pollini, Gilels, Béroff and others, there is none of the version for two pianos (made by Victor Babin). It is marvellously exhilarating in the hands of the Labèque sisters and, like the *Concerto for two pianos* of 1935, sounds brilliant and lifelike in the acoustic of The Maltings at Snape. The latter work with its self-conscious neoclassicism is very much in sparkling monochrome, as opposed to the vivid, brittle, kaleidoscopic colours of the *Petrushka* arrangement. Marvellous playing and recording – though with a playing time of just over a half an hour, this is very short measure indeed.

3 Movements from Petrushka; Piano rag music; Serenade in A; Sonata; Tango.
*(**) Tel. **ZK8 43417** [id.]. Dezsö Ránki – BARTÓK: *Suite; Out of doors*.*(**)

3 Movements from Petrushka.
*** DG **419 202-2** [id.]. Maurizio Pollini – *Recital*.***
(M) * Pickwick Dig. **PCD 818**. Geoffrey Saba – MUSSORGSKY: *Pictures*.*(*)

The piano plays a relatively peripheral role in Stravinsky's output: the *Capriccio*, the *Concerto for piano and wind*, and the late *Movements* are the only works where it takes on a solo role, and this Teldec disc comprises all his music for solo piano except the early *Sonata* and the Op. 7 *Studies*. Ránki recorded this recital in 1979 in a rather dry studio that may not be wholly inappropriate to Stravinsky's music. (Stravinsky's own pioneering record of his *Capriccio* was even drier than this.) However, it does Ránki less than full justice and prevents his normally wide dynamic range making its full effect. The CD transfer is more present and makes one even more aware of the acoustic. The playing is excellent, but the recording is a serious handicap.

Staggering, electrifying playing from Pollini, creating the highest degree of excitement. This is part of an outstandingly generous recital of twentieth-century piano music.

Geoffrey Saba is eccentrically wayward and the *Shrove-tide fair* sequence is rhythmically laboured. He is well recorded, but this is not competitive.

VOCAL MUSIC

(i) *Mass;* (ii) *Les Noces.*

*** DG **423 251-2** [id.]. (i) Trinity Boys' Ch., E. Bach Fest. O; (i; ii) E. Bach Fest. Ch.; (ii) Mory, Parker, Mitchinson, Hudson; Argerich, Zimerman, Katsaris, Francesch (pianos), percussion; cond. Bernstein.

Bernstein directs characterful performances of both works, unexpectedly but imaginatively coupled. He reinforces the point that both the *Mass* and the much earlier ballet illustrating a folk wedding ceremony are intensely Russian in their inspiration. In the *Mass* the style is overtly expressive, with the boys of Trinity Choir responding freshly, but it is in *Les Noces* that Bernstein conveys an electricity and a dramatic urgency which at last on record give the work its rightful stature as one of Stravinsky's supreme masterpieces, totally original and even today unexpected, not least in its black-and-white instrumentation for four pianos and percussion. The star pianists here make a superb, imaginative team. Good atmospheric recording effectively transferred to CD.

Le Roi des étoiles (*The King of stars*); *Symphony of Psalms.*

** Decca Dig. **414 078-2** [id.]. Berlin R. Ch. & SO, Chailly – *Le Chant du rossignol; Fireworks.***

Symphony of Psalms.

*(*) Telarc Dig. **CD 80105** [id.]. Atlanta Ch. & SO, Shaw – POULENC: *Gloria.**(*)

The Decca recording is first class, but the ambience of the Jesus-Christus Church in West Berlin emphasizes the expressive lyricism of Chailly's approach; although the *Laudate Dominum* has a spectacular dynamic expansion, overall this performance is soft-centred. The inclusion by Chailly of the short but dramatic motet *Le Roi des étoiles* is most welcome; this piece has greater intensity. The Decca CD is very impressive as sound.

Like the Poulenc on the reverse, Robert Shaw's Atlanta version is well disciplined and brilliantly recorded, but it misses the energetic bite and sharpness of focus so necessary in this work, before it finds its resolution at the end in heavenly *Alleluias.*

Oedipus Rex (opera/oratorio).

*** Orfeo Dig. *M 071831A* [id.]. Moser, Norman, Nimsgern, Bracht, Piccoli (nar.), Bav. R. Male Ch. & SO, C. Davis.

Recorded live in Munich in 1983, Davis's Orfeo performance is unerringly paced, with rhythms crisply sprung and detail finely touched in. Though the low-level sound is no help, the orchestral playing is first rate, and the cast is excellent, with Jessye Norman a commanding figure as Jocasta, firm and dramatic, making one wish the role was longer. Thomas Moser is both expressive and cleanly faithful to Stravinsky, and it is only partially his fault that the culminating moment of *Lux facta est* is rather understated. Michel Piccoli as narrator uses the original Cocteau text in French with fine dramatic emphasis. All in all, this is the most satisfactory recording available of Stravinsky's opera/oratorio, and we hope it will soon find its way on to CD.

The Rake's progress (complete).
(*) Decca Dig. **411 644-2 (2) [id.]. Langridge, Pope, Walker, Ramey, Dean, Dobson, L. Sinf. Ch. & O, Chailly.

Riccardo Chailly draws from the London Sinfonietta playing of a clarity and brightness to set the piece aptly on a chamber scale without reducing the power of this elaborately neoclassical piece, so cunningly based on Mozartian models by the librettists, W. H. Auden and Chester Kallman. Philip Langridge is excellent as the Rake himself, very moving when Tom is afflicted with madness. Samuel Ramey as Nick, Stafford Dean as Trulove and Sarah Walker as Baba the Turk are all first rate, but Cathryn Pope's soprano as recorded is too soft-grained for Anne. Charming as the idea is of getting the veteran Astrid Varnay to sing Mother Goose, the result is out of style. The recording is exceptionally full and vivid but the balances are sometimes odd: the orchestra recedes behind the singers and the chorus sounds congested, with little air round the sound. As an interpretation, the composer's own version is more subtly varied and therefore more dramatic, and this is no doubt earmarked for CD before too long.

Suk, Josef (1874–1935)

Asrael symphony, Op. 27.
*** Sup. Dig. **C37 7404** [id.]. Czech PO, Neumann.

It is astonishing that a work of this stature has been so neglected outside Czechoslovakia. Only a few months after the first performance of his *G minor Fantasy* in 1904, Suk suffered a double bereavement: first, the death of Dvořák the same year, quickly followed by that of his wife, Dvořák's daughter, Otilia. Suk poured all his grief into this *Symphony*, which is a work of rare vision and compelling power. In its organization it owes a good deal to the 'cyclic' principle fashionable at the end of the last century. A sense of numbness in the face of grief comes across, yet there is much that is fiery, vigorous and exciting. Asrael is the Angel of Death – hence the title – and touches real depths; but it is more than a moving human document, it is a great work. The predominant influences, apart from his countrymen, are Liszt and, above all in the Scherzo, Mahler. The performance is a very fine one; though those who have Vaclav Talich's classic account will surely never part with it, this is its first recording for almost thirty years and a must for all serious collectors.

A Fairy-tale, Op. 16; Praga (symphonic poem), Op. 26.
*** Sup. Dig. **C37 7509** [id.]. Czech PO, Libor Pešek.

Suk's *A Fairy-tale* is a concert suite drawn from the incidental music to Julius Zeyer's fairy-tale drama, *Raduz and Nahulena.* The music comes from 1898 and tells of a prince and princess, subject to all sorts of trials; it must have appealed to the young composer then poised on the brink of marriage. The invention is full of charm and originality, and is persuasively played here. On this compact disc it is coupled with *Praga* (1904), a patriotic tone-poem reflecting a more public, out-going figure than *Asrael*, which was to follow it. Libor Pešek secures an excellent response from the Czech Philharmonic; the recordings, which date from 1981–2, are reverberant but good.

(i) *Fantasy in G min. for violin and orchestra, Op. 24; Symphony in E, Op. 14.*
*** Sup. Dig. **C37 7540** [id.]. Czech PO, Neumann; (i) with Josef Suk.

A well-filled record (the *Symphony* takes 46′ 06″ and the *Fantasy* 22′ 30″). The *Symphony in E major* comes from 1898 when Suk was in his mid-twenties, and he took great trouble over its composition. For the third movement, for instance, he wrote no fewer than three Scherzos before deciding on this one – all one can say is that he made a splendid choice. He likewise rejected his first thoughts for the second movement in favour of the present *Adagio*. The *Symphony* sounds marvellously fresh; though much of it is Dvořákian in outward appearance, there is much that one recognizes from Suk's maturity. This is a delightfully inventive and astonishingly accomplished *Symphony* that will captivate all who enjoy Dvořák, who became his father-in-law during the latter stages of its composition. The *G minor Fantasy*, Op. 24, was first performed in 1904; Josef Suk first recorded it for Supraphon way back in the late 1960s, and this is a worthy successor. It is an ardent, life-loving work – a kind of one-movement concerto, full of imaginative ideas and variety of invention. Suk is rather forwardly placed, but the somewhat reverberant recording is generally well balanced and the performance is very good indeed.

Serenade for strings, Op. 6.
*** ASV *ZCALH 969* [id.]. RCO of Poland, Duczmal – TCHAIKOVSKY: *Serenade*.***

Suk's *Serenade* is a gorgeous work and it receives a lovely performance from the Polish Radio Chamber Orchestra under Agnieszka Duczmal. The opening is immediately winning, light and gracious, yet the orchestra can produce a rich body of timbre when needed. The *Adagio* is very beautifully played indeed; it follows Suk's unusual *Allegro ma non troppo e grazioso*, which is nearly a waltz but not quite. The orchestra's sparkling articulation and subtle rhythmic feeling here are most distinctive. This is altogether first rate; and the recording is full textured and well balanced, bringing out Duczmal's many fine shadings of colour.

Serenade for strings in E flat, Op. 6; (i) *Under the apple tree, Op. 20.*
(*) Sup. **33CO 1372. (i) Eva Depoltova; Czech PO, Libor Pešek.

Libor Pešek gives an unhurried and dignified reading of the *Serenade*, far more leisurely than the Duczmal version listed above, though, as in so many recordings made in the House of Artists, the sound is a bit top-heavy. Suk's suite, *Under the apple tree*, written a few years later, is a charming work indebted to Dvořák and the Czech nationalists, but with a distinctive feel to it. It is very well performed and the recording, though not in the demonstration class, is well balanced.

Elegy, Op. 23.
(*) Sup. Dig. **C37 7057 [id.]. Suk Trio – DVOŘÁK: *Piano trio No. 4*.**(*)

Suk's *Elegy* comes from the turn of the century, begun in 1899 and finished the following year. It is a fine piece with a particularly impassioned middle section. The performance is by Josef Suk, the composer's grandson (and Dvořák's great-grandson), and his distinguished partners, Jan Panenka and Josef Chuchro, and could hardly be more authoritative or persuasive.

Sullivan, Arthur (1842–1900)

Cello concerto (reconstructed Mackerras and Mackie).
*** HMV Dig. **CDC7 47622-2** [id.]; *EL 270430-4*. Julian Lloyd Webber, LSO, Mackerras – HERBERT: *Concerto No. 2*; ELGAR: *Romance*.***

Sullivan's *Cello concerto* is a curiosity. Written when he was nineteen, soon after he returned from study in Leipzig, it had an initial success but, unpublished, was then neglected for the rest of the composer's life. It was given solitary performances in 1910 and 1953; but then in 1964 the one surviving score was destroyed in the fire at Chappell's publishing house. Thanks to Sir Charles Mackerras and the Sullivan scholar, David Mackie, it has been reconstructed with the help of the solo cello part. Sadly, the end result hardly justifies such labours. Curiously proportioned, with the first movement too brief for any symphonic pretensions and with themes less memorable than those Sullivan was going to write in the operettas, it is a lightweight divertissement, pleasant but undistinguished. Julian Lloyd Webber and Sir Charles, very well recorded, do all they can to give the flimsy inspiration some bite. There is an acceptable cassette, but the sound is rather over-resonant in the bass.

Overtures: *Di Ballo; The Gondoliers; HMS Pinafore; Iolanthe; Patience; The Pirates of Penzance; Princess Ida; Ruddigore; The Sorcerer; The Yeomen of the Guard* (all arr. Geoffrey Toye).
(M) *** Nimbus Dig. **NIM 5066** [id.]. SCO, Alexander Faris.

A well-played and well-recorded collection of Sullivan overtures. Mostly they are little more than pot-pourris, but *The Yeoman of the Guard* is an exception, and the gay *Di Ballo* is vivacious and tuneful and shows Sullivan's scoring at its most felicitous.

Pineapple Poll (ballet music, arr. Mackerras).
*** Ara. **Z 8016** [id.]. RPO, Mackerras.

Pineapple Poll; Overture: Di Ballo.
*** Decca Dig. *KSXDC 7619*. Philh. O, Mackerras.

The new Decca digital recording of *Pineapple Poll* was made in the Kingsway Hall, and its glowing ambience casts a pleasing bloom over the spirited and elegantly polished playing of the Philharmonia Orchestra. Mackerras conducts with great warmth and finds space for a delightful performance of *Di Ballo*, showing a fine delicacy of approach. The chrome cassette is first class. We look forward to a CD version in due course.

Mackerras's earlier record is not entirely superseded. Considered definitive in its day (1962), it is still striking for its sheer brio. The RPO is in excellent form and the HMV recording still sounds extremely well; the playing has a real feeling of the ballet theatre, even if the later version gains in breadth and atmosphere. As can be seen, the enterprising Arabesque company have made a CD of this earlier account for the American market and this is available in the UK as an import. The transfer is remarkably successful. Most of the background noise has been vanquished and the bright, vivid sound suits the music, while in the lyrical sections (*Poll's solo* and *Jasper's solo*, scene ii) the strings retain their body. However, the fortissimos have a degree of hardness on top, the string sound is tighter and there is a touch of shrillness at times, though not beyond control. This makes an excellent stopgap until the Decca recording arrives on CD.

Songs: *The absent-minded beggar; The Dove song; Gone!; Let me dream again; The lost chord; The Marquis de Mincepie; Mary Morison; The moon in silent brightness; Shakespeare songs: O mistress mine; Orpheus with his lute; Willow song; St Agnes' Eve; Sweethearts; What does the little birdie say?; Winter.*
*** Conifer Dig. **CDCFC 156**; *MCFC 156* [id.]. Jeanne Ommerle, Sanford Sylvan, Gary Wedow.

It has taken a pair of American singers (with a pianist who is also chorus master of the Sante Fe Opera) to discover the delights of these Sullivan songs and bring them to our attention in an admirably planned recital which offers singing to catch their style superbly. The ballads have all the melodic resource of the Savoy Operas and the duet *Sweethearts* could almost have come from *Patience*, although it has an appropriate link with Victor Herbert in its added sentimentality. The Shakespeare settings are memorable, particularly the unexpected soaring line of *Orpheus with his lute*, though the gentle *Willow song* is equally lovely. *The Marquis de Mincepie* comes from a forgotten 'drawing-room extravaganza' that Sullivan wrote in collaboration with F. C. Burnand (the librettist of *Cox and Box*) and its humour is concerned with the possible indigestion of over-indulgence. *Mary Morison* is a fine Burns setting (delightfully sung by Sanford Sylvan, although his transatlantic pronunciation of the name strikes the ear strangely) and *The Dove song* is a charming polka written for a Christmas pantomime. *What does the little birdie say?* is a children's lullaby, while the splendid Kipling narrative of *The absent-minded beggar* reminds one of the repertoire Peter Dawson made famous. Jeanne Ommerle sings with full involvement with the words and her voice gives consistent pleasure in her simplicity of line and tonal beauty. Sanford Sylvan is very good, too, and, after opening restraint in *The lost chord*, then builds a resplendent climax, aided and abetted by spectacular accompaniment from the pianist, Gary Wedow; one understands how the Victorians could be bowled over by the sheer eloquence of the piece. Elsewhere the reverberant acoustic of the recording is less than ideal, but the words come over clearly (on tape as well as disc) and certainly there is plenty of bloom on the voices. A most involving and entertaining collection without one dull number.

OPERAS

As can be seen below, both Decca and – more particularly – EMI have been regrouping their major Gilbert and Sullivan recordings to make them attractively economical in their CD layout. On cassette their reissue in pairs by EMI (and in one case a trio) puts them into the bargain category, with the snag that they are no longer available singly in this format. The distinction of both the Godfrey/D'Oyly Carte series and the rather different and more operatic Sargent recordings means that newer competition (linked to current live performances) can seldom match the earlier versions in panache and style, to say nothing of overall polish.

(i) *Cox and Box* (libretto by F. C. Burnand) complete; (ii) *Ruddigore* (complete, without dialogue).
(M) *** Decca *417 355-4* (2). (i) Styler, Riordan, Adams; New SO of L.; (ii) J. Reed, Round, Sandford, Riley, Adams, Hindmarsh, Knight, Sansom, Allister, D'Oyly Carte Op. Ch., ROHCGO, Godfrey.

Cox and Box is a superb performance in every way. It is given a recording which without sacrificing clarity conveys with perfect balance the stage atmosphere. Those who feel that Sullivan's genius could operate only with the catalyst of Gilbert's words will be surprised to find here that the music is almost as delightful as any written for Gilbert. In fact *Cox and Box* has words by F. C. Burnand and is based very closely on Maddison Morton's farce *Box and Cox*. It was written in 1867 and thus pre-dates the first G & S success, *Trial by Jury*, by eight years. One must notice the lively military song *Rataplan* – splendidly sung by Donald Adams, an ideal Bouncer – which was to set the style for many similar and later pieces with words by Gilbert, and also the captivating *Bacon 'Lullaby'*, so ravishingly sung by Joseph Riordan. Later on, in Box's recitative telling how he 'committed suicide', Sullivan makes one of his first and most impressive parodies of grand opera, which succeeds also in being effective in its own right.

Ruddigore, too, comes up surprisingly freshly. It was a pity the dialogue was omitted; in the famous Act II duet for the reformed Mad Margaret and Sir Despard, the scene is incomplete without the delightful spoken interchange about Basingstoke. The performance includes *The battle's roar is over*, which is (for whatever reason) traditionally omitted. There is much to enjoy here (especially Gillian Knight and Donald Adams, whose *Ghosts' high noon* song is a marvellous highlight). Godfrey is his inimitable, sprightly self and the chorus and orchestra are excellent. A fine traditional D'Oyly Carte set, then, brightly recorded, even if in this instance the Sargent version is generally even finer.

The Gondoliers (complete, with dialogue).
*(**) Decca **417 254-2**; *417 254-4* (2) [id.]. Reed, Skitch, Sandford, Round, Styler, Knight, Toye, Sansom, Wright, D'Oyly Carte Op. Ch., New SO of L., Godfrey.

One welcomes back *The Gondoliers* to the catalogue, especially as it is now complete on two CDs and tapes, whereas previously it needed a third. Isidore Godfrey's conducting is vividly alive. Decca provided a large and excellent orchestra. The solo singing throughout is consistently good. Jeffrey Skitch and Jennifer Toye are a well-matched pair of lovers, and the two Gondoliers and their wives are no less effective. Thomas Round sings *Take a pair of sparkling eyes* very well indeed. The ensemble singing is very well balanced and always both lively and musical. The *Cachucha* is captivating and goes at a sparkling pace. Everywhere one can feel the conductor's guiding hand. The dialogue is for the most part well spoken, and Kenneth Sandford, who is a rather light-voiced Don Alhambra, makes much of his spoken part, as well as singing his songs with fine style. John Reed is a suitably dry Duke of Plaza-Toro: he makes the part his own and is well partnered by Gillian Knight. The snag lies in the digitally remastered recording which has been miscalculated – the treble is fierce, making the strings edgy and the female voices peaky.

The Gondoliers (complete, without dialogue).
(*) HMV **CDS7 47775-8 [Ang. **CDCB 47775**] (2). Evans, Young, Brannigan, Lewis, Cameron, Milligan, M. Sinclair, Graham, Morison, Thomas, Watts, Glyndebourne Fest. Ch., Pro Arte O, Sargent.

(i) *The Gondoliers;* (ii) *The Mikado;* (iii) *Trial by Jury.*
(B) **(*) HMV *EX 749696-4* (3). (i) Young, Watts, Graham, Milligan; (i; ii) Evans, Thomas, M. Sinclair; (ii) Wallace, J. Sinclair; (iii) G. Baker; (i; ii; iii) Brannigan, Lewis, Cameron, Morison, Glyndebourne Fest. Ch., Pro Arte O, Sargent.

The snag to the Sargent set of *The Gondoliers* is the curiously slow tempo he chooses for the *Cachucha*, while the long opening scene is rather relaxed and leisurely. At the entrance of the Duke of Plaza-Toro things wake up considerably and, early in the opera, Owen Brannigan as a perfectly cast Don Alhambra sings a masterly *No possible doubt whatever*. From then on and throughout the rest of the opera, there is much to captivate the ear. Edna Graham's Casilda is charmingly small-voiced (by the same token, Elsie Morison is a little heavy in her song, *Kind sir, you cannot have the heart*). But there is a great deal of musical pleasure to be had from this set. It is very well transferred to CD. The age of the 1957 recording shows in the orchestra, but the voices sound fresh, and there is a pleasing overall bloom – sonically this is far preferable to the Decca D'Oyly Carte version.

The chrome tapes are smoothly transferred and offer excellent sound in their own right, more readily disguising the recording date. The drawback is that the layout does not place one opera complete on each of the three cassettes. *The Mikado* comes first, occupying 2½ sides; *The Gondoliers* commences in the middle of side 3, with Act I concluding at the end of side 4. Act II is on side 5 and *Trial by Jury* complete on side 6. The three cassettes are offered in a slimline box at a very reasonable price, with an overall playing time of 3 hours 41 minutes. *The Mikado* and *Trial by Jury* are discussed below, in their CD formats.

(i) *The Grand Duke;* (ii) *The Zoo* (libretto by Bolton Rowe).
*** Decca *417 342-4* (2). M. Reed, Sandford, Ayldon, Goss, Metcalfe; (i) John Reed, Rayner, Ellison, Lilley; (ii) nar. Geoffrey Shovelton; D'Oyly Carte Op. Ch., RPO, Nash.

The Grand Duke was the fourteenth and last of the Savoy operas. In spite of a spectacular production and a brilliant first night on 7 March 1896, the work played for only 123 performances and then lapsed into relative oblivion, although it has been revived by amateur societies. The present recording came after a successful concert presentation in 1975, and the recorded performance, which has both polish and vigour, represents perhaps the ideal way to sample Sullivan's least-known major score. Less than first-rate Sullivan can still make rewarding listening, even though, compared with the sparkle and melodic inspiration of *HMS Pinafore*, the music shows a sad decline. Gilbert's libretto is impossibly complicated, but there are many felicities in the lyrics to reward the dedicated enthusiast. The recording is characteristically brilliant.

The Zoo (with a libretto by Bolton Rowe, a pseudonym of B. C. Stevenson) dates from June 1875, only three months after the success of *Trial by Jury*, which it obviously seeks to imitate, as the music more than once reminds us. With some initial success the piece was restaged in 1879, but after eighteen performances was withdrawn. Unpublished, the score lay neglected for nearly a century in the vaults of a London bank. This recorded performance is the first to be associated with the D'Oyly Carte Company. Although the libretto lacks the finesse and whimsicality of Gilbert, it is not without humour, and many of the situations presented by the plot (and indeed the actual combinations of words and music) are typical of the later Savoy Operas. Thomas Brown (the disguised Duke of Islington) has a charmingly pompous number, *Ladies and gentlemen*, in which he addresses the crowd and requires their good-humoured prompting in the presentation of his speech; and Eliza's song *I'm a simple little child* catches the metre and style of the Victorian music hall. The musical invention itself is often delightful and shows Sullivan's characteristic craftsmanship. The two couples are given a fetching double-duet, with a romantic melody and a patter song ingeniously combined. The plot contains reminders of Offenbach's *La Périchole*, which at the time of the first production of *The Zoo* was playing at another theatre in London, in harness with *Trial by Jury*. As the piece has no spoken dialogue it is provided here with a stylized narration, well enough presented by Geoffrey Shovelton. A recording of the animals at London Zoo sets the scene fairly effectively, but the return of the animal noises at the end is an unnecessary intrusion. The performance, however, is first class, splendidly sung, fresh as paint, and admirably recorded, with a natural and lively tape transfer.

HMS Pinafore (complete, with dialogue).

❀ *** Decca *414 283-4* (2) [*OSA5-1209*]. J. Reed, Skitch, Round, Adams, Hindmarsh, Wright, Knight, D'Oyly Carte Op. Ch., New SO of L., Godfrey.

There is a marvellous spontaneity about the invention in *Pinafore* and somehow the music has a genuine briny quality. It would be difficult to imagine a better-recorded performance than the 1960 Decca D'Oyly Carte set. It is complete with dialogue, and here it is vital in establishing the character of Dick Deadeye, since much of his part is spoken rather than sung. Donald Adams is a totally memorable Deadeye and his larger-than-life personality underpins the whole piece. Among the others, Jeffrey Skitch is a first-class Captain; Jean Hindmarsh is absolutely convincing as Josephine (it was a pity she stayed with the company for so short a time), and she sings with great charm. Thomas Round is equally good as Ralph Rackstraw. Little Buttercup could be slightly more colourful, but this is a small blemish; among the minor parts, George Cook is a most personable Bill Bobstay. The choral singing is excellent, the orchestral playing good and Isidore Godfrey conducts with marvellous spirit and lift. The recording has splendid atmosphere and its vintage qualities are very apparent in this remastered form. The sound is bright and open, words are clear and the ambience is splendidly calculated. The tapes (two of them, packed in a double-width hinged library box) use only iron-oxide stock and, though the transfers are good, the relatively modest level means that the upper range is slightly attenuated. We hope this is scheduled for CD issue soon.

HMS Pinafore (complete, without dialogue).
*** That's Entertainment Dig. **CDTER2 1150** [id.]. Grace, Sandison, Ormiston, Ritchie, Roebuck, Gillett, Lawlor, Parfitt, Thomson, New Sadler's Wells Ch. & O, Phipps.

The digital recording of the recent new Sadler's Wells Opera production has a splendid theatrical atmosphere. It is consistently well cast, with Linda Ormiston a particularly characterful Buttercup and Nickolas Grace making an appropriately aristocratic Sir Joseph Porter. The lovers sing well together and the briny choral numbers of Act I have plenty of zest. Simon Phipps paces the music fluently, if without quite the unerring timing of Godfrey, and this is very enjoyable from first to last. Alongside the classic Godfrey set, however, the characterization is just that bit less sharp; if you want a fine modern recording, this new one is very entertaining; but the D'Oyly Carte set under Godfrey remains a clear first choice on tape, and the Sargent version on CD. Both offer a surer sense of style and are also considerably more polished. Three different endings are offered (separately banded so that listeners can choose their own).

HMS Pinafore (complete, without dialogue); *Trial by Jury*.
*** HMV **CDS7 47798-8** (2). G. Baker, Cameron, Lewis, Brannigan, Milligan, Morison, Thomas, M. Sinclair, Glyndebourne Fest. Ch., Pro Arte O, Sargent.

(i) *HMS Pinafore;* (ii) *The Yeomen of the Guard* (both without dialogue).
(B) *** HMV EX *749594-4* (2). (i) G. Baker, Milligan; (ii) Dowling, Carol Case, Young, Evans; (i; ii) Lewis, Morison, Thomas, Brannigan, Cameron, M. Sinclair, Glyndebourne Fest. Ch., Pro Arte O, Sargent.

It is to Owen Brannigan's great credit that, little as he had to do here, without the dialogue, he conveyed the force of Deadeye's personality so strongly. For those who find the dialogue tedious in repetition this is a very happy set, offering some good solo singing and consistently lovely ensemble singing and chorus work. The whole of the final scene is musically quite ravishing, and throughout if Sir Malcolm fails to find quite all the wit in the music he is never less than lively. George Baker is of course splendid as Sir Joseph, and John Cameron, Richard Lewis and (especially) Monica Sinclair, as Buttercup, make much of their songs. Elsie Morison is rather disappointing; she spoils the end of her lovely song in Act I by singing sharp. However, she brings plenty of drama to her *Scena* in Act II. The male trio near the end of Act I is outstandingly well sung – full of brio and personality. The coupling with *Trial by Jury* makes this a fine bargain. The recording is bright and lively and does not lack atmosphere. For the cassette issue the coupling is with *The Yeomen of the Guard*. The chrome tapes produce excellent quality, but the layout means that the second opera begins with its overture at the end of side 2 and with Act I opening on side 3.

Iolanthe (complete, with dialogue).
(M) *** Decca *414 145-4* (2) [id.]. Sansom, J. Reed, Adams, Round, Sandford, Styler, Knight, Newman, D'Oyly Carte Op. Ch., Grenadier Guards Band, New SO, Godfrey.

This was the first (1960) stereo *Iolanthe*, not the later and generally inferior remake under Nash. Even though Decca's budget had not yet stretched to the Royal Philharmonic Orchestra, the production was given added panache by introducing the Grenadier Guards Band into the *March of the Peers*, with spectacular effect. The only real gain in the later version was that John Reed had refined his portrayal of the Lord Chancellor, but here the characterization is wittily immediate, and the famous *Nightmare song* undoubtedly has greater freshness. (There is still a hint that its virtuosity is not surmounted without considerable concentration.) Mary Sansom is a convincing Phyllis, and if her singing has not the sense of style Elsie Morison brings to the

Sargent HMV set, she is marvellous with the dialogue. Her discourse with the two Earls – portrayed to perfection by Donald Adams and Thomas Round – at the beginning of side 4 is sheer delight. Alan Styler makes a vivid personal identification with the role of Strephon. To create a convincing portrayal of an Arcadian shepherd is no mean feat in itself, but the individuality of Styler's vocal personality and inflexions is curiously appropriate to this role. Iolanthe's final aria (sung by Yvonne Newman) is a shade disappointing: it is a lovely song and it needs a ravishing, melancholy timbre, whereas here the voice does not sound quite secure. But this is a minor lapse in a first-rate achievement. The chorus is excellent, and the orchestral detail has the usual light Godfrey touch. Indeed, his spirited direction keeps the whole cast on their toes, and the engaging Act I finale (with both composer and librettist at their most inspired) is wonderfully infectious. The remastering is very successful, the sound bright but with an admirable acoustic ambience which allows every word to project clearly.

(i) *Iolanthe* (complete, without dialogue); (ii) *Overture Di ballo*.

*** HMV **CDC7 47831-8** [Ang. **CDCB 47831**] (2). (i) G. Baker, Wallace, Young, Brannigan, Cameron, M. Sinclair, Thomas, Cantelo, Harper, Morison, Glyndebourne Fest. Ch., Pro Arte O, Sargent; (ii) Royal Liverpool PO, Groves.

(i) *Iolanthe;* (ii) *Patience* (without dialogue).

(B) *** HMV *EX 749597-4* (2). (i) Wallace, Brannigan, Cantelo; (i; ii) Morison, G. Baker, Young, Cameron, M. Sinclair, Thomas, Harper; (ii) Harwood; Glyndebourne Fest. Ch., Pro Arte O, Sargent.

There is much to praise in this HMV set, and EMI have refurbished the recording very successfully; it suits the studio-based performance and projects the music brightly without loss of inner warmth. The climax of Act I, the scene of the Queen of the Fairies' curse on members of both Houses of Parliament, shows most excitingly what can be achieved with the 'full operatic treatment': this is a dramatic moment indeed. George Baker too is very good as the Lord Chancellor; his voice is fuller and more baritonal than the dry monotone we are used to from John Reed, yet he provides an equally individual characterization. For some listeners John Cameron's dark timbre may not readily evoke an Arcadian Shepherd, although he sings stylishly. Nevertheless there is much to enjoy. The two Earls and Private Willis are excellent, the famous *Nightmare song* is very well and clearly sung, and all of Act II (except perhaps Iolanthe's recitative and ballad near the end) goes very well. The famous *Trio* with the Lord Chancellor and the two Earls is a joy. The opening scene of Act I is effectively atmospheric, with Monica Sinclair a splendid Fairy Queen. The *Di ballo overture* acts as an attractive encore at the end of the opera. The chrome tapes offer very good sound, smooth and full yet not lacking presence. However, the layout places *Iolanthe* on 2½ sides so that *Patience* begins in the middle of side 3.

The Mikado (complete, without dialogue).

*** Decca **417 296-2** (2) [id.]. Ayldon, Wright, J. Reed, Sandford, Masterson, Holland, D'Oyly Carte Op. Ch., RPO, Nash.

(*) HMV **CDS7 47773-8 (2). Brannigan, Lewis, Evans, Wallace, Cameron, Morison, Thomas, J. Sinclair, M. Sinclair, Glyndebourne Fest. Ch., Pro Arte O, Sargent.

The 1973 stereo re-recording of *The Mikado* by the D'Oyly Carte company directed by Royston Nash is a complete success in every way and shows the Savoy tradition at its most attractive. The digital remastering for CD adds to the brightness: its effect is like a coat of new paint, so that the G & S masterpiece emerges with a pristine sparkle. Musically this is the finest version the D'Oyly Carte company have ever put on disc. The choral singing is first rate, with much refinement of detail. The glees, *Brightly dawns* and *See how the fates*, are robust in the D'Oyly Carte manner but more polished than usual. The words are exceptionally clear throughout.

This applies to an important early song in Act I, *Our great Mikado*, which contains the seeds of the plot and is sometimes delivered in a throaty, indistinct way. Not so here: every word is crystal clear. Of the principals, John Reed is a splendid Ko-Ko, a refined and individual characterization, and his famous *Little list* song has an enjoyable lightness of touch. Kenneth Sandford gives his customary vintage projection of Pooh-Bah – a pity none of his dialogue has been included. Valerie Masterson is a charming Yum-Yum; *The sun whose rays* has rarely been sung with more feeling and charm, and it is followed by a virtuoso account of *Here's a how-de-do* which one can encore, for each number is separately cued (there are 37 separate bands on the two CDs). Colin Wright's vocal production has a slightly nasal quality, but one soon adjusts to it and his voice has the proper bright freshness of timbre for Nanki-Poo. John Ayldon's Mikado has not quite the satanic glitter of Donald Adams's classic version, but he provides a laugh of terrifying bravura. Katisha (Lyndsie Holland) is commanding, and her attempts to interrupt the chorus in the finale of Act I are superbly believable and dramatic. On CD the singers are given striking presence, though the bright lighting of the sound has brought more sibilance. As a CD transfer this is less successful than *The Pirates*.

The Sargent set, the first of his series, dates from as early as 1957 and the recording has been given remarkable vividness and presence by the digital remastering. Words are wonderfully crisp and clear. There is much to enjoy. The grand operatic style to the finales of both Acts, the trio about the 'death' of Nanki-Poo and the glee that follows are characteristic of the stylish singing, even if the humour is less readily caught than in the D'Oyly Carte production. Owen Brannigan is a fine Mikado, but the star performance is that of Richard Lewis who sings most engagingly throughout as Nanki-Poo. Elsie Morison is a charming Yum-Yum and Monica Sinclair a generally impressive Katisha, although she could sound more convinced when she sings *These arms shall thus enfold you.*

The Mikado: highlights.
(*) That's Entertainment **CDTER 1121; *ZCTER 1121* [MCA **MCAD 6215**]. Angas, Bottone, Idle, Garrett, Van Allan, Palmer, E. Nat. Op. Ch. & O, Peter Robinson.

This selection is generous (62′) and includes virtually all the important music; but it will appeal primarily to those wanting a memento of the English National Opera production. As is normal, the performance is dominated by Ko-Ko, and Eric Idle's characterization will not be to all tastes; moreover the libretto is often considerably altered – most notably in the 'little list' – not always to advantage. Without the stage action the performance is less than racy with Peter Robinson generally adopting very relaxed tempi, although there are memorable moments: the *Three little maids from School*, for instance, and indeed the Act I finale with Felicity Palmer a positively malignant Katisha. Here the dramatically wide dynamic range of the recording is very telling. It is naturally balanced, set back in a nice theatrical ambience, and the words are mostly clear (though the choral singing is at times surprisingly slack); but this does not displace either the D'Oyly Carte or the earlier Sadler's Wells recording (not yet issued on CD).

Patience (complete, with dialogue).
*** Decca **414 429-2**; *414 429-4* (2) [id.]. Sansom, Adams, Cartier, Potter, J. Reed, Sandford, Newman, Lloyd-Jones, Toye, Knight, D'Oyly Carte Op. Ch. & O, Godfrey.

Patience comes up superbly in its digitally remastered format. The military numbers are splendidly projected and vividly coloured – *When I first put this uniform on* and *The soldiers of our Queen* have an unforgettable vigour and presence, with Donald Adams in glorious voice. Everything seems to be freshened, and the D'Oyly Carte soloists, chorus and orchestra have never sounded better. Mary Sansom takes the lead charmingly and she is especially good in the dialogue. Both Bunthorne and Grosvenor are very well played. The dialogue is at a slightly lower dynamic level than the music, but that only reflects the reality of the theatre. Overall, this is irresistible.

(i) *Patience* (complete, without dialogue); (ii) *Symphony in E* (*Irish*).
*** HMV **CDC7 47783-8** [Ang. **CDCB 47783**] (2). (i) Morison, Young, G. Baker, Cameron, Thomas, M. Sinclair, Harper, Harwood, Glyndebourne Fest. Ch., Pro Arte O, Sargent; (ii) Royal Liverpool PO, Groves.

It seems a curious idea to couple *Patience* with Sullivan's *Irish symphony*. Yet it is a pleasing work, lyrical, with echoes of Schumann as much as the more predictable Mendelssohn and Schubert. The jaunty *Allegretto* of the third movement with its 'Irish' tune on the oboe is nothing less than haunting. Groves and the Royal Liverpool Philharmonic give a fresh and affectionate performance, and the CD transfer of the 1968 recording is generally well managed.

Patience was another of the great successes of the Sargent series and (like the Decca set) emerges freshly minted in its new transfer. Although there is no dialogue, there is more business than is usual from HMV and a convincing theatrical atmosphere. The recording is vivid, with no lack of warmth, and the singing is consistently good. The chorus is a strong feature throughout, and where the men and women sing different melodic lines the clarity of each is admirable. Elsie Morison's Patience, George Baker's Bunthorne and John Cameron's Grosvenor are all admirably characterized, while the military men are excellent too. The many concerted items continually beguile the ear and Sir Malcolm's accompaniments tell splendidly. All in all, this is the sort of production we anticipated when HMV first began their 'Glyndebourne' series, and it can be heartily recommended.

The Pirates of Penzance (complete, with dialogue).
*** Decca **414 286-2**; *414 286-4* [id.]. J. Reed, Adams, Potter, Masterson, Palmer, Brannigan, D'Oyly Carte Op. Ch., RPO, Godfrey.

For compact disc issue, Decca have chosen the second (1968) D'Oyly Carte recording, and Isidore Godfrey is helped by a more uniformly excellent cast than was present on the earlier set. The dialogue is included, theatrical spontaneity is well maintained, and the spoken scenes with the Pirate King are particularly effective. Donald Adams has a great gift for Gilbertian inflexion – some of his lines give as much pleasure as his splendidly characterized singing. Christene Palmer's Ruth is not quite so poised, but her singing is first rate – her opening aria has never been better done. John Reed's characterization of the part of the Major-General is strong, while Valerie Masterson is an excellent Mabel; if her voice is not creamy throughout its range, she controls it with great skill. Her duet with Frederic, *Leave me not to pine alone*, is enchanting, sung very gently. Godfrey has prepared us for it in the overture, and it is one of the highlights of the set. Godfrey's conducting is as affectionate as ever, more lyrical here without losing the rhythmic buoyancy; one can hear him revelling in the many touches of colour in the orchestration, which the Royal Philharmonic Orchestra present with great sophistication. But perhaps the greatest joy of the set is Owen Brannigan's Sergeant of Police, a part this artist was surely born to play. It is a marvellously humorous performance, yet the humour is never clumsy; the famous *Policeman's song* is so fresh that it is almost like hearing it for the first time. The recording is superbly spacious and clear throughout, with a fine sense of atmosphere. The cassettes are also of excellent quality, although only iron-oxide stock is used. The CD transfer is remarkable in its added presence. While a slight degree of edge appears on the voices at times, the sense of theatrical feeling is greatly enhanced and the dialogue interchanges have an uncanny realism. This is markedly more successful technically than the companion CD transfer of *The Mikado*.

(i) *The Pirates of Penzance* (complete, without dialogue)*; Overtures: Cox and Box; Princess Ida; The Sorcerer*. (ii) *Overture in C* (*In Memoriam*).

*** HMV **CDC7 47785-8**. G. Baker, Milligan, Cameron, Lewis, Brannigan, Morison, Harper, Thomas, M. Sinclair, Glyndebourne Fest. Ch., Pro Arte O, Sargent; (ii) CBSO, Dunn.

(i) *The Pirates of Penzance;* (ii) *Ruddigore* (both without dialogue).

(B) *** HMV *EX 749693-4* (2). (i) Milligan, Cameron, Harper, Thomas; (ii) Blackburn, Bowden, Harwood, Rouleau; (i; ii) G. Baker, Lewis, Brannigan, Morison, M. Sinclair, Glyndebourne Fest. Ch., Pro Arte O, Sargent.

The Pirates was one of the finest of Sir Malcolm Sargent's G & S sets. Besides a performance which is stylish as well as lively, conveying both the fun of the words and the charm of the music, the HMV recording has more atmosphere than usual in this series. Undoubtedly the star of the piece is George Baker; he is a splendid Major-General. Here is an excellent example of a fresh approach yielding real dividends, and Sargent's slower than usual tempo for his famous patter song means that the singer can relax and add both wit and polish to the words. As in the Decca D'Oyly Carte set, Owen Brannigan gives a rich portrayal of the Sergeant of Police. The performance takes a little while to warm up: Sargent's accompaniment to the Pirate King's song is altogether too flaccid. Elsie Morison is a less than ideal Mabel: her opening cadenza of *Poor wandering one* is angular and over-dramatic. However, elsewhere she is much more convincing, especially in the famous duet, *Leave me not to pine alone*. The choral contributions (the opening of Act II, for instance) are pleasingly refined, yet have no lack of vigour. *Hail poetry* is resplendent, while the choral finale is managed with poise and a balance which allows the inner parts to emerge pleasingly. The whole performance is in fact more than the sum of its parts. The recording has transferred with fine presence and realism to CD; but the chrome cassettes are extremely successful, too, the sound mellower but very natural, if with slightly less projection. Both operas are complete on one tape; and the pairing with *Ruddigore*, also one of the very best of the Sargent series, makes this both economical and highly desirable. The CDs include some overtures as fillers on the second disc, including *In Memoriam*, a somewhat inflated religious piece written for the 1866 Norwich Festival.

Ruddigore (complete recording of original score, without dialogue).

*** That's Entertainment **CDTER2 1128**; *ZCTED 1128*. Hill Smith, Sandison, Davies, Ayldon, Hillman, Innocent, Hann, Ormiston, Lawlor, New Sadler's Wells Op. Ch. & O, Simon Phipps.

What is exciting about the New Sadler's Wells production of *Ruddigore* is that it includes the original finale, created by the logic of Gilbert's plot which brought *all* the ghosts back to life, rather than just the key figure. This idea had a poor reception from the first night audience and a new ending was hastily substituted. In the theatre the original dénouement works admirably as it does on record. The opera is strongly cast, with Marilyn Hill Smith and David Hillman in the principal roles and Joan Davies a splendid Dame Hannah, while Harold Innocent as Sir Despard and Linda Ormiston as Mad Margaret almost steal the show. Simon Phipps conducts brightly and keeps everything moving forward, even if his pacing is not always as assured as in the classic Sargent version. The recording is first class, with fine theatrical atmosphere.

(i) *Ruddigore* (complete, without dialogue)*;* (ii) *The Merchant of Venice* (suite)*; The Tempest* (incidental music).

*** HMV **CDC7 47787-8** (2). (i) Lewis, G. Baker, Brannigan, Blackburn, Morison, Bowden, M. Sinclair, Harwood, Rouleau, Glyndebourne Fest. Ch., Pro Arte O, Sargent; (ii) CBSO, Dunn.

The HMV set has been most successfully remastered and offers first-class sound, the voices natural and well balanced with the orchestra, and much warmth and bloom on the recording.

This matches Sargent's essentially lyrical approach and emphasizes the associations this lovely score so often finds with the music of Schubert. The performance is beautifully sung and the excellence is uniform. Perhaps George Baker sounds a little old in voice for Robin Oakapple, but he does the *Poor little man . . . poor little maid* duet in Act I with great charm and manages his 'character transformation' later in the opera splendidly. Pamela Bowden is a first-class Mad Margaret, and her short Donizettian *Scena* is superbly done. Equally Richard Lewis is an admirably bumptious Richard. Perhaps, surprisingly, Owen Brannigan does not make quite as much of the *Ghosts' high noon* song as Donald Adams on the D'Oyly Carte set, but his delicious Act II duet with Mad Margaret has an irresistible gentility (and one can visualize their traditional little dance-movements, so evocatively is this section managed). The drama of the score is well managed too: Sir Despard's Act I entry has real bravado (the words of the chorus here are wonderfully crisp), and later the scene in the picture gallery (given a touch of added resonance by the recording) is effectively sombre. Even the slightly prissy crowd effects in Act I seem to fall into place, giving an attractive feeling of stylization. A superb reissue, sounding splendid on CD, which brings some interesting bonuses.

The longer orchestral work, the suite of incidental music for *The Tempest*, dates from 1861, when the student composer was only nineteen. Not surprisingly it made him an overnight reputation, for it displays an astonishing flair and orchestral confidence. The *Introduction* may be melodramatic but it is memorably atmospheric too, and although some of the other items are conventional, the *Banquet dance* is charmingly scored and the *Dance of the Nymphs and Shepherds* is already anticipating *Iolanthe*. The shorter *Merchant of Venice* suite was composed five years later, and almost immediately the writing begins to anticipate the lively style which was so soon to find a happy marriage with Gilbert's words. The performance here is highly infectious, and the sound is first class, bright yet with plenty of depth and a spacious ambience.

Utopia Ltd: complete. *Imperial march.*

**(*) Decca *414 359-4* (2). Field, Holland, Ayldon, M. Reed, Sandford, Ellison, Buchan, Conroy-Ward, D'Oyly Carte Op. Ch., RPO, Nash.

Utopia Ltd was first performed in 1893, ran for 245 performances and then remained unheard (except for amateur productions) until revived for the D'Oyly Carte centenary London season in 1974, which led to this recording. Its complete neglect is unaccountable; the piece stages well, and if the music is not as consistently fine as the best of the Savoy Operas, it contains much that is memorable. Moreover, Gilbert's libretto shows him at his most wittily ingenious, and the idea of a Utopian society *inevitably* modelled on British constitutional practice suggests Victorian self-confidence at its most engaging. Also the score offers a certain nostalgic quality in recalling earlier successes. Apart from a direct quote from *Pinafore* in the Act I finale, the military number of the First Light Guards has a strong flavour of *Patience*, and elsewhere *Iolanthe* is evoked. *Make way for the Wise Men*, near the opening, immediately wins the listener's attention, and the whole opera is well worth having in such a lively and vigorous account. Royston Nash shows plenty of skill in the matter of musical characterization, and the solo singing is consistently assured. When Meston Reed as Captain Fitz-Battleaxe sings 'You see I can't do myself justice' in *Oh, Zara*, he is far from speaking the truth – this is a performance of considerable bravura. The ensembles are not always as immaculately disciplined as one is used to from the D'Oyly Carte, and *Eagle high* is disappointingly focused: the intonation here is less than secure. However, the sparkle and spontaneity of the performance as a whole are irresistible. As there is no overture as such, the recording uses Sullivan's *Imperial march*, written for the opening – by the Queen – of the Imperial Institute, five months before the première of the opera. It is an effective enough piece, but not a patch on the *March of the Peers* from *Iolanthe*. The cassettes, which have been remastered, are curiously uneven in quality for Decca. The first two sides are transferred at fractionally too high a level, bringing a hint of peakiness on climaxes; the second two go to the other extreme and lack something in presence and clarity in the upper range.

The Yeomen of the Guard (complete, without dialogue).
*** HMV **CDS7 47781-2** [Ang. **CDCB 47781**] (2). Dowling, Lewis, Evans, Brannigan, Morison, M. Sinclair, Glyndebourne Fest. Ch., Pro Arte O, Sargent.

(i) *The Yeomen of the Guard* (complete, without dialogue); (ii) *Trial by Jury*.
*** Decca *417 358-4* [id.]. Hood, J. Reed, Sandford, Adams, Raffell; (i) Harwood, Knight; (ii) Round; D'Oyly Carte Opera Ch.; (i) RPO, Sargent; (ii) ROHCG O, Godfrey.

Sir Malcolm Sargent recorded *The Yeomen of the Guard* in stereo twice very successfully. The later Decca set has marginally the finer recording, but the solo singing in the HMV version is by no means outclassed by the Decca. In the latter, Sir Malcolm's breadth of approach is at once apparent in the overture, and when the chorus enters (*Tower warders*) the feeling of opera rather than operetta is striking. Indeed one has seldom heard the choruses expand with such power, nor indeed has the orchestra (especially the brass) produced such a regal sound. As the work proceeds the essential lyricism of Sargent's reading begins to emerge more and more, and the ensemble singing is especially lovely. There is no lack of drama either, and indeed the only aspect of the work to be played down somewhat is the humorous side. The interjections of Jack and Wilfred in the Act I finale are obviously seen as part of the whole rather than a suggestion of the humour that somehow seems to intrude into the most serious of human situations. The pathos of the famous Jester's song in Act II is played up, and the only moment to raise a real smile is the duet which follows, *Tell a tale of cock and bull*. But with consistently fine singing throughout from all the principals (and especially Elizabeth Harwood as Elsie), this *Yeomen* is unreservedly a success with its brilliant and atmospheric Decca recording. The cassette transfer has splendid presence and immediacy.

The singing on Sargent's HMV recording (which dates from 1960) is very persuasive. As on his Decca set, the trios and quartets with which this score abounds are most beautifully performed and skilfully balanced, and the ear is continually beguiled. Owen Brannigan's portrayal of Wilfred is splendidly larger than life and Monica Sinclair is a memorable Dame Carruthers. The finales to both Acts have striking breadth, and the delightfully sung trio of Elsie, Phoebe and the Dame in the finale of Act II is a good example of the many individual felicities of this set. *Strange adventure*, too, is most beautifully done. As in the Decca recording there is very little feeling of humour, but the music triumphs. The sound is excellent, with the CDs bringing greater presence and definition. However, the Decca set also includes Godfrey's immaculately stylish and affectionate *Trial by Jury* with John Reed as the Judge.

'A Gilbert & Sullivan Gala': Arias, duets and trios from: *The Gondoliers; The Grand Duke; Haddon Hall; HMS Pinafore; Iolanthe; The Mikado; Patience; The Pirates of Penzance; Ruddigore; The Sorcerer; The Yeomen of the Guard.*
*** HMV Dig. **CDC7 47763-2**. Masterson, Armstrong, Tear, Luxon, Bournemouth Sinf., Alwyn, or N. Sinfonia, Hickox.

This superb collection combines the best part of two recitals of G & S, the first made by Valerie Masterson and Robert Tear with Kenneth Alwyn in 1982 and recorded at the Guildhall, Southampton, and the second, where the balance is even more realistic, in EMI's No. 1 Studio at Abbey Road, with Sheila Armstrong, Tear and Benjamin Luxon under the direction of Richard Hickox in 1984. The result is one of the most successful (and generous – nearly 73′) anthologies of this repertoire ever put on disc. Quite apart from the excellence of the singing and the sparkling accompaniments, the programme is notable for the clever choice of material, with items from different operas engagingly juxtaposed instead of being just gathered together in sequence. The singing from the first group is particularly fine. Valerie Masterson's upper range is ravishingly fresh and free. It is a pity her *Pinafore* number had to be omitted, but the final cadence of *Leave me not to pine alone* (*Pirates*) is very touching, and she sings Yum-Yum's famous song from *The Mikado, The sun, whose rays*, with a captivating, ingenuous charm. Robert Tear too is in excellent form and his *A wandering minstrel* is wonderfully stylish, while *A magnet hung in a hardware shop* has fine sparkle. The *Prithee, pretty maiden* duet (also from *Patience*) is hardly less endearing. In the second recital it is the ensemble items that score, notably the duets from *Ruddigore, The Gondoliers* and the vivacious *Hereupon we're both agreed* from *The Yeomen of the Guard*; the star here is Benjamin Luxon. He is splendid in the principal novelty, *I've heard it said*, from *Haddon Hall*, a vintage Sullivan number even if the words are not by Gilbert, and he is left to end the concert superbly with a bravura account of *My name is John Wellington Wells* from *The Sorcerer*, and a splendidly timed, beguilingly relaxed account of *When you find you're a broken-down critter* from *The Grand Duke*, in which Richard Hickox and the Northern Sinfonia make the very most of Sullivan's witty orchestral comments.

Suppé, Franz von (1819–95)

Overtures: *Beautiful Galathea; Fatinitza; Jolly robbers; Light cavalry; Morning, noon and night in Vienna; Pique dame; Poet and peasant.*
*** Decca Dig. **414 408-2** [id.]. Montreal SO, Dutoit.

Decca have previously relied on Solti for their Suppé overtures – indeed, he was first disconcertingly asked to record this repertoire, when he would have much preferred Wagner. As we know, that came later. Dutoit's approach could hardly be further removed from Solti's electrifyingly hard-driven performances. There is no lack of bravura but, as the dignified opening of *Poet and peasant* demonstrates, there is breadth, too. Indeed, the pacing is splendid, combining warmth and geniality with brilliance and wit, as in the closing galop of *Fatinitza*. The orchestral playing is admirably polished, the violins sounding comfortable even in the virtuoso passages of *Light cavalry*, one of the most infectious of the performances here. It is difficult to imagine these being bettered, even by Karajan, while the Decca sound is superb, well up to the usual Montreal standards.

Overtures: *Light cavalry; Morning, noon and night in Vienna; Poet and peasant.*
(*) DG **415 377-2 [id.]. BPO, Karajan – ROSSINI: *Overtures.***(*)

Karajan's performances are taken from a 1970 collection and are coupled with four Rossini overtures. The playing is swaggeringly brilliant, but the sound is just a little fierce at fortissimo level, although the overall balance is warm and natural.

Svendsen, Johan Severin (1840–1912)

Symphonies Nos 1 in D, Op. 4; 2 in B flat, Op. 15; 2 Swedish folk-melodies, Op. 27.
*** BIS Dig. **CD 347** [id.]. Gothenburg SO, Neeme Järvi.

Together with the four symphonies of Berwald, Svendsen's two (1867, 1876) are the finest to have appeared in Scandinavia before Sibelius. His invention blends liveliness and exuberance with a vein of poetic fantasy not unworthy of the best Grieg, but while Grieg's interest in Norwegian folk-music resulted in his cultivation of the miniature, Svendsen excelled (where Grieg did not) in the larger forms. As befits a conductor, Svendsen was a master of the orchestra – for which Grieg had no particular flair. Listening to the two symphonies, one can't help feeling regret that his creative fires burned themselves out and that, after the famous *Romance* for violin and orchestra, he became what we would call nowadays a 'star' conductor. The *D major Symphony* is a student work, written while he was at the Leipzig Conservatoire and a pupil of Reinecke, a work of astonishing assurance and freshness, in some ways even more remarkable than the *B flat*. There is much of him in Nielsen, who played under his baton in the 1890s and eventually succeeded him. Neeme Järvi is a splendid guide to this terrain; these are first-class performances, sensitive and vital, and the excellent recordings earn them a strong recommendation.

Szymanowski, Karol (1882–1937)

Violin concertos Nos 1, Op. 35; 2, Op. 61.
(M) **(*) EMI *ED 291215-4*. Konstanty Kulka, Polish RSO, Maksymiuk.

These glorious concertos have been less well served on record than they deserve. These are accomplished and dedicated accounts that convey a great deal of the atmosphere of this extraordinary music. Its sound-world is completely distinctive: there is an exotic, Amazon-like luxuriance, a sense of ecstasy and longing, a heightened awareness of colour and glowing, almost luminous textures as if one is perceiving the world in a dreamlike state which, while it lasts, seems far more vivid than the real thing. The *First Concerto* of 1917 is arguably Szymanowski's masterpiece: its extraordinary refinement and melancholy intensity linger in the memory, and its closing bars are among the most poignant – even fragrant – music written in the present century. The *Second* was his last work, and occupied him during 1932–3 when he was sinking into ill-health and penury. The recordings would gain from a less contrived balance but they are still very good and, if the performances offer more sensuousness than spirituality, they are sufficiently impressive to deserve recommendation, particularly at this price.

Études, Op. 4; Études, Op. 33; Masques, Op. 34; Mazurkas, Op. 50/1, 2, 3, 7, 11, 15 & 18; Mazurkas, Op. 62.
*(*) Delos Dig. **D/CD 1002** [id.]. Carole Rosenberger.

This compilation ranges from the early Op. 4 *Studies* of 1902, the rarely heard Op. 33 (1917), seven of the wonderful *Mazurkas*, Op. 50, which occupied Szymanowski in the mid-1920s, and the two *Mazurkas*, Op. 62, he composed three years before his death. Thus one can follow his development from the Scriabinesque early works and observe his fascination with Debussy and Stravinsky, whose influence can certainly be discerned as late as the *Tantris* movement of *Masques*. All the same, this issue can only be recommended *faute de mieux*. Carole Rosenberger has none of the hypersensitivity and range of colour and dynamics that this music calls for, though the highly unflattering, dry and cramped acoustic must bear much of the blame for this. Indeed, this is the kind of studio that makes perfectly accomplished playing sound inelegant. This scores higher marks for enterprise than for achievement.

Tallis, Thomas (*c.* 1505–85)

Absterge Domine; Candidid facti sunt; Nazareri; Derelinquat impius; Dum transsiset Sabbatum; Gaude gloriosa Dei mater; Magnificat and Nunc dimittis; Salvator mundi.
*** CRD **CRD 3429**; *CRDC 4129* [id.]. New College, Oxford, Ch., Higginbottom.

Many of the Latin settings on this fine record were included in the *Cantiones sacrae* (1575). The performances by the Choir of New College, Oxford – recorded in the splendid acoustic of the College Chapel – are eminently well prepared, with good internal balance, excellent intonation, ensemble and phrasing. The *Gaude gloriosa* is one of Tallis's most powerful and eloquent works. The exact date of composition of this votive antiphon is not established, but it has been suggested that it was composed during the reign of Queen Mary and was intended to glorify the Queen as well as the Virgin Mary. An invaluable addition to the Tallis discography, and excellently recorded in both media.

Anthems: *Blessed are those that be undefiled; Christ, rising again; Hear the voice and prayer; If ye love me; A new commandment; O Lord, in Thee is all my trust; O Lord, give thy holy spirit; Out from the deep, Purge me. Remember not, O Lord God; Verily, verily I say: 9 Psalm Tunes for Archbishop Parker's Psalter.*
*** Gimell Dig. **CDGIM 007**; *1585T-07* [id.]. Tallis Scholars, Phillips.

This disc collects the complete English anthems of Tallis and is thus a valuable complement to the disc listed above. Here, of course, women's voices are used instead of boys', but the purity of the sound they produce is not in question. There is ample evidence here of the richness and diversity of Tallis's inventive powers, and the performances could hardly be more committed or more totally inside this repertoire. Strongly recommended. The chrome cassette, as usual with Gimell, is a state-of-the-art transfer.

Gaude gloriosa; Loquebantur variis linguis; Miserere nostri; Salvator mundi, salva nos, I and II; Sancte Deus; Spem in alium (40-part motet).
❀ *** Gimell **CDGIM 006**; *1585T-06* [id.]. Tallis Scholars, Phillips.

On the splendid Gimell issue the Tallis Scholars at once celebrate the Quatercentenary of the composer's death and provide a Tallis collection for the CD era to match – and surpass – the Argo recordings of the 1960s. Within the admirably suitable acoustics of Merton College Chapel, Oxford, they give a thrilling account of the famous 40-part motet, *Spem in alium*, in which the astonishingly complex polyphony is spaciously separated over a number of point sources, yet blending as a satisfying whole to reach a massive climax. The *Gaude gloriosa* is also a magnificent piece, while the soaring *Sancte Deus* and the two very contrasted settings of the *Salvator mundi* are hardly less beautiful. Throughout, the music is paced spontaneously, the vocal line is beautifully shaped and the singing combines ardour with serenity. On CD, the breadth and depth of the sound is spectacular; the cassette is a model of its kind, full and smooth, with the focus never slipping.

The Lamentations of Jeremiah the Prophet; Spem in alium (40-part motet).
(M) ** Pickwick Dig. **PCD 806** [MCA **MCAD 25847**]. Pro Cantione Antiqua, Mark Brown – ALLEGRI: *Miserere.***

On Pickwick, a strong, generally well-sung performance (although there are moments in the motet when intonation is not absolutely secure). Tempi are well judged but there is less light and shade than would be ideal. The microphone balance brings a thickening of tone to the expansive climax of *Spem in alium* and less than ideal transparency of texture. But this CD comes at mid-price and may be counted good value.

Taneyev, Sergei (1856–1915)

Piano quartet in E, Op. 20.
(*) Pro Arte Dig. **CDD 301 [id.]. Cantilena Chamber Players.

Although the *Piano quartet* (1908) is not quite as memorable or as powerful as the *Piano quintet* of two years later – its last movement outstays its welcome – it is still a finely wrought and often subtle work. Its language is closer to that of Brahms or Fauré than to the Russians, though Taneyev's piano writing is highly original. What a superbly sensitive pianist the Cantilena Chamber Players have in the person of Frank Glazer! The performance is altogether first rate, though the acoustic in which it is recorded is not quite big enough.

Piano quintet in G min., Op. 30.
*** Ara. Dig. **Z 6539** [id.]. Jerome Lowenthal, Rosenthal, Kamei, Thompson, Kates.

The *Piano quintet* (1908–10) is something of a rarity, yet it is a powerfully made and ambitious score running to nearly 43′. It is more original than the two *String quartets* listed below, and indeed if any work is likely to persuade the music lover that Taneyev is a master, this is it. Not only is it well structured and its motivic organization subtle, its melodic ideas are strong and individual. It is arguably the greatest Russian chamber work between Tchaikovsky and Shostakovich. The recording is not in the demonstration bracket, but it is very good; and the playing, particularly of the pianist Jerome Lowenthal, is excellent. Strongly recommended.

Piano trio in D, Op. 22.
** Pro Arte Dig. **CDD 303** [id.]. Odeon Trio – TCHEREPNIN: *Trio.***

Taneyev's *D major Trio* comes from 1907, at a time when the composer had resumed work as a concert pianist. Its musical debts are to Tchaikovsky's *Trio* and to the Brahms/Dvořák tradition, though he disliked Brahms's music. But Taneyev is his own man and there is much of interest here. The Odeon Trio play well, too, but they are not well served by the engineers. The recording comes from 1980 and there is little space round the three instruments; tonally, the sound is wanting in range and colour.

String quartets Nos 8 in C; 9 in A.
(M) **(*) Olympia **OCD 128** [id.]. Leningrad Taneyev Qt.

Taneyev was a composer of wide-ranging talents whose creative achievements were to some extent overshadowed by his prodigious pianistic talents – he gave the first performance of Tchaikovsky's *First Concerto* – as well as his academic attainments. He was made a professor at the Moscow Conservatoire in his twenties and became its director in 1885. (His pupils included Scriabin, Medtner, Rachmaninov and Glière.) Yet his output was not inconsiderable in terms of either quality or quantity; his choral music is particularly impressive. Both these quartets are large-scale works in the classical mould, and both are beautifully crafted, though they are not strongly personal: No. 8 takes almost 40′ and No. 9 the best part of 35′. The minuet of No. 8 and the scherzo of No. 9 are highly attractive. They are well played, though the violin tone above the stave has a tendency to harden.

String quintet in D, Op. 14.
(M) *** Olympia **OCD 138** [id.]. Leningrad Taneyev Qt with Benjamin Morozow – BORODIN: *String quartet No. 2.****

This *String quintet* may lack the strong personal profile of Taneyev's great teacher, Tchaikovsky, or his finest pupils, but closer acquaintance reveals a strong and resourceful musical mind. It is beautifully proportioned, in three movements, the last of which is a theme and variations. (One of them is quite magical and has enormous delicacy and atmosphere.) The performance by the eponymous quartet and the cellist, Benjamin Morozow, is extremely fine and so, too, is the recording. A rewarding disc.

The Oresteia (opera): complete.
(*) Olympia **OCD 195 A/B [id.]. Chernobayev, Galushkina, Bukov, Dubrovin, Belorussian State Ch. & O, Kolomizheva.

Taneyev regarded *The Oresteia* as his *chef d'œuvre* and took some seven years over its composition. It was warmly received at its première in 1895 but was never again performed in his lifetime. (Napravnik wanted to cut it and Taneyev refused.) Not surprisingly, considering he was the author of a masterly study on Invertible Counterpoint, he was, as Gerald Abraham put it, 'more interested in Josquin than Chopin', and it hardly seems possible that he should have composed so effective an opera: to compress the whole of the *Oresteia* into the space of 147 minutes and the idiom of a nineteenth-century Russian opera is no mean feat. Taneyev's reputation as an academic must be reassessed in the light of this piece, for this is not only a finely wrought work; it is full of imaginative touches and effective musical drama. Rimsky-Korsakov spoke of its 'pages of unusual beauty and expressiveness'. This performance, recorded in 1978, was briefly available on DG in a rather smoother transfer than on these Olympia CDs, vivid though they are. There are some splendid singers. There is a tendency for the sound to coarsen on climaxes, though some of the blame for this must be laid at the feet of the orchestra. A most worthwhile issue.

Tarrega, Francisco (1852–1909)

Music for guitar: *Adelita; La Cartagenera; Columpio; Danza mora; Endecha; Estudio de velocidad; Estudio en forma de minuetto; Jota; Lagrima; La Mariposa; Minuetto; Oremus; Pavana; Preludio in G; Recuerdos de la Alhambra; Sueno.*
*** DG Dig. **410 655-2**; *410 655-4* [id.]. Narciso Yepes.

Although much of Tarrega's music is slight, he was a key figure in the movement to restore the guitar to it rightful place as a concert instrument, and stands as the link between Sor and the composers of the early part of our own century. Narciso Yepes made a special study of Tarrega's manuscripts (there is more than one version of each piece) and plays them very persuasively. The recording, excellent in its cassette format, has even finer definition on CD.

Tartini, Giuseppe (1692–1770)

Concertino for clarinet.
*** ASV Dig. **CDDCA 585**; *ZCDCA 585* [id.]. Emma Johnson, ECO, Yan Pascal Tortelier – CRUSELL: *Introduction, theme & variations*; DEBUSSY: *Rapsodie*; WEBER: *Concerto No. 1.****

Gordon Jacob's arrangement of sonata movements by Tartini as a brief, four-movement *Clarinet concerto* is a delightful oddity. Inevitably it seems strange to have such baroque ideas associated with clarinet tone; but with sprightly, characterful playing, it is an attractive and unusual makeweight in Emma Johnson's mixed collection of concertante pieces, well recorded. There is a very good tape.

Violin concertos: in E min. D.56; in A, D.96; in A min., D.113.
*** Erato Dig. **ECD 88096** [id.]. Uto Ughi, I Solisti Veneti, Scimone.

Tartini is a composer of unfailing originality, and the three violin concertos on this record are all rewarding. Uto Ughi's performances are distinguished by excellent taste and refinement of tone, and the Solisti Veneti are hardly less polished. The harpsichord continuo is somewhat reticent but otherwise the recording is exemplary.

Tavener, John (born 1944)

Funeral Ikos; Ikon of Light; Carol: The Lamb.
*** Gimell **CDGIM 005**; *1585T-05* [id.]. Tallis Scholars, Chilingirian Qt, Phillips.

Both the major works on the disc, *Funeral Ikos* and *Ikon of Light*, represent Tavener's more recent style at its most compelling, simple and consonant to the point of bareness but with sensuous overtones. *Ikon of Light*, first performed at the Cheltenham Festival in 1984, is a setting of Greek mystical texts, with chant-like phrases repeated hypnotically. The string trio provides the necessary textural variety. More concentrated is *Funeral Ikos*, an English setting of the Greek funeral sentences in six linked sections, often yearningly beautiful. Both in these and in the brief setting of Blake's *The Lamb*, the Tallis Scholars give immaculate performances, atmospherically recorded in the chapel of Merton College, Oxford. The CD improves the definition and presence, but the tape also offers sound of the greatest realism.

Taverner, John (*c.* 1495–1545)

Missa gloria tibi Trinitas; Audivi vocem (responsory); ANON.: *Gloria tibi Trinitas.*
*** Hyp. **CDA 66134** [id.]. The Sixteen, Harry Christophers.

Missa gloria tibi Trinitas; Dum transisset sabbatum; Kyrie a 4 (*Leroy*).
*** Gimell Dig. **CDGIM 004**; *1585T-04* [id.]. Tallis Scholars, Phillips.

This six-voice setting of the Mass is one of the great glories of Tudor music, richly varied in its invention (not least in rhythm) and expressive in a deeply personal way very rare for its period. Harry Christophers and The Sixteen underline the beauty with an exceptionally pure and clear account, superbly recorded and made the more brilliant by having the pitch a minor third higher than modern concert pitch.

Peter Phillips and the Tallis Scholars give an intensely involving performance of this glorious example of Tudor music. The recording may not be so clear as on the rival Hyperion version, but Phillips rejects all idea of reserve or cautiousness of expression; the result reflects the emotional basis of the inspiration the more compellingly. The motet, *Dum transisset sabbatum*, is then presented more reflectively, another rich inspiration. On CD, textures are further clarified yet the attractive ambient effect remains.

Tchaikovsky, Peter (1840–93)

Andante cantabile, Op. 11; Nocturne, Op. 19/4; Pezzo capriccioso, Op. 62 (1887 version)*: 2 Songs: Legend; Was I not a little blade of grass; Variations on a rococo theme, Op. 33* (1876 version).
*** Chan. Dig. **CHAN 8347**; *ABTD 1080* [id.]. Wallfisch, ECO, Simon.

This delightful record gathers together all of Tchaikovsky's music for cello and orchestra – including his arrangements of such items as the famous *Andante cantabile* and two songs. The major item is the original version of the *Rococo variations* with an extra variation and the earlier variations put in a more effective order, as Tchaikovsky wanted. The published version, radically different, was not sanctioned by him. Geoffrey Simon, following up the success of his record of the original version of the *Little Russian symphony*, draws lively and sympathetic playing from the ECO, with Wallfisch a vital if not quite flawless soloist. Excellent recording, with the CD providing fine presence and an excellent perspective. The cassette transfer approaches demonstration standard on side one, but is much softer-grained on side two, which rather suits the music. Rostropovich's analogue recording, with Karajan, of the *Rococo variations* is also available on CD – see below – but he uses the published score.

Capriccio italien, Op. 45.
*** RCA Dig. **RCD 14439**; [**RCD1 4439**]. Dallas SO, Mata (with *Concert****).

Capriccio italien; 1812 overture; Francesca da Rimini, Op. 32; Romeo and Juliet.
(B) ** DG *419 842-4* [id.]. Chicago SO, Barenboim.

Capriccio italien; 1812 overture; Hamlet (fantasy overture); Marche slave.
** DG Dig. **415 379-2** [id.]. Israel PO, Bernstein.

Capriccio italien; 1812 overture; Marche slave.
** DG Dig. **400 035-2** [id.]. Chicago SO, Barenboim.

Capriccio italien; 1812 overture; Marche slave; Nutcracker suite.
(*) Decca Dig. **417 300-2; *417 300-4* [id.]. Montreal SO, Dutoit.
(M) **(*) DG **423 225-2**; *423 225-4* [id.]. BPO, Karajan (with Don Cossack Ch.).

(i) *Capriccio italien; 1812 overture; Marche slave;* (ii) *Romeo and Juliet.*
(M) ** Decca **417 742-2** [id.]. (i) Detroit SO; (ii) Nat. SO of Washington, Dorati.

Capriccio italien; 1812 overture; Mazeppa: Cossack dance.
** Telarc Dig. **CD 80041** [id.]. Cincinnati SO, Kunzel.

(i) *Capriccio italien; Marche slave; Mazeppa: Gopak. Romeo and Juliet* (fantasy overture); (ii) *Sleeping Beauty: Waltz and Polacca.* (i) *Suite No. 3 in G, Op. 55.*
(B) ** HMV *TCC2-POR 290114-9.* (i) LPO; (ii) RPO, Boult.

Tchaikovsky's *Capriccio italien* was given an extraordinarily successful compact disc début on Mata's Dallas disc. The concert-hall effect of the recording is very impressive indeed, with the opening fanfares as sonically riveting as the silences when the reverberation dies away naturally. The performance is colourful and exciting, and the piece is issued within an attractive compilation of favourite orchestral showpieces (see Concerts section below).

Dutoit's performances are individually characterized and by no means conventional in approach. The *Capriccio italien* is particularly successful, with even a touch of nostalgia in the string tune that follows the opening fanfare, but there are also high spirits and elegance and the coda is well prepared and nicely paced. In the *Nutcracker suite* there is almost a chamber music refinement, not only in the *Miniature overture* but in the characteristic dances which have both a piquant sense of colour and delicacy of articulation; the *Waltz of the flowers* is pleasing but rather restrained. *Marche slave* is sombre and dignified, while *1812* (complete with cannon provided by the 22nd Regiment of Quebec) is exciting without making one sit on the edge of one's chair. The sound is refined and luminous but lacks the sumptuous weight which is needed to give Tchaikovsky's climaxes a physical thrill. The cassette is first class in every way, although the end of *1812* is slightly congested.

Karajan's collection was one of his eightieth-birthday celebratory reissues. The *1812 overture* is very professional and quite exciting, although the chorus used to open the piece is not ideally sonorous, and the closing pages have the cannon balanced in a calculated fashion rather than showing a touch of engineering flair. The *Capriccio italien* is played with splendid panache and with exhilarating orchestral bravura at the close, and the *Nutcracker suite* offers similar polish, spick-and-span and vividly coloured; only the *Waltz of the flowers* seems a shade glossy. *Marche slave* has a fine combination of dignity and flair. The remastered recording is brilliant, yet does not lack depth, and the brass fanfares of the *Capriccio* are superbly telling.

Barenboim is too ready to let the tension relax to be entirely convincing throughout this programme, although his affection for the music is never in doubt. He is slinkily persuasive in the *Capriccio*, but by the finest Chicago standards *1812* is much less impressively played, although not without excitement. The recording could expand more and the violin sound has a distinct digital edge. The *Capriccio* is more agreeable overall. In *Romeo and Juliet* Barenboim conveys a sensuous quality in the love theme but the ardour of the performance is sporadic, though there is a burst of excitement in the feud music. The middle section of *Francesca da Rimini* yields some fine solo wind playing, notably from the clarinet; but the full nervous tension of the outer sections is partly subdued by the conductor's partiality for breadth, although the coda is exciting enough. The sound is always vivid and the tape transfer is very well managed. The *Capriccio* and *1812* are also available on CD with *Marche slave* (**400 035-2**), but this hardly justifies its premium price.

Dorati's reissue is not a digital recording and the sound-quality does not compare with his more recent Decca CDs. It represented the return of the Detroit orchestra to the international recording scene at the beginning of 1979. The performance of the *Capriccio* is not without elegance, but the steadily paced *Marche slave* seems rather sombre until the coda, which is taken briskly. This is underlined by an over-emphasis to the bass response. The account of *1812* is not especially exciting, nor is it helped by the lack of a really sharp focus in the sound. The original LP was excessively bright; this has now been tempered in the remastering. There are guns and bells at the end, all well contained. *Romeo and Juliet* had been added to make the CD more competitive.

Even more than in Bernstein's Stravinsky series, here the Tel Aviv acoustic is too dry for music which needs a warmly expansive resonance. The performances have plenty of excitement and are well paced, although the oboe solo in *Hamlet* could have been more beguiling. The CD is greatly preferable to the original LP; with the extra presence and definition, the ear can accept – though not revel in – the chosen ambience. At the end of *1812* the cannon make a spectacular effect, though the sudden peal of bells near the end seems contrived. Overall, this cannot be recommended with great enthusiasm.

The Telarc compact disc gives due warning that on this record the cannon dwarf the orchestra in *1812* – indeed, at the time of the sessions many windows nearby were shattered. So if you need a recording of cannon, plus *1812*, and your speakers can accommodate the dynamic range and amplitude, both impressively wide, then this issue is for you. In the *Capriccio* there are no cannon – so the engineers substitute the bass drum, which is very prominent. The orchestral contribution throughout is lively but not memorable, and the playing simply does not generate enough adrenalin to compensate for the relative lack of projection of the orchestral tone. At the end of *1812*, Tchaikovsky's carefully contrived climax, with its full-blooded scalic descent, seriously lacks weight. The most enjoyable item here is the lively *Cossack dance*.

Boult's 'Portrait of the Artist' double-length tape offers a reasonably attractive complete version of Tchaikovsky's *Third Orchestral suite*, with its famous *Theme and variations*. Boult displays less than his usual flair in this final section of the work, although the first three movements are lyrically persuasive. *Romeo and Juliet* was one of his best Tchaikovsky recordings, but the other performances are unexpectedly idiosyncratic at times, quite volatile in their control of the forward momentum, especially *Marche slave*. The recording is resonant, which means that the focus is smooth rather than sharp; on our copy, the opening trumpet solo of the *Capriccio italien* produced a moment of discoloration. Otherwise the sound is good.

Piano concerto No. 1 in B flat minor, Op. 23.

*** RCA **RD 85912** [**RCA 5912-2-RC**]. Van Cliburn, RCA SO, Kondrashin – RACHMANINOV: *Concerto No. 2.****

*** DG **415 062-2** [id.]. Martha Argerich, RPO, Dutoit – PROKOFIEV: *Concerto No. 3.****

(M) *** Decca **417 750-2** [id.]. Ashkenazy, LSO, Maazel – CHOPIN: *Concerto No. 2.****

*** Decca **417 555-2** [id.]. Ashkenazy, LSO, Maazel – SCHUMANN: *Concerto.****

(*) RCA Dig. **RD 89968 [RCA 5708-2-RC]. Barry Douglas, LSO, Slatkin.
(M) **(*) DG Dig. **415 122-2** [id.]. Ivo Pogorelich, LSO, Abbado.
(*) CBS Dig. **CD 36660 [id.]. Emil Gilels, NYPO, Mehta (with BACH: *Well-tempered Clavier: Prelude No. 10*, arr. Siloti***).
(*) RCA **RD 85363 [RCD1 5363]. Rubinstein, Boston SO, Leinsdorf – GRIEG: *Concerto*.*(*)
(*) Ph. Dig. **411 057-2 [id.]. Martha Argerich, Bav. RSO, Kondrashin.
(M) *(**) Decca **417 676-2**; *417 676-4* [id.]. Curzon, VPO, Solti – GRIEG: *Concerto*.*(**)
** Decca Dig. **417 294-2**; *417 294-4* [id.]. Schiff, Chicago SO, Solti: DOHNÁNYI: *Variations*.**(*)
(M) *(*) DG **419 068-2**; *419 068-4* [id.]. Sviatoslav Richter, VSO, Karajan (with RACHMANINOV: *Preludes****).
*(*) Telarc Dig. **CD 80124** [id.]. Parker, RPO, Previn – PROKOFIEV: *Concerto No. 3*.**
*(*) Decca Dig. **421 181-2**; *421 181-4* [id.]. Bolet, Montreal SO, Dutoit – RACHMANINOV: *Concerto No. 2*.**

The Van Cliburn is (after the Horowitz/Toscanini version) one of the most brilliant recordings of this work ever made. The young American pianist lives up to his reputation as Moscow Prize-winner with playing which has great virtuosity, but much else besides. There is spontaneity and a natural feeling for the phrasing which usually comes only with long experience. Van Cliburn and the Soviet conductor Kondrashin in short give an inspired performance with as much warmth as glitter. The 1958 recording is forward and could do with more atmosphere, but the digital remastering has brought a firmer orchestral image – Kondrashin sees that the orchestral detail is never swamped – and the piano timbre too is improved. Coupled with an equally outstanding version of the Rachmaninov *C minor*, this is a very distinguished reissue indeed, even if the piano timbre here is shallower than in the coupling.

Argerich's 1971 recording of the Tchaikovsky *First Piano concerto* with Dutoit remains a strong recommendation. Not quite all the background hiss has been eliminated, and the digital remastering cannot provide the inner clarity which is more apparent in her 1980 version for Philips. Nor are the strings as rich in timbre as on the DG/Pogorelich version. But the sound is firm, with excellent presence, and its ambience is more attractive than the later version. The weight of the opening immediately sets the mood for a big, broad performance, with the kind of music making in which the personalities of both artists are complementary. Argerich's conception encompasses the widest range of tonal shading. In the finale she often produces a scherzando-like effect; then the orchestra thunders in with the Russian dance theme to create a real contrast. The tempo of the first movement is comparatively measured, but satisfyingly so; the slow movement is strikingly atmospheric, yet delicate, its romanticism light-hearted. The Argerich performance is also available on a particularly attractive Walkman tape (see below) where the couplings are even more generous.

Ashkenazy's version with Maazel has also stood the test of time and is now offered in alternative couplings: the Chopin is the more attractive, being at mid-price. Ashkenazy's performance is not high-powered but it is lyrically satisfying. The soloist refuses to be stampeded by Tchaikovsky's rhetoric and the biggest climaxes of the first movement are made to grow naturally out of the music. In the *Andantino* too, Ashkenazy refuses to play flashily and he uses the middle section rather as a contrasting episode to set in the boldest relief the delicate return of the opening tune. The finale is very fast and brilliant, yet the big tune is broadened at the end in the most convincing way. The remastering is highly successful: the piano sounds splendidly bold and clear while the orchestral balance is realistic.

Barry Douglas's CD plays for 36′ 41″ and it would have to provide a pretty stunning performance to be considered good value at premium price. Douglas, outright winner of the 1986 Moscow Tchaikovsky competition, in the event proves an admirable soloist; like Van Cliburn, his bravura is always at the service of the music and he provides many imaginative touches, especially in the first-movement cadenzas and the *Andante*, which is beautifully done.

Slatkin accompanies capably but the orchestral contribution is altogether more routine, with a rather heavy reprise of the big tune in the finale. The sound is excellent, well balanced and full, with a concert-hall ambience; but until this is coupled with another work it remains uncompetitive.

The opening of the Pogorelich/Abbado account has an impressive sweep and, provided one accepts the forward balance of the piano – on CD it is so tangible that one feels almost able to reach out and touch it – the recording is superbly full-bodied and wide-ranging. The orchestra, set back in the spacious acoustic of Watford Town Hall, makes an impressive impact, even if pianissimos seem a shade recessed. The dramatic contrasts of the first movement are thus underlined, with the poetic secondary material beautifully and thoughtfully played by soloist and orchestra alike. But after the first big climax, Pogorelich puts the brakes on; here, and again in the cadenza, his ruminative (some might say narcissistic) introspection holds up the music's forward flow. The movement overall takes 23′ 18″, which must be something of a record. The *Andante* is a delight, with the delicately agile LSO strings matching the soloist's nimbleness in the central *Prestissimo*; and the finale is similarly exhilarating in its crisp articulation, producing no real barnstorming until the closing section after Abbado's very positive broadening for the final statement of the big tune. The charisma of the performance is undeniable and, in spite of Pogorelich's eccentricities, his partnership with Abbado is a convincing one; but many will find the first movement too wilful to live with – and with no fill-up, the CD seems poor value, running for only 37 minutes.

Any Gilels record is an event, and his CBS recording appears a quarter of a century after his first account with Fritz Reiner and the Chicago Symphony Orchestra. Gilels has an outsize musical personality, and this is a performance of leonine calibre, with nobility and fire. There is no want of virtuosity – the double octaves leap off the CD – and there are the inward-looking qualities we associate with Gilels, too. The music making was recorded live at Carnegie Hall, and the claims of Gilels' artistry have to be weighed against less than distinguished recorded sound and second-rate orchestral playing: the wind (bar 186) are not in tune and do not blend, and at no point does the orchestra respond as alertly or sensitively as it did in the days of Bernstein. The digital recording reproduces clean detail, although the upper string timbre is rather crude – and the relationship between soloist and orchestra is well balanced. But the sound is not top drawer. The compact disc offers very marginally greater refinement and the obvious advantage of background silence. However, Gilels is Gilels, and the quality of his playing cannot be too highly praised. The Siloti arrangement of the Bach *Prelude* was his encore on the occasion of the recording, and it is affecting in its direct eloquence.

Many older readers will remember Rubinstein's famous 78 r.p.m. recording of this work. The present account is no less magnetic, with fine bravura in the outer movements and a poetic *Andante*. There is a mercurial quality here, not only in the central section of the slow movement but also in the finale. Leinsdorf is obviously caught up in the music making and the orchestra opens the work splendidly and provides plenty of excitement throughout. The 1963 recording is less than ideal, but the digital remastering has taken some of the brashness out of the close-microphoned strings and provided a piano image impressively bold and clear. The result is very enjoyable.

Argerich's Philips issue comes from a live performance given in October 1980, full of animal excitement, with astonishingly fast speeds in the outer movements. The impetuous virtuosity is breathtaking, even if passagework is not always as cleanly articulated as in her superb studio performance for DG. That earlier version also brings more variety of tone; but you will find few more satisfying performances on record than either of these. The CD version clarifies and intensifies the already vivid sound, but is poor value without a coupling.

Clifford Curzon's 1969 recording with Solti has resurfaced on a Decca CD and tape, but the remastering makes the orchestral sound rather dated, although the piano retains its fullness.

It is a characteristically fine version. Curzon matches thoughtfulness to unostentatious bravura, and Solti ensures that the performance overall has fine zest and spontaneity.

Schiff's approach puts the concerto nearer to the Romantic tradition of Schumann than to Liszt. Both he and Solti make the most of the lyrical side of the first movement, but with the cadenzas introspective rather than flamboyant there is a missing dimension. The *Andantino* opens with the most hushed of pianissimos and the soloist is fastidiously delicate throughout – the scherzando middle section is very light and graceful. The essentially lightweight approach extends to the finale, too, which is underpowered, even if the reprise is strong in Solti's hands. The recording, set slightly back, with a mellow timbred piano, matches the music making very well.

Unlike his partnership with Lazar Berman (see below), Karajan and Richter failed to agree on a uniform interpretation. The element of struggle for which this work is famous is only too clear in the finale, with soloist and conductor each choosing a different tempo for the second subject and maintaining it in spite of the other. In both the dramatic opening and closing pages of the work they produce a very mannered approach and the main body of the first movement is made to sound unspontaneous by Richter's excessive rubato in the second subject group. Clearly two major artists are involved, but the result is only fitfully exciting. The remastered recording sounds bold and clear. The coupling of five Rachmaninov *Preludes* is admirably played.

Jon Kimura Parker and Previn give a spaciously relaxed reading, with no lack of poetry in the lyrical moments of the first movement and an agreeably intimate *Andantino*. The finale is effective, but the adrenalin does not run very high and the rich Telarc recording, somewhat opaque, with a resonant bass, helps to make the closing sections of both outer movements sound somewhat ponderous.

Bolet's is essentially an epic view but, with the opening square and solid and the first movement very deliberate, the end effect is heavy rather than conveying grandeur. The *Andantino* too is measured and the finale is by far the most effective movement, with a lighter mood introduced in the second subject so that the closing peroration makes a striking contrast. The sound is sumptuous, with the piano larger than life.

Piano concertos Nos 1; 3 in E flat, Op. 75.
(B) ** CfP Dig. **CD-CFP 9010**; *TC-CFP 4518*. Philip Fowke, LPO, Boettcher.
*(*) Decca Dig. **410 112-2** [id.]. Victoria Postnikova, VSO, Rozhdestvensky.

It is a pity that the least successful part of Philip Fowke's two performances is the grand introduction to the *First Concerto*, plain and four-square at a stolid tempo. After that, much of the first movement is plain too, lacking in sparkle; paradoxically, however, the bravura passages with their extra challenge lift the performance, and the soloist promptly sounds more relaxed and spontaneous. The slow movement is coolly presented, effectively so, with the central scherzando delightfully clean and light; but it is the finale which really sets the performance alight, with the orchestra, like the soloist, warming to the exuberance of inspiration. Fowke then gives a dazzling performance of the *Third Concerto*, full of joyful bravura. At CfP price, this alone is worth the money, and the digital recording is excellent on CD, though disappointingly the cassette lacks brightness in the upper range.

The collaboration of wife and husband in the Postnikova/Rozhdestvensky performances makes for very personal readings, marked by spacious speeds. The very introduction is disconcertingly slow and so is the basic tempo for the central *Andante*. There and in other places Postnikova's expressive fluctuations sound studied, but the clarity of articulation will for some make up for the lack of adrenalin. The long single movement of the *Third Concerto* also needs more consistently persuasive treatment, though the dactylic dance-theme is delectably pointed. Close balance for the piano in a firm, clear recording, enhanced on CD – but the performances remain unenticing.

Piano concerto No. 1; Concert fantasia in G, Op. 56.
(*) HMV Dig. **CDC7 47718-2 [id.]; *EL 270537-4*. Dmitri Sgouros, LPO, Weller.

A big, bold performance of the *B flat minor Concerto* from Sgouros, the mood set by the spacious opening. Sgouros's articulation of the main subject of the allegro is particularly appealing and he is highly responsive to the work's balancing poetic elements. But Weller's accompaniment lacks fire and it is left to the soloist to carry the first movement. The *Andante* brings out the best in soloist and orchestra alike, and the finale has fine flair and a satisfying apotheosis, with some breathtaking bravura from the pianist. The coupling, with its engaging affinities with Tchaikovsky's ballet music, but with a strong central solo cadenza, comes over splendidly, with the performers clearly enjoying themselves. Why this work is so neglected in the concert hall is difficult to determine after hearing a performance as convincing as this. The HMV recording is realistically full-bodied, the piano tangibly out in front on CD, but with the orchestra well in the picture. The cassette is comparatively opaque.

(i) *Piano concerto No. 1;* (ii) *Violin concerto in D, Op. 35;* (iii) *Serenade for strings: Waltz;* (iv) *Variations on a rococo theme, Op. 33.*
(B) ❀ *** DG Walkman *413 161-4*. (i) Argerich, RPO, Dutoit; (ii) Milstein, VPO, Abbado; (iii) BPO, Karajan; (iv) Rostropovich, Leningrad PO, Rozhdestvensky.

This extended-length chrome tape is the jewel in the crown of DG's Walkman series, always generous but here exceptionally so, both in quality of performances and recording, as well as in the amount of music offered. We award it a Rosette as the outstanding Tchaikovsky bargain. Argerich's account of the *B flat minor Piano concerto* is second to none, Milstein's (1973) performance of the *Violin concerto* is equally impressive, undoubtedly one of the finest available, while Abbado secures playing of genuine sensitivity and scale from the Vienna Philharmonic. Rostropovich's earlier (1961) version of the *Rococo variations* offers playing with just the right amount of jaunty elegance as regards the theme and the first few variations; and when the virtuoso fireworks are let off, they are brilliant, effortless and breathtaking in their éclat. Indeed, Rostropovich needs no superlatives and his accompanist shows a mastery all his own. Karajan provides a stylishly polished account of one of Tchaikovsky's most memorable (and original) waltzes, here an elegant interlude between the *Variations* and the first movement of the *Piano concerto*. The only slight drawback is that the turnover then follows, before the *Andantino*. But it is difficult to see how this could have been avoided within the chosen format. The sound is first class.

Piano concerto No. 1; (ii) *Violin concerto in D, Op. 35.*
(M) **(*) DG **423 224-2**; *423 224-4* [id.]. (i) Lazar Berman; (ii) Christian Ferras, BPO, Karajan.
(M) **(*) Ph. **420 717-2**; *420 717-4* [id.]. (i) Claudio Arrau, Boston SO; (ii) Accardo, BBC SO; C. Davis.
(M) **(*) RCA **GD 86526**; *GK 86526* [**RC-6526-RG**]. (i) Mischa Dichter; (ii) Itzhak Perlman, Boston SO, Leinsdorf.

Berman's 1976 recording with Karajan has been reissued at mid-price, generously coupled with Christian Ferras's much earlier version of the *Violin concerto*. It is interesting that credit for its incandescence must go almost as much to the conductor as to the pianist – and yet the conductor is Karajan, who has sometimes seemed too aloof as a concerto accompanist. Berman's character is firmly established in the massive chords of the introduction (though, curiously, he hustles the first group of all); from there his revelling in dramatic contrast – whether of texture, tone colour, dynamic or tempo – makes this one of the most exciting readings ever put on record. It is not just a question of massive bravura but of extreme delicacy too, so that in the central scherzando of the slow movement it almost sounds as though Berman is merely breathing on the keyboard, hardly depressing the notes at all. The ripe playing of the Berlin Philharmonic backs up the individuality of Berman's reading, and the recording is massively brilliant to match. Consideration of the Ferras/Karajan performance must be affected by personal reactions to Ferras's characteristic tone, with its rather close vibrato in lyrical passages and tendency to emphasize the schmalz on the G string. One finds too that Ferras's playing tends to lack charm, but some may react differently, and this is a well-conceived reading, with Karajan shaping the work as a whole very convincingly. The recording is excellent, the brilliance emphasizing the style of the soloist.

Arrau, splendidly accompanied, gives a direct and unexaggerated performance of the *B flat minor Concerto* which is in general most refreshing. The temperature is not high, excitement is shunned, and with a seventy-year-old soloist double octaves do not run quite so freely as once they did. There is also a strange agogic hesitation in Arrau's enunciation of the main theme of the finale, but with clean recording this version will appeal to those who like a thoughtful reading. The sound is full and clear. Salvatore Accardo's account of the *Violin concerto* combines poise and freshness with flair. He has a keen lyricism and a fine sense of line, as one would expect, and he is sensitively accompanied by Sir Colin Davis and the BBC Symphony Orchestra. He plays the *Concerto* complete. Accardo's reading has a refinement and restraint that mark it off from the traditional virtuoso approach, and no doubt for some collectors it will lack the passionate sweep they look for. His playing has a marvellous purity, and if the recording was as good, it would carry a three-star grading. As it is, the soloist is a shade too close to the microphone to do his tone full justice, otherwise the remastered sound is very good.

The RCA digital remastering brings very brightly lit sound in both concertos and this suits the work for piano better than the *Violin concerto*. Nevertheless Perlman is in good form in the latter: he plays the *Canzonetta* with much feeling and the finale has fine bravura. The performance of the *Piano concerto* is a good one, with no lack of adrenalin, and there is poetry too. But the sound is lacking in bloom and in the *Violin concerto* tuttis could be better focused. This is very much a third choice in this coupling.

Piano concerto No. 2 in G, Op. 44.
❀ *** HMV Dig. **CDC7 49124-2** [id.]; *EL 270603-4*. Peter Donohoe, Bournemouth SO, Barshai.

In the past, Tchaikovsky's *Second Piano concerto* has usually been recorded in an abridged form dictated by its first soloist, Siloti. Now comes a superb recording of the full original score which in every way justifies the work's length and the unusual format of the slow movement where the piece temporarily becomes a triple concerto, with its extended solos for violin and cello. Here these are played with beguiling warmth by Nigel Kennedy and Steven Isserlis, the latter slightly less extrovert but still very sensitive. The success of the first movement depends on a fairly brisk tempo, which allows the division of the basic rhythm into duple time rather than a ponderous four-in-a-bar. Barshai's pacing is not only perfectly calculated but he gives the opening tune an engaging rhythmic lift. The whole movement goes with a splendid impetus, yet the central orchestral episode is effectively broadened. The slow movement has one of Tchaikovsky's very best tunes, and the performance is a delight from beginning to end. But if Peter Donohoe plays marvellously in the first two movements – he is quite melting in the *Andante* – in the finale he is inspired to playing which recalls Horowitz in the *B flat minor Concerto*. The main theme, shooting off with the velocity of a ball in a pinball machine is exhilarating and the orchestral response has a matching excitement. The coda, with its cascading octaves, is a *tour de force* and brings one to the edge of one's seat in admiration. The recording has a fine, spacious ambience and is admirably realistic and very well balanced. Tchaikovsky's work has never before received such convincing advocacy on record. Alas, the tape is muffled and cannot be recommended.

Piano concertos Nos 2 in G, Op. 44; 3 in E flat, Op. 75.
*** Ara. Dig. **Z 6583** [id.]. Jerome Lowenthal, LSO, Comissiona.

In an obviously attractive coupling of two unjustly neglected works, the energy and flair of Lowenthal and Comissiona combine to give highly spontaneous performances, well balanced and recorded. If the *G major Concerto* has not quite the distinction of the HMV version, it is still satisfyingly alive; the solist brings an individual, poetic response as well as bravura. With very good sound, this is well worth investigating, as the account of the *Third Concerto* is comparably spontaneous.

Violin concerto in D, Op. 35.
*** Decca Dig. **410 011-2** [id.]. Kyung Wha Chung, Montreal SO, Dutoit – MENDELSSOHN: *Concerto.****
(M) *** Decca **417 707-2** (id.]. Kyung Wha Chung, LSO, Previn – BRUCH: *Concerto No. 1*; SAINT-SAËNS: *Havanaise.****
*** Ph. Dig. **416 821-2**; *416 821-4* [id.]. Mullova, Boston SO, Ozawa – SIBELIUS: *Concerto.****
(M) *** DG **419 067-2**; *419 067-4* [id.]. Milstein, VPO, Abbado – MENDELSSOHN: *Concerto.****
(*) HMV Dig. **CDC7 47623-2 [id.]; (M) *TC-EMX 2100*. Nigel Kennedy, LPO, Kamu – CHAUSSON: *Poème.***(*)
(*) Erato **ECD 88109 [id.]. Amoyal, Philh. O, Dutoit – SIBELIUS: *Concerto.***(*)
(M) **(*) Decca **417 687-2**; *417 687-4* [id.]. Ricci, Netherlands R. PO, Fournet – MENDELSSOHN: *Concerto.***(*)
** PRT **CDPCD 14**. Yaron, LPO, Soundant – SIBELIUS: *Concerto.***(*)

Violin concerto in D, Op. 35; Sérénade mélancolique, Op. 26; String serenade: Waltz.
(*) RCA **RD 85933 [**RCA 5933-2-RC**]. Heifetz, Chicago SO, Reiner, or CO – MENDELSSOHN: *Concerto.***(*)

Violin concerto in D; Sérénade mélancolique; Melodie, Op. 42/3.
(*) CBS Dig. **MK 39563 [id.]. Zukerman, Israel PO, Mehta.

Violin concerto; Sérénade mélancolique.
(*) HMV **CDC7 47106-2 [id.]. Perlman, Phd. O, Ormandy.
** DG Dig. **400 027-2** [id.]. Kremer, BPO, Maazel.

Chung's earlier recording of the Tchaikovsky *Concerto* with Previn conducting has remained one of the strongest recommendations for a much-recorded work ever since it was made, right at the beginning of her career. The remake with Dutoit is amazingly consistent. Though on the concert platform she is so volatile a performer, responding to the inspiration of the moment, she is a deeply thoughtful interpreter. Here, as before, she refuses to sentimentalize the central *Canzonetta*, choosing a flowing, easily songful speed. The result is the more tenderly affecting, though this time the violin is balanced more closely than before. The finale has, if anything, even more exhilaration, with technical problems commandingly overcome at a very fast speed.

Those preferring the alternative coupling with Bruch and Saint-Saëns should be well satisfied with Chung's 1970 version of the Tchaikovsky which is still among the finest in the catalogue. Her technique is impeccable and her musicianship of the highest order, and Previn's accompanying is highly sympathetic and responsive. This has warmth, spontaneity and discipline, every detail is beautifully shaped and turned without a trace of sentimentality. The recording is well balanced and detail is clean, though the acoustic is warm. This is a very distinguished reissue.

Viktoria Mullova made the headlines some years ago by winning the Sibelius Competition and subsequently making a dramatic escape to the West. Her first commercial recording couples the Sibelius and Tchaikovsky *Concertos* and is a resounding success. Her performance of the

Tchaikovsky *Concerto* is immaculate and finely controlled – as is the coupling – but she does not always succeed in achieving the combination of warmth and nobility that this score above all requires. However, her playing has an undeniable splendour and an effortless virtuosity. Ozawa and the Boston orchestra give excellent support and the recording is exemplary. Not perhaps a first recommendation, but there is much to enjoy here. There is a good cassette, but it is rather bass-orientated.

Milstein's fine 1973 version with Abbado is more attractively coupled on the Walkman cassette – see above – but those for whom the Mendelssohn *Concerto* is more suitable will find that on Galleria the recording has been digitally remastered, bringing greater clarity, although the sound on the Walkman tape is fuller.

Zukerman's Israel version with Mehta was recorded at a live performance, which inevitably makes it marginally less perfect on detail and overall less disciplined than the superb account he recorded in London (also for CBS) at the very beginning of his recording career. However, that was relatively disappointing technically, while this new CD sounds extremely well. The sound is less dry and enclosed than in most recordings made in the Mann Auditorium in Tel Aviv, freer, better defined and with more bloom. The soloist is balanced closely, but only at one point in the first movement is the impact of bow on string given a touch of aggressiveness, while in the cadenza the violin image is very tangible indeed. The new reading of the central *Canzonetta* is certainly preferable to the old – faster, less heavily expressive – but the first movement is more self indulgent in its expressive lingering. Yet Zukerman's warmth is endearing and the intensity of the live music-making prevents the result from being slack. Zukerman, unlike most other soloists in recent versions, does not open out the once-traditional tiny cuts in the finale, but the playing here certainly conveys the excitement and thrills of a live performance, with extremes of speed in both directions – although the soloist's habit of stamping his foot may irritate some listeners. The fill-ups are brief, if apt, and are tenderly played: Zukerman's G string tone in the *Sérénade mélancolique* is ravishing, without being too schmaltzy. All in all, a most rewarding issue.

Heifetz's recording was made in the earliest years of stereo (1957). He was balanced very near the microphone; on the original LP, this tended to make the performance sound over-intense and also provided the listener with some uncomfortable sounds, as bow met strings in the many florid moments in which this concerto abounds. Now the recording (like the Brahms, made during the same period) has been digitally remastered and, with the upper range smoothed and the orchestral presence enhanced, the magic of Heifetz can be enjoyed more fully. There is some gorgeous lyrical playing and the slow movement marries deep feeling and tenderness in ideal proportions, while the finale scintillates. Reiner accompanies understandingly, producing fierily positive tuttis. A fine performance of the *Sérénade mélancolique* makes an attractive encore.

Taken from an analogue original of the late 1970s, Perlman's Philadelphia version sounds all the fuller and more natural in its CD format, with the soloist balanced less aggressively forward than usual; in clarity and openness, however, it cannot match the finest digital recordings on compact disc. Perlman's expressive warmth goes with a very bold orchestral texture from Ormandy and the Philadelphia Orchestra, and anyone who follows Perlman – in so many ways the supreme violin virtuoso of our time – is not likely to be disappointed. The coupling is not very generous, though beguilingly played.

Nigel Kennedy gives a warmly romantic reading of the Tchaikovsky *Concerto*, full of temperament with one of the most expansive readings of the first movement ever put on disc. In ample sound it could for many be a good first choice, though equally its idiosyncrasies will not please everyone. Slow as Kennedy's basic tempo for the first movement is, he takes every opportunity to linger lovingly. The result would sound self-indulgent, except that Kennedy's total commitment vividly conveys the impression of a live experience, naturally free in expression. For all his many *tenutos* and *rallentandos*, he is not sentimental, and his range of tone is exceptionally rich and wide, so that the big moments are powerfully sensual. The *Canzonetta* is taken at a flowing speed, while the finale brings extremes of expression similar to those in the first movement. Though Okku Kamu and the LPO are recorded in exceptionally rich and full sound, and the playing is excellent, their style does not always match that of the soloist; it sometimes sounds a little stiff in tuttis, though the final coda is thrilling. The (mid-priced) tape is acceptably full, but lacks the upper range of the CD.

Pierre Amoyal gives a fine account of the Tchaikovsky, though without opening out the traditional cuts. However, there is an aristocratic quality about his playing and great warmth, too. The Philharmonia Orchestra under Charles Dutoit are in excellent form and eminently well recorded. Erato scores over such rivals as Perlman and Kremer, both coupled with the *Sérénade mélancolique*, in offering the Sibelius *Concerto*.

Ricci made an outstanding record of this concerto in the early days of mono LP. He then recorded it in stereo with rather less success, but his newer (originally Phase Four) recording with Fournet restores his reputation fully. The characteristic intense vibrato may not be to all tastes, but the ear readily submits to the compulsion and colour of the playing, which shows a rock-steady technique and a splendid lyrical feeling. Even though Ricci is very near the microphone, so secure is his left hand that the rich stream of tone is always securely based, and the larger-than-life image is attractive when the orchestral impact and detail are so vividly conveyed. The new CD transfer is full and clear and there is a very good tape.

Yuval Yaron gives an impressive performance. Like Zukerman, he takes the first movement at a comparatively spacious tempo and revels in its lyrical detail; however, unlike Zukerman, he does not enjoy the extra intensity engendered by a live performance. The *Canzonetta* is played most tenderly – he uses a mute at the opening and is given an elegiac atmosphere; then Soudant prepares the finale rather deliberately, so that the start of the allegro makes a striking contrast. The woodwind interchanges in the finale are very relaxed, and the soloist too brings out the lyricism of these interludes between the bravura very pleasingly. Thus the performance as a whole is imaginatively thought out and individual. Yaron is balanced well forward, but his technique stands up to the spotlight thus provided. The 1978 analogue recording has been successfully remastered; but those seeking a coupling with the Sibelius will find that Amoyal's more modern version on Erato is even finer, though that also has an analogue source.

Kremer's was the first digital recording of the concerto and the first CD version. This artist blends keen nervous energy with controlled lyrical feeling, and it goes without saying that his virtuosity is impressive. Self-regarding agogic distortions are few (bars 50–58 and the first-movement cadenza are instances), and there is no lack of warmth. Yet both here and in the *Sérénade mélancolique* there is something missing. A great performance of this work refreshes the spirit and resonates in the mind. Here, although both the recording and the playing of the Berlin Philharmonic for Maazel are undoubtedly excellent, there is not the special kind of humanity and perception that are needed if a newcomer is to displace the superb versions already available.

(i) *Violin concerto in D;* (ii) *Variations on a rococo theme for cello and orchestra, Op. 33.*
(B) ** Sup. **2SUP 0004**. (i) Ishikawa, Czech PO, Kosler; (ii) Apolin, Prague SO, Smetaček.

Ishikawa opens the *Violin concerto* impressively and the presentation of the main themes is unforced and eloquent. She plays songfully in the *Andante* and the finale is vivacious, with the conductor making strong contrasts of tempo for the lyrical secondary material. With fine playing throughout from soloist and orchestra alike, this is enjoyable even though Kosler, perhaps guided by his soloist, takes the latter part of the first movement at rather too relaxed a tempo and the tension slips somewhat. Stanislav Apolin's account of the *Rococo variations* is first class. He has a fine, full tone and plays with eloquence and fire; yet he does not miss the essential elegance of the writing. In both works the recording (from 1978 and 1974 respectively) has transferred vividly to CD with plenty of presence, warmth and colour. The coupling is unusual and effective, and this is excellent value at the modest price asked.

1812 Overture, Op. 49.
* HMV **CDC7 47022-2** [id.]. Phd. O, Muti – LISZT: *Les Préludes***; RAVEL: *Boléro.**

1812 Overture; Francesca da Rimini; Marche slave; Eugene Onegin: Polonaise.
(*) HMV Dig. **CDC7 47375-2 [id.]. BPO, Ozawa.

1812 Overture; Francesca da Rimini; Romeo and Juliet.
(*) HMV Dig. **CDC7 49141-2 [id.]; *EL 749141-4.* Oslo PO, Jansons.

1812 Overture; Marche slave.
*(*) CBS **CD 37252** [id.]. V. State Op. Ch., VPO, Maazel – BEETHOVEN: *Wellington's victory.***

(i) *1812 Overture;* (ii) *Marche slave;* (iii) *Romeo and Juliet.*
(*) HMV **CDC7 47843-2 [id.]. LSO, Previn.
(B) **(*) DG Walkman *412 153-4.* (i) Boston Pops O, Fiedler; (ii) BPO, Karajan; (iii) San Francisco SO, Ozawa – MUSSORGSKY: *Pictures* etc.***
(M) ** Pickwick Dig. **PCD 801** [MCA **MCAD 25851**]. LSO, Ahronovich.

1812 Overture; Nutcracker (ballet): suite; Romeo and Juliet.
(*) Decca Dig. **417 400-2; *417 400-4* [id.]. Chicago SO, Solti.

(i) *1812 Overture; Romeo and Juliet;* (ii) *Eugene Onegin: Polonaise; Waltz; Écossaise. The Oprichnik: Dances.*
*** Ph. **411 448-2** [id.]. (i) Boston SO, with Tanglewood Fest. Ch. (in *1812*); (ii) ROHCGO; C. Davis.

(i) *1812 Overture; Serenade for strings, Op. 48; Eugene Onegin: Polonaise and waltz.*
(M) **(*) DG **415 855-2**; *415 855-4* [id.]. (i) Don Cossack Ch.; BPO, Karajan.

Sir Colin Davis is not renowned as a Tchaikovskian, yet here he provides one of the most satisfying versions of *1812* ever recorded. Though he departs from the original score – to great effect – by including a chorus, it is musical values rather than any sense of gimmickry that make this version so successful. Men's voices alone are used to introduce softly the Russian hymn at the opening, with the ladies freshening the reprise. In the closing spectacle, the chorus soars above the bells, and the effect is exhilarating. The music in between is splendidly played and satisfyingly alert. On CD, the initial choral entry is enhanced by the absence of background and the balance in the closing peroration is superbly managed, the choral sound a little thicker than it would be in a digital master, but impressively full-bodied; and the very believable cannon are superbly placed. What is especially striking is how the resonantly firm support of the middle and lower strings adds to the effect of the Tchaikovsky sound, to make a consistently satisfying impact throughout, as it does in *Romeo and Juliet*. This is a slightly reserved performance, but one which in its minor degree of introversion misses neither the noble passion of the lovers nor the clash of swords in the feud sequences. The elegiac closing pages are particularly telling. The colourful operatic dances are a generous makeweight and are played with élan; while the two most famous *Eugene Onegin* items tend to overshadow what follows, the *Oprichnik* excerpts show the composer's orchestral skill at its most felicitous. Here the ear notices, slightly more than in *Romeo and Juliet*, that the recording balance has lost just a degree of sparkle in the upper range, with the removal of virtually all the background noise.

Previn takes a clear-headed, totally unsentimental view of three of Tchaikovsky's most popular orchestral works. As a result the music emerges stronger in design (even *1812*) and no less exciting than usual. The 1973 recording has losses and gains in its digital remastering. The upper range seems slightly restricted, yet there is a striking gain in ambience and warmth, with a resonant bass providing the necessary sumptuousness and the massed violins singing richly. Internal detail is not sharp but the overall balance is very convincing. With only 47′ of music offered, this record is perhaps overpriced, but the performances are undoubtedly among the finest available of all three works; Previn's overall control of structure and tension is very impressive. There is both vigour and spontaneity and *1812* is exciting without getting out of hand at the end.

Jansons does not have quite the kind of success in his association with EMI that he consistently achieved in his Chandos Tchaikovsky series. Not that there is anything wrong with the recording balance: the sound here is rich, vivid and weighty, with a natural upper range; there is also a first-class chrome cassette, even if not as transparent in texture as the CD. The highlight is *Romeo and Juliet*. The performance has genuine breadth and the love theme shows characteristic Oslo eloquence. The main allegro lacks the last degree of physical excitement but there is plenty of vigour. The one idiosyncrasy is Jansons' interpolation of a tam tam alongside the explosive timpani roll in the coda, an effect which suits *Francesca da Rimini* more readily than *Romeo and Juliet*. In *Francesca* there is a frenzied evocation of Dante's Inferno in the outer sections of the work and the orchestral imitation of the whirlwinds in the reprise is very telling; the idyllic central section, too, is beautifully played. However, the overwhelming passion of the lovers and the complex polyphonic representation of their discovery by Francesca's husband does not communicate here with the power of Stokowski's famous performance. *1812* combines brilliance with a rather dignified grandiloquence, but the last degree of fervour is missing in the orchestral response.

Characteristically, Solti provides an exciting and spectacular *1812*, and the bold immediacy of the Chicago sound – thrusting violins in the allegro, powerful, sonorous brass at climaxes – brings compulsive music-making throughout. At the end the cannon-shots are placed precisely, but the bells are curiously blurred (even more so on the otherwise well-managed chrome tape), but the conductor's overall tautness in holding the piece together is undoubtedly commanding. *Romeo and Juliet* has an unexpected element of restraint: the battle sequences have plenty of bite in the strings, and at the climax the trumpets ring out resplendently. The structural symmetry is underlined by the mirroring in the coda of the elegiac melancholy of the opening; and the love theme, very tender and gentle when it first appears on the cor anglais, finds a yearning passion without histrionics. The *Nutcracker suite* produces marvellously characterful solo playing and much subtle detail from Solti, while the ear is struck by the vivid colours of Tchaikovsky's scoring, so realistic when the sound of the individual instruments is very tangible on CD. All in all, this is an excellent collection, even if other versions of *Romeo and Juliet* have a more striking spontaneity.

Ozawa's *1812* has the advantage of strikingly vivid digital recording, full-blooded, but not without a degree of edge on the brass. The reading is thrustful and certainly exciting, with the Berlin Philharmonic strings singing their lyrical melodies eloquently. The cannon are very spectacular: their first fusillade is so engulfing that one is surprised to discover the orchestra still sitting in their places afterwards, to reassert the musical line! In the final cannonade, however, the joyous bells are drowned, unlike the Davis/Philips version where all the 'ad lib' additions to the orchestra are well balanced. Ozawa's *Marche slave* is nicely paced, dignified yet spirited, and the *Eugene Onegin Polonaise* is attractively buoyant. The reading of *Francesca da Rimini*, however, is essentially neurotic. Tchaikovsky's portrayal of Dante's Inferno is vividly realized, with superb bravura playing from the orchestra. The beautifully scored middle section is also seductive, but Ozawa begins his accelerando much too early (at the cor anglais scalic figure) and, while what follows is undeniably thrilling, it turns Tchaikovsky's construction into melodrama. On CD the sound is enhanced at both ends of the spectrum, the bass full and firm, the upper range just as clear but with added body and smoothness. This approaches demonstration quality, but the cannon in *1812* remain overwhelmingly noisy.

The Galleria disc is a further reshuffling of performances from the late 1960s and early 1970s, digitally remastered to brilliant effect. Karajan's *1812* (with chorus) is also available with different couplings – see above – but here one reflects again that while the closing fusillade is spectacular, the precision seems calculated. Karajan's reading of the *Serenade* is brilliantly played. The two central movements are superb, the *Waltz* bringing masterly control of rubato and colour (the strings make a lovely sound) while the *Élégie* is freely passionate. The brightness of the sound brings a slight feeling of aggressiveness to the outer movements and especially to the finale. The *Polonaise* and *Waltz* from *Eugene Onegin* have fine panache.

Fiedler's account of *1812* has plenty of adrenalin and is brilliantly recorded, with the effective display of pyrotechnics at the end adding spectacle without drowning the music. The direct manner of the performance does all Tchaikovsky asks, if with no special individuality. Nevertheless, with Karajan's *March slave* and Ozawa's excellent *Romeo and Juliet* and first-class sound throughout, this Walkman chrome tape coupled with Mussorgsky is certainly good value.

The Pickwick CD is offered at mid-price, and the recording is very spectacular. The balance is truthful, the ambience a little dry but with a convincing perspective. The dynamic range is wide and the fusillade of cannon at the end of *1812* impressively realistic, without ruining the musical focus. Yuri Ahronovich's readings are extremely wilful. He moulds the lyrical music idiosyncratically and drives on the allegros with the acceleration in constant flux. The LSO ensemble suffers, but the thrust is undeniable. There is no doubt that this music making creates bursts of excitement, and the sound is physically very involving. The CD is superior in this respect.

Maazel's performance of *1812* is in no way distinctive, with the chorus failing to add a frisson of excitement at the opening, as it does in Sir Colin Davis's Philips version. Moreover, the CD adds little to one's enjoyment, serving only to emphasize the relative lack of ambient richness, with brass sharply defined and upper strings very brightly lit. The closing pages, with chorus, orchestra and cannon, certainly make a spectacle, but there is nothing really involving about the music making itself. *Marche slave* is rather more successful; but there are other, better versions.

Muti gives an urgent, crisply articulated version of *1812*, concentrated in its excitement. The Philadelphia Orchestra takes the fast speed of the main allegro in its stride, and the coda produces a spectacular climax. The snag is the recording which – like the coupled *Boléro* – has a shrill upper range in its CD format, with the violins glassy above the stave, and the brilliance sounding wholly artificial.

Festival coronation march in D; (i) *Romeo and Juliet:* duet (orch. Taneyev).
*** Chan. Dig. **CHAN 8476**; *ABTD 1187* [id.]. (i) Murphy, Lewis, Wilson-Johnson; SNO, Järvi – RACHMANINOV: *The Bells* etc.**(*)

Tchaikovsky's *Festival coronation march* was written for open-air performance before the Tsar in 1883. It is suitably grandiloquent but has a rather engaging trio, plus a whiff of the Tsarist hymn we recognize from *1812*. It is very well played here and superbly recorded. The vocalization of *Romeo and Juliet*, with the music drawn from the famous fantasy overture, was left in the form of posthumous sketches, which Taneyev completed and scored. The effect is more like a symphonic poem with vocal obbligatos, rather than operatic. It is well sung here but is mainly of curiosity value.

Festival overture on the Danish national anthem, Op. 15. (i) *Hamlet: Overture and incidental music, Op. 67 bis. Mazeppa: Battle of Poltava and Cossack dance; Romeo and Juliet* (fantasy overture; 1869 version)*; Serenade for Nikolai Rubinstein's saint's day.*
❀ *** Chan. Dig. **CD8310/1**; *DBRT 2003* (2) [id.]. LSO, Simon, (i) with Janis Kelly, Hammond-Stroud.

The credit for the appearance of this enterprising set, indispensable for any true Tchaikovskian, lies with Edward Johnson, a keen enthusiast and Tchaikovsky expert. He spent many months trying to persuade one of the major recording companies to make an investment in this repertoire, and it was Chandos which finally responded, producing a resplendent digital recording fully worthy of the occasion. Tchaikovsky himself thought his *Danish Festival overture* superior to *1812*, and though one cannot agree with his judgement it is well worth hearing. The *Hamlet* incidental music is another matter. The overture is a shortened version of the *Hamlet Fantasy overture*, but much of the rest of the incidental music is unknown, and the engaging *Funeral march* and the two poignant string elegies show the composer's inspiration at its most memorable. Ophelia's mad scene is partly sung and partly spoken, and Janis Kelly's performance is most sympathetic, while Derek Hammond-Stroud is suitably robust in the *Gravedigger's song*. The music from *Mazeppa* and the tribute to Rubinstein make engaging bonuses, but the highlight of the set is the 1869 version of *Romeo and Juliet*, very different from the final 1880 version we know so well. It may be less sophisticated in construction, but it uses its alternative ideas with confidence and flair. It is fascinating to hear the composer's early thoughts before he finalized a piece which was to become one of the most successful of all his works. The performances here under Geoffrey Simon are excitingly committed and spontaneous; the orchestral playing is nearly always first rate, and the digital recording has spectacular resonance and depth to balance its brilliance. Edward Johnson provides the excellent notes and a translation of the vocal music, which is sung (as the original production of *Hamlet* was performed) in French. The compact discs are among Chandos's most impressive, with the strings in the *Hamlet* incidental music sounding attractively refined, although the forward balance of the vocal soloists is made more noticeable.

Francesca da Rimini; Hamlet (fantasy overture), *Op. 67a.*
❀ *** Dell'Arte **CDDA 9006** [id.]. NY Stadium O, Stokowski.

Stokowski's famous Everest coupling – one of his greatest records – is here remastered for CD with great success, with the sound cleaner and clearer, yet remarkably expansive in the bass in *Hamlet*. Stokowski's inspired performance is quite sensational. He plays the central lyrical tune so convincingly that, if it has not quite the romantic panache of *Romeo and Juliet*, it has instead the proper sombre passion suitable to the altogether different atmosphere of Shakespeare's *Hamlet*. It is the dignity of the music and its close identification with the play that come over so strikingly. And, fascinatingly, Stokowski shows us how intensely Russian the music is: this is Shakespeare played in the vernacular of that great country, with its national feeling for epic drama; the funeral march at the end is extremely moving. *Francesca* is hardly less exciting. Surely the opening whirlwinds have seldom roared at such tornado speeds before, and the skilful way Stokowski builds up the climax out of the fragmentation of Tchaikovsky's score is thrilling indeed. The central section is played with the beguiling care for detail and balance for which this conductor was famous. When the great polyphonic climax comes, and the themes for the lovers' passion intertwine with music to suggest they are discovered, the tension is tremendous. The recording throughout is astonishingly vivid when one considers that it was made three decades ago: this is an outstanding reissue in every way. The New York Stadium Orchestra drew on the New York Philharmonic for its players and the tremendous commitment of their response more than makes up for any slight imperfections of ensemble. An indispensable record for all Tchaikovskians.

Francesca da Rimini, Op. 32. Romeo and Juliet (fantasy overture).
*(*) Decca Dig. **414 159-2** [id.]. Cleveland O, Chailly.

Chailly's coupling is superbly recorded in Decca's best manner, the sound wonderfully vivid and spacious, with the spectacle of the Tchaikovskian climaxes even more telling on CD. But Chailly, who secures excellent playing from the Cleveland Orchestra, especially in the middle section of *Francesca da Rimini*, displays no interpretative flair in this repertoire. *Romeo and Juliet* is not without life and ardour, yet the performance lacks individuality, while the outer climaxes of *Francesca* are underpowered, and the overall effect gives the impression as much of the ballet as of a symphonic poem.

Manfred symphony, Op. 58.
❀ *** Chan. Dig. **CHAN 8535**; *ABTD 1245* [id.]. Oslo PO, Jansons.
*** HMV Dig. **CDC7 47412-2** [id.]. Phd. O, Muti.
(M) ** Vox Prima **MWCD 7123** [id.]. Utah SO, Abravanel.

Jansons' performance of *Manfred* with the Oslo Philharmonic crowns his outstanding series in an electrifying account of this difficult, unconventionally structured work. Except in a relatively relaxed view of the *vivace* second movement, relating the Fairy of the Alps to Mendelssohn's fairy music, Jansons favours speeds flowing faster than usual, bringing out the drama but subtly varying the tensions to press each climax home to the full, and always showing his mastery of Tchaikovskian rubato: his warmly expressive phrasing never sounds self-conscious when it is regularly given the freshness of folksong. The performance culminates in a thrilling account of the finale, leading up to the entry of the organ, gloriously resonant and supported by luxuriant string sound. The Chandos recording is among the finest in the Oslo series, atmospheric but with fine inner detail. The tape does not match the disc in this respect although it is full and well balanced.

Muti's recording of Tchaikovsky's *Manfred*, released in 1982, was one of EMI's spectacular early digital LPs. Recorded in Kingsway Hall, it remains one of this company's most impressive digital issues. At the close of the first movement. Tchaikovsky's memorable climactic statement of the principal Manfred theme heard on the massed strings (*sul G*) brings a tremendous physical excitement, and when it is similarly reprised in the finale, capped with cymbals, the effect is electrifying. The weight of the sound emphasizes the epic style of Muti's reading, forceful and boldly dramatic throughout. Muti's Scherzo has a quality of exhilarating bravura, rather than concentrating on delicacy; the lovely central melody is given a sense of joyous vigour. The *Andante*, after a refined opening, soon develops a passionate forward sweep; in the finale the amplitude and brilliant detail of the recording, combined with magnificent playing from the Philharmonia Orchestra, brings a massively compulsive projection of Tchaikovsky's bacchanale and a richly satisfying dénouement. The CD adds to the weight and definition of the recording, but the result is slightly less sumptuous than the original LP, and sonically the new Oslo version on Chandos is even more spectacular.

Abravanel and the Utah Symphony Orchestra give a highly satisfactory account of Tchaikovsky's epic work, with the Byronic atmosphere of the first movement well managed and the central movements nicely paced and effectively characterized. The finale could do with more force and glitter, although the resonant ambience of the Utah auditorium gives plenty of amplitude. But on the whole this account sounds relatively routine by the side of the Jansons and Muti versions.

Marche slave, Op. 31.
(M) *** DG *419 873-4* [id.]. Chicago SO, Barenboim – MUSSORGSKY: *Night on the bare mountain*; RIMSKY-KORSAKOV: *Capriccio espagnol; Easter Festival overture*.***

This is part of a first-rate concert of Russian music showing Barenboim at his finest, and very well recorded.

Méditation (for violin and orchestra, arr. Glazunov), *Op. 42/1.*
*** HMV **CDC7 47087-2** [id.]. Perlman, Israel PO, Mehta – KHACHATURIAN: *Violin concerto.***(*)

A charming Tchaikovskian trifle, arranged for violin and orchestra by Glazunov, makes an agreeable balm to the ear, following on, as it does, after the brilliant finale of the Khachaturian *Concerto.*

The Nutcracker (ballet), *Op. 71* (complete).
*** HMV Dig. **CDS7 47267-8** (2) [Ang. **CDCB 47267**]; *EX 270457-5.* Amb. S., RPO, Previn.
*** Telarc Dig. **CD 8137** (2) [id.]. LSO & Ch., Mackerras.
*** HMV Dig. **CDS7 49399-2** (2) [id.]. Amb. S., Philh. O, Lanchbery.
*** CBS Dig. **M2K 42173** (2) [id.]. Philh. O & Ch., Tilson Thomas.
(B) *** CfP *TC-CFPD 4706* (2). LSO & Ch., Previn.
(*) RCA Dig. **RD 87005 [RCD-2 7005]. St Louis SO & Ch., Slatkin.

The Nutcracker (ballet) complete; *Eugene Onegin: Introduction; Waltz; Polonaise.*
*** Ph. Dig. **420 237-2**; *420 237-4* (2) [id.]. BPO, Bychkov.
** Capriccio **10071/2** [id.] (without *Introduction*). Dresden State O & Boys' Ch., Vonk.

Splendid versions of Tchaikovsky's enchanting Christmas ballet come in profusion and it is almost impossible to suggest a clear first choice. Previn's digital version is superbly played and its freshness is immediately apparent in the opening children's party. With the magic beginning at the growth of the Christmas tree there is a fine toy bang to set off the sparkling battle sequence. The Snowflakes scene is captivating with lovely vocal timbre from the Ambrosians in the delectable *Waltz*. When we arrive at the series of dances which form the *Divertissement* of Act II, the orchestral playing is marvellously elegant and polished, with rhythms lifted and colours glowing. The EMI recording, made at EMI's No. 1 Studio at Abbey Road, has warm ambience, yet detail is cleanly focused and the orchestra is given fine presence.

The Telarc set was recorded in Watford Town Hall, bringing the extra resonance of the concert hall which adds a little glamour to the violins and a glowing warmth in the middle and lower range. Yet the reverberation is nicely calculated to prevent an 'empty hall' feeling. When the magic spell begins, the spectacularly wide dynamic range and the extra amplitude make for a physical frisson in the climaxes, while the glorious climbing melody, as Clara and the Prince travel through the pine forest, sounds richly expansive. Before that, the battle has some real cannon-shots interpolated but is done good-humouredly, for this is a toy battle. In the earlier party scene, Mackerras presses forward more than Previn and this creates added intensity in Act I, but in the Act II *Divertissement* Mackerras's sparkling vivacity is sometimes less telling than Previn's easy elegance, and here the latter is preferable (note how his *Dance of the flutes* has more finesse when it is so nicely relaxed). Yet the great *Pas de deux* brings the most sumptuous climax, with superb sonority from the brass on the Telarc version. The Telarc presentation, too, with a detailed synopsis, is far superior to the much more meagre EMI documentation.

Semyon Bychkov has the services of the Berlin Philharmonic (an orchestra that always identifies readily with Tchaikovsky) and they offer superlative playing, of striking flair and character. The *Miniature overture* is brisk and crisply accented, almost like Mozart, and the events of Act I are strongly dramatized (the gun-shot which opens the battle makes one jump). Although a concert-hall ambience is favoured, the strings seem more forward, inner detail is very clear and the cymbals have a thrilling metallic clash. The strings produce plenty of body in the climbing melody of the Pine forest and they provide great intensity in the passionate climax of the Act II *Pas de deux*. There is some superbly stylish playing in the *Divertissement* and here Mackerras, though not Previn, is upstaged: the latter's *Waltz of the flowers* has a more beguiling lilt. There are many moments when the extra vividness of the Berlin recording is especially compelling, and, of course, Bychkov offers a bonus, for the *Eugene Onegin* excerpts are brilliantly done. The Philips notes are extensive but not so conveniently matched to the CD cues.

Lanchbery has the feeling of ballet music in his very bones, and his account, if not pictorially as evocative in Act I as some of his competitors, nevertheless has an attractive momentum and sweep, so that the narrative line is strongly projected. There are many nuances and touches of detail that could only come from a conductor who knows the score inside out, yet the freshness of his performance is a consistent pleasure too. The Philharmonia Orchestra is on its topmost form; the famous characteristic dances bring engagingly polished solo contributions from throughout the orchestra; and the consistent vitality of the playing is striking when the digital recording is brilliant in a glittering way (yet without edge), while there is no lack of bloom.

Michael Tilson Thomas also has the advantage of fine Philharmonia playing, recorded in rather similar acoustics to the EMI set. The CBS balance is very good too, and this account lies between those of Previn and Mackerras, with a touch more spectacle than the former. The clock striking midnight makes for quite a sinister effect after a feeling of skilfully created tension. The party scene before this has been pressed on strongly, but there is a pleasing relaxation after the battle and the *Waltz of the snowflakes* has real radiance. Tempi are generally a fraction brisker on CBS but the brighter rhythmic feeling often pays dividends. Generally, however, this would not be a first choice and the CBS documentation is inadequate, with only a brief synopsis.

Those looking for a bargain on cassette should be well pleased with Previn's earlier analogue set with the LSO, admirably remastered and sounding freshly minted. As in the later version, the famous dances in Act II are played with much sophistication, and indeed the orchestral playing throughout is of very high quality, often directly comparable in excellence with the much more expensive CD set (which also has a faithful tape equivalent). However, with Act I sounding brighter and more dramatic than originally, this CfP reissue makes a splendid investment, packed in a chunky box, handy for the car.

Slatkin's RCA version and the Vonk Capriccio set are both very well recorded with the Dresden acoustics more sumptuous than those of St Louis. Slatkin's brightly paced reading is not short on vitality and the orchestral playing has plenty of character; Vonk is more wayward and there is too often a feeling of routine (this also applies to the two bonuses from *Eugene Onegin* which have little panache). In the *Waltz of the snowflakes* the chaste Dresden choirboys bring an agreeably cool effect; but generally neither of these sets could be strongly recommended against the competition, although the RCA documentation is excellent.

Nutcracker suite, Op. 71a.

*** Ph. Dig. **412 559-2 [412 556-2]**; *412 559-4* Boston Pops O, John Williams – PROKOFIEV: *Peter and the wolf.****

A vividly crisp performance of Tchaikovsky's marvellous score from John Williams and the Boston Pops. Tempi are brisk and the style is rather metrical, but the playing has plenty of rhythmic lift and only in the closing *Waltz of the flowers* is there a slight lack of lyrical freedom, but not of flair. The characteristic dances are strong on personality: the piccolo in the *Chinese dance* provides superb bravura, and the freely sinuous wind solos in the *Arab dance* are equally engaging. The *Russian dance* is exhilarating, and the Sugar plum fairy is gently seductive. With vivid three-dimensional recording within the glowing Boston acoustic, this makes a first-rate coupling for a splendid version of *Peter and the wolf.*

Nutcracker suite; Romeo and Juliet.
(*) DG Dig. **410 873-2 [id.]. BPO, Karajan.
(*) Telarc Dig. **CD 80068 [id.]. Cleveland O, Maazel.

Originally designed to accompany a picture biography of Karajan, this surprisingly rare Tchaikovsky coupling brings superbly played performances. The suite is delicate and detailed, yet perhaps lacks a little in charm, notably the *Arab dance* which, taken fairly briskly, loses something of its gentle sentience. The overture is both polished and dramatic, but Karajan draws out the climax of the love theme with spacious moulding, and there is marginally less spontaneity here than in his earlier recordings. The sound, characteristic of Berlin, is truthfully balanced; but alongside greater clarity, the CD brings a certain dryness of timbre in *Romeo and Juliet*, while adding a degree of hardness on the high violins in the *Nutcracker*, although the wind and brass solos have good definition and presence.

With vivid orchestral playing and bright, crisply focused recording within a natural ambience, Maazel's *Nutcracker suite* is enjoyably colourful. His manner is affectionate (especially in the warmly lilting *Waltz of the flowers*), and the only idiosyncrasy is the sudden accelerando at the close of the *Russian dance*. *Romeo and Juliet* is given a spaciously romantic performance, reaching a climax of considerable passion. However, the almost overwhelming impact of the percussion in the (undoubtedly exciting) feud music is obviously designed for those who like to say 'Listen to that bass drum!' Others may feel that the balance is not exactly what one would experience in the concert hall.

Nutcracker suite; Romeo and Juliet (fantasy overture); Sleeping Beauty: suite.
(M) *** DG *419 481-4* [id.]. BPO, Karajan.

If not quite as striking as the Decca VPO recording he made a decade earlier (see below), Karajan's DG *Romeo and Juliet* is very telling, with passion and dignity nicely blended. The *Nutcracker suite* is full of character and the *Sleeping Beauty* shows him at his finest, with a high level of tension and orchestral playing that is full of imagination as well as excitement. The remastering for this Galleria triptych seems less severe than the effect created by the *Sleeping Beauty* on CD (the same recordings of the ballet music are used, with *Swan Lake* added – see below). The strings sound fuller and sweeter, yet the freshness remains. The big climax of *Romeo and Juliet* is excitingly caught.

Nutcracker suite; Serenade for strings.
** Ph. Dig. **411 471-2** [id.]. ASMF, Marriner.

A good if not especially individual account of the *Nutcracker suite* is here coupled with a new version of the *Serenade* which is no match for Sir Neville Marriner's Decca account, recorded when the Academy was at an early peak. By the side of this, the new performance, though well played, seems a routine affair. The recording is vivid and full-bodied, with detail slightly more refined on the CD, though the difference is not very striking.

Nutcracker suite; Sleeping Beauty: Introduction and Waltz; Swan Lake: suite.
** ASV Dig. **CDDCA 583**; *ZCDCA 583* [id.]. RPO, Bátiz.
(M) ** Pickwick Dig. **PCD 884** (with *Sleeping Beauty: Adagio – Pas d'action*). LSO, Richard Williams.

Nutcracker suite; Sleeping Beauty: suite; Swan Lake: suite.
(M) *** HMV **CDM7 69044-2** [id.]. LSO, Previn.
(M) **(*) Decca **417 700-2**; *417 274-4* [id.]. VPO, Karajan.
*(**) DG **419 175** [id.]. BPO, Karajan.

The best buy here is the generously full EMI Studio collection, described as 'highlights' from the three ballets. The digital remastering has been very successful, freshening the sound of these excellent analogue recordings, taken from Previn's complete sets (which means that the *Dance of the Sugar Plum Fairy* in *The Nutcracker* has the longer coda rather than the ending Tchaikovsky devised for the *Suite*). The performances are at once vivid and elegant, warm and exciting.

Karajan's DG collection is also generous (74′) but here the digital remastering has brought very bright lighting indeed, with the massed strings inclined to be shrill above the stave at fortissimo levels. The 1972 analogue coupling of *Sleeping Beauty* and *Swan Lake* was outstanding musically. Karajan immediately creates an electrifying climax in the *Introduction* to *The Sleeping Beauty*, and throughout the orchestral solos are wonderfully polished and beguiling, though perhaps the *Little Swans* are made to sound rather reserved. But with the bright treble and a meagre supporting bass response, sonically this is less than the whole Tchaikovskian sound-picture. Interestingly, the earlier (1967) *Nutcracker* is fuller and the *Waltz of the flowers* with its velvety horn timbre demonstrates a greater ambient effect. All three recordings were made in the Jesus-Christus Church, Berlin, which produced so many fine recordings for DG.

The VPO triptych was made during Karajan's Decca period in the 1960s. Again the *Nutcracker suite* (1962) sounds best, but the *Sleeping Beauty* selection, as sound, is much preferable to the DG. Both this and *Swan Lake* were originally paired together in a fine 1965 coupling; if tuttis in the latter are rather sharply focused by the digital transfer, overall this record offers fine playing, even if the VPO textures seem more leonine, less sumptuous than that of the Berlin Philharmonic. The equivalent cassette is first rate without losing vividness, notably so in *Swan Lake*.

Bátiz offers modern digital recording, well balanced within the attractive acoustics of the Henry Wood Hall and the performances are well paced and fresh, certainly spontaneous. Yet the effect has a certain lack of idiosyncrasy (the famous violin and cello duet in *Swan Lake* is rather cool); although enjoyable in its way, this issue seems overpriced.

In his brightly recorded compilation for Pickwick, Richard Williams offers one more *Sleeping Beauty* item than Bátiz. The LSO respond well to the conductor's direct approach, and both playing and sound make a vivid if slightly anonymous impression. The *Nutcracker suite* in particular has less individual characterization than usual, although the *Waltz of the flowers* has a nice lilt. This is good value (58′) but not distinctive.

Nutcracker suite; Swan Lake: excerpts.
(*) Pro Arte Dig. **CDD 121 [id.]. Minnesota SO, Slatkin.
* CBS **MYK 42549** [**MYK 37238**]. NYPO, Bernstein.

Nutcracker suite; Swan Lake: suite.
** Decca Dig. **410 551-2** [id.] Israel PO, Mehta.

Splendid playing from the wind soloists in the excellent Minnesota orchestra and attractively vivid recording, with a very wide dynamic range, the orchestra attractively set out in a concert-hall acoustic. The usual *Swan Lake suite* is augmented to include eight items and, in the closing *Wedding dance*, Slatkin's hitherto spirited direction becomes positively boisterous. There is much attractive detail in both *Suites*, although in the Swan Queen's famous orchestral duet the principal violin (Lea Foli) displays more poetic flair than the cellist (Robert Jamieson). The cornet soloist in the *Neapolitan dance* perhaps slightly overdoes the rubato, while Slatkin's rhythms in the *Waltz of the flowers* are a shade metrical; but otherwise this is a most enjoyable coupling and the playing is generally more spontaneous and imaginative than Mehta's Decca selection.

Mehta's compact disc is markedly superior to the LP recording of the same performances. The sound is fuller and much more refined and, in the *Nutcracker*, textures have more delicacy.

The Mann Auditorium in Tel Aviv, where this recording was made, does not usually provide a flattering ambience, but on the CD it is caught most successfully. Climaxes swell up thrillingly and the brass is especially vivid. Even with the help of CD brilliance, however, the performances are not distinctive enough to command a strong recommendation: there are better versions.

Bernstein's are superbly polished and vividly played performances and the selection from *Swan Lake* is generous. But the glassy upper strings and the lack of a real pianissimo brought about by the forward balance (especially noticeable in the *Miniature overture* of the *Nutcracker*) mean that this cannot be given a full recommendation.

Romeo and Juliet (fantasy overture).

(M) *** Decca **417 722-2** [id.]. VPO, Karajan – GRIEG: *Peer Gynt**** (with R. STRAUSS: *Till Eulenspiegel****).

*** DG **423 068-2** [id.]. San Francisco SO, Ozawa – BERLIOZ: *Romeo.****

Karajan's Decca recording of *Romeo and Juliet* comes from the early 1960s. The performance is marvellously shaped and has superb ardour and excitement: his later DG accounts never quite recaptured the spontaneous freshness of this version. Well coupled with an equally impressive *Till Eulenspiegel* and fine set of excerpts from *Peer Gynt*, this vintage Decca reissue is excellent value. The remastered sound is full, firm and clear.

Ozawa draws from the San Francisco orchestra warmly committed playing, and the vivid new CD transfer increases the impact of the climaxes without losing the Boston ambient atmosphere, although the focus is not absolutely sharp.

Serenade for strings in C, Op. 48.

*** DG Dig. **400 038-2** [id.]. BPO, Karajan – DVOŘÁK: *Serenade.****

(B) **(*) DG Dig. *423 258-4* [id.]. BPO, Karajan – DVOŘÁK: *Serenade*; R. STRAUSS: *Metamorphosen.****

*** ASV *ZCALH 969* [id.]. Polish R. CO, Duczmal – SUK: *Serenade.****

(M) **(*) Ph. **420 883-2** *420 883-4* [id.] ECO, Leppard – DVOŘÁK: *Serenade.* **(*)

(M) **(*) Decca **417 736-2**; *417 736-4* [id.]. ASMF, Marriner – DVOŘÁK: *Serenade*** (with SIBELIUS: *Valse triste.****)

(*) Ph. Dig. **422 031-2; *422 031-4* [id.]. Bav. RSO, C. Davis – DVOŘÁK: *Serenade.***(*)

** DG Dig. **423 060-2**; *423 060-4* [id.]. Orpheus CO – GRIEG: *Holberg suite* etc.*(*)

A vigorously extrovert reading from Karajan, with taut, alert and superbly polished playing in the first movement, an elegant *Waltz*, a passionately intense *Élégie* and a bustling, immensely spirited finale. The compact disc is one of the finest to come from DG. Although there is just a hint of digital edge on the violins, this is offset by the extension of the middle and lower range which is gloriously full and resonant, far superior to the LP. The refinement of inner detail is remarkable. Tchaikovsky often wrote antiphonally (when he was not using his strings in unison), and so clear is the definition that the effect almost becomes visual as ideas move back and forth within the string groupings. This performance and its Dvořák coupling are also available on a DG Pocket Music tape at bargain price. The programme also includes Karajan's superb digital version of Richard Strauss's *Metamorphosen* and must be counted a keen bargain, even though the Tchaikovsky transfer brings a rather over-resonant bass response, not too well focused. The upper range remains clear, but softer-grained than the CD.

The Polish Radio Chamber Orchestra is a first-class body of players and they give a highly individual reading, full of subtlety and grace. The conductor's imaginative nuancing of dynamic shading is most winning and this account often finds a rare quality of tenderness alongside its vigour and expansiveness. The very opening leads to a hint of nostalgia before the main theme of the allegro is gently ushered in, while later the orchestra's lightness of articulation in the busy second subject is delightfully intimate. The *Waltz* is relaxed and gentle, very refined, even thoughtful, with radiant violin timbre; later there is a wistful delicacy in the *Élégie* as Tchaikovsky's lovely cantilena is floated over gentle pizzicatos. Yet there is no lack of temperament or romantic ardour. The finale is exquisitely prepared, then the allegro is off with the wind, very fast, light and balletic, again with engagingly crisp articulation. Altogether this is the kind of performance that makes one appreciate this as one of the composer's greatest works, with its Mozartian elegance and perfection of form. The recording is excellent, full, transparent, yet with a fine overall bloom.

Leppard's remastered Philips recording sounds more leonine than before, yet his warm, direct manner is very attractive, and the Waltz is beautifully done. In general this is preferable to the Marriner alternative. Marriner's 1969 performance came from the Academy's vintage years, and its glowing sense of joy combined with the finest pointing and precision of ensemble put it in a class of its own. The unanimity of phrasing of the violins in the intense slow movement is breathtaking in its expressiveness, but the brightening of the treble response inherent in the digital remastering draws the ear to notice, more than on the original analogue LP, the lack of sheer tonal weight that a bigger body of strings can afford. The performance overall is now made to sound more athletic, less warmly expansive, though the playing in the *Waltz* remains poised and elegant and the *Élégie* is both nostalgic and passionate.

Like the Dvořák coupling, Sir Colin Davis's performance is on the heavy side, with rich timbres from the Bavarian Radio strings and a resonant bass amplifying the breadth and warmth of the reading. While rhythms are resilient, and this is warmly attractive in its way, at times a lighter touch would have been welcome.

No one could accuse the Orpheus Chamber Orchestra of lack of energy in the outer movements; indeed the finale has tremendous bustle and vigour, the sheer nervous energy communicating in exhilarating fashion. Overall it is an impressive performance, even if the problems of rubato without a conductor are not always easily solved. The *Waltz* is nicely relaxed, but the sudden slowing at its coda is not quite convincing, nor is a spurt of accelerando towards the end of the *Élégie*. At the end of the first movement when the great striding opening tune is reprised it is heavily accented for no apparent reason. Yet there is much that is fresh here, and one cannot but admire the precision of ensemble. The sound is first class, with the acoustics of the Performing Arts Center at New York State University providing plenty of warmth as well as clarity and a full, firm bass-line, very important in this work. There is an excellent cassette.

The Sleeping Beauty (ballet), *Op. 66*.
*** BBC **CD 3003X** (3) [id.]. BBC SO, Rozhdestvensky.
** Ph. **420 792-2** (3) [id.]. Concg. O, Dorati.

Rozhdestvensky's set was made as part of the BBC Symphony Orchestra's fiftieth anniversary celebrations and is fully worthy of the occasion. It is superb in every way, marvellously played and very well recorded in an excellent acoustic that is neither too dry nor too resonant for comfort (a problem with this particular score). There is occasional minor spotlighting of wind soloists, but who would cavil when all the solo playing is so outstanding – as indeed are the contributions of the strings and brass: the trumpet and horn fanfares are splendid. Rozhdestvensky uses the original Russian score, which is absolutely complete, even including music omitted from the ballet's première. There are those who hold that this is Tchaikovsky's greatest ballet score, finer even than *Swan Lake*; and these discs do much to support that view. The work could not be entrusted to more caring or sensitive direction, and the ear is continually amazed by the consistent quality of Tchaikovsky's inspiration. Rozhdestvensky's loving attention to detail and his response to the textural colouring are matched by his feeling for the narrative drama, yet he never overplays his hand, so that the big moments of spectacle – the *Rose adagio*, for instance – have ardour without becoming emotionally aggressive. Tchaikovsky's continuously fertile imagination in matters of scoring is readily demonstrated, and the lighter characteristic dances sound as fresh as the day they were written. There is atmosphere too, and the magical *Sleep entr'acte* before the happy ending of the story is given a haunting sense of anticipation and fantasy. In CD form this is an outstanding achievement in every way.

Dorati's is a vibrant and dramatic account, supported by firm, rich recording and splendid orchestral playing (especially in the last Act, which gives the orchestral wind soloists many chances to shine). Yet this is a score that – for all its melodic inspiration – can momentarily disengage the listener's attention; and here in spite of the drama this does happen. Everything is well characterized, but at times there is a lack of magic.

Sleeping Beauty: extended suite; *Swan Lake:* extended suite.
(*) Telarc Dig. **CD 80151 [id.]. RPO, Mackerras.

(i) *Sleeping Beauty: suite*; (ii) *Swan Lake, Op. 20:* excerpts.
(B) **(*) DG Walkman *413 430-4* [id.]. (i) BPO, Rostropovich; (ii) Boston SO, Ozawa – PROKOFIEV: *Romeo and Juliet.****

Sleeping Beauty: suite; Swan Lake: suite.
(*) HMV Dig. **CDC7 47075-2 [id.]. Phd. O, Muti.

Those who enjoy Telarc recording of Tchaikovsky with its wide dynamic range, rich, sweet violins, ripe middle sonorities, spectacular brass (and the bass drum never forgotten) will enjoy this greatly. The richly resonant sound-picture adds much to the recording; indeed in the *Introduction* to the *Sleeping Beauty* it is more the impact of the recording than any special fervour in the playing itself that creates the excitement; Karajan's Berlin Philharmonic version produces more real intensity here. Similarly in the overwhelming finale of *Swan Lake* the recording is at its most thrillingly weighty. But elsewhere Mackerras's penchant for brisk tempi does not always find all the magic and colour. The gorgeous *Panorama* from *Sleeping Beauty*, with its melody floated over a rocking bass, sounds much more beguiling at Previn's relaxed tempo; similarly the famous oboe theme of *Swan Lake* is attractively nubile but could be more serene. The violin/cello duet of the *Dance of the Swans* is a highlight, but overall an element of routine hovers over this music making, for all its surface vivacity. Previn's HMV disc offering selections from all three major ballets remains preferable, except for those who want to wallow in Telarc's sumptuous sonic histrionics.

Rostropovich's *Sleeping Beauty suite* is highly distinguished, as fine as any in the catalogue. The recording is wonderfully expansive and the performances admirably combine Slavonic intensity with colour. The whimsical portrait of the cats contrasts with the glorious *Panorama* melody, floated over its gently rocking bass with magical delicacy. The collection of *Swan Lake* excerpts from Ozawa is generous. Here the sophistication of playing and recording, within the warm Boston acoustic, is impressive; while the individual items have less individuality of approach than with Rostropovich, the orchestral response is first class and the final climax expands magnificently. Combined with an excellent selection from Prokofiev's *Romeo and Juliet*, this Walkman tape is splendid value.

From HMV, one of the first recordings made by the Philadelphia Orchestra in the Fairmount Park Memorial Hall, which at last provides a flattering ambience for this great orchestra. The layout has a convincing concert-hall perspective so that the placing of the solo string players in the beautifully phrased *Swan Queen's dance* is naturally distanced. The only snag (if it is that) is the very wide dynamic range, which means that when one achieves a satisfactory level for the violin/cello duet the spectacular climaxes are almost overwhelming. The order of items in *Swan Lake* is unconventional, ending with the Act III *Mazurka* instead of the (perhaps more suitable) grandiloquent finale. Muti's approach is essentially spacious and he concentrates on the elegance of the music, achieving an excellent response from his orchestra. There is not the Slavonic intensity of Rostropovich here, nor quite the electricity of Karajan in the *Rose Adagio*, yet the recording makes a thrilling effect at fortissimo level, and its amplitude is considerable. The CD is transferred at the highest level; this increases the presence of the orchestra even further and emphasizes the resonance of the loudest moments, with the textures glowingly rich.

Souvenir de Florence (orchestral version), *Op. 70.*
*** Tel. Dig. **ZK8 43311**; *AZ4 43311* [id.]. Israel CO, Talmi – SCHOENBERG: *Verklaerte Nacht.****

Souvenir de Florence, Op. 70.
(*) Claves Dig. **CD 50-8507 [id.]. Camerata Lysy (with ATTERBERG: *Suite No. 3, Op. 19/1.* BLOCH: *From Jewish life: Prayer.* PUCCINI: *Crisantemi.* WAGNER: *Träume.***(*)).

Souvenir de Florence; Serenade for strings.
** Erato Dig. **ECD 88237** [id.]. Berne Camerata, Füri.

It is high time that Tchaikovsky's sextet, the *Souvenir de Florence*, left the chamber for the concert hall. It can sound well enough with one instrument to a part when played as well and as sympathetically as by the Camerata Lysy of Gstaad, but it is transformed when it is performed with a full orchestral string section within a spacious ambience. The account by the Israel Chamber Orchestra under Yoav Talmi is the finest on record (and not forgetting the old ASMF version under Marriner, which was cut to fit on a single LP side). The Israeli strings play with superb sweep and make one realize that the piece is brimming over with memorable Tchaikovsky tunes, as luscious as any in the *Serenade*. The second subject of the first movement is quite haunting, and the *Andante cantabile* is equally lovely, rhapsodic in the way of the *Élégie* from the *Serenade*. With yet another swinging melody in the finale, played with fine verve here, this fine work must surely find a niche in the standard repertoire. Talmi is a true Tchaikovskian and his shaping and control of the ebb and flow of tension are masterly. The sound too is splendidly full-bodied, brighter on CD than on the chrome tape (which is excellent in its own right). The Schoenberg coupling is equally involving.

Of the two chamber versions the Camerata Lysy is preferable, with fine ensemble and plenty of fervour; but six string players are not enough for this piece. The couplings are all highly romantic and enjoyable, but a bit insubstantial.

The Berne performances are polished and characterful, but there is more of an element of routine in the playing. The coupling is apt and if the music making had been more imaginative this would have been an ideal pairing.

Suites Nos 1 in D min., Op. 45; 4 (Mozartiana), Op. 61.
(M) *** Olympia Dig. **OCD 109** [id.]. USSR Academic SO, Svetlanov.

Tchaikovsky's *Orchestral suites* are directly descended from the dance suites of the Baroque era and Svetlanov shows his understanding of this link by his engagingly light touch. He is particularly successful in *Mozartiana*, where Tchaikovsky's neat scoring is always respectful of the music. Even so, the *Preghiera*, based on Mozart's *Ave verum*, can sometimes sound too opulent, but not here. The *Variations* which end the suite are a delight, while the opening *Gigue* finds a ready parallel with the closing *Gavotte* of the *First Suite*, Tchaikovsky's own music, when both are articulated so buoyantly. The earlier D minor work suffers from the charismatic personality of its central movement, a deliciously orchestrated *Marche miniature* which tends to dwarf everything else, except perhaps the *Introduction* where Tchaikovsky's innate melancholy at the opening is effectively dispersed by the following fugato. With such sympathetic playing and excellent digital sound, this is a prime recommendation for all keen Tchaikovskians.

(i) *Suite No. 2 in C, Op. 53;* (ii) *Symphony No. 2 in C min.,* (*Little Russian*), *Op. 17.*
(M) *** Olympia **OCD 153** [id.]. (i) USSR Academic SO, Svetlanov; (ii) USSR RSO, Fedoseyev.

Svetlanov's inspirational recording of the *Second Suite* is doubly distinctive for making the listener realize that this is a far more substantial and attractive work than was previously thought. The first movement, subtitled *Jeu de son* ('Play of sounds'), after the Introduction (which itself has two striking ideas) contrasts three separate themes, the first essentially rhythmic, the second lyrical and scored for flutes and clarinets, the third contrasted again, with more movement. They are thrown together in an exuberant free fantasia, which includes an ingenious fugato. Clearly Tchaikovsky was seeking a strong baroque association here, although his lyrical strain triumphs and the *Introduction* returns to make a coda. The second movement is a graceful *Waltz*, but by no means conventional in treatment, while the *Scherzo burlesque* bustles with energy (the playing here is exhilarating). It has a part for accordions in its central section, but here they are covered with folksy woodwind sounds: the effect is highly piquant. Then comes a charming *Rêves d'enfant*, a pensive lullaby, developed most imaginatively, and finally a vivacious *Danse baroque* (in the style of Dargomizhky, suggested the composer) where the energy of the performance bubbles right over. The Russian orchestral playing is full of character and affection throughout and the vivid recording is a joy in projecting this multi-coloured music.

Fedoseyev's version of the *Little Russian symphony* may not be the most brilliant available: the finale is paced in a very relaxed way and the further broadening at the end is overdone. But the very Russian character of the woodwind and the bright, clean string articulation give the music making plenty of character and impulse. The opening melody of the first movement, scored first for the horn and then the bassoon, has the melancholy of the genuine folksong, and the playing is gently responsive in a special way, quite unlike a West European performance. With a total playing time of 73′ 55″ this bright-hued disc is well worth having, even if it means duplicating the symphony.

Suite No. 3 in G, Op. 55.
(M) *** Olympia Dig. **OCD 106** [id.]. USSR Academic SO, Svetlanov – ARENSKY: *Violin concerto.****

When Tchaikovsky began work on his *Third Suite* in 1884 he thought a symphony was in gestation, but in the end he contented himself with the present work. 'The title is of no consequence,' he suggested to Taneyev, but one senses that the music had taken on a life of its own and produced a hybrid structure which didn't entirely satisfy its composer. The first movement is lyrically rhapsodic and Svetlanov treats it very freely, supported by the most eloquent response from one of the premier Soviet orchestras; then comes a bitter-sweet *Valse mélancolique*, its nostalgia curiously dark for all its grace and lightness of form. The Scherzo, deliciously scored, is almost too purposefully gay, but the work is capped by the masterly final theme and variations, which quite outbalances the structure but justifies itself by its inspired melodic invention, and in its unsurpassed use of orchestral colour. Here some of Svetlanov's tempi are unexpected, notably in variations 3 and 4, while the woodwind chorale which precedes the lovely variation 8 is lightly articulated rather than preparing for the dark melancholy of the cor anglais solo to follow. This is beautifully played in a full-throated Russian way, as is the Mazurka violin solo which forms variation 10. The finale *Polacca* is less overwhelming than in some previous versions, Svetalanov emphasizing its dance rhythms rather than seeking to be grandiose. With excellent, vivid digital recording and an attractive concert-hall ambience, this is highly recommendable, particularly in view of the tempting Arensky coupling and an overall playing time of 65′ 12″.

Suites Nos 3 in G, Op. 55; 4 in G (Mozartiana), Op. 61.
** Capriccio Dig. **10 200** [id.]. Stuttgart RSO, Marriner.

Marriner's performances are cultured and polished; the playing of the Stuttgart orchestra can hardly be faulted in ensemble and they are not unresponsive. Yet, compared to the Svetlanov versions, the musiç making here is mellow to the point of blandness. The vitality and life which make the Russian performances so vivid appear only fitfully in Stuttgart and both sets of variations which make up the final movement of each *Suite* are disappointingly under-characterized; moreover, neither has cues provided for the individual variations. The Stuttgart recording is very naturally balanced, but this coupling remains a great disappointment.

Swan Lake (ballet), *Op. 20* (complete).
(*) HMV **CDS7 49531-2 (2) [id.]. LSO, Previn.
** DG **415 367-2** (2) [id.]. Boston SO, Ozawa.

Previn's set, like his recordings of the other Tchaikovsky ballets, offers extremely polished orchestral playing, with beautiful wind solos, helped by a full, resonant recording which gives plenty of bloom to the overall sound-picture. Miss Haendel's contribution is first class, and there is much refined detail and no lack of drama when the music calls for it. As in his recording of *The Nutcracker*, Previn is at his finest in the Act III *Divertissement* with its variety of national dances where the orchestral soloists all excel themselves. The recording, originally a little contained and plushy, has been admirably opened out by the digital remastering and sounds very fresh, with little loss of ambient warmth. But it would have been more generous of EMI to reissue this 1976 set at mid-price; the focus is not always absolutely clear.

Ozawa omits the Act III *Pas de deux* but otherwise plays the original score as Tchaikovsky conceived it. It is now generously fitted on to a pair of CDs, against the three LPs of the original issue. The performance was by no means a first choice in its LP format: Previn has far more character. But the playing of the Boston orchestra is strikingly polished and sympathetic, and there are many impressive things here, with wind (and violin) solos that always give pleasure. The 1979 analogue recording is spectacular and wide-ranging, and it has been enhanced in this transfer to CD, but the end result is just a little faceless, without quite the verve or the seductive elegance of Previn and the LSO.

Swan Lake (ballet), *Op. 20:* highlights.
(M) ❀ *** Decca *417 881-4* [id.]. Concg. O, Fistoulari.
(M) *** HMV *EG 290305-4* [id.]. LSO, Previn.
(M) **(*) Ph. **420 872-2**; *420 872-4* [id.]. LSO, Monteux.
** Denon Dig. **C37 7479** [id.]. VSO, Soltesz.

Fistoulari was a marvellous ballet conductor; in Tchaikovsky he could be inspired, as he was here on this magnificent Decca tape, recorded in 1961, certainly the finest *Swan Lake* selection in the catalogue and probably the most distinguished single set of highlights (or 'Scenes' as they are described) from any Tchaikovsky ballet. The Concertgebouw playing is wonderfully responsive and Fistoulari's always apt tempi and his consistent care for detail go along with a thrillingly 'live' quality to the music making. The recording was of a demonstration standard when it first appeared and still sounds extremely vivid in its Weekend tape format, although the remastering has not produced an absolutely clean focus in fortissimos.

Previn's selection is both generous and felicitous. It is superbly played and shows the very best qualities of his complete set, with splendid wind solos and a rich-toned contribution from the violinist, Ida Haendel. The recording has been digitally remastered; the quality is full, slightly drier than the original, but still impressive. At mid-price, this is highly recommendable.

Monteux is also a master of this repertoire and his 1962 recording has been made to seem more vivid, while the weight of the sound remains especially effective in the finale, which Monteux takes broadly and grandly. The LSO playing is lively and responsive, if perhaps not quite as fetching as on the Previn selection. But those looking for an inexpensive CD of this repertoire should find this very satisfactory. There is also a good tape.

The Hungarian-born Stefan Soltesz is Viennese by upbringing and is a former soloist in the Vienna Boys' Choir. As conductor of the Vienna National Opera Ballet, he is obviously familiar with this repertoire; he secures meticulously rehearsed playing from the VSO, which has no lack of life. The orchestral solo contributions are sensitive, if not displaying the personality of the LSO under Previn, and at times the music making is just a little lacking in flair. The recording is wide-ranging and its ambience pleasing. The selection is fairly generous, but CD collectors will find that other couplings of the *Suite* with music from the *Nutcracker* and *Sleeping Beauty* are more rewarding than this.

Symphony No. 1 in G min. (Winter daydreams), Op. 13.
❀ *** Chan. Dig. **CHAN 8402**; *ABTD 1139* [id.]. Oslo PO, Jansons.
*** HMV **CDC7 47866-2** [id.]. New Philh. O, Muti.

Symphony No. 1; Marche slave, Op. 31; Eugene Onegin: Polonaise and Waltz.
*** DG **419 176-2** [id.]. BPO, Karajan.

Refreshingly direct in style and for the most part avoiding the romantically expressive moulding common in Tchaikovsky interpretations, Jansons with his brilliant orchestra gives an electrically compelling performance of this earliest of the symphonies. The focus is sharp, both of the playing and of the recording, which is both brilliant and atmospheric. Structurally strong, the result tingles with excitement, most of all in the finale, faster than usual, with the challenge of the complex fugato passages superbly taken. Jansons' directness is conveyed with such involvement that there is no question of the performance sounding cold, least of all in the lyrical outpouring of the slow movement. The recording is highly successful in both media. Our Rosette is a token not only of this performance but also of the others in Jansons' outstandingly successful Chandos cycle of the Tchaikovsky *Symphonies*, a remarkable combined achievement for conductor, orchestral players and recording engineers alike.

Having recorded the last three Tchaikovsky symphonies three times over in little more than ten years, Karajan finally turned to the earlier symphonies (before returning for the fourth time to the later works, with video in mind, this time using the VPO – see below). In the first three of the Tchaikovsky canon, displaying the same superlative refined qualities he produced performances with the great Berlin orchestra which proved equally illuminating. The orchestral playing is marvellous and it is typical that, though the opening *Allegro tranquillo* of the first movement of No. 1 is taken fast, there is no feeling of breathlessness, as there usually is: it is genuinely *tranquillo*, though the rhythmic bite of the syncopated passages, so important in these early symphonies, could hardly be sharper. The high polish may give a hint of the ballroom to some of the dance movements, with the folk element underplayed, but the fugato in the last movement is given classical strength (there is never any sign that Karajan sees the first three symphonies as immature), and the peroration has regality and splendour. The sound is excellent, brilliant and with a wide dynamic range. The CD transfer is one of DG's best: there is little suggestion that this is not a modern recording; the sound has refinement and transparency in the slow movement. However, the quality is very much brasher in all three fill-ups, with the upper range bright to the point of glare in the *Eugene Onegin* excerpts; and the overall sound is shallow by the side on the symphony.

Tchaikovsky's marking *Allegro tranquillo* for the first movement presents problems of interpretation for any conductor. If the metronome marking is observed faithfully the result sounds rather tense and breathless, until sixty or so bars later the music comes to need that urgency. Muti, like Karajan, has a fast tempo from the start, and needs no speed-change. It is the only questionable point of tension in a beautiful reading, which is helped by fine recording quality and warmly sympathetic playing. There is no mistaking the way the performance takes wing, with a glorious climax to the horn melody in the slow movement, a light and lilting Scherzo, and an urgent finale. The remastered sound is full and the sense of orchestral presence is enhanced; but without a coupling this could not be recommended in preference to either Karajan or Jansons.

Symphony No. 2 in C min. (*Little Russian*), *Op. 17* (original 1872 score).
*** Chan. Dig. **CHAN 8304**; *ABTD 1071* [id.]. LSO, Simon.

This is the first recording of Tchaikovsky's original score of the *Little Russian symphony* and probably the first performance outside Russia. It was prompted (like the earlier Chandos set of rare Tchaikovsky – see above) by the enterprising enthusiasm of Edward Johnson, who provides an admirably exhaustive sleeve-note (included with the cassette too). Although the 1872 score gained considerable success at its early performances, it gave the composer immediate and serious doubts, principally about the construction of the first movement and the length of the finale. Fortunately the work had only been published in piano-duet form, and so in 1879 Tchaikovsky retrieved the score and immediately set to work to rewrite the first movement. He left the *Andante* virtually unaltered, touched up the scoring of the Scherzo, made minor excisions and added repeats, and made a huge cut of 150 bars (some two minutes of music) in the finale. He then destroyed the original. (The present performance has been possible because of the surviving orchestral parts.) There can be no question that Tchaikovsky was right. The reworked first movement is immensely superior to the first attempt and the finale – delightful though it is – seems quite long enough shorn of the extra bars. However, to hear the composer's first thoughts (as with the original version of *Romeo and Juliet*) is fascinating, and this is an indispensable recording for all Tchaikovskians. The original first movement begins and ends much like the familiar version with its andante horn theme based on the folksong, *Down by Mother Volga*, but the first subject of the exposition offers unfamiliar lyrical material. The working out is more self-consciously 'symphonic', and clearly there is more rhetoric than development. There are some exciting moments of course, but in the end one remains unconvinced. Geoffrey Simon secures a committed response from the LSO, there is some splendid string playing in the finale, and the brass is bitingly sonorous as recorded. Indeed, the sound is first class and the chrome tape is very impressive, too, in its range and impact. The compact disc is striking in its inner orchestral detail and freshness, and although the lower range is without the resonant richness of some CDs, the balance remains very good and the bass drum is telling without swamping the fortissimos.

Symphony No. 2 in C min. (*Little Russian*), *Op. 17* (*see also above, under Suite No. 2*).
*** Telarc Dig. **CD 80131** [id.]. Pittsburgh SO, Maazel – RIMSKY-KORSAKOV: *Antar*.***

Symphony No. 2 (*Little Russian*); *Capriccio italien, Op. 45.*
*** Chan. Dig. **CHAN 8460**; *ABTD 1173* [id.]. Oslo PO, Jansons.

Symphony No. 2 (*little Russian*); *Overture 1812, Op. 49.*
*** DG **419 177-2** [id.]. BPO, Karajan.

Symphony No. 2 (*Little Russian*); *Romeo and Juliet* (fantasy overture).
*** HMV **CDC7 47867-2** [id.]. Philh. O, Muti.

Symphony No. 2 (*Little Russian*); *The Tempest, Op. 18.*
(*) CBS Dig. **MK 39359 [id.]. Chicago SO, Abbado.

Jansons and the Oslo Philharmonic in their outstanding Tchaikovsky series give a characteristically warm and affectionate, yet unmannered reading. Like other Soviet conductors, Jansons prefers a fastish speed for the *Andantino* second movement, but what above all distinguishes this version is the joyful exuberance both of the bouncy Scherzo – fresh and folk-like in the Trio – and of the finale. Jansons' handling of the syncopated idea in the development section of that movement is a delight, and the final coda brings a surge of excitement, making most others seem stiff. The coupling is a fizzing performance of the *Capriccio italien*, bringing a gloriously uninhibited account of the coda with its deliberately vulgar reprise of the Neapolitan tune. With some edge on violin tone, this is not the finest of the Chandos Oslo recordings, but still fresh and atmospheric. The cassette smoothes a little of the edge and is otherwise full and vivid.

Muti's account is characteristically fresh. His warmth brings an agreeable geniality to the first movement, which does not lack excitement but is not too aggressively pointed. His *Andantino* takes Tchaikovsky's *marziale* rather literally, but its precise rhythmic beat has character without heaviness. Perhaps here, as in the finale, there is less than the full degree of charm, but the Scherzo is vivacious and clean. In the finale Muti's degree of relaxed affection produces much colour, and the movement has strong character, even if the performance lacks a strong forward thrust of excitement. The recording is rich and full. The digital remastering has brought added presence without loss of body; indeed, the bass seems more extended and more resonant. Muti's *Romeo and Juliet* is distinguished, one of the finest available, full of imaginative touches. The opening has just the right degree of atmospheric restraint and immediately creates a sense of anticipation; the great romantic climax is noble in contour yet there is no lack of passion, while the main allegro is crisply and dramatically pointed. The repeated figure on the timpani at the coda is made to suggest a tolling bell, and the expressive woodwind playing which follows gently underlines the feeling of tragedy. The full, rich recording suits the interpretation and this generous coupling can be strongly recommended alongside Jansons.

Karajan's performance of the *Little Russian symphony* is superbly played. Everything is in perfect scale; the tempo for the engaging *Andante* is very nicely judged, and the outer movements have plenty of drama and fire. The articulation in the finale is a joy, and the sound balance is excellent. The recording is not as richly resonant as Muti's and the ambient effect seems slightly drier than in the *First Symphony*, but there is no lack of weight. Karajan's *1812* is also exciting and brilliantly transferred, but many will not count this an ideal coupling.

Maazel has broadened his view since he made his first recording of the work as part of his Decca series with the Vienna Philharmonic in the 1960s. The slow introduction is now weightier and much more measured. From then on, as before, Maazel believes in treating Tchaikovsky directly and without sentimentality, but there is a degree more relaxation in this fine Pittsburgh account, incisive of attack, refined of texture. The undistracting freshness of his view – never too tense – is enhanced by excellent, well-balanced recording. If the fine *Antar* coupling is suitable, this is thoroughly worth while.

Abbado's version is the first in a projected new Tchaikovsky series from CBS, and its advantage over direct rivals is the interest of its fill-up, Tchaikovsky's large-scale *Fantasy* on Shakespeare's *The Tempest* – not to be confused with the much less ambitious piece, based on Ostrovsky's *The Storm*. In that work, Abbado's performance, dramatic and passionate as well as evocative in the opening seascape, is likely to be unrivalled on record: in the *Symphony*, too, he is most persuasive, with virtuoso playing from the Chicago orchestra. With speeds generally faster than usual, he conveys lightness and sparkle, so that the *Andantino marziale* of the second movement becomes a sharply pointed miniature march and in the Scherzo the cross-rhythms are incisively sprung. Only in the finale does he adopt a restrained basic speed; effectively so, except that he slows perceptibly in the jaunty syncopated counter-subject. The recording is warm with the sound a little distanced, natural and undistracting but not ideally clear on detail.

The CD, disappointingly, brings no improvement, with the lower range not too well focused and the bass drum balanced too prominently at times, especially in the finale of the *Symphony*. There are no dividing bands for individual movements.

Symphony No. 3 in D (Polish), Op. 29.
*** Chan. Dig. **CHAN 8463**; *ABTD 1179* [id.]. Oslo PO, Jansons.
*** HMV **CDC7 47868-2** [id.]. Philh. O, Muti.

Symphony No. 3 in D (Polish); Capriccio italien, Op. 45.
*** DG **419 178-2** [id.]. BPO, Karajan.

A clear first choice for Tchaikovsky's *Polish symphony* is difficult to determine. Karajan, Jansons and Muti each have their own virtues and the digital remastering of the HMV issue is particularly successful, with rich, resonant sound that brings out all the warmth and colour of Tchaikovsky's scoring.

Jansons' performance of Tchaikovsky's least tractable symphony glows with freshness and vitality; it certainly deserves its share of the token Rosette given to the companion performance of the *Winter daydreams symphony*. Like that account, the *Third* is given a clear, refreshingly direct reading, totally unsentimental, yet conveying the warmth as well as the exuberance of Tchaikovsky's inspiration. The likeness with *Swan Lake* in the first movement is delectably pointed, but it is the irresistible sweep of urgency with which Jansons builds the development section that puts his performance apart, with the basic tempo varied less than usual. The second movement is beautifully relaxed, light and lilting in *Alla tedesca*. The *Andante elegiaco* brings a heartwarming performance, expressive, tender and refined. The fourth-movement Scherzo has a Mendelssohnian elfin quality, but it is the swaggering reading of the finale, always in danger of sounding bombastic, which sets the seal on the whole performance. Even the anthem-like second subject has a lightness of touch, avoiding any sense of squareness or coarseness. Though the recording does not convey a genuinely hushed pianissimo for the strings, it brings full, rich and brilliant sound, like the others in the series. The CD adds a touch of extra precision in the overall focus, but the cassette sounds very impressive too, strikingly warm and full, yet not lacking range and transparency, and with particularly convincing violin tone.

The playing of the Berlin orchestra is wonderfully polished and committed; Karajan's first movement is full of flair and in the central movements he is ever conscious of the variety of Tchaikovsky's colouring. He even finds an affinity with Brahms in the second movement, and yet the climax of the *Andante* is full of Tchaikovskian fervour. In the finale the articulation of the *Polacca* is both vigorous and joyful, and it brings a sense of symphonic strength, often lacking in other versions. The recording is bold, brilliant and clear, with the CD refining detail without loss of weight. After the close of the symphony, the spectacular entry of the brass in the *Capriccio* brings a certain glare to the sound, but this is a sparkling performance and the recording is generally well balanced.

Muti is at his finest in the three central movements, with the Philharmonia playing full of charm, the ballet associations acknowledged, and the soloists revelling in the colour and warmth of Tchaikovsky's felicitous scoring. The *Andante* is admirably volatile, and while the outer movements have not quite the forward impulse of the Jansons version, the playing is alert and sparkling. The wide dynamic range of HMV recording brings powerful climaxes, but in the grandiose peroration at the close of the finale, Muti does not match Karajan in minimizing the sense of rhetoric.

Symphonies Nos 4–6 (Pathétique).
❀ *** DG **419 745-2** (2) [id.]. Leningrad PO, Mravinsky.

Few reissues give greater cause for rejoicing than this, the last three Tchaikovsky symphonies by the late Yevgeny Mravinsky and the Leningrad Philharmonic Orchestra. They have never been surpassed – save, perhaps, by their classic 1956 mono accounts – and rarely equalled. The DG remastering produces a much cleaner and better-defined sound than we have ever had before and is a vast improvement particularly over the cassette version which appeared a couple of years ago. These are very exciting performances which bring one closer to the soul of this music than almost any other accounts: and it is good to have them with several layers of murkiness removed. They cannot be recommended too strongly.

Symphony No. 4 in F min., Op. 36.
*** Chan Dig. **CHAN 8361**; *ABTD 1124* [id.]. Oslo PO, Jansons.
(*) DG Dig. **415 348-2 [id.]. VPO, Karajan.
(*) Telarc Dig. **CD 80047 [id.]. Cleveland O, Maazel.
** Ph. Dig. **400 090-2** [id.]. Pittsburgh SO, Previn.
*(*) Decca Dig. **414 192-2** [id.]. Chicago SO, Solti.

Symphony No. 4; Capriccio italien.
(M) *** DG **419 872-2**; *419 872-4* [id.]. BPO, Karajan.

Symphony No. 4; Marche slave.
(M) **(*) Pickwick Dig. **PCD 867**. LSO, Rozhdestvensky.

In his outstanding Tchaikovsky series with the Oslo Philharmonic, Jansons conducts a dazzling performance of the *Fourth*, unusually fresh and natural in its expressiveness, yet with countless subtleties of expression, as in the balletic account of the second-subject group of the first movement. So idiomatic-sounding is Jansons' handling that the transitions between sections are totally unobtrusive, with steady rather than fluctuating speeds. The *Andantino* flows lightly and persuasively, the Scherzo is very fast and lightly sprung, while the finale reinforces the impact of the whole performance: fast and exciting, but with no synthetic whipping-up of tempo. That is so until the very end of the coda, which finds Jansons pressing ahead just fractionally as he would in a concert, a thrilling conclusion made the more so by the wide-ranging, brilliant and realistic recording in which the reverberant background brings warmth of atmosphere and little or no obscuring of detail. The CD adds impressively to the orchestra's sense of presence within the characterful ambience of the Oslo Philharmonic Hall, although the lower end of the sound spectrum is less expansive than Maazel's Telarc Cleveland recording. The chrome cassette is highly successful; tape collectors can be assured that its loss of range and clarity of detail, compared with the CD, is marginal.

Karajan's 1977 version is undoubtedly more compelling than his previous recordings (one for DG and two for EMI) and is in most respects preferable to the new Vienna version too. After a dramatically robust fanfare at the start of the first movement, the theme of the *Allegro* steals in and although its atmosphere has a tinge of melancholy, there is a hint of suaveness also. But any doubts are swept away by the vitality and drive of the performance as as whole, and the beauty of the wind playing at the opening and close of the slow movement can give nothing but pleasure. The finale has tremendous force to sweep the listener along, and the wide dynamic range of the recording makes the most dramatic effect. The CD transfer is extremely vivid and there is an excellent tape. The ubiquitous *Capriccio italien* is offered as a filler.

The *Fourth* is the most successful of the last three Tchaikovsky symphony recordings which Karajan made in 1985 in connection with the Telemodial video project. Although the playing of the Vienna orchestra does not match that of the Berlin Philharmonic in earlier versions, the performance itself has greater flexibility and more spontaneity. The freer control of tempo in the first movement brings a more relaxed second-subject group, while in the *Andantino* the

Vienna oboist is fresher (though the timbre is edgier) than his Berlin counterpart, the phrasing less calculated. The Scherzo is attractively bright, if less precise, and the finale has splendid urgency and excitement. With the extra depth in the bass that CD can provide, the sound is fuller than before, and the warmly resonant acoustic is attractive, even if detail remains a little clouded. But the Chandos version has even greater electricity and the Oslo recording is richer still, and clearer.

Maazel's Telarc Cleveland disc was one of the first digital recordings of any Tchaikovsky symphony; in its initial LP format it established a reputation for sound of spectacular depth and brilliance within natural concert-hall acoustics. The CD is even more impressive in its amplitude and range. It was made, not in the Severance Hall – scene of other Telarc early successes – but in the Masonic Auditorium. Maazel's reading is very similar to his 1965 Decca record, and only in the finale does the new version differ markedly from the old, by seeking amplitude and breadth in preference to uninhibited extrovert excitement. Maazel's is a less subtle approach than Jansons', but it generates a strong forward momentum in the first movement and is consistently involving in its directness. Yet he lightens the tension effectively (like Jansons) by his balletic approach to the second-subject group. The slow movement, with a plaintive oboe solo, is distinctly appealing, and at the *Più mosso* Maazel makes a swift, bold tempo change, whereas here Jansons makes the transition more flexibly. On the whole, Jansons' is the more imaginative reading, and his finale generates more adrenalin, but the Cleveland Orchestra produces not only a richer body of timbre in the upper strings but has a fuller, more resonant response from the lower strings and brass. This is immediately apparent at the first big fortissimo chord at the end of the – comparatively mellow – opening fanfare of the first movement.

After the fanfare, Rozhdestvensky's performance takes a little while to warm up, but when the first climax arrives it is very impressive, and the big unison horn entry at bar 169 is thrilling. The lyrical secondary material is presented very beguilingly and the rocking string theme at the *Ben sostenuto* is positively sensuous. The slow movement is basically simple, although Rozhdestvensky allows himself a mannered emphasis at its climax. The Scherzo, light and gentle, has the feeling of an arabesque and the finale is strongly articulated and expansive. With first-class digital recording and a powerful response from the LSO in both the symphony and the coupled *Marche slave*, this is certainly worth considering in the mid-price range.

Previn's view is distinctive. His preference in Tchaikovsky is for directness and no mannerism: with unusually slow speeds for the first three movements, this produces little excitement and some lack of charm, however. The finale makes up for that with a very fast tempo, which is a formidable challenge for the Pittsburgh orchestra, here distinguishing itself with fine playing, well recorded. The CD is a major improvement on the original LP issue, the sound brighter and fresher, with no unnatural edge on the violins; but other versions are more involving.

Solti's basic speed for the first movement is surprisingly slow, yet it remains a clear-headed, straightforward reading rather than an affectionate one. The *Andantino* is then slow to the point of sounding sluggish, while in the third and fourth movements, taken very fast, he finally goes for brilliance at all costs. In brilliant sound, lacking a little in depth and perspective, emphasized on CD, it is not a version to warm to.

Symphony No. 5 in E min., Op. 64.

*** Chan. Dig. **CHAN 8351**; *ABTD 1111* [id.]. Oslo PO, Jansons.

*** Telarc Dig. **CD 80107** [id.]. RPO, Previn – RIMSKY-KORSAKOV: *Tsar Saltan: March.****

*** HMV **CDC7 47859-2** [id.]. Philh. O, Muti.

(*) DG Dig. **415 094-2 [id.]. VPO, Karajan.

** ASV Dig. *ZCDCA 550* [id.]. LPO, Bátiz.

** Decca Dig. **410 232-2** [id.]. VPO, Chailly.

*(*) CBS Dig. **CD 36700** [id.]. Cleveland O, Maazel.
*(*) Delos **D/CD 3015** [id.]. Phd. O, Ormandy.
(M) *(*) Decca **417 723-2** [id.]. Chicago SO, Solti – GLINKA: *Russian overture*; MUSSORGSKY: *Night on the bare mountain.****

Symphony No. 5 Capriccio italien.
(M) **(*) Pickwick Dig. **PCD 875.** LSO, Rozhdestvensky.

(i) *Symphony No. 5;* (ii) *Francesca da Rimini.*
(M) *(*) Olympia Dig. **OCD 139** [id.]. USSR RSO, (i) Fedoseyev, (ii) Ovchinnikov.

Symphony No. 5; Marche slave.
(M)*** DG **419 066-2**; *419 066-4* [id.]. BPO, Karajan.

Symphony No. 5; The Voyevoda, Op. 78.
*** CBS Dig. [**MK 42094**]; **(*) *IMT 42094* [id.]. Chicago SO, Abbado.

With speeds fast but never breathless and with a manner fresh and direct but never rigid, Jansons conducts the Oslo Philharmonic in a brilliant and exciting performance which is full and vivid in its sound. This was the first to be recorded in an outstanding Tchaikovsky series, in which Jansons, Leningrad-trained, revealed something of the debt he held to the example of Yevgeny Mravinsky, a master among Russian interpreters. Jansons is notably less wilful than Mravinsky tended to be but is no less intense and electrifying. In the first movement, Jansons' refusal to linger never sounds anything but warmly idiomatic, lacking only a little in charm. The slow movement again brings a steady tempo, with climaxes built strongly and patiently but with enormous power, the final culmination topping everything. In the finale, taken very fast, Jansons tightens the screw of the excitement without ever making it a scramble, following Tchaikovsky's notated slowings rather than allowing extra rallentandos. The sound is excellent, specific and well focused within a warmly reverberant acoustic, with digital recording on CD reinforcing any lightness of bass. A warm recommendation – unless charm or wayward sensuousness are essentials. There is an excellent chrome cassette.

Karajan's 1976 recording stands out from his other recordings of the *Fifth.* For many (including I.M.), this will be a first choice. The first movement is unerringly paced and has great romantic flair; in Karajan's hands the climax of the slow movement is grippingly intense, though with a touchingly elegiac preparation for the horn solo at the opening. The *Waltz* has character and charm too – the Berlin Philharmonic string playing is peerless – and in the finale Karajan drives hard, creating an electrifying forward thrust. The remastered recording brings a remarkable improvement over the analogue LP; the bass is more expansive and, although the overall sound-picture is brilliantly lit, it has depth and weight too, besides strong projection and impact. There is an excellent cassette, but the CD at mid-price makes a fine bargain.

Previn's version brought his first recording with the RPO, the orchestra of which he was already the musical director designate, and the quality of the playing is a tribute to a fast-blossoming relationship. Previn's fine concern for detail is well illustrated by the way that the great horn melody in the slow movement (superbly played by Jeff Bryant with firmly focused tone and immaculate control of phrasing) contains the implication of a quaver rest before each three-quarter group, where normally it sounds like a straight triplet. In the first movement rhythms are light and well sprung, and the third movement is sweet and lyrical yet with no hint of mannerism, for Previn adopts a naturally expressive style within speeds generally kept steady, even in the great climax of the slow movement which then subsides into a coda of breathtaking delicacy. Not that Previn misses any of the drama or excitement; and the finale, taken very fast indeed, crowns an outstandingly satisfying reading. The Telarc recording is full and wide-ranging, not as detailed as some, but very naturally balanced. The Rimsky-Korsakov coupling makes a delightful fill-up, brief but charming.

Muti underlines the symphonic strength of the first movement rather than immediate excitement. The approach is direct and unmannered but with no stiffness of phrasing. The *Waltz* may lack a little in charm, and certain passages perhaps let the tension relax too far, but the slow movement is beautifully controlled, with the second theme genuinely *con nobilita* when the violins first play it, and passion kept in hand for the second half of the movement. As for the finale, it presents a sharp contrast with its fast tempo and controlled excitement. The recording is full, in the EMI manner, the digital remastering has brought a natural transparency without loss of body, although the effect is less sumptuous than in the early symphonies.

Abbado's fine CBS Chicago version is not yet issued in Britain on CD (as we go to press) but it is available in the USA. The performance is admirably fresh and superbly played. All Tchaikovsky's markings are scrupulously yet imaginatively observed, and the reading is full of contrast. Thus, in the second subject group of the first movement, the firmly articulated crotchet/quaver motive is the more striking in its emphasis, leading, as it does, to the lyrical legato of the *Molto più tranquillo*. Other versions of the slow movement have more extrovert passion, but Abbado shows that the climaxes can be involving without being histrionic. After an elegant *Waltz,* with the orchestra in sparkling form, the finale has fine energy and momentum. If it does not have quite the gripping excitement of Jansons' version, the moment of the composer's self-doubt, before the *Poco più animato*, is the more effectively characterized. *The Voyevoda* was discarded by Tchaikovsky after an unsuccessful première, and he was probably right to do so. It is a melodramatic piece, lacking strong thematic interest. The plot has something in common with *Francesca da Rimini* – only here it is the betrayed husband who (literally and audibly) gets the bullet at the end, instead of the wife's lover. The CBS recording is made in a convincingly resonant acoustic; if inner detail is not always sharply defined, the balance is very good, with full strings and a supporting weight in the bass; but it is less rich than the Jansons Chandos version. On cassette the sound is more restricted.

Karajan's latest VPO version of the *Fifth* brings a characteristically strong and expressive performance; however, neither in the playing of the Vienna Philharmonic nor even in the recorded sound can it quite match his earlier Berlin Philharmonic version for DG. Like Karajan's most recent recordings of the Beethoven symphonies, this was done with video as part of the project; though the long takes have brought extra spontaneity, the recording of the strings in the Musikvereinsaal (a difficult venue for the engineers) is inconsistent, with front-desk players sharply focused but not the whole body of strings behind them, and with woodwind set at a distance. The slack ensemble and control of rhythm in the waltz movement is specially disappointing. All this is emphasized with the extra definition of the CD.

Though less brightly recorded than its companions in Rozhdestvensky's LSO series for Pickwick, with strings a little cloudy, this version of the *Fifth* brings a strong, passionate performance, with the middle movements in particular beautifully done. The *Capriccio italien* is also given a sunny and relaxed reading at relatively spacious speeds.

Fedoseyev's latest digital recording shows the USSR Radio Symphony Orchestra in a good light. The strings create a fine body of tone and the wind playing is vivid in a Russian way, without being coarse. The reading is idiosyncratic and the ebb and flow of tension is not always spontaneous, with the slow movement dangerously slow. But there are some exciting moments and the finale has a fine sweep with a burst of adrenalin at the coda. The *Francesca* coupling is exciting too and brilliantly played, but the remastered analogue sound brings upper strings too shrill for comfort.

Bátiz's performance is enjoyably direct and exciting, and he secures a lively response from the LPO. It is an extrovert reading, and his control of the music's ebb and flow of tension has an attractive ardour. The recording, though made in a resonant hall with the orchestra set back, has transferred richly and clearly to tape.

Chailly's is a relatively lightweight and somewhat idiosyncratic reading which gives the impression of inexperience in this repertoire. There are some attractive things here, notably the exhilarating tempo for the finale, but the reading does not make a very convincing whole. The VPO playing is not always immaculate, and the horn solo in the slow movement is not really distinguished. Yet the lyrical momentum of the performance is certainly enjoyable; the Decca digital recording, which has considerable richness and brilliance, is very attractive, especially in its enhanced CD format.

Though the reading remains direct, Maazel's Cleveland version is less fresh-sounding than his earlier Vienna version for Decca (also rather lightweight, and now deleted). Cleveland virtuosity is impressive but, with a disappointing slow movement and aggressive digital recording, the result is cold. The CD is unimpressive, with poorly focused strings. Chailly's Decca version has far superior sound.

Ormandy in his heyday was an outstanding Tchaikovskian, warmly expressive but always keeping emotion firmly under control. This Delos version, recorded not long before he died, characteristically has plenty of excitement and no hysteria, but the fires were burning lower and the recorded sound takes away the bite that might have been there, with textures unattractively thick. The one benefit of that is that for once the horn solo in the slow movement is not spotlit.

Solti's Chicago version is disappointing: the tension seems too forced and the pulse too rigid. Of course there is some brilliant orchestral playing on this reissue and Tchaikovsky's score certainly makes an impact, but the brightly lit sound adds to the impression of inflexibility and also brings a hint of fierceness.

Symphonies Nos 5–6 (Pathétique)
(B) *** HMV *TCC2-POR 54284*. Phil. O, Muti.
(B) **(*) DG Walkman *413 429-4*. LSO, VPO, Abbado.

Muti's recordings of these two symphonies are both highly successful, the *Fifth* strong, direct and exciting, the *Pathétique* persuasive in its easy expressiveness (see below). This double-length tape in EMI's 'Portrait of the Artist' series allows each work to be heard uninterrupted. The transfers are both first class, the wide dynamic range admirably caught, with the sound vivid and full throughout.

The Walkman chrome cassette couples Abbado's lightweight but refreshingly individual DG accounts of Tchaikovsky's two most popular symphonies. The performance of the *Fifth* is both sophisticated and sparkling: there is lyrical intensity and the outer movements have plenty of vigour; the finale is genuinely exciting, yet with no sense of rhetoric. There are more powerful accounts available but none more spontaneously volatile. The *Pathétique* is also slightly underpowered but may have many attractions for those who prefer a reading that is not too intense. There is a strong impulse throughout, with the third movement essentially a Scherzo, the march-rhythms never becoming weighty and pontifical. The recordings have transferred well to tape, that of the *Fifth* richer than the *Sixth*, which is slightly dry.

Symphony No. 6 in B min. (Pathétique), Op. 74.
*** Chan. Dig. **CHAN 8446**; *ABTD 1158* [id.]. Oslo PO, Jansons.
*** Decca **411 615-2** [id.]. Philh. O, Ashkenazy.
(M) *** DG *419 486-4* [id.]. BPO, Karajan.
*** HMV **CDC7 47858-2** [id.]. Philh. O, Muti.
(M) *(**) HMV **CDM7 69043-2** [id.]. BPO, Karajan.
(*) DG Dig. **419 604-2; *419 604-4* [id.]. NYPO, Bernstein.
(*) DG Dig. **415 095-2 [id.]. VPO, Karajan.
** DG Dig. **400 029-2** [id.]. LAPO, Giulini.
(B) ** DG Dig. *419 841-4* [id.]. LAPO, Giulini – RACHMANINOV: *Isle of the dead* etc.***
** ASV Dig. *ZCDCA 566* [id.]. LPO, Bátiz.

** Erato Dig. **ECD 88242** [id.]. Boston SO, Ozawa.
(M) *(*) Decca **417 708-2** [id.]. Chicago SO, Solti.
*(*) Tel. Dig. **ZK8 43340** [id.]. Leipzig GO, Masur.
*(*) Delos **D/CD 3016** [id.]. Phd. O, Ormandy.
* Ph. Dig. **420 925-2** [id.]. Concg. O, Bychkov.
RCA **RD 85355** [**RCD1 5355**]. Chicago SO, Levine.

Symphony No. 6 (Pathétique); Marche slave.
*(*) CBS Dig. **MK 42368** [id.]. Chicago SO, Abbado.

Symphony No. 6 (Pathétique); Romeo and Juliet (fantasy overture).
(M) *** DG **423 223-2**; *423 223-4* [id.]. BPO, Karajan.
(M) * RCA **GD 86527**; *GK 86527* [**RCA 6527-2-RG**]. Boston SO, Munch.

Symphony No. 6 (Pathétique); The Storm, Op. 76.
(M) **(*) Pickwick Dig. **PCD 878**. LSO, Rozhdestvensky.

(i) *Symphony No. 6 (Pathétique)*; (ii) *Variations on a rococo theme, Op. 33.*
(M) *** Decca *417 463-4* [id.]. (i) Philh. O, Ashkenazy; (ii) Harrell, Cleveland O, Maazel.

Mariss Jansons and the Oslo Philharmonic crown their magnetically compelling Tchaikovsky series with a superbly concentrated account of the last and greatest of the symphonies. It is characteristic of Jansons that the great second-subject melody is at once warm and passionate yet totally unsentimental, with rubato barely noticeable. Yet look at the score, and you will find remarkable fidelity in detail to the specified ebb and flow. The very fast speed for the third-movement march stretches the players to the very limit, but the exhilaration is infectious, leading to the simple dedication of the slow finale, unexaggerated but deeply felt. Fine warm recording as in the rest of the series, although the cassette is less well defined than the CD.

After an arresting account of the sombre introduction, the urgency with which Ashkenazy and his Philharmonia players attack the *Allegro* of the first movement of the *Pathétique* belies the composer's *non troppo* marking. The directness and intensity of the music making are supported by remarkably crisp articulation, producing an electrifying forward thrust. The emergence of the beautiful second subject offers the more striking contrast, with Ashkenazy's characteristic lyrical ardour bringing a natural warmth to the great melody. As in his other Tchaikovsky records, this whole performance is pervaded by freshness and spontaneity, through the balletic 5/4 movement, with its essentially Russian quality of melancholy, and the vigorous Scherzo/march, rhythmically buoyant and joyful rather than relentlessly high-powered, as under Karajan. The finale combines passion with tenderness, and the total absence of expressive hysteria brings a more poignant culmination than usual. With superb Decca Kingsway Hall sound, this is among the finest *Pathétiques* ever recorded. The Philharmonia is on peak form and, although the Berlin Philharmonic playing under Karajan is even more polished, the Decca version gains by its greater amplitude, warmth and colour. The CD retains the analogue atmosphere while detail is clarified and intensified. Ashkenazy's performance is offered at mid-price on cassette, very generously coupled with Lynn Harrell's fine account of the *Rococo variations*. With state-of-the-art sound quality, this is a bargain.

Karajan has a very special affinity with Tchaikovsky's *Pathétique symphony* (and – remembering Furtwängler's famous 78 r.p.m. set – so has the Berlin Philharmonic Orchestra). He has recorded it five times in stereo. For many the 1977 version is the finest. With a brilliant recording of the widest dynamic range (though not an especially sumptuous lower resonance) the impact of Tchaikovsky's climaxes – notably those of the first and third movements – is tremendously powerful, the articulation of the Berlin players precise and strong. The climactic peaks are created with fierce bursts of tension, and the effect on the listener is almost overwhelming. In the 5/4 movement Karajan allows the middle section to increase the elegiac feeling, against a background of remorseless but distanced drum-beats, like a tolling bell. The finale has great passion and eloquence, with two gentle sforzandos at the very end to emphasize the finality of the closing phrase. This is currently available only on tape (*419 486-4*).

Turning back to Karajan's 1964 CD, one finds a reading that is no less exciting but more consistent in its overall control of tension. For some ears this is the finest version of all, the steady tempo of the *Moderato mosso* in the first movement leading the ear on as the conductor builds towards the movement's climax with a steady emotional thrust. At the climactic point the deeply committed playing creates a quality of expressive fervour to send shivers down the spine, with a noble resolution from the Berlin brass. The sound has more bloom than in the later version, and this brings a lighter, elegant quality to the 5/4 movement. The march/Scherzo has an exhilaratingly consistent forward momentum, and with demonic playing from the Berlin orchestra, wonderfully sharp in ensemble, the aggressive force of the climaxes communicates the greatest excitement. The physical thrill of the closing pages is very gripping indeed. Karajan's consistency is carried through to the passionate last movement, concluded, as in the later version, with those gentle stabbing chordal emphases. It is overall an engulfing experience and the remastered sound is first rate, brilliant but with a balancing warmth and weight, the violin timbre, bright but full, too. Now offered paired with Karajan's 1967 version of *Romeo and Juliet*, also a very fine performance, this mid-priced CD is extraordinary value.

In between his two DG versions, in 1972 Karajan returned to the Jesus-Christus Kirche in Berlin to record the work yet again, this time for EMI. It is another superlative performance, in some ways the most spontaneous of all in its deep feeling and onward flow. In the first movement the beautiful second subject is less consciously moulded than in the 1964 version and the *Allegro con grazia* is gentler and has a poignant combination of warmth and nostalgia. The Scherzo/march has enormous energy, yet remains exuberantly joyful; the finale brings the deepest intensity of feeling. Once again the Berlin Philharmonic rise to the occasion and play with great commitment and create a superb body of tone. The snag is the recording itself which, in its remastered format, is uncomfortably shrill in fortissimos: massed violins don't sound like this in real life. But otherwise the sound has plenty of body and the ambience of the famous Berlin church adds to the overall sonority.

Muti adopts characteristically fast tempi, yet the result is fresh and youthful, not over-hectic. The lyrical second subject, flowing swifter than usual, has easy expressiveness without a hint of mannerism, and the 5/4 movement, also taken at a speed faster than usual, is most persuasive. The march, for all its urgency, never sounds brutal, and the finale has real eloquence. HMV have been particularly successful in transferring Muti's Tchaikovsky cycle to CD and the *Pathétique* is no exception; although inner detail is not as sharp as it would be on a digital recording, the analogue master is revealed in its full glory, the sound rich and naturally balanced, with no lack of weight and with a truthful upper range, fresh but without edge.

The timings in Bernstein's version make you suspect that someone has made a mistake with the stopwatch. At 59 minutes overall, it is the slowest *Pathétique* ever, over a quarter of an hour longer than Jansons' (by no means rushed) version. To an amazing degree the conductor's magnetism and his ability to sustain electric tension, not least in hushed pianissimos of fine delicacy, justify his view, but this is an eccentric version by any count, a live recording that is fascinating to hear once but not for repeated listening. The wide-ranging DG recording is one of the best made in Avery Fisher Hall. The cassette, however, is rather ill-defined and opaque.

Recorded, like the VPO *Fourth* and *Fifth*, with video as part of the project, Karajan's latest version of the *Pathétique* has many characteristically strong points; however, although the reading is not without intensity or spontaneity, it lacks the grip of the earlier Berlin Philharmonic recordings and, with the Vienna ensemble noticeably slacker than that of the Berliners, it is a flawed experience. The 5/4 movement is slower than before and rather heavy in style; though the speed of the march movement remains as fast as previously, the result is less tense, breathless rather than exuberant in virtuosity. The sound is curiously inconsistent, with violins edgy in tuttis, while the heavy brass jangles aggressively. There are distracting knocks and rustles in the *pppppp* passage at the end of the exposition just before the fortissimo start to the development.

Rozhdestvensky's performance with the LSO on the mid-price Pickwick label, generously coupled and very well recorded in modern digital sound, makes an obvious bargain. His passionate reading fails to match the finest in precision of ensemble – the slow finale is warm rather than tense or tragic – but the sense of spontaneity is most compelling.

Giulini's digital *Pathétique* is curiously lightweight, the mood set with the almost *scherzando* quality of the opening *Allegro*. The 5/4 movement is relatively unlilting, and though the march is impressive, it is no match for the Ashkenazy version. The finale does not lack eloquence, but Giulini's Philharmonia version of two decades earlier had more individuality than this. The digital recording is impressive, if slightly dry. The compact disc tends to emphasize rather than disguise the recording's faults, especially the close balance. Giulini's digital *Pathétique* is also available very well transferred on to an economically priced Pocket Music chrome tape, a much better investment, particularly as it is coupled with outstanding Maazel performances of Rachmaninov's symphonic poems.

Bátiz is usually successful in creating the feeling of a live performance in the recording studio; here he secures a first-rate response from the LSO, who swagger splendidly in the Scherzo/march with the brass blazing. However, taken overall this reading is just a little matter-of-fact and at full price it cannot compete with the best versions available. The cassette is of good but not outstanding quality.

Ozawa's Boston account, appearing unexpectedly on the Erato label, takes a balletic view, playful in the first-movement *Allegro*, lilting and waltz-like in the 5/4 second movement. The result lacks a little in weight, particularly when the undistractingly natural recording balances the violins a little too backwardly to bring out the full glory of the big melodies.

With dangerously fast tempi throughout the first and third movements, the element of hysteria is never far away in Solti's intense reading; and the element of nobility, so necessary to provide emotional balance, is missing. The March/Scherzo loses all charm at this hectic pace; indeed the march element almost disappears altogether. The finale is more controlled in feeling but does not resolve the performance in any satisfactory way. Brilliantly clear recording to match the playing.

Masur's reading is at the opposite extreme to Solti's, well laid out but with a very low level of tension in spite of consistently fine playing from the Leipzig orchestra. The recording is rich and natural, but the Leipzig acoustics do not provide the necessary brilliance and projection.

Ormandy made several fine recordings of the *Pathétique* before this final account for Delos which found the veteran conductor lacking some of his earlier fire. The reading remains warmly romantic, strong and unexaggerated, with steady, generally rather measured speeds. Only in the yearning lyricism of the slow finale is there the full flavour of Ormandy in his prime. The recording is dull, strangely damped down and restricted on top.

Abbado's version, bringing the benefit of a coupling, the rumbustious *Marche slave*, still is unsuccessful in the relative lack of tension and less-than-pinpoint precision in ensemble. It cannot match Abbado's own earlier Vienna version for DG. The recorded sound is a little muffled, lacking full bite.

Bychkov's disc is disappointing, not only for the self-indulgence of the reading, generally ponderous with sudden spurts of energy, but for the often opaque sound of tuttis.

Munch's Boston version suffers from a recording that seems to put everything on an unvarying dynamic, partly the result of a close balance and partly the recording system which sought to make everything uniformly vivid. There is some fine Boston playing, but without a pianissimo the *Pathétique* loses several dimensions. *Romeo and Juliet* sounds much better; but this cannot be recommended.

Levine's reading is dramatic and direct, but his version is totally ruled out by the indifferent quality of the recording, strident on the brass, scratchy on high violin timbre.

The Tempest (fantasy), Op. 18 (see also above, under *Symphony No. 2*).
(*) ASV Dig. **CDDCA 586; *ZCDCA 586* [id.]. LSO, Yondani Butt – LISZT: *Ce qu'on entend sur la montagne.***(*)*

The Tempest is a comparatively early work (1873) but it has great imaginative force and is greatly superior to its Liszt coupling, although clearly Tchaikovsky's symphonic poems show a strong Lisztian influence. The opening seascape here, with its highly evocative horn passage, is matched later by the passionate intensity of Miranda and Ferdinand's love theme, with its soaring upward leap. Yondani Butt gives an impressively controlled performance, holding back for the final climax, and on CD the spectacular digital recording produces some thrilling sounds within its resonant acoustic – the effect is not unlike a Telarc recording. The cassette is much more restricted in range and impact.

Variations on a rococo theme for cello and orchestra, Op. 33.
*** DG **413 819-2** [id.]. Rostropovich, BPO, Karajan – DVOŘÁK: *Concerto.****
*** RCA Dig. **RD 71003**. Ofra Harnoy, Victoria SO, Freeman – OFFENBACH: *Concerto*; SAINT-SAËNS: *Concerto No. 1.****
(B) *** DG Walkman *423 290-4* [id.]. Rostropovich, Leningrad PO, Rozhdestvensky – LALO; SCHUMANN: *Concertos*; SAINT-SAËNS: *Concerto No. 1.****

No grumbles about Rostropovich's performance in partnership with Karajan. He plays as if this were one of the greatest works for the cello, and he receives glowing support from Karajan and the Berlin Philharmonic. The *Rococo variations* is a delightful work, and it has never sounded finer than it does here. Rostropovich uses the published score, not Tchaikovsky's quite different original version as played by Wallfisch on Chandos; the latter also has the advantage of modern digital sound, whereas the DG version is analogue from as early as 1969. But it is rich and refined and sounds fresh in its digitally remastered form (if less transparent than its RCA competitor). Those seeking the Dvořák coupling should be well satisfied.

Ofra Harnoy is a singularly decorative lady, judging by her picture on her CD, generously combining Offenbach, Saint-Saëns and Tchaikovsky, but she is just as much a pleasure to listen to as to look at. Her account of the *Rococo variations* is quite different from Rostropovich's but no less rewarding. The scale is smaller, the style essentially elegant, letting the eighteenth-century feel of Tchaikovsky's inspiration dominate the work's atmosphere, not missing its colour or ardour but never forgetting the word 'rococo' in the title. It is a considerable performance, stylish yet emotionally responsive, and Paul Freeman's accompaniment is first class, too, with some engaging woodwind solos from his excellent Victoria players. The CD gives a forward balance to the cello, but this is more than acceptable when the playing is so enticing.

Rostropovich's earlier and vibrant Leningrad recording is also available in an exceptionally attractive coupling with the *Piano* and *Violin concertos* – see above. But the present anthology of no fewer than four major works for cello, all in outstanding performances, makes a quite unbelievable bargain in DG's same Walkman series. The sound is admirable.

CHAMBER AND INSTRUMENTAL MUSIC

Album for the young, Op. 39: (i) original piano version; (ii) trans. for string quartet by Dubinsky.
*** Chan. **CHAN 8365**; *ABTD 1129* [id.]. (i) Luba Edlina; (ii) augmented Borodin Trio.

These twenty-four pieces are all miniatures, with many playing for approximately a minute only, but they have great charm; their invention is often memorable, with quotations from

Russian folksongs and one French, plus a brief reminder of *Swan Lake*. Here they are presented twice, in their original piano versions, sympathetically played by Luba Edlina, and in effective string quartet transcriptions arranged by her husband, Rostislav Dubinsky. Some of the arrangements are more telling on the piano, but others transcribe so well that one could imagine that was how their composer conceived them. The Borodin group play them with both affection and finesse. The CD has plenty of presence; this collection is rather attractive, however, in its excellent cassette format, for late evening listening or as a background in the car.

Piano trio in A min., Op. 50.
*** HMV **CDC7 47988-2** [id.]. Ashkenazy, Perlman, Harrell.
(M) **(*) Olympia **OCD 157** [id.]. Leningrad Philharmonic Trio – GLAZUNOV: *String quartet No. 1.****
** Tel. Dig. **ZK8 43209** [id.]. Vienna Haydn Trio.
** Chan. Dig. **CHAN 8348**; *ABTD 1049* [id.]. Borodin Trio.

Although no coupling is offered, Ashkenazy, Perlman and Harrell remain first choice. The dominating keyboard role of the first movement can so easily sound rhetorical, as well as gripping and commanding – and that element is not entirely avoided here. But the *Variations* which form the second part of the work are very successful, with engaging characterization and a great deal of electricity in the closing pages. Indeed, generally this group carry all before them with their sense of artistic purpose and through their warmth and ardour. As far as the quality of sound is concerned, the HMV CD was recorded in the CBS studios in New York in 1981 and the sound is on the dry side, with the digital remastering increasing the sharpness of focus, where a little more ambience would have been a more attractive addition.

The Leningrad Philharmonic Trio are first-rate players; both Vladimir Ovcharek, the violinist, and Benjamin Morosov, the cellist, produce a rich timbre and they have a natural feeling for Tchaikovsky's melodic lines, particularly when there is a touch of melancholy. The balance of the trio is much more integrated than in the HMV version, with the piano placed among the strings rather than taking a concertante role. While Tamara Fidler can play boldly when required, she does not dominate the tuttis in quite the way Ashkenazy does. But the intimacy of the performance has its own appeal – the very opening is enticing – and this is a real performance, albeit much more relaxed in the first movement (20′ 02″ against 18′ 20″ on HMV). The variations are done with sparkle and a good deal of charm, and the *Fugue* is not left out. The recording is modern (1986), balanced a shade closely but truthful, and it does not make the strings sound edgy. With its handsome Glazunov coupling, this is excellent value.

The Vienna Haydn Trio (Heinz Medjimorec, Michael Schnitzler, Walther Schulz) play all the variations but make the usual cut in the finale. It is a good performance in every respect, with finesse and clean articulation, though they are not as Slavonic in temperament as their Leningrad rivals. The recording is not made in quite as lively an acoustic as for the Borodins on Chandos, though it has more space and warmth than the EMI. All the same, it gives a good deal of pleasure and, though not a first choice, can be recommended.

The Borodins on Chandos omit, not the *Fugue*, variation 8, a practice sanctioned by the score, but the variation preceding it, which is not. The performance is eloquent and the variations have spontaneity and are not without charm, but the first movement is less convincing. The clear digital recording serves to spotlight the string sounds, which are less polished and less rich than on the rival versions. The added presence of CD is undeniable but ideally one needs a warmer string timbre to balance the large-scale piano writing.

String quartets Nos 1 in D, Op. 11; 2 in F, Op. 22; 3 in E flat min., Op. 30; (i) *Souvenir de Florence* (string sextet), *Op. 70.*
*** HMV Dig. **CDS7 49775-2**; *EX 749775-4* (2). Borodin Qt, (i) with Y. Bashmet, N. Gutman.

This set assembles all three Tchaikovsky quartets together with the glorious *Souvenir de Florence*. Given performances of this distinction and music of this quality of inspiration, the set is self-recommending. The digital recording is very nearly as outstanding as the performances, and there is no reason to qualify the strength and warmth of our recommendation. There are excellent chrome tapes. It is difficult to understand why the Tchaikovsky *Quartets* are not played and recorded more often. They are fine, cultivated works, inventive and tuneful, with the proper intimacy of their genre, and they are highly rewarding.

PIANO MUSIC

Nutcracker: suite (arr. for 2 pianos).
** DG Dig. **410 616-2** [id.]. Argerich, Economou – RACHMANINOV: *Symphonic dances*.**

Nicolas Economou is a Cypriot pianist and composer born in 1953 who now lives in Munich. His arrangement of the *Nutcracker suite* for two pianos works well though it does not banish memories of the transcription made by Mikhail Pletnyev, the 1978 Tchaikovsky Competition prizewinner, and recorded by him on HMV (now deleted) – dazzlingly brilliant and wonderfully imaginative playing that made one forget this music could ever exist in any other form. This is very good indeed but not quite so breathtaking – nor, for that matter, quite as well recorded. Nevertheless this playing is of a very high order and will give corresponding pleasure.

The Seasons, Op. 37a.
(*) Chan. Dig. **CHAN 8349; *ABTD 1070* [id.]. Lydia Artymiw.

The Seasons: January; May; June; November.
*** MMG Dig. **MCD 10031** [id.]. Sviatoslav Richter – RACHMANINOV: *Études-tableaux*.***

Tchaikovsky's twelve *Seasons* (they would better have been called months) were written to a regular deadline for publication in the St Petersburg music magazine, *Nuvellist*. They are lightweight but attractively varied in character and style. It is the gentler, lyrical pieces that are most effective in the hands of Lydia Artymiw, and she plays them thoughtfully and poetically. Elsewhere, she sometimes has a tendency marginally to over-characterize the music, which is slight, but she also notices and brings out the orchestral feeling in fuller-sustained textures, and she is rhythmically alert and sparkling. The digital recording is truthful, and on CD the fairly close balance (pedal noises are faintly audible) gives striking presence to the piano which might ideally have been a little further back; but the image is real. The chrome tape is first class.

Richter chose four very contrasting movements, including the most famous, *June*, a Barcarolle. He plays each of them with great character and enhances their stature. The 1983 Melodiya recording is excellent; the internal focus is not always absolutely sharp, but the piano timbre is naturally coloured and the instrument given realistic presence.

The Seasons, Op. 37; Piano sonata in G, Op. 37.
(M) *(*) Olympia **OCD 192** [id.]. Peter Katin.

Those who have heard such keyboard lions as Richter or Pletyev in the *G major Sonata* will find Peter Katin's admirably recorded account a little small-scale. It goes without saying that there are many sensitive touches, but the *Sonata* is just a little wanting in fire and concentration. Although the work is not held in high esteem by some specialists, it is a finer piece than appears here. The *Seasons* suits Katin's talents much more readily.

OPERA

Eugene Onegin (complete).
*** Decca **417 413-2** (2) [id.]. Kubiak, Weikl, Burrows, Reynolds, Ghiaurov, Hamari, Sénéchal, Alldis Ch., ROHCGO, Solti.
(M) *(*) Olympia **OCD 115 A/B** [id.]. Milashkina, Masurok, Atlantov, Sinyavskaya, Nesterenko, Ermler, Bolshoi Theatre Ch. & O, Ermler.

Solti's version comes up all the fresher on CD with the fine focus of the Decca recording, as well as its bloom and atmosphere, all the more impressive. It is a great benefit having the whole opera on two CDs instead of three LPs, with Act I complete on the first disc, Acts II and III on the second. In addition to the superb sound, the orchestral playing is a delight. This set satisfies an important need. Solti, characteristically crisp in attack, has plainly warmed to the score, allowing his singers full rein in rallentando and rubato to a degree one might not have expected of him. The Tatiana of Teresa Kubiak is most moving – rather mature-sounding for the *ingénue* of Act I, but with her golden, vibrant voice rising to the final confrontation of Act III most impressively. The Onegin of Bernd Weikl may have too little variety of tone, but again this is firm singing that yet has authentic Slavonic tinges. Onegin becomes something like a first-person story-teller. The rest of the cast is excellent, with Stuart Burrows as Lensky giving one of his finest performances on record yet. Here for the first time the full range of musical expression in this most atmospheric of operas is superbly caught, with the Decca recording capturing every subtlety – including the wonderful off-stage effects.

On two mid-price Olympia discs, the mid-1970s Melodiya recording from the Bolshoi offers a performance including some fine Soviet singers. Though not often imaginative, Yuri Masurok has a voice exceptionally well suited to the role of Onegin in its range and timbre. Atlantov as Lensky has his ringingly exciting moments and Nesterenko as Gremin sings magnificently. The snag is Milashkina's seriously flawed singing as Tatiana, made to sound shriller and less girlish by the closeness of balance. Only in Act III is her performance acceptable. Mark Ermler is a lively, understanding conductor, but the close balance of all the voices makes this a disappointing set.

Queen of Spades (complete).
** Ph. **420 375-2**; *420 375-4* (3) [id.]. Atlantov, Milashkina, Fedoseyev, Levko, Bolshoi Theatre Ch. & O, Ermler.

This Bolshoi recording of the *Queen of Spades*, made in 1974, brings a strong if unsubtle reading, atmospherically set against a warmly reverberant acoustic. The sense of presence and atmosphere makes up for shortcomings in the singing, with Vladimir Atlantov as Herman too taut and strained, singing consistently loudly, and with Tamara Milashkina producing curdled tone at the top, not at all girlish. Both those singers, for all their faults, are archetypally Russian, and so – in a much more controlled way – is Valentina Levko, a magnificent Countess, firm and sinister. The CD transfer makes the helpfully vibrant sound the more specific and real-sounding, though a degree of tape hiss is audible. There is also a good cassette equivalent.

Yolanta (complete).
(*) Erato Dig. **ECD 88147 (2) [id.]. Vishnevskaya, Gedda, Groenroos, Petkov, Krause, Group Vocale de France, O de Paris, Rostropovich.

Tchaikovsky's one-act opera *Yolanta* (*Iolanthe*) is a much later (1892) work than *Eugene Onegin*. Recorded at a live concert performance in the Salle Pleyel in December 1984, with excellent, spacious sound. Rostropovich's performance has a natural expressive warmth to make one tolerant of vocal shortcomings. This is the fairy-tale story of a blind princess in medieval

Provence who is finally cured by the arrival of the knight who falls in love with her. The libretto may be flawed but the lyrical invention is a delight. Though Vishnevskaya's voice is not naturally suited to the role of a sweet young princess, she does wonders in softening her hardness of tone, bringing fine detail of characterization. Gedda equally by nature sounds too old for his role, but again the artistry is compelling, and ugly sounds few. More questionable is the casting of Dimiter Petkov as the King, far too wobbly as recorded.

Tcherepnin, Alexander (1899–1977)

Piano trio in D, Op. 34.
** Pro Arte Dig. **CDD 303**. Odeon Trio – TANEYEV: *Trio.***

Alexander Tcherepnin grew up in the musical atmosphere of pre-war St Petersburg where the family home was the meeting-place for many of the most illustrious names of the day (Glazunov, Stravinsky, Prokofiev and Liadov). He was a true cosmopolitan: after spending some time in Tiflis (1917–21), he settled first in Paris then in Shanghai, before dividing his time between Paris and America. His engaging *Piano trio* comes from 1925 and its three movements take all of seven minutes! As with the weightier Taneyev work with which it is coupled, there is too little space round the three instruments and tonally the sound is wanting in range and colour.

Telemann, Georg Philipp (1681–1767)

Concertos: for 2 chalumeaux in D min.; for flute in D; for 3 oboes, 3 violins in B flat; for recorder & flute in E min.; for trumpet in D; for trumpet & violin in D.
*** DG Dig. **419 633-2** [id.]. Soloists, Col. Mus. Ant., Goebel.

This well-filled disc offers half a dozen splendid concertos by this unfailingly inventive composer. The opening *Flute concerto* is typical of the diversity and freshness of Telemann's composition and there are two for trumpet, played with much sensitivity here. As Reinhard Goebel points out, Telemann 'displayed immense audacity in the imaginative and ingenious mixing of the colours from the palette of the baroque orchestra', and these are heard to excellent effect here. Those who know the vital *B flat concerto* – or, rather, A major for that is how it actually sounds – for three oboes and violins, from earlier versions, will find the allegro very fast indeed and the slow movement quite thought-provoking. The chalumeau is the precursor of the clarinet, and the concerto for two chalumeaux recorded here is full of unexpected delights. Marvellously alive and accomplished playing, even if one occasionally tires of the bulges and nudges on the first beats of bars.

Concerto for flute, oboe d'amore and viola d'amore in E; Concerto polonois; Double concerto for recorder and flute in E min.; Triple trumpet concerto in D; Quadro in B flat.
*** O-L Dig. **411 949-2** [id.]. AAM with soloists, Hogwood.

In the early years of the eighteenth century, Telemann had served as kapellmeister to Count Erdmann II of Promnitz at Sorau in Poland. During the summer the Court moved to Pless, one of the Promnitz estates in Upper Silesia, and the folk music he heard there made a great impression on him. 'An attentive observer could gather from these folk musicians enough ideas in eight days to last a lifetime,' he wrote; in three of the concertos recorded here, Polish ideas are to be found – indeed, one of the pieces is called *Concerto polonois*. As always, Telemann has a refined ear for sonority and the musical discourse with which he diverts us is unfailingly intelligent and delightful. The performances are excellent and readers will not find cause for disappointment in either the recording or presentation.

Horn concerto in D; Double horn concerto in D; Triple horn concerto in D; Suite in F for 2 horns and strings; Tafelmusik, Book 3: *Double horn concerto in E flat*.
*** Ph. Dig. **412 226-2** [id.]. Baumann, Timothy Brown, Hill, ASMF, Iona Brown.

The *E flat Concerto* comes from the third set of *Tafelmusik* (1733) and is the best-known of the four recorded here. The playing here and in the other concertos is pretty dazzling, not only from Hermann Baumann but also from his colleagues, Timothy Brown and Nicholas Hill. Mention should also be made of the concertante contributions from the two violinists. Telemann's invention rarely fails to hold the listener, and the recording has warm ambience and excellent clarity in all its three forms. The usual advantages of compact disc must be noted and readers with an interest in this much-underrated and unfailingly intelligent composer should acquire this rewarding issue.

Double concerto in F for 2 horns; Concerto in B flat for 3 oboes & 3 violins; Double concerto in F for recorder, bassoon & strings; Concerto in G for 4 violins.
(M) *** Tel. **ZS8 43773** [id.]. Soloists, VCM, Harnoncourt.

One of the best Telemann discs currently available. The *Concerto for two horns* shows the composer at his most characteristic (natural horns are used), and the performances are most persuasive. The oboes also sound splendidly in tune, which is not always the case with the baroque instrument, and phrasing is alive and sensitive. Indeed these performances are extremely fine, and only the *Concerto for recorder and bassoon* lets the disc down a little; it is also not as well played as the others. The quality is good and the digital remastering has not tried to clarify artificially what is basically a resonant recording with inner detail mellowed by the ambience. Outlines, however, are cleaner and one would not guess that this dates from 1966.

Oboe concertos: in C min.; D; D min.; E min.; F min.
*** Ph. Dig. **412 879-2** [id.]. Holliger, ASMF, Iona Brown.

The *C minor Concerto* with its astringent opening dissonance is the most familiar of the concertos on Holliger's record and the *E minor* has also been recorded before, but the remaining three are all new to the catalogue. Telemann was himself proficient on the oboe and wrote with particular imagination and poignancy for this instrument. The performances are all vital and sensitively shaped and a valuable addition to the Telemann discography. Well worth investigation.

Recorder concerto in C. (i) *Double concerto for recorder and bassoon.*
*** BIS Dig. **CD 271** [id.]. Pehrsson, (i) McGraw, Drottningholm Bar. Ens. – VIVALDI: *Concertos.****

Clas Pehrsson and Michael McGraw are most expert players, as indeed are their colleagues of the Drottningholm Baroque Ensemble. Readers wanting these two Telemann concertos need not hesitate; the recordings are well balanced and fresh.

Double concerto in F, for recorder, bassoon & strings; Double concerto in E min., for recorder, flute & strings; Suite in A min., for recorder & strings.
*** Ph. Dig. **410 041-2** [id.]. Petri, Bennett, Thunemann, ASMF, Iona Brown.

The *E minor Concerto* for recorder, flute and strings is also included on the Academy of Ancient Music's anthology (O-L **411 949-2**) but is played on modern instruments on the Philips record. This is a delightful piece and is beautifully played, even though period instrument addicts will doubtless find William Bennett's tone a little fruity. The playing throughout is highly accomplished and the *Suite in A minor*, Telemann's only suite for treble recorder, comes off beautifully. Excellently played and recorded throughout. The compact disc brings out the forward balance of the soloists in the *Double concerto*, but the effect is not unattractive. The orchestral focus is not absolutely clean, though quite agreeable.

(i) *Double concerto in A min. for recorder, viola & strings; Duet in C for recorder & violin.* (ii) *Trio in C for recorder, violin & continuo; Trio in F for recorder, viola & continuo.*
*** Ph. Dig. **420 243-2**; *420 243-4* [id.]. Petri, Zukerman, (i) St Paul CO; (ii) James (with HERBERLE: *Recorder concerto in G* ***).

The liveliness of Telemann's invention is heard at its finest here, not only in the two *Trios*, which are further enlivened by some deliciously nimble decoration from Michala Petri, but in the *Duet*. Here one is amazed at the diversity of colour and interplay of timbre Telemann achieves in this exceedingly entertaining four-movement piece. Of course the partnership of Petri and Zukerman is a joy: they play with a smiling vivacity and elegance that it is impossible to resist. The forward, truthful recording helps with good projection, on tape as well as disc. The concert is completed with a *Concerto* by Anton Herberle, an obscure musician who lived around the turn of the nineteenth century. His *galant* three-movement work is undeniably engaging and it has a winning virtuoso finale in the form of a fast Minuet with two Trios – the sort of infectious piece that James Galway might wish he had discovered before Ms Petri. Needless to say, she plays it with enormous flair: it is the kind of lollipop that remains in the memory.

Concerto for 3 trumpets, 2 oboes & strings.
** Erato Dig. **ECD 88007** [id.]. M. André, Touvron, L. André, Arrignon, Chavana, Pontet, Paris O Ens., Wallez – HUMMEL; NERUDA: *Concertos.***

This Telemann work has some very attractive textures and the invention is fresh. The soloists, led by Maurice André, are excellent but the orchestral support is less impressive. The recording is good, though not as clearly defined as one usually expects from a digital source.

Overtures (*Suites*)*: in G min.; D min.*
*** Tel. **ZK8 42986** [id.]. VCM, Harnoncourt.

One hundred and thirty-four *Overtures* (or *Suites*) by Telemann survive, though he composed many more. The two recorded here were first issued during 1981, the tercentenary of his birth. The performances have plenty of liveliness to recommend them; they communicate fully the vitality and wit of this music. As always, Telemann's invention has freshness and intelligence and, at times, unpredictability: there is, for example, an extraordinary modulation in the *Loure* of the *D minor*, from B minor to F major in its middle section. The balance is rather close but the sound has plenty of presence, even though this brings out the nasal sound of the strings.

Suite in A min. for flute & strings.
(B) ** CBS **MK 35133** [id.]. Rampal, Jerusalem Music Centre CO – VIVALDI: *Concertos.***

Telemann's *Suite in A minor*, which has so much in common with Bach's *B minor Suite*, is available on CD in a splendid performance by Michala Petri with the ASMF – see above. Rampal is very spirited, even racy, even if his performance is not authentic in style (the orchestra is distinctly big band). Not for purists by any means, and it is perhaps too brisk and wanting in dignity to enjoy the widest appeal.

Tafelmusik: Overtures (Suites): in E min. (from Part I); in D (from Part II); in B flat (from Part III).
(M) *** Tel. **ZS8 43776** [id.]. Concerto Amsterdam, Brüggen.

These three agreeable *Suites*, each of which introduces one part of Telemann's ambitious *Tafelmusik*, have something in common with the Bach *Orchestral suites*. Essentially, they are made up of French dance-movements of considerable diversity, and the *E minor Suite* is engagingly scored for a pair of recorders with strings; although it has no *Badinerie*, its sound is not unlike Bach's B minor work; while Telemann's *D major*, with its forthright use of a trumpet, similarly reminds one of the Bach *Third suite*, even though its invention has nothing in it as memorable as Bach's famous *Air*. The third suite here is perhaps the most agreeable of all, using two oboes with considerable flair. All this music is expertly played by the Concerto Amsterdam under Frans Brüggen, and the remastered 1970 recording is fresh and full, so that the disc sounds hardly dated at all. Offered at mid-price, it represents first-rate value with an overall playing time of 75′ 31″.

Water Music (Hamburg Ebb and Flow); Concertos in A min.; B flat; F.
*** DG Dig. **413 788-2** [id.]. Col. Mus. Ant., Goebel.

Telemann's *Water Music* was written for the centenary celebrations of the Hamburg Admiralty in 1723, and this lively and inventive suite was performed during the festivities. It is one of Telemann's best-known works and, save for the very opening *overture*, is given a very lively performance, with sprightly rhythms and vital articulation. The eccentric opening is less than half the speed of Marriner's (deleted) version on Argo, or Wenzinger's famous old Archiv account. Of particular interest are the three concertos which form the coupling, two of which (in F major and A minor) are new to records. The invention is of unfailing interest, as is the diversity of instrumental colouring. The balance is admirably judged and the recording excellent, with the compact disc offering additional presence.

CHAMBER MUSIC

Essercizii musici: Sonatas in C; D min. Der getreue Musik-Meister: Sonatas in A; C; F; F min.
*** HMV Dig. **CDC7 47653-2** [id.]. Cologne Camerata.

Half a dozen sonatas that give a splendid picture of the variety and resource this inventive composer possessed. Michael Schneider's recorder playing is sensitive and accomplished, and his two partners (Rainer Zipperling, cello and viola da gamba, and Harald Hoeren, harpsichord and organ) are hardly less impressive. *Der getreue Musik-Meister* was a subscription series of twenty-five lessons which Telemann published fortnightly and which Archiv recorded complete for the first time in the 1960s. The four sonatas are of high quality, as indeed are the two from the *Essercizii musici* (1739). Splendidly alive playing and good recording – though obviously they are best heard separately rather than all at one sitting.

Essercizii musici: Sonata in B flat. Der getreue Musik-Meister: Suite in G min. Die kleine Kammermusik: Partita No. 2 in G. Tafelmusik: Sonata in G min.
** Accent **ACC 48013D**. Dombrecht, Kuijken, Kohnen.

This recital of oboe music by Telemann first appeared in 1980 and has been digitally remastered for CD. Paul Dombrecht is a sensitive player who offers pieces from the *Tafelmusik* and *Der getreue Musik-Meister* as well as a rather remarkable *Sonata in B flat* from the *Essercizii musici* of 1739. Enthusiasts will doubtless want everything; for a basic Telemann collection, however, the non-specialist collector will probably turn first to Holliger's anthology from *Der getreue*

Musik-Meister listed below, particularly as there is the occasional insecurity of intonation here. Generally speaking, however, these are good performances and are well recorded.

Der getreue Musik-Meister: Nos 4, 7, 13, 20, 28, 31, 35, 50, 53, 59, 62.
*** Denon Dig. **C37 7052** [id.]. Holliger, Thunemann, Jaccottet.

This compact disc offers three of the most important works from *Der getreue Musik-Meister* for oboe and continuo, two *Sonatas* and a *Suite*, as well as the *F minor Sonata*, designated for recorder or bassoon and played here by Klaus Thunemann. They are interspersed with various miniatures, all well played and recorded. Holliger's playing is unusually expressive and his eloquence makes this selection alone worth having. Those who don't possess the complete set on LP might well consider obtaining this selection.

Sonatas for two recorders Nos 1 in F; 2 in B flat; 3 in C; 4 in G min.; 5 in D min.; 6 in G; Duetto in B flat.
*** BIS Dig. **CD 334** [id.]. Clas Pehrsson, Dan Laurin.

Canon sonatas Nos 1 in B flat; 2 in F; 3 in D min.; 4 in G min.; 5 in C; 6 in C min.; Duettos Nos 1 in B flat; 2 in C min.; 3 in D min,; 4 in G min.; 5 in C; 6 in G.
*** BIS Dig. **CD 335** [id.]. Clas Pehrsson, Dan Laurin.

The *Sonatas sans basse* appeared in Hamburg in 1727. All the sonatas are in four movements, the second being a fugue; the *Canon sonatas* come from the following decade (1738) and are for two flutes, violins or bass viols. Needless to say, listening to two recorders for longer than one piece at a time imposes a strain on one's powers of endurance, however expert the playing – and expert it certainly is.

Tiomkin, Dimitri (1894–1979)

Film music: *The Fall of the Roman Empire: Overture: Pax Romana. The Guns of Navarone: Prologue-Prelude; Epilogue. A President's country. Rhapsody of steel. Wild is the wind.*
(*) Unicorn **DKPCD 9047; *DKPC 9047* [id.]. Royal College of Music O, Willcocks; D. King (organ).

Dimitri Tiomkin was one of a number of émigré musicians who made a considerable contribution to the music of Hollywood. He was born in the Ukraine, studied under Glazunov and was still in St Petersburg at the time of the Russian Revolution. Later in Berlin he was a pupil of Busoni and made appearances as a solo pianist with the Berlin Philharmonic. His musical pedigree, then, is impressive and it is not surprising that his film career was distinguished. He contributed scores to some of the most famous movies of all time, for Hitchcock and Frank Capra among others. But it was Carl Foreman's *High noon* that produced his most memorable idea, and he quotes its famous theme, among others in *A President's country*, a well-crafted medley used as background music for a documentary about President Johnson's Texas. *Wild is the wind* is another familiar melody; Christopher Palmer's arrangement makes a tastefully scored showcase. The latter has arranged and orchestrated all the music here except *Rhapsody of steel*, a complex pseudo-symphonic score written for another documentary, which lasts some 22 minutes. It is an ambitious piece; while aficionados of this repertoire will welcome its inclusion, others may decide that the rhetoric outbalances the fresher material: this includes a nonchalant theme in the style of a popular song and a scherzando section which comes about halfway through. The music of *Pax Romana* has the robust character of a typical epic Hollywood costume spectacular, featuring a bold contribution from the organ. All the music is played with obvious enjoyment by the Orchestra of the Royal College of Music; no apologies need be made for their technique, which is fully professional. Sir David Willcocks conducts with understanding of the idiom and great personal conviction. The music could hardly be better presented. The recording is very impressive too, though the balance gives brass and percussion rather too much prominence. Such a degree of spectacle obviously has a maximum effect in the CD format, and the chrome tape is a little disappointing, lacking ultimate brilliance, though wide in amplitude.

Tippett, Michael (born 1905)

Concerto for double string orchestra.
(M) **(*) Nimbus Dig. **NI 5097** [id.]. E. String O, Boughton – STRAVINSKY: *Apollo.***(*)

Concerto for double string orchestra; The Midsummer Marriage: Ritual dances.
** HMV Dig. **CDC7 47330-2** [id.]. Bournemouth SO, Barshai.

In 1963 Rudolf Barshai made a fine recording of the *Concerto for double string orchestra* with the combined Moscow Chamber and Bath Festival orchestras, but this 1985 Bournemouth version brings a slowing and a thickening which take away the natural impulse of the music and even undermine the radiant lyricism of the slow movement. The *Ritual dances* sound cautious, too, and the weight of brass obscures the detail in other sections. Nevertheless the digital recording is weightily impressive, full and realistic.

Like the Stravinsky ballet with which it is coupled, Boughton's account of the Tippett *Concerto* is fresh, warm and punchy, marginally faster in all three movements than the composer himself on his Virgin Classics disc. It is just as sympathetic, with idiomatically jazzy rhythms brought out in the outer movements, as well as the tender poetry of the middle movement and with the opening viola solo very beautiful indeed. Though the violin ensemble is a little edgy, the reverberant recording smooths it acceptably.

Concerto for double string orchestra; Fantasia concertante on a theme of Corelli. (i) *Songs for Dov.*
*** Virgin Dig. **VC 790701-2**; *VC 790701-4* [id.]. Scottish CO, composer; (i) Nigel Robson.

The very first list of Virgin Classics releases brought this heartwarming record of Tippett conducting his own music. It is particularly valuable to have the richest and most immediately appealing of his works, the *Concerto for double string orchestra*, which he had never previously recorded himself. Interpreting his own youthful inspiration, the octogenarian gives delightfully pointed readings of the outer movements, bringing out the jazzy implications of the cross-rhythms, not taking them too literally, while the lovely melody of the slow movement has never sounded more warmly expressive. The Scottish Chamber Orchestra plays with comparable passion in the *Fantasia concertante*, a related work from Tippett's middle period, while Nigel Robson is a wonderfully idiomatic and convincing tenor soloist in the difficult vocal lines of the three *Songs for Dov*. This is an exceptionally generous coupling, representing Tippett at all periods. Warm, full recording, with the chrome cassette lacking the extra range and definition of the CD although offering a pleasing enough sound-balance.

Fantasia concertante on a theme of Corelli.
** ASV Dig. **CDDCA 518**; *ZCDCA 518* [id.]. ASMF, Marriner – ELGAR: *Serenade***; VAUGHAN WILLIAMS: *Tallis fantasia* etc.**(*)

The *Fantasia concertante on a theme of Corelli* was the first Tippett work to appear on CD and the ASV recording has fine clarity and detail. The new performance is certainly successful – but the composer's account is finer still and has preferable couplings.

(i) *Symphonies Nos 1–2;* (i; ii) *Symphony No. 3;* (iii) *Symphony No. 4.*
*** Decca *414 091-4* (3). (i) LSO, C. Davis; (ii) with Heather Harper; (iii) Chicago SO, Solti.

All four symphonies have been available separately, the *First* and *Third* on Philips, the *Second* on Argo, and the *Fourth* on Decca itself. One welcome result of the Polygram merger is this kind of venture, marking the composer's eightieth birthday, which enables all four symphonies to be accommodated in one box, albeit shorn of their original couplings. (Since possessing the *First* and *Fourth* originally involved duplication as they were both coupled with the *Suite for the birthday of Prince Charles*, this new format is obviously attractive.) However, as we go to press this invaluable set is marked for deletion in its tape format.

Piano sonatas Nos 1 (Fantasy sonata); 2; 3; 4.
*** CRD Dig. *CRDC 4130/1* (2) [id.]. Paul Crossley.

More than two decades separate the first two sonatas, and the remaining two have appeared at ten-year intervals. The *Fantasy sonata* is one of Tippett's very first published works and was written in 1937. The two middle sonatas are related to other Tippett works: the *Second* (1962) to the opera, *King Priam*, from which it quotes; and the *Third* (1973) comes from the same world as the *Third Symphony*. Paul Crossley has been strongly identified with the Tippett sonatas; he recorded the first three for Philips in the mid-1970s: indeed, No. 3 was written for him. The *Fourth* and most recent (1983–4) started life as a set of five bagatelles. Crossley contributes an informative and illuminating note on the sonata and its relationship with, among other things, Ravel's *Miroirs*; his performance has all the lucidity and subtlety one would expect from him. These masterly accounts supersede the earlier recording and their excellence is matched by truthful and immediate sound-quality, with chrome cassettes of high quality.

String quartet No. 4.
*** ASV Dig. **CDDCA 608**; *ZCDCA 608* [id.]. Lindsay Qt – BRITTEN: *Quartet No. 3.****

Tippett's *Fourth quartet*, here given a fine performance by the Lindsays for whom it was written, is a formidably tough, uncompromising work in four linked movements. Together they develop even more rigorously the birth-to-death theme of his *Fourth Symphony*, written at about the same time. The two fast movements, second and fourth in the scheme, are the longest in the span, underlining the composer's urgency of inspiration in this product of his mid-seventies. But the emotional core lies in the slow and still abrasive movement which comes third, bringing no easy solution. The Lindsay Quartet give a powerful, deeply committed reading of music far thornier than the late Britten *Quartet* with which it is coupled. Fine, vivid reading, with the players presented rather close, so that extraneous playing noises sometimes intrude. There is an excellent cassette.

VOCAL MUSIC

A Child of our time (oratorio).
(*) Ph. **420 075-2 [id.]. Norman, J. Baker, Cassilly, Shirley-Quirk, BBC Singers, BBC Ch. Society, BBC SO, C. Davis.
(*) ASV Dig. **CDRPO 8005; *ZCRPO 8005* [id.]. Armstrong, Palmer, Langridge, Shirley Quirk, Brighton Fest. Ch., RPO, Previn.

Davis's is a tough performance of the Tippett oratorio. His speeds tend to be on the fast side, both in the spirituals (taking the place which Bach gave to chorales) and in the other numbers. He may miss some of the tenderness; by avoiding all suspicion of sentimentality, however, the result is incisive and very powerful, helped by excellent solo and choral singing. With the CD transfer of 1975 analogue sound even fuller and more atmospheric than the much later Previn recording, Davis also gains in the firmness and power of the soloists, Jessye Norman and Dame Janet Baker among them. Ensemble is a degree more precise, even if jazz rhythms are less idiomatically done.

Previn's is a colourful and winning performance, warmer and more expressive than Davis's, predictably helped by the conductor's natural understanding of jazz rhythms. This is a reading which leaves you in no doubt as to the depth of emotion felt by the composer; but ensemble is not always ideally crisp, the chorus is set rather backwardly and the soloists, a less polished if just as characterful a team as Davis's, have uneven moments. The digital recording is unobtrusively natural, if slightly recessed. There is a good tape.

The Mask of Time.
*** HMV Dig. **CDS7 47707-8** (2); *EX 270567-5.* Robinson, Sarah Walker, Tear, Cheek, BBC Singers, BBC Ch., BBC SO, Andrew Davis.

The Mask of Time is among the most remarkable works that even Sir Michael Tippett has written in his extraordinarily fruitful old age, a piece bursting with exuberant invention. There are richness, generosity and overwhelming vigour in this Seven Days of Creation for a Nuclear Age, astounding in a composer who was nearing eighty when he wrote it. If initially it seemed that Tippett's characteristic wildness both of concept and of invention had gone too far, this live performance, vividly captured on record by EMI, rebuts any doubts. With his BBC forces, Andrew Davis brilliantly clarifies and sharpens the ever-busy score, and the fine discipline brings out a creative, purposeful control behind the wildness. Not only is the energy of the writing given more force, the poetry of the piece emerges the more intensely, culminating in the lovely setting for soprano and humming chorus of lines by Anna Akhmatova in *Hiroshima, mon amour*. The final wordless chorus then projects the role of music into eternity, under the title, *The singing will never be done*. Davis draws incandescent singing from the BBC Symphony Chorus and attendant professionals. The quartet of soloists too is outstanding, three of them in the original Boston performance – Faye Robinson rich and vibrant, Robert Tear and John Cheek – with Sarah Walker characterful and incisive even in the whimsy of the dragon-turned-snake episode in the Paradise Garden. CD helps in clarifying the complex textures and presenting the performers in a natural and believable ensemble. No finer recording has ever been made in the difficult acoustics of the Royal Festival Hall. On tape the work is transferred on to a single iron-oxide cassette, but the lack of range at the top and the blurred inner detail mean that it is a very poor relation of the CD.

Tomasi, André (1901–71)

Trumpet concerto.
*** CBS **MK 42096**; *IMT 42096* [id.]. Wynton Marsalis, Philh. O, Salonen – JOLIVET: *Concertos.****

Like the Jolivet couplings, this is essentially crossover music, if with a neoclassical flavour. The structure is chimerical, but not without spontaneity and, with Wynton Marsalis offering scintillating bravura throughout and an easy affinity with the swiftly changing moods, the result is quite attractive. It is all very slight but, at less than 14′, does not outstay its welcome. The recording, however, is not ideally clear in either format, and in playing time this issue is singularly ungenerous.

Tosti, Francesco (1846–1916)

Songs: *L'alba sepàra della luce l'ombra; Aprile; 'A vucchella; Chanson de L'adieu; Goodbye; Ideale; Malia; Marechiare; Non t'amo; Segreto; La serenata; Sogno; L'ultima canzone; Vorrei morire.*
*** Ph. **416 900-2** [id.]. José Carreras, ECO, Muller.

Tosti (knighted by Queen Victoria for his services to music) had a gently charming lyric gift in songs like these, and it is good to have a tenor with such musical intelligence – not to mention such a fine, pure voice – tackling once-popular trifles like *Marechiare* and *Goodbye*. The arrangements are sweetly done, and the recording is excellent.

Tubin, Eduard (1905–82)

(i) *Balalaika concerto; Music for strings; Symphony No. 1.*
*** BIS Dig. **CD 351** [id.]. (i) Sheynkman; Swedish RSO, Järvi.

It is an astonishing and gratifying thought that during the lifetime of this book all ten symphonies of this composer plus the first movement of his unfinished *Eleventh* will be available on CD. Tubin was born in Estonia and fled his country in 1944 to settle in Sweden where only now are amends being made for his neglect. The *First Symphony*, composed when Tubin was in his late twenties, apparently caused something of a stir on its first performance in Tallinn. The opening almost puts one in mind of Bax and there is a Sibelian breadth; but for the most part it is a symphony apart from its fellows, perhaps in a way that *Kullervo* is apart from the seven Sibelius symphonies. The quality of the musical substance is high, though its personal profile is perhaps less developed than in its immediate successor. Yet the feeling for form is every bit as strong, and its presentation is astonishingly assured for a young man still in his twenties; indeed, the scoring is quite masterly. The other two works are much later: the *Balalaika concerto* of 1964 was written for Nicolaus Zwetnow, not only a leading exponent of the balalaika but professor of neurosurgery in Oslo! Emanuil Sheynkman's account with Neeme Järvi is every bit as good as – and both tauter and more concentrated than – the Caprice version (which is not available on CD).

Violin concerto No. 1; Suite on Estonian dances for violin and orchestra; Prélude solennel.
** BIS Dig. **CD 286** [id.]. Lubotsky, Gothenburg SO, Järvi.

All the music on the present disc derives from the period before Tubin settled in Sweden in 1944: the *Suite* (1943) is a rather slight and folksy piece, originally for violin and piano, which Tubin scored later in life. But no one approaching this *Suite* or the empty and bombastic *Prélude solennel* without foreknowledge of any of Tubin's other music should judge him on either of these pieces. The *Violin concerto No. 1* is a good deal better – though, again, it is no match for the *Fourth Symphony*, composed only a year later. The solo line is lyrical and the melodic ideas are not unappealing or lacking in character, but the orchestra often provides rather simple harmonic support and the writing is somehow wanting in interest. It was recorded at a public concert in Gothenburg, and both the performance and sound engineering are eminently acceptable. However, this is emphatically not Tubin at his best.

Symphonies Nos 2 (The Legendary); 6.
*** BIS **CD 304** [id.]. Swedish RSO, Järvi.

The *Second Symphony* was written during the summer of 1937, which Tubin spent on the high north-eastern coastline of Estonia; despite its title, there is no specific programme. The opening is quite magical: there are soft luminous string chords that evoke a strong atmosphere of wide vistas and white summer nights, but the music soon gathers power and reveals a genuine feeling for proportion and of organic growth. In some ways this makes a more attractive and interesting introduction to Tubin's music than the *Fourth Symphony*, and it is certainly better played. If there is a Sibelian strength in the *Second Symphony*, the *Sixth*, written after he had settled in Sweden, has obvious resonances of Prokofiev – even down to instrumentation – and yet his rhythmic vitality and melodic invention are quietly distinctive. The music is always pursuing a purposeful course and the ear is always engaged by the diversity of musical incident. The Swedish Radio Symphony Orchestra play with great commitment under Neeme Järvi, and the engineers have done a magnificent job.

Symphonies Nos 3; 8.
*** BIS Dig. **CD 342** [id.]. Swedish RSO, Järvi.

The first two movements of the wartime *Third Symphony* are vintage Tubin, but the heroic finale approaches bombast. The *Eighth* (1966) is his masterpiece; its opening movement has a sense of vision and mystery, and the atmosphere stays with you. This is the darkest of the symphonies and the most intense in feeling, music of real substance and importance. Järvi and the Swedish orchestra play it marvellously and the recording is in the demonstration bracket.

Symphonies (i) *Nos 4* (*Sinfonia lirica*)*;* (ii) *9* (*Sinfonia semplice*)*; Toccata.*
❀ *** BIS Dig. **CD 227** [id.]. (i) Bergen SO, (ii) Gothenburg SO, Järvi.

The *Fourth* (1943) was the last symphony Tubin composed while he was still living in Estonia. He took it with him to Sweden the following year and later in life revised it. A highly attractive piece, immediately accessible, the music is well argued and expertly crafted. The opening has a Sibelian feel to it but, the closer one comes to it, the more individual it seems. The recording comes from a concert performance and has an exceptionally well-behaved audience. The *Ninth Symphony* dates from 1969 and is in two movements: its mood is elegiac and a restrained melancholy permeates the slower sections. Its musical language is direct, tonal and, once one gets to grips with it, quite personal. If its spiritual world is clearly Nordic, the textures are transparent and luminous, and its argument unfolds naturally and cogently. It is strong in both concentration of feeling and melodic invention; the playing of the Gothenburgers under Järvi is totally committed in all sections of the orchestra. The performances are authoritative and the recording altogether excellent.

Symphony No. 5 in B minor; Kratt (ballet suite).
*** BIS Dig. **CD 315** [id.]. Bamberg SO, Järvi.

The *Fifth* makes as good a starting point as any to investigate the Tubin canon. Written after he had settled in Sweden, it finds him at his most neoclassic; the music is finely paced and full of energy and invention. The ballet suite is a work of much character, tinged with folk-inspired ideas and some echoes of Prokofiev.

Symphony No. 10; (i) *Requiem for fallen soldiers.*
*** BIS Dig. **CD 297** [id.]. Gothenburg SO, Järvi; (i) with Lundin, Rydell, Hardenberger, Lund Students' Ch., Järvi.

Tubin began his *Requiem for fallen soldiers* as early as 1950, but work on it did not proceed well and so, in the middle of the second movement, he put it aside. It was only in the late 1970s that he returned to it, finishing the *Requiem* in 1979, almost thirty years after its original conception. He conducted its first performance himself in 1981, the year before his death. The work is austere in character and is for two soloists (a contralto and baritone) and male chorus. The instrumental forces are merely an organ, piano, drums, timpani and trumpet. The simplicity and directness of the language are affecting and the sense of melancholy is finely controlled, without the slightest trace of self-pity. The final movement is prefaced by a long trumpet solo, played here with stunning control and a masterly sense of line by the young Håkan Hardenberger. It is an impressive and dignified work, even if the quality of the choral singing is less than first rate. The *Tenth Symphony* is a one-movement piece, some 25 minutes in duration and quite unlike its rather elegiac predecessor. It begins with a sombre string idea which is soon interrupted by a horn call that periodically recurs – and which resonates in the mind long afterwards. It shows that Tubin's imaginative vitality and strong feeling for structure remained unimpaired. The recordings are absolutely first class and in the best traditions of the house.

Turina, Joaquín (1882–1949)

Rapsodia sinfónica, Op. 66.

*** Decca Dig. **410 289-2**; *410 289-4* [id.]. De Larrocha, LPO, Frühbeck de Burgos – FALLA: *Nights in the gardens of Spain* *** (with ALBÉNIZ: *Rapsodia****).

Turina's *Rapsodia sinfónica* has been recorded by others, but in the hands of Alicia de Larrocha it is played with such éclat that it becomes almost memorable and thoroughly entertaining. The Falla coupling is poetic and atmospheric, while the delightfully chimerical Albéniz companion piece glitters most engagingly. Excellent, vivid sound out of Decca's top drawer.

Vaňhal, Jan (1739–1813)

(i) *Double bassoon concerto in F; Sinfonias: in A min.; F.*

** BIS **CD 288** [id.]. (i) Wallin, Nilsson; Umeå Sinf., Saraste.

The best thing here is the *Concerto*, which is an arresting and inventive piece. The opening allegro is conceived on a broader canvas than one expects, and the slow movement has real distinction, touching a deeper vein of feeling than anything else on this record. The work is not only beautifully crafted and well laid out, which one expects, but its invention is fresh. It is not too fanciful to detect in some of the harmonic suspensions the influence of Gluck, with whose music Vaňhal came into contact in the late 1760s. The two *Sinfonias* are less musically developed but far from uninteresting: the minuet of the *F major* has a distinctly '*Sturm und Drang*' feel to it: Vaňhal's symphonies may well have paved the way for Haydn at this period; they were certainly given by Haydn while Kapellmeister at the Esterhazy palace. The recording is good, as one has come to expect from this source, and detail is clean and fresh, even if the acoustic is on the dry side. The playing of the Umeå ensemble is eminently respectable, even if the upper strings occasionally sound a little lacking in bloom. The balance is well judged, though perhaps the accomplished young soloists are placed just a little too forward.

Violin concerto in G.

(*) Sup. Dig. **C37 7571 [id.]. Josef Suk, Suk CO, Vlach – HAYDN: *Concerto in G.***(*)*

Jan Vaňhal was Haydn's contemporary, Bohemian by birth but active in Vienna. His *G major Concerto* is every bit as good as Haydn's in the same key – which, of course, is not saying a great deal. In fact, it is quite an engaging little work, with a busy first movement, a rather solemn *Adagio* which Suk plays with characteristic warmth, and a brilliant *presto* finale, which both soloist and orchestra dive into with great vivacity and spirit. The recording is truthful if forwardly balanced, but this is short measure for CD – room could easily have been found for a third concerto.

Vaughan Williams, Ralph (1872–1958)

(i) *Concerto accademico;* (ii) *Oboe concerto; Fantasia on Greensleeves; 5 variants of Dives and Lazarus; Hymn tune preludes: Hyfrydol; Rhosymedre.*
*** HMV Dig. **CDC7 49745-2** [id.]; *EL 749745-4.* (i) Bradley Creswick; (ii) Roger Winfield; N. Sinfonia, Hickox.

A particularly attractive compilation, splendidly recorded in the rich (yet not blurring) ambience of All Saints' Quayside Church, Newcastle-upon-Tyne. Bradley Creswick's account of the *Concerto accademico* is the finest available, with the complex mood of the *Adagio*, both ethereal and ecstatic, caught on the wing. Roger Winfield is hardly less persuasive in the engaging *Oboe concerto*, his timbre full of pastoral colour, while he displays a deliciously light touch in the finale. Hickox takes *Greensleeves* very spaciously, in the American way, and brings out the breadth as well as the lyrical beauty of the melody. The *Dives and Lazarus fantasia* and two *Hymn tune preludes* sustain the elegiac mood, and the rich string timbres add to the pleasure this record brings throughout. The chrome tape is also a state-of-the-art transfer, vivid, full and admirably clear.

(i) *Concerto accademico in D min. for violin & orchestra;* (ii) *Flos campi.*
(M) (***) HMV mono *EH 291276-4.* (i) Menuhin, LPO, Boult; (ii) Primrose, BBC Ch., Philh. O, Boult – WALTON: *Viola concerto* etc.(***)

The art of William Primrose, unmatched as a viola player in his generation, is superbly brought out in his cassette of *Flos campi* – not to mention the Walton *Concerto* on the reverse – even if the instrument is balanced unnaturally close. This first ever recording still brings a uniquely persuasive account of a rare, elusive masterpiece and comes fascinatingly coupled with not only the two Walton concertante works but also a Menuhin recording of the *Concerto accademico*, made in 1952 but never previously issued. Not immaculate, it yet gives a strong sense of purpose to this curious example of V.W. in neoclassical mood. Good transfers of obviously limited mono sound. The ear soon adjusts, so magnetic are the performances.

Concerto grosso; (i) *Oboe concerto; Fantasia on Greensleeves; Fantasia on a theme of Thomas Tallis; Five variants of Dives and Lazarus.*
(M) **(*) Nimbus Dig. **NIM 5019** [id.]. (i) Bourgue; E. String O, Boughton.

Recorded in the spacious acoustic of the Great Hall of Birmingham University, Boughton's sympathetic performances of an attractive group of Vaughan Williams works are presented amply and atmospherically. That is particularly effective in the *Tallis fantasia*, and the *Greensleeves fantasia* – with the flute solo nicely distanced – is equally beautiful. Though the reverberation thickens the textures of the *Concerto grosso*, reducing its neoclassic lightness, that too loses little from the weight of sound. More questionable is the *Oboe concerto* with the superb French soloist, Maurice Bourgue, balanced too close, so that the strings in the background do little more than comment distantly. Nevertheless Bourgue's playing, rich in tone and sharply rhythmic, makes a persuasive case for a neglected piece.

(i) *Oboe concerto;* (ii) *The Lark ascending.*
*** DG **419 748-2** [id.]. (i) Neil Black; (ii) Zukerman, ECO, Barenboim – DELIUS: *Aquarelles* etc.; WALTON: *Henry V.****

Neil Black's creamy tone is particularly suited to Vaughan Williams's *Oboe concerto* and he gives a wholly persuasive performance of what is not one of the composer's strongest works. Zukerman's account of *The Lark ascending* is full of pastoral rapture – even if perhaps not totally idiomatic, the effect is ravishing. The recordings from 1977 and 1975 respectively have not lost their allure or atmospheric warmth in the digital remastering. It is a pity that the *Fantasia on Greensleeves* (included in the original LP collection instead of the *Oboe concerto*) was omitted here there was room for it.

English folksongs suite; Fantasia on Greensleeves; In the Fen Country. (i) *The Lark ascending. Norfolk rhapsody No. 1.* (ii) *Serenade to music.*
*** HMV **CDC7 47218-2** [id.]. LPO, Boult, with (i) Bean; (ii) 16 vocal soloists.

An attractive coupling of four works that originally appeared as fill-ups to Boult versions of the symphonies, all beautifully performed and recorded. Hugh Bean understands the spirit of *The Lark ascending* perfectly and his performance is wonderfully serene. For the CD reissue two others works have been added, the colourful *English folksongs suite* and Vaughan Williams's fine arrangement of one of the loveliest of all traditional melodies, *Greensleeves*. The transfers are highly successful, fresh yet not losing body and atmosphere; the vocal version of the *Serenade to music* sounds particularly lovely.

English folksongs suite; Toccata marziale.
(M) *** ASV **CDQS 6021**; *ZCQS 6021* [id.]. London Wind O, Denis Wick – HOLST: *Military band suites* etc.***

As in the Holst suites, the pace of these performances is attractively zestful, and if the slow movement of the *English folksongs suite* could have been played more reflectively, the bounce of *Seventeen come Sunday* is irresistible. The *Toccata marziale*, written in 1924 for the British Empire Exhibition at Wembley, has plenty of flourish. The first-class analogue recording has been transferred vividly to CD.

Fantasia on Sussex folk tunes for cello and orchestra.
*** RCA Dig. **RD 70800**; *RK 70800*. Lloyd Webber, Philh. O, Handley – DELIUS: *Cello concerto*; HOLST: *Invocation.****

The *Fantasia on Sussex folk tunes* is new to the gramophone. It was composed for Casals, who gave its first performance in 1930 at a Royal Philharmonic Society concert, and comes from the same period as *Job* and the *Piano concerto*. The piece has lain neglected since its first performance, and it proves something of a discovery. This is a highly appealing work, most persuasively performed too by Lloyd Webber and the Philharmonia and Vernon Handley. The recording is first class: the CD transfer is bright and vivid, yet admirably refined too. There is a good tape.

Fantasia on Greensleeves.
(B) *** HMV *TCC2-POR 54290*. LSO, Previn – HOLST: *The Planets* etc.*** (with BUTTERWORTH: *Banks of green willow****).

Fantasia on Greensleeves; Fantasia on a theme of Thomas Tallis.
*** HMV **CDC7 47537-2** [id.]. Sinf. of L., Allegri Qt, Barbirolli – ELGAR: *Introduction and allegro; Serenade.****
* DG Dig. **419 191-2**; *419 191-4* [id.]. Orpheus CO – ELGAR: Elegy; Introduction & allegro; Serenade.*

Fantasia on Greensleeves; Fantasia on a theme of Thomas Tallis; Five Variants of Dives and Lazarus; (i) *The Lark ascending.*
*** Argo **414 595-2** [id.]. ASMF, Marriner (i) with Iona Brown.

Fantasia on a theme of Thomas Tallis; Five variants of Dives and Lazarus; In the Fen Country; Norfolk rhapsody.
*** Chan. Dig. **CHAN 8502**; *ABTD 1212* [id.]. LPO, Bryden Thomson.

Fantasia on a theme of Thomas Tallis; (i) *The Lark ascending.*
(*) ASV Dig. **CDDCA 518; *ZCDCA 518* [id.]. (i) Iona Brown; ASMF, Marriner – ELGAR: *String serenade;* TIPPETT: *Fantasia concertante.***

The Chandos collection is generous and now leads the field in this repertoire. It offers a well-recorded anthology of (save for the *Tallis fantasia*) lesser-known Vaughan Williams. *In the Fen Country* (1904–7) is an early work which V.W. revised no fewer than four times, on the last occasion just after the *Fourth Symphony*; so, too, is the *Norfolk rhapsody* (1905). Boult recorded them successfully, but neither is otherwise available in modern digital sound. Bryden Thomson is a thoroughly persuasive guide in all this repertoire, and in the other two pieces more than holds his own with most of the opposition although Barbirolli achieves a unique intensity in the *Tallis fantasia*. There is a first-rate tape, although the sound is resonant in the bass.

The rich projection of the Tallis theme on which Vaughan Williams based his *Fantasia* when it first appears in full, after the pizzicato introduction, sets the seal on Barbirolli's quite outstanding performance of the *Tallis fantasia*, one of the great masterpieces of all music. The wonderfully ethereal and magically quiet playing of the second orchestra is another very moving feature of this remarkable performance. On CD the sound retains its warmth, amplitude and bloom, but the disposal of background has also taken off a little of the recording's upper range, which is slightly restricted. The delightful *Greensleeves fantasia* makes a pleasing bonus, and here the quality is pleasingly fresh.

On Argo, superbly balanced and refined performances of four favourite Vaughan Williams works, which with the help of full, clear recorded sound here have great power and intensity. A rewarding record, made in 1972, but enhanced in its CD format; detail is more refined and the fullness retained, but the massed upper strings now have a slight edge in climaxes.

On ASV, Iona Brown offers her second recording of *The Lark ascending* and she has the advantage here of digital recording. The present version, though not finer than the old, is both eloquent and evocative; the silent background of the CD, plus the internal clarity, makes it highly competitive. The *Tallis fantasia* is beautifully played too, but the effect here is relatively bland beside the earlier Argo account, now also transferred to CD. The acoustic is warm but not quite as expansive as the Argo and HMV versions. Couplings are also important with a record of this kind (called 'The English connection'), and neither shows these artists at their very best.

Even more than in the coupled Elgar, the Orpheus performance of the *Tallis fantasia* suggests a lack of the kind of familiarity and innate understanding of the music which comes with frequent performance. Though there are moments of passion, they are short-lived and the overall pacing is unconvincing. The bright, vividly clear recording confirms the need for a greater weight and body of tone to help the work to expand emotionally.

Previn's excellent account of the *Greensleeves fantasia* is part of a double-length tape in HMV's 'Portrait of the Artist' series, of which the major contents are by Holst. The sound is first rate.

Five variants of Dives and Lazarus; (i) *The Lark ascending; The Wasps: Overture and suite.*
(M) *** EMI Dig. **CD-EMX 9508**; *EMX 41 2082-4*. (i) David Nolan; LPO, Handley.

Handley, like his mentor, Sir Adrian Boult, is an outstanding interpreter of Vaughan Williams, and here on the Eminence label he conducts an unusual and attractive collection in which rarities spice the two central, popular items, *The Lark ascending* and *The Wasps overture*. The immediacy of the brilliant, full recorded sound allows no mistiness in the former piece, but it is still a warm, understanding performance. The overture is here spaciously conceived and it leads to charming colourful accounts of the other, less well-known pieces in the suite, tuneful and lively. The *Five Variants of Dives and Lazarus* finds Vaughan Williams using his folksong idiom at its most poetic, here superbly played and recorded. The CD transfer is highly successful, the sound fresh and clear, if rather brightly lit. *The Wasps overture* is a demonstration item.

Hymn-tune preludes: Nos 1, Eventide (arr. of Monk); *2, Dominus regit me* (arr. of Dykes); *The Poisoned Kiss: overture; The Running Set; Sea Songs: Quick march.*
*** Chan. **CHAN 8432**; (M) *CBT 1004* [id.]. Bournemouth Sinf., Hurst – ELGAR: *Adieu* etc.***

George Hurst directs no fewer than three first recordings on the Vaughan Williams side of a delightful collection of minor pieces. The overture to the opera *The Poisoned Kiss* is merely a pot-pourri, but it whets the appetite for a complete recording of a piece neglected simply because of its poor libretto. *The Running Set* is an exhilarating fantasy on jig rhythms, while the *March on sea songs*, with its bounding rhythms and surging melody in the trio, would make an ideal Prom item. Ripe performances and recording which has been admirably transferred to CD. There is some lack of weight in the upper strings but otherwise this sounds splendid. The excellent cassette is offered at mid-price.

Job (masque for dancing).
(M) ❀ *** EMI Dig. **CD-EMX 9506**; *TC-EMX 41 2056-4*. LPO, Handley

Job is undeniably one of Vaughan Williams's very greatest compositions. It shows his inspiration at its most deeply characteristic and at its most consistently noble. The Eminence digital recording by the LPO, playing with inspired fervour under Vernon Handley – made in St Augustine's Church, London – offers sound of superlative quality, very much in the demonstration class. The breadth of dynamic range is used to enormous effect by Handley to increase the dramatic effect – the organ entry representing Satan enthroned in heaven has overwhelming impact and power – and one feels that had Diaghilev heard this record he would not have rejected Vaughan Williams's masterly score. The ravishingly luminous espressivo playing in the work's quieter lyrical pages is movingly beautiful, with the music's evocative feeling memorably captured. Even at full price this CD would be irresistible, one of Handley's major achievements in the recording studio. The cassette is also very impressive but the CD has added range and definition.

Suite for viola and orchestra; (i) *Flos campi.*
(*) Chan. **CHAN 8374; (M) *CBT 1019* [id.]. Riddle, Bournemouth Sinf., Del Mar; (i) with Ch.

Originally issued in 1978 by RCA, this valuable coupling has been digitally remastered by Chandos with the choral sound enhanced on CD. Neither work is over-familiar and the evocation of the Song of Solomon contained in *Flos campi* shows Vaughan Williams at his most rarefied and imaginative. The *Suite* is lightweight but engaging, unpretentious music to be enjoyed, with its charming *Carol* and quirky *Polka mélancolique*. Frederick Riddle is an eloquent soloist, even if the playing is not always technically immaculate, and Norman Del Mar directs sympathetically. On the otherwise good chrome tape the choral sound is a little misty. However, the cassette is in the mid-price range.

A Sea symphony (No. 1).
*** HMV **CDC7 47212-2** [id.]. Armstrong, Carol Case, LPO Ch., LPO, Boult.
*** RCA **RD 89689**; (M) *GK 89689*. Harper, Shirley-Quirk, LSO Ch., LSO, Previn.
** Pinnacle Dig. **DSCD 1005**. Bickers, Blooding, Atlanta Ch., O des Jeunes, Noll

Boult's is a warm, relaxed reading of Vaughan Williams's expansive symphony. If the ensemble is sometimes less perfect than one would like, the flow of the music consistently holds the listener, and this is matched by warmly atmospheric recorded sound. Boult, often thought of as a 'straight' interpreter, here demonstrates his affectionate style, drawing consistently expressive but never sentimental phrasing from his singers and players. John Carol Case's baritone does not sound well on disc with his rather plaintive tone-colour, but his style is right, and Sheila Armstrong sings most beautifully. The set has been remastered and freshened, but perhaps this series ought now to be put on EMI's mid-priced CD label.

Previn's is a fresh, youthful reading of a young composer's symphony. If his interpretation lacks some of the honeyed sweetness that Boult brings to music he has known and loved for half a century and more, Previn's view provides a clearer focus. His nervous energy is obvious from the very start. He does not always relax as Boult does, even where, as in the slow movement, he takes a more measured tempo than the older conductor. In the Scherzo, Boult concentrates on urgency, the emotional surge of the music, even at the expense of precision of ensemble, where Previn is lighter and cleaner, holding more in reserve. The finale similarly is built up over a longer span, with less deliberate expressiveness. The culminating climax with Previn is not allowed to be swamped with choral tone, but has the brass and timpani still prominent. The *Epilogue* may not be so deliberately expressive, but it is purer in its tenderness and exact control of dynamics. Even if Vaughan Williams devotees will disagree over the relative merits of the interpretations, Previn has clear advantages in his baritone soloist and his choir. The recording has been digitally remastered and detail clarified, yet the rich ambience remains, with the performers set slightly back, which means that the famous opening section is more spacious but has a less dramatic bite than in Boult's version. The chrome cassette matches the disc closely and loses only a little of the inner definition, although the soloists are slightly more present on CD.

Though the Atlanta version on Pinnacle is too distantly recorded, the performance is strong and committed, with particularly fine singing from the Atlanta Choral Guild, ably backed by the very proficient youth orchestra. The soloists are fair enough, but are seriously obscured by bad balance.

A London symphony (*No. 2*).
(M) *** PRT **PVCD 8375** [id.]. Hallé O, Barbirolli.

A London symphony (*No. 2*); (i) *Concerto accademico; The Wasps: Overture.*
*** RCA **RD 89826**. LSO, Previn; (i) with James Buswell.

A London symphony (*No. 2*); *Fantasia on a theme of Thomas Tallis.*
*** HMV **CDC7 49394-2**; [id.]; *EL 749394-4*. LPO, Haitink.
*** HMV **CDC7 47213-2**; [id.]; (M) *ED 290331-4*. LPO, Boult.

A London symphony (*No. 2*); (i) *The Lark ascending.*
*** Telarc Dig. **CD 80138** [id.]. RPO, Previn; (i) with Barry Griffiths.

There is a very special place in the catalogue for Barbirolli's wonderful 1957 recording of the *London symphony*. It is an inspirational performance, entirely throwing off the fetters of the studio. The spontaneity of the music making means that the reading gathers power as it proceeds, and the slow movement has great intensity and eloquence with the Hallé strings surpassing themselves. The recording is somewhat dated, but it has a wide dynamic range and plenty of atmosphere and warmth, and the great string climax of the slow movement sounds surprisingly rich. Indeed the digital remastering is wholly successful with background subdued; admirers of this great conductor should not miss it.

Those seeking a modern digital recording will probably turn to Previn's newest recording, which has typically rich Telarc quality, even if his earlier RCA version has remarkable freshness and, if not as refined as a recording, is by no means to be dismissed – his early set of Vaughan Williams symphonies was one of his finest achievements in the recording studio. However, the Telarc version brings an exceptionally spacious reading, marked by a vivid and refined sound-balance. The atmospheric beauty of this lovely score has rarely been brought out more intensely, and the slow movement in particular brings a radiant, deeply poetic performance, caressing the ear. The faster movements consistently bring out the conductor's natural idiomatic feeling for this music, with rhythms nicely sprung – not least the sharp syncopations – and with melodies warmly moulded, though without sentimentality. In the fast movements Previn's earlier RCA version is crisper and more intense in its dramatic flow. On Telarc Barry Griffiths' account of *The Lark ascending* is a welcome bonus, but it is not as instinctively rapturous a performance as those by Iona Brown or indeed Zukerman.

Haitink's is a characteristically powerful, even monumental reading of the *London symphony*, less concerned with the evocative programme (although this is by no means ignored) than with symphonic proportions. Like Haitink's other readings of British music, this one is more literal in its rhythmic manners, less obviously idiomatic; but many will find it the more refreshing for that, and the incisiveness certainly makes a powerful impact. In jaunty themes Haitink's straight manner at times brings an unexpected Stravinskian quality, and the expansively serene handling of the lovely melodies of the slow movement brings elegiac nobility rather than romantic warmth. Syncopated themes at times sound a little stiff with this treatment, and the *Lento* sections in the last movement are taken dangerously slowly; but that is set against a fast, intense treatment of the allegro, and the tension is powerfully maintained. In the *Tallis fantasia*, a generous fill-up, the straight rhythmic manners make the result sound somewhat unidiomatic, too, but very powerful in its monumental directness. The recording has spectacular range, though it is not quite as transparent or as atmospheric as Previn on Telarc. But these are individually involving accounts and any reader who already has Barbirolli, Previn or Boult will discover that this HMV record finds a new and different dimension in both works. There is an excellent cassette.

On RCA Previn underlines the greatness of this work as a symphony, as more than a sequence of programmatic impressions. Though the actual sonorities are subtly and beautifully realized, the architecture is equally convincingly presented, with the great climaxes of the first and last movements powerful and incisive. Most remarkable of all are the pianissimos which here have great intensity, a quality of frisson as in a live performance. The LSO play superbly and the digitally remastered recording, made in Kingsway Hall, is still sounding well, with its wide range of dynamic the more effectively projected on CD. The fill-ups are welcome, especially James Buswell's fine account of the concerto.

Boult's 1970 LP has also been remastered; though detail is sharper and the sound remains spacious, the upper strings sound less rich than before. (On the XDR tape the slight loss of range at the top means that they seem smoother and fuller, though the focus is slightly less clear-cut.) The orchestral playing is outstandingly fine. The outer movements are expansive, less taut than in his much earlier mono version for Decca. The central *tranquillo* episode of the first movement, for instance, is very relaxed; but here, as in the slow movement, the orchestra produces lovely sounds, the playing deeply committed; and criticism is disarmed. The Scherzo is light as thistledown and the gentle melancholy which underlies the solemn pageantry of the finale is coloured with great subtlety. With Boult's noble, gravely intense account of the *Tallis fantasia* offered as a coupling, this remains an attractive alternative to Previn. The CD impressively refines textures (especially in *Tallis*), but lightens the bass.

(i) *A London symphony;* (ii) *Symphony No. 5 in D.* (iii) *Fantasia on Greensleeves.*
(B) *** HMV *TCC2-POR 54280.* (i) Hallé O; (ii) Philh. O; (iii) Sinf. of L., Barbirolli.

This is among the finest of HMV's enterprising 'Portrait of the Artist' tape-only series. Barbirolli was a great Vaughan Williams conductor, and his account of the *Fifth Symphony* is unforgettable, with the Philharmonia strings and brass making the most ravishing sounds. The account of the *London Symphony* is more uneven but still rewarding, and *Greensleeves* is offered as an attractive encore at the end of the latter work. Both symphonies are heard without a break. The XDR transfers have lost a little of the sharpness of detail of the original LPs, but the sound remains very good.

(i) *A Pastoral symphony* (*No. 3*)*; Symphony No. 4 in F min.*
*** RCA **RD 89827 [6780-2-RG]**. (i) Heather Harper; LSO, Previn.

One tends to think of Vaughan Williams's pastoral music as essentially synonymous with the English countryside, and it is something of a shock to discover that in fact the *Pastoral symphony* was sketched in Northern France while the composer was on active service in 1916, and the initial inspiration was a Corot-like landscape in the sunset. But the music remains English in essence, and its gentle rapture is not easily evoked.

Previn draws an outstandingly beautiful and refined performance from the LSO, the bare textures sounding austere but never thin, the few climaxes emerging at full force with purity undiminished. In the third movement the final coda – the only really fast music in the whole work – brings a magic tracery of pianissimo in this performance, lighter, faster and even clearer than in Boult's version. The digitally remastered recording adds to the beauty in its atmospheric distancing, not least in the trumpet cadenza of the second movement and the lovely melismas for the soprano soloist in the last movement. Previn secures a fine performance of the *F minor Symphony*; only the somewhat ponderous tempo he adopts for the first movement lets it down. But on the whole this is a powerful reading, and it is vividly recorded. A good alternative to Boult's version, though not superior to it.

(i) *A Pastoral symphony* (*No. 3*)*;* (ii) *Symphony No. 5 in D.*
*** HMV **CDC7 47214-2** [id.]. (i) Margaret Price, New Philh. O; (ii) LPO, Boult.

In the *Pastoral symphony* Boult is not entirely successful in controlling the tension of the short but elusive first movement, although it is beautifully played. The opening of the *Lento moderato*, however, is very fine, and its close is sustained with a perfect blend of restraint and intensity. After the jovial third movement, the orchestra is joined by Margaret Price, whose wordless contribution is blended into the texture most skilfully. Boult gives a loving performance of the *Fifth Symphony*, one which links it directly with the great opera *The Pilgrim's Progress*, from which (in its unfinished state) the composer drew much of the material. It is a gentler performance, easier, more flowing than Previn's, and some may prefer it for that reason, but the emotional involvement is a degree less intense, particularly in the slow movement. Both recordings have been successfully remastered, retaining the fullness and atmosphere (while refining detail) to help the tranquil mood which is striking in both works.

Symphonies Nos (*i*) 4 in F min.; (*ii*) *5 in D.*
(M) (***) HMV mono *EH 769168-4*. (i) BBC SO, composer; (ii) Hallé O, Barbirolli.

The composer's own 1937 recording of the *Fourth Symphony* and Barbirolli's 1944 version of the *Fifth* were both first recordings and, quite apart from being historic on that account, they have rarely if ever been surpassed since in thrust and passionate involvement. V.W.'s own speeds for No. 4 are surprisingly brisk, notably in the first movement, but never feel rushed or perfunctory, quite the opposite. In no way does this bear out the idea of V.W. as a meandering conductor. The Barbirolli *Fifth* is passionate too, building to superb climaxes in the first and third movements. The transfer of the *Fourth* is a little drier than it was originally but remains fresh enough. The Barbirolli – one of his first Hallé recordings – is rather rough for an EMI transfer and, though acceptable, hardly does justice to the original sound. His later stereo version is also available on tape (coupled with the *London symphony*) and sounds marvellously opulent – see above.

Symphonies Nos 4 in F min.; 6 in E min.
(*) HMV **CDC7 47215-2 [id.]. New Philh. O, Boult.

Boult's was the first stereo recording of the *Fourth*; although it would be possible to imagine a performance of greater fire and tenacity, few will find much to disappoint them in this persuasive account. Sir Adrian procures orchestral playing of the highest quality from the New Philharmonia, and the slow movement, one of the composer's finest inspirations, is particularly successful. The recording, too, is first class; in this remastered form it sounds admirably fresh and combines body and clarity with spaciousness. There is an element of disappointment in discussing Boult's re-recording of the powerful *Sixth Symphony*; perhaps one expected too much. The performance is without the tension of the earlier mono recording Boult made for Decca, with the composer present. The sound of that record cannot of course compare with that of the newer version, but Boult's comparative mellowness here means that the reading is not as searching as the score demands. The strange finale is beautifully played, with a finely sustained pianissimo, but the atmosphere, if not without a sense of mystery, is somehow too complacent.

Symphony No. 5 in D; The England of Elizabeth: 3 Portraits (arr. Mathieson).
*** RCA **RD 89882 [6780-2-RG]**. LSO, Previn.

Symphony No. 5 in D; (i) *Flos campi* (suite).
(M) ❀ *** EMI Dig. **CD-EMX 9512** [Ang. **CDM 62029**]; *TC-EMX 2112.* Royal Liverpool PO, Handley; (i) with Christopher Balmer & Liverpool Philharmonic Ch.

Symphony No. 5 in D; (i) *The Lark ascending.*
(*) Chan. Dig. **CHAN 8554; *ABTD 1260* [id.]. LSO, Bryden Thomson.

Vernon Handley's disc, winner of the BPI Classical Award in 1988, is outstanding in every way, a spacious yet concentrated reading, superbly played and recorded, which masterfully holds the broad structure of this symphony together, building to massive climaxes. The warmth and poetry of the work are also beautifully caught. The rare and evocative *Flos Campi*, inspired by the Song of Solomon, makes a generous and attractive coupling, equally well played, though the viola solo is rather closely balanced. The sound is outstandingly full, giving fine clarity of texture. Adding to the record's attractions, it comes on the Eminence label at mid-price, every bit as fine as any full-price EMI issue. What is especially fascinating about this reading of the symphony is the way it stands almost halfway between the more restrained lyricism of Boult's approach and Barbirolli's, but leaning rather more towards the more passionate feeling of the latter, with which – Handley tells us – the composer himself more readily identified. There is a good cassette, but the CD is well worth the extra cost, especially in the first two movements where the wide dynamic range against the silent background gives the music making a profound projection and emotional force.

If anyone ever doubted the dedication of Previn as an interpreter of Vaughan Williams, this glowing disc will provide the clearest rebuttal. In this most characteristic – and many would say greatest – of the Vaughan Williams symphonies, Previn refuses to be lured into pastoral byways. His tempi may – rather surprisingly – be consistently on the slow side, but the purity of tone he draws from the LSO, the precise shading of dynamic and phrasing, and the sustaining of tension through the longest, most hushed passages produce results that will persuade many not normally convinced of the greatness of this music. In the first movement Previn builds the great climaxes of the second subject with much warmth, but he reserves for the climax of the slow movement his culminating thrust of emotion, a moment of visionary sublimity, after which the gentle urgency of the *Passacaglia* finale and the stillness of the *Epilogue* seem a perfect happy conclusion. It is some tribute to Previn's intensity that he can draw out the diminuendi at the ends of movements with such refinement and no sense of exaggeration. This is an outstanding performance, very well transferred to CD. The *England of Elizabeth suite* is a film score of no great musical interest but is undoubtedly pleasant to listen to; both performance and recording are first class.

Thomson's version with the LSO, very beautifully played and recorded in spacious sound, brings out the darkness behind this work, inspired by, and dedicated to, Sibelius. It may be less warm or sympathetic than more outward-going readings, less beautiful than others, but it stands as a strong, refreshing reading, superbly recorded, if not quite as cleanly as the very finest. Michael Davis makes a rich-toned soloist in *The Lark ascending*, presented as more than a pastoral evocation. The cassette is one of Chandos's very best, warm and full, yet refined and clear.

Symphonies Nos 6 in E min.; 9 in E min.
*** RCA **RD 89883** [**6779-2-RG**]. LSO, Previn.

Previn's coupling of the two E minor symphonies was a happy choice. The *Sixth Symphony*, with its moments of darkness and brutality contrasted against the warmth of the second subject or the hushed intensity of the final other-worldly slow movement, is a work for which Previn has a natural affinity. In the first three movements his performance is superbly dramatic, clear-headed and direct with natural understanding. His account of the mystic final movement with its endless pianissimo is not, however, on the same level, for the playing is not quite hushed enough, and the tempo is a little too fast. In its closely wrought contrapuntal texture this is a movement which may seem difficult to interpret, but which should be allowed to flow along on its own intensity. Boult here achieves a more vital sense of mystery, even though his account is not ideal. The *Ninth*, Vaughan Williams's last symphony, stimulates Previn to show a freshness and sense of poetry which prove particularly thought-provoking and rewarding. He secures smooth contours in the first movement and, as a result of refined string playing, he produces attractively transparent textures. The RCA recording is highly successful, and the string tone is expansive, well balanced in relation to the rest of the orchestra and free from the slight hint of hardness that sometimes disturbs this cycle. Listening to this reading reinforces the view that the critics of the day were unfairly harsh to this fine score. On the whole, this version is better than Boult's HMV account.

Sinfonia Antartica (*No. 7*).
*** HMV Dig. **CDC7 47516-2** [id.]; *EL 270318-4*. Sheila Armstrong, LPO Ch., LPO, Haitink.

(i) *Sinfonia Antartica* (*No. 7*); *The Wasps* (incidental music): *Overture & suite*.
*** HMV **CDC7 47216-3**; (M) *ED 291204* [id.]. (i) Norma Burrows, LPO Ch.; LPO, Boult.

With stunningly full and realistic recording, among the finest EMI has ever produced, Haitink directs a revelatory performance of what has long been thought of as merely a programmatic symphony. Based on material from V.W.'s film music for *Scott of the Antarctic*, the symphony is in fact a work which, as Haitink demonstrates, stands powerfully as an original inspiration in absolute terms. When it first appeared in 1953, its avoidance of conventional symphonic argument seemed a weakness; however, in a performance whose generally measured speeds and weighty manner bring out the inherent power of the writing, mere structural points seem irrelevant in the face of so strong a concept. Only in the second movement does the 'penguin' music seem heavier than it should be, but even that acquires new and positive qualities, thanks to Haitink. There is a first-class cassette equivalent.

Sir Adrian gives a stirring account and is well served by the EMI engineers. There is not really a great deal to choose between this and Previn's version as performances: both are convincing. Perhaps the EMI recording has slightly greater range and a more natural balance; but both are technically put in the shade by the new Haitink CD. However, the inclusion of Vaughan Williams's Aristophanic suite, *The Wasps,* with its endearing participation of the kitchen utensils plus its indelibly tuneful *Overture*, is a bonus for the Boult issue, although in the *Overture* the upper strings sound a bit thin. Otherwise the CD transfer is very impressive and the cassette sounds opaque by comparison.

(i) *Sinfonia Antartica* (*No. 7*)*; Symphony No. 8 in D min.*
*** RCA **RD 89884 [6781-2-RG].** (i) Heather Harper, Ralph Richardson, LSO Ch., LSO, Previn.

The coupling of the *Sinfonia Antartica* with the *Eighth* is the most generous in Previn's cycle. In the former, the RCA recording in its relatively distant balance, as well as Previn's interpretation, concentrates on atmosphere rather than drama in a performance that is sensitive and literal. Because of the recessed effect of the sound the portrayal of the ice fall (represented by the sudden entry of the organ) has a good deal less impact than on Haitink's version. Before each movement Sir Ralph Richardson speaks the superscriptions written by the composer on his score. Previn's account of the *Eighth* brings no reservations, with finely pointed playing, the most precise control of dynamic shading, and a delightfully Stravinskian account of the bouncing Scherzo for woodwind alone. Excellent recording, which has been opened up by the digital remastering and made to sound more expansive.

Symphony No. 8 in D min.
(M) **(*) PRT **PVCD 8380** [id.]. Hallé O, Barbirolli – BAX: *Garden of Fand*; BUTTERWORTH: *Shropshire Lad.* **(*)

Vaughan Williams identified very readily with Barbirolli's passionately extrovert approach to his music and 'Glorious John', as he called him affectionately, was invited to give the première of the *Eighth Symphony* (more a sinfonietta, really) and became its dedicatee. It is an inspired and much underrated work, as Barbirolli's marvellous recording, made in 1956 soon after the first performance, readily demonstrates. It is the most valuable of the three works included on this indispensable mid-priced PRT reissue; and Michael Dutton's digital remastering is a great success, adding vividness and presence without losing the body of the orchestral sound, the extra clarity of focus revealing only the merest hints of congestion at one or two big climaxes. The absence of documentation, however, is deplorable.

Symphonies Nos 8 in D min.; 9 in E min.
*** HMV **CDC7 47217-2** [id.]; (M) *ED 290239-4*. LPO, Boult.

The coupling of Vaughan Williams's *Eighth* and *Ninth Symphonies* is generous and apt, both having been seriously underestimated. Boult's account of the *Eighth* is an essentially genial one. It may not be as sharply pointed as Previn's version, but some will prefer the extra warmth of the Boult interpretation with its rather more lyrical approach. The *Ninth* contains much noble and arresting intervention, and Boult's performance is fully worthy of it. He gets most committed playing from the LPO, and the recording is splendidly firm in tone. The digital remastering is well up to the high standard EMI have set with reissuing Boult's recordings. There is a good cassette, offered at mid-price, so costing far less than the CD.

The Wasps: Overture. Serenade to music (orchestral version).
*** Chan. **CHAN 8330**; *ABTD 1106* [id.]. LPO, Handley – DELIUS: *Collection.****

Exceptionally well recorded and vividly impressive on CD, Handley's readings of the *Wasps overture* and the *Serenade to music* in its orchestral version are most sympathetically done. The overture is here more urgent than in Handley's more recent version for Eminence (as part of the complete suite), and though the *Serenade* inevitably lacks a dimension without voices, this is most persuasive, beautifully played by the LPO. As usual with Chandos, the chrome-tape transfer is exceptionally sophisticated, the sound beautifully refined yet firm.

VOCAL MUSIC

(i) *Epithalamion; 4 Hymns;* (ii) *Merciless beauty.*
*** HMV Dig. **CDC7 47769-2** [id.]; *EL 270569-4.* (i) Stephen Roberts, Howard Shelley, Bach Ch., LPO, Willcocks; (ii) Philip Langridge, Endellion Qt.

There are no rivals here: all three pieces are not otherwise available and are rarities. Vaughan Williams's setting of *Epithalamion* began life as a masque in the late 1930s and, only a year before he died, he expanded it into the coolly lyrical cantata recorded here. Scored for baritone and small orchestra with piano (Howard Shelley quite superb), solo parts for flute and viola, it is an eloquent and thoroughly characteristic piece. Stephen Roberts gives a beautiful account of it, and Philip Langridge is hardly less impressive in *Merciless beauty*, three much earlier settings for voice and string trio. A most valuable addition to the Vaughan Williams discography; splendid performances and recording. The chrome cassette sounds very impressive too.

(i) *Flos campi;* (ii) *5 Mystical songs;* (iii) *O clap your hands;* (iv) *5 Tudor portraits.*
(B) *** HMV *TCC2-POR 54294.* (i) Aronowitz, Jacques O; (ii) Shirley-Quirk; (i; iii) King's College Ch.; (iii) ECO; (iv) Bainbridge, Carol Case, Bach Ch., New Philh. O, Willcocks.

In an earlier edition, we dismissed this imaginative issue in EMI's 'Portrait of the Artist' tape series for poor technology. We are glad to report that the XDR reissue has been remastered and now sounds well. The performances are admirable, with the *Five Tudor portraits* particularly attractive, very well performed and recorded.

(i) *In Windsor Forest (cantata);* (ii) *Towards the unknown region.*
*** HMV **CDC7 49738-2**. (i) Helen Fields, Bournemouth SO Ch. & SO; (ii) CBSO Ch. & O; Del Mar – ELGAR: *From the Bavarian Highlands.****

The cantata *In Windsor Forest*, which Vaughan Williams adapted from his Falstaff opera, *Sir John in Love*, makes the perfect coupling for Elgar's suite of part-songs. The movements are not always exact transcriptions from the opera, for the composer rethought and amplified certain passages. As in the Elgar, Del Mar directs warmly sympathetic performances, given excellent sound. *Towards the unknown region* is digitally recorded. It is an early cantata (1907) to words of Walt Whitman; aptly, the chorus is presented at an evocative distance, although the work's big climax is admirably vivid.

Mass in G min.; Te Deum in C.
*** Hyp. **CDA 66076**; *KA 66076* [id.]. Corydon Singers, Best – HOWELLS: *Requiem.****

The only alternative version of Vaughan Williams's masterly *Mass in G minor* is nearly twenty years old and this newcomer is a worthy rival. It has the additional attraction of Herbert Howells's *Requiem*, a work of great depth and tranquillity of spirit. Matthew Best and the

Corydon Singers give as committed an account as King's College Choir and, despite the spacious acoustic, there is admirable clarity of texture. This has now also been made available on a well-transferred tape, not issued when the original LP appeared.

(ii) *On Wenlock Edge* (song-cycle from A. E. Housman's *A Shropshire Lad*); (i) *10 Blake songs for voice and oboe.*
(M) ❀ *** HMV **CDM7 69170-2**; *ED 769170-4*. Ian Partridge, (i) Janet Craxton; (ii) Music Group of London – WARLOCK: *The Curlew.****

The HMV mid-priced CD is an outstandingly beautiful record, with Ian Partridge's intense artistry and lovely individual tone-colour used with compelling success in Vaughan Williams songs both early and late. The Housman cycle has an accompaniment for piano and string quartet which can sound ungainly, but here, with playing from the Music Group of London which matches the soloist's sensitivity, the result is atmospheric and moving. The *Ten Blake songs* come from just before the composer's death, bald, direct settings that with the artistry of Partridge and Craxton are darkly moving. The tenor's sister accompanies with fine understanding in two favourite songs as a welcome extra. The cassette equivalent is splendidly transferred using chrome stock – it is beautifully clear and vivid.

(i) *On Wenlock Edge*; (ii) *Songs of travel* (song-cycles)
*** HMV Dig. **CDC7 47220-2** [id.]. (i) Robert Tear; (ii) Thomas Allen, CBSO, Rattle.

Orchestral arrangements of two song-cycles originally written for lighter accompaniment make an attractive and apt coupling. The more revelatory is the collection of *Songs of travel*, to words by Robert Louis Stevenson, originally written with piano accompaniment and here discreetly orchestrated. The orchestral version brings home the aptness of treating the nine songs as a cycle, particularly when the soloist is as characterful and understanding a singer as Thomas Allen. Only in 1960 was the epilogue song finally published (after the composer's death), drawing together the two sets of four songs that had previously been published separately. The Housman settings in the other cycle are far better known, and Robert Tear – who earlier recorded this same orchestral version with Vernon Handley and the Birmingham orchestra – again proves a deeply perceptive soloist, with his sense of atmosphere, feeling for detailed word-meaning and flawless breath control. Warm, understanding conducting and playing, and excellent sound.

Songs of travel; *The House of Life* (6 sonnets); *4 Poems by Fredegond Shove*; *4 Last songs:* No. 2, *Tired*; Songs: *In the spring*; *Linden Lea.*
(*) Chan. Dig. **CHAN 8475; *ABTD 1186* [id.]. Benjamin Luxon, David Williams.

Though Benjamin Luxon's vibrato is distractingly wide, the warmth and clarity of the recording help to make his well-chosen collection of Vaughan Williams songs very attractive, including as it does not only the well-known Stevenson travel cycle but the Rossetti cycle, *The House of Life* (including *The Water mill*), as well as the most famous song of all, *Linden Lea*. The cassette is well up to Chandos's usual high standard.

(i) *5 Tudor portraits;* (ii) *Benedicte;* (iii) *Five variants of Dives and Lazarus.*
*** HMV **CDC7 49023-2** [id.]; (M) *ED 291263-4*. (i) Bainbridge, Carol Case, Bach Ch., New Philh. O; (ii) Heather Harper, Bach Ch. LSO; (iii) Jacques O; Willcocks.

Another of EMIs generous re-assemblies of fine performances of British music from the analogue era, dating from 1968/9 and playing for 71′. Ursula Vaughan Williams reports in her biography of the composer that the first performance of the *Five Tudor portraits* – in Norwich in

1936 – was remarkable for shocking many of the audience. ('The elderly Countess of Albemarle sat in the front row getting pinker and pinker in the face', says Mrs Vaughan Williams, and after the old lady had departed, the composer complimented the chorus on its diction.) The composer deliberately chose bawdy words by the early Tudor poet, John Skelton, and set them in his most rumbustious style. This is a good, strong performance, but the soloists are not earthy enough for such music. It is a pity that the humour was not more strongly underlined, but the musical invention is still more than strong enough to sustain compelling interest and the digital remastering has brought splendid bite and projection to the chorus without losing too much of the original ambience. The *Benedicte* is another strong work, compressed in its intensity, too brief to be accepted easily into the choral repertory, but a fine addition to the R.V.W. discography. The *Five variants of Dives and Lazarus* is beautifully played and warmly recorded and adds a touch of serenity and balm after the vigour of the vocal works. The cassette is acceptable but has patches of exaggerated bass resonance – especially in the climaxes of *Dives and Lazarus*.

Verdi, Giuseppe (1813–1901)

Overtures and Preludes: *Un Ballo in maschera* (prelude); *La Battaglia di Legnano*; *Il Corsaro* (sinfonias); *Ernani* (prelude); *La Forza del destino*; *Luisa Miller* (overtures); *Macbeth; I Masnadieri* (preludes); *Nabucco* (overture); *Rigoletto*; *La Traviata* (preludes); *I vespri siciliani* (sinfonia).
*** **DG 419 622-2** [id.]. BPO, Karajan.

Overtures and Preludes: *Aïda* (prelude); *Un ballo in maschera* (prelude); *La Forza del destino* (overture); *Nabucco* (overture); *La Traviata* (prelude to Act I); *I vespri siciliani* (sinfonia).
(M) **(*) DG **423 218-2**; *423 218-4* [id.]. BPO, Karajan – ROSSINI: *Overtures.***(*)

Make no mistake, this playing is in a class of its own and has an electricity, refinement and authority that sweep all before it. Some of the overtures are little known (*Il Corsaro* and *La Battaglia di Legnano*), and are given with tremendous panache and virtuosity. These are performances of real spirit and are vividly recorded, even if the climaxes could expand more. On the shorter selection which is offered at mid-price, the bright lighting which has been brought to the digital remastering is increased to the point of glare and the strings playing loudly above the stave have an added element of harshness.

Overtures and Preludes: *Aïda; Attila; Un Ballo in maschera; La Forza del destino; Luisa Miller; Nabucco; La Traviata: Preludes, Acts I and III; I vespri siciliani.*
*** DG **411 469-2** [id.]. VPO, Sinopoli.

Overtures: *Aroldo; La Forza del destino; Giovanna d'Arco; Luisa Miller; Nabucco; Oberto, Conte di San Bonifacio; I vespri siciliani.*
*** Decca Dig. **410 141-2** [id.]. Nat. PO, Chailly.

Sinopoli's preference for sharp contrasts and precise rhythms makes for dramatic accounts of these Verdi overtures and preludes, which (like other rivals) include the four finest: *Forza, Vespri siciliano, Luisa Miller* and *Nabucco. Forza,* the finest of all, brings a less fierce account than one would have expected from this conductor, with delicate textures, rhythms and phrasing, but *Luisa Miller* is very characteristic, finely chiselled and exciting in its contrasts, with the Vienna cellos in particular adding lustre. The four items chosen for makeweight represent the most popular choice. The refined recording is matched by warm recorded sound, with the sweetness of string timbre the more striking on CD.

In his collection, Chailly has the advantage of brilliant Decca recording, with the four most obviously desirable – *Nabucco, I vespri siciliani, Luisa Miller* and *Forza* – plus three rarities, including the overture to his very first opera, *Oberto*, and the most substantial of the early ones, *Aroldo*. Crisp and incisive, Chailly draws vigorous and polished playing from the National Philharmonic. The admirable compact disc clarifies the texture without loss of bloom.

String quartet in E min.

*** CRD *CRD 4066* [id.]. Alberni Qt – DONIZETTI: *Quartet No. 13;* PUCCINI: *Crisantemi.****

** Denon Dig. **CO 1029** [id.]. Nuovo Qt – BOCCHERINI: *Quartets.***

** Tel. Dig. **ZK8 43105** [id.]. Vermeer Qt – DVOŘÁK: *Quartet No. 10.**(*)

It is odd that Verdi, having written his *String quartet* as an exercise about the time he completed *Aïda*, should then have refused to let it be heard or published for many years. To us today its skill and finesse are what strike home; it is a unique work in Verdi's output, with a distinctive tone of voice and only one excursion into a recognizably vocal style – in the Neapolitan tune of the trio in the third movement. The Alberni Quartet's performance is strong and compelling, not as polished as the old Amadeus version but in many ways the more effective for that; and it is most imaginatively and attractively coupled with the Puccini and Donizetti pieces. The excellent recording is matched by one of CRD's best cassette transfers; it offers demonstration sound, full and with splendid detail and presence.

The Nuovo Quartet play Verdi's music with considerable character and a good deal of intensity. Their attack and rhythmic energy are in no doubt and ensemble is precise, but one feels that this music needs to be more expansive, although the fugal finale comes off impressively. The recording is very present and realistic, perhaps a shade too close, but the image is very believable.

The Vermeer Quartet on Telefunken are coupled with the Dvořák *Quartet*, Op. 51, and give a well-groomed and affectionate account of Verdi's charming *E minor Quartet*. As was the case with the coupling, the acoustic is small and does not expand, and the CD rather enhances its dryness. However, the Vermeer have a splendid range of dynamics and colour, and their performance is persuasive.

Requiem Mass.

*** Decca **411 944-2** (2) [id.]. Sutherland, Horne, Pavarotti, Talvela, V. State Op. Ch., VPO, Solti.

(*) DG Dig. **415 091-2 (2) [id.]. Tomowa-Sintow, Baltsa, Carreras, Van Dam, V. State Op. Concert Assoc. Ch., Sofia Nat. Op. Ch., VPO, Karajan.

** HMV Dig. **CDS7 49390-2** [id.]; *EX 749390-4* (2). Studer, Zajic, Pavarotti, Ramey, La Scala, Milan, Ch. & O, Muti.

*(*) DG **415 976-2** (2) [id.]. Ricciarelli, Verrett, Domingo, Ghiaurov, La Scala, Milan, Ch. and O, Abbado.

(i) *Requiem Mass;* (ii) *4 Sacred pieces.*

(*) HMV **CDS7 47257-8 (2) [id.]. (i) Schwarzkopf, Ludwig, Gedda, Ghiaurov; (ii) J. Baker; Philh. Ch. & O, Giulini.

(i) *Requiem Mass. Choruses* from: *Aïda; Don Carlo; Macbeth; Nabucco; Otello.*

❀ *** Telarc Dig. **CD 80152** (2) [id.]. Dunn, Curry, Hadley, Plishka, Atlanta Ch. & SO, Shaw.

Robert Shaw, who first made his name in the recording world as the chorus-master for some of Toscanini's finest recordings, here in the finest of his Atlanta recordings reflects consistently what he learned from the great maestro in the Verdi *Requiem*. It may not have quite the same searing electricity as Toscanini's rough old NBC recording, but it regularly echoes it in power and the well-calculated pacing. In the *Dies irae* for example, like Toscanini he gains in thrust and power from a speed marginally slower than usual. With sound of spectacular quality, beautifully balanced and clear, the many felicities of the performance, not least the electricity of the choral singing and the consistency of the solo singing, add up to an exceptionally satisfying reading, more recommendable than those of even the most eminent conductors. Only the Giulini has choral singing that might be counted finer; and Shaw also has the advantage of the outstanding modern digital recording. Though none of the singers are international stars, their clear, fresh, well-focused voices are beautifully suited to recording, and they make a fine team. The fill-up of five Verdi opera choruses is not as generous as Giulini's but is more colourful, and again brings superb choral singing. This is a fine tribute to Shaw's training with this chorus and orchestra over twenty years. An outstanding issue.

By its side Giulini's set is technically rather less satisfactory as a recording. Yet Giulini's combination of refinement and elemental strength remains totally memorable. Such passages as the *Dies irae* are overwhelmingly exciting (though never merely frenetic), but the hushed tension of the chorus's whispers in the same movement and the warm lyricism of the solo singing are equally impressive. What Giulini proves is that refinement added to power can provide an even more intense experience than the traditional Italian approach. In this concept a fine English chorus and orchestra prove exactly right: better disciplined than their Italian counterparts, less severe than the Germans. The array of soloists could hardly be bettered. Schwarzkopf caresses each phrase, and the exactness of her voice matches the firm mezzo of Christa Ludwig in their difficult octave passages. Again with Ludwig you have to throw aside conventional Italian ideas of performance, but the result is undeniably more musical. Gedda is at his most reliable, and Ghiaurov with his really dark bass actually manages to sing the almost impossible *Mors stupebit* in tune without a suspicion of wobble. Giulini's set also finds space to include the *Four Sacred pieces* and there is no doubt that in a performance as polished and dramatic as this the element of greatness in these somewhat uneven works is magnified. The CD transfer does its best to freshen the sound and is successful enough in the *Sacred pieces*; but it tends to emphasize the occasional roughness of the heavy climaxes in the *Requiem*, even though generally the quality is fully acceptable.

Solti's Decca performance is not really a direct rival to any other for, with the wholehearted co-operation of the Decca engineers, he has played up the dramatic side of the work at the expense of the spiritual. There is little or nothing reflective about this account, and those who criticize the work for being too operatic will find plenty of ammunition here. The team of soloists is a very strong one, though the matching of voices is not always ideal. It is a pity that the chorus is not nearly as incisive as the Philharmonia on the HMV set – a performance which conveys far more of the work's profundity than this. But if you want an extrovert performance, the firmness of focus and precise placing of forces in the Decca engineering of 1967 make for exceptionally vivid results on CD. The detail is much clearer than on most modern versions, and signs of age are minimal.

Recorded in conjunction with live performances in Vienna, Karajan's digital recording of 1984 certainly conveys a sense of occasion. With speeds slower than usual, the weight of the music is powerfully conveyed and much of its spiritual intensity. Though Karajan's smooth style has altered relatively little since he recorded this work before for DG, the overall impression is notably fresher – and would be even more so, were the recording more sharply focused and more consistent. Balances change between sections, though the soloists are more backwardly placed than is common, merging into the generally rich texture. The lack of brilliance in the recording also diminishes the element of Italian fire, so that the *Dies irae* is less sharply dramatic than in the finest versions. Soloists are good, naturally and warmly expressive. Though Tomowa-Sintow's un-Italian soprano timbre sometimes brings a hint of flutter, she sings most beautifully in the final rapt account of *Libera me*. The CDs bring sharper definition and an improvement in presence and range, but the basic recording faults remain.

Muti's recording, made live at La Scala barely eight years after his fine studio account with

Philharmonia forces, is inevitably flawed, but has many memorable ingredients, not least the singing of Luciano Pavarotti, who proves very persuasive in live performance. He brings a masterly breadth of expression and tonal range to the *Ingemisco*. But generally Muti's reading is less intense in its brisk pursuit of dramatic effect, opera-style, than his earlier version, let alone the finest of the recent CD versions. It is less precise in ensemble too, with Dolora Zajic a tremulous soloist letting the three other soloists down, though Cheryl Studer is well below her best, and Ramey's bass-baritone is barely dark enough.

Abbado's version was recorded at La Scala, Milan, when an opera project was abandoned at the last moment. So far from making the result operatic – as, for example, Muti's highly charged version is – it seems to have sapped tensions. It is a pity that so intense a Verdian did not have a more committed team of performers. The choral entry on *Te decet hymnus* gives an early indication of the slackness and lack of bite, and though the *Dies irae* is exactly in place there is no excitement whatever, with the chorus sounding too small. The soloists too are often below their best, but, balances apart, the recording is very good. The CD transfer undoubtedly brings enhancement but the focus is not especially sharp at pianissimo level, although there is an attractive ambient bloom.

4 Sacred pieces (*Ave Maria; Stabat Mater; Laudi alla Vergine; Te Deum*).
*** HMV Dig. **CDC7 47066-2** [id.]. Augér, Stockholm Chamber Ch., BPO, Muti.

4 Sacred pieces: Te Deum (only).
** Telarc Dig. **CD 80109** [id.]. Morehouse-Spelman Ch., Atlanta Ch. & SO, Shaw – BERLIOZ: *Requiem*; BOITO: *Mefistofele: Prologue*.**

Verdi's *Four Sacred pieces* form his very last work – or, to be precise, group of works. There are echoes of the great *Requiem*, and many of the ideas have a genuine Verdian originality, but in general they mark a falling-off after the supreme achievement of the last two operas after Shakespeare, *Otello* and *Falstaff*. Muti directs a characteristically dramatic yet thoughtful reading of these late pieces, keenly attentive to Verdi's markings. The two big outward-going pieces, the *Te Deum* and *Stabat Mater*, suit him perfectly, and the incisiveness of the professional Swedish choir, freshly yet atmospherically recorded, is an asset. In the first and third pieces the performances are hushed and devotional, without hint of sentimentality. The digital recording is full and bright, and the extra clarity of CD brings out the range more impressively, with the finely balanced choral singing made all the fresher and more beautiful.

Shaw conducts a finely disciplined reading of the Verdi *Te Deum* as the second of two generous fill-ups on the CD version of his recording of the Berlioz *Requiem*. As in the rest of the set, however, tension and mystery are lacking, despite firmly focused recording.

On an Erato CD, Scimone conducts his Portuguese forces in an urgently devotional account of the *Four Sacred pieces*, but fast speeds make for poor ensemble, and the recording is not transparent enough (**ECD 88170**).

Songs: *Ad una stella; Ave Maria; Chi i bei di m'adduce ancora; Deh pietoso, oh Addolorata; L'esule; Il poveretto; In solitaria stanza; Lo spazzacamino; Nell'orror di notte oscura; Non t'accostare all'urna; Perduta ho la pace; La seduzione; Stornello; Il tramonto; La zingara*.
(*) DG Dig. **419 621-2; *419 621-4* [id.]. Margaret Price, Geoffrey Parsons.

Margaret Price sings beautifully in these two delightful sets of Verdi songs, not always giving them the dramatic point that they ask for but always persuasive and intelligent. Fine recording and an excellent cassette.

OPERA

Aïda (complete).

(M) *** HMV **CMS7 69300-2** (3) [id.]; *EX 290808-5*. Freni, Carreras, Baltsa, Cappuccilli, Raimondi, Van Dam, V. State Op. Ch., VPO, Karajan.
*** Decca **417 416-2** (3) [id.]. Leontyne Price, Gorr, Vickers, Merrill, Tozzi, Rome Op. Ch. & O, Solti.
(M) (***) RCA mono **GD 86652** (3). Milanov, Bjoerling, Barbieri, Warren, Christoff, Rome Op. Ch. & O, Perlea.
(*) DG Dig. **410 092-2 (3) [id.]. Ricciarelli, Domingo, Obraztsova, Nucci, Raimondi, Ghiaurov, La Scala, Milan, Ch. & O, Abbado.
(*) HMV **CDS7 47271-8 (3) [id.]. Caballé, Domingo, Cossotto, Ghiaurov, ROHCG Ch., New Philh. O, Muti.
(**) HMV mono **CDS7 49030-8** [id.]; (M) *EX 270976-5* (3). Callas, Tucker, Barbieri, Gobbi, La Scala, Milan, Ch. & O, Serafin.

Karajan's is a performance of *Aïda* that carries splendour and pageantry to the point of exaltation. At the very end of the Triumphal Scene, when the march resumes with brass bands, there is a lift, a surge of emotion, such as is captured only rarely on record. Plainly the success of the performance – more urgent if less poised than Karajan's earlier account – owes much to its being conceived in conjunction with a Salzburg Festival production. And for all the power of the pageantry, Karajan's fundamental approach is lyrical, the moulding of phrase warmly expressive from the prelude onwards. Arias are often taken at a slow speed, taxing the singers more, yet Karajan's controversial choice of soloists is amply justified. On record at least, there can be little question of Freni lacking power in a role normally given to a larger voice, and there is ample gain (as on stage) in the tender beauty of her singing. Carreras makes a fresh, sensitive Radames, Raimondi a darkly intense Ramphis and Van Dam a cleanly focused King, his relative lightness no drawback. Cappuccilli here gives a more detailed performance than he did for Muti on HMV, while Baltsa as Amneris crowns the whole performance with her fine, incisive singing. Despite some overbrightness on cymbals and trumpet (betraying an analogue original), the Berlin sound for Karajan, as transferred to CD, is richly and involvingly atmospheric, both in the intimate scenes and, most strikingly, in the scenes of pageant which have rarely been presented on record in greater splendour. It makes an outstanding choice, the more attractive for being at mid-price.

The earlier Price version, recorded by Decca in Rome, has been refurbished to fine effect, for it actually outshines the later Price version, recorded at Walthamstow ten years later, in sound as in performance. Price is an outstandingly assured Aïda, rich, accurate and imaginative, while Solti's direction is superbly dramatic, notably in the Nile Scene. Merrill is a richly secure Amonasro, Rita Gorr a characterful Amneris, and Jon Vickers is splendidly heroic as Radames. Though the tizzy sound of the cymbals in the digital transfer betrays the age of the recording (1962), making the result fierce at times to match the reading, Solti's version otherwise brings full, spacious sound, finer, more open and with greater sense of presence than most versions since.

Like the EMI set with Callas and Gobbi, the RCA version in the mid-price Victor Opera series brings a classic performance, more than adequately vital to make you forget any limitations of mono sound, particularly when it is transferred with plenty of body. All four principals are at their very finest, notably Milanov, whose poise and control in *O patria mia* are a marvel. Barbieri as Amneris is even finer here than in the Callas set, and it is good to hear the young Christoff resonant as Ramfis. Perlea too conducts with great panache.

Fresh and intelligent, unexaggerated in its pacing, Abbado's version from La Scala lacks a little in excitement. It is stronger on the personal drama than on the ceremonial. Domingo gives a superb performance as Radames, not least in the Nile Scene, and the two bass roles are cast from strength in Raimondi and Ghiaurov. Leo Nucci makes a dramatic Amonasro, not always pure of line, while Elena Obraztsova produces too much curdled tone as Amneris, dramatic as she is. In many ways Ricciarelli is an appealing Aïda, but the voice grows impure above the stave, and floating legatos are marred. The digital recording – cleaner on compact disc than in the other formats – fails to expand for the ceremonial, and voices are highlighted, but it is acceptably fresh. The layout is improved on compact disc, but the increased clarity serves only to emphasize the confined acoustic.

Caballé's portrait of the heroine is superb, full of detailed insight into the character and with countless examples of superlative singing. The set is worth having for her alone, and Cossotto makes a fine Amneris. Domingo produces glorious sound, but this is not one of his most imaginative recordings, while the Amonasro of Piero Cappuccilli is prosaic. So is much of Muti's direction – no swagger in the Triumphal Scene, unfeeling metrical rhythms in the Death Scene – and the CD transfer, though faithful enough, brings out the relatively small scale of the sound, underlining the fierceness of Muti's reading; but solo voices are generally well caught.

Though 1950s mono sound inevitably is inadequate in representing the splendours of this opera, Callas's voice and that of Gobbi, two of the most characterful of the century, are vividly caught, to make the set essential for their admirers. The Nile Scene – focus of the central emotional conflict in a masterpiece which is only incidentally a pageant – has never been more powerfully and characterfully performed on record than in this vintage La Scala set. Though Callas is hardly as sweet-toned as some will think essential for an Aïda, her detailed imagination is irresistible, and she is matched by Tito Gobbi at the very height of his powers. Tucker gives one of his very finest performances on record, and Barbieri is a commanding Amneris.

Aïda: highlights.
(M) *** Decca **417 763-2**; *417 338-4* [id.]. Tebaldi, Bergonzi, Simionato, MacNeil, V. Singverein, VPO, Karajan.
(*) DG **415 286-2 [id.] (from above set, cond. Abbado).
(M) **(*) HMV **CDM7 69058-2** [id.] (from above set, cond. Muti).

Although DG have gathered together a generous collection of highlights from Abbado's set, lasting well over an hour, and Muti's similar selection is offered at mid-price, by far the most interesting compilation is the Decca 'Scenes and arias' from John Culshaw's Karajan recording from the early stereo era. With fine singing from the principals and vintage Decca sound quality, this remastered CD and cassette serves to remind us of an outstanding set.

Alzira (complete).
*** Orfeo **CO 57832** (2) [id.]. Cotrubas, Araiza, Bruson, George, Bonilla, Bav. R. Ch., Munich R. O, Gardelli.

Of all the operas that Verdi wrote in his years slaving 'in the galleys', this was the one he most vigorously rejected, yet this fine, beautifully sung and superbly paced reading brings out the formidable merits of this very compact piece. It is the shortest of the Verdi operas, but its concision is on balance an advantage on record, intensifying the adaptation of Voltaire's story of Inca nobles defying the conformity of Christian conquerors. In musical inspiration it is indistinguishable from other typical 'galley' operas, with Verdian melodies less distinctive than they became later, but consistently pleasing. Gardelli is a master with early Verdi, and the cast is strong, helped by warm and well-balanced recording supervised by Munich Radio engineers.

Attila (complete).
*** Ph. **412 875-2** (2) [id.]. Raimondi, Deutekom, Bergonzi, Milnes, Amb. S., Finchley Children's Music Group, RPO, Gardelli.

** Hung. Dig. **HCD 12934/35** (2). Nesterenko, Miller, Sass, Nagy, Kovats, Hungarian R. & RV Ch., Hungarian State O, Gardelli.

It is easy to criticize the music Verdi wrote during his 'years in the galleys', but a youthfully urgent work like this makes you marvel not at its musical unevenness but at the way Verdi consistently entertains you. The dramatic anticipations of *Macbeth*, with Attila himself far more than a simple villain, the musical anticipations of *Rigoletto*, the compression which on record if not on the stage becomes a positive merit – all these qualities, helped by a fine performance under Gardelli, makes this an intensely enjoyable Philips set. Deutekom, not the most sweet-toned of sopranos, has never sung better on record, and the rest of the cast is outstandingly good. The 1973 recording is well balanced and atmospheric, but the remastering for CD has been able to make only a marginal improvement in definition, with the chorus less sharply focused than one would expect on a modern digital set. However, the absence of appreciable background noise and the access provided by the generous cueing are obvious advantages of the new format.

The Hungaroton set, conducted (like the Philips) by the ever-responsive Gardelli, brings the advantage of clean, brilliant digital sound of a quality now expected from Budapest. There is also the magisterial Evgeni Nesterenko in the name-part, and in this bass role a Slavonic rather than an Italianate timbre helps to characterize the invading barbarian. Lajos Miller is a strong Ezio, and Sylvia Sass a characterful Odabella though, like Deutekom on the Philips set, she has her squally moments. The snag is the principal tenor, the strained and unstylish Janos B. Nagy as Foresto, the knight from Aquileia. He is no match at all for Carlo Bergonzi on the earlier set. Though the role for tenor is less central than in most operas, his singing is a serious blemish.

Un Ballo in maschera (complete).

*** Decca Dig. **410 210-2** (2) [id.]. Margaret Price, Pavarotti, Bruson, Ludwig, Battle, L. Op. Ch., Royal College of Music Junior Dept Ch., Nat. PO, Solti.

*** DG **415 685-2** (2) [id.]. Ricciarelli, Domingo, Bruson, Obraztsova, Gruberova, Raimondi, La Scala, Milan, Ch. & O, Abbado.

(***) HMV mono **CDS7 47498-8**; (M) *EX 290925-5* (2). Callas, Di Stefano, Gobbi, Barbieri, Ratti, La Scala, Milan, Ch. & O, Serafin.

Shining out from the cast of Solti's set of *Ballo* is the gloriously sung Amelia of Margaret Price in one of her richest and most commanding performances on record, ravishingly beautiful, flawlessly controlled and full of unforced emotion. The role of Riccardo, pushy and truculent, is well suited to the extrovert Pavarotti, who swaggers through the part, characteristically clear of diction, challenged periodically by Price to produce some of his subtlest tone-colours. Bruson makes a noble Renato, Christa Ludwig an unexpected but intense and perceptive Ulrica, while Kathleen Battle is an Oscar whose coloratura is not just brilliant but sweet too. Solti is far more relaxed than he often is on record, presenting a warm and understanding view of the score. The recording is extremely vivid within a reverberant acoustic, with orchestra as well as singers given added presence on the pair of CDs with excellent cueing.

Abbado's powerful reading, admirably paced and with a splendid feeling for the sparkle of the comedy, remains highly recommendable. The cast is very strong, with Ricciarelli at her very finest and Domingo sweeter of tone and more deft of characterization than on the Muti set of five years earlier. Bruson as the wronged husband Renato (a role he again takes for Solti) sings magnificently and only Obraztsova as Ulrica and Gruberova as Oscar are less consistently convincing. The analogue recording clearly separates the voices and instruments in different acoustics, which is distracting only initially and after that brings the drama closer. Certainly on the CD transfer the overall effect is marvellously vivid, with solo voices firmly placed and the chorus realistically full-bodied and clear. Internal access is excellent, with 26 cues provided over the two discs.

The 1957 recording, with voices as ever set rather close but with a fair amount of space round them, is among the best of the sets with Callas from La Scala, and CD focuses its qualities the more sharply. Cast from strength with all the principals – notably Gobbi and Giuseppe di Stefano – on top form, this is indispensable for Callas's admirers. It is also available on cassette at mid-price with generally good, full sound.

Il Corsaro (complete).
*** Ph. **416 398-2** (2) [id.]. Norman, Caballé, Carreras, Grant, Mastromei, Noble, Amb. S., New Philh. O, Gardelli.

Verdi did not even bother to attend the first performance of *Il Corsaro* in Trieste in 1848, despite the inclusion in the cast of four of his favourite singers. It seemed as though his 'years in the galleys' had caught up with him in this, the thirteenth of his operas. By the time he had completed the score, Verdi had fallen out of love with his subject, an adaptation of Byron. Only latterly has the composer's own poor view of the piece, predictably parroted through the years, been revised in the light of closer study. The two-disc format points to one of the first merits of the piece, its compactness, and Piave's treatment of Byron is not nearly so clumsy as has been thought. Though the characterization is rudimentary, the contrast of the two heroines is effective, with Gulnara, the Pasha's slave, carrying conviction in the *coup de foudre* which has her promptly worshipping the Corsair, an early example of the Rudolph Valentino figure. The rival heroines are splendidly taken here, with Jessye Norman as the faithful wife, Medora, actually upstaging Montserrat Caballé as Gulnara. Likenesses in many of the numbers to some of the greatest passages in *Rigoletto*, *Trovatore* and *Traviata* give the opera vintage Verdian flavour, and the orchestration is often masterly. Gardelli, as in his previous Philips recordings of early Verdi, directs a vivid performance, with fine singing from the hero, portrayed by José Carreras. Gian-Piero Mastromei, not rich in tone, still rises to the challenge of the Pasha's music. On two compact discs, with Act III complete on the second, the CD transfer brings not only extra convenience but a clarification of the excellent, firmly focused and well-balanced Philips sound.

Don Carlos (complete).
*** HMV **CDS7 47701-8** [id.]; (M) *EX 290712-5* (3). Domingo, Caballé, Raimondi, Verrett, Milnes, Amb. Op. Ch., ROHCGO, Giulini.
(M) *** HMV **CMS7 69304-2** [id.]; *EX 769304-4* (3). Carreras, Freni, Ghiaurov, Baltsa, German Op. Berlin Ch., BPO, Karajan.
(*) DG Dig. **415 316-2 (4); *415 316-4* (3) [id.]. Ricciarelli, Domingo, Valentini-Terrani, Nucci, Raimondi, Ghiaurov, La Scala, Milan, Ch. & O, Abbado.

Giulini was the conductor who in the Covent Garden production of 1958 demonstrated in the opera house the supreme mastery of Verdi's score. Here he is conducting the same orchestra as Solti directed in the Decca version five years earlier, and predictably he is more flowing, more affectionate in his phrasing, while conveying the quiet dramatic intensity which made his direction so irresistible in the opera house. There is extra joy for example in the Auto da fé scene as it is pointed by Giulini. Generally the new cast is a little stronger than the old, but each is admirably consistent. The only major vocal disappointment among the principals lies in Caballé's account of the big aria *Tu che la vanità* in the final Act. Like the Decca set this one uses the full five-Act text. The CD transfer of the 1971 analogue recording brings astonishing vividness and realism, a tribute to the original engineering of Christopher Parker. Even in the big ensembles of the Auto da fé scene the focus is very precise, yet atmospheric too, not just analytic. The extra bite of realism enhances an already fine version to make it the finest, irrespective of age.

As in the Salzburg Festival production on which his recording is based, Karajan opts firmly for the later four-Act version of the opera, merely opening out the cuts he adopted on stage. The results could hardly be more powerfully dramatic, one of his most involving opera performances, comparable with his vivid HMV *Aïda*. Though a recording can hardly convey the full grandeur of a stage peopled with many hundreds of singers, the Auto da fé scene is here superb, while Karajan's characteristic choice of singers for refinement of voice rather than sheer size consistently pays off. Both Carreras and Freni are most moving, even if *Tu che la vanità* has its raw moments. Baltsa is a superlative Eboli and Cappuccilli an affecting Rodrigo, though neither Carreras nor Cappuccilli is at his finest in the famous oath duet. Raimondi and Ghiaurov as the Grand Inquisitor and Philip II provide the most powerful confrontation. Though many collectors will naturally resist the idea of the four-Act rather than the five-Act version on record, having so vivid a Karajan set at mid-price on fewer discs than before makes a superb bargain. Though the sound is not as analytically detailed as the earlier EMI version with Giulini, it is both rich and atmospheric, giving great power to Karajan's uniquely taut account of the four-Act version.

For the dedicated Verdian, Abbado's set brings new authenticity and new revelation. This is the first recording to use the language which Verdi originally set, French; in addition to the full five-Act text in its composite 1886 form including the Fontainebleau scene (recorded twice before), there are half a dozen appendices from the original 1867 score, later cut or recomposed. These include a substantial prelude and introduction to Act I, an introduction and chorus to Act III, the Queen's ballet from that same Act (15 minutes long), a duet for the Queen and Eboli in Act IV (even longer), and extra material for the finales of Acts IV and V. By rights, this should be the definitive recording of the opera, for, as has often been promised, the French text brings an apt darkening of tone compared with the open sounds of Italian, and Abbado is a masterly interpreter of Verdi. The first disappointment lies in the variable quality of the sound, with odd balances, so that although the Fontainebleau opening, with its echoing horns, is arrestingly atmospheric, the Auto da fé scene lacks bite, brilliance and clarity. In addition, the very weight of the project, the extra stress on soloists and chorus working on music they know in a language they do not, has tended to prevent the drama from taking flight. Large-scale flair and urgency are missing; once that is said, however, the cast of singers is a strong one (even if they are variable in their French), with Placido Domingo outstanding. Domingo easily outshines his earlier recording with Giulini (in Italian), while Katia Ricciarelli as the Queen gives a tenderly moving performance, if not quite commanding enough in the Act V aria. Ruggero Raimondi is a finely focused Philip II, nicely contrasted with Nicolai Ghiaurov as the Grand Inquisitor in the other black-toned bass role. Lucia Valentini-Terrani as Eboli is warm-toned if not very characterful, and Leo Nucci makes a noble Posa. Whatever the reservations, this most costly of all opera recordings to date remains a fine historic document. The three chrome cassettes represent the highest state of the art, vividly transferred and having no problems with the varying perspectives.

Don Carlos: highlights.
*** DG Dig. **415 981-2**; *415 981-4* [id.] (from above recording, cond. Abbado).

A generous selection from the impressive Abbado set, following the narrative throughout all five Acts. There is well over an hour of music here. The cassette transfer is particularly well managed.

Ernani (complete).
(*) HMV Dig. **CDS7 47082-2 (3) [Ang. **CDC 47082**]. Domingo, Freni, Bruson, Ghiaurov, Ch. & O of La Scala, Milan, Muti.

(B) **(*) RCA **GD 86503** (2) [**6503-2-RG**]. Leontyne Price, Bergonzi, Sereni, Flagello, RCA Italiana Op. Ch. & O, Schippers.
** Hung. Dig. **HCD 12259/61** [id.]. Lamberti, Sass, Kovats, Miller, Takacs, Hungarian State Op. Ch. and O, Gardelli.

Ernani, the fifth of Verdi's operas, was the first to achieve international success. At this stage of his career Verdi was still allowing himself the occasional imitation of Rossini in a crescendo, or of Bellini in parallel thirds and sixths; but the control of tension is already masterly, the ensembles even more than the arias giving the authentic Verdian flavour. The great merit of Muti's set, recorded live at a series of performances at La Scala, is that the ensembles have an electricity rarely achieved in the studio. The results may not always be so precise and stage noises are often obtrusive with a background rustle of stage movement rarely absent for long, but the result is vivid and atmospheric. The singing, generally strong and characterful, is yet flawed. The strain of the role of Elvira for Mirella Freni is plain from the big opening aria, *Ernani involami*, onwards. Even in that aria there are cautious moments. Bruson is a superb Carlo, Ghiaurov a characterful Silva, but his voice now betrays signs of wear. Ernani himself, Placido Domingo, gives a commandingly heroic performance, but under pressure there are hints of tight tone such as he nowadays rarely produces in the studio. The recording inevitably has odd balances which will disturb some more than others. The CD version gives greater immediacy and presence, but also brings out the inevitable flaws of live recording the more clearly.

At mid-price in RCA's Victor Opera series on two CDs instead of three LPs, Schippers' set, recorded in Rome in 1967, is an outstanding bargain. Leontyne Price may take the most celebrated aria, *Ernani involami*, rather cautiously, but the voice is gloriously firm and rich, and Bergonzi is comparably strong and vivid, though Mario Sereni, vocally reliable, is dull, and Ezio Flagello gritty-toned. Nevertheless, with Schippers drawing the team powerfully together, it is a highly enjoyable set, with the digital transfer making voices and orchestra sound full and vivid.

Gardelli's conducting is most sympathetic and idiomatic in the Hungarian version, and like Muti's it is strong on ensembles. Sylvia Sass is a sharply characterful Elvira, Callas-like in places, and Lamberti a bold Ernani, but their vocal flaws prevent this from being a first choice. Capable rather than inspired or idiomatic singing from the rest. The digital recording is bright and well balanced, although the CD transfer brings out the fact that the recording acoustics are very resonant.

Ernani: highlights.
** Hung. Dig. **HCD 12609** [id.] (from above recording, cond. Gardelli).

A useful selection of items from the complete Hungaroton set, flawed but most sympathetically conducted.

Falstaff (complete).
*** DG Dig. **410 503-2** (2) [id.]. Bruson, Ricciarelli, Hendricks, Egerton, Valentini-Terrani, Boozer, LA Master Chorale, LAPO, Giulini.
*** CBS **M2K 42535** (2) [id.]. Fischer-Dieskau, Panerai, Ligabue, Sciutti, Rossl-Majdan, Resnik, Oncina, V. State Op. Ch., VPO, Bernstein.
(*) HMV **CDS7 49668-2 [id.]; (M) *EX 749668-4*. (2) Gobbi, Schwarzkopf, Zaccaria, Moffo, Panerai, Philh. Ch. & O, Karajan.
(*) Ph. Dig. **412 263-2 (2). Taddei, Kabaivanska, Perry, Panerai, Ludwig, Araiza, V. State Op. Ch., VPO, Karajan.

Recorded at a series of live performances in the Chandler Pavilion in Los Angeles, Giulini's reading combines the tensions and atmosphere of live performance with a precision normally achieved only in the studio. This was Giulini's first essay in live opera-conducting in fourteen years, and he treated the piece with a care for musical values which at times undermined the knockabout comic element. On record that is all to the good, for the clarity and beauty of the playing are superbly caught by the DG engineers, and though the parallel with Toscanini is an obvious one – also recorded at a live performance – Giulini is far more relaxed. Here the CD emphasizes the success of the engineers in the matter of balance, besides adding to the refinement of detail and the tangibility of the overall sound-picture. The voices are given fine bloom but in a contrasted stage acoustic. Bruson, hardly a comic actor, is impressive on record for his fine incisive singing, giving tragic implications to the monologue at the start of Act III after Falstaff's dunking. The Ford of Leo Nucci, impressive in the theatre, is thinly caught, where the heavy-weight quality of Ricciarelli as Alice comes over well, though in places one would wish for a purer sound. Barbara Hendricks is a charmer as Nannetta, but she hardly sounds fairy-like in her Act III aria. The full women's ensemble, though precise, is not always quite steady in tone, though the conviction of the whole performance puts it among the most desirable of modern readings.

The CBS set is based on a production at the Vienna State Opera, and the fleetness of execution in hair-raisingly fast speeds suggests that Bernstein was intent on out-Toscanini-ing Toscanini. The allegros may be consistently faster than Toscanini's, but they never sound rushed, and always Bernstein conveys a sense of fun; while in relaxed passages, helped by warm Viennese sensitivity, he allows a full rotundity of phrasing, at least as much so as any rival. It does not really matter, any more than it did in the Toscanini set, that the conductor is the hero rather than Falstaff himself. Fischer-Dieskau does wonders in pointing the humour. In his scene with Mistress Quickly arranging an assignation with Alice, he can inflect a simple *Ebben?* to make it intensely funny, but he finally suffers from having a voice one inevitably associates with baritonal solemnity, whether heroic or villainous. Just how noble Falstaff should seem is a matter for discussion. The others are first rate – Panerai singing superbly as Ford, Ilva Ligabue (also the Alice of the Solti set), Regina Resnik as Mistress Quickly, and Graziella Sciutti and Juan Oncina as the young lovers. Excellent engineering by Decca together with effective re-mastering have produced a sound-balance which is far fuller and more attractive than the remastered EMI Karajan set.

This earlier 1956 Karajan recording presents not only the most pointed account orchestrally of Verdi's comic masterpiece (the Philharmonia Orchestra at its very peak) but the most sharply characterful cast ever gathered for a recording. If you relish the idea of Tito Gobbi as Falstaff (his many-coloured voice, not quite fat-sounding in humour, presents a sharper character than usual), then this is clearly the best choice, for the rest of the cast is a delight, with Schwarzkopf a tinglingly masterful Mistress Ford, Anna Moffo sweet as Nannetta and Rolando Panerai a formidable Ford. One reason why the whole performance hangs together so stylishly is the production of Walter Legge: this is a vintage example of his work. Unfortunately the digital remastering has been mismanaged. While the precision and placing of voices on the stereo stage, a model even today, comes out the more clearly on CD, the transfer itself, at a low level and with high hiss, has lost the bloom and warmth of the original analogue master which was outstanding for its time (indeed, an excerpt from it was included on EMI's first Stereo Demonstration Disc). The cassettes, although more restricted, sound far fuller in sound – and of course cost much less than the CDs at full price.

Karajan's second recording of Verdi's last opera, made over twenty years after his classic Philharmonia set, has lower standards of precision, yet conveys a relaxed and genial atmosphere. With the exception of Kabaivanska whose voice is not steady enough for the role of Alice, it is a good cast, with Ludwig fascinating as Mistress Quickly. Most amazing of all is Taddei's performance as Falstaff himself, full and characterful and vocally astonishing from a man in his sixties. The recording is not as beautifully balanced as the Philharmonia set, but the digital sound is faithful and wide-ranging. The CD version captures the bloom of the original, reverberant recording so vividly, one worries less about any oddities of balance, while textures are to a degree clarified.

La Forza del destino (complete).

*** DG Dig. **419 203-2**; *419 203-4* (3) [id.]. Plowright, Carreras, Bruson, Burchuladze, Baltsa, Amb. Op. Ch., Philh. O, Sinopoli.

*** RCA **RD 81864** (3) [**RCD3-1864**]. Leontyne Price, Domingo, Milnes, Cossotto, Giaiotti, Bacquier, Alldis Ch., LSO, Levine.

(*) HMV Dig. **CDS7 47485-8 (3) [**Ang. CDCC 47485**]. Freni, Domingo, Zancanaro, Zajic, Bruscantini, Plishka, La Scala, Milan, Ch. & O, Muti.

Sinopoli's is an exceptionally spacious view of *Forza*, in many ways akin to the similarly distinctive reading of *Il Trovatore* recorded for DG by Giulini. Like the Giulini performance, this one is refined in its expressive warmth rather than traditionally Italian. Sinopoli draws out phrases lovingly, sustaining pauses to the limit, putting extra strain on the singers. Happily, the whole cast seems to thrive on the challenge, and the spaciousness of the recording acoustic not only makes the dramatic interchanges the more realistic, it brings out the bloom on all the voices, above all the creamy soprano of Rosalind Plowright, here giving a performance to match the one she gave as Verdi's other Leonora, in the Giulini *Trovatore*. Though José Carreras is sometimes too conventionally histrionic, even strained, it is a strong, involved performance. Renato Bruson is a thoughtful Carlo, while some of the finest singing of all comes from Agnes Baltsa as Preziosilla and Paata Burchuladze as the Padre Guardiano, uniquely resonant. Though the speeds will not please all Verdians, Sinopoli's is a distinctive, deeply felt view that in its breadth conveys the epic nobility of the piece with great authority. There are excellent cassettes. Incidentally, it is ironic that this fine set was recorded in sessions originally set up for a Philharmonia recording with Muti.

James Levine directs a superb performance of an opera which in less purposeful hands can seem too episodic. The results are electrifying, and rarely if ever does Levine cut across the natural expressiveness of an outstanding cast. Leontyne Price recorded the role of Leonora in an earlier RCA version made in Rome in 1956, but the years have hardly touched her voice, and details of the reading have been refined. The roles of Don Alvaro and Don Carlo are ideally suited to the regular team of Placido Domingo and Sherrill Milnes, so that their confrontations are the cornerstones of the dramatic structure. Fiorenza Cossotto makes a formidable rather than a jolly Preziosilla, while on the male side the line-up of Bonaldo Giaiotti, Gabriel Bacquier, Kurt Moll and Michel Sénéchal is far stronger than on rival sets. In a good, vivid transfer of the mid-1970s sound, this strong, well-paced version will for many provide a safe middle course between Sinopoli and Muti, with an exceptionally good and consistent cast. Voices come over with fine immediacy, but with plenty of bloom.

Placido Domingo is the glory of the Muti set recorded at La Scala, giving a performance even more commanding and detailed than in the earlier RCA version with Levine. Mirella Freni is an appealing Leonora, though she is vocally stressed; she is not helped by the recording, which is depressingly boxy and presents the voices unflatteringly in close-up. Though many Verdians will welcome Muti's fast, even hectic speeds, echoing Toscanini, the antithesis of the Sinopoli view, the recorded sound is the factor that puts the set out of court. Giorgio Zancanaro is a powerful Carlo, but Paul Plishka is disappointing as the Padre Guardiano, affected even more than the others by the dry, unhelpful acoustic which removes the bloom from all the voices.

La Forza del destino (slightly abridged).

(***) HMV mono **CDS7 47581-8** (3) [Ang. **CDCC 47581**]; (M) *EX 290921-5* (2). Callas, Tucker, Tagliabue, Clabassi, Nicolai, Rossi-Lemeni, Capecchi, La Scala, Milan, Ch. & O, Serafin.

Callas was at her very peak when she took the role of Leonora in the Scala recording. Hers is an electrifying performance, providing a focus for an opera normally regarded as diffuse. Though there are classic examples of Callas's raw tone on top notes, they are insignificant next to the wealth of phrasing which sets a totally new and individual stamp on even the most familiar passages. Apart from his tendency to disturb his phrasing with sobs, Richard Tucker sings superbly; but not even he and certainly none of the others – including the baritone Carlo Tagliabue, well past his prime – begin to rival the dominance of Callas. Serafin's direction is crisp, dramatic and well paced, again drawing the threads together. The 1955 mono sound is less aggressive than many La Scala recordings of this vintage and has been freshened on CD. The tape transfer (on to four sides) is also vivid and clear, though the libretto offers very small print. For those wanting the uniquely intense Callas version and not minding a seriously cut text, this can be strongly recommended.

I Lombardi (complete).
(*) Hung. Dig. **HCD 12498/500 [id.]. Kovats, Sass, Lamberti, Misura, Gregor, Jasz, Janosi, Hungarian R. & TV Ch., Hungarian State Op. O, Gardelli.

The Hungaroton set makes a very acceptable alternative to the earlier Philips set conducted by Lamberti Gardelli with warmth and finesse; it brings the benefit of modern digital recording and a CD alternative. One of the principal glories of the Budapest performance is the brilliant and committed singing of the chorus, turning the Crusaders Hymn of Act II into a sort of Verdian *Csardas*. The big ensembles have a warmth and thrust to suggest stage experience, and though the line-up of principals is not quite as strong as on that earlier Philips set, there is no serious weakness; Sylvia Sass, singing with a new evenness and purity, is certainly preferable to the fluttery Deutekom on Philips. Giorgio Lamberti as the hero is no match for Placido Domingo, heroic of tone but unsubtle; similarly, Kolos Kovats as the Hermit has a glorious natural voice, a really firm bass, but musically is no rival to Raimondi on the earlier set. The sound is excellent, clean and well balanced.

Luisa Miller (complete).
*** Decca **417 420-2** (2) [id.]. Caballé, Pavarotti, Milnes, Reynolds, L. Op. Ch., Nat. PO, Maag.
*** DG **423 144-2** (2) [id.]. Ricciarelli, Obraztsova, Domingo, Bruson, ROHCG Ch. & O, Maazel.

Lorin Maazel, making his Covent Garden début in this opera – belatedly in 1978 – went on to record this generally enjoyable set for DG. Though not as affectionate as Peter Maag on the earlier Decca version, Maazel is unfailingly strong and intense in his treatment of an extraordinary opera in the Verdi canon – predating *Rigoletto* but with flavours of much later: *Don Carlo*, even *Forza*. Though taut in his control, Maazel uses his stage experience of working with these soloists to draw them out to their finest, most sympathetic form. Ricciarelli gives one of her tenderest and most beautiful performances on record, Domingo is in glorious voice – having just established *Otello* in his central repertory – and Bruson as Luisa's father sings with velvet tone. Gwynne Howell is impressive as the Conte di Walter and Wladimiro Ganzarolli's vocal roughness is apt for the character of Wurm. The snag is the abrasive Countess Federica of Elena Obraztsova. This DG set now comes very economically packaged on two discs only.

On Decca, Caballé, though not as flawless vocally as one would expect, gives a splendidly dramatic portrait of the heroine and Pavarotti's performance is full of creative, detailed imagination. As Federica, Anna Reynolds is distinctly preferable to Obraztsova, and Maag's sympathetic reading, by underlining the light and shade, consistently brings out the atmospheric qualities of Verdi's conception. Also on a pair of CDs, vividly transferred, this Decca recording has the balance of advantage.

Macbeth (complete).

*** Ph. Dig. **412 133-2** (3) [id.]. Bruson, Zampieri, Shicoff, Lloyd, German Op. Berlin Ch. & O, Sinopoli.

*** DG **415 688-2** (3) [id.]. Cappuccilli, Verrett, Ghiaurov, Domingo, Ch. & O of La Scala, Milan, Abbado.

(M) **(*) RCA **GD 85416** (2) [**4516-2-RG**]. Warren, Rysanek, Bergonzi, Hines, Met. Op. Ch. & O, Leinsdorf.

** Decca Dig. **417 525-2**; *417 525-4* (2). Nucci, Verrett, Luchetti, Ramey, Ch. & O of Teatro Communale di Bologna, Chailly.

*(*) Hung. **HCD 12738/40** [id.]. Cappuccilli, Sass, Kovats, Kleen, Hungarian R. & TV Ch., Budapest SO, Gardelli.

A vital element in Sinopoli's conducting of Verdi – maybe the Toscanini inheritance – is an electrifying fierceness of expression. Here it has one sitting up in surprise over the choruses for witches and murderers, but equally relishing the absence of apology. Even more than his finest rivals, Sinopoli presents this opera as a searing Shakespearean inspiration, scarcely more uneven than much of the work of the Bard himself. In the Banqueting scene, for example, he creates extra dramatic intensity by his concern for detail and by his preference for extreme dynamics, as in the vital stage-whispered phrases from Lady Macbeth to her husband, marked *sotto voce*, which heighten the sense of horror and disintegration over the appearance of the ghost. Detailed word-meaning is a key factor in this, and Renato Bruson and Mara Zampieri respond vividly. Zampieri's voice may be biting rather than beautiful, occasionally threatening to come off the rails, but, with musical precision as an asset, she matches exactly Verdi's request for the voice of a she devil. Neil Schicoff as Macduff and Robert Lloyd as Banquo make up the excellent quartet of principals, while the high voltage of the whole performance clearly reflects Sinopoli's experience with the same chorus and orchestra at the Deutsche Oper in Berlin. Some of the unusually slow speeds for the big ensembles make the result all the more tellingly ominous. CD adds vividly to the realism of a recording that is well balanced and focused but atmospheric.

In Abbado's scintillating performance the diamond precision of ensemble also has one thinking of Toscanini. The conventional rum-ti-tum of witches' and murderers' choruses is transformed, and becomes tense and electrifying, helped by the immediacy of sound. At times Abbado's tempi are unconventional, but with slow speeds he springs the rhythm so infectiously that the results are the more compelling. Based on the Giorgio Strehler production at La Scala, the whole performance gains from superb teamwork, for each of the principals is far more meticulous than is common about observing Verdi's detailed markings, above all those for *pianissimo* and *sotto voce*. Verrett, hardly powerful above the stave, yet makes a virtue out of necessity in floating glorious half-tones, and with so firm and characterful a voice she makes a highly individual, not at all conventional Lady Macbeth. As for Cappuccilli, he has never sung with such fine range of tone and imagination on record as here, and José Carreras makes a real, sensitive character out of the small rôle of Macduff. Excellent, clean recording, impressively remastered for CD.

On two mid-price discs in the Victor Opera series the Leinsdorf version makes a good bargain, bringing a large-scale performance featuring three favourite principals from the Met. Leonie Rysanek here gives one of her finest performances on record, producing her firmest, creamiest sound for the Sleepwalking scene, even though the coloratura taxes her severely. Leonard Warren, much admired in this part before his untimely death – on stage, singing this very role – gives a strong, thoughtful reading, marred by the way the microphone exaggerates his vibrato. Carlo Bergonzi is a stylish, clear-toned Macduff. Good sound for its period.

Chailly's recording, made for the pretentious French film of the opera, cannot compare with other modern versions. Except for Samuel Ramey as a fine Banquo, none of the principals are at their best, and the ensemble of the Bologna orchestra falls well short of international standards. Shirley Verrett's is a powerful performance as Lady Macbeth, but she was far firmer and just as perceptive ten years earlier in the Abbado version on DG. Leo Nucci gives a generally well-sung, sometimes forced, but undercharacterized portrait of Macbeth himself. Luchetti is not at his freshest either. Good, atmospheric Decca sound hardly sways the balance.

Well conducted and well recorded as it is, the Hungaroton version is not competitive. Both Cappuccilli in the name-part and Sylvia Sass as Lady Macbeth – potentially an exciting combination – are both well past their best, and though there are some fine contributions from the others, the flaws are irretrievable.

Nabucco (complete).

*** DG Dig. **410 512-2** (2) [id.]. Cappuccilli, Dimitrova, Nesterenko, Domingo, Ch. & O of German Op., Berlin, Sinopoli.

*** Decca **417 407-2** (2) [id.]. Gobbi, Suliotis, Cava, Previdi, V. State Op. Ch. & O, Gardelli.

(*) HMV **CDS7 47488-8 (2) [Ang. **CDCB 47488**]. Manuguerra, Scotto, Ghiaurov, Luchetti, Obraztsova, Amb. Op. Ch., Philh. O, Muti.

This was Sinopoli's first opera recording and it suggests in its freshness, its electricity and its crystal clarification the sort of insight that Toscanini must once have brought. Sinopoli makes Verdi sound less comfortable than traditional conductors, but he never lets the 'grand guitar' accompaniments of early Verdi churn along automatically. One keeps hearing details normally obscured. Even the thrill of the great chorus *Va, pensiero* is the greater when the melody first emerges at a hushed pianissimo, as marked, sound almost offstage. Strict as he is, Sinopoli encourages his singers to relish the great melodies to the full. Dimitrova is superb in Abigaille's big Act II aria, noble in her evil, as is Cappuccilli as Nabucco, less intense than Gobbi was on Gardelli's classic set for Decca, but stylistically pure. The rest of the cast is strong too, including Domingo in a relatively small role and Nesterenko superb as the High Priest, Zaccaria. Bright and forward digital sound, less atmospheric than the 1965 Decca set with Gobbi and Suliotis, conducted by Gardelli. The CD layout of the Sinopoli recording is on two discs and brings added presence and sharper detail, while emphasizing the dramatic dynamic range.

The vividly real and atmospheric sound in the 1965 Decca recording comes up very three-dimensionally on CD, even though tape hiss is at a higher level than usual. There is more presence than in Sinopoli's DG, but that digital recording copes better with big ensembles. The Viennese choral contribution was less committed than one would ideally like in a work which contains a chorus unique in Verdi's output, *Va, pensiero*; but in every other way this is a masterly performance, with dramatically intense and deeply imaginative contributions from Tito Gobbi as Nabucco and Elena Suliotis as the evil Abigaille. Gobbi was already nearing the end of his full career, but even he rarely recorded a performance so full of sharply dramatic detail, while Suliotis made this the one totally satisfying performance of an all-too-brief recording career, wild in places but no more than is dramatically necessary. Though Carlo Cava as Zaccaria is not ideally rich of tone, it is a strong performance, and Gardelli, as in his later Verdi recordings for both Decca and Philips, showed what a master he is at pointing Verdian inspiration, whether in the individual phrase or over a whole scene, simply and naturally without ever forcing.

Muti's 1978 set does not match either Sinopoli's newest DG version or the Gardelli set on Decca. The HMV cast, as impressive as could be gathered at the time, with Manuguerra an imaginative choice as Nabucco, failed nevertheless to equal the three-dimensional characterizations of its competitors. Renata Scotto sang well but was not entirely inside her role; Manuguerra proved strong and reliable but lacked something in flair. Even the recording quality failed to improve on the earlier Decca set, although it is clarified and more vivid than before in its CD format.

Oberto (complete).
*** Orfeo **C 105843 F** (3) [id.]. Dimitrova, Bergonzi, Panerai, Baldani, Bav. R. Ch., Munich R. O, Gardelli.

It was left to the enterprising Orfeo label to round off the series of early Verdi operas, with Gardelli conducting, that Philips for so long promoted. In every way this issue matches the success of those other recordings, despite the change of venue to Munich. Gardelli is a master of pacing and pointing Verdi effortlessly; here he presents a strong case for this first of the Verdi canon, revealing in such ensembles as the Trio towards the end of Act I clear forecasts of full mastery to come. Otherwise there is much that reflects the manners and style of Donizetti, as one would expect of a 26-year-old writing in Italy at the time; but the underlying toughness regularly provides a distinctive flavour. Gardelli successfully papers over the less convincing moments, helped by fine playing from the orchestra, an outstanding chorus and first-rate principals. Ghena Dimitrova makes a very positive heroine, powerful in attack in her moment of fury in the Act I finale, but also gently expressive when necessary. Only in cabalettas is she sometimes ungainly. The veterans, Carlo Bergonzi and Rolando Panerai, more than make up in stylishness and technical finesse for any unevenness of voice, and Ruza Baldani is a warm-toned Cuniza, the mezzo role. First-rate recording.

Otello (complete).
*** RCA **RD 82951** (2) [**RCD2-2951**]. Domingo, Scotto, Milnes, Amb. Op. Ch., Nat. PO, Levine.
(M) *** HMV **CMS7 69308-2** (2) [id.]; *EX 769308-4*. Vickers, Freni, Glossop, Ch. of German Op., Berlin, BPO, Karajan.
(*) HMV Dig. **CDS7 47450-2 (2) [Ang. **CD 47450**]. Domingo, Ricciarelli, Diaz, La Scala, Milan, Ch. & O, Maazel.
(*) Decca **411 618-2; (M) *411 618-4* (2). Del Monaco, Tebaldi, Protti, V. State Op. Ch., VPO, Karajan.

Otello: highlights.
(M) **(*) HMV Dig. **CDM7 69059-2** (from above recording, cond. Maazel).

Levine's is the most consistently involving version of *Otello*; on balance, it has the best cast and is superbly conducted, as well as magnificently sung. Levine combines a Toscanini-like thrust with a Karajan-like sensuousness, pointing rhythms to heighten mood, as in the Act II confrontation between hero and heroine over Cassio. Domingo as Otello combines glorious heroic tone with lyrical tenderness. If anyone thought he would be overstrained, here is proof to the contrary: he himself has claimed that singing Otello has helped and benefited his voice. Scotto is not always sweet-toned in the upper register, and the big ensemble at the end of Act III brings obvious strain; nevertheless, it is a deeply felt performance which culminates in a most beautiful account of the all-important Act IV solos, the *Willow song* and *Ave Maria*, most affecting. Milnes too is challenged by the role of Iago. His may not be a voice which readily conveys extremes of evil, but his view is far from conventional: this Iago is a handsome, virile creature beset by the biggest of chips on the shoulder. In the digital transfer for CD of the 1977 analogue original, the voices are vividly and immediately caught, and with ample bloom. The orchestral sound too is fuller and cleaner than in many more recent versions, though there is an occasional hint of roughness in big tuttis.

Karajan directs a big, bold and brilliant account, for the most part splendidly sung, and with all the dramatic contrasts (above all, those in the orchestra) strongly underlined. There are several tiny, but irritating, statutory cuts, but otherwise on two mid-price CDs this makes an outstanding bargain. Freni's Desdemona is delightful, delicate and beautiful, while Vickers and Glossop are both positive and characterful, only occasionally forcing their tone and losing focus. The recording is clarified on CD, with better focus and more bloom than on the much more recent EMI set under Maazel. There are splendid cassettes, too.

Maazel's version, used as soundtrack for the Zeffirelli film but with the text uncut (unlike that of the film), brings a fine performance from Domingo and taut, subtle control from Maazel, particularly good in the spacious, tenderly emotional treatment of the final scene. In many ways Domingo shows how he has developed since he made his earlier recording with Levine; but with a disappointingly negative, unsinister Iago in Justino Diaz, the result often loses in dramatic bite, and Maazel's direction occasionally sags, as in the closing pages of Act II at the end of the oath duet. Ricciarelli, though not the ideal Desdemona, sings most affectingly, with pianissimos beautifully caught in the *Willow song* and *Ave Maria*. One snag is the sound, which is curiously recessed, with the voices often not quite in focus and little sense of presence. On tape the opening is muddled by the almost oppressive held-bass-note, but after that the sound is pleasingly warm and natural.

Karajan's 1961 version, flawed as it is in its casting, yet brings remarkably fine sound to match and even outshine any version since – a tribute to the artistry of the producer, John Culshaw, and his team of Decca engineers. Protti is admittedly not as inadequate an Iago as one had expected. He is always reliable if never imaginative and never sinister – and that is a drawback in an opera whose plot hinges on Iago's machinations. Del Monaco is hardly a subtle Otello, although both he and Tebaldi give one of their finest gramophone performances. There is a good tape set offered at mid-price, and highlights are also available on an excellent cassette (Decca *417 538-4*).

Rigoletto (complete).

*** Ph. Dig. **412 592-2** (2); *412 592-4* (3) [id.]. Bruson, Gruberova, Shicoff, Fassbaender, Lloyd, Rome St Cecilia Ac. Ch. & O, Sinopoli.

*** Decca **414 296-2** (2) [id.]. Milnes, Sutherland Pavarotti, Talvela, Tourangeau, Amb. Op. Ch., LSO, Bonynge.

(*) DG **415 288-2 (2) [id.]. Cappuccilli, Cotrubas, Domingo, Obraztsova, Ghiaurov, Moll, Schwarz, V. State Op. Ch., VPO, Giulini.

(M) **(*) RCA **GD 86506** (2) [**6506-2-RG**]. Merrill, Moffo, Kraus, Elias, Flagello, RCA Italiana Op. Ch. & O, Solti.

(***) HMV mono **CDS7 47469-8** (2) [id.]; (M) *EX 290928-5*. Gobbi, Callas, Di Stefano, Zaccaria, La Scala, Milan, Ch. & O, Serafin.

(B) ** CfP *TC-CFPD 4700* (2). MacNeil, Grist, Gedda, Ferrin, Rome Op. Ch. & O, Molinari-Pradelli.

Sinopoli conducts a tensely dramatic reading which, in its detailed concentration from first to last, brings out the unity of Verdi's inspiration. Unlike many other conductors who present Verdi freshly at white heat, Sinopoli here has close concern for his singers, with full potential drawn from each in what is on record the most consistent cast yet. Edita Gruberova might have been considered an unexpected choice for Gilda, remarkable for her brilliant coloratura rather than for deeper expression, yet here she makes the heroine a tender, feeling creature, emotionally vulnerable yet vocally immaculate. As a stickler for the text, Sinopoli eliminates a top note or two, as in *Caro nome*. Similarly, Renato Bruson as Rigoletto does far more than produce a stream of velvety tone, detailed and intense, responding to the conductor and combining beauty with dramatic bite. Even more remarkable is the brilliant success of Neil Shicoff as the Duke, more than a match for his most distinguished rivals. Here the Quartet becomes a genuine climax as it rarely has been in complete recordings. Like the others, Shicoff brings out unexpected detail, as does Brigitte Fassbaender as Maddalena, sharply unconventional but vocally most satisfying. Sinopoli's speeds, too, are unconventional at times, but the fresh look he provides makes this one of the most exciting of recent Verdi operas on disc, helped by full and vivid recording, consistently well balanced and particularly impressive on CD, fitted on two discs as against three LPs. Cassettes follow the layout of the LPs, with no attempt to tailor Acts to side-ends. However, the quality is outstandingly vibrant and clear.

Just over ten years after her first recording of this opera, Sutherland appeared in it again – and this set was far more than a dutiful remake. Richard Bonynge from the very start shows his feeling for the resilient rhythms; the result is fresh and dramatic, underlining the revolutionary qualities in the score which we nowadays tend to ignore. Pavarotti is an intensely characterful Duke: an unmistakable rogue but an unmistakable charmer, too. Thanks to him and to Bonynge above all, the Quartet, as on the Sinopoli set, becomes a genuine musical climax. Sutherland's voice has acquired a hint of a beat, but there is little of the mooning manner which disfigured her earlier assumption, and the result is glowingly beautiful as well as being technically supremely assured. Milnes makes a strong Rigoletto, vocally masterful and with good if hardly searching presentation of character. Urgently enjoyable, the digital transfer on two compact discs is exceptionally vivid and atmospheric, underlining the excellence of the original engineering with its finely judged balances, but also enhancing the superimposed crowd noises and the like, which not everyone will welcome.

Giulini, ever thoughtful for detail, directs a distinguished performance. Speeds tend to be slow, phrases are beautifully shaped and, with fine playing from the Vienna Philharmonic, the dynamics are subtle rather than dramatic. The conductor seems determined to get away from any conception of *Rigoletto* as melodrama; however, in doing that he misses the red-blooded theatricality of Verdi's concept, the basic essential. Although it may be consistent with Giulini's view, it further reduces the dramatic impact that Cappuccilli (with his unsinister voice) makes the hunchback a noble figure from first to last, while Domingo, ever intelligent, makes a reflective rather than extrovert Duke. Cotrubas is a touching Gilda, but the close balance of her voice is not helpful, and the topmost register is not always comfortable. The recording, made in the Musikverein in Vienna, has the voices well to the fore, with much reverberation on the instruments behind. CD focuses the voices even more vividly than before, but that makes the closeness of balance all the more apparent, even if the orchestral sound is cleaner.

Anna Moffo makes a charming Gilda in the Solti set of 1963, well transferred on two mid-price CDs in the Victor Opera series. Solti at times presses too hard but this is a strong and dramatic reading, with Robert Merrill producing a glorious flow of dark, firm tone in the name-part. Alfredo Kraus is as stylish as ever as the Duke, and this rare example of his voice at its freshest should not be missed. A good bargain, though there are statutory cuts in the text.

There has never been a more compelling performance of the title role in *Rigoletto* than that of Gobbi on his classic Scala set of the 1950s. At every point, in almost every single phrase, Gobbi finds extra meaning in Verdi's vocal lines, with the widest range of tone-colour employed for expressive effect. Callas, though not naturally suited to the role of the wilting Gilda, is compellingly imaginative throughout, and Di Stefano gives one of his finer performances. The digital transfer of the original mono recording (no stereo transcription as in earlier LP reissues) is astonishingly vivid in capturing the voices which are sharply focused, given a fine sense of presence, so that you miss stereo spread remarkably little. With fair bloom on the sound, the highly distinctive timbres of all three principals, notably Gobbi, are superbly caught. The set is the more attractive for appearing on two discs instead of the original three LPs. The (mid-priced) tapes are also generally well managed, though there is inevitably some peaking on Callas's high notes, for instance in *Caro nome*. The Acts are tailored to side-ends and there is a good slimline libretto with small but dark print.

The CfP set is not really distinguished, but it is well transferred, inexpensive and offered in a chunky box handy for the car. Reri Grist's Gilda is lightweight and not strong on charm, but Gedda has some good moments: he gives a strong dramatic lead, and because of this the *Quartet* is a highlight. MacNeil sings well and even if he is not a very dominent Rigoletto the performance is still musically enjoyable. With vivid sound this is fair value.

Rigoletto: highlights.
*** Decca **421 303-2** [id.] (from above recording, cond. Bonynge).
(*) DG **423 114-2 [id.] (from above recording, cond. Giulini).

Two useful and generous sets of highlights for those who do not want to go to the expense of a complete set.

Simon Boccanegra (complete).
❀ *** DG **415 692-2** (2) [id.]. Cappuccilli, Freni, Ghiaurov, Van Dam, Carreras, La Scala, Milan, Ch. & O, Abbado.
** RCA **RD 70729** (2). Cappuccilli, Raimondi, Mastromei, Mazzieri, Ricciarelli, Domingo, RCA Ch. & O, Gavazzeni.

Abbado's 1977 recording of *Simon Boccanegra*, directly reflecting the superb production which the La Scala company brought to London at the time, is one of the most beautiful Verdi sets ever made, and the virtual background silence of the CDs enhances the warmth and beauty of the sound, the orchestra fresh and glowing in ambient warmth, the voices vivid and the perspectives always believable. From this one can appreciate not just the vigour of the composer's imagination but the finesse of the colouring, instrumental as well as vocal. Under Abbado the playing of the orchestra is brilliantly incisive as well as refined, so that the drama is underlined by extra sharpness of focus. The cursing of Paolo after the great Council Chamber scene makes the scalp prickle, with the chorus muttering in horror and the bass clarinet adding a sinister comment, here beautifully moulded. Cappuccilli, always intelligent, gives a far more intense and illuminating performance than the one he recorded for RCA earlier in his career. He may not match Gobbi in range of colour and detail, but he too gives focus to the performance; and Ghiaurov as Fiesco sings beautifully too, though again not as characterfully as Christoff on the deleted HMV set. Freni as Maria Boccanegra sings with freshness and clarity, while Van Dam is an impressive Paolo. With electrically intense choral singing too, this is a set to outshine even Abbado's superb *Macbeth* with the same company. The CD layout is on two discs, with 29 access points provided by the internal cueing. The libretto is clear, if in small print.

Gavazzeni's version cannot compare with the Abbado set on DG whether in conducting, singing or recorded sound. On paper the cast seems very strong but, except for Placido Domingo, magnificent as Gabriele, they all bring disappointments, with Cappuccilli surprisingly coarse in the name-part, not helped by Gavazzeni's unimaginative, often rushed direction. In the digital transfer the sound is rough, too.

Simon Boccanegra: highlights.
** Hung. Dig. **HCD 12611** [id.]. Kincses, Nagy, Miller, Gregor, Hungarian State Op. Ch. & O, Patane.

Though the complete set from which these excerpts are taken (LP only) is a non-starter compared with Abbado's masterly DG version, this makes a useful collection on CD, bringing together some of the finest passages of a still-undervalued masterpiece. Lajos Miller as Boccanegra gives the only performance of real stature, strong and expressive if not always smooth of tone; and the admirable bass, Josef Gregor, sings Fiesco. Disappointing singing from soprano and tenor, but excellent recording.

La Traviata (complete).
*** Decca Dig. **410 154-2** (2) [id.]. Sutherland, Pavarotti, Manuguerra, L. Op. Ch., Nat. PO, Bonynge.
(*) HMV Dig. **CDS7 47059-8 [id.]. Scotto, Kraus, Bruson, Amb. Op. Ch., Philh. O, Muti.
(*) HMV **CDS7 49578-2; (B) CfP *CFPD 41 4450-4* (2). De los Angeles, Del Monte, Sereni, Ch. & O of Rome Op., Serafin.

(*) DG **415 132-2 (2) [id.]. Cotrubas, Domingo, Milnes, Bav. State Op. Ch. & O, Carlos Kleiber.
(***) HMV mono **CDS7 49187-8** (2) [id.]; (M) *EX 291315-5*. Callas, Kraus, Sereni, Ch. & O of San Carlos Op., Lisbon, Ghione.

Sutherland's second recording of the role of Violetta has a breadth and exuberance beyond what she achieved in her earlier version of 1963 conducted by John Pritchard. This *Traviata* is dominated by the grand lady that Sutherland makes her. Some of the supremely tender moments of her earlier recording – *Ah dite alla giovine* in the Act II duet with Germont, for example – are more straightforward this time, but the mooning manner is dispelled, the words are clearer, and the richness and command of the singing put this among the very finest of Sutherland's later recordings. Pavarotti too, though he overemphasizes *Di miei bollenti spiriti*, sings with splendid panache as Alfredo. Manuguerra as Germont lacks something in authority, but the firmness and clarity are splendid. Bonynge's conducting is finely sprung, the style direct, the speeds often spacious in lyrical music, generally undistracting. The digital recording is outstandingly vivid and beautifully balanced. The CD booklet is a reduction and is not ideal.

Muti as a Verdi interpreter believes in clearing away performance traditions not sanctioned in the score, so cadential top notes and extra decorations are ruthlessly eliminated; Muti, with no concern for tradition, insists on speeds, generally fast, for which he quotes the score as authority. Thus, at the start of the Act I party music, he is even faster than Toscanini, but the result is dazzling; and when he needs to give sympathetic support to his soloists, above all in the great Act II duet between Violetta and Germont, there is no lack of tenderness. Overall, it is an intensely compelling account, using the complete text (like Bonynge), and it gains from having three Italy-based principals. Scotto and Kraus have long been among the most sensitive and perceptive interpreters of these roles, and so they are here; with bright digital recording, however, it is obvious that these voices are no longer young, with Scotto's soprano spreading above the stave and Kraus's tenor often sounding thin. Scotto gives a view of Violetta which even amid the gaiety of Act I points forward to tragedy, with wonderful expansion in *Ah fors'è lui* on the phrase *Ah quell'amor*. Kraus takes *Di miei bollenti spiriti* slowly, but effectively so, with plenty of extra expression. Bruson makes a fine, forthright Germont, though it does not add to dramatic conviction that his is the youngest voice. Small parts are well taken and the stage picture is vivid. The breadth and range of sound, as well as the firm placing of instruments and voices, are the more present on CD, with the pleasant reverberation clarified.

Even when Victoria de los Angeles made this EMI recording in the late 1950s, the role of Violetta lay rather high for her voice. Nevertheless, it drew from her much beautiful singing, not least in the coloratura display at the end of Act I which, though it may lack easily ringing top notes, has delightful sparkle and flexibility. As to the characterization, De los Angeles was a far more sympathetically tender heroine than is common; though neither the tenor nor the baritone begins to match her in artistry, their performances are both sympathetic and feeling, thanks in part to the masterly conducting of Serafin. All the traditional cuts are made, not just the second stanzas. The sound on tape is vivid and clear, seldom betraying the age of the recording. Reissued on two cassettes at CfP's extreme budget price, the set makes an outstanding bargain, both for newcomers and for those who have another set already, though no libretto is provided. It is now also available on CD, costing about four to five times as much.

For some, Cotrubas makes an ideal heroine in this opera; but what is disappointing in the DG recording is that the microphone-placing exaggerates technical flaws, so that not only is her breathing too often audible but also her habit of separating coloratura with intrusive aitches is underlined, and the vibrato becomes too obvious at times. Such is her magic that some will forgive the faults, for her characterization combines strength with vulnerability. But Carlos Kleiber's direction is equally controversial, with more than a hint of Toscanini-like rigidity in the party music, and an occasionally uncomfortable insistence on discipline. The characteristic contributions of Domingo and Milnes, both highly commendable, hardly alter the issue. The recording suggests over-reliance on multi-channel techniques, and the closeness of the microphone-placing, spotlighting not only the soloists but members of the orchestra, is the more apparent on CD, underlining the fierce side of Kleiber's conducting which contrasts strongly with his ripely romantic side.

Recorded at a live performance in March 1958, Callas's Lisbon-made version is uniquely valuable in spite of very rough sound. Here far more than in her earlier Cetra recording of this opera one can appreciate the intensity which made this one of her supreme roles, with exquisite detail conveying fleeting emotions even in such an obvious passage as the *Brindisi*. Kraus is a fresh, stylish Alfredo, Sereni a positive Germont, more characterful than in the HMV set with De los Angeles. For Callas admirers – who will not object to the occasional ugliness – it is an essential set. However, the extraneous noises in this live recording – like the prompter's constant groaning – as well as the tape background and the crumbling at climaxes, are made all the clearer on CD; what matters is the vivid sense of presence, with Callas at her most vibrant. A unique historical document.

La Traviata: highlights.
*** Decca Dig. **400 057-2** [id.] (from above set with Sutherland, cond. Bonynge).

This Decca highlights disc was the first operatic issue on compact disc, and pointed forward to the extra immediacy possible with the new medium. One item is omitted compared with the LP – Germont's *Di Provenza* – but it remains a generous selection at just on an hour of music; CD irresistibly brings the sense of being face to face with the singers even while it brings out the forward balance of voices against orchestra. Pavarotti is less individual than Sutherland, but well placed, and the whole selection brings highly enjoyable performances. There is also available on tape a similar selection from Sutherland's earlier set with Bergonzi and Merrill, conducted by Sir John Pritchard (Decca *417 331-4*).

Il Trovatore (complete).
❀ *** RCA **RD 86194** (2) **[6194-2-RC]**. Leontyne Price, Domingo, Milnes, Cossotto, Amb. Op. Ch., New Philh. O, Mehta.
*** DG Dig. **423 858-2** (2) [id.]. Plowright, Domingo, Fassbaender, Zancanaro, Nesterenko, Ch. & O of St Cecilia Academy, Rome, Giulini.
(M) (***) RCA mono **GD 86643** (2). Milanov, Bjoerling, Warren, Barbieri, Robert Shaw Chorale, RCA Victor O, Cellini.
(M) (***) HMV **CDS7 49347-2** (2); *EX 749347-4*. Callas, Barbieri, Di Stefano, Panerai, La Scala, Milan, Ch. & O, Karajan.
(M) **(*) HMV **CMS7 69311-2** [id.]; *EX 290953-5*. Leontyne Price, Bonisolli, Obraztsova, Cappuccilli, Raimondi, German Op., Berlin, Ch., BPO, Karajan.
** Decca **417 137-2** (3) [id.]. Sutherland, Pavarotti, Horne, Wixell, Ghiaurov, L. Op. Ch. & Nat. PO, Bonynge.

Caruso once said of *Il Trovatore* that all it needs is 'the four greatest singers in the world'. Abounding as the opera does in great and memorable tunes, the orchestration is comparatively primitive, often like a kind of orchestral guitar. The support for the voices is a framework only, a dramatic framework to be sure, but it covers up nothing. The singers alone have to create the necessary breadth and beauty of tone, and the proper dramatic projection. That is not to say the conductor is not important: red-blooded conducting is vital. This is why *Trovatore* is difficult to bring off in the opera house, and even more so on record.

The soaring curve of Leontyne Price's rich vocal line (almost too ample for some ears) is immediately thrilling in her famous Act I aria, and it sets the style of the performance, full-blooded, the tension consistently held at the highest levels. The choral contribution is superb; the famous *Soldiers'* and *Anvil choruses* are marvellously fresh and dramatic. When *Di quella pira* comes, the orchestra opens with tremendous gusto and Domingo sings with a ringing, heroic quality worthy of Caruso himself. There are many dramatic felicities, and Sherill Milnes is in fine voice throughout, but perhaps the highlight of the set is the opening section of Act III, when Azucena finds her way to Conte di Luna's camp. The ensuing scene with Fiorenza Cossotto is vocally and dramatically quite electrifying. Unfortunately this set has been out of the British catalogue for some years, but now it returns on CD vibrantly transferred to make one of the most thrilling of all early Verdi operas on record.

In an intensely revelatory performance, one which is richly red-blooded but which transforms melodrama into a deeper experience, Giulini flouts convention at every point. The opera's white-hot inspiration comes out in the intensity of the playing and singing, but the often slow tempi and refined textures present the whole work in new and deeper detail, product of the conductor's intense study of the work afresh. Even Giulini has rarely matched this achievement among his many fine Verdi records. More than any previous conductor on record, Giulini brings out the kinship between *Il Trovatore* and *La Forza del destino*, above all in the heroine's music, in which inspired casting presents Rosalind Plowright triumphantly in her first international opera recording. Sensuous yet ethereal in *Tacea la notte*, she masterfully brings together the seemingly incompatible qualities demanded, not just sweetness and purity but brilliant coloratura, flexibility and richly dramatic bite and power. Placido Domingo sings Manrico as powerfully as he did in the richly satisfying Mehta set on RCA (perhaps still a safer choice for the unadventurous), but the voice is even more heroic in an Otello-like way, only very occasionally showing strain. Giorgio Zancanaro proves a gloriously firm and rounded Count di Luna and Evgeny Nesterenko a dark, powerful Ferrando, while Brigitte Fassbaender, singing her first Azucena, finds far greater intensity and detail than the usual roaring mezzo, matching Giulini's freshness. The recording is warm and atmospheric with a pleasant bloom on the voices, naturally balanced and not spotlit. Now on a pair of CDs, it sounds all the firmer and more vivid.

Though dating from 1952, using a cut text as in the Met. production, the Cellini version brings a vivid reminder of that great opera house at a key period. It was recorded not at the old Met, but in the Manhattan Center, and as transferred the mono recording has plenty of body, bringing out the beauty of the voices with plenty of presence. Milanov, though at times a little raw in Leonora's coloratura, gives a glorious, commanding performance, never surpassed on record, with the voice at its fullest. Bjoerling and Warren too are in ringing voice, and Barbieri is a superb Azucena, with Cellini – rarely heard on record – proving an outstanding Verdian.

The combination of Karajan and Callas is formidably impressive. There is toughness and dramatic determination in Callas's singing, whether in the coloratura or in the dramatic passages, and this gives the heroine an unsuspected depth of character which culminates in Callas's fine singing of an aria which used often to be cut entirely – *Tu vedrai che amore in terra*, here with its first stanza alone included. Barbieri is a magnificent Azucena, Panerai a strong, incisive Count, and Di Stefano at his finest as Manrico. On CD the 1957 mono sound, though dry and unatmospheric, is one of the more vivid from La Scala at that period, with the voices given bloom as well as immediacy and with Karajan's balancing of the orchestra more clearly defined than in his later stereo version.

The new Karajan set with Leontyne Price promised much but proved disappointing, largely because of the thickness and strange balances of the recording, the product of multi-channel techniques exploited over-enthusiastically. So the introduction to Manrico's aria *Di quella pira* provides full-blooded orchestral sound, but then the orchestra fades down for the entry of the tenor, who in any case is in coarse voice. In other places he sings more sensitively, but at no point does this version match that of Mehta on RCA. CD clarifies the sound, but makes the flaws in the original recording all the more evident.

Bonynge in most of his opera sets has been unfailingly urgent and rhythmic, but his account of *Il Trovatore* is at an altogether lower level of intensity, with elegance rather than dramatic power the dominant quality. Nor does the role of Leonora prove very apt for the present-day Sutherland; the coloratura passages are splendid, but a hint of unsteadiness is present in too much of the rest. Pavarotti for the most part sings superbly, but he falls short, for example, in the semi-quaver groups of *Di quella pira*, and, like Sutherland, Marilyn Horne as Azucena does not produce consistently firm tone. Wixell as the Count sings intelligently, but a richer tone is needed. Most recommendable in the set is the complete ballet music, more brilliantly recorded as well as better played than the rest. On CD the 1977 recording sounds even more vivid and atmospheric than before, with voices very naturally balanced against an open acoustic.

Il Trovatore: highlights.
*** DG Dig. **415 285-2**; *415 285-4* [id.] (from above recording, cond. Giulini).
(*) Ph. Dig. **411 447-2 [id.]. Ricciarelli, Toczyska, Carreras, Lloyd, ROHCG Ch. & O, C. Davis.

This generous and well-chosen DG collection of excerpts celebrates Giulini's masterly and highly individual interpretation, with the sound again excellent, but the warning given in the *Gramophone* review might be repeated: 'listening to these highlights may make you regret not having invested in the whole set'.

Sir Colin Davis's complete set is a refreshing and direct reading, refined in sound but rather wanting in dramatic impact; a highlights disc seems an excellent way to approach it. Ricciarelli's Leonora is most moving and if Carreras lacks the full confidence of a natural Manrico, he is at his best in the more lyrical moments.

COLLECTIONS

'Pavarotti premières': Aïda: overture. Attila: Oh dolore. I due Foscari: Si lo cento; (ii) *Dal più remoto esilio.* (ii) *Ernani: Odi il voto. Simon Boccanegra: Prelude. I Vespri siciliani: A toi que j'ai chérie.* (i) *Scene for two tenors and orchestra.*
(*) CBS **MK 37228 [id.]. Pavarotti, La Scala O, Abbado; (i) A. Savastano; (ii) Morresi; Giacomotti.

This fascinating collection brings a series of alternative versions and additions generally forgotten, two orchestral, four vocal. The *Overture* to *Aïda* and the *Prelude* to *Boccanegra*, later cut, are both worth hearing, but the vocal items, splendidly sung by Pavarotti (with two head-voice top E flats in the *Due Foscari* item), are even more cherishable. The voice is presented in a different acoustic from that of the orchestra, and the strings sound insubstantial.

Arias: *Aïda: Se quel guerrier io fossi! . . . Celeste Aïda; Pur ti riveggo, mia dolce Aïda . . . Tu! Amonasro! Don Carlos: Fontainebleau! Forêt immense et solitaire . . . Je l'ai vue; Écoute. Les portes du couvent . . . Dieu, tu seras dans nos âmes. Nabucco: Che si vuol? Il Trovatore: Quale d'armi . . . Ah! si, ben mio . . . Di quella pira.*
*** DG Dig. **413 785-2** [id.]. Placido Domingo with various orchestras & conductors – PUCCINI: *Arias.****

Domingo's Verdi recital, supplemented by Puccini items from *Manon Lescaut* and *Turandot*, brings an excellent collection of recordings taken from different sources. When working on a complete opera recording there is no danger of big arias like this simply being churned out without apt characterization. The sound is most vivid throughout.

Arias: *Aïda: Ritorna vincitor . . . l'insana parola . . . I sacri nomi; Qui Radamès verra . . . O patria mia. Un ballo in maschera: Morrò, ma prima in grazia. Ernani: Sorta e la notte . . . Ernani,*

volami. La Forza del destino: Pace, pace, mio Dio! Don Carlos: Tu che le vanità. Macbeth: Una macchia è qui tuttora! Otello: Mi parea . . . Piange cantando . . . Ave Maria. Il Trovatore: Tacea la notte placida.
*** HMV Dig. **CDC7 47396-2** [id.]. Aprile Millo, LPO, Patanè.

Acclaimed as the successor of Leontyne Price, Aprile Millo in this first major recording gives an impressive display of her generous soprano, rich, vibrant and masterfully controlled with fearless attack on exposed notes. She tackles each of these formidable arias in total confidence, with only the occasional slight uncertainty – as in the final item, *O patria mia* – to reflect her relative inexperience. All the items – a generous collection lasting 73 minutes – bring warmly satisfying singing, and when the repertory is so wide, that itself indicates the only significant shortcoming, a lack of variety in the approach, whether in characterization or in vocal colouring. Lady Macbeth for example does not emerge as very different from Desdemona. That reflects a slight lack of temperament too, if you judge at the highest level, which is where the publicists have been asking us to place Miss Millo – a lady of American birth and upbringing but of Italian parentage. Though the recording brings its odd orchestral balances of detail, it is warm and atmospheric, and catches the voice beautifully. An impressive début record.

Arias: *Aïda: Ritorna vincitor; L'insana parola. Un Ballo in maschera: Ecco l'orrido campo . . . Ma dall'arido stelo divulsa; Solo un detto acora a te . . . Morrò ma prima in grazia. Don Carlos: Tu che le vanità, conoscesti del mondo. Ernani: Sorta è la notte . . . Ernani, Ernani involami. Rigoletto: Gualtier Maldè . . . Caro nome. Simon Boccanegra: Come in quest'ora bruna. La Traviata: Teneste la promessa . . . Addio, del passato bei sogni ridenti.*
*** PRT Nixa Dig. **NIXC 1**; *NIXM 1.* Carol Vaness, British Concert O, Frank Renton.

Having started her recording career in Mozart with Glyndebourne colleagues, Carol Vaness here expands into the full Verdian repertory, using her natural, rich, warm timbre very positively. The recording catches a rawness above the stave but, with fine differentiation of character and a sense of challenge well taken, this is one of the most impressive of recent Verdi recital.

Arias: *ι*
.sluticeeste Aïda. Un Ballo in maschera: La rivedra; Di'tu se fedele; Ma se m'è forza perderti. I due Foscari: Dal più remote esilio. Luisa Miller: Quando le sere. Macbeth: Ah, la paterna mano. Rigoletto: Questa o quella; Parmi veder; La donna è mobile. La Traviata: De'miei bollenti. Il Trovatore: Di quella pira.
(M) *** Decca **417 570-2**; *417 570-4.* Luciano Pavarotti (with various orchestras & conductors).

Taken mainly from a recital which Pavarotti recorded early in his career with Edward Downes and the Vienna State Opera Orchestra, this Verdi collection on the mid-price Opera Gala label can be warmly recommended, a generous collection of favourite items, plus one or two rarer arias.

'Heroines': Aïda: Ritorna vincitor! O patria mia. Un Ballo in maschera: Ma dall'arido. Ernani: Ernani involami. La Forza del destino: Madre, pietosa; La Vergine; Pace, pace, mio Dio. Macbeth: Sleepwalking scene. Otello: Willow song; Ave Maria. La Traviata: Addio del passato. Il Trovatore: Tacea la motte; D'amor sull'ali rosee.
*** RCA **RD 87016 [RCD1 7016]**. Leontyne Price (various orchestras & conductors).

Leontyne Price, peerless in her generation in the more dramatic Verdi roles, is here at her finest in a generous collection of arias recorded at the peak of her career, with the glorious voice well caught in the transfers.

Arias: *Aïda: Ritorna vincitor. Un Ballo in maschera: Ecco l'orrido campo. Don Carlos: Tu che le vanità. Ernani: Ernani involami. I Lombardi: O Madre dal cielo. Macbeth: Nel di della vittoria; La luce langue una macchia. Nabucco: Anch'io dischiuso un giorno. I vespri siciliani: Arrigo! Oh parli.*
*** HMV **CDC7 47730-2** [id.]. Maria Callas, Philh. O, Rescigno.

In this first of two Verdi recital records issued to commemorate the tenth anniversary of Callas's death, the great soprano is at her most commanding, not flawless but thrilling, both in her creative musicianship and in her characterizations, powerfully Shakespearean in the Lady Macbeth arias presented as a sequence, and holding tension masterfully in the long *Don Carlos* scene. Both those performances date from the late 1950s, when the voice was still in fine condition. Though the later items here come from a period when the voice had deteriorated (done in the 1960s but issued only in 1972), Aïda's *Ritorna vincitor*, vehemently done, is magnificent for one. Generally good transfers and clean sound.

Arias (Vol. 2): *Aroldo: Ciel! ch'io respiri! . . . Salvami, salvami; O Cielo! Attila: Liberamente or piangi . . . Oh! nel fuggente nuvolo. Un Ballo in maschera: Morrò, ma prima in grazia. Il Corsaro: Egli non riede ancora . . . Non so le tetre immagini; Ne sulla terra . . . Vola talor dal carcere. Don Carlos: Non pianger, mia compagna; O don fatale. Otello: Mia madre aveva una povera ancella; Piangea cantando; Ave Maria piena di grazia. Il Trovatore: Tacea la notte placida . . . Di tale amor.*
** HMV **CDC7 47943-2** [id.]. Maria Callas, Paris Conservatoire O, Rescigno.

Though this second of the two Callas commemorative issues of Verdi is essential for the singer's devotees, it can be recommended to others only with severe reservations. The Shakespearean challenge of the Desdemona sequence from *Otello* is commandingly taken, very distinctive, and all the singing is dramatic, but too many allowances have to be made, particularly in the items recorded as late as 1969. Good transfers.

Arias & duets: *Un Ballo in maschera: Teco io sto. Il Corsaro: Egli non riede ancora! Don Carlos: Non pianger, mia compagna. Giovanna d'Arco: Qui! Qui! Dove più s'apre libero il ciela; O fatidica foresta. Jérusalem: Ave Maria. I Masnadieri: Dall'infame banchetto io m'involai; Tu del mio; Carlo vive. Otello: Già nella notte densa; Ave Maria. Il Trovatore: Timor di me; D'amor sull'ali rosee; Tu vedrai che amor in terr. I vespri siciliani: Arrigo! Ah, parli a un cor.*
(M) *** RCA **GD 86534**; *GK 86534* **[6534-2-RG]**. Katia Ricciarelli, Placido Domingo, Rome PO or St Cecilia Academy O, Gavazzeni.

At mid-price this collection of Verdi arias and duets from two star singers, both in fresh voice, makes a good bargain. The inclusion of rarities adds to the attractions, and though the sound is not the most modern, it is more than acceptable in the digital transfer. The sound is very bright; although the orchestral sound is a bit thin, both voices are given a good presence.

Arias: *Don Carlos: Tu che le vanità. La Traviata: Ah fors'è lui. Il Trovatore: Timor di me.*
*** CBS Dig. **CD 37298** [id.]. Kiri Te Kanwa, LPO, Pritchard – PUCCINI: *Arias.****

The Verdi side of Kiri Te Kanawa's Verdi–Puccini recital brings three substantial items less obviously apt for the singer, but in each the singing is felt as well as beautiful. The coloratura of the *Traviata* and *Trovatore* items is admirably clean, and it is a special joy to hear Elisabetta's big aria from *Don Carlos* sung with such truth and precision. Good recording, enhanced on CD.

Choruses: *Aïda: Triumphal march and ballet music. Attila: Urli rapine. La Battaglia di Legnano: Giuriam d'Italia. I Lombardi: O Signore dal tetto natio. Nabucco: Gli arredi festivi; Va pensiero. Otello: Fuoco di gloria. Il Trovatore: Vedi! le fosche; Squilli, echeggi.*

(M) ** Decca **417 721-2**; *417 721-4* [id.]. Ch. & O of St Cecilia Ac., Rome, Carlo Franci.

When this collection was first issued in 1965 we wondered (in the first *Penguin Stereo Record Guide*) whether the engineers had brightened the sound artificially. This impression still remains with the remastered reissue, for the upper range of chorus and orchestra has an unnatural brightness, and this applies to both disc and tape. In all other respects the quality is very good, inner detail is sharp and the big climaxes open up well. The performances are vivid, with a willingness to sing softly and, indeed, sometimes a degree of refinement in the approach surprising in an Italian chorus. The *I Lombardi* excerpts are especially appealing, but all the little-known items come up freshly. The trumpets in the *Aïda* Triumphal scene get the full stereo treatment.

Choruses: *Aïda: Gloria all'Egitto. Don Carlos: Spuntato ecco il dì. Ernani: Si, ridesti il leon di Castiglia. I Lombardi: Gerusalem. Macbeth: Patria oppressa. Nabucco: Gli arredi festivi; Va, pensiero. Otello: Fuoco di gioia. Il Trovatore: Vedi, le fosche.*
*(**) DG **413 448-2** [id.]. Ch. & O of La Scala, Milan, Abbado.

The combination of precision and tension in these La Scala performances is riveting, and the recording has a strikingly wide dynamic range. The diminuendo at the end of the *Anvil chorus* is most subtly managed, while the rhythmic bounce of *Si, ridesti* is matched by the expansive brilliance of the excerpts from *Aïda* (with fruity trumpets) and *Don Carlos*, and by the atmospheric power of *Patria oppressa* from *Macbeth*. One's praise, however, has to be tempered with disappointment, for this is one instance when the analogue recording from the mid-1970s has lost something in its digital remastering for CD. On the original LP and cassette, pianissimo detail registered convincingly and the upper range was free and open. On CD, definition at lower dynamic levels is disappointingly dim and there is a fierce edge on fortissimos, though the pleasing ambience remains.

Choruses: *Aïda: Gloria all'Egitto. Don Carlos: Spuntato ecco il dì. I Lombardi: Gerusalem!; O Signore, dal tetto natio. Macbeth: Patria oppressa! Nabucco: Va, pensiero; Gli arredi festivi. Otello: Fuoco di gioia! Il Trovatore. Vedi! le fosche; Or co' dadi . . . Squilli, echeggi.*
(*) Ph. Dig. **412 235-2 [id.]. Dresden State Op. Ch. & State O, Varviso.

Varviso's collection of choruses brings polished but soft-grained performances, beautifully supported by the magnificent Dresden orchestra. Gentler choruses are excellent, but the dramatic ones lack something in bite. One of the highlights is the *Fire chorus* from *Otello* in which the choral and woodwind detail suggests the flickering flames of bonfires burning in Otello's honour. The recording is warmly atmospheric, with CD adding a degree more presence and definition.

Choruses and ballet music: *Aïda: Gloria all'Egitto and Ballet. Don Carlos: Ce jour heureux; Ballet of the Queen. Macbeth: Ballet music. Nabucco: Va, pensiero. Il Trovatore: Vedi! le fosche notturne, spoglie* (*Anvil chorus*).
(M) **(*) DG **419 487-2**; *419 487-4* [id.]. La Scala, Milan, Ch. & O, Abbado.

A lively selection taken from various complete sets. The remastering has brightened the sound and the choral timbre is clean and incisive – in *Va, pensiero* the climax has a touch of fierceness, and here as elsewhere the ear notices that the bass is dry too. Both the *Anvil chorus* and the *Grand march* from *Aïda* have impressive vividness and projection. The tape is just a little smoother than the CD, with the bass that bit fuller; many will prefer the sense of added weight.

Choruses, overtures and ballet music from: *Aïda; La Forza del destino; I Lombardi; Macbeth; Nabucco; Il Trovatore; I vespri siciliani.*
** HMV **CDC7 47274-2** [id.]. Amb. Op. Ch., ROHCG Ch., Philh. and New Philh. O, Muti.

Though the element of fierceness in some of Muti's interpretations here will not please all Verdians, this useful compilation of different late 1970s recordings, all in excellent sound, can be warmly recommended to those who want a mixed collection of choruses and overtures. At 55′ it provides good if not exceptional measure.

Victoria, Tomás Luis de (*c.* 1548–1611)

Ascendens Christus (motet); *Missa Ascendis Christus in altum; O Magnum mysterium* (motet); *Missa O Magnum mysterium.*
*** Hyp. Dig. **CDA 66190**; *KA 66190* [id.]. Westminster Cathedral Ch., David Hill.

Missa Ave maris stella; O quam gloriosum est regnum (motet); *Missa O quam gloriosum.*
❀ *** Hyp. **CDA 66114**; *KA 66114* [id.]. Westminster Cathedral Ch., David Hill.

Winner of a *Gramophone* award in 1984, David Hill's superb coupling of *Ave maris stella* and *O quam gloriosum* gave Tomás Luis de Victoria a splendid CD début. The Latin fervour of the singing is very involving; some listeners may be surprised initially at the volatile way David Hill moves the music on, with the trebles eloquently soaring aloft on the line of the music. *Ave maris stella* is particularly fine, Hill's mastery of the overall structure producing a cumulative effect as the choir moves towards the magnificent closing *Agnus Dei.* The recording balance is perfectly judged, with the Westminster acoustic adding resonance in both senses of the word to singing of the highest calibre, combining a sense of timelessness and mystery with real expressive power. Throughout, the choral line remains firm without clouding. While the CD with its silent background marginally increases the tangibility of the sound, the cassette transfer also is flawless – this too is in the demonstration class.

The companion disc and tape are hardly less recommendable, the singing at once fervent and serene. Tempi are consistently fresh. The spirited presentation of the motet *Ascendens Christus in altum* prepares the way for a performance of the Mass that is similarly invigorating. The spontaneous ebb and flow of the pacing is at the heart of David Hill's understanding of this superb music, and the listener is thrillingly involved when the sound so successfully combines immediacy and body, yet remains admirably coloured by the Westminster resonance. Again the cassette is of demonstration standard.

Ave Maria; Ave Maris stella (hymn). *Missa Vidi speciosam. Ne timeas, Maria; Sancta Maria, succurre miseris; Vidi speciosam* (motets).
*** Hyp. Dig. **CDA 66129**; *KA 66129* [id.]. Westminster Cathedral Ch., David Hill.

An outstanding collection of some of Victoria's most beautiful music celebrating the Virgin Mary. The four-part *Ave Maria* may not be authentic, but the composer would surely not be reluctant to own it; and the hymn *Ave maris stella* is also a memorable setting. The three motets were all published in 1572. *Vidi speciosam* derives from the Song of Songs and its secular language inspires a special kind of expressive radiance, which could only come from a Latin composer. The Westminster Choir again show their flexibly volatile response to this music with that special amalgam of fervour and serenity that Victoria's writing demands. Throughout, the line is firmly contoured, yet sounds free, and the sensuous side of the music is balanced with its spirituality. The Mass based on the motet was published in 1592; its effect is much more controlled, although its use of the same musical material creates an affinity with its emotionally more exuberant source. David Hill's performance cannot be faulted; it is a most satisfying account, making a clear contrast with the other works in the programme. The acoustics of Westminster Cathedral add the right degree of resonance to the sound without clouding, and the choral textures are gloriously rich and yet refined too. The cassette is also highly recommendable.

Officium defunctorum.
*** Gimell Dig. **CDGIM 012**; *1585 T* [id.]. Tallis Scholars, Phillips (with LOBO: Motet: *Versa est in luctum****).
*** Hyp. Dig. **CDA 66250**; *KA 66250* [id.]. Westminster Cathedral Ch., David Hill.

Victoria's *Officium defunctorum* was his last publication and was written to honour the Dowager Empress Maria whose chaplain he was between 1587 and 1603 after his return from Rome. The *Officium defunctorum* comprises his *Requiem for six voices*, the Responsory *Libera me* and two motets. He spoke of it in his dedication to Princess Margaret as a swan-song, not in regard to his own composing but for the Empress – though in fact he died only six years later. It is a work of great serenity and beauty. Honours are fairly evenly divided between the Westminster Cathedral Choir on Hyperion and the Tallis Scholars under Peter Phillips. The Westminster Choir has the advantage of boys' voices and larger forces; they are recorded in a warmer, more spacious acoustic. By comparison with the Gimell recording the sound seems a little less well focused, but on its own terms it is thoroughly convincing. They permit themselves greater expressiveness, too. Moreover the *Requiem* is set in the wider liturgical context by the use of some chants.

The Tallis Scholars achieve great clarity of texture; they are twelve in number and as a result the polyphony is clearer and so, too, are their words. The lines are slightly harder-etched, as indeed are those of Spanish choirs, and their intonation is always true. There are no chants but they offer a short and deeply felt motet by Alonso Lobo (*c.* 1555–1617). The recording has a warm, glowing sound which almost persuades you that you are in the imperial chapel. Both the Tallis and Westminster versions can be strongly recommended but the added item may well tempt some readers towards the former. Here the state-of-the-art cassette loses very little indeed against the excellent CD.

Mass and Motet – O quam gloriosum.
(*) Argo Dig. **410 149-2 [id.]. King's College Ch., Cleobury – PALESTRINA: *Tu es Petrus.***(*)

This coupling with Palestrina offers eloquent, if slightly reserved performances in the King's tradition, the voices finely blended to produce an impressive range of sonority. The recording is admirably faithful and, while there is an element of introspection here, the singing also offers moments of affecting serenity. The CD adds slightly to the presence, but the recording is basically 'live' and well balanced. However, by the side of David Hill's Westminster Cathedral performance, the King's approach sounds relatively static.

Vierne, Louis (1870–1937)

Suite No. 3, Op. 54: Carillon de Westminster.
*** DG Dig. **413 438-2** [id.]. Simon Preston (organ of Westminster Abbey) – WIDOR: *Symphony No. 5.****

The Vierne *Carillon de Westminster* is splendidly played by Simon Preston and sounds appropriately atmospheric in this spacious acoustic and well-judged recording. It makes an attractive makeweight to the Widor *Fifth Symphony*.

Vieuxtemps, Henry (1820–81)

Violin concertos Nos 4 in D min., Op. 31; 5 in A min., Op. 37.
*** HMV **CDC7 47165-2** [id.]. Perlman, O de Paris, Barenboim.

Vieuxtemps wrote six violin concertos, and it is surprising that so few violinists have attempted to resurrect more than the odd one. This coupling of the two best-known is not only apt; it presents superbly stylish readings, with Perlman both aristocratically pure of tone and intonation and passionate of expression. In his accompaniments Barenboim draws warmly romantic playing from the Paris Orchestra. The 1978 recording, balancing the soloist well forward, now sounds a little dated in its clear, clean CD transfer.

Violin concerto No. 5 in A min., Op. 57.

*** RCA **RD 86214** [**RCA 6214-2-RC**]. Heifetz, New SO of L., Sargent – BRUCH: *Concerto No. 1; Scottish fantasia.****

(*) CBS Dig. **CD 37796 [id.]. Cho-Liang Lin, Minnesota SO, Marriner – HAYDN: *Concerto.***

The quicksilver of Heifetz is well suited to the modest but attractive *Fifth Concerto* of Vieuxtemps, and Sir Malcolm provides a musical and well-recorded accompaniment. The balance of the soloist is rather close, but the digital remastering is successful and the couplings are both attractive and generous.

Cho-Liang Lin is a Taiwanese-born player whose formidable technique is well able to meet the demands of this concerto. He plays it with flair and zest, and is well supported by Sir Neville Marriner and the Minnesota Orchestra. The recording is first class, and the enhancement provided by the CD is striking. However, the coupling, though well played, is not a very appropriate one. Now that Lin's reputation has been established by his splendid CD of the Mendelssohn and Saint-Saëns concertos, CBS would do well to find another pairing for his Vieuxtemps.

Villa-Lobos, Heitor (1887–1959)

(i) *Bachianas Brasileiras Nos 1–9* (complete); (ii) *Guitar concerto.*

*** HMV Dig. **CDS7 47901-8** (3) [id.]; *EX 270580-5.* (i) Barbara Hendricks, Osorio; (ii) Alfonso Moreno; (i) RPO; (ii) Mexico City PO; Bátiz.

In 1930 Villa-Lobos returned to Brazil after seven years in Paris; in the next fifteen years he composed a series of suites called *Bachianas Brasileiras*, which combine his lifelong love of Bach with all the colour and vitality of Brazil. They are scored for a variety of ensembles: No. 1 is for an orchestra of cellos, No. 3 is a kind of concertante for piano and orchestra, the celebrated No. 5 is for soprano and cellos, 6 for flute and bassoon, 7 and 8 for full orchestra, and so on. This is music not only of tremendous colour and energy but of considerable musical ingenuity – as, for example, the fugure of No. 9. There is abundant spirit here and the performances under Enrique Bátiz are thoroughly persuasive; the popular last movement of No. 2, *The little train of the Caipira*, moves on its track with evident zest. Jorge Fredrico Osorio is an excellent soloist in No. 3, and it goes without saying that Barbara Hendricks is her appealing self in No. 5. The *Guitar concerto*, written for Segovia, is not Villa-Lobos at his best: an amiable but inconsequential piece, it makes a useful fill-up to the last CD. A very worthwhile issue and good recorded sound on CD. The cassettes are acceptable, but the orchestral sound is not very transparent.

Bachianas Brasileiras Nos (i) *1* (*Prelude* only); (ii) *2* (includes *The little train of the Caipira*), (i; iii) *5* (*Aria* only); (iv) *Cirenda of the seven notes, for bassoon and strings;* (v) *Chôro No. 4, for 3 horns and trombone.*

(**) Chant du Monde **278 644** [id.]. (i) Rostropovich with Cello Ens.; (ii) USSR SO, Bakarev; (iii) Vishnevskaya; (iv) Pecherski, Leningrad CO, Gozman; (v) Bouyanovski, Evstigneyev, Sukorov, Benglovski.

Although this collection looks enticing and the cast list is strong, the results are often less than captivating. The digital remastering has brought a pungency to the treble response which affects the strings adversely in the most substantial item, the *Bachianas Brasileiras No. 2*, and also makes the percussive effects in *The little train of the Caipira* sound tinselly. The result is unevocative. The programme opens with Vishnevskaya's unlovely account of the *Aria* from *No. 5*, which is made the more abrasive by the forward balance and the edgy sound. Rostropovich languishes ravishingly in his solo in the *Prelude* to *No. 1* and here the recording is much more agreeable, as it is in the attractive brass quartet and the *Cirenda*, a fine piece, very well played. Thus the latter half of the concert, which includes these three items together, is far more attractive than the earlier part; it was not a good idea to open the disc with Vishnevskaya.

Bachianas Brasileiras Nos 1; 5; (i) *Suite for voice and guitar.* Arr. of Bach: *The Well-tempered clavier: Prelude in D min., BWV 583; Fugue in B flat, BWV 846; Prelude in G min., BWV 867; Fugue in D, BWV 874.*
*** Hyp. Dig. **CDA 66257**; *KA 66257* [id.]. Pleeth Cello Octet; (i) Jill Gomez, Peter Manning.

Jill Gomez is outstanding in the popular *Fifth Bachianas Brasileiras* and with the violinist, Peter Manning, in the *Suite* (1923). His favourite 'orchestra of cellos' produce sumptuous sounds in both the *Bachianas Brasileiras*, and an added point of interest is the effective transcriptions for cellos of unrelated Bach preludes and fugues. An eminently attractive introduction to this most colourful of composers for those who feel disinclined to buy the three-CD set listed above. There is an excellent cassette, and this is a particularly winning collection in both formats.

Bachianas Brasileiras Nos 1; 2 (includes *The little train of the Caipira*)*;* (i) *5* (for soprano & 8 cellos)*;* (ii) *6* (for flute & bassoon)*; 9.*
(***) EMI mono **CDH7 61015-2** [id.]. French Nat. R.O, composer, with (i) De los Angeles; (ii) Fernand Dufrêne, René Plessier.

It is good to have on EMI's historic Références label this generous collection of the composer's own recordings, not immaculate in performance and with depressingly dry and boxy recording, but full of colour and life. Though even Victoria de los Angeles' golden voice loses some of its bloom, her account of the famous No. 5 is ravishing, and no one has been more persuasive than the composer himself in the other favourite, the *Little train of the Caipira.*

Bachianas Brasileiras Nos 2 (includes *The little train of the Caipira*)*;* (i) *5, 6 & 9.*
** HMV Dig. **CDC7 47357** [id.]. (i) Mady Mesplé; O de Paris, Capolongo.

Duplicating four of the *Bachianas Brasileiras* that the composer himself recorded, Paul Capolongo conducts far more refined, though still flawed performances, infinitely better recorded. Such complex passages as the fugue in No. 9 are transformed, but the *Little train of the Caipira* lacks magic, and Mady Mesplé's bright, tinkly soprano is far from ideal for the sensuous lines of No. 5.

Bachianas Brasileiras No. 5 for soprano and cellos.
*** Decca Dig. **411 730-2** [id.]. Te Kanawa, Harrell and instrumental ens. – CANTELOUBE: *Songs of the Auvergne.***(*)

The Villa-Lobos piece makes an apt fill-up for the Canteloube songs completing Kiri Te Kanawa's recording of all five books. It is, if anything, even more sensuously done, well sustained at a speed far slower than one would normally expect. Rich recording to match.

Choros Nos 1, 2 (includes also piano version), *3* (*Picapau*), *4, 5* (*Alma Brasileira*), *7; Quinteto en forma de choros*.
** Chant du Monde **LDC 278 835** [id.]. Various artists.

In all Villa-Lobos composed sixteen *Choros* which try to evoke something of the improvised serenades of Brazilian street-life. They are written for an extraordinary variety of instruments and instrumental combinations – and, in this instance, one can add recordings. The *Quinteto en forma de choros* was recorded in 1968, the *First Choros for guitar* in 1986 and most of the rest in 1977. The disc makes an attractive introduction to the *Choros*; the performances, though not the last word in finesse, have plenty of character.

Guitar concerto.
*** Ph. Dig. **416 357-2**; *416 357-4* [id.]. Pepe Romero, ASMF, Marriner – CASTELNUOVO-TEDESCO: *Concerto*; RODRIGO: *Sones en la Giralda.****
(B) *** CBS *MGT 39017*. John Williams, ECO, Barenboim – CASTELNUOVO-TEDESCO: *Concerto.***(*); RODRIGO: *Concierto*; *Fantasia.****

(i) *Guitar concerto; Preludes Nos 1–5.*
*** RCA **RD 89813**; [(d.) **6525-2-RG**]. Julian Bream; (i) LSO, Previn.

Helped by attractively atmospheric recording, Romero and Marriner join to give an outstanding account of the Villa-Lobos *Concerto* and make it seem more substantial than usual while losing nothing of its poetic atmosphere. With equally recommendable couplings, this is first choice in this repertoire.

A highly distinguished account of the *Guitar concerto* from Bream, a work more striking for its atmosphere than for its actual invention. The rest of the programme also shows Bream in inspirational form; several of the *Preludes* are hauntingly memorable when the concentration of the playing is so readily communicated.

John Williams, too, makes the most of the work's finer points, especially the rhapsodic quality of the *Andantino*. The CBS recording is lively and immediate, and this extended-length tape is an undoubted bargain.

12 Études; 5 Preludes (for guitar).
*** Decca Dig. **414 616-2**; *414 616-4* [id.]. Eduard Fernández – GINASTERA: *Sonata.****

Excellent playing from this notable Uruguayan guitarist in the *Five Preludes*, while in the diverse *Études* there is some exhilarating bravura. He produces subtle and refined colours, and characterizes these pieces with artistry. This must be recommended alongside the very best, and he is given very natural and realistic recorded sound, with a very good cassette to match the CD.

Étude No. 1 in E min.; 5 Préludes; Suite populaire brésilienne.
(*) Ph. Dig. **420 245-2; *420 245-4* [id.]. Pepe Romero (with BUSTAMANTE: *Misionera.* MANGORÉ: *Una limosna por el amor de Dios.***(*)).

Romero's concert opens with the best-known of the *Studies* and then includes the *Five Préludes*, which are very well played indeed, and the more exotic *Suite populaire brésilienne* with its diverse chôros based on different European formal dances. Here the playing is agreeable but relaxed, and others have found more piquancy in this music. The recording is truthful but resonant. Romero ends his recital with a romantic piece by the Argentinian composer, Fernando Bustamante, and another by the Paraguayan, Agustin Barrios Mangoré, which features the tremolo accompanying device which is so effective on the guitar.

Piano music: *As três Maria; Bachianas Brasileiras No. 4; Caixinha de música quebrada; Ciclo Brasileiro; Cirandas Nos 4 & 14; Cuia prático; Poema singelo; Saudades das selvas Brasileiras No. 2; Valsa da dor.*
*** Decca Dig. **417 650-2**; *417 650-4* [id.]. Cristina Ortiz.

Cristina Ortiz, herself Brazilian, is a natural choice for this repertoire. Her anthology embraces the piano version of the *Bachianas Brasileiras No. 4* and a well-chosen collection of other pieces, the main work on her well-filled disc (67 minutes) being the *Ciclo Brasileiro*. She has a good ear for sonority and her phrasing is subtle and sensitive. As a single-disc introduction to Villa-Lobos's piano music this can be strongly recommended. The piano sound is clean and bright and there is a striking vivid cassette.

Bachianas Brasileiras No. 4; Choros No. 5: Alma Brasileira; Ciclo Brasileiro; Valsa da dor.
(*) ASV Dig. **CDDCA 607; *ZCDCA 607* [id.]. Alma Petchersky.

Alma Petchersky's style is more romantic than that of Cristina Ortiz, and some might find her thoughtful deliberation in the *Preludio* of the *Bachianas Brasileira No. 4* overdone. Her very free rubato is immediately apparent in the *Valsa da dor* which opens the recital. Yet she clearly feels all this music deeply and the playing is strong in personality and – with fuller piano than on the Decca collection – her timbre is often richly coloured. She is at her finest in the *Brazilian cycle* and makes much of the opening *Plantio de Caboclo* which, with its repeated figuration in the treble anticipates minimalist techniques, if remaining harmonically far more individual than most pieces in this style. In the dance-inspired pieces there is felicitous articulation and a nice feeling for rhythmic inflexion. The recording is first class, with more body and resonance than in the Decca collection. There is an excellent cassette.

Viotti, Giovanni Battista (1755–1824)

Violin concerto No. 13 in A.
*** Hyp. Dig. **CDA 66210**; *KA 66210* [id.]. Oprean, European Community CO, Faerber – FIORILLO: *Violin concerto No. 1.****

Viotti wrote a great many violin concertos in much the same mould, but this is one of his best. Its first movement has agreeable facility; the charming central *Andante* is more ambitious than that in the coupled Fiorillo concerto, and the jaunty rondo/polonaise finale is quite infectious, having much in common with a Paganini finale. Adelina Oprean's quicksilver style and light lyrical touch give much pleasure – she has the exact measure of this repertoire and she is splendidly accompanied by Faerber and this first-class chamber orchestra. Recorded in London's Sir Henry Wood Hall, the sound is most realistic (on tape as well as disc) and well balanced; one's only reservation is that there would easily have been room for another concerto of the period.

Vivaldi, Antonio (1675–1741)

L'Estro armonico (12 Concertos), Op. 3.
*** DG Dig. **423 094-2**; *423 094-4* (2) [id.]. Standage & soloists, E. Concert, Trevor Pinnock.
*** O-L **414 554-2** (2) [id.]. Holloway, Huggett, Mackintosh, Wilcock, AAM, Hogwood.
*** Ph. Dig. **412 128-2** [id.]. Carmirelli, I Musici.

Vivaldi's *L'Estro armonico* was published in 1711. The set includes some of his finest music and had great influence: Bach made creative arrangements of half the concertos for various combinations, from solo organ to a quadruple harpsichord concerto. Some of them are solo works, others are for two or four violins; probably more works are extracted from this set to be played and recorded individually than from any other of Vivaldi's collections – save Op. 8 with its ubiquitous *Four Seasons*. Previously we have had admirable recordings (utterly different in style) from Marriner and his Academy, I Musici, and, much more astringently, from Hogwood and his Academy of Ancient Music. This new chamber version from Pinnock (with one instrument to a part) seems instinctively to summarize and amalgamate the best features from past versions: there is as much sparkle and liveliness as with Hogwood, for rhythms are consistently resilient, ensemble crisp and vigorous. Yet in slow movements there is that expressive radiance and sense of enjoyment of beauty without unstylish indulgence that one expects from the ASMF; there is a touch of sunshine too, which was the speciality of I Musici (who could also veer towards blandness). The only aspect that one might cavil at is the use of harpsichord continuo throughout (Hogwood used organ as well; Marriner additionally featured the lute). However, this is a small point; everything else here gives delight, not least the sound itself, which is totally free from vinegar. The recording was made in EMI's Abbey Road studios and the balance and ambient effect are perfectly judged: there is bloom and internal clarity and a realistic but not exaggerated sense of presence. The chrome cassettes are also of a high standard.

There is no question about the sparkle of Christopher Hogwood's performance with the Academy of Ancient Music. The captivating lightness of the solo playing and the crispness of articulation of the accompanying group bring music making that combines joyful vitality with the authority of scholarship. Textures are always transparent, but there is no lack of body to the ripieno (even though there is only one instrument to each part). Hogwood's continuo is first class, varying between harpsichord and organ, the latter used to add colour as well as substance. The balance is excellent, and the whole effect is exhilarating. While some listeners may need to adjust to the style of playing in slow movements, the underlying expressive feeling is never in doubt, and in the allegros the nimble flights of bravura from the four soloists are a constant delight. The recording is superb; apart from the truthfulness of individual timbres, there is a striking depth of acoustic, with the solo instruments given a backward and forward perspective as well as the expected antiphonal interplay. The extra range that the compact disc can encompass helps to give the aural image the impression of greater definition.

Readers allergic to the Academy of Ancient Music are well served, too. I Musici are thoroughly fresh and alive, and few will find much to quarrel with in their interpretation. They may not have the dash and sparkle of the Academy – but they do not have any rough edges either. The Philips recording has great warmth and the texture is well ventilated, allowing detail to register clearly within a realisic perspective. The non-specialist collector will find much to enjoy here. Recommended alongside – but not in preference to – the Academy.

L'Estro armonico: Double violin concerto in A min.; Quadruple violin concerto in B min.; Triple concerto in D min., for 2 violins and cello, Op. 3/8, 10 and 11. Triple violin concerto in F.
(M) **(*) Pickwick Dig. **PCD 809** [id.]. Soloists, Scottish CO, Laredo.

The three concertos from *L'Estro armonico* are among Vivaldi's finest; they receive vigorous performances from members of the Scottish Chamber Orchestra, with their director, Jaime Laredo, again creating the lively spontaneity that informs his successful version of *The Four Seasons*. While the solo playing occasionally lacks the last touch of polish, there is an excellent team spirit, and the phrasing has more light and shade than in Laredo's companion collection of wind concertos. The recording is a shade overbright, but there is a firm supporting bass line and the acoustic is attractive, adding ambience and warmth without blurring detail. The *Triple concerto in F* has an unusual pizzicato-based *Andante*, showing the composer at his most imaginative. On Pickwick's mid-priced CD label, this seems excellent value.

L'Estro armonico: Double violin concerto No. 8 in A min.
** CBS Dig. [**MK 37278**]. Zukerman, Stern, St Paul CO, James – BACH: *Double concertos*.**

This lovely *Double concerto* makes an apt coupling for the two Bach *Double concertos* on this record from Minnesota, but the same reservations have to be made about the excessive weight of bass, alongside comparable praise for the solo playing.

La Stravaganza (12 Violin concertos), *Op. 4*.
*** O-L Dig. **417 502-2** (2); *417 502-4* [id.]. Huggett, AAM, Hogwood.

As we go to press, Monica Huggett and the Academy of Ancient Music with Christopher Hogwood have no current rivals. Even so, it would be difficult to see any newcomer easily displacing this excellently played set. Five of the concertos of Op. 4 look, not to the concerto grosso form of Corelli, but to the true solo concerto form of Torelli and Albinoni, which Vivaldi himself presaged in *L'Estro armonico*. Monica Huggett brings not only virtuosity but considerable warmth to the solo concertos and the Academy are both spirited and sensitive. Those who think of Vivaldi's music as predictable will find much to surprise them in *La Stravaganza*; his invention is unflagging and of high quality. Strongly recommended.

The Trial between harmony and invention (*Il Cimento dell'armonia e dell' invenzione*) (12 Concertos), *Op. 8*.
(*) O-L Dig. **417 515-2 (2) [id.]. Bury, Hirons, Holloway, Huggett, Mackintosh, Piguet, AAM, Hogwood.
(*) CRD **CRD 3325; *CRDC 4025* (*Nos 1–4*); **CRD 3410**; *CRDC 4048* (*Nos 5–10*); **CRD 3411**; *CRD 4049* (*Nos 11–12* and *Cello concerto in B min., RV 424*; *Flute concerto in D, RV 429*) [id.]. Simon Standage, Pleeth, Preston, E. Concert, Pinnock – C. P. E. BACH: *Harpsichord concerto* **(*)
(*) Tel. **ZK8 42985 (*Nos 1–6*); **ZK8 43094** (*Nos 7–12*) [id.]. Alice Harnoncourt, Schaeftlein, VCM, Harnoncourt.
**(*) Chan. *DBTD 3003* (3) [id.]. Ronald Thomas, Digney, Bournemouth Sinf.

The first four concertos of Op. 8 are a set within a set, forming what is (understandably) Vivaldi's most popular work, *The Four Seasons*. Their imaginative power and their eloquence and tunefulness tend to dwarf the remaining eight concertos, but there is some splendid music throughout the complete work, well worth exploring.

There is no want of zest in the Academy of Ancient Music's accounts of Op. 8. These are likeable and, generally speaking, well-prepared versions and differ from some rivals in choosing the oboe in two of the concertos, where Vivaldi has indicated an option. There are moments where more polish would not have come amiss (in the *G minor Concerto*, for example) and intonation is not above reproach either. However, admirers of the Academy will find much to enjoy here – as, indeed, will those who are not always in tune with period-instrument performances. In *The Four Seasons*, Pinnock is not displaced, however. The recordings are well up to standard and are given fine presence, complete on a pair of CDs.

CRD have anticipated the needs of many collectors, who either may not wish to duplicate *The Four Seasons* or may prefer to choose an alternative account, by making available the remaining eight concertos on two CDs, filling up the available space with two other Vivaldi works, and on CD offering a harpsichord concerto by C. P. E. Bach as a bonus. The *Flute concerto* (played by Simon Preston on a baroque flute) is particularly attractive. These 1981 performances are alert and full of character; they established a new style, using original instruments, which was to become even more famous when Pinnock and his English Concert later moved over to DG's Archiv label. Slow movements remain expressively eloquent, and a chamber organ is used in the continuo to add extra colour, although without the imaginative touches or sense of fantasy which Marriner finds in this repertoire. Indeed, the playing is a little short on charm. On the cassettes, the sound has a certain astringency, but in the remastering for CD this has been slightly smoothed off, and in tuttis there is at times some loss of focus. The separate concertos are banded, but there is no cueing of individual movements. *The Four Seasons* from this set are available on CD also, well transferred, but buying all twelve concertos is uneconomical as it involves three discs, even if you get a good deal of extra music.

The Telefunken complete set is undoubtedly original in approach and full of character; there is, however, an element of eccentricity in Harnoncourt's control of dynamics and tempi, with allegros often aggressively fast and chimerical changes of mood that are not always convincing. Alice Harnoncourt's timbre is leonine, and her tone production somewhat astringent, bringing out the pithiness of timbre inherent in her baroque instrument. The dramatic style of the solo playing is certainly at one with the vivid pictorialism of Vivaldi's imagery. The shepherd's dog in *Spring* barks vociferously, and the dance rhythms at the finale of the same concerto are extremely invigorating. The interpretative approach throughout emphasizes this element of contrast. The languorous opening of *Summer* makes a splendid foil for the storm and the buzzing insects, yet the zephyr breezes are wistfully gentle. The continuo uses a chamber organ to great effect, and picaresque touches of colour are added to the string textures. Concertos Nos 9 and 12 are played on the oboe by Jurg Schaeftlein, who makes a first-class contribution; and this choice of instrumentation further varies the colouring of Vivaldi's score. The sound is bright, vivid and clean, if dry-textured and sometimes fierce in the Telefunken manner. As can be seen, this 1978 analogue recording has been reissued on a pair of CDs, digitally remastered. The two discs are available separately; the first includes *The Four Seasons* plus two other characterful works: No. 5, subtitled *La Tempesta di mare*, and No. 6, called, with no special significance, *Il Piacere*.

The Bournemouth Sinfonietta set on Chandos is beautifully recorded and has much in its favour. The use of modern instruments does not preclude a keen sense of style, and the balance is convincing, with the continuo coming through not too insistently. The later concertos are particularly successful; Nos 5 (*La Tempesta di mare*) and 6 (*Il piacere*) are excellent, and there is some delectable oboe playing from John Digney in the final group. Allegros are alert without being rigid and slow movements are expressive, with musical phrasing and a fine sense of atmosphere. The drawback for most listeners will be the account of *The Four Seasons*, which is seen as part of the whole cycle rather than as individually dramatic. Ronald Thomas's approach emphasizes the music's breadth and lyricism rather than its colourful pictorialism, so that the shepherd's dog barks gently and the winds blow amiably, certainly never reaching gale force. In its way this is pleasing, but there remains an element of disappointment in the under-characterization. The cassette transfer is very variable in level (the second side of *The Four Seasons* registers a big drop after side one), and the degree of immediacy and range varies accordingly.

The Four Seasons, Op. 8/1–4.
*** Argo **414 486-2**; *KZRC 654* [id.]. Alan Loveday, ASMF, Marriner.
*** DG Dig. **400 045-2** [id.]. Simon Standage, E. Concert, Pinnock.
*** BIS Dig. **CD 275** [id.]. Nils-Erik Sparf, Drottningholm Bar. Ens.
*** DG Dig. **419 214-2**; *419 214-4* [id.]. Stern, Zukerman, Mintz, Perlman, Israel PO, Mehta.
(M) *** HMV **CDM7 69046-2** [id.]. Itzhak Perlman, LPO.
*** Ph. Dig. **410 001-2** [id.]. Pina Carmirelli, I Musici.
(M) *** Pickwick Dig. **PCD 800** [MCA **MCAD 25843**]. Jaime Laredo, Scottish CO.
*** DG **413 726-2** [id.]. Gidon Kremer, LSO, Abbado.
*** O-L Dig. **410 126-2** [id.]. Hirons, Holloway, Bury, Mackintosh, AAM, Hogwood.
*** Ph. Dig. **420 216-2**; *420 216-4* [id.]. Viktoria Mullova, COE, Abbado.
(*) CBS **CD 36710 [id.]. Pinchas Zukerman, St Paul CO.
(*) HMV **CDC7 47319-2 [id.]. Perlman, Israel PO.
(B) **(*) CfP **CD-CFP 9001**; *TC-CFP 40016*. Kenneth Sillito, Virtuosi of England, Davison.

(M) **(*) Decca **417 712-2**; *417 226-4* [id.]. Konstanty Kulka, Stuttgart CO, Münchinger – ALBINONI: *Adagio****; PACHELBEL: *Canon.****

(M) ** DG **415 301-2** [id.]. Michel Schwalbé, BPO, Karajan – CORELLI: *Concerto grosso, Op. 6/8*; ALBINONI: *Adagio.***

(M) ** DG *419 488-4* [id.]. Schwalbé, BPO, Karajan – PACHELBEL: *Canon and Gigue*; ALBINONI: *Adagio.***

** HMV Dig. **CDC7 47043-2** [id.]. Anne-Sophie Mutter, VPO, Karajan.

** Ph. **420 482-2** [id.]. Iona Brown, ASMF.

(M) ** Decca *417 873-4* [id.]. Krotzinger, Stuttgart CO, Münchinger (with CORELLI: *Concerto grosso in G min., Op. 6/8.* PERGOLESI: *Flute concerto No. 2* (with Rampal)***).

** Delos Dig. **D/CD 3007** [id.]. Elmar Oliveira, LACO, Schwarz.

The Four Seasons; Violin concertos: in B flat (*La Caccia*), *Op. 8/10; in A* (*per eco in lontana*), *RV 552.*

(M) **(*) Ph. **420 356-2**; *420 356-4* [id.]. Roberto Michelucci, I Musici.

(i) *The Four Seasons;* (ii) *Flute concertos, Op. 10/1–3.*

(M) **(*) RCA **GD 86533**; *GK 86533.* (i) La Petite Bande, Kuijken; (ii) Brüggen, O of 18th Century.

Vivaldi's *Four Seasons* is currently the most often recorded of any piece of classical music. It seems extraordinary that Sir Neville Marriner's 1970 Academy of St Martin-in-the-Fields version with Alan Loveday, having dominated the LP and tape catalogues for nearly two decades, should now establish its place at the top of the list of recommended compact discs. It was made during a vintage Argo recording period and the digital remastering has been completely successful, retaining the fullness and bloom of the original, besides slightly refining its inner detail, already excellent on the original LP. The performance is as satisfying as ever, and will surely delight all but those who are ruled by the creed of authenticity. It has an element of fantasy that makes the music sound utterly new; it is full of imaginative touches, with Simon Preston subtly varying the continuo between harpsichord and organ. The opulence of string tone may have a romantic connotation, but there is no self-indulgence in the interpretation, no sentimentality, for the contrasts are made sharper and fresher, not smoothed over. The cassette is not quite as clean as the CD (especially on side two) but is still thoroughly recommendable alongside it.

The Archiv version by Simon Standage with the English Concert, directed from the harpsichord by Trevor Pinnock, has the advantage of using a newly discovered set of parts found in Manchester's Henry Watson Music Library – which has additionally brought the correction of minor textual errors in the Le Cène text in normal use. The Archiv performance also (minimally) introduces a second soloist and is played on period instruments. The players create a relatively intimate sound, though their approach is certainly not without drama, while the solo contribution has impressive flair and bravura. The overall effect is essentially refined, treating the pictorial imagery with subtlety. The result is less voluptuous than with Marriner and less vibrant than Kremer's version under Abbado, but it finds a natural balance between vivid projection and atmospheric feeling. The digital recording is first class, while the compact disc offers the usual additional virtues of background silence, added clarity and refinement. Authenticists should be well satisfied.

The BIS recording by Nils-Erik Sparf and the Drottningholm Baroque Ensemble is in a rather special category. As a recording, it has astonishing clarity and presence; and as playing, it is hardly less remarkable in its imaginative vitality. These Swedish players make the most of all the pictorial characterization without ever overdoing anything: they achieve the feat of making one hear this eminently familiar repertoire as if for the very first time. In a crowded discography, this *Four Seasons* demands to be heard, for its freshness and enthusiasm are infectious. Many will feel it deserves to be at the very top of the list.

The recording made at the 1982 Huberman Festival in Tel Aviv took the opportunity offered by a stellar gathering of fiddlers to give each of the four concertos to a different soloist. It makes one wonder why only one other record company had thought of doing this before. The result is an unqualified success, with each artist revelling in writing that offers equal opportunities for bravura and espressivo playing, plus a chance for the imagination to find a similar balance between the musical and pictorial aspects of Vivaldi's remarkable conception. The playing has striking freshness and spontaneity throughout. With outstanding recording quality (CD and tape are almost identical) this is an example of 'live' music-making at its finest.

Those looking for an outstanding mid-priced CD should be well satisfied with Perlman and the LPO. His finesse as a great violinist is evident from first to last. Though some will demand more reticence in baroque concertos, Perlman's imagination holds the sequence together superbly, and there are many passages of pure magic, as in the central *Adagio* of *Summer*. The digital remastering of the 1976 recording is admirably managed, the sound firm, clear and well balanced, with plenty of detail.

The new Philips digital recording is the third in stereo by I Musici, and it is undoubtedly the finest of the three. Musical values as ever are paramount; this time, however, there is more vitality and the programmatic implications are more strikingly realized (indeed, the bark of the shepherd's dog in *Spring* is singularly insistent). Yet Pina Carmirelli's expressive playing maintains the lyrical feeling and beauty of tone for which I Musici versions are remembered, and he combines it with attractively alert and nimble bravura in the allegros. The gentle breezes are as effectively caught as the summer storms, and the slow movement of *Autumn* (helped by especially atmospheric recording) makes an elegiac contrast. The opening of *Winter* is certainly chilly. The recording is outstandingly natural and is most impressive on CD, with its added refinement of detail.

Jaime Laredo's Pickwick CD is a fine bargain. The performance has great spontaneity and vitality, emphasized by the forward balance which is nevertheless admirably truthful. The bright upper range is balanced by a firm, resonant bass. Laredo plays with bravura and directs polished, strongly characterized accompaniments. Pacing tends to be on the fast side; although the reading is extrovert, and the lyrical music – played responsively – is made to offer a series of interludes to the vigour of the allegros, the effect is exhilarating rather than aggressive. The compact disc gives tangibility to the soloist and body to the orchestra.

In the DG version by Gidon Kremer with the LSO under Claudio Abbado, it is obvious from the first bar that Abbado is the dominating partner. This is an enormously vital account, with great contrasts of tempo and dynamic. The dramatization of Vivaldi's detailed pictorial effects has never been more vivid; the vigour of the dancing peasants is surpassed by the sheer fury and violence of the summer storms. Yet the delicacy of the gentle zephyrs is matched by the hazy somnolence of the beautiful *Adagio* of *Autumn*. After a freezingly evocative opening to *Winter*, Abbado creates a mandolin-like pizzicato effect in the slow movement (taken faster than the composer's marking) to simulate a rain shower. The finale opens delicately, but at the close the listener is almost blown away by the winter gales. Kremer matches Abbado's vigour with playing that combines sparkling bravura and suitably evocative expressive moments. Given the projection of a brilliantly lit recording, the impact of this version is considerable. Leslie Pearson's nimble continuo, alternating organ and harpsichord, sometimes gets buried, but drama rather than subtlety is the keynote of this arresting account. The 1982 analogue recording has been effectively remastered for CD, sounding fresh and clean, its brilliance very apparent.

With a different soloist for each of the four concertos, Hogwood directs the Academy of Ancient Music in lively performances with exceptionally imaginative use of continuo contrasts, guitar with harpsichord in *Spring* and *Autumn*, lute and chamber organ in *Summer* and *Winter*. These performances have a high place among authentic versions, a shade more abrasive than most; however, they cannot quite match the subtly responsive approach of Trevor Pinnock's Archiv set with the English Concert. The CD has striking presence; a state-of-the-art transfer.

Viktoria Mullova's Philips record with the Chamber Orchestra of Europe under Claudio Abbado is well worth considering. As one would expect, she is vibrant and vital in the outer movements and imaginative and eloquent in the slow movements. She is given excellent support by Abbado and his players, and the recording, as always from this source, is very well balanced in both formats. There is a bonus in the form of the *G minor concerto*, RV 577, one of two Vivaldi composed for Dresden, whose orchestra boasted a strong wind department.

Another fine modern version comes from Zukerman. The playing has character throughout, with the music's programmatic associations well observed but not overemphasized. The conception has a strong lyrical feeling; perhaps the relaxed approach does minimize the drama, but there is a compensating refinement and, as with I Musici, musical values are paramount here. The sound of the orchestra gives a degree of bass emphasis, but the continuo comes through well and the overall effect is believable with the added presence afforded by CD.

Fine as was Perlman's 1976 recording of *The Four Seasons*, a modern virtuoso performance that held the sequence together with perceptive artistry and immaculate virtuosity, he decided that he wanted to record the four concertos again. There are certainly gains, in that the harpsichord continuo is more readily audible, but the closeness of sound, as recorded in the Mann Auditorium in Tel Aviv, also brought an unwanted harshness on LP. However, as so often with recordings made in this venue, the CD brings a remarkable improvement. The balance remains close, but the sound is opened out, the effect much more natural and congenial. The accompanying string group has more body and the imagery is altogether more believable. As an interpretation, this is a masterly example of a virtuoso's individual artistry, but the account does not convey quite the warmth and spontaneity of the earlier set.

Among versions in the mid-priced and bargain range, that by Kenneth Sillito with the Virtuosi of England under Arthur Davison stands out for its bold, clear sound, beautifully focused and full of presence. Indeed the soloist is a shade too present, and this detracts a little from gentler expressiveness. Yet Sillito's playing is both poetic and assured and, with such vivid projection, this music making is full of personality in its CD format.

On RCA La Petite Band (soloist unnamed) offer an authentic version of considerable appeal. Although the accompanying group can generate plenty of energy when Vivaldi's winds are blowing, this is essentially a small-scale reading, notable for its delicacy. The small, pure violin line is particularly appealing in slow movements and one notes how closely the soloist follows Vivaldi's instructions in the second movement of *Spring: Largo e pianissimo sempre*. But this mid-priced issue offers not just the four concertos of Op. 8 (which on cassette are heard complete on one side) but also three favourite *Flute concertos* from Op. 10: *Tempesta di mare*, *La notte* and *Il gardinello*. With the master-instrumentalist, Frans Brüggen, playing a period instrument and directing the Orchestra of the 18th Century, the excellence of these performances, vividly recorded, can be taken for granted.

Philips have also reissued Michelucci's 1970 version at mid-price, sounding extremely well. I Musici must have played this work countless times and probably find it more difficult than most groups to bring freshness to each new recording. Roberto Michelucci is a first-class soloist, displaying bursts of bravura in the outer movements but often musingly thoughtful in the slower ones. His expressiveness is finely judged, and the group are naturally balanced, with the harpsichord coming through in the right way, without exaggeration. The last degree of spontaneity is sometimes missing, but this is certainly enjoyable. This version is made the more tempting by the inclusion of two extra named violin concertos, both very well played and recorded.

On Decca Kulka gives a first-class solo performance, while Münchinger and the Stuttgart Chamber Orchestra, whose early LPs did so much to reawaken interest in Vivaldi, bring a stylish and lively manner to the accompaniments. This was always a strong recommendation in the mid-price range, but with digital remastering the brightly lit recording has become vivid to the point of astringency in its CD format, and the ear is drawn to this when the bonus items sound much mellower.

Karajan's 1973 version was an undoubted success, even if unlikely to appeal to authenticists. Its tonal beauty is not achieved at the expense of vitality and, although the harpsichord hardly ever comes through, the overall scale is acceptable. Michel Schwalbé is a memorable soloist. His playing is neat, precise and very musical, with a touch of Italian sunshine in the tone. His sparkling playing is set against polished Berlin Philharmonic string textures, although in the digital remastering the sound seems to have been dried out a little and is not as expansive or as natural-sounding as before. Choice lies between the CD and a cassette which costs around a third as much. The couplings are slightly different, although Albinoni's *Adagio* is common to both.

As with his previous recording, made in Berlin, Karajan's HMV version with Mutter offers much to admire, not least the beautiful playing of his young soloist. A reduced string group from the Vienna orchestra is used, but the warmly reverberant acoustic makes the sound plushy, although the effect is richly agreeable. The balance sometimes drowns the continuo (to which Karajan contributes himself); detail registers more clearly on the CD, but this medium serves also to emphasize the anachronism of the conception.

The Academy of St Martin's earlier Argo recording under Neville Marriner, unauthentically sumptuous, had irresistible magic; but Iona Brown's version with the same band fails to repeat that. The mannered style, with exaggerated dynamic contrasts, suggests that she may have been attempting to do so, but not even in refinement of playing is this among the Academy's finest issues. The recording is rich, yet has good detail.

Münchinger's first stereo recording with Krotzinger had lost the freshness of new discovery of the earlier mono set. This is a straightforward, rather German account, somewhat phlegmatic, although very well played and recorded. What makes this Weekend tape attractive are the Corelli and (especially) the Pergolesi concertos, the latter with Rampal on his best form. The sound is really very good throughout a tape obviously intended for the car.

The Delos recording by Elmar Oliveira and the excellent Los Angeles Chamber Orchestra under Gerard Schwarz made the digital début of *The Four Seasons* in 1980. The recording is extremely brilliant, the sharp spotlighting of the soloist bringing a degree of steeliness to his upper range. Tempi too are extremely brisk throughout: extrovert bravura is the keynote here, rather than atmosphere. The recording balance ensures that the continuo comes through well. But – as the opening of *Winter* demonstrates – this is not an especially imaginative version, although the alert vivacity of the playing of soloist and orchestra alike is undoubtedly exhilarating, and slow movements are expressive and sympathetic.

Other versions of Vivaldi's masterpiece abound. Denon have three different CDs: the first by Gunars Larsens and Baumgartner, which is well played but not especially imaginative; the second a state-of-the-art digital recording by John Holloway and the Taverner Players under Andrew Parrott, which suffers from moments of uncertain tuning (**C37 7283**). This is authenticity at its bleakest. The most recent (**CO 1471**) by I Solisti Italiani offers, in fact, six concertos from Op. 8, and brings playing which though perhaps better than routine falls very short of anything approaching inspiration. Equally, the RCA recording by Garcia and Slatkin (**RD 85827**) and an earlier RCA Erato issue by Piero Tosos and Scimone (Erato **ECD 88003**) are not distinctive enough to be competitive at full price.

(i; ii) *The Four Seasons;* (iii) *Recorder concerto in C, RV 443;* (ii) *Double violin concerto in A* (*Echo*), *RV 552*.

(B) **(*) DG Walkman *413 142-4*. (i) Schneiderhan; (ii) Lucerne Fest. Strings, Baumgartner; (iii) Linde, Emil Seiler CO, Hofmann (with: ALBINONI: *Adagio* (arr. Giazotto). CORELLI:

Concerto grosso in G min. (Christmas), Op. 6/8. PACHELBEL: *Canon and Gigue in D****).

Schneiderhan favours fast tempi in the *Seasons*, but his playing is assured and the performance has plenty of character. The recording, from the beginning of the 1960s, is rather light in the bass. On the Walkman tape the couplings are generous and include Vivaldi's ingenious *Echo concerto*, where the echo effects are not just confined to the soloists but feature the ripieno too; plus the engaging *Concerto for sopranino recorder*, RV 443. Then to make the concert doubly generous, this bargain-priced Walkman tape offers three other Baroque favourites. Performances are of high quality throughout and the transfer is consistently vivid, although there is a slight edge on the solo violin in *The Four Seasons*.

The Four Seasons, Op. 8/1–4 (arr. for flute and strings).
*** RCA **RD 70161 [RCD1 2264]**. Galway, I Solisti di Zagreb.

James Galway's transcription is thoroughly musical and so convincing that at times one is tempted to believe that the work was conceived in this form. The playing itself is marvellous, full of detail and imagination, and the recording is excellent, even if the flute is given a forward balance, the more striking on CD.

The Four Seasons, Op. 8/1–4 (arr. for recorder)*; Recorder concerto in C, RV 443.*
*** RCA Dig. **RD 86656**; *RK 86656*. Michala Petri, Guildhall String Ens., Malcolm.

No question as to the virtuosity of Michala Petri or the excellence and musicianship of the Guildhall Strings. The question is not how but why. Who wants to hear this eminently violinistically conceived music played on any other instrument, even if by as accomplished an artist as Galway or Petri? Well, those who do are unlikely to be disappointed by the results here, even if there are some ear-piercing moments. The RCA recording is eminently clean and well detailed. Three stars for that and the skill and accomplishment of the playing . . . but for the idea itself none.

La Cetra (12 Violin concertos), Op. 9.
*** HMV Dig. **CDS7 47829-8** [id.]; *EX 270557-5* (2). Huggett, Raglan Bar. Players, Kraemer.

La Cetra (The Lyre) was the last set of violin concertos Vivaldi published: they appeared in Amsterdam in 1727, by which time his reputation was well established in Europe. Monica Huggett and the Raglan Baroque Players have the field to themselves at present on CD, and theirs is the first set of *La Cetra* to be made on period instruments. Even so, as in the case of her recording of *La Stravaganza* on the Oiseau-Lyre label, the performances are so accomplished and in such good style that – even if they were to be equalled – they are unlikely to be surpassed. She is in excellent form and her virtuosity always appears effortless. Even if *La Cetra* as a set is not as consistently inspired as *La Stravaganza* or *Il cimento*, in these performances it almost sounds their equal. The Raglan Baroque Players are of the same size as the Academy of Ancient Music, and some players are common to both this and the Oiseau-Lyre Op. 4. First-class recording on CD. The iron-oxide tapes, however, are not really recommendable; the sound is patchy: at times bass-heavy, at others ill-focused in the treble.

6 Flute concertos, Op. 10 (complete).
*** O-L **414 685-2** [id.]. Stephen Preston, AAM.
*** Ph. **412 874-2** [id.]. Michala Petri, ASMF, Marriner.
(M) **(*) EMI Dig. **CD-EMX 9504**; *TC-EMX 2105*. William Bennett, ECO, Malcolm.
(*) Ph. Dig. **420 188-2; *420 188-4* [id.]. Aurèle Nicolet, I Musici.
** CBS Dig. **MK 39062** [id.]. Rampal, Sol. Ven., Scimone.
** RCA Dig. **RD 85316 [RCD1 5316]**. Galway, New Irish CO.

Stephen Preston plays a period instrument, a Schuchart, and the Academy of Ancient Music likewise play old instruments. Their playing is eminently stylish, yet both spirited and expressive, and they are admirably recorded, with the analogue sound enhanced further in the CD format.

Whereas Stephen Preston uses a baroque flute and Jean-Pierre Rampal a modern instrument, the young Danish virtuoso Michala Petri uses a modern recorder. At least this, like Rampal's set, gives us the opportunity of hearing these concertos at present-day pitch. Michala Petri plays with breathtaking virtuosity and impeccable control, and she has the advantage of superb recording. In the slow movements – and occasionally elsewhere – there is more in the music than she finds, but the sheer virtuosity of this gifted young artist is most infectious. She uses a sopranino recorder in three of the concertos. Generally speaking, this Philips recording is to be preferred to any of the recent newcomers, and sounds even fresher on the digitally remastered compact disc.

Though beefier in approach than some rival versions, William Bennett's issue on the mid-price Eminence label brings highly enjoyable performances, marked by fine solo playing and sparkling and imaginative continuo from George Malcolm. Good, warm, modern recording.

Like Bennett's set with Malcolm, Aurèle Nicolet's with I Musici is, of course, a modern instrument version and there is no lack of expertise. There are some touches which will not please purists (some flutter-tonguing in *Il gardellino* sounds out-of-period) but there is no want of virtuosity and charm. The recording is very well balanced on CD. The cassette is slightly bass-orientated and not very transparent.

Jean-Pierre Rampal was one of the first to record these concertos, way back in the early 1950s, but this CBS account, his third, is somewhat more glamorized than its predecessors. Dynamic contrasts are rather extreme and the results a little overblown. Of course, as flute playing this is pretty spectacular; if you want a frankly modern virtuoso approach, rather than a more scaled-down reading with a greater sense of period, this excellently recorded version will not disappoint. The CD has the advantage of a digital master and sounds admirably fresh and transparent.

James Galway directs the New Irish Chamber Orchestra from the flute – and to generally good effect. The playing is predictably brilliant but the sweet vibrato is all a bit too much. This record is directed towards the broader public, and it is for Galway rather than Vivaldi that one will want it. No complaints about the recording quality or the orchestral contribution, but those who do buy it are warned that the pauses between movements are absurdly short.

Bassoon concertos: in C, RV 466; in C, RV 467; in F, RV 486; in F, RV 491; in A min., RV 499; in A min., RV 500.
(*) ASV Dig. **CDDCA 565; *ZCDCA 565* [id.]. Daniel Smith, ECO, Ledger.

Bassoon concertos in C, RV 469; in C, RV 470; in C, RV 474; in C, RV 476; in F, RV 487; in G, RV 494.
(*) ASV Dig. **CDDCA 571; *ZCDCA 571* [id.]. Daniel Smith, ECO, Ledger.

Bassoon concertos: in C, RV 473; in E flat, RV 483; in F, RV 485; in G, RV 492; in A min., RV 497; in B flat, RV 503.
*** Ph. Dig. **416 355-2**; *416 355-4* [id.]. Klaus Thunemann, I Musici.

The bassoon seems to have uncovered a particularly generous fund of inspiration in Vivaldi, for few of his concertos for that instrument are in any way routine and they number almost forty. None of the six recorded on Philips is second rate: they are all inventive, fresh and at times inspired, and Klaus Thunemann and I Musici give most appealing accounts of them. No complaints either about the quality or balance of the Philips recording. Even those not usually responsive to Vivaldi will find these refreshing and original.

Daniel Smith is a genial and personable player and he has considerable facility; even if some of the more complicated roulades are not executed with exact precision, his playing has undoubted flair. He is balanced well forward, but the orchestral accompaniment has plenty of personality and registers well enough. He appears to be working his way steadily through the Vivaldi concertos for his instrument and this (on the second volume, particularly) has led to the juxtaposition of several concertos in the same key, something Thunemann avoids. Even so, this is enjoyably spontaneous music-making, although the concertos should be approached singly, a facility which CD readily provides. Of the two tapes, *ZCDCA 565* is on iron-oxide stock, and *ZCDCA 571* on chrome: the difference is very apparent, with the sound-picture mellow on the one, bright and fresh (even slightly astringent in the strings) and more immediate on the other.

Bassoon concerto in F, RV 485; (i) *Double concerto in G min., for recorder and bassoon* (*La Notte*)*, RV 104.*
*** BIS Dig. **CD 271** [id.]. McGraw, (i) Pehrsson, Drottningholm Bar. Ens. – TELEMANN: *Concertos.****

The concerto subtitled *La Notte* exists in three versions: one for flute (the most familiar), RV 439, another for bassoon, RV 501 and the present version, RV 104. Clas Pehrsson, Michael McGraw and the Drottningholm Baroque Ensemble give a thoroughly splendid account of it, and the *Bassoon concerto in F major* also fares well. Excellent recording.

Cello concertos: in G, RV 413; in B min., RV 424; (i) *Double cello concerto in G min., RV 531.*
*(*) Chan. Dig. *ABTD 1145* [id.]. Turovsky, (i) Aubut, I Musici di Montreal – BOCCHERINI: *Cello concerto.**(*)

There is nothing here really to detail to the collector. The performances are acceptable, though the solo playing in the *Double concerto* is a bit scrappy. Good sound.

Chamber concertos: in A min., RV 86; in C, RV 87; in D, RV 92 & 95 (*La Pastorella*)*; in G, RV 101; in G min., RV 103 & RV 105; in A min., RV 108.*
*** Ph. Dig. **411 356-2** (2) [id.]. Petri, Holliger, Ayo, Pellegrino, Jaccottet, Thunemann, Demenga, Rubin.

These are what later generations might have called concertante works, concertos exploiting the interplay of several soloists. They are all given performances of the highest accomplishment and recordings that are natural in both timbre and perspective. As usual, Philips give us warm, excellently focused sound with admirable detail and realism, particularly in the compact disc format, which is delightfully fresh and immediate. The playing of these artists is eminently fine, though in one or two of the slow movements there is just a suggestion of the routine. However, so rich is Vivaldi's invention and resource and so brilliant are these performances that it would be curmudgeonly to deny them a warm recommendation.

(i) *Flute concertos: in D, RV 84 & RV 89; in G, RV 102;* (ii) *Recorder concerto in A min., RV 108* (with (ii) VALENTINE: *Recorder concerto in B flat;* SARRI: *Recorder concerto in A min.*).
* DG **415 299-2** [id.]. (i) Hazelzet; (ii) Heyens, Col. Mus. Ant., Goebel.

Both Gudrun Heyens and Wilbert Hazelzet are masters of their authentic instruments. With fast pacing from Goebel, their bravura is in no doubt either. But the edgy accompaniments, using only a string quartet plus continuo, are not helped by a recording focus that is less than sharp, and there is a total absence of charm here, with allegros made to sound aggressive by the close balance. The concertos by Roberto Valentine (1680–1735) and Domenico Sarri (1679–

1744), each of four movements, open the concert, with the Sarri work the more attractive of the two. But the lack of bloom on the recording does not entice the listener to return to them.

Concertos for flute and strings: in G, RV 435; in F, RV 442; Chamber concertos with flute or recorder: in D (Il Gardellino), RV 90; in F (La Tempesta di mare), RV 98; in G, RV 101; in G min. (La Notte), RV 104.
*** RCA **RD 70951**; (M) *GK 70951*. Brüggen, O of 18th Century.

An interesting disc. When Vivaldi prepared his set of six concertos, Op. 10, he drew on earlier works (except in the case of the *G major*, RV 435), and on this record Frans Brüggen presents the composer's earlier working of the material. The results are uniformly fresh and delightful and both his solo playing on treble recorder or transverse flute and that of the Orchestra of the 18th Century is remarkably alive and vibrant, completely attuned to the sensibility of the period. Good recording too.

Guitar concertos: in D, RV 93; in A min. (from Op. 3/6), RV 356; in C, RV 425. Double guitar concerto in G, RV 532; Quadruple guitar concerto in B min. (from Op. 3/10), RV 580.
*** Ph. Dig. **412 624-2** [id.]. Los Romeros, ASMF, Iona Brown.

Two of these concertos are transcriptions from *L'Estro armonico* and, though they are in themselves pleasing, they are probably more enjoyable in their original form, particularly the slow movements with their sustained melodic lines. However, no less a composer than Bach transcribed them for keyboard, and there is no doubting the expertise and musicianship of the four Romeros and the Academy, nor the excellence of the Philips engineering. The other concertos for lute and mandolin come off excellently. Probably not an issue that would have high priority in a Vivaldi collection, but none the less enjoyable, and this could provide evocative listening for the late evening. The *Largo* of RV 93, which ends the programme, is particularly haunting.

Guitar concertos in D, RV 93; in B flat, RV 524; in G min., RV 531; in G, RV 532. Trios: in C, RV 82; in G min., RV 85.
*** DG Dig. **415 487-2** [id.]. Söllscher, Bern Camerata, Füri.

Four of these works are for two mandolins (RV 532) or lute (RV 82, 85, 93), and the remaining two are for two violins (RV 524) and two cellos (RV 531). Göran Söllscher further enhances his reputation both as a master-guitarist and as an artist on this excellently recorded issue, in which he has first-class support from the Camerata Bern under Thomas Füri. In RV 532, Söllscher resorts to technology and plays both parts. Throughout, this gifted young Swedish artist plays with the taste and intelligence one has come to expect from him. The DG balance is admirably judged, and in the compact disc format the results are remarkably clean and finely focused.

Mandolin concerto in C, RV 425; Double mandolin concerto in G, RV 532; (Soprano) Lute concerto in D, RV 93; Double concerto in D min. for viola d'amore and lute, RV 540. Trios: in C, RV 82; in G min., RV 85.
*** Hyp. **CDA 66160**; *KA 66160* [id.]. Jeffrey, O'Dette, Parley of Instruments, Goodman and Holman.

These are chamber performances, with one instrument to each part, and this obviously provides an ideal balance for the *Mandolin concertos*. There are other innovations, too. An organ continuo replaces the usual harpsichord, and very effective it is; in the *Trios* and the *Lute concerto* (but not in the *Double concerto*, RV 540) Paul O'Dette uses a gut-strung soprano lute. This means that in passages with the lute doubling the violin, the two instruments play in unison and the effect is piquant, with the lute giving a delicate edge to the more sustained string articulation. The *Double concerto* features a normal baroque lute, and Peter Holman argues the case for the use of these alternatives in his interesting notes. Any practice of this kind is bound to be conjectural, but the delightful sounds here, with all players using original instruments or copies, are very convincing. Certainly the mandolin concertos are more telling (plucked with a plectrum) than they are in guitar transcriptions. The recording is realistically balanced within an attractively spacious acoustic, and the scale is most convincing. There is an excellent tape.

Oboe concertos: in C, RV 446 & RV 452; in D min. (from Op. 8), RV 454; in G for oboe and bassoon, RV 545.
*** Ph. Dig. **411 480-2** [id.]. Holliger, Thunemann, I Musici.

A collection of this kind is self-recommending. Holliger is in superb form, matching his expressive flexibility with infectious bravura in allegros and providing nicely judged ornamentation. All the music is attractively inventive, especially the *Double concerto for oboe and bassoon* which is nicely scored and has a memorable slow movement. The recording is balanced most realistically and sounds especially well in its newest compact disc format.

Piccolo concertos: in C, RV 433; in C min., RV 441; in C, RV 444; in A min., RV 445.
** Denon Dig. **C37 7076** [id.]. Dünschede, augmented Berlin Philh. Qt.

These are chamber performances using modern instruments, and the resonance of the sound adds substance to the accompanying string quintet, plus harpsichord, without in any way blurring inner detail. The playing is eminently musical, tempi are steady, articulation is clean and Hans Wolfgang Dünschede plays expertly and adds judicious ornamentation. But four piccolo concertos in a row is not very good planning, particularly when two are in C major, and the performances have no striking flair to render them individual or give them special charm. Michael Copley's rather similar collection, using recorders – see below – is a much better recommendation.

Recorder concertos: in C min., RV 441; in F, RV 442; in C, RV 443 & RV 444; in A min., RV 445.
*** DG Dig. **415 275-2** [id.]. Copley, Bern Camerata, Füri.

The first two concertos (RV 441–2) are for alto recorder and strings, the remaining three are for an instrument Vivaldi called the *flautino*, which the majority of expert opinion believes to be the sopranino recorder. This plays an octave above the alto recorder. The music is not to be taken at one sitting but, as always with this composer, one is often taken by surprise by the quality and range of the invention. The *F major*, RV 442, is a delight, the material of all three movements deriving from operatic arias written twenty years earlier in the 1720s. The slow movement in particular is quite inspired. These performances by Michael Copley and the Camerata Bern lack nothing in virtuosity and dash; and the recording is excellent in every way, well balanced and truthful in perspective.

Concertos for strings: in D, RV 121; in D min., RV 127; in E min., RV 133; in F, RV 142; in G, RV 145; in G, RV 151; in G min., RV 152; in A min., RV 161; in B flat, RV 166.
*** Ph. **411 035-2** [id.]. I Musici.

There are nine string concertos on this excellent anthology. Although Vivaldi is often thought to be routine, more often than not he is unpredictable and one is surprised by the freshness of his inspiration. The present disc is one such case and finds I Musici in excellent form.

Violin concertos: L'Estro armonico: in A min., Op. 3/6; La Stravaganza: in A, Op. 4/5; in C min. (Il Sospetto), RV 199; in G min., Op. 12/1.
*** HMV Dig. **CDC7 47076-2** [id.]. Perlman, Israel PO.

Virtuoso performances of a representative set of Vivaldi violin concertos, given with Perlman's customary aplomb and effortless virtuosity. Unlike, say, Galway or Rampal in the Op. 10 *Flute concertos*, Perlman scales down the virtuoso display, and those who want sweet modern string-tone and warmth in the slow movements need look no further. The string playing of the Israel Philharmonic is expressive without becoming overladen with sentiment. The only handicap is the somewhat dryish acoustic, a factor that is underlined in the clarity achieved on compact disc, which also lends a trace of hardness in tutti. However, the ear rapidly adjusts, and it is worth stressing that this is not sufficiently disturbing to stand in the way of a strong recommendation.

Violin concertos, Op. 8, Nos 5 in E flat (La Tempesta di mare), RV 253; 6 in C (Il Piacere), RV 180; 10 in B flat (La Caccia), RV 362; 11 in D, RV 210; in C min. (Il Sospetto), RV 199.
*** CfP Dig. *TC-CFP 4522.* Menuhin, Polish CO, Maksymiuk.

Menuhin's collection of five concertos – four of them with nicknames and particularly delightful – brings some of his freshest, most intense playing in recent years. Particularly in slow movements – notably that of *Il Piacere*, ('Pleasure') – he shows afresh his unique insight in shaping a phrase. Fresh, alert accompaniment and full digital recording. The sound on the cassette is admirably wide-ranging and full.

Violin concertos: in E flat (La Tempesta di mare), Op. 8/5, RV 253; in E (L'Amoroso), RV 271; in E min. (Il Favorito), RV 277; in A, RV 253.
*(*) ASV Gaudeamus **CDGAU 105**; *ZCGAU 105* [id.]. Monica Huggett, L. Vivaldi O.

This collection is strictly for confirmed authenticists. Monica Huggett has a justified reputation in this repertoire, but the playing here, with spiky timbres and squeezed phrasing, is charmless, lacking any feeling of Italian sunshine in works that can sound highly beguiling.

Violin concertos: in D min. (Senza cantin), RV 243; in E (Il Riposo), RV 270; in E min. (Il Favorito), RV 277; in F (Per la solennità di San Lorenzo), RV 286.
*** HMV Dig. **CDC7 49320-2** [id.]; (B) *TC-CFP 4536.* Accardo, I Solisti delle Settimane Musicali Internazionali di Napoli.

Salvatore Accardo plays each of the four concertos on this record on different instruments from the collection of the Palazzo Communale, Cremona. He plays the *E major*, *Il Riposo*, on the Niccolo Amati, *Il Favorito* on the Cremonose of 1715, the darker-hued *Concerto senza cantin* (without using the E string) on the Guarnieri del Gesù, and the *Concerto per la solennità di San Lorenzo* on the Andrea Amati of Charles IX of France. But this is more than a record for violin specialists; it offers playing of the highest order by one of the finest violinists of our time. Accardo himself directs the excellent ensemble, and the EMI recording is first class in every respect. A very distinguished record and an essential CD for any Vivaldi collection. The tape quality is dry and clear, but not lacking in bloom. Issued on EMI's cheapest label, the cassette costs about a quarter the price of the CD, yet is a completely acceptable alternative.

Double violin concertos: in C min., RV 509; in D min., RV 514.
** CBS **MK 35133** [id.]. Rampal, Stern, Jerusalem Music Centre CO – TELEMANN: *Suite in A min.***

These arrangements of concertos written for two violins were presumably made for a special occasion when Rampal and Stern joined forces, and then recorded. The playing has plenty of charisma: it is very fast and brilliant, and will give many of the authentic lobby a seizure. Bright recording to match.

Double violin concerto in C min., RV 510; Triple concerto for 2 violins and cello in D min., Op. 3/11; Quadruple violin concerto in D, Op. 3/1.
** HMV Dig. **CDC7 47900-2** [id.]. Yehudi Menuhin, Hu Kun, Mi-Kyung Li, Vassallo, Camerata Lysy Gstaad – BACH: *Double concerto* etc.**

Three multiple string concertos by Vivaldi make an attractive coupling for Bach concertos on the reverse. With Menuhin the most persuasive leader, the performances are fresh and understanding if not immaculate, but suffer from a disagreeable dryness of sound, unflattering to all.

Triple concerto for 2 violins and cello in C min. (San Lorenzo), RV 556.
(*) ASV Dig. **CDCOE 803; *ZCCOE 803* [id.]. COE, Schneider – BACH: *Double concerto*; MOZART: *Sinfonia concertante*.**(*)

Vivaldi's *San Lorenzo concerto* for two violins and cello makes an attractive makeweight for the two other multiple concertos on the Chamber Orchestra of Europe's disc. In a performance recorded live at St John's, Smith Square, the outer movements are inflated in scale but bring winningly resilient playing.

Double concerto for violin and oboe in G min., RV 576; Violin concerto in D (per la S.S.ma Assontione di Maria Vergine), RV 582.
(*) Ph. Dig. **411 466-2 [id.]. Holliger, Kremer, ASMF – BACH: *Double concerto* and *Sinfonia*.***

As in the Bach coupling, Holliger dominates the performance of the *Double concerto*, especially in the slow movement, where Kremer's timbre is expressively less expansive. But Kremer comes into his own in the delightful *D major concerto*, showing Vivaldi at his most inspired and imaginative. This features a double orchestra in the accompaniment sometimes used antiphonally and, although the effects are well brought off here, the stereo separation is not as clear as might have been expected. Otherwise the sound, clear and resonant, is finely judged; Kremer's sparkling articulation in the allegros is balanced by his serenely beautiful playing in the delicate cantilena of the central *Largo*.

MISCELLANEOUS CONCERTO COLLECTIONS

Bassoon concerto in A min., RV 498; Cello concerto in C min., RV 401; Oboe concerto in F, RV 455; Concerto for strings in A, RV 158; Violin concerto in E min., RV 278; Concerto for 2 violins and 2 cellos, RV 575.
*** Novalis Dig. **150 016-21**; *150 106-4* [id.]. Camerata Bern.

The majority of the concertos on this disc are not otherwise available and most of them are highly inventive. The Camerata Bern is an excellent ensemble, playing on modern instruments with great expertise and a sure sense of style. There is some particularly good playing from the bassoon soloist in the *A minor Concerto*, RV 498; but throughout the disc there is much to divert and delight the listener, and there is no cause for complaint so far as the recording is concerned.

Basson concerto in E min., RV 484; Flute concerto in G, RV 436; Concerto for oboe and bassoon in G, RV 545; Concerto for strings in A, RV 159; Concerto for viola d'amore and lute in D min., RV 540; Violin concerto in E (L'Amoroso), RV 271.
*** DG Dig. **419 615-2**; *419 615-4* [id.]. Soloists, E. Concert, Pinnock.

Entitled '*L'Amoroso*' after the fine *E major Violin concerto* which is one of the six varied concertos on the disc, this collection brings lively, refreshing performances with fine solo playing from wind and string players alike using period instruments in the most enticing way. *L'Amoroso* itself is almost too vigorous in its outer movements, but the variety of Vivaldi is what is consistently established, totally contradicting the old idea that he wrote just one concerto hundreds of times over. The *Concerto for oboe and bassoon* is particularly engaging. The recording is well balanced within a pleasingly warm acoustic. There is also a very good cassette.

(i) *Bassoon concerto in E min., RV 584;* (ii) *Double horn concerto in F, RV 539;* (iii) *Double trumpet concerto in D, RV 537; Concerto for 2 violins, 2 cellos in D, RV 564;* (iv) *Concerto for 2 violins and lute, RV 93.*
*(*) Erato Dig. **ECD 88009** [id.]. (i) Allard; (ii) Magnardi, Both; (iii) Touvron, Boisson; (iv) Hubscher (lute), Sol. Ven., Scimone.

A disappointing collection, often lacking in vitality. The most characterful of the soloists is Maurice Allard (bassoon) whose woody timbre is attractive; he finds a nice balance between geniality and lyricism. The two string concertos are also well done, with plenty of antiphonal interplay; much use is made of echo phrasing. The string soloists are drawn from the orchestra, while Jürgen Hubscher's lute adds an extra constituent to RV 93. The 1981 recording does not provide the presence and inner definition one would expect from a digital master, though it is naturally balanced.

Cello concerto in B min., RV 424; Oboe concerto in A min., RV 461; Double concerto in C min. for oboe and violin, RV Anh.17; Violin concerto in D, RV 208; Sinfonia in B min., RV 169; Sonata à 4 in E flat for 2 violins, viola and continuo, RV 130.
(M) ** Tel. **ZS8 43630** [id.]. Soloists, Concerto Amsterdam, Schröder.

There is an element of too much rectitude here, and the forward balance seems to emphasize the somewhat stiff approach, although allegros are alert and lively. The recording readily captures the robust and somewhat pungent timbres, and those who favour Vivaldi played on baroque instruments will certainly find the sound faithful; the digital remastering is clean without loss of ambience, and the 1978 analogue recording sounds quite modern.

Double cello concerto in G min., RV 531; Double flute concerto in C, RV 533; Concertos for strings in D min. (Madrigalesco), RV 129; in G (Alla rustica), RV 151; Double trumpet concerto in C, RV 537; Concerto for 2 violins and 2 cellos in D, RV 564.
*** O-L **414 588-2** [id.]. AAM, Hogwood.

Not everything in this issue is of equal substance: the invention in the *Double trumpet concerto*, for example, is not particularly strong; but for the most part it is a rewarding and varied programme. It is especially appealing in that authenticity is allied to musical spontaneity. The best-known concertos are the *Madrigalesco* and the *Alla rustica*, but some of the others are just as captivating. The *Concerto for two flutes* has great charm and is dispatched with vigour and aplomb. Readers with an interest in this often unexpectedly rewarding composer, whose unpredictability continues to astonish, should not hesitate. Performances and recording alike are first rate, with added clarity and presence on CD.

(i) *Flute concerto in F (La Tempesta di mare), Op. 10/1;* (ii) *Oboe concertos: in C (from Op. 8/12), RV 449; in D min., RV 454;* (i) *Recorder concerto in C, RV 444; Concertos for strings: in D min., RV 127; in A, RV 158.*
(*) Chan. Dig. **CHAN 8444; *ABTD 1156* [id.]. (i) Hutchins, (ii) Baskin; I Musici di Montreal, Turovsky.

I Musici di Montreal is a Canadian group that has been working under its present conductor since the autumn of 1983. They are recorded in the resonant acoustic of St Madeleine's Church, Montreal, and the balance produces a fresh bright sound from the fourteen strings, just a shade lacking in body. Their spirited musicianship brings plenty of life to the two attractive string concertos, while the rather beautiful *Largo* of the *A major*, RV 158, enjoys a nicely judged expressive response. The programme opens buoyantly with Timothy Hutchins's brilliant account of *La Tempesta di mare*, expertly presented on a sopranino recorder; but the highlight of the concert is the pair of oboe concertos, beautifully played by Theodore Baskin. Like Hutchins, he is a principal of the Montreal Symphony. Readers who possess Dutoit's Montreal Ravel recordings will not be surprised to discover that he is a superb soloist in every respect. His articulation of allegros is a delight, while phrasing in slow movements combines elegance and finesse with a stylish approach to ornamentation. The recording places him realistically in relation to the accompaniment; allowing for the reverberation, the sound is first class.

Flute concerto in G min. (La Notte), Op. 10/2, RV 439; Concertos for strings: in D min. (Madrigalesco), RV 129; in G (Alla rustica), RV 151; Violin concertos: in D (L'Inquietudine), RV 234; in E (L'Amoroso), RV 271; Double violin concerto in A, RV 523; Sinfonia in B min. (Al Santo Sepolcro), RV 169.
(M) **(*) DG **423 226-2**; *423 226-4* [id.]. Soloists, BPO, Karajan.

This collection dates from 1971 (except for the *Flute concerto*, which was recorded a decade later) and shows Karajan indulging himself in repertoire which he clearly loves but for which he does not have the stylistic credentials. Yet the sheer charisma of the playing and the glorious body of tone the orchestra creates within a resonant acoustic, notably in the extraordinary *Sinfonia al Santo Sepolcro*, is difficult to resist. The orchestra dominates even the solo concertos and the soloists seem to float, concertante style, within the resonantly glowing ambience. The refinement of execution is remarkable and all the music comes to life, if in an inflated way. The remastered sound is bright and takes an initial adjustment for it is not quite natural, but if this music making is perhaps too sweet for frequent repetition, it is a considerable and unique listening experience, a Vivaldi record like no other.

(i) *Flute concerto in D (Il Cardellino), Op. 10/3; Triple violin concerto in F, RV 551.*
*(*) Denon Dig. **C37 7178** [id.]. Susan Milan; Lucerne Fest. Strings, Baumgartner MOZART: *Divertimento, K.138* etc.*(*)

Recorded very realistically in the attractive ambience of the new Symphony Hall in Osaka, Baumgartner and his group give eminently musical accounts of these two concertos. However, the German manner in Vivaldi is not always totally convincing, and in the slow movement of the *Flute concerto* the soloist's phrasing seems very deliberate. Acceptable, but not really distinctive, in spite of the excellent sound.

Double flute concerto in C, RV 533; Double oboe concerto in D min., RV 535; Double horn concerto in F, RV 539; Double trumpet concerto in C, RV 537; Concerto for 2 oboes, 2 clarinets and strings, RV 560.
(M) **(*) Pickwick Dig. **PCD 811**. Soloists, Scottish CO, Laredo.

An attractive mid-priced compilation, with soloists and orchestra set back in good perspective in a believable acoustic. The resonance tends to make the trumpet timbre spread, but otherwise the sound is very good. The solo playing is accomplished, although rather more light and shade between phrases would have made the performances even more enticing, while Jaime Laredo's direction of the slow movements is not especially imaginative. But there is some highly engaging music here, not least the outer movements of RV 560 where the sounds of oboes and clarinets chatter in alternation like excited children chasing each other. In RV 539, the horn playing is robust; while modern instruments are used, the effect is not over-sophisticated, though remaining secure.

Double flute concerto in C, RV 533; Double horn concerto in F, RV 539; Double mandolin concerto in G, RV 536; Double oboe concerto in A min., RV 536; Concerto for oboe and bassoon in G, RV 545; Double trumpet concerto in D, RV 563.
*** Ph. Dig. **412 892-2** [id.]. Soloists, ASMF, Marriner.

This collection repeats the success of the Academy's recordings of Vivaldi wind concertos made in the late 1970s for Argo. Apart from the work for two horns, where the focus of the soloists lacks a degree of sharpness, the recording often reaches demonstration standard. On CD, the concerto featuring a pair of mandolins is particularly tangible, with the balance near perfect, the solo instruments in proper scale yet registering admirable detail. The concertos for flutes and oboes are played with engaging finesse, conveying a sense of joy in the felicity of the writing. Throughout, the accompaniments are characteristically polished and especially imaginative in their use of light and shade in alternating phrases. In this respect the music making here is of a different calibre from the Scottish collection on Pickwick – see above – but, as it happens, only two of the concertos are duplicated. Once again Marriner makes a very good case for the use of modern wind instruments in this repertoire.

Double mandolin concerto in G, RV 532; Oboe concertos: in A min., RV 461; in B flat, RV 548; Concertos for strings: in G (Alla rustica), RV 151; in C (con molti stromenti), RV 558; Double violin concerto in G, RV 516.
*** DG Dig. **415 674-2**; *415 674-4* [id.]. Soloists, E. Concert, Pinnock.

Taking its title, '*Alla rustica*', from the charming little *G major Concerto*, RV 151, with its drone in the finale, this collection of six varied Vivaldi concertos finds Pinnock and the English Concert at their liveliest and most refreshing. Outstanding in a nicely balanced programme is the *C major Concerto*, RV 558, involving an astonishing array of concertino instruments including two violins (curiously labelled *in tromba marina*) and pairs of recorders, mandolins and theorbos, plus one cello. Excellent recording, giving a most realistic impression on CD. The high-level chrome cassette is impressive too, though textures are not quite so clean and free.

Double concerto for oboe and violin in B flat, RV 548; Triple concerto in C for violin, oboe and organ, RV 554; Double concertos for violin and organ: in D min., RV 541; in C min. & F, RV 766–7.
*** Unicorn Dig. **DKPCD 9050**; *DKPC 9050* [id.]. Francis, Studt, Bate, Tate Music Group, Studt.

An engaging clutch of concertos, two of which (RV 766–7) are first recordings. The works featuring the organ in a concertante role are in the concerto grosso tradition and are notable for their imaginative juxtaposition of colours – which is not to say that they lack vitality of invention. The highlight is RV 541 with its fine *Grave* slow movement and exhilaratingly busy finale, while the *Double concerto for oboe* (in the ascendant role) *and violin* is hardly less engaging, and offers some captivating oboe playing from Richard Studt, whose timbre seems exactly right for this repertoire. The recording is very attractive in ambience and the balance is admirable, with the sound first class in both media – the chrome cassette is outstandingly realistic.

Concertos for strings: in D min. (Concerto madrigalesco), RV 129; in G (Alla rustica), RV 151; in

G min., RV 157. (i) Motet: *In turbato mare irato, RV 627;* Cantata: *Lungi dal vago volto, RV 680. Magnificat, RV 610.*
*** Hyp. Dig. **CDA 66247**; *KA 66247* [id.]. (i) Kirkby, Leblanc, Forget, Cunningham, Ingram, Tafelmusik Ch. & Bar. O, Lamon.

Mingling vocal and instrumental items, and works both well-known and unfamiliar, Jean Lamon provides a delightful collection, with Emma Kirkby a sparkling, pure-toned soloist in two items never recorded before: the motet, *In turbato mare irato*, and the chamber cantata, *Lungi dal vago volto*. The *Magnificat* comes in the second of the three versions, for double chorus with strings and oboes. The performance is lively, with fresh choral sound. The Tafelmusik performers come from Canada, and though the use of period instruments has some roughness, the vigour and alertness amply make up for that. Good, clear recorded sound on CD; the cassette is less sharply focused in the vocal music, but still fully acceptable.

VOCAL MUSIC

Beatus vir, RV 597; Dixit dominus, RV 594.
*** Argo Dig. **414 495-2** [id.]. Buchanan, Jennifer Smith, Watts, Partridge, Shirley-Quirk, King's College Ch., ECO, Cleobury.

When discussing this issue in *Gramophone*, the reviewer, Nicholas Anderson, recalled the mono LP début of this setting of *Beatus vir*, conducted on Vox by the late Hans Grischat. We remember it too, and especially the discovery of Vivaldi's magically gleaming phrase on the trebles with which the piece opens so memorably. Those were the days when the gramophone was just beginning to reveal the genius and diversity of a composer whose music had lain largely unperformed for well over two centuries. In the early 1950s even *The Four Seasons* was fresh to most ears, and there was so much else to come; nothing, however, more refreshing than these two delightfully spontaneous and original psalm settings. *Dixit dominus* cannot fail to attract those who have enjoyed the better-known *Gloria*. Both works are powerfully inspired and are here given vigorous and sparkling performances with King's College Choir in excellent form under its latest choirmaster. The soloists are a fine team, fresh, stylish and nimble – for much of the florid music calls for technical bravura – and the reverberant recording remains atmospheric, without detail becoming clouded. There is plenty of clean articulation from the choristers, nicely projected, especially in the CD format, with its extra sharpness of definition.

Motets: *Canto in prato, RV 623; In furore giustissimae irae, RV 626; Longa mala umbrae tertores, RV 640; Vos aurae per montes (per la solennita di S.Antonio), RV 634.*
*** Erato Dig. **ECD 88094**; *NUM 75181* [id.]. Cecilia Gasdia, Sol. Ven., Scimone.

Though the booklet for this collection of Vivaldi rarities fails to provide texts for these four solo motets, they make a delightful collection, also displaying the formidable talent of a rising star among Italian sopranos, Cecilia Gasdia. Vivaldi's solo motets might be described structurally as concertos for voice, but generally with a recitative between first movement and slow movement. *Canto in prato* is the exception, with three jolly, rustic allegros in succession. Lively performances and well-balanced recording.

Dixit dominus, RV 594; Gloria in D, RV 589.
*** DG Dig. **423 386-2** [id.]. Argenta, Attrot, Denley, Stafford, Varcoe, E. Concert & Ch., Pinnock.

Pinnock's versions of the better-known of Vivaldi's two settings of the *Gloria* and the grander of his two settings of the psalm, *Dixit dominus* (the one for double chorus), make an attractive and strong coupling. His fresh, vigorous performances, beautifully recorded, add impressively to his developing reputation as a choral conductor on record, with first-rate playing and singing.

Introduzione al Gloria, RV 642; Gloria, RV 589; Lauda Jerusalem, RV 609; Laudate pueri, RV 602; Laudate Dominum, RV 606; Nisi Dominus, RV 608.
*** Ph. **420 648-2** [id.]. Soloists, John Alldis Ch., ECO, Negri.

These recordings were made in the late 1970s and were first included in the Vivaldi Edition of which we wrote with some enthusiasm in our 1982 *Guide*. It is good to have some performances on modern instruments and to reaffirm that style does not depend on the means but springs from imaginative musicianship. The performances under the direction of Vittorio Negri, for long a Philips producer, are vital, intelligent and sensitive. The music itself is of high quality and the recordings still sound admirable. There is a warmth about this music that is likeable and it is good to see that other transfers from the eight-LP set are planned.

Gloria in D, RV 589.
*** O-L **414 678-2** [id.]. Nelson, Watkinson, Christ Church Cathedral Ch., AAM, Preston – BACH: *Magnificat.****
(M) **(*) Decca *417 457-4* [id.]. Vaughan, J. Baker, King's College Ch., ASMF, Willcocks – BACH: *Magnificat.***(*)

The freshness and point of the Christ Church performance of the *Gloria* are irresistible; anyone who normally doubts the attractiveness of authentic string technique should sample this, for the absence of vibrato adds a tang exactly in keeping with the performance. The soloists too keep vibrato to the minimum, adding to the freshness, yet Carolyn Watkinson rivals even Dame Janet Baker in the dark intensity of the Bach-like central aria for contralto, *Domine Deus, Agnus Dei*. The choristers of Christ Church Cathedral excel themselves and the recording is outstandingly fine.

The Willcocks version, with small forces, is very stylish and the soloists include Dame Janet Baker on very good form. A very acceptable tape alternative, well coupled with Bach.

Gloria in D, RV 588; Gloria in D, RV 589.
*** Argo Dig. **410 018-2** [id.]. Russell, Kwella, Wilkens, Bowen, St John's College, Cambridge, Ch., Wren O, Guest.

The two settings of the *Gloria* make an apt and illuminating coupling. Both in D major, they have many points in common, presenting fascinating comparisons, when RV 588 is as inspired as its better-known companion. Guest directs strong and well-paced readings, with RV 588 the more lively. Good, warm recording to match the performances. On compact disc the added clarity is never clinical in sharpening detail, and the ambient atmosphere is most appealing.

Gloria in D, RV 589; Kyrie, RV 587 and Credo, R 591; Magnificat, RV 610.
*** Erato **ECD 88070** [id.]. Jennifer Smith, Staempfli, Rossier, Schaer, Lausanne Vocal & Instrumental Ens., Corboz.

Michel Corboz, a fine choral conductor, gives a lively performance of the *Gloria*, and his version is aptly coupled with three other richly rewarding liturgical settings by Vivaldi. The *Magnificat* is given in its simpler first version, on a relatively small scale with the chorus singing the alto solo, *Fecit potentiam*. The *Kyrie* with its double chorus and double string orchestra, plus four soloists, makes a fine contrast in its magnificence. This is very welcome as the first in a whole series of Vivaldi's choral music. The professional singers of the Lausanne choir are generally admirable, and the soloists are sweet-toned. Good, clear recording, well transferred to CD. The disc plays for over 70′.

Gloria in D, RV 589; Magnificat, RV 611.
** HMV **CDC7 47990-2** [id.]. Berganza, Valentini-Terrani, New Philh. Ch. & O, Muti.

Muti offers the more expansive version of the *Magnificat*, including extended solo arias. His approach, both in the *Magnificat* and in the *Gloria*, is altogether blander than the more authentic style adopted by Preston and Guest, let alone Pinnock. Muti's expansiveness undoubtedly suits the larger-scaled *Magnificat* better than the *Gloria*, which lacks incisiveness. The 1977 analogue recording has been effectively remastered, the freshening not interfering with the ambient effect; but the acoustics do not present the clearest sound-image for the chorus, although the soloists are well projected.

Laudate pueri dominum, RV 601; Nisi Dominus, RV 608.
*** Mer. Dig. **CDE 84129**; *KE 77129* [id.]. Lynne Dawson, Christopher Robson, King's Consort, Robert King.

There are in all four Vivaldi settings of Psalm 113, *Laudate pueri dominum*, two of them for soloists and chorus and orchestra. The present setting, RV 601, is a strong work whose inspiration runs at a consistently high level, and the performance by Lynne Dawson with the King's Consort, a period-instrument group, is very accomplished. Dawson sings with an excellent sense of style and she is given splendid support. Vivaldi is so prolific and the inventive diversity of his best work is much underrated. The coupling, the *Nisi Dominus*, a setting of Psalm 126, is much better known but makes an attractive makeweight. It is also given an excellent performance by Christopher Robson. Good recording.

(i) *Nisi Dominus (Psalm 126), RV 608; Stabat Mater, RV 621; Concerto for strings in G min., RV 153.*
(*) O-L Dig. **414 329-2 [id.]. AAM, Hogwood; (i) with Bowman.

These performances are vital enough and there is no want of stylistic awareness. James Bowman is a persuasive soloist. But since Vivaldi probably wrote these for the Pietà, a Venetian orphanage for girls, readers might prefer to wait for Helen Watts in the *Nisi Dominus*, as her beautiful Erato version is not yet available on compact disc. The *Concerto* is an engaging work whose charms benefit from the authentic instruments. The CD is altogether excellent; the sound is marvellously fresh and present.

OPERA

Catone in Utica (partially complete).
*(*) Erato Dig. **ECD 88142** (2) [id.]. Gasdia, Schmiege, Zimmermann, Lendi, Palaccio, Sol. Ven., Scimone.

When so few Vivaldi operas have been recorded, it is disappointing that this set can be given only a limited recommendation. It is a curious choice, when the first Act is missing, and the other two Acts are not as musically rich as other Vivaldi operas. Cecilia Gasdia sings impressively, and Scimone conducts a fair, middle-of-the-road interpretation, but more is needed if the cause of the music is to be argued effectively. Good sound.

L'Incoronazione di Dario (complete).
(*) HM Dig. **HMC 901235/7 [id.]. Elwes, Lesne, Ledroit, Verschaeve, Poulenard, Mellon, Visse, Nice Bar. Ens., Bezzina.

Set in the fifth century BC at the Persian court, this Vivaldi opera involves the conflict which followed the death of King Cyrus and the succession of Darius. Written in 1717, it is one of

Vivaldi's earlier operas, in places reflecting the great oratorio he had written the year before, *Juditha triumphans*, reworking three numbers. The opera here receives a lively performance, generally well sung. John Elwes as Darius himself, though stylish, does not sound as involved as some of the others, notably the male alto, Dominique Visse, who is superb both vocally and dramatically as the female confidante, Flora. Reliable singing from the whole cast, and first-rate recording. The full libretto is provided only in Italian, with translated summaries of the plot in English, French and German.

Orlando Furioso (complete).
*** Erato **ECD 88190** (3) [id.]. Horne, De los Angeles, Valentini-Terrani, Gonzales, Kozma, Bruscantini, Zaccaria, Sol. Ven., Scimone.

Though the greater part of this opera consists of recitative – with only fifteen arias included on the three discs, plus one for Orlando borrowed from a chamber cantata – it presents a fascinating insight into this totally neglected area of Vivaldi's work. Scimone has heavily rearranged the order of items as well as cutting many, but, with stylish playing and excellent recording, it is a set well worth a Vivaldi enthusiast's attention. Outstanding in a surprisingly star-studded cast is Marilyn Horne in the title role, rich and firm of tone, articulating superbly in divisions, notably in the hero's two fiery arias. In the role of Angelica, Victoria de los Angeles has many sweetly lyrical moments, and though Lucia Valentini-Terrani is less strong as Alcina, she gives an aptly clean, precise performance. The remastering has somewhat freshened a recording which was not outstanding in its analogue LP form, and a good booklet with translation is provided with the CD set.

Wagner, Richard (1813–83)

Overtures: Die Feen; Der fliegende Holländer; Tannhäuser (with *Bacchanale*).
** Ph. Dig. **400 089-2** [id.]. Concg. O, De Waart.

The special interest here is the rarely heard (and rarely recorded) *Die Feen overture*, written, when Wagner was twenty, for his first completed opera (see below). It is agreeable music, cast in the same melodic mould as *Rienzi*, if less rumbustious in feeling. All the performances here are warmly spacious, lacking something in electricity (the *Flying Dutchman* – which uses the original ending – sounds too cultured). The digital recording faithfully reflects the acoustic of the Concertgebouw, with its richly textured strings and brass, and resonant lower range; but some listeners might feel a need for a more telling upper range.

Overtures: Polonia: Rule Britannia. Marches: Grosser Festmarsch; Kaisermarsch.
*(*) Marco Polo **HK 8220114** [id.]. Hong Kong PO, Kojian.

The *Polonia overture* (1836) is the best piece here. Although its basic style is Weberian, there is a hint of the Wagner of *Rienzi* in the slow introduction. The *Grosser Festmarsch* (*American Centennial march*) was commissioned from Philadelphia, and for this inflated piece Wagner received a cool five thousand dollars! The *Rule Britannia overture* is even more overblown and the famous tune, much repeated, outstays its welcome. The *Kaisermarsch* is also empty and loud. The Hong Kong orchestra play all this with great enthusiasm, if without much finesse. The recording is vividly bright, but on CD it is not a priority item, even for the most dedicated Wagnerian.

Siegfried idyll.
*** DG **419 196-2** (2) [id.]. BPO, Karajan – BRUCKNER: *Symphony No. 8.****

*** Decca Dig. **410 111-2** [id.]. ECO, Ashkenazy – SCHOENBERG: *Verklaerte Nacht.***(*)
*** Ph. **412 465-2** (2) [id.]. Concg. O, Haitink – BRUCKNER: *Symphony No. 8.****
(*) CBS **M2K 42036 (2) [id.]. Columbia SO, Walter – BRUCKNER: *Symphony No. 7.**(*)

Karajan's account of Wagner's wonderful birthday present to Cosima is unsurpassed and is available coupled with Bruckner's *Eighth*. Ashkenazy makes a fine alternative, bringing out the honeyed warmth of Wagner's domestic inspiration, its flow of melodies and textures caressing the ear. Warm, full recording to match the playing, especially on compact disc.

Haitink gives a simple, unaffected reading and draws playing of great refinement from the Concertgebouw Orchestra. Like Karajan's version this has a simplicity of expression and a tenderness that will leave few listeners unmoved. The sound is first class, with the 1980 analogue recording most successfully remastered.

Walter's is essentially a gentle performance; the opening is quite lovely, and though the 1963 recording loses just a little of its bloom at the climax – which has no lack of ardour – the rapt quality of the closing ritenuto is magical, with the ambience just right for the music.

Siegfried idyll. Der fliegende Holländer: Overture; Lohengrin: Preludes to Acts I and III; Die Meistersinger: Overture.
*** DG Dig. **419 169-2**; *419 169-4* [id.]. NYPO, Sinopoli.

Superbly spacious performances from Sinopoli with *Der fliegende Holländer* seeming less melodramatic than usual, yet played with free rubato in the most effective way. The emotional arch of the *Lohengrin* Act I *Prelude* is superbly graduated with the New York violins finding radiant tone for the closing pianissimo. *Die Meistersinger* is massively stately, helped by the full reverberation of the Performing Arts Centre at Purchase, New York State University. Sinopoli opens and closes the *Siegfried idyll* with the greatest delicacy, and the end is wonderfully serene and romantic; the middle section is fast and volatile, moving to its climax with passionate thrust. Nothing Sinopoli does is without imaginative grip and this concert is a fine example of his most charismatic music-making. The cassette is even more sumptuous than the disc.

Siegfried idyll; Rienzi: Overture; Tannhäuser: Overture and Venusberg music.
(*) Eurodisc **257 845 [id.]. Bamberg SO, Horst Stein (with chorus).

If *Rienzi* has had more unbuttoned performance elsewhere, here the polish and sophistication of the Bambergers brings a mellower and equally attractive view. Stein gives a powerful account of the Paris version of *Tannhäuser* with the chorus refined yet sensuous in the *Venusberg music*. The *Siegfried idyll* offers beautiful, cultured string playing, with the central climax like a summer storm then relaxing into an agreeable languor, gently romantic in feeling. The sound is warm and naturally balanced, lacking something in detail. But there is no documentation at all with this CD, just music titles!

Siegfried idyll; Tristan und Isolde: Prelude and Liebestod: Die Walküre: (i) *Act I, scene iii; Act II: Ride of the Valkyries.*
(***) RCA mono **RD 84751 [RCA 5751-2-RC]**. (i) Helen Traubel, Lauritz Melchior, NBC SO, Toscanini.

It is sad that Toscanini never recorded a Wagner opera complete. Despite harsh, limited mono recording, this CD makes it clear just how incandescent were the Toscanini performances of Wagner and how, with his ear for balance, he brought brightness and transparency to the scores. It is good that CD has restored to currency long-buried historic recordings like these, featuring two of the finest Wagner singers of their time.

ORCHESTRAL EXCERPTS FROM THE OPERAS

Der fliegende Holländer: Overture. Götterdämmerung: Dawn and Siegfried's Rhine journey; Funeral march; Finale, Act III. Die Meistersinger: Overture. Siegfried: Forest murmurs. Tristan und Isolde: Prelude and Liebestod. Die Walküre: Ride of the Valkyries.
(B) *(*) DG Dig. *419 847-4* [id.]. O de Paris, Barenboim.

Barenboim provides here a useful collection of orchestral items including the *Ring* excerpts which he recorded in 1984 before his appearances conducting the *Ring* cycle. The snag is that the Paris orchestra – particularly the brass section, with its excessive vibrato – does not sound authentic, and the recording acoustic is not helpful, failing to give the necessary resonance to the deeper brass sounds. The cassette transfer, with its very bright upper range and somewhat dry bass, tends to emphasize this disparity.

Der fliegende Holländer: Overture. Götterdämmerung: Siegfried's Rhine journey. Die Meistersinger: Overture. Rienzi: Overture.
** Telarc **CD 80083** [id.]. Minnesota SO, Marriner.

Marriner is at his best in the earlier overtures and notably in *Rienzi*, played with plenty of spirit, with the Minneapolis Hall adding richness and bloom. However, in *Die Meistersinger*, while the effect is agreeably spacious, the contrapuntal detail in the middle section is clouded in a way one does not expect in a digital recording. The overall perspective is truthful, but the muddying of the resonance is not ideal. *Siegfried's Rhine journey* is very well played, but is in no way distinctive.

Der fliegende Holländer: Overture. Lohengrin: Prelude to Act I. Die Meistersinger: Overture. (i) *Tannhäuser: Overture and Venusberg music.*
*** CBS **MK 42050** [id.]. Columbia SO, Bruno Walter, (i) with Occidental College Ch.

These performances all date from 1959. When the *Tannhäuser Overture and Venusberg music* was first issued at the beginning of the 1960s, we described it – in an early edition of the *Stereo Record Guide* – as one of Walter's greatest recordings. The years have not diminished its impact. The poise of the opening of the *Pilgrim's chorus* is arresting, and the reprise of this famous melody, before the introduction of the Venusberg section, is wonderfully gentle. With the central section thrillingly sensuous, the closing pages – the Occidental College Choir distantly balanced – bring a radiant hush. In digitally remastered form, the recording is most impressive. The sound in the *Flying Dutchman* and the *Mastersinger* overtures is fiercer in the upper range and, ideally, the latter could do with more amplitude; but the performances are mellowed by the conductor's spacious approach. The detail in the fugato middle section of *Die Meistersinger* is characteristically affectionate, and all the threads are satisfyingly drawn together in the expansive closing pages. The *Lohengrin Prelude* is rather relaxed, but beautifully controlled. With fine orchestral playing throughout, this stands among the most rewarding of all available compilations of Wagnerian orchestral excerpts.

Der fliegende Holländer: Overture. Lohengrin: Preludes, Acts I & III. Rienzi: Overture. Tristan und Isolde: Prelude and Liebestod.
(*) HMV **CDC7 47254-2 [id.]. Philh. O, Klemperer.

It is good to have Klemperer's view of Wagner. Most of the performances here and on the companion issue have the kind of incandescent glow found only in the interpretations of really great conductors, and the Philharmonia plays immaculately. But judged by the highest standards Klemperer falls just a degree short, and the *Tristan Prelude and Liebestod* does not have the sense of wonder that Toscanini brought, though the feeling of ennobled passion at its climax cannot fail to communicate. Throughout there is never any doubt that one is in the presence of a great conductor and no one could complain about the lack of zest in the *Lohengrin Prelude to Act III*. The remastered recording is drier and cleaner, but still reasonably expansive.

Der fliegende Holländer: Overture. Lohengrin: Prelude to Act III. Die Meistersinger: Overture. Rienzi: Overture. Tannhäuser: Overture. Die Walküre: Ride of the Valkyries.
(M) ** Pickwick Dig. **PCD 860** [MCA **MCAD 25968**]. LSO, Tuckwell.

An enjoyable concert, well played and given excellent modern digital recording. This is value for money, but the performances, although polished and not lacking spontaneity, are in no way distinctive.

Der fliegende Holländer: Overture. Lohengrin: Preludes to Acts I & III. Tristan und Isolde: Prelude and Liebestod.
(*) DG **413 733-2 [id.]. VPO, Boehm.

This companion to Boehm's earlier collection of Wagner overtures and preludes (see below) follows very much the same spacious pattern, with speeds broad rather than urgent. Not all the balances seem quite natural, but sound quality is not one's first concern in one of Boehm's last records. However, although the CD transfers are successful, this is not especially generous measure.

Overtures: Der fliegende Holländer; Die Meistersinger; Tannhäuser (original version). *Tristan und Isolde: Prelude and Liebestod.*
(M) **(*) Decca **417 752-2** [id.]. Chicago SO, Solti.

A quite attractive collection of Wagner overtures, very well played. Except for the *Flying Dutchman overture*, these are newly made recordings, not taken from Solti's complete opera sets. So this is the self-contained *Tannhäuser overture* from the Dresden version, and the *Liebestod* comes in the purely orchestral version. Perhaps surprisingly, comparison between Solti in Chicago and Solti in Vienna shows him warmer in America. The compact disc has been digitally remastered and emphasizes the different recording balances: *Fliegende Holländer* very brightly lit, *Die Meistersinger* appropriately mellower, *Tannhäuser* somewhat two-dimensional, and *Tristan* the most effective, with an impressive ambience. Overall, however, this is not a compilation to show any striking advantages from CD remastering.

Der fliegende Holländer: Overture. Die Meistersinger: Overture. (i) *Tannhäuser: Overture and Venusberg music. Tristan: Prelude and Liebestod.*
(M) *** HMV **CDM7 69019-2** [id.]; *EG 769019-4*. BPO, Karajan; (i) with German Op. Ch.

This mid-priced collection is assembled from two LPs quadraphonically recorded by Karajan in 1975, one slightly more successful than the other in terms of electricity and excitement. All the music is superbly played, but the *Overture and Venusberg music* from *Tannhäuser* (Paris version, using chorus) and the *Prelude and Liebestod* from *Tristan* are superb. In the *Liebestod* the climactic culmination is overwhelming in its sentient power, while *Tannhäuser* has comparable spaciousness and grip. There is an urgency and edge to *The Flying Dutchman overture*, and *Die Meistersinger* has weight and dignity, but the last degree of tension is missing. Moreover, the digitally remastered sound produces a touch of fierceness in the upper range of these pieces; the *Tannhäuser* and *Tristan* excerpts are fuller, though some of the original bloom has gone. But the glorious playing of the Berlin orchestra still ensures a firm recommendation at mid-price.

Götterdämmerung: Dawn and Siegfried's Rhine journey; Funeral march. Lohengrin: Preludes to Acts I & III. Die Meistersinger: Overture; Dance of the apprentices. Die Walküre: Ride of the Valkyries.
(B) *** CfP Dig. **CD-CFP 9008**; *TC-CFP 41 4412-4*. LPO, Rickenbacher.

Karl Anton Rickenbacher, formerly principal conductor with the BBC Scottish Symphony Orchestra, here makes an impressive recording début. He secures first-class playing from the LPO with the strings at their peak in the radiant opening of the *Lohengrin Prelude* and the brilliantly articulated scalic passage at the opening of the *Dance of the apprentices*. This is chosen – rather ineffectively – to end the concert, but this is the only real criticism of a first-rate bargain collection. Rickenbacher's tempi are far from stoically Teutonic and he presses the music on convincingly, yet retains a sense of breadth. Some might feel his pacing of the *Die Meistersinger overture* is fractionally fast. The CD improves remarkably on the sound of the original LP: the sound is firmer and fuller, with a more expansive bass response; indeed the *Prelude to Act III* of *Lohengrin* makes a splendid demonstration recording; an exciting performance, particularly vividly projected.

Götterdämmerung: Siegfried's Rhine journey; Siegfried's funeral march. Die Meistersinger: Overture; Dance of the apprentices; Entry of the masters. Parsifal: Prelude. Das Rheingold: Entry of the gods into Valhalla. Siegfried: Forest murmurs. Die Walküre: Ride of the Valkyries.
(*) HMV **CDC7 47255-2 [id.]. Philh. O, Klemperer.

The second of the CDs compiled from Klemperer's Wagner recordings offers characteristically spacious music-making, with the superbly played *Parsifal Prelude* a highlight. The *Ride of the Valkyries* without the concert coda ends rather abruptly and in the other items, although the orchestral playing is peerless, the level of tension is more variable. But Klemperer's readings are always solidly concentrated, even if this means that the plodding *Mastersingers* seem a bit too full of German pudding. Even with reservations expressed, however, there is no doubt that a great conductor is at the helm. The remastering has dried out the sound a little, but most of the ambience remains and the balance is good.

Götterdämmerung: Dawn music; Siegfried's Rhine journey, death and funeral music; Finale. Die Meistersinger: Prelude, Act III; Dance of the apprentices; Entry of the masters. Das Rheingold: Entry of the gods into Valhalla. Tannhäuser: Overture and Venusberg music.
(*) Delos Dig. **D/CD 3040 [id.]. Seattle SO, Schwarz.

This is a generous collection (69′) and it is well planned to span Wagner's career from *Tannhäuser* to the end of the *Ring* cycle. The excerpts are well chosen and well tailored. The Seattle orchestra – particularly the strings which can produce a rich sensuous sheen – play this repertoire most convincingly; and Gerard Schwarz's pacing is convincing, except perhaps in the *Prelude to Act III* of *Die Meistersinger*, where he presses on a shade too strongly. The violins are allowed to be a good deal more sprightly in the music for the *Mastersingers'* apprentices than are the Philharmonia in Klemperer's version. The recording, made in Seattle Opera House, is expansive and clear with the right spacious ambience. It is a pity there is no chorus for the *Venusberg music* in *Tannhäuser*.

Götterdämmerung: Dawn and Siegfried's Rhine journey; Siegfried's death and funeral march. Das Rheingold: Entry of the gods into Valhalla. Siegfried: Forest murmurs. Die Walküre: Ride of the Valkyries; Wotan's farewell and Magic fire music.
(*) HMV Dig. **CDC7 47007-2 [id.]. BPO, Tennstedt.
** **CBS MK 37795** [id.]. NYPO, Mehta (with Peter Wimberger in the *Magic fire music*).

This HMV Berlin Philharmonic CD was the first digital orchestral collection from *The Ring*, and it was recorded with demonstrable brilliance. With steely metallic cymbal clashes in the *Ride of the Valkyries* and a splendid drum thwack at the opening of the *Entry of the gods into Valhalla*, the sense of spectacle is in no doubt. There is weight too: the climax of *Siegfried's funeral march* has massive penetration. There is also fine detail, especially in the atmospheric *Forest murmurs*. The playing itself is of the finest quality throughout and Tennstedt maintains a high level of tension. But the brass recording is rather dry and at times the ear feels some lack of amplitude and resonance in the bass. However, the grip of the playing is extremely well projected, and the degree of fierceness at the top is tameable. The compact disc seems to emphasize the dryness in the bass, and while detail is clear there is a lack of richness and bloom.

Mehta's performances are spacious and there is plenty of surface excitement. The playing of the New York Philharmonic has fervour; in the *Magic fire music* from *Die Walküre*, the orchestra is joined briefly by Peter Wimberger as Wotan, which has the effect of increasing the level of tension. *Siegfried's funeral music* is paced slowly with a sombre pianissimo at the opening, but Mehta's grip here is not ideally taut. Elsewhere, the very brilliant CBS sound gives a brashness to the brass which is not always quite comfortable.

Götterdämmerung: Siegfried's funeral music. Die Meistersinger: Overture. Parsifal: Good Friday music. Tannhäuser: Overture. Tristan und Isolde: Prelude and Liebestod.
(**) DG mono **415 663-2** [id.]. BPO, Furtwängler.

Furtwängler's account of the *Tristan Prelude and Liebestod* is electrifying, and the 1954 recording is good. However, the collection opens with a 1949 version of the *Mastersingers overture* (notable for a memorably spacious broadening at the close) and a 1951 *Tannhäuser overture* (with splendidly clean articulation from the Berlin strings, but rather blatant brass), where the recording is no more than acceptable, and the harsh timbres are at odds with the music's amplitude. The *Parsifal* and *Götterdämmerung* excerpts sound much better, and again offer characteristic tension, but the bronchial afflictions of the audience in the *Good Friday music* are disturbingly intrusive.

Götterdämmerung: Siegfried's Rhine journey. Die Meistersinger: Overture. Tannhäuser: Overture. Tristan: Prelude and Liebestod.
(B) *** Cirrus **CICD 1005**. LSO, Wyn Morris.

A splendid bargain collection of four favourite Wagner excerpts. The LSO playing is first rate, with the strings producing real fervour in the *Liebestod*. *Tannhäuser*, too, is a most exciting performance, very well structured. The recording, made at EMI's Abbey Road studios, is rich and lively, creating ripe string and brass sounds, ideal for this music. It is good to see Wyn Morris recording again and he could hardly have celebrated his return more effectively. A bargain.

Lohengrin: Preludes to Acts I & III. Die Meistersinger: Overture. Rienzi: Overture. Tannhäuser: Overture.
(*) HMV Dig. **CDC7 47030-2 [id.]. BPO, Tennstedt.

Klaus Tennstedt here shows something of the Klemperer tradition with these essentially broad and spacious readings, yet the voltage is consistently high. The opening and closing sections of the *Tannhäuser overture* are given a restrained nobility of feeling (and there is absolutely no hint of vulgarity) without any loss of power or impact. Similarly the gorgeous string melody at the opening of *Rienzi* is elegiacally moulded, and later when the brass enter in the allegro there is no suggestion of the bandstand. In the Act I *Lohengrin Prelude*, Tennstedt lingers in the pianissimo sections, creating radiant detail, then presses on just before the climax, a quite different approach from Furtwängler's, but no less telling. The Berlin Philharmonic are on top form throughout and the digital recording is both refined and brilliant, if without a glowing resonance in the middle and bass frequencies. This is emphasized by the CD, which adds clarity of detail, brightens the treble, and makes the ear aware that a greater overall richness and amplitude would have been welcome. But these are fine performances, superbly played.

Die Meistersinger: Overture. Parsifal: Prelude to Act I. Rienzi: Overture. Tannhäuser: Overture.
(*) DG **413 551-2 [id.]. VPO, Boehm.

Under Boehm the Vienna Philharmonic play beautifully in a choice of overtures spanning Wagner's full career from *Rienzi* to *Parsifal.* The performance of *Rienzi* has striking life and vigour; *Die Meistersinger* has both grandeur and detail, the *Parsifal Prelude* is superbly eloquent and spacious in feeling, and both show a compulsive inevitability in their forward flow. The recording is full, but its beauty is slightly marred by the aggressiveness of trumpet tone, although this is slightly less disturbing on CD. The programme is not very generous either.

Die Meistersinger: Prelude to Act III. Tannhäuser: Overture and Venusberg music. Tristan und Isolde: Prelude and Liebestod.
(*) DG Dig. **413 754-2 [id.]. BPO, Karajan.

HMV issued much the same compilation from Karajan and the Berlin Philharmonic in the mid-1970s in quadraphony, the difference being that on the present occasion the *Prelude* to Act III of *Die Meistersinger* replaces that to Act I of *Lohengrin*, and the Dresden rather than the Paris version of the *Venusberg music* is used in *Tannhäuser*. As can be seen above, EMI have reissued the earlier *Tannhäuser* and *Tristan* performances at mid-price in a different collection, with the digitally remastered sound a good deal less opulent than the original. In the new CD concert the orchestral playing, as before, is altogether superlative; artistically, there need be no reservations here. But the upper strings lack an ideal amount of space in which to open out and climaxes are not altogether free. The overall effect is slightly more clinical in its detail, instead of offering a resonant panoply of sound. But Brangaene's potion still remains heady, and the playing is eloquent and powerful.

Parsifal: Prelude and Good Friday music.
*** CBS **MK 42038** [id.]. Columbia SO, Bruno Walter – DVOŘÁK: *Symphony No. 8.****

A glorious account of the *Prelude and Good Friday music* from Walter, recorded in 1959, but with the glowingly rich recording never hinting at its age. The digital remastering is a superb achievement. This is one of the most beautiful orchestral recordings of Wagner yet available on CD, and the sound-balance is preferable to nearly all the modern digital collections of Wagner orchestral excerpts. The coupling with Walter's outstanding account of Dvořák's *Eighth Symphony* – another very fine performance and recording – makes this CD an indispensable acquisition for any admirer of this great conductor.

Parsifal: Good Friday music.
(B) *** DG Walkman *419 391-4* [id.]. Bav. RSO, Jochum – BRUCKNER: *Symphony No. 7; Te Deum.****

Jochum's inspirational account of the *Good Friday music* was a famous early highlight of the stereo catalogue: the recording dates from 1958. It still sounds spacious and full in the present Walkman transfer, where it is a bonus for a highly recommendable coupling of Bruckner's *Seventh Symphony* and *Te Deum.*

PIANO MUSIC

Opera transcriptions: *Die Meistersinger: Prelude* (arr. Kocsis). *Lohengrin: Elsa's bridal procession* (arr. Liszt). *Parsifal: Festive march* (arr. Liszt). *Tristan und Isolde: Einleitung; Liebestod.*
(*) Ph. **416 452-2 [id.]. Zóltan Kocsis.

These digital recordings come from 1982. To the Liszt transcriptions, Kocsis adds a couple of his own – most notably the *Prelude* to *The Mastersingers*, which is quite a *tour de force.* He shows his considerable mastery of pianistic colour and an impressive keyboard control, though the idea of hearing the *Tristan Prelude and Liebestod* in this form will inevitably strike some listeners as bizarre when the real thing is so readily available. The recording is very good, but not many collectors – apart from Kocsis's wide circle of admirers – will want this.

Wesendonk Lieder.
*** HMV **CDC7 47854-2** [id.]. Dame Janet Baker, LPO, Boult – BRAHMS: *Alto rhapsody****; R. STRAUSS: *Lieder.***(*)
*** Decca **414 624-2** [id.]. Kirsten Flagstad, VPO, Knappertsbusch – MAHLER: *Kindertotenlieder; Lieder eines fahrenden Gesellen.***
*(*) Ph. Dig. **416 807-2**; *416 807-4* [id.]. Agnes Baltsa, LSO, Tate – BERLIOZ: *Nuits d'été.**(*)

Wesendonk Lieder. Tristan und Isolde: Prelude und Liebestod.
(*) Ph. **412 655-2 [id.]. Jessye Norman, LSO, C. Davis.

Dame Janet Baker gives a radiant performance of the *Wesendonk Lieder*. From the very first phrase the concentration and imagination are firmly established, and the expansive view of *Stehe still* makes that song far deeper than usual, with no hint of sentimentality. The range of tone-colour is ravishing, and Sir Adrian draws comparably beautiful sounds from the LPO. Glowing recording quality.

Flagstad's glorious voice is perfectly suited to the rich inspiration of the *Wesendonk Lieder. Im Treibhaus* is particularly beautiful. Fine accompaniment, with the 1956 recording sounding remarkable for its vintage and skilfully remastered to give the voice added character and presence. However, the Mahler couplings recorded during the same period are rather less successful.

The poised phrases of the *Wesendonk Lieder* drew from Jessye Norman in this 1976 recording a glorious range of tone-colour, though in detailed imagination she falls short of some of the finest rivals on record. The coupling is most apt, since two of the *Wesendonk* songs were written as studies for *Tristan*. Though the role of Isolde would no doubt strain a still-developing voice, and this is not the most searching of *Liebestods*, it is still the vocal contribution which crowns this conventional linking of first and last in the opera. Good, refined recording, made the more vivid on CD with an excellent digital transfer and silent background.

Baltsa is powerful and very individual in the five songs; but, as in the Berlioz on the reverse, a tough, characterful voice cannot encompass the necessary sensuousness in this music. The view is often illuminating on detail but cannot be generally recommended. Excellent accompaniment and recording on an intimate scale.

OPERA

Die Feen (complete).
*** Orfeo Dig. **C063833** (3) [id.]. Gray, Lovaas, Laki, Studer, Alexander, Hermann, Moll, Rootering, Bracht, Bav. R. Ch. & SO, Sawallisch.

Wagner was barely twenty when he wrote *Die Feen*, his first opera, a story of a fairy who marries a mortal and is threatened with separation from him. It is amazing how confident the writing is, regularly echoing Weber but stylistically more consistent than Wagner's next two operas, *Das Liebesverbot* and *Rienzi*. The piece is through-composed in what had become the new, advanced manner, and even when he bows to convention and has a buffo duet between the second pair of principals, the result is distinctive and fresh, delightfully sung here by Cheryl Studer and Jan-Hendrik Rootering. This first complete recording was edited together from live performances given in Munich in 1983, and has few of the usual snags of live performance and plenty of its advantages. Sawallisch gives a strong and dramatic performance, finely paced; and central to the total success is the singing of Linda Esther Gray as Ada, the fairy-heroine, powerful and firmly controlled. John Alexander as the tenor hero, King Arindal – finally granted immortality to bring a happy ending – sings cleanly and capably; the impressive cast-list boasts such excellent singers as Kurt Moll, Kari Lovaas and Krisztina Laki in small but vital roles. Ensembles and choruses – with the Bavarian Radio Chorus finely disciplined – are particularly impressive, and the recording is generally first rate. On CD the realism is enhanced, with the sound more vivid and sharply focused.

Der fliegende Holländer (complete).

*** Ph. Dig. **416 300-2**; *416 300-4* (2) [id.]. Estes, Balslev, Salminen, Schunk, Bayreuth Fest. (1985) Ch. & O, Nelsson.

*** HMV Dig. **CDS7 47054-8** (3) [id.]. Van Dam, Vejzovic, Moll, Hofmann, Moser, Borris, V. State Op. Ch., BPO, Karajan.

(*) Decca **414 551-2 (3) [id.]. Bailey, Martin, Talvela, Kollo, Krenn, Isola Jones, Chicago SO Ch. & O, Solti.

The biting intensity of a Bayreuth performance has rarely been more thrillingly caught than in the fine Philips recording of a 1985 performance. Woldemar Nelsson, with the team he had worked with intensively through the season, conducts a performance even more glowing and responsively paced than those of his starrier rivals. The cast, also less starry than some, is yet more consistent than any, with Lisbeth Balslev as Senta firmer, sweeter and more secure than any current rival, raw only occasionally, and Simon Estes a strong, ringing Dutchman, clear and noble of tone. Matti Salminen is a dark and equally secure Daland and Robert Schunk an ardent, idiomatic Erik. The veteran, Anny Schlemm, as Mary, though vocally overstressed, adds pointful character, and the chorus is superb, wonderfully drilled and passionate with it. Though inevitably stage noises are obtrusive at times, the recording is exceptionally vivid and atmospheric. On two discs only, it makes an admirable first choice. There are also excellent cassettes.

The extreme range of dynamics in EMI's recording for Karajan, not ideally clear but rich, matches the larger-than-life quality of the conductor's reading. He firmly and convincingly relates this early work not so much to such seminal earlier works as Weber's *Der Freischütz* as to later Wagner, *Tristan* above all. His choice of José van Dam as the Dutchman, thoughtful, finely detailed and lyrical, strong but not at all blustering, goes well with this. The Dutchman's Act I monologue is turned into a prayer as well as a protest in its extra range of expression. Van Dam is superbly matched and contrasted with the finest Daland on record, Kurt Moll, gloriously biting and dark in tone yet detailed in his characterization. Neither the Erik of Peter Hofmann, nor – more seriously – the Senta of Dunja Vejzovic matches such a standard, for Hofmann has his strained and gritty moments and Vejzovic her shrill ones. They were both better cast in Karajan's *Parsifal* recording. Nevertheless, for all her variability Vejzovic is wonderfully intense in *Senta's Ballad* and she matches even Van Dam's fine legato in the Act II duet. The CD version underlines the heavyweight quality of the recording, with the *Sailors' chorus* for example made massive, but effectively so, when Karajan conducts it with such fine spring. The banding is not generous, making the issue less convenient to use than most Wagner CD sets.

Solti's first Wagner opera recording in Chicago marked a change from the long series he made in Vienna. The playing is superb, the singing cast is generally impressive, and the recording is vividly immediate to the point of aggressiveness. What will disappoint some who admire Solti's earlier Wagner sets is that this most atmospheric of the Wagner operas is presented with no Culshaw-style production whatever. Characters halloo to one another when evidently standing elbow to elbow, and even the Dutchman's ghostly chorus sounds very close and earthbound. But with Norman Bailey a deeply impressive Dutchman, Janis Martin a generally sweet-toned Senta, Martti Talvela a splendid Daland, and Kollo, for all his occasional coarseness, an illuminating Erik, it remains well worth hearing. The brilliance of the recording is all the more striking on CD, but the precise placing so characteristic of the new medium reinforces the clear impression of a concert performance, not an atmospheric re-creation.

Götterdämmerung (complete).

*** Decca **414 115-2** (4); *414 115-4* [id.]. Nilsson, Windgassen, Fischer-Dieskau, Frick, Neidlinger, Watson, Ludwig, V. State Op. Ch., VPO, Solti.

*** DG **415 155-2** (4) [id.]. Dernesch, Janowitz, Brilioth, Stewart, Kelemen, Ludwig, Ridderbusch, German Op. Ch., BPO, Karajan.

*** Ph. **412 488-2** (4) [id.]. Nilsson, Windgassen, Greindl, Mödl, Stewart, Neidlinger, Dvořáková, Bayreuth Fest. (1967) Ch. & O, Boehm.

(*) Eurodisc Dig. **610081 (5). Altmeyer, Kollo, Salminen, Wenkel, Nocker, Nimsgern, Sharp, Popp, Leipzig R. Ch., Berlin R. Ch., Dresden State Op. Ch., Dresden State O, Janowski.

In Decca's formidable task of recording the whole *Ring* cycle under Solti, *Götterdämmerung* provided the most daunting challenge of all; characteristically, Solti, and with him the Vienna Philharmonic and the Decca recording team under John Culshaw, were inspired to heights even beyond earlier achievements. Even the trifling objections raised on earlier issues have been eliminated here. The balance between voices and orchestra has by some magic been made perfect, with voices clear but orchestra still rich and near-sounding. On CD, the weight of sound in this 1964 recording comes out with satisfying power in its digital transfer, so giving the brilliance of the upper range its proper support. The big ensembles come over particularly well, and Culshaw's carefully planned, highly atmospheric sound staging is the more sharply focused, exhilaratingly so in the fall of the Gibichung Hall at the end. Access to the set is first class, with rather more generous cueing than in rival versions. Solti's reading had matured before the recording was made. He presses on still, but no longer is there any feeling of over-driving, and even the *Funeral march*, which in his early Covent Garden performances was brutal in its power, is made into a natural, not a forced, climax. There is not a single weak link in the cast. Nilsson surpasses herself in the magnificence of her singing: even Flagstad in her prime would not have been more masterful as Brünnhilde. As in *Siegfried*, Windgassen is in superb voice; Frick is a vivid Hagen, and Fischer-Dieskau achieves the near impossible in making Gunther an interesting and even sympathetic character. As for the recording quality, it surpasses even Decca's earlier achievement. No more magnificent set has appeared in the whole history of the gramophone, and Decca have also surpassed themselves in the excellence of the tape transfer, with remarkably little background noise.

Recorded last in Karajan's *Ring* series, *Götterdämmerung* has the finest, fullest sound, less brilliant than Solti's on Decca but with glowing purity in the CD transfer to match the relatively lyrical approach of the conductor, with Helga Dernesch's voice in the Immolation scene given satisfying richness and warmth. His singing cast is marginally even finer than Solti's, and his performance conveys the steady flow of recording sessions prepared in relation to live performances. But ultimately he falls short of Solti's achievement in the orgasmic quality of the music, the quality which finds an emotional culmination in such moments as the end of Brünnhilde's and Siegfried's love scene, the climax of the *Funeral march* and the culmination of the Immolation. At each of these points Karajan is a degree less committed, beautifully as the players respond, and warm as his overall approach is. Dernesch's Brünnhilde is warmer than Nilsson's, with a glorious range of tone. Brilioth as Siegfried is fresh and young-sounding, while the Gutrune of Gundula Janowitz is far preferable to that of Claire Watson on Decca. The matching is otherwise very even. The balance of voices in the recording may for some dictate a choice: DG brings the singers closer, gives less brilliance to the orchestral texture. Nevertheless, next to Solti's Decca set, such scenes as the summoning of the vassals in Act II lack weight.

Boehm's urgently involving reading of *Götterdämmerung*, very well cast, is crowned by an incandescent performance of the final Immolation scene from Birgit Nilsson as Brünnhilde. Small wonder that she herself has always preferred this version to the fine one she recorded three years earlier for Solti in the studio. It is an astonishing achievement that she could sing with such biting power and accuracy in a live performance, coming to it at the very end of a long evening. The excitement of that is matched by much else in the performance, so that incidental stage noises and the occasional inaccuracy, almost inevitable in live music-making, matter hardly at all. This recording, which appeared on LP in the early 1970s, has been transformed in its CD version. The voices are well forward of the orchestra, but the result gives a magnetically real impression of hearing the opera in the Festspielhaus, with the stage movements adding to that sense of reality. Balances are inevitably variable, and at times Windgassen as Siegfried is less well treated by the microphones than Nilsson. Generally his performance for Solti is fresher – but there are points of advantage, too. Josef Greindl is rather unpleasantly nasal in tone as Hagen, and Martha Mödl as Waltraute is unsteady; but both are dramatically involving. Thomas Stewart is a gruff but convincing Gunther and Dvořáková, as Gutrune, strong if not ideally pure-toned. Neidlinger as ever is a superb Alberich. Anyone preferring a live recording of the *Ring* will find Boehm's final instalment the most satisfying culmination.

With sharply focused digital sound, Janowski's studio recording hits refreshingly hard, at least as much so as in the earlier *Ring* operas. Speeds rarely linger but, with some excellent casting – consistent with the earlier operas – the result is rarely lightweight. Jeanine Altmeyer as Brünnhilde rises to the challenges not so much in strength as in feeling and intensity, ecstatic in Act I, bitter in Act II, dedicated in the Immolation scene. Kollo is a fine heroic Siegfried, only occasionally raw-toned, and Salminen is a magnificent Hagen, with Nimsgern again an incisive Alberich on his brief appearances. Despite an indifferent Gunther and Gutrune and a wobbly if characterful Waltraute, the impression is of clean vocalization matched by finely disciplined and dedicated playing, all recorded in faithful studio sound with no sonic tricks. On the five CDs the background silence adds to the dramatic presence and overall clarity, which is strikingly enhanced, but on ten sides the layout is less satisfactory than that of its rivals, to say nothing of the price disadvantage this incurs.

The Twilight of the Gods (*Götterdämmerung*)*: Act III:* excerpts in English.
*** Chan. **CHAN 8534**; *ABTD 1244* [id.]. Rita Hunter, Alberto Remedios, Norman Bailey, Grant, Curphey, Sadler's Wells Opera Ch. & O, Goodall.

Originally recorded by Unicorn in the early 1970s, even before the Sadler's Wells company had changed its name to the English National Opera, the single Chandos CD brings an invaluable reminder of Reginald Goodall's performance of the *Ring* cycle when it was in its first flush of success. The two-LP set is here transferred on to a single CD, lasting 66 minutes, covering the closing two scenes. In many ways it possesses an advantage over even the complete live recording of the opera, made at the Coliseum five years later, when Rita Hunter and Alberto Remedios are here obviously fresher and less stressed than at the end of a full evening's performance. It is good too to have this sample, however brief, of Clifford Grant's Hagen and Norman Bailey's Gunther, fine performances both. Fresh, clear recording, not as full as it might be.

Lohengrin (complete).

❀ *** Decca Dig. **421 053-2**; *421 053-4* (4) [id.]. Domingo, Norman, Nimsgern, Randova, Sotin, Fischer-Dieskau, V. State Op. Concert Ch., VPO, Solti.

*** HMV **CDS7 49017-2** [id.]; (M) *EX 290955-5* (3). Jess Thomas, Grümmer, Fischer-Dieskau, Ludwig, Frick, Wiener, V. State Op. Ch., VPO, Kempe.

(M) **(*) HMV **CMS7 69314-2** [id.]; *EX 769314-4* (4). Kollo, Tomowa-Sintow, Nimsgern, Vejzovic, Ridderbusch, German Op., Berlin, Ch., BPO, Karajan.

Solti rounded off his complete cycle of the Wagner operas in the Bayreuth canon (the first conductor to do so) with this incandescent performance of *Lohengrin*. It was also the last recording made by the Decca engineers in their favourite Vienna venue, the Sofiensaal, where most of Solti's earlier Wagner sets, including the *Ring* cycle, had been recorded. With its massive ensembles, *Lohengrin* presents special problems, and the engineers here excel themselves in well-aerated sound that still has plenty of body. Solti presents those ensemble moments with rare power and panache, but he also appreciates the chamber-like delicacy of much of the writing, relaxing far more than he might have done earlier in his career, bringing out the endless lyricism warmly and naturally. It was bold to choose for the principal roles two of today's superstar singers. It is Placido Domingo's achievement singing Lohengrin that the lyrical element blossoms so consistently, with no hint of Heldentenor barking; at whatever dynamic level, Domingo's voice is firm and unstrained. In the Act III aria, *In fernem Land*, for example, he uses the widest, most beautiful range of tonal colouring, with ringing heroic tone dramatically contrasted against a whisper of head voice, finely controlled. Jessye Norman, not naturally suited to the role of Elsa, yet gives a warm, commanding performance, always intense, full of detailed insights into words and character. Eva Randova's grainy mezzo does not take so readily to recording, but as Ortrud she provides a pointful contrast, even if she never matches the firm, biting malevolence of Christa Ludwig on the Kempe set. Siegmund Nimsgern, Telramund for Solti as for Karajan, equally falls short of his rival on the Kempe set, Fischer-Dieskau; but it is still a strong, cleanly focused performance. Fischer-Dieskau here sings the small but vital role of the Herald, while Hans Sotin makes a comparably distinctive King Henry. Radiant playing from the Vienna Philharmonic, and committed chorus work too. This is one of the crowning glories of Solti's long recording career.

Kempe's is a rapt account of *Lohengrin* which has been surpassed on record only by Solti's Decca set, and remains one of his finest monuments in sound. After all, Kempe looked at Wagner very much from the spiritual side, giving *Lohengrin* perspectives deeper than is common. The link with early Wagner is less obvious than usual; instead one sees the opera as the natural pair with *Parsifal*, linked no doubt in Wagner's mind too, since in mythology Parsifal was the father of Lohengrin. The intensity of Kempe's conducting lies even in its very restraint, and throughout this glowing performance one senses a gentle but sure control, with the strings of the Vienna Philharmonic playing radiantly. The singers too seem uplifted, Jess Thomas singing more clearly and richly than usual, Elisabeth Grümmer unrivalled as Elsa in her delicacy and sweetness, Gottlob Frick gloriously resonant as the king. But it is the partnership of Christa Ludwig and Fischer-Dieskau as Ortrud and Telramund that sets the seal on this superb performance, giving the darkest intensity to their machinations in Act II, their evil heightening the beauty and serenity of so much in this opera. Though the digital transfer on CD reveals roughness (even occasional distortion) in the original recording, the glow and intensity of

Kempe's reading comes out all the more involvingly in the new format. The set is also very economically contained on three CDs instead of the four for all rivals, though inevitably breaks between discs come in the middle of Acts. The cassettes are quite well transferred on iron-oxide stock, which has resulted in the upper range being restricted, while there is a fair amount of background hiss.

Karajan, whose DG recording of *Parsifal* was so naturally intense, failed in this earlier but related opera to capture comparable spiritual depth. So some of the big melodies sound a degree over-inflected; and the result though warm and expressive and dramatically powerful, with wide-ranging recording, misses an important dimension. Nor is much of the singing as pure-toned as it might be, with René Kollo too often straining and Tomowa-Sintow not always able to scale down in the necessary purity her big dramatic voice. Even so, with strong and beautiful playing from the Berlin Philharmonic, it remains a powerful performance, and it makes a fair bargain version on four mid-priced CDs – though remember that the Kempe version, on one disc fewer, is comparable in price. There are outstandingly successful chrome cassettes of the Karajan set. Both the CDs and tapes share the same booklet, which offers the libretto without an English translation, but a synopsis instead.

Die Meistersinger von Nürnberg (complete).

*** DG **415 278-2** (4) [id.]. Fischer-Dieskau, Ligendza, Lagger, Hermann, Domingo, Laubenthal, Ludwig, German Op., Berlin, Ch. & O, Jochum.

(*) Decca **417 497-2 (4) [id.]. Bailey, Bode, Moll, Weikl, Kollo, Dallapozza, Hamari, Gumpoldskirchner Spatzen, V. State Op. Ch., VPO, Solti.

(*) HMV **CDS7 49683-2 [id.]; (M) *EX 749683-4* (4). Adam, Evans, Kelemen, Riddersbusch, Kollo, Schreier, Donath, Hess, Leipzig R. Ch., Dresden State Op. Ch. & State O, Karajan.

Jochum's is a performance which, more than any, captures the light and shade of Wagner's most warmly approachable score, its humour and tenderness as well as its strength. The recording was made at the same time as live opera-house performances in Berlin, and the sense of a comedy being enacted is irresistible. With Jochum the processions at the start of the final Festwiese have sparkling high spirits, not just German solemnity, while the poetry of the score is radiantly brought out, whether in the incandescence of the Act III *Prelude* (positively Brucknerian in hushed concentration) or the youthful magic of the love music for Walther and Eva. Above all, Jochum is unerring in building long Wagnerian climaxes and resolving them – more so than his recorded rivals. The cast is the most consistent yet assembled on record. Though Caterina Ligendza's big soprano is a little ungainly for Eva, it is an appealing performance, and the choice of Domingo for Walther is inspired. The key to the set is of course the searching and highly individual Sachs of Fischer-Dieskau, a performance long awaited. Obviously controversial (you can never imagine this sharp Sachs sucking on his boring old pipe), Fischer-Dieskau with detailed word-pointing and sharply focused tone gives new illumination in every scene. The Masters – with not one woolly-toned member – make a superb team, and Horst Laubenthal's finely tuned David matches this Sachs in applying Lieder style. The recording balance favours the voices, but on CD they are made to sound just slightly ahead of the orchestra. There is a lovely bloom on the whole sound and, with a recording which is basically wide-ranging and refined, the ambience brings an attractively natural projection of the singers.

The great glory of Solti's long-awaited set is not the searing brilliance of the conductor but rather the mature and involving portrayal of Sachs by Norman Bailey. For his superb singing the set is well worth investigating, and there is much else to enjoy, not least the bright and detailed sound which the Decca engineers have, as so often in the past, obtained with the Vienna Philharmonic, recording Wagner in the Sofiensaal. Kurt Moll as Pogner, Bernd Weikl as Beckmesser (really singing the part) and Julia Hamari as Magdalene (refreshingly young-sounding) are all excellent, but the shortcomings are comparably serious. Both Hannelore Bode and René Kollo fall short of their far-from-perfect contributions to earlier sets, and Solti for all his energy gives a surprisingly square reading of this most appealing of Wagner scores, exaggerating the four-square rhythms with even stressing, pointing his expressive lines too heavily and failing to convey real spontaneity. It remains an impressive achievement, and those who must at all costs hear Bailey's marvellous Sachs should not be deterred, for the Decca sound comes up very vividly on CD. Yet that merit is hardly enough to compensate for the vocal shortcomings.

HMV, in setting up their star-studded version, fell down badly in the choice of Sachs. Theo Adam, promising in many ways, has quite the wrong voice for the part, in one way too young-sounding, in another too grating, not focused enough. After that keen disappointment there is much to enjoy, for in a modestly reverberant acoustic (a smallish church was used) Karajan draws from the Dresden players and chorus a rich performance which retains a degree of bourgeois intimacy. Anyone wanting an expansive sound may be disappointed, but Karajan's thoughtful approach and sure command of phrasing are most enjoyable. Donath is a touching, sweet-toned Eva, Kollo here is as true and ringing a Walther as one could find today, Geraint Evans an incomparably vivid Beckmesser, and Ridderbusch a glorious-toned Pogner. The extra clarity of CD gives new realism and sense of presence to a recording not specially impressive on LP. With the finest Eva on any current set, it is a good choice for those who are not upset by Adam's ungenial Sachs. There are admirable chrome cassettes of the Karajan set. There is some occasional excess bass resonance (noticeable in the *Overture*) but the transfer generally is fresh, clear and wide-ranging.

Parsifal (complete).

❀ *** DG Dig. **413 347-2** (4) [id.]. Hofmann, Vejzovic, Moll, Van Dam, Nimsgern, Von Halem, German Op. Ch., BPO, Karajan.

*** Decca **417 143-2** (4) [id.]. Kollo, Ludwig, Fischer-Dieskau, Hotter, Kelemen, Frick, V. Boys' Ch., V. State Op. Ch., VPO, Solti.

(*) Ph. Dig. **416 842-2; *416 842-4* (4) [id.]. Hofmann, Meier, Estes, Sotin, Salminen, Mazura, Bayreuth Fest. (1985) Ch. & O, Levine.

(*) Ph. **416 390-2 (4). Jess Thomas, Dalis, London, Talvela, Neidlinger, Hotter, Bayreuth Fest. (1962) Ch. & O, Knappertsbusch.

(*) HMV Dig. **CDS7 49182-8 (5) [id.]. Ellsworth, Meier, Joll, Gwynne, McIntyre, Folwell, Welsh Nat. Op. Ch. & O, Goodall.

Communion, musical and spiritual, is what this intensely beautiful Karajan set provides, with pianissimos shaded in magical clarity and the ritual of bells and offstage choruses heard as in ideal imagination. If, after the Solti recording for Decca, it seemed doubtful whether a studio recording could ever match in spiritual intensity earlier ones made on stage at Bayreuth, Karajan proves otherwise, his meditation the more intense because the digital sound allows total silences. The playing of the Berlin orchestra – preparing for performance at the Salzburg Easter Festival of 1980 – is consistently beautiful; but the clarity and refinement of sound prevent this from emerging as a lengthy serving of Karajan soup. He has rarely sounded so spontaneously involved in opera on record. Kurt Moll as Gurnemanz is the singer who, more than any other, anchors the work vocally, projecting his voice with firmness and subtlety. José van Dam as Amfortas is also splendid: the *Lament* is one of the glories of the set, enormously wide in dynamic and expressive range. The Klingsor of Siegmund Nimsgern could be more sinister, but the singing is admirable. Dunja Vejzovic makes a vibrant, sensuous Kundry who rises superbly to the moment in Act II where she bemoans her laughter in the face of Christ. Only Peter Hofmann as Parsifal leaves any disappointment; at times he develops a gritty edge on the voice, but his natural tone is admirably suited to the part – no one can match him today –

and he is never less than dramatically effective. He is not helped by the relative closeness of the solo voices, but otherwise the recording is near the atmospheric ideal, a superb achievement. The four CDs, generously full and offering an improved layout, are among DG's finest so far, with the background silence adding enormously to the concentration of the performance.

It was natural that, after Solti's other magnificent Wagner recordings for Decca, he should want to go on to this last of the operas. In almost every way it is just as powerful an achievement as any of his previous Wagner recordings in Vienna, with the Decca engineers surpassing themselves in vividness of sound and the Vienna Philharmonic in radiant form. The singing cast could hardly be stronger, every one of them pointing words with fine, illuminating care for detail. The complex balances of sound, not least in the *Good Friday music*, are beautifully caught; throughout, Solti shows his sustained intensity in Wagner. There remains just one doubt, but that rather serious: the lack of that spiritual quality which makes Knappertsbusch's live version so involving. However, the clear advantage of a studio recording is the absence of intrusive audience noises which, in an opera such as this with its long solos and dialogues, can be very distracting. The remastering for CD, as with Solti's other Wagner recordings, opens up the sound, and the choral climaxes are superb. On CD, the break between the second and third discs could have been better placed. Cueing is generous but the libretto is poor, the typeface minuscule and in places no pleasure to read.

James Levine's conducting of *Parsifal* at Bayreuth brought a landmark in an already distinguished career. With this spacious, dedicated performance he completely shook off any earlier associations as an American whizzkid conductor which, even after many years at the Met., still clung to him. Of all the Wagner operas this is the one that gains most and loses least from being recorded live at Bayreuth, and the dedication of the reading, the intensity as in an act of devotion, comes over consistently, if not with quite the glow that so marks Karajan's inspired studio performance. Unfortunately the singing is flawed. Peter Hofmann, in far poorer voice than for Karajan, is often ill-focused, and even Hans Sotin as Gurnemanz is vocally less reliable than usual. The rest are excellent, with Franz Mazura as Klingsor, Simon Estes as Amfortas and Matti Salminen as Titurel all giving resonant, finely projected performances, well contrasted with each other. Waltraud Meier is an outstanding Kundry here, as in Goodall's studio performance, singing at Bayreuth with more dramatic thrust, for Goodall with more security. The recording, though not the clearest from this source, captures the Bayreuth atmosphere well.

Knappertsbusch's expansive and dedicated reading is superbly caught in the Philips set, arguably the finest live recording ever made in the Festspielhaus at Bayreuth, with outstanding singing from Jess Thomas as Parsifal and Hans Hotter as Gurnemanz. Though Knappertsbusch chooses consistently slow tempi, there is no sense of excessive squareness or length, so intense is the concentration of the performance, its spiritual quality, and the sound has undoubtedly been further enhanced in the remastering for CD. The snag is that the stage noises and coughs are also emphasized and the bronchial afflictions are particularly disturbing in the *Prelude*. However, the recording itself is most impressive, with the choral perspectives particularly convincing and the overall sound warmly atmospheric.

It is sad that EMI opted to spread the Goodall version on to five CDs, when all the rivals take only four, even the Levine which is barely less spacious in its speeds. Goodall's devotees will perhaps not worry over expense, when the extra vividness of the sound and the absence of background add to the immediacy and dedication. Goodall in his plain, unvarnished, patiently expansive reading characteristically finds deep intensity in a strong, rough-hewn way. He may lack the ethereal beauties of Karajan, for here *Parsifal* is brought down to earth, thanks not just to Goodall but to the cast which with one exception stands up well to international competition. It was plainly a help that these same singers had appeared together under Goodall on stage in the Welsh National Opera production. Donald McIntyre gives one of his very finest performances as Gurnemanz, with more bloom than usual. Waltraud Meier's powerful, penetrating voice suits the role of Kundry well, while the American, Warren Ellsworth, has power and precision, if little beauty, as Parsifal. Only the ill-focused Amfortas of Phillip Joll is disappointing, too gritty of tone, though he too makes the drama compelling.

Das Rheingold (complete).
*** Decca **414 101-2** (3); *414 101-4* (2). London, Flagstad, Svanholm, Neidlinger, VPO, Solti.
(*) DG **415 141-2 (3) [id.]. Fischer-Dieskau, Veasey, Stolze, Kelemen, BPO, Karajan.
(*) Ph. **412 475-2 (2) [id.]. Adam, Nienstedt, Windgassen, Neidlinger, Talvela, Böhme, Silja, Soukupová, Bayreuth Fest. (1967) Ch. & O, Boehm.
(*) Eurodisc Dig. **610058 (3). Adam, Nimsgern, Stryczek, Schreier, Bracht, Salminen, Vogel, Buchner, Minton, Popp, Priew, Schwarz, Dresden State O, Janowski.

The first of Solti's cycle, recorded in 1958, *Rheingold* remains in terms of engineering the most spectacular, an ideal candidate for transfer to CD with its extra clarity and range. Noises and movements in the lowest bass register, virtually inaudible on LP, become clearly identifiable on CD; but the immediacy and precise placing of sound are thrilling, while the sound-effects of the final scenes, including Donner's hammer-blow and the Rainbow bridge, have never been matched since. The sound remains of demonstration quality, to have one cherishing all the more this historic recording with its unique vignette of Flagstad as Fricka. Solti gives a magnificent reading of the score, crisp, dramatic and direct. He somehow brings a freshness to the music without ever overdriving or losing an underlying sympathy. Vocally, the set is held together by the unforgettable singing of Neidlinger as Alberich. Too often the part – admittedly ungrateful on the voice – is spoken rather than sung, but Neidlinger vocalizes with wonderful precision and makes the character of the dwarf develop from the comic creature of the opening scene to the demented monster of the last. Flagstad learnt the part of Fricka specially for this recording, and her singing makes one regret that she never took the role on the stage; but regret is small when a singer of the greatness of Flagstad found the opportunity during so-called retirement to extend her reputation with performances such as this. Only the slightest trace of hardness in the upper register occasionally betrays her, and the golden power and richness of her singing are for the rest unimpaired – enhanced even, when recorded quality is as true as this. As Wotan, George London is sometimes a little rough – a less brilliant recording might not betray him – but this is a dramatic portrayal of the young Wotan. Svanholm could be more characterful as Loge, but again it is a relief to hear the part really sung. Much has been written on the quality of the recording, and without a shadow of a doubt it deserves the highest star rating. Decca went to special trouble to produce the recording as for a stage performance and to follow Wagner's intentions as closely as possible. They certainly succeeded. An outstanding achievement, and so is the cassette version, complete on four sides.

Karajan's account is more reflective than Solti's; the very measured pace of the *Prelude* indicates this at the start and there is often an extra bloom on the Berlin Philharmonic playing. But Karajan's very reflectiveness has its less welcome side, for the tension rarely varies. One finds such incidents as Alberich's stealing of the gold or Donner's hammer-blow passing by without one's pulse quickening as it should. Unexpectedly, Karajan is not as subtle as Solti in shaping phrases and rhythms. There is also no doubt that the DG recording managers were not as painstaking as John Culshaw's Decca team, and that too makes the end result less compellingly dramatic. On the credit side, however, the singing cast has hardly any flaw at all, and Fischer-Dieskau's Wotan is a brilliant and memorable creation, virile and expressive. Among the others, Veasey is excellent, though obviously she cannot efface memories of Flagstad; Gerhard Stolze with his flickering, almost *Sprechstimme* as Loge gives an intensely vivid if, for some, controversial interpretation. The 1968 sound has been clarified in the digital transfer, but while the compact discs bring out the beauty of Fischer-Dieskau's singing as the young Wotan the more vividly, generally the lack of bass brings some thinness.

The transfer to CD of Boehm's 1967 live recording made at Bayreuth is outstandingly successful. His preference for fast speeds (consistently through the whole cycle) here brings the benefit that the whole of the *Vorabend* is contained on two CDs, a considerable financial advantage. The pity is that the performance is marred by the casting of Theo Adam as Wotan, keenly intelligent but rarely agreeable on the ear, at times here far too wobbly. On the other hand, Gustav Neidlinger as Alberich is superb, even more involving here than he is for Solti, with the curse made spine-chilling. It is good too to have Loge cast from strength in Wolfgang Windgassen, cleanly vocalized; among the others, Anja Silja makes an attractively urgent Freia. Though a stage production brings nothing like the sound-effects which make Solti's set so involving, the atmosphere of the theatre in its way is just as potent.

The Eurodisc set of *Das Rheingold*, also part of a complete cycle, comes from East Germany, with Marek Janowski a direct, alert conductor of the Dresden State Orchestra, and more recently of the Royal Liverpool Philharmonic. This performance is treated to a digital recording totally different from Solti's. The studio sound has the voices close and vivid, with the orchestra rather in the background. Some Wagnerians prefer that kind of balance, but the result here rather lacks the atmospheric qualities which make the Solti *Rheingold* still the most compelling in sound, thanks to the detailed production of the late John Culshaw. With Solti, Donner's hammer-blow is overwhelming; but the Eurodisc set comes up with only a very ordinary 'ping' on an anvil, and the grandeur of the moment is missing. Theo Adam as Wotan has his grittiness of tone exaggerated here, but otherwise it is a fine set, consistently well cast, including Peter Schreier, Matti Salminen, Yvonne Minton and Lucia Popp, as well as East German singers of high calibre. The CDs sharpen the focus even further, with clarity rather than atmosphere the keynote.

Siegfried (complete).

*** Decca **414 110-2** (4); *414 110-4* (3). Windgassen, Nilsson, Hotter, Stolze, Neidlinger, Böhme, Hoffgen, Sutherland, VPO, Solti.

*** Ph. **412 483-2** (4) [id.]. Windgassen, Nilsson, Adam, Neidlinger, Soukupová, Köth, Böhme, Bayreuth Fest. (1967) Ch. & O, Boehm.

(*) Eurodisc Dig. **610070 (5). Kollo, Altmeyer, Adam, Schreier, Nimsgern, Wenkel, Salminen, Sharp, Dresden State O, Janowski.

** DG **415 150-2** (4) [id.]. Dernesch, Dominguez, Jess Thomas, Stolze, Stewart, Kelemen, BPO, Karajan.

Culshaw tackled this second recording in Solti's *Ring* series after a gap of four years following *Das Rheingold*. By then he was using what he called the 'Sonicstage' technique, which on compact disc makes the sepulchral voice of Fafner as Dragon all the more chilling. On CD, this 1962 recording comes out very well, with full brilliance and weight as well as extra clarity. The gimmicks may be made the more obvious, but they are good ones. *Siegfried* has too long been thought of as the grimmest of the *Ring* cycle, with dark colours predominating. It is true that the preponderance of male voices till the very end, and Wagner's deliberate matching of this in his orchestration, gives a special colour to the opera, but a performance as buoyant as Solti's reveals that, more than in most Wagner, the message is one of optimism. Each of the three Acts ends with a scene of triumphant optimism – the first Act in Siegfried's forging song, the second with him in hot pursuit of the woodbird, and the third with the most opulent of love duets. Solti's array of singers could hardly be bettered. Windgassen is at the very peak of his form, lyrical as well as heroic. Hotter has never been more impressive on records, his Wotan at last captured adequately. Stolze, Neidlinger and Böhme are all exemplary, and predictably Joan Sutherland makes the most seductive of woodbirds. Only the conducting of Solti leaves a tiny margin of doubt. In the dramatic moments he could hardly be more impressive, but that very woodbird scene shows up the shortcomings: the bird's melismatic carolling is plainly intended to have a degree of freedom, whereas Solti allows little or no lilt in the music at all. But it is a minute flaw in a supreme achievement. With singing finer than any opera house could normally provide, with masterly playing from the Vienna Philharmonic and Decca's most opulent recording, this is a set likely to stand comparison with anything the rest of the century may provide. The tape transfer is of outstanding quality. Decca have digitally remastered the recording on cassette as well as on disc, and the quality of the tapes is first class, with an almost silent background and remarkable overall clarity.

The natural-sounding quality of Boehm's live recording from Bayreuth, coupled with his determination not to let the music lag, makes his account of *Siegfried* as satisfying as the rest of his cycle, vividly capturing the atmosphere of the Festspielhaus, with voices well ahead of the orchestra. Windgassen is at his peak here, if anything more poetic in Acts II and III than he is in Solti's studio recording, and just as fine vocally. Nilsson, as in *Götterdämmerung*, gains over her studio recording from the extra flow of adrenalin in a live performance; and Gustav Neidlinger is unmatchable as Alberich. Erika Köth is disappointing as the woodbird, not sweet enough, and Soukupová is a positive, characterful Erda. Theo Adam is at his finest as the Wanderer, less wobbly than usual, clean and incisive.

Dedication and consistency are the mark of the Eurodisc *Ring*, recorded with German thoroughness in collaboration with the East German state record company. The result – with Janowski, direct and straight in his approach, securing superb playing from the Dresdeners – lacks a degree of dramatic tension, but he does not always build the climaxes cumulatively, so there is no compensation for any loss of immediate excitement. So the final scene of Act II just scurries to a close, with Siegfried in pursuit of a rather shrill woodbird in Norma Sharp. The singing is generally first rate, with Kollo a fine Siegfried, less strained than he has sometimes been, and Peter Schreier a superb Mime, using Lieder-like qualities in detailed characterization. Siegmund Nimsgern is a less characterful Alberich, but the voice is excellent; and Theo Adam concludes his portrayal of Wotan/Wanderer with his finest performance of the series. The relative lightness of Jeannine Altmeyer's Brünnhilde comes out in the final love-duet more strikingly than in *Walküre*. She may be reduced from goddess to human, but the musical demands are greater. Nevertheless, the tenderness and femininity are most affecting as at the entry of the idyll motif, where Janowski in his dedicated simplicity is also at his most compelling. Clear, beautifully balanced digital sound, with voices and instruments firmly placed. On CD, the opera's dark colouring is given an even sharper focus against the totally silent background, but the layout on five compact discs, against four for all the competitors, is a distinct disadvantage.

When Siegfried is outsung by Mime, it is time to complain, and though the DG set has many fine qualities – not least the Brünnhilde of Helga Dernesch – it hardly rivals the Solti or Boehm versions. Windgassen on Decca gave a classic performance, and any comparison highlights the serious shortcomings of Jess Thomas. Even when voices are balanced forward – a point the more apparent on CD – the digital transfer helps little to make Thomas's singing as Siegfried any more acceptable. Otherwise, the vocal cast is strong, and Karajan provides the seamless playing which characterizes his cycle. Recommended only to those irrevocably committed to the Karajan cycle.

Tannhäuser (Paris version; complete).

*** Decca **414 581-2** (3) [id.]. Kollo, Dernesch, Ludwig, Sotin, Braun, Hollweg, V. State Op. Ch., VPO, Solti.

Tannhäuser (Dresden version; complete).

(*) Ph. **420 122-2 (3) [id.]. Windgassen, Waechter, Silja, Stolze, Bumbry, Bayreuth Fest. (1962) Ch. & O, Sawallisch.

** HMV Dig. **CDS7 47296-8** (3) [id.]. König, Popp, Weikl, Meier, Moll, Jerusalem, Bav. R. Ch. & O, Haitink.

Solti provides an electrifying experience, demonstrating beyond a shadow of doubt how much more effective the Paris revision of *Tannhäuser* is, compared with the usual Dresden version. The differences lie mainly – though not entirely – in Act I in the scene between Tannhäuser and Venus. Wagner rewrote most of the scene at a time when his style had developed enormously. The love music here is closer to *Walküre* and *Tristan* than to the rest of *Tannhäuser*. The hero's harp song enters each time in its straight diatonic style with a jolt; but this is only apt, and the richness of inspiration, the musical intensification – beautifully conveyed here – transform the opera. The Paris version has never been recorded before, and that alone should dictate choice. Quite apart from that, however, Solti gives one of his very finest Wagner performances to date, helped by superb playing from the Vienna Philharmonic and an outstanding cast, superlatively recorded. Dernesch as Elisabeth and Ludwig as Venus outshine all rivalry; and Kollo, though not ideal, makes as fine a Heldentenor as we are currently likely to hear. The compact disc transfer reinforces the brilliance and richness of the performance. The sound is outstanding for its period (1971), and Ray Minshull's production adds to the atmospheric quality, with the orchestra given full weight and with the placing and movement of the voices finely judged.

Sawallisch's version, recorded at the 1962 Bayreuth Festival, comes up very freshly on CD. Though the new medium brings out all the more clearly the thuds, creaks and audience noises of a live performance (most distracting at the very start), the dedication of the reading is very persuasive, notably in the Venusberg scene where Grace Bumbry is a superb, sensuous Venus and Windgassen – not quite in his sweetest voice, often balanced rather close – is a fine, heroic Tannhäuser. Anja Silja controls the abrasiveness of her soprano well, to make this her finest performance on record, not ideally sweet but very sympathetic. Voices are set well forward of the orchestra, in which strings have far more bloom than brass; but the atmosphere of the Festspielhaus is vivid and compelling throughout.

Haitink's unexpected pursuit of lightness and refinement, almost as though this is music by Mendelssohn, makes for a reading which, for all its beauties, lacks an essential dramatic bite. Consistently he refines the piece, until you can hardly believe that this is an opera which deeply shocked early Victorians with its noisy vulgarity. Haitink's performance tends to sound like a studio run-through, carefully done with much intelligence, but largely uninvolved. It is not helped by a strained hero in Klaus König and a shrewish-sounding Venus in Waltraud Meier. The serious disappointment of the first Act then tends to colour one's response to the rest too, though Lucia Popp, stretched to the limit in a role on the heavy side for her, produces some characteristically beautiful singing as Elisabeth. Bernd Weikl is an intelligent but uningratiating Wolfram. Finely balanced sound, the more impressive on CD, beautifully atmospheric in the processional scenes. Banding is sparse, with limited index points added.

Tristan und Isolde (complete).

(M) *** HMV **CMS7 69319-2** [id.]; *EX 769319-4* (4). Vickers, Dernesch, Ludwig, Berry, Ridderbusch, German Op., Berlin, Ch., BPO, Karajan.

*** DG **419 889-2** (3) [id.]. Windgassen, Nilsson, Ludwig, Talvela, Waechter, Bayreuth Fest. (1966) Ch. & O, Boehm.

*** Ph. Dig. **410 447-2** (5) [id.]. Hofmann, Behrens, Minton, Weikl, Sotin, Bav. R. Ch. & SO, Bernstein.

(***) HMV mono **CDS7 47322-8** (4) [Ang. **CDC47321**]. Suthaus, Flagstad, Thebom, Greindl, Fischer-Dieskau, ROHCG Ch., Philh. O, Furtwängler.

(*) DG Dig. **413 315-2 (4) [id.]. Kollo, Margaret Price, Fassbaender, Fischer-Dieskau, Moll, Dresden State O, Carlos Kleiber.

Karajan's is a sensual performance of Wagner's masterpiece, caressingly beautiful and with superbly refined playing from the Berlin Philharmonic. At the climactic points of each Act Karajan is a tantalizing deceiver, leading you to expect that the moment of resolution will not be fully achieved, but then punching home with a final crescendo of supreme force. He is helped by a recording (not ideally balanced, but warmly atmospheric) which copes with an enormous dynamic range. Dernesch as Isolde is seductively feminine, not as noble as Flagstad, not as tough and unflinching as Nilsson, but the human quality makes this account if anything more moving still, helped by glorious tone-colour through every range. Jon Vickers matches her, in what is arguably his finest performance on record, allowing himself true pianissimo shading. The rest of the cast is excellent too. Though CD brings out more clearly the occasional oddities of balance – the distancing of the chorus at the end of Act I, and of the lovers themselves during the gentler parts of the love-duet – the 1972 sound has plenty of body, making this (on four mid-price CDs) an excellent first choice, with inspired conducting and the most satisfactory cast of all.

Boehm's Bayreuth performance, recorded at the 1966 Festival, has a cast that for consistency has seldom been bettered on disc. Now on only three CDs, one disc per Act, the benefit is enormous in presenting one of the big Wagner operas for the first time on disc without any breaks at all, with each Act uninterrupted. The performance is a fine one. Boehm is on the urgent side in this opera (one explanation for the economical layout), and the orchestral ensemble is not always immaculate; but the performance glows with intensity from beginning to end, carried through in the longest spans. Birgit Nilsson is in astonishingly rich and powerful voice. She sings the *Liebestod* at the end of the long evening as though she was starting out afresh, radiant and with not a hint of tiredness, rising to an orgasmic climax and bringing a heavenly pianissimo on the final rising octave to F sharp. Opposite Nilsson is Wolfgang Windgassen, the most mellifluous of Heldentenoren; though the microphone balance sometimes puts him at a disadvantage to his Isolde, the realism and sense of presence of the whole set has you bathing in the authentic atmosphere of Bayreuth. The darkness of the opening of Act III on lower strings has never sounded more sepulchrally threatening. Making up an almost unmatchable cast are Christa Ludwig as Brangaene, Eberhard Waechter as Kurwenal and Martii Talvela as King Mark, with the young Peter Schreier as the Young Sailor.

Bernstein's was the first *Tristan* on CD; worthily so, though at that point the art of fitting Wagner operas on to at most four discs was not pursued and, beside most other Wagner offerings in the new medium, this five-disc set is not only expensive but cumbersome in five separate 'jewel-boxes'. Nevertheless, the fine quality of the recording is all the more ravishing in the transfer, the sound rich, full and well detailed, a tribute to the Bavarian engineers working in the Herkulesaal in Munich. 'For the first time someone dares to perform this music as Wagner wrote it,' was Karl Boehm's comment when he visited Bernstein during rehearsals for this *Tristan* recording, made live at three separate concert performances. The surprise is that Bernstein, over-emotional in some music, here exercises restraint to produce the most spacious reading ever put on disc, more expansive even than Furtwängler's. His rhythmic sharpness goes with warmly expressive but unexaggerated phrasing, to give unflagging concentration and deep commitment. The love-duet has rarely if ever sounded so sensuous, with supremely powerful climaxes – as at the peak of *O sink'hernieder*. Nor in the *Liebestod* is there any question of Bernstein rushing ahead, for the culmination comes naturally and fully at a taxingly slow speed. Behrens makes a fine Isolde, less purely beautiful than her finest rivals but with reserves of power giving dramatic bite. The contrast of tone with Yvonne Minton's Brangaene (good, except for flatness in the warning solo) is not as great as usual, and there is likeness too between

Peter Hofmann's Tristan, often baritonal, and Bernd Weikl's Kurwenal, lighter than usual. The King Mark of Hans Sotin is superb.

It was one of the supreme triumphs of the recording producer, Walter Legge, when in 1952 with his recently formed Philharmonia Orchestra he teamed the incomparable Wagnerian, Wilhelm Furtwängler, with Kirsten Flagstad as the heroine in *Tristan und Isolde*. It was no easy matter, when Furtwängler was resentful of Legge at the time for sponsoring his rival, Karajan, and he agreed to the arrangement only because Flagstad insisted. The result has an incandescent intensity, typical of the conductor at his finest, and caught all too rarely in his studio recordings. The concept is spacious from the opening *Prelude* onwards, but equally the bite and colour of the drama are vividly conveyed, matching the nobility of Flagstad's portrait of Isolde. Some of the sensuousness of the character is missing, but the richly commanding power of her singing and her always distinctive timbre make it a uniquely compelling performance. Suthaus is not of the same calibre as Heldentenor, but he avoids ugliness and strain, which is rare in Tristan. Among the others, the only remarkable performance is from the young Fischer-Dieskau as Kurwenal, not ideally cast but keenly imaginative. One endearing oddity is that – on Flagstad's insistence – the top Cs at the opening of the love-duet were sung by Mrs Walter Legge (Elisabeth Schwarzkopf). The Kingsway Hall recording was admirably balanced, catching the beauty of the Philharmonia Orchestra at its peak. The CDs have opened up the original mono sound and it is remarkable how little constriction there is in the biggest climaxes, mostly shown in the *fortissimo* violins above the stave. The voices ride triumphantly over the orchestra (the balance is superbly judged) and at *mezzo forte* and *piano* levels there is striking atmosphere and bloom, with the vocal timbres firm and realistically focused. CD cueing is not especially generous (24 bands over the four discs) and the libretto typeface, though clear, is minuscule.

Kleiber directs a compellingly impulsive reading crowned by the glorious Isolde, the most purely beautiful of any complete interpretation on record, of Margaret Price. Next to more spacious readings, his at times sounds excitable, almost hysterical, with fast speeds tending to get faster, for all his hypnotic concentration. But the lyricism of Margaret Price, feminine and vulnerable, is well contrasted against the heroic Tristan of Kollo, at his finest in Act III. Kurt Moll makes a dark, leonine King Mark, but Fischer-Dieskau is at times gritty as Kurwenal and Brigitte Fassbaender is a clear but rather cold Brangaene. On CD the oddities and inconsistencies of sound (including odd bumps) are the more apparent; but with voices set well back in a spacious acoustic, the sound is still sensuously beautiful.

Die Walküre (complete).

*** Decca **414 105-2** (4); *414 105-4* (3) [id.]. Nilsson, Crespin, Ludwig, King, Hotter, Frick, VPO, Solti.

*** Ph. **412 478-2** (4) [id.]. King, Rysanek, Nienstedt, Nilsson, Adam, Burmeister, Bayreuth Fest. (1967) Ch. & O, Boehm.

*** Eurodisc **610064** (5). Altmeyer, Norman, Minton, Jerusalem, Adam, Moll, Dresden State O, Janowski.

(*) DG **415 145-2 (4) [id.]. Crespin, Janowitz, Veasey, Vickers, Stewart, Talvela, BPO, Karajan.

Recorded last in Solti's series, *Die Walküre* in some ways had the most refined sound, to make the CD version particularly impressive, amazingly fine for 1965, with voices and orchestral detail all the more precisely placed. Solti's conception is more lyrical than one would have expected from his recordings of the other three *Ring* operas. He sees Act II as the kernel of the work, perhaps even of the whole cycle. Acts I and III have their supremely attractive set-pieces which must inevitably make them more popular as entertainment, but here one appreciates that in Act II the conflict of wills, between Wotan and Fricka makes for one of Wagner's most deeply searching scenes. That is the more apparent when the greatest of latterday Wotans, Hans Hotter, takes the role, and Christa Ludwig sings with searing dramatic sense as his wife. Before that, Act I seems a little underplayed. This is partly because of Solti's deliberate lyricism – apt enough when love and spring greetings are in the air – but also (on the debit side) because James King fails both to project the character of Siegmund and to delve into the word-meanings as all the other members of the cast consistently do. Crespin has never sung more beautifully on record, but even that cannot cancel out the shortcoming. As for Nilsson's Brünnhilde, it has grown mellower, the emotions are clearer, and under-the-note attack is almost eliminated. Some may hesitate in the face of Hotter's obvious vocal trials; but the unsteadiness is, if anything, less marked than in his EMI recordings of items done many years ago. Like the CDs, the cassettes have been remastered and the background virtually eliminated.

Anyone wondering whether to invest in the Boehm *Ring* cycle, recorded live at Bayreuth in 1967, should sample the end of Act I of this account of *Die Walküre*, where the white heat of the occasion makes the scalp prickle. When Siegmund pulls the sword, Nothung, from the tree – James King in heroic voice – the Sieglinde, Leonie Rysanek, utters a shriek of joy to delight even the least susceptible Wagnerian, matching the urgency of the whole performance as conducted by Boehm. Rarely if ever does his preference for fast speeds undermine the music; on the contrary, it adds to the involvement of the performance, which never loses its concentration. Theo Adam is in firmer voice here as Wotan than he is in *Rheingold*, hardly sweet of tone but always singing with keen intelligence. As ever, Nilsson is in superb voice as Brünnhilde. Though the inevitable roughnesses of a live performance occasionally intrude, this presents a more involving experience than any rival complete recording. The CD transfer transforms what on LP seemed a rough recording, even if passages of heavy orchestration still bring some constriction of sound.

The Eurodisc *Ring* cycle is one for Wagnerians who want to concentrate on the score, undistracted by stereo staging or even by strongly characterful conducting. Janowski's direct approach matches the relative dryness of the acoustic, with voices fixed well forward of the orchestra – but not aggressively so. That balance allows full presence for the singing from a satisfyingly consistent cast. Jessye Norman might not seem an obvious choice for Sieglinde, but the sound is glorious, the expression intense and detailed, making her a superb match for the fine, if rather less imaginative Siegmund of Siegfried Jerusalem. The one snag with so commanding a Sieglinde is that she overtops the Brünnhilde of Jeannine Altmeyer who, more than usual, conveys a measure of feminine vulnerability in the leading Valkyrie even in her godhead days. Miss Altmeyer, born in Los Angeles of a German father and an Italian mother, may be slightly overparted, but the beauty and frequent sensuousness of her singing are the more telling, next to the gritty Wotan of Theo Adam. With its slow vibrato under pressure, his is rarely a pleasing voice, but the clarity of the recording makes it a specific, never a woolly sound, so that the illumination of the narrative is consistent and intense. Kurt Moll is a gloriously firm Hunding, and Yvonne Minton a searingly effective Fricka. On CD, the drama and urgency of the recording have even greater bite; but, as with the others in this series, the use of five discs is uncompetitive.

The great merits of Karajan's version in competition with those of Solti are the refinement of the orchestral playing and the heroic strength of Jon Vickers as Siegmund. With that underlined, one cannot help but note that the vocal shortcomings here are generally more marked, and the total result does not add up to quite so compelling a dramatic experience: one is less involved. Thomas Stewart may have a younger, firmer voice than Hotter, but the character of Wotan emerges only partially; it is not just that he misses some of the word-meaning, but that on occasion – as in the kissing away of Brünnhilde's godhead – he underlines too crudely. A fine performance, none the less; and Josephine Veasey as Fricka matches her rival Ludwig in conveying the biting intensity of the part. Gundula Janowitz's Sieglinde has its beautiful moments, but the singing is ultimately a little static. Crespin's Brünnhilde is impressive, but nothing like as satisfying as her study of Sieglinde on the Decca set. The voice is at times strained into unsteadiness, which the microphone seems to exaggerate. The DG recording is good, but not quite in the same class as the Decca – its slightly recessed quality is the more apparent in the CD transfer. The bass is relatively light, but an agreeable bloom is given to the voices, set in an atmospheric acoustic, all made the more realistic on CD.

VOCAL COLLECTIONS

Der fliegende Holländer: Senta's ballad. Götterdämmerung: Brünnhilde's immolation. Lohengrin: Elsa's dream; Euch Lüften. Tannhäuser: Elisabeth's greeting; Elisabeth's prayer, Tristan: Isolde's Liebestod. Die Walküre: Die Männer Sippe.
(*) HMV Dig. **CDC7 47436-2 [id.]. Hildegard Behrens, Munich RO, Schneider.

Hildegard Behrens's Wagner collection brings much powerful dramatic singing. She is more successful with Brünnhilde and Isolde than the more sweetly lyrical inspirations for Elsa and Elisabeth. Though, as usual, the microphone exaggerates the edge and unevenness, the voice is here more firmly controlled than on many of her other records, helped by sympathetic conducting from Peter Schneider. Though the sound is not ideally clear, the voice is well caught.

Der fliegende Holländer: Senta's ballad. Götterdämmerung: Brünnhilde's immolation. Tannhäuser: Dich teure Halle. Tristan und Isolde: Prelude and Liebestod.
*(*) CBS **CD 37294**. Caballé, NYPO, Mehta.

There are moments of tender intensity in Caballé's recital, illuminatingly perceptive of detail; but the singing is too often flawed, when the voice is not well suited to the heavier roles, and Caballé disguises her weakness in mannerism. The recording is only fair; and this is a collection for Caballé admirers, rather than for the general collector.

Der fliegende Holländer: Die Frist ist um. Parsifal: Mein Sohn, Amfortas, bist du am Amt . . . Wehel Wehe der Qual! Die Walküre: Lass isch's verlauten . . . Was keinem in Worten ich hünde; Leb wohl du kühnes herrliches Kindl.
*** Ph. Dig. **412 271-2** [id.]. Simon Estes (with Bundschuh, Reeh), Berlin State Op. O, Fricke.

Simon Estes with his dark bass-baritone has proved an impressive Dutchman at Bayreuth, and the firmness and tonal clarity of his singing contrasts strongly with the woolly Wagner sound often delivered in these roles. His enunciation of German is excellent, but the relative youthfulness of the timbre may disconcert some who expect Wotan or Amfortas or even the Dutchman to sound old. Variety of expression is a little limited; but it is rare for the music to be heard with such freshness and clarity in all four of these substantial excerpts – *Wotan's Narration* 25 minutes long. Eva-Maria Bundschuh as Brünnhilde in that passage and Hein Reeh as Titurel in *Amfortas's Lament* provide capable support, as does the Berlin State Opera Orchestra. First-rate recording, particularly clear and vivid on CD.

Götterdämmerung: Dawn and Siegfried's Rhine journey; Siegfried's funeral march. Parsifal: Ich sah' das Kind. Tristan und Isolde: Prelude; Liebestod. Die Walküre: Wotan's farewell and Magic fire music.
(*) Decca **414 625-2 [id.]. Flagstad, Nilsson, London, VPO, Knappertsbusch.

This is a splendid reminder of Hans Knappertsbusch's mastery as a Wagnerian, recorded in the period when Decca was working up to the idea of tackling a complete *Ring* cycle. The much younger Solti was finally chosen for that big project, but the veteran Knappertsbusch in the preliminary period did these glowing performances, collaborating with the two greatest Wagnerian sopranos of their generations, Nilsson in the *Liebestod*, Flagstad in the *Parsifal* item. George London is the Wotan, firmer than he later became. Though the digital transfers are bright, the vividness of sound is amazing, with the voices particularly well caught.

Lohengrin: In fernem Land. Die Meistersinger: Fanget an!; Morgenlich leuchtend im rosigen Schein, Rienzi: Allmacht'ger Vater. Siegfried: Nothung! (i) *Tannhäuser: Unbrunst im Herzen. Die Walküre: Ein Schwert verhiess mir der Vater; Winterstürme wichen dem Wonnemond.*
(*) CBS Dig. **CD 38931 [id.]. Peter Hofmann, Stuttgart RSO, Ivan Fischer; (i) with Doernberger.

Hofmann's Wagner recital, extending over a wide range of heroes, is as fine as any from today's Heldentenoren. The voice as recorded is a little gritty in lyrical music, and the high tessitura of Walther's *Prize song* brings strain, but the heroic power is impressive in everything. The *Tannhäuser* excerpt is not limited to the hero's solo but also includes his exchanges with Wolfram (Victor Doernberger). Sympathetic accompaniment, not brilliant in ensemble or sound.

OTHER COLLECTIONS

(i) *Siegfried idyll;* (ii) *Der fliegende Holländer: Overture; Lohengrin:* (i) *Prelude to Act I;* (iii) *Bridal Chorus;* (i) *Die Meistersinger: Prelude;* (iv) *Tannhäuser: Overture;* (i) *Tristan und Isolde: Prelude and Liebestod;* (v) *Die Walküre: Ride of the Valkyries.*
(B) **(*) DG Walkman *413 849-4* [id.]. (i) BPO, Kubelik; (ii) Bayreuth Fest. O, Boehm; (iii) Bayreuth Fest. Ch., Pitz; (iv) cond. Gerdes; (v) cond. Karajan.

This Wagner Walkman tape centres on some fine performances made in 1963 by Kubelik and the Berlin Philharmonic, including the *Siegfried idyll.* Karajan contributes a lively *Ride of the Valkyries* (taken from his complete *Die Walküre*); Gerdes's *Tannhäuser overture* also comes from his (deleted) complete set; while the *Bridal chorus* from *Lohengrin* has a Bayreuth hallmark, although in fact recorded in the studio. The sound is generally very good; only the opening *Flying Dutchman overture*, actually made at Bayreuth under Boehm, sounds slightly less refined than the rest of the concert.

Waldteufel, Emil (1837–1915)

Waltzes: *Dolores; España; Estudiantina; Les Patineurs; Plus de diamants; Les Sirènes; Très jolie.*
** Ph. Dig. **400 012-2** [id.]. V. Volksoper O, Bauer-Theussl.

Waldteufel's waltzes have a direct, breezy vivacity. They lack the underlying poetic feeling that takes the works of Johann Strauss into the concert hall, but their spontaneity and wit more than compensate for any lack of distinction in the tunes. Undoubtedly *The Skaters* is Waldteufel's masterpiece, but *Pomone*, *Mon Rêve* and the less well-known *Toujours ou jamais* all show the composer at his best. *España* is, of course, a direct crib from Chabrier, but is enjoyable enough, even if it does not match the original score in exuberance. Franz Bauer-Theussl's performances with the excellent Vienna Volksoper Orchestra are amiable and recorded in a generously warm acoustic. The effect is pleasing, but slightly bland. Moreover, the opening of *Les Patineurs* is truncated. The famous horn solo is omitted; instead, there is just a snatch of the main theme on the cello. The compact disc makes admirable if rather expensive background music, but does not differ a great deal from the LP.

Walton, William (1902–83)

Capriccio burlesco; Crown imperial (march); Johannesburg festival overture; Orb and sceptre (march); Scapino: comedy overture. Spitfire prelude & fugue.
(M) **(*) HMV *ED 291053-4*. Royal Liverpool PO, Groves – BLISS: *Things to come*.**(*)

An attractive collection of Walton's popular shorter orchestral pieces. The playing is excellent and, if Groves is a little phlegmatic in the two marches with the *nobilmente* feeling tending to undermine the bite, the *Johannesburg festival overture* has a sparkling scherzando quality. The stirring music for the Leslie Howard film, *The First of the Few*, is also very effective, helped by the recording, originally a high-fi-orientated Studio Two master, yet resonant and sonorous as well as bright. The tape transfer takes a little of the edge off the top, but this is not nearly as striking here as on the Bliss coupling. We hope this will arrive on a Studio CD in due course.

Cello concerto.
*** CBS **MK 39541**; *IMT 39541* [id.]. Yo-Yo Ma, LSO, Previn – ELGAR: *Concerto*.***
*(*) Chan. Dig. **CHAN 8384**; *ABTD 1007* [id.]. Kirshbaum, SNO, Gibson – ELGAR: *Concerto*.*(*)

Yo-Yo Ma and Previn give a sensuously beautiful performance. With speeds markedly slower than usual in the outer movements, the meditation is intensified to bring a mood of ecstasy, quite distinct from other Walton. In turn, with spacious outer movements, the toughness and power of the central allegro is made the more marked. It becomes the symphonic kernel of the work, far more than just a scherzo. In the excellent CBS recording the soloist is less forwardly and more faithfully balanced than is common. The CD is one of CBS's most impressive, refining detail and increasing tangibility.

The reading of Kirshbaum and Gibson is disappointing, lacking the warmth, weight and expressiveness that so ripe an example of late romanticism demands. The digital recording is also disappointingly lacking in body in CD, while the cassette has a restricted upper range.

(i) *Viola concerto*; (ii) *Sinfonia concertante for piano and orchestra.*
(M) (***) HMV mono *EH 291276-4*. (i) William Primrose, Philh. O; (ii) Phyllis Sellick, CBSO; composer – VAUGHAN WILLIAMS: *Concerto accademico; Flos campi*.(***)

An indispensable reissue, sounding remarkably well in its tape format. No one has ever surpassed Phyllis Sellick in this first ever recording of the *Sinfonia concertante*, with the composer conducting. The 1945 mono sound is limited, but in a modern transfer this grossly under-appreciated piece comes out very convincingly. William Primrose's 1946 recording of the *Viola concerto*, also with the composer conducting, is even more vivid, though the soloist is placed well forward and is never really allowed to play softly. It is a strong, involving performance, in most ways preferable to his later LP versions. With the V.W. concertante works, it makes an exceptionally generous tape, lasting well over 75 minutes.

Viola concerto; Violin concerto.
❀ *** HMV Dig. **CDC7 49628-2** [id.]; *EL 749628-4*. Nigel Kennedy, RPO, Previn.

Few works written this century can match Walton's two pre-war string concertos in richness and warmth of melody. They mirror each other in their broadly similar structures, each starting with the slowest, most lyrical movement, followed by a Scherzo and a strongly argued sonata-form finale, ending in an epilogue. Kennedy's achievement in giving performances of both works equally rich and expressive makes for an ideal coupling, helped by the unique insight of André Previn as Waltonian. Kennedy on the viola produces tone as rich and firm as on his usual violin. His double-stopping is wonderfully firm and true, and though in the first movement of the *Viola concerto* he opts for a dangerously slow tempo, drawing the lovely first melody out more spaciously than the score would strictly allow, he justifies it with his concentration at a steady, undistorted pace. The Scherzo has never been recorded with more panache than here, and the finale brings a magic moment in the return of the main theme from the opening, hushed and intense. In the *Violin concerto* too, Kennedy gives a warmly relaxed reading, in which he dashes off the bravura passages with a flair that suggests he knows the original Heifetz recordings. He may miss some of the more searchingly introspective manner of Chung in her 1971 version (which must return on CD before long), but there are few Walton records as richly rewarding as this, helped by warm, atmospheric sound. There is a first-class cassette too.

Violin concerto.
(M) *** HMV *ED 290353-4.* Ida Haendel, Bournemouth SO, Berglund – BRITTEN: *Violin concerto.****

The *Violin concerto*, written for Heifetz in 1939, shows Walton at his most distinctively compelling. Even he has rarely written melodies so ravishingly beautiful, so hauntedly romantic, yet his equally personal brand of spikiness has rarely if ever been presented with more power. A sunny, glowing, Mediterranean-like view of the *Concerto* comes from Ida Haendel, with brilliant playing from the soloist and eloquent orchestral support from the Bournemouth orchestra under Paavo Berglund. Kyung Wha Chung's version is wirier and in some ways more in character, but many collectors will respond equally (or even more) positively to Miss Haendel's warmth. There is an unrelieved lyricism about her tone that may not be to all tastes but, given the quality of both playing and recording (as well as the interest of the no less successful performance of the Britten coupling), this is an eminently desirable issue. On the cassette, which is generally impressively transferred, the resonance does slightly cloud some of the more exuberant orchestral tuttis, but the soloist is beautifully caught.

Coronation marches: Crown Imperial; Orb and sceptre. Façade: suites 1 & 2; (i; ii) *Gloria;* (ii) *Te Deum.*
*** HMV **CDC7 47512-2** [id.]. CBSO, Louis Frémaux, (i) with Robotham, Rolfe Johnson, Rayner Cook, CBSO Ch. (ii) Choristers of Worcester Cathedral.

'Shatteringly apt displays of pomp and circumstance' is the delightful description of Frank Howes for the three Walton works inspired by coronations, and here they are splendidly coupled with the grand setting of the *Gloria* which Walton wrote in 1961 for a double celebration at Huddersfield, the 125th anniversary of the Choral Society and the 30th anniversary of its association with Sir Malcolm Sargent. That last work, the longest of the four, has not quite the same concentration as the others, for it represents Walton tending to repeat himself in his jagged Alleluia rhythms and jazzy fugatos. Frémaux directs a highly enjoyable performance nevertheless; but it rather pales before the Coronation *Te Deum*, which may use some of the same formulas but has Walton electrically inspired. It is a grand setting which yet has a superb formal balance (almost a sonata form) while exploiting every tonal and atmospheric effect imaginable between double choirs and semi-choruses. The two splendid marches are marvellously done too. Frémaux uses the original full version of *Crown Imperial* instead of observing the cuts suggested by Walton, which reduce it by about a third, and that is the right decision. The rich, resonant recording is apt for the music, spacious with excellent perspectives, and it has transferred splendidly to CD, with the brass both sonorous and biting and the choral sound fresh as well as with plenty of weight. The *Façade suites* have been added for the CD (total playing time 67′) and here the remastering is even more telling, adding point to playing which is already affectionately witty. Frémaux's rhythmic control gives a fresh, new look to familiar music: his jaunty jazz inflexions in *Old Sir Faulk* are deliciously whimsical.

(i) *Façade suites;* (ii) *Henry V: Death of Falstaff; Touch her soft lips and part;* (iii) *Scapino: comedy overture;* (i) *Siesta;* (iv) *Spitfire prelude & fugue;* (v) *Belshazzar's Feast.*
(***) HMV mono *ED 290715-4.* (i) LPO; (ii) Philh. Strings; (iii) Philh. O; (iv) Hallé O; (v) Dennis Noble, Huddersfield Ch. Soc., Liverpool PO; composer.

Walton's original wartime recording of *Belshazzar's Feast* in some ways remains unsurpassed by any of the many versions that have been recorded since. The fervour of chorus and orchestra alike, working under stress, is still electrifying in this excellent if limited transfer of the 78s. That leaves room for the other recordings that the composer made of his own music, before the age of LP. The pre-war recordings of the *Façade suites* are among the finest of their period and still sound remarkably well.

Film music: *As you like it: suite. The Battle of Britain: suite. Henry V: suite. History of the English speaking peoples: March. Troilus and Cressida* (opera): *Interlude.*
*** HMV Dig. **CDC7 47944-2** [id.]; *EL 290591-4.* LPO Ch. & O, Carl Davis.

No composer has followed on the Elgar ceremonial tradition with such brilliance and panache as Walton. Here, with many items never recorded before, is a heartwarming celebration of that side of his work, helped by red-blooded performances from the LPO under the tireless advocate, Carl Davis. *The Battle of Britain suite* presents the music that (for trumpery reasons) was rejected for the original film, including a Wagnerian send-up and a splendid final march. Another vintage Walton march here was written for a television series based on Churchill's history, but again was never used. It is a pity the *Henry V suite* does not include the Agincourt charge, but it is good to have the choral contributions to the opening and closing sequences. Best of all, perhaps, is the long-buried music for the 1926 Paul Czinner film of *As you like it.* Walton, having just had great success with his *First Symphony,* here exuberantly does some joyful cribbing from Respighi, Ravel and others, but remains gloriously himself, making one regret that as a serious composer he was self-critical to the point of inhibition. If only he had allowed himself to throw off music like this rather more often, we would all have gained by it. Warm, opulent recording. There is quite a good tape, but the CD is immeasurably superior in such spectacular music.

Henry V (film music): *Passacaglia; The Death of Falstaff; Touch her soft lips and part.*
*** DG **419 748-2** [id.]. ECO, Barenboim – DELIUS: *Aquarelles* etc.; VAUGHAN WILLIAMS: *Lark ascending; Oboe concerto.****

These two fine Walton string pieces make an admirable complement to a sensuously beautiful collection of English music, with Barenboim at his most affectionately inspirational and the ECO very responsive. The 1975 recording has been remastered most successfully, retaining its warmth and bloom.

Symphony No. 1 in B flat min.
** Chan. Dig. **CHAN 8313**; *ABTD 1095* [id.]. SNO, Gibson.

Symphony No. 1 in B flat min.; Coronation marches: Crown Imperial; Orb and sceptre.
(*) Telarc Dig. **CD 80125 [id.]. RPO, Previn.

Previn's view of Walton's electrifying *First Symphony* has grown broader and less biting with the years. The sumptuous Telarc recording also makes for warmth rather than incisiveness. Those who know Previn's incomparable earlier reading for RCA – surely due for CD transfer – may well be disappointed; however, with fine playing from the RPO and with the slow movement more richly luxuriant than before, this is still a most enjoyable reading. The two *Coronation marches* make a colourful and welcome fill-up.

Gibson's is a convincingly idiomatic view, well paced but with ensemble not always bitingly precise enough for this darkly intense music (malice prescribed for the Scherzo, melancholy for the slow movement). Recording first rate, but with less body than usual from Chandos and with timpani resonantly obtrusive. The compact disc is somewhat disappointing, bringing out the thinness on top, and this probably sounds best in its excellent cassette format. This is only a stop-gap until Previn's intermittently available RCA version is transferred to CD.

Passacaglia for solo cello.
*** Chan. Dig. **CHAN 8499**; *ABTD 1209* [id.]. Raphael and Peter Wallfisch – BAX: *Rhapsodic ballad*; BRIDGE: *Cello sonata*; DELIUS: *Cello sonata.****

William Walton's *Passacaglia* for solo cello was composed in the last year of his life. It has restraint and eloquence, and Raphael Wallfisch gives a thoroughly sympathetic account of it. Excellent recording, on tape as well as CD.

(i) *Piano quartet; String quartet in A min.*
(*) Mer. Dig. **CDE 84139; *KE 84139* [id.]. John McCabe, English Qt.

The *Piano quartet* is a work of Walton's immaturity: it dates from his days as an undergraduate and reflects enthusiasm for Ravel and Stravinsky, though there are many indications of what is to come. It is coupled with the mature *Quartet*, written immediately after the war; this is a substantial piece with stronger claims on the repertoire than it seems to have realized. McCabe and the English Quartet give a convincing enough account of the early piece, but the latter's account of the *String quartet* does not present a strong challenge to that of the Gabrielis on Chandos. If you want this particular coupling rather than the Elgar, this is certainly worth investigating.

String quartet in A min.
*** Chan. Dig. **CHAN 8474**; *ABTD 1185* [id.]. Gabrieli Qt – ELGAR: *String quartet.****

Walton planned to start work on what turned out to be his only string quartet immediately after the *Violin concerto*; but the war turned his thoughts elsewhere (particularly in the direction of film music) and it was not finished until 1947. It must rank as one of his best works and, in hands such as these, sounds far more effective than in the version for full strings that he made in the early 1970s. The performance was given at The Maltings, Snape, and the excellence of both the playing and the recorded sound must earn this a strong recommendation on the excellent chrome cassette as well as the CD, which is in the demonstration bracket.

Violin sonata.
(*) ASV Dig. *ZCDCA 548* [id.]. McAslan, Blakely – ELGAR: *Sonata.*(*)

Lorraine McAslan gives a warmly committed performance of Walton's often wayward *Sonata*, coping well with the sharp and difficult changes of mood in both of the two long movements. The romantic melancholy of the piece suits her well, and though the recording does not make her tone as rounded as it should be, she produces some exquisite pianissimo playing, making this a most impressive début recording. John Blakely is a most sympathetic partner, particularly impressive in crisply articulated scherzando passages.

(i) *Belshazzar's Feast; Henry V (film score): suite.*
*** ASV Dig. **CDRPO 8001**; *ZCRPO 8001* [id.]. (i) Luxon, Brighton Fest. Ch., L. Coll. Mus., RPO, Previn.

(i) *Belshazzar's Feast; Improvisations on an impromptu of Benjamin Britten; Overtures: Portsmouth Point; Scapino.*
*** HMV **CDC7 47624-2** [id.]. LSO, Previn, (i) with John Shirley-Quirk, LSO Ch.

Previn's HMV version of *Belshazzar's Feast* remains the most spectacular yet recorded. The digital remastering has not lost the body and atmosphere of the sound, but has increased its impact. This fine performance was recorded with Walton present on his seventieth birthday, and though Previn's tempi are occasionally slower than those set by Walton himself in his two recordings, the authenticity is clear, with consistently sharp attack and with dynamic markings meticulously observed, down to the tiniest hairpin markings. Chorus and orchestra are challenged to their finest standards, and John Shirley-Quirk proves a searching and imaginative soloist. The *Improvisations*, given a first recording, make a generous fill-up alongside the two overtures in which Previn, the shrewdest and most perceptive of Waltonians, finds more light and shade than usual. Again the remastered sound is excellent.

André Previn's new digital version of Walton's oratorio was the first issue on the Royal Philharmonic Orchestra's own RPO label, providing a first-class start to the project in a performance in some ways even sharper and more urgent than his fine earlier version for EMI with the LSO. The recording is very clear, bringing out details of Walton's brilliant orchestration as never before. The chorus, singing with biting intensity, is set realistically behind the orchestra, and though that gives the impression of a smaller group than is ideal, clarity and definition are enhanced. Benjamin Luxon – who earlier sang in Solti's Decca version – is a characterful soloist, but his heavy vibrato is exaggerated by too close a balance. The five-movement suite from Walton's film music for *Henry V* makes a generous and attractive coupling. Previn was the first conductor on record since Walton himself to capture the full dramatic bite and colour of this music, with the cavalry charge at Agincourt particularly vivid. The iron-oxide cassette cannot be recommended. The transfer level is low and there is little choral bite with the upper range blunted.

The Bear (opera: complete).
**(*) Chan. *ABT 1052* [id.]. Harris, Yurisich, Mangin, Melbourne SO, Cavdarski.

Walton's brilliant adapatation of Chekhov's one-Act farce with its array of parodies makes ideal material for recording. This Australian version lacks some of the wit of the original-cast recording (not currently available), but with first-rate sound and clean-cut, youthful-sounding singing it is well worth investigating. The tape is vivid, but there is an occasional hint of peaking.

Ward, John (1571–1638)

Madrigals: *Come sable night*; *Cruel unkind; Die not, fond man*; *Hope of my heart; If heaven's just wrath*; *If the deep sighs*; *I have retreated*; *My breast I'll set*; *Oft have I tender'd*; *Out from the vale*; *Retire, my troubled soul*; *Sweet Philomel*.
*** Hyp. Dig. **CDA 66256**; *KA 66256* [id.]. Consort of Musicke, Anthony Rooley.

Ward's music speaks with a distinctive voice free from the self-conscious melancholy that afflicts some of his contemporaries. This is not to say that his output is wanting in depth of feeling or elegiac sentiment, but rather that his language is freer from artifice. He chooses poetry of high quality and his music is always finely proportioned and organic in conception. His achievement is well summed up by Richard Luckett's note about the poems: 'Together they make up an exploration of a sombre, pastoral world, a darkened Arcadia where the shepherds' eclogues are predominantly elegiac, and pain and loss in love are shaded by a sense of the pain and loss of death.' John Ward served the Honourable Henry Fanshawe as both Attorney and Musician, and the madrigals are dedicated to him. They appeared at the end of the period in which the madrigal flourished (in 1613, to be exact) but are by no means to be regarded as representing the tradition at anything less than its finest. Readers who possess the earlier Oiseau-Lyre set made in 1981, in which madrigals were interspersed with instrumental fantasies, may wonder whether to replace it in the new format. These new performances do have a distinctly finer tonal blend and in many ways are now to be preferred. Newcomers have no choice, since the earlier set is deleted; such is the quality of this music and the accomplishment with which it is presented that there should be no hesitation. In addition, there are three previously unpublished madrigals.

Warlock, Peter (1894–1930)

The Curlew (song cycle for tenor, flute, cor anglais & strings).
(M) *** HMV **CDM7 69170-2** [id.]; *ED 769170-4.* Ian Partridge, Music Group of London – VAUGHAN WILLIAMS: *On Wenlock Edge; 10 Blake Songs.*** ❀

The Curlew is Warlock's most striking and ambitious work, a continuous setting of a sequence of poems by Yeats, which reflect the darker side of the composer's complex personality. Ian Partridge, with the subtlest shading of tone-colour and the most sensitive response to word-meaning, gives an intensely poetic performance, beautifully recorded, and transferred to CD with striking presence. The chrome cassette is also exceptionally clear and vivid and costs proportionately less than the compact disc.

The Curlew (song cycle). Songs: *The Birds; Chopcherry; The fairest May; Mourne no more; My ghostly fader; Nursery jingles* (*How many miles to Babylon?; O, my kitten; Little Jack Jingle; Suky, you shall be my wife; Jenny Gray*)*; Sleep; The Water Lily.*
(*) *Pearl* **SHECD 510 [id.]. Griffet, Haffner Qt, Murdoch, Ryan.

Though this performance of *The Curlew* is not so beautiful or quite so imaginative as Ian Partridge's version, it is good to have a whole record of songs by a composer with a strikingly distinctive feeling for English verse. Each one of these songs is a miniature of fine sensitivity, and James Griffett sings them with keen insight, pointing the words admirably. Good recording.

Wassenaer, Unico (1692–1766)

6 Concerti armonici.
*** Argo Dig. **410 205-2**. ASMF, Marriner.
** Chan. Dig. **CHAN 8481**; *ABTD 1193* [id.]. I Musici di Montreal, Turovsky.

For years these eloquent concertos were attributed to Pergolesi, and in the 1950s their authorship migrated from him to Riccioti, De Fesch and others. In 1981, however, an autograph manuscript came to light in the hand of a Dutch nobleman, which would appear to have settled the matter. Sir Neville Marriner and the Academy of St Martin-in-the-Fields are nothing if not spacious. They bring both dignity and warmth to these remarkable pieces, and they are sumptuously recorded, too. They combine opulence of tone with genuine feeling and make a clear first choice in this repertoire. The compact disc is first class.

I Musici de Montreal have admirable spirit and produce a rich, robust sonority. In terms of finesse, however, they do not displace the Academy, whose version must remain a first recommendation.

Waxman, Franz (1906–67)

Film scores: *Bride of Frankenstein: Creation of the female monster. Mr Skeffington: excerpts. Old acquaintance: Elegy for strings. Objective Burma: excerpts. Peyton Place: suite. Philadelphia story: Fanfare; True love. A Place in the Sun: Suite. Prince Valiant: suite. Rebecca: suite. Sunset Boulevard: suite. Taras Bulba: The ride to Dublo. To have and have not: excerpts. The two Mrs Carrolls: suite.*
*** RCA **RD 87017 [RCD1 7017]**. Nat. PO, Gerhardt.

Of the many European musicians who crossed the Atlantic to make careers in Hollywood, Franz Waxman was among the most distinguished. Born in Upper Silesia, he had his early musical training in Germany. He was immensely gifted, and much of his music can stand on its own without the screen images it originally served to accompany. His first important score was for James Whale's *Bride of Frankenstein*, a horror movie to which many film buffs give classic status. His marvellously evocative music (a haunting, almost Wagnerian crescendo built over a throbbing timpani beat) for *The creation of the female monster* (visually most compelling in the film sequence) was restored by the conductor, mainly from listening to the film soundtrack, as the orchestral parts are lost. It builds on a memorable three-chord motif which seems instantly familiar. Readers will soon discover its associations for themselves: sufficient to say that the more familiar use of this melodic fragment comes from a score written by another composer some fourteen years later. The *Bride of Frankenstein* music dates from 1935. Waxman stayed on to write for 188 films over thirty-two years. The opening of the first item on this tape, the *Suite* from *Prince Valiant*, immediately shows the vigour of Waxman's invention and the brilliance of his Richard Straussian orchestration, and this score includes one of those sweeping string tunes which are the very epitome of Hollywood film music. Perhaps the finest of these comes in *A Place in the Sun*, and in the *Suite* it is used to preface an imaginative rhapsodical movement for solo alto sax (brilliantly played here by Ronnie Chamberlain). The reprise of the main tune, also on the alto sax but decorated by a characteristic counter-theme in the upper strings, is a moment of the utmost magic. In this work, incidentally, there is another curious anticipation of music written by another composer: a fugal section of Waxman's score is remarkably like the end of the second movement of Shostakovich's *Eleventh Symphony* (written seven years after the film, which was not shown in the Soviet Union). To make the coincidence complete, it was Waxman who conducted the West Coast première of the symphony in 1958. All the music on this CD is of high quality, and for any movie buff this is desert-island material. It nostalgically includes the famous MGM introductory title fanfare, which Waxman wrote as a backcloth for Leo the Lion. The orchestral playing throughout is marvellously eloquent, and the conductor's dedication is obvious. The recording is rich and full, with no lack of brilliance in this very successful transfer to compact disc.

Weber, Carl (1786–1826)

Clarinet concertino in C min., Op. 26.
*** ASV Dig. **CDDCA 559**; *ZCDCA 559* [id.]. Emma Johnson, ECO, Groves – CRUSELL: *Concerto No. 2* *** ❀; BAERMANN: *Adagio* ***; ROSSINI: *Introduction, theme and variatons.****

Emma Johnson is in her element in Weber's delightful *Concertino*. Her phrasing is wonderfully beguiling and her use of light and shade agreeably subtle, while she finds a superb lilt in the final section, pacing the music to bring out its charm rather than achieve breathless bravura. Sir Charles Groves provides an admirable accompaniment, and the recording is eminently realistic and naturally balanced. There is a good tape.

Clarinet concerto No. 1 in F min., Op. 73.
*** ASV Dig. **CDDCA 585**; *ZCDCA 585* [id.]. Emma Johnson, ECO, Yan Pascal Tortelier – DEBUSSY: *Rapsodie*; CRUSELL: *Introduction, theme and variations*; TARTINI: *Concertino*.***
(*) RCA **RD 89831. Stoltzman, Mostly Mozart O, Schneider – MOZART: *Concerto*.**

Clarinet concertos Nos 1 in F min., Op. 73; 2 in E flat, Op. 74; Concertino in C min., Op. 26.
(*) Chan. **CHAN 8305; *ABTD 1058* [id.]. Hilton, CBSO, Järvi.
(*) HM Orfeo **CO 67831A. Brunner, Bamberg SO, Caetani.

Clarinet concerto No. 2.
*** Hyp. **CDA 66088**; *KA 66088* [id.]. Thea King, LSO, Francis – CRUSELL: *Concerto No. 2*.***

Emma Johnson's fine, inspired version of the Weber *First Concerto* takes up one half of an attractive mixed-bag collection of concertante pieces which reveal many sides of her winning artistry. The subtlety of her expression, even in relation to most of her older rivals. is astonishing, with pianissimos more daringly extreme and with distinctively persuasive phrasing in the slow movement, treated warmly and spaciously. In the sparkling finale she is wittier than any, plainly enjoying herself to the full. With undistracting and natural sound, set in a helpful acoustic, it makes an excellent version, particularly if you fancy the unusual coupling. There is a good chrome cassette, although the orchestral bass seems a shade over-resonant.

Stylish, understanding performances of both concertos from Janet Hilton, spirited and rhythmic (particularly in No. 1), but erring just a little on the side of caution next to her finest virtuoso rivals. With full, well-balanced digital recording and nice matching between soloist and orchestra, it certainly outshines its main competitor in sound, with an excellent matching cassette. This record is generous in including the engaging *Concertino* alongside the two concertos, a piece made famous in far-off 78 r.p.m. days by a Columbia record by the Garde Républicain Band of France, the solo part played with great bravura by all members of the first clarinet line in unison.

Eduard Brunner offers the same couplings as Janet Hilton. His performances are often more romantically ardent, with a firmer line. Both slow movements come off especially well, with the horn chorale in the *Adagio* of the *First Concerto* producing some lovely playing from the Bamberg orchestra. However, articulation of the fast running passages is sometimes less characterful and Janet Hilton finds rather more humour in the finales, especially the *Alla Polacca* of No. 2. Yet Brunner is at his best in the last movement of the *Concertino*, his bravura agreeably extrovert here. Where the Chandos issue scores is in the recording which, especially on the compact disc, is more open and transparent, whereas on the Orfeo CD orchestral textures are thick in tuttis.

Readers content with the *E flat Concerto* alone will find the Hyperion coupling with Crusell a delectable combination. Thea King with her beautiful range of tone-colours is an outstandingly communicative artist on record and here gives a totally delightful account of the second of the two Weber concertos, particularly lovely in the G minor slow movement and seductively pointed in the *Polacca* rhythms of the finale, never pressed too hard. She is admirably accompanied by Alun Francis and the LSO in a warmly reverberant recording that CD makes very realistic indeed.

The wit of Richard Stoltzman's playing of the *First Concerto* with his clean, distinctive tone is well brought out in his account of the Weber. The finale, sparkling and light, is particularly winning. It makes a fair recommendation if you fancy the Mozart coupling, though that is less completely recommendable.

Horn concertino in E min., Op. 45.
*** Ph. Dig. **412 237-2** [id.]. Baumann, Leipzig GO, Masur – R. STRAUSS: *Horn concertos*.**(*)

Baumann plays Weber's opening lyrical melody so graciously that the listener is made to feel this is a more substantial work than it is. At the end of the *Andante* Baumann produces an undulating series of chords (by gently singing the top note as he plays) and the effect is spine-tingling, while the easy virtuosity of the closing *Polacca* is hardly less breathtaking. The bravura, is essentially easy-going, and Masur's accompaniment has matching warmth, while the Leipzig Hall adds its usual flattering ambience. The soloist is given fine presence on CD.

Introduction, theme and variations (for clarinet and orchestra).
*** Denon **C37 7038** [id.]. Meyer, Berlin Philh. Qt – MOZART: *Clarinet Quintet.****

This piece attributed to Weber is now known to be the work of Joseph Küffner (1777–1856) and is listed here for convenience. It is an effective but unimportant brief display work, essentially lightweight. The recording by Sabine Meyer and the Berlin Philharmonia is first rate, very well balanced and recorded.

Invitation to the dance (orch. Berlioz).
*** Decca Dig. **411 898-2** [id.]. Nat. PO, Bonynge – BERLIOZ: *Les Troyens ballet***; LECOCQ: *Mam'zelle Angot.****

Bonynge's account has elegance and polish and the waltz rhythms are nicely inflected. The Kingsway Hall recording is first class, if slightly sharper in focus on CD. The Lecocq coupling is vivaciously tuneful; but the Berlioz ballet sequence is not really memorable heard out of context.

Bonynge's performance is also available on a generous and well-transferred medium-price cassette, coupled with Chopin's *Les Sylphides* and Rossini's *La Boutique fantasque* (Decca *417 600-4*).

Konzertstück in F min., Op. 79.
*** Ph. **412 251-2** [id.]. Brendel, LSO, Abbado – SCHUMANN: *Piano concerto.****

Weber's programmatic *Konzertstück* is seldom heard in the concert hall these days, and it is a rarity in the recording studio. This Philips version is very brilliant indeed, and finds the distinguished soloist in his very best form: he is wonderfully light and invariably imaginative. In every respect, including the recording quality, this is unlikely to be surpassed for a long time. As in the case of the Schumann concerto with which it is coupled, on CD Weber emerges in brighter, firmer focus than on LP; collectors wanting this delightful work in the new format need not hesitate.

Overtures: *Abu Hassan; Beherrscher der Geister; Euryanthe; Der Freischütz; Oberon; Peter Schmoll. Invitation to the dance* (orch. Berlioz), *Op. 65.*
(M) *** DG **419 070-2**; *419 069-4* [id.]. BPO, Karajan.

A self-recommending reissue from 1973, digitally remastered. The performances have great style and refinement. Weber's overtures are superbly crafted and there are no better examples of the genre than *Oberon* and *Der Freischütz*. While epitomizing the spirit of the operas which they serve to introduce, each also shows the composer's special feeling for the romantic possibilities of the French horn, heard as soloist in *Oberon* and in a marvellously crafted quartet in *Der Freischütz*. Here, by scoring the four parts for a pair each of horns, crooked in C and F, Weber achieves a lengthy four-part melody, with almost every note available on the natural harmonics of the valveless instrument of his time. Needless to say, the Berlin horn playing is peerless. For this reissue, Karajan's stylish performance of another Weberian innovation, the *Invitation to the dance* (in Berlioz's orchestration), makes a valuable bonus. On CD the sound is drier and brighter than originally, with a loss of weight in the bass.

Overtures: *Der Freischütz; Oberon.*
(M) *** DG **415 840-2**; *415 840-4* [id.]. Bav. RSO, Kubelik – MENDELSSOHN: *Midsummer Night's Dream.****

Kubelik offers Weber's two greatest overtures as a fine bonus for his extended selection from Mendelssohn's *Midsummer Night's Dream* incidental music. The playing is first class and compares favourably with the Karajan versions.

Symphonies Nos 1 in C; 2 in C.
*** ASV Dig. **CDDCA 515**; *ZCDCA 515* [id.]. ASMF, Marriner.
(*) Orfeo **C 091841A [id.]. Bav. RSO, Sawallisch.

Weber's two symphonies were written within a period of two months between December 1806 amd the end of January 1807. Curiously, both are in C major, yet each has its own individuality and neither lacks vitality or invention. Sir Neville Marriner has their full measure; these performances combine vigour and high spirits with the right degree of gravitas (not too much) in the slow movements. The orchestral playing throughout is infectiously lively and catches the music's vibrant character. The recording is bright and fresh, with excellent detail. It is full in the bass, but the bright upper range brings a touch of digital edge to the upper strings, and this is slightly more apparent on the CD. The cassette is smoother on top, yet still bright and full.

Sawallisch's is also a fine, well-played coupling. His approach is more romantic, with rather more atmosphere. Allegros are alert; and both slow movements go well, although there is heaviness in the minuet of No. 2, taken rather ponderously. On the whole, Marriner is fresher and the Academy playing has greater resilience. The Orfeo recording is smoother on top but not so clear.

Clarinet quintet in B flat, Op. 34.
(*) Tel. **ZA8 48262 (2) [id.]. Benny Goodman, Berkshire Qt – BEETHOVEN: *Trio*; BRAHMS: *Quintet*; *Trio.***(*)

(i) *Clarinet quintet in B flat*; (ii) *Flute trio in G min.* (for flute, cello and piano), *Op. 63.*
*** CRD **CRD 3398**; *CRDC 4098* [id.]. (i) Anthony Pay; (ii) Judith Pearce, Nash Ens.

(i) *Clarinet quintet in B flat, Op. 34;* (ii) *Grand Duo concertante, Op. 48; 7 Variations on a theme from Silvana, Op. 33.*
(*) Chan. Dig. **CHAN 8366; *ABTD 1131* [id.]. Hilton, (i) Lindsay Qt; (ii) Keith Swallow.

Weber's *Clarinet quintet* is very much dominated by the clarinet; on the CRD version Anthony Pay makes the very most of its bravura, catching the exuberance of the *Capriccio* third movement (as unlike a classical minuet as could possibly be managed) and the breezy gaiety of the finale. The Nash players provide an admirable partnership and then adapt themselves readily to the different mood of the *Trio*, another highly engaging work with a picturesque slow movement, described as a *Shepherd's lament*. The recording is first class, vivid yet well balanced, and the cassette transfer is also exceptionally lively.

Benny Goodman is in his element in the Weber *Quintet*, finding a genial bravura in the outer movements, a serene line for the *Adagio*, and chirruping away most engagingly in the minuet. He dominates the performance, as he is intended to, but the Berkshire players give excellent support. The recording is fresh and faithful, if a little dry.

The Chandos issue with Janet Hilton and the Lindsays is also very enjoyable. She plays with considerable authority and spirit though she is not always as mellifluous as her rivals. This version does not entirely sweep the board even though it is very good indeed. Janet Hilton's account of the *Grand Duo concertante*, which Weber wrote for himself and Baermann to play, is a model of fine ensemble, as are the *Variations on a theme from Silvana*, of 1811, in both of which Keith Swallow is an equally expert partner. At times the acoustic seems almost too reverberant in the two pieces for clarinet and piano, but the sound in the *Quintet* is eminently satisfactory. There is a first-class cassette.

Clarinet quintet in B flat (arr. for clarinet & string orchestra).
*** HMV Dig. **CDC7 47233-2**; *EL 270220-4*. Meyer, Württemberg CO, Faerber – BAERMANN: *Adagio;* MENDELSSOHN: *Concert pieces.****

Weber's *Clarinet quintet* was written for Baermann, whose *Adagio* is one of the couplings of the HMV issue. The *Quintet* is recorded in an orchestral transcription, a course which Weber himself authorized. Sabine Meyer is, of course, the highly accomplished clarinettist whom Karajan invited to join the Berlin Philharmonic, and her account of this quintet leaves no doubts as to her expertise and musicianship. The recording is warm and bright, and the balance between soloist and orchestra well judged.

7 Variations on a theme from Silvana in B flat, Op. 33.
*** Chan. Dig. **CHAN 8566**; *ABTD 1216* [id.]. Gervase de Peyer, Gwenneth Pryor – SCHUBERT: *Arpeggione sonata*; SCHUMANN: *Fantasiestücke* etc.***

These engaging Weber *Variations* act as a kind of encore to Schubert's *Arpeggione sonata* and with their innocent charm they follow on naturally. They are most winningly played by Gervase de Peyer who is on top form; Gwenneth Pryor accompanies admirably. The recording is first class in both media.

Folksong settings: *The gallant troubadour; John Anderson; My love is like a red, red rose; O poor tithe cauld and restless love; Robin is my joy; A soldier am I; The soothing shades of gloaming; True hearted was he; Yes, thou may'st walk; Where ha'e ye been a' the day.*
*** HMV Dig. **CDC7 47420-2**; *EL 270323-4* [Ang. *4DS 37352*]. Robert White, Sanders, Peskanov, Rosen, Wilson – BEETHOVEN: *Folksongs.****

It was an inspiration for Robert White to unearth, as an ideal coupling for Beethoven, ten of the folksong settings which Weber in the last months of his life composed (like Beethoven before him) for the Scottish publisher, George Thomson. This first recording, winningly sung with heady tenor tone and fine characterization, brings out the poetry and imagination that the dying composer gave to his well-paid commission. *The gallant troubadour* is a lilting setting of the Walter Scott poem; but just as attractive – with specially original use of the flute obbligato – are such items as the four Burns settings, including a honeyed one of *My love is like a red, red rose*. Warm, helpful recording on CD, with a first-class cassette.

OPERA

Der Freischütz (complete).
*** DG **415 432-2** (2) [id.]. Janowitz, Mathis, Schreier, Adam, Vogel, Crass, Leipzig R. Ch., Dresden State O, Carlos Kleiber.
(*) Decca **417 119-2 (2) [id.]. Behrens, Donath, Meven, Kollo, Moll, Brendel, Bav. R. Ch. & SO, Kubelik.
** Denon Dig. **C37 6433/5** [id.]. Smitková, Ihle, Goldberg, Wlaschiha, Adam, Dresden State Op. Ch. & O, Hauschild.

The DG set marked Carlos Kleiber's first major recording venture. The young conductor, son of a famous father, had already won himself a reputation for inspiration and unpredictability, and this fine, incisive account of Weber's atmospheric and adventurous score fulfilled all expectations. With the help of an outstanding cast, excellent work by the recording producer, and electrically clear recording, this is a most compelling version of an opera which transfers well to the gramophone. Only occasionally does Kleiber betray a fractional lack of warmth, but the full drama of the work is splendidly projected in the enhanced CD format. Not only is there added presence for the voices; but Weber's inspired orchestral colouring is the more vivid, while the famous Wolf's Glen scene is made superbly atmospheric.

Kubelik takes a direct view of Weber's high romanticism. The result has freshness but lacks something in dramatic bite and atmosphere. There is far less tension than in the finest earlier versions, not least in the Wolf's Glen scene which, in spite of full-ranging brilliant recording, seems rather tame, even with the added projection of CD. The singing is generally good – René Kollo as Max giving one of his best performances on record – but Hildegard Behrens, superbly dramatic in later German operas, here seems clumsy as Agathe in music that often requires a pure lyrical line. The 1981 recording has been vividly remastered on to a pair of CDs.

On 13 February 1985 the Semper opera house in Dresden was re-opened, lovingly rebuilt and restored after wartime destruction thirty years earlier. Japanese engineers from Denon worked with East German colleagues to record this first performance in the theatre, capturing the atmosphere very vividly. Those who like live recordings of opera will not mind the occasional odd balance and the bouts of coughing from the audience, but the conducting of Wolf-Dieter Hauschild is not always electrifying enough to make compensation. The Wolf's Glen scene, when the magic bullets are cast, lacks the full tingle of horror, though Ekkehard Wlaschiha, as Kasper, and Rainer Goldberg are both first rate. Jana Smitková makes a tender and vulnerable Agathe, though she is not always steady of tone. Much of the rest of the singing is indifferent, though the chorus work is lively. Moreover the set is uneconomically laid out on three CDs.

Webern, Anton (1883–1945)

Concerto for nine instruments, Op. 24.
*** Chan. *ABT 1046* [id.]. Nash Ens., Rattle – SCHOENBERG: *Pierrot Lunaire.****

This late Webern piece, tough, spare and uncompromising, makes a valuable fill-up for Jane Manning's outstanding version of Schoenberg's *Pierrot Lunaire*, a 1977 recording originally made for the Open University. First-rate sound.

5 Movements for string orchestra, Op. 5; Passacaglia; 6 Pieces for orchestra, Op. 6; Symphony, Op. 21.
(M) *** DG **423 254-2** [id.]. BPO, Karajan.

Taken from Karajan's four-LP collection of music of the Second Viennese School made in the early 1970s, this collection, devoted to four compact and chiselled Webern works, is in many ways the most remarkable of all. Karajan's expressive refinement reveals the emotional undertones behind this seemingly austere music, and the results are riveting – as for example in the dramatic and intense *Funeral march* of Op. 6. Op 21 is altogether more difficult to grasp, but Karajan still conveys the intensity of argument even to the unskilled ear. Indeed, if Webern always sounded like this, he might even enjoy real popularity. Karajan secures a highly sensitive response from the Berlin Philharmonic, who produce sonorities as seductive as Debussy. Incidentally, he plays the 1928 version of Op. 6. Only the Berg Op. 6 still remains untransferred to

CD and could have been accommodated on this disc. All the same a strong recommendation, with excellent sound.

5 Pieces, Op. 5.
*** HMV Dig. **CDC7 47923-2** [id.]; *EL 169588-4.* Junge Deutsch Philharmonie CO, Gulke – BERG: *Lyric suite*; SCHOENBERG: *Quartet No. 2.****

This arrangement, like its companions on this record, was the outcome of a request from Universal Edition; and Webern's transcription is if anything even more effective than the original. These young players bring enormous intensity and poetic feeling to these pieces, and even those who normally find Webern an alien spirit might be surprised how compelling this music can be. All those taking part in these performances play as if their very lives depended upon it. The recording has a splendidly wide dynamic range and tremendous presence. This is altogether superb on CD. There is also a first-class cassette.

5 Pieces for orchestra, Op. 6.
*** DG Dig. **419 781-2** [id.]. BPO, Levine – BERG: *3 Pieces*; SCHOENBERG: *5 Pieces.****

Levine, as in the other pieces by Schoenberg and Berg (the aptest of couplings), brings out the expressive warmth of Webern's writing, with no chill in the spare fragmentation of argument and much tender poetry. Not all Webern devotees will like such a reading; but with the longest of the six tiny movements, the *Funeral march*, particularly powerful, it complements the other works perfectly. Ripe recording, with some spotlighting of individual lines.

6 Bagatelles for string quartet, Op. 9; 5 Movements for string quartet, Op. 5; Slow movement for string quartet (1905); String quartet (1905); String quartet, Op. 28.
*** Ph. **420 796-2** [id.]. Italian Qt.

Readers who quail at the name of Webern need not tremble at the prospect of hearing this record. The early music in particular is most accessible, and all of it is played with such conviction and beauty of tone that its difficulties melt away or at least become manageable. The recording is of outstanding vividness and presence, and it is difficult to imagine a more eloquent or persuasive introduction to Webern's chamber music than this. Although the recording dates from 1970, one would never guess that it was not fairly recent. The players are given remarkable presence – they might well be at the end of the room.

(i) *Piano quintet; String trio, Op. 20; Movement for string trio, Op. posth.; Rondo.*
*** DG Dig. **415 982-2** [id.]. Stefan Litwin, LaSalle Qt – SCHOENBERG: *Ode to Napoleon.***

The LaSalle Quartet's collection of miscellaneous chamber works, well coupled with Schoenberg's *Ode to Napoleon*, makes a valuable supplement to their formidable collection of the quartet music of the Second Viennese School. The *String trio* is one of Webern's strongest and most characteristic chamber works, but the other pieces are rarities. The *Movement* of 1927 was written in preparation for the full-scale *Trio*; while the two early works are fascinating too, particularly the single-movement *Piano quintet* of 1907, eleven minutes long, in a powerful, post-romantic style. The LaSalle performance brings out the emotional thrust without compromise, but the commitment of the players in all these pieces will immediately help the new listener to respond. First-rate recording.

Weill, Kurt (1900–50)

Little threepenny music: suite (arr. David Purser).
** Decca Dig. **417 354-2**; *417 354-4* [id.]. Philip Jones Brass Ensemble – BERNSTEIN: *West Side story: suite.***

Klemperer has been successful with an orchestral suite from *The Threepenny Opera*, but the Philip Jones brass fail to catch its seedy atmosphere here, notably *Mack the Knife*. But the playing itself is expert and the recording vividly present.

Silverlake (complete).
** None. Dig. **CD 79003** (2) [id.]. Grey, Neill, Hynes, Bonazzi, NY City Op. Ch. & O, Rudel.

Textually this is a travesty of Weill's intentions in *Der Silbersee*, the play in three Acts 'with extensive musical score' which he wrote to a text by Georg Kaiser. For a highly successful production at the New York City Opera, *Silverlake* was given an entirely new book by Hugh Wheeler with lyrics by Lys Symonette, who also drew on Weill's earlier incidental music for a Strindberg play to provide support for spoken dialogue. Such is the vitality of Weill's inspiration that much of the authentic bite comes over in this lively performance, which is presented in recorded sound as in performing style on the lines of a Broadway musical. The acoustic is dry and unflattering, the placing of voices and instruments close.

Widor, Charles-Marie (1844–1937)

Organ symphony No. 5 in F min., Op. 42/1.
*** DG Dig. **413 438-2** [id.]. Simon Preston (organ of Westminster Abbey) – VIERNE: *Carillon de Westminster.****
(B) *** DG Dig. *419 839-4* [id.]. Simon Preson (as above) – SAINT-SAËNS: *Symphony No. 3.**

Organ symphonies Nos 5 in F, Op. 42/1; 6 in G, Op. 42/2.
*** Novalis Dig. **150015-2** [id.]. Günther Kaunzinger (Klais organ of Limburg Cathedral).

Organ symphonies Nos 5; 10 (Romane), Op. 73.
*** Ph. Dig. **410 054-2** [id.]. Chorzempa (organ of Saint-Sernin Basilica, Toulouse).

Günther Kaunzinger's Novalis coupling is now a clear first choice in this repertoire. He plays with great vigour and commitment and makes Widor's opening allegro of the *Fifth Symphony* more substantial and involving than usual; similarly the *Andante quasi allegretto* does not sound in the least bland. The famous *Toccata* is second to none in its rhythmic vivacity. In his hands, the *Sixth Symphony* is an equally impressive piece; in the two slow movements, the *Adagio* and *Cantabile*, he produces some delicious sounds from his woodwind stops. The West German organ has plenty of bite, even a hint of harshness in its fortissimos which help to add character to this music. But the clarity of detail permitted by the acoustics of Limburg Cathedral lets one relish Kaunzinger's bravura and the clarity of his articulation, especially in the outer movements and Intermezzo of No. 6.

Simon Preston, too, gives a masterly account of the Widor *Fifth Symphony*, with a fine sense of pace and command of colour. The Westminster Abbey organ may lack something of the Gallic acerbity of the Cavaillé-Coll used by Chorzempa, but there is a marvellous sense of space in this DG recording. On compact disc, detail seems far more sharply focused and one benefits from the wider dynamic range CD encompasses. However, cassette collectors will find that DG's chrome Pocket Music tape offers very good sound indeed, with the closing *Toccata* brilliantly projected. Although the Saint-Saëns coupling is unrecommendable, this is the cheapest way to purchase a first-class recording of the Widor *Symphony*.

Daniel Chorzempa provides a massive demonstration of CD opulence which should send the neighbours scurrying for cover if this CD is played at full volume. He chooses some agreeable registration for the amiable earlier music of the *Fifth Symphony*; but at times one wonders if he does not overdo the dynamic range for domestic listening, for the gentle music is distanced and atmospheric to a great degree. Nevertheless, he provides a highly energetic account of the famous *Toccata* which exudes a nice mixture of power and exuberance. The *Tenth Symphony* has its structure bound together by the Easter plainchant, *Haec Dies*, and after a pleasant *Cantilène* third movement the composer gathers up the threads of the music for another weighty finale; then the rhetoric suddenly evaporates and the piece ends gently. Chorzempa makes much of this effect (and the CD background silence helps) and seems entirely at home in this repertoire. The Cavaillé-Coll organ is well chosen.

Organ symphony No. 5: Toccata.
*** Argo Dig. **410 165-2** [id.]. Hurford (organ of Ratzeburg Cathedral) – *Recital.****

Those wanting the *Toccata* alone could not do better than choose Peter Hurford's exhilarating version, recorded with great presence and impact on a most attractive organ, and giving demonstration quality.

Organ symphonies: No. 5: Toccata (only); *6 in G min., Op. 42/2; 9 in C min.* (*Gothic*), *Op. 70.*
*** Erato **ECD 88111** [id.]. Marie-Claire Alain (Cavaillé-Coll organs).

Marie-Claire Alain plays Cavaillé-Coll organs, using the instrument at Orléans Cathedral for the famous *Toccata* (recorded in 1980) and the organ of Saint Germain-en-Laye for the later symphonies. Her performances are first class, that of the *Toccata* spacious and bold, rather like the composer's own 78 r.p.m. version. Both the later symphonies are much more impressive works than the earlier group of Op. 13. The *Gothic symphony* has a specially fine third movement, where a Christmas chant (*Puer natus est nobis*) is embroidered fugally. The final section is a set of variations, and in the closing *Toccata* the Gregorian chant is reintroduced on the pedals. Both this and the hardly less inventive *Sixth Symphony* were recorded in 1977, but the analogue master yields splendid results. However, the *Symphonie gothique* is cut at a lower level than the *Toccata*, and having raised the volume it is important to remember to turn it down again, otherwise one is engulfed in a flood of sound at the opening of No. 6.

Wieniawski, Henryk (1835–80)

Violin concertos Nos 1 in F sharp min., Op. 14; 2 in D min., Op. 22.
*** HMV **CDC7 47107-2** [id.]. Perlman, LPO, Ozawa.

Violin concerto No. 2 in D min., Op. 22.
*** DG Dig. **410 526-2** [id.]. Perlman, O de Paris, Barenboim – SAINT-SAËNS: *Violin concerto No. 3.****
(B) *** DG *423 261-4* [id.]. Perlman, O de Paris, Barenboim – SAINT-SAËNS: *Concerto No. 3*; LALO: *Symphonie espagnole.****

Those who have enjoyed the relatively well-known *Second Concerto* of this contemporary of Tchaikovsky should investigate this coupling of his two concertos. The *First* may not be as consistently memorable as the *Second*, but the central *Preghiera* is darkly intense, and the finale is full of the showmanship that was the mark of the composer's own virtuosity on the violin. Perlman gives scintillating performances, full of flair, and is excellently accompanied. The recording, from 1973, has similar admirable qualities to the companion remastered CD, from the same period, of Paganini's *First Concerto*. The sound is warm, vivid and well balanced, and all the clearer and more realistic in its compact disc format. It is preferable to Perlman's digital re-make of the *Second Concerto*. This offers playing that is effortlessly dazzling, while he and Barenboim create an attractively songful *Andante*, so that the scintillating bravura of the *moto perpetuo* finale sounds even more dashing by contrast. Generally good recording, with a moderately forward balance for the soloist. The compact disc offers the usual advantages but, as so often with DG, emphasizes that the balance is artificially contrived, with the soloist too close. Cassette collectors are offered a special bargain: Perlman's performance is also available on a DG Pocket Music tape, coupled with not only Saint-Saëns but also Lalo's *Symphonie espagnole*. The sound is less brilliant than the compact disc, but well balanced.

Williams, Grace (1906–77)

Ave maris stella; The Dancers; Harp song of the Dane women; Mariners' song. The 6 Gerard Manley Hopkins poems.
*** Chan. Dig. *ABTD 1116* [id.]. Eiddwen Harrhy, Helen Watts, Thomas, Richard Hickox Singers, City of L. Sinfonia, Hickox.

Hickox presents a delightful collection of the choral music of Grace Williams, one of the most sensitive of Welsh composers. With overtones of Britten and early Tippett, the writing yet has freshness and originality, with rich textures supporting open melodies, often crisply rhythmic. The resonant acoustic does not always allow for ideally clear textures, but the performances are as fresh as the inspirations. Helen Watts is the eloquent contralto soloist in the Hopkins cycle with its complex rhythmic patterning.

Williams, John (born 1932)

Close encounters of the third kind: suite; Star Wars: suite.
(*) RCA **RCD 13650. Nat. PO, Gerhardt.

Film music: *Close encounters of the third kind; E. T.; Raiders of the lost ark; Star Wars trilogy; Superman* (with COURAGE: *Star Trek: theme*).
** Telarc Dig. **CD 80094** [id.]. Cincinnati Pops O, Kunzel.

Gerhardt has the full measure of this music and the National Philharmonic plays marvellously for him: the sweeping strings have an eloquence in the best Hollywood tradition. He shows particular skill in the *Close encounters* sequence, creating genuine tension and evocative feeling. In *Star Wars*, the theme for Princess Leia includes a horn solo which is played quite gorgeously, while the closing section has a *nobilmente* swagger. The RCA recording is bright and well balanced, but it could ideally be richer.

The Telarc recording is certainly spectacular and the concert has a synthesized prologue and epilogue to underline the sci-fi associations. The inclusion of the famous *Star Trek* signature theme (a splendid tune) is wholly appropriate. The orchestra plays this music with striking verve, and the sweeping melody of *E.T.* is especially effective; but the overall effect is brash, with the microphones seeking brilliance in the sound-balance.

Wirén, Dag (1905–83)

Serenade for strings, Op. 11.
*** RCA Dig. **RD 85362**. Canadian Nat. Arts Centre O, Mata – R. STRAUSS: *Le bourgeois gentilhomme.****

An unexpected but welcome coupling for a very attractive account of Strauss's delectable

Bourgeois gentilhomme. Mata's touch is a light one: this is essentially a chamber performance, but it is very well played and recorded. There is an alternative version by the Stockholm Sinfonietta on BIS (**CD 285** – see Concerts, below) using a larger string group, where the conductor, Salonen, gives even more point to the famous *Alla marcia* at a slightly faster tempo; but Mata's account remains attractive in its smaller scale.

Wolf, Hugo (1860–1903)

Goethe-Lieder: Anakreons Grab; Erschaffen und Beleben; Frech und Froh I; Ganymed; Kophtisches Lied I & II; Ob der Koran; Der Rattenfänger; Trunken müssen wir alle sein. Mörike-Lieder: Abschied; An die Geliebte; Auf ein altes Bild; Begegnung; Bei einer Trauung; Denk' es, O Seele!; Er ist's; Der Feuerreiter; Fussreise; Der Gärtner; In der Frühe; Jägerlied; Nimmersatte Liebe; Selbstgeständnis; Storchenbotschaft; Der Tambour; Verborgenheit.
*** DG **415 192-2** [id.]. Dietrich Fischer-Dieskau, Daniel Barenboim.

This generous collection of seventeen of Wolf's Mörike songs and nine Goethe settings (65 minutes in all, with each song separately banded) was issued on CD to celebrate the singer's sixtieth birthday, a masterly example of his art. Barenboim's easily spontaneous style goes beautifully with Fischer-Dieskau's finely detailed singing, matching the sharp and subtle changes of mood. The mid-1970s analogue recording has been very well transferred, with the voice vividly immediate. Full texts and translations are given in the accompanying booklet.

Italian Lieder Book (abridged).
*** Chan. Dig. *ABTD 1130* [id.]. Ileana Cotrubas, Thomas Allen, Geoffrey Parsons.

Only 33 of the 46 songs making up Wolf's *Italian Songbook* are included here, but among them are virtually all the favourite items. With two such positive and characterful artists, recorded in a live performance at Covent Garden, the result is most compelling – not flawless, but full of life and spontaneous imagination. The lighter pieces go mainly to the soprano, who brings out the vein of irony. With the help of Geoffrey Parsons, the humour of *Wie lange schon*, for example, is delightfully touched in. The warmth and resonance of Thomas Allen's baritone makes a fine contrast in the weightier songs. The recording catches the bloom of voices at Covent Garden very effectively.

Mörike Lieder: An die Geliebt; Auf ein altes Bild; Auf eine Christblume I & II; Auf einer Wanderung; Auftrag; Begegnung; Bei einer Trauung; Er ist's; Der Gärtner; Gebet; In Frühling; Der Jäger; Jägerlied; Lied eines Verliebted; Neue Liebe; Nimmersatte Liebe; Peregrina I & II; Schlafendes Jesuskind; Selbstgeständnis; Störchebotschaft; Verborgenheit; Zum Neuen Jahr.
*** HMV Dig. **CDC7 49054-2** [id.]; *EL 270628-4*. Olaf Bär, Geoffrey Parsons.

Wolf's songs to words by Mörike include many of his finest and most memorable. This generous collection presents the youthful but refined artistry of Olaf Bär in this challenging repertory. Though on detail one may prefer this or that great liedersinger of the past, Bär's is an exceptionally intelligent and unforced view of these songs, helped by a superb natural voice. Geoffrey Parsons is an ever-helpful accompanist, and the recording is beautifully balanced.

Wyner, Yehudi (born 1929)

Intermezzi (for piano quartet).
** Pro Arte Dig. **CDD 120** [id.]. Frank Glazer, Cantilena Chamber Players – FOSS: *Round a common center*; COPLAND: *Piano quartet*.**

The notes offer no biographical information about Wyner – but then what do you expect when the front cover proclaims the *Piano quartet* to be by 'Copeland'! Wyner was Canadian-born and became a pupil of Walter Piston at Harvard before teaching at Yale (1964–77). He has written liturgical music for the Jewish synagogue, Torah Service, and various instrumental works, the best known of which is a *Serenade for seven instruments*. The composer calls the *Intermezzi* 'in a curious way a museum piece', assembling as it does numerous allusions to music of the past (Schubert, Chausson, Brahms, Schoenberg and so on) without indulging in any direct quotations. A serious, often deeply felt piece, with very committed playing.

Ysäye, Eugene (1858–1931)

(Unaccompanied) *Violin sonata in D min.* (*Ballade*), *Op. 27/3.*
(M) *** Ph. **420 777-2** [id.]. D Oistrakh – DEBUSSY; RAVEL: *Sonatas*; PROKOFIEV: *5 Melodies*.***

All the music on this record was written within a decade, the Debussy *Sonata* in 1917, the Ravel from 1923 to 1927, the Prokofiev in 1920; and this Ysaÿe *Sonata* appeared in 1924. David Oistrakh won the first prize at the International Ysaÿe Concours in Brussels in 1937, and it would be difficult to imagine his account of the best-known of Ysaÿe's six solo sonatas being surpassed even by the composer himself.

Zamfir, Gheorghe (born 1941)

Concerto No. 1 in G for panpipes and orchestra; Rumanian rhapsody (*Spring*); *Autumn colours; Black waltz.*
(*) Ph. Dig. **412 221-2 [id.]. Zamfir, Monte Carlo PO, Foster.

Gheorghe Zamfir is famous, not only as a virtuoso of the panpipes which he plays with unique flair and skill, but also as performer/composer, notably providing a haunting score for the Australian film, *Picnic at Hanging Rock*. These two concertante works are fluently written, tunefully based on folk material. Unfortunately, the *Rumanian rhapsody* outlasts its welcome; but the *Concerto* is better judged and more economically constructed. It is entertaining, if lightweight. Of the two encores, the *Black waltz* is almost indelible and reminds one of Khachaturian. The recording is first class – though, understandably, the soloist dominates the sound-picture.

Zelenka, Jan (1649–1745)

6 Sonatas for 2 oboes and bassoon with continuo.
Capriccio **10074/5** [id.]. Glaetzner, Goritzki, Sonstevold, Beyer, Pank, Bernstein.

Working only seventy miles away from Bach, Zelenka in these sonatas was demonstrating the sort of originality and mastery of contrapuntal technique that had the great JSB putting this long-underestimated colleague among his most esteemed contemporaries. These superb performances from East German musicians make light of the technical problems in six striking works, all but one of them in the four-movement *sonata da chiesa* form. The chromatic writing, quite different from Bach's, is yet amazingly advanced for its time. First-rate recording. Highly recommended.

Requiem in C min.
(*) Claves Dig. **CD 50-8501 [id.]. Brigitte Fournier, Balleys, Ishii, Tüller, Berne Chamber Ch. and O, Dahler.

The DG Archiv recordings of the orchestral works and the *Trio sonatas* (currently withdrawn) left no doubt as to the individuality of Zelenka's mind. This record of the *Requiem in C minor*, like the settings of the *Lamentations of the Prophet Jeremiah* which Supraphon recorded in the late 1970s, confirms his originality. *The Last Trump*, for example, is a thoughtful soprano solo without any of the dramatic gestures one might expect; and the *Agnus Dei* is quite unlike any other setting of his period – or of any other – austere, intent and mystical. There is hardly a moment that is not of compelling interest here; the only qualification that needs to be made concerns the balance, which places the solo singers too forward. The performance is well prepared and thoroughly committed. On CD, one might have expected the choral focus to be sharper, but in all other respects the sound is very good, wih the ambience nicely judged.

Zemlinsky, Alexander von (1871–1942)

Lyric symphony, Op. 18.
*** DG Dig. **419 261-2** [id.]. Varady, Fischer-Dieskau, BPO, Maazel.

Zemlinsky was an influential figure in Viennese musical life and numbered Schoenberg among his pupils and Berg among his admirers. He was a friend and protégé of Mahler, who appointed him conductor of the Vienna Court Opera in 1907. His *Lyric symphony* dates from 1922 and inhabits much the same world as Mahler. It is a symphony song-cycle, modelled on *Das Lied von der Erde* and based on Eastern poetry, and its lush textures and refined scoring make it immediately accessible. The idiom is that of early Schoenberg (*Verklaerte Nacht* and *Gurrelieder*), Mahler and figures such as Strauss and Franz Schreker. Yet it is not just derivative but has something quite distinctive to say. Its sound-world is imaginative, the vocal writing graceful and the orchestration masterly. Both soloists and the orchestra sound thoroughly convinced and convincing, and Maazel's refined control of texture prevents the sound from cloying, as does his incisive manner. Varady and Fischer-Dieskau make an outstanding pair of soloists, keenly responsive to the words, and the engineering is first class, the voices being well balanced against the orchestra.

Die Seejungfrau (*The Mermaid*); *Psalm 13, Op. 24.*
*** Decca Dig. **417 450-2**; *417 450-4* [id.]. Ernest Senff Chamber Ch., Berlin RSO, Chailly.

Zemlinsky, three years older than his brother-in-law, Schoenberg, was in his early thirties when he wrote this three-movement symphonic fantasy based on the Hans Andersen story of the mermaid. It is comparable with Schoenberg's high romantic *Pelleas and Melisande*, written at the same period, an exotic piece full of sumptuous orchestral writing. It is beautifully performed here, with ample recording to match. The choral setting of *Psalm 13* dates from three decades later, but still reveals the urgency of Zemlinsky's inspiration – never a revolutionary in the way that Schoenberg was, but always inventive and imaginative. The choral sound is not as full as that of the orchestra. There is an excellent cassette.

Eine florentinische Tragödie (opera; complete).
*** Schwann Dig. **CD 11625** [id.]. Soffel, Riegel, Sarabia, Berlin RSO, Albrecht.

The Florentine Tragedy is the more pretentious and less effective of the two Wilde-based one-act pieces which have been turned into a highly successful Zemlinsky double-bill. Dramatically it is pure hokum. It presents a simple love triangle: a Florentine merchant returns home to find his sluttish wife with the local prince. Zemlinsky in 1917 may have been seeking to repeat the shock tactics of Richard Strauss in *Salome* (another Wilde story) a decade earlier; but the musical syrup which flows over all the characters makes them far more repulsive, with motives only dimly defined. The score itself is most accomplished; it is here compellingly performed, more effective on disc than it is in the opera house. First-rate sound.

Der Gerburtstag der Infantin (opera; complete).
*** Schwann Dig. **CD 11626** [id]. Nielsen, Riegel, Haldas, Weller, Berlin RSO, Albrecht.

The Birthday of the Infanta, like its companion one-acter, was inspired by a story of Oscar Wilde, *The Dwarf*. Analysed coldly, it is the repellent story of a hideous dwarf caught in the forest and given to the Infanta as a birthday present. Even after realizing his own hideousness, he declares his love to the princess and is casually rejected. He dies of a broken heart, with the Infanta untroubled – 'Oh dear, my present already broken.' Zemlinsky, dwarfish himself, gave his heart to the piece, reproducing his own rejection at the hands of Alma Mahler. In this performance, based on a much-praised stage production, Kenneth Riegel gives a heartrendingly passionate performance as the dwarf declaring his love. His genuine passion is intensified by being set against lightweight, courtly music to represent the Infanta and her attendants. With the conductor and others in the cast also experienced in the stage production, the result is a deeply involving performance, beautifully recorded.

Collections

A selective list – we have included only the outstanding compilations from the many which are available

Concerts of Orchestral and Concertante Music

Academy of Ancient Music, Hogwood or Schröder

PACHELBEL: *Canon and gigue.* VIVALDI: *Concerto in B min. for 4 violins, Op. 3/10. Double trumpet concerto in C, RV 537.* GLUCK: *Orfeo: Dance of the Furies; Dance of the Blessed Spirits.* HANDEL: *Solomon: Arrival of the Queen of Sheba. Berenice: Overture; Minuet. Water music: Air; Hornpipe.*
** O-L **410 553-2** [id.].

It seems a curious idea to play popular Baroque repertoire with a severe manner. Pachelbel's *Canon* here sounds rather abrasive and lacking charm; and the *Arrival of the Queen of Sheba* is altogether more seductive in Beecham's or Marriner's hands. But those who combine a taste for these pieces with a desire for authenticity at all costs should be satisfied. The highlight here is the pair of Gluck dances, very strongly characterized and making a splendid foil for each other. The sound is extremely vivid, especially on compact disc.

'Christmas concertos': CORELLI: *Concerto grosso, Op. 6/8.* WERNER: *Christmas pastorella.* GOSSEC: *Christmas suite* (with chorus). HANDEL: *Messiah: Pifa (Pastoral symphony).* VEJVANOVSKÝ: *Sonata Natalis.* BACH: *Christmas oratorio.* TORELLI: *Concerto grosso, Op. 8/6.*
(*) O-L Dig. **410 179-2 [id.].

For those needing a touch of acerbity to prevent their Christmas pastorellas becoming too bland, the present collection provides the answer. The playing has a suitably light touch (the Corelli especially so) and the programme is imaginative, though the invention in some of the lesser-known pieces is somewhat ingenuous, notably the Vejvanovský (which has the compensation of trumpets to add colour), or the Gossec, which surprises with a chorus of shepherds as its finale. The sound is first class, with the compact disc adding extra presence.

Academy of St Martin-in-the-Fields, Iona Brown

'Concerti da caccia' (with Hermann Baumann, Radovan Vlatkovic, Timothy Brown, Nicholas Hill: horns; Les Trompes de France): L. MOZART: *Hunt symphony; Concerto in E flat.* FASCH: *Concerto in D (Hunt).* MOURET: *2nd Suite de Symphonies.*
** Ph. Dig. **416 815-2**; *416 815-4* [id.].

The main interest here is Leopold Mozart's *Jagd-Symphonie*, which comes complete with barking dogs (how was that managed in the eighteenth-century concert hall?), and the Mouret second *Suite de Symphonies* which features five French players of *trombes de chasse*, a primitive predecessor of the hand horn. They play robustly, with great confidence, ignoring out-of-tune harmonics and often producing a wailing vibrato on sustained notes. The effect is almost bizarre, but undoubtedly authentic. A little of this goes a long way, but on CD the seven movements are banded, so one need not take them all at once. The other works have limited, if often agreeable, invention and are conventional, although the Fasch has a detailed programme following the progress of the hunt. Expert playing from Baumann and his group, and accompaniments that are stylish as well as enthusiastic: the opening of the Leopold Mozart work, with its exuberant fanfares, is very effective indeed. The recording is excellent, although the cassette is not quite as cleanly focused as the CD.

Academy of St Martin-in-the-Fields, Marriner

HANDEL: *Solomon: Arrival of the Queen of Sheba; Berenice: Minuet. Messiah: Pastoral symphony.* BACH: *Cantatas Nos 147: Jesu, joy of man's desiring; 208: Sheep may safely graze; Christmas oratorio: Sinfonia.* GRIEG: *Holberg suite: Prelude.* SCHUBERT: *Rosamunde: Entr'acte No. 2.* GLUCK: *Orfeo: Dance of the Blessed Spirits.* BORODIN: *Nocturne for strings* (arr. Marriner).
(*) HMV **CDC7 47027-2 [id.]; (M) *TC-EMX 2131.*

The sound of Sir Neville Marriner's CD is a striking improvement on the equivalent tape, fresher and more transparent – very good indeed – and while the two Bach chorales are still given considerable warmth of texture, the suggestion of romanticism is less overt than on the more ample-sounding cassette. As a whole, however, this programme is less memorable than many earlier Academy analogue collections. Handel's Queen of Sheba trots in very briskly but the polished playing prevents a feeling of breathlessness. The *Pastoral symphony* is stylish and the noble contour of the famous *Berenice* melody is warmly phrased. But it is the Schubert *Entr'acte* and the passionately expressive Borodin *Nocturne* that resonate in the memory.

English string music: HOLST: *St Paul's suite, Op. 29/2.* DELIUS (arr. Fenby): *2 Aquarelles.* PURCELL: *Chacony in G min.* VAUGHAN WILLIAMS: *Rhosymedre: Prelude.* WALTON: *Henry V* (incidental music): *Death of Falstaff* (*Passacaglia*); *Touch her soft lips and part.* BRITTEN: *Simple symphony, Op. 4.*
*** HMV **CDC7 47842-2** [id.].

This attractively varied disc was recorded in 1972, but so expert was the chosen balance of producer Christopher Bishop and engineer Neville Boyling that the quality is hardly dated at all. The sound is fresh and full-bodied. The digital remastering has not lost the truthfulness of timbre, yet there is an improved focus and background is hardly noticeable. The playing is at once refined and resilient, delicately tough and warmly expressive by turns. Britten's *Simple symphony* sounds bigger than usual in fast movements, more openly romantic in the *Sentimental sarabande.* Holst's *St Paul suite* brings wonderfully pointed rhythms in all four movements; while the Vaughan Williams (an arrangement of a haunting organ piece) and the Walton are finely atmospheric, against a rich acoustic. The Delius, too – atmosphere music *par excellence* – prepares the way for the comparative astringency of the magnificent Purcell *Chacony.* Although the straight transfer of the original programme means that the programme is not particularly generous, the quality of both music making and recording ensures a firm recommendation.

'The sound of the Academy': PONCHIELLI: *La Gioconda: Dance of the hours.* NICOLAI: *Overture: The merry wives of Windsor.* SUPPÉ: *Overture: Light cavalry.* SHOSTAKOVICH: *The Gadfly; Barrel organ music; Romance.* MUSSORGSKY: *Khovanshchina: Dance of the Persian*

Slaves. RIMSKY-KORSAKOV: *Snow Maiden: Dance of the tumblers. Tsar Saltan: Flight of the bumble bee.* BERLIOZ: *Damnation de Faust: Dance of the Sylphs.*
*** HMV Dig. **CDC7 49043-2** [id.]; *EL 270617-4.*

Delicately introduced by the harp and the gentle striking of the morning hour, Marriner's version of the *Dance of the hours* has characteristic finesse and colour, the recording wide in range and with plenty of sparkle. The two overtures are especially attractive, genial in mood and with gracious phrasing in *Merry wives of Windsor*. With the Shostakovich *Barrel organ music* providing a touch of piquancy and the *Persian slaves* suitably sinuous and sentient, this makes a most agreeable entertainment, ending with gusto with Rimsky's *Tumblers*. The overall programme is lightweight in the best sense.

'The Academy plays opera': Orchestral excerpts from: VERDI: *Aïda; Rigoletto; Il Trovatore; La Traviata.* PUCCINI: *Madama Butterfly; Tosca; Turandot; La Bohème.*
*(*) HMV Dig. **CDC7 49552-2** [id.]; *EL 749552-4.*

With outrageous orchestration, even featuring the ondes martenot – admittedly used discreetly – in *Madama Butterfly*, this selection of opera without words becomes refined kitsch. It is agreeable in its way, and the recording is sumptuous; but this is little more than wallpaper music, although the effect is undoubtedly pleasant.

'The French connection': RAVEL: *Le Tombeau de Couperin.* DEBUSSY: *Danses sacrée et profane* (with Ellis, harp). IBERT: *Divertissement.* FAURÉ: *Dolly suite, Op. 56.*
*** ASV Dig. **CDDCA 517**; *ZCDCA 517* [id.].

An excellent collection. The spirited account of Ibert's *Divertissement* is matched by the warmth of Fauré's *Dolly suite* in the Rabaud orchestration. The remainder of the record is hardly less appealing. Ravel's *Le Tombeau de Couperin* is nicely done, though the *Forlane* is kept on too tight a rein and one feels the need for a slightly bigger body of strings. But though not a first choice, there is no denying that it is very well played indeed, as is the Debussy *Danses sacrée et profane*. One would welcome more space round the orchestra and, considering the disc was made in Studio One, Abbey Road, greater use could have been made of the location's ambience. This apart, however, everything is very clear with the sound even more refined and present on CD. The cassette has slightly less bite.

'The English connection': ELGAR: *Serenade for strings, Op. 20.* TIPPETT: *Fantasia concertante on a theme of Corelli.* VAUGHAN WILLIAMS: *Fantasia on a theme of Thomas Tallis; The Lark ascending* (with Iona Brown).
(*) ASV Dig. **CDDCA 518; *ZCDCA 518* [id.].

Sir Neville Marriner's newer performances of the Elgar *Serenade* and the *Tallis Fantasia* are less intense (and less subtle) than his earlier versions; the highlight of this concert is Iona Brown's radiant account of *The Lark ascending*. The sound is rich and very well defined, especially in its CD format, while the cassette is only marginally less sharply detailed. Readers will note, however, that Marriner's 1972 Argo recordings of the Vaughan Williams *Tallis fantasia* and *The Lark ascending* (also with Iona Brown) are also available on CD (see above, under the composer).

French music: BERLIOZ: *Damnation de Faust: Hungarian march.* DUKAS: *The Sorcerer's apprentice.* SAINT-SAËNS: *Danse macabre, Op. 40.* DEBUSSY: *Prélude à l'après-midi d'un faune.* CHABRIER: *Joyeuse marche.* RAVEL: *Pavane pour une infante défunte.*
(*) Ph. Dig. **412 131-2; *412 131-4* [id.].

Marriner may not have quite the panache of Beecham in lollipops like these, but with the Academy's 'big band' it makes a succulent collection, if ungenerous in length (42′). The Saint-Saëns, taken fast, has brilliant solo work from Alan Loveday; the Debussy and Ravel are sensuously beautiful; and the Chabrier is full of flair, the most Beechamesque of the performances here. By comparison, the Berlioz lacks something in spectacle, neat and rhythmic rather than expansive (though on CD the bass drum is impressively caught). *L'apprenti sorcier* has a sparkling scherzando quality, though rather less of a sense of drama, and the tempo could be more consistent. The sound is the more transparent on compact disc; but the cassette is less impressive and has problems with the bass drum.

'Famous overtures': J. STRAUSS Jnr: *Die Fledermaus*. SUPPÉ: *Morning, noon and night in Vienna*. AUBER: Fra Diavolo. SMETANA: *The Bartered bride*. OFFENBACH: *La Belle Hélène*. SULLIVAN: *The Mikado*.
*** Ph. Dig. **411 450-2** [id.].

Sparkling performances, the pacing often brilliantly fast, with *Die Fledermaus* convincing in its dash, even though tempi are wayward. The effect is exhilarating, particularly in the bustle of *The Bartered bride*, where string detail is attractively refined, as it is at the engaging opening of *Fra Diavolo*. It is good to have Sullivan included. Even if the overture to *The Mikado* was not one of his best, it receives most persuasive advocacy here. For the Offenbach piece, Sir Neville uses an arrangement by Alan Boustead which is less effective than the Haensch version that we usually hear. However, with playing of much finesse and extremely vivid sound, approaching demonstration standard, this is all most enjoyable.

'Scandinavian music': GRIEG: *Holberg suite; 2 Elegiac melodies, Op. 34*. SIBELIUS: *Kuolema: Valse triste, Op. 44. Rakastava, Op. 14*. NIELSEN: *Little suite, Op. 1*. WIRÉN: *Serenade for strings, Op. 11*.
*** Argo **417 132-2** [id.].

A splendid collection of appealing and attractive music from the north. It gives us a splendid account of Sibelius's magical *Rakastava* (there is an eloquent version by the Finnish Chamber Ensemble on BIS) as well as the perennially fresh Dag Wirén *Serenade*. These are good, vividly recorded performances from 1980, to which the splendid vintage (1970) version of the *Holberg suite* has been added for the CD issue. The sound is full with a keen upper range.

Adni, Daniel (piano)

'Music from the movies' (with Bournemouth SO, Alwyn): ADDINSELL: *Warsaw concerto*. WILLIAMS: *The Dream of Olwen*. ROZSA: *Spellbound concerto*. BATH: *Cornish rhapsody*. GERSHWIN: *Rhapsody in Blue*.
(B) **(*) CfP **CD-CFP 9020**; *CFP 41 4493-4*.

By far the finest of these film 'concertos' is Addinsell's *Warsaw concerto*, written for *Dangerous Moonlight*. The other pieces here have less distinction but are taken seriously and presented with commitment and flair. The performance of the Gershwin *Rhapsody* (also used in a biopic of the same title) is not as distinctive as the rest of the programme. Excellent, vivid sound on CD; on cassette, however, the warmly resonant acoustic blunts the upper range.

André, Maurice (trumpet)

Trumpet concertos (with ASMF, Marriner): STÖLZEL: *Concerto in D.* TELEMANN: *Concerto in C min. Concerto in D for trumpet, 2 oboes and strings* (with Nicklin and Miller). VIVALDI: *Double trumpet concerto in C, RV 537* (with Soustrot); *Double concerto in B flat for trumpet and violin, RV 548* (with I. Brown).
*** HMV Dig. **CDC7 47012-2**.

Maurice André has recorded a number of such collections for EMI but they have all been swiftly deleted. He is peerless in this kind of repertoire and the accompaniments under Marriner are attractively alert and stylish. The Academy provides expert soloists to match André on the concertante works by Telemann (*in D*) and Vivaldi (*RV 548*) which come together towards the end and offer much the most interesting invention. The concerto by Stölzel is conventional, but has a fine slow movement. Throughout, André's smooth, rich timbre and highly musical phrasing give pleasure. The recording is first class, with the CD adding extra definition and presence.

Baroque suites and concertos (with Paris O Ens., Wallez): MOURET: *Suites de symphonies.* VIVALDI: *Concertos: in C, RV 534; in D min., RV 535.* LALANDE: *Symphonies pour les souper du Roy: 1st Caprice;* STÖLZEL: *Concerto grosso in D.* TORELLI: *Sinfonia a 4 in C.*
** HMV Dig. **CDC7 47140-2** [id.].

Maurice André plays here as brilliantly as ever. However, in the Vivaldi arrangements (the works were conceived for a pair of oboes), for all the combined balancing skill of the soloist and the engineers, the effect is not completely convincing. The CD offers brilliant sound and a forward balance and is best not played in a single session. André's other compact discs are more rewarding than this, where at times the dominating trumpet timbre becomes a little tiring.

Concertos (with Philh. O, Muti.): BACH: *Brandenburg concerto No. 2 in F, BWV 1047.* TELEMANN: *Concerto in D.* TORELLI: *Concerto in D.* HAYDN: *Concerto in E flat.*
*** HMV Dig. **CDC7 47311-2** [id.].

André is a big star on the continent, which accounts for the allocation of many compact discs to him in EMI's CD catalogue. It seems a curious idea to include the Bach *Brandenburg*, for, although André plays the solo part most stylishly and the balance with his Philharmonia colleagues is expertly managed, most collectors will have already acquired this work within a complete set. Otherwise this is an admirable concert, for André's performance of the Haydn is particularly pleasing, with a gentle *Andante* to offset the sparkle of the outer movements; the Telemann is also a fine piece. With first-class accompaniments throughout and an excellently balanced recording, this is all enjoyable. The CD is striking for its added presence.

'Trumpet concertos' (with BPO, Karajan): HUMMEL: *Concerto in E flat.* L. MOZART: *Concerto in C.* TELEMANN: *Concerto in D.* VIVALDI: *Concerto in A flat* (arr. Thilde).
(*) HMV **CDC7 49237-2 [id.].

Another attractive collection of trumpet concertos, brilliantly played by André. His security in the upper register in the work by Leopold Mozart and the fine Telemann concerto is impressive, with Karajan and the BPO wonderfully serene and gracious in the opening *Adagio* and the *Grave* slow movement of the latter. The jaunty quality of the Hummel is not missed, and the finale of this work, taken at breakneck pace, is certainly exhilarating, while the cantilena of the *Andante* is nobly contoured. The Vivaldi work is arranged from the *Sonata in F major for violin and continuo*, RV 20, and makes a very effective display piece. The 1974 recording has generally been well transferred to CD. Although the trumpet timbre is very bright and the violins are not absolutely clean in focus, there is plenty of ambience. However, this reissue would have been even more tempting at mid-price, with only 47′ of music on offer.

Trumpet concertos (with (i) Maurice Bourgue, oboe; (ii) Maurice Allard (bassoon); Württemberg CO, Faerber): HERTEL: (i) *Double concerto in E flat for trumpet and oboe*. STÖLZEL: *Sonata in D* (arr. Thilde). HANDEL: *Concerto in B flat*. (i; ii) BISCOGLI: *Concerto for trumpet, oboe and bassoon*.
*** HMV Dig. **CDC7 49572-2** [id.].

It is the use of texture rather than melodic invention that gives the pleasure here. Hertel's *Double concerto* is thematically conventional, but the interplay of oboe and trumpet is most felicitous and in the *Arioso* slow movement Maurice Bourgue is given ample opportunities to shine in his solo passages. The *Triple concerto* by Francesco Biscogli (*c*. 1750) is even more ingenious, and the extended *Grazioso* second movement (8′ 28″) is delightful; the *Largo e staccato* also produces some piquant sounds, and the finale is attractively spirited. The Stölzel *Sonata* is agreeable enough; the Handel is a transcription of an oboe concerto with a song-like *Siciliana* as its centrepiece. André's contribution throughout is appealingly stylish and the balance with the other instruments is expertly managed: he fines his tone down appropriately and the engineers do the rest with clever balancing. The sound is very good, the orchestral contribution clean and clear.

Trumpet concertos (with Württemberg CO, Faerber): LUIGI OTTO: *Concerto in E flat*. BARSANTI: *Concerto grosso in D, Op. 3/10*. ALBINONI: *Concerto a cinque in D min. Op. 9/2*. HANDEL: *Sonata in F, Op. 1/12*.
(*) HMV Dig. **CDC7 49573-2 [id.].

Maurice André's problem is that there are not enough trumpet concertos of distinction to provide him with a repertoire adequate to demonstrate his astounding technique and natural musicality, so he has to rely on transcriptions. He plays the *Adagio* of Albinoni's *Concerto a cinque in D minor* (intended for the oboe) with a ravishing line, and his articulation of the finale is similarly appealing and stylish. He is impressive, too, in the *Largo* of Handel's Opus 1, No. 12, but fails overall to convince us that this work gains from being transcribed for the trumpet. In the Barsanti *Concerto grosso*, there is some engaging interplay with the orchestra in the slow movement (although surely more use could have been made of dynamic light and shade), while the high lyrical tessitura of the Otto *Concerto* demonstrates his uncanny control; the finale is gay and splendidly done. Good, clean accompaniments from Faerber and clear – yet not too dry – recording.

Trumpet concertos (with various orchestras & conductors): HAYDN: *Concerto in E Flat*. M. HAYDN: *Concerto in D*. HANDEL: *Concerto in G min.* (from *Oboe concerto No. 3*). VIVALDI: *Double trumpet concerto in C, RV 537*. VIVIANI: *Sonata in C*. TELEMANN: *Concerto/Sonata in D*.
*** DG **415 980-2**; (M) *419 874-4* [id.].

Recorded between 1967 and 1977, this is a generous anthology of consistently high quality. Michael Haydn's *Concerto*, a concertante section of a seven-movement *Serenade*, has incredibly high tessitura, with the D trumpet taken up to high A (the fourth ledger-line above the treble stave), the highest note in any classical trumpet concerto. It is just a peep but, characteristically, Maurice André reaches up for it with consummate ease. He is completely at home in all this repertoire: his version of the Joseph Haydn *Concerto* is stylish and elegant, with a memorably eloquent account of the slow movement, the line gracious and warmly serene. These are the earliest of the recordings included and the sound is slightly less clean than in the three works accompanied by Mackerras and the ECO. These include the very effective Viviani *Sonata* with organ obbligato, and the fine Telemann piece, where in the second movement André makes impressive use of a long controlled crescendo. In the Vivaldi *Double concerto* André plays both parts by electronic means. As can be seen, the CD is offered at full price, while the excellently transferred tape is on DG's mid-priced Galleria label.

Ballet

'Nights at the ballet' (with (i) RPO, Weldon; (ii) Philh. O; (iii) Kurtz; (iv) Irving; (v) RPO, Fistoulari; (vi) CBSO, Frémaux; (vii) New Philh. O, Mackerras): excerpts from: (i) TCHAIKOVSKY: *Nutcracker; Swan Lake.* (ii; iii) PROKOFIEV: *Romeo and Juliet.* (ii; iv) ADAM: *Giselle.* (v) LUIGINI: *Ballet Égyptien* (suite). (vi) SATIE: *Gymnopédies Nos 1 and 3.* (vii) DELIBES: *Coppélia.* GOUNOD: *Faust* (suite).
(B) *** EMI *TC2-MOM 111.*

Here (on tape only) is nearly an hour and a half of the most tuneful and colourful ballet music ever written. Kurtz's three excerpts from *Romeo and Juliet* are most distinguished, the inclusion of the Fistoulari recording of *Ballet Égyptien* is most welcome, and Mackerras is at his sparkling best in the *Coppélia* and *Faust* selections. Weldon's Tchaikovsky performances lack the last degree of flair, but they are alert and well played. The sound is admirable both for home listening and in the car.

Baroque music

'The sound of baroque' (with (i) Royal Liverpool PO, Groves; (ii) Scottish CO, Tortelier; (iii) LPO, Boult; (iv) Menuhin, Ferras, Bath Fest. O; (v) Bournemouth Sinf., Montgomery; (vi) Reginald Kilbey and Strings; (vii) RPO, Weldon, (viii) ASMF, Marriner): (i) ALBINONI: *Adagio for strings and organ* (arr. Giazotto). (ii) BACH: *Suite No. 3 in D, BWV 1068: Air.* (iii) *Brandenburg concerto No. 3 in G, BWV 1048.* (iv) *Double violin concerto in D, BWV 1043.* (i) GLUCK: *Orfeo: Dance of the Blessed Spirits.* (v) HANDEL: *Messiah: Pastoral symphony. Berenice overture.* (v) *Solomon: Arrival of the Queen of Sheba.* (vi) *Serse: Largo.* (vii) *Water music: suite* (arr. Harty). (viii) PACHELBEL: *Canon.*
(B) *** EMI *TC2-MOM 103.*

One of the first of EMI's 'Miles of Music' tapes, planned for motorway listening as well as at home, and offering about 80 minutes of favourite baroquerie, this is recommendable in every way. The sound is lively, the performances are first class, with Bach's *Double violin concerto* and *Brandenburg No. 3* (Boult) bringing substance among the lollipops.

Baumann, Hermann (horn)

Concertos (with Leipzig GO, Masur): GLIÈRE: *Concerto in B flat, Op. 91.* SAINT-SAËNS: *Morceau de concert, Op. 94.* CHABRIER: *Larghetto, Op. posth.* DUKAS: *Villanelle.*
(*) Ph. Dig. **416 380-2; *416 380-4* [id.].

The Glière *Concerto* is ambitious, playing for nearly 23 minutes. It is floridly romantic, supposedly modelled on the Tchaikovsky *Violin concerto* – but the two pieces find an affinity only in their Russian dance finales; it is agreeable if somewhat ingenuous in invention. Both the Dukas *Villanelle* and the two-part Saint-Saëns *Morceau* are elegantly crafted and have character; but the discovery here is the Chabrier *Larghetto*, which is distinctly memorable. Baumann's playing is confident and stylish, although he favours the use of vibrato. The accompaniments are alive and polished and the sound good, though the resonant acoustics of the Leipzig Auditorium prevent a great deal of internal clarity. A useful if not indispensable disc.

BBC Symphony Orchestra, Sir Colin Davis

'The Last Night of the Proms' (with BBC Chorus & Choral Society, Jessye Norman): ELGAR: *Cockaigne overture, Op. 40; Pomp and circumstance march No. 1, Op. 39.* BERLIOZ: *Les Troyens: Hail, all hail to the Queen.* WAGNER: *Wesendonk Lieder: Schmerzen; Träume.* MENDELSSOHN: *Octet: Scherzo.* WOOD: *Fantasia on British sea songs.* HANDEL: *Judas Maccabaeus: See, the conqu'ring hero comes.* ARNE: *Rule Britannia.* PARRY: *Jerusalem* (arr. Elgar).
*** Ph. **420 085-2.**

Although the vociferous clapping is sometimes almost overwhelming, this CD (recorded on two 'last nights', in 1969 and 1972) fully captures the exuberant atmosphere of the occasion. Only the *Cockaigne overture* is slightly below par. The full humour of the *Sea songs* extravaganza is well caught, with the clapping coming totally to grief in the *Sailor's hornpipe*. But the fervour of the singing in *Land of hope and glory* and *Rule Britannia* is superbly caught, and the entry of the organ crowns a frisson-making version of Parry's *Jerusalem*.

Berlin Philharmonic Orchestra, Herbert von Karajan

'Operatic overtures and intermezzi': MASSENET: *Thaïs: Méditation* (with Mutter). CHERUBINI: *Anacreon overture.* WEBER: *Der Freischütz: overture.* SCHMIDT: *Notre Dame: Intermezzo.* PUCCINI: *Suor Angelica; Manon Lescaut: Intermezzi.* MASCAGNI: *L'amico Fritz: Intermezzo.* HUMPERDINCK: *Hansel and Gretel: Overture.*
(M) *(*) Dig. **CDM7 69020-2** [id.].

A curiously planned programme, opening with the *Méditation* from *Thaïs* played gently and dreamily by Anne-Sophie Mutter, immediately followed by Cherubini's *Anacreon overture* which is made to sound heavily anachronistic. The performances of the other overtures, by Weber and Humperdinck, are disappointing too, not helped by the resonantly overblown recording. Best are the intermezzi, played with the utmost passion, where the sumptuous sound is more flatteringly suitable.

ALBINONI: *Adagio in G min.* (arr. Giazotto). VIVALDI: *Flute concerto in G min.* (*La Notte*), *Op. 10/3, RV 439.* BACH: *Suite No. 3 in D: Air.* PACHELBEL: *Canon and Gigue in D.* GLUCK: *Orfeo: Dance of the Blessed Spirits.* MOZART: *Serenata notturna, K.239.*
** DG Dig. **413 309-2**; *413 309-4.*

Karajan's digital Baroque collection is given the benefit of beautiful sound, rich and refined. His mood is solemn, both in the famous *Adagio* and in his stately, measured view of the Pachelbel *Canon*, with the *Gigue* sprightly to provide contrast. The rest of the programme is very polished, but the effect is enervating rather than spirited. The CD is exceptionally vivid, approaching demonstration standard. The chrome cassette, too, is of high quality, smooth, yet full and clear.

'Encore': WEBER: *Invitation to the dance, Op. 65* (arr. Berlioz). SMETANA: *Má Vlast: Vltava.* ROSSINI: *William Tell: overture.* LISZT: *Les Préludes, G.97; Hungarian rhapsody No. 5, G. 359.*
(*) DG Dig. **413 587-2 [id.].

Karajan has recorded all these pieces before, so *'Encore'* is an appropriate title. Moreover the concert plays for over 63 minutes and is generous value. Karajan is at his finest in *Vltava*: there is some radiant playing from the Berlin orchestra in the moonlit stillness before the river approaches the St John's Rapids. *Les Préludes* is vibrant, but a little brash; however, the dark colouring of the *Fifth Hungarian rhapsody* is finely caught. The *William Tell overture* has fine panache, and *Invitation to the dance* a characteristically suave elegance. The Berlin Philharmonie provides a less flattering ambience than in some of Karajan's earlier analogue recordings, and this is even more striking with the sharper, brighter image of the compact disc.

Opera intermezzi and ballet music: PONCHIELLI: *La Gioconda: Dance of the hours.* Intermezzi from: MASCAGNI: *Cavalleria Rusticana; L'amico Fritz.* GIORDANO: *Fedora.* SCHMIDT: *Notre Dame.* MUSSORGSKY: *Khovanshchina.* MASSENET: *Thaïs: Méditation* (with Schwalbé). VERDI: *Aïda: ballet suite.* BERLIOZ: *Damnation de Faust: Danse des Sylphes; Menuet des Follets.* SMETANA: *Bartered bride: Polka.* GOUNOD: *Faust: Waltz.*
(M) *** DG **415 856-2**; *415 856-4* [id.].

This generous and attractive programme (63 minutes) is assembled from recordings made between 1968 and 1972. The playing is marvellous and Karajan consistently displays both warmth and flair: the *Dance of the hours* is captivating, as are the two Berlioz pieces and the *Polka* from the *Bartered Bride* with its affectionate rubato. The various intermezzi sound wonderfully fresh and vivid, and in the *Thaïs Méditation* Michel Schwalbé plays the violin solo exquisitely. In short, this is more than the sum of its parts; and the analogue recordings, although brightly lit in their digitally remastered form, have the advantage of a more flattering and congenial ambience than many of Karajan's more recent sessions made digitally in the Philharmonie. The cassette also sounds first class – but there is an even more generous selection (with a slightly different programme) available on an outstanding bargain Walkman tape; see below.

Karajan: *Opera intermezzi and ballet music: Intermezzi* from: SCHMIDT: *Notre Dame.* MASCAGNI: *Cavalleria Rusticana.* LEONCAVALLO: *I Pagliacci.* PUCCINI: *Suor Angelica; Manon Lescaut. Ballet music* from: VERDI: *Otello; Aïda.* SMETANA: *Bartered Bride: Polka and Dance of the comedians.* TCHAIKOVSKY: *Eugene Onegin: Waltz and Polonaise.* VERDI: *La Traviata: Prelude to Act III.* BORODIN: *Prince Igor: Polovtsian dances.* MASSENET: *Thaïs: Méditation* (with Schwalbé).
(B) *** DG Walkman *419 394-4* [id.].

This excellent Walkman programme is comparable with the similar collection on Galleria (see above) – only here there is 83′ of music. As before, everything is done with characteristic panache; the chrome-tape transfer is very sophisticated, and all in all this is marvellous entertainment, ideal for the car.

Christmas concertos: CORELLI: *Concerto grosso in G min., Op. 6/8.* MANFREDINI: *Concerto grosso in C, Op. 3/12.* TORELLI: *Concerto a 4 in forma di pastorale per il santissimo natale.* LOCATELLI: *Concerto grosso in F min., Op. 1/8.* G. GABRIELI: *Canzona a 8.* SCHEIDT: *In dulci jubilo.* ECCARD: *Vom Himmel hoch; Es ist ein Ros' entsprungen.* GRUBER: *Stille Nacht.*
(M) **(*) DG **419 413-2**; *419 413-4*.

Karajan's collection of baroque Christmas concertos brings first-class playing from the Berlin Philharmonic; but concentration on sensuous beauty of texture (the string sonorities are often ravishing) does tend to be self-defeating when four pieces with a similar pastoral inspiration are heard together. So DG had the bright idea of interspersing the concertos with carol-like chorales played by the Berlin Philharmonic brass, ending the concert with Gruber's *Silent Night*. While purists and authenticists are warned to stay clear, others may find a good deal to enjoy here. The remastered 1970s recording is still very good.

LISZT: *Hungarian rhapsody No. 5.* SMETANA: *Má Vlast: Vltava.* SIBELIUS: *Valse triste, Op. 44; Finlandia, Op. 26.* GRIEG: *Peer Gynt: Morning.* TCHAIKOVSKY: *Nutcracker: Waltz of the flowers. String serenade: Waltz. Symphony No. 5: Waltz.* OFFENBACH: *Contes d'Hoffmann: Barcarolle.* J. STRAUSS Jnr.: *Die Fledermaus: overture.* ROSSINI: *William Tell: overture.*
(B) *** DG Dig. *419 843-4* [id.].

A self-recommending bargain-priced collection (originally offered at the launch of the Pocket Music tape series at super-bargain price). The charisma of Karajan and his orchestra lights up all these performances and the collection overall makes excellent entertainment. The brilliant recording is consistent throughout.

BORODIN: *Prince Igor: Polovtsian dances.* BRAHMS: *Hungarian dances Nos 1 in G min.; 3 in F; 5 in G min.; 6 in D; 17 in F sharp min.; 18 in D; 19 in B min.; 20 in E min.* TCHAIKOVSKY: *Eugene Onegin: Polonaise and Waltz.* SMETANA: *Bartered bride: Polka; Furiant; Dance of the Comedians.*
(M) **(*) DG **423 207-2**; *423 207-4* [id.].

DVORAK: *Scherzo capriccioso, Op. 66.* LISZT: *Les Préludes, G.97; Hungarian rhapsody No. 4, G.359.* SMETANA: *Má Vlast: Vyšehrad; Vltava.*
(M) **(*) DG **423 220-2**; *423 220-4* [id.].

Two collections of popular orchestral favourites, many of which are available coupled with other works in the composer index. The analogue recordings have been digitally remastered brightly – and sometimes, as in the case of the Brahms *Hungarian dances*, sound very bright indeed.

Boston Pops Orchestra, Williams

'Pops round the world': KABALEVSKY: *Overture: Colas Breugnon.* SUPPÉ: *Overture: Boccaccio.* AUBER: *Overture: The bronze horse.* GLINKA: *Overture: Ruslan and Ludmilla.* WILLIAMS: *Overture: The Cowboys.* ROSSINI: *Overture: L'Italiana in Algeri.* BERNSTEIN: *Overture: Candide.*
(*) Ph. Dig. **400 071-2 [id.].

During the 78 r.p.m. era, Arthur Fiedler created in the Boston 'Pops' a musical tradition, enduring and influential, comparable with, though quite different from, Sir Henry Wood's London Promenade Concerts. In assuming Fiedler's role, John Williams brings not only his brilliant talents as a composer of film music, but a natural understanding of the lighter orchestral repertoire, whether derived from the European concert hall and musical theatre, or from the rhythm and blues tradition of American popular music. This lively collection, played and recorded with brash brilliance, brings together a fizzing musical cocktail. There are subtler versions of most of these pieces, but Williams can in no way be faulted for lack of bounce or vigour. The bright, extrovert qualities of performance and recording come out even more vividly on compact disc.

'On stage': BERLIN: *There's no business like show business*. HAMLISCH: *A Chorus line: Overture*. MANN/WEIL: *Here you come again*. ELLINGTON: *Sophisticated lady; Mood indigo; It don't mean a thing*. STRAYHORN: *Take the 'A' train*. LLOYD WEBBER: *Cats: Memory*. BERLIN: *Top hat, white tie and tails*. YOUMANS: *The Carioca*. SCHWARZ: *Dancing in the dark*. KERN: *I won't dance*. CONRAD: *The Continental*. RODGERS: *On your toes: Slaughter on 10th Avenue* (arr. Bennett).
*** Ph. **412 132-2** [id.].

John Williams is completely at home in this repertoire. He is especially good in bringing out detail in the *Overture* for *A Chorus line*, and in the ballet score, *Slaughter on 10th Avenue*, which is heard complete and contains two of the most memorable tunes the composer ever wrote – fully worthy of Gershwin. The other items are offered in groups, tailored sophisticatedly as tributes to Duke Ellington and Fred Astaire; but equally enjoyable is the highlight of Bob Fosse's *Dancin'*, the engaging *Here you come again*. Splendid orchestral playing and excellent sound, although the body of strings is not made to seem sumptuous, and this is even more striking on CD. Even so, this is a highly recommendable collection.

'We wish you a merry Christmas': TRAD.: *We wish you a merry Christmas*. ANDERSON: *Medley: Christmas festival*. BURT: *Medley: A Christmas greeting*. MAY: *Medley: Holiday cheer*. IVES: *A Christmas carol*. DAVIS: *Carol of the drum*. Arr. MAY: *The twelve days of Christmas*.
*** Ph. Dig. **416 287-2** [id.].

Leroy Anderson's arrangements of nine famous carols are predictably stylish and lively. There are also some attractive cross-over carols by Alfred Burt plus a group more positively derived from the idiom of the Pop world by Billy May. The piece by Ives was an interesting choice; but what makes this CD irresistible is Billy May's tongue-in-cheek version of *The twelve days of Christmas* featuring orchestral instruments as the gifts: 'three French horns; four golden strings . . . and a bell high up in a pear tree'. The whole conception is delightfully witty and not too long. With splendid choral singing (though the words could be clearer) in the warm Boston ambience, this is a most attractive entertainment for Christmas Eve.

'Pops in love': FAURÉ: *Pavane*. DEBUSSY: *Suite bergamasque: Clair de lune. Prelude: The girl with the flaxen hair*. ALBINONI: *Adagio in G min*. (arr. Giazotto). SAINT-SAËNS: *Carnival of the animals: The Swan*. SATIE: *Gymnopédies 1–2*. TCHAIKOVSKY: *Andante cantabile*. RAVEL: *Pavane pour une infante défunte*. VAUGHAN WILLIAMS: *Greensleeves fantasia*. PACHELBEL: *Canon*.
** Ph. Dig. **416 361-2**; *416 361-4* [id.].

The title seems wildly inappropriate for a programme of classical lollipops, but the playing is warmly affectionate, even if such a collection of slow, often languorous pieces inevitably lacks variety of mood. The recording is suitably warm and resonant, and there is a very good matching cassette.

'That's entertainment': excerpts from: *That's Entertainment; Fiddler on the Roof; A Little Night Music; Chorus Line; Annie; Evita; Gigi*. RODGERS: *Waltz medley*.
*** Ph. Dig. **416 499-2** [id.].

This is music John Williams does splendidly and there are plenty of really memorable tunes here which many will enjoy in full orchestral dress, not least those by Richard Rodgers and Stephen Sondheim.

Bournemouth Sinfonietta, Hurst

'English music for strings': HOLST: *St Paul's suite, Op. 29/2.* ELGAR: *Serenade for strings, Op. 20.* WARLOCK: *Capriol suite.* IRELAND: *Concertino pastorale.*
(*) Chan. **CHAN 8375; (M) *CBT 1020* [id.].

The novelty here is Ireland's *Concertino pastorale*, a gently persuasive piece, perhaps a shade long for its unambitious material, but always attractive. It is very sympathetically presented. The rest of the programme is well played but less strongly characterized. There are better versions of the Elgar and Warlock suites available, although the *St Paul's suite* of Holst is most enjoyable, with the outer sections of the *Intermezzo* beautifully done. The 1977 sound has plenty of body and atmosphere, but detail at pianissimo level is not as clear as one would have in a modern digital recording, and this is especially true of the pizzicato section of the *Capriol suite*. There is an excellent cassette which costs a good deal less than the CD, as it is in the medium-price range.

Bournemouth Sinfonietta or Symphony Orchestra, Norman Del Mar

HOLST: *Brook Green suite; A Somerset rhapsody.* DELIUS: *Air and dance.* VAUGHAN WILLIAMS: *Concerto grosso; The Wasps: Overture and suite.* WARLOCK: *Serenade.*
*** HMV **CDC7 47812-2** [id.].

This CD generously combines the contents of two previously issued LPs of English music, omitting only one work. Holst's *Brook Green suite* was originally written for the St Paul's School for Girls, where Holst was in charge of music. It emerged as far more than an exercise for students, as Del Mar's dedicated performance demonstrates, most strikingly in the vigorous final dance. The *Concerto grosso* of Vaughan Williams on the other hand was written for a jamboree at the Royal Albert Hall with hundreds of string players of the Rural Music Schools Association. Here (in its début recording) it is given as a straight work for double string orchestra. The enchanting Delius miniatures, the hazily atmospheric Warlock and the evocative Holst *Somerset rhapsody* make an excellent contrast, while the *Wasps Overture* – here dashingly performed – and the other items in the suite are delightful, too. Del Mar brings out the wit in the *March of the kitchen utensils* with his mock pomposity. The recording throughout is splendid.

Brüggen, Frans (recorder)

Recorder concertos (with VCM, Harnoncourt): VIVALDI: *Concerto in C min., RV 441.* SAMMARTINI: *Concerto in F.* TELEMANN: *Concerto in C.* NAUDOT: *Concerto in G.*
(M) *** Tel. **ZS8 43777** [id.].

Frans Brüggen is an unsurpassed master of his instrument, and he gives the four assorted concertos on this excellent reissued record from 1968 his keen advocacy. (In the Vivaldi he even takes part in the tutti.) In his hands, phrases are turned with the utmost sophistication, intonation is unbelievably accurate and matters of style exact. There is spontaneity too and, with superb musicianship, good recording and a well-balanced orchestral contribution, this mid-priced CD can earn nothing but praise. The soloist is given fine presence and the spare string-sounds characteristic of 'authentic' performance techniques are as striking here as they are in recordings made two decades later. The violins are a little raw in timbre, but respond to a little softening of the treble with the controls.

Burns, Stephen (trumpet)

'Music for trumpet and strings' (with Ensemble): PURCELL: *Sonata No. 1 in D.* STANLEY: *Trumpet voluntary* (from *Organ Voluntary, Op. 6/5,* arr. Bergler). CLARKE: *Suite in D.* CORELLI: *Sonata in D.* BALDASSARE: *Sonata in F.* TORELLI: *Sonata a cinque in D, G. 1.*
*** ASV Dig. **CDDCA 528**; *ZCDCA 528* [id.].

Stephen Burns plays a rotary piccolo trumpet in the East German style by Scherzer, and his freedom and smoothness of timbre in the instrument's highest tessitura are breathtaking. With crisp ornamentation (often florid, in short decorative bursts of filigree), the playing is attractively stylish: the timbre gleams and the exhilarating articulation of the allegros is balanced by a natural expressive lyricism in slow movements. Whether in the beautiful *Grave* sections of the Corelli and Torelli *Sonatas* or in the faster movements of the latter piece, this is playing to delight the ear with its combination of sensitivity and bravura. The opening of Purcell's *Sonata* is marked 'Pomposo' and Burns catches its character perfectly: it is a most engaging work overall, as is the *Suite* of Jeremiah Clarke which includes the *Trumpet voluntary* (entitled *The Prince of Denmark's march*). The other movements are inventive too, notably the *Prelude*, another catchy march for the Duke of Gloucester. The recording balances the soloist well forward and the CD projects him almost into the room, although it also emphasizes the rather insubstantial sound of the accompaniment and the ineffective harpsichord balance. But this collection is Stephen Burns' triumph, and it would be churlish to withhold the fullest recommendation. Alongside the Marsalis/Gruberova CBS compact disc, this is strongly recommended to trumpet aficionados.

Chamber Orchestra of Europe, Judd

'Music of the Masters': BEETHOVEN: *Creatures of Prometheus overture, Op. 43.* MOZART: *Divertimento No. 1 in D for strings, K.136.* ROSSINI: *Il Barbiere di Siviglia: overture.* FAURÉ: *Pavane, Op. 50.* WAGNER: *Siegfried idyll.*
(M) **(*) Pickwick Dig. **PCD 805**.

An enjoyable and well-balanced programme with first-class ensemble from these young players and excellently balanced digital recording. The presence and naturalness of the sound are especially striking in the Fauré *Pavane* (with a beautiful flute solo) and the *Siegfried idyll*, using only a small string group. James Judd brings stylish, thoroughly musical direction, although the overall presentation is a shade anonymous.

Chandos: 'The special sound of Chandos'

Digital demonstration recordings: (i) SNO, Gibson; (ii) Janis Kelly, LSO, Simon; (iii) Janet Hilton, CBSO, Järvi; (iv) Taverner Players, Parrott; (v) Ulster O, Thomson; (vi) J. Strauss O,

Rothstein; (vii) Cantilena, Shepherd; (viii) ECO, Gibson; (ix) BBC SO, Schurmann: (i) HOLST: *The Planets: Jupiter*. (ii) TCHAIKOVSKY: *Hamlet: Scène d'Ophélie*. (iii) WEBER: *Clarinet concertino, Op. 73: Finale*. (iv) PURCELL: *Dido and Aeneas: Overture*. (v) HARTY: *Irish symphony: 3rd movt*. (i) ARNOLD: *Tam O'Shanter, Op. 51*. (vi) J. STRAUSS, Jnr: *Egyptian march*. (vii) HANDEL: *Solomon: Arrival of the Queen of Sheba:* (viii): STRAVINSKY: *Pulcinella: Serenata and Scherzino*. (ix) SCHURMANN: *6 Studies: No. 5*.
*** Chan. Dig. **CHAN 8301**; *CBTD 1008* [id.].

It is surprising that a smaller company should make the first digital demonstration issue in compact disc form, rather than one of the majors. The result is a spectacular success. All the recordings are impressive (though the Purcell sounds spiky, and the oboes are balanced too closely in the *Arrival of the Queen of Sheba*). On CD, there is a thrilling impact and sense of orchestral presence in the pieces by Holst and Malcolm Arnold, while the delightful Tchaikovsky vocal scena (a perfect item for a musical quiz), the Harty excerpt from the *Irish symphony* (*In the Antrim Hills*) and the Johann Strauss *March* are equally impressive and enjoyable with their different kinds of evocation. The sound is demonstration-worthy on the chrome cassette but the CD is breathtaking in its vividness.

Chicago Symphony Orchestra, Barenboim

SMETANA: *Má Vlast: Vltava*. DVOŘÁK: *Slavonic dances, Op. 46/1 and 8*. BRAHMS: *Hungarian dances Nos 1, 3 & 10*. BORODIN: *Prince Igor: Polovtsian dances*. LISZT: *Les Préludes*.
(M) *** DG **415 851-2**; *415 851-4* [id.].

When this collection was first issued at the end of the 1970s, we commented that the measure was short. For the reissue, DG have added the *Polovtsian dances* which has splendid life and impetus. Indeed one hardly misses the chorus, so lively is the orchestral playing. Both *Vltava* and *Les Préludes* show Barenboim and the Chicago orchestra at their finest. *Vltava* is highly evocative – especially the moonlight sequence – and beautifully played; *Les Préludes* has dignity and poetry, as well as excitement. The Brahms and Dvořák *Dances* make attractive encores (especially the delightfully phrased *Hungarian dance No. 3 in F*). The only slight snag is that, in the digital remastering, the recording has lost some of its original glow and the strings sound thinner above the stave. But this is only striking in the violin timbre of the big tune of *Vltava*. There is a first-class cassette equivalent.

TCHAIKOVSKY: *1812 overture, Op. 49*; *Romeo and Juliet* (fantasy overture). MUSSORGSKY: *Night on the bare mountain*. BORODIN: *Prince Igor: Polovtsian dances*. RIMSKY-KORSAKOV: *Russian Easter festival overture, Op. 36*.
(M) ** DG **419 407-2** [id.].

The programme is generous (72′) but this is a mixed bag. The highlight is the superb account of Rimsky-Korsakov's *Russian Easter festival overture*. The Borodin and Mussorgsky pieces are also very successful, the Tchaikovsky items less so. The sound is uniformly good, full-bodied and brilliant with the Rimsky-Korsakov in the demonstration class.

Cincinnati Pops Orchestra, Kunzel

'Time warp': DORSEY: *Ascent*. R. STRAUSS: *Also sprach Zarathustra: Opening*. GOLDSMITH: *Star Trek the Movie: Main theme. The Alien: Closing title*. COURAGE: *The Menagerie: suite*.

PHILIPS: *Battlestar Galactica: Main theme.* WILLIAMS: *Superman: Love theme. Star wars: Throne room and end-title.* J. STRAUSS, Jnr: *Blue Danube waltz.* KHACHATURIAN: *Gayaneh: Adagio.*
*** Telarc Dig. **CD 80106** [id.].

This sumptuously recorded CD is well established as a demonstration disc *par excellence* and needs no fillip from us. Sufficient to say that the playing is first class and the sound superb, the rich ambient effect just right for this music, with particularly gorgeous string and brass timbres, Telarc's concert-hall balance at its most impressive. There are plenty of indelible tunes too and John Williams's music for *Superman* and *Star wars* (the latter in the Elgar/Walton nobilmente tradition) has never been recorded to more telling effect. Aficionados of *Star Trek* (who are not already knowledgeable Trekkies) will be interested to read in the excellent sleeve-notes that *The Menagerie* was the hour-long pilot for the series and that the only familiar face in its cast was that of Leonard Nimoy: the others all came later. Alexander Courage's music is of excellent quality. The collection opens with an electronic spectacular to put the Cincinnati orchestra in orbit.

'Orchestral spectaculars': RIMSKY-KORSAKOV: *Mlada: Procession of the nobles. Snow Maiden: Dance of the Tumblers.* DUKAS: *L'apprenti sorcier.* WEINBERGER: *Svanda the Bagpiper: Polka and fugue.* SAINT-SAËNS: *Samson et Dalila: Bacchanale.* LISZT: *Les Préludes.*
(*) Telarc Dig. **CD 80115 [id.].

Some of the earlier records made by the Cincinnati orchestra in their Music Hall have been ineffectively balanced by the Telarc engineers, but this collection is very successful. The title is not belied by the sound, which has a sparkling but not exaggerated percussive constituent. The side drum which introduces the colourful Rimsky *Procession of the nobles* is strikingly well focused, and this clarity comes within a believable overall perspective. There is much fine orchestral playing, with the string detail in the *Svanda Polka and fugue* particularly pleasing, and the horns sounding agreeably strong and rich-timbred in the introductory Rimsky-Korsakov piece. The Saint-Saëns *Bacchanale* has plenty of adrenalin, with the timpani and bass drum adding to the climax without swamping it. The account of *Les Préludes* is lightweight until the end, which is almost solemn in its spacious broadening. The one disappointment is *The Sorcerer's apprentice,* an elusive piece in the recording studio, here bright and well paced, but lacking cumulative excitement. The CD has a subtle added presence and the advantage of background silence.

'The Stokowski sound' (orchestral transcriptions): BACH: *Toccata and fugue in D min., BWV 565; Fugue in G min., BWV 578.* BOCCHERINI: *Quintet in E: Minuet.* DEBUSSY: *Suite bergamasque: Clair de lune; Prélude: La cathédrale engloutie.* BEETHOVEN: *Piano sonata No. 14 (Moonlight): 1st movement.* ALBÉNIZ: *Sevilla.* RACHMANINOV: *Prelude in C sharp min., Op. 3/2.* MUSSORGSKY: *Night on the bare mountain.*
❀ *** Telarc Dig. **CD 80129** [id.].

Stokowski began his conducting career in Cincinnati in 1909, moving on to Philadelphia three years later; so a collection of his orchestral transcriptions from his first orchestra is appropriate, particularly when the playing is so committed and polished and the recording so sumptuous. Indeed, none of Stokowski's own recordings can match this Telarc disc in sheer glamour of sound. The *'Little' G minor Fugue* of Bach hardly sounds diminutive here, matching the famous *D minor Toccata and fugue* at its resplendent climax. By contrast, Boccherini's *Minuet* is played as a miniature, tenderly and gracefully. Spectacle is paramount in the Albéniz and Rachmaninov pieces, the latter vulgarly larger than life but irresistible. Schoenberg apparently thought

Stokowski's sentient arrangement of *Clair de lune* so convincing that he decided it was Debussy's original version; no wonder he liked it, with its element of ecstasy, complete with shimmering vibraphone. The arrangement of *La cathédrale engloutie* is very free and melodramatically telling. Most interesting is *Night on the bare mountain*, which has a grandiloquent brass chorale added as a coda. Any admirer of Stokowski should regard this superbly engineered CD as an essential purchase.

Cleveland Symphonic Winds, Fennell

'Stars and stripes': ARNAUD: *3 Fanfares*. BARBER: *Commando march*. LEEMANS: *Belgian Paratroopers*. FUČIK: *Florentine march, Op. 214*. KING: *Barnum and Bailey's favourite*. ZIMMERMAN: *Anchors aweigh*. J. STRAUSS Snr: *Radetzky march*. VAUGHAN WILLIAMS: *Sea songs; Folk songs suite*. SOUSA: *The Stars and Stripes forever*. GRAINGER: *Lincolnshire posy*.
*** Telarc Dig. **CD 80099** [id.].

This vintage collection from Frederick Fennell and his superb Cleveland wind and brass group is one of the finest of its kind ever made. Severance Hall, Cleveland, has ideal acoustics for this programme and the playing has wonderful virtuosity and panache. Leo Arnaud, the composer of the opening *Fanfares* (which are agreeably concise), flew to Cleveland 'with his side drum under his arm' to make a personal contribution, and the result is most attractive. What is also unusual about the programme is its variety. Both the Barber and Leemans pieces mix subtlety with spectacle; the Barnum and Bailey circus march is predictably exuberant; while *The Stars and Stripes* is not overblown, with the piccolo solo in natural perspective. Add, to all this, digital engineering of Telarc's highest calibre – and you have a very special issue, with the Grainger and Vaughan Williams suites adding just the right amount of ballast.

'Country gardens'

English music (various artists, including Bournemouth SO, Silvestri; Hallé O, Barbirolli; Royal Liverpool PO, Groves; E. Sinfonia, Dilkes): VAUGHAN WILLIAMS: *The Wasps: Overture. Rhosymedre*. WARLOCK: *Capriol suite*. DELIUS: *Summer night on the river. A Song before sunset*. GRAINGER: *Country gardens. Mock Morris; Shepherd's Hey*. arr. BRIDGE: *Cherry Ripe*. COLERIDGE TAYLOR: *Petite suite de concert* (excerpts). GERMAN: *Nell Gwyn: 3 Dances*. COATES: *Meadow to Mayfair: In the country. Summer Days: At the dance. Wood Nymphs*. ELGAR: *Chanson de matin. Salut d'amour*.
(B) **(*) EMI *TC2-MOM 123*.

A recommendable tape-only collection, essentially lightweight but never trivial. Barbirolli's Delius and Neville Dilkes's *Capriol suite* are among the highlights, and certainly it makes a most entertaining concert for use on a long journey, with the lively Grainger, Coates and German pastoral dances providing an excellent foil for the lyrical music. On domestic equipment the quality is slightly variable, with side two noticeably brighter than side one. Thus the opening *Wasps overture* is a little bass-heavy and the attractive *Capriol suite* has a more restricted upper range here than when it appears on EMI's companion tape collection *'Serenade'* (see below). But the rest of the programme sounds well.

Czech Philharmonic Orchestra, Neumann

'Festival concert': Bohemian polkas, waltzes and marches by NOVÁČEK; KRÁL; KOMZÁK; LABITSKY; BISKUP; HILMAR; HAŠLER; LABSKÝ; KAŠPAR; VACKAR; NEDBAL; FUČÍK; KMOCH.
*** HM **C 107101A**; **C 107201A** (2 CDs, available separately).

These recordings are the Bohemian equivalent of the music of the Strauss family. Although the discs contain no masterpieces of the calibre of *The Blue Danube*, the music is consistently tuneful and agreeably inventive in its scoring. Performances and recording are excellent. If you want something lightheartedly different, try one or other of these two CDs, which are available separately.

Dallas Symphony Orchestra, Mata

Concert: MUSSORGSKY: *Night on the bare mountain.* DUKAS: *L'apprenti sorcier.* TCHAIKOVSKY: *Capriccio italien.* ENESCU: *Rumanian rhapsody No. 1.*
*** RCA Dig. **RCD 14439 [RCD1 4439]**.

One of the outstanding early digital orchestral demonstration CDs. The acoustic of the Dallas Hall produces a thrilling resonance without too much clouding of detail. The opening of Tchaikovsky's *Capriccio italien* is stunning in its amplitude, with lustrous string timbres and brass fanfares riveting in their impact. The silences when the music pauses are hardly less telling, both here and in the equally sumptuous Enescu *Rhapsody*. These are the two most effective performances; the Mussorgsky piece is rather lacking in menace when textures are so ample. *The Sorcerer's apprentice* is spirited and affectionately characterized, yet there is no sense of real calamity at the climax. But the Tchaikovsky and Enescu are richly enjoyable, even if the latter lacks the last degree of unbuttoned exuberance in its closing pages.

Dichter, Misha (piano), Philharmonia Orchestra, Marriner

Concertante works: ADDINSELL: *Warsaw concerto.* GERSHWIN: *Rhapsody in blue.* LITOLFF: *Concerto symphonique, Op. 102: Scherzo.* CHOPIN: *Fantasia on Polish airs, Op. 13.* LISZT: *Polonaise brillante* (arr. of WEBER: *Polacca brillante, Op. 72*).
*** Ph. Dig. **411 123-2**; *411 123-4* [id.].

Addinsell's indelible pastiche is here promoted up-market, away from the usual film-music anthologies into a collection of pieces written for the concert hall, and how well it holds its own. Never before has the orchestral detail emerged so beguilingly on record as it does under Marriner; he and Misha Dichter combine to give the music genuine romantic memorability, within a warmly sympathetic acoustic. Gershwin's famous *Rhapsody* is hardly less successful, the performance spirited yet glowing. To make a foil, the Litolff *Scherzo* is taken at a sparkingly brisk tempo and projected with great flair. The Chopin *Fantasia* has a lower voltage, but the closing Liszt arrangement of Weber glitters admirably. The sound is first rate (with an excellent tape) and is very believable in its CD format.

Dresden State Orchestra, Varviso

Overtures and intermezzi: ROSSINI: *La gazza ladra: overture.* PONCHIELLI: *La Gioconda: Dance of the hours.* MASCAGNI: *Cavalleria Rusticana: Intermezzo.* PUCCINI: *Manon Lescaut: Intermezzo.* BIZET: *Carmen: Prelude to Act I.* SAINT-SAËNS: *Samson et Dalila: Bacchanale.* SCHMIDT: *Notre-Dame: Intermezzo.* MASSENET: *Thaïs: Méditation* (with Mirring). OFFENBACH: *Contes d'Hoffmann: Barcarolle.*
(*) Ph. Dig. **412 236-2; *412 236-4* [id.].

The highlight here is a splendid version of the *Dance of the hours,* the most beguiling in the catalogue. The rich Dresden ambience adds to the colour of the elegant woodwind chirruping, and the recording provides a fine dynamic expansion for the climax before the scintillating finale. Otherwise, the mood is very relaxed and atmospheric; in the ripely romantic account of the *Thaïs Méditation* (with a fine violin solo from Peter Mirring), the Dresden State Opera Chorus creates a soupily religiose backing. The atmospheric timbre of the strings and the warmly sentient playing are certainly very agreeable; and if the Saint-Saëns *Bacchanale* becomes unbuttoned only at the very close, the *Carmen Prelude* does not lack dash. With the background silence especially telling in the Ponchielli ballet, the CD enhances refinement of detail, although the chrome tape sounds well too, even if not transferred at the highest level.

English Chamber Orchestra, Paul Tortelier

'French impressions': DEBUSSY: *Petite suite: En bateau. Prélude à l'après-midi d'un faune.* FAURÉ: *Pavane, Op. 50. Elégie in C min., Op. 24.* PIERNE: *Marche des petites soldats de plomb.* MASSENET: *Thaïs: Méditation. La Vierge: Le dernier sommeil de la Vierge.* SATIE: *2 Gymnopédies* (arr. Debussy). SAINT-SAËNS: *Carnival of the animals: Le cygne.* TORTELIER: *Alla Maud* (valse – Paul & Maud Tortelier: cellos).
** Virgin Dig. **VC 790707-2**; *VC 790707-4.*

A pleasant but not distinctive concert of evocative French music, well played and very well recorded. The gentle Satie *Gymnopédies* are among the highlights.

English Concert, Pinnock

PACHELBEL: *Canon and gigue in D.* VIVALDI: *Sinfonia in G min., RV 149.* ALBINONI: *Concerto a cinque in D min. for oboe and strings, Op. 9/2.* PURCELL: *Chacony in G min.* HANDEL: *Solomon: Arrival of the Queen of Sheba.* AVISON: *Concerto Grosso No. 9 in A min.* HAYDN: *Concerto for harpsichord in D, Hob. XVIII/2.*
*** DG Dig. **415 518-2** [id.].

The English Concert is one of the acceptable faces of the authentic-instrument movement, and these vital accounts will give unalloyed pleasure. There are many good things here, particularly the Albinoni *Concerto* (with David Reichenberg the eloquent soloist) and the Avison, which comes from the set that draws on Scarlatti keyboard sonatas. Although there are popular items too, such as Handel's *Arrival of the Queen of Sheba* from *Solomon* and the Pachelbel *Canon*, there are others of considerable substance, the Purcell *Chacony* and Haydn's *D major Concerto* brilliantly played on the harpsichord by Trevor Pinnock. The performances are crisp and thoroughly alive, and beautifully recorded.

'The best of Baroque': HANDEL: *Water music*: excerpts. *Solomon: Arrival of the Queen of Sheba.* PACHELBEL: *Canon and Gigue.* VIVALDI: *Concerto all rustica, RV 151*; *Concerto for 2 mandolins, RV 532.* BACH: *Brandenburg concerto No. 3 in G. BWV 1048*; excerpts from *Suites Nos. 2–3. BWV 1067/1068.*
(*) DG Dig. **419 410-2.

Anyone wanting to try a representative baroque programme, played in authentic style on original instruments, should find this a good sampler. The playing has much spirit and polish and does not shirk expressive feeling; witness the *Air* from the Bach *Suite No. 3 in D*. The brass sounds in Handel's *Water music* are much less opulent than performances on modern instruments; and certain items, like Pachelbel's *Canon*, seem just a trifle bleak; but the recording is clean and believable and this is excellent of its kind. The disc plays for 71′.

European Community Chamber Orchestra, Faerber

'The Symphony is Europe', 1785': BOCCHERINI: *Symphony in B flat, G. 514.* MALDERE: *Symphony in G min., Op. 4/1.* SCHWINDL: *Symphony périodique in F.* SAMUEL WESLEY: *Symphony No. 5 in A.*
(*) Hyp. Dig. **CDA 66156; *KA 66156* [id.].

Four amiable symphonies, written at about the same time, but otherwise chosen arbitrarily from four different European countries, given lively, polished but not especially distinctive performances. The Maldere, in the unusual key of G minor, is quite an impressive little work; the Schwindl *Symphony périodique* is certainly a charming, if lightweight, piece; but on the whole the English work, Samuel Wesley's No. 5, is as attractive as any, and its *Brillante* finale is in the form of a rondo with a main theme that remains in the memory. The recording is good, but the acoustic of St James's Church, Clerkenwell, is perhaps a shade too resonant. There is, nevertheless, a good cassette.

'Fantasia on Greensleeves'

English music (with (i) Boston Pops O, Fiedler; (ii) ASMF, Marriner; (iii) ECO, Britten or (iv) Steuart Bedford): VAUGHAN WILLIAMS: (i) *English folksongs suite*; (ii) *Fantasia on Greensleeves.* TRAD: *The oak and the ash.* (iii) ELGAR: *Introduction and allegro for strings, Op. 47.* DELIUS: *2 Aquarelles.* BRIDGE: *Sir Roger de Coverley.* GRAINGER: *Shepherd's Hey:* (iv) *Green bushes; Molly on the shore.*
(M) *** Decca *411 639-4.*

An attractive anthology centring on Britten's ECO recordings made in 1968 at The Maltings. In the Delius, the delicacy of evocation is delightful; while the *Introduction and allegro* is a fascinating performance, with the structure of the piece brought out far more clearly than is common and the music deeply felt. Among the lighter pieces, Frank Bridge's delicious arrangement of *Sir Roger de Coverley* is particularly memorable with its unexpected introduction of *Auld lang syne* near the end. The sound is admirably fresh on cassette.

Film classics

'Film Classics': WAGNER: *Ride of the Valkyries* (*Apocalypse Now*) O de Paris, Barenboim. MYERS: *Cavatina* (*Deerhunter*) Söllscher. BACH: *Double violin concerto: Vivace*; *Harpsichord concerto No. 5 in F min.* (*Hannah and her Sisters*) Soloists, E. Concert, Pinnock. R. STRAUSS: *Also sprach Zarathustra*: opening. J. STRAUSS: *Blue Danube* (*2001*) VPO, Maazel/Boehm. DONIZETTI: *L'Elisir d'amore: Una furtiva lagrima* (*Prizzi's honor*). PUCCINI: *Turandot: Nessun dorma* (*Killing Fields*) Placido Domingo. MOZART: *Clarinet concerto: Adagio* (*Out of Africa*) Prinz, VPO, Boehm. PACHELBEL: *Canon* (*Ordinary People*) E. Concert. Pinnock. BARBER: *Adagio for Strings* (*Elephant Man; Platoon*) LAPO, Bernstein. RAVEL: *Boléro* (*10*) LSO, Abbado.
(*) DG **419 630-2 [id.].

The main purpose of a collection like this is to identify music for those who 'know the tune' but not the title. Most of the items included were used to good effect in the films with which they are identified, and no one could fault the performances. The sound too is uniformly good. Newcomers to classical music will find this a useful starting point for further exploration.

Galway, James (flute)

'In the Pink' (with Nat. PO Mancini): MANCINI: *The Pink Panther. The Thorn Birds: Meggie's theme; Theme. Breakfast at Tiffany's. The Molly Maguires: Pennywhistle jig; Theme. Victor Victoria: Crazy world. The Great Race: Pie in the face polka. Baby elephant walk. Two for the road. Speedy Gonzales. Medley: Days of wine and roses – Charade – Moon River. Cameo for flute 'for James'.*
❀ *** RCA Dig. **RCD 85315 [RCD1-5315]**.

Of the several fine composers who have dominated post-war film music (including Ron Goodwin, John Williams and John Barry) Henry Mancini stands out in providing the most indelible melodies of all. If Sir Arthur Bliss was the pioneer with his famous *March* for the H. G. Wells film, *Things to come* (1936), it was Max Steiner who, in *Gone with the Wind* (1939), first established the idea of associating a film in the public mind with an unforgettable musical 'theme' (in this case representing Tara, the home of the heroine – from which all the action derives). More recently came Maurice Jarre's *Dr Zhivago*, where the music (as David Lean commented appreciatively) had the effect of drawing the public – who had heard the music first – into the cinema to see the film. But the prolifically talented Henry Mancini has provided a whole string of superb musical ideas. It is interesting to reflect that a century ago he and his colleagues would have found an outlet for their invention in the ballet theatre and concert hall. But today's avant garde, often surrounded by musical barbed wire, eschews (or is incapable of) the direct musical communication of melody. Mancini's tunes are often unashamedly romantic (*Moon River* and *Charade* are superb examples); but the delicate *Meggie's theme* from *The Thorn Birds* or the similar *Theme* from *The Molly Maguires* (which Galway phrases with magical Irish inflexion) have an agreeable understated lyricism. Other no less striking examples make their impact with a quirky rhythmic felicity: no one easily forgets *The Pink Panther* or *The Baby Elephant Walk*. Mancini is admirably served here by Galway's superb artistry. His advocacy is wonderfully stylish and sympathetic to the melodic lines, while he can add an attractive touch of Irish whimsy to a piece like the *Pennywhistle jig*. Mancini himself directs the accompaniment using an orchestra of top London sessions players and creating an appropriately silky string timbre. The atmospheric recording is nicely balanced, Galway forwardly miked in the Pop manner, and the whole concoction makes a delightful entertainment, with an encore especially written for the soloist.

'Greensleeves'

English music (with (i) Sinfonia of L. or Hallé O, Barbirolli; (ii) New Philh. O, LPO or LSO, Boult; (iii) Williams, Bournemouth SO, Berglund; (iv) E. Sinfonia, Dilkes): (i) VAUGHAN WILLIAMS: *Fantasia on Greensleeves.* (ii) *The Lark ascending* (with Hugh Bean). (iii) *Oboe concerto in A min.* (ii) *English folksongs suite.* (i) DELIUS: *A Village Romeo and Juliet: Walk to the Paradise Garden. On hearing the first cuckoo in spring.* (iv) BUTTERWORTH: *The Banks of green willow.* (ii) ELGAR: *Serenade for strings, Op. 20.* (iii) MOERAN: *Lonely Waters.*
(B) *** EMI *TC2-MOM 104.*

Looking at the programme and artists' roster, the reader will hardly need the confirmation that this is a very attractive tape anthology. Performances never disappoint, the layout is excellent, and for the car this is ideal. On domestic equipment the sound is a little variable, although the tape has been remastered since its first issue and now sounds pleasantly smooth on top. Often the quality is both vivid and rich, as in the title-piece and the Elgar *Serenade*. Vaughan Williams's *Oboe concerto*, stylishly played by John Williams, is admirably fresh. This is excellent value.

Hallé Orchestra, Maurice Handford

'Hallé encores': COPLAND: *Fanfare for the Common Man.* KHACHATURIAN: *Spartacus: Adagio of Spartacus and Phrygia.* GOUNOD: *Mors et Vita: Judex.* MACCUNN: *Overture: Land of the Mountain and the Flood.* SATIE: *Gymnopédies Nos 1 and 3* (orch. Debussy). MASSENET: *Thaïs: Meditation.* TRAD.: *Suo Gan.* BARBER: *Adagio for strings.*
(B) *** CfP **CD-CFP 4543**; *TC-CFP 4543.*

Maurice Handford and the Hallé offer an exceptionally attractive collection of miscellaneous pieces, beautifully recorded. Many of the items have achieved popularity almost by accident through television and the other media (how else would the MacCunn overture have come – so rightly – to notice?), but the sharpness of the contrasts adds to the charm. The Hallé violins sound a little thin in Barber's beautiful *Adagio*, but otherwise the playing is first rate. What is particularly attractive about this concert is the way the programme is laid out so that each piece follows on naturally after its predecessor. The CD transfer is vivid and there is an excellent tape.

Hallé Orchestra and Choir, Arwel Hughes

'Much loved music': ARNOLD: *English dances,* Set 2, No. 5. VAUGHAN WILLIAMS: *Fantasia on Greensleeves.* VERDI: *Il Trovatore: Anvil chorus. Nabucco: Chorus of Hebrew slaves.* HANDEL: *Solomon: Arrival of the Queen of Sheba. Samson: Let the bright seraphim; Let their celestial concerts* (with Pamela Coburn). BACH: *Cantata No. 147: Jesu, joy of man's desiring. Orchestral suite No. 3 in D, BWV 1068: Air.* MASCAGNI: *Cavalleria Rusticana: Easter hymn* (with Coburn). SHOSTAKOVICH: *The Gadfly: Romance.* CANTELOUBE: *Songs of the Auvergne: Baïlèro* (with Coburn). ROSSINI: *Petite messe solennelle: Cum sancto spiritu.*
(B) ** CfP Dig. **CD-CFP 9009**; *CFP 41 4474-4.*

Arwel Hughes here offers the sort of concert which he has frequently presented on British TV with marked popular success. The programme is effectively chosen and the performances are well made and direct. But there is an element of routine here – the production seems somewhat studio-bound and, unexpectedly, the choruses lack the high degree of fervour one would expect to be generated by a Welsh conductor. The digital sound is excellent: clear, well balanced and full.

Hallé Orchestra, James Loughran

'French music': RAVEL: *Boléro.* DUKAS: *L'Apprenti sorcier.* CHABRIER: *España. Marche joyeuse.* BERLIOZ: *La Damnation de Faust: Hungarian march; Dance of the Sylphs; Minuet of the will-o'-the-wisps.*
(B) ** CfP **CD-CFP 9011**; *TC-CFP 40312.*

Although lacking something in charisma, these pieces are well played and vividly recorded. Chabrier's *España* has plenty of life, and the pictorial effects of the Dukas symphonic poem are well brought off. Ravel's *Boléro* is built steadily to its climax, but undoubtedly the highlight of the concert is the suite from *The Damnation of Faust*, with each piece very strongly characterized. The CD brings fresh, bright sound and the tape is generally well managed, although the wide dynamic range has meant that the quiet opening side-drum in *Boléro* is almost inaudible at normal playback level.

Harvey, Richard (recorder)

Chamber concertos (with Huggett, Goodman, Caudle, Roberts, or Ross), VIVALDI: *Recorder concerto in A min., RV 108.* BASTON: *Concerto No. 2 in C for descant recorder.* NAUDOT: *Concerto in G for treble recorder.* TELEMANN: *Concerto in G min. for treble recorder.*
(*) ASV **CDDCA 523; *ZCDCA 523* [id.].

Both the Naudot *Concerto for treble recorder* and the delightful Baston piece for descant recorder have also been recorded by Michala Petri, although they are in two separate collections. She is accompanied by the ASMF, whereas the present performances are on a more intimate scale, with one instrument to each part. However, the solo balance is forward; and this is especially striking on the CD, which is very clearly focused, so the feeling of a chamber partnership is diluted. The performances have strong character and the Telemann *Concerto*, a fine piece, comes off especially well. The cassette uses iron-oxide stock and in consequence the focus is less sharp.

'Italian recorder concertos' (with L. Vivaldi O, Huggett): VIVALDI: *Concerto in C min., RV 441; Concerto in C, RV 444.* SAMMARTINI: *Concerto in F.* A. SCARLATTI: *Sinfonia di concerto grosso No. 3.*
*** Gaudeamus **CDGAU 111**; *ZCGAU 111* [id.].

Richard Harvey plays with persuasive style and flair. Moreover the accompaniments are unusually authentic and in exactly the right scale. The Sammartini *Concerto* is a charmer and, of the two Vivaldi works, RV 444, for sopranino recorder, is especially engaging. The Scarlatti *Sinfonia* in five movements is hardly less winning. The recording has excellent presence and a good balance, with a very lively cassette. Highly recommended.

Holliger, Heinz (oboe), I Musici

Oboe concertos: MARCELLO: *Concerto in D min.* SAMMARTINI: *Concerto in D.* ALBINONI: *Concerto a cinque in G min., Op. 9/8.* LOTTI: *Concerto in A.* CIMAROSA (arr. Benjamin): *Concerto in C.*
*** Ph. Dig. **420 189-2**; *420 189-4.*

A collection like this is self-recommending, with five concertos offered, all of them attractive. The Lotti has a very agreeable extended *Affettuoso* slow movement, and the *Adagio* of the Sammartini is richly memorable too, while the central movement of Albinoni's Op. 9, No. 8, is wonderfully serene here. Holliger's timbre is enticingly coloured throughout and his phrasing is always supple and sensitive; some might feel that his ornamentation is at times a shade prolix, but this is a small point. In the Cimarosa his articulation of the allegros is engagingly neat and clean (although here Evelyn Rothwell in her famous PRT version – see composer index displays an even lighter touch), and the lovely *Siciliana* is radiantly presented. I Musici accompany with characteristic finesse and Italian warmth: there are no squeezed lines or acerbic timbres here, only sunshine, especially with the recording warm and realistically balanced. There is a very good tape. The overall playing time is just short of an hour.

Johann Strauss Orchestra, Rothstein

'Vienna première': MILLÖCKER: *Die Sieben Schwaben* (march). *Jonathan* (march). J. STRAUSS Jnr: *Concurrenzen waltz; L'Inconnue* (polka); *Hoch Österreich!* (march); *Alexandrine polka; Die Fledermaus: New Czardas.* E. STRAUSS: *Knall und Fall* (polka); *Leuchtkäferln waltz; Hectograph* (polka). JOSEF STRAUSS: *Frohes Leben* (waltz). *Vorwärts!* (polka); *Nachtschatten* (polka); *Elfen* (polka).
** Chan. Dig. **CHAN 8381**; *ABTD 1087* [id.].

Quite apart from the variety offered, virtually none of this repertoire is otherwise available. The present record was sponsored by the Johann Strauss Society of Great Britain. Jack Rothstein gives polished, spirited performances, with rhythms well sprung and touches of rubato nicely sophisticated. He uses a comparatively small orchestral group; the recording is balanced fairly well forward, so that, even though the ambient effect is good, the strings are made to sound very bright and not too full-bodied, though detail is admirably clear. The result tends to be aurally tiring and this is best taken a few items at a time. Not all the music is inspired, although the highlights (such as the *Vorwärts!* and *Elfen* polkas of Josef Strauss) are well worth a hearing. Marilyn Hill Smith makes a brief appearance to sing an alternative *Czardas* for *Die Fledermaus* (distinctly inferior to the famous one); the microphone is not too kind to her voice, although the performance has plenty of character.

Philip Jones Brass Ensemble

'Lollipops': LANGFORD: *London miniatures.* RIMSKY-KORSAKOV: *Flight of the bumble bee.* ARBAN: *Variations on a Tyrolean theme.* KOETSIER: *Little circus march, Op. 79.* GRIEG: *Norwegian dance, Op. 35/2.* JOPLIN: *Bethena.* PARKER: *A Londoner in New York.* TRAD. (arr. Iveson): *Song of the Seahorse.*
*** Claves **CD 50 8503** [id.].

Recorded in St Luke's Church, Hampstead, this Claves CD makes an ideal demonstration showcase for the superb British group that is in some ways the brass equivalent of the Academy of St Martin-in-the-Fields. A collection of 'originals' – music written or arranged specifically for these players, the concert is admirably framed by two suites of descriptive miniatures, both considerable additions to the brass repertoire. In between come many entertaining examples of musical bravura, including Rimsky's descriptive piece, sounding like a jumbo-sized bumble bee on John Fletcher's incredibly nimble tuba, and Arban's more conventional, but no less breathtaking *Variations on a Tyrolean theme*, where the horn player Frank Lloyd is featured; while Jan Koetsier's *Kleiner Zirkusmarsch* has wonderfully deft articulation from the whole group. Gordon Langford's set of six *London miniatures* shows this composer at his most inventive. Each cameo catches the spirit of a famous London landmark, with Nelson dominating *Trafalgar Square* in an ingenious kaleidoscope of sea-songs. The contrasting *Elegy*, evoking the Cenotaph, is touchingly sombre, while the brilliant *Horse Guards Parade* march is in the best Eric Coates tradition. Jim Parker's *A Londoner in New York* provides a transatlantic mirror-image in his five-movement suite, with lively jazzy imagery not only in the second movement, *Harlem* (with a strong Scott Joplin flavour), but also in the finale, *Radio City*, which provides an exuberant contrast after the nostalgic little waltz representing *Central Park*. Tony Faulkner, the recording producer, deserves a credit for the wonderful tangibility of the sound balance, which combines bite and clarity with fine, rich sonority. The presence of the instrumentalists on CD is very real.

'PJBE Finale': PREVIN: *Triolet for brass*. M. BERKELEY: *Music from Chaucer*. LUTOSLAWSKI: *Mini overture*. DURKÓ: *Sinfonietta*. RAUTAVAARA: *Playgrounds for angels*.
*** Chan. Dig. **CHAN 8490**; *ABTD 1190* [id.].

As usual, the Jones Brass play these complex scores with superb musicianship and with often breathtaking freedom from any suggestion of technical problems. The writing of both the avant-garde works, Zsolt Durkó's *Sinfonietta*, and Einojuhani Rautavaara's *Playgrounds for angels*, with its separate clustering of different brass textures, is very complex; but both are presented with an easy virtuosity which is most compelling. The Previn *Triolet*, in eight, often brief sections, is amiably diverse. It was written in 1984 and its finale proved to be a favourite piece of the conductor's one-year-old son. The finale of Berkeley's *Music from Chaucer* is even catchier, and this too is very agreeable in its invention. The recording is very much in the demonstration bracket, and there is an excellent tape.

'Music for the courts of Europe': HENRY VIII: *Rose without a thorn* (suite). FARNABY: *Mal Sims; His dream; His humour*. BULL: *The King's hunting jig*. GIBBONS: *In nomine a 5*. D. SCARLATTI: *3 Sonatas*. BACH: *Suite for brass* (arr. Mowat); *Brandenburg concerto No. 3*.
(*) Decca Dig. **417 524-2 [id.].

Music of this kind in brass transcriptions sounds utterly different from its origination, with the Scarlatti *Sonatas*, in particular, having little in common with their keyboard formats. Henry VIII's *Suite* offers some most agreeable music and the Gibbons *In nomine* has splendid sonority. The Bach too transcribes effectively, but this is primarily a programme for admirers of expert brass playing and fine sound.

Kremer Ensemble

Viennese dance music: LANNER: *Die Weber, Op. 103; Marien Waltz; Steyrische-Tänze*. J. STRAUSS, Snr: *Eisle und Beisle Sprünge (polka). Kettenbrücke Waltz; Beliebte Annen-Polka;*

Wiener Gemüts Waltz; Schwarz'sche Ball-Tänze. KLAUSER: *Nationalländler Nos 1, 2, 5–6, 12.*
*** Ph. **410 395-2** [id.].

Gidon Kremer, not just a brilliant and individual virtuoso, is a devotee of chamber playing. It is good to have such superb performances of this charming Viennese dance repertoire using an authentic small-scale group. Much of the music is slight, and Johann Strauss senior emerges as the strongest musical personality, with his *Eisele und Beisle Sprünge polka* – delivered here with great élan – and the engaging *Kettenbrücke Waltz* among the more memorable items. The recording is most realistic in its CD format, although somewhat dry, and its intimacy is heard most effectively if the volume control is not too high.

Lloyd Webber, Julian (cello)

'Travels with my cello' (with ECO, Cleobury): J. STRAUSS, Jnr: *Pizzicato polka.* LEHÁR: *Vilja.* DEBUSSY: *Golliwog's cakewalk.* SCHUMANN: *Träumerei.* ALBÉNIZ: *Puerta de tierra.* SAINT-SAËNS: *The swan.* BACH/GOUNOD *Ave Maria.* LLOYD WEBBER: *Andante.* ALBINONI: *Adagio.* KHACHATURIAN: *Sabre dance.* GRAINGER: *Londonderry air.* RIMSKY-KORSAKOV: *Flight of the bumble bee.*
(*) Ph. Dig. **412 231-2; *412 231-4* [id.].

This collection is issued in connection with Julian Lloyd Webber's autobiographical book, which shares the same title. The colourful orchestral arrangements were specially made by Christopher Palmer; the recording balance, by not projecting the cello too far forward, ensures that orchestral detail is very good. The solo playing has considerable flair, although the swooping lyrical style in *Vilja* and, notably, *The swan* may not appeal to all tastes. But there is no lack of personality here.

'Encore: Travels with my cello, Vol. 2' (with RPO, Cleobury): GERSHWIN: *Bess, you is my woman.* DEBUSSY: *Clair de lune.* MOZART: *Turkish Rondo.* TAUBE: *Nocturne.* BIZET: *Habañera.* LEHÁR: *You are my heart's delight.* VANGELIS: *Après-midi.* BACH: *Jesu, joy of man's desiring.* BERNSTEIN: *Somewhere.* MCCARTNEY: *When I'm 64.* RIMSKY-KORSAKOV: *Song of India,* etc.
*** Ph. Dig. **416 698-2**; *416 698-4.*

If anything, Julian Lloyd Webber's second travel album is even more attractive than the first. His warm singing cantilena always gives pleasure and there are some effective crossover items, notably Vangelis's synthesized *Un après-midi* and the McCartney song. The orchestra clearly enjoy themselves, and the recording is suitably vivid and atmospheric. Very entertaining of its kind.

Locke Brass Consort, Lake

'Miniatures for brass': PEZEL: *Suite.* SPEER: *Sonata No. 1.* HOLBORNE: *3 Pieces.* BRADE: *Suite.* STEELE-PERKINS: *Intrada.* GRIEG: *Bridal song. Op. 17/24; Ballad, Op. 65/5; Wedding day in Troldhaugen, Op. 65/6.* GUBBY: *The great Panathenaea.* BARTÓK: *For Children: 3 Pieces.* WALTON: *2 Duets for children.*
**(*) Chan. Dig. *ABTD 1038* [id.].

Although expertly presented, with admirable use of dynamic light and shade, the early (seventeenth-century) music has an element of blandness played on modern brass instruments. Yet its invention remains attractive. The twentieth-century items are all most entertaining. Alan Civil's Grieg arrangements, too, are highly diverting; and throughout the second side of this impressive chrome cassette the sparkle of the music making combines with sound of vivid realism to give much pleasure.

London Brass

'Impressions of brass': BIZET: *Carmen (suite).* FAURÉ: *Requiem: Pié Jesu.* DEBUSSY: *Le petit nègre; Golliwog's cakewalk; Clair de lune; Masques.* RAVEL: *Le Tombeau de Couperin: Rigaudon. Alborada del gracioso; Pavane pour une infante défunte. Mother Goose: Entry of Beauty and the Beast. Boléro.*
(M) ** Pickwick Dig. **PCD 836** [id.].

It is difficult to fault such a programme: cleverly arranged, expertly played and given most realistic recording in the right kind of ambience; the sound of the brass is most tangible. However, much of the music here, for all the cleverness of the scoring and playing, sounds infinitely more effective in its original format; *Boléro* really goes on too long, even though the climax is remorselessly achieved. If you enjoy the sound of brass and admire polished bravura playing, this is a fine example of both.

London Collegiate Brass, Stobart

ELGAR: *Severn suite, Op. 87* (arr. Geehl and Brand). VAUGHAN WILLIAMS: *Henry V overture.* HOLST: *A Moorside suite.* IRELAND: *A comedy overture.*
*** CRD Dig. **CRD 3434**; *CRDC 4134* [id.].

Elgar's *Severn suite* was a late work, commissioned as a brass band test piece in 1930. He was aided in the scoring by Henry Geehl, but the performing version was lost for half a century. When it was rediscovered, in 1980, it was found to be in a key a tone higher than the published score. The piece was then further edited by Geoffrey Brand, who favoured the original pitch but took into account the composer's own revisions made for his orchestral arrangement. The result is very convincing and here the opening theme is given a swagger and feeling of pageantry that remain obstinately in the memory. The rest of the work is also impressive, though the quality of the music is uneven. Vaughan Williams's *Henry V overture* dates from 1933/4 but remained unpublished until 1981, again in an edited version, by Roy Douglas. It stirringly quotes both French and English traditional melodies. Holst's *Moorside suite* demonstrates the composer's usual mastery when writing for wind and brass; while John Ireland's jaunty *Comedy overture*, played with striking rhythmic felicity, also shows the composer at his finest. The performances here (by a group drawn mainly from the London music colleges, and using trumpets rather than cornets, French horns rather than the tenor horns of the brass band world) produce a fine rich sonority. The execution has impressively polished ensemble; timbres are vibratoless to give an orchestral character to the sound. CRD's recording is superbly spacious and realistic, and the focus is only slightly less sharp on the chrome tape which handles the wide amplitude impressively. Even on CD the upper range, at times, seems not absolutely clean, probably an effect created by the reverberation.

WALTON: *The First shoot.* TIPPETT: *Festal brass with blues.* BRITTEN: *Russian funeral music.* IRELAND: *A Downland suite.*
*** CRD Dig. **CRD 3444**; *CRDC 4144* [id.].

Only the John Ireland suite is (deservedly) well known. Walton's *First shoot*, a mock ballet originally part of a C. B. Cochran review, is characteristically witty – the composer made the brass arrangement not long before he died. In spite of its title, the Tippett piece is stronger and more ambitious; and Britten's *Funeral music* makes a good foil. All the music is played expertly and with considerable intensity, if not always wth the greatest subtlety. The recording is excellent, with a very good matching tape.

London Gabrieli Brass Ensemble

'The splendour of baroque brass': SUSATO: *La Danserye: suite.* G. GABRIELI: *Canzona per sonare a 4: La Spiritata.* SCHEIDT: *Suite.* PEZEL: *Ceremonial brass music.* BACH: *The Art of fugue: Contrapunctus IX.* CHARPENTIER: *Te Deum: Prelude in D.* arr. James: *An Elizabethan suite.* CLARKE: *The Prince of Denmark's march.* HOLBORNE: *5 Dances.* STANLEY: *Trumpet tune.* LOCKE: *Music for His Majesty's sackbutts and cornetts.* PURCELL: *Trumpet tune and ayre. Music for the funeral of Queen Mary* (with Chorus).
(M) ❀ *** ASV **CDQS 6013**; *ZCQS 6013* [id.].

This is one of the really outstanding brass anthologies. With 73 minutes of music it is exceptionally generous, and the digitally remastered analogue recording is very realistic. The brass group is comparatively small: two trumpets, two trombones, horn and tuba; and that brings internal clarity, while the ambience adds fine sonority. The opening Susato *Danserye* is splendid music, and the Scheidt *Suite* is similarly inventive. Pezel's *Ceremonial brass music* is also in effect a suite – it includes a particularly memorable *Sarabande*; while Matthew Locke's *Music for His Majesty's Sackbutts and Cornetts* opens with a very striking *Air* and offers six diverse movements overall. (All these works are indexed.) With the Gabrieli *Canzona,* Purcell's *Trumpet tune and Ayre* and the Jeremiah Clarke *Prince of Denmark's march* (better known as the *Trumpet voluntary*) all familiar, this makes a superb entertainment to be dipped into at will. The closing *Music for the Funeral of Queen Mary* brings an eloquent choral contribution. Introduced by solemn drum-beats, it is one of Purcell's finest short works and the performance here is very moving. The arrangements throughout the concert (usually made by Crispian Steele-Perkins, who leads the group both sensitively and resplendently) are felicitous and the documentation is excellent. This is a very real bargain at mid-price. There is a faithful chrome cassette; but a relatively modest transfer level means that some of the bite and presence are missing here. However, it still sounds impressively rich.

London Philharmonic Orchestra, Mackerras

TCHAIKOVSKY: *1812 overture, Op. 49* (with Welsh Guards Band). GLINKA: *Ruslan and Ludmilla: Overture.* WAGNER: *Lohengrin: Prelude to Act III.* MUSSORGSKY: *Night on the bare mountain.* TCHAIKOVSKY: *Marche slave* (cond. Davison). BORODIN: *Prince Igor: Polovtsian dances* (cond. Susskind).
(B) ** CfP **CD-CFP 9000.**

It is appropriate that this should be the first CD from Classics for Pleasure, for the equivalent LP (CFP 101) was the very first issue on this label, and its 1970 recording has stood the test of time. Now digitally remastered, it still sounds well, although *1812* could ideally be more expansive – the gunfire and bells at the end give rather a dry effect. The performances are racy and alert, very well played, with the Glinka and Wagner items particularly vivid. For the CD *Marche slave*, vigorously conducted by Arthur Davison, and a set of *Polovtsian dances* from Walter Susskind have been added.

London Sinfonietta, Rattle

'The Jazz Album': MILHAUD: *La Création du monde*. GERSHWIN: *Rhapsody in blue* (with Peter Donohoe). STRAVINSKY: *Ebony concerto*. BERNSTEIN: *Prelude fugue and riffs* (both with Michael Collins). Songs: *After you've gone*; *Nobody's sweetheart*; *Sweet Sue*; *Dardanella*; *Makin' whoopee*; *My blue heaven*; *San*.
** HMV Dig. **CDC7 47991-2** [id.]; *EL 747991-4*.

Rattle consistently reveals his natural sympathy for jazz and jazz rhythms in this colourful collection of jazz-inspired works. The London Sinfonietta soloists, Michael Collins (in Stravinsky and Bernstein) on the clarinet and John Harle (in Milhaud) on the saxophone, are every bit as inspired as the piano virtuoso Peter Donohoe in the jazz-band version of the Gershwin *Rhapsody*. The snags are, first, that the recording, made in a Pop studio, is uncomfortably close and dry and, second, that the vocal contributions of Harvey and the Wallbangers in the songs associated with Paul Whiteman fall into a stylistic limbo, embarrassing rather than effective.

London Symphony Orchestra, Ahronovich

'Russian spectacular': KHACHATURIAN: *Gayaneh: Sabre dance. Spartacus: Adagio of Spartacus and Phyrigia. Masquerade: Waltz*. PROKOFIEV: *Lieutenant Kijé: Troika. Love of 3 Oranges: March*. BORODIN: *Prince Igor: Polovtsian dances*. GLINKA: *Overture: Ruslan and Ludmilla*. MUSSORGSKY: *Night on the bare mountain*. SHOSTAKOVICH: *The Gadfly: Folk festival*.
(M) **(*) Pickwick Dig. **PCD 804**.

An excellent collection of characteristically vivid Russian orchestral genre pieces, played with plenty of spirit and polish by the LSO who are in excellent form. Yuri Ahronovich may not be a subtle conductor, but his pacing here is notably convincing in Mussorgsky's *Night on the bare mountain*, while the piquant Prokofiev *March* is crisply rhythmic and nicely pointed. The *Sabre dance* and *Polovtsian dances* have no lack of energy and fire. The recording combines brilliance with weight; this CD is excellent value in Pickwick's mid-priced series, even though the ambience is a little dry.

Los Angeles Chamber Orchestra, Schwarz

'American string music': BARBER: *Serenade, Op. 1*. CARTER: Elegy. DIAMOND: *Rounds*. FINE: *Serious song*.
*** None. Dig. **CD 79002** [id.].

The Barber *Serenade* was first recorded in the 1960s, but its long absence from the catalogue is at last rectified by this excellent issue. It is a winning piece with all the freshness of youth. The *Rounds* for strings by David Diamond is another fertile and inventive piece, which has not been available since the early days of LP. Elliot Carter's *Elegy* was originally written for cello and piano, then arranged for string quartet, and dates from 1939. It is a long-breathed and noble piece, while Irving Fine, like Carter a pupil of Boulanger and Walter Piston, composed his *Serious song* in the mid-1950s. A worthwhile issue for all who have inquiring tastes, excellently played and recorded.

Los Angeles Philharmonic Orchestra, André Previn

GLINKA: *Ruslan and Ludmilla: overture.* MUSSORGSKY: *Night on the bare mountain* (orch. Rimsky-Korsakov). SMETANA: *Má Vlast: Vltava.* TCHAIKOVSKY: *Romeo and Juliet* (*fantasy overture*).
** Ph. Dig. **416 382-2**; *416 382-4* [id.].

Sumptuously recorded in UCLA's Royce Hall, Los Angeles, this CD brings rich sound and vivid orchestral colour, with bright trumpets and sonorous trombones and tuba in the Mussorgsky. The performances are polished and characterful, if without the last degree of spontaneity: *Ruslan* lacks the infectious zest of the famous Solti version, and this *Vltava* and *Romeo and Juliet* cannot be counted among the more memorable versions of either piece.

Marsalis, Wynton (trumpet), Edita Gruberova (soprano)

'Let the bright Seraphim' (with ECO, Leppard): FASCH: *Concerto for trumpet and 2 oboes in D.* TORELLI: *2 Sonatas for trumpet and strings a 5.* HANDEL: *Samson: Let the bright Seraphim. Birthday Ode for Queen Anne: Eternal source of Light divine.* PURCELL: *Come ye sons of art: Sound the trumpet; Chaconne. Indian Queen: Trumpet overture; Intrada; Air. King Arthur: Trumpet tune.* MOLTER: *Concerto No. 2 in D.*
*** CBS Dig. **MK 39061**; *IMT 39061* [id.].

Although Edita Gruberova makes an important contribution to the success of this anthology, it must be listed here, rather than in the vocal section, for Wynton Marsalis is clearly the star. His superb, sometimes slightly restrained virtuosity is ideal for this programme and his cool sense of classical style brings consistently memorable results. So often in a trumpet anthology the ear wearies of the timbre, but never here. Marsalis scales down his tone superbly to match the oboes in the delightful Fasch *Concerto* (especially as they are backwardly balanced), and he plays the *Sonatas* of Torelli and the sharply characterized Purcell miniatures with winning finesse. With Edita Gruberova he achieves a complete symbiosis in *Sound the trumpet* from *Come ye sons of art*, with the voice and instrumental melismas uncannily imitative; and he forms a comparable partnership in the two Handel arias, where Gruberova's agile and beautifully focused singing is hardly less admirable. The recording balance is excellent and the CD, as usual, adds an indefinable extra sense of presence, making the trumpet very tangible, especially in the upper tessitura of the Molter *Concerto*, where the solo playing makes the hairs at the nape of one's neck tingle.

Menuhin, Yehudi and Stéphane Grappelli (violins)

'For all seasons' (with Instrumental Ens. and rhythm): HARRIS: *Winter set.* HENDERSON: *Button up your overcoat.* BERLIN: *I've got my love to keep me warm; Heat wave.* JOHNSTON: *I'll remember April.* LOESSER: *Spring will be a little late this year.* GRAPPELLI: *Giboulées de Mars;* Automne. DUKE: *April in Paris.* MCHUGH: *On the sunny side of the street.* STYNE: *The things we did last summer.* WARREN: *September in the rain.* KOSMA: *Autumn leaves.* DUKE: *Autumn in New York.*
*** HMV Dig. **CDC7 47144-2** [id.].

The unexpected but rewarding collaboration of Menuhin and Grappelli has produced a whole series of highly individual 'crossover' records of which this is the first on CD (although the sixth overall). It returns to the original, more intimate format where, in Menuhin's words, he and

Grappelli 'exchange comments and solo passages with others, accompanied by the incredibly intense, precise rhythmic commentary'. The others include Martin Taylor and Marc Fosset (guitars) and David Snell (harp), plus a small instrumental group of strings and horns. The arrangements are by Max Harris and in two numbers Grappelli makes a contribution on the piano. Everything combines to make an excellent example of the sweet-sour genre, and the many hits are spiced with some unusual items. There is no better example of this fruitful partnership than Irving Berlin's *Heat wave*, with plenty of warmth generated by the interplay of these two quite different musical personalities. On CD, the recording is full and forwardly balanced, with plenty of presence. The earlier analogue reissues are listed under instrumental Recitals – see below, page 1318.

Moscow Philharmonic Orchestra, Lawrence Leighton Smith; Dmitiri Kitalenko

'The Moscow Sessions': TCHAIKOVSKY: *Symphony No. 5*. MUSSORGSKY: *Khovanshchina: Prelude*. SHOSTAKOVICH: *Symphony No. 1 in F min., Op. 10*. PISTON: *The incredible flutist* (ballet suite). BARBER: *Essay for orchestra, Op. 12*. SHOSTAKOVICH: *Festival overture, Op. 96*. COPLAND: *Appalachian spring*. GERSHWIN: *Lullaby*. GRIFFES: *The White peacock* (ballet). GLAZUNOV: *Concert waltz No. 1 in D, Op. 47*. IVES: *Contemplation No. 1; The unanswered question*.
** Sheffield Lab Dig. **CD 25/7** (3) [id.].

As audiophiles well know, Sheffield Lab is one of those small specialist labels that in the days of analogue LPs sought for the highest technical quality with special mastering techniques and custom pressing. Now, with CDs manufactured by an internationally similar system, they are seeking to find a new niche, and one of the results has been this USA/USSR joint recording project, using an American recording team and the resources of the USSR state TV and radio. To complete the cultural interchange, an American conductor is featured in Russian music and his Russian counterpart in transatlantic repertoire, with mixed success. On the first disc Lawrence Leighton Smith's account of Tchaikovsky's *Fifth Symphony* is direct but produces an eccentric ritardando in the finale. The playing of the Russian brass also leaves something to be desired in the closing peroration, very brazen and fierce. Leighton Smith is much more successful in Shostakovich on the second disc, and here the playing is compulsive. Then Kitalenko brings plenty of feeling and colour to the Barber *Essay* and Piston's *Incredible flutist*. The third disc is easily the most successful, with the Russian players responding readily to Copland and Ives, and the Glazunov *Waltz* sounding suitably elegant. The sound is first class throughout.

I Musici

ALBINONI: *Adagio in G min.* (arr. Giazotto). BEETHOVEN: *Minuet in G, WoO.10/2*. BOCCHERINI: *Quintet in E, Op. 13/5: Minuet*. HAYDN (attrib.): *Quartet, Op. 3/5; Serenade*. MOZART: *Serenade No. 13 in G* (*Eine kleine Nachtmusik*), *K.525*. PACHELBEL: *Canon*.
*** Ph. Dig. **410 606-2**; *410 606-4* [id.].

An exceptionally successful concert, recorded with remarkable naturalness and realism. The compact disc is very believable indeed, but the cassette also offers demonstration quality. The playing combines warmth and freshness, and the oft-played Mozart *Night music* has no suggestion whatsoever of routine: it combines elegance, warmth and sparkle. The Boccherini *Minuet* and (especially) the Hofstetter (attrib. Haydn) *Serenade* have an engaging lightness of touch.

'Christmas concertos': CORELLI: *Concerto grosso in G min., Op. 6/8.* TORELLI: *Concerto in G min. (in forma di pastorale per il Santissimo Natale), Op. 8/6.* MANFREDINI: *Concerto in C, Op. 3/12.* LOCATELLI: *Concerto in F min., Op. 1/8.*
(*) Ph. Dig. **412 739-2.

These concertos sustain a similar mood and atmosphere; together, they fail to offer a great deal of variety. Performances are warmly responsive, and I Musici bring great lightness of touch to this Christmas anthology. While some listeners will prefer this repertoire in more self-consciously 'authentic' performances, there is still much to be said for the richer sonority and body that this expert ensemble bring to bear on these concertos. The recording is excellent.

BARBER: *Adagio for strings, Op. 11.* ELGAR: *Serenade in E min., Op. 20.* RESPIGHI: *Ancient airs and dances: suite No. 3.* ROTA: *Concerto.*
*(*) Ph. Dig. **416 356-2**; *416 356-4* [id.].

A disappointing concert. The Barber *Adagio* lacks real tension, the Respighi is pleasant but rather characterless, though well played technically, and the Elgar needs more strings and a riper feeling. The strongest performance by far is the Rota *Concerto for strings*, written for I Musici in 1964/5, accurately described in the notes as 'an animated neoclassical piece'.

I Musici de Montreal, Yuri Turovsky

'In Concert': BARBER: *Adagio for strings.* BARTÓK: *Divertimento for strings.* STRAVINSKY: *Concerto in D for strings.* PREVOST: *Scherzo.*
** Chan. Dig. **CHAN 8515**; *ABTD 1125*.

Good playing from this small Canadian group, well recorded (if in a somewhat resonant acoustic.) They give very acceptable accounts of the Bartók and Stravinsky. André Prevost is a Canadian composer now in his fifties; but this short *Scherzo* is not substantial enough to give any definite impression of his musical personality.

NBC Symphony Orchestra, Arturo Toscanini

'Light classics': BIZET: *Carmen suite No. 1.* DUKAS: *L'apprenti sorcier.* BRAHMS: *Hungarian dances Nos 1, 17, 20 & 21.* ROSSINI: *William Tell: Overture.* SAINT-SAËNS: *Danse macabre.* SMETANA: *Má Vlast: Vltava.* SOUSA: *The Stars and stripes forever.*
(***) RCA RD 86205 [RCA 6205-2-RC].

Few if any apologies need be made about the quality of the sound here. Apart from *The Stars and stripes* (1945) the transfers come from LPs made between 1950 and 1953. The *Bizet, Brahms and the charismatic account of the William Tell overture* were recorded in Carnegie Hall with obvious ambient advantage, although the balance is close. *Danse macabre* is a surprisingly affectionate account and Toscanini is obviously enjoying himself in the Brahms *Hungarian dances. Vltava* has fine detail but is not as picturesque as some versions, and the highlight is undoubtedly *L'apprenti sorcier*, with its brilliantly paced exuberance. In the *Carmen* suite, which has pungent rhythms and lots of flair, Toscanini adds a harp cadenza to link the 'Fate' motive at the end of the Act I Prelude to the *Intermezzo*, and this is most seductively played. He makes changes too to the Toreador music at the end, using additional material from the opera's final act. This collection, even more than some of his hard-driven 'serious' recordings, shows why Toscanini was considered the greatest living conductor in the 1930s and '40s.

New York Trumpet Ensemble, 'Y' Chamber Orchestra, Schwarz

'The sound of trumpets': ALTENBURG: *Concerto in D for 7 trumpets.* VIVALDI: *Double trumpet concerto, RV 537.* BIBER: *Sonata (Sancti Polcarpi).* TORELLI: *Sonata a 5.* TELEMANN: *Concerto in D.*
(*) Delos Dig. **D/CD 3002 [id.].

As we know from his outstanding version of the Haydn *Trumpet concerto*, Gerard Schwarz is an accomplished soloist and musician, and both the Telemann and Vivaldi performances (where he is joined by Norman Smith) are first class. The Altenburg *Concerto* features seven soloists, the Biber *Sonata* eight in two antiphonal groups. Both come off splendidly: neither is too long to outstay its welcome. The balance places the brass well forward, but the chamber orchestra is backward, and detail might have been better defined. Otherwise the sound is very good.

Odense Symphony Orchestra, Ole Schmidt

'Music inspired by Hans Christian Andersen Fairy Tales': ENNA: *The little match-seller: overture.* WEYSE: *Kenilworth: Gipsy dance.* SCHIERBECK: *In Denmark I was born.* HARTMANN: *The Raven: overture.* LOUIS GLASS: *The hill of the elves: suite.* HOFFDING: *It's absolutely true.*
*** Unicorn Dig. *DKPC 9036* [id.].

A most attractive programme of Danish music. The only living composer represented here is Finn Hoffding, eighty-eight and still composing. *It's absolutely true* is an inventive and witty piece from the 1940s, unfailingly imaginative and most expertly scored. However, Glass's suite, *The hill of the elves*, is the real discovery here. Louis Glass (1864–1936) does not feature in many musical encyclopaedias, though he was regarded as important in his time. His suite transports one immediately into a fairy-tale world, full of childlike wonder and magic. His scoring is elegant and polished and there is some French influence, though he is his own man. The other music is not quite so memorable, though the *Overture* by August Enna, who was four years older than Glass and lived to be eighty-nine, has charm. But this issue is well worth its cost for the sake of the Glass and Hoffding pieces; the recordings and performances throughout are excellent.

Orchestra of St John's, Smith Square, John Lubbock

'On hearing the first cuckoo in spring': VAUGHAN WILLIAMS: *Fantasia on Greensleeves. Rhosymedre.* GRIEG: *Peer Gynt: Morning.* RAVEL: *Pavane.* DELIUS: *On Hearing the First Cuckoo in Spring.* FAURÉ: *Masques et bergamasques: overture. Berceuse, Op. 56.* SCHUBERT:

Rosamunde: Entr'acte No. 2; Ballet music No. 2. MOZART: *Divertimento in D, K.136: Presto.*
(M) **(*) ASV Dig. **CDQS 6007**; *ZCQS 6007* [id.].

An enjoyable bargain collection of essentially atmospheric music for late evening. Fine playing throughout: tempi are very relaxed, notably in the Grieg, Fauré and Schubert items, but the evocation is persuasive. The digital recording is first class, full and clear, yet not too clinical in its detail. Some might feel that the music making here verges on the somnolent in its consistently easy-going manner – the Delius piece is indicative of the conductor's style – but the closing Mozart *Presto* ends the concert with a sparkle. There is a good chrome cassette which, with its smoother sound – not as wide-ranging as the CD – brings an even softer focus to the music making.

Orchestral fireworks

'Orchestral Fireworks': excerpts (played by various orchestras & conductors) from: R. STRAUSS: *Also sprach Zarathustra.* PROKOFIEV: *Romeo and Juliet.* MENDELSSOHN: *A Midsummer Night's Dream.* ORFF: *Carmina Burana.* TCHAIKOVSKY: *Swan Lake.* RAVEL: *Daphnis and Chloé.* PUCCINI: *Manon Lescaut* (Intermezzo). FALLA: *3-Cornered hat.* MUSSORGSKY: *Pictures from an exhibition.* J. STRAUSS Jnr: *Unter Donner und Blitz.* J. STRAUSS Snr: *Radetzky march.* OFFENBACH: *Orpheus in the Underworld: overture.*
** DG **419 409-2** [id.].

It seems curious to include in a CD spectacular so many analogue recordings, but often these offer the most attractive sound. However, a series of snippets like this will surely appeal mostly to inexperienced collectors trying to find their way about the classical repertoire. Among the highlights here are Sinopoli's *Manon Lescaut Intermezzo* and the atmospheric excerpts from Rostropovich's CD of Prokofiev's *Romeo and Juliet.* The selection plays for 70 minutes.

Petri, Michala (recorder), ASMF

Recorder concertos (directed I. Brown): VIVALDI: *Sopranino recorder concerto in C, RV 443.* SAMMARTINI: *Descant recorder concerto in F.* TELEMANN: *Treble recorder concerto in C.* HANDEL: *Treble recorder concerto in F* (arr. of *Organ concerto, Op. 4/5*).
*** Ph. **400 075-2** [id.].

Michala Petri plays her various recorders with enviable skill, and her nimble piping creates some delightful sounds in these four attractively inventive concertos. This is not a record to be played all at once; taken in sections, it has unfailing charm; the sound is of demonstration quality. The CD retains the analogue ambient warmth, while detail seems marginally cleaner. While the upper range is not quite as open as on recordings with a digital source, the quality remains very impressive.

'English concertos' (directed K. Sillito): BABEL: *Concerto in C for descant recorder, Op. 3/1.* HANDEL: *Concerto in B flat for treble recorder and bassoon, Op. 4/6* (with G. Sheene). BASTON: *Concerto No. 2 for descant recorder in D.* JACOB: *Suite for treble recorder and strings.*
❀ *** Ph. Dig. **411 056-2** [id.].

The *Concerto* by William Babel (*c.* 1690–1723) is a delight, with Petri's sparkling performance of the outer movements full of good humour and high spirits, matched by Kenneth Sillito's alert accompaniments. The Handel is yet another arrangement of Op. 4/6, with the organ part felicitously re-scored for recorder and bassoon. The two instruments are nicely balanced and thus a familiar work is given an attractive new look. Not a great deal is known about John Baston, except that he lived in eighteenth-century London. But his *Concerto* has individuality, its *Adagio* has distinct charm, and the finale is quirkily infectious. Gordon Jacob's *Suite* of seven movements balances a gentle bitter-sweet melancholy in the lyrical writing with a rumbustious extrovert quality in the dances. Altogether a highly rewarding concert, beautifully played and recorded. On CD, the quality of the string timbre in the Gordon Jacob *Suite* is especially real and beautiful.

Recorder concertos (directed K. Sillito): VIVALDI: *Concerto in C, RV 44.* MARCELLO: *Concerto in D min.* TELEMANN: *Concerto in F.* NAUDOT: *Concerto in G.*
(*) Ph. **412 630-2 [id.].

The Vivaldi *Concerto* is the most familiar work for sopranino recorder and has been frequently recorded, though never more winningly than here. The Marcello is better known in its original format for oboe; Michala Petri plays it convincingly on the descant recorder and makes it her own. The Telemann is also a good piece, but the Naudot is rather less memorable. Admirers of this fine artist will be glad to have this new collection, notable for splendid accompaniments, with slow movements particularly attractive in their expressive warmth, without being romanticized. Overall, however, this is a less memorable programme than the collection listed above. The recording is excellent, with the compact disc adding marginally to the clarity of detail within a pleasing ambience.

(i) Philharmonia Orchestra (ii) LSO; Geoffrey Simon

'Gala': (i) WAGNER: *Lohengrin: Prelude to Act III.* TCHAIKOVSKY: *Violin concerto* (with Shkolnikova). BEETHOVEN: *Symphony No. 5.* (ii) ROSSINI: *Overture: William Tell.* DEBUSSY: *Prélude a l'après-midi d'un faune.* PAGANINI: *Introduction, theme and variations on a theme from Rossini's Mosè* (with Gary Karr). GERSHWIN: *Rhapsody in blue* (with James Tocco). VAUGHAN WILLIAMS: *Fantasia on Greensleeves.* RIMSKY-KORSAKOV: *Capriccio espagnol.*
** HM Dig. **CACD 1/2**; *CAMC 1/2* [id.].

The presentation here is, so far, unique for the CD format in that the two discs are suspended in a package resembling a book (size $10\frac{3}{4}'' \times 8''$), handsomely bound in deep crimson rexine with gold lettering. The enclosed booklet even has a colour print (Calame's *Am Ujersee*) to make it appear more luxurious. This is like a souvenir concert programme, with detailed notes about music and performers. The listener is offered two complete concerts, one with overture, concerto and symphony, the other a collection of classical pops. The first is very successful, with Geoffrey Simon giving well-paced and spontaneous readings and Nelli Shkolnikova a commanding and sympathetic soloist. The second collection has a lower voltage and is much less distinctive, but the recording throughout (produced by Chandos, although the set is marketed by Harmonia Mundi) is spectacular, made in All Saints, Tooting. This would make a good de-luxe gift for a newcomer to classical music, but many experienced collectors will find such an arbitrary selection less enticing.

Philharmonia and **Pro Arte Orchestras, George Weldon**

British light music: VAUGHAN WILLIAMS: *Fantasia on Greensleeves.* COLERIDGE TAYLOR: *Petite suite de concert, Op. 77.* ELGAR: *Bavarian dance No. 1, Op. 27.* GERMAN: *Gipsy suite: Menuetto – Love duet.* COLLINS: *Vanity Fair.* COATES: *London Bridge.* QUILTER: *Where the rainbow ends* (suite): *Rosamund.* CURZON: *Puncinello: miniature overture.* GRAINGER: *Mock Morris.* DELIUS: *Koanga: La Calinda.*
(B) *** CfP *TC-CFP 4510.*

An exceptionally attractive concert of lighter English music showing George Weldon as a lively and sympathetic advocate. Coleridge Taylor's *Petite suite de concert* is known for its engaging second movement, *Demande et reponse* but, as played by the Philharmonia, the whole work has plenty of vitality. Anthony Collins was a famous Sibelius conductor for Decca in the mono LP era, but he also left us the indelibly attractive miniature, *Vanity Fair*. The whole programme is admirably chosen and well laid out to provide contrast and give pleasure. The orchestral playing is first class and the recordings from the early 1960s sound good. The high-level iron-oxide tape is well managed, though chrome stock would have added a bit of range at the top and clarified the bass.

Ragossnig, Konrad (lute), **Ulsamer Collegium, Ulsamer**

'Terpsichore': Renaissance dance music by: ATTAINGNANT; DALZA; PETRUCCI; NEUSIDLER; SUSATO; GERVAISE; PHALESE. *Early Baroque dance music by:* MAINERIO; RESARD; MOLINARO; DA VENOSA; CAROSO; CAROUBEL; HOLBOURNE; DOWLAND; SIMPSON; GIBBONS; PRAETORIUS; HAUSSMANN.
*** DG **415 294-2** [id.].

There are in all 43 items on this compact disc which collects material from the recordings made by this ensemble, issued on two LPs in 1971 and 1972. Although on the face of it this music is of specialist interest, it is in fact highly attractive and could (and should) enjoy wide appeal. The performances are crisp and vital, and the DG engineers have made a first-class job of the digital remastering. Readers who recall the originals will not hesitate, and newcomers will find it full of delights.

Reilly, Tommy (harmonica), **ASMF Chamber Ensemble**

'Serenade': MOODY: *Bulgarian wedding dance; Sonata* (arr. from HANDEL: *Flute sonatas*). FAURÉ: *Pavane, Op. 50; Romance; Au bord de l'eau, Op. 8/1.* GRIEG: *Norwegian dance, Op. 35/2.* MARTIN: *Adagietto.* D. REILLY: *Aviator.* T. REILLY: *Serenade.* DEBUSSY: *Bruyères.* MENDELSSOHN: *On wings of song.* TRAD.: *My Lagen love.* MCCARTNEY: *2 Beatle girls: Eleanor and Michelle.*
*** Chan. Dig. **CHAN 8486**; *ABTD 1202* [id.].

The slightly acerbic edge of the harmonica can add piquancy to a romantic programme like this, and Tommy Reilly is a very stylish player. Moody's two contributions are particularly engaging and so is Reilly's own *Serenade*, while all the other light pieces are predictably appealing, if you like the harmonica timbre, projected against a small accompanying group. The effect is consistently refined (even in the Handel arrangement, which is the very opposite of 'authentic') and the pleasingly atmospheric sound makes this a very agreeable concert. There is an excellent tape, although here the harmonica focus is slightly less consistently sharp.

Royal Philharmonic Orchestra, Sir Thomas Beecham

'Beecham favourites': HANDEL: *Solomon: Arrival of the Queen of Sheba.* ROSSINI: *Overtures: La Cambiale di matrimonio; Semiramide.* SIBELIUS: *Kuolema: Valse triste, Op. 44.* GRIEG: *In Autumn: concert overture. Symphonic dance in A, Op. 64/2.* DVOŘÁK: *Legend in G min., Op. 59/3.* MENDELSSOHN: *Fair Melusina: overture, Op. 32.*
(M) *** EMI *TC-EMX 2013.*

Altogether delicious performances from the old magician. They come up remarkably fresh, too, after more than two decades, a tribute not only to the artistry of Beecham and the RPO but the quality of the EMI engineering. Notable are the Grieg items: the *Symphonic dance* is utterly delectable, while his little-known overture displays an unexpected degree of colour and charm. The sound on the cassette is generally well balanced and full, but there is a tendency for the bass to be slightly over-resonant.

Royal Philharmonic Orchestra or (i) French National Radio Orchestra, Beecham

'Popular French repertoire': CHABRIER: *Marche joyeuse.* DEBUSSY: *L'enfant prodigue; Cortège et Air de danse. Prélude à l'après-midi d'un faune.* SAINT-SAËNS: *Samson et Dalila: Danse des prêtresses de Dagon; Bacchanale. Le rouet d'Omphale, Op. 31.* GOUNOD: *Roméo et Juliette: Le sommeil de Juliette.* (i) FAURÉ: *Dolly suite, Op. 56; Pavane, Op. 50.*
(M) ❀ *** EMI *EMX 41 2077–4.*

This is an enchanting concert, full of the imaginative and poetic phrasing that distinguishes the best Beecham performances. The delicacy of the wind playing (notably the flute) in *Le rouet d'Omphale* and Debussy's *Cortège et Air de danse* is exquisite, but this is only one of many delights to be found here. Both the Saint-Saëns *Bacchanale* and the *Marche joyeuse* of Chabrier have wonderful dash and flair, and one can visualize the twinkle in Sir Thomas's eye. After Delius, this is repertoire which showed him at his very finest. The recording is always good and sometimes excellent. The cassette is first class in every way, but this is a prime candidate for compact disc issue.

St Louis Symphony Orchestra, Slatkin

PACHELBEL: *Canon.* BORODIN: *Nocturne for strings* (arr. Sargent). VAUGHAN WILLIAMS: *Fantasia on Greensleeves.* TCHAIKOVSKY: *Serenade for strings in C, Op. 48.*
(*) Telarc Dig. **CD 80080 [id.].

A winning account of Tchaikovsky's *Serenade* from Slatkin, essentially sunny, with the *Elégie* warmly controlled, the histrionics not emphasized. The finale is nicely prepared; if it lacks the last degree of incandescent energy, its good-humoured mood fits in with the overall conception, as does the genially elegant account of the *Waltz*. The Borodin *Nocturne* is volatile, with accelerando treatment of the middle section to point the contrast. *Greensleeves* is slow and stately, in the American manner, endearingly respectful in its spaciousness. There are two climaxes in Pachelbel's *Canon*, which some may feel is one too many – but better this than the unimaginative approach of some German performances. All in all, a successful concert, given a rich, naturally balanced concert-hall sound-balance, slightly recessed, with inner detail less than ideally sharp.

Savijoki, Pekka (saxophone), New Stockholm Chamber Orchestra, Panula

LARSSON: *Concerto for saxophone and string orchestra, Op. 14.* GLAZUNOV: *Concerto in E flat, Op. 109.* PANULA: *Adagio and allegro for string orchestra.*
*** BIS **CD 218** [id.].

The find here for most collectors outside Scandinavia will be Lars-Erik Larsson's *Saxophone concerto*, written in the 1930s for Sigurd Rascher (and indeed recorded by him in the days of 78s, but neglected since). It is a very fine and inventive work; the slow movement with its beautiful canonic opening is of particular distinction. The Glazunov, written at the same time, is more original and imaginative than it at first appears. Accomplished performances and good recording.

Scandinavian Brass Ensemble, Jorma Panula

HALLBERG: *Blacksmith's tune.* HOLMBOE: *Concerto for brass, Op. 157.* MADSEN: *Divertimento for brass and percussion, Op. 47.* GRIEG: *Funeral march.* ALMILA: *Te Pa Te Pa, Op. 26.* DANIELSSON: *Suite No. 3.*
*** BIS Dig. **CD 265** [id.].

The sound is quite spectacular and has superb presence and body: in short a demonstration disc. However, not all the music is spectacular, but the collection is worth having for Holmboe's *Concerto*, a short but finely wrought piece that towers over everything else here. Grieg's *Funeral march* was written for Richard Nordraak and was originally intended for piano, though Grieg arranged it for military band. The arrangement used here is by Geoffrey Emerson. The Norwegian Trygve Madsen's piece begins attractively enough with some lively syncopation but turns out to be pretty cheap. Christer Danielsson is a Swedish trombonist of note and his *Suite* is craftsmanlike and musicianly.

Scottish Baroque Ensemble, Leonard Friedman

'Scandinavian serenade': GRIEG: *Holberg suite, Op. 40.* NIELSEN: *Little suite for string orchestra, Op. 1.* SIBELIUS: *Canzonetta, Op. 62a.* WIRÉN: *Serenade for strings, Op. 11.*
** CRD **CRD 3342**; *CRDC 4042* [id.].

Good accounts of all these pieces, let down by a rather forward balance which prevents the players making the most of pianissimo markings. The Sibelius *Canzonetta*, which derives from the incidental music to *Kuolema*, is beguilingly played. The first movement of the Dag Wirén *Serenade* sounds a shade untidy at times and the quality above the stave is spiky. The cassette, while not quite as impressive as is usual with this label, remains perfectly acceptable.

Scottish Chamber Orchestra, Laredo

'String masterpieces': ALBINONI: *Adagio in G min.* (arr. Giazotto). HANDEL: *Berenice: Overture. Solomon: Arrival of the Queen of Sheba.* BACH: *Suite No. 3, BWV 1068: Air. Violin concerto No. 1 in A min., BWV 1041: Finale.* PACHELBEL: *Canon.* PURCELL: *Abdelazer: Rondo. Chacony in G min.*
(M) *** Pickwick Dig. **PCD 802.**

An excellent issue. The playing is alive, alert, stylish and committed without being overly expressive, yet the Bach *Air* has warmth and Pachelbel's *Canon* is fresh and unconventional in approach. The sound is first class, especially spacious and convincing in CD, well detailed without any clinical feeling. The Purcell *Rondo* is the tune made familiar by Britten's orchestral guide; the *Chaconne* is played with telling simplicity.

Scottish National Orchestra, Gibson

'Land of the mountain and the flood': MENDELSSOHN: *The Hebrides overture (Fingal's Cave), Op. 26.* BERLIOZ: *Waverley overture, Op. 2.* ARNOLD: *Tam O'Shanter overture.* VERDI: *Macbeth: Ballet music.* MACCUNN: *Overture: Land of the Mountain and the Flood.*
(*) Chan. Dig. **CHAN 8379; *ABTD 1032* [id.].

The MacCunn overture, made popular by a television programme (*Sutherland's Law*), here provides an attractive foil for the Scottish National Orchestra's collection of short pieces inspired by Scotland. These performances are not as refined as the best available versions – significantly, the most dashing performance is of Arnold's difficult and rumbustious overture – but make an attractive recital. On CD, the spectacularly vivid orchestration of *Tam O'Shanter* produces sound that is in the demonstration bracket; and the MacCunn piece is pretty impressive, too. The Berlioz is vivid, and Gibson's approach to *Fingal's Cave* attractively romantic. The cassette transfer is of good quality, but the comparatively unadventurous level brings a less sparkling upper range than the CD.

'Serenade for strings'

Serenades (with (i) Philh. O, C. Davis; (ii) LSO, Barbirolli; (iii) N. Sinfonia, Tortelier; (iv) RPO, Sargent; (v) E. Sinfonia, Dilkes; (vi) Bournemouth Sinf., Montgomery; (vii) LPO, Boult): (i) MOZART: *Serenade No. 13 in G (Eine kleine Nachtmusik), K.525.* (ii) TCHAIKOVSKY: *String serenade, Op. 48: Waltz.* (iii) GRIEG: *Holberg suite, Op. 40. Elegiac melody: Heart's wounds, Op. 34/1.* (iv) DVOŘÁK: *String serenade, Op. 11: March.* (vii) ELGAR: *Introduction and allegro for strings, Op. 47.*
(B) *** EMI *TC2-MOM 108.*

This was the finest of EMI's first release of 'Miles of Music' tapes with an attractive programme, good (and sometimes distinguished) performances and consistent sound-quality, slightly restricted in the upper range, but warm, full and clear. Tortelier's Grieg and Boult's complete version of Elgar's *Introduction and allegro* are obvious highlights, and this certainly makes an attractive background for a car journey, yet can be enjoyed at home too.

Smith, Daniel (bassoon), English Chamber Orchestra, Ledger

3 Bassoon concertos: VIVALDI: *Concerto in C, RV 472.* J. C. BACH: *Concerto in B flat.* GRAUPNER: *Concerto in G.*
*** ASV Dig. *ZCDCA 545* [id.].

Anyone thinking that a combination of three bassoon concertos might be a shade dull will be pleasantly surprised by this entertaining ASV collection. Daniel Smith is principal with the New York Virtuosi Chamber Symphony and a well-known orchestra player on the East Coast of the USA. He is also a first-class concerto soloist with a strong personality, an enviable technical command and a mastery of colour and mood. The J. C. Bach *Concerto* is the most substantial piece here, but the work by Christopher Graupner (1683–1760) springs readily to life when played so winningly. With alert, responsive accompaniments from the ECO under Philip Ledger and vivid sound on the excellent tape (although the soloist is balanced perhaps a shade too forwardly), this can be strongly recommended.

I Solisti Veneti, Claudio Scimone

Baroque mandolin concertos (with Ugo Orlandi): PAISIELLO: *Concertos: in E flat; in C.* LECCE: *Concerto in G.* ANTONIO MARIA GIULIANI: *Concerto in E for 2 mandolins and viola* (with D. Frati and J. Levitz).
(*) Erato Dig. **ECD 88165 [id.].

The Giuliani on this record is not Mauro but Antonio Maria; neither he nor Francesco Lecce are exactly household names and they are not liberally documented in the accompanying liner-notes. However, whatever their stature, the music is appealing and its invention far from pale. Pleasant out-of-the-way repertoire, nicely played and recorded.

Baroque concertos: DURANTE: *Concerto in A* (*La Pazzia*). PERGOLESI: *Violin concerto in B flat* (with B. Mussumeli); *Double harpsichord concerto in C* (with Buckley, Scimone); PORPORA: *Cello concerto in G* (with S. Moses).
** Erato Dig. **ECD 88172** [id.].

The Durante derives its name from its abrupt changes of mood in the first movement, but it is an attractive and interesting piece – while the (probably spurious) Pergolesi *Double concerto* is not. The best piece on the disc is the four-movement Porpora *Cello concerto* whose two slow movements are most eloquently played by Susan Moses and this fine ensemble. Good recording.

Soloists of Australia, Ronald Thomas (violin)

BACH: *Violin concerto No. 2 in E, BWV 1042.* MOZART: *Serenade No. 6 in D* (*Serenata notturna*), *K. 239.* TIPPETT: *Little Music.* HOWARD: *Sun and steel.* ELGAR: *Serenade in E min. for strings, Op. 20.*
** Chan. Dig. **CHAN 8498**; *ABTD 1208* [id.].

The Soloists of Australia is an ad hoc group of a dozen players who come together for special occasions such as the Perth Festival, where these recordings were made. They are a very respectable ensemble and produce a good, well-blended sound. The Elgar is sensitively done. Brian Howard is a young Australian composer in his mid-thirties and his *Sun and steel*, commissioned for the group, is a tribute to the Japanese writer, Mishima. Good though the performances are, collectors wanting the Elgar, the Mozart or the Bach are more likely to gravitate elsewhere. The Tippett, however, is not otherwise available on CD.

Steele-Perkins, Crispian (trumpet)

'Shore's trumpet' (with City of L. Baroque Sinfonia, Hickox): PURCELL: *The Indian Queen: incidental music. Trumpet sonata in D. King Arthur: Act V tunes. Suite in C.* CLARKE: *Ayres for the theatre: Cebel; Trumpet song; 3 Minuets; Round-O* (*Prince of Denmark's march*); *Serenade: Gigue.* ANON.: (*Mr Shore's tunes*): *Shore's trumpet; Trumpett; Prince Eugene's march; Song* (*Prince Eugene's march into Italy*); *Shore's tune.* FINGER: *Trumpet and oboe sonata in C* (with A. Robson, oboe). BIBER: *Sonata in G min. for trumpet, violin and 2 violas* (with D. Woodcock, R. Nalden & M. Kelly).
*** HMV Dig. **CDC7 47664-2** [id.]; *EL 270556-4.*

The title of this collection derives from the name of Purcell's trumpeter, John Shore, and some of the repertoire comes from Shore's personal collection. Both the *Sonatas* of Biber and Gottfried Finger are excellent works; and the programme is agreeably diverse, including an engaging account of *Shore's Tune*, allotted to the treble recorder. The famous *Trumpet voluntary* by Jeremiah Clarke is stirringly done and, with excellent accompaniments from Hickox and fine recording, this record is highly recommendable for trumpet fanciers.

Stern, Isaac (violin)

'Sixtieth anniversary celebration' (with Perlman, Zukerman, NYPO, Mehta): BACH: *Double violin concerto in D min., BWV 1043.* MOZART: *Sinfonia concertante in E flat, K.364.* VIVALDI: *Triple violin concerto in F, RV 551.*
(*) CBS Dig. **CD 36692 [id.].

At a time when the pursuit of authenticity has accustomed us to pinched sound in Bach and Vivaldi it is good to have such rich performances as these, recorded live at Stern's sixtieth-birthday concert in the autumn of 1980. Stern nobly cedes first place to Perlman in the Bach *Double concerto*, and in the Vivaldi he plays third violin, though there he has the bonus of playing the melody in the lovely slow movement. With Zukerman on the viola this account of the *Sinfonia concertante* is even more alive than the studio recording made ten years earlier by the same artists, heartfelt and beautifully sprung. The recording is a little thin, but digitally clear. Mehta and the New York orchestra are not ideal in this music, but the flavour of the live occasion is most compelling.

Stockholm Sinfonietta, Salonen

'A Swedish serenade'. WIRÉN: *Serenade for strings, Op. 11.* LARSSON: *Little serenade for strings, Op. 12.* SÖDERLUNDH: *Oboe concertino* (with A. Nilsson). LIDHOLM: *Music for strings.*
*** BIS Dig. **CD 285** [id.].

The most familiar piece here is the Dag Wirén *Serenade for strings.* Lille Bror Söderlundh will be a new name to collectors. He began his career in the world of light music, and it was some time before he gained acceptance (albeit limited) as a more serious composer in the 1950s. The *Concertino for oboe and orchestra* comes from 1944, when he was in his early thirties: he died just over a decade later in 1957. By far the best movement is the lovely *Andante*, whose melancholy is winning and has a distinctly Gallic feel to it. By contrast, the finale is rather thin and naïve, but the piece is still worth hearing and is certainly played with splendid artistry by Alf Nilsson and the Stockholm Sinfonietta, one of the best small chamber orchestras in the

Nordic countries. The Lidholm piece, the *Music for strings* (from 1952) is somewhat grey and anonymous though it is expertly wrought. It reveals a greater debt to Bartók than is desirable. Esa-Pekka Salonen gets good results from this ensemble and the recording lives up to the high standards of the BIS label, with the CD enjoying an impressive immediacy and presence. It is forwardly balanced but has splendid body and realism.

Stuttgart Chamber Orchestra, Münchinger

Baroque music: PACHELBEL: *Canon.* GLUCK: *Orfeo: Dance of the Blessed Spirits.* HANDEL: *Water music: suite No. 3; Organ concerto in F* (*Cuckoo and the nightingale*; with M. Haselböck). L. MOZART: *Toy symphony.* ALBINONI: *Adagio in G min.* (arr. Giazotto). BACH: *Suite No. 3, BMV 1068: Air.* BOCCHERINI: *Minuet* (from *String quintet in E. Op. 13/5*).
(*) Decca Dig. **411 973-2; *411 973-4* [id.].

Beautifully recorded – the CD is particularly fine – this is an attractive concert with a very well-played suite from Handel's *Water music*, and the engaging *Cuckoo and the nightingale Organ concerto* (with Martin Haselböck an excellent soloist) to give a little ballast. The performance of Pachelbel's *Canon* is a little heavy-handed, but the strongly expressive account of Albinoni's *Adagio* is convincing. The *Toy symphony* has some piquant special effects, and the shorter lollipops are quite elegantly played. The overall mood is a trifle serious, but that is Münchinger's way. The cassette is transferred at a high level and the upper range is less smooth than the disc version; although the sound is vivid, the violins are slightly fierce above the stave.

'Swedish rhapsody'

'Swedish Rhapsody and other Scandinavian Favourites' (with (i) Bournemouth SO, Gerlund; (ii) Copenhagen SO, Frisholm; (iii) Stockholm PO, Bjorlin; (iv) Bournemouth Sinf., Montgomery; (v) Philh. O, Weldon): (i) HALVORSEN: *Entry of the Boyars.* BULL: *Herd girls' Sunday.* ALFVÉN: *Swedish rhapsody, Op. 19.* JÄRNEFELT: *Praeludium.* (ii) LUMBYE: *Copenhagen Steam Railway galop.* (iii) LARSSON: *Pastoral suite, Op. 19.* (iv) WIRÉN: *Serenade for Strings, Op. 11.* NIELSEN: *Little suite for strings, Op. 1: Intermezzo.* (v) GRIEG: *Sigurd Jorsalfar suite, Op. 56: Homage march.*
(B) *** Cf P *TC-CFP 4524.*

A useful and rewarding anthology of music that often recalls an earlier gramophone era. Several of these pieces, because of their brevity, fitted conveniently on to a 78 r.p.m. disc. They are tunefully memorable and nicely scored. Järnefelt's *Praeludium* and Halvorsen's *Entry of the Boyars* are engaging examples, while Alfvén's *Swedish rhapsody* which became famous for its opening melody has a less familiar but equally attractive middle section. All are played with character and are well recorded, and this tape becomes more than the sum of its parts. But what makes it indispensable is the inclusion of Lumbye's *Copenhagen Steam Railway galop*, an enchanting pictorialization of a railway train, which has a Disneyesque sense of fantasy and a deliciously light touch and which overshadows the more portentous piece of Honegger and Villa-Lobos's rather similar portrait. The performance is first rate and the effect irresistible. The cassette is not ideally focused – notably in the *Railway galop*, where the upper range is restricted, but the sound generally is fully acceptable, although chrome tape would have brought greater detail and transparency. However, this concert is a worthy candidate for CD.

Thames Chamber Orchestra, Michael Dobson

'The baroque concerto in England' (with Black, Bennett): ANON. (probably HANDEL): *Concerto grosso in F.* BOYCE: *Concerti grossi: in E min. for strings; in B min. for 2 solo violins, cello and strings.* WOODCOCK: *Oboe concerto in E flat; Flute concerto in D.*
*** CRD **CRD 3331**; *CRDC 4031* [id.].

A wholly desirable collection, beautifully played and recorded. Indeed the recording, on both CD and tape, has splendid life and presence and often offers demonstration quality – try the opening of the Woodcock *Flute concerto*, for instance. The music is all highly rewarding. The opening concerto was included in Walsh's first edition of Handel's Op. 3 (as No. 4) but was subsequently replaced by another work. Whether or not it is by Handel, it is an uncommonly good piece, and it is given a superbly alert and sympathetic performance here. Neil Black and William Bennett are soloists of the highest calibre, and it is sufficient to say that they are on top form throughout this most enjoyable concert.

Touvron, Guy and Bernard Soustrot (trumpets)

Trumpet concertos (with Lucerne Fest. Strings, Baumgartner): HAYDN: *Concerto in E flat.* MANFREDINI: *Double concerto in D.* M. HAYDN: *Concerto in C.* ALBINONI: *Concerto a cinque, Op. 9/9.*
(*) Denon Dig. **C37 7544 [id.].

A generally attractive collection, recorded in Zurich. Both soloists are French, and the style of their playing is admirable in all respects, with no intrusive vibrato. Guy Touvron's account of Joseph Haydn's famous concerto is fresh, lightly articulated and pleasingly stylish. Bravura is always at the service of the music, the nicely paced *Andante* has a hint of melancholy and the finale is contrastingly gay. The Manfredini is a more conventional piece but, like Michael Haydn's two-movement work, also has a memorable finale, dispatched with easy flair by Soustrot. Albinoni's *Concerto a cinque* was intended for a pair of solo violins, but the trumpeters make it seem otherwise and the overlapping imitation of the *Adagio* and finale is particularly effective. The Denon recording is well balanced and orchestral detail is good (although the harpsichord is almost inaudible), while the soloists are given a fine presence against a suitably resonant acoustic.

Tuckwell, Barry (horn)

'Baroque horn concertos from the Court of Dresden' (with ASMF, Iona Brown): KNECHTL: *Concerto in D.* REINHARDT: *Concerto in E flat.* QUANTZ: *Concertos Nos 3 in E flat; 9 in E flat.* GRAUN: *Concerto in D.* ROLLIG: *Concertos Nos 14 in E flat; 15 in D.*
*** Decca Dig. **417 406-2**; *417 406-4* [id.].

None of this is great music, but it is all played by a master-soloist, and electricity is readily created from the bravura demands of the writing, so easily met by Barry Tuckwell. There is plenty of high tessitura (as in the Knechtl and both the Rollig *Concertos*) while Reinhardt's florid writing, with leaps as well as prolix textures, is very testing indeed. This concerto, like those of Quantz and Rollig, favours a siciliano slow movement, which brings lyrical contrast. Probably the best works here are the Graun, short and strong in character (particularly the finale with its crisp decoration), and Quantz's No. 9. This features a concertante oboe soloist, who echoes the horn's solo line most appealingly. Polished and stylish accompaniments from the Academy under Iona Brown, and bright, clear recording, with the overall balance well managed and the harpsichord continuo not lost. There is an excellent chrome tape.

Vienna Volksoper Orchestra, Bauer-Theussl

'Famous waltzes': WEBER: *Invitation to the dance, Op. 65* (arr. Berlioz). LANNER: *Die Schönbrunner.* IVANOVICI: *Donauwellen* (*Waves of the Danube*). KOMZAK: *Bad'ner Mad'ln.* JOSEF STRAUSS: *Dynamiden.* ZIEHRER: *Herreinspaziert* (arr. Schönnherr).
(*) Ph. Dig. **400 013-2 [id.].

The first of two collections, this record admirably gathers together some waltzes from contemporaries of the Johann Strauss family. Each has a striking main theme and the performances, if sometimes lacking the last degree of vitality, have an agreeable warmth. Franz Bauer-Theussl's rubato is not always subtle but is often effective in its way. He is good with the atmospheric openings – indeed, he shapes the main theme of Ivanovici's *Donauwellen* (*Danube waves*) very persuasively. *Invitation to the dance* lacks the last degree of characterization although, like the rest of the programme, it is well played. The resonant acoustic is effective and the digital recording ensures good detail, although the CD adds comparatively little to the LP quality, apart from the silent background.

'Famous waltzes', Vol. 2: ZIEHRER: *Faschingskinder; Wiener Burger.* LEHÁR: *Gold and silver; Ballsirenen.* ROSAS: *Uber den Wellen.* LANNER: *Hofballtänze; Der Romantiker.*
(*) Ph. Dig. **412 883-2 [id.].

There is some worthwhile repertoire in Volume 2, and Franz Bauer-Theussl and his excellent Vienna Volksoper Orchestra are warmly sympathetic. The rhythmic emphasis is perhaps a little stylized, but there is an engaging geniality of spirit and the phrasing of the lyrical melodies (and there are some memorable ones) is both polished and nicely timed. The recording is within an attractively resonant acoustic and the excellent digital recording provides good detail. This should bring a ready response from listeners familiar with the music of the Strauss family wanting to do a little exploring in the Viennese hinterland. Ziehrer and Lanner were accomplished tune-masters, and the Lehár waltzes are first rate.

Wallace, John (trumpet)

'Man – the measure of all things' (with Philh. O, Warren-Green): MONTEVERDI: *Orfeo: Toccata.* TORELLI: *Sinfonia a 4 in C.* ALBINONI: *2 Concerti a 6 in C; Sonata di concerto a 7 in D.* VIVALDI: *Double concerto in C.* FRANCHESCINI: *Sonata in D.* PURCELL: *Sonata in D.* BONONCINE: *Sinfonia decima a 7.* ALBERTI: *Sinfonia teatrale a 4.*
(*) Nimbus Dig. **NIM 5017 [id.].

The title of this collection aims to epitomize the spirit of the Italian Renaissance, which produced a great flowering of the arts. The collection covers a period of nearly two centuries of trumpet music. The total playing time (at nearly 67′) almost defeats its own object of showing the diversity of baroque style, for during this period trumpet devices did not change very much. The music explores all the possibilities of one, two and four trumpets, and the ear finds welcome relief in Albinoni's *Concerto a 6* for trumpet, oboes and bassoon. John Wallace is a splendid soloist; in the multiple works he is joined by John Miller, David Mason and William Stokes, who play with comparable bravura. The recording was made in the resonant acoustics of All

Saints, Tooting, which tend to blur the opening Monteverdi *Toccata* and the following Torelli *Sinfonia*, which features all four soloists. On another occasion, in an Albinoni *Grave*, the harpsichordist is left sounding lonely in the distance, against reiterated string chords. But for the most part the reverberation colours the music attractively.

Wickens, Derek (oboe)

'The classical oboe' (with RPO, Howarth): VIVALDI: *Oboe concerto in A min., RV 461.* ALESSANDRO. MARCELLO: *Oboe concerto in D min.* HAYDN: *Oboe concerto in C.*
*** ASV **CDDCA 1003** [id.].

The Haydn concerto may be spurious, but it makes an attractive item in this collection, and the Vivaldi, a lively, compact piece, and the Marcello (by Alessandro, not his more famous brother Benedetto), with its lovely slow movement, make up a good mixture. During his years with the RPO, Wickens repeatedly demonstrated in yearningly beautiful solos that he was one of the most characterful of London's orchestral players. Though at times he seems to be looking for his back desk rather than his solo spot, his artistry comes out vividly on this well-recorded disc, with the CD providing believable projection for the oboe against Howarth's sympathetic accompaniments.

Instrumental Recitals

Amsterdam Loeki Stardust Quartet

'Virtuoso recorder music': ANON.: *Istampita: Tre Fontane*. PALESTRINA: *Ricercar del secundo tuono*. FRESCOBALDI: *Canzon prima*. MERULA: *Canson: La Lusignuola*. VIVALDI: *Recorder concerto in C, RV 443*. LOCKE: *Suite in G min*. GIBBONS: *In Nomine*. SIMPSON: *Ricercar: Bonny Sweet Robin*. BLACK: *Report upon When shall my sorrowful sighing slake*. JOHNSON: *The Temporiser*. BYRD: *Sermone blande*.
*** O-L Dig. **414 277-2** [id.].

The Amsterdam Loeki Stardust Quartet are superbly expert players: their blend is rich in colour and their ensemble wonderfully polished. There are many piquant sounds here: the virtuosity of Robert Johnson's transcribed lute piece, *The Temporiser*, is a delicious *tour de force* with the following *Sermone blande* of Byrd aptly named; the Vivaldi *Concerto* transcribes successfully to an all-recorder group. It is surprising – although this is not a collection to be played all at once – that the ear does not readily weary of the timbre, even after several pieces heard consecutively. The recording has striking presence and realism.

Barenboim, Daniel (piano)

'Träumerei': BEETHOVEN: *Sonata No. 14 (Moonlight): 1st movt. Sonata No. 8 (Pathétique): Adagio*. CHOPIN: *Nocturnes: in E flat, Op. 9/2; in F sharp, Op. 15/2*. LISZT: *Années de pèlerinage: Au lac de Wallenstadt; Petrarch sonnet No. 123*. MENDELSSOHN: *Songs without words: Venetian gondola song; Spring song; Spinning song; Cradle song*. SCHUMANN: *Kinderszenen: Träumerei. Arabesque, Op. 18*. SCHUBERT: *Moments musicaux, D.780/2–3; Impromptu in G flat, D.899/3*. LISZT: *Liebestraum No. 3; Consolation No. 3*.
*** DG **419 408-2** [id.].

It would be difficult to imagine a more attractive collection of piano lollipops than this. Purists may object to the Beethoven sonata movements being extracted, but otherwise the choice makes an admirable programme, with favourite pieces by Liszt, Chopin and Schubert, beautifully played and recorded, nicely placed within the recital, and with Mendelssohn's *Songs without words* and Schumann's *Arabesque* bringing variety to an essentially romantic programme. The recordings were made between 1974 and 1986, and the transfers achieve remarkable consistency of sound-quality. Highly recommended as a gift to anyone who likes romantic piano music but finds the names of the individual pieces elusive. There is 72′ of music here.

Bate, Jennifer (organ)

Organ of St James's Church, Muswell Hill, London: *'Two centuries of British organ music'*: STANLEY: *Voluntary in F*. RUSSELL: *Voluntary in A min*. SAMUEL WESLEY: *A Scrap*. SAMUEL SEBASTIAN WESLEY: *Holsworthy Church bells; Introduction and fugue in C sharp min*. WOOD: *Prelude on St Mary's*. STANFORD: *Prelude and postlude on a theme of Orlando Gibbons, Op. 105/2; Andante tranquillo; Allegro non troppo e pesante, Op. 101/4 & 2*.
*** Hyp. Dig. **CDA 66180**; *KA 66180* [id.].

French organ music is currently very fashionable, but this fine collection of British repertoire can stand alongside most French compilations for quality and variety of invention. The *Voluntaries* of Charles John Stanley (1713–86) and William Russell (1777–1813) are most personable, and their cheerfulness is striking. Samuel Wesley's *Scrap for organ*, a delightful moto perpetuo in binary form, is even more fetching; and the set of rather gentle variations on *Holsworthy Church bells* by his son, Samuel Sebastian, has great charm. The *Introduction and fugue* is strongly argued and very well structured, but less flamboyant than the comparable piece by Parry. Charles Wood's *Prelude on St Mary's* opens elegiacally and brings an association with the opening of Elgar's *First Symphony*. The three Stanford pieces are strongly characterized and round the collection off satisfyingly. The organ of St James, Muswell Hill, is perfectly chosen for the programme, the effect warmly atmospheric yet vivid and clear; and Jennifer Bate's choice of tempi and registration is admirable, with all the music sounding spontaneous. The excellent recording sounds almost equally well on the very impressive cassette.

Organ of Beauvais Cathedral: *'Virtuoso French organ music'*: BOËLLMANN: *Suite gothique*. GUILMANT: *Cantilène pastorale; March on 'Lift up your heads'*. SAINT-SAËNS: *Improvisation No. 7*. GIGOUT: *Toccata in B min.; Scherzo; Grand chœur dialogué*.
(*) Unicorn Dig. **DKPCD 9041; *DKPC* 9041 [id.].

The playing here has enormous flair and thrilling bravura. Jennifer Bate's imaginative touch makes Boëllmann's *Suite gothique* sound far better music than it is. In the closing *Toccata*, as in the spectacular Guilmant march based on Handel's famous chorus, the panache and excitement of the playing grip the listener firmly, and the clouding of the St Beauvais acoustic is forgotten. But in the swirling Saint-Saëns *Improvisation* and the Gigout *Scherzo*, detail is masked. In the massive *Grand chœur dialogué*, the clever timing makes the firm articulation register, but although the Unicorn engineers achieve a splendidly sumptuous sound-image, elsewhere there is blurring caused by the wide reverberation of the empty cathedral. There is an excellent chrome tape.

Baumann, Hermann (horn), **Leonard Hokanson** (piano)

BEETHOVEN: *Sonata for horn and piano, Op. 17*. CZERNY: *Andante e polacca*. KRUFFT: *Sonata in E*. ROSSINI: *Prelude, theme and variations*. R. STRAUSS: *Andante, Op. posth.*
(*) Ph. Dig. **416 816-2; *416 816-4* [id.].

If Beethoven's *Sonata* is the most substantial work here, Rossini's is the most entertaining, with its ample opportunities for bravura which Baumann seizes readily. The Krufft *Sonata* is agreeable but insubstantial; the Czerny, which opens the recital, is another effective opportunity for display. Richard Strauss wrote his *Andante cantabile* for his parents' silver wedding, so a touch of solemnity is added to the romanticism of the melodic line; he also makes his own comment on the occasion by quoting a motive from Verdi's *Forza del destino* at the opening. The playing here has characteristic aplomb; Baumann's timbre is ample, and not only because of the resonant recording, and he indulges in refined vibrato at times. The piano is backwardly balanced.

Bell, Joshua (violin), **Samuel Sanders** (piano)

'Presenting Joshua Bell': WIENIAWSKI: *Variations on an original theme, Op. 15; Scherzo tarantelle, Op. 16.* SIBELIUS: *Romance, Op. 78/2; Mazurka, Op. 81/1.* BRAHMS: *Hungarian dance No. 1.* PAGANINI: *Cantabile.* BLOCH: *Nigun.* NOVÁČEK: *Moto perpetuo.* SCHUMANN: *The Prophet bird.* FALLA: *La vide breve: Spanish dance.* GRASSE: *Waves at play.* SARASATE: *Carmen fantasy.*
*** Decca Dig. **417 891-2**; *417 891-4* [id.].

Bell's début recital was issued at the same time as his coupling of the Bruch and Mendelssohn *Concertos*; the recording has a similar forward balance, which brings striking presence but also just a hint of edge to the violin timbre. He plays all these pieces with an equal measure of style and easy bravura; often the playing is dazzling, and in the lyrical melodies he produces a comparable amalgam of warmth amd elegance. In short, this is first-class playing and passionately felt, too, when required, as in the Bloch *Nigun*. *Waves at play* is an engaging picaresque novelty, and the *Carmen fantasy* provides plenty of opportunities for sparkle and dash.

Bergen Wind Quintet

BARBER: *Summer music, Op. 31.* SAEVERUD: *Tunes and dances from Siljustøl, Op. 21a.* JOLIVET: *Serenade for wind quintet with principal oboe.* HINDEMITH: *Kleine Kammermusik, Op. 24/2.*
*** BIS **CD 291** [id.].

Barber's *Summer music* is a glorious piece dating from the mid-1950s; it is in a single movement. Saeverud's *Tunes and dances from Siljustøl* derive from piano pieces of great charm and sound refreshing in their transcribed format. Jolivet's *Serenade* is hardly less engaging, while Hindemith's *Kleine Kammermusik*, when played with such character and finesse, is no less welcome. Throughout, the fine blend and vivacious ensemble give consistent pleasure, and the recording seems ideally balanced within an ambience that brings bloom and atmosphere without being too reverberant. On CD, the illusion of realism is very striking. Highly recommended.

Bolet, Jorge (piano)

'Encores': MENDELSSOHN: *Rondo capriccioso, Op. 14; Song without words* (*Jägerlied*), *Op. 19/3.* CHOPIN: *Nocturnes: in F sharp, Op. 15/2; in E flat, Op. 9/2; Waltzes: in D flat* (*Minute*), *Op. 64/1; in E min., Op. posth. Études: in A flat; F min., Op. 25/1–2; in A min., Op. 25/11.* DEBUSSY: *Prélude: La fille aux cheveux de lin.* SCHUBERT: *Rosamunde: Ballet music* (arr. Godowsky). ALBÉNIZ: *Tango. Op. 165/2* (arr. Godowsky). GODOWSKY: *Elégie* (*for left hand*). R. STRAUSS: *Ständchen* (arr. Godowsky). BIZET: *L'Arlésienne: Adagio* (arr. Godowsky). MOSZKOWSKI: *En automne, Op. 36/4; La Jongleuse, Op. 52/4.* SCHLOZER: *Étude, Op. 1/2.*
*** Decca Dig. **417 361-2**; *417 361-4* [id.].

An attractively generous and imaginatively varied recital which, if in essence lightweight, is certainly not without substance and offers much to delight the ear. In the opening Mendelssohn *Rondo capriccioso* Bolet immediately establishes his credentials of easy bravura applied with the lightest of touch. Later in the Chopin *Études* he offers even more dazzling playing but never employs virtuosity for its own sake, while the decorative element in Godowsky's attractive arrangement of Strauss's *Ständchen* is deliciously articulated. Debussy's lovely portrait of the flaxen-haired maid is beautifully done, and the Schubert *Rosamunde ballet music* has considerable charm (again with Godowsky's additions). The sound is most realistic (on tape as well as CD), and this can be recommended strongly on all counts.

Bonell, Carlos (guitar)

WALTON: *20th-Century music:* WALTON: *5 Bagatelles.* FALLA: *Homenaje pour la tombeau de Claude Debussy.* BRITTEN: *Nocturnal after John Dowland, Op. 70.* GINASTERA: *Sonata, Op. 47.*
*** HMV Dig. **CDC7 49512-2** [id.]; *EL 270560-4.*

Like his *Suite for harp*, Britten's *Nocturnal* is like no other music written for the specified instrument. It is a dream-like fantasy in seven contrasting 'moods', with a culminating *Passacaglia*, based on a descending scale of six notes, at the climax of which Dowland's tune appears for the first time in full. The mood of the close has something in common with Ives's *Unanswered question*. It is a haunting piece, and very well played – as is the rest of the programme. Walton's *Bagatelles* (written with the aid of a chart showing the positions of the notes on the fingerboard) is a series of arabesques, also conveying a sense of reverie – pictures in the fire. The second piece, *Lento*, is reminiscent of the *Waltz* from Constant Lambert's *Horoscope*; the *Sempre espressivo*, too, has a delicate romanticism; and both act as effective contrast to the livelier numbers. Ginastera's *Sonata* has a few avant-garde effects, but is readily accessible and inventive music, while Falla's *Homenaje* avoids being too sombre by the use of a habañera as its basis. The recording is real and with fine presence, and there is an excellent cassette.

Bream, Julian (guitar)

'Homage to Segovia': TURINA: *Fandanguillo, Op. 36; Sevillana, Op. 20.* MOMPOU: *Suite compostelana.* TÓRROBA: *Sonatina.* GERHARD: *Fantasia.* FALLA: *Homenaje pour le tombeau de Claude Debussy; Three-cornered hat: Miller's dance.* OHANA: *Tiento*
*** RCA Dig. **RD 85306 [RCD1 5306]**.

Readers who have already acquired Bream's earlier digital recital concentrating on the music of Albéniz and Granados (see the Composer section, above) will find this hardly less impressive, both musically and technically. The programme here is even more diverse, with the Gerhard *Fantasia* adding a twentieth-century dimension while Ohana's *Tiento* has a comparable imaginative approach to texture. The Mompou *Suite compostelana* is most attractive in its diversity and the Tórroba *Sonatina* is perhaps this composer's finest work for guitar. Throughout, Bream plays with his usual flair and spontaneity, constantly imaginative in his use of a wide dynamic range and every possible colouristic effect. The recording has the most tangible realism and presence, and the background silence of the compact disc adds much.

'Guitarra': MUDARRA: *Fantasias Nos 10 and 14.* MILAN: *Fantasia No. 22.* NARVAEZ: *La canción del Emperador; Conde Claros.* SANZ: *Galliardas; Pasacalles; Canarios.* GUERAU: *Villano; Canario.* MURCIA: *Prelude and allegro.* SOR: *Variations on a theme by Mozart, Op. 9.* AQUADO: *Rondo in A, Op. 2/3.* TARREGA: *Prelude in A min; Recuerdos de la Alhambra.* GRANADOS: *La Maja de Goya. Danza española No. 5.* ALBÉNIZ: *Suite española: Cádiz.* TÓRROBA: *Sonata in A.* TURINA: *Fandanguillo.* FALLA: *Homenaje pour le tombeau de Claude Debussy. Three-cornered hat: Miller's dance.*
*** RCA Dig. **RD 86206.**

A wholly admirable survey of Spanish guitar music covering four hundred years and featuring four different instruments, all especially built by José Ramanillos: a Renaissance guitar, vihuela, baroque guitar and a modern classical guitar. Bream's natural dexterity is matched by his remarkable control of colour and unerring sense of style. Many of the early pieces are quite simple but have considerable magnetism. Three of the items included in the latter part of the recital come from his Albéniz/Granados coupling reviewed in the Composer section, others from the shorter collection above dedicated to Segovia, notably the exciting Turina *Fandanguillo*, a real highlight. The presence of the recordings is remarkable, the focus sharp and believable; while one again registers the background silence of the CD as bringing a subtle additional sense of realism. This collection was originally issued on a pair of discs, but now, with five items taken out, has been generously fitted on to a single CD.

Bream, Julian and **John Williams** (guitars)

'Together': LAWES: *Suite for 2 guitars*. CARULLI: *Duo in G, Op. 34*. SOR: *L'Encouragement, Op. 34*. ALBÉNIZ: *Córdoba*. GRANADOS: *Goyescas: Intermezzo*. FALLA: *La vida breve: Spanish dance No. 1*. RAVEL: *Pavane pour une infante défunte*.
*** RCA **RD 83257**.

'Together again': CARULLI: *Serenade, Op. 96*. GRANADOS: *Danzas españolas Nos 6 and 11*. ALBÉNIZ: *Bajo la Palmera, Op. 32. Iberia: Evocación*. GIULIANI: *Variazioni concertanti, Op. 130*.
*** RCA **RD 80456**.

In this case two guitars are better than one; these two fine artists clearly strike sparks off each other. In the first recital, Albéniz's *Córdoba* is hauntingly memorable and the concert closes with a slow, stately version of Ravel's *Pavane* which is unforgettable. Here Bream justifies a tempo which he did not bring off so effectively in his solo version (now deleted). On the second disc, it is again music of Albéniz that one remembers for the haunting atmosphere the two artists create together. The sound of these reissues is truthful and atmospheric, although the digital remastering for CD does not succeed in removing all the background hiss. This is distinctly noticeable in the first collection, but in the second is only very slight, and the effect is not intrusive. Moreover, the digital remastering of **RD 80456** brings striking presence.

'Live': JOHNSON: *Pavane and Galliard*. TELEMANN: *Partie polonaise*. SOR: *Fantaisie, Op. 54*. BRAHMS: *Theme and variations, Op. 18* (trans. Williams). FAURÉ: *Dolly suite, Op. 56*. DEBUSSY: *Rêverie. Children's Corner: Golliwog's cakewalk. Suite bergamasque: Clair de lune*. ALBÉNIZ: *Castilla*. GRANADOS: *Spanish dance No. 2* (*Oriental*).
(*) RCA **RD 89654.

This recital was recorded live in Boston and New York during a North American tour. The recording is well balanced and eminently realistic, but the drawback is the applause which, though shortened in the editing, is still very intrusive on repeated hearings. The playing is of the highest quality although perhaps at times slightly self-conscious (the Granados encore has an almost narcissistic tonal beauty). As a whole there is not quite the electricity of this team's other recitals. Fauré's *Dolly suite* sounds a little cosy and the transcription of the *Variations* from Brahms's *B flat major Sextet* is not entirely effective. But the *Golliwog's cakewalk* and the Albéniz *Castilla* are highly enjoyable. The compact disc transfer provides a very quiet but not absolutely silent background (though the very slight hiss is not distracting); it offers the contents of the pair of LPs or tapes on a single disc (over 70′), so is good value; and the documentation is adequate.

Byzantine, Julian (guitar)

'Baroque guitar music': BACH: *Lute suite No. 1 in E min., BWV 996; Prelude, fugue and allegro in D, BWV 998.* WEISS: *Tombeau sur la mort de M. Compte De Logy; Fantasie; Suite No. 14: Passacaille.* D. SCARLATTI: *Keyboard sonatas: in A, Kk. 332; in E, Kk. 380.*
** CfP Dig. **CD-CFP 9014**; *CFP 41 4486-4.*

Julian Byzantine's thoughtful, somewhat self-effacing style produces a thoroughly musical account of the Bach *Suite* and in the Weiss *Tombeau sur la mort de M. Compte De Logy* his restraint is telling. Overall, however, one would have liked a little more projection of personality, although the music making itself, if somewhat considered, is never lifeless. The digital recording is eminently realistic and well balanced, and the CD brings fine presence. The cassette is good, too.

Cambridge Buskers

'Classic Busking'.
(B) *** DG Walkman *415 337-4.*

This highly diverting collection is ideal entertainment for a long car journey – though, for all its effervescence and wit, it is best taken a side at a time. The Cambridge Buskers are a duo, Michael Copley (who plays the flute, piccolo and various recorders, with often astonishing bravura) and Dag Ingram, the hardly less fluent accordionist. They met at Cambridge, and these recordings date from the end of the 1970s. There are thirty-four items here, including a remarkably wide range of classical lollipops. The recital immediately establishes the stylistic credentials of the players by opening with an engaging account of the *Rondo* from Mozart's *Eine kleine Nachtmusik*. The programme ranges from Chopin and Praetorius to Bach and Vivaldi, with ear-tickling operatic excerpts by Bizet, Gluck, Rossini, Mozart and Verdi. With tongue-in-cheek irreverence, they manage to include not only the Quartet from *Rigoletto*, but even the *Ride of the Valkyries* – which sounds a good deal more enticing than some over-enthusiastic orchestral versions. The players clearly delight in their more outrageous transcriptions, and they are such natural musicians that good taste comes easily. With crisp, clean recording and 83 minutes of music, this is certainly value for money.

Chung, Kyung Wha (violin), **Phillip Moll** (piano)

'Con amore': KREISLER: *La Gitana; Liebeslied; Praeludium and allegro in the style of Pugnani. Liebesfreud.* POLDINI: *Dancing doll.* WIENIAWSKI: *Scherzo-Tarantelle; Caprice in A min.* ELGAR: *Salut d'amor, Op. 12; La Capricieuse, Op. 17.* TCHAIKOVSKY: *Valse sentimentale.* NOVAČEK: *Moto perpetuo.* DEBUSSY: *Beau soir.* CHOPIN: *Nocturne in C sharp min.* GOSSEC: *Gavotte.* CHAMINADE: *Sérénade espagnole.* SAINT-SAËNS: *Caprice (after a study in the form of a waltz), Op. 52/6.* BRAHMS: *Hungarian dance No. 1.*
*** Decca Dig. **417 289-2**; *417 289-4* [id.].

Kyung Wha Chung's collection, '*Con amore*', reflects that title in a delightfully varied choice of items, sweet as well as brilliant. When she claims in all seriousness that she does not think of herself as a virtuoso violinist, she really means that technical brilliance is only an incidental for her, and the poise and flair of all these items show her at her most winningly characterful, helped by Phillip Moll's very sympathetic accompaniment, and well-balanced recording, which has fine presence on CD and sounds pretty good on chrome cassette, too.

Clarion Ensemble

'Trumpet collection': FANTINI: *Sonata; Brando; Balletteo; Corrente.* MONTEVERDI: *Et e pur dunque vero.* FRESCOBALDI: *Canzona a canto solo.* PURCELL: *To arms, heroic prince.* A. SCARLATTI: *Si suoni la tromba.* BISHOP: *Arietta and Waltz; Thine forever.* DONIZETTI: *Lo L'udia.* KOENIG: *Post horn galop.* ARBAN: *Fantasia on Verdi's Rigoletto.* CLARKE: *Cousins.* ENESCU: *Legende.*
❀ *** Amon Ra **CD-SAR 30** [id.].

The simple title *'Trumpet collection'* covers a fascinating recital of music for trumpet written over three centuries and played with great skill and musicianship by Jonathan Impett, using a variety of original instruments, from a keyed bugle and clapper shake-key cornopean to an English slide trumpet and a posthorn. Impett is a complete master of all these instruments, never producing a throttled tone; indeed in the Purcell and Scarlatti arias he matches the soaring soprano line of Deborah Roberts with uncanny mirror-image precision. In the duet, *Thine forever*, by Sir Henry Bishop, the two artists produce an interplay of voice and trumpet timbre comparable with the writing for voice and flute in a Donizetti mad scene. Miss Roberts also gives a ravishing account of the Monteverdi scene, to show her remarkable range. Accompaniments are provided by other members of the Clarion Ensemble, including Paul Nicholson who plays a fortepiano with great flair and with the slightly dry timbre particularly suited to act as a foil to the brass sounds. The Frescobaldi *Canzona* brings a duet for trumpet and trombone, with a background harpsichord filigree, which is most effective. With demonstration-worthy recording – one could readily believe the instrumentalists to be at the end of one's room – this is as enjoyable as it is interesting, with the *Post horn galop* and Arban's *Rigoletto variations* producing exhilarating bravura.

Craxton, Janet (oboe)

'The Art of Janet Craxton': MOZART: *Oboe quartet in F, K.370;* LUTYENS: *O Absalom, Op. 122* (both with London Oboe Qt.) MUSGRAVE: *Impromptu No. 1 for flute and oboe* (with D. Whittaker); POULENC: *Sonata.* BRITTEN: *Temporal variations* (both with Ian Brown, piano). RICHARDSON: *Allegretto* (with composer).
*** BBC **CD 635X**; (M) *ZCN 635X* [id.].

This compilation of BBC broadcasts was made as a tribute to Janet Craxton (1929–81). She was a remarkable chamber musician and also served in the BBC Symphony Orchestra (1954–63), the London Sinfonietta (1969–81) and the Royal Opera House Orchestra (1979–81). The performance of the Mozart *Oboe quartet* enjoys (and deserves) a great reputation within the BBC, and the other performances (mainly drawn from 1979 to 1981) are hardly less fine. The earliest piece, the charming Alan Richardson *Allegretto*, comes from 1966.

Davies, Philippa (flute), Thelma Owen (harp)

'The Romance of the flute and harp': HASSELMANS: *La Source, Op. 44; Feuilles d'automne.* GODARD: *Suite, Op. 16: Allegretto.* GODEFROID: *Étude de concert.* FAURÉ: *Berceuse, Op. 16;*

Impromptu, Op. 86. DÖPPLER: *Mazurka.* MENDELSSOHN: *Spring song, Op. 62/3.* THOMAS: *Watching the wheat.* SAINT-SAËNS: *Le Cygne.* BIZET: *Fair maid of Perth: Intermezzo.* PARISH-ALVARS: *Serenade.* DEBUSSY: *Syrinx; Suite bergamasque: Clair de lune.*
(M) *** Pickwick Dig. **PCD 835.**

An unexpectedly successful recital which effectively intersperses harp solos with music in which the flute takes the leading role. The playing is most sensitive and the recording is very realistic indeed. The programme, too, is well chosen and attractively laid out, besides being very generous in playing time (59′). Highly recommended for playing on a pleasant summer evening.

Drake, Susan (harp)

'Echoes of a waterfall'. HASSELMANS: *La Source, Op. 44; Prelude, Op. 52; Chanson de mai, Op. 40.* ALVARS: *Divertissement, Op. 38.* GODEFROID: *Bois solitaire; Étude de concert in E flat min., Op. 193.* GLINKA: *Variations on a theme of Mozart.* THOMAS: *Echoes of a waterfall: Watching the wheat; Megan's daughter.* SPOHR: *Variations on Je suis encore, Op. 36.*
*** Hyp. **CDA 66038**; *KA 66038* [id.].

The music is lightweight and sometimes facile, but the young Welsh harpist, Susan Drake, is a beguiling exponent, and her technique is as impressive as her feeling for atmosphere. Those intrigued by the title of the collection will not be disappointed by the sounds here (the recording is excellent) which balance evocation with a suitable degree of flamboyance when the music calls for it. The Thomas evocation of watery effects is certainly picturesque, as is Hasselmans' charming *La Source,* and both the Spohr and (especially) the Glinka *Variations* have considerable appeal. This is a case where the background quiet of the CD must be an advantage, but the cassette too has little background noise and manages the resonance well; the sound is warm and mellow, yet definition remains quite good.

Ensemble Wien–Berlin

HAYDN: *Divertimento in B flat, Hob. II/46.* DANZI: *Wind quintet in B flat, Op. 51/1.* BOZZA: *Scherzo for wind, Op. 48.* IBERT: *3 Pièces brêves.* VILLA-LOBOS: *Quintet en forme de chôros.*
*** CBS Dig. **MK 39558** [id.].

The Vienna/Berlin Ensemble happily combine elegance and a lightness of touch with technical polish, and it is difficult to imagine these pieces being better played. Haydn's *Divertimento* is engaging, if not of the calibre of similar works by Mozart, but its main interest is in indicating the source of the chorale used in Brahms's famous orchestral variations. It has great character heard in Haydn's original wind scoring. The Danzi is facile but pleasing, the Bozza *Scherzo* highly felicitous, even memorable. Probably the best work is the set of *Pièces brêves* of Ibert (given here with considerable flair); the most original, though not the most agreeable – it is a little spiky – is the Villa-Lobos *Chôros.* The recording is first class, well balanced and eminently realistic.

Equale Brass

'Baccanales': WARLOCK: *Capriol suite* (arr. Gout). POULENC: *Suite* (arr. Jenkins): *Mouvement perpétuel No. 1; Novellette No. 1 in C; Impromptu No. 3; Suite française.* ARNOLD: *Brass quintet.* F. COUPERIN: *Suite* (arr. Wallace). BARTÓK: *4 Hungarian pictures* (arr. Sears).
*** Nimbus **NIM 5004.**

This was one of the first Nimbus compact discs to be issued without an LP equivalent. It offers sound of striking presence and realism and the programme (56′ including the silences between items) is quite generous and certainly imaginative. The arrangements are cleverly scored and produce highly diverting results. Warlock's *Capriol suite* and the music of François Couperin seem unlikely to adapt well for brass, yet they are the highlights of the programme, alongside the engaging Poulenc *Mouvement perpétuel* and the colourful Bartók *Hungarian pictures*. The Equale Brass is a quintet (two trumpets, horn, trombone and tuba); besides immaculate ensemble, their playing is infectiously spirited and readily conveys the enjoyment of the participants so that the music making has the atmosphere of a live concert. Each of the twenty-one items is banded. A demonstration issue.

Fernández, Eduardo (guitar)

Spanish music: TURINA: *Homenaje a Tárrega.* GRANADOS: *La maja de Goya.* ALBÉNIZ: *Torre bermeja; Rumores de la caleta; Cádiz.* TÓRROBA: *Sonatina.* RODRIGO: *2 Spanish pieces.* FALLA: *Homenaje pour le tombeau de Claude Debussy. Three-cornered hat: Miller's dance.*
*** Decca Dig. **414 161-2** [id.].

Eduardo Fernández is a thoughtful, often intimate player and while he creates less sheer electricity than Julian Bream in much of this recital, the playing has fine musicianship and is always alive. He sees the Tórroba *Sonatina* as classical in feeling and makes the very most of the variety within the *Passacaglia*, second of the two *Spanish pieces* of Rodrigo. Then he treats the last two items, Albéniz's *Cádiz*, played with great charm, and the spectacular *Miller's dance* of Falla, which is dramatically arresting, as encores, and the latter would surely receive an ovation at a live recital. The recording is most believable, the acoustic somewhat drier than that favoured by Bream and Williams on RCA, but this increases the feeling of intimacy without detracting from the immediacy and realism on CD.

Francis, Sarah (oboe), Peter Dickinson (piano)

HARTY: *3 Pieces.* HOWELLS: *Sonata* (1942). RUBBRA: *Sonata, Op. 100.*
**(*) Hyp. *KA 66206* [id.].

The Howells *Sonata* was written for Léon Goossens, but the latter had reservations about its structure and the composer decided to rework it. When he borrowed it in 1978, Christopher Palmer fortunately photocopied the manuscript, which did not survive at Howells's death. It is a long, rather diffuse but not uninteresting piece and well worth having on record. The Rubbra *Sonata* of 1958 is a more substantial piece, its first movement inspired. The performances are thoughtful but not helped by the recording, which is made in a rather resonant acoustic.

Fretwork

'In nomine': 16th-century English music for viols: TALLIS: *In nomine a 4, Nos 1 & 2; Solfaing song a 5; Fantasia a 5; In nomine a 4, No. 2; Libera nos, salva nos a 5.* TYE: *In nomine a 5 (Crye); In nomine a 5 (Trust).* CORNYSH: *Fa la sol a 3.* BALDWIN: *In nomine a 4.* BULL: *In nomine a 5.* BYRD: *In nomine a 4, No. 2. Fantasia a 3, No. 3.* TAVERNER: *In nomine; In nomine a 4;* PRESTON: *O lux beata Trinitas a 3.* JOHNSON: *In nomine a 4.* PARSONS: *In nomine a 5; Ut re mi fa sol la a 4.* FERRABOSCO: *In nomine a 5; Lute fantasia No. 5; Fantasia a 4.*
*** Amon Ra **CD-SAR 29** [id.].

This was Fretwork's début CD; it immediately demonstrates their special combination of musical understanding, warmth and refinement in this repertoire. They play with polish and elegance and there is a certain aristocratic melancholy here that gives this music great character. The collection is not so obviously of strong popular appeal as the later collection for Virgin but is nevertheless very rewarding and distinguished, and it includes the complete consort music of Thomas Tallis. The sound is naturally pleasing in a fairly rich acoustic and readers can be assured that there is no vinegar in the string-timbre here; indeed, the sound itself is quite lovely in its gentle, austere atmosphere.

'Heart's ease': HOLBORNE: *The Honiesuckle; Countess of Pembroke's paradise; The Fairie round.* BYRD: *Fantasia a 5 (Two in one); Fancy in C.* DOWLAND: *Mr Bucton, his galliard; Captaine Digorie Piper, his galliard; Lachrimae antiquae pavan; Mr Nicholas Gryffith, his galliard.* BULL: *Fantasia a 4.* FERRABOSCO: *In nomine a 5.* GIBBONS: *In nomine a 5; Fantasia a 4 for the great dooble base.* LAWES: *Airs for 2 division viols in C: Pavan of Alfonso; Almain of Alfonso. Consort sett a 5 in C: Fantasia; Pavan; Almain.*
*** Virgin Dig. **VC 790706-2**; *VC 790706-4* [id.].

An outstanding collection of viol consort music from the late Tudor and early Stuart periods, this was one of the notable issues in the first release on Virgin's classical label. The playing is both stylish and vivacious, with a fine sense of the most suitable tempo for each piece. The more lyrical music is equally sensitive. This is a tuneful entertainment, not just for the specialist collector, and Fretwork convey their pleasure in all this music. The William Byrd *Fancy* (from *My Ladye Nevells Booke*) is exuberantly played on the organ by Paul Nicholson, to bring some contrast before the closing Lawes *Consort set*. The recording is agreeably warm, yet transparent too; however, the cassette, though pleasing, has a much more limited range and is middle- and bass-orientated.

Galway, James (flute), Kazuhito Yamashita (guitar)

'Italian serenade': GIULIANI/MOSCHELES: *Grand duo concertante in A, Op. 85.* ROSSINI: *Andante with variations.* BAZZINI: *La ronde des lutins, Op. 25.* CIMAROSA: *Serenade.* PAGANINI: *Sonata concertata.*
*** RCA Dig. **RD 85679**; *RK 85679*.

This is a lightweight concert; the clear realistic recording and the polished, elegant playing, plus the fine rapport between these two artists, make for music making of the highest quality, realistically projected. The Cimarosa *Serenade* is in fact the *Concerto* arranged for oboe by Arthur Benjamin, but it sounds beguiling enough in this alternative scoring for flute and harp. Both the Giuliani and Paganini works are quite extended pieces and, with attractive if ingenuous invention, they do not outstay their welcome; and the Rossini and Bazzini show Galway's easy virtuosity. While the CD has very striking presence, the cassette is excellent too.

'Guitar favourites'

(i) Diaz; (ii) Parkening; (iii) Angel Romero; (iv) Costano: (i) RODRIGO: *Concierto de Aranjuez* (with Professors of Spanish Nat. O, Frühbeck de Burgos). SOR: *Variations on a theme from Die Zauberflöte.* (ii) BACH: *Jesu, joy of man's desiring. Sheep may safely graze. Sleepers, awake.* (iii) GRANADOS: *La maja de Goya.* RODRIGO: *Fandango.* ALBÉNIZ: *Tango.* (iv) VILLA-LOBOS:

Preludes Nos 1–3. TURINA: *Sevillana. Fandanguillo. Rafaga. Homenaje a Tarrega*. (i) MOMPOU: *Canción*.
(B) *** EMI *TC2-MOM 117*.

At the centre of this tape-only collection is a warmly attractive performance of Rodrigo's *Concierto de Aranjuez* from Alirio Diaz and a Spanish orchestral ensemble. Diaz is good too in the Sor and Mompou items. The contribution from Angel Romero has less electricity, but Christopher Parkening's group of Bach transcriptions is most enjoyable, especially *Sleepers, awake*, which is presented with great flair. Irma Costanto provides the most memorable playing of all, her style very free but compellingly spontaneous and full of atmosphere and colour. The sound is excellent throughout.

Hardenberger, Håken (trumpet)

'The virtuoso trumpet' (with Roland Pöntinen): ARBAN: *Variations on themes from Bellini's 'Norma'*. FRANÇAIX: *Sonatine*. TISNÉ: *Héraldiques*. HONEGGER: *Intrada*. MAXWELL DAVIES: *Sonata*. RABE: *Shazam!*. HARTMANN: *Fantasia brillante on the air Rule Britannia*.
*** BIS **CID 287** [id.].

This collection includes much rare and adventurous repertoire, not otherwise available and very unlikely to offer frequent access in live performance. Moreover, Hardenberger is a superb trumpeter, playing with electrifying bravura in the Maxwell Davies *Sonata* and the virtuoso miniatures. Antoine Tisné's five *Héraldiques* are eclectic but highly effective on the lips of such an assured player; *Scandé* and the following *Elégiaque* are notably characterful. Two sets of nineteenth-century airs with variations are used to flank the serious content: they are agreeably ingenuous and, like Folke Rabe's florid *Shazam!*, are quite entertaining when presented with such flair. But easily the most memorable item is the Françaix *Sonatine* (originally for violin and piano) in which two delicious brief outer movements frame a pleasing central *Sarabande*. Honegger's improvisatory *Intrada* is an effective encore piece. The recording is eminently realistic, with the CD giving superb presence, so that at the finale of the Tisné suite one almost believes the trumpet to be in the room. The balance with the piano is expertly managed.

Herrick, Christopher (organ)

Organ of Westminter Abbey: *'Organ fireworks'*: BONNET: *Variations de concert, Op. 1*. GUILMANT: *Grand chœur triomphale in A, Op. 47/2; March upon Handel's 'Lift up your heads', Op. 16*. WHITLOCK: *Fanfare*. BREWER: *Marche héroïque*. MONNIKENDAM: *Toccata*. JOHNSON: *Trumpet tune in D*. WIDOR: *Symphony No. 7: Finale*. PRESTON: *Alleluyas*. HOVLAND: *Toccata on 'Now thank we all our God'*.
(*) Hyp. **CDA 66121; *KA 66121* [id.].

Fireworks there are in plenty in Egil Hovland's *Toccata*, based on *Now thank we all our God*, where the florid brilliance in the treble counteracts the wide Westminster reverberation. The performance is a *tour de force* of dexterity, but Christopher Herrick is less exciting than Jennifer Bate (see above) in Guilmant's treatment of Handel. Those who like a hugely expansive organ sound, with thundering pedals, will be well satisfied here, while the Whitlock *Fanfare*, which depends on the trumpet stop, brings a welcome relief in its brighter, lighter texture. The engineering is faultless, and there is a remarkably good cassette.

Horowitz, Vladimir (piano)

Recital: SCHUMANN: *Kinderszenen, Op. 15; Toccata in C, Op. 7.* D. SCARLATTI: *Sonatas: in G, Kk.-455; in E, Kk. 531; in A, Kk. 322.* SCHUBERT: *Impromptu No. 3 in G flat, D. 889.* SCRIABIN: *Poème, Op. 32/1; Études: in C sharp min., Op. 2/1; in D sharp min, Op. 8/12.*
(M) **(*) CBS **MYK 42534.**

Horowitz's 1968 recital offers marvellous playing of repertoire he knows and loves, recorded when he was still at his technical peak. The recording is dry (there is a hint of wow, but it appears only once or twice); even so, this is magical playing: the Schumann and Scarlatti are superb – but then so is the Scriabin, and Schubert's *G flat Impromptu* is infinitely subtle in its gradations of dynamic and colour.

'At the Met.': D. SCARLATTI: *Sonatas: in A flat, Kk. 127; in F min., Kk. 184 & 466; in A, Kk. 101; in B min., Kk. 87; in E, Kk. 135.* CHOPIN: *Ballade No. 4 in F min., Op. 52; Waltz No. 9 in A flat, Op. 69/1.* LISZT: *Ballade No. 2 in B min., G. 171.* RACHMANINOV: *Prelude No. 6 in G min., Op. 23/5.*
*** RCA Dig. **RCD 14585 [RCD1 4585].**

The sound Horowitz makes has not previously been fully captured on record, particularly in some of his RCA mono issues of the 1940s and 1950s. The playing is in a class of its own and all one needs to know is that this recording (especially on compact disc) reproduces the highly distinctive tone-quality he commands. This recital, given at the Metropolitan Opera House and issued here at the time of his London Festival Hall appearance in 1982, comes closer to the real thing than anything else on record, except his DG recitals – see below. The quality of the playing is quite extraordinary.

'In London': God save the Queen (arr. Horowitz). CHOPIN: *Ballade No. 1 in G min., Op. 23; Polonaise No. 7 in A flat (Polonaise-Fantasie), Op. 61.* SCHUMANN: *Kinderszenen, Op. 15.* SCRIABIN: *Étude in D sharp min., Op. 8/12.*
*** RCA Dig. **RD 84572.**

Highlights from the memorable London recital Horowitz gave in 1982, though omitting the elegant Scarlatti sonatas he played on that occasion, doubtless because it would duplicate *'Horowitz at the Met.'* – see above. However, room could surely have been found for the Rachmaninov *Sonata*, or his encores, as the CD is not generously filled. As those who attended this electrifying recital will know, there were idiosyncratic touches, particularly in the *Kinderszenen* (and also in the Chopin *Ballade*), but this is remarkable testimony to his wide dynamic range and his refined *pianopianissimo*. There are many fascinating points of detail in both works (but notably the Chopin) which give one the feeling of hearing the music for the first time.

Recital: BACH/BUSONI: *Chorale prelude: Nun komm der Heiden Heiland.* MOZART: *Piano sonata No. 10 in C, K. 330.* CHOPIN: *Mazurka in A min., Op. 17/4; Scherzo No. 1 in B min., Op. 20; Polonaise No. 6 in A flat, Op. 53.* LISZT: *Consolation No. 3 in D flat.* SCHUBERT: *Impromptu in A flat, D. 899/4.* SCHUMANN: *Novellette in F, Op. 21/1.* RACHMANINOV: *Prelude in G sharp min., Op. 32/12.* SCRIABIN: *Étude in C sharp min., Op. 2/1.* MOSZKOWSKI: *Étude in F, Op. 72/6* (recording of performances featured in the film *Vladimir Horowitz – The Last Romantic*).
*** DG Dig. **419 045-2** [id.].

Possibly the best recording Horowitz has received so far, in all three media, though his RCA compact discs have also given a splendid sense of his *pp* tone. Recorded when he was over eighty, this playing betrays remarkably little sign of frailty. The Mozart is beautifully elegant and the Chopin *A minor Mazurka*, Op. 17, No. 4, could hardly be more delicate. The only sign of age comes in the *B minor Scherzo* which does not have the leonine fire and tremendous body of his famous 1950 recording. However, it is pretty astonishing for all that.

'The studio recordings': SCHUMANN: *Kreisleriana, Op. 16.* D. SCARLATTI: *Sonatas: in B min., Kk. 87; in E, Kk. 135.* LISZT: *Impromptu (Nocturne) in F sharp; Valse oubliée No. 1.* SCRIABIN: *Étude in D sharp min., Op. 812.* SCHUBERT: *Impromptu in B flat, D. 935/3.* SCHUBERT/TAUSIG: *Marche militaire, D. 733/1.*
❀ *** DG **419 217-2** [id.].

Those who have watched Horowitz's televised recitals will be familiar with much of this music. He plays it in the studio just as if he were in front of an audience, and the freshness and accuracy would be astonishing if we had not already heard him repeating the trick. The pianism is marvellous. The subtle range of colour and articulation in the Schumann is matched in his Schubert *Impromptu,* and the Liszt *Valse oubliée* offers the most delicious, twinking rubato. Hearing Scarlatti's *E major Sonata* played with such crispness, delicacy and grace must surely convert even the most dedicated authenticist to the view that this repertoire can be totally valid in terms of the modern instrument. The Schubert–Tausig *Marche militaire* makes a superb encore, played with the kind of panache that would be remarkable in a pianist half Horowitz's age. With the passionate Scriabin *Étude* as the central romantic pivot, this recital is uncommonly well balanced to show Horowitz's special range of sympathies. Only Mozart is missing, and he is featured elsewhere. The recording is extremely realistic and present in its CD format. It belies the suggestion, made to support the harsh timbre of some of the pianist's older American recordings, that he sought a dry, close sound-balance.

'In Moscow': D. SCARLATTI: *Sonata in E, Kk. 380.* MOZART: *Sonata No. 10 in C, K. 330.* RACHMANINOV: *Preludes: in G, Op. 32/5; in G sharp min. Op. 32/12.* SCRIABIN: *Études: in C sharp min., Op. 2/1; in D sharp min., Op. 8/12.* LISZT/SCHUBERT: *Soirées de Vienne; Petrarch Sonnet 104.* CHOPIN: *Mazurkas, Op. 30/4; Op. 7/3.* SCHUMANN: *Kinderszenen: Träumerei.*
*** DG Dig. **419 499-2**; *419 499-4* [id.].

This is familiar Horowitz repertoire, played with characteristic musical discernment and spontaneity. Technically the pianism may not quite match his finest records of the analogue era, but it is still both melting and dazzling. The sound too is really excellent, much better than he ever received from his American engineers in earlier days. There is a very good tape.

Hurford, Peter (organ)

Ratzeburg Cathedral organ: *'Romantic organ music':* WIDOR: *Symphony No. 5, Op. 42: Toccata.* VIERNE: *Pièces en style libre: Berceuse.* ALAIN: *Litanies.* FRANCK: *Chorale No. 3.* KARG-ELERT: *Marche triomphale; Nun danket alle Gotte, Op. 65.* BRAHMS: *Chorale preludes: O wie selig, seid, ihr doch; Schmücke dich; Es ist ein' Ros' entsprungen, Op. 122.* MENDELSSOHN: *Organ sonata in A, Op. 65/3.* REGER: *Introduction and passacaglia in D min.*
*** Argo Dig. **410 165-2** [id.].

There are not many records of Romantic organ music to match this in colour, breadth of repertory and brilliance of performance, superbly recorded. The ever-popular Widor item leads to pieces just as efficient at bringing out the variety of organ sound, such as the Karg-Elert or the Alain. These are performances which defy all thought of Victorian heaviness, and the

Ratzeburg organ produces piquant and beautiful sounds. On CD the presence and range are breathtaking.

Sydney Opera House organ: *'Great organ works'*: BACH: *Toccata and fugue in D min., BWV 565; Jesu, joy of man's desiring.* ALBINONI: *Adagio* (arr. Giazotto). PURCELL: *Trumpet tune in D.* MENDELSSOHN: *A Midsummer Night's Dream: Wedding march.* FRANCK: *Chorale No. 2 in B min.* MURRILL: *Carillon.* WALFORD DAVIES: *Solemn melody.* WIDOR: *Organ symphony No. 5: Toccata.*
(*) Argo Dig. **411 929-2 [id.].

Superb sound here, wonderfully free and never oppressive, even in the most spectacular moments. The Widor is spiritedly genial when played within the somewhat mellower registration of the magnificent Sydney instrument (as contrasted with the Ratzeburg Cathedral organ – see above), and the pedals have great sonority and power. The Murrill *Carillon* is equally engaging alongside the Purcell *Trumpet tune*, while Mendelssohn's wedding music has never sounded more resplendent. The Bach is less memorable, and the Albinoni *Adagio*, without the strings, is not an asset to the collection either.

Organ of Bethlehemkerk, Papendrecht, Holland: *'Baroque organ music'*: BÖHM: *Prelude and fugue in C;* Chorales: *Vater unser im Himmelreich; Auf meinen lieben Gott; Vom himmel hoch da komm' ich her.* COUPERIN: *Branle de basque; Fantaisie in G min.* KERLL: *Capriccio sopra il cucu.* BUXTEHUDE: *Mensch, willt du leben seliglich; Wir danken dir, Herr Jesu Christ; Vater unser im Himmelreich.* WALOND: *Voluntary No. 5 in G.* PESCETTI: *Sonata in C min.* PACHELBEL: *Ciaccona in D min.* SWEELINCK: *Unter der Linden grüne.* STANLEY: *Voluntary in C.*
*** Argo **414 496-2** [id.].

This beautifully recorded recital seems to gather emotional pace as it proceeds. To be truthful, the Böhm pieces are just a little bland, but the Louis Couperin miniatures have plenty of flavour and Johann Kerll's *Capriccio* with its piquant cuckoo simulations is ingenuously charming. Pescetti's *Sonata* is ambitiously inventive with fine interplay of part writing, and Pachelbel's *Ciaccona* builds to a powerful climax on a memorable tune; this will not disappoint admirers of his *Canon*. Sweelinck's variants on a very famous tune are most effective and John Stanley ends the concert with a martial voluntary. As usual, Peter Hurford's registration is unendingly imaginative in its control of the many piquant colours this Dutch organ has available, and his playing from first to last is not only stylish but brings everything to life as at a live recital.

Jacobs, Paul (piano)

American piano music: BOLCOM: *3 Ghost rags.* COPLAND: *4 Piano blues.* RZEWSKI: *4 North American Ballads.*
** None. Dig. **CD 79006** [id.].

The death of Paul Jacobs in 1983 robbed us of a versatile and enterprising artist, who has enriched the catalogue with much out-of-the-way material. The best music here is the Copland, also available in Leo Smit's two-record Copland set on CBS, and Jacobs plays these pieces with thoroughly idiomatic style; the most interesting is Frederick Rzewski's brilliant and effective *Ballads*. The composer, now in his forties, is new to the catalogue and is eminently worth watching. The Bolcom *Rags* are not particularly strong pieces, but Jacobs makes out as persuasive a case for them as he can. Good recording, slightly reverberant but given convincing presence on CD.

Kayath, Marcello (guitar)

'Guitar classics from Latin America': PONCE: *Valse.* PIAZZOLA: *La muerte del angel.* BARRIOS: *Vals. Op. 8/3; Choro de saudade; Julia florida.* LAURO: *Vals venezolanos No. 2; El negrito; El marabino.* BROUWER: *Canción de cuna; Ojos brujos.* PERNAMBUCO: *Sons de carrilhões; Interrogando; Sono de maghia.* REIS: *Si ela perguntar.* VILLA-LOBOS: *5 Preludes.*
(M) *** Pickwick Dig. **PCD 853.**

Marcello Kayath studied in Rio de Janeiro and is the winner of many awards, including the Segovia Prize at the International Villa-Lobos Competition. He is a master of this repertoire – and indeed his flexibly inspirational accounts of the Villa-Lobos *Preludes* can stand comparison with the finest performances on record. He has the rare gift of playing in the studio as at a live recital; obviously he soon becomes unaware of his surroundings, for he plays everything here with consummate technical ease and the most appealing spontaneity. His rubato in the Barrios *Vals* is particularly effective, and he is a fine advocate too of the engaging Lauro pieces and the picaresque writing of João Pernambuco, a friend of Villa-Lobos. The recording, made in a warm, but not too resonant acoustic, is first class, and there is a fine illusion of presence. Even though this is a mid-priced issue, it carries excellent notes.

Kremer, Gidon (violin)

'A Paganini': MILSTEIN: *Paganiniana.* SCHNITTKE: *A Paganini.* H. ERNST: *Étude No. 6: Die letzte Rose.* G. ROCHBERG: *Caprice variations Nos 5, 7–8, 16, 18–19, 21, 23–25, 31, 34–36, 38, 41–46, 49–51.*
*** DG Dig. **415 484-2** [id.].

This is playing of extraordinary virtuosity and command. The programme, in a real sense, starts where Paganini left off. The recital begins and ends with the famous *Caprice No. 24* which has inspired so much subsequent music by others, of which Milstein's is an entertainingly light-weight example, with seven variations very much in the Paganini manner. Heinrich Ernst's *Variations* on *The last rose of summer* show the nineteenth-century inheritance of the format quite pleasingly, while Alfred Schnittke and George Rochberg bring the music's ethos into the twentieth century. In his mighty set of 51 variations (of which 24 are included here) Rochberg moves backwards and forwards in his eclecticism: some of his variations (like the opening *Nocturnal*) are relatively avant garde; others are more conventional. The variety of the music here is remarkable, and so is Gidon Kremer's identification with it. The recording gives him an absolutely natural presence (though it is important not to set the volume level too high), which is very tangible indeed on CD.

Kroumata Percussion Ensemble

CAGE: *Second construction.* COWELL: *Pulse.* LUNDQUIST: *Sisu.* TAÏRA: *Hiérophonie.*
*** BIS Dig. **CD 232** [id.].

A well-constructed programme (lasting only 39′ 29″ – but perhaps that is long enough), demonstrating the range of a percussion group performing without other 'melodic' instruments. That is not perhaps strictly true, for the Lundquist piece introduces simplistic melodic ideas (rather attractively) using xylophone, vibraphone, xylorimba and marimba. Cage relies on imaginative textures, and as his piece is not too extended (6′ 44″) it is very successful. The

Cowell is not dissimilar, but the *Hiérophonie* of Yoshihisa Taïra is another matter. The CD draws attention to the layout of the music on the disc, with the Cage quietly atmospheric, but warns that this final piece has a very wide dynamic range. The work opens with vigorous and highly involved shouts, making an interplay with the percussive sounds, and one cannot help but associate the effect with Kung Fu. The structure moves steadily and strongly towards a spectacular climax whose sheer physical thrill is undeniable, even if the listener might feel a lack of patience on the way, as the experience lasts 19′ 32″. But the skill and commitment of the performers are very impressive throughout this collection, which is a classic of its kind. The recording itself is superbly realistic, with the instruments set back in an atmospheric acoustic. The sound engineers have resisted the temptation to emphasize the transient bite.

'Music with flute' (with Manuela Wiesler): JOLIVET: *Suite en concert for flute and percussion.* L. HARRISON: *Concerto No. 1 for flute and percussion.* CAGE: *Amores.* SANDSTRÖM: *Drums.*
(*) BIS Dig. **CD 272 [id.].

It is the gentle music which comes off best here, with the many delicate *piano* and *pianissimo* passages greatly enhanced by the silent background of the CD. Not many readers would expect that an avant garde piece by a composer like John Cage would make atmospheric listening suitable for the late evening, but his four-part *Amores* has an ear-tickling fascination, especially the two central *Trios* for nine tom-toms and pod rattle(!) or seven woodblocks, 'not Chinese', respectively, used with the utmost discretion. Of the two works featuring the concertante flute, the Jolivet has a haunting second-movement *Stabile* and an improvisatory *Calme* finale, where flute and exotically soft percussion sounds make a memorable impression; similarly, Lou Harrison's *Concerto* had a middle movement, marked *Slow and poignant*, which is quite indelible. All this music is lightweight, in both implications of the adjective; however, the final item, which (at 14′ 40″) is far too long, makes a thunderous contrast. Even the most resilient pair of speaker cones will surely shudder at the weight of *fortissimos* heaped upon them by Sandström's *Drums*: it is all physically thrilling in projecting animal vitality, but its only real purpose is surely to provide hi-fi buffs with noisy demonstration sound, *par excellence*. The recording handles the widest dynamic ranges with the utmost realism throughout the concert.

Labèque, Katia and Marielle (piano duet)

'Glad rags': GERSHWIN/DONALDSON: *Rialto ripples.* MAYERL: *Honky-tonk.* JOHNSON: *Carolina shout.* JOPLIN: *The Entertainer; Antoinette; Magnetic rag; Maple leaf rag; Elite syncopations; Strenuous life; Stop-time; Bethena.*
*** EMI Dig. **CDC7 47093-2** [id.].

The Labèque duo play with irresistible bravura and dash. Scott Joplin may have frowned on their tempi (he favoured slow speeds), but the playing has such wit and conveyed enjoyment that criticism is silenced. The recording has sparkle but depth too and fine presence in CD. This is by far the most recommendable collection of this repertoire.

Larrocha, Alicia de (piano)

'Favourite Spanish encores': MATEO ALBÉNIZ: *Sonata in D.* ISAAC ALBÉNIZ: *Recuerdos de Viaje, Nos 5, Puerta de Tierra (Bolero); 6, Rumores de la Caleta (Malaguena). Pavana – Capricho, Op. 12. Tango, Op. 165/2; Malaguena, Op. 165/3; Suite espagnole: No. 3, Sevillanas.* SOLER: *Sonatas in G min.; in D.* GRANADOS: *Danzas espanolas Nos 5 (Andaluza); 7 (Valenciana*

O Calesera). TURINA: *5 Danzas Gitanas,* 1st series. *No. 5, Sacro-monte, Op. 55. 3 danzas Andaluzas, No. 3, Zapateado Op. 8.* MOMPOU: *Impresiones intimas.*
*** Decca **417 639-2** [id.].

This compilation has been made from various recital records Mme de Larrocha made over the years. The Mompou *Impresiones intimas* is the most recent (1984) but the others come from the mid-1970s. We must hope that her LP of Mompou's music, including the Fourth Book of the *Musica Callada*, written especially for her, will be transferred to CD. She plays the *Impresiones* and the Albéniz and Soler superbly, with finesse and subtlety; and the recordings are very natural and lifelike. In every way a delightful record.

LaSalle Quartet

Chamber music of the Second Viennese School: BERG: *Lyric suite; String quartet, Op. 3.* SCHOENBERG: *String quartets: in D; No. 1 in D min., Op. 7; No. 2 in F sharp min., Op. 10/3* (with Margaret Price); *No. 3, Op. 30; No. 4, Op. 37.* WEBERN: *5 Movements, Op. 5; String quartet (1905); 6 Bagatelles, Op. 9; String quartet, Op. 28.*
(M) *** DG **419 994-2** (4) [id.].

DG have compressed their 1971 five-LP set on to four CDs, offering them at a reduced and competitive price. They have also retained the invaluable and excellent documentary study edited by Ursula Rauchhaupt – which runs to 340 pages! It is almost worth having this set for the documentation alone. Now that the Juilliard version on CBS is out of circulation, this is the only complete survey of the Schoenberg *Four Quartets* plus the early *D major* before the public. The LaSalle Quartet give splendidly expert performances, even if at times their playing seems a little cool; and they are very well recorded. An invaluable issue for all who care about twentieth-century music.

'Liebesträume'

'Romantic piano music': (i) Bolet; (ii) Ashkenazy; (iii) De Larrocha; (iv) Lupu: (i) LISZT: *Liebestraum No. 3; Étude de concert No. 3 (Un sospiro).* (ii) RACHMANINOV: *Prelude in C sharp min., Op. 3/2.* CHOPIN: *Nocturne in F min., Op. 55/1; Étude in E, Op. 10/3.* BEETHOVEN: *Piano sonata No. 14 in C sharp min. (Moonlight).* (iii) CHOPIN: *Prelude No. 15 in D flat (Raindrop).* SCHUBERT: *Impromptu in A flat, D. 899/4.* SCHUMANN: *Romance, Op. 28/2.* (iv) BRAHMS: *Rhapsody in G min., Op. 79/2.*
*** Decca **411 934-2** [id.].

Jorge Bolet's warmly romantic account of Liszt gives this specially assembled compact disc its title and is also the only true digital recording included in the programme. But the sound is generally excellent and the digital remastering, if producing a rather forward image, offers truthful quality throughout. The performances are distinguished and there is passionate contrast in Ashkenazy's Rachmaninov. Lupu's Brahms is rather less extrovert in feeling; generally, the recital has a nicely relaxed atmosphere.

Lin, Cho-Liang (violin), Sandra Rivers (piano)

'Bravura': FALLA: *Suite populaire espagnole.* KREISLER: *Liebeslied; Liebesfreud. Tambourin chinois.* MOZART: *Serenade, K. 250: Rondo.* RACHMANINOV: *Vocalise.* WIENIAWSKI: *Capriccio-valse in E, Op. 7.* SARASATE: *Introduction and Tarantella, Op. 43.*
*** CBS Dig. **MK 39133**; *IMT 39133* [id.].

Some first-rate playing here from this remarkable young virtuoso. He tosses off these pieces with great aplomb and brilliance. But besides his pyrotechnics, he is also able to find poetry in these miniatures and is well supported by Sandra Rivers. A most attractive recital, as well recorded as it is played.

Lipatti, Dinu (piano)

BACH: *Partita No. 1 in B flat, BWV 825; Chorale preludes: Nun komm' der Heiden Heiland; Ich ruf'zu dir; Cantata No. 147: Jesu, joy of man's desiring* (arr. Hess); *Siciliana.* D. SCARLATTI: *Sonatas, Kk. 380; Kk. 9.* MOZART: *Sonata No. 8 in A min., K. 310.*
(***) HMV mono **CDC7 47517-2** [id.].

No collector should overlook this Lipatti CD. Most of the performances have scarcely been out of circulation since their first appearance: the haunting account of the Mozart *A minor Sonata* and the Bach *B flat Partita* have both had more than one incarnation on LP. The remastering is well done; and one notices that, among his other subtleties, Lipatti creates a different timbre for the music of each composer.

Lloyd Webber, Julian (cello)

'British cello music' (with (i) John McCabe, piano): (i) RAWSTHORNE: *Sonata for cello and piano.* ARNOLD: *Fantasy for cello.* (i) IRELAND: *The Holy Boy.* WALTON: *Passacaglia.* BRITTEN: *Teme* (*Sacher*); (on CD only: *Cello suite No. 3*).
*** ASV Dig. **CDDCA 592**; *ZCDDCA 592* [id.].

A splendid recital and a most valuable one. Julian Lloyd Webber has championed such rarities as the Bridge *Oration* at a time when it was unrecorded and now devotes this present issue to English music that needs strong advocacy; there is no alternative version of the Rawsthorne *Sonata*, in which he is most ably partnered by John McCabe. He gives this piece – and, for that matter, the remainder of the programme – with full-blooded commitment. The Britten *Cello suite* is offered only in the CD format. Good recording.

'The romantic cello' (with Yitkin Seow, piano): POPPER: *Elfentanz, Op. 39.* SAINT-SAËNS: *Carnival of the Animals: The Swan. Allegro appassionato, Op. 43.* FAURÉ: *Après un rêve.* MENDELSSOHN: *Song without Words, Op. 109.* RACHMANINOV: *Cello sonata, Op. 19:* slow movt. DELIUS: *Romance.* CHOPIN: *Introduction and polonaise brillante, Op. 3.* ELGAR: *Salut d'amour, Op. 12.*
(M) **(*) ASV **CDQS 6014**; *ZCQS 6014* [id.].

Julian Lloyd Webber has gathered together a most attractive collection of showpieces for the cello, romantic as well as brilliant. Such dazzling pieces as the Popper – always a favourite with virtuoso cellists – is on record a welcome rarity. The recording, a little edgy, if with undoubted presence, favours the cello; the cassette transfer is vivid, with good body and range.

Longhurst, John (organ)

Organ of Mormon Tabernacle, Salt Lake City: GIGOUT: *Grand chœur dialogué; Toccata.* HERON: *Trumpet voluntary.* WIDOR: *Symphony No. 9 (Gothique), Op. 70: Andante.* VIERNE: *Carillon de Westminster.* CLARKE: *Trumpet voluntary.* HANDEL: *Xerxes: Largo.* FRANCK: *Pièce héroïque.* BACH: *Chorale prelude: Wachet auf, BWV 645; Jesu, joy of man's desiring. Bist du bei mir.*
*** Ph. Dig. **412 217-2** [id.].

Although John Longhurst is a most accomplished organist who plays and registers with admirable taste and understanding of the potential of his instrument, it is the huge Mormon Tabernacle organ that is the star here (flattered by the Tabernacle ambience). There is spectacle when called for – in the Franck, for instance – but one is never overwhelmed. Most enjoyable.

Menuhin, Yehudi and **Stéphane Grappelli** (violins)

(see also above, in Orchestral and Concertante Music)

'Menuhin and Grappelli play Berlin, Kern, Porter and Rodgers & Hart': BERLIN: *Cheek to cheek; Isn't this a lovely day; The Piccolino; Change partners; Top Hat; I've got my love to keep me warm; Heat wave.* KERN: *The way you look tonight; Pick yourself up; A fine romance; All the things you are; Why do I love you?* C. PORTER: *I get a kick out of you; Night and day; Looking at you; Just one of those things.* RODGERS: *My funny valentine; Thou swell; The lady is a tramp; Blue moon.*
(M) **(*) HMV **CDM7 69219-2** [id.].

'Jealousy and other great standards': Jealousy; Tea for two; Limehouse blues; These foolish things; The Continental; A Nightingale sang in Berkeley Square; Sweet Sue; Skylark; Laura; Sweet Georgia Brown; I'll remember April; April in Paris; The things we did last summer; September in the rain; Autumn leaves; Autumn in New York; Button up your overcoat.
(M) **(*) HMV **CDM7 69220-2** [id.].

The partnership of Menuhin and Grappelli started in the television studio; their brief duets (tagged on to interviews) were so successful that the idea came of recording a whole recital, which between 1973 and 1985 became a series of five. These two CDs offer some of the best numbers extracted from all five. One of the secrets of the partnership's success lies in the choice of material. All these items started out as first-class songs with striking melodies which live in whatever guise, and here with ingenious arrangements they spark off the individual genius of each violinist, both as a challenge and towards the players' obvious enjoyment. The high spirits of each occasion are caught beautifully with no intimidation from the recording studio ambience; while the playing styles of each artist are different, they are also complementary and remarkably close in such matters as tone and balance. The result is delightful, particularly in such numbers as *Pick yourself up,* where the arrangement directly tips a wink towards Bachian figuration, or in lyrical tunes, like *Laura*, which are memorably phrased. The snag is that the digital re-mastering, in an attempt to add presence, has made the overall sound drier and, more noticeably in the second collection (entitled *'Jealousy'*) there is a degree of edge on the violin timbre.

'Top Hat' (with Orchestra, Nelson Riddle): BERLIN: *Puttin' on the Ritz; Isn't this a lovely day; The Piccolino; Change partners; Top Hat.* KERN: *The way you look tonight.* GERSHWIN: *He loves and she loves; They can't take that away from me; They all laughed; Funny face.* GRAPPELLI: *Alison; Amanda.* CONRAD: *The Continental.* YOUMANS: *Carioca.*
(B) **(*) CfP *TC-CFP 4509.*

This was their fifth collection and Menuhin and Grappelli are joined by a small orchestral group directed by Nelson Riddle. Aficionados might fear that this will dilute the jazz element of the playing, and perhaps it does a little at times; but Riddle's arrangements are witty and understanding and some of these tunes undeniably have an orchestral feeling. The result is just as lively and entertaining as previous collections in this series. The music itself is associated with Fred Astaire, although Grappelli contributes two numbers himself. The sound is as crisp and lively as ever on the excellent chrome tape.

Ortiz, Cristina (piano)

'French impressionist piano music': DEBUSSY: *2 Arabesques; Prélude: La Cathédrale engloutie. Images: Reflets dans l'eau. Children's corner: Golliwog's cakewalk. Suite bergamasque: Clair de lune; L'isle joyeuse.* CHABRIER: *Pièce pittoresque No. 7: Danse villageoise.* SATIE: *Gymnopédie No. 1.* FAURÉ: *Impromptu No. 3, Op. 34.* IBERT: *10 Histoires: Le petite âne blanc.* POULENC: *Mélancolie.* MILHAUD: *Saudades de Brasil: Copacabana, Op. 67/4.* RAVEL: *Jeux d'eau; Alborada del gracioso.*
(M) **(*) Pickwick Dig. **PCD 846**.

As usual with Pickwick, this is a very generous recital and it is most realistically recorded. Cristina Ortiz shows her versatility in this wide-ranging French repertoire and projects plenty of charm – Ibert's *Little white donkey* is a notable highlight, while Ravel's *Jeux d'eau* is full of evocative feeling. Sometimes in the bravura her playing goes a little over the top, and one would have liked more poise, but there is no lack of commitment and spontaneity, and there is much to reward here. The Debussy pieces come off especially well, and *Reflets dans l'eau* and *La Cathédrale engloutie* are as atmospheric as the Ravel pieces.

Ousset, Cécile (piano)

'French piano music': FAURÉ: *Impromptus Nos 2 in F min., Op. 31; 3 in A flat, Op. 34.* DEBUSSY: *Estampes.* RAVEL: *Miroirs; Alborada del gracioso.* CHABRIER: *Pièces pittoresques: Nos 6, Idyll; 10, Scherzo-valse.* SATIE: *3 Gymnopédies.* SAINT-SAËNS: *Allegro appassionato, Op. 70; Étude en forme de valse, Op. 52/6.*
*** HMV Dig. **CDC7 47225-2** [id.].

An admirable recital by this highly proficient and often impressive French pianist whose reputation has suddenly soared during the last few years. There is much to satisfy the connoisseur here, even if not all details will be to all tastes: the Saint-Saëns *Allegro appassionato* is rather shallow but she gives it with panache and style. The Satie pieces could have slightly more sense of movement, perhaps, but few will have quarrels with her Debussy or Ravel. The quality of the recording is very truthful and realistic, and admirers of Miss Ousset will find this issue a rewarding introduction to her playing. The CD adds presence and reality to what is already an excellent and believable recording.

Parker-Smith, Jane (organ)

Organ of Coventry Cathedral: *'Popular French Romantics':* WIDOR: *Symphony No. 1: March pontifical. Symphony No 9 (Gothique), Op. 70: Andante sostenuto.* GUILMANT: *Sonata No. 5 in*

C min., Op. 80; Scherzo. GIGOUT: *Toccata in B min.* BONNET: *Elfes, Op. 7.* LEFÉBURE-WÉLY: *Sortie in B flat.* VIERNE: *Pièces de fantaisie: Clair de lune, Op. 53/5; Carillon de Westminster, Op. 54/6.*
*** ASV Dig. **CDDCA 539**; *ZCDCA 539* [id.].

The modern organ in Coventry Cathedral (built by Harrison and Harrison of Durham) is surprisingly well suited to French repertoire. Its bright, full-blooded tutti, with just a touch of harshness, adds a nice bite to Jane Parker-Smith's very pontifical performance of the opening Widor *March* and creates a blaze of splendour at the close of the famous Vierne *Carillon de Westminster*, the finest performance on record. The detail of the fast, nimble articulation in the engagingly Mendelssohnian *Elfes* of Joseph Bonnet is not clouded; yet here, as in the splendid Guilmant *Scherzo* with its wider dynamic range, there is a nice atmospheric effect, too. Hardly less enjoyable is the robustly jocular *Sortie* of Lefébure-Wély, which is delivered with fine geniality and panache. Overall, a most entertaining recital, made the more vivid on the boldly focused compact disc.

Perahia, Murray (piano)

'Portrait': BEETHOVEN: *Sonata No. 23 (Appassionata), Op. 57;* SCHUBERT: *Impromptu in G flat, D.899/3.* SCHUMANN: *Papillons, Op. 2.* CHOPIN: *Fantaisie-Impromptu, Op. 66; Preludes, Op. 28 Nos 6, 7 & 15.* MENDELSSOHN: *Rondo capriccioso, Op. 14.* MOZART: *Rondo for piano and orchestra in D, K.382* (with ECO).
*** CBS **MK 42448**; *IMT 42448* [id.].

A self-recommending recital, with the single proviso that being a sampler it includes excerpts from a number of CDs which many readers may wish to consider separately. Bearing in mind the variety of sources and that some are remastered analogue and some digital, the sound is remarkably consistent and, for the most part, excellent.

Petri, Michala (recorder), George Malcolm (harpsichord)

Recorder sonatas: VIVALDI: *Il Pastor fido: Sonata No. 6 in G min., RV 58.* CORELLI: *Sonata in C, Op. 5/9.* D. BIGAGLIA: *Sonata in A min.* BONONCINI: *Divertimento da camera No. 6 in C min.* SAMMARTINI: *Sonata in G, Op. 13/4.* B. MARCELLO: *Sonata in F, Op. 2/1.*
❀ *** Ph. Dig. **412 632-2** [id.].

Six recorder sonatas in a row might seem too much of a good thing, but the playing is so felicitous and the music has such charm that the collection is immensely enjoyable, even taken complete, and if sensibly dipped into is a source of much delight. There are many individual highlights. The Corelli *Sonata* has a memorable *Tempo di gavotta* as its finale which reminds one a little of Handel's *Harmonious blacksmith*; the work in A minor by the composer with the unlikely name of Diogenio Bigaglia (*c.* 1676–*c.* 1745) is a winner, with a nimble minuet and sparkling finale. Bononcini's *Divertimento da camera* alternates slow and fast sections, and in the third-movement *Largo* George Malcolm makes the delicate accompaniment sound like a harp. Sammartini's *Sonata* is enchanting, with its opening *Andante* in siciliano form and three more delectable movements to follow. Throughout, Michala Petri's playing is wonderfully fresh: she has made many records for Philips, but none more enticing than this. George Malcolm proves an equally imaginative partner, and both artists embellish with admirable flair and taste, never overdoing it. The music making combines geniality and finesse with spontaneity and a direct communication of pleasure in a lightweight but consistently rewarding programme. The Philips recording is quite perfectly balanced and wonderfully tangible.

Recorder sonatas: BACH: *Sonata in G min., BWV 1034.* SCHICKHARDT: *Sonata in E, Op. 30/9.* TELEMANN: *Partita in E flat.* HANDEL: *Sonata in G min., Op. 1/1.* FREDERICK THE GREAT: *Sonata No. 3 in D.*
** Ph. Dig. **416 369-2**; *416 369-4.*

Both the Bach and Handel sonatas were written for transverse flute, but sound well enough on the recorder, if demonstrating no valid reason for the change. The Schickhardt is a virtuoso piece for sopranino recorder, and here Michala Petri is in her element. The Telemann *Partita* also comes off well; however, in spite of fine support from George Malcolm and excellent sound, this is not as enticing a recital as its companion above.

Petrov, Nikolai (piano)

C. P. E. BACH: *Fantasy in C.* MOZART: *Fantasia in C, K.475.* MENDELSSOHN: *Fantasy in F sharp min. (Sonate écossaise), Op. 28.* BRAHMS: *Fantasias, Op. 116.* LISZT: *Réminiscences de Don Juan, G. 148.*
(M) ** Olympia **OCD 198** [id.].

A programme of *Fantasies* for the piano played with great brilliance. Nikolai Petrov is a big player with a formidable technique, and in fortissimo passages his tone can be pretty thunderous. He can play with great delicacy, as in the opening of the Mozart, but is basically a virtuoso player and he is not fully attuned to the Mendelssohnian sensibility. His virtuosity in the Liszt *Don Juan* is really quite stunning and undoubtedly exciting, but those who recall Arrau in this know that the climaxes can be achieved without any loss of beauty of tone. He is very truthfully recorded.

Pinnock, Trevor (harpsichord)

'The harmonious blacksmith'. HANDEL: *Suite 5: The Harmonious blacksmith.* FISCHER: *Urania: Passacaglia in D min.* COUPERIN: *Les baricades mystérieuses.* BACH: *Italian concerto in F, BWV 971.* RAMEAU: *Gavotte in A min.* D. SCARLATTI: *2 Sonatas Kk.380/1.* FIOCCO: *Suite 1: Adagio in F.* DAQUIN: *Le Coucou.* BALBASTHE: *La Suzanne in E min.*
(*) DG **413 591-2 [id.].

A delightful collection of harpsichord lollipops, superbly and stylishly played and brilliantly – if aggressively – recorded. If one samples the famous title-piece, being careful to set the volume control at a realistic level, in the CD format the presence and tangibility of the instrument are spectacular. However, the bright sharpness of focus can become just a little tiring if the recital is taken all at once.

Pollini, Maurizio (piano)

PROKOFIEV: *Piano sonata No. 7 in B flat, Op. 83.* STRAVINSKY: *Three movements from Petrushka.* BOULEZ: *Piano sonata No. 2.* WEBERN: *Variations for piano, Op. 27.*
*** DG **419 202-2**.

The Prokofiev is a great performance, one of the finest ever committed to disc; and the Stravinsky *Petrushka* is electrifying. Not all those responding to this music will do so quite so readily to the Boulez, fine though the playing is; but the Webern also makes a very strong impression. This is the equivalent of two LPs and is outstanding value.

Pöntinen, Roland (piano)

Russian piano music. STRAVINSKY: *3 Movements from Petrushka.* SCRIABIN: *Sonata No. 7 in F sharp (White Mass), Op. 64.* SHOSTAKOVICH: *3 Fantastic dances.* RACHMANINOV: *Études-tableaux, Opp. 33 & 39.* PROKOFIEV: *Toccata.* KHACHATURIAN: *Toccata.*
*** BIS Dig. **CD 276** [id.].

Roland Pöntinen is a young Swedish pianist who is beginning to make a name for himself. The name sounds Finnish rather than Swedish: his father hails from the Baltic and settled in Sweden in 1946. He gives a suitably ardent and inflammable account of the *Seventh Sonata*, the so-called *'White Mass'*, and is fully attuned to the Scriabin sensibility, conveying its wild, excitable character to good effect. His playing has real temperament and sense of colour, and this well-recorded recital shows his very considerable technique and prowess to advantage. A very enjoyable programme.

Preston, Simon (organ)

English organ music (with organs of (i) Knole Chapel, Sevenoaks, (ii) St John the Baptist, Armitage; (iii) with Trevor Pinnock): (i) ANON.: *I smile to see how you devise.* BYRD: *Fantasia in C.* TOMKINS: *Voluntary (Fancy) in C.* GIBBONS: *Fantasia in A min.* PURCELL: *Voluntary in G.* FARRANT: *Felix namque.* BULL: *Prelude in D min.* and *In nomine in A min.* (ii) STANLEY: *Voluntary in A min.* GREENE: *Voluntary in G.* BOYCE: *Voluntary in D.* (ii; iii) WESLEY: *Duet in C.*
*(**) DG Dig. **415 675-2** [id.].

An attractive idea, but one that will offer aural problems for some listeners. The programme played on the Knole Chapel organ with its engagingly bright timbre is attractive enough, although none of the music is of great moment. The Armitage organ, however, has a very individual temperament so that the major thirds are all slightly wider than pure, and the fifths down from C are slightly wider than those upwards. This produces an 'out of tune' impression in some of the music, and while the very personable *Voluntary* of Maurice Greene (with its effective exploitation of the cornet stop) is a highlight, the Wesley *Duet* (where Simon Preston is joined at the keyboard by Trevor Pinnock) produces some clashes of tuning that some may find piquant but other ears will resist.

Rawsthorne, Noel (organ)

Organ of Coventry Cathedral: *'Organ spectacular':* VERDI: *Aïda: Grand march.* CLARKE: *Trumpet voluntary.* BACH: *Suite No. 3 in D; Air.* SCHUBERT: *Marche militaire.* SULLIVAN: *The lost chord.* MENDELSSOHN: *Midsummer Night's Dream: Wedding march.* SOUSA: *The Stars and stripes forever.* ELGAR: *Pomp and circumstance march No. 1.* TRAD: *Londonderry air.* HANDEL: *Messiah: Hallelujah.* WAGNER: *Die Walküre: Ride of the Valkyries.*
*** HMV Dig. **CDC7 47764-2** [id.].

This collection is aptly named, for the digital recording captures some splendid sounds from the modern Coventry organ. With all the transcriptions arranged by Rawsthorne himself, obviously with the instrument in mind, he shows great flair in both playing and registration. It is a frankly popular programme, well laced with marches, balancing expansive tunes with opportunities for bravura, as in the *Aïda* march or the boisterous *Stars and stripes*. The resonance is well controlled by player and engineers alike, and this is very impressive on CD.

Rev, Livia (piano)

'For children': BACH: *Preludes in E, BWV 939; in G min., BWV 930*. DAQUIN: *Le coucou*. MOZART: *Variations on Ah vous dirai-je maman, K.265*. BEETHOVEN: *Für Elise*. SCHUMANN: *Album for the young Op. 63*: excerpts. CHOPIN: *Nocturne in C min., Op. posth.* LISZT: *Études G. 136/1 & 2*. BIZET: *Jeux d'enfants: La Toupie*. FAURÉ: *Dolly: Berceuse*. TCHAIKOVSKY: *Album for the young, Op. 39: Maman; Waltz*. VILLA-LOBOS: *Prole do bebê*: excerpts. JOLIVET: *Chansons naïve 1 & 2*. PROKOFIEV: *Waltz, Op. 65*. BARTÓK: *Evening in the country; For Children*: excerpts. DEBUSSY: *Children's corner*: excerpts. MAGIN: *3 Pieces*. MATAČIĆ: *Miniature variations*.
*** Hyp. **CDA 66185**; *KA 66185*.

A wholly delectable recital, and not just for children either. The whole is more than the sum of its many parts, and the layout provides excellent variety, with the programme stimulating in mixing familiar with unfamiliar. The recording is first class, on cassette as well as CD. Highly recommended for late evening listening, with the tape a fine entertainment for the car.

Richter, Sviatoslav (piano)

CHOPIN: *Préludes, Op. 28/2; 4–11; 13; 19; 21 & 23*. TCHAIKOVSKY: *Nocturne in F, Op. 10/1; Valse-scherzo in A, Op. 7*. RACHMANINOV: *Études-Tableaux, Op. 33/3, 5 & 6; Op. 39 1–4; 7 & 9*.
(M) *** Olympia **OCD 112** [id.].

Some marvellous playing here from Richter. He plays an odd assortment of Chopin *Preludes*, Nos 4 through to 10 in the published sequence, then 23, 19, 11, 2, 23 and 21! These obviously derive from a public concert, as there is applause. He is distinctly ruminative and wayward at times. The two Tchaikovsky pieces are done with extraordinary finesse and the Rachmaninov is masterly. The piano does not sound fresh, either in the *C sharp minor Étude-Tableau* of Op. 33 or (not surprisingly) in the last of Op. 39 where one or two octaves sound 'tired', but it is all right elsewhere in the set. There is some magical playing in the *A minor* piece and some dazzling virtuosity elsewhere. The recordings are not top drawer and the disc gives no details of their provenance; but the sound is perfectly acceptable.

DEBUSSY: *Estampes; Préludes, Book I: Voiles; Le vent dans la plaine; Les collines d'Anacapri*. PROKOFIEV: *Visions fugitives, Op. 22, Nos 3, 6 & 9; Sonata No. 8 in B flat, Op. 84*. SCRIABIN: *Sonata No. 5 in F sharp, Op. 53*.
(M) ❀ *** DG **423 573-2** [id.].

The Debussy *Préludes* and the Prokofiev *Sonata* were recorded at concerts during an Italian tour in 1962, while the remainder were made the previous year in Wembley Town Hall. The former sound more open than the rather confined studio acoustic – but what playing! The Scriabin is demonic and the Debussy could not be more atmospheric. The performance of the Prokofiev *Sonata* is, like the legendary Gilels account, a classic of the gramophone.

Romero, Pepe (guitar)

'Famous Spanish guitar music': ANON.: *Jeux interdits.* ALBÉNIZ: *Asturias.* MALATS: *Serenata española.* TARREGA: *Capricho Ababe.* SOR: *Introduction and variations on a theme of Mozart, Op. 9.* TARREGA: *Recuerdos de la Alhambra; Tango (Maria); Marieta; Las dos hermanitas.* TÓRROBA: *Romance de los pinos.* C. ROMERO: *Malagueña; Fantasia.*
** Ph. Dig. **411 033-2** [id.].

A thoroughly professional and immaculately played collection of favourites. The effect is rather calculated and sometimes a little chocolate-boxy – the virtuoso showing his paces in familiar vehicles. Of course a bravura piece like Tarrega's *Recuerdos de la Alhambra* cannot fail to make a strong impression, and the Tórroba *Romance* is very beguiling too. The Flamenco-based pieces by the artist's father, Celedonio, bring a sudden hint of fire, but for the most part the easy style of the playing does not generate a great deal of electricity. The recording is very natural and sounds well, but even the compact disc gives a touch of blandness to the focus. No information is provided about the music (except titles).

Rubinstein, Artur (piano)

'A French programme': RAVEL: *Valses nobles et sentimentales Nos 1–8; La vallée des cloches. Le tombeau: Forlane.* POULENC: *Mouvements perpetuels (Assez modéré; Tres modéré; Alerte); Intermezzo in A flat; Intermezzo No. 2 in D flat.* FAURÉ: *Nocturne in A flat, Op. 33/3.* CHABRIER: *10 Pièces pittoresques: Scherzo-Valse.*
*** RCA **RD 85665**.

This recital dates from the mid-1960s. The playing is eminently aristocratic and the Ravel pieces and the Poulenc could hardly be bettered. The recording, like the rest of Rubinstein's analogue records, has been enhanced in its new format and is fully acceptable; admirers of this artist need have no qualms about investigating this disc.

Scott Whiteley, John (organ)

Organ of York Minster: *'Great Romantic organ music':* TOURNEMIRE: *Improvisation on the Te Deum.* JONGEN: *Minuet-Scherzo, Op. 53.* MULET: *Tu es Petra.* DUPRÉ: *Prelude and fugue in G min., Op. 3/7.* R. STRAUSS: *Wedding prelude.* KARG-ELERT: *Pastel in B, Op. 92/1.* BRAHMS: *Chorale prelude: O Gott, du frommer Gott, Op. 122/7.* LISZT: *Prelude and fugue on BACH, G.260.*
*** York **CD 101**; *MC 101.*

A superb organ recital, with the huge dynamic range of the York Minster organ spectacularly captured on CD and pianissimo detail registering naturally. John Scott Whiteley's playing is full of flair: the attractively complex and sparklingly florid *Prelude and fugue* of Marcel Dupré is exhilarating and reaches a high climax, while the grand Liszt piece is hardly less overwhelming. The shorter lyrical pieces add serenity and proper contrast at the centre of a recital that is as well planned as it is played and recorded. The opening Tournemire *Improvisation* is very arresting indeed, while Jongen's *Minuet-Scherzo* displays Scott Whiteley's splendidly clear articulation.

Organ of St Paul's Cathedral: *'Favourite organ works':* BACH: *Toccata and fugue in D min.,*

BWV 565. MOZART: *Fantasia in F min., K.608.* S. S. WESLEY: *Air and Gavotte.* MENDELSSOHN: *Sonata No. 3 in A, Op. 65.* SCHUMANN: *Canon in B min., Op. 56.* FRANCK: *Choral No. 2 in B min.* SAINT-SAËNS: *Fantaisie in E flat.* GIGOUT: *Scherzo.* BOËLLMANN: *Suite gothique, Op. 25: Toccata.*
(B) ** Cirrus **CICD 1007** [id.].

The huge panoply of sound, resounding around St Paul's Cathedral, is magnificently caught here, but the resonance offers considerable musical problems: in the opening Bach *Toccata*, John Scott Whiteley has to pause to allow cadences to register. He manages to project detail remarkably well in the florid Gigout *Scherzo*; and the big *Toccata in C minor*, with its thundering pedals, is a *tour de force*; but the Mozart piece is overwhelmed by this degree of amplitude, and the French music, well played as it is, needs more bite. The programme is generous and the recording itself in the demonstration class.

Söllscher, Göran (guitar)

'Cavatina': MYERS: *Cavatina; Portrait.* ALBÉNIZ: *Granada.* TÁRREGA: *Maria; Rosita.* BARRIOS: *Villancico de Navidad.* YOCOH: *Sakura.* LLOBET: arr. of Catalan folksongs: *La filla del marxant; La canço del lladre; El noi de la mare.* LAURO: *El Marabino.* CRESPO: *Norteña.* PATIÑO: *Nevando está.* NEUMANN: *Karleksvals.* CARMICHAEL: *Georgia on my mind.* ANON.: *Romance d'amour.*
*** DG Dig. **413 720-2** [id.].

Göran Söllscher is at his finest here. The programme is essentially Romantic and very tuneful and atmospheric. The indelible opening Myers *Cavatina* is of course the justly famous *Deerhunter* theme, while even the anonymous *Romance* will be familiar. Whether in the attractive Llobet arrangements of Catalan folksongs, the two evocative portraits from Tárrega, or Yocoh's colourful *Sakura* (from Japan), this is the kind of music making that remains in the memory, for even while the playing is relaxed there is no doubt about Söllscher's magnetism. Hoagy Carmichael's *Georgia on my mind* gives the feeling of a final lollipop as the stylish closing encore. The sound is most naturally balanced, and the immediacy and realism are apparent.

'Greensleeves': ANON./CUTTING: *Greensleeves.* ANON.: *Kemp's Jig; Packington's round; Watkin's ale; Romance d'amour.* DOWLAND: *Lachrimae pavan; Frogg galliard.* GALILEI: *Toccata; Corrente; Volta.* WEISS: *Fantasia; Ciacona.* ALBÉNIZ: *Granada.* TÁRREGA: *Maria; Rosita.* BACH: *Chaconne* (arr. Segovia). MYERS: *Cavatina.* SOR: *Introduction and variations on Marlborough.* BARRIOS: *Villancico de Navidad; La filla del marxant.* YOCOH: *Sakura.* LAURO: *El Marabino* (*Vals venezolano*). PATIÑO: *Nevando está; La canço del Lladre; El noi de la mare* (Catalan folksongs). NEUMANN: *Kärleksvals.* CARMICHAEL: *Georgia on my mind.*
(B) ❀ *** DG Dig. *423 263-4.*

This outstanding DG Pocket Music tape is well engineered and represents a very generous and attractive recital, offering a good deal more music than the CD listed above. After opening with the famous title-piece, there is English music, then a Spanish interlude, and an excellent performance of Bach's *Chaconne* (transcribed by Segovia). Then come Sor's finest set of variations, some haunting Barrios and various, more exotic pieces, ending with Hoagy Carmichael. The whole recital is as engaging as it is diverse, and is very highly recommendable.

Stringer, Alan (trumpet), **Noel Rawsthorne** (organ)

Organ of Liverpool Cathedral: *'Trumpet and organ'*: M.-A. CHARPENTIER: *Te Deum: Prelude.* STANLEY: *Voluntary No. 5 in D.* PURCELL: *Sonata in C. Two Trumpet tunes and Air.* BOYCE: *Voluntary in D.* CLARKE: *Trumpet voluntary.* BALDASSARE: *Sonata No. 1 in F.* ROMAN: *Keyboard suite in D: Non troppo allegro; Presto (Gigue).* FIOCCO: *Harpsichord suite No. 1: Andante.* BACH: *Cantata No. 147: Jesu, joy of man's desiring.* attrib. GREENE: *Introduction and trumpet tune.* VIVIANI: *Sonata No. 1 in C.*
(*) CRD **CRD 3308; *CRDC 4008.*

This collection is extremely well recorded. The reverberation of Liverpool Cathedral is under full control and both trumpet and organ are cleanly focused, while the trumpet has natural timbre and bloom. Alan Stringer is at his best in the classical pieces, the *Voluntary* of Boyce, the *Trumpet tunes* and *Sonata* of Purcell and the stylishly played *Sonata* of Viviani, a most attractive little work. He also gives a suitably robust performance of the famous *Trumpet voluntary.* Elsewhere he is sometimes a little square: the Bach chorale is rather too stiff and direct. But admirers of this repertoire will find much to enjoy, and the *Andante* of Fiocco has something in common with the more famous *Adagio* attributed to Albinoni in Giazotto's famous arrangement. The CD transfer improves definition satisfactorily. There is a very good cassette.

Turovsky, Eleonora (violin), **Yuli Turovsky** (cello)

French music for violin and cello: RAVEL: *Sonata.* J. RIVIER: *Sonatine.* HONEGGER: *Sonatine.* MARTINŮ: *Duo.*
*** Chan. Dig. **CHAN 8358**; *ABTD 1121* [id.].

An enterprising issue, albeit one that is unlikely to top the charts. Yuli Turovsky is best known as the cellist of the Borodin Trio, but his partner is hardly less fine. The most substantial piece here is the Ravel *Sonata*, which opens magically and is beautifully played by these two artists. Jean Rivier is little known outside France though his *Third* and *Fifth Symphonies* were recorded in the 1950s. His *Sonatine* lasts ten minutes and is slight but charming; while the Honegger and Martinů works are more challenging. There is over an hour's music here, repertoire that one seldom encounters in the concert hall. A very well-recorded programme, designed rather for the connoisseur of French music than for the wider record-collecting public, but well worth investigating. Tape collectors will find that the chrome cassette is admirably smooth and faithful.

Williams, John (guitar)

'Portrait': LAURO: *Seis por perecho; El Negrito.* CLARE: *Castilla.* TARREGA: *Recuerdos de la Alhambra.* BACH: *Cello suite No. 1 in G, BWV 1007: Prelude.* VIVALDI: *Concerto in D* (with orchestra). LENNON/MCCARTNEY: *Fool on the hill.* BARRIOS: *Vals, Op. 8/4.* BROUWER: *Guajira; Danza caracteristica.* MYERS: *Cavatina.* YOCOH: *Sakura.*
(*) CBS Dig. **MK 37791 [id.].

John Williams's digital début is a little disappointing. The solo items are forwardly balanced and the sound is somewhat clinical. The Vivaldi *Concerto*, recorded with a chamber orchestra, also sounds rather meagre in texture. The highlights are the famous *Recuerdos de la Alhambra*, the engaging version of *Fool on the hill* and the Myers *Cavatina*, which are given a string accompaniment and recorded more atmospherically. But most memorable of all is the delicious

Sakura, a traditional Japanese melody with variations where, as John Williams aptly comments, the spaces between the notes are as important as the notes themselves.

Yepes, Narciso (guitar)

Spanish guitar music: TÁRREGA: *Recuerdos de la Alhambra; Capricho arabe; Serenata; Tango; Alborada; Marieta mazurka.* SOR: *Theme and variations, Op. 9; Minuet in G, Op. 11/1. Variations on Marlborough, Op. 28;* SANZ: *Spanish suite.* RODRIGO: *En los trigales.* GRANADOS: *Spanish Dance No. 4.* ALBÉNIZ: *Rumores de la Caleta; Malagueña, Op. 165. Suite española: Asturias (Leyenda).* arr. LLOBET: *La canço del lladre; La filla del marxant* (Catalan folksongs). SEGOVIA: *El noi de la mare.* YEPES: *Forbidden games* (film score): *Romance.* VILLA-LOBOS: *Prelude No. 1.* RUIZ PIPÓ: *Canción and Danza No. 1.*
(B) ⊛ *** DG Walkman *413 434-4.*

This can be recommended with the utmost enthusiasm to anyone wanting an inexpensive, generous (88 minutes) and representative programme of Spanish guitar music. Narciso Yepes is not only an outstanding exponent of this repertoire, he also has the rare gift of consistently creating electricity in the recording studio, and all this music springs vividly to life. In popular favourites like the famous opening *Recuerdos de la Alhambra* of Tárrega, the exciting transcription of Falla's *Miller's dance*, the earlier Baroque repertoire (the *Suite* of Sanz is particularly appealing), and in the communicative twentieth-century items by Rodrigo and Ruiz Pipó, Yepes' assured and always stylish advocacy brings consistent pleasure. The tape transfer level is quite high and the attendant hiss is not a problem. A real bargain in every sense of the word.

Vocal Recitals and Choral Collections

Ameling, Elly (soprano)

'Serenata' (with Rudolf Jansen, piano): TOSTI: *La Serenata.* CASTELNUOVO-TEDESCO: *Ninna nanna.* DOWLAND: *Weep you no more, sad fountaines.* QUILTER: *Weep you no more.* NAKADA: *Watakushi no kono kami.* MARX: *Hat dich die Liebe berührt.* SCHUMANN: *Du bist wie eine Blume.* WOLF: *Verborgenheit.* SATIE: *La diva de L'Empire.* HAHN: *L'amité; La vie belle.* BIZET: *Adieux de l'hôtesse arabe.* GOUNOD; *Viens! Les gazons sont verts!* CHABRIER: *L'île heureuse.* OBRADORS: *Del cabello mas sutil; El vito.* CIMAGLIA: *Niebla portena.*
*** Ph. Dig. **412 216-2** [id.].

The charm of the Dutch soprano in lighter music is vividly caught in this attractive collection, taking its title from the song which receives the most memorable performance, Tosti's *Serenade*, enchantingly done. With an obvious exception in the Satie song, most items are slow, but the variety of expression makes up for that. Warm recording.

'18th-Century Bel Canto' (with Leipzig GO, Masur): GIORDANI: *Caro mio ben.* VIVALDI: *Juditha triumphana: Jam no procul ab axe . . . Armatae face.* PAISIELLO: *L'Amor contrastato: Nel cor più.* HEINICHEN: *Diana sull' Elba: Mille belve dalle selve.* HANDEL: *Giulio Cesare: E pur così . . . Piangero ì a sorte mia. V'adoro pupille.* GLUCK: *Paride ed Elena: Oh, del mio dolce ardor.* PERGOLESI: *Tre giorní son che Nina.* MOZART: *Non più! Tutto ascoltai . . . Non temer amato bene, K.490.* PURCELL: *Dido and Aeneas: Thy hand, Belinda . . . When I am laid in earth.*
*** Ph. Dig. **412 233-2**; *412 233-4* [id.].

With warm playing from the Leipzig Gewandhaus Orchestra, opulently recorded, Elly Ameling's collection of Baroque opera arias and arie antiche brings out sweetness as well as purity. With such a winning singer, it is a delightful disc, so long as you have no stylistic objections – this is a modern rather than an 'authentic' approach. The cassette is admirably smooth and kind to the voice, but the CD has more striking presence.

'Sentimental me' (with Louis van Dijk, piano, John Clayton, double bass): GERSHWIN: *I've got a crush on you; But not for me.* GOEMANS: *Aan de Amsterdames gratchen.* PORTER: *I get a kick out of you; What is this thing called love?; You do something to me; Begin the beguine; Night and day.* KERN: *All the things you are.* SONDHEIM: *Can that boy foxtrot!.* JOBIM: *Garota de Ipanema.* GIRAUD: *Sous le ciel de Paris.* ELLINGTON: *Caravan; Sophisticated lady; Solitude; It don't mean a thing; In a sentimental mood.*
*** Ph. Dig. **412 433-2** [id.].

If anyone thought of Elly Ameling as just a staid singer in the Dutch manner, this frothy 'crossover' collection completely counters that. More than most who attempt to turn popular numbers into art songs, she finds a happy stylistic compromise. Although she is most obviously at home in a song like *Aan de Amsterdames gratchen*, numbers like *Night and day* and *Begin the beguine* bring an idiomatic response; and she is particularly good in the Ellington items. The recording is suitably intimate and atmospheric, and the balance with the piano is nicely judged. The sound is very good.

'Soirée française' (with Rudolf Jansen, piano): DEBUSSY: *Beau soir.* FAURÉ: *Mandoline.* GOUNOD: *Chanson de printemps.* POULENC: *Métamorphoses: C'est ainsi que tu es.* CANTELOUSE: *Chants d'Auvergne: Baïlèro; Oi Aaï.* ROUSSEL: *Réponse d'un épouse sage.* MESSIAEN: *La fiancée perdue.* CHAUSSON: *Le temps des lilas.* CAPLET: *Le corbeau et le renard.* HONEGGER: *Trois chansons de la Petite Sirène.* FRANCK: *Nocturne.* BIZET: *Chanson d'Avril.* DUPARC: *Romance de Mignon.* SATIE: *Ludions.*
*** Ph. Dig. **412 628-2**; *412 628-4* [id.].

Elly Ameling's collection of French mélodies is a charming selection, linking well-known songs by Debussy and Fauré to much rarer, just as delightful items, all performed in the consistently pure style which makes this artist a timeless singer. The sweet songs are nicely contrasted with the lighter, more pointed items by Bizet, Gounod, Roussel and Satie; while it is fascinating to have Duparc's setting of *Mignon's song*, originally withdrawn by the composer. Well-balanced recording. The cassette is faithful but the sound is rather soft-grained.

Angeles, Victoria de los, Elisabeth Schwarzkopf (sopranos), Dietrich Fischer-Dieskau (baritone), Gerald Moore (piano)

'Gerald Moore: A tribute': MOZART: *Più non si trovano.* SCHUBERT: *Nachtviolen; Schwanengesang; Abschied; Im Abendroth; An die Musik.* ROSSINI: *Cats' duet; Serate musicale: La Regata Veneziana; La Pesca.* BRAHMS: *Der Gang zum Liebchen; Vergebliches Ständchen.* SCHUMANN: *Tanzlied; Er und Sie.* WOLF: *Sonne der Schlummerlosen; Das verlassene Mägdlein; Der Zigeunerin; Kennst du das Land.* MENDELSSOHN: *Ich wollt' meine Lieb'; Gruss; Lied aus Ruy Blas; Abendlied; Wasserfahrt.* HAYDN: *An den Vetter; Daphnens einziger Fehler.*
*** HMV **CDC7 49238-2**.

This masterly collection, at once superbly stylish yet sparkling and at times comic too, comes from the live concert which these artists gave at the Festival Hall on Moore's retirement. The full recital set of two discs is long deleted, but this selection has most of the finest and most delectable items, including Schwarzkopf's unforgettable account of Wolf's greatest song, *Kennst du das Land.* The recital is perhaps most famous for the performance of the *Duetto buffo di due gatti,* attributed to Rossini. The recording, slightly distanced, sounds very real in its digitally remastered CD format, and it is good that a speech by Gerald Moore is included before the recital ends with *An die Musik.*

Atlanta Chorus and Symphony Orchestra, Robert Shaw

'The many moods of Christmas' (arr. R. Russell Bennett): *Good Christian men, rejoice; Patapan; O come all ye faithful; O Sanctissima; Away in a manger; Fum fum fum; March of the Kings; What Child is this?; Bring a torch, Jeanette, Isabella; Angels we have heard on high; The first nowell; I saw three ships; Deck the halls.* GRÜBER: *Silent night.* MENDELSSOHN: *Hark the herald angels sing.* BACH: *Break forth, O beauteous heav'nly light.* REDNER-BROOKS: *O little town of Bethlehem.*
*** Telarc **CD 80087** [id.].

The carols here are arranged into four groups, each lasting about 12 minutes, and the scoring and use of both chorus and orchestra is as flamboyantly imaginative as one would expect from a musician of the calibre of Robert Russell Bennett. Moreover, the dynamic range of the recording is dramatically wide and the expansion of sound for the climaxes of *O come all ye faithful* and *Hark the herald angels sing*, with thrillingly realistic brass, is almost overwhelming. The chorus is backwardly balanced and with some choral pianissimos the words are barely audible, but the musical effect remains impressive. This is not a concert that can be treated as background music; one has to stop and listen, whether to the gentle solo lute playing of the *Greensleeves* melody by George Petsch (*What Child is this?*), the charming detail in *Bring a torch, Jeanette, Isabella*, or the impressive choral interplay in the splendid arrangement of *Angels we have heard on high*. Technically this is vintage Telarc, with the hall's ambience seen as of primary importance in its warm colouring of the rich-hued sounds from voices and instrumentalists alike. Highly recommended on all counts.

Augér, Arleen (soprano), Irwin Gage (piano)

Lieder: MOZART: *Die Verschweigung; Un moto di gioia; Das Veilchen; Das Lied der Trennug; Als Luise die Briefe; Abendempfindung.* R. STRAUSS: *Morgen; Hat gessagt-bleibt's nich dabei; Glückes genug; Gefunden.* WOLF: *Die vier Lieder der Mignon.*
*** CBS Dig. **MK 42447**; *MT 42447* [id.].

Arleen Augér, always a keenly intelligent and imaginative artist, here uses her sweet, light, bright soprano in consistently satisfying readings of songs by three composers for whom she has special affinity. Irwin Gage is a totally sympathetic accompanist, helped by well-balanced recording.

Bach Choir, Sir David Willcocks

'Family carols' (with Philip Jones Brass Ens.): *O come, all ye faithful; Gabriel's message; Angelus and Virginem; Ding dong merrily on high; A virgin most pure; God rest ye merry gentlemen; In dulci jubilo; Unto us a son is born; Once in Royal David's city; Hush, my dear, lie still and slumber.* WILLCOCKS: *Fanfare.* RUTTER: *Shepherd's pipe carol; Star carol.* KIRKPATRICK: *Away in a manger.* GRUBER: *Stille Nacht.* arr. VAUGHAN WILLIAMS: *Sussex carol.* MENDELSSOHN: *Hark! the herald angels sing.*
(M) *** Decca Dig. **417 898-2**; *417 898-4*.

An admirably chosen and beautifully recorded collection of traditional carols. Fresh simplicity is the keynote here; the brass fanfares bring a touch of splendour but the music is not overscored. *Silent Night* has seldom sounded more serene, and Rutter's infectiously rhythmic *Shepherd's pipe carol* makes a refreshing contrast. The digital sound is in no way clinical; indeed the resonance is perfectly judged. The excellent cassette is only marginally less sharply focused.

Baker, Dame Janet (mezzo-soprano)

Song recital: BERLIOZ: *Nuits d'été: Villanelle; Les Troyens: Pluton, semble, m'être propice.* FAURÉ: *Clair de lune.* GOUNOD: *Sérénade.* MASSENET: *Crépuscule.* CHABRIER: *Villanelle des petits canards.* CAMPION: *Fain would I wed.* TRAD: *Drink to me only; I know where I'm going.* ELGAR: *Sea pictures: Where corals lie.* MENDELSSOHN: *Elijah: O rest in the Lord.* BACH: *Cantata No. 82: Aria: Ich habe genug.* R. STRAUSS: *Morgen.* MAHLER: *Ich bin der Welt abhanden gekommen.*
(B) ❀ *** CfP *CFP 41 4487-4*.

Compiled from some of Dame Janet's finest records of the 1960s and early 1970s, including some – like the Strauss – long unavailable, this CfP collection is a total delight. The variety of expression combined with keenly consistent intensity makes this a superb portrait of a great artist. The sound is transferred with commendable consistency; this is an excellent tape. An outstanding bargain.

'Songs for Sunday' (with Philip Ledger, piano): BRAHE: *Bless this house.* PARRY: *Jerusalem.* TRAD.: *Were you there.* PLUMSTEAD: *A grateful heart; Close thine eyes.* EASTHOPE MARTIN: *The holy child.* THOMPSON: *The knights of Bethlehem.* LIDDLE: *How lovely are Thy dwellings; The Lord is my shepherd; Abide with me.* VAUGHAN WILLIAMS: *The call.* FORD: *A prayer to Our Lady.* BACH/GOUNOD: *Ave Maria.* WALFORD DAVIES: *God be in my head.*
(M) *** EMI *EMX 41 2088-4.*

Dame Janet Baker's total dedication makes this a moving experience, transforming songs that would as a rule seem merely sentimental. Sensitive accompaniment by Philip Ledger and excellent recording, which has transferred admirably to tape, where the atmospheric sound remains clear, with only slight loss of definition at the top.

Baltsa, Agnes (mezzo-soprano)

Arias (with Munich RO, Zedda): DONIZETTI: *Mary Stuart: Elisabeth's cavatina; Eche! Non amiche ad insolita gioia; Oh nube!* MOZART: *Così fan tutte: Temerari, sortite fuori . . . Come scoglio.* VERDI: *Macbeth: Nel di dela vittoria; Sleepwalking scene.* BERLIOZ: *Les Troyens: Je vais mourir; Adieu, fière cité.*
(*) HMV Dig. **CDC7 47627-2 [id.]; *EL 270478-4.*

Agnes Baltsa is nothing if not characterful in this surprising collection of arias which take her well into the soprano range, even as far as a pianissimo top D flat at the end of Lady Macbeth's *Sleepwalking scene*, an extraordinary sound. Vocally the joys are mixed, with Donizetti hardly suited to the abrasive tang of the Baltsa timbre. But this is a fearsome, fire-breathing, Lady Macbeth; and though Mozartians may raise eyebrows at a Fiordiligi presented as that character's first cousin, she is certainly magnetic. Zedda's accompaniments are lacklustre, but the recording captures the voice well, and there is an excellent chrome cassette. Well worth exploring.

'Songs my country taught me' (with Kostas Papadopoulos, bouzouki; Athens Experimental O, Xarhakos): HADJIDAKIS: *A carnation behind your ear; Dream of urban children; The postman.* THEODORAKIS: *A day in May; The train leaves at eight; I gave you rosewater to drink.* XARHAKOS: *When Otto was king; There will be better days; Barcarolle; The trains which left.* TSITSANIS: *Princess of my heart.*
(*) DG Dig. **419 236-2; *419 236-4* [id.].

Although this collection is folk-based, it becomes crossover music too, by virtue of the sultry and at times hypnotic arrangements by Stavros Xarhakos for his Athens Experimental Orchestra which, if dominated by bouzouki rhythms, create sumptuously atmospheric textures, producing a distinctly Greek form of kitsch. Over all this rides the pungent vocal timbre of Agnes Baltsa, delivering the words and melodic lines with a passion which is both personal and wholly idiomatic. The recorded sound overall makes a strong impact (even on the tape, which is less sharply defined than the CD). The music itself is sometimes somewhat cheap, but always potent; and in its way this is distinctly memorable, if not for ethnic purists.

Battle, Kathleen (soprano)

'The pleasures of their company' (with Christopher Parkening, guitar): DOWLAND: *Come again; Allemande; What if I never speed; Galliard; Fine knacks for ladies.* VILLA-LOBOS: *Bachianas brasileiras No. 5: Aria.* GRANADOS: *La Maja de Goya.* HENRIQUE: *Boi-Bumba.* OVALLE: *Azulao.* BARROSO: *Para ninar.* FALLA: *3 Spanish folksongs; 6 spirituals.*
*** HMV Dig. **CDC7 47196-2** [id.]; *EL 270307-4.*

With Christopher Parkening a sympathetic accompanist on the guitar, Kathleen Battle is at her most individual in this unexpected but apt and attractive mixture of Elizabethan lute songs, Spanish guitar songs and spirituals. The vivacity of the singer is well caught, with the animated facial expression consistently suggested. Immediate, vivid recording. The cassette, too, has fine presence.

'Salzburg Recital (with James Levine, piano): PURCELL: *Come all ye songsters; Music for a while; Sweeter than roses.* HANDEL: *O had I Jubal's lyre.* MENDELSSOHN: *Bei der Wiege; Neue Liebe.* R. STRAUSS: *Schlagende Herzen; Ich wollt'ein Sträusslein binden; Säusle, liebe Myrte.* MOZART: *Ridente la calma; Das Veilchen; Un moto di gioia.* FAURÉ: *Mandoline; Les roses d'Ispahan; En prière; Notre amour.* Spirituals: *Honour, honour; His name so sweet; Witness; He's got the whole world in his hands.*
*** DG Dig. **415 361-2**; *415 361-4* [id.].

Kathleen Battle is at her most characterful and provocative in this recital with Levine, recorded live in the Mozarteum in Salzburg as part of the 1984 Festival. Her singing of Susanna's little alternative aria from *Figaro*, *Un moto di gioia*, is a particular delight, and Levine – from Ohio, like Battle herself – proves a splendidly pointed and provocative accompanist. Helpfully atmospheric recording. The chrome cassette is smooth and pleasing, not quite as sharply defined as the CD but fully acceptable.

Berganza, Teresa (mezzo-soprano)

Venetian concert (with Yasunori Imamura, lute, theorbo, chitarra; Joerg Ewald, harpsichord or organ; and continuo): STROZZI: *Non ti doler mio cor; Rissolvetevi pensieri.* SANCES: *Misera, hor si ch'il pianto; O perduti diletti.* MONTEVERDI: *Confitebor tibi Domine.* MILANUZZI: *Ut re mi.* FONTEI: *Auree stelle.* MINISCALCHI: *Fuggir pur mi convien; Fuggir voglio.* LAMORETTI: *Bell'il vana tua beltade.* (Instrumental): MOLINARO: *Fantasia nono.* PALESTRINA: *Vestiva i colli.* RORE: *Anchor che col partire.*
*** Claves **CD 8206** [id.].

Teresa Berganza is the star of this attractive concert of Venetian music, with little of the included repertoire at all familiar. The vocal contributions are characteristically intelligent and stylish – but expressively telling, too. The instrumental numbers provide suitable contrast and are very well done; the recording has fine presence, although the CD offers only a marginal gain except in the matter (not a small one here) of freedom from intrusive background noises. The collection is well documented.

Berlin German Opera Chorus and Orchestra, Sinopoli

Opera choruses: MOZART: *Die Zauberflöte: O Isis und Osiris.* BEETHOVEN: *Fidelio: O welche Lust.* WEBER: *Der Freischütz: Huntsmen's chorus; Viktoria! Viktoria!* WAGNER: *Tannhäuser: Grand march.* VERDI: *Nabucco: Va, pensiero. I Lombardi: O Signore, dal tetto natio. Macbeth: Patria oppressa. Il Trovatore: Anvil chorus. Aïda: Gloria all'Egitto . . . Vieni, a guerriero vindice.*
*** DG Dig. **415 283-2** [id.].

A splendid collection of choruses, full of character, the atmosphere of each opera distinctive. The pianissimo at the beginning of the famous *Fidelio Prisoners' chorus* has striking intensity, while the exuberant *Hunting chorus* from *Freischütz* is irresistible in its buoyancy. On the other hand, Sinopoli's broadening of the sustained tune in the short *Aïda* excerpt may for some seem too deliberate. Needless to say, the orchestral playing is first class; the balance, with the orchestra placed vividly forward and the chorus set back within a warmly resonant acoustic, is most convincing, although words are not always sharply clear. A well-balanced and rewarding compilation in all other respects, especially vivid in its compact disc format.

Bowman, James (alto), King's Consort, Robert King

VIVALDI: *Salve regina in C min., RV 616.* TELEMANN: *Weg mit Sodoms gift'gen Fruchter.* PERGOLESI: *Salve regina in F min.* BACH: *Cantata No. 54; Widerstehe doch der Sunde.*
*** Mer. Dig. **CDE 84138**; *KE 77138.*

James Bowman's collection of four varied items suited to the countertenor voice makes for an unusual and attractive mixture, beautifully performed by singer and instrumentalists alike. Maybe beauty is brought out too much in the Bach *Cantata* with its severe text, but the singer's artistry is consistent throughout, helped by full, well-balanced recording.

Bjoerling, Jussi (tenor)

Opera arias from: DONIZETTI: *L'Elisir d'amore.* VERDI: *Il Trovatore; Un Ballo in maschera; Aïda.* LEONCAVALLO: *I Pagliacci.* PUCCINI: *La Bohème; Tosca; La Fanciulla del West; Turandot.* GIORDANO: *Fedora.* CILEA: *L'Arlesiana.* MEYERBEER: *L'Africana.* GOUNOD: *Faust.* MASSENET: *Manon.* FLOTOW: *Martha.* ROSSINI: *Stabat mater.*
(M) (***) EMI mono **CDH7 61053-2.**

Unlike the disappointing Bjoerling CD from RCA, the EMI collection on the Références label brings excellent transfers of material recorded between 1936 and 1947 on the tenor's home-ground in Stockholm. The voice was then at its very peak, well caught in those final years of 78 r.p.m. discs, with artistry totally assured over this wide range of repertory.

Opera arias from: VERDI: *Aïda; Rigoletto.* PUCCINI: *Manon Lescaut; Turandot; La Bohème; Tosca.* MASCAGNI: *Cavalleria Rusticana.* BORODIN: *Prince Igor.* GIORDANO: *Andrea Chénier.* FLOTOW: *Martha.* DONIZETTI: *L'Elisir d'amore.* TCHAIKOVSKY: *Eugene Onegin.* GOUNOD: *Faust.* LEONCAVALLO: *Pagliacci.*
*(**) RCA **RD 85934 [RCA 5934-2-RC]**.

The lack of care in RCA's transfer of these superb Bjoerling items is little short of a disgrace. The transfers are rough but, just as seriously, the extracting of items from complete sets is extraordinarily clumsy. Nevertheless the actual singing is a delight, a fine representation of one of the great tenor voices of the century.

Burchuladze, Paata (bass)

Arias (with ECO, London Opera Chorus, Edward Downes): MUSSORGSKY: *Boris Godunov: Coronation scene; Monologue; Clock scene; Death of Boris.* VERDI: *Simon Boccanegra: A te l'estremo addio . . . Il lacerato spirito. Macbeth: Studia il passo . . . Come dal ciel precipita. Don Carlos: Ella giamma m'amò. Ernani: Che mai vegg'io! . . . Infelice! . . . Infin che.*
*** Decca Dig. **414 335-2** [id.].

This exciting Russian bass from Georgia sings each one of these items with gloriously firm tone from top to bottom of the register. In every sense a great voice is revealed, and the repertory could hardly be more apt, one half comprising Verdi's finest bass arias, the other Boris's principal solos. If little depth of feeling is conveyed as yet, the sensuous beauty of the sound is enough to make this a very special bass recital record, strongly accompanied by Downes and his team and briliantly recorded.

Callas, Maria (soprano)

Operatic recital: CILEA: *Adriana Lecouvreur: Ecco, respiro appena . . . Io son l'umile; Poveri fiori.* GIORDANO: *Andrea Chénier: La mamma morta.* CATALANI: *La Wally: Ebben? Ne andro lontana.* BOITO: *Mefistofele: L'altra notte.* ROSSINI: *Il barbiere di Siviglia: Una voce poco fa.* MEYERBEER: *Dinorah: Shadow song.* DELIBES: *Lakmé: Bell song.* VERDI: *I vespri siciliani: Boléro.* CHERUBINI: *Medea: Dei tuoi figli.* SPONTINI: *La Vestale: Tu che invoco; O Nume tutelar; Caro oggetto.*
❀ (***) HMV mono **CDC7 47282-2** [id.].

This fine recital disc is a conflation of two of Callas's most successful earlier LPs. The *Medea* and *Vestale* items were originally coupled with extracts from complete opera sets and might otherwise have been left in limbo. These are recordings from the 1950s, when the voice was still in fine condition and the artistry at its most magnetic. Callas's portrait of Rosina in *Una voce* was never more sparklingly viperish than here, and she never surpassed the heart-felt intensity of such numbers as *La mamma morta* and *Poveri fiori.* Some items may reveal strain – the *Bell song* from *Lakmé*, for example – but this has many claims to be the finest single Callas recital on CD, very well transferred.

'Mad scenes and Bel canto arias' (with Philh. O. Rescigno): DONIZETTI: *Anna Bolena: Piangete voi; Al dolce guidami. La figlia del reggimento: Convienpartir. Lucrezia Borgia: Tranquillo ei possa . . . Come' è bello. L'Elisir d'amore: Prendi, per me sei libero.* THOMAS: *Hamlet: À vos jeux; Partagez-vous mes fleurs; Et maintenant écoutez ma chanson.* BELLINI: *Il Pirata: Oh! s'io potessi . . . Col sorriso d'innocenza; Sorgete, Lo sognai ferito esangue.*
*** HMV **CDC7 47283-2** [id.].

If, as ever, the rawness of exposed top-notes mars the sheer beauty of Callas's singing, few recital records ever made can match, let alone outshine, her collection of mad scenes in vocal and dramatic imagination. This is Callas at her very peak; Desmond Shawe-Taylor suggested this as the collection which, more than any other, summed up the essence of Callas's genius. For the CD reissue further arias have been added, notably excerpts from Donizetti's *La figlia del reggimento, L'Elisir d'amore* and *Lucrezia Borgia* (from the mid-1960s), a fair example of the latter-day Callas, never very sweet-toned, yet displaying the usual Callas fire. However, the singing here is less imaginative and there are few phrases that stick in the memory by their sheer individuality. Nevertheless, the main part of the recital is indispensable; the digital remastering has enhanced the originally excellent recordings and given the voice striking presence.

'Callas à Paris' (with French Nat.R.O, Prêtre): GLUCK: *Orphée et Eurydice: J'ai perdu mon Eurydice. Alceste: Divinités du Styx.* BIZET: *Carmen: Habañera; Séguedilla.* SAINT-SAËNS: *Samson et Dalila: Printemps qui commence; Amour! Viens aider; mon cœur s'ouvre à ta voix.* MASSENET: *Manon: Adieu, notre petite table; Je marche sur tous les chemins. Le Cid: Pleurez, mes yeux.* GOUNOD: *Roméo et Juliette: Je veux vivre.* THOMAS: *Mignon: Je suis Titania.* CHARPENTIER: *Louise: Depuis le jour.*
*** HMV **CDC7 49059-2**.

The original LP collection, *'Callas à Paris'*, dating from 1961 with the singer at her most commanding and characterful, is here augmented with five items from the sequel disc of two years later, when the voice was in decline. The vocal contrast is clear enough, and the need at the time to patch and re-patch the takes in the later sessions makes the results sound less spontaneous and natural. But the earlier portraits of Carmen, Alceste, Dalila and Juliette find Callas still supreme. Her mastery of the French repertory provides a fascinating slant on her artistry.

'The incomparable Callas': BELLINI: *Norma: Casta diva.* DONIZETTI: *Lucia: Regnava nei silenzio.* VERDI: *Ernani: Surta à la notte . . . Ernani involami. Aïda: Ritorna vincitor.* PONCHIELLI: *La Gioconda: Suicidio!* PUCCINI: *Tosca: Vissi d'arte.* GLUCK: *Orphée et Eurydice: L'ai perdu mon Eurydice.* GOUNOD: *Roméo et Juliette: Je veux vivre.* THOMAS: *Mignon: Je suis Titania.* MASSENET: *Le Cid: Pleurez, mes yeux.* BIZET: *Carmen: Les tringles des sistres tintaient; Carreau, pique . . . la mort!* SAINT-SAËNS: *Samson et Dalila: Mon cœur s'ouvre à ta voix.*
*** HMV **CDC7 49393-2** [id.]; (M) *EG 749393-4*.

One might quibble whether the title *'The incomparable Callas'* is aptly applied to these particular items, mostly taken from complete operas and recitals recorded in the 1960s. Her later sets of *Lucia* and *Norma* are both well represented here, but even finer is the *Suicidio!* from her second version of Ponchielli's *La Gioconda*, among her finest achievements. The *Carmen* items taken from the complete set are more questionable in their fierceness but are totally individual as indeed, flawed or not, is the last-recorded item here, Aïda's *Ritorna vincitor*, made in 1972. The transfers capture the voice well. The tape is offered at mid-price and is vividly transferred.

'The unknown recordings': WAGNER: *Tristan: Liebestod.* VERDI: *Don Carlos: Tu che la vanità. I Lombardi: Te vergin santa. I vespri siciliani: Arrigo! Ah, parli a un core, Attila: Liberamente or piangi.* BELLINI: *Il Pirata: Col sorriso d'innocenza.* ROSSINI: *Cenerentola: Non più mesta. Guglielmo Tell: Selva opaca. Semiramide: Bel raggio lusinger.*
*** HMV **CDC7 49428-2** [id.], *EL 749428-4*.

The collection brings together unpublished material from several sources, mainly alternative recordings of arias which appeared earlier in other versions, but also live recordings made in Athens and Amsterdam. The alternative readings all bring us fresh illumination of a supreme artist who was both deeply thoughtful and spontaneous in that she never merely repeated herself. These items of early Verdi, Rossini and Bellini are all most cherishable, but just as fascinating is her very early Athens account of Isolde's *Liebestod* in Italian and her 1959 Holland Festival performances of passages from Bellini's *Il Pirata* and Verdi's *Don Carlos*. Variable recording, helped by skilled and refined EMI transfers.

'Callas at Juilliard' (masterclasses): performances, with students, of arias from: MOZART: *Don Giovanni.* BEETHOVEN: *Fidelio.* CHERUBINI: *Medea.* BELLINI: *Norma.* ROSSINI: *Il barbiere di*

Siviglia. VERDI: *Rigoletto; Don Carlos.* MASSENET: *Werther.* PUCCINI: *La Bohème; Madama Butterfly.*
(*) HMV **CDS7 49600-2 [id.]; (M) *EX 749600-4* (3).

No devotee of Callas will want to miss the collection of masterclass excerpts from 1972, interspersed with vintage Callas recordings, that John Ardoin has painstakingly helped to put together. The personality as it emerges is not always attractive, tough yet vulnerable; but the moments of illumination are many, with the living presence of the diva vividly conveyed. There are some particularly fascinating insights in the Rossini items and in the outline of nuances possible in *Sì, mi chiamano Mimì*. Many will wish that the editing had been even more severe, but Callas's personality is endlessly fascinating, and this set provides a unique portrait in close-up.

Arias: ROSSINI: *Il barbiere di Siviglia: Una voce poco fa.* VERDI: *Macbeth: La luce langue. Don Carlos: Tu che le vanità.* PUCCINI: *Tosca: Vissi d'arte.* GLUCK: *Alceste: Divinités du Styx.* BIZET: *Carmen: Habañera; Séguedilla* (with Nicolai Gedda). SAINT-SAËNS: *Samson et Dalila: Printemps qui commence.* MASSENET: *Manon: Je ne suis faiblesse* (*Adieu, notre petite table*). CHARPENTIER: *Louise: Depuis le jour.*
(M) *** EMI *TC-EMX 2123.*

This compilation on the EMI Eminence label brings together at bargain price some of Callas's most cherishable performances, mostly taken from recital material. An excellent sampler, well recorded and satisfactorily transferred on to a mid-priced tape. No doubt a CD will follow.

Cambridge Singers, John Rutter

'There is sweet music' (English choral songs): STANFORD: *The blue bird.* DELIUS: *To be sung of a summer night on the water I & II.* ELGAR: *There is sweet music; My love dwelt in a Northern land.* VAUGHAN WILLIAMS: *3 Shakespearean songs: Full fathom five; The cloud-capp'd towers; Over hill, over dale.* BRITTEN: *5 Flower songs, Op. 47.* Folksongs: arr. MOERAN: *The sailor and young Nancy.* arr. GRAINGER: *Brigg Fair: Londonderry air.* arr. CHAPMAN: *Three ravens.* arr. HOLST: *My sweetheart's like Venus.* arr. BAIRSTOW: *The oak and the ash.* arr. STANFORD: *Quick! We have but a second.*
❀ *** Coll. Dig. **COLCD 104**; *COLC 104* [id.].

Opening with an enchanting performance of Stanford's *The blue bird* and followed by equally expressive accounts of Delius's two wordless summer evocations, this most attractive recital ranges from Elgar and Vaughan Williams, both offering splendid performances, to various arrangements of folksongs, less fashionable today than they once were, but giving much pleasure here. The recording, made in the Great Hall of University College, London, has an almost ideal ambience: words are clear, yet the vocal timbre is full and natural. A highly recommendable anthology, with an excellent cassette equivalent.

'Flora gave me fairest flowers' (English madrigals): MORLEY: *My bonny lass she smileth; Fyer, fyer! Now is the month of Maying.* EAST: *Quick, quick, away dispatch!* GIBBONS: *Dainty fine bird; Silver swan.* BYRD: *Though Amaryllis dance in green; This sweet and merry month of May; Lullaby.* WEELKES: *Hark, all ye lovely saints.* WILBYE: *Weep, weep, mine eyes; Flora gave me; Draw on sweet night; Adieu sweet Amaryllis.* TOMKINS: *Too much I once lamented; Adieu ye city-prisoning towers.* FARMER: *Little pretty bonny lass.* BENNETT: *Round about.* WEELKES: *Ha ha! this world doth pass; Death hath deprived me.* RAMSEY: *Sleep, fleshly birth.*
*** Coll. Dig. **COLCD 105;** *COLC 105* [id.].

John Rutter's Cambridge Singers bring consistent unanimity of ensemble and a natural expressive feeling to this very attractive programme of madrigals. Perhaps the first group, devoted to love and marriage, may be thought rather consistently mellifluous, but the second, *'Madrigals of times and season'*, is nicely contrasted, with the clean articulation of Morley's *Now is the month of Maying* made the more telling by the lightness of the vocal production. John Wilbye's lovely *Draw on sweet night*, which follows, makes a perfect contrast. After two items about *'Fairies, spirits and conceits'*, the concert closes in a mood of moving Elizabethan melancholy with a group devoted to mourning and farewell. Superb recording in a most flattering acoustic makes this collection the more enjoyable, though one to be dipped into rather than heard all at once. There is a first-class cassette.

'Faire is the Heaven' (Music of the English Church): PARSONS: *Ave Maria.* TALLIS: *Loquebantur variis linguis; If ye love me.* BYRD: *Misere mei; Haec dies; Ave verum corpus; Bow thine ear.* FARRANT: *Hide not thou thy face; Lord, not thou thy face; Lord for thy tender mercy's sake.* GIBBONS: *O clap your hands; Hosanna to the Son of David.* PURCELL: *Lord, how long wilt thou be angry; Thou knowest, Lord; Hear my prayer, O Lord.* STANFORD: *Beati quorum via.* arr. WOOD: *This joyful Eastertide.* HOWELLS: *Sing lullaby; A spotless rose.* WALTON: *What cheer?.* VAUGHAN WILLIAMS: *O taste and see.* BRITTEN: *Hymn to the Virgin.* POSTON: *Jesus Christ the apple tree.* HARRIS: *Faire is the Heaven.*
*** Coll. **COLCD 107;** *COLC 107* [id.].

These recordings were made in 1982 and originally issued on a pair of Word LPs. The digital remastering on to a single compact disc is entirely successful; the quality is first class and the choral sound very much in the demonstration class. It was made in the Lady Chapel of Ely Cathedral, and the ambience adds beauty to the sound without in any way impairing clarity of focus. The music ranges from examples of the Roman Catholic Rite as set by Tallis, Byrd and Robert Parsons (with a touch of almost Latin eloquence in the presentation), through widely varied Reformation music, to the Restoration, represented by three Purcell anthems, and on to the Anglican revival and the twentieth century. The Reformation group is particularly successful, with the opening Tallis and closing Gibbons works rich in polyphony and Byrd's *Bow thine ear* wonderfully serene. Of the modern items, the Howells pieces are quite lovely and Walton's *What cheer?*, with its engaging imitation, is attractively genial. The Britten and Poston items, both well known, are hardly less engaging; and the concert ends with the ambitious title-number, William Harris's *Faire is the Heaven*, sung with great feeling and considerable power. Indeed, throughout, the Cambridge Singers under Rutter show a natural response to the many changing moods, yet establish a continuing Anglican tradition throughout the programme. There is no more successful survey of English church music in the current catalogue and certainly not one presented with more conviction; at 69′ the value is obvious.

Carreras, José (tenor)

Neapolitan songs (with ECO, Muller): DENZA: *Funiculi, funicula; I'te vurria vasà.* CARDILLO: *Core 'ngrato.* D'ANNIBALE: *'O paese d'o sole.* FALVO: *Dicitencello vuie.* LAMA: *Silenzio cantatore.* MARIO: *Santa Lucia luntana.* DI CURTIS: *Tu, ca nun chiagne! Torna a Surriento.* DI CAPUA: *'O sole mio.* BOVIO/TAGLIAFERRI: *Passione.* CIOFFI: *'Na sera 'e maggio.* CANNIO: *'O surdato 'nnamurato.*
(*) Ph. Dig. **400 015-2 [id.].

José Carreras produces refined tone here. The performances have plenty of lyrical fervour and are entirely lacking in vulgarity. The opening *Funiculi, funicula* is attractively lilting, but elsewhere some listeners will wish for a more gutsy style. The recording is first class. The compact disc combines naturalness with added presence, yet the sound remains warmly atmospheric.

'You belong to my heart' (with ECO, Asensio): LARA: *You belong to my heart*. LEONCAVALLO: *Mattinata*. BELLINI: *Fenesta che lucive*. LECOUNA: *Siboney*. ROSSINI: *La danza*. GARDEL: *El Dia que me quieras*. BARGONI: *Concerto d'autonno*. GREVER: *Te quiero*. D'HARDELOT: *Because*. ROIG: *Quiéreme mucho*. EPOSITO: *Anema e core*. MENENDEZ: *Aquellos ojos*.
(*) Ph. Dig. **411 422–2 [id.].

Following his rivals Domingo and Pavarotti, Carreras here presents a collection of love-songs coming from European popular repertoire as distinct from the American-derived rhythm-and-blues idiom presented below. They are all done with commendable taste and attractively presented – if with only a few hints of their earthier, more robust side. The recording is bright and lively.

Spanish songs (with Martin Katz, piano): FALLA: *7 Spanish popular songs*. MOMPOU: *Combat del somni*. GINASTERA: *Canción al arbol del olivido*. GUASTAVINO: *La rosa y el sauce; Se equivicó la paloma*. OBRADORS: *Corazón, porqué pasáis; Del cabelle mas sutil*. TURINA: *Poema en forma de cançiones, Op. 19*.
*** Ph. Dig. **411 478-2** [id.].

José Carreras's collection of Spanish songs provides an attractive slant on repertory both rare and well known. It is interesting to have the Falla *Spanish popular songs* sung by a male voice, predictably with new insights, and there is much lively and imaginative singing in the rest too, with the voice recorded in close-up.

'Love is' (with Orchestra, Farnon): BRODSZKY: *Because you're mine*. HUPFELD: *As time goes by*. FAIN: *Love is a many-splendoured thing*. HAMLISCH: *The way we were*. BERNSTEIN: *West Side story: Tonight*. GROSS: *Tenderly*. STEINER: *My own true love*. MANDEL: *The sandpiper*. LLOYD WEBBER: *Cats: Memory*. LEGRAND: *The summer knows*. DARION: *Man of La Mancha: The impossible dream*. FRANÇOIS: *My way*.
(*) Ph. Dig. **412 270-2 [id.].

The potency of such a splendid tenor voice unleashed in standards like *The impossible dream* and *My way* is undeniable, yet José Carreras is most impressive of all in the ballads, bringing considerable nostalgia to *The way we were*. The very opening number is given a feeling of Hollywood kitsch by his slight accent, yet lyrics are admirably clear throughout, and *Tonight* from *West Side story* projects splendidly. Robert Farnon's accompaniments are stylishly made and the recording is first class.

Caruso, Enrico (tenor)

'Opera arias and songs': Arias from: VERDI: *Rigoletto; Aïda*. MASSENET: *Manon*. DONIZETTI: *L'Elisir d'amore*. BOITO: *Mefistofele*. PUCCINI: *Tosca*. MASCAGNI: *Iris; Cavalleria Rusticana*. GIORDANO: *Fedora*. PONCHIELLI: *La Gioconda*. LEONCAVALLO: *I Pagliacci*. CILEA: *Adriana Lecouvreur*. BIZET: *Les pêcheurs de perles*. MEYERBEER: *Les Huguenots*. Songs.
(M) (***) EMI mono **CDH7 61046-2** [id.].

The EMI collection on the Références label brings together Caruso's earliest recordings, made in 1902 and 1904 in Milan with misty piano accompaniment. The very first were done impromptu in Caruso's hotel, and the roughness of presentation reflects that; but the voice is glorious in its youth, amazingly well caught for that period. It was that sound of these very recordings which, more than anything else, first convinced a wide public that the gramophone was more than a toy.

'21 Favourite arias': from LEONCAVALLO: *I Pagliacci.* PUCCINI: *Tosca; La Bohème.* VERDI: *Rigoletto; Aïda; La Forza del destino; Otello; Il Trovatore.* MEYERBEER: *L'Africana.* HALÉVY: *La Juive.* GIORDANO: *Andrea Chénier.* DONIZETTI: *La Favorita; L'Elisir d'amore.* BIZET: *Les Pêcheurs de perles; Carmen.* PONCHIELLI: *La Gioconda.* GOUNOD: *Faust.* FLOTOW: *Martha.* HANDEL: *Serse.*
(***) RCA **RD 85911 [RCA 5911-2-RC]**.

Taken from RCA's earlier Caruso reissue series using the digital Soundstream system (which sought to eliminate the unnatural resonances of the acoustic recording horn, well before the age of general digital recording), these transfers are far preferable to those of the same company's Bjoerling selection, even though the recordings are much earlier. The selection, unlike EMI's Références disc of Caruso, ranges widely over the great tenor's career, with some fine examples of his work in the French repertory as well as in popular Italian items. An outstanding disc, with the voice remarkably fresh; few technical apologies need to be made here.

Chaliapin, Feodor (bass)

Russian opera arias: MUSSORGSKY: *Boris Godunov: Coronation scene; Clock scene; Farewell and Death of Boris.* GLINKA: *Life for the Tsar: They guess the truth. Ruslan and Ludmilla: Farlaf's Rondo; Field O field.* DARGOMINSKY: *Russalka: You young girls are all alike; Mad scene and death of the miller.* RUBINSTEIN: *The Demon; Do not weep, child.* BORODIN: *Prince Igor: Khan Konchak's aria.* RIMSKY-KORSAKOV: *Sadko: Song of the Viking guest.* RACHMANINOV: *Aleko: The moon is high.*
(M) ❀ (***) EMI mono **CDH7 61009-2** [id.].

Not only the glory of the voice, amazingly rich and consistent as recorded here between 1908 (aged 35) and 1931, but also the electrifying personality is vividly caught in this superb Références CD. The range of expression is astonishing. If posterity tends to think of this megastar among basses in the role of Mussorgsky's *Boris* (represented here in versions previously unissued), he is just as memorable in such an astonishing item as *Farlaf's Rondo* from *Ruslan and Ludmilla*, with its tongue-twisting chatter made thrilling at such speed and with such power. The presence of the singer is unwaveringly vivid in model transfers, whether the original recording was acoustic or electric.

Chiara, Maria (soprano)

(with Vienna Volksoper O, Nello Santi): *'Grandi voci':* DONIZETTI: *Anna Bolena: Piangete voi . . . Al dolce guidami castel natio.* BELLINI: *I Puritani: Qui la voce sua soave . . . Vien, diletto.* VERDI: *Aïda: Qui Radames verrà . . . O patria mia.* BOITO: *Mefistofele: L'altra notte in fondo al mare.* PUCCINI: *La Bohème: Si, mi chiamano Mimi; Donde lieta usci. Suor Angelica: Senza mamma. O bimbo, tu sei morto. Manon Lescaut: In quelle trine morbide. Turandot: Signore ascolta.* MASCAGNI: *Lodoletta: Ah! il suo nome . . . Flammen perdonami.*
(M) ❀ *** Decca *417 454-4* [id.].

Few début recitals can match this wonderfully satisfying anthology. In many ways Maria Chiara's voice recalls the rich sweetness of the youthful Tebaldi, but here the artistic personality is already fuller than Tebaldi's first disc, the sense of line and control of phrase pointing the way to early maturity. In the whole catalogue of soprano recitals it is difficult to think of many issues which so consistently bring the listener to catch his breath at a magical turn of phrase, or such freedom and bloom on the voice itself. The limpid flexibility is immediately apparent in the opening Donizetti arias: the floating quality of the line, the exquisitely free pianissimo; but these qualities are matched by the marvellous legato phrasing in *O patria mia* and the frisson created by the sudden darkening of tone at the cadence of the excerpt from *Mefistofele*. Miss Chiara is the Mimi of one's dreams: here is singing of great poignancy: and indeed her voice is the perfect instrument for Puccini. But the highlight of side two is the ravishing performance of the aria from *Lodoletta*. What a voice, and what spontaneity of style! The recording throughout is Decca's best: this is a tape not to be missed.

Christ Church Cathedral Choir, Oxford, Francis Grier

'O, for the wings of a dove': MENDELSSOHN: *Hear my prayer*. S. WESLEY: *In exitu Israel*. STANFORD: *For lo I raise up, Op. 145; Beati quorum via integra est, Op. 38; Evening service in A, Op. 12*. MOZART: *Ave verum corpus, K.618*. WOOD: *Hail gladdening light*. BACH: *Cantata No. 147: Jesu, joy of man's desiring*.
(M) **(*) ASV **CDQS 6019**; *ZCQS 6019* [id.].

This is a record centring on English music, but adding some more familiar items. (Mozart, Bach and Mendelssohn) to tempt a wider audience. The recording is distanced but effective and the singing expressively strong, notably so in the music by Stanford and Wesley. The analogue recording is effectively remastered.

Domingo, Placido (tenor)

Operatic recital (1970–80 recordings): VERDI: *Aïda: Se quel guerrier ... Celeste Aïda. Giovanna d'Arco: Sotto una quercia ... Pondo è letal, martiro. Un Ballo in maschera: Forse la soglia ... Ma se m'è forza perderti. Don Carlos; Fontainebleau! ... Io la vidi, al suo sorriso; Ascolta! ... Dio che nell'alma infondere*. GOUNOD: *Faust: Quel trouble inconnu ... Salut! Demeure chaste et pure; Il se fait tard*. BOITO: *Mefistofele: Dai campi, dai prati*. PUCCINI: *Manon Lescaut: Donna non vidi mai! Ah, Manon, mi tradisce. Tosca: Dammi i colori ... Recondita armonia; È lucevan le stelle; Ah! Franchigia a Floria Tosca ... O dolci mani ... Amaro*.
*** HMV Dig. **CDC7 47257-2** [id.].

Compiled from Domingo's contributions to EMI opera sets in the 1970s, this CD includes some 71 minutes of music. The remastering brings the advantage of negligible background noise, but otherwise there is no great gain in presence; however, the sound is admirably clear and well balanced. If Domingo has recorded such items as the *Manon Lescaut* excerpt more perceptively, and if his singing of *Faust* is less stylish here than it usually is in French music, the range of achievement is formidable and the beauties great. The Puccini arias sound especially real, combining a fresh clarity with a pleasing atmosphere.

'Vienna, city of my dreams' (with Amb. S., ECO, Rudel): *Arias* from: LEHÁR:*Paganini; Merry Widow; Land of smiles*. ZELLER: *Vogelhändler*. KÁLMÁN: *Gräfin Mariza*. FALL: *Rose von Stambul: Der fidele Bauer*. O. STRAUSS: *Walzerträume*. J. STRAUSS: *Nacht in Venedig*. SIECZYNSKI: *Wien, du Stadt*.
*** HMV Dig. **CDC7 47398-2** [id.]; *EL 270408-4*.

Having such a golden tenor sound in Viennese operetta makes a winning combination, and Domingo, always the stylist, rebuts the idea that only a German tenor can be really idiomatic. A delightful selection including one or two rarities, very well recorded. There is a good tape, full and clear, and this is attractive music for the car.

'Ave Maria' (with Vienna Boys' Choir, VSO, Froschauer): HERBECK: *Pueri concinite.* TRAD.: *Adeste fidelis.* FRANCK: *Panis angelicus.* SCHUBERT: *Ave Maria.* KIENZL: *Der Evangelimann: Selig sind, die Verfolgung leiden.* HANDEL: *Xerxes: Ombra mai fù.* EYBLER: *Omnes de Saba venient.* BACH–GOUNOD: *Ave Maria.* FAURÉ: *Crucifix.* BIZET: *Agnus Dei.* LUTHER: *A mighty fortress is our God* (*Ein feste Burg*).
*** RCA **RD 70760 [RCD1 3835]**.

This collection dates from 1979 and can be recommended unreservedly. Domingo is in freshest voice and these famous religious 'pops' are sung with golden tone and a simple eloquence that is most engaging. Nothing sounds routine and the Vienna Boys make a considerable contribution, not only by providing a treble soloist to share Schubert's *Ave Maria* but in the dialogue of the excerpt from Kienzl's *Evangelimann* (an attractive novelty and a highlight of the programme). In the closing chorale (*Ein feste Burg*) the Chorus Viennensis join the group to excellent effect. Attractively atmospheric recording, with Domingo's voice given fine presence and bloom.

'Bravissimo, Domingo': VERDI: *Il Trovatore: Di quella pira. Un Ballo in maschera: Teco io sto* (with Leontyne Price). *Rigoletto: La donna è mobile. Otello: Ah! Mille vite; Si, pel ciel marmoreo giuro! Don Carlos: Dio, che nell'alma infondere* (both with Sherrill Milnes). *Aïda: Se quel guerrier io fossi . . . Celeste Aïda. La Traviata: Lunge da lei . . . De'miei bollenti spiriti.* PUCCINI: *Tosca: È lucevan le stelle. Manon Lescaut: Oh, sarò la più bella!; Tu, tu, amore tu?* (with Leontyne Price). *Turandot: Non piangere Liù.* LEONCAVALLO: *Pagliacci: Recitar! Mente preso . . . Vesti la giubba.* CILEA: *Adriana Lecouvreur: L'anima ho stanco.* GOUNOD: *Roméo et Juliette: L'amour! L'amour! Ah! Lève-toi, soleil. Faust: Quel trouble inconnu; Salut! Demeure chaste et pure.* GIORDANO: *Andrea Chènier: Un di all'azzurro spazio.* MASCAGNI: *Cavalleria Rusticana: Mamma; mamma! Quel vino è generoso.* BIZET: *Carmen: Flower song.*
*** RCA **RD 87020**.

This selection of recordings ranges wide over Domingo's recording career. The opening items come from complete sets and *Di quella pira* immediately establishes the ringing vocal authority. The excerpts from *Cav.* and *Pag.* are equally memorable, as are the duets with Sherrill Milnes. With over 72 minutes offered, this is generous enough; although the remastered recordings sometimes show their age in the orchestra, the voice always remains fresh.

'Bravissimo Domingo!', Volume 2: VERDI: *Rigoletto: Questa o quella; Ella mi fu rapita!; Parmi veder le lagrime. I vespri siciliani: Giorno di pianto, di fier dolore. Il Trovatore: Ah, sì ben mio. Luisa Miller: Oh! fede negar potessi; Quando le sere al placido. La forma del destino: Oh, te che in agno agli angeli.* PUCCINI: *Tosca: Dammi i colori; Recondita armonia. La Bohème: Che gelida manina.* BELLINI: *Norma: Meco all'altar de Venere* (with Amb. Op. Ch.). MASCAGNI: *Brindisi; Viva il vina spumeggiante* (with John Alldis Ch.). WAGNER: *Lohengrin: In fernem Land.* MASSENET: *Werther: Pourquoi me réveiller?.* DONIZETTI: *L'Elisir d'amore: Una furtiva lagrima.* TCHAIKOVSKY: *Eugene Onegin: Lensky's aria.* FLOTOW: *Martha: M'apparì tutt'amor.* GIORDANO: *Andrea Chénier: Come un bel dì di Maggio.*
*** RCA **RD 86211 [RCA-6211-2-RC]**.

Opening stylishly with *Questa o quella*, and always establishing his sense of Verdian line, this second RCA collection is if anything even more attractive than the first. There is not a single below-par performance, and Domingo seems as at home in Tchaikovsky's and Wagner's lyricism as he is in the Italian repertoire. *Che gelida manina* (after an engaging little gasp from Mimi) is noble as well as eloquent, and the Donizetti and Flotow arias show the warm timbre of this remarkably consistent artist. Excellent remastering throughout the 72′ of music offered.

'Great love scenes' (with Renata Scotto, Kiri Te Kanawa, Ileana Cotrubas): PUCCINI: *Madama Butterfly: Love Duet. La rondine: Tu madre!* CILEA: *Adriana Lecouvreur: La dolcissima effigie.* MASSENET: *Manon: Toi!* GOUNOD: *Roméo et Juliette: Va, je t'ai pardonné.* CHARPENTIER: *Louise: Vois la ville qui s'eclaire.*
*** CBS **MK 39030** [id.].

This compilation from various CBS opera sets brings an attractively varied group of love duets, with Domingo matched against three splendid heroines. Scotto is the principal partner, better as Adriana than as Butterfly, Juliette or Manon, but still warmly individual, responding to the glory of Domingo's singing which is unfailingly beautiful and warmly committed. The wonder is that his exceptional consistency never falls into routine; these are all performances to have one wanting to go back to the complete operas. Good recording.

'Gala opera concert' (with LAPO, Giulini): DONIZETTI: *L'Elisir d'amore: Una furtiva lagrima. Lucia di Lammermoor: Tombe degl'avi miei . . . Fra poco.* VERDI: *Ernani: Mercé, diletti amici . . . Come rugiada; Dell'esilio nel dolore . . . O tu che l'alma adora. Il Trovatore: Ah si, ben mio; Di quella pira. Aïda: Se quel guerrier io fossi . . . Celeste Aïda.* HALÉVY: *La Juive: Rachel, quand du Seigneur.* MEYERBEER: *L'Africaine: Pays merveilleux . . . O Paradis.* BIZET: *Les Pêcheurs de perles: Je crois entendre encore. Carmen: La fleur que tu m'avais jetée* (with R. Wagner Chorale).
*** DG Dig. **400 030-2** [id.].

Recorded in 1980 in connection with a gala in San Francisco, this is as noble and resplendent a tenor recital as you will find. Domingo improves in detail even on the fine versions of some of these arias he had recorded earlier, and the finesse of the whole gains greatly from the sensitive direction of Giulini, though the orchestra is a little backward. Otherwise excellent recording, with tingling digital brass in the *Aïda* excerpt; on the compact disc the honeyed beauty of the voice is given the greatest immediacy. The orchestra too gains resonance in the bass and this added weight improves the balance.

'The best of Domingo': VERDI: *Aïda: Se quel guerrier . . . Celeste Aïda. Rigoletto: La donna è mobile. Luisa Miller: Oh! fede negar . . . Quando le sere. Un Ballo in maschera: Forse la soglia . . . Ma se m'è forza perderti; Di tu se fedele. La Traviata: Lunge de lai . . . De miei bollenti spiriti.* BIZET: *Carmen: Flower song.* FLOTOW: *Martha: Ach so fromm.* DONIZETTI: *L'Elisir d'amore: Una furtiva lagrima.* OFFENBACH: *Contes d'Hoffmann: Legend of Kleinzach.*
*** DG **415 366-2** [id.].

A popular recital showing Domingo in consistent form, the voice and style vibrant and telling, as the opening *Celeste Aïda* readily shows, followed by an agreeably relaxed *La donna è mobile*. In the lyric arias, the *Flower song* and the excerpts from *Martha* and *L'Elisir d'amore* there is not the honeyed sweetness of a Gigli, but in the closing *Hoffmann* scena the sheer style of the singing gives special pleasure. The sound is vivid throughout and the CD brings the usual enhancement, though marginally.

Arias from: VERDI: *Rigoletto; Aïda; Il Trovatore; La Traviata; Ernani; Macbeth.* DONIZETTI: *L'Elisir d'amore; Lucia di Lammermoor.* BIZET: *Carmen; Les Pêcheurs de perles.* MEYERBEER: *L'Africaine.* PUCCINI: *La Fanciulla del West.* LEHÁR: *Land des Lächelns.* Songs: LEON-

CAVALLO: *Mattinata.* LARA: *Granada.* CURTIS: *Nonti scorda.* GREVER: *Mucho.* CARDILLO: *Catari, catari.*
(B) *** DG Walkman *419 091-4* [id.].

A self-recommending Walkman tape offering nearly an hour and a half of Domingo on excellent operatic form. The programme includes obvious favourites but some less-expected items too, and the songs are welcome in showing the great tenor in lighter mood. A bargain, very useful for the car.

Early Music Consort of London, Munrow

'Music of the Gothic era': Notre Dame period: LEONIN: *Organum Viderunt omnes.* PEROTIN: *Organum Viderunt omnes.* Ars Antiqua: *Motets from the Bamberg and Montpellier Codices* by Petrus de Cruce, Adam de la Halle and Anon. Ars Nova: *Motets from the Roman de Fauvel. Chantilly/Ivrea Codices* by Machaut: De Vitry.
*** DG **415 292-2.**

This issue draws on the fine three-LP set, *'Music of the Gothic Era'*, made by the late lamented David Munrow just before his death in 1976. It offers two items from the first LP, one each by Leonin and Perotin, and gives us more from the other two, from the so-called *Ars antiqua* (1250–1320) and includes two motets of Adam de la Halle, and the *Ars nova* (1320–80), representing such figures as Philippe de Vitry and Machaut. David Munrow had exceptional powers both as a scholar-performer and as a communicator, and it is good that his work is remembered on compact disc. The performances are wonderfully alive and vital, and the digital remastering as expert as one would expect. A strong recommendation.

Estes, Simon (bass-baritone)

Spirituals (with Howard Roberts Chorale, Orchestra, Roberts): *Ride on, King Jesus; Swing low, sweet chariot; Ezekiel saw thy wheel; City called Heaven; Plenty good room; Let us break bread together; Go down, Moses; No hiding place; Nobody knows the trouble I've seen; Every time I feel the spirit; Steal away to Jesus; Witness; Sometimes I feel like a motherless child; Standin' in the need of prayer; He's got the whole world in His hands.*
(*) Ph. Dig. **412 631-2.

With his heroic baritone, Estes makes this an outstanding recital of spirituals, tastefully done, if with the accompaniment overblown in some items. First-rate sounds. Some listeners may feel that the music, with the chorus consistently acting as a ripieno to the solo voice, is over-arranged.

Ferrier, Kathleen (contralto)

Lieder, arias and songs: MAHLER: *Kindertotenlieder* (with VPO, Walter). GLUCK: *Orfeo ed Euridice:* excerpts including *Che faro.* PURCELL: *Ode for Queen Mary: Sound the trumpet. Indian Queen: Let us not wander* (with I. Baillie). HANDEL: *Ottone: Spring is coming; Come to me.* GREEN: *O praise the Lord; I will lay me down in peace.* MENDELSSOHN: *I would that my love* (with I. Baillie, G. Moore).
(M) (***) EMI mono **CDH7 61003-2.**

It was especially tragic that Kathleen Ferrier made so few recordings in which the technical quality matched her magical artistry. This disc includes many of her EMI mono records, which generally sound much better than the Decca repertoire listed below. The Gluck *Orfeo* excerpts (deriving from a broadcast) have undoubtedly been enhanced and the 1949 *Kindertotenlieder* comes over very well, too. Particularly worth having are the duets with Isobel Baillie, as these artists obviously worked especially well together. Generally, the new transfers are vivid and show a considerable enhancement of their previous LP incarnations.

'Blow the wind southerly' (with Phyllis Spurr, piano): arr. WHITTAKER: *Ma bonny lad; The Keel Row; Blow the wind southerly*. arr. HUGHES: *I have a bonnet trimmed with blue; I will walk with my love; The stuttering lovers; Down by the Sally gardens; The lover's curse*. arr. SHARPE: *My boy Willie*. HUGHES/GRAY: *I know where I'm going*. arr. JACOBSON: *Ca' the yowes*. arr. BRITTEN: *O Waly Waly*. arr. ROBERTON: *The fidgety bairn*. arr. WARLOCK: *Willow, Willow*. QUILTER: *Now sleeps the crimson petal; Fair house of joy; To daisies; Over the mountains*. arr. QUILTER: *Ye banks and braes; Drink to me only*. arr. GREW: *Have you seen but a white lillie grow?*.
(***) Decca mono **417 192-2** [id.].

This is Ferrier at her most magical. Apart from the famous *Blow the wind southerly*, songs like *I will walk with my love* show her artistic radiance to the full, and throughout she makes the words tell wonderfully. Her consistent freshness and warmth give enormous pleasure and, if the sound itself is variable – the CD tending to emphasize the faults more than the original LP and tape – the voice comes over very realistically . . . and what a voice!

Ferrier, Kathleen (contralto), Bruno Walter (piano)

Edinburgh Festival recital, 1949: SCHUBERT: *Die junge Nonne. Rosamunde: Romance. Du liebst mich nicht: Der Tod und das Mädchen; Suleika; Du bist die Ruh'*. BRAHMS: *Immer leiser wird mein Schlummer; Der Tod das ist die kuhle Nacht; Botschaft; Von ewiger Liebe*. SCHUMANN: *Frauenliebe und Leben, Op. 42*.
(M) (***) Decca mono **414 611-2** [id.].

Though the mono recording – taken from a BBC tape of 1949 – leaves much to be desired, with the piano sound often hazy, this historic issue gives a wonderful idea of the intensity of a Ferrier recital. Her account here of *Frauenliebe* is freer and even more compelling than the performance she recorded earlier. Walter's accompaniments may not be flawless, but they are comparably inspirational. The recital is introduced by a brief talk on Walter and the Edinburgh Festival given by Ferrier. The CD transfer does not seek to 'enhance' the sound, but most of the background has been cleaned up. There are moments when the vocal focus slips – and this is not exactly hi-fi, even in mono terms, but the ear adjusts readily.

'French Operetta'

OFFENBACH: Overtures: *Orpheus in the Underworld; La Belle Hélène* (SRO, Ansermet). *La Grande-Duchesse de Gérolstein: Dites-moi qu'on l'a remarqué; Vous aimez le danger . . . Ah! qui j'aime les Militaires! Robinson Crusoë: Conduisez-moi vers celui que j'adore*. MASSÉ: *Les noces de Jeannette: Au bord du chemin qui passe à ma porte*. LECOCQ: *Le Cœur et la main: Un soir Pérez le capitaine* (Joan Sutherland). OFFENBACH: *Belle Hélène: Dis-moi, Vénus. La Périchole: O mon cher amant; Ah! Quel diner*. MESSAGER: *L'Amour masqué: J'ai deux amants*. HAHN: *Ciboulette:*

Moi, je m'appelle Ciboulette; Y'a des arbres . . . C'est sa banlieue. CHRISTINE: *Phi-Phi: Ah! Cher monsieur, excusez-moi* (Régine Crespin).
(M) *** Decca *417 337-4.*

Apart from the overtures, which are not really an asset, this is superb entertainment, with Joan Sutherland and Régine Crespin both in scintillating form and the programme full of fascinating novelties which do not disappoint. A tape to be snapped up quickly before it disappears.

Gigli, Beniamino (tenor)

Opera arias from: GOUNOD: *Faust.* BIZET: *Carmen; Les Pêcheurs de perles.* MASSENET: *Manon.* HANDEL: *Serse.* DONIZETTI: *Lucia di Lammermoor; L'Elisir d'amore.* VERDI: *Rigoletto; Aïda.* LEONCAVALLO: *I Pagliacci.* MASCAGNI: *Cavalleria Rusticana.* PUCCINI: *La Bohème; Tosca.* GIORDANO: *Andrea Chénier.* PIETRI: *Maristella.*
❀ (***) EMI mono **CDH7 61051-2** [id.].

No Italian tenor has sung with more honeyed beauty than Beniamino Gigli. His status in the inter-war period as a singing superstar at a time when the media were less keenly organized is vividly reflected in this Références collection of eighteen items, the cream of his recordings made between 1927 and 1937. It is specially welcome to have two historic ensemble recordings, made in New York in 1927 and originally coupled on a short-playing 78 r.p.m. disc – the *Quartet* from *Rigoletto* and the *Sextet* from *Lucia di Lammermoor.* In an astonishing line-up Gigli is joined by Galli-Curci, Pinza, De Luca and Louise Homer. Excellent transfers.

Gothic Voices, Christopher Page

'The Guardian of Zephirus' (*Courtly songs of the 15th century*, with Imogen Barford, medieval harp): DUFAY: *J'atendray tant qu'il vous playra; Adieu ces bons vins de Lannoys; mon cuer me fait tous dis penser.* BRIQUET: *Ma seul amour et ma belle maistresse.* DE CASERTA: *Amour ma' le cuer mis.* LANDINI: *Nessun ponga speranza; Giunta vaga bilta.* REYNEAU: *Va t'en mon cuer, avent mes yeux.* MATHEUS DE SACTO JOHANNE: *Fortune, faulce, parverse.* DE INSULA: *Amours n'ont cure le tristesse.* BROLLO: *Qui le sien vuelt bien maintenir.* ANON: *N'a pas long temps que trouvay Zephirus; Je la remire, la belle.*
*** Hyp. **CDA 66144**; *KA 66144* [id.].

Most of this repertoire is unfamiliar, with Dufay the only famous name, but everything here is of interest and the listener inexperienced in medieval music will be surprised at the strength of its character. The performances are naturally eloquent and, although the range of colour is limited compared with later writing, it still has immediacy of appeal, especially if taken in short bursts. The recording balance is faultless and the sound first rate, with a splendid matching cassette. With complete security of intonation and a chamber-music vocal blend, the presentation is wholly admirable. There is full back-up documentation.

Gruberova, Edita (soprano)

(see also Orchestral Concerts under Marsalis, Wynton)

Italian and French opera arias (with Munich R.O, Kuhn): DELIBES: *Lakmé: Bell song.* MEYERBEER: *Les Huguenots: Nobles seigneurs, salut!* GOUNOD: *Roméo et Juliette: Waltz song.*

THOMAS: *Hamlet: Mad scene.* DONIZETTI: *Lucia di Lammermoor: Mad scene.* ROSSINI: *Semiramide: Bel raggio lusinghier. Il barbiere di Siviglia: Una voce poco fa.*
*** HMV Dig. **CDC7 47047-2** [id.].

Gruberova, for long type-cast in the roles of Queen of the Night and Zerbinetta, here formidably extends her range of repertory in a dazzling display of coloratura, impressive not only in the Italian repertory but in the French too, notably the *Hamlet* mad scene. The agility is astonishing, but the tone as recorded often hardens on top. CD provides extra fullness and clarity.

Hendricks, Barbara (soprano), Dmitri Alexeev (piano)

Spirituals: *Deep river; Ev'ry time I feel the spirit; Fix me, Jesus; Git on boa'd little child'n; His name is so sweet; Hold on!; Joshua fit de battle of Jericho; Nobody knows de trouble I've seen; Oh what a beautiful city!; Plenty good room; Roun' about de mountain; Sometimes I feel like a motherless child; Swing low, sweet chariot; Talk about a child that do love Jesus; Were you there?; When I lay my burden down.*
*** HMV Dig. **CDC7 47026-2** [id.].

So often spirituals can be made to seem too ingenuous, their deep reserve of feeling degraded into sentimentality. Not so here. Barbara Hendricks' vibrant identification with the words is thrilling, the jazz inflexions adding natural sophistication, yet not robbing the music of its directness of communication. Her lyrical singing is radiant, operatic in its eloquence of line, yet retaining the ecstasy of spirit, while the extrovert numbers – *Joshua fit de battle of Jericho* a superb example – are full of joy in their gutsy exuberance. Dmitri Alexeev accompanies superbly and the very well-balanced recording has remarkable presence on disc and tape alike. A rare example of a record that feels like a 'live' experience. *Roun' about de mountain* is unforgettable in its impact, although on CD the forward projection of the voice almost overdoes the sense of presence.

Hilliard Ensemble, Paul Hillier

'The Singing Club': RAVENSCROFT: *A round of three country dances; There were three ravens.* HILTON: *Call George again, boys.* W. LAWES: *Drink to the knight of the moonshine bright; She weepeth sore in the night; Dainty, fine aniseed water; Gather ye rosebuds.* WILSON: *Where the bee sucks.* PURCELL: *'Tis woman makes us love; Sir Walter enjoying his damsel.* BATTISHILL: *Epitaph.* ARNE: *The singing club; To soften care; Elegy on the death of Mr Shenstone; Sigh no more, ladies.* BISHOP: *Foresters sound the cheerful horn.* J. S. SMITH: *The Ancreontick song.* PEARSALL: *There is a paradise on earth; O who will o'er the downs so free.* BARNBY: *Sweet and low.*
(*) HM Dig **HMC 901153 [id.].

This collection of part-songs, glees, catches and rounds embraces a period of English song stretching from the beginning of the seventeenth century to the end of the nineteenth. The Hilliard Ensemble are particularly at home in the earlier songs: their blending and intonation cannot be faulted and they show a nice feeling for the gentle melancholy of the period. They manage the more robust glees with panache, notably the *Wedding night song* of Inigo Jones, whose lyrics make a ribald pun on the writer's name, and Purcell's risqué narrative based on a true story of Sir Walter Raleigh's first conquest in the woods. Words are admirably clear throughout and the recording, made in London's Henry Wood Hall, gives a very real impression of the group standing back just behind the speakers. In some of the later nineteenth-century items the style, though not insensitive, is just a little pale.

'Summer is icumen in': ST GODRIC: *Sainte Marie viergene, Crist and Sainte Marie; Saint Nicholas*. Medieval anonymous English songs, including: *Summer is icumen in; Fuweles in the Frifth; Edi be thu; Worldes blisse; Gabriel fram heven-king; Mater ora filium; Gaude virgo mater Christi*. Motets; Mass: excerpts.
*** HM **HMC 901154** [id.].

The Hilliard Ensemble's collection, *'Sumer is icumen in'*, is an attractive issue both for the non-specialist who wants to learn about early-fourteenth-century music in England and for scholars of the period. *Sumer is icumen in* is given twice, in Latin as well as in the Early English version, as is *Campanis cum cymbalis*. Even more valuable are the motets and movements from the Mass, among the earliest transcribed polyphonic works from this country, sung here with persuasive intensity. Paul Hillier gives a helpful, highly informed commentary in the booklet, which also provides full texts. Excellent, well-balanced recording.

Hill Smith, Marilyn (soprano), Peter Morrison (baritone)

'Treasures of operetta' (with Concert O, Barry): ZIEHRER: *Der Schatzmeister; Do re mi fa sol la si*. J. STRAUSS Jnr: *Casanova: O Queen of my delight*. KÁLMÁN: *Gypsy Princess: Let me dance and let me sing*. STRAUS: *Chocolate Soldier: My hero*. TAUBER: *Old Chelsea: My heart and I*. MESSAGER: *Veronique: Trot here and there*. HERBERT: *Naughty Marietta: Tramp! tramp! tramp! tramp!* LEHAR: *The Merry Widow: Love unspoken; I'm off to Chez Maxim. Giuditta: On my lips every kiss is like wine*. ZELLER: *Der Obersteiger: Don't be cross*. MONCKTON: *The Arcadians: Charming weather*.
(*) Chan. Dig. **CHAN 8362; *LBTD 013* [id.].

One has to make an initial adjustment to a style of performance which is very English, evoking memories of the Palm Court tradition of Anne Ziegler and Webster Booth. Marilyn Hill Smith sings freshly and often very sweetly, and she is genially partnered by the warm, easy-going baritone of Peter Morrison. Moreover, the orchestral accompaniments have plenty of flexibility and lilt, and the resonantly rich recording is exactly right for the music. With almost every number a 'hit', this is very attractive of its kind. While the voices are given slightly more presence on CD, the chrome cassette too is first class and costs considerably less.

'Treasures of operetta' Vol. 2 (with Amb. S., Concert O, Barry): JACOBI: *Sybil: The Colonel of the Crimson Hussars*. POSFORD: *Balalaika: At the Balalaika*. MONCKTON: *The Quaker Girl: A bad boy and a good girl*. MILLOCKER: *Der arme Jonathan: The doleful prima-donna*. ZIEHRER: *Der Schatzmeister: O let me hold your tiny little hand. Der Fremdenfuhrer: Military life*. GERMAN: *Merrie England: The yeoman of England*. LEHÁR: *The Merry widow: Vilja. Paganini: Girls were made to love and kiss*. STOLZ/BENATSKY: *White Horse Inn: My song of love*. MESSAGER: *Monsieur Beaucaire: Lightly, lightly*. J. STRAUSS Jnr: *Casanova: Nuns' chorus*.
(*) Chan. Dig. **CHAN 8561; *LBTD 019* [id.].

If anything, this is more successful than the first collection, with many novelties among the more familiar items, and the charming duet from *The Quaker Girl* an obvious highlight. Extra support is given by the excellent Ambrosian Singers, and the presentation and recording are both of a high standard.

Hirst, Linda (mezzo-soprano)

'Songs Cathy sang': (with L. Sinf., Masson): CAGE: *Aria*. BERIO: *Folksongs; Sequenza 3.* POUSSEUR: *Phonemes for Cathy*. BERBERIAN: *Stripsody*.
** Virgin Dig. **VC 790704-2**; *VC 790704-4* [id.].

Linda Hirst's collection with the London Sinfonietta on the Virgin Classics label makes an attractive group of works directly reflecting the vibrant personality of Cathy Berberian. But not even an artist as sharp and sensitive as Linda Hirst – who, as a member of Swingles Two, studied Cathy's art from close up – can provide more than a pale echo of the original. So the delightful Berio *Folksongs* sound oddly unidiomatic; and the rendering of the weird avant-garde effects of Pousseur or Berberian herself sound a degree inhibited, though they were recorded live at the Almeida Theatre. The Berio *Folksongs*, done in the studio, brings fuller, more helpfully atmospheric sound.

Horne, Marilyn (mezzo-soprano)

French opera arias (with Monte Carlo PO, Lawrence Foster): AUBER: *Zerline: O Palerme! O Sicile*. SAINT-SAËNS: *Samson et Dalila: Mon cœur s'ouvre à ta voix*. OFFENBACH: *La Grande Duchesse de Gérolstein: Ah! que j'aime les militaires*. GOUNOD: *Sapho: O ma lyre immortelle; Héro sur la tour solitaire*. GODARD: *La Vivandière: Viens avec nous, petit*. MASSENET: *Hérodiade: Venge-moi d'une suprême offense*. DONIZETTI: *La Favorita: L'ai-je bien entendu? . . . Oh, mon Fernand*. CHERUBINI: *Médée: Ah! nos peines*.
*** Erato Dig. **ECD 88085** [id.].

With a fair proportion of rare items, Horne's French recital is highly recommendable. The voice may have lost some of the firm focus that was so impressive at the beginning of her career, but the brilliance and command are unfailing over the widest range of repertory. The classical poise of the Cherubini aria is as impressive as the zest of the Offenbach or the rich resonance of the Massenet. Excellent sound, made the more vivid on CD.

'Beautiful dreamer' (*The Great American Songbook*, with ECO, Carl Davis): FOSTER: *Jeannie with the light brown hair; Beautiful dreamer; If you've only got a moustache; Camptown Races*. COPLAND: *5 Old American Songs*. TRAD.: *Sometimes I feel like a motherless child; I've just come from the fountain; Shenandoah*, etc.
*** Decca Dig. **417 242-2**; *417 242-4* [id.].

Marilyn Horne is tangily characterful in this American repertory which draws from her a glorious range of tone, and she bridges the stylistic gaps between popular and concert repertory with supreme confidence. The Copland songs are particularly delightful, and the Decca recording is outstandingly vivid.

Kanawa, Dame Kiri Te (soprano)

'Come to the fair' (with Medici Qt; Nat. PO, Gamley): EASTHOPE MARTIN: *Come to the fair*. LAMBERT: *She is far from the land*. TRAD.: *Early one morning; The last rose of summer; Island spinning song; The ash grove; The Keel Row; Comin' thro' the rye; Annie Laurie; O can ye sew cushions; The Sally gardens; Greensleeves; The gentle maiden; I have a bonnet trimmed with blue; Danny Boy*.
*** HMV Dig. **CDC7 47080-2** [id.].

Very much following in the Kathleen Ferrier tradition, Dame Kiri Te Kanawa sings this repertoire with infectious charm. She can be exhilaratingly robust, as in the title piece and *The Keel Row*, yet at the next moment provide a ravishing lyricism, as in *The last rose of summer* or *The Sally gardens*. The orchestral accompaniments are decorative but simple (*Greensleeves*, a highlight, is especially felicitous). The recording has splendid presence. A captivating recital in every way.

'Portrait': PUCCINI: *Tosca: Vissi d'arte. Gianni Schicchi: O mio babbino caro.* VERDI: *La Traviata: È strano . . . Ah, fors'è lui.* HUMPERDINCK: *Hänsel und Gretel: Der kleine Sandmann.* MOZART: *Don Giovanni: Ah, fuggi il traditor; Mi tradi.* R. STRAUSS: *Morgen; Ruhe, meine Seele.* SCHUBERT: *Gretchen am Spinnrade.* SCHUMANN: *Du bist wie eine Blume.* FAURÉ: *Après un rêve.* WALTON: *Façade: Old Sir Faulk; Daphne; Through gilded trellises.*
(*) CBS **MK 39208 [id.].

CBS's sampler portrait of Dame Kiri may not be as representative of her usual repertory as the rival Decca disc, but the rarities – such as the Walton songs – are just as winning as the more predictable items. Recordings not all of the most vivid, but made reasonably compatible.

'Ave Maria' (with St Paul's Cathedral Choir, ECO, Rose): GOUNOD: *Messe solennelle à Sainte Cécile: Sanctus. O divine Redeemer.* MOZART: *Ave verum, K. 618; Solemn Vespers: Laudate Dominum.* FRANCK: *Panis angelicus.* HANDEL: *Solomon: Let the bright Seraphim; Let their celestial concert.* MENDELSSOHN: *On wings of song.* BACH: *Jesu, joy of man's desiring.* SCHUBERT: *Ave Maria.*
(*) Ph. Dig. **412 629-2; *412 629-4* [id.].

Countless music-lovers who heard Dame Kiri sing *Let the bright Seraphim* at the wedding of the Prince and Princess of Wales were kept waiting for this record to appear, and they will not be disappointed, for the trumpet playing, too, is suitably resplendent. This comes at the end, and the rest of the programme lacks something in variety, although the voice always sounds beautiful and the naturally expressive singing gives much pleasure. The chorus, backwardly balanced, might have been more clearly focused, however. Obviously the recording producer intended to sustain a devotional atmosphere throughout, and in this he has succeeded. The CD hardly improves the definition. There is an excellent cassette.

'Blue skies' (with Nelson Riddle and his orchestra): BERLIN: *Blue skies.* WEILL: *Speak low.* RODGERS: *It might as well be spring; I didn't know what time it was.* VAN HEUSEN: *Here's that rainy day.* KERN: *Yesterdays; The folk who live on the hill.* PORTER: *So in love; True love.* LEWIS: *How high the moon.* WRUBEL: *Gone with the wind.* ROMBERG: *When I grow too old to dream.*
*(*) Decca Dig. **414 666-2** [id.].

This is disappointing – more a disc for those who like crossover records than for the general devotee of Dame Kiri. Nelson Riddle provides characteristic arrangements of the numbers, but there is a curious lack of vitality. The tempi lack sufficient variety and what is intended to sound sultry too often becomes soporific; *True love*, for instance, is much too languorous. There is plenty of atmosphere (helped by the background silence of the CD) but a curiously inert feeling overall.

'Kiri – A Portrait': CANTALOUBE: *Chants d'Auvergne: Baïlèro.* GAY: *Beggar's opera: Virgins are like the fair flow'r; Cease your funning.* HANDEL: *Messiah: Rejoice greatly; I know that my Redeemer liveth.* BRAHMS: *German Requiem: Ihr habt nun Traurigkeit.* MOZART: *Concert aria: Vado, ma dove? oh Dei!, K. 583. Le nozze di Figaro: Dove sono.* BIZET: *Carmen: Je dis*

que rien ne m'épouvante. PUCCINI: *Tosca: Vissi d'arte.* VILLA-LOBOS: *Bachianas brasileiras No. 5.*
*** Decca **417 645-2**; *417 645-4.*

Decca's portrait of Dame Kiri gathers together many of her most delectable recordings of recent years, a winning compendium of her art, whether seductive in Canteloube and Villa-Lobos, dazzling in Handel, or sparkling in *The Beggar's opera.* The recordings capture the voice at its fullest and most golden.

King's College, Cambridge, Choir, Cleobury

ALLEGRI: *Miserere mei, Deus.* FRESCOBALDI: *Messa sopra l'aria della Monica.* MARENZIO: *Magnificat.* NANINO: *Adoramus te, Christe.* UGOLINI: *Beata es Virgo Maria.*
(*) HMV **CDC7 47065-2 [id.].

An attractively planned concert of Renaissance choral music. The opening *Adoramus te, Christe* is movingly serene, and both Marenzio's fine *Magnificat* and the stirring *Beata es Virgo Maria* of Ugolini (a contemporary of Allegri) make a strong impression – the latter reminding the listener of Andrea Gabrieli. The performances are generally excellent and the King's acoustic provides its usual beautiful aura. The account of Allegri's *Miserere*, although effective, lacks the ethereal memorability of the finest versions, its treble soloist, Timothy Beasley-Murray, is made to sound almost over-confident, with his upward leap commandingly extrovert. The CD gains much from the background silence, but the choral focus is mistier than one might have expected.

'O come all ye faithful' (with David Briggs, organ): *Once in Royal David's city; Up! good Christian folk; On Christmas night; Ding dong merrily on high; O little town of Bethlehem; In the bleak midwinter; The first nowell; Away in a manger; The seven joys of Mary; The infant king; God rest ye merry, gentlemen; The holly and the ivy; I saw three ships; O come all ye faithful:* GRÜBER: *Silent night.* MENDELSSOHN: *Hark! the herald angels sing.*
*** Decca Dig. **414 042-2** [id.].

King's College Choir make their digital Christmas début with a programme of tested favourites. The usual opening is varied, with *Once in Royal David's city* done not as a processional but as an interplay between the treble solo and full choir. The atmosphere overall is slightly subdued; but *Hark the herald angels* comes in a spectacular arrangement by Philip Ledger, and Stephen Cleobury's version of *Silent night* takes an original turn after the opening verse. The digital recording does not seek to clarify textures but concentrates on capturing the ambient atmosphere.

King's College, Cambridge, Choir, Ledger and Willcocks

'Christmas carols from King's College': Once in Royal David's city; O little town of Bethlehem; The first nowell; I saw three ships; Personent Hodie; Myn Lyking; A spotless rose; Away in a manger; I sing of a maiden; O come, O come Emanuel; While shepherds watched; Up! good Christian folk; In the bleak midwinter; Silent night; The holly and the ivy; It came upon a midnight clear; Three kings; On Christmas night; A child is born in Bethlehem; In dulci jubilo; O come all ye faithful; Hark! the herald angels sing.
(M) *** HMV **CDC7 47500-2** [id.]; *ED 290701-4.*

With over an hour of music and twenty-two carols included, this is formidable value. The recordings were made between 1969 and 1976 and have been digitally remastered. The sound is excellent on CD, although the tape focus is not always absolutely clean; but this is an ideal programme for cassette listening, and the King's acoustic is generally well caught in both media. The closing two carols are made particularly resplendent.

King's College, Cambridge, Choir, Philip Ledger

'Festival of lessons and carols' (1979).
*** HMV **CDC7 49620-2** [id.].

This most recent version on record of the annual King's College ceremony has the benefit of modern recording, even more atmospheric than before. Under Philip Ledger the famous choir keeps its beauty of tone and incisive attack. The opening processional, *Once in Royal David's city*, is even more effective heard against the background quiet of CD and this remains a unique blend of liturgy and music.

'Procession with carols on Advent Sunday'.
*** HMV Dig. **CDC7 49619-2** [id.].

This makes an attractive variant to the specifically Christmas-based service, though the carols themselves are not quite so memorable. Beautiful singing and richly atmospheric recording; the wide dynamic range is demonstrated equally effectively by the atmospheric opening and processional and the sumptuous closing hymn.

King's College, Cambridge, Choir, Sir David Willcocks

ALLEGRI: *Miserere* (with Roy Goodman). PALESTRINA: *Magnificat in 8 parts* (*Primi toni*); *Stabat mater*. BLOW: *Anthems: Let Thy hand be strengthened; Behold; O God our defender*. CROFT: *Burial service*. TALLIS: *Spem in alium* (40-part motet) (with Cambridge University Musical Society Chorus).
(M) *** Argo *417 160-4* [id.].

A splendid summation of Sir David Willcocks' era with the King's Choir, recording for Argo in the 1960s. The inclusion of the famous performance of Allegri's *Miserere* is especially welcome (with Roy Goodman's soaring treble solos still unsurpassed) as is Croft's *Burial service* with its evocative opening processional. The two Palestrina items show this partnership at its finest, as does the 1965 version of Tallis's glorious 40-part motet, *Spem in alium*, although here the attempt to clarify the textures in the remastering has not been entirely successful. Nevertheless, with consistently excellent chrome-tape transfers, the sound is first rate throughout the programme.

Lehman, Lotte (soprano)

Opera arias from: BEETHOVEN: *Fidelio*, WEBER: *Der Freischütz; Oberon*. NICOLAI: *Die lustigen Weiber von Windsor*. WAGNER: *Lohengrin; Tannhäuser; Tristan und Isolde*. R. STRAUSS: *Der Rosenkavalier; Ariadne auf Naxos; Arabella*. KORNGOLD: *Die tote Stadt; Das Wunder der Heliane*. J. STRAUSS, Jnr: *Die Fledermaus*. LEHÁR: *Eva*.
(M) (***) EMI mono **CDH7 610422** [id.].

Lehmann's celebrated account of the Marschallin's monologue from the classic set of *Rosenkavalier* excerpts recorded in Vienna in 1933 is an essential item here. Otherwise this collection of fourteen of her recordings, made in the days of 78s, concentrates on the Parlophone issues done in Berlin in the 1920s and early '30s. The earliest has the young George Szell accompanying her in Korngold (the only pre-electric here), but there are many other treasures. The Richard Strauss items are particularly valuable, with Arabella's *Mein Elemer* recorded within months of the opera's première in 1933. Though Isolde was not a role she would ever have considered singing on stage, the *Liebestod* here has wonderful poise and beauty, while it is good to hear her speaking voice in the 1928 recording of Lehár's *Eva*.

Lott, Felicity (soprano), Graham Johnson (piano)

Mélodies on Victor Hugo poems: GOUNOD: *Sérénade.* BIZET: *Feuilles d'album: Guitare. Adieux de l'hôtesse arabe.* LALO: *Guitare.* DELIBES: *Eclogue.* FRANCK: *S'il est un charmant gazon.* FAURÉ: *L'absent; Le papillon et la fleur; Puisqu'ici bas.* WAGNER: *L'attente.* LISZT: *O quand je dors; Comment, disaint-ils.* SAINT-SAËNS: *Soirée en mer; La fiancée du timbalier.* M. V. WHITE: *Chantez, chantez jeune inspirée.* HAHN: *Si mes vers avaient des ailes. Rêverie.*
*** HM **HMC 901138** [id.].

Felicity Lott's collection of Hugo settings relies mainly on sweet and charming songs, freshly and unsentimentally done, with Graham Johnson an ideally sympathetic accompanist. The recital is then given welcome stiffening with fine songs by Wagner and Liszt, as well as two by Saint-Saëns that have a bite worthy of Berlioz.

Melba, Dame Nellie (soprano)

Arias and songs: Arias from DONIZETTI: *Lucia di Lammermoor.* VERDI: *Rigoletto: La Traviata; Otello.* GOUNOD: *Roméo et Juliette; Faust.* PUCCINI: *La Bohème.* Songs by: TOSTI; BEMBERG. BISHOP: *Lo, hear the gentle lark; Home, sweet home.* CHAUSSON: *Le temps de lilas.* SZULC: *Clair de lune.*
(**) EMI mono **CDH7 61070-2** [id.].

Puccini disparagingly called Melba 'the Centenarian'. That was long before she retired in 1926 at the age of sixty-five and, as the excerpts here from her Covent Garden Farewell demonstrate, the voice remained astonishingly bright, firm and true. Yet equally it shows very clearly how little emotion she seems to have felt, or at least was able to convey. There is that same limitation throughout these twenty items (including the two done with piano accompaniment after her retirement). But the security of her technique and the elarity and precision of her voice are amazing in one dazzling performance after another. Excellent transfers.

Methodist Central Hall, Westminster, Choir, John Chapman

'20 Favourite hymns' (with the Epworth Choir): includes: *O for a thousand tongues to sing; Father of everlasting grace; All praise to our redeeming Lord; Jesu, lover of my soul; Come, sinners, to the gospel feast; Christ, whose glory fills the skies; Jesus, the first and last; O Thou, who comest from above; And can it be that I should gain.*
(*) Abbey Dig. **CDMVP 828 [id.].

The Methodist hymn-singing tradition is justly famous, and these hymns are sung with characteristic fervour. The presentation is straightforward and the recording first rate.

Monteverdi Choir, English Baroque Soloists, Gardiner

'Sacred choral music': D. SCARLATTI: *Stabat Mater.* CAVALLI: *Salve regina.* GESUALDO: *Ave, dulcissima Maria:* CLÉMENT: *O Maria vernana rosa.*
*** Erato Dig. **ECD 88087** [id.].

This collection is centred round Domenico Scarlatti's *Stabat Mater*, which is praised in the Composer section. The shorter works which fill out this collection are no less worth while, notably the rewarding Gesualdo motet from the *Sacrae cantiones*, whose remarkably expressive opening has few precedents in its harmonic elequence, and another Marian motet by Jacques Clément, better known as Clemens non Papa. The recording is very good indeed without being in the demonstration bracket.

New College, Oxford, Choir, Higginbottom

'Carols from New College': O come all ye faithful; The angel Gabriel; Ding dong merrily on high; The holly and the ivy; I wonder as I wander; Sussex carol; This is the truth; A Virgin most pure; Rocking carol; Once in Royal David's city; ORD: *Adam lay y-bounden;* BENNETT: *Out of your sleep.* HOWELLS: *A spotless rose; Here is the litle door.* DARKE: *In the bleak midwinter.* MATHIAS: *A babe is born; Wassail carol.* WISHART: *Alleluya, a new work is come on hand.* LEIGHTON: *Lully, lulla, thou little tiny child.* JOUBERT: *There is no rose of such virtue.*
*** CRD **CRD 3443**; *CRDC 4143* [id.].

A beautiful Christmas record, the mood essentially serene and reflective. Apart from the lovely traditional arrangements, from the Czech *Rocking carol* to the Appalachian *I wonder as I wander*, many of the highlights are more recently composed. Both the Mathias settings are memorable and spark a lively response from the choir; Howell's *Here is the little door* is matched by Wishart's *Alleluya* and Kenneth Leighton's *Lully, lulla, thou little tiny child* in memorability. In some of these and in the opening *O come all ye faithful* and the closing *Once in Royal David's city*, Howerd Moody adds weight with excellent organ accompaniments, but fifteen of the twenty-one items here are sung unaccompanied, to maximum effect. The recording acoustic seems ideal and the balance is first class. The documentation, however, consists of just a list of titles and sources – and the CD (using the unedited artwork from the LP) lists them as being divided on to side one and side two!

Norman, Jessye (soprano)

'Sacred songs' (with Amb. S., RPO, Gibson): GOUNOD: *Messe solennelle à Sainte Cécile: Sanctus. O Divine Redeemer.* FRANCK: *Panis angelicus.* ADAMS: *The Holy City.* ANON: *Amazing grace. Greensleeves. Let us break bread. I wonder.* MAGGIMSEY: *Sweet little Jesus Boy.* YON: *Gesù Bambino.*
*** Ph. Dig. **400 019-2** [id.].

Miss Norman's restraint is very telling here; she sings with great eloquence, but her simplicity and sincerity shine through repertoire that can easily sound sentimental. The Gounod *Sanctus* is especially fine, but the simpler traditional songs are also very affecting. The compact disc is very much in the demonstration class, strikingly natural and giving the soloist remarkable presence, especially when she is singing unaccompanied.

'With a song in my heart' (with Boston Pops O, Williams): RODGERS: *Falling in love with love; Spring is here; With a song in my heart.* PORTER: *In the still of the night; I love Paris; I love you.* KERN: *I'm old fashioned; The song is you; All the things you are.* ARLEN: *The sleeping bee.* GERSHWIN: *Love is here to stay; Love walked in.*
*(*) Ph. Dig. **412 625-2** [id.].

Though the big, rich voice is as glorious to hear as ever, this crossover record is a disappointment, with the singer caught between operatic and Pop styles, and the accompaniments generally too aggressive. Bright, forwardly balanced recording.

French songs (with Dalton Baldwin, piano): DUPARC: *La vie antérieure; Phidylé; Chanson triste; L'invitation au voyage.* RAVEL: *2 mélodies hébraïques.* POULENC: *Voyage à Paris; Montparnasse; La Grenouillère; Les chemins de l''amour.* SATIE: *3 mélodies; Je le veux.*
(*) Ph. **416 445-2 [id.].

Recorded in 1976, Jessye Norman's delightful collection of French songs reveals the great voice already glowing in its distinctive range of tone and expression. But at that point in her career she was still a shade inhibited in the studio; though the interpretative subtleties are many, she was later to give even deeper and more searching performances in this repertory. The analogue sound has been transferred very well.

Operatic Duets: 'Duets from famous operas'

Duets sung by: (i) Nicolai Gedda, (ii) Ernest Blanc, (iii) Jussi Bjoerling and Victoria de los Angeles, (iv) Carlo Bergonzi, (v) Maria Callas, (vi) Mirella Freni, (vii) Eberhard Waechter and Graziella Sciutti, (viii) Tito Gobbi, (ix) Gabriella Tucci, (x) Franco Corelli, (xi) Evelyn Lear and D. Ouzounov, (xii) Antonietta Stella; (i; ii) BIZET: *Les Pêcheurs de perles: Au fond du temple saint.* (iii) PUCCINI: *Madama Butterfly: Bimba dagli occhi.* (iv; v) *Tosca: O dolci mani.* (i; vi) *La Bohème: O soave fanciulla.* (vii) MOZART: *Don Giovanni: Là ci darem la mano.* (v; viii) ROSSINI: *Il barbiere di Siviglia: Dunque io son'* (ix; x) VERDI: *Il Trovatore: Miserere d'un'alma già vicina.* (xi) MUSSORGSKY: *Boris Godunov: O Tsarevich I beg you.* (x; xii) GIORDANO: *Andrea Chénier: Vicini a te.*
(B) **(*) CfP **CD-CFP 9013**; *CFP 41 4498-4.*

There are not many operas that hold their reputation in the public memory by means of a male duet, but *The pearl fishers* is one, and a sturdy performance of *Au fond du temple saint* makes a suitable centre-point of this collection of purple duos. The CD, however, opens with the genial lyricism of *Là ci darem la mano*, from the 1961 Giulini set of *Don Giovanni* with Eberhard Waechter and Graziella Sciutti singing most winningly. The star quality of the artists is noticeable through most of these extracts. Highlights include this beautifully relaxed *Là ci darem*, the short Rossini item, and the *La Bohème* duet (which seldom fails). There is also a blaze of melodrama from *Andrea Chénier*. As a programme, the effect of a series of such full-blooded passionate vocal embraces is perhaps a little wearing. But otherwise, with generally lively recording, few will be disappointed. The cassette is smoothly transferred, if without quite the range of the CD. This has been admirably remastered to make the most of the different recording sources – the vocal timbres are particularly smooth and natural, without loss of projection.

Operetta: 'Golden operetta'

'Golden operetta': J. STRAUSS, Jnr: *Die Fledermaus: Mein Herr Marquis* (Gueden); *Csardas* (Janowitz). *Eine Nacht in Venedig: Lagunen waltz* (Krenn). *Wiener Blut: Wiener Blut* (Gueden). *Der Zigeunerbaron: O habet Acht* (Lorengar). *Casanova: Nuns' chorus* (Sutherland, Ambrosian Singers). ZELLER: *Der Obersteiger: Sei nicht bös* (Gueden). LEHÁR: *Das Land des Lächelns: Dein ist mein ganzes Herz* (Bjoerling). *Die lustige Witwe: Vilja-Lied* (Sutherland); *Lippen schweigen* (Holm, Krenn). *Schön ist die Welt* (Krenn). *Der Graf von Luxemburg: Lieber Freund . . . Bist du's, Lachendes Gluck* (Holm, Krenn). *Giuditta: Du bist meine Sonne* (Kmentt). LECOCQ: *Le Cœur et la main: Bonsoir Perez le capitaine* (Sutherland). OFFENBACH: *La Périchole: Letter song*. *La Grande Duchesse de Gérolstein: J'aime les militaires* (Crespin).
(M) *** Decca *414 466-4*.

A valuable and generous anthology, not just for the obvious highlights: Joan Sutherland's *Vilja* and the delightful contributions from Hilde Gueden – notably a delicious *Sei nicht bös* – recorded in 1961 when the voice was at its freshest; but also Régine Crespin at her finest in Offenbach – the duchess reviewing her troops, and the charming *Letter song* from *La Périchole*. In their winningly nostalgic account of the *Merry Widow waltz* Renate Holm and Werner Krenn hum the melody, having sung the words, giving the impression of dancing together. The recording throughout is very good.

Pavarotti, Luciano (tenor)

'The world's favourite arias' from: LEONCAVALLO: *I Pagliacci*. FLOTOW: *Martha*. BIZET: *Carmen*. PUCCINI: *La Bohème; Tosca; Turandot*. VERDI: *Rigoletto; Aïda; Il Trovatore*. GOUNOD: *Faust*.
(*) Decca **400 053-2 [id.]; *KSXC 6649* [Lon. *OSA 5-26384*].

As one would expect from Pavarotti, there is much to enjoy in his ripe and resonant singing of these favourite arias, but it is noticeable that the finest performances are those which come from complete sets, conducted by Karajan (*Bohème*), Mehta (*Turandot*) and Bonynge (*Rigoletto*), where with character in mind Pavarotti's singing is more intense and imaginative. The rest remains very impressive, though at under 40 minutes the measure is short. The transfer to compact disc has involved digital remastering, which has resulted in slight limitation of the upper range to take out background noise. However, the vividness of the voice is enhanced in the process. The cassette is slightly more uneven in quality than the CD, most noticeably in the *Turandot* excerpt where the chorus is none too clear.

'Digital recital' (with Nat. PO, Chailly or Fabritiis): GIORDANO: *Fedora: Amor ti vieta. Andrea Chénier: Colpito qui m'avete . . . Un di all'azzuro spazio; Come un bel dì di maggio; Si, fui soldata*. BOITO: *Mefistofele: Dai campi, dai prati; Ogni mortal . . . Giunto sul passo estremo*. CILEA: *Adriana Lecouvreur: La dolcissima effigie; L'anima ho stanca*. MASCAGNI: *Iris: Apri la tua finestra!* MEYERBEER: *L'Africana: Mi batti il cor . . . O Paradiso*. MASSENET: *Werther: Pourquoi me réveiller*. PUCCINI: *La Fanciulla del West: Ch'ella mi creda. Manon Lescaut: Tra voi belle; Donna non vidi mai; Ah! non v'avvicinate! . . . No! No! pazzo son!* (with Howlett).
(*) Decca Dig. **400 083-2 [id.]; *KSXDC 7504* [Lon. *LDR 5-10020*].

This first digital recital record from Pavarotti has the voice more resplendent than ever. The passion with which he tackles Des Grieux's Act III plea from *Manon Lescaut* is devastating, and the big breast-beating numbers are all splendid, imaginative as well as heroic. But the slight pieces,

Des Grieux's *Tra voi belle* and the *Iris Serenade*, could be lighter and more charming. The compact disc gives the voice even greater projection, with its full resonance and brilliance admirably caught, but it does also make the listener more aware of the occasional lack of subtlety of the presentation. The cassette transfer is vibrant and clear, if losing a little of the CD projection.

Neapolitan songs (with Ch. and O of Teatro Comunale, Bologna, Guadagno, or Nat. PO, Chiaramello): DI CAPUA: *O sole mio; Maria, Mari.* TOSTI: *A vuchella. Marechiare.* CANNIO: *O surdato 'nnamurato.* GAMBARDELLA: *O Marenariello.* ANON.: *Fenesta vascia.* DE CURTIS: *Torna a Surriento. Tu, ca nun chiagne.* PENNINO: *Pecchè . . .* D'ANNIBALE: *O paese d'o sole.* TAGLIAFERRI: *Piscatore 'e pusilleco.* DENZA: *Funiculi, funicula.*
*** Decca **410 015-2** [id.]; *KSXC 6870* [Lon. *OSA 5-26560*].

Neapolitan songs given grand treatment in passionate Italian performances, missing some of the charm but none of the red-blooded fervour. The recording is both vivid and atmospheric. The tape transfer is well managed although there is slight loss of presence in the items with chorus. This certainly does not apply to the compact disc, where the recording is most successfully digitally remastered.

'Mamma' (Italian and Neapolitan popular songs with O and Ch., Henry Mancini): BIXIO: *Mamma; Vivere; Mia canzone al vento; Parlai, d'amore.* DE CURTIS: *Non ti scordar di me.* BUZZI-PECCIA: *Lolita:* excerpts. GASTALDON: *Musica proibita.* CESARINI: *Firenza sogna.* KRAMER: *In un palco della scala.* RIVI: *Addio, sogni di gloria!* D'ANZI: *Voglio vivere cosi.* DI LAZZARO: *Chitarra romana.* DE CRESCENZO: *Rondine al nido.* TRAD.: *Ghirlandeina.* CALIFONA: *Vieni sul mar'.* ARONA: *Campana di San Giusto.*
(*) Decca Dig. **411 959-2; *411 959-4* [id.].

Larger-than-life arrangements by Henry Mancini of popular Italian and Neapolitan songs with larger-than-life singing to match. Vulgarity is welcomed rather than skirted, which is fair enough in this music. Larger-than-life recording, too.

'O Holy night' (with Wandsworth School Boys' Ch., Nat. PO, Adler): ADAM: *Cantique noël* (*O holy night*). STRADELLA: *Pieta Signore.* FRANCK: *Panis angelicus.* MERCADANTE: *Parola quinta.* SCHUBERT: *Ave Maria.* BACH–GOUNOD: *Ave Maria.* BIZET: *Agnus Dei.* BERLIOZ: *Requiem: Sanctus.* TRAD.: *Adeste fidelis.* YON: *Jesù bambino.* SCHUBERT, arr. Melichar: *Mille cherubini in coro.*
(*) Decca **414 044-2 [id.]; *KSXC 6781.*

It is a long-established tradition for great Italian tenors to indulge in such songs as these, most of them overtly sugary in their expression of (no doubt) sincere religious fervour. Pavarotti is hardly a model of taste but, more than most of his rivals (even a tenor as intelligent as Placido Domingo), he avoids the worst pitfalls; and if this sort of recital is what you are looking for, then Pavarotti is a good choice, with his beautiful vocalizing helped by full, bright recording. Note too that one or two of these items are less hackneyed than the rest, for instance the title setting by Adam, Mercadante's *Parola quinta* and the *Sanctus* from Berlioz's *Requiem Mass.* The analogue recording has transferred well to CD; the cassette too is admirably clear and clean, the chorus naturally caught.

'Mattinata': CALDARA: *Alma del core.* CIAMPI: Tre giorni. BELLINI: Vaga luna che inargenti. DURANTE: *Danza danza, fanciulla.* GIORDANI: *Caro mio ben.* ROSSINI: *La promessa.* GLUCK: *Orfeo: Che farò.* TOSTI: *L'alba separa; Aprile; Chanson de l'adieu; L'Ultima canzone.* DONIZETTI: *Il barcaiolo.* LEONCAVALLO: *Mattinata.* BEETHOVEN: *In questo tomba.*
(*) Decca **414 454-2 [id.]; *KSXC 7013* [Lon. *OSA 5-26669*].

Pavarotti is at home in the lightweight items. *Caro mio ben* is very nicely done and the romantic songs have a well-judged ardour. *Che farò* is rather less impressive. The tone is not always golden, but most of the bloom remains. The recording is vividly faithful in both media.

'Pavarotti's greatest hits': PUCCINI: *Turandot: Nessun dorma. Tosca: Recondita armonia; È lucevan le stelle. La Bohème: Che gelida manina.* DONIZETTI: *La fille du régiment: O mes amis . . . Pour mon âme. La Favorita: Spirito gentil. L'Elisir d'amore: Una furtiva lagrima.* R. STRAUSS: *Der Rosenkavalier: Di rigori armato.* LEONCAVALLO: *Mattinata.* ROSSINI: *La danza.* DE CURTIS: *Torna a Surriento.* BIZET: *Carmen: Flower song.* BELLINI: *I Puritani: A te O cara. Vanne, O rose fortunata.* VERDI: *Il Trovatore: Di qual tetra . . . Ah, si ben, mio; Di quella pira. Rigoletto; La donna è mobile; Questa o quella. Requiem: Ingemisco. Aïda: Celeste Aïda.* FRANCK: *Panis angelicus.* GOUNOD: *Faust: Salut! Demeure.* SCHUBERT: *Ave Maria.* LEONCAVALLO: *I Pagliacci: Vesti la giubba.* PONCHIELLI: *La Gioconda: Cielo e mar.* DENZA: *Funiculi, funicula.*
*** Decca **417 011-2** (2) [id.]; *K236 K22* [Lon. *PAV 5-2003/4*].

This collection of 'greatest hits' can safely be recommended to all who have admired the golden beauty of Pavarotti's voice. Including as it does a fair proportion of earlier recordings, the two discs demonstrate the splendid consistency of his singing. Songs are included as well as excerpts from opera, including *Torna a Surriento, Funiculi, funicula,* Leoncavallo's *Mattinata* and Rossini's *La Danza*. The sound is especially vibrant on CD, but sometimes a little fierce on cassette.

'Passione' (with Bologna Teatro Comunale O, Chiaramello): TAGLIAFERRI: *Passione.* COSTA: *Era de maggio.* ANON: *Fenesta che lucive; La Palummella; Te voglio bene assaje.* NARDELLA: *Chiove.* FALVO: *Dicitencello vuie.* DE CURTIS: *Voce 'e notte.* DI PAPUA: *I 'te vurria vasa.* MARIO: *Santa Lucia luntana.* LAMA: *Silenzio cantatore.* CARDILLO: *Core 'ngrato.*
*** Decca Dig. **417 117-2**; *417 117-4* [id.].

With the advantage of first-class recording, this perhaps is the most attractive of Pavarotti's Neapolitan collections. The voice sounds fresh, the singing is ardent and the programme is chosen imaginatively. The great tenor obviously identifies with this repertoire and sings everything with the kind of natural response that skirts vulgarity. The orchestrations by Giancarlo Chiaramello show a feeling for the right kind of orchestral colour: they may be sophisticated, but they undoubtedly enhance the melodic lines. If the title of the collection suggests hyperbole, there is in fact a well-judged balance here between passionate romanticism and concern for phrasing and detail. There is an excellent high-level cassette.

'Anniversary': PUCCINI: *La Bohème: Che gelida manina. Tosca: Recondita armonia; È lucevan le stelle.* GIORDANO: *Andrea Chénier: Colpito qui m'avete . . . Un dì all'azzuro spazio; Si, fui soldato; Come un bel dì di maggio.* BELLINI: *La Sonnambula: Ah! perchè non posso odiarti.* PONCHIELLI: *La Gioconda: Cielo e mar.* VERDI: *La Traviata: Lunge da lei . . . De'miei bollenti spiriti. Un Ballo in maschera: Di' tu se fedele; Forse la soglia attinse . . . Ma se m'è forsa perderti.* LEONCAVALLO: *Pagliacci: Vesti la giubba.* BOITO: *Mefistofele: Dai campi; Giunto sui passo estremo.* ROSSINI: *Gugliemo Tell: Non mi . . . Oh muto asil.* MASCAGNI: *Cavalleria Rusticana: Addio.*
(*) Decca **417 362-2; *417 362-4* [id.].

Pavarotti's recital celebrated the 25th anniversary of his operatic début. It is a good compilation of mixed items from complete opera sets, some of them relatively rare and mostly imaginatively done, though the *Andrea Chénier* items could be subtler. Good, bright recording of various vintages.

'Volare' (*popular Italian songs*, with Ch. & O of Teatro Comunale di Bologna, Mancini): MODUGNO: *Volare*. DENZA: *Occhi di fata*. BIXIO: *La strada nel bosco; Chi è più felice di me; La canzone dell'amore; Cantate con me; Bimmi tu primavera*. SIBELLA: *La girometta*. D'ANZI: *Malinconia d'amore*. BONAGURA: *Luna marinara*. CASSARINI: *Fra tanta gente*. MASCHERONI: *Fiorin fiorello*. DE CURTIS: *Ti voglio tanto bene*. RUCCIONE: *Una chitarra nella notte*. MASCAGNI: *Serenata*. FERILLI: *Un amore così grande*.
(*) Decca Dig. **421 052-2; *421 052-4* [id.].

Supported by Henry Mancini in characteristically colourful arrangements, Pavarotti throws his considerable weight into these popular Neapolitan songs, not the most tasteful renderings but very satisfying for aficionados, helped by aptly ripe recording.

Donizetti and Verdi arias (with Vienna Op. O, Downes): DONIZETTI: *Dom Sébastien, roi de Portugal: Deserto in terra. Il Duca d'Alba: inosservato, penetrava . . . Angelo casto e bel. La Favorita: Spirito gentil. Lucia di Lammermoor: Tombe degli avi miei . . . Fra poce a me*. VERDI: *Un Ballo in maschera: Forse la soglia . . . Me se m'è forza perderti. I due Foscari: Ah si, ch'io sento ancora . . . Dal più remoto esiglio. Luisa Miller: Oh! fede negar potessi . . . Quando le sere al placido. Macbeth: O figli . . . Ah, la paterna mano.*
(M) *** Decca **421 304-2**; *417 001-4* [id.].

Though not as distinguished as either the Sutherland or the Marilyn Horne (Rossini) recitals in Decca's mid-price series. Pavarotti's 'Opera Gala' issue of Verdi and Donizetti represents the tenor in impressive performances of mainly rare arias, recorded early in his career in 1968, with the voice fresh and golden. Good, full recording.

Price, Leontyne (soprano)

'Christmas with Leontyne Price' (with V. Singverein, VPO, Karajan); GRÜBER: *Silent night*. MENDELSSOHN: *Hark! the herald angels*. HOPKINS: *We three kings*. TRAD.: *Angels we have heard on high; O Tannenbaum; God rest ye merry, gentlemen; Sweet li'l Jesus*. WILLIS: *It came upon the midnight clear*. BACH: *Vom Himmel hoch*. BACH–GOUNOD: *Ave Maria*. SCHUBERT: *Ave Maria*. ADAM: *O holy night*. MOZART: *Alleluja, K.165*.
(*) Decca **421 103-2 [id.].

There is much beautiful singing here, but the style is essentially operatic. The rich, ample voice, when scaled down (as for instance in *We three kings*), can be very beautiful, but at full thrust it does not always catch the simplicity of melodic line which is characteristic of many of these carols. Yet the vibrant quality of the presentation is undoubtedly thrilling, and it can charm too, as in *God rest ye merry, gentlemen*, with its neat harpsichord accompaniment. The sound is admirably full, clear and vivid in its CD format.

Robeson, Paul (bass)

'Favourites': KERN: *Ol' Man River; Roll away, clouds; The lonesome road; Got the south in my soul; Hush-a-bye lullaby; Round the bend of the road; Carry me back to green pastures; Blue prelude; Wagon wheels; So shy; St Louis blues; Little man, you've had a busy day; I ain't lazy, I'm just dreaming; All through the night; Shenandoah*. ELLINGTON: *Solitude. Song of the Volga Boatman; Dear old Southland; Nothin'; A perfect day.*
(***) HMV **CDC7 47839-2** [id.].

A welcome reissue from the HMV archives offering recordings made between 1928 and 1939 when the great singer was in his prime, vocally and artistically. There is an innocence in the singing of the simpler songs (*So shy*, for instance) which he would perhaps not have captured so easily later in his life. Throughout, the Robeson magic projects readily and there is little complaint about the technical quality of the originals, although the digital remastering has brought a touch of dryness to the voice in its most resonant low notes.

Royal Naval College Chapel, Greenwich, Choir, Gordon St John Clarke

'20 favourite hymns' (with brass ensemble): includes: *Lead us, Heavenly Father; All people that on earth do dwell; Love divine; O God our help in ages past; Eternal father strong to save; Praise to the holiest in the height; Dear Lord and Father of mankind; The day thou gavest, Lord, is ended.*
(*) Abbey Dig. **CDMVP 826.

The combination of choir, congregation and brass ensemble is a familiar one on Sunday evenings on BBC TV, and this excellently recorded CD captures such an occasion faithfully with strongly committed singing, even if *Eternal father strong to save* might have been expected to raise an even higher degree of fervour at such a venue.

St George's Canzona, John Sothcott

Medieval songs and dances. Lamento di Tristano, L'autrier m'iere levaz. 4 Estampies real; Edi beo thu hevene quene; Eyns ne soy ke plente fu; Tre fontane; PERRIN D'AGINCOURT: *Quant voi en la fin d'este.* Cantigas de Santa Maria: *Se ome fezer; Nas mentes semper teer; Como poden per sas culpas; Maravillosos et piadosos.*
*** CRD **CRD 3421**; *CRDC 4121* [id.].

As so often when early music is imaginatively re-created, one is astonished at the individuality of many of the ideas. This applies particularly to the second item in this collection, *Quant voi en la fin d'este*, attributed to the mid-thirteenth-century trouvère, Perrin d'Agincourt, but no less to the four Cantigas de Santa Maria. The fruity presentation of *Como poden per sas culpas* ('As men may be crippled by their sins, so they may afterwards be made sound by the Virgin') is admirably contrasted with the strong lyrical appeal of the following *Maravillosos et piadosos*, directly extolling the virtues and compassion of Saint Mary. Among the four *Estampies real* the one presented last (band 11 on the CD) is haunting in its lilting melancholy. The instrumentation is at times suitably robust but does not eschew good intonation and subtle effects. The group is vividly recorded and the acoustics of St James, Clerkenwell, are never allowed to cloud detail. The sound is admirably firm and real in its CD format, but the cassette is very lively and clear also. The documentation is first class.

St George's Chapel, Windsor Castle, Choir, Christopher Robinson

20 Christmas carols (with John Porter, organ): *Once in Royal David's city; Hark! the herald angels sing; God rest you merry, gentlemen; The holly and the ivy; Gabriel's message; It came upon the midnight clear; People, look east; There is no rose of such virtue; Away in a manger; A stable in Bethlehem; The first nowell; O come all ye faithful; On Christmas night; Silent night;*

Jesus Christ the apple tree; In the bleak mid-winter; While shepherds watched their flocks; Ding dong merrily on high; In dulci jubilo; O little town of Bethlehem.
(*) Abbey Dig. **CD MVP 827; *MVPC 827* [id.].

The opening *Once in Royal David's city* is treated as a processional, but otherwise these are no-frills performances, the singing direct and eloquent, the arrangements straightforward. With such generous measure and many favourites included, this is very good value – even if some other carol collections are more imaginatively presented. The digital recording is excellent.

Schwarzkopf, Elisabeth (soprano)

'Elisabeth Schwarzkopf sings operetta' (with Philharmonia Ch. and O, Ackermann): HEUBERGER: *Der Opernball: Im chambre séparée.* ZELLER: *Der Vogelhändler: Ich bin die Christel; Schenkt man sich Rosen Der Obersteiger; Sei nicht bös.* LEHÁR: *Der Zarewitsch: Einer wird kommen. Der Graf von Luxembourg: Hoch Evoë, Heut noch werd ich Ehefrau. Giuditta: Meine Lippen.* J. STRAUSS, Jnr: *Casanova: Nuns' chorus; Laura's song.* MILLÖCKER: *Die Dubarry: Ich schenk mein Herz; Was ich im Leben beginne.* SUPPÉ: *Boccaccio: Hab ich nur deine Liebe.* SIECZYŃSKY: *Wien, du Stadt meiner Träume* (*Vienna, city of my dreams;* song).
❀ *** HMV **CDC7 47284-2** [id.].

This is one of the most delectable recordings of operetta arias ever made, and it is here presented with excellent sound. Schwarzkopf's 'whoopsing' manner (as Philip Hope-Wallace called it) is irresistible, authentically catching the Viennese style, languor and sparkle combined. Try for sample the exquisite *Im chambre séparée* or *Sei nicht bös*; but the whole programme is performed with supreme artistic command and ravishing tonal beauty. This outstanding example of the art of Elisabeth Schwarzkopf at its most enchanting is a disc which ought to be in every collection. The compact disc transfer enhances the superbly balanced recording even further, manages to cut out nearly all the background, give the voice a natural presence, and retain the orchestral bloom.

Soviet Army Chorus, Soloists and Band, Colonel Boris Alexandrov

DUNAYEVSKY: *Song of youth.* TRAD.: *A birch tree in a field; Volga boat song; Along Peter's Street; Ah! lovely night; Kamarinskaya; Annie Laurie; Kalinka; Bandura; Oh No! John; Snowflakes.* ALEXANDROV: *Ukrainian poem.* SHAPORIN: *The Decembrists: Soldiers' chorus.* MOKROUSOV: *You are always beautiful.* WILLIAMS-JUDGE: *Tipperary.* KNIPPER: *Song of the plains.*
*** HMV **CDC7 47833-2** [id.].

This anthology caused something of a sensation on its first issue, and it has still not lost its power to electrify. The sheer vitality of the music making is at times almost overwhelming, yet there is much magic too. The unnamed tenor's performance of *Annie Laurie* is meltingly lovely and although the words of *Oh No! John* are not sharply clear, the singer's vocal production and bluff humour are memorable. *Tipperary*, learnt especially for the 1956 visit, has irresistible gusto. The Russian items, with the balalaika often to the fore, are often very exciting too, with *Ah! lovely night* another frisson-creating lyrical number. The recordings come from 1956 and 1963. The remastering has added clarity and presence, plus some fierceness, but has also lost some of the original ambient atmosphere.

Stade, Frederica von (mezzo-soprano)

'Portrait': MOZART: *Le nozze di Figaro: Non so più.* ROSSINI: *Semiramide: Bel raggio lusinghier.* THOMAS: *Mignon: C'est moi . . . Me voici.* MASSENET: *Cendrillon: Que mes sœurs.* OFFENBACH: *La Grande Duchesse: Dites-lui.* CHAUSSON: *Chanson perpétuelle.* SCHUMANN: *Botschaft; Das Glück.* BRAHMS: *6 Duets* (with Judith Blegen).
*** CBS **MK 39315** [id.].

This *'Portrait'*, compiled from a variety of sources, gives a good idea of the wide range of this characterful and charming singer. Though she is appreciated most as a superb Cherubino, the French items are the ones that stand out here for their extra intensity. The Chausson and the items taken from the complete sets of *Cendrillon* and *Mignon* are enchantingly done, while the Offenbach brings out the full fun of the piece lightly with point and wit. Intelligent singing too in Rossini and the duets with Blegen. Recording from different sources is generally well transferred, with the CD improving definition and presence.

Opera arias: ROSSINI: *Otello: Quanto son fieri i palpiti; Che amania. Ohimè! che affano! Assisa a piè d'un salice; Deh calma, o Ciel.* HAYDN: *La fedelta premiata: Per te m'accesse amore; Vanne . . . fuggi . . . traditore! Barbaro conte . . . Dell'amor mio fedele. Il mondo della luna: Una donna come me; Se lo commando ci veniro.* MOZART: *La clemenza di Tito: Torna di Tito a lato; Tu tosti tradito.*
*** Ph. **420 084-2** [id.].

Von Stade's Philips recital is a splendid compilation of some of her finest performances from complete sets of rare operas. It is sad that the Philips Haydn series did not achieve wider circulation, when it included such delectable items as those here; it is also valuable to have reminders of her contribution to the Rossini *Otello* set and to Colin Davis's recording of Mozart's *Clemenza di Tito*. Good original sound, well transferred.

Sutherland, Dame Joan (soprano)

'The art of the prima donna': ARNE: *Artaxerxes: The soldier tir'd.* HANDEL: *Samson: Let the bright seraphim.* BELLINI: *Norma: Casta diva. I Puritani: Son vergin vezzosa; Qui la voce. La Sonnambula: Come per me sereno.* ROSSINI: *Semiramide: Bel raggio lusinghier.* GOUNOD: *Faust: Jewel song. Roméo et Juliette: Waltz song.* VERDI: *Otello: Willow song. Rigoletto: Caro nome. La Traviata: Ah fors è lui; Sempre libera.* MOZART: *Die Entführung aus dem Serail: Marten aller Arten.* THOMAS: *Hamlet: Mad scene.* DELIBES: *Lakmé: Bell song.* MEYERBEER: *Les Huguenots: O beau pays.*
❀ *** Decca **414 450-2**; (M) *414 450-4* (2) [id.].

This ambitious early two-disc recital (from 1960) remains one of Joan Sutherland's outstanding gramophone achievements, and it is a matter of speculation whether even Melba or Tetrazzini in their heyday managed to provide sixteen consecutive recordings quite as dazzling as these performances. Indeed, it is the Golden Age that one naturally turns to rather than to current singers when making any comparisons. Sutherland herself by electing to sing each one of these fabulously difficult arias in tribute to a particular soprano of the past, from Mrs Billington in the eighteenth century, through Grisi, Malibran, Pasta and Jenny Lind in the nineteenth century, to Lilli Lehmann, Melba, Tetrazzini and Galli-Curci in this, is asking to be judged by the standards of the Golden Age. On the basis of recorded reminders she comes out with flying colours, showing a greater consistency and certainly a wider range of sympathy than even the greatest Golden Agers possessed. The sparkle and delicacy of the *Puritani Polonaise*, the freshness and lightness of the mad scene from Thomas's *Hamlet*, the commanding power of the *Entführung* aria and the breathtaking brilliance of the Queen's aria from *Les Huguenots* are all among the high spots here, while the arias which Sutherland later recorded in her complete opera sets regularly bring performances just as fine – and often finer – than the later versions. The freshness of the voice is caught superbly in the recording, which on CD is amazingly full, firm and realistic, far more believable than many new digital recordings. The cassettes, too, are very well managed and at mid-price cost considerably less than the CDs.

'Bel canto Arias' (with Welsh Nat. Op. O, Bonynge): DONIZETTI: *Il castello di Kenilworth: Par che me dica ancora. Betley: In questo semplice. La Favorita: L'ai-je bien entendu . . . O mon Fernand.* VERDI: *Attila: Liberamente or piangi . . . Oh! nel fuggente nuvolo.* MEYERBEER: *L'Africaine: Sur mes genoux.* BELLINI: *I Capuleti ed i Montecchi: Eccomi in lieta vesta . . . Oh! quante volte.* ROSSINI: *Guillaume Tell: Sombre forêt. Il barbiere di Siviglia: Una voce poco fa.*
** Decca Dig. **417 253-2**; *417 253-4* [id.].

Recorded in the mid-1980s, Sutherland's *'Bel canto'* collection with the Welsh National Opera Orchestra finds the voice in variable form, less firm than when in pristine condition, whether early or late. As long as you are not distracted by the beat on sustained notes, however, there is much to relish of Sutherland at her warmest, here exploring new repertory, even though, for all its brilliance, this *Una voce* is not the most sparkling. Full, vivid recording.

'Romantic French arias' (with Geneva Grand Theatre Ch., SRO, Bonynge): OFFENBACH: *Robinson Crusoé: Conduisez-moi vers celui que j'adore. La Grande-Duchesse de Gérolstein: Dites-lui qu'on l'a remarqué; Vous aimez le danger . . . Ah! que j'aime les militaires. Contes d'Hoffmann: Les oiseaux* (*Doll song*). CHARPENTIER: *Louise: Depuis le jour.* MEYERBEER: *Dinorah: Bellah! ma chèvre chérie . . . Dors, petite. L'Etoile du Nord: C'est bien lui . . . La, la, la, air chéri; Veille sur eux . . . Vaisseau que le flot balance. Robert le Diable; En vain j'espère . . . Idole de ma vie.* AUBER: *Manon Lescaut: C'est l'histoire amoureuse; Fra Diavolo: Non temete milord . . . Or son sola.* BIZET: *Les Pêcheurs de perles: Me voilà seule . . . Comme autrefois. Carmen: La marquerite a fermé . . . Ouvre ton cœur.* MASSENET: *Cendrillon: Ah que mes sœurs sont heureuses.* GOUNOD: *Mireille: O légère hirondelle; Le tribut de Zamora: Ce Sarrasin disait. Faust: Si le bonheur.* LECOCQ: *Le cœur et la main: Un soir Pérez le capitaine.* MASSENET: *Les noces de Jeannette: Au bord du chemin qui passe à ma porte.*
(M) *** Decca *417 490-4* (2) [id.].

It will come as a delightful surprise to many that Offenbach's *Robinson Crusoé* includes an irresistible waltz song for the heroine as she steps ashore on Crusoe's island and is met by cannibals (*Take me to the man I adore*). Sutherland sings that and all the other brilliant numbers with great flair and abandon, relishing her virtuosity, while the romantic side is represented by such enchanting items as Massenet's sad little *Cinderella* aria, Dinorah's sweet lullaby for her pet goat, a nightingale aria from Massenet's *Les noces de Jeannette* and a ravishing account of *Depuis le jour* from *Louise*. Among Sutherland's recitals overall, this stands out for the freshness of the voice, with its wide range of tone and dynamic. Except in the arias from *Les Pêcheurs de perles*, Sutherland is in first-rate form. The pair of cassettes are well transferred and make a fine mid-priced bargain, but we hope a CD is planned. On tape, some of this repertoire is also included in Decca's anthology of *'French operetta'* – see above.

'Joy to the world' (Christmas carols) (with Amb. S., New Philh. O, Bonynge) (all arr. Gamley): HANDEL: *Joy to the world.* WILLIS: *It came upon the midnight clear.* ADAM: *O holy night.* GOUNOD: *O Divine Redeemer.* TRAD.: *What child is this?; Adeste Fidelis; The 12 days of Christmas; Good King Wenceslas; The holly and the ivy; Angels we have heard on high; Deck the*

hall. REGER: *The Virgin's slumber song.* MENDELSSOHN: *Hark! the herald angels sing.* SCHUBERT: *Ave Maria.*
(*) Decca **421 095-2 [id.].

These are sugar-coated arrangements of carols made by Douglas Gamley – but who is going to complain when the result cocoons the listener in a web of atmospheric sound? A popular carol record like this may be hard to take at a single sitting, but of its kind this is very good indeed with an unforgettable, resilient performance of *The 12 days of Christmas.* The brisk carols come off best. The digital remastering offers clear, vivid sound, with the voice caught naturally.

'Opera gala': BELLINI: *Norma: Sediziose voce . . . Casta diva . . . Ah! bello a me ritorna.* DONIZETTI: *Lucia di Lammermoor: Ancor non giunse . . . Regnava nel silenzio. Il dolce suono mi colpi di sua voce! . . . Ardon gl'incensi. Linda di Chamounix: Ah! tardai troppo . . . O luce di quest'anima.* VERDI: *Ernani: Surta è la notte . . . Ernani involami. I vespri siciliani: Merce, dilette.*
(M) ⊛ *** Decca **421 305-2** [id.].

Sutherland's 'Opera Gala' disc is one of the most cherishable of all operatic recital records, bringing together the glorious, exuberant items from her very first recital disc, made within weeks of her first Covent Garden success in 1959 and – as a valuable supplement – the poised account of *Casta diva* she recorded the following year as part of the *'Art of the Prima Donna'.* It was this 1959 recital which at once put Sutherland firmly on the map among the great recording artists of all time. Even she has never surpassed the freshness of these versions of the two big arias from *Lucia di Lammermoor*, sparkling in immaculate coloratura, while the lightness and point of the jaunty *Linda di Chamounix* aria and the *Boléro* from *I vespri Siciliani* are just as winning. The sound is exceptionally vivid and immediate, though the accompaniments under Nello Santi are sometimes rough in ensemble.

Sutherland, Dame Joan (soprano), Marilyn Horne (mezzo-soprano) and Luciano Pavarotti (tenor)

'Duets and trios from the Lincoln Center' (with NY City Op. O, Bonynge): excerpts from VERDI: *Ernani; Otello; Il Trovatore.* BELLINI: *Norma.* PONCHIELLI: *La Gioconda.*
(*) Decca Dig. **417 587-2 [id.].

Not all gala concerts make good records, but this is an exception; almost every item here puts an important gloss on the achievements of the three principal stars in the concerted numbers. These have been extracted from the original two-LP set to make a single CD playing for 72′. It is good to have a sample not only of Sutherland's Desdemona but of Pavarotti's Otello in their account of the Act I duet. The final scene from *Il Trovatore* is more compelling here than in the complete set made by the same soloists five years earlier. The microphone catches a beat in the voices of both Sutherland and Horne, but not as obtrusively as on some studio discs. Lively accompaniment under Bonynge; bright, vivid digital recording, but over-loud applause.

Sutherland, Dame Joan and Luciano Pavarotti (tenor)

Operatic duets (with Nat. PO, Bonynge) from: VERDI: *La Traviata; Otello; Aïda* (with chorus). BELLINI: *La Sonnambula.* DONIZETTI: *Linda di Chamounix.*
*** Decca **400 058-2** [id.]; *KSXC 6828* [Lon. *OSA5-26437*].

This collection offers a rare sample of Sutherland as Aïda (*La fatale pietra . . . O terra, addio* from Act IV), a role she sang only once on stage, well before her international career began; and with this and her sensitive impersonations of Desdemona, Violetta and the Bellini and Donizetti heroines, Sutherland might have been expected to steal first honours here. In fact these are mainly duets to show off the tenor, and it is Pavarotti who runs away with the main glory, though both artists were plainly challenged to their finest and the result, with excellent accompaniment, is among the most attractive and characterful duet recitals. The recording is admirably clear and well focused, and the sophistication of orchestral detail is striking in the *Otello* and *Aïda* scenes which close the recital; and this is especially striking on the compact disc which, though a remastered analogue recording, gives the artists remarkable presence. The cassette too is extremely well managed.

Tallis Scholars, Peter Phillips

'Christmas carols and motets': Ave Maria settings by JOSQUIN DES PRES; VERDELOT; VICTORIA. *Coventry carol* (2 settings). BYRD: *Lullaby*. PRAETORIUS: *Es ist ein Ros'entsprungen; Joseph lieber, Joseph mein; In dulci jubilo; Wachet auf*. BACH: *Wachet auf*. Medieval carols: *Angelus ad virginem; There is no rose; Nowell sing we.*
*** Gimell Dig. **CDGIM 010**; *1585T-10* [id.].

Wonderfully serene singing from the Tallis Scholars, recorded with superb naturalness and presence, makes this a very special Christmas record. There is something unique about a carol and even the very early music here has that special intensity of inspiration which brings memorability. There are some familiar melodies too, notably those set by Praetorius; but much of this repertoire will come as refreshingly new to most ears. The singing has a purity of spirit that is wonderfully communicative in its simplicity and spontaneous eloquence. There is a first-class matching tape, though the CD is very much in the demonstration class for the clear choral image, heard against the ideal acoustics of St Pierre et St Paul, Salle, Norfolk.

Vienna Boys' Choir

'Folksongs and songs for children' (with V. CO, Harrer; Farnberger, Miller).
*** Ph. Dig. **400 014-2** [id.].

Here are some two dozen songs, many traditional, and all of great charm. They are presented artlessly, but the singing is polished and the simply scored accompaniments are very effective. The recording is admirably natural, with the CD offering a marginal improvement in definition. There is a good deal of moderately paced music here, and sometimes one feels that the direction could be more spirited; yet the overall effect is undoubtedly beguiling and, not taken all at once, this recital will give much pleasure. With the CD comes an excellent booklet, complete with all translations.

Walker, Sarah (mezzo-soprano), Thomas Allen (baritone)

'The Sea' (with Roger Vignoles, piano): IRELAND: *Sea fever*. HAYDN: *Mermaid's song; Sailor's song*. DIBDIN: *Tom Bowling*. WALTON: *Song for the Lord Mayor's table; Wapping Old Stairs*. WOLF: *Seemanns Abschied*. FAURÉ: *Les Berceaux; Au cimetière; L'horizon chimerique*. SCHUBERT: *Lied eines Schiffers an die Dioskuren*. BORODIN: *The Sea; The Sea Princess*. DEBUSSY: *Proses lyriques: De grêve*. IVES: *Swimmers*. SCHUMANN: *Die Meerfee*. BERLIOZ:

Nuits d'été: L'ile inconnue. MENDELSSOHN: *Wasserfahrt.* BRAHMS: *Die Meere.* TRAD.; *The Mermaid.* arr. BRITTEN: *Sail on, sail on.*
❀ *** Hyp. **CDA 66165**; *KA 66165* [id.].

With Roger Vignoles as master of ceremonies in a brilliantly devised programme, ranging wide, this twin-headed recital celebrating The Sea is a delight from beginning to end. Two outstandingly characterful singers are mutually challenged to their very finest form, whether in solo songs or duets. As sample, try the setting of the sea-song, *The Mermaid*, brilliantly arranged by Vignoles, with hilarious key-switches on the comic quotations from *Rule Britannia*. Excellent recording in both media.

Welitsch, Ljuba (soprano)

Arias: TCHAIKOVSKY: *Eugene Onegin: Tatiana's letter scene.* VERDI: *Aïda: Ritorna vincitor.* PUCCINI: *Tosca: Vissi d'arte. La Bohème: Musetta's waltz song.* WEBER: *Der Freischütz: Wie nacht mire der Schlummer . . . Leise, leise.* R. STRAUSS: *Salome: Closing scene.*
(M) (***) EMI mono **CDH7 61007-2** [id.].

It is sad that Ljuba Welitsch's career was far shorter than it should have been. The voice itself, strikingly individual in its timbre, conveys fire and intensity and, as these classic recordings consistently show, the vibrant personality matches that. This immaculately transferred collection gathers together the handful of studio recordings she made for EMI after the Second World War (notably *Tatiana's letter song* from 1948, done in German). As a splendid bonus comes the radio recording, made in Vienna in 1944, of the closing scene from Strauss's *Salome*, where the extra vibrancy of live performance is vividly caught, despite the fuzziness of sound, here reasonably clarified in the digital transfer.

Westminster Abbey Choir, Preston

Christmas carols: TRAD.: *Up! awake; There stood in heaven a linden tree; The holly and the ivy; Ding dong merrily on high; Up! good Christian folk; In dulci jubilo; Rocking; Illuminare Jerusalem; Good King Wenceslas.* OLDHAM: *Remember O thou man.* WISHART: *Alleluya, a new work.* CHARPENTIER: *Salve puerule.* POSTON: *Jesus Christ the apple tree.* PRAETORIUS: *Resonet in laudibus.* MAXWELL DAVIES: *Nowell* (*Out of your sleep arise*). HAMMERSCHMIDT: *Alleluja! Freuet euch.* MENDELSSOHN: *Hark! the herald angels sing.* SCHEIDT: *Puer natus.* GARDNER: *Tomorrow shall be my dancing day.* BRITTEN: *Shepherd's carol.*
*** DG Dig. **413 590-2**; *413 590-4*.

An excellent concert in every way. The programme is nicely balanced between old favourites and rewarding novelty, the traditional material spiced with modern writing, which readily captures the special essence that makes a carol instantly recognizable as a Christmas celebration. Fresh singing of fine vigour, expressively responsive, is combined with first-class sound in both media, the ambience nicely judged.

Westminster Cathedral Choir, Hill

'Treasures of the Spanish Renaissance': GUERRERO: *Surge propera amica mea; O altitudo divitiarum; O Domine Jesu Christe; O sacrum convivium; Ave, Virgo sanctissima; Regina coeli*

laetare. LOBO: *Versa est in luctum; Ave Maria; O quam suavis est. Domine*. VIVANCO: *Magnificat octavi toni.*
*** Hyp. **CDA 66168**; *KA 66168* [id.].

This immensely valuable collection reminds us vividly that Tomas Luis de Victoria was not the only master of church music in Renaissance Spain. Francisco Guerrero is generously represented here, and the spacious serenity of his polyphonic writing (for four, six and, in *Regina coli laetare*, eight parts) creates the most beautiful sounds. A criticism might be made that tempi throughout this collection, which also includes fine music by Alonso Lobo and a superb eight-part *Magnificat* by Sebastian de Vivanco, are too measured, but the tension is well held, and David Hill is obviously concerned to convey the breadth of the writing. The singing is gloriously firm, with the long melismatic lines admirably controlled. Discreet accompaniments (using Renaissance double harp, bass dulcian and organ) do not affect the essentially a cappella nature of the performances. The Westminster Cathedral acoustic means the choral tone is richly upholstered, but the focus is always firm and clear. There is a first-rate cassette which shares the excellent documentation of the other formats.

White, Robert (tenor)

'Favourite Irish songs of Princess Grace' (with Monte Carlo PO, Stapleton): *Danny Boy; Pretty Kitty Kelly; Galway Bay; MacNamara's Band; Oft in the stilly night; Molly Malone; The last rose of summer; The foggy dew; Mother Machree; Off to Philadelphia; I hear you calling me; My wild Irish rose; The Sally gardens; She is far from the land; The star of County Down; Macushla; Mistress Biddy was a giddy little witch; The Rose of Tralee; I'll take you home again, Kathleen.*
*** Virgin **VC 790705-2;** *VC 790705-4* [id.].

Princess Grace of Monaco was the sponsor for a Foundation to support a comprehensive archive of Irish music in Monte Carlo, from which these songs are taken; the colourful orchestral arrangements are by Peter Hope and Robert Docker. Among contemporary singers, Robert White is unsurpassed in this repertoire. His golden tenor and wonderfully free upper range make the lyrical numbers, like *I hear you calling me* and *The Sally gardens*, sound quite ravishing, while the light-hearted *MacNamara's Band* and *The star of the County Down* sparkle splendidly. The total lack of artifice in the singing, combined with an obvious emotional response, brings consistent pleasure. A superb voice, naturally caught by the engineers and very well balanced with the warmly recorded orchestral accompaniments, sympathetically directed by Robin Stapleton. This is outstanding of its kind. There is an excellent cassette.

FOR THE BEST IN PAPERBACKS, LOOK FOR THE 

In every corner of the world, on every subject under the sun, Penguin represents quality and variety – the very best in publishing today.

For complete information about books available from Penguin – including Pelicans, Puffins, Peregrines and Penguin Classics – and how to order them, write to us at the appropriate address below. Please note that for copyright reasons the selection of books varies from country to country.

In the United Kingdom: For a complete list of books available from Penguin in the U.K., please write to *Dept E.P., Penguin Books Ltd, Harmondsworth, Middlesex, UB7 0DA*

In the United States: For a complete list of books available from Penguin in the U.S., please write to *Dept BA, Penguin, 299 Murray Hill Parkway, East Rutherford, New Jersey 07073*

In Canada: For a complete list of books available from Penguin in Canada, please write to *Penguin Books Canada Ltd, 2801 John Street, Markham, Ontario L3R 1B4*

In Australia: For a complete list of books available from Penguin in Australia, please write to the *Marketing Department, Penguin Books Australia Ltd, P.O. Box 257, Ringwood, Victoria 3134*

In New Zealand: For a complete list of books available from Penguin in New Zealand, please write to the *Marketing Department, Penguin Books (NZ) Ltd, Private Bag, Takapuna, Auckland 9*

In India: For a complete list of books available from Penguin, please write to *Penguin Overseas Ltd, 706 Eros Apartments, 56 Nehru Place, New Delhi, 110019*

In Holland: For a complete list of books available from Penguin in Holland, please write to *Penguin Books Nederland B.V., Postbus 195, NL–1380AD Weesp, Netherlands*

In Germany: For a complete list of books available from Penguin, please write to *Penguin Books Ltd, Friedrichstrasse 10 – 12, D–6000 Frankfurt Main 1, Federal Republic of Germany*

In Spain: For a complete list of books available from Penguin in Spain, please write to *Longman Penguin España, Calle San Nicolas 15, E–28013 Madrid, Spain*

FOR THE BEST IN PAPERBACKS, LOOK FOR THE 

PENGUIN OMNIBUSES

Author's Choice: Four Novels by Graham Greene

Four magnificent novels by an author whose haunting and distinctive 'entertainments' and fiction have captured the moral and spiritual dilemmas of our time: *The Power and the Glory*, *The Quiet American*, *Travels with My Aunt* and *The Honorary Consul.*

The Collected Stories of Colette

Edited with and Introduction by Robert Phelps

'Poetry and passion' – *Daily Telegraph.* A sensuous feast of one hundred short stories, shot through with the colours and flavours of the Parisian world and fertile French countryside, they reverberate with the wit and acuity that made Colette unique.

The Penguin Complete Novels of George Orwell

The six novels of one of England's most original and significant writers. Collected in this volume are the novels which brought George Orwell world fame: *Animal Farm*, *Burmese Days*, *A Clergyman's Daughter*, *Coming Up for Air*, *Keep the Aspidistra Flying* and *Nineteen Eighty-Four*.

The Great Novels of D. H. Lawrence

The collection of the masterworks of one of the greatest writers in the English language of any time – *Women in Love*, *Sons and Lovers* and *The Rainbow*.

Frank Tuohy: The Collected Stories

'The time has come for him to be honoured for what he is: a great short-story writer, an absolute master of the form' – Paul Bailey in the *Standard*. From Poland to Brazil, from England to Japan, Tuohy maps the intricate contours of personal and racial misunderstanding, shock and embarrassment. 'Exhilarating fiction' – *Sunday Times*

The Nancy Mitford Omnibus

Nancy Mitford's immortal, unforgettable world in one scintillating volume: *The Pursuit of Love*, *Love in a Cold Climate*, *The Blessing* and *Don't Tell Alfred.*

PENGUIN REFERENCE BOOKS

The Penguin English Dictionary

Over 1,000 pages long and with over 68,000 definitions, this cheap, compact and totally up-to-date book is ideal for today's needs. It includes many technical and colloquial terms, guides to pronunciation and common abbreviations.

The Penguin Reference Dictionary

The ideal comprehensive guide to written and spoken English the world over, with detailed etymologies and a wide selection of colloquial and idiomatic usage. There are over 100,000 entries and thousands of examples of how words are actually used – all clear, precise and up-to-date.

The Penguin English Thesaurus

This unique volume will increase anyone's command of the English language and build up your word power. Fully cross-referenced, it includes synonyms of every kind (formal or colloquial, idiomatic and figurative) for almost 900 headings. It is a must for writers and utterly fascinating for any English speaker.

The Penguin Dictionary of Quotations

A treasure-trove of over 12,000 new gems and old favourites, from Aesop and Matthew Arnold to Xenophon and Zola.

The Penguin Wordmaster Dictionary Manser and Turton

This dictionary puts the pleasure back into word-seeking. Every time you look at a page you get a bonus – a panel telling you everything about a particular word or expression. It is, therefore, a dictionary to be read as well as used for its concise and up-to-date definitions.

PENGUIN REFERENCE BOOKS

The Penguin Guide to the Law

This acclaimed reference book is designed for everyday use, and forms the most comprehensive handbook ever published on the law as it affects the individual.

The Penguin Medical Encyclopedia

Covers the body and mind in sickness and in health, including drugs, surgery, history, institutions, medical vocabulary and many other aspects. 'Highly commendable' – *Journal of the Institute of Health Education*

The Penguin French Dictionary

This invaluable French-English, English-French dictionary includes both the literary and dated vocabulary needed by students, and the up-to-date slang and specialized vocabulary (scientific, legal, sporting, etc) needed in everyday life. As a passport to the French language, it is second to none.

A Dictionary of Literary Terms

Defines over 2,000 literary terms (including lesser known, foreign language and technical terms) explained with illustrations from literature past and present.

The Penguin Map of Europe

Covers all land eastwards to the Urals, southwards to North Africa and up to Syria, Iraq and Iran. Scale – 1:5,500,000, 4-colour artwork. Features main roads, railways, oil and gas pipelines, plus extra information including national flags, currencies and populations.

The Penguin Dictionary of Troublesome Words

A witty, straightforward guide to the pitfalls and hotly disputed issues in standard written English, illustrated with examples and including a glossary of grammatical terms and an appendix on punctuation.